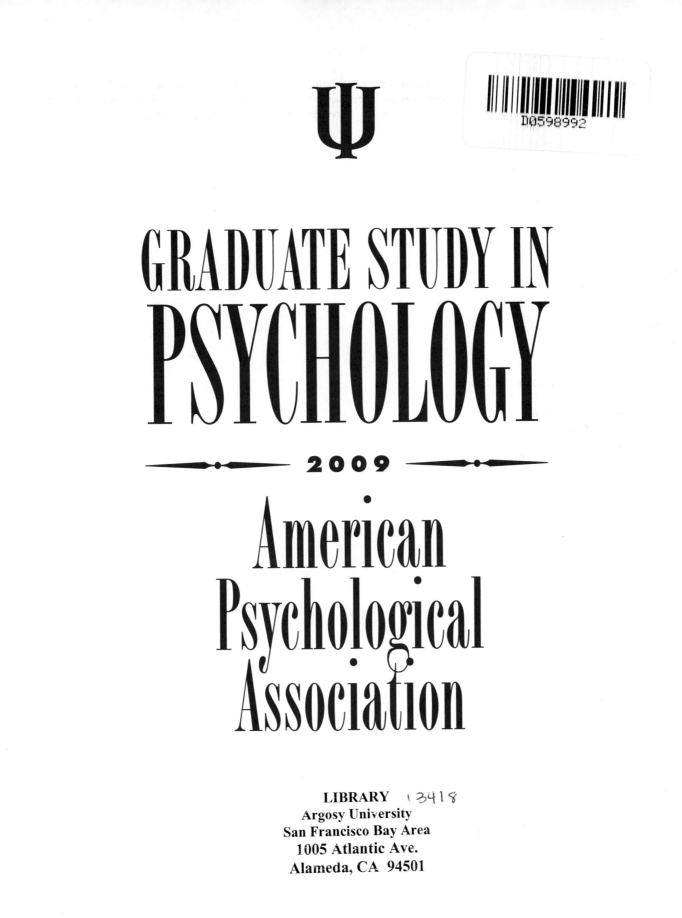

GRADUATE STUDY IN PSYCHOLOGY

2009

American Psychological Association

American Psychological Association
Washington, DC

Published by
American Psychological Association
750 First Street, NE
Washington, DC 20002

www.apa.org

ISBN-13: 978-1-4338-0395-6
ISBN-10: 1-4338-0395-X
ISSN: 0742-7220
42nd edition

To order
APA Order Department
P.O. Box 92984
Washington, DC 20090-2984
Tel: (800) 374-2721, Direct: (202) 336-5510
Fax: (202) 336-5502, TDD/TTY: (202) 336-6123
Online: www.apa.org/books/
E-mail: order@apa.org

Printed in the United States of America

Contents

Foreword

This is the 42nd edition of a book prepared to assist individuals interested in graduate study in psychology. The current edition provides information for more than 600 graduate departments, programs, and schools of psychology in the United States and Canada. The information was obtained from questionnaires sent to graduate departments and schools of psychology and was provided voluntarily. The American Psychological Association (APA) is not responsible for the accuracy of the information reported.

The purpose of this publication is to provide an information service, offering in one book information about the majority of graduate programs in psychology. Inclusion in this publication does not signify APA approval or endorsement of a graduate program, nor should it be assumed that a listing of a program in *Graduate Study in Psychology* means that its graduates are automatically qualified to sit for licensure as psychologists or are eligible for positions requiring a psychology degree.

However, programs listed in this publication have agreed to the following quality assurance provisions:

1. They have agreed to honor April 15 as the date allowed for graduate applicants to accept or reject an offer of admission and financial assistance for fall matriculation. This date adheres to national policy guidelines as stated by the Council of Graduate Schools and the Council of Graduate Departments of Psychology.

2. They have satisfied the following criteria: The program offers a graduate degree and is sponsored by a public or private higher education institution accredited by one of six regional accrediting bodies recognized by the U.S. Secretary of Education or, in the case of Canadian programs, the institution is publicly recognized by the Association of Universities and Colleges of Canada as a member in good standing, or the program indicates that it meets *all* of the following criteria:

A. The graduate program, wherever it may be administratively housed, is publicly labeled as a psychology program in pertinent institutional catalogs and brochures.

B. The psychology program stands as a recognizable, coherent organizational entity within the institution.

C. There is an identifiable core of full-time psychology faculty.

D. Psychologists have clear authority and primary responsibility for the academic core and specialty preparation, whether or not the program involves multiple administrative lines.

E. There is an identifiable body of graduate students who are enrolled in the program for the attainment of the graduate degree offered.

F. The program is an organized, integrated sequence of study designed by the psychology faculty responsible for the program.

G. Programs leading to a doctoral degree require at least the equivalent of 3 full-time academic years of graduate study.

H. Doctoral programs ensure appropriate breadth and depth of education and training in psychology as follows:

1) Methodology and history, including systematic preparation in scientific standards and responsibilities, research design and methodology, quantitative methods (e.g., statistics, psychometric methods), and historical foundations in psychology.

2) Foundations in psychology, including

a. biological bases of behavior (e.g., physiological psychology, comparative psychology, neuropsychology, psychopharmacology);

b. cognitive–affective bases of behavior (e.g., learning, memory, perception, cognition, thinking, motivation, emotion);

c. social bases of behavior (e.g., social psychology; cultural, ethnic, and group processes; sex roles; organizational behavior); and

d. individual differences (e.g., personality theory, human development, individual differences, abnormal psychology, psychology of women, psychology of persons with disabilities, psychology of the minority experience).

3) Additional preparation in the program's area of specialization, to include

a. knowledge and application of ethical principles and guidelines and standards as may apply to scientific and professional practice activities;

b. supervised practicum and/or laboratory experiences appropriate to the area of practice, teaching, or research in psychology; and

c. advanced preparation appropriate to the area of specialization.

This publication may not answer all questions you have about graduate education in psychology. Some questions you may want to direct to particular graduate departments, programs, or schools of psychology. *For more information about general policies and information related to graduate education, visit the APA Education Web site (http://www.apa.org/ed).*

Producing this annual publication involves the cooperation of many individuals each year. We wish to express appreciation to all graduate departments, programs, and schools that contributed information. We also wish to acknowledge the support and contributions by individuals in the Education Directorate, Internet Services, Publications and Databases, and the Center for Psychology Workforce Analysis and Research.

Joan Freund
Assistant Director
Office of Graduate Education and Training
Education Directorate
American Psychological Association

Considering Graduate Study

Psychology is a broad scientific discipline bridging the social and biological sciences. Psychology's applications include education and human development, health and human resilience, family and community relations, organizations and other work environments, engineering and technology, the arts and architecture, communications, and political and judiciary systems.

There are many types of graduate programs in psychology. Selecting a graduate program that is best for you requires thoughtful consideration. The American Psychological Association (APA) does not rank graduate programs in psychology. Rather, APA encourages selecting graduate programs based on the best match for you. Some programs focus on preparing students for an academic research career, while others focus on preparing students for applied research outside the university. Other programs prepare students to provide psychological services as licensed professional psychologists. Some programs offer professional development in addition to a focus in psychology to prepare students for a college teaching career. Psychology subfields of recent master's and doctoral graduates are illustrated in Figures 1 and 2.

Figure 1. Master's Degrees Awarded by Selected Psychology Subfield: 2006–2007

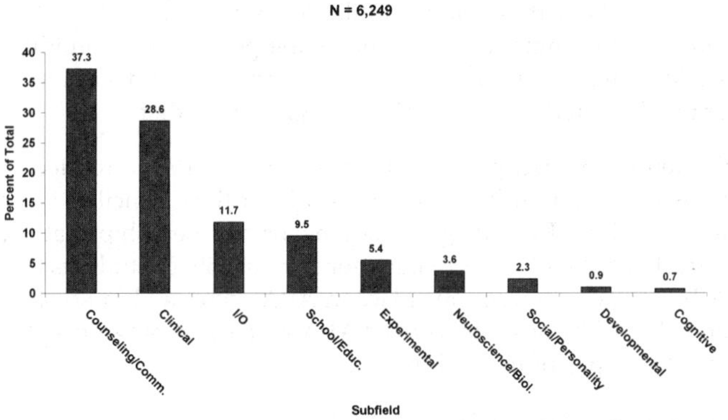

Source: *Graduate Study in Psychology, 2009 Edition* data. Prepared by APA Office of Graduate and Postgraduate Education and Training.

Figure 2. Doctoral Degrees Awarded by Selected Psychology Subfield: 2006–2007

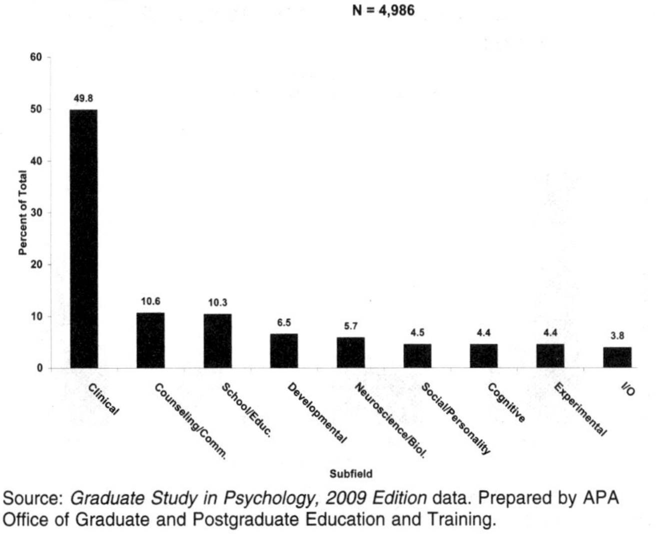

Source: *Graduate Study in Psychology, 2009 Edition* data. Prepared by APA Office of Graduate and Postgraduate Education and Training.

Programs, Degrees, and Employment

Although employment in research, teaching, and human service positions is possible for those with a master's degree in psychology, the doctoral degree is generally considered the entry-level degree in psychology for the independent, licensed practice of psychology as a profession. The doctoral degree is the preferred degree for college and university faculty, and it has long been a requirement for faculty positions in research universities. For specific information about employment outcomes of a program's graduates, review the section entitled "Employment of Department Graduates" in each listing in this publication.

Figures 3 and 4 summarize the types of post-degree outcomes of graduates of master's and doctoral degree programs. About one fourth of those awarded a baccalaureate degree in psychology continue in graduate or professional education in psychology or other fields.

Doctoral programs differ in the type of doctoral degree awarded. The two most common doctoral degrees are the PhD (Doctor of

Figure 3. Employment and Outcomes of Master's Recipients: 2006–2007

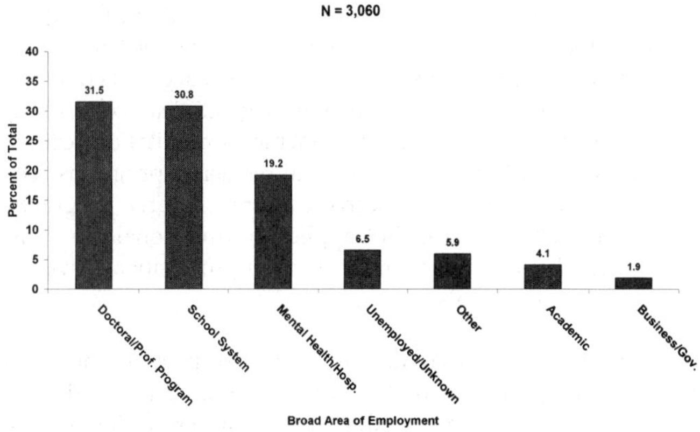

Source: *Graduate Study in Psychology, 2009 Edition* data. Prepared by APA Office of Graduate and Postgraduate Education and Training.

Figure 4. Employment and Outcomes of Doctorate Recipients: 2006–2007

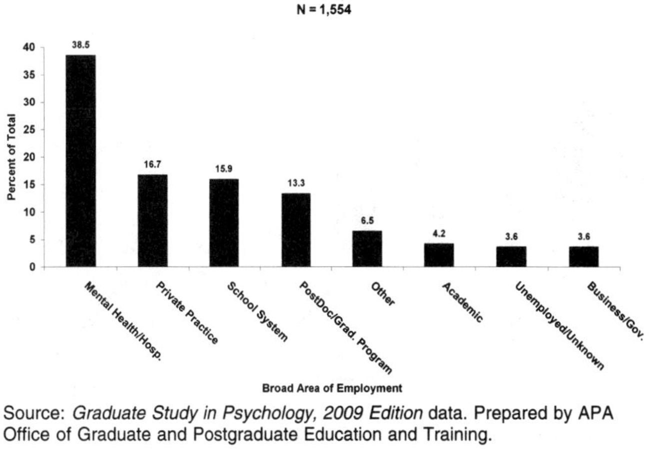

Source: *Graduate Study in Psychology, 2009 Edition* data. Prepared by APA Office of Graduate and Postgraduate Education and Training.

Philosophy) and the PsyD (Doctor of Psychology). Programs in Colleges of Education may offer the EdD (Doctor of Education) degree. The PhD is generally regarded as the research degree. Although many professional psychology programs award the PhD degree, especially those in university academic departments, these programs typically have an emphasis on research training integrated with applied or practice training. The PsyD is a professional degree in psychology (similar to the MD in medicine). Programs awarding the PsyD emphasize preparing their graduates for professional practice with less extensive research training. About 70% of all doctoral degrees in psychology are PhDs; of the degrees awarded in clinical psychology, however, only 50% are PhDs, while the others are PsyDs. Figure 5 gives a profile of initial employment outcomes for PhD and PsyD program graduates. For more information about degrees, employment, and salaries in psychology, visit the APA Center for Workforce Studies Web site (http://research.apa.org).

Accreditation in Professional Psychology

Accreditation in the United States is the mechanism by which students and the public are assured of the general quality of the education provided according to a set of educational and/or professional standards. Accreditation bodies include those that review and accredit at the institutional level and those that accredit at the program or area level. Institutions that confer advanced degrees (i.e., colleges, universities, and professional schools) are ruled eligible for accreditation by regional accrediting bodies. The APA Commission on Accreditation (CoA) accredits at the program level and only reviews doctoral programs in regionally accredited institutions. The CoA accredits doctoral programs in professional psychology (e.g., clinical, counseling, school, and combinations of areas in which accreditation occurs), as well as internship and postdoctoral residency programs. The APA Commission does not accredit master's degree programs. Accreditation by the APA CoA applies to educational programs (i.e., doctoral programs or internships in professional psychology), not to individuals.

Graduation from an accredited institution or program does not guarantee employment or licensure for individuals, although being a graduate of an accredited program may facilitate such achievement and is required in some jurisdictions.

All programs listed in this publication are, at a minimum, situated in regionally accredited institutions. The doctoral programs that are APA-accredited are identified as such. For more information and the most current lists of accredited programs, see the APA Office of Program Consultation and Accreditation Web site (http://www.apa.org/ed/accreditation).

Doctoral Internship Training in Professional Psychology

Doctoral programs that prepare their graduates for the practice of psychology, especially in health service provision, typically require a doctoral internship prior to the awarding of the doctorate. The doctoral internship is often considered the capstone experience in professional psychology education and training and consists of 1 year (or the equivalent) of full-time supervised practice training. The internship is completed in a professional service agency training program that is typically not affiliated with the student's graduate program. Students sometimes relocate geographically to complete their internships. All accredited internship programs select students through a nationwide matching process that has a standardized application and fixed deadlines. Some nonaccredited programs participate as well. To learn more about this process and other valuable information related to internship training, refer to the Association of Psychology Postdoctoral and Internship Centers Web site (APPIC; http://www.appic.org). Internship programs vary widely in terms of the settings and populations served as well as their models of training. Figure 6 shows the percentage of graduate students who were matched to an internship by doctoral program characteristics (accredited program vs. other).

Students obtained placements in either an APA-accredited internship, an internship listed by APPIC or the Council of Directors of School Psychology Programs, or an internship that was not affiliated with any organization. About 65% of students from APA-accredited programs place in APA-accredited internships, and about 35% of students from APA-accredited programs place in other types of internships.

Admission Requirements

Requirements for admission vary from program to program. Psychology programs may require significant undergraduate

Figure 5. Employment and Outcomes of PhD and PsyD Recipients: 2006–2007

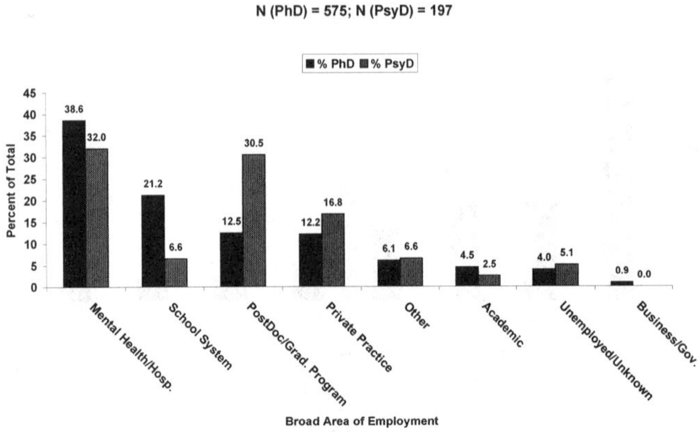

Source: *Graduate Study in Psychology, 2009 Edition* data. Prepared by APA Office of Graduate and Postgraduate Education and Training.

Figure 6. Internship Placement by Doctoral Program Type: 2006–2007

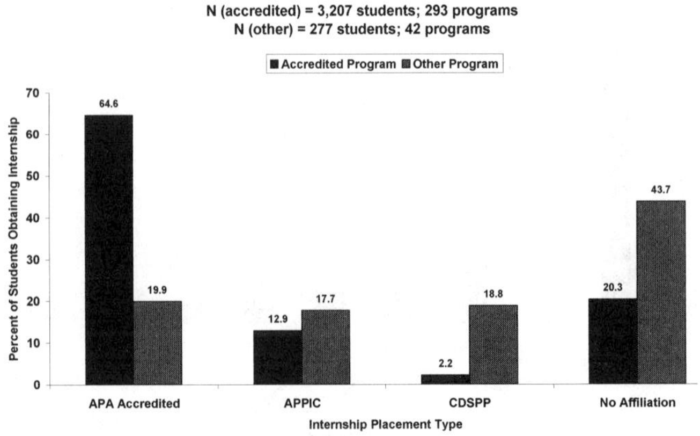

Source: *Graduate Study in Psychology, 2009 Edition* data. Prepared by APA Office of Graduate and Postgraduate Education and Training.

coursework in psychology, often the equivalent of a major or minor, while others do not. Sixty-five percent of recent psychology PhD recipients have also received a bachelor's degree in psychology.

Of the graduate departments listed in this publication that offer master's degrees, 53% require the Graduate Record Examination (GRE) Verbal and Quantitative sections and 8% require the GRE-Subject (Psychology); 4% require the Miller Analogies Test (MAT). Sixty-one percent of the doctoral programs listed require the GRE-Verbal and Quantitative sections, 15% require the GRE-Subject (Psychology), and 1% the MAT. If the programs in which you are interested require these standardized tests, you should take the GRE-V, GRE-Q and GRE-Subject (Psychology), and the MAT in time for the scores to be included with your application materials. The overall median GRE scores reported for applicants admitted to master's degree programs listed in this publication are 510 (GRE-V), 580 (GRE-Q), and 600 (GRE-Subject). The overall median GRE scores reported for applicants admitted to doctoral degree programs listed in this publication are 575 (GRE-V), 640 (GRE-Q), and 650 (GRE-Subject).

Other criteria considered as admission factors may include previous research activities, work experience, clinically related public service, extracurricular activities, letters of recommendation, statement of goals and objectives, an interview, a major or minor in psychology or a record of specific courses in psychology, and undergraduate GPA. Figure 7 shows the ratings of importance of these other admissions criteria by master's and doctoral programs listed in this publication. A rating of 3 indicates that the individual admissions criterion is considered to be of high importance, while a rating of 0 indicates that the admissions criterion plays no importance in a program's admissions process. The three admissions criteria rated as of highest importance for both master's and doctoral programs are undergraduate GPA, letters of recommendation, and a statement of goals and interests. The overall median undergraduate GPA reported for applicants admitted to master's degree programs listed in this publication is 3.37, while that for doctoral programs is 3.55.

The number of graduate school applicants typically exceeds the number of student openings. The number of applications received by a program and the number of students accepted provide a sense of the expected competition when applying to a particular department, program, or school. Figure 8 shows the percent of students admitted in relationship to the number of applications for psychology programs in different areas. For more information, review the section entitled "Student Applications/Admissions" for each of the programs of interest to you listed in this publication.

Application Information

An application to a department or program of study is a very important document. Always confirm (a) the deadline for filing the application, (b) what documents are required, and (c) who should receive the application. Include the admission fee required when filing an application.

Most graduate programs in psychology accept students only for fall admission. However, if you are interested in winter, spring, or summer admission, check the application information listed in this publication for the program to which you are applying. Information about application deadlines in this publication are listed in the section entitled "Application Information".

Time to Degree

Programs should be clear about the average number of years in full-time study (or part-time equivalent) required to complete the degree requirements. On average, graduate students take 7 years from entrance into a graduate program to complete the doctoral degree. Eighty percent of recent psychology PhD recipients also have master's degrees.

Figure 7. Mean Rating of Importance of Various Admissions Criteria: 2006–2007

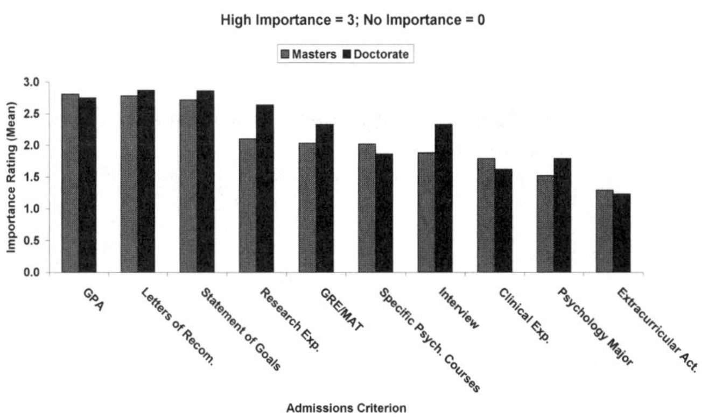

Source: *Graduate Study in Psychology, 2009 Edition* data. Prepared by APA Office of Graduate and Postgraduate Education and Training.

Figure 8. Percent of Applicants Admitted to Graduate Programs by Selected Psychology Subfield: 2006–2007

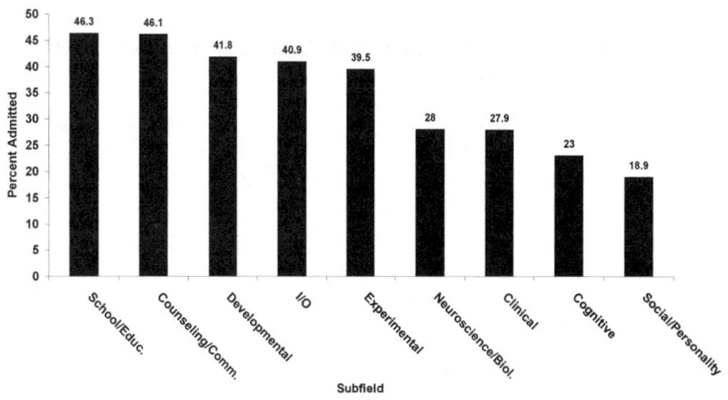

Source: *Graduate Study in Psychology, 2009 Edition* data. Prepared by APA Office of Graduate and Postgraduate Education and Training.

Tuition and Financial Assistance

Graduate education can be expensive. Figure 9 shows the average in-state and out-of-state public university and private university tuition rates for master's and doctoral level programs in psychology.

Many students require loans even when working part time to pay for their graduate education. Indeed, the amount of debt incurred by doctoral graduate students can be significant, as illustrated by Figure 10.

Financial assistance in various forms is available to students. You can apply for a fellowship, scholarship, assistantship, or another type of financial assistance. Many fellowships and scholarships are grants that do not require service to the department or university. For departments and programs listed in this publication, 64% indicate that they offer some form of fellowship or scholarship to 1st-year students, and 62% indicate that they offer some form of fellowship or scholarship to advanced students. Assistantships in teaching and research are also available in many programs. These are forms of employment for services in a department. Teaching assistantships may require teaching a class or assisting a professor by grading papers, acting as a laboratory assistant, or performing other such supporting work. Research assistants ordinarily work on research projects being conducted by program faculty. Among departments and programs reporting for this publication, 81% indicate that they offer teaching and research assistantships to 1st-year students and 87% report offering teaching and research assistantships to advanced students.

Figure 9. Median Tuition by Type of Institution/Residency: 2006–2007

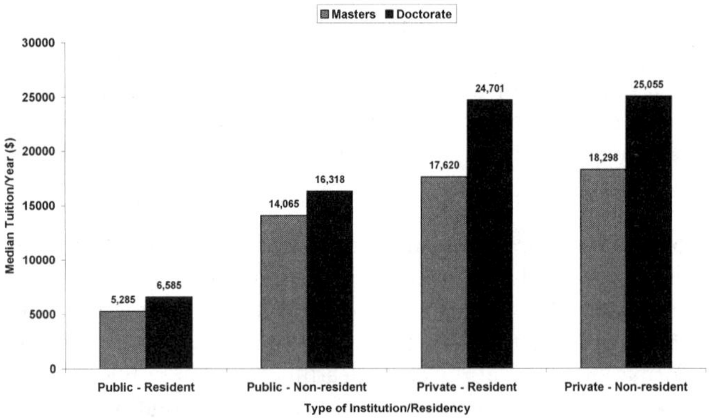

Source: *Graduate Study in Psychology, 2009 Edition* data. Prepared by APA Office of Graduate and Postgraduate Education and Training.

Figure 10. Graduate School Debt for Recent Doctorate Recipients: 2005

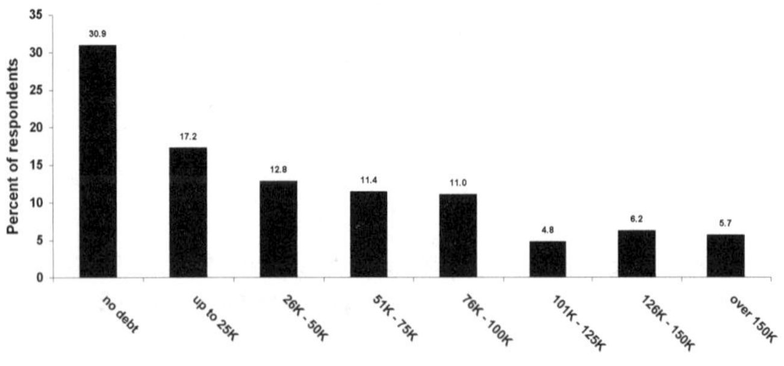

Source: *Graduate Study in Psychology, 2009 Edition* data. Prepared by APA Center for Workforce Studies.

The amount of work required for fellowships, assistantships, and traineeships is expressed in hours per week. Stipends are expressed in terms of total stipend for an academic year of 9 months. Students should inquire, when receiving an offer of financial assistance, as to the amount to be given in terms of tuition remission (not requiring the student to pay tuition) versus a stipend (actual cash in hand).

For information about tuition costs and the types of assistance offered by departments and programs, review the section entitled "Financial Information/Assistance" for the programs of interest listed in this publication. You can review information listed on the APA Education Web site (http://www.apa.org/ed/graduate) for information about scholarships, fellowships, grants, and other funding opportunities.

The summary information presented in this introduction is based on the responses provided by the graduate programs listed in this publication. This information is not exhaustive in that a number of graduate programs in the United States and Canada are not listed in this publication and not all programs listed provide complete information to all questions. For this reason, you should look closely at the information provided by a specific program of interest to you and not rely exclusively on the group averages presented in this introduction.

Catherine Grus, PhD
Clare Porac, PhD
Associate Executive Directors

Joan Freund
Assistant Director
Office of Graduate and Postgraduate Education and Training
APA Education Directorate

Rules for Acceptance of Offers for Admission and Financial Aid

The Council of Graduate Schools has adopted the following policy that provides guidance to students and graduate programs regarding offers of financial support. The policy was adopted by the Council of Graduate Schools in 1965 and reaffirmed in 1992. It was endorsed by the Council of Graduate Departments of Psychology in 1981 and reaffirmed in 2000. Graduate programs and schools currently listed in the book have agreed to honor the policy. The policy reads as follows:

> Acceptance of an offer of financial support (such as graduate scholarship, fellowship, traineeship, or assistantship) for the next academic year by a prospective or enrolled graduate student completes an agreement that both student and graduate school expect to honor. In that context, the conditions affecting such offers and their acceptance must be defined carefully and understood by all parties.

Students are under no obligation to respond to offers of financial support prior to April 15; earlier deadlines for acceptance of such offers violate the intent of this Resolution. In those instances in which the student accepts the offer before April 15 and subsequently desires to withdraw that acceptance, the student may submit in writing a resignation of the appointment at any time through April 15. However, an acceptance given or left in force after April 15 commits the student not to accept another offer without first obtaining a written release from the institution to which a commitment has been made. Similarly, an offer by an institution after April 15 is conditional on presentation by the student of the written release from any previously accepted offer. It is further agreed by the institutions and organizations subscribing to the above Resolution that a copy of this Resolution should accompany every scholarship, fellowship, traineeship, and assistantship offer.

Explanation of Program Listings

The following summarizes the information solicited from each program:

Contact Information

The name of the university or school, address, telephone number, fax number, e-mail, and World Wide Web address are provided. There may be more than one department in an institution that offers degrees in psychology, and if so, each department is listed separately.

Department Information

The year the department was established is provided, including the name of the department chairperson, and the number of full-time and part-time faculty members including information on the number of minority faculty employees.

Programs and Degrees Offered

This heading highlights the program areas in which degrees are offered by the department or school, and includes the type of degree awarded and the number of degrees awarded.

APA Accreditation Status

Whether a department or school has a program accredited in clinical psychology, counseling psychology, school psychology, or combined professional–scientific psychology is noted. Because changes in accreditation status may occur after publication, please contact the APA Office of Program Consultation and Accreditation, or review the Web site (http://www.apa.org/ed).

Student Applications/Admissions

This section includes information about the number of applications received by the individual program areas of departments and schools. Also listed are the number of applicants accepted into the program and the number of openings anticipated in the next year. In addition, the information reflects the median number of years required for a degree and the number of students enrolled who were dismissed or voluntarily withdrew from the program before completing their degree requirements.

Information on standardized test scores and other criteria considered during admission decisions are rated according to their importance.

This section also includes characteristics of students enrolled in the department or psychology program.

Financial Information/Assistance

Tuition figures per year and per academic unit are indicated. Note that some schools and institutions have different fee structures for doctoral and master's students. The words *non-state residents* are used by state universities that charge more for out-of-state residents than students who reside in the state. These fees should be used as rough guidelines and are subject to change.

Teaching assistantships, research assistantships, traineeships, or fellowships and scholarships are reported. The data for each type of assistance are listed for 1st-year and advanced students. The average amount awarded to each student and the average number of hours that must be worked each week are included in the listing. Contact information for financial assistance is also listed.

Information has been added by departments on those programs that require a professional internship of doctoral students prior to graduation. Information is included on the number of students who applied for an internship, the number who obtained an internship, and if the internship was paid or unpaid. In addition, the department was asked to indicate whether the student achieved an APA- or CPA-accredited internship, and if the internship was listed by the Association of Psychology Postdoctoral Internship Centers or by the Council of Directors of School Psychology Programs. Lastly, many departments provided additional information about the types of settings where students were located, the number of hours spent weekly at the internship site, and other information.

Employment of Department Graduates

This section provides information about employment activities of graduates. Data presented by departments or schools include information about master's and doctoral degree graduates, such as enrollment in psychology doctoral programs, and employment in academic positions, business, and government.

Additional Information

This section provides an opportunity for the department or school to present the orientation, objectives, and emphasis of the department or school. Information is also presented about the special facilities or resources offered by the school or institution.

Also included in this section are statements related to personal behavior and religious beliefs statements that are considered a condition for admission and retention with the program. All information in *Graduate Study in Psychology* is self-reported. In the interest of full disclosure to prospective students, therefore, departments, programs, or institutions by which they are governed that have a statement to this effect are requested to cite the statement or provide a Web site or address at which it can be found.

Application Information

This last section provides the addresses, deadlines, and fees for the submission of applications for each department or school.

2009

Graduate Study in Psychology

Alabama, University of

Department of Psychology
College of Arts and Sciences
P.O. Box 870348
Tuscaloosa, AL 35487-0348
Telephone: (205) 348-1919
Fax: (205) 348-8648
E-mail: *mbhubbard@as.ua.edu*
Web: *http://www.psychology.ua.edu*

Department Information:

1937. Chairperson: Kenneth L. Lichstein. Number of faculty: total—full-time 26, part-time 2; women—full-time 10, part-time 1; total—minority—full-time 4; women minority—full-time 4; faculty subject to the Americans With Disabilities Act 1.

Programs and Degrees Offered:

Listed in the following order: Program area, degree type (T if terminal Master's), number awarded 7/06–6/07. Clinical PhD (Doctor of Philosophy) 12, Cognitive PhD (Doctor of Philosophy) 2, Social PhD (Doctor of Philosophy) 0, Developmental PhD (Doctor of Philosophy) 0.

APA Accreditation: Clinical PhD (Doctor of Philosophy).

Student Applications/Admissions:

Student Applications

Clinical PhD (Doctor of Philosophy)—Applications 2007–2008, 189. Total applicants accepted 2007–2008, 17. Number full-time enrolled (new admits only) 2007–2008, 10. Total enrolled 2007–2008 full-time, 72, part-time, 1. Openings 2008–2009, 12. The median number of years required for completion of a degree in 2006–2007 were 6. The number of students enrolled full- and part-time who were dismissed or voluntarily withdrew from this program area in 2007–2008 were 0. *Cognitive PhD (Doctor of Philosophy)*—Applications 2007–2008, 7. Total applicants accepted 2007–2008, 2. Number full-time enrolled (new admits only) 2007–2008, 2. Openings 2008–2009, 2. The median number of years required for completion of a degree in 2006–2007 were 6. The number of students enrolled full- and part-time who were dismissed or voluntarily withdrew from this program area in 2007–2008 were 1. *Social PhD (Doctor of Philosophy)*—Applications 2007–2008, 22. Total applicants accepted 2007–2008, 2. Number full-time enrolled (new admits only) 2007–2008, 2. Number part-time enrolled (new admits only) 2007–2008, 0. Openings 2008–2009, 2. The number of students enrolled full- and part-time who were dismissed or voluntarily withdrew from this program area in 2007–2008 were 0. *Developmental PhD (Doctor of Philosophy)*—Applications 2007–2008, 13. Total applicants accepted 2007–2008, 2. Number full-time enrolled (new admits only) 2007–2008, 2. Number part-time enrolled (new admits only) 2007–2008, 0. Openings 2008–2009, 2. The number of students enrolled full- and part-time who were dismissed or voluntarily withdrew from this program area in 2007–2008 were 0.

Admissions Requirements:

Scores: Entries appear in this order: required test or GPA, minimum score (if required), median score of students entering in 2007–2008. Doctoral Programs: GRE-V 500, 590; GRE-Q 500, 650; overall undergraduate GPA 3.0, 3.6. GRE subject is preferred for the clinical program—500 minimum score.

Other Criteria: (importance of criteria rated low, medium, or high): GRE/MAT scores—high, research experience—high, work experience—low, extracurricular activity—low, clinically related public service—low, GPA—medium, letters of recommendation—high, interview—medium, statement of goals and objectives—high. Interview not typical for cognitive program. For additional information on admission requirements, go to http://psychology.ua.edu/admission.html.

Student Characteristics: The following represents characteristics of students in 2007–2008 in all graduate psychology programs in the department: Female—full-time 76, part-time 1; Male—full-time 19, part-time 0; African American/Black—full-time 8, part-time 0; Hispanic/Latino(a)—full-time 6, part-time 0; Asian/Pacific Islander—full-time 4, part-time 0; American Indian/Alaska Native—full-time 1, part-time 0; Caucasian/White—full-time 76, part-time 1; Multi-ethnic—full-time 0, part-time 0; students subject to the Americans With Disabilities Act—full-time 0, part-time 0; Unknown ethnicity—full-time 0, part-time 0; International students who hold an F-1 or J-1 Visa—full-time 4, part-time 0.

Financial Information/Assistance:

Tuition for Full-Time Study: *Doctoral:* State residents: per academic year $5,700; Nonstate residents: per academic year $16,518. Tuition is subject to change.

Financial Assistance:

First-Year Students: Teaching assistantships available for first year. Average amount paid per academic year: $11,142. Average number of hours worked per week: 20. Tuition remission given: full. Research assistantships available for first year. Average amount paid per academic year: $11,142. Average number of hours worked per week: 20. Tuition remission given: full. Fellowships and scholarships available for first year. Average amount paid per academic year: $16,000. Tuition remission given: full.

Advanced Students: Teaching assistantships available for advanced students. Average amount paid per academic year: $11,142. Average number of hours worked per week: 20. Tuition remission given: full. Research assistantships available for advanced students. Average amount paid per academic year: $11,142. Average number of hours worked per week: 20. Tuition remission given: full. Traineeships available for advanced students. Average amount paid per academic year: $11,142. Average number of hours worked per week: 20. Tuition remission given: full. Fellowships and scholarships available for advanced students. Average amount paid per academic year: $16,000. Tuition remission given: full.

Additional Information: Of all students currently enrolled full time, 90% benefited from one or more of the listed financial assistance programs.

Internships/Practica: Doctoral Degree (PhD clinical): For those doctoral students for whom a professional internship was required in this program prior to graduation, (10) students applied for an internship in 2006–2007, with (9) students obtaining an internship. Of those students who obtained an internship, (9) were paid internships. Of those students who obtained an internship, (9) students placed in APA/CPA-accredited internships, (0) students placed in internships not APA/CPA-accredited but listed with the Association of Psychology Postdoctoral and Internship Centers (APPIC), (0) students placed in internships conforming to guidelines of the Council of Directors of School Psychology Programs (CDSPP), (0) students placed in internships that were not APA/CPA-accredited, APPIC or CDSPP listed. There are a number of practica available to graduate students. Most doctoral students take PY695/696, a teaching internship, in which the student teaches an introductory psychology class under the supervision of a faculty member. Two semesters of basic psychotherapy practicum are required of every doctoral student in clinical psychology. In this practicum, students conduct psychotherapy with 4 to 6 clients in the Department's Psychological Clinic. Students complete approximately 100 hours of direct client contact to fulfill this requirement. After basic psychotherapy practicum, doctoral clinical psychology students take either one or two (depending on specialty area) advanced practica in their area of specialization. Many of these practica are housed in community service agencies (e.g., state psychiatric hospital, community mental health center, University operated treatment center for disturbed children). In addition to these formal practica, most doctoral students in the clinical program are financially supported at some time during their graduate school years through field placements in various community agencies. These students are supervised by either licensed psychologists employed by these agencies or by Department of Psychology clinical faculty. In addition to the intervention practica discussed above, all clinical doctoral students must take two of the three graduate psychological assessment courses offered. These courses have a significant practicum component, requiring approximately five administrations of commonly used psychological assessment instruments with Psychological Clinic clients.

Housing and Day Care: On-campus housing is available. See the following Web site for more information: http://www.catalogs.ua.edu/graduate/10440.html. On-campus day care facilities are available. See the following Web site for more information: http://www.ches.ua.edu/backup/children.

Employment of Department Graduates:

Master's Degree Graduates: Of those who graduated in the academic year 2006–2007, the following categories and numbers represent the postgraduate activities and employment of master's degree graduates: Enrolled in a postdoctoral residency/fellowship (n/a), employed in independent practice (n/a), total from the above (master's) (0).

Doctoral Degree Graduates: Of those who graduated in the academic year 2006–2007, the following categories and numbers represent the postgraduate activities and employment of doctoral degree graduates: Enrolled in a psychology doctoral program (n/a), enrolled in a postdoctoral residency/fellowship (1), employed in an academic position at a university (2), employed in other positions at a higher education institution (1), employed in business or industry (1), employed in government agency (6), employed in a community mental health/counseling center (1), not seeking employment (1), do not know (1), total from the above (doctoral) (14).

Additional Information:

Orientation, Objectives, and Emphasis of Department: The University of Alabama doctoral program in psychology was founded in 1957 and trains students in clinical and experimental psychology. The clinical program has been continually accredited by the American Psychological Association since 1959. The department trains scientists and scientist–practitioners for a variety of roles: research, teaching, and applied practice. Both the clinical and the experimental programs strongly emphasize furthering psychology as a science. The clinical program has specialty areas in psychology-law, clinical-child, gerontology, and health and the experimental program has specialty areas in cognitive, social, and developmental. The social and developmental training areas involve exciting collaborations with other units on campus. The doctoral programs emphasize core knowledge in the social, cognitive, developmental, and biological aspects of behavior as well as methodological/statistical foundations. All students take additional courses designed to prepare them with the necessary knowledge and skills in their chosen specialty area. A further objective of the department is to promote independent scholarship and professional development. Coursework is supplemented by the active collaboration of faculty and students in ongoing research projects and clinical activities. The department maintains access to a wide range of settings in which students can refine their research and applied skills.

Special Facilities or Resources: The department is housed in a four-story building that it shares with the Department of Mathematics. It is directly connected to the department's Psychological Clinic and the University's Seebeck Computer Center. Facilities include faculty offices, student offices, classroom and seminar space, and research laboratories. Graduate students have access to microcomputers for research and word processing and videotaping capabilities for instruction and training. A major resource is the Psychological Clinic, which provides psychological assessment, referral, treatment planning, and direct intervention for a variety of clinical populations. The department's Child and Family Research Clinic serves as a specialized training and research laboratory. Both clinics include observation facilities. Also affiliated with the department is the brand new Child Development Research Center, which has research, office, and training space, and runs a state-of-the-art preschool. Other affiliations on campus include the Center for Mental Health and Aging, the Institute for Social Science Research, the Brewer-Porch Childrens Center, the Student Counseling Center, and the University Medical Center. In the community, the department maintains research and clinical relationships with DCH Regional Medical Center, VA Medical Center, Bryce Hospital, Family Counseling Services, city and county school systems, Indian Rivers Mental Health Center, Partlow Developmental Center, and the Taylor Hardin Forensic Medical Facility.

Information for Students With Physical Disabilities: See the following Web site for more information: http://www.ods.ua.edu.

Application Information:

Send to Office of the Graduate School, University of Alabama, Box 870118, Tuscaloosa, AL 35487-0118. Application available online. URL of online application: http://www.graduate.ua.edu/application/

index.htm. Students are admitted in the Fall, application deadline December 1. Deadline for the applications to the clinical program is December 1; January 15 is the deadline for the cognitive, social, and developmental programs. *Fee:* $30. Application fee is waived for McNair Scholars.

Alabama, University of, at Birmingham

Department of Psychology
School of Social and Behavioral Sciences
415 Campbell Hall
Birmingham, AL 35294-1170
Telephone: (205) 934-3850
Fax: (205) 975-6110
E-mail: *cmcfarla@uab.edu*
Web: *http://www.psy.uab.edu*

Department Information:

1969. Chairperson: Carl E. McFarland, Jr. Number of faculty: total—full-time 29, part-time 58; women—full-time 9, part-time 16; total—minority—full-time 5, part-time 5; women minority—full-time 1, part-time 2.

Programs and Degrees Offered:

Listed in the following order: Program area, degree type (T if terminal Master's), number awarded 7/06–6/07. Behavioral Neuroscience PhD (Doctor of Philosophy) 1, Developmental PhD (Doctor of Philosophy) 3, Medical/Clinical PhD (Doctor of Philosophy) 7.

APA Accreditation: Clinical PhD (Doctor of Philosophy).

Student Applications/Admissions:

Student Applications

Behavioral Neuroscience PhD (Doctor of Philosophy)—Applications 2007–2008, 15. Total applicants accepted 2007–2008, 2. Number full-time enrolled (new admits only) 2007–2008, 2. Openings 2008–2009, 2. The median number of years required for completion of a degree in 2006–2007 were 5. The number of students enrolled full- and part-time who were dismissed or voluntarily withdrew from this program area in 2007–2008 were 0. *Developmental PhD (Doctor of Philosophy)*—Applications 2007–2008, 17. Total applicants accepted 2007–2008, 3. Number full-time enrolled (new admits only) 2007–2008, 3. Number part-time enrolled (new admits only) 2007–2008, 0. Openings 2008–2009, 4. The median number of years required for completion of a degree in 2006–2007 were 5. The number of students enrolled full- and part-time who were dismissed or voluntarily withdrew from this program area in 2007–2008 were 0. *Medical/Clinical PhD (Doctor of Philosophy)*—Applications 2007–2008, 57. Total applicants accepted 2007–2008, 7. Number full-time enrolled (new admits only) 2007–2008, 7. Number part-time enrolled (new admits only) 2007–2008, 0. Openings 2008–2009, 7. The median number of years required for completion of a degree in 2006–2007 were 6. The number of students enrolled full- and part-time who were dismissed or voluntarily withdrew from this program area in 2007–2008 were 0.

Admissions Requirements:

Scores: Entries appear in this order: required test or GPA, minimum score (if required), median score of students entering in 2007–2008. Doctoral Programs: GRE-V no minimum stated, 580; GRE-Q no minimum stated, 650; GRE-Subject (Psychology) no minimum stated; overall undergraduate GPA 3.00, 3.57; last 2 years GPA 3.20, 3.82.

Other Criteria: (importance of criteria rated low, medium, or high): GRE/MAT scores—high, research experience—high, work experience—low, extracurricular activity—low, clinically related public service—medium, GPA—high, letters of recommendation—medium, interview—medium, statement of goals and objectives—medium. For additional information on admission requirements, go to http://www.psy.uab.edu.

Student Characteristics: The following represents characteristics of students in 2007–2008 in all graduate psychology programs in the department: Female—full-time 51, part-time 0; Male—full-time 15, part-time 0; African American/Black—full-time 11, part-time 0; Hispanic/Latino(a)—full-time 1, part-time 0; Asian/Pacific Islander—full-time 2, part-time 0; American Indian/Alaska Native—full-time 0, part-time 0; Caucasian/White—full-time 52, part-time 0; Multi-ethnic—full-time 0, part-time 0; students subject to the Americans With Disabilities Act—full-time 2, part-time 0; Unknown ethnicity—full-time 0, part-time 0.

Financial Information/Assistance:

Tuition for Full-Time Study: *Doctoral:* State residents: per academic year $5,824, $182 per credit hour; Nonstate residents: per academic year $14,560, $455 per credit hour. Tuition is subject to change. See the following Web site for updates and changes in tuition costs: http://www.main.uab.edu.

Financial Assistance:

First-Year Students: Fellowships and scholarships available for first year. Average amount paid per academic year: $16,590. Average number of hours worked per week: 15. Apply by February 1. Tuition remission given: full.

Advanced Students: Teaching assistantships available for advanced students. Average amount paid per academic year: $18,500. Average number of hours worked per week: 20. Tuition remission given: partial. Research assistantships available for advanced students. Average amount paid per academic year: $17,500. Average number of hours worked per week: 20. Tuition remission given: partial. Traineeships available for advanced students. Average amount paid per academic year: $20,770. Average number of hours worked per week: 20. Tuition remission given: partial. Fellowships and scholarships available for advanced students. Average amount paid per academic year: $17,500. Average number of hours worked per week: 20. Tuition remission given: partial.

Additional Information: Of all students currently enrolled full time, 100% benefited from one or more of the listed financial assistance programs. Application and information available online at http://www.psy.uab.edu.

Internships/Practica: Doctoral Degree (PhD medical/clinical): For those doctoral students for whom a professional internship was required in this program prior to graduation, (4) students applied for an internship in 2006–2007, with (4) students obtaining an internship. Of those students who obtained an internship, (4) were paid internships. Of those students who obtained an internship, (4) students placed in APA/CPA-accredited internships, (0) students placed in internships not APA/CPA-accredited but listed with the Association of Psychology Postdoctoral and Internship Centers (APPIC), (0) students placed in internships conforming to guidelines of the Council of Directors of School Psychology Programs (CDSPP), (0) students placed in internships that were not APA/CPA-accredited, APPIC or CDSPP listed. Students in the Medical/Clinical Psychology Program have opportunities for clinical/research practicas at multiple sites across the UAB campus as well as off-campus sites, including Departments of Psychology, Anesthesiology, Neurology, Pediatrics, Psychiatry, Rehabilitation Medicine, Center for Aging, Sparks Center for Developmental and Learning Disorders, VA Medical Center, Hill Crest Hospital, and several private practices. For additional information on education and training outcomes for our programs, see the following Web site: http://www.students.uab.edu/services/show/.asp?durki=40136.

Housing and Day Care: On-campus housing is available. UAB Student Housing, 1604 9th Avenue South, DNMH 101G, Birmingham, AL 35294, Phone: (205) 934-2092. On-campus day care facilities are available. UAB Child Care Center, 1113 15th Street South, Birmingham, AL 35294-4553, Phone: (205) 934-7353.

Employment of Department Graduates:

Master's Degree Graduates: Of those who graduated in the academic year 2006–2007, the following categories and numbers represent the postgraduate activities and employment of master's degree graduates: Enrolled in a postdoctoral residency/fellowship (n/a), employed in independent practice (n/a), total from the above (master's) (0).

Doctoral Degree Graduates: Of those who graduated in the academic year 2006–2007, the following categories and numbers represent the postgraduate activities and employment of doctoral degree graduates: Enrolled in a psychology doctoral program (n/a), enrolled in a postdoctoral residency/fellowship (6), employed in a hospital/medical center (1), total from the above (doctoral) (7).

Additional Information:

Orientation, Objectives, and Emphasis of Department: The Department offers three doctoral programs: Clinical/Medical Psychology, Behavioral Neuroscience, and Developmental Psychology. Each program promotes rigorous scientific training for students pursuing basic or applied research careers. The programs are designed to produce scholars who will engage in independent research, practice, and teaching. Medical Psychology is a specialty within clinical psychology that focuses on psychological factors in health care. It is cosponsored by the UAB School of Medicine. The Behavioral Neuroscience Program provides individualized, interdisciplinary training for research on the biological bases of behavior. The Developmental Program trains students to conduct research to discover and apply basic principles of developmental psychology across the lifespan in an interdisciplinary context. Students are exposed to the issues of development in its natural and social contexts, as well as in laboratories. Faculty research interests include health psychology, substance abuse, clinical neuropsychology, psychopharmacology, human psychophysiology, brain imaging, sensation and perception, spinal cord injury, control of movement, aging, mental retardation/developmental disabilities, motivation, pediatric psychology, social ecology, cognitive development, developmental psychopathology, psychosocial influences on cancer, pain, and clinical outcomes evaluation.

Special Facilities or Resources: The University of Alabama at Birmingham is a comprehensive, urban research university, recently ranked by U.S. News and World Report as the number one up-and-coming university in the country. The UAB Psychology Department, in the School of Social and Behavioral Sciences, ranks among the top 20 psychology departments in the U.S. in federal/research funding. The UAB campus encompasses a 75-block area on Birmingham's Southside, offering all of the advantages of a university within a highly supportive city. Resources are available from the School of Medicine, Department of Physiological Optics, School of Public Health, Civitan International Research Center, Sparks Center for Developmental and Learning Disorders, Center for Aging, Department of Pediatrics, Department of Psychiatry and Behavioral Neurobiology, Neurobiology Research Center, School of Education, School of Nursing, Department of Computer and Information Sciences, Department of Biocommunications, University Hospital, a psychiatric hospital, and Children's Hospital.

Information for Students With Physical Disabilities: See the following Web site for more information: http://www.dss@uab.edu.

Application Information:

Send to The Graduate School, University of Alabama at Birmingham, Birmingham, AL 35294. Application available online. URL of online application: http://www.main.uab.edu/show.asp?durki=24740. Students are admitted in the Fall, application deadline January 15. Medical/Clinical—November 30. *Fee:* $35. Waived for U.S. citizens.

Alabama, University of, at Huntsville

Department of Psychology
Liberal Arts
Morton Hall 335, University of Alabama in Huntsville
Huntsville, AL 35899
Telephone: (256) 824-6191
Fax: (256) 824-6949
E-mail: *carpens@email.uah.edu*
Web: *http://www.uah.edu/colleges/liberal/psychology/*

Department Information:

1968. Chairperson: Sandra Carpenter. Number of faculty: total—full-time 5, part-time 2; women—full-time 2, part-time 1; total—minority—full-time 1; women minority—full-time 1.

Programs and Degrees Offered:

Listed in the following order: Program area, degree type (T if terminal Master's), number awarded 7/06–6/07. Experimental–General MA/MS (Master of Arts/Science) (T) 4.

Student Applications/Admissions:

Student Applications

Experimental–General MA/MS (Master of Arts/Science)—Applications 2007–2008, 9. Total applicants accepted 2007–2008, 6. Number full-time enrolled (new admits only) 2007–2008, 3. Number part-time enrolled (new admits only) 2007–

2008, 3. Total enrolled 2007–2008 full-time, 5, part-time, 6. Openings 2008–2009, 10. The median number of years required for completion of a degree in 2006–2007 were 2. The number of students enrolled full- and part-time who were dismissed or voluntarily withdrew from this program area in 2007–2008 were 0.

Admissions Requirements:

Scores: Entries appear in this order: required test or GPA, minimum score (if required), median score of students entering in 2007–2008. Master's Programs: GRE-V no minimum stated, 500; GRE-Q no minimum stated, 500; overall undergraduate GPA 3.25, 3.5.

Other Criteria: (importance of criteria rated low, medium, or high): GRE/MAT scores—high, research experience—high, work experience—low, clinically related public service—low, GPA—high, letters of recommendation—high, interview—low, statement of goals and objectives—high, empirical paper—high, undergraduate major in psychology—low, specific undergraduate psychology courses taken—high.

Student Characteristics: The following represents characteristics of students in 2007–2008 in all graduate psychology programs in the department: Female—full-time 3, part-time 6; Male—full-time 2, part-time 0; African American/Black—full-time 0, part-time 0; Hispanic/Latino(a)—full-time 0, part-time 1; Asian/Pacific Islander—full-time 0, part-time 0; American Indian/Alaska Native—full-time 0, part-time 0; Caucasian/White—full-time 5, part-time 5; Multi-ethnic—full-time 0, part-time 0; students subject to the Americans With Disabilities Act—full-time 0, part-time 0; Unknown ethnicity—full-time 0, part-time 0.

Financial Information/Assistance:

Tuition for Full-Time Study: *Master's:* State residents: per academic year $5,132, $285 per credit hour; Nonstate residents: per academic year $10,532, $585 per credit hour. Tuition is subject to change.

Financial Assistance:

First-Year Students: Fellowships and scholarships available for first year. Average number of hours worked per week: 0. Apply by June 1. Tuition remission given: full.

Advanced Students: Teaching assistantships available for advanced students. Average amount paid per academic year: $8,400. Average number of hours worked per week: 20. Apply by June 1. Tuition remission given: full. Research assistantships available for advanced students. Average amount paid per academic year: $8,400. Average number of hours worked per week: 20. Apply by June 1. Tuition remission given: partial. Traineeships available for advanced students. Average amount paid per academic year: $4,000. Average number of hours worked per week: 10. Apply by June 1. Fellowships and scholarships available for advanced students. Average amount paid per academic year: $4,000. Average number of hours worked per week: 0. Apply by June 1. Tuition remission given: full and partial.

Additional Information: Of all students currently enrolled full time, 75% benefited from one or more of the listed financial assistance programs.

Internships/Practica: Internships in academic student advising and in psychological test administration may be available for some students.

Housing and Day Care: On-campus housing is available. On-campus day care facilities are available.

Employment of Department Graduates:

Master's Degree Graduates: Of those who graduated in the academic year 2006–2007, the following categories and numbers represent the postgraduate activities and employment of master's degree graduates: Enrolled in a psychology doctoral program (2), enrolled in a postdoctoral residency/fellowship (n/a), employed in independent practice (n/a), employed in an academic position at a university (1), employed in other positions at a higher education institution (1), total from the above (master's) (4).

Doctoral Degree Graduates: Of those who graduated in the academic year 2006–2007, the following categories and numbers represent the postgraduate activities and employment of doctoral degree graduates: Enrolled in a psychology doctoral program (n/a), total from the above (doctoral) (0).

Additional Information:

Orientation, Objectives, and Emphasis of Department: The content of our program is directed toward the study of psychology as an intellectual and scientific pursuit, as contrasted with training directly applicable to counselor or psychologist licensure and practice. Specialization areas include applied psychology, social/personality, cognitive, developmental and biopsychological psychology. The program is designed for a small number of students who will work in close interaction with individual faculty members and with each other. Although there are a few structured courses that are required of all students, a substantial portion of the students program focuses on individual readings, research, and thesis.

Special Facilities or Resources: Access to research facilities at NASA's-Marshall Space Flight Center is available via an existing Space Act Agreement. Students also have access to archives at the National Children's Advocacy Center. Some students work collaboratively with the scientists in the Center for Simulation and Modeling on the UAH campus.

Application Information:

Send to Department Chair, Department of Psychology, Morton Hall 335, University of Alabama in Huntsville, Huntsville, AL 35899. Application available online. URL of online application: http://www.uah.edu/gradschool/forms.php. Students are admitted in the Fall, application deadline July 1; Spring, application deadline December 1; Summer, application deadline May 1; Programs have rolling admissions. *Fee:* $35.

Auburn University

Counselor Education, Counseling Psychology, and School Psychology
College of Education
2084 Haley Center
Auburn University, AL 36849-5222
Telephone: (334) 844-5160
Fax: (334) 844-2860
E-mail: *pipesrb@auburn.edu*
Web: *http://www.auburn.edu/coun*

Department Information:

1965. Professor and Head of Department: Holly A. Stadler. Number of faculty: total—full-time 9, part-time 1; women—full-time 5, part-time 1; women minority—full-time 2.

Programs and Degrees Offered:

Listed in the following order: Program area, degree type (T if terminal Master's), number awarded 7/06–6/07. School Psychology EdS/MEd (School Psychology) 0, Counseling Psychology PhD (Doctor of Philosophy) 5, Counselor Education PhD (Doctor of Philosophy) 6, School Psychology PhD (Doctor of Philosophy) 1, Community Agency Counseling Other 11, School Counseling Other 5.

APA Accreditation: Counseling PhD (Doctor of Philosophy).

Student Applications/Admissions:

Student Applications

School Psychology EdS/MEd (School Psychology)—Applications 2007–2008, 9. Total applicants accepted 2007–2008, 5. Number full-time enrolled (new admits only) 2007–2008, 2. Number part-time enrolled (new admits only) 2007–2008, 0. Openings 2008–2009, 5. The median number of years required for completion of a degree in 2006–2007 were 3. The number of students enrolled full- and part-time who were dismissed or voluntarily withdrew from this program area in 2007–2008 were 0. *Counseling Psychology PhD (Doctor of Philosophy)*—Applications 2007–2008, 84. Total applicants accepted 2007–2008, 6. Number full-time enrolled (new admits only) 2007–2008, 5. Number part-time enrolled (new admits only) 2007–2008, 0. Openings 2008–2009, 5. The median number of years required for completion of a degree in 2006–2007 were 5. The number of students enrolled full- and part-time who were dismissed or voluntarily withdrew from this program area in 2007–2008 were 1. *Counselor Education PhD (Doctor of Philosophy)*—Applications 2007–2008, 15. Total applicants accepted 2007–2008, 5. Number full-time enrolled (new admits only) 2007–2008, 5. Number part-time enrolled (new admits only) 2007–2008, 0. Openings 2008–2009, 6. The median number of years required for completion of a degree in 2006–2007 were 4. The number of students enrolled full- and part-time who were dismissed or voluntarily withdrew from this program area in 2007–2008 were 2. *School Psychology PhD (Doctor of Philosophy)*—Applications 2007–2008, 11. Total applicants accepted 2007–2008, 6. Number full-time enrolled (new admits only) 2007–2008, 3. Number part-time enrolled (new admits only) 2007–2008, 0. Total enrolled 2007–2008 full-time, 12. Openings 2008–2009, 5. The median number of years required for completion of a degree in 2006–2007 were 5. The number of students enrolled full- and part-time who were dismissed or voluntarily withdrew from this program area in 2007–2008 were 1. *Community Agency Counseling Other*—Applications 2007–2008, 41. Total applicants accepted 2007–2008, 31. Number full-time enrolled (new admits only) 2007–2008, 17. Total enrolled 2007–2008 full-time, 35. Openings 2008–2009, 25. The median number of years required for completion of a degree in 2006–2007 were 2. The number of students enrolled full- and part-time who were dismissed or voluntarily withdrew from this program area in 2007–2008 were 1. *School Counseling Other*—Applications 2007–2008, 12. Total applicants accepted 2007–2008, 0. Number full-time enrolled (new admits only) 2007–2008, 0. Number part-time enrolled (new admits only) 2007–2008, 0. Openings 2008–2009, 15. The median number of years required for completion of a degree in 2006–2007 were 2. The number of students enrolled full- and part-time who were dismissed or voluntarily withdrew from this program area in 2007–2008 were 0.

Admissions Requirements:

Scores: Entries appear in this order: required test or GPA, minimum score (if required), median score of students entering in 2007–2008. Master's Programs: GRE-V no minimum stated; GRE-Q no minimum stated; overall undergraduate GPA no minimum stated; last 2 years GPA no minimum stated; psychology GPA no minimum stated. Contact Director of particular Master's program in which you are interested for more specific data. Doctoral Programs: GRE-V no minimum stated; GRE-Q no minimum stated; overall undergraduate GPA no minimum stated; last 2 years GPA no minimum stated; psychology GPA no minimum stated. This information in item 12 is for the PhD program in Counseling Psychology—last 2 years of admissions.

Other Criteria: (importance of criteria rated low, medium, or high): GRE/MAT scores—medium, research experience—medium, work experience—medium, extracurricular activity—low, clinically related public service—low, GPA—high, letters of recommendation—high, interview—high, statement of goals and objectives—high, clinical experience—medium, This pattern of criteria is generally the same across program areas. For additional information on admission requirements, go to http://www.auburn.edu/coun.

Student Characteristics: The following represents characteristics of students in 2007–2008 in all graduate psychology programs in the department: Female—full-time 104, part-time 0; Male—full-time 12, part-time 0; African American/Black—full-time 12, part-time 0; Hispanic/Latino(a)—full-time 1, part-time 0; Asian/Pacific Islander—full-time 1, part-time 0; American Indian/Alaska Native—full-time 1, part-time 0; Caucasian/White—full-time 100, part-time 0; Multi-ethnic—full-time 1, part-time 0; students subject to the Americans With Disabilities Act—full-time 0, part-time 0; Unknown ethnicity—full-time 0, part-time 0; International students who hold an F-1 or J-1 Visa—full-time 7, part-time 0.

Financial Information/Assistance:

Tuition for Full-Time Study: *Master's:* State residents: per academic year $5,786; Nonstate residents: per academic year $16,286. *Doctoral:* State residents: per academic year $5,786; Nonstate residents: per academic year $16,286. Tuition is subject to change. See the following Web site for updates and changes in tuition costs: http://www,auburn.edu/coun. Doctoral students on assistantships typically receive full tuition remission-though not guaranteed.

Financial Assistance:

First-Year Students: Teaching assistantships available for first year. Average amount paid per academic year: $5,500. Average number of hours worked per week: 10. Apply by April 1. Tuition remission given: full. Research assistantships available for first year. Average amount paid per academic year: $5,500. Average number of hours worked per week: 10. Apply by April 1. Tuition remission given: full. Fellowships and scholarships available for first year. Average amount paid per academic year: $15,000. Average number of hours worked per week: 10. Apply by varies. Tuition remission given: full.

Advanced Students: Teaching assistantships available for advanced students. Average amount paid per academic year: $5,500. Average number of hours worked per week: 10. Apply by April 1. Tuition remission given: full. Research assistantships available for advanced students. Average amount paid per academic year: $5,500. Average number of hours worked per week: 10. Apply by April 1. Tuition remission given: full. Fellowships and scholarships available for advanced students. Average amount paid per academic year: $15,000. Average number of hours worked per week: 10. Apply by varies. Tuition remission given: full.

Additional Information: Of all students currently enrolled full time, 30% benefited from one or more of the listed financial assistance programs. Application and information available online at http://www.auburn.edu/coun.

Internships/Practica: Doctoral Degree (PhD Counseling Psychology): For those doctoral students for whom a professional internship was required in this program prior to graduation, (5) students applied for an internship in 2006–2007, with (5) students obtaining an internship. Of those students who obtained an internship, (5) were paid internships. Of those students who obtained an internship, (4) students placed in APA/CPA-accredited internships, (1) students placed in internships not APA/CPA accredited, but listed with the Association of Psychology Postdoctoral and Internship Centers (APPIC), (0) students placed in internships conforming to guidelines of the Council of Directors of School Psychology Programs (CDSPP), (0) students placed in internships that were not APA/CPA-accredited, APPIC or CDSPP listed. Doctoral Degree (PhD School Psychology): For those doctoral students for whom a professional internship was required in this program prior to graduation, (3) students applied for an internship in 2006–2007, with (3) students obtaining an internship. Of those students who obtained an internship, (3) were paid internships. Of those students who obtained an internship, (0) students placed in APA/CPA-accredited internships, (0) students placed in internships not APA/CPA-accredited, but listed with the Association of Psychology Postdoctoral and Internship Centers (APPIC), (3) students placed in internships conforming to guidelines of the Council of Directors of School Psychology Programs (CDSPP), (0) students placed in internships that were not APA/CPA-accredited, APPIC or CDSPP listed. University counseling centers; community mental health centers; community counseling agencies.

Housing and Day Care: On-campus housing is available. Typically the only graduate students living in university housing are those who work for university housing. These positions include both financial remuneration as well as free housing. Contact Departmental Administrative Assistant or University Housing. No on-campus day care facilities are available.

Employment of Department Graduates:

Master's Degree Graduates: Of those who graduated in the academic year 2006–2007, the following categories and numbers represent the postgraduate activities and employment of master's degree graduates: Enrolled in a postdoctoral residency/fellowship (n/a), employed in independent practice (n/a), total from the above (master's) (0).

Doctoral Degree Graduates: Of those who graduated in the academic year 2006–2007, the following categories and numbers represent the postgraduate activities and employment of doctoral degree graduates: Enrolled in a psychology doctoral program (n/a), employed in other positions at a higher education institution (1), employed in government agency (1), employed in a community mental health/counseling center (1), employed in a hospital/medical center (1), not seeking employment (1), total from the above (doctoral) (5).

Additional Information:

Orientation, Objectives, and Emphasis of Department: The Department offers graduate education programs for counseling psychologists, school psychologists, counselors, and counselor educators. Graduates will develop the competencies to address psychological, social, and environmental barriers to educational achievement and personal development. In this process students will engage in rigorous and challenging educational experiences in order to fashion their own unique contributions to society. The department values teaching, research, and outreach that contributes to the missions of the College and University. Further, the department seeks to foster a culture in which individual creativity and scholarship is reinforced and nurtured. Diversity is considered a core value in all that we do.

Special Facilities or Resources: Interdisciplinary community. University partnership serving underserved, rural minority communities devoted to education, research, and service. We also partner with University Student Affairs, Housing, and the Athletic Department.

Information for Students With Physical Disabilities: See the following Web site for more information: http://www.auburn.edu/academic/disabilities.

Application Information:

Send to (Program Name), Counselor Education, Counseling Psychology, & School Psychology, 2084 Haley Center, Auburn University, AL 36849-5222. Application available online. URL of online application: http://www.auburn.edu/coun. Students are admitted in the Fall, application deadline January 15. PhD in Counseling Psychology—January 15. PhD in School Psychology, Counselor Education—February 1. MA in Community Agency Counseling, School Counseling, EdS in School Counseling, School Psychology—March 15. *Fee:* $25.

Auburn University

Department of Psychology
College of Liberal Arts
226 Thach Hall
Auburn University, AL 36849-5214
Telephone: (334) 844-4412
Fax: (334) 844-4447
E-mail: *bryangt@auburn.edu*
Web: *http://www.auburn.edu/psychology*

Department Information:

1948. Chairperson: Barry Burkhart. Number of faculty: total—full-time 22, part-time 1; women—full-time 5, part-time 1; total—minority—full-time 3; women minority—full-time 2; faculty subject to the Americans With Disabilities Act 1.

Programs and Degrees Offered:

Listed in the following order: Program area, degree type (T if terminal Master's), number awarded 7/06–6/07. Clinical PhD (Doctor of Philosophy) 7, Experimental PhD (Doctor of Philosophy) 6, Industrial/Organizational PhD (Doctor of Philosophy) 2, Applied Behavior Analysis in Developmental Disabilities MA/MS (Master of Arts/Science) (T) 13.

APA Accreditation: Clinical PhD (Doctor of Philosophy).

Student Applications/Admissions:

Student Applications

Clinical PhD (Doctor of Philosophy)—Applications 2007–2008, 172. Total applicants accepted 2007–2008, 12. Number full-time enrolled (new admits only) 2007–2008, 9. Number part-time enrolled (new admits only) 2007–2008, 0. Openings 2008–2009, 7. The median number of years required for completion of a degree in 2006–2007 were 6. The number of students enrolled full- and part-time who were dismissed or voluntarily withdrew from this program area in 2007–2008 were 0. *Experimental PhD (Doctor of Philosophy)*—Applications 2007–2008, 27. Total applicants accepted 2007–2008, 6. Number full-time enrolled (new admits only) 2007–2008, 6. Number part-time enrolled (new admits only) 2007–2008, 0. Openings 2008–2009, 5. The median number of years required for completion of a degree in 2006–2007 were 5. The number of students enrolled full- and part-time who were dismissed or voluntarily withdrew from this program area in 2007–2008 were 0. *Industrial/Organizational PhD (Doctor of Philosophy)*—Applications 2007–2008, 48. Total applicants accepted 2007–2008, 4. Number full-time enrolled (new admits only) 2007–2008, 4. Number part-time enrolled (new admits only) 2007–2008, 0. Openings 2008–2009, 4. The median number of years required for completion of a degree in 2006–2007 were 7. The number of students enrolled full- and part-time who were dismissed or voluntarily withdrew from this program area in 2007–2008 were 0. *Applied Behavior Analysis in Developmental Disabilities MA/MS (Master of Arts/Science)*—Applications 2007–2008, 38. Total applicants accepted 2007–2008, 15. Number full-time enrolled (new admits only) 2007–2008, 15. Number part-time enrolled (new admits only) 2007–2008, 0. Openings 2008–2009, 15. The median number of years required for completion of a degree in 2006–2007 was 1. The number of students enrolled full- and part-time who were dismissed or voluntarily withdrew from this program area in 2007–2008 were 0.

Admissions Requirements:

Scores: Entries appear in this order: required test or GPA, minimum score (if required), median score of students entering in 2007–2008. Master's Programs: GRE-V no minimum stated, 500; GRE-Q no minimum stated, 630; overall undergraduate GPA no minimum stated, 3.1. The above data are for the Master's Concentration in Applied Behavior Analysis in Developmental Disabilities. Doctoral Programs: GRE-V no minimum stated, 570; GRE-Q no minimum stated, 640; overall undergraduate GPA no minimum stated, 3.7; psychology GPA no minimum stated, 3.8. The above data are for the clinical doctoral program.

Other Criteria: (importance of criteria rated low, medium, or high): GRE/MAT scores—medium, research experience—high, work experience—medium, extracurricular activity—low, clinically related public service—medium, GPA—high, letters of recommendation—high, interview—high, statement of goals and objectives—medium, For I/O and EXP programs, clinically related public service has less significance. For additional information on admission requirements, go to http://www.auburn.edu/psychology.

Student Characteristics: The following represents characteristics of students in 2007–2008 in all graduate psychology programs in the department: Female—full-time 63, part-time 0; Male—full-time 36, part-time 0; African American/Black—full-time 5, part-time 0; Hispanic/Latino(a)—full-time 3, part-time 0; Asian/Pacific Islander—full-time 2, part-time 0; American Indian/Alaska Native—full-time 0, part-time 0; Caucasian/White—full-time 87, part-time 0; Multi-ethnic—full-time 2, part-time 0; students subject to the Americans With Disabilities Act—full-time 1, part-time 0; Unknown ethnicity—full-time 0, part-time 0; International students who hold an F-1 or J-1 Visa—full-time 1, part-time 0.

Financial Information/Assistance:

Tuition for Full-Time Study: *Master's:* State residents: per academic year $7,875, $217 per credit hour; Nonstate residents: per academic year $23,625, $651 per credit hour. *Doctoral:* State residents: per academic year $7,875, $217 per credit hour; Nonstate residents: per academic year $23,625, $651 per credit hour. Tuition is subject to change. See the following Web site for updates and changes in tuition costs: http://www.auburn.edu/finaid/special-information/cost-of-attendance.html.

Financial Assistance:

First-Year Students: Teaching assistantships available for first year. Average amount paid per academic year: $12,600. Average number of hours worked per week: 13. Apply by December 1. Tuition remission given: full.

Advanced Students: Teaching assistantships available for advanced students. Average number of hours worked per week: 13. Tuition remission given: full. Research assistantships available for advanced students. Average amount paid per academic year: $14,600. Average number of hours worked per week: 13. Tuition remission given: full.

Additional Information: Of all students currently enrolled full time, 80% benefited from one or more of the listed financial assistance programs. Application and information available online at http://www.auburn.edu/psychology.

Internships/Practica: Master's Degree (MA/MS Applied Behavior Analysis in Developmental Disabilities): An internship experience, such as, a final research project or "capstone" experience is required of graduates. Doctoral Degree (PhD clinical): For those doctoral students for whom a professional internship was required in this program prior to graduation, (10) students applied for an internship in 2006–2007, with (10) students obtaining an internship. Of those students who obtained an internship, (10) were paid internships. Of those students who obtained an internship, (10) students placed in APA/CPA-accredited internships, (0) students placed in internships not APA/CPA-accredited, but listed with the Association of Psychology Postdoctoral and Internship Centers (APPIC), (0) students placed in internships conforming to guidelines of the Council of Directors of School Psychology Programs (CDSPP), (0) students placed in internships that were not APA/CPA-accredited, APPIC or CDSPP listed. Current practicum sites that offer assistantships for clinical graduate students are Auburn University Psychological Services Center, Auburn University Student Services Counseling, Mt. Meigs Adolescent Correctional Facility (Mt. Meigs, AL), Lee County Youth

Development Center (Opelika, AL), Head Start Program of Lee County (Auburn and Opelika, AL), the Auburn University School of Pharmacy, the Auburn University College of Veterinary Medicine, and UAB/Montgomery Internal Medicine/Family Medicine Residency Program (Montgomery, AL), and the Central Alabama Veterans Health Care System. Industrial/Organizational psychology students receive paid practicum training at a number of area organizations, including Auburn University's Center for Governmental Services, Auburn University at Montgomery's Center for Business and Economic Development, and the Fort Benning Field Station of the Army Research Institute. I/O students participate in consulting internship work before completing their doctoral work. Experimental students have participated in practica at the Bancroft Center (NJ), Warm Springs Rehabilitation Center (GA), and the Army Research Institute (GA). Students in the Masters Program in Applied Behavior Analysis in Developmental Disabilities participate in a practicum program that involves various sites serving individuals with developmental disabilities, including Opelika City Schools, the Little Tree Preschool, the Learning Tree Tallassee Campus, Lee County Department of Human Resources, and the Macon County Retardation and Rehabilitation Activity Center.

Housing and Day Care: On-campus housing is available. See the following Web site for more information: https://fp.auburn.edu/housing/. No on-campus day care facilities are available.

Employment of Department Graduates:

Master's Degree Graduates: Of those who graduated in the academic year 2006–2007, the following categories and numbers represent the postgraduate activities and employment of master's degree graduates: Enrolled in a postdoctoral residency/fellowship (n/a), employed in independent practice (n/a), employed in a professional position in a school system (2), employed in a community mental health/counseling center (2), other employment position (9), total from the above (master's) (13).

Doctoral Degree Graduates: Of those who graduated in the academic year 2006–2007, the following categories and numbers represent the postgraduate activities and employment of doctoral degree graduates: Enrolled in a psychology doctoral program (n/a), enrolled in a postdoctoral residency/fellowship (4), employed in independent practice (2), employed in an academic position at a university (1), employed in an academic position at a 2-year/4-year college (3), employed in business or industry (1), employed in government agency (3), employed in a hospital/medical center (1), total from the above (doctoral) (15).

Additional Information:

Orientation, Objectives, and Emphasis of Department: Graduate education in Auburn's psychology program offers training in basic research and in the application of knowledge and theory to societal problems. Faculty are committed to the premise that inquiry, breadth, and respect for the research process and the application of behavioral science knowledge are valued elements in graduate education. Students work closely in laboratories with fellow students and faculty mentors. Students interested in applied work are provided with direct experience and supervision within community agencies and organizations where theory and technique can be practiced and refined. The Clinical Psychology training program applies a scientist–practitioner model that blends an empirical approach to knowledge within an experiential context. The Experimental program provides training opportunities in the fundamentals of behavior and cognition. Excellent animal and human laboratories are available in a number of settings. The Industrial/Organizational program emphasizes a scientist–practitioner approach in which research is used to improve both organizational effectiveness and the quality of work life of individual employees. The Applied Behavior Analysis in Developmental Disabilities program (Master's) trains students to provide programmatic habilitative services to individuals with developmental disorders and prepares students to qualify for certification by the Behavior Analyst Certification Board. This 1-year program integrates foundational and specialized coursework with carefully designed practicum experiences.

Special Facilities or Resources: A substantial clinical psychology training grant from the State of Alabama, university teaching assistantships, a wide variety of contracts with community agencies, and faculty research contracts and grants have typically provided all doctoral psychology graduate students with financial support throughout their graduate careers. The department administers a multipurpose psychological services center. Relationships with extra-university agencies and organizations facilitate training in applied research.

Information for Students With Physical Disabilities: See the following Web site for more information: http://www.auburn.edu/academic/disabilities/.

Application Information:

Send to Thane Bryant, Department of Psychology, 226 Thach Hall, Auburn University, AL 36849-5214; bryangt@auburn.edu. Application available online. URL of online application: http://www.auburn.edu/psychology. Students are admitted in the Fall, application deadline December 1. Clinical PhD: December 1; Industrial–Organizational and Experimental PhD: January 15; Master's Concentration in Applied Behavior Analysis in Developmental Disabilities: February 15. *Fee:* $25.

Auburn University at Montgomery (2007 data)

Department of Psychology
School of Sciences
P.O. Box 244023
Montgomery, AL 36124-4023
Telephone: (334) 244-3306
Fax: (334) 244-3947
E-mail: *slobello@mail.aum.edu*
Web: *http://www.aum.edu/Academics/Schools/Sciences/Graduate_Programs/MS_in_Psychology/index.aspx?id=4852*

Department Information:

1969. Chairperson: Peter Zachar, PhD. Number of faculty: total—full-time 10, part-time 6; women—full-time 3, part-time 5; faculty subject to the Americans With Disabilities Act 1.

Programs and Degrees Offered:

Listed in the following order: Program area, degree type (T if terminal Master's), number awarded 7/06–6/07. Applied/Clinical Counseling MA/MS (Master of Arts/Science) (T) 7.

Student Applications/Admissions:

Student Applications

Applied/Clinical Counseling MA/MS (Master of Arts/Science)—Applications 2007–2008, 40. Total applicants accepted 2007–2008, 31. Total enrolled 2007–2008 full-time, 25, part-time, 5. Openings 2008–2009, 25. The median number of years required for completion of a degree in 2006–2007 were 2. The number of students enrolled full- and part-time who were dismissed or voluntarily withdrew from this program area in 2007–2008 were 3.

Admissions Requirements:

Scores: Entries appear in this order: required test or GPA, minimum score (if required), median score of students entering in 2007–2008. Master's Programs: GRE-V no minimum stated; GRE-Q no minimum stated; MAT no minimum stated; overall undergraduate GPA 3.0. We require either the MAT or the GRE, plus undergraduate transcripts. We also require two letters of reference and a statement of interest.

Other Criteria: (importance of criteria rated low, medium, or high): GRE/MAT scores—high, research experience—low, work experience—low, extracurricular activity—low, clinically related public service—medium, GPA—high, letters of recommendation—medium, interview—low, statement of goals and objectives—high. Research experience, work experience, and extracurricular activities are valued, but not required for consideration for admission. A formal interview is not required, but campus visits to meet faculty and view the facilities are encouraged. When coming to campus is not possible, telephone contacts with faculty are welcome.

Student Characteristics: The following represents characteristics of students in 2007–2008 in all graduate psychology programs in the department: Female—full-time 17, part-time 7; Male—full-time 6, part-time 1; African American/Black—full-time 5, part-time 2; Hispanic/Latino(a)—full-time 0, part-time 1; Asian/Pacific Islander—full-time 1, part-time 0; American Indian/Alaska Native—full-time 0, part-time 0; Caucasian/White—full-time 11, part-time 4; Multi-ethnic—full-time 0, part-time 0; students subject to the Americans With Disabilities Act—full-time 0, part-time 0; Unknown ethnicity—full-time 6, part-time 1.

Financial Information/Assistance:

Tuition for Full-Time Study: *Master's:* State residents: $186 per credit hour; Nonstate residents: $546 per credit hour. Tuition is subject to change. See the following Web site for updates and changes in tuition costs: http://www.aum.edu/Students/Financial_Information/Financial_Aid/index.aspx?id=2225.

Financial Assistance:

First-Year Students: Teaching assistantships available for first year. Tuition remission given: partial. Fellowships and scholarships available for first year. Tuition remission given: full.

Advanced Students: Teaching assistantships available for advanced students. Average number of hours worked per week: 15. Tuition remission given: partial. Fellowships and scholarships available for advanced students. Tuition remission given: full.

Additional Information: Of all students currently enrolled full time, 50% benefited from one or more of the listed financial assistance programs. Application and information available online. See Department Chair for information.

Internships/Practica: Internship and practica are available at several local agencies and organizations. Practica are often tailored to the interests and career objectives of the student. The practicum is required for students who do not write a thesis. It is optional for students who complete a thesis.

Housing and Day Care: On-campus housing is available. Contact Kevin Schaudt, Senior Director at (334) 244-3573 or kschaudt@mail.aum.edu See the following Web site for more information: http://www.aum.edu/Students/Student_Affairs/Housing_Residence_Life/Housing_Residence_Life_1/index.aspx?id=4719. On-campus day care facilities are available. Contact Jannett Baggett, Director (334) 244-3772; Kathy Glass, Secretary (334) 244-3441. See the following Web site for more information: http://www.aum.edu/Education/Early Childhood Center/.

Employment of Department Graduates:

Master's Degree Graduates: Of those who graduated in the academic year 2006–2007, the following categories and numbers represent the postgraduate activities and employment of master's degree graduates: Enrolled in a psychology doctoral program (5), enrolled in another graduate/professional program (1), enrolled in a postdoctoral residency/fellowship (n/a), employed in independent practice (n/a), employed in an academic position at a university (0), employed in an academic position at a 2-year/4-year college (0), employed in other positions at a higher education institution (0), employed in a professional position in a school system (0), employed in business or industry (0), employed in government agency (0), employed in a community mental health/counseling center (4), employed in a hospital/medical center (0), still seeking employment (0), other employment position (0), total from the above (master's) (10).

Doctoral Degree Graduates: Of those who graduated in the academic year 2006–2007, the following categories and numbers represent the postgraduate activities and employment of doctoral degree graduates: Enrolled in a psychology doctoral program (n/a), total from the above (doctoral) (0).

Additional Information:

Orientation, Objectives, and Emphasis of Department: Our MS program is designed to provide a core curriculum for those intending to pursue doctoral studies and to offer course and practicum experiences for those wishing to enter direct service positions.

Special Facilities or Resources: Computer facilities are available for student use.

Application Information:

Send to Office of Enrollment Services, 130 Taylor Center, Auburn University Montgomery, P.O. Box 244023, Montgomery, AL 36124-4023. Application available online in Acrobat format (pdf) at http://www.aum.edu/Prospective_Students/Admissions/Application_Form/index.cfm?id=761. Application available online. URL of online application: https://www.senator.aum.edu/prod/bwskalog.P_DispLoginNon. Students are admitted in the Fall, application deadline July 1; Spring, application deadline November 1; Summer, application deadline April 1; Programs have rolling admissions. The pdf form of the application may be downloaded, completed, and mailed to the university. Access this application form at http://www.aum.edu/uploadedfiles/grad.pdf. *Fee:* $25.

Jacksonville State University
Department of Psychology
College of Graduate Studies
700 Pelham Road, North
Jacksonville, AL 36265-1602
Telephone: (256) 782-5402
Fax: (256) 782-5637
E-mail: *sdworkin@jsu.edu*
Web: *http://www.jsu.edu/depart/psychology/welcome.html*

Department Information:

1971. Department Head: Steven I. Dworkin, PhD. Number of faculty: total—full-time 9, part-time 4; women—full-time 5, part-time 3.

Programs and Degrees Offered:

Listed in the following order: Program area, degree type (T if terminal Master's), number awarded 7/06–6/07. Applied MA/MS (Master of Arts/Science) (T) 14, Applied MA/MS (Master of Arts/Science) (T) 6.

Student Applications/Admissions:

Student Applications

Applied MA/MS (Master of Arts/Science)—Applications 2007–2008, 48. Total applicants accepted 2007–2008, 40. Number full-time enrolled (new admits only) 2007–2008, 11. Number part-time enrolled (new admits only) 2007–2008, 10. Total enrolled 2007–2008 full-time, 15, part-time, 16. Openings 2008–2009, 20. The median number of years required for completion of a degree in 2006–2007 were 2. The number of students enrolled full- and part-time who were dismissed or voluntarily withdrew from this program area in 2007–2008 were 4. *Applied MA/MS (Master of Arts/Science)*—Applications 2007–2008, 3. Total applicants accepted 2007–2008, 3. Number full-time enrolled (new admits only) 2007–2008, 2. Number part-time enrolled (new admits only) 2007–2008, 0. The median number of years required for completion of a degree in 2006–2007 were 3. The number of students enrolled full- and part-time who were dismissed or voluntarily withdrew from this program area in 2007–2008 were 0.

Admissions Requirements:

Scores: Entries appear in this order: required test or GPA, minimum score (if required), median score of students entering in 2007–2008. Master's Programs: overall undergraduate GPA no minimum stated; psychology GPA no minimum stated; 450 times undergraduate GPA + GRE V + Q = 1600 or more OR 15 times undergraduate GPA + MAT = 60 or more.

Other Criteria: (importance of criteria rated low, medium, or high): GRE/MAT scores—high, GPA—high, letters of recommendation—medium.

Student Characteristics: The following represents characteristics of students in 2007–2008 in all graduate psychology programs in the department: Female—full-time 10, part-time 13; Male—full-time 5, part-time 3; African American/Black—full-time 4, part-time 2; Hispanic/Latino(a)—full-time 1, part-time 2; Asian/Pacific Islander—full-time 1, part-time 0; American Indian/Alaska Native—full-time 0, part-time 0; Caucasian/White—full-time 9, part-time 12; Multi-ethnic—full-time 0, part-time 0; students subject to the Americans With Disabilities Act—full-time 0, part-time 1; Unknown ethnicity—full-time 0, part-time 0.

Financial Information/Assistance:

Tuition for Full-Time Study: *Master's:* State residents: per academic year $4,725, $225 per credit hour; Nonstate residents: per academic year $9,550, $450 per credit hour. Tuition is subject to change. See the following Web site for updates and changes in tuition costs: http://www.jsu.edu/depart/graduate/bulletin/index.html.

Financial Assistance:

First-Year Students: Teaching assistantships available for first year. Average amount paid per academic year: $5,000. Average number of hours worked per week: 20. Apply by August 28. Tuition remission given: partial. Research assistantships available for first year. Average amount paid per academic year: $5,000. Average number of hours worked per week: 20. Apply by August 28. Tuition remission given: partial. Fellowships and scholarships available for first year. Apply by August 28. Tuition remission given: partial.

Advanced Students: No information provided.

Additional Information: Of all students currently enrolled full time, 0% benefited from one or more of the listed financial assistance programs. Application and information available online at http://www.jsu.edu/depart/finaid/finaid.html.

Internships/Practica: Clinical and Behavior Analysis and Instructional Practica are offered. The Clinical Practicum includes supervised clinical assessment, report writing, ethical principles, as well as the design and implementation of psychological treatment programs with a client population, in an on-campus clinic. The Behavior Analysis Practicum includes the application of psychological principles in areas such as developmental disabilities, organizational behavior management, remediation of academic behavior, and environmental psychology. The Instructional Practicum allows students to gain teaching experience assisting a professor.

Housing and Day Care: On-campus housing is available. See the following Web site for more information: http://www.jsu.edu/depart/rlmn/. On-campus day care facilities are available.

Employment of Department Graduates:

Master's Degree Graduates: Of those who graduated in the academic year 2006–2007, the following categories and numbers represent the postgraduate activities and employment of master's degree graduates: Enrolled in a psychology doctoral program (3), enrolled in a postdoctoral residency/fellowship (n/a), employed in independent practice (n/a), employed in a community mental health/counseling center (5), employed in a hospital/medical center (1), total from the above (master's) (9).

Doctoral Degree Graduates: Of those who graduated in the academic year 2006–2007, the following categories and numbers represent the postgraduate activities and employment of doctoral degree graduates: Enrolled in a psychology doctoral program (n/a), total from the above (doctoral) (0).

Additional Information:

Orientation, Objectives, and Emphasis of Department: The objective of the program is to provide students with the requisite methodological skills as well as the theoretical and ethical background necessary for practice or research. Consistent with this objective is a 15-hour core sequence of courses covering biological, quantitative, methodological, and preprofessional areas. Students can then tailor the remaining coursework, research program, and practicum–internship experiences to fit their career objectives. Overall, the courses reflect a behavioral emphasis. Training is available to prepare students for state Master's level licensure or national certification as a behavior analyst. Student research and thesis is encouraged, especially for students preparing to pursue doctoral-level studies.

Special Facilities or Resources: Practicum arrangements with a variety of agencies allow students to gain experience in a variety of applications of behavior analysis. Special facilities include an animal room, a running room with 15 chambers, student offices, and a seminar computer room. A network of control computers (which were developed at JSU and used in many other universities) runs experiments and provides interactive graphical analyses. Social Design: In the Center for Social Design, students apply principles of environmental design to affect behavior. Precision Teaching: The Learning Skills Department is affiliated with the Psychology Department and offers students opportunities to apply psychological principles in an instructional setting using computer assisted instruction.

Information for Students With Physical Disabilities: See the following Web site for more information: http://www.jsu.edu/depart/dss/index.html.

Application Information:

Send to Jacksonville State University, College of Graduate Studies, 700 Pelham Road North, Jacksonville, AL 36265-1602. Application available online. URL of online application: http://www.webhost.jsu.edu/Scripts/WebEncore.dll?Application-Graduate.html. Students are admitted in the Fall, application deadline August 27; Spring, application deadline January 2; Summer, application deadline April 28. *Fee:* $20.

South Alabama, University of

Department of Psychology
Arts and Sciences
LSCB Room 326
Mobile, AL 36688
Telephone: (251) 460-6371
Fax: (251) 460-6320
E-mail: *lchriste@usouthal.edu*
Web: *http://www.southalabama.edu/psychology*

Department Information:

1964. Chairperson: Larry Christensen. Number of faculty: total—full-time 14, part-time 10; women—full-time 6, part-time 4; total—minority—full-time 1, part-time 2; women minority—full-time 1.

Programs and Degrees Offered:

Listed in the following order: Program area, degree type (T if terminal Master's), number awarded 7/06–6/07. Clinical MA/MS (Master of Arts/Science) (T) 5, Experimental MA/MS (Master of Arts/Science) (T) 1.

Student Applications/Admissions:

Student Applications

Clinical MA/MS (Master of Arts/Science)—Applications 2007–2008, 19. Total applicants accepted 2007–2008, 10. Number full-time enrolled (new admits only) 2007–2008, 8. Openings 2008–2009, 12. The median number of years required for completion of a degree in 2006–2007 were 3. The number of students enrolled full- and part-time who were dismissed or voluntarily withdrew from this program area in 2007–2008 were 0. *Experimental MA/MS (Master of Arts/Science)*—Applications 2007–2008, 4. Total applicants accepted 2007–2008, 3. Number full-time enrolled (new admits only) 2007–2008, 3. Openings 2008–2009, 3. The median number of years required for completion of a degree in 2006–2007 were 2.

Admissions Requirements:

Scores: Entries appear in this order: required test or GPA, minimum score (if required), median score of students entering in 2007–2008. Master's Programs: GRE-V 380, 480; GRE-Q 490, 555; overall undergraduate GPA 2.9, 3.52; psychology GPA 3.29, 3.8.

Other Criteria: (importance of criteria rated low, medium, or high): GRE/MAT scores—medium, research experience—medium, work experience—low, extracurricular activity—low, clinically related public service—medium, GPA—high, letters of recommendation—high, interview—medium, statement of goals and objectives—medium.

Student Characteristics: The following represents characteristics of students in 2007–2008 in all graduate psychology programs in the department: Female—full-time 17, part-time 0; Male—full-time 5, part-time 0; African American/Black—full-time 1, part-time 0; Hispanic/Latino(a)—part-time 0; Asian/Pacific Islander—full-time 1, part-time 0; American Indian/Alaska Native—full-time 0, part-time 0; Caucasian/White—full-time 20, part-time 0; Multi-ethnic—full-time 0, part-time 0; students subject to the Americans With Disabilities Act—full-time 0, part-time 0; Unknown ethnicity—full-time 0, part-time 0.

Financial Information/Assistance:

Tuition for Full-Time Study: *Master's:* State residents: per academic year $3,674, $167 per credit hour; Nonstate residents: per academic year $7,348, $334 per credit hour. Tuition is subject to change.

Financial Assistance:

First-Year Students: Research assistantships available for first year. Average amount paid per academic year: $6,000. Average number of hours worked per week: 20. Apply by March 1. Tuition remission given: full.

Advanced Students: Research assistantships available for advanced students. Average amount paid per academic year: $6,000. Apply by March 1. Tuition remission given: full.

Additional Information: Of all students currently enrolled full time, 75% benefited from one or more of the listed financial assistance programs.

Internships/Practica: Graduate students receive practical experience in the application of psychological assessment and treatment procedures in a variety of clinical settings. Emphasis is given to ethical and professional issues with intensive individual and group supervision. The Department of Psychology operates an outpatient teaching clinic where a variety of children and adults are seen for short-term assessment and treatment. External practicum placements are also available in a variety of community settings including a state mental hospital, a mental retardation facility, and community substance abuse programs.

Housing and Day Care: On-campus housing is available. See the following Web site for more information: http://www.southalabama.edu/housing. No on-campus day care facilities are available.

Employment of Department Graduates:

Master's Degree Graduates: Of those who graduated in the academic year 2006–2007, the following categories and numbers represent the postgraduate activities and employment of master's degree graduates: Enrolled in a psychology doctoral program (1), enrolled in a postdoctoral residency/fellowship (n/a), employed in independent practice (n/a), employed in a professional position in a school system (1), employed in a community mental health/counseling center (3), do not know (1), total from the above (master's) (6).

Doctoral Degree Graduates: Of those who graduated in the academic year 2006–2007, the following categories and numbers represent the postgraduate activities and employment of doctoral degree graduates: Enrolled in a psychology doctoral program (n/a), total from the above (doctoral) (0).

Additional Information:

Orientation, Objectives, and Emphasis of Department: The University of South Alabama offers a master's program in general psychology that allows the student to choose either an applied or experimental focus. All students complete a core curriculum designed to provide them with knowledge of current theories, principles, and methods of experimental and applied psychology. This is followed by courses in either clinical or experimental areas. The clinical courses are designed to equip students with basic psychological assessment and treatment skills that will enable them to function later in an applied employment setting under supervision of a licensed psychologist. Courses for the experimental student are designed to provide more extensive information in research design and experimental methods as well as theoretical background related to the student's thesis research. Both programs, as well as the core curriculum, are designed to provide students with the necessary theoretical and research background to pursue further graduate study, if they so choose. Graduate students in both areas receive individual attention and close supervision by departmental faculty.

Special Facilities or Resources: The Comparative Hearing Laboratory maintains exceptional sound room, computer, and animal facilities. Through the comparison of human, monkey, gerbil, and computer simulations of perception, the laboratory seeks to study how the brain has become specialized for language, and what has gone wrong with particular classes of communication and learning disorders. In addition to the Psychological Clinic and the Comparative Hearing Laboratory, the Department has laboratory facilities for neuropsychological and behavioral research, and has access to both mainframe and personal computer facilities. An EEG/ERP laboratory exists that is used for conducting research requiring the utilization of a dense array electrode cap. This laboratory is available for both faculty and graduate student research. A family interaction laboratory exists for studying parent–child interactions with the goal of enhancing parenting skills. A cognitive laboratory exists with the capability of studying linguistic enhancement. This laboratory also has an eye-tracking apparatus capable of being integrated into a variety of research projects. A social interaction and a sound attenuation laboratory has recently been constructed to provide a laboratory for research into the dynamics of phenomena such as echolocation and social interactions.

Information for Students With Physical Disabilities: See the following Web site for more information: http://www.southalabama.edu/dss.

Application Information:

Send to Director of Admission, Meisler Hall Suite 2500, University of South Alabama, Mobile, AL 36688-0002. Students are admitted in the Fall, application deadline March 1. *Fee:* $35.

Alaska Pacific University

Master of Science in Counseling Psychology (MSCP)
4101 University Drive
Anchorage, AK 99508
Telephone: (907) 564-8225
Fax: (907) 564-8396
E-mail: *ecole@alaskapacific.edu*
Web: *http://www.alaskapacific.edu*

Department Information:

1990. Chairperson: Kim Kjaersgaard, PhD. Number of faculty: total—full-time 3, part-time 4; women—full-time 4, part-time 1.

Programs and Degrees Offered:

Listed in the following order: Program area, degree type (T if terminal Master's), number awarded 7/06–6/07. Master of Science Counseling Psychology MA/MS (Master of Arts/Science) (T) 20.

Student Applications/Admissions:

Student Applications

Master of Science Counseling Psychology MA/MS (Master of Arts/Science)—Applications 2007–2008, 32. Total applicants accepted 2007–2008, 26. Number full-time enrolled (new admits only) 2007–2008, 22. Number part-time enrolled (new admits only) 2007–2008, 0. Total enrolled 2007–2008 full-time, 46, part-time, 4. Openings 2008–2009, 21. The median number of years required for completion of a degree in 2006–2007 were 2. The number of students enrolled full- and part-time who were dismissed or voluntarily withdrew from this program area in 2007–2008 were 1.

Admissions Requirements:

Scores: Entries appear in this order: required test or GPA, minimum score (if required), median score of students entering in 2007–2008. Master's Programs: MAT no minimum stated; overall undergraduate GPA 3.0, 3.2; psychology GPA 3.0, 3.0.
Other Criteria: (importance of criteria rated low, medium, or high): GRE/MAT scores—medium, research experience—low, work experience—high, extracurricular activity—medium, clinically related public service—medium, GPA—medium, letters of recommendation—high, interview—high, statement of goals and objectives—high, undergraduate major in psychology—low, specific undergraduate psychology courses taken—medium.

Student Characteristics: The following represents characteristics of students in 2007–2008 in all graduate psychology programs in the department: Female—full-time 37, part-time 0; Male—full-time 9, part-time 0; African American/Black—full-time 1, part-time 0; Hispanic/Latino(a)—full-time 1, part-time 0; Asian/Pacific Islander—full-time 2, part-time 0; American Indian/Alaska Native—full-time 3, part-time 0; Caucasian/White—full-time 28, part-time 0; Multi-ethnic—full-time 3, part-time 0; students subject to the Americans With Disabilities Act—full-time 0, part-time 0; Unknown ethnicity—full-time 0, part-time 0.

Financial Information/Assistance:

Tuition for Full-Time Study: *Master's:* State residents: $575 per credit hour; Nonstate residents: $575 per credit hour.

Financial Assistance:

First-Year Students: No information provided.

Advanced Students: Teaching assistantships available for advanced students. Apply by March 15. Tuition remission given: partial. Traineeships available for advanced students. Apply by March 15. Tuition remission given: partial. Fellowships and scholarships available for advanced students. Tuition remission given: partial.

Additional Information: Of all students currently enrolled full time, 10% benefited from one or more of the listed financial assistance programs.

Internships/Practica: A significant part of a counselor's education occurs outside the classroom through an internship experience. This is a 600-hour opportunity for students to begin to apply theories and techniques of their classroom education as well as to focus their professional development in a specialized area of counseling. Internship opportunities are diverse in clientele and therapeutic context. In collaboration with the MSCP director and faculty, students identify internship sites consistent with their interests and needs. Examples of internship sites are Southcentral Foundation (Alaska Native services), Anchorage Center for Families, Alaska Children's Services, Southcentral Counseling Center (state mental health services), Alaska Human Services, Salvation Army Clitheroe Center, Alaska Native Hospital, McLaughlin Youth Center, Catholic Social Services, and private practitioners.

Housing and Day Care: On-campus housing is available. Housing available for graduate students. See the following Web site for more information: http://www.alaskapacific.edu. No on-campus day care facilities are available.

Employment of Department Graduates:

Master's Degree Graduates: Of those who graduated in the academic year 2006–2007, the following categories and numbers represent the postgraduate activities and employment of master's degree graduates: Enrolled in a postdoctoral residency/fellowship (n/a), employed in independent practice (n/a), employed in a community mental health/counseling center (18), total from the above (master's) (18).
Doctoral Degree Graduates: Of those who graduated in the academic year 2006–2007, the following categories and numbers represent the postgraduate activities and employment of doctoral degree graduates: Enrolled in a psychology doctoral program (n/a), total from the above (doctoral) (0).

Additional Information:

Orientation, Objectives, and Emphasis of Department: The master of science in counseling psychology (MSCP) program at Alaska Pacific University is a selective, rigorous program for the creative adult who plans to become a mental health practitioner or enter a doctoral program. Main objectives of the MSCP program are to foster the knowledge and skills needed to succeed as a professional counselor, to promote the integration of learning with practical "real life" issues in the field, and to encourage the development of leadership skills. To accomplish these educational objectives, the MSCP program is committed to providing individual attention to students, a personal and supportive atmosphere, and a mentorship approach to education. The curriculum is eclectic in theoretical orientation and celebrates diversity within the range of professional mental health approaches and techniques. A "hands on" approach to learning is emphasized along with an integration of theory and practice throughout the program. The program is committed to the centrality of multicultural awareness, ethical responsibility, and each student's personal growth and development. When students graduate from the MSCP program, they will have acquired a better understanding of themselves as human beings, greater sensitivity for others, and professional competence in theory, research, practice, skills, and ethics.

Special Facilities or Resources: Our special resources lie in our unique blend of theoretical knowledge and practical experience that make up our counselor education program. This is enhanced by the diverse faculty and unique internship sites available in Alaska. Further, a cooperative rather than a competitive spirit is fostered. Because MSCP students progress through the program as an intact group, they develop a strong spirit of community. Class assignments and projects often are completed in a small-group format, with each member taking active responsibility for the final product of all. The MSCP curriculum includes a variety of course styles, with greatest emphasis given to seminar-style classroom interactions, experiential activities, and student-designed projects. Even in lecture-oriented courses, students engage in small-group learning activities and personal discovery. Practicing counselors and psychologists are regularly brought into the classroom as visitors and also serve on a regular basis as adjunct faculty. And faculty doors are open to students all of the time. Further, the curriculum is responsive to current factors that influence the profession, such as managed care and certification and licensure laws throughout the United States, and cutting edge therapies and techniques.

Information for Students With Physical Disabilities: See the following Web site for more information: http://www.alaskapacific.edu/.

Application Information:

Send to Graduate Admissions Office, Alaska Pacific University, 4101 University Drive, Anchorage, AK 99508. Application available online. URL of online application: http://www.alaskapacific.edu. Students are admitted in the Fall, application deadline February 1. *Fee:* $25.

Alaska, University of, Anchorage

Psychology/MS in Clinical Psychology
Arts and Sciences
3211 Providence Drive
Anchorage, AK 99508
Telephone: (907) 786-1795
Fax: (907) 786-4898
E-mail: *afprs@uaa.alaska.edu*
Web: *http://www.psych.uaa.alaska.edu*

Department Information:

1967. Chairperson: John Petraitis. Number of faculty: total—full-time 11; women—full-time 7.

Programs and Degrees Offered:

Listed in the following order: Program area, degree type (T if terminal Master's), number awarded 7/06–6/07. Clinical Psychology MA/MS (Master of Arts/Science) (T) 9.

Student Applications/Admissions:

Student Applications

Clinical Psychology MA/MS (Master of Arts/Science)—Applications 2007–2008, 40. Total applicants accepted 2007–2008, 10. Number full-time enrolled (new admits only) 2007–2008, 10. Number part-time enrolled (new admits only) 2007–2008, 0. Total enrolled 2007–2008 full-time, 20, part-time, 2. Openings 2008–2009, 10. The median number of years required for completion of a degree in 2006–2007 were 2. The number of students enrolled full- and part-time who were dismissed or voluntarily withdrew from this program area in 2007–2008 were 1.

Admissions Requirements:

Scores: Entries appear in this order: required test or GPA, minimum score (if required), median score of students entering in 2007–2008. Master's Programs: GRE-V no minimum stated; GRE-Q no minimum stated; overall undergraduate GPA no minimum stated, 3.5; psychology GPA no minimum stated, 3.5. The GRE Psychology Subtest is only required if students do not have an undergraduate psychology major.

Other Criteria: (importance of criteria rated low, medium, or high): GRE/MAT scores—medium, research experience—low, work experience—medium, extracurricular activity—medium, clinically related public service—medium, GPA—medium, letters of recommendation—medium, statement of goals and objectives—medium, undergraduate major in psychology—low, specific undergraduate psychology courses taken—medium. For additional information on admission requirements, go to http://www.psych.uaa.alaska.edu.

Student Characteristics: The following represents characteristics of students in 2007–2008 in all graduate psychology programs in the department: Female—full-time 18, part-time 1; Male—full-time 2, part-time 1; African American/Black—full-time 1, part-time 0; Hispanic/Latino(a)—full-time 0, part-time 0; Asian/Pacific Islander—full-time 0, part-time 0; American Indian/Alaska Native—full-time 3, part-time 0; Caucasian/White—full-time 13, part-time 2; Multi-ethnic—full-time 3, part-time 0; students subject to the Americans With Disabilities Act—full-time 0, part-time 0; Unknown ethnicity—full-time 0, part-time 0; International students who hold an F-1 or J-1 Visa—full-time 0, part-time 0.

Financial Information/Assistance:

Financial Assistance:

First-Year Students: Teaching assistantships available for first year. Average amount paid per academic year: $3,000. Average number of hours worked per week: 15. Apply by June 1. Tuition remission given: partial. Research assistantships available for first year. Average amount paid per academic year: $3,000. Average number of hours worked per week: 15. Apply by June 1. Tuition remission given: partial.

Advanced Students: No information provided.

Additional Information: Of all students currently enrolled full time, 60% benefited from one or more of the listed financial

assistance programs. Application and information available online at http://www.uaa.alaska.edu/psych.

Internships/Practica: Master's Degree (MA/MS Clinical Psychology): An internship experience such as a final research project or "capstone" experience is required of graduates. All students complete one semester of practicum in the Psychological Services Center, which is run by the Psychology Department. This closely supervised experience involves direct clinical contact with psychotherapy clients of all ages and backgrounds. Students spend an average of 20 hours per week on practicum and typically schedule 5 or 6 hours of face-to-face contact time with clients. All students also complete two semesters of internship at a community agency. Internship sites are selected on the basis of student preferences and their professional goals. Potential internship sites include private or public psychiatric inpatient facilities; private or public psychiatric outpatient facilities, including those that specialize in the treatment of Alaskan Natives, college students, or families; the school district; and residential homes for adolescents or the elderly. As with practicum, students typically spend 20 hours per week on internship and receive close supervision.

Housing and Day Care: On-campus housing is available. See the following Web site for more information: http://www.uaa.alaska.edu/housing/. On-campus day care facilities are available. Contact tanaina@alaska.net.

Employment of Department Graduates:

Master's Degree Graduates: Of those who graduated in the academic year 2006–2007, the following categories and numbers represent the postgraduate activities and employment of master's degree graduates: Enrolled in a psychology doctoral program (4), enrolled in a postdoctoral residency/fellowship (n/a), employed in independent practice (n/a), employed in an academic position at a university (1), employed in a professional position in a school system (2), employed in business or industry (2), employed in government agency (2), employed in a community mental health/counseling center (10), employed in a hospital/medical center (5), total from the above (master's) (26).

Doctoral Degree Graduates: Of those who graduated in the academic year 2006–2007, the following categories and numbers represent the postgraduate activities and employment of doctoral degree graduates: Enrolled in a psychology doctoral program (n/a), total from the above (doctoral) (0).

Additional Information:

Orientation, Objectives, and Emphasis of Department: The MS degree in Clinical Psychology is designed to be responsive to the needs of a variety of Alaska mental health service settings and to meet prerequisites for licensing at the master's level in the state of Alaska. The MS degree allows graduates to pursue either the Licensed Professional Counselor (LPC) or the Licensed Psychological Associate (LPA) license. The goal of the program is to provide students with a well-rounded education that includes an evidence-based background in the best practices applicable to community mental health settings. The curriculum addresses local behavioral health needs in a context that is culturally sensitive and community focused. An important program goal is the recruitment and retention of nontraditional students.

Special Facilities or Resources: The Psychology Department runs an experimental research laboratory and a mental health clinic. Both settings have computer facilities for audio-visual recording or one-way observation. In addition, the department maintains close ties to the Center for Human Development: University Affiliated Program, which provides interdisciplinary training, research, and support for people with developmental disabilities by collaborating with a variety of state agencies and community providers. The Consortium Library is the major research library for Southcentral Alaska, with a collection of more than 694,00 volumes and subscriptions to more than 3,600 journals, including a well-maintained selection of psychology resources. The UAA Information Technology Services provides microcomputer, mainframe, and Internet resources, and it maintains four general access computer labs across the campus. The university also houses the Center for Alcohol and Addiction Studies, which addresses the problem of substance abuse in Alaska through educational, research, and public service programs; the Institute for Circumpolar Health Studies, which addresses health problems in Alaska and the Circumpolar North through instruction, information services, and basic and applied research in health and medicine; and the Institute of Social and Economic Research, which is devoted to studying economic and social conditions in Alaska.

Application Information:

Send to Enrollment Services, University of Alaska Anchorage, 3211 Providence Drive, Anchorage, AK 99508. Application available online. URL of online application: http://www.psych.uaa.alaska.edu. Students are admitted in the Fall, application deadline April 1. Application for the MS clinical psychology program is separate from the joint UAF/UAA PhD Psychology program. Students may apply to both programs if desired. *Fee:* $45. Fee will go up after April 1, 2009.

Alaska, University of, Fairbanks/Anchorage

Department of Psychology/Joint PhD Program in Clinical–Community Psychology
UAF College of Liberal Arts/UAA College of Arts and Sciences
P.O. Box 756480/3211 Providence Drive
Fairbanks, AK 99775
Telephone: (907) 474-7012/561-2880
Fax: (907) 474-578
E-mail: *anaeh@uaa.alaska.edu*
Web: *http://www.psyphd.alaska.edu*

Department Information:

1984. Co-Directors of Clinical Training: UAF TBA and UAA Dr. Christiane Brems. Number of faculty: total—full-time 9, part-time 8; women—full-time 4, part-time 5; total—minority—full-time 3, part-time 1; women minority—full-time 1.

Programs and Degrees Offered:

Listed in the following order: Program area, degree type (T if terminal Master's), number awarded 7/06–6/07. Joint PhD Program in Clinical–Community Psychology PhD (Doctor of Philosophy) 0.

Student Applications/Admissions:

Student Applications

Joint PhD Program in Clinical–Community Psychology (Doctor of Philosophy)—Applications 2007–2008, 50. Total applicants accepted 2007–2008, 8. Number full-time enrolled (new admits only) 2007–2008, 7. Number part-time enrolled (new admits only) 2007–2008, 0. Openings 2008–2009, 8. The number of students enrolled full- and part-time who were dismissed or voluntarily withdrew from this program area in 2007–2008 were 1.

Admissions Requirements:

Scores: Entries appear in this order: required test or GPA, minimum score (if required), median score of students entering in 2007–2008. Doctoral Programs: overall undergraduate GPA 3.0; psychology GPA 3.0. If an applicant holds an undergraduate degree and a master's degree, they may use the higher GPA of the two degrees for this requirement.

Other Criteria: (importance of criteria rated low, medium, or high): GRE/MAT scores—low, research experience—medium, work experience—medium, extracurricular activity—medium, clinically related public service—medium, GPA—medium, letters of recommendation—high, interview—high, statement of goals and objectives—high, Rural/indigenous interest—medium, undergraduate major in psychology—low, specific undergraduate psychology courses taken—high. For additional information on admission requirements, go to http://psyphd.alaska.edu.

Student Characteristics: The following represents characteristics of students in 2007–2008 in all graduate psychology programs in the department: Female—full-time 12, part-time 0; Male—full-time 7, part-time 0; African American/Black—full-time 1, part-time 0; Hispanic/Latino(a)—full-time 2, part-time 0; Asian/Pacific Islander—full-time 0, part-time 0; American Indian/Alaska Native—full-time 3, part-time 0; Caucasian/White—full-time 12, part-time 0; Multi-ethnic—full-time 1, part-time 0; students subject to the Americans With Disabilities Act—full-time 0, part-time 0; Unknown ethnicity—full-time 0, part-time 0.

Financial Information/Assistance:

Tuition for Full-Time Study: *Doctoral:* State residents: $287 per credit hour; Nonstate residents: $586 per credit hour. Tuition is subject to change. See the following Web site for updates and changes in tuition costs: http://www.uaf.edu/uaf/costs/.

Financial Assistance:

First-Year Students: Teaching assistantships available for first year. Average amount paid per academic year: $13,710. Average number of hours worked per week: 20. Apply by February 1. Tuition remission given: partial. Research assistantships available for first year. Average amount paid per academic year: $13,710. Average number of hours worked per week: 20. Apply by February 1. Tuition remission given: partial.

Advanced Students: Teaching assistantships available for advanced students. Average amount paid per academic year: $14,760. Average number of hours worked per week: 20. Apply by February 1. Tuition remission given: partial. Research assistantships available for advanced students. Average amount paid per academic year: $14,760. Average number of hours worked per week: 20. Apply by February 1. Tuition remission given: partial.

Additional Information: Of all students currently enrolled full time, 100% benefited from one or more of the listed financial assistance programs. Application and information available online at http://psyphd.alaska.edu.

Internships/Practica: Both campuses provide clinical practica through on-campus clinics and placements in local behavioral health centers. Community practica in a variety of community settings are also provided to all students. Internship placements in Alaska will also be available to students.

Housing and Day Care: On-campus housing is available. See the following Web site for more information: UAA on-campus housing: http://www.uaa.alaska.edu/housing/. UAF on-campus housing: http://www.uaf.edu/reslife/. On-campus day care facilities are available. See the following Web site for more information: UAA child care center: http://www.tanainachildren.org/. UAF child care center: http://www.tvc.uaf.edu/programs/BunnellHouse/.

Employment of Department Graduates:

Master's Degree Graduates: Of those who graduated in the academic year 2006–2007, the following categories and numbers represent the postgraduate activities and employment of master's degree graduates: Enrolled in a postdoctoral residency/fellowship (n/a), employed in independent practice (n/a), total from the above (master's) (0).

Doctoral Degree Graduates: Of those who graduated in the academic year 2006–2007, the following categories and numbers represent the postgraduate activities and employment of doctoral degree graduates: Enrolled in a psychology doctoral program (n/a), total from the above (doctoral) (0).

Additional Information:

Orientation, Objectives, and Emphasis of Department: The PhD Program in Clinical–Community Psychology is a program jointly delivered and administered by the Departments of Psychology at the University of Alaska Fairbanks and the University of Alaska Anchorage. All program courses are co-taught across campuses via video conference and all program components are delivered by faculty at both campuses. The student experience is identical regardless of students' city of residence (Fairbanks or Anchorage). The PhD Program integrates clinical and community psychology and focuses on rural, indigenous, and cultural psychology with an applied emphasis. The program uniquely combines the spirit of clinical and community psychology. As such, it places strong emphasis on nontraditional service delivery and social action, as well as clinical service delivery to individuals, groups, families, and communities. The program is on the forefront of creative and enriching knowledge dissemination that is locally relevant; focused on public service; sensitive to the unique environments of Alaska; and concerned with acknowledging, fostering, and celebrating diversity. The program has many unique features that combine to make for a rigorous training experience that requires a student's full-time commitment.

Personal Behavior Statement: Prior to admission, students must submit a disclosure statement and a criminal background check. The disclosure statement is located by clicking on the Disclosure Form link at this site: http://psyphd.alaska.edu/appprocedures.htm.

Special Facilities or Resources: In Fairbanks, the program is housed in the Gruening Building on the UAF campus, a seven-story structure completed in 1970. Facilities available to graduate students include two high-definition video classrooms, individual study areas, and a newly renovated clinic with individual therapy rooms, a family/group therapy room, a child therapy room, and a telehealth therapy room. Other facilities available to graduate students include a departmental lab and several university labs with PCs and Macs. UAF is an international center for research in the Arctic and the North. In Anchorage, the academic facilities available to graduate students include two high-definition video classrooms; individual study areas; clinical space in the Psychological Service Center consisting of individual, family/group, child, and telehealth therapy rooms; and the Consortium Library, the major research library for Southcentral Alaska. Research facilities available to graduate students include the Behavioral Health Research and Services, a departmental laboratory and several university computer labs with PCs and Macs.

Information for Students With Physical Disabilities: See the following Web site for more information: http://www.uaa.alaska.edu/dss/ or http://www.uaf.edu/chc/disabilityr.html.

Application Information:
Send to UAF Co-Director of Clinical Training, University of Alaska Fairbanks, P.O. Box 756480, Fairbanks, AK 99775-6480 or Christiane Brems, UAA Co-Director of Clinical Training, University of Alaska Anchorage, 3211 Providence Drive, Anchorage, AK 99508. Application available online. URL of online application: http://www.psyphd.alaska.edu. Students are admitted in the Fall, application deadline February 1. *Fee:* $100. If a student receives a teaching or research assistantship or a fellowship, he or she also receives a tuition waiver.

Argosy University/Phoenix, American School of Professional Psychology

Clinical Psychology, Sport–Exercise Psychology, Professional Counseling, School Psychology
2233 West Dunlap Avenue, Suite 150
Phoenix, AZ 85021
Telephone: (866) 216-2777 (toll-free)
Fax: (602) 216-2601
E-mail: *ahughes@argosy.edu*
Web: *http://www.argosy.edu*

Department Information:

1997. Vice President of Academic Affairs: Norma J. H. Patterson, PhD. Number of faculty: total—full-time 16, part-time 1; women—full-time 11, part-time 1; total—minority—full-time 5, part-time 1; women minority—full-time 3, part-time 1.

Programs and Degrees Offered:

Listed in the following order: Program area, degree type (T if terminal Master's), number awarded 7/06–6/07. Counseling MA/MS (Master of Arts/Science) (T) 30, Sport–Exercise Psychology MA/MS (Master of Arts/Science) (T) 6, Clinical Psychology PsyD (Doctor of Psychology) 25, Clinical Psychology MA/MS (Master of Arts/Science) (T) 34, School Psychology PsyD (Doctor of Psychology) 5, Forensic Psychology MA/MS (Master of Arts/Science) (T) 15, School Psychology MA/MS (Master of Arts/Science) (T) 4.

APA Accreditation: Clinical PsyD (Doctor of Psychology).

Student Applications/Admissions:

Student Applications

Counseling MA/MS (Master of Arts/Science)—Applications 2007–2008, 72. Total applicants accepted 2007–2008, 65. Number full-time enrolled (new admits only) 2007–2008, 65. Number part-time enrolled (new admits only) 2007–2008, 0. Openings 2008–2009, 40. The median number of years required for completion of a degree in 2006–2007 were 2. The number of students enrolled full- and part-time who were dismissed or voluntarily withdrew from this program area in 2007–2008 were 7. *Sport–Exercise Psychology MA/MS (Master of Arts/Science)*—Applications 2007–2008, 19. Total applicants accepted 2007–2008, 16. Number full-time enrolled (new admits only) 2007–2008, 16. Total enrolled 2007–2008 full-time, 18, part-time, 2. Openings 2008–2009, 17. The median number of years required for completion of a degree in 2006–2007 were 2. The number of students enrolled full- and part-time who were dismissed or voluntarily withdrew from this program area in 2007–2008 were 1. *Clinical Psychology PsyD (Doctor of Psychology)*—Applications 2007–2008, 115. Total applicants accepted 2007–2008, 32. Number full-time enrolled (new admits only) 2007–2008, 32. Number part-time enrolled (new admits only) 2007–2008, 0. Total enrolled 2007–2008 full-time, 163. Openings 2008–2009, 45. The median number of years required for completion of a degree in 2006–2007 were 5. The number of students enrolled full- and part-time who were dismissed or voluntarily withdrew from this program area in 2007–2008 were 3. *Clinical Psychology MA/MS (Master of Arts/Science)*—Applications 2007–2008, 18. Total applicants accepted 2007–2008, 7. Number full-time enrolled (new admits only) 2007–2008, 16. Number part-time enrolled (new admits only) 2007–2008, 0. Openings 2008–2009, 15. The median number of years required for completion of a degree in 2006–2007 were 2. The number of students enrolled full- and part-time who were dismissed or voluntarily withdrew from this program area in 2007–2008 were 2. *School Psychology PsyD (Doctor of Psychology)*—Applications 2007–2008, 17. Total applicants accepted 2007–2008, 6. Number full-time enrolled (new admits only) 2007–2008, 6. Number part-time enrolled (new admits only) 2007–2008, 0. Openings 2008–2009, 15. The median number of years required for completion of a degree in 2006–2007 were 5. The number of students enrolled full- and part-time who were dismissed or voluntarily withdrew from this program area in 2007–2008 were 0. *Forensic Psychology MA/MS (Master of Arts/Science)*—Applications 2007–2008, 53. Total applicants accepted 2007–2008, 47. Number full-time enrolled (new admits only) 2007–2008, 47. Total enrolled 2007–2008 full-time, 47. Openings 2008–2009, 40. The median number of years required for completion of a degree in 2006–2007 were 2. The number of students enrolled full- and part-time who were dismissed or voluntarily withdrew from this program area in 2007–2008 were 0. *School Psychology MA/MS (Master of Arts/Science)*—Applications 2007–2008, 21. Total applicants accepted 2007–2008, 10. Number full-time enrolled (new admits only) 2007–2008, 10. Total enrolled 2007–2008 full-time, 10. Openings 2008–2009, 20. The median number of years required for completion of a degree in 2006–2007 were 2. The number of students enrolled full- and part-time who were dismissed or voluntarily withdrew from this program area in 2007–2008 were 0.

Other Criteria: (importance of criteria rated low, medium, or high): research experience—low, work experience—high, extracurricular activity—medium, clinically related public service—high, GPA—high, letters of recommendation—medium, interview—high, statement of goals and objectives—high, resume—medium. For additional information on admission requirements, go to http://www.argosy.edu.

Student Characteristics: The following represents characteristics of students in 2007–2008 in all graduate psychology programs in the department: Female—full-time 192, part-time 38; Male—full-time 70, part-time 29; African American/Black—full-time 18, part-time 6; Hispanic/Latino(a)—full-time 28, part-time 2; Asian/Pacific Islander—full-time 7, part-time 4; American Indian/Alaska Native—full-time 10, part-time 0; Caucasian/White—full-time 185, part-time 49; Multi-ethnic—full-time 14, part-time 6; students subject to the Americans With Disabilities Act—full-time 9, part-time 0; Unknown ethnicity—full-time 0, part-time 0.

Financial Information/Assistance:

Tuition for Full-Time Study: *Master's:* State residents: per academic year $10,800, $560 per credit hour; Nonstate residents: per

academic year $10,800, $560 per credit hour. *Doctoral:* State residents: per academic year $14,400, $780 per credit hour; Non-state residents: per academic year $14,400, $780 per credit hour. Tuition is subject to change. Additional fees are assessed to students beyond the costs of tuition for the following: graduation, internship, practica fee, technology fee, student activity fee, late registration fee. Tuition costs vary by program. Contact Department of Admissions toll free (866) 216-2777. Higher tuition cost for this program: Clinical Psychology programs are $895 per credit hour.

Financial Assistance:

First-Year Students: Fellowships and scholarships available for first year. Average amount paid per academic year: $3,000. Apply by rolling.

Advanced Students: Teaching assistantships available for advanced students. Average number of hours worked per week: 4. Tuition remission given: partial.

Additional Information: Of all students currently enrolled full time, 80% benefited from one or more of the listed financial assistance programs. Application and information available online at http://www.argosy.edu.

Internships/Practica: Doctoral Degree (PsyD Clinical Psychology): For those doctoral students for whom a professional internship was required in this program prior to graduation, (28) students applied for an internship in 2006–2007, with (27) students obtaining an internship. Of those students who obtained an internship, (27) were paid internships. Of those students who obtained an internship, (27) students placed in APA/CPA-accredited internships, (0) students placed in internships not APA/CPA accredited, but listed with the Association of Psychology Postdoctoral and Internship Centers (APPIC), (0) students placed in internships conforming to guidelines of the Council of Directors of School Psychology Programs (CDSPP), (0) students placed in internships that were not APA/CPA-accredited, APPIC or CDSPP listed. Doctoral Degree (PsyD School Psychology): For those doctoral students for whom a professional internship was required in this program prior to graduation, (0) students applied for an internship in 2006–2007, with (0) students obtaining an internship. Of those students who obtained an internship, (0) were paid internships. Of those students who obtained an internship, (0) students placed in APA/CPA-accredited internships, (0) students placed in internships not APA/CPA-accredited, but listed with the Association of Psychology Postdoctoral and Internship Centers (APPIC), (0) students placed in internships conforming to guidelines of the Council of Directors of School Psychology Programs (CDSPP), (0) students placed in internships that were not APA/CPA-accredited, APPIC or CDSPP listed. The School maintains an extensive clinical training network including public and private hospitals, community mental health agencies, private practices, substance abuse and rehabilitation agencies, correctional facilities, and the Indian Health Service.

Housing and Day Care: No on-campus housing is available. No on-campus day care facilities are available.

Employment of Department Graduates:

Master's Degree Graduates: Of those who graduated in the academic year 2006–2007, the following categories and numbers represent the postgraduate activities and employment of master's degree graduates: Enrolled in a psychology doctoral program (30), enrolled in a postdoctoral residency/fellowship (n/a), employed in independent practice (n/a), employed in a professional position in a school system (10), employed in a community mental health/counseling center (15), still seeking employment (6), total from the above (master's) (61).

Doctoral Degree Graduates: Of those who graduated in the academic year 2006–2007, the following categories and numbers represent the postgraduate activities and employment of doctoral degree graduates: Enrolled in a psychology doctoral program (n/a), enrolled in a postdoctoral residency/fellowship (11), employed in a professional position in a school system (5), still seeking employment (2), total from the above (doctoral) (18).

Additional Information:

Orientation, Objectives, and Emphasis of Department: The mission of Argosy University/Phoenix is to educate and train students in the major areas of clinical psychology, sport–exercise psychology, and professional counseling, and to prepare students for successful practitioner careers. The curriculum integrates theory, training, research, and practice and prepares students to work with a wide range of populations in need of psychological services. Faculty are both scholars and practitioners and guide students through coursework and field experiences so that they might understand how formal knowledge and practice operate to inform and enrich each other. The School follows a generalist practitioner–scholar orientation exposing students to a broad array of clinical theories and interventions. Sensitivity to diverse populations, populations with specific needs, and multicultural awareness are important components of the school's training model.

Personal Behavior Statement: When students sign an enrollment agreement, they agree to all the policies of the academic catalog where the statements of expected student behavior are stated.

Special Facilities or Resources: Concentration in Sport–Exercise Psychology within the clinical doctoral program.

Information for Students With Physical Disabilities: See the following Web site for more information: http://www.argosy.edu.

Application Information:

Send to Andy Hughes, Director of Admissions, Argosy University/Phoenix, 2233 Dunlap Avenue, Phoenix, AZ 85021. Phone Number: toll free (866) 216-2777 ext. 3110; e-mail: ahughes@argosy.edu. Application available online. URL of online application: http://www.argosy.edu/admissions. Students are admitted in the Fall, application deadline May 15; Spring, application deadline October 15; Programs have rolling admissions. Deadlines vary by program, contact the Department of Admissions toll free at (866) 216-2777 for more information. Priority deadline of January 15 for fall admission. *Fee:* $50.

Arizona State University (2007 data)

Applied Psychology
7001 East Williams Field Road
Mesa, AZ 85212
Telephone: (480) 727-1177
Fax: (480) 727-1538
E-mail: *Deanna.Lara@asu.edu*
Web: *http://www.poly.asu.edu/ecollege/appliedpsych/*

Department Information:

1999. Chairperson: Rob Gray. Number of faculty: total—full-time 6, part-time 10; women—full-time 1, part-time 3.

Programs and Degrees Offered:

Listed in the following order: Program area, degree type (T if terminal Master's), number awarded 7/06–6/07. Ms in Applied Psychology MA/MS (Master of Arts/Science) (T) 2.

Student Applications/Admissions:

Student Applications

Applied Psychology MA/MS (Master of Arts/Science)—Applications 2007–2008, 8. Total applicants accepted 2007–2008, 3. Number full-time enrolled (new admits only) 2007–2008, 2. Number part-time enrolled (new admits only) 2007–2008, 0. Openings 2008–2009, 4. The median number of years required for completion of a degree in 2006–2007 were 2. The number of students enrolled full- and part-time who were dismissed or voluntarily withdrew from this program area in 2007–2008 were 0.

Admissions Requirements:

Scores: Entries appear in this order: required test or GPA, minimum score (if required), median score of students entering in 2007–2008. Master's Programs: GRE-V no minimum stated; GRE-Q no minimum stated; overall undergraduate GPA no minimum stated; last 2 years GPA no minimum stated.

Other Criteria: (importance of criteria rated low, medium, or high): GRE/MAT scores—medium, research experience—high, work experience—medium, extracurricular activity—medium, GPA—medium, letters of recommendation—medium, interview—low, statement of goals and objectives—high.

Student Characteristics: The following represents characteristics of students in 2007–2008 in all graduate psychology programs in the department: Female—full-time 8, part-time 0; Male—full-time 4, part-time 0; African American/Black—full-time 0, part-time 0; Hispanic/Latino(a)—full-time 0, part-time 0; Asian/Pacific Islander—full-time 0, part-time 0; American Indian/Alaska Native—full-time 0, part-time 0; Caucasian/White—full-time 12, part-time 0; Multi-ethnic—full-time 0, part-time 0; students subject to the Americans With Disabilities Act—full-time 0, part-time 0; Unknown ethnicity—full-time 0, part-time 0.

Financial Information/Assistance:

Tuition for Full-Time Study: *Master's:* State residents: per academic year $6,028, $335 per credit hour; Nonstate residents: per academic year $16,074, $713 per credit hour. Tuition is subject to change. See the following Web site for updates and changes in tuition costs: http://www.asu.edu/sbs/fees.html.

Financial Assistance:

First-Year Students: Research assistantships available for first year. Average amount paid per academic year: $16,000. Average number of hours worked per week: 20. Tuition remission given: full and partial.

Advanced Students: Research assistantships available for advanced students. Average amount paid per academic year: $17,000. Tuition remission given: full and partial.

Additional Information: Of all students currently enrolled full time, 100% benefited from one or more of the listed financial assistance programs.

Internships/Practica: Students currently work on projects at the Air Force Research Laboratory, at Intel, and at Motorola. Other opportunities are continually being sought as the program develops.

Housing and Day Care: On-campus housing is available. See the following Web site for more information: http://www.poly.asu.edu/housing/. On-campus day care facilities are available.

Employment of Department Graduates:

Master's Degree Graduates: Of those who graduated in the academic year 2006–2007, the following categories and numbers represent the postgraduate activities and employment of master's degree graduates: Enrolled in a psychology doctoral program (1), enrolled in a postdoctoral residency/fellowship (n/a), employed in independent practice (n/a), employed in government agency (4), total from the above (master's) (8).

Doctoral Degree Graduates: Of those who graduated in the academic year 2006–2007, the following categories and numbers represent the postgraduate activities and employment of doctoral degree graduates: Enrolled in a psychology doctoral program (n/a), total from the above (doctoral) (0).

Additional Information:

Orientation, Objectives, and Emphasis of Department: The Applied Psychology Department has adopted a strong research emphasis as a major goal in addition to providing a first-rate education for both graduate and undergraduate students. Research in the unit is motivated by applied issues, but our goal is to seek answers to fundamental issues within the applied framework. Some research appears in the best journals publishing basic empirical and theoretical research. Other projects will find more appropriate audiences in the best applied journals. Students studying for the MS degree are prepared both for further graduate study and for employment in government and industry.

Special Facilities or Resources: Excellent research facilities in a newly completed laboratory building.

Application Information:

Send to Admissions Secretary. Application available online. URL of online application: http://www.asu.edu/graduate/prospective/index.htm. Programs have rolling admissions. *Fee:* $50.

Arizona State University

Department of Psychology
College of Liberal Arts and Sciences
P.O. Box 871104
Tempe, AZ 85287-1104
Telephone: (480) 965-7598
Fax: (480) 965-8544
E-mail: *laurie.chassin@asu.edu*
Web: *http://www.asu.edu/clas/psych*

Department Information:

1932. Chairperson: Keith Crnic. Number of faculty: total—full-time 55, part-time 2; women—full-time 21; total—minority—full-time 6; women minority—full-time 2; faculty subject to the Americans With Disabilities Act 1.

Programs and Degrees Offered:

Listed in the following order: Program area, degree type (T if terminal Master's), number awarded 7/06–6/07. Clinical PhD (Doctor of Philosophy) 5, Developmental PhD (Doctor of Philosophy) 1, Quantitative PhD (Doctor of Philosophy) 0, Social PhD (Doctor of Philosophy) 1, Behavioral Neuroscience PhD (Doctor of Philosophy) 0, Cognition and Behavior PhD (Doctor of Philosophy) 0, Law and Psychology Other 0.

APA Accreditation: Clinical PhD (Doctor of Philosophy).

Student Applications/Admissions:

Student Applications

Clinical PhD (Doctor of Philosophy)—Applications 2007–2008, 248. Total applicants accepted 2007–2008, 7. Number full-time enrolled (new admits only) 2007–2008, 7. Openings 2008–2009, 8. The median number of years required for completion of a degree in 2006–2007 were 7. The number of students enrolled full- and part-time who were dismissed or voluntarily withdrew from this program area in 2007–2008 were 1. *Developmental PhD (Doctor of Philosophy)*—Applications 2007–2008, 32. Total applicants accepted 2007–2008, 2. Number full-time enrolled (new admits only) 2007–2008, 2. Number part-time enrolled (new admits only) 2007–2008, 0. Openings 2008–2009, 4. The median number of years required for completion of a degree in 2006–2007 were 4. The number of students enrolled full- and part-time who were dismissed or voluntarily withdrew from this program area in 2007–2008 were 1. *Quantitative PhD (Doctor of Philosophy)*—Applications 2007–2008, 22. Total applicants accepted 2007–2008, 1. Number full-time enrolled (new admits only) 2007–2008, 1. Number part-time enrolled (new admits only) 2007–2008, 0. Openings 2008–2009, 4. The number of students enrolled full- and part-time who were dismissed or voluntarily withdrew from this program area in 2007–2008 were 0. *Social PhD (Doctor of Philosophy)*—Applications 2007–2008, 104. Total applicants accepted 2007–2008, 5. Number full-time enrolled (new admits only) 2007–2008, 5. Number part-time enrolled (new admits only) 2007–2008, 0. Openings 2008–2009, 5. The median number of years required for completion of a degree in 2006–2007 were 7. The number of students enrolled full- and part-time who were dismissed or voluntarily withdrew from this program area in 2007–2008 were 2. *Behavioral Neuroscience PhD (Doctor of Philosophy)*—Applications 2007–2008, 33. Total applicants accepted 2007–2008, 5. Number full-time enrolled (new admits only) 2007–2008, 5. Total enrolled 2007–2008 full-time, 12. Openings 2008–2009, 6. The number of students enrolled full- and part-time who were dismissed or voluntarily withdrew from this program area in 2007–2008 were 1. *Cognition and Behavior PhD (Doctor of Philosophy)*—Applications 2007–2008, 25. Total applicants accepted 2007–2008, 4. Number full-time enrolled (new admits only) 2007–2008, 4. Total enrolled 2007–2008 full-time, 21. Openings 2008–2009, 4. The number of students enrolled full- and part-time who were dismissed or voluntarily withdrew from this program area in 2007–2008 were 1. *Law and Psychology Other*—Applications 2007–2008, 1. Total applicants accepted 2007–2008, 1. Number full-time enrolled (new admits only) 2007–2008, 1. Total enrolled 2007–2008 full-time, 1. Openings 2008–2009, 3. The number of students enrolled full- and part-time who were dismissed or voluntarily withdrew from this program area in 2007–2008 were 0.

Admissions Requirements:

Scores: Entries appear in this order: required test or GPA, minimum score (if required), median score of students entering in 2007–2008. Doctoral Programs: GRE-V no minimum stated; GRE-Q no minimum stated; GRE-Subject (Psychology) no minimum stated; overall undergraduate GPA no minimum stated; last 2 years GPA no minimum stated. Subject test is strongly for clinical applicants only. Scores vary across programs.

Other Criteria: (importance of criteria rated low, medium, or high): GRE/MAT scores—medium, research experience—high, work experience—low, extracurricular activity—low, clinically related public service—medium, GPA—medium, letters of recommendation—high, interview—high, statement of goals and objectives—high. Weightings vary across programs. For additional information on admission requirements, go to http://www.asu.edu/clas/psych/.

Student Characteristics: The following represents characteristics of students in 2007–2008 in all graduate psychology programs in the department: Female—full-time 92, part-time 0; Male—full-time 41, part-time 0; African American/Black—full-time 1, part-time 0; Hispanic/Latino(a)—full-time 19, part-time 0; Asian/Pacific Islander—full-time 12, part-time 0; American Indian/Alaska Native—full-time 2, part-time 0; Caucasian/White—full-time 99, part-time 0; Multi-ethnic—part-time 0; students subject to the Americans With Disabilities Act—full-time 0, part-time 0; Unknown ethnicity—full-time 0, part-time 0; International students who hold an F-1 or J-1 Visa—full-time 11, part-time 0.

Financial Information/Assistance:

Tuition for Full-Time Study: *Doctoral:* State residents: per academic year $7,039, $565 per credit hour; Nonstate residents: per academic year $19,604, $1,633 per credit hour. Tuition is subject to change. See the following Web site for updates and changes in tuition costs: http://www.asu.edu.

Financial Assistance:

First-Year Students: Teaching assistantships available for first year. Average amount paid per academic year: $14,300. Average number of hours worked per week: 20. Tuition remission given: full. Research assistantships available for first year. Average amount paid per academic year: $14,300. Average number of hours worked per week: 20. Tuition remission given: full. Fellowships and scholarships available for first year.

Advanced Students: Teaching assistantships available for advanced students. Average amount paid per academic year: $15,300. Average number of hours worked per week: 20. Tuition remission given: full. Research assistantships available for advanced students. Average amount paid per academic year: $15,300. Average number of hours worked per week: 20. Tuition remission given: full. Traineeships available for advanced students. Fellowships and scholarships available for advanced students.

Additional Information: Of all students currently enrolled full time, 100% benefited from one or more of the listed financial assistance programs.

Internships/Practica: Doctoral Degree (PhD Clinical): For those doctoral students for whom a professional internship was required

in this program prior to graduation, (6) students applied for an internship in 2006–2007, with (5) students obtaining an internship. Of those students who obtained an internship, (5) were paid internships. Of those students who obtained an internship, (4) students placed in APA/CPA-accredited internships, (1) student placed in internships not APA/CPA-accredited, but listed with the Association of Psychology Postdoctoral and Internship Centers (APPIC), (0) students placed in internships conforming to guidelines of the Council of Directors of School Psychology Programs (CDSPP), (0) students placed in internships that were not APA/CPA-accredited, APPIC or CDSPP listed. Doctoral clinical students complete practica in community agencies and in our in-house training clinic.

Housing and Day Care: On-campus housing is available. On-campus day care facilities are available.

Employment of Department Graduates:

Master's Degree Graduates: Of those who graduated in the academic year 2006–2007, the following categories and numbers represent the postgraduate activities and employment of master's degree graduates: Enrolled in a postdoctoral residency/fellowship (n/a), employed in independent practice (n/a), total from the above (master's) (0).

Doctoral Degree Graduates: Of those who graduated in the academic year 2006–2007, the following categories and numbers represent the postgraduate activities and employment of doctoral degree graduates: Enrolled in a psychology doctoral program (n/a), enrolled in a postdoctoral residency/fellowship (1), employed in an academic position at a university (5), not seeking employment (1), do not know (1), total from the above (doctoral) (8).

Additional Information:

Orientation, Objectives, and Emphasis of Department: The department seeks to instill in students knowledge, skills, and an appreciation of psychology as a science and as a profession. To do so, it offers undergraduate and graduate programs emphasizing theory, research, and applied practice. The department encourages a multiplicity of theoretical viewpoints and research interests. The behavioral neuroscience area emphasizes the neural bases of motor disorders, drug abuse, and recovery of function following brain damage. The clinical program includes areas of emphasis in health psychology, child–clinical psychology, and community–prevention. Also offered are classes in psychopathology, prevention, assessment, and psychotherapy. The cognitive systems area includes cognitive psychology, adaptive systems, learning, sensation and perception, and cognitive development. The developmental area includes coursework and research experience in the core areas of cognitive and social development. The environmental area emphasizes the application of psychological research to environmental and population problems, including architectural design, urban planning, and human ecology. The quantitative area focuses on design, measurement, and statistical analysis issues that arise in diverse areas of psychological research. The social area emphasizes theoretical and laboratory skills combined with program evaluation and applied social psychology. New interdisciplinary training opportunities are in Arts, Media, and Engineering, and Law and Psychology. See the following Web site for more information: http://www.asu.edu/jointprograms/lawpsych/.

Special Facilities or Resources: The department has the Child Study Laboratory for training and research in developmental psychology, including both normal and clinical groups, particularly of preschool age; the Clinical Psychology Center, whose clients represent a wide range of psychological disorders and are not limited to the university community; and the experimental laboratories, with exceptional computer facilities for the study of speech perception, neural networks, categorization, memory, sensory processes, and learning. The clinical and social programs maintain continuing liaison with a wide range of off-campus agencies for research applications of psychological theory and research. Our NIMH-funded Preventive Intervention Research Center provides a site for training in the design, implementation, and evaluation of preventative interventions. Quantitatively oriented students receive methodological experience in large-scale research programs and in our statistical laboratory.

Application Information:

Send to Admissions Secretary, Department of Psychology, Arizona State University, P.O. Box 871104, Tempe, AZ 85287-1104. Application materials must also be sent directly to the Divsion of Graduate Studies, Arizona State University, Tempe, AZ 85287 (see Web site). Application available online. URL of online application: http://www.asu.edu/clas/psych/gprogram/apply.htm. Students are admitted in the Fall, application deadline. December 15 for Clinical, January 5 for all other programs. *Fee:* $65.

Arizona State University

Division of Psychology in Education
Mary Lou Fulton College of Education
Payne Hall 302, P.O. Box 870611
Tempe, AZ 85287-0611
Telephone: (480) 965-3384
Fax: (480) 965-0300
E-mail: *james.klein@asu.edu*
Web: *http://www.coe.asu.edu/psyched/*

Department Information:

1968. Interim Division Director: James D. Klein. Number of faculty: total—full-time 30, part-time 5; women—full-time 14, part-time 2; total—minority—full-time 6; women minority—full-time 3.

Programs and Degrees Offered:

Listed in the following order: Program area, degree type (T if terminal Master's), number awarded 7/06–6/07. Educational: Learning PhD (Doctor of Philosophy) 3, Counseling Psychology PhD (Doctor of Philosophy) 7, Master of Counseling MA/MS (Master of Arts/Science) (T) 58, Master of Education in Counseling (Other) 2, Educational Psychology (Other) 10, Educational: Measurement, Statistics PhD (Doctor of Philosophy) 1, Educational: Lifespan Development PhD (Doctor of Philosophy) 4, Educational Technology Other 11, Educational: School Psychology PhD (Doctor of Philosophy) 1, Educational Technology PhD (Doctor of Philosophy) 5.

APA Accreditation: Counseling PhD (Doctor of Philosophy). School PhD (Doctor of Philosophy).

Student Applications/Admissions:

Student Applications

Educational: Learning PhD (Doctor of Philosophy)—Applications 2007–2008, 4. Total applicants accepted 2007–2008, 1. Number full-time enrolled (new admits only) 2007–2008, 1. Number part-time enrolled (new admits only) 2007–2008, 0. Total enrolled 2007–2008 full-time, 5, part-time, 8. Openings 2008–2009, 6. The median number of years required for completion of a degree in 2006–2007 were 4. The number of students enrolled full- and part-time who were dismissed or voluntarily withdrew from this program area in 2007–2008 were 0. *Counseling Psychology PhD (Doctor of Philosophy)*—Applications 2007–2008, 100. Total applicants accepted 2007–2008, 9. Number full-time enrolled (new admits only) 2007–2008, 6. Number part-time enrolled (new admits only) 2007–2008, 1. Total enrolled 2007–2008 full-time, 29, part-time, 29. Openings 2008–2009, 9. The median number of years required for completion of a degree in 2006–2007 were 6. The number of students enrolled full- and part-time who were dismissed or voluntarily withdrew from this program area in 2007–2008 were 0. *Master of Counseling MA/MS (Master of Arts/Science)*—Applications 2007–2008, 144. Total applicants accepted 2007–2008, 44. Number full-time enrolled (new admits only) 2007–2008, 27. Number part-time enrolled (new admits only) 2007–2008, 5. Total enrolled 2007–2008 full-time, 86, part-time, 37. Openings 2008–2009, 50. The median number of years required for completion of a degree in 2006–2007 were 3. The number of students enrolled full- and part-time who were dismissed or voluntarily withdrew from this program area in 2007–2008 were 2. *Master of Education in Counseling Other*—Applications 2007–2008, 0. Total applicants accepted 2007–2008, 0. Number full-time enrolled (new admits only) 2007–2008, 0. Number part-time enrolled (new admits only) 2007–2008, 0. Openings 2008–2009, 4. The median number of years required for completion of a degree in 2006–2007 were 2. The number of students enrolled full- and part-time who were dismissed or voluntarily withdrew from this program area in 2007–2008 were 0. *Educational Psychology Other*—Applications 2007–2008, 17. Total applicants accepted 2007–2008, 10. Number full-time enrolled (new admits only) 2007–2008, 3. Number part-time enrolled (new admits only) 2007–2008, 4. Total enrolled 2007–2008 full-time, 10, part-time, 17. Openings 2008–2009, 10. The median number of years required for completion of a degree in 2006–2007 were 2. The number of students enrolled full- and part-time who were dismissed or voluntarily withdrew from this program area in 2007–2008 were 0. *Educational: Measurement, Statistics PhD (Doctor of Philosophy)*—Applications 2007–2008, 14. Total applicants accepted 2007–2008, 8. Number full-time enrolled (new admits only) 2007–2008, 3. Number part-time enrolled (new admits only) 2007–2008, 2. Total enrolled 2007–2008 full-time, 5, part-time, 17. Openings 2008–2009, 6. The median number of years required for completion of a degree in 2006–2007 were 6. The number of students enrolled full- and part-time who were dismissed or voluntarily withdrew from this program area in 2007–2008 were 2. *Educational: Lifespan Development PhD (Doctor of Philosophy)*—Applications 2007–2008, 6. Total applicants accepted 2007–2008, 5. Number full-time enrolled (new admits only) 2007–2008, 1. Number part-time enrolled (new admits only) 2007–2008, 1. Total enrolled 2007–2008 full-time, 8, part-time, 13. Openings 2008–2009, 5. The median number of years required for completion of a degree in 2006–2007 were 4. The number of students enrolled full- and part-time who were dismissed or voluntarily withdrew from this program area in 2007–2008 were 1. *Educational Technology Other*—Applications 2007–2008, 15. Total applicants accepted 2007–2008, 15. Number full-time enrolled (new admits only) 2007–2008, 3. Number part-time enrolled (new admits only) 2007–2008, 9. Total enrolled 2007–2008 full-time, 9, part-time, 22. Openings 2008–2009, 15. The median number of years required for completion of a degree in 2006–2007 were 2. The number of students enrolled full- and part-time who were dismissed or voluntarily withdrew from this program area in 2007–2008 were 1. *Educational: School Psychology PhD (Doctor of Philosophy)*—Applications 2007–2008, 35. Total applicants accepted 2007–2008, 10. Number full-time enrolled (new admits only) 2007–2008, 6. Number part-time enrolled (new admits only) 2007–2008, 1. Total enrolled 2007–2008 full-time, 25, part-time, 24. Openings 2008–2009, 7. The median number of years required for completion of a degree in 2006–2007 were 6. The number of students enrolled full- and part-time who were dismissed or voluntarily withdrew from this program area in 2007–2008 were 1. *Educational Technology PhD (Doctor of Philosophy)*—Applications 2007–2008, 23. Total applicants accepted 2007–2008, 14. Number full-time enrolled (new admits only) 2007–2008, 5. Number part-time enrolled (new admits only) 2007–2008, 6. Total enrolled 2007–2008 full-time, 11, part-time, 14. Openings 2008–2009, 10. The median number of years required for completion of a degree in 2006–2007 were 4. The number of students enrolled full- and part-time who were dismissed or voluntarily withdrew from this program area in 2007–2008 were 1.

Admissions Requirements:

Scores: Entries appear in this order: required test or GPA, minimum score (if required), median score of students entering in 2007–2008. Master's Programs: GRE-V no minimum stated, 520; GRE-Q no minimum stated, 600; MAT no minimum stated; overall undergraduate GPA no minimum stated; last 2 years GPA 3.00, 3.62. The GRE is required by all programs. Doctoral Programs: GRE-V no minimum stated, 570; GRE-Q no minimum stated, 640; overall undergraduate GPA no minimum stated; last 2 years GPA 3.0, 3.60. Educational Technology PhD requires a 3.2 or above undergraduate GPA.

Other Criteria: (importance of criteria rated low, medium, or high): GRE/MAT scores—medium, research experience—high, work experience—medium, extracurricular activity—low, clinically related public service—medium, GPA—medium, letters of recommendation—low, interview—medium, statement of goals and objectives—medium. Programs use the FRK index which combines GRE V+Q with undergraduate GPA. Minimum FRKs are set by faculty admissions committees. For additional information on admission requirements, go to http://education.asu.edu; http://www.asu.edu/graduate.

Student Characteristics: The following represents characteristics of students in 2007–2008 in all graduate psychology programs in the department: Female—full-time 135, part-time 132; Male—full-time 53, part-time 53; African American/Black—full-time 11, part-time 6; Hispanic/Latino(a)—full-time 21, part-time 23; Asian/Pacific Islander—full-time 21, part-time 16; American Indian/Alaska Native—full-time 3, part-time 2; Caucasian/White—full-time 122, part-time 132; students subject to the Americans With Disabilities Act—full-time 1, part-time 2; Unknown ethnicity—full-time 10, part-time 6; International students who hold an F-1 or J-1 Visa—full-time 21, part-time 12.

Financial Information/Assistance:

Tuition for Full-Time Study: *Master's:* State residents: per academic year $7,042, $443 per credit hour; Nonstate residents: per academic year $19,606, $894 per credit hour. *Doctoral:* State residents: per academic year $7,042, $443 per credit hour; Nonstate residents: per academic year $19,606, $894 per credit hour. Tuition is subject to change. See the following Web site for updates and changes in tuition costs: http://www.asu.edu/sbs/GraduateFees.html.

Financial Assistance:

First-Year Students: Teaching assistantships available for first year. Average amount paid per academic year: $6,342. Average number of hours worked per week: 10. Apply by April 15. Tuition remission given: partial. Research assistantships available for first year. Average amount paid per academic year: $6,342. Average number of hours worked per week: 10. Apply by April 15. Tuition remission given: partial.

Advanced Students: Teaching assistantships available for advanced students. Average amount paid per academic year: $6,342. Average number of hours worked per week: 10. Apply by April 15. Tuition remission given: partial. Research assistantships available for advanced students. Average amount paid per academic year: $6,342. Average number of hours worked per week: 10. Apply by April 15. Tuition remission given: partial.

Additional Information: Of all students currently enrolled full time, 26% benefited from one or more of the listed financial assistance programs. Application and information available online at http://www.asu.edu/graduate.

Internships/Practica: Doctoral Degree (PhD Counseling Psychology): For those doctoral students for whom a professional internship was required in this program prior to graduation, (14) students applied for an internship in 2006–2007, with (14) students obtaining an internship. Of those students who obtained an internship, (14) were paid internships. Of those students who obtained an internship, (13) students placed in APA/CPA-accredited internships, (1) student placed in internships not APA/CPA accredited, but listed with the Association of Psychology Postdoctoral and Internship Centers (APPIC), (0) students placed in internships conforming to guidelines of the Council of Directors of School Psychology Programs (CDSPP), (0) students placed in internships that were not APA/CPA-accredited, APPIC or CDSPP listed. Doctoral Degree (PhD Educational: School Psychology): For those doctoral students for whom a professional internship was required in this program prior to graduation, (5) students applied for an internship in 2006–2007, with (5) students obtaining an internship. Of those students who obtained an internship, (5) were paid internships. Of those students who obtained an internship, (1) student placed in APA/CPA-accredited internships, (1) student placed in internships not APA/CPA accredited, but listed with the Association of Psychology Postdoctoral and Internship Centers (APPIC), (3) students placed in internships conforming to guidelines of the Council of Directors of School Psychology Programs (CDSPP), (0) students placed in internships that were not APA/CPA-accredited, APPIC or CDSPP listed. Our doctoral internships include APA-approved sites throughout the nation. Sites include university counseling centers, community mental health clinics, and hospitals. Practica for doctoral and master's students typically are local (the greater Phoenix area) and include university counseling centers, community mental health clinics, and hospitals.

Housing and Day Care: No on-campus housing is available. No on-campus day care facilities are available.

Employment of Department Graduates:

Master's Degree Graduates: Of those who graduated in the academic year 2006–2007, the following categories and numbers represent the postgraduate activities and employment of master's degree graduates: Enrolled in a postdoctoral residency/fellowship (n/a), employed in independent practice (n/a), total from the above (master's) (0).

Doctoral Degree Graduates: Of those who graduated in the academic year 2006–2007, the following categories and numbers represent the postgraduate activities and employment of doctoral degree graduates: Enrolled in a psychology doctoral program (n/a), total from the above (doctoral) (0).

Additional Information:

Orientation, Objectives, and Emphasis of Department: The Division adheres to a scientist–practitioner model across all areas. The Counseling Psychology and School Psychology doctoral programs are APA accredited. Less than half of the doctoral graduates accept positions in colleges and universities, the remainder function in applied settings.

Special Facilities or Resources: The department staffs and operates a large-scale psychological assessment laboratory, and most students are currently assigned research and study space. Strong research relations exist with local schools, agencies, and private industry. The Counseling Training Center is a training facility for Master's and PhD level counseling students. The center serves clients from both the university and the general public.

Information for Students With Physical Disabilities: See the following Web site for more information: http://www.asu.edu/drs.

Application Information:

Supplemental materials should be sent to Admissions Secretary, Psychology in Education, Arizona State University, Payne Hall 302, P.O. Box 870611, Tempe, AZ 85287-0611. Application available online. URL of online application: http://www.asu.edu/graduate/admissions. Students are admitted in the Fall and Spring. Counseling Psychology—December 1 for Fall; School Psychology—January 1 for fall; Master of Counseling—January 15 for Fall; Educational Psychology, Learning, Lifespan, Measurement, and Educational Technology—February 15 for Fall and October 15 for Spring. *Fee:* $65. The application fee cannot be waived. Application fee for international students is $80.

Arizona, University of

Department of Psychology
Social and Behavioral Sciences
P.O. Box 210068
Tucson, AZ 85721
Telephone: (520) 621-7447
Fax: (520) 621-9306
E-mail: *kaszniak@u.arizona.edu*
Web: *http://www.psychology.arizona.edu/*

Department Information:

1914. Head: Alfred W. Kaszniak. Number of faculty: total—full-time 40, part-time 12; women—full-time 15, part-time 5; total—minority—full-time 3, part-time 1; women minority—full-time 2.

Programs and Degrees Offered:

Listed in the following order: Program area, degree type (T if terminal Master's), number awarded 7/06–6/07. Clinical PhD (Doctor of Philosophy) 4, Cognition and Neural Systems PhD (Doctor of Philosophy) 6, Ethology and Evolutionary PhD (Doctor of Philosophy) 1, Psychology, Policy, and Law PhD (Doctor of Philosophy) 0, Social PhD (Doctor of Philosophy) 0, Undeclared/General PhD (Doctor of Philosophy) 1.

APA Accreditation: Clinical PhD (Doctor of Philosophy).

Student Applications/Admissions:

Student Applications

Clinical PhD (Doctor of Philosophy)—Applications 2007–2008, 220. Total applicants accepted 2007–2008, 7. Number full-time enrolled (new admits only) 2007–2008, 7. Number part-time enrolled (new admits only) 2007–2008, 0. Openings 2008–2009, 8. The median number of years required for completion of a degree in 2006–2007 were 6. The number of students enrolled full- and part-time who were dismissed or voluntarily withdrew from this program area in 2007–2008 were 0. *Cognition and Neural Systems PhD (Doctor of Philosophy)*—Applications 2007–2008, 65. Total applicants accepted 2007–2008, 6. Number full-time enrolled (new admits only) 2007–2008, 6. Openings 2008–2009, 7. The median number of years required for completion of a degree in 2006–2007 were 7. The number of students enrolled full- and part-time who were dismissed or voluntarily withdrew from this program area in 2007–2008 were 0. *Ethology and Evolutionary PhD (Doctor of Philosophy)*—Applications 2007–2008, 18. Total applicants accepted 2007–2008, 0. Number full-time enrolled (new admits only) 2007–2008, 0. Total enrolled 2007–2008 full-time, 5, part-time, 2. Openings 2008–2009, 2. The median number of years required for completion of a degree in 2006–2007 were 6. The number of students enrolled full- and part-time who were dismissed or voluntarily withdrew from this program area in 2007–2008 were 2. *Psychology, Policy, and Law PhD (Doctor of Philosophy)*—Applications 2007–2008, 67. Total applicants accepted 2007–2008, 1. Number full-time enrolled (new admits only) 2007–2008, 2. Number part-time enrolled (new admits only) 2007–2008, 0. Total enrolled 2007–2008 full-time, 5, part-time, 1. Openings 2008–2009, 1. The number of students enrolled full- and part-time who were dismissed or voluntarily withdrew from this program area in 2007–2008 were 1. *Social PhD (Doctor of Philosophy)*—Applications 2007–2008, 62. Total applicants accepted 2007–2008, 3. Number full-time enrolled (new admits only) 2007–2008, 3. Openings 2008–2009, 2. The number of students enrolled full- and part-time who were dismissed or voluntarily withdrew from this program area in 2007–2008 were 0. *Undeclared/General PhD (Doctor of Philosophy)*—Applications 2007–2008, 0. Total applicants accepted 2007–2008, 0. Number full-time enrolled (new admits only) 2007–2008, 0. Number part-time enrolled (new admits only) 2007–2008, 0. Total enrolled 2007–2008 full-time, 6, part-time, 1. The median number of years required for completion of a degree in 2006–2007 were 15. The number of students enrolled full- and part-time who were dismissed or voluntarily withdrew from this program area in 2007–2008 were 0.

Admissions Requirements:

Scores: Entries appear in this order: required test or GPA, minimum score (if required), median score of students entering in 2007–2008. Master's Programs: We do not offer a terminal Master's. Doctoral Programs: GRE-V no minimum stated, 560; GRE-Q no minimum stated, 720; GRE-Subject (Psychology) no minimum stated, 677; overall undergraduate GPA 3.0, 3.89. The Clinical Program requires the GRE subject score. For other programs, this score is recommended, but not required.
Other Criteria: (importance of criteria rated low, medium, or high): GRE/MAT scores—medium, research experience—high, work experience—low, extracurricular activity—low, clinically related public service—low, GPA—medium, letters of recommendation—high, interview—medium, statement of goals and objectives—high, subject scores for the Clinical Program would be—medium. For additional information on admission requirements, go to http://psychology.arizona.edu/programs/g_each.php?option=12.

Student Characteristics: The following represents characteristics of students in 2007–2008 in all graduate psychology programs in the department: Female—full-time 55, part-time 9; Male—full-time 31, part-time 3; African American/Black—full-time 2, part-time 0; Hispanic/Latino(a)—full-time 9, part-time 1; Asian/Pacific Islander—full-time 5, part-time 1; American Indian/Alaska Native—full-time 1, part-time 0; Caucasian/White—full-time 45, part-time 10; Multi-ethnic—full-time 0, part-time 0; students subject to the Americans With Disabilities Act—full-time 1, part-time 0; Unknown ethnicity—full-time 12, part-time 0; International students who hold an F-1 or J-1 Visa—full-time 12, part-time 0.

Financial Information/Assistance:

Tuition for Full-Time Study: *Doctoral:* State residents: per academic year $2,772, $290 per credit hour; Nonstate residents: per academic year $5,403, $391 per credit hour. Tuition is subject to change. See the following Web site for updates and changes in tuition costs: http://www.bursar.arizona.edu/students/fees/index.asp.

Financial Assistance:

First-Year Students: Teaching assistantships available for first year. Average amount paid per academic year: $13,710. Average number of hours worked per week: 20. Tuition remission given: partial. Research assistantships available for first year. Average amount paid per academic year: $13,710. Average number of hours worked per week: 20. Tuition remission given: partial. Traineeships available for first year. Average amount paid per academic year: $13,710. Average number of hours worked per week: 20. Tuition remission given: partial. Fellowships and scholarships available for first year. Average amount paid per academic year: $13,300. Average number of hours worked per week: 20. Tuition remission given: partial.

Advanced Students: Teaching assistantships available for advanced students. Average amount paid per academic year: $13,710. Average number of hours worked per week: 20. Tuition remission given: partial. Research assistantships available for advanced students. Average amount paid per academic year: $13,710. Average number of hours worked per week: 20. Tuition remission given: partial. Traineeships available for advanced students. Average amount paid per academic year: $13,710. Average number of hours worked per week: 20. Tuition remission given: partial. Fellowships and scholarships available for advanced students. Average amount paid per academic year: $13,300. Average number of hours worked per week: 20. Tuition remission given: partial.

Additional Information: Of all students currently enrolled full time, 96% benefited from one or more of the listed financial assistance programs. Application and information available online at http://psychology.arizona.edu/programs/g_each.php?option=12.

Internships/Practica: Doctoral Degree (PhD clinical): For those doctoral students for whom a professional internship was required in this program prior to graduation, (6) students applied for an internship in 2006–2007, with (3) students obtaining an internship. Of those students who obtained an internship, (3) were paid internships. Of those students who obtained an internship, (3) students placed in APA/CPA-accredited internships, (0) students placed in internships not APA/CPA-accredited, but listed with the Association of Psychology Postdoctoral and Internship Centers (APPIC), (0) students placed in internships conforming to guidelines of the Council of Directors of School Psychology Programs (CDSPP), (0) students placed in internships that were not APA/CPA-accredited, APPIC or CDSPP listed. Clinical students are required to do a 1-year internship. UMC medical school does offer internship positions, although most of our students leave campus for the internship. All of the clinical students are placed in APA-accredited internships. There are also various externships and practica available within the department as well as throughout the community.

Housing and Day Care: On-campus housing is available. See the following Web site for more information: http://www.life.arizona.edu/graduate/cl/index.asp. On-campus day care facilities are available. See the following Web site for more information: http://www.lifework.arizona.edu/cc/.

Employment of Department Graduates:

Master's Degree Graduates: Of those who graduated in the academic year 2006–2007, the following categories and numbers represent the postgraduate activities and employment of master's degree graduates: Enrolled in a postdoctoral residency/fellowship (n/a), employed in independent practice (n/a), total from the above (master's) (0).

Doctoral Degree Graduates: Of those who graduated in the academic year 2006–2007, the following categories and numbers represent the postgraduate activities and employment of doctoral degree graduates: Enrolled in a psychology doctoral program (n/a), enrolled in another graduate/professional program (0), enrolled in a postdoctoral residency/fellowship (0), employed in independent practice (0), employed in an academic position at a university (9), employed in an academic position at a 2-year/4-year college (0), employed in other positions at a higher education institution (1), employed in a professional position in a school system (0), employed in business or industry (1), employed in government agency (0), employed in a community mental health/counseling center (0), employed in a hospital/medical center (1), still seeking employment (0), not seeking employment (0), other employment position (0), do not know (0), total from the above (doctoral) (12).

Additional Information:

Orientation, Objectives, and Emphasis of Department: Our objectives as a department include contributing to the growth of knowledge about the mind and its workings, and the training of students to participate in this pursuit, as well as using this knowledge to benefit society. The department emphasizes research and training students headed toward both academic and applied careers. Required courses provide breadth of coverage, but emphasis is on research within the area of specialization, relying on independent work with individual faculty members. The interdisciplinary nature of the department fosters specialization in areas that cut across program boundaries and permits work with faculty members in various programs. The cognition and neural systems area emphasizes language, perception, attention, memory, aging, ensemble recording of neural activity, and human neuroimaging; the clinical area emphasizes clinical neuropsychology, psychotherapy research, sleep disorders, psychophysiology, and assessment; the social area emphasizes prejudice and stereotyping, cognitive dissonance, self-esteem, and motivational factors in thought and behavior; the psychology, policy, and law area emphasizes the contributions of psychological science to legal and policy decisions; and the ethology and evolutionary area emphasizes quantitative ethology, invertebrate behavior, and human behavioral ecology. In addition to these formal programs, the department also offers specialization in evaluation and research methods. The department is the administrative home for the Center for Consciousness Studies, and the Cognition and Neuroimaging Laboratory.

Special Facilities or Resources: The department has modern laboratories devoted to research in various areas of cognitive, clinical, neuroscientific, social, and comparative research. The department employs five technicians available for assistance with computers and other equipment. There are a number of clinics within the department, bringing in patients associated with research projects on aging, sleep disorders, memory disorders, depression, and others. The department has ties with a number of other programs on campus, including the departments of Anatomy, Family and Community Medicine, Neurology, Ophthalmology, Pediatrics, Pharmacology, Physiology and Psychiatry in the College of Medicine, and the departments of Ecology and Evolutionary Biology, Family Studies, Linguistics, Management and Policy, Mathematics, Philosophy, Renewable and Natural Resources, Speech and Hearing Sciences, and Physics on the main campus. Ties also exist with various interdisciplinary programs, including Cognitive Science (many of whose laboratories are located in the Psychology Building), Applied Mathematics, and Neuroscience. Most of the department's faculty members are holders of research grants, permitting a significant proportion of the graduate students to serve as research assistants at various times during their training.

Information for Students With Physical Disabilities: See the following Web site for more information: http://www.drc.arizona.edu/.

Application Information:
Send to The Univeristy of Arizona Department of Psychology, Graduate Admissions 1503 East University Boulevard, Room 312, P.O. Box 210068 Tucson, AZ 85721-0068. Application available online. URL of online application: https://www.sbs.arizona.edu/project/admission/psych/login.php. Students are admitted in the Fall, application deadline December 15. *Fee:* $50. The Psychology Department does not charge a fee to apply to our program. The $50 fee is a charge they pay to the Graduate College to apply.

Midwestern University

Clinical Psychology
College of Health Sciences
19555 North 59th Avenue
Glendale, AZ 85308
Telephone: (623) 572-3860
Fax: (623) 572-3830
E-mail: *phutch@midwestern.edu*
Web: *http://www.midwestern.edu*

Department Information:
2006. Program Director: Philinda Smith Hutchings, PhD, ABPP. Number of faculty: total—full-time 5; women—full-time 4; total—minority—full-time 2; women minority—full-time 2.

Programs and Degrees Offered:
Listed in the following order: Program area, degree type (T if terminal Master's), number awarded 7/06–6/07. Clinical Psychology PsyD (Doctor of Psychology) 0.

Student Applications/Admissions:
Student Applications
Clinical Psychology PsyD (Doctor of Psychology)—Number full-time enrolled (new admits only) 2007–2008, 5. Number part-time enrolled (new admits only) 2007–2008, 0. Openings 2008–2009, 15. The number of students enrolled full- and part-time who were dismissed or voluntarily withdrew from this program area in 2007–2008 were 0.

Admissions Requirements:
Scores: Entries appear in this order: required test or GPA, minimum score (if required), median score of students entering in 2007–2008. Doctoral Programs: GRE-V no minimum stated, 455; GRE-Q no minimum stated, 600; overall undergraduate GPA 2.75, 3.23. GRE or other standardized test scores, such as MAT, are required.
Other Criteria: (importance of criteria rated low, medium, or high): GRE/MAT scores—medium, research experience—low, work experience—medium, extracurricular activity—medium, clinically related public service—high, GPA—high, letters of recommendation—high, interview—high, statement of goals and objectives—high, undergraduate major in psychology—medium, specific undergraduate psychology courses taken—high. For additional information on admission requirements, go to http://www.midwestern.edu/az-psych/.

Student Characteristics: The following represents characteristics of students in 2007–2008 in all graduate psychology programs in the department: Female—full-time 3, part-time 0; Male—full-time 2, part-time 0; African American/Black—full-time 1, part-time 0; Hispanic/Latino(a)—full-time 0, part-time 0; Asian/Pacific Islander—full-time 0, part-time 0; American Indian/Alaska Native—full-time 0, part-time 0; Caucasian/White—full-time 4, part-time 0; Multi-ethnic—full-time 0, part-time 0; students subject to the Americans With Disabilities Act—full-time 0, part-time 0; Unknown ethnicity—full-time 0, part-time 0; International students who hold an F-1 or J-1 Visa—full-time 0, part-time 0.

Financial Information/Assistance:
Tuition for Full-Time Study: *Doctoral:* State residents: per academic year $22,750; Nonstate residents: per academic year $22,750.

Financial Assistance:
First-Year Students: Fellowships and scholarships available for first year. Apply by varies. Tuition remission given: full and partial.
Advanced Students: Fellowships and scholarships available for advanced students. Tuition remission given: full and partial.
Additional Information: Of all students currently enrolled full time, 0% benefited from one or more of the listed financial assistance programs. Application and information available online at: http://www.midwestern.edu/az-psych/.

Internships/Practica: Students begin their clinical experiences with a clerkship in the first year of the program, which exposes them to clinical practice. The specific clinical focus of the experience varies according to the student's needs, interests, and availability of sites. Students complete a minimum of eight quarters of practicum in the 2nd and 3rd years, approximately 16 to 20 hours per week in a clinical setting. The practicum experiences in psychodiagnostics and psychotherapy total a minimum of 1,000 hours over 2 years. A variety of practicum sites are available, including Midwestern University's Clinic on campus. Internship is completed in the 4th year of the program, and may be completed at any APPIC-member internship site in the United States or Canada. For additional information on education and training outcomes for our programs, see the following Web site: http://www.midwestern.edu/az-psych/.

Housing and Day Care: On-campus housing is available. See the following Web site for more information: http://www.midwestern.edu/az-psych/. No on-campus day care facilities are available.

Employment of Department Graduates:
Master's Degree Graduates: Of those who graduated in the academic year 2006–2007, the following categories and numbers represent the postgraduate activities and employment of master's degree graduates: Enrolled in a postdoctoral residency/fellowship (n/a), employed in independent practice (n/a), total from the above (master's) (0).
Doctoral Degree Graduates: Of those who graduated in the academic year 2006–2007, the following categories and numbers represent the postgraduate activities and employment of doctoral degree graduates: Enrolled in a psychology doctoral program (n/a), total from the above (doctoral) (0).

Additional Information:

Orientation, Objectives, and Emphasis of Department: The clinical psychology program at Midwestern University offers generalist training in clinical psychology, with an emphasis on integrated healthcare, offering psychological services in primary care settings. Midwestern University provides an environment of collaborative training in the healthcare professions, so that as you pursue your studies, you will be surrounded by students of osteopathic medicine, pharmacy, podiatry, physician's assistance, nurse-anesthesia, occupational therapy, cardiovascular science/perfusion, dentistry, and biomedical sciences. The program curriculum includes the foundations of psychological science and emphasizes professional skills in relationship, assessment, intervention, research and evaluation, consultation and education, management and supervision, and diversity. In 3 years of full-time academic coursework and practicum experiences, and 1 year of internship, students gain the knowledge, skill, and values to practice clinical psychology in primary care settings, hospitals, outpatient clinics, schools, and private practice. The knowledgeable and dedicated faculty members are accessible and available to students in small classes, seminars, and individually.

Information for Students With Physical Disabilities: See the following Web site for more information: http://www.midwestern.edu/az-psych/.

Application Information:

Send to Office of Admissions Midwestern University 19555 North 59th Avenue, Glendale, AZ 85308. Application available online. URL of online application: http://www.midwestern.edu/az-psych/. Students are admitted in the Fall. Programs have rolling admissions. *Fee:* $50.

Northcentral University (2007 data)

School of Psychology
Behavioral and Social Sciences
505 West Whipple
Prescott, AZ 86301
Telephone: (888) 327-2877
Fax: (928) 541-7817
E-mail: *aperry@ncu.edu*
Web: *http://www.ncu.edu*

Department Information:

1999. Chairperson: Anthony R. Perry. Number of faculty: total—full-time 6, part-time 68; women—part-time 26.

Programs and Degrees Offered:

Listed in the following order: Program area, degree type (T if terminal Master's), number awarded 7/06–6/07. General Psychology PhD (Doctor of Philosophy) 34, Health Psychology PhD (Doctor of Philosophy), Industrial/Organizational Psychology PhD (Doctor of Philosophy), Marriage and Family Therapy MA/MS (Master of Arts/Science) 0, Psychology MA/MS (Master of Arts/Science) 22.

Student Applications/Admissions:

Student Applications

General Psychology PhD (Doctor of Philosophy)—Number part-time enrolled (new admits only) 2007–2008, 98. Total enrolled 2007–2008 part-time, 424. The median number of years required for completion of a degree in 2006–2007 were 3. *Health Psychology PhD (Doctor of Philosophy)—Industrial/Organizational Psychology PhD (Doctor of Philosophy)—Marriage and Family Therapy MA/MS (Master of Arts/Science)*—Number part-time enrolled (new admits only) 2007–2008, 16. Total enrolled 2007–2008 part-time, 16. *Psychology MA/MS (Master of Arts/Science)*—Number part-time enrolled (new admits only) 2007–2008, 53. Total enrolled 2007–2008 part-time, 154. The median number of years required for completion of a degree in 2006–2007 were 2.

Admissions Requirements:

Scores: Entries appear in this order: required test or GPA, minimum score (if required), median score of students entering in 2007–2008. Master's Programs: last 2 years GPA 2.0, 3.0. Doctoral Programs: last 2 years GPA 2.0, 3.0.

Other Criteria: (importance of criteria rated low, medium, or high): research experience—low, work experience—medium, extracurricular activity—low, clinically related public service—medium, GPA—low, letters of recommendation—low, interview—low, statement of goals and objectives—medium. For additional information on admission requirements, go to http://www.ncu.edu.

Student Characteristics: The following represents characteristics of students in 2007–2008 in all graduate psychology programs in the department: Female—part-time 350; Male—part-time 244; African American/Black—part-time 43; Hispanic/Latino(a)—part-time 17; Asian/Pacific Islander—part-time 18; American Indian/Alaska Native—part-time 8; Caucasian/White—full-time 0, part-time 508; Unknown ethnicity—full-time 0, part-time 0.

Financial Information/Assistance:

Financial Assistance:

First-Year Students: No information provided.

Advanced Students: No information provided.

Additional Information: Application and information available online at http://www.ncu.edu.

Internships/Practica: Learners may enroll in supervised practica.

Housing and Day Care: No on-campus housing is available. No on-campus day care facilities are available.

Employment of Department Graduates:

Master's Degree Graduates: Of those who graduated in the academic year 2006–2007, the following categories and numbers represent the postgraduate activities and employment of master's degree graduates: Enrolled in a postdoctoral residency/fellowship (n/a), employed in independent practice (n/a), total from the above (master's) (0).

Doctoral Degree Graduates: Of those who graduated in the academic year 2006–2007, the following categories and numbers represent the postgraduate activities and employment of doctoral degree graduates: Enrolled in a psychology doctoral program (n/a), total from the above (doctoral) (0).

Additional Information:

Orientation, Objectives, and Emphasis of Department: The department emphasizes applications of psychology. All instruction is carried out via distance learning in which learners and mentors work together in one-on-one relationship. Learners need to be highly motivated, independent, and conscientious.

Application Information:
Application available online. URL of online application: https://www.ncu.edu/applicant/. Programs have rolling admissions.

Northern Arizona University

Department of Psychology
Social and Behavioral Sciences
NAU Box 15106
Flagstaff, AZ 86011
Telephone: (520) 523-3063
Fax: (520) 523-6777
E-mail: *laurie.dickson@nau.edu*
Web: *http://www.nau.edu*

Department Information:
1967. Chairperson: K. Laurie Dickson. Number of faculty: total—full-time 11, part-time 1; women—full-time 10, part-time 3.

Programs and Degrees Offered:
Listed in the following order: Program area, degree type (T if terminal Master's), number awarded 7/06–6/07. Clinical Health Psychology MA/MS (Master of Arts/Science) (T) 4, Predoctoral Training in General Psychology MA/MS (Master of Arts/Science) (T) 10, Teaching of Psychology MA/MS (Master of Arts/Science) (T) 1, Predoctoral Training in Clinical Health Psychology MA/MS (Master of Arts/Science) (T) 5.

Student Applications/Admissions:
Student Applications
Clinical Health Psychology MA/MS (Master of Arts/Science)—Applications 2007–2008, 12. Total applicants accepted 2007–2008, 5. Number full-time enrolled (new admits only) 2007–2008, 1. Total enrolled 2007–2008 full-time, 3. Openings 2008–2009, 4. *Predoctoral Training in General Psychology MA/MS (Master of Arts/Science)*—Applications 2007–2008, 18. Total applicants accepted 2007–2008, 10. Number full-time enrolled (new admits only) 2007–2008, 9. Total enrolled 2007–2008 full-time, 19. Openings 2008–2009, 8. The median number of years required for completion of a degree in 2006–2007 were 2. The number of students enrolled full- and part-time who were dismissed or voluntarily withdrew from this program area in 2007–2008 were 0. *Teaching of Psychology MA/MS (Master of Arts/Science)*—Total enrolled 2007–2008 full-time, 1. Openings 2008–2009, 2. The median number of years required for completion of a degree in 2006–2007 were 2. *Predoctoral Training in Clinical Health Psychology MA/MS (Master of Arts/Science)*—Applications 2007–2008, 18. Total applicants accepted 2007–2008, 6. Number full-time enrolled (new admits only) 2007–2008, 4. Total enrolled 2007–2008 full-time, 10. Openings 2008–2009, 6. The median number of years required for completion of a degree in 2006–2007 were 2.

Admissions Requirements:
Scores: Entries appear in this order: required test or GPA, minimum score (if required), median score of students entering in 2007–2008. Master's Programs: GRE-V no minimum stated, 510; GRE-Q no minimum stated, 580; overall undergraduate GPA no minimum stated, 3.5; last 2 years GPA no minimum stated, 3.6; psychology GPA no minimum stated, 3.7. Preference is for a combined GRE-V + GRE-Q of 1000 or more. An overall undergraduate GPA of 3.0 or above is preferred.
Other Criteria: (importance of criteria rated low, medium, or high): GRE/MAT scores—high, research experience—high, work experience—low, extracurricular activity—low, clinically related public service—low, GPA—high, letters of recommendation—high, interview—medium, statement of goals and objectives—high. Clinically related public service used only for Clinical Health Psychology program. Work experience and extracurricular activity given somewhat higher importance for Clinical Health Psychology program. Phone interviews are conducted for selected applicants for the Clinical Health and Predoctoral training in Clinical Health Psychology. For additional information on admission requirements, go to http://www.nau.edu/~psych/grad.html.

Student Characteristics: The following represents characteristics of students in 2007–2008 in all graduate psychology programs in the department: Female—full-time 24, part-time 3; Male—full-time 9, part-time 1; African American/Black—full-time 1, part-time 0; Hispanic/Latino(a)—full-time 1, part-time 1; Asian/Pacific Islander—full-time 1, part-time 0; American Indian/Alaska Native—full-time 0, part-time 0; Caucasian/White—full-time 30, part-time 3; Multi-ethnic—full-time 0, part-time 0; students subject to the Americans With Disabilities Act—full-time 0, part-time 0; Unknown ethnicity—full-time 0, part-time 0.

Financial Information/Assistance:
Tuition for Full-Time Study: *Master's:* State residents: per academic year $4,562, $239 per credit hour; Nonstate residents: per academic year $9,910, $550 per credit hour. Tuition is subject to change. See the following Web site for updates and changes in tuition costs: http://www4.nau.edu/bursar/fees_spring.htm.

Financial Assistance:
First-Year Students: Teaching assistantships available for first year. Average number of hours worked per week: 10. Apply by February 15. Tuition remission given: partial. Research assistantships available for first year. Average number of hours worked per week: 10. Apply by February 15. Tuition remission given: partial.
Advanced Students: Teaching assistantships available for advanced students. Average number of hours worked per week: 10. Apply by n/a. Tuition remission given: partial. Research assistantships available for advanced students. Average number of hours worked per week: 10. Apply by n/a. Tuition remission given: partial.
Additional Information: Of all students currently enrolled full time, 80% benefited from one or more of the listed financial assistance programs.

Internships/Practica: Master's Degree (MA/MS Clinical Health Psychology): An internship experience, such as, a final research project or "capstone" experience is required of graduates. Master's Degree (MA/MS Predoctoral Training in General Psychology): An internship experience, such as, a final research project or "capstone" experience is required of graduates. Master's Degree

(MA/MS Teaching of Psychology): An internship experience, such as a final research project or "capstone" experience is required of graduates. Master's Degree (MA/MS Predoctoral Training in Clinical Health Psychology): An internship experience, such as a final research project or "capstone" experience is required of graduates. Clinical Health and Predoctoral Clinical Health Psychology students are required to take two or three semesters of practicum in the department's Health Psychology Center. Our multipurpose training and service facility serves NAU students, faculty, and staff as well as community residents. In the Center, supervised graduate students in applied health psychology work to promote wellness and healthy lifestyles in adults and children through a variety of educational and treatment modalities. The Center offers programs on such topics as stress management, healthy eating and weight control, exercise, and smoking cessation, as well as group and individual interventions for these topics. The Center also provides psychological evaluation and behavioral management for health-related problems such as headaches, high blood pressure, cardiovascular disease, obesity, premenstrual syndrome, ulcers, diabetes, asthma, smoking, cancer, and chronic pain. Health Psychology students are also encouraged to take one or more semesters of fieldwork placement at a variety of agencies in the surrounding communities (including ethnic and rural communities). Predoctoral General Psychology students also may enroll in fieldwork placement. Teaching of Psychology students are required to enroll in a Teaching Practicum and Teaching Fieldwork.

Housing and Day Care: On-campus housing is available. See the following Web site for more information: http://www4.nau.edu/reslife/reslife/. No on-campus day care facilities are available.

Employment of Department Graduates:

Master's Degree Graduates: Of those who graduated in the academic year 2006–2007, the following categories and numbers represent the postgraduate activities and employment of master's degree graduates: Enrolled in a psychology doctoral program (4), enrolled in another graduate/professional program (1), enrolled in a postdoctoral residency/fellowship (n/a), employed in independent practice (n/a), employed in an academic position at a 2-year/4-year college (1), employed in other positions at a higher education institution (1), employed in business or industry (2), employed in a community mental health/counseling center (6), other employment position (1), do not know (3), total from the above (master's) (19).

Doctoral Degree Graduates: Of those who graduated in the academic year 2006–2007, the following categories and numbers represent the postgraduate activities and employment of doctoral degree graduates: Enrolled in a psychology doctoral program (n/a), total from the above (doctoral) (0).

Additional Information:

Orientation, Objectives, and Emphasis of Department: The Psychology Department is committed to excellence in education at the graduate level, emphasizing teaching, scholarship, and service to the university and to the larger community. The department emphasizes theoretical foundations, empirical research, innovative curriculum, and practical hands-on applications of psychological knowledge. Four graduate programs are offered. First, the Predoctoral General Psychology Training program, which involves study of the theoretical and methodological foundations of general (Clinical, Cognitive, Developmental, Experimental, Industrial/Organizational, Social, Personality, Neurosciences) psychology, is appropriate if you plan to pursue a doctoral degree or to conduct research and data management in a variety of settings. Second, the Predoctoral Clinical Health Psychology Training program, which involves study of the theoretical and methodological foundations of Clinical Health psychology, is appropriate if you plan to pursue a doctoral degree or to conduct research and data management in a variety of settings. Third, the Teaching of Psychology graduate program provides extensive training in the theoretical and methodological foundations of psychology and affords students a variety of teaching experiences and skills in face-to-face, Web, and hybrid settings. This program prepares students to pursue a teaching career at the high school or community college level. Fourth, the Clinical Health Psychology program is appropriate if you plan to work in a master's-level position using skills related to the promotion of health and wellness and the prevention and treatment of illness.

Special Facilities or Resources: The Department of Psychology has over 1,500 square feet of clinic space dedicated to training in Health Psychology and a state-of-the-art psychophysiology/biofeedback laboratory. Other well-equipped research facilities are available in an adjunct building and are assigned to faculty members engaged in research. A computer laboratory used for teaching purposes is also available for data collection. The department is housed in a modern building at the south end of the Flagstaff Mountain Campus. All teaching rooms are equipped with up-to-date technology. NAU is located in the city of Flagstaff, a four-season community of approximately 50,000 residents at the base of the majestic, 12,670-foot-high San Francisco Peaks. Flagstaff and the surrounding area offer excellent hiking and mountain-biking trails as well as cross-country and downhill skiing. Students enjoy the nearby diversity of Arizona's climate and attractions, from Grand Canyon National Park to metropolitan Phoenix in the Sonoran desert.

Information for Students With Physical Disabilities: See the following Web site for more information: http://www2.nau.edu/dss/.

Application Information:

Send to Departmental Application: Department of Psychology, Graduate Programs, Northern Arizona University, NAU Box 15106, Flagstaff, AZ 86011. Graduate Application: NAU Graduate College, P.O. Box 4125, Flagstaff, AZ 86011-4125. Application available online. URL of online application: http://www.nau.edu/gradcol/. Students are admitted in the Fall, application deadline February 15. *Fee:* $45.

Northern Arizona University

Educational Psychology
College of Education
COE 5774
Flagstaff, AZ 86011
Telephone: (928) 523-7103
Fax: (928) 523-9284
E-mail: *Eugene.Moan@nau.edu*
Web: *http://www.coe.nau.edu/academics/eps*

Department Information:

1962. Chairperson: Eugene R. Moan. Number of faculty: total—full-time 21, part-time 3; women—full-time 15, part-time 3; women minority—full-time 4.

Programs and Degrees Offered:

Listed in the following order: Program area, degree type (T if terminal Master's), number awarded 7/06–6/07. Community Counseling MA/MS (Master of Arts/Science) (T) 18, Certification in School Psychology MA/MS (Master of Arts/Science) (T) 8, School Counseling Other 44, Student Affairs MA/MS (Master of Arts/Science) (T) 1, Counseling Psychology PhD (Doctor of Philosophy) 42, School Psychology PhD (Doctor of Philosophy) 7, Learning and Instruction PhD (Doctor of Philosophy) 0, Counseling–Human Relations MA/MS (Master of Arts/Science) (T) 12.

Student Applications/Admissions:

Student Applications

Community Counseling MA/MS (Master of Arts/Science)—Applications 2007–2008, 74. Total applicants accepted 2007–2008, 40. Number full-time enrolled (new admits only) 2007–2008, 28. Number part-time enrolled (new admits only) 2007–2008, 4. Total enrolled 2007–2008 full-time, 62, part-time, 38. Openings 2008–2009, 35. The median number of years required for completion of a degree in 2006–2007 were 2. The number of students enrolled full- and part-time who were dismissed or voluntarily withdrew from this program area in 2007–2008 were 0. *Certification in School Psychology MA/MS (Master of Arts/Science)*—Applications 2007–2008, 33. Total applicants accepted 2007–2008, 12. Number full-time enrolled (new admits only) 2007–2008, 11. Number part-time enrolled (new admits only) 2007–2008, 0. Total enrolled 2007–2008 full-time, 22, part-time, 10. Openings 2008–2009, 12. The median number of years required for completion of a degree in 2006–2007 were 3. The number of students enrolled full- and part-time who were dismissed or voluntarily withdrew from this program area in 2007–2008 were 0. *School Counseling Other*—Applications 2007–2008, 70. Total applicants accepted 2007–2008, 40. Number full-time enrolled (new admits only) 2007–2008, 30. Number part-time enrolled (new admits only) 2007–2008, 6. Total enrolled 2007–2008 full-time, 57, part-time, 78. Openings 2008–2009, 50. The median number of years required for completion of a degree in 2006–2007 were 2. The number of students enrolled full- and part-time who were dismissed or voluntarily withdrew from this program area in 2007–2008 were 1. *Student Affairs MA/MS (Master of Arts/Science)*—Applications 2007–2008, 11. Total applicants accepted 2007–2008, 6. Number full-time enrolled (new admits only) 2007–2008, 4. Number part-time enrolled (new admits only) 2007–2008, 2. Total enrolled 2007–2008 full-time, 12, part-time, 4. Openings 2008–2009, 10. The median number of years required for completion of a degree in 2006–2007 were 2. The number of students enrolled full- and part-time who were dismissed or voluntarily withdrew from this program area in 2007–2008 were 1. *Counseling Psychology PhD (Doctor of Philosophy)*—Applications 2007–2008, 5. Total applicants accepted 2007–2008, 2. Number full-time enrolled (new admits only) 2007–2008, 1. Number part-time enrolled (new admits only) 2007–2008, 1. Total enrolled 2007–2008 full-time, 14, part-time, 8. Openings 2008–2009, 5. The median number of years required for completion of a degree in 2006–2007 were 5. The number of students enrolled full- and part-time who were dismissed or voluntarily withdrew from this program area in 2007–2008 were 3. *School Psychology PhD (Doctor of Philosophy)*—Applications 2007–2008, 5. Total applicants accepted 2007–2008, 2. Number full-time enrolled (new admits only) 2007–2008, 2. Number part-time enrolled (new admits only) 2007–2008, 0. Total enrolled 2007–2008 full-time, 8, part-time, 9. Openings 2008–2009, 5. The median number of years required for completion of a degree in 2006–2007 were 4. The number of students enrolled full- and part-time who were dismissed or voluntarily withdrew from this program area in 2007–2008 were 0. *Learning and Instruction PhD (Doctor of Philosophy)*—Applications 2007–2008, 3. Total applicants accepted 2007–2008, 2. Number full-time enrolled (new admits only) 2007–2008, 1. Number part-time enrolled (new admits only) 2007–2008, 0. Total enrolled 2007–2008 full-time, 4, part-time, 3. Openings 2008–2009, 3. The median number of years required for completion of a degree in 2006–2007 were 5. The number of students enrolled full- and part-time who were dismissed or voluntarily withdrew from this program area in 2007–2008 were 0. *Counseling–Human Relations MA/MS (Master of Arts/Science)*—Applications 2007–2008, 20. Total applicants accepted 2007–2008, 16. Number full-time enrolled (new admits only) 2007–2008, 8. Number part-time enrolled (new admits only) 2007–2008, 6. Total enrolled 2007–2008 full-time, 18, part-time, 21. Openings 2008–2009, 10. The median number of years required for completion of a degree in 2006–2007 were 2. The number of students enrolled full- and part-time who were dismissed or voluntarily withdrew from this program area in 2007–2008 were 0.

Admissions Requirements:

Scores: Entries appear in this order: required test or GPA, minimum score (if required), median score of students entering in 2007–2008. Master's Programs: GRE-V no minimum stated, 478; GRE-Q no minimum stated, 544; overall undergraduate GPA no minimum stated, 3.47; last 2 years GPA no minimum stated, 3.4. Doctoral Programs: GRE-V no minimum stated, 519; GRE-Q no minimum stated, 521.

Other Criteria: (importance of criteria rated low, medium, or high): GRE/MAT scores—high, research experience—low, work experience—medium, extracurricular activity—low, clinically related public service—low, GPA—high, letters of recommendation—medium, statement of goals and objectives—high. For additional information on admission requirements, go to http://coe.nau.edu/academics/eps.

Student Characteristics: The following represents characteristics of students in 2007–2008 in all graduate psychology programs in the department: Female—full-time 151, part-time 153; Male—full-time 44, part-time 22; African American/Black—full-time 5, part-time 4; Hispanic/Latino(a)—full-time 32, part-time 30; Asian/Pacific Islander—full-time 5, part-time 0; American Indian/Alaska Native—full-time 7, part-time 22; Caucasian/White—full-time 142, part-time 118; Multi-ethnic—full-time 0, part-time 0; students subject to the Americans With Disabilities Act—full-time 1, part-time 1; Unknown ethnicity—full-time 4, part-time 1.

Financial Information/Assistance:

Tuition for Full-Time Study: *Master's:* State residents: per academic year $5,214, $328 per credit hour; Nonstate residents: per academic year $14,896, $591 per credit hour. *Doctoral:* State residents: per academic year $4,736, $328 per credit hour; Nonstate residents: per academic year $14,896, $591 per credit hour. Tuition is subject to change. See the following Web site for updates and changes in tuition costs: http://www.home.nau.edu/bursar/tuition_fees.asp.

Financial Assistance:

First-Year Students: Teaching assistantships available for first year. Average amount paid per academic year: $8,910. Average number of hours worked per week: 20. Apply by April 15. Tuition remission given: partial.

Advanced Students: Teaching assistantships available for advanced students. Average amount paid per academic year: $9,900. Average number of hours worked per week: 20. Apply by April 15. Tuition remission given: partial. Research assistantships available for advanced students. Average amount paid per academic year: $9,575. Average number of hours worked per week: 20. Apply by April 15. Tuition remission given: partial.

Additional Information: Of all students currently enrolled full time, 25% benefited from one or more of the listed financial assistance programs. Application and information available online at: http://www4.nau.edu/finaid/.

Internships/Practica: Master's Degree (MA/MS Community Counseling): An internship experience such as a final research project or "capstone" experience is required of graduates. Master's Degree (MA/MS Certification in School Psychology): An internship experience such as a final research project or "capstone" experience is required of graduates. Doctoral Degree (PhD Counseling Psychology): For those doctoral students for whom a professional internship was required in this program prior to graduation, (2) students applied for an internship in 2006–2007, with (2) students obtaining an internship. Of those students who obtained an internship, (2) were paid internships. Of those students who obtained an internship, (0) students placed in APA/CPA accredited internships, (1) student placed in internships not APA/CPA-accredited, but listed with the Association of Psychology Postdoctoral and Internship Centers (APPIC), (0) students placed in internships conforming to guidelines of the Council of Directors of School Psychology Programs (CDSPP), (1) student placed in internships that were not APA/CPA-accredited, APPIC or CDSPP listed. Our programs are built on competency-based models and include closely supervised experiential practica and internship components. Many of these experiences are offered in NAU's Counseling and Testing Center and the Institute for Human Development; student service facilities; public-school settings; reservation schools and communities; rural settings; and community agencies. In addition, the College of Education houses a Skills Lab Network that includes comprehensive testing and curriculum libraries and a practicum facility that uses both videotape and direct live feedback in the supervision of students working with clients.

Housing and Day Care: On-campus housing is available. See the following Web site for more information: http://www.nau.edu/reslife/ These include family housing, fraternities/sororities, apartment-style halls, suite-style halls, graduate, over 21-year old floors, over 25-year old floor, nonsmoking floor/halls, honors/scholars halls, 12-month contract option, 24-hour quiet floors, and freshmen halls. On-campus day care facilities are available. See the following Web site for more information: http://www4.nau.edu/stulife/ChildCare/FAQ.htm. The NAU Child Care Voucher Program is a subsidy program designed to assist NAU students with child care expenses while they attend the University.

Employment of Department Graduates:

Master's Degree Graduates: Of those who graduated in the academic year 2006–2007, the following categories and numbers represent the postgraduate activities and employment of master's degree graduates: Enrolled in a postdoctoral residency/fellowship (n/a), employed in independent practice (n/a), total from the above (master's) (0).

Doctoral Degree Graduates: Of those who graduated in the academic year 2006–2007, the following categories and numbers represent the postgraduate activities and employment of doctoral degree graduates: Enrolled in a psychology doctoral program (n/a), enrolled in a postdoctoral residency/fellowship (0), employed in an academic position at a 2-year/4-year college (0), total from the above (doctoral) (0).

Additional Information:

Orientation, Objectives, and Emphasis of Department: Because of the barriers to learning and living in our society, there is an increasing need for professionally trained counseling and school psychology personnel. Our graduate programs are based on a developmental, experiential training model that includes understanding theory, learning assessment and intervention skills, practicing skills in a supervised clinical setting, and performing skills in like settings. Integrated throughout our programs is a scientist–practitioner orientation that prepares students to ascertain the efficacy of assessment and intervention techniques.

Special Facilities or Resources: Students in School Psychology programs complete portions of their practicum at sites located on the Indian reservations and work with children and schools affiliated with the Navajo, Hopi, and Supai tribes. The MA Community Counseling and the MEd School Counseling programs are also available at select sites in Arizona (i.e., Phoenix, Tucson and Yuma).

Information for Students With Physical Disabilities: See the following Web site for more information: http://www.nau.edu/dss.

Application Information:

Graduate and Department Application is combined and can only be completed online: http://www.applyweb.com/apply/northazg/. Application available online. URL of online application: http://www.applyweb.com/apply/northazg/. Students are admitted in the Fall, application deadline September 15; Spring, application deadline February 15. PhD—Counseling Psychology and School Psychology—January 15. PhD—Learning and Instruction—Rolling deadline. MA and Certification in School Psychology—February 15. MA Community Counseling, MEd School Counseling—Dates above for Fall and Spring apply. MA Student Affairs—September 15 snd April 1 for MA Community Counseling and MEd School Counseling located at statewide sites (Phoenix, Tucson, and Yuma), deadlines vary each year. Please call department office (928) 523-7103 for more information or visit our Web site (http://coe.nau.edu/academics/eps). *Fee:* $50.

Arkansas, University of

Department of Psychology
J. William Fulbright College of Arts and Science
216 Memorial Hall
Fayetteville, AR 72701
Telephone: (479) 575-4256
Fax: (479) 575-3219
E-mail: *psycapp@uark.edu*
Web: *http://www.uark.edu/depts/psyc*

Department Information:
1926. Chairperson: Douglas A. Behrend. Number of faculty: total—full-time 15; women—full-time 5.

Programs and Degrees Offered:
Listed in the following order: Program area, degree type (T if terminal Master's), number awarded 7/06–6/07. Clinical PhD (Doctor of Philosophy) 6, Experimental PhD (Doctor of Philosophy) 2.

APA Accreditation: Clinical PhD (Doctor of Philosophy).

Student Applications/Admissions:
Student Applications
Clinical PhD (Doctor of Philosophy)—Applications 2007–2008, 96. Total applicants accepted 2007–2008, 4. Number full-time enrolled (new admits only) 2007–2008, 4. Openings 2008–2009, 5. The median number of years required for completion of a degree in 2006–2007 were 5. The number of students enrolled full- and part-time who were dismissed or voluntarily withdrew from this program area in 2007–2008 were 0. *Experimental PhD (Doctor of Philosophy)*—Applications 2007–2008, 16. Total applicants accepted 2007–2008, 3. Number full-time enrolled (new admits only) 2007–2008, 3. Openings 2008–2009, 3. The median number of years required for completion of a degree in 2006–2007 were 5. The number of students enrolled full- and part-time who were dismissed or voluntarily withdrew from this program area in 2007–2008 were 1.

Admissions Requirements:
Scores: Entries appear in this order: required test or GPA, minimum score (if required), median score of students entering in 2007–2008. Doctoral Programs: GRE-V 500, 620; GRE-Q 500, 630; overall undergraduate GPA 3.0, 3.80.
Other Criteria: (importance of criteria rated low, medium, or high): GRE/MAT scores—high, research experience—high, work experience—low, extracurricular activity—low, clinically related public service—medium, GPA—high, letters of recommendation—high, interview—high, statement of goals and objectives—high. Clinically relevant service only considered for clinical applicants.

Student Characteristics: The following represents characteristics of students in 2007–2008 in all graduate psychology programs in the department: Female—full-time 30, part-time 0; Male—full-time 17, part-time 0; African American/Black—full-time 1, part-time 0; Hispanic/Latino(a)—full-time 1, part-time 0; Asian/Pacific Islander—full-time 0, part-time 0; American Indian/Alaska Native—full-time 0, part-time 0; Caucasian/White—full-time 44, part-time 0; Multi-ethnic—full-time 0, part-time 0; students subject to the Americans With Disabilities Act—full-time 0, part-time 0; Unknown ethnicity—full-time 0, part-time 0.

Financial Information/Assistance:
Tuition for Full-Time Study: *Doctoral:* State residents: per academic year $6,744, $321 per credit hour; Nonstate residents: per academic year $14,793, $704 per credit hour. Tuition is subject to change. See the following Web site for updates and changes in tuition costs: http://www.uark.edu/depts/gradinfo.

Financial Assistance:
First-Year Students: Teaching assistantships available for first year. Average amount paid per academic year: $9,300. Average number of hours worked per week: 20. Apply by December 1. Tuition remission given: full. Research assistantships available for first year. Average amount paid per academic year: $9,300. Average number of hours worked per week: 20. Apply by December 1. Tuition remission given: full. Fellowships and scholarships available for first year. Average amount paid per academic year: $20,000. Average number of hours worked per week: 20. Apply by December 1. Tuition remission given: full.
Advanced Students: Teaching assistantships available for advanced students. Average amount paid per academic year: $9,300. Average number of hours worked per week: 20. Tuition remission given: full. Research assistantships available for advanced students. Average amount paid per academic year: $9,300. Average number of hours worked per week: 20. Tuition remission given: full. Fellowships and scholarships available for advanced students. Average amount paid per academic year: $20,000. Average number of hours worked per week: 20. Tuition remission given: full.
Additional Information: Of all students currently enrolled full time, 100% benefited from one or more of the listed financial assistance programs. Application and information available online at http://www.uark.edu/depts/psyc.

Internships/Practica: Doctoral Degree (PhD Clinical): For those doctoral students for whom a professional internship was required in this program prior to graduation, (9) students applied for an internship in 2006–2007, with (8) students obtaining an internship. Of those students who obtained an internship, (8) were paid internships. Of those students who obtained an internship, (8) students placed in APA/CPA-accredited internships, (0) students placed in internships not APA/CPA-accredited, but listed with the Association of Psychology Postdoctoral and Internship Centers (APPIC), (0) students placed in internships conforming to guidelines of the Council of Directors of School Psychology Programs (CDSPP), (0) students placed in internships that were not APA/CPA-accredited, APPIC or CDSPP listed. Doctoral students in the Clinical Training Program have always been able to obtain high-quality, APA-accredited predoctoral internships. Additionally, our students have numerous mental health agency placement opportunities throughout their tenure with us. These

AMERICAN PSYCHOLOGICAL ASSOCIATION

Affiliate Membership Application

Students | High School Teachers | Community College Teachers | International

Please complete the required information below. Return your completed application with payment to:
American Psychological Association, Service Center/Membership, 750 First Street, NE, Washington, DC 20002-4242

Applicant Information

Please print clearly or type.

Name (First/Middle/Last) ______________________

Contact Address ______________________

____

City ______________________

State/Province/Country ______________________ Zip/Postal/Country Code ______________________

Phone (________) ______________________ Fax (________) ______________________

Add phone (include area/ country code), e-mail and school or institution.

▶ E-mail ______________________

▶ Name of School or Institution ______________________

▶ ☐ Your contact information will be listed in the APA Membership Directory. If you wish to publish only your name in the directory, please check here.

Membership Category

Please check the affiliate type that best describes you. See reverse side for requirements.

Student: ☐ Graduate $51.00* Undergraduate ☐ $27.00 or ☐ $51.00* ☐ High School $27.00
☐ Please check here if you attend a community college

*Includes membership in the American Psychological Association of Graduate Students (APAGS) and a subscription to *gradPSYCH*

Teacher: ☐ High School $32.00 ☐ Community College $35.00

International: ☐ Psychologists residing outside the U.S. or Canada $27.00
Name of the psychological association of the country of which you are a member; or give highest degree in psychology, date, institution and major field of study (required) ______________________

____

For Students Only

All U.S. graduate and undergraduate student applicants must complete sections A, B, and C.

A **Licensure/Ethics**
If the graduate degree for which you are currently enrolled is a health service provider subfield (i.e., clinical, child clinical, counseling, school, geropsychology, or health), do you intend to seek licensure/certification by a state or provincial board of psychologist examiners for the independent practice of psychology?
☐ Yes, within the next year ☐ Yes, eventually ☐ No
☐ N/A, already licensed for the independent practice of psychology

B Have you at any time been convicted of a felony, sanctioned by any professional ethics body, licensing board, or other regulatory body or by any professional or scientific organization? ☐ Yes *If yes, please provide an explanation on a separate sheet of paper.* ☐ No

In submitting this application, I subscribe to and will support the objectives of the American Psychological Association as set forth in Article 1 of the Bylaws, and the Ethical Principles of Psychologists and Code of Conduct, as adopted by the Association, and I affirm that the statements made in this application correctly represent my qualifications for election, and understand that if they do not, my affiliation may be voided.

The Ethical Principles of Psychologists and Code of Conduct is available on APA's Web site at http://www.apa.org/ethics/. The Bylaws are available at http://www.apa.org/governance/. Copies of these documents are also available to me upon request.

All students must sign the ethics statement (section C).

C Signature ______________________ Date ______________________

Additional Information

The following items are voluntary and are used for research purposes only.

☐ Male ☐ Female ☐ Transgender Date of birth (MM/DD/YY) ________

What is your race/ethnicity? *(U.S. residents, mark all that apply)*

☐ American Indian or Alaska Native ☐ Hispanic/Latino(a) ☐ African American/Black
☐ Caucasian/White ☐ Asian or Pacific Islander ☐ Other (Specify) ________

Payment Method

Applications will not be processed without payment. All payments must be drawn on a U.S. bank in U.S. dollars.

APA membership is based on the calendar year (January–December).

I am paying my total of $ ________ by:

☐ Check or money order Check # ________ payable to the American Psychological Association

☐ American Express ☐ MasterCard ☐ Visa

Account Number ______________________ Expiration Date ________

Cardholder Name ______________________

Credit Card Billing Address ______________________

City/State/ZIP Code/Country ______________________

Daytime Telephone Number **(include area code)** ______________________

Signature of Credit Card Holder (Required) ______________________

GS09

AMERICAN PSYCHOLOGICAL ASSOCIATION

Affiliate Membership Requirements Summary

Student requirements: High school, undergraduate, and graduate students taking psychology courses can become APA student affiliates. Graduate student affiliates are automatically enrolled in the American Psychological Association of Graduate Students (APAGS). Undergraduate affiliates may choose to join APAGS by paying the same rate as graduate students.

Teacher requirements: Teachers of psychology in high schools, junior colleges, and community colleges qualify as APA teacher affiliates. High school teacher affiliates are automatically members of Teachers of Psychology in Secondary Schools (TOPSS), an APA organization. Community college teacher affiliates receive membership in Psychology Teachers at Community Colleges (PT@CC), an APA organization.

Psychologists residing in countries other than the United States or Canada: May become APA international affiliates by providing required documentation indicating membership in your country's national psychology organization or evidence of appropriate qualifications.

Complete membership requirements: Requirements are available from APA's Service Center/Membership (see below for contact information).

Dues: Payment must accompany application. Applications without payment can not be processed. Payment must be made in U.S. dollars, drawn on a U.S. bank. APA affiliate dues (stated on the front of this application) are substantially discounted, over 75% off full member rates.

Membership term: APA membership is based on the calendar year (January–December). If your application is approved in September through December of the current year, your membership (including your subscriptions to the *Monitor on Psychology* and the *American Psychologist*) will automatically be extended to the end of the following year.

Standard inclusions: All APA affiliates receive a subscription to the *Monitor on Psychology* (11 issues*). Undergraduate and graduate students receive a subscription to *American Psychologist* (9 issues*). APAGS members receive a subscription to *gradPSYCH* (4 issues*).

Membership also includes substantial discounts (up to 60%) on various APA publications and electronic products. A detailed list of publications will be sent to you upon acceptance of your application.

Delivery of products and services: Allow 3–4 weeks for the processing of your application and 6–8 weeks for the initial delivery of your APA publications. International orders are sent via surface mail and may take longer.

APA Member and Affiliate Directory: Upon acceptance, your contact information will automatically be included in the official directory, which is a main source of member-to-member communication. To publish only your name in the directory, please check the appropriate box on the front of this application.

For questions or additional information:

Service Center/Membership: (202) 336-5580 or (800) 374-2721 or TDD/TTY: (202) 336-6123; Fax: (202) 336-5568; E-mail: membership@apa.org; Web: http://www.apa.org

Return your completed application to: American Psychological Association, Service Center/Membership, 750 First Street, NE, Washington, DC 20002-4242

*$6.00 of APA dues is allocated towards the *Monitor on Psychology* subscription and $12.00 of APA dues is allocated towards the *American Psychologist* subscription. If you receive *gradPSYCH*, $3.00 of APA dues is allocated towards the subscription.

clerkship placements include local community mental health centers, the University Health Service, inpatient psychiatric hospitals, and several facilities dealing with disabilities, neuropsychology, and other clinical specialties.

Housing and Day Care: On-campus housing is available. Additional housing information may be obtained from University Housing, 900 Hotz Hall, University of Arkansas, Fayetteville, AR 72701, by telephone at (479) 575-3951, or at http://housing.uark.edu. On-campus day care facilities are available. Limited on-campus child care is available.

Employment of Department Graduates:

Master's Degree Graduates: Of those who graduated in the academic year 2006–2007, the following categories and numbers represent the postgraduate activities and employment of master's degree graduates: Enrolled in a postdoctoral residency/fellowship (n/a), employed in independent practice (n/a), total from the above (master's) (0).

Doctoral Degree Graduates: Of those who graduated in the academic year 2006–2007, the following categories and numbers represent the postgraduate activities and employment of doctoral degree graduates: Enrolled in a psychology doctoral program (n/a), employed in independent practice (2), employed in an academic position at a 2-year/4-year college (2), employed in a hospital/medical center (1), other employment position (1), total from the above (doctoral) (6).

Additional Information:

Orientation, Objectives, and Emphasis of Department: The PhD program in Clinical Psychology follows the scientist–practitioner model of training. Although some of our graduates obtain applied, direct service provision positions, our training curriculum is such that those students whose career aspirations have been directed toward academic and research positions also have been successful. The Clinical Training Program is based on the premise that clinical psychologists should be skilled practitioners and mental health service providers as well as competent researchers. To facilitate these goals, we strive to maximize the match between the clinical and research interests of the faculty with those of the graduate students. The academic courses and clinical experiences are designed to promote the development in both areas. The objective of the Clinical Training Program is to graduate clinical psychologists capable of applying psychological theory, research methodology, and clinical skills to complex clinical problems and diverse populations. The program is fully accredited by the American Psychological Association. The PhD program in experimental psychology provides students with a broad knowledge of psychology via a core curriculum, with a specialized training emphasis in our Social and Cognitive Processes focus area via research team meetings, colloquia, and advanced seminars. Training in social, developmental, and cognitive psychology within the focus area includes independent research experience, and extensive and supervised classroom teaching experience. The program provides students with a thorough understanding of psychological principles and prepares them for careers as academicians and researchers.

Special Facilities or Resources: The Department of Psychology is housed in Memorial Hall, a multilevel building with 58,000 square feet of office and research space for faculty and students. The building contains modern facilities for both human and small animal research, including specialized space for use with individuals and small groups of children and adults. The on-site Psychological Clinic is a state-of-the-art training and research facility dedicated to providing practicum and applied research experiences for clinical students. The Clinic's treatment, testing, and research rooms are equipped with a closed-circuit videotaping system. Memorial Hall has comprehensive data analysis facilities, including personal computers networked to the University and Internet. Finally, the Department is the beneficiary of a generous bequest that established the Marie Wilson Howells Fund, which provides funding for thesis and dissertation research, numerous research assistantships, student travel, and departmental colloquia. The Department also nominates qualified students for supplemental Doctoral Fellowships available through the Graduate School.

Information for Students With Physical Disabilities: See the following Web site for more information: http://www.uark.edu/ua/csd/.

Application Information:

Send to Admissions Coordinator, Department of Psychology, University of Arkansas, Memorial Hall 216, Fayetteville, AR 72701. Application available online. URL of online application: http://www.uark.edu/depts/psyc/application.html. Students are admitted in the Fall, application deadline December 1. Experimental Program will continue to consider applications received after January 1. *Fee:* $0. U.S. applicants should apply directly to the Department of Psychology and have all application materials (e.g., transcripts, GRE scores, letters of recommendation) for most efficient consideration; application materials of students accepted by the Department for admission will be submitted to the Graduate School for processing. The Department will pay the Graduate School application fees for admitted students. EXCEPTION: International applicants must apply to the Graduate School and pay a $50 application fee.

Central Arkansas, University of

Department of Psychology and Counseling
Health and Behavioral Sciences
201 Donaghey Avenue
Conway, AR 72035-0001
Telephone: (501) 450-3193
Fax: (501) 450-5424
E-mail: *DavidS@.uca.edu*
Web: *http://www.uca.edu/psychology*

Department Information:

1967. Chairperson: David Skotko. Number of faculty: total—full-time 22, part-time 4; women—full-time 7, part-time 3; total—minority—full-time 1, part-time 1; women minority—part-time 1.

Programs and Degrees Offered:

Listed in the following order: Program area, degree type (T if terminal Master's), number awarded 7/06–6/07. School Psychology PhD (Doctor of Philosophy) 1, School Psychology MA/MS (Master of Arts/Science) (T) 5, Counseling Psychology MA/MS (Master of Arts/Science) (T) 6, Community Counseling MA/MS (Master of Arts/Science) (T) 5.

APA Accreditation: School PhD (Doctor of Philosophy).

Student Applications/Admissions:

Student Applications

School Psychology PhD (Doctor of Philosophy)—Applications 2007–2008, 12. Total applicants accepted 2007–2008, 4. Number full-time enrolled (new admits only) 2007–2008, 4. Number part-time enrolled (new admits only) 2007–2008, 0. Total enrolled 2007–2008 full-time, 13, part-time, 10. Openings 2008–2009, 5. The median number of years required for completion of a degree in 2006–2007 were 5. The number of students enrolled full- and part-time who were dismissed or voluntarily withdrew from this program area in 2007–2008 were 1. *School Psychology MA/MS (Master of Arts/Science)*—Applications 2007–2008, 14. Total applicants accepted 2007–2008, 6. Number full-time enrolled (new admits only) 2007–2008, 6. Number part-time enrolled (new admits only) 2007–2008, 0. Openings 2008–2009, 7. The median number of years required for completion of a degree in 2006–2007 were 3. The number of students enrolled full- and part-time who were dismissed or voluntarily withdrew from this program area in 2007–2008 were 1. *Counseling Psychology MA/MS (Master of Arts/Science)*—Applications 2007–2008, 20. Total applicants accepted 2007–2008, 15. Number full-time enrolled (new admits only) 2007–2008, 15. Number part-time enrolled (new admits only) 2007–2008, 0. Openings 2008–2009, 15. The median number of years required for completion of a degree in 2006–2007 were 2. The number of students enrolled full- and part-time who were dismissed or voluntarily withdrew from this program area in 2007–2008 were 0. *Community Counseling MA/MS (Master of Arts/Science)*—Applications 2007–2008, 21. Total applicants accepted 2007–2008, 18. Number full-time enrolled (new admits only) 2007–2008, 18. Total enrolled 2007–2008 full-time, 34. Openings 2008–2009, 18. The median number of years required for completion of a degree in 2006–2007 were 2. The number of students enrolled full- and part-time who were dismissed or voluntarily withdrew from this program area in 2007–2008 were 1.

Admissions Requirements:

Scores: Entries appear in this order: required test or GPA, minimum score (if required), median score of students entering in 2007–2008. Master's Programs: GRE-V 360, 470; GRE-Q 370, 525; GRE-Subject (Psychology) no minimum stated; overall undergraduate GPA 3.0, 3.5; last 2 years GPA no minimum stated; psychology GPA no minimum stated. Only School Psychology program requires GRE-Subject. Doctoral Programs: GRE-V 520, 570; GRE-Q 460, 520; GRE-Subject (Psychology) 550, 550; overall undergraduate GPA 2.6, 3.5.

Other Criteria: (importance of criteria rated low, medium, or high): GRE/MAT scores—medium, research experience—medium, work experience—low, extracurricular activity—medium, clinically related public service—low, GPA—high, letters of recommendation—medium, interview—high, statement of goals and objectives—high, undergraduate major in psychology—low, specific undergraduate psychology courses taken—low. Doctoral program places greater emphasis on research experience.

Student Characteristics: The following represents characteristics of students in 2007–2008 in all graduate psychology programs in the department: Female—full-time 88, part-time 10; Male—full-time 19, part-time 0; African American/Black—full-time 6, part-time 1; Hispanic/Latino(a)—full-time 1, part-time 0; Asian/Pacific Islander—full-time 0, part-time 0; American Indian/Alaska Native—full-time 3, part-time 0; Caucasian/White—full-time 96, part-time 9; Multi-ethnic—full-time 1, part-time 0; students subject to the Americans With Disabilities Act—full-time 1, part-time 0; Unknown ethnicity—full-time 0, part-time 0; International students who hold an F-1 or J-1 Visa—full-time 1, part-time 1.

Financial Information/Assistance:

Tuition for Full-Time Study: *Master's:* State residents: $239 per credit hour; Nonstate residents: $496 per credit hour. *Doctoral:* State residents: $239 per credit hour; Nonstate residents: $496 per credit hour. Tuition is subject to change. See the following Web site for updates and changes in tuition costs: http://www.uca.edu/divisions/admin/finserv/studentaccounts/tuitionfees.asp.

Financial Assistance:

First-Year Students: Teaching assistantships available for first year. Average amount paid per academic year: $5,700. Average number of hours worked per week: 20. Research assistantships available for first year. Average amount paid per academic year: $8,000. Average number of hours worked per week: 20.

Advanced Students: Teaching assistantships available for advanced students. Average amount paid per academic year: $5,000. Average number of hours worked per week: 10. Research assistantships available for advanced students. Average amount paid per academic year: $8,000. Average number of hours worked per week: 20.

Additional Information: Of all students currently enrolled full time, 50% benefited from one or more of the listed financial assistance programs. Application and information available online at http://www.uca.edu/divisions/academic/graduate/pdf/GA%20application.pdf.

Internships/Practica: Master's Degree (MA/MS Counseling Psychology): An internship experience such as a final research project or "capstone" experience is required of graduates. Master's Degree (MA/MS Community Counseling): An internship experience such as a final research project or "capstone" experience is required of graduates. Doctoral Degree (PhD School Psychology): For those doctoral students for whom a professional internship was required in this program prior to graduation, (3) students applied for an internship in 2006–2007, with (3) students obtaining an internship. Of those students who obtained an internship, (3) were paid internships. Of those students who obtained an internship, (2) students placed in APA/CPA-accredited internships, (0) students placed in internships not APA/CPA-accredited, but listed with the Association of Psychology Postdoctoral and Internship Centers (APPIC), (1) students placed in internships conforming to guidelines of the Council of Directors of School Psychology Programs (CDSPP), (0) students placed in internships that were not APA/CPA-accredited, APPIC or CDSPP listed. Students are placed in a wide range of practica and internships depending on their program of study, career aspirations, and match between the practica/internship site and our program objectives. Examples of placements include schools, community agencies, hospitals, and clinics.

Housing and Day Care: On-campus housing is available. See the following Web site for more information: http://www.uca.edu/divisions/admin/housing/. On-campus day care facilities are available. See the following Web site for more information:

http://www.uca.edu/divisions/academic/coe/ecse/pages/ChildStudy.htm.

Employment of Department Graduates:

Master's Degree Graduates: Of those who graduated in the academic year 2006–2007, the following categories and numbers represent the postgraduate activities and employment of master's degree graduates: Enrolled in a psychology doctoral program (0), enrolled in another graduate/professional program (0), enrolled in a postdoctoral residency/fellowship (n/a), employed in independent practice (n/a), employed in an academic position at a university (0), employed in an academic position at a 2-year/4-year college (0), employed in other positions at a higher education institution (0), employed in a professional position in a school system (5), employed in business or industry (0), employed in government agency (0), employed in a community mental health/counseling center (11), employed in a hospital/medical center (0), still seeking employment (0), not seeking employment (0), other employment position (0), do not know (0), total from the above (master's) (16).

Doctoral Degree Graduates: Of those who graduated in the academic year 2006–2007, the following categories and numbers represent the postgraduate activities and employment of doctoral degree graduates: Enrolled in a psychology doctoral program (n/a), enrolled in another graduate/professional program (0), enrolled in a postdoctoral residency/fellowship (1), employed in independent practice (0), employed in an academic position at a university (0), employed in an academic position at a 2-year/4-year college (0), employed in other positions at a higher education institution (0), employed in a professional position in a school system (0), employed in business or industry (0), employed in government agency (0), employed in a community mental health/counseling center (0), employed in a hospital/medical center (0), still seeking employment (0), not seeking employment (0), other employment position (0), do not know (0), total from the above (doctoral) (1).

Additional Information:

Orientation, Objectives, and Emphasis of Department: The MS programs in Counseling Psychology, Community Counseling, and School Psychology are designed to serve as terminal degrees with professional employment opportunities or as a firm foundation for prospective doctoral candidates. Broad training is offered in understanding of psychological theories, assessment, and mental health interventions to enable graduates to function successfully in a variety of mental health and educational settings. The PhD in School Psychology is grounded in the scientist–practitioner model of training. Strong emphasis is placed on child mental health promotion, primary prevention, and intervention with a broad range of community related problems involving children, families, and schools. The program is responsive to ongoing societal concerns and issues pertaining to children, families, and schools. It prepares its graduates to function in schools, clinics, community agencies, and hospitals. A PhD in Counseling Psychology will be offered beginning in Fall 2008. The program is based on the scientist–practitioner model of training and emphasizes community mental health prevention and intervention services for clients with a wide variety of mental health problems. Graduates will be prepared to provide evidence-based assessment and treatment services and to conduct research in clinical and university settings. Accreditation by APA will be sought at the earliest possible opportunity.

Special Facilities or Resources: The department has (a) a fully operational computer instruction/research room that can be used for onsite research purposes; (b) human and animal research labs; (c) a multi-media computer system for research-related editing (e.g., self-modeling, therapy tapes).

Information for Students With Physical Disabilities: See the following Web site for more information: http://www.uca.edu/divisions/student/disability/.

Application Information:

Send to Department Chair, Department of Psychology and Counseling, Box 4915, UCA, Conway, AR 72035. Application available online. URL of online application: http://www.uca.edu/psychology/. Students are admitted in the Fall, application deadline March 15; July 15; Summer, application deadline March 15. School Psychology PhD Program deadline: February 10. *Fee:* $25.

Alliant International University: Fresno/Sacramento

Programs in Clinical Psychology
California School of Professional Psychology
5130 East Clinton Way
Fresno, CA 93727
Telephone: (559) 456-2777
Fax: (559) 253-2267
E-mail: *brianevans@alliant.edu*
Web: *http://www.alliant.edu/cspp/*

Department Information:

1973. Dean, California School of Professional Psychology: Morgan T. Sammons, PhD, ABPP. Number of faculty: total—full-time 8, part-time 23; women—full-time 5, part-time 12; total—minority—full-time 1, part-time 5; women minority—part-time 3.

Programs and Degrees Offered:

Listed in the following order: Program area, degree type (T if terminal Master's), number awarded 7/06–6/07. Clinical Psychology PsyD (Doctor of Psychology) 25, Clinical Psychology PhD (Doctor of Philosophy) 12, Clinical Psychology–Advanced Standing/Online PsyD (Doctor of Psychology) 0.

APA Accreditation: Clinical PsyD (Doctor of Psychology). Clinical PhD (Doctor of Philosophy).

Student Applications/Admissions:

Student Applications

Clinical Psychology PsyD (Doctor of Psychology)—Applications 2007–2008, 96. Total applicants accepted 2007–2008, 42. Number full-time enrolled (new admits only) 2007–2008, 32. Number part-time enrolled (new admits only) 2007–2008, 0. Total enrolled 2007–2008 full-time, 113, part-time, 5. Openings 2008–2009, 39. The median number of years required for completion of a degree in 2006–2007 were 4. The number of students enrolled full- and part-time who were dismissed or voluntarily withdrew from this program area in 2007–2008 were 1. *Clinical Psychology PhD (Doctor of Philosophy)*—Applications 2007–2008, 25. Total applicants accepted 2007–2008, 10. Number full-time enrolled (new admits only) 2007–2008, 6. Number part-time enrolled (new admits only) 2007–2008, 1. Total enrolled 2007–2008 full-time, 34, part-time, 5. Openings 2008–2009, 12. The median number of years required for completion of a degree in 2006–2007 were 4. The number of students enrolled full- and part-time who were dismissed or voluntarily withdrew from this program area in 2007–2008 were 1. *Clinical Psychology–Advanced Standing/Online PsyD (Doctor of Psychology)*—Applications 2007–2008, 30. Total applicants accepted 2007–2008, 10. Number full-time enrolled (new admits only) 2007–2008, 6. Number part-time enrolled (new admits only) 2007–2008, 1. Total enrolled 2007–2008 full-time, 16, part-time, 2. Openings 2008–2009, 10. The number of students enrolled full- and part-time who were dismissed or voluntarily withdrew from this program area in 2007–2008 were 2.

Admissions Requirements:

Scores: Entries appear in this order: required test or GPA, minimum score (if required), median score of students entering in 2007–2008. Doctoral Programs: overall undergraduate GPA 3.00, 3.32; psychology GPA 3.00. A master's degree is not required for entry, but if a master's degree is held at the time of application, the minimum 3.0 GPA applies.

Other Criteria: (importance of criteria rated low, medium, or high): research experience—medium, work experience—medium, extracurricular activity—low, clinically related public service—medium, GPA—high, letters of recommendation—high, interview—high, statement of goals and objectives—high. For additional information on admission requirements, go to http://www.alliant.edu/wps/wcm/connect/website/Home/Admissions/Graduate+Student+Admissions/.

Student Characteristics: The following represents characteristics of students in 2007–2008 in all graduate psychology programs in the department: Female—full-time 129, part-time 8; Male—full-time 34, part-time 4; African American/Black—full-time 9, part-time 0; Hispanic/Latino(a)—full-time 11, part-time 2; Asian/Pacific Islander—full-time 17, part-time 0; American Indian/Alaska Native—full-time 1, part-time 0; Caucasian/White—full-time 94, part-time 9; Multi-ethnic—full-time 6, part-time 0; students subject to the Americans With Disabilities Act—full-time 3, part-time 1; Unknown ethnicity—full-time 25, part-time 1; International students who hold an F-1 or J-1 Visa—full-time 5, part-time 0.

Financial Information/Assistance:

Tuition for Full-Time Study: *Doctoral:* State residents: $915 per credit hour; Nonstate residents: $915 per credit hour. Tuition is subject to change. See the following Web site for updates and changes in tuition costs: http://www.alliant.edu/wps/wcm/connect/website/Home/Admissions/Tuition+and+Fees/.

Financial Assistance:

First-Year Students: Research assistantships available for first year. Average amount paid per academic year: $1,000. Average number of hours worked per week: 10. Apply by see department. Fellowships and scholarships available for first year. Average amount paid per academic year: $1,500. Apply by February 15.

Advanced Students: Teaching assistantships available for advanced students. Average amount paid per academic year: $3,000. Average number of hours worked per week: 10. Apply by see department. Research assistantships available for advanced students. Average amount paid per academic year: $1,000. Average number of hours worked per week: 10. Apply by see department. Fellowships and scholarships available for advanced students. Average amount paid per academic year: $1,500. Apply by April 15.

Additional Information: Of all students currently enrolled full time, 56% benefited from one or more of the listed financial assistance programs. Application and information available online at https://www.e-fao.com/eFAO_site.html?OEID=011117&ViewID={10EF815B-422E-4C55-B8CD-BDBD3063BA18}.

Internships/Practica: Doctoral Degree (PsyD Clinical Psychology): For those doctoral students for whom a professional internship was required in this program prior to graduation, (24) students applied for an internship in 2006–2007, with (24) students obtaining an internship. Of those students who obtained an internship, (18) were paid internships. Of those students who obtained an internship, (11) students placed in APA/CPA-accredited internships, (10) students placed in internships not APA/CPA accredited, but listed with the Association of Psychology Postdoctoral and Internship Centers (APPIC), (0) students placed in internships conforming to guidelines of the Council of Directors of School Psychology Programs (CDSPP), (3) students placed in internships that were not APA/CPA-accredited, APPIC or CDSPP listed. Doctoral Degree (PhD Clinical Psychology): For those doctoral students for whom a professional internship was required in this program prior to graduation, (10) students applied for an internship in 2006–2007, with (10) students obtaining an internship. Of those students who obtained an internship, (10) were paid internships. Of those students who obtained an internship, (2) students placed in APA/CPA-accredited internships, (4) students placed in internships not APA/CPA-accredited, but listed with the Association of Psychology Postdoctoral and Internship Centers (APPIC), (0) students placed in internships conforming to guidelines of the Council of Directors of School Psychology Programs (CDSPP), (4) students placed in internships that were not APA/CPA-accredited, APPIC or CDSPP listed. The clinical psychology programs at Fresno and Sacramento emphasize the integration of academic coursework and research with clinical practice. In order to integrate appropriate skills with material learned in the classroom, students participate in a professional training placement experience beginning in the first year. The settings where students complete the professional training requirements include community mental health centers, clinics, inpatient mental health facilities, medical settings, specialized service centers, rehabilitation programs, residential/day care programs, forensic/correctional facilities, and educational programs. Third year students will spend 15 hours per week in a practicum either at CSPP's Psychological Service Center or at some other CSPP-approved agency. During their final year, clinical students complete a full-year internship at an appropriate APA or APPIC internship. CSPP also has formed the Central California Psychology Internship Consortium for students working to complete their internship in Central California. PhD students must also complete teaching practica.

Housing and Day Care: No on-campus housing is available. No on-campus day care facilities are available.

Employment of Department Graduates:

Master's Degree Graduates: Of those who graduated in the academic year 2006–2007, the following categories and numbers represent the postgraduate activities and employment of master's degree graduates: Enrolled in a postdoctoral residency/fellowship (n/a), employed in independent practice (n/a), total from the above (master's) (0).

Doctoral Degree Graduates: Of those who graduated in the academic year 2006–2007, the following categories and numbers represent the postgraduate activities and employment of doctoral degree graduates: Enrolled in a psychology doctoral program (n/a), total from the above (doctoral) (0).

Additional Information:

Orientation, Objectives, and Emphasis of Department: The clinical psychology PsyD program emphasizes training in clinical skills and clinical application of research knowledge and is designed for students who are interested in careers as practitioners but it also includes a research component. The program is multisystemically or ecosystemically oriented and trains students to consider the role of diverse systems in creating and/or remedying individual and social problems. An empirical PsyD dissertation is required and may focus on program development and/or evaluation, test development, survey research, or therapeutic outcomes. The program in Sacramento is offered in an evening/weekend format for working professionals. The Advanced Standing Online Clinical PsyD Program offers a new method of completing requirements for the Clinical PsyD program for those who already hold master's degrees and are certified or licensed in their field (LMFT, LCSW, and School Psychologists); note that this program is not accredited by the APA. Approximately 1 year of coursework is transferred in based on course equivalencies, and documented supervised clinical experience and 1 year is taking in an online format with four in residence sessions during the year. The remainder of the program is taken on location at Sacramento or Fresno; an internship is also required. The clinical psychology PhD program puts equal weight on training in clinical, research, and teaching skills. The program is for students whose goal is a teaching career in psychology. Emphasis areas offered are ecosystemic clinical child emphasis—trains students to work with infants, children, and adolescents, as well as with the adults in these clients' lives; health psychology emphasis—provides students with exposure to the expanding field of health psychology and behavioral medicine; forensic clinical psychology emphasis—prepares students to practice clinical psychology in a forensic environment. All courses required for an emphasis may not be available in Sacramento; students interested in an emphasis may need to travel to Fresno for courses.

Special Facilities or Resources: The Psychological Service Center serves the dual purpose of offering high-quality psychological services to the community, particularly underserved segments, and continuing the tradition of education, training, and service. The facility consists of eight therapy and two play therapy rooms, large conference room, student work room, TV/monitor, and staff offices. The campus is also home to the Association for Play Therapy.

Information for Students With Physical Disabilities: Go to About Alliant > Student Life and Athletics > Disability Services at the following Web site: http://www.alliant.edu.

Application Information:

Send to Alliant International University Admissions Processing Center, 10455 Pomerado Road, San Diego, CA 92131-1799. Application available online. URL of online application: http://www.alliant.edu/applyonline/. Students are admitted in the Fall, application deadline January 15; Spring, application deadline November 15. Programs have rolling admissions. The programs have a January 15 priority deadline in order to provide a response by April 1 for applicants who need a decision by that date. Programs accept and admit appliants on a space available basis after any stated deadlines. For updated information on deadlines, contact the admissions office at 1-866-U-ALLIANT. *Fee:* $70. A limited number of application fee waivers are available for students with significant financial need.

Alliant International University: San Francisco

Programs in Clinical Psychology and Clinical Psychopharmacology
California School of Professional Psychology
One Beach Street
San Francisco, CA 94133-1221
Telephone: (415) 955-2146
Fax: (415) 955-2179
E-mail: *jaquino@alliant.edu*
Web: *http://www.alliant.edu/cspp/*

Department Information:

1969. Dean, California School of Professional Psychology: Morgan T. Sammons, PhD, ABPP. Number of faculty: total—full-time 27, part-time 50; women—full-time 13, part-time 20; total—minority—full-time 6, part-time 12; women minority—full-time 2, part-time 5; faculty subject to the Americans With Disabilities Act 2.

Programs and Degrees Offered:

Listed in the following order: Program area, degree type (T if terminal Master's), number awarded 7/06–6/07. Clinical Psychology PsyD (Doctor of Psychology) 43, Clinical Psychology PhD (Doctor of Philosophy) 9, Clinical Psychology Respecialization Diploma 0, Clinical Psychopharmacology MA/MS (Master of Arts/Science) (T) 55.

APA Accreditation: Clinical PsyD (Doctor of Psychology). Clinical PhD (Doctor of Philosophy).

Student Applications/Admissions:

Student Applications

Clinical Psychology PsyD (Doctor of Psychology)—Applications 2007–2008, 217. Total applicants accepted 2007–2008, 131. Number full-time enrolled (new admits only) 2007–2008, 58. Number part-time enrolled (new admits only) 2007–2008, 1. Total enrolled 2007–2008 full-time, 293, part-time, 60. Openings 2008–2009, 66. The median number of years required for completion of a degree in 2006–2007 were 4. The number of students enrolled full- and part-time who were dismissed or voluntarily withdrew from this program area in 2007–2008 were 2. *Clinical Psychology PhD (Doctor of Philosophy)*—Applications 2007–2008, 82. Total applicants accepted 2007–2008, 44. Number full-time enrolled (new admits only) 2007–2008, 24. Number part-time enrolled (new admits only) 2007–2008, 0. Total enrolled 2007–2008 full-time, 129, part-time, 25. Openings 2008–2009, 25. The median number of years required for completion of a degree in 2006–2007 were 5. The number of students enrolled full- and part-time who were dismissed or voluntarily withdrew from this program area in 2007–2008 were 2. *Clinical Psychology Respecialization Diploma*—Applications 2007–2008, 1. Total applicants accepted 2007–2008, 1. Number full-time enrolled (new admits only) 2007–2008, 0. Number part-time enrolled (new admits only) 2007–2008, 1. Total enrolled 2007–2008 full-time, 2, part-time, 2. Openings 2008–2009, 3. The number of students enrolled full- and part-time who were dismissed or voluntarily withdrew from this program area in 2007–2008 were 0. *Clinical Psychopharmacology MA/MS (Master of Arts/Science)*—Number full-time enrolled (new admits only) 2007–2008, 0. Number part-time enrolled (new admits only) 2007–2008, 0. Openings 2008–2009, 60. The median number of years required for completion of a degree in 2006–2007 were 4. The number of students enrolled full- and part-time who were dismissed or voluntarily withdrew from this program area in 2007–2008 were 0.

Admissions Requirements:

Scores: Entries appear in this order: required test or GPA, minimum score (if required), median score of students entering in 2007–2008. Master's Programs: Admission to the postdoctoral master's program in clinical psychopharmacology requires written proof from the State Board of Examiners that the applicant holds a current, valid license in good standing as a doctoral-level psychologist. Doctoral Programs: overall undergraduate GPA 3.00, 3.33; psychology GPA 3.00.

Other Criteria: (importance of criteria rated low, medium, or high): GRE/MAT scores—low, research experience—high, work experience—high, extracurricular activity—low, clinically related public service—high, GPA—high, letters of recommendation—high, interview—high, statement of goals and objectives—high. Admissions requirements vary by program. PhD programs place more emphasis on prior research experience; PsyD programs place more emphasis on clinical/work experience. For additional information on admission requirements, go to http://www.alliant.edu/wps/wcm/connect/website/Home/Admissions/Graduate+Student+Admissions/.

Student Characteristics: The following represents characteristics of students in 2007–2008 in all graduate psychology programs in the department: Female—full-time 334, part-time 113; Male—full-time 90, part-time 42; African American/Black—full-time 21, part-time 9; Hispanic/Latino(a)—full-time 48, part-time 11; Asian/Pacific Islander—full-time 60, part-time 14; American Indian/Alaska Native—full-time 1, part-time 0; Caucasian/White—full-time 244, part-time 109; Multi-ethnic—full-time 16, part-time 0; students subject to the Americans With Disabilities Act—full-time 18, part-time 2; Unknown ethnicity—full-time 34, part-time 12; International students who hold an F-1 or J-1 Visa—full-time 21, part-time 2.

Financial Information/Assistance:

Tuition for Full-Time Study: *Master's:* State residents: per academic year $5,900; Nonstate residents: per academic year $5,900. *Doctoral:* State residents: $915 per credit hour; Nonstate residents: $915 per credit hour. Tuition is subject to change. Tuition costs vary by program. See the following Web site for updates and changes in tuition costs: http://www.alliant.edu/wps/wcm/connect/website/Home/Admissions/Tuition+and+Fees/.

Financial Assistance:

First-Year Students: Research assistantships available for first year. Average amount paid per academic year: $1,500. Average number of hours worked per week: 10. Apply by see department. Fellowships and scholarships available for first year. Average amount paid per academic year: $1,500. Apply by February 15.

Advanced Students: Teaching assistantships available for advanced students. Average amount paid per academic year: $3,000. Average number of hours worked per week: 10. Apply by see department. Research assistantships available for advanced students. Average amount paid per academic year: $1,000. Average number of hours worked per week: 10. Apply by see department. Fellowships and scholarships available for advanced students. Average amount paid per academic year: $1,500. Apply by April 15.

Additional Information: Of all students currently enrolled full time, 58% benefited from one or more of the listed financial assistance programs. Application and information available online at https://www.e-fao.com/eFAO_site.html?OEID=011117&ViewID={10EF815B-422E-4C55-B8CD-BDBD3063BA18}.

Internships/Practica: Doctoral Degree (PsyD Clinical Psychology): For those doctoral students for whom a professional internship was required in this program prior to graduation, (72) students applied for an internship in 2006–2007, with (72) students obtaining an internship. Of those students who obtained an internship, (46) were paid internships. Of those students who obtained an internship, (12) students placed in APA/CPA-accredited internships, (7) students placed in internships not APA/CPA accredited, but listed with the Association of Psychology Postdoctoral and Internship Centers (APPIC), (0) students placed in internships conforming to guidelines of the Council of Directors of School Psychology Programs (CDSPP), (53) students placed in internships that were not APA/CPA-accredited, APPIC or CDSPP listed. Doctoral Degree (PhD Clinical Psychology): For those doctoral students for whom a professional internship was required in this program prior to graduation, (23) students applied for an internship in 2006–2007, with (23) students obtaining an internship. Of those students who obtained an internship, (20) were paid internships. Of those students who obtained an internship, (10) students placed in APA/CPA-accredited internships, (3) students placed in internships not APA/CPA-accredited, but listed with the Association of Psychology Postdoctoral and Internship Centers (APPIC), (0) students placed in internships conforming to guidelines of the Council of Directors of School Psychology Programs (CDSPP), (10) students placed in internships that were not APA/CPA-accredited, APPIC or CDSPP listed. During the first three years of the PsyD program and during the second and third years of the PhD program, students are engaged in field practica 8–16 hours per week. All students get experience working with adults, children/adolescents, and persons with severe mental illness as well as more moderate forms of dysfunction. The tremendous ethnic/racial diversity of the San Francisco Bay Area insures that all students get exposure to working with clients from a variety of cultural groups. Practica are selected and approved by CSPP based on the quality of training and supervision provided for the students. They include community mental health centers, neuropsychology clinics, hospitals, child guidance clinics, college counseling centers, forensic settings, couple and family therapy agencies, residential treatment centers, infant/toddler mental health programs, corporate settings, and school programs for children and adolescents. Students begin the required internship in the 4th year (PsyD program) or the 5th year (PhD program). Full-time internship options include APA-accredited or APPIC-member training programs pursued through the national selection process, or local internship programs approved by the California Psychology Internship Council (CAPIC). Students have the option of completing the internship requirement in 2 years of half-time experience.

Housing and Day Care: No on-campus housing is available. No on-campus day care facilities are available.

Employment of Department Graduates:

Master's Degree Graduates: Of those who graduated in the academic year 2006–2007, the following categories and numbers represent the postgraduate activities and employment of master's degree graduates: Enrolled in a postdoctoral residency/fellowship (n/a), employed in independent practice (n/a), total from the above (master's) (0).

Doctoral Degree Graduates: Of those who graduated in the academic year 2006–2007, the following categories and numbers represent the postgraduate activities and employment of doctoral degree graduates: Enrolled in a psychology doctoral program (n/a), total from the above (doctoral) (0).

Additional Information:

Orientation, Objectives, and Emphasis of Department: CSPP's clinical psychology programs combine supervised field experiences with study of psychological theory, clinical techniques, and applied research. The PsyD is a practitioner-oriented program. The PhD provides a balance of clinical and research training and is intended for students who expect independent research, teaching, and scholarship to be a significant part of their professional careers in addition to clinical work. In addition to the usual offerings, special training opportunities are available in five areas: family-child-adolescent psychology, health psychology, multicultural-community psychology, psychodynamic psychology, and gender studies (which includes psychology of women and men, and lesbian, gay, bisexual and transgender issues). The PsyD program also offers an intensive Child and Family Track (which focuses on child assessment, child therapy, and family therapy) and a Forensic Family/Child Track (which focuses on child abuse, child custody, delinquency, and family court services). Students in the PsyD tracks are required to complete a specific sequence of courses, a dissertation, and an internship related to their track's focus. Other students in the PhD and PsyD programs can take many of these same training experiences on an elective basis. Multicultural/diversity issues are infused throughout the entire curriculum. Three major theoretical orientations are strongly represented in the program: cognitive–behavioral, family systems, and psychodynamic.

Special Facilities or Resources: Students can elect to receive supervised clinical experience through CSPP's Psychological Services Center (PSC)—a community mental health clinic that serves children, adults, couples, and families. The PSC enables faculty to model professional service delivery and to directly supervise and evaluate students' clinical work. Clinical services provided at the PSC include psychodiagnostic assessment and individual, couple, family, and group psychotherapy. The PSC has both Adult–Clinical and Child/Family–Clinical training programs. The Rockway Institute works to counter antigay prejudice and inform public policies affecting lesbian, gay, bisexual, and transgender (LGBT) people. Primary goals of the Institute is to convey accurate scientific and professional information about LGBT issues to the media, legislatures, and the courts, and conduct research relevant to LGBT public policy questions in the areas of family relations, education, healthcare, social services, and the workplace. Computer labs are available to students and are fully equipped with SPSS and other statistical programs for research purposes. Designated space is available on campus for research activities (such as data collection), and the library is equipped with the major searchable databases for the research literature in psychology and related areas. The campus occupies approximately 31,000 square feet of space in an historic building near the San Francisco waterfront across from Pier 39.

Information for Students With Physical Disabilities: Go to About Alliant > Student Life and Athletics > Disability Services at the following Web site: http://www.alliant.edu.

Application Information:
Send to Alliant International University, Admissions Processing Center, 10455 Pomerado Road, San Diego, CA 92131. Application available online. URL of online application: http://www.alliant.edu/applyonline/. Students are admitted in the Fall, application deadline January 15; Spring, application deadline varies. Programs have rolling admissions. The priority deadline for doctoral programs is January 15; applicants who complete an application by that date are guaranteed notification by April 1. Applications submitted after that date will be reviewed on a space-available basis. Applications to the clinical psychopharmacology master's programs vary by location and cohort start date. For more information contact the admissions office at 1-866-U-ALLIANT. *Fee:* $70. A limited number of fee waivers are available for those with significant financial need.

Alliant International University: Fresno

Forensic Psychology Programs
Center for Forensic Studies
5130 East Clinton Way
Fresno, CA 93727-2014
Telephone: (559) 456-2777
Fax: (559) 253-2267
E-mail: *brianevans@alliant.edu*
Web: *http://www.alliant.edu/*

Department Information:
1996. Program Director: William Holcomb, PhD. Number of faculty: total—full-time 4, part-time 10; women—full-time 3, part-time 4; minority—part-time 1; women minority—part-time 1.

Programs and Degrees Offered:
Listed in the following order: Program area, degree type (T if terminal Master's), number awarded 7/06–6/07. Forensic Psychology PhD (Doctor of Philosophy) 8, Forensic Psychology PsyD (Doctor of Psychology) 10.

Student Applications/Admissions:
Student Applications
Forensic Psychology PhD (Doctor of Philosophy)—Applications 2007–2008, 44. Total applicants accepted 2007–2008, 30. Number full-time enrolled (new admits only) 2007–2008, 23. Number part-time enrolled (new admits only) 2007–2008, 0. Total enrolled 2007–2008 full-time, 66, part-time, 4. Openings 2008–2009, 20. The median number of years required for completion of a degree in 2006–2007 were 4. The number of students enrolled full- and part-time who were dismissed or voluntarily withdrew from this program area in 2007–2008 were 2. *Forensic Psychology PsyD (Doctor of Psychology)*—Applications 2007–2008, 20. Total applicants accepted 2007–2008, 13. Number full-time enrolled (new admits only) 2007–2008, 10. Number part-time enrolled (new admits only) 2007–2008, 1. Total enrolled 2007–2008 full-time, 28, part-time, 8. Openings 2008–2009, 15. The median number of years required for completion of a degree in 2006–2007 were 4. The number of students enrolled full- and part-time who were dismissed or voluntarily withdrew from this program area in 2007–2008 were 2.

Admissions Requirements:
Scores: Entries appear in this order: required test or GPA, minimum score (if required), median score of students entering in 2007–2008. Doctoral Programs: overall undergraduate GPA 3.0, 3.34; psychology GPA 3.0. The master's degree is not required for admission, but if held at the time of application, the minimum 3.0 GPA is required.
Other Criteria: (importance of criteria rated low, medium, or high): research experience—high, work experience—high, extracurricular activity—low, clinically related public service—medium, GPA—high, letters of recommendation—high, interview—high, statement of goals and objectives—high. Requirements vary by program. The PhD program puts more emphasis on prior research experience; the PsyD program on prior clinically related experience. For additional information on admission requirements, go to http://www.alliant.edu/wps/wcm/connect/website/Home/Admissions/.

Student Characteristics: The following represents characteristics of students in 2007–2008 in all graduate psychology programs in the department: Female—full-time 72, part-time 9; Male—full-time 22, part-time 3; African American/Black—full-time 3, part-time 1; Hispanic/Latino(a)—full-time 10, part-time 0; Asian/Pacific Islander—full-time 9, part-time 0; American Indian/Alaska Native—full-time 1, part-time 0; Caucasian/White—full-time 63, part-time 8; Multi-ethnic—full-time 1, part-time 2; students subject to the Americans With Disabilities Act—full-time 2, part-time 0; Unknown ethnicity—full-time 7, part-time 1; International students who hold an F-1 or J-1 Visa—full-time 0, part-time 0.

Financial Information/Assistance:
Tuition for Full-Time Study: *Doctoral:* State residents: $915 per credit hour; Nonstate residents: $915 per credit hour. Tuition is subject to change. Tuition costs vary by program. See the following Web site for updates and changes in tuition costs: http://www.alliant.edu/wps/wcm/connect/website/Home/Admissions/Tuition+and+Fees/.

Financial Assistance:
First-Year Students: Research assistantships available for first year. Average amount paid per academic year: $1,000. Average number of hours worked per week: 10. Apply by see department. Fellowships and scholarships available for first year. Average amount paid per academic year: $1,500. Apply by January 2.

Advanced Students: Teaching assistantships available for advanced students. Average amount paid per academic year: $3,000. Average number of hours worked per week: 20. Apply by see department. Research assistantships available for advanced students. Average amount paid per academic year: $1,000. Average number of hours worked per week: 10. Apply by see department. Fellowships and scholarships available for advanced students. Average amount paid per academic year: $1,500. Apply by April 15.

Additional Information: Of all students currently enrolled full time, 51% benefited from one or more of the listed financial

assistance programs. Application and information available online at https://www.e-fao.com/efao_site.html?OEID=011117&ViewID={10EF815B-422E-4C55-B8CD-BDBD3063BA18}.

Internships/Practica: Doctoral Degree (PsyD Forensic Psychology): For those doctoral students for whom a professional internship was required in this program prior to graduation, (19) students applied for an internship in 2006–2007, with (18) students obtaining an internship. Of those students who obtained an internship, (12) were paid internships. Of those students who obtained an internship, (4) students placed in APA/CPA-accredited internships, (11) students placed in internships not APA/CPA accredited, but listed with the Association of Psychology Postdoctoral and Internship Centers (APPIC), (0) students placed in internships conforming to guidelines of the Council of Directors of School Psychology Programs (CDSPP), (3) students placed in internships that were not APA/CPA-accredited, APPIC or CDSPP listed. Students in the PhD program complete a research internship in a law enforcement or other forensic setting. Students in the PsyD program complete a predoctoral internship. For full-time students, these internships typically occur in the 4th year and involve full-time or close to full-time activity.

Housing and Day Care: No on-campus housing is available. No on-campus day care facilities are available.

Employment of Department Graduates:

Master's Degree Graduates: Of those who graduated in the academic year 2006–2007, the following categories and numbers represent the postgraduate activities and employment of master's degree graduates: Enrolled in a postdoctoral residency/fellowship (n/a), employed in independent practice (n/a), total from the above (master's) (0).

Doctoral Degree Graduates: Of those who graduated in the academic year 2006–2007, the following categories and numbers represent the postgraduate activities and employment of doctoral degree graduates: Enrolled in a psychology doctoral program (n/a), employed in a community mental health/counseling center (1), employed in a hospital/medical center (6), still seeking employment (1), other employment position (1), do not know (10), total from the above (doctoral) (19).

Additional Information:

Orientation, Objectives, and Emphasis of Department: The forensic psychology PhD program prepares students for roles in administration in a variety of mental health agencies, correctional facilities and organizations, and law enforcement departments. Students are prepared to conduct research in both academic and government institutions; examine policy initiatives; and provide advocacy, lobbying, and mediation skills to agencies and organizations. The PsyD program has an applied psychology orientation. This curriculum prepares students to conduct assessments for the courts, to serve as expert witnesses, or to work as mental health treatment providers in a variety of forensic settings, including prisons, jails, offender treatment groups, and youth facilities among many others. Core areas in both programs include forensic psychology, theories of crime and justice, industrial and organizational psychology, legal research, psychopathology, research design and data analysis, forensic mediation and dispute resolution, ethics, and substance abuse theory and treatment. Although the programs are not specifically designed to train licensed psychologists, some students who enter the program may wish to seek clinical licensure after graduation. Arrangements can be made to take additional psychology courses required for licensing exams, and both PsyD and PhD students have become licensed.

Information for Students With Physical Disabilities: Go to About Alliant > Student Life > Disability Services at http://www.alliant.edu..

Application Information:

Send to Alliant International University, Admissions Processing Center, 10455 Pomerado Road, San Diego, CA 92131-1799. Application available online. URL of online application: http://www.alliant.edu/applyonline/. Students are admitted in the Fall, application deadline varies; Spring, application deadline varies. Programs have rolling admissions. Applicants wishing notification by April 1 should submit their applications in January. Applications are welcomed on a rolling basis and will be processed on a space-available basis. *Fee:* $70. A limited number of fee waivers are available for those with significant financial need.

Alliant International University: Fresno/Sacramento

Programs in Organizational Psychology
Marshall Goldsmith School of Management
5130 East Clinton Way
Fresno, CA 93727-2014
Telephone: (559) 253-2262
Fax: (559) 253-2267
E-mail: *mjones@alliant.edu*
Web: *http://www.mgsm.alliant.edu*

Department Information:

1995. Program Director: Toni A Knott, PhD. Number of faculty: total—full-time 2, part-time 7; women—full-time 1, part-time 5; total—minority—full-time 1.

Programs and Degrees Offered:

Listed in the following order: Program area, degree type (T if terminal Master's), number awarded 7/06–6/07. Organization Development PsyD (Doctor of Psychology) 8, Orgranizational Behavior MA/MS (Master of Arts/Science) (T) 6.

Student Applications/Admissions:

Student Applications

Organization Development PsyD (Doctor of Psychology)—Applications 2007–2008, 3. Total applicants accepted 2007–2008, 1. Number full-time enrolled (new admits only) 2007–2008, 0. Number part-time enrolled (new admits only) 2007–2008, 1. Total enrolled 2007–2008 full-time, 21, part-time, 21. Openings 2008–2009, 10. The median number of years required for completion of a degree in 2006–2007 were 4. The number of students enrolled full- and part-time who were dismissed or voluntarily withdrew from this program area in 2007–2008 were 0. *Orgranizational Behavior MA/MS (Master of Arts/Science)*—Applications 2007–2008, 15. Total applicants accepted 2007–2008, 10. Number full-time enrolled (new admits only) 2007–2008, 5. Number part-time enrolled (new admits only) 2007–2008, 0. Total enrolled 2007–2008 full-time, 11, part-time, 2. Openings 2008–2009, 18. The median number of years required for completion of a degree in

2006–2007 were 2. The number of students enrolled full- and part-time who were dismissed or voluntarily withdrew from this program area in 2007–2008 were 1.

Admissions Requirements:
Scores: Entries appear in this order: required test or GPA, minimum score (if required), median score of students entering in 2007–2008. Master's Programs: overall undergraduate GPA 3.0, 3.0; psychology GPA 3.0. Doctoral Programs: overall undergraduate GPA 3.0, 3.34; psychology GPA 3.0.
Other Criteria: (importance of criteria rated low, medium, or high): research experience—low, work experience—high, extracurricular activity—medium, GPA—high, letters of recommendation—high, interview—high, statement of goals and objectives—high. For additional information on admission requirements, go to http://www.alliant.edu/wps/wcm/connect/website/Home/Admissions/.

Student Characteristics: The following represents characteristics of students in 2007–2008 in all graduate psychology programs in the department: Female—full-time 9, part-time 9; Male—full-time 23, part-time 14; African American/Black—full-time 5, part-time 4; Hispanic/Latino(a)—full-time 6, part-time 1; Asian/Pacific Islander—full-time 6, part-time 3; American Indian/Alaska Native—full-time 0, part-time 0; Caucasian/White—full-time 11, part-time 12; Multi-ethnic—full-time 1, part-time 0; students subject to the Americans With Disabilities Act—full-time 0, part-time 1; Unknown ethnicity—full-time 3, part-time 3; International students who hold an F-1 or J-1 Visa—full-time 0, part-time 0.

Financial Information/Assistance:
Tuition for Full-Time Study: *Doctoral:* State residents: $700 per credit hour; Nonstate residents: $915 per credit hour. Tuition is subject to change. Tuition costs vary by program. See the following Web site for updates and changes in tuition costs: http://www.alliant.edu/wps/wcm/connect/website/Home/Admissions/Tuition+and+Fees/.

Financial Assistance:
First-Year Students: Research assistantships available for first year. Average amount paid per academic year: $1,000. Average number of hours worked per week: 10. Apply by see department. Fellowships and scholarships available for first year. Average amount paid per academic year: $1,500. Apply by February 1.
Advanced Students: Teaching assistantships available for advanced students. Average amount paid per academic year: $3,000. Average number of hours worked per week: 10. Apply by see department. Research assistantships available for advanced students. Average amount paid per academic year: $1,000. Average number of hours worked per week: 10. Apply by see department. Fellowships and scholarships available for advanced students. Average amount paid per academic year: $1,500. Apply by April 15.
Additional Information: Of all students currently enrolled full time, 51% benefited from one or more of the listed financial assistance programs. Application and information available online at https://www.e-fao.com/efao_site.html?OEID=011117&ViewID={10EF815B-422E-4C55-B8CD-BDBD3063BA18}.

Internships/Practica: The 2nd and 3rd years of the doctoral program involves a professional placement in organizational studies.

Housing and Day Care: No on-campus housing is available. No on-campus day care facilities are available.

Employment of Department Graduates:
Master's Degree Graduates: Of those who graduated in the academic year 2006–2007, the following categories and numbers represent the postgraduate activities and employment of master's degree graduates: Enrolled in a psychology doctoral program (2), enrolled in a postdoctoral residency/fellowship (n/a), employed in independent practice (n/a), employed in an academic position at a university (0), employed in an academic position at a 2-year/4-year college (0), employed in other positions at a higher education institution (0), employed in a professional position in a school system (0), employed in business or industry (0), employed in government agency (0), employed in a community mental health/counseling center (0), employed in a hospital/medical center (0), still seeking employment (0), not seeking employment (0), other employment position (0), do not know (0), total from the above (master's) (2).
Doctoral Degree Graduates: Of those who graduated in the academic year 2006–2007, the following categories and numbers represent the postgraduate activities and employment of doctoral degree graduates: Enrolled in a psychology doctoral program (n/a), enrolled in another graduate/professional program (0), enrolled in a postdoctoral residency/fellowship (0), employed in independent practice (3), employed in an academic position at a university (1), employed in an academic position at a 2-year/4-year college (2), employed in other positions at a higher education institution (0), employed in a professional position in a school system (0), employed in business or industry (1), employed in government agency (0), employed in a community mental health/counseling center (0), employed in a hospital/medical center (0), still seeking employment (0), not seeking employment (0), other employment position (0), do not know (0), total from the above (doctoral) (7).

Additional Information:
Orientation, Objectives, and Emphasis of Department: The doctoral program prepares students for careers as consultants, leaders/managers, or faculty in community college or other academic institutions. The program is 3 years postmasters and accessible to working adults. Students focus on the individual as a scholar–practitioner, themes and cultures of organizations, and practice in the global community. During the program they learn about managing change in complex organizations, examine and assess organizational procedures and processes, design interventions at the system/group/individual levels, and learn skills for Organization Development consulting and conducting applied research. A PsyD project is a required part of the program. The master's program is a 2-year program for working professionals and may be taken jointly with another doctoral program at Alliant in Fresno. The program has a practical curriculum related to management issues involving people and organizational processes. The PsyD program is accredited by the Organization Development Institute.

Special Facilities or Resources: The Marshall Goldsmith School of Management operates the Organizational Consulting Center (OCC). Students may have opportunities to participate with faculty and OCC associates on consulting projects during their programs.

Information for Students With Physical Disabilities: Go to About Alliant > Student Life and Athletics > Disability Services at the following Web site: http://www.alliant.edu.

Application Information:
Send to Alliant International University, Admissions Processing Center, 10455 Pomerado Road, San Diego, CA 92131-1799. Application available online. URL of online application: http://www.alliant.edu/applyonline/. Students are admitted in the Fall, application deadline February 1; Winter, application deadline November 1; Spring, application deadline varies. Programs have rolling admissions. Doctoral program has a February 1 deadline in order to provide a response by April 1 for applicants who need a decision by that date. The program accepts applications and admits students on a space-available basis after any stated deadlines. For complete information on deadlines visit www.alliant.edu/admissions/gradtimelines.htm or contact the admissions office at 1-866-U-ALLIANT. *Fee:* $70. A limited number of fee waivers are available to those with significant financial need.

Alliant International University: Irvine

Forensic Psychology Program
Center for Forensic Studies
2500 Michelson Drive, Building 400
Irvine, CA 92612-1548
Telephone: (949) 833-2651
Fax: (949) 833-3507
E-mail: *bpiquet@alliant.edu*
Web: *http://www.alliant.edu*

Department Information:
2007. Program Director: William Holcomb, PhD. Number of faculty: total—full-time 1, part-time 4; women—part-time 1.

Programs and Degrees Offered:
Listed in the following order: Program area, degree type (T if terminal Master's), number awarded 7/06–6/07. Forensic Psychology PsyD (Doctor of Psychology) 0.

Student Applications/Admissions:
Student Applications
Forensic Psychology PsyD (Doctor of Psychology)—Applications 2007–2008, 26. Total applicants accepted 2007–2008, 18. Number full-time enrolled (new admits only) 2007–2008, 15. Number part-time enrolled (new admits only) 2007–2008, 0. Openings 2008–2009, 15. The number of students enrolled full- and part-time who were dismissed or voluntarily withdrew from this program area in 2007–2008 were 0.

Admissions Requirements:
Scores: Entries appear in this order: required test or GPA, minimum score (if required), median score of students entering in 2007–2008. Doctoral Programs: overall undergraduate GPA 3.0; psychology GPA 3.0. A master's degree is not required for entry, but if held at the time of entry, the 3.0 minimum GPA applies.
Other Criteria: (importance of criteria rated low, medium, or high): research experience—medium, work experience—high, extracurricular activity—low, clinically related public service—high, GPA—high, letters of recommendation—high, interview—high, statement of goals and objectives—high. For additional information on admission requirements, go to http://www.alliant.edu/wps/wcm/connect/website/Home/Admissions/.

Student Characteristics: The following represents characteristics of students in 2007–2008 in all graduate psychology programs in the department: Female—full-time 13, part-time 0; Male—full-time 2, part-time 0; African American/Black—full-time 1, part-time 0; Hispanic/Latino(a)—full-time 3, part-time 0; Asian/Pacific Islander—full-time 1, part-time 0; American Indian/Alaska Native—full-time 0, part-time 0; Caucasian/White—full-time 7, part-time 0; Multi-ethnic—full-time 0, part-time 0; students subject to the Americans With Disabilities Act—full-time 0, part-time 0; Unknown ethnicity—full-time 3, part-time 0; International students who hold an F-1 or J-1 Visa—full-time 0, part-time 0.

Financial Information/Assistance:
Tuition for Full-Time Study: *Doctoral:* State residents: $915 per credit hour; Nonstate residents: $915 per credit hour. Tuition is subject to change. See the following Web site for updates and changes in tuition costs: http://www.alliant.edu/wps/wcm/connect/website/Home/Admissions/Tuition+and+Fees/.

Financial Assistance:
First-Year Students: Research assistantships available for first year. Average amount paid per academic year: $1,000. Average number of hours worked per week: 10. Apply by see department. Fellowships and scholarships available for first year. Average amount paid per academic year: $1,500. Apply by February 15.
Advanced Students: Teaching assistantships available for advanced students. Average amount paid per academic year: $3,000. Apply by see department. Research assistantships available for advanced students. Average amount paid per academic year: $1,000. Apply by see department. Fellowships and scholarships available for advanced students. Average amount paid per academic year: $1,500. Apply by February 15.
Additional Information: Application and information available online at https://www.e-fao.com/efao_site.html?OEID=011117&ViewID={10EF815B-422E-4C55-B8CD-BDBD3063BA18}.

Internships/Practica: Doctoral Degree (PsyD Forensic Psychology): For those doctoral students for whom a professional internship was required in this program prior to graduation, (0) students applied for an internship in 2006–2007, with (0) students obtaining an internship. Of those students who obtained an internship, (0) were paid internships. Of those students who obtained an internship, (0) students placed in APA/CPA-accredited internships, (0) students placed in internships not APA/CPA accredited, but listed with the Association of Psychology Postdoctoral and Internship Centers (APPIC), (0) students placed in internships conforming to guidelines of the Council of Directors of School Psychology Programs (CDSPP), (0) students placed in internships that were not APA/CPA-accredited, APPIC or CDSPP listed. A 1-year predoctoral internship is part of the program; this occurs in the 4th or 5th year of the program, depending on the student's pace through the program.

Housing and Day Care: No on-campus housing is available. No on-campus day care facilities are available.

Employment of Department Graduates:

Master's Degree Graduates: Of those who graduated in the academic year 2006–2007, the following categories and numbers represent the postgraduate activities and employment of master's degree graduates: Enrolled in a postdoctoral residency/fellowship (n/a), employed in independent practice (n/a), total from the above (master's) (0).

Doctoral Degree Graduates: Of those who graduated in the academic year 2006–2007, the following categories and numbers represent the postgraduate activities and employment of doctoral degree graduates: Enrolled in a psychology doctoral program (n/a), total from the above (doctoral) (0).

Additional Information:

Orientation, Objectives, and Emphasis of Department: The PsyD program has an applied psychology orientation and is offered in a part-time 5-year curriculum. This format attracts students with prior work experience from a variety of fields. The curriculum prepares students to conduct assessments for the courts, to serve as expert witnesses, or to work as mental health treatment providers in a variety of forensic settings, including prisons, jails, offender treatment groups, and youth facilities among many others. Core areas include forensic psychology, theories of crime and justice, industrial and organizational psychology, legal research, psychopathology, research design and data analysis, forensic mediation and dispute resolution, ethics, and substance abuse theory and treatment. Although licensure is not required for most forensic careers, some students who enter the program may choose to seek clinical licensure after graduating from the program. These students take additional courses in psychology that are required in order to be eligible to sit for the psychology licensing exam.

Information for Students With Physical Disabilities: Go to About Alliant > Student Life and Athletics > Disability Services at the following Web site: http://www.alliant.edu.

Application Information:

Send to Alliant International University, Admissions Processing Center, 10455 Pomerado Road, San Diego, CA 92131-1799. URL of online application: https://www.alliant.edu/applyonline/. Students are admitted in the Fall, application deadline January 2. Programs have rolling admissions. Applicants wishing for notification by April 1 should submit their applications in January. Applications are welcomed on a rolling basis and will be processed on a space-available basis. *Fee:* $70.

Alliant International University: Irvine

Marital and Family Therapy Program
California School of Professional Psychology
2500 Michelson Drive, Building 400
Irvine, CA 92612-1548
Telephone: (949) 833-2651
Fax: (949) 833-3507
E-mail: *rpettay@alliant.edu*
Web: *http://www.alliant.edu/cspp/*

Department Information:

1973. Program Director: Scott Woolley, PhD. Number of faculty: total—full-time 6, part-time 4; women—full-time 1, part-time 2; total—minority—full-time 1.

Programs and Degrees Offered:

Listed in the following order: Program area, degree type (T if terminal Master's), number awarded 7/06–6/07. Marital and Family Therapy MA/MS (Master of Arts/Science) (T) 5, Marital and Family Therapy PsyD (Doctor of Psychology) 3.

Student Applications/Admissions:

Student Applications

Marital and Family Therapy MA/MS (Master of Arts/Science)—Applications 2007–2008, 78. Total applicants accepted 2007–2008, 36. Number full-time enrolled (new admits only) 2007–2008, 20. Number part-time enrolled (new admits only) 2007–2008, 2. Total enrolled 2007–2008 full-time, 27, part-time, 6. Openings 2008–2009, 20. The median number of years required for completion of a degree in 2006–2007 were 2. The number of students enrolled full- and part-time who were dismissed or voluntarily withdrew from this program area in 2007–2008 were 0. *Marital and Family Therapy PsyD (Doctor of Psychology)*—Applications 2007–2008, 40. Total applicants accepted 2007–2008, 24. Number full-time enrolled (new admits only) 2007–2008, 12. Number part-time enrolled (new admits only) 2007–2008, 4. Total enrolled 2007–2008 full-time, 50, part-time, 55. Openings 2008–2009, 20. The median number of years required for completion of a degree in 2006–2007 were 4. The number of students enrolled full- and part-time who were dismissed or voluntarily withdrew from this program area in 2007–2008 were 0.

Admissions Requirements:

Scores: Entries appear in this order: required test or GPA, minimum score (if required), median score of students entering in 2007–2008. Master's Programs: overall undergraduate GPA 3.00, 3.09; psychology GPA 3.00. Doctoral Programs: overall undergraduate GPA 3.00, 3.20; psychology GPA 3.00. Although a master's degree is not required for entry into the PsyD program, if master's level work has been taken, a 3.0 GPA is required.

Other Criteria: (importance of criteria rated low, medium, or high): GRE/MAT scores—low, research experience—medium, work experience—medium, clinically related public service—medium, GPA—high, letters of recommendation—medium, interview—high, statement of goals and objectives—high. For additional information on admission requirements, go to http://www.alliant.edu/wps/wcm/connect/website/Home/Admissions/Graduate+Student+Admissions/.

Student Characteristics: The following represents characteristics of students in 2007–2008 in all graduate psychology programs in the department: Female—full-time 69, part-time 48; Male—full-time 8, part-time 13; African American/Black—full-time 3, part-time 3; Hispanic/Latino(a)—full-time 5, part-time 6; Asian/Pacific Islander—full-time 11, part-time 9; American Indian/Alaska Native—full-time 2, part-time 2; Caucasian/White—full-time 43, part-time 27; Multi-ethnic—full-time 3, part-time 0; students subject to the Americans With Disabilities Act—full-time 0, part-time 0; Unknown ethnicity—full-time 10, part-time 14; International students who hold an F-1 or J-1 Visa—full-time 1, part-time 0.

Financial Information/Assistance:

Tuition for Full-Time Study: *Master's:* State residents: $915 per credit hour; Nonstate residents: $915 per credit hour. *Doctoral:*

State residents: $915 per credit hour; Nonstate residents: $915 per credit hour. Tuition is subject to change. Tuition costs vary by program. See the following Web site for updates and changes in tuition costs: http://www.alliant.edu/wps/wcm/connect/website/Home/Admissions/Tuition+and+Fees/.

Financial Assistance:

First-Year Students: Research assistantships available for first year. Average amount paid per academic year: $1,000. Average number of hours worked per week: 10. Apply by see department. Fellowships and scholarships available for first year. Average amount paid per academic year: $750. Apply by varies.

Advanced Students: Teaching assistantships available for advanced students. Average amount paid per academic year: $3,000. Average number of hours worked per week: 10. Apply by see department. Research assistantships available for advanced students. Average amount paid per academic year: $1,000. Average number of hours worked per week: 10. Apply by see department. Fellowships and scholarships available for advanced students. Average amount paid per academic year: $750. Apply by varies.

Additional Information: Of all students currently enrolled full time, 58% benefited from one or more of the listed financial assistance programs. Application and information available online at https://www.e-fao.com/eFAO_site.html?OEID=011117&ViewID={10EF815B-422E-4C55-B8CD-BDBD3063BA18}.

Internships/Practica: As part of the practicum experience, students complete 500 client contact hours, 250 of which must be with couples and families. Students receive at least 100 hours of individual and group supervision, 50 hours of which are based on direct observation, videotape, or audiotape. At least 25 of those hours must be videotape or direct observation. When students are ready to begin practicum, experienced faculty and staff assist students through each step in obtaining a field placement site approved by Alliant. While students are doing practicum training they are required to perform marriage and family therapy under a California state licensed, AAMFT-approved supervisor or the equivalent.

Housing and Day Care: No on-campus housing is available. No on-campus day care facilities are available.

Employment of Department Graduates:

Master's Degree Graduates: Of those who graduated in the academic year 2006–2007, the following categories and numbers represent the postgraduate activities and employment of master's degree graduates: Enrolled in a postdoctoral residency/fellowship (n/a), employed in independent practice (n/a), total from the above (master's) (0).

Doctoral Degree Graduates: Of those who graduated in the academic year 2006–2007, the following categories and numbers represent the postgraduate activities and employment of doctoral degree graduates: Enrolled in a psychology doctoral program (n/a), total from the above (doctoral) (0).

Additional Information:

Orientation, Objectives, and Emphasis of Department: The mission of the Marital and Family Therapy Program is to prepare graduate students who are skilled in the theory, research, and clinical practice of the field of Marriage and Family Therapy and can integrate individual and systemic therapeutic models in an international, multicultural environment. The marital and family therapy (MFT) programs provide students with the essential training needed to pursue a career as a professional marriage and family therapist. The Master of Arts in MFT allows students to be licensed as a marital and family therapist and the Doctor of Psychology in MFT allows a student to be licensed as a marital and family therapist and as a psychologist. Students who complete the MFT masters at Alliant can apply all of their masters degree coursework and practicum hours toward the doctoral program. The programs are accredited by COAMFTE.

Information for Students With Physical Disabilities: Go to About Alliant > Student Life and Athletics > Disability Services at the following Web site: http://www.alliant.edu.

Application Information:

Send to Alliant International University Admissions Processing Center, 10455 Pomerado Road, San Diego, CA 92131-1799. Application available online. URL of online application: http://www.alliant.edu/applyonline/. Students are admitted in the Fall, application deadline January 15; Spring, application deadline varies; Summer, application deadline varies. Programs have rolling admissions. Applications for the Fall semester are due January 15 (priority deadline), March 1, and April 16. Applications received after the priority deadline are considered on a space-available basis. For complete information on deadlines, contact the admissions office at 1-866-U-ALLIANT. *Fee:* $70. A limited number of fee waivers are available for those with significant financial need.

Alliant International University: Irvine

Programs in Educational and School Psychology
Graduate School of Education
2500 Michelson Drive, Building 400
Irvine, CA 92612-1548
Telephone: (949) 833-2651
Fax: (949) 833-3507
E-mail: *bpiquet@alliant.edu*
Web: *http://www.alliant.edu/gsoe/*

Department Information:

2002. Systemwide Program Director: Donald Wofford, PsyD. Number of faculty: total—full-time 1, part-time 4; women—part-time 3; minority—part-time 1; women minority—part-time 1.

Programs and Degrees Offered:

Listed in the following order: Program area, degree type (T if terminal Master's), number awarded 7/06–6/07. Educational Psychology PsyD (Doctor of Psychology) 9, School Psychology MA/MS (Master of Arts/Science) (T) 14.

Student Applications/Admissions:

Student Applications

Educational Psychology PsyD (Doctor of Psychology)—Applications 2007–2008, 7. Total applicants accepted 2007–2008, 6. Number full-time enrolled (new admits only) 2007–2008, 4. Number part-time enrolled (new admits only) 2007–2008, 2. Total enrolled 2007–2008 full-time, 5, part-time, 10. Openings 2008–2009, 15. The median number of years required for completion of a degree in 2006–2007 were 3. The number of students enrolled full- and part-time who were dismissed or voluntarily withdrew from this program area in 2007–2008 were 1. *School Psychology MA/MS (Master of Arts/Science)*—Applications 2007–2008, 21. Total applicants accepted 2007–2008, 12. Number full-time enrolled (new admits only) 2007–2008, 11. Number part-time enrolled (new admits only) 2007–2008, 0. Total enrolled 2007–2008 full-time, 18, part-time, 8. Openings 2008–2009, 18. The median number of years required for completion of a degree in 2006–2007 were 2. The number of students enrolled full- and part-time who were dismissed or voluntarily withdrew from this program area in 2007–2008 were 0.

Admissions Requirements:

Scores: Entries appear in this order: required test or GPA, minimum score (if required), median score of students entering in 2007–2008. Master's Programs: overall undergraduate GPA 2.5, 2.84; psychology GPA 2.5. Doctoral Programs: overall undergraduate GPA 3.0, 3.6; psychology GPA 3.0. A master's degree is not required for the 5-year PsyD program, but if the degree is held at the time of application, the 3.0 minimum GPA applies.

Other Criteria: (importance of criteria rated low, medium, or high): research experience—medium, work experience—medium, extracurricular activity—low, clinically related public service—high, GPA—high, letters of recommendation—high, interview—high, statement of goals and objectives—high. Criteria differ by program and level. For additional information on admission requirements, go to http://www.alliant.edu/wps/wcm/connect/website/Home/Admissions/.

Student Characteristics: The following represents characteristics of students in 2007–2008 in all graduate psychology programs in the department: Female—full-time 21, part-time 17; Male—full-time 2, part-time 1; African American/Black—full-time 2, part-time 0; Hispanic/Latino(a)—full-time 4, part-time 3; Asian/Pacific Islander—full-time 1, part-time 2; Caucasian/White—full-time 14, part-time 9; Multi-ethnic—full-time 0, part-time 1; students subject to the Americans With Disabilities Act—full-time 1, part-time 0; Unknown ethnicity—full-time 2, part-time 3; International students who hold an F-1 or J-1 Visa—full-time 0, part-time 0.

Financial Information/Assistance:

Tuition for Full-Time Study: *Master's:* State residents: $525 per credit hour; Nonstate residents: $525 per credit hour. *Doctoral:* State residents: $855 per credit hour; Nonstate residents: $855 per credit hour. Tuition is subject to change. Tuition costs vary by program. See the following Web site for updates and changes in tuition costs: http://www.alliant.edu/wps/wcm/connect/website/Home/Admissions/Tuition+and+Fees/.

Financial Assistance:

First-Year Students: Research assistantships available for first year. Average amount paid per academic year: $1,000. Average number of hours worked per week: 10. Apply by see department. Fellowships and scholarships available for first year. Average amount paid per academic year: $750. Apply by June 1.

Advanced Students: Teaching assistantships available for advanced students. Average amount paid per academic year: $3,000. Average number of hours worked per week: 10. Apply by see department. Research assistantships available for advanced students. Average amount paid per academic year: $1,000. Average number of hours worked per week: 10. Apply by see department. Fellowships and scholarships available for advanced students. Average amount paid per academic year: $750. Apply by April 1.

Additional Information: Of all students currently enrolled full time, 40% benefited from one or more of the listed financial assistance programs. Application and information available online at https://www.e-fao.com/efao_site.html?OEID=011117&ViewID={10EF815B-422E-4C55-B8CD-BDBD3063BA18}.

Internships/Practica: Students in the master's program have practica tied to their coursework beginning in the first semester of their programs. Internships are required of students seeking a Pupil Personnel Services (PPS) credential postmasters or as part of the doctoral program in educational psychology. The 1,200 required internship hours are completed at a public school district. Students interested in seeking clinical licensure must complete a separate psychology internship.

Housing and Day Care: No on-campus housing is available. No on-campus day care facilities are available.

Employment of Department Graduates:

Master's Degree Graduates: Of those who graduated in the academic year 2006–2007, the following categories and numbers represent the postgraduate activities and employment of master's degree graduates: Enrolled in a postdoctoral residency/fellowship (n/a), employed in independent practice (n/a), total from the above (master's) (0).

Doctoral Degree Graduates: Of those who graduated in the academic year 2006–2007, the following categories and numbers represent the postgraduate activities and employment of doctoral degree graduates: Enrolled in a psychology doctoral program (n/a), total from the above (doctoral) (0).

Additional Information:

Orientation, Objectives, and Emphasis of Department: Programs train students with the skills necessary to work with students, teachers, parents, and other school professionals in today's school environments. Curriculum includes professional skills, professional roles courses, applied research, and professional concepts. The master's degree program prepares students to gain the PPS (Pupil Personnel Services) credential that allows them to practice in California's schools. Students take afternoon, evening, and weekend classes and engage in fieldwork. At the doctoral level, students complete special focus area courses, examples of which include adolescent stress and coping, school culture and administration, pediatric psychology, infant and preschool mental health, child neuropsychology, and provision of services for children in alternative placement. Students also complete a PsyD project.

Information for Students With Physical Disabilities: Go to About Alliant > Student Life and Athletics > Disability Services at the following Web site: http://www.alliant.edu.

Application Information:

Send to Alliant International University, Admissions Processing Center, 10455 Pomerado Road, San Diego, CA 92131-1799. Application available online. URL of online application: http://www.alliant.edu/applyonline/. Students are admitted in the Fall, application deadline

June 1; Spring, application deadline varies; Summer, application deadline varies. *Fee:* $55. A limited number of fee waivers are available to those with significant financial need.

Alliant International University: Los Angeles

Forensic Psychology Programs
Center for Forensic Studies
1000 South Fremont Avenue
Alhambra, CA 91803-1360
Telephone: (626) 284-2777
Fax: (626) 284-0550
E-mail: *skim@alliant.edu*
Web: *http://www.alliant.edu/*

Department Information:

1999. Program Director: William Holcomb, PhD. Number of faculty: total—full-time 3, part-time 7; women—full-time 1, part-time 1; minority—part-time 1; women minority—part-time 1.

Programs and Degrees Offered:

Listed in the following order: Program area, degree type (T if terminal Master's), number awarded 7/06–6/07. Forensic Psychology PsyD (Doctor of Psychology) 4.

Student Applications/Admissions:

Student Applications

Forensic Psychology PsyD (Doctor of Psychology)—Applications 2007–2008, 47. Total applicants accepted 2007–2008, 36. Number full-time enrolled (new admits only) 2007–2008, 28. Number part-time enrolled (new admits only) 2007–2008, 2. Total enrolled 2007–2008 full-time, 62, part-time, 8. Openings 2008–2009, 25. The median number of years required for completion of a degree in 2006–2007 were 5. The number of students enrolled full- and part-time who were dismissed or voluntarily withdrew from this program area in 2007–2008 were 3.

Admissions Requirements:

Scores: Entries appear in this order: required test or GPA, minimum score (if required), median score of students entering in 2007–2008. Master's Programs: overall undergraduate GPA no minimum stated; psychology GPA no minimum stated. Doctoral Programs: overall undergraduate GPA 3.0, 3.25; psychology GPA 3.0. master's degree is not required for entry, but if held at time entry, 3.0 minimum GPA applies.

Other Criteria: (importance of criteria rated low, medium, or high): research experience—medium, work experience—high, extracurricular activity—low, clinically related public service—high, GPA—high, letters of recommendation—high, interview—high, statement of goals and objectives—high. For additional information on admission requirements, go to http://www.alliant.edu/wps/wcm/connect/website/Home/Admissions/.

Student Characteristics: The following represents characteristics of students in 2007–2008 in all graduate psychology programs in the department: Female—full-time 49, part-time 6; Male—full-time 13, part-time 2; African American/Black—full-time 4, part-time 1; Hispanic/Latino(a)—full-time 12, part-time 1; Asian/Pacific Islander—full-time 3, part-time 0; American Indian/Alaska Native—full-time 0, part-time 0; Caucasian/White—full-time 32, part-time 3; Multi-ethnic—full-time 3, part-time 2; students subject to the Americans With Disabilities Act—full-time 0, part-time 1; Unknown ethnicity—full-time 8, part-time 1; International students who hold an F-1 or J-1 Visa—full-time 0, part-time 0.

Financial Information/Assistance:

Tuition for Full-Time Study: *Doctoral:* State residents: $915 per credit hour; Nonstate residents: $915 per credit hour. Tuition is subject to change. See the following Web site for updates and changes in tuition costs: http://www.alliant.edu/wps/wcm/connect/website/Home/Admissions/Tuition+and+Fees/.

Financial Assistance:

First-Year Students: Research assistantships available for first year. Average amount paid per academic year: $1,000. Average number of hours worked per week: 10. Apply by see department. Fellowships and scholarships available for first year. Average amount paid per academic year: $1,500. Apply by February 15.

Advanced Students: Teaching assistantships available for advanced students. Average amount paid per academic year: $3,000. Average number of hours worked per week: 20. Apply by see department. Research assistantships available for advanced students. Average amount paid per academic year: $1,000. Average number of hours worked per week: 10. Apply by see department. Fellowships and scholarships available for advanced students. Average amount paid per academic year: $1,500. Apply by February 15.

Additional Information: Of all students currently enrolled full time, 52% benefited from one or more of the listed financial assistance programs. Application and information available online at https://www.e-fao.com/efao_site.html?OEID=011117&ViewID={10EF815B-422E-4C55-B8CD-BDBD3063BA18}.

Internships/Practica: Doctoral Degree (PsyD Forensic Psychology): For those doctoral students for whom a professional internship was required in this program prior to graduation, (0) students applied for an internship in 2006–2007, with (0) students obtaining an internship. Of those students who obtained an internship, (0) were paid internships. Of those students who obtained an internship, (0)students placed in APA/CPA-accredited internships, (0) students placed in internships not APA/CPA accredited, but listed with the Association of Psychology Postdoctoral and Internship Centers (APPIC), (0) students placed in internships conforming to guidelines of the Council of Directors of School Psychology Programs (CDSPP), (0) students placed in internships that were not APA/CPA-accredited, APPIC or CDSPP listed. A 1-year predoctoral internship is part of the program; this occurs in the 5th year of the program.

Housing and Day Care: No on-campus housing is available. No on-campus day care facilities are available.

Employment of Department Graduates:

Master's Degree Graduates: Of those who graduated in the academic year 2006–2007, the following categories and numbers represent the postgraduate activities and employment of master's degree graduates: Enrolled in a postdoctoral residency/fellowship (n/a), employed in independent practice (n/a), total from the above (master's) (0).

Doctoral Degree Graduates: Of those who graduated in the academic year 2006–2007, the following categories and numbers represent the postgraduate activities and employment of doctoral degree graduates: Enrolled in a psychology doctoral program (n/a), total from the above (doctoral) (0).

Additional Information:

Orientation, Objectives, and Emphasis of Department: The PsyD program has an applied psychology orientation and is offered in a part-time 5-year curriculum. This format attracts students with prior work experience from a variety of fields. The curriculum prepares students to conduct assessments for the courts, to serve as expert witnesses, or to work as mental health treatment providers in a variety of forensic settings, including prisons, jails, offender treatment groups, and youth facilities among many others. Core areas include forensic psychology, theories of crime and justice, industrial and organizational psychology, legal research, psychopathology, research design and data analysis, forensic mediation and dispute resolution, ethics, and substance abuse theory and treatment. Although licensure is not required for most forensic careers, some students who enter the program may choose to seek clinical licensure after graduating from the program. These students take additional courses in psychology that are required in order to be eligible to sit for the psychology licensing exam.

Information for Students With Physical Disabilities: Go to About Alliant > Student Life and Athletics > Disability Services at the following Web site: http://www.alliant.edu.

Application Information:

Send to Alliant International University, Admissions Processing Center, 10455 Pomerado Road, San Diego, CA 92131-1799. Application available online. URL of online application: https://www.ais1.alliant.edu/apply/. Students are admitted in the Fall, application deadline January 2. Programs have rolling admissions. Applicants wishing notification by April 1 should submit their applications in January. Applications are welcomed on a rolling basis and will be processed on a space-available basis. *Fee:* $70. A limited number of fee waivers are available for those with significant financial need. Please contact the Director of Admissions for details.

Alliant International University: Los Angeles

Programs in Clinical Psychology and Marital and Family Therapy

California School of Professional Psychology
1000 South Fremont Avenue, Unit 5
Alhambra, CA 91803-1360
Telephone: (626) 284-2777 x3126
Fax: (626) 284-0550
E-mail: *sbyers-bell@alliant.edu*
Web: *http://www.alliant.edu/cspp/*

Department Information:

1970. Dean, California School of Professional Psychology: Morgan Sammons, PhD, ABPP. Number of faculty: total—full-time 30, part-time 14; women—full-time 15, part-time 9; total—minority—full-time 9, part-time 3; women minority—full-time 6, part-time 2; faculty subject to the Americans With Disabilities Act 1.

Programs and Degrees Offered:

Listed in the following order: Program area, degree type (T if terminal Master's), number awarded 7/06–6/07. Clinical Psychology PsyD (Doctor of Psychology) 53, Clinical Psychology PhD (Doctor of Philosophy) 17, Marital and Family Therapy MA/MS (Master of Arts/Science) (T).

APA Accreditation: Clinical PsyD (Doctor of Psychology). Clinical PhD (Doctor of Philosophy).

Student Applications/Admissions:

Student Applications

Clinical Psychology PsyD (Doctor of Psychology)—Applications 2007–2008, 197. Total applicants accepted 2007–2008, 85. Number full-time enrolled (new admits only) 2007–2008, 63. Number part-time enrolled (new admits only) 2007–2008, 0. Total enrolled 2007–2008 full-time, 286, part-time, 3. Openings 2008–2009, 67. The median number of years required for completion of a degree in 2006–2007 were 4. The number of students enrolled full- and part-time who were dismissed or voluntarily withdrew from this program area in 2007–2008 were 0. *Clinical Psychology PhD (Doctor of Philosophy)*—Applications 2007–2008, 77. Total applicants accepted 2007–2008, 37. Number full-time enrolled (new admits only) 2007–2008, 22. Number part-time enrolled (new admits only) 2007–2008, 0. Total enrolled 2007–2008 full-time, 155, part-time, 1. Openings 2008–2009, 25. The median number of years required for completion of a degree in 2006–2007 were 6. The number of students enrolled full- and part-time who were dismissed or voluntarily withdrew from this program area in 2007–2008 were 0. *Marital and Family Therapy MA/MS (Master of Arts/Science)*.

Admissions Requirements:

Scores: Entries appear in this order: required test or GPA, minimum score (if required), median score of students entering in 2007–2008. Master's Programs: overall undergraduate GPA 3.0; psychology GPA 3.0, Doctoral Programs: overall undergraduate GPA 3.0, 3.36; psychology GPA 3.0. The master's degree is not required for admission to doctoral programs; however, if the master's degree is held at the time of application, the 3.0 minimum GPA applies.

Other Criteria: (importance of criteria rated low, medium, or high): GRE/MAT scores—low, research experience—medium, work experience—medium, clinically related public service—medium, GPA—high, letters of recommendation—medium, interview—high, statement of goals and objectives—high. Admissions criteria and their importance vary by program and degree level. PhD programs place more emphasis on prior research experience; PsyD programs place more emphasis on clinical/work experience. For additional information on admission requirements, go to http://www.alliant.edu/wps/wcm/connect/website/Home/Admissions/Graduate+Student+Admissions/.

Student Characteristics: The following represents characteristics of students in 2007–2008 in all graduate psychology programs in the department: Female—full-time 357, part-time 3; Male—full-time 84, part-time 1; African American/Black—full-time 30, part-time 0; Hispanic/Latino(a)—full-time 72, part-time 0; Asian/Pacific Islander—full-time 60, part-time 0; American Indian/Alaska Native—full-time 1, part-time 0; Caucasian/White—

full-time 202, part-time 4; Multi-ethnic—full-time 11, part-time 0; students subject to the Americans With Disabilities Act—full-time 6, part-time 0; Unknown ethnicity—full-time 65, part-time 0; International students who hold an F-1 or J-1 Visa—full-time 11, part-time 0.

Financial Information/Assistance:

Tuition for Full-Time Study: *Master's:* State residents: $915 per credit hour; Nonstate residents: $915 per credit hour. *Doctoral:* State residents: $915 per credit hour; Nonstate residents: $915 per credit hour. Tuition is subject to change. See the following Web site for updates and changes in tuition costs: http://www.alliant.edu/wps/wcm/connect/website/Home/Admissions/Tuition+and+Fees/.

Financial Assistance:

First-Year Students: Research assistantships available for first year. Average amount paid per academic year: $1,000. Average number of hours worked per week: 10. Apply by see department. Fellowships and scholarships available for first year. Average amount paid per academic year: $1,500. Apply by April 15.

Advanced Students: Teaching assistantships available for advanced students. Average amount paid per academic year: $3,000. Average number of hours worked per week: 10. Apply by see department. Research assistantships available for advanced students. Average amount paid per academic year: $1,000. Average number of hours worked per week: 10. Apply by see department. Traineeships available for advanced students. Average number of hours worked per week: 25. Apply by variable. Fellowships and scholarships available for advanced students. Average amount paid per academic year: $1,500. Apply by April 15.

Additional Information: Of all students currently enrolled full time, 57% benefited from one or more of the listed financial assistance programs. Application and information available online at https://www.e-fao.com/eFAO_site.html?OEID=011117&ViewID={10EF815B-422E-4C55-B8CD-BDBD3063BA18}.

Internships/Practica: Doctoral Degree (PsyD Clinical Psychology): For those doctoral students for whom a professional internship was required in this program prior to graduation, (157) students applied for an internship in 2006–2007, with (157) students obtaining an internship. Of those students who obtained an internship, (36) were paid internships. Of those students who obtained an internship, (0) students placed in APA/CPA-accredited internships, (4) students placed in internships not APA/CPA-accredited, but listed with the Association of Psychology Postdoctoral and Internship Centers (APPIC), (0) students placed in internships conforming to guidelines of the Council of Directors of School Psychology Programs (CDSPP), (153) students placed in internships that were not APA/CPA-accredited, APPIC or CDSPP listed. Doctoral Degree (PhD Clinical Psychology): For those doctoral students for whom a professional internship was required in this program prior to graduation, (68) students applied for an internship in 2006–2007, with (68) students obtaining an internship. Of those students who obtained an internship, (31) were paid internships. Of those students who obtained an internship, (7) students placed in APA/CPA-accredited internships, (3) students placed in internships not APA/CPA-accredited, but listed with the Association of Psychology Postdoctoral and Internship Centers (APPIC), (0) students placed in internships conforming to guidelines of the Council of Directors of School Psychology Programs (CDSPP), (58) students placed in internships that were not APA/CPA-accredited, APPIC or CDSPP listed. All students engage in practica and internships. Clinical psychology students complete 2,000 predoctoral internship hours as part of their programs. The majority of the professional training sites are within 40 miles of the campus. These agencies serve a diverse range of individuals across ethnicity, culture, religion, and sexual orientation. These sites provide excellent training, offering a variety of theoretical orientations related to children, adolescents, adults, families and the elderly. Students who wish to pursue full-time internships are encouraged to make applications throughout the country. Marital and Family Therapy students complete 500 client contact hours, 250 of which must be with couples and families. Students receive at least 100 hours of individual and group supervision, 50 hours of which are based on direct observation, videotape, or audiotape. At least 25 of those hours must be videotape or direct observation. When students are ready to begin practicum, experienced faculty and staff assist students through each step in obtaining a field placement site approved by Alliant. While students are doing practicum training they are required to perform marriage and family therapy under a California state licensed, AAMFT-approved supervisor or the equivalent.

Housing and Day Care: No on-campus housing is available. No on-campus day care facilities are available.

Employment of Department Graduates:

Master's Degree Graduates: Of those who graduated in the academic year 2006–2007, the following categories and numbers represent the postgraduate activities and employment of master's degree graduates: Enrolled in a postdoctoral residency/fellowship (n/a), employed in independent practice (n/a), total from the above (master's) (0).

Doctoral Degree Graduates: Of those who graduated in the academic year 2006–2007, the following categories and numbers represent the postgraduate activities and employment of doctoral degree graduates: Enrolled in a psychology doctoral program (n/a), total from the above (doctoral) (0).

Additional Information:

Orientation, Objectives, and Emphasis of Department: The clinical psychology PsyD and PhD programs at the California School of Professional Psychology prepare students to function as multifaceted clinical psychologists through a curriculum based on an integration of psychological theory, research, and practice. Students develop competencies in seven areas: clinical health psychology; interpersonal/relationship; assessment; multifaceted multimodal intervention; research and evaluation; consultation/teaching; management/supervision/training; and quality assurance. The PsyD program is a practitioner program where candidates gain relatively greater mastery in assessment, intervention, and management/supervision. The PhD program is a based on a scholar–practitioner model where practice and scholarship receive equal emphasis and includes the following guiding principles: the generation and application of knowledge must occur with an awareness of the sociocultural and sociopolitical contexts of mental health and mental illness; scholarship and practice must not only build upon existing literature but also maintain relevance to the diverse elements in our society and assume the challenges of attending to the complex social issues associated with psychological functioning; and methods of research and intervention must be appropriate to the culture in which they are conducted. Practica and internship experiences are integrated throughout the programs. Students have the opportunity to choose a curricular emphasis in clinical health psychology, multicultural community clinical, or family and couple clinical psychology. The mission of the Marital and Family Therapy Program is to prepare graduate students who are skilled in the theory, research, and clinical practice of the field of Marriage and Family Therapy and can integrate individual and systemic therapeutic models in an international, multicultural environment. The marital and family therapy (MFT) programs provide students with the essential training needed to pursue a career as a professional marriage and family therapist. The Master of Arts in MFT allows students to be licensed as a marital and family therapist and the Doctor of Psychology in MFT allows a student to be licensed as a marital and family therapist and as a psychologist. Students who complete the MFT masters at Alliant can apply all of their master's degree coursework and practicum hours toward the doctoral program. The programs are accredited by COAMFTE.

Special Facilities or Resources: The Psychological Services Center (PSC) is charged with the mission of developing professional training, research, and consultation opportunities for CSPP faculty and students while providing services to a variety of public/private agencies. It is committed to developing effective and innovative service strategies and resources that address the needs of a wide range of clients with a particular focus on ethnically diverse, underserved populations. As a center "without walls," the PSC is the administrative umbrella for two major community-based programs: the Children, Youth, and Family Consortium and the School Court Accountability Project. These projects are designed to provide hands-on research, consulting, and clinical experience for students and to enhance the critically needed services to school-aged youth within the court system and school-aged populations. These programs enable participating CSPP faculty, staff, students, alumni/ae, and external consultant associates to provide services few other institutions can offer. Students also receive unique training and supervision that prepares them for critically needed roles as community advocates and leaders.

Information for Students With Physical Disabilities: Go to About Alliant > Student Life and Athletics > Disability Services at the following Web site: http://www.alliant.edu.

Application Information:

Send to Alliant International University, Admissions Processing Center, 10455 Pomerado Road, San Diego, CA 92131-1799. Application available online. URL of online application: http://www.alliant.edu/applyonline/. Students are admitted in the Fall, application deadline January 15; Spring, application deadline November 15. Programs have rolling admissions. The programs have a January 15 priority deadline in order to provide a response by April 1 for applicants who need a decision by that date. Programs accept applications and admit students on a space-available basis after any stated deadlines. For complete information on deadlines visit http://www.alliant.edu/wps/wcm/connect/website/Home/Admissions/Graduate+Student+Admissions/Admission+Deadlines or contact the admissions office at 1-866-U-ALLIANT. *Fee:* $70. A limited number of application fee waivers are available for students with significant financial need.

Alliant International University: Los Angeles

Programs in Educational and School Psychology
Graduate School of Education
1000 South Fremont Avenue
Alhambra, CA 91803-1360
Telephone: (626) 284-2777
Fax: (626) 284-0550
E-mail: *sbyers-bell@alliant.edu*
Web: *http://www.alliant.edu/gsoe/*

Department Information:

1999. Systemwide Program Director: Donald Wofford, PsyD. Number of faculty: total—full-time 1, part-time 8; women—part-time 3; total—minority—full-time 1, part-time 2; women minority—part-time 1.

Programs and Degrees Offered:

Listed in the following order: Program area, degree type (T if terminal Master's), number awarded 7/06–6/07. School Psychology MA/MS (Master of Arts/Science) (T) 2, Educational Psychology PsyD (Doctor of Psychology) 4.

Student Applications/Admissions:

Student Applications

School Psychology MA/MS (Master of Arts/Science)—Applications 2007–2008, 20. Total applicants accepted 2007–2008, 14. Number full-time enrolled (new admits only) 2007–2008, 8. Number part-time enrolled (new admits only) 2007–2008, 0. Total enrolled 2007–2008 full-time, 16, part-time, 8. Openings 2008–2009, 18. The median number of years required for completion of a degree in 2006–2007 were 2. The number of students enrolled full- and part-time who were dismissed or voluntarily withdrew from this program area in 2007–2008 were 0. *Educational Psychology PsyD (Doctor of Psychology)*—Applications 2007–2008, 6. Total applicants accepted 2007–2008, 5. Number part-time enrolled (new admits only) 2007–2008, 5. Total enrolled 2007–2008 full-time, 1, part-time, 18. Openings 2008–2009, 10. The median number of years required for completion of a degree in 2006–2007 were 3. The number of students enrolled full- and part-time who were dismissed or voluntarily withdrew from this program area in 2007–2008 were 1.

Admissions Requirements:

Scores: Entries appear in this order: required test or GPA, minimum score (if required), median score of students entering in 2007–2008. Master's Programs: overall undergraduate GPA 2.5, 2.84; psychology GPA 2.5. Doctoral Programs: overall undergraduate GPA 3.0; psychology GPA 3.0. Master's degree is not required for entry to the 5-year PsyD program, but it the degree is held at the time of application, the 3.0 minimum GPA applies.

Other Criteria: (importance of criteria rated low, medium, or high): research experience—medium, work experience—high, extracurricular activity—low, clinically related public service—high, GPA—high, letters of recommendation—high, interview—high, statement of goals and objectives—high. Criteria differ by program and level. For additional information on admission requirements, go to http://www.alliant.edu/wps/wcm/connect/website/Home/Admissions/.

Student Characteristics: The following represents characteristics of students in 2007–2008 in all graduate psychology programs in the department: Female—full-time 15, part-time 16; Male—full-time 2, part-time 10; African American/Black—full-time 2, part-time 3; Hispanic/Latino(a)—full-time 7, part-time 9; Asian/Pacific Islander—full-time 4, part-time 2; American Indian/Alaska Native—full-time 0, part-time 0; Caucasian/White—full-time 3, part-time 7; Multi-ethnic—full-time 1, part-time 0; students subject to the Americans With Disabilities Act—full-time 1, part-time 0; Unknown ethnicity—full-time 0, part-time 5; International students who hold an F-1 or J-1 Visa—full-time 0, part-time 0.

Financial Information/Assistance:

Tuition for Full-Time Study: *Master's:* State residents: $525 per credit hour; Nonstate residents: $525 per credit hour. *Doctoral:* State residents: $855 per credit hour; Nonstate residents: $855 per credit hour. Tuition is subject to change. Tuition costs vary by program. See the following Web site for updates and changes in tuition costs: http://www.alliant.edu/wps/wcm/connect/website/Home/Admissions/Tuition+and+Fees/.

Financial Assistance:

First-Year Students: Research assistantships available for first year. Average amount paid per academic year: $1,000. Average number of hours worked per week: 10. Apply by see department. Fellowships and scholarships available for first year. Average amount paid per academic year: $1,500. Apply by June 1.

Advanced Students: Teaching assistantships available for advanced students. Average amount paid per academic year: $3,000. Average number of hours worked per week: 10. Apply by see department. Research assistantships available for advanced students. Average amount paid per academic year: $1,000. Average number of hours worked per week: 10. Apply by see department. Fellowships and scholarships available for advanced students. Average amount paid per academic year: $1,500. Apply by April 1.

Additional Information: Of all students currently enrolled full time, 40% benefited from one or more of the listed financial assistance programs. Application and information available online at https://www.e-fao.com/efao_site.html?OEID=011117&ViewID={10EF815B-422E-4C55-B8CD-BDBD3063BA18}.

Internships/Practica: Students in the master's program have practica tied to their coursework beginning in the first semester of their programs. Internships are required of any students seeking the Pupil Personnel Services (PPS) credential postmasters or as part of the doctoral program in educational psychology. The 1,200 internship hours are completed at a public school district. Those in the doctoral program who are interested in clinical licensure must complete a separate psychology internship.

Housing and Day Care: No on-campus housing is available. No on-campus day care facilities are available.

Employment of Department Graduates:

Master's Degree Graduates: Of those who graduated in the academic year 2006–2007, the following categories and numbers represent the postgraduate activities and employment of master's degree graduates: Enrolled in a postdoctoral residency/fellowship (n/a), employed in independent practice (n/a), total from the above (master's) (0).

Doctoral Degree Graduates: Of those who graduated in the academic year 2006–2007, the following categories and numbers represent the postgraduate activities and employment of doctoral degree graduates: Enrolled in a psychology doctoral program (n/a), total from the above (doctoral) (0).

Additional Information:

Orientation, Objectives, and Emphasis of Department: Programs train students with the skills necessary to work with students, teachers, parents, and other school professionals in today's school environments. The curriculum includes professional skills, professional roles courses, applied research, and professional concepts. The master's degree program prepares students to gain the PPS (Pupil Personnel Services) credential that allow them to practice in California's schools. Students take afternoon, evening, and weekend classes and engage in fieldwork. At the doctoral level students complete special focus area courses, examples of which include adolescent stress and coping, school culture and administration, pediatric psychology, infant and preschool mental health, child neuropsychology, and provision of services for children in alternative placement. Students also complete a PsyD project.

Information for Students With Physical Disabilities: Go to About Alliant > Student Life and Athletics > Disability Services at the following Web site: http://www.alliant.edu.

Application Information:

Send to Alliant International University, Admissions Processing Center, 10455 Pomerado Road, San Diego, CA 93121-1799. Application available online. URL of online application: http://www.alliant.edu/applyonline/. Students are admitted in the Fall, application deadline June 1; Spring, application deadline varies. Programs have rolling admissions. *Fee:* $70. A limited number of fee waivers are available for those with significant financial need.

Alliant International University: Los Angeles

Programs in Organizational Psychology
Marshall Goldsmith School of Management
1000 South Fremont Avenue
Alhambra, CA 91803-1360
Telephone: (626) 284-2777
Fax: (626) 284-0550
E-mail: *sbyers-bell@alliant.edu*
Web: *http://www.mgsm.alliant.edu*

Department Information:

1981. Systemwide Associate Dean and Program Director: Jay M. Finkelman, PhD. Number of faculty: total—full-time 5, part-time 2; women—full-time 2, part-time 1; total—minority—full-time 2; women minority—full-time 2.

Programs and Degrees Offered:

Listed in the following order: Program area, degree type (T if terminal Master's), number awarded 7/06–6/07. Industrial-Organizational PhD (Doctor of Philosophy) 5, Industrial-Organizational MA/MS (Master of Arts/Science) (T) 6, Industrial-Organizational Respecialization Diploma 0.

Student Applications/Admissions:

Student Applications

Industrial-Organizational PhD (Doctor of Philosophy)—Applications 2007–2008, 14. Total applicants accepted 2007–2008, 10. Number full-time enrolled (new admits only) 2007–2008, 9. Number part-time enrolled (new admits only) 2007–2008, 0. Total enrolled 2007–2008 full-time, 46, part-time, 5. Openings 2008–2009, 12. The median number of years required for completion of a degree in 2006–2007 were 6. The number of students enrolled full- and part-time who were dismissed or voluntarily withdrew from this program area in 2007–2008 were 0. *Industrial-Organizational MA/MS (Master of Arts/Science)*—Applications 2007–2008, 26. Total applicants accepted 2007–2008, 15. Number full-time enrolled (new admits only) 2007–2008, 10. Number part-time enrolled (new admits only) 2007–2008, 2. Total enrolled 2007–2008 full-time, 17, part-time, 3. Openings 2008–2009, 15. The median number of years required for completion of a degree in 2006–2007 were 2. The number of students enrolled full- and part-time who were dismissed or voluntarily withdrew from this program area in 2007–2008 were 0. *Industrial-Organizational Respecialization Diploma*—Applications 2007–2008, 0. Total applicants accepted 2007–2008, 0. Number full-time enrolled (new admits only) 2007–2008, 0. Number part-time enrolled (new admits only) 2007–2008, 0. Openings 2008–2009, 2. The number of students enrolled full- and part-time who were dismissed or voluntarily withdrew from this program area in 2007–2008 were 0.

Admissions Requirements:

Scores: Entries appear in this order: required test or GPA, minimum score (if required), median score of students entering in 2007–2008. Master's Programs: overall undergraduate GPA 3.0, 3.10; psychology GPA 3.0. Doctoral Programs: overall undergraduate GPA 3.0, 3.04; psychology GPA 3.0. The master's degree is not required for doctoral program admission; however if a master's is held at the time of application, the 3.0 minimum GPA applies.

Other Criteria: (importance of criteria rated low, medium, or high): research experience—high, work experience—high, extracurricular activity—low, clinically related public service—low, GPA—high, letters of recommendation—high, interview—high, statement of goals and objectives—high. Criteria vary by program. For additional information on admission requirements, go to http://www.alliant.edu/wps/wcm/connect/website/Home/Admissions/.

Student Characteristics: The following represents characteristics of students in 2007–2008 in all graduate psychology programs in the department: Female—full-time 48, part-time 3; Male—full-time 15, part-time 5; African American/Black—full-time 7, part-time 1; Hispanic/Latino(a)—full-time 5, part-time 1; Asian/Pacific Islander—full-time 11, part-time 0; American Indian/Alaska Native—full-time 0, part-time 0; Caucasian/White—full-time 23, part-time 4; Multi-ethnic—full-time 1, part-time 0; students subject to the Americans With Disabilities Act—full-time 2, part-time 0; Unknown ethnicity—full-time 16, part-time 2; International students who hold an F-1 or J-1 Visa—full-time 2, part-time 0.

Financial Information/Assistance:

Tuition for Full-Time Study: *Master's:* State residents: $915 per credit hour; Nonstate residents: $915 per credit hour. *Doctoral:* State residents: $915 per credit hour; Nonstate residents: $915 per credit hour. Tuition is subject to change. Tuition costs vary by program. See the following Web site for updates and changes in tuition costs: http://www.alliant.edu/wps/wcm/connect/website/Home/Admissions/Tuition+and+Fees/.

Financial Assistance:

First-Year Students: Research assistantships available for first year. Average amount paid per academic year: $1,000. Average number of hours worked per week: 10. Apply by see department. Fellowships and scholarships available for first year. Average amount paid per academic year: $1,500. Apply by varies.

Advanced Students: Teaching assistantships available for advanced students. Average amount paid per academic year: $3,000. Average number of hours worked per week: 10. Apply by see department. Research assistantships available for advanced students. Average amount paid per academic year: $1,000. Average number of hours worked per week: 10. Apply by see department. Fellowships and scholarships available for advanced students. Average amount paid per academic year: $1,500. Apply by April 15.

Additional Information: Of all students currently enrolled full time, 53% benefited from one or more of the listed financial assistance programs. Application and information available online at https://www.e-fao.com/efao_site.html?OEID=011117&ViewID={10EF815B-422E-4C55-B8CD-BDBD3063BA18}.

Internships/Practica: Doctoral students may begin their practical training though the Center for Innovation and Change, working with faculty on pro bono consulting projects. A doctoral level field placement/internship is completed typically in the 4th year. Students spend 8–40 hours per week in a corporate, business, governmental, or nonprofit setting. The majority of these are local to the student's campus; a few are outside the area, and are usually identified as part of a student's own career development interests. Students in the organizational psychology master's program have a one semester practicum in organizational studies.

Housing and Day Care: No on-campus housing is available. No on-campus day care facilities are available.

Employment of Department Graduates:

Master's Degree Graduates: Of those who graduated in the academic year 2006–2007, the following categories and numbers represent the postgraduate activities and employment of master's degree graduates: Enrolled in a postdoctoral residency/fellowship (n/a), employed in independent practice (n/a), total from the above (master's) (0).

Doctoral Degree Graduates: Of those who graduated in the academic year 2006–2007, the following categories and numbers represent the postgraduate activities and employment of doctoral degree graduates: Enrolled in a psychology doctoral program (n/a), total from the above (doctoral) (0).

Additional Information:

Orientation, Objectives, and Emphasis of Department: The doctoral program is based on the philosophy that the foundations of effective organizational change are science based, especially the science of human behavior in work settings. The program is designed to address both sides of the consultant–client relationship. The program integrates a strong foundation in the behavioral and organizational sciences; an understanding of intrapersonal and self-reflective approaches for examining human behavior; knowledge of interpersonal dynamics and political processes in professional practice, organizational interventions and consultant–clients relations; and professional experiential training. Graduates are prepared for careers in a wide variety of practice areas including management consulting, organizational assessment and design, human resources development, organizational development, diversity training, and change management. The master's degree program is for those seeking preparation to begin or continue careers in organizational leadership and management. Some master's students are seeking an academic foundation for future doctoral work. Students in the programs are hired in the field as early as the first year of the program. Doctoral students find employment in such companies as Disney, JPL, City of Hope, IBM Business Consulting Services, and Korn Ferry International.

Special Facilities or Resources: At the Center for Innovation and Change in Los Angeles, graduate students apply what they are learning in the classroom by providing consulting services to nonprofit organizations. Through the Center 1st- and 2nd-year students form consulting teams that provide pro bono service to clients in the Los Angeles area. Each consulting team works with a faculty supervisor. Thus students get practical training beginning early on in their programs.

Information for Students With Physical Disabilities: Go to About Alliant > Student Life and Athletics, > Disability Services at the following Web site: http://www.alliant.edu.

Application Information:
Send to Alliant International University, Admissions Processing Center, 10455 Pomerado Road, San Diego, CA 92131-1799. Application available online. URL of online application: http://www.alliant.edu/applyonline/. Students are admitted in the Fall, application deadline varies; Spring, application deadline varies. Programs have rolling admissions. The doctoral program has a February 1 priority deadline in order to provide a response by April 1 for applicants who need a decision by that date. Master's programs have later deadlines. Programs accept and admit applicants on a space-available basis after any stated deadlines. For updates on deadlines and programs contact the admission office at 1-866-U-ALLIANT. *Fee:* $70. A limited number of fee waivers are available to those with significant financial need.

Alliant International University: Sacramento

Forensic Psychology Program
Center for Forensic Studies
425 University Avenue, Suite 201
Sacramento, CA 95825-6509
Telephone: (916) 565-2955
Fax: (916) 565-2959
E-mail: *pschafer@alliant.edu*
Web: *http://www.alliant.edu*

Department Information:
2008. Program Director: William Holbomb, PhD. Number of faculty: total—full-time 1, part-time 3; women—part-time 1; minority—part-time 1; women minority—part-time 1.

Programs and Degrees Offered:
Listed in the following order: Program area, degree type (T if terminal Master's), number awarded 7/06–6/07. Forensic Psychology PsyD (Doctor of Psychology) 0.

Student Applications/Admissions:
Student Applications
Forensic Psychology PsyD (Doctor of Psychology)—Applications 2007–2008, 16. Total applicants accepted 2007–2008, 11. Number full-time enrolled (new admits only) 2007–2008, 8. Number part-time enrolled (new admits only) 2007–2008, 2. Total enrolled 2007–2008 full-time, 8, part-time, 2. Openings 2008–2009, 15. The number of students enrolled full- and part-time who were dismissed or voluntarily withdrew from this program area in 2007–2008 were 0.

Admissions Requirements:
Scores: Entries appear in this order: required test or GPA, minimum score (if required), median score of students entering in 2007–2008. Doctoral Programs: overall undergraduate GPA 3.0; psychology GPA 3.0. Master's degree is not required for entry, but if held at time entry, 3.0 minimum GPA applies.
Other Criteria: (importance of criteria rated low, medium, or high): research experience—medium, work experience—high, extracurricular activity—low, clinically related public service—high, GPA—high, letters of recommendation—high, interview—high, statement of goals and objectives—high. For additional information on admission requirements, go to http://www.alliant.edu/wps/wcm/connect/website/Home/Admissions/.

Student Characteristics: The following represents characteristics of students in 2007–2008 in all graduate psychology programs in the department: Female—full-time 8, part-time 2; Male—full-time 0, part-time 0; African American/Black—full-time 0, part-time 0; Hispanic/Latino(a)—full-time 2, part-time 0; Asian/Pacific Islander—full-time 0, part-time 0; American Indian/Alaska Native—full-time 0, part-time 0; Caucasian/White—full-time 6, part-time 2; Multi-ethnic—full-time 0, part-time 0; students subject to the Americans With Disabilities Act—full-time 0, part-time 0; Unknown ethnicity—full-time 0, part-time 0; International students who hold an F-1 or J-1 Visa—full-time 0, part-time 0.

Financial Information/Assistance:
Tuition for Full-Time Study: *Doctoral:* State residents: $915 per credit hour; Nonstate residents: $915 per credit hour. Tuition is subject to change. See the following Web site for updates and changes in tuition costs: http://www.alliant.edu/wps/wcm/connect/website/Home/Admissions/Tuition+and+Fees/.

Financial Assistance:
First-Year Students: Research assistantships available for first year. Average amount paid per academic year: $1,000. Average number of hours worked per week: 10. Apply by see department. Fellowships and scholarships available for first year. Average amount paid per academic year: $1,500. Apply by February 15.
Advanced Students: Teaching assistantships available for advanced students. Average amount paid per academic year: $3,000. Average number of hours worked per week: 20. Apply by see department. Research assistantships available for advanced students. Average amount paid per academic year: $1,000. Average number of hours worked per week: 10. Apply by see depart-

ment. Fellowships and scholarships available for advanced students. Average amount paid per academic year: $1,500. Apply by February 15.

Additional Information: Application and information available online at: https://www.e-fao.com/efao_site.html?OEID=011117&ViewID={10EF815B-422E-4C55-B8CD-BDBD3063BA18}.

Internships/Practica: Doctoral Degree (PsyD Forensic Psychology): For those doctoral students for whom a professional internship was required in this program prior to graduation, (0) students applied for an internship in 2006–2007, with (0) students obtaining an internship. Of those students who obtained an internship, (0) were paid internships. Of those students who obtained an internship, (0)students placed in APA/CPA-accredited internships, (0) students placed in internships not APA/CPA accredited, but listed with the Association of Psychology Postdoctoral and Internship Centers (APPIC), (0) students placed in internships conforming to guidelines of the Council of Directors of School Psychology Programs (CDSPP), (0) students placed in internships that were not APA/CPA-accredited, APPIC or CDSPP listed. A 1-year predoctoral internship is part of the program; this occurs in the 4th or 5th year of the program, depending on student pace thorugh the curriculum.

Housing and Day Care: No on-campus housing is available. No on-campus day care facilities are available.

Employment of Department Graduates:

Master's Degree Graduates: Of those who graduated in the academic year 2006–2007, the following categories and numbers represent the postgraduate activities and employment of master's degree graduates: Enrolled in a postdoctoral residency/fellowship (n/a), employed in independent practice (n/a), total from the above (master's) (0).

Doctoral Degree Graduates: Of those who graduated in the academic year 2006–2007, the following categories and numbers represent the postgraduate activities and employment of doctoral degree graduates: Enrolled in a psychology doctoral program (n/a), total from the above (doctoral) (0).

Additional Information:

Orientation, Objectives, and Emphasis of Department: The PsyD program has an applied psychology orientation and is offered in a part-time 5-year curriculum. This format attracts students with prior work experience from a variety of fields. The curriculum prepares students to conduct assessments for the courts, to serve as expert witnesses, or to work as mental health treatment providers in a variety of forensic settings, including prisons, jails, offender treatment groups, and youth facilities among many others. Core areas include forensic psychology, theories of crime and justice, industrial and organizational psychology, legal research, psychopathology, research design and data analysis, forensic mediation and dispute resolution, ethics, and substance abuse theory and treatment. Although licensure is not required for most forensic careers, some students who enter the program may choose to seek clinical licensure after graduating from the program. These students take additional courses in psychology that are required in order to be eligible to sit for the psychology licensing exam.

Information for Students With Physical Disabilities: Go to About Alliant > Student Life and Athletics > Disability Services at the following Web site: http://www.alliant.edu.

Application Information:

Send to Alliant International University, Admissions Processing Center, 10455 Pomerado Road, San Diego, CA 92131-1799. URL of online application: https://www.ais1.alliant.edu/apply/. Students are admitted in the Fall, application deadline; Spring, application deadline. Applicants wishing notification by April 1 should submit their applications in January. Applications are welcomed on a rolling basis and will be processed on a space-available basis. *Fee:* $70. A limited number of fee waivers are available for those with significant financial need. Please contact the Director of Admissions for details.

Alliant International University: Sacramento

Marital and Family Therapy Program
California School of Professional Psychology
425 University Avenue, Suite 201
Sacramento, CA 95825-6509
Telephone: (916) 565-2955
Fax: (916) 565-2959
E-mail: *cmateo@alliant.edu*
Web: *http://www.alliant.edu/cspp*

Department Information:

2005. Program Director: Scott Woolley, PhD. Number of faculty: total—full-time 2, part-time 4; women—part-time 2.

Programs and Degrees Offered:

Listed in the following order: Program area, degree type (T if terminal Master's), number awarded 7/06–6/07. Marital and Family Therapy MA/MS (Master of Arts/Science) (T) 3.

Student Applications/Admissions:

Student Applications

Marital and Family Therapy MA/MS (Master of Arts/Science)—Applications 2007–2008, 46. Total applicants accepted 2007–2008, 18. Number full-time enrolled (new admits only) 2007–2008, 10. Number part-time enrolled (new admits only) 2007–2008, 1. Total enrolled 2007–2008 full-time, 18, part-time, 3. Openings 2008–2009, 15. The median number of years required for completion of a degree in 2006–2007 were 2. The number of students enrolled full- and part-time who were dismissed or voluntarily withdrew from this program area in 2007–2008 were 0.

Admissions Requirements:

Scores: Entries appear in this order: required test or GPA, minimum score (if required), median score of students entering in 2007–2008. Master's Programs: overall undergraduate GPA 3.00; last 2 years GPA 3.00; psychology GPA 3.00. Doctoral Programs: overall undergraduate GPA 3.00; last 2 years GPA 3.00. A master's degree is not required for entry to the doctoral program, but if a master's degree is held at the time of application, the minimum 3.0 GPA applies.

Other Criteria: (importance of criteria rated low, medium, or high): research experience—medium, work experience—medium, clinically related public service—medium, GPA—high, letters of recommendation—medium, interview—high, statement of goals and objectives—high. For additional information on admission requirements, go to http://www.alliant.

edu/wps/wcm/connect/website/Home/Admissions/Graduate+Student+Admissions/.

Student Characteristics: The following represents characteristics of students in 2007–2008 in all graduate psychology programs in the department: Female—full-time 16, part-time 2; Male—full-time 2, part-time 1; African American/Black—full-time 0, part-time 2; Hispanic/Latino(a)—full-time 1, part-time 0; Asian/Pacific Islander—full-time 5, part-time 0; American Indian/Alaska Native—full-time 0, part-time 0; Caucasian/White—full-time 9, part-time 1; Multi-ethnic—full-time 0, part-time 0; students subject to the Americans With Disabilities Act—full-time 0, part-time 0; Unknown ethnicity—full-time 3, part-time 0; International students who hold an F-1 or J-1 Visa—full-time 0, part-time 0.

Financial Information/Assistance:

Tuition for Full-Time Study: *Master's:* State residents: $915 per credit hour; Nonstate residents: $915 per credit hour. *Doctoral:* State residents: $915 per credit hour; Nonstate residents: $915 per credit hour. Tuition is subject to change. Tuition costs vary by program. See the following Web site for updates and changes in tuition costs: http://www.alliant.edu/wps/wcm/connect/website/Home/Admissions/Tuition+and+Fees/.

Financial Assistance:

First-Year Students: Fellowships and scholarships available for first year. Average amount paid per academic year: $750. Apply by varies.

Advanced Students: Fellowships and scholarships available for advanced students. Average amount paid per academic year: $750. Apply by varies.

Additional Information: Of all students currently enrolled full time, 65% benefited from one or more of the listed financial assistance programs. Application and information available online at https://www.e-fao.com/eFAO_site.html?OEID=011117&ViewID={10EF815B-422E-4C55-B8CD-BDBD3063BA18}.

Internships/Practica: As part of the practicum experience, students complete 500 client contract hours, 250 of which must be with couples and families. Students recieve at least 100 hours of individual and group supervision, 50 hours of which are based on direct observation, videotape, or audiotape. At least 25 of those hours must be videotaped or direct observation. When student are ready to begin practicum, experienced faculty and staff assist students through each step in obtaining a field placement site approved by Alliant. While students are doing practicum training they are required to perform marriage and family therapy under a California state licensed AAMFT approved supervisor or the equivalent.

Housing and Day Care: No on-campus housing is available. No on-campus day care facilities are available.

Employment of Department Graduates:

Master's Degree Graduates: Of those who graduated in the academic year 2006–2007, the following categories and numbers represent the postgraduate activities and employment of master's degree graduates: Enrolled in a postdoctoral residency/fellowship (n/a), employed in independent practice (n/a), total from the above (master's) (0).

Doctoral Degree Graduates: Of those who graduated in the academic year 2006–2007, the following categories and numbers represent the postgraduate activities and employment of doctoral degree graduates: Enrolled in a psychology doctoral program (n/a), total from the above (doctoral) (0).

Additional Information:

Orientation, Objectives, and Emphasis of Department: The mission of the Marital and Family Therapy Program is to prepare graduate students who are skilled in the theory, research, and clinical practice of the field of Marriage and Family Therapy and can integrate individual and systemic therapeutic models in an international, multicultural environment. The marital and family therapy (MFT) programs provide students with the essential training needed to pursue a career as a professional marriage and family therapist. The Master of Arts in MFT allows students to be licensed as a marital and family therapist and the Doctor of Psychology in MFT allows a student to be licensed as a marital and family therapist and as a psychologist. Students who complete the MFT masters at Alliant can apply all of their masters degree coursework and practicum hours toward the doctoral program. The programs are accredited by COAMFTE.

Information for Students With Physical Disabilities: Go to About Alliant > Student Life and Athletics > Disability Services at the following Web site: http://www.alliant.edu.

Application Information:

Send to Alliant International University Admissions Processing Center, 10455 Pomerado Road, San Diego, CA 92131-1799. Application available online. URL of online application: http://www.alliant.edu/applyonline/. Students are admitted in the Fall, application deadline January 15; Spring, application deadline varies. Programs have rolling admissions. Applications for the Fall semester are due January 15 (priority deadline), March 15, and April 16. Applications received after the priority deadline will be accepted on a space-available basis. For complete information on deadlines, contact the system admissions office at 1-866-U-ALLIANT. *Fee:* $70. A limited number of fee waivers are available for those with significant financial need.

Alliant International University: San Diego

Programs in Clinical Psychology and Marital and Family Therapy

California School of Professional Psychology
10455 Pomerado Road
San Diego, CA 92131-1799
Telephone: (858) 635-4442
Fax: (858) 635-4739
E-mail: *kjanowsky@alliant.edu*
Web: *http://www.alliant.edu/cspp/*

Department Information:

1972. Dean, California School of Professional Psychology: Morgan Sammons, PhD, ABPP. Number of faculty: total—full-time 34, part-time 46; women—full-time 16, part-time 16; total—minority—full-time 4, part-time 6; women minority—full-time 3, part-time 2.

Programs and Degrees Offered:

Listed in the following order: Program area, degree type (T if terminal Master's), number awarded 7/06–6/07. Clinical Psychology PhD (Doctor of Philosophy) 27, Dual Clinical/Industrial-Organizational PhD (Doctor of Philosophy) 2, Clinical Psychology PsyD (Doctor of Psychology) 21, Marital and Family Therapy MA/MS (Master of Arts/Science) (T) 22, Marital and Family Therapy PsyD (Doctor of Psychology) 6, Clinical Psychology Respecialization Diploma 0.

APA Accreditation: Clinical PhD (Doctor of Philosophy). Clinical PsyD (Doctor of Psychology).

Student Applications/Admissions:

Student Applications

Clinical Psychology PhD (Doctor of Philosophy)—Applications 2007–2008, 113. Total applicants accepted 2007–2008, 49. Number full-time enrolled (new admits only) 2007–2008, 30. Number part-time enrolled (new admits only) 2007–2008, 0. Total enrolled 2007–2008 full-time, 189, part-time, 58. Openings 2008–2009, 35. The median number of years required for completion of a degree in 2006–2007 were 5. The number of students enrolled full- and part-time who were dismissed or voluntarily withdrew from this program area in 2007–2008 were 3. *Dual Clinical/Industrial-Organizational PhD (Doctor of Philosophy)*—Applications 2007–2008, 27. Total applicants accepted 2007–2008, 6. Number full-time enrolled (new admits only) 2007–2008, 4. Number part-time enrolled (new admits only) 2007–2008, 0. Total enrolled 2007–2008 full-time, 18, part-time, 7. Openings 2008–2009, 5. The median number of years required for completion of a degree in 2006–2007 were 7. The number of students enrolled full- and part-time who were dismissed or voluntarily withdrew from this program area in 2007–2008 were 0. *Clinical Psychology PsyD (Doctor of Psychology)*—Applications 2007–2008, 124. Total applicants accepted 2007–2008, 54. Number full-time enrolled (new admits only) 2007–2008, 42. Number part-time enrolled (new admits only) 2007–2008, 1. Total enrolled 2007–2008 full-time, 199, part-time, 39. Openings 2008–2009, 45. The median number of years required for completion of a degree in 2006–2007 were 4. The number of students enrolled full- and part-time who were dismissed or voluntarily withdrew from this program area in 2007–2008 were 1. *Marital and Family Therapy MA/MS (Master of Arts/Science)*—Applications 2007–2008, 82. Total applicants accepted 2007–2008, 50. Number full-time enrolled (new admits only) 2007–2008, 34. Number part-time enrolled (new admits only) 2007–2008, 0. Total enrolled 2007–2008 full-time, 58, part-time, 12. Openings 2008–2009, 35. The median number of years required for completion of a degree in 2006–2007 were 2. The number of students enrolled full- and part-time who were dismissed or voluntarily withdrew from this program area in 2007–2008 were 2. *Marital and Family Therapy PsyD (Doctor of Psychology)*—Applications 2007–2008, 37. Total applicants accepted 2007–2008, 24. Number full-time enrolled (new admits only) 2007–2008, 17. Number part-time enrolled (new admits only) 2007–2008, 3. Total enrolled 2007–2008 full-time, 50, part-time, 25. Openings 2008–2009, 20. The median number of years required for completion of a degree in 2006–2007 were 5. The number of students enrolled full- and part-time who were dismissed or voluntarily withdrew from this program area in 2007–2008 were 1. *Clinical Psychology Respecialization Diploma*—Applications 2007–2008, 0. Total applicants accepted 2007–2008, 0. Number full-time enrolled (new admits only) 2007–2008, 0. Number part-time enrolled (new admits only) 2007–2008, 0. Openings 2008–2009, 2. The number of students enrolled full- and part-time who were dismissed or voluntarily withdrew from this program area in 2007–2008 were 0.

Admissions Requirements:

Scores: Entries appear in this order: required test or GPA, minimum score (if required), median score of students entering in 2007–2008. Master's Programs: overall undergraduate GPA 3.0, 3.19; psychology GPA 3.0. Doctoral Programs: overall undergraduate GPA 3.0, 3.43; psychology GPA 3.0. The master's degree is not required for admission to doctoral programs; however, if the master's degree is held at the time of application, the 3.0 minimum GPA applies.

Other Criteria: (importance of criteria rated low, medium, or high): GRE/MAT scores—low, research experience—medium, work experience—medium, clinically related public service—medium, GPA—high, letters of recommendation—medium, interview—high, statement of goals and objectives—high. Admissions criteria and their importance vary by program and degree level. PhD programs place more emphasis on prior research experience; PsyD programs place more emphasis on clinical/work experience. For additional information on admission requirements, go to http://www.alliant.edu/wps/wcm/connect/website/Home/Admissions/Graduate+Student+Admissions/.

Student Characteristics: The following represents characteristics of students in 2007–2008 in all graduate psychology programs in the department: Female—full-time 425, part-time 108; Male—full-time 89, part-time 33; African American/Black—full-time 21, part-time 3; Hispanic/Latino(a)—full-time 44, part-time 15; Asian/Pacific Islander—full-time 30, part-time 12; American Indian/Alaska Native—full-time 5, part-time 3; Caucasian/White—full-time 328, part-time 89; Multi-ethnic—full-time 11, part-time 0; students subject to the Americans With Disabilities Act—full-time 9, part-time 6; Unknown ethnicity—full-time 75, part-time 19; International students who hold an F-1 or J-1 Visa—full-time 10, part-time 2.

Financial Information/Assistance:

Tuition for Full-Time Study: *Master's:* State residents: $915 per credit hour; Nonstate residents: $915 per credit hour. *Doctoral:* State residents: $915 per credit hour; Nonstate residents: $915 per credit hour. Tuition is subject to change. Tuition costs vary by program. See the following Web site for updates and changes in tuition costs: http://www.alliant.edu/wps/wcm/connect/website/Home/Admissions/Tuition+and+Fees/.

Financial Assistance:

First-Year Students: Research assistantships available for first year. Average amount paid per academic year: $1,000. Average number of hours worked per week: 10. Apply by see department. Fellowships and scholarships available for first year. Average amount paid per academic year: $1,500. Apply by varies.

Advanced Students: Teaching assistantships available for advanced students. Average amount paid per academic year: $3,000. Average number of hours worked per week: 10. Apply by see department. Research assistantships available for advanced students. Average amount paid per academic year: $1,000. Average number of hours worked per week: 10. Apply by see department. Fellowships and scholarships available for advanced students. Average amount paid per academic year: $1,500. Apply by April 15.

Additional Information: Of all students currently enrolled full time, 62% benefited from one or more of the listed financial assistance programs. Application and information available online at https://www.e-fao.com/eFAO_site.html?OEID=011117&ViewID={10EF815B-422E-4C55-B8CD-BDBD3063BA18}.

Internships/Practica: Doctoral Degree (PhD Clinical Psychology): For those doctoral students for whom a professional internship was required in this program prior to graduation, (60) students applied for an internship in 2006–2007, with (57) students obtaining an internship. Of those students who obtained an internship, (45) were paid internships. Of those students who obtained an internship, (7) students placed in APA/CPA-accredited internships, (0) students placed in internships not APA/CPA accredited, but listed with the Association of Psychology Postdoctoral and Internship Centers (APPIC), (0) students placed in internships conforming to guidelines of the Council of Directors of School Psychology Programs (CDSPP), (50) students placed in internships that were not APA/CPA-accredited, APPIC or CDSPP listed. Doctoral Degree (PsyD Clinical Psychology): For those doctoral students for whom a professional internship was required in this program prior to graduation, (80) students applied for an internship in 2006–2007, with (78) students obtaining an internship. Of those students who obtained an internship, (60) were paid internships. Of those students who obtained an internship, (5) students placed in APA/CPA-accredited internships, (0) students placed in internships not APA/CPA-accredited, but listed with the Association of Psychology Postdoctoral and Internship Centers (APPIC), (0) students placed in internships conforming to guidelines of the Council of Directors of School Psychology Programs (CDSPP), (73) students placed in internships that were not APA/CPA-accredited, APPIC or CDSPP listed. Clinical psychology doctoral students receive practicum and internship experience at more than 80 agencies that meet the requirements for licensure set by the California Board of Psychology. Assignments to these agencies result from an application process conducted by year level, with 3rd-, 4th-, and 5th-year students receiving priority for licensable placements. The option of doing an APA-accredited full-time internship in the 4th or 5th years (depending on the program and year level requirements) is available and encouraged. Marital and family therapy students complete a required practicum including 500 client contact hours, 250 of which must be with couples and families. Students receive at least 100 hours of individual and group supervision, 50 hours of which are based on direct observation, videotape, or audiotape. At least 25 of those hours must be videotape or direct observation. While students are doing practicum training, they are required to perform marraige and family therapy under a California state licensed AAMFT-approved supervisor or the equivalent. MFT doctoral students complete a predoctoral internship.

Housing and Day Care: On-campus housing is available. See the following Web site for more information: On-campus housing is available for graduate students at the San Diego campus. For more information visit http://www.alliant.edu/wps/wcm/connect/website/Home/Campuses/San+Diego+Campus/Housing+%26+Food+Service/Graduate+Housing. No on-campus day care facilities are available.

Employment of Department Graduates:

Master's Degree Graduates: Of those who graduated in the academic year 2006–2007, the following categories and numbers represent the postgraduate activities and employment of master's degree graduates: Enrolled in a postdoctoral residency/fellowship (n/a), employed in independent practice (n/a), total from the above (master's) (0).

Doctoral Degree Graduates: Of those who graduated in the academic year 2006–2007, the following categories and numbers represent the postgraduate activities and employment of doctoral degree graduates: Enrolled in a psychology doctoral program (n/a), employed in independent practice (0), employed in an academic position at a university (0), employed in an academic position at a 2-year/4-year college (0), employed in a professional position in a school system (0), employed in a community mental health/counseling center (0), employed in a hospital/medical center (0), total from the above (doctoral) (0).

Additional Information:

Orientation, Objectives, and Emphasis of Department: The California School of Professional Psychology (CSPP) at Alliant International University offers comprehensive PhD and PsyD program of instruction in professional psychology with an emphasis on doctoral training in clinical psychology in which academic requirements are integrated with supervised field experience. Students are evaluated by instructors and field supervisors on the basis of their performance and participation throughout the year. Theory, personal growth, professional skill, humanities, investigatory skills courses, and field experience are designed to stimulate the graduate toward a scholarly as well as a professional contribution to society. Elective areas of emphasis in health psychology (PhD only), family and child psychology, clinical forensic psychology, psychodynamic, multicultural and international, and integrative psychology (PsyD only) are available within the clinical programs. Students in CSPP's Marital and Family Therapy MA and PsyD are trained to treat individuals, couples, and families with relational mental health issues from a systemic perspective. Skills are developed in mental health assessment, diagnosis, and treatment of individuals and relationship systems. The PsyD is based on the scholar–practitioner model; both degrees are offered in a format for working professionals. The MFT programs are accredited by COAMFTE. The dual clinical/industrial–organizational psychology PhD program is offered jointly with the Marshall Goldsmith School of Management; students fulfill the requirements of both specialties.

Special Facilities or Resources: The Center for Applied Behavioral Services (CABS) is a multiservice and training center. The Center incorporates the expertise of CSPP faculty in the delivery of direct services and in modeling specific techniques of treatment and service for practicum and interns. This is currently accomplished through an array of clinical and community services that are directed by faculty members.

Information for Students With Physical Disabilities: Go to About Alliant > Student Life and Athletics > Disability Services at the following Web site: http://www.alliant.edu.

Application Information:
Send to Alliant International University Admissions Processing Center, 10455 Pomerado Road, San Diego, CA 92131-1799. Application available online. URL of online application: http://www.alliant.edu/applyonline/. Students are admitted in the Fall, application deadline varies; Spring, application deadline open. Programs have rolling admissions. Deadlines vary by program. Most doctoral programs have priority deadlines in January in order to provide a response by April 1 to applicants who need a decision by that date. Some doctoral programs and most master's programs have later deadlines. Programs accept applications and admit students on a space-available basis after any stated deadlines. For complete information on deadlines contact the admissions office at 1-866-U-ALLIANT. *Fee:* $70. A limited number of fee waivers are available for those with significant financial need.

Alliant International University: San Diego

Programs in Educational and School Psychology
Graduate School of Education
10455 Pomerado Road
San Diego, CA 92131-1799
Telephone: (858) 635-4772
Fax: (858) 635-4555
E-mail: *lcruz@alliant.edu*
Web: *http://www.alliant.edu/gsoe/*

Department Information:
2002. Systemwide Program Director: Donald Wofford, PsyD. Number of faculty: total—full-time 1, part-time 6; women—part-time 4; minority—part-time 1; women minority—part-time 1.

Programs and Degrees Offered:
Listed in the following order: Program area, degree type (T if terminal Master's), number awarded 7/06–6/07. Educational Psychology PsyD (Doctor of Psychology) 1, School Psychology MA/MS (Master of Arts/Science) (T) 11.

Student Applications/Admissions:
Student Applications
Educational Psychology PsyD (Doctor of Psychology)—Applications 2007–2008, 11. Total applicants accepted 2007–2008, 10. Number full-time enrolled (new admits only) 2007–2008, 6. Number part-time enrolled (new admits only) 2007–2008, 4. Total enrolled 2007–2008 full-time, 8, part-time, 8. Openings 2008–2009, 15. The median number of years required for completion of a degree in 2006–2007 were 4. The number of students enrolled full- and part-time who were dismissed or voluntarily withdrew from this program area in 2007–2008 were 0. *School Psychology MA/MS (Master of Arts/Science)*—Applications 2007–2008, 36. Total applicants accepted 2007–2008, 21. Number full-time enrolled (new admits only) 2007–2008, 17. Number part-time enrolled (new admits only) 2007–2008, 0. Total enrolled 2007–2008 full-time, 28, part-time, 10. Openings 2008–2009, 18. The median number of years required for completion of a degree in 2006–2007 were 2. The number of students enrolled full- and part-time who were dismissed or voluntarily withdrew from this program area in 2007–2008 were 2.

Admissions Requirements:
Scores: Entries appear in this order: required test or GPA, minimum score (if required), median score of students entering in 2007–2008. Master's Programs: overall undergraduate GPA 2.5, 3.07; psychology GPA 2.5. Doctoral Programs: overall undergraduate GPA 3.0, 3.23; psychology GPA 3.0. Master's degree is not required for the 5-year PsyD program, but if the degree is held at the time of application, the 3.0 minimum GPA applies.
Other Criteria: (importance of criteria rated low, medium, or high): research experience—medium, work experience—medium, extracurricular activity—low, clinically related public service—high, GPA—high, letters of recommendation—high, interview—high, statement of goals and objectives—high. Criteria differ by program and level. For additional information on admission requirements, go to http://www.alliant.edu/wps/wcm/connect/website/Home/Admissions/.

Student Characteristics: The following represents characteristics of students in 2007–2008 in all graduate psychology programs in the department: Female—full-time 28, part-time 14; Male—full-time 8, part-time 4; African American/Black—full-time 2, part-time 0; Hispanic/Latino(a)—full-time 10, part-time 3; Asian/Pacific Islander—full-time 0, part-time 0; American Indian/Alaska Native—full-time 1, part-time 0; Caucasian/White—full-time 17, part-time 10; Multi-ethnic—full-time 0, part-time 2; students subject to the Americans With Disabilities Act—full-time 1, part-time 0; Unknown ethnicity—full-time 6, part-time 3; International students who hold an F-1 or J-1 Visa—full-time 1, part-time 0.

Financial Information/Assistance:
Tuition for Full-Time Study: *Master's:* State residents: $525 per credit hour; Nonstate residents: $525 per credit hour. *Doctoral:* State residents: $855 per credit hour; Nonstate residents: $855 per credit hour. Tuition is subject to change. Tuition costs vary by program. See the following Web site for updates and changes in tuition costs: http://www.alliant.edu/wps/wcm/connect/website/Home/Admissions/Tuition+and+Fees/.

Financial Assistance:
First-Year Students: Research assistantships available for first year. Average amount paid per academic year: $1,000. Average number of hours worked per week: 10. Apply by see department. Fellowships and scholarships available for first year. Average amount paid per academic year: $750. Apply by June 1.
Advanced Students: Teaching assistantships available for advanced students. Average amount paid per academic year: $3,000. Average number of hours worked per week: 10. Apply by see department. Research assistantships available for advanced students. Average amount paid per academic year: $1,000. Average number of hours worked per week: 10. Apply by see department. Fellowships and scholarships available for advanced students. Average amount paid per academic year: $750. Apply by April 1.
Additional Information: Of all students currently enrolled full time, 40% benefited from one or more of the listed financial assistance programs. Application and information available online at https://www.e-fao.com/efao_site.html?OEID=011117&ViewID={10EF815B-422E-4C55-B8CD-BDBD3063BA18}.

Internships/Practica: Students in the master's program have practica tied to their coursework beginning in the first semester of their programs. Internships are required of students seeking a Pupil Personnel Services (PPS) credential postmasters or as part of the doctoral program in educational psychology. The 1,200 required internship hours are completed at a public school district. Students interested in seeking clinical licensure must complete a separate psychology internship.

Housing and Day Care: On-campus housing is available. See the following Web site for more information: Housing is available for graduate students who are interested in living on the San Diego campus. For information, visit http://www.alliant.edu/wps/wcm/connect/website/Home/Campuses/San+Diego+Campuses/Housing+%26+Food+Service/. No on-campus day care facilities are available.

Employment of Department Graduates:

Master's Degree Graduates: Of those who graduated in the academic year 2006–2007, the following categories and numbers represent the postgraduate activities and employment of master's degree graduates: Enrolled in a postdoctoral residency/fellowship (n/a), employed in independent practice (n/a), total from the above (master's) (0).

Doctoral Degree Graduates: Of those who graduated in the academic year 2006–2007, the following categories and numbers represent the postgraduate activities and employment of doctoral degree graduates: Enrolled in a psychology doctoral program (n/a), total from the above (doctoral) (0).

Additional Information:

Orientation, Objectives, and Emphasis of Department: Programs train students with the skills necessary to work with students, teachers, parents, and other school professionals in today's school environments. Curriculum includes professional skills, professional roles courses, applied research, and professional concepts. The master's degree program prepares students to gain the PPS (Pupil Personnel Services) credential that allows them to practice in California's schools. Students take afternoon, evening, and weekend classes and engage in fieldwork. At the doctoral level, students complete special focus area courses, examples of which include adolescent stress and coping, school culture and administration, pediatric psychology, infant and preschool mental health, child neuropsychology, and provision of services for children in alternative placement. Students also complete a PsyD project.

Special Facilities or Resources: The Graduate School of Education at the San Diego campus houses the World Council of Curriculum and Instruction.

Information for Students With Physical Disabilities: Go to About Alliant > Student Life and Athletics > Disability Services at the following Web site: http://www.alliant.edu.

Application Information:

Send to Alliant International University, Admissions Processing Center, 10455 Pomerado Road, San Diego, CA 92131-1799. Application available online. URL of online application: http://www.alliant.edu/applyonline/. Students are admitted in the Fall, application deadline June 1; Spring, application deadline varies; Summer, application deadline varies. Programs have rolling admissions. *Fee:* $70. A limited number of fee waivers are available for those with significant financial need.

Alliant International University: San Diego

Programs in Organizational Psychology
Marshall Goldsmith School of Management
10455 Pomerado Road
San Diego, CA 92131-1799
Telephone: (858) 635-4772
Fax: (858) 635-4739
E-mail: *lcruz@alliant.edu*
Web: *http://mgsm.alliant.edu*

Department Information:

1981. Program Director: Herbert George Baker, PhD. Number of faculty: total—full-time 8, part-time 19; women—full-time 2, part-time 7; total—minority—full-time 2, part-time 3; women minority—full-time 1, part-time 1.

Programs and Degrees Offered:

Listed in the following order: Program area, degree type (T if terminal Master's), number awarded 7/06–6/07. Industrial-Organizational PhD (Doctor of Philosophy) 9, Consulting Psychology PhD (Doctor of Philosophy) 2, Industrial-Organizational MA/MS (Master of Arts/Science) (T) 4, Industrial-Organizational Respecialization Diploma 0, Dual Clinical/Industrial-Organizational PhD (Doctor of Philosophy) 1.

Student Applications/Admissions:

Student Applications

Industrial-Organizational PhD (Doctor of Philosophy)—Applications 2007–2008, 18. Total applicants accepted 2007–2008, 15. Number full-time enrolled (new admits only) 2007–2008, 13. Number part-time enrolled (new admits only) 2007–2008, 0. Total enrolled 2007–2008 full-time, 42, part-time, 25. Openings 2008–2009, 12. The median number of years required for completion of a degree in 2006–2007 were 6. The number of students enrolled full- and part-time who were dismissed or voluntarily withdrew from this program area in 2007–2008 were 0. *Consulting Psychology PhD (Doctor of Philosophy)*—Applications 2007–2008, 10. Total applicants accepted 2007–2008, 6. Number full-time enrolled (new admits only) 2007–2008, 6. Number part-time enrolled (new admits only) 2007–2008, 0. Total enrolled 2007–2008 full-time, 28, part-time, 10. Openings 2008–2009, 12. The median number of years required for completion of a degree in 2006–2007 were 5. The number of students enrolled full- and part-time who were dismissed or voluntarily withdrew from this program area in 2007–2008 were 1. *Industrial-Organizational MA/MS (Master of Arts/Science)*—Applications 2007–2008, 20. Total applicants accepted 2007–2008, 9. Number full-time enrolled (new admits only) 2007–2008, 6. Number part-time enrolled (new admits only) 2007–2008, 3. Total enrolled 2007–2008 full-time, 18, part-time, 4. Openings 2008–2009, 15. The median number of years required for completion of a degree in 2006–2007 were 3. The number of students enrolled full- and part-time who were dismissed or voluntarily withdrew from this program area in 2007–2008 were 0. *Industrial-Organizational Respecialization Diploma*—Applications 2007–2008, 0. Total applicants accepted 2007–2008, 0. Number full-time enrolled (new admits only) 2007–2008, 0. Number part-time enrolled (new admits only) 2007–2008, 0. Openings 2008–2009, 2. The number of students enrolled full- and part-time who were dismissed or voluntarily withdrew from this program area in 2007–2008 were 0. *Dual Clinical/Industrial-Organizational PhD (Doctor of Philosophy)*—Applications 2007–2008, 20. Total applicants accepted 2007–2008, 12. Number full-time enrolled (new admits only) 2007–2008, 5. Number part-time enrolled (new admits only) 2007–2008, 0. Total enrolled 2007–2008 full-time, 20, part-time, 7. Openings 2008–2009, 5. The median number of years required for completion of a degree in 2006–2007 were 5. The number of students enrolled full- and part-time who were dismissed or voluntarily withdrew from this program area in 2007–2008 were 0.

Admissions Requirements:

Scores: Entries appear in this order: required test or GPA, minimum score (if required), median score of students entering in 2007–2008. Master's Programs: overall undergraduate GPA 3.0, 3.20; psychology GPA 3.0. Doctoral Programs: overall undergraduate GPA 3.0, 3.31; last 2 years GPA 3.0. A master's degree is not required for admission to the doctoral programs, but if held at the time of application, the minimum 3.0 GPA applies.

Other Criteria: (importance of criteria rated low, medium, or high): research experience—high, work experience—medium, extracurricular activity—low, clinically related public service—low, GPA—high, letters of recommendation—high, interview—high, statement of goals and objectives—high. Criteria vary by program. Research experience is more important for doctoral applicants; work experience is more important for some master's programs. For additional information on admission requirements, go to http://www.alliant.edu/wps/wcm/connect/website/Home/Admissions/.

Student Characteristics: The following represents characteristics of students in 2007–2008 in all graduate psychology programs in the department: Female—full-time 68, part-time 32; Male—full-time 42, part-time 18; African American/Black—full-time 4, part-time 4; Hispanic/Latino(a)—full-time 10, part-time 2; Asian/Pacific Islander—full-time 7, part-time 10; American Indian/Alaska Native—full-time 0, part-time 0; Caucasian/White—full-time 55, part-time 27; Multi-ethnic—full-time 4, part-time 0; students subject to the Americans With Disabilities Act—full-time 1, part-time 2; Unknown ethnicity—full-time 30, part-time 7; International students who hold an F-1 or J-1 Visa—full-time 10, part-time 2.

Financial Information/Assistance:

Tuition for Full-Time Study: *Master's:* State residents: $915 per credit hour; Nonstate residents: $915 per credit hour. *Doctoral:* State residents: $915 per credit hour; Nonstate residents: $915 per credit hour. Tuition is subject to change. Tuition costs vary by program. See the following Web site for updates and changes in tuition costs: http://www.alliant.edu/wps/wcm/connect/website/Home/Admissions/Tuition+and+Fees/.

Financial Assistance:

First-Year Students: Research assistantships available for first year. Average amount paid per academic year: $1,000. Average number of hours worked per week: 10. Apply by see department. Fellowships and scholarships available for first year. Average amount paid per academic year: $1,500. Apply by April 1.

Advanced Students: Teaching assistantships available for advanced students. Average amount paid per academic year: $3,000. Average number of hours worked per week: 10. Apply by see department. Research assistantships available for advanced students. Average amount paid per academic year: $1,000. Average number of hours worked per week: 10. Apply by see department. Fellowships and scholarships available for advanced students. Average amount paid per academic year: $1,500. Apply by April 15.

Additional Information: Of all students currently enrolled full time, 51% benefited from one or more of the listed financial assistance programs. Application and information available online at https://www.e-fao.com/efao_site.html?OEID=011117&ViewID={10EF815B-422E-4C55-B8CD-BDBD3063BA18}.

Internships/Practica: Doctoral students participate in two half-time internships in the 3rd and 4th years of the program; this allows for the integration of professional training with courses, seminars, and research. Consulting psychology doctoral students' internships have an individual/group focus in the 3rd year and systemwide interventions focus in the 4th year. Master's students in Industrial-Organizational psychology have a one-semester practicum in the last term of their programs. The majority of these interships are local to the students' campus.

Housing and Day Care: On-campus housing is available. See the following Web site for more information: http://www.alliant.edu/wps/wcm/connect/website/Home/Campuses/San+Diego+Campus/Housing+%26+Food+Service/. No on-campus day care facilities are available.

Employment of Department Graduates:

Master's Degree Graduates: Of those who graduated in the academic year 2006–2007, the following categories and numbers represent the postgraduate activities and employment of master's degree graduates: Enrolled in a postdoctoral residency/fellowship (n/a), employed in independent practice (n/a), total from the above (master's) (0).

Doctoral Degree Graduates: Of those who graduated in the academic year 2006–2007, the following categories and numbers represent the postgraduate activities and employment of doctoral degree graduates: Enrolled in a psychology doctoral program (n/a), total from the above (doctoral) (0).

Additional Information:

Orientation, Objectives, and Emphasis of Department: The consulting psychology doctoral program combines individual, group, organization, and systemic consultation skills to produce specialists in the psychological aspects of organizational consulting. The individual focus includes career assessment and executive coaching; the group focus includes team building and assisting dysfunctional work groups; the organizational/systemic focus includes the understanding, diagnosis, and intervention with organizational systems. The industrial-organizational doctoral program is patterned after the doctoral-level training guidelines prepared by the Educational and Training Committee of the Society for Industrial and Organizational Psychology (Division 14 of the APA). The programs emphasize personnel selections, work motivation, design of compensation systems, measurement, and productivity. Master's programs lead to careers as internal consultants within organizations or other master's-level or entry-level careers in organizations and provide foundations for further study if desired. These programs stress leadership, management, and organizational skills.

Some master's programs are structured specifically for working professionals.

Special Facilities or Resources: The Marshall Goldsmith School of Management houses an Organizational Consulting Center (OCC). Some students may have opportunities to work with faculty or consultant associates from the Center during their programs.

Information for Students With Physical Disabilities: Go to About Alliant > Student Life and Athletics > Disability Services at the following Web site: http://www.alliant.edu.

Application Information:

Send to Alliant International University, Admissions Processing Center, 10455 Pomerado Road, San Diego, CA 92121-1799. Application available online. URL of online application: http://www.alliant.edu/applyonline/. Students are admitted in the Fall, application deadline February 1; Spring, application deadline varies; Summer, application deadline varies. Programs have rolling admissions. Doctoral programs have a February 1 priority deadline in order to provide a response by April 1 for applicants who need a decision by that date. Master's programs have later deadlines. Programs accept and admit applicants on a space-available basis after any stated deadlines. For updated information on deadlines and programs open, contact the local admissions office or application processing center at 1-866-U-ALLIANT. *Fee:* $70. A limited number of fee waivers are available to those with significant financial need.

Alliant International University: San Francisco

Programs in Educational and School Psychology
Graduate School of Education
One Beach Street
San Francisco, CA 94133-1221
Telephone: (415) 955-2146
Fax: (415) 955-2179
E-mail: *jaquino@alliant.edu*
Web: *http://www.alliant.edu/gsoe/*

Department Information:

2002. Systemwide Program Director: Donald Wofford, PsyD. Number of faculty: total—full-time 1, part-time 11; women—part-time 8; total—minority—full-time 1, part-time 2; women minority—part-time 2.

Programs and Degrees Offered:

Listed in the following order: Program area, degree type (T if terminal Master's), number awarded 7/06–6/07. School Psychology MA/MS (Master of Arts/Science) (T) 8, Educational Psychology PsyD (Doctor of Psychology) 0.

Student Applications/Admissions:

Student Applications

School Psychology MA/MS (Master of Arts/Science)—Applications 2007–2008, 12. Total applicants accepted 2007–2008, 7. Number full-time enrolled (new admits only) 2007–2008, 3. Number part-time enrolled (new admits only) 2007–2008, 2. Total enrolled 2007–2008 full-time, 6, part-time, 12. Openings 2008–2009, 15. The median number of years required for completion of a degree in 2006–2007 were 3. The number of students enrolled full- and part-time who were dismissed or voluntarily withdrew from this program area in 2007–2008 were 0. *Educational Psychology PsyD (Doctor of Psychology)*—Applications 2007–2008, 3. Total applicants accepted 2007–2008, 3. Number full-time enrolled (new admits only) 2007–2008, 0. Number part-time enrolled (new admits only) 2007–2008, 2. Openings 2008–2009, 5. The number of students enrolled full- and part-time who were dismissed or voluntarily withdrew from this program area in 2007–2008 were 0.

Admissions Requirements:

Scores: Entries appear in this order: required test or GPA, minimum score (if required), median score of students entering in 2007–2008. Master's Programs: overall undergraduate GPA 2.5, 3.32; psychology GPA 2.5. Doctoral Programs: overall undergraduate GPA 3.0; psychology GPA 3.0. A master's degree is not required for entry into the 5 year PsyD program; however, if a master's degree is held at the time of application, the 3.0 minimum GPA applies.

Other Criteria: (importance of criteria rated low, medium, or high): research experience—medium, work experience—high, extracurricular activity—low, clinically related public service—high, GPA—high, letters of recommendation—high, interview—high, statement of goals and objectives—high. Criteria differ for master's and doctoral programs. For additional information on admission requirements, go to http://www.alliant.edu/wps/wcm/connect/website/Home/Admissions/.

Student Characteristics: The following represents characteristics of students in 2007–2008 in all graduate psychology programs in the department: Female—full-time 5, part-time 16; Male—full-time 1, part-time 1; African American/Black—full-time 1, part-time 2; Hispanic/Latino(a)—full-time 0, part-time 1; Asian/Pacific Islander—full-time 0, part-time 0; American Indian/Alaska Native—full-time 0, part-time 0; Caucasian/White—full-time 4, part-time 10; Multi-ethnic—full-time 0, part-time 0; students subject to the Americans With Disabilities Act—full-time 0, part-time 0; Unknown ethnicity—full-time 1, part-time 4; International students who hold an F-1 or J-1 Visa—full-time 0, part-time 0.

Financial Information/Assistance:

Tuition for Full-Time Study: *Master's:* State residents: $525 per credit hour; Nonstate residents: $525 per credit hour. *Doctoral:* State residents: $855 per credit hour; Nonstate residents: $855 per credit hour. Tuition is subject to change. See the following Web site for updates and changes in tuition costs: http://www.alliant.edu/wps/wcm/connect/website/Home/Admissions/Tuition+and+Fees/.

Financial Assistance:

First-Year Students: Research assistantships available for first year. Average amount paid per academic year: $1,000. Average number of hours worked per week: 10. Apply by see department. Fellowships and scholarships available for first year. Average amount paid per academic year: $750. Apply by June 1.

Advanced Students: Teaching assistantships available for advanced students. Average amount paid per academic year: $3,000. Average number of hours worked per week: 10. Apply by see department. Research assistantships available for advanced students. Average amount paid per academic year: $1,000. Average number of hours worked per week: 10. Apply by see department. Fellowships and scholarships available for advanced students. Average amount paid per academic year: $750. Apply by April 1.

Additional Information: Of all students currently enrolled full time, 40% benefited from one or more of the listed financial assistance programs. Application and information available online at https://www.e-fao.com/efao_site.html?OEID=011117&ViewID={10EF815B-422E-4C55-B8CD-BDBD3063BA18}.

Internships/Practica: Students in the master's program have practica tied to their coursework beginning in the first semester of their programs. Internships are required of any students seeking a Pupil Personnel Services (PPS) credential postmasters or as part of the doctoral program in educational psychology. The 1,200 internships hours are completed at a public school district. Those in the doctoral program who are interested in clinical licensure must complete a separate psychology internship.

Housing and Day Care: No on-campus housing is available. No on-campus day care facilities are available.

Employment of Department Graduates:

Master's Degree Graduates: Of those who graduated in the academic year 2006–2007, the following categories and numbers represent the postgraduate activities and employment of master's degree graduates: Enrolled in a postdoctoral residency/fellowship (n/a), employed in independent practice (n/a), total from the above (master's) (0).

Doctoral Degree Graduates: Of those who graduated in the academic year 2006–2007, the following categories and numbers represent the postgraduate activities and employment of doctoral degree graduates: Enrolled in a psychology doctoral program (n/a), total from the above (doctoral) (0).

Additional Information:

Orientation, Objectives, and Emphasis of Department: Programs train students with the skills necessary to work with students, teachers, parents, and other school professionals in today's school environments. The curriculum includes professional skills, professional roles courses, applied research, and professional concepts. The master's degree program prepares students to gain the PPS (Pupil Personnel Services) credential that allows them to practice in California's schools. Students take afternoon, evening, and weekend classes and engage in fieldwork. At the doctoral level students complete special focus area courses, examples of which include adolescent stress and coping, school culture and administration, pediatric psychology, infant and preschool mental health, child neuropsychology, and provision of services for children in alternative placement. Students also complete a PsyD project.

Information for Students With Physical Disabilities: Go to About Alliant > Student Life and Athletics > Disability Services at the following Web site: http://www.alliant.edu.

Application Information:

Send to Alliant International University, Admissions Processing Center, 10455 Pomerado Road, San Diego, CA 92131-1799. Application available online. URL of online application: http://www.alliant.edu/applyonline/. Students are admitted in the Fall, application deadline June 1; Spring, application deadline varies; Summer, application deadline varies. Programs have rolling admissions. See information about timelines at http://www.alliant.edu/admissions/gradtimelines.htm or contact the admissions office at 1-866-U-ALLIANT. *Fee:* $70. A limited number of fee waivers are available for those with significant financial need.

Alliant International University: San Francisco

Programs in Organizational Psychology
Marshall Goldsmith School of Management
One Beach Street
San Francisco, CA 94133-1221
Telephone: (415) 955-2146
Fax: (415) 955-2179
E-mail: *jaquino@alliant.edu*
Web: *http://www.mgsm.alliant.edu/*

Department Information:

1983. Program Director: Ira Levin, PhD. Number of faculty: total—full-time 5, part-time 11; women—full-time 3, part-time 5; minority—part-time 3; women minority—part-time 1.

Programs and Degrees Offered:

Listed in the following order: Program area, degree type (T if terminal Master's), number awarded 7/06–6/07. Organizational Psychology PhD (Doctor of Philosophy) 4, Organizational Psychology MA/MS (Master of Arts/Science) (T) 2, Organizational Development MA/MS (Master of Arts/Science) (T) 5, Organizational Psychology Respecialization Diploma 0.

Student Applications/Admissions:

Student Applications

Organizational Psychology PhD (Doctor of Philosophy)—Applications 2007–2008, 19. Total applicants accepted 2007–2008, 11. Number full-time enrolled (new admits only) 2007–2008, 9. Number part-time enrolled (new admits only) 2007–2008, 1. Total enrolled 2007–2008 full-time, 21, part-time, 32. Openings 2008–2009, 12. The median number of years required for completion of a degree in 2006–2007 were 4. The number of students enrolled full- and part-time who were dismissed or voluntarily withdrew from this program area in 2007–2008 were 0. *Organizational Psychology MA/MS (Master of Arts/Science)*—Applications 2007–2008, 5. Total applicants accepted 2007–2008, 3. Number full-time enrolled (new admits only) 2007–2008, 0. Number part-time enrolled (new admits only) 2007–2008, 0. Openings 2008–2009, 15. The median number of years required for completion of a degree in 2006–2007 were 4. *Organizational Development MA/MS (Master of Arts/Science)*—Applications 2007–2008, 3. Total applicants accepted 2007–2008, 1. Number full-time enrolled (new admits only) 2007–2008, 0. Number part-time enrolled (new admits only) 2007–2008, 0. Total enrolled 2007–2008 full-time, 1, part-time, 4. Openings 2008–2009, 5. The median number of years required for completion of a degree in 2006–2007 were 2. The number of students enrolled full- and part-time who were dismissed or voluntarily withdrew from this program area in 2007–2008 were 0. *Organizational Psychology Respecialization Diploma*—Applications 2007–2008, 1. Total applicants accepted 2007–2008, 1. Number part-time enrolled (new admits only) 2007–2008, 0. Openings 2008–2009, 2.

The number of students enrolled full- and part-time who were dismissed or voluntarily withdrew from this program area in 2007–2008 were 0.

Admissions Requirements:

Scores: Entries appear in this order: required test or GPA, minimum score (if required), median score of students entering in 2007–2008. Master's Programs: overall undergraduate GPA 3.0; psychology GPA 3.0. Doctoral Programs: overall undergraduate GPA 3.0; psychology GPA 3.0. A master's degree is not required for entry to the doctoral program; however, if a master's degree is held at the time of admissions, the minimum 3.0 GPA applies.

Other Criteria: (importance of criteria rated low, medium, or high): research experience—high, work experience—high, extracurricular activity—low, clinically related public service—low, GPA—high, letters of recommendation—high, interview—high, statement of goals and objectives—high. Admission criteria vary by program and program level. For additional information on admission requirements, go to http://www.alliant.edu/wps/wcm/connect/website/Home/Admissions/.

Student Characteristics: The following represents characteristics of students in 2007–2008 in all graduate psychology programs in the department: Female—full-time 12, part-time 29; Male—full-time 13, part-time 12; African American/Black—full-time 3, part-time 4; Hispanic/Latino(a)—full-time 0, part-time 3; Asian/Pacific Islander—full-time 3, part-time 8; American Indian/Alaska Native—full-time 0, part-time 0; Caucasian/White—full-time 13, part-time 22; Multi-ethnic—full-time 0, part-time 0; students subject to the Americans With Disabilities Act—full-time 1, part-time 1; Unknown ethnicity—full-time 6, part-time 4; International students who hold an F-1 or J-1 Visa—full-time 3, part-time 1.

Financial Information/Assistance:

Tuition for Full-Time Study: *Master's:* State residents: $915 per credit hour; Nonstate residents: $915 per credit hour. *Doctoral:* State residents: $915 per credit hour; Nonstate residents: $915 per credit hour. Tuition is subject to change. Tuition costs vary by program. See the following Web site for updates and changes in tuition costs: http://www.alliant.edu/wps/wcm/connect/website/Home/Admissions/Tuition+and+Fees/.

Financial Assistance:

First-Year Students: Research assistantships available for first year. Average amount paid per academic year: $1,000. Average number of hours worked per week: 10. Apply by see department. Fellowships and scholarships available for first year. Average amount paid per academic year: $1,500. Apply by February 15.

Advanced Students: Teaching assistantships available for advanced students. Average amount paid per academic year: $3,000. Average number of hours worked per week: 10. Apply by see department. Research assistantships available for advanced students. Average amount paid per academic year: $1,000. Average number of hours worked per week: 10. Apply by see department. Fellowships and scholarships available for advanced students. Average amount paid per academic year: $1,500. Apply by April 15.

Additional Information: Of all students currently enrolled full time, 53% benefited from one or more of the listed financial assistance programs. Application and information available online at https://www.e-fao.com/efao_site.html?OEID=011117&ViewID={10EF815B-422E-4C55-B8CD-BDBD3063BA18}.

Internships/Practica: Organizational doctoral students develop skills through practical training experiences during the 3rd and 4th years of the program. Students usually devote 8–40 hours per week to field placement assignments. Some training sites are local to the student's campus location; occasionally students find internships at out-of-area or out-of-state sites that meet their professional training needs. Placements are available in a variety of settings including consulting firms, major corporations, government agencies, healthcare organizations, and nonprofit agencies. Students in the master's programs have a one semester applied experience with supervision.

Housing and Day Care: No on-campus housing is available. No on-campus day care facilities are available.

Employment of Department Graduates:

Master's Degree Graduates: Of those who graduated in the academic year 2006–2007, the following categories and numbers represent the postgraduate activities and employment of master's degree graduates: Enrolled in a postdoctoral residency/fellowship (n/a), employed in independent practice (n/a), total from the above (master's) (0).

Doctoral Degree Graduates: Of those who graduated in the academic year 2006–2007, the following categories and numbers represent the postgraduate activities and employment of doctoral degree graduates: Enrolled in a psychology doctoral program (n/a), total from the above (doctoral) (0).

Additional Information:

Orientation, Objectives, and Emphasis of Department: Doctoral students gain exposure to three core areas of study: organizational theory, grounded in the behavioral sciences; quantitative and qualitative research methods; and professional practice skill development. The program focuses on research and practice in organizational consulting at the individual, team, and system levels; collaborative strategic change; organizational culture and leadership; multicultural competence; executive coaching and mentoring; organizational innovation, creativity, and knowledge management. Programs are structured so students can attend at a moderated pace—this allows students to continue working while in their programs. Master's-level programs provide solid education in organizational psychology and behavior; they are suitable for students who may wish to continue on to doctoral education. The master's in organization development is primarily for those who have backgrounds in other fields and wish to move into a managerial or organizational development position; three concentrations are offered in systemic change in a global context, building healthy organizations, and applied research. The master's in organizational psychology provides a stronger research foundation.

Special Facilities or Resources: Marshall Goldsmith School of Management offers the Organizational Consulting Center (OCC). Students may have opportunities to participate with faculty and OCC associates on consulting projects during their programs.

Information for Students With Physical Disabilities: Go to About Alliant > Student Life and Athletics > Disability Services at the following Web site: http://www.alliant.edu.

Application Information:
Send to Alliant International University, Admissions Processing Center, 10455 Pomerado Road, San Diego, CA 92131-1799. Application available online. URL of online application: http://www.alliant.edu/applyonline/. Students are admitted in the Fall, application deadline February 1; Spring, application deadline varies. Programs have rolling admissions. Doctoral program has a February 1 deadline in order to provide a response by April 1 for applicants who need a decision by that date. Master's programs have later deadlines. Programs accept applications and admit students on a space-available basis after any stated deadlines. For complete information on deadlines contact the admissions office at 1-866-U-ALLIANT. *Fee:* $70. A limited number of fee waivers are available for those with significant financial need.

Antioch University, Santa Barbara

Graduate Psychology Programs
801 Garden Street, Suite 101
Santa Barbara, CA 93101
Telephone: (805) 962-8179
Fax: (805) 962-4786
E-mail: *mharway@antiochsb.edu*
Web: *http://www.antiochsb.edu*

Department Information:
1977. Chairperson: Catherine Radecki-Bush, PhD Number of faculty: total—full-time 8, part-time 44; women—full-time 6, part-time 22; total—minority—full-time 1, part-time 11; women minority—part-time 6; faculty subject to the Americans With Disabilities Act 1.

Programs and Degrees Offered:
Listed in the following order: Program area, degree type (T if terminal Master's), number awarded 7/06–6/07. Clinical Psychology PsyD (Doctor of Psychology) 0, Clinical Psychology MA/MS (Master of Arts/Science) (T) 55.

Student Applications/Admissions:
Student Applications
Clinical Psychology PsyD (Doctor of Psychology)—Applications 2007–2008, 48. Total applicants accepted 2007–2008, 24. Number full-time enrolled (new admits only) 2007–2008, 16. Number part-time enrolled (new admits only) 2007–2008, 0. Openings 2008–2009, 16. The median number of years required for completion of a degree in 2006–2007 were 4. The number of students enrolled full- and part-time who were dismissed or voluntarily withdrew from this program area in 2007–2008 were 0. *Clinical Psychology MA/MS (Master of Arts/Science)*—Applications 2007–2008, 95. Total applicants accepted 2007–2008, 69. Number full-time enrolled (new admits only) 2007–2008, 50. Number part-time enrolled (new admits only) 2007–2008, 9. Total enrolled 2007–2008 full-time, 116, part-time, 27. Openings 2008–2009, 70. The median number of years required for completion of a degree in 2006–2007 were 2. The number of students enrolled full- and part-time who were dismissed or voluntarily withdrew from this program area in 2007–2008 were 2.

Admissions Requirements:
Scores: Entries appear in this order: required test or GPA, minimum score (if required), median score of students entering in 2007–2008. Master's Programs: overall undergraduate GPA no minimum stated; last 2 years GPA no minimum stated; psychology GPA no minimum stated. No minimum GPA for MA Program but usually 3.0. Doctoral Programs: last 2 years GPA no minimum stated; psychology GPA no minimum stated. We also accept outstanding narrative evaluations from institutions like Antioch that do not calculate GPAs.
Other Criteria: (importance of criteria rated low, medium, or high): research experience—low, work experience—medium, extracurricular activity—low, clinically related public service—medium, GPA—high, letters of recommendation—medium, interview—high, statement of goals and objectives—high, writing sample—high. The doctoral program requires two essays in lieu of GREs that are used to assess analytic and critical thinking. These are heavily weighted. For additional information on admission requirements, go to http://www.antiochsb.edu.

Student Characteristics: The following represents characteristics of students in 2007–2008 in all graduate psychology programs in the department: Female—full-time 130, part-time 25; Male—full-time 29, part-time 2; African American/Black—full-time 5, part-time 1; Hispanic/Latino(a)—full-time 30, part-time 5; Asian/Pacific Islander—full-time 7, part-time 1; American Indian/Alaska Native—full-time 0, part-time 0; Caucasian/White—full-time 108, part-time 18; Multi-ethnic—full-time 6, part-time 1; students subject to the Americans With Disabilities Act—full-time 6, part-time 2; Unknown ethnicity—full-time 3, part-time 1; International students who hold an F-1 or J-1 Visa—full-time 6, part-time 0.

Financial Information/Assistance:
Tuition for Full-Time Study: *Master's:* State residents: per academic year $21,764, $545 per credit hour; Nonstate residents: per academic year $21,764, $545 per credit hour. *Doctoral:* State residents: per academic year $19,959, $530 per credit hour; Nonstate residents: per academic year $19,959, $530 per credit hour. Tuition is subject to change. Tuition costs vary by program. See the following Web site for updates and changes in tuition costs: http://www.antiochsb.edu.

Financial Assistance:
First-Year Students: No information provided.
Advanced Students: No information provided.
Additional Information: Of all students currently enrolled full time, 70% benefited from one or more of the listed financial assistance programs. Note: above are for the doctoral program.

Internships/Practica: Traineeships are available in community agencies, schools, and clinics, in Santa Barbara, San Luis Obispo, and Ventura Counties. Students may find placements working with children, adolescents, and seniors; with clients in recovery from chemical dependency; with survivors of sexual abuse, domestic violence, and child abuse; with mental health clients; with court-referred clients; and with adults, couples, and families. Doctoral practica have been developed in a variety of settings also in Santa Barbara, San Luis Obispo, and Ventura Counties but also in Los Angeles County where some of our students reside. Our doctoral students are not yet at the internship stage.

Housing and Day Care: No on-campus housing is available. No on-campus day care facilities are available.

Employment of Department Graduates:

Master's Degree Graduates: Of those who graduated in the academic year 2006–2007, the following categories and numbers represent the postgraduate activities and employment of master's degree graduates: Enrolled in a postdoctoral residency/fellowship (n/a), employed in independent practice (n/a), total from the above (master's) (0).

Doctoral Degree Graduates: Of those who graduated in the academic year 2006–2007, the following categories and numbers represent the postgraduate activities and employment of doctoral degree graduates: Enrolled in a psychology doctoral program (n/a), total from the above (doctoral) (0).

Additional Information:

Orientation, Objectives, and Emphasis of Department: The MA Clinical Psychology program is committed to the education and training of students to develop (a) critical thinking and reflective learning in the acquisition of psychological knowledge; (b) basic skills in clinical psychology required to become ethical, professional therapists; (c) self-awareness, particularly as it pertains to professional clinical, practice; (d) awareness of self as an integral part of families, the mental health community, and local communities; and (e) understanding of diversity, including culture, ethnicity, gender, sexual orientation, age, and theoretical orientation. The MA Psychology—Individualized Concentration allows students, to define and develop expertise in a particular area of interest. Past students have completed concentrations in Human Development, Feminist Psychology, and Interpersonal Relationships. For some areas of concentration such as Organizational Psychology and Professional, Development, and Career Counseling, a core curriculum has been developed. This nonclinical degree program is for students interested in pursuing professional careers in consulting, education, program development, business, and government, as well as for students interested in applying to doctoral degree programs. The doctoral program is a postmaster's PsyD degree in Clinical Psychology with a Family Psychology emphasis and a Family Forensic Concentration. We also have a post bachelor's entry track (PrePsyD).

Special Facilities or Resources: Faculty are all practicing professionals in their respective areas of expertise. We are seeking funds for a training clinic to serve a primarily Spanish-speaking clientele with training to be done in Spanish.

Application Information:

Send to Admissions Office, Antioch University Santa Barbara, 801 Garden Street, Santa Barbara, CA 93101. Application available online. URL of online application: http://www.antiochsb.edu. Students are admitted in the Fall, application deadline January 31 and July 15; Winter, application deadline November 16; Programs have rolling admissions. PsyD Program Fall admit only. Priority application deadline is January 31. MA Psychology programs have rolling admissions. *Fee:* $60. Financial need.

Argosy University/Orange County

Psychology
School of Psychology and Behavioral Sciences
3501 West Sunflower Avenue
Santa Ana, CA 92704
Telephone: (714) 338-6200
Fax: (714) 437-1284
E-mail: *gbruss@argosy.edu*
Web: *http://www.argosy.edu*

Department Information:

2001. Program Chair, Clinical Psychology: Gary Bruss, PhD. Number of faculty: total—full-time 13, part-time 24; women—full-time 7, part-time 17; total—minority—full-time 7, part-time 11; women minority—full-time 5, part-time 8; faculty subject to the Americans With Disabilities Act 7.

Programs and Degrees Offered:

Listed in the following order: Program area, degree type (T if terminal Master's), number awarded 7/06–6/07. PsyD (Doctor of Psychology) 9, Counseling Psychology EdD (Doctor of Education), Counseling Psychology MA/MS (Master of Arts/Science) (T), Clinical Psychology MA/MS (Master of Arts/Science) (T), Forensic Psychology MA/MS (Master of Arts/Science) (T) 0.

Student Applications/Admissions:

Student Applications

PsyD (Doctor of Psychology)—Applications 2007–2008, 90. Number full-time enrolled (new admits only) 2007–2008, 24. Number part-time enrolled (new admits only) 2007–2008, 0. Openings 2008–2009, 35. The median number of years required for completion of a degree in 2006–2007 were 5. The number of students enrolled full- and part-time who were dismissed or voluntarily withdrew from this program area in 2007–2008 were 7. *Counseling Psychology EdD (Doctor of Education)*—The median number of years required for completion of a degree in 2006–2007 were 4. *Counseling Psychology MA/MS (Master of Arts/Science)*—The median number of years required for completion of a degree in 2006–2007 were 3. *Clinical Psychology MA/MS (Master of Arts/Science)*—Applications 2007–2008, 48. Total applicants accepted 2007–2008, 39. Number full-time enrolled (new admits only) 2007–2008, 24. Number part-time enrolled (new admits only) 2007–2008, 3. Total enrolled 2007–2008 full-time, 55, part-time, 13. Openings 2008–2009, 30. The median number of years required for completion of a degree in 2006–2007 were 2. The number of students enrolled full- and part-time who were dismissed or voluntarily withdrew from this program area in 2007–2008 were 1. *Forensic Psychology MA/MS (Master of Arts/Science)*—The median number of years required for completion of a degree in 2006–2007 were 2.

Admissions Requirements:

Scores: Entries appear in this order: required test or GPA, minimum score (if required), median score of students entering in 2007–2008. Master's Programs: overall undergraduate GPA 3.0, 3.1; last 2 years GPA 3.0, 3.1; psychology GPA 3.0, 3.1. Doctoral Programs: overall undergraduate GPA 3.25, 3.45; last 2 years GPA 3.25, 3.5; psychology GPA 3.25, 3.5. PsyD program requires a minimum GPA of 3.25 in total undergraduate, last 2 years undergraduate, and undergraduate psychology courses. EdD Counseling Psychology program requires a minimum GPA of 3.25 in Master's Programs (required for admission to the program). MA programs require 3.0 minimum undergraduate psychology GPA and last 2 years of course work.

Other Criteria: (importance of criteria rated low, medium, or high): research experience—low, work experience—medium, extracurricular activity—medium, clinically related public service—medium, GPA—high, letters of recommendation—high, interview—high, statement of goals and objectives—high. High emphasis on work experience for doctoral programs, although outstanding presentation in areas related to GPA, recommendation letters, interview, and personal statement can offset a deficit in work experience. Letters of recommendation from work, prior training, and/or academic references are expected for all programs. Emphasis on both clinical and academic references for doctoral applicants. For additional information on admission requirements, go to http://www.argosy.edu.

Student Characteristics: The following represents characteristics of students in 2007–2008 in all graduate psychology programs in the department: Caucasian/White—full-time 0, part-time 0; students subject to the Americans With Disabilities Act—full-time 4, part-time 2; Unknown ethnicity—full-time 0, part-time 0.

Financial Information/Assistance:

Tuition for Full-Time Study: *Master's:* State residents: per academic year $12,500, $500 per credit hour; Nonstate residents: per academic year $12,500, $500 per credit hour. *Doctoral:* State residents: per academic year $13,000, $650 per credit hour; Nonstate residents: per academic year $13,000, $650 per credit hour. Tuition is not available at this time. Tuition is subject to change. Tuition costs vary by program. See the following Web site for updates and changes in tuition costs: http://www.argosy.edu. Higher tuition cost for this program: Clinical Programs: MA, PsyD, $895; MA Counseling, $500; EdD Counseling, $650.

Financial Assistance:

First-Year Students: Teaching assistantships available for first year. Fellowships and scholarships available for first year. Average amount paid per academic year: $2,000. Average number of hours worked per week: 3. Apply by June 30. Tuition remission given: partial.

Advanced Students: Teaching assistantships available for advanced students. Average amount paid per academic year: $1,000. Average number of hours worked per week: 6. Apply by June 30. Tuition remission given: partial. Research assistantships available for advanced students. Average amount paid per academic year: $2,000. Average number of hours worked per week: 3. Apply by June 30. Tuition remission given: partial. Fellowships and scholarships available for advanced students. Average amount paid per academic year: $3,000. Average number of hours worked per week: 5. Apply by June 30. Tuition remission given: partial.

Additional Information: Of all students currently enrolled full time, 7% benefited from one or more of the listed financial assistance programs. Application and information available online at http://www.argosy.edu.

Internships/Practica: Doctoral Degree (PsyD): For those doctoral students for whom a professional internship was required in this program prior to graduation, (19) students applied for an internship in 2006–2007, with (19) students obtaining an internship. Of those students who obtained an internship, (12) were paid internships. Of those students who obtained an internship, (2) students placed in APA/CPA-accredited internships, (7) students placed in internships not APA/CPA-accredited, but listed with the Association of Psychology Postdoctoral and Internship Centers (APPIC), (0) students placed in internships conforming to guidelines of the Council of Directors of School Psychology Programs (CDSPP), (10) students placed in internships that were not APA/CPA-accredited, APPIC or CDSPP listed. The specific clinical focus of the practicum varies according to the student's program, training needs, professional interests and goals, and the availability of practicum sites. MA Counseling and Clinical practica focus on training students in couples/family counseling and therapy skills. The PsyD Clinical Psychology practica provide 1 year of psychodiagnostic assessment training and 1 year of therapy training. The program is committed to finding a wide range of practicum sites to provide many options for student professional exposure and development.

Housing and Day Care: No on-campus housing is available. No on-campus day care facilities are available.

Employment of Department Graduates:

Master's Degree Graduates: Of those who graduated in the academic year 2006–2007, the following categories and numbers represent the postgraduate activities and employment of master's degree graduates: Enrolled in a psychology doctoral program (0), enrolled in another graduate/professional program (0), enrolled in a postdoctoral residency/fellowship (n/a), employed in independent practice (n/a), employed in an academic position at a university (0), employed in an academic position at a 2-year/4-year college (0), employed in other positions at a higher education institution (0), employed in a professional position in a school system (0), employed in business or industry (0), employed in government agency (0), employed in a community mental health/counseling center (0), employed in a hospital/medical center (0), still seeking employment (0), other employment position (0), total from the above (master's) (0).

Doctoral Degree Graduates: Of those who graduated in the academic year 2006–2007, the following categories and numbers represent the postgraduate activities and employment of doctoral degree graduates: Enrolled in a psychology doctoral program (n/a), enrolled in a postdoctoral residency/fellowship (0), employed in independent practice (1), employed in an academic position at a university (0), employed in an academic position at a 2-year/4-year college (0), employed in other positions at a higher education institution (0), employed in a professional position in a school system (0), employed in business or industry (0), employed in government agency (0), employed in a community mental health/counseling center (6), employed in a hospital/medical center (2), still seeking employment (0), other employment position (0), total from the above (doctoral) (9).

Additional Information:

Orientation, Objectives, and Emphasis of Department: The graduate programs in psychology are designed to educate and train practitioners, with an additional emphasis on scholarly training in the doctoral programs. Courses and fieldwork experiences embrace multiple theoretical and intervention approaches, and a range of psychodiagnostic techniques (in the clinical programs), all of which are designed to serve a wide and diverse range of populations. Two PsyD concentrations are available in Forensic Psychology and in Child/Adolescent Psychology. Students are taught by faculty with strong teaching and practitioner skills, with a strong focus on developing students with the fundamental clinical, counseling, and relevant scholarly competencies required to pursue careers in psychology. Courses in applied and academic areas are considered to be critical in the development of practioners with the skills to develop, innovate, implement, and assess delivery of services to clientele in clinical, counseling, and educational types of settings.

Information for Students With Physical Disabilities: See the following Web site for more information: http://www.argosyu.edu.

Application Information:
Send to Director of Admissions, c/o Argosy University/Orange County, 3501 West Sunflower Avenue, Santa Ana, CA 92704. Application available online. URL of online application: http://www.argosyu.edu. Students are admitted in the Fall, application deadline May 15; Spring, application deadline October 15; Summer, application deadline March 30. We offer a year-round rolling admissions process for both the EdD-CP and MACP programs, with admissions points for Fall, Spring, and Summer semesters. PsyD and MA Clinical applicant deadlines are January 15 for fall, with a May 15 deadline if spaces are available, and October 15 for Spring term with a November 15 deadline if spaces are still available. *Fee:* $50.

Argosy University/San Francisco Bay Area

Clinical Psychology
College of Psychology and Behavioral Sciences
1005 Atlantic Avenue
Alameda, CA 94501
Telephone: (510) 217-4700
Fax: (510) 217-4800
E-mail: *plytle@argosy.edu*
Web: *http://www.argosy.edu*

Department Information:
1999. Program Chair: Pauline Lytle, PhD. Number of faculty: total—full-time 10, part-time 23; women—full-time 8, part-time 16; total—minority—full-time 2, part-time 6; women minority—full-time 1, part-time 4; faculty subject to the Americans With Disabilities Act 1.

Programs and Degrees Offered:
Listed in the following order: Program area, degree type (T if terminal Master's), number awarded 7/06–6/07. Clinical Psychology MA/MS (Master of Arts/Science) (T) 2, Clinical Psychology PsyD (Doctor of Psychology) 27.

APA Accreditation: Clinical PsyD (Doctor of Psychology).

Student Applications/Admissions:
Student Applications
Clinical Psychology MA/MS (Master of Arts/Science)—Applications 2007–2008, 64. Total applicants accepted 2007–2008, 36. Number full-time enrolled (new admits only) 2007–2008, 11. Number part-time enrolled (new admits only) 2007–2008, 1. Total enrolled 2007–2008 full-time, 17, part-time, 2. Openings 2008–2009, 8. The median number of years required for completion of a degree in 2006–2007 were 2. The number of students enrolled full- and part-time who were dismissed or voluntarily withdrew from this program area in 2007–2008 were 1. *Clinical Psychology PsyD (Doctor of Psychology)*—Applications 2007–2008, 231. Total applicants accepted 2007–2008, 126. Number full-time enrolled (new admits only) 2007–2008, 58. Number part-time enrolled (new admits only) 2007–2008, 0. Total enrolled 2007–2008 full-time, 228, part-time, 12. Openings 2008–2009, 80. The median number of years required for completion of a degree in 2006–2007 were 4. The number of students enrolled full- and part-time who were dismissed or voluntarily withdrew from this program area in 2007–2008 were 1.

Admissions Requirements:
Scores: Entries appear in this order: required test or GPA, minimum score (if required), median score of students entering in 2007–2008. Master's Programs: overall undergraduate GPA 3.0; last 2 years GPA 3.0; psychology GPA 3.0. Doctoral Programs: overall undergraduate GPA 3.25; last 2 years GPA 3.25; psychology GPA no minimum stated.
Other Criteria: (importance of criteria rated low, medium, or high): research experience—medium, work experience—medium, extracurricular activity—medium, clinically related public service—medium, GPA—high, letters of recommendation—high, interview—high, statement of goals and objectives—high, TOEFL as needed—high, undergraduate major in psychology—medium, specific undergraduate psychology courses taken—medium. For additional information on admission requirements, go to http://www.argosy.edu.

Student Characteristics: The following represents characteristics of students in 2007–2008 in all graduate psychology programs in the department: Female—full-time 198, part-time 10; Male—full-time 47, part-time 4; African American/Black—full-time 28, part-time 3; Hispanic/Latino(a)—full-time 19, part-time 0; Asian/Pacific Islander—full-time 27, part-time 1; American Indian/Alaska Native—full-time 2, part-time 0; Caucasian/White—full-time 151, part-time 8; Multi-ethnic—full-time 0, part-time 0; students subject to the Americans With Disabilities Act—full-time 8, part-time 0; Unknown ethnicity—full-time 18, part-time 2; International students who hold an F-1 or J-1 Visa—full-time 8, part-time 1.

Financial Information/Assistance:
Tuition for Full-Time Study: *Master's:* State residents: $895 per credit hour; Nonstate residents: $895 per credit hour. *Doctoral:* State residents: $895 per credit hour; Nonstate residents: $895 per credit hour. Tuition is subject to change. Additional fees are assessed to students beyond the costs of tuition for the following: Child Abuse Reporting Class, Professional Liability Insurance, Student Activity Fee, Technology Fee. See the following Web site for updates and changes in tuition costs: http://www.argosy.edu.

Financial Assistance:
First-Year Students: Fellowships and scholarships available for first year. Average amount paid per academic year: $1,000. Apply by August 25. Tuition remission given: full and partial.

Advanced Students: Teaching assistantships available for advanced students. Average amount paid per academic year: $800. Average number of hours worked per week: 12. Research assistantships available for advanced students. Traineeships available for advanced students. Fellowships and scholarships available for advanced students. Average amount paid per academic year: $1,000. Apply by August 25.

Additional Information: Of all students currently enrolled full time, 90% benefited from one or more of the listed financial assistance programs. Application and information available online at http://www.argosy.edu.

Internships/Practica: Doctoral Degree (Clinical Psychology PsyD): For those doctoral students for whom a professional internship was required in this program prior to graduation, (45) students applied for an internship in 2006–2007, with (45) students obtaining an internship. Of those students who obtained an internship, (16) were paid internships. Of those students who obtained an internship, (9) students placed in APA/CPA-accredited internships, (7) students placed in internships not APA/CPA accredited, but listed with the Association of Psychology Postdoctoral and Internship Centers (APPIC), (0) students placed in internships conforming to guidelines of the Council of Directors of School Psychology Programs (CDSPP), (29) students placed in internships that were not APA/CPA-accredited, APPIC or CDSPP listed. Argosy University SFBA students are encouraged to choose the internship experience that best meets their long term training goals. Students from our program are able to apply to both APPIC (including APA internships) and CAPIC (California Psychology Internship Council) internship agencies. CAPIC is a collaboration between Bay Area psychology graduate programs and internship programs in California. This allows students to have the option of applying to either a full-time or a half-time internship. Argosy University SFBA's database of approved San Francisco Bay Area practicum sites includes community mental health centers; consortiums; state, community, and private psychiatric hospitals, medical and trauma centers; university counseling centers; schools; correctional facilities; residential treatment programs; independent and group practices; and corporate settings. Some sites serve the general population while others service specific populations (e.g., children, adolescents, geriatrics, particular ethnic or racial groups, criminal offenders, etc.) or clinical problems (e.g., chemical dependency, eating disorders, medical and psychiatric rehabilitation, etc.). Students are required to seek a combination of practicum placements that will provide a breadth of experience including working with severely disordered clients, children or adolescents, and adults. The Training Department works throughout the year to maintain positive relationships with existing sites and to affiliate itself with new sites throughout the Bay Area. Argosy University SFBA strongly encourages students to complete their training in settings that provide opportunities to work with diverse populations. It is essential that students learn to work with people who are different from themselves (e.g., race, ethnicity, disability, sexual orientation, etc.) in a supervised setting where they can learn the skills, knowledge, and attitudes necessary to practice as a competent clinician. For additional information on education and training outcomes for our programs, see the following Web site: (http://www.argosy.edu/colleges/ProgramDetail.aspx?ID=732.

Housing and Day Care: No on-campus housing is available. No on-campus day care facilities are available.

Employment of Department Graduates:

Master's Degree Graduates: Of those who graduated in the academic year 2006–2007, the following categories and numbers represent the postgraduate activities and employment of master's degree graduates: Enrolled in a psychology doctoral program (0), enrolled in another graduate/professional program (0), enrolled in a postdoctoral residency/fellowship (n/a), employed in independent practice (n/a), do not know (0), total from the above (master's) (0).

Doctoral Degree Graduates: Of those who graduated in the academic year 2006–2007, the following categories and numbers represent the postgraduate activities and employment of doctoral degree graduates: Enrolled in a psychology doctoral program (n/a), enrolled in another graduate/professional program (0), total from the above (doctoral) (0).

Additional Information:

Orientation, Objectives, and Emphasis of Department: The clinical orientation of the program is integrative. All major theoretical orientations are presented including psychodynamic, family systems, developmental, cognitive, and humanistic.

Special Facilities or Resources: Argosy University San Francisco Bay Area campus emphasizes specialized hands-on clinical training through our Intensive Clinical Training facility. Through the Intensive Clinical Training series, students work directly with clients referred from the community while being observed by a team through a one-way mirror. The team consists of the instructor and/or clinical assistant and fellow students who participate in pre- and posttherapy sessions in which they provide input and feedback about the therapeutic process. Each client session is guided by the instructor/assistant who, through the use of a microphone, provides clinical guidance and interventions directly to the student therapist through an earpiece worn by the student. As the session progresses, the instructor/assistant educates the team about the dynamics of the therapist/client interaction and the treatment approach. Students may participate on three levels: (a) as a clinical observer and a member of the team; (b) as a student therapist working directly with clients, and (c) as a clinical assistant in concert with our Supervision/Consultation course.

Information for Students With Physical Disabilities: Contact lbundy@argosy.edu.

Application Information:

Send to Admissions Department Argosy University, San Francisco Bay Area, 1005 Atlantic Avenue, Alameda, CA 94501. Application available online. URL of online application: https://www.app.applyyourself.com/?id=arg-grad. Students are admitted in the Fall, application deadline January; Spring, application deadline October; Programs have rolling admissions. January 15 priority deadline for Fall. May 15 final deadlline depending on space availability. Rolling admissions depending on availability. *Fee:* $50.

Azusa Pacific University
Department of Graduate Psychology
901 East Alosta, P.O. Box 7000
Azusa, CA 91702-7000
Telephone: (626) 815-5008
Fax: (626) 815-5015
E-mail: *sscott@apu.edu*
Web: *http://www.apu.edu/ Search: Clinical Psychology*

Department Information:

1976. Chairperson: Sheryn T. Scott, PhD. Number of faculty: total—full-time 12, part-time 15; women—full-time 6, part-time 10; total—minority—full-time 2, part-time 1; women minority—full-time 1.

Programs and Degrees Offered:

Listed in the following order: Program area, degree type (T if terminal Master's), number awarded 7/06–6/07. Clinical Psychology MA/MS (Master of Arts/Science) (T) 48, Clinical Psychology PsyD (Doctor of Psychology) 7, Clinical Psychology MA/MS (Master of Arts/Science) 20.

APA Accreditation: Clinical PsyD (Doctor of Psychology).

Student Applications/Admissions:

Student Applications

Clinical Psychology MA/MS (Master of Arts/Science)—Applications 2007–2008, 150. Total applicants accepted 2007–2008, 89. Number full-time enrolled (new admits only) 2007–2008, 63. Number part-time enrolled (new admits only) 2007–2008, 3. Total enrolled 2007–2008 full-time, 148, part-time, 16. Openings 2008–2009, 65. The median number of years required for completion of a degree in 2006–2007 were 3. The number of students enrolled full- and part-time who were dismissed or voluntarily withdrew from this program area in 2007–2008 were 2. *Clinical Psychology PsyD (Doctor of Psychology)*—Applications 2007–2008, 49. Total applicants accepted 2007–2008, 29. Number full-time enrolled (new admits only) 2007–2008, 25. Number part-time enrolled (new admits only) 2007–2008, 0. Total enrolled 2007–2008 full-time, 65, part-time, 43. Openings 2008–2009, 28. The median number of years required for completion of a degree in 2006–2007 were 5. The number of students enrolled full- and part-time who were dismissed or voluntarily withdrew from this program area in 2007–2008 were 2. *Clinical Psychology MA/MS (Master of Arts/Science)*—Applications 2007–2008, 121. Total applicants accepted 2007–2008, 33. Number full-time enrolled (new admits only) 2007–2008, 23. Number part-time enrolled (new admits only) 2007–2008, 0. Openings 2008–2009, 25. The median number of years required for completion of a degree in 2006–2007 were 2. The number of students enrolled full- and part-time who were dismissed or voluntarily withdrew from this program area in 2007–2008 were 0.

Admissions Requirements:

Scores: Entries appear in this order: required test or GPA, minimum score (if required), median score of students entering in 2007–2008. Master's Programs: overall undergraduate GPA 3.0; psychology GPA 3.0. Doctoral Programs: GRE-V no minimum stated; GRE-Q no minimum stated; overall undergraduate GPA 3.0; last 2 years GPA 3.0, 3.0; psychology GPA 3.0. Note: The GRE General exam, including verbal, quantitative, and analytical writing assessment is required. Scores are one consideration in the entire application. Verbal ability is important to succeed in the PsyD program. GRE Analytical Writing Score is required, so if applicant took GRE prior to inclusion of that section, she or he must take that section of the restructured exam.

Other Criteria: (importance of criteria rated low, medium, or high): GRE/MAT scores—medium, research experience—medium, work experience—medium, extracurricular activity—medium, clinically related public service—medium, GPA—high, letters of recommendation—high, interview—high, statement of goals and objectives—high. No GRE/MAT scores required for MA; Work experience of medium importance for MA; Research experience of medium importance for MA; Clinically Related Public Service low for MA. For additional information on admission requirements, go to http://www.apu.edu/educabs/graduatepsychology/.

Student Characteristics: The following represents characteristics of students in 2007–2008 in all graduate psychology programs in the department: Female—full-time 174, part-time 47; Male—full-time 62, part-time 12; African American/Black—full-time 17, part-time 4; Hispanic/Latino(a)—full-time 49, part-time 9; Asian/Pacific Islander—full-time 35, part-time 7; American Indian/Alaska Native—full-time 3, part-time 1; Caucasian/White—full-time 106, part-time 36; Multi-ethnic—full-time 16, part-time 2; students subject to the Americans With Disabilities Act—full-time 2, part-time 0; Unknown ethnicity—full-time 10, part-time 0; International students who hold an F-1 or J-1 Visa—full-time 6, part-time 2.

Financial Information/Assistance:

Tuition for Full-Time Study: *Master's:* State residents: $495 per credit hour; Nonstate residents: $495 per credit hour. *Doctoral:* State residents: $695 per credit hour; Nonstate residents: $695 per credit hour. Tuition is subject to change. Tuition costs vary by program. See the following Web site for updates and changes in tuition costs: http://www.apu.edu/graduatecenter/services/sfs/costs/.

Financial Assistance:

First-Year Students: Teaching assistantships available for first year. Average amount paid per academic year: $6,250. Average number of hours worked per week: 15. Apply by April 15. Tuition remission given: partial. Research assistantships available for first year. Average amount paid per academic year: $6,250. Average number of hours worked per week: 15. Apply by April 15. Tuition remission given: partial.

Advanced Students: No information provided.

Additional Information: Of all students currently enrolled full time, 5% benefited from one or more of the listed financial assistance programs.

Internships/Practica: Doctoral Degree (PsyD Clinical Psychology): For those doctoral students for whom a professional internship was required in this program prior to graduation, (9) students applied for an internship in 2006–2007, with (7) students obtaining an internship. Of those students who obtained an internship, (7) were paid internships. Of those students who obtained an internship, (5) students placed in APA/CPA-accredited internships, (1) student placed in internships not APA/CPA-accredited, but listed with the Association of Psychology Postdoctoral and Internship Centers (APPIC), (1) student placed in internships conforming to guidelines of the Council of Directors of School Psychology Programs (CDSPP), (0) students placed in internships that were not APA/CPA-accredited, APPIC or CDSPP listed. PsyD students are required to complete 6 semesters of practicum experience. These experiences are gained in placements throughout Los Angeles, Orange, and San Bernardino Counties, which provide diverse clinical and multicultural experiences. A Counseling Center on the Azusa Pacific University campus also serves as a practicum site for doctoral students. A sequence of clinical practicum courses is offered simultaneously with the field placement experience. All doctoral students are required to complete one full year of psychology internship. APU places interns in a variety of sites (must be APA approved or those meeting APPIC standards) across the country. Students enrolled in the MA Program in Clinical Psychology complete a clinical training sequence that meets all requirements for future licensure as a Marital and Family Therapist (MFT) in the state of California. Students complete 150 hours of direct client contact in diverse, multicultural settings such as community counseling centers, domestic violence clinics, and schools. Students receive training in individual, marital, and group therapy and exposure to treatments that have been demonstrated to be effective with specific problems. A sequence of clinical placement courses is offered simultaneously with the field placement experience.

Housing and Day Care: No on-campus housing is available. No on-campus day care facilities are available.

Employment of Department Graduates:

Master's Degree Graduates: Of those who graduated in the academic year 2006–2007, the following categories and numbers represent the postgraduate activities and employment of master's degree graduates: Enrolled in a postdoctoral residency/fellowship (n/a), employed in independent practice (n/a), do not know (36), total from the above (master's) (36).

Doctoral Degree Graduates: Of those who graduated in the academic year 2006–2007, the following categories and numbers represent the postgraduate activities and employment of doctoral degree graduates: Enrolled in a psychology doctoral program (n/a), enrolled in a postdoctoral residency/fellowship (4), do not know (3), total from the above (doctoral) (7).

Additional Information:

Orientation, Objectives, and Emphasis of Department: The PsyD in Clinical Psychology with an emphasis in Family Psychology (APA accredited) prepares students for the practice of professional psychology. The program adheres to a practitioner–scholar model of training and emphasizes development of the core competencies in clinical psychology adopted by the National Council of Schools and Programs of Professional Psychology. The program requires completion of a rigorous sequence of courses in the science and practice of psychology. Requirements include 3 years of clinical training, successful demonstration of clinical competency through examination, completion of a clinical dissertation, and a predoctoral internship. Prespecialty education in family psychology and an emphasis in interdisciplinary studies, relating psychology to ethics, theology, and philosophy, are included. The program was designed to be consistent with the requirements of the Guidelines and Principles for Accreditation of Programs in Professional Psychology (APA, 1996). The MA in Clinical Psychology with an emphasis in Marriage and Family Therapy meets requirements for California MFT licensure. Concepts of individual psychology are integrated with interpersonal and ecological concepts of systems theory. Goals include cultivating the examined life, fostering theoretical mastery, developing practical clinical skills, encouraging clinically integrative strategies, and preparing psychotherapists to work in a culturally diverse world.

Special Facilities or Resources: All students have access to the APA PsycINFO database and all APA journals full-text online as part of their student library privileges. The new Darling Library provides an attractive and functional set of resources for the APU PsyD and MA. The library is technology friendly and includes the Ahmanson Information Technology Center, an area with 75 computer desks. Each computer is wired into the university system for Internet and library catalog system searches. PsycINFO, as well as over 100 additional licensed databases, are available for student literature and subject searches. Eight "scholar rooms" were designed as a part of the Darling Graduate Library to be used for conducting research and writing. Doctoral students in the dissertation phase of their program are given priority in the reservation of these rooms. There are also several conference rooms in the Darling Library that may be reserved for student study groups or research teams. The Department of Graduate Psychology runs the Child and Family Development Center (CFDC), which offers psychological services to the surrounding community as well as to faculty, staff, and university students. The CFDC also contracts to provide services to the surrounding 12 schools in the Azusa Unified School District. The CFDC currently trains 25 MA and PsyD graduate students and has provided data for two doctoral dissertations.

Information for Students With Physical Disabilities: See the following Web site for more information: http://www.apu.edu/lec/language/.

Application Information:

Send to Azusa Pacific University, Graduate Admissions, 901 East Alosta, P.O. Box 7000, Azusa, CA 91702-7000. Application available online. URL of online application: http://www.apu.edu/apply/. Students are admitted in the Fall, application deadline February 15; Spring, application deadline October 15. PsyD (and the PrePsyD) application deadline is February 15 (if space is available, extended case by case with a deadline of April 15). Application deadlines for MA are as follows: Fall deadline is March 15 and Spring deadline is October 15. *Fee:* $45 domestic, $65 international.

California Institute of Integral Studies (2007 data)

PsyD Program
School of Professional Psychology
1453 Mission Street
San Francisco, CA 94103
Telephone: (415) 575-6100
Fax: (415) 575-1266
E-mail: *hvoigt@ciis.edu*
Web: *http://www.ciis.edu*

Department Information:

1979. Director of Clinical Training: Harrison Voigt. Number of faculty: total—full-time 18, part-time 35; women—full-time 10, part-time 20; faculty subject to the Americans With Disabilities Act 1.

Programs and Degrees Offered:

Listed in the following order: Program area, degree type (T if terminal Master's), number awarded 7/06–6/07. Clinical Psychology PsyD (Doctor of Psychology) 16, Counseling Psychology MA/MS (Master of Arts/Science) (T) 58.

APA Accreditation: Clinical PsyD (Doctor of Psychology).

Student Applications/Admissions:

Student Applications

Clinical Psychology PsyD (Doctor of Psychology)—Applications 2007–2008, 141. Total applicants accepted 2007–2008, 63. Number full-time enrolled (new admits only) 2007–2008, 38. Number part-time enrolled (new admits only) 2007–2008, 0. Total enrolled 2007–2008 full-time, 139, part-time, 35. Openings 2008–2009, 32. The number of students enrolled full- and part-time who were dismissed or voluntarily withdrew from this program area in 2007–2008 were 4. *Counseling Psychology MA/MS (Master of Arts/Science)*—Applications 2007–2008, 274. Total applicants accepted 2007–2008, 124. Number full-time enrolled (new admits only) 2007–2008, 100. Number part-time enrolled (new admits only) 2007–2008, 24. Total enrolled 2007–2008 full-time, 287, part-time, 70. Openings 2008–2009, 125. The median number of years required for completion of a degree in 2006–2007 were 3. The number of students enrolled full- and part-time who were dismissed or voluntarily withdrew from this program area in 2007–2008 were 6.

Admissions Requirements:

Scores: Entries appear in this order: required test or GPA, minimum score (if required), median score of students entering in 2007–2008. Master's Programs: overall undergraduate GPA 3.0, 3.3. Doctoral Programs: GRE-V no minimum stated, 571; GRE-Q no minimum stated, 589; overall undergraduate GPA 3.1, 3.6; Doctoral program GRE-Analytic no minimum stated, 4.87. GRE (verbal, quantitative and analytic) required but there is no minimum qualifying score.

Other Criteria: (importance of criteria rated low, medium, or high): GRE/MAT scores—high, research experience—low, work experience—medium, extracurricular activity—medium, clinically related public service—high, GPA—high, letters of recommendation—high, interview—high, statement of goals and objectives—high, written work sample—high. Admissions criteria listed above apply to PsyD program. For the MA program, criteria are similar but may vary and GRE is not required. For additional information on admission requirements, go to http://www.ciis.edu.

Student Characteristics: The following represents characteristics of students in 2007–2008 in all graduate psychology programs in the department: Female—full-time 319, part-time 86; Male—full-time 107, part-time 21; African American/Black—full-time 15, part-time 2; Hispanic/Latino(a)—full-time 36, part-time 9; Asian/Pacific Islander—full-time 20, part-time 6; American Indian/Alaska Native—full-time 1, part-time 0; Caucasian/White—full-time 349, part-time 87; Multi-ethnic—full-time 5, part-time 3; students subject to the Americans With Disabilities Act—full-time 2, part-time 0; Unknown ethnicity—full-time 0, part-time 0.

Financial Information/Assistance:

Tuition for Full-Time Study: *Master's:* State residents: per academic year $15,270, $725 per credit hour; Nonstate residents: per academic year $15,270, $725 per credit hour. *Doctoral:* State residents: per academic year $24,700, $860 per credit hour; Nonstate residents: per academic year $24,700, $860 per credit hour. Tuition is subject to change. See the following Web site for updates and changes in tuition costs: http://www.ciis.edu.

Financial Assistance:

First-Year Students: Teaching assistantships available for first year. Fellowships and scholarships available for first year. Average amount paid per academic year: $5,000. Apply by May 1. Tuition remission given: partial.

Advanced Students: Teaching assistantships available for advanced students. Apply by varies. Fellowships and scholarships available for advanced students. Average amount paid per academic year: $5,000. Apply by May 1. Tuition remission given: partial.

Additional Information: Of all students currently enrolled full time, 15% benefited from one or more of the listed financial assistance programs. Application and information available online at http://www.ciis.edu.

Internships/Practica: Internship and practicum placements are available throughout the greater San Francisco Bay Area at a broad variety of mental health service agencies. All doctoral internship sites are approved by APPIC or CAPIC. Not all internship positions are funded.

Housing and Day Care: No on-campus housing is available. No on-campus day care facilities are available.

Employment of Department Graduates:

Master's Degree Graduates: Of those who graduated in the academic year 2006–2007, the following categories and numbers represent the postgraduate activities and employment of master's degree graduates: Enrolled in a postdoctoral residency/fellowship (n/a), employed in independent practice (n/a), total from the above (master's) (0).

Doctoral Degree Graduates: Of those who graduated in the academic year 2006–2007, the following categories and numbers represent the postgraduate activities and employment of doctoral degree graduates: Enrolled in a psychology doctoral program (n/a), total from the above (doctoral) (0).

Additional Information:

Orientation, Objectives, and Emphasis of Department: The Institute offers a unique program of education and training, broadening the usual conceptual framework for graduate training in psychology by including in the curriculum some exposure to Asian philosophic, humanistic, and transpersonal approaches to understanding human experience. The educational philosophy simultaneously values scholarly knowledge, inner development, applied research, and human service. Psychology programs at CIIS flourish within a fertile and broadening climate provided by other social science graduate programs in philosophy/religion, anthropology, and women's spirituality, along with online degree programs. Within the practitioner–scholar training model, the APA-accredited PsyD program provides knowledge of the foundations of scientific and professional psychology while emphasizing the understanding of consciousness, self-knowledge, and human evolution embodied in the philosophical and psychological traditions of both East and West. The clinical specialization prepares students for work with the broad range of clientele and systems found across the range of multidisciplinary service settings and the spectrum of populations served by the clinical psychologist. Experiential growth work is required in all programs. Several clinical concentrations are available. CIIS has a 35,000-volume library and a well-developed Placement Office to support academic studies.

Special Facilities or Resources: CIIS operates four separate community-based counseling centers: the on-campus Psychological Services Center operated by the PsyD Clinical Psychology program, and three counseling centers operated by the MA Counseling program. All counseling centers serve as primary training sites for the MA and PsyD programs.

Information for Students With Physical Disabilities: See the following Web site for more information: http://www.ciis.edu.

Application Information:
Send to Office of Admissions. Students are admitted in the Fall, application deadline January 15. MA programs: April 15 for Fall, September 15 for Spring (not all programs). *Fee:* $65.

California Lutheran University

Psychology Department
60 West Olsen Road
Thousand Oaks, CA 91360-2787
Telephone: (805) 493-3528
Fax: (805) 493-3479
E-mail: *mpuopolo@clunet.edu*
Web: *http://www.clunet.edu*

Department Information:
1959. Director, Graduate Programs in Psychology: Mindy Puopolo, PsyD. Number of faculty: total—full-time 3, part-time 15; women—full-time 1, part-time 10; total—minority—full-time 1, part-time 2; women minority—part-time 1.

Programs and Degrees Offered:
Listed in the following order: Program area, degree type (T if terminal Master's), number awarded 7/06–6/07. Clinical MA/MS (Master of Arts/Science) (T) 8, Marital and Family Therapy MA/MS (Master of Arts/Science) (T) 19.

Student Applications/Admissions:
Student Applications
Clinical MA/MS (Master of Arts/Science)—Applications 2007–2008, 70. Total applicants accepted 2007–2008, 18. Number full-time enrolled (new admits only) 2007–2008, 16. Number part-time enrolled (new admits only) 2007–2008, 2. Total enrolled 2007–2008 full-time, 29, part-time, 4. Openings 2008–2009, 20. The median number of years required for completion of a degree in 2006–2007 were 2. The number of students enrolled full- and part-time who were dismissed or voluntarily withdrew from this program area in 2007–2008 were 0. *Marital and Family Therapy MA/MS (Master of Arts/Science)*—Applications 2007–2008, 108. Total applicants accepted 2007–2008, 30. Number full-time enrolled (new admits only) 2007–2008, 24. Number part-time enrolled (new admits only) 2007–2008, 2. Total enrolled 2007–2008 full-time, 52, part-time, 14. Openings 2008–2009, 40. The median number of years required for completion of a degree in 2006–2007 were 2. The number of students enrolled full- and part-time who were dismissed or voluntarily withdrew from this program area in 2007–2008 were 2.

Admissions Requirements:
Scores: Entries appear in this order: required test or GPA, minimum score (if required), median score of students entering in 2007–2008. Master's Programs: last 2 years GPA 3.0. GRE is required only if upper division undergraduate GPA is below 3.0.
Other Criteria: (importance of criteria rated low, medium, or high): GRE/MAT scores—medium, research experience—medium, work experience—medium, extracurricular activity—low, clinically related public service—medium, GPA—high, letters of recommendation—medium, interview—high, statement of goals and objectives—high. Counseling Psychology (MFT) program emphasizes clinically related public service and paraprofessional volunteer experiences.

Student Characteristics: The following represents characteristics of students in 2007–2008 in all graduate psychology programs in the department: Female—full-time 71, part-time 14; Male—full-time 10, part-time 4; African American/Black—full-time 1, part-time 0; Hispanic/Latino(a)—full-time 11, part-time 1; Asian/Pacific Islander—full-time 4, part-time 0; American Indian/Alaska Native—full-time 1, part-time 0; Caucasian/White—full-time 48, part-time 12; Multi-ethnic—full-time 5, part-time 0; students subject to the Americans With Disabilities Act—full-time 2, part-time 0; Unknown ethnicity—full-time 11, part-time 5; International students who hold an F-1 or J-1 Visa—full-time 4, part-time 0.

Financial Information/Assistance:
Tuition for Full-Time Study: *Master's:* State residents: $535 per credit hour; Nonstate residents: $535 per credit hour. Tuition is subject to change.

Financial Assistance:
First-Year Students: Teaching assistantships available for first year. Average amount paid per academic year: $2,480. Average number of hours worked per week: 8. Apply by August 15. Tuition remission given: partial. Research assistantships available for first year. Average amount paid per academic year: $2,480. Average number of hours worked per week: 8. Apply by August 15. Tuition remission given: partial.
Advanced Students: Teaching assistantships available for advanced students. Average amount paid per academic year: $2,480. Average number of hours worked per week: 8. Apply by May 1. Tuition remission given: partial. Research assistantships available for advanced students. Average amount paid per academic year: $2,480. Average number of hours worked per week: 8. Apply by May 1. Tuition remission given: partial. Fellowships and scholarships available for advanced students. Average amount paid per academic year: $2,000. Average number of hours worked per week: 0. Apply by none. Tuition remission given: partial.

Additional Information: Of all students currently enrolled full time, 15% benefited from one or more of the listed financial assistance programs.

Internships/Practica: A special feature of the Counseling Psychology Marital and Family Therapy Program is a 12-month practicum placement in the University's Community Counseling Services Center. Students may also choose an external practicum in a local community agency. CLU's Community Counseling Services is a low-cost community counseling facility, which provides an intensive on-site clinical training experience. Individual supervision, group supervision, staff training, peer support, and sharing of learning experiences in an atmosphere designed to facilitate growth as a therapist create exceptional opportunities. Approximately 500 hours applicable to the California licensing requirement can be obtained through the MFT practicum experience.

Housing and Day Care: No on-campus housing is available. No on-campus day care facilities are available.

Employment of Department Graduates:

Master's Degree Graduates: Of those who graduated in the academic year 2006–2007, the following categories and numbers represent the postgraduate activities and employment of master's degree graduates: Enrolled in a postdoctoral residency/fellowship (n/a), employed in independent practice (n/a), total from the above (master's) (0).

Doctoral Degree Graduates: Of those who graduated in the academic year 2006–2007, the following categories and numbers represent the postgraduate activities and employment of doctoral degree graduates: Enrolled in a psychology doctoral program (n/a), total from the above (doctoral) (0).

Additional Information:

Orientation, Objectives, and Emphasis of Department: The Master of Science degree in Clinical Psychology provides both a scientific and practitioner foundation, with courses in research as well as clinical and assessment training. Students choose either a two-course sequence in Child and Adolescent Therapy or a two-course sequence in Psychiatric Rehabilitation, which focuses on clients who have serious mental illnesses. The Master of Science in Clinical Psychology provides excellent preparation for application to doctoral programs, provides skills leading toward careers in the mental health profession, and qualifies the graduate to teach in community colleges. The Master of Science Degree in Counseling Psychology prepares the student to become a professional Marital and Family Therapist. The program is designed to meet all academic requirements for the state license in marriage and family therapy, administered by the California Board of Behavioral Sciences. Over the years, graduates of this program have an outstanding record of successfully passing the California state licensing examination. Graduates have built successful practices in private and institutional fields. All of the Master's degree programs can be completed in 2 years, or 3 years on a part-time basis.

Special Facilities or Resources: Students who obtain research assistantships may work with psychology faculty on individual and collaborative interdisciplinary research projects.

Application Information:

Send to Michelle Saucedo, Graduate Admission Counselor, 60 West Olsen Road, Thousand Oaks, CA 91360. Programs have rolling admissions. Master's program in Counseling Psychology (Marital and Family Therapy) and Master's program in Clinical Psychology generally only admit students in the Fall semester. *Fee:* $50. Candidates who attend the regularly scheduled Information Meetings are eligible for an application fee waiver.

California Polytechnic State University

Psychology/Master of Science in Psychology
Liberal Arts
Cal Poly Psychology/Child Development Department
San Luis Obispo, CA 93407
Telephone: (805) 756-2456
Fax: (805) 756-1134
E-mail: *mbooker@calpoly.edu*
Web: *http://www.calpoly.edu/~psychhd*

Department Information:

1969. Chairperson: Basil A. Fiorito. Number of faculty: total—full-time 19, part-time 22; women—full-time 12, part-time 13; total—minority—full-time 6, part-time 2; women minority—full-time 4, part-time 1; faculty subject to the Americans With Disabilities Act 1.

Programs and Degrees Offered:

Listed in the following order: Program area, degree type (T if terminal Master's), number awarded 7/06–6/07. Counseling Marriage and Family MA/MS (Master of Arts/Science) (T) 19.

Student Applications/Admissions:

Student Applications

Counseling Marriage and Family MA/MS (Master of Arts/Science)—Applications 2007–2008, 66. Total applicants accepted 2007–2008, 24. Number full-time enrolled (new admits only) 2007–2008, 11. Number part-time enrolled (new admits only) 2007–2008, 1. Total enrolled 2007–2008 full-time, 23, part-time, 9. Openings 2008–2009, 20. The median number of years required for completion of a degree in 2006–2007 were 3. The number of students enrolled full- and part-time who were dismissed or voluntarily withdrew from this program area in 2007–2008 were 8.

Admissions Requirements:

Scores: Entries appear in this order: required test or GPA, minimum score (if required), median score of students entering in 2007–2008. Master's Programs: GRE-V no minimum stated, 517; GRE-Q no minimum stated, 597; last 2 years GPA 3.0, 3.64; Masters GRE-Analytical no minimum stated, 5.

Other Criteria: (importance of criteria rated low, medium, or high): GRE/MAT scores—high, research experience—low, work experience—medium, extracurricular activity—medium, clinically related public service—medium, GPA—high, letters of recommendation—high, statement of goals and objectives—high, undergraduate major in psychology—low, specific undergraduate psychology courses taken—low.

Student Characteristics: The following represents characteristics of students in 2007–2008 in all graduate psychology programs in the department: Female—full-time 19, part-time 9; Male—full-time 4, part-time 0; African American/Black—full-time 1,

part-time 0; Hispanic/Latino(a)—full-time 3, part-time 0; Asian/Pacific Islander—full-time 1, part-time 1; American Indian/Alaska Native—full-time 0, part-time 0; Caucasian/White—full-time 12, part-time 6; Multi-ethnic—full-time 0, part-time 0; students subject to the Americans With Disabilities Act—full-time 0, part-time 0; Unknown ethnicity—full-time 6, part-time 2; International students who hold an F-1 or J-1 Visa—full-time 0, part-time 0.

Financial Information/Assistance:

Tuition for Full-Time Study: *Master's:* State residents: per academic year $5,055; Nonstate residents: per academic year $5,055, $226 per credit hour. Tuition is subject to change. See the following Web site for updates and changes in tuition costs: http://www.fees.calpoly.edu/.

Financial Assistance:

First-Year Students: No information provided.

Advanced Students: No information provided.

Additional Information: Of all students currently enrolled full time, 0% benefited from one or more of the listed financial assistance programs. Application and information available online at http://www.ess.calpoly.edu/_finaid.

Internships/Practica: Master's Degree (MA/MS Counseling Marriage and Family): An internship experience such as a final research project or "capstone" experience is required of graduates. The Central Coast of California offers numerous well-supervised clinical internships in public and private nonprofit agencies with a variety of client populations. Internships are selected based on their ability to provide (a) quality supervision by a state-qualified licensed clinician; (b) clients with a wide variety of psychological disorders; (c) a variety of treatment modalities (i.e., individual, couple, family, and group therapy); and (d) a wide variety of clients who represent the diversity of the community. Most internship students are placed at public agency sites that serve the country's entire range of ethnic and minority populations. For additional information on education and training outcomes for our programs, see the following Web site: http://www.cla.calpoly.edu/psychhd/masters.html.

Housing and Day Care: On-campus housing is available. See the following Web site for more information: http://www.housing.calpoly.edu/. On-campus day care facilities are available. See the following Web site for more information: http://www.asi.calpoly.edu/childrens_center.

Employment of Department Graduates:

Master's Degree Graduates: Of those who graduated in the academic year 2006–2007, the following categories and numbers represent the postgraduate activities and employment of master's degree graduates: Enrolled in a postdoctoral residency/fellowship (n/a), employed in independent practice (n/a), total from the above (master's) (0).

Doctoral Degree Graduates: Of those who graduated in the academic year 2006–2007, the following categories and numbers represent the postgraduate activities and employment of doctoral degree graduates: Enrolled in a psychology doctoral program (n/a), total from the above (doctoral) (0).

Additional Information:

Orientation, Objectives, and Emphasis of Department: The MS in Psychology is designed for persons who desire to practice in the field of clinical/counseling psychology. The program's mission is to provide the state of California with highly competent master-level clinicians who are academically prepared for the Marriage and Family Therapist (MFT) license and counseling with individuals, couples, families, and groups in a multicultural society. The program fulfills the educational requirements for the state of California's MFT license. Its mission is also to provide students who want to proceed on to doctoral programs in clinical or counseling psychology with sound research skills, thesis experience, and clinical intervention training. Graduates find career opportunities in public social service agencies such as Mental Health and Departments of Social Services as well as in private nonprofit and private practice counseling centers. Ten to twenty percent of graduates go on to doctoral programs in clinical or counseling psychology.

Special Facilities or Resources: Closely supervised on-campus practicum experiences leading to challenging internships in community agencies are the cornerstone of Cal Poly's preparation for the future clinician. The program runs a community counseling services clinic with three counseling offices and an observation room that provides direct viewing through one-way mirrors and remotely controlled video equipment. Closely supervised experience in Cal Poly's practicum clinic serving clients from the community provides trainees with the opportunity to develop skills and confidence before undertaking an internship.

Information for Students With Physical Disabilities: See the following Web site for more information: http://www.drc.calpoly.edu/.

Application Information:

Send to Admissions Office, California Polytechnic State University, San Luis Obispo, CA 93407. Application available online. URL of online application: http://www.csumentor.edu/. Students are admitted in the Fall, application deadline January 15. Portfolio deadline is February 15. *Fee:* $55.

California State University, Bakersfield

Department of Psychology
School of Humanities and Social Sciences
9001 Stockdale Highway
Bakersfield, CA 93311-1099
Telephone: (661) 654-2363
Fax: (661) 654-6955
E-mail: *tboone@csub.edu*
Web: *http://www.csub.edu/*

Department Information:

1970. Chairperson: Steve Bacon, PhD. Number of faculty: total—full-time 15, part-time 1; women—full-time 8, part-time 1; total—minority—full-time 4, part-time 1; women minority—full-time 1, part-time 1.

Programs and Degrees Offered:

Listed in the following order: Program area, degree type (T if terminal Master's), number awarded 7/06–6/07. Psychology MA/MS (Master of Arts/Science) (T) 3, Marriage, Family, and Child MA/MS (Master of Arts/Science) (T) 13.

Student Applications/Admissions:

Student Applications

Psychology MA/MS (Master of Arts/Science)—Number full-time enrolled (new admits only) 2007–2008, 5. Number part-time enrolled (new admits only) 2007–2008, 0. Openings 2008–2009, 10. The median number of years required for completion of a degree in 2006–2007 were 2. The number of students enrolled full- and part-time who were dismissed or voluntarily withdrew from this program area in 2007–2008 were 0. *Marriage, Family, and Child MA/MS (Master of Arts/Science)*—Applications 2007–2008, 40. Total applicants accepted 2007–2008, 26. Number full-time enrolled (new admits only) 2007–2008, 9. Number part-time enrolled (new admits only) 2007–2008, 15. Total enrolled 2007–2008 full-time, 9, part-time, 30. Openings 2008–2009, 20. The median number of years required for completion of a degree in 2006–2007 were 3. The number of students enrolled full- and part-time who were dismissed or voluntarily withdrew from this program area in 2007–2008 were 0.

Admissions Requirements:

Scores: Entries appear in this order: required test or GPA, minimum score (if required), median score of students entering in 2007–2008. Master's Programs: GRE-V 420, 530; GRE-Q 350, 600; last 2 years GPA 3.00; psychology GPA 3.00. For the MS in Counseling Psychology the GRE is NOT required.

Other Criteria: (importance of criteria rated low, medium, or high): GRE/MAT scores—low, research experience—high, work experience—low, extracurricular activity—medium, GPA—high, letters of recommendation—high, statement of goals and objectives—high. Above are admission criteria weightings for the MA in Counseling Psychology. Admission criteria weightings for the M.S. in Counseling Psychology: GRE scores—none, research experience—low, work experience—medium, extracurricular activities—medium, clinically related public service—high, GPA—medium, letters of recommendation—high, interview—low, statement of goals and objectives—high. For additional information on admission requirements for MA in Psychology, go to http://www.csub.edu/psychology/grcourse.htm; for MS in Counseling, go to http://www.csub.edu/cpsy.

Student Characteristics: The following represents characteristics of students in 2007–2008 in all graduate psychology programs in the department: Female—full-time 3, part-time 0; Male—full-time 3, part-time 0; Hispanic/Latino(a)—full-time 1, part-time 0; Caucasian/White—full-time 5, part-time 0; students subject to the Americans With Disabilities Act—full-time 0, part-time 0; Unknown ethnicity—full-time 0, part-time 0.

Financial Information/Assistance:

Tuition for Full-Time Study: *Master's:* State residents: per academic year $3,102; Nonstate residents: per academic year $13,960. Tuition is subject to change. Tuition costs vary by program. See the following Web site for updates and changes in tuition costs: http://www.calstate.edu/PA/Info/fees.shtml.

Financial Assistance:

First-Year Students: Research assistantships available for first year. Average number of hours worked per week: 10. Apply by varies. Fellowships and scholarships available for first year. Apply by ASAP. Tuition remission given: partial.

Advanced Students: Research assistantships available for advanced students. Average number of hours worked per week: 10. Apply by varies. Fellowships and scholarships available for advanced students. Apply by ASAP.

Additional Information: Of all students currently enrolled full time, 75% benefited from one or more of the listed financial assistance programs. Application and information available online at http://www.csub.edu/FinAid/.

Internships/Practica: Master's Degree (MA/MS in Psychology): An internship experience such as a final research project or "capstone" experience is required of graduates. The MS program features practica in human communication, diagnostic interviewing, and individual, child, family and group treatment in a university counselor training clinic. Two quarters of training in a modern, well-equipped on-campus training clinic is required. With approval, this is followed by two quarters of traineeship in one of a wide variety of community placements including substance abuse, dual diagnosis, perinatal intervention, child guidance, domestic violence, forensics, and college counseling. Students must be available during weekday, day-time hours during their final two quarters to engage (volunteer or paid) in traineeship.

Housing and Day Care: On-campus housing is available. See the following Web site for more information: http://www.csub.edu/housing/ed_program.html or call (661) 664-3014. On-campus day care facilities are available. See the following Web site for more information: http://www.csub.edu/childrenscenter/ or call (661) 664-3165.

Employment of Department Graduates:

Master's Degree Graduates: Of those who graduated in the academic year 2006–2007, the following categories and numbers represent the postgraduate activities and employment of master's degree graduates: Enrolled in a psychology doctoral program (1), enrolled in a postdoctoral residency/fellowship (n/a), employed in independent practice (n/a), employed in an academic position at a university (1), do not know (1), total from the above (master's) (3).

Doctoral Degree Graduates: Of those who graduated in the academic year 2006–2007, the following categories and numbers represent the postgraduate activities and employment of doctoral degree graduates: Enrolled in a psychology doctoral program (n/a), enrolled in a postdoctoral residency/fellowship (0), total from the above (doctoral) (0).

Additional Information:

Orientation, Objectives, and Emphasis of Department: We offer a 45-unit, 2-year MA program that offers training for either doctoral preparation or teaching psychology in community college settings. Students take courses in a broad range of areas of psychological research and participate in both research and teaching. Students must complete an empirical thesis at the end of their 2nd year. The 90-unit MS is jointly sponsored by the Psychology Department and Advanced Educational Studies in the School of Education. Faculty teach principles and skills for the developing professional to work effectively and ethically with children, adolescents, adults, couples, and families from diverse populations. The curriculum emphasizes a balance between content and application, theory and practice, and science and art. It is designed to meet the academic requirements established by the Board of

Behavioral Sciences (BBS), Section 4980.37 of the Business and Professions Code for the California license in Marriage and Family Therapy (MFT). See Web site for more information: http://www.csub.edu/cpsy.

Special Facilities or Resources: For MA students there are active programs in vision research, psycholinguistics, biopsychology, social psychology, and developmental psychology. On-site labs include a vision laboratory with extensive spatial frequency presentation and measuring equipment, an animal laboratory meeting stringent Federal standards, a cognitive processes/psycholinguistics laboratory with recording and eye-tracking equipment and computer stations for both voice activated and keypad responses, and observational labs. The department also maintains a file of psychological tests. For MS students, three of the four full-time clinical faculty are licensed in the state of California. The university counselor training clinic is supervised by a licensed MFT.

Information for Students With Physical Disabilities: See the following Web site for more information: http://www.csub.edu/UnivServices/SSD/.

Application Information:
For MA send to Tanya Boone, PhD, Psychology Graduate Coordinator, Psychology Department, California State University, Bakersfield, CA 93311-1022; for MS: Ms. Barbara Espinosa, 24DDH, Psychology Department, California State University, 9001 Stockdale Highway, Bakersfield, CA 93311-1022. Application available online. URL of online application: http://www.csub.edu/Psychology/grcourse.htm for MA; http://www.csub.edu/cpsy for MS Students are admitted in the Fall, application deadline April 1. For MA deadline is April 1 for subsequent Fall admission. There is no rolling application. For MS application deadlines are located on Web site. *Fee:* $0. There is a separate application process for university admission. Contact: Admissions and Records, California State University Bakersfield, 9001 Stockdale Highway, Bakersfield, CA 93311-1099.

California State University, Chico (2007 data)

Psychology Department
College of Behavioral and Social Sciences
Chico, CA 95929-0234
Telephone: (530) 898-5147
Fax: (530) 898-4740
E-mail: *pspear@csuchico.edu*
Web: *http://www.csuchico.edu/psy*

Department Information:
1961. Chairperson: Paul Spear. Number of faculty: total—full-time 19, part-time 20; women—full-time 9, part-time 11.

Programs and Degrees Offered:
Listed in the following order: Program area, degree type (T if terminal Master's), number awarded 7/06–6/07. MA/PPS MA/MS (Master of Arts/Science) (T) 9, MA/Psychological Science MA/MS (Master of Arts/Science) (T), MS/MFT MA/MS (Master of Arts/Science) (T).

Student Applications/Admissions:

Student Applications

MA/PPS *MA/MS (Master of Arts/Science)*—Applications 2007–2008, 35. Total applicants accepted 2007–2008, 13. Total enrolled 2007–2008 full-time, 23. Openings 2008–2009, 12. The median number of years required for completion of a degree in 2006–2007 were 3. *MA/Psychological Science MA/MS (Master of Arts/Science)*—Applications 2007–2008, 26. Total applicants accepted 2007–2008, 18. Total enrolled 2007–2008 full-time, 34. Openings 2008–2009, 15. *MS/MFT MA/MS (Master of Arts/Science)*—Applications 2007–2008, 48. Total applicants accepted 2007–2008, 26. Total enrolled 2007–2008 full-time, 45. Openings 2008–2009, 25.

Admissions Requirements:

Scores: Entries appear in this order: required test or GPA, minimum score (if required), median score of students entering in 2007–2008. Master's Programs: last 2 years GPA 2.75. Completion of either GRE V+Q+A or MAT. GRE-Subject (Psychology) not required but is considered if available. Last 60 units GPA—2.75 minimum; Last 30 units GPA—3.00 minimum

Other Criteria: (importance of criteria rated low, medium, or high): GRE/MAT scores—medium, research experience—low, work experience—low, extracurricular activity—low, clinically related public service—medium, GPA—high, letters of recommendation—high, statement of goals and objectives—high.

Student Characteristics: The following represents characteristics of students in 2007–2008 in all graduate psychology programs in the department: Female—full-time 60, part-time 0; Male—full-time 30, part-time 0; African American/Black—full-time 3, part-time 0; Hispanic/Latino(a)—full-time 12, part-time 0; Asian/Pacific Islander—full-time 3, part-time 0; American Indian/Alaska Native—full-time 1, part-time 0; Caucasian/White—full-time 57, part-time 0; Unknown ethnicity—full-time 14, part-time 0.

Financial Information/Assistance:

Tuition for Full-Time Study: *Master's:* State residents: per academic year $3,994; Nonstate residents: per academic year $7,045, $339 per credit hour. Tuition is subject to change.

Financial Assistance:

First-Year Students: No information provided.
Advanced Students: No information provided.
Additional Information: No information provided.

Internships/Practica: For the MS degree: Individual and Child Counseling, Group Counseling, and Family Therapy practica are offered as well as postpracticum traineeships. School Psychology internships are required of all students seeking the School Psychology Credential.

Housing and Day Care: On-campus housing is available. See the following Web site for more information: http://www.csuchico.edu.hfs. On-campus day care facilities are available. Call (530) 898-5865.

Employment of Department Graduates:

Master's Degree Graduates: Of those who graduated in the academic year 2006–2007, the following categories and numbers

represent the postgraduate activities and employment of master's degree graduates: Enrolled in a postdoctoral residency/fellowship (n/a), employed in independent practice (n/a), total from the above (master's) (0).

Doctoral Degree Graduates: Of those who graduated in the academic year 2006–2007, the following categories and numbers represent the postgraduate activities and employment of doctoral degree graduates: Enrolled in a psychology doctoral program (n/a), total from the above (doctoral) (0).

Additional Information:

Orientation, Objectives, and Emphasis of Department: The Department offers three graduate programs. The Master of Science Degree prepares students to meet the educational requirements for Marriage and Family Therapy licensure in the State of California. It is designed to train competent professional counselors to work in mental health agencies and private practice. The curriculum is competency based and includes laboratory courses and practica, culminating in a family practicum and/or a postpracticum internship in a counseling agency. The Master of Arts Degree, Psychological Science Option, is designed to prepare students for doctoral work or teaching at the community college level. It offers extensive research experience, supervised teaching, and advanced coursework in experimental psychology and statistics. The Master of Arts Degree, Applied Psychology Option, is designed for students intending to enter our Pupil Personnel Services Credential program, which meets California requirements for a School Psychology Credential. The program has a prevention-oriented philosophy, is competency based, and provides practice in a variety of skills which enable school psychologists to serve all children. Trainees work in schools several days a week during 2 years of fieldwork.

Special Facilities or Resources: The Department of Psychology has modern, up-to-date laboratories, classrooms, and seminar rooms, including laboratories in biopsychology, perception, learning, and statistics, and a counseling training center.

Information for Students With Physical Disabilities: See the following Web site for more information: http://www.csuchico.edu/dss.

Application Information:

Send to Graduate Coordinator California State University, Chico, Psychology Department, Chico, CA 95929-0234; http://www.csuchico.edu/psy/. Application available online. Students are admitted in the Fall, application deadline March 1. *Fee:* $55.

California State University, Dominguez Hills

Department of Psychology/MA in Psychology Program—Clinical Option
Natural and Behavioral Sciences
1000 East Victoria Street
Carson, CA 90747
Telephone: (310) 243-3427
Fax: (310) 516-3642
E-mail: *kmason@csudh.edu*
Web: *http://www.nbs.csudh.edu/psychology*

Department Information:

1969. Coordinator, MA in Psychology Program: Karen I. Mason, PhD. Number of faculty: total—full-time 10, part-time 20; women—full-time 6, part-time 6; total—minority—full-time 7, part-time 10; women minority—full-time 6, part-time 2.

Programs and Degrees Offered:

Listed in the following order: Program area, degree type (T if terminal Master's), number awarded 7/06–6/07. Clinical Emphasis MA/MS (Master of Arts/Science) (T) 7.

Student Applications/Admissions:

Student Applications

Clinical Emphasis MA/MS (Master of Arts/Science)—Applications 2007–2008, 64. Total applicants accepted 2007–2008, 15. Number full-time enrolled (new admits only) 2007–2008, 8. Number part-time enrolled (new admits only) 2007–2008, 0. Total enrolled 2007–2008 full-time, 30, part-time, 3. Openings 2008–2009, 20. The median number of years required for completion of a degree in 2006–2007 were 2. The number of students enrolled full- and part-time who were dismissed or voluntarily withdrew from this program area in 2007–2008 were 0.

Admissions Requirements:

Scores: Entries appear in this order: required test or GPA, minimum score (if required), median score of students entering in 2007–2008. Master's Programs: GRE-V no minimum stated; GRE-Q no minimum stated; last 2 years GPA 3.00, 3.5; Masters GRE-Analytical no minimum stated.

Other Criteria: (importance of criteria rated low, medium, or high): GRE/MAT scores—medium, research experience—medium, work experience—low, clinically related public service—medium, GPA—high, letters of recommendation—high, interview—low, statement of goals and objectives—high. For additional information on admission requirements, go to http://www.nbs.csudh.edu/psychology/maprogram.html.

Student Characteristics: The following represents characteristics of students in 2007–2008 in all graduate psychology programs in the department: Female—full-time 23, part-time 2; Male—full-time 7, part-time 1; African American/Black—full-time 8, part-time 2; Hispanic/Latino(a)—full-time 12, part-time 0; Asian/Pacific Islander—full-time 1, part-time 0; American Indian/Alaska Native—full-time 0, part-time 0; Caucasian/White—full-time 9, part-time 1; Unknown ethnicity—full-time 0, part-time 0; International students who hold an F-1 or J-1 Visa—full-time 1, part-time 0.

Financial Information/Assistance:

Tuition for Full-Time Study: *Master's:* State residents: per academic year $3,784; Nonstate residents: $339 per credit hour. Tuition is subject to change.

Financial Assistance:

First-Year Students: Fellowships and scholarships available for first year. Average amount paid per academic year: $2,000. Apply by March/October.

Advanced Students: Teaching assistantships available for advanced students. Research assistantships available for advanced students. Fellowships and scholarships available for advanced students. Average amount paid per academic year: $2,000. Apply by March/October.

Additional Information: Of all students currently enrolled full time, 10% benefited from one or more of the listed financial assistance programs.

Internships/Practica: Master's Degree (MA/MS Clinical Emphasis): An internship experience such as a final research project or "capstone" experience is required of graduates. The Master of Arts in Psychology offers 550 supervised hours of practicum experience in a variety of settings.

Housing and Day Care: On-campus housing is available. See the following Web site for more information: http://www.csudh.edu. On-campus day care facilities are available.

Employment of Department Graduates:

Master's Degree Graduates: Of those who graduated in the academic year 2006–2007, the following categories and numbers represent the postgraduate activities and employment of master's degree graduates: Enrolled in a psychology doctoral program (0), enrolled in another graduate/professional program (0), enrolled in a postdoctoral residency/fellowship (n/a), employed in independent practice (n/a), employed in an academic position at a university (1), employed in a community mental health/counseling center (3), other employment position (2), do not know (1), total from the above (master's) (7).

Doctoral Degree Graduates: Of those who graduated in the academic year 2006–2007, the following categories and numbers represent the postgraduate activities and employment of doctoral degree graduates: Enrolled in a psychology doctoral program (n/a), total from the above (doctoral) (0).

Additional Information:

Orientation, Objectives, and Emphasis of Department: The Clinical Psychology Master of Arts Program provides you with a solid academic background in clinical psychology as it is applied within a community mental health framework. This program prepares you for a career in counseling, teaching, and research in community settings, which includes public or private agencies. Eighteen units of additional coursework prepare you for practice as a marriage and family therapist. Our graduates are successful in gaining admission to and graduating from the doctoral programs of their choice.

Special Facilities or Resources: Special resources include laboratory facilities, a course and experience in teaching psychology, computer facilities, and online PsychLIT retrieval system.

Application Information:

Send to Department of Psychology, California State University, Dominguez Hills, 1000 East Victoria Street, Carson, CA 90747. Application available online. URL of online application: http://www.nbs.csudh.edu/psychology/maprogram.html. Students are admitted in the Fall, application deadline March 1. *Fee:* $55.

California State University, Fullerton

Department of Psychology
Humanities and Social Sciences
P.O. Box 6846
Fullerton, CA 92834-6846
Telephone: (714) 278-3589
Fax: (714) 278-7134
E-mail: *kkarlson@fullerton.edu*
Web: *http://www.Psych.fullerton.edu/*

Department Information:

1957. Chairperson: Jack Mearns. Number of faculty: total—full-time 29, part-time 32; women—full-time 17, part-time 26; total—minority—full-time 7, part-time 7; women minority—full-time 4, part-time 4.

Programs and Degrees Offered:

Listed in the following order: Program area, degree type (T if terminal Master's), number awarded 7/06–6/07. Clinical Psychology MA/MS (Master of Arts/Science) (T) 16, Psychological Research MA/MS (Master of Arts/Science) (T) 13.

Student Applications/Admissions:

Student Applications

Clinical Psychology MA/MS (Master of Arts/Science)—Applications 2007–2008, 55. Total applicants accepted 2007–2008, 18. Number full-time enrolled (new admits only) 2007–2008, 17. Number part-time enrolled (new admits only) 2007–2008, 0. The median number of years required for completion of a degree in 2006–2007 were 2. The number of students enrolled full- and part-time who were dismissed or voluntarily withdrew from this program area in 2007–2008 were 1. *Psychological Research MA/MS (Master of Arts/Science)*—Applications 2007–2008, 59. Total applicants accepted 2007–2008, 17. Number full-time enrolled (new admits only) 2007–2008, 17. Number part-time enrolled (new admits only) 2007–2008, 0. Openings 2008–2009, 17. The median number of years required for completion of a degree in 2006–2007 were 2.

Admissions Requirements:

Scores: Entries appear in this order: required test or GPA, minimum score (if required), median score of students entering in 2007–2008. Master's Programs: GRE-V 300, 500; GRE-Q 300, 600; GRE-Subject (Psychology) 300, 580; overall undergraduate GPA 2.5, 3.35; last 2 years GPA 2.5, 3.5; psychology GPA 3.0, 3.5.

Other Criteria: (importance of criteria rated low, medium, or high): GRE/MAT scores—high, research experience—high, clinically related public service—high, GPA—high, letters of recommendation—high, interview—high, statement of goals and objectives—high, specific undergraduate psychology courses taken—high. The Master of Science Program requires an interview. There is no interview required for the Master of Arts Program. For additional information on admission requirements, go to http://psych.fullerton.edu.

Student Characteristics: The following represents characteristics of students in 2007–2008 in all graduate psychology programs in the department: Female—full-time 46, part-time 13; Male—full-time 14, part-time 4; African American/Black—full-time 1, part-time 0; Hispanic/Latino(a)—full-time 6, part-time 3; Asian/Pacific Islander—full-time 9, part-time 1; American Indian/Alaska Native—full-time 0, part-time 0; Caucasian/White—full-time 44, part-time 13; Unknown ethnicity—full-time 0, part-time 0; International students who hold an F-1 or J-1 Visa—full-time 4, part-time 0.

Financial Information/Assistance:

Tuition for Full-Time Study: *Master's:* State residents: per academic year $4,024; Nonstate residents: $339 per credit hour. Tuition is subject to change. See the following Web site for updates and changes in tuition costs: http://www.fullerton.edu/.

Financial Assistance:

First-Year Students: No information provided.

Advanced Students: No information provided.

Additional Information: Of all students currently enrolled full time, 0% benefited from one or more of the listed financial assistance programs.

Internships/Practica: Master's Degree (MA/MS Clinical Psychology): An internship experience, such as, a final research project or "capstone" experience is required of graduates. Master's Degree (MA/MS Psychological Research): An internship experience such as, a final research project or "capstone" experience is required of graduates. A majority of the internships are done in agencies that do family therapy and substance abuse prevention and training. Most internships have live and videotape supervision. Students have done internships in policy psychology, county clinics, and inpatient settings as well. Most agencies combine clinical and community work and serve low income and minority populations.

Housing and Day Care: On-campus housing is available. See the following Web site for more information: http://www.fullerton.edu/ or call the Housing Office (714) 278-2168. On-campus day care facilities are available. See the following Web site for more information: http://www.fullerton.edu/ or call the Children's Center (714) 278-2961.

Employment of Department Graduates:

Master's Degree Graduates: Of those who graduated in the academic year 2006–2007, the following categories and numbers represent the postgraduate activities and employment of master's degree graduates: Enrolled in a psychology doctoral program (6), enrolled in another graduate/professional program (1), enrolled in a postdoctoral residency/fellowship (n/a), employed in independent practice (n/a), employed in an academic position at a 2-year/4-year college (1), employed in business or industry (7), employed in a community mental health/counseling center (9), total from the above (master's) (24).

Doctoral Degree Graduates: Of those who graduated in the academic year 2006–2007, the following categories and numbers represent the postgraduate activities and employment of doctoral degree graduates: Enrolled in a psychology doctoral program (n/a), total from the above (doctoral) (0).

Additional Information:

Orientation, Objectives, and Emphasis of Department: The MA program provides advanced coursework and research training in core areas of psychology. Completion of the MA can facilitate application to PhD programs in psychology and provides skills important to careers in education, the health professions, and industry. The MS program in clinical psychology is intended to prepare students for work in a variety of mental health settings, and the program contains coursework relevant for the MFT license in California. The program is also designed to prepare students for PhD work in both academic and professional schools of clinical psychology.

Special Facilities or Resources: The department has laboratories for research in cognitive psychology, conditioning, perception, biopsychology, social psychology, psychological testing, and developmental psychology. The department also has extensive computer facilities.

Application Information:

Send department application to Graduate Office, Department of Psychology, California State Fullerton, P.O. Box 6846, Fullerton, CA 92834-6846; CSU Fullerton application only available online at http://www.fullerton.edu. Department of Psychology Application available online. URL of online application: http://www.psych.fullerton.edu. Students are admitted in the Fall, application deadline March 1. *Fee:* $55. Application fee for university application; there is no fee for the department application. The fee waiver process is built in CSU Mentor (online application) so you will not need to file a separate Request for an Application Fee Waiver. In some cases where the online application is unable to determine your eligibility to apply for a fee waiver, you will have to submit the request to the campus. The campus will inform you if you do not qualify for the waiver. Only California residents are eligible.

California State University, Long Beach

Department of Psychology
1250 Bellflower Boulevard
Long Beach, CA 90840-0901
Telephone: (562) 985-5000
E-mail: *psygrad@csulb.edu*
Web: *http://www.csulb.edu/~psych/*

Department Information:

1949. Chairperson: Kenneth F. Green. Number of faculty: total—full-time 22, part-time 22; women—full-time 14, part-time 18; total—minority—full-time 10, part-time 9; women minority—full-time 5, part-time 7.

Programs and Degrees Offered:

Listed in the following order: Program area, degree type (T if terminal Master's), number awarded 7/06–6/07. Research MA/MS (Master of Arts/Science) (T) 7, Industrial/Organizational MA/MS (Master of Arts/Science) (T) 6, Human Factors MA/MS (Master of Arts/Science) (T) 1.

Student Applications/Admissions:

Student Applications

Research MA/MS (Master of Arts/Science)—Applications 2007–2008, 64. Total applicants accepted 2007–2008, 30. Number full-time enrolled (new admits only) 2007–2008, 18. Number part-time enrolled (new admits only) 2007–2008, 1. Total enrolled 2007–2008 full-time, 37, part-time, 12. Openings 2008–2009, 25. The median number of years required for completion of a degree in 2006–2007 were 2. The number of students enrolled full- and part-time who were dismissed or voluntarily withdrew from this program area in 2007–2008 were 1. *Industrial/Organizational MA/MS (Master of Arts/Science)*—Applications 2007–2008, 69. Total applicants accepted 2007–2008, 20. Number full-time enrolled (new admits only) 2007–2008, 12. Number part-time enrolled (new admits only) 2007–2008, 0. Total enrolled 2007–2008 full-time, 14, part-time, 9. Openings 2008–2009, 16. The median number of years required for completion of a degree in 2006–2007 were 2. The number of students enrolled full- and part-time who were dismissed or voluntarily withdrew from this program area in 2007–2008 were 1. *Human Factors MA/MS (Master of Arts/Science)*—Applications 2007–2008, 21. Total applicants accepted 2007–2008, 9. Number full-time enrolled (new admits only) 2007–2008, 5. Number part-time enrolled (new admits only) 2007–2008, 0. Total enrolled 2007–2008 full-time, 6, part-time, 4. Openings 2008–2009, 10. The median number of years required for completion of a degree in 2006–2007 were 2.

Admissions Requirements:

Scores: Entries appear in this order: required test or GPA, minimum score (if required), median score of students entering in 2007–2008. Master's Programs: GRE-V no minimum stated, 494; GRE-Q no minimum stated, 575; last 2 years GPA no minimum stated, 3.55; psychology GPA no minimum stated, 3.50. GRE-Subject (Psychology) not required.

Other Criteria: (importance of criteria rated low, medium, or high): GRE/MAT scores—high, research experience—high, work experience—low, extracurricular activity—low, GPA—high, letters of recommendation—high, statement of goals and objectives—high. For additional information on admission requirements, go to http://www.csulb.edu/~psych/gradprgm/prostud/gradapp.html.

Student Characteristics: The following represents characteristics of students in 2007–2008 in all graduate psychology programs in the department: Female—full-time 46, part-time 4; Male—full-time 11, part-time 21; African American/Black—full-time 1, part-time 2; Hispanic/Latino(a)—full-time 14, part-time 3; Asian/Pacific Islander—full-time 8, part-time 0; American Indian/Alaska Native—full-time 1, part-time 0; Caucasian/White—full-time 33, part-time 20; students subject to the Americans With Disabilities Act—full-time 2, part-time 1; Unknown ethnicity—full-time 0, part-time 0.

Financial Information/Assistance:

Tuition for Full-Time Study: *Master's:* State residents: per academic year $3,790; Nonstate residents: per academic year $3,790, $339 per credit hour. Tuition is subject to change. See the following Web site for updates and changes in tuition costs: http://www.csulb.edu/depts/enrollment/registration/fees_basics.html.

Financial Assistance:

First-Year Students: Research assistantships available for first year. Average amount paid per academic year: $5,500. Average number of hours worked per week: 10. Apply by April 15. Fellowships and scholarships available for first year. Average amount paid per academic year: $2,500. Apply by March 1.

Advanced Students: Research assistantships available for advanced students. Average amount paid per academic year: $5,500. Average number of hours worked per week: 10. Apply by April 15. Fellowships and scholarships available for advanced students. Average amount paid per academic year: $2,500. Apply by March 1.

Additional Information: Of all students currently enrolled full time, 29% benefited from one or more of the listed financial assistance programs. Application and information available online at http://www.csulb.edu/depts/enrollment/financial_aid/.

Internships/Practica: Master's Degree (MA/MS Research): An internship experience such as a final research project or "capstone" experience is required of graduates. Master's Degree (MA/MS Industrial/Organizational): An internship experience such as a final research project or "capstone" experience is required of graduates. Master's Degree (MA/MS Human Factors): An internship experience such as a final research project or "capstone" experience is required of graduates. Graduate assistantship positions provide teaching, computer, and internship experiences to selected students in all the master's programs. Applications for graduate assistantships are available through the Graduate Office and are included in the application packet and online. Graduate assistantship assignments are based upon the pairing of each applicant's academic background, interests, and experience with current department needs. Specific assignments are geared toward providing educational experiences most appropriate for students in each program. Appointments are for 10 hours per week. Available teaching assignments include assistance to the introductory and intermediate statistics, psychological assessment, critical thinking, program evaluation, computer applications, and research methods courses. In addition to the aforementioned paid departmental positions, volunteer and/or externally funded research positions can be arranged with individual faculty members. Such research opportunities are often available in the physiological, cognition, language, human factors, language acquisition, and social psychology laboratories. Various internships in outside industrial and organizational settings are options for 2nd-year MSIO students. Internships are available through Boeing for MSHF students.

Housing and Day Care: On-campus housing is available. See the following Web site for more information: http://www.csulb.edu/divisions/students2/housing/. On-campus day care facilities are available. See the following Web site for more information: http://www.csulb.edu/divisions/students2/child_dev_ctr/index.html.

Employment of Department Graduates:

Master's Degree Graduates: Of those who graduated in the academic year 2006–2007, the following categories and numbers represent the postgraduate activities and employment of master's degree graduates: Enrolled in a postdoctoral residency/fellowship (n/a), employed in independent practice (n/a), total from the above (master's) (0).

Doctoral Degree Graduates: Of those who graduated in the academic year 2006–2007, the following categories and numbers represent the postgraduate activities and employment of doctoral degree graduates: Enrolled in a psychology doctoral program (n/a), total from the above (doctoral) (0).

Additional Information:

Orientation, Objectives, and Emphasis of Department: California State University Long Beach has three master's programs in psychology. The Master of Science in Human Factors prepares students to apply knowledge of psychology to the design of jobs, information systems, consumer products, workplaces, and equipment in order to improve user performance, safety, and comfort. Students acquire a background in the core areas of experimental psychology, research design and methodology, human factors, computer applications, and applied research methods. The Master of Arts, Research Option (MA-R) prepares students for doctoral work in any psychology field or for master's-level research or teaching positions. Core seminars include cognition, learning, physiological and sensory psychology, social, personality, developmental psychology, and quantitative methods. MA-R graduates who apply to doctoral programs have high acceptance rates with financial support. The Master of Science, Industrial and Organizational option (MSIO) offers preparation for careers for which a background in industrial–organizational psychology is essential. These fields include personnel, organizational development, industrial relations, employee training, and marketing research.

Special Facilities or Resources: The psychology building has extensive facilities available without charge. Computer facilities with microcomputers and mainframe stations include many current software packages. The physiological research lab, with a staffed animal compound, is used to study conditioned analgesia and neurotransmission. For research in stress and coping, interpersonal relations, social influence, gender psychology, and the biopsychology of mood, there are many research suites and a test materials center. These facilities, located in the psychology building, are for research and training in interviewing and case studies, forensic psychology, program and treatment evaluation, assessment of social support and family systems, self-management, and intervention strategies for hard-to-reach populations. Computer facilities are central to research in decision analysis, human–computer interface, statistical theory, assessment, and computer-aided instruction. A computerized human-factors lab is used to study auditory and visual perception. Our diversified facilities also accommodate a large AIDS-education project, research in managing diversity in the workplace, and other topics in industrial–organizational psychology. Outstanding CSULB Library facilities are available.

Information for Students With Physical Disabilities: See the following Web site for more information: http://www.csulb.edu/divisions/students2/dss.

Application Information:
Send Department application to Psychology Graduate Office, 1250 Bellflower Boulevard, Long Beach, CA 90840-0901 Must also apply to the university by March 1: http://www.csumentor.edu. Application available online. URL of online application: http://www.csulb.edu/~psych/gradprgm/prostud/gradapp.html. Students are admitted in the Fall, application deadline February 14–March 1; Spring, application deadline November 1. Spring 2009 admission deadline for MAR/MSHF: November 1, 2008 (tentative); Fall 2009 admission deadline for MAIO: February 14, 2009; MAR: February 12, 2009; MSHF: March 1, 2009. Department application available online at http://www.csulb.edu/~psych/gradprgm/prostud/gradapp.html or by writing or sending an e-mail request. *Fee:* $55. Fee for University application only.

California State University, Northridge (2007 data)

Department of Psychology
Social and Behavioral Sciences
18111 Nordhoff Street
Northridge, CA 91330-8255
Telephone: (818) 677-2827
Fax: (818) 677-2829
E-mail: *paul.skolnick@csun.edu*
Web: *http://www.csun.edu/psychology*

Department Information:
1958. Chair: Paul Skolnick. Number of faculty: total—full-time 29, part-time 31; women—full-time 16, part-time 12; faculty subject to the Americans With Disabilities Act 2.

Programs and Degrees Offered:
Listed in the following order: Program area, degree type (T if terminal Master's), number awarded 7/06–6/07. Clinical Psychology MA/MS (Master of Arts/Science) (T) 7, General Psychology MA/MS (Master of Arts/Science) 6, Human Factors MA/MS (Master of Arts/Science) (T) 4.

Student Applications/Admissions:
Student Applications
Clinical Psychology MA/MS (Master of Arts/Science)—Applications 2007–2008, 52. Total applicants accepted 2007–2008, 15. Number full-time enrolled (new admits only) 2007–2008, 11. Number part-time enrolled (new admits only) 2007–2008, 0. Openings 2008–2009, 12. The median number of years required for completion of a degree in 2006–2007 were 2. The number of students enrolled full- and part-time who were dismissed or voluntarily withdrew from this program area in 2007–2008 were 1. *General Psychology MA/MS (Master of Arts/Science)*—Applications 2007–2008, 41. Total applicants accepted 2007–2008, 15. Number full-time enrolled (new admits only) 2007–2008, 13. Number part-time enrolled (new admits only) 2007–2008, 0. Openings 2008–2009, 12. The median number of years required for completion of a degree in 2006–2007 were 2. The number of students enrolled full- and part-time who were dismissed or voluntarily withdrew from this program area in 2007–2008 were 2. *Human Factors MA/MS (Master of Arts/Science)*—Applications 2007–2008, 42. Total applicants accepted 2007–2008, 13. Number full-time enrolled (new admits only) 2007–2008, 11. Number part-time enrolled (new admits only) 2007–2008, 0. Openings 2008–2009, 10. The median number of years required for completion of a degree in 2006–2007 were 2. The number of students enrolled full- and part-time who were dismissed or voluntarily withdrew from this program area in 2007–2008 were 2.

Admissions Requirements:
Scores: Entries appear in this order: required test or GPA, minimum score (if required), median score of students entering in 2007–2008. Master's Programs: GRE-V 500, 500; GRE-Q 540, 540; GRE-Subject (Psychology) 540, 540; overall undergraduate GPA 3.0, 3.5; last 2 years GPA 3.0, 3.5; psychology GPA 3.0, 3.5. GRE-Subject (Psychology) required for Clinical option. GRE-V, GRE-Q, and Analytic Writing required for all options.
Other Criteria: (importance of criteria rated low, medium, or high): GRE/MAT scores—low, research experience—high, work experience—medium, extracurricular activity—medium, clinically related public service—high, GPA—medium, letters of recommendation—high, interview—low, statement of goals and objectives—high. Clinically Related Public Services is rated high by the Clinical option; low relevance for the General Experimental and Human Factors options. Interviews are required by the Clinical option, either in-person (preferred) or via telephone (if necessary due to geographical restrictions). For additional information on admission requirements, go to http://www.csun.edu/psychology.

Student Characteristics: The following represents characteristics of students in 2007–2008 in all graduate psychology programs in the department: Female—full-time 67, part-time 0; Male—full-time 40, part-time 0; African American/Black—full-time 2, part-time 0; Hispanic/Latino(a)—full-time 15, part-time 0; Asian/Pacific Islander—full-time 12, part-time 0; American Indian/Alaska Native—full-time 0, part-time 0; Caucasian/White—full-time 50, part-time 0; Multi-ethnic—full-time 28, part-time 0; Unknown ethnicity—full-time 0, part-time 0.

Financial Information/Assistance:
Tuition for Full-Time Study: *Master's:* State residents: per academic year $3,624; Nonstate residents: per academic year $3,624,

$339 per credit hour. Tuition is subject to change. See the following Web site for updates and changes in tuition costs: http://www-admn.csun.edu/ucs/tuition.html.

Financial Assistance:

First-Year Students: Research assistantships available for first year. Fellowships and scholarships available for first year.

Advanced Students: Teaching assistantships available for advanced students. Apply by March 13. Research assistantships available for advanced students. Fellowships and scholarships available for advanced students.

Additional Information: Application and information available online at http://www.csun.edu/~gripact/06_ScholarshipsAndAwards/01_GeneralInformation.html.

Internships/Practica: Graduate students in applied fields have available an array of practicum experiences in the area. Direct clinical practicum experience is required of the Clinical students, who receive supervised training in three campus clinics specializing in Parent–Child Interaction Training, Child and Adolescent Diagnostic Assessment, and Cognitive–Behavioral Psychotherapy. In addition, clinical internships are available in many community sites including the University Counseling Services and local mental health care facilities. Human Factors students are connected with research and applications positions in the region. General Experimental students work with departmental faculty as well as with those at neighboring universities.

Housing and Day Care: On-campus housing is available. Contact the CSUN Housing Office at (818) 677-2160 or see the following Web site for more information: http://housing.csun.edu. On-campus day care facilities are available.

Employment of Department Graduates:

Master's Degree Graduates: Of those who graduated in the academic year 2006–2007, the following categories and numbers represent the postgraduate activities and employment of master's degree graduates: Enrolled in a postdoctoral residency/fellowship (n/a), employed in independent practice (n/a), total from the above (master's) (0).

Doctoral Degree Graduates: Of those who graduated in the academic year 2006–2007, the following categories and numbers represent the postgraduate activities and employment of doctoral degree graduates: Enrolled in a psychology doctoral program (n/a), total from the above (doctoral) (0).

Additional Information:

Orientation, Objectives, and Emphasis of Department: The Department of Psychology has, as a primary goal, the assurance that students receive a strong theoretical foundation as well as rigorous methodological and statistical coursework. In addition, all students must complete a project or a thesis in order to display their knowledge of their content area and their methodological sophistication. The applied Human Factors program emphasizes both job-related skills and general skills should students desire to continue their education at the doctoral level (and many do). The General Experimental and Clinical programs emphasize the basic research and content knowledge required to enhance students' opportunities for entry into doctoral programs.

Special Facilities or Resources: Some professors have federal or private grants that employ graduate students as research assistants. In addition, we have laboratories in Physiological Psychology (NeuroScan, BioPac), computer applications for Cognitive and Human Factors Psychology, multiple child-care sites for observation of children, and extensive research space. In addition, we also have a state-of-the-art Statistics Laboratory that can be used for data analyses for theses or projects.

Information for Students With Physical Disabilities: See the following Web site for more information: http://www.csun.edu/cod/index.htm.

Application Information:

Send to Psychology Graduate Office, California State University Northridge, 18111 Nordhoff Street, Northridge, CA 91330-8255. Students are admitted in the Fall, application deadline February 15; Spring, application deadline November 1. The Clinical Psychology Program accepts Fall applications only. General–Experimental and Human Factors will accept Spring and Fall applications, space permitting. *Fee:* $55. Contact Admissions and Records Office for details (818) 677-3700.

California State University, Sacramento

Department of Psychology
6000 J Street
Sacramento, CA 95819-6007
Telephone: (916) 278-6254
Fax: (916) 278-6820
E-mail: *youngl@csus.edu*
Web: *http://www.csus.edu/psyc*

Department Information:

1947. Chairperson: Bruce Behrman. Number of faculty: total—full-time 22, part-time 21; women—full-time 11, part-time 11; total—minority—full-time 6, part-time 5; women minority—full-time 3, part-time 4; faculty subject to the Americans With Disabilities Act 1.

Programs and Degrees Offered:

Listed in the following order: Program area, degree type (T if terminal Master's), number awarded 7/06–6/07. Counseling Psychology MA/MS (Master of Arts/Science) (T), Doctoral Preparation MA/MS (Master of Arts/Science) (T), Industrial/Organizational MA/MS (Master of Arts/Science) (T), Behavior Analysis MA/MS (Master of Arts/Science) (T), General Master's MA/MS (Master of Arts/Science) (T).

Student Applications/Admissions:

Student Applications

Counseling Psychology MA/MS (Master of Arts/Science)—Total applicants accepted 2007–2008, 15. The median number of years required for completion of a degree in 2006–2007 were 4. *Doctoral Preparation MA/MS (Master of Arts/Science)*—Total applicants accepted 2007–2008, 14. The median number of years required for completion of a degree in 2006–2007 were 3. *Industrial/Organizational MA/MS (Master of Arts/Science)*—Total applicants accepted 2007–2008, 8. The median number of years required for completion of a degree in 2006–2007 were 3. *Behavior Analysis MA/MS (Master of Arts/Science)*—*General Master's MA/MS (Master of Arts/Science)*—

Admissions Requirements:

Scores: Entries appear in this order: required test or GPA, minimum score (if required), median score of students entering in 2007–2008. Master's Programs: GRE-V no minimum stated, 580; GRE-Q no minimum stated, 580; GRE-Subject (Psychology) no minimum stated, 580.

Other Criteria: (importance of criteria rated low, medium, or high): GRE/MAT scores—high, GPA—high, letters of recommendation—high. For additional information on admission requirements, go to http://www.csus.edu/psyc.

Student Characteristics: The following represents characteristics of students in 2007–2008 in all graduate psychology programs in the department: Female—full-time 40, part-time 30; Male—full-time 30, part-time 20; African American/Black—full-time 8, part-time 0; Hispanic/Latino(a)—full-time 6, part-time 0; Asian/Pacific Islander—full-time 10, part-time 0; American Indian/Alaska Native—full-time 1, part-time 0; Caucasian/White—full-time 30, part-time 0; students subject to the Americans With Disabilities Act—full-time 3, part-time 0; Unknown ethnicity—full-time 15, part-time 0.

Financial Information/Assistance:

Financial Assistance:

First-Year Students: No information provided.

Advanced Students: Teaching assistantships available for advanced students. Fellowships and scholarships available for advanced students.

Additional Information: Of all students currently enrolled full time, 10% benefited from one or more of the listed financial assistance programs.

Internships/Practica: Students following both the Industrial/Organizational (I/O) and the Counseling Psychology programs will gain supervised on-site experience. I/O students typically enroll for several semesters of internship supervised by one of our faculty members. Opportunities are available in public sector organizations (e.g., state, county, and city personnel departments; public utilities) as well as private sector consulting firms, small businesses, and large corporations. Counseling Psychology students must also enroll for additional fieldwork in a community mental health setting with an on-site supervisor. Students may choose from more than a hundred sites in the Sacramento metropolitan area. These community sites must enter into a formal arrangement with the department, and the student's supervision hours must be officially logged.

Housing and Day Care: On-campus housing is available. See the following Web site for more information: http://www.csus.edu. On-campus day care facilities are available.

Employment of Department Graduates:

Master's Degree Graduates: Of those who graduated in the academic year 2006–2007, the following categories and numbers represent the postgraduate activities and employment of master's degree graduates: Enrolled in a psychology doctoral program (15), enrolled in a postdoctoral residency/fellowship (n/a), employed in independent practice (n/a), employed in an academic position at a university (2), employed in an academic position at a 2-year/4-year college (8), employed in business or industry (8), employed in government agency (12), employed in a community mental health/counseling center (20), total from the above (master's) (65).

Doctoral Degree Graduates: Of those who graduated in the academic year 2006–2007, the following categories and numbers represent the postgraduate activities and employment of doctoral degree graduates: Enrolled in a psychology doctoral program (n/a), total from the above (doctoral) (0).

Additional Information:

Orientation, Objectives, and Emphasis of Department: Our major programs are Doctoral Preparation, Industrial/Organizational (I/O), and Counseling Psychology. Doctoral preparation students take a strong research methods and quantitative course sequence in addition to content coursework in their interest area. They also engage in research during most of their program and are encouraged to become teaching assistants. Our I/O program has been designed to meet the competencies specified by SIOP and involved both classroom and fieldwork experience. Students take both general survey and current literature I/O courses in addition to their research, statistics, and measurement/testing courses, and are also expected to gain job experience as an intern. The Counseling Psychology program meets the state licensing requirements for Marriage and Family Therapy; students are exposed to a variety of therapeutic orientations and must participate in multiple practicum courses. In addition, graduate students can supplement their program with a Teaching of Psychology miniprogram in which they enroll in a formal teaching course and are then eligible to team teach an introductory psychology course in a subsequent semester. Those oriented toward a teaching career in a community college are advised to supplement their main course of study with this miniprogram. We also have a program in Behavior Analysis, which partially fulfills the requirements to become a Board Certified Behavior Analyst.

Special Facilities or Resources: The department occupies much of a relatively large building. Extensive facilities for human and animal research are available. We have a modern surgery room, animal colony, small group rooms with capabilities for audiovisual monitoring and recording, and a perception lab. A multiroom counseling suite within the building also has audiovisual capabilities; students enrolled in our practicum course provide services in this suite (under supervision) to clients from the community. One room in the building is maintained by the computer center; it contains 30 workstations.

Information for Students With Physical Disabilities: See the following Web site for more information: http://www.csus.edu.

Application Information:

Send to Graduate Coordinator, Psychology Department, CSU, Sacramento, 6000 J Street, Sacramento, CA 95819-6007. Application available online. URL of online application: http://www.csus.edu/psyc. Students are admitted in the Fall, application deadline March 1; Spring, application deadline November 1. *Fee:* $0.

California State University, San Marcos
Psychology
San Marcos, CA 92096
Telephone: (760) 750-4102
Fax: (760) 750-3418
E-mail: *smohseni@csusm.edu*
Web: *http://www.csusm.edu/psychology/*

Department Information:
1989. Chairperson: Sharon Hamill. Number of faculty: total—full-time 13, part-time 12; women—full-time 8, part-time 8; total—minority—full-time 2, part-time 2; women minority—full-time 1, part-time 1.

Programs and Degrees Offered:
Listed in the following order: Program area, degree type (T if terminal Master's), number awarded 7/06–6/07. Master of Arts in General Experimental Psychology MA/MS (Master of Arts/Science) (T) 5.

Student Applications/Admissions:
Student Applications
Master of Arts in General Experimental Psychology MA/MS (Master of Arts/Science)—Applications 2007–2008, 38. Total applicants accepted 2007–2008, 12. Number full-time enrolled (new admits only) 2007–2008, 6. Number part-time enrolled (new admits only) 2007–2008, 0. Total enrolled 2007–2008 full-time, 20, part-time, 2. Openings 2008–2009, 10. The median number of years required for completion of a degree in 2006–2007 were 3. The number of students enrolled full- and part-time who were dismissed or voluntarily withdrew from this program area in 2007–2008 were 0.

Admissions Requirements:
Scores: Entries appear in this order: required test or GPA, minimum score (if required), median score of students entering in 2007–2008. Master's Programs: GRE-V no minimum stated; GRE-Q no minimum stated; overall undergraduate GPA 3.0, 3.35; last 2 years GPA 3.0, 3.45; psychology GPA 3.0, 3.53; Masters GRE-Analytical no minimum stated. GRE-Subject (Psychology) is recommended but not required. Median GRE scores vary widely across years and so are not reported here.
Other Criteria: (importance of criteria rated low, medium, or high): GRE/MAT scores—medium, research experience—high, work experience—low, extracurricular activity—low, clinically related public service—low, GPA—high, letters of recommendation—high, statement of goals and objectives—high, match with faculty research—high, undergraduate major in psychology—high, specific undergraduate psychology courses taken—high. In the statement of goals and objectives, students must identify one or more faculty members in our department with whom they would like to work. We closely match students with faculty research interests. For additional information on admission requirements, go to http://www.csusm.edu/psychology/.

Student Characteristics: The following represents characteristics of students in 2007–2008 in all graduate psychology programs in the department: Female—full-time 17, part-time 1; Male—full-time 3, part-time 1; African American/Black—full-time 1, part-time 1; Hispanic/Latino(a)—full-time 4, part-time 0; Asian/Pacific Islander—full-time 0, part-time 0; American Indian/Alaska Native—full-time 0, part-time 0; Caucasian/White—full-time 15, part-time 1; Multi-ethnic—full-time 0, part-time 0; students subject to the Americans With Disabilities Act—full-time 0, part-time 0; Unknown ethnicity—full-time 0, part-time 0.

Financial Information/Assistance:
Tuition for Full-Time Study: *Master's:* State residents: per academic year $4,016; Nonstate residents: per academic year $7,067. Tuition is subject to change. See the following Web site for updates and changes in tuition costs: http://www.csusm.edu.

Financial Assistance:
First-Year Students: Teaching assistantships available for first year. Average number of hours worked per week: 5. Apply by varies. Research assistantships available for first year. Apply by varies. Fellowships and scholarships available for first year. Apply by varies. Tuition remission given: partial.
Advanced Students: Teaching assistantships available for advanced students. Apply by varies. Research assistantships available for advanced students. Apply by varies. Fellowships and scholarships available for advanced students. Apply by varies.
Additional Information: Of all students currently enrolled full time, 50% benefited from one or more of the listed financial assistance programs. Application and information available online at http://www.csusm.edu/psychology/ and http://www.csumentor.edu.

Internships/Practica: Master's Degree (MA/MS Master of Arts in General Experimental Psychology): An internship experience such as a final research project or "capstone" experience is required of graduates. Teaching of Psychology (PSYC 680) is designed for students who hope someday to teach at either a community college or a 4-year institution. Students learn pedagogical techniques associated with the discipline of psychology and will become eligible for teaching assignments in the university.

Housing and Day Care: On-campus housing is available. See the following Web site for more information: http://www.csusm.edu/srl/ (note: on-campus housing is very limited for graduate students, but private housing is available near campus). On-campus day care facilities are available. A new, state-of-the-art child care facility opened on campus in Fall 2007.

Employment of Department Graduates:
Master's Degree Graduates: Of those who graduated in the academic year 2006–2007, the following categories and numbers represent the postgraduate activities and employment of master's degree graduates: Enrolled in a psychology doctoral program (2), enrolled in another graduate/professional program (0), enrolled in a postdoctoral residency/fellowship (n/a), employed in independent practice (n/a), employed in an academic position at a 2-year/4-year college (1), employed in other positions at a higher education institution (2), employed in business or industry (0), total from the above (master's) (5).
Doctoral Degree Graduates: Of those who graduated in the academic year 2006–2007, the following categories and numbers represent the postgraduate activities and employment of doctoral degree graduates: Enrolled in a psychology doctoral program (n/a), total from the above (doctoral) (0).

Additional Information:

Orientation, Objectives, and Emphasis of Department: Our program is designed to accommodate students with different goals. The active research programs of our faculty, and our recognition of psychology as a scientific enterprise, provides students with the intensive research training and course work in primary content areas that are central to preparation for more advanced graduate work in any area of psychology. Likewise, students who have in mind careers in community college teaching, community service, mental health, or business and industry, will benefit from our program's emphasis on critical thinking, research methods, and advanced course work. It is our belief that excellent graduate education is best accomplished in an atmosphere in which graduate students are closely mentored by the faculty. The program is best suited for students who can attend full time, at least in the first 2 years, although exceptions are occasionally made. Note that our emphasis is on research training; we do not offer training leading to the Marriage and Family Therapy license in California.

Special Facilities or Resources: Established in 1989, CSUSM is the 20th campus of the California State University system. Our facilities are new and are growing to meet the demands of our increasing student population. In Psychology, we offer excellent computer support and shared research space for graduate students. Our faculty provide research opportunities for graduate students in a number of off-campus settings in the San Diego area.

Information for Students With Physical Disabilities: See the following Web site for more information: http://www.csusm.edu/dss/.

Application Information:

Send to Ms. Soheyla Darvish-Mohseni, Administrative Coordinator, Department of Psychology, California State University San Marcos, San Marcos, CA 92096. Application available online. URL of online application: http://www.csusm.edu/psychology and http://www.csumentor.edu. Students are admitted in the Fall, application deadline February 1. Review of applications begins February 1 and continues until all openings are filled or until March 15. *Fee:* $55. Fee may be waived for a limited number of low-income applicants. Ask for a Request for Application Fee Waiver Form. Out-of-state tuition may be waived in a small number of cases.

California, University of, Merced

Psychology
Social Sciences, Humanities, and Arts
P.O. Box 2039
Merced, CA 95344
Telephone: (209) 228-4372
Fax: (209) 228-4390
E-mail: *wshadish@ucmerced.edu*

Department Information:

2007. Chairperson: William R. Shadish. Number of faculty: total—full-time 4, part-time 5; women—full-time 1, part-time 3; minority—part-time 1; women minority—part-time 1.

Programs and Degrees Offered:

Listed in the following order: Program area, degree type (T if terminal Master's), number awarded 7/06–6/07. Developmental Psychology PhD (Doctor of Philosophy) 0, Health Psychology PhD (Doctor of Philosophy) 0, Quantitative Psychology PhD (Doctor of Philosophy) 0.

Student Applications/Admissions:

Student Applications

Developmental Psychology PhD (Doctor of Philosophy)—Applications 2007–2008, 7. Total applicants accepted 2007–2008, 3. Number full-time enrolled (new admits only) 2007–2008, 3. Number part-time enrolled (new admits only) 2007–2008, 0. Openings 2008–2009, 4. The number of students enrolled full- and part-time who were dismissed or voluntarily withdrew from this program area in 2007–2008 were 0. *Health Psychology PhD (Doctor of Philosophy)*—Applications 2007–2008, 3. Total applicants accepted 2007–2008, 0. Number full-time enrolled (new admits only) 2007–2008, 0. Number part-time enrolled (new admits only) 2007–2008, 0. Openings 2008–2009, 4. The number of students enrolled full- and part-time who were dismissed or voluntarily withdrew from this program area in 2007–2008 were 0. *Quantitative Psychology PhD (Doctor of Philosophy)*—Applications 2007–2008, 1. Total applicants accepted 2007–2008, 0. Number full-time enrolled (new admits only) 2007–2008, 0. Number part-time enrolled (new admits only) 2007–2008, 0. Openings 2008–2009, 5. The number of students enrolled full- and part-time who were dismissed or voluntarily withdrew from this program area in 2007–2008 were 1.

Admissions Requirements:

Scores: Entries appear in this order: required test or GPA, minimum score (if required), median score of students entering in 2007–2008. Doctoral Programs: GRE-V 510, 550; GRE-Q 470, 585; overall undergraduate GPA 2.88, 3.32.

Other Criteria: (importance of criteria rated low, medium, or high): GRE/MAT scores—medium, research experience—medium, work experience—low, extracurricular activity—low, clinically related public service—low, GPA—medium, letters of recommendation—medium, statement of goals and objectives—medium, undergraduate major in psychology—medium, specific undergraduate psychology courses taken—low. Admission decisions are based on a combination of factors, including academic degrees and records, the statement of purpose, letters of recommendation, test scores, and relevant work experience. We also consider the appropriateness of your goals to the degree program in which you are interested and to the research interests of the program's faculty. In addition, consideration may be given to how your background and life experience would contribute significantly to an educationally beneficial blend of students.

Student Characteristics: The following represents characteristics of students in 2007–2008 in all graduate psychology programs in the department: Female—full-time 4, part-time 0; Male—full-time 2, part-time 0; African American/Black—full-time 0, part-time 0; Hispanic/Latino(a)—full-time 2, part-time 0; Asian/Pacific Islander—full-time 0, part-time 0; American Indian/Alaska Native—full-time 0, part-time 0; Caucasian/White—full-time 4, part-time 0; Multi-ethnic—full-time 0, part-time 0; students subject to the Americans With Disabilities Act—full-time 0, part-time 0; Unknown ethnicity—full-time 0, part-time 0; International students who hold an F-1 or J-1 Visa—full-time 0, part-time 0.

Financial Information/Assistance:

Tuition for Full-Time Study: *Doctoral:* State residents: per academic year $9,328; Nonstate residents: per academic year $24,316. Tuition is subject to change. See the following Web site for updates and changes in tuition costs: http://www.registrar.ucmerced.edu/2.asp?uc=1&lvl2=76&contentid=114.

Financial Assistance:

First-Year Students: Teaching assistantships available for first year. Average amount paid per academic year: $18,000. Average number of hours worked per week: 20. Apply by March 2. Tuition remission given: full. Research assistantships available for first year. Average amount paid per academic year: $18,000. Average number of hours worked per week: 20. Apply by March 2. Tuition remission given: full. Fellowships and scholarships available for first year. Average amount paid per academic year: $18,000. Average number of hours worked per week: 20. Apply by March 2. Tuition remission given: full.

Advanced Students: Teaching assistantships available for advanced students. Average amount paid per academic year: $18,000. Average number of hours worked per week: 20. Apply by March 2. Tuition remission given: full. Research assistantships available for advanced students. Average amount paid per academic year: $18,000. Average number of hours worked per week: 20. Apply by March 2. Tuition remission given: full. Fellowships and scholarships available for advanced students. Average amount paid per academic year: $18,000. Average number of hours worked per week: 20. Apply by March 2. Tuition remission given: full.

Additional Information: Of all students currently enrolled full time, 100% benefited from one or more of the listed financial assistance programs. Application and information available online at http://graduatedivision.ucmerced.edu/2.asp?uc=1&lvl2=174&contentid=65.

Internships/Practica: None.

Housing and Day Care: No on-campus housing is available. No on-campus day care facilities are available.

Employment of Department Graduates:

Master's Degree Graduates: Of those who graduated in the academic year 2006–2007, the following categories and numbers represent the postgraduate activities and employment of master's degree graduates: Enrolled in a psychology doctoral program (6), enrolled in a postdoctoral residency/fellowship (n/a), employed in independent practice (n/a), total from the above (master's) (6). ***Doctoral Degree Graduates:*** Of those who graduated in the academic year 2006–2007, the following categories and numbers represent the postgraduate activities and employment of doctoral degree graduates: Enrolled in a psychology doctoral program (n/a), total from the above (doctoral) (0).

Additional Information:

Orientation, Objectives, and Emphasis of Department: University of California Merced is the first research university built in the United States this century. Our graduate training started in 2006, and is growing very rapidly in developmental, health, and quantitative psychology. We are highly research oriented, and do not offer any clinical training. We place priority on graduate students who desire a research career, but welcome applications from students with other aspirations as well. Applicants should review University of California Merced psychology faculty research interests before applying, and then indicate when applying how their interests fit within our faculty's interests.

Special Facilities or Resources: We are currently housed in a general office building, but will be housed in a new Social Sciences and Management building to be completed in 2011.

Information for Students With Physical Disabilities: See the following Web site for more information: http://www.disability.ucmerced.edu/.

Application Information:

Application available online. URL of online application: http://www.graduatedivision.ucmerced.edu/. Students are admitted in the Fall, application deadline January 15. *Fee:* $60.

California, University of, Berkeley (2007 data)

Psychology Department
Letters and Sciences
3210 Tolman Hall MC 1650
Berkeley, CA 94720-1650
Telephone: (510) 642-1382
Fax: (510) 642-5293
E-mail: *jtupper@berkeley.edu*
Web: *http://www.psychology.berkeley.edu/*

Department Information:

1921. Chairperson: Stephen Hinshaw. Number of faculty: total—full-time 45; women—full-time 16; faculty subject to the Americans With Disabilities Act 1.

Programs and Degrees Offered:

Listed in the following order: Program area, degree type (T if terminal Master's), number awarded 7/06–6/07. Cognition, Brain, and Behavior PhD (Doctor of Philosophy) 6, Social/Personality PhD (Doctor of Philosophy) 5, Change, Plasticity, and Development PhD (Doctor of Philosophy) 3, Clinical Science PhD (Doctor of Philosophy) 5.

APA Accreditation: Clinical PhD (Doctor of Philosophy).

Student Applications/Admissions:

Student Applications

Cognition, Brain, and Behavior PhD (Doctor of Philosophy)—Applications 2007–2008, 131. Total applicants accepted 2007–2008, 11. Number full-time enrolled (new admits only) 2007–2008, 9. Total enrolled 2007–2008 full-time, 35. Openings 2008–2009, 12. The median number of years required for completion of a degree in 2006–2007 were 5. *Social/Personality PhD (Doctor of Philosophy)*—Applications 2007–2008, 176. Total applicants accepted 2007–2008, 11. Number full-time enrolled (new admits only) 2007–2008, 3. Total enrolled 2007–2008 full-time, 27. Openings 2008–2009, 10. The median number of years required for completion of a degree in 2006–2007 were 5. *Change, Plasticity, and Development PhD (Doctor of Philosophy)*—Applications 2007–2008, 48. Total applicants accepted 2007–2008, 6. Number full-time enrolled (new admits only) 2007–2008, 3. Total enrolled 2007–2008 full-time, 21. Openings 2008–2009, 8. The number of students enrolled full- and part-time who were dismissed or voluntarily withdrew from this program area in 2007–2008 were 1. *Clinical Science PhD (Doctor of Philosophy)*—Applications 2007–2008, 321. Total applicants accepted 2007–2008, 8. Number full-time enrolled (new admits only) 2007–2008, 3. Total enrolled 2007–2008 full-time, 34. Openings 2008–2009, 8. The median number of years required for completion of a degree in 2006–2007 were 6.

Admissions Requirements:

Scores: Entries appear in this order: required test or GPA, minimum score (if required), median score of students entering in 2007–2008. Master's Programs: We do not have a Master's Program. Doctoral Programs: GRE-V no minimum stated; GRE-Q no minimum stated; overall undergraduate GPA 3.0; last 2 years GPA 3.0; psychology GPA 3.0; Doctoral program GRE-Analytic no minimum stated.

Other Criteria: (importance of criteria rated low, medium, or high): GRE/MAT scores—medium, research experience—high, work experience—high, extracurricular activity—medium, clinically related public service—high, GPA—medium, letters of recommendation—high, interview—high, statement of goals and objectives—high.

Student Characteristics: The following represents characteristics of students in 2007–2008 in all graduate psychology programs in the department: Female—full-time 71, part-time 0; Male—full-time 46, part-time 0; African American/Black—full-time 2, part-time 0; Hispanic/Latino(a)—full-time 4, part-time 0; Asian/Pacific Islander—full-time 14, part-time 0; American Indian/Alaska Native—full-time 0, part-time 0; Caucasian/White—full-time 77, part-time 0; Multi-ethnic—full-time 3, part-time 0; students subject to the Americans With Disabilities Act—full-time 0, part-time 0; Unknown ethnicity—full-time 17, part-time 0.

Financial Information/Assistance:

Tuition for Full-Time Study: *Doctoral:* State residents: per academic year $8,438; Nonstate residents: per academic year $18,904. Tuition is subject to change. See the following Web site for updates and changes in tuition costs: http://www.registrar.berkeley.edu/.

Financial Assistance:

First-Year Students: Teaching assistantships available for first year. Average amount paid per academic year: $14,445. Tuition remission given: partial. Research assistantships available for first year. Average amount paid per academic year: $18,904. Tuition remission given: partial. Fellowships and scholarships available for first year. Apply by December 1. Tuition remission given: full.

Advanced Students: Teaching assistantships available for advanced students. Average amount paid per academic year: $14,445. Tuition remission given: partial. Research assistantships available for advanced students. Average amount paid per academic year: $16,785. Tuition remission given: partial. Fellowships and scholarships available for advanced students.

Additional Information: Of all students currently enrolled full time, 90% benefited from one or more of the listed financial assistance programs.

Internships/Practica: The sole practicum experience on-site is the Psychology Clinic, a pre-internship site for 2nd and 3rd year students in the Clinical Science program. A community clinic, operating on a sliding scale basis, for individuals and families in the Bay Area, the Clinic offers assessment, individual therapy, couples therapy, child/family therapy, and consultations.

Housing and Day Care: On-campus housing is available. See the following Web site for more information: http://www.housing.berkeley.edu. On-campus day care facilities are available. See the following Web site for more information: http://www.housing.berkeley.edu/child/families/.

Employment of Department Graduates:

Master's Degree Graduates: Of those who graduated in the academic year 2006–2007, the following categories and numbers represent the postgraduate activities and employment of master's degree graduates: Enrolled in a postdoctoral residency/fellowship (n/a), employed in independent practice (n/a), total from the above (master's) (0).

Doctoral Degree Graduates: Of those who graduated in the academic year 2006–2007, the following categories and numbers represent the postgraduate activities and employment of doctoral degree graduates: Enrolled in a psychology doctoral program (n/a), total from the above (doctoral) (0).

Additional Information:

Orientation, Objectives, and Emphasis of Department: The goal of the graduate program in Psychology at Berkeley is to produce scholar–researchers with sufficient breadth to retain perspective on the field of psychology and sufficient depth to permit successful independent and significant research. The members of the Department have organized themselves into four graduate training areas. These areas reflect a sense of intellectual community among the faculty and correspond, in general, with traditional designations in the field. However, each graduate training area has a distinctive stamp placed upon it by the faculty and students that make up the program. The majority of our students enter graduate training and fulfill the requirements established by the existent training areas listed below. These requirements vary from area to area but always involve a combination of courses, seminars, and supervised independent research. Students are also encouraged to take courses outside the Psychology Department, using the unique faculty strengths found on the Berkeley campus to enrich their graduate training.

Special Facilities or Resources: The Department of Psychology is housed in Tolman Hall, a building shared with the Graduate School of Education. A library devoted to books and journals in psychology and education is maintained on the second floor of this building. The main office of the Psychology Department, as well as faculty and teaching assistant offices are on the third floor of Tolman Hall. Research rooms for carrying out a variety of studies with human subjects are on the basement, ground, fourth, and fifth floors. The basement also houses a human audition laboratory, an electronics shop, and a machine and woodworking shop. A photographic darkroom is on the fifth floor. The Institute of Human Development is housed on the first floor of Tolman Hall, the Psychology Clinic on the second floor, and the Institute of Personality and Social Research on the fourth floor. The remaining research units—The Institute for Cognitive and Brain Sciences, the Field Station for the Study of Behavior, Ecology and Reproduction, the Institute of Industrial Relations, the Helen Wills Neuroscience Institute, the Henry H. Wheeler Center for Brain Imaging, and the Northwest Animal Facility are located elsewhere on campus and in the adjacent areas.

Information for Students With Physical Disabilities: See the following Web site for more information: http://vdsp.berkeley.edu/.

Application Information:

Send to Graduate Assistant, Department of Psychology, 3210 Tolman Hall, University of California at Berkeley, Berkeley, CA 94720-1652. Application available online. URL of online application: https://www.gradadm.berkeley.edu:7200/gapappl/grd_login_menu. Students are admitted in the Fall, application deadline December 1. Web applications strongly encouraged. Web application available October 1. *Fee:* $60.

California, University of, Berkeley

School Psychology Program
Graduate School of Education
4511 Tolman Hall
Berkeley, CA 94720-1670
Telephone: (510) 642-7581
Fax: (510) 642-3555
E-mail: *frankc@berkeley.edu*
Web: *http://www-gse.berkeley.edu/program/sp/sp.html*

Department Information:

1966. Program Director: Frank C. Worrell. Number of faculty: total—full-time 2, part-time 5; women—full-time 1, part-time 5.

Programs and Degrees Offered:

Listed in the following order: Program area, degree type (T if terminal Master's), number awarded 7/06–6/07. School Psychology Program PhD (Doctor of Philosophy) 7.

APA Accreditation: School PhD (Doctor of Philosophy).

Student Applications/Admissions:

Student Applications

School Psychology Program PhD (Doctor of Philosophy)—Applications 2007–2008, 67. Total applicants accepted 2007–2008, 8. Number full-time enrolled (new admits only) 2007–2008, 5. Total enrolled 2007–2008 full-time, 44. Openings 2008–2009, 8. The median number of years required for completion of a degree in 2006–2007 were 6. The number of students enrolled full- and part-time who were dismissed or voluntarily withdrew from this program area in 2007–2008 were 0.

Admissions Requirements:

Scores: Entries appear in this order: required test or GPA, minimum score (if required), median score of students entering in 2007–2008. Doctoral Programs: GRE-V no minimum stated, 600; GRE-Q no minimum stated, 640; overall undergraduate GPA 3.00, 3.8; Doctoral program GRE-Analytic no minimum stated.

Other Criteria: (importance of criteria rated low, medium, or high): GRE/MAT scores—high, research experience—high, work experience—medium, extracurricular activity—medium, clinically related public service—medium, GPA—high, letters of recommendation—high, interview—medium, statement of goals and objectives—high, undergraduate major in psychology—medium.

Student Characteristics: The following represents characteristics of students in 2007–2008 in all graduate psychology programs in the department: Female—full-time 38, part-time 0; Male—full-time 6, part-time 0; African American/Black—full-time 6, part-time 0; Hispanic/Latino(a)—full-time 3, part-time 0; Asian/Pacific Islander—full-time 5, part-time 0; American Indian/Alaska Native—full-time 1, part-time 0; Caucasian/White—full-time 29, part-time 0; Multi-ethnic—full-time 0, part-time 0; students subject to the Americans With Disabilities Act—full-time 0, part-time 0; Unknown ethnicity—full-time 0, part-time 0; International students who hold an F-1 or J-1 Visa—full-time 1, part-time 0.

Financial Information/Assistance:

Tuition for Full-Time Study: *Doctoral:* State residents: per academic year $9,578; Nonstate residents: per academic year $24,566. Tuition is subject to change. See the following Web site for updates and changes in tuition costs: http://www.registrar.berkeley.edu/Registration/feesched.html.

Financial Assistance:

First-Year Students: Teaching assistantships available for first year. Average amount paid per academic year: $16,391. Average number of hours worked per week: 20. Apply by before Fall and Spring. Tuition remission given: partial. Research assistantships available for first year. Average amount paid per academic year: $16,212. Average number of hours worked per week: 20. Apply by varies. Tuition remission given: full. Fellowships and scholarships available for first year. Average amount paid per academic year: $12,500. Apply by December 1.

Advanced Students: Teaching assistantships available for advanced students. Average amount paid per academic year: $16,391. Average number of hours worked per week: 20. Apply by before Fall and Spring. Tuition remission given: partial. Research assistantships available for advanced students. Average amount paid per academic year: $16,212. Average number of hours worked per week: 20. Apply by before Fall and Spring. Tuition remission given: full. Fellowships and scholarships available for advanced students. Average amount paid per academic year: $10,000. Apply by March 1.

Additional Information: Of all students currently enrolled full time, 80% benefited from one or more of the listed financial assistance programs. Application and information available online at http://gse.berkeley.edu.

Internships/Practica: Doctoral Degree (PhD School Psychology Program): For those doctoral students for whom a professional internship was required in this program prior to graduation, (15) students applied for an internship in 2006–2007, with (14) students obtaining an internship. Of those students who obtained an internship, (11) were paid internships. Of those students who obtained an internship, (0)students placed in APA/CPA-accredited internships, (0) students placed in internships not APA/CPA-accredited, but listed with the Association of Psychology Postdoctoral and Internship Centers (APPIC), (6) students placed in internships conforming to guidelines of the Council of Directors of School Psychology Programs (CDSPP), (8) students placed in internships that were not APA/CPA accredited, APPIC or CDSPP listed. Students on school-based internships are usually paid on the basis of school-district schedule for half to three-quarter time usually from $13,000–$17,000 per school year.

Housing and Day Care: On-campus housing is available. See the following Web site for more information: http://www.calrentals.housing.berkeley.edu. On-campus day care facilities are available. See the following Web site for more information: http://www.housing.berkeley.edu/child.

Employment of Department Graduates:

Master's Degree Graduates: Of those who graduated in the academic year 2006–2007, the following categories and numbers represent the postgraduate activities and employment of master's degree graduates: Enrolled in a postdoctoral residency/fellowship (n/a), employed in independent practice (n/a), total from the above (master's) (0).

Doctoral Degree Graduates: Of those who graduated in the academic year 2006–2007, the following categories and numbers represent the postgraduate activities and employment of doctoral degree graduates: Enrolled in a psychology doctoral program (n/a), employed in a professional position in a school system (7), total from the above (doctoral) (7).

Additional Information:

Orientation, Objectives, and Emphasis of Department: The school psychology program is a doctoral program within the cognition and development area. The program emphasizes the scientist–professional model of school psychological services, linking strong preparation in theory and research to applications in the professional context of schools and school systems. Through the thoughtful application of knowledge and skills, school psychologists work together with teachers and other school professionals to clarify and resolve problems regarding the educational and mental health needs of children in classrooms. Working as consultants and collaborators, school psychologists help others to accommodate the social systems of schools to the individual differences of students, with the ultimate goal of promoting academic and social development. Graduate work within the program is supervised by professors from the Departments of Education and Psychology. Students fulfill all requirements for the academic PhD in human development, with additional coursework representing professional preparation for the specialty practice of school psychology. The program is accredited by APA. A program brochure is available for anyone wishing further information.

Special Facilities or Resources: The school psychology program is based at the University of California, Berkeley, which is a major research university in a large metropolitan area of the country. Students have access to faculty research and university resources in countless topics and areas of specialization. The university and department sponsor numerous colloquia, speakers, and visiting lecturers from around the world throughout the year. Both intellectual and cultural resources abound. Ongoing research programs of faculty offer students opportunities to engage in applications of psychology to educational problems during their first three years of the program and in their dissertation research.

Information for Students With Physical Disabilities: See the following Web site for more information: http://www.dsp.berkeley.edu.

Application Information:

Send to Admission Office, Graduate School of Education. Application available online. URL of online application: http://www.gse.berkeley.edu. Students are admitted in the Fall, application deadline December 1. *Fee:* $60.

California, University of, Davis (2007 data)

Department of Psychology
College of Letters and Science
One Shields Avenue
Davis, CA 95616-8686
Telephone: (530) 752-9362
Fax: (530) 752-2087
E-mail: *kfwidaman@ucdavis.edu*
Web: *http://www.psychology.ucdavis.edu*

Department Information:

1957. Chairperson: Keith Widaman. Number of faculty: total—full-time 40, part-time 1; women—full-time 12, part-time 1.

Programs and Degrees Offered:

Listed in the following order: Program area, degree type (T if terminal Master's), number awarded 7/06–6/07. Cognition and Cognitive Neuroscience PhD (Doctor of Philosophy) 0, Psychobiology PhD (Doctor of Philosophy) 2, Developmental PhD (Doctor of Philosophy) 2, Social Personality PhD (Doctor of Philosophy) 4, Quantitative PhD (Doctor of Philosophy) 0.

Student Applications/Admissions:

Student Applications

Cognition and Cognitive Neuroscience PhD (Doctor of Philosophy)—Applications 2007–2008, 94. Total applicants accepted 2007–2008, 16. Number full-time enrolled (new admits only) 2007–2008, 9. Number part-time enrolled (new admits only) 2007–2008, 0. Openings 2008–2009, 8. The median number of years required for completion of a degree in 2006–2007 were 5. The number of students enrolled full- and part-time who were dismissed or voluntarily withdrew from this program area in 2007–2008 were 0. *Psychobiology PhD (Doctor of Philosophy)*—Applications 2007–2008, 19. Total applicants accepted 2007–2008, 6. Number full-time enrolled (new admits only) 2007–2008, 3. Openings 2008–2009, 2. The median number of years required for completion of a degree in 2006–2007 were 5. The number of students enrolled full- and part-time who were dismissed or voluntarily withdrew from this program area in 2007–2008 were 0. *Developmental PhD (Doctor of Philosophy)*—Applications 2007–2008, 54. Total applicants accepted 2007–2008, 8. Number full-time enrolled (new admits only) 2007–2008, 4. Number part-time enrolled (new admits only) 2007–2008, 0. Openings 2008–2009, 4. The median number of years required for completion of a degree in 2006–2007 were 5. The number of students enrolled full- and part-time who were dismissed or voluntarily withdrew from this program area in 2007–2008 were 0. *Social Personality PhD (Doctor of Philosophy)*—Applications 2007–2008, 71. Total applicants accepted 2007–2008, 15. Number full-time enrolled (new admits only) 2007–2008, 7. Number part-time enrolled (new admits only) 2007–2008, 0. Openings 2008–2009, 5. The median number of years required for completion of a degree in 2006–2007 were 5. The number of students enrolled full- and part-time who were dismissed or voluntarily withdrew from this program area in 2007–2008 were 0. *Quantitative PhD (Doctor of Philosophy)*—Applications 2007–2008, 16. Total applicants accepted 2007–2008, 7. Number full-time enrolled (new admits only) 2007–2008, 3. Total enrolled 2007–2008 full-time, 4. Openings 2008–2009, 2. The median number of years required for completion of a degree in 2006–2007 were 5. The number of students enrolled full- and part-time who were dismissed or voluntarily withdrew from this program area in 2007–2008 were 0.

Admissions Requirements:

Scores: Entries appear in this order: required test or GPA, minimum score (if required), median score of students entering in 2007–2008. Doctoral Programs: GRE-V no minimum stated, 660; GRE-Q no minimum stated, 720; overall undergraduate GPA 3.00, 3.58; psychology GPA no minimum stated, 3.76.

Other Criteria: (importance of criteria rated low, medium, or high): GRE/MAT scores—high, research experience—high, work experience—low, extracurricular activity—low, GPA—high, letters of recommendation—high, statement of goals and objectives—high. For additional information on admission requirements, go to http://psychology.ucdavis.edu.

Student Characteristics: The following represents characteristics of students in 2007–2008 in all graduate psychology programs in the department: Female—full-time 44, part-time 0; Male—full-time 32, part-time 0; African American/Black—full-time 2, part-time 0; Hispanic/Latino(a)—full-time 1, part-time 0; Asian/Pacific Islander—full-time 9, part-time 0; American Indian/Alaska Native—full-time 0, part-time 0; Caucasian/White—full-time 63, part-time 0; students subject to the Americans With Disabilities Act—full-time 2, part-time 0; Unknown ethnicity—full-time 1, part-time 0.

Financial Information/Assistance:

Tuition for Full-Time Study: *Doctoral:* State residents: per academic year $9,142; Nonstate residents: per academic year $24,103. Tuition is subject to change. See the following Web site for updates and changes in tuition costs: http://www.registrar.ucdavis.edu.

Financial Assistance:

First-Year Students: Teaching assistantships available for first year. Average amount paid per academic year: $15,610. Average number of hours worked per week: 20. Tuition remission given: full. Research assistantships available for first year. Average amount paid per academic year: $15,438. Average number of hours worked per week: 20. Tuition remission given: full. Traineeships available for first year. Average amount paid per academic year: $16,265. Tuition remission given: partial. Fellowships and scholarships available for first year. Average amount paid per academic year: $5,000. Apply by January 15.

Advanced Students: Teaching assistantships available for advanced students. Average amount paid per academic year: $15,610. Average number of hours worked per week: 20. Tuition remission given: full. Research assistantships available for advanced students. Average amount paid per academic year: $18,450. Average number of hours worked per week: 20. Tuition remission given: full. Fellowships and scholarships available for advanced students. Average amount paid per academic year: $5,000. Apply by January 15.

Additional Information: Of all students currently enrolled full time, 95% benefited from one or more of the listed financial assistance programs. Application and information available online at http://psychology.ucdavis.edu.

Internships/Practica: No information provided.

Housing and Day Care: On-campus housing is available. See the following Web site for more information: http://www.housing.ucdavis.edu. On-campus day care facilities are available. See the following Web site for more information: http://www.hr.ucdavis.edu/childcare.

Employment of Department Graduates:

Master's Degree Graduates: Of those who graduated in the academic year 2006–2007, the following categories and numbers represent the postgraduate activities and employment of master's degree graduates: Enrolled in a postdoctoral residency/fellowship (n/a), employed in independent practice (n/a), total from the above (master's) (0).

Doctoral Degree Graduates: Of those who graduated in the academic year 2006–2007, the following categories and numbers represent the postgraduate activities and employment of doctoral degree graduates: Enrolled in a psychology doctoral program (n/a), enrolled in a postdoctoral residency/fellowship (4), employed in an academic position at a university (5), employed in other positions at a higher education institution (1), employed in government agency (1), total from the above (doctoral) (11).

Additional Information:

Orientation, Objectives, and Emphasis of Department: The department places strong emphasis on empirical research in five broad areas: (a) psychobiology (e.g., animal behavior, primatology, hormones and behavior, brain bases of social attachments, eating and obesity); (b) perception, cognition, and cognitive neuroscience (e.g., memory, attention, language, consciousness); (c) personality, social psychology, and social neuroscience (e.g., emotions, attitudes, prejudice, close relationships, cultural psychology, psychology of religion, brain bases of personality traits); (d) developmental psychology (cognitive, affective, and social development, personality development, effects of child abuse, brain bases of developmental disorders); and (e) quantitative psychology (e.g., psychometrics, multivariate statistics, hierarchical linear models, statistical models used in areas as diverse as neuroscience and longitudinal developmental research). Weekly colloquia in these five areas provide students with opportunities to hear about new research and present their own ideas and findings. Each student selects a three-person faculty advisory committee, which guides and evaluates the student's progress through the program. Major exams are tailored to each student by his or her advisory committee. Every faculty member has an active lab, permitting students to learn about anything from cellular recording and brain imaging to behavioral studies of development, perception, cognition, language, emotion, and both individual and social behavior, in both humans and nonhuman animals.

Special Facilities or Resources: The Psychology Department, which contains numerous state-of-the-art laboratories, computer facilities, and a survey research facility, overlaps with several other major research centers on campus: a regional Primate Research

Center, a Center for Neuroscience, a Center for Mind and Brain, and the M.I.N.D. Institute for research on developmental disorders. Departmental faculty members participate in campuswide graduate groups in psychology, human development, animal behavior, neuroscience, and other fields, and in a cross-university Bay Area Affective Sciences Training Program. The university includes a medical school, a veterinary school, a business school, and a law school, as well as exceptionally strong programs in all of the biological and social sciences. The Department of Psychology offers graduate students an education that is intellectually exciting, personally challenging, and very forward-looking, one that prepares new teacher–scientist–scholars to advance the study of mind, brain, and behavior.

Information for Students With Physical Disabilities: See the following Web site for more information: http://www.sdc.ucdavis.edu.

Application Information:
Send to Anna Libonati, Graduate Program Coordinator, Psychology Department, University of California, One Shields Avenue, Davis, CA 95616-8686. Application available online. URL of online application: http://www.gradstudies.ucdavis.edu. Students are admitted in the Fall, application deadline December 15. Fellowship deadline is December 15. *Fee:* $60.

California, University of, Davis

Human Development
Agricultural and Environmental Sciences
One Shields Avenue
Davis, CA 95616-8523
Telephone: (530) 754-4109
Fax: (530) 752-5660
E-mail: *effie@ucdavis.edu*
Web: *http://www.humandevelopment.ucdavis.edu*

Department Information:

1971. Chair, Human and Child Development Graduate Groups: Rand Conger. Number of faculty: total—full-time 29; women—full-time 24; faculty subject to the Americans With Disabilities Act 1.

Programs and Degrees Offered:

Listed in the following order: Program area, degree type (T if terminal Master's), number awarded 7/06–6/07. Child Development MA/MS (Master of Arts/Science) (T) 5, Human Development PhD (Doctor of Philosophy) 6.

Student Applications/Admissions:

Student Applications

Child Development MA/MS (Master of Arts/Science)—Applications 2007–2008, 16. Total applicants accepted 2007–2008, 4. Number full-time enrolled (new admits only) 2007–2008, 2. Openings 2008–2009, 12. The median number of years required for completion of a degree in 2006–2007 were 3. The number of students enrolled full- and part-time who were dismissed or voluntarily withdrew from this program area in 2007–2008 were 0. *Human Development PhD (Doctor of Philosophy)*—Applications 2007–2008, 18. Total applicants accepted 2007–2008, 12. Number full-time enrolled (new admits only) 2007–2008, 6. Total enrolled 2007–2008 full-time, 31. Openings 2008–2009, 12. The median number of years required for completion of a degree in 2006–2007 were 7. The number of students enrolled full- and part-time who were dismissed or voluntarily withdrew from this program area in 2007–2008 were 1.

Admissions Requirements:

Scores: Entries appear in this order: required test or GPA, minimum score (if required), median score of students entering in 2007–2008. Master's Programs: GRE-V no minimum stated, 515; GRE-Q no minimum stated, 538; overall undergraduate GPA 3.0, 3.81; last 2 years GPA 3.0; psychology GPA 3.0; Masters GRE-Analytical no minimum stated, 5.0. Doctoral Programs: GRE-V no minimum stated, 525; GRE-Q no minimum stated, 642; overall undergraduate GPA 3.0, 3.62; last 2 years GPA 3.0; psychology GPA 3.0; Doctoral program GRE-Analytic no minimum stated, 4.5. GRE subject test is recommended but not required.

Other Criteria: (importance of criteria rated low, medium, or high): GRE/MAT scores—high, research experience—high, work experience—high, extracurricular activity—low, clinically related public service—low, GPA—high, letters of recommendation—high, interview—high, statement of goals and objectives—high, undergraduate major in psychology—medium, specific undergraduate psychology courses taken—high. For the Human Development PhD, we require a writing sample/paper. This can be a MS Thesis but more often it is a past publication where the applicant is considered a major author. For additional information on admission requirements, go to http://humandevelopment.ucdavis.edu/.

Student Characteristics: The following represents characteristics of students in 2007–2008 in all graduate psychology programs in the department: Female—full-time 42, part-time 0; Male—full-time 3, part-time 0; African American/Black—full-time 4, part-time 0; Hispanic/Latino(a)—full-time 6, part-time 0; Asian/Pacific Islander—full-time 9, part-time 0; American Indian/Alaska Native—full-time 0, part-time 0; Caucasian/White—full-time 0, part-time 0; Multi-ethnic—full-time 1, part-time 0; students subject to the Americans With Disabilities Act—full-time 2, part-time 0; Unknown ethnicity—full-time 25, part-time 0.

Financial Information/Assistance:

Tuition for Full-Time Study: *Master's:* State residents: per academic year $9,142; Nonstate residents: per academic year $24,103. *Doctoral:* State residents: per academic year $9,142; Nonstate residents: per academic year $24,103. Tuition is subject to change. See the following Web site for updates and changes in tuition costs: http://www.ormp.ucdavis.edu/studentfees.

Financial Assistance:

First-Year Students: Teaching assistantships available for first year. Average number of hours worked per week: 20. Apply by open. Tuition remission given: full. Research assistantships available for first year. Average number of hours worked per week: 20. Apply by open. Tuition remission given: full. Fellowships and scholarships available for first year. Apply by January 15. Tuition remission given: full and partial.

Advanced Students: Teaching assistantships available for advanced students. Average number of hours worked per week: 20. Apply by open. Tuition remission given: full. Research assistantships available for advanced students. Average number of hours worked per week: 20. Apply by open. Tuition remission given: full. Fellowships and scholarships available for advanced students. Apply by January 15. Tuition remission given: full and partial.

Additional Information: Of all students currently enrolled full time, 90% benefited from one or more of the listed financial assistance programs. Application and information available online at http://humandevelopment.ucdavis.edu/.

Internships/Practica: For Child Development MS: students' application of theories of learning and development to interaction with children 6 months to 5 years at the Center for Child and Family Studies and field studies with children and adolescents. Study of children's affective, cognitive, and social development within the context of family/school environments, hospitals, and foster group homes. Child Life internships through the University of California Davis Medical Center. Internships through the 4-H Center for Youth Development, includng 4-H and CE-sponsored out-of-school childcare, and the M.I.N.D. Institute.

Housing and Day Care: No on-campus housing is available. On-campus day care facilities are available. See the following Web site for more information: http://www.hr.ucdavis.edu/childcare/.

Employment of Department Graduates:

Master's Degree Graduates: Of those who graduated in the academic year 2006–2007, the following categories and numbers represent the postgraduate activities and employment of master's degree graduates: Enrolled in a psychology doctoral program (3), enrolled in a postdoctoral residency/fellowship (n/a), employed in independent practice (n/a), do not know (1), total from the above (master's) (4).

Doctoral Degree Graduates: Of those who graduated in the academic year 2006–2007, the following categories and numbers represent the postgraduate activities and employment of doctoral degree graduates: Enrolled in a psychology doctoral program (n/a), enrolled in a postdoctoral residency/fellowship (1), employed in an academic position at a university (1), employed in business or industry (2), employed in a community mental health/counseling center (1), do not know (1), total from the above (doctoral) (6).

Additional Information:

Orientation, Objectives, and Emphasis of Department: Both the Child Development Master of Science and Human Development PhD are offered by a graduate group that is interdisciplinary in nature, with a core faculty housed in the Department of Human and Community Development, and other graduate group faculty housed in education, law, medicine, psychiatry, M.I.N.D. Institute, and psychology. Child Development MS students will be prepared to teach at the community college level in developmental and to do applied/evaluation research, or pursue higher degrees. The Human Development PhD students will be prepared to teach at the university level to do basic or applied research in lifespan, cognitive, and social–emotional development from an interdisciplinary perspective with an appreciation of the contexts of development (family, school, health, social–cultural, and social policy). There are extensive student research opportunities within all the departments from which faculty are drawn, as well as the Center for Child and Family Studies, the 4-H Extension Program's Center for Youth Development, the M.I.N.D. Institute, and the Center for Neuroscience.

Special Facilities or Resources: Center for Child and Family Studies, Infant Sleep Lab, Parent and Child Lab, Center for Neuroscience, Center for Youth Development, Cooperative Research and Extension Services for Schools, M.I.N.D. Institute. Extensive community placements in education, and social welfare.

Information for Students With Physical Disabilities: See the following Web site for more information: http://www.sdc.ucdavis.edu.

Application Information:

Send to Effie Kolbeins, Graduate Adviser, Human Development Graduate Group, University of California Davis, One Shields Avenue, Davis, CA 65616-8523. Application available online. URL of online application: https://www.apply.embark.com/grad/UCDavis/30/. Students are admitted in the Fall, application deadline January 1. Fellowship deadline for the next September—January 1. *Fee:* $60.

California, University of, Irvine

Department of Cognitive Sciences
3151 Social Science Plaza
Irvine, CA 92697-5100
Telephone: (949) 824-6692
Fax: (949) 824-2307
E-mail: *cogsci@uci.edu*
Web: *http://www.cogsci.uci.edu/*

Department Information:

1986. Chairperson: Michael D'Zmura. Number of faculty: total—full-time 29, part-time 12; women—full-time 7, part-time 5; total—minority—full-time 1, part-time 3; women minority—part-time 1; faculty subject to the Americans With Disabilities Act 2.

Programs and Degrees Offered:

Listed in the following order: Program area, degree type (T if terminal Master's), number awarded 7/06–6/07. Cognitive PhD (Doctor of Philosophy) 6.

Student Applications/Admissions:

Student Applications

Cognitive PhD (Doctor of Philosophy)—Applications 2007–2008, 75. Total applicants accepted 2007–2008, 18. Number full-time enrolled (new admits only) 2007–2008, 16. Openings 2008–2009, 15. The median number of years required for completion of a degree in 2006–2007 were 5. The number of students enrolled full- and part-time who were dismissed or voluntarily withdrew from this program area in 2007–2008 were 0.

Admissions Requirements:

Scores: Entries appear in this order: required test or GPA, minimum score (if required), median score of students entering in 2007–2008. Doctoral Programs: GRE-V no minimum stated;

GRE-Q no minimum stated; overall undergraduate GPA 3.0; last 2 years GPA 3.5. Applicants whose first language is not English must also take the Test of English as a Foreign Language (TOEFL) and achieve a score of 213 or higher on the computer-based exam or 550 or higher on the paper-based exam. As an alternative, candidates for admission may submit scores from the Academic Modules of the International English Language Testing System (IELTS), in which case an overall minimum score of 7 is required, with a score of no less than 6 on any individual module.

Other Criteria: (importance of criteria rated low, medium, or high): GRE/MAT scores—high, research experience—high, work experience—low, GPA—medium, letters of recommendation—high, interview—high, statement of goals and objectives—high.

Student Characteristics: The following represents characteristics of students in 2007–2008 in all graduate psychology programs in the department: Female—full-time 30, part-time 0; Male—full-time 33, part-time 0; African American/Black—full-time 0, part-time 0; Hispanic/Latino(a)—full-time 5, part-time 0; Asian/Pacific Islander—full-time 20, part-time 0; American Indian/Alaska Native—full-time 0, part-time 0; Caucasian/White—full-time 38, part-time 0; Multi-ethnic—full-time 0, part-time 0; students subject to the Americans With Disabilities Act—full-time 0, part-time 0; Unknown ethnicity—full-time 0, part-time 0; International students who hold an F-1 or J-1 Visa—full-time 12, part-time 0.

Financial Information/Assistance:

Tuition for Full-Time Study: *Doctoral:* State residents: per academic year $10,715; Nonstate residents: per academic year $25,703. Tuition is subject to change. See the following Web site for updates and changes in tuition costs: http://www.rgs.uci.edu/grad/prospective/deadline.htm.

Financial Assistance:

First-Year Students: Teaching assistantships available for first year. Average amount paid per academic year: $16,390. Average number of hours worked per week: 20. Apply by April 15. Tuition remission given: full. Research assistantships available for first year. Average amount paid per academic year: $12,159. Average number of hours worked per week: 20. Apply by April 15. Tuition remission given: full. Fellowships and scholarships available for first year. Apply by April 15. Tuition remission given: full and partial.

Advanced Students: Teaching assistantships available for advanced students. Average amount paid per academic year: $16,390. Average number of hours worked per week: 20. Apply by see Web site. Tuition remission given: full. Research assistantships available for advanced students. Average amount paid per academic year: $15,696. Average number of hours worked per week: 20. Tuition remission given: full. Fellowships and scholarships available for advanced students. Apply by varies. Tuition remission given: full.

Additional Information: Of all students currently enrolled full time, 99% benefited from one or more of the listed financial assistance programs. Application and information available online at http://www.fao.uci.edu.

Internships/Practica: None.

Housing and Day Care: On-campus housing is available. See the following Web site for more information: http://www.rgs.uci.edu/grad/prospective/housing.htm. On-campus day care facilities are available. See the following Web site for more information: http://www.rgs.uci.edu/grad/students/childcare.htm.

Employment of Department Graduates:

Master's Degree Graduates: Of those who graduated in the academic year 2006–2007, the following categories and numbers represent the postgraduate activities and employment of master's degree graduates: Enrolled in a postdoctoral residency/fellowship (n/a), employed in independent practice (n/a), total from the above (master's) (0).

Doctoral Degree Graduates: Of those who graduated in the academic year 2006–2007, the following categories and numbers represent the postgraduate activities and employment of doctoral degree graduates: Enrolled in a psychology doctoral program (n/a), employed in an academic position at a university (2), employed in other positions at a higher education institution (3), employed in business or industry (1), total from the above (doctoral) (6).

Additional Information:

Orientation, Objectives, and Emphasis of Department: The Department of Cognitive Sciences offers a PhD degree program in Psychology, with a specialization in cognitive science, to prepare students for research and teaching careers in academia, industry, and government. The emphasis is on modern techniques of experimentation and theory construction. Special attention is given to providing hands-on research experience and equipping students with sophisticated mathematical and computing skills. Of the Department faculty, two are members of the National Academy of Sciences, and many have served as editors or editorial board members of leading professional journals and as members of NSF and NIH study panels. Many Cognitive Sciences faculty are also members of UCI's Institute of Mathematical Behavioral Sciences, and the Department is generally regarded as one of the world?s leading centers for mathematically oriented research in cognitive psychology. The Department is also allied closely to the school's Center for Cognitive Neuroscience. Some Cognitive Sciences faculty participate in the Interdepartmental Neuroscience Program. For information about other psychology degree programs at UCI, visit Psychology at UCI, a joint website of the Departments of Psychology and Social Behavior and Cognitive Sciences.

Special Facilities or Resources: The facilities of the Department of Cognitive Sciences are housed in three buildings with teaching labs, lecture rooms, and instructional computing equipment. Its research laboratories are on the technological forefront and highly computerized. A research-dedicated 4.0T whole body MR Imaging/Spectroscopy System supports research in cognitive neuroscience.

Information for Students With Physical Disabilities: See the following Web site for more information: http://www.disability.uci.edu/.

Application Information:

Send to Graduate Advisor, Department of Cognitive Sciences, 3151 Social Science Plaza, University of California, Irvine, CA 92697-5100. Application available online. URL of online application: http://www.rgs.uci.edu/grad/. Students are admitted in the Fall, application deadline December 15. To receive full consideration for fellowship and assistantship awards, applications must be received by December 15. *Fee:* $60.

California, University of, Irvine

Department of Psychology and Social Behavior
3340 Social Ecology II, University of California, Irvine
Irvine, CA 92697-7085
Telephone: (949) 824-5574
Fax: (949) 824-3002
E-mail: *samorris@uci.edu*
Web: *http://www.seweb.uci.edu/psb/*

Department Information:

1992. Chairperson: David Dooley, PhD. Number of faculty: total—full-time 25, part-time 8; women—full-time 18, part-time 8; total—minority—full-time 1, part-time 3; women minority—part-time 2.

Programs and Degrees Offered:

Listed in the following order: Program area, degree type (T if terminal Master's), number awarded 7/06–6/07. Psychology and Social Behavior PhD (Doctor of Philosophy) 7.

Student Applications/Admissions:

Student Applications

Psychology and Social Behavior PhD (Doctor of Philosophy)—Applications 2007–2008, 207. Total applicants accepted 2007–2008, 23. Number full-time enrolled (new admits only) 2007–2008, 12. Total enrolled 2007–2008 full-time, 73, part-time, 1. Openings 2008–2009, 14. The median number of years required for completion of a degree in 2006–2007 were 5. The number of students enrolled full- and part-time who were dismissed or voluntarily withdrew from this program area in 2007–2008 were 1.

Admissions Requirements:

Scores: Entries appear in this order: required test or GPA, minimum score (if required), median score of students entering in 2007–2008. Doctoral Programs: GRE-V no minimum stated, 660; GRE-Q no minimum stated, 670; overall undergraduate GPA no minimum stated, 3.70; Doctoral program GRE-Analytic no minimum stated, 5.0.

Other Criteria: (importance of criteria rated low, medium, or high): GRE/MAT scores—high, research experience—high, work experience—low, extracurricular activity—low, GPA—high, letters of recommendation—high, interview—high, statement of goals and objectives—high. For additional information on admission requirements, go to http://www.seweb.uci.edu/psb/gradprog.uci.

Student Characteristics: The following represents characteristics of students in 2007–2008 in all graduate psychology programs in the department: Female—full-time 55, part-time 0; Male—full-time 17, part-time 1; African American/Black—full-time 0, part-time 0; Hispanic/Latino(a)—full-time 2, part-time 0; Asian/Pacific Islander—full-time 9, part-time 1; American Indian/Alaska Native—full-time 0, part-time 0; Caucasian/White—full-time 56, part-time 0; Multi-ethnic—full-time 5, part-time 0; students subject to the Americans With Disabilities Act—full-time 0, part-time 1; Unknown ethnicity—full-time 1, part-time 0.

Financial Information/Assistance:

Tuition for Full-Time Study: *Doctoral:* State residents: per academic year $10,715; Nonstate residents: per academic year $25,703. Tuition is subject to change. See the following Web site for updates and changes in tuition costs: http://www.reg.uci.edu/registrar/soc/fees.html.

Financial Assistance:

First-Year Students: Teaching assistantships available for first year. Average amount paid per academic year: $16,391. Average number of hours worked per week: 20. Tuition remission given: partial. Research assistantships available for first year. Average amount paid per academic year: $12,159. Average number of hours worked per week: 20. Tuition remission given: full. Fellowships and scholarships available for first year. Average amount paid per academic year: $18,000. Average number of hours worked per week: 0. Tuition remission given: full.

Advanced Students: Teaching assistantships available for advanced students. Average amount paid per academic year: $16,391. Average number of hours worked per week: 20. Tuition remission given: partial. Research assistantships available for advanced students. Average amount paid per academic year: $12,159. Average number of hours worked per week: 20. Tuition remission given: full. Fellowships and scholarships available for advanced students. Average amount paid per academic year: $18,000. Tuition remission given: full.

Additional Information: Of all students currently enrolled full time, 100% benefited from one or more of the listed financial assistance programs. Application and information available online at http://www.rgs.uci.edu/grad/prospective/finance_edu.htm.

Internships/Practica: The school places a strong emphasis on field experiences as part of the education of students and maintains an extensive list of community agencies where students may seek various forms of research involvement. All students are required to take the course "Applied Psychological Research." An optional course "Applied Psychological Research in Community Settings" is available to students who would like to have field placement experience.

Housing and Day Care: On-campus housing is available. See the following Web site for more information: http://www.housing.uci.edu/gfh/. On-campus day care facilities are available. See the following Web site for more information: http://www.childcare.uci.edu/.

Employment of Department Graduates:

Master's Degree Graduates: Of those who graduated in the academic year 2006–2007, the following categories and numbers represent the postgraduate activities and employment of master's degree graduates: Enrolled in a postdoctoral residency/fellowship (n/a), employed in independent practice (n/a), total from the above (master's) (0).

Doctoral Degree Graduates: Of those who graduated in the academic year 2006–2007, the following categories and numbers represent the postgraduate activities and employment of doctoral degree graduates: Enrolled in a psychology doctoral program (n/a), enrolled in a postdoctoral residency/fellowship (2), employed in an academic position at a university (1), employed in an academic position at a 2-year/4-year college (1), total from the above (doctoral) (4).

Additional Information:

Orientation, Objectives, and Emphasis of Department: The Department of Psychology and Social Behavior is united by an overarching interest in human adaptation in various sociocultural and developmental contexts. The department has emphases in four areas (Health Psychology, Developmental Psychology, Social and Personality Psychology, and Psychopathology and Behavioral Disorder). The multidisciplinary faculty, whose training is mainly in social, developmental, clinical, and community psychology, examines human health, well-being, and the ways in which individuals respond and adjust to changing circumstances over the life span. Faculty interests include stress and coping, cognitive and biobehavioral processes in health behavior, subjective well-being, cognition and emotion, social development and developmental transitions across the life span, cultural influences on cognition and behavior, psychology and law, aging and health, and societal problems such as violence and unemployment.

Special Facilities or Resources: In-house laboratories, including the Consortium for Integrative Health Studies, the Family Studies Lab, the Development in Cultural Contexts Lab, and the Health Psychology Lab, provide graduate students with direct access to state-of-the-art facilities and opportunities for research training. In addition, the department maintains strong ties with psychologists at other campuses in the area, including UC Los Angeles, UC Riverside, and UC San Diego (each approximately 1 hour away), and the UCI College of Medicine. For example, we participate in the Consortium on Families and Human Development, a joint undertaking of faculty members and graduate students at UCLA, UCR, UCI, and the University of Southern California. Selected students participate as predoctoral fellows in the Department's NIMH Training Program, and opportunities continually arise for all students to become involved in many ongoing faculty research projects.

Information for Students With Physical Disabilities: See the following Web site for more information: http://www.disability.uci.edu/.

Application Information:

Send to Suzy Morrison, Graduate Coordinator, 3340 Social Ecology II, Psychology and Social Behavior, School of Social Ecology UCI, Irvine, CA 92697-7085. Application available online. URL of online application: http://www.rgs.uci.edu/grad/prospective/admissions.htm. Students are admitted in the Fall, application deadline December 15. *Fee:* $60.

California, University of, Los Angeles

Department of Psychology
Letters and Science
405 Hilgard Avenue
Los Angeles, CA 90095-1563
Telephone: (310) 825-2617
Fax: (310) 206-5895
E-mail: *Herbert@psych.ucla.edu*
Web: *http://www.psych.ucla.edu*

Department Information:

1937. Chairperson: Robert A. Bjork. Number of faculty: total—full-time 64; women—full-time 24; total—minority—full-time 14; women minority—full-time 5.

Programs and Degrees Offered:

Listed in the following order: Program area, degree type (T if terminal Master's), number awarded 7/06–6/07. Behavioral Neuroscience PhD (Doctor of Philosophy) 2, Clinical PhD (Doctor of Philosophy) 15, Cognitive PhD (Doctor of Philosophy) 2, Developmental PhD (Doctor of Philosophy) 2, Learning and Behavior PhD (Doctor of Philosophy) 0, Quantitative PhD (Doctor of Philosophy) 2, Social PhD (Doctor of Philosophy) 5, Health PhD (Doctor of Philosophy) 0.

APA Accreditation: Clinical PhD (Doctor of Philosophy).

Student Applications/Admissions:

Student Applications

Behavioral Neuroscience PhD (Doctor of Philosophy)—Applications 2007–2008, 17. Total applicants accepted 2007–2008, 3. Number full-time enrolled (new admits only) 2007–2008, 5. Number part-time enrolled (new admits only) 2007–2008, 0. Openings 2008–2009, 3. The median number of years required for completion of a degree in 2006–2007 were 6. The number of students enrolled full- and part-time who were dismissed or voluntarily withdrew from this program area in 2007–2008 were 0. *Clinical PhD (Doctor of Philosophy)*—Applications 2007–2008, 378. Total applicants accepted 2007–2008, 12. Number full-time enrolled (new admits only) 2007–2008, 13. Openings 2008–2009, 12. The median number of years required for completion of a degree in 2006–2007 were 6. The number of students enrolled full- and part-time who were dismissed or voluntarily withdrew from this program area in 2007–2008 were 0. *Cognitive PhD (Doctor of Philosophy)*—Applications 2007–2008, 55. Total applicants accepted 2007–2008, 6. Number full-time enrolled (new admits only) 2007–2008, 6. Openings 2008–2009, 6. The median number of years required for completion of a degree in 2006–2007 were 6. The number of students enrolled full- and part-time who were dismissed or voluntarily withdrew from this program area in 2007–2008 were 0. *Developmental PhD (Doctor of Philosophy)*—Applications 2007–2008, 57. Total applicants accepted 2007–2008, 6. Number full-time enrolled (new admits only) 2007–2008, 7. Openings 2008–2009, 6. The median number of years required for completion of a degree in 2006–2007 were 6. The number of students enrolled full- and part-time who were dismissed or voluntarily withdrew from this program area in 2007–2008 were 0. *Learning and Behavior PhD (Doctor of Philosophy)*—Applications 2007–2008, 12. Total applicants accepted 2007–2008, 2. Number full-time enrolled (new admits only) 2007–2008, 0. Openings 2008–2009, 2. The median number of years required for completion of a degree in 2006–2007 were 6. The number of students enrolled full- and part-time who were dismissed or voluntarily withdrew from this program area in 2007–2008 were 0. *Quantitative PhD (Doctor of Philosophy)*—Applications 2007–2008, 11. Total applicants accepted 2007–2008, 2. Number full-time enrolled (new admits only) 2007–2008, 4. Openings 2008–2009, 2. The median number of years required for completion of a degree in 2006–2007 were 6. The number of students enrolled full- and part-time who were dismissed or voluntarily withdrew from this program area in 2007–2008 were 0. *Social PhD (Doctor of Philosophy)*—Applications 2007–2008, 90. Total applicants accepted 2007–2008, 6. Number full-time enrolled (new admits only) 2007–2008, 4. Openings 2008–2009, 6. The median number of years required for completion of a degree in

2006–2007 were 6. The number of students enrolled full- and part-time who were dismissed or voluntarily withdrew from this program area in 2007–2008 were 0. *Health PhD (Doctor of Philosophy)*—Applications 2007–2008, 34. Total applicants accepted 2007–2008, 5. Number full-time enrolled (new admits only) 2007–2008, 0. Number part-time enrolled (new admits only) 2007–2008, 0. Openings 2008–2009, 5. The median number of years required for completion of a degree in 2006–2007 were 6. The number of students enrolled full- and part-time who were dismissed or voluntarily withdrew from this program area in 2007–2008 were 0.

Admissions Requirements:

Scores: Entries appear in this order: required test or GPA, minimum score (if required), median score of students entering in 2007–2008. Doctoral Programs: GRE-V no minimum stated, 649; GRE-Q no minimum stated, 724; GRE-Subject (Psychology) no minimum stated, 725; overall undergraduate GPA no minimum stated, 3.68; Doctoral program GRE-Analytic no minimum stated, 5.3. Note: Analytical median score prior to October 2002 is 721.

Other Criteria: (importance of criteria rated low, medium, or high): GRE/MAT scores—high, research experience—high, work experience—medium, extracurricular activity—medium, clinically related public service—medium, GPA—high, letters of recommendation—high, interview—high, statement of goals and objectives—high. The Clinical area also requires an interview as part of the admissions process. After an initial screening of applications, the areas invites selected candidates to an on-campus interview. For additional information on admission requirements, go to http://www.psych.ucla.edu/Grads/Prospective/.

Student Characteristics: The following represents characteristics of students in 2007–2008 in all graduate psychology programs in the department: Female—full-time 120, part-time 0; Male—full-time 64, part-time 0; African American/Black—full-time 7, part-time 0; Hispanic/Latino(a)—full-time 18, part-time 0; Asian/Pacific Islander—full-time 33, part-time 0; American Indian/Alaska Native—full-time 0, part-time 0; Caucasian/White—full-time 117, part-time 0; Multi-ethnic—full-time 0, part-time 0; students subject to the Americans With Disabilities Act—full-time 1, part-time 0; Unknown ethnicity—full-time 9, part-time 0; International students who hold an F-1 or J-1 Visa—full-time 12, part-time 0.

Financial Information/Assistance:

Tuition for Full-Time Study: *Doctoral:* State residents: per academic year $8,967; Nonstate residents: per academic year $23,955. Tuition is subject to change. See the following Web site for updates and changes in tuition costs: http://www.registrar.ucla.edu/fees/grad.htm.

Financial Assistance:

First-Year Students: Teaching assistantships available for first year. Average amount paid per academic year: $16,389. Average number of hours worked per week: 20. Tuition remission given: partial. Research assistantships available for first year. Average amount paid per academic year: $13,104. Average number of hours worked per week: 20. Tuition remission given: partial. Traineeships available for first year. Average amount paid per academic year: $20,000. Average number of hours worked per week: 0. Fellowships and scholarships available for first year. Average amount paid per academic year: $20,000. Average number of hours worked per week: 0. Apply by December 15.

Advanced Students: Teaching assistantships available for advanced students. Average amount paid per academic year: $18,288. Average number of hours worked per week: 20. Tuition remission given: partial. Research assistantships available for advanced students. Average amount paid per academic year: $16,740. Average number of hours worked per week: 20. Tuition remission given: partial. Traineeships available for advanced students. Average amount paid per academic year: $20,000. Average number of hours worked per week: 0. Fellowships and scholarships available for advanced students. Average amount paid per academic year: $20,000. Average number of hours worked per week: 0. Apply by varies.

Additional Information: Of all students currently enrolled full time, 100% benefited from one or more of the listed financial assistance programs. Application and information available online at http://www.gdnet.ucla.edu/prospective.html.

Internships/Practica: Doctoral Degree (PhD clinical): For those doctoral students for whom a professional internship was required in this program prior to graduation, (10) students applied for an internship in 2006–2007, with (10) students obtaining an internship. Of those students who obtained an internship, (10) were paid internships. Of those students who obtained an internship, (10) students placed in APA/CPA-accredited internships, (0) students placed in internships not APA/CPA-accredited, but listed with the Association of Psychology Postdoctoral and Internship Centers (APPIC), (0) students placed in internships conforming to guidelines of the Council of Directors of School Psychology Programs (CDSPP), (0) students placed in internships that were not APA/CPA-accredited, APPIC or CDSPP listed. VA Hospitals; San Fernando Valley Child Guidance Center; St. John's Child Development Center; Neuropsychiatric Institute/UCLA; UCLA Student Psychological Services.

Housing and Day Care: On-campus housing is available. See the following Web site for more information: http://www.housing.ucla.edu. On-campus day care facilities are available. gmacdonald@be.ucla.edu.

Employment of Department Graduates:

Master's Degree Graduates: Of those who graduated in the academic year 2006–2007, the following categories and numbers represent the postgraduate activities and employment of master's degree graduates: Enrolled in a postdoctoral residency/fellowship (n/a), employed in independent practice (n/a), total from the above (master's) (0).

Doctoral Degree Graduates: Of those who graduated in the academic year 2006–2007, the following categories and numbers represent the postgraduate activities and employment of doctoral degree graduates: Enrolled in a psychology doctoral program (n/a), enrolled in another graduate/professional program (0), enrolled in a postdoctoral residency/fellowship (15), employed in independent practice (0), employed in an academic position at a university (4), employed in an academic position at a 2-year/4-year college (0), employed in other positions at a higher education institution (2), employed in a professional position in a school system (0), employed in business or industry (2), employed in government agency (0), employed in a community mental health/counseling center (2), employed in a hospital/medical center (1), still seeking employment (0), not seeking employment (0), other employment position (0), do not know (1), total from the above (doctoral) (27).

Additional Information:

Orientation, Objectives, and Emphasis of Department: Rigorous scientific training is the foundation of the PhD program. The graduate curriculum focuses on the usage of systematic methods of investigation to understand and quantify general principles of human behavior, pathology, cognition, and emotion. More specifically, the department includes such research clusters as psychobiology and the brain; child–clinical and developmental psychology; adult psychopathology and family dynamics; cognition and memory; health, community, and political psychology; minority mental health; social cognition and intergroup relations; quantitative; and learning and behavior. In all these areas, the department's central aim is to train researchers dedicated to expanding the scientific knowledge upon which the discipline of psychology rests. This orientation also applies to the clinical program; although it offers excellent clinical training, its emphasis is on training researchers rather than private practitioners. In sum, the graduate training is designed to prepare research psychologists for careers in academic and applied settings—as college and university instructors; for leadership roles in community, government, and business organizations; and as professional research psychologists.

Special Facilities or Resources: The department is one of the largest on campus. Our three-connected buildings (known collectively as Franz Hall) provide ample space (over 120,000 square feet) for psychological research. Laboratory facilities are of the highest quality. Precision equipment is available for electrophysiological stimulation and recording, magnetic resonance imaging (MRI), and for all major areas of sensory study. Specially designed laboratories exist for studies of group behavior and naturalistic observation. An extensive vivarium contains facilities for physiological animal studies. Computing facilities are leading-edge at all levels, from microcomputers to supercomputer clusters. The department also houses the Psychology Clinic, a training and research center for psychotherapy and diagnostics. Other resources include the Fernald Child Study Center (a research facility committed to investigating childhood behavioral disorders); the National Research Center for Asian American Mental Health; the California Self-Help Center; and the Center for Computer-Based Behavioral Studies. Departmental affiliations with the Brain Research Institute, the University Elementary School, the Neuropsychiatric Institute, and the local Veterans Administration also provide year-round research opportunities.

Information for Students With Physical Disabilities: Contact kmolini@saonet.ucla.edu.

Application Information:

Send to Graduate Admissions Advisor, Psychology Department, 1285 Franz Hall, Box 951563, Los Angeles, CA 90095-1563. Application available online. URL of online application: http://www.psych.ucla.edu/Grads/Prospective/instructions.php. Students are admitted in the Fall, application deadline December 15. Only clinical and social areas have a different deadline—December 15 for clinical and social; December 30 for other areas. *Fee:* $60.

California, University of, Riverside

Department of Psychology
College of Humanties, Arts, and Social Sciences
Olmsted Hall
Riverside, CA 92521-0426
Telephone: (951) 827-6306
Fax: (951) 827-3985
E-mail: *dianne.fewkes@ucr.edu*
Web: *http://www.psych.ucr.edu*

Department Information:

1962. Chairperson: Glenn Stanley. Number of faculty: total—full-time 29; women—full-time 13; total—minority—full-time 3; women minority—full-time 3.

Programs and Degrees Offered:

Listed in the following order: Program area, degree type (T if terminal Master's), number awarded 7/06–6/07. Cognitive PhD (Doctor of Philosophy) 0, Developmental PhD (Doctor of Philosophy) 3, Social/Personality PhD (Doctor of Philosophy) 2, Systems Neuroscience PhD (Doctor of Philosophy) 2.

Student Applications/Admissions:

Student Applications

Cognitive PhD (Doctor of Philosophy)—Applications 2007–2008, 34. Total applicants accepted 2007–2008, 3. Number full-time enrolled (new admits only) 2007–2008, 1. Openings 2008–2009, 6. The median number of years required for completion of a degree in 2006–2007 were 5. The number of students enrolled full- and part-time who were dismissed or voluntarily withdrew from this program area in 2007–2008 were 0. *Developmental PhD (Doctor of Philosophy)*—Applications 2007–2008, 40. Total applicants accepted 2007–2008, 11. Number full-time enrolled (new admits only) 2007–2008, 4. Openings 2008–2009, 6. The median number of years required for completion of a degree in 2006–2007 were 5. The number of students enrolled full- and part-time who were dismissed or voluntarily withdrew from this program area in 2007–2008 were 0. *Social/Personality PhD (Doctor of Philosophy)*—Applications 2007–2008, 95. Total applicants accepted 2007–2008, 14. Number full-time enrolled (new admits only) 2007–2008, 7. Openings 2008–2009, 7. The median number of years required for completion of a degree in 2006–2007 were 5. The number of students enrolled full- and part-time who were dismissed or voluntarily withdrew from this program area in 2007–2008 were 0. *Systems Neuroscience PhD (Doctor of Philosophy)*—Applications 2007–2008, 5. Total applicants accepted 2007–2008, 1. Number full-time enrolled (new admits only) 2007–2008, 0. Openings 2008–2009, 4. The median number of years required for completion of a degree in 2006–2007 were 5. The number of students enrolled full- and part-time who were dismissed or voluntarily withdrew from this program area in 2007–2008 were 0.

Admissions Requirements:

Scores: Entries appear in this order: required test or GPA, minimum score (if required), median score of students entering in 2007–2008. Doctoral Programs: GRE-V no minimum stated; GRE-Q no minimum stated; overall undergraduate GPA no minimum stated; last 2 years GPA 3.4, 3.84. A strong GPA in science courses is recommended for applicants to the Systems Neuroscience area.

Other Criteria: (importance of criteria rated low, medium, or high): GRE/MAT scores—medium, research experience—high, work experience—low, extracurricular activity—low, GPA—medium, letters of recommendation—high, interview—high, statement of goals and objectives—high. For additional information on admission requirements, go to http://www.psych.ucr.edu/grad/admissions.html.

Student Characteristics: The following represents characteristics of students in 2007–2008 in all graduate psychology programs in the department: Female—full-time 40, part-time 0; Male—full-time 23, part-time 0; African American/Black—full-time 0, part-time 0; Hispanic/Latino(a)—full-time 5, part-time 0; Asian/Pacific Islander—full-time 11, part-time 0; American Indian/Alaska Native—full-time 0, part-time 0; Caucasian/White—full-time 47, part-time 0; Multi-ethnic—full-time 0, part-time 0; students subject to the Americans With Disabilities Act—full-time 1, part-time 0; Unknown ethnicity—full-time 0, part-time 0; International students who hold an F-1 or J-1 Visa—full-time 1, part-time 0.

Financial Information/Assistance:

Tuition for Full-Time Study: *Doctoral:* State residents: per academic year $8,619; Nonstate residents: per academic year $23,580. Tuition is subject to change. See the following Web site for updates and changes in tuition costs: http://www.graddiv.ucr.edu/FinSupport.html.

Financial Assistance:

First-Year Students: Teaching assistantships available for first year. Average amount paid per academic year: $15,400. Average number of hours worked per week: 20. Apply by January 2. Tuition remission given: full. Research assistantships available for first year. Average amount paid per academic year: $16,314. Average number of hours worked per week: 20. Apply by January 2. Tuition remission given: full. Fellowships and scholarships available for first year. Average amount paid per academic year: $17,000. Average number of hours worked per week: 0. Apply by January 2. Tuition remission given: full.

Advanced Students: Teaching assistantships available for advanced students. Average amount paid per academic year: $15,400. Average number of hours worked per week: 20. Apply by January 2. Tuition remission given: full. Research assistantships available for advanced students. Average amount paid per academic year: $19,542. Average number of hours worked per week: 20. Apply by January 2. Tuition remission given: full.

Additional Information: Of all students currently enrolled full time, 100% benefited from one or more of the listed financial assistance programs. Application and information available online at http://www.psych.ucr.edu/grad/index.html.

Internships/Practica: No information provided.

Housing and Day Care: On-campus housing is available. See the following Web site for more information: http://www.housing.ucr.edu. On-campus day care facilities are available. See the following Web site for more information: http://www.childrenservices.ucr.edu or call (951) 827-3854.

Employment of Department Graduates:

Master's Degree Graduates: Of those who graduated in the academic year 2006–2007, the following categories and numbers represent the postgraduate activities and employment of master's degree graduates: Enrolled in a postdoctoral residency/fellowship (n/a), employed in independent practice (n/a), total from the above (master's) (0).

Doctoral Degree Graduates: Of those who graduated in the academic year 2006–2007, the following categories and numbers represent the postgraduate activities and employment of doctoral degree graduates: Enrolled in a psychology doctoral program (n/a), enrolled in a postdoctoral residency/fellowship (5), employed in an academic position at a university (1), employed in other positions at a higher education institution (1), do not know (0), total from the above (doctoral) (7).

Additional Information:

Orientation, Objectives, and Emphasis of Department: The orientation is toward theoretical and research training. Objectives are to provide the appropriate theoretical, quantitative, and methodological background to enable graduates of the program to engage in high-quality research. Additionally, training and experience in university-level teaching are provided. We also offer a minor in quantitative psychology which may be completed by any student in the PhD program in Psychology regardless of main area of interest. A concentration in health psychology is also offered in the social and developmental areas. The cognitive area has a strong concentration in cognitive modeling.

Special Facilities or Resources: A new building for the psychology department is currently under construction. The department has equipment and support systems to help students conduct research in all aspects of behavior. The neuroscience laboratories are equipped with the latest instrumentation for hormonal assays, extracellular and intracellular electrophysiology, and microscopic analysis of neuronal morphology. Research in the cognitive area incorporates computer-assisted experimental control for most any kind of reaction time experiment and has facilities for video and speech digitization, and infrared eye-tracking. The developmental faculty have laboratory facilities to study parents and children, have access to the campus day-care center for studies that involve toddlers and preschool children, and have been very successful in conducting research in a culturally diverse local school system. The developmental faculty all participate in the Center for Family Studies, an interdisciplinary center. The social/personality psychology labs support research in social perception, nonverbal communication, health psychology, emotional expression, and attribution processes using audiovisual laboratories and observation rooms. Direct, free, access is available to PsycInfo, PubMed, and many other online journals and databases.

Information for Students With Physical Disabilities: See the following Web site for more information: http://www.specialservices.ucr.edu; TTY (951) 827-4538.

Application Information:

Send to Graduate Admissions Psychology Department, University of California, Riverside, Riverside, CA 92521. Application available online. URL of online application: http://www.graddiv.ucr.edu/HowApply.html. Students are admitted in the Fall, application deadline January 2. *Fee:* $60. No waivers possible for foreign applicants. Specific critieria apply for waiver of application. Contact Graduate

Admissions in the Graduate Division, (951) 827-3313; grdadmis@pop.ucr.edu.

California, University of, San Diego (2007 data)

Department of Psychology
La Jolla, CA 92093-0109
Telephone: (858) 534-3002
Fax: (858) 534-7190
E-mail: *jwixted@ucsd.edu*
Web: *http://www.psy.ucsd.edu/*

Department Information:

1965. Chairperson: John T. Wixted. Number of faculty: total—full-time 30, part-time 10; women—full-time 7, part-time 5.

Programs and Degrees Offered:

Listed in the following order: Program area, degree type (T if terminal Master's), number awarded 7/06–6/07. Experimental PhD (Doctor of Philosophy) 4.

Student Applications/Admissions:

Student Applications

Experimental PhD (Doctor of Philosophy)—Applications 2007–2008, 234. Total applicants accepted 2007–2008, 20. Number full-time enrolled (new admits only) 2007–2008, 16. Openings 2008–2009, 14. The median number of years required for completion of a degree in 2006–2007 were 7. The number of students enrolled full- and part-time who were dismissed or voluntarily withdrew from this program area in 2007–2008 were 2.

Admissions Requirements:

Scores: Entries appear in this order: required test or GPA, minimum score (if required), median score of students entering in 2007–2008. Doctoral Programs: GRE-V 600, 620; GRE-Q 600, 720; overall undergraduate GPA 3.0, 3.8. Minimum GRE is more accurately stated as a percentile: 50%.

Other Criteria: (importance of criteria rated low, medium, or high): GRE/MAT scores—high, research experience—high, work experience—medium, extracurricular activity—low, clinically related public service—low, GPA—high, letters of recommendation—high, interview—high, statement of goals and objectives—high.

Student Characteristics: The following represents characteristics of students in 2007–2008 in all graduate psychology programs in the department: Female—full-time 45, part-time 0; Male—full-time 32, part-time 0; African American/Black—full-time 0, part-time 0; Hispanic/Latino(a)—full-time 6, part-time 0; Asian/Pacific Islander—full-time 8, part-time 0; American Indian/Alaska Native—full-time 1, part-time 0; Caucasian/White—full-time 0, part-time 0; Unknown ethnicity—full-time 0, part-time 0.

Financial Information/Assistance:

Tuition for Full-Time Study: *Doctoral:* Nonstate residents: per academic year $14,694. See the following Web site for updates and changes in tuition costs: http://www.ogs.ucsd.edu/financialinfo/gradstudent/tuition_fees/index.htm.

Financial Assistance:

First-Year Students: Teaching assistantships available for first year. Average amount paid per academic year: $15,611. Tuition remission given: full.

Advanced Students: Teaching assistantships available for advanced students. Average amount paid per academic year: $15,611. Tuition remission given: full.

Additional Information: Application and information available online at http://psy.ucsd.edu/.

Internships/Practica: No information provided.

Housing and Day Care: On-campus housing is available. See the following Web site for more information: http://www.hds.ucsd.edu/hsgaffil/index.html. On-campus day care facilities are available. See the following Web site for more information: http://www.blink.ucsd.edu/Blink/External/Topics/Policy/1,1162,227,00.html?coming_from=Content.

Employment of Department Graduates:

Master's Degree Graduates: Of those who graduated in the academic year 2006–2007, the following categories and numbers represent the postgraduate activities and employment of master's degree graduates: Enrolled in a postdoctoral residency/fellowship (n/a), employed in independent practice (n/a), total from the above (master's) (0).

Doctoral Degree Graduates: Of those who graduated in the academic year 2006–2007, the following categories and numbers represent the postgraduate activities and employment of doctoral degree graduates: Enrolled in a psychology doctoral program (n/a), enrolled in a postdoctoral residency/fellowship (2), employed in an academic position at a university (1), do not know (1), total from the above (doctoral) (4).

Additional Information:

Orientation, Objectives, and Emphasis of Department: The Department of Psychology at the University of California San Diego provides advanced training in research on most aspects of experimental psychology. Modern laboratories and an attractive physical setting combine with a distinguished faculty, both within the Department of Psychology and in supporting disciplines, to provide research opportunities and training at the frontiers of psychological science. The graduate training program emphasizes and supports individual research, starting with the first year of study. The Department offers the following emphases: behavior analysis, biopsychology, cognitive psychology, developmental psychology, sensation and perception, and social psychology.

Special Facilities or Resources: The Department shares research space and facilities with the Center for Brain and Cognition. Within the joint facilities, there are two computing facilities, a computational laboratory, visual and auditory laboratories, social psychology laboratories, cognitive laboratories, developmental laboratories, a clinic for autistic children, animal facilities, and extensive contacts with hospitals, industry, and the legal system. In addition to the numerous impressive libraries on campus, the Department also keeps a large selection of literature within our Mandler Library. Collaborative research is carried on with members of the Departments of Linguistics (who share our building), Cognitive Science, Computer Science and Engineering, Sociology, Music, Ophthalmology, Neurosciences, members of the UCSD School of Medicine, Scripps Clinic and Research Foundation, and with the Salk Institute for Biological Studies. The Scripps Institution of Oceanography, located on campus, provides facilities in neurosciences as does the School of Medicine. For a complete tour of the university and its facilities, visit http://www.ucsd.edu/visit.

Information for Students With Physical Disabilities: See the following Web site for more information: http://www.orpheus.ucsd.edu/osd/.

Application Information:
Send to Graduate Admission, Department of Psychology-0109, University of California-San Diego, La Jolla, CA 92093. Application available online. URL of online application: http://www.graduateapp.ucsd.edu/. Students are admitted in the Fall, application deadline January 5. *Fee:* $60.

California, University of, Santa Barbara

Counseling, Clinical, and School Psychology
Gevirtz Graduate School of Education
Phelps Hall 1110, University of California, Santa Barbara
Santa Barbara, CA 93106-9490
Telephone: (805) 893-3375
Fax: (805) 893-3375
E-mail: *cosden@education.ucsb.edu*
Web: *http://www.education.ucsb.edu/Graduate-Studies/CCSP/CCSP-home.html*

Department Information:
1965. Chairperson: Michael Furlong. Number of faculty: total—full-time 8, part-time 1; women—full-time 7; women minority—full-time 3.

Programs and Degrees Offered:
Listed in the following order: Program area, degree type (T if terminal Master's), number awarded 7/06–6/07. Counseling/Clinical/School PhD (Doctor of Philosophy) 10, School EdS/MEd (School Psychology) 2.

APA Accreditation: Combination PhD (Doctor of Philosophy).

Student Applications/Admissions:
Student Applications
Counseling/Clinical/School PhD (Doctor of Philosophy)—Applications 2007–2008, 331. Total applicants accepted 2007–2008, 28. Number full-time enrolled (new admits only) 2007–2008, 19. Number part-time enrolled (new admits only) 2007–2008, 0. Openings 2008–2009, 20. The median number of years required for completion of a degree in 2006–2007 were 6. The number of students enrolled full- and part-time who were dismissed or voluntarily withdrew from this program area in 2007–2008 were 0. *School EdS/MEd (School Psychology)*—Applications 2007–2008, 31. Total applicants accepted 2007–2008, 8. Number full-time enrolled (new admits only) 2007–2008, 6. Number part-time enrolled (new admits only) 2007–2008, 0. Openings 2008–2009, 6. The median number of years required for completion of a degree in 2006–2007 were 2. The number of students enrolled full- and part-time who were dismissed or voluntarily withdrew from this program area in 2007–2008 were 0.

Admissions Requirements:
Scores: Entries appear in this order: required test or GPA, minimum score (if required), median score of students entering in 2007–2008. Master's Programs: GRE-V no minimum stated, 537; GRE-Q no minimum stated, 598; MAT no minimum stated; overall undergraduate GPA no minimum stated; last 2 years GPA 3.0, 3.57. Doctoral Programs: GRE-V no minimum stated, 591; GRE-Q no minimum stated, 675; MAT no minimum stated; overall undergraduate GPA no minimum stated; last 2 years GPA 3.0, 3.72.
Other Criteria: (importance of criteria rated low, medium, or high): GRE/MAT scores—high, research experience—high, work experience—high, extracurricular activity—medium, clinically related public service—high, GPA—high, letters of recommendation—high, interview—high, statement of goals and objectives—high. Research experience less important for MEd. Match of interests with faculty very important. For additional information on admission requirements, go to http://education.ucsb.edu/Graduate-Studies/CCSP/prospective-students/how-to-apply-checklist.htm.

Student Characteristics: The following represents characteristics of students in 2007–2008 in all graduate psychology programs in the department: Female—full-time 62, part-time 0; Male—full-time 13, part-time 0; African American/Black—full-time 1, part-time 0; Hispanic/Latino(a)—full-time 15, part-time 0; Asian/Pacific Islander—full-time 14, part-time 0; American Indian/Alaska Native—full-time 1, part-time 0; Caucasian/White—full-time 30, part-time 0; Multi-ethnic—full-time 6, part-time 0; students subject to the Americans With Disabilities Act—full-time 3, part-time 0; Unknown ethnicity—full-time 8, part-time 0; International students who hold an F-1 or J-1 Visa—full-time 2, part-time 0.

Financial Information/Assistance:
Tuition for Full-Time Study: *Master's:* State residents: per academic year $10,108; Nonstate residents: per academic year $25,096. *Doctoral:* State residents: per academic year $10,108; Nonstate residents: per academic year $25,096. Tuition is subject to change. See the following Web site for updates and changes in tuition costs: http://www.registrar.ucsb.edu/feechart-grad.htm.

Financial Assistance:
First-Year Students: Teaching assistantships available for first year. Research assistantships available for first year. Average amount paid per academic year: $11,872. Average number of hours worked per week: 20. Apply by November 15. Tuition remission given: full and partial. Fellowships and scholarships available for first year. Average amount paid per academic year: $22,000. Average number of hours worked per week: 0. Apply by November 15. Tuition remission given: full.
Advanced Students: Teaching assistantships available for advanced students. Average amount paid per academic year: $8,195. Average number of hours worked per week: 10. Tuition remission given: full and partial. Research assistantships available for advanced students. Average amount paid per academic year: $14,183. Average number of hours worked per week: 20. Tuition remission given: full and partial. Fellowships and scholarships available for advanced students. Average amount paid per aca-

demic year: $22,548. Average number of hours worked per week: 0. Tuition remission given: full.

Additional Information: Of all students currently enrolled full time, 90% benefited from one or more of the listed financial assistance programs. Application and information available online at http://education.ucsb.edu/Graduate-Studies/Student-Services/prospective-students/financial-aid.htm.

Internships/Practica: Doctoral Degree (PhD Counseling/Clinical/School): For those doctoral students for whom a professional internship was required in this program prior to graduation, (8) students applied for an internship in 2006–2007, with (8) students obtaining an internship. Of those students who obtained an internship, (8) were paid internships. Of those students who obtained an internship, (8) students placed in APA/CPA-accredited internships, (0) students placed in internships not APA/CPA-accredited, but listed with the Association of Psychology Postdoctoral and Internship Centers (APPIC), (0) students placed in internships conforming to guidelines of the Council of Directors of School Psychology Programs (CDSPP), (0) students placed in internships that were not APA/CPA-accredited, APPIC or CDSPP listed. We provide supervised training in our Hosford Clinic, a sliding scale agency that serves clients from the community. Students in the clinical emphasis have external practica in community-based agencies, including one that serves families and children exposed to violence, a local hospital, and county alcohol, drug, and mental health services; students in the counseling emphasis have external practica at our Counseling and Career Services Center; and students in the school emphasis have external practica in the schools. The school psychology MEd students receive their degree in 2 years and have a 3rd year of school internship for their credential.

Housing and Day Care: On-campus housing is available. See the following Web site for more information: http://www.housing.ucsb.edu/. On-campus day care facilities are available. See the following Web site for more information: http://www.childrenscenter.sa.ucsb.edu/ http://www.housing.ucsb.edu/.

Employment of Department Graduates:

Master's Degree Graduates: Of those who graduated in the academic year 2006–2007, the following categories and numbers represent the postgraduate activities and employment of master's degree graduates: Enrolled in a postdoctoral residency/fellowship (n/a), employed in independent practice (n/a), total from the above (master's) (0).

Doctoral Degree Graduates: Of those who graduated in the academic year 2006–2007, the following categories and numbers represent the postgraduate activities and employment of doctoral degree graduates: Enrolled in a psychology doctoral program (n/a), enrolled in a postdoctoral residency/fellowship (4), employed in other positions at a higher education institution (2), employed in a professional position in a school system (1), employed in a community mental health/counseling center (3), total from the above (doctoral) (10).

Additional Information:

Orientation, Objectives, and Emphasis of Department: The primary goal of the combined psychology program is to prepare graduates who will (a) conduct research and teach in university settings and (b) assume leadership roles in the academic community and in the helping professions. The program has a secondary goal of training students to provide psychological services in university, school, and community agency settings.

Special Facilities or Resources: The UCSB Combined Psychology Program has its own training clinic, the Hosford Clinic, which serves community clients and which is equipped with state-of-the-art video equipment for recording, reviewing, editing, and live monitoring of assessment and counseling sessions. Part of the Hosford Clinic is the Psychology Assessment Center, which provides psychological assessment services for the measurement of disorders that affect psychological, emotional, academic, and occupational functioning. The Autism Center is also available for student training and research. Computer laboratories equipped with Macintosh and IBM personal computers are available for student use. Faculty have research labs in different areas of interest.

Information for Students With Physical Disabilities: See the following Web site for more information: http://www.dsp.sa.ucsb.edu/.

Application Information:

Send to Student Affairs Office, Gevirtz Graduate School of Education, University of California, Santa Barbara, CA 93106-9490. Application available online. URL of online application: http://www.education.ucsb.edu/Graduate-Studies/CCSP/prospective-students/how-to-apply-checklist.htm. Students are admitted in the Fall, application deadline November 15. *Fee:* $60.

California, University of, Santa Barbara (2007 data)

Department of Psychology
Santa Barbara, CA 93106-9660
Telephone: (805) 893-2793
Fax: (805) 893-4303
E-mail: *cunningh@psych.ucsb.edu*
Web: *http://www.psych.ucsb.edu*

Department Information:

1953. Chairperson: Daphne Bugental. Number of faculty: total—full-time 30; women—full-time 9.

Programs and Degrees Offered:

Listed in the following order: Program area, degree type (T if terminal Master's), number awarded 7/06–6/07. Cognitive,Perception, Cognitive Neuroscience PhD (Doctor of Philosophy) 3, Development and Evolution PhD (Doctor of Philosophy) 1, Neuroscience and Behavior PhD (Doctor of Philosophy) 2, Social PhD (Doctor of Philosophy) 6.

Student Applications/Admissions:

Student Applications

Cognitive, Perception, Cognitive Neuroscience PhD (Doctor of Philosophy)—Applications 2007–2008, 65. Total applicants accepted 2007–2008, 11. Number full-time enrolled (new admits only) 2007–2008, 4. Openings 2008–2009, 6. The median number of years required for completion of a degree in 2006–2007 were 6. The number of students enrolled full- and part-time who were dismissed or voluntarily withdrew from this program area in 2007–2008 were 0. *Development and Evolu-*

tion PhD (Doctor of Philosophy)—Applications 2007–2008, 46. Total applicants accepted 2007–2008, 4. Number full-time enrolled (new admits only) 2007–2008, 1. Openings 2008–2009, 3. The median number of years required for completion of a degree in 2006–2007 were 6. The number of students enrolled full- and part-time who were dismissed or voluntarily withdrew from this program area in 2007–2008 were 0. *Neuroscience and Behavior PhD (Doctor of Philosophy)*—Applications 2007–2008, 36. Total applicants accepted 2007–2008, 7. Number full-time enrolled (new admits only) 2007–2008, 4. Openings 2008–2009, 4. The median number of years required for completion of a degree in 2006–2007 were 6. The number of students enrolled full- and part-time who were dismissed or voluntarily withdrew from this program area in 2007–2008 were 0. *Social PhD (Doctor of Philosophy)*—Applications 2007–2008, 112. Total applicants accepted 2007–2008, 14. Number full-time enrolled (new admits only) 2007–2008, 6. Openings 2008–2009, 5. The median number of years required for completion of a degree in 2006–2007 were 6. The number of students enrolled full- and part-time who were dismissed or voluntarily withdrew from this program area in 2007–2008 were 0.

Admissions Requirements:

Scores: Entries appear in this order: required test or GPA, minimum score (if required), median score of students entering in 2007–2008. Master's Programs: We do not admit MA students. Doctoral Programs: GRE-V no minimum stated, 643; GRE-Q no minimum stated, 712; last 2 years GPA no minimum stated, 3.75; Doctoral program GRE-Analytic no minimum stated, 728. Please note that the anayltic score is no longer a part of the GRE. This should be changed to GRE-writing.

Other Criteria: (importance of criteria rated low, medium, or high): GRE/MAT scores—high, research experience—high, work experience—medium, GPA—high, letters of recommendation—high, statement of goals and objectives—high. If applicant is interviewed (not required), this can be very important.

Student Characteristics: The following represents characteristics of students in 2007–2008 in all graduate psychology programs in the department: Female—full-time 39, part-time 0; Male—full-time 36, part-time 0; African American/Black—full-time 2, part-time 0; Hispanic/Latino(a)—full-time 2, part-time 0; Asian/Pacific Islander—full-time 4, part-time 0; American Indian/Alaska Native—full-time 0, part-time 0; Caucasian/White—full-time 65, part-time 0; Multi-ethnic—full-time 2, part-time 0; students subject to the Americans With Disabilities Act—full-time 1, part-time 0; Unknown ethnicity—full-time 0, part-time 0.

Financial Information/Assistance:

Financial Assistance:

First-Year Students: Teaching assistantships available for first year. Average amount paid per academic year: $15,611. Average number of hours worked per week: 20. Apply by December 1. Tuition remission given: partial. Research assistantships available for first year. Average amount paid per academic year: $15,943. Average number of hours worked per week: 20. Apply by December 1. Tuition remission given: full. Fellowships and scholarships available for first year. Average amount paid per academic year: $20,000. Average number of hours worked per week: 0. Apply by December 1. Tuition remission given: full.

Advanced Students: Teaching assistantships available for advanced students. Average amount paid per academic year: $15,611. Average number of hours worked per week: 20. Tuition remission given: partial. Research assistantships available for advanced students. Average amount paid per academic year: $15,943. Average number of hours worked per week: 20. Tuition remission given: full. Fellowships and scholarships available for advanced students. Average amount paid per academic year: $20,000. Average number of hours worked per week: 0. Tuition remission given: full.

Additional Information: Of all students currently enrolled full time, 98% benefited from one or more of the listed financial assistance programs.

Internships/Practica: No information provided.

Housing and Day Care: On-campus housing is available. See the following Web site for more information: http://www.housing.ucsb.edu. On-campus day care facilities are available. See the following Web site for more information: http://www.sa.ucsb.edu/childcare/uchildcenter/index.asp.

Employment of Department Graduates:

Master's Degree Graduates: Of those who graduated in the academic year 2006–2007, the following categories and numbers represent the postgraduate activities and employment of master's degree graduates: Enrolled in a postdoctoral residency/fellowship (n/a), employed in independent practice (n/a), total from the above (master's) (0).

Doctoral Degree Graduates: Of those who graduated in the academic year 2006–2007, the following categories and numbers represent the postgraduate activities and employment of doctoral degree graduates: Enrolled in a psychology doctoral program (n/a), enrolled in a postdoctoral residency/fellowship (3), employed in an academic position at a university (7), employed in business or industry (2), total from the above (doctoral) (12).

Additional Information:

Orientation, Objectives, and Emphasis of Department: The major graduate program of the Department of Psychology consists of work leading to the PhD degree; however, the MA is also awarded to PhD students who are continuing in the PhD program, or PhD students who elect to leave the program with a terminal MA The Department does not admit MA students. Specialized training is offered in neuroscience and behavior, cognition, perception and cognitive neuroscience, developmental and evolutionary psychology, and social psychology.

Information for Students With Physical Disabilities: See the following Web site for more information: http://www.sa.ucsb.edu/dsp/.

Application Information:

Send to Graduate Admissions. Application available online. URL of online application: http://www.graddiv.ucsb.edu. Students are admitted in the Fall, application deadline December 1. It is very likely that we will change our application deadline from December 15 to December 1. *Fee:* $60.

California, University of, Santa Cruz

Psychology Department
273 Social Sciences 2
Santa Cruz, CA 95064
Telephone: (831) 459-4932
Fax: (831) 459-3519
E-mail: *allison@ucsc.edu*
Web: *http://www.psych.ucsc.edu/*

Department Information:

1965. Chairperson: Martin M. Chemers. Number of faculty: total—full-time 23; women—full-time 14; ; women minority—full-time 5.

Programs and Degrees Offered:

Listed in the following order: Program area, degree type (T if terminal Master's), number awarded 7/06–6/07. Developmental PhD (Doctor of Philosophy) 0, Social PhD (Doctor of Philosophy) 0, Cognitive PhD (Doctor of Philosophy) 4.

Student Applications/Admissions:

Student Applications

Developmental PhD (Doctor of Philosophy)—Applications 2007–2008, 40. Total applicants accepted 2007–2008, 6. Number full-time enrolled (new admits only) 2007–2008, 5. Total enrolled 2007–2008 full-time, 25. Openings 2008–2009, 8. The median number of years required for completion of a degree in 2006–2007 were 5. The number of students enrolled full- and part-time who were dismissed or voluntarily withdrew from this program area in 2007–2008 were 0. *Social PhD (Doctor of Philosophy)*—Applications 2007–2008, 83. Total applicants accepted 2007–2008, 4. Number full-time enrolled (new admits only) 2007–2008, 6. Total enrolled 2007–2008 full-time, 20. Openings 2008–2009, 7. The median number of years required for completion of a degree in 2006–2007 were 6. The number of students enrolled full- and part-time who were dismissed or voluntarily withdrew from this program area in 2007–2008 were 0. *Cognitive PhD (Doctor of Philosophy)*—Applications 2007–2008, 39. Total applicants accepted 2007–2008, 8. Number full-time enrolled (new admits only) 2007–2008, 3. Total enrolled 2007–2008 full-time, 20, part-time, 1. Openings 2008–2009, 8. The median number of years required for completion of a degree in 2006–2007 were 6. The number of students enrolled full- and part-time who were dismissed or voluntarily withdrew from this program area in 2007–2008 were 3.

Admissions Requirements:

Scores: Entries appear in this order: required test or GPA, minimum score (if required), median score of students entering in 2007–2008. Doctoral Programs: GRE-V 50%, 560; GRE-Q 50%, 620; overall undergraduate GPA 2.75, 3.6; last 2 years GPA no minimum stated, 3.5.

Other Criteria: (importance of criteria rated low, medium, or high): GRE/MAT scores—high, research experience—high, work experience—medium, extracurricular activity—medium, GPA—high, letters of recommendation—high, statement of goals and objectives—high.

Student Characteristics: The following represents characteristics of students in 2007–2008 in all graduate psychology programs in the department: Female—full-time 48, part-time 1; Male—full-time 17, part-time 0; African American/Black—full-time 1, part-time 0; Hispanic/Latino(a)—full-time 15, part-time 0; Asian/Pacific Islander—full-time 7, part-time 0; American Indian/Alaska Native—full-time 1, part-time 0; Caucasian/White—full-time 38, part-time 1; Multi-ethnic—full-time 0, part-time 0; students subject to the Americans With Disabilities Act—full-time 0, part-time 0; Unknown ethnicity—full-time 3, part-time 0; International students who hold an F-1 or J-1 Visa—full-time 1, part-time 0.

Financial Information/Assistance:

Financial Assistance:

First-Year Students: Teaching assistantships available for first year. Average number of hours worked per week: 20. Research assistantships available for first year. Traineeships available for first year. Fellowships and scholarships available for first year. Apply by December 15.

Advanced Students: Teaching assistantships available for advanced students. Average number of hours worked per week: 20. Research assistantships available for advanced students.

Additional Information: Of all students currently enrolled full time, 95% benefited from one or more of the listed financial assistance programs.

Internships/Practica: None.

Housing and Day Care: On-campus housing is available. See the following Web site for more information: Graduate Student Housing, http://www.housing.ucsc.edu/sponsored-housing/grad-index.html, or call (831) 458-2462; Family Students Housing, http://housing.ucsc.edu/sponsored-housing/family-index.html, or call (831) 459-2549; Off-campus Housing, http://housing.ucsc.edu/cro/index.html, or call (831) 459-4435. On-campus day care facilities are available. See the following Web site for more information: http://www.housing.ucsc.edu/childcare/index.html, or call Child Care Services, (831) 459-5664.

Employment of Department Graduates:

Master's Degree Graduates: Of those who graduated in the academic year 2006–2007, the following categories and numbers represent the postgraduate activities and employment of master's degree graduates: Enrolled in a postdoctoral residency/fellowship (n/a), employed in independent practice (n/a), total from the above (master's) (0).

Doctoral Degree Graduates: Of those who graduated in the academic year 2006–2007, the following categories and numbers represent the postgraduate activities and employment of doctoral degree graduates: Enrolled in a psychology doctoral program (n/a), enrolled in another graduate/professional program (0), enrolled in a postdoctoral residency/fellowship (1), employed in independent practice (0), employed in an academic position at a university (1), employed in an academic position at a 2-year/4-year college (0), employed in other positions at a higher education institution (0), employed in a professional position in a school system (0), employed in business or industry (1), employed in government agency (0), employed in a community mental health/counseling center (0), employed in a hospital/medical center (0), still seeking employment (0), not seeking employment (0), other employment position (0), do not know (0), total from the above (doctoral) (3).

Additional Information:

Orientation, Objectives, and Emphasis of Department: The Psychology Department at UC Santa Cruz offers a PhD degree with areas of specialization in cognitive, developmental, and social psychology. Students are prepared for research, teaching, and administrative positions in colleges and universities, as well as positions in schools, government, and other public and private organizations. The PhD is a research degree. Students are required to demonstrate the ability to carry through to completion rigorous empirical research and to be active in research throughout their graduate career. Course requirements establish a foundation for critical evaluation of research literature and the design of conceptually important empirical research. To support students in achieving these goals, each student must be associated with one of the faculty, who serves as academic advisor and research sponsor. The program requires full-time enrollment. Important notes: The program does not offer courses, training, or supervision in counseling or clinical psychology. Students are not admitted to pursue only a Master's degree. However, students may be awarded a Master's degree as part of their studies for the PhD.

Special Facilities or Resources: The department provides training to prepare the student for academic and applied settings. Graduate students have the use of a variety of research facilities, including a number of computer-controlled experimental laboratories. Electronic equipment is available to allow the generation of sophisticated written and pictorial vision displays, musical sequences, and synthesized and visual speech patterns. There are observational facilities for developmental psychological research, and a discourse analysis lab. A bilingual survey unit is under development which will utilize public opinion survey technology to study significant public policy, legal, and political issues that are critical to California's emerging majority population. Research opportunities exist with diverse sample groups in both laboratory and natural settings. The department has collaborative relationships with the National Center for Research on Cultural Diversity, Second Language Learning, and the Bilingual Research Center.

Information for Students With Physical Disabilities: See the following Web site for more information: http://www.ucsc.edu/drc/.

Application Information:

Send to Psychology Department, Graduate Program, 1156 High Street, University of California, Santa Cruz, CA 95064-1077, phone: (831) 459-4932. Paper application materials are no longer available, you will need to find access to the http://graddiv.ucsc.edu/admissions/ Web site. It is preferable that you submit your application online so that the information you submit can be imported into a database for all faculty to review. Application available online. URL of online application: http://www.graddiv.ucsc.edu/admissions/. Students are admitted in the Fall, application deadline December 15. *Fee:* $60. Fee waivers for cases of hardship are available to U.S. citizens and permanent residents only; international students are not eligible. Funds for waivers are limited; if you feel you qualify for a waiver, complete the Request for Graduate Application Fee Waiver form and return it to the Graduate Admissions office for approval. For more information go to http://graddiv.ucsc.edu/admissions/reqs.php#fee.

Claremont Graduate University

Graduate Department of Psychology
School of Behavioral and Organizational Sciences
123 East Eighth Street
Claremont, CA 91711-3955
Telephone: (909) 621-8084
Fax: (909) 621-8905
E-mail: *Stewart.Donaldson@cgu.edu*
Web: *http://www.cgu.edu/sbos*

Department Information:

1926. Dean: Stewart I. Donaldson. Number of faculty: total—full-time 17, part-time 39; women—full-time 7, part-time 24; total—minority—full-time 2, part-time 12; women minority—full-time 1, part-time 6.

Programs and Degrees Offered:

Listed in the following order: Program area, degree type (T if terminal Master's), number awarded 7/06–6/07. Applied Social Psychology/Evaluation Co-Concentration MA/MS (Master of Arts/Science) (T) 6, Cognitive Psychology/Evaluation Co-Concentration MA/MS (Master of Arts/Science) (T) 0, Organizational/Evaluation Co-Concentration MA/MS (Master of Arts/Science) (T) 15, Developmental Psychology/Evaluation Co-Concentration MA/MS (Master of Arts/Science) (T) 0, Human Resources Design MA/MS (Master of Arts/Science) (T) 14, Applied Cognitive Psychology PhD (Doctor of Philosophy) 5, Applied Developmental Psychology PhD (Doctor of Philosophy) 5, Applied Social Psychology PhD (Doctor of Philosophy) 7, Evaluation and Applied Research Methods PhD (Doctor of Philosophy) 0, Organizational Behavior, Industrial/Organizational PhD (Doctor of Philosophy) 6, Health Behavior Research MA/MS (Master of Arts/Science) (T) 0, Positive Developmental Psychology (New in 07) PhD (Doctor of Philosophy), Positive Organizational Psychology (New in 07) PhD (Doctor of Philosophy), Positive Developmental Psychology/Evaluation Co-Concentration MA/MS (Master of Arts/Science) (T), Positive Organizational Psychology/Evaluation Co-Concentration MA/MS (Master of Arts/Science) (T).

Student Applications/Admissions:

Student Applications

Applied Social Psychology/Evaluation Co-Concentration MA/MS (Master of Arts/Science)—Applications 2007–2008, 47. Number full-time enrolled (new admits only) 2007–2008, 10. Total enrolled 2007–2008 full-time, 19. Openings 2008–2009, 9. The median number of years required for completion of a degree in 2006–2007 were 2. The number of students enrolled full- and part-time who were dismissed or voluntarily withdrew from this program area in 2007–2008 were 0. *Cognitive Psychology/Evaluation Co-Concentration MA/MS (Master of Arts/Science)*—Applications 2007–2008, 9. Number full-time enrolled (new admits only) 2007–2008, 1. Total enrolled 2007–2008 full-time, 2. Openings 2008–2009, 3. The median number of years required for completion of a degree in 2006–2007 were 2. The number of students enrolled full- and part-time who were dismissed or voluntarily withdrew from this program area in 2007–2008 were 0. *Organizational/Evaluation Co-Concentration MA/MS (Master of Arts/Science)*—Applications 2007–2008, 86. Number full-time enrolled (new admits only) 2007–2008, 11. Total enrolled 2007–2008 full-time, 20. Openings 2008–2009, 10. The median number of years required for completion of a degree in 2006–2007 were 2. The number of students enrolled full- and part-time who were dismissed or voluntarily withdrew from this program area in 2007–2008 were 0. *Developmental Psychology/Evaluation Co-Concentration MA/MS (Master of Arts/Science)*—Applications 2007–2008, 15. Number full-time enrolled (new admits only) 2007–2008, 2. Total enrolled 2007–2008 full-time, 5. Openings 2008–2009, 6. The median number of years required for completion of a degree in 2006–2007 were 2. The number of students enrolled full- and part-time who were dismissed or voluntarily withdrew from this program area in 2007–2008 were 0. *Human Resources Design MA/MS (Master of Arts/Science)*—Applications 2007–2008, 23. Total applicants accepted 2007–2008, 13. Number full-time enrolled (new admits only) 2007–2008, 10. Number part-time enrolled (new admits only) 2007–2008, 0. Openings 2008–2009, 10. The median number of years required for completion of a degree in 2006–2007 were 2. The number of students enrolled full- and part-time who were dismissed or voluntarily withdrew from this program area in 2007–2008 were 2. *Applied Cognitive Psychology PhD (Doctor of Philosophy)*—Applications 2007–2008, 14. Number full-time enrolled (new admits only) 2007–2008, 4. Total enrolled 2007–2008 full-time, 21. Openings 2008–2009, 6. The median number of years required for completion of a degree in 2006–2007 were 7. The number of students enrolled full- and part-time who were dismissed or voluntarily withdrew from this program area in 2007–2008 were 0. *Applied Developmental Psychology PhD (Doctor of Philosophy)*—Applications 2007–2008, 32. Number full-time enrolled (new admits only) 2007–2008, 3. Total enrolled 2007–2008 full-time, 21. Openings 2008–2009, 8. The median number of years required for completion of a degree in 2006–2007 were 6. The number of students enrolled full- and part-time who were dismissed or voluntarily withdrew from this program area in 2007–2008 were 0. *Applied Social Psychology PhD (Doctor of Philosophy)*—Applications 2007–2008, 54. Number full-time enrolled (new admits only) 2007–2008, 7. Total enrolled 2007–2008 full-time, 50. Openings 2008–2009, 9. The median number of years required for completion of a degree in 2006–2007 were 6. The number of students enrolled full- and part-time who were dismissed or voluntarily withdrew from this program area in 2007–2008 were 2. *Evaluation and Applied Research Methods PhD (Doctor of Philosophy)*—Applications 2007–2008, 5. Number full-time enrolled (new admits only) 2007–2008, 2. Total enrolled 2007–2008 full-time, 11. Openings 2008–2009, 6. The median number of years required for completion of a degree in 2006–2007 were 6. The number of students enrolled full- and part-time who were dismissed or voluntarily withdrew from this program area in 2007–2008 were 1. *Organizational Behavior, Industrial/Organizational PhD (Doctor of Philosophy)*—Applications 2007–2008, 74. Number full-time enrolled (new admits only) 2007–2008, 9. Total enrolled 2007–2008 full-time, 32. Openings 2008–2009, 4. The median number of years required for completion of a degree in 2006–2007 were 7. The number of students enrolled full- and part-time who were dismissed or voluntarily withdrew from this program area in 2007–2008 were 0. *Health Behavior Research MA/MS (Master of Arts/Science)*—Applications 2007–2008, 9. Number full-time enrolled (new admits only) 2007–2008, 1. Total enrolled 2007–2008 full-time, 1. Openings 2008–2009, 5. The number of students enrolled full- and part-time who were dismissed or voluntarily withdrew from this program area in 2007–2008 were 0. *Positive Developmental Psychology (New in 07) PhD (Doctor of Philosophy)*—Applications 2007–2008, 31. Number full-time enrolled (new admits only) 2007–2008, 1. Total enrolled 2007–2008 full-time, 1. Openings 2008–2009, 3. *Positive Organizational Psychology (New in 07) PhD (Doctor of Philosophy)*—Applications 2007–2008, 26. Number full-time enrolled (new admits only) 2007–2008, 1. Total enrolled 2007–2008 full-time, 1. Openings 2008–2009, 3. *Positive Developmental Psychology/Evaluation Co-Concentration MA/MS (Master of Arts/Science)*—Applications 2007–2008, 18. Number full-time enrolled (new admits only) 2007–2008, 2. Total enrolled 2007–2008 full-time, 2. Openings 2008–2009, 3. *Positive Organizational Psychology/Evaluation Co-Concentration MA/MS (Master of Arts/Science)*—Applications 2007–2008, 26. Number full-time enrolled (new admits only) 2007–2008, 0. Openings 2008–2009, 3.

Admissions Requirements:

Scores: Entries appear in this order: required test or GPA, minimum score (if required), median score of students entering in 2007–2008. Master's Programs: GRE-V no minimum stated, 488; GRE-Q no minimum stated, 612; overall undergraduate GPA 3.00, 3.4; Masters GRE-Analytical no minimum stated, 4.38. HRD program requires either GRE or GMAT scores and weights work experience more heavily in admissions. Doctoral Programs: GRE-V no minimum stated, 581; GRE-Q no minimum stated, 650; overall undergraduate GPA 3.00, 3.63; Doctoral program GRE-Analytic no minimum stated, 4.67.

Other Criteria: (importance of criteria rated low, medium, or high): GRE/MAT scores—high, research experience—medium, work experience—medium, extracurricular activity—medium, GPA—high, letters of recommendation—high, statement of goals and objectives—high, undergraduate major in psychology—medium, specific undergraduate psychology courses taken—medium. Human Resource Design program does not require research experience but emphasizes work experience more strongly. For additional information on admission requirements, go to http://www.cgu.edu/sbos.

Student Characteristics: The following represents characteristics of students in 2007–2008 in all graduate psychology programs in the department: Female—full-time 151, part-time 20; Male—full-time 46, part-time 6; African American/Black—full-time 13, part-time 4; Hispanic/Latino(a)—full-time 12, part-time 4; Asian/Pacific Islander—full-time 23, part-time 4; American Indian/Alaska Native—full-time 1, part-time 0; Caucasian/White—full-time 74, part-time 3; Multi-ethnic—full-time 0, part-time 2; students subject to the Americans With Disabilities Act—full-time 0, part-time 0; Unknown ethnicity—full-time 74, part-time 9.

Financial Information/Assistance:

Tuition for Full-Time Study: *Master's:* State residents: per academic year $33,698, $1,465 per credit hour; Nonstate residents: per academic year $33,698, $1,465 per credit hour. *Doctoral:* State residents: per academic year $33,698, $1,465 per credit hour; Nonstate residents: per academic year $33,698, $1,465 per credit hour. Tuition is subject to change. See the following Web site for updates and changes in tuition costs: http://www.cgu.edu/new_tuition.

Financial Assistance:

First-Year Students: Teaching assistantships available for first year. Average amount paid per academic year: $5,200. Average number of hours worked per week: 10. Research assistantships available for first year. Average amount paid per academic year: $5,200. Average number of hours worked per week: 12. Fellowships and scholarships available for first year. Average amount paid per academic year: $8,425. Apply by January 15. Tuition remission given: partial.

Advanced Students: Teaching assistantships available for advanced students. Average amount paid per academic year: $5,200. Average number of hours worked per week: 10. Research assistantships available for advanced students. Average amount paid per academic year: $5,200. Average number of hours worked per week: 12. Fellowships and scholarships available for advanced students. Average amount paid per academic year: $7,910. Apply by January 15. Tuition remission given: partial.

Additional Information: Of all students currently enrolled full time, 100% benefited from one or more of the listed financial assistance programs. Application and information available online at http://www.cgu.edu/pages/102.asp.

Internships/Practica: Research and consulting internships are available and encouraged for all students. Appropriate settings and roles are arranged according to the interests of individual students within the wide range of opportunities available in a large urban area. Typical settings include social service agencies; business and industrial organizations; hospitals, clinics, and mental health agencies; schools; governmental and regulatory agencies; and nonacademic research institutions, as well as numerous onsite research institutes.

Housing and Day Care: On-campus housing is available. See the following Web site for more information: http://www.cgu.edu/pages/1156.asp. On-campus day care facilities are available.

Employment of Department Graduates:

Master's Degree Graduates: Of those who graduated in the academic year 2006–2007, the following categories and numbers represent the postgraduate activities and employment of master's degree graduates: Enrolled in another graduate/professional program (1), enrolled in a postdoctoral residency/fellowship (n/a), employed in independent practice (n/a), employed in an academic position at a university (1), employed in an academic position at a 2-year/4-year college (1), employed in other positions at a higher education institution (1), employed in a professional position in a school system (3), employed in business or industry (2), employed in a community mental health/counseling center (2), employed in a hospital/medical center (1), other employment position (1), total from the above (master's) (13).

Doctoral Degree Graduates: Of those who graduated in the academic year 2006–2007, the following categories and numbers represent the postgraduate activities and employment of doctoral degree graduates: Enrolled in a psychology doctoral program (n/a), enrolled in a postdoctoral residency/fellowship (4), employed in an academic position at a university (2), employed in an academic position at a 2-year/4-year college (3), employed in other positions at a higher education institution (2), employed in a professional position in a school system (1), employed in business or industry (3), employed in a community mental health/counseling center (2), employed in a hospital/medical center (2), other employment position (3), total from the above (doctoral) (22).

Additional Information:

Orientation, Objectives, and Emphasis of Department: The program emphasizes contemporary human problems and social issues, and the organizations and systems involved in such issues, as well as on basic substantive research in social, organizational, developmental, and cognitive psychology and health behavior. Unusual specialty opportunities are available in organizational behavior, applied cognitive psychology, applied social psychology, health psychology, and program evaluation research. The program offers preparation for careers in public service and business and industry as well as teaching and research. Research, theory, and practice are stressed in such policy and program areas as organizations and work; human social and physical environments; social service systems; psychological effects of educational computer technology; health and mental health systems; crime, delinquency, and law; aging and life span education. Many opportunities are available for research, consulting, and field experiences in these and related areas. Strong emphasis is given to training in a broad range of research methodologies, from naturalistic observation to experimental design, with special attention to field research methods. Seminars, tutorials, independent research, individualized student program plans, practical field experience, and close advisory and collaborative relations with the faculty are designed to foster clarifications of individual goals, intellectual and professional growth, self-pacing, and attractive career opportunities.

Special Facilities or Resources: The school is equipped with labs for social, developmental, and cognitive research, supplies and equipment for field research, a student lounge, and department library. The computer facilities are excellent, conveniently located, and include a wide variety of application programs. The department cooperates in overseeing research institutes for student–faculty grant or contract research, focusing on major problems of organizational and program evaluation research as well as research on social issues. Claremont Graduate University is a free-standing graduate institution within the context of the Claremont University Consortium of five colleges, the Graduate University, and the Keck Graduate Institute. This context allows the department to concentrate exclusively on graduate education in a relaxed, intimate context while enjoying the resources of a major university. In addition to the full-time graduate psychology faculty, there are more than 40 full-time faculty members from the undergraduate Claremont Colleges who participate in the graduate program and who are available to students for research, advising, and instruction. Resources from other programs within the Graduate University are also available to psychology students, in such areas as public policy, education, information sciences, business administration, executive management, economics, and government. The nearby Los Angeles basin is a major urban area that offers rich and varied opportunities for interesting research, field placements and internships, part-time employment, and career development.

Application Information:

Send to Admissions Office, McManus Hall 131, Claremont Graduate University, Claremont, CA 91711. Application available online. URL of online application: http://www.cgu.edu/pages/102.asp. Students are admitted in the Fall, application deadline January 15; Spring, application deadline November 15. The Human Resources Design MS program accepts applications throughout the year on a space-available basis. *Fee:* $60. Fee waived or deferred if need is certified.

Fielding Graduate University
School of Psychology
2112 Santa Barbara Street
Santa Barbara, CA 93105
Telephone: (805) 687-1099
Fax: (805) 687-9793
E-mail: *psyadmissions@fielding.edu*
Web: *http://www.fielding.edu*

Department Information:

1974. Dean, Psychology: Raymond J. Trybus. Number of faculty: total—full-time 40; women—full-time 17; total—minority—full-time 4.

Programs and Degrees Offered:

Listed in the following order: Program area, degree type (T if terminal Master's), number awarded 7/06–6/07. Clinical Psychology Respecialization Diploma 2, Clinical PhD (Doctor of Philosophy) 41, Media Psychology PhD (Doctor of Philosophy) 1, Postdoctorate Neuropsychology Certificate Other 22.

APA Accreditation: Clinical PhD (Doctor of Philosophy).

Student Applications/Admissions:

Student Applications

Clinical Psychology Respecialization Diploma—Applications 2007–2008, 14. Total applicants accepted 2007–2008, 9. Number full-time enrolled (new admits only) 2007–2008, 6. Total enrolled 2007–2008 full-time, 25. Openings 2008–2009, 6. The median number of years required for completion of a degree in 2006–2007 were 5. The number of students enrolled full- and part-time who were dismissed or voluntarily withdrew from this program area in 2007–2008 were 2. *Clinical PhD (Doctor of Philosophy)*—Applications 2007–2008, 391. Total applicants accepted 2007–2008, 129. Number full-time enrolled (new admits only) 2007–2008, 96. Number part-time enrolled (new admits only) 2007–2008, 0. Openings 2008–2009, 80. The median number of years required for completion of a degree in 2006–2007 were 8. The number of students enrolled full- and part-time who were dismissed or voluntarily withdrew from this program area in 2007–2008 were 27. *Media Psychology PhD (Doctor of Philosophy)*—Applications 2007–2008, 43. Total applicants accepted 2007–2008, 43. Number full-time enrolled (new admits only) 2007–2008, 28. Number part-time enrolled (new admits only) 2007–2008, 0. Openings 2008–2009, 30. The median number of years required for completion of a degree in 2006–2007 were 4. The number of students enrolled full- and part-time who were dismissed or voluntarily withdrew from this program area in 2007–2008 were 5. *Postdoctorate Neuropsychology Certificate Other*—Applications 2007–2008, 30. Total applicants accepted 2007–2008, 29. Number full-time enrolled (new admits only) 2007–2008, 0. Number part-time enrolled (new admits only) 2007–2008, 23. Openings 2008–2009, 25. The median number of years required for completion of a degree in 2006–2007 were 2. The number of students enrolled full- and part-time who were dismissed or voluntarily withdrew from this program area in 2007–2008 were 8.

Admissions Requirements:

Scores: Entries appear in this order: required test or GPA, minimum score (if required), median score of students entering in 2007–2008. Doctoral Programs: overall undergraduate GPA 3.0. A minimum GPA of 3.0 for the highest degree earned is recommended.

Other Criteria: (importance of criteria rated low, medium, or high): research experience—high, work experience—high, extracurricular activity—medium, clinically related public service—high, GPA—medium, letters of recommendation—high, interview—high, statement of goals and objectives—high, autobiography and writing sample—medium, Watson-Glaser for Clinical program only. For additional information on admission requirements, go to http://www.fielding.edu/admission.

Student Characteristics: The following represents characteristics of students in 2007–2008 in all graduate psychology programs in the department: Female—full-time 443, part-time 58; Male—full-time 172, part-time 35; African American/Black—full-time 43, part-time 6; Hispanic/Latino(a)—full-time 48, part-time 9; Asian/Pacific Islander—full-time 27, part-time 3; American Indian/Alaska Native—full-time 5, part-time 0; Caucasian/White—full-time 452, part-time 62; Multi-ethnic—full-time 11, part-time 2; students subject to the Americans With Disabilities Act—full-time 5, part-time 0; Unknown ethnicity—full-time 29, part-time 11; International students who hold an F-1 or J-1 Visa—full-time 0, part-time 0.

Financial Information/Assistance:

Tuition for Full-Time Study: *Doctoral:* State residents: per academic year $19,695; Nonstate residents: per academic year $19,695. Tuition is subject to change. See the following Web site for updates and changes in tuition costs: http://www.fielding.edu/policies/financial/tuitinfo.htm.

Financial Assistance:

First-Year Students: No information provided.

Advanced Students: Fellowships and scholarships available for advanced students. Average amount paid per academic year: $5,000.

Additional Information: Of all students currently enrolled full time, 10% benefited from one or more of the listed financial assistance programs. Application and information available online at http://www.fielding.edu/financialaid/index.htm.

Internships/Practica: Doctoral Degree (PhD Clinical): For those doctoral students for whom a professional internship was required in this program prior to graduation, (35) students applied for an internship in 2006–2007, with (32) students obtaining an internship. Of those students who obtained an internship, (23) were paid internships. Of those students who obtained an internship, (18) students placed in APA/CPA-accredited internships, (8) students placed in internships not APA/CPA-accredited, but listed with the Association of Psychology Postdoctoral and Internship Centers (APPIC), (0) students placed in internships conforming to guidelines of the Council of Directors of School Psychology Programs (CDSPP), (6) students placed in internships that were not APA/CPA-accredited, APPIC or CDSPP listed. Students apply to APA or APPIC approved or comparable internship sites that offer organized training programs lasting 1 year full-time or 2 consecutive years half-time. Such internships provide a planned, integrated sequence of clinical and didactic experiences with the goal of providing sufficient training and supervision so that upon completion our graduates can function responsibly as a postdoctoral psychologists.

Housing and Day Care: No on-campus housing is available. No on-campus day care facilities are available.

Employment of Department Graduates:

Master's Degree Graduates: Of those who graduated in the academic year 2006–2007, the following categories and numbers represent the postgraduate activities and employment of master's degree graduates: Enrolled in a postdoctoral residency/fellowship (n/a), employed in independent practice (n/a), total from the above (master's) (0).

Doctoral Degree Graduates: Of those who graduated in the academic year 2006–2007, the following categories and numbers represent the postgraduate activities and employment of doctoral degree graduates: Enrolled in a psychology doctoral program (n/a), enrolled in a postdoctoral residency/fellowship (7), employed in independent practice (6), employed in an academic position at a university (1), employed in other positions at a higher education institution (2), employed in a professional position in a school system (1), employed in business or industry (1), employed in government agency (1), employed in a community mental health/counseling center (4), employed in a hospital/medical center (4), still seeking employment (1), other employment position (2), do not know (14), total from the above (doctoral) (44).

Additional Information:

Orientation, Objectives, and Emphasis of Department: Fielding Graduate University's School of Psychology enables mid-career adults with mental health and human service experience to earn the PhD in clinical or media psychology as well as postdoctoral certificates in neuropsychology or respecialization in clinical psychology. Our students bring a sense of autonomy, extensive personal and professional experience to their studies. The programs' scholar–pracitioner model accommodates the special characteristics of adult students. Through seminars and guided study, the adult learner pursues study at whatever location life circumstances permit. Each of our programs are described in detail on our Web site at http://www.fielding.edu/schoolpsy.

Special Facilities or Resources: Students become members of a "cluster" in their geographical area consisting of a Regional Faculty member and other students. Meetings are held regularly and consist of a variety of learning activities including seminars, clinical and research training, faculty supervision consultation, as well as peer contact and support. Each student is assigned to an Associate Dean who is located in Santa Barbara, CA, and who oversees the student's academic program. Two intensive week-long residential sessions are offered each year that bring together students, faculty, and other scholars who offer seminars and other educational and training events. Two residential research sessions are held each year. These include research training, dissertation seminars, instruction in the use of research libraries and electronic databases, and lectures by invited research scholars. Psychological assessment laboratories are offered several times each year to provide training in conducting comprehensive psychodiagnostic evaluations.

Information for Students With Physical Disabilities: See the following Web site for more information: http://www.fielding.edu/policies/institut/adastmt.htm.

Application Information:
Send to Psychology Admission Counselor, Fielding Graduate University, 2112 Santa Barbara Street, Santa Barbara, CA 93105. Application available online. URL of online application: http://www.fielding.edu/admission. Students are admitted in the Fall, application deadline February 27; Spring, application deadline August 22. Clinical and Respecialization, February 27 and August 22; Media, April 25 and October 25. *Fee:* $75.

Fuller Theological Seminary

Graduate School of Psychology
180 North Oakland Avenue
Pasadena, CA 91101
Telephone: (626) 584-5500
Fax: (626) 584-9630
E-mail: *lwagener@fuller.edu*
Web: *http://www.fuller.edu/sop/main*

Department Information:

1965. Associate Dean: Linda Wagener, PhD Number of faculty: total—full-time 7, part-time 5; women—full-time 5, part-time 1; ; women minority—full-time 1.

Programs and Degrees Offered:

Listed in the following order: Program area, degree type (T if terminal Master's), number awarded 7/06–6/07. Clinical Psychology PhD (Doctor of Philosophy) 17, Clinical Psychology PsyD (Doctor of Psychology) 11.

APA Accreditation: Clinical PhD (Doctor of Philosophy). Clinical PsyD (Doctor of Psychology).

Student Applications/Admissions:

Student Applications

Clinical Psychology PhD (Doctor of Philosophy)—Applications 2007–2008, 66. Total applicants accepted 2007–2008, 44. Number full-time enrolled (new admits only) 2007–2008, 27. Number part-time enrolled (new admits only) 2007–2008, 0. Openings 2008–2009, 25. The median number of years required for completion of a degree in 2006–2007 were 7. The number of students enrolled full- and part-time who were dismissed or voluntarily withdrew from this program area in 2007–2008 were 2. *Clinical Psychology PsyD (Doctor of Psychology)*—Applications 2007–2008, 46. Total applicants accepted 2007–2008, 27. Number full-time enrolled (new admits only) 2007–2008, 12. Number part-time enrolled (new admits only) 2007–2008, 0. Openings 2008–2009, 20. The median number of years required for completion of a degree in 2006–2007 were 6. The number of students enrolled full- and part-time who were dismissed or voluntarily withdrew from this program area in 2007–2008 were 0.

Admissions Requirements:

Scores: Entries appear in this order: required test or GPA, minimum score (if required), median score of students entering

in 2007–2008. Doctoral Programs: GRE-V 430, 520; GRE-Q 460, 610; overall undergraduate GPA 3.0, 3.5; psychology GPA 3.0, 3.66.

Other Criteria: (importance of criteria rated low, medium, or high): GRE/MAT scores—high, research experience—high, work experience—medium, extracurricular activity—low, clinically related public service—medium, GPA—high, letters of recommendation—high, interview—high, statement of goals and objectives—high. Research experience is less important for PsyD candidate than for PhD.

Student Characteristics: The following represents characteristics of students in 2007–2008 in all graduate psychology programs in the department: Female—full-time 163, part-time 0; Male—full-time 85, part-time 0; African American/Black—full-time 18, part-time 0; Hispanic/Latino(a)—full-time 14, part-time 0; Asian/Pacific Islander—full-time 47, part-time 0; American Indian/Alaska Native—full-time 0, part-time 0; Caucasian/White—full-time 169, part-time 0; Multi-ethnic—full-time 0, part-time 0; students subject to the Americans With Disabilities Act—full-time 0, part-time 0; Unknown ethnicity—full-time 0, part-time 0.

Financial Information/Assistance:

Tuition for Full-Time Study: *Doctoral:* State residents: per academic year $27,556, $508 per credit hour; Nonstate residents: per academic year $27,556, $508 per credit hour. Tuition is subject to change. Tuition costs vary by program. See the following Web site for updates and changes in tuition costs: http://www.fuller.edu/registrar/tuition.asp.

Financial Assistance:

First-Year Students: Research assistantships available for first year. Average amount paid per academic year: $12,000. Average number of hours worked per week: 15. Apply by variable. Fellowships and scholarships available for first year. Average amount paid per academic year: $2,045. Average number of hours worked per week: 0. Apply by application.

Advanced Students: Teaching assistantships available for advanced students. Average amount paid per academic year: $10,000. Average number of hours worked per week: 10. Apply by variable. Research assistantships available for advanced students. Average amount paid per academic year: $12,000. Average number of hours worked per week: 15. Apply by variable. Traineeships available for advanced students. Average amount paid per academic year: $10,000. Average number of hours worked per week: 10. Apply by variable. Fellowships and scholarships available for advanced students. Average amount paid per academic year: $2,045. Average number of hours worked per week: 0. Apply by March 31.

Additional Information: Of all students currently enrolled full time, 60% benefited from one or more of the listed financial assistance programs. Application and information available online at http://www.fuller.edu/finaid/.

Internships/Practica: Doctoral Degree (PhD Clinical Psychology): For those doctoral students for whom a professional internship was required in this program prior to graduation, (26) students applied for an internship in 2006–2007, with (24) students obtaining an internship. Of those students who obtained an internship, (22) were paid internships. Of those students who obtained an internship, (21) students placed in APA/CPA-accredited internships, (3) students placed in internships not APA/CPA accredited, but listed with the Association of Psychology Postdoctoral and Internship Centers (APPIC), (0) students placed in internships conforming to guidelines of the Council of Directors of School Psychology Programs (CDSPP), (0) students placed in internships that were not APA/CPA-accredited, APPIC or CDSPP listed. Doctoral Degree (PsyD Clinical Psychology): For those doctoral students for whom a professional internship was required in this program prior to graduation, (12) students applied for an internship in 2006–2007, with (12) students obtaining an internship. Of those students who obtained an internship, (11) were paid internships. Of those students who obtained an internship, (8) students placed in APA/CPA-accredited internships, (4) students placed in internships not APA/CPA-accredited, but listed with the Association of Psychology Postdoctoral and Internship Centers (APPIC), (0) students placed in internships conforming to guidelines of the Council of Directors of School Psychology Programs (CDSPP), (0) students placed in internships that were not APA/CPA-accredited, APPIC or CDSPP listed. Students are placed in field training sites throughout their program beginning in year one with clinical foundations, through 2 years of practicum, 1 year of assessment clerkships, 1 year of pre-internship (PhD only), and a full-time clinical internship. Students are placed at Fuller Psychological and Family Services clinic as well as in over 50 sites throughout the Los Angeles metropolitan area. Because of our location students are exposed to multiple methods of service delivery as well as to diverse ethnic, clinical, and age populations. Students obtain internships throughout the United States and Canada.

Housing and Day Care: On-campus housing is available. See the following Web site for more information: http://www.fuller.edu/housing/. No on-campus day care facilities are available.

Employment of Department Graduates:

Master's Degree Graduates: Of those who graduated in the academic year 2006–2007, the following categories and numbers represent the postgraduate activities and employment of master's degree graduates: Enrolled in a postdoctoral residency/fellowship (n/a), employed in independent practice (n/a), total from the above (master's) (0).

Doctoral Degree Graduates: Of those who graduated in the academic year 2006–2007, the following categories and numbers represent the postgraduate activities and employment of doctoral degree graduates: Enrolled in a psychology doctoral program (n/a), do not know (28), total from the above (doctoral) (28).

Additional Information:

Orientation, Objectives, and Emphasis of Department: The purpose of the Graduate School of Psychology is to prepare a distinctive kind of clinical psychologist: men and women whose understanding and action are deeply informed by both psychology and the Christian faith. It is based on the conviction that the coupling of Christian understanding with refined clinical and research skills will produce a psychologist with a special ability to help persons of faith on their journeys to wholeness. The school has adopted the scientist–practitioner model for its PhD program and the clinical scientist model for its PsyD program.

Special Facilities or Resources: The Lee Edward Travis Research Institute (TRI) in the School of Psychology at Fuller Theological Seminary is committed to fostering interdisciplinary research into the relationships between social systems, environmental situations, personality, mental and affective states, biological processes, and spiritual and religious states and practices. Please go to our Web site at http://www.fuller.edu/sop/travis to learn more. Fuller Psychological and Family Services: This outpatient clinic provides assistance to individuals, couples, and families, including services to children and adolescents. Psychological interventions are offered for adjustment disorders, anxiety, depression, stress management, abuse and domestic violence, and physical conditions affected by psychological factors. Student trainees may be placed in the clinic for practicum, clerkship, or pre-internship. Please see http://www.fuller.edu/sop/main/psychological_center.asp.

Information for Students With Physical Disabilities: See the following Web site for more information: http://www.oss-office@dept.fuller.edu.

Application Information:
Send to Office of Admissions, Fuller Theological Seminary, 135 North Oakland Avenue, Pasadena, CA 91182. Application available online. URL of online application: https://www.applyweb.com/apply/fuller/menu.html. Students are admitted in the Fall, application deadline January 10. Early admission deadline is November 30. *Fee:* $100. Fee is waived for early admission. On line application fee is $75.

Humboldt State University

Department of Psychology
College of Natural Resources and Sciences
1 Harpst Street
Arcata, CA 95521
Telephone: (707) 826-3755
Fax: (707) 826-4993
E-mail: *bbd1@humboldt.edu*
Web: *http://www.humboldt.edu/~psych*

Department Information:
1964. Professor: Brent Duncan. Number of faculty: total—full-time 12, part-time 7; women—full-time 4, part-time 6; total—minority—full-time 2; women minority—full-time 1.

Programs and Degrees Offered:
Listed in the following order: Program area, degree type (T if terminal Master's), number awarded 7/06–6/07. Academic Research MA/MS (Master of Arts/Science) (T) 1, Counseling MA/MS (Master of Arts/Science) (T) 8, School Psychology MA/MS (Master of Arts/Science) (T) 6.

Student Applications/Admissions:
Student Applications
Academic Research MA/MS (Master of Arts/Science)—Applications 2007–2008, 15. Total applicants accepted 2007–2008, 9. Number full-time enrolled (new admits only) 2007–2008, 8. Number part-time enrolled (new admits only) 2007–2008, 0. Total enrolled 2007–2008 full-time, 15, part-time, 5. Openings 2008–2009, 14. The median number of years required for completion of a degree in 2006–2007 were 5. The number of students enrolled full- and part-time who were dismissed or voluntarily withdrew from this program area in 2007–2008 were 0. *Counseling MA/MS (Master of Arts/Science)*—Applications 2007–2008, 26. Total applicants accepted 2007–2008, 11. Number full-time enrolled (new admits only) 2007–2008, 8. Number part-time enrolled (new admits only) 2007–2008, 0. Total enrolled 2007–2008 full-time, 13, part-time, 9. Openings 2008–2009, 13. The median number of years required for completion of a degree in 2006–2007 were 3. The number of students enrolled full- and part-time who were dismissed or voluntarily withdrew from this program area in 2007–2008 were 4. *School Psychology MA/MS (Master of Arts/Science)*—Applications 2007–2008, 29. Total applicants accepted 2007–2008, 10. Number full-time enrolled (new admits only) 2007–2008, 10. Number part-time enrolled (new admits only) 2007–2008, 0. Total enrolled 2007–2008 full-time, 31, part-time, 1. Openings 2008–2009, 13. The median number of years required for completion of a degree in 2006–2007 were 3. The number of students enrolled full- and part-time who were dismissed or voluntarily withdrew from this program area in 2007–2008 were 0.

Admissions Requirements:
Scores: Entries appear in this order: required test or GPA, minimum score (if required), median score of students entering in 2007–2008. Master's Programs: overall undergraduate GPA 3.00. The Academic Research program requires a 3.25 GPA in Psychology courses and General GRE scores. The School Psychology Program requires the General GRE scores.
Other Criteria: (importance of criteria rated low, medium, or high): GRE/MAT scores—medium, research experience—medium, work experience—medium, extracurricular activity—medium, clinically related public service—medium, GPA—high, letters of recommendation—high, interview—medium, statement of goals and objectives—high. An interview is required for Counseling and School Psychology; research experience is important for Academic Research; clinically related public service or work experience is highly important for Counseling and School Psychology; school/child related work experience highly important for School Psychology. For additional information on admission requirements, go to http://www.humboldt.edu/~psych/.

Student Characteristics: The following represents characteristics of students in 2007–2008 in all graduate psychology programs in the department: Female—full-time 49, part-time 13; Male—full-time 10, part-time 2; African American/Black—full-time 1, part-time 0; Hispanic/Latino(a)—full-time 4, part-time 0; Asian/Pacific Islander—full-time 3, part-time 0; American Indian/Alaska Native—full-time 3, part-time 0; Caucasian/White—full-time 44, part-time 14; Multi-ethnic—full-time 3, part-time 0; students subject to the Americans With Disabilities Act—full-time 0, part-time 0; Unknown ethnicity—full-time 1, part-time 1.

Financial Information/Assistance:
Tuition for Full-Time Study: *Master's:* State residents: per academic year $3,760; Nonstate residents: per academic year $3,760, $339 per credit hour. Tuition is subject to change. See the following Web site for updates and changes in tuition costs: http://www.humboldt.edu.

Financial Assistance:
First-Year Students: Fellowships and scholarships available for first year. Average amount paid per academic year: $1,500. Apply by variable.

Advanced Students: Fellowships and scholarships available for advanced students. Average amount paid per academic year: $1,500. Apply by variable.

Additional Information: Of all students currently enrolled full time, 0% benefited from one or more of the listed financial assistance programs.

Internships/Practica: Humboldt's Future Faculty Training Program provides teaching internship opportunities (some paid) at the local community college. School Psychology internships (usually paid) are required of all students seeking the School Psychology credential. Counseling MA students are provided the opportunity to do fieldwork/practica in the department's psychology clinic, as well as in several local mental heath agencies.

Housing and Day Care: On-campus housing is available. Housing Office (707) 826-3451 (on campus) or (707) 826-3455 (off campus). On-campus day care facilities are available. Children's Center House (707) 826-3838.

Employment of Department Graduates:

Master's Degree Graduates: Of those who graduated in the academic year 2006–2007, the following categories and numbers represent the postgraduate activities and employment of master's degree graduates: Enrolled in a psychology doctoral program (2), enrolled in a postdoctoral residency/fellowship (n/a), employed in independent practice (n/a), employed in an academic position at a 2-year/4-year college (0), employed in a professional position in a school system (6), employed in business or industry (1), employed in a community mental health/counseling center (5), other employment position (1), total from the above (master's) (15).

Doctoral Degree Graduates: Of those who graduated in the academic year 2006–2007, the following categories and numbers represent the postgraduate activities and employment of doctoral degree graduates: Enrolled in a psychology doctoral program (n/a), total from the above (doctoral) (0).

Additional Information:

Orientation, Objectives, and Emphasis of Department: The objectives of our department of psychology are to provide students with an understanding of principles and theories concerning human behavior and to the processes by which such information is obtained; to provide a sound academic education for those working for degrees in psychology with a future goal of professional work in psychology; to offer a liberal arts major and minor in psychology for students seeking a quality liberal education; to provide quality professional graduate education for students working toward California School Psychologist credentials, Marriage and Family Therapist licenses, and other specialized occupational fields; and to provide flexibility in our offerings that responds to changing societal agenda and student needs. Our Academic Research Masters Program provides specializations in the following areas: Developmental Psychopathology, Biological Psychology, and Social and Environmental Psychology. Students should select one of these areas when they apply to the AR program.

Special Facilities or Resources: The department has an on-campus clinic staffed by MA counseling students, an electronic equipment shop, a lab with biofeedback and EEG equipment, a lab equipped for research on motion sickness, observation and research access to an on-campus demonstration nursery school, a test library, and a computer laboratory. Our new Behavioral and Social Sciences Building provides exceptional research, instruction, and faculty and student space for the Department of Psychology.

Information for Students With Physical Disabilities: Student Disability Resource Center (SDRC) (707) 826-4678.

Application Information:

Send to Office of Admissions, Humboldt State University, Arcata, CA 95521 for general admissions; Department of Psychology, Humboldt State University, Arcata, CA 95521 for specific admissions requirements for each of the three programs. Contact Graduate Secretary, (707) 826-5264. Application available online. URL of online application: http://www.humboldt.edu/%7Egradst/new_student.html. Students are admitted in the Fall, application deadline see below. Deadline for Academic Research MA program is March 1. Deadline for Counseling MA program is February 15. Deadline for School Psychology MA program is February 15. *Fee:* $55. Partial out-of-state tuition waiver available most semesters.

Institute of Transpersonal Psychology (2007 data)

Department of Psychology
1069 East Meadow Circle
Palo Alto, CA 94303
Telephone: (650) 493-4430, ext. 216
Fax: (650) 493-6835
E-mail: *jhofmann@itp.edu*
Web: *http://www.itp.edu*

Department Information:

1975. Chairperson: Dr. Christopher Dryer. Number of faculty: total—full-time 19, part-time 5; women—full-time 8, part-time 2.

Programs and Degrees Offered:

Listed in the following order: Program area, degree type (T if terminal Master's), number awarded 7/06–6/07. Transpersonal Clinical Psychology PhD (Doctor of Philosophy) 0, Counseling Psychology MA/MS (Master of Arts/Science) (T) 20, Psychology PhD (Doctor of Philosophy) 0, Distance Learning Master's MA/MS (Master of Arts/Science) 19, Distance Learning Certificates Other 19, Transpersonal Psychology PhD (Doctor of Philosophy) 18.

Student Applications/Admissions:

Student Applications

Transpersonal Clinical Psychology PhD (Doctor of Philosophy)—Applications 2007–2008, 0. Total applicants accepted 2007–2008, 0. Number full-time enrolled (new admits only) 2007–2008, 0. Number part-time enrolled (new admits only) 2007–2008, 0. Openings 2008–2009, 40. The number of students enrolled full- and part-time who were dismissed or voluntarily withdrew from this program area in 2007–2008 were 0. *Counseling Psychology MA/MS (Master of Arts/Science)*—Applications 2007–2008, 53. Total applicants accepted 2007–2008, 39. Number full-time enrolled (new admits only) 2007–2008, 35. Number part-time enrolled (new admits only) 2007–2008, 0. Total enrolled 2007–2008 full-time, 78, part-time, 8. Openings 2008–2009, 30. The median number of years required for completion of a degree in 2006–2007 were 3. The number of students enrolled full- and part-time who were dismissed or voluntarily withdrew from this program area in 2007–2008 were 2. *Psychology PhD (Doctor of Philosophy)*—Applications 2007–2008, 39. Total applicants accepted 2007–2008, 32. Number full-time enrolled (new admits only) 2007–2008, 25. Openings 2008–2009, 30. The number of students enrolled full- and part-time who were dismissed or voluntarily withdrew from this program area in 2007–2008 were 9. *Distance Learning Master's MA/MS (Master of Arts/Science)*—Applications 2007–2008, 38. Total applicants accepted 2007–2008, 29. Number full-time enrolled (new admits only) 2007–2008, 27. Number part-time enrolled (new admits only) 2007–2008, 0. Openings 2008–2009, 50. The median number of years required for completion of a degree in 2006–2007 were 2. The number of students enrolled full- and part-time who were dismissed or voluntarily withdrew from this program area in 2007–2008 were 3. *Distance Learning Certificates Other*—Applications 2007–2008, 15. Total applicants accepted 2007–2008, 14. Number full-time enrolled (new admits only) 2007–2008, 13. Openings 2008–2009, 50. The median number of years required for completion of a degree in 2006–2007 was 1. The number of students enrolled full- and part-time who were dismissed or voluntarily withdrew from this program area in 2007–2008 were 9. *Transpersonal Psychology PhD (Doctor of Philosophy)*—Applications 2007–2008, 67. Total applicants accepted 2007–2008, 40. Number full-time enrolled (new admits only) 2007–2008, 47. Total enrolled 2007–2008 full-time, 122, part-time, 8. Openings 2008–2009, 40. The median number of years required for completion of a degree in 2006–2007 were 5. The number of students enrolled full- and part-time who were dismissed or voluntarily withdrew from this program area in 2007–2008 were 8.

Admissions Requirements:

Scores: Entries appear in this order: required test or GPA, minimum score (if required), median score of students entering in 2007–2008. Master's Programs: overall undergraduate GPA 3.0. Doctoral Programs: overall undergraduate GPA 3.0.

Other Criteria: (importance of criteria rated low, medium, or high): research experience—medium, work experience—medium, extracurricular activity—medium, clinically related public service—medium, GPA—medium, letters of recommendation—high, interview—high, statement of goals and objectives—high. The Academic Writing Sample is required for applications to the Residential PhD and the Distance Learning PhD; it is not required for any of the MA or Certificate programs. Research experience is not a criteria for admission to any of the MA programs. For additional information on admission requirements, go to http://www.itp.edu/admissions/application2.cfm.

Student Characteristics: The following represents characteristics of students in 2007–2008 in all graduate psychology programs in the department: Female—full-time 269, part-time 4; Male—full-time 94, part-time 24; African American/Black—full-time 9, part-time 0; Hispanic/Latino(a)—full-time 6, part-time 0; Asian/Pacific Islander—full-time 12, part-time 1; American Indian/Alaska Native—full-time 3, part-time 0; Caucasian/White—full-time 211, part-time 14; Multi-ethnic—full-time 56, part-time 9; students subject to the Americans With Disabilities Act—full-time 0, part-time 0; Unknown ethnicity—full-time 0, part-time 0.

Financial Information/Assistance:

Tuition for Full-Time Study: *Master's:* State residents: per academic year $10,875, $476 per credit hour; Nonstate residents: per academic year $10,875, $476 per credit hour. *Doctoral:* State residents: per academic year $21,201, $498 per credit hour; Nonstate residents: per academic year $21,201, $498 per credit hour. Tuition is subject to change. Tuition costs vary by program. See the following Web site for updates and changes in tuition costs: http://www.itp.edu/admissions/tuition.cfm.

Financial Assistance:

First-Year Students: Teaching assistantships available for first year. Average amount paid per academic year: $1,368. Average number of hours worked per week: 6. Apply by August 1. Research assistantships available for first year. Average amount paid per academic year: $1,368. Average number of hours worked per week: 6. Apply by August 1. Fellowships and scholarships available for first year. Average amount paid per academic year: $875. Apply by August 1.

Advanced Students: Teaching assistantships available for advanced students. Average amount paid per academic year: $1,368. Average number of hours worked per week: 6. Apply by August 1. Research assistantships available for advanced students. Average amount paid per academic year: $1,368. Average number of hours worked per week: 6. Apply by August 1. Fellowships and scholarships available for advanced students. Average amount paid per academic year: $875. Apply by August 1.

Additional Information: Of all students currently enrolled full time, 19% benefited from one or more of the listed financial assistance programs. Application and information available online at http://www.itp.edu/admissions/finAid.cfm.

Internships/Practica: The Transpersonal Counseling Center is a nonprofit community counseling center and training institute affiliated with the nation's leading institution of transpersonal studies. Clinical PhD students gain hands-on psychotherapy experience providing individual, couples, family, and group psychotherapy to children, adolescents, and adults. Traditional models of assessment and treatment are combined with transpersonal approaches. Applicants for internship must meet the criteria set out by the CAPIC uniform application process. Placement offers an opportunity to gain hours (SPEs) toward licensure as a Clinical Psychologist. The initial contract is for a 1-year half-time internship (20 hours/week) beginning in July and running to the next July, with renewal of contract possible. Each week at the Center comprises approximately 6–8 direct client therapy hours, 1 hour of individual supervision, and 2 and a half hours of group supervision and training. Two hours of service to the center and community outreach work is also expected weekly. Within an outpatient psychotherapy setting, interns are offered an opportunity to utilize any number of contemporary therapeutic modalities while working from a transpersonal framework that includes attention to multiple layers of consciousness, spirituality, mind–body wellness, and the relationship of the individual to the community in each of the aforementioned contexts.

Housing and Day Care: No on-campus housing is available. No on-campus day care facilities are available.

Employment of Department Graduates:

Master's Degree Graduates: Of those who graduated in the academic year 2006–2007, the following categories and numbers represent the postgraduate activities and employment of master's degree graduates: Enrolled in a postdoctoral residency/fellowship (n/a), employed in independent practice (n/a), total from the above (master's) (0).

Doctoral Degree Graduates: Of those who graduated in the academic year 2006–2007, the following categories and numbers represent the postgraduate activities and employment of doctoral degree graduates: Enrolled in a psychology doctoral program (n/a), total from the above (doctoral) (0).

Additional Information:

Orientation, Objectives, and Emphasis of Department: The mission of ITP's graduate programs is to produce skillful, well-rounded psychologists, counselors, teachers, and educators through disciplined inquiry, scholarly research, and self-discovery in the context of a supportive community environment. Transpersonal Psychology applies the methods and tools of psychology to investigate experiences, developmental processes, and levels of identity that go beyond or transcend the ordinary personality. To adequately prepare students for this line of inquiry, ITP's curriculum is informed by a whole-person learning model that maintains that a student's education must attend to all aspects of his or her experience, including the mental, emotional, physical, spiritual, creative, and social dimensions. Besides integrating theory, research, and professional training, each degree program encourages students to cultivate transpersonal values, such as mindfulness, compassion, discernment, and an appreciation of differences, and to integrate these principles into their personal and professional lives. Collaborative learning is emphasized in order to understand the powerful role that others play in shaping one's education. Graduates are well prepared to follow traditional career paths while contributing an innovative transpersonal approach to their respective field. Students not only build a strong foundation of psychotherapeutic skills but also learn how to communicate in a variety of complex relational circumstances.

Special Facilities or Resources: Named in honor of the illustrious American psychologist, philosopher, and writer, the William James Center for Consciousness Studies was established in 1994 as the research arm of the Institute of Transpersonal Psychology. The Center's projects emphasize exceptional human experiences, both psychic and mystical, psychospiritual transformation, and physical and psychological well-being and growth. These themes were of keen interest to William James throughout his life, and today, more than ever before, they provoke far-reaching questions for humanity. The aim of the Center is to foster and support studies that have clear implications for the field of transpersonal psychology. Researchers at the Center are encouraged to develop, initiate, and evaluate practical applications of the principles emerging from their work (for example, in education, business, wellness, counseling, therapy, and spiritual guidance). Research projects are designed and conducted primarily by Institute faculty, doctoral, and postdoctoral students; however, the Center is also designed to provide an umbrella for work by adjunct and visiting researchers and by outside investigators. Work at the William James Center for Consciousness Studies is carried out through narrative, empirical, and theoretical investigations; meetings and discussions; sponsorship of special projects; and funding applications.

Information for Students With Physical Disabilities: See the following Web site for more information: Please contact ITP's Dean of Students at http://www.pyue@itp.edu for assistance.

Application Information:

Send to Institute of Transpersonal Psychology, Admissions Office, 1069 East Meadow Circle, Palo Alto, CA 94303. Application available online. URL of online application: http://www.itp.edu/admissions/application2.cfm. Students are admitted in the Fall, application deadline February 1; Programs have rolling admissions. ITP's Distance Learning Master's and Certificate programs enroll students each quarter (Fall, Winter, Spring, and Summer), and applications are accepted up to 3 weeks prior to the start of the term. ITP's Distance Learning PhD program enrolls each July, and its application deadline is February 1. *Fee:* $55.

John F. Kennedy University

Graduate School of Professional Psychology
100 Ellinwood Way
Pleasant Hill, CA 94523
Telephone: (925) 969-3400
Fax: (925) 969-3401
E-mail: *wdparham@jfku.edu*
Web: *http://www.jfku.edu*

Department Information:

1965. Dean: William D. Parham. Number of faculty: total—full-time 8, part-time 89; women—full-time 8, part-time 76; faculty subject to the Americans With Disabilities Act 2.

Programs and Degrees Offered:

Listed in the following order: Program area, degree type (T if terminal Master's), number awarded 7/06–6/07. Counseling Psychology MA/MS (Master of Arts/Science) (T) 82, Organizational Psychology MA/MS (Master of Arts/Science) (T) 9, PsyD (Doctor of Psychology) 20, Sport Psychology MA/MS (Master of Arts/Science) (T) 13.

APA Accreditation: Clinical PsyD (Doctor of Psychology).

Student Applications/Admissions:

Student Applications

Counseling Psychology MA/MS (Master of Arts/Science)—Applications 2007–2008, 164. Total applicants accepted 2007–2008, 125. Number full-time enrolled (new admits only) 2007–2008, 25. Number part-time enrolled (new admits only) 2007–2008, 49. Total enrolled 2007–2008 full-time, 90, part-time, 193. Openings 2008–2009, 75. The median number of years required for completion of a degree in 2006–2007 were 2. The number of students enrolled full- and part-time who were dismissed or voluntarily withdrew from this program area in 2007–2008 were 9. *Organizational Psychology MA/MS (Master of Arts/Science)*—Applications 2007–2008, 27. Total applicants accepted 2007–2008, 18. Number full-time enrolled (new admits only) 2007–2008, 6. Number part-time enrolled (new admits only) 2007–2008, 12. Total enrolled 2007–2008 full-time, 10, part-time, 33. Openings 2008–2009, 15. The median number of years required for completion of a degree in 2006–2007 were 2. The number of students enrolled full-

and part-time who were dismissed or voluntarily withdrew from this program area in 2007–2008 were 0. *PsyD (Doctor of Psychology)*—Applications 2007–2008, 151. Total applicants accepted 2007–2008, 78. Number full-time enrolled (new admits only) 2007–2008, 24. Number part-time enrolled (new admits only) 2007–2008, 5. Total enrolled 2007–2008 full-time, 75, part-time, 40. Openings 2008–2009, 30. The median number of years required for completion of a degree in 2006–2007 were 5. The number of students enrolled full- and part-time who were dismissed or voluntarily withdrew from this program area in 2007–2008 were 2. *Sport Psychology MA/MS (Master of Arts/Science)*—Applications 2007–2008, 31. Total applicants accepted 2007–2008, 29. Number full-time enrolled (new admits only) 2007–2008, 7. Number part-time enrolled (new admits only) 2007–2008, 10. Total enrolled 2007–2008 full-time, 15, part-time, 35. Openings 2008–2009, 20. The median number of years required for completion of a degree in 2006–2007 were 2.

Admissions Requirements:

Scores: Entries appear in this order: required test or GPA, minimum score (if required), median score of students entering in 2007–2008. Master's Programs: overall undergraduate GPA 3.0. Doctoral Programs: overall undergraduate GPA 3.0.

Other Criteria: (importance of criteria rated low, medium, or high): research experience—medium, work experience—high, extracurricular activity—high, clinically related public service—high, GPA—high, letters of recommendation—high, interview—high, statement of goals and objectives—high, undergraduate major in psychology—medium, specific undergraduate psychology courses taken—low. The PsyD Program puts more emphasis on the GPA than do the MA Programs. For additional information on admission requirements, go to http://www.jfku.edu.

Student Characteristics: The following represents characteristics of students in 2007–2008 in all graduate psychology programs in the department: Female—full-time 149, part-time 241; Male—full-time 41, part-time 60; African American/Black—full-time 16, part-time 26; Hispanic/Latino(a)—full-time 13, part-time 30; Asian/Pacific Islander—full-time 20, part-time 24; American Indian/Alaska Native—full-time 0, part-time 3; Caucasian/White—full-time 120, part-time 190; Multi-ethnic—full-time 3, part-time 5; students subject to the Americans With Disabilities Act—full-time 4, part-time 2; Unknown ethnicity—full-time 18, part-time 23.

Financial Information/Assistance:

Tuition for Full-Time Study: *Master's:* State residents: $475 per credit hour; Nonstate residents: $475 per credit hour. *Doctoral:* State residents: $610 per credit hour; Nonstate residents: $610 per credit hour. Tuition is subject to change. Additional fees are assessed to students beyond the costs of tuition for the following: Comprehensive exams, petition to graduate, student services, and technology fees. Tuition costs vary by program. See the following Web site for updates and changes in tuition costs: http://www.jfku.edu.

Financial Assistance:

First-Year Students: No information provided.

Advanced Students: No information provided.

Additional Information: Of all students currently enrolled full time, 0% benefited from one or more of the listed financial assistance programs. Application and information available online at http://www.jfku.edu.

Internships/Practica: The Graduate School of Professional Psychology has three community counseling centers, located near one of our two campuses, which provide state of the art supervision for students and provide thousands of hours of low-fee counseling each year. Additionally, approximately 150 external fieldwork sites, monitored by our faculty, are available in the surrounding counties. Students in the Counseling MA program and the PsyD program accumulate hours toward their respective licenses at both the community counseling centers and the external sites. The MA in Sport Psychology and Expressive Art programs offer summer camps for children that also serve as additional field placement sites for graduate students.

Housing and Day Care: No on-campus housing is available. No on-campus day care facilities are available.

Employment of Department Graduates:

Master's Degree Graduates: Of those who graduated in the academic year 2006–2007, the following categories and numbers represent the postgraduate activities and employment of master's degree graduates: Enrolled in a postdoctoral residency/fellowship (n/a), employed in independent practice (n/a), total from the above (master's) (0).

Doctoral Degree Graduates: Of those who graduated in the academic year 2006–2007, the following categories and numbers represent the postgraduate activities and employment of doctoral degree graduates: Enrolled in a psychology doctoral program (n/a), total from the above (doctoral) (0).

Additional Information:

Orientation, Objectives, and Emphasis of Department: The mission of the Graduate School of Professional Psychology is to create an innovative, diverse, and responsive environment for students that supports personal and professional learning. We are committed to active learning and community service, and are guided by a commitment to traditionally underserved populations. Students acquire excellence in both traditional and emerging competencies and are taught by faculty who are practicing professionals in their field. The MA Counseling Psychology program offers specializations in Child and Adolescent Therapy, Addiction Studies, Cross-Cultural Issues, Expressive Arts, Couples and Families, and Sport Psychology. In addition to the MA degree, the Organizational Psychology program offers certificates in Coaching and Conflict Management. Students may also enroll in the Link Program and receive both the MA in Sports Psychology and the PsyD in Clinical Psychology.

Special Facilities or Resources: As noted, the Graduate School of Professional Psychology community counseling centers serve a broad-based clientele throughout the surrounding communities. The programs in the school are actively engaged in community service. For example, the Sports Psychology program is an active participant in the Life Enhancement Through Athletic and Academic Participation (LEAP) in numerous Bay Area schools. The Expressive Arts specialization in the Counseling Psychology MA program works with elementary school children from a variety of sites.

Information for Students With Physical Disabilities: See the following Web site for more information: http://www.accomm@jfku.edu.

Application Information:
Send to Olga Lepilina, Office of Admissions, John F. Kennedy University, 100 Ellinwood Way, Pleasant Hill, CA 94523. Application available online. URL of online application: http://www.jfku.edu. Students are admitted in the Fall, application deadline rolling; Winter, application deadline rolling; Spring, application deadline rolling; Summer, application deadline rolling. January 2 for PsyD (Fall admissions only) MA Counseling Program takes new students in Fall and Spring; MA in Organizational Psychology and Sport Psychology take new students each quarter. *Fee:* $55. $75 application fee for PsyD Program.

La Verne, University of (2007 data)

Psychology Department
Arts and Sciences
1950 Third Street
La Verne, CA 91750
Telephone: (909) 593-3511, ext. 4413
Fax: (909) 392-2745
E-mail: *bperlmutter@ulv.edu*
Web: *http://www.ulv.edu/psychology/*

Department Information:
1968. Chairperson: Glenn Gamst, PhD. Number of faculty: total—full-time 12, part-time 14; women—full-time 4, part-time 7.

Programs and Degrees Offered:
Listed in the following order: Program area, degree type (T if terminal Master's), number awarded 7/06–6/07. Clinical–Community PsyD (Doctor of Psychology) 6, Marriage and Family Therapy MA/MS (Master of Arts/Science) (T) 20, Counseling (College Counseling and Student Services) MA/MS (Master of Arts/Science) (T) 5.

APA Accreditation: Clinical PsyD (Doctor of Psychology).

Student Applications/Admissions:
Student Applications
Clinical–Community PsyD (Doctor of Psychology)—Applications 2007–2008, 90. Total applicants accepted 2007–2008, 35. Number full-time enrolled (new admits only) 2007–2008, 19. Openings 2008–2009, 20. The median number of years required for completion of a degree in 2006–2007 were 5. The number of students enrolled full- and part-time who were dismissed or voluntarily withdrew from this program area in 2007–2008 were 5. *Marriage and Family Therapy MA/MS (Master of Arts/Science)*—Applications 2007–2008, 40. Total applicants accepted 2007–2008, 32. Number full-time enrolled (new admits only) 2007–2008, 18. Number part-time enrolled (new admits only) 2007–2008, 14. Total enrolled 2007–2008 full-time, 35, part-time, 35. Openings 2008–2009, 25. The median number of years required for completion of a degree in 2006–2007 were 3. The number of students enrolled full- and part-time who were dismissed or voluntarily withdrew from this program area in 2007–2008 were 3. *Counseling (College Counseling and Student Services) MA/MS (Master of Arts/Science)*—Applications 2007–2008, 10. Total applicants accepted 2007–2008, 7. Number full-time enrolled (new admits only) 2007–2008, 4. Number part-time enrolled (new admits only) 2007–2008, 3. Total enrolled 2007–2008 full-time, 11, part-time, 9. Openings 2008–2009, 15. The median number of years required for completion of a degree in 2006–2007 were 3. The number of students enrolled full- and part-time who were dismissed or voluntarily withdrew from this program area in 2007–2008 were 1.

Admissions Requirements:
Scores: Entries appear in this order: required test or GPA, minimum score (if required), median score of students entering in 2007–2008. Master's Programs: overall undergraduate GPA 3.0, 3.3. Doctoral Programs: overall undergraduate GPA 3.25, 3.50; last 2 years GPA 3.25, 3.50; psychology GPA 3.25, 3.50.
Other Criteria: (importance of criteria rated low, medium, or high): research experience—medium, work experience—high, extracurricular activity—low, clinically related public service—high, GPA—high, letters of recommendation—high, interview—high, statement of goals and objectives—high. Research experience is considered more strongly for admission to the PsyD program compared to the MS programs. For additional information on admission requirements, go to http://www.ulv.edu/psychology/.

Student Characteristics: The following represents characteristics of students in 2007–2008 in all graduate psychology programs in the department: Female—full-time 91, part-time 35; Male—full-time 19, part-time 9; African American/Black—full-time 13, part-time 5; Hispanic/Latino(a)—full-time 39, part-time 17; Asian/Pacific Islander—full-time 11, part-time 5; American Indian/Alaska Native—full-time 0, part-time 1; Caucasian/White—full-time 44, part-time 16; Multi-ethnic—full-time 3, part-time 0; students subject to the Americans With Disabilities Act—full-time 2, part-time 0; Unknown ethnicity—full-time 0, part-time 0.

Financial Information/Assistance:
Tuition for Full-Time Study: *Master's:* State residents: $550 per credit hour; Nonstate residents: $550 per credit hour. *Doctoral:* State residents: $680 per credit hour; Nonstate residents: $680 per credit hour. Tuition is subject to change. See the following Web site for updates and changes in tuition costs: http://www.ulv.edu.

Financial Assistance:
First-Year Students: Teaching assistantships available for first year. Average amount paid per academic year: $2,000. Average number of hours worked per week: 8. Apply by June. Tuition remission given: partial. Research assistantships available for first year. Average amount paid per academic year: $2,000. Average number of hours worked per week: 8. Apply by June. Tuition remission given: partial.

Advanced Students: Teaching assistantships available for advanced students. Average amount paid per academic year: $2,000. Average number of hours worked per week: 8. Apply by June. Tuition remission given: partial. Research assistantships available for advanced students. Average amount paid per academic year: $2,000. Average number of hours worked per week: 8. Apply by June. Tuition remission given: partial. Traineeships available for advanced students. Average amount paid per academic year: $4,000. Average number of hours worked per week: 20. Apply by March. Tuition remission given: partial.

Additional Information: Of all students currently enrolled full time, 20% benefited from one or more of the listed financial assistance programs.

Internships/Practica: The PsyD program includes required supervised practica in the 2nd and 3rd years of the program, with an optional 4th year practicum available. A minimum of 1,500 hours of clinical–community practicum activities is required for the PsyD. The culminating predoctoral internship in the 5th and final year of the program consists of an additional 1,500 clinical hours, which is typically completed as a 1-year full-time internship. Although most students follow this track, a 2-year, half-time internship option is available. The PsyD program participates in a regional consortium of program and training site directors for doctoral programs, and is a graduate program member of CAPIC and NCSPP. The MS programs include 1 year of supervised fieldwork, typically in the 2nd year of the program. Hours vary by program. The Psychology department has an extensive network of practica, fieldwork, and internship sites with mental health and educational settings throughout the San Gabriel and Pomona valleys and the Inland Empire region. The on-campus Counseling Center is part of the Psychology department, is staffed by PsyD and Masters students, and is one of the largest practicum training sites.

Housing and Day Care: No on-campus housing is available. No on-campus day care facilities are available.

Employment of Department Graduates:

Master's Degree Graduates: Of those who graduated in the academic year 2006–2007, the following categories and numbers represent the postgraduate activities and employment of master's degree graduates: Enrolled in a psychology doctoral program (1), enrolled in another graduate/professional program (0), enrolled in a postdoctoral residency/fellowship (n/a), employed in independent practice (n/a), employed in an academic position at a university (0), employed in an academic position at a 2-year/4-year college (0), employed in other positions at a higher education institution (4), employed in a professional position in a school system (0), employed in business or industry (0), employed in government agency (0), employed in a community mental health/counseling center (14), employed in a hospital/medical center (4), still seeking employment (0), not seeking employment (2), other employment position (0), do not know (0), total from the above (master's) (25).

Doctoral Degree Graduates: Of those who graduated in the academic year 2006–2007, the following categories and numbers represent the postgraduate activities and employment of doctoral degree graduates: Enrolled in a psychology doctoral program (n/a), enrolled in another graduate/professional program (0), enrolled in a postdoctoral residency/fellowship (0), employed in independent practice (0), employed in an academic position at a university (0), employed in an academic position at a 2-year/4-year college (0), employed in other positions at a higher education institution (0), employed in a professional position in a school system (0), employed in business or industry (0), employed in government agency (0), employed in a community mental health/counseling center (5), employed in a hospital/medical center (2), still seeking employment (0), not seeking employment (0), other employment position (0), do not know (0), total from the above (doctoral) (7).

Additional Information:

Orientation, Objectives, and Emphasis of Department: The clinical faculty consists of psychologists whose theoretical orientations include psychodynamic, humanist, cognitive–behavioral, family systems, and community psychology, and who are clinically active in a range of clinical settings and populations. Faculty research interests include topics such as multiculturalism, juvenile delinquency and adult forensic issues, substance abuse, psychotherapy outcome research, racial identity and acculturation, professional violations of mental health professionals, child and family development, moral development and decision making, and violence and victimization. The curriculum of the PsyD program in Clinical–Community psychology is anchored in an ecological and multicultural perspective, and involves a multidisciplinary faculty who are actively involved in clinical and research activities. The curriculum of the MS programs is anchored primarily in the family systems model although students are exposed to multiple theoretical perspectives. The PsyD program meets all predoctoral requirements for California psychology licensure. The program received APA accreditation in 2003. Students proceed through the program in a cohort model, taking all but elective courses together with their entering group. This fosters a high level of cooperation among students. Student–faculty ratios are relatively small, resulting in multiple opportunities for mentoring by faculty, and for student–faculty collaboration.

Special Facilities or Resources: Masters and doctoral students have access to a wide network of local and regional clinical, research, and library facilities in the metropolitan Los Angeles and Southern California area. The campus University Counseling Center is directed by the Psychology department and provides counseling services to university students and staff. The Center is equipped with videotape and biofeedback equipment. ULV's Wilson Library contains 200,000 volumes and over 2,000 current journal subscriptions. Access to library resources is available through reciprocal borrowing privileges at many academic libraries in the Southern California area, as well as through online catalogs and CD-ROM databases.

Information for Students With Physical Disabilities: See the following Web site for more information: http://www.ulv.edu/gaas/contact.phtml.

Application Information:

Send to Graduate Student Services, 1950 Third Street, University of La Verne, La Verne, CA 91750. PsyD application deadline: January 15 for yearly admission. Students will be considered for the PsyD program after the deadline on a space-available basis. MS programs: April 1 for Fall admission and December 1 for Spring admission. *Fee:* $75. Fee for MS programs is $50. Fee for PsyD program is $75. The application fee is waived for current ULV students.

Loma Linda University

Department of Psychology
School of Science and Technology
11130 Anderson Street, Suite 106
Loma Linda, CA 92350
Telephone: (909) 558-8577
Fax: (909) 558-0971
E-mail: *sLane@llu.edu*
Web: *http://www.llu.edu/llu/grad/psychology*

Department Information:

1994. Chairperson: Louis E Jenkins, PhD, ABPP. Number of faculty: total—full-time 10, part-time 3; women—full-time 3, part-time 1; total—minority—full-time 2, part-time 1.

Programs and Degrees Offered:

Listed in the following order: Program area, degree type (T if terminal Master's), number awarded 7/06–6/07. Clinical Psychology PhD (Doctor of Philosophy) 6, Clinical Psychology PsyD (Doctor of Psychology) 7, Experimental Psychology PhD (Doctor of Philosophy) 2, Experimental Psychology MA/MS (Master of Arts/Science) (T) 1.

APA Accreditation: Clinical PhD (Doctor of Philosophy). Clinical PsyD (Doctor of Psychology).

Student Applications/Admissions:

Student Applications

Clinical Psychology PhD (Doctor of Philosophy)—Applications 2007–2008, 33. Total applicants accepted 2007–2008, 11. Number full-time enrolled (new admits only) 2007–2008, 11. Number part-time enrolled (new admits only) 2007–2008, 0. The median number of years required for completion of a degree in 2006–2007 were 7. The number of students enrolled full- and part-time who were dismissed or voluntarily withdrew from this program area in 2007–2008 were 2. *Clinical Psychology PsyD (Doctor of Psychology)*—Applications 2007–2008, 24. Total applicants accepted 2007–2008, 7. Number full-time enrolled (new admits only) 2007–2008, 12. Number part-time enrolled (new admits only) 2007–2008, 0. The median number of years required for completion of a degree in 2006–2007 were 5. The number of students enrolled full- and part-time who were dismissed or voluntarily withdrew from this program area in 2007–2008 were 1. *Experimental Psychology PhD (Doctor of Philosophy)*—Applications 2007–2008, 2. Total applicants accepted 2007–2008, 2. Number full-time enrolled (new admits only) 2007–2008, 2. Openings 2008–2009, 3. The median number of years required for completion of a degree in 2006–2007 were 5. The number of students enrolled full- and part-time who were dismissed or voluntarily withdrew from this program area in 2007–2008 were 1. *Experimental Psychology MA/MS (Master of Arts/Science)*—Applications 2007–2008, 5. Total applicants accepted 2007–2008, 2. Number full-time enrolled (new admits only) 2007–2008, 2. Number part-time enrolled (new admits only) 2007–2008, 0. Openings 2008–2009, 8. The median number of years required for completion of a degree in 2006–2007 were 2. The number of students enrolled full- and part-time who were dismissed or voluntarily withdrew from this program area in 2007–2008 were 2.

Admissions Requirements:

Scores: Entries appear in this order: required test or GPA, minimum score (if required), median score of students entering in 2007–2008. Master's Programs: GRE-V 500; GRE-Q 500; overall undergraduate GPA 3.0; Masters GRE-Analytical 4.0. Doctoral Programs: GRE-V 500; GRE-Q 500; overall undergraduate GPA 3.0; last 2 years GPA 3.0; psychology GPA 3.0; Doctoral program GRE-Analytic 4.0.

Other Criteria: (importance of criteria rated low, medium, or high): GRE/MAT scores—high, research experience—high, work experience—medium, extracurricular activity—medium, clinically related public service—high, GPA—high, letters of recommendation—high, interview—high, statement of goals and objectives—high, undergraduate major in psychology—high, specific undergraduate psychology courses taken—high. For PhD applicants, research experience is highly desirable. For PsyD applicants, clinical related experience is highly desirable.

Student Characteristics: The following represents characteristics of students in 2007–2008 in all graduate psychology programs in the department: Female—full-time 92, part-time 0; Male—full-time 46, part-time 0; African American/Black—full-time 11, part-time 0; Hispanic/Latino(a)—full-time 14, part-time 0; Asian/Pacific Islander—full-time 22, part-time 0; American Indian/Alaska Native—full-time 0, part-time 0; Caucasian/White—full-time 92, part-time 0; Multi-ethnic—full-time 6, part-time 0; students subject to the Americans With Disabilities Act—full-time 5, part-time 0; Unknown ethnicity—full-time 0, part-time 0.

Financial Information/Assistance:

Tuition for Full-Time Study: *Master's:* State residents: per academic year $25,600; Nonstate residents: per academic year $25,600. *Doctoral:* State residents: per academic year $25,600; Nonstate residents: per academic year $25,600. Tuition is subject to change. Tuition costs vary by program. See the following Web site for updates and changes in tuition costs: http://www.llu.edu/ssweb/finaid.

Financial Assistance:

First-Year Students: Research assistantships available for first year. Average amount paid per academic year: $3,280. Average number of hours worked per week: 5. Fellowships and scholarships available for first year. Average amount paid per academic year: $3,000. Apply by August 15. Tuition remission given: partial.

Advanced Students: Teaching assistantships available for advanced students. Average amount paid per academic year: $1,950. Average number of hours worked per week: 7. Research assistantships available for advanced students. Average amount paid per academic year: $6,560. Average number of hours worked per week: 10. Fellowships and scholarships available for advanced students. Average amount paid per academic year: $3,000. Apply by August 15. Tuition remission given: partial.

Additional Information: Of all students currently enrolled full time, 35% benefited from one or more of the listed financial assistance programs.

Internships/Practica: Doctoral Degree (PhD Clinical Psychology): For those doctoral students for whom a professional internship was required in this program prior to graduation, (8) students applied for an internship in 2006–2007, with (7) students obtaining an internship. Of those students who obtained an internship, (7) were paid internships. Of those students who obtained an internship, (6) students placed in APA/CPA-accredited internships, (1) student placed in internships not APA/CPA-accredited, but listed with the Association of Psychology Postdoctoral and Internship Centers (APPIC), (0) students placed in internships conforming to guidelines of the Council of Directors of School Psychology Programs (CDSPP), (0) students placed in internships that were not APA/CPA-accredited, APPIC or CDSPP listed. Doctoral Degree (PsyD Clinical Psychology): For those doctoral students for whom a professional internship was required in this program prior to graduation, (12) students applied for an internship in 2006–2007, with (12) students obtaining an internship. Of those students who obtained an internship, (12) were paid internships. Of those students who obtained an internship, (6) students placed in APA/CPA-accredited internships, (6) students placed in internships not APA/CPA-accredited, but listed with the Association of Psychology Postdoctoral and Internship Centers (APPIC), (0) students placed in internships conforming to guidelines of the Council of Directors of School Psychology Programs (CDSPP), (0) students placed in internships that were not APA/CPA-accredited, APPIC or CDSPP listed. Second-year practicum experiences are obtained in the departmental clinic and in a satellite clinic that reaches a previously underserved area of the City of San Bernardino. Other department training experiences include the LLU Craniofacial Team Clinic and Growing Fit Multidisciplinary clinic for obese children. Second-year practicum students may also receive some supervised clinical training in area public and private school settings. The external practicum (20 hours per week, normally in the 3rd year of the program) is entirely off the departmental campus. Students are expected to accumulate 950 to 1,000 hours of supervised experience while on external practicum, with an absolute minimum of 250 hours being spent in direct service experiences with patients. External practicum students are presently placed in six settings: (a) The Rehabilitation Unit of the Loma Linda University Medical Center; (b) the California Institution for Women; (c) the California Youth Authority; (d) the Riverside County Department of Mental Health; (e) The San Bernardino County Department of Mental Health; and (f) the Casa Colina Hospital for Rehabilitative Medicine. A full-year (40 hours per week) of internship is required with sites available across the country. All acceptable internship sites must meet the criteria for membership in the Association of Psychology Postdoctoral and Internship Centers.

Housing and Day Care: On-campus housing is available. See the following Web site for more information: http://www.llu.edu/student services. On-campus day care facilities are available.

Employment of Department Graduates:

Master's Degree Graduates: Of those who graduated in the academic year 2006–2007, the following categories and numbers represent the postgraduate activities and employment of master's degree graduates: Enrolled in a psychology doctoral program (11), enrolled in another graduate/professional program (3), enrolled in a postdoctoral residency/fellowship (n/a), employed in independent practice (n/a), employed in an academic position at a university (0), employed in an academic position at a 2-year/4-year college (0), employed in other positions at a higher education institution (0), employed in a professional position in a school system (0), employed in business or industry (0), employed in government agency (0), employed in a community mental health/counseling center (0), employed in a hospital/medical center (0), still seeking employment (0), other employment position (0), total from the above (master's) (14).

Doctoral Degree Graduates: Of those who graduated in the academic year 2006–2007, the following categories and numbers represent the postgraduate activities and employment of doctoral degree graduates: Enrolled in a psychology doctoral program (n/a), enrolled in a postdoctoral residency/fellowship (9), employed in independent practice (0), employed in an academic position at a university (0), employed in an academic position at a 2-year/4-year college (0), employed in other positions at a higher education institution (1), employed in a professional position in a school system (0), employed in business or industry (0), employed in government agency (0), employed in a community mental health/counseling center (12), employed in a hospital/medical center (4), still seeking employment (0), other employment position (1), total from the above (doctoral) (27).

Additional Information:

Orientation, Objectives, and Emphasis of Department: Doctoral training at Loma Linda University takes place within the context of a holistic approach to human health and welfare. The university motto to make man whole takes in every aspect of being human—the physical, psychological, spiritual, and social. Building on a university tradition of health sciences research, training, and service, the doctoral programs in the department offer a combination of traditional and innovative training opportunities. The PhD in clinical psychology follows the traditional scientist–practitioner model and emphasizes research and clinical training. The PsyD is oriented toward clinical practice with emphasis on the understanding and application of the principles and research of psychological science. The PsyD/PhD dual degree program offers an innovative combination of education in psychology and the health sciences to train practitioners who are highly qualified in the application of psychology to health promotion, preventive medicine, and health care as well as clinical practice and research. The PhD in experimental psychology is designed to train a small number of individuals for careers in research and academia. Students in the experimental PhD program work closely with a research mentor; a current list of faculty and their research interests may be obtained from the department.

Special Facilities or Resources: As a health sciences university, Loma Linda provides an ideal environment with resources for research and clinical training in such areas as health psychology/behavioral medicine and the delivery of health services. LLU Medical Center has nearly 900 beds, is staffed by more than 5,000 people, and is the "flagship" of a system including hundreds of health care institutions around the world. In addition, a number of institutions in the area, such as the LLU Behavioral Medicine Center, Jerry L. Pettis VA Hospital, Patton State Hospital, and the San Bernardino County Mental Health Department represent numerous opportunities for research and clinical training in psychology. In the area of teaching and research the department has a consortial agreement with the department of psychology at California State University, San Bernardino. By this agreement, students at a postmaster's level have TA opportunities to get experience teaching undergraduate courses. At the same time, a select group of graduate faculty members at CSUSB have appointments at LLU significantly enhancing advanced seminar offerings and opportunities for research training in a number of areas, strengthening and complementing those available at LLU.

Information for Students With Physical Disabilities: See the following Web site for more information: http://www.llu.edu/graduate school/psychology.

Application Information:
Send to Minerva Sitompul, Director Enrollment Management Loma Linda University School of Science and Technology 11226 Campus Street (Nelson House), Loma Linda, CA 92350. Application available online. URL of online application: http://www.llu.edu/apply. Students are admitted in the Fall, application deadline December 31. Applicants to our dual-degree program, PsyD/PhD, must apply to our School of Public Health concurrently with their application to our PsyD program in the Department of Psychology. *Fee:* $60. Waivers must be approved by the Department of Psychology. It is necessary to have information about your GPA and GRE scores to make an adequate decision on fee waiver requests.

Mount St. Mary's College

Graduate Program in Counseling Psychology
Mount St. Mary's College
10 Chester Place
Los Angeles, CA 90007-2598
Telephone: (213) 477-2654
Fax: (213) 477-2659
E-mail: *cmabry@msmc.la.edu*
Web: *http://www.msmc.la.edu*

Department Information:
Graduate Director: Dr. Corinne Hay Mabry. Number of faculty: total—full-time 4, part-time 5; women—full-time 3, part-time 4; minority—part-time 1; women minority—part-time 1.

Programs and Degrees Offered:
Listed in the following order: Program area, degree type (T if terminal Master's), number awarded 7/06–6/07. Counseling Psychology MA/MS (Master of Arts/Science) (T) 18.

Student Applications/Admissions:

Student Applications

Counseling Psychology MA/MS (Master of Arts/Science)—Applications 2007–2008, 20. Total applicants accepted 2007–2008, 13. Number full-time enrolled (new admits only) 2007–2008, 13. Total enrolled 2007–2008 full-time, 44. Openings 2008–2009, 20. The median number of years required for completion of a degree in 2006–2007 were 3. The number of students enrolled full- and part-time who were dismissed or voluntarily withdrew from this program area in 2007–2008 were 2.

Admissions Requirements:

Scores: Entries appear in this order: required test or GPA, minimum score (if required), median score of students entering in 2007–2008. Master's Programs: GRE-V no minimum stated; GRE-Q no minimum stated; overall undergraduate GPA 3.00; Masters GRE-Analytical no minimum stated.

Other Criteria: (importance of criteria rated low, medium, or high): GRE/MAT scores—high, research experience—medium, work experience—medium, extracurricular activity—medium, clinically related public service—medium, GPA—high, letters of recommendation—high, interview—high, statement of goals and objectives—high. For additional information on admission requirements, go to http://www.msmc.la.edu.

Student Characteristics: The following represents characteristics of students in 2007–2008 in all graduate psychology programs in the department: Female—full-time 40, part-time 0; Male—full-time 4, part-time 0; African American/Black—full-time 10, part-time 0; Hispanic/Latino(a)—full-time 17, part-time 0; Asian/Pacific Islander—full-time 2, part-time 0; Caucasian/White—full-time 15, part-time 0; Unknown ethnicity—full-time 0, part-time 0.

Financial Information/Assistance:

Tuition for Full-Time Study: *Master's:* State residents: $708 per credit hour; . Tuition is subject to change. See the following Web site for updates and changes in tuition costs: http://www.msmc.la.edu.

Financial Assistance:

First-Year Students: No information provided.
Advanced Students: No information provided.
Additional Information: No information provided.

Internships/Practica: Field Experiences in Counseling Practicum relates counseling principles to a variety of clinical settings. Assessment, differential diagnosis, and short-term and long-term interventions are emphasized. For each course 120 hours of field work are required, and 90 of those hours must be face-to-face with clients. Fieldwork must take place in a site approved by the instructor and department.

Housing and Day Care: No on-campus housing is available. No on-campus day care facilities are available.

Employment of Department Graduates:

Master's Degree Graduates: Of those who graduated in the academic year 2006–2007, the following categories and numbers represent the postgraduate activities and employment of master's degree graduates: Enrolled in a postdoctoral residency/fellowship (n/a), employed in independent practice (n/a), total from the above (master's) (0).

Doctoral Degree Graduates: Of those who graduated in the academic year 2006–2007, the following categories and numbers represent the postgraduate activities and employment of doctoral degree graduates: Enrolled in a psychology doctoral program (n/a), total from the above (doctoral) (0).

Additional Information:

Orientation, Objectives, and Emphasis of Department: Mount St. Mary's College offers a Master of Science in counseling psychology, with a specialization in Marriage and Family Therapy (MFT). The student-centered faculty emphasize leadership, service, and training geared toward preparing students for later professional practice.

Special Facilities or Resources: The Doheny campus, where psychology graduate students study, was originally an estate of private Victorian homes. To meet the growing needs of Doheny students, the new Sister Magdalen Coughlin Learning Complex, which houses a library, Cultural Fluency Center, Academic Building, and Learning Resource Center, was built. Doheny affords easy access to neighboring University of Southern California and downtown Los Angeles, while housing classrooms and offices in a secure, park-like setting.

Information for Students With Physical Disabilities: See the following Web site for more information: http://www.msmc.la.edu.

Application Information:
Send to The Graduate Division, Mount St. Mary's College, 10 Chester Place, Los Angeles, California 90007-2598. Application available on-line. URL of online application: http://www.msmc.la.edu/pages/140.asp. Students are admitted in the Fall, application deadline July 15; Spring, application deadline November 15; Summer, application deadline April 15; Programs have rolling admissions. *Fee:* $50.

Pacific Graduate School of Psychology

Clinical Psychology Program
935 East Meadow Drive
Palo Alto, CA 94303
Telephone: (650) 843-3419 & (800) 818-6136
Fax: (650) 493-6147
E-mail: *dsims@pgsp.edu*
Web: *http://www.pgsp.edu*

Department Information:
1975. Director of Admissions: Dacien Sims. Number of faculty: total—full-time 9, part-time 3; women—full-time 7, part-time 2; total—minority—full-time 2; women minority—full-time 1.

Programs and Degrees Offered:
Listed in the following order: Program area, degree type (T if terminal Master's), number awarded 7/06–6/07. Clinical Psychology PhD (Doctor of Philosophy) 35, Psychology and Law Other 2, MBA/PhD Other 0, PsyD (Doctor of Psychology) 0, Distance Learning Master's Program MA/MS (Master of Arts/Science) (T) 6.

APA Accreditation: Clinical PhD (Doctor of Philosophy). Clinical PsyD (Doctor of Psychology).

Student Applications/Admissions:
Student Applications
Clinical Psychology PhD (Doctor of Philosophy)—Applications 2007–2008, 135. Total applicants accepted 2007–2008, 120. Number full-time enrolled (new admits only) 2007–2008, 68. Openings 2008–2009, 65. The median number of years required for completion of a degree in 2006–2007 were 6. The number of students enrolled full- and part-time who were dismissed or voluntarily withdrew from this program area in 2007–2008 were 4. *Psychology and Law Other*—Applications 2007–2008, 8. Total applicants accepted 2007–2008, 6. Number full-time enrolled (new admits only) 2007–2008, 2. Openings 2008–2009, 5. The median number of years required for completion of a degree in 2006–2007 were 7. The number of students enrolled full- and part-time who were dismissed or voluntarily withdrew from this program area in 2007–2008 were 0. *MBA/PhD Other*—Applications 2007–2008, 2. Total applicants accepted 2007–2008, 1. Number full-time enrolled (new admits only) 2007–2008, 0. Total enrolled 2007–2008 full-time, 3. Openings 2008–2009, 5. The median number of years required for completion of a degree in 2006–2007 were 6. The number of students enrolled full- and part-time who were dismissed or voluntarily withdrew from this program area in 2007–2008 were 0. *PsyD (Doctor of Psychology)*—Applications 2007–2008, 90. Total applicants accepted 2007–2008, 45. Number full-time enrolled (new admits only) 2007–2008, 22. Openings 2008–2009, 30. The number of students enrolled full- and part-time who were dismissed or voluntarily withdrew from this program area in 2007–2008 were 1. *Distance Learning Master's Program MA/MS (Master of Arts/Science)*—Applications 2007–2008, 19. Total applicants accepted 2007–2008, 19. Number part-time enrolled (new admits only) 2007–2008, 13. Total enrolled 2007–2008 part-time, 20. Openings 2008–2009, 30. The median number of years required for completion of a degree in 2006–2007 were 2. The number of students enrolled full- and part-time who were dismissed or voluntarily withdrew from this program area in 2007–2008 were 2.

Admissions Requirements:
Scores: Entries appear in this order: required test or GPA, minimum score (if required), median score of students entering in 2007–2008. Doctoral Programs: GRE-V no minimum stated; GRE-Q no minimum stated; Doctoral program GRE-Analytic no minimum stated.
Other Criteria: (importance of criteria rated low, medium, or high): GRE/MAT scores—high, research experience—medium, work experience—medium, extracurricular activity—medium, clinically related public service—medium, GPA—high, letters of recommendation—high, interview—medium, statement of goals and objectives—medium. Interview required for the following programs: PGSP-Stanford PsyD Consortium, JD/PhD Program, and MBA/PhD Programs. For additional information on admission requirements, go to http://www.pgsp.edu.

Student Characteristics: The following represents characteristics of students in 2007–2008 in all graduate psychology programs in the department: Female—full-time 249, part-time 19; Male—full-time 75, part-time 3; African American/Black—full-time 15, part-time 3; Hispanic/Latino(a)—full-time 25, part-time 4; Asian/Pacific Islander—full-time 41, part-time 4; American Indian/Alaska Native—full-time 2, part-time 0; Caucasian/White—full-time 198, part-time 11; Multi-ethnic—full-time 43, part-time 0; students subject to the Americans With Disabilities Act—full-time 0, part-time 0; Unknown ethnicity—full-time 0, part-time 0.

Financial Information/Assistance:
Tuition for Full-Time Study: *Master's:* State residents: per academic year $18,420; Nonstate residents: per academic year $18,420. *Doctoral:* State residents: per academic year $35,154; Nonstate residents: per academic year $35,154. Tuition is subject to change. Tuition costs vary by program. See the following Web site for updates and changes in tuition costs: http://www.pgsp.edu. Higher tuition cost for this program: PGSP-Stanford PsyD Consortium.

Financial Assistance:
First-Year Students: Fellowships and scholarships available for first year. Average amount paid per academic year: $5,000.

Average number of hours worked per week: 0. Apply by January 15.

Advanced Students: Teaching assistantships available for advanced students. Average amount paid per academic year: $3,000. Average number of hours worked per week: 25. Apply by N/A. Research assistantships available for advanced students. Average amount paid per academic year: $4,000. Average number of hours worked per week: 30. Apply by N/A.

Additional Information: Of all students currently enrolled full time, 25% benefited from one or more of the listed financial assistance programs. Application and information available online at http://www.pgsp.edu.

Internships/Practica: Doctoral Degree (PhD Clinical Psychology): For those doctoral students for whom a professional internship was required in this program prior to graduation, (29) students applied for an internship in 2006–2007, with (26) students obtaining an internship. Of those students who obtained an internship, (16) were paid internships. Of those students who obtained an internship, (21) students placed in APA/CPA-accredited internships, (0) students placed in internships not APA/CPA accredited, but listed with the Association of Psychology Postdoctoral and Internship Centers (APPIC), (0) students placed in internships conforming to guidelines of the Council of Directors of School Psychology Programs (CDSPP), (5) students placed in internships that were not APA/CPA-accredited, APPIC or CDSPP listed. All students take their 2nd year of practicum in our Kurt and Barbara Gronowski Clinic and the 3rd and 4th years in local agencies. All students are expected to complete an APA-accredited, APPIC or CAPIC-approved internship.

Housing and Day Care: No on-campus housing is available. No on-campus day care facilities are available.

Employment of Department Graduates:

Master's Degree Graduates: Of those who graduated in the academic year 2006–2007, the following categories and numbers represent the postgraduate activities and employment of master's degree graduates: Enrolled in a postdoctoral residency/fellowship (n/a), employed in independent practice (n/a), total from the above (master's) (0).

Doctoral Degree Graduates: Of those who graduated in the academic year 2006–2007, the following categories and numbers represent the postgraduate activities and employment of doctoral degree graduates: Enrolled in a psychology doctoral program (n/a), enrolled in a postdoctoral residency/fellowship (21), employed in a community mental health/counseling center (1), employed in a hospital/medical center (1), other employment position (2), do not know (4), total from the above (doctoral) (29).

Additional Information:

Orientation, Objectives, and Emphasis of Department: Pacific Graduate School of Psychology is a freestanding graduate school offering doctoral degrees in clinical psychology to students from diverse backgrounds. The program is designed to integrate academic work, research, and clinical experiences at every level of the student's training. All students must develop a thorough understanding of a systematic body of knowledge that comprises the current field of psychology. They are expected to carry out an independent investigation that makes an original contribution to scientific knowledge in psychology and to demonstrate excellence in the application of specific clinical skills. PGSP considers this integration of scholarship, research, and practical experience the best training model for preparing psychologists to meet the highest standards of scholarly research and community service. Graduates are expected to enter the community at large prepared to do research, practice, and teach in culturally and professionally diverse settings.

Special Facilities or Resources: PGSP's setting as a free-standing graduate school of psychology is much enhanced by our San Francisco Bay Area location. We provide students with access to local university libraries (e.g., Stanford, UC Berkeley). The range of clinical experience available to students is inexhaustible. All faculty have active research programs in which students participate. Furthermore, PGSP has a close relationship with local Veteran Administration medical centers.

Information for Students With Physical Disabilities: See the following Web site for more information: http://www.pgsp.edu.

Application Information:

Send to Office of Admissions, Pacific Graduate School of Psychology, 935 East Meadow Drive, Palo Alto, CA 94303. Application available online. URL of online application: http://www.pgsp.edu. Students are admitted in the Fall; programs have rolling admissions, however application is due January 15 for those who want to be considered for a PGSP fellowship. *Fee:* $50.

Pacific Graduate School of Psychology and Stanford University School of Medicine, Department of Psychiatry and Behavioral Sciences

PGSP-Stanford PsyD Consortium
405 Broadway Street
Redwood City, CA 94063
Telephone: (650) 421-4836
Fax: (650) 421-4890
E-mail: *acastrillo@pgsp.edu*
Web: *http://www.pgsp.edu/program_stanford_psyd_home.php*

Department Information:

2002. Directors of Clinical Training: James N. Breckenridge, PhD and Bruce Arnow, PhD. Number of faculty: total—full-time 9, part-time 19; women—full-time 4, part-time 12; total—minority—full-time 2, part-time 3; women minority—full-time 1, part-time 3.

Programs and Degrees Offered:

Listed in the following order: Program area, degree type (T if terminal Master's), number awarded 7/06–6/07. PGSP–Stanford PsyD Consortium PsyD (Doctor of Psychology) 0.

APA Accreditation: Clinical PsyD (Doctor of Psychology).

Student Applications/Admissions:

Student Applications

PGSP–Stanford PsyD Consortium PsyD (Doctor of Psychology)—Applications 2007–2008, 185. Total applicants accepted 2007–2008, 31. Number full-time enrolled (new admits only)

2007–2008, 30. Number part-time enrolled (new admits only) 2007–2008, 0. Openings 2008–2009, 30. The median number of years required for completion of a degree in 2006–2007 were 5. The number of students enrolled full- and part-time who were dismissed or voluntarily withdrew from this program area in 2007–2008 were 1.

Admissions Requirements:

Scores: Entries appear in this order: required test or GPA, minimum score (if required), median score of students entering in 2007–2008. Doctoral Programs: GRE-V 550; GRE-Q 550; GRE-Subject (Psychology) 600; overall undergraduate GPA 3.3; last 2 years GPA 3.4; psychology GPA 3.4; Doctoral program GRE-Analytic 5.0. The PGSP institutional code for receipt of GRE scores is 4638.

Other Criteria: (importance of criteria rated low, medium, or high): GRE/MAT scores—medium, research experience—low, work experience—high, extracurricular activity—medium, clinically related public service—high, GPA—high, letters of recommendation—high, interview—high, statement of goals and objectives—high, undergraduate major in psychology—medium, specific undergraduate psychology courses taken—medium. For additional information on admission requirements, go to http://www.pgsp.edu/program_stanford_psyd_home.php.

Student Characteristics: The following represents characteristics of students in 2007–2008 in all graduate psychology programs in the department: Female—full-time 98, part-time 0; Male—full-time 24, part-time 0; African American/Black—full-time 3, part-time 0; Hispanic/Latino(a)—full-time 5, part-time 0; Asian/Pacific Islander—full-time 12, part-time 0; American Indian/Alaska Native—full-time 1, part-time 0; Caucasian/White—full-time 83, part-time 0; Multi-ethnic—full-time 0, part-time 0; students subject to the Americans With Disabilities Act—full-time 0, part-time 0; Unknown ethnicity—full-time 18, part-time 0; International students who hold an F-1 or J-1 Visa—full-time 5, part-time 0.

Financial Information/Assistance:

Tuition for Full-Time Study: *Doctoral:* State residents: per academic year $32,000; Nonstate residents: per academic year $32,000. Tuition is subject to change. See the following Web site for updates and changes in tuition costs: http://www.pgsp.edu/program_stanford_psyd_home.php.

Financial Assistance:

First-Year Students: Research assistantships available for first year. Average amount paid per academic year: $1,000. Average number of hours worked per week: 5. Apply by rolling. Fellowships and scholarships available for first year. Average amount paid per academic year: $3,000. Average number of hours worked per week: 8. Apply by April 1. Tuition remission given: partial.

Advanced Students: Teaching assistantships available for advanced students. Average amount paid per academic year: $750. Average number of hours worked per week: 6. Apply by rolling. Research assistantships available for advanced students. Average amount paid per academic year: $1,000. Average number of hours worked per week: 5. Apply by rolling. Fellowships and scholarships available for advanced students. Average amount paid per academic year: $3,000. Average number of hours worked per week: 8. Apply by March 31. Tuition remission given: partial.

Additional Information: Of all students currently enrolled full time, 20% benefited from one or more of the listed financial assistance programs.

Internships/Practica: Doctoral Degree (PGSP–Stanford PsyD Consortium): For those doctoral students for whom a professional internship was required in this program prior to graduation, (25) students applied for an internship in 2006–2007, with (18) students obtaining an internship. Of those students who obtained an internship, (18) were paid internships. Of those students who obtained an internship, (15) students placed in APA/CPA accredited internships, (3) students placed in internships not APA/CPA-accredited, but listed with the Association of Psychology Postdoctoral and Internship Centers (APPIC), (0) students placed in internships conforming to guidelines of the Council of Directors of School Psychology Programs (CDSPP), (0) students placed in internships that were not APA/CPA-accredited, APPIC or CDSPP listed. The PGSP-Stanford Consortium training program provides students with experiences that are sequenced with increasing amounts of time spent in clinical work during each year of graduate training, with a total of approximately 2,000 clinical hours obtained prior to internship. Graduate students begin working in clinical settings as a volunteer during their 1st year; during their 2nd and 3rd years, students enroll in field practica that may take place in a variety of settings, such as Stanford and UCSF medical school hospitals and programs, community mental health centers, the Palo Alto VA Health Care System medical centers, county mental health systems, AIDS prevention project, and child/family psychiatric clinics. In the 4th year students will work on a clinical dissertation, and a 4th year practicum is optionl but highly recommended. In the 5th year, following advancement to the candidacy for the Doctor of Psychology (PsyD) degree, the student is required to complete a 2,000-hour external predoctoral internship that provides high-quality professional supervision and experience.

Housing and Day Care: No on-campus housing is available. No on-campus day care facilities are available.

Employment of Department Graduates:

Master's Degree Graduates: Of those who graduated in the academic year 2006–2007, the following categories and numbers represent the postgraduate activities and employment of master's degree graduates: Enrolled in a postdoctoral residency/fellowship (n/a), employed in independent practice (n/a), total from the above (master's) (0).

Doctoral Degree Graduates: Of those who graduated in the academic year 2006–2007, the following categories and numbers represent the postgraduate activities and employment of doctoral degree graduates: Enrolled in a psychology doctoral program (n/a), total from the above (doctoral) (0).

Additional Information:

Orientation, Objectives, and Emphasis of Department: This training program emphasizes a biopsychosocial understanding of psychological disorders (i.e., a model that conceptualizes psychological disorders and problems as having biological, psychological, and social components). In addition, the program provides "cutting edge" training for student psychologist–practitioners in the use of empirically supported treatments for a wide variety of psychiatric illnesses and behavioral disorders. There are four primary training goals for the PGSP–Stanford Consortium: (a) to develop psychologists who can effectively evaluate sophisticated social research and apply empirically supported psychological intervention in their practice of psychology; (b) to educate highly trained psychologists who can contribute to the advancement of clinical psychology; (c) to produce clinical psychologists who are competent in psychological assessment, consultation, and supervision; and (d) to provide theory, skills, and supervision necessary to enable students to confidentially and effectively engage in treatment interventions in response to our societal needs.

Special Facilities or Resources: The PGSP–Stanford Doctor of Psychology program draws upon nationally renowned faculty and resources from the Pacific Graduate School and the Stanford University School of Medicine's Department of Psychiatry and Behavioral Sciences. The 5-year Doctor of Psychology degree program consists of 3 years of graduate coursework, a year spent working on a clinical dissertation, followed by a year-long internship in clinical psychology. As a practitioner-oriented graduate program, the focus is on intensive clinical training and will utilize the rich resources of the San Francisco Bay area mental health community for pre-internship basic and advanced supervised clinical experiences. The program strives for the earliest possible full recognition of the first-year class (entering in 2002–2003) for licensure in all 50 states, as well as interstate mobility through the "Certificate of Professional Qualification in Psychology" from the Association of State and Provincial Psychology Boards.

Application Information:

Send to Office of Admissions, PGSP–Stanford PsyD Consortium, 405 Broadway Street, Redwood City, CA 94063 Application information available online: http://www.pgsp.edu/consortium/conapply.htm. Application available online. URL of online application: http://www.pgsp.edu/pdf_docs/form_pgsp_psyd_application_for_admission.pdf. Students are admitted in the Fall, application deadline January 2. *Fee:* $50.

Pacific, University of the

Department of Psychology
3601 Pacific Avenue
Stockton, CA 95211
Telephone: (209) 946-2133
Fax: (209) 946-2454
E-mail: *ckohn@pacific.edu*
Web: *http://www.pacific.edu/college/psychology http://www.theskinnerbox.com/Pacific/*

Department Information:

1960. Chairperson: Roseann Hannon, PhD. Number of faculty: total—full-time 7; women—full-time 4.

Programs and Degrees Offered:

Listed in the following order: Program area, degree type (T if terminal Master's), number awarded 7/06–6/07. Applied Behavior Analysis MA/MS (Master of Arts/Science) 4, Doctoral Preparation MA/MS (Master of Arts/Science).

Student Applications/Admissions:

Student Applications

Applied Behavior Analysis MA/MS (Master of Arts/Science)—Number full-time enrolled (new admits only) 2007–2008, 4. Number part-time enrolled (new admits only) 2007–2008, 0. Openings 2008–2009, 4. The median number of years required for completion of a degree in 2006–2007 were 3. The number of students enrolled full- and part-time who were dismissed or voluntarily withdrew from this program area in 2007–2008 were 1. *Doctoral Preparation MA/MS (Master of Arts/Science)*—Number full-time enrolled (new admits only) 2007–2008, 2. Number part-time enrolled (new admits only) 2007–2008, 0. Openings 2008–2009, 4. The median number of years required for completion of a degree in 2006–2007 were 2. The number of students enrolled full- and part-time who were dismissed or voluntarily withdrew from this program area in 2007–2008 were 0.

Admissions Requirements:

Scores: Entries appear in this order: required test or GPA, minimum score (if required), median score of students entering in 2007–2008. Master's Programs: GRE-V no minimum stated, 490; GRE-Q no minimum stated, 550; overall undergraduate GPA 3.0, 3.60; last 2 years GPA 3.0, 3.70; psychology GPA 3.0, 3.75.

Other Criteria: (importance of criteria rated low, medium, or high): GRE/MAT scores—low, research experience—high, work experience—medium, clinically related public service—low, GPA—high, letters of recommendation—high, statement of goals and objectives—high, applied experience—high, undergraduate major in psychology—medium, specific undergraduate psychology courses taken—medium. Those applying to the Behavior Analysis track should have some relevant course work and applied experiences in this area. For additional information on admission requirements, go to http://www.theskinnerbox.com/Pacific/ or http://www.pacific.edu/college/psychology.

Student Characteristics: The following represents characteristics of students in 2007–2008 in all graduate psychology programs in the department: Female—full-time 9, part-time 0; Male—full-time 2, part-time 0; African American/Black—full-time 0, part-time 0; Hispanic/Latino(a)—full-time 2, part-time 0; Asian/Pacific Islander—full-time 3, part-time 0; American Indian/Alaska Native—full-time 0, part-time 0; Caucasian/White—full-time 6, part-time 0; Multi-ethnic—full-time 0, part-time 0; students subject to the Americans With Disabilities Act—full-time 0, part-time 0; Unknown ethnicity—full-time 0, part-time 0; International students who hold an F-1 or J-1 Visa—full-time 1, part-time 0.

Financial Information/Assistance:

Tuition for Full-Time Study: *Master's:* State residents: per academic year $13,840, $890 per credit hour; Nonstate residents: per academic year $13,840, $890 per credit hour. See the following Web site for updates and changes in tuition costs: http://www.web.pacific.edu/x18683.xml.

Financial Assistance:

First-Year Students: Teaching assistantships available for first year. Average amount paid per academic year: $9,474. Average number of hours worked per week: 20. Apply by February 15. Tuition remission given: partial. Traineeships available for first year. Average amount paid per academic year: $12,400. Average number of hours worked per week: 20. Apply by February 15. Tuition remission given: partial.

Advanced Students: Teaching assistantships available for advanced students. Average amount paid per academic year: $9,474. Average number of hours worked per week: 20. Apply by February 15. Tuition remission given: partial. Traineeships available for advanced students. Average amount paid per academic year: $12,400. Average number of hours worked per week: 20. Apply by February 15. Tuition remission given: partial.

Additional Information: Of all students currently enrolled full time, 100% benefited from one or more of the listed financial assistance programs. Application and information available online at http://www.pacific.edu/homepage/graduate/funding.asp.

Internships/Practica: Contained directly within the department is the Psychology Clinic, which provides services for families and children (e.g., behavioral interventions; evaluations for child custody, attention deficit disorder, etc.; parent training). All students are required to complete 2 years of experience working in the Clinic during their MA studies, or else to complete an appropriate alternative applied experience (e.g., business settings, educational settings). The department also directs the Community Re-entry Program (contracted directly with the local county), which provides a wide range of behaviorally based programs to assist the mentally disabled/ill in becoming independent. This program provides half-time employment for eight graduate students per year. Students interested in developmental disabilities can work with the Behavioral Instructional Service (in cooperation with Valley Mountain Regional Center, which serves these clients), and part-time employment is available with this program. We also have contracts with several outside agencies at which students can obtain practica experience, including the Stockton Unified School District (ABA assessment and interventions for school problem behaviors) and BEST (early ABA interventions with children diagnosed with autism).

Housing and Day Care: On-campus housing is available. See the following Web site for more information: http://www.web.pacific.edu/x3887.xml. No on-campus day care facilities are available.

Employment of Department Graduates:

Master's Degree Graduates: Of those who graduated in the academic year 2006–2007, the following categories and numbers represent the postgraduate activities and employment of master's degree graduates: Enrolled in a psychology doctoral program (2), enrolled in another graduate/professional program (1), enrolled in a postdoctoral residency/fellowship (n/a), employed in independent practice (n/a), employed in a professional position in a school system (2), employed in business or industry (3), employed in a community mental health/counseling center (1), other employment position (2), total from the above (master's) (11).

Doctoral Degree Graduates: Of those who graduated in the academic year 2006–2007, the following categories and numbers represent the postgraduate activities and employment of doctoral degree graduates: Enrolled in a psychology doctoral program (n/a), total from the above (doctoral) (0).

Additional Information:

Orientation, Objectives, and Emphasis of Department: The Psychology Department offers a program of graduate study leading to the MA degree in Psychology. We offer two tracks: (a) Applied Behavior Analysis track (MA or doctoral preparation) or (b) Clinical/Counseling Doctoral Preparation track. Students wishing to pursue a doctorate in applied behavior analysis should apply under the applied behavior analysis track, but indicate in a cover letter that they ultimately wish to apply to a doctorate program in ABA. We do not offer an MFT or a Counseling MA. Overall program focus for both tracks note that coursework involvement overlaps substantially for both tracks, while specific types of research and applied experiences differ. Wide variety of applied experience in a number of different settings. Intensive involvement in designing, conducting, and evaluating research. Coursework in theoretical and research foundations of applied behavior analysis and cognitive behavior theory. Commitment to the development of student potential by active, supportive, involved faculty.

Special Facilities or Resources: The department provides office space for faculty and graduate students, computing equipment, and video equipment for research projects. Applied research projects are also conducted in community settings (e.g., schools, medical settings). The Community Re-entry Program and Valley Mountain Regional Center (described above) also provide rich opportunities for research in community settings.

Information for Students With Physical Disabilities: See the following Web site for more information: http://www.web.pacific.edu/x10591.xml.

Application Information:

Send to Dean of the Graduate School, University of the Pacific, 3601 Pacific Avenue, Stockton, CA 95211. Application available online. URL of online application: https://www.applyweb.com/apply/uopg/menu.html. Students are admitted in the Fall, application deadline February 15. Although the deadline for applications is February 15, on occasion we accept late applications. However, applying after the deadline decreases an applicant's chances to receive funding. *Fee:* $75.

Pacifica Graduate Institute

PhD in Clinical Psychology with emphasis in Depth Psychology
Department of Psychology
249 Lambert Road
Carpinteria, CA 93013
Telephone: (805) 969-3626 ext. 305
Fax: (805) 879-7391
E-mail: *admissions@pacifica.edu*
Web: *http://www.pacifica.edu*

Department Information:

1989. Chairperson: James L. Broderick, PhD. women—full-time 2, part-time 21; ; women minority—part-time 2.

Programs and Degrees Offered:

Listed in the following order: Program area, degree type (T if terminal Master's), number awarded 7/06–6/07. PhD in Clinical Psychology PhD (Doctor of Philosophy).

Student Applications/Admissions:

Student Applications

Clinical Psychology PhD (Doctor of Philosophy).

Admissions Requirements:

Scores: Entries appear in this order: required test or GPA, minimum score (if required), median score of students entering in 2007–2008. Master's Programs: overall undergraduate GPA no minimum stated; last 2 years GPA no minimum stated. Doctoral Programs: overall undergraduate GPA no minimum stated; last 2 years GPA no minimum stated.

Other Criteria: (importance of criteria rated low, medium, or high): GRE/MAT scores—low, research experience—medium, work experience—medium, extracurricular activity—medium, clinically related public service—medium, GPA—medium, letters of recommendation—high, interview—high, statement of goals and objectives—medium, undergraduate major in psychology—low, specific undergraduate psychology courses taken—low. For additional information on admission requirements, go to http://www.pacifica.edu/admissions.html.

Student Characteristics: The following represents characteristics of students in 2007–2008 in all graduate psychology programs in the department: Caucasian/White—full-time 0, part-time 0; Unknown ethnicity—full-time 0, part-time 0.

Financial Information/Assistance:

Tuition for Full-Time Study: *Doctoral:* State residents: per academic year $23,400. Tuition is subject to change. Tuition costs vary by program. See the following Web site for updates and changes in tuition costs: http://www.pacifica.edu/admissions_fee_schedule.html.

Financial Assistance:

First-Year Students: No information provided.

Advanced Students: No information provided.

Additional Information: Application and information available online at http://www.pacifica.edu/admissions_financial.html.

Internships/Practica: The practicum sites are to serve as laboratory settings that allow students the opportunity for mastering the fundamental skills and knowledge being taught in the introductory courses in psychopathology, assessment, and intervention. The internship experience follows from both this practicum experience and the successful completion of three core practicum courses. Internship training requires more responsibility on the part of the students, with interns viewed as junior colleagues who perform, under supervision, all the duties of staff psychologists. The internship years are designed to prepare the students for the assumption of an autonomous professional role by allowing for the participation in the full repertoire of activities in which psychologists engage. Interns are expected to refine and to coordinate the skills acquired in the first three years of practica training, as well as to acquire new skills that are specifically related to supervision, care management, decision making, and treatment team leadership. For additional information on education and training outcomes for our programs, see the following Web site: http://www.online.pacifica.edu/phdintern/.

Housing and Day Care: On-campus housing is available. See the following Web site for more information: http://www.pacifica.edu/housing.html. No on-campus day care facilities are available.

Employment of Department Graduates:

Master's Degree Graduates: Of those who graduated in the academic year 2006–2007, the following categories and numbers represent the postgraduate activities and employment of master's degree graduates: Enrolled in a postdoctoral residency/fellowship (n/a), employed in independent practice (n/a), total from the above (master's) (0).

Doctoral Degree Graduates: Of those who graduated in the academic year 2006–2007, the following categories and numbers represent the postgraduate activities and employment of doctoral degree graduates: Enrolled in a psychology doctoral program (n/a), total from the above (doctoral) (0).

Additional Information:

Orientation, Objectives, and Emphasis of Department: Pacifica Graduate Institute's doctoral program in Clinical Psychology offers a course of study situated within the depth psychological traditions.

Application Information:

Send to Department of Admissions Wendy Overend, Director; e-mail admissions@pacifica.edu; call (805) 969-3626 ext. 305. Students are admitted in the Fall, application deadline availability. *Fee:* $60.

Pepperdine University

Division of Psychology
Graduate School of Education and Psychology
6100 Center Drive, 5th Floor
Los Angeles, CA 90045
Telephone: (800) 888-4849
Fax: (310) 568-5609
E-mail: *psyd@pepperdine.edu*
Web: *http://www.gsep.pepperdine.edu*

Department Information:

1951. Associate Dean: Robert A. deMayo. Number of faculty: total—full-time 27, part-time 60; women—full-time 13, part-time 40; total—minority—full-time 7, part-time 12; women minority—full-time 4, part-time 10; faculty subject to the Americans With Disabilities Act 1.

Programs and Degrees Offered:

Listed in the following order: Program area, degree type (T if terminal Master's), number awarded 7/06–6/07. Clinical MA/MS (Master of Arts/Science) (T) 122, Clinical (Malibu Campus) MA/MS (Master of Arts/Science) (T) 39, General MA/MS (Master of Arts/Science) (T) 92, Clinical PsyD (Doctor of Psychology) 25.

APA Accreditation: Clinical PsyD (Doctor of Psychology).

Student Applications/Admissions:

Student Applications

Clinical MA/MS (Master of Arts/Science)—Applications 2007–2008, 211. Total applicants accepted 2007–2008, 182. Number full-time enrolled (new admits only) 2007–2008, 100. Number part-time enrolled (new admits only) 2007–2008, 8. Total enrolled 2007–2008 full-time, 364, part-time, 110. Openings 2008–2009, 135. The median number of years required for completion of a degree in 2006–2007 were 3. The number of students enrolled full- and part-time who were dismissed or voluntarily withdrew from this program area in 2007–2008 were 28. *Clinical (Malibu Campus) MA/MS (Master of Arts/ Science)*—Applications 2007–2008, 178. Total applicants accepted 2007–2008, 130. Number full-time enrolled (new admits only) 2007–2008, 49. Number part-time enrolled (new admits only) 2007–2008, 0. Openings 2008–2009, 44. The median number of years required for completion of a degree in 2006–2007 were 2. The number of students enrolled full- and part-time who were dismissed or voluntarily withdrew from this program area in 2007–2008 were 2. *General MA/MS (Master of Arts/Science)*—Applications 2007–2008, 87. Total applicants accepted 2007–2008, 81. Number full-time enrolled (new admits only) 2007–2008, 47. Number part-time enrolled (new admits only) 2007–2008, 1. Total enrolled 2007–2008 full-time, 172, part-time, 29. Openings 2008–2009, 60. The median number of years required for completion of a degree in 2006–2007 were 2. The number of students enrolled full- and part-time who were dismissed or voluntarily withdrew from this program area in 2007–2008 were 7. *Clinical PsyD (Doctor of Psychology)*—Applications 2007–2008, 151. Total applicants accepted 2007–2008, 44. Number full-time enrolled (new admits only) 2007–2008, 26. Number part-time enrolled (new admits only) 2007–2008, 0. Openings 2008–2009, 26. The median number of years required for completion of a degree in 2006–2007 were 5. The number of students enrolled full- and part-time who were dismissed or voluntarily withdrew from this program area in 2007–2008 were 1.

Admissions Requirements:

Scores: Entries appear in this order: required test or GPA, minimum score (if required), median score of students entering in 2007–2008. Master's Programs: GRE-V no minimum stated, 474; GRE-Q no minimum stated, 510; MAT no minimum stated, 40; overall undergraduate GPA no minimum stated, 3.32. For the Evening Format MA programs, the GRE or MAT may be waived for applicants with seven or more years of qualified full-time work experience or a cumulative undergraduate GPA of 3.7 or higher. Doctoral Programs: GRE-V 500, 562; GRE-Q 500, 615; GRE-Subject (Psychology) 600, 664; overall undergraduate GPA 3.00, 3.35; Doctoral program GRE-Analytic 4.5, 4.87.

Other Criteria: (importance of criteria rated low, medium, or high): GRE/MAT scores—medium, research experience—medium, work experience—low, extracurricular activity—low, clinically related public service—low, GPA—high, letters of recommendation—high, interview—high, statement of goals and objectives—high, clinical experience—high. For the MA in Psychology and the MA in Clinical Psychology, work experience, letters of recommendation, and personal statements have medium importance, whereas previous research or clinical experience has low importance. For additional information on admission requirements, go to http://gsep.pepperdine.edu/admission/.

Student Characteristics: The following represents characteristics of students in 2007–2008 in all graduate psychology programs in the department: Female—full-time 611, part-time 178; Male—full-time 99, part-time 29; African American/Black—full-time 66, part-time 21; Hispanic/Latino(a)—full-time 86, part-time 17; Asian/Pacific Islander—full-time 54, part-time 16; American Indian/Alaska Native—full-time 5, part-time 3; Caucasian/White—full-time 283, part-time 97; Multi-ethnic—full-time 27, part-time 8; students subject to the Americans With Disabilities Act—full-time 5, part-time 0; Unknown ethnicity—full-time 189, part-time 45; International students who hold an F-1 or J-1 Visa—full-time 13, part-time 0.

Financial Information/Assistance:

Tuition for Full-Time Study: *Master's:* State residents: $840 per credit hour; Nonstate residents: $840 per credit hour. *Doctoral:* State residents: $1,055 per credit hour; Nonstate residents: $1,055 per credit hour. See the following Web site for updates and changes in tuition costs: http://www.gsep.pepperdine.edu/financialaid/costs. Higher tuition cost for this program: Tuition for MA Clinical (Malibu, daytime format) is $1,055 per credit hour.

Financial Assistance:

First-Year Students: Teaching assistantships available for first year. Average amount paid per academic year: $6,042. Average number of hours worked per week: 10. Apply by variable. Research assistantships available for first year. Average amount paid per academic year: $6,042. Average number of hours worked per week: 10. Apply by variable. Traineeships available for first year. Average amount paid per academic year: $6,042. Average number of hours worked per week: 10. Apply by variable. Fellowships and scholarships available for first year. Average number of hours worked per week: 0. Apply by variable. Tuition remission given: partial.

Advanced Students: Teaching assistantships available for advanced students. Average amount paid per academic year: $6,593. Average number of hours worked per week: 10. Apply by variable. Research assistantships available for advanced students. Average amount paid per academic year: $6,593. Average number of hours worked per week: 10. Apply by variable. Traineeships available for advanced students. Average amount paid per academic year: $6,593. Average number of hours worked per week: 10. Apply by variable. Fellowships and scholarships available for advanced students. Average amount paid per academic year: $7,200. Average number of hours worked per week: 0. Apply by April 15. Tuition remission given: partial.

Additional Information: Of all students currently enrolled full time, 30% benefited from one or more of the listed financial assistance programs. Application and information available online at http://gsep.pepperdine.edu/financialaid/.

Internships/Practica: Master's Degree (MA/MS Clinical): An internship experience, such as, a final research project or "capstone" experience is required of graduates. Doctoral Degree (PsyD Clinical): For those doctoral students for whom a professional internship was required in this program prior to graduation, (29) students applied for an internship in 2006–2007, with (28) students obtaining an internship. Of those students who obtained an internship, (27) were paid internships. Of those students who obtained an internship, (22) students placed in APA/CPA accredited internships, (4) students placed in internships not APA/CPA-accredited, but listed with the Association of Psychology Postdoctoral and Internship Centers (APPIC), (0) students placed in internships conforming to guidelines of the Council of Directors of School Psychology Programs (CDSPP), (2) students placed in internships that were not APA/CPA-accredited, APPIC or CDSPP listed. Students in the PsyD and MA in Clinical Psychology programs complete practicum requirements at Pepperdine clinics or affiliated agencies in the community. PsyD students complete predoctoral internships in approved agencies. Pepperdine clinical training staff assist students in locating training positions. For additional information on education and training outcomes for our programs, see the following website: (For PsyD program: http://www.gsep.pepperdine.edu/psychology/psyd-clinical-psy.

Housing and Day Care: On-campus housing is available. See the following Web site for more information: http://www.pepperdine.edu/housing. No on-campus day care facilities are available.

Employment of Department Graduates:

Master's Degree Graduates: Of those who graduated in the academic year 2006–2007, the following categories and numbers represent the postgraduate activities and employment of master's degree graduates: Enrolled in a postdoctoral residency/fellowship (n/a), employed in independent practice (n/a), total from the above (master's) (0).

Doctoral Degree Graduates: Of those who graduated in the academic year 2006–2007, the following categories and numbers represent the postgraduate activities and employment of doctoral degree graduates: Enrolled in a psychology doctoral program (n/a), enrolled in another graduate/professional program (0), enrolled in a postdoctoral residency/fellowship (6), employed in independent practice (1), employed in an academic position at a university (0), employed in an academic position at a 2-year/4-year college (0), employed in other positions at a higher education institution (1), employed in a professional position in a school system (0), employed in business or industry (0), employed in government agency (0), employed in a community mental health/counseling center (8), employed in a hospital/medical center (1), other employment position (3), do not know (5), total from the above (doctoral) (25).

Additional Information:

Orientation, Objectives, and Emphasis of Department: The psychology degree programs are designed to provide the student with a theoretical and practical understanding of the principles of psychology within the framework of a strong clinical emphasis. Courses present various aspects of the art and science of psychology as it is applied to the understanding of human behavior, and to the prevention, diagnosis, and treatment of mental and emotional problems. The MA in psychology serves as the prerequisite for the PsyD degree, or for students seeking human services positions in community agencies and organizations. The MA in clinical psychology provides the academic preparation for the Marriage and Family Therapist license. The PsyD program ascribes to a practitioner–scholar model of training.

Special Facilities or Resources: The Master of Arts in Psychology and Clinical Psychology programs at Pepperdine University are offered at four campuses throughout Southern California. Computer laboratories and libraries are available at all four campuses offering the psychology program. Psychology clinics are located at the West Los Angeles Graduate Campus, the Irvine Graduate Campus and the Encino Graduate Campus, as well as a student counseling center on the Malibu Campus.

Information for Students With Physical Disabilities: See the following Web site for more information: http://www.pepperdine.edu/studentaffairs/disabilityservices.

Application Information:

Send to Pepperdine University, Graduate School of Education and Psychology, Office of Admissions, 6100 Center Drive, Los Angeles, CA 90045. Application available online. URL of online application: http://www.gsep.pepperdine.edu/admission/application. Students are admitted in the Fall, application deadline June 1; Spring, application deadline October 1; Summer, application deadline February 1. PsyD and MA Clinical (Malibu, daytime format) programs: Fall admission only: January 7 application deadline for PsyD; February 1 application deadline for MA Clinical (Malibu, daytime format). Evening format MA Clinical and General programs: Fall admission, June 1 application deadline; Spring admission, October 1 application deadline; Summer admission, February 1 application deadline. *Fee:* $55.

Phillips Graduate Institute

Clinical Psychology Doctoral Program
5445 Balboa Boulevard
Encino, CA 91316
Telephone: (818) 386-5600
Fax: (818) 386-5699
E-mail: *rbkennedy@pgi.edu*
Web: *http://www.pgi.edu*

Department Information:

2001. Interim Program Chair, Clinical Psychology Doctoral Program: Rhonda Brinkley-Kennedy, PsyD. Number of faculty: total—full-time 6, part-time 18; women—full-time 3, part-time 11; total—minority—full-time 3, part-time 1; women minority—full-time 2; faculty subject to the Americans With Disabilities Act 3.

Programs and Degrees Offered:

Listed in the following order: Program area, degree type (T if terminal Master's), number awarded 7/06–6/07. Clinical Psychology PsyD (Doctor of Psychology) 13.

Student Applications/Admissions:

Student Applications

Clinical Psychology PsyD (Doctor of Psychology)—Applications 2007–2008, 61. Total applicants accepted 2007–2008, 46. Number full-time enrolled (new admits only) 2007–2008, 23. Number part-time enrolled (new admits only) 2007–2008, 0. Total enrolled 2007–2008 full-time, 71, part-time, 19. Openings 2008–2009, 20. The median number of years required for completion of a degree in 2006–2007 were 5. The number of students enrolled full- and part-time who were dismissed or voluntarily withdrew from this program area in 2007–2008 were 6.

Admissions Requirements:

Scores: Entries appear in this order: required test or GPA, minimum score (if required), median score of students entering in 2007–2008. Master's Programs: overall undergraduate GPA no minimum stated. Doctoral Programs: overall undergraduate GPA 3.0.

Other Criteria: (importance of criteria rated low, medium, or high): research experience—low, work experience—medium, extracurricular activity—medium, clinically related public service—high, GPA—high, letters of recommendation—medium, interview—high, statement of goals and objectives—medium, undergraduate major in psychology—medium, specific undergraduate psychology courses taken—low. For additional information on admission requirements, go to http://www.pgi.edu.

Student Characteristics: The following represents characteristics of students in 2007–2008 in all graduate psychology programs in the department: Female—full-time 56, part-time 13; Male—full-time 15, part-time 6; African American/Black—full-time 6, part-time 2; Hispanic/Latino(a)—full-time 9, part-time 4; Asian/Pacific Islander—full-time 7, part-time 0; American Indian/Alaska Native—full-time 1, part-time 0; Caucasian/White—full-time 34, part-time 9; Multi-ethnic—full-time 6, part-time 2; students subject to the Americans With Disabilities Act—full-time 0, part-time 0; Unknown ethnicity—full-time 8, part-time 2.

Financial Information/Assistance:

Tuition for Full-Time Study: *Doctoral:* Nonstate residents: per academic year $19,440, $810 per credit hour. Tuition is subject to change. Additional fees are assessed to students beyond the costs of tuition for the following: Administrative fee: $300 per semester. See the following Web site for updates and changes in tuition costs: http://www.pgi.edu.

Financial Assistance:

First-Year Students: No information provided.

Advanced Students: Teaching assistantships available for advanced students. Average amount paid per academic year: $5,000. Average number of hours worked per week: 10. Apply by May 30.

Additional Information: Of all students currently enrolled full time, 4% benefited from one or more of the listed financial assistance programs.

Internships/Practica: Doctoral Degree (PsyD Clinical Psychology): For those doctoral students for whom a professional internship was required in this program prior to graduation, (22) students applied for an internship in 2006–2007, with (22) students obtaining an internship. Of those students who obtained an internship, (16) were paid internships. Of those students who obtained an internship, (3) students placed in APA/CPA-accredited internships, (4) students placed in internships not APA/CPA accredited, but listed with the Association of Psychology Postdoctoral and Internship Centers (APPIC), (0) students placed in internships conforming to guidelines of the Council of Directors of School Psychology Programs (CDSPP), (15) students placed in internships that were not APA/CPA-accredited, APPIC or CDSPP listed. The Clinical Placement Office provides students information and guidance in the choice of practica and internship experiences.

Housing and Day Care: No on-campus housing is available. No on-campus day care facilities are available.

Employment of Department Graduates:

Master's Degree Graduates: Of those who graduated in the academic year 2006–2007, the following categories and numbers represent the postgraduate activities and employment of master's degree graduates: Enrolled in a postdoctoral residency/fellowship (n/a), employed in independent practice (n/a), total from the above (master's) (0).

Doctoral Degree Graduates: Of those who graduated in the academic year 2006–2007, the following categories and numbers represent the postgraduate activities and employment of doctoral degree graduates: Enrolled in a psychology doctoral program (n/a), enrolled in another graduate/professional program (0), enrolled in a postdoctoral residency/fellowship (5), employed in independent practice (0), employed in an academic position at a university (1), employed in an academic position at a 2-year/4-year college (0), employed in other positions at a higher education institution (0), employed in a professional position in a school system (0), employed in business or industry (0), employed in government agency (0), employed in a community mental health/counseling center (5), employed in a hospital/medical center (0), still seeking employment (3), not seeking employment (1), other employment position (2), do not know (0), total from the above (doctoral) (17).

Additional Information:

Orientation, Objectives, and Emphasis of Department: The Doctor of Psychology in Clinical Psychology provides the education and training to be eligible to apply for licensure in the state of California. The program integrates ecosystemic and family systems theory throughout the curriculum. In addition, students select advanced coursework in either diversity or forensic psychology to fulfill concentration area requirements.

Information for Students With Physical Disabilities: See the following Web site for more information: http://www.pgi.edu.

Application Information:

Send to Office of Admissions, Phillips Graduate Institute, 5445 Balboa Boulevard, Encino, CA 91316. Students are admitted in the Fall, application deadline January 31; Programs have rolling admissions. *Fee:* $75.

San Diego State University (2007 data)

Counseling and School Psychology
Education
5500 Campanille Drive
San Diego, CA 92182-1179
Telephone: (619) 594-6109
Fax: (619) 594-7025
E-mail: *gmonk@mail.sdsu.edu*
Web: ***http://www.edweb.sdsu.edu/csp/***

Department Information:

1965. Chairperson: Carol Robinson-Zañartu, PhD. Number of faculty: total—full-time 13, part-time 26; women—full-time 11, part-time 14.

Programs and Degrees Offered:

Listed in the following order: Program area, degree type (T if terminal Master's), number awarded 7/06–6/07. School Psychology EdS/MEd (School Psychology) 12, Marriage and Family Therapy MA/MS (Master of Arts/Science) (T) 25, School Counseling MA/MS (Master of Arts/Science) (T) 10, Community-Based Counseling MA/MS (Master of Arts/Science) (T) 24, Culture and Community Trauma Studies Certificate Other.

Student Applications/Admissions:

Student Applications

School Psychology EdS/MEd (School Psychology)—Applications 2007–2008, 102. Total applicants accepted 2007–2008, 12. Number full-time enrolled (new admits only) 2007–2008, 12. Openings 2008–2009, 12. The median number of years required for completion of a degree in 2006–2007 were 4. The number of students enrolled full- and part-time who were dismissed or voluntarily withdrew from this program area in 2007–2008 were 1. *Marriage and Family Therapy MA/MS (Master of Arts/Science)*—Applications 2007–2008, 130. Total applicants accepted 2007–2008, 18. Number full-time enrolled (new admits only) 2007–2008, 12. Number part-time enrolled (new admits only) 2007–2008, 12. Total enrolled 2007–2008 full-time, 69, part-time, 6. Openings 2008–2009, 24. The median number of years required for completion of a degree in 2006–2007 were 3. The number of students enrolled full- and part-time who were dismissed or voluntarily withdrew from this program area in 2007–2008 were 2. *School Counseling MA/MS (Master of Arts/Science)*—Applications 2007–2008, 86. Total applicants accepted 2007–2008, 14. Number full-time enrolled (new admits only) 2007–2008, 10. Number part-time enrolled (new admits only) 2007–2008, 2. Total enrolled 2007–2008 full-time, 23, part-time, 3. Openings 2008–2009, 12. The median number of years required for completion of a degree in 2006–2007 were 2. The number of students enrolled full- and part-time who were dismissed or voluntarily withdrew from this program area in 2007–2008 were 2. *Community-Based Counseling MA/MS (Master of Arts/Science)*—Applications 2007–2008, 118. Total applicants accepted 2007–2008, 24. Number full-time enrolled (new admits only) 2007–2008, 24. Total enrolled 2007–2008 full-time, 24. Openings 2008–2009, 27. The median number of years required for completion of a degree in 2006–2007 was 1. The number of students enrolled full- and part-time who were dismissed or voluntarily withdrew from this program area in 2007–2008 were 0. *Culture and Community Trauma Studies Certificate Other.*

Admissions Requirements:

Scores: Entries appear in this order: required test or GPA, minimum score (if required), median score of students entering in 2007–2008. Master's Programs: GRE-V no minimum stated; GRE-Q no minimum stated; overall undergraduate GPA no minimum stated; last 2 years GPA no minimum stated.

Other Criteria: (importance of criteria rated low, medium, or high): GRE/MAT scores—medium, research experience—medium, work experience—high, extracurricular activity—medium, clinically related public service—high, GPA—high, letters of recommendation—high, interview—high, statement of goals and objectives—high, portfolio applications—high. Porfolio applications are assessed on multiple criteria, and include professional, personal, and cross cultural readiness for graduate study. A percentage of applicants is selected from the portfolios for a day-long interview, from which the cohort is selected annually. Criteria vary a bit by program (see Web sites). For additional information on admission requirements, go to http://edweb.sdsu.edu/csp/.

Student Characteristics: The following represents characteristics of students in 2007–2008 in all graduate psychology programs in the department: Female—full-time 95, part-time 14; Male—full-time 50, part-time 2; African American/Black—full-time 22, part-time 1; Hispanic/Latino(a)—full-time 42, part-time 3; Asian/Pacific Islander—full-time 13, part-time 1; American Indian/Alaska Native—full-time 8, part-time 0; Caucasian/White—full-time 44, part-time 3; Multi-ethnic—full-time 22, part-time 1; students subject to the Americans With Disabilities Act—full-time 8, part-time 0; Unknown ethnicity—full-time 0, part-time 0.

Financial Information/Assistance:

Tuition for Full-Time Study: *Master's:* State residents: per academic year $3,422; Nonstate residents: $339 per credit hour. Tuition is subject to change. See the following Web site for updates and changes in tuition costs: http://www.sdsu.edu.

Financial Assistance:

First-Year Students: Research assistantships available for first year. Average amount paid per academic year: $4,000. Average number of hours worked per week: 10. Apply by varies. Fellowships and scholarships available for first year. Average amount paid per academic year: $7,000. Apply by varies. Tuition remission given: partial.

Advanced Students: Research assistantships available for advanced students. Average amount paid per academic year: $4,000. Average number of hours worked per week: 10. Apply by varies. Fellowships and scholarships available for advanced students. Average amount paid per academic year: $7,000. Apply by varies. Tuition remission given: partial.

Additional Information: Of all students currently enrolled full time, 18% benefited from one or more of the listed financial assistance programs. Application and information available online; contact each program office for detailed information about annual availability.

Internships/Practica: Internships in school psychology are consistent with the standards outlined by the National Association of School Psychologists (NASP) and are integrated into the final year of that program. Internships in School Counseling are consistent with the standards of the California Commission on Teacher Credentialing (CCTC) and occur in year two of that program. Traineeships in Marriage and Family Therapy are consistent with the standards of the American Association for Marriage and Family Therapy (AAMFT).

Housing and Day Care: On-campus housing is available. See the following Web site for more information: http://www.sa.sdsu.edu/hrlo/. On-campus day care facilities are available. See the following Web site for more information: http://www.sdsu.edu.

Employment of Department Graduates:

Master's Degree Graduates: Of those who graduated in the academic year 2006–2007, the following categories and numbers represent the postgraduate activities and employment of master's degree graduates: Enrolled in a psychology doctoral program (2), enrolled in another graduate/professional program (15), enrolled in a postdoctoral residency/fellowship (n/a), employed in independent practice (n/a), employed in an academic position at a 2-year/4-year college (2), employed in other positions at a higher education institution (3), employed in a professional position in a school system (16), employed in a community mental health/counseling center (16), employed in a hospital/medical center (2), other employment position (6), do not know (5), total from the above (master's) (67).

Doctoral Degree Graduates: Of those who graduated in the academic year 2006–2007, the following categories and numbers represent the postgraduate activities and employment of doctoral degree graduates: Enrolled in a psychology doctoral program (n/a), total from the above (doctoral) (0).

Additional Information:

Orientation, Objectives, and Emphasis of Department: The Department of Counseling and School Psychology is a graduate level professional preparation community that prepares school psychologists, family therapists, and school and community counselors. We promote critical inquiry, reflection, self-development, and social action in its faculty and students, and are committed to work towards equity and economic and social justice. Our graduates are prepared to work in a multicultural and changing world in leadership roles in family, educational, and social systems.

Special Facilities or Resources: The department has a clinical training facility located in a highly diverse section of the urban community. Known as the Community Counseling Center, we serve the local community with students under faculty supervision, and sponsor continuing education activities. Students in the Marriage and Family Therapy Program are supervised by AAMFT-Approved supervisors; students in community counseling are supervised by university faculty members.

Information for Students With Physical Disabilities: See the following Web site for more information: http://www.sa.sdsu.edu/dss/dss_home.html.

Application Information:

Each program has its own admissions process in addition to the application to the university. Please visit the Web site for specific application information: http://edweb.sdsu.edu/csp/. Application available online. URL of online application: http://www.edweb.sdsu.edu/csp. Students are admitted in the Spring, application deadline February 1. Most programs currently list February 1 as the application deadline. Some begin review on that date. Check Web site for most current information. *Fee:* $55. University application fee is $55. Departmental fee of $25 in 2005–2006. Out-of-state tuition may occasionally be waived for 1 year should an applicant be selected as graduate assistant and be awarded the waiver.

San Diego State University

Department of Psychology
College of Sciences
5500 Campanile Drive
San Diego, CA 92182-4611
Telephone: (619) 594-5358
Fax: (619) 594-1332
E-mail: *mcrawfor@sciences.sdsu.edu*
Web: *http://www.psychology.sdsu.edu/new-web/gradprograms.htm*

Department Information:

1947. Chair: Claire Murphy. Number of faculty: total—full-time 45, part-time 25; women—full-time 21, part-time 12; total—minority—full-time 4, part-time 3; women minority—full-time 2, part-time 2.

Programs and Degrees Offered:

Listed in the following order: Program area, degree type (T if terminal Master's), number awarded 7/06–6/07. Master of Arts MA/MS (Master of Arts/Science) 21, Master of Sciences MA/MS (Master of Arts/Science) (T) 7.

Student Applications/Admissions:

Student Applications

Master of Arts MA/MS (Master of Arts/Science)—Applications 2007–2008, 82. Total applicants accepted 2007–2008, 47. Number full-time enrolled (new admits only) 2007–2008, 45. Number part-time enrolled (new admits only) 2007–2008, 0. Openings 2008–2009, 35. The median number of years required for completion of a degree in 2006–2007 were 2. The number of students enrolled full- and part-time who were dismissed or voluntarily withdrew from this program area in 2007–2008 were 1. *Master of Sciences MA/MS (Master of Arts/Science)*—Applications 2007–2008, 41. Total applicants accepted 2007–2008, 12. Number full-time enrolled (new admits only) 2007–2008, 7. Number part-time enrolled (new admits only) 2007–2008, 0. Total enrolled 2007–2008 full-time, 17. Openings 2008–2009, 8. The median number of years required for completion of a degree in 2006–2007 were 3. The number of students enrolled full- and part-time who were dismissed or voluntarily withdrew from this program area in 2007–2008 were 0.

Admissions Requirements:

Scores: Entries appear in this order: required test or GPA, minimum score (if required), median score of students entering in 2007–2008. Master's Programs: GRE-V no minimum stated; GRE-Q no minimum stated; GRE-Subject (Psychology) no minimum stated; overall undergraduate GPA 2.85; last 2 years GPA 3.0; psychology GPA 3.0. We require a score above 50th percentile in GRE in Verbal, Quantitative, and Psychology subject test of GRE.

Other Criteria: (importance of criteria rated low, medium, or high): GRE/MAT scores—medium, research experience—high, work experience—medium, extracurricular activity—medium, clinically related public service—low, GPA—high, letters of recommendation—high, statement of goals and objectives—high, undergraduate major in psychology—low, specific undergraduate psychology courses taken—high. Work experience is viewed more closely by the Applied Psychology (MS) faculty than by the MA faculty. Research experience is particularly important in the MA program as this is a predoctoral program. For additional information on admission requirements, go to http://www.psychology.sdsu.edu/admisReq.html.

Student Characteristics: The following represents characteristics of students in 2007–2008 in all graduate psychology programs in the department: Female—full-time 75, part-time 0; Male—full-time 34, part-time 0; African American/Black—full-time 3, part-time 0; Hispanic/Latino(a)—full-time 10, part-time 0; Asian/Pacific Islander—full-time 9, part-time 0; American Indian/Alaska Native—full-time 0, part-time 0; Caucasian/White—full-time 78, part-time 0; Multi-ethnic—full-time 2, part-time 0; students subject to the Americans With Disabilities Act—full-time 0, part-time 0; Unknown ethnicity—full-time 7, part-time 0; International students who hold an F-1 or J-1 Visa—full-time 3, part-time 0.

Financial Information/Assistance:

Tuition for Full-Time Study: *Master's:* State residents: per academic year $4,070; Nonstate residents: per academic year $4,070. Tuition is subject to change. Additional fees are assessed to students beyond the costs of tuition for the following: Out-of-state and international students pay $339/unit unless awarded a waiver. See Financial Assistance. See the following Web site for updates and changes in tuition costs: http://www.bfa.sdsu.edu/fm/co/sfs/studentfees.html.

Financial Assistance:

First-Year Students: Teaching assistantships available for first year. Average amount paid per academic year: $10,126. Average number of hours worked per week: 20. Apply by February 1. Research assistantships available for first year. Average amount paid per academic year: $11,042. Average number of hours worked per week: 20. Apply by February 1.

Advanced Students: Teaching assistantships available for advanced students. Average amount paid per academic year: $10,126. Average number of hours worked per week: 20. Apply by January 15. Research assistantships available for advanced students. Average amount paid per academic year: $11,042. Average number of hours worked per week: 20. Apply by January 15.

Additional Information: Of all students currently enrolled full time, 70% benefited from one or more of the listed financial assistance programs. Application and information available online at http://www.psychology.sdsu.edu/gradprograms.html.

Internships/Practica: An essential component of graduate training in Applied Psychology is an internship experience that provides students with an opportunity to apply their classroom training and acquire new skills in a field setting. Interns are placed in a variety of settings, such as community-based organizations, consulting firms, city and county organizations, education, hospitality and high-tech and private industry. Through the internship experience students also develop close contacts with other psychologists and practitioners working in their field. Internships are normally undertaken during the summer following the 1st year in the program and during the fall semester of the 2nd year.

Housing and Day Care: On-campus housing is available. See the following Web site for more information: http://www.sa.sdsu.edu/housing. On-campus day care facilities are available. See the following Web site for more information: http://www-rohan.sdsu.edu/dept/childfam/Childstudy.html#center.

Employment of Department Graduates:

Master's Degree Graduates: Of those who graduated in the academic year 2006–2007, the following categories and numbers represent the postgraduate activities and employment of master's degree graduates: Enrolled in a psychology doctoral program (8), enrolled in another graduate/professional program (0), enrolled in a postdoctoral residency/fellowship (n/a), employed in independent practice (n/a), employed in an academic position at a university (0), employed in an academic position at a 2-year/4-year college (2), employed in other positions at a higher education institution (1), employed in a professional position in a school system (0), employed in business or industry (3), employed in government agency (0), employed in a community mental health/counseling center (0), employed in a hospital/medical center (0), still seeking employment (0), not seeking employment (1), other employment position (0), do not know (2), total from the above (master's) (17).

Doctoral Degree Graduates: Of those who graduated in the academic year 2006–2007, the following categories and numbers represent the postgraduate activities and employment of doctoral degree graduates: Enrolled in a psychology doctoral program (n/a), total from the above (doctoral) (0).

Additional Information:

Orientation, Objectives, and Emphasis of Department: The MA degree program provides graduate level studies and preparation for PhD programs in several areas. It is particularly appropriate for students who need advanced work to strengthen their profiles for application to PhD programs, or for those wishing to explore graduate-level work before committing to PhD training. Areas of emphasis within the MA are Behavioral Psychology, Social Psychology, Physical and or Mental Health Psychology, Social Psychology, Developmental Psychology, and Learning/Cognition Psychology. Areas of emphasis within the MS are Industrial/Organization Psychology and Program Evaluation. Our research-oriented program does not offer instruction in technical skills (e.g., intelligence testing) and does not have a counseling practicum or provide opportunities for development of clinical skills. Students gain valuable research experience, which may involve working with humans in nonclinical areas. Upon admission to the program students are assigned a faculty research mentor who guides them through the research process leading to the thesis. Students take core classes in the major areas of psychology and electives in their areas of specialization. The MS Degree program in Applied Psychology has emphases in Program Evaluation and Industrial/Organizational Psychology. Students are prepared for professional careers in the public and private sectors or for doctoral-level training in Applied Psychology. All MS students take core courses in statistics and measurement and complete an internship.

Special Facilities or Resources: The following research labs welcome master's students: Anxiety and Depression in Children/Adolescents; Stereotype Threat, Aging/Dementia, Active Living/Healthy Eating; Alcohol Research; Behavioral Teratology; Brain Development Imaging; Categorical Distortions; Child Language/Emotion; Child and Adolescent Mental Health; Cognitive Development; Culture, Work Values/Organizational Behavior; Generational Differences; Child Abuse/Neglect; Health Outcomes; Intergroup Relations; Life-Span Human Senses; Measurement and Evaluation; Minority Community Health Intervention; Organizational Leadership/Citizenship; Organizational Research; Personality Assessment/Psychometrics; Personality Measurement Binge Drinking/Intervention; Family Library Use/Lifelong Learning; Social Support and Education on Health/Well Being of People With Chronic Diseases; Psychosocial Factors in Coronary Heart Disease; Language/Cognitive Studies; Psychosocial, Chronic Illness Adjustment; Smoking; Social Development; Social Influence and Group Dynamics; Social Rejection; Stress/Coping; and Activity for Adolescent Girls. Students may conduct research at Children's Hospital, where several faculty members have their offices. Other resources include a community psychology clinic, the Center for Behavioral and Community Health Studies, Center for Behavioral Teratology, and the Center for Research in Mathematics and Science Education. Also available is an exchange program with the University of Mannheim, Germany. Students can choose to spend a semester or a year attending classes in Mannheim, and graduate students from Mannheim can spend a semester or a year taking classes here.

Information for Students With Physical Disabilities: See the following Web site for more information: http://www.sa.sdsu.edu/dss/dss_home.html.

Application Information:
Send to Master's Programs Admissions Coordinator, Department of Psychology San Diego State University, 5500 Campanile Drive, San Diego, CA 92182-4611. Application available online. URL of online application: http://www.psychology.sdsu.edu/MasApp2004-05.pdf. Students are admitted in the Fall, application deadline February 1. At this time departmental application is available online. Details about the program, as well as the departmental application, can be found at http://www.psychology.sdsu.edu/gradprograms.html. There are two steps to the application process: (a) Part 1: University application. Complete and submit the online university application at http://www.csumentor.com, follow payment instructions, electronically transmit your GRE scores to institution 4682 department 2016, and mail one set of official transcripts for every college-level institution you have to: Enrollment Services, Graduate Admissions Document Processing Unit, San Diego State University, San Diego, CA 92182-7416. (b) Part 2: Psychology department application. The departmental application must be printed and submitted to the Department of Psychology, Master's Programs Coordinator, 5500 Campanile Drive, San Diego, CA 92182-4611. Please include in the application packet: Psychology Department application, one set of unofficial transcripts transcripts for every college-level institution ever attended, three sealed and signed letters of recommendation, a copy of your GRE scores, and a statement of purpose. If recommenders prefer, they can submit their letters of recommendation directly to the Master's Programs Coordinator at the above address. Please do not send items to the Psychology department that need to go to Enrollment Services (e.g., checks, official transcripts.). *Fee:* $55.

San Diego State University/University of California, San Diego Joint Doctoral Program in Clinical Psychology

SDSU Department of Psychology/UCSD Department of Psychiatry
SDSU: College of Sciences UCSD: School of Medicine
San Diego State University
6363 Alvarado Court, Suite 103
San Diego, CA 92120-4913
Telephone: (619) 594-2246
Fax: (619) 594-6780
E-mail: *sscott@sciences.sdsu.edu*
Web: *http://www.psychology.sdsu.edu/doctoral*

Department Information:
1985. Codirectors: Elizabeth Klonoff, PhD; Robert Heaton, PhD. Number of faculty: total—full-time 40, part-time 33; women—full-time 15, part-time 17; total—minority—full-time 5, part-time 1; women minority—full-time 2.

Programs and Degrees Offered:
Listed in the following order: Program area, degree type (T if terminal Master's), number awarded 7/06–6/07. SDSU/UCSD Joint Doctoral Program in Clinical Psychology PhD (Doctor of Philosophy) 13.

APA Accreditation: Clinical PhD (Doctor of Philosophy).

Student Applications/Admissions:
Student Applications
SDSU/UCSD Joint Doctoral Program in Clinical Psychology PhD (Doctor of Philosophy)—Applications 2007–2008, 373. Total applicants accepted 2007–2008, 10. Number full-time enrolled (new admits only) 2007–2008, 10. Number part-time enrolled (new admits only) 2007–2008, 0. Openings 2008–2009, 15. The median number of years required for completion of a degree in 2006–2007 were 6. The number of students enrolled full- and part-time who were dismissed or voluntarily withdrew from this program area in 2007–2008 were 0.

Admissions Requirements:
Scores: Entries appear in this order: required test or GPA, minimum score (if required), median score of students entering in 2007–2008. Doctoral Programs: GRE-V 550, 590; GRE-Q 550, 705; GRE-Subject (Psychology) no minimum stated, 705; overall undergraduate GPA 3.0, 3.7; last 2 years GPA 3.25, 3.88. Master's not required for this program. JDP usually requires much higher scores and GPAs than the Graduate Admissions minimum.
Other Criteria: (importance of criteria rated low, medium, or high): GRE/MAT scores—medium, research experience—high, work experience—low, clinically related public service—medium, GPA—high, letters of recommendation—high, interview—high, statement of goals and objectives—high, undergraduate major in psychology—medium, specific undergraduate psychology courses taken—medium. These criteria are for the Joint Doctoral Program only. For additional information on admission requirements, go to http://www.psychology.sdsu.edu/doctoral.

Student Characteristics: The following represents characteristics of students in 2007–2008 in all graduate psychology programs in the department: Female—full-time 62, part-time 0; Male—full-time 12, part-time 0; African American/Black—full-time 3, part-time 0; Hispanic/Latino(a)—full-time 16, part-time 0; Asian/Pacific Islander—full-time 11, part-time 0; American Indian/Alaska Native—full-time 0, part-time 0; Caucasian/White—full-time 40, part-time 0; Multi-ethnic—full-time 0, part-time 0; students subject to the Americans With Disabilities Act—full-time 0, part-time 0; Unknown ethnicity—full-time 4, part-time 0; International students who hold an F-1 or J-1 Visa—full-time 11, part-time 0.

Financial Information/Assistance:
Tuition for Full-Time Study: *Doctoral:* State residents: per academic year $3,758; Nonstate residents: per academic year $3,758, $339 per credit hour. Tuition is subject to change. See the following Web site for updates and changes in tuition costs: Go to SDSU home page and click on cashiers office link; http://www.bfa.sdsu.edu/fm/co/sfs/registration.

Financial Assistance:
First-Year Students: Research assistantships available for first year. Average amount paid per academic year: $14,000. Average number of hours worked per week: 20. Apply by N/A. Tuition

remission given: full. Fellowships and scholarships available for first year. Average amount paid per academic year: $14,000. Average number of hours worked per week: 20. Apply by varies. Tuition remission given: full.

Advanced Students: Teaching assistantships available for advanced students. Average amount paid per academic year: $15,954. Average number of hours worked per week: 20. Apply by N/A. Tuition remission given: full. Research assistantships available for advanced students. Average amount paid per academic year: $16,000. Average number of hours worked per week: 20. Apply by N/A. Tuition remission given: full.

Additional Information: Of all students currently enrolled full time, 100% benefited from one or more of the listed financial assistance programs. Application and information available online at http://www.psychology.sdsu.edu/doctoral.

Internships/Practica: Doctoral Degree (PhD SDSU/UCSD Joint Doctoral Program in Clinical Psychology): For those doctoral students for whom a professional internship was required in this program prior to graduation, (13) students applied for an internship in 2006–2007, with (12) students obtaining an internship. Of those students who obtained an internship, (12) were paid internships. Of those students who obtained an internship, (12) students placed in APA/CPA-accredited internships, (0) students placed in internships not APA/CPA-accredited, but listed with the Association of Psychology Postdoctoral and Internship Centers (APPIC), (0) students placed in internships conforming to guidelines of the Council of Directors of School Psychology Programs (CDSPP), (0) students placed in internships that were not APA/CPA-accredited, APPIC or CDSPP listed. For doctoral students only SDSU: Primary placement for all students in their 2nd year is the Psychology Clinic. Students are taught general clinical skills. Therapy sessions are routinely videotaped for review in intensive weekly supervision session. UCSD: VA Outpatient Clinic: psychiatric outpatients—assessment and individual and group therapy. VA Medical Center: psychiatric inpatients—assessment, individual and group therapy. UCSD Outpatient Psychiatric Clinic: psychiatric outpatients—neuropsychological assessment and individual and group therapy. UCSD Medical Center: assessment and therapy of all types. All practicum placements are assigned for 1 full year beginning in the student's 2nd year.

Housing and Day Care: On-campus housing is available. Both universities provide housing and child care. Information will be available at interviews. On-campus day care facilities are available.

Employment of Department Graduates:

Master's Degree Graduates: Of those who graduated in the academic year 2006–2007, the following categories and numbers represent the postgraduate activities and employment of master's degree graduates: Enrolled in a postdoctoral residency/fellowship (n/a), employed in independent practice (n/a), total from the above (master's) (0).

Doctoral Degree Graduates: Of those who graduated in the academic year 2006–2007, the following categories and numbers represent the postgraduate activities and employment of doctoral degree graduates: Enrolled in a psychology doctoral program (n/a), enrolled in a postdoctoral residency/fellowship (13), total from the above (doctoral) (13).

Additional Information:

Orientation, Objectives, and Emphasis of Department: Our PhD program is a cooperative venture of an academic Department of Psychology (SDSU) and a medical school Department of Psychiatry (UCSD). This partnership between two different departments in two universities provides unusual opportunities for interdisciplinary research. We currently offer concentrations in behavioral medicine, neuropsychology, and experimental psychopathology. The scientist–practitioner model on which the program is based involves a strong commitment to research as well as clinical training. The program aims to prepare students for leadership roles in academic and research settings. Our program is designed as a 5-year curriculum with a core of classroom instruction followed by apprenticeship training in specialty areas with appropriate seminars and tutorials. Clinical experiences are integrated with formal instruction throughout. The program as a whole is designed to satisfy the criteria for APA accreditation.

Special Facilities or Resources: The UCSD Department of Psychiatry, through the medical school, UCSD hospitals, and the VA Medical Center, has available all of the modern research and clinical facilities consistent with the School of Medicine's ranking among the top 10 in the country in biomedical research. These include specialty laboratories (e.g., sleep labs), access to clinical trials, supercomputing facilities, and state-of-the-art neurochemical and biochemical laboratory facilities. Qualified students interested in MRI studies have access to a number of fully supported imagers. At SDSU, the Department of Psychology has a state-of-the-art video-equipped therapy training complex, as well as experiment rooms, equipment (e.g., computerized test administration capabilities), and supplies available for research, including computerized physiological assessment and biofeedback laboratories. Animal research can be conducted on campus, where small animals are housed in a modern vivarium staffed with a veterinarian. SDSU faculty also supervise research on more exotic species at Sea World and the San Diego Zoo. The College of Sciences maintains a completely equipped electronics shop, a wood shop, a metal shop, and computer support facilities with several high-end Unix servers, all staffed with full-time technicians. Collaborative relationships with faculty in the Graduate School of Public Health allow access to resources there as well.

Information for Students With Physical Disabilities: See the following Web site for more information: http://www.sdsu.edu/dss.

Application Information:

Send to Student Selection Committee, 6363 Alvarado Court, Suite 103, San Diego, CA 92120-4913. Students must also apply to the SDSU Office of Admissions and Records, 5500 Campanile Drive, San Diego, CA 92182. The application for SDSU Admissions and Records can be submitted online at http://www.csumentor.edu. JDP application Part I can be submitted on line, print out Part II, sign and mail copies of both parts to Selection Committee address. Application available online. URL of online application: http://www.psychology.sdsu.edu/doctoral. Students are admitted in the Fall, application deadline December 15. Please note that this information only applies to the SDSU/UCSD Joint Doctoral Program in Clinical Psychology. It does not include information about any other program. *Fee:* $55. Applicants may secure a waiver form from SDSU Admissions and Records. Must demonstrate financial need. The CSU Mentor application has space for requesting fee waiver at the end of the form.

San Francisco State University
Psychology
Behavioral and Social Science
1600 Holloway Avenue
San Francisco, CA 94132
Telephone: (415) 338-2167
Fax: (415) 338-2398
E-mail: *psych@sfsu.edu*
Web: *http://www.sfsu.edu/~psych/*

Department Information:

1923. Chairperson: Dr. Kathleen Mosier. Number of faculty: total—full-time 20, part-time 22; women—full-time 14, part-time 9; women minority—full-time 5, part-time 2.

Programs and Degrees Offered:

Listed in the following order: Program area, degree type (T if terminal Master's), number awarded 7/06–6/07. Clinical Psychology MA/MS (Master of Arts/Science) (T) 12, Developmental Psychology MA/MS (Master of Arts/Science) (T) 6, Industrial/Organizational Psychology MA/MS (Master of Arts/Science) (T) 12, School Psychology MA/MS (Master of Arts/Science) (T) 10, Social Psychology MA/MS (Master of Arts/Science) (T) 6, Research Psychology MA/MS (Master of Arts/Science) (T) 9.

Student Applications/Admissions:

Student Applications

Clinical Psychology MA/MS (Master of Arts/Science)—Applications 2007–2008, 160. Total applicants accepted 2007–2008, 12. Number full-time enrolled (new admits only) 2007–2008, 12. Total enrolled 2007–2008 full-time, 25. Openings 2008–2009, 12. The median number of years required for completion of a degree in 2006–2007 were 2. *Developmental Psychology MA/MS (Master of Arts/Science)*—Applications 2007–2008, 36. Total applicants accepted 2007–2008, 7. Number full-time enrolled (new admits only) 2007–2008, 7. Openings 2008–2009, 12. The median number of years required for completion of a degree in 2006–2007 were 3. *Industrial/Organizational Psychology MA/MS (Master of Arts/Science)*—Applications 2007–2008, 86. Total applicants accepted 2007–2008, 12. Number full-time enrolled (new admits only) 2007–2008, 12. Openings 2008–2009, 12. The median number of years required for completion of a degree in 2006–2007 were 3. *School Psychology MA/MS (Master of Arts/Science)*—Applications 2007–2008, 130. Total applicants accepted 2007–2008, 12. Number full-time enrolled (new admits only) 2007–2008, 12. Openings 2008–2009, 12. The median number of years required for completion of a degree in 2006–2007 were 3. *Social Psychology MA/MS (Master of Arts/Science)*—Applications 2007–2008, 33. Total applicants accepted 2007–2008, 10. Number full-time enrolled (new admits only) 2007–2008, 10. Total enrolled 2007–2008 full-time, 15. Openings 2008–2009, 7. The median number of years required for completion of a degree in 2006–2007 were 2. *Research Psychology MA/MS (Master of Arts/Science)*—Applications 2007–2008, 48. Total applicants accepted 2007–2008, 9. Number full-time enrolled (new admits only) 2007–2008, 9. Total enrolled 2007–2008 full-time, 18. Openings 2008–2009, 10. The median number of years required for completion of a degree in 2006–2007 were 3.

Admissions Requirements:

Scores: Entries appear in this order: required test or GPA, minimum score (if required), median score of students entering in 2007–2008. Master's Programs: GRE-V no minimum stated; GRE-Q no minimum stated; overall undergraduate GPA no minimum stated; last 2 years GPA no minimum stated; psychology GPA no minimum stated.

Other Criteria: (importance of criteria rated low, medium, or high): GRE/MAT scores—medium, research experience—medium, work experience—medium, extracurricular activity—low, clinically related public service—medium, GPA—medium, letters of recommendation—high, interview—high, statement of goals and objectives—high, undergraduate major in psychology—medium, specific undergraduate psychology courses taken—medium. Clinical: clinical and community experience, interview. School: clinical and school experience, interview. Industrial/Organizational: interview. The three MA programs (Developmental, Social, and Research) emphasize research experience.. For additional information on admission requirements, go to http://bss.sfsu.edu./psych/.

Student Characteristics: The following represents characteristics of students in 2007–2008 in all graduate psychology programs in the department: Female—full-time 99, part-time 0; Male—full-time 25, part-time 0; African American/Black—full-time 5, part-time 0; Hispanic/Latino(a)—full-time 13, part-time 0; Asian/Pacific Islander—full-time 20, part-time 0; American Indian/Alaska Native—full-time 0, part-time 0; Caucasian/White—full-time 43, part-time 0; Multi-ethnic—full-time 0, part-time 0; Unknown ethnicity—full-time 43, part-time 0; International students who hold an F-1 or J-1 Visa—full-time 1, part-time 0.

Financial Information/Assistance:

Tuition for Full-Time Study: *Master's:* State residents: per academic year $4,098; Nonstate residents: per academic year $8,166, $339 per credit hour. Tuition is subject to change. See the following Web site for updates and changes in tuition costs: http://www.sfsu.edu/prospect/costs.htm.

Financial Assistance:

First-Year Students: Teaching assistantships available for first year.

Advanced Students: Teaching assistantships available for advanced students. Research assistantships available for advanced students.

Additional Information: Of all students currently enrolled full time, 14% benefited from one or more of the listed financial assistance programs.

Internships/Practica: Master's Degree (MA/MS Clinical Psychology): An internship experience such as a final research project or "capstone" experience is required of graduates. Master's Degree (MA/MS Developmental Psychology): An internship experience such as a final research project or "capstone" experience is required of graduates. Master's Degree (MA/MS I/O Psychology): An internship experience such as a final research project or "capstone" experience is required of graduates. Master's Degree (MA/MS School Psychology): An internship experience such as a final research project or "capstone" experience is required of graduates. Master's Degree (MA/MS Social Psychology): An internship experience such as a final research project or "capstone" experience is required of graduates. Master's Degree (MA/MS Research Psychology): An internship experience such as a final research project or "capstone" experience is required of graduates. For clinical students, practica in the first year is provided in the Psychology Clinic. Second-year internships are located throughout the San Francisco Bay area. For Industrial/Organizational students, an internship is required during the 2nd year of study. Students are placed in various work organizations throughout the San Francisco Bay area. Students enrolled in the School Psychology program are required to complete a 3rd year paid internship. The Social Psychology students have a year-long field placement.

Housing and Day Care: On-campus housing is available. See the following Web site for more information: http://www.sfsu.edu/~housing/. On-campus day care facilities are available. See the following Web site for more information: http://www.sfsu.edu/prospect/child.htm.

Employment of Department Graduates:

Master's Degree Graduates: Of those who graduated in the academic year 2006–2007, the following categories and numbers represent the postgraduate activities and employment of master's degree graduates: Enrolled in a postdoctoral residency/fellowship (n/a), employed in independent practice (n/a), total from the above (master's) (0).

Doctoral Degree Graduates: Of those who graduated in the academic year 2006–2007, the following categories and numbers represent the postgraduate activities and employment of doctoral degree graduates: Enrolled in a psychology doctoral program (n/a), total from the above (doctoral) (0).

Additional Information:

Orientation, Objectives, and Emphasis of Department: Clinical: The theoretical orientation of the Clinical program is based on psychodynamic, developmental theory within a family and community systems framework. The Clinical program emphasizes training in psychotherapy and applied clinical experience. Developmental: The Developmental program takes a lifespan approach. Research and courses emphasize family systems; attachment; social, cognitive, and emotional development; and the development of diverse populations. Training is provided on developmental research methods. Industrial/Organizational: The I/O MS program has a science–practice approach to workplace issues. The program prepares graduates for professional work in business, industry, and government and for continuing education in I/O psychology. School: The School Psychology program emphasizes, within a cultural context, developmental and psychodynamic theories with an applied interpersonal relations and family systems approach. Research: The Research Psychology program takes a basic scientific approach, including study of physiological issues. Social: The Social Psychology program, oriented toward research and applications in the public interest, prepares students for MA-level careers and doctoral study with training in both qualitative and quantitative methods.

Special Facilities or Resources: The Psychology Department Training Clinic is a full-service clinic offering psychotherapy to the campus and the larger community. The Clinic is staffed by graduate students under the supervision of licensed clinicians. The Psychology Department Test Library is available to qualified users including students with faculty permission and supervision. Many faculty-led research laboratories are in operation.

Information for Students With Physical Disabilities: See the following Web site for more information: http://www.sfsu.edu/~dprc/welcome.html.

Application Information:

Send to Graduate Secretary, Department of Psychology, San Francisco State University, 1600 Holloway Avenue, San Francisco, CA 94132. Application available online. URL of online application: http://www.sfsu.edu/~psych/psygrdap.htm. Students are admitted in the Fall, application deadline February 1; Spring, application deadline October 15. Only the Developmental Psychology program accepts students for the Spring semester. The application deadline is October 15. *Fee:* $55. Processing fee applies to the University application only. There is no fee for the Departmental application.

San Jose State University (2007 data)

Department of Psychology
Social Sciences
One Washington Square
San Jose, CA 95192-0120
Telephone: (408) 924-5600
Fax: (408) 924-5605
E-mail: *nakamura@email.sjsu.edu*
Web: *http://www.psych.sjsu.edu*

Department Information:

1944. Chairperson: Sheila Bienenfeld. Number of faculty: total—full-time 21, part-time 11; women—full-time 12, part-time 5; faculty subject to the Americans With Disabilities Act 1.

Programs and Degrees Offered:

Listed in the following order: Program area, degree type (T if terminal Master's), number awarded 7/06–6/07. Clinical MA/MS (Master of Arts/Science) (T) 13, Experimental MA/MS (Master of Arts/Science) (T) 5, Industrial/Organizational MA/MS (Master of Arts/Science) (T) 7.

Student Applications/Admissions:

Student Applications

Clinical MA/MS (Master of Arts/Science)—Applications 2007–2008, 58. Total applicants accepted 2007–2008, 14. Number full-time enrolled (new admits only) 2007–2008, 8. Number part-time enrolled (new admits only) 2007–2008, 0. Total enrolled 2007–2008 full-time, 18, part-time, 7. Openings 2008–2009, 14. The median number of years required for completion of a degree in 2006–2007 were 2. The number of students enrolled full- and part-time who were dismissed or voluntarily withdrew from this program area in 2007–2008 were 0. *Experimental MA/MS (Master of Arts/Science)*—Applications 2007–2008, 32. Total applicants accepted 2007–2008, 17. Number full-time enrolled (new admits only) 2007–2008, 12. Number part-time enrolled (new admits only) 2007–2008, 0. Openings 2008–2009, 11. The median number of years required for completion of a degree in 2006–2007 were 2. The number of students enrolled full- and part-time who were dismissed or voluntarily withdrew from this program area in 2007–2008 were 1. *Industrial/Organizational MA/MS (Master of Arts/Science)*—Applications 2007–2008, 45. Total applicants accepted 2007–2008, 13. Number full-time enrolled (new admits only) 2007–2008, 12. Number part-time enrolled (new admits only) 2007–2008, 0. Openings 2008–2009, 15. The median number of years required for completion of a degree in 2006–2007 were 3. The number of students enrolled full- and part-time who were dismissed or voluntarily withdrew from this program area in 2007–2008 were 1.

Admissions Requirements:

Scores: Entries appear in this order: required test or GPA, minimum score (if required), median score of students entering in 2007–2008. Master's Programs: GRE-V no minimum stated; GRE-Q no minimum stated; overall undergraduate GPA no minimum stated; last 2 years GPA 3.0; psychology GPA 3.0. GRE required for I/O and MA General only; no GRE for MS Clinical Program. MS Clinical GPA averages: 3.58 (Psychology GPA), 3.61 (Last 2 years GPA). Doctoral Programs: different scores/GPAs are required for different program areas. There are both university as well as department and program-specific criteria.

Other Criteria: (importance of criteria rated low, medium, or high): Clinical Program has specific course requirements for admission and requires minimum 1 year of applied clinical experience and 100 hours. Admission criteria vary by program. For additional information on admission requirements, go to http://www.psych.sjsu.edu/grad.

Student Characteristics: The following represents characteristics of students in 2007–2008 in all graduate psychology programs in the department: Female—full-time 35, part-time 7; Male—full-time 14, part-time 2; African American/Black—full-time 1, part-time 0; Hispanic/Latino(a)—full-time 3, part-time 0; Asian/Pacific Islander—full-time 5, part-time 0; American Indian/Alaska Native—full-time 0, part-time 0; Caucasian/White—full-time 0, part-time 0; Multi-ethnic—full-time 2, part-time 0; students subject to the Americans With Disabilities Act—full-time 0, part-time 0; Unknown ethnicity—full-time 0, part-time 0.

Financial Information/Assistance:

Tuition for Full-Time Study: *Master's:* State residents: per academic year $4,274; Nonstate residents: per academic year $4,274, $339 per credit hour. Tuition is subject to change. Additional fees are assessed to students beyond the costs of tuition for the following: international students pay base and additional per unit fee. See the following Web site for updates and changes in tuition costs: http://www.sjsu.edu/bursar/.

Financial Assistance:

First-Year Students: Teaching assistantships available for first year. Research assistantships available for first year. Fellowships and scholarships available for first year.

Advanced Students: Teaching assistantships available for advanced students. Research assistantships available for advanced students. Fellowships and scholarships available for advanced students.

Additional Information: Of all students currently enrolled full time, 50% benefited from one or more of the listed financial assistance programs. Application and information available online at http://www2.sjsu.edu/depts/finaid/.

Internships/Practica: An internship is required for students in the Industrial/Organizational Psychology program. The program coordinator works with each student to determine the student's interests and helps find a placement site for each student. Some students in the Experimental Program are offered internships at NASA/Ames Research Center.

Housing and Day Care: On-campus housing is available. See the following Web site for more information: http://www.housing.sjsu.edu/oncampus.stm. On-campus day care facilities are available. See the following Web site for more information: http://www.as.sjsu.edu/childcare/index.jsp.

Employment of Department Graduates:

Master's Degree Graduates: Of those who graduated in the academic year 2006–2007, the following categories and numbers represent the postgraduate activities and employment of master's degree graduates: Enrolled in a psychology doctoral program (4), enrolled in a postdoctoral residency/fellowship (n/a), employed in independent practice (n/a), employed in business or industry (3), employed in government agency (4), employed in a community mental health/counseling center (10), total from the above (master's) (28).

Doctoral Degree Graduates: Of those who graduated in the academic year 2006–2007, the following categories and numbers represent the postgraduate activities and employment of doctoral degree graduates: Enrolled in a psychology doctoral program (n/a), total from the above (doctoral) (0).

Additional Information:

Orientation, Objectives, and Emphasis of Department: The mission of the University is to enrich the lives of its students, to transmit knowledge to its students along with the necessary skills for applying it in the service of our society, and to expand the base of knowledge through research and scholarship. It emphasizes the following goals for both undergraduate and graduate students: in-depth knowledge of a major field of study; broad understanding of the sciences, social sciences, humanities, and the arts; skills in communication and in critical inquiry; multicultural and global perspectives gained through intellectual and social exchange with people of diverse economic and ethnic backgrounds; active participation in professional, artistic, and ethnic communities, responsible citizenship and an understanding of ethical choices inherent in human development.

Special Facilities or Resources: The department maintains a variety of facilities and support staff to enhance instruction and research. For biological and cognitive research and instruction, the department has a number of laboratories and specialized laboratory equipment on campus, and lab technicians are available to construct additional equipment. For work in clinical and counseling psychology, the department has a Psychology Clinic consisting of therapy rooms and adjoining observation rooms equipped with audio and video equipment. These rooms are also available to individuals working in other areas, such as developmental, personality, and social psychology. In addition, students interested in counseling-related activities have access to a number of off-campus organizations. Three computer laboratories containing microcomputers and terminals hooked up to minicomputers and mainframes are available for students. These labs have extensive software, and computer consultants are on call to help with software and hardware problems, design and interpretation of statistical analyses, and computer exercises. There is a child care center on campus.

Information for Students With Physical Disabilities: See the following Web site for more information: http://www.drc.sjsu.edu.

Application Information:
Send to Program coordinator (program name). All information and application materials are available online at http:www.psych.sjsu.edu/grad. A separate concurrent university application is required. Application available online. URL of online application: http://www.psych.sjsu.edu/grad. Students are admitted in the Fall, application deadline January 15; February 1. Deadline for Clinical/Counseling is January 15; for the Experimental Psychology Program and the Industrial/Organizational Psychology Program it is February 1. *Fee:* $55. Separate applications go to the university and to the department.

Santa Clara University (2007 data)

Department of Counseling Psychology
Counseling Psychology, Education, and Pastoral Ministries
500 El Camino Real, Bannan Hall 243
Santa Clara, CA 95053-0201
Telephone: (408) 554-4355
Fax: (408) 554-4367
E-mail: *sbabbel@scu.edu*
Web: *http://www.scu.edu/ecppm/*

Department Information:
1970. Chairperson: Jerrold Lee Shapiro, PhD. Number of faculty: total—full-time 9, part-time 22; women—full-time 4, part-time 16.

Programs and Degrees Offered:
Listed in the following order: Program area, degree type (T if terminal Master's), number awarded 7/06–6/07. Counseling Psychology MA/MS (Master of Arts/Science) (T) 44, Counseling MA/MS (Master of Arts/Science) 9.

Student Applications/Admissions:
Student Applications
Counseling Psychology MA/MS (Master of Arts/Science)—Applications 2007–2008, 120. Total applicants accepted 2007–2008, 101. Number full-time enrolled (new admits only) 2007–2008, 38. Number part-time enrolled (new admits only) 2007–2008, 27. Total enrolled 2007–2008 full-time, 117, part-time, 137. Openings 2008–2009, 60. The median number of years required for completion of a degree in 2006–2007 were 3. The number of students enrolled full- and part-time who were dismissed or voluntarily withdrew from this program area in 2007–2008 were 3. *Counseling MA/MS (Master of Arts/Science)*—Applications 2007–2008, 9. Total applicants accepted 2007–2008, 8. Number full-time enrolled (new admits only) 2007–2008, 1. Number part-time enrolled (new admits only) 2007–2008, 4. Total enrolled 2007–2008 full-time, 4, part-time, 5. Openings 2008–2009, 20. The median number of years required for completion of a degree in 2006–2007 were 2. The number of students enrolled full- and part-time who were dismissed or voluntarily withdrew from this program area in 2007–2008 were 0.

Admissions Requirements:
Scores: Entries appear in this order: required test or GPA, minimum score (if required), median score of students entering in 2007–2008. Master's Programs: GRE-V no minimum stated; GRE-Q no minimum stated; MAT no minimum stated; overall undergraduate GPA 3.0; Masters GRE-Analytical no minimum stated. We require either the GRE or MAT. We do not have cut off or minimum scores.
Other Criteria: (importance of criteria rated low, medium, or high): GRE/MAT scores—low, research experience—low, work experience—medium, extracurricular activity—medium, clinically related public service—high, GPA—medium, letters of recommendation—high, statement of goals and objectives—high. For additional information on admission requirements, go to http://www.scu.edu/cp/.

Student Characteristics: The following represents characteristics of students in 2007–2008 in all graduate psychology programs in the department: Female—full-time 103, part-time 123; Male—full-time 18, part-time 19; African American/Black—full-time 2, part-time 4; Hispanic/Latino(a)—full-time 22, part-time 19; Asian/Pacific Islander—full-time 17, part-time 9; American Indian/Alaska Native—full-time 0, part-time 0; Caucasian/White—full-time 61, part-time 88; Multi-ethnic—full-time 0, part-time 0; students subject to the Americans With Disabilities Act—full-time 2, part-time 1; Unknown ethnicity—full-time 19, part-time 22.

Financial Information/Assistance:
Tuition for Full-Time Study: *Master's:* State residents: $411 per credit hour; Nonstate residents: $411 per credit hour. Tuition is subject to change. See the following Web site for updates and changes in tuition costs: http://www.scu.edu/ecppm/about/financialinformation.

Financial Assistance:
First-Year Students: Teaching assistantships available for first year. Average amount paid per academic year: $1,200. Average number of hours worked per week: 3. Apply by quarterly. Research assistantships available for first year. Average amount paid per academic year: $600. Average number of hours worked per week: 6. Apply by varies. Fellowships and scholarships available for first year. Average amount paid per academic year: $1,400. Average number of hours worked per week: 0. Apply by quarterly.
Advanced Students: Teaching assistantships available for advanced students. Average amount paid per academic year: $1,200. Average number of hours worked per week: 3. Apply by quarterly. Research assistantships available for advanced students. Average amount paid per academic year: $600. Average number of hours worked per week: 6. Apply by varies. Fellowships and scholarships available for advanced students. Average amount paid per academic year: $1,400. Average number of hours worked per week: 0. Apply by quarterly.
Additional Information: Of all students currently enrolled full time, 26% benefited from one or more of the listed financial assistance programs. Application and information available online at http://www.scu.edu/ecppm/about/financialinformation.

Internships/Practica: Counseling Practicum: Marriage and Family Therapy. Supervised counseling experience designed specifically to meet California MFT licensing requirements. Weekly seminars for consultation and discussion with a licensed supervisor on such topics as case management and evaluation, referral procedures, ethical practices, professional and client interaction, confidential communication, and interprofessional ethical considerations.

Housing and Day Care: No on-campus housing is available. On-campus day care facilities are available. Kids on Campus, Santa Clara University, 500 El Camino Real, Santa Clara, CA 95053-0858; Phone: 408-554-4771; See the following Web site for more information: http://www.scu.edu/koc/.

Employment of Department Graduates:

Master's Degree Graduates: Of those who graduated in the academic year 2006–2007, the following categories and numbers represent the postgraduate activities and employment of master's degree graduates: Enrolled in a psychology doctoral program (4), enrolled in another graduate/professional program (1), enrolled in a postdoctoral residency/fellowship (n/a), employed in independent practice (n/a), employed in an academic position at a 2-year/4-year college (2), employed in other positions at a higher education institution (4), employed in a professional position in a school system (4), employed in a community mental health/counseling center (8), employed in a hospital/medical center (1), other employment position (6), do not know (19), total from the above (master's) (54).

Doctoral Degree Graduates: Of those who graduated in the academic year 2006–2007, the following categories and numbers represent the postgraduate activities and employment of doctoral degree graduates: Enrolled in a psychology doctoral program (n/a), total from the above (doctoral) (0).

Additional Information:

Orientation, Objectives, and Emphasis of Department: Santa Clara University's graduate programs in counseling and counseling psychology are offered through the School of Education, Counseling Psychology, and Pastoral Ministries. Programs lead to the Master of Arts in Counseling or the Master of Arts in Counseling Psychology, with the option of an emphasis in Health Psychology, Career Counseling, Latino Counseling, and Correctional Psychology. All of the Counseling Psychology (78-unit) programs prepare students for MFT licensure through the California Board of Behavioral Sciences (BBS). Santa Clara is accredited by the Western Association of Schools and Colleges and is approved by the Board of Behavioral Science, Department of Consumer Affairs (California) to prepare students for MFT licensure. The faculty represent a diverse set of clinical theories and perspectives, and students gain a broad exposure to a range of theories and practical applications in counseling.

Special Facilities or Resources: Santa Clara University is located in the heart of Silicon Valley, with close connection to major business and academic resources in this area. The University has a complete complement of facilities including an excellent library, theatre, museum, and state-of-the-art physical fitness center. The University has a dedication to educating the whole person and includes Centers of Distinction, which explore diversity, ethics, and the interface of technology and society.

Information for Students With Physical Disabilities: See the following Web site for more information: http://www.scu.edu/advising/learning/disabilities/index.cfm.

Application Information:

Send to Graduate Admissions School of ECPPM, Bannan 243, Santa Clara University, 500 El Camino Real, Santa Clara, CA 95053-0201. Application available online. URL of online application: https://www.scu.edu/apply/edcp/handler.cfm?event=home. Students are admitted in the Fall, application deadline April 1; Winter, application deadline October 1; Spring, application deadline February 1; Summer, application deadline April 1. *Fee:* $50.

Saybrook Graduate School and Research Center

Graduate School
747 Front Street, Third Floor
San Francisco, CA 94111-1920
Telephone: (415) 433-9200
Fax: (415) 433-9271
E-mail: *ecooper@saybrook@saybrook.edu*
Web: *http://www.saybrook.edu*

Department Information:

1971. Vice President for Academic Affairs: Ed Cooper. Number of faculty: total—full-time 13, part-time 40; women—full-time 9, part-time 30.

Programs and Degrees Offered:

Listed in the following order: Program area, degree type (T if terminal Master's), number awarded 7/06–6/07. Human Science MA/MS (Master of Arts/Science) 0, Human Science PhD (Doctor of Philosophy) 5, Organizational Systems MA/MS (Master of Arts/Science) 0, Psychology MA/MS (Master of Arts/Science) 23, Psychology PhD (Doctor of Philosophy) 37, Organizational Systems PhD (Doctor of Philosophy) 3, Psychology Licensure MA/MS (Master of Arts/Science) 0.

Student Applications/Admissions:

Student Applications

Human Science MA/MS (Master of Arts/Science)—Applications 2007–2008, 3. Total applicants accepted 2007–2008, 3. Number full-time enrolled (new admits only) 2007–2008, 2. Total enrolled 2007–2008 full-time, 7. Openings 2008–2009, 10. The number of students enrolled full- and part-time who were dismissed or voluntarily withdrew from this program area in 2007–2008 were 2. *Human Science PhD (Doctor of Philosophy)*—Applications 2007–2008, 17. Total applicants accepted 2007–2008, 9. Number full-time enrolled (new admits only) 2007–2008, 15. Total enrolled 2007–2008 full-time, 30. Openings 2008–2009, 20. The number of students enrolled full- and part-time who were dismissed or voluntarily withdrew from this program area in 2007–2008 were 9. *Organizational Systems MA/MS (Master of Arts/Science)*—Applications 2007–2008, 9. Total applicants accepted 2007–2008, 3. Number full-time enrolled (new admits only) 2007–2008, 1. Total enrolled 2007–2008 full-time, 6. Openings 2008–2009, 20. The number of students enrolled full- and part-time who were dismissed or voluntarily withdrew from this program area in 2007–2008 were 1. *Psychology MA/MS (Master of Arts/Science)*—Applications 2007–2008, 54. Total applicants accepted 2007–2008, 31. Number full-time enrolled (new admits only) 2007–2008, 40. Total enrolled 2007–2008 full-time, 55. Openings 2008–2009, 30. The number of students enrolled full- and part-time who were dismissed or voluntarily withdrew from this program area in 2007–2008 were 15. *Psychology PhD (Doctor of Philosophy)*—Applications 2007–2008, 158. Total applicants accepted 2007–2008, 81. Number full-time enrolled (new admits only) 2007–2008, 83. Total enrolled 2007–2008 full-time, 296. Openings 2008–2009, 45. The number of students enrolled full- and part-time who were dismissed or voluntarily withdrew from this program area in 2007–2008 were 41. *Organizational Systems PhD (Doctor of Philosophy)*—Applications 2007–2008, 38. Total applicants accepted 2007–2008, 26. Number full-time enrolled (new admits only) 2007–2008, 9. Total enrolled 2007–2008 full-time, 56. Openings 2008–2009, 30. The number of students enrolled full- and part-time who were dismissed or voluntarily withdrew from this program area in 2007–2008 were 5. *Psychology Licensure MA/MS (Master of Arts/Science)*—Applications 2007–2008, 54. Total applicants accepted 2007–2008, 31. Openings 2008–2009, 30.

Admissions Requirements:

Scores: Entries appear in this order: required test or GPA, minimum score (if required), median score of students entering in 2007–2008. Doctoral Programs: GRE scores are only required for admission to Saybrook's PsyD program. If GRE scores are less than 500 in each of the three parts of verbal reasoning, quantitative reasoning, critical thinking, and analytical writing skills, other evidence of academic promise in the applicant's history will be expected.

Other Criteria: (importance of criteria rated low, medium, or high): GRE/MAT scores—low, research experience—high, work experience—high, extracurricular activity—medium, clinically related public service—medium, GPA—high, letters of recommendation—high, interview—low, statement of goals and objectives—high. GRE score is only required for admission to Saybrook's clinical PsyD degree program. Saybrook does not require the GRE for other MA or PhD degrees. For additional information on admission requirements, go to http://www.saybrook.edu/admissions/apply_to_saybrook.asp.

Student Characteristics: The following represents characteristics of students in 2007–2008 in all graduate psychology programs in the department: Female—full-time 333, part-time 0; Male—full-time 146, part-time 0; African American/Black—full-time 30, part-time 0; Hispanic/Latino(a)—full-time 18, part-time 0; Asian/Pacific Islander—full-time 13, part-time 0; American Indian/Alaska Native—full-time 1, part-time 0; Caucasian/White—full-time 278, part-time 0; Multi-ethnic—full-time 0, part-time 0; Unknown ethnicity—full-time 139, part-time 0.

Financial Information/Assistance:

Tuition for Full-Time Study: *Master's:* State residents: per academic year $17,600; Nonstate residents: per academic year $17,600. *Doctoral:* State residents: per academic year $17,600; Nonstate residents: per academic year $17,600. Additional fees are assessed to students beyond the costs of tuition for the following: Residential Conferences for food and lodging. See the following Web site for updates and changes in tuition costs: http://www.saybrook.edu/student_resources/business_office/tuition_fees.asp.

Financial Assistance:

First-Year Students: Fellowships and scholarships available for first year. Average amount paid per academic year: $2,500.

Advanced Students: Fellowships and scholarships available for advanced students. Average amount paid per academic year: $2,000.

Additional Information: Of all students currently enrolled full time, 43% benefited from one or more of the listed financial assistance programs. Application and information available online at http://www.saybrook.edu/student_resources/financial_aid/how_to_apply.asp.

Internships/Practica: Saybrook graduate students are distributed throughout the United States and the world. Because of the distance learning format, it is impractical for Saybrook to offer internship and practica training based at Saybrook. Saybrook graduate students are often successful midlife professionals who are accomplished in their first careers. The Clinical Training Coordinator works with doctoral students to find training experiences that will provide solid clinical training while drawing upon the strengths and clinical interests of these mature students.

Housing and Day Care: No on-campus housing is available. No on-campus day care facilities are available.

Employment of Department Graduates:

Master's Degree Graduates: Of those who graduated in the academic year 2006–2007, the following categories and numbers represent the postgraduate activities and employment of master's degree graduates: Enrolled in a psychology doctoral program (11), enrolled in a postdoctoral residency/fellowship (n/a), employed in independent practice (n/a), employed in an academic position at a university (1), employed in an academic position at a 2-year/4-year college (1), employed in other positions at a higher education institution (1), employed in business or industry (2), employed in a community mental health/counseling center (3), total from the above (master's) (19).

Doctoral Degree Graduates: Of those who graduated in the academic year 2006–2007, the following categories and numbers represent the postgraduate activities and employment of doctoral degree graduates: Enrolled in a psychology doctoral program (n/a), employed in independent practice (21), employed in an academic position at a 2-year/4-year college (2), employed in other positions at a higher education institution (2), employed in a professional position in a school system (5), employed in government agency (1), employed in a community mental health/counseling center (5), employed in a hospital/medical center (2), total from the above (doctoral) (38).

Additional Information:

Orientation, Objectives, and Emphasis of Department: The mission of Saybrook Graduate School and Research Center is to provide a unique and creative environment for graduate study, research, and communication in humanistic psychology, focused on understanding the human experience, in a distance learning format. Applying the highest standards of scholarship, Saybrook is dedicated to fostering the full expression of the human spirit and humanistic values in society.

Application Information:

Send to Saybrook Graduate School, Admissions Department, 747 Front Street, 3rd floor, San Francisco, CA 94111-1920. Application available online. URL of online application: https://www.mars.saybrook.edu/SMS/MainAdmissionsLogin.jsp. Students are admitted in the Fall, application deadline June 1; Spring, application deadline December 15; Programs have rolling admissions. For clincial PsyD degree, apply by April 15. *Fee:* $50.

Sonoma State University

Department of Counseling
1801 East Cotati Avenue
Rohnert Park, CA 94928
Telephone: (707) 664-2544
Fax: (707) 664-2038
E-mail: *carolyn.saarni@sonoma.edu*
Web: *http://www.sonoma.edu/counseling*

Department Information:

1973. Chairperson: Carolyn Saarni. Number of faculty: total—full-time 5, part-time 5; women—full-time 4, part-time 4; ; women minority—part-time 1.

Programs and Degrees Offered:

Listed in the following order: Program area, degree type (T if terminal Master's), number awarded 7/06–6/07. Community Counseling/Marriage and Family Therapy MA/MS (Master of Arts/Science) (T) 19, School Counseling MA/MS (Master of Arts/Science) (T) 13.

Student Applications/Admissions:

Student Applications

Community Counseling/Marriage and Family Therapy MA/MS (Master of Arts/Science)—Applications 2007–2008, 79. Total applicants accepted 2007–2008, 24. Number full-time enrolled (new admits only) 2007–2008, 16. Number part-time enrolled (new admits only) 2007–2008, 8. Total enrolled 2007–2008 full-time, 30, part-time, 18. Openings 2008–2009, 24. The median number of years required for completion of a degree in 2006–2007 were 3. The number of students enrolled full- and part-time who were dismissed or voluntarily withdrew from this program area in 2007–2008 were 2. *School Counseling MA/MS (Master of Arts/Science)*—Applications 2007–2008, 31. Total applicants accepted 2007–2008, 12. Number full-time enrolled (new admits only) 2007–2008, 9. Number part-time enrolled (new admits only) 2007–2008, 4. Total enrolled 2007–2008 full-time, 17, part-time, 8. Openings 2008–2009, 12. The median number of years required for completion of a degree in 2006–2007 were 2. The number of students enrolled full- and part-time who were dismissed or voluntarily withdrew from this program area in 2007–2008 were 0.

Admissions Requirements:

Scores: Entries appear in this order: required test or GPA, minimum score (if required), median score of students entering in 2007–2008. Master's Programs: overall undergraduate GPA 3.0, 3.0; last 2 years GPA 3.0, 3.5.

Other Criteria: (importance of criteria rated low, medium, or high): research experience—low, work experience—medium, extracurricular activity—medium, clinically related public service—high, GPA—medium, letters of recommendation—high, interview—high, statement of goals and objectives—high, undergraduate major in psychology—medium, specific undergraduate psychology courses taken—high. School counseling program looks for school-related service or clinical/social work with children or youth. Specific course prerequisites include Personality, Abnormal Psychology, Statistics, and Child Development. For additional information on admission requirements, go to http://www.sonoma.edu/counseling.

Student Characteristics: The following represents characteristics of students in 2007–2008 in all graduate psychology programs in the department: Female—full-time 27, part-time 31; Male—full-time 8, part-time 13; African American/Black—full-time 0, part-time 1; Hispanic/Latino(a)—full-time 5, part-time 8; Asian/Pacific Islander—full-time 1, part-time 0; American Indian/Alaska Native—full-time 1, part-time 0; Caucasian/White—full-time 25, part-time 33; Multi-ethnic—full-time 3, part-time 2; students subject to the Americans With Disabilities Act—full-time 1, part-time 1; Unknown ethnicity—full-time 0, part-time 0.

Financial Information/Assistance:

Tuition for Full-Time Study: *Master's:* State residents: per academic year $4,588; Nonstate residents: per academic year $12,724. Tuition is subject to change. See the following Web site for updates and changes in tuition costs: http://www.sonoma.edu/ar/registration/fees.shtml.

Financial Assistance:

First-Year Students: Fellowships and scholarships available for first year. Average amount paid per academic year: $1,400. Apply by February 15.

Advanced Students: Fellowships and scholarships available for advanced students. Average amount paid per academic year: $1,400. Apply by January 15.

Additional Information: Of all students currently enrolled full time, 40% benefited from one or more of the listed financial assistance programs. Application and information available online at http://www.sonoma.edu/FinAid/.

Internships/Practica: Master's Degree (MA/MS School Counseling): An internship experience such as a final research project or "capstone" experience is required of graduates. Our students generally have several internship options to choose from, and they are highly sought by agencies and schools as interns. We do limit the internship sites to Sonoma State University's service area, which is the North Bay/tri-county region of the San Francisco Bay Area. For additional information on education and training outcomes for our programs, see the following Web site: http://www.sonoma.edu/counseling/life-after.htm.

Housing and Day Care: On-campus housing is available. See the following Web site for more information: http://www.sonoma.edu/housing or (707) 664-2541. On-campus day care facilities are available. See the following Web site for more information: http://www.sonoma.edu. Or call the Children's School (707) 664-2230.

Employment of Department Graduates:

Master's Degree Graduates: Of those who graduated in the academic year 2006–2007, the following categories and numbers represent the postgraduate activities and employment of master's degree graduates: Enrolled in a postdoctoral residency/fellowship

(n/a), employed in independent practice (n/a), employed in other positions at a higher education institution (1), employed in a professional position in a school system (14), employed in a community mental health/counseling center (18), other employment position (2), do not know (1), total from the above (master's) (36). ***Doctoral Degree Graduates:*** Of those who graduated in the academic year 2006–2007, the following categories and numbers represent the postgraduate activities and employment of doctoral degree graduates: Enrolled in a psychology doctoral program (n/a), total from the above (doctoral) (0).

Additional Information:

Orientation, Objectives, and Emphasis of Department: The 60-unit graduate program in counseling (nationally accredited through CACREP, affiliated with the American Counseling Association) prepares students for entry into the profession of counseling or student personnel services. The Marriage and Family Therapy (MFT) program prepares students for licensure as MFTs in California; the School Counseling students obtain a Pupil Personnel Services Credential. The program relies heavily on interpersonal skill training and field experience, beginning during the first semester and culminating with an intensive supervised internship in some aspect of counseling, permitting the integration of theoretical constructs and research appraisal with practical application during the second year. The department is prepared to assist students in obtaining field placements relevant to their projected professional goals. These placements include, but are not limited to, family service agencies, mental health clinics, counseling centers, public schools, community colleges, and college-level student counseling centers. Special characteristics of the program include the following: (a) early involvement in actual counseling settings, (b) development of a core of knowledge and experience in both individual and group counseling theory and practice, (c) encouragement in the maintenance and development of individual counseling styles, and (d) commitment to self-exploration and personal growth through participation in peer counseling, individual counseling, and group experiences. This aspect of the program is seen as crucial to the development of counseling skills and is given special consideration by the faculty as part of its evaluation of student readiness to undertake internship responsibilities.

Special Facilities or Resources: Center for Community Counseling (on campus).

Information for Students With Physical Disabilities: See the following Web site for more information: http://www.sonoma.edu/sas/drc/drc.html, (707) 664-2677, or (707) 664-2958 (text).

Application Information:

Send to Counseling Department, Sonoma State University, 1801 East Cotati Avenue, N220, Rohnert Park, CA 94928. Application available online. URL of online application: http://www.sonoma.edu/counseling/application-process.htm. Students are admitted in the Fall, application deadline January 31. *Fee:* $80. $25 fee for application to the Counseling Department, $55 fee for application to Sonoma State University, Total: $80.

Sonoma State University (2007 data)

Department of Psychology
1801 East Cotati Avenue
Rohnert Park, CA 94928
Telephone: (707) 664-2682
Fax: (707) 664-3113
E-mail: *laurel.mccabe@sonoma.edu*
Web: *http://www.sonoma.edu/exed/programs.html*

Department Information:

1961. Chairperson: Laurel McCabe, PhD. Number of faculty: total—full-time 12, part-time 10; women—full-time 9, part-time 9.

Programs and Degrees Offered:

Listed in the following order: Program area, degree type (T if terminal Master's), number awarded 7/06–6/07. Art Therapy MA/MS (Master of Arts/Science) (T) 7, Depth Psychology MA/MS (Master of Arts/Science) 8, Organization Development MA/MS (Master of Arts/Science) 10.

Student Applications/Admissions:

Student Applications

Art Therapy MA/MS (Master of Arts/Science)—Applications 2007–2008, 25. Total applicants accepted 2007–2008, 10. Number full-time enrolled (new admits only) 2007–2008, 0. Number part-time enrolled (new admits only) 2007–2008, 0. Total enrolled 2007–2008 full-time, 20, part-time, 5. The median number of years required for completion of a degree in 2006–2007 were 3. The number of students enrolled full- and part-time who were dismissed or voluntarily withdrew from this program area in 2007–2008 were 0. *Depth Psychology MA/MS (Master of Arts/Science)*—Applications 2007–2008, 25. Total applicants accepted 2007–2008, 12. Number full-time enrolled (new admits only) 2007–2008, 11. Number part-time enrolled (new admits only) 2007–2008, 0. Total enrolled 2007–2008 full-time, 22, part-time, 6. Openings 2008–2009, 14. The median number of years required for completion of a degree in 2006–2007 were 3. The number of students enrolled full- and part-time who were dismissed or voluntarily withdrew from this program area in 2007–2008 were 1. *Organization Development MA/MS (Master of Arts/Science)*—Applications 2007–2008, 25. Total applicants accepted 2007–2008, 15. Number full-time enrolled (new admits only) 2007–2008, 14. Total enrolled 2007–2008 full-time, 30, part-time, 5. Openings 2008–2009, 16. The median number of years required for completion of a degree in 2006–2007 were 2. The number of students enrolled full- and part-time who were dismissed or voluntarily withdrew from this program area in 2007–2008 were 1.

Admissions Requirements:

Scores: Entries appear in this order: required test or GPA, minimum score (if required), median score of students entering in 2007–2008. Master's Programs: last 2 years GPA 3.00, 3.45. ***Other Criteria:*** (importance of criteria rated low, medium, or high): research experience—low, work experience—high, extracurricular activity—medium, clinically related public service—medium, GPA—high, letters of recommendation—high, interview—high, statement of goals and objectives—

high. Demonstrated graduate-level writing ability in all programs.

Student Characteristics: The following represents characteristics of students in 2007–2008 in all graduate psychology programs in the department: Female—full-time 55, part-time 10; Male—full-time 17, part-time 5; African American/Black—full-time 2, part-time 0; Hispanic/Latino(a)—full-time 2, part-time 0; Asian/Pacific Islander—full-time 0, part-time 0; American Indian/Alaska Native—full-time 0, part-time 0; Caucasian/White—full-time 68, part-time 15; Multi-ethnic—full-time 0, part-time 0; students subject to the Americans With Disabilities Act—full-time 0, part-time 0; Unknown ethnicity—full-time 0, part-time 0.

Financial Information/Assistance:

Tuition for Full-Time Study: *Master's:* State residents: per academic year $8,100, $450 per credit hour; Nonstate residents: per academic year $8,100, $450 per credit hour. Tuition is subject to change. Tuition costs vary by program. See the following Web site for updates and changes in tuition costs: http://www.sonoma.edu/exed/programs.html.

Financial Assistance:

First-Year Students: Fellowships and scholarships available for first year. Average amount paid per academic year: $700. Apply by January 15.

Advanced Students: No information provided.

Additional Information: Of all students currently enrolled full time, 80% benefited from one or more of the listed financial assistance programs. Application and information available online at http://www.sonoma.edu/finaid/.

Internships/Practica: Internships are optional in the Depth Psychology program. About half of the students engage in a supervised internship teaching an undergraduate psychology class at SSU. Internships are required as part of the Art Therapy program. Field projects working as a team of two or three students studying an organization are required in the Organization Development program.

Housing and Day Care: On-campus housing is available. Contact Housing Office at (707) 664-2541; The University mainly supports undergraduate housing, but it is possible for a single graduate student to share housing. Housing must be vacated in June. No married student housing. On-campus day care facilities are available. Child Care Center (707) 664-2230.

Employment of Department Graduates:

Master's Degree Graduates: Of those who graduated in the academic year 2006–2007, the following categories and numbers represent the postgraduate activities and employment of master's degree graduates: Enrolled in a psychology doctoral program (5), enrolled in another graduate/professional program (1), enrolled in a postdoctoral residency/fellowship (n/a), employed in independent practice (n/a), employed in an academic position at a university (3), employed in an academic position at a 2-year/4-year college (4), employed in other positions at a higher education institution (3), employed in a professional position in a school system (2), employed in business or industry (20), employed in government agency (0), employed in a community mental health/counseling center (4), employed in a hospital/medical center (0), still seeking employment (10), not seeking employment (10), other employment position (10), total from the above (master's) (80).

Doctoral Degree Graduates: Of those who graduated in the academic year 2006–2007, the following categories and numbers represent the postgraduate activities and employment of doctoral degree graduates: Enrolled in a psychology doctoral program (n/a), total from the above (doctoral) (0).

Additional Information:

Orientation, Objectives, and Emphasis of Department: Art Therapy: Offers 36-units of coursework that meets both the educational standards of the American Art Therapy Association and continues the humanistic tradition of the SSU Psychology Department. To become professionally registered as an ATR, an additional 1,500 postmaster's supervised hours of work are required. Depth Psychology: An embodied 36-unit curriculum that integrates intensive personal process work in Jungian and archetypal psychology with conceptual learning and practical skills development. A small group environment enables students to develop skills in process work, group facilitation, arts expressions, dream work, personal growth facilitation, and cross-cultural awareness. Organization Development: Provides professional preparation for midcareer individuals interested in learning how to develop more effective and humane organizations. A 36-unit program of seminar discussions, skill-building activities, and extensive field projects under faculty guidance. Participants gain the practical skills, conceptual knowledge, and field-tested experience to successfully lead organization improvement efforts.

Special Facilities or Resources: Facilities include a biofeedback lab and computer lab. The faculty are open to investigations in depth psychology and organization development. The department has excellent interdisciplinary cooperation with sociology, gerontology, business, and other related programs. Sonoma State University has a state-of-the-art new library and information center.

Information for Students With Physical Disabilities: See the following Web site for more information: http://www.sonoma.edu/sas/dss/.

Application Information:

Send to MA Programs in Psychology, Department of Psychology, Sonoma State University, 1801 East Cotati Avenue, Rohnert Park, CA 94928. Students are admitted in the Fall, application deadline January 31. Programs have rolling admissions. Applications accepted on a rolling basis until quota reached. *Fee:* $55. No waiver or deferral of fees. Programs do qualify for low-interest federal government loans.

Southern California, University of

Department of Psychology
College of Letters, Arts and Sciences
University Park, SGM 501
Los Angeles, CA 90089-1061
Telephone: (213) 740-2203
Fax: (213) 746-9082
E-mail: *itakarag@usc.edu*
Web: *http://www.usc.edu/schools/college/psyc*

Department Information:

1929. Chairperson: Margaret Gatz. Number of faculty: total—full-time 34; women—full-time 9; total—minority—full-time 5.

Programs and Degrees Offered:

Listed in the following order: Program area, degree type (T if terminal Master's), number awarded 7/06–6/07. Brain and Cognitive Sciences PhD (Doctor of Philosophy) 1, Clinical Science PhD (Doctor of Philosophy) 5, Developmental PhD (Doctor of Philosophy) 1, Quantitative Methods PhD (Doctor of Philosophy) 1, Social PhD (Doctor of Philosophy) 1.

APA Accreditation: Clinical PhD (Doctor of Philosophy).

Student Applications/Admissions:

Student Applications

Brain and Cognitive Sciences PhD (Doctor of Philosophy)—Applications 2007–2008, 57. Total applicants accepted 2007–2008, 5. Number full-time enrolled (new admits only) 2007–2008, 3. Openings 2008–2009, 6. The median number of years required for completion of a degree in 2006–2007 were 6. The number of students enrolled full- and part-time who were dismissed or voluntarily withdrew from this program area in 2007–2008 were 1. *Clinical Science PhD (Doctor of Philosophy)*—Applications 2007–2008, 283. Total applicants accepted 2007–2008, 14. Number full-time enrolled (new admits only) 2007–2008, 6. Openings 2008–2009, 7. The median number of years required for completion of a degree in 2006–2007 were 6. The number of students enrolled full- and part-time who were dismissed or voluntarily withdrew from this program area in 2007–2008 were 0. *Developmental PhD (Doctor of Philosophy)*—Applications 2007–2008, 34. Total applicants accepted 2007–2008, 2. Number full-time enrolled (new admits only) 2007–2008, 2. Openings 2008–2009, 2. The median number of years required for completion of a degree in 2006–2007 were 5. The number of students enrolled full- and part-time who were dismissed or voluntarily withdrew from this program area in 2007–2008 were 3. *Quantitative Methods PhD (Doctor of Philosophy)*—Applications 2007–2008, 12. Total applicants accepted 2007–2008, 4. Number full-time enrolled (new admits only) 2007–2008, 2. Openings 2008–2009, 2. The median number of years required for completion of a degree in 2006–2007 were 6. The number of students enrolled full- and part-time who were dismissed or voluntarily withdrew from this program area in 2007–2008 were 0. *Social PhD (Doctor of Philosophy)*—Applications 2007–2008, 60. Total applicants accepted 2007–2008, 3. Number full-time enrolled (new admits only) 2007–2008, 3. Openings 2008–2009, 2. The median number of years required for completion of a degree in 2006–2007 were 5. The number of students enrolled full- and part-time who were dismissed or voluntarily withdrew from this program area in 2007–2008 were 1.

Admissions Requirements:

Scores: Entries appear in this order: required test or GPA, minimum score (if required), median score of students entering in 2007–2008. Doctoral Programs: GRE-V no minimum stated, 595; GRE-Q 560, 735; overall undergraduate GPA no minimum stated, 3.6.

Other Criteria: (importance of criteria rated low, medium, or high): GRE/MAT scores—high, research experience—high, work experience—medium, extracurricular activity—low, clinically related public service—medium, GPA—high, letters of recommendation—high, statement of goals and objectives—high. Interview and clinically related public service are very important for the Clinical Science program but less so for other areas. For additional information on admission requirements, go to http://www.usc.edu/schools/college/psyc/graduate.

Student Characteristics: The following represents characteristics of students in 2007–2008 in all graduate psychology programs in the department: Female—full-time 62, part-time 0; Male—full-time 33, part-time 0; African American/Black—full-time 5, part-time 0; Hispanic/Latino(a)—full-time 9, part-time 0; Asian/Pacific Islander—full-time 34, part-time 0; American Indian/Alaska Native—full-time 0, part-time 0; Caucasian/White—full-time 47, part-time 0; Multi-ethnic—full-time 0, part-time 0; students subject to the Americans With Disabilities Act—full-time 0, part-time 0; Unknown ethnicity—full-time 0, part-time 0; International students who hold an F-1 or J-1 Visa—full-time 18, part-time 0.

Financial Information/Assistance:

Tuition for Full-Time Study: *Doctoral:* State residents: per academic year $28,440, $1,185 per credit hour; Nonstate residents: per academic year $28,440, $1,185 per credit hour. Tuition is subject to change. Additional fees are assessed to students beyond the costs of tuition for the following: Orientation fee (one time only) plus additional nominal fees (about $50) each semester. See the following Web site for updates and changes in tuition costs: http://www.usc.edu/students/enrollment/classes/.

Financial Assistance:

First-Year Students: Teaching assistantships available for first year. Average amount paid per academic year: $18,570. Average number of hours worked per week: 20. Tuition remission given: full. Research assistantships available for first year. Average amount paid per academic year: $18,570. Average number of hours worked per week: 20. Tuition remission given: full. Traineeships available for first year. Average amount paid per academic year: $20,772. Average number of hours worked per week: 0. Tuition remission given: full. Fellowships and scholarships available for first year. Average amount paid per academic year: $19,000. Average number of hours worked per week: 0. Tuition remission given: full.

Advanced Students: Teaching assistantships available for advanced students. Average amount paid per academic year: $18,570. Average number of hours worked per week: 20. Tuition remission given: full. Research assistantships available for advanced students. Average amount paid per academic year: $18,570. Average number of hours worked per week: 20. Tuition remission given: full. Traineeships available for advanced students. Average amount paid per academic year: $20,772. Average number of hours worked per week: 0. Tuition remission given: full. Fellowships and scholarships available for advanced students. Average amount paid per academic year: $19,000. Average number of hours worked per week: 0. Tuition remission given: full.

Additional Information: Of all students currently enrolled full time, 80% benefited from one or more of the listed financial assistance programs. Application and information available online at http://www.usc.edu/schools/college/psyc/graduate.

Internships/Practica: Doctoral Degree (PhD Clinical Science): For those doctoral students for whom a professional internship was required in this program prior to graduation, (3) students applied for an internship in 2006–2007, with (3) students obtaining an internship. Of those students who obtained an internship, (3) were paid internships. Of those students who obtained an internship, (3) students placed in APA/CPA-accredited internships, (0) students placed in internships not APA/CPA-accredited, but listed with the Association of Psychology Postdoctoral and Internship Centers (APPIC), (0) students placed in internships conforming to guidelines of the Council of Directors of School Psychology Programs (CDSPP), (0) students placed in internships that were not APA/CPA-accredited, APPIC or CDSPP listed. Students in the clinical psychology area take at least six semesters of clinical didactic practica, each of which involves instruction and supervised clinical service provision. Students receive both group and individual supervision of their cases. The 1st year practica focus on clinical interviewing and formal assessment. In the 2nd and 3rd year, students take practica based on their interests and specialty track. Practica are offered in general adult psychotherapy, psychotherapy with older adults, and child/family psychotherapy. After admission to doctoral candidacy, all students must complete a 1-year, APA-approved, clinical internship for which students separately apply at the time.

Housing and Day Care: On-campus housing is available. See the following Web site for more information: http://www.housing.usc.edu/. On-campus day care facilities are available. See the following Web site for more information: http://www.usc.edu/dept/adminops/childcare/.

Employment of Department Graduates:

Master's Degree Graduates: Of those who graduated in the academic year 2006–2007, the following categories and numbers represent the postgraduate activities and employment of master's degree graduates: Enrolled in a postdoctoral residency/fellowship (n/a), employed in independent practice (n/a), total from the above (master's) (0).

Doctoral Degree Graduates: Of those who graduated in the academic year 2006–2007, the following categories and numbers represent the postgraduate activities and employment of doctoral degree graduates: Enrolled in a psychology doctoral program (n/a), enrolled in a postdoctoral residency/fellowship (7), employed in an academic position at a university (2), total from the above (doctoral) (9).

Additional Information:

Orientation, Objectives, and Emphasis of Department: Though oriented toward research and teaching, graduate training in psychology also shows concern for the applications of psychology. In addition to completing the required coursework, students in all specialty areas are expected to engage in empirical research throughout graduate study. Areas of specialization include clinical psychology, child development, adult development and aging, cognitive psychology, behavioral neuroscience, quantitative, and social psychology. Within the clinical science program, there are formal tracks in clinical aging and child and family. The APA-approved clinical program incorporates the scientist–practitioner model and prepares students for careers in teaching and research, as well as in empirically oriented applied settings.

Special Facilities or Resources: We are housed in the upper six floors of a 10 story building. Ample laboratory and office space are supplemented by facilities in the Hedco Neurosciences building that is adjacent to the main Psychology building. The Dornsife Cognitive Neuroscience Imaging Center, attached to the Psychology building, makes available a state-of-the-art fMRI imaging facility for faculty and student research.

Information for Students With Physical Disabilities: See the following Web site for more information: http://www.usc.edu/student-affairs/asn/DSP/.

Application Information:

Send to Irene Takaragawa, Graduate Advisor, Department of Psychology/SGM 508, University of Southern California, Los Angeles, CA 90089-1061. Application available online. URL of online application: http://www.usc.edu/admission/graduate/apply/. Students are admitted in the Fall, application deadline December 1. *Fee:* $85. Must send to the Office of Graduate and International Admissions, USC, Los Angeles, CA 90089-0915, the most current financial aid statement from current/last school of enrollment.

Southern California, University of, Keck School of Medicine

Department of Preventive Medicine, Division of Health Behavior Research
USC/IPR, 1000 South Fremont Avenue, Unit 8
Attn: Marny Barovich
Alhambra, CA 91803
Telephone: (626) 457-6648
Fax: (626) 457-4012
E-mail: *barovich@usc.edu*
Web: *http://www.usc.edu/medicine/hbrphd*

Department Information:

1984. Director: Mary Ann Pentz. Number of faculty: total—full-time 17, part-time 1; women—full-time 13, part-time 1; ; women minority—full-time 1.

Programs and Degrees Offered:

Listed in the following order: Program area, degree type (T if terminal Master's), number awarded 7/06–6/07. Health Behavior Research PhD (Doctor of Philosophy) 3.

Student Applications/Admissions:

Student Applications

Health Behavior Research PhD (Doctor of Philosophy)—Applications 2007–2008, 30. Total applicants accepted 2007–2008, 2. Number full-time enrolled (new admits only) 2007–2008, 2. Number part-time enrolled (new admits only) 2007–2008, 0. Openings 2008–2009, 4. The median number of years required for completion of a degree in 2006–2007 were 4. The number of students enrolled full- and part-time who were dismissed or voluntarily withdrew from this program area in 2007–2008 were 0.

Admissions Requirements:

Scores: Entries appear in this order: required test or GPA, minimum score (if required), median score of students entering in 2007–2008. Doctoral Programs: GRE-V 500, 550; GRE-Q 500, 620; overall undergraduate GPA 3.0, 3.54. A master's degree is not required. The 3.4 minimum master's GPA is preferred.

Other Criteria: (importance of criteria rated low, medium, or high): GRE/MAT scores—high, research experience—medium, work experience—low, extracurricular activity—low, GPA—high, letters of recommendation—high, interview—low, statement of goals and objectives—high, undergraduate major in psychology—low. Students are invited to interview (via telephone is OK), but interviews are not required. For additional information on admission requirements, go to http://www.usc.edu/medicine/hbrphd.

Student Characteristics: The following represents characteristics of students in 2007–2008 in all graduate psychology programs in the department: Female—full-time 23, part-time 0; Male—full-time 5, part-time 0; African American/Black—full-time 1, part-time 0; Hispanic/Latino(a)—full-time 3, part-time 0; Asian/Pacific Islander—full-time 8, part-time 0; American Indian/Alaska Native—full-time 1, part-time 0; Caucasian/White—full-time 13, part-time 0; Multi-ethnic—full-time 2, part-time 0; students subject to the Americans With Disabilities Act—full-time 0, part-time 0; Unknown ethnicity—full-time 0, part-time 0; International students who hold an F-1 or J-1 Visa—full-time 0, part-time 0.

Financial Information/Assistance:

Tuition for Full-Time Study: *Doctoral:* State residents: per academic year $18,960, $1,185 per credit hour; Nonstate residents: per academic year $18,960, $1,185 per credit hour. Tuition is subject to change.

Financial Assistance:

First-Year Students: Teaching assistantships available for first year. Average amount paid per academic year: $28,222. Average number of hours worked per week: 20. Apply by February 1. Tuition remission given: full. Research assistantships available for first year. Average amount paid per academic year: $28,222. Average number of hours worked per week: 20. Apply by February 1. Tuition remission given: full. Traineeships available for first year. Average amount paid per academic year: $28,222. Average number of hours worked per week: 20. Apply by as available. Tuition remission given: full. Fellowships and scholarships available for first year. Average amount paid per academic year: $28,222. Average number of hours worked per week: 20. Apply by December 1. Tuition remission given: full.

Advanced Students: Teaching assistantships available for advanced students. Average amount paid per academic year: $28,222. Average number of hours worked per week: 20. Apply by no deadline. Tuition remission given: full. Research assistantships available for advanced students. Average amount paid per academic year: $28,222. Average number of hours worked per week: 20. Apply by no deadline. Tuition remission given: full. Traineeships available for advanced students. Average amount paid per academic year: $28,222. Average number of hours worked per week: 20. Apply by as available. Tuition remission given: full. Fellowships and scholarships available for advanced students. Average amount paid per academic year: $28,222. Average number of hours worked per week: 20. Apply by as available. Tuition remission given: full.

Additional Information: Of all students currently enrolled full time, 92% benefited from one or more of the listed financial assistance programs. Application and information available online at http://www.usc.edu/dept/GRADSCHL/.

Internships/Practica: Three practica in health behavior are available to doctoral students: prevention, compliance, and health behavior topics. Through the practica, students gain practical experience in a variety of field settings to gain a certain type of skill such as curriculum development, media production, and patient education.

Housing and Day Care: On-campus housing is available. See the following Web site for more information: http://www.housing.usc.edu. On-campus day care facilities are available. See the following Web site for more information: http://www.usc.edu/dept/admin ops/childcare/.

Employment of Department Graduates:

Master's Degree Graduates: Of those who graduated in the academic year 2006–2007, the following categories and numbers represent the postgraduate activities and employment of master's degree graduates: Enrolled in a postdoctoral residency/fellowship (n/a), employed in independent practice (n/a), total from the above (master's) (0).

Doctoral Degree Graduates: Of those who graduated in the academic year 2006–2007, the following categories and numbers represent the postgraduate activities and employment of doctoral degree graduates: Enrolled in a psychology doctoral program (n/a), enrolled in a postdoctoral residency/fellowship (1), employed in other positions at a higher education institution (1), employed in business or industry (1), total from the above (doctoral) (3).

Additional Information:

Orientation, Objectives, and Emphasis of Department: The University of Southern California (USC) School of Medicine, Department of Preventive Medicine, Division of Health Behavior Research, offers a doctorate in health behavior research (HBR), providing academic and research training for students interested in pursuing career opportunities in the field of health promotion and disease prevention research. The specific objective of the program is to train exceptional researchers and scholars in the multidisciplinary field of health behavior research who will apply this knowledge creatively to the goal of primary and secondary prevention of disease. Students receive well-rounded training that encompasses theory and methods from many allied fields, including communication, psychology, preventive medicine, statistics, public health, and epidemiology. Students receive research experience participating in projects conducted through the USC Institute for Health Promotion and Disease Prevention Research (IPR). Required core courses: foundations of health behavior, data analysis, behavioral epidemiology, biological basis of disease, basic theory and strategies in prevention, basic theories and strategies for compliance/adaptation, health behavior research methods, and research seminar in health behavior. In addition to core course requirements, the curriculum includes content courses from the Department of Preventive Medicine, Divisions of Biostatistics, Epidemiology, or Occupational Medicine.

Special Facilities or Resources: Faculty and other researchers at IPR are recognized leaders in community-based approaches to health promotion and disease prevention. The research at IPR integrates the scientific perspectives of epidemiology, the behavioral sciences, biology, communication, and policy research in disease etiology and prevention. IPR enjoys research collaborations in 10 schools and 35 departments within USC and with noted researchers and public health leaders in leading universities across the United States, Europe, Latin America, and Asia. IPR's faculty and researchers are world leaders in school- and community-based prevention, cancer epidemiology, tobacco control, drug abuse, childhood obesity, nutrition, physical activity, cardiovascular disease, diabetes, health disparities, and health communication campaigns for chronic disease prevention. IPR has three National Institutes of Health (NIH) funded transdisciplinary research centers that integrate theories and methods across multiple disciplines to approach the complex problems of tobacco use, drug abuse, and obesity prevention within diverse communities. Supported by the NCI, the National Institute on Drug Abuse (NIDA), and the Robert Wood Johnson Foundation, the USC Transdisciplinary Tobacco Use Research Center studies tobacco use and prevention among ethnically diverse adolescents in California, Hawaii, and China. The USC Center for Transdisciplinary Research on Energetics and Cancer, funded by NIDDK, addresses the physiological, metabolic, behavioral, genetic, and environmental influences on obesity, metabolic health and cancer risk with a focus on minority children. And the new Comprehensive Center of Excellence in Minority Health, funded by MCMHD, focuses on understanding why obesity and associated factors increase the risk for type-2 diabetes and cardiovascular disease within minority populations. All three centers also train students and faculty in transdisciplinary approaches to research.

Information for Students With Physical Disabilities: See the following Web site for more information: http://www.usc.edu/student-affairs/asn/dsp/index.htm.

Application Information:

Applications should be submitted online. If desired, any supplemental materials, copies of GRE and TOEFL scores, and letters of recommendation may be sent to Doctoral Program Admissions (attn: Marny Barovich), USC/IPR, 1000 South Fremont Avenue, Unit 8 (suite #4203 if sending via express mail), Alhambra, CA 91803. Application available online. URL of online application: http://www.usc.edu/admission/graduate. Students are admitted in the Fall, application deadline February 1. The official deadline is February 1. We fund the majority of our students through graduate assistantships, although a few students have received All-University Predoctoral Diversity Fellowships. Students are also eligible for the Provost Graduate Fellowships (see online application information) and some are eligible for the Chen fellowship. To be considered for these awards, applications must be submitted by December 1. *Fee:* $85.

Stanford University

Department of Psychology
Humanities & Sciences
Building 420
Stanford, CA 94305-2130
Telephone: (650) 725-2400
Fax: (650) 736-2029
E-mail: *wandell@stanford.edu*
Web: *http://www.psychology.stanford.edu/*

Department Information:

1892. Chairperson: Brian Wandell. Number of faculty: total—full-time 29, part-time 1; women—full-time 11; total—minority—full-time 4; women minority—full-time 2.

Programs and Degrees Offered:

Listed in the following order: Program area, degree type (T if terminal Master's), number awarded 7/06–6/07. Concentration in Cognitive Psychology PhD (Doctor of Philosophy) 3, Concentration in Social Psychology PhD (Doctor of Philosophy) 3, Concentration in Area of Neuroscience PhD (Doctor of Philosophy) 2, Concentration in Personality Psychology PhD (Doctor of Philosophy) 1, Concentration in Developmental Psychology PhD (Doctor of Philosophy) 0.

Student Applications/Admissions:

Student Applications

Concentration in Cognitive Psychology PhD (Doctor of Philosophy)—Applications 2007–2008, 73. Total applicants accepted 2007–2008, 3. Number full-time enrolled (new admits only) 2007–2008, 3. Number part-time enrolled (new admits only) 2007–2008, 0. Openings 2008–2009, 3. The median number of years required for completion of a degree in 2006–2007 were 5. The number of students enrolled full- and part-time who were dismissed or voluntarily withdrew from this program area in 2007–2008 were 0. *Concentration in Social Psychology PhD (Doctor of Philosophy)*—Applications 2007–2008, 109. Total applicants accepted 2007–2008, 3. Number full-time enrolled (new admits only) 2007–2008, 3. Number part-time enrolled (new admits only) 2007–2008, 0. Openings 2008–2009, 3. The median number of years required for completion of a degree in 2006–2007 were 5. The number of students enrolled full- and part-time who were dismissed or voluntarily withdrew from this program area in 2007–2008 were 0. *Concentration in Area of Neuroscience PhD (Doctor of Philosophy)*—Applications 2007–2008, 41. Total applicants accepted 2007–2008, 0. Number full-time enrolled (new admits only) 2007–2008, 0. Number part-time enrolled (new admits only) 2007–2008, 0. Openings 2008–2009, 3. The median number of years required for completion of a degree in 2006–2007 were 5. The number of students enrolled full- and part-time who were dismissed or voluntarily withdrew from this program area in 2007–2008 were 0. *Concentration in Personality Psychology PhD (Doctor of Philosophy)*—Applications 2007–2008, 52. Total applicants accepted 2007–2008, 4. Number full-time enrolled (new admits only) 2007–2008, 4. Number part-time enrolled (new admits only) 2007–2008, 0. Openings 2008–2009, 3. The median number of years required for completion of a degree in 2006–2007 were 5. The number of students enrolled full- and part-time who were dismissed or voluntarily withdrew from this program area in 2007–2008 were 1. *Concentration in Developmental Psychology PhD (Doctor of Philosophy)*—Applications 2007–2008, 34. Total applicants accepted 2007–2008, 2. Number full-time enrolled (new admits only) 2007–2008, 2. Number part-time enrolled (new admits only) 2007–2008, 0. Openings 2008–2009, 3. The median number of years required for completion of a degree in 2006–2007 were 5. The number of students enrolled full- and part-time who were dismissed or voluntarily withdrew from this program area in 2007–2008 were 1.

Admissions Requirements:

Scores: Entries appear in this order: required test or GPA, minimum score (if required), median score of students entering in 2007–2008. Doctoral Programs: GRE-V no minimum stated; GRE-Q no minimum stated; overall undergraduate GPA no minimum stated; psychology GPA no minimum stated; Doctoral program GRE-Analytic no minimum stated.

Other Criteria: (importance of criteria rated low, medium, or high): GRE/MAT scores—medium, research experience—high, work experience—low, extracurricular activity—low, clinically related public service—low, GPA—high, letters of recommendation—high, interview—high, statement of goals and objectives—high. For additional information on admission requirements, go to http://www.gradadmissions.stanford.edu.

Student Characteristics: The following represents characteristics of students in 2007–2008 in all graduate psychology programs in the department: Female—full-time 48, part-time 0; Male—full-time 33, part-time 0; African American/Black—full-time 4, part-time 0; Hispanic/Latino(a)—full-time 6, part-time 0; Asian/Pacific Islander—full-time 8, part-time 0; American Indian/Alaska Native—full-time 1, part-time 0; Caucasian/White—full-time 36, part-time 0; Multi-ethnic—full-time 0, part-time 0; students subject to the Americans With Disabilities Act—full-time 0, part-time 0; Unknown ethnicity—full-time 26, part-time 0; International students who hold an F-1 or J-1 Visa—full-time 11, part-time 0.

Financial Information/Assistance:

Financial Assistance:

First-Year Students: Teaching assistantships available for first year. Average amount paid per academic year: $27,569. Average number of hours worked per week: 20. Tuition remission given: full. Research assistantships available for first year. Average amount paid per academic year: $27,569. Average number of hours worked per week: 20. Tuition remission given: full. Traineeships available for first year. Average amount paid per academic year: $27,569. Average number of hours worked per week: 20. Tuition remission given: full. Fellowships and scholarships available for first year. Average amount paid per academic year: $27,569. Average number of hours worked per week: 20. Tuition remission given: full.

Advanced Students: Teaching assistantships available for advanced students. Average amount paid per academic year: $27,569. Average number of hours worked per week: 20. Tuition remission given: full. Research assistantships available for advanced students. Average amount paid per academic year: $27,569. Average number of hours worked per week: 20. Tuition remission given: full. Traineeships available for advanced students. Average amount paid per academic year: $27,569. Average number of hours worked per week: 20. Tuition remission given: full. Fellowships and scholarships available for advanced students. Average amount paid per academic year: $27,569. Average number of hours worked per week: 20. Tuition remission given: full.

Additional Information: Of all students currently enrolled full time, 90% benefited from one or more of the listed financial assistance programs. Application and information available online at http://www.psychology.stanford.edu.

Internships/Practica: No information provided.

Housing and Day Care: On-campus housing is available. See the following Web site for more information: http://www.stanford.edu/dept/hds/has/. On-campus day care facilities are available. See the following Web site for more information: http://www.worklife.stanford.edu/children_prog.html.

Employment of Department Graduates:

Master's Degree Graduates: Of those who graduated in the academic year 2006–2007, the following categories and numbers represent the postgraduate activities and employment of master's degree graduates: Enrolled in a postdoctoral residency/fellowship (n/a), employed in independent practice (n/a), total from the above (master's) (0).

Doctoral Degree Graduates: Of those who graduated in the academic year 2006–2007, the following categories and numbers represent the postgraduate activities and employment of doctoral degree graduates: Enrolled in a psychology doctoral program (n/a), total from the above (doctoral) (0).

Additional Information:

Orientation, Objectives, and Emphasis of Department: Please visit our Web site at http://www.psychology.stanford.edu for more information regarding our program.

Special Facilities or Resources: The department comprises facilities and personnel housed in Jordan Hall, where it maintains a psychology library and extensive laboratory and shop facilities, supervised by specialized technical assistants. Most of the laboratories are equipped with computer terminals linked directly to the university's computer center. Others are equipped with their own computers. In addition, the department has its own computer and a computer programmer on the psychology staff. The department maintains a nursery school close to the married students' housing area. This provides a laboratory for child observation, for training in nursery school practice, and for research.

Information for Students With Physical Disabilities: See the following Web site for more information: http://www.stanford.edu/group/DRC/.

Application Information:

Application will be accepted through our online application system, found at http://www.gradadmissions.stanford.edu. The rest of our program information can be found at the department Web site at http://psychology.stanford.edu/graduate_admissions.html. The department cannot provide any paper materials for admissions. Application available online. URL of online application: http://www.gradadmissions.stanford.edu. Students are admitted in the Fall, application deadline November 25. All materials (recommendations, transcripts, GRE general test scores and TOEFL test scores) must be in by the November 25 deadline. *Fee:* $105. Fee waiver from U.S. institutions only. Contact http://www.gradadmissions.stanford.edu for more information.

Vanguard University of Southern California

Graduate Program in Clinical Psychology
55 Fair Drive
Costa Mesa, CA 92626
Telephone: (714) 556-3610
Fax: (714) 662-5226
E-mail: *gradpsych@vanguard.edu*
Web: *http://www.vanguard.edu/gradpsych/*

Department Information:

1998. Director: Jerre White. Number of faculty: total—full-time 2, part-time 3; women—full-time 2, part-time 1.

Programs and Degrees Offered:

Listed in the following order: Program area, degree type (T if terminal Master's), number awarded 7/06–6/07. Clinical Psychology MA/MS (Master of Arts/Science) (T) 17.

Student Applications/Admissions:

Student Applications

Clinical Psychology MA/MS (Master of Arts/Science)—Applications 2007–2008, 95. Total applicants accepted 2007–2008, 46. Number full-time enrolled (new admits only) 2007–2008, 18. Number part-time enrolled (new admits only) 2007–2008, 9. Total enrolled 2007–2008 full-time, 45, part-time, 21. Openings 2008–2009, 25. The median number of years required for completion of a degree in 2006–2007 were 3. The number of students enrolled full- and part-time who were dismissed or voluntarily withdrew from this program area in 2007–2008 were 5.

Admissions Requirements:

Scores: Entries appear in this order: required test or GPA, minimum score (if required), median score of students entering in 2007–2008. Master's Programs: overall undergraduate GPA 2.5, 3.3; psychology GPA 3.0, 3.5.

Other Criteria: (importance of criteria rated low, medium, or high): research experience—low, work experience—medium, extracurricular activity—low, clinically related public service—medium, GPA—high, letters of recommendation—high, interview—medium, statement of goals and objectives—high, undergraduate major in psychology—low, specific undergraduate psychology courses taken—low. For additional information on admission requirements, go to http://www.vanguard.edu/GradPsych/.

Student Characteristics: The following represents characteristics of students in 2007–2008 in all graduate psychology programs in the department: Female—full-time 37, part-time 17; Male—full-time 8, part-time 4; African American/Black—full-time 1, part-time 0; Hispanic/Latino(a)—full-time 6, part-time 4; Asian/Pacific Islander—full-time 2, part-time 0; American Indian/Alaska Native—full-time 0, part-time 0; Caucasian/White—full-time 33, part-time 14; Multi-ethnic—full-time 0, part-time 1; students subject to the Americans With Disabilities Act—full-time 0, part-time 0; Unknown ethnicity—full-time 3, part-time 2.

Financial Information/Assistance:

Tuition for Full-Time Study: *Master's:* State residents: $674 per credit hour; Nonstate residents: $674 per credit hour. Tuition is subject to change. See the following Web site for updates and changes in tuition costs: http://www.vanguard.edu/gradadmissions/detail.aspx?doc_id=2458.

Financial Assistance:

First-Year Students: Fellowships and scholarships available for first year. Average amount paid per academic year: $1,200. Average number of hours worked per week: 0.

Advanced Students: Teaching assistantships available for advanced students. Average amount paid per academic year: $2,400. Average number of hours worked per week: 5. Research assistantships available for advanced students. Average amount paid per academic year: $2,400. Average number of hours worked per week: 5. Fellowships and scholarships available for advanced students. Average amount paid per academic year: $2,400. Average number of hours worked per week: 5.

Additional Information: Of all students currently enrolled full time, 65% benefited from one or more of the listed financial assistance programs. Application and information available online at http://www.vanguard.edu/gradadmissions/.

Internships/Practica: Master's Degree (MA/MS Clinical Psychology): An internship experience such as a final research project or "capstone" experience is required of graduates. Each student is required to complete a minimum of 150 client contact hours at approved practicum sites. These sites currently include domestic violence shelters, county agencies, community clinics, and student counseling centers serving a variety of populations.

Housing and Day Care: No on-campus housing is available. No on-campus day care facilities are available.

Employment of Department Graduates:

Master's Degree Graduates: Of those who graduated in the academic year 2006–2007, the following categories and numbers represent the postgraduate activities and employment of master's degree graduates: Enrolled in a psychology doctoral program (2), enrolled in another graduate/professional program (0), enrolled in a postdoctoral residency/fellowship (n/a), employed in independent practice (n/a), employed in an academic position at a university (0), employed in an academic position at a 2-year/4-year college (0), employed in other positions at a higher education institution (1), employed in a professional position in a school system (0), employed in business or industry (2), employed in government agency (0), employed in a community mental health/counseling center (12), employed in a hospital/medical center (2), still seeking employment (0), other employment position (0), do not know (0), total from the above (master's) (19).

Doctoral Degree Graduates: Of those who graduated in the academic year 2006–2007, the following categories and numbers represent the postgraduate activities and employment of doctoral degree graduates: Enrolled in a psychology doctoral program (n/a), total from the above (doctoral) (0).

Additional Information:

Orientation, Objectives, and Emphasis of Department: Vanguard University of Southern California is a university of Christian liberal arts and sciences. It is within this faith-based context that we offer a Master of Science in Clinical Psychology degree, which meets the educational requirements for licensure as a Marriage and Family Therapist in the state of California. The goal of the Graduate Program in Clinical Psychology is to equip its students to serve with excellence as Christian mental health professionals. Our goal is met by providing the highest quality of rigorous academic training, guided professional development, and integrative faith-based learning in a collaborative and supportive environment.

Special Facilities or Resources: None applicable.

Application Information:

Send to Graduate Admissions, 55 Fair Drive, Costa Mesa, CA 92626. Application available online. URL of online application: http://www.vanguard.edu/gradpsych/application/. Students are admitted in the Fall, application deadline April 1. *Fee:* $45.

Wright Institute
Graduate School of Psychology
2728 Durant Avenue
Berkeley, CA 94704
Telephone: (510) 841-9230
Fax: (510) 841-0167
E-mail: *info@wrightinst.edu*
Web: *http://www.wrightinst.edu*

Department Information:

1969. Dean: Charles Alexander, PhD. Number of faculty: total—full-time 7, part-time 23; women—full-time 5, part-time 19; women minority—full-time 3, part-time 3; faculty subject to the Americans With Disabilities Act 1.

Programs and Degrees Offered:

Listed in the following order: Program area, degree type (T if terminal Master's), number awarded 7/06–6/07. Clinical PsyD (Doctor of Psychology) 47.

APA Accreditation: Clinical PsyD (Doctor of Psychology).

Student Applications/Admissions:

Student Applications

Clinical PsyD (Doctor of Psychology)—Applications 2007–2008, 333. Total applicants accepted 2007–2008, 102. Number full-time enrolled (new admits only) 2007–2008, 68. Number part-time enrolled (new admits only) 2007–2008, 0. Openings 2008–2009, 57. The median number of years required for completion of a degree in 2006–2007 were 5. The number of students enrolled full- and part-time who were dismissed or voluntarily withdrew from this program area in 2007–2008 were 3.

Admissions Requirements:

Scores: Entries appear in this order: required test or GPA, minimum score (if required), median score of students entering in 2007–2008. Doctoral Programs: overall undergraduate GPA 3.0, 3.39. Because the Wright Institute seeks applicants with significant life accomplishment rather than those who simply test well, GRE scores are not factored into our admissions decision-making process. For research purposes, students are required to take the GRE General Test (which includes the analytic writing section) prior to matriculation.

Other Criteria: (importance of criteria rated low, medium, or high): research experience—medium, work experience—medium, extracurricular activity—medium, clinically related public service—high, GPA—medium, letters of recommendation—high, interview—high, statement of goals and objectives—high. For additional information on admission requirements, go to www.wrightinst.edu/ad/procedures.html.

Student Characteristics: The following represents characteristics of students in 2007–2008 in all graduate psychology programs in the department: Female—full-time 237, part-time 0; Male—full-time 82, part-time 0; African American/Black—full-time 9, part-time 0; Hispanic/Latino(a)—full-time 27, part-time 0; Asian/Pacific Islander—full-time 28, part-time 0; American Indian/Alaska Native—full-time 2, part-time 0; Caucasian/White—full-time 238, part-time 0; Multi-ethnic—full-time 15, part-time 0; students subject to the Americans With Disabilities Act—full-time 5, part-time 0; Unknown ethnicity—full-time 0, part-time 0; International students who hold an F-1 or J-1 Visa—full-time 5, part-time 0.

Financial Information/Assistance:

Tuition for Full-Time Study: *Doctoral:* State residents: per academic year $23,050; Nonstate residents: per academic year $23,050. Tuition is subject to change. See the following Web site for updates and changes in tuition costs: http://www.wrightinst.edu/ad/tuition.html.

Financial Assistance:

First-Year Students: Research assistantships available for first year. Average amount paid per academic year: $1,600. Average number of hours worked per week: 4. Apply by open.

Advanced Students: Teaching assistantships available for advanced students. Average amount paid per academic year: $1,980. Average number of hours worked per week: 5. Apply by open. Research assistantships available for advanced students. Average amount paid per academic year: $1,600. Average number of hours worked per week: 4. Apply by open. Fellowships and scholarships available for advanced students. Average amount paid per academic year: $2,000. Apply by December 1.

Additional Information: Of all students currently enrolled full time, 38% benefited from one or more of the listed financial assistance programs. Application and information available online at http://www.wrightinst.edu/admissions_aid.html.

Internships/Practica: Doctoral Degree (PsyD Clinical): For those doctoral students for whom a professional internship was required in this program prior to graduation, (60) students applied for an internship in 2006–2007, with (57) students obtaining an internship. Of those students who obtained an internship, (36) were paid internships. Of those students who obtained an internship, (18) students placed in APA/CPA-accredited internships, (11) students placed in internships not APA/CPA-accredited, but listed with the Association of Psychology Postdoctoral and Internship Centers (APPIC), (0) students placed in internships conforming to guidelines of the Council of Directors of School Psychology Programs (CDSPP), (28) students placed in internships that were not APA/CPA-accredited, APPIC or CDSPP listed. The goal of the Wright Institute's field training program, which culminates with the clinical internship, is to enable students to integrate theoretical knowledge with professional clinical experience. Beginning with the 1st-year practicum, and in conjunction with the weekly case conference/professional development seminar, students learn how to work with a wide range of populations, treatment modalities, and professional roles. The Institute's Field Placement Office furnishes information and support to students in the practicum and internship application and selection processes. Students are encouraged to conduct their internships at APA-approved agencies. Wright Institute students are highly valued by the nation's most well-regarded internship sites, as they are by local Bay Area hospitals, clinics, and community mental health centers. The broad range of internship and practicum sites allows sudents to receive training in a variety of clinical settings serving the ethnically and culturally diverse populations of the greater Bay Area. The SF Bay Area has an established internship community, most of whom are members of the California Psychology Internship Council (CAPIC). The Board of Psychology in California recognizes a formal internship as a program accredited by the APA or which is a member of or meets the membership requirements of APPIC or CAPIC. Because many of our students are established residents of the SF Bay Area, we allow students to apply to APPIC and CAPIC member programs. Our students who apply throughout the nation for APA internships are generally successful. For additional information on education and training outcomes for our programs, see the following Web site: http://www.wrightinst.edu/admissions_internships.html.

Housing and Day Care: No on-campus housing is available. No on-campus day care facilities are available.

Employment of Department Graduates:

Master's Degree Graduates: Of those who graduated in the academic year 2006–2007, the following categories and numbers represent the postgraduate activities and employment of master's degree graduates: Enrolled in a psychology doctoral program (0), enrolled in a postdoctoral residency/fellowship (n/a), employed in independent practice (n/a), total from the above (master's) (0).

Doctoral Degree Graduates: Of those who graduated in the academic year 2006–2007, the following categories and numbers represent the postgraduate activities and employment of doctoral degree graduates: Enrolled in a psychology doctoral program (n/a), enrolled in another graduate/professional program (0), enrolled in a postdoctoral residency/fellowship (37), employed in independent practice (1), employed in an academic position at a university (1), employed in an academic position at a 2-year/4-year college (0), employed in other positions at a higher education institution (0), employed in a professional position in a school system (0), employed in business or industry (0), employed in government agency (0), employed in a community mental health/counseling center (1), employed in a hospital/medical center (0), still seeking employment (0), not seeking employment (0), other employment position (0), do not know (6), total from the above (doctoral) (46).

Additional Information:

Orientation, Objectives, and Emphasis of Department: The Wright Institute teaches the scientific knowledge base of clinical psychology, and enriches that learning by exploring the meanings of students' experiences with clients. This unique learning method enables students to formulate and address clinical problems by examining the lenses through which they filter experience. The Institute promotes that educational endeavor by teaching students to think rigorously and critically. The program helps students apply critical thinking skills to three fundamental areas: clinical theory and research, understanding of the self in social context, and appreciation of the interaction between clinician and client. The curriculum at the Institute solidly grounds students in science and research methods, while challenging them to explore the conscious and unconscious ways in which they and their clients influence the creation and direction of therapy. Coursework is integrated with practical experience, providing for the systematic, progressive acquisition of skills and knowledge. Weekly case conferences/professional development seminars, begun in the 1st year, and continuing over the course of the full 3 years of residency, provide a rich forum for developing and integrating theory, technique, and reflective judgment. Practica and internship experiences consolidate the applied aspects of theoretical knowledge. Education about the multiple roles of the modern psychologist—clinician, supervisor, consultant and advocate—prepares students for working in fulfilling ways amid the changing realities of the healthcare field.

Special Facilities or Resources: The Wright Institute is located in a three-story English Tudor-style building that underwent a $3.5 million dollar renovation in 2001. The building meets the highest seismic safety standards, is ADA compliant, and has completely new, environmentally sound electrical, plumbing, heating and air-conditioning systems. The Institute operates a well-respected, low-fee, on-site clinic that has been providing community mental health outpatient services for nearly 40 years. Services include intake diagnostic reports, individual and couples psychotherapy. Second-year Wright Institute students who are supervised by highly experienced adjunct clinical faculty staff the Clinic. Students also participate in a weekly 2-hour training conference. A database is maintained for research on the therapeutic process and related areas. The Institute's library provides free online access to major bibliographic databases including PsycINFO, the Dissertations and Theses database, and Mental Measurements Yearbook. These online resources are also available to students from their home computers.

Application Information:

Send to Admissions Director, The Wright Institute, 2728 Durant Avenue, Berkeley, CA 94704. Application available online. URL of online application: http://www.wrightinst.edu/ad/admissions.html. Students are admitted in the Fall, application deadline January 15. *Fee:* $50.

Colorado State University
Department of Psychology
Natural Sciences
200 West Lake Street, 1876 Campus Delivery
Fort Collins, CO 80523-1876
Telephone: (970) 491-6363
Fax: (970) 491-1032
E-mail: *ernest.chavez@colostate.edu*
Web: *http://www.colostate.edu/Depts/Psychology/graduate*

Department Information:

1962. Chairperson: Ernest L. Chavez. Number of faculty: total—full-time 31, part-time 4; women—full-time 16, part-time 3; total—minority—full-time 3; women minority—full-time 1.

Programs and Degrees Offered:

Listed in the following order: Program area, degree type (T if terminal Master's), number awarded 7/06–6/07. Counseling PhD (Doctor of Philosophy) 5, Industrial/Organizational PhD (Doctor of Philosophy) 1, Cognitive PhD (Doctor of Philosophy) 1, Applied Social PhD (Doctor of Philosophy) 2, Perceptual and Brian Science PhD (Doctor of Philosophy) 0.

APA Accreditation: Counseling PhD (Doctor of Philosophy).

Student Applications/Admissions:

Student Applications

Counseling PhD (Doctor of Philosophy)—Applications 2007–2008, 220. Total applicants accepted 2007–2008, 20. Number full-time enrolled (new admits only) 2007–2008, 11. Number part-time enrolled (new admits only) 2007–2008, 0. Total enrolled 2007–2008 full-time, 37, part-time, 6. Openings 2008–2009, 7. The median number of years required for completion of a degree in 2006–2007 were 6. The number of students enrolled full- and part-time who were dismissed or voluntarily withdrew from this program area in 2007–2008 were 1. *Industrial/Organizational PhD (Doctor of Philosophy)*—Applications 2007–2008, 58. Total applicants accepted 2007–2008, 13. Number full-time enrolled (new admits only) 2007–2008, 5. Number part-time enrolled (new admits only) 2007–2008, 0. Total enrolled 2007–2008 full-time, 22, part-time, 1. Openings 2008–2009, 5. The median number of years required for completion of a degree in 2006–2007 were 5. The number of students enrolled full- and part-time who were dismissed or voluntarily withdrew from this program area in 2007–2008 were 0. *Cognitive PhD (Doctor of Philosophy)*—Applications 2007–2008, 19. Total applicants accepted 2007–2008, 6. Number full-time enrolled (new admits only) 2007–2008, 5. Number part-time enrolled (new admits only) 2007–2008, 0. Openings 2008–2009, 3. The median number of years required for completion of a degree in 2006–2007 were 5. The number of students enrolled full- and part-time who were dismissed or voluntarily withdrew from this program area in 2007–2008 were 0. *Applied Social PhD (Doctor of Philosophy)*—Applications 2007–2008, 56. Total applicants accepted 2007–2008, 2. Number full-time enrolled (new admits only) 2007–2008, 0. Number part-time enrolled (new admits only) 2007–2008, 0. Total enrolled 2007–2008 full-time, 23, part-time, 1. Openings 2008–2009, 4. The median number of years required for completion of a degree in 2006–2007 were 5. The number of students enrolled full- and part-time who were dismissed or voluntarily withdrew from this program area in 2007–2008 were 0. *Perceptual and Brian Science PhD (Doctor of Philosophy)*—Applications 2007–2008, 23. Total applicants accepted 2007–2008, 4. Number full-time enrolled (new admits only) 2007–2008, 2. Number part-time enrolled (new admits only) 2007–2008, 0. Openings 2008–2009, 4. The median number of years required for completion of a degree in 2006–2007 were 5. The number of students enrolled full- and part-time who were dismissed or voluntarily withdrew from this program area in 2007–2008 were 0.

Admissions Requirements:

Scores: Entries appear in this order: required test or GPA, minimum score (if required), median score of students entering in 2007–2008. Master's Programs: GRE-V 500; GRE-Q 560; overall undergraduate GPA 3.6; last 2 years GPA no minimum stated; psychology GPA no minimum stated; Masters GRE-Analytical no minimum stated. GRE Psychology Subject score required for Industrial/Organizational Program, optional for all others Doctoral Programs: GRE-V 500; GRE-Q 560; GRE-Subject (Psychology) no minimum stated; overall undergraduate GPA 3.6; last 2 years GPA no minimum stated; psychology GPA no minimum stated; Doctoral program GRE-Analytic no minimum stated. GRE Psychology Subject score required for Industrial/Organizational Program; optional for all others.

Other Criteria: (importance of criteria rated low, medium, or high): GRE/MAT scores—medium, research experience—high, work experience—medium, extracurricular activity—medium, clinically related public service—medium, GPA—high, letters of recommendation—high, statement of goals and objectives—high. Scientific writing sample required by Applied Social and Industrial/Organizational Programs; optional for Cognitive.

Student Characteristics: The following represents characteristics of students in 2007–2008 in all graduate psychology programs in the department: Female—full-time 71, part-time 9; Male—full-time 26, part-time 5; African American/Black—full-time 0, part-time 0; Hispanic/Latino(a)—full-time 4, part-time 3; Asian/Pacific Islander—full-time 2, part-time 2; American Indian/Alaska Native—full-time 6, part-time 1; Caucasian/White—full-time 77, part-time 10; Multi-ethnic—full-time 0, part-time 0; students subject to the Americans With Disabilities Act—full-time 0, part-time 0; Unknown ethnicity—full-time 0, part-time 0; International students who hold an F-1 or J-1 Visa—full-time 3, part-time 0.

Financial Information/Assistance:

Tuition for Full-Time Study: *Master's:* State residents: per academic year $4,887, $346 per credit hour; Nonstate residents: per academic year $16,425, $987 per credit hour. *Doctoral:* State residents: per academic year $4,887, $346 per credit hour; Nonstate residents: per academic year $16,425, $987 per credit hour. Tuition is subject to change. See the following Web site for updates and changes in tuition costs: http://www.colostate.edu.

Financial Assistance:

First-Year Students: Teaching assistantships available for first year. Average amount paid per academic year: $12,169. Average number of hours worked per week: 20. Apply by January 15. Tuition remission given: full. Research assistantships available for first year. Average amount paid per academic year: $11,875. Average number of hours worked per week: 20. Apply by January 15. Tuition remission given: full. Fellowships and scholarships available for first year. Average amount paid per academic year: $1,500. Average number of hours worked per week: 0. Apply by January 15. Tuition remission given: partial.

Advanced Students: Teaching assistantships available for advanced students. Average amount paid per academic year: $12,169. Average number of hours worked per week: 20. Apply by January 15. Tuition remission given: full. Research assistantships available for advanced students. Average amount paid per academic year: $11,875. Average number of hours worked per week: 20. Apply by January 15. Tuition remission given: full. Traineeships available for advanced students. Tuition remission given: full. Fellowships and scholarships available for advanced students. Average amount paid per academic year: $1,500. Average number of hours worked per week: 0. Apply by January 15. Tuition remission given: partial.

Additional Information: Of all students currently enrolled full time, 98% benefited from one or more of the listed financial assistance programs. Application and information available online at http://www.colostate.edu/Depts/Psychology.

Internships/Practica: Doctoral Degree (PhD Counseling): For those doctoral students for whom a professional internship was required in this program prior to graduation, (6) students applied for an internship in 2006–2007, with (6) students obtaining an internship. Of those students who obtained an internship, (6) were paid internships. Of those students who obtained an internship, (6) students placed in APA/CPA-accredited internships, (0) students placed in internships not APA/CPA-accredited, but listed with the Association of Psychology Postdoctoral and Internship Centers (APPIC), (0) students placed in internships conforming to guidelines of the Council of Directors of School Psychology Programs (CDSPP), (0) students placed in internships that were not APA/CPA-accredited, APPIC or CDSPP listed. Completion of a five year excellence award (1998-2003) by the Colorado Commission on Higher Education allowed for the development of health-related practica for Counseling students throughout Northern Colorado. The following are examples: neuropsychology, local community college, primary health care, and school districts. Industrial Organizational students consult with a variety of businesses throughout the state including United Airlines, HP, Sun Systems, IBM, micorbreweries, and hospitals. The Tri Ethnic Center for Prevention Research (TEC) and the Colorado Injury Control Research Center (CICRC) are a part of the department. TEC was designated a Center of Research and Scholarly Excellence by the University in 1991, 1998, and again in 2004.

Housing and Day Care: On-campus housing is available. See the following Web site for more information: http://www.colostate.edu. On-campus day care facilities are available.

Employment of Department Graduates:

Master's Degree Graduates: Of those who graduated in the academic year 2006–2007, the following categories and numbers represent the postgraduate activities and employment of master's degree graduates: Enrolled in a psychology doctoral program (17), enrolled in a postdoctoral residency/fellowship (n/a), employed in independent practice (n/a), total from the above (master's) (17).

Doctoral Degree Graduates: Of those who graduated in the academic year 2006–2007, the following categories and numbers represent the postgraduate activities and employment of doctoral degree graduates: Enrolled in a psychology doctoral program (n/a), enrolled in a postdoctoral residency/fellowship (7), employed in a community mental health/counseling center (2), employed in a hospital/medical center (0), do not know (1), total from the above (doctoral) (10).

Additional Information:

Orientation, Objectives, and Emphasis of Department: Colorado State University offers graduate training leading to the MS and PhD degrees in applied social, cognitive, counseling, industrial/organizational psychology, and perceptual and brain science. A core program of study is required of all students in the first years of graduate work to insure a broad and thorough grounding in psychology. Graduate students in applied social, cognitive, and behavioral neuroscience areas take positions in academic, research, or government agencies. Industrial/organizational has opportunities for students to have experiences in selection techniques, occupational health psychology, assessment centers, organizational climate and structure, and consultation. Counseling students are trained in academic and applied skills with opportunities in behavior therapy, group techniques, assessment, outreach, consultation, and supervision. Emphasis is on diversity and breadth. In addition to the adult specialty, a program is available that will lead to a PhD in counseling psychology with advanced courses that deal with children and adolescents.

Special Facilities or Resources: Tri Ethnic Center for Prevention research, a NIDA, CDC, and Justice Department funded research center, focuses on adolescent issues such as substance use, violence, rural issues, and culturally appropriate prevention strategies. The CICR is currently in Year 1 of a 5-year second cycle of funding by the CDC, National Center for Injury Prevention and Control. CICR's focus is to address the prevention and control of injuries among rural and underserved populations.

Information for Students With Physical Disabilities: See the following Web site for more information: http://www.colostate.edu.

Application Information:

Send to Graduate Admissions Committee, Department of Psychology, Colorado State University, 1876 Campus Delivery, Fort Collins, CO 80526-1876. Application available online. URL of online application: http://www.colostate.edu/Depts/Psychology. Students are admitted in the Fall, application deadline January 15. Counseling—December 15 application deadline; Industrial/Organizational—January 1 application deadline. Please note that deadlines are strictly adhered to. *Fee:* $50.

Colorado, University of, at Colorado Springs (2007 data)

Department of Psychology
Letters, Arts, and Sciences
1420 Austin Bluffs Parkway, P.O. Box 7150
Colorado Springs, CO 80933-7150
Telephone: (719) 262-4500
Fax: (719) 262-4166
E-mail: *ddubois@uccs.edu*
Web: *http://www.uccs.edu/psych*

Department Information:

1965. Chairperson: Dr. Robert L. Durham. Number of faculty: total—full-time 14, part-time 14; women—full-time 6, part-time 7.

Programs and Degrees Offered:

Listed in the following order: Program area, degree type (T if terminal Master's), number awarded 7/06–6/07. Clinical Psychology MA/MS (Master of Arts/Science) (T) 8, General Experimental Psychology MA/MS (Master of Arts/Science) (T) 4, Clinical Psychology With Emphasis in Geropsychology PhD (Doctor of Philosophy) 0.

Student Applications/Admissions:

Student Applications

Clinical Psychology MA/MS (Master of Arts/Science)—Applications 2007–2008, 42. Total applicants accepted 2007–2008, 14. Number full-time enrolled (new admits only) 2007–2008, 5. Openings 2008–2009, 12. The number of students enrolled full- and part-time who were dismissed or voluntarily withdrew from this program area in 2007–2008 were 1. *General Experimental Psychology MA/MS (Master of Arts/Science)*—Applications 2007–2008, 10. Total applicants accepted 2007–2008, 6. Number full-time enrolled (new admits only) 2007–2008, 3. Total enrolled 2007–2008 full-time, 12. Openings 2008–2009, 5. The number of students enrolled full- and part-time who were dismissed or voluntarily withdrew from this program area in 2007–2008 were 0. *Clinical Psychology With Emphasis in Geropsychology PhD (Doctor of Philosophy)*—Applications 2007–2008, 21. Total applicants accepted 2007–2008, 6. Number full-time enrolled (new admits only) 2007–2008, 3. Openings 2008–2009, 5. The number of students enrolled full- and part-time who were dismissed or voluntarily withdrew from this program area in 2007–2008 were 0.

Admissions Requirements:

Scores: Entries appear in this order: required test or GPA, minimum score (if required), median score of students entering in 2007–2008. Master's Programs: GRE-V no minimum stated, 485; GRE-Q no minimum stated, 565; overall undergraduate GPA 2.75, 3.54. Doctoral Programs: GRE-V no minimum stated, 485; GRE-Q no minimum stated, 565; overall undergraduate GPA 2.75, 3.54.

Other Criteria: (importance of criteria rated low, medium, or high): GRE/MAT scores—medium, research experience—high, work experience—low, extracurricular activity—medium, clinically related public service—high, GPA—medium, letters of recommendation—high, statement of goals and objectives—high. Clinically related public service is not required for experimental.

Student Characteristics: The following represents characteristics of students in 2007–2008 in all graduate psychology programs in the department: Female—full-time 33, part-time 0; Male—full-time 10, part-time 0; African American/Black—full-time 0, part-time 0; Hispanic/Latino(a)—full-time 1, part-time 0; Asian/Pacific Islander—full-time 3, part-time 0; American Indian/Alaska Native—full-time 0, part-time 0; Caucasian/White—full-time 39, part-time 0; Multi-ethnic—full-time 0, part-time 0; students subject to the Americans With Disabilities Act—full-time 1, part-time 0; Unknown ethnicity—full-time 0, part-time 0.

Financial Information/Assistance:

Tuition for Full-Time Study: *Master's:* State residents: $232 per credit hour; Nonstate residents: $915 per credit hour. *Doctoral:* State residents: $232 per credit hour; Nonstate residents: $915 per credit hour. Tuition is subject to change. Tuition costs vary by program. See the following Web site for updates and changes in tuition costs: http://www.uccs.edu/%7Ebursar/site/tuition.htm.

Financial Assistance:

First-Year Students: Teaching assistantships available for first year. Research assistantships available for first year. Fellowships and scholarships available for first year.

Advanced Students: Teaching assistantships available for advanced students. Research assistantships available for advanced students. Fellowships and scholarships available for advanced students.

Additional Information: Of all students currently enrolled full time, 65% benefited from one or more of the listed financial assistance programs. Application and information available online at http://www.uccs.edu/%7Efinaidse/index.html.

Internships/Practica: Practicum experiences are completed at the departmental CU Aging Center, the CU Counseling Center, or in community placements under licensed supervision (e.g., school settings, community health centers, state mental health facility, domestic violence center, inpatient psychiatric hospital). The goal of these experiences is to expose students to clinical settings, to roles of clinical psychologists, and to begin the development of clinical skills.

Housing and Day Care: On-campus housing is available. See the following Web site for more information: http://www.web.uccs.edu/housing/. On-campus day care facilities are available. See the following Web site for more information: http://www.web.uccs.edu/fdc/default.htm.

Employment of Department Graduates:

Master's Degree Graduates: Of those who graduated in the academic year 2006–2007, the following categories and numbers represent the postgraduate activities and employment of master's degree graduates: Enrolled in a postdoctoral residency/fellowship (n/a), employed in independent practice (n/a), total from the above (master's) (0).

Doctoral Degree Graduates: Of those who graduated in the academic year 2006–2007, the following categories and numbers represent the postgraduate activities and employment of doctoral

degree graduates: Enrolled in a psychology doctoral program (n/a), total from the above (doctoral) (0).

Additional Information:

Orientation, Objectives, and Emphasis of Department: The program places special emphasis in general areas of applied clinical practice and general experimental psychology. The training will enable a student to prepare for a doctoral program, teach in community colleges, work under a licensed psychologist in private and public agencies, or work in university counseling centers. A research thesis is required of all students. There is a broad range of faculty research interests including aging (e.g., psychopathology and psychological treatment of older adults, family dynamics, self-concept development, memory, cognition, and personality), social psychology, psychology and the law, personality, program evaluation, prevention of child abuse, and psychological trauma. Please see our Web site for additional information.

Special Facilities or Resources: Research facilities include clinical training laboratories with observational capabilities, laboratories for individual and small group research, a psychophysiological laboratory, and a computer laboratory. Columbine Hall houses a 50-station computer lab that is available for general use. The CU Aging Center, administered through the Psychology Department, is a community-based nonprofit mental health clinic designed to serve the mental health needs of older adults and their families. The mission of the Center is to provide state-of-the-art psychological assessment and treatment services to older persons and their families, to study psychological aging processes, and to train students in clinical psychology and related disciplines.

Application Information:

Send to Dr. Hasker P. Davis, Director of Graduate Studies/Psychology Department. Application available online. URL of online application: http://www.web.uccs.edu/gradschl/app/. Students are admitted in the Fall, application deadline January 1. *Fee:* $60.

Colorado, University of, Boulder

Department of Psychology
Arts and Sciences
Muenzinger D244, UCB 345
Boulder, CO 80309-0345
Telephone: (303) 492-8662
Fax: (303) 492-2967
E-mail: *asst.to.chair@psych.Colorado.EDU*
Web: *http://www.psych.colorado.edu*

Department Information:

1910. Chairperson: Lewis O. Harvey, Jr. Number of faculty: total—full-time 20, part-time 1; women—full-time 20; ; women minority—full-time 4.

Programs and Degrees Offered:

Listed in the following order: Program area, degree type (T if terminal Master's), number awarded 7/06–6/07. Behavioral Genetics PhD (Doctor of Philosophy) 2, Behavior Neuroscience PhD (Doctor of Philosophy) 2, Clinical Psychology PhD (Doctor of Philosophy) 4, Cognitive Psychology PhD (Doctor of Philosophy) 1, Social Psychology PhD (Doctor of Philosophy) 1.

APA Accreditation: Clinical PhD (Doctor of Philosophy).

Student Applications/Admissions:

Student Applications

Behavioral Genetics PhD (Doctor of Philosophy)—Applications 2007–2008, 91. Total applicants accepted 2007–2008, 4. Number full-time enrolled (new admits only) 2007–2008, 3. Openings 2008–2009, 3. The median number of years required for completion of a degree in 2006–2007 were 4. *Behavior Neuroscience PhD (Doctor of Philosophy)*—Applications 2007–2008, 59. Total applicants accepted 2007–2008, 4. Number full-time enrolled (new admits only) 2007–2008, 4. Openings 2008–2009, 3. The median number of years required for completion of a degree in 2006–2007 were 5. The number of students enrolled full- and part-time who were dismissed or voluntarily withdrew from this program area in 2007–2008 were 0. *Clinical Psychology PhD (Doctor of Philosophy)*—Applications 2007–2008, 199. Total applicants accepted 2007–2008, 6. Number full-time enrolled (new admits only) 2007–2008, 1. Openings 2008–2009, 5. The median number of years required for completion of a degree in 2006–2007 were 6. The number of students enrolled full- and part-time who were dismissed or voluntarily withdrew from this program area in 2007–2008 were 0. *Cognitive Psychology PhD (Doctor of Philosophy)*—Applications 2007–2008, 78. Total applicants accepted 2007–2008, 8. Number full-time enrolled (new admits only) 2007–2008, 3. Total enrolled 2007–2008 full-time, 24. Openings 2008–2009, 4. The median number of years required for completion of a degree in 2006–2007 were 5. The number of students enrolled full- and part-time who were dismissed or voluntarily withdrew from this program area in 2007–2008 were 0. *Social Psychology PhD (Doctor of Philosophy)*—Applications 2007–2008, 102. Total applicants accepted 2007–2008, 4. Number full-time enrolled (new admits only) 2007–2008, 4. Openings 2008–2009, 3. The median number of years required for completion of a degree in 2006–2007 were 5. The number of students enrolled full- and part-time who were dismissed or voluntarily withdrew from this program area in 2007–2008 were 1.

Admissions Requirements:

Scores: Entries appear in this order: required test or GPA, minimum score (if required), median score of students entering in 2007–2008. Doctoral Programs: GRE-V no minimum stated, 600; GRE-Q no minimum stated, 670; overall undergraduate GPA no minimum stated, 3.5. GRE Subject test is required for the clinical program; for the other programs it is recommended but not required.

Other Criteria: (importance of criteria rated low, medium, or high): GRE/MAT scores—high, research experience—high, work experience—medium, extracurricular activity—medium, clinically related public service—medium, GPA—high, letters of recommendation—high, interview—high, statement of goals and objectives—high. Clinical work experience is only relevant in clinical program. Research experience is critical to admissions to all programs. For additional information on admission requirements, go to http://psych.colorado.edu.

Student Characteristics: The following represents characteristics of students in 2007–2008 in all graduate psychology programs

in the department: Female—full-time 60, part-time 0; Male—full-time 35, part-time 0; African American/Black—full-time 1, part-time 0; Hispanic/Latino(a)—full-time 8, part-time 0; Asian/Pacific Islander—full-time 3, part-time 0; American Indian/Alaska Native—full-time 1, part-time 0; Caucasian/White—full-time 75, part-time 0; Multi-ethnic—full-time 1, part-time 0; students subject to the Americans With Disabilities Act—full-time 1, part-time 0; Unknown ethnicity—full-time 6, part-time 0; International students who hold an F-1 or J-1 Visa—full-time 4, part-time 0.

Financial Information/Assistance:

Tuition for Full-Time Study: *Doctoral:* State residents: $335 per credit hour; Nonstate residents: $717 per credit hour. Tuition is not available at this time. Tuition is subject to change. See the following Web site for updates and changes in tuition costs: http://www.bursar.colorado.edu/now/tuitfeebill.html.

Financial Assistance:

First-Year Students: Teaching assistantships available for first year. Average number of hours worked per week: 20. Tuition remission given: full. Research assistantships available for first year. Average number of hours worked per week: 20. Tuition remission given: full. Traineeships available for first year. Average amount paid per academic year: $20,000. Average number of hours worked per week: 20. Tuition remission given: full. Fellowships and scholarships available for first year.

Advanced Students: Teaching assistantships available for advanced students. Average number of hours worked per week: 20. Tuition remission given: full. Research assistantships available for advanced students. Average amount paid per academic year: $13,334. Average number of hours worked per week: 20. Tuition remission given: full. Traineeships available for advanced students. Average amount paid per academic year: $20,000. Average number of hours worked per week: 20. Tuition remission given: full. Fellowships and scholarships available for advanced students.

Additional Information: Of all students currently enrolled full time, 98% benefited from one or more of the listed financial assistance programs. Application and information available online at: http://psych.colorado.edu.

Internships/Practica: No information provided.

Housing and Day Care: On-campus housing is available. See the following Web site for more information: http://www.housing.colorado.edu. On-campus day care facilities are available. See the following Web site for more information: http://www.housing.colorado.edu/fh/fh_childrens_center.cfm.

Employment of Department Graduates:

Master's Degree Graduates: Of those who graduated in the academic year 2006–2007, the following categories and numbers represent the postgraduate activities and employment of master's degree graduates: Enrolled in a postdoctoral residency/fellowship (n/a), employed in independent practice (n/a), total from the above (master's) (0).

Doctoral Degree Graduates: Of those who graduated in the academic year 2006–2007, the following categories and numbers represent the postgraduate activities and employment of doctoral degree graduates: Enrolled in a psychology doctoral program (n/a), enrolled in a postdoctoral residency/fellowship (8), employed in an academic position at a university (5), employed in an academic position at a 2-year/4-year college (1), employed in other positions at a higher education institution (5), employed in a community mental health/counseling center (4), do not know (1), total from the above (doctoral) (24).

Additional Information:

Orientation, Objectives, and Emphasis of Department: Our emphasis is on training graduate students who have the capability to advance knowledge in the field and who are committed to applying their knowledge. We emphasize rigorous training in both the theory and methods of psychological research.

Special Facilities or Resources: The department is housed in a large and modern four-story building that contains ample space for offices, a clinic, and research laboratories. There are extensive research facilities available to students, both in individual laboratories and from the department generally. The department maintains its own network of Macintosh, Linux, and Windows computers used for data collection, data analysis, and manuscript preparation. There is also a departmental laboratory of Macintosh and DOS personal computers for real-time data collection. In addition, numerous laboratories in the department have their own computing capabilities. The facilities of the Institute of Behavioral Genetics, the Institute of Behavioral Science, the Institute of Cognitive Science, and the Center for Neuroscience are available to students. Each of these institutes has its own laboratory space and specialized computer facilities. In addition, they attract a number of scholars from other disciplines on the campus.

Information for Students With Physical Disabilities: See the following Web site for more information: http://www.colorado.edu/disabilityservices/.

Application Information:

Send to Department of Psychology, Muenzinger Psychology Building, UCB 345, Boulder, CO 80309-0345. Application available online. URL of online application: http://www.psych.colorado.edu/grad-appinfo.html. Students are admitted in the Fall, application deadline December 15. Clinical: December 15; others January 1. *Fee:* $50; $70 foreign students.

Colorado, University of, Boulder (2007 data)

Educational Psychological Studies
School of Education
249 UCB
Boulder, CO 80309-0249
Telephone: (303) 492-8391
Fax: (303) 492-7090
E-mail: *Steven.Guberman@Colorado.EDU*
Web: *http://www.colorado.edu/education*

Department Information:

Program Chair: Steven R. Guberman. Number of faculty: total—full-time 5; women—full-time 2.

Programs and Degrees Offered:

Listed in the following order: Program area, degree type (T if terminal Master's), number awarded 7/06–6/07. Educational Psychological Studies MA/MS (Master of Arts/Science) (T) 0, Educational Psychological Studies PhD (Doctor of Philosophy) 0.

Student Applications/Admissions:

Student Applications

Educational Psychological Studies MA/MS (Master of Arts/Science)—Applications 2007–2008, 4. Total applicants accepted 2007–2008, 0. Number full-time enrolled (new admits only) 2007–2008, 0. Total enrolled 2007–2008 full-time, 2. Openings 2008–2009, 3. The median number of years required for completion of a degree in 2006–2007 were 2. The number of students enrolled full- and part-time who were dismissed or voluntarily withdrew from this program area in 2007–2008 were 0. *Educational Psychological Studies PhD (Doctor of Philosophy)*—Applications 2007–2008, 10. Total applicants accepted 2007–2008, 2. Number full-time enrolled (new admits only) 2007–2008, 1. Total enrolled 2007–2008 full-time, 15. Openings 2008–2009, 5. The median number of years required for completion of a degree in 2006–2007 were 6. The number of students enrolled full- and part-time who were dismissed or voluntarily withdrew from this program area in 2007–2008 were 1.

Admissions Requirements:

Scores: Entries appear in this order: required test or GPA, minimum score (if required), median score of students entering in 2007–2008. Master's Programs: GRE-V no minimum stated; GRE-Q no minimum stated; overall undergraduate GPA 3.0; last 2 years GPA no minimum stated; Masters GRE-Analytical no minimum stated. Doctoral Programs: GRE-V no minimum stated; GRE-Q no minimum stated; overall undergraduate GPA 3.0; last 2 years GPA no minimum stated; Doctoral program GRE-Analytic no minimum stated.

Other Criteria: (importance of criteria rated low, medium, or high): GRE/MAT scores—high, research experience—medium, work experience—medium, extracurricular activity—low, GPA—high, letters of recommendation—high, interview—medium, statement of goals and objectives—high. Interviews (in person or by phone) are not generally required; however, when scheduled, are helpful in the selection process. For additional information on admission requirements, go to http://www.colorado.edu/education/prospective/gradprograms.html.

Student Characteristics: The following represents characteristics of students in 2007–2008 in all graduate psychology programs in the department: Female—full-time 13, part-time 0; Male—full-time 4, part-time 0; African American/Black—full-time 0, part-time 0; Hispanic/Latino(a)—full-time 1, part-time 0; Asian/Pacific Islander—full-time 0, part-time 0; American Indian/Alaska Native—full-time 0, part-time 0; Caucasian/White—full-time 16, part-time 0; Multi-ethnic—full-time 0, part-time 0; students subject to the Americans With Disabilities Act—full-time 0, part-time 0; Unknown ethnicity—full-time 0, part-time 0.

Financial Information/Assistance:

Tuition for Full-Time Study: *Master's:* State residents: per academic year $6,570, $365 per credit hour; Nonstate residents: per academic year $21,726, $1,207 per credit hour. *Doctoral:* State residents: per academic year $6,570, $365 per credit hour; Nonstate residents: per academic year $21,726, $1,207 per credit hour. Tuition is subject to change. See the following Web site for updates and changes in tuition costs: http://www.colorado.edu/prospective/graduate/finances/index.html.

Financial Assistance:

First-Year Students: Teaching assistantships available for first year. Average amount paid per academic year: $15,200. Average number of hours worked per week: 10. Apply by January 1. Tuition remission given: full and partial. Research assistantships available for first year. Average amount paid per academic year: $15,200. Average number of hours worked per week: 10. Apply by January 1. Tuition remission given: full and partial. Fellowships and scholarships available for first year. Average amount paid per academic year: $15,200. Average number of hours worked per week: 10. Apply by January 1. Tuition remission given: full and partial.

Advanced Students: Teaching assistantships available for advanced students. Average amount paid per academic year: $15,200. Average number of hours worked per week: 20. Tuition remission given: full and partial. Research assistantships available for advanced students. Average amount paid per academic year: $15,200. Average number of hours worked per week: 20. Tuition remission given: full and partial. Fellowships and scholarships available for advanced students. Average amount paid per academic year: $15,200. Average number of hours worked per week: 20. Tuition remission given: full and partial.

Additional Information: Of all students currently enrolled full time, 47% benefited from one or more of the listed financial assistance programs. Application and information available online at http://www.colorado.edu/education/prospective/gradprograms.html.

Internships/Practica: Because we do not offer a clinical program, we do not require internships or practica.

Housing and Day Care: On-campus housing is available. See the following Web site for more information: http://www.colorado.edu/prospective/graduate/studentlife/housing.html. On-campus day care facilities are available. See the following Web site for more information: http://www.colorado.edu/humres/childcare.

Employment of Department Graduates:

Master's Degree Graduates: Of those who graduated in the academic year 2006–2007, the following categories and numbers represent the postgraduate activities and employment of master's degree graduates: Enrolled in a psychology doctoral program (2), enrolled in a postdoctoral residency/fellowship (n/a), employed in independent practice (n/a), total from the above (master's) (2).

Doctoral Degree Graduates: Of those who graduated in the academic year 2006–2007, the following categories and numbers represent the postgraduate activities and employment of doctoral degree graduates: Enrolled in a psychology doctoral program (n/a), total from the above (doctoral) (0).

Additional Information:

Orientation, Objectives, and Emphasis of Department: Within the Educational and Psychological Studies Program, faculty and students collaborate to facilitate the development of research, theory, and professional knowledge with an emphasis on learning and teaching in K–12 educational settings. The Educational and Psychological Studies Program is structured in accordance with a scientist–practitioner model with primary emphasis given to academic study and research. Whether students are preparing for university research and teaching, work in K–12 education, or employment in the private sector, all develop an academic foundation in educational psychology. Onto that base, students and faculty advisors build programs of study that meet both the program goals and the student's interests. (Please note the School of Education does not offer programs in school psychology or counseling.) The educational psychology program is the only psychology-related program in the School of Education. Other programs are located in the College of Arts and Sciences.

Information for Students With Physical Disabilities: See the following Web site for more information: http://www.colorado.edu/disabilityservices/.

Application Information:
Send to Office of Student Services, School of Education, 249 UCB, University of Colorado, Boulder, CO 80309-0249. Application available online. URL of online application: http://www.colorado.edu/education/prospective/gradprograms.html. Students are admitted in the Fall, application deadline January 1. MA program: Summer and Fall admission deadline: February 1; Spring admission deadline: September 1. PhD program: Fall admission only, deadline: January 1. *Fee:* $50.

Colorado, University of, Denver

Department of Psychology
College of Liberal Arts and Sciences
Campus Box 173, P.O. Box 173364
Denver, CO 80217-3364
Telephone: (303) 556-8565
Fax: (303) 556-3520
E-mail: *gay.freebern@cudenver.edu*
Web: *http://www.thunder1.cudenver.edu/clas/psychology/gradPrograms.html*

Department Information:
1960. Director of Clinical Training: Allison Bashe, PhD. Number of faculty: total—full-time 13, part-time 2; women—full-time 6, part-time 1; total—minority—full-time 2; women minority—full-time 1.

Programs and Degrees Offered:
Listed in the following order: Program area, degree type (T if terminal Master's), number awarded 7/06–6/07. Clinical Psychology MA/MS (Master of Arts/Science) (T) 8, Clinical Health Psychology PhD (Doctor of Philosophy).

Student Applications/Admissions:
Student Applications
Clinical Psychology MA/MS (Master of Arts/Science)—Applications 2007–2008, 80. Total applicants accepted 2007–2008, 10. Number full-time enrolled (new admits only) 2007–2008, 10. Number part-time enrolled (new admits only) 2007–2008, 0. Openings 2008–2009, 10. The median number of years required for completion of a degree in 2006–2007 were 2. The number of students enrolled full- and part-time who were dismissed or voluntarily withdrew from this program area in 2007–2008 were 0. *Clinical Health Psychology PhD (Doctor of Philosophy)*—Applications 2007–2008, 20. Total applicants accepted 2007–2008, 5. Openings 2008–2009, 5.

Admissions Requirements:
Scores: Entries appear in this order: required test or GPA, minimum score (if required), median score of students entering in 2007–2008. Master's Programs: GRE-V 500, 580; GRE-Q 500, 650; overall undergraduate GPA 3.0, 3.74; last 2 years GPA 3.0, 3.76; psychology GPA 3.0, 3.91; Masters GRE-Analytical no minimum stated. Doctoral Programs: GRE-V 550; GRE-Q 550; GRE-Subject (Psychology) 550; overall undergraduate GPA 3.0; last 2 years GPA 3.5; psychology GPA 3.5; Doctoral program GRE-Analytic no minimum stated.
Other Criteria: (importance of criteria rated low, medium, or high): GRE/MAT scores—medium, research experience—high, work experience—medium, extracurricular activity—low, clinically related public service—low, GPA—high, letters of recommendation—high, interview—high, statement of goals and objectives—high, undergraduate major in psychology—low, specific undergraduate psychology courses taken—low. For additional information on admission requirements, go to http://thunder1.cudenver.edu/clas/psychology/gradPrograms.html.

Student Characteristics: The following represents characteristics of students in 2007–2008 in all graduate psychology programs in the department: Female—full-time 21, part-time 0; Male—full-time 9, part-time 0; African American/Black—full-time 0, part-time 0; Hispanic/Latino(a)—full-time 4, part-time 0; Asian/Pacific Islander—full-time 1, part-time 0; American Indian/Alaska Native—full-time 0, part-time 0; Caucasian/White—full-time 20, part-time 0; Multi-ethnic—full-time 2, part-time 0; students subject to the Americans With Disabilities Act—full-time 0, part-time 0; Unknown ethnicity—full-time 3, part-time 0; International students who hold an F-1 or J-1 Visa—full-time 1, part-time 0.

Financial Information/Assistance:
Tuition for Full-Time Study: *Master's:* State residents: per academic year $6,284, $337 per credit hour; Nonstate residents: per academic year $17,188, $1,029 per credit hour. *Doctoral:* State residents: per academic year $6,284, $337 per credit hour; Nonstate residents: per academic year $14,188, $1,029 per credit hour. Tuition is subject to change. Additional fees are assessed to students beyond the costs of tuition for the following: Transportation, technology, student services, etc. Tuition costs vary by program. See the following Web site for updates and changes in tuition costs: http://www.cudenver.edu/Admissions/Bursar/Tuition/Graduate/default.htm.

Financial Assistance:
First-Year Students: Teaching assistantships available for first year. Average amount paid per academic year: $5,800. Average number of hours worked per week: 10. Research assistantships available for first year. Average amount paid per academic year: $6,000. Average number of hours worked per week: 10. Fellowships and scholarships available for first year. Average amount paid per academic year: $15,000.
Advanced Students: Teaching assistantships available for advanced students. Average amount paid per academic year: $5,800. Average number of hours worked per week: 10. Research

assistantships available for advanced students. Average amount paid per academic year: $6,000. Average number of hours worked per week: 10.

Additional Information: Of all students currently enrolled full time, 100% benefited from one or more of the listed financial assistance programs. Application and information available online at: http://www.cudenver.edu/Admissions/Financial+Aid/default.htm.

Internships/Practica: Master's Degree (MA/MS Clinical Psychology): An internship experience such as a final research project or "capstone" experience is required of graduates. Internships and practica are widely available at several community agencies. Past students have completed internships at local hospitals, mental health centers, residential treatment centers, and the division of corrections. Funding (in the form of tuition vouchers) is available through the Americorps program. MA students may elect to complete both an internship and a thesis. Students electing the internship option may begin internships after completing the first year of courses. A total of 800 hours of supervised field experience is required for the full-time internship, and students may elect to do 200-, 400-, or 600-hour internships in addition to a thesis. All field placements must be approved by the director of clinical training in advance.

Housing and Day Care: On-campus housing is available. See the following Web site for more information: http://www.thunder1.cudenver.edu/housing/. On-campus day care facilities are available. See the following Web site for more information: http://www.tivoli.org/earlylearning/index.html.

Employment of Department Graduates:

Master's Degree Graduates: Of those who graduated in the academic year 2006–2007, the following categories and numbers represent the postgraduate activities and employment of master's degree graduates: Enrolled in a psychology doctoral program (5), enrolled in another graduate/professional program (2), enrolled in a postdoctoral residency/fellowship (n/a), employed in independent practice (n/a), employed in an academic position at a university (1), employed in other positions at a higher education institution (1), employed in a professional position in a school system (2), employed in business or industry (3), employed in a community mental health/counseling center (1), employed in a hospital/medical center (2), total from the above (master's) (17).

Doctoral Degree Graduates: Of those who graduated in the academic year 2006–2007, the following categories and numbers represent the postgraduate activities and employment of doctoral degree graduates: Enrolled in a psychology doctoral program (n/a), total from the above (doctoral) (0).

Additional Information:

Orientation, Objectives, and Emphasis of Department: Both programs adhere to the scientist–practitioner model, and training emphasizes the contribution of research to the understanding, treatment, and prevention of human problems, and the application of knowledge that is grounded in scientific evidence. Students in our clinical health PhD program will be trained to work within the community to use psychological tools and techniques to promote health, prevent and treat illness, and improve the health care system. In addition to coursework, students acquire expertise in research by completing a master's thesis and doctoral dissertation, and demonstrate competence in clinical assessment and intervention through several applied practicum experiences and a predoctoral internship. We will be seeking accreditation by the APA as a Clinical PhD. The principal objective of the clinical MA program is to prepare graduates for doctoral-level work. The program offers rigorous training in diagnostic evaluation, psychological assessment, and empirically based psychotherapy. After 1 year of coursework, students have the option of completing a thesis and/or an internship. Applied practicum and internship experiences can be completed with a wide variety of populations in the area. With the introduction of our PhD program, changes may occur to the MA program so please check our Web site frequently for updates.

Special Facilities or Resources: In July 2004, the University of Colorado, Downtown Denver Campus (our campus) merged with the University of Colorado Health Sciences Center. There are numerous possibilities for research collaborations with faculty at the Health Sciences Center (renamed Anschutz Medical Campus) in addition to the faculty members in our own department. There are also several affiliated institutions (e.g., AMC Cancer Research Center, The Children's Hospital and Kempe Center, Denver Health Medical Center, and National Jewish) in the area that provide additional opportunities for research collaborations and applied clinical work.

Information for Students With Physical Disabilities: See the following Web site for more information: http://www.cudenver.edu/Admissions/Registrar/Student+Resources/default.htm.

Application Information:

Send to Kimberly Hill, Program Assistant, Department of Psychology, University of Colorado Denver, Campus Box 173, P.O. Box 173364, Denver, CO 80217-3364. Application available online. URL of online application: http://www.cudenver.edu/Admissions/Graduate+Admissions/default.htm. Students are admitted in the Fall, application deadline December 15. PhD application deadline is December 15; MA application deadline for Fall enrollment is February 15; international students should send application materials at least 2 weeks before posted deadlines to ensure timely processing. *Fee:* $50. International student application fee: $75.

Denver, University of

Child, Family, and School Psychology Program
Morgridge College of Education
2450 South Vine Street
Denver, CO 80208
Telephone: (303) 871-2509
Fax: (303) 871-4456
E-mail: *edinfo@du.edu*
Web: *http://www.du.edu/education/programs/cfsp/index.html*

Department Information:

2003. Program Chair: Karin Dittrick-Nathan, PhD. Number of faculty: total—full-time 4, part-time 1; women—full-time 4, part-time 1.

Programs and Degrees Offered:

Listed in the following order: Program area, degree type (T if terminal Master's), number awarded 7/06–6/07. MA/MS (Master of Arts/Science) 4, EdS/MEd (School Psychology) 5, PhD (Doctor of Philosophy) 6.

Student Applications/Admissions:

Student Applications

MA/MS (Master of Arts/Science)—Applications 2007–2008, 12. Number full-time enrolled (new admits only) 2007–2008, 3. Number part-time enrolled (new admits only) 2007–2008, 1. Total enrolled 2007–2008 full-time, 5, part-time, 1. Openings 2008–2009, 5. The median number of years required for completion of a degree in 2006–2007 were 2. The number of students enrolled full- and part-time who were dismissed or voluntarily withdrew from this program area in 2007–2008 were 0. *EdS/MEd (School Psychology)*—Applications 2007–2008, 39. Number full-time enrolled (new admits only) 2007–2008, 10. Number part-time enrolled (new admits only) 2007–2008, 0. Total enrolled 2007–2008 full-time, 30, part-time, 1. Openings 2008–2009, 16. The median number of years required for completion of a degree in 2006–2007 were 4. The number of students enrolled full- and part-time who were dismissed or voluntarily withdrew from this program area in 2007–2008 were 0. *PhD (Doctor of Philosophy)*—Applications 2007–2008, 22. Total applicants accepted 2007–2008, 0. Number full-time enrolled (new admits only) 2007–2008, 4. Number part-time enrolled (new admits only) 2007–2008, 0. Total enrolled 2007–2008 full-time, 7, part-time, 2. Openings 2008–2009, 6. The median number of years required for completion of a degree in 2006–2007 were 4. The number of students enrolled full- and part-time who were dismissed or voluntarily withdrew from this program area in 2007–2008 were 0.

Admissions Requirements:

Scores: Entries appear in this order: required test or GPA, minimum score (if required), median score of students entering in 2007–2008. Master's Programs: GRE-V no minimum stated; GRE-Q no minimum stated; Masters GRE-Analytical no minimum stated. Doctoral Programs: GRE-V no minimum stated; GRE-Q no minimum stated; Doctoral program GRE-Analytic no minimum stated.

Other Criteria: (importance of criteria rated low, medium, or high): GRE/MAT scores—medium, research experience—medium, work experience—medium, extracurricular activity—medium, clinically related public service—medium, GPA—medium, letters of recommendation—medium, interview—high, statement of goals and objectives—medium. For additional information on admission requirements, go to http://www.du.edu/education/calls/admission.html.

Student Characteristics: The following represents characteristics of students in 2007–2008 in all graduate psychology programs in the department: Female—full-time 38, part-time 3; Male—full-time 4, part-time 1; African American/Black—full-time 0, part-time 0; Hispanic/Latino(a)—full-time 4, part-time 0; Asian/Pacific Islander—full-time 1, part-time 0; American Indian/Alaska Native—full-time 1, part-time 0; Caucasian/White—full-time 35, part-time 4; Multi-ethnic—full-time 0, part-time 0; students subject to the Americans With Disabilities Act—full-time 0, part-time 0; Unknown ethnicity—full-time 1, part-time 0; International students who hold an F-1 or J-1 Visa—full-time 0, part-time 0.

Financial Information/Assistance:

Tuition for Full-Time Study: *Master's:* State residents: $874 per credit hour; Nonstate residents: $874 per credit hour. *Doctoral:* State residents: $874 per credit hour; Nonstate residents: $874 per credit hour. Tuition is subject to change. Additional fees are assessed to students beyond the costs of tuition for the following: Technology Fee of $4 per credit hour. See the following Web site for updates and changes in tuition costs: http://www.du.edu/registrar.

Financial Assistance:

First-Year Students: Teaching assistantships available for first year. Research assistantships available for first year. Traineeships available for first year. Fellowships and scholarships available for first year.

Advanced Students: Teaching assistantships available for advanced students. Research assistantships available for advanced students. Traineeships available for advanced students. Fellowships and scholarships available for advanced students.

Additional Information: No information provided.

Internships/Practica: Clinic practicum is an advanced formative supervised experience to enhance and extend knowledge and skills developed during ongoing assessment, intervention, and consultation coursework. Most students complete an on-campus clinic practicum during their 2nd year at one of two on-campus clinics associated with the CFSP Program. MA and C F Leadership tract Doctoral students are supervised at the Child and Family Clinic (CFC) located in the Fisher Early Learning Center and most EdS and School Psychology Licensure tract Doctoral students are supervised at the Counseling and Educational Services Clinic (CESC) located in the Ammi Hyde Building. EdS students in the EC Certification tract must complete a clinic practicum at both clinics. Further descriptions of these clinics can be found in the Program Resources section of this Handbook and also in the Clinic Practicum manual. Both clinics serve clients from the DU and surrounding metro community; the CFC primarily serves early childhood populations from birth to age 5 using a play-based team assessment approach, and the CESC primarily serves families and students in elementary to college settings using a more traditional individualized clinical diagnostic approach.

Housing and Day Care: On-campus housing is available. See the following Web site for more information: http://www.du.edu/housing/. On-campus day care facilities are available. See the following Web site for more information: http://www.du.edu/felc/.

Employment of Department Graduates:

Master's Degree Graduates: Of those who graduated in the academic year 2006–2007, the following categories and numbers represent the postgraduate activities and employment of master's degree graduates: Enrolled in a postdoctoral residency/fellowship (n/a), employed in independent practice (n/a), total from the above (master's) (0).

Doctoral Degree Graduates: Of those who graduated in the academic year 2006–2007, the following categories and numbers represent the postgraduate activities and employment of doctoral degree graduates: Enrolled in a psychology doctoral program (n/a), total from the above (doctoral) (0).

Additional Information:

Orientation, Objectives, and Emphasis of Department: The Child, Family, and School Psychology program, which stresses serving children in the context of their families and communities, teaches students about psychological factors that influence human development and learning. Students can be prepared for licensure as school psychologists through the National Association of School Psychologists (NASP) conditionally approved EdS degree program, or for professional careers in a broad range of educational, medical, research, or treatment-oriented service systems serving children from birth through age 21. The program offers a distinctive opportunity to interested students to develop a specialization in early childhood education. The curriculum emphasizes strategies for supporting and intervening with children and families with diverse needs, as well as policy development, research, and program development and evaluation.

Special Facilities or Resources: Doctoral students are supervised at the Child and Family Clinic (CFC) located in the Fisher Early Learning Center and most EdS and School Psychology Licensure tract Doctoral students are supervised at the Counseling and Educational Services Clinic (CESC) located in the Ammi Hyde Building.

Information for Students With Physical Disabilities: See the following Web site for more information: http://www.du.edu/disability/.

Application Information:
Send to Morgridge College of Education, Child, Family, and School Psychology, 2450 South Vine Street, Denver, CO 80208. Application available online. URL of online application: http://www.du.edu/education/calls/admission.html. Students are admitted in the Fall, application deadline December 15. *Fee:* $60.

Denver, University of

Counseling Psychology
Morgridge College of Education
2450 South Vine Street
Denver, CO 80208
Telephone: (303) 871-2509
Fax: (303) 871-4456
E-mail: *edinfo@du.edu*
Web: *http://www.du.edu/education*

Department Information:
1980. Program Chair: Maria Riva. Number of faculty: total—full-time 6; women—full-time 4; total—minority—full-time 2; women minority—full-time 1.

Programs and Degrees Offered:
Listed in the following order: Program area, degree type (T if terminal Master's), number awarded 7/06–6/07. Counseling MA/MS (Master of Arts/Science) (T) 24, Counseling Psychology PhD (Doctor of Philosophy) 7.

APA Accreditation: Counseling PhD (Doctor of Philosophy).

Student Applications/Admissions:

Student Applications
Counseling MA/MS (Master of Arts/Science)—Applications 2007–2008, 100. Total applicants accepted 2007–2008, 56. Number full-time enrolled (new admits only) 2007–2008, 25. Number part-time enrolled (new admits only) 2007–2008, 1. Total enrolled 2007–2008 full-time, 43, part-time, 3. Openings 2008–2009, 26. The median number of years required for completion of a degree in 2006–2007 were 2. The number of students enrolled full- and part-time who were dismissed or voluntarily withdrew from this program area in 2007–2008 were 2. *Counseling Psychology PhD (Doctor of Philosophy)*—Applications 2007–2008, 66. Total applicants accepted 2007–2008, 14. Number full-time enrolled (new admits only) 2007–2008, 7. Number part-time enrolled (new admits only) 2007–2008, 0. Total enrolled 2007–2008 full-time, 29, part-time, 7. Openings 2008–2009, 7. The median number of years required for completion of a degree in 2006–2007 were 5. The number of students enrolled full- and part-time who were dismissed or voluntarily withdrew from this program area in 2007–2008 were 0.

Admissions Requirements:
Scores: Entries appear in this order: required test or GPA, minimum score (if required), median score of students entering in 2007–2008. Master's Programs: GRE-V 500, 530; GRE-Q 500, 560; overall undergraduate GPA 3.25. Doctoral Programs: GRE-V 550, 575; GRE-Q 550, 617; overall undergraduate GPA 3.5, 3.5.
Other Criteria: (importance of criteria rated low, medium, or high): GRE/MAT scores—medium, research experience—high, work experience—high, extracurricular activity—low, clinically related public service—medium, GPA—medium, letters of recommendation—high, interview—high, statement of goals and objectives—high, undergraduate major in psychology—medium, specific undergraduate psychology courses taken—low.

Student Characteristics: The following represents characteristics of students in 2007–2008 in all graduate psychology programs in the department: Female—full-time 58, part-time 8; Male—full-time 11, part-time 5; African American/Black—full-time 2, part-time 0; Hispanic/Latino(a)—full-time 6, part-time 0; Asian/Pacific Islander—full-time 2, part-time 0; American Indian/Alaska Native—full-time 1, part-time 0; Caucasian/White—full-time 59, part-time 8; Multi-ethnic—full-time 0, part-time 0; students subject to the Americans With Disabilities Act—full-time 0, part-time 0; Unknown ethnicity—full-time 3, part-time 1; International students who hold an F-1 or J-1 Visa—full-time 0, part-time 4.

Financial Information/Assistance:
Tuition for Full-Time Study: *Master's:* State residents: $874 per credit hour; Nonstate residents: $874 per credit hour. *Doctoral:* State residents: $874 per credit hour; Nonstate residents: $874 per credit hour. Tuition is subject to change. Additional fees are assessed to students beyond the costs of tuition for the following: Technology Fee of $4 per credit hour. See the following Web site for updates and changes in tuition costs: http://www.du.edu/registrar/.

Financial Assistance:

First-Year Students: Teaching assistantships available for first year. Average amount paid per academic year: $5,000. Average number of hours worked per week: 10. Apply by April 1. Tuition remission given: partial. Research assistantships available for first year. Average amount paid per academic year: $5,000. Average number of hours worked per week: 10. Apply by April 1. Tuition remission given: partial. Fellowships and scholarships available for first year. Average number of hours worked per week: 0. Tuition remission given: partial.

Advanced Students: Teaching assistantships available for advanced students. Average amount paid per academic year: $5,000. Average number of hours worked per week: 10. Apply by April 1. Tuition remission given: partial. Research assistantships available for advanced students. Average number of hours worked per week: 10. Apply by April 1. Tuition remission given: partial. Fellowships and scholarships available for advanced students. Average amount paid per academic year: $5,000. Average number of hours worked per week: 0. Apply by April 1. Tuition remission given: partial.

Additional Information: Of all students currently enrolled full time, 90% benefited from one or more of the listed financial assistance programs.

Internships/Practica: Master's Degree (MA/MS Counseling): An internship experience such as a final research project or "capstone" experience is required of graduates. Doctoral Degree (PhD Counseling Psychology): For those doctoral students for whom a professional internship was required in this program prior to graduation, (5) students applied for an internship in 2006–2007, with (5) students obtaining an internship. Of those students who obtained an internship, (5) were paid internships. Of those students who obtained an internship, (5) students placed in APA/CPA-accredited internships, (0) students placed in internships not APA/CPA-accredited, but listed with the Association of Psychology Postdoctoral and Internship Centers (APPIC), (0) students placed in internships conforming to guidelines of the Council of Directors of School Psychology Programs (CDSPP), (0) students placed in internships that were not APA/CPA accredited, APPIC or CDSPP listed. Both Doctoral and Master's student complete practica and internship as well as hours in a campus clinic. Most practica and internships are off campus. Doctoral students must complete APA-approved internships (exceptions made in unusual circumstances). Doctoral students have opportunities to complete advanced practica in variety of settings including college counseling centers, hospitals, and mental health agencies. MA students complete practica and internships in the Denver area including adolescent treatment facilities, mental health centers, womens crisis centers, schools, etc.

Housing and Day Care: On-campus housing is available. Department of Residence (303) 871-2246. Very few students live in campus housing as we are located in a neighborhood setting. On-campus day care facilities are available. Fisher Early Learning Center (303) 871-2723.

Employment of Department Graduates:

Master's Degree Graduates: Of those who graduated in the academic year 2006–2007, the following categories and numbers represent the postgraduate activities and employment of master's degree graduates: Enrolled in a psychology doctoral program (3), enrolled in a postdoctoral residency/fellowship (n/a), employed in independent practice (n/a), employed in an academic position at a university (0), employed in an academic position at a 2-year/4-year college (0), employed in other positions at a higher education institution (2), employed in a professional position in a school system (4), employed in business or industry (0), employed in government agency (0), employed in a community mental health/counseling center (12), total from the above (master's) (21).

Doctoral Degree Graduates: Of those who graduated in the academic year 2006–2007, the following categories and numbers represent the postgraduate activities and employment of doctoral degree graduates: Enrolled in a psychology doctoral program (n/a), enrolled in a postdoctoral residency/fellowship (3), employed in an academic position at a university (1), employed in a professional position in a school system (1), employed in business or industry (1), employed in a community mental health/counseling center (1), total from the above (doctoral) (7).

Additional Information:

Orientation, Objectives, and Emphasis of Department: As a graduate student in the Counseling Psychology Program, you'll develop the skills necessary to become an effective practitioner, researcher, and/or leader in your field. Our goal is to develop professionals who are insightful and self-reflective, who are innovative risk takers and superior critical thinkers. Our highly selective doctoral program is accredited by the American Psychological Association and is well known for providing access to high-quality internships for our students. We want our students not only to demonstrate accurate and current knowledge but to have expertise related to the many issues confronting society and to have the skills to create effective strategies and approaches to address these challenges. To work professionally in counseling psychology at the master's or doctoral level, you will need a strong background in the practice of counseling and psychotherapy, as well as a knowledge of the scientific foundations of psychology in order to evaluate and think critically about your practice.

Special Facilities or Resources: PhD students are required to complete a minor in one of two APA-approved clinical psychology programs on campus. Microcomputers and video equipment are available for use in conjunction with coursework. In-house clinic is available. Students are required to spend one evening a week for two quarters in clinic. Intensive supervision provided.

Information for Students With Physical Disabilities: Disability Services Program (303) 871-4333.

Application Information:

Send to Graduate Studies, Office of Admission, 2199 South University Boulevard, Denver, CO 80208-0302. Application available online. URL of online application: http://www.du.edu/education/calls/admission.html. Students are admitted in the Fall, application deadline December 15. Master's Degree in Counseling application deadline is January 15. For the Doctorate in Counseling Psychology, the deadline is December 15. *Fee:* $60.

Denver, University of

Department of Psychology
Frontier Hall, 2155 South Race Street
Denver, CO 80208
Telephone: (303) 871-3803
Fax: (303) 871-4747
E-mail: *rroberts@du.edu*
Web: *http://www.du.edu/psychology*

Department Information:

1952. Chairperson: Ralph J. Roberts. Number of faculty: total—full-time 15, part-time 3; women—full-time 8, part-time 1; total—minority—full-time 1, part-time 2; women minority—part-time 1.

Programs and Degrees Offered:

Listed in the following order: Program area, degree type (T if terminal Master's), number awarded 7/06–6/07. Clinical Child PhD (Doctor of Philosophy) 5, Developmental PhD (Doctor of Philosophy) 0, Psychology and the Law MA/MS (Master of Arts/Science) (T) 1, Social PhD (Doctor of Philosophy) 2, Cognitive PhD (Doctor of Philosophy) 1, Developmental Cognitive Neuroscience PhD (Doctor of Philosophy) 5, Affective Science PhD (Doctor of Philosophy) 0.

APA Accreditation: Clinical PhD (Doctor of Philosophy).

Student Applications/Admissions:

Student Applications

Clinical Child PhD (Doctor of Philosophy)—Applications 2007–2008, 215. Total applicants accepted 2007–2008, 10. Number full-time enrolled (new admits only) 2007–2008, 6. Openings 2008–2009, 6. The median number of years required for completion of a degree in 2006–2007 were 6. The number of students enrolled full- and part-time who were dismissed or voluntarily withdrew from this program area in 2007–2008 were 0. *Developmental PhD (Doctor of Philosophy)*—Applications 2007–2008, 18. Total applicants accepted 2007–2008, 3. Number full-time enrolled (new admits only) 2007–2008, 2. Openings 2008–2009, 2. The median number of years required for completion of a degree in 2006–2007 were 6. The number of students enrolled full- and part-time who were dismissed or voluntarily withdrew from this program area in 2007–2008 were 0. *Psychology and The law MA/MS (Master of Arts/Science)*—Applications 2007–2008, 0. Total applicants accepted 2007–2008, 0. Number full-time enrolled (new admits only) 2007–2008, 0. Openings 2008–2009, 1. The median number of years required for completion of a degree in 2006–2007 were 3. The number of students enrolled full- and part-time who were dismissed or voluntarily withdrew from this program area in 2007–2008 were 0. *Social PhD (Doctor of Philosophy)*—Applications 2007–2008, 28. Total applicants accepted 2007–2008, 2. Number full-time enrolled (new admits only) 2007–2008, 1. Total enrolled 2007–2008 full-time, 3. Openings 2008–2009, 2. The median number of years required for completion of a degree in 2006–2007 were 6. The number of students enrolled full- and part-time who were dismissed or voluntarily withdrew from this program area in 2007–2008 were 0. *Cognitive PhD (Doctor of Philosophy)*—Applications 2007–2008, 21. Total applicants accepted 2007–2008, 2. Number full-time enrolled (new admits only) 2007–2008, 0. Total enrolled 2007–2008 full-time, 6. Openings 2008–2009, 2. The median number of years required for completion of a degree in 2006–2007 were 6. The number of students enrolled full- and part-time who were dismissed or voluntarily withdrew from this program area in 2007–2008 were 0. *Developmental Cognitive Neuroscience PhD (Doctor of Philosophy)*—Applications 2007–2008, 40. Total applicants accepted 2007–2008, 9. Number full-time enrolled (new admits only) 2007–2008, 1. Total enrolled 2007–2008 full-time, 13. Openings 2008–2009, 6. The median number of years required for completion of a degree in 2006–2007 were 6. The number of students enrolled full- and part-time who were dismissed or voluntarily withdrew from this program area in 2007–2008 were 0. *Affective Science PhD (Doctor of Philosophy)*—Applications 2007–2008, 28. Total applicants accepted 2007–2008, 2. Number full-time enrolled (new admits only) 2007–2008, 1. Total enrolled 2007–2008 full-time, 1. Openings 2008–2009, 2. The number of students enrolled full- and part-time who were dismissed or voluntarily withdrew from this program area in 2007–2008 were 0.

Admissions Requirements:

Scores: Entries appear in this order: required test or GPA, minimum score (if required), median score of students entering in 2007–2008. Master's Programs: GRE-V 550, 580; GRE-Q 600, 660; overall undergraduate GPA 3.0, 3.71. Doctoral Programs: GRE-V 550, 580; GRE-Q 600, 660; overall undergraduate GPA 3.0, 3.71.

Other Criteria: (importance of criteria rated low, medium, or high): GRE/MAT scores—high, research experience—high, work experience—medium, extracurricular activity—medium, clinically related public service—high, GPA—high, letters of recommendation—high, interview—high, statement of goals and objectives—high. For additional information on admission requirements, go to http://www.du.edu/psychology.

Student Characteristics: The following represents characteristics of students in 2007–2008 in all graduate psychology programs in the department: Female—full-time 44, part-time 0; Male—full-time 5, part-time 0; African American/Black—full-time 2, part-time 0; Hispanic/Latino(a)—full-time 3, part-time 0; Asian/Pacific Islander—full-time 4, part-time 0; American Indian/Alaska Native—full-time 0, part-time 0; Caucasian/White—full-time 39, part-time 0; Multi-ethnic—full-time 1, part-time 0; students subject to the Americans With Disabilities Act—full-time 0, part-time 0; Unknown ethnicity—full-time 0, part-time 0.

Financial Information/Assistance:

Tuition for Full-Time Study: *Master's:* State residents: per academic year $27,480, $916 per credit hour; Nonstate residents: per academic year $27,480, $916 per credit hour. *Doctoral:* State residents: per academic year $27,480, $916 per credit hour; Nonstate residents: per academic year $27,480, $916 per credit hour. See the following Web site for updates and changes in tuition costs: http://www.du.edu/registrar.

Financial Assistance:

First-Year Students: Teaching assistantships available for first year. Average amount paid per academic year: $16,000. Average number of hours worked per week: 20. Tuition remission given: full. Research assistantships available for first year. Average amount paid per academic year: $16,000. Average number of hours worked per week: 20. Tuition remission given: full.

Advanced Students: Teaching assistantships available for advanced students. Average amount paid per academic year: $16,000. Average number of hours worked per week: 20. Tuition remission given: full. Research assistantships available for advanced students. Average amount paid per academic year: $16,000. Average number of hours worked per week: 20. Tuition remission given: full.

Additional Information: Of all students currently enrolled full time, 100% benefited from one or more of the listed financial assistance programs. Application and information available online at http://www.du.edu/psychology.

Internships/Practica: Doctoral Degree (PhD Clinical Child): For those doctoral students for whom a professional internship was required in this program prior to graduation, (6) students applied for an internship in 2006–2007, with (6) students obtaining an internship. Of those students who obtained an internship, (6) were paid internships. Of those students who obtained an internship, (6) students placed in APA/CPA-accredited internships, (0) students placed in internships not APA/CPA accredited, but listed with the Association of Psychology Postdoctoral and Internship Centers (APPIC), (0) students placed in internships conforming to guidelines of the Council of Directors of School Psychology Programs (CDSPP), (0) students placed in internships that were not APA/CPA-accredited, APPIC or CDSPP listed. The department offers two clinical training facilities: the Child Study Center (CSC) and the Developmental Neuropsychology Clinic. The CSC provides training in assessment and psychotherapy with children, families, and adults. The Neuropsychology Clinic provides specialized training in assessment of learning disorders, mainly in school-age children. Thus, a considerable amount of clinical training is provided within our Department by faculty supervisors, ensuring that each clinical student is solidly grounded in both assessment and treatment. Clinical students also typically do externships in the community, such as local hospitals, day treatment programs, and other community agencies. Graduate students who are not in clinical can also get experience with patient populations either by internships in the neuropsychology clinic, by attending rounds at a local rehab center, or through practica in neuroimaging and other research with abnormal populations.

Housing and Day Care: On-campus housing is available. Contact Department of Residence (303) 871-2246. On-campus day care facilities are available. Contact Fisher Early Learning Center (303) 871-2723 for more information.

Employment of Department Graduates:

Master's Degree Graduates: Of those who graduated in the academic year 2006–2007, the following categories and numbers represent the postgraduate activities and employment of master's degree graduates: Enrolled in a postdoctoral residency/fellowship (n/a), employed in independent practice (n/a), total from the above (master's) (0).

Doctoral Degree Graduates: Of those who graduated in the academic year 2006–2007, the following categories and numbers represent the postgraduate activities and employment of doctoral degree graduates: Enrolled in a psychology doctoral program (n/a), enrolled in a postdoctoral residency/fellowship (1), employed in independent practice (1), employed in an academic position at a university (1), employed in business or industry (1), employed in a community mental health/counseling center (1), employed in a hospital/medical center (2), do not know (1), total from the above (doctoral) (8).

Additional Information:

Orientation, Objectives, and Emphasis of Department: Programs are oriented toward training students to pursue careers in research, teaching, and professional practice. They include a new program in Affective Science, and established programs in Clinical Child, Cognitive, Developmental, and Social, as well as Developmental Cognitive Neuroscience, a program open to students in any of the other programs, and that fosters an interdisciplinary approach to cognitive, affective, and social neuroscience. The department has one of the few APA-accredited child clinical programs, and has been ranked very highly in past rankings by the American Psychological Society for publication impact. The department offers close collaborative relationships between faculty and students, with an emphasis on individualized tutorial relationships. The atmosphere encourages and offers students the freedom to seek out and work with multiple faculty members as fits the student's evolving interests. Our students are successful in publishing in prestigious journals, in winning predoctoral grants, and obtaining their first choice for clinical internships. Situated at the foot of the Rocky Mountains, Denver combines urban culture with readily accessible skiing, hiking, and biking in a climate that has over 300 days of sunshine.

Special Facilities or Resources: Our labs are custom-designed for the kinds of research conducted in our department. They include the Center for Marital and Family Studies, the Relationship Center, the Developmental Neuropsychology Center, the Cognitive Neuroscience Lab, the Reading and Language Lab, the Emotion Regulation Lab, the Center for Infant Development, the Center for Research on Family Stress, the Center for the Study of Self and Others, the Perception/Action Lab, the Emotion and Coping Lab, the Traumatic Stress Studies Lab, the Developmental Cognitive Neuroscience Lab, and the Child Health and Development Lab. Labs are equipped with computers for controlling the presentation of stimuli and the collection of data. Some labs include equipment to measure EDA, ECG, and EMG. The DCN lab includes a high-density electrophysiology system for measuring ERPs and EEG in infants and young children. The Perception-Action Lab employs eye movement recording methods in children and adults. The Child Health and Development Lab is equipped with a modified wet lab for processing saliva samples including a −80 freezer for storage. In addition, we have a host of conventional laboratory rooms with one-way observation windows and up-to-date audio and video recording equipment. Finally, we are closely partnered with the neuroimaging facilities at the University of Colorado Health Sciences Center and a genotyping facility at the Institute for Behavioral Genetics at CU Boulder. The neuroimaging facilities allow us to conduct fMRI and MEG studies. Genotype data allow us to test directly genetic effects on behavior. In addition to research laboratories, the department also maintains its own clinical training facility, the Child Study Center, and it houses a Neuropsychology Clinic. The department enjoys excellent computer facilities. It maintains a local area computer network (LAN) that interconnects over 100 departmental PCs. Many graduate student offices are equipped with computers, and there is also a graduate student computer lab with 10 PCs, printers, and scanners. Research subjects are available from undergraduate classes, and from nearby schools and the university daycare center, and local hospitals and rehab centers for patients with neuropsychological disorders. Classrooms are smart-to-the-seat, allowing Internet access for students' laptops.

Information for Students With Physical Disabilities: See the following Web site for more information: http://www.du.edu/uds.

Application Information:
Send to Graduate Studies Office, University of Denver, 2199 South University Boulevard, Denver, CO 80208 (self-addressed envelope is enclosed in application materials). Application available online. URL of online application: http://www.du.edu/grad. Students are admitted in the Fall, application deadline December 1 for all programs. *Fee:* $60.

Denver, University of

Graduate School of Professional Psychology
2460 South Vine Street, MSC 4101
Denver, CO 80208-3626
Telephone: (303) 871-3736
Fax: (303) 871-7656
E-mail: *gsppinfo@du.edu*
Web: *http://www.du.edu/gspp*

Department Information:

1976. Dean: Dr. Peter Buirski. Number of faculty: total—full-time 13, part-time 6; women—full-time 8, part-time 2; total—minority—full-time 3, part-time 1; women minority—full-time 1, part-time 1.

Programs and Degrees Offered:

Listed in the following order: Program area, degree type (T if terminal Master's), number awarded 7/06–6/07. Clinical Psychology PsyD (Doctor of Psychology) 26, Forensic Psychology MA/MS (Master of Arts/Science) (T) 23, International Disaster Psychology MA/MS (Master of Arts/Science) (T) 0, Sport and Performance Psychology MA/MS (Master of Arts/Science) (T) 0.

APA Accreditation: Clinical PsyD (Doctor of Psychology).

Student Applications/Admissions:

Student Applications

Clinical Psychology PsyD (Doctor of Psychology)—Applications 2007–2008, 324. Total applicants accepted 2007–2008, 66. Number full-time enrolled (new admits only) 2007–2008, 36. Openings 2008–2009, 35. The median number of years required for completion of a degree in 2006–2007 were 4. The number of students enrolled full- and part-time who were dismissed or voluntarily withdrew from this program area in 2007–2008 were 1. *Forensic Psychology MA/MS (Master of Arts/Science)*—Applications 2007–2008, 100. Total applicants accepted 2007–2008, 51. Number full-time enrolled (new admits only) 2007–2008, 28. Openings 2008–2009, 25. The median number of years required for completion of a degree in 2006–2007 were 2. The number of students enrolled full- and part-time who were dismissed or voluntarily withdrew from this program area in 2007–2008 were 0. *International Disaster Psychology MA/MS (Master of Arts/Science)*—Applications 2007–2008, 40. Total applicants accepted 2007–2008, 14. Number full-time enrolled (new admits only) 2007–2008, 14. Total enrolled 2007–2008 full-time, 11. Openings 2008–2009, 15. The median number of years required for completion of a degree in 2006–2007 were 2. The number of students enrolled full- and part-time who were dismissed or voluntarily withdrew from this program area in 2007–2008 were 3. *Sport and Performance Psychology MA/MS (Master of Arts/Science)*—Applications 2007–2008, 7. Total applicants accepted 2007–2008, 7. Openings 2008–2009, 14. The median number of years required for completion of a degree in 2006–2007 were 2.

Admissions Requirements:

Scores: Entries appear in this order: required test or GPA, minimum score (if required), median score of students entering in 2007–2008. Master's Programs: GRE-V no minimum stated, 550; GRE-Q no minimum stated, 550; overall undergraduate GPA no minimum stated, 3.5; Masters GRE-Analytical no minimum stated, 4.5. GRE-Subject (Psychology) is optional for MA applicants. Doctoral Programs: GRE-V no minimum stated, 550; GRE-Q no minimum stated, 570; overall undergraduate GPA no minimum stated, 3.5; Doctoral program GRE-Analytic no minimum stated, 5.0. GRE Psychology subject test is optional for PsyD applicants.

Other Criteria: (importance of criteria rated low, medium, or high): GRE/MAT scores—high, research experience—medium, work experience—high, extracurricular activity—high, clinically related public service—high, GPA—high, letters of recommendation—high, interview—high, statement of goals and objectives—high, required essay responses—high. For additional information on admission requirements, go to http://www.du.edu/gspp.

Student Characteristics: The following represents characteristics of students in 2007–2008 in all graduate psychology programs in the department: Female—full-time 206, part-time 0; Male—full-time 44, part-time 0; African American/Black—full-time 3, part-time 0; Hispanic/Latino(a)—full-time 10, part-time 0; Asian/Pacific Islander—full-time 8, part-time 0; American Indian/Alaska Native—full-time 2, part-time 0; Caucasian/White—full-time 195, part-time 0; Multi-ethnic—full-time 0, part-time 0; students subject to the Americans With Disabilities Act—full-time 0, part-time 0; Unknown ethnicity—full-time 19, part-time 0.

Financial Information/Assistance:

Tuition for Full-Time Study: *Master's:* State residents: per academic year $32,976, $916 per credit hour; Nonstate residents: per academic year $32,976, $916 per credit hour. *Doctoral:* State residents: per academic year $43,968, $916 per credit hour; Nonstate residents: per academic year $43,968, $916 per credit hour. Tuition is subject to change. See the following Web site for updates and changes in tuition costs: http://www.du.edu.

Financial Assistance:

First-Year Students: Research assistantships available for first year. Average amount paid per academic year: $2,500. Tuition remission given: partial. Fellowships and scholarships available for first year. Average amount paid per academic year: $2,500.

Advanced Students: Research assistantships available for advanced students. Average amount paid per academic year: $2,500. Tuition remission given: partial.

Additional Information: Of all students currently enrolled full time, 45% benefited from one or more of the listed financial assistance programs.

Internships/Practica: Doctoral Degree (PsyD Clinical Psychology): For those doctoral students for whom a professional internship was required in this program prior to graduation, (34) students applied for an internship in 2006–2007, with (31) students obtaining an internship. Of those students who obtained an internship, (31) were paid internships. Of those students who obtained an internship, (31) students placed in APA/CPA-accredited internships, (0) students placed in internships not APA/CPA accredited, but listed with the Association of Psychology Postdoctoral and Internship Centers (APPIC), (0) students placed in internships conforming to guidelines of the Council of Directors of School Psychology Programs (CDSPP), (0) students placed in internships that were not APA/CPA-accredited, APPIC or CDSPP listed. In addition to participation in the APPIC internship match, the GSPP offers an exclusive consortium of internship sites for which appropriate students may apply. For additional information on education and training outcomes for our programs, see the following Web site: http://www.du.edu/gspp.

Housing and Day Care: On-campus housing is available. See the following Web site for more information: http://www.slife.du.edu/housing/. On-campus day care facilities are available.

Employment of Department Graduates:

Master's Degree Graduates: Of those who graduated in the academic year 2006–2007, the following categories and numbers represent the postgraduate activities and employment of master's degree graduates: Enrolled in a postdoctoral residency/fellowship (n/a), employed in independent practice (n/a), total from the above (master's) (0).

Doctoral Degree Graduates: Of those who graduated in the academic year 2006–2007, thc following categories and numbers represent the postgraduate activities and employment of doctoral degree graduates: Enrolled in a psychology doctoral program (n/a), total from the above (doctoral) (0).

Additional Information:

Orientation, Objectives, and Emphasis of Department: The Graduate School of Professional Psychology focuses on scientifically based training for applied professional work rather than on the more traditional academic–scientific approach to clinical training. In addition to the basic clinical curriculum, special emphases are available in several areas. Our students should have a probing, questioning stance toward human problems and, therefore, should be (a) knowledgeable about intra- and interpersonal theories, including assessment and intervention; (b) conversant with relevant issues and techniques in research; (c) sensitive to self and to interpersonal interactions as primary clinical tools; (d) skilled in assessing and effectively intervening in human problems; (e) able to assess effectiveness of outcomes; and (f) aware of current professional and ethical issues. To these ends the programs focus on major social and psychological theories; research training directed toward the consumer rather than the producer of research; technical knowledge of assessment; and intervention in problems involving individuals, families, groups, and institutional systems. Strong emphasis is placed on practicum training. There are no requirements for empirical research output. The Master's degree in Forensic Psychology supplements graduate-level clinical training with course work and practicum experiences in the legal, criminal justice, and law enforcement systems. The Master's degree in International Disaster psychology supplements graduate-level clinical training with coursework and practicum experiences in trauma, community building, and international field experience.

Special Facilities or Resources: The program offers its own in-house community psychological services center, and varied opportunities are available in many community facilities for the required practicum experiences.

Information for Students With Physical Disabilities: See the following Web site for more information: http://www.du.edu/gspp.

Application Information:

Send to University of Denver, Graduate Admissions Office 216, 2197 South University Boulevard, Denver, CO 80208. Application available online. URL of online application: http://www.du.edu/gspp. Students are admitted in the Fall, application deadline January. *Fee:* $60.

Northern Colorado, University of (2007 data)

School of Applied Psychology and Counselor Education
College of Education
501 20th Street
Greeley, CO 80639
Telephone: (970) 351-2731
Fax: (970) 351-2625
E-mail: *brian.johnson@unco.edu*
Web: *http://www.unco.edu/cebs/counspsych/about.html*

Department Information:

1911. School Director: Fred Hanna. Number of faculty: total—full-time 16, part-time 5; women—full-time 11, part-time 3.

Programs and Degrees Offered:

Listed in the following order: Program area, degree type (T if terminal Master's), number awarded 7/06–6/07. School Counseling MA/MS (Master of Arts/Science) (T) 19, Community Counseling MA/MS (Master of Arts/Science) (T) 44, Community Counseling Marriage MA/MS (Master of Arts/Science) 20, School Psychology EdS/MEd (School Psychology) 31, Counseling Psychology PsyD (Doctor of Psychology) 5, School Psychology PhD (Doctor of Philosophy) 11, Counselor Education and Supervision PhD (Doctor of Philosophy) 6, School Psychology Endorsement Respecialization Diploma 0.

APA Accreditation: Counseling PsyD (Doctor of Psychology). School PhD (Doctor of Philosophy).

Student Applications/Admissions:

Student Applications

School Counseling MA/MS (Master of Arts/Science)—Applications 2007–2008, 72. Total applicants accepted 2007–2008, 27. Number full-time enrolled (new admits only) 2007–2008,

14. Total enrolled 2007–2008 full-time, 55, part-time, 2. Openings 2008–2009, 25. The median number of years required for completion of a degree in 2006–2007 were 2. The number of students enrolled full- and part-time who were dismissed or voluntarily withdrew from this program area in 2007–2008 were 0. *Community Counseling MA/MS (Master of Arts/Science)*—Applications 2007–2008, 109. Total applicants accepted 2007–2008, 57. Number full-time enrolled (new admits only) 2007–2008, 52. Total enrolled 2007–2008 full-time, 130, part-time, 21. Openings 2008–2009, 35. The median number of years required for completion of a degree in 2006–2007 were 2. The number of students enrolled full- and part-time who were dismissed or voluntarily withdrew from this program area in 2007–2008 were 0. *Community Counseling Marriage MA/MS (Master of Arts/Science)*—Applications 2007–2008, 34. Total applicants accepted 2007–2008, 18. Number full-time enrolled (new admits only) 2007–2008, 18. Total enrolled 2007–2008 full-time, 28, part-time, 5. Openings 2008–2009, 20. The median number of years required for completion of a degree in 2006–2007 were 2. The number of students enrolled full- and part-time who were dismissed or voluntarily withdrew from this program area in 2007–2008 were 0. *School Psychology EdS/MEd (School Psychology)*—Applications 2007–2008, 39. Total applicants accepted 2007–2008, 28. Number full-time enrolled (new admits only) 2007–2008, 25. Total enrolled 2007–2008 full-time, 52, part-time, 3. Openings 2008–2009, 30. The median number of years required for completion of a degree in 2006–2007 were 3. The number of students enrolled full- and part-time who were dismissed or voluntarily withdrew from this program area in 2007–2008 were 0. *Counseling Psychology PsyD (Doctor of Psychology)*—Applications 2007–2008, 63. Total applicants accepted 2007–2008, 8. Number full-time enrolled (new admits only) 2007–2008, 8. Total enrolled 2007–2008 full-time, 37. Openings 2008–2009, 8. The median number of years required for completion of a degree in 2006–2007 were 4. The number of students enrolled full- and part-time who were dismissed or voluntarily withdrew from this program area in 2007–2008 were 0. *School Psychology PhD (Doctor of Philosophy)*—Applications 2007–2008, 38. Total applicants accepted 2007–2008, 10. Number full-time enrolled (new admits only) 2007–2008, 9. Total enrolled 2007–2008 full-time, 30, part-time, 2. Openings 2008–2009, 8. The median number of years required for completion of a degree in 2006–2007 were 4. The number of students enrolled full- and part-time who were dismissed or voluntarily withdrew from this program area in 2007–2008 were 0. *Counselor Education and Supervision PhD (Doctor of Philosophy)*—Applications 2007–2008, 10. Total applicants accepted 2007–2008, 7. Number full-time enrolled (new admits only) 2007–2008, 6. Number part-time enrolled (new admits only) 2007–2008, 0. Total enrolled 2007–2008 full-time, 17, part-time, 3. Openings 2008–2009, 8. The median number of years required for completion of a degree in 2006–2007 were 4. *School Psychology Endorsement Respecialization Diploma*—Applications 2007–2008, 12. Total applicants accepted 2007–2008, 10. Number full-time enrolled (new admits only) 2007–2008, 0. Number part-time enrolled (new admits only) 2007–2008, 9. Openings 2008–2009, 10. The number of students enrolled full- and part-time who were dismissed or voluntarily withdrew from this program area in 2007–2008 were 0.

Admissions Requirements:

Scores: Entries appear in this order: required test or GPA, minimum score (if required), median score of students entering in 2007–2008. Master's Programs: overall undergraduate GPA 3.0; last 2 years GPA 3.0. GREs are required for master's degree applicants with a GPA lower than 3.0 (1000 GRE V & Q total) Doctoral Programs: GRE-V 400, 580; GRE-Q 400, 600; last 2 years GPA 3.5, 3.7; Doctoral program GRE-Analytic 3.5, 5.

Other Criteria: (importance of criteria rated low, medium, or high): GRE/MAT scores—high, research experience—medium, work experience—high, extracurricular activity—low, clinically related public service—medium, GPA—high, letters of recommendation—high, interview—high, statement of goals and objectives—high. Research experience is of low importance for the master's degree programs, but of medium importance for the other programs. For additional information on admission requirements, go to http://www.unco.edu/cebs/ppsy/.

Student Characteristics: The following represents characteristics of students in 2007–2008 in all graduate psychology programs in the department: Female—full-time 361, part-time 0; Male—full-time 82, part-time 0; African American/Black—full-time 2, part-time 0; Hispanic/Latino(a)—full-time 12, part-time 0; Asian/Pacific Islander—full-time 14, part-time 0; American Indian/Alaska Native—full-time 8, part-time 0; Caucasian/White—full-time 406, part-time 0; Multi-ethnic—full-time 1, part-time 0; students subject to the Americans With Disabilities Act—full-time 2, part-time 0; Unknown ethnicity—full-time 0, part-time 0.

Financial Information/Assistance:

Tuition for Full-Time Study: *Master's:* State residents: per academic year $5,118, $213 per credit hour; Nonstate residents: per academic year $14,832, $618 per credit hour. *Doctoral:* State residents: per academic year $5,118, $213 per credit hour; Nonstate residents: per academic year $14,832, $618 per credit hour. Tuition is subject to change. See the following Web site for updates and changes in tuition costs: http://www.unco.edu/acctservices/budget/costs.htm.

Financial Assistance:

First-Year Students: Research assistantships available for first year. Average amount paid per academic year: $6,000. Average number of hours worked per week: 8. Apply by April 15. Tuition remission given: partial. Fellowships and scholarships available for first year. Average amount paid per academic year: $1,500. Apply by April 15. Tuition remission given: partial.

Advanced Students: Teaching assistantships available for advanced students. Average amount paid per academic year: $6,000. Average number of hours worked per week: 8. Apply by variable. Tuition remission given: partial. Research assistantships available for advanced students. Average amount paid per academic year: $6,000. Average number of hours worked per week: 8. Apply by April 15. Tuition remission given: partial. Fellowships and scholarships available for advanced students. Average amount paid per academic year: $1,500. Apply by variable. Tuition remission given: partial.

Additional Information: Of all students currently enrolled full time, 80% benefited from one or more of the listed financial

assistance programs. Application and information available online at http://www.unco.edu/cebs/ppsy/.

Internships/Practica: Master's and doctoral practica take place within our in-house clinic. Master's internships are in mental health agencies or schools. Doctoral internships are APPIC and/or APA accredited.

Housing and Day Care: On-campus housing is available. See the following Web site for more information: http://www.unco.edu. No on-campus day care facilities are available.

Employment of Department Graduates:

Master's Degree Graduates: Of those who graduated in the academic year 2006–2007, the following categories and numbers represent the postgraduate activities and employment of master's degree graduates: Enrolled in a postdoctoral residency/fellowship (n/a), employed in independent practice (n/a), total from the above (master's) (0).

Doctoral Degree Graduates: Of those who graduated in the academic year 2006–2007, the following categories and numbers represent the postgraduate activities and employment of doctoral degree graduates: Enrolled in a psychology doctoral program (n/a), enrolled in a postdoctoral residency/fellowship (2), employed in independent practice (6), employed in an academic position at a university (2), employed in a professional position in a school system (8), employed in a community mental health/counseling center (4), total from the above (doctoral) (22).

Additional Information:

Orientation, Objectives, and Emphasis of Department: The School of Applied Psychology and Counselor Education offers graduate programs in the fields of Counseling and School Psychology that prepare students for careers in schools, community agencies, industry, higher education, and private practice. The school offers professional psychological services to the university and the local community through its departmental clinic, a research and training facility. The School Psychology program is based on the scientist–practitioner model of training and focuses on the interaction of content knowledge, process and assessment skills, the educational and community context, and research. The Counseling Psychology program is based on the scientist–practitioner model with a greater emphasis on practice. Its training focuses on content knowledge, the educational and community context, therapeutic/assessment skills and their interaction. Students can be part of a cluster of outstanding psychology training programs. All programs are nestled within the School of Applied Psychology and Counselor Education with training in Counseling Psychology, School Psychology, Counselor Education, School Counseling, Community Counseling, and Family Therapy. Students have the opportunity to pursue elective course work in any or all of these areas.

Special Facilities or Resources: The school maintains a laboratory facility for use by the counseling and school psychology programs. This facility is built around a central observation area, from which eight counseling rooms, five testing rooms, two family therapy, one group therapy, one neuropsychology lab, and three play therapy rooms can be observed and videotaped through one-way windows. All are furnished appropriately for the specific functions of each. All rooms are equipped with ceiling-mounted microphones with the observation area for each room supplied with an amplifier and earphone jacks. Several observation areas are also equipped with speakers. The main university library has provided excellent support for the professional psychology programs. Sufficient funding is provided annually for the purchase of relevant books, tapes, microforms, and microfiche. The journal collection is also updated annually, and facilities are available for several types of computer literature searches. Additionally, funding is available for purchasing tests listed in the Mental Measurements Yearbook.

Information for Students With Physical Disabilities: See the following Web site for more information: http://www.unco.edu/dss/geninfo.asp.

Application Information:

Send to Admissions Secretary, Division of Professional Psychology, University of Northern Colorado, Greeley, CO 80639. Application available online. URL of online application: http://www.unco.edu/cebs/ppsy/ and http://www.unco.edu/grad/admissions/home.htm. Students are admitted in the Fall, application deadline (see below); Programs have rolling admissions. Counseling Psychology, PsyD—December 15; School Psychology, EdS and PhD—December 15; Counselor Education PhD—January 1; Community Counseling and Marriage/Family, School Counseling, MA degrees—December 15. *Fee:* $50. Fee is for the Graduate School Application Process. Graduates from the University of Northern Colorado can get this fee waived.

Northern Colorado, University of

School of Psychological Sciences
Education and Behavioral Sciences
501 20th Street
Greeley, CO 80639-0001
Telephone: (970) 351-2957
Fax: (970) 351-1103
E-mail: *Roberta.ochsner@unco.edu*
Web: *http://www.unco.edu/psychology/*

Department Information:

1982. Director: Mark Alcorn. Number of faculty: total—full-time 19; women—full-time 7.

Programs and Degrees Offered:

Listed in the following order: Program area, degree type (T if terminal Master's), number awarded 7/06–6/07. Educational Psychology PhD (Doctor of Philosophy) 2, Educational Psychology MA/MS (Master of Arts/Science) (T) 3.

Student Applications/Admissions:

Student Applications

Educational Psychology PhD (Doctor of Philosophy)—Applications 2007–2008, 10. Total applicants accepted 2007–2008, 6. Number full-time enrolled (new admits only) 2007–2008, 3. Total enrolled 2007–2008 full-time, 21. Openings 2008–2009, 6. The median number of years required for completion of a degree in 2006–2007 were 4. The number of students enrolled full- and part-time who were dismissed or voluntarily withdrew from this program area in 2007–2008 were 0. *Educational Psychology MA/MS (Master of Arts/Science)*—Applications 2007–2008, 28. Total applicants accepted 2007–2008,

17. Number full-time enrolled (new admits only) 2007–2008, 7. Total enrolled 2007–2008 full-time, 12. Openings 2008–2009, 10. The median number of years required for completion of a degree in 2006–2007 was 1. The number of students enrolled full- and part-time who were dismissed or voluntarily withdrew from this program area in 2007–2008 were 0.

Admissions Requirements:

Scores: Entries appear in this order: required test or GPA, minimum score (if required), median score of students entering in 2007–2008. Master's Programs: overall undergraduate GPA 3.00. Doctoral Programs: GRE-V no minimum stated, 500; GRE-Q no minimum stated, 575; overall undergraduate GPA 3.0.

Other Criteria: (importance of criteria rated low, medium, or high): GRE/MAT scores—medium, research experience—medium, work experience—medium, extracurricular activity—medium, clinically related public service—low, GPA—high, letters of recommendation—high, statement of goals and objectives—high.

Student Characteristics: The following represents characteristics of students in 2007–2008 in all graduate psychology programs in the department: Female—full-time 33, part-time 0; Male—full-time 10, part-time 0; African American/Black—full-time 2, part-time 0; Hispanic/Latino(a)—full-time 2, part-time 0; Asian/Pacific Islander—full-time 8, part-time 0; American Indian/Alaska Native—full-time 0, part-time 0; Caucasian/White—full-time 31, part-time 0; Multi-ethnic—full-time 0, part-time 0; students subject to the Americans With Disabilities Act—full-time 0, part-time 0; Unknown ethnicity—full-time 0, part-time 0; International students who hold an F-1 or J-1 Visa—full-time 4, part-time 0.

Financial Information/Assistance:

Tuition for Full-Time Study: *Master's:* State residents: per academic year $4,704; Nonstate residents: per academic year $11,989. *Doctoral:* State residents: per academic year $4,704; Nonstate residents: per academic year $11,989. Tuition is subject to change. See the following Web site for updates and changes in tuition costs: http://www.unco.edu/acctservices/budget/costs.htm.

Financial Assistance:

First-Year Students: Research assistantships available for first year. Average amount paid per academic year: $5,532. Average number of hours worked per week: 9. Apply by March 15. Tuition remission given: partial. Fellowships and scholarships available for first year. Average amount paid per academic year: $1,200. Average number of hours worked per week: 0. Apply by March 1.

Advanced Students: Teaching assistantships available for advanced students. Average amount paid per academic year: $7,554. Average number of hours worked per week: 11. Apply by Spring. Tuition remission given: partial. Research assistantships available for advanced students. Average amount paid per academic year: $6,536. Average number of hours worked per week: 9. Apply by Fall. Tuition remission given: partial.

Additional Information: Application and information available online at http://www.unco.edu/grad/general/home.htm.

Internships/Practica: Doctoral students in Educational Psychology are given priority by the School in hiring Teaching Assistants. TAs are instructors of record, administering their own undergraduate classes, such as introductory psychology, human growth and development, and educational psychology. No internship is required. Doctoral students in Educational Psychology. Our practica experiences for both MA and PhD students include a seminar in college teaching, individually scheduled directed studies, apprenticeships in teaching or research, as well as research practica that are closely supervised by faculty members. No internship is required.

Housing and Day Care: On-campus housing is available. See the following Web site for more information: http://www.housing.unco.edu/. No on-campus day care facilities are available.

Employment of Department Graduates:

Master's Degree Graduates: Of those who graduated in the academic year 2006–2007, the following categories and numbers represent the postgraduate activities and employment of master's degree graduates: Enrolled in a psychology doctoral program (5), enrolled in another graduate/professional program (1), enrolled in a postdoctoral residency/fellowship (n/a), employed in independent practice (n/a), employed in an academic position at a university (0), employed in an academic position at a 2-year/4-year college (0), employed in other positions at a higher education institution (0), employed in a professional position in a school system (0), employed in business or industry (2), employed in government agency (1), employed in a community mental health/counseling center (0), employed in a hospital/medical center (0), still seeking employment (0), other employment position (0), total from the above (master's) (9).

Doctoral Degree Graduates: Of those who graduated in the academic year 2006–2007, the following categories and numbers represent the postgraduate activities and employment of doctoral degree graduates: Enrolled in a psychology doctoral program (n/a), enrolled in a postdoctoral residency/fellowship (0), employed in independent practice (0), employed in an academic position at a university (2), employed in an academic position at a 2-year/4-year college (0), employed in other positions at a higher education institution (0), employed in a professional position in a school system (2), employed in business or industry (0), employed in government agency (0), employed in a community mental health/counseling center (0), employed in a hospital/medical center (0), still seeking employment (0), other employment position (0), total from the above (doctoral) (4).

Additional Information:

Orientation, Objectives, and Emphasis of Department: Our society faces many critical educational issues, such as how to make learning meaningful and authentic, develop critical thinking skills and creativity in individuals of various ages, and effectively educate special populations, including minorities and gifted students. These issues fall under the purview of Educational Psychology, which is the study of human learning and motivation. It encompasses investigations of cognition and the brain; the influence of affect, goals, and interest on learning; the role of assessment in learning; the psychology of teaching; the effectiveness of instructional interventions; the relationship between cognition and technology; the social psychology of learning organizations; and methods for conducting educational research. It addresses such issues in school contexts, work contexts, and everyday contexts such as the home or museums. The MA and PhD program at UNC prepares individuals to become leaders in addressing these issues.

Students are trained in the art of reading, writing, and empirically researching such issues through course work and collaboration on research projects with faculty members. Our program is flexible and we help students design a course of study that best suits their needs. Faculty members take pride in mentoring students and building lasting professional relationships as both scholars and teachers.

Special Facilities or Resources: The University of Northern Colorado is accredited by the North Central Association of Colleges and Schools (NCA), the National Council for Accreditation of Teacher Education (NCATE) and the Colorado Department of Education (CDE). The Michener Library, a 150,000 sq ft facility is named for and endowed by James A. Michener. It houses almost 1.5 million hardbound volumes, periodicals, monographs, government documents, filmstrips, slides, and software programs. The university's Research Consulting Laboratory is located in the College of Education and Behavioral Sciences (CEBS) and supports faculty, students, and community agencies by offering consultation on research design and statistical analyses. The university also has several computer labs, both MAC and PC, available for student use, and the School of Psychological Sciences has its own laboratory with computers equipped with a software program to construct experimental paradigms. The School also has a fully equipped physiological and experimental psychology laboratory, and access to the University Animal Facility. The Sponsored Program and Academic Research Center (SPARC) administers and oversees the Internal Review Board (IRB) of the university and employs grants and contracts specialists who have expertise in grant development, as well as monitoring the day-to-day financial aspects of grant administration.

Information for Students With Physical Disabilities: See the following Web site for more information: http://www.unco.edu/dss/.

Application Information:
Send to Graduate School, University of Northern Colorado, Greeley, CO 80639. Application available online. Programs have rolling admissions. To be considered for financial assistance, a statement of intent is due to the School of Psychological Sciences by March 15: Graduate Coordinator, School of Psychological Sciences, Campus Box 94, University of Northern Colorado, Greeley, CO 80639. *Fee:* $50.

Central Connecticut State University

Department of Psychology
1615 Stanley Street
New Britain, CT 06050-4010
Telephone: (860) 832-3100
Fax: (860) 832-3123
E-mail: *waite@ccsu.edu*
Web: *http://www.psychology.ccsu.edu*

Department Information:

1967. Chairperson: Dr. Bradley Waite. Number of faculty: total—full-time 21, part-time 21; women—full-time 11, part-time 9; total—minority—full-time 4, part-time 2.

Programs and Degrees Offered:

Listed in the following order: Program area, degree type (T if terminal Master's), number awarded 7/06–6/07. Community MA/MS (Master of Arts/Science) (T) 0, General MA/MS (Master of Arts/Science) (T) 9, Health MA/MS (Master of Arts/Science) 2.

Student Applications/Admissions:

Student Applications

Community MA/MS (Master of Arts/Science)—Applications 2007–2008, 5. Total applicants accepted 2007–2008, 3. Number full-time enrolled (new admits only) 2007–2008, 1. Number part-time enrolled (new admits only) 2007–2008, 1. Total enrolled 2007–2008 full-time, 3, part-time, 2. Openings 2008–2009, 5. The median number of years required for completion of a degree in 2006–2007 were 6. The number of students enrolled full- and part-time who were dismissed or voluntarily withdrew from this program area in 2007–2008 were 0. *General MA/MS (Master of Arts/Science)*—Applications 2007–2008, 23. Total applicants accepted 2007–2008, 10. Number full-time enrolled (new admits only) 2007–2008, 5. Number part-time enrolled (new admits only) 2007–2008, 0. Total enrolled 2007–2008 full-time, 9, part-time, 10. Openings 2008–2009, 10. The median number of years required for completion of a degree in 2006–2007 were 6. *Health MA/MS (Master of Arts/Science)*—Applications 2007–2008, 14. Total applicants accepted 2007–2008, 4. Number full-time enrolled (new admits only) 2007–2008, 2. Number part-time enrolled (new admits only) 2007–2008, 0. Total enrolled 2007–2008 full-time, 7, part-time, 4. Openings 2008–2009, 7.

Admissions Requirements:

Scores: Entries appear in this order: required test or GPA, minimum score (if required), median score of students entering in 2007–2008. Master's Programs: overall undergraduate GPA 2.75; psychology GPA 3.0.

Other Criteria: (importance of criteria rated low, medium, or high): research experience—medium, work experience—medium, extracurricular activity—low, clinically related public service—medium, GPA—high, letters of recommendation—high, statement of goals and objectives—high, 18 credits in psychology—medium. For additional information on admission requirements, go to http://www.psychology.ccsu.edu/graduate.html.

Student Characteristics: The following represents characteristics of students in 2007–2008 in all graduate psychology programs in the department: Female—full-time 13, part-time 15; Male—full-time 8, part-time 5; African American/Black—full-time 0, part-time 1; Hispanic/Latino(a)—full-time 2, part-time 2; Asian/Pacific Islander—full-time 0, part-time 0; American Indian/Alaska Native—full-time 0, part-time 0; Caucasian/White—full-time 14, part-time 17; Multi-ethnic—full-time 0, part-time 0; students subject to the Americans With Disabilities Act—full-time 0, part-time 0; Unknown ethnicity—full-time 2, part-time 0; International students who hold an F-1 or J-1 Visa—full-time 3, part-time 0.

Financial Information/Assistance:

Tuition for Full-Time Study: *Master's:* State residents: per academic year $7,491, $416 per credit hour; Nonstate residents: per academic year $16,171, $898 per credit hour. Tuition is subject to change. See the following Web site for updates and changes in tuition costs: http://www.bursar.ccsu.edu/FT_Fees.htm.

Financial Assistance:

First-Year Students: Teaching assistantships available for first year. Average amount paid per academic year: $2,700. Average number of hours worked per week: 10. Apply by April 25. Tuition remission given: partial.

Advanced Students: Teaching assistantships available for advanced students. Average amount paid per academic year: $2,700. Average number of hours worked per week: 10. Apply by April 25. Tuition remission given: partial.

Additional Information: Of all students currently enrolled full time, 7% benefited from one or more of the listed financial assistance programs. Application and information available online at http://www.ccsu.edu/grad/Assistantships.html.

Internships/Practica: We offer a variety of internships. For students in the community specialization, there are internships in prevention-oriented community programs dealing with substance abuse, teen pregnancy, etc. We also offer internships in developmental and counseling areas.

Housing and Day Care: On-campus housing is available. See the following Web site for more information: http://www.ccsu.edu/reslife/. On-campus day care facilities are available. See the following Web site for more information: http://www.ccsu.edu/Elp/.

Employment of Department Graduates:

Master's Degree Graduates: Of those who graduated in the academic year 2006–2007, the following categories and numbers represent the postgraduate activities and employment of master's degree graduates: Enrolled in a postdoctoral residency/fellowship (n/a), employed in independent practice (n/a), total from the above (master's) (0).

Doctoral Degree Graduates: Of those who graduated in the academic year 2006–2007, the following categories and numbers represent the postgraduate activities and employment of doctoral

degree graduates: Enrolled in a psychology doctoral program (n/a), total from the above (doctoral) (0).

Additional Information:

Orientation, Objectives, and Emphasis of Department: The psychology department includes 21 faculty members whose interests cover a wide range of psychological areas. Collectively, the orientation of the department is toward applied areas (clinical, community, health, applied, developmental), with generally little emphasis on animal learning and behavior. The specialization in community psychology focuses heavily on primary prevention. The general specialization is intended to expose students to a broad range of applied areas in psychology, whereas the one in health psychology prepares students for careers in the field of health psychology. The three specializations have a strong research emphasis.

Special Facilities or Resources: The psychology department has limited space available for human experimental research. The department has a computer laboratory, and the university has very good computer facilities available for student use. Students may also work on applied research projects with faculty through the Center for Social Research at the University.

Application Information:

Send to Office of Graduate Admissions, Central Connecticut State University, 1615 Stanley Street, New Britain, CT 06050-4010. Application available online. URL of online application: http://www.ccsu.edu/grad/admissions.htm. Students are admitted in the Fall, application deadline April 25; Spring, application deadline December 1. *Fee:* $50.

Connecticut College (2007 data)

Department of Psychology
270 Mohegan Avenue
New London, CT 06320
Telephone: (860) 439-2330
Fax: (860) 439-5300
E-mail: *nmmac@conncoll.edu*
Web: *http://www.camel.conncoll.edu/ccacad/psycholgy/ind*

Department Information:

1960. Chairperson: Joan C. Chrisler, PhD. Number of faculty: total—full-time 10, part-time 5; women—full-time 6, part-time 1.

Programs and Degrees Offered:

Listed in the following order: Program area, degree type (T if terminal Master's), number awarded 7/06–6/07. General MA/MS (Master of Arts/Science) (T) 4.

Student Applications/Admissions:

Student Applications

General MA/MS (Master of Arts/Science)—Applications 2007–2008, 15. Total applicants accepted 2007–2008, 8. Total enrolled 2007–2008 full-time, 6, part-time, 4. Openings 2008–2009, 7. The median number of years required for completion of a degree in 2006–2007 were 2. The number of students enrolled full- and part-time who were dismissed or voluntarily withdrew from this program area in 2007–2008 were 1.

Admissions Requirements:

Scores: Entries appear in this order: required test or GPA, minimum score (if required), median score of students entering in 2007–2008. Master's Programs: GRE-V no minimum stated, 620; GRE-Q no minimum stated, 625; GRE-Subject (Psychology) no minimum stated, 580; overall undergraduate GPA no minimum stated, 3.33; psychology GPA no minimum stated, 3.72; Masters GRE-Analytical no minimum stated, 4.5.

Other Criteria: (importance of criteria rated low, medium, or high): GRE/MAT scores—medium, research experience—high, work experience—low, extracurricular activity—low, clinically related public service—low, GPA—high, letters of recommendation—high, statement of goals and objectives—high.

Student Characteristics: The following represents characteristics of students in 2007–2008 in all graduate psychology programs in the department: Female—full-time 6, part-time 3; Male—full-time 0, part-time 0; African American/Black—full-time 0, part-time 0; Hispanic/Latino(a)—full-time 0, part-time 0; Asian/Pacific Islander—full-time 0, part-time 0; American Indian/Alaska Native—full-time 0, part-time 0; Caucasian/White—full-time 6, part-time 3; Multi-ethnic—full-time 0, part-time 0; students subject to the Americans With Disabilities Act—full-time 0, part-time 0; Unknown ethnicity—full-time 0, part-time 0.

Financial Information/Assistance:

Tuition for Full-Time Study: *Master's:* State residents: per academic year $9,975, $367 per credit hour; Nonstate residents: per academic year $9,975, $367 per credit hour. Tuition is subject to change.

Financial Assistance:

First-Year Students: Fellowships and scholarships available for first year. Average amount paid per academic year: $4,275. Tuition remission given: partial.

Advanced Students: Fellowships and scholarships available for advanced students. Average amount paid per academic year: $2,850. Tuition remission given: partial.

Additional Information: Of all students currently enrolled full time, 75% benefited from one or more of the listed financial assistance programs.

Internships/Practica: The Master's Program offers two types of practicum courses—a research practicum or a clinical practicum. Each of these practicum courses lasts two semesters and requires a commitment of two 8-hour days a week. The research practicum is conducted under the supervision of an experienced scientist (typically a PhD or MD) in a setting outside the Psychology Department. This research is distinct from and in addition to both the student's Master's thesis and any involvement in Connecticut College faculty research. Past examples include research work at Yale University, University of Massachusetts Medical Center, Pfizer Pharmaceuticals Inc., the United States Naval Base in Groton, and Whiting Forensic Institute. The Clinical practicum consists of clinical experience in a variety of modalities and therapeutic settings. All clinical work is conducted under the supervision of experienced clinicians (typically a PhD or licensed MSW). Students perform evaluations, facilitate groups, engage in individual and family therapy, and conduct clinical research, depending upon the type of setting. Students also participate in case conferences, in-services, and research seminars at their settings, as well as a weekly seminar conducted in the Psychology Department. Examples of clinical settings include the West Haven VA Health Psychology Program, St. Francis Hospital, Child Guidance Clinic, Lawrence and Memorial Hospital Adolescent Partial Hospitalization program, University of Massachusetts Medical Center, University of Connecticut Medical Center, Waterford Country School, Rhode Island College Counseling Center, among many others.

Housing and Day Care: No on-campus housing is available. No on-campus day care facilities are available.

Employment of Department Graduates:

Master's Degree Graduates: Of those who graduated in the academic year 2006–2007, the following categories and numbers represent the postgraduate activities and employment of master's degree graduates: Enrolled in a psychology doctoral program (1), enrolled in another graduate/professional program (0), enrolled in a postdoctoral residency/fellowship (n/a), employed in independent practice (n/a), employed in other positions at a higher education institution (1), do not know (1), total from the above (master's) (3).

Doctoral Degree Graduates: Of those who graduated in the academic year 2006–2007, the following categories and numbers represent the postgraduate activities and employment of doctoral degree graduates: Enrolled in a psychology doctoral program (n/a), total from the above (doctoral) (0).

Additional Information:

Orientation, Objectives, and Emphasis of Department: The department offers both clinical and research orientations. Concentrations are available in behavioral medicine, clinical, behavioral neuroscience, and personality–social. The faculty is diversified in their theoretical emphases. We provide training in traditional fields of experimental and clinical psychology and in special areas such as behavioral neuroscience, health psychology, environmental psychology, women and gender, behavior analysis, and personality research. The aim of most graduating students is to pursue the PhD, primarily in clinical psychology.

Special Facilities or Resources: In addition to shop and laboratory space for social, neuroscience, and conditioning and learning psychology, the Psychology Department has one-way observation suites and biofeedback and video equipment. The college's computer is housed in Bill Hall, the home of the Psychology Department, and graduate students have access to the building's computer terminals and microprocessors. Each graduate student is assigned desk space within Bill Hall.

Application Information:

Send to Nancy M. MacLeod, Academic Assistant, Department of Psychology, Connecticut College 5516, 270 Mohegan Avenue, New London, CT 06320. Students are admitted in the Fall, application deadline February 15. *Fee:* $60.

Connecticut, University of

Department of Psychology
College of Liberal Arts and Sciences
406 Babbidge Road, Unit 1020
Storrs, CT 06269-1020
Telephone: (860) 486-3515
Fax: (860) 486-2760
E-mail: *charles.lowe@uconn.edu*
Web: *http://www.web.uconn.edu/psychology/*

Department Information:

1939. Head: Charles A. Lowe. Number of faculty: total—full-time 56, part-time 4; women—full-time 25, part-time 4; total—minority—full-time 2, part-time 1; women minority—full-time 1, part-time 1.

Programs and Degrees Offered:

Listed in the following order: Program area, degree type (T if terminal Master's), number awarded 7/06–6/07. Behavioral Neuroscience PhD (Doctor of Philosophy) 8, Developmental PhD (Doctor of Philosophy) 1, Clinical PhD (Doctor of Philosophy) 6, Perception, Action, Cognition PhD (Doctor of Philosophy) 2, Industrial/Organizational PhD (Doctor of Philosophy) 3, Social PhD (Doctor of Philosophy) 3.

APA Accreditation: Clinical PhD (Doctor of Philosophy).

Student Applications/Admissions:

Student Applications

Behavioral Neuroscience PhD (Doctor of Philosophy)—Applications 2007–2008, 24. Total applicants accepted 2007–2008, 7. Number full-time enrolled (new admits only) 2007–2008, 6. Number part-time enrolled (new admits only) 2007–2008, 0. Openings 2008–2009, 4. The median number of years required for completion of a degree in 2006–2007 were 6. The number of students enrolled full- and part-time who were dismissed or voluntarily withdrew from this program area in 2007–2008 were 0. *Developmental PhD (Doctor of Philosophy)*—Applications 2007–2008, 28. Total applicants accepted 2007–2008, 4. Number full-time enrolled (new admits only) 2007–2008, 3. Number part-time enrolled (new admits only) 2007–2008, 0. Openings 2008–2009, 3. The median number of years required for completion of a degree in 2006–2007 were 7. The number of students enrolled full- and part-time who were dismissed or voluntarily withdrew from this program area in 2007–2008 were 0. *Clinical PhD (Doctor of Philosophy)*—Applications 2007–2008, 311. Total applicants accepted 2007–2008, 11. Number full-time enrolled (new admits only) 2007–2008, 7. Number part-time enrolled (new admits only) 2007–2008, 0. Openings 2008–2009, 9. The median number of years required for completion of a degree in 2006–2007 were 6. The number of students enrolled full- and part-time who were dismissed or voluntarily withdrew from this program area in 2007–2008 were 1. *Perception, Action, Cognition PhD (Doctor of Philosophy)*—Applications 2007–2008, 23. Total applicants accepted 2007–2008, 10. Number full-time enrolled (new admits only) 2007–2008, 6. Number part-time enrolled (new admits only) 2007–2008, 1. Total enrolled 2007–2008 full-time, 32, part-time, 2. Openings 2008–2009, 5. The median number of years required for completion of a degree in

2006–2007 were 6. The number of students enrolled full- and part-time who were dismissed or voluntarily withdrew from this program area in 2007–2008 were 3. *Industrial/Organizational PhD (Doctor of Philosophy)*—Applications 2007–2008, 53. Total applicants accepted 2007–2008, 10. Number full-time enrolled (new admits only) 2007–2008, 4. Number part-time enrolled (new admits only) 2007–2008, 0. Openings 2008–2009, 9. The median number of years required for completion of a degree in 2006–2007 were 7. The number of students enrolled full- and part-time who were dismissed or voluntarily withdrew from this program area in 2007–2008 were 0. *Social PhD (Doctor of Philosophy)*—Applications 2007–2008, 88. Total applicants accepted 2007–2008, 11. Number full-time enrolled (new admits only) 2007–2008, 6. Number part-time enrolled (new admits only) 2007–2008, 0. Openings 2008–2009, 5. The median number of years required for completion of a degree in 2006–2007 were 5. The number of students enrolled full- and part-time who were dismissed or voluntarily withdrew from this program area in 2007–2008 were 1.

Admissions Requirements:

Scores: Entries appear in this order: required test or GPA, minimum score (if required), median score of students entering in 2007–2008. Doctoral Programs: GRE-V no minimum stated; GRE-Q no minimum stated; overall undergraduate GPA 3.0; Doctoral program GRE-Analytic no minimum stated. GPA requirement: A cumulative GPA of 3.0 for the entire undergraduate record, a GPA of at least 3.0 for the last two undergraduate years, a GPA of 3.5 or better in the entire final undergraduate year, or graduate work with a minimum GPA of 3.0 or better is required.

Other Criteria: (importance of criteria rated low, medium, or high): GRE/MAT scores—medium, research experience—high, work experience—low, clinically related public service—low, GPA—medium, letters of recommendation—high, interview—medium, statement of goals and objectives—high. Check the department Web site at http://web.uconn.edu/psychology/academics/graduate/graduate_program.html for admissions requirements for specific program areas. The Clinical Division interviews applicants by invitation only. The clinical interviews are considered to be high in importance of criteria used for offering admission. The Behavioral Neuroscience Division may interview by invitation or by applicant request, however interviews are not required. The Developmental, Experimental, Industrial/Organizational, and Social divisions do not interview applicants as part of the admissions process. For additional information on admission requirements, go to http://web.uconn.edu/psychology/academics/graduate/graduate_program.html.

Student Characteristics: The following represents characteristics of students in 2007–2008 in all graduate psychology programs in the department: Female—full-time 116, part-time 0; Male—full-time 60, part-time 2; African American/Black—full-time 10, part-time 1; Hispanic/Latino(a)—full-time 11, part-time 0; Asian/Pacific Islander—full-time 16, part-time 0; American Indian/Alaska Native—full-time 0, part-time 0; Caucasian/White—full-time 131, part-time 1; students subject to the Americans With Disabilities Act—full-time 0, part-time 0; Unknown ethnicity—full-time 8, part-time 0; International students who hold an F-1 or J-1 Visa—full-time 22, part-time 0.

Financial Information/Assistance:

Tuition for Full-Time Study: *Doctoral:* State residents: per academic year $8,910; Nonstate residents: per academic year $23,130. Tuition is subject to change. See the following Web site for updates and changes in tuition costs: http://www.grad.uconn.edu/tuition.html.

Financial Assistance:

First-Year Students: Teaching assistantships available for first year. Average amount paid per academic year: $9,549. Average number of hours worked per week: 10. Apply by January 1st. Tuition remission given: full. Research assistantships available for first year. Average amount paid per academic year: $9,459. Average number of hours worked per week: 10. Apply by January 1. Tuition remission given: full. Fellowships and scholarships available for first year. Average amount paid per academic year: $2,000. Average number of hours worked per week: 0. Apply by January 1.

Advanced Students: Teaching assistantships available for advanced students. Average amount paid per academic year: $11,171. Average number of hours worked per week: 10. Tuition remission given: full. Research assistantships available for advanced students. Average amount paid per academic year: $11,171. Average number of hours worked per week: 10. Tuition remission given: full. Fellowships and scholarships available for advanced students. Average amount paid per academic year: $2,000. Average number of hours worked per week: 0.

Additional Information: Of all students currently enrolled full time, 90% benefited from one or more of the listed financial assistance programs. No separate financial aid application for Department funding; Federal funding. Application and information available online at http://www.financialaid.uconn.edu.

Internships/Practica: No information provided.

Housing and Day Care: On-campus housing is available. See the following Web site for more information: http://www.reslife.uconn.edu/graduate_housing.html and http://www.grad.uconn.edu/housing.html. On-campus day care facilities are available. The Child Development Laboratories, which are part of the Department of Human Development and Family Studies, offer full day and half day programs for children from 6 weeks to 5 years of age. For information, e-mail the Child Development Labs at childlabs@uconn.edu, or check on their Web site: http://childlabs.uconn.edu/general.html.

Employment of Department Graduates:

Master's Degree Graduates: Of those who graduated in the academic year 2006–2007, the following categories and numbers represent the postgraduate activities and employment of master's degree graduates: Enrolled in a postdoctoral residency/fellowship (n/a), employed in independent practice (n/a), total from the above (master's) (0).

Doctoral Degree Graduates: Of those who graduated in the academic year 2006–2007, the following categories and numbers represent the postgraduate activities and employment of doctoral degree graduates: Enrolled in a psychology doctoral program (n/a), enrolled in a postdoctoral residency/fellowship (8), employed in an academic position at a university (6), employed in an academic position at a 2-year/4-year college (2), employed in other positions at a higher education institution (2), employed in business or industry (3), employed in a hospital/medical center (1), do not know (1), total from the above (doctoral) (23).

Additional Information:

Orientation, Objectives, and Emphasis of Department: The department is focused on a dual mission of pursuing excellence in both research and teaching, while not losing sight of its broader mission to engage in meaningful outreach. The department is comprised of six divisions, each of which offers doctoral training in one or more areas of concentration as follows: (a) Behavioral Neuroscience (biopsychology, neuroscience); (b) Clinical Psychology; (c) Developmental Psychology; (d) Perception, Action, Cognition (ecological psychology, language and cognition); (e) Industrial/Organizational Psychology; and (f) Social Psychology. Interdivisional areas of strength, and targets for future growth, include (a) quantitative research methods, (b) health psychology, (c) cognitive science, (d) neuropsychology, and (e) developmental psychopathology. The pursuit of new knowledge (i.e., discovery through research) is the dominant emphasis of the department. This emphasis relies heavily on the interactive contributions from faculty, graduate students, and undergraduate students. In addition, the department's Graduate Student Teacher Training Program provides multiple, mentored teaching experiences for graduate students interested in pursuing a teaching/research career. Despite these varied emphases and endeavors, the department continues to maintain a collegial and supportive atmosphere where individual contributions are both recognized and rewarded.

Special Facilities or Resources: Multiple facilities, resources, and opportunities for research and training endeavors are not only available but also are encouraged, fostered, and strongly supported by the department. These opportunities include existing and strong research collaborations with the University of Connecticut Health Center, with Haskins Laboratories in New Haven, with the Olin Neuropsychiatry Research Center at the Institute of Living in Hartford, and with a wide variety of research and internship opportunities available at multiple industries, hospitals, mental institutions, and school systems located in Connecticut. In addition, the department makes available and encourages research and training opportunities with units located within the department and/or within the University, including the Center for Health Intervention and Prevention, the Psychological Services Clinic (PSC), the Industrial Psychology Applications Center (IPAC), and the Center for the Ecological Study of Perception and Action (CESPA). Collectively, these collaborative relationships provide graduate students with a myriad of opportunities to pursue their research and training experience objectives.

Information for Students With Physical Disabilities: See the following Web site for more information: http://www.csd.uconn.edu.

Application Information:

Send to University of Connecticut Graduate School, 438 Whitney Road Extension, Unit 1006, Storrs, CT 06269-1006. Application available online. URL of online application: http://www.grad.uconn.edu/apply.html. Students are admitted in the Fall, application deadline Janaury 1. Clinical Psychology program: December 1; Social Psychology and Industrial/Organizational Psychology programs: December 15; all other programs: January 1. *Fee:* $75; $55 fee for applications submitted using online application system.

Connecticut, University of

School Psychology Program
NEAG School of Education
249 Glenbrook Road, Unit 2064
Storrs, CT 06269-2064
Telephone: (860) 486-4031
Fax: (860) 486-0180
E-mail: *thomas.kehle@uconn.edu*
Web: *http://www.ucc.uconn.edu/~wwwepsy*

Department Information:

1960. Director, School Psychology Program: Thomas J. Kehle. Number of faculty: total—full-time 4, part-time 1; women—full-time 3, part-time 1; total—minority—full-time 2.

Programs and Degrees Offered:

Listed in the following order: Program area, degree type (T if terminal Master's), number awarded 7/06–6/07. School Psychology PhD (Doctor of Philosophy) 8, School Psychology, MA/MS (Master of Arts/Science) 6.

APA Accreditation: School PhD (Doctor of Philosophy).

Student Applications/Admissions:

Student Applications

School Psychology PhD (Doctor of Philosophy)—Applications 2007–2008, 37. Total applicants accepted 2007–2008, 10. Number full-time enrolled (new admits only) 2007–2008, 4. Number part-time enrolled (new admits only) 2007–2008, 0. Total enrolled 2007–2008 full-time, 15, part-time, 2. Openings 2008–2009, 5. The median number of years required for completion of a degree in 2006–2007 were 5. The number of students enrolled full- and part-time who were dismissed or voluntarily withdrew from this program area in 2007–2008 were 1. *School Psychology MA/MS (Master of Arts/Science)*—Applications 2007–2008, 59. Total applicants accepted 2007–2008, 10. Number full-time enrolled (new admits only) 2007–2008, 3. Number part-time enrolled (new admits only) 2007–2008, 0. Openings 2008–2009, 5. The median number of years required for completion of a degree in 2006–2007 were 3. The number of students enrolled full- and part-time who were dismissed or voluntarily withdrew from this program area in 2007–2008 were 1.

Admissions Requirements:

Scores: Entries appear in this order: required test or GPA, minimum score (if required), median score of students entering in 2007–2008. Master's Programs: GRE-V 500, 560; GRE-Q 500, 620; overall undergraduate GPA 3.0; last 2 years GPA 3.0; Masters GRE-Analytical 4.0. GRE-V and Q required for School Psychology Masters/Sixth-Year and Doctoral Programs. Doctoral Programs: GRE-V 550, 573; GRE-Q 550, 640; overall undergraduate GPA 3.0, 3.6; last 2 years GPA 3.0; Doctoral program GRE-Analytic 4.0.

Other Criteria: (importance of criteria rated low, medium, or high): GRE/MAT scores—high, research experience—medium, work experience—medium, extracurricular activity—low, clinically related public service—low, GPA—medium, letters of recommendation—high, interview—high, statement of goals and objectives—high, undergraduate major in psychology—low, specific undergraduate psychology courses taken—low. School Psychology Masters/Sixth Year and Doctoral programs require interviews.

Student Characteristics: The following represents characteristics of students in 2007–2008 in all graduate psychology programs in the department: Female—full-time 23, part-time 0; Male—full-time 2, part-time 2; African American/Black—full-time 0, part-time 0; Hispanic/Latino(a)—full-time 0, part-time 0; Asian/Pacific Islander—full-time 1, part-time 0; American Indian/Alaska Native—full-time 1, part-time 0; Caucasian/White—full-time 23, part-time 2; Multi-ethnic—full-time 0, part-time 0; students subject to the Americans With Disabilities Act—full-time 0, part-time 0; Unknown ethnicity—full-time 0, part-time 0; International students who hold an F-1 or J-1 Visa—full-time 0, part-time 0.

Financial Information/Assistance:

Tuition for Full-Time Study: *Master's:* State residents: per academic year $8,442, $469 per credit hour; Nonstate residents: per academic year $21,924, $1,218 per credit hour. *Doctoral:* State residents: per academic year $8,442, $469 per credit hour; Nonstate residents: per academic year $21,942, $1,218 per credit hour. Additional fees are assessed to students beyond the costs of tuition for the following: General University, Infrastructure/Maintenance, Graduate Matriculation, Activity, Transit, Student Union. See the following Web site for updates and changes in tuition costs: http://www.grad.uconn.edu/.

Financial Assistance:

First-Year Students: Research assistantships available for first year. Average amount paid per academic year: $18,817. Average number of hours worked per week: 20. Apply by September 1. Tuition remission given: full.

Advanced Students: Research assistantships available for advanced students. Average amount paid per academic year: $22,012. Average number of hours worked per week: 20. Apply by September 1. Tuition remission given: full.

Additional Information: Of all students currently enrolled full time, 90% benefited from one or more of the listed financial assistance programs.

Internships/Practica: Doctoral Degree (PhD School Psychology): For those doctoral students for whom a professional internship was required in this program prior to graduation, (4) students applied for an internship in 2006–2007, with (4) students obtaining an internship. Of those students who obtained an internship, (4) were paid internships. Of those students who obtained an internship, (0) students placed in APA/CPA-accredited internships, (0) students placed in internships not APA/CPA accredited, but listed with the Association of Psychology Postdoctoral and Internship Centers (APPIC), (4) students placed in internships conforming to guidelines of the Council of Directors of School Psychology Programs (CDSPP), (0) students placed in internships that were not APA/CPA-accredited, APPIC or CDSPP listed. There are a number of practica and internship placement opportunities for school psychology students at the University of Connecticut, affiliated sites, and school districts. The overwhelming majority of internship placements are paid, as are many of the practicum placements.

Housing and Day Care: On-campus housing is available. See the following Web site for more information: http://www.drl.uconn.edu. On-campus day care facilities are available. See the following Web site for more information: http://www.childlabs.uconn.edu or call the Child Development Center (860) 486-2865.

Employment of Department Graduates:

Master's Degree Graduates: Of those who graduated in the academic year 2006–2007, the following categories and numbers represent the postgraduate activities and employment of master's degree graduates: Enrolled in a psychology doctoral program (3), enrolled in another graduate/professional program (0), enrolled in a postdoctoral residency/fellowship (n/a), employed in independent practice (n/a), employed in an academic position at a university (0), employed in an academic position at a 2-year/4-year college (0), employed in other positions at a higher education institution (0), employed in a professional position in a school system (8), employed in business or industry (0), employed in government agency (0), employed in a community mental health/counseling center (0), employed in a hospital/medical center (0), still seeking employment (0), other employment position (0), do not know (0), total from the above (master's) (11).

Doctoral Degree Graduates: Of those who graduated in the academic year 2006–2007, the following categories and numbers represent the postgraduate activities and employment of doctoral degree graduates: Enrolled in a psychology doctoral program (n/a), enrolled in another graduate/professional program (0), enrolled in a postdoctoral residency/fellowship (0), employed in independent practice (0), employed in an academic position at a university (0), employed in an academic position at a 2-year/4-year college (0), employed in other positions at a higher education institution (0), employed in a professional position in a school system (0), employed in business or industry (0), employed in government agency (0), employed in a community mental health/counseling center (0), employed in a hospital/medical center (0), still seeking employment (0), other employment position (0), do not know (0), total from the above (doctoral) (0).

Additional Information:

Orientation, Objectives, and Emphasis of Department: The Department of Educational Psychology sponsors master of arts/sixth year and doctor of philosohpy programs in school psychology. The programs are an integrated and organized preparation of psychologists whose primary professional interests involve children, families, and the educational process. The programs adhere to the scientist–practitioner model of training that assumes the effective practice of school psychology is based on knowledge gained from established methods of scientific inquiry. The faculty are committed to a learning environment that stresses an organized and explicit curriculum with clear expectations. In addition, the programs are designed to acquaint students with the diversity of theories and practices of school psychology, allowing students sufficient intellectual freedom to experiment with different delivery systems and various theoretical bases. The atmosphere is intended to foster informal student–faculty interactions, critical debate, and respect for theoretical diversity of practice, thus creating a more intense and exciting learning experience. It is believed that such a philosophy encourages and reinforces students' creatvity and intellectual risk taking that are fundamental in the further development of the professional practice of school psychology.

Special Facilities or Resources: Research space, equipment and/or opportunities exist in the following center/labs: Center for Behavioral and Educational Research, the National Research

Center for Gifted and Talented the Pappanikou Special Education Center, the University Program for Students With Learning Disabilities, the University of Connecticut Educational Microcomputing Laboratory, the Hartford Professional Development Academy.

Information for Students With Physical Disabilities: See the following Web site for more information: http://www.csd.uconn.edu/policies.html.

Application Information:
Send to Graduate Admissions, Room 108, Whetten Center Box U-6A, 438 Whitney Road Extension, Storrs, CT 06269-1006. Application available online. Students are admitted in the Fall, application deadline January 1. January 1 deadline for all admissions—Fall admits only. *Fee:* $55 for electronic submission, $75 for paper submission.

Hartford, University of

Department of Psychology
Arts and Sciences
200 Bloomfield Avenue
West Hartford, CT 06117
Telephone: (860) 768-4544
Fax: (860) 768-5292
E-mail: *jpowell@hartford.edu*

Department Information:
1953. Chair: Jack Powell, PhD. Number of faculty: total—full-time 12, part-time 2; women—full-time 6.

Programs and Degrees Offered:
Listed in the following order: Program area, degree type (T if terminal Master's), number awarded 7/06–6/07. Clinical Practices in Psychology MA/MS (Master of Arts/Science) (T) 12, General Psychology MA/MS (Master of Arts/Science) (T) 5, School Psychology MA/MS (Master of Arts/Science) 12, Organizational Psychology MA/MS (Master of Arts/Science) (T) 7.

Student Applications/Admissions:
Student Applications
Clinical Practices in Psychology MA/MS (Master of Arts/Science)—Applications 2007–2008, 51. Total applicants accepted 2007–2008, 25. Number full-time enrolled (new admits only) 2007–2008, 12. Total enrolled 2007–2008 full-time, 23. Openings 2008–2009, 12. The median number of years required for completion of a degree in 2006–2007 were 2. *General Psychology MA/MS (Master of Arts/Science)*—Applications 2007–2008, 12. Total applicants accepted 2007–2008, 5. Number full-time enrolled (new admits only) 2007–2008, 2. Total enrolled 2007–2008 full-time, 2, part-time, 16. Openings 2008–2009, 10. The median number of years required for completion of a degree in 2006–2007 were 2. *School Psychology MA/MS (Master of Arts/Science)*—Applications 2007–2008, 25. Total applicants accepted 2007–2008, 16. Number full-time enrolled (new admits only) 2007–2008, 12. Total enrolled 2007–2008 full-time, 33. Openings 2008–2009, 12. The median number of years required for completion of a degree in 2006–2007 were 3. The number of students enrolled full- and part-time who were dismissed or voluntarily withdrew from this program area in 2007–2008 were 0. *Organizational Psychology MA/MS (Master of Arts/Science)*—Applications 2007–2008, 28. Total applicants accepted 2007–2008, 24. Number full-time enrolled (new admits only) 2007–2008, 6. Number part-time enrolled (new admits only) 2007–2008, 14. Total enrolled 2007–2008 full-time, 6, part-time, 37. Openings 2008–2009, 12. The median number of years required for completion of a degree in 2006–2007 were 2. The number of students enrolled full- and part-time who were dismissed or voluntarily withdrew from this program area in 2007–2008 were 0.

Admissions Requirements:
Scores: Entries appear in this order: required test or GPA, minimum score (if required), median score of students entering in 2007–2008. Master's Programs: GRE-V no minimum stated, 440; GRE-Q no minimum stated, 500; GRE-Subject (Psychology) no minimum stated, 510; overall undergraduate GPA no minimum stated, 3.3; last 2 years GPA no minimum stated; psychology GPA no minimum stated, 3.2.
Other Criteria: (importance of criteria rated low, medium, or high): GRE/MAT scores—medium, research experience—medium, work experience—medium, extracurricular activity—low, clinically related public service—medium, GPA—medium, letters of recommendation—high, statement of goals and objectives—high.

Student Characteristics: The following represents characteristics of students in 2007–2008 in all graduate psychology programs in the department: Female—full-time 53, part-time 43; Male—full-time 11, part-time 10; African American/Black—full-time 3, part-time 1; Hispanic/Latino(a)—full-time 3, part-time 3; Asian/Pacific Islander—full-time 0, part-time 1; American Indian/Alaska Native—full-time 0, part-time 0; Caucasian/White—full-time 58, part-time 48; Multi-ethnic—full-time 0, part-time 0; Unknown ethnicity—full-time 0, part-time 0.

Financial Information/Assistance:
Tuition for Full-Time Study: *Master's:* State residents: $390 per credit hour; Nonstate residents: $390 per credit hour.

Financial Assistance:
First-Year Students: Teaching assistantships available for first year. Average amount paid per academic year: $2,550. Average number of hours worked per week: 15. Research assistantships available for first year. Average amount paid per academic year: $2,000. Average number of hours worked per week: 10.
Advanced Students: Teaching assistantships available for advanced students. Average amount paid per academic year: $2,550. Average number of hours worked per week: 15. Research assistantships available for advanced students. Average amount paid per academic year: $2,000. Average number of hours worked per week: 10.
Additional Information: Of all students currently enrolled full time, 25% benefited from one or more of the listed financial assistance programs.

Internships/Practica: All Clinical Practices in Psychology students are assigned a half-time practicum throughout the 2nd year of their academic program. The assignments for practica include mental health clinics, in- and outpatient services in hospitals, community centers, schools, and correctional institutions. Students are supervised both onsite by professional psychologists and at the University by the faculty. All School Psychology students are assigned a half-time practicum throughout their 2nd year in a school setting and a full-time internship in their 3rd year. Students are supervised by school psychologists on site and at the university by the faculty. Organizational Behavior students have an option of a one semester practicum and General Experimental students have an option of a two semester, half-time practicum at a facility in an area relevant to the student's training.

Housing and Day Care: No on-campus housing is available. No on-campus day care facilities are available.

Employment of Department Graduates:

Master's Degree Graduates: Of those who graduated in the academic year 2006–2007, the following categories and numbers represent the postgraduate activities and employment of master's degree graduates: Enrolled in a postdoctoral residency/fellowship (n/a), employed in independent practice (n/a), total from the above (master's) (0).

Doctoral Degree Graduates: Of those who graduated in the academic year 2006–2007, the following categories and numbers represent the postgraduate activities and employment of doctoral degree graduates: Enrolled in a psychology doctoral program (n/a), total from the above (doctoral) (0).

Additional Information:

Orientation, Objectives, and Emphasis of Department: The primary orientation of the department in terms of undergraduate training might be best described as eclectic, and the goal is to provide a broadly based foundation in psychology for both the student who will graduate with an undergraduate major and the student who will use the major as a building block for further graduate training in the field. At the level of graduate training, the emphasis varies with the separate programs. The Clinical Practices in Psychology, Organizational Behavior, and School Psychology programs tend to be precisely focused in terms of professional preparation at the master's level of training, whereas the General Experimental program is more broadly based and is viewed as being preparatory to doctoral training.

Special Facilities or Resources: In addition to mock therapy observational studios located within the Department of Psychology, there are research labs dedicated to the study of stress management, pain management, and attachment. Numerous on-campus and community organizations are available for student internships and practica.

Application Information:

Send to Center for Graduate and Adult Academic Services, University of Hartford, 200 Bloomfield Avenue, West Hartford, CT 06117. Application available online. URL of online application: http://www.hartford.edu. Students are admitted in the Fall, application deadline February 15. All programs: review begins February 15. Rolling admission until filled. *Fee:* $45.

Hartford, University of

Graduate Institute of Professional Psychology
200 Bloomfield Avenue
West Hartford, CT 06117-1599
Telephone: (860) 768-4778
Fax: (860) 768-4814
E-mail: *viereck@hartford.edu*
Web: *http://www.hartford.edu/gipppsyd*

Department Information:

1993. Director: Otto Wahl. Number of faculty: total—full-time 7, part-time 20; women—full-time 4, part-time 9; total—minority—full-time 1, part-time 3; women minority—full-time 1, part-time 1.

Programs and Degrees Offered:

Listed in the following order: Program area, degree type (T if terminal Master's), number awarded 7/06–6/07. Graduate Institute of Professional Psychology PsyD (Doctor of Psychology) 19.

APA Accreditation: Clinical PsyD (Doctor of Psychology).

Student Applications/Admissions:

Student Applications

Psychology PsyD (Doctor of Psychology)—Applications 2007–2008, 164. Total applicants accepted 2007–2008, 23. Number full-time enrolled (new admits only) 2007–2008, 23. Total enrolled 2007–2008 full-time, 140. Openings 2008–2009, 25. The median number of years required for completion of a degree in 2006–2007 were 5. The number of students enrolled full- and part-time who were dismissed or voluntarily withdrew from this program area in 2007–2008 were 4.

Admissions Requirements:

Scores: Entries appear in this order: required test or GPA, minimum score (if required), median score of students entering in 2007–2008. Doctoral Programs: GRE-V no minimum stated, 550; GRE-Q no minimum stated, 550; GRE-Subject (Psychology) no minimum stated, 550; overall undergraduate GPA no minimum stated, 3.6.

Other Criteria: (importance of criteria rated low, medium, or high): GRE/MAT scores—medium, research experience—medium, work experience—medium, extracurricular activity—low, clinically related public service—medium, GPA—high, letters of recommendation—high, interview—high, statement of goals and objectives—high.

Student Characteristics: The following represents characteristics of students in 2007–2008 in all graduate psychology programs in the department: Female—full-time 120, part-time 0; Male—full-time 20, part-time 0; African American/Black—full-time 6, part-time 0; Hispanic/Latino(a)—full-time 6, part-time 0; Asian/Pacific Islander—full-time 8, part-time 0; American Indian/Alaska Native—full-time 0, part-time 0; Caucasian/White—full-time 117, part-time 0; Multi-ethnic—part-time 0; students subject to the Americans With Disabilities Act—full-time 2, part-time 0; Unknown ethnicity—full-time 3, part-time 0; International students who hold an F-1 or J-1 Visa—full-time 6, part-time 0.

Financial Information/Assistance:

Tuition for Full-Time Study: *Doctoral:* State residents: per academic year $21,375; Nonstate residents: per academic year $21,375. Tuition is subject to change. See the following Web site for updates and changes in tuition costs: http://www.uhaweb.hartford.edu/bursar.

Financial Assistance:

First-Year Students: Research assistantships available for first year. Average amount paid per academic year: $3,100. Average number of hours worked per week: 6. Apply by varies. Fellowships and scholarships available for first year. Average amount paid per academic year: $4,000. Average number of hours worked per week: 0. Apply by none. Tuition remission given: partial.

Advanced Students: Teaching assistantships available for advanced students. Average amount paid per academic year: $6,200. Average number of hours worked per week: 12. Apply by varies. Research assistantships available for advanced students. Average amount paid per academic year: $3,100. Average number of hours worked per week: 6. Apply by varies. Fellowships and scholarships available for advanced students. Average amount paid per academic year: $3,100. Apply by none.

Additional Information: Of all students currently enrolled full time, 40% benefited from one or more of the listed financial assistance programs. Application and information available online at http://www.hartford.edu.

Internships/Practica: Doctoral Degree (PsyD Psychology): For those doctoral students for whom a professional internship was required in this program prior to graduation, (31) students applied for an internship in 2006–2007, with (28) students obtaining an internship. Of those students who obtained an internship, (28) were paid internships. Of those students who obtained an internship, (26) students placed in APA/CPA-accredited internships, (2) students placed in internships not APA/CPA-accredited, but listed with the Association of Psychology Postdoctoral and Internship Centers (APPIC), (0) students placed in internships conforming to guidelines of the Council of Directors of School Psychology Programs (CDSPP), (0) students placed in internships that were not APA/CPA-accredited, APPIC or CDSPP listed. Practica network is extensive (approximately 75 sites in 4 states), and includes child, adolescent, and adult placements. Students generally get their first or second choice of sites. Practica placement is coordinated with Professional Practice Seminar (2nd year) and Case Conference Seminar (3rd year) to insure student's clinical training needs are being met. Emphasis is placed upon the concept of "self-in-role" learning.

Housing and Day Care: No on-campus housing is available. No on-campus day care facilities are available.

Employment of Department Graduates:

Master's Degree Graduates: Of those who graduated in the academic year 2006–2007, the following categories and numbers represent the postgraduate activities and employment of master's degree graduates: Enrolled in a postdoctoral residency/fellowship (n/a), employed in independent practice (n/a), total from the above (master's) (0).

Doctoral Degree Graduates: Of those who graduated in the academic year 2006–2007, the following categories and numbers represent the postgraduate activities and employment of doctoral degree graduates: Enrolled in a psychology doctoral program (n/a), total from the above (doctoral) (0).

Additional Information:

Orientation, Objectives, and Emphasis of Department: The primary mission of the program is to prepare students for effective functioning in the multiple roles they will need to fill as practicing psychologists in these rapidly changing times. The program also espouses the principle of affirmative diversity, defined as upholding the fundamental values of human differences and the belief that respect for individual and cultural differences enhances and increases the quality of educational and interpersonal experiences.

Special Facilities or Resources: The Graduate Institute added a Child and Adolescent Proficiency Track in the Fall of 2003. The goal of the track is to allow students to develop not only broad clinical skills but also strong therapeutic, assessment, and program development skills in working specifically with children, adolescents, and families.

Information for Students With Physical Disabilities: See the following Web site for more information: http://www.hartford.edu/support.

Application Information:

Send to Center for Graduate and Adult Services, University of Hartford, 200 Bloomfield Avenue, Hartford, CT 06107. Application available online. URL of online application: http://www.hartford.edu/gipppsyd. Students are admitted in the Fall, application deadline December 15. *Fee:* $35.

New Haven, University of

Graduate Psychology
College of Arts and Sciences, University of New Haven
300 Boston Post Road
West Haven, CT 06516
Telephone: (203) 932-7339
Fax: (203) 931-6032
E-mail: *ssidle@newhaven.edu*
Web: *http://www.newhaven.edu*

Department Information:

1972. Graduate Program Directors: Stuart Sidle, PhD and Mike Morris, PhD. Number of faculty: total—full-time 9, part-time 11; women—full-time 2, part-time 6; total—minority—full-time 1, part-time 1; women minority—part-time 1.

Programs and Degrees Offered:

Listed in the following order: Program area, degree type (T if terminal Master's), number awarded 7/06–6/07. Industrial/Organizational Psychology MA/MS (Master of Arts/Science) (T) 35, Community Psychology MA/MS (Master of Arts/Science) 20.

Student Applications/Admissions:

Student Applications

Industrial/Organizational Psychology MA/MS (Master of Arts/Science)—Applications 2007–2008, 140. Total applicants accepted 2007–2008, 112. Number full-time enrolled (new admits only) 2007–2008, 47. Number part-time enrolled (new admits only) 2007–2008, 26. Total enrolled 2007–2008 full-time, 78, part-time, 38. Openings 2008–2009, 40. The median number of years required for completion of a degree in 2006–2007 were 2. The number of students enrolled full- and part-time who were dismissed or voluntarily withdrew from this program area in 2007–2008 were 3. *Community Psychology MA/MS (Master of Arts/Science)*—Applications 2007–2008, 50. Total applicants accepted 2007–2008, 38. Number full-time enrolled (new admits only) 2007–2008, 11. Number part-time enrolled (new admits only) 2007–2008, 6. Total enrolled 2007–2008 full-time, 17, part-time, 6. Openings 2008–2009, 25. The median number of years required for completion of a degree in 2006–2007 were 2.

Admissions Requirements:

Scores: Entries appear in this order: required test or GPA, minimum score (if required), median score of students entering in 2007–2008. Master's Programs: overall undergraduate GPA 3.0, 3.4.

Other Criteria: (importance of criteria rated low, medium, or high): research experience—medium, work experience—medium, extracurricular activity—medium, clinically related public service—low, GPA—high, letters of recommendation—high, statement of goals and objectives—high. For additional information on admission requirements, go to http://www.newhaven.edu.

Student Characteristics: The following represents characteristics of students in 2007–2008 in all graduate psychology programs in the department: Female—full-time 72, part-time 33; Male—full-time 23, part-time 11; African American/Black—full-time 13, part-time 4; Hispanic/Latino(a)—full-time 6, part-time 2; Asian/Pacific Islander—full-time 9, part-time 0; American Indian/Alaska Native—full-time 0, part-time 0; Caucasian/White—full-time 54, part-time 18; students subject to the Americans With Disabilities Act—full-time 0, part-time 0; Unknown ethnicity—full-time 13, part-time 20; International students who hold an F-1 or J-1 Visa—full-time 6, part-time 0.

Financial Information/Assistance:

Tuition for Full-Time Study: *Master's:* State residents: $630 per credit hour; Nonstate residents: $630 per credit hour. See the following Web site for updates and changes in tuition costs: http://www.newhaven.edu.

Financial Assistance:

First-Year Students: Teaching assistantships available for first year. Average number of hours worked per week: 15. Tuition remission given: partial. Research assistantships available for first year. Average number of hours worked per week: 15. Tuition remission given: partial.

Advanced Students: Teaching assistantships available for advanced students. Tuition remission given: partial. Research assistantships available for advanced students. Tuition remission given: partial.

Additional Information: Of all students currently enrolled full time, 90% benefited from one or more of the listed financial assistance programs.

Internships/Practica: Most of the full-time students complete an internship that allows the student to acquire special skills through coordinating formal coursework with an internship or practicum in an organizational setting. The internship gives the student with limited work experience the opportunity to work in cooperating organizations or consulting firms. We have longstanding relationships with a wide variety of business organizations that seek our students as interns.

Housing and Day Care: On-campus housing is available. No on-campus day care facilities are available.

Employment of Department Graduates:

Master's Degree Graduates: Of those who graduated in the academic year 2006–2007, the following categories and numbers represent the postgraduate activities and employment of master's degree graduates: Enrolled in a postdoctoral residency/fellowship (n/a), employed in independent practice (n/a), total from the above (master's) (0).

Doctoral Degree Graduates: Of those who graduated in the academic year 2006–2007, the following categories and numbers represent the postgraduate activities and employment of doctoral degree graduates: Enrolled in a psychology doctoral program (n/a), total from the above (doctoral) (0).

Additional Information:

Orientation, Objectives, and Emphasis of Department: The primary goal of the Master of Arts in Industrial and Organizational Psychology program is to provide students with the knowledge and experience necessary to improve the satisfaction and productivity of people at work. Graduates obtain challenging and rewarding positions in public and private corporations, consulting firms, and government agencies. Even though our program has a strong applied/career orientation, we have been quite successful in providing those students who wish to pursue doctoral study with a strong research foundation.

Information for Students With Physical Disabilities: See the following Web site for more information: http://www.newhaven.edu/show.asp?durki=1589.

Application Information:

Send to Graduate Admissions 300 Boston Post Road, University of New Haven, West Haven, CT 06516. Application available online. URL of online application: http://www.estrada2.newhaven.edu/admissions/gradadmissions/17944/. Students are admitted in the Fall, Winter, and Spring; Programs have rolling admissions. *Fee:* $50.

Southern Connecticut State University

Department of Psychology
501 Crescent Street
New Haven, CT 06515
Telephone: (203) 392-6868
Fax: (203) 392-6805
E-mail: *hauseltw1@southernct.edu*
Web: *http://www.southernct.edu/departments/psychology/*

Department Information:

1893. Graduate Coordinator: W. J. Hauselt.

Programs and Degrees Offered:

Listed in the following order: Program area, degree type (T if terminal Master's), number awarded 7/06–6/07. Psychology MA/MS (Master of Arts/Science) (T) 16.

Student Applications/Admissions:

Student Applications

Psychology MA/MS (Master of Arts/Science)—Applications 2007–2008, 52. Total applicants accepted 2007–2008, 35. Number full-time enrolled (new admits only) 2007–2008, 7. Number part-time enrolled (new admits only) 2007–2008, 15. Total enrolled 2007–2008 full-time, 25, part-time, 54. Openings 2008–2009, 20. The number of students enrolled full- and part-time who were dismissed or voluntarily withdrew from this program area in 2007–2008 were 4.

Admissions Requirements:

Scores: Entries appear in this order: required test or GPA, minimum score (if required), median score of students entering in 2007–2008. Master's Programs: overall undergraduate GPA 2.5, 3.3; psychology GPA 3.0, 3.4.

Other Criteria: (importance of criteria rated low, medium, or high): research experience—low, work experience—low, GPA—high, letters of recommendation—high, statement of goals and objectives—high, undergraduate major in psychology—low, specific undergraduate psychology courses taken—medium. For additional information on admission requirements, go to http://www.southernct.edu/psychology/graduate/.

Student Characteristics: The following represents characteristics of students in 2007–2008 in all graduate psychology programs in the department: Caucasian/White—full-time 0, part-time 0; Unknown ethnicity—full-time 0, part-time 0.

Financial Information/Assistance:

Tuition for Full-Time Study: *Master's:* State residents: per academic year $7,370, $483 per credit hour; Nonstate residents: per academic year $16,050, $483 per credit hour. Tuition is subject to change. See the following Web site for updates and changes in tuition costs: http://www.southernct.edu/bursar/tuitionfees/.

Financial Assistance:

First-Year Students: Teaching assistantships available for first year. Average amount paid per academic year: $4,400. Average number of hours worked per week: 20. Apply by May 1. Tuition remission given: partial.

Advanced Students: Teaching assistantships available for advanced students. Average amount paid per academic year: $4,400. Average number of hours worked per week: 20. Apply by May 1. Tuition remission given: partial.

Additional Information: Of all students currently enrolled full time, 20% benefited from one or more of the listed financial assistance programs.

Internships/Practica: With departmental permission, MA students may arrange a one- or two-semester clinical internship (three credits for one semester; six credits for two semesters).

Housing and Day Care: On-campus housing is available. See the following Web site for more information: http://www.southernct.edu/departments/graduatestudies/adreslife.php3. On-campus day care facilities are available. See the following Web site for more information: http://www.southernct.edu/services/?file=services.html.

Employment of Department Graduates:

Master's Degree Graduates: Of those who graduated in the academic year 2006–2007, the following categories and numbers represent the postgraduate activities and employment of master's degree graduates: Enrolled in a psychology doctoral program (2), enrolled in another graduate/professional program (1), enrolled in a postdoctoral residency/fellowship (n/a), employed in independent practice (n/a), employed in other positions at a higher education institution (1), employed in business or industry (3), employed in a community mental health/counseling center (5), do not know (4), total from the above (master's) (16).

Doctoral Degree Graduates: Of those who graduated in the academic year 2006–2007, the following categories and numbers represent the postgraduate activities and employment of doctoral degree graduates: Enrolled in a psychology doctoral program (n/a), total from the above (doctoral) (0).

Additional Information:

Orientation, Objectives, and Emphasis of Department: This rigorous, research-based program is designed to develop creative, problem-solving skills that graduates can apply to a variety of clinical, industrial, and educational settings. Leading to a master of arts degree, this program is flexible enough to be completed on either a full-or part-time basis, meeting the needs of a wide range of candidates. For potential doctoral candidates who can enter neither a PhD nor a PsyD program at the present time, this program may provide the basis for later acceptance into a doctoral program. For those who are already working in clinical, educational, or industrial settings, it offers updating and credentials. In addition, this program provides ideal training for people who want to explore their personal interest in careers related to psychology. High school teachers may use the program to prepare themselves to teach psychology in addition to their current certification. The program emphasizes faculty advisement to help tailor the program to the needs of each individual student.

Information for Students With Physical Disabilities: See the following Web site for more information: http://www.southernct.edu/departments/dro/.

Application Information:

Send to School of Graduate Studies, Southern Connecticut State University, New Haven, CT 06515. Application available online. URL of online application: http://www.southernct.edu/grad/admissions/admissionprocedures/. Students are admitted in the Fall, application deadline June 1; Spring, application deadline November 1. *Fee:* $50.

Wesleyan University

Psychology
207 High Street
Middletown, CT 06459-0408
Telephone: (860) 685-2342
Fax: (860) 685-2761
E-mail: *tvelasquez@wesleyan.edu*
Web: *http://www.wesleyan.edu/psyc/*

Department Information:

1913. Chairperson: Ruth Striegel-Moore. Number of faculty: total—full-time 7; women—full-time 7.

Programs and Degrees Offered:

Listed in the following order: Program area, degree type (T if terminal Master's), number awarded 7/06–6/07. General MA/MS (Master of Arts/Science) (T) 3.

Student Applications/Admissions:

Student Applications

General MA/MS (Master of Arts/Science)—Applications 2007–2008, 28. Total applicants accepted 2007–2008, 3. Number full-time enrolled (new admits only) 2007–2008, 3. Openings 2008–2009, 3. The median number of years required for completion of a degree in 2006–2007 were 2. The number of students enrolled full- and part-time who were dismissed or voluntarily withdrew from this program area in 2007–2008 were 0.

Admissions Requirements:

Scores: Entries appear in this order: required test or GPA, minimum score (if required), median score of students entering in 2007–2008. Master's Programs: GRE-V no minimum stated; GRE-Q no minimum stated; overall undergraduate GPA no minimum stated; Masters GRE-Analytical no minimum stated.

Other Criteria: (importance of criteria rated low, medium, or high): GRE/MAT scores—high, research experience—high, work experience—low, extracurricular activity—low, clinically related public service—medium, GPA—high, letters of recommendation—high, statement of goals and objectives—high. For additional information on admission requirements, go to http://www.wesleyan.edu/psyc/programs.htm#ma.

Student Characteristics: The following represents characteristics of students in 2007–2008 in all graduate psychology programs in the department: Female—full-time 3, part-time 0; Male—full-time 0, part-time 0; African American/Black—full-time 1, part-time 0; Hispanic/Latino(a)—full-time 0, part-time 0; Asian/Pacific Islander—full-time 0, part-time 0; American Indian/Alaska Native—full-time 0, part-time 0; Caucasian/White—full-time 1, part-time 0; Multi-ethnic—full-time 0, part-time 0; students subject to the Americans With Disabilities Act—full-time 0, part-time 0; Unknown ethnicity—full-time 1, part-time 0; International students who hold an F-1 or J-1 Visa—full-time 0, part-time 0.

Financial Information/Assistance:

Financial Assistance:

First-Year Students: Teaching assistantships available for first year. Average amount paid per academic year: $14,000. Average number of hours worked per week: 10. Tuition remission given: full.

Advanced Students: Teaching assistantships available for advanced students. Average amount paid per academic year: $14,000. Average number of hours worked per week: 10. Tuition remission given: full.

Additional Information: Of all students currently enrolled full time, 100% benefited from one or more of the listed financial assistance programs. Application and information available online at http://www.wesleyan.edu/grad/StudentServ/.

Internships/Practica: No information provided.

Housing and Day Care: On-campus housing is available. See the following Web site for more information: http://www.wesleyan.edu/grad/. Contact graduate office for this information: gradoffice@wesleyan.edu. No on-campus day care facilities are available.

Employment of Department Graduates:

Master's Degree Graduates: Of those who graduated in the academic year 2006–2007, the following categories and numbers represent the postgraduate activities and employment of master's degree graduates: Enrolled in a psychology doctoral program (3), enrolled in a postdoctoral residency/fellowship (n/a), employed in independent practice (n/a), other employment position (1), do not know (1), total from the above (master's) (5).

Doctoral Degree Graduates: Of those who graduated in the academic year 2006–2007, the following categories and numbers represent the postgraduate activities and employment of doctoral degree graduates: Enrolled in a psychology doctoral program (n/a), total from the above (doctoral) (0).

Additional Information:

Orientation, Objectives, and Emphasis of Department: The department of Psychology at Wesleyan University offers a 2-year program of study culminating in the master of arts degree. The hallmarks of the program are its selectivity, small size, and research orientation. Most students go on to pursue doctoral studies. Toward this end, the program is designed to provide a solid foundation of training in general psychology and additional experience in the fundamentals of research in a more specialized area of interest. Areas of expertise represented in the department include clinical, cognitive, developmental, educational, neuroscience, personality, social, and women's studies.

Special Facilities or Resources: Most faculty have research laboratories within the Psychology Department. All MA students who are between their first and second year of study have the option of receiving a summer research stipend of approximately $3,000.

Application Information:

Send to Graduate Coordinator, Psychology Department, Wesleyan University, 207 High Street, Middletown, CT 06459-0408. Application available online. URL of online application: http://www.wesleyan.edu/psyc/grad_MA.html. Students are admitted in the Spring, application deadline February 8. *Fee:* $0.

Yale University

Department of Psychology
P.O. Box 208205
New Haven, CT 06520-8205
Telephone: (203) 432-4518
Fax: (203) 432-7172
E-mail: *lauretta.olivi@yale.edu*
Web: *http://www.yale.edu/psychology*

Department Information:

1928. Chair: Marcia Johnson. Number of faculty: total—full-time 12, part-time 1; women—full-time 11; women minority—full-time 2.

Programs and Degrees Offered:

Listed in the following order: Program area, degree type (T if terminal Master's), number awarded 7/06–6/07. Behavioral Neuroscience PhD (Doctor of Philosophy) 3, Clinical PhD (Doctor of Philosophy) 3, Cognitive PhD (Doctor of Philosophy) 1, Developmental PhD (Doctor of Philosophy) 3, Social Personality PhD (Doctor of Philosophy) 5.

APA Accreditation: Clinical PhD (Doctor of Philosophy).

Student Applications/Admissions:

Student Applications

Behavioral Neuroscience PhD (Doctor of Philosophy)—Applications 2007–2008, 35. Total applicants accepted 2007–2008, 3. Number full-time enrolled (new admits only) 2007–2008, 1. Number part-time enrolled (new admits only) 2007–2008, 0. Openings 2008–2009, 5. The median number of years required for completion of a degree in 2006–2007 were 6. The number of students enrolled full- and part-time who were dismissed or voluntarily withdrew from this program area in 2007–2008 were 0. *Clinical PhD (Doctor of Philosophy)*—Applications 2007–2008, 324. Total applicants accepted 2007–2008, 3. Number full-time enrolled (new admits only) 2007–2008, 1. Number part-time enrolled (new admits only) 2007–2008, 0. Openings 2008–2009, 6. The median number of years required for completion of a degree in 2006–2007 were 6. The number of students enrolled full- and part-time who were dismissed or voluntarily withdrew from this program area in 2007–2008 were 0. *Cognitive PhD (Doctor of Philosophy)*—Applications 2007–2008, 83. Total applicants accepted 2007–2008, 4. Number full-time enrolled (new admits only) 2007–2008, 1. Number part-time enrolled (new admits only) 2007–2008, 0. Openings 2008–2009, 7. The median number of years required for completion of a degree in 2006–2007 were 6. The number of students enrolled full- and part-time who were dismissed or voluntarily withdrew from this program area in 2007–2008 were 0. *Developmental PhD (Doctor of Philosophy)*—Applications 2007–2008, 32. Total applicants accepted 2007–2008, 3. Number full-time enrolled (new admits only) 2007–2008, 3. Number part-time enrolled (new admits only) 2007–2008, 0. Openings 2008–2009, 6. The median number of years required for completion of a degree in 2006–2007 were 6. The number of students enrolled full- and part-time who were dismissed or voluntarily withdrew from this program area in 2007–2008 were 0. *Social Personality PhD (Doctor of Philosophy)*—Applications 2007–2008, 134. Total applicants accepted 2007–2008, 5. Number full-time enrolled (new admits only) 2007–2008, 2. Number part-time enrolled (new admits only) 2007–2008, 0. Openings 2008–2009, 6. The median number of years required for completion of a degree in 2006–2007 were 6. The number of students enrolled full- and part-time who were dismissed or voluntarily withdrew from this program area in 2007–2008 were 0.

Admissions Requirements:

Scores: Entries appear in this order: required test or GPA, minimum score (if required), median score of students entering in 2007–2008. Master's Programs: We do not offer a terminal Master's Program. Doctoral Programs: GRE-V 600, 650; GRE-Q 600, 700; overall undergraduate GPA no minimum stated, 3.76; psychology GPA no minimum stated; Doctoral program GRE-Analytic 4.0, 5.0.

Other Criteria: (importance of criteria rated low, medium, or high): GRE/MAT scores—high, research experience—high, work experience—low, extracurricular activity—low, clinically related public service—low, GPA—high, letters of recommendation—high, interview—medium, statement of goals and objectives—high, undergraduate major in psychology—medium, specific undergraduate psychology courses taken—medium. For additional information on admission requirements, go to http://www.yale.edu/graduateschool/admissions.

Student Characteristics: The following represents characteristics of students in 2007–2008 in all graduate psychology programs in the department: Female—full-time 50, part-time 0; Male—full-time 28, part-time 0; African American/Black—full-time 2, part-time 0; Hispanic/Latino(a)—full-time 0, part-time 0; Asian/Pacific Islander—full-time 10, part-time 0; American Indian/Alaska Native—full-time 0, part-time 0; Caucasian/White—full-time 57, part-time 0; Multi-ethnic—full-time 9, part-time 0; students subject to the Americans With Disabilities Act—full-time 0, part-time 0; Unknown ethnicity—full-time 0, part-time 0; International students who hold an F-1 or J-1 Visa—full-time 3, part-time 0.

Financial Information/Assistance:

Financial Assistance:

First-Year Students: No information provided.

Advanced Students: Teaching assistantships available for advanced students. Average amount paid per academic year: $14,000. Average number of hours worked per week: 15. Apply by June 30. Tuition remission given: full. Research assistantships available for advanced students. Average number of hours worked per week: 10. Tuition remission given: full. Traineeships available for advanced students. Tuition remission given: full. Fellowships and scholarships available for advanced students. Tuition remission given: full.

Additional Information: Of all students currently enrolled full time, 100% benefited from one or more of the listed financial assistance programs. Application and information available online at http://www.yale.edu/graduateschool/financial/index.html.

Internships/Practica: Doctoral Degree (PhD Clinical): For those doctoral students for whom a professional internship was required in this program prior to graduation, (3) students applied for an internship in 2006–2007, with (3) students obtaining an internship. Of those students who obtained an internship, (3) were paid internships. Of those students who obtained an internship, (3) students placed in APA/CPA-accredited internships, (0) students placed in internships not APA/CPA-accredited, but listed with the Association of Psychology Postdoctoral and Internship Centers (APPIC), (0) students placed in internships conforming to guidelines of the Council of Directors of School Psychology Programs (CDSPP), (0) students placed in internships that were not APA/CPA-accredited, APPIC or CDSPP listed. Students are required to assist in teaching an average of 10–15 hours per week in their 2nd, 3rd, and 4th years as part of their educational program. Local facilities for predoctoral internships are the Veterans Administration Center in West Haven, Yale Psychological Services Clinic, the Yale Child Study Center, and Yale Department of Psychiatry, with placement in the Connecticut Mental Health Center, Yale-New Haven Hospital, or the Yale Psychiatric Institute. Also, internships are arranged in accredited facilities throughout the United States.

Housing and Day Care: On-campus housing is available. See the following Web site for more information: http://www.yale.edu/

hronline/gho/. On-campus day care facilities are available. See the following Web site: http://www.yale.edu/daycare.

Employment of Department Graduates:

Master's Degree Graduates: Of those who graduated in the academic year 2006–2007, the following categories and numbers represent the postgraduate activities and employment of master's degree graduates: Enrolled in another graduate/professional program (0), enrolled in a postdoctoral residency/fellowship (n/a), employed in independent practice (n/a), total from the above (master's) (0).

Doctoral Degree Graduates: Of those who graduated in the academic year 2006–2007, the following categories and numbers represent the postgraduate activities and employment of doctoral degree graduates: Enrolled in a psychology doctoral program (n/a), enrolled in a postdoctoral residency/fellowship (10), employed in independent practice (0), employed in an academic position at a university (2), employed in an academic position at a 2-year/4-year college (0), employed in other positions at a higher education institution (0), employed in a professional position in a school system (0), employed in business or industry (0), employed in government agency (0), employed in a community mental health/counseling center (0), employed in a hospital/medical center (0), still seeking employment (0), not seeking employment (0), other employment position (0), do not know (0), total from the above (doctoral) (12).

Additional Information:

Orientation, Objectives, and Emphasis of Department: The chief goal of graduate education in psychology at Yale University is the training of research workers in academic and other settings who will broaden the basic scientific knowledge on which the discipline of psychology rests. Major emphasis is given to preparation for research; a definite effort is made to give students a background for teaching. The concentration of doctoral training on research and teaching is consistent with a variety of career objectives in addition to traditional academics. The department believes that rigorous and balanced exposure to basic psychology is the best preparation for research careers. The first important aspect of graduate training is advanced study of general psychology, including method and psychological theory. The second is specialized training within a subfield. Third, the student is encouraged to take advantage of opportunities for wider training emphasizing research rather than practice. For the clinical area, research and practica are strongly integrated. Training is geared to the expectation that the majority of students will have research careers.

Special Facilities or Resources: Facilities available as adjuncts to research and teaching include the Yale Capuchin Cognition Lab, the Yale Parenting Center and Child Conduct Clinic, the Rudd Center for Food Policy and Obesity, and the Yale Center for Eating and Weight Disorders as well as the Behavioral Alcohol Research for Clinical Advancement (BARCA) Lab. Other facilities include special rooms equipped for observation, intercommunication, and recording as required for clinical supervision or testing or for interview training and research. Also available to our students is an fMRI facility in the Yale University School of Medicine.

Information for Students With Physical Disabilities: See the following Web site for more information: http://www.yale.edu/rod/.

Application Information:

Send to Graduate School, Yale University, Office of Admissions, P.O. Box 208323, New Haven, CT 06520-8323. Application available online. URL of online application: http://www.yale.edu/graduateschool/admissions. Students are admitted in the Fall, application deadline December 15. Our applications are available only online. *Fee:* $85.

Delaware, University of
Department of Psychology
College of Arts and Science
108 Wolf Hall
Newark, DE 19716
Telephone: (302) 831-2271
Fax: (302) 831-3645
E-mail: *mchermol@psych.udel.edu*
Web: *http://www.psych.udel.edu/graduate/index.php*

Department Information:

1946. Chairperson: Thomas DiLorenzo. Number of faculty: total—full-time 28; women—full-time 10; total—minority—full-time 3; women minority—full-time 1.

Programs and Degrees Offered:

Listed in the following order: Program area, degree type (T if terminal Master's), number awarded 7/06–6/07. Clinical PhD (Doctor of Philosophy) 2, Behavioral Neuroscience PhD (Doctor of Philosophy) 0, Social PhD (Doctor of Philosophy) 2, Cognitive PhD (Doctor of Philosophy) 1.

APA Accreditation: Clinical PhD (Doctor of Philosophy).

Student Applications/Admissions:

Student Applications

Clinical PhD (Doctor of Philosophy)—Applications 2007–2008, 180. Total applicants accepted 2007–2008, 9. Number full-time enrolled (new admits only) 2007–2008, 3. Number part-time enrolled (new admits only) 2007–2008, 0. The number of students enrolled full- and part-time who were dismissed or voluntarily withdrew from this program area in 2007–2008 were 0. *Behavioral Neuroscience PhD (Doctor of Philosophy)*—Applications 2007–2008, 22. Total applicants accepted 2007–2008, 5. Number full-time enrolled (new admits only) 2007–2008, 1. Number part-time enrolled (new admits only) 2007–2008, 0. The number of students enrolled full- and part-time who were dismissed or voluntarily withdrew from this program area in 2007–2008 were 0. *Social PhD (Doctor of Philosophy)*—Applications 2007–2008, 39. Total applicants accepted 2007–2008, 2. Number full-time enrolled (new admits only) 2007–2008, 3. Number part-time enrolled (new admits only) 2007–2008, 0. The number of students enrolled full- and part-time who were dismissed or voluntarily withdrew from this program area in 2007–2008 were 0. *Cognitive PhD (Doctor of Philosophy)*—Applications 2007–2008, 18. Total applicants accepted 2007–2008, 1. Number full-time enrolled (new admits only) 2007–2008, 2. Number part-time enrolled (new admits only) 2007–2008, 0. The number of students enrolled full- and part-time who were dismissed or voluntarily withdrew from this program area in 2007–2008 were 0.

Admissions Requirements:

Scores: Entries appear in this order: required test or GPA, minimum score (if required), median score of students entering in 2007–2008. Master's Programs: Admission is for doctoral program only. Above information is not applicable. Doctoral Programs: GRE-V 410, 595; GRE-Q 400, 670; overall undergraduate GPA 3.25, 3.88.

Other Criteria: (importance of criteria rated low, medium, or high): GRE/MAT scores—high, research experience—medium, work experience—low, extracurricular activity—low, clinically related public service—medium, GPA—high, letters of recommendation—high, interview—high, statement of goals and objectives—high. In the behavioral neuroscience, cognitive, and social areas, GRE scores are emphasized less (medium) and research experience is emphasized more (high) relative to the clinical area.

Student Characteristics: The following represents characteristics of students in 2007–2008 in all graduate psychology programs in the department: Female—full-time 33, part-time 0; Male—full-time 15, part-time 0; African American/Black—full-time 4, part-time 0; Hispanic/Latino(a)—full-time 0, part-time 0; Asian/Pacific Islander—full-time 1, part-time 0; American Indian/Alaska Native—full-time 0, part-time 0; Caucasian/White—full-time 39, part-time 0; Multi-ethnic—full-time 0, part-time 0; students subject to the Americans With Disabilities Act—full-time 0, part-time 0; Unknown ethnicity—full-time 1, part-time 0; International students who hold an F-1 or J-1 Visa—full-time 3, part-time 0.

Financial Information/Assistance:

Tuition for Full-Time Study: *Doctoral:* State residents: per academic year $6,980, $291 per credit hour; Nonstate residents: per academic year $17,690, $737 per credit hour. Tuition is not available at this time. See the following Web site for updates and changes in tuition costs: http://www.udel.edu/bill_coll/tuition worksite.html.

Financial Assistance:

First-Year Students: Teaching assistantships available for first year. Average amount paid per academic year: $15,262. Average number of hours worked per week: 20. Apply by January 7. Tuition remission given: full. Research assistantships available for first year. Average amount paid per academic year: $16,479. Average number of hours worked per week: 20. Apply by January 7. Tuition remission given: full. Fellowships and scholarships available for first year. Average amount paid per academic year: $15,262. Apply by January 7. Tuition remission given: full.

Advanced Students: Teaching assistantships available for advanced students. Average amount paid per academic year: $15,803. Average number of hours worked per week: 20. Apply by N/A. Tuition remission given: full. Research assistantships available for advanced students. Average amount paid per academic year: $15,803. Average number of hours worked per week: 20. Apply by N/A. Tuition remission given: full. Fellowships and scholarships available for advanced students. Average amount paid per academic year: $15,803. Apply by February 29. Tuition remission given: full.

Additional Information: Of all students currently enrolled full time, 100% benefited from one or more of the listed financial assistance programs.

Internships/Practica: Doctoral Degree (PhD Clinical): For those doctoral students for whom a professional internship was required in this program prior to graduation, (2) students applied for an internship in 2006–2007, with (2) students obtaining an internship. Of those students who obtained an internship, (2) were paid internships. Of those students who obtained an internship, (2) students placed in APA/CPA-accredited internships, (0) students placed in internships not APA/CPA-accredited, but listed with the Association of Psychology Postdoctoral and Internship Centers (APPIC), (0) students placed in internships conforming to guidelines of the Council of Directors of School Psychology Programs (CDSPP), (0) students placed in internships that were not APA/CPA-accredited, APPIC or CDSPP listed. A wide range of practica experiences are available for clinical graduate students.

Housing and Day Care: On-campus housing is available. See the following Web site for more information: http://www.udel.edu/housing/. On-campus day care facilities are available.

Employment of Department Graduates:

Master's Degree Graduates: Of those who graduated in the academic year 2006–2007, the following categories and numbers represent the postgraduate activities and employment of master's degree graduates: Enrolled in a postdoctoral residency/fellowship (n/a), employed in independent practice (n/a), total from the above (master's) (0).

Doctoral Degree Graduates: Of those who graduated in the academic year 2006–2007, the following categories and numbers represent the postgraduate activities and employment of doctoral degree graduates: Enrolled in a psychology doctoral program (n/a), total from the above (doctoral) (0).

Additional Information:

Orientation, Objectives, and Emphasis of Department: The department fosters a scientific approach to all areas of psychology. The training is organized around clinical, cognitive, behavioral neuroscience, and social areas, as well as an integrative developmental focus that cuts across areas. All first-year students are required to complete 1st and 2nd year research projects as well as take seminars in their program area of study. In the 3rd and 4th year students take additional seminars, take a comprehensive qualifying exam or prepare a comprehensive paper, and prepare dissertation proposals. Clinical students also participate in the training of practice skills. Beyond the first year, students work out their own research programs with faculty advisors. The goal of this training is to prepare students to function as scientists and teachers in academic, applied, and clinical settings. Major current research interests in these areas are as follows: (a) clinical: evaluation of therapy, social development of children, community mental health, theory of emotions, communication of emotions, organic brain syndromes, family therapy, sex roles, sensation seeking, and sexuality; (b) cognitive: attention, pattern recognition, psycholinguistics, visual information processing, memory, and cognitive development; (c) behavioral neuroscience: neuroanatomy, developmental psychobiology, psychopharmacology, and neurobiology of learning; and (d) social: interpersonal conflict, racism, helping behavior, nonverbal communications, social power and influence, and decision making. The program is flexible and encourages each student to develop his or her unique interests. The clinical program emphasizes empirically supported intervention and prevention techniques. A particular strength of the program is in child–clinical research, intervention, and prevention, but students with interests in adult psychopathology and intervention would be equally at home and well served. The department has strengths in early experience and developmental processes, visual cognition, and brain plasticity during development and learning.

Special Facilities or Resources: The University's mainframe computing needs are met by several Unix timesharing systems. These systems are used primarily for administraive purposes, some special statistical analysis applications and for cognitive model simulations. The Department of Psychology is well equipped to handle department computing needs with a large assortment of Windows and MacIntosh microcomputers and several department servers that bear the brunt of department computing needs. Graduate students will find generous laboratory resources aimed to meet their scientific and computing needs individually. There is also a state-of-the-art computer classroom used for instructional purposes and available to graduate students around the clock for data reduction, statistical analysis and general word processing. The department laboratories are well equipped for the online control of experiments for human and animal subjects as well as for data analysis and modeling. Laboratories are generously equipped with videotape, acoustic, behavioral, and physiological recording systems. The department also operates the Psychological Services Training Center for practicum training in clinical psychology.

Application Information:

Send to Office of Graduate Studies, 234 Hullihen Hall, University of Delaware, Newark, DE 19716. Application available online. URL of online application: http://www.udel.edu/gradoffice/applicants/index.html. Students are admitted in the Fall, application deadline January 7. *Fee:* $60. The fee may be waived or deferred by the Department of Psychology.

American University
Department of Psychology
College of Arts and Sciences
321 Asbury, 4400 Massachusetts Avenue, Northwest
Washington, DC 20016-8062
Telephone: (202) 885-1710
Fax: (202) 885-1023
E-mail: *psychology@american.edu*
Web: *http://www.american.edu/cas/psychology*

Department Information:

1929. Chairperson: Anthony L. Riley. Number of faculty: total—full-time 9; women—full-time 6; ; women minority—full-time 1.

Programs and Degrees Offered:

Listed in the following order: Program area, degree type (T if terminal Master's), number awarded 7/06–6/07. Behavior, Cognition, and Neuroscience (BCAN) PhD (Doctor of Philosophy) 6, Clinical PhD (Doctor of Philosophy) 9, General MA/MS (Master of Arts/Science) (T) 27.

APA Accreditation: Clinical PhD (Doctor of Philosophy).

Student Applications/Admissions:

Student Applications

Behavior, Cognition, and Neuroscience (BCAN) PhD (Doctor of Philosophy)—Applications 2007–2008, 32. Total applicants accepted 2007–2008, 6. Number full-time enrolled (new admits only) 2007–2008, 5. Number part-time enrolled (new admits only) 2007–2008, 0. Total enrolled 2007–2008 full-time, 13, part-time, 9. Openings 2008–2009, 6. The median number of years required for completion of a degree in 2006–2007 were 7. The number of students enrolled full- and part-time who were dismissed or voluntarily withdrew from this program area in 2007–2008 were 0. *Clinical PhD (Doctor of Philosophy)*—Applications 2007–2008, 220. Total applicants accepted 2007–2008, 14. Number full-time enrolled (new admits only) 2007–2008, 6. Number part-time enrolled (new admits only) 2007–2008, 0. Total enrolled 2007–2008 full-time, 22, part-time, 20. Openings 2008–2009, 6. The median number of years required for completion of a degree in 2006–2007 were 7. The number of students enrolled full- and part-time who were dismissed or voluntarily withdrew from this program area in 2007–2008 were 1. *General MA/MS (Master of Arts/Science)*—Applications 2007–2008, 153. Total applicants accepted 2007–2008, 57. Number full-time enrolled (new admits only) 2007–2008, 19. Number part-time enrolled (new admits only) 2007–2008, 5. Total enrolled 2007–2008 full-time, 28, part-time, 28. Openings 2008–2009, 20. The median number of years required for completion of a degree in 2006–2007 were 2. The number of students enrolled full- and part-time who were dismissed or voluntarily withdrew from this program area in 2007–2008 were 1.

Admissions Requirements:

Scores: Entries appear in this order: required test or GPA, minimum score (if required), median score of students entering in 2007–2008. Master's Programs: GRE-V no minimum stated, 530; GRE-Q no minimum stated, 600; overall undergraduate GPA no minimum stated, 3.5. Doctoral Programs: GRE-V no minimum stated, 680; GRE-Q no minimum stated, 720; GRE-Subject (Psychology) no minimum stated, 740; overall undergraduate GPA no minimum stated, 3.75; Doctoral program GRE-Analytic no minimum stated, 5.5.

Other Criteria: (importance of criteria rated low, medium, or high): GRE/MAT scores—high, research experience—high, work experience—medium, clinically related public service—medium, GPA—high, letters of recommendation—high, interview—high, statement of goals and objectives—high. Interview, clinically related public service not required for Behavior, Cognition, and Neuroscience program. For additional information on admission requirements, go to http://www.american.edu/cas/admissions/index.html.

Student Characteristics: The following represents characteristics of students in 2007–2008 in all graduate psychology programs in the department: Female—full-time 48, part-time 49; Male—full-time 15, part-time 8; African American/Black—full-time 5, part-time 7; Hispanic/Latino(a)—full-time 4, part-time 0; Asian/Pacific Islander—full-time 5, part-time 2; American Indian/Alaska Native—full-time 0, part-time 0; Caucasian/White—full-time 30, part-time 37; Multi-ethnic—full-time 5, part-time 0; students subject to the Americans With Disabilities Act—full-time 0, part-time 0; Unknown ethnicity—full-time 14, part-time 11; International students who hold an F-1 or J-1 Visa—full-time 1, part-time 2.

Financial Information/Assistance:

Tuition for Full-Time Study: *Master's:* State residents: $1,111 per credit hour; Nonstate residents: $1,111 per credit hour. *Doctoral:* State residents: $1,111 per credit hour; Nonstate residents: $1,111 per credit hour. Tuition is subject to change. See the following Web site for updates and changes in tuition costs: http://www.admissions.american.edu/.

Financial Assistance:

First-Year Students: Teaching assistantships available for first year. Average amount paid per academic year: $7,488. Average number of hours worked per week: 20. Apply by January 1. Tuition remission given: full. Fellowships and scholarships available for first year. Average amount paid per academic year: $12,000. Tuition remission given: full.

Advanced Students: Teaching assistantships available for advanced students. Average amount paid per academic year: $7,488. Average number of hours worked per week: 20. Apply by January 1. Tuition remission given: full. Fellowships and scholarships available for advanced students. Average amount paid per academic year: $12,000. Tuition remission given: full.

Additional Information: Of all students currently enrolled full time, 75% benefited from one or more of the listed financial assistance programs. Application and information available online at http://www.american.edu/cas/admissions/financial_aid.cfm.

Internships/Practica: Doctoral Degree (PhD Clinical): For those doctoral students for whom a professional internship was required

in this program prior to graduation, (10) students applied for an internship in 2006–2007, with (10) students obtaining an internship. Of those students who obtained an internship, (10) were paid internships. Of those students who obtained an internship, (7) students placed in APA/CPA-accredited internships, (3) students placed in internships not APA/CPA-accredited, but listed with the Association of Psychology Postdoctoral and Internship Centers (APPIC), (0) students placed in internships conforming to guidelines of the Council of Directors of School Psychology Programs (CDSPP), (0) students placed in internships that were not APA/CPA-accredited, APPIC or CDSPP listed. The greater Washington, DC metropolitan area provides a wealth of applied and research resources to complement our students' work in the classroom and faculty laboratories. These include the university's Counseling Center, local hospitals (Children's, St. Elizabeth's, Walter Reed, Georgetown University, National Rehabilitation), the Kennedy Institute, Gallaudet University, the NIH (NIMH, NINDS, NIA, NCI), the National Zoo, and the national offices of many agencies (e.g., APA, APS, NAMI). Field work and short-term externships are available in many city, county, and private organizations, such as the Alexandria, VA Community Mental Health Center; the Montgomery County, MD Department of Addiction, Victim, and Mental Health Services; and the DC Rape Crisis Center. MA and PhD students can also earn degree credit while obtaining practical experience working in the private sector with autistic children, teaching self-management skills, or volunteering at shelters for battered women or the homeless. Many of these positions sometimes can provide funding. Clinical students participate in Rogerian, cognitive–behavioral, and psychodynamic therapy practica.

Housing and Day Care: On-campus housing is available. See the following Web site for more information: http://www.american.edu/ocl/housing/index1.html. On-campus day care facilities are available. See the following Web site for more information: http://www.american.edu/hr/cdc.html.

Employment of Department Graduates:

Master's Degree Graduates: Of those who graduated in the academic year 2006–2007, the following categories and numbers represent the postgraduate activities and employment of master's degree graduates: Enrolled in a psychology doctoral program (3), enrolled in another graduate/professional program (6), enrolled in a postdoctoral residency/fellowship (n/a), employed in independent practice (n/a), employed in business or industry (1), employed in government agency (2), employed in a community mental health/counseling center (1), total from the above (master's) (13).

Doctoral Degree Graduates: Of those who graduated in the academic year 2006–2007, the following categories and numbers represent the postgraduate activities and employment of doctoral degree graduates: Enrolled in a psychology doctoral program (n/a), enrolled in a postdoctoral residency/fellowship (3), employed in independent practice (1), employed in an academic position at a university (1), employed in other positions at a higher education institution (1), employed in business or industry (1), employed in government agency (3), employed in a community mental health/counseling center (3), employed in a hospital/medical center (2), total from the above (doctoral) (15).

Additional Information:

Orientation, Objectives, and Emphasis of Department: The psychology department of American University offers two graduate programs. The PhD program has separate tracks in clinical psychology and behavior, cognition, and neuroscience. The MA program has tracks in general, personality/social, and biological/experimental psychology. The doctoral program in clinical psychology trains psychologists to do therapy, assessment, research, university teaching, and consultation. The theoretical orientation is eclectic and follows the Boulder scientist–practitioner model. The doctoral program in behavioral neuroscience/experimental psychology involves intensive training in both pure and applied research settings. Students can work in laboratories exploring conditioning and learning, the experimental analysis of behavior, cognition and memory, physiological psychology, neuropsychology, and neuropharmacology. Study at the master's level provides the basis for further doctoral-level work and prepares students for immediate employment in a variety of careers including clinical–medical research, teaching, counseling and policy formulation, law enforcement, and government work. Our graduate students are expected to be professional, ethical, committed, full-time members of our psychology community. This concept of community implies an atmosphere of mutual support rather than competition, communication rather than isolation, and stimulation rather than disinterest.

Special Facilities or Resources: Nine well-equipped laboratories investigate conditioning and learning, clinical and experimental neuropsychology, human cognition and memory, neuropharmacology, physiological psychology, rodent olfaction, social behavior, psychopathology, depression, anxiety disorders, emotion, eating disorders, parent–child interaction, addictive behavior, child development, and various other issues in applied and experimental psychology. Students also train in the Department's cognitive behavioral training clinic. Close working relationships with laboratories at the National Institutes of Health, the Walter Reed Army Institutes of Research, and Georgetown University's Hospital and School of Medicine allow additional training opportunities. The Washington Research Library Consortium (WRLC) provides access to six local college and university libraries in addition to AU's Bender Library, the National Library of Medicine, and the Library of Congress. AU's computing center supports IBM, Macintosh, and Unix systems, has dial-in access, and maintains 15 computing labs. EagleNet, a campus-wide network service, runs on Novell Netware 4.x and 5.0. Applications include WordPerfect, Quattro Pro, Presentations, Paradox, SAS, SPSS, Photoshop, Netscape, and e-mail as well as many Internet applications and services (Usenet newsgroups, electronic discussion lists-Listserv, file transfer, FTP, the ALADIN online catalog of the WRLC).

Information for Students With Physical Disabilities: See the following Web site for more information: http://www.american.edu/ocl/dss/index1.html.

Application Information:

Send to College of Arts and Sciences, Graduate Admissions, McKinley Building, 4400 Massachusetts Avenue, Northwest, Washington, DC 20016-8107. Application available online. URL of online application: https://www.my.american.edu/cgi/mvi.exe/A26.APPL.LOGIN?SCH=CAS. Students are admitted in the Fall, application deadline. Clinical, January 1; Behavior, Cognition, and Neuroscience, January 1; MA, March 1. *Fee:* $50. Fall deadlines—Clinical, January 1; Behavior, Cognition, and Neuroscience, January 1; MA, March 1 The online application fee is $50. The fee for paper mailed applications is $80.

Catholic University of America, The

Department of Psychology
O'Boyle Hall, Room 314
4001 Harewood Road, Northeast
Washington, DC 20064
Telephone: (202) 319-5750
Fax: (202) 319-6263
E-mail: *sebrechts@cua.edu*
Web: *http://www.psychology.cua.edu*

Department Information:

1891. Chairperson: Marc M. Sebrechts. Number of faculty: total—full-time 7, part-time 1; women—full-time 7, part-time 1; women minority—full-time 2.

Programs and Degrees Offered:

Listed in the following order: Program area, degree type (T if terminal Master's), number awarded 7/06–6/07. General Ma MA/MS (Master of Arts/Science) (T) 12, Clinical PhD (Doctor of Philosophy) 7, Applied Experimental PhD (Doctor of Philosophy) 2, Human Development (accepting for MA degree only) PhD (Doctor of Philosophy) 0, Psychology/Law MA/MS (Master of Arts/Science) (T) 1, Human Factors MA/MS (Master of Arts/Science) (T) 1.

APA Accreditation: Clinical PhD (Doctor of Philosophy).

Student Applications/Admissions:

Student Applications

General MA/MS (Master of Arts/Science)—Applications 2007–2008, 49. Total applicants accepted 2007–2008, 25. Number full-time enrolled (new admits only) 2007–2008, 17. Number part-time enrolled (new admits only) 2007–2008, 2. Openings 2008–2009, 16. The median number of years required for completion of a degree in 2006–2007 were 3. The number of students enrolled full- and part-time who were dismissed or voluntarily withdrew from this program area in 2007–2008 were 1. *Clinical PhD (Doctor of Philosophy)*—Applications 2007–2008, 181. Total applicants accepted 2007–2008, 13. Number full-time enrolled (new admits only) 2007–2008, 6. Number part-time enrolled (new admits only) 2007–2008, 0. Openings 2008–2009, 6. The median number of years required for completion of a degree in 2006–2007 were 6. The number of students enrolled full- and part-time who were dismissed or voluntarily withdrew from this program area in 2007–2008 were 1. *Applied Experimental PhD (Doctor of Philosophy)*—Applications 2007–2008, 11. Total applicants accepted 2007–2008, 4. Number full-time enrolled (new admits only) 2007–2008, 1. Number part-time enrolled (new admits only) 2007–2008, 0. Openings 2008–2009, 3. The median number of years required for completion of a degree in 2006–2007 were 6. The number of students enrolled full- and part-time who were dismissed or voluntarily withdrew from this program area in 2007–2008 were 0. *Human Development PhD (Doctor of Philosophy)*—Applications 2007–2008, 6. Total applicants accepted 2007–2008, 0. Number full-time enrolled (new admits only) 2007–2008, 0. Number part-time enrolled (new admits only) 2007–2008, 0. The number of students enrolled full- and part-time who were dismissed or voluntarily withdrew from this program area in 2007–2008 were 1. *Psychology/Law MA/MS (Master of Arts/Science)*—Applications 2007–2008, 4. Total applicants accepted 2007–2008, 2. Number full-time enrolled (new admits only) 2007–2008, 1. Number part-time enrolled (new admits only) 2007–2008, 0. Openings 2008–2009, 2. The median number of years required for completion of a degree in 2006–2007 were 2. The number of students enrolled full- and part-time who were dismissed or voluntarily withdrew from this program area in 2007–2008 were 0. *Human Factors MA/MS (Master of Arts/Science)*—Applications 2007–2008, 6. Total applicants accepted 2007–2008, 3. Number full-time enrolled (new admits only) 2007–2008, 1. Number part-time enrolled (new admits only) 2007–2008, 1. Total enrolled 2007–2008 full-time, 1, part-time, 1. Openings 2008–2009, 2. The median number of years required for completion of a degree in 2006–2007 were 5. The number of students enrolled full- and part-time who were dismissed or voluntarily withdrew from this program area in 2007–2008 were 0.

Admissions Requirements:

Scores: Entries appear in this order: required test or GPA, minimum score (if required), median score of students entering in 2007–2008. Master's Programs: GRE-V no minimum stated, 500; GRE-Q no minimum stated, 630; overall undergraduate GPA no minimum stated, 3.4. Doctoral Programs: GRE-V no minimum stated, 600; GRE-Q no minimum stated, 650; GRE-Subject (Psychology) no minimum stated; overall undergraduate GPA no minimum stated, 3.5. Psychology Subject Test is required for clinical program only (mean of 756).

Other Criteria: (importance of criteria rated low, medium, or high): GRE/MAT scores—medium, research experience—high, work experience—medium, extracurricular activity—low, clinically related public service—medium, GPA—high, letters of recommendation—high, interview—high, statement of goals and objectives—high. Interview only for clinical PhD program. For additional information on admission requirements, go to http://psychology.cua.edu/graduate/.

Student Characteristics: The following represents characteristics of students in 2007–2008 in all graduate psychology programs in the department: Female—full-time 65, part-time 2; Male—full-time 18, part-time 1; African American/Black—full-time 5, part-time 0; Hispanic/Latino(a)—full-time 5, part-time 0; Asian/Pacific Islander—full-time 2, part-time 0; American Indian/Alaska Native—full-time 0, part-time 0; Caucasian/White—full-time 41, part-time 1; Multi-ethnic—part-time 0; students subject to the Americans With Disabilities Act—full-time 1, part-time 0; Unknown ethnicity—full-time 30, part-time 2; International students who hold an F-1 or J-1 Visa—full-time 1, part-time 0.

Financial Information/Assistance:

Tuition for Full-Time Study: *Master's:* State residents: per academic year $30,520, $1,195 per credit hour; Nonstate residents: per academic year $30,520, $1,195 per credit hour. *Doctoral:* State residents: per academic year $30,520, $1,195 per credit hour; Nonstate residents: per academic year $30,520, $1,195 per credit hour. See the following Web site for updates and changes in tuition costs: http://www.financialaid.cua.edu.

Financial Assistance:

First-Year Students: Research assistantships available for first year. Average amount paid per academic year: $13,000. Average number of hours worked per week: 20. Apply by Rolling. Tuition remission given: full. Fellowships and scholarships available for first year. Apply by January 15. Tuition remission given: full.

Advanced Students: Teaching assistantships available for advanced students. Average amount paid per academic year: $4,000. Average number of hours worked per week: 10. Apply by March 1. Tuition remission given: full. Research assistantships available for advanced students. Average amount paid per academic year: $13,000. Average number of hours worked per week: 20. Apply by Rolling. Tuition remission given: full. Fellowships and scholarships available for advanced students. Apply by March 1. Tuition remission given: full.

Additional Information: Of all students currently enrolled full time, 85% benefited from one or more of the listed financial assistance programs. Application and information available online at http://www.psychology.cua.edu/graduate/ and http://www.admissions.cua.edu.

Internships/Practica: Master's Degree (MA/MS General MA): An internship experience such as a final research project or "capstone" experience is required of graduates. Doctoral Degree (PhD Clinical): For those doctoral students for whom a professional internship was required in this program prior to graduation, (8) students applied for an internship in 2006–2007, with (8) students obtaining an internship. Of those students who obtained an internship, (8) were paid internships. Of those students who obtained an internship, (7) students placed in APA/CPA-accredited internships, (0) students placed in internships not APA/CPA-accredited, but listed with the Association of Psychology Postdoctoral and Internship Centers (APPIC), (0) students placed in internships conforming to guidelines of the Council of Directors of School Psychology Programs (CDSPP), (1) students placed in internships that were not APA/CPA-accredited, APPIC or CDSPP listed. Students in the Clinical doctoral program begin practicum experience in their first year as a part of their courses in assessment and psychotherapy. Advanced courses are available in objective personality assessment and projective personality assessment. Both of these courses incorporate practicum experience. In their 2nd year, clinical students do a practicum in individual psychotherapy in the university's counseling center, in which the clients are undergraduate and graduate students. The core clinical faculty supervises this year long practicum. An advanced psychotherapy practicum, supervised by a core clinical faculty member, is available in family therapy. All on-campus practica are supervised very closely. For example, in the 2nd-year psychotherapy practicum, students are given 3.5 hours of supervision a week while they are seeing 2 or 3 clients. Additionally, in their 3rd and 4th year, clinical students do 16-hour-a-week externships, supervised by licensed clinical psychologists, in one of many community settings in the area, such as community mental health centers, clinics, and hospitals. The clinical training culminates in a year-long internship, preferably an APA-accredited internship. Applied Experimental and MA students have a number of research opportunities in the Washington, DC area. Recent opportunities have included positions at the National Institutes of Health, the Army Research Institute, and National Defense University.

Housing and Day Care: On-campus housing is available. See the following Web site for more information: http://www.housing.cua.edu. No on-campus day care facilities are available.

Employment of Department Graduates:

Master's Degree Graduates: Of those who graduated in the academic year 2006–2007, the following categories and numbers represent the postgraduate activities and employment of master's degree graduates: Enrolled in a psychology doctoral program (4), enrolled in another graduate/professional program (1), enrolled in a postdoctoral residency/fellowship (n/a), employed in independent practice (n/a), employed in business or industry (2), do not know (6), total from the above (master's) (13).

Doctoral Degree Graduates: Of those who graduated in the academic year 2006–2007, the following categories and numbers represent the postgraduate activities and employment of doctoral degree graduates: Enrolled in a psychology doctoral program (n/a), enrolled in a postdoctoral residency/fellowship (2), employed in independent practice (3), employed in an academic position at a university (2), do not know (2), total from the above (doctoral) (9).

Additional Information:

Orientation, Objectives, and Emphasis of Department: Two PhD programs, clinical and applied experimental, are offered. Further specialization is offered in Children, Families, and Cultures and in the Cognitive, Affective, and Neural Sciences. The objectives of the clinical program are to train according to the scientist–practitioner model in clinical and applied areas. The Children, Families, and Cultures specialization provides interdisciplinary training in both normal and abnormal developmental processes in the clinical program or in the MA human development program. The applied experimental program emphasizes research in human cognition: current areas of interest include cognitive aging (serial pattern learning, Alzheimer's), spatial mental models (virtual reality, information visualization, and memory applied to health issues). The Cognitive, Affective, and Neural Sciences track focuses on a range of cognitive deficits across the lifespan. Additional Master's programs are offered in Human Factors and General Psychology. A dual degree program MA Psychology/JD Law is available. Admission to CUA Columbus School of Law is a prerequisite.

Special Facilities or Resources: The department maintains several well-equipped laboratories for both cognitive science and clinical research. Capabilities exist for studies on auditory and visual perception, attention and memory, simulation, human computer interaction, virtual reality, and social interaction, including family interaction.

Information for Students With Physical Disabilities: See the following Web site for more information: http://www.disabilityservices.cua.edu/.

Application Information:

Send to Office of Graduate Admissions, The Catholic University of America, 102 McMahon Hall, Washington, DC 20064. Application available online. Students are admitted in the Fall, application deadline January 15; Spring, application deadline October 1. Admission to clinical program available for Fall only. *Fee:* $55. We waive the application fee for those with serious financial difficulties that make it a hardship to pay the fee, and for others who would increase diversity in the student body, such as veterans and ethnic minorities. To request an application fee waiver, applicants must write a letter explaining the basis for their request and send it by U.S. Post to the Office of

Graduate Admissions, 102 McMahon Hall, The Catholic University of America, Washington, DC 20064.

Gallaudet University

Department of Psychology
College of Liberal Arts, Sciences and Technologies
800 Florida Avenue, Northeast
Washington, DC 20002
Telephone: (202) 651-5540
Fax: (202) 651-5747
E-mail: *Virginia.Gutman@gallaudet.edu*
Web: *http://www.depts.gallaudet.edu/psychology/*

Department Information:

1955. Chairperson: Virginia Gutman, PhD. Number of faculty: total—full-time 13, part-time 1; women—full-time 10, part-time 1; women minority—full-time 2; faculty subject to the Americans With Disabilities Act 6.

Programs and Degrees Offered:

Listed in the following order: Program area, degree type (T if terminal Master's), number awarded 7/06–6/07. Clinical PhD (Doctor of Philosophy) 3, School Psychology Other 11.

APA Accreditation: Clinical PhD (Doctor of Philosophy).

Student Applications/Admissions:

Student Applications

Clinical PhD (Doctor of Philosophy)—Applications 2007–2008, 23. Total applicants accepted 2007–2008, 6. Number full-time enrolled (new admits only) 2007–2008, 5. Number part-time enrolled (new admits only) 2007–2008, 0. Openings 2008–2009, 6. The median number of years required for completion of a degree in 2006–2007 were 6. The number of students enrolled full- and part-time who were dismissed or voluntarily withdrew from this program area in 2007–2008 were 1. *School Psychology Other*—Applications 2007–2008, 11. Total applicants accepted 2007–2008, 7. Number full-time enrolled (new admits only) 2007–2008, 6. Number part-time enrolled (new admits only) 2007–2008, 0. Openings 2008–2009, 10. The median number of years required for completion of a degree in 2006–2007 were 3. The number of students enrolled full- and part-time who were dismissed or voluntarily withdrew from this program area in 2007–2008 were 2.

Admissions Requirements:

Scores: Entries appear in this order: required test or GPA, minimum score (if required), median score of students entering in 2007–2008. Master's Programs: GRE-V no minimum stated, 533; GRE-Q no minimum stated, 575; overall undergraduate GPA 3.0, 3.5; Masters GRE-Analytical no minimum stated, 4.5. Occasionally, applicants with a GPA lower than 3.0 may be admitted conditionally. Doctoral Programs: GRE-V no minimum stated, 630; GRE-Q no minimum stated, 690; overall undergraduate GPA 3.0, 3.59; psychology GPA no minimum stated. Occasionally, students with GPAs below this level may be admitted conditionally.

Other Criteria: (importance of criteria rated low, medium, or high): GRE/MAT scores—medium, research experience—high, work experience—medium, extracurricular activity—medium, clinically related public service—high, GPA—medium, letters of recommendation—medium, interview—high, statement of goals and objectives—medium, psychology courses—high. Varies by program. Students with little experience with deaf people or sign language may be required to take sign language (ASL) courses prior to enrolling. Prior research experience is highly valued in doctoral program admissions, but has a medium weight for the Specialist program. For additional information on admission requirements, go to https://securedgspp.gallaudet.edu/gradschool/inquiry/.

Student Characteristics: The following represents characteristics of students in 2007–2008 in all graduate psychology programs in the department: Female—full-time 39, part-time 0; Male—full-time 13, part-time 0; African American/Black—full-time 6, part-time 0; Hispanic/Latino(a)—full-time 4, part-time 0; Asian/Pacific Islander—full-time 2, part-time 0; American Indian/Alaska Native—full-time 0, part-time 0; Caucasian/White—full-time 39, part-time 0; Multi-ethnic—full-time 1, part-time 0; students subject to the Americans With Disabilities Act—full-time 18, part-time 0; Unknown ethnicity—full-time 0, part-time 0; International students who hold an F-1 or J-1 Visa—full-time 2, part-time 0.

Financial Information/Assistance:

Tuition for Full-Time Study: *Master's:* State residents: per academic year $11,930, $663 per credit hour; Nonstate residents: per academic year $11,930, $663 per credit hour. *Doctoral:* State residents: per academic year $11,930, $663 per credit hour; Nonstate residents: per academic year $11,930, $663 per credit hour. Tuition is subject to change. Additional fees are assessed to students beyond the costs of tuition for the following: Unit fee, room/board, health insurance, and services. See the following Web site for updates and changes in tuition costs: http://www.gallaudet.edu/af/Documents/finance_schedule_fall_2008_spring_. International students pay higher tuition.

Financial Assistance:

First-Year Students: Teaching assistantships available for first year. Average amount paid per academic year: $4,500. Average number of hours worked per week: 8. Research assistantships available for first year. Average amount paid per academic year: $4,500. Average number of hours worked per week: 8. Fellowships and scholarships available for first year. Average amount paid per academic year: $7,000. Average number of hours worked per week: 10. Tuition remission given: full.

Advanced Students: Teaching assistantships available for advanced students. Average amount paid per academic year: $4,500. Average number of hours worked per week: 8. Research assistantships available for advanced students. Average amount paid per academic year: $4,500. Average number of hours worked per week: 8. Fellowships and scholarships available for advanced students. Average amount paid per academic year: $7,000. Average number of hours worked per week: 10. Tuition remission given: full.

Additional Information: Of all students currently enrolled full time, 90% benefited from one or more of the listed financial assistance programs. Application and information available online at http://www.gallaudet.edu/x582.xml.

Internships/Practica: Doctoral Degree (PhD clinical): For those doctoral students for whom a professional internship was required

in this program prior to graduation, (5) students applied for an internship in 2006–2007, with (5) students obtaining an internship. Of those students who obtained an internship, (5) were paid internships. Of those students who obtained an internship, (4) students placed in APA/CPA-accredited internships, (0) students placed in internships not APA/CPA-accredited, but listed with the Association of Psychology Postdoctoral and Internship Centers (APPIC), (0) students placed in internships conforming to guidelines of the Council of Directors of School Psychology Programs (CDSPP), (1) student placed in internships that were not APA/CPA-accredited, APPIC or CDSPP listed. Students in the School Psychology Specialist Program (which includes the MA as a nonterminal degree), begin with a practicum experience in their first semester, visiting and observing school programs as part of their Introduction to School Psychology course. During their second semester they are involved in Practicum I (3-credit course), which involves closely supervised practicum doing cognitive assessments of deaf and hearing children (if appropriate) at laboratory schools on campus and a Washington, DC neighborhood school. Practicum II (3 credits) is taken the third semester and requires 2 full days per week for a minimum of 14 weeks in which they work with a school psychologist in the Washington, DC metropolitan area doing comprehensive assessments, some counseling if opportunities are available, and observation on a limited basis during their fourth semester (an option). The 3rd year (semesters 5 and 6) are spent in a full-time internship in a school program approved by the program. These internships are typically located in both residential schools for the deaf as well as public school systems serving mainstreamed deaf youngsters. Internship sites are located in all parts of the United States. Students in the Clinical Psychology Doctoral Program begin practicum in their 2nd year, conducting psychological assessments and psychotherapy at the Gallaudet University Mental Health Center. Advanced students can apply for any of the more than 80 externships available in the Washington, DC area. These externships allow students to work with a wide variety of settings and populations in assessment, psychotherapy, and other psychological interventions. Experiences with both deaf and hearing clients are available. A full-time, 1-year doctoral level internship (typically in an APA-accredited internship program) is required. For additional information on education and training outcomes for our programs, see the following Web site: http://www.psychology.gallaudet.edu/.

Housing and Day Care: On-campus housing is available. See the following Web site for more information: http://www.gallaudet.edu/x531.xml. On-campus day care facilities are available. See the following Web site for more information: http://www.clerccenter.gallaudet.edu/cdc/.

Employment of Department Graduates:

Master's Degree Graduates: Of those who graduated in the academic year 2006–2007, the following categories and numbers represent the postgraduate activities and employment of master's degree graduates: Enrolled in a postdoctoral residency/fellowship (n/a), employed in independent practice (n/a), employed in a professional position in a school system (11), total from the above (master's) (11).

Doctoral Degree Graduates: Of those who graduated in the academic year 2006–2007, the following categories and numbers represent the postgraduate activities and employment of doctoral degree graduates: Enrolled in a psychology doctoral program (n/a), enrolled in a postdoctoral residency/fellowship (2), employed in independent practice (0), employed in a hospital/medical center (1), total from the above (doctoral) (3).

Additional Information:

Orientation, Objectives, and Emphasis of Department: The Psychology department at Gallaudet University offers graduate programs in school psychology and clinical psychology. The school psychology program awards a nonterminal Master of Arts degree in developmental psychology plus a Specialist in School Psychology degree with specialization in deafness. The clinical psychology program is a scholar–practitioner model PhD program, and trains generalist clinical psychologists to work with deaf, hard-of-hearing, and hearing populations. The school psychology program is both NCATE/NASP and NASDTEC-approved, and leads to certification as a school psychologist in the District of Columbia and approximately 24 states with reciprocity of certification. The full-time, 3-year program requires completion of at least 72 graduate semester hours, including a 1-year internship. The APA accredited clinical psychology doctoral program is a 5-year program providing balanced training in research and clinical skills with a variety of age groups, including deaf and hard-of-hearing children, adults, and older adults. The 5th year is designed as a full-time clinical psychology internship. A research-based dissertation is required.

Special Facilities or Resources: Gallaudet University is an internationally recognized center for research and training in areas related to deafness. With a diverse student body of approximately 1,600, the university trains deaf, hard-of-hearing, and hearing students in a variety of fields at the bachelor, master's, and doctoral levels. Gallaudet programs are located on historic Kendall Green, in northeast Washington, DC near the U.S. Capitol, the Library of Congress, and the Smithsonian Institute. Also located on the campus are the Gallaudet University Mental Health Center, the Kendall Demonstration Elementary School, the Model Secondary School for the Deaf, the Gallaudet Research Institute, the Kellogg Conference Center, and the Gallaudet Library, which contains the largest collection of references on deafness in the world. Gallaudet faculty, including both deaf and hearing individuals, possess a unique combination of scholarly activity in their respective disciplines and experience with deaf clients and research on deafness. The University is committed to a working model of a bilingual (American Sign Language and English), multicultural community, where deaf, hard-of-hearing, and hearing people can work together without communication barriers. Gallaudet University is accredited by the Middle States Association of Colleges and Secondary Schools and is a member of the Consortium of Universities of the Washington Metropolitan Area and the Washington Research Library Consortium.

Information for Students With Physical Disabilities: See the following Web site for more information: http://www.depts.gallaudet.edu/oswd/.

Application Information:

Send to Office of Graduate Admissions, Gallaudet University, 800 Florida Avenue Northeast, Washingon, DC 20002. Application available online. URL of online application: https://www.securedgspp.gallaudet.edu/gradschool/inquiry/. Students are admitted in the Fall, application deadline February 1. *Fee:* $50. Waived for McNair Scholars.

George Washington University
Department of Psychology
2125 G Street, Northwest
Washington, DC 20052
Telephone: (202) 994-6320
Fax: (202) 994-1602
E-mail: *pjp@gwu.edu*
Web: *http://www.gwu.edu/~psycdept*

Department Information:

1922. Chairperson: Paul Poppen. Number of faculty: total—full-time 20, part-time 3; women—full-time 11, part-time 3; total—minority—full-time 7; women minority—full-time 6.

Programs and Degrees Offered:

Listed in the following order: Program area, degree type (T if terminal Master's), number awarded 7/06–6/07. Applied Social Psychology PhD (Doctor of Philosophy) 2, Clinical PhD (Doctor of Philosophy) 5, Cognitive Neuroscience PhD (Doctor of Philosophy) 2.

APA Accreditation: Clinical PhD (Doctor of Philosophy).

Student Applications/Admissions:

Student Applications

Applied Social Psychology PhD (Doctor of Philosophy)—Applications 2007–2008, 70. Total applicants accepted 2007–2008, 2. Number full-time enrolled (new admits only) 2007–2008, 2. Number part-time enrolled (new admits only) 2007–2008, 0. Openings 2008–2009, 2. The median number of years required for completion of a degree in 2006–2007 were 5. *Clinical PhD (Doctor of Philosophy)*—Applications 2007–2008, 300. Total applicants accepted 2007–2008, 5. Number full-time enrolled (new admits only) 2007–2008, 5. Number part-time enrolled (new admits only) 2007–2008, 0. Openings 2008–2009, 5. The median number of years required for completion of a degree in 2006–2007 were 6. *Cognitive Neuroscience PhD (Doctor of Philosophy)*—Applications 2007–2008, 45. Total applicants accepted 2007–2008, 2. Number full-time enrolled (new admits only) 2007–2008, 2. Openings 2008–2009, 2. The median number of years required for completion of a degree in 2006–2007 were 5.

Admissions Requirements:

Scores: Entries appear in this order: required test or GPA, minimum score (if required), median score of students entering in 2007–2008. Doctoral Programs: GRE-V no minimum stated, 670; GRE-Q no minimum stated, 650; overall undergraduate GPA no minimum stated, 3.80.

Other Criteria: (importance of criteria rated low, medium, or high): GRE/MAT scores—medium, research experience—high, work experience—medium, extracurricular activity—medium, clinically related public service—medium, GPA—high, letters of recommendation—medium, interview—high, statement of goals and objectives—high, undergraduate major in psychology—low, specific undergraduate psychology courses taken—medium. Interview and clinical public service apply to Clinical program.

Student Characteristics: The following represents characteristics of students in 2007–2008 in all graduate psychology programs in the department: Female—full-time 41, part-time 0; Male—full-time 10, part-time 0; African American/Black—full-time 6, part-time 0; Hispanic/Latino(a)—full-time 6, part-time 0; Asian/Pacific Islander—full-time 9, part-time 0; American Indian/Alaska Native—full-time 0, part-time 0; Caucasian/White—full-time 30, part-time 0; students subject to the Americans With Disabilities Act—full-time 0, part-time 0; Unknown ethnicity—full-time 0, part-time 0; International students who hold an F-1 or J-1 Visa—full-time 1, part-time 0.

Financial Information/Assistance:

Tuition for Full-Time Study: *Doctoral:* State residents: per academic year $18,000, $1,000 per credit hour; Nonstate residents: per academic year $18,000, $1,000 per credit hour. Tuition is subject to change.

Financial Assistance:

First-Year Students: Teaching assistantships available for first year. Average amount paid per academic year: $18,000. Tuition remission given: full. Research assistantships available for first year. Average amount paid per academic year: $18,000. Tuition remission given: full. Fellowships and scholarships available for first year. Average amount paid per academic year: $20,000. Tuition remission given: full.

Advanced Students: Teaching assistantships available for advanced students. Average amount paid per academic year: $18,000. Tuition remission given: full. Research assistantships available for advanced students. Average amount paid per academic year: $18,000. Tuition remission given: full. Fellowships and scholarships available for advanced students. Average amount paid per academic year: $20,000. Tuition remission given: full.

Additional Information: Of all students currently enrolled full time, 100% benefited from one or more of the listed financial assistance programs.

Internships/Practica: Doctoral Degree (PhD Clinical): For those doctoral students for whom a professional internship was required in this program prior to graduation, (7) students applied for an internship in 2006–2007, with (7) students obtaining an internship. Of those students who obtained an internship, (7) were paid internships. Of those students who obtained an internship, (7) students placed in APA/CPA-accredited internships, (0) students placed in internships not APA/CPA-accredited, but listed with the Association of Psychology Postdoctoral and Internship Centers (APPIC), (0) students placed in internships conforming to guidelines of the Council of Directors of School Psychology Programs (CDSPP), (0) students placed in internships that were not APA/CPA-accredited, APPIC or CDSPP listed. There is a wide variety of placements available in the DC Metro area. Placements are required part of training in the clinical programs.

Housing and Day Care: On-campus housing is available. On-campus day care facilities are available.

Employment of Department Graduates:

Master's Degree Graduates: Of those who graduated in the academic year 2006–2007, the following categories and numbers represent the postgraduate activities and employment of master's degree graduates: Enrolled in a postdoctoral residency/fellowship

(n/a), employed in independent practice (n/a), total from the above (master's) (0).

Doctoral Degree Graduates: Of those who graduated in the academic year 2006–2007, the following categories and numbers represent the postgraduate activities and employment of doctoral degree graduates: Enrolled in a psychology doctoral program (n/a), enrolled in a postdoctoral residency/fellowship (3), employed in independent practice (0), employed in an academic position at a university (1), employed in other positions at a higher education institution (1), employed in business or industry (2), employed in government agency (2), total from the above (doctoral) (9).

Additional Information:

Orientation, Objectives, and Emphasis of Department: The department provides training in the basic science of psychology for each of its graduate programs. Specialized training is offered in three program areas: applied social, clinical, and cognitive neuropsychology. The applied social program focuses on theory and methods of addressing current social problems such as in health care, education, and the prevention of high-risk social behaviors. The clinical program is an APA-approved program emphasizing both the basic science and applied aspects of clinical psychology. The focus of the program is Health Promotion and Disease Prevention in Diverse Urban Communities. The cognitive neuroscience program focuses on cognition, learning, and memory with emphasis on the psychobiological determinants of these functions. The training in each program addresses both scientific and professional objectives: Students are trained for careers in academic institutions, applied research, and professional practice.

Special Facilities or Resources: Excellent on-campus computer facilities; laboratories for child study, group studies, cognitive testing, and small animal research. Convenient access to staff, libraries, and facilities at national health and mental health institutes (NIH); mental health training centers for clinical students. See home page for information: http://www.gwu.edu.

Application Information:

Send to Graduate School, CCAS, George Washington University, Washington, DC 20052. Students are admitted in the Fall, application deadline December 15. Cognitive Neuropscience and Applied Social, January 1. Cognitive Neuropsychology and Applied Social, February 1. *Fee:* $65.

George Washington University

Doctoral Program in Clinical Psychology
Columbian College of Arts and Sciences
2300 M Street, Northwest, Suite 910
Washington, DC 20037
Telephone: (202) 496-6260
Fax: (202) 496-6263
E-mail: *crescent@gwu.edu*
Web: *http://www.gwu.edu/~psyd*

Department Information:

1996. Director: Dorothy E. Holmes, PhD. Number of faculty: total—full-time 3, part-time 5; women—full-time 2, part-time 2; total—minority—full-time 1, part-time 1; women minority—full-time 1.

Programs and Degrees Offered:

Listed in the following order: Program area, degree type (T if terminal Master's), number awarded 7/06–6/07. Clinical PsyD (Doctor of Psychology) 33.

APA Accreditation: Clinical PsyD (Doctor of Psychology).

Student Applications/Admissions:

Student Applications

Clinical PsyD (Doctor of Psychology)—Applications 2007–2008, 325. Total applicants accepted 2007–2008, 35. Number full-time enrolled (new admits only) 2007–2008, 33. Openings 2008–2009, 36. The median number of years required for completion of a degree in 2006–2007 were 4. The number of students enrolled full- and part-time who were dismissed or voluntarily withdrew from this program area in 2007–2008 were 1.

Admissions Requirements:

Scores: Entries appear in this order: required test or GPA, minimum score (if required), median score of students entering in 2007–2008. Doctoral Programs: GRE-V 500; GRE-Q 500; overall undergraduate GPA 3.0, 3.26.

Other Criteria: (importance of criteria rated low, medium, or high): GRE/MAT scores—medium, research experience—medium, work experience—medium, clinically related public service—high, GPA—medium, letters of recommendation—high, interview—high, statement of goals and objectives—high. For additional information on admission requirements, go to http://columbian.gwu.edu/grad/index.php/id/44.

Student Characteristics: The following represents characteristics of students in 2007–2008 in all graduate psychology programs in the department: Female—full-time 108, part-time 0; Male—full-time 30, part-time 0; African American/Black—full-time 4, part-time 0; Hispanic/Latino(a)—full-time 8, part-time 0; Asian/Pacific Islander—full-time 6, part-time 0; American Indian/Alaska Native—full-time 0, part-time 0; Caucasian/White—full-time 118, part-time 0; Multi-ethnic—full-time 2, part-time 0; students subject to the Americans With Disabilities Act—full-time 0, part-time 0; Unknown ethnicity—full-time 0, part-time 0; International students who hold an F-1 or J-1 Visa—full-time 3, part-time 0.

Financial Information/Assistance:

Tuition for Full-Time Study: *Doctoral:* State residents: $1,000 per credit hour; Nonstate residents: $1,000 per credit hour. Tuition is subject to change.

Financial Assistance:

First-Year Students: Fellowships and scholarships available for first year. Average amount paid per academic year: $9,000. Average number of hours worked per week: 0. Apply by none. Tuition remission given: partial.

Advanced Students: Fellowships and scholarships available for advanced students. Average amount paid per academic year: $5,000. Average number of hours worked per week: 0. Apply by none. Tuition remission given: partial.

Additional Information: Of all students currently enrolled full time, 20% benefited from one or more of the listed financial assistance programs.

Internships/Practica: Doctoral Degree (PsyD Clinical): For those doctoral students for whom a professional internship was required in this program prior to graduation, (38) students applied for an internship in 2006–2007, with (38) students obtaining an internship. Of those students who obtained an internship, (33) were paid internships. Of those students who obtained an internship, (30) students placed in APA/CPA-accredited internships, (6) students placed in internships not APA/CPA-accredited, but listed with the Association of Psychology Postdoctoral and Internship Centers (APPIC), (0) students placed in internships conforming to guidelines of the Council of Directors of School Psychology Programs (CDSPP), (2) students placed in internships that were not APA/CPA-accredited, APPIC or CDSPP listed. The principal practica/externships are provided in the Program's Center Clinic, which is administered by core faculty, postdoctoral fellows, and clinical facult. Students staff the clinic under supervision. We have Clinic Affiliate Settings, which provide patients and clinical opportunities under our supervision. Special interests and needs as served by independent externship settings.

Housing and Day Care: No on-campus housing is available. No on-campus day care facilities are available.

Employment of Department Graduates:

Master's Degree Graduates: Of those who graduated in the academic year 2006–2007, the following categories and numbers represent the postgraduate activities and employment of master's degree graduates: Enrolled in a postdoctoral residency/fellowship (n/a), employed in independent practice (n/a), total from the above (master's) (0).

Doctoral Degree Graduates: Of those who graduated in the academic year 2006–2007, the following categories and numbers represent the postgraduate activities and employment of doctoral degree graduates: Enrolled in a psychology doctoral program (n/a), enrolled in a postdoctoral residency/fellowship (10), employed in independent practice (8), employed in other positions at a higher education institution (4), employed in a community mental health/counseling center (4), employed in a hospital/medical center (4), other employment position (4), do not know (3), total from the above (doctoral) (37).

Additional Information:

Orientation, Objectives, and Emphasis of Department: The George Washington University PsyD program in Clinical Psychology has a broadly based psychodynamic orientation. After completing the core curriculum in the first year, students choose from among three advanced tracks: (a) psychodynamic psychotherapy, (b) child and adolscent clinical psychology, and (c) diagnostic assessment. Students choose major and minor areas of concentration, with the goal of obtaining advanced, in-depth training in their specialties. The principal emphasis from the first semester of the program is on high-quality clinical training. For all 3 years of class work students participate in case seminars, practica, and externships, culminating in a 4th-year internship. In the 3rd year the student writes a major area paper on a clinical topic of interest. Additional emphases of the program include: in-depth understanding of the empirical research literature pertaining to psychodynamic treatments, including the opportunity to participate in research studies conducted in the program clinic; group and organizational dynamics; community intervention; psychodynamic theory; psychodynamic child development and intervention; psychology and law; and comprehensive (biopsychosocial) diagnosis.

Special Facilities or Resources: In August 1997 our PsyD Program moved into a facility designed specifically for our needs, with all faculty and program offices, classrooms, training clinics, lounges and study areas in one location.

Information for Students With Physical Disabilities: See the following Web site for more information: http://www.gwu.edu/~dss.

Application Information:

Send to Graduate Admissions, Columbian School of Arts and Sciences, The George Washington University, 801 22nd Street, Northwest, Suite 107, Washington, DC 20052; (202) 994-6211, fax: (202) 994-6213, e-mail: askccas@gwu.edu. Application available online. URL of online application: http://www.columbian.gwu.edu/grad/index.php/id/44. Students are admitted in the Fall, application deadline December 1. Programs have rolling admissions. Prior to enrollment in the PsyD program, students are expected to have completed an introductory level statistics course. *Fee:* $60.

Georgetown University (2007 data)

Department of Psychology
Graduate School of Arts and Sciences
306 White Gravenor Hall
3700 O Street, Northwest
Washington, DC 20057
Telephone: (202) 687-4042
Fax: (202) 687-6050
E-mail: *psychology@georgetown.edu*
Web: *http://www.psychology.georgetown.edu*

Department Information:

2003. Chairperson: Sandra L Calvert, PhD. Number of faculty: total—full-time 15, part-time 4; women—full-time 7, part-time 2.

Programs and Degrees Offered:

Listed in the following order: Program area, degree type (T if terminal Master's), number awarded 7/06–6/07. Lifespan Cognitive Neuroscience PhD (Doctor of Philosophy), Human Development and Public Policy PhD (Doctor of Philosophy) 0.

Student Applications/Admissions:

Student Applications

Lifespan Cognitive Neuroscience PhD (Doctor of Philosophy)—Applications 2007–2008, 13. Total applicants accepted 2007–2008, 1. Number full-time enrolled (new admits only) 2007–2008, 1. Number part-time enrolled (new admits only) 2007–2008, 0. Openings 2008–2009, 2. *Human Development and Public Policy PhD (Doctor of Philosophy)*—Applications 2007–2008, 30. Total applicants accepted 2007–2008, 3. Number full-time enrolled (new admits only) 2007–2008, 3. Number part-time enrolled (new admits only) 2007–2008, 0. Openings 2008–2009, 2. The number of students enrolled full- and part-time who were dismissed or voluntarily withdrew from this program area in 2007–2008 were 0.

Admissions Requirements:

Scores: Entries appear in this order: required test or GPA, minimum score (if required), median score of students entering

in 2007–2008. Doctoral Programs: GRE-V 650; GRE-Q 650; overall undergraduate GPA 3.50; Doctoral program GRE-Analytic 4.5. A minimum score of 1300 is required on two sections of the GRE—Verbal and Quantitative. A minimum score of 4.5 is required on the Analytical Writing Exam. Applicants who took the GRE prior to the new format should have scored at least at 1300 on two sections of the exam—Verbal, Quantitative, or Analytical.

Other Criteria: (importance of criteria rated low, medium, or high): GRE/MAT scores—high, research experience—high, work experience—low, extracurricular activity—low, clinically related public service—low, GPA—high, letters of recommendation—high, interview—high, statement of goals and objectives—high. The 500-word statement of academic, professional, and personal goals should (a) include a discussion of how graduate school in Developmental Science will help you to achieve these goals, (b) specify your interest in one of the two areas of concentration, and (c) indicate which faculty member/s you would want to work with and how you see their interests meshing with yours. This latter information is very important because the fit between student and faculty research interests is a key component in admissions decisions. Please identify your name, program to which you are applying, term of application, U.S. social security number (if applicable), and birthdate on your submitted statement. The Writing Sample, typically chosen from your undergraduate work, should best reflect your abilities and interests as they relate to your chosen concentration in the PhD program. For additional information on admission requirements, go to http://psychology.georgetown.edu.

Student Characteristics: The following represents characteristics of students in 2007–2008 in all graduate psychology programs in the department: Female—full-time 12, part-time 0; Male—full-time 0, part-time 0; African American/Black—full-time 0, part-time 0; Hispanic/Latino(a)—full-time 0, part-time 0; Asian/Pacific Islander—full-time 0, part-time 0; American Indian/Alaska Native—full-time 0, part-time 0; Caucasian/White—full-time 10, part-time 0; Multi-ethnic—full-time 1, part-time 0; students subject to the Americans With Disabilities Act—full-time 0, part-time 0; Unknown ethnicity—full-time 1, part-time 0.

Financial Information/Assistance:

Tuition for Full-Time Study: *Doctoral:* State residents: per academic year $31,512, $1,313 per credit hour; Nonstate residents: per academic year $31,512, $1,313 per credit hour. Tuition is subject to change. See the following Web site for updates and changes in tuition costs: http://www.finaid.georgetown.edu/coagrad.htm.

Financial Assistance:

First-Year Students: Teaching assistantships available for first year. Average amount paid per academic year: $17,000. Average number of hours worked per week: 15. Tuition remission given: full. Fellowships and scholarships available for first year. Average amount paid per academic year: $17,000. Tuition remission given: full.

Advanced Students: Teaching assistantships available for advanced students. Average amount paid per academic year: $17,000. Average number of hours worked per week: 15. Tuition remission given: full. Fellowships and scholarships available for advanced students. Average amount paid per academic year: $17,000. Tuition remission given: full.

Additional Information: Of all students currently enrolled full time, 100% benefited from one or more of the listed financial assistance programs. Application and information available online at http://www.georgetown.edu/students/student-aid/grmenu.htm.

Internships/Practica: No information provided.

Housing and Day Care: No on-campus housing is available. On-campus day care facilities are available. Georgetown University has a campus child care center, Hoya Kids. See the following Web site for more information: http://www3.georgetown.edu/hr/hoya_kids/index.html.

Employment of Department Graduates:

Master's Degree Graduates: Of those who graduated in the academic year 2006–2007, the following categories and numbers represent the postgraduate activities and employment of master's degree graduates: Enrolled in a postdoctoral residency/fellowship (n/a), employed in independent practice (n/a), total from the above (master's) (0).

Doctoral Degree Graduates: Of those who graduated in the academic year 2006–2007, the following categories and numbers represent the postgraduate activities and employment of doctoral degree graduates: Enrolled in a psychology doctoral program (n/a), total from the above (doctoral) (0).

Additional Information:

Orientation, Objectives, and Emphasis of Department: This new program enrolled its first class in 2003. Its two concentrations provide an interdisciplinary education in the sciences concerned with the processes and contexts of development across the lifespan. It offers training in the theories and methods of the Developmental Sciences, enabling students to place the study of development into broader contexts—biological, familial, social, cultural, economic, historical, and political. The concentration in Human Development and Public Policy and the joint degree in Psychology and Public Policy link students to Georgetown's extensive network of policy scholars and programs, integrating a grounding in Developmental Science with instruction in quantitative and policy analysis skills, the policy process, and additional perspectives common to policy studies, notably economics and political science. The concentration in Lifespan Cognitive Neuroscience integrates grounding in Developmental Science with preparation for teaching and research on cognition and its neural bases. Students may focus their research on the behavioral–cognitive level, or may add neuroimaging techniques to explore brain bases of cognition. This concentration maintains ties with Georgetown's Interdisciplinary Program in Neuroscience PhD program. Both concentrations prepare students for postdegree positions in institutions of higher education, research institutes, medical settings, nonprofit organizations, government agencies, and other policy settings.

Special Facilities or Resources: Graduate students have office space in a graduate student suite (first years) or faculty laboratory space (later years). They enter a rich interdisciplinary community in which psychology graduate students take courses with graduate students from public policy, neuroscience, linguistics, and other related disciplines. The Psychology Department contains an observational laboratory facility as well as faculty laboratories investigating a range of areas including children and the media, cognitive aging, social reasoning, developmental cognitive neuroscience, infant cognition, child care, animal models of developmental disorders, and research on adolescence, women, and the law. The Psychology Department also maintains the Georgetown Research Volunteer Project, a university-funded, Web-based facility for recruiting research participants across the lifespan. The Medical Center, which is immediately adjacent to the Main Campus, contains the Center for Functional and Molecular Imaging, affording the opportunity to conduct research using fMRI and other state-of-the-art neuroimaging technology. Georgetown University is situated in the nation's capitol and has among its unique mix of resources a public policy institute, medical school, law school, and school of foreign policy, each of which is among the leading programs in the nation. The two graduate concentrations take full advantage of these resources.

Information for Students With Physical Disabilities: See the following Web site for more information: http://www12.georgetown.edu/student-affairs/arc/services.cfm.

Application Information:
Send to Office of Graduate Admissions, Graduate School of Arts and Sciences, Georgetown University, Attention: Credentials—Department of Psychology Graduate Program, Box 571004, 3700 O Street, Northwest, ICC-302, Washington, DC 20057-1004. Application available online. URL of online application: https://www.app.applyyourself.com/?id=gtu-g. Students are admitted in the Fall, application deadline December 1. *Fee:* $70. Georgetown University Graduate School of Arts and Sciences offers a preferred, online application and recommendation system that allows for submission of most required application materials online. For applicants who cannot utilize this system, a downloadable paper application and self-assembled application package procedure is available. The online application is $70; paper application is $80. The Office of Graduate Admissions offers an online application and recommendation system for submission of the application form and supporting electronic documents, such as the statement of purpose, writing sample, resume, and official online recommendations. Documents submitted online should not be sent in hard copy format to the Office of Graduate Admissions. For submission of hard copy supporting documents not submitted online, such as official transcripts and supplemental data forms, applicants should submit a self-assembled application package. The application fee may be paid online by credit card or may be submitted by check or money order with the supporting application package. Please note that cash is not accepted as a form of payment.

Howard University (2007 data)

Department of Psychology
The Graduate School
525 Bryant Street, Northwest
Washington, DC 20059
Telephone: (202) 806-6805
Fax: (202) 806-4873
E-mail: *aroberts@howard.edu*
Web: *http://www.howard.edu*

Department Information:
1928. Acting Chairman: Dr. Jules P. Harrell. Number of faculty: total—full-time 24, part-time 2; women—full-time 12, part-time 2.

Programs and Degrees Offered:
Listed in the following order: Program area, degree type (T if terminal Master's), number awarded 7/06–6/07. Clinical PhD (Doctor of Philosophy) 4, Developmental PhD (Doctor of Philosophy) 1, Neuropsychology PhD (Doctor of Philosophy) 1, Personality PhD (Doctor of Philosophy) 0, Social PhD (Doctor of Philosophy) 1.

APA Accreditation: Clinical PhD (Doctor of Philosophy).

Student Applications/Admissions:
Student Applications
Clinical PhD (Doctor of Philosophy)—Applications 2007–2008, 135. Total applicants accepted 2007–2008, 10. Total enrolled 2007–2008 full-time, 26, part-time, 4. Openings 2008–2009, 6. The median number of years required for completion of a degree in 2006–2007 were 6. The number of students enrolled full- and part-time who were dismissed or voluntarily withdrew from this program area in 2007–2008 were 1. *Developmental PhD (Doctor of Philosophy)*—Applications 2007–2008, 36. Total applicants accepted 2007–2008, 7. Total enrolled 2007–2008 full-time, 18, part-time, 6. Openings 2008–2009, 4. The median number of years required for completion of a degree in 2006–2007 were 5. The number of students enrolled full- and part-time who were dismissed or voluntarily withdrew from this program area in 2007–2008 were 4. *Neuropsychology PhD (Doctor of Philosophy)*—Applications 2007–2008, 7. Total applicants accepted 2007–2008, 3. Total enrolled 2007–2008 full-time, 4, part-time, 2. Openings 2008–2009, 2. The median number of years required for completion of a degree in 2006–2007 were 5. The number of students enrolled full- and part-time who were dismissed or voluntarily withdrew from this program area in 2007–2008 were 0. *Personality PhD (Doctor of Philosophy)*—Applications 2007–2008, 15. Total applicants accepted 2007–2008, 5. Total enrolled 2007–2008 full-time, 6, part-time, 2. Openings 2008–2009, 2. The median number of years required for completion of a degree in 2006–2007 were 6. The number of students enrolled full- and part-time who were dismissed or voluntarily withdrew from this program area in 2007–2008 were 0. *Social PhD (Doctor of Philosophy)*—Applications 2007–2008, 16. Total applicants accepted 2007–2008, 6. Total enrolled 2007–2008 full-time, 6, part-time, 3. Openings 2008–2009, 3. The median number of years required for completion of a degree in 2006–2007 were 6. The number of students enrolled full- and part-time who were dismissed or voluntarily withdrew from this program area in 2007–2008 were 1.

Admissions Requirements:
Scores: Entries appear in this order: required test or GPA, minimum score (if required), median score of students entering in 2007–2008. Master's Programs: GRE-V no minimum stated; GRE-Q no minimum stated; overall undergraduate GPA 3.0, 3.4. You cannot receive an assistantship with a grade point average less than 3.26. Doctoral Programs: GRE-V no minimum stated; GRE-Q no minimum stated; overall undergraduate GPA 3.00, 3.5.
Other Criteria: (importance of criteria rated low, medium, or high): GRE/MAT scores—low, research experience—medium, GPA—high, letters of recommendation—high, interview—high, statement of goals and objectives—medium. Interview is of high importance for the clinical area only.

Student Characteristics: The following represents characteristics of students in 2007–2008 in all graduate psychology programs in the department: Female—full-time 48, part-time 12; Male—full-time 12, part-time 5; African American/Black—full-time 52, part-time 13; Hispanic/Latino(a)—full-time 1, part-time 0; Asian/Pacific Islander—full-time 1, part-time 0; American Indian/Alaska Native—full-time 0, part-time 0; Caucasian/White—full-time 6, part-time 0; students subject to the Americans With Disabilities Act—full-time 0, part-time 0; Unknown ethnicity—full-time 0, part-time 0.

Financial Information/Assistance:

Tuition for Full-Time Study: *Master's:* State residents: per academic year $11,195, $644 per credit hour; Nonstate residents: per academic year $11,195, $644 per credit hour. *Doctoral:* State residents: per academic year $11,195, $644 per credit hour; Nonstate residents: per academic year $11,195, $644 per credit hour. Tuition is subject to change. See the following Web site for updates and changes in tuition costs: http://www.Howard.edu.

Financial Assistance:

First-Year Students: Teaching assistantships available for first year. Average amount paid per academic year: $10,000. Average number of hours worked per week: 20. Apply by May 1. Tuition remission given: full. Fellowships and scholarships available for first year. Average amount paid per academic year: $13,500. Average number of hours worked per week: 20. Apply by May 1. Tuition remission given: full.

Advanced Students: Teaching assistantships available for advanced students. Average amount paid per academic year: $13,500. Average number of hours worked per week: 20. Apply by May 1. Fellowships and scholarships available for advanced students. Average amount paid per academic year: $15,000. Average number of hours worked per week: 20. Apply by May 1.

Additional Information: Of all students currently enrolled full time, 45% benefited from one or more of the listed financial assistance programs.

Internships/Practica: Internships and practica are available at various clinical sites in the District of Columbia, Maryland, and Virginia for students beginning in their first year of study.

Housing and Day Care: On-campus housing is available. Howard University, Office of Residence Life, 2401 4th Street, Northwest, Washington, DC 20059; (202) 806-6135. On-campus day care facilities are available. Howard University Early Learning Center, Howard Place, Washington, DC 20059.

Employment of Department Graduates:

Master's Degree Graduates: Of those who graduated in the academic year 2006–2007, the following categories and numbers represent the postgraduate activities and employment of master's degree graduates: Enrolled in a postdoctoral residency/fellowship (n/a), employed in independent practice (n/a), total from the above (master's) (0).

Doctoral Degree Graduates: Of those who graduated in the academic year 2006–2007, the following categories and numbers represent the postgraduate activities and employment of doctoral degree graduates: Enrolled in a psychology doctoral program (n/a), total from the above (doctoral) (0).

Additional Information:

Orientation, Objectives, and Emphasis of Department: The Graduate Program at Howard prepares students for careers in research, teaching, and the practice of psychology. Advanced study in clinical, developmental, social, personality, and neuropsychology is offered. A major emphasis of the program is research training, and students are expected to conduct research throughout their graduate study.

Application Information:

Send to Graduate Admissions, Graduate School of Arts and Sciences, Howard University, Washington, DC 20059. Application available online. URL of online application: http://www.gs.howard.edu. Students are admitted in the Fall, application deadline February 1. February 15 all other areas except clinical. *Fee:* $45.

Argosy University/Tampa

Clinical Psychology
American School of Professional Psychology
4410 North Himes Avenue, Suite 150
Tampa, FL 33614
Telephone: (800) 850-6488
Fax: (813) 246-4045
E-mail: *jpeterson@argosy.edu*
Web: *http://www.argosy.edu*

Department Information:

1995. Dean: Jeanne Peterson, PsyD. Number of faculty: total—full-time 10, part-time 1; women—full-time 7; total—minority—full-time 3; women minority—full-time 2.

Programs and Degrees Offered:

Listed in the following order: Program area, degree type (T if terminal Master's), number awarded 7/06–6/07. Clinical Psychology PsyD (Doctor of Psychology) 19.

APA Accreditation: Clinical PsyD (Doctor of Psychology).

Student Applications/Admissions:

Student Applications

Clinical Psychology PsyD (Doctor of Psychology)—Applications 2007–2008, 123. Total applicants accepted 2007–2008, 55. Number full-time enrolled (new admits only) 2007–2008, 45. Number part-time enrolled (new admits only) 2007–2008, 0. Openings 2008–2009, 45. The median number of years required for completion of a degree in 2006–2007 were 5. The number of students enrolled full- and part-time who were dismissed or voluntarily withdrew from this program area in 2007–2008 were 7.

Admissions Requirements:

Scores: Entries appear in this order: required test or GPA, minimum score (if required), median score of students entering in 2007–2008. Master's Programs: overall undergraduate GPA 3.0; last 2 years GPA 3.0; psychology GPA 3.0. Doctoral Programs: GRE-V no minimum stated; GRE-Q no minimum stated; MAT no minimum stated; overall undergraduate GPA 3.25, 3.53; last 2 years GPA 3.25; psychology GPA 3.25.

Other Criteria: (importance of criteria rated low, medium, or high): research experience—medium, work experience—high, extracurricular activity—medium, clinically related public service—high, GPA—high, letters of recommendation—high, interview—high, statement of goals and objectives—high. For additional information on admission requirements, go to http://www.argosy.edu/admissions/admissions-downloads.aspx.

Student Characteristics: The following represents characteristics of students in 2007–2008 in all graduate psychology programs in the department: Female—full-time 144, part-time 0; Male—full-time 32, part-time 0; African American/Black—full-time 12, part-time 0; Hispanic/Latino(a)—full-time 18, part-time 0; Asian/Pacific Islander—full-time 9, part-time 0; American Indian/Alaska Native—full-time 2, part-time 0; Caucasian/White—full-time 123, part-time 0; Multi-ethnic—full-time 0, part-time 0; Unknown ethnicity—full-time 12, part-time 0.

Financial Information/Assistance:

Tuition for Full-Time Study: *Master's:* State residents: $905 per credit hour; Nonstate residents: $905 per credit hour. *Doctoral:* State residents: $905 per credit hour; Nonstate residents: $905 per credit hour. Tuition is subject to change. See the following Web site for updates and changes in tuition costs: http://www.argosy.edu.

Financial Assistance:

First-Year Students: Research assistantships available for first year. Average amount paid per academic year: $3,000. Average number of hours worked per week: 5. Tuition remission given: partial. Fellowships and scholarships available for first year. Average amount paid per academic year: $1,000. Tuition remission given: partial.

Advanced Students: Teaching assistantships available for advanced students. Average amount paid per academic year: $3,000. Average number of hours worked per week: 10. Tuition remission given: partial. Research assistantships available for advanced students. Average amount paid per academic year: $3,000. Average number of hours worked per week: 10. Tuition remission given: partial. Fellowships and scholarships available for advanced students. Average amount paid per academic year: $1,000.

Additional Information: Of all students currently enrolled full time, 35% benefited from one or more of the listed financial assistance programs.

Internships/Practica: Doctoral Degree (PsyD Clinical Psychology): For those doctoral students for whom a professional internship was required in this program prior to graduation, (21) students applied for an internship in 2006–2007, with (19) students obtaining an internship. Of those students who obtained an internship, (19) were paid internships. Of those students who obtained an internship, (8) students placed in APA/CPA-accredited internships, (11) students placed in internships not APA/CPA accredited, but listed with the Association of Psychology Postdoctoral and Internship Centers (APPIC), (0) students placed in internships conforming to guidelines of the Council of Directors of School Psychology Programs (CDSPP), (0) students placed in internships that were not APA/CPA-accredited, APPIC or CDSPP listed. All students are required to complete a 800-hour diagnostic practicum and a 800-hour therapy practicum. Opportunities for practicum experience are available at many sites throughout the community including community mental health centers, hospitals, schools, college counseling centers, private practices, forensic, geriatric and child treatment centers, medical centers, and rehabilitation centers. Supplemental and specialty practicum sites are developed based on student interest and availability.

Housing and Day Care: No on-campus housing is available. No on-campus day care facilities are available.

Employment of Department Graduates:

Master's Degree Graduates: Of those who graduated in the academic year 2006–2007, the following categories and numbers represent the postgraduate activities and employment of master's degree graduates: Enrolled in a postdoctoral residency/fellowship (n/a), employed in independent practice (n/a), total from the above (master's) (0).

Doctoral Degree Graduates: Of those who graduated in the academic year 2006–2007, the following categories and numbers represent the postgraduate activities and employment of doctoral degree graduates: Enrolled in a psychology doctoral program (n/a), total from the above (doctoral) (0).

Additional Information:

Orientation, Objectives, and Emphasis of Department: The American School of Professional Psychology—Tampa Campus is a practitioner-oriented program, based on the local clinical scientist model, established with the aim of training highly qualified clinical psychologists. In the belief that it is the responsibility of each clinician to determine his or her approach to therapy, the program strives to introduce students to a variety of clinical orientations. Emphasis is on clinical skills, particularly psychological assessment, diagnosis, and psychotherapy. Students have the opportunity to focus on neuropsychology, geropsychology, child psychology, or marriage and family therapy.

Special Facilities or Resources: All faculty are experienced clinicians as well as educators. A number of general and specialized practicum sites are available to students. The departmental library houses a focused collection of monographs and journals and provides students access to electronic library resources throughout the Argosy University and state of Florida library systems. There is an observation room with one-way mirror and videotaping facilities on campus.

Information for Students With Physical Disabilities: Contact nirodriguez@argosy.edu.

Application Information:

Send to Assistant Director of Admissions/ASPP Argosy University—Tampa Campus, 4410 North Himes Avenue, Suite 150, Tampa, FL 33614. Application available online. URL of online application: http://www.argosy.edu/admissions/admissions-downloads.aspx. Students are admitted in the Fall, application deadline March 15; Spring, application deadline November 15; Summer, application deadline March 30; Programs have rolling admissions. Applications are also accepted on a rolling admissions basis depending on the availability of seats for the next entering class. *Fee:* $50.

Barry University

Department of Psychology
School of Arts and Sciences
11300 Northeast 2nd Avenue
Miami Shores, FL 33161
Telephone: (305) 899-3270
Fax: (305) 899-3279
E-mail: *lszuchman@mail.barry.edu*
Web: *http://www.barry.edu*

Department Information:

1978. Chairperson: Lenore T. Szuchman. Number of faculty: total—full-time 9, part-time 14; women—full-time 6, part-time 9; total—minority—full-time 2, part-time 6; women minority—full-time 1, part-time 4.

Programs and Degrees Offered:

Listed in the following order: Program area, degree type (T if terminal Master's), number awarded 7/06–6/07. Clinical Psychology MA/MS (Master of Arts/Science) (T) 3, School Psychology Other 10, Psychology MA/MS (Master of Arts/Science) 5.

Student Applications/Admissions:

Student Applications

Clinical Psychology MA/MS (Master of Arts/Science)—Applications 2007–2008, 16. Total applicants accepted 2007–2008, 15. Number full-time enrolled (new admits only) 2007–2008, 12. Total enrolled 2007–2008 full-time, 28, part-time, 8. Openings 2008–2009, 15. The median number of years required for completion of a degree in 2006–2007 were 3. The number of students enrolled full- and part-time who were dismissed or voluntarily withdrew from this program area in 2007–2008 were 6. *School Psychology Other*—Applications 2007–2008, 10. Total applicants accepted 2007–2008, 7. Number full-time enrolled (new admits only) 2007–2008, 1. Total enrolled 2007–2008 full-time, 8, part-time, 1. Openings 2008–2009, 15. The median number of years required for completion of a degree in 2006–2007 were 2. The number of students enrolled full- and part-time who were dismissed or voluntarily withdrew from this program area in 2007–2008 were 5. *Psychology MA/MS (Master of Arts/Science)*—Applications 2007–2008, 20. Total applicants accepted 2007–2008, 11. Number full-time enrolled (new admits only) 2007–2008, 5. Number part-time enrolled (new admits only) 2007–2008, 2. Total enrolled 2007–2008 full-time, 22, part-time, 5. Openings 2008–2009, 15. The median number of years required for completion of a degree in 2006–2007 was 1. The number of students enrolled full- and part-time who were dismissed or voluntarily withdrew from this program area in 2007–2008 were 5.

Admissions Requirements:

Scores: Entries appear in this order: required test or GPA, minimum score (if required), median score of students entering in 2007–2008. Master's Programs: GRE-V no minimum stated; GRE-Q no minimum stated; overall undergraduate GPA 3.0; Masters GRE-Analytical no minimum stated. Master's GPA 3.4 required for admission to Specialist in School Psychology Program.

Other Criteria: (importance of criteria rated low, medium, or high): GRE/MAT scores—medium, research experience—medium, work experience—medium, extracurricular activity—low, clinically related public service—medium, GPA—high, letters of recommendation—high, statement of goals and objectives—medium, undergraduate major in psychology—medium, specific undergraduate psychology courses taken—high. For additional information on admission requirements, go to http://www.barry.edu/psychologyclinical/admissions/requirements.asp.

Student Characteristics: The following represents characteristics of students in 2007–2008 in all graduate psychology programs in the department: Female—full-time 48, part-time 9; Male—full-time 10, part-time 5; African American/Black—full-time 14, part-time 4; Hispanic/Latino(a)—full-time 16, part-time 4; Asian/

Pacific Islander—full-time 0, part-time 0; American Indian/Alaska Native—full-time 0, part-time 0; Caucasian/White—full-time 24, part-time 6; Multi-ethnic—full-time 0, part-time 0; students subject to the Americans With Disabilities Act—full-time 0, part-time 0; Unknown ethnicity—full-time 4, part-time 0.

Financial Information/Assistance:

Tuition for Full-Time Study: *Master's:* State residents: $765 per credit hour; Nonstate residents: $765 per credit hour. Tuition is subject to change. See the following Web site for updates and changes in tuition costs: http://www.barry.edu/admissions FinancialAid/graduate/admissions/tuitionFees.htm.

Financial Assistance:

First-Year Students: Teaching assistantships available for first year. Average amount paid per academic year: $3,675. Average number of hours worked per week: 14. Apply by April 30. Tuition remission given: partial.

Advanced Students: Teaching assistantships available for advanced students. Average amount paid per academic year: $3,675. Average number of hours worked per week: 14. Apply by April 30. Tuition remission given: partial.

Additional Information: Of all students currently enrolled full time, 15% benefited from one or more of the listed financial assistance programs.

Internships/Practica: All students enrolled in the MS in Clinical Psychology Program must complete a one-semester practicum. Students in the 60-credit program must also complete a two-semester, full-time clinical internship. Because Barry University is located in a large, multicultural metropolitan area, the program is able to offer more than the usual number and variety of settings for the internship experience. Sites include but are not limited to community mental health centers, assessment centers (primarily for the assessment of children), psychiatric hospitals, addiction treatment programs, nursing homes, and prison settings. Supervision is provided both at the site and by a clinical supervisor on campus. Students in the SSP program complete a practicum and an internship in the public schools. The internship is full-time for two semesters and can be done locally or at a distance from the campus.

Housing and Day Care: No on-campus housing is available. No on-campus day care facilities are available.

Employment of Department Graduates:

Master's Degree Graduates: Of those who graduated in the academic year 2006–2007, the following categories and numbers represent the postgraduate activities and employment of master's degree graduates: Enrolled in a psychology doctoral program (2), enrolled in a postdoctoral residency/fellowship (n/a), employed in independent practice (n/a), employed in a professional position in a school system (8), total from the above (master's) (10).

Doctoral Degree Graduates: Of those who graduated in the academic year 2006–2007, the following categories and numbers represent the postgraduate activities and employment of doctoral degree graduates: Enrolled in a psychology doctoral program (n/a), total from the above (doctoral) (0).

Additional Information:

Orientation, Objectives, and Emphasis of Department: In the MS Program in Clinical Psychology, students are expected to achieve competence in theory, assessment, therapy, and research. All clinical psychology students complete a thesis and a practicum. The 36-credit option, a 2-year program, is designed for students who want to go directly into a doctoral program. Students who complete the 3-year, 60-credit program meet licensure requirements for the Mental Health Counselor in Florida. The MS in Psychology is designed for the student who wishes to go on to the Specialist degree in School Psychology (SSP). The SSP program follows the scientist–practitioner model and integrates theoretical and practical training to prevent and remediate academic and emotional problems in the schools. Students gain expertise in evaluation, diagnosis, prescription, interventions, psychometric applications, research, consultation, and professional ethics and standards. Students who successfully complete the MS in Psychology and the SSP program will be prepared to meet licensure requirements for the private practice of school psychology in the state of Florida as well as certification requirements of the Florida State Board of Education. The School Psychology Program has been approved by the Department of Education of the State of Florida and the National Association of School Psychologists.

Special Facilities or Resources: The psychology department is normally composed of 11 full-time faculty members. Classes are small, and the students are given individual attention and supervision.

Information for Students With Physical Disabilities: See the following Web site for more information: http://www.barry.edu/DisabilityServices/default.htm.

Application Information:

Send to Office of Enrollment Services, Barry University, 11300 Northeast 2nd Avenue, Miami FL 33161. Application available online. URL of online application: http://www.barry.edu/psychologyclinical/admissions/applyNow.asp. Students are admitted in the Fall, application deadline February 15. Rolling admissions for MS Psychology and SSP. MS Clinical deadline is February 15 with review continuing as long as space is available. Applicants may be admitted at other times but are urged to enroll in Fall term with undergraduate prerequisites completed in order to finish programs in timely fashion. *Fee:* $30. Waived for Barry University alumni.

Carlos Albizu University, Miami Campus (2007 data)

Doctoral Program, Terminal Master's Programs

2173 Northwest 99th Avenue
Miami, FL 33172-2209
Telephone: (305) 593-1223
Fax: (305) 629-8052
E-mail: *grodriguez@albizu.edu*
Web: *http://www.albizu.edu*

Department Information:

1980. Chancellor: Gerardo Rodriguez-Menendez, PhD. Number of faculty: total—full-time 18, part-time 34; women—full-time 10, part-time 18.

Programs and Degrees Offered:

Listed in the following order: Program area, degree type (T if terminal Master's), number awarded 7/06–6/07. Industrial/Organizational MA/MS (Master of Arts/Science) (T) 9, Clinical PsyD (Doctor of Psychology) 30, Counseling MA/MS (Master of Arts/Science) (T) 49.

APA Accreditation: Clinical PsyD (Doctor of Psychology).

Student Applications/Admissions:

Student Applications

Industrial/Organizational MA/MS (Master of Arts/Science)—Applications 2007–2008, 30. Total applicants accepted 2007–2008, 21. Number full-time enrolled (new admits only) 2007–2008, 19. Number part-time enrolled (new admits only) 2007–2008, 2. Total enrolled 2007–2008 full-time, 32, part-time, 11. Openings 2008–2009, 40. The median number of years required for completion of a degree in 2006–2007 were 3. The number of students enrolled full- and part-time who were dismissed or voluntarily withdrew from this program area in 2007–2008 were 2. *Clinical PsyD (Doctor of Psychology)*—Applications 2007–2008, 106. Total applicants accepted 2007–2008, 80. Number full-time enrolled (new admits only) 2007–2008, 70. Number part-time enrolled (new admits only) 2007–2008, 8. Total enrolled 2007–2008 full-time, 304, part-time, 12. Openings 2008–2009, 33. The median number of years required for completion of a degree in 2006–2007 were 7. The number of students enrolled full- and part-time who were dismissed or voluntarily withdrew from this program area in 2007–2008 were 21. *Counseling MA/MS (Master of Arts/Science)*—Applications 2007–2008, 121. Total applicants accepted 2007–2008, 105. Number full-time enrolled (new admits only) 2007–2008, 75. Number part-time enrolled (new admits only) 2007–2008, 23. Total enrolled 2007–2008 full-time, 190, part-time, 94. Openings 2008–2009, 75. The median number of years required for completion of a degree in 2006–2007 were 3. The number of students enrolled full- and part-time who were dismissed or voluntarily withdrew from this program area in 2007–2008 were 20.

Admissions Requirements:

Scores: Entries appear in this order: required test or GPA, minimum score (if required), median score of students entering in 2007–2008. Master's Programs: overall undergraduate GPA 3.00, 3.04. Doctoral Programs: overall undergraduate GPA 3.00, 3.40.

Other Criteria: (importance of criteria rated low, medium, or high): GRE/MAT scores—low, research experience—low, work experience—medium, extracurricular activity—low, clinically related public service—medium, GPA—high, letters of recommendation—high, interview—high, statement of goals and objectives—high. For terminal MS Programs only: GRE/MAT scores—none, extracurricular activity—medium.

Student Characteristics: The following represents characteristics of students in 2007–2008 in all graduate psychology programs in the department: Female—full-time 420, part-time 90; Male—full-time 106, part-time 27; African American/Black—full-time 55, part-time 14; Hispanic/Latino(a)—full-time 373, part-time 95; Asian/Pacific Islander—full-time 2, part-time 0; American Indian/Alaska Native—full-time 2, part-time 0; Caucasian/White—full-time 83, part-time 5; Multi-ethnic—full-time 0, part-time 0; students subject to the Americans With Disabilities Act—full-time 1, part-time 3; Unknown ethnicity—full-time 11, part-time 3.

Financial Information/Assistance:

Tuition for Full-Time Study: *Master's:* State residents: per academic year $9,090, $505 per credit hour; Nonstate residents: per academic year $9,090, $505 per credit hour. *Doctoral:* State residents: per academic year $11,520, $640 per credit hour; Nonstate residents: per academic year $11,520, $640 per credit hour. Tuition is subject to change. Tuition costs vary by program.

Financial Assistance:

First-Year Students: Fellowships and scholarships available for first year. Average amount paid per academic year: $2,700. Apply by June 1.

Advanced Students: Teaching assistantships available for advanced students. Average amount paid per academic year: $2,500. Average number of hours worked per week: 10. Research assistantships available for advanced students. Average amount paid per academic year: $2,500. Average number of hours worked per week: 10. Fellowships and scholarships available for advanced students. Average amount paid per academic year: $2,850. Apply by June 1.

Additional Information: Of all students currently enrolled full time, 7% benefited from one or more of the listed financial assistance programs.

Internships/Practica: Carlos Albizu University, Miami Campus, operates the Goodman Psychological Services Center, which provides low-cost services to the community and functions as both a Practicum and internship site for doctoral students. All PsyD students begin their practicum work in the Center and later have the option of moving on to any of about 35 practicum sites in the community. The Goodman Center is also an APPIC member and offers a predoctoral internship. The majority of internship candidates seek outside internships with the support and assistance of the Department of Field Placement. Terminal Master's students are placed during their senior year (8–12 months) at a variety of corporations, schools, and human services settings with diverse client populations. Sixty practicum sites are available in the tri-county area (Miami-Dade, Broward, Palm Beach).

Housing and Day Care: No on-campus housing is available. No on-campus day care facilities are available.

Employment of Department Graduates:

Master's Degree Graduates: Of those who graduated in the academic year 2006–2007, the following categories and numbers represent the postgraduate activities and employment of master's degree graduates: Enrolled in a psychology doctoral program (3), enrolled in a postdoctoral residency/fellowship (n/a), employed in independent practice (n/a), employed in a professional position in a school system (6), employed in business or industry (5), employed in a community mental health/counseling center (20), employed in a hospital/medical center (2), do not know (20), total from the above (master's) (58).

Doctoral Degree Graduates: Of those who graduated in the academic year 2006–2007, the following categories and numbers represent the postgraduate activities and employment of doctoral degree graduates: Enrolled in a psychology doctoral program (n/a), enrolled in a postdoctoral residency/fellowship (9), employed in independent practice (10), employed in an academic position at a university (1), employed in a community mental health/counseling center (2), employed in a hospital/medical center (5), total from the above (doctoral) (30).

Additional Information:

Orientation, Objectives, and Emphasis of Department: Carlos Albizu University (CAU) has as its primary objective the training of psychologists, mental health counselors, marriage and family therapists, school counselors, and master's level industrial and organizational psychology practitioners at the highest level of professional competence with a special sensitivity to multicultural issues. The academic curriculum emphasizes a core of traditional courses, including training in theory and research methodology. Academic courses are sequenced to foster steady growth in conceptual mastery and technical skills within a multicultural context. Clinical training provides for the opportunity of applied practice in the areas of psychotherapy, psychodiagnostics, school counseling, and industrial and organizational services within settings serving a multicultural population. The PsyD Program curriculum offers four concentrations: Child Psychology, Clinical Neuropsychology, Forensic Psychology, and General Practice.

Special Facilities or Resources: The University has its own Psychological Services Center, which is an on-campus facility that provides varied clinical services to the community while serving as a training site for practicum and predoctoral interns enrolled in the PsyD Program. Throughout their internship and practica, students are supervised by licensed psychologists who monitor their work and evaluate their performance. Tools such as two-way mirrors and audiovisual equipment are used to provide supervision and feedback to the students.

Application Information:

Send to Mr. Rafael Vásquez, Assistant Director of Recruitment and Admissions, Carlos Albizu University, Miami Campus, 2173 Northwest 99th Avenue, Miami, FL 33172-2209. Application available online. URL of online application: http://www.mia.albizu.edu. Students are admitted in the Fall, application deadline; Spring, application deadline; Summer, application deadline; Programs have rolling admissions. *Fee:* $50. Fee waived for on-site applications during select institutional events (i.e., Open House).

Central Florida, University of

Department of Psychology
College of Sciences
P.O. Box 161390
Orlando, FL 32816-1390
Telephone: (407) 823-4344
Fax: (407) 823-5862
E-mail: *psychinfo@mail.ucf.edu*
Web: *http://www.psych.ucf.edu/*

Department Information:

1968. Chairperson: Robert L. Dipboye. Number of faculty: total—full-time 48; women—full-time 19; total—minority—full-time 9; women minority—full-time 2; faculty subject to the Americans With Disabilities Act 1.

Programs and Degrees Offered:

Listed in the following order: Program area, degree type (T if terminal Master's), number awarded 7/06–6/07. Clinical MA/MS (Master of Arts/Science) (T) 11, Industrial/Organizational MA/MS (Master of Arts/Science) (T) 25, Applied Experimental and Human Factors PhD (Doctor of Philosophy) 8, Clinical PhD (Doctor of Philosophy) 6, Industrial-Organizational PhD (Doctor of Philosophy) 6.

APA Accreditation: Clinical PhD (Doctor of Philosophy).

Student Applications/Admissions:

Student Applications

Clinical MA/MS (Master of Arts/Science)—Applications 2007–2008, 86. Total applicants accepted 2007–2008, 16. Number full-time enrolled (new admits only) 2007–2008, 9. Total enrolled 2007–2008 full-time, 21. Openings 2008–2009, 12. The median number of years required for completion of a degree in 2006–2007 were 2. The number of students enrolled full- and part-time who were dismissed or voluntarily withdrew from this program area in 2007–2008 were 2. *Industrial/Organizational MA/MS (Master of Arts/Science)*—Applications 2007–2008, 85. Total applicants accepted 2007–2008, 27. Number full-time enrolled (new admits only) 2007–2008, 16. Total enrolled 2007–2008 full-time, 31. Openings 2008–2009, 15. The median number of years required for completion of a degree in 2006–2007 were 2. The number of students enrolled full- and part-time who were dismissed or voluntarily withdrew from this program area in 2007–2008 were 0. *Applied Experimental and Human Factors PhD (Doctor of Philosophy)*—Applications 2007–2008, 42. Total applicants accepted 2007–2008, 9. Number full-time enrolled (new admits only) 2007–2008, 8. Number part-time enrolled (new admits only) 2007–2008, 0. Openings 2008–2009, 12. The median number of years required for completion of a degree in 2006–2007 were 5. The number of students enrolled full- and part-time who were dismissed or voluntarily withdrew from this program area in 2007–2008 were 1. *Clinical PhD (Doctor of Philosophy)*—Applications 2007–2008, 140. Total applicants accepted 2007–2008, 7. Number full-time enrolled (new admits only) 2007–2008, 6. Openings 2008–2009, 7. The median number of years required for completion of a degree in 2006–2007 were 6. The number of students enrolled full- and part-time who were dismissed or voluntarily withdrew from this program area in 2007–2008 were 1. *Industrial-Organizational PhD (Doctor of Philosophy)*—Applications 2007–2008, 74. Total applicants accepted 2007–2008, 18. Number full-time enrolled (new admits only) 2007–2008, 7. Number part-time enrolled (new admits only) 2007–2008, 0. Openings 2008–2009, 7. The median number of years required for completion of a degree in 2006–2007 were 5. The number of students enrolled full- and part-time who were dismissed or voluntarily withdrew from this program area in 2007–2008 were 2.

Admissions Requirements:

Scores: Entries appear in this order: required test or GPA, minimum score (if required), median score of students entering in 2007–2008. Master's Programs: GRE-V no minimum stated; GRE-Q no minimum stated; overall undergraduate GPA 3.0; last 2 years GPA 3.0, 3.5; psychology GPA 3.0, 3.5; Masters GRE-Analytical no minimum stated. Doctoral Programs: GRE-V no minimum stated; GRE-Q no minimum stated; overall undergraduate GPA no minimum stated; last 2 years GPA 3.0, 3.7; psychology GPA 3.0, 3.7; Doctoral program GRE-Analytic no minimum stated. GRE of 1000 or 3.0 GPA are minimum requirements to apply to Clinical PhD, Clinical

MA, I/O MS, and I/O PhD program. For AEHF, the minimum GRE is 1100 and GPA 3.2.

Other Criteria: (importance of criteria rated low, medium, or high): GRE/MAT scores—high, research experience—high, work experience—low, extracurricular activity—medium, clinically related public service—medium, GPA—high, letters of recommendation—high, interview—high, statement of goals and objectives—high, undergraduate major in psychology—low, specific undergraduate psychology courses taken—medium. Criteria vary by program.

Student Characteristics: The following represents characteristics of students in 2007–2008 in all graduate psychology programs in the department: Female—full-time 117, part-time 0; Male—full-time 57, part-time 0; African American/Black—full-time 14, part-time 0; Hispanic/Latino(a)—full-time 19, part-time 0; Asian/Pacific Islander—full-time 12, part-time 0; American Indian/Alaska Native—full-time 1, part-time 0; Caucasian/White—full-time 128, part-time 0; Multi-ethnic—full-time 0, part-time 0; students subject to the Americans With Disabilities Act—full-time 0, part-time 0; Unknown ethnicity—full-time 0, part-time 0; International students who hold an F-1 or J-1 Visa—full-time 10, part-time 0.

Financial Information/Assistance:

Tuition for Full-Time Study: *Master's:* State residents: per academic year $4,863, $270 per credit hour; Nonstate residents: per academic year $17,953, $997 per credit hour. *Doctoral:* State residents: per academic year $4,863, $270 per credit hour; Nonstate residents: per academic year $17,953, $997 per credit hour. Tuition is subject to change. See the following Web site for updates and changes in tuition costs: http://www.graduate.ucf.edu.

Financial Assistance:

First-Year Students: Teaching assistantships available for first year. Average amount paid per academic year: $10,000. Average number of hours worked per week: 20. Tuition remission given: full and partial. Research assistantships available for first year. Average amount paid per academic year: $15,000. Average number of hours worked per week: 20. Tuition remission given: full and partial. Fellowships and scholarships available for first year. Average amount paid per academic year: $13,500. Average number of hours worked per week: 20. Tuition remission given: full and partial.

Advanced Students: Teaching assistantships available for advanced students. Average amount paid per academic year: $10,000. Average number of hours worked per week: 20. Tuition remission given: full and partial. Research assistantships available for advanced students. Average amount paid per academic year: $15,000. Average number of hours worked per week: 20. Tuition remission given: full and partial. Fellowships and scholarships available for advanced students. Average amount paid per academic year: $13,500. Average number of hours worked per week: 20. Tuition remission given: full and partial.

Additional Information: Of all students currently enrolled full time, 90% benefited from one or more of the listed financial assistance programs. Application and information available online at http://www.graduate.ucf.edu.

Internships/Practica: Doctoral Degree (Clinical PhD): For those doctoral students for whom a professional internship was required in this program prior to graduation, (6) students applied for an internship in 2006–2007, with (6) students obtaining an internship. Of those students who obtained an internship, (6) were paid internships. Of those students who obtained an internship, (6) students placed in APA/CPA-accredited internships, (0) students placed in internships not APA/CPA-accredited, but listed with the Association of Psychology Postdoctoral and Internship Centers (APPIC), (0) students placed in internships conforming to guidelines of the Council of Directors of School Psychology Programs (CDSPP), (0) students placed in internships that were not APA/CPA-accredited, APPIC or CDSPP listed. Clinical: Internships for clinical masters students exist in community mental health centers and other agencies throughout Central Florida. Doctoral students complete their practica in our on-campus clinic as well as in a variety of community-based clinical agencies. Human Factors: Human Factors students complete internships in a variety of government, business, and industry settings. Industrial/Organizational: I/O master's students complete practica placements in a variety of government, business, and industry settings. Doctoral students complete an internship in a variety of business, industry, and government settings.

Housing and Day Care: On-campus housing is available. See the following Web site for more information: http://www.housing.ucf.edu/. On-campus day care facilities are available. See the following Web site for more information: http://www.csc.sdes.ucf.edu/.

Employment of Department Graduates:

Master's Degree Graduates: Of those who graduated in the academic year 2006–2007, the following categories and numbers represent the postgraduate activities and employment of master's degree graduates: Enrolled in a psychology doctoral program (4), enrolled in a postdoctoral residency/fellowship (n/a), employed in independent practice (n/a), employed in business or industry (16), employed in a community mental health/counseling center (12), total from the above (master's) (32).

Doctoral Degree Graduates: Of those who graduated in the academic year 2006–2007, the following categories and numbers represent the postgraduate activities and employment of doctoral degree graduates: Enrolled in a psychology doctoral program (n/a), enrolled in a postdoctoral residency/fellowship (2), employed in an academic position at a university (5), employed in business or industry (9), employed in government agency (2), employed in a hospital/medical center (2), total from the above (doctoral) (20).

Additional Information:

Orientation, Objectives, and Emphasis of Department: The PhD program in clinical psychology is an APA-accredited program, designed for individuals seeking a research-oriented career in the field of clinical psychology. The program also emphasizes training in consultation, teaching, supervision, and the design/evaluation of mental health programs. The MA program in clinical psychology has major emphases in assessment and evaluation skills; intervention, counseling, and psychotherapy skills; and an academic foundation in research methods. The program is designed to provide training and preparation for persons desiring to deliver clinical services at the master's level through community agencies. Graduates of this program meet the educational requirements for the mental health counselor state license. The MS program in Industrial/Organizational psychology has major emphases in selection and training of employees, applied theories of organizational behavior, job satisfaction, test theory and construction, assessment center technology, statistics, and experimental design. As of Fall

2000 a PhD in Industrial/Organizational was approved and admitted an initial class of 10 students. I/O students receive training in the 21 competence areas detailed by Division 14 of the APA. The PhD program in applied experiment/human factors is patterned on the scientist–practitioner model of the APA. It adheres to the guidelines for education and training established by the committee for Education and Training of APA's Division 21 (Applied Experimental and Engineering Psychology). The Applied Experimental and Human Factors program is accredited by the Educational Committee of the Human Factors and Ergonomics Society. Concentration areas include human–computer interaction, human performance, and human factors in simulation and training.

Special Facilities or Resources: The department's facilities and resources include extensive videotape capability, an intelligence and personality testing library, a statistics library, computer facilities within the department and in the computer center, a counseling and testing center, a creative school for children, and a communicative disorders clinic. Doctoral students have use of specialized equipment in the department-based Human Visual Performance Laboratory and Team Performance Laboratory. The clinical program has extensive ties to a number of community agencies for practica and assistantship as well as an on-site clinic.

Information for Students With Physical Disabilities: See the following Web site for more information: http://www.sds.sdes.ucf.edu/.

Application Information:
Send online application to University of Central Florida, Office of Graduate Studies, P.O. Box 160112, Orlando, FL 32816-0112. Web address: http://www.graduate.ucf.edu. Application materials should be sent to: University of Central Florida, Department of Psychology, ATTN: Graduate Admissions, P.O. Box 161390, Orlando, FL 32816-1390. Application available online. URL of online application: http://www.graduate.ucf.edu/gradonlineapp/. Students are admitted in the Fall, application deadline December 15. *Fee:* $30.

Embry-Riddle Aeronautical University (2007 data)

Human Factors and Systems
600 South Clyde Morris Boulevard
Daytona Beach, FL 32114
Telephone: (386) 226-6790
Fax: (386) 226-7050
E-mail: *boque007@erau.edu*
Web: *http://www.humanfactorsandsystems.com*

Department Information:
1997. Chairperson: Albert Boquet, PhD. Number of faculty: total—full-time 11; women—full-time 5.

Programs and Degrees Offered:
Listed in the following order: Program area, degree type (T if terminal Master's), number awarded 7/06–6/07. Human Factors and Systems MA/MS (Master of Arts/Science) (T) 8.

Student Applications/Admissions:

Student Applications

Human Factors and Systems MA/MS (Master of Arts/Science)—Applications 2007–2008, 20. Total applicants accepted 2007–2008, 16. Number full-time enrolled (new admits only) 2007–2008, 10. Number part-time enrolled (new admits only) 2007–2008, 2. Total enrolled 2007–2008 full-time, 16, part-time, 30. Openings 2008–2009, 25. The median number of years required for completion of a degree in 2006–2007 were 2. The number of students enrolled full- and part-time who were dismissed or voluntarily withdrew from this program area in 2007–2008 were 3.

Admissions Requirements:

Scores: Entries appear in this order: required test or GPA, minimum score (if required), median score of students entering in 2007–2008. Master's Programs: GRE-V 500; GRE-Q 500; overall undergraduate GPA 3.0.

Other Criteria: (importance of criteria rated low, medium, or high): GRE/MAT scores—high, research experience—high, work experience—medium, extracurricular activity—low, GPA—high, letters of recommendation—high, interview—low, statement of goals and objectives—high.

Student Characteristics: The following represents characteristics of students in 2007–2008 in all graduate psychology programs in the department: Female—full-time 7, part-time 24; Male—full-time 9, part-time 6; African American/Black—full-time 1, part-time 1; Hispanic/Latino(a)—full-time 0, part-time 5; Asian/Pacific Islander—full-time 0, part-time 1; American Indian/Alaska Native—full-time 0, part-time 0; Caucasian/White—full-time 14, part-time 23; Multi-ethnic—full-time 1, part-time 0; students subject to the Americans With Disabilities Act—full-time 0, part-time 0; Unknown ethnicity—full-time 0, part-time 0.

Financial Information/Assistance:

Tuition for Full-Time Study: *Master's:* State residents: $1,020 per credit hour; Nonstate residents: $1,020 per credit hour.

Financial Assistance:

First-Year Students: Teaching assistantships available for first year. Average amount paid per academic year: $5,700. Average number of hours worked per week: 20. Tuition remission given: partial. Research assistantships available for first year. Average amount paid per academic year: $5,700. Average number of hours worked per week: 20. Tuition remission given: partial. Fellowships and scholarships available for first year. Tuition remission given: partial.

Advanced Students: Teaching assistantships available for advanced students. Average amount paid per academic year: $6,300. Average number of hours worked per week: 20. Tuition remission given: partial. Research assistantships available for advanced students. Average amount paid per academic year: $6,300. Average number of hours worked per week: 20. Tuition remission given: partial. Fellowships and scholarships available for advanced students. Tuition remission given: partial.

Additional Information: Of all students currently enrolled full time, 20% benefited from one or more of the listed financial assistance programs.

Internships/Practica: The Master's Degree program at Embry-Riddle provides extensive opportunities for students to engage in paid and/or credit-based internship or co-op placements. Master's students are strongly encouraged, although not required, to take advantage of these placements. Previous placements of graduate students include premiere companies such as Lockheed Martin, IBM, Veritas Software, Sikorsky Helicopter, the FAA, NTSB, and the United States Air Force. Placements typically range from 3–6 months and can be done at any time during the student's program.

Housing and Day Care: On-campus housing is available. However, due to the limited amount of housing for graduate students we recommend you also explore these Web sites regarding off-campus housing: http://www.springstreet.com/apartments/home.jhtml?source=a1rnft2t117; http://www.rent.net/cgi-bin/chome/RentNet/scripts/home.jsp; and http://www.rent-usa.com/rent-fl. No on-campus day care facilities are available.

Employment of Department Graduates:

Master's Degree Graduates: Of those who graduated in the academic year 2006–2007, the following categories and numbers represent the postgraduate activities and employment of master's degree graduates: Enrolled in another graduate/professional program (0), enrolled in a postdoctoral residency/fellowship (n/a), employed in independent practice (n/a), employed in an academic position at a university (1), not seeking employment (1), total from the above (master's) (8).

Doctoral Degree Graduates: Of those who graduated in the academic year 2006–2007, the following categories and numbers represent the postgraduate activities and employment of doctoral degree graduates: Enrolled in a psychology doctoral program (n/a), total from the above (doctoral) (0).

Additional Information:

Orientation, Objectives, and Emphasis of Department: Embry-Riddle Aeronautical University prides itself on being the largest Aviation and Aerospace-based university in the world. As such, the focus of education is oriented to issues related to those domains and in other technologically advanced areas. The Human Factors and Systems Master's Degree program provides a fundamental, theoretical, and applied education in the fields of human factors and systems. Electives in the program are then oriented toward exploring human factors and systems principles within aviation domains. Faculty interests and research opportunities for students in the program are diverse. Current research interests range from personnel selection to motivational issues to design of cockpits. The diversity of faculty backgrounds adds to the eclectic nature of the research interests at Embry-Riddle. As such, students in the program can choose from a wide array of projects or thesis topics to pursue. Particular areas of faculty and student research currently include development of heads-up displays, tunnel in the sky technology, pilot selection, pilot motivation, prediction of flight performance, virtual and augmented reality displays, security screening, human–computer interaction, and air traffic management systems. The University facilities include flight simulation laboratories, an air traffic management laboratory, and other computer laboratories. The overall goal of the Embry-Riddle program is to train an individual to move directly into a career as a Human Factors or Systems Engineering specialist in industry, government, or the military. In order to achieve this goal, the program provides training in research methodology and human factors applications. In addition, classes emphasize teamwork and development, as well as refinement of writing and oral communication skills.

Special Facilities or Resources: A fleet of more than 100 single- and multiengine general aviation aircraft flying over 80,000 hours per year on various levels of training missions; 20 dedicated procedural trainers and simulators ranging from FRASCA 141s through a Level D Boeing 737-300. The department has access to flight faculty/instructors with extensive background and experience and over 1,500 students enrolled at various levels of flight training. The Human Performance Lab also contains equipment related to augmented reality, eye tracking, and flight performance meaurement. The laboratory contains a core set of PC-based flight simulation tools including an elite flight simulation device for the investigation of a variety of information display issues, augmented by measurement tools such as the SeeingMachines FaceLab gaze monitoring tool. The department also has access to multiple air traffic control training and research laboratories on campus in coordination with faculty who have an extensive background and experience in civilian and military air traffic control both in the United States and internationally.

Application Information:

Send to Graduate Programs, Embry-Riddle Aeronautical University, 600 South Clyde Morris Boulevard, Daytona Beach, FL 32114-3900. Application available online. URL of online application: https://www.erau.edu/db/gradadmissions/apply.html. Students are admitted in the Fall, application deadline July 1. *Fee:* $50.

Florida Atlantic University

Psychology
Charles E. Schmidt College of Science
777 Glades Road, P.O. Box 3091
Boca Raton, FL 33431-0991
Telephone: (561) 297-3360
Fax: (561) 297-2160
E-mail: *laursen@fau.edu or tuller@fau.edu*
Web: *http://www.psy.fau.edu*

Department Information:

1965. Chairperson: David L. Wolgin. Number of faculty: total—full-time 33; women—full-time 11; total—minority—full-time 1; women minority—full-time 1.

Programs and Degrees Offered:

Listed in the following order: Program area, degree type (T if terminal Master's), number awarded 7/06–6/07. Psychology MA/MS (Master of Arts/Science) (T) 10, Psychology PhD (Doctor of Philosophy) 8.

Student Applications/Admissions:

Student Applications

Psychology MA/MS (Master of Arts/Science)—Applications 2007–2008, 60. Total applicants accepted 2007–2008, 30. Number full-time enrolled (new admits only) 2007–2008, 15. Number part-time enrolled (new admits only) 2007–2008, 0. Openings 2008–2009, 20. The median number of years required for completion of a degree in 2006–2007 were 2. The number of students enrolled full- and part-time who were dismissed or voluntarily withdrew from this program area in 2007–2008 were 5. *Psychology PhD (Doctor of Philosophy)*—Applications 2007–2008, 75. Total applicants accepted 2007–2008, 19. Number full-time enrolled (new admits only) 2007–2008, 10. Number part-time enrolled (new admits only) 2007–2008, 0. Total enrolled 2007–2008 full-time, 39, part-time, 1. Openings 2008–2009, 8. The median number of years required for completion of a degree in 2006–2007 were 5. The number of students enrolled full- and part-time who were dismissed or voluntarily withdrew from this program area in 2007–2008 were 2.

Admissions Requirements:

Scores: Entries appear in this order: required test or GPA, minimum score (if required), median score of students entering in 2007–2008. Master's Programs: GRE-V 500, 550; GRE-Q 500, 550; overall undergraduate GPA 3.0, 3.5; last 2 years GPA 3.00, 3.60. GRE-Subject (Psychology) recommended but not required. Doctoral Programs: GRE-V 500, 580; GRE-Q 500, 660; last 2 years GPA 3.00, 3.9. GRE-Subject (Psychology) recommended but not required.

Other Criteria: (importance of criteria rated low, medium, or high): GRE/MAT scores—high, research experience—high, work experience—low, extracurricular activity—low, clinically related public service—low, GPA—high, letters of recommendation—high, statement of goals and objectives—high.

Student Characteristics: The following represents characteristics of students in 2007–2008 in all graduate psychology programs in the department: Female—full-time 47, part-time 0; Male—full-time 20, part-time 1; African American/Black—full-time 1, part-time 1; Hispanic/Latino(a)—full-time 4, part-time 0; Asian/Pacific Islander—full-time 3, part-time 0; American Indian/Alaska Native—full-time 0, part-time 0; Caucasian/White—full-time 59, part-time 0; students subject to the Americans With Disabilities Act—full-time 1, part-time 0; Unknown ethnicity—full-time 0, part-time 0.

Financial Information/Assistance:

Tuition for Full-Time Study: *Master's:* State residents: $256 per credit hour; Nonstate residents: $915 per credit hour. *Doctoral:* State residents: $256 per credit hour; Nonstate residents: $915 per credit hour. Tuition is subject to change. See the following Web site for updates and changes in tuition costs: http://www.iea.fau.edu/factbk/tuition07.htm.

Financial Assistance:

First-Year Students: Teaching assistantships available for first year. Average amount paid per academic year: $20,000. Average number of hours worked per week: 20. Apply by August 1. Tuition remission given: partial. Research assistantships available for first year. Average amount paid per academic year: $20,000. Average number of hours worked per week: 20. Apply by August 1. Tuition remission given: partial.

Advanced Students: Teaching assistantships available for advanced students. Average amount paid per academic year: $20,000. Average number of hours worked per week: 20. Apply by August 1. Tuition remission given: partial. Research assistantships available for advanced students. Average amount paid per academic year: $20,000. Average number of hours worked per week: 20. Apply by August 1. Tuition remission given: partial.

Additional Information: Of all students currently enrolled full time, 100% benefited from one or more of the listed financial assistance programs.

Internships/Practica: No information provided.

Housing and Day Care: On-campus housing is available. See the following Web site for more information: http://www.fau.edu. On-campus day care facilities are available.

Employment of Department Graduates:

Master's Degree Graduates: Of those who graduated in the academic year 2006–2007, the following categories and numbers represent the postgraduate activities and employment of master's degree graduates: Enrolled in a postdoctoral residency/fellowship (n/a), employed in independent practice (n/a), total from the above (master's) (0).

Doctoral Degree Graduates: Of those who graduated in the academic year 2006–2007, the following categories and numbers represent the postgraduate activities and employment of doctoral degree graduates: Enrolled in a psychology doctoral program (n/a), enrolled in a postdoctoral residency/fellowship (1), employed in an academic position at a university (4), employed in an academic position at a 2-year/4-year college (4), employed in a professional position in a school system (1), total from the above (doctoral) (10).

Additional Information:

Orientation, Objectives, and Emphasis of Department: The PhD program emphasizes research in several areas of experimental psychology. Students may select courses and conduct research in five areas: cognitive psychology, developmental psychology, evolutionary psychology, psychobiology/neuroscience, and social/personality psychology. Current research by faculty includes psycholinguistics, sentence processing, visual perception, and speech production and perception; conflict in married couples, the relationship between tool use and style of play in preschool children, psychological adaptations to sperm competition in humans, and mental synchronization in social interaction; neural mechanisms in recovery of function from brain damage, psychopharmacology, and nonlinear dynamics of brain and behavior; the use of traits to predict behavior, sex differences in mating, domestic violence, and the dynamics of social influence. The MA program is designed to prepare students for entry into doctoral-level programs in all areas of psychology. Research in developmental psychology uses a campus laboratory school for children in kindergarten through the eighth grade. Research in social/personality psychology uses laboratories with video and online computer facilities. The cognitive psychology laboratories include testing rooms with a network of PCs for online control of experiments in perception, learning, language, and cognition. The EEG laboratory includes an acoustic isolation chamber and a variety of amplifying and recording systems.

Special Facilities or Resources: Additional information and online application forms are available at http://www.psy.fau.edu.

Information for Students With Physical Disabilities: See the following Web site for more information: http://www.psy.fau.edu.

Application Information:

Send to (a) FAU Admissions Office, 777 Glades Road, Boca Raton, FL 33431; (b) Department of Psychology Florida Atlantic University,

777 Glades Road, Boca Raton, FL 33431. Application available online. URL of online application: http://www.cosserv3.fau.edu/~kersten/fau/graduate/application2.html. Students are admitted in the Spring, application deadline January 15. PhD application deadline January 15; MA application deadline April 15. *Fee:* $30.

Florida Institute of Technology

School of Psychology
College of Psychology and Liberal Arts
150 West University Boulevard
Melbourne, FL 32901-6988
Telephone: (321) 674-8104
Fax: (321) 674-7105
E-mail: *mkenkel@fit.edu*
Web: *http://www.cpla.fit.edu/psych/*

Department Information:

1978. Dean: Mary Beth Kenkel. Number of faculty: total—full-time 11, part-time 2; women—full-time 9, part-time 5; women minority—full-time 2, part-time 1.

Programs and Degrees Offered:

Listed in the following order: Program area, degree type (T if terminal Master's), number awarded 7/06–6/07. Applied Behavior Analysis MA/MS (Master of Arts/Science) (T) 43, Clinical PsyD (Doctor of Psychology) 14, Industrial/Organizational MA/MS (Master of Arts/Science) (T) 6, Industrial/Organizational PhD (Doctor of Philosophy) 2, Organizational Behavioral Management MA/MS (Master of Arts/Science) 0.

APA Accreditation: Clinical PsyD (Doctor of Psychology).

Student Applications/Admissions:

Student Applications

Applied Behavior Analysis MA/MS (Master of Arts/Science)—Applications 2007–2008, 58. Total applicants accepted 2007–2008, 29. Number full-time enrolled (new admits only) 2007–2008, 30. Number part-time enrolled (new admits only) 2007–2008, 2. Total enrolled 2007–2008 full-time, 62, part-time, 3. Openings 2008–2009, 25. The median number of years required for completion of a degree in 2006–2007 were 2. The number of students enrolled full- and part-time who were dismissed or voluntarily withdrew from this program area in 2007–2008 were 3. *Clinical PsyD (Doctor of Psychology)*—Applications 2007–2008, 154. Total applicants accepted 2007–2008, 47. Number full-time enrolled (new admits only) 2007–2008, 27. Number part-time enrolled (new admits only) 2007–2008, 0. Openings 2008–2009, 25. The median number of years required for completion of a degree in 2006–2007 were 5. The number of students enrolled full- and part-time who were dismissed or voluntarily withdrew from this program area in 2007–2008 were 1. *Industrial/Organizational MA/MS (Master of Arts/Science)*—Applications 2007–2008, 53. Total applicants accepted 2007–2008, 34. Number full-time enrolled (new admits only) 2007–2008, 6. Number part-time enrolled (new admits only) 2007–2008, 0. Total enrolled 2007–2008 full-time, 17, part-time, 1. Openings 2008–2009, 12. The median number of years required for completion of a degree in 2006–2007 were 2. The number of students enrolled full- and part-time who were dismissed or voluntarily withdrew from this program area in 2007–2008 were 0. *Industrial/Organizational PhD (Doctor of Philosophy)*—Applications 2007–2008, 47. Total applicants accepted 2007–2008, 25. Number full-time enrolled (new admits only) 2007–2008, 6. Number part-time enrolled (new admits only) 2007–2008, 0. Total enrolled 2007–2008 full-time, 17, part-time, 3. Openings 2008–2009, 6. The median number of years required for completion of a degree in 2006–2007 were 4. The number of students enrolled full- and part-time who were dismissed or voluntarily withdrew from this program area in 2007–2008 were 0. *Organizational Behavioral Management MA/MS (Master of Arts/Science)*—Applications 2007–2008, 16. Total applicants accepted 2007–2008, 12. Number full-time enrolled (new admits only) 2007–2008, 3. Number part-time enrolled (new admits only) 2007–2008, 0. Openings 2008–2009, 15. The median number of years required for completion of a degree in 2006–2007 were 2. The number of students enrolled full- and part-time who were dismissed or voluntarily withdrew from this program area in 2007–2008 were 0.

Admissions Requirements:

Scores: Entries appear in this order: required test or GPA, minimum score (if required), median score of students entering in 2007–2008. Master's Programs: GRE-V no minimum stated, 510; GRE-Q no minimum stated, 590; overall undergraduate GPA no minimum stated, 3.52; last 2 years GPA no minimum stated, 3.69; psychology GPA no minimum stated, 3.66. Doctoral Programs: GRE-V no minimum stated, 530; GRE-Q no minimum stated, 630; GRE-Subject (Psychology) no minimum stated, 625; overall undergraduate GPA 3.0, 3.71. GRE subject test required for PsyD program only.

Other Criteria: (importance of criteria rated low, medium, or high): GRE/MAT scores—medium, research experience—medium, work experience—high, extracurricular activity—medium, clinically related public service—high, GPA—high, letters of recommendation—high, interview—medium, statement of goals and objectives—medium. For additional information on admission requirements, go to http://www.fit.edu/admission/graduate/.

Student Characteristics: The following represents characteristics of students in 2007–2008 in all graduate psychology programs in the department: Female—full-time 144, part-time 4; Male—full-time 39, part-time 3; African American/Black—full-time 8, part-time 2; Hispanic/Latino(a)—full-time 12, part-time 1; Asian/Pacific Islander—full-time 10, part-time 1; American Indian/Alaska Native—full-time 1, part-time 0; Caucasian/White—full-time 119, part-time 1; Multi-ethnic—full-time 0, part-time 2; students subject to the Americans With Disabilities Act—full-time 3, part-time 0; Unknown ethnicity—full-time 33, part-time 0; International students who hold an F-1 or J-1 Visa—full-time 4, part-time 0.

Financial Information/Assistance:

Tuition for Full-Time Study: *Master's:* State residents: per academic year $17,640, $980 per credit hour; Nonstate residents: per academic year $17,640, $980 per credit hour. *Doctoral:* State residents: per academic year $27,045, $980 per credit hour; Nonstate residents: per academic year $27,045, $980 per credit hour. Tuition is subject to change. Tuition costs vary by program.

Financial Assistance:

First-Year Students: Fellowships and scholarships available for first year. Average amount paid per academic year: $6,477. Average number of hours worked per week: 10. Apply by June 1. Tuition remission given: partial.

Advanced Students: Teaching assistantships available for advanced students. Average amount paid per academic year: $8,000. Average number of hours worked per week: 15. Apply by March 15. Research assistantships available for advanced students. Average amount paid per academic year: $4,000. Average number of hours worked per week: 5. Apply by March 15. Fellowships and scholarships available for advanced students. Average amount paid per academic year: $6,477. Average number of hours worked per week: 10. Apply by June 1. Tuition remission given: partial.

Additional Information: Of all students currently enrolled full time, 43% benefited from one or more of the listed financial assistance programs. Application and information available online at http://www.fit.edu/admission/graduate/.

Internships/Practica: Doctoral Degree (PsyD clinical): For those doctoral students for whom a professional internship was required in this program prior to graduation, (16) students applied for an internship in 2006–2007, with (15) students obtaining an internship. Of those students who obtained an internship, (15) were paid internships. Of those students who obtained an internship, (13) students placed in APA/CPA-accredited internships, (2) students placed in internships not APA/CPA-accredited, but listed with the Association of Psychology Postdoctoral and Internship Centers (APPIC), (0) students placed in internships conforming to guidelines of the Council of Directors of School Psychology Programs (CDSPP), (0) students placed in internships that were not APA/CPA-accredited, APPIC or CDSPP listed. Students in the PsyD program complete a sequence of three or more separate practicum placements prior to internship. These include the Florida Tech's Community Psychological Services Center, and then options at other outpatient and inpatient facilities. Inpatient sites include adult psychiatric hospitals, rehabilitation hospitals, children and adolescent inpatient units, behavioral medicine practica within a medical hospital, and a prison setting. Outpatient sites include mental health centers, private practice settings, VA outpatient clinics, and neuropsychological practices. Students gain experience in assessment and treatment of individuals, groups, couples and families, consultation, and psychoeducational presentations. Treatment specialties include neuropsychology, aging, sexual abuse, domestic violence, PTSD, and drug and alcohol abuse. The I/O program has strong ties to local business in Brevard County. Students have been placed in a wide range of practicum sites including county and federal departments, aerospace and electronics industries, financial institutions, health care organizations, and management consulting firms. The Applied Behavior Analysis program has practicum sites with private and public agencies working with children with developmental disabilities, serious emotional and behavioral disorders, and autism. Students receive on-site supervision as well as ancillary supervision by program faculty. The Organizational Behavior Management program has internships with local businesses as well as with national consulting firms. For additional information on education and training outcomes for our programs, see the following Web site: http://wwwcpla.fit.edu/clinical/PsyDProgramOutcomes.htm.

Housing and Day Care: On-campus housing is available. See the following Web site for more information: http://www.auxservices.fit.edu/housing.html. No on-campus day care facilities are available.

Employment of Department Graduates:

Master's Degree Graduates: Of those who graduated in the academic year 2006–2007, the following categories and numbers represent the postgraduate activities and employment of master's degree graduates: Enrolled in a psychology doctoral program (7), enrolled in another graduate/professional program (4), enrolled in a postdoctoral residency/fellowship (n/a), employed in independent practice (n/a), employed in an academic position at a university (0), employed in an academic position at a 2-year/4-year college (0), employed in other positions at a higher education institution (1), employed in a professional position in a school system (6), employed in business or industry (15), employed in government agency (1), employed in a community mental health/counseling center (0), employed in a hospital/medical center (1), still seeking employment (0), not seeking employment (0), other employment position (14), do not know (3), total from the above (master's) (52).

Doctoral Degree Graduates: Of those who graduated in the academic year 2006–2007, the following categories and numbers represent the postgraduate activities and employment of doctoral degree graduates: Enrolled in a psychology doctoral program (n/a), enrolled in another graduate/professional program (0), enrolled in a postdoctoral residency/fellowship (9), employed in independent practice (1), employed in an academic position at a university (0), employed in an academic position at a 2-year/4-year college (0), employed in other positions at a higher education institution (0), employed in a professional position in a school system (0), employed in business or industry (2), employed in government agency (0), employed in a community mental health/counseling center (0), employed in a hospital/medical center (3), still seeking employment (1), not seeking employment (0), other employment position (0), do not know (0), total from the above (doctoral) (16).

Additional Information:

Orientation, Objectives, and Emphasis of Department: The School of Psychology at Florida Institute of Technology offers the MS and PhD in Industrial/Organizational Psychology, the MS in Behavior Analysis and the MS in Organizational Behavior Management, and the PsyD in Clinical Psychology. The clinical PsyD program trains students based on a practitioner–scientist model focused on development of clinical skills. The program incorporates multiple theoretical orientations and has emphases in neuropsychology and health psychology, child and family therapy, and forensic psychology. In the Industrial/Organizational Psychology program, students are trained in advanced statistics, organizational research, industrial training and development, personnel selection, performance appraisal, group and team development, and organizational research methodology. The program prepares graduates for a wide variety of careers in academics, management, human resources, and consulting. The master's program in Behavioral Psychology offers two degrees: one in Applied Behavior Analysis (ABA) and one in Organizational Behavior Management (OBM). The program prepares graduates for employment as Board Certified Behavior Analysts (BCBA) and/or as internal or external consultants in business and industry. Students from the ABA program upon graduation meet all the educational and supervised practicum requirements to seek certification as a BCBA.

Special Facilities or Resources: The facilities of the School of Psychology include the Psychology building, the Community Psychological Services Center, the Children's House, the Neuropsychology Lab, the Industrial/Organizational Psychology Lab, and the Applied Research Lab. The academic building contains offices, classrooms, and computer facilities. The University's Academic Computing Services Microcenter provides computers and software, media conversion, digital graphic assistance, and professional editing of theses and papers for publication. The counseling centers include group and individual treatment rooms. Additionally students receive training and conduct research in several community service programs operated by the School of Psychology. These include Center for Professional Services, a campus-based consulting and research organization; East Central Florida Memory Clinic, through a contract with Holmes Regional Medical Center serves individuals with memory disorders by providing memory screenings, case management, education, and wellness and support groups; Family Learning Program offers psychological assessment and treatment to child victims of sexual abuse and their family members. The School of Psychology's Center for Autism Treatment scheduled to open in 2009 provides behavioral and clinical services for individuals with Autism Spectrum Disorder.

Information for Students With Physical Disabilities: See the following Web site for more information: http://www.fit.edu/asc/handbook/Section_6.html.

Application Information:

Send to Florida Institute of Technology, Office of Graduate Admissions, 150 West University Boulevard, Melbourne, FL 32901. Application available online. URL of online application: http://www.fit.edu/admission/graduate/. Students are admitted in the Fall, application deadline. PsyD deadline is January 15. Industrial/Organizational Psychology deadline is February 1. ABA deadline is February 15. *Fee:* PsyD $60; PhD $60; MS $50.

Florida International University

Psychology
Arts and Sciences
11200 Southwest 8th Street
Miami, FL 33199
Telephone: (305) 348-2881
Fax: (305) 348-3879
E-mail: *levittmj@fiu.edu*
Web: *http://www.psych.fiu.edu*

Department Information:

1972. Chairperson: Mary J Levitt. Number of faculty: total—full-time 23; women—full-time 9; total—minority—full-time 3; women minority—full-time 2.

Programs and Degrees Offered:

Listed in the following order: Program area, degree type (T if terminal Master's), number awarded 7/06–6/07. Life Span Developmental Science PhD (Doctor of Philosophy) 9, Industrial/Organizational Psychology PhD (Doctor of Philosophy) 0, Legal Psychology PhD (Doctor of Philosophy) 0, Counseling MA/MS (Master of Arts/Science) (T) 7, Behavior Analysis MA/MS (Master of Arts/Science) (T) 2.

Student Applications/Admissions:

Student Applications

Life Span Developmental Science PhD (Doctor of Philosophy)—Applications 2007–2008, 13. Total applicants accepted 2007–2008, 6. Number full-time enrolled (new admits only) 2007–2008, 6. Total enrolled 2007–2008 full-time, 35. The median number of years required for completion of a degree in 2006–2007 were 4. *Industrial/Organizational Psychology PhD (Doctor of Philosophy)*—Applications 2007–2008, 8. Total applicants accepted 2007–2008, 3. Number full-time enrolled (new admits only) 2007–2008, 2. Total enrolled 2007–2008 full-time, 11. The number of students enrolled full- and part-time who were dismissed or voluntarily withdrew from this program area in 2007–2008 were 1. *Legal Psychology PhD (Doctor of Philosophy)*—Applications 2007–2008, 19. Total applicants accepted 2007–2008, 3. Number full-time enrolled (new admits only) 2007–2008, 3. Total enrolled 2007–2008 full-time, 14. The number of students enrolled full- and part-time who were dismissed or voluntarily withdrew from this program area in 2007–2008 were 0. *Counseling MA/MS (Master of Arts/Science)*—Applications 2007–2008, 21. Total applicants accepted 2007–2008, 12. Number full-time enrolled (new admits only) 2007–2008, 12. Total enrolled 2007–2008 full-time, 49. Openings 2008–2009, 22. The median number of years required for completion of a degree in 2006–2007 were 3. The number of students enrolled full- and part-time who were dismissed or voluntarily withdrew from this program area in 2007–2008 were 0. *Behavior Analysis MA/MS (Master of Arts/Science)*—Applications 2007–2008, 7. Total applicants accepted 2007–2008, 2. Number full-time enrolled (new admits only) 2007–2008, 2. Total enrolled 2007–2008 full-time, 14. The median number of years required for completion of a degree in 2006–2007 were 3. The number of students enrolled full- and part-time who were dismissed or voluntarily withdrew from this program area in 2007–2008 were 0.

Admissions Requirements:

Scores: Entries appear in this order: required test or GPA, minimum score (if required), median score of students entering in 2007–2008. Master's Programs: GRE-V 500, 550; GRE-Q 500, 560; last 2 years GPA 3.00, 3.66. Doctoral Programs: GRE-V 560, 526; GRE-Q 560, 606; last 2 years GPA 3.50, 3.80.
Other Criteria: (importance of criteria rated low, medium, or high): GRE/MAT scores—high, research experience—high, work experience—medium, extracurricular activity—low, GPA—high, letters of recommendation—high, interview—medium, statement of goals and objectives—high, undergraduate major in psychology—medium, specific undergraduate psychology courses taken—low. For additional information on admission requirements, go to http://www.psych.fiu.edu.

Student Characteristics: The following represents characteristics of students in 2007–2008 in all graduate psychology programs in the department: Female—full-time 101, part-time 0; Male—full-time 41, part-time 0; African American/Black—full-time 14, part-time 0; Hispanic/Latino(a)—full-time 61, part-time 0; Asian/Pacific Islander—full-time 8, part-time 0; American Indian/Alaska Native—full-time 0, part-time 0; Caucasian/White—full-time 50, part-time 0; Multi-ethnic—full-time 0, part-time 0;

students subject to the Americans With Disabilities Act—full-time 0, part-time 0; Unknown ethnicity—full-time 9, part-time 0; International students who hold an F-1 or J-1 Visa—full-time 0, part-time 0.

Financial Information/Assistance:

Tuition for Full-Time Study: *Master's:* State residents: per academic year $5,224, $273 per credit hour; Nonstate residents: per academic year $14,296, $777 per credit hour. *Doctoral:* State residents: per academic year $5,224, $273 per credit hour; Nonstate residents: per academic year $14,296, $777 per credit hour. Tuition is subject to change. Additional fees are assessed to students beyond the costs of tuition for the following: athletic, health, photo ID, and parking fees. See the following Web site for updates and changes in tuition costs: http://www.fiu.edu/orgs/controller/UG%20Calculator.htm.

Financial Assistance:

First-Year Students: Teaching assistantships available for first year. Average amount paid per academic year: $16,000. Average number of hours worked per week: 20. Apply by December 15. Tuition remission given: full. Research assistantships available for first year. Average amount paid per academic year: $16,000. Average number of hours worked per week: 20. Apply by December 15. Tuition remission given: full.

Advanced Students: Teaching assistantships available for advanced students. Average amount paid per academic year: $16,900. Average number of hours worked per week: 20. Apply by December 15. Tuition remission given: full. Research assistantships available for advanced students. Average amount paid per academic year: $16,900. Average number of hours worked per week: 20. Apply by December 15. Tuition remission given: full.

Additional Information: Of all students currently enrolled full time, 40% benefited from one or more of the listed financial assistance programs.

Internships/Practica: No information provided.

Housing and Day Care: On-campus housing is available. See the following Web site for more information: http://www.housing.fiu.edu/. On-campus day care facilities are available. See the following Web site for more information: http://www.fiu.edu/~children/info.htm.

Employment of Department Graduates:

Master's Degree Graduates: Of those who graduated in the academic year 2006–2007, the following categories and numbers represent the postgraduate activities and employment of master's degree graduates: Enrolled in a postdoctoral residency/fellowship (n/a), employed in independent practice (n/a), total from the above (master's) (0).

Doctoral Degree Graduates: Of those who graduated in the academic year 2006–2007, the following categories and numbers represent the postgraduate activities and employment of doctoral degree graduates: Enrolled in a psychology doctoral program (n/a), total from the above (doctoral) (0).

Additional Information:

Orientation, Objectives, and Emphasis of Department: The mission of the Department of Psychology at Florida International University is to create new knowledge about human behavior, apply what is known to improve the human condition, and educate and train students. Our graduate programs are designed to foster a commitment both to basic research and application as an integral part of the student's specialty area.

Application Information:

Send to Graduate Studies Admissions Committee, Department of Psychology, Florida International University, DM 256, Miami, FL 33199. Application available online. URL of online application: http://www.gradschool.fiu.edu/admissions.html. Students are admitted in the Fall, application deadline December 15. Masters in Behavior Analysis and Masters in Life Span Developmental deadline for Fall admission is June 1 and for Spring admission is October 1. *Fee:* $30.

Florida State University

Department of Psychology
Arts and Sciences
1107 West Call Street
P.O. Box 3064301
Tallahassee, FL 32306-4301
Telephone: (850) 644-2499
Fax: (850) 644-7739
E-mail: *plant@psy.fsu.edu*
Web: *http://www.psy.fsu.edu*

Department Information:

1918. Chairperson: Janet A. Kistner. Number of faculty: total—full-time 44, part-time 1; women—full-time 15; total—minority—full-time 3, part-time 1; women minority—full-time 1.

Programs and Degrees Offered:

Listed in the following order: Program area, degree type (T if terminal Master's), number awarded 7/06–6/07. Cognitive Psychology PhD (Doctor of Philosophy) 2, Clinical Psychology PhD (Doctor of Philosophy) 6, Neuroscience PhD (Doctor of Philosophy) 2, Applied Behavior Analysis MA/MS (Master of Arts/Science) (T) 21, Social Psychology PhD (Doctor of Philosophy) 1, Developmental Psychology PhD (Doctor of Philosophy) 0.

APA Accreditation: Clinical PhD (Doctor of Philosophy).

Student Applications/Admissions:

Student Applications

Cognitive Psychology PhD (Doctor of Philosophy)—Applications 2007–2008, 27. Total applicants accepted 2007–2008, 8. Number full-time enrolled (new admits only) 2007–2008, 5. Openings 2008–2009, 6. The median number of years required for completion of a degree in 2006–2007 were 6. The number of students enrolled full- and part-time who were dismissed or voluntarily withdrew from this program area in 2007–2008 were 0. *Clinical Psychology PhD (Doctor of Philosophy)*—Applications 2007–2008, 189. Total applicants accepted 2007–2008, 13. Number full-time enrolled (new admits only) 2007–2008, 10. Number part-time enrolled (new admits only) 2007–2008, 0. Openings 2008–2009, 10. The median number of years required for completion of a degree in 2006–2007 were

6. The number of students enrolled full- and part-time who were dismissed or voluntarily withdrew from this program area in 2007–2008 were 1. *Neuroscience PhD (Doctor of Philosophy)*—Applications 2007–2008, 23. Total applicants accepted 2007–2008, 8. Number full-time enrolled (new admits only) 2007–2008, 5. Openings 2008–2009, 6. The median number of years required for completion of a degree in 2006–2007 were 5. The number of students enrolled full- and part-time who were dismissed or voluntarily withdrew from this program area in 2007–2008 were 0. *Applied Behavior Analysis MA/MS (Master of Arts/Science)*—Applications 2007–2008, 54. Total applicants accepted 2007–2008, 30. Number full-time enrolled (new admits only) 2007–2008, 13. Openings 2008–2009, 16. The median number of years required for completion of a degree in 2006–2007 were 2. The number of students enrolled full- and part-time who were dismissed or voluntarily withdrew from this program area in 2007–2008 were 0. *Social Psychology PhD (Doctor of Philosophy)*—Applications 2007–2008, 88. Total applicants accepted 2007–2008, 9. Number full-time enrolled (new admits only) 2007–2008, 5. Total enrolled 2007–2008 full-time, 18. Openings 2008–2009, 6. The median number of years required for completion of a degree in 2006–2007 were 7. The number of students enrolled full- and part-time who were dismissed or voluntarily withdrew from this program area in 2007–2008 were 0. *Developmental Psychology PhD (Doctor of Philosophy)*—Applications 2007–2008, 14. Total applicants accepted 2007–2008, 0. Number full-time enrolled (new admits only) 2007–2008, 0. Total enrolled 2007–2008 full-time, 10. Openings 2008–2009, 4. The number of students enrolled full- and part-time who were dismissed or voluntarily withdrew from this program area in 2007–2008 were 0.

Admissions Requirements:

Scores: Entries appear in this order: required test or GPA, minimum score (if required), median score of students entering in 2007–2008. Master's Programs: GRE-V 500, 490; GRE-Q 500, 580; last 2 years GPA 3.0, 3.71. Above GRE/GPA requirements are for the Applied Behavior Analysis master's program. Doctoral Programs: GRE-V 500, 590; GRE-Q 500, 700; last 2 years GPA 3.0, 3.79. The required minimum GRE and GPA vary slightly across the doctoral programs.

Other Criteria: (importance of criteria rated low, medium, or high): GRE/MAT scores—high, research experience—high, work experience—low, extracurricular activity—low, clinically related public service—low, GPA—high, letters of recommendation—high, interview—medium, statement of goals and objectives—high, match with faculty research interest—high, undergraduate major in psychology—medium, specific undergraduate psychology courses taken—medium. Research experience is not an important factor for admission to the Applied Behavior Analysis master's program; work or volunteer experience in behavior analysis is of high importance for this program. For additional information on admission requirements, go to http://www.psy.fsu.edu.

Student Characteristics: The following represents characteristics of students in 2007–2008 in all graduate psychology programs in the department: Female—full-time 109, part-time 0; Male—full-time 49, part-time 0; African American/Black—full-time 8, part-time 0; Hispanic/Latino(a)—full-time 13, part-time 0; Asian/Pacific Islander—full-time 3, part-time 0; American Indian/Alaska Native—full-time 1, part-time 0; Caucasian/White—full-time 133, part-time 0; Multi-ethnic—full-time 0, part-time 0; students subject to the Americans With Disabilities Act—full-time 0, part-time 0; Unknown ethnicity—full-time 0, part-time 0; International students who hold an F-1 or J-1 Visa—full-time 5, part-time 0.

Financial Information/Assistance:

Tuition for Full-Time Study: *Master's:* State residents: per academic year $4,464, $248 per credit hour; Nonstate residents: per academic year $15,840, $880 per credit hour. *Doctoral:* State residents: per academic year $4,464, $248 per credit hour; Nonstate residents: per academic year $15,840, $880 per credit hour. Tuition is subject to change. See the following Web site for updates and changes in tuition costs: http://www.sfs.fsu.edu/tuition.html.

Financial Assistance:

First-Year Students: Teaching assistantships available for first year. Average amount paid per academic year: $15,000. Average number of hours worked per week: 16. Tuition remission given: full. Research assistantships available for first year. Average amount paid per academic year: $18,000. Average number of hours worked per week: 20. Tuition remission given: full. Traineeships available for first year. Average amount paid per academic year: $20,000. Average number of hours worked per week: 20. Tuition remission given: full. Fellowships and scholarships available for first year. Average amount paid per academic year: $20,000. Average number of hours worked per week: 0. Tuition remission given: full.

Advanced Students: Teaching assistantships available for advanced students. Average amount paid per academic year: $15,000. Average number of hours worked per week: 16. Tuition remission given: full. Research assistantships available for advanced students. Average amount paid per academic year: $18,000. Average number of hours worked per week: 20. Tuition remission given: full. Traineeships available for advanced students. Average amount paid per academic year: $20,000. Average number of hours worked per week: 20. Tuition remission given: full. Fellowships and scholarships available for advanced students. Average amount paid per academic year: $20,000. Average number of hours worked per week: 0. Tuition remission given: full.

Additional Information: Of all students currently enrolled full time, 92% benefited from one or more of the listed financial assistance programs. Application and information available online at http://www.psy.fsu.edu/.

Internships/Practica: Doctoral Degree (PhD Clinical Psychology): For those doctoral students for whom a professional internship was required in this program prior to graduation, (12) students applied for an internship in 2006–2007, with (11) students obtaining an internship. Of those students who obtained an internship, (11) were paid internships. Of those students who obtained an internship, (11) students placed in APA/CPA-accredited internships, (0) students placed in internships not APA/CPA-accredited, but listed with the Association of Psychology Postdoctoral and Internship Centers (APPIC), (0) students placed in internships conforming to guidelines of the Council of Directors of School Psychology Programs (CDSPP), (0) students placed in internships that were not APA/CPA-accredited, APPIC or CDSPP listed. Community facilities provide a multitude of settings for practicum placements for clinical students and for master's students in applied behavior analysis. Clinical students receive a stipend and tuition waivers for their practicum work in the community as well as excellent supervised experience and opportunities for research. Practicum settings for clinical students include an inpatient psychiatric hospital, a comprehensive evaluation center for children, a juvenile treatment program, forensic facilities, and other agencies in the community. Clinical psychology students complete a required unpaid practicum at our nationally recognized on-campus Psychology Clinic during the 2nd and typically 3rd year of study. The clinic provides empirically based assessment and therapy services to adults, children, and families in the north Florida region. Psychology faculty provides supervision. The clinical program culminates in a required 1-year internship in an APA-approved facility. Clinical students from the FSU program have, over the years, been highly successful in obtaining excellent internships throughout the country. Applied Behavior Analysis master's students have diverse practicum sites from which to choose, including public schools, family homes, residential treatment facilities, businesses, consulting firms, and state agencies. Stipends and tuition waivers are available for many of the applied behavior analysis practicum settings. For additional information on education and training outcomes for our programs, see the following Web site: http://www.psy.fsu.edu.

Housing and Day Care: On-campus housing is available. See the following Web site for more information: http://www.housing.fsu.edu/. On-campus day care facilities are available. See the following Web site for more information: http://www.childcare.fsu.edu/.

Employment of Department Graduates:

Master's Degree Graduates: Of those who graduated in the academic year 2006–2007, the following categories and numbers represent the postgraduate activities and employment of master's degree graduates: Enrolled in a psychology doctoral program (1), enrolled in a postdoctoral residency/fellowship (n/a), employed in independent practice (n/a), employed in a professional position in a school system (1), employed in business or industry (14), do not know (5), total from the above (master's) (21). ***Doctoral Degree Graduates:*** Of those who graduated in the academic year 2006–2007, the following categories and numbers represent the postgraduate activities and employment of doctoral degree graduates: Enrolled in a psychology doctoral program (n/a), enrolled in a postdoctoral residency/fellowship (6), employed in an academic position at a university (2), employed in a community mental health/counseling center (2), employed in a hospital/medical center (1), total from the above (doctoral) (11).

Additional Information:

Orientation, Objectives, and Emphasis of Department: This is a scientifically oriented department with over $6 million in annual grant funding, fourth highest in the nation among all psychology departments. The Clinical Psychology program promotes a scientifically based approach to understanding, assessing, and ameliorating cognitive, emotional, behavioral, and health problems. Integrative training in clinical science and clinical service delivery is provided. Cognitive Psychology students develop research and analytical skills while learning to coordinate basic research with theory development and application. Current research includes expert performance, skill acquisition, reading, memory, attention, language processing, and cognitive aging. Students in the Developmental Psychology program conduct basic and applied research. A developmental perspective is interdisciplinary; consequently members of the developmental faculty routinely hold appointments in one of our other doctoral programs. The Social Psychology program provides students with in-depth training in personality and social psychology, focusing on basic and applied research. Current research areas include the self, prejudice and stereotyping, and evolutionary perspectives on various topics. The interdisciplinary Neuroscience program offers students broad training in brain and behavior research. Areas of emphasis include sensory processes, neural development and plasticity, behavioral and molecular genetics, regulation of energy balance and hormonal control of behavior. The terminal master's program in Applied Behavior Analysis focuses on analyzing and modifying behavior using well-established principles of learning.

Special Facilities or Resources: The department's technical staff and support facilities are some of the best in the country. Fully staffed and equipped electronic and machine shops support faculty and graduate student research. Highly trained staff provides assistance in graphic arts, photography, instrument and computer software design, and electronic communication services. A neurosurgical operating room and a neurohistological laboratory are available. Faculty and students have available to them a supercomputer and workstations offering human eyetracking and brain wave and psychophysiological recording, among others. A molecular neuroscience laboratory provides equipment and training for studies of gene cloning and gene expression, as well as techniques to measure levels of hormones and neurotransmitters. The Clinical program administers an on-campus outpatient clinic that offers empirically based assessment and therapy services to members of the Tallahassee and surrounding communities. The department was one of four in the United States recognized in 2003 by APA for innovative practices in graduate education in psychology. This recognition was for the on-campus clinic, which is a full-fledged clinical research laboratory. Based on research and case studies conducted at the clinic, faculty and students have published many books and peer-reviewed articles. The department and clinic are housed in a new, state-of-the-art building.

Information for Students With Physical Disabilities: See the following Web site for more information: http://www.disabilitycenter.fsu.edu.

Application Information:

Send to Graduate Program, Department of Psychology, Florida State University, 1107 West Call Street, P.O. Box 3064301, Tallahassee, FL 32306-4301. Application available online. URL of online application: http://www.psy.fsu.edu. Students are admitted in the Fall, application deadline. The application deadline is December 1 for Clinical Psychology and Neuroscience; December 15 for Social Psychology; and January 15 for Cognitive and Developmental Psychology. The Applied Behavior Analysis application deadline is February 1. Applicants should confirm these dates on the department's Web site. *Fee:* $30. No waivers or deferrals of fee are available.

Florida State University
Psychological Services in Education: PhD Combined Counseling/School Psychology
Education
306 Stone Building
Tallahassee, FL 32306-4453
Telephone: (850) 644-4592
Fax: (850) 644-8776
E-mail: *pfeiffer@coe.fsu.edu*
Web: *http://www.fsu.edu/~coe/departments/epls/cpsp.html*

Department Information:

2002. Director of Clinical Training: Steven Pfeiffer. Number of faculty: total—full-time 8; women—full-time 4; faculty subject to the Americans With Disabilities Act 1.

Programs and Degrees Offered:

Listed in the following order: Program area, degree type (T if terminal Master's), number awarded 7/06–6/07. Combined Counseling and School Psychology PhD (Doctor of Philosophy) 9, Mental Health Counseling MA/MS (Master of Arts/Science) (T) 14, School Psychology EdS/MEd (School Psychology) 14.

APA Accreditation: Combined Counseling and School Psychology PhD (Doctor of Philosophy).

Student Applications/Admissions:

Student Applications

Combined Counseling and School Psychology PhD (Doctor of Philosophy)—Applications 2007–2008, 66. Total applicants accepted 2007–2008, 8. Number full-time enrolled (new admits only) 2007–2008, 8. Number part-time enrolled (new admits only) 2007–2008, 0. Openings 2008–2009, 8. The median number of years required for completion of a degree in 2006–2007 were 6. The number of students enrolled full- and part-time who were dismissed or voluntarily withdrew from this program area in 2007–2008 were 3. *Mental Health Counseling MA/MS (Master of Arts/Science)*—Applications 2007–2008, 60. Total applicants accepted 2007–2008, 15. Number full-time enrolled (new admits only) 2007–2008, 15. Number part-time enrolled (new admits only) 2007–2008, 0. Openings 2008–2009, 15. The median number of years required for completion of a degree in 2006–2007 were 2. The number of students enrolled full- and part-time who were dismissed or voluntarily withdrew from this program area in 2007–2008 were 2. *School Psychology EdS/MEd (School Psychology)*—Applications 2007–2008, 70. Total applicants accepted 2007–2008, 14. Number full-time enrolled (new admits only) 2007–2008, 14. Number part-time enrolled (new admits only) 2007–2008, 0. Openings 2008–2009, 15. The median number of years required for completion of a degree in 2006–2007 were 3. The number of students enrolled full- and part-time who were dismissed or voluntarily withdrew from this program area in 2007–2008 were 2.

Admissions Requirements:

Scores: Entries appear in this order: required test or GPA, minimum score (if required), median score of students entering in 2007–2008. Master's Programs: GRE-V no minimum stated, 500; GRE-Q no minimum stated, 500; overall undergraduate GPA 3.0, 3.4; last 2 years GPA 3.0, 3.5; Masters GRE-Analytical no minimum stated. Doctoral Programs: GRE-V 500, 600; GRE-Q 500, 600; overall undergraduate GPA 3.0, 3.5; last 2 years GPA 3.0, 3.6; Doctoral program GRE-Analytic no minimum stated.

Other Criteria: (importance of criteria rated low, medium, or high): GRE/MAT scores—high, research experience—medium, work experience—medium, extracurricular activity—low, clinically related public service—medium, GPA—high, letters of recommendation—high, interview—high, statement of goals and objectives—high, undergraduate major in psychology—low, specific undergraduate psychology courses taken—low.

Student Characteristics: The following represents characteristics of students in 2007–2008 in all graduate psychology programs in the department: Female—full-time 96, part-time 12; Male—full-time 20, part-time 9; African American/Black—full-time 19, part-time 3; Hispanic/Latino(a)—full-time 9, part-time 1; Asian/Pacific Islander—full-time 5, part-time 0; American Indian/Alaska Native—full-time 1, part-time 0; Caucasian/White—full-time 82, part-time 17; students subject to the Americans With Disabilities Act—full-time 3, part-time 0; Unknown ethnicity—full-time 0, part-time 0.

Financial Information/Assistance:

Tuition for Full-Time Study: *Master's:* State residents: per academic year $6,900, $230 per credit hour; Nonstate residents: per academic year $25,830, $861 per credit hour. *Doctoral:* State residents: per academic year $6,900, $230 per credit hour; Nonstate residents: per academic year $25,830, $861 per credit hour. Tuition is subject to change.

Financial Assistance:

First-Year Students: Teaching assistantships available for first year. Average amount paid per academic year: $3,200. Average number of hours worked per week: 10. Apply by open. Tuition remission given: full. Research assistantships available for first year. Average amount paid per academic year: $3,600. Average number of hours worked per week: 10. Apply by open. Tuition remission given: full. Fellowships and scholarships available for first year. Average amount paid per academic year: $6,300. Average number of hours worked per week: 10. Apply by January 3. Tuition remission given: full.

Advanced Students: Teaching assistantships available for advanced students. Average amount paid per academic year: $3,400. Average number of hours worked per week: 10. Apply by open. Tuition remission given: full. Research assistantships available for advanced students. Average amount paid per academic year: $3,800. Average number of hours worked per week: 10. Apply by open. Tuition remission given: full. Fellowships and scholarships available for advanced students. Average amount paid per academic year: $6,400. Average number of hours worked per week: 10. Apply by January 3. Tuition remission given: full.

Additional Information: Of all students currently enrolled full time, 60% benefited from one or more of the listed financial assistance programs.

Internships/Practica: Master's Degree (MA/MS Mental Health Counseling): An internship experience such as a final research project or "capstone" experience is required of graduates. Doctoral Degree (PhD Combined Counseling and School Psychology): For those doctoral students for whom a professional internship was required in this program prior to graduation, (7) students applied for an internship in 2006–2007, with (7) students obtaining an internship. Of those students who obtained an internship, (7) were paid internships. Of those students who obtained an internship, (6) students placed in APA/CPA-accredited internships, (1) student placed in internships not APA/CPA-accredited, but listed with the Association of Psychology Postdoctoral and Internship Centers (APPIC), (0) students placed in internships conforming to guidelines of the Council of Directors of School Psychology Programs (CDSPP), (0) students placed in internships that were not APA/CPA-accredited, APPIC or CDSPP listed. The program has available both on-campus and off-campus practica experiences; on-campus clinical practica include a mental health clinic serving clients from the community, adult learning disability clinic serving college students and the community, student career counseling center, and multidisciplinary center serving K–12 grade students from a number of school districts. Off-campus practica include a wide range of mental health, psychiatric, educational, and behavioral healthcare agencies.

Housing and Day Care: On-campus housing is available. See the following Web site for more information: http://www.fsu.edu/housing. On-campus day care facilities are available. See the following Web site for more information: http://www.fsu.edu/child care Note: facilities are limited, so please apply early.

Employment of Department Graduates:

Master's Degree Graduates: Of those who graduated in the academic year 2006–2007, the following categories and numbers represent the postgraduate activities and employment of master's degree graduates: Enrolled in a psychology doctoral program (4), enrolled in another graduate/professional program (2), enrolled in a postdoctoral residency/fellowship (n/a), employed in independent practice (n/a), total from the above (master's) (6).

Doctoral Degree Graduates: Of those who graduated in the academic year 2006–2007, the following categories and numbers represent the postgraduate activities and employment of doctoral degree graduates: Enrolled in a psychology doctoral program (n/a), employed in independent practice (4), employed in an academic position at a university (2), employed in an academic position at a 2-year/4-year college (1), employed in other positions at a higher education institution (2), employed in a professional position in a school system (2), employed in government agency (1), employed in a community mental health/counseling center (2), employed in a hospital/medical center (2), other employment position (2), do not know (1), total from the above (doctoral) (19).

Additional Information:

Orientation, Objectives, and Emphasis of Department: The Combined Doctoral Program in Counseling Psychology and School Psychology is fully accredited by the American Psychological Association. This unique program allows students to acquire knowledge and skills necessary for leadership positions in the practice of counseling psychology and school psychology in a variety of academic and applied settings. Students acquire basic competency in counseling psychology and school psychology, and advanced expertise in either counseling psychology or school psychology. The program prepares graduates for appropriate national certification and state licensure. Within the combined program, all students share a common core of experience in research and practice in counseling psychology and school psychology; students also are afforded the opportunity to concentrate in counseling psychology or school psychology (a few students decide to concentrate in both). The Combined Program embraces a scientist–practitioner model consistent with the mission of the College of Education and University. The program faculty enjoy diverse research and clinical interests, providing students with a range of opportunities for professional development in the areas of mental health counseling, school psychology, career counseling, prevention and early intervention, wellness, and psychology of the gifted.

Special Facilities or Resources: The program uses the following clinic facilities for the development of assessment, counseling, and consultation skills: (a) the Human Services Center. The Human Services Center is a mental health training clinic that provides counseling services at no cost to residents of Tallahassee and surrounding communities. This center offers counseling for a wide range of mental health and psychiatric problems, social skill trianing, anger management, relationship counseling, family counseling, and personal growth and development. The center works with the juvenile justice system in providing services to court referred cases. (b) The Adult Learning and Evaluation Center is a referral source for FSU and our other two local colleges, FAMU and TCC, and the community. It serves to assist adults in identifying learning disabilities and related problems that may compromise the attainment of educational and career progress. It offers students practica and assistantships in psychological assessment and consultation. (c) The Career Center is located in the Student Services Center and provides one of the most technologically advanced career facilities in the nation. The Career Center provides opportunities for practica and internships as well as for student employment opportunities as career advisors. This Center serves as many as 6,000 students per year with a variety of career concerns from choice of major to job placement. The philosophy is one of a full-service career center that is able to address not only presenting career concerns but related mental health issues as well.

Information for Students With Physical Disabilities: See the following Web site for more information: http://www.fsu.edu/StudentDisabilitiesResourceCenter.

Application Information:

Send to Admissions Committee, Psychological Services in Education, Florida State University, 307 Stone Building, Tallahassee, FL 32306-4453. NOTE: Please specify program that you are applying to. Application available online. URL of online application: http://www.epls.fsu.edu/psych__services/index.htm. Students are admitted in the Fall, application deadline January 15. Applications are reviewed as early as November 15. Finalists are invited to campus for personal interviews. *Fee:* $30.

Florida, University of

Department of Clinical and Health Psychology
Public Health and Health Professions
Box 100165 HSC
Gainesville, FL 32610-0165
Telephone: (352) 273-6455
Fax: (352) 273-6156
E-mail: *soltvl@phhp.ufl.edu*
Web: *http://www.phhp.ufl.edu/chp/*

Department Information:

1959. Chairperson: Russell M Bauer. Number of faculty: total—full-time 33; women—full-time 13; total—minority—full-time 2; faculty subject to the Americans With Disabilities Act 1.

Programs and Degrees Offered:

Listed in the following order: Program area, degree type (T if terminal Master's), number awarded 7/06–6/07. Clinical PhD (Doctor of Philosophy) 14.

APA Accreditation: Clinical PhD (Doctor of Philosophy).

Student Applications/Admissions:

Student Applications

Clinical PhD (Doctor of Philosophy)—Applications 2007–2008, 350. Total applicants accepted 2007–2008, 19. Number full-time enrolled (new admits only) 2007–2008, 15. Number part-time enrolled (new admits only) 2007–2008, 0. Total enrolled 2007–2008 full-time, 80, part-time, 7. Openings 2008–2009, 12. The median number of years required for completion of a degree in 2006–2007 were 6. The number of students enrolled full- and part-time who were dismissed or voluntarily withdrew from this program area in 2007–2008 were 1.

Admissions Requirements:

Scores: Entries appear in this order: required test or GPA, minimum score (if required), median score of students entering in 2007–2008. Master's Programs: We do not offer a terminal master's degree program. Doctoral Programs: GRE-V 500, 610; GRE-Q 500, 650; last 2 years GPA 3.00, 3.80.

Other Criteria: (importance of criteria rated low, medium, or high): GRE/MAT scores—medium, research experience—high, work experience—medium, extracurricular activity—medium, clinically related public service—high, GPA—medium, letters of recommendation—high, interview—high, statement of goals and objectives—high. For additional information on admission requirements, go to http://chp.phhp.ufl.edu/programs/doctoral/.

Student Characteristics: The following represents characteristics of students in 2007–2008 in all graduate psychology programs in the department: Female—full-time 63, part-time 1; Male—full-time 19, part-time 0; African American/Black—full-time 4, part-time 0; Hispanic/Latino(a)—full-time 3, part-time 0; Asian/Pacific Islander—full-time 5, part-time 0; American Indian/Alaska Native—full-time 0, part-time 0; Caucasian/White—full-time 64, part-time 1; Multi-ethnic—full-time 0, part-time 0; students subject to the Americans With Disabilities Act—full-time 0, part-time 0; Unknown ethnicity—full-time 6, part-time 0.

Financial Information/Assistance:

Tuition for Full-Time Study: *Doctoral:* State residents: per academic year $7,478, $311 per credit hour; Nonstate residents: per academic year $22,602, $941 per credit hour. Tuition is subject to change. See the following Web site for updates and changes in tuition costs: http://www.fa.ufl.edu/ufs/cashiers/feecalc.asp.

Financial Assistance:

First-Year Students: Research assistantships available for first year. Average amount paid per academic year: $12,000. Average number of hours worked per week: 20. Apply by December 1. Tuition remission given: full. Fellowships and scholarships available for first year. Average amount paid per academic year: $15,000. Apply by December 1. Tuition remission given: full.

Advanced Students: Teaching assistantships available for advanced students. Average amount paid per academic year: $12,000. Average number of hours worked per week: 20. Tuition remission given: full and partial. Research assistantships available for advanced students. Average amount paid per academic year: $12,000. Average number of hours worked per week: 20. Tuition remission given: full and partial. Fellowships and scholarships available for advanced students. Average amount paid per academic year: $18,000. Tuition remission given: full.

Additional Information: Of all students currently enrolled full time, 99% benefited from one or more of the listed financial assistance programs. Application and information available online at http://chp.phhp.ufl.edu/programs/doctoral/.

Internships/Practica: Doctoral Degree (PhD Clinical): For those doctoral students for whom a professional internship was required in this program prior to graduation, (17) students applied for an internship in 2006–2007, with (17) students obtaining an internship. Of those students who obtained an internship, (17) were paid internships. Of those students who obtained an internship, (17) students placed in APA/CPA-accredited internships, (0) students placed in internships not APA/CPA-accredited, but listed with the Association of Psychology Postdoctoral and Internship Centers (APPIC), (0) students placed in internships conforming to guidelines of the Council of Directors of School Psychology Programs (CDSPP), (0) students placed in internships that were not APA/CPA-accredited, APPIC or CDSPP listed. The Department of Clinical and Health Psychology runs a Psychology Clinic that is part of the Shands Hospital within the University of Florida Health Science Center. This Clinic provides consultation, assessment, and intervention services to medical–surgical inpatients and outpatients, as well as community patients with emotional and behavioral problems. Major services include clinical health psychology, child/pediatric psychology, and clinical neuropsychology.

Housing and Day Care: On-campus housing is available. See the following Web site for more information: http://www.housing.ufl.edu/housing/. On-campus day care facilities are available. See the following Web site for more information: http://www.coe.ufl.edu/Departments/BabyGator/.

Employment of Department Graduates:

Master's Degree Graduates: Of those who graduated in the academic year 2006–2007, the following categories and numbers

represent the postgraduate activities and employment of master's degree graduates: Enrolled in a postdoctoral residency/fellowship (n/a), employed in independent practice (n/a), total from the above (master's) (0).

Doctoral Degree Graduates: Of those who graduated in the academic year 2006–2007, the following categories and numbers represent the postgraduate activities and employment of doctoral degree graduates: Enrolled in a psychology doctoral program (n/a), enrolled in a postdoctoral residency/fellowship (6), employed in independent practice (2), employed in an academic position at a university (2), employed in government agency (1), employed in a hospital/medical center (2), do not know (1), total from the above (doctoral) (14).

Additional Information:

Orientation, Objectives, and Emphasis of Department: The program is designed to develop doctoral-level professional psychologists in the scientist–practitioner model through development of broad clinical skills and competencies, through mastery of broad areas of knowledge in psychology and clinical psychology, and through demonstrated competencies in contributing to that knowledge by research. Within these program objectives particular emphases can be identified: clinical health psychology, clinical neuropsychology, and clinical child/pediatric psychology. Courses, practica, conferences, committees, supervision, and settings are designed to augment each emphasis.

Special Facilities or Resources: The Department and its parent College, the College of Public Health and Health Professions, recently moved into a new building that houses faculty offices, student work spaces, and state-of-the-art classroom facilities. Department faculty currently occupy several thousand square feet of laboratory space for clinical and basic research. The Department is particularly strong in instrumentation and methodology for clinical research in pediatric psychology, health psychology, and neuropsychology. Psychophysiological and neuroimaging capabilities are present and utilized by many faculty. The clinical psychology program uses the extensive resources of the campus and community. The primary focus is in the Center for Clinical and Health Psychology of the University of Florida Health Science Center with its six colleges, and Shands Teaching Hospital and Clinics. Other sites utilized for clinical training include the university student health services, the university counseling center, and the VA Medical Center in Gainesville. Agencies and centers throughout the state and nation are also used, principally for intern training for students. The use of these varied resources is consonant with the program objectives. The trainee is directly involved with a broad scope of clinical and health problems, professionals, agencies, and settings.

Information for Students With Physical Disabilities: See the following Web site for more information: http://www.dso.ufl.edu/OSD/.

Application Information:

Send to Graduate Admissions, Department of Clinical and Health Psychology, Box 100165 HSC, University of Florida, Gainesville, FL 32610-0165. Application available online. URL of online application: http://www.chp.phhp.ufl.edu/programs/doctoral/. Students are admitted in the Fall, application deadline December 1. *Fee:* $30. Application fee cannot be waived, this is a University of Florida fee.

Florida, University of

Department of Psychology
Liberal Arts and Sciences
P.O. Box 112250
Gainesville, FL 32611-2250
Telephone: (352) 392-0601
Fax: (352) 392-7985
E-mail: *west51@ufl.edu*
Web: *http://www.psych.ufl.edu*

Department Information:

1947. Professor and Chair: Neil Rowland. Number of faculty: total—full-time 38, part-time 1; women—full-time 10; total—minority—full-time 2; women minority—full-time 2.

Programs and Degrees Offered:

Listed in the following order: Program area, degree type (T if terminal Master's), number awarded 7/06–6/07. Behavior Analysis PhD (Doctor of Philosophy) 8, Cognitive PhD (Doctor of Philosophy) 3, Counseling PhD (Doctor of Philosophy) 5, Developmental PhD (Doctor of Philosophy) 1, Social PhD (Doctor of Philosophy) 1, Behavioral Neuroscience PhD (Doctor of Philosophy) 2.

APA Accreditation: Counseling PhD (Doctor of Philosophy).

Student Applications/Admissions:

Student Applications

Behavior Analysis PhD (Doctor of Philosophy)—Applications 2007–2008, 46. Total applicants accepted 2007–2008, 7. Number full-time enrolled (new admits only) 2007–2008, 7. Number part-time enrolled (new admits only) 2007–2008, 0. Openings 2008–2009, 8. The median number of years required for completion of a degree in 2006–2007 were 5. The number of students enrolled full- and part-time who were dismissed or voluntarily withdrew from this program area in 2007–2008 were 0. *Cognitive PhD (Doctor of Philosophy)*—Applications 2007–2008, 19. Total applicants accepted 2007–2008, 2. Number full-time enrolled (new admits only) 2007–2008, 3. Number part-time enrolled (new admits only) 2007–2008, 0. Openings 2008–2009, 2. The median number of years required for completion of a degree in 2006–2007 were 4. The number of students enrolled full- and part-time who were dismissed or voluntarily withdrew from this program area in 2007–2008 were 1. *Counseling PhD (Doctor of Philosophy)*—Applications 2007–2008, 150. Total applicants accepted 2007–2008, 7. Number full-time enrolled (new admits only) 2007–2008, 6. Number part-time enrolled (new admits only) 2007–2008, 0. Total enrolled 2007–2008 full-time, 47, part-time, 14. Openings 2008–2009, 6. The median number of years required for completion of a degree in 2006–2007 were 4. The number of students enrolled full- and part-time who were dismissed or voluntarily withdrew from this program area in 2007–2008 were 2. *Developmental PhD (Doctor of Philosophy)*—Applications 2007–2008, 21. Total applicants accepted 2007–2008, 4. Number full-time enrolled (new admits only) 2007–2008, 2. Number part-time enrolled (new admits only) 2007–2008, 0. Total enrolled 2007–2008 full-time, 13, part-time, 2. Openings 2008–2009, 4. The median number of years required for completion of a degree in 2006–2007 were 6. The number of students enrolled full- and part-time who were dismissed or voluntarily withdrew from this program area in 2007–2008 were 1. *Social PhD (Doctor of Philosophy)*—Applications 2007–2008, 44. Total applicants accepted 2007–2008, 3. Number full-time enrolled (new admits only) 2007–2008, 1. Number part-time enrolled (new admits only) 2007–2008, 0. Openings 2008–2009, 4. The median number of years required for completion of a degree in 2006–2007 were 5. The number of students enrolled full- and part-time who were dismissed or voluntarily withdrew from this program area in 2007–2008 were 3. *Behavioral Neuroscience PhD (Doctor of Philosophy)*—Applications 2007–2008, 20. Total applicants accepted 2007–2008, 3. Number full-time enrolled (new admits only) 2007–2008, 5. Number part-time enrolled (new admits only) 2007–2008, 0. Openings 2008–2009, 3. The median number of years required for completion of a degree in 2006–2007 were 5. The number of students enrolled full- and part-time who were dismissed or voluntarily withdrew from this program area in 2007–2008 were 1.

Admissions Requirements:

Scores: Entries appear in this order: required test or GPA, minimum score (if required), median score of students entering in 2007–2008. Master's Programs: no separate masters program offered. Doctoral Programs: GRE-V 450; GRE-Q 450; overall undergraduate GPA 3.0.

Other Criteria: (importance of criteria rated low, medium, or high): GRE/MAT scores—medium, research experience—high, work experience—low, extracurricular activity—medium, clinically related public service—high, GPA—high, letters of recommendation—high, interview—medium, statement of goals and objectives—medium, match to faculty interest—high, undergraduate major in psychology—medium, specific undergraduate psychology courses taken—medium. Only the Counseling Psychology program requires clinically related experience. Weight given to these criteria varies from program to program. Some programs do not conduct interviews every year. For additional information on admission requirements, go to http://www.psych.ufl.edu.

Student Characteristics: The following represents characteristics of students in 2007–2008 in all graduate psychology programs in the department: Female—full-time 88, part-time 9; Male—full-time 45, part-time 7; African American/Black—full-time 3, part-time 1; Hispanic/Latino(a)—full-time 5, part-time 1; Asian/Pacific Islander—full-time 15, part-time 2; American Indian/Alaska Native—full-time 0, part-time 0; Caucasian/White—full-time 98, part-time 12; Multi-ethnic—full-time 12, part-time 0; students subject to the Americans With Disabilities Act—full-time 0, part-time 0; Unknown ethnicity—full-time 0, part-time 0; International students who hold an F-1 or J-1 Visa—full-time 16, part-time 0.

Financial Information/Assistance:

Tuition for Full-Time Study: *Master's:* State residents: per academic year $5,700, $312 per credit hour; Nonstate residents: per academic year $17,000, $942 per credit hour. *Doctoral:* State residents: per academic year $5,700, $312 per credit hour; Nonstate residents: per academic year $17,000, $942 per credit hour. Tuition is subject to change. See the following Web site for updates and changes in tuition costs: http://www.fa.ufl.edu/ufs/cashiers/feecalc.asp.

Financial Assistance:

First-Year Students: Teaching assistantships available for first year. Average amount paid per academic year: $12,500. Average number of hours worked per week: 14. Apply by January 15. Tuition remission given: full. Research assistantships available for first year. Average amount paid per academic year: $12,500. Average number of hours worked per week: 14. Apply by January 15. Tuition remission given: full. Fellowships and scholarships available for first year. Average amount paid per academic year: $17,000. Average number of hours worked per week: 14. Apply by January 15. Tuition remission given: full.

Advanced Students: Teaching assistantships available for advanced students. Average amount paid per academic year: $12,500. Average number of hours worked per week: 14. Tuition remission given: full. Research assistantships available for advanced students. Average amount paid per academic year: $12,500. Average number of hours worked per week: 14. Tuition remission given: full. Fellowships and scholarships available for advanced students. Average amount paid per academic year: $14,500. Average number of hours worked per week: 14. Tuition remission given: full.

Additional Information: Of all students currently enrolled full time, 95% benefited from one or more of the listed financial assistance programs. Application and information available online at http://www.psych.ufl.edu.

Internships/Practica: Doctoral Degree (PhD Counseling): For those doctoral students for whom a professional internship was required in this program prior to graduation, (8) students applied for an internship in 2006–2007, with (7) students obtaining an internship. Of those students who obtained an internship, (7) were paid internships. Of those students who obtained an internship, (6) students placed in APA/CPA-accredited internships, (1) student placed in internships not APA/CPA-accredited, but listed with the Association of Psychology Postdoctoral and Internship Centers (APPIC), (0) students placed in internships conforming to guidelines of the Council of Directors of School Psychology Programs (CDSPP), (0) students placed in internships that were not APA/CPA-accredited, APPIC or CDSPP listed. University Counseling Center, University of Florida Student Health Service, Family Practice Medical Group, Meridian Behavioral Healthcare, Alachua County Crisis Center, VA Medical Center, North Florida Treatment and Evaluation Center, and Northeast Florida State Hospital.

Housing and Day Care: On-campus housing is available only for married graduate students. See the following Web site for more information: http://www.housing.ufl.edu. On-campus day care facilities are available. Baby Gator daycare is located on campus and is available to all graduate students. See the following Web site for more information: http://www.coe.ufl.edu/BabyGator.

Employment of Department Graduates:

Master's Degree Graduates: Of those who graduated in the academic year 2006–2007, the following categories and numbers represent the postgraduate activities and employment of master's degree graduates: Enrolled in a postdoctoral residency/fellowship (n/a), employed in independent practice (n/a), employed in business or industry (2), total from the above (master's) (2).

Doctoral Degree Graduates: Of those who graduated in the academic year 2006–2007, the following categories and numbers represent the postgraduate activities and employment of doctoral

degree graduates: Enrolled in a psychology doctoral program (n/a), enrolled in a postdoctoral residency/fellowship (3), employed in independent practice (1), employed in an academic position at a university (4), employed in an academic position at a 2-year/4-year college (1), employed in other positions at a higher education institution (4), employed in business or industry (1), employed in government agency (1), employed in a community mental health/counseling center (2), other employment position (1), total from the above (doctoral) (18).

Additional Information:

Orientation, Objectives, and Emphasis of Department: The graduate program in Psychology at the University of Florida is designed for those planning careers as researchers, teacher–scholars, and scientist–practitioners in psychology. In addition to specialized training in one or more areas, a core program of theories, methods, and research in general psychology insures that each student will be well prepared in the basic areas of psychology. The primary goal of the department is educating scientists who will help advance psychology as a science through teaching, research, and professional practice. Because the University of Florida is a broad spectrum university, including almost all the major academic departments as well as professional schools on a single campus, a unique atmosphere exists for the evolution of the general program and the development of personal programs of study. Each student also receives specialized training in at least one of the areas of specialization including cognition and sensory processes, counseling psychology, developmental, experimental analysis of behavior, psychobiology (comparative–physiological), and social. One of the fundamental goals of the doctoral program is to engage the student as early as possible in the area of interest while assuring a sound background of knowledge of theory, methodology, and major content areas so that maximum integration may be achieved. All students participate in various ongoing aspects of the academic community such as teaching, research, field experience, and professional activities. Seminars are offered in techniques of teaching accompanied by supervised undergraduate teaching. Continuous research experience is required. The Department participates in a number of interdisciplinary programs including sensory studies, neurobiological sciences, and gerontological studies.

Special Facilities or Resources: Special facilities in the department include laboratories in comparative, developmental, experimental analysis of behavior, cognitive and information processing, perception, personality, psychobiology, sensory, and social; an animal colony; a statistical computation laboratory; a laboratory in neuropsychology and developmental learning disabilities; the Communication Sciences Laboratory; and the Computing Center.

Information for Students With Physical Disabilities: See the following Web site for more information: http://www.ufl.edu.

Application Information:

Send to Graduate Studies Secretary, Psychology Department, University of Florida, Gainesville, FL 32611-2250. Application available online. URL of online application: http://www.psych.ufl.edu. Students are admitted in the Fall, application deadline January 15. Department is considering earlier application deadline in the future. *Fee:* $30.

Miami, University of

Department of Educational and Psychological Studies/Area of Counseling Psychology
Education
P.O. Box 248065
Coral Gables, FL 33124-2040
Telephone: (305) 284-3001
Fax: (305) 284-3003
E-mail: *blewis@miami.edu*
Web: *http://www.education.miami.edu*

Department Information:

1967. Director of Training, Counseling Psychology Program: Brian L. Lewis. Number of faculty: total—full-time 7, part-time 2; women—full-time 2, part-time 2; total—minority—full-time 2; women minority—full-time 1.

Programs and Degrees Offered:

Listed in the following order: Program area, degree type (T if terminal Master's), number awarded 7/06–6/07. Counseling Psychology PhD (Doctor of Philosophy) 4, Marriage and Family Therapy MA/MS (Master of Arts/Science) (T) 5, Mental Health Counseling MA/MS (Master of Arts/Science) (T) 14.

APA Accreditation: Counseling PhD (Doctor of Philosophy).

Student Applications/Admissions:

Student Applications

Counseling Psychology PhD (Doctor of Philosophy)—Applications 2007–2008, 108. Total applicants accepted 2007–2008, 10. Number full-time enrolled (new admits only) 2007–2008, 5. Total enrolled 2007–2008 full-time, 25, part-time, 7. Openings 2008–2009, 6. The median number of years required for completion of a degree in 2006–2007 were 6. The number of students enrolled full- and part-time who were dismissed or voluntarily withdrew from this program area in 2007–2008 were 1. *Marriage and Family Therapy MA/MS (Master of Arts/Science)*—Applications 2007–2008, 40. Total applicants accepted 2007–2008, 13. Number full-time enrolled (new admits only) 2007–2008, 4. Number part-time enrolled (new admits only) 2007–2008, 1. Total enrolled 2007–2008 full-time, 12, part-time, 8. Openings 2008–2009, 15. The median number of years required for completion of a degree in 2006–2007 were 2. The number of students enrolled full- and part-time who were dismissed or voluntarily withdrew from this program area in 2007–2008 were 1. *Mental Health Counseling MA/MS (Master of Arts/Science)*—Applications 2007–2008, 45. Total applicants accepted 2007–2008, 15. Number full-time enrolled (new admits only) 2007–2008, 8. Number part-time enrolled (new admits only) 2007–2008, 3. Total enrolled 2007–2008 full-time, 20, part-time, 10. Openings 2008–2009, 15. The median number of years required for completion of a degree in 2006–2007 were 2. The number of students enrolled full- and part-time who were dismissed or voluntarily withdrew from this program area in 2007–2008 were 1.

Admissions Requirements:

Scores: Entries appear in this order: required test or GPA, minimum score (if required), median score of students entering in 2007–2008. Master's Programs: GRE-V no minimum stated,

510; GRE-Q no minimum stated, 610; overall undergraduate GPA no minimum stated, 3.24. Doctoral Programs: GRE-V no minimum stated, 560; GRE-Q no minimum stated, 640; overall undergraduate GPA no minimum stated, 3.42.

Other Criteria: (importance of criteria rated low, medium, or high): GRE/MAT scores—high, research experience—medium, work experience—medium, extracurricular activity—low, clinically related public service—medium, GPA—high, letters of recommendation—high, interview—high, statement of goals and objectives—high. For doctoral program.

Student Characteristics: The following represents characteristics of students in 2007–2008 in all graduate psychology programs in the department: Female—full-time 20, part-time 7; Male—full-time 5, part-time 1; African American/Black—full-time 1, part-time 1; Hispanic/Latino(a)—full-time 7, part-time 1; Asian/Pacific Islander—full-time 0, part-time 0; American Indian/Alaska Native—full-time 0, part-time 0; Caucasian/White—full-time 16, part-time 6; Multi-ethnic—full-time 1, part-time 0; students subject to the Americans With Disabilities Act—full-time 1, part-time 0; Unknown ethnicity—full-time 0, part-time 0; International students who hold an F-1 or J-1 Visa—full-time 1, part-time 0.

Financial Information/Assistance:

Tuition for Full-Time Study: *Master's:* State residents: $1,350 per credit hour; Nonstate residents: $1,350 per credit hour. *Doctoral:* State residents: $1,350 per credit hour; Nonstate residents: $1,350 per credit hour.

Financial Assistance:

First-Year Students: Teaching assistantships available for first year. Average amount paid per academic year: $18,000. Average number of hours worked per week: 20. Apply by January 2. Tuition remission given: full. Research assistantships available for first year. Average amount paid per academic year: $18,000. Average number of hours worked per week: 20. Apply by January 2. Tuition remission given: full. Fellowships and scholarships available for first year. Average amount paid per academic year: $20,000. Average number of hours worked per week: 0. Apply by January 2. Tuition remission given: full.

Advanced Students: Teaching assistantships available for advanced students. Average amount paid per academic year: $18,000. Average number of hours worked per week: 20. Apply by April 15. Tuition remission given: full. Research assistantships available for advanced students. Average amount paid per academic year: $18,000. Average number of hours worked per week: 20. Apply by April 15. Tuition remission given: full. Fellowships and scholarships available for advanced students. Average amount paid per academic year: $20,000. Average number of hours worked per week: 0. Apply by February 1. Tuition remission given: full.

Additional Information: Of all students currently enrolled full time, 100% benefited from one or more of the listed financial assistance programs. Application and information available online at http://www.education.miami.edu/ProgramReq/ProgramRep.asp?ID=1&PgmID=47.

Internships/Practica: Doctoral Degree (PhD Counseling Psychology): For those doctoral students for whom a professional internship was required in this program prior to graduation, (4) students applied for an internship in 2006–2007, with (4) students obtaining an internship. Of those students who obtained an internship, (4) were paid internships. Of those students who obtained an internship, (4) students placed in APA/CPA-accredited internships, (0) students placed in internships not APA/CPA accredited, but listed with the Association of Psychology Postdoctoral and Internship Centers (APPIC), (0) students placed in internships conforming to guidelines of the Council of Directors of School Psychology Programs (CDSPP), (0) students placed in internships that were not APA/CPA-accredited, APPIC or CDSPP listed. Students complete 2 academic years of practicum: the 1st year in our on-campus training clinic and the 2nd year in an agency or hospital setting located in the community. Program faculty supervise the practicum through weekly one-to-one meetings and group supervision meetings. Therapeutic modalities in these placements include individual, couple, and group therapies. The off-campus placement is tailored to the student's career goals. Many students also complete an optional advanced practicum in their 3rd year with placements tailored to their career goals. Placements include university counseling centers, psychiatric facilities, VA hospitals, behavioral medicine settings, correctional facilities, schools, among others.

Housing and Day Care: On-campus housing is available. See the following Web site for more information: http://www.miami.edu/. On-campus day care facilities are available.

Employment of Department Graduates:

Master's Degree Graduates: Of those who graduated in the academic year 2006–2007, the following categories and numbers represent the postgraduate activities and employment of master's degree graduates: Enrolled in a postdoctoral residency/fellowship (n/a), employed in independent practice (n/a), total from the above (master's) (0).

Doctoral Degree Graduates: Of those who graduated in the academic year 2006–2007, the following categories and numbers represent the postgraduate activities and employment of doctoral degree graduates: Enrolled in a psychology doctoral program (n/a), enrolled in a postdoctoral residency/fellowship (3), employed in a hospital/medical center (1), total from the above (doctoral) (4).

Additional Information:

Orientation, Objectives, and Emphasis of Department: The multicultural, health psychology, and family areas are foci in the doctoral program that is designed to educate counseling psychologists following the scientist–practitioner model to prepare individuals who will contribute to knowledge in psychology and who will be exemplary practitioners of psychological science. A sequence of research experiences is required as well as at least four semesters of supervised practicum and a full-year internship. In addition to coursework in the psychological foundations, requirements include the study of human development and personality (including career development), theories of therapy and the change process, therapeutic methodologies, and psychological assessment. We offer a five-course sequence leading to a certificate in bilingual counseling (Spanish/English). The titles of the courses are: Professional Psychological Spanish, Hispanic and Latino Psychology, Community Interventions for Latino and Hispanic Populations, and Supervised Practice in Bilingual Counseling. Two of the five courses can be taken as required electives in the program.

Special Facilities or Resources: The Institute for Individual and Family Counseling, an on-campus clinic, is used as the primary practicum site. It is equipped with facilities for audio, video, and live supervision. The multicultural clientele of the Institute and the other agencies and schools in the Miami area are available for practica and fieldwork. Computer laboratories are available to students in the department. A microcomputer laboratory is available to all students in the department. In addition, an assessment laboratory is an integral part of assessment training in the program.

Information for Students With Physical Disabilities: See the following Web site for more information: http://www.miami.edu/academic-development/addisab01.html.

Application Information:
Send to Coordinator of Graduate Studies, School of Education, 312 Merrick Building, University of Miami, P.O. Box 248065, Coral Gables, FL 33124. Application available online. URL of online application: https://www.applyweb.com/aw?mgred/. Students are admitted in the Fall, application deadline January 2; Winter, application deadline August 1. January 2 deadline is for Doctoral program applicants. August 1 deadline is for master's degree applicants. *Fee:* $50.

Miami, University of

Department of Psychology
College of Arts and Sciences
P.O. Box 248185
Coral Gables, FL 33124
Telephone: (305) 284-2814
Fax: (305) 284-8469
E-mail: *rwellens@miami.edu*
Web: *http://www.psy.miami.edu*

Department Information:
1937. Chairperson: A. Rodney Wellens. Number of faculty: total—full-time 35; women—full-time 20; total—minority—full-time 6; women minority—full-time 4.

Programs and Degrees Offered:
Listed in the following order: Program area, degree type (T if terminal Master's), number awarded 7/06–6/07. Developmental PhD (Doctor of Philosophy) 2, Behavioral Neuroscience PhD (Doctor of Philosophy) 1, Clinical PhD (Doctor of Philosophy) 12.

APA Accreditation: Clinical PhD (Doctor of Philosophy).

Student Applications/Admissions:
Student Applications
Developmental PhD (Doctor of Philosophy)—Applications 2007–2008, 16. Total applicants accepted 2007–2008, 1. Number full-time enrolled (new admits only) 2007–2008, 0. Number part-time enrolled (new admits only) 2007–2008, 0. Openings 2008–2009, 4. The median number of years required for completion of a degree in 2006–2007 were 6. The number of students enrolled full- and part-time who were dismissed or voluntarily withdrew from this program area in 2007–2008 were 0. *Behavioral Neuroscience PhD (Doctor of Philosophy)*—Applications 2007–2008, 7. Total applicants accepted 2007–2008, 0. Number full-time enrolled (new admits only) 2007–2008, 0. Number part-time enrolled (new admits only) 2007–2008, 0. Openings 2008–2009, 1. The median number of years required for completion of a degree in 2006–2007 were 6. The number of students enrolled full- and part-time who were dismissed or voluntarily withdrew from this program area in 2007–2008 were 0. *Clinical PhD (Doctor of Philosophy)*—Applications 2007–2008, 317. Total applicants accepted 2007–2008, 21. Number full-time enrolled (new admits only) 2007–2008, 14. Number part-time enrolled (new admits only) 2007–2008, 0. Openings 2008–2009, 14. The median number of years required for completion of a degree in 2006–2007 were 6. The number of students enrolled full- and part-time who were dismissed or voluntarily withdrew from this program area in 2007–2008 were 0.

Admissions Requirements:
Scores: Entries appear in this order: required test or GPA, minimum score (if required), median score of students entering in 2007–2008. Doctoral Programs: GRE-V 500, 630; GRE-Q 500, 650; overall undergraduate GPA 3.2, 3.5.
Other Criteria: (importance of criteria rated low, medium, or high): GRE/MAT scores—high, research experience—high, work experience—medium, extracurricular activity—medium, clinically related public service—medium, GPA—high, letters of recommendation—high, interview—high, statement of goals and objectives—high, undergraduate major in psychology—medium, specific undergraduate psychology courses taken—medium. Clinically related public service not weighted for non-clinical programs. For additional information on admission requirements, go to http://www.psy.miami.edu.

Student Characteristics: The following represents characteristics of students in 2007–2008 in all graduate psychology programs in the department: Female—full-time 76, part-time 0; Male—full-time 20, part-time 0; African American/Black—full-time 5, part-time 0; Hispanic/Latino(a)—full-time 21, part-time 0; Asian/Pacific Islander—full-time 9, part-time 0; American Indian/Alaska Native—full-time 0, part-time 0; Caucasian/White—full-time 60, part-time 0; Multi-ethnic—full-time 1, part-time 0; students subject to the Americans With Disabilities Act—full-time 0, part-time 0; Unknown ethnicity—full-time 0, part-time 0; International students who hold an F-1 or J-1 Visa—full-time 2, part-time 0.

Financial Information/Assistance:
Tuition for Full-Time Study: *Doctoral:* State residents: per academic year $31,328, $1,424 per credit hour; Nonstate residents: per academic year $31,328, $1,424 per credit hour.

Financial Assistance:
First-Year Students: Teaching assistantships available for first year. Average amount paid per academic year: $20,000. Average number of hours worked per week: 15. Apply by December 1. Tuition remission given: full. Research assistantships available for first year. Average amount paid per academic year: $22,660. Average number of hours worked per week: 20. Apply by December 1. Tuition remission given: full. Traineeships available for first

year. Average amount paid per academic year: $22,660. Average number of hours worked per week: 15. Apply by December 1. Tuition remission given: full. Fellowships and scholarships available for first year. Average amount paid per academic year: $22,660. Average number of hours worked per week: 0. Apply by December 1. Tuition remission given: full.

Advanced Students: Teaching assistantships available for advanced students. Average amount paid per academic year: $20,000. Average number of hours worked per week: 15. Tuition remission given: full. Research assistantships available for advanced students. Average amount paid per academic year: $22,660. Average number of hours worked per week: 20. Tuition remission given: full. Traineeships available for advanced students. Average amount paid per academic year: $22,660. Average number of hours worked per week: 15. Tuition remission given: full. Fellowships and scholarships available for advanced students. Average amount paid per academic year: $22,660. Average number of hours worked per week: 0. Tuition remission given: full.

Additional Information: Of all students currently enrolled full time, 100% benefited from one or more of the listed financial assistance programs. Application and information available online at http://www.psy.miami.edu.

Internships/Practica: Doctoral Degree (PhD Clinical): For those doctoral students for whom a professional internship was required in this program prior to graduation, (6) students applied for an internship in 2006–2007, with (6) students obtaining an internship. Of those students who obtained an internship, (6) were paid internships. Of those students who obtained an internship, (6) students placed in APA/CPA-accredited internships, (0) students placed in internships not APA/CPA-accredited, but listed with the Association of Psychology Postdoctoral and Internship Centers (APPIC), (0) students placed in internships conforming to guidelines of the Council of Directors of School Psychology Programs (CDSPP), (0) students placed in internships that were not APA/CPA-accredited, APPIC or CDSPP listed. Practica sites are available for students enrolled in our APA-approved clinical program on the Coral Gables campus, Medical School campus and throughout Miami-Dade County. The department's Psychological Services Center and the University Counseling Center represent primary sites for students developing skills in psychological assessment and empirically based interventions. Additional specialty practica are located in the Department of Pediatrics at Medical School, the Veterans Administration Medical Center and various clinics throughout Miami-Dade County.

Housing and Day Care: No on-campus housing is available. On-campus day care facilities are available: UM/Canterbury Preschool, 1150 Stanford Drive, Coral Gables, FL 33124, (305) 284-5437.

Employment of Department Graduates:

Master's Degree Graduates: Of those who graduated in the academic year 2006–2007, the following categories and numbers represent the postgraduate activities and employment of master's degree graduates: Enrolled in a postdoctoral residency/fellowship (n/a), employed in independent practice (n/a), total from the above (master's) (0).

Doctoral Degree Graduates: Of those who graduated in the academic year 2006–2007, the following categories and numbers represent the postgraduate activities and employment of doctoral degree graduates: Enrolled in a psychology doctoral program (n/a), enrolled in a postdoctoral residency/fellowship (6), employed in an academic position at a university (4), employed in other positions at a higher education institution (1), employed in business or industry (2), employed in a community mental health/counseling center (1), do not know (1), total from the above (doctoral) (15).

Additional Information:

Orientation, Objectives, and Emphasis of Department: The Department of Psychology's mission is to acquire, advance, and disseminate knowledge within the Psychological and Biobehavioral Sciences. The Department seeks a balance among several academic endeavors including basic scientific research, applied research, undergraduate teaching, graduate teaching, professional training, and community service. The department offers courses leading to the degree of Doctor of Philosophy. The Clinical Psychology Program, with tracks in adult, child, pediatric health, and health, uses a scientist–practitioner model of training with somewhat greater emphasis on the clinical science component. A mentor–model method of research training is employed. Prospective students in Psychology are admitted to graduate study within the Adult, Child, or Health Divisions. The Adult Division houses the adult clinical track that includes a focus on personality–social psychology in addition to adult psychopathology and treatment. The Child Division houses the clinical child and pediatric heath tracks of the clinical program and also the developmental program. The Health Division houses the health clinical track and the behavioral neuroscience program. All students teach at least one undergraduate course as part of their graduate training. Students are supported via training grants, fellowships, teaching assistantships, and research assistantships.

Special Facilities or Resources: The Psychological Services Center serves as a community-based mental health training clinic for clinical students. The Behavioral Medicine Research Building provides excellent research facilities for students in behavioral neuroscience and health psychology. The Behavioral Medicine Research Center located at the UM Miller School of Medicine Clinical Research Building provides state-of-the-art facilities for research in psychoneuroimmunology. The Linda Ray Intervention Center and the Center for Autism and Related Disabilities provide excellent research opportunities for students in our child programs. Faculty research is supported by more than $14 million yearly in federal and state funding. The department recently moved to a new state-of-the-art research and teaching facility constructed for its use in 2003.

Information for Students With Physical Disabilities: See the following Web site for more information: http://www.miami.edu/umar/.

Application Information:

Send to Graduate Admissions, Department of Psychology, P.O. Box 248185, Coral Gables, FL 33124. To access our online application go to https://www.applyweb.com/aw?mgrpsy/. Application available online. URL of online application: http://www.psy.miami.edu. Students are admitted in the Fall, application deadline December 1. *Fee:* $50.

North Florida, University of
Department of Psychology
College of Arts and Sciences
4567 St. John's Bluff Road, South
Jacksonville, FL 32224-2673
Telephone: (904) 620-2807
Fax: (904) 620-3814
E-mail: *lfoley@unf.edu*
Web: *http://www.unf.edu*

Department Information:

1972. Interim Chair: Linda A Foley. Number of faculty: total—full-time 21, part-time 18; women—full-time 9, part-time 9; total—minority—full-time 6; women minority—full-time 4; faculty subject to the Americans With Disabilities Act 2.

Programs and Degrees Offered:

Listed in the following order: Program area, degree type (T if terminal Master's), number awarded 7/06–6/07. General Psychology MA/MS (Master of Arts/Science) (T) 4, Counseling Psychology MA/MS (Master of Arts/Science) (T) 18.

Student Applications/Admissions:

Student Applications

General Psychology MA/MS (Master of Arts/Science)—Applications 2007–2008, 39. Total applicants accepted 2007–2008, 17. Number full-time enrolled (new admits only) 2007–2008, 16. Number part-time enrolled (new admits only) 2007–2008, 0. Openings 2008–2009, 12. The median number of years required for completion of a degree in 2006–2007 were 2. The number of students enrolled full- and part-time who were dismissed or voluntarily withdrew from this program area in 2007–2008 were 1. *Counseling Psychology MA/MS (Master of Arts/Science)*—Applications 2007–2008, 87. Total applicants accepted 2007–2008, 18. Number full-time enrolled (new admits only) 2007–2008, 18. Number part-time enrolled (new admits only) 2007–2008, 0. Total enrolled 2007–2008 full-time, 38, part-time, 3. Openings 2008–2009, 18. The median number of years required for completion of a degree in 2006–2007 were 2. The number of students enrolled full- and part-time who were dismissed or voluntarily withdrew from this program area in 2007–2008 were 1.

Admissions Requirements:

Scores: Entries appear in this order: required test or GPA, minimum score (if required), median score of students entering in 2007–2008. Master's Programs: GRE-V no minimum stated, 540; GRE-Q no minimum stated, 550; overall undergraduate GPA 3.0, 3.4; last 2 years GPA 3.0, 3.7; psychology GPA 3.0, 3.4. A low performance on one criterion can be offset by a high performance on another.

Other Criteria: (importance of criteria rated low, medium, or high): GRE/MAT scores—high, research experience—high, work experience—medium, extracurricular activity—low, clinically related public service—medium, GPA—high, letters of recommendation—medium, interview—high, statement of goals and objectives—high, volunteerism—low. Research experience weighted more heavily for MAGP. Interview and clinically related public service for MACP. For additional information on admission requirements, go to http://www.unf.edu/coas/psychology/Programs.html#GradProgs.

Student Characteristics: The following represents characteristics of students in 2007–2008 in all graduate psychology programs in the department: Female—full-time 49, part-time 3; Male—full-time 7, part-time 0; African American/Black—full-time 2, part-time 0; Hispanic/Latino(a)—full-time 2, part-time 0; Asian/Pacific Islander—full-time 2, part-time 0; American Indian/Alaska Native—full-time 0, part-time 0; Caucasian/White—full-time 50, part-time 3; Multi-ethnic—full-time 0, part-time 0; students subject to the Americans With Disabilities Act—full-time 0, part-time 0; Unknown ethnicity—full-time 0, part-time 0.

Financial Information/Assistance:

Tuition for Full-Time Study: *Master's:* State residents: $206 per credit hour; Nonstate residents: $966 per credit hour.

Financial Assistance:

First-Year Students: Teaching assistantships available for first year. Research assistantships available for first year. Traineeships available for first year. Average amount paid per academic year: $5,000. Apply by September 30. Fellowships and scholarships available for first year. Average amount paid per academic year: $2,000. Apply by September 30. Tuition remission given: partial.

Advanced Students: Teaching assistantships available for advanced students. Average amount paid per academic year: $1,800. Apply by June 1. Research assistantships available for advanced students. Traineeships available for advanced students. Average amount paid per academic year: $10,000. Apply by April 1. Fellowships and scholarships available for advanced students. Tuition remission given: partial.

Additional Information: Of all students currently enrolled full time, 15% benefited from one or more of the listed financial assistance programs.

Internships/Practica: MACP students take part in a required 1,000-hour practicum/internship that provides application experience. The greater Jacksonville area allows for a great variety of internship placements with a diverse set of clientele and clinical/contextual issues.

Housing and Day Care: On-campus housing is available. See the following Web site for more information: http://www.unf.edu. On-campus day care facilities are available.

Employment of Department Graduates:

Master's Degree Graduates: Of those who graduated in the academic year 2006–2007, the following categories and numbers represent the postgraduate activities and employment of master's degree graduates: Enrolled in a psychology doctoral program (3), enrolled in another graduate/professional program (1), enrolled in a postdoctoral residency/fellowship (n/a), employed in independent practice (n/a), employed in an academic position at a university (1), employed in an academic position at a 2-year/4-year college (1), employed in other positions at a higher education institution (3), employed in a professional position in a school system (1), employed in business or industry (0), employed in government agency (1), employed in a community mental health/counseling center (8), do not know (3), total from the above (master's) (22).

Doctoral Degree Graduates: Of those who graduated in the academic year 2006–2007, the following categories and numbers represent the postgraduate activities and employment of doctoral degree graduates: Enrolled in a psychology doctoral program (n/a), total from the above (doctoral) (0).

Additional Information:

Orientation, Objectives, and Emphasis of Department: The Master of Arts in Counseling Psychology program is designed to prepare students for emerging professional roles as Florida licensed master's level practitioners. The program consists of 60 semester hours of course work, including a two-semester practicum in a community mental health agency. The program balances theory and practice and is designed to provide the prospective practitioner with a firm theoretical foundation for developing counseling strategies as well as the ability to apply particular goal-oriented intervention tactics. The Master of Arts in General Psychology program is a broad-based, research-oriented program intended to equip students with the critical skills and knowledge necessary for continued occupation and educational advancement in fields related to psychology. The program consists of 37 semester hours of course work designed around a core curriculum of statistics, research design, substantive areas of psychology, and a research-based thesis.

Special Facilities or Resources: The Department of Psychology moved into an aesthetically pleasing facility in Fall 2006, located on the edge of scenic wetlands and hosting cutting-edge technology, including closed-circuit digital recording capabilities for research and counselor training purposes and student response technology for an interactional classroom environment. Several teaching laboratories are housed within the psychology department. The counseling lab and the psychometric lab each consist of a large observation room, three small rooms for individual counseling/testing, and one large seminar/classroom. A computer applications lab has 24 individual computer work stations and an instructor's server, with a local area network and connections to the university mainframe, with hardware updated frequently. An animal lab allows for research with rodents. Finally, a department conference room serves as a comfortable gathering place for graduate training. In addition to these teaching laboratories, individual faculty research labs also are housed within the Department. Laboratory emphases include preschool education, cognitive development, child–father interactions, adolescent psychopathology, psychometrics, psychophysiology, human performance, human factors, social cognition, social interaction, and psychology and law.

Application Information:

Send to Gabriel J. Ybarra, PhD, Coordinator, Master of Arts in Counseling Psychology; Randall Russac, PhD, Coordinator, Master of Arts in General Psychology. Application available online. URL of online application: https://www.csdweb.unf.edu/access/htdoes/onlineapp.htm. Students are admitted in the Fall, application deadline March 1. Application deadlines: MACP March 1; MAGP March 1. *Fee:* $20. $20 online; $30 paper.

Nova Southeastern University

Center for Psychological Studies
3301 College Avenue
Fort Lauderdale, FL 33314
Telephone: (954) 262-5700
Fax: (954) 262-3859
E-mail: *karol@nsu.nova.edu*
Web: *http://www.cps.nova.edu*

Department Information:

1967. Dean: Karen S. Grosby. Number of faculty: total—full-time 34, part-time 68; women—full-time 11, part-time 32; total—minority—full-time 6, part-time 11; women minority—full-time 3, part-time 6; faculty subject to the Americans With Disabilities Act 1.

Programs and Degrees Offered:

Listed in the following order: Program area, degree type (T if terminal Master's), number awarded 7/06–6/07. Mental Health Counseling MA/MS (Master of Arts/Science) (T) 113, Clinical Psychology PhD (Doctor of Philosophy) 15, Clinical Psychology PsyD (Doctor of Psychology) 54, Clinical Psychopharmacology MA/MS (Master of Arts/Science) (T) 0, School Guidance Counseling MA/MS (Master of Arts/Science) (T) 50, School Psychology Other 36, Counseling MA/MS (Master of Arts/Science) (T) 19.

APA Accreditation: Clinical PhD (Doctor of Philosophy). Clinical PsyD (Doctor of Psychology).

Student Applications/Admissions:

Student Applications

Mental Health Counseling MA/MS (Master of Arts/Science)—Applications 2007–2008, 201. Total applicants accepted 2007–2008, 132. Number full-time enrolled (new admits only) 2007–2008, 165. Total enrolled 2007–2008 full-time, 311, part-time, 34. Openings 2008–2009, 200. The median number of years required for completion of a degree in 2006–2007 were 3. The number of students enrolled full- and part-time who were dismissed or voluntarily withdrew from this program area in 2007–2008 were 15. *Clinical Psychology PhD (Doctor of Philosophy)*—Applications 2007–2008, 115. Total applicants accepted 2007–2008, 30. Number full-time enrolled (new admits only) 2007–2008, 22. Number part-time enrolled (new admits only) 2007–2008, 0. Openings 2008–2009, 16. The median number of years required for completion of a degree in 2006–2007 were 6. The number of students enrolled full- and part-time who were dismissed or voluntarily withdrew from this program area in 2007–2008 were 1. *Clinical Psychology PsyD (Doctor of Psychology)*—Applications 2007–2008, 232. Total applicants accepted 2007–2008, 154. Number full-time enrolled (new admits only) 2007–2008, 73. Number part-time enrolled (new admits only) 2007–2008, 0. Openings 2008–2009, 72. The median number of years required for completion of a degree in 2006–2007 were 5. The number of students enrolled full- and part-time who were dismissed or voluntarily withdrew from this program area in 2007–2008 were 8. *Clinical Psychopharmacology MA/MS (Master of Arts/Science)*—Applications 2007–2008, 20. Total applicants accepted 2007–2008, 20. Number full-time enrolled (new admits only) 2007–2008,

20. Number part-time enrolled (new admits only) 2007–2008, 0. Openings 2008–2009, 25. The median number of years required for completion of a degree in 2006–2007 were 2. The number of students enrolled full- and part-time who were dismissed or voluntarily withdrew from this program area in 2007–2008 were 8. *School Guidance Counseling MA/MS (Master of Arts/Science)*—Applications 2007–2008, 214. Total applicants accepted 2007–2008, 128. Number full-time enrolled (new admits only) 2007–2008, 78. Number part-time enrolled (new admits only) 2007–2008, 0. Total enrolled 2007–2008 full-time, 191. Openings 2008–2009, 150. The median number of years required for completion of a degree in 2006–2007 were 2. The number of students enrolled full- and part-time who were dismissed or voluntarily withdrew from this program area in 2007–2008 were 0. *School Psychology Other*—Applications 2007–2008, 92. Total applicants accepted 2007–2008, 43. Number full-time enrolled (new admits only) 2007–2008, 52. Number part-time enrolled (new admits only) 2007–2008, 0. Openings 2008–2009, 55. The median number of years required for completion of a degree in 2006–2007 were 4. The number of students enrolled full- and part-time who were dismissed or voluntarily withdrew from this program area in 2007–2008 were 18. *Counseling MA/MS (Master of Arts/Science)*—Applications 2007–2008, 98. Total applicants accepted 2007–2008, 52. Number full-time enrolled (new admits only) 2007–2008, 115. Number part-time enrolled (new admits only) 2007–2008, 0. Openings 2008–2009, 120. The median number of years required for completion of a degree in 2006–2007 were 3. The number of students enrolled full- and part-time who were dismissed or voluntarily withdrew from this program area in 2007–2008 were 21.

Admissions Requirements:

Scores: Entries appear in this order: required test or GPA, minimum score (if required), median score of students entering in 2007–2008. Doctoral Programs: GRE-V no minimum stated, 523; GRE-Q no minimum stated, 606; overall undergraduate GPA 3.0, 3.4. GRE-V + Q > 1000 is preferred. GPA requirement may be satisfied by a Master's GPA> 3.5. GRE-P is recommended, but not required.

Other Criteria: (importance of criteria rated low, medium, or high): GRE/MAT scores—high, work experience—medium, extracurricular activity—low, clinically related public service—medium, GPA—high, letters of recommendation—high, interview—high, statement of goals and objectives—high. The importance of research is high for the PhD program.

Student Characteristics: The following represents characteristics of students in 2007–2008 in all graduate psychology programs in the department: Female—full-time 1014, part-time 0; Male—full-time 205, part-time 0; African American/Black—full-time 278, part-time 0; Hispanic/Latino(a)—full-time 269, part-time 0; Asian/Pacific Islander—full-time 30, part-time 0; American Indian/Alaska Native—full-time 5, part-time 0; Caucasian/White—full-time 794, part-time 0; Multi-ethnic—full-time 2, part-time 0; students subject to the Americans With Disabilities Act—full-time 8, part-time 0; Unknown ethnicity—full-time 71, part-time 0; International students who hold an F-1 or J-1 Visa—full-time 24, part-time 0.

Financial Information/Assistance:

Tuition for Full-Time Study: *Master's:* State residents: $525 per credit hour; Nonstate residents: $525 per credit hour. *Doctoral:* State residents: $815 per credit hour; Nonstate residents: $815 per credit hour. Tuition is subject to change. Additional fees are assessed to students beyond the costs of tuition for the following: online counseling program—one-time fee $750 for practicum. Tuition costs vary by program. See the following Web site for updates and changes in tuition costs: http://www.cps.nova.edu. Higher tuition cost for this program: Specialist in School Psychology, $580 per credit hour.

Financial Assistance:

First-Year Students: Research assistantships available for first year. Average amount paid per academic year: $5,600. Average number of hours worked per week: 15.

Advanced Students: Teaching assistantships available for advanced students. Average amount paid per academic year: $2,000. Average number of hours worked per week: 6. Research assistantships available for advanced students. Average amount paid per academic year: $5,600. Average number of hours worked per week: 15. Traineeships available for advanced students. Average amount paid per academic year: $5,800. Average number of hours worked per week: 15. Fellowships and scholarships available for advanced students. Apply by varies. Tuition remission given: partial.

Additional Information: Of all students currently enrolled full time, 12% benefited from one or more of the listed financial assistance programs. Assistantship and scholarship information available at http://www.cps.nova.edu.

Internships/Practica: Doctoral Degree (PhD Clinical Psychology): For those doctoral students for whom a professional internship was required in this program prior to graduation, (17) students applied for an internship in 2006–2007, with (16) students obtaining an internship. Of those students who obtained an internship, (16) were paid internships. Of those students who obtained an internship, (14) students placed in APA/CPA-accredited internships, (2) students placed in internships not APA/CPA accredited, but listed with the Association of Psychology Postdoctoral and Internship Centers (APPIC), (0) students placed in internships conforming to guidelines of the Council of Directors of School Psychology Programs (CDSPP), (0) students placed in internships that were not APA/CPA-accredited, APPIC or CDSPP listed. Doctoral Degree (PsyD Clinical Psychology): For those doctoral students for whom a professional internship was required in this program prior to graduation, (62) students applied for an internship in 2006–2007, with (56) students obtaining an internship. Of those students who obtained an internship, (54) were paid internships. Of those students who obtained an internship, (38) students placed in APA/CPA-accredited internships, (18) students placed in internships not APA/CPA-accredited, but listed with the Association of Psychology Postdoctoral and Internship Centers (APPIC), (0) students placed in internships conforming to guidelines of the Council of Directors of School Psychology Programs (CDSPP), (0) students placed in internships that were not APA/CPA-accredited, APPIC or CDSPP listed. Accredited by the American Psychological Association, the Psychology Services Center Internship Program offers doctoral candidates in psychology the opportunity to develop professionally, to enhance their ability to use scholarly research for informed practice, to develop proficiency in psychological assessment and psychotherapeutic intervention, and to acquire basic competence in the provision of supervision and consultation. In addition, the Center for Psychological Studies sponsors the Consortium Internship Program (APPIC member) that provides internship experiences in hospital and other settings within the South Florida Community. In addition to the extensive practicum placements available in the community, practicum opportunities for more than 100 students are provided through various CPS faculty supervised, applied research clinical programs located within the NSU Psychology Services Center. Areas of research include ADHD, alcohol and substance abuse, anxiety treatment, child and adolescent traumatic stress, clinical biofeedback, interpersonal violence, neuropsychological assessment, older adults, school psychology assessment and testing, the seriously emotionally disturbed, and trauma resolution integration.

Housing and Day Care: On-campus housing is available. See the following Web site for more information regarding off-campus housing: http://www.nova.edu/cwis/studentaffairs/reslife. On-campus day care facilities are available. See the following Web site for more information: http://www.nova.edu/cwis/studentaffairs/reslife.

Employment of Department Graduates:

Master's Degree Graduates: Of those who graduated in the academic year 2006–2007, the following categories and numbers represent the postgraduate activities and employment of master's degree graduates: Enrolled in a psychology doctoral program (2), enrolled in a postdoctoral residency/fellowship (n/a), employed in independent practice (n/a), employed in a professional position in a school system (54), employed in a community mental health/counseling center (2), other employment position (1), total from the above (master's) (59).

Doctoral Degree Graduates: Of those who graduated in the academic year 2006–2007, the following categories and numbers represent the postgraduate activities and employment of doctoral degree graduates: Enrolled in a psychology doctoral program (n/a), enrolled in a postdoctoral residency/fellowship (31), employed in independent practice (7), employed in an academic position at a university (4), employed in other positions at a higher education institution (3), employed in a professional position in a school system (3), employed in business or industry (2), employed in government agency (4), employed in a community mental health/counseling center (6), employed in a hospital/medical center (6), other employment position (4), do not know (2), total from the above (doctoral) (72).

Additional Information:

Orientation, Objectives, and Emphasis of Department: The Center for Psychological Studies (CPS) is committed to providing the highest quality educational experience to future psychologists and counseling professionals. These training experiences provide individuals with a sophisticated understanding of psychological research and the delivery of the highest quality mental health care. Through the intimate interplay between CPS academic programs and the Nova Southeastern University (NSU) Psychology Services Center, learning becomes rooted in real problems, and research activities attempt to find answers to extant concerns. The center offers master's programs in counseling, mental health counseling, school guidance and counseling, clinical psychopharmacology, and a specialist program (PsyS) in school psychology, two APA-accredited doctoral programs in clinical psychology. The doctor of psychology (PsyD) program provides emphasis on training professionals to do service while the doctor of philosophy (PhD) program provides greater emphasis on applied research. In response to changes in health care delivery and the profession of psychology, the center developed concentrations at the doctoral level. Concentrations/tracks based on the existing PsyD and PhD curriculum are available in the areas of Clinical Neuropsychology, Clinical Health Psychology, Forensic Psychology, Psychodynamic Psychology, Psychology of Long-Term Mental Illness, Multicultural/diversity, and Child, Adolescent, and Family.

Special Facilities or Resources: The Center for Psychological Studies is housed in the Maltz Psychology Building, a 65,000 sq. ft. facility that includes classrooms with state-of-the-art computer technology, a microcomputer lab with 30 multimedia computers connected to major databases and the Internet, study carrels, lounges and meeting rooms, and the Psychology Services Center where there are therapy rooms with audio and video monitoring capability, play-therapy rooms, and workstations for practicum students assigned to faculty specialty clinical programs. As a university-based professional school, CPS provides access to the NSU 325,000 sq. ft. Library, Research, and Information Technology Center, as well as NSU's Schools of Law, Business, and Systemic Studies; the colleges of its Health Professions Division (Medicine, Dentistry, Pharmacy, Allied Health, and Optometry); and its Family and School Center. Also included on NSU's 232-acre campus are five residence halls, recreation facilities, and the Miami Dolphins Training Center.

Application Information:

Send to Enrollment Processing Services, Attn: Center for Psychological Studies, P.O. Box 299000, Ft. Lauderdale, FL 33329-9905. URL of online application: http://www.cps.nova.edu/. Students are admitted in the Fall, application deadline January 8. Applications for the doctoral programs are accepted only for the Fall; the deadline is January 8. Application deadlines for master's and school psychology programs vary by site. Visit our Web site at http://www.cps.nova.edu for further information. *Fee:* $50.

South Florida, University of

Department of Psychological and Social Foundations
College of Education
EDU 162
Tampa, FL 33620-7750
Telephone: (813) 974-3246
Fax: (813) 974-5814
E-mail: *kbradley@tempest.coedu.usf.edu*
Web: *http://www.coedu.usf.edu/schoolpsych*

Department Information:

1970. Interim Department Chair: Herbert Exum, PhD. Number of faculty: total—full-time 22; women—full-time 14; total—minority—full-time 7; women minority—full-time 3.

Programs and Degrees Offered:

Listed in the following order: Program area, degree type (T if terminal Master's), number awarded 7/06–6/07. School Psychology PhD (Doctor of Philosophy) 7, School Psychology EdS/MEd (School Psychology) 9.

APA Accreditation: School Psychology PhD (Doctor of Philosophy).

Student Applications/Admissions:

Student Applications

School Psychology PhD (Doctor of Philosophy)—Applications 2007–2008, 46. Total applicants accepted 2007–2008, 7. Number full-time enrolled (new admits only) 2007–2008, 6. Number part-time enrolled (new admits only) 2007–2008, 0. Openings 2008–2009, 6. The median number of years required for completion of a degree in 2006–2007 were 5. The number of students enrolled full- and part-time who were dismissed or voluntarily withdrew from this program area in 2007–2008 were 1. *School Psychology EdS/MEd (School Psychology)*—Applications 2007–2008, 49. Total applicants accepted 2007–2008, 4. Number full-time enrolled (new admits only) 2007–2008, 2. Number part-time enrolled (new admits only) 2007–2008, 0. Openings 2008–2009, 4. The median number of years required for completion of a degree in 2006–2007 were 3. The number of students enrolled full- and part-time who were dismissed or voluntarily withdrew from this program area in 2007–2008 were 0.

Admissions Requirements:

Scores: Entries appear in this order: required test or GPA, minimum score (if required), median score of students entering in 2007–2008. Master's Programs: GRE-V no minimum stated; GRE-Q no minimum stated; overall undergraduate GPA 3.0, 3.6; last 2 years GPA 3.0, 3.7. Doctoral Programs: GRE-V no minimum stated, 490; GRE-Q no minimum stated, 590; last 2 years GPA 3.00, 3.80; Doctoral program GRE-Analytic no minimum stated, 4.5.

Other Criteria: (importance of criteria rated low, medium, or high): GRE/MAT scores—medium, research experience—high, work experience—medium, extracurricular activity—medium, clinically related public service—medium, GPA—high, letters of recommendation—high, interview—high, statement of goals and objectives—high, writing sample—high, undergraduate major in psychology—medium, specific undergraduate psychology courses taken—high. For additional information on admission requirements, go to http://coedu.usf.edu/schoolpsych.

Student Characteristics: The following represents characteristics of students in 2007–2008 in all graduate psychology programs in the department: Female—full-time 45, part-time 0; Male—full-time 11, part-time 0; African American/Black—full-time 11, part-time 0; Hispanic/Latino(a)—full-time 5, part-time 0; Asian/Pacific Islander—full-time 1, part-time 0; American Indian/Alaska Native—full-time 0, part-time 0; Caucasian/White—full-time 33, part-time 0; Multi-ethnic—full-time 6, part-time 0; students subject to the Americans With Disabilities Act—full-time 0, part-time 0; Unknown ethnicity—full-time 0, part-time 0; International students who hold an F-1 or J-1 Visa—full-time 6, part-time 0.

Financial Information/Assistance:

Tuition for Full-Time Study: *Master's:* State residents: per academic year $9,904, $275 per credit hour; Nonstate residents: per academic year $33,085, $919 per credit hour. *Doctoral:* State residents: per academic year $9,904, $275 per credit hour; Nonstate residents: per academic year $33,085, $919 per credit hour. Tuition is subject to change. Additional fees are assessed to students beyond the costs of tuition for the following: Athletic fees, service fees, and student union fees. See the following Web site for updates and changes in tuition costs: http://www.registrar.usf.edu.

Financial Assistance:

First-Year Students: Research assistantships available for first year. Average amount paid per academic year: $10,200. Average number of hours worked per week: 16. Apply by May 1. Tuition remission given: partial. Fellowships and scholarships available for first year. Average amount paid per academic year: $10,000. Average number of hours worked per week: 0. Apply by February 15. Tuition remission given: full and partial.

Advanced Students: Teaching assistantships available for advanced students. Average amount paid per academic year: $10,200. Average number of hours worked per week: 16. Apply by May 1. Tuition remission given: partial. Research assistantships available for advanced students. Average amount paid per academic year: $10,200. Average number of hours worked per week: 16. Apply by May 1. Tuition remission given: partial. Fellowships and scholarships available for advanced students. Average amount paid per academic year: $10,000. Average number of hours worked per week: 0. Apply by February 15. Tuition remission given: full and partial.

Additional Information: Of all students currently enrolled full time, 100% benefited from one or more of the listed financial assistance programs. Application and information available online at http://www.coedu.usf.edu/schoolpsych.

Internships/Practica: Doctoral Degree (PhD School Psychology): For those doctoral students for whom a professional internship was required in this program prior to graduation, (8) students applied for an internship in 2006–2007, with (8) students obtaining an internship. Of those students who obtained an internship, (8) were paid internships. Of those students who obtained an internship, (2) students placed in APA/CPA-accredited internships, (0) students placed in internships not APA/CPA accredited, but listed with the Association of Psychology Postdoctoral and Internship Centers (APPIC), (6) students placed in internships conforming to guidelines of the Council of Directors of School Psychology Programs (CDSPP), (0) students placed in internships that were not APA/CPA-accredited, APPIC or CDSPP listed. Our practica and internships integrate home, school, and community service programs for students at risk for educational failure and their families, including students with disabilities. We focus especially on the priorities of researching and promoting effective educational and mental health practices for all children, youth, and their families. All doctoral students participate in practica during the first three years of the program. Practica settings include schools (public, charter, alternative), hospital settings, research settings, special agencies (e.g., Tampa Children's Cancer Center) and special programs (e.g., Early Intervention Program). Doctoral students participate in approximately 1,000 hours of practicum prior to internship. All doctoral students complete a 2,000-hour predoctoral internship in an APA-accredited/APPIC site or one that meets the APA/APPIC criteria. For additional information on education and training outcomes for our programs, see the following Web site: http://www.coedu.usf.edu/schoolpsych/.

Housing and Day Care: On-campus housing is available. See the following Web site for more information: http://www.reserv.usf.edu. On-campus day care facilities are available. See the following

Web site for more information: http://www.usf.edu/about-usf/child-care.asp.

Employment of Department Graduates:

Master's Degree Graduates: Of those who graduated in the academic year 2006–2007, the following categories and numbers represent the postgraduate activities and employment of master's degree graduates: Enrolled in a psychology doctoral program (4), enrolled in a postdoctoral residency/fellowship (n/a), employed in independent practice (n/a), total from the above (master's) (4). ***Doctoral Degree Graduates:*** Of those who graduated in the academic year 2006–2007, the following categories and numbers represent the postgraduate activities and employment of doctoral degree graduates: Enrolled in a psychology doctoral program (n/a), employed in independent practice (1), employed in an academic position at a university (1), employed in a professional position in a school system (5), total from the above (doctoral) (7).

Additional Information:

Orientation, Objectives, and Emphasis of Department: Thorough admissions procedures result in the selection of outstanding students. This makes possible a faculty commitment to do everything possible to guide each student to a high level of professional competence. The curriculum is well organized and explicit such that students are always aware of program expectations and their progress in relation to these expectations. The student body is kept small, resulting in greater student–faculty contact than would otherwise be possible. Skills of practice are developed through nonthreatening apprenticeship networks established with local school systems. This model encourages students to assist several professors and practicing school psychologists throughout their training. The notion here is to provide positive environments, containing rich feedback, in which competent psychological skills develop. We emphasize a scientist–practitioner model representing primarily a cognitive–behavioral orientation. Further, we support comprehensive school psychology, including consultation, prevention, intervention, and program evaluation.

Special Facilities or Resources: The University of South Florida is a comprehensive Research I (FL) and Doctoral/Research Universities-Extensive (Carnegie) university that has over 44,000 students on a 1,700 acre campus 10 miles northeast of downtown Tampa, a city of over 350,000 people. Amongst its faculty, the School Psychology Program has one APA Fellows, two past presidents of the National Association of School Psychologists, and faculty who have received over $25 million in federal and state grants over the past years. Students collaborate with professors and researchers in the program, the College of Education, Departments of Psychology and Psychiatry, the Florida Mental Health Institute, the Department of Pediatrics, Shriner's Hospital, Tampa General and St. Joseph's hospitals, the Florida Department of Education, and other settings. The program is housed in a new College of Education physical plant that has the latest fiber optic based technology, clinical and research observation areas, and strong technology support. Strong links exist with community schools and agencies.

Information for Students With Physical Disabilities: See the following Web site for more information: http://www.usf.edu/sds.

Application Information:

Send to Linda Raffaele Mendez, Coordinator of Admissions, School Psychology Program, EDU 162, University of South Florida, Tampa, FL 33620-7750. Application available online. URL of online application: http://www.grad.usf.edu. Students are admitted in the Fall, application deadline January 1. All application materials should be submitted directly to the Coordinator of Admissions, School Psychology Program (address above). *Fee:* $30. Contact Program Director/Admissions Coordinator, School Psychology Program (raffaele @tempest.coedu.usf.edu).

South Florida, University of

Department of Psychology
Arts and Sciences
4202 East Fowler Avenue, PCD 4118G
Tampa, FL 33620-7200
Telephone: (813) 974-2492
Fax: (813) 974-4617
E-mail: *lpierce@cas.usf.edu*
Web: *http://www.psychology.usf.edu/*

Department Information:

1964. Chairperson: Emanuel Donchin. Number of faculty: total—full-time 36; women—full-time 11; total—minority—full-time 3; women minority—full-time 1.

Programs and Degrees Offered:

Listed in the following order: Program area, degree type (T if terminal Master's), number awarded 7/06–6/07. Clinical PhD (Doctor of Philosophy) 10, Cognition, Neurocience, and Social Psychology PhD (Doctor of Philosophy) 1, Industrial/Organizational PhD (Doctor of Philosophy) 10.

APA Accreditation: Clinical PhD (Doctor of Philosophy).

Student Applications/Admissions:

Student Applications

Clinical PhD (Doctor of Philosophy)—Applications 2007–2008, 237. Total applicants accepted 2007–2008, 13. Number full-time enrolled (new admits only) 2007–2008, 7. Number part-time enrolled (new admits only) 2007–2008, 0. Openings 2008–2009, 7. The median number of years required for completion of a degree in 2006–2007 were 6. The number of students enrolled full- and part-time who were dismissed or voluntarily withdrew from this program area in 2007–2008 were 1. *Cognition, Neurocience, and Social Psychology PhD (Doctor of Philosophy)*—Applications 2007–2008, 60. Total applicants accepted 2007–2008, 7. Number full-time enrolled (new admits only) 2007–2008, 4. Number part-time enrolled (new admits only) 2007–2008, 0. Openings 2008–2009, 5. The median number of years required for completion of a degree in 2006–2007 were 12. The number of students enrolled full- and part-time who were dismissed or voluntarily withdrew from this program area in 2007–2008 were 0. *Industrial/Organizational PhD (Doctor of Philosophy)*—Applications 2007–2008, 107. Total applicants accepted 2007–2008, 15. Number full-time enrolled (new admits only) 2007–2008, 8. Number part-time enrolled (new admits only) 2007–2008, 0. Openings 2008–2009, 5. The median number of years required for completion of a degree in 2006–2007 were 6. The number of students enrolled full- and part-time who were dismissed or voluntarily withdrew from this program area in 2007–2008 were 0.

Admissions Requirements:

Scores: Entries appear in this order: required test or GPA, minimum score (if required), median score of students entering in 2007–2008. Doctoral Programs: GRE-V 500, 600; GRE-Q 600, 720; last 2 years GPA 3.00, 3.91; Doctoral program GRE-Analytic no minimum stated, 5.0. Our Clinical Program recommends that GRE-Subject (Psychology) be taken.

Other Criteria: (importance of criteria rated low, medium, or high): GRE/MAT scores—high, research experience—high, work experience—low, clinically related public service—low, GPA—high, letters of recommendation—high, interview—medium, statement of goals and objectives—high. For additional information on admission requirements, go to http://psychology.usf.edu/grad/admission/adminreq/.

Student Characteristics: The following represents characteristics of students in 2007–2008 in all graduate psychology programs in the department: Female—full-time 82, part-time 0; Male—full-time 47, part-time 0; African American/Black—full-time 5, part-time 0; Hispanic/Latino(a)—full-time 8, part-time 0; Asian/Pacific Islander—full-time 10, part-time 0; American Indian/Alaska Native—full-time 0, part-time 0; Caucasian/White—full-time 106, part-time 0; Multi-ethnic—full-time 0, part-time 0; students subject to the Americans With Disabilities Act—full-time 2, part-time 0; Unknown ethnicity—full-time 0, part-time 0; International students who hold an F-1 or J-1 Visa—full-time 17, part-time 0.

Financial Information/Assistance:

Tuition for Full-Time Study: *Master's:* State residents: per academic year $6,602, $275 per credit hour; Nonstate residents: per academic year $22,056, $919 per credit hour. *Doctoral:* State residents: per academic year $4,951, $275 per credit hour; Nonstate residents: per academic year $16,542, $919 per credit hour. Tuition is subject to change. Additional fees are assessed to students beyond the costs of tuition for the following: $37 flat fee per semester and a one-time first semester new graduate student orientaton fee of $35. See the following Web site for updates and changes in tuition costs: http://www.usfweb.usf.edu/controller/cashaccounting/tuition.

Financial Assistance:

First-Year Students: Teaching assistantships available for first year. Average amount paid per academic year: $13,500. Average number of hours worked per week: 20. Tuition remission given: partial. Research assistantships available for first year. Average amount paid per academic year: $13,500. Average number of hours worked per week: 20. Tuition remission given: partial. Fellowships and scholarships available for first year. Average amount paid per academic year: $15,500. Average number of hours worked per week: 10. Tuition remission given: partial.

Advanced Students: Teaching assistantships available for advanced students. Average amount paid per academic year: $13,500. Average number of hours worked per week: 20. Tuition remission given: partial. Research assistantships available for advanced students. Average amount paid per academic year: $13,500. Average number of hours worked per week: 20. Tuition remission given: partial. Fellowships and scholarships available for advanced students. Average amount paid per academic year: $15,500. Average number of hours worked per week: 10. Tuition remission given: partial.

Additional Information: Of all students currently enrolled full time, 87% benefited from one or more of the listed financial assistance programs. No application needed for assistantships. For financial aid information, go to http://usfweb2.usf.edu/finaid/.

Internships/Practica: Doctoral Degree (PhD Clinical): For those doctoral students for whom a professional internship was required in this program prior to graduation, (4) students applied for an internship in 2006–2007, with (4) students obtaining an internship. Of those students who obtained an internship, (4) were paid internships. Of those students who obtained an internship, (4) students placed in APA/CPA-accredited internships, (0) students placed in internships not APA/CPA-accredited, but listed with the Association of Psychology Postdoctoral and Internship Centers (APPIC), (0) students placed in internships conforming to guidelines of the Council of Directors of School Psychology Programs (CDSPP), (0) students placed in internships that were not APA/CPA-accredited, APPIC or CDSPP listed. Doctoral Degree (PhD Industrial/Organizational): For those doctoral students for whom a professional internship was required in this program prior to graduation, (3) students applied for an internship in 2006–2007, with (3) students obtaining an internship. Of those students who obtained an internship, (3) were paid internships. Of those students who obtained an internship, (0) students placed in APA/CPA-accredited internships, (0) students placed in internships not APA/CPA-accredited, but listed with the Association of Psychology Postdoctoral and Internship Centers (APPIC), (0) students placed in internships conforming to guidelines of the Council of Directors of School Psychology Programs (CDSPP), (3) students placed in internships that were not APA/CPA accredited, APPIC or CDSPP listed. The Clinical Program operates its own Psychology Clinic within the Psychology Department, providing opportunities for practical training in clinical assessment and clinical psychological interventions. Students are active in the Psychology Clinic throughout their training. Clinical core faculty provide most of the supervision of clinic cases. The Clinical Psychology Program is fortunate to have a unique cluster of campus and community training facilities available for student placement. For example, we have student placements at or near such campus facilities as the USF Florida Mental Health Research Institute, the USF Counseling Center for Human Development, the Moffitt Cancer Center and Research Institute, and the Tampa Veterans Administration Hospital, as well as carefully selected community agencies. Students in the Industrial/Organizational Program are required to complete a predoctoral internship. Placements are made in numerous governmental, corporate, and consulting firms both locally and nationally. Recent placements have included Cities of Tampa and Clearwater, GTE, Tampa Electric Company, Personnel Decisions Research Institute, Personnel Decisions, Inc., Florida Power, and USF&G.

Housing and Day Care: On-campus housing is available. See the following Web site for more information: http://www.housing.usf.edu/. On-campus day care facilities are available. See the following Web site for more information: http://www.usf.edu/About-USF/child-care.asp.

Employment of Department Graduates:

Master's Degree Graduates: Of those who graduated in the academic year 2006–2007, the following categories and numbers represent the postgraduate activities and employment of master's degree graduates: Enrolled in a postdoctoral residency/fellowship

(n/a), employed in independent practice (n/a), total from the above (master's) (0).

Doctoral Degree Graduates: Of those who graduated in the academic year 2006–2007, the following categories and numbers represent the postgraduate activities and employment of doctoral degree graduates: Enrolled in a psychology doctoral program (n/a), enrolled in a postdoctoral residency/fellowship (4), employed in independent practice (0), employed in an academic position at a university (5), employed in an academic position at a 2-year/4-year college (1), employed in other positions at a higher education institution (2), employed in business or industry (7), employed in a hospital/medical center (1), still seeking employment (1), total from the above (doctoral) (21).

Additional Information:

Orientation, Objectives, and Emphasis of Department: The department attempts to educate graduate students to a high level of proficiency in research and in practice. The department expects its doctoral students to be of such quality as to take their place at major institutions of learning if they choose academic careers and to assume roles of responsibility and importance if they choose professional careers. The doctoral program in clinical psychology provides broad-based professional and research training to prepare students for careers in a variety of applied, research, and teaching settings. The doctoral program in cognition, neuroscience, and social psychology prepares students for research careers in both applied and academic environments. This program also offers an interdisciplinary degree in Speech, Language, and Hearing Science, which is offered in conjunction with the Department of Communication Sciences and Disorders. The doctoral program in Industrial/Organizational Psychology provides professional and research training to prepare students for careers in industrial, governmental, academic, and related organizational settings.

Special Facilities or Resources: State-of-the-art facilities and equipment houses the Psychology Department. There is ample research space for faculty, graduate, and advanced undergraduate students, including a large vivarium. An open-use lab has been equipped with computer terminals that access the mainframe computer on campus. The University Computer Center is available. The Psychological Services Center is operated as the department's facility for clinical practicum work. A state-of-the-art video system permits supervisory capabilities for clinical practica.

Information for Students With Physical Disabilities: See the following Web site for more information: http://www.usfweb2.usf.edu/SDS/.

Application Information:

Send to Graduate Admissions Coordinator, Psychology Department, University of South Florida, 4202 East Fowler Avenue, PCD4118G, Tampa, FL 33620-7200. Application available online. URL of online application: http://www.grad.usf.edu/newsite/admissions/grad_app.asp. Students are admitted in the Fall, application deadline December 15 and January 15. Clinical deadline for international and U.S. residents is December 15. CNS and I/O deadlines are January 2 for international and January 15 for U.S. residents. *Fee:* $30. McNair Scholars Program, FAMU Feeder Program, RISE Program, USTAR-MARC Program. Application Fee Waiver Verification Request Form submission required prior to application submission.

West Florida, The University of

Department of Psychology
College of Arts and Sciences
11000 University Parkway
Pensacola, FL 32514-5751
Telephone: (850) 474-2363
Fax: (850) 857-6060
E-mail: *psych@uwf.edu*
Web: *http://www.uwf.edu/psychology*

Department Information:

1967. Chairperson: Laura L. Koppes. Number of faculty: total—full-time 14, part-time 1; women—full-time 5.

Programs and Degrees Offered:

Listed in the following order: Program area, degree type (T if terminal Master's), number awarded 7/06–6/07. Counseling Psychology MA/MS (Master of Arts/Science) (T) 7, General Psychology MA/MS (Master of Arts/Science) (T) 5, Industrial/Organizational Psychology MA/MS (Master of Arts/Science) (T) 9.

Student Applications/Admissions:

Student Applications

Counseling Psychology MA/MS (Master of Arts/Science)—Applications 2007–2008, 54. Total applicants accepted 2007–2008, 21. Number full-time enrolled (new admits only) 2007–2008, 14. Openings 2008–2009, 18. The median number of years required for completion of a degree in 2006–2007 were 2. The number of students enrolled full- and part-time who were dismissed or voluntarily withdrew from this program area in 2007–2008 were 6. *General Psychology MA/MS (Master of Arts/Science)*—Applications 2007–2008, 27. Total applicants accepted 2007–2008, 16. Number full-time enrolled (new admits only) 2007–2008, 10. Openings 2008–2009, 15. The median number of years required for completion of a degree in 2006–2007 were 2. The number of students enrolled full- and part-time who were dismissed or voluntarily withdrew from this program area in 2007–2008 were 3. *Industrial/Organizational Psychology MA/MS (Master of Arts/Science)*—Applications 2007–2008, 42. Total applicants accepted 2007–2008, 23. Number full-time enrolled (new admits only) 2007–2008, 7. Openings 2008–2009, 18. The median number of years required for completion of a degree in 2006–2007 were 2. The number of students enrolled full- and part-time who were dismissed or voluntarily withdrew from this program area in 2007–2008 were 1.

Admissions Requirements:

Scores: Entries appear in this order: required test or GPA, minimum score (if required), median score of students entering in 2007–2008. Master's Programs: GRE-V no minimum stated, 459; GRE-Q no minimum stated, 540; overall undergraduate GPA 3.00.

Other Criteria: (importance of criteria rated low, medium, or high): GRE/MAT scores—high, research experience—medium, work experience—medium, extracurricular activity—medium, clinically related public service—medium, GPA—high, letters of recommendation—high, interview—high, statement of goals and objectives—high, coursework—high, undergraduate major in psychology—high, specific undergraduate psychology courses taken—medium. Counseling applicants are required to comple an interview. For additional information on admission requirements, go to http://uwf.edu/psychology/graduate/.

Student Characteristics: The following represents characteristics of students in 2007–2008 in all graduate psychology programs in the department: Female—full-time 87, part-time 0; Male—full-time 25, part-time 0; African American/Black—full-time 10, part-time 0; Hispanic/Latino(a)—full-time 5, part-time 0; Asian/Pacific Islander—full-time 3, part-time 0; American Indian/Alaska Native—full-time 0, part-time 0; Caucasian/White—full-time 0, part-time 0; Multi-ethnic—full-time 0, part-time 0; students subject to the Americans With Disabilities Act—full-time 0, part-time 0; Unknown ethnicity—full-time 94, part-time 0; International students who hold an F-1 or J-1 Visa—full-time 3, part-time 0.

Financial Information/Assistance:

Tuition for Full-Time Study: *Master's:* State residents: $252 per credit hour; Nonstate residents: $912 per credit hour. Tuition is subject to change. See the following Web site for updates and changes in tuition costs: http://www.uwf.edu/enrserv/fees.htm.

Financial Assistance:

First-Year Students: Teaching assistantships available for first year. Average amount paid per academic year: $3,280. Average number of hours worked per week: 10. Apply by April 15. Tuition remission given: partial. Research assistantships available for first year. Average amount paid per academic year: $3,760. Average number of hours worked per week: 10. Apply by April 15. Tuition remission given: partial. Fellowships and scholarships available for first year. Average amount paid per academic year: $2,000. Apply by April 15.

Advanced Students: Teaching assistantships available for advanced students. Average amount paid per academic year: $3,760. Average number of hours worked per week: 10. Apply by April 15. Tuition remission given: partial. Fellowships and scholarships available for advanced students. Average amount paid per academic year: $750. Apply by April 15.

Additional Information: Of all students currently enrolled full time, 65% benefited from one or more of the listed financial assistance programs.

Internships/Practica: Master's students may elect either thesis or 600-hour internship (850-hour for mental health counseling licensure option). Faculty assist in finding suitable placements in field settings under qualified supervision. The student also prepares a portfolio demonstrating mastery of several specific competencies and includes an integrative paper reflecting on professional development. Practica (required for counseling students, optional for other students) are completed earlier in the program and involve more limited applied experience and closer supervision by faculty. Internship placements for Counseling students include a variety of local mental health agencies providing inpatient, outpatient and community outreach services. Internship placements for Industrial/Organizational students include a variety of business and healthcare settings.

Housing and Day Care: On-campus housing is available. See the following Web site for more information: http://www.uwf.edu/housing/. On-campus day care facilities are available. See the following Web site for more information: http://www.uwf.edu/childdev.

Employment of Department Graduates:

Master's Degree Graduates: Of those who graduated in the academic year 2006–2007, the following categories and numbers represent the postgraduate activities and employment of master's degree graduates: Enrolled in a psychology doctoral program (4), enrolled in a postdoctoral residency/fellowship (n/a), employed in independent practice (n/a), employed in business or industry (9), employed in government agency (1), employed in a community mental health/counseling center (7), total from the above (master's) (21).

Doctoral Degree Graduates: Of those who graduated in the academic year 2006–2007, the following categories and numbers represent the postgraduate activities and employment of doctoral degree graduates: Enrolled in a psychology doctoral program (n/a), total from the above (doctoral) (0).

Additional Information:

Orientation, Objectives, and Emphasis of Department: The department is a member of the Council of Applied Master's Programs in Psychology and is committed to the philosophy of training with a foundation in general psychology (individual, social, biological, and learned bases of behavior) as the basis for training in application of psychology. Applied students receive significant supervised field experience. The departmental mission is preparation of master's level practitioners and preparation of students for doctoral work as well. The programs in Counseling Psychology and Industrial/Organizational Psychology are accredited by the Master's in Psychology Accreditation Council (MPAC). The department also offers a certificate in Health Psychology and Cognitive Psychology. The Counseling Psychology program offers a 60-hour option with coursework comparable to requirements for licensure as a Mental Health Counselor in Florida.

Special Facilities or Resources: The department is housed in a modern, 22,000 sq. ft. building with excellent research facilities, including a neurocognition lab with a 128-channel Neuroscan ESI System. The University of West Florida Center for Applied Psychology (CAP) is a consulting group within the Department of Psychology aimed at optimizing human performance across the lifespan in educational, health, and workplace contexts. Other University resources include Institute for Business and Economic Research and the Institute for Human and Machine Cognition. We have links with CMHCs and local health/mental health professionals and organizations. Community resources include three major hospitals and a large Naval training facility. The department hosts student chapters of Psi Chi, Society for Human Resource Management (SHRM), and Student Psychological Association.

Information for Students With Physical Disabilities: See the following Web site for more information: http://www.uwf.edu/dss/.

Application Information:

Send to Department of Psychology, Graduate Admissions, University of West Florida, 11000 University Parkway, Pensacola, FL 32514-5751. Application available online. URL of online application: http://www.uwf.edu/admissions/gap.htm. Students are admitted in the Fall, application deadline February 1; Summer, application deadline February 1. GREQ, GREV required by February 1. Departmental Supplemental Form, letter of intent, and three letters of recommendation required by February 1. Counseling applicants with complete applications are required to complete a formal interview. *Fee:* $30.

Argosy University/Atlanta

Clinical Psychology
Georgia School of Professional Psychology
980 Hammond Drive, Building 2, Suite 100
Atlanta, GA 30328
Telephone: (888) 671-4777
Fax: (770) 671-0476
E-mail: *tcbrown@argosy.edu*
Web: *http://www.argosy.edu*

Department Information:

1990. Chairperson: Timothy C. Brown, PhD. Number of faculty: total—full-time 15, part-time 2; women—full-time 9, part-time 1; total—minority—full-time 3; women minority—full-time 2.

Programs and Degrees Offered:

Listed in the following order: Program area, degree type (T if terminal Master's), number awarded 7/06–6/07. Clinical Psychology MA/MS (Master of Arts/Science) (T) 15, Clinical Psychology PsyD (Doctor of Psychology) 26.

APA Accreditation: Clinical PsyD (Doctor of Psychology).

Student Applications/Admissions:

Student Applications

Clinical Psychology MA/MS (Master of Arts/Science)—Applications 2007–2008, 52. Total applicants accepted 2007–2008, 29. Number full-time enrolled (new admits only) 2007–2008, 17. Number part-time enrolled (new admits only) 2007–2008, 0. Total enrolled 2007–2008 full-time, 29, part-time, 6. Openings 2008–2009, 15. The median number of years required for completion of a degree in 2006–2007 were 2. The number of students enrolled full- and part-time who were dismissed or voluntarily withdrew from this program area in 2007–2008 were 3. *Clinical Psychology PsyD (Doctor of Psychology)*—Applications 2007–2008, 182. Total applicants accepted 2007–2008, 75. Number full-time enrolled (new admits only) 2007–2008, 48. Number part-time enrolled (new admits only) 2007–2008, 0. Total enrolled 2007–2008 full-time, 129, part-time, 109. Openings 2008–2009, 50. The median number of years required for completion of a degree in 2006–2007 were 6. The number of students enrolled full- and part-time who were dismissed or voluntarily withdrew from this program area in 2007–2008 were 10.

Admissions Requirements:

Scores: Entries appear in this order: required test or GPA, minimum score (if required), median score of students entering in 2007–2008. Master's Programs: overall undergraduate GPA 3.0. Doctoral Programs: overall undergraduate GPA 3.25, 3.35.
Other Criteria: (importance of criteria rated low, medium, or high): GRE/MAT scores—medium, research experience—low, work experience—high, extracurricular activity—low, clinically related public service—high, GPA—high, letters of recommendation—medium, interview—high, statement of goals and objectives—high. For additional information on admission requirements, go to http://www.argosy.edu.

Student Characteristics: The following represents characteristics of students in 2007–2008 in all graduate psychology programs in the department: Female—full-time 132, part-time 91; Male—full-time 26, part-time 24; African American/Black—full-time 31, part-time 23; Hispanic/Latino(a)—full-time 4, part-time 2; Asian/Pacific Islander—full-time 4, part-time 3; American Indian/Alaska Native—full-time 1, part-time 1; Caucasian/White—full-time 114, part-time 82; Multi-ethnic—full-time 0, part-time 0; students subject to the Americans With Disabilities Act—full-time 5, part-time 0; Unknown ethnicity—full-time 4, part-time 4; International students who hold an F-1 or J-1 Visa—full-time 2, part-time 0.

Financial Information/Assistance:

Tuition for Full-Time Study: *Master's:* State residents: $895 per credit hour; Nonstate residents: $895 per credit hour. *Doctoral:* State residents: $895 per credit hour; Nonstate residents: $895 per credit hour. Tuition is subject to change. See the following Web site for updates and changes in tuition costs: http://www.argosy.edu.

Financial Assistance:

First-Year Students: Research assistantships available for first year. Average amount paid per academic year: $1,000. Average number of hours worked per week: 5. Apply by anytime. Fellowships and scholarships available for first year. Average amount paid per academic year: $3,000. Average number of hours worked per week: 0. Apply by June 30.

Advanced Students: Teaching assistantships available for advanced students. Average amount paid per academic year: $1,500. Average number of hours worked per week: 7. Apply by September 1. Research assistantships available for advanced students. Average amount paid per academic year: $1,000. Average number of hours worked per week: 5. Apply by anytime. Fellowships and scholarships available for advanced students. Average amount paid per academic year: $3,000. Average number of hours worked per week: 0. Apply by June 30.

Additional Information: Of all students currently enrolled full time, 30% benefited from one or more of the listed financial assistance programs. Application and information available online at http://www.argosy.edu.

Internships/Practica: Doctoral Degree (PsyD Clinical Psychology): For those doctoral students for whom a professional internship was required in this program prior to graduation, (38) students applied for an internship in 2006–2007, with (28) students obtaining an internship. Of those students who obtained an internship, (27) were paid internships. Of those students who obtained an internship, (23) students placed in APA/CPA-accredited internships, (5) students placed in internships not APA/CPA accredited, but listed with the Association of Psychology Postdoctoral and Internship Centers (APPIC), (0) students placed in internships conforming to guidelines of the Council of Directors of School Psychology Programs (CDSPP), (0) students placed in internships that were not APA/CPA-accredited, APPIC or

CDSPP listed. Practica and internship involve supervised clinical field training in which students work with clinical populations in health delivery settings. Practica offer opportunities to apply classroom knowledge, increase assessment and therapeutic skills, and develop professional and personal attitudes important to the identity of a professional psychologist. Although all doctoral students complete a minimum of 2 years of practicum training, many elect to complete an additional 1-year advanced practicum to gain further experience before internship. Students are placed at a diverse set of training sites formally affiliated with the MA and PsyD programs. The specific content and training vary according to the setting and expertise of supervisors. Training sites include state mental health facilities, outpatient clinics, private psychiatric hospitals, psychiatric units in community hospitals, university counseling centers, and private practice settings, as well as treatment facilities for developmentally disabled, behavior disordered, and/or emotionally disturbed adults and children. In addition, a variety of specialized placements are available in facilities such as children's/pediatric hospitals, treatment centers for eating disorders, and neuropsychiatric rehabilitation programs.

Housing and Day Care: No on-campus housing is available. No on-campus day care facilities are available.

Employment of Department Graduates:

Master's Degree Graduates: Of those who graduated in the academic year 2006–2007, the following categories and numbers represent the postgraduate activities and employment of master's degree graduates: Enrolled in a psychology doctoral program (5), enrolled in another graduate/professional program (2), enrolled in a postdoctoral residency/fellowship (n/a), employed in independent practice (n/a), employed in a community mental health/counseling center (2), still seeking employment (2), do not know (4), total from the above (master's) (15).

Doctoral Degree Graduates: Of those who graduated in the academic year 2006–2007, the following categories and numbers represent the postgraduate activities and employment of doctoral degree graduates: Enrolled in a psychology doctoral program (n/a), enrolled in a postdoctoral residency/fellowship (20), employed in a community mental health/counseling center (1), employed in a hospital/medical center (1), do not know (4), total from the above (doctoral) (26).

Additional Information:

Orientation, Objectives, and Emphasis of Department: The primary purpose of the Clinical Psychology doctoral program is to educate and train students in the major aspects of clinical practice. The curriculum integrates theory, training, research, and practice, preparing graduates to work in a broad range of roles and to work with a wide range of populations in need of psychological services. Students who graduate from the doctoral program earn a Doctor of Psychology degree, indicating that the recipient has completed academic and training experiences essential to pursuing professional endeavors in the field of clinical psychology.

Special Facilities or Resources: See Internships/Practica.

Application Information:

Send to Office of Admissions, Argosy University, 980 Hammond Drive, Building 2, Suite 100, Atlanta, GA 30328. Applications may be submitted online. URL of online application: http://www.argosy.edu. Students are admitted in the Fall, application deadline January 15. *Fee:* $50.

Augusta State University

Department of Psychology
2500 Walton Way
Augusta, GA 30904-2200
Telephone: (706) 737-1694
Fax: (706) 737-1538
E-mail: *cbradley@aug.edu*
Web: *http://www.aug.edu/psychology/*

Department Information:

1963. Chairperson: Deborah S. Richardson. Number of faculty: total—full-time 11, part-time 11; women—full-time 7, part-time 3.

Programs and Degrees Offered:

Listed in the following order: Program area, degree type (T if terminal Master's), number awarded 7/06–6/07. Applied Psychology MA/MS (Master of Arts/Science) (T) 5, Experimental Psychology MA/MS (Master of Arts/Science) (T) 2.

Student Applications/Admissions:

Student Applications

Applied Psychology MA/MS (Master of Arts/Science)—Applications 2007–2008, 30. Total applicants accepted 2007–2008, 16. Number full-time enrolled (new admits only) 2007–2008, 11. Number part-time enrolled (new admits only) 2007–2008, 0. Openings 2008–2009, 16. The median number of years required for completion of a degree in 2006–2007 were 2. The number of students enrolled full- and part-time who were dismissed or voluntarily withdrew from this program area in 2007–2008 were 2. *Experimental Psychology MA/MS (Master of Arts/Science)*—Applications 2007–2008, 3. Total applicants accepted 2007–2008, 3. Number full-time enrolled (new admits only) 2007–2008, 3. Number part-time enrolled (new admits only) 2007–2008, 0. Openings 2008–2009, 6. The median number of years required for completion of a degree in 2006–2007 were 2. The number of students enrolled full- and part-time who were dismissed or voluntarily withdrew from this program area in 2007–2008 were 0.

Admissions Requirements:

Scores: Entries appear in this order: required test or GPA, minimum score (if required), median score of students entering in 2007–2008. Master's Programs: GRE-V 400*, 420; GRE-Q 450*, 500; overall undergraduate GPA 2.5, 3.10. *Applicant must have taken the Graduate Record Examination (GRE) within the past 5 years with a minimum score of 400 on one of the subtests and at least 450 on the remaining two. If the GRE was taken after October 1, 2002, the analytical score must be 3.5 or higher, one of the remaining scores must be 400 or better, and one score must reach 450 or better.

Other Criteria: (importance of criteria rated low, medium, or high): GRE/MAT scores—high, research experience—medium, work experience—medium, extracurricular activity—low, clinically related public service—low, GPA—high, letters of recommendation—high, statement of goals and objectives—medium.

Student Characteristics: The following represents characteristics of students in 2007–2008 in all graduate psychology programs

in the department: Female—full-time 21, part-time 0; Male—full-time 5, part-time 0; African American/Black—full-time 8, part-time 0; Hispanic/Latino(a)—full-time 0, part-time 0; Asian/Pacific Islander—full-time 0, part-time 0; American Indian/Alaska Native—full-time 0, part-time 0; Caucasian/White—full-time 18, part-time 0; Multi-ethnic—full-time 0, part-time 0; students subject to the Americans With Disabilities Act—full-time 0, part-time 0; Unknown ethnicity—full-time 0, part-time 0; International students who hold an F-1 or J-1 Visa—full-time 0, part-time 0.

Financial Information/Assistance:

Tuition for Full-Time Study: *Master's:* State residents: per academic year $4,221, $133 per credit hour; Nonstate residents: per academic year $14,391, $509 per credit hour. Tuition is subject to change. See the following Web site for updates and changes in tuition costs: http://www.aug.edu.

Financial Assistance:

First-Year Students: Traineeships available for first year. Average amount paid per academic year: $2,400. Average number of hours worked per week: 10. Tuition remission given: partial.

Advanced Students: Traineeships available for advanced students. Average amount paid per academic year: $2,400. Average number of hours worked per week: 10. Tuition remission given: partial.

Additional Information: Of all students currently enrolled full time, 75% benefited from one or more of the listed financial assistance programs. Application and information available online at http://www.aug.edu/psychology.

Internships/Practica: Institutions that provide unique opportunities for fieldwork and internship experiences include two Veterans Administration hospitals, a regional psychiatric hospital, the Medical College of Georgia, Gracewood State School and Hospital, Dwight David Eisenhower Medical Center, and various other agencies. Internships are also available in business, education, and private practice settings.

Housing and Day Care: On-campus housing is available. No on-campus day care facilities are available.

Employment of Department Graduates:

Master's Degree Graduates: Of those who graduated in the academic year 2006–2007, the following categories and numbers represent the postgraduate activities and employment of master's degree graduates: Enrolled in a psychology doctoral program (1), enrolled in another graduate/professional program (0), enrolled in a postdoctoral residency/fellowship (n/a), employed in independent practice (n/a), employed in an academic position at a university (0), employed in other positions at a higher education institution (1), employed in a professional position in a school system (1), employed in business or industry (0), employed in government agency (0), employed in a community mental health/counseling center (2), employed in a hospital/medical center (1), total from the above (master's) (6).

Doctoral Degree Graduates: Of those who graduated in the academic year 2006–2007, the following categories and numbers represent the postgraduate activities and employment of doctoral degree graduates: Enrolled in a psychology doctoral program (n/a), total from the above (doctoral) (0).

Additional Information:

Orientation, Objectives, and Emphasis of Department: The graduate program in psychology at Augusta State University provides intensive training oriented toward the local and regional job markets. A secondary emphasis of the program is to provide an opportunity for graduate work in experimental psychology. The MS program is, for most students, a 2-year program consisting of equal amounts of advanced experimental and theoretical coursework combined with courses relevant to professional psychology. Supervised internship experience in approved treatment or research facilities is also required.

Personal Behavior Statement: See http://www.aug.edu/psychology/Plagiarism.html.

Special Facilities or Resources: The department maintains an active human and animal research laboratory and a clinical facility with video taping and closed circuit television capabilities, and the university provides easy access to advanced computer resources. Students and faculty additionally engage in collaborative research at the Medical College of Georgia and Veterans Medical Center. Social and Developmental labs available for teaching and research.

Information for Students With Physical Disabilities: See the following Web site for more information: http://www.aug.edu/counseling_and_testing_center.

Application Information:

Send to Director of Graduate Studies, Department of Psychology, 2500 Walton Way, Augusta State University, Augusta, GA 30904-2200. Application available online. URL of online application: http://www.aug.edu/psychology/. Students are admitted in the Fall, application deadline June 1; Summer, application deadline Rolling. *Fee:* $30.

Emory University

Department of Psychology
532 Kilgo Circle Northeast
Atlanta, GA 30322
Telephone: (404) 727-7438
Fax: (404) 727-0372
E-mail: *paula.mitchell@emory.edu*
Web: *http://www.psychology.emory.edu/*

Department Information:

1945. Chairperson: Robyn Fivush. Number of faculty: total—full-time 39; women—full-time 17; total—minority—full-time 1.

Programs and Degrees Offered:

Listed in the following order: Program area, degree type (T if terminal Master's), number awarded 7/06–6/07. Clinical PhD (Doctor of Philosophy) 4, Cognition and Development PhD (Doctor of Philosophy) 2, Neuroscience and Animal Behavior PhD (Doctor of Philosophy) 1.

APA Accreditation: Clinical PhD (Doctor of Philosophy).

Student Applications/Admissions:

Student Applications

Clinical PhD (Doctor of Philosophy)—Applications 2007–2008, 238. Total applicants accepted 2007–2008, 7. Number full-time enrolled (new admits only) 2007–2008, 7. Number part-time enrolled (new admits only) 2007–2008, 0. Openings 2008–2009, 6. The median number of years required for completion of a degree in 2006–2007 were 6. The number of students enrolled full- and part-time who were dismissed or voluntarily withdrew from this program area in 2007–2008 were 0. *Cognition and Development PhD (Doctor of Philosophy)*—Applications 2007–2008, 45. Total applicants accepted 2007–2008, 5. Number full-time enrolled (new admits only) 2007–2008, 5. Openings 2008–2009, 12. The median number of years required for completion of a degree in 2006–2007 were 6. The number of students enrolled full- and part-time who were dismissed or voluntarily withdrew from this program area in 2007–2008 were 1. *Neuroscience and Animal Behavior PhD (Doctor of Philosophy)*—Applications 2007–2008, 64. Total applicants accepted 2007–2008, 2. Number full-time enrolled (new admits only) 2007–2008, 2. Number part-time enrolled (new admits only) 2007–2008, 0. Openings 2008–2009, 4. The median number of years required for completion of a degree in 2006–2007 were 6. The number of students enrolled full- and part-time who were dismissed or voluntarily withdrew from this program area in 2007–2008 were 0.

Admissions Requirements:

Scores: Entries appear in this order: required test or GPA, minimum score (if required), median score of students entering in 2007–2008. Doctoral Programs: GRE-V 600, 647; GRE-Q 600, 720; overall undergraduate GPA 3.5, 3.79; Doctoral program GRE-Analytic 4.5, 5.5. The Clinical program requires the verbal, quantitative, and analytical GRE scores. The Cognition and Development program and the Neuroscience and Animal Behavior program requires the verbal, quantitative, and analytical/written scores. For international students, the TOEFL score must be submitted as well.

Other Criteria: (importance of criteria rated low, medium, or high): GRE/MAT scores—high, research experience—high, work experience—low, extracurricular activity—low, clinically related public service—medium, GPA—high, letters of recommendation—high, interview—high, statement of goals and objectives—high, faculty interest—high, undergraduate major in psychology—high, specific undergraduate psychology courses taken—low. Faculty research interest is a big factor. Clinically related public service is less pertinent to the Cognition and Development and the Neuroscience and Animal Behavior programs. For additional information on admission requirements, go to http://www.psychology.emory.edu/graduate/admission.html.

Student Characteristics: The following represents characteristics of students in 2007–2008 in all graduate psychology programs in the department: Female—full-time 61, part-time 0; Male—full-time 19, part-time 0; African American/Black—full-time 7, part-time 0; Hispanic/Latino(a)—full-time 1, part-time 0; Asian/Pacific Islander—full-time 3, part-time 0; American Indian/Alaska Native—full-time 0, part-time 0; Caucasian/White—full-time 69, part-time 0; Multi-ethnic—full-time 0, part-time 0; students subject to the Americans With Disabilities Act—full-time 0, part-time 0; Unknown ethnicity—full-time 0, part-time 0; International students who hold an F-1 or J-1 Visa—full-time 3, part-time 0.

Financial Information/Assistance:

Tuition for Full-Time Study: *Doctoral:* State residents: per academic year $31,900, $1,440 per credit hour; Nonstate residents: per academic year $31,900, $1,440 per credit hour. Tuition is subject to change. See the following Web site for updates and changes in tuition costs: http://www.emory.edu/GSOAS/current/financial_information/tuition_fees/.

Financial Assistance:

First-Year Students: Fellowships and scholarships available for first year. Average amount paid per academic year: $19,125. Average number of hours worked per week: 20. Apply by January 3. Tuition remission given: full.

Advanced Students: Teaching assistantships available for advanced students. Average amount paid per academic year: $19,125. Average number of hours worked per week: 20. Apply by January 25. Tuition remission given: full. Fellowships and scholarships available for advanced students. Average amount paid per academic year: $19,125. Average number of hours worked per week: 20. Apply by varies. Tuition remission given: full.

Additional Information: Of all students currently enrolled full time, 100% benefited from one or more of the listed financial assistance programs. Application and information available online at: http://www.emory.edu/GSOAS/current/financial_information/.

Internships/Practica: Doctoral Degree (PhD Clinical): For those doctoral students for whom a professional internship was required in this program prior to graduation, (2) students applied for an internship in 2006–2007, with (2) students obtaining an internship. Of those students who obtained an internship, (2) were paid internships. Of those students who obtained an internship, (2) students placed in APA/CPA-accredited internships, (0) students placed in internships not APA/CPA-accredited, but listed with the Association of Psychology Postdoctoral and Internship Centers (APPIC), (0) students placed in internships conforming to guidelines of the Council of Directors of School Psychology Programs (CDSPP), (0) students placed in internships that were not APA/CPA-accredited, APPIC or CDSPP listed. Clinical students generally go through a series of interviews to find the best match for their internships. For additional information on education and training outcomes for our programs, see the following Web site: http://www.psychology.emory.edu/clinical/admission.html.

Housing and Day Care: On-campus housing is available. See the following Web site for more information: http://www.emory.edu/RES_LIFE/GRAD/. On-campus day care facilities are available. See the following Web site for more information: http://www.emory.edu/FMD/web/kidcare.htm.

Employment of Department Graduates:

Master's Degree Graduates: Of those who graduated in the academic year 2006–2007, the following categories and numbers represent the postgraduate activities and employment of master's degree graduates: Enrolled in a postdoctoral residency/fellowship (n/a), employed in independent practice (n/a), do not know (0), total from the above (master's) (0).

Doctoral Degree Graduates: Of those who graduated in the academic year 2006–2007, the following categories and numbers

represent the postgraduate activities and employment of doctoral degree graduates: Enrolled in a psychology doctoral program (n/a), enrolled in a postdoctoral residency/fellowship (2), employed in an academic position at a university (2), employed in a hospital/medical center (1), do not know (2), total from the above (doctoral) (7).

Additional Information:

Orientation, Objectives, and Emphasis of Department: The primary emphasis of our clinical curriculum is to provide students with the knowledge and skills they need to function as productive clinical researchers in psychology. This requires a basic understanding of the determinants of human behavior, including biological, psychological, and social factors, and a strong background in research design and quantitative methods. The program in cognition and development at Emory is committed to the principle that cognition and its development are best studied together. The research interests of the faculty span a wide range, and are reflected in our graduate courses, which include memory, emotion, language, perception, and concepts and categories. The program in neuroscience and animal behavior approaches topics within the areas of neuroscience, physiological psychology, acquired behavior, and ethology as a unified entity. Thus, the emphasis is on behavior as a biological phenomenon. Research in neuroscience and physiological psychology explores brain–behavior relationships, research on acquired behavior studies the ongoing and evolutionary factors influenced in individual adaptations; and ethological studies are concerned with understanding how animals function in their natural environment.

Special Facilities or Resources: The department has affiliations with the Emory Medical School, Yerkes National Primate Center, and the Center for Behavioral Neuroscience. In addition, faculty and students from many of the universities in the Atlanta area meet formally and informally to discuss common research interests.

Information for Students With Physical Disabilities: See the following Web site for more information: http://www.emory.edu/EEO/ODS/.

Application Information:

Send inquiries to Mrs. Paula Mitchell, Graduate Program Specialist, Department of Psychology, Emory University, 532 Kilgo Circle, Atlanta, GA 30322. Application available online. URL of online application: https://www.apply.embark.com/grad/emory/gsas/21/. Students are admitted in the Fall, application deadline December 1. Clinical: December 1; Cognition and Development: January 3; Neuroscience and Animal Behavior: January 3. *Fee:* $50.

Georgia Institute of Technology (2007 data)

School of Psychology
J. S. Coon Building
Atlanta, GA 30332-0170
Telephone: (404) 894-2680
Fax: (404) 894-8905
E-mail: *randall.engle@psych.gatech.edu*
Web: *http://www.psychology.gatech.edu*

Department Information:

1945. Chairperson: Randall W. Engle. Number of faculty: total—full-time 25, part-time 2; women—full-time 6, part-time 1.

Programs and Degrees Offered:

Listed in the following order: Program area, degree type (T if terminal Master's), number awarded 7/06–6/07. General Experimental PhD (Doctor of Philosophy) 3, Engineering PhD (Doctor of Philosophy) 1, Industrial/Organizational PhD (Doctor of Philosophy) 2, Human Computer Interaction MA/MS (Master of Arts/Science) (T) 3, Quantitative PhD (Doctor of Philosophy) 0.

Student Applications/Admissions:

Student Applications

General Experimental PhD (Doctor of Philosophy)—Applications 2007–2008, 36. Total applicants accepted 2007–2008, 12. Number full-time enrolled (new admits only) 2007–2008, 8. Openings 2008–2009, 10. The median number of years required for completion of a degree in 2006–2007 were 5. The number of students enrolled full- and part-time who were dismissed or voluntarily withdrew from this program area in 2007–2008 were 0. *Engineering PhD (Doctor of Philosophy)*—Applications 2007–2008, 17. Total applicants accepted 2007–2008, 7. Number full-time enrolled (new admits only) 2007–2008, 2. Openings 2008–2009, 6. The median number of years required for completion of a degree in 2006–2007 were 5. The number of students enrolled full- and part-time who were dismissed or voluntarily withdrew from this program area in 2007–2008 were 0. *Industrial/Organizational PhD (Doctor of Philosophy)*—Applications 2007–2008, 43. Total applicants accepted 2007–2008, 10. Number full-time enrolled (new admits only) 2007–2008, 8. Openings 2008–2009, 6. The median number of years required for completion of a degree in 2006–2007 were 5. The number of students enrolled full- and part-time who were dismissed or voluntarily withdrew from this program area in 2007–2008 were 0. *Human Computer Interaction MA/MS (Master of Arts/Science)*—Applications 2007–2008, 10. Total applicants accepted 2007–2008, 5. Number full-time enrolled (new admits only) 2007–2008, 2. Openings 2008–2009, 3. The median number of years required for completion of a degree in 2006–2007 were 2. The number of students enrolled full- and part-time who were dismissed or voluntarily withdrew from this program area in 2007–2008 were 0. *Quantitative PhD (Doctor of Philosophy)*—Applications 2007–2008, 2. Total applicants accepted 2007–2008, 2. Number full-time enrolled (new admits only) 2007–2008, 2. Total enrolled 2007–2008 full-time, 2. Openings 2008–2009, 6. The number of students enrolled full- and part-time who were dismissed or voluntarily withdrew from this program area in 2007–2008 were 0.

Admissions Requirements:

Scores: Entries appear in this order: required test or GPA, minimum score (if required), median score of students entering in 2007–2008. Master's Programs: GRE-V no minimum stated; GRE-Q no minimum stated; Masters GRE-Analytical no minimum stated. Doctoral Programs: GRE-V 550, 600; GRE-Q 550, 640; overall undergraduate GPA 3.0, 3.6.

Other Criteria: (importance of criteria rated low, medium, or high): GRE/MAT scores—high, research experience—high, work experience—low, GPA—high, letters of recommendation—medium, statement of goals and objectives—high.

Student Characteristics: The following represents characteristics of students in 2007–2008 in all graduate psychology programs in the department: Female—full-time 40, part-time 0; Male—

full-time 31, part-time 0; African American/Black—full-time 2, part-time 0; Hispanic/Latino(a)—full-time 1, part-time 0; Asian/Pacific Islander—full-time 7, part-time 0; American Indian/Alaska Native—full-time 0, part-time 0; Caucasian/White—full-time 59, part-time 0; Multi-ethnic—full-time 2, part-time 0; students subject to the Americans With Disabilities Act—full-time 0, part-time 0; Unknown ethnicity—full-time 0, part-time 0.

Financial Information/Assistance:

Tuition for Full-Time Study: *Master's:* State residents: per academic year $4,630, $193 per credit hour; Nonstate residents: per academic year $18,394, $767 per credit hour. *Doctoral:* State residents: per academic year $4,630, $193 per credit hour; Nonstate residents: per academic year $18,394, $767 per credit hour. Tuition is subject to change. See the following Web site for updates and changes in tuition costs: http://www.finaid.gatech.edu/costs/#gr0607.

Financial Assistance:

First-Year Students: Teaching assistantships available for first year. Average amount paid per academic year: $14,000. Average number of hours worked per week: 20. Apply by January 1. Tuition remission given: full. Research assistantships available for first year. Average amount paid per academic year: $14,000. Average number of hours worked per week: 20. Apply by January 1. Tuition remission given: full. Traineeships available for first year. Average amount paid per academic year: $16,500. Average number of hours worked per week: 20. Apply by January 1. Tuition remission given: full.

Advanced Students: Teaching assistantships available for advanced students. Average amount paid per academic year: $14,000. Apply by January 1. Tuition remission given: full. Research assistantships available for advanced students. Average amount paid per academic year: $14,000. Apply by January 1. Tuition remission given: full. Traineeships available for advanced students. Average amount paid per academic year: $16,500. Apply by January 1. Tuition remission given: full.

Additional Information: Of all students currently enrolled full time, 100% benefited from one or more of the listed financial assistance programs.

Internships/Practica: Internships are available for Industrial/Organizational and Engineering Psychology doctoral students in local corporations.

Housing and Day Care: On-campus housing is available. See the following Web site for more information: http://www.housing.gatech.edu/. No on-campus day care facilities are available.

Employment of Department Graduates:

Master's Degree Graduates: Of those who graduated in the academic year 2006–2007, the following categories and numbers represent the postgraduate activities and employment of master's degree graduates: Enrolled in a postdoctoral residency/fellowship (n/a), employed in independent practice (n/a), total from the above (master's) (0).

Doctoral Degree Graduates: Of those who graduated in the academic year 2006–2007, the following categories and numbers represent the postgraduate activities and employment of doctoral degree graduates: Enrolled in a psychology doctoral program (n/a), employed in an academic position at a university (2), employed in other positions at a higher education institution (2), employed in business or industry (4), total from the above (doctoral) (8).

Additional Information:

Orientation, Objectives, and Emphasis of Department: Programs are offered leading to the MS and PhD degrees with four areas of specialization: Engineering, Experimental (including cognitive psychology, cognitive aging, and animal behavior), Industrial/Organizational, and Quantitative psychology. Each program of study involves intensive exposure to the experimental and theoretical foundations of psychology with a strong emphasis on quantitative methods. It is the basic philosophy of the faculty that the student is trained as a psychologist first and a specialist second. Individual initiative in research and study is strongly encouraged and supported by close faculty–student contact.

Special Facilities or Resources: Special facilities or resources include affiliations with Southeast Center for Applied Cognitive Research on Aging, Georgia State Gerontology Center, Zoo Atlanta, close ties with College Computing (Graphics, Visualization and Usability Center), and the Georgia Tech Research Institute.

Application Information:

Send to Graduate Coordinator, School of Psychology, Georgia Institute of Technology, Atlanta, GA 30332-0170. URL of online application: http://www.grad.gatech.edu/admissions. Students are admitted in the Fall, application deadline January 1. for all programs and degrees. *Fee:* $50. The Institute has a preapplication form without fee to determine the student's potential for acceptance into the program.

Georgia Southern University

Department of Psychology
College of Liberal Arts and Social Sciences
P.O. Box 8041
Statesboro, GA 30460-8041
Telephone: (912) 478-5539
Fax: (912) 478-0751
E-mail: *JMurray@georgiasouthern.edu*
Web: *http://www.class.georgiasouthern.edu/psychology/*

Department Information:

1967. Chairperson: Dr. John Murray. Number of faculty: total—full-time 15; women—full-time 9.

Programs and Degrees Offered:

Listed in the following order: Program area, degree type (T if terminal Master's), number awarded 7/06–6/07. Psychology MA/MS (Master of Arts/Science) (T) 4, Clinical Psychology PsyD (Doctor of Psychology) 0.

Student Applications/Admissions:

Student Applications

Psychology MA/MS (Master of Arts/Science)—Applications 2007–2008, 18. Total applicants accepted 2007–2008, 9. Number full-time enrolled (new admits only) 2007–2008, 5. Openings 2008–2009, 12. The median number of years required for completion of a degree in 2006–2007 were 2. The number of students enrolled full- and part-time who were dismissed or voluntarily withdrew from this program area in 2007–2008 were 1. *Clinical Psychology PsyD (Doctor of Psychology)*—Applications 2007–2008, 10. Total applicants accepted 2007–2008, 4. Number full-time enrolled (new admits only) 2007–2008, 4. Total enrolled 2007–2008 full-time, 4. Openings 2008–2009, 6. The number of students enrolled full- and part-time who were dismissed or voluntarily withdrew from this program area in 2007–2008 were 1.

Admissions Requirements:

Scores: Entries appear in this order: required test or GPA, minimum score (if required), median score of students entering in 2007–2008. Master's Programs: GRE-V 450, 510; GRE-Q 450, 600; overall undergraduate GPA 3.00, 3.35. Applicants failing to meet one of the three requirements (GRE-V, GRE-Q, or GPA) but meeting the other may be admitted provisionally upon the recommendation of the graduate admissions committee. Doctoral Programs: GRE-V 550, 550; GRE-Q 550, 505; GRE-Subject (Psychology) 550, 600.

Other Criteria: (importance of criteria rated low, medium, or high): GRE/MAT scores—high, research experience—medium, clinically related public service—medium, GPA—high, letters of recommendation—medium, interview—medium, statement of goals and objectives—high, undergraduate major in psychology—low, specific undergraduate psychology courses taken—high. For MS: GRE, grades, research experience are all important; for PsyD: GRE, grades, statement most important. For additional information on admission requirements, go to http://class.georgiasouthern.edu/psychology/.

Student Characteristics: The following represents characteristics of students in 2007–2008 in all graduate psychology programs in the department: Female—full-time 19, part-time 0; Male—full-time 6, part-time 0; African American/Black—full-time 4, part-time 0; Hispanic/Latino(a)—full-time 1, part-time 0; Asian/Pacific Islander—part-time 0; American Indian/Alaska Native—full-time 0, part-time 0; Caucasian/White—full-time 20, part-time 0; Multi-ethnic—full-time 0, part-time 0; students subject to the Americans With Disabilities Act—full-time 0, part-time 0; Unknown ethnicity—full-time 0, part-time 0; International students who hold an F-1 or J-1 Visa—full-time 0, part-time 0.

Financial Information/Assistance:

Tuition for Full-Time Study: *Master's:* State residents: per academic year $4,640, $193 per credit hour; Nonstate residents: per academic year $15,184, $632 per credit hour. *Doctoral:* State residents: per academic year $4,640; Nonstate residents: per academic year $15,184. Tuition is subject to change. See the following Web site for updates and changes in tuition costs: http://www.services.georgiasouthern.edu/bursar/tuitionandfees/main.htm.

Financial Assistance:

First-Year Students: Research assistantships available for first year. Average amount paid per academic year: $6,850. Average number of hours worked per week: 20. Apply by April 15. Tuition remission given: full.

Advanced Students: Research assistantships available for advanced students. Average amount paid per academic year: $6,850. Average number of hours worked per week: 20. Apply by April 15. Tuition remission given: full.

Additional Information: Of all students currently enrolled full time, 40% benefited from one or more of the listed financial assistance programs. Application and information available online at http://cogs.georgiasouthern.edu/appsforms.htm.

Internships/Practica: No information provided.

Housing and Day Care: On-campus housing is available. See the following Web site for more information: http://www.students.georgiasouthern.edu/housing/. On-campus day care facilities are available. See the following Web site for more information: http://www.georgiasouthernhealthscience.com/departments/htfcs/resources/centers_cdc_overview.html.

Employment of Department Graduates:

Master's Degree Graduates: Of those who graduated in the academic year 2006–2007, the following categories and numbers represent the postgraduate activities and employment of master's degree graduates: Enrolled in a psychology doctoral program (2), enrolled in a postdoctoral residency/fellowship (n/a), employed in independent practice (n/a), do not know (1), total from the above (master's) (3).

Doctoral Degree Graduates: Of those who graduated in the academic year 2006–2007, the following categories and numbers represent the postgraduate activities and employment of doctoral degree graduates: Enrolled in a psychology doctoral program (n/a), total from the above (doctoral) (0).

Additional Information:

Orientation, Objectives, and Emphasis of Department: The MS program focuses on general psychology and prepares students for doctoral study in any area of psychology. The program consists of coursework and supervised research in traditional areas of interest such as social, developmental, learning, cognitive, physiological, and industrial/organizational and has a thesis requirement. The PsyD program in clinical psychology is new (beginning Fall, 2007) and follows the practitioner–scholar model of training. The program is 5 years (including internship) and is consistent with the guidelines for accreditation set forth by the APA (although is not yet accredited). The program emphasizes training in psychotherapy and assessment with indivdiuals in rural settings.

Special Facilities or Resources: The department houses faculty research laboraties in a variety of subdisciplines in psychology (social, cognitive, physiological). The department also houses a community psychology clinic, where students in the clinical program are supervised in seeing adults from the Statesboro community and surrounding rural areas.

Information for Students With Physical Disabilities: See the following Web site for more information: http://www.students.georgiasouthern.edu/disability/.

Application Information:

Send to Office of Graduate Admissions, Georgia Southern University, P.O. Box 8113, Statesboro, GA 30460-8113. Application available online. URL of online application: http://www.cogs.georgiasouthern.edu/grad_application.html. Students are admitted in the Winter, application deadline January 15; Spring, application deadline March 1; Summer, application deadline July 1. PsyD: Deadline: January 15; MS: priority deadline: March 1, final deadline: July 1. *Fee:* $50.

Georgia State University
Department of Psychology
College of Arts and Sciences
Georgia State University Department of Psychology
P.O. Box 5010
Atlanta, GA 30302-5010
Telephone: (404) 413.6200
Fax: (404) 413.6207
E-mail: *GradAdmissions@langate.gsu.edu*
Web: *http://www2.gsu.edu/~wwwpsy/*

Department Information:

1955. Chairperson: David Washburn. Number of faculty: total—full-time 27; women—full-time 22; women minority—full-time 4.

Programs and Degrees Offered:

Listed in the following order: Program area, degree type (T if terminal Master's), number awarded 7/06–6/07. Clinical PhD (Doctor of Philosophy) 6, Community PhD (Doctor of Philosophy) 2, Developmental PhD (Doctor of Philosophy) 1, Neuropsychology and Behavioral Neurosciences PhD (Doctor of Philosophy) 1, Social/Cognitive PhD (Doctor of Philosophy) 0.

APA Accreditation: Clinical PhD (Doctor of Philosophy).

Student Applications/Admissions:

Student Applications

Clinical PhD (Doctor of Philosophy)—Applications 2007–2008, 339. Total applicants accepted 2007–2008, 17. Number full-time enrolled (new admits only) 2007–2008, 7. Number part-time enrolled (new admits only) 2007–2008, 0. Openings 2008–2009, 10. The median number of years required for completion of a degree in 2006–2007 were 6. The number of students enrolled full- and part-time who were dismissed or voluntarily withdrew from this program area in 2007–2008 were 1. *Community PhD (Doctor of Philosophy)*—Applications 2007–2008, 27. Total applicants accepted 2007–2008, 2. Number full-time enrolled (new admits only) 2007–2008, 2. Number part-time enrolled (new admits only) 2007–2008, 0. Openings 2008–2009, 4. The median number of years required for completion of a degree in 2006–2007 were 6. The number of students enrolled full- and part-time who were dismissed or voluntarily withdrew from this program area in 2007–2008 were 0. *Developmental PhD (Doctor of Philosophy)*—Applications 2007–2008, 15. Total applicants accepted 2007–2008, 5. Number full-time enrolled (new admits only) 2007–2008, 1. Number part-time enrolled (new admits only) 2007–2008, 0. Openings 2008–2009, 4. The median number of years required for completion of a degree in 2006–2007 were 5. The number of students enrolled full- and part-time who were dismissed or voluntarily withdrew from this program area in 2007–2008 were 0. *Neuropsychology and Behavioral Neurosciences PhD (Doctor of Philosophy)*—Applications 2007–2008, 26. Total applicants accepted 2007–2008, 5. Number full-time enrolled (new admits only) 2007–2008, 4. Number part-time enrolled (new admits only) 2007–2008, 0. Openings 2008–2009, 4. The median number of years required for completion of a degree in 2006–2007 were 5. The number of students enrolled full- and part-time who were dismissed or voluntarily withdrew from this program area in 2007–2008 were 1. *Social/Cognitive PhD (Doctor of Philosophy)*—Applications 2007–2008, 38. Total applicants accepted 2007–2008, 1. Number full-time enrolled (new admits only) 2007–2008, 1. Number part-time enrolled (new admits only) 2007–2008, 0. Openings 2008–2009, 4. The number of students enrolled full- and part-time who were dismissed or voluntarily withdrew from this program area in 2007–2008 were 1.

Admissions Requirements:

Scores: Entries appear in this order: required test or GPA, minimum score (if required), median score of students entering in 2007–2008. Doctoral Programs: GRE-V no minimum stated, 560; GRE-Q no minimum stated, 631; overall undergraduate GPA no minimum stated, 3.61.

Other Criteria: (importance of criteria rated low, medium, or high): GRE/MAT scores—high, research experience—high, work experience—medium, extracurricular activity—low, clinically related public service—medium, GPA—high, letters of recommendation—high, interview—high, statement of goals and objectives—high, undergraduate major in psychology—medium, specific undergraduate psychology courses taken—high. For additional information on admission requirements, go to http://www2.gsu.edu/~wwwpsy/HowToApply.htm.

Student Characteristics: The following represents characteristics of students in 2007–2008 in all graduate psychology programs in the department: Female—full-time 93, part-time 0; Male—full-time 27, part-time 0; African American/Black—full-time 15, part-time 0; Hispanic/Latino(a)—full-time 4, part-time 0; Asian/Pacific Islander—full-time 13, part-time 0; American Indian/Alaska Native—full-time 0, part-time 0; Caucasian/White—full-time 84, part-time 0; Multi-ethnic—full-time 3, part-time 0; students subject to the Americans With Disabilities Act—full-time 0, part-time 0; Unknown ethnicity—full-time 1, part-time 0; International students who hold an F-1 or J-1 Visa—full-time 6, part-time 0.

Financial Information/Assistance:

Tuition for Full-Time Study: *Doctoral:* State residents: per academic year $7,947, $147 per credit hour; Nonstate residents: per academic year $31,773, $588 per credit hour. Tuition is subject to change. See the following Web site for updates and changes in tuition costs: http://www.gosolar.gsu.edu/webforstudent.htm.

Financial Assistance:

First-Year Students: Teaching assistantships available for first year. Average amount paid per academic year: $15,054. Average number of hours worked per week: 20. Tuition remission given: full. Research assistantships available for first year. Average amount paid per academic year: $15,054. Average number of hours worked per week: 20. Tuition remission given: full. Fellowships and scholarships available for first year. Average amount paid per academic year: $21,000.

Advanced Students: Teaching assistantships available for advanced students. Average amount paid per academic year: $15,614. Average number of hours worked per week: 20. Tuition remission given: full. Research assistantships available for advanced students. Average amount paid per academic year: $15,614. Average number of hours worked per week: 20. Tuition remission given: full. Fellowships and scholarships available for advanced students. Average amount paid per academic year: $21,000. Tuition remission given: full.

Additional Information: Of all students currently enrolled full time, 95% benefited from one or more of the listed financial assistance programs. Application and information available online at http://www2.gsu.edu/~wwwpsy/Financial.htm.

Internships/Practica: Doctoral Degree (PhD Clinical): For those doctoral students for whom a professional internship was required in this program prior to graduation, (10) students applied for an internship in 2006–2007, with (10) students obtaining an internship. Of those students who obtained an internship, (10) were paid internships. Of those students who obtained an internship, (10) students placed in APA/CPA-accredited internships, (0) students placed in internships not APA/CPA-accredited, but listed with the Association of Psychology Postdoctoral and Internship Centers (APPIC), (0) students placed in internships conforming to guidelines of the Council of Directors of School Psychology Programs (CDSPP), (0) students placed in internships that were not APA/CPA-accredited, APPIC or CDSPP listed. Practicum experiences are an important component of the clinical training program. Supervised therapy and assessment practica are available in a variety of settings. For clinical students, one source of training is the Psychology Clinic, which is located within the department. It provides services to students and members of the community in a variety of modalities, including assessment, individual therapy, group therapy, and family therapy. Another facility within the department is the Regent's Center for Learning Disorders, which offers comprehensive psychoeducational assessments to students and members of the community. Student clinicians are the primary providers of services in both of these clinics. In addition, there are numerous off-campus settings that offer supervised practicum experiences in a variety of areas including health psychology, neuropsychological assessment, personality assessment, psychiatric emergency room services, day treatment programs, etc. Many of these practica are available at Grady Memorial Hospital, a major metropolitan full-service facility located two blocks from the center of campus. Community students likewise do practica at various community-based organizations. Often this research takes the form of needs assessment, program development, and program evaluation.

Housing and Day Care: On-campus housing is available. See the following Web site for more information: http://www.gsu.edu/housing/. On-campus day care facilities are available. See the following Web site for more information: http://www.education.gsu.edu/cdc/.

Employment of Department Graduates:

Master's Degree Graduates: Of those who graduated in the academic year 2006–2007, the following categories and numbers represent the postgraduate activities and employment of master's degree graduates: Enrolled in a postdoctoral residency/fellowship (n/a), employed in independent practice (n/a), total from the above (master's) (0).

Doctoral Degree Graduates: Of those who graduated in the academic year 2006–2007, the following categories and numbers represent the postgraduate activities and employment of doctoral degree graduates: Enrolled in a psychology doctoral program (n/a), total from the above (doctoral) (0).

Additional Information:

Orientation, Objectives, and Emphasis of Department: The department is eclectic, and many philosophical perspectives and research interests are represented. The policy of the department is to promote the personal and professional development of students. This includes the discovery of individual interests and goals, the growth of independent scholarship and research skills, the mastery of fundamental psychological knowledge and methodology, and the development of various professional skills (e.g., clinical skills, community intervention).

Special Facilities or Resources: The facilities of the department permit work in cognition, development, neuroscience and neuropsychology, learning, infant behavior, sensation and perception, motivation, aging, social psychology, assessment, individual, group and family therapy, behavior therapy, and community psychology. Students may work with both human and nonhuman populations. Human populations include all age ranges and a variety of ethnic and socioeconomic backgrounds. Nonhuman populations include a variety of rodent and nonhuman primates.

Information for Students With Physical Disabilities: See the following Web site for more information: http://www.gsu.edu/~wwwods/.

Application Information:

Applications sent via USPS should be sent to Office of Graduate Studies, College of Arts and Sciences, Georgia State University, P.O. Box 3993, Atlanta, GA 30302-3993 If submitting application via UPS or FedEx, please send to: Office of Graduate Studies, College of Arts and Sciences, Haas Howell Building, 75 Poplar Street, Suite 800, Atlanta, GA 30303. Application available online. URL of online application: https://www.apply.embark.com/Grad/GAState/50/. Students are admitted in the Fall, application deadline December 5. The following programs have an application deadline of December 5: CLG (General Clinical), CLN (Joint Clinical and Neuropsychology), CLC (Joint Clinical and Community), NBN (Neuropsychology and Behavioral Neuroscience), SCG (Social/Cogntive). The following programs have an application deadline of January 5: COR (Community), DEV (Developmental). *Fee:* $50.

Georgia, University of

Department of Counseling and Human Development Services, Counseling Psychology Program
College of Education
402 Aderhold Hall
Athens, GA 30602
Telephone: (706) 542-1812
Fax: (706) 542-4130
E-mail: *edelgado@uga.edu*
Web: *http://www.uga.edu/chds*

Department Information:

1946. Department Head: Rosemary E. Phelps. Number of faculty: total—full-time 20, part-time 1; women—full-time 14, part-time 1; total—minority—full-time 5, part-time 1; women minority—full-time 2, part-time 1.

Programs and Degrees Offered:

Listed in the following order: Program area, degree type (T if terminal Master's), number awarded 7/06–6/07. Counseling Psychology PhD (Doctor of Philosophy) 9.

APA Accreditation: Counseling PhD (Doctor of Philosophy).

Student Applications/Admissions:

Student Applications

Counseling Psychology PhD (Doctor of Philosophy)—Applications 2007–2008, 82. Total applicants accepted 2007–2008, 21. Number full-time enrolled (new admits only) 2007–2008, 10. Number part-time enrolled (new admits only) 2007–2008, 0. Openings 2008–2009, 14. The median number of years required for completion of a degree in 2006–2007 were 4. The number of students enrolled full- and part-time who were dismissed or voluntarily withdrew from this program area in 2007–2008 were 2.

Admissions Requirements:

Scores: Entries appear in this order: required test or GPA, minimum score (if required), median score of students entering in 2007–2008. Master's Programs: GRE-V no minimum stated, 510; GRE-Q no minimum stated, 610. MAT also accepted Doctoral Programs: GRE-V no minimum stated, 510; GRE-Q no minimum stated, 550; overall undergraduate GPA no minimum stated, 3.29.

Other Criteria: (importance of criteria rated low, medium, or high): GRE/MAT scores—medium, research experience—high, work experience—high, extracurricular activity—low, clinically related public service—medium, GPA—medium, letters of recommendation—high, interview—high, statement of goals and objectives—high, undergraduate major in psychology—low. For additional information on admission requirements, go to http://www.uga.edu/chds.

Student Characteristics: The following represents characteristics of students in 2007–2008 in all graduate psychology programs in the department: Female—full-time 24, part-time 0; Male—full-time 17, part-time 0; African American/Black—full-time 14, part-time 0; Hispanic/Latino(a)—full-time 0, part-time 0; Asian/Pacific Islander—full-time 2, part-time 0; American Indian/Alaska Native—full-time 0, part-time 0; Caucasian/White—full-time 22, part-time 0; Multi-ethnic—full-time 1, part-time 0; students subject to the Americans With Disabilities Act—full-time 1, part-time 0; Unknown ethnicity—full-time 2, part-time 0; International students who hold an F-1 or J-1 Visa—full-time 1, part-time 0.

Financial Information/Assistance:

Tuition for Full-Time Study: *Master's:* State residents: per academic year $5,792, $242 per credit hour; Nonstate residents: per academic year $20,996, $875 per credit hour. *Doctoral:* State residents: per academic year $5,792, $242 per credit hour; Nonstate residents: per academic year $20,996, $822 per credit hour. Tuition is subject to change. Additional fees are assessed to students beyond the costs of tuition for the following: See Student fees breakdown at http://www.busfin.uga.edu/bursar/sched subject to change. See the following Web site for updates and changes in tuition costs: http://www.busfin.uga.edu/bursar/sched.

Financial Assistance:

First-Year Students: Teaching assistantships available for first year. Average amount paid per academic year: $10,645. Average number of hours worked per week: 13. Apply by December 1. Tuition remission given: full. Research assistantships available for first year. Average amount paid per academic year: $10,645. Average number of hours worked per week: 13. Apply by December 1. Tuition remission given: full.

Advanced Students: Teaching assistantships available for advanced students. Average amount paid per academic year: $10,645. Average number of hours worked per week: 13. Apply by December 1. Tuition remission given: full. Research assistantships available for advanced students. Average amount paid per academic year: $10,645. Average number of hours worked per week: 13. Apply by December 1. Tuition remission given: full.

Additional Information: Of all students currently enrolled full time, 100% benefited from one or more of the listed financial assistance programs. Application and information available online at http://www.uga.edu/chds.

Internships/Practica: Doctoral Degree (PhD Counseling Psychology): For those doctoral students for whom a professional internship was required in this program prior to graduation, (9) students applied for an internship in 2006–2007, with (9) students obtaining an internship. Of those students who obtained an internship, (9) were paid internships. Of those students who obtained an internship, (7) students placed in APA/CPA-accredited internships, (2) students placed in internships not APA/CPA accredited, but listed with the Association of Psychology Postdoctoral and Internship Centers (APPIC), (0) students placed in internships conforming to guidelines of the Council of Directors of School Psychology Programs (CDSPP), (0) students placed in internships that were not APA/CPA-accredited, APPIC or CDSPP listed. Practica opportunities are provided in two on-campus clinics: the Counseling and Personal Evaluation Center and Counseling Psychological Services and surrounding areas.

Housing and Day Care: On-campus housing is available. See the following Web site for more information: http://www.ses.uga.edu. On-campus day care facilities are available.

Employment of Department Graduates:

Master's Degree Graduates: Of those who graduated in the academic year 2006–2007, the following categories and numbers represent the postgraduate activities and employment of master's degree graduates: Enrolled in a postdoctoral residency/fellowship (n/a), employed in independent practice (n/a), total from the above (master's) (0).

Doctoral Degree Graduates: Of those who graduated in the academic year 2006–2007, the following categories and numbers represent the postgraduate activities and employment of doctoral degree graduates: Enrolled in a psychology doctoral program (n/a), enrolled in a postdoctoral residency/fellowship (4), employed in independent practice (1), employed in an academic position at a university (1), employed in government agency (1), employed in a hospital/medical center (1), still seeking employment (1), total from the above (doctoral) (9).

Additional Information:

Orientation, Objectives, and Emphasis of Department: The goal of the program is to educate students in the scientist–practitioner model of training in professional counseling psychology. The program focuses on professional competency development in three areas: teaching, research, and clinical service. The theoretical orientations of faculty members vary widely including representatives of most major schools of thought. The broad emphases of the program include developmental perspectives, cultural diversity perspectives, cognitive–behavioral approaches, and psychodynamic therapies.

Special Facilities or Resources: The University, the College, and the Department separately and collectively offer a number of services and fully equipped facilities to assist students in conducting academic inquiry, including special computer labs, research assistance centers, and major libraries. Several members of the university's Counseling and Testing Center are adjunct faculty members, thereby offering consultation and instructional assistance.

Information for Students With Physical Disabilities: See the following Web site for more information: http://www.ses.uga.edu.

Application Information:
Send to Admissions Committee, Department of Counseling and Human Development Services, 402 Aderhold Hall, The University of Georgia, Athens, GA 30602-7142. Application available online. URL of online application: http://www.uga.edu/chds. Students are admitted in the Fall, application deadline December 1. *Fee:* $50. Fee is for Graduate School application only, subject to change.

Georgia, University of

Department of Psychology
Franklin College of Arts and Sciences
Athens, GA 30602-3013
Telephone: (706) 542-2174
Fax: (706) 542-3275
E-mail: *bhammond@uga.edu*
Web: *http://www.uga.edu/psychology*

Department Information:
1921. Chairperson: Patricia Miller. Number of faculty: total—full-time 42, part-time 6; women—full-time 18, part-time 3; total—minority—full-time 2; women minority—full-time 2.

Programs and Degrees Offered:
Listed in the following order: Program area, degree type (T if terminal Master's), number awarded 7/06–6/07. Applied PhD (Doctor of Philosophy) 6, Clinical PhD (Doctor of Philosophy) 10, Cognitive Experimental PhD (Doctor of Philosophy) 2, Lifespan Developmental PhD (Doctor of Philosophy) 3, Social PhD (Doctor of Philosophy) 2, Neuroscience and Behavior PhD (Doctor of Philosophy) 3.

APA Accreditation: Clinical PhD (Doctor of Philosophy).

Student Applications/Admissions:
Student Applications
Applied PhD (Doctor of Philosophy)—Applications 2007–2008, 34. Total applicants accepted 2007–2008, 11. Number full-time enrolled (new admits only) 2007–2008, 6. Total enrolled 2007–2008 full-time, 18. Openings 2008–2009, 5. The number of students enrolled full- and part-time who were dismissed or voluntarily withdrew from this program area in 2007–2008 were 0. *Clinical PhD (Doctor of Philosophy)*—Applications 2007–2008, 186. Total applicants accepted 2007–2008, 16. Number full-time enrolled (new admits only) 2007–2008, 5. Total enrolled 2007–2008 full-time, 28, part-time, 5. Openings 2008–2009, 12. The median number of years required for completion of a degree in 2006–2007 were 5. The number of students enrolled full- and part-time who were dismissed or voluntarily withdrew from this program area in 2007–2008 were 0. *Cognitive Experimental PhD (Doctor of Philosophy)*—Applications 2007–2008, 26. Total applicants accepted 2007–2008, 6. Number full-time enrolled (new admits only) 2007–2008, 4. Total enrolled 2007–2008 full-time, 14, part-time, 2. Openings 2008–2009, 4. The median number of years required for completion of a degree in 2006–2007 were 5. *Lifespan Developmental PhD (Doctor of Philosophy)*—Applications 2007–2008, 15. Total applicants accepted 2007–2008, 3. Number full-time enrolled (new admits only) 2007–2008, 1. Openings 2008–2009, 23. The median number of years required for completion of a degree in 2006–2007 were 6. The number of students enrolled full- and part-time who were dismissed or voluntarily withdrew from this program area in 2007–2008 were 0. *Social PhD (Doctor of Philosophy)*—Applications 2007–2008, 32. Total applicants accepted 2007–2008, 4. Number full-time enrolled (new admits only) 2007–2008, 2. The median number of years required for completion of a degree in 2006–2007 were 5. *Neuroscience and Behavior PhD (Doctor of Philosophy)*—Applications 2007–2008, 25. Total applicants accepted 2007–2008, 8. Number full-time enrolled (new admits only) 2007–2008, 5. Total enrolled 2007–2008 full-time, 17, part-time, 1. Openings 2008–2009, 5.

Admissions Requirements:
Scores: Entries appear in this order: required test or GPA, minimum score (if required), median score of students entering in 2007–2008. Master's Programs: No MS program alone. Doctoral Programs: GRE-V no minimum stated; GRE-Q no minimum stated.
Other Criteria: (importance of criteria rated low, medium, or high): GRE/MAT scores—medium, research experience—high, work experience—high, extracurricular activity—medium, clinically related public service—medium, GPA—medium, letters of recommendation—medium, interview—medium, statement of goals and objectives—high. Each program weighs according to its own criteria. Interviews are only required by Clinical. For additional information on admission requirements, go to http://www.uga.edu/psychology/.

Student Characteristics: The following represents characteristics of students in 2007–2008 in all graduate psychology programs in the department: Female—full-time 64, part-time 10; Male—full-time 30, part-time 1; African American/Black—full-time 6, part-time 1; Hispanic/Latino(a)—full-time 4, part-time 1; Asian/Pacific Islander—full-time 11, part-time 0; American Indian/Alaska Native—full-time 0, part-time 0; Caucasian/White—full-time 71, part-time 8; Multi-ethnic—full-time 2, part-time 0; students subject to the Americans With Disabilities Act—full-time 2, part-time 1; Unknown ethnicity—full-time 0, part-time 1; International students who hold an F-1 or J-1 Visa—full-time 10, part-time 0.

Financial Information/Assistance:

Tuition for Full-Time Study: *Master's:* State residents: per academic year $5,044, $211 per credit hour; Nonstate residents: per academic year $20,298, $846 per credit hour. *Doctoral:* State residents: per academic year $5,044, $211 per credit hour; Nonstate residents: per academic year $20,298, $846 per credit hour. Tuition is subject to change. Additional fees are assessed to students beyond the costs of tuition for the following: transportation, activity, athletic, health, student facilities, and technology (total: $563 per semester). See the following Web site for updates and changes in tuition costs: htps://www.busfin1.busfin.uga.edu/bursar/schedule.cfm.

Financial Assistance:

First-Year Students: Teaching assistantships available for first year. Average amount paid per academic year: $13,856. Average number of hours worked per week: 17. Tuition remission given: partial. Research assistantships available for first year. Average amount paid per academic year: $13,856. Average number of hours worked per week: 17. Tuition remission given: partial. Fellowships and scholarships available for first year. Average amount paid per academic year: $15,817. Average number of hours worked per week: 20. Tuition remission given: partial.

Advanced Students: Teaching assistantships available for advanced students. Average amount paid per academic year: $14,780. Average number of hours worked per week: 17. Tuition remission given: partial. Research assistantships available for advanced students. Average amount paid per academic year: $14,780. Average number of hours worked per week: 17. Tuition remission given: partial. Fellowships and scholarships available for advanced students. Average amount paid per academic year: $16,875. Average number of hours worked per week: 20. Tuition remission given: partial.

Additional Information: Of all students currently enrolled full time, 80% benefited from one or more of the listed financial assistance programs. Application and information available online at http://www.gradsch.edu/.

Internships/Practica: No information provided.

Housing and Day Care: On-campus housing is available. See the following Web site for more information: http://www.uga.edu/housing. On-campus day care facilities are available. See the following Web site for more information: http://www.fcs.uga.edu/cfd/mcphaul.

Employment of Department Graduates:

Master's Degree Graduates: Of those who graduated in the academic year 2006–2007, the following categories and numbers represent the postgraduate activities and employment of master's degree graduates: Enrolled in a postdoctoral residency/fellowship (n/a), employed in independent practice (n/a), total from the above (master's) (0).

Doctoral Degree Graduates: Of those who graduated in the academic year 2006–2007, the following categories and numbers represent the postgraduate activities and employment of doctoral degree graduates: Enrolled in a psychology doctoral program (n/a), enrolled in a postdoctoral residency/fellowship (8), employed in independent practice (1), employed in an academic position at a university (6), employed in an academic position at a 2-year/4-year college (2), employed in business or industry (1), do not know (8), total from the above (doctoral) (26).

Additional Information:

Orientation, Objectives, and Emphasis of Department: Our emphasis is on research and the basic science aspects of psychology with a focus on doctoral education. A few state and private facilities provide internships. We have a cooperative liaison with several mental health facilties in the region as well as other universities.

Personal Behavior Statement: All applicants must sign a statement that includes the following text: "I will be academically honest in all my academic work and will not tolerate academic dishonesty of others. I understand that by signing this Application for Graduate Admission, I am subscribing to the Honor Code. http://www.uga.edu/honesty/."

Special Facilities or Resources: Facilities include a research and Regents Center for Learning Disabilities and the Institute for Behavioral Research, Psychology Clinic, and the Vision Sciences Laboratory. We recently opened a new center (9,000 square feet) for Bioimaging (see http://www.uga.edu/psychology/neuro/), which contains equipment for high-density EEG, MEG, MRI, and fMRI. We are also part of the Biomedical and Health Sciences Institute (see http://www.biomed.uga.edu/), which focuses on the neurosciences and biomedical applications.

Information for Students With Physical Disabilities: See the following Web site for more information: http://www.dissvcs.uga.edu.

Application Information:

Please send supplemental application and reference letters to Department of Psychology, c/o Graduate Coordinator, University of Georgia, Athens, GA 30602-3013. Please send admission application to the attention of the Graduate Admissions office. Application available online. URL of online application: http://www.gradsch.uga.edu. Students are admitted in the Fall, application deadline December 1. The deadline for receipt of admission materials for Fall semester is December 1 for all programs. *Fee:* $50.

Georgia, University of (2007 data)

School Psychology Program
Education
630 Aderhold Hall
Athens, GA 30602-7143
Telephone: (706) 542-4110
Fax: (706) 542-4240
E-mail: *mlease@uga.edu*
Web: *http://www.coe.uga.edu/epit/spy/*

Department Information:

1968. Program Coordinator: Michele Lease. Number of faculty: total—full-time 4; women—full-time 2.

Programs and Degrees Offered:

Listed in the following order: Program area, degree type (T if terminal Master's), number awarded 7/06–6/07. School Psychology PhD (Doctor of Philosophy) 7.

APA Accreditation: School Psychology PhD (Doctor of Philosophy).

Student Applications/Admissions:

Student Applications

School Psychology PhD (Doctor of Philosophy)—Applications 2007–2008, 70. Total applicants accepted 2007–2008, 10. Number full-time enrolled (new admits only) 2007–2008, 5. Openings 2008–2009, 6. The median number of years required for completion of a degree in 2006–2007 were 5. The number of students enrolled full- and part-time who were dismissed or voluntarily withdrew from this program area in 2007–2008 were 0.

Admissions Requirements:

Scores: Entries appear in this order: required test or GPA, minimum score (if required), median score of students entering in 2007–2008. Doctoral Programs: GRE-V 500, 585; GRE-Q 500, 623; overall undergraduate GPA 3.0, 3.5.

Other Criteria: (importance of criteria rated low, medium, or high): GRE/MAT scores—medium, research experience—high, work experience—low, extracurricular activity—low, clinically related public service—medium, GPA—high, letters of recommendation—high, interview—medium, statement of goals and objectives—medium.

Student Characteristics: The following represents characteristics of students in 2007–2008 in all graduate psychology programs in the department: Female—full-time 33, part-time 0; Male—full-time 6, part-time 0; African American/Black—full-time 3, part-time 0; Hispanic/Latino(a)—full-time 1, part-time 0; Asian/Pacific Islander—full-time 2, part-time 0; American Indian/Alaska Native—full-time 0, part-time 0; Caucasian/White—full-time 33, part-time 0; students subject to the Americans With Disabilities Act—full-time 0, part-time 0; Unknown ethnicity—full-time 0, part-time 0.

Financial Information/Assistance:

Tuition for Full-Time Study: *Doctoral:* State residents: per academic year $4,368; Nonstate residents: per academic year $18,768. Tuition is subject to change.

Financial Assistance:

First-Year Students: Teaching assistantships available for first year. Average amount paid per academic year: $12,623. Average number of hours worked per week: 13. Apply by February 1. Tuition remission given: full. Research assistantships available for first year. Average amount paid per academic year: $12,623. Average number of hours worked per week: 13. Apply by February 1. Tuition remission given: full.

Advanced Students: Teaching assistantships available for advanced students. Average amount paid per academic year: $13,643. Average number of hours worked per week: 13. Apply by February 1. Tuition remission given: full. Research assistantships available for advanced students. Average amount paid per academic year: $13,643. Average number of hours worked per week: 13. Apply by February 1. Tuition remission given: full.

Additional Information: Of all students currently enrolled full time, 88% benefited from one or more of the listed financial assistance programs.

Internships/Practica: No information provided.

Housing and Day Care: On-campus housing is available. On-campus day care facilities are available.

Employment of Department Graduates:

Master's Degree Graduates: Of those who graduated in the academic year 2006–2007, the following categories and numbers represent the postgraduate activities and employment of master's degree graduates: Enrolled in a postdoctoral residency/fellowship (n/a), employed in independent practice (n/a), total from the above (master's) (0).

Doctoral Degree Graduates: Of those who graduated in the academic year 2006–2007, the following categories and numbers represent the postgraduate activities and employment of doctoral degree graduates: Enrolled in a psychology doctoral program (n/a), enrolled in a postdoctoral residency/fellowship (1), employed in independent practice (0), employed in an academic position at a university (2), employed in an academic position at a 2-year/4-year college (0), employed in other positions at a higher education institution (0), employed in a professional position in a school system (3), employed in business or industry (0), employed in government agency (0), employed in a community mental health/counseling center (0), employed in a hospital/medical center (0), still seeking employment (0), other employment position (0), total from the above (doctoral) (6).

Additional Information:

Orientation, Objectives, and Emphasis of Department: The PhD program in school psychology trains research-oriented school psychologists for work in educational settings, hospitals, clinics, and universities in which they can provide leadership in applied practice, research, and teaching. The school psychology program follows the scientist–practitioner model, and emphasizes human development and developmental psychopathology and the central core elements of training.

Special Facilities or Resources: Special facilities and resources include access to a superior computer center, decentralized computational equipment, a major research library, and faculty members who are extraordinarily accessible to students. The department is strongly committed to affirmative action and fair treatment. Despite the suburban setting (a small urban area of 75,000 over an hour from Atlanta), we attract ethnic minority as well as out-of-state and out-of-region students and faculty. NASP and APA requirements and full accreditation from APA and NCATE form the foundation of our programs.

Application Information:

Send to Graduate Admissions Office, Graduate Studies Building, The University of Georgia, Athens, GA 30602. Students are admitted in the Fall, application deadline January 1. Deadline dates are unrelated to degree; all applications are considered only for Fall admission. *Fee:* $30.

Valdosta State University (2007 data)

Psychology and Counseling
1500 North Patterson Street
Valdosta, GA 31698-0100
Telephone: (229) 333-5930
Fax: (229) 259-5576
E-mail: *bbauer@valdosta.edu*
Web: *http://www.coefaculty.valdosta.edu/psych/*

Department Information:

1965. Chairperson: Robert E. L. Bauer. Number of faculty: total—full-time 19, part-time 2; women—full-time 5, part-time 1.

Programs and Degrees Offered:

Listed in the following order: Program area, degree type (T if terminal Master's), number awarded 7/06–6/07. Clinical/Counseling MA/MS (Master of Arts/Science) (T) 7, Industrial/Organizational MA/MS (Master of Arts/Science) (T) 5, School Counseling Other 1, School Psychology EdS/MEd (School Psychology) 5, School Counseling Other 14.

Student Applications/Admissions:

Student Applications

Clinical/Counseling MA/MS (Master of Arts/Science)—Applications 2007–2008, 23. Total applicants accepted 2007–2008, 9. Number full-time enrolled (new admits only) 2007–2008, 5. Number part-time enrolled (new admits only) 2007–2008, 3. Total enrolled 2007–2008 full-time, 13, part-time, 9. Openings 2008–2009, 15. The median number of years required for completion of a degree in 2006–2007 were 2. The number of students enrolled full- and part-time who were dismissed or voluntarily withdrew from this program area in 2007–2008 were 0. *Industrial/Organizational MA/MS (Master of Arts/Science)*—Applications 2007–2008, 19. Total applicants accepted 2007–2008, 9. Number full-time enrolled (new admits only) 2007–2008, 5. Number part-time enrolled (new admits only) 2007–2008, 3. Total enrolled 2007–2008 full-time, 15, part-time, 3. Openings 2008–2009, 15. The median number of years required for completion of a degree in 2006–2007 were 2. The number of students enrolled full- and part-time who were dismissed or voluntarily withdrew from this program area in 2007–2008 were 0. *School Counseling Other*—Applications 2007–2008, 4. Total applicants accepted 2007–2008, 2. Number full-time enrolled (new admits only) 2007–2008, 0. Number part-time enrolled (new admits only) 2007–2008, 2. Openings 2008–2009, 5. The median number of years required for completion of a degree in 2006–2007 were 2. The number of students enrolled full- and part-time who were dismissed or voluntarily withdrew from this program area in 2007–2008 were 0. *School Psychology EdS/MEd (School Psychology)*—Applications 2007–2008, 10. Total applicants accepted 2007–2008, 4. Number full-time enrolled (new admits only) 2007–2008, 0. Number part-time enrolled (new admits only) 2007–2008, 4. Total enrolled 2007–2008 full-time, 3, part-time, 14. Openings 2008–2009, 13. The median number of years required for completion of a degree in 2006–2007 were 2. The number of students enrolled full- and part-time who were dismissed or voluntarily withdrew from this program area in 2007–2008 were 1. *School Counseling Other*—Applications 2007–2008, 22. Total applicants accepted 2007–2008, 17. Number full-time enrolled (new admits only) 2007–2008, 3. Number part-time enrolled (new admits only) 2007–2008, 17. Total enrolled 2007–2008 full-time, 10, part-time, 34. Openings 2008–2009, 12. The median number of years required for completion of a degree in 2006–2007 were 2. The number of students enrolled full- and part-time who were dismissed or voluntarily withdrew from this program area in 2007–2008 were 0.

Admissions Requirements:

Scores: Entries appear in this order: required test or GPA, minimum score (if required), median score of students entering in 2007–2008. Master's Programs: GRE-V 400; GRE-Q 400; overall undergraduate GPA 3.00. MS in Psychology (reported here) differs from MEd and EdS in admissions criteria. Please write for details.

Other Criteria: (importance of criteria rated low, medium, or high): GRE/MAT scores—high, research experience—medium, work experience—medium, extracurricular activity—low, clinically related public service—low, GPA—high, letters of recommendation—medium, interview—low, statement of goals and objectives—low. Because criteria vary by program, please write for details by program. For additional information on admission requirements, go to http://www.valdosta.edu/GRADSCHOOL/.

Student Characteristics: The following represents characteristics of students in 2007–2008 in all graduate psychology programs in the department: Female—full-time 29, part-time 50; Male—full-time 12, part-time 14; African American/Black—full-time 6, part-time 6; Hispanic/Latino(a)—full-time 0, part-time 4; Asian/Pacific Islander—full-time 0, part-time 0; American Indian/Alaska Native—full-time 0, part-time 0; Caucasian/White—full-time 32, part-time 52; Multi-ethnic—full-time 0, part-time 0; students subject to the Americans With Disabilities Act—full-time 1, part-time 0; Unknown ethnicity—full-time 3, part-time 2.

Financial Information/Assistance:

Tuition for Full-Time Study: *Master's:* State residents: per academic year $3,044, $127 per credit hour; Nonstate residents: per academic year $12,172, $508 per credit hour. Tuition is subject to change. See the following Web site for updates and changes in tuition costs: http://www.valdosta.edu/admissions/documents/grad.pdf.

Financial Assistance:

First-Year Students: Research assistantships available for first year. Average amount paid per academic year: $2,452. Average number of hours worked per week: 15. Apply by July 15. Tuition remission given: full.

Advanced Students: Research assistantships available for advanced students. Average amount paid per academic year: $2,452. Average number of hours worked per week: 15. Apply by July 15. Tuition remission given: full.

Additional Information: Of all students currently enrolled full time, 15% benefited from one or more of the listed financial assistance programs. Application and information available online at: http://www.valdosta.edu/GRADSCHOOL/Student_Forms.htm.

Internships/Practica: Master's Degree students are assigned to appropriate practica sites, related to their programs of study. Some sites offer stipends. All School Psychology EdS students work in schools during their internships and receive a stipend.

Housing and Day Care: On-campus housing is available. See the following Web site for more information: http://www.services.valdosta.edu/housing/. No on-campus day care facilities are available.

Employment of Department Graduates:

Master's Degree Graduates: Of those who graduated in the academic year 2006–2007, the following categories and numbers represent the postgraduate activities and employment of master's degree graduates: Enrolled in a psychology doctoral program (3), enrolled in another graduate/professional program (3), enrolled in a postdoctoral residency/fellowship (n/a), employed in independent practice (n/a), employed in an academic position at a university (0), employed in an academic position at a 2-year/4-year college (1), employed in other positions at a higher education institution (0), employed in a professional position in a school system (14), employed in business or industry (0), employed in government agency (0), employed in a community mental health/counseling center (6), employed in a hospital/medical center (1), still seeking employment (0), not seeking employment (0), other employment position (0), total from the above (master's) (33).

Doctoral Degree Graduates: Of those who graduated in the academic year 2006–2007, the following categories and numbers represent the postgraduate activities and employment of doctoral degree graduates: Enrolled in a psychology doctoral program (n/a), total from the above (doctoral) (0).

Additional Information:

Orientation, Objectives, and Emphasis of Department: The Department of Psychology and Counseling serves the citizens of the region and state by offering instruction, research, and services designed to advance the understanding of behavioral and cognitive processes and to improve the quality of life. The principle function of the department is to prepare students at the undergraduate and graduate levels to pursue careers within the discipline and affiliated areas. A related purpose is to provide courses for programs in education, nursing, and other disciplines. At the baccalaureate level, the students develop basic skills in scientific research, knowledge of psychological nomenclature and concepts, and are introduced to the diverse applications of psychology. The graduate programs prepare students to apply skills in schools, mental health agencies, government, industry, and other settings. Training at the graduate level is designed to prepare qualified, responsible professionals who may provide assessment, consulting, counseling, and other services to the citizenry of the region.

Information for Students With Physical Disabilities: See the following Web site for more information: http://www.valdosta.edu/access/.

Application Information:

Send to Graduate School, Valdosta State University, 1500 North Patterson Street, Valdosta, GA 31698-0005. Application available online. URL of online application: http://www.valdosta.edu/GRADSCHOOL/index_of_application_forms.htm. Students are admitted in the Fall, application deadline July 15; Spring, application deadline November 15; Summer, application deadline May 1. Programs have rolling admissions. *Fee:* $20. Filing application online, $25.

West Georgia, University of (2007 data)

Counseling and Educational Psychology
Education
237 Education Annex
Carrollton, GA 30118
Telephone: (638) 839-6554
Fax: (638) 839-6099
E-mail: *bsnow@westga.edu*
Web: *http://www.coe.westga.edu/cep/*

Department Information:

1969. Chairperson: Brent M. Snow, PhD. Number of faculty: total—full-time 12; women—full-time 8.

Programs and Degrees Offered:

Listed in the following order: Program area, degree type (T if terminal Master's), number awarded 7/06–6/07. Counseling EdS/MEd (School Psychology), Counseling (MEd) Other.

Student Applications/Admissions:

Student Applications

Counseling EdS/MEd (School Psychology)—Counseling (MEd) Other—No information provided.

Admissions Requirements:

Scores: Entries appear in this order: required test or GPA, minimum score (if required), median score of students entering in 2007–2008. Master's Programs: GRE-V 450; GRE-Q 450; GRE-Analytical 3.5; overall undergraduate GPA 2.7.

Other Criteria: (importance of criteria rated low, medium, or high): GRE/MAT scores—high, research experience—low, work experience—medium, extracurricular activity—low, clinically related public service—low, GPA—high, letters of recommendation—high, interview—high, statement of goals and objectives—high.

Student Characteristics: The following represents characteristics of students in 2007–2008 in all graduate psychology programs in the department: Caucasian/White—full-time 0, part-time 0; Unknown ethnicity—full-time 0, part-time 0.

Financial Information/Assistance:

Tuition for Full-Time Study: *Master's:* State residents: per academic year $1,480, $101 per credit hour; Nonstate residents: per academic year $5,098, $402 per credit hour. Tuition is subject to change. See the following Web site for updates and changes in tuition costs: http://www.westga.edu.

Financial Assistance:

First-Year Students: Research assistantships available for first year. Average amount paid per academic year: $6,000. Average number of hours worked per week: 13. Apply by July. Tuition remission given: full.

Advanced Students: Research assistantships available for advanced students. Average amount paid per academic year: $6,000. Average number of hours worked per week: 13. Apply by July. Tuition remission given: full.

Additional Information: Of all students currently enrolled full time, 5% benefited from one or more of the listed financial assistance programs.

Internships/Practica: Practicum (100 hours) and Internship (600 hours) are required of all graduate students in school and community counseling.

Housing and Day Care: On-campus housing is available. Residence Life Director, jclower@westga.edu. On-campus day care facilities are available.

Employment of Department Graduates:

Master's Degree Graduates: Of those who graduated in the academic year 2006–2007, the following categories and numbers represent the postgraduate activities and employment of master's degree graduates: Enrolled in a postdoctoral residency/fellowship (n/a), employed in independent practice (n/a), total from the above (master's) (0).

Doctoral Degree Graduates: Of those who graduated in the academic year 2006–2007, the following categories and numbers represent the postgraduate activities and employment of doctoral degree graduates: Enrolled in a psychology doctoral program (n/a), total from the above (doctoral) (0).

Additional Information:

Orientation, Objectives, and Emphasis of Department: The Department's identity is in training professional counselors for schools and community agencies. Master's programs are accredited by the Council for Accreditation of Counseling and Related Educational Programs (CACREP)—the largest and most prestigious accreditation in the field of counseling. Professional identity of faculty and students is the American Counseling Association (ACA) and it's various divisions. Depending on the program emphasis, graduates qualify for the following credentials: licensed professional counselor, nationally certified counselor, and state certification in school counseling.

Special Facilities or Resources: The Department is nationally prominent and recognized as a leader in the transforming school counseling initiative. Excellent lab facilities.

Application Information:

Send to Graduate School, University of West Georgia, Carrollton, GA 30118. Application available online. Students are admitted in the Fall, application deadline June 3; Spring, application deadline November 5; Summer, application deadline March 4.

West Georgia, University of

Department of Psychology
Arts and Sciences
1600 Maple Street
Carrollton, GA 30118
Telephone: (678) 839-6510
Fax: (678) 839-0611
E-mail: *drice@westga.edu*
Web: *http://www.westga.edu~psydept http://www.westga.edu/~psydoc*

Department Information:

1967. Professor and Chair: Donadrian L. Rice. Number of faculty: total—full-time 3, part-time 2; women—full-time 4, part-time 2.

Programs and Degrees Offered:

Listed in the following order: Program area, degree type (T if terminal Master's), number awarded 7/06–6/07. Humanistic/Transpersonal/Critical Psychology MA/MS (Master of Arts/Science) (T) 15, Individual, Organizational, and Community Transform PsyD (Doctor of Psychology) 0.

Student Applications/Admissions:

Student Applications

Humanistic/Transpersonal/Critical Psychology MA/MS (Master of Arts/Science)—Applications 2007–2008, 65. Total applicants accepted 2007–2008, 49. Number full-time enrolled (new admits only) 2007–2008, 45. Number part-time enrolled (new admits only) 2007–2008, 1. Total enrolled 2007–2008 full-time, 80, part-time, 6. Openings 2008–2009, 35. The median number of years required for completion of a degree in 2006–2007 were 3. The number of students enrolled full- and part-time who were dismissed or voluntarily withdrew from this program area in 2007–2008 were 2. *Individual, Organizational, and Community Transform PsyD (Doctor of Psychology)*—Applications 2007–2008, 0. Total applicants accepted 2007–2008, 0. Number full-time enrolled (new admits only) 2007–2008, 0. Number part-time enrolled (new admits only) 2007–2008, 0. Openings 2008–2009, 10. The number of students enrolled full- and part-time who were dismissed or voluntarily withdrew from this program area in 2007–2008 were 0.

Admissions Requirements:

Scores: Entries appear in this order: required test or GPA, minimum score (if required), median score of students entering in 2007–2008. Master's Programs: GRE-V 500; GRE-Q 500; overall undergraduate GPA 2.5. Doctoral Programs: GRE-V no minimum stated; GRE-Q no minimum stated.

Other Criteria: (importance of criteria rated low, medium, or high): GRE/MAT scores—medium, research experience—high, work experience—high, extracurricular activity—medium, clinically related public service—high, GPA—high, letters of recommendation—high, interview—high, statement of goals and objectives—high. For additional information on admission requirements, go to http://www.westga.edu/~psydept/.

Student Characteristics: The following represents characteristics of students in 2007–2008 in all graduate psychology programs in the department: Female—full-time 57, part-time 15; Male—full-time 29, part-time 20; African American/Black—full-time 3, part-time 0; Hispanic/Latino(a)—full-time 4, part-time 0; Asian/Pacific Islander—full-time 3, part-time 0; American Indian/Alaska Native—full-time 0, part-time 0; Caucasian/White—full-time 67, part-time 11; students subject to the Americans With Disabilities Act—full-time 0, part-time 0; Unknown ethnicity—full-time 0, part-time 0.

Financial Information/Assistance:

Tuition for Full-Time Study: *Master's:* State residents: per academic year $3,370, $117 per credit hour; Nonstate residents: per academic year $11,730, $465 per credit hour. *Doctoral:* State residents: per academic year $3,370, $117 per credit hour; Nonstate residents: per academic year $11,730, $465 per credit hour. Tuition is subject to change. Tuition costs vary by program. See the following Web site for updates and changes in tuition costs: http://www.westga.edu/policies/gradcat_2001.pdf.

Financial Assistance:

First-Year Students: Teaching assistantships available for first year. Research assistantships available for first year. Average amount paid per academic year: $3,000. Average number of hours worked per week: 13. Tuition remission given: full.

Advanced Students: No information provided.

Additional Information: Of all students currently enrolled full time, 25% benefited from one or more of the listed financial assistance programs.

Internships/Practica: Internships are available at local facilities.

Housing and Day Care: On-campus housing is available. See the following Web site for more information: http://www.westga.edu/~psydept. No on-campus day care facilities are available.

Employment of Department Graduates:

Master's Degree Graduates: Of those who graduated in the academic year 2006–2007, the following categories and numbers represent the postgraduate activities and employment of master's degree graduates: Enrolled in a psychology doctoral program (5), enrolled in another graduate/professional program (7), enrolled in a postdoctoral residency/fellowship (n/a), employed in independent practice (n/a), employed in an academic position at a university (4), employed in an academic position at a 2-year/4-year college (5), employed in other positions at a higher education institution (3), employed in a professional position in a school system (8), employed in business or industry (3), employed in a community mental health/counseling center (10), other employment position (5), total from the above (master's) (50).

Doctoral Degree Graduates: Of those who graduated in the academic year 2006–2007, the following categories and numbers represent the postgraduate activities and employment of doctoral degree graduates: Enrolled in a psychology doctoral program (n/a), total from the above (doctoral) (0).

Additional Information:

Orientation, Objectives, and Emphasis of Department: The department is a pioneer of humanistic–transpersonal psychology. It differs from other programs in that it goes beyond conventional subjects and approaches a holistic and integrative understanding of human experience. Alongside demanding academic work, student growth and personal awareness are inherent to this venture because such reflection is considered an important factor in human understanding. Individual programs are designed according to personal needs and interests; the overall atmosphere is communal, encouraging personal and intellectual dialogue and encounter. Most conventional topic areas are taught. Beyond these are areas almost uniquely explorable in a program such as this: the horizons of consciousness through such vantages as Eastern and transpersonal psychologies, hermeneutics, existential and phenomenological psychologies, and critical psychology. Specific areas include women's studies; aesthetic and sacred experience; myths, dreams, and symbols; and creativity. Areas of applied interest are viewed as correlates of the learning process: skill courses related to human services, prevention and community psychology, counseling psychology, cross-cultural psychology, organizational development, and growth therapies. The department offers training in qualitative and traditional methodologies of research. Practicum and internship experience along with individual research and reading are highly encouraged for those who can profit from these. Interest areas include human science research; parapsychology; transpersonal and Eastern psychologies; counseling, clinical, community, and organizational development; and psychology in the classroom.

Special Facilities or Resources: Special resources include large library holdings in the areas of humanistic, parapsychology, transpersonal, philosophical, and Asian psychology. The library holds papers of Sidney M. Jourard, Edith Weiskoff-Joelsen, and the Psychical Research Foundation Library. The department hosts major conferences, and faculty are associated with several journals and newsletters exploring orientation areas.

Information for Students With Physical Disabilities: See the following Web site for more information: http://www.westga.edu/~sdev.

Application Information:

Send to Graduate Coordinator, Department of Psychology, State University of West Georgia, Carrollton, GA 30118. Application available online. URL of online application: http://www.westga.edu/~gradsch/. Students are admitted in the Fall, application deadline February 17; Spring, application deadline September 22. *Fee:* $20.

Argosy University, Hawaii Campus

Clinical Psychology
American School of Professional Psychology
400 ASB Tower, 1001 Bishop Street
Honolulu, HI 96813
Telephone: (808) 536-5555
Fax: (808) 536-5505
E-mail: *santhony@argosyuedu*
Web: *http://www.argosy.edu*

Department Information:

1994. Chairperson: Suzanne Anthony, PhD. Number of faculty: total—full-time 11, part-time 1; women—full-time 6, part-time 1; total—minority—full-time 7, part-time 1; women minority—full-time 5, part-time 1.

Programs and Degrees Offered:

Listed in the following order: Program area, degree type (T if terminal Master's), number awarded 7/06–6/07. Clinical PsyD (Doctor of Psychology) 39, Marriage and Family MA/MS (Master of Arts/Science) (T) 34, Clinical Respecialization Program Respecialization Diploma 0, Postdoctoral/Clinical Psychopharmacology Other 4, Clinical MA/MS (Master of Arts/Science) (T) 20, School Psychology MA/MS (Master of Arts/Science) (T) 6.

APA Accreditation: Clinical PsyD (Doctor of Psychology).

Student Applications/Admissions:

Student Applications

Clinical PsyD (Doctor of Psychology)—Applications 2007–2008, 120. Total applicants accepted 2007–2008, 35. Number full-time enrolled (new admits only) 2007–2008, 35. Number part-time enrolled (new admits only) 2007–2008, 0. Openings 2008–2009, 40. The median number of years required for completion of a degree in 2006–2007 were 5. The number of students enrolled full- and part-time who were dismissed or voluntarily withdrew from this program area in 2007–2008 were 7. *Marriage and Family MA/MS (Master of Arts/Science)*—Applications 2007–2008, 79. Total applicants accepted 2007–2008, 56. Number full-time enrolled (new admits only) 2007–2008, 56. Number part-time enrolled (new admits only) 2007–2008, 0. Total enrolled 2007–2008 full-time, 77, part-time, 7. Openings 2008–2009, 45. The median number of years required for completion of a degree in 2006–2007 were 2. The number of students enrolled full- and part-time who were dismissed or voluntarily withdrew from this program area in 2007–2008 were 8. *Clinical Respecialization Program Respecialization Diploma*—Applications 2007–2008, 1. Total applicants accepted 2007–2008, 1. Number full-time enrolled (new admits only) 2007–2008, 1. Number part-time enrolled (new admits only) 2007–2008, 0. Openings 2008–2009, 1. The median number of years required for completion of a degree in 2006–2007 were 3. The number of students enrolled full- and part-time who were dismissed or voluntarily withdrew from this program area in 2007–2008 were 0. *Postdoctoral/Clinical Psychopharmacology Other*—Applications 2007–2008, 6. Total applicants accepted 2007–2008, 6. Number full-time enrolled (new admits only) 2007–2008, 6. Number part-time enrolled (new admits only) 2007–2008, 0. Openings 2008–2009, 15. The median number of years required for completion of a degree in 2006–2007 was 1. The number of students enrolled full- and part-time who were dismissed or voluntarily withdrew from this program area in 2007–2008 were 2. *Clinical MA/MS (Master of Arts/Science)*—Applications 2007–2008, 33. Total applicants accepted 2007–2008, 12. Number full-time enrolled (new admits only) 2007–2008, 12. Number part-time enrolled (new admits only) 2007–2008, 0. Openings 2008–2009, 10. The median number of years required for completion of a degree in 2006–2007 were 2. The number of students enrolled full- and part-time who were dismissed or voluntarily withdrew from this program area in 2007–2008 were 1. *School Psychology MA/MS (Master of Arts/Science)*—Applications 2007–2008, 19. Total applicants accepted 2007–2008, 8. Number full-time enrolled (new admits only) 2007–2008, 5. Number part-time enrolled (new admits only) 2007–2008, 3. Total enrolled 2007–2008 full-time, 15, part-time, 4. Openings 2008–2009, 5. The median number of years required for completion of a degree in 2006–2007 were 3. The number of students enrolled full- and part-time who were dismissed or voluntarily withdrew from this program area in 2007–2008 were 1.

Admissions Requirements:

Scores: Entries appear in this order: required test or GPA, minimum score (if required), median score of students entering in 2007–2008. Master's Programs: overall undergraduate GPA 3.00, 3.70; last 2 years GPA 3.00; psychology GPA 3.00. No set GPA requirement for professional counseling program. Doctoral Programs: overall undergraduate GPA 3.25, 3.70; last 2 years GPA 3.25.

Other Criteria: (importance of criteria rated low, medium, or high): research experience—low, work experience—medium, extracurricular activity—low, clinically related public service—high, GPA—medium, letters of recommendation—medium, interview—high, statement of goals and objectives—high, diversity focus—high.

Student Characteristics: The following represents characteristics of students in 2007–2008 in all graduate psychology programs in the department: Female—full-time 246, part-time 9; Male—full-time 61, part-time 2; African American/Black—full-time 12, part-time 0; Hispanic/Latino(a)—full-time 14, part-time 0; Asian/Pacific Islander—full-time 143, part-time 0; American Indian/Alaska Native—full-time 5, part-time 0; Caucasian/White—full-time 127, part-time 0; Multi-ethnic—full-time 0, part-time 0; students subject to the Americans With Disabilities Act—full-time 2, part-time 0; Unknown ethnicity—full-time 6, part-time 11; International students who hold an F-1 or J-1 Visa—full-time 2, part-time 0.

Financial Information/Assistance:

Financial Assistance:

First-Year Students: Fellowships and scholarships available for first year. Average amount paid per academic year: $3,000. Apply by April 30. Tuition remission given: partial.

Advanced Students: Teaching assistantships available for advanced students. Average amount paid per academic year: $600. Average number of hours worked per week: 4. Apply by not available. Fellowships and scholarships available for advanced students. Average amount paid per academic year: $3,000. Apply by April 30. Tuition remission given: partial.

Additional Information: Of all students currently enrolled full time, 10% benefited from one or more of the listed financial assistance programs. Application and information available online at http://www.argosy.edu.

Internships/Practica: Master's Degree (MA/MS Clinical): An internship experience such as a final research project or "capstone" experience is required of graduates. Doctoral Degree (Clinical PsyD): For those doctoral students for whom a professional internship was required in this program prior to graduation, (30) students applied for an internship in 2006–2007, with (28) students obtaining an internship. Of those students who obtained an internship, (28) were paid internships. Of those students who obtained an internship, (12) students placed in APA/CPA accredited internships, (16) students placed in internships not APA/CPA-accredited, but listed with the Association of Psychology Postdoctoral and Internship Centers (APPIC), (0) students placed in internships conforming to guidelines of the Council of Directors of School Psychology Programs (CDSPP), (0) students placed in internships that were not APA/CPA-accredited, APPIC or CDSPP listed. Programs at Argosy University/Honolulu provide training in assessment and intervention through placement in community practica on O'ahu and throughout the Hawaiian Islands. Supervision is provided by licensed psychologists at these settings, and students are simultaneously enrolled in practicum seminars led by faculty with relevant expertise. These seminars combine teaching and case consultation to train students in specific clinical skills. Students are currently placed at settings that include university counseling centers, community mental health centers, outpatient treatment centers, residential adolescent treatment centers, day treatment and hospice programs, developmental evaluation clinics, substance abuse treatment centers, public and private schools, state courts, parole agencies, prisons, and psychiatric, medical, and veteran's hospitals. Argosy University Hawaii Campus maintains a predoctoral internship consortium for its Doctoral Program students that is listed with the Association of Psychology Postdoctoral and Internship Centers (APPIC). Both practicum and consortium internship sites serve client populations that are culturally diverse.

Housing and Day Care: No on-campus housing is available. No on-campus day care facilities are available.

Employment of Department Graduates:

Master's Degree Graduates: Of those who graduated in the academic year 2006–2007, the following categories and numbers represent the postgraduate activities and employment of master's degree graduates: Enrolled in a postdoctoral residency/fellowship (n/a), employed in independent practice (n/a), total from the above (master's) (0).

Doctoral Degree Graduates: Of those who graduated in the academic year 2006–2007, the following categories and numbers represent the postgraduate activities and employment of doctoral degree graduates: Enrolled in a psychology doctoral program (n/a), total from the above (doctoral) (0).

Additional Information:

Orientation, Objectives, and Emphasis of Department: The Argosy University/Honolulu Doctoral Program in Clinical Psychology (PsyD) prepares practitioners–scholars for both contemporary and emerging roles in professional psychology. The program supports the development of core competencies in psychological assessment, intervention, consultation/education, and management/supervision. Training emphasizes attention to human diversity and difference, self-reflexivity in clinical relationships, and critical evaluation and application of empirical literature to guide clinical decision making. Concentrations may be selected in areas such as Diversity and Clinical Practice, Child and Family Clinical Practice, and Health Psychology. The Master of Arts in Clinical Psychology Program is designed to meet the needs of both those students seeking a terminal degree for work in the mental health field and those students who eventually plan to pursue a doctoral degree. The Clinical Respecialization Postdoctoral Program provides doctoral-level psychologists with clinical courses and experiences. The Postdoctoral Program in Clinical Psychopharmacology integrates relevant knowledge from medicine, pharmacology, nursing, and psychology. The Master of Arts in Professional Counseling—Marriage and Family Therapy Specialty Program is offered through weekend courses that are scheduled to allow concurrent employment; the format provides students an opportunity to continue professional development or to pursue a career change.

Information for Students With Physical Disabilities: See the following Web site for more information: http://www.argosy.edu/.

Application Information:

Send to Admissions Office, Argosy University, Hawaii Campus, 400 ASB Tower, 1001 Bishop Street, Honolulu, HI 96813. Application available online. URL of online application: http://www.argosy.edu/. Students are admitted in the Fall, application deadline January 15, May 15. MA School Psychology and Marriage and Family MA Programs have rolling admissions. *Fee:* $50.

Hawaii, University of (2007 data)

Department of Educational Psychology
College of Education
1776 University Avenue
Honolulu, HI 96822-2463
Telephone: (808) 956-7775
Fax: (808) 956-6615
E-mail: *abayer@hawaii.edu*
Web: *http://www.hawaii.edu/edpsych/*

Department Information:

1965. Chairperson: Ann Bayer. Number of faculty: total—full-time 7; women—full-time 5.

Programs and Degrees Offered:

Listed in the following order: Program area, degree type (T if terminal Master's), number awarded 7/06–6/07. Educational Psychology (Med) Other 8, Educational Psychology PhD (Doctor of Philosophy) 7.

Student Applications/Admissions:

Student Applications

Educational Psychology (Med) Other—Applications 2007–2008, 20. Total applicants accepted 2007–2008, 8. Number part-time enrolled (new admits only) 2007–2008, 8. Total enrolled 2007–2008 part-time, 25. The median number of years required for completion of a degree in 2006–2007 were 2. The number of students enrolled full- and part-time who were dismissed or voluntarily withdrew from this program area in 2007–2008 were 0. *Educational Psychology PhD (Doctor of Philosophy)*—Applications 2007–2008, 12. Total applicants accepted 2007–2008, 3. Total enrolled 2007–2008 part-time, 29. The median number of years required for completion of a degree in 2006–2007 were 6. The number of students enrolled full- and part-time who were dismissed or voluntarily withdrew from this program area in 2007–2008 were 0.

Admissions Requirements:

Scores: Entries appear in this order: required test or GPA, minimum score (if required), median score of students entering in 2007–2008. Master's Programs: last 2 years GPA 3.0, 3.23. Doctoral Programs: GRE-V no minimum stated, 640; GRE-Q no minimum stated, 630; last 2 years GPA 3.0, 3.35.

Other Criteria: (importance of criteria rated low, medium, or high): GRE/MAT scores—high, research experience—medium, work experience—low, extracurricular activity—medium, GPA—high, letters of recommendation—high, statement of goals and objectives—high. Criteria above pertain to the PhD program. The MEd program does not require the GRE or research experience.

Student Characteristics: The following represents characteristics of students in 2007–2008 in all graduate psychology programs in the department: Female—full-time 0, part-time 34; Male—full-time 0, part-time 14; African American/Black—full-time 0, part-time 0; Hispanic/Latino(a)—full-time 0, part-time 0; Asian/Pacific Islander—full-time 0, part-time 22; American Indian/Alaska Native—full-time 0, part-time 0; Caucasian/White—full-time 0, part-time 18; Multi-ethnic—part-time 8; students subject to the Americans With Disabilities Act—full-time 0, part-time 0; Unknown ethnicity—full-time 0, part-time 0.

Financial Information/Assistance:

Tuition for Full-Time Study: *Master's:* State residents: per academic year $4,814, $193 per credit hour; Nonstate residents: per academic year $11,030, $452 per credit hour. *Doctoral:* State residents: per academic year $4,814, $193 per credit hour; Nonstate residents: per academic year $11,030, $452 per credit hour. See the following Web site for updates and changes in tuition costs: http://www.hawaii.edu/admrec/tuition.html.

Financial Assistance:

First-Year Students: Teaching assistantships available for first year. Average amount paid per academic year: $15,558. Average number of hours worked per week: 20. Apply by automatic with application. Tuition remission given: full.

Advanced Students: No information provided.

Additional Information: Of all students currently enrolled full time, 10% benefited from one or more of the listed financial assistance programs. Application and information available online at http://www.hawaii.edu/fas/.

Internships/Practica: Research and teaching internships are highly recommended for doctoral students; however, financial support continues to be very limited.

Housing and Day Care: On-campus housing is available. See the following Web site for more information: http://www.housing.hawaii.edu/. No on-campus day care facilities are available.

Employment of Department Graduates:

Master's Degree Graduates: Of those who graduated in the academic year 2006–2007, the following categories and numbers represent the postgraduate activities and employment of master's degree graduates: Enrolled in a postdoctoral residency/fellowship (n/a), employed in independent practice (n/a), total from the above (master's) (0).

Doctoral Degree Graduates: Of those who graduated in the academic year 2006–2007, the following categories and numbers represent the postgraduate activities and employment of doctoral degree graduates: Enrolled in a psychology doctoral program (n/a), total from the above (doctoral) (0).

Additional Information:

Orientation, Objectives, and Emphasis of Department: The primary objective of graduate training is the development of competent scholars in the discipline of Educational Psychology. Therefore, the faculty seeks students with research interests and abilities, independence of thought, and a willingness to actively participate in both formal and informal teaching and learning experiences. The students' efforts may be directed toward the attainment of the MEd or the PhD degree. Thesis (Plan A) and nonthesis (Plan B) options are available at the MEd level. Members of the faculty share a commitment to a model of graduate education that is humanistic and inquiry oriented. An extensive core of quantitative coursework—measurement, statistics, and research methodology—underlies most programs of study, especially at the doctoral level. In addition, core courses in human learning and development give the student a contextual framework within which inquiry methodologies are applied. The small size of the department ensures a high level of interaction among students and faculty in and out of class. Working closely with the faculty, each student creates a degree plan uniquely suited to his or her academic goals. Interdisciplinary study is particularly encouraged.

Special Facilities or Resources: The college's Curriculum Research and Development Group affords opportunities for involvement in a wide variety of educational research and program evaluation activities, many of which are centered in the K–12 laboratory school on campus.

Information for Students With Physical Disabilities: See the following Web site for more information: http://www.catalog.hawaii.edu/general_information/student-life/support.htm.

Application Information:

Send to Department of Educational Psychology, College of Education, 1776 University Avenue, Honolulu, HI 96822. Students are admitted in the Fall, application deadline February 1; Spring, application deadline September 1. PhD program has Fall admission only. Applications from foreign students have deadlines of January 15 and August 1 for Fall and Spring admission, respectively. *Fee:* $50. Application fee for non-U.S. citizens is $50. Separate applications materials are submitted to the department and to the Graduate Division.

Hawaii, University of, Manoa (2007 data)

Department of Psychology
College of Social Sciences
2430 Campus Road
Honolulu, HI 96822-2294
Telephone: (808) 956-8414
Fax: (808) 956-4700
E-mail: *amaynard@hawaii.edu*
Web: *http://www.hawaii.edu/psychology*

Department Information:

1939. Chairperson: Ashley E. Maynard, PhD. Number of faculty: total—full-time 22, part-time 4; women—full-time 8, part-time 3.

Programs and Degrees Offered:

Listed in the following order: Program area, degree type (T if terminal Master's), number awarded 7/06–6/07. Behavioral Neuroscience PhD (Doctor of Philosophy) 1, Clinical PhD (Doctor of Philosophy) 6, Community and Cultural PhD (Doctor of Philosophy) 2, Developmental PhD (Doctor of Philosophy) 0, Experimental Psychopathology PhD (Doctor of Philosophy) 1, Social–Personality PhD (Doctor of Philosophy) 2, Cognition PhD (Doctor of Philosophy) 0.

APA Accreditation: Clinical PhD (Doctor of Philosophy).

Student Applications/Admissions:

Student Applications

Behavioral Neuroscience PhD (Doctor of Philosophy)—Applications 2007–2008, 14. Total applicants accepted 2007–2008, 3. Number full-time enrolled (new admits only) 2007–2008, 2. Openings 2008–2009, 3. The median number of years required for completion of a degree in 2006–2007 were 6. The number of students enrolled full- and part-time who were dismissed or voluntarily withdrew from this program area in 2007–2008 were 0. *Clinical PhD (Doctor of Philosophy)*—Applications 2007–2008, 119. Total applicants accepted 2007–2008, 9. Number full-time enrolled (new admits only) 2007–2008, 9. Number part-time enrolled (new admits only) 2007–2008, 0. Openings 2008–2009, 10. The median number of years required for completion of a degree in 2006–2007 were 8. The number of students enrolled full- and part-time who were dismissed or voluntarily withdrew from this program area in 2007–2008 were 0. *Community and Cultural PhD (Doctor of Philosophy)*—Applications 2007–2008, 13. Total applicants accepted 2007–2008, 2. Number full-time enrolled (new admits only) 2007–2008, 1. Openings 2008–2009, 2. The median number of years required for completion of a degree in 2006–2007 were 6. The number of students enrolled full- and part-time who were dismissed or voluntarily withdrew from this program area in 2007–2008 were 0. *Developmental PhD (Doctor of Philosophy)*—Applications 2007–2008, 8. Total applicants accepted 2007–2008, 2. Number full-time enrolled (new admits only) 2007–2008, 1. Openings 2008–2009, 2. The number of students enrolled full- and part-time who were dismissed or voluntarily withdrew from this program area in 2007–2008 were 0. *Experimental Psychopathology PhD (Doctor of Philosophy)*—Applications 2007–2008, 1. Total applicants accepted 2007–2008, 1. Number full-time enrolled (new admits only) 2007–2008, 1. Openings 2008–2009, 2. The median number of years required for completion of a degree in 2006–2007 were 6. The number of students enrolled full- and part-time who were dismissed or voluntarily withdrew from this program area in 2007–2008 were 0. *Social–Personality PhD (Doctor of Philosophy)*—Applications 2007–2008, 27. Total applicants accepted 2007–2008, 3. Number full-time enrolled (new admits only) 2007–2008, 3. Openings 2008–2009, 5. The median number of years required for completion of a degree in 2006–2007 were 6. The number of students enrolled full- and part-time who were dismissed or voluntarily withdrew from this program area in 2007–2008 were 0. *Cognition PhD (Doctor of Philosophy)*—Applications 2007–2008, 3. Total applicants accepted 2007–2008, 0. Number full-time enrolled (new admits only) 2007–2008, 1. Openings 2008–2009, 2. The number of students enrolled full- and part-time who were dismissed or voluntarily withdrew from this program area in 2007–2008 were 0.

Admissions Requirements:

Scores: Entries appear in this order: required test or GPA, minimum score (if required), median score of students entering in 2007–2008. Master's Programs: GRE-V no minimum stated, 620; GRE-Q no minimum stated, 640; overall undergraduate GPA 3.0, 3.5; last 2 years GPA 3.0. Doctoral Programs: GRE-V no minimum stated, 620; GRE-Q no minimum stated, 640; overall undergraduate GPA 3.0, 3.5; last 2 years GPA 3.0. Numbers are same for MA and PhD. Most students are initially admitted into MA program and proceed to doctoral candidacy.

Other Criteria: (importance of criteria rated low, medium, or high): GRE/MAT scores—high, research experience—high, work experience—low, extracurricular activity—low, clinically related public service—low, GPA—high, letters of recommendation—high, statement of goals and objectives—high. For additional information on admission requirements, go to http://www.psychology.hawaii.edu/.

Student Characteristics: The following represents characteristics of students in 2007–2008 in all graduate psychology programs in the department: Female—full-time 71, part-time 0; Male—full-time 25, part-time 0; African American/Black—full-time 1, part-time 0; Hispanic/Latino(a)—full-time 6, part-time 0; Asian/Pacific Islander—full-time 30, part-time 0; American Indian/Alaska Native—full-time 0, part-time 0; Caucasian/White—full-time 55, part-time 0; Multi-ethnic—full-time 4, part-time 0; students subject to the Americans With Disabilities Act—full-time 1, part-time 0; Unknown ethnicity—full-time 0, part-time 0.

Financial Information/Assistance:

Tuition for Full-Time Study: *Master's:* State residents: per academic year $6,864; Nonstate residents: per academic year $16,320. *Doctoral:* State residents: per academic year $6,864; Nonstate residents: per academic year $16,320, $462 per credit hour. Tuition is subject to change. See the following Web site for updates and changes in tuition costs: http://www.hawaii.edu/graduatestudies/.

Financial Assistance:

First-Year Students: Teaching assistantships available for first year. Average amount paid per academic year: $13,296. Average number of hours worked per week: 20. Apply by January 1. Tuition remission given: full. Research assistantships available for first year. Average amount paid per academic year: $13,296. Average number of hours worked per week: 20. Apply by January 1. Tuition remission given: full. Fellowships and scholarships available for first year. Average amount paid per academic year: $0. Apply by January 1. Tuition remission given: full.

Advanced Students: Teaching assistantships available for advanced students. Average amount paid per academic year: $14,382. Average number of hours worked per week: 20. Apply by January 1. Tuition remission given: full. Research assistantships available for advanced students. Average amount paid per academic year: $14,382. Average number of hours worked per week: 20. Apply by January 1. Tuition remission given: full. Fellowships and scholarships available for advanced students. Average amount paid per academic year: $0. Apply by January 1. Tuition remission given: full.

Additional Information: Of all students currently enrolled full time, 30% benefited from one or more of the listed financial assistance programs. Application and information available online at http://www.hawaii.edu/graduate/financial/html/assistantships.htm.

Internships/Practica: A minimum of 2 years of practica experience (18 to 20 hours per week) are required for all 2nd- through 4th-year graduate students in the clinical studies program. A variety of practica sites are available throughout the state and most include stipend support (average $14,000 per academic year). Sites include the department's Cognitive Behavior Therapy Clinic, community mental health outpatient centers, VA (including PTSD specialty clinics), mental health hospitals, child mental health institutions, UH counseling center, and state-supported work with the seriously mentally disabled population.

Housing and Day Care: On-campus housing is available. See the following Web site for more information: http://www.housing.hawaii.edu/. On-campus day care facilities are available. See the following Web site for more information: http://www.hawaii.edu/osa/Childrens_Center.html.

Employment of Department Graduates:

Master's Degree Graduates: Of those who graduated in the academic year 2006–2007, the following categories and numbers represent the postgraduate activities and employment of master's degree graduates: Enrolled in a postdoctoral residency/fellowship (n/a), employed in independent practice (n/a), total from the above (master's) (0).

Doctoral Degree Graduates: Of those who graduated in the academic year 2006–2007, the following categories and numbers represent the postgraduate activities and employment of doctoral degree graduates: Enrolled in a psychology doctoral program (n/a), total from the above (doctoral) (0).

Additional Information:

Orientation, Objectives, and Emphasis of Department: The Department of Psychology's orientation is best characterized as a synthesis of biological, behavioral, and cognitive areas, with an overriding emphasis on empiricism (i.e., the study of psychological phenomena based on sound research findings). The graduate concentrations in clinical, developmental, community and cultural, behavioral neuroscience, experimental psychopathology, social–personality, and cognition emphasize the development of research skills and knowledge that are applicable to a wide range of academic and applied settings. The clinical program adheres to the scientist–practitioner model of training, wherein research and clinical skills are equally emphasized. Research opportunities in all graduate concentrations are available. The faculty is particularly interested in admitting students who are interested in pursuing academically related careers.

Special Facilities or Resources: The Psychology Department is mainly housed in Gartley Hall, a historic campus building. Gartley Hall is devoted to facilities for office space, research, and teaching in psychology. Faculty members have specialized laboratories for research, including equipment to support cognitive, social, and developmental work. Graduate students are assigned shared office space in Gartley Hall and have access to most departmental facilities. The computing facilities in the department and university are of a high standard, and the campus has good wireless Internet coverage. Opportunities for study and research also exist elsewhere at the university and in the community. These include the Pacific Biosciences Research Center, the John A. Burns School of Medicine, the Center for Disability Studies, the Hawaii State Hospital at Kaneohe, Leahi Hospital, the State Departments of Health and Education, and the Osher Lifelong Learning Institute. Beyond the physical facilities available to the department is the unusual opportunity for research provided by the unique social and environmental structure of Hawaii. An important dimension is also provided by the East–West Center for Cultural Interchange, which provides fellowships for Asian and U.S. students and for senior scholars from mainland and foreign universities.

Information for Students With Physical Disabilities: See the following Web site for more information: http://www.hawaii.edu/osa/KOKUA.html.

Application Information:

Send to Graduate Studies Chair, Department of Psychology, University of Hawaii at Manoa, 2430 Campus Road, Honolulu, HI 96822. Application available online. URL of online application: http://www.hawaii.edu/graduate/admissions/html/apply.htm. Students are admitted in the Fall, application deadline January 1. *Fee:* $50.

Idaho State University

Department of Psychology
Arts and Sciences
921 South 8th Avenue, Stop 8112
Pocatello, ID 83209
Telephone: (208) 282-2462
Fax: (208) 282-4832
E-mail: *turlkand@isu.edu*
Web: *http://www.isu.edu/departments/psych*

Department Information:

1968. Chairperson: Kandi Turley-Ames. Number of faculty: total—full-time 7, part-time 6; women—full-time 7, part-time 4; ; women minority—full-time 1; faculty subject to the Americans With Disabilities Act 1.

Programs and Degrees Offered:

Listed in the following order: Program area, degree type (T if terminal Master's), number awarded 7/06–6/07. Clinical PhD (Doctor of Philosophy) 4, Experimental General MA/MS (Master of Arts/Science) (T) 0.

APA Accreditation: Clinical PhD (Doctor of Philosophy).

Student Applications/Admissions:

Student Applications

Clinical PhD (Doctor of Philosophy)—Applications 2007–2008, 73. Total applicants accepted 2007–2008, 12. Number full-time enrolled (new admits only) 2007–2008, 6. Number part-time enrolled (new admits only) 2007–2008, 0. Total enrolled 2007–2008 full-time, 29, part-time, 5. Openings 2008–2009, 6. The median number of years required for completion of a degree in 2006–2007 were 6. The number of students enrolled full- and part-time who were dismissed or voluntarily withdrew from this program area in 2007–2008 were 0. *Experimental General MA/MS (Master of Arts/Science)*—Applications 2007–2008, 6. Total applicants accepted 2007–2008, 3. Number full-time enrolled (new admits only) 2007–2008, 1. Number part-time enrolled (new admits only) 2007–2008, 0. Total enrolled 2007–2008 full-time, 2, part-time, 3. Openings 2008–2009, 5. The number of students enrolled full- and part-time who were dismissed or voluntarily withdrew from this program area in 2007–2008 were 0.

Admissions Requirements:

Scores: Entries appear in this order: required test or GPA, minimum score (if required), median score of students entering in 2007–2008. Master's Programs: GRE-V no minimum stated, 550; GRE-Q no minimum stated, 680; GRE-Subject (Psychology) no minimum stated, 640; last 2 years GPA 3.0, 3.78; Masters GRE-Analytical no minimum stated, 4.5. GREs at the 50th percentile or higher are preferred, but not required, on two of three aptitude tests and on the advanced subject test in psychology. All applicants must submit both the GRE aptitude tests and the GRE Advanced Subject Test in Psychology to be considered for admission. Doctoral Programs: GRE-V no minimum stated, 580; GRE-Q no minimum stated, 680; GRE-Subject (Psychology) no minimum stated, 665; last 2 years GPA 3.0, 3.84; Doctoral program GRE-Analytic no minimum stated, 4.75. GREs at the 50th percentile or higher are preferred, but not required, on two of three aptitude tests and on the advanced subject test in psychology. All applicants must submit both the GRE aptitude tests and the GRE Advanced Subject Test in Psychology to be considered for admission.

Other Criteria: (importance of criteria rated low, medium, or high): GRE/MAT scores—medium, research experience—medium, work experience—low, extracurricular activity—low, clinically related public service—medium, GPA—medium, letters of recommendation—medium, interview—medium, statement of goals and objectives—medium, undergraduate major in psychology—medium, specific undergraduate psychology courses taken—low. For the Experimental General MS program, clinically related public service is not relevant. For additional information on admission requirements, go to http://www.isu.edu/psych.

Student Characteristics: The following represents characteristics of students in 2007–2008 in all graduate psychology programs in the department: Female—full-time 24, part-time 6; Male—full-time 7, part-time 2; African American/Black—full-time 0, part-time 0; Hispanic/Latino(a)—full-time 1, part-time 0; Asian/Pacific Islander—full-time 0, part-time 0; American Indian/Alaska Native—full-time 0, part-time 0; Caucasian/White—full-time 30, part-time 8; Multi-ethnic—full-time 0, part-time 0; students subject to the Americans With Disabilities Act—full-time 0, part-time 0; Unknown ethnicity—full-time 0, part-time 0; International students who hold an F-1 or J-1 Visa—full-time 1, part-time 0.

Financial Information/Assistance:

Tuition for Full-Time Study: *Master's:* State residents: per academic year $5,160, $259 per credit hour; Nonstate residents: per academic year $13,844, $379 per credit hour. *Doctoral:* State residents: per academic year $5,160, $259 per credit hour; Nonstate residents: per academic year $13,844, $379 per credit hour. Tuition is subject to change. Additional fees are assessed to students beyond the costs of tuition for the following: $523 health insurance premium per semester, unless waived by proof of insurance. See the following Web site for updates and changes in tuition costs: http://www.isu.edu/finserv/costinfo.shtml.

Financial Assistance:

First-Year Students: Teaching assistantships available for first year. Average amount paid per academic year: $11,924. Average number of hours worked per week: 18. Apply by March 1. Tuition remission given: full. Traineeships available for first year. Average amount paid per academic year: $6,500. Average number of hours worked per week: 15. Apply by March 1. Tuition remission given: partial. Fellowships and scholarships available for first year. Average amount paid per academic year: $1,800. Average number of hours worked per week: 0. Apply by March 1.

Advanced Students: Teaching assistantships available for advanced students. Average amount paid per academic year: $11,924. Average number of hours worked per week: 18. Apply by March 1. Tuition remission given: full. Traineeships available for advanced students. Average amount paid per academic year: $12,000. Average number of hours worked per week: 15. Apply by March 1. Tuition remission given: partial. Fellowships and scholarships available for advanced students. Average amount paid per academic year: $1,800. Average number of hours worked per week: 0. Apply by March 1.

Additional Information: Of all students currently enrolled full time, 100% benefited from one or more of the listed financial assistance programs. Application and information available online at http://www.isu.edu/psych/apply.shtml.

Internships/Practica: Doctoral Degree (PhD Clinical): For those doctoral students for whom a professional internship was required in this program prior to graduation, (3) students applied for an internship in 2006–2007, with (3) students obtaining an internship. Of those students who obtained an internship, (3) were paid internships. Of those students who obtained an internship, (2) students placed in APA/CPA-accredited internships, (1) students placed in internships not APA/CPA-accredited, but listed with the Association of Psychology Postdoctoral and Internship Centers (APPIC), (0) students placed in internships conforming to guidelines of the Council of Directors of School Psychology Programs (CDSPP), (0) students placed in internships that were not APA/CPA-accredited, APPIC or CDSPP listed. Clinical practica are required for doctoral students admitted into the MS PhD clinical program. First- and second-year students complete practica in the ISU Psychology Clinic under the supervision of clinical faculty. Third- and fourth-year students, however, often participate in community practica and/or clinical externships under the supervision of licensed psychologists employed by local mental health providers/agencies. One semester participation on the ISU Interdisciplinary Evaluation Team is also required. Currently, eight clinical externships sites provide stipends and supervised practice in applied settings for 10 students. The average student entering APPIC internships from ISU during 2007–2008 accumulated 1,945 hours of supervised professional activities (median = 1,816 hours).

Housing and Day Care: On-campus housing is available. See the following Web site for more information: http://www.isu.edu/housing or call the University Housing Office (208) 282-2120. On-campus day care facilities are available. See the following Web site for more information: http://www.isu.edu/earlylc or call the Early Leaning Center (208) 282-2769.

Employment of Department Graduates:

Master's Degree Graduates: Of those who graduated in the academic year 2006–2007, the following categories and numbers represent the postgraduate activities and employment of master's degree graduates: Enrolled in a postdoctoral residency/fellowship (n/a), employed in independent practice (n/a), total from the above (master's) (0).

Doctoral Degree Graduates: Of those who graduated in the academic year 2006–2007, the following categories and numbers represent the postgraduate activities and employment of doctoral degree graduates: Enrolled in a psychology doctoral program (n/a), enrolled in a postdoctoral residency/fellowship (1), employed in government agency (1), employed in a hospital/medical center (2), total from the above (doctoral) (4).

Additional Information:

Orientation, Objectives, and Emphasis of Department: The master of science program in general/experimental psychology provides students with an education in core areas of psychological science, such as personality–social, perception–cognitive, and sensory–physiological. This program of study, culminating in defense of a thesis, is designed to prepare students for doctoral work in psychology or careers in psychology or related fields that require mastery of the principles and methods of general experimental psychology. The experimental MS in psychology is not intended to prepare students for careers in mental health. The department anticipates offering the doctoral degree in experimental psychology, pending final approval by the State Board of Education. The mission of the clinical doctoral program is to train competent clinical psychologists who can apply and adapt general conceptual and technical skills in diverse regional and professional settings. An effective clinical psychologist possesses a strong professional identity that includes (a) a firm grounding in the science of psychology, and (b) knowledge of relevant theories and technical skills that aid in the amelioration of human suffering. Most important, a clinical psychologist understands the interactive relationship between science and practice. As such, the educational philosophy of the clinical training program at ISU is based on the traditional scientist–practitioner model of clinical training.

Special Facilities or Resources: The Psychology Department has office and laboratory space for all faculty. The ISU Psychology Clinic, housed in the same building, provides four individual therapy rooms, two child/family rooms, two testing rooms, and a group therapy room, all equipped with observation systems and videotape capabilities. Office space is provided to all graduate students. Computer access is available in offices, in the department, the clinic, and a university center located nearby. The university maintains an animal colony at which one Psychology faculty member participates, an Office of Sponsored Programs (grant assistance), and an instructional technical resource center (website assistance).

Information for Students With Physical Disabilities: See the following Web site for more information: http://www.isu.edu/ada4isu/.

Application Information:

Send to Admissions Committee, 921 South 8th Avenue, Stop 8112 Idaho State University, Pocatello, ID 83209. Application available online. URL of online application: http://www.isu.edu/psych/apply.shtml. Students are admitted in the Fall, application deadline January 1; Spring, application deadline November 1. For clinical students the deadline is January 1. Clinical students are only admitted to enter Fall semester. For general MS students the fall admission deadline is March 1, and the spring admission deadline is November 1. All application forms can be obtained online. There are two steps to the application process. The Graduate School application (http://www.isu.edu/graduate/graduate-application.shtml) can be completed online. The Psychology Department application (http://www.isu.edu/psych/apply.shtml) requires downloading the forms and mailing the forms plus requested materials to the Psychology Department. *Fee:* $55.

Idaho, University of

Department of Psychology and Communication Studies
Letters, Arts, and Social Sciences
University of Idaho
Moscow, ID 83844-3043
Telephone: (208) 885-6324
Fax: (208) 885-7710
E-mail: *cberreth@uidaho.edu*
Web: *http://www.class.uidaho.edu/psychcomm*

Department Information:

Chairperson: Kenneth Locke. Number of faculty: total—full-time 15, part-time 1; women—full-time 4; total—minority—full-time 2; women minority—full-time 1.

Programs and Degrees Offered:

Listed in the following order: Program area, degree type (T if terminal Master's), number awarded 7/06–6/07. General Experimental MA/MS (Master of Arts/Science) (T) 1, Human Factors MA/MS (Master of Arts/Science) (T) 2, Industrial/Organizational MA/MS (Master of Arts/Science) (T) 5, Neuroscience PhD (Doctor of Philosophy) 0.

Student Applications/Admissions:

Student Applications

General Experimental MA/MS (Master of Arts/Science)—Applications 2007–2008, 2. Total applicants accepted 2007–2008, 2. Number full-time enrolled (new admits only) 2007–2008, 2. Total enrolled 2007–2008 full-time, 2. Openings 2008–2009, 1. The median number of years required for completion of a degree in 2006–2007 were 2. The number of students enrolled full- and part-time who were dismissed or voluntarily withdrew from this program area in 2007–2008 were 0. *Human Factors MA/MS (Master of Arts/Science)*—Applications 2007–2008, 15. Total applicants accepted 2007–2008, 7. Number full-time enrolled (new admits only) 2007–2008, 1. Number part-time enrolled (new admits only) 2007–2008, 2. Total enrolled 2007–2008 full-time, 5, part-time, 16. Openings 2008–2009, 7. The median number of years required for completion of a degree in 2006–2007 were 2. The number of students enrolled full- and part-time who were dismissed or voluntarily withdrew from this program area in 2007–2008 were 0. *Industrial/Organizational MA/MS (Master of Arts/Science)*—Applications 2007–2008, 10. Total applicants accepted 2007–2008, 6. Number full-time enrolled (new admits only) 2007–2008, 2. Number part-time enrolled (new admits only) 2007–2008, 0. Openings 2008–2009, 4. The median number of years required for completion of a degree in 2006–2007 were 2. The number of students enrolled full- and part-time who were dismissed or voluntarily withdrew from this program area in 2007–2008 were 0. *Neuroscience PhD (Doctor of Philosophy)*—Applications 2007–2008, 1. Total applicants accepted 2007–2008, 1. Number full-time enrolled (new admits only) 2007–2008, 1. Total enrolled 2007–2008 full-time, 2. Openings 2008–2009, 1. The median number of years required for completion of a degree in 2006–2007 were 5. The number of students enrolled full- and part-time who were dismissed or voluntarily withdrew from this program area in 2007–2008 were 0.

Admissions Requirements:

Scores: Entries appear in this order: required test or GPA, minimum score (if required), median score of students entering in 2007–2008. Master's Programs: GRE-V no minimum stated; GRE-Q no minimum stated; overall undergraduate GPA 3.0, 3.5. Doctoral Programs: GRE-V no minimum stated; GRE-Q no minimum stated.

Other Criteria: (importance of criteria rated low, medium, or high): GRE/MAT scores—high, research experience—high, work experience—medium, extracurricular activity—low, GPA—high, letters of recommendation—high, statement of goals and objectives—high, undergraduate major in psychology—low, specific undergraduate psychology courses taken—low. Work experience more important for Human Factors and Industrial/Organizational candidates than General Experimental candidates.

Student Characteristics: The following represents characteristics of students in 2007–2008 in all graduate psychology programs in the department: Female—full-time 5, part-time 8; Male—full-time 10, part-time 8; African American/Black—full-time 0, part-time 0; Hispanic/Latino(a)—full-time 0, part-time 1; Asian/Pacific Islander—full-time 1, part-time 0; American Indian/Alaska Native—full-time 0, part-time 0; Caucasian/White—full-time 12, part-time 12; Multi-ethnic—full-time 0, part-time 0; students subject to the Americans With Disabilities Act—full-time 0, part-time 0; Unknown ethnicity—full-time 0, part-time 0; International students who hold an F-1 or J-1 Visa—full-time 2, part-time 3.

Financial Information/Assistance:

Tuition for Full-Time Study: *Master's:* State residents: per academic year $4,740, $227 per credit hour; Nonstate residents: per academic year $14,340, $367 per credit hour. Tuition is subject to change. See the following Web site for updates and changes in tuition costs: http://www.students.uidaho.edu/futurestudents/.

Financial Assistance:

First-Year Students: Teaching assistantships available for first year. Average amount paid per academic year: $4,900. Average number of hours worked per week: 10. Apply by March 1. Tuition remission given: partial. Research assistantships available for first year. Average amount paid per academic year: $10,000. Average number of hours worked per week: 20. Apply by March 1. Tuition remission given: partial.

Advanced Students: Teaching assistantships available for advanced students. Average amount paid per academic year: $10,000. Average number of hours worked per week: 20. Apply by March 1. Tuition remission given: partial. Research assistantships available for advanced students. Average amount paid per academic year: $10,500. Average number of hours worked per week: 20. Apply by March 1. Tuition remission given: partial.

Additional Information: Of all students currently enrolled full time, 100% benefited from one or more of the listed financial assistance programs.

Internships/Practica: A few internships are available locally (e.g., human resources, usability testing, Web analytics).

Housing and Day Care: On-campus housing is available. See the following Web site for more information: http://www.resnet.uidaho.edu/. On-campus day care facilities are available.

Employment of Department Graduates:

Master's Degree Graduates: Of those who graduated in the academic year 2006–2007, the following categories and numbers represent the postgraduate activities and employment of master's degree graduates: Enrolled in a psychology doctoral program (1), enrolled in another graduate/professional program (0), enrolled in a postdoctoral residency/fellowship (n/a), employed in independent practice (n/a), employed in an academic position at a university (0), employed in an academic position at a 2-year/4-year college (0), employed in other positions at a higher education institution (1), employed in a professional position in a school system (0), employed in business or industry (3), employed in a community mental health/counseling center (0), employed in a hospital/medical center (0), still seeking employment (1), other employment position (1), total from the above (master's) (7).

Doctoral Degree Graduates: Of those who graduated in the academic year 2006–2007, the following categories and numbers represent the postgraduate activities and employment of doctoral degree graduates: Enrolled in a psychology doctoral program (n/a), total from the above (doctoral) (0).

Additional Information:

Orientation, Objectives, and Emphasis of Department: In the Land Grant tradition of providing a "practical education," the Department of Psychology at the University of Idaho offers the MS degree in psychology with emphases in either Industrial/Organizational psychology (human resources, personnel, selection, organizational behavior) or Human Factors psychology (human technology interaction, ergonomics, human performance). The Department also provides off-campus and distance educational outreach by offering the MS in Psychology (Human Factors option only) through video and compressed video. The intent of both emphases is to develop knowledge and skills germane to a professional position. However, both programs also provide appropriate preparation for further graduate study. Thus, students are encouraged to develop analytical and problem-solving skills that will serve them well in whatever they choose to do after graduation. Student placement figures show that most graduates have been very successful in obtaining positions in technical industries. The Department is small, but it is able to address the broad needs of its students through working relationships with the College of Business and Economics, the College of Engineering, and the Department of Psychology at nearby (10 miles) Washington State University. Department will consider, and has occasionally admitted, students for the general experimental MS. General experimental students typically use the program to prepare for admission to doctoral programs elsewhere. Starting in 2004, the Department began admitting students seeking a PhD degree in Neuroscience. This degree is interdisciplinary, and our primary partner is the Department of Biological Sciences.

Special Facilities or Resources: The Department is in temporary quarters, but is still able to provide approximately 2,500 square feet of research space. Labs are equipped with up-to-date computers, graphics displays, and other apparatus. Research opportunities are available at remote sites, such as the Motion Analysis Lab at Shriners Hospital in Spokane, WA.

Information for Students With Physical Disabilities: See the following Web site for more information: http://www.access.uidaho.edu/.

Application Information:

Send to Graduate Admissions. Application available online. URL of online application: http://www.students.uidaho.edu/gradadmissions. Students are admitted in the Fall, application deadline March 1. Applications will be considered after the deadline, but availability of funding declines with passage of time. *Fee:* $30.

Adler School of Professional Psychology

Professional School
65 East Wacker Place, Suite 2100
Chicago, IL 60601-7203
Telephone: (312) 201-5900
Fax: (312) 201-5917
E-mail: *twilson@adler.edu*
Web: *http://www.adler.edu*

Department Information:

1952. Chairperson: Torrey Wilson, PhD. Number of faculty: total—full-time 31; women—full-time 15; total—minority—full-time 8; women minority—full-time 7; faculty subject to the Americans With Disabilities Act 3.

Programs and Degrees Offered:

Listed in the following order: Program area, degree type (T if terminal Master's), number awarded 7/06–6/07. Clinical Psychology PsyD (Doctor of Psychology) 23, Counseling Psychology MA/MS (Master of Arts/Science) (T) 81, Marriage and Family Counseling MA/MS (Master of Arts/Science) (T) 7, Substance Abuse Counseling Other 3, Art Therapy/Counseling MA/MS (Master of Arts/Science) (T) 6, Organizational MA/MS (Master of Arts/Science) (T) 3, Police Psychology MA/MS (Master of Arts/Science) 0.

APA Accreditation: Clinical PsyD (Doctor of Psychology).

Student Applications/Admissions:

Student Applications

Clinical Psychology PsyD (Doctor of Psychology)—Applications 2007–2008, 240. Total applicants accepted 2007–2008, 98. Number full-time enrolled (new admits only) 2007–2008, 65. Total enrolled 2007–2008 full-time, 267. Openings 2008–2009, 45. The median number of years required for completion of a degree in 2006–2007 were 5. The number of students enrolled full- and part-time who were dismissed or voluntarily withdrew from this program area in 2007–2008 were 5. *Counseling Psychology MA/MS (Master of Arts/Science)*—Applications 2007–2008, 94. Total applicants accepted 2007–2008, 47. Number full-time enrolled (new admits only) 2007–2008, 22. Total enrolled 2007–2008 full-time, 65. Openings 2008–2009, 40. The number of students enrolled full- and part-time who were dismissed or voluntarily withdrew from this program area in 2007–2008 were 3. *Marriage and Family Counseling MA/MS (Master of Arts/Science)*—Applications 2007–2008, 35. Total applicants accepted 2007–2008, 17. Number full-time enrolled (new admits only) 2007–2008, 9. Total enrolled 2007–2008 full-time, 28. Openings 2008–2009, 20. The number of students enrolled full- and part-time who were dismissed or voluntarily withdrew from this program area in 2007–2008 were 0. *Substance Abuse Counseling Other*—Applications 2007–2008, 5. Total applicants accepted 2007–2008, 4. Openings 2008–2009, 10. The median number of years required for completion of a degree in 2006–2007 was 1. The number of students enrolled full- and part-time who were dismissed or voluntarily withdrew from this program area in 2007–2008 were 0. *Art Therapy/Counseling MA/MS (Master of Arts/Science)*—Applications 2007–2008, 44. Total applicants accepted 2007–2008, 34. Number full-time enrolled (new admits only) 2007–2008, 17. Total enrolled 2007–2008 full-time, 21, part-time, 20. Openings 2008–2009, 20. The number of students enrolled full- and part-time who were dismissed or voluntarily withdrew from this program area in 2007–2008 were 0. *Organizational MA/MS (Master of Arts/Science)*—Applications 2007–2008, 25. Total applicants accepted 2007–2008, 12. Number full-time enrolled (new admits only) 2007–2008, 8. Total enrolled 2007–2008 full-time, 17. Openings 2008–2009, 15. *Police Psychology MA/MS (Master of Arts/Science)*—Applications 2007–2008, 20. Total applicants accepted 2007–2008, 20. Total enrolled 2007–2008 full-time, 44. Openings 2008–2009, 30. The median number of years required for completion of a degree in 2006–2007 were 2.

Admissions Requirements:

Scores: Entries appear in this order: required test or GPA, minimum score (if required), median score of students entering in 2007–2008. Master's Programs: overall undergraduate GPA 3.00; last 2 years GPA 3.00; psychology GPA 3.00. Doctoral Programs: overall undergraduate GPA 3.25; last 2 years GPA 3.25; psychology GPA 3.25.

Other Criteria: (importance of criteria rated low, medium, or high): research experience—low, work experience—medium, extracurricular activity—high, clinically related public service—high, GPA—high, letters of recommendation—high, interview—high, statement of goals and objectives—high, mission consistant—high. Masters in Art Therapy must also have 18 studio credits of art and present a portfolio at the time of interview. For additional information on admission requirements, go to http://www.adler.edu.

Student Characteristics: The following represents characteristics of students in 2007–2008 in all graduate psychology programs in the department: Female—full-time 138, part-time 190; Male—full-time 44, part-time 62; African American/Black—full-time 11, part-time 14; Hispanic/Latino(a)—full-time 8, part-time 8; Asian/Pacific Islander—full-time 3, part-time 4; American Indian/Alaska Native—full-time 1, part-time 0; Caucasian/White—full-time 66, part-time 92; Multi-ethnic—full-time 2, part-time 0; students subject to the Americans With Disabilities Act—full-time 4, part-time 6; Unknown ethnicity—full-time 3, part-time 19.

Financial Information/Assistance:

Tuition for Full-Time Study: *Master's:* State residents: $740 per credit hour; Nonstate residents: $740 per credit hour. *Doctoral:* State residents: $740 per credit hour; Nonstate residents: $740 per credit hour. Tuition is subject to change. See the following Web site for updates and changes in tuition costs: http://www.adler.edu. Higher tuition cost for this program: Vancouver campus tuition is $550 canadian dollars per credit and the MAP tuition is $890.

Financial Assistance:

First-Year Students: Fellowships and scholarships available for first year. Average amount paid per academic year: $5,000. Apply by February 15.

Advanced Students: Teaching assistantships available for advanced students. Average amount paid per academic year: $5,200. Average number of hours worked per week: 10. Apply by varies. Traineeships available for advanced students. Average amount paid per academic year: $0. Average number of hours worked per week: 20. Fellowships and scholarships available for advanced students. Average amount paid per academic year: $5,000. Apply by June 1.

Additional Information: Of all students currently enrolled full time, 6% benefited from one or more of the listed financial assistance programs. Application and information available online at: http://www.adler.edu.

Internships/Practica: Doctoral Degree (PsyD Clinical Psychology): For those doctoral students for whom a professional internship was required in this program prior to graduation, (41) students applied for an internship in 2006–2007, with (39) students obtaining an internship. Of those students who obtained an internship, (36) were paid internships. Of those students who obtained an internship, (11) students placed in APA/CPA-accredited internships, (28) students placed in internships not APA/CPA accredited, but listed with the Association of Psychology Postdoctoral and Internship Centers (APPIC), (0) students placed in internships conforming to guidelines of the Council of Directors of School Psychology Programs (CDSPP), (0) students placed in internships that were not APA/CPA-accredited, APPIC or CDSPP listed. Practicum students, predoctoral interns, and postdoctoral interns have the opportunity to receive training at the school's licensed Psychological Services Center, which serves more than 250 clients weekly. Students under faculty supervision provide a wide range of services to the public including psychotherapy, psychological testing, art therapy, neurological assessments, forensic evaluations, support groups, and parenting classes. In addition to the counseling center on campus, students are placed in a number of satellite locations throughout the Chicago area in settings such as elementary and high schools, prisons, Veterans Administration Medical Centers, transitional homes, and gerontological facilities.

Housing and Day Care: No on-campus housing is available. No on-campus day care facilities are available.

Employment of Department Graduates:

Master's Degree Graduates: Of those who graduated in the academic year 2006–2007, the following categories and numbers represent the postgraduate activities and employment of master's degree graduates: Enrolled in a postdoctoral residency/fellowship (n/a), employed in independent practice (n/a), total from the above (master's) (0).

Doctoral Degree Graduates: Of those who graduated in the academic year 2006–2007, the following categories and numbers represent the postgraduate activities and employment of doctoral degree graduates: Enrolled in a psychology doctoral program (n/a), employed in independent practice (8), employed in a hospital/medical center (10), total from the above (doctoral) (18).

Additional Information:

Orientation, Objectives, and Emphasis of Department: The Adler School of Professional Psychology is a private, not-for-profit, institution of higher education. Founded in 1952 by Rudolf Dreikers, MD, the Adler School is the oldest psychology school in the country and the only accredited doctoral institution in the world having Alfred Adler's Individual Psychology as its major educational orientation. The reputation of the school has been built by an outstanding faculty who combine professional practice with their research, instructional, and clinical supervision responsibilities. Located in Chicago's Loop, the Adler School has an established reputation for providing educational programs, publications, and clinical services. The student body comprises persons of diverse cultures, ages, educational backgrounds, and professional experiences. The Adler School continues to apply Adler's vision to today's social problems with an emphasis on the training of soically responsible psychologists. The School's curricula prepare professionals to address social and global challenges as well as the needs of marginalized and underserved populations. Our on-campus, full-service clinic offers an opportunity for students to train with faculty in a clinical setting. Degrees offered include Masters of Arts in Counseling, Art Therapy, Marriage and Family Counseling, Organizational Psychology, Substance Abuse Counseling, Gerontological Psychology and a Doctor of Psychology (PsyD) as well as a number of specialization certificates such as clinical neuropsychology, substance abuse, clinical hypnosis, and Adlerian psychology. The doctoral program is accredited by the American Psychological Association.

Special Facilities or Resources: An especially valuable asset to the programs offered is the school's licensed Psychological Services Center, which serves more than 250 clients weekly. Students under faculty supervision provide a wide range of services to the public including psychotherapy, psychological testing, art therapy, neuropsycholgical assessments, forensic evaluations, support groups, and parenting classes. Practicum students, predoctoral interns, and postdoctoral interns are involved at the counseling center on campus and at a number of satellite locations throughout the Chicago area in settings such as elementary and high schools, prisons, churches, transitional homes, and gerontological facilities. The Adler School of Professional Psychology is located in the center of downtown Chicago on the Chicago River. The School's location provides easy access to libraries and related facilities of some of the nation's best educational institutions, some with whom the library maintains cooperative lending agreements. The building is handicap accessible, available 365 days of the year, and has 24-hour security.

Information for Students With Physical Disabilities: See the following Web site for more information: http://www.adler.edu.

Application Information:

Send to Office of Admissions, 65 East Wacker Place, Suite 2100, Chicago, IL 60601. Application available online. URL of online application: http://www.adler.edu. Students are admitted in the Fall, application deadline February 15; Winter, application deadline November 1; Programs have rolling admissions. PsyD priority deadline is February 15 for Fall and November 1 for Winter. All programs are on rolling admissions basis. *Fee:* $50. Documentation from social service agency documenting financial hardship. Fee is waived for McNair Scholars.

Argosy University/American School of Professional Psychology, Schaumburg Campus

Clinical Psychology
American School of Professional Psychology
999 Plaza Drive, Suite 111
Schaumburg, IL 60173
Telephone: (847) 969-4900
Fax: (847) 969-4999
E-mail: *jwasner@argosy.edu*
Web: *http://www.argosy.edu*

Department Information:

1994. Dean, ASPP and Chair, Clinical Psychology: Jim Wasner, PhD. Number of faculty: total—full-time 13, part-time 10; women—full-time 5, part-time 5; total—minority—full-time 1, part-time 2; women minority—full-time 1, part-time 1; faculty subject to the Americans With Disabilities Act 1.

Programs and Degrees Offered:

Listed in the following order: Program area, degree type (T if terminal Master's), number awarded 7/06–6/07. Clinical Psychology MA/MS (Master of Arts/Science) (T) 27, Clinical Psychology PsyD (Doctor of Psychology) 36.

APA Accreditation: Clinical PsyD (Doctor of Psychology).

Student Applications/Admissions:

Student Applications

Clinical Psychology MA/MS (Master of Arts/Science)—Applications 2007–2008, 60. Total applicants accepted 2007–2008, 35. Number full-time enrolled (new admits only) 2007–2008, 18. Number part-time enrolled (new admits only) 2007–2008, 6. Total enrolled 2007–2008 full-time, 33, part-time, 13. Openings 2008–2009, 19. The median number of years required for completion of a degree in 2006–2007 were 2. The number of students enrolled full- and part-time who were dismissed or voluntarily withdrew from this program area in 2007–2008 were 1. *Clinical Psychology PsyD (Doctor of Psychology)*—Applications 2007–2008, 151. Total applicants accepted 2007–2008, 75. Number full-time enrolled (new admits only) 2007–2008, 50. Number part-time enrolled (new admits only) 2007–2008, 3. Total enrolled 2007–2008 full-time, 129, part-time, 68. Openings 2008–2009, 42. The median number of years required for completion of a degree in 2006–2007 were 5. The number of students enrolled full- and part-time who were dismissed or voluntarily withdrew from this program area in 2007–2008 were 2.

Admissions Requirements:

Scores: Entries appear in this order: required test or GPA, minimum score (if required), median score of students entering in 2007–2008. Master's Programs: overall undergraduate GPA 3.00, 3.19; last 2 years GPA 3.00, 3.36; psychology GPA 3.00, 3.37. Above requirements for the MA Clinical Program. Doctoral Programs: overall undergraduate GPA 3.25, 3.57; last 2 years GPA 3.25, 3.66; psychology GPA 3.25, 3.68. Students may be admitted into the doctoral program with only a BA/BS degree.

Other Criteria: (importance of criteria rated low, medium, or high): research experience—low, work experience—medium, extracurricular activity—low, clinically related public service—medium, GPA—high, letters of recommendation—high, interview—high, statement of goals and objectives—high. For additional information on admission requirements, go to http://www.argosy.edu.

Student Characteristics: The following represents characteristics of students in 2007–2008 in all graduate psychology programs in the department: Female—full-time 132, part-time 68; Male—full-time 30, part-time 13; African American/Black—full-time 11, part-time 9; Hispanic/Latino(a)—full-time 8, part-time 4; Asian/Pacific Islander—full-time 6, part-time 3; American Indian/Alaska Native—full-time 1, part-time 0; Caucasian/White—full-time 131, part-time 62; Multi-ethnic—full-time 0, part-time 0; students subject to the Americans With Disabilities Act—full-time 10, part-time 0; Unknown ethnicity—full-time 5, part-time 3.

Financial Information/Assistance:

Tuition for Full-Time Study: *Master's:* State residents: per academic year $22,375, $895 per credit hour; Nonstate residents: per academic year $22,375, $895 per credit hour. *Doctoral:* State residents: per academic year $21,480, $895 per credit hour; Nonstate residents: per academic year $21,480, $895 per credit hour. Tuition is subject to change.

Financial Assistance:

First-Year Students: Teaching assistantships available for first year. Average amount paid per academic year: $2,000. Average number of hours worked per week: 5. Apply by vAries. Traineeships available for first year. Average amount paid per academic year: $2,000. Average number of hours worked per week: 7. Apply by varies. Fellowships and scholarships available for first year. Average amount paid per academic year: $2,000. Apply by varies.

Advanced Students: Teaching assistantships available for advanced students. Average amount paid per academic year: $2,000. Average number of hours worked per week: 5. Apply by varies. Traineeships available for advanced students. Average amount paid per academic year: $2,000. Average number of hours worked per week: 7. Apply by varies. Fellowships and scholarships available for advanced students. Average amount paid per academic year: $2,000. Apply by varies.

Additional Information: Of all students currently enrolled full time, 25% benefited from one or more of the listed financial assistance programs. Application and information available online at http://www.argosy.edu.

Internships/Practica: Doctoral Degree (PsyD Clinical Psychology): For those doctoral students for whom a professional internship was required in this program prior to graduation, (23) students applied for an internship in 2006–2007, with (22) students obtaining an internship. Of those students who obtained an internship, (19) were paid internships. Of those students who obtained an internship, (7) students placed in APA/CPA-accredited internships, (10) students placed in internships not APA/CPA accredited, but listed with the Association of Psychology Postdoctoral and Internship Centers (APPIC), (0) students placed in internships conforming to guidelines of the Council of Directors of School Psychology Programs (CDSPP), (5) students placed in internships that were not APA/CPA-accredited, APPIC or CDSPP listed. Clinical field training is a required component of all programs at the Argosy University American School of

Professional Psychology/Schaumburg Campus and is a direct outgrowth of the practitioner emphasis of professional psychology. The school provides advisement and assistance in placing students in a wide variety of clinical sites, including hospitals, schools, mental health facilities, treatment centers, and social service agencies. The MA in clinical psychology requires a minimum of 750 hours of practicum experience. The PsyD program includes 2 years of practicum experience, including separate practica for diagnosis and assessment, and psychotherapy, with a minimum of 900 hours per year; plus an additional 1-year full-time clinical internship.

Housing and Day Care: No on-campus housing is available. No on-campus day care facilities are available.

Employment of Department Graduates:

Master's Degree Graduates: Of those who graduated in the academic year 2006–2007, the following categories and numbers represent the postgraduate activities and employment of master's degree graduates: Enrolled in a psychology doctoral program (21), enrolled in a postdoctoral residency/fellowship (n/a), employed in independent practice (n/a), employed in a community mental health/counseling center (3), employed in a hospital/medical center (1), other employment position (1), do not know (1), total from the above (master's) (27).

Doctoral Degree Graduates: Of those who graduated in the academic year 2006–2007, the following categories and numbers represent the postgraduate activities and employment of doctoral degree graduates: Enrolled in a psychology doctoral program (n/a), enrolled in another graduate/professional program (0), enrolled in a postdoctoral residency/fellowship (10), employed in independent practice (5), employed in an academic position at a university (3), employed in an academic position at a 2-year/4-year college (3), employed in other positions at a higher education institution (3), employed in a professional position in a school system (5), employed in a community mental health/counseling center (5), employed in a hospital/medical center (2), total from the above (doctoral) (36).

Additional Information:

Orientation, Objectives, and Emphasis of Department: The primary purpose of the Argosy University/American School of Professional Psychology, Schaumburg Campus programs in Clinical Psychology is to educate and train students in the major aspects of clinical practice and prepare students for careers as practitioners. To ensure that students are prepared adequately, the curriculum integrates theory, training, research, and practice in preparing students to work with a wide range of populations in need of psychological services. Faculty are both scholars and practitioners and guide students through coursework and field experiences so that they might learn the work involved in professional psychology and understand how formal knowledge and practice operate to inform and enrich each other. The emphasis of the school is a scholar–practitioner orientation, with faculty skilled in all major theories of assessment and intervention. Working closely with faculty, students are provided with exposure to a variety of diagnostic and therapeutic approaches. Sensitivity to diverse populations, populations with specific needs, and multicultural issues are important components of all programs. The program also has emphasis areas in forensic psychology, clinical health psychology, child and family psychology, clinical hypnosis, and multicultural psychology. A Forensic Certificate Program and a Clinical Health Psychology Certificate Program is available to both PsyD and postgraduate students.

Special Facilities or Resources: Faculty members actively encourage student involvement in research projects as a means of fostering mentoring relationships. The Argosy University/American School of Professional Psychology, Schaumburg Campus has core faculty with extensive experience, enthusiasm, and expertise in the following areas: clinical research, forensic psychology, clinical health and rehabilitation psychology, brief therapy, cognitive–behavioral therapy, client-centered and experiential therapy, emotion-focused therapy, severe psychopathology, substance abuse, addictive disorders, family and couples therapy, child development and therapy, psychodiagnostics, psychology of women, sexual orientation diversity, domestic violence, neuropsychology, clinical hypnosis, and psychoanalysis. In addition, the clinical training department has contracts with the Illinois Department of Correction at several correctional facilities to provide training in forensic psychology to practicum students, interns, and postdoctoral fellows. These training contracts allow students to blend the knowledge attained in the classroom with professional on-site training in correctional and forensic psychology.

Information for Students With Physical Disabilities: See the following Web site for more information: http://www.argosy.edu.

Application Information:

Send to Jeffrey Rockenfield, Director of Admissions, 999 North Plaza Drive, Suite 111, Schaumburg, Illinois 60173. Applicants may also e-mail inquiries regarding admissions to jrockenfield@argosy.edu. Application available online. URL of online application: http://www.argosy.edu. Students are admitted in the Fall, application deadline May 15; Spring, application deadline November 15. Programs have rolling admissions. Deadlines may be extended dependent upon space availability. *Fee:* $50.

Argosy University/Illinois School of Professional Psychology, Chicago Campus (2007 data)

Clinical Psychology Department
Merchandise Mart, 350 North Orleans
Chicago, IL 60654
Telephone: (800) 626-4123
Fax: (312) 777-7600
E-mail: *adelaney@argosyu.edu*
Web: *http://www.argosyu.edu*

Department Information:

1976. Dean of the Clinical Program: Annemarie Slobig. Number of faculty: total—full-time 26, part-time 55; women—full-time 16, part-time 30.

Programs and Degrees Offered:

Listed in the following order: Program area, degree type (T if terminal Master's), number awarded 7/06–6/07. Clinical MA/MS (Master of Arts/Science) 46, Clinical Psychology Respecialization Diploma 1, Professional Counseling MA/MS (Master of Arts/Science) 19, Clinical Psychology PsyD (Doctor of Psychology) 71.

APA Accreditation: Clinical PsyD (Doctor of Psychology).

Student Applications/Admissions:

Student Applications

Clinical MA/MS (Master of Arts/Science)—Applications 2007–2008, 113. Total applicants accepted 2007–2008, 97. Number full-time enrolled (new admits only) 2007–2008, 51. Number part-time enrolled (new admits only) 2007–2008, 3. Total enrolled 2007–2008 full-time, 95, part-time, 40. Openings 2008–2009, 45. The median number of years required for completion of a degree in 2006–2007 were 2. The number of students enrolled full- and part-time who were dismissed or voluntarily withdrew from this program area in 2007–2008 were 16. *Clinical Psychology Respecialization Diploma*—Applications 2007–2008, 0. Total applicants accepted 2007–2008, 0. Openings 2008–2009, 5. The median number of years required for completion of a degree in 2006–2007 were 3. *Professional Counseling MA/MS (Master of Arts/Science)*—Applications 2007–2008, 73. Total applicants accepted 2007–2008, 41. Number full-time enrolled (new admits only) 2007–2008, 34. Number part-time enrolled (new admits only) 2007–2008, 1. Total enrolled 2007–2008 full-time, 89, part-time, 21. Openings 2008–2009, 40. The median number of years required for completion of a degree in 2006–2007 were 2. The number of students enrolled full- and part-time who were dismissed or voluntarily withdrew from this program area in 2007–2008 were 10. *Clinical Psychology PsyD (Doctor of Psychology)*—Applications 2007–2008, 388. Total applicants accepted 2007–2008, 174. Number full-time enrolled (new admits only) 2007–2008, 80. Number part-time enrolled (new admits only) 2007–2008, 8. Total enrolled 2007–2008 full-time, 266, part-time, 164. Openings 2008–2009, 80. The median number of years required for completion of a degree in 2006–2007 were 5. The number of students enrolled full- and part-time who were dismissed or voluntarily withdrew from this program area in 2007–2008 were 8.

Admissions Requirements:

Scores: Entries appear in this order: required test or GPA, minimum score (if required), median score of students entering in 2007–2008. Master's Programs: overall undergraduate GPA 3.0, 3.06; last 2 years GPA 3.0, 3.16; psychology GPA 3.0, 3.17. Doctoral Programs: overall undergraduate GPA 3.25, 3.29. For PsyD, require at least one of GPA categories to be 3.25 minimum.

Other Criteria: (importance of criteria rated low, medium, or high): research experience—medium, work experience—high, extracurricular activity—medium, clinically related public service—high, GPA—high, letters of recommendation—high, interview—high, statement of goals and objectives—high. MA Professional Counseling Program admits students after successful completion (including faculty review) of first four courses in program.

Student Characteristics: The following represents characteristics of students in 2007–2008 in all graduate psychology programs in the department: Female—full-time 395, part-time 129; Male—full-time 102, part-time 47; African American/Black—full-time 63, part-time 32; Hispanic/Latino(a)—full-time 28, part-time 9; Asian/Pacific Islander—full-time 29, part-time 9; American Indian/Alaska Native—full-time 3, part-time 0; Caucasian/White—full-time 339, part-time 105; Multi-ethnic—full-time 35, part-time 21; students subject to the Americans With Disabilities Act—full-time 3, part-time 0; Unknown ethnicity—full-time 0, part-time 0.

Financial Information/Assistance:

Tuition for Full-Time Study: *Master's:* State residents: per academic year $22,400, $800 per credit hour; Nonstate residents: per academic year $22,400, $800 per credit hour. *Doctoral:* State residents: per academic year $27,200, $800 per credit hour; Nonstate residents: per academic year $27,200, $800 per credit hour. Tuition is subject to change.

Financial Assistance:

First-Year Students: Fellowships and scholarships available for first year. Average amount paid per academic year: $2,000. Average number of hours worked per week: 5. Apply by May 15. Tuition remission given: partial.

Advanced Students: Teaching assistantships available for advanced students. Average amount paid per academic year: $765. Average number of hours worked per week: 5. Apply by no deadline. Tuition remission given: partial. Research assistantships available for advanced students. Average amount paid per academic year: $2,000. Average number of hours worked per week: 5. Apply by May 15. Tuition remission given: partial. Fellowships and scholarships available for advanced students. Average amount paid per academic year: $2,000. Average number of hours worked per week: 5. Apply by May 15. Tuition remission given: partial.

Additional Information: Of all students currently enrolled full time, 7% benefited from one or more of the listed financial assistance programs.

Internships/Practica: The School approves and monitors over 200 practica sites and assists students in locating and applying for internships across the country and in Canada. Both practica and internship sites offer a wide range of training populations and approaches to students in the school programs.

Housing and Day Care: No on-campus housing is available. No on-campus day care facilities are available.

Employment of Department Graduates:

Master's Degree Graduates: Of those who graduated in the academic year 2006–2007, the following categories and numbers represent the postgraduate activities and employment of master's degree graduates: Enrolled in a psychology doctoral program (58), enrolled in a postdoctoral residency/fellowship (n/a), employed in independent practice (n/a), employed in an academic position at a university (0), employed in an academic position at a 2-year/4-year college (0), employed in other positions at a higher education institution (2), employed in a professional position in a school system (0), employed in business or industry (0), employed in government agency (0), employed in a community mental health/counseling center (5), employed in a hospital/medical center (0), still seeking employment (58), not seeking employment (16), total from the above (master's) (139).

Doctoral Degree Graduates: Of those who graduated in the academic year 2006–2007, the following categories and numbers represent the postgraduate activities and employment of doctoral degree graduates: Enrolled in a psychology doctoral program (n/a), enrolled in a postdoctoral residency/fellowship (14), employed in an academic position at a university (3), employed in an academic position at a 2-year/4-year college (0), employed in other positions at a higher education institution (4), employed in a professional position in a school system (0), employed in business or industry (1), employed in government agency (0), employed in a community mental health/counseling center (7), employed in a hospital/medical center (7), not seeking employment (3), other employment position (0), do not know (22), total from the above (doctoral) (72).

Additional Information:

Orientation, Objectives, and Emphasis of Department: The Illinois School of Professional Psychology/Chicago programs prepare students for contemporary practice through a clinically focused curriculum, taught by practitioner–scholar faculty, with a strong commitment to quality teaching and supervision. The current curricula have been structured to provide students with the fundamental knowledge and skills in psychological assessment and psychotherapy necessary to work with a wide range of traditional clinical populations. In addition, the required curricula include courses and perspectives designed to prepare students for emerging populations from diverse backgrounds and contemporary practice approaches now addressed by clinical psychology. PsyD students may satisfy basic requirements that address the learning of fundamental knowledge and competencies in intervention, assessment, population diversity, and professional practice areas through elective clusters that also provide choices that may conform to their individualized professional goals. As part of the commitment to providing both general and concentrated education and training for doctoral students, the PsyD program offers nine minors, or optional areas of electives choices for students wishing to focus their predoctoral studies in particular areas.

Special Facilities or Resources: The Illinois School of Professional Psychology offers predoctoral minors that support students' interests in the following areas: Child/Adolescent Psychology, Health Psychology, Family Psychology, Forensic Psychology, Psychoanalytic Psychology, Psychology of Maltreatment and Trauma, Client-Centered and Experiential Psychology, and Psychology and Spirituality. The School has over 200 practicum sites available for student training in agencies, schools, clinics, hospitals, and practice organizations. Several faculty at the School have ongoing research projects in the following areas, in which students are invited to participate as they engage in their Clinical Research Projects: Effects of mindfulness meditation techniques on medical residents, intergenerational patterns related to sexual abuse, psychology of women, psychology in the schools, intergenerational cultural patterns in mother–daughter relationships, client-centered therapy with the severely mentally ill, personality disorders.

Application Information:

Send to Admissions Department, Argosy University/Chicago Campus, ISPP, 3rd Floor, 20 South Clark Street, Chicago, IL 60603. Application available online. URL of online application: http://www.argosyu.edu. Students are admitted in the Fall, application deadline January 15; Spring, application deadline October 15; Summer, application deadline April 15. Professional Counseling—Spring deadline, October 15; Fall deadline, June 30; Summer deadline, February 28. *Fee:* $50.

Benedictine University

Graduate Department of Clinical Psychology
College of Liberal Arts
5700 College Road
Lisle, IL 60532
Telephone: (630) 829-6230
Fax: (630) 829-6231
E-mail: *jbooth@ben.edu*
Web: *http://www.ben.edu*

Department Information:

1967. Chairperson: James K. Crissman. Number of faculty: total—full-time 3, part-time 2; women—full-time 3, part-time 5.

Programs and Degrees Offered:

Listed in the following order: Program area, degree type (T if terminal Master's), number awarded 7/06–6/07. Clinical Psychology MA/MS (Master of Arts/Science) (T) 17.

Student Applications/Admissions:

Student Applications

Clinical Psychology MA/MS (Master of Arts/Science)—Total applicants accepted 2007–2008, 16. Number full-time enrolled (new admits only) 2007–2008, 3. Number part-time enrolled (new admits only) 2007–2008, 10. Total enrolled 2007–2008 full-time, 35, part-time, 45. Openings 2008–2009, 25. The median number of years required for completion of a degree in 2006–2007 were 3. The number of students enrolled full- and part-time who were dismissed or voluntarily withdrew from this program area in 2007–2008 were 2.

Admissions Requirements:

Scores: Entries appear in this order: required test or GPA, minimum score (if required), median score of students entering in 2007–2008. Master's Programs: MAT no minimum stated; overall undergraduate GPA 3.0; last 2 years GPA no minimum stated.

Other Criteria: (importance of criteria rated low, medium, or high): GRE/MAT scores—medium, research experience—low, work experience—medium, extracurricular activity—medium, clinically related public service—high, GPA—medium, letters of recommendation—high, interview—high, statement of goals and objectives—high. For additional information on admission requirements, go to http://www.ben.edu/admissions/graduate.

Student Characteristics: The following represents characteristics of students in 2007–2008 in all graduate psychology programs in the department: Female—full-time 32, part-time 39; Male—full-time 5, part-time 6; African American/Black—full-time 1, part-time 0; Hispanic/Latino(a)—full-time 2, part-time 1; Asian/Pacific Islander—full-time 2, part-time 0; American Indian/Alaska Native—full-time 0, part-time 0; Caucasian/White—full-time 30, part-time 44; Multi-ethnic—full-time 0, part-time 0; students subject to the Americans With Disabilities Act—full-time 0, part-time 2; Unknown ethnicity—full-time 0, part-time 0.

Financial Information/Assistance:

Tuition for Full-Time Study: *Master's:* State residents: $450 per credit hour; Nonstate residents: $450 per credit hour. Tuition is subject to change. See the following Web site for updates and changes in tuition costs: http://www.ben.edu/admissions/tuition_fees.asp.

Financial Assistance:

First-Year Students: No information provided.

Advanced Students: No information provided.

Additional Information: Of all students currently enrolled full time, 0% benefited from one or more of the listed financial assistance programs. Application and information available online at http://www.ben.edu/resources/financialaid/GradProgramTable03.htm.

Internships/Practica: The program has established relationships with over 100 mental health agencies, in-patient, out-patient, and social service agencies in the Chicago metropolitan area.

Housing and Day Care: On-campus housing is available. We do have an apartment community on campus that has one-, two-, and four-bedroom units. See the following Web site for more information: http://www.founderswoods.com. Or contact Founder's Woods at (630) 829-6436. No on-campus day care facilities are available.

Employment of Department Graduates:

Master's Degree Graduates: Of those who graduated in the academic year 2006–2007, the following categories and numbers represent the postgraduate activities and employment of master's degree graduates: Enrolled in a psychology doctoral program (5), enrolled in a postdoctoral residency/fellowship (n/a), employed in independent practice (n/a), total from the above (master's) (5).

Doctoral Degree Graduates: Of those who graduated in the academic year 2006–2007, the following categories and numbers represent the postgraduate activities and employment of doctoral degree graduates: Enrolled in a psychology doctoral program (n/a), total from the above (doctoral) (0).

Additional Information:

Orientation, Objectives, and Emphasis of Department: Our program is a rigorous one, offering two clinical internship experiences that more than meet the number of hours required for state licensure. Our program has a curriculum in place that satisfies all Licensed Clinical Professional Counselor (LCPC) licensure requirements. To date, more than 90% of our alumni have successfully passed the licensure exam. Our program is approved by the Illinois Department of Professional Regulation.

Special Facilities or Resources: The department has lab space provided for role play and audio and video taping. The university opened the state-of-art Kindlon Hall of Learning in Fall 2001. The building has a beautiful new library and teaching facilities.

Information for Students With Physical Disabilities: See the following Web site for more information: http://www.ben.edu.

Application Information:

Send to Graduate Admissions, Benedictine University, 5700 College Road, Lisle, IL 60532. Application available online. URL of online application: http://www.ben.edu/admissions/graduate/application.asp. Students are admitted in the Fall, application deadline August; Winter, application deadline November; Spring, application deadline February; Summer, application deadline April; Programs have rolling admissions. *Fee:* $40. Application fee waived for Benedictine University, Illinois Benedictine College, or St. Procopius College alumni.

Chicago, University of

Department of Psychology
5848 South University Avenue
Chicago, IL 60637
Telephone: (773) 702-8861
Fax: (773) 702-0886
E-mail: *marj@uchicago.edu*
Web: *http://www.psychology.uchicago.edu/*

Department Information:

1893. Chairperson: Howard Nusbaum. Number of faculty: total—full-time 19; women—full-time 8; total—minority—full-time 1.

Programs and Degrees Offered:

Listed in the following order: Program area, degree type (T if terminal Master's), number awarded 7/06–6/07. Social PhD (Doctor of Philosophy) 0, Developmental PhD (Doctor of Philosophy) 4, Integrative Neuroscience PhD (Doctor of Philosophy) 0, Language PhD (Doctor of Philosophy) 0, Perception PhD (Doctor of Philosophy) 1, Biopsychology PhD (Doctor of Philosophy) 0, Cognition Program PhD (Doctor of Philosophy) 6.

Student Applications/Admissions:

Student Applications

Social PhD (Doctor of Philosophy)—Applications 2007–2008, 106. Total applicants accepted 2007–2008, 6. Number full-time enrolled (new admits only) 2007–2008, 1. Number part-time enrolled (new admits only) 2007–2008, 0. Openings 2008–2009, 5. The number of students enrolled full- and part-time who were dismissed or voluntarily withdrew from this program area in 2007–2008 were 0. *Developmental PhD (Doctor of Philosophy)*—Applications 2007–2008, 32. Total applicants accepted 2007–2008, 7. Number full-time enrolled (new admits only) 2007–2008, 3. Number part-time enrolled (new admits only) 2007–2008, 0. Openings 2008–2009, 7. The median number of years required for completion of a degree in 2006–2007 were 5. The number of students enrolled full- and part-time who were dismissed or voluntarily withdrew from this program area in 2007–2008 were 0. *Integrative Neuroscience PhD (Doctor of Philosophy)*—Applications 2007–2008, 23. Total applicants accepted 2007–2008, 7. Number full-time enrolled (new admits only) 2007–2008, 5. Number part-time enrolled (new admits only) 2007–2008, 0. Openings 2008–2009, 7. The number of students enrolled full- and part-time who were dismissed or voluntarily withdrew from this program area in 2007–2008 were 0. *Language PhD (Doctor of Philosophy)*—Applications 2007–2008, 0. Total applicants accepted 2007–2008, 0. Number full-time enrolled (new admits only) 2007–2008, 0. Total enrolled 2007–2008 full-time, 1. The number of students enrolled full- and part-time who were dismissed or voluntarily withdrew from this program area in 2007–2008 were 0. *Perception PhD (Doctor of Philosophy)*—Applications 2007–2008, 0. Total applicants accepted 2007–2008, 0. Number full-time enrolled (new admits only) 2007–2008, 0. Total enrolled 2007–2008 full-time, 5. The median number of years required for completion of a degree in 2006–

2007 were 5. The number of students enrolled full- and part-time who were dismissed or voluntarily withdrew from this program area in 2007–2008 were 0. *Biopsychology PhD (Doctor of Philosophy)*—Applications 2007–2008, 15. Total applicants accepted 2007–2008, 0. Number full-time enrolled (new admits only) 2007–2008, 0. Total enrolled 2007–2008 full-time, 6. The number of students enrolled full- and part-time who were dismissed or voluntarily withdrew from this program area in 2007–2008 were 0. *Cognition Program PhD (Doctor of Philosophy)*—Applications 2007–2008, 34. Total applicants accepted 2007–2008, 5. Number full-time enrolled (new admits only) 2007–2008, 1. Number part-time enrolled (new admits only) 2007–2008, 0. Openings 2008–2009, 5. The median number of years required for completion of a degree in 2006–2007 were 6. The number of students enrolled full- and part-time who were dismissed or voluntarily withdrew from this program area in 2007–2008 were 0.

Admissions Requirements:

Scores: Entries appear in this order: required test or GPA, minimum score (if required), median score of students entering in 2007–2008. Doctoral Programs: GRE-V no minimum stated, 661; GRE-Q no minimum stated, 737; overall undergraduate GPA no minimum stated; Doctoral program GRE-Analytic no minimum stated, 5.25. Scores listed above are the average GRE of students who matriculated in Autumn 2007.

Other Criteria: (importance of criteria rated low, medium, or high): GRE/MAT scores—high, research experience—high, work experience—low, extracurricular activity—low, GPA—high, letters of recommendation—high, interview—medium, statement of goals and objectives—high, undergraduate major in psychology—medium, specific undergraduate psychology courses taken—medium. Some science background is helpful for the Integrative Neuroscience program. For additional information on admission requirements, go to http://psychology.uchicago.edu.

Student Characteristics: The following represents characteristics of students in 2007–2008 in all graduate psychology programs in the department: Female—full-time 37, part-time 0; Male—full-time 23, part-time 0; African American/Black—full-time 1, part-time 0; Hispanic/Latino(a)—full-time 4, part-time 0; Asian/Pacific Islander—full-time 10, part-time 0; American Indian/Alaska Native—full-time 1, part-time 0; Caucasian/White—full-time 43, part-time 0; Multi-ethnic—full-time 1, part-time 0; students subject to the Americans With Disabilities Act—full-time 0, part-time 0; Unknown ethnicity—full-time 0, part-time 0; International students who hold an F-1 or J-1 Visa—full-time 14, part-time 0.

Financial Information/Assistance:

Tuition for Full-Time Study: *Doctoral:* State residents: per academic year $36,666; Nonstate residents: per academic year $36,666. Tuition is subject to change. Additional fees are assessed to students beyond the costs of tuition for the following: activity fee and a health and wellness fee. See the following Web site for updates and changes in tuition costs: http://www.bursar.uchicago.edu/tuition.html#schedule.

Financial Assistance:

First-Year Students: Fellowships and scholarships available for first year. Average amount paid per academic year: $19,000. Apply by December 10. Tuition remission given: full.

Advanced Students: Teaching assistantships available for advanced students. Average amount paid per academic year: $1,500. Average number of hours worked per week: 15. Tuition remission given: full. Research assistantships available for advanced students. Average amount paid per academic year: $19,000. Average number of hours worked per week: 15. Tuition remission given: full. Fellowships and scholarships available for advanced students. Average amount paid per academic year: $19,000. Tuition remission given: full.

Additional Information: Of all students currently enrolled full time, 85% benefited from one or more of the listed financial assistance programs. Application and information available online at http://grad-application.uchicago.edu/.

Internships/Practica: For additional information on education and training outcomes for our programs, see the following Web site: http://www.psychology.uchicago.edu.

Housing and Day Care: On-campus housing is available. See the following Web site for more information: http://www.reo.uchicago.edu/gradhousing-list.shtml. No on-campus day care facilities are available.

Employment of Department Graduates:

Master's Degree Graduates: Of those who graduated in the academic year 2006–2007, the following categories and numbers represent the postgraduate activities and employment of master's degree graduates: Enrolled in a postdoctoral residency/fellowship (n/a), employed in independent practice (n/a), total from the above (master's) (0).

Doctoral Degree Graduates: Of those who graduated in the academic year 2006–2007, the following categories and numbers represent the postgraduate activities and employment of doctoral degree graduates: Enrolled in a psychology doctoral program (n/a), enrolled in a postdoctoral residency/fellowship (4), employed in an academic position at a university (3), employed in other positions at a higher education institution (1), employed in government agency (1), other employment position (1), total from the above (doctoral) (10).

Additional Information:

Orientation, Objectives, and Emphasis of Department: The Department of Psychology at the University of Chicago has been for a century a leading center of scholarship, research, and teaching in psychology and related fields. The department is organized into specialized programs that reflect the contemporary state of the discipline as well as the wide-ranging interests of its own faculty. The four areas are the Cognition Program, the Developmental Psychology Program, the Integrative Neuroscience Program, and the Social Psychology Program. The interdisciplinary character of the University is further reflected in the close connections the Department of Psychology maintains with other departments in the University.

Special Facilities or Resources: Facilities include a Laboratory for Conceptual Psychology, an Audio Visual Laboratory, an Early Childhood Initiative, Institute for Mind and Biology, and a Center for Cognitive and Social Neuroscience.

Information for Students With Physical Disabilities: See the following Web site for more information: http://www.disabilities.uchicago.edu/.

Application Information:
Send to Social Science Division, Office of Admissions, Foster Hall 105, 1130 East 59th Street, University of Chicago, Chicago, IL 60637. Application available online. URL of online application: https://www.grad-application.uchicago.edu/. Students are admitted in the Fall, application deadline December 10. *Fee:* $55. In special circumstances, applicants may contact the Associate Dean of Students.

DePaul University

Department of Psychology
2219 North Kenmore, Room 420
Chicago, IL 60614
Telephone: (773) 325-7887
Fax: (773) 325-7888
E-mail: *lrapp@depaul.edu*
Web: *http://www.condor.depaul.edu/~psych/*

Department Information:
1936. Chairperson: Christopher B. Keys, PhD. Number of faculty: total—full-time 33, part-time 4; women—full-time 20, part-time 2; total—minority—full-time 7, part-time 1; women minority—full-time 5, part-time 1.

Programs and Degrees Offered:
Listed in the following order: Program area, degree type (T if terminal Master's), number awarded 7/06–6/07. Clinical PhD (Doctor of Philosophy) 11, Experimental PhD (Doctor of Philosophy) 2, Industrial/Organizational PhD (Doctor of Philosophy) 7, Community PhD (Doctor of Philosophy) 0, General Psychology MA/MS (Master of Arts/Science) (T) 4.

APA Accreditation: Clinical PhD (Doctor of Philosophy).

Student Applications/Admissions:
Student Applications
Clinical PhD (Doctor of Philosophy)—Applications 2007–2008, 284. Total applicants accepted 2007–2008, 6. Number full-time enrolled (new admits only) 2007–2008, 6. Number part-time enrolled (new admits only) 2007–2008, 0. Openings 2008–2009, 6. The median number of years required for completion of a degree in 2006–2007 were 6. The number of students enrolled full- and part-time who were dismissed or voluntarily withdrew from this program area in 2007–2008 were 1. *Experimental PhD (Doctor of Philosophy)*—Applications 2007–2008, 30. Total applicants accepted 2007–2008, 3. Number full-time enrolled (new admits only) 2007–2008, 3. Number part-time enrolled (new admits only) 2007–2008, 0. Openings 2008–2009, 3. The median number of years required for completion of a degree in 2006–2007 were 7. The number of students enrolled full- and part-time who were dismissed or voluntarily withdrew from this program area in 2007–2008 were 0. *Industrial/Organizational PhD (Doctor of Philosophy)*—Applications 2007–2008, 101. Total applicants accepted 2007–2008, 3. Number full-time enrolled (new admits only) 2007–2008, 3. Number part-time enrolled (new admits only) 2007–2008, 0. Openings 2008–2009, 3. The median number of years required for completion of a degree in 2006–2007 were 7. The number of students enrolled full- and part-time who were dismissed or voluntarily withdrew from this program area in 2007–2008 were 1. *Community PhD (Doctor of Philosophy)*—Applications 2007–2008, 34. Total applicants accepted 2007–2008, 3. Number full-time enrolled (new admits only) 2007–2008, 3. Number part-time enrolled (new admits only) 2007–2008, 0. Openings 2008–2009, 3. The number of students enrolled full- and part-time who were dismissed or voluntarily withdrew from this program area in 2007–2008 were 0. *General Psychology MA/MS (Master of Arts/Science)*—Applications 2007–2008, 27. Total applicants accepted 2007–2008, 6. Number full-time enrolled (new admits only) 2007–2008, 6. Number part-time enrolled (new admits only) 2007–2008, 0. Openings 2008–2009, 5. The median number of years required for completion of a degree in 2006–2007 were 3. The number of students enrolled full- and part-time who were dismissed or voluntarily withdrew from this program area in 2007–2008 were 1.

Admissions Requirements:
Scores: Entries appear in this order: required test or GPA, minimum score (if required), median score of students entering in 2007–2008. Master's Programs: GRE-V no minimum stated, 467; GRE-Q no minimum stated, 612; GRE-Subject (Psychology) no minimum stated, 580; overall undergraduate GPA no minimum stated, 3.16. Doctoral Programs: GRE-V no minimum stated, 566; GRE-Q no minimum stated, 639; GRE-Subject (Psychology) no minimum stated, 650; overall undergraduate GPA no minimum stated, 3.6.
Other Criteria: (importance of criteria rated low, medium, or high): GRE/MAT scores—high, research experience—high, work experience—medium, extracurricular activity—medium, clinically related public service—medium, GPA—high, letters of recommendation—high, interview—high, statement of goals and objectives—high. Clinically related public service is not applicable for the Community, Experimental, I/O, or General MS programs. Only the Clinical and Community programs require interviews. For additional information on admission requirements, go to http://www.depaul.edu/admission/types_of_admission/graduate/psychology/index.asp.

Student Characteristics: The following represents characteristics of students in 2007–2008 in all graduate psychology programs in the department: Female—full-time 88, part-time 0; Male—full-time 38, part-time 0; African American/Black—full-time 18, part-time 0; Hispanic/Latino(a)—full-time 5, part-time 0; Asian/Pacific Islander—full-time 7, part-time 0; American Indian/Alaska Native—full-time 2, part-time 0; Caucasian/White—full-time 85, part-time 0; Multi-ethnic—full-time 5, part-time 0; students subject to the Americans With Disabilities Act—full-time 0, part-time 0; Unknown ethnicity—full-time 3, part-time 0; International students who hold an F-1 or J-1 Visa—full-time 5, part-time 0.

Financial Information/Assistance:
Tuition for Full-Time Study: *Master's:* State residents: per academic year $17,208, $478 per credit hour; Nonstate residents: per academic year $17,208, $478 per credit hour. *Doctoral:* State residents: per academic year $17,208, $478 per credit hour; Nonstate residents: per academic year $17,208, $478 per credit hour. Tuition is subject to change. See the following Web site for updates and changes in tuition costs: http://www.depaul.edu/admission/tuition/index.asp.

Financial Assistance:

First-Year Students: Teaching assistantships available for first year. Average amount paid per academic year: $15,500. Average number of hours worked per week: 20. Tuition remission given: full. Research assistantships available for first year. Average amount paid per academic year: $15,500. Average number of hours worked per week: 20. Tuition remission given: full.

Advanced Students: Teaching assistantships available for advanced students. Average amount paid per academic year: $15,500. Average number of hours worked per week: 20. Tuition remission given: full. Research assistantships available for advanced students. Average amount paid per academic year: $15,500. Average number of hours worked per week: 20. Tuition remission given: full. Traineeships available for advanced students. Average amount paid per academic year: $15,500. Average number of hours worked per week: 20. Tuition remission given: full.

Additional Information: Of all students currently enrolled full time, 100% benefited from one or more of the listed financial assistance programs. Application and information available online at http://www.depaul.edu/admissions/types_of_admission/graduate/psychology/index.asp.

Internships/Practica: Doctoral Degree (PhD Clinical): For those doctoral students for whom a professional internship was required in this program prior to graduation, (7) students applied for an internship in 2006–2007, with (5) students obtaining an internship. Of those students who obtained an internship, (5) were paid internships. Of those students who obtained an internship, (5) students placed in APA/CPA-accredited internships, (0) students placed in internships not APA/CPA-accredited, but listed with the Association of Psychology Postdoctoral and Internship Centers (APPIC), (0) students placed in internships conforming to guidelines of the Council of Directors of School Psychology Programs (CDSPP), (0) students placed in internships that were not APA/CPA-accredited, APPIC or CDSPP listed. All of our clinical students are required to take a practicum course every quarter in their 2nd and 3rd years. Though DePaul does not have an internship program, our students fulfill their internship requirement at top facilities in Chicago and across the nation.

Housing and Day Care: On-campus housing is available. See the following Web site for more information: http://www.housing.depaul.edu/. No on-campus day care facilities are available.

Employment of Department Graduates:

Master's Degree Graduates: Of those who graduated in the academic year 2006–2007, the following categories and numbers represent the postgraduate activities and employment of master's degree graduates: Enrolled in a postdoctoral residency/fellowship (n/a), employed in independent practice (n/a), total from the above (master's) (0).

Doctoral Degree Graduates: Of those who graduated in the academic year 2006–2007, the following categories and numbers represent the postgraduate activities and employment of doctoral degree graduates: Enrolled in a psychology doctoral program (n/a), enrolled in a postdoctoral residency/fellowship (1), employed in an academic position at a university (1), employed in an academic position at a 2-year/4-year college (2), employed in other positions at a higher education institution (2), total from the above (doctoral) (6).

Additional Information:

Orientation, Objectives, and Emphasis of Department: Our Clinical program has two separate tracks: Clinical–Child and Clinical–Community. When applying to the graduate program, students indicate their intent to focus on one track or the other. Students in the Clinical–Child track focus on treatment methods with children, family therapy, and behavior change. Research is developmental, systems-oriented, and applied in focus. Students in the Clinical–Community track are encouraged to be innovative designers of interventions, practitioners, and evaluators. Rather than emphasizing treatment, training focuses on health promotion, empowerment, and prevention within a range of populations. All students in the Clinical program do take some courses in both areas, and following admission into either track, students may combine elements of both areas of emphasis. The educational philosophy of the Department of Psychology is based upon a recognition of three components of modern psychology. The first of these is academic: the accumulated body of knowledge and theory relevant to the many areas of psychological study. The second is research: the methodologies and skills whereby the science of psychology is advanced. The third is application: the use of psychology for individuals and society. A major function of the graduate curriculum in psychology is to bring to the student an awareness of the real unity of psychological study and practice, despite apparent diversity. The student must come to appreciate the fact that psychology is both a pure science and an applied science, and that these aspects are not mutually exclusive. This educational philosophy underlies all programs within the department. Each seeks to incorporate the three interrelated components of psychology at the graduate and professional levels; hence each program contains an academic, a research, and an applied component. It is the emphasis given to each component that is distinctive for each of our graduate programs. Students are strongly encouraged to work with faculty in research and tutorial settings. Doctoral candidates are given opportunities to gain teaching experience. Many students work in applied or research settings in the metropolitan Chicago area so that they can apply their graduate education to practical settings. Our Experimental Program has three tracks: Cognitive, Developmental, and Social Psychology. Students specialize in one of these areas, but are free to change areas during their graduate careers or to work with faculty in multiple areas. Faculty research interests are described on the department Web pages.

Special Facilities or Resources: Extensive facilities are available to support the graduate programs and research projects. We have state-of-the-art classrooms and computer facilities. The university also has a new library, recreation center, athletic facility, and student center. The community Mental Health Center, which is located in the same building as the psychology department, serves approximately 150,000 people. Our clinical students gain their initial practicum experiences in the Mental Health Center. In addition, the center serves as a venue for community and applied research. The university has prominent law and business colleges, which are well reputed in the midwestern business community and provide work opportunities for our experimental and industrial/organizational students. The department maintains an active network of our PhD graduates to help in obtaining jobs. There are many educational opportunities in this area, including colloquia, lectures, and regional and national organizations and conferences. We have an active graduate student organization that maintains contact with graduate students from other universities, providing opportunities to share educational experiences and recreational activities.

Information for Students With Physical Disabilities: See the following Web site for more information: http://www.studentaffairs.depaul.edu/studentdisabilities.html.

Application Information:
Send to Department of Psychology, DePaul University, 2219 North Kenmore, Chicago, IL 60614-3504. Application available online. URL of online application: https://www.depaul.edu/admission/index.asp. Students are admitted in the Fall, application deadline see below. Clinical Child and Clinical Community—December 1; Industrial/Organizational—January 5; Community—January 5; Experimental—February 15; General (MS)—May 1. *Fee:* $40. A student in need of financial aid may request a waiver of the application fee by submitting a personal letter requesting this consideration, a letter from the financial aid office of the institution attended outlining need, and official copies of financial aid transcripts. These materials must be sent with the other application materials.

Eastern Illinois University

Department of Psychology
College of Sciences
Department of Psychology, Eastern Illinois University
Charleston, IL 61920
Telephone: (217) 581-2127
Fax: (217) 581-6764
E-mail: *jmhavey@eiu.edu; asharma@eiu.edu*
Web: *http://www.psych.eiu.edu/*

Department Information:
1963. Chairperson: William A. Addison. Number of faculty: total—full-time 21; women—full-time 8; total—minority—full-time 4; women minority—full-time 3.

Programs and Degrees Offered:
Listed in the following order: Program area, degree type (T if terminal Master's), number awarded 7/06–6/07. Clinical MA/MS (Master of Arts/Science) (T) 10, School Psychology Other 11.

Student Applications/Admissions:
Student Applications
Clinical MA/MS (Master of Arts/Science)—Applications 2007–2008, 45. Total applicants accepted 2007–2008, 20. Number full-time enrolled (new admits only) 2007–2008, 10. Total enrolled 2007–2008 full-time, 19. Openings 2008–2009, 10. The median number of years required for completion of a degree in 2006–2007 were 2. The number of students enrolled full- and part-time who were dismissed or voluntarily withdrew from this program area in 2007–2008 were 0. *School Psychology Other*—Applications 2007–2008, 55. Total applicants accepted 2007–2008, 20. Number full-time enrolled (new admits only) 2007–2008, 10. Openings 2008–2009, 12. The median number of years required for completion of a degree in 2006–2007 were 3.

Admissions Requirements:
Scores: Entries appear in this order: required test or GPA, minimum score (if required), median score of students entering in 2007–2008. Master's Programs: overall undergraduate GPA 3.00, 3.44; last 2 years GPA no minimum stated; psychology GPA 3.25, 3.54.
Other Criteria: (importance of criteria rated low, medium, or high): GRE/MAT scores—high, research experience—medium, work experience—medium, extracurricular activity—medium, clinically related public service—medium, GPA—high, letters of recommendation—high, interview—low, statement of goals and objectives—high.

Student Characteristics: The following represents characteristics of students in 2007–2008 in all graduate psychology programs in the department: Female—full-time 37, part-time 1; Male—full-time 13, part-time 0; African American/Black—full-time 0, part-time 0; Hispanic/Latino(a)—full-time 0, part-time 0; Asian/Pacific Islander—full-time 5, part-time 0; American Indian/Alaska Native—full-time 0, part-time 0; Caucasian/White—full-time 47, part-time 1; Multi-ethnic—full-time 0, part-time 0; Unknown ethnicity—full-time 0, part-time 0; International students who hold an F-1 or J-1 Visa—full-time 5, part-time 0.

Financial Information/Assistance:
Tuition for Full-Time Study: *Master's:* State residents: per academic year $5,670, $189 per credit hour; Nonstate residents: $569 per credit hour. Additional fees are assessed to students beyond the costs of tuition for the following: assessment courses. See the following Web site for updates and changes in tuition costs: http://www.eiu.edu/%7Egraduate/prospective_students/admissions_tuitionfees.php.

Financial Assistance:
First-Year Students: Research assistantships available for first year. Average amount paid per academic year: $7,900. Average number of hours worked per week: 18. Apply by February 15. Tuition remission given: full.
Advanced Students: Research assistantships available for advanced students. Average amount paid per academic year: $7,900. Average number of hours worked per week: 18. Apply by February 15. Tuition remission given: full.
Additional Information: Of all students currently enrolled full time, 90% benefited from one or more of the listed financial assistance programs.

Internships/Practica: A two-semester clinical internship in the 2nd year of graduate study is required for the Master of Arts degree. The 12 semester hour internship includes a weekly seminar emphasizing treatment planning, ethical practice, and case management, and requires 600 hours of supervised clinical practice in an approved community agency setting with regular on-campus clinical supervision coordinated with on-site supervision provided by an approved agency supervisor. Some internships carry a stipend and tuition waiver. During the 2 years of on-campus study required by the school psychology program, students participate in three practica. First-semester students complete a school-based practicum that is designed to orient them to the workings of the public education system. During the first semester of the 2nd year students participate in an assessment practicum centered in the on-campus psychological assessment center. A field-based component of this practicum allows students to also complete assessment activities in a public school setting. During their last semester on campus, students participate in a field-based practicum devoted to enhancing counseling and consultation skills.

Housing and Day Care: On-campus housing is available. See the following Web site for more information: http://www.eiu.edu/~housing/. No on-campus day care facilities are available.

Employment of Department Graduates:

Master's Degree Graduates: Of those who graduated in the academic year 2006–2007, the following categories and numbers represent the postgraduate activities and employment of master's degree graduates: Enrolled in a psychology doctoral program (1), enrolled in another graduate/professional program (0), enrolled in a postdoctoral residency/fellowship (n/a), employed in independent practice (n/a), employed in other positions at a higher education institution (1), employed in a professional position in a school system (11), employed in a community mental health/counseling center (8), still seeking employment (0), total from the above (master's) (21).

Doctoral Degree Graduates: Of those who graduated in the academic year 2006–2007, the following categories and numbers represent the postgraduate activities and employment of doctoral degree graduates: Enrolled in a psychology doctoral program (n/a), total from the above (doctoral) (0).

Additional Information:

Orientation, Objectives, and Emphasis of Department: The Master of Arts degree in Clinical Psychology at Eastern Illinois University is designed to provide graduate training with a solid foundation in the science and practice of clinical psychology. The program is a terminal master's degree training experience, which is approved by the Council of Applied Master's Programs in Psychology. The emphases highlight training and instruction in psychological interventions and therapy, assessment, and research. EIU graduates in Clinical Psychology possess a combination of skills in assessment, data management, and analysis that uniquely position them amongst other master's-level practitioners when it comes to assisting mental health organizations to meet the increasing demands of accurate evaluation, current, state-of-the-art programming, timely treatment protocols, and accountability. The Clinical Psychology program also provides solid preparation for further graduate study. The purpose of the school psychology program is to prepare students to deliver high-quality services to students, parents, and professional personnel in public school settings. The program offers a generalist curriculum designed to allow students to develop the flexibility to practice in varied settings. Particular emphasis is placed on assessment, consultation, behavior management, and counseling. The importance of applied experiences is stressed.

Special Facilities or Resources: The Department of Psychology has a computer/statistics lab, as well as faculty-directed research labs, one currently in use as setting for a NIH Grant. Training facilities include a three-room suite used as a Psychology Assessment Center with one-way mirror viewing for testing and interviews and video taping facilities. A further clinical observation research suite, with video and one-way mirror equipment is available for clinical training and supervised community services. Both applied programs enjoy viable cooperative agreements with a number of area educational, correctional, and mental health agencies that serve as training and practica sites for graduate clinical experiences in addition to the internship sites.

Application Information:

Send to Michael Havey, Coordinator, School Psychology Program; Anu Sharma, Coordinator, Graduate Program in Clinical Psychology, Department of Psychology, Eastern Illinois University, Charleston, IL 61920. Application available online. URL of online application: http://www.psych.eiu.edu/. Students are admitted in the Fall, application deadline February 15. *Fee:* $30.

Governors State University (2007 data)

Division of Psychology and Counseling
College of Education
1 University Parkway
University Park, IL 60466-0975
Telephone: (708) 534-4840
Fax: (708) 534-8451
E-mail: *gsunow@govst.edu*
Web: *http://www.govst.edu/coe*

Department Information:

1979. Division Chairperson: Lonn Wolf. Number of faculty: total—full-time 20, part-time 3; women—full-time 13, part-time 1.

Programs and Degrees Offered:

Listed in the following order: Program area, degree type (T if terminal Master's), number awarded 7/06–6/07. Counseling MA/MS (Master of Arts/Science) (T) 42, General MA/MS (Master of Arts/Science) (T) 28.

Student Applications/Admissions:

Student Applications

Counseling MA/MS (Master of Arts/Science)—Applications 2007–2008, 217. Total applicants accepted 2007–2008, 169. Number full-time enrolled (new admits only) 2007–2008, 2. Number part-time enrolled (new admits only) 2007–2008, 14. Total enrolled 2007–2008 full-time, 22, part-time, 191. Openings 2008–2009, 52. The number of students enrolled full- and part-time who were dismissed or voluntarily withdrew from this program area in 2007–2008 were 2. *General MA/MS (Master of Arts/Science)*—Applications 2007–2008, 36. Total applicants accepted 2007–2008, 5. Number part-time enrolled (new admits only) 2007–2008, 3. Total enrolled 2007–2008 full-time, 7, part-time, 25. Openings 2008–2009, 40. The number of students enrolled full- and part-time who were dismissed or voluntarily withdrew from this program area in 2007–2008 were 0.

Admissions Requirements:

Scores: Entries appear in this order: required test or GPA, minimum score (if required), median score of students entering in 2007–2008. Master's Programs: GRE-Subject (Psychology) 400; last 2 years GPA 3.0; psychology GPA 3.0. Counseling has different requirements, which are as follows: (a) have a GPA of 2.75 or higher for all undergraduate course work attempted, a GPA of 3.0 for the last 60 hours of undergraduate course work attempted, or a GPA of 2.5 or higher for all undergraduate course work attempted and a score of at least 1050 on the verbal and quantitative portions of the Graduate Record Examination General Test; (b) recommendation of the faculty based on the submission of supplementary application packet that includes official transcripts of all previous college work, Counseling Application Form, three letters of recommendation, Statement of Character form; (c) have completed all prerequisite courses with a GPA of 3.0 or higher. Prerequisite courses for the Community Counseling and Marriage and Family Counseling sequences include statistics (STAT468), a course in research methodology (PSYC560), a course in abnormal psychology (PSYC430), and course work in Addictions Studies at the 500 level (Marriage and Family sequence must complete ADDS630) or above totaling three semester hours. Applicants for the School Counseling sequence must have completed a course in statistics (STAT468), a course in research methodology (PSYC560), and course work in Addictions Studies at the 500 level or above totaling three semester hours. Applicants may be conditionally admitted after meeting criteria (a) and (b). The conditional status will be removed after criteria (c) has been met.

Other Criteria: (importance of criteria rated low, medium, or high): GRE/MAT scores—low, work experience—low, GPA—high, letters of recommendation—high, interview—medium, statement of goals and objectives—high. For additional information on admission requirements, go to http://www.govst.edu/admissions.

Student Characteristics: The following represents characteristics of students in 2007–2008 in all graduate psychology programs in the department: Female—full-time 23, part-time 189; Male—full-time 6, part-time 27; African American/Black—full-time 14, part-time 85; Hispanic/Latino(a)—full-time 2, part-time 8; Asian/Pacific Islander—part-time 1; American Indian/Alaska Native—part-time 1; Caucasian/White—full-time 13, part-time 121; Multi-ethnic—part-time 0; Unknown ethnicity—full-time 0, part-time 0.

Financial Information/Assistance:

Tuition for Full-Time Study: *Master's:* State residents: $157 per credit hour; Nonstate residents: $471 per credit hour. Tuition is subject to change. See the following Web site for updates and changes in tuition costs: http://www.govst.edu/catalog.

Financial Assistance:

First-Year Students: No information provided.

Advanced Students: Research assistantships available for advanced students. Tuition remission given: full.

Additional Information: Application and information available online at http://www.govst.edu/financial/.

Internships/Practica: Counseling internships are readily available in a wide variety of community mental health and human service agencies.

Housing and Day Care: No on-campus housing is available. On-campus day care facilities are available. See the following Web site for more information: http://www.govst.edu/.

Employment of Department Graduates:

Master's Degree Graduates: Of those who graduated in the academic year 2006–2007, the following categories and numbers represent the postgraduate activities and employment of master's degree graduates: Enrolled in a postdoctoral residency/fellowship (n/a), employed in independent practice (n/a), total from the above (master's) (0).

Doctoral Degree Graduates: Of those who graduated in the academic year 2006–2007, the following categories and numbers represent the postgraduate activities and employment of doctoral degree graduates: Enrolled in a psychology doctoral program (n/a), total from the above (doctoral) (0).

Additional Information:

Orientation, Objectives, and Emphasis of Department: The graduate programs in the Division of Psychology and Counseling are appropriate for the returning adult student. Required classes are primarily offered during the early evening or evening hours. Most students work and are completing their program of studies on a part-time basis. Some classes are scheduled on the weekend.

Information for Students With Physical Disabilities: See the following Web site for more information: http://www.govst.edu/sas/t_stu_dev.asp?id=997.

Application Information:

Send to Office of Admissions and Student Recruitment, Governors State University, 1 University Parkway, University Park, IL 60466. Application available online. URL of online application: http://www.govst.edu/application. Students are admitted in the Fall, application deadline April 15; Winter, application deadline September 15. *Fee:* $25.

Illinois Institute of Technology

Institute of Psychology
3105 South Dearborn, LS-252
Chicago, IL 60616
Telephone: (312) 567-3500
Fax: (312) 567-3493
E-mail: *mitchelle@iit.edu*
Web: *http://www.iit.edu/colleges/psych/*

Department Information:

1929. Dean: M. Ellen Mitchell. Number of faculty: total—full-time 18, part-time 13; women—full-time 9, part-time 10; total—minority—full-time 2, part-time 4; women minority—full-time 1, part-time 3.

Programs and Degrees Offered:

Listed in the following order: Program area, degree type (T if terminal Master's), number awarded 7/06–6/07. Clinical PhD (Doctor of Philosophy) 8, Industrial/Organizational PhD (Doctor of Philosophy) 2, Personal and Human Resources Development MA/MS (Master of Arts/Science) (T) 6, Rehabilitation PhD (Doctor of Philosophy) 2, Rehabilitation Counseling MA/MS (Master of Arts/Science) (T) 11.

APA Accreditation: Clinical PhD (Doctor of Philosophy).

Student Applications/Admissions:

Student Applications

Clinical PhD (Doctor of Philosophy)—Applications 2007–2008, 110. Total applicants accepted 2007–2008, 22. Number full-time enrolled (new admits only) 2007–2008, 13. Number part-time enrolled (new admits only) 2007–2008, 0. Openings 2008–2009, 13. The median number of years required for completion of a degree in 2006–2007 were 6. The number of students enrolled full- and part-time who were dismissed or voluntarily withdrew from this program area in 2007–2008 were 1. *Industrial/Organizational PhD (Doctor of Philosophy)*—Applications 2007–2008, 69. Total applicants accepted 2007–2008, 21. Number full-time enrolled (new admits only) 2007–2008, 5. Number part-time enrolled (new admits only) 2007–2008, 0. Total enrolled 2007–2008 full-time, 64, part-time, 3. Openings 2008–2009, 10. The median number of years required for completion of a degree in 2006–2007 were 8. The number of students enrolled full- and part-time who were dismissed or voluntarily withdrew from this program area in 2007–2008 were 1. *Personal and Human Resources Development MA/MS (Master of Arts/Science)*—Applications 2007–2008, 38. Total applicants accepted 2007–2008, 29. Number full-time enrolled (new admits only) 2007–2008, 6. Number part-time enrolled (new admits only) 2007–2008, 0. Total enrolled 2007–2008 full-time, 16, part-time, 1. Openings 2008–2009, 10. The median number of years required for completion of a degree in 2006–2007 were 2. The number of students enrolled full- and part-time who were dismissed or voluntarily withdrew from this program area in 2007–2008 were 1. *Rehabilitation PhD (Doctor of Philosophy)*—Applications 2007–2008, 0. Total applicants accepted 2007–2008, 0. Number full-time enrolled (new admits only) 2007–2008, 0. Number part-time enrolled (new admits only) 2007–2008, 0. Openings 2008–2009, 3. The median number of years required for completion of a degree in 2006–2007 were 6. The number of students enrolled full- and part-time who were dismissed or voluntarily withdrew from this program area in 2007–2008 were 1. *Rehabilitation Counseling MA/MS (Master of Arts/Science)*—Applications 2007–2008, 40. Total applicants accepted 2007–2008, 16. Number full-time enrolled (new admits only) 2007–2008, 11. Number part-time enrolled (new admits only) 2007–2008, 0. Total enrolled 2007–2008 full-time, 26, part-time, 12. Openings 2008–2009, 15. The median number of years required for completion of a degree in 2006–2007 were 2. The number of students enrolled full- and part-time who were dismissed or voluntarily withdrew from this program area in 2007–2008 were 1.

Admissions Requirements:

Scores: Entries appear in this order: required test or GPA, minimum score (if required), median score of students entering in 2007–2008. Master's Programs: overall undergraduate GPA 3.0, 3.63. The Master's in Rehabilitation does not require a GRE. Doctoral Programs: overall undergraduate GPA 3.0, 3.7. Rehabilitation Counseling MS does not require a GRE score.

Other Criteria: (importance of criteria rated low, medium, or high): GRE/MAT scores—high, research experience—high, work experience—high, extracurricular activity—low, clinically related public service—medium, GPA—high, letters of recommendation—high, interview—high, statement of goals and objectives—high. GPA and GRE are less important for MS programs; MS in rehabilitation does not require the GRE.

Student Characteristics: The following represents characteristics of students in 2007–2008 in all graduate psychology programs in the department: Female—full-time 191, part-time 16; Male—full-time 52, part-time 5; African American/Black—full-time 11, part-time 2; Hispanic/Latino(a)—full-time 7, part-time 3; Asian/Pacific Islander—full-time 18, part-time 4; American Indian/Alaska Native—full-time 0, part-time 0; Caucasian/White—full-time 131, part-time 4; Multi-ethnic—full-time 0, part-time 0; students subject to the Americans With Disabilities Act—full-time 5, part-time 2; Unknown ethnicity—full-time 2, part-time 1; International students who hold an F-1 or J-1 Visa—full-time 22, part-time 2.

Financial Information/Assistance:

Tuition for Full-Time Study: *Master's:* State residents: $778 per credit hour; Nonstate residents: $778 per credit hour. *Doctoral:* State residents: $778 per credit hour; Nonstate residents: $778 per credit hour. Tuition is subject to change. Tuition costs vary by program. See the following Web site for updates and changes in tuition costs: http://www.grad.iit.edu/admission/tuition.html.

Financial Assistance:

First-Year Students: Fellowships and scholarships available for first year. Tuition remission given: partial.

Advanced Students: Teaching assistantships available for advanced students. Average amount paid per academic year: $3,517. Average number of hours worked per week: 20. Apply by April 1. Tuition remission given: partial. Research assistantships available for advanced students. Average number of hours worked per week: 15. Apply by varies. Tuition remission given: partial. Traineeships available for advanced students. Average number of hours worked per week: 0. Apply by varies. Tuition remission given: partial. Fellowships and scholarships available for advanced students. Apply by varies. Tuition remission given: partial.

Additional Information: Of all students currently enrolled full time, 54% benefited from one or more of the listed financial assistance programs.

Internships/Practica: Doctoral Degree (PhD Clinical): For those doctoral students for whom a professional internship was required in this program prior to graduation, (12) students applied for an internship in 2006–2007, with (8) students obtaining an internship. Of those students who obtained an internship, (8) were paid internships. Of those students who obtained an internship, (8) students placed in APA/CPA-accredited internships, (0) students placed in internships not APA/CPA-accredited, but listed with the Association of Psychology Postdoctoral and Internship Centers (APPIC), (0) students placed in internships conforming to guidelines of the Council of Directors of School Psychology Programs (CDSPP), (0) students placed in internships that were not APA/CPA-accredited, APPIC or CDSPP listed. All students are required to complete fieldwork internships and practica. Experiences vary by program. As one of the largest cities in the United States, Chicago provides access to diverse practicum and internship sites.

Housing and Day Care: On-campus housing is available. See the following Web site for more information: http://www.iit.edu. No on-campus day care facilities are available.

Employment of Department Graduates:

Master's Degree Graduates: Of those who graduated in the academic year 2006–2007, the following categories and numbers represent the postgraduate activities and employment of master's degree graduates: Enrolled in a postdoctoral residency/fellowship (n/a), employed in independent practice (n/a), total from the above (master's) (0).

Doctoral Degree Graduates: Of those who graduated in the academic year 2006–2007, the following categories and numbers represent the postgraduate activities and employment of doctoral

degree graduates: Enrolled in a psychology doctoral program (n/a), total from the above (doctoral) (0).

Additional Information:

Orientation, Objectives, and Emphasis of Department: The primary emphasis in the Institute is on a scientist–practitioner model of training. Our APA-approved clinical psychology program offers intensive clinical and research training with an emphasis on a cognitive theoretical framework, community involvement, and exposure to underserved populations. The MS in rehabilitation counseling prepares students to function as rehabilitation counselors for disabled persons. The PhD program in rehabilitation psychology prepares students for careers in rehabilitation education, research, and the practice of rehabilitation psychology. Our industrial/organizational program provides a solid scientific background as well as knowledge and expertise in personnel selection, evaluation, training and development, motivation, and organizational behavior.

Special Facilities or Resources: Facilities include laboratories for human behavior studies, psychophysiological research, infant and maternal attachment, and a testing and interviewing laboratory with attached one-way viewing rooms. Equipment includes programming apparatus for learning studies, specialized computer facilities, and videotaping and other audiovisual equipment. There are graduate student offices, a testing library of assessment equipment, and a student lounge. The Disabilities Resource Center is housed within psychology.

Information for Students With Physical Disabilities: See the following Web site for more information: http://www.iit.edu/~cdr/ Contact: nnoffsin@iit.edu.

Application Information:

Send to Admissions, Institute of Psychology, Illinois Institute of Technology, 3101 South Dearborn, Suite 252, Chicago, IL 60616. Application available online. URL of online application: http://www.grad.iit.edu/admission/apforms.html. Students are admitted in the Fall, application deadline January 15. Clinical deadline is January 15, I/O and PHRD deadline is February 15, Rehabilitation deadline is March 15. *Fee:* $40.

Illinois State University

Department of Psychology
College of Arts and Sciences
Campus Box 4620
Normal, IL 61790-4620
Telephone: (309) 438-8701
Fax: (309) 438-5789
E-mail: *psygrad@ilstu.edu*
Web: *http://www.psychology.ilstu.edu/*

Department Information:

1966. Interim Chair: Neil T. Skaggs. Number of faculty: total—full-time 17, part-time 3; women—full-time 14, part-time 2; ; women minority—full-time 1; faculty subject to the Americans With Disabilities Act 1.

Programs and Degrees Offered:

Listed in the following order: Program area, degree type (T if terminal Master's), number awarded 7/06–6/07. Clinical–Counseling Psychology MA/MS (Master of Arts/Science) (T) 13, Developmental Psychology MA/MS (Master of Arts/Science) (T) 2, Cognitive and Behavioral Sciences MA/MS (Master of Arts/Science) (T) 0, School Psychology PhD (Doctor of Philosophy) 7, Quantitative MA/MS (Master of Arts/Science) (T) 2, Industrial/Organizational—Social MA/MS (Master of Arts/Science) (T) 6, School Psychology Other 7.

APA Accreditation: School Psychology PhD (Doctor of Philosophy).

Student Applications/Admissions:

Student Applications

Clinical–Counseling Psychology MA/MS (Master of Arts/Science)—Applications 2007–2008, 52. Total applicants accepted 2007–2008, 21. Number full-time enrolled (new admits only) 2007–2008, 12. Number part-time enrolled (new admits only) 2007–2008, 0. Total enrolled 2007–2008 full-time, 22, part-time, 2. Openings 2008–2009, 14. The median number of years required for completion of a degree in 2006–2007 were 2. The number of students enrolled full- and part-time who were dismissed or voluntarily withdrew from this program area in 2007–2008 were 0. *Developmental Psychology MA/MS (Master of Arts/Science)*—Applications 2007–2008, 15. Total applicants accepted 2007–2008, 5. Number full-time enrolled (new admits only) 2007–2008, 4. Number part-time enrolled (new admits only) 2007–2008, 0. Total enrolled 2007–2008 full-time, 9, part-time, 3. Openings 2008–2009, 4. The median number of years required for completion of a degree in 2006–2007 were 3. The number of students enrolled full- and part-time who were dismissed or voluntarily withdrew from this program area in 2007–2008 were 0. *Cognitive and Behavioral Sciences MA/MS (Master of Arts/Science)*—Applications 2007–2008, 17. Total applicants accepted 2007–2008, 4. Number full-time enrolled (new admits only) 2007–2008, 2. Number part-time enrolled (new admits only) 2007–2008, 0. Total enrolled 2007–2008 full-time, 7, part-time, 5. Openings 2008–2009, 5. The number of students enrolled full- and part-time who were dismissed or voluntarily withdrew from this program area in 2007–2008 were 0. *School Psychology PhD (Doctor of Philosophy)*—Applications 2007–2008, 22. Total applicants accepted 2007–2008, 14. Number full-time enrolled (new admits only) 2007–2008, 5. Number part-time enrolled (new admits only) 2007–2008, 0. Total enrolled 2007–2008 full-time, 29, part-time, 10. Openings 2008–2009, 7. The median number of years required for completion of a degree in 2006–2007 were 8. The number of students enrolled full- and part-time who were dismissed or voluntarily withdrew from this program area in 2007–2008 were 0. *Quantitative MA/MS (Master of Arts/Science)*—Applications 2007–2008, 6. Total applicants accepted 2007–2008, 3. Number full-time enrolled (new admits only) 2007–2008, 3. Number part-time enrolled (new admits only) 2007–2008, 0. Total enrolled 2007–2008 full-time, 4, part-time, 2. Openings 2008–2009, 2. The median number of years required for completion of a degree in 2006–2007 were 4. The number of students enrolled full- and part-time who were dismissed or voluntarily withdrew from this program area in 2007–2008 were 1. *Industrial/Organizational—Social MA/MS (Master of Arts/Science)*—Applications 2007–2008, 52. Total applicants accepted 2007–2008, 10. Number full-time enrolled (new admits only) 2007–2008, 5. Number part-time enrolled (new admits only) 2007–2008, 1. Total enrolled 2007–2008 full-time, 11, part-time, 13. Openings 2008–2009, 5. The median number of years required for completion of a degree in 2006–2007 were 3. The number of students enrolled full- and part-time who were dismissed or voluntarily withdrew from this program area in 2007–2008 were 0. *School Psychology Other*—Applications 2007–2008, 69. Total applicants accepted 2007–2008, 16. Number full-time enrolled (new admits only) 2007–2008, 8. Number part-time enrolled (new admits only) 2007–2008, 0. Total enrolled 2007–2008 full-time, 22, part-time, 1. Openings 2008–2009, 7. The median number of years required for completion of a degree in 2006–2007 were 3. The number of students enrolled full- and part-time who were dismissed or voluntarily withdrew from this program area in 2007–2008 were 0.

Admissions Requirements:

Scores: Entries appear in this order: required test or GPA, minimum score (if required), median score of students entering in 2007–2008. Master's Programs: GRE-V no minimum stated, 510; GRE-Q no minimum stated, 620; overall undergraduate GPA no minimum stated, 3.51; last 2 years GPA 3.0, 3.65; psychology GPA no minimum stated, 3.64. SSP degree figures have been included in the figures for the master's degree. Doctoral Programs: GRE-V no minimum stated, 490; GRE-Q no minimum stated, 670; overall undergraduate GPA no minimum stated, 3.39; last 2 years GPA 3.0, 3.65; psychology GPA no minimum stated, 3.56.

Other Criteria: (importance of criteria rated low, medium, or high): GRE/MAT scores—high, research experience—medium, work experience—medium, extracurricular activity—low, clinically related public service—medium, GPA—high, letters of recommendation—medium, interview—high, statement of goals and objectives—medium, undergraduate major in psychology—medium, specific undergraduate psychology courses taken—medium, Interview required only for the PhD degree. Interview (in person,preferably, or by phone) for master's degree. For additional information on admission requirements, go to http://www.psychology.ilstu.edu/grad/admreq.html.

Student Characteristics: The following represents characteristics of students in 2007–2008 in all graduate psychology programs in the department: Female—full-time 80, part-time 26; Male—full-time 24, part-time 10; African American/Black—full-time 3, part-time 0; Hispanic/Latino(a)—full-time 1, part-time 2; Asian/Pacific Islander—full-time 7, part-time 1; American Indian/Alaska Native—full-time 1, part-time 0; Caucasian/White—full-time 83, part-time 32; Multi-ethnic—full-time 0, part-time 0; students subject to the Americans With Disabilities Act—full-time 0, part-time 0; Unknown ethnicity—full-time 9, part-time 1; International students who hold an F-1 or J-1 Visa—full-time 9, part-time 2.

Financial Information/Assistance:

Tuition for Full-Time Study: *Master's:* State residents: per academic year $4,656, $194 per credit hour; Nonstate residents: per academic year $9,696, $404 per credit hour. *Doctoral:* State residents: per academic year $5,044, $194 per credit hour; Nonstate residents: per academic year $10,504, $404 per credit hour. Tuition is subject to change. Additional fees are assessed to students beyond the costs of tuition for the following: General fees and Student Insurance (which may be waived if other coverage is in place). See the following Web site for updates and changes in tuition costs: http://www.comptroller.ilstu.edu/studentaccounts/tuition-rates/graduate_table.shtml.

Financial Assistance:

First-Year Students: Teaching assistantships available for first year. Average amount paid per academic year: $3,755. Average number of hours worked per week: 10. Apply by January 5. Tuition remission given: full. Research assistantships available for first year. Average amount paid per academic year: $4,950. Average number of hours worked per week: 10. Apply by January 5. Tuition remission given: full. Traineeships available for first year. Average amount paid per academic year: $4,705. Average number of hours worked per week: 10. Apply by January 5. Tuition remission given: full. Fellowships and scholarships available for first year. Average amount paid per academic year: $3,366. Average number of hours worked per week: 0. Apply by variable.

Advanced Students: Teaching assistantships available for advanced students. Average amount paid per academic year: $4,782. Average number of hours worked per week: 10. Apply by March 15. Tuition remission given: full. Research assistantships available for advanced students. Average amount paid per academic year: $5,805. Average number of hours worked per week: 10. Apply by March 15. Tuition remission given: full. Traineeships available for advanced students. Average amount paid per academic year: $5,354. Average number of hours worked per week: 10. Apply by March 15. Tuition remission given: full. Fellowships and scholarships available for advanced students. Average amount paid per academic year: $3,600. Average number of hours worked per week: 0. Apply by variable.

Additional Information: Of all students currently enrolled full time, 70% benefited from one or more of the listed financial assistance programs. Application and information available online at http://www.fao.ilstu.edu.

Internships/Practica: Doctoral Degree (PhD School Psychology): For those doctoral students for whom a professional internship was required in this program prior to graduation, (4) students applied for an internship in 2006–2007, with (4) students obtaining an internship. Of those students who obtained an internship, (4) were paid internships. Of those students who obtained an internship, (4) students placed in APA/CPA-accredited internships, (0) students placed in internships not APA/CPA accredited, but listed with the Association of Psychology Postdoctoral and Internship Centers (APPIC), (0) students placed in internships conforming to guidelines of the Council of Directors of School Psychology Programs (CDSPP), (0) students placed in internships that were not APA/CPA-accredited, APPIC or CDSPP listed. Students in the clinical-counseling master's program are provided with extensive supervised experience in practica in external mental health agencies. Students in the School Psychology specialist (SSP) and doctoral (PhD) programs participate from their first semester in supervised practica in public and private schools, Head Start centers, and the on-campus Psychological Services Center. Full-time internships are required for all school psychology students.

Housing and Day Care: On-campus housing is available. See the following Web site for more information: Housing: http://www.housing.ilstu.edu/. On-campus day care facilities are available.

See the following Web site for more information: http://www.childcarecenter.ilstu.edu/.

Employment of Department Graduates:

Master's Degree Graduates: Of those who graduated in the academic year 2006–2007, the following categories and numbers represent the postgraduate activities and employment of master's degree graduates: Enrolled in a psychology doctoral program (4), enrolled in another graduate/professional program (0), enrolled in a postdoctoral residency/fellowship (n/a), employed in independent practice (n/a), employed in an academic position at a university (0), employed in an academic position at a 2-year/4-year college (0), employed in other positions at a higher education institution (1), employed in a professional position in a school system (8), employed in business or industry (7), employed in government agency (0), employed in a community mental health/counseling center (10), employed in a hospital/medical center (0), still seeking employment (0), not seeking employment (0), other employment position (0), do not know (1), total from the above (master's) (31).

Doctoral Degree Graduates: Of those who graduated in the academic year 2006–2007, the following categories and numbers represent the postgraduate activities and employment of doctoral degree graduates: Enrolled in a psychology doctoral program (n/a), enrolled in another graduate/professional program (0), employed in independent practice (0), employed in an academic position at a university (1), employed in an academic position at a 2-year/4-year college (0), employed in other positions at a higher education institution (0), employed in a professional position in a school system (5), employed in business or industry (0), employed in government agency (0), employed in a community mental health/counseling center (0), still seeking employment (0), other employment position (0), do not know (0), total from the above (doctoral) (6).

Additional Information:

Orientation, Objectives, and Emphasis of Department: The department provides training in professional areas supplemented by options in developmental, cognitive and behavioral sciences, and quantitative. Training in the professional areas takes advantage of the professional experience of the faculty in human service settings and industry so that instruction is both practical and theoretical. Programs require a master's thesis, doctoral dissertation, an applied research apprenticeship, or a comprehensive examination project.

Special Facilities or Resources: The department has computer facilities and human and animal laboratories. The department also has a Psychological Services Center for assessment and treatment of children and families. For the clinical–counseling and school psychology programs, a large number of community agencies participate in the 1-year practicum (schools, hospitals, mental health centers, and alcohol and drug rehabilitation centers).

Information for Students With Physical Disabilities: See the following Web site for more information: http://www.ilstu.disabilityconcerns.edu/depts/; e-mail: ableisu@ilstu.edu.

Application Information:

Send to Illinois State University, Department of Psychology, Graduate Psychology Programs, Campus Box 4620, Normal, IL 61790-4620. Application available online. URL of online application: http://www.admissions.ilstu.edu/apply/. Students are admitted in the Fall, application deadline November 15. Fall and Summer application deadline for the PhD program in School Psychology only is November 15. Fall and Summer application deadline for SSP program in School Psychology only is December 1. Fall application deadline for all master's programs is January 5. *Fee:* $40. Fee waiver based on documented financial need, re-enrollment at same level as prior enrollment at ISU, veteran service (active duty for 1 year or more), McNair, Project 1000, and Fulbright Scholar applicants.

Illinois, University of, Chicago

Department of Psychology (M/C 285)
Liberal Arts and Sciences
1007 West Harrison Street
Chicago, IL 60607-7137
Telephone: (312) 996-2434
Fax: (312) 413-4122
E-mail: *geraney@uic.edu*
Web: *http://www.psch.uic.edu/*

Department Information:

1965. Chairperson: Gary E. Raney. Number of faculty: total—full-time 31, part-time 12; women—full-time 14, part-time 7; total—minority—full-time 2; women minority—full-time 2.

Programs and Degrees Offered:

Listed in the following order: Program area, degree type (T if terminal Master's), number awarded 7/06–6/07. Behavioral Neuroscience PhD (Doctor of Philosophy) 0, Clinical PhD (Doctor of Philosophy) 4, Cognitive PhD (Doctor of Philosophy) 3, Community and Prevention Research PhD (Doctor of Philosophy) 3, Social and Personality PhD (Doctor of Philosophy) 0.

APA Accreditation: Clinical PhD (Doctor of Philosophy).

Student Applications/Admissions:

Student Applications

Behavioral Neuroscience PhD (Doctor of Philosophy)—Applications 2007–2008, 17. Total applicants accepted 2007–2008, 2. Total enrolled 2007–2008 full-time, 11. Openings 2008–2009, 2. The median number of years required for completion of a degree in 2006–2007 were 6. The number of students enrolled full- and part-time who were dismissed or voluntarily withdrew from this program area in 2007–2008 were 0. *Clinical PhD (Doctor of Philosophy)*—Applications 2007–2008, 202. Total applicants accepted 2007–2008, 9. Total enrolled 2007–2008 full-time, 33. Openings 2008–2009, 9. The median number of years required for completion of a degree in 2006–2007 were 7. The number of students enrolled full- and part-time who were dismissed or voluntarily withdrew from this program area in 2007–2008 were 2. *Cognitive PhD (Doctor of Philosophy)*—Applications 2007–2008, 12. Total applicants accepted 2007–2008, 7. Total enrolled 2007–2008 full-time, 13. Openings 2008–2009, 7. The median number of years required for completion of a degree in 2006–2007 were 6. The number of students enrolled full- and part-time who were dismissed or voluntarily withdrew from this program area in 2007–2008 were 0. *Community and Prevention Research PhD (Doctor of Philosophy)*—Applications 2007–2008, 45. Total applicants accepted 2007–2008, 9. Total enrolled 2007–2008 full-time, 27. Openings 2008–2009, 9. The median number of years required for completion of a degree in 2006–2007 were 7. The number of students enrolled full- and part-time who were dismissed or voluntarily withdrew from this program area in 2007–2008 were 0. *Social and Personality PhD (Doctor of Philosophy)*—Applications 2007–2008, 29. Total applicants accepted 2007–2008, 2. Total enrolled 2007–2008 full-time, 17. Openings 2008–2009, 2. The median number of years required for completion of a degree in 2006–2007 were 6. The number of students enrolled full- and part-time who were dismissed or voluntarily withdrew from this program area in 2007–2008 were 0.

Admissions Requirements:

Scores: Entries appear in this order: required test or GPA, minimum score (if required), median score of students entering in 2007–2008. Doctoral Programs: GRE-V no minimum stated, 570; GRE-Q no minimum stated, 670; GRE-Subject (Psychology) no minimum stated, 630; last 2 years GPA 3.2, 3.8.

Other Criteria: (importance of criteria rated low, medium, or high): GRE/MAT scores—medium, research experience—high, work experience—medium, extracurricular activity—medium, clinically related public service—low, GPA—high, letters of recommendation—high, interview—high, statement of goals and objectives—high, fit with faculty research—high, undergraduate major in psychology—medium, specific undergraduate psychology courses taken—medium. For additional information on admission requirements, go to http://www.psch.uic.edu/.

Student Characteristics: The following represents characteristics of students in 2007–2008 in all graduate psychology programs in the department: Female—full-time 71, part-time 0; Male—full-time 33, part-time 0; African American/Black—full-time 7, part-time 0; Hispanic/Latino(a)—full-time 4, part-time 0; Asian/Pacific Islander—full-time 10, part-time 0; American Indian/Alaska Native—full-time 0, part-time 0; Caucasian/White—full-time 81, part-time 0; Multi-ethnic—full-time 0, part-time 0; students subject to the Americans With Disabilities Act—full-time 0, part-time 0; Unknown ethnicity—full-time 1, part-time 0; International students who hold an F-1 or J-1 Visa—full-time 1, part-time 0.

Financial Information/Assistance:

Tuition for Full-Time Study: *Doctoral:* State residents: per academic year $7,114; Nonstate residents: per academic year $19,112. Tuition is subject to change. See the following Web site for updates and changes in tuition costs: http://www.uic.edu/depts/oar/grad/tuition_grad.html.

Financial Assistance:

First-Year Students: Teaching assistantships available for first year. Average amount paid per academic year: $13,500. Average number of hours worked per week: 20. Apply by January 1. Tuition remission given: full. Research assistantships available for first year. Average amount paid per academic year: $13,500. Average number of hours worked per week: 20. Apply by January 1. Tuition remission given: full. Traineeships available for first year. Average amount paid per academic year: $13,500. Average number of hours worked per week: 0. Apply by January 1. Tuition remission given: full. Fellowships and scholarships available for first year. Average amount paid per academic year: $20,000. Average number of hours worked per week: 0. Apply by January 1. Tuition remission given: full.

Advanced Students: Teaching assistantships available for advanced students. Average amount paid per academic year: $14,000. Average number of hours worked per week: 20. Tuition remission given: full. Research assistantships available for advanced students. Average amount paid per academic year: $14,000. Average number of hours worked per week: 20. Tuition remission given: full. Traineeships available for advanced students. Average amount paid per academic year: $14,000. Average number of hours worked per week: 0. Tuition remission given: full. Fellowships and scholarships available for advanced students. Average amount paid per academic year: $20,000. Average number of hours worked per week: 0. Tuition remission given: full.

Additional Information: Of all students currently enrolled full time, 100% benefited from one or more of the listed financial assistance programs. Application and information available online at http://www.psch.uic.edu/.

Internships/Practica: Doctoral Degree (PhD Clinical): For those doctoral students for whom a professional internship was required in this program prior to graduation, (2) students applied for an internship in 2006–2007, with (2) students obtaining an internship. Of those students who obtained an internship, (2) were paid internships. Of those students who obtained an internship, (1) student placed in APA/CPA-accredited internships, (1) student placed in internships not APA/CPA-accredited, but listed with the Association of Psychology Postdoctoral and Internship Centers (APPIC), (0) students placed in internships conforming to guidelines of the Council of Directors of School Psychology Programs (CDSPP), (0) students placed in internships that were not APA/CPA-accredited, APPIC or CDSPP listed. Access to a wide variety of practicum and research sites is available to advanced students. These include the UIC Counseling Service, Cook County Hospital, Rush–Presbyterian–St. Lukes Medical Center, the Institute for Juvenile Research, the Institute on Disabilities and Human Development, several Veterans Administration hospitals and mental health clinics, schools, and diverse community agencies throughout the Chicago area, in addition to our own Office of Applied Psychology.

Housing and Day Care: On-campus housing is available. See the following Web site for more information: http://www.vcsa.uic.edu/MainSite/departments/campus_housing/home/. On-campus day care facilities are available. See the following Web site for more information: http://www.vcsa.uic.edu/MainSite/departments/children_center/home/.

Employment of Department Graduates:

Master's Degree Graduates: Of those who graduated in the academic year 2006–2007, the following categories and numbers represent the postgraduate activities and employment of master's degree graduates: Enrolled in a postdoctoral residency/fellowship (n/a), employed in independent practice (n/a), total from the above (master's) (0).

Doctoral Degree Graduates: Of those who graduated in the academic year 2006–2007, the following categories and numbers represent the postgraduate activities and employment of doctoral degree graduates: Enrolled in a psychology doctoral program (n/a), enrolled in a postdoctoral residency/fellowship (1), employed in an academic position at a university (2), employed in other positions at a higher education institution (1), employed in government agency (1), employed in a hospital/medical center (0), other employment position (1), do not know (4), total from the above (doctoral) (10).

Additional Information:

Orientation, Objectives, and Emphasis of Department: The goal of the psychology department's doctoral program is to educate scholars and researchers who will contribute to the growth of psychological knowledge whether they work in academic, applied, or policy settings. Within the framework of satisfying the requirements of a major division and a minor, the department encourages students in consultation with their advisors to construct programs individually tailored to their research interests. The psychology department has more than 30 faculty and over 100 graduate students. It has five major divisions: biopsychology, clinical, cognitive, community and prevention research, and social and personality. It has a psychology and law minor; a statistics, methods, and measurement minor; and an interdepartmental specialization in neuroscience. We have close collaborations with the Institute for Juvenile Research, the Institute for Disabilities and Human Development, the School of Public Health, the Center for Urban Educational Research and Development, the Center for the Study of Learning, Instruction and Teacher Development, the Center for Literacy, and the Institute of Government and Public Affairs. These partnerships provide students and faculties having interest in interdisciplinary research an opportunity to work with scholars from diverse fields.

Special Facilities or Resources: The department is located in the Behavioral Sciences Building, a fully equipped facility designed to serve the needs of the behavioral and social sciences. Physical facilities include seminar rooms; animal laboratories; human research labs; clinical observation rooms with one-way observational windows and video-recording and biofeedback equipment; a well-equipped electronics and mechanics shop with an on-staff engineer; a department library; the Office of Applied Psychological Services, which coordinates clinical and community interventions; the Office of Social Science Research, which provides research support; and faculty-student lounge. The Department maintains its own computer lab, in which personal computer workstations connected to a mainframe and stand-alone PCs (MS-DOS based and Macintosh) are offered for student use. The department also offers wireless Internet access.

Information for Students With Physical Disabilities: See the following Web site for more information: http://www.uic.edu/index.html/disability.shtml.

Application Information:

Send to Graduate Admissions, University of Illinois at Chicago, Department of Psychology, MC 285, 1007 West Harrison Street, Chicago, IL 60607-7137. Application available online. Students are admitted in the Fall, application deadline December 15. *Fee:* $50. McNair application fee waivers.

Illinois, University of, Urbana Champaign

Department of Educational Psychology
College of Education
226 Education Building, 1310 South Sixth Street
Champaign, IL 61820
Telephone: (217) 333-2245
Fax: (217) 244-7620
E-mail: *edpsy@uiuc.edu*
Web: *http://www.ed.uiuc.edu/edpsy*

Department Information:

1962. Chairperson: Thomas A. Schwandt. Number of faculty: total—full-time 15, part-time 6; women—full-time 10, part-time 2; total—minority—full-time 1, part-time 3; women minority—full-time 1, part-time 2; faculty subject to the Americans With Disabilities Act 1.

Programs and Degrees Offered:

Listed in the following order: Program area, degree type (T if terminal Master's), number awarded 7/06–6/07. Counseling Psychology PhD (Doctor of Philosophy) 5, Child Development PhD (Doctor of Philosophy) 2, Measurement and Evaluation PhD (Doctor of Philosophy) 4, Cognitive Science of Teaching and Learning (CSTL) PhD (Doctor of Philosophy) 3, Curriculum, Technology and Education Reform (CTER) Other 15.

APA Accreditation: Counseling PhD (Doctor of Philosophy).

Student Applications/Admissions:

Student Applications

Counseling Psychology PhD (Doctor of Philosophy)—Applications 2007–2008, 63. Total applicants accepted 2007–2008, 4. Number full-time enrolled (new admits only) 2007–2008, 3. Number part-time enrolled (new admits only) 2007–2008, 0. Openings 2008–2009, 5. The median number of years required for completion of a degree in 2006–2007 were 5. The number of students enrolled full- and part-time who were dismissed or voluntarily withdrew from this program area in 2007–2008 were 1. *Child Development PhD (Doctor of Philosophy)*—Applications 2007–2008, 11. Total applicants accepted 2007–2008, 4. Number full-time enrolled (new admits only) 2007–2008, 4. Number part-time enrolled (new admits only) 2007–2008, 0. Openings 2008–2009, 3. The median number of years required for completion of a degree in 2006–2007 were 7. The number of students enrolled full- and part-time who were dismissed or voluntarily withdrew from this program area in 2007–2008 were 0. *Measurement and Evaluation PhD (Doctor of Philosophy)*—Applications 2007–2008, 22. Total applicants accepted 2007–2008, 7. Number full-time enrolled (new admits only) 2007–2008, 4. Number part-time enrolled (new admits only) 2007–2008, 0. Openings 2008–2009, 8. The median number of years required for completion of a degree in 2006–2007 were 5. The number of students enrolled full- and part-time who were dismissed or voluntarily withdrew from this program area in 2007–2008 were 0. *Cognitive Science of Teaching and Learning (CSTL) PhD (Doctor of Philosophy)*—Applications 2007–2008, 25. Total applicants accepted 2007–2008, 8. Number full-time enrolled (new admits only) 2007–2008, 2. Number part-time enrolled (new admits only) 2007–2008, 0. Openings 2008–2009, 8. The median number of years required for completion of a degree in 2006–2007 were 7. The number of students enrolled full- and part-time who were dismissed or voluntarily withdrew from this program area in 2007–2008 were 1. *Curriculum, Technology and Education Reform (CTER) Other*—Applications 2007–2008, 38. Total applicants accepted 2007–2008, 32. Number full-time enrolled (new admits only) 2007–2008, 0. Number part-time enrolled (new admits only) 2007–2008, 31. Openings 2008–2009, 30. The median number of years required for completion of a degree in 2006–2007 were 2. The number of students enrolled full- and part-time who were dismissed or voluntarily withdrew from this program area in 2007–2008 were 3.

Admissions Requirements:

Scores: Entries appear in this order: required test or GPA, minimum score (if required), median score of students entering in 2007–2008. Master's Programs: last 2 years GPA 3.0, 3.5. Doctoral Programs: GRE-V no minimum stated, 600; GRE-Q no minimum stated, 600; last 2 years GPA 3.0, 3.5.

Other Criteria: (importance of criteria rated low, medium, or high): GRE/MAT scores—medium, research experience—high, work experience—medium, extracurricular activity—medium, clinically related public service—medium, GPA—medium, letters of recommendation—high, interview—low, statement of goals and objectives—high. GRE scores and research experience are not required or evaluated for CTER applicants. For additional information on admission requirements, go to http://www.ed.uiuc.edu/edpsy.

Student Characteristics: The following represents characteristics of students in 2007–2008 in all graduate psychology programs in the department: Female—full-time 89, part-time 27; Male—full-time 32, part-time 16; African American/Black—full-time 12, part-time 1; Hispanic/Latino(a)—full-time 8, part-time 0; Asian/Pacific Islander—full-time 43, part-time 3; American Indian/Alaska Native—full-time 0, part-time 0; Caucasian/White—full-time 45, part-time 38; Multi-ethnic—full-time 0, part-time 0; students subject to the Americans With Disabilities Act—full-time 0, part-time 0; Unknown ethnicity—full-time 13, part-time 1; International students who hold an F-1 or J-1 Visa—full-time 54, part-time 0.

Financial Information/Assistance:

Tuition for Full-Time Study: *Doctoral:* State residents: per academic year $9,000; Nonstate residents: per academic year $22,000. Tuition is subject to change. See the following Web site for updates and changes in tuition costs: http://www.oar.uiuc.edu.

Financial Assistance:

First-Year Students: Teaching assistantships available for first year. Average amount paid per academic year: $14,000. Average number of hours worked per week: 20. Apply by varies. Tuition remission given: full. Research assistantships available for first year. Average amount paid per academic year: $14,000. Average number of hours worked per week: 20. Apply by varies. Tuition remission given: full. Fellowships and scholarships available for first year. Apply by varies. Tuition remission given: full.

Advanced Students: Teaching assistantships available for advanced students. Average amount paid per academic year: $15,000. Average number of hours worked per week: 20. Apply by varies. Tuition remission given: full. Research assistantships available for advanced students. Average amount paid per academic year: $15,000. Average number of hours worked per week: 20. Apply by varies. Tuition remission given: full. Fellowships and scholarships available for advanced students. Apply by varies. Tuition remission given: full.

Additional Information: Of all students currently enrolled full time, 90% benefited from one or more of the listed financial assistance programs. Application and information available online at http://www.ed.uiuc.edu/edpsy.

Internships/Practica: Doctoral Degree (PhD Counseling Psychology): For those doctoral students for whom a professional internship was required in this program prior to graduation, (7) students applied for an internship in 2006–2007, with (7) students obtaining an internship. Of those students who obtained an internship, (7) were paid internships. Of those students who obtained an internship, (7) students placed in APA/CPA-accredited internships, (0) students placed in internships not APA/CPA-accredited, but listed with the Association of Psychology Postdoctoral and Internship Centers (APPIC), (0) students placed in internships conforming to guidelines of the Council of Directors of School Psychology Programs (CDSPP), (0) students placed in internships that were not APA/CPA-accredited, APPIC or CDSPP listed. The Counseling Psychology Division offers a variety of practica and students are placed for practicum work within University-affiliated agencies, such as the Counseling Centers at UIUC and Illinois State University, the Career Development and Placement Center, McKinley Health Center, and the Psychological Services Center or in a variety of community agencies such as the Champaign County Mental Health Center, Carle Clinic, Veterans Administration Medical Center, Cunningham Children's Home, and the Illinois State University Counseling Center. Supervision is provided by on-site supervisors and by faculty members. Each Counseling Psychology doctoral student is required to complete a year-long, full-time predoctoral internship at an outside service agency that is approved by the Association of Psychology Internship Centers, or the equivalent. Sites to which students apply for internships include university counseling centers, hospitals, and community mental health agencies across the nation.

Housing and Day Care: On-campus housing is available. See the following Web site for more information: http://www.housing.uiuc.edu. On-campus day care facilities are available. See the following Web site for more information: http://www.cdl.uiuc.edu.

Employment of Department Graduates:

Master's Degree Graduates: Of those who graduated in the academic year 2006–2007, the following categories and numbers represent the postgraduate activities and employment of master's degree graduates: Enrolled in a postdoctoral residency/fellowship (n/a), employed in independent practice (n/a), employed in a professional position in a school system (15), total from the above (master's) (15).

Doctoral Degree Graduates: Of those who graduated in the academic year 2006–2007, the following categories and numbers represent the postgraduate activities and employment of doctoral degree graduates: Enrolled in a psychology doctoral program (n/a), employed in an academic position at a university (5), employed in other positions at a higher education institution (2), employed in business or industry (1), employed in a hospital/medical center (1), do not know (5), total from the above (doctoral) (14).

Additional Information:

Orientation, Objectives, and Emphasis of Department: The Department of Educational Psychology has been a leader in placing students as university/college professors, researchers, professional psychologists, and administrators in educational, private and government settings. The Department comprises four divisions, each with a with distinctive program of doctoral study: (a) Counseling Psychology, offering an APA-accredited program, in which students are trained in the scientist–practitioner model from a multicultural perspective; (b) Child Development, focused on the development of children and adolescents, especially as it is relevant to education and educationally relevant outcomes; (c) Studies in Interpretive, Statistical, Measurement, and Evaluative Methodologies for Education (QUERIES), focused on developing and applying new methodologies in educational measurement, statistics, research design, and evaluation; and (d) the Cognitive Science of Teaching and Learning (CSTL), which is concerned with the study of basic processes in learning, cognition, and language understanding, and the principles through which learning is optimized in diverse contexts across the life span, among individuals who vary with respect to abilities, interests, and goals.

Special Facilities or Resources: The Department of Educational Psychology is under the purview of the College of Education, rated one of the nation's top education colleges, with research and support facilities that include the Graduate Research and Instructional Computing Lab, Children's Research Center, Bureau of Educational Research, Council on Teacher Education, Office of Educational Technology, Adult Learning Lab (with eyetracking equipment), Center for the Study of Reading, and interview and experimental rooms equipped with video and audio taping, classrooms for video demonstration, telecommunications, and computer-based education. The University of Illinois offers a rich academic environment with top-ranked Departments of Psychology, Computer Science, Anthropology, and Speech Communication, as well as the third-largest academic library system in the United States, ranking only behind Harvard and Yale. There are also strong programs in Cognitive Neuroscience (Brain and Cognition Program), Artificial Intelligence (Computer Science), Human and Community Development, Gender and Women's Studies, Afro-American Studies and Research Program, and Center for Latin American and Caribbean Studies. Research and support facilities on campus include Beckman Institute for Advanced Science and Technology, Statistical Laboratory for Educational and Psychological Measurement, Language Learning Lab, Model-Based Measurement Laboratory, Survey Research Laboratory, and Illinois Statistical Office (consulting services).

Information for Students With Physical Disabilities: See the following Web site for more information: http://www.disability.uiuc.edu/.

Application Information:

Send to Admissions Secretary, Department of Educational Psychology, 226 Education, 1310 South Sixth Street, Champaign, IL 61820. Application available online. URL of online application: http://www.grad.uiuc.edu/admissions/apply/. Students are admitted in the Fall, application deadline December 1 and January 15; Spring, application deadline October 10; Summer, application deadline March 15. Fall deadline is for PhD program only. December 1 is deadline for international applicants and applicants who want to be considered for fellowships. January 15 is for all other domestic applicants. Summer and Spring deadlines are for the CTER online master's program only. Exact dates vary from year to year. *Fee:* $60. Domestic fee $60. International fee $75.

Illinois, University of, Urbana–Champaign

Human and Community Development/Human Development and Family Studies/Community Studies and Outreach
Agricultural, Consumer, and Environmental Sciences
274 Bevier Hall, MC-180
Urbana, IL 61801
Telephone: (217) 333-3790
Fax: (217) 244-7877
E-mail: *roswald@uiuc.edu*
Web: *http://www.hcd.uiuc.edu/*

Department Information:

1996. Department Head: Robert Hughes, Jr., PhD. Number of faculty: total—full-time 18; women—full-time 11; total—minority—full-time 5; women minority—full-time 3; faculty subject to the Americans With Disabilities Act 1.

Programs and Degrees Offered:

Listed in the following order: Program area, degree type (T if terminal Master's), number awarded 7/06–6/07. Human Development and Family Studies PhD (Doctor of Philosophy) 9, Marriage and Family Services (MS/MSW) MA/MS (Master of Arts/Science) (T) 1, Community Studies and Outreach PhD (Doctor of Philosophy) 0.

Student Applications/Admissions:

Student Applications

Human Development and Family Studies PhD (Doctor of Philosophy)—Applications 2007–2008, 20. Total applicants accepted 2007–2008, 4. Number full-time enrolled (new admits only) 2007–2008, 2. Number part-time enrolled (new admits only) 2007–2008, 0. Openings 2008–2009, 5. The median number of years required for completion of a degree in 2006–2007 were 5. The number of students enrolled full- and part-time who were dismissed or voluntarily withdrew from this program area in 2007–2008 were 0. *Marriage and Family Services (MS/MSW) MA/MS (Master of Arts/Science)*—Applications 2007–2008, 9. Total applicants accepted 2007–2008, 4. Number full-time enrolled (new admits only) 2007–2008, 4. Number part-time enrolled (new admits only) 2007–2008, 0. Openings 2008–2009, 4. The median number of years required for completion of a degree in 2006–2007 were 2. The number of students enrolled full- and part-time who were dismissed or voluntarily withdrew from this program area in 2007–2008 were 0. *Community Studies and Outreach PhD (Doctor of Philosophy)*—Applications 2007–2008, 15. Total applicants accepted 2007–2008, 4. Number full-time enrolled (new admits only) 2007–2008, 3. Number part-time enrolled (new admits only) 2007–2008, 0. Openings 2008–2009, 3. The median number of years required for completion of a degree in 2006–2007 were 5. The number of students enrolled full- and part-time who were dismissed or voluntarily withdrew from this program area in 2007–2008 were 0.

Admissions Requirements:

Scores: Entries appear in this order: required test or GPA, minimum score (if required), median score of students entering

in 2007–2008. Master's Programs: GRE-V 500, 545; GRE-Q 500, 690; last 2 years GPA 3.0, 3.71; Masters GRE-Analytical 4.0, 4.5. Doctoral Programs: GRE-V 550, 550; GRE-Q 550, 630; last 2 years GPA 3.0, 3.72; Doctoral program GRE-Analytic 4.5, 4.5.

Other Criteria: (importance of criteria rated low, medium, or high): GRE/MAT scores—medium, research experience—high, GPA—medium, letters of recommendation—high, statement of goals and objectives—high, fit with program—high. For additional information on admission requirements, go to http://www.hcd.uiuc.edu/grad/.

Student Characteristics: The following represents characteristics of students in 2007–2008 in all graduate psychology programs in the department: Female—full-time 19, part-time 0; Male—full-time 5, part-time 0; African American/Black—full-time 5, part-time 0; Hispanic/Latino(a)—full-time 0, part-time 0; Asian/Pacific Islander—full-time 2, part-time 0; American Indian/Alaska Native—full-time 0, part-time 0; Caucasian/White—full-time 9, part-time 0; Multi-ethnic—full-time 1, part-time 0; students subject to the Americans With Disabilities Act—full-time 0, part-time 0; Unknown ethnicity—full-time 1, part-time 0; International students who hold an F-1 or J-1 Visa—full-time 6, part-time 0.

Financial Information/Assistance:

Tuition for Full-Time Study: *Master's:* State residents: per academic year $10,831; Nonstate residents: per academic year $31,353. *Doctoral:* State residents: per academic year $10,831; Nonstate residents: per academic year $31,353. Tuition is subject to change. See the following Web site for updates and changes in tuition costs: http://www.oar.uiuc.edu/current/index.html.

Financial Assistance:

First-Year Students: Teaching assistantships available for first year. Average amount paid per academic year: $13,300. Average number of hours worked per week: 20. Tuition remission given: full. Research assistantships available for first year. Average amount paid per academic year: $13,300. Average number of hours worked per week: 20. Tuition remission given: full. Fellowships and scholarships available for first year. Average amount paid per academic year: $17,500. Average number of hours worked per week: 0. Tuition remission given: full.

Advanced Students: Teaching assistantships available for advanced students. Average amount paid per academic year: $13,500. Average number of hours worked per week: 20. Tuition remission given: full. Research assistantships available for advanced students. Average amount paid per academic year: $13,500. Average number of hours worked per week: 20. Tuition remission given: full. Fellowships and scholarships available for advanced students. Average amount paid per academic year: $20,000. Average number of hours worked per week: 0. Tuition remission given: full.

Additional Information: Of all students currently enrolled full time, 100% benefited from one or more of the listed financial assistance programs. Application and information available online at http://www.hcd.uiuc.edu/grad/fellow.html.

Internships/Practica: Master's Degree (MA/MS Marriage and Family Services (MS/MSW)): An internship experience such as a final research project or "capstone" experience is required of graduates. Master's students and doctoral students with the applied option complete at least one semester-long internship, usually within a human services setting.

Housing and Day Care: On-campus housing is available. See the following Web site for more information: http://www.housing.uiuc.edu/. On-campus day care facilities are available. See the following Web site for more information: http://www.cdl.uiuc.edu/ http://www.aces.uiuc.edu/%7ECCRSCare/.

Employment of Department Graduates:

Master's Degree Graduates: Of those who graduated in the academic year 2006–2007, the following categories and numbers represent the postgraduate activities and employment of master's degree graduates: Enrolled in a postdoctoral residency/fellowship (n/a), employed in independent practice (n/a), employed in an academic position at a university (1), employed in a community mental health/counseling center (2), total from the above (master's) (3).

Doctoral Degree Graduates: Of those who graduated in the academic year 2006–2007, the following categories and numbers represent the postgraduate activities and employment of doctoral degree graduates: Enrolled in a psychology doctoral program (n/a), enrolled in a postdoctoral residency/fellowship (4), employed in an academic position at a university (1), still seeking employment (1), other employment position (1), total from the above (doctoral) (7).

Additional Information:

Orientation, Objectives, and Emphasis of Department: Our doctoral program focuses on the positive development and resilience of children, youth, and families within everyday life contexts. Emphases include the social and emotional development of children and youth; parent–child and sibling relationships; racial, ethnic, and sexual orientation diversity. All topics are studied within specific settings. Faculty have expertise in both qualitative and quantitative research. Students may choose an applied supporting option in program development, evaluation, and outreach.

Special Facilities or Resources: Our department includes two Laboratory Preschool facilities, a Child Care Resource and Referral Service, a Lab for Community and Economic Development, and the Family Resiliency Center.

Information for Students With Physical Disabilities: See the following Web site for more information: http://www.disability.uiuc.edu/.

Application Information:

Send to Graduate Secretary, 274 Bevier Hall, 905 South Goodwin, Urbana, IL, 61801. Application available online. URL of online application: http://www.hcd.uiuc.edu/grad/app-process.html. Students are admitted in the Winter, application deadline January 15. *Fee:* $50 for domestic applicants; $60 for international applicants.

Illinois, University of, Urbana–Champaign
Department of Psychology
Liberal Arts and Sciences
Psychology Building, 603 East Daniel Street
Champaign, IL 61820
Telephone: (217) 333-2169
Fax: (217) 244-5876
E-mail: *cberger@cyrus.psych.uiuc.edu*
Web: *http://www.psych.uiuc.edu*

Department Information:

1904. Head: David E. Irwin. Number of faculty: total—full-time 49, part-time 11; women—full-time 17, part-time 4; total—minority—full-time 9, part-time 2; women minority—full-time 4, part-time 1.

Programs and Degrees Offered:

Listed in the following order: Program area, degree type (T if terminal Master's), number awarded 7/06–6/07. Applied Measurement MA/MS (Master of Arts/Science) (T) 0, Applied Personnel MA/MS (Master of Arts/Science) (T) 0, Biological PhD (Doctor of Philosophy) 0, Clinical PhD (Doctor of Philosophy) 15, Cognitive PhD (Doctor of Philosophy) 3, Developmental PhD (Doctor of Philosophy) 9, Social–Personality–Organizational PhD (Doctor of Philosophy) 12, Quantitative PhD (Doctor of Philosophy) 4, Brain and Cognition PhD (Doctor of Philosophy) 3, Visual Cognition and Human Performance PhD (Doctor of Philosophy) 4.

APA Accreditation: Clinical PhD (Doctor of Philosophy).

Student Applications/Admissions:

Student Applications

Applied Measurement MA/MS (Master of Arts/Science)—Applications 2007–2008, 2. Total applicants accepted 2007–2008, 2. Number full-time enrolled (new admits only) 2007–2008, 2. The median number of years required for completion of a degree in 2006–2007 were 2. The number of students enrolled full- and part-time who were dismissed or voluntarily withdrew from this program area in 2007–2008 were 0. *Applied Personnel MA/MS (Master of Arts/Science)*—Applications 2007–2008, 5. Total applicants accepted 2007–2008, 0. Number full-time enrolled (new admits only) 2007–2008, 0. The median number of years required for completion of a degree in 2006–2007 were 2. The number of students enrolled full- and part-time who were dismissed or voluntarily withdrew from this program area in 2007–2008 were 0. *Biological PhD (Doctor of Philosophy)*—Applications 2007–2008, 13. Total applicants accepted 2007–2008, 2. Number full-time enrolled (new admits only) 2007–2008, 2. The median number of years required for completion of a degree in 2006–2007 were 6. The number of students enrolled full- and part-time who were dismissed or voluntarily withdrew from this program area in 2007–2008 were 0. *Clinical PhD (Doctor of Philosophy)*—Applications 2007–2008, 200. Total applicants accepted 2007–2008, 18. Number full-time enrolled (new admits only) 2007–2008, 7. The median number of years required for completion of a degree in 2006–2007 were 6. *Cognitive PhD (Doctor of Philosophy)*—Applications 2007–2008, 34. Total applicants accepted 2007–2008, 6. Number full-time enrolled (new admits only) 2007–2008, 2. The median number of years required for completion of a degree in 2006–2007 were 6. *Developmental PhD (Doctor of Philosophy)*—Applications 2007–2008, 39. Total applicants accepted 2007–2008, 11. Number full-time enrolled (new admits only) 2007–2008, 6. The median number of years required for completion of a degree in 2006–2007 were 6. *Social–Personality–Organizational PhD (Doctor of Philosophy)*—Applications 2007–2008, 139. Total applicants accepted 2007–2008, 9. Number full-time enrolled (new admits only) 2007–2008, 4. The median number of years required for completion of a degree in 2006–2007 were 6. *Quantitative PhD (Doctor of Philosophy)*—Applications 2007–2008, 22. Total applicants accepted 2007–2008, 6. Number full-time enrolled (new admits only) 2007–2008, 3. The median number of years required for completion of a degree in 2006–2007 were 6. *Brain and Cognition PhD (Doctor of Philosophy)*—Applications 2007–2008, 56. Total applicants accepted 2007–2008, 10. Number full-time enrolled (new admits only) 2007–2008, 5. Total enrolled 2007–2008 full-time, 22. The median number of years required for completion of a degree in 2006–2007 were 6. *Visual Cognition and Human Performance PhD (Doctor of Philosophy)*—Applications 2007–2008, 26. Total applicants accepted 2007–2008, 5. Number full-time enrolled (new admits only) 2007–2008, 4. The median number of years required for completion of a degree in 2006–2007 were 6.

Admissions Requirements:

Scores: Entries appear in this order: required test or GPA, minimum score (if required), median score of students entering in 2007–2008. Master's Programs: GRE-V no minimum stated, 640; GRE-Q no minimum stated, 730; GRE-Subject (Psychology) no minimum stated; last 2 years GPA 3.0, 3.39. Subject test is recommended but not required. GPA above a B average. Doctoral Programs: GRE-V no minimum stated, 632; GRE-Q no minimum stated, 714; GRE-Subject (Psychology) no minimum stated, 672; last 2 years GPA 3.0, 3.75. Subject test is recommended but not required.

Other Criteria: (importance of criteria rated low, medium, or high): GRE/MAT scores—high, research experience—high, work experience—medium, clinically related public service—high, GPA—high, letters of recommendation—high, interview—high, statement of goals and objectives—high, TSE, iBT, or IELTS scores—high. International applicants must present documentation for one of the following English Language Proficiency Tests at the time of application: TSE, iBT, or IELTS. Applicants need a minimum score of 24 on the speak section of the TOEFL-iBT; minimum score of 8 on the speak section of the IELTS; or a minimum score of 50 on TSE.. For additional information on admission requirements, go to http://www.psych.uiuc.edu.

Student Characteristics: The following represents characteristics of students in 2007–2008 in all graduate psychology programs in the department: Female—full-time 119, part-time 0; Male—full-time 64, part-time 0; African American/Black—full-time 8, part-time 0; Hispanic/Latino(a)—full-time 12, part-time 0; Asian/Pacific Islander—full-time 16, part-time 0; American Indian/Alaska Native—full-time 0, part-time 0; Caucasian/White—full-time 94, part-time 0; Multi-ethnic—part-time 0; students subject to the Americans With Disabilities Act—part-time 0; Unknown ethnicity—full-time 53, part-time 0; International students who hold an F-1 or J-1 Visa—full-time 53, part-time 0.

Financial Information/Assistance:

Tuition for Full-Time Study: *Master's:* State residents: per academic year $8,374; Nonstate residents: per academic year $21,214. *Doctoral:* State residents: per academic year $8,374; Nonstate residents: per academic year $21,214. Tuition is subject to change. See the following Web site for updates and changes in tuition costs: http://www.oar.uiuc.edu.

Financial Assistance:

First-Year Students: Teaching assistantships available for first year. Average amount paid per academic year: $15,749. Average number of hours worked per week: 20. Apply by January 2. Tuition remission given: full. Research assistantships available for first year. Average amount paid per academic year: $15,749. Average number of hours worked per week: 20. Apply by January 2. Tuition remission given: full. Traineeships available for first year. Average amount paid per academic year: $20,772. Apply by January 2. Tuition remission given: full. Fellowships and scholarships available for first year. Average amount paid per academic year: $15,000. Apply by January 2. Tuition remission given: full.

Advanced Students: Teaching assistantships available for advanced students. Average amount paid per academic year: $15,749. Average number of hours worked per week: 20. Tuition remission given: full. Research assistantships available for advanced students. Average amount paid per academic year: $15,749. Average number of hours worked per week: 20. Tuition remission given: full. Traineeships available for advanced students. Average amount paid per academic year: $20,772. Tuition remission given: full. Fellowships and scholarships available for advanced students. Average amount paid per academic year: $15,000. Tuition remission given: full.

Additional Information: Of all students currently enrolled full time, 100% benefited from one or more of the listed financial assistance programs. Application and information available online at http://www.psych.uiuc.edu.

Internships/Practica: Doctoral Degree (PhD Clinical): For those doctoral students for whom a professional internship was required in this program prior to graduation, (8) students applied for an internship in 2006–2007, with (7) students obtaining an internship. Of those students who obtained an internship, (7) were paid internships. Of those students who obtained an internship, (7) students placed in APA/CPA-accredited internships, (0) students placed in internships not APA/CPA-accredited, but listed with the Association of Psychology Postdoctoral and Internship Centers (APPIC), (0) students placed in internships conforming to guidelines of the Council of Directors of School Psychology Programs (CDSPP), (0) students placed in internships that were not APA/CPA-accredited, APPIC or CDSPP listed. Laboratories in Clinical Psychology—Intensive practice in techniques of clinical assessment and behavior modification with emphasis on recent innovations; small sections of the course formed according to the specialized interests of students and staff.

Housing and Day Care: On-campus housing is available. See the following Web site for more information: http://www.housing.uiuc.edu/ or e-mail Family and Graduate Housing: famhous@uiuc.edu. On-campus day care facilities are available. See the following for more information: Child Care Resource Service, 314 Bevier, 905 South Goodwin, Urbana, IL 61801 or call (217) 333-3252; Early Child Development Laboratory, 100 Early Child Development Lab, 1005 West Nevada, Urbana, IL 61801, or call (217) 244-6883; Web site: http://www.cdl.uiuc.edu.

Employment of Department Graduates:

Master's Degree Graduates: Of those who graduated in the academic year 2006–2007, the following categories and numbers represent the postgraduate activities and employment of master's degree graduates: Enrolled in a postdoctoral residency/fellowship (n/a), employed in independent practice (n/a), total from the above (master's) (0).

Doctoral Degree Graduates: Of those who graduated in the academic year 2006–2007, the following categories and numbers represent the postgraduate activities and employment of doctoral degree graduates: Enrolled in a psychology doctoral program (n/a), total from the above (doctoral) (0).

Additional Information:

Orientation, Objectives, and Emphasis of Department: The department trains students at the doctoral level for basic research in all areas. Students are admitted in one of the eight divisions: biological, brain and cognition, cognitive, clinical–community, developmental, quantitative, social–personality–organizational, and visual cognition and human performance. Interactions with faculty in other divisions are quite common; interdisciplinary training is encouraged. Applied research training is offered in measurement and personnel psychology. There is a strong emphasis on individualized training programs in an apprenticeship model. Each student's program is tailored to his or her research interests. Wide opportunities exist for students to participate in ongoing research programs. Students are encouraged to develop their own programs.

Special Facilities or Resources: The department has extensive laboratory facilities in all areas, including biological psychology. Excellent departmental and university computer facilities are readily available to graduate students. Most faculty laboratories are computerized. The department maintains a computer system that supports text processing, data management, and communication between laboratories and campus computers. There are very advanced facilities for research in all areas, including psychophysiology, cognitive psychology, neurochemistry, and neuroanatomy. A first-rate animal colony is maintained by the department. There is an excellent machine shop and a fine electronics shop. Programs are coordinated with other campus departments and institutes, including life sciences, communications, labor, education, and child study.

Information for Students With Physical Disabilities: See the following Web site for more information: http://www.rehab.uiuc.edu/.

Application Information:

Send to Graduate Student Affairs Office, 314 Psychology Building, 603 East Daniel Street, Champaign, IL 61820. Application available online. URL of online application: http://www.psych.uiuc.edu. Students are admitted in the Fall, application deadline January 2. *Fee:* $60. The fee for an international application is $75.

Lewis University
Department of Psychology
One University Parkway
Romeoville, IL 60446
Telephone: (815) 836-5594
Fax: (815) 836-5032
E-mail: *Helmka@lewisu.edu*
Web: *http://www.lewisu.edu*

Department Information:

1993. Director of Graduate Programs in Psychology: Katherine Helm. Number of faculty: total—full-time 10, part-time 9; women—full-time 9; ; women minority—full-time 2.

Programs and Degrees Offered:

Listed in the following order: Program area, degree type (T if terminal Master's), number awarded 7/06–6/07. Counseling Psychology MA/MS (Master of Arts/Science) 20, School Counseling MA/MS (Master of Arts/Science) (T) 78.

Student Applications/Admissions:

Student Applications

Counseling Psychology MA/MS (Master of Arts/Science)—Applications 2007–2008, 47. Total applicants accepted 2007–2008, 33. Number full-time enrolled (new admits only) 2007–2008, 7. Number part-time enrolled (new admits only) 2007–2008, 9. Total enrolled 2007–2008 full-time, 17, part-time, 70. Openings 2008–2009, 40. The median number of years required for completion of a degree in 2006–2007 were 3. The number of students enrolled full- and part-time who were dismissed or voluntarily withdrew from this program area in 2007–2008 were 5. *School Counseling MA/MS (Master of Arts/Science)*—Applications 2007–2008, 78. Total applicants accepted 2007–2008, 68. Number full-time enrolled (new admits only) 2007–2008, 65. Number part-time enrolled (new admits only) 2007–2008, 134. Total enrolled 2007–2008 full-time, 88, part-time, 112. Openings 2008–2009, 55. The median number of years required for completion of a degree in 2006–2007 were 2. The number of students enrolled full- and part-time who were dismissed or voluntarily withdrew from this program area in 2007–2008 were 8.

Admissions Requirements:

Scores: Entries appear in this order: required test or GPA, minimum score (if required), median score of students entering in 2007–2008. Master's Programs: overall undergraduate GPA no minimum stated, 3.0; last 2 years GPA no minimum stated, 3.0; psychology GPA no minimum stated, 3.0.

Other Criteria: (importance of criteria rated low, medium, or high): research experience—low, work experience—high, extracurricular activity—medium, clinically related public service—high, GPA—high, letters of recommendation—high, interview—low, statement of goals and objectives—high, undergraduate major in psychology—medium, specific undergraduate psychology courses taken—medium. The counseling psychology program requires that applicants have taken 15 hours of undergraduate psychology courses prior to being considered for the program. The school counseling program is a joint program in Psychology and Education. There are no prerequisite psychology courses for this program. For additional information on admission requirements, go to http://www.lewisu.edu.

Student Characteristics: The following represents characteristics of students in 2007–2008 in all graduate psychology programs in the department: Female—full-time 68, part-time 152; Male—full-time 38, part-time 84; African American/Black—full-time 0, part-time 28; Hispanic/Latino(a)—full-time 0, part-time 14; Asian/Pacific Islander—full-time 0, part-time 6; American Indian/Alaska Native—full-time 0, part-time 0; Caucasian/White—full-time 0, part-time 0; Multi-ethnic—part-time 4; students subject to the Americans With Disabilities Act—full-time 2, part-time 0; Unknown ethnicity—full-time 0, part-time 0.

Financial Information/Assistance:

Tuition for Full-Time Study: *Master's:* State residents: per academic year $34,080, $710 per credit hour; Nonstate residents: per academic year $34,080, $710 per credit hour. Tuition is subject to change. Tuition costs vary by program. See the following Web site for updates and changes in tuition costs: http://www.lewisu.edu.

Financial Assistance:

First-Year Students: Research assistantships available for first year. Average amount paid per academic year: $12,780. Average number of hours worked per week: 15. Tuition remission given: partial.

Advanced Students: Research assistantships available for advanced students. Average amount paid per academic year: $12,780. Average number of hours worked per week: 15. Tuition remission given: partial.

Additional Information: Of all students currently enrolled full time, 5% benefited from one or more of the listed financial assistance programs.

Internships/Practica: Numerous practica and internship sites available in the community.

Housing and Day Care: No on-campus housing is available. No on-campus day care facilities are available.

Employment of Department Graduates:

Master's Degree Graduates: Of those who graduated in the academic year 2006–2007, the following categories and numbers represent the postgraduate activities and employment of master's degree graduates: Enrolled in a postdoctoral residency/fellowship (n/a), employed in independent practice (n/a), total from the above (master's) (0).

Doctoral Degree Graduates: Of those who graduated in the academic year 2006–2007, the following categories and numbers represent the postgraduate activities and employment of doctoral degree graduates: Enrolled in a psychology doctoral program (n/a), total from the above (doctoral) (0).

Additional Information:

Orientation, Objectives, and Emphasis of Department: The program in counseling psychology is oriented toward individuals who have some experience or great interest in mental health, behavioral, social service, or educational interventions or assessment. It is designed primarily as part-time with courses offered primarily in the evenings and on occasional weekends. The Program has two subspecialty areas: (a) Mental Health counseling; (b) Child and Adolescent Counseling. There is a second program in School Counseling and Guidance designed for those individuals who want to work in the public or private school systems. The School Counseling program has several sites including the main campus, Chicago, and Tinley Park.

Application Information:
Send to Graduate Program Director, Department of Psychology, Lewis University, One University Parkway, Romeoville, IL 60446. Application available online. Students are admitted in the Fall, application deadline rolling; Spring, application deadline rolling; Summer, application deadline rolling; Programs have rolling admissions. Students can apply year round. *Fee:* $35. Need-based waiver.

Loyola University of Chicago

Counseling Psychology Program
School of Education
820 North Michigan Avenue
Chicago, IL 60611
Telephone: (312) 915-6836
Fax: (312) 915-6660
E-mail: *sbrown@luc.edu*
Web: *http://www.luc.edu*

Department Information:
1969. Graduate Program Director: Steven D. Brown. Number of faculty: total—full-time 5, part-time 12; women—full-time 4, part-time 6; total—minority—full-time 3, part-time 3; women minority—full-time 3, part-time 2.

Programs and Degrees Offered:
Listed in the following order: Program area, degree type (T if terminal Master's), number awarded 7/06–6/07. Counseling Psychology PhD (Doctor of Philosophy) 10, Community Counseling MA/MS (Master of Arts/Science) (T) 16, School Counseling Other 10.

APA Accreditation: Counseling PhD (Doctor of Philosophy).

Student Applications/Admissions:
Student Applications
Counseling Psychology PhD (Doctor of Philosophy)—Applications 2007–2008, 70. Total applicants accepted 2007–2008, 7. Number full-time enrolled (new admits only) 2007–2008, 4. Openings 2008–2009, 4. The median number of years required for completion of a degree in 2006–2007 were 6. The number of students enrolled full- and part-time who were dismissed or voluntarily withdrew from this program area in 2007–2008 were 0. *Community Counseling MA/MS (Master of Arts/Science)*—Applications 2007–2008, 66. Total applicants accepted 2007–2008, 48. Number full-time enrolled (new admits only) 2007–2008, 10. Number part-time enrolled (new admits only) 2007–2008, 0. Total enrolled 2007–2008 full-time, 33, part-time, 2. Openings 2008–2009, 25. The median number of years required for completion of a degree in 2006–2007 were 2. The number of students enrolled full- and part-time who were dismissed or voluntarily withdrew from this program area in 2007–2008 were 0. *School Counseling Other*—Applications 2007–2008, 52. Total applicants accepted 2007–2008, 40. Number full-time enrolled (new admits only) 2007–2008, 10. Number part-time enrolled (new admits only) 2007–2008, 4. Total enrolled 2007–2008 full-time, 40, part-time, 6. Openings 2008–2009, 25. The median number of years required for completion of a degree in 2006–2007 were 2. The number of students enrolled full- and part-time who were dismissed or voluntarily withdrew from this program area in 2007–2008 were 0.

Admissions Requirements:
Scores: Entries appear in this order: required test or GPA, minimum score (if required), median score of students entering in 2007–2008. Master's Programs: GRE-V no minimum stated; GRE-Q no minimum stated; overall undergraduate GPA 3.00. Doctoral Programs: GRE-V no minimum stated, 600; GRE-Q no minimum stated, 600; GRE-Subject (Psychology) no minimum stated, 550; overall undergraduate GPA 3.00, 3.25; Doctoral program GRE-Analytic no minimum stated. These scores refer to the PhD program in Counseling Psychology.
Other Criteria: (importance of criteria rated low, medium, or high): GRE/MAT scores—medium, research experience—high, work experience—medium, clinically related public service—high, GPA—medium, letters of recommendation—high, interview—high, statement of goals and objectives—high, match w/ faculty interest—high. These are for the PhD program in Counseling Psychology. For additional information on admission requirements, go to http:///www.luc.edu/.

Student Characteristics: The following represents characteristics of students in 2007–2008 in all graduate psychology programs in the department: Female—full-time 81, part-time 10; Male—full-time 18, part-time 2; African American/Black—full-time 6, part-time 0; Hispanic/Latino(a)—full-time 6, part-time 3; Asian/Pacific Islander—full-time 4, part-time 0; American Indian/Alaska Native—full-time 0, part-time 0; Caucasian/White—full-time 80, part-time 8; Multi-ethnic—full-time 0, part-time 0; students subject to the Americans With Disabilities Act—full-time 0, part-time 0; Unknown ethnicity—full-time 3, part-time 1.

Financial Information/Assistance:
Tuition for Full-Time Study: *Master's:* State residents: $710 per credit hour; Nonstate residents: $710 per credit hour. *Doctoral:* State residents: $710 per credit hour; Nonstate residents: $710 per credit hour. Tuition is subject to change. See the following Web site for updates and changes in tuition costs: http:///www.luc.edu/.

Financial Assistance:
First-Year Students: Teaching assistantships available for first year. Average amount paid per academic year: $12,000. Average number of hours worked per week: 20. Apply by December 1. Tuition remission given: full. Research assistantships available for first year. Average amount paid per academic year: $12,000. Average number of hours worked per week: 20. Apply by December 1. Tuition remission given: full. Traineeships available for first year. Average amount paid per academic year: $11,000. Average number of hours worked per week: 20. Apply by December 1. Tuition remission given: full. Fellowships and scholarships available for first year. Average amount paid per academic year: $12,000. Average number of hours worked per week: 20. Apply by varies. Tuition remission given: full.

Advanced Students: Teaching assistantships available for advanced students. Average amount paid per academic year: $14,000. Average number of hours worked per week: 20. Apply by December 1. Tuition remission given: full. Research assistantships available for advanced students. Average amount paid per academic year: $12,000. Average number of hours worked per week: 20. Apply by December 1. Tuition remission given: full. Traineeships available for advanced students. Average amount paid per academic year: $12,000. Average number of hours worked per week: 20. Apply by December 1. Tuition remission given: full. Fellowships and scholarships available for advanced students. Average amount paid per academic year: $12,000. Average number of hours worked per week: 20. Apply by varies. Tuition remission given: full.

Additional Information: Of all students currently enrolled full time, 75% benefited from one or more of the listed financial assistance programs. Application and information available online at http://www.luc.edu/.

Internships/Practica: Doctoral Degree (PhD Counseling Psychology): For those doctoral students for whom a professional internship was required in this program prior to graduation, (6) students applied for an internship in 2006–2007, with (4) students obtaining an internship. Of those students who obtained an internship, (4) were paid internships. Of those students who obtained an internship, (4) students placed in APA/CPA-accredited internships, (0) students placed in internships not APA/CPA accredited, but listed with the Association of Psychology Postdoctoral and Internship Centers (APPIC), (0) students placed in internships conforming to guidelines of the Council of Directors of School Psychology Programs (CDSPP), (0) students placed in internships that were not APA/CPA-accredited, APPIC or CDSPP listed. Internships and practica are available at many excellent training facilities in the greater Chicago-land area, including university counseling centers, hospitals, VA Centers, and mental health clinics. There are both therapy-oriented and diagnostic/assessment-oriented practica. Most practicum sites serve a diverse clientele.

Housing and Day Care: On-campus housing is available. Apartment style housing is available for graduate students. No on-campus day care facilities are available.

Employment of Department Graduates:

Master's Degree Graduates: Of those who graduated in the academic year 2006–2007, the following categories and numbers represent the postgraduate activities and employment of master's degree graduates: Enrolled in a postdoctoral residency/fellowship (n/a), employed in independent practice (n/a), total from the above (master's) (0).

Doctoral Degree Graduates: Of those who graduated in the academic year 2006–2007, the following categories and numbers represent the postgraduate activities and employment of doctoral degree graduates: Enrolled in a psychology doctoral program (n/a), enrolled in a postdoctoral residency/fellowship (1), employed in an academic position at a university (1), employed in other positions at a higher education institution (1), employed in government agency (1), employed in a community mental health/counseling center (4), employed in a hospital/medical center (1), total from the above (doctoral) (9).

Additional Information:

Orientation, Objectives, and Emphasis of Department: The PhD program, accredited by APA, is based on the scientist–practitioner model of graduate education and emphasizes the interdependence of science and practice. Doctoral students are provided with opportunities to collaborate with faculty in terms of research, prevention/intervention, and teaching activites from the first year of enrollment. Faculty research concentrates in three areas: multicultural psychology, preventive psychology, and vocational psychology. Applicant interest in one of these three areas is a major admission criterion because students are expected to apprentice themselves with a faculty member throughout their tenure in the program. Regardless of the field of interest, each student is exposed to the scientist–practitioner model. Graduates are prepared for teaching, research, and professional practice.

Special Facilities or Resources: The school has excellent library and research facilities and computer resources available to students.

Information for Students With Physical Disabilities: See the following Web site for more information: http://www.luc.edu.

Application Information:

Send to Graduate Enrollment Management Loyola University Chicago 820 North Michigan Avenue, Chicago, IL 60611. Application available online. URL of online application: http://www.luc.edu/schools/grad/homedata/9applica/applica.htm/. Students are admitted in the Fall, application deadline December 1. Master's programs have an application deadline of February 15. *Fee:* $40. Waived if submitted on line.

Loyola University of Chicago

Department of Psychology
Arts and Sciences
6525 North Sheridan Road
Chicago, IL 60626
Telephone: (773) 508-3001
Fax: (773) 508-8713
E-mail: *prupert@luc.edu*
Web: *http://www.luc.edu*

Department Information:

1930. Chairperson: Patricia A. Rupert. Number of faculty: total—full-time 31, part-time 8; women—full-time 15, part-time 3; total—minority—full-time 6, part-time 1; women minority—full-time 3.

Programs and Degrees Offered:

Listed in the following order: Program area, degree type (T if terminal Master's), number awarded 7/06–6/07. Developmental PhD (Doctor of Philosophy) 3, Social PhD (Doctor of Philosophy) 7, Clinical PhD (Doctor of Philosophy) 7, Applied Social MA/MS (Master of Arts/Science) (T) 4.

APA Accreditation: Clinical PhD (Doctor of Philosophy).

Student Applications/Admissions:

Student Applications

Developmental PhD (Doctor of Philosophy)—Applications 2007–2008, 12. Total applicants accepted 2007–2008, 3. Number full-time enrolled (new admits only) 2007–2008, 3. Openings 2008–2009, 2. The median number of years required for completion of a degree in 2006–2007 were 6. The number of students enrolled full- and part-time who were dismissed or voluntarily withdrew from this program area in 2007–2008 were 1. *Social PhD (Doctor of Philosophy)*—Applications 2007–2008, 66. Total applicants accepted 2007–2008, 7. Number full-time enrolled (new admits only) 2007–2008, 4. Number part-time enrolled (new admits only) 2007–2008, 0. Openings 2008–2009, 4. The median number of years required for completion of a degree in 2006–2007 were 6. The number of students enrolled full- and part-time who were dismissed or voluntarily withdrew from this program area in 2007–2008 were 0. *Clinical PhD (Doctor of Philosophy)*—Applications 2007–2008, 327. Total applicants accepted 2007–2008, 15. Number full-time enrolled (new admits only) 2007–2008, 6. Number part-time enrolled (new admits only) 2007–2008, 0. Openings 2008–2009, 6. The median number of years required for completion of a degree in 2006–2007 were 6. The number of students enrolled full- and part-time who were dismissed or voluntarily withdrew from this program area in 2007–2008 were 0. *Applied Social MA/MS (Master of Arts/Science)*—Applications 2007–2008, 24. Total applicants accepted 2007–2008, 7. Number full-time enrolled (new admits only) 2007–2008, 2. Openings 2008–2009, 4. The median number of years required for completion of a degree in 2006–2007 were 2. The number of students enrolled full- and part-time who were dismissed or voluntarily withdrew from this program area in 2007–2008 were 0.

Admissions Requirements:

Scores: Entries appear in this order: required test or GPA, minimum score (if required), median score of students entering in 2007–2008. Master's Programs: GRE-V no minimum stated, 510; GRE-Q no minimum stated, 670; GRE-Subject (Psychology) no minimum stated, 550; overall undergraduate GPA 3.00, 3.8. These are the scores for the Terminal Master's Program in applied social psychology. Doctoral Programs: GRE-V no minimum stated, 620; GRE-Q no minimum stated, 650; GRE-Subject (Psychology) no minimum stated, 620; overall undergraduate GPA 3.00, 3.78. Scores vary slightly for different program areas.

Other Criteria: (importance of criteria rated low, medium, or high): GRE/MAT scores—high, research experience—high, work experience—low, extracurricular activity—low, clinically related public service—medium, GPA—high, letters of recommendation—high, interview—high, statement of goals and objectives—high. Only the Clinical Program requires an interview and clinically related public service. For additional information on admission requirements, go to http://www.luc.edu/psychology/.

Student Characteristics: The following represents characteristics of students in 2007–2008 in all graduate psychology programs in the department: Female—full-time 80, part-time 0; Male—full-time 17, part-time 0; African American/Black—full-time 7, part-time 0; Hispanic/Latino(a)—full-time 8, part-time 0; Asian/Pacific Islander—full-time 8, part-time 0; American Indian/Alaska Native—full-time 1, part-time 0; Caucasian/White—full-time 71, part-time 0; Multi-ethnic—full-time 2, part-time 0; students subject to the Americans With Disabilities Act—full-time 1, part-time 0; Unknown ethnicity—full-time 0, part-time 0; International students who hold an F-1 or J-1 Visa—full-time 8, part-time 0.

Financial Information/Assistance:

Tuition for Full-Time Study: *Master's:* State residents: per academic year $15,750, $750 per credit hour; *Doctoral:* State residents: per academic year $15,750, $750 per credit hour. Tuition is subject to change. See the following Web site for updates and changes in tuition costs: http://www.luc.edu.

Financial Assistance:

First-Year Students: Research assistantships available for first year. Average amount paid per academic year: $15,000. Average number of hours worked per week: 20. Apply by December 1. Tuition remission given: full.

Advanced Students: Teaching assistantships available for advanced students. Average amount paid per academic year: $15,000. Average number of hours worked per week: 20. Apply by March 1. Tuition remission given: full. Research assistantships available for advanced students. Average amount paid per academic year: $15,000. Average number of hours worked per week: 20. Apply by March 1. Tuition remission given: full.

Additional Information: Of all students currently enrolled full time, 80% benefited from one or more of the listed financial assistance programs. Application and information available online at http://www.luc.edu/psychology/.

Internships/Practica: Doctoral Degree (PhD Clinical): For those doctoral students for whom a professional internship was required in this program prior to graduation, (6) students applied for an internship in 2006–2007, with (6) students obtaining an internship. Of those students who obtained an internship, (6) were paid internships. Of those students who obtained an internship, (6) students placed in APA/CPA-accredited internships, (0) students placed in internships not APA/CPA-accredited, but listed with the Association of Psychology Postdoctoral and Internship Centers (APPIC), (0) students placed in internships conforming to guidelines of the Council of Directors of School Psychology Programs (CDSPP), (0) students placed in internships that were not APA/CPA-accredited, APPIC or CDSPP listed. Externship experiences are available for clinical psychology students through our in-house Training Clinic at the Wellness Center. In addition, numerous externship training opportunities are available throughout the Chicago metropolitan area and clinical students apply nationally for APA-accredited internships. Students in the doctoral applied social psychology program serve a 1,000-hour planning, research, and evaluation internship during their 3rd year, whereas students in the developmental program complete a 250-hour internship. These positions are usually found in health-related, governmental, and research organizations in the Chicago area.

Housing and Day Care: On-campus housing is available. See the following Web site for more information: http://www.luc.edu. On-campus day care facilities are available.

Employment of Department Graduates:

Master's Degree Graduates: Of those who graduated in the academic year 2006–2007, the following categories and numbers

represent the postgraduate activities and employment of master's degree graduates: Enrolled in a psychology doctoral program (3), enrolled in another graduate/professional program (1), enrolled in a postdoctoral residency/fellowship (n/a), employed in independent practice (n/a), employed in an academic position at a university (0), employed in an academic position at a 2-year/4-year college (0), employed in other positions at a higher education institution (0), employed in a professional position in a school system (0), employed in business or industry (0), employed in government agency (0), employed in a community mental health/counseling center (0), employed in a hospital/medical center (0), still seeking employment (0), total from the above (master's) (4). ***Doctoral Degree Graduates:*** Of those who graduated in the academic year 2006–2007, the following categories and numbers represent the postgraduate activities and employment of doctoral degree graduates: Enrolled in a psychology doctoral program (n/a), enrolled in a postdoctoral residency/fellowship (8), employed in independent practice (0), employed in an academic position at a university (1), employed in an academic position at a 2-year/4-year college (1), employed in other positions at a higher education institution (0), employed in a professional position in a school system (0), employed in business or industry (0), employed in government agency (1), employed in a community mental health/counseling center (1), employed in a hospital/medical center (0), still seeking employment (0), other employment position (1), total from the above (doctoral) (13).

Additional Information:

Orientation, Objectives, and Emphasis of Department: Graduate study is organized into three areas: clinical, developmental, and social. All programs offer the PhD; only the social program offers a terminal MA in applied social psychology. The clinical program emphasizes the scientist–practitioner model, with students receiving extensive training in both areas. Students may specialize in work with children or adults. The developmental program provides training for students wishing to pursue the study of human development, particularly among infants, children, and adolescents. Cognition, social, gender role, and personality development are covered. The social psychology program includes training in both basic and applied social psychology. The emphasis in the applied program is on developing social psychologists who are capable of conducting applied research on the planning, evaluating, and modification of social programs in the areas of law and criminal justice, educational systems, health and/or community services, and organizational behavior.

Special Facilities or Resources: Excellent libraries and computer support are available. Departmental facilities include specialized laboratories for audition, vision, and neurophysiology research; a general purpose laboratory for sensory processes; suites of research and observation rooms for clinical research; observation and videotaping rooms and equipment; an extensive psychological test library; a psychophysiology and biofeedback laboratory; and computer facilities.

Information for Students With Physical Disabilities: See the following Web site for more information: http://www.luc.edu.

Application Information:

Send to Department of Psychology, [Name of Program,] Loyola University Chicago, 6525 North Sheridan Road, Chicago, IL 60626. Application available online. URL of online application: http://www.luc.edu. Students are admitted in the Fall, application deadline December 1. For the Fall semester the deadlines for each program are as follows: Developmental, February 1; Social, January 15; Clinical, December 1. *Fee:* $40.

Midwestern University

Department of Behavioral Medicine/Clinical Psychology Program
College of Health Sciences
555 31st Street
Downers Grove, IL 60515
Telephone: (630) 515-7650
Fax: (630) 515-7655
E-mail: *fprero@midwestern.edu*
Web: *http://www.midwestern.edu*

Department Information:

2001. Chairperson: Frank J. Prerost, PhD. Number of faculty: total—full-time 9, part-time 10; women—full-time 6, part-time 5; total—minority—full-time 2, part-time 2; women minority—full-time 1, part-time 1.

Programs and Degrees Offered:

Listed in the following order: Program area, degree type (T if terminal Master's), number awarded 7/06–6/07. Clinical Psychology PsyD (Doctor of Psychology) 8, Clinical Psychology MA/MS (Master of Arts/Science) 17.

Student Applications/Admissions:

Student Applications

Clinical Psychology PsyD (Doctor of Psychology)—Applications 2007–2008, 98. Total applicants accepted 2007–2008, 40. Number full-time enrolled (new admits only) 2007–2008, 24. Number part-time enrolled (new admits only) 2007–2008, 0. Openings 2008–2009, 22. The median number of years required for completion of a degree in 2006–2007 were 4. The number of students enrolled full- and part-time who were dismissed or voluntarily withdrew from this program area in 2007–2008 were 0. *Clinical Psychology MA/MS (Master of Arts/Science)*—Applications 2007–2008, 0. Total applicants accepted 2007–2008, 0. Number full-time enrolled (new admits only) 2007–2008, 0. The median number of years required for completion of a degree in 2006–2007 were 2. The number of students enrolled full- and part-time who were dismissed or voluntarily withdrew from this program area in 2007–2008 were 0.

Admissions Requirements:

Scores: Entries appear in this order: required test or GPA, minimum score (if required), median score of students entering in 2007–2008. Master's Programs: overall undergraduate GPA 2.75. Students only admitted to doctoral program at this time. Doctoral Programs: overall undergraduate GPA 2.75, 3.50. GRE scores are required with application, but the Clinical Psychology Program will accept scores on the MCAT, GMAT, LSAT or Millers Analogy in lieu of the GRE. Personal interview is a central component of the admission process.

Other Criteria: (importance of criteria rated low, medium, or high): GRE/MAT scores—medium, research experience—

medium, work experience—medium, extracurricular activity—medium, clinically related public service—high, GPA—high, letters of recommendation—high, interview—high, statement of goals and objectives—medium, health care experience—medium, undergraduate major in psychology—medium, specific undergraduate psychology courses taken—low. For additional information on admission requirements, go to http://www.midwestern.edu.

Student Characteristics: The following represents characteristics of students in 2007–2008 in all graduate psychology programs in the department: Female—full-time 70, part-time 0; Male—full-time 11, part-time 0; African American/Black—full-time 8, part-time 0; Hispanic/Latino(a)—full-time 5, part-time 0; Asian/Pacific Islander—full-time 6, part-time 0; American Indian/Alaska Native—full-time 1, part-time 0; Caucasian/White—full-time 61, part-time 0; Multi-ethnic—full-time 0, part-time 0; students subject to the Americans With Disabilities Act—full-time 1, part-time 0; Unknown ethnicity—full-time 0, part-time 0.

Financial Information/Assistance:

Tuition for Full-Time Study: *Doctoral:* State residents: per academic year $21,462; Nonstate residents: per academic year $21,462. Tuition is subject to change. See the following Web site for updates and changes in tuition costs: http://www.midwestern.edu.

Financial Assistance:

First-Year Students: No information provided.

Advanced Students: No information provided.

Additional Information: Application and information available online at http://www.midwestern.edu (work study is available for most students).

Internships/Practica: Doctoral Degree (PsyD Clinical Psychology): For those doctoral students for whom a professional internship was required in this program prior to graduation, (14) students applied for an internship in 2006–2007, with (14) students obtaining an internship. Of those students who obtained an internship, (12) were paid internships. Of those students who obtained an internship, (0) students placed in APA/CPA-accredited internships, (13) students placed in internships not APA/CPA accredited, but listed with the Association of Psychology Postdoctoral and Internship Centers (APPIC), (0) students placed in internships conforming to guidelines of the Council of Directors of School Psychology Programs (CDSPP), (1) student placed in internships that were not APA/CPA-accredited, APPIC or CDSPP listed. Students participate in clerkships during their 1st year under the supervision of program core faculty. These are clinical experiences at various direct service sites. A diagnostic practicum is completed in the 2nd year and is followed with a therapy practicum. The 4th year of study consists of a full-time internship. Students may opt for an advanced practicum in their 3rd year while postponing internship into the next year. Students are given individualized attention to help secure appropriate clinical training experiences in practica and internship. Midwestern University has numerous affiliation agreements with clinical sites throughout the metropolitan area of Chicago. For additional information on education and training outcomes for our programs, see the following Web site: http://www.midwestern.edu.

Housing and Day Care: On-campus housing is available. See the following Web site for more information: A variety of housing options are available on campus, but students are advised to request on-campus housing at the earliest possible time. In addition to on-campus housing, a number of off-campus housing sites are in close proximity to the campus. Additional information is available at http://www.midwestern.edu. No on-campus day care facilities are available.

Employment of Department Graduates:

Master's Degree Graduates: Of those who graduated in the academic year 2006–2007, the following categories and numbers represent the postgraduate activities and employment of master's degree graduates: Enrolled in a psychology doctoral program (0), enrolled in another graduate/professional program (0), enrolled in a postdoctoral residency/fellowship (n/a), employed in independent practice (n/a), employed in an academic position at a university (0), employed in an academic position at a 2-year/4-year college (0), employed in other positions at a higher education institution (0), employed in a professional position in a school system (0), employed in business or industry (0), employed in government agency (0), employed in a community mental health/counseling center (0), employed in a hospital/medical center (0), still seeking employment (0), not seeking employment (0), other employment position (0), do not know (0), total from the above (master's) (0).

Doctoral Degree Graduates: Of those who graduated in the academic year 2006–2007, the following categories and numbers represent the postgraduate activities and employment of doctoral degree graduates: Enrolled in a psychology doctoral program (n/a), enrolled in a postdoctoral residency/fellowship (8), total from the above (doctoral) (8).

Additional Information:

Orientation, Objectives, and Emphasis of Department: The program follows a practitioner–scholar model of training entry-level mental health professionals with an eclectic focus who can serve a diverse population. The training model adheres to a competency approach in the development of knowledge, skills, and attitudes related to the practice of clinical psychology. Students are systematically evaluated in the development of competency areas including relationship, assessment, intervention, professionalism, diversity, management and supervision, consultation and education, and research and evaluation. The Program emphasizes first-year supervised clinical experiences to produce a foundation for later clinical training. The Program provides an individualized mentoring experience for its students.

Special Facilities or Resources: The clinical psychology program has the full support of the resources available from the Midwestern University Osteopathic Medical School and School of Pharmacy, including research scientists and practicing clinicians. The program is housed on a large wooded campus with numerous buildings and research facilities including a state-of-the-art library. The majority of the physical resources have been constructed or remodelled in the past 3 years.

Information for Students With Physical Disabilities: See the following Web site for more information: http://www.midwestern.edu.

Application Information:
Send to Office of Admissions, Midwestern University, 555 31st Street, Downers Grove, IL 60515. Application available online. URL of online application: http://www.midwestern.edu. Programs have rolling admissions. *Fee:* $50.

Northern Illinois University

Department of Psychology
College of Liberal Arts and Sciences
DeKalb, IL 60115-2892
Telephone: (815) 753-0372
Fax: (815) 753-8088
E-mail: *mholliday@niu.edu*
Web: *http://www.niu.edu/psyc*

Department Information:
1959. Chairperson: Greg Waas. Number of faculty: total—full-time 31; women—full-time 14; total—minority—full-time 1.

Programs and Degrees Offered:
Listed in the following order: Program area, degree type (T if terminal Master's), number awarded 7/06–6/07. Clinical PhD (Doctor of Philosophy) 5, Neuroscience and Behavior PhD (Doctor of Philosophy) 0, Social and Industrial/Organizational PhD (Doctor of Philosophy) 5, Cognitive PhD (Doctor of Philosophy) 1, Developmental PhD (Doctor of Philosophy) 0, School PhD (Doctor of Philosophy) 2.

APA Accreditation: Clinical PhD (Doctor of Philosophy).

Student Applications/Admissions:
Student Applications
Clinical PhD (Doctor of Philosophy)—Applications 2007–2008, 191. Total applicants accepted 2007–2008, 11. Number full-time enrolled (new admits only) 2007–2008, 7. Number part-time enrolled (new admits only) 2007–2008, 0. Openings 2008–2009, 8. The median number of years required for completion of a degree in 2006–2007 were 8. The number of students enrolled full- and part-time who were dismissed or voluntarily withdrew from this program area in 2007–2008 were 1. *Neuroscience and Behavior PhD (Doctor of Philosophy)*—Applications 2007–2008, 16. Total applicants accepted 2007–2008, 3. Number full-time enrolled (new admits only) 2007–2008, 2. Openings 2008–2009, 2. The number of students enrolled full- and part-time who were dismissed or voluntarily withdrew from this program area in 2007–2008 were 0. *Social and Industrial/Organizational PhD (Doctor of Philosophy)*—Applications 2007–2008, 62. Total applicants accepted 2007–2008, 9. Number full-time enrolled (new admits only) 2007–2008, 6. Openings 2008–2009, 6. The median number of years required for completion of a degree in 2006–2007 were 5. The number of students enrolled full- and part-time who were dismissed or voluntarily withdrew from this program area in 2007–2008 were 0. *Cognitive PhD (Doctor of Philosophy)*—Applications 2007–2008, 6. Total applicants accepted 2007–2008, 1. Number full-time enrolled (new admits only) 2007–2008, 1. Total enrolled 2007–2008 full-time, 11. Openings 2008–2009, 2. The median number of years required for completion of a degree in 2006–2007 were 5. The number of students enrolled full- and part-time who were dismissed or voluntarily withdrew from this program area in 2007–2008 were 0. *Developmental PhD (Doctor of Philosophy)*—Applications 2007–2008, 6. Total applicants accepted 2007–2008, 1. Number full-time enrolled (new admits only) 2007–2008, 1. Openings 2008–2009, 2. The number of students enrolled full- and part-time who were dismissed or voluntarily withdrew from this program area in 2007–2008 were 0. *School PhD (Doctor of Philosophy)*—Applications 2007–2008, 82. Total applicants accepted 2007–2008, 10. Number full-time enrolled (new admits only) 2007–2008, 7. Openings 2008–2009, 7. The median number of years required for completion of a degree in 2006–2007 were 8. The number of students enrolled full- and part-time who were dismissed or voluntarily withdrew from this program area in 2007–2008 were 0.
Other Criteria: (importance of criteria rated low, medium, or high): GRE/MAT scores—high, research experience—high, work experience—low, extracurricular activity—low, clinically related public service—low, GPA—high, letters of recommendation—high, interview—medium, statement of goals and objectives—high. Clinical and School programs interview students; other programs generally do not.

Student Characteristics: The following represents characteristics of students in 2007–2008 in all graduate psychology programs in the department: Female—full-time 101, part-time 0; Male—full-time 48, part-time 0; African American/Black—full-time 5, part-time 0; Hispanic/Latino(a)—full-time 6, part-time 0; Asian/Pacific Islander—full-time 13, part-time 0; American Indian/Alaska Native—full-time 5, part-time 0; Caucasian/White—full-time 117, part-time 0; Multi-ethnic—full-time 0, part-time 0; Unknown ethnicity—full-time 3, part-time 0; International students who hold an F-1 or J-1 Visa—full-time 5, part-time 0.

Financial Information/Assistance:
Tuition for Full-Time Study: *Master's:* State residents: $226 per credit hour; Nonstate residents: $452 per credit hour. *Doctoral:* State residents: $226 per credit hour; Nonstate residents: $452 per credit hour. Tuition is subject to change. Additional fees are assessed to students beyond the costs of tuition for the following: General university student fees.

Financial Assistance:
First-Year Students: Teaching assistantships available for first year. Average amount paid per academic year: $11,500. Average number of hours worked per week: 20. Tuition remission given: full. Research assistantships available for first year. Average amount paid per academic year: $11,500. Average number of hours worked per week: 20. Tuition remission given: full. Traineeships available for first year. Tuition remission given: full. Fellowships and scholarships available for first year. Tuition remission given: full.

Advanced Students: Teaching assistantships available for advanced students. Average amount paid per academic year: $11,500. Average number of hours worked per week: 20. Tuition remission given: full. Research assistantships available for advanced students. Average amount paid per academic year: $11,500. Average number of hours worked per week: 20. Tuition remission given: full. Traineeships available for advanced students. Tuition remission given: full. Fellowships and scholarships available for advanced students. Tuition remission given: full.

Additional Information: Of all students currently enrolled full time, 91% benefited from one or more of the listed financial assistance programs. Application and information available online at http://www.grad.niu.edu.

Internships/Practica: Doctoral Degree (PhD Clinical): For those doctoral students for whom a professional internship was required in this program prior to graduation, (9) students applied for an internship in 2006–2007, with (8) students obtaining an internship. Of those students who obtained an internship, (8) were paid internships. Of those students who obtained an internship, (8) students placed in APA/CPA-accredited internships, (0) students placed in internships not APA/CPA-accredited, but listed with the Association of Psychology Postdoctoral and Internship Centers (APPIC), (0) students placed in internships conforming to guidelines of the Council of Directors of School Psychology Programs (CDSPP), (0) students placed in internships that were not APA/CPA-accredited, APPIC or CDSPP listed. Clinical and school psychology internships are required for students in those areas. Clinical externships (equivalent to in-residence assistantships) are available and recommended.

Housing and Day Care: On-campus housing is available. See the following Web site for more information: http://www.niu.edu; then "A–Z Index," and "Campus Child Care Services" or "Student Housing and Dining Services." On-campus day care facilities are available.

Employment of Department Graduates:

Master's Degree Graduates: Of those who graduated in the academic year 2006–2007, the following categories and numbers represent the postgraduate activities and employment of master's degree graduates: Enrolled in a postdoctoral residency/fellowship (n/a), employed in independent practice (n/a), total from the above (master's) (0).

Doctoral Degree Graduates: Of those who graduated in the academic year 2006–2007, the following categories and numbers represent the postgraduate activities and employment of doctoral degree graduates: Enrolled in a psychology doctoral program (n/a), employed in government agency (1), employed in a community mental health/counseling center (2), employed in a hospital/medical center (2), total from the above (doctoral) (5).

Additional Information:

Orientation, Objectives, and Emphasis of Department: The PhD program in psychology is designed to prepare graduate students to function in a variety of settings such as academic institutions, which emphasize research and/or teaching, nonacademic institutions, which emphasize research on mental health, human factors, or skill acquisition, and various consultative modalities, which emphasize practitioner applications and the delivery of human services. Doctorates in psychology are awarded in four specialty areas: a fully accredited APA program in clinical psychology; cognitive/instructional, developmental, and school psychology (NASP approved); neuroscience and behavior; and social and organizational psychology. Faculty in all areas endorse the value of well-trained researchers and practitioners. Students are equipped to conduct sophisticated theoretically based empirical research and to teach at the graduate or undergraduate level. In addition to academic placements, students can also find suitable employment as applied researchers or service practitioners in a variety of mental health (clinical), educational (instructional, developmental, school), physical health (neuroscience), or business (social and organizational) settings. The overall goal of the graduate program is to produce doctoral graduates who appreciate and are deeply committed to the study of psychological processes and behavior, who are familiar with fundamental knowledge in the field, and who are well-trained in methodology and modern techniques of data analysis.

Special Facilities or Resources: The department has a modern psychology building with offices for faculty, staff, and graduate students; classrooms; shops; a six-story research wing with research equipment, including minicomputers and direct access to the university computer and Internet applications; and a Psychological Services Center for practicum training in clinical, school, organizational, and other applied psychological areas.

Application Information:

Send to The Graduate School, Northern Illinois University, DeKalb, IL 60115-2864. Application available online. URL of online application: http://www.grad.niu.edu. Students are admitted in the Fall, application deadline December 15; Spring, application deadline October 1. Spring admissions are rare. December 15 deadline for Clinical applicants. January 15 deadline for Social and Industrial/Organizational. February 1 deadline for Cognitive/Instructional, Developmental, or School. March 1 deadline for Neuroscience and Behavior. *Fee:* $30. Fees waived/deferred if applicant was exempt from GRE fees, is NIU employee, or is currently enrolled in graduate program at NIU.

Northwestern University

Department of Psychology
102 Swift Hall, 2029 Sheridan Road
Evanston, IL 60208-2710
Telephone: (847) 491-5190
Fax: (847) 491-7859
E-mail: *f-sales@northwestern.edu*
Web: *http://www.wcas.northwestern.edu/psych/*

Department Information:

1909. Chairperson: Alice H. Eagly. Number of faculty: total—full-time 33, part-time 1; women—full-time 12, part-time 1; total—minority—full-time 3; women minority—full-time 3.

Programs and Degrees Offered:

Listed in the following order: Program area, degree type (T if terminal Master's), number awarded 7/06–6/07. Clinical Psychology PhD (Doctor of Philosophy) 1, Cognitive Psychology PhD (Doctor of Philosophy) 2, Personality Psychology PhD (Doctor of Philosophy) 0, Brain, Behavior, and Cognition PhD (Doctor of Philosophy) 1, Social Psychology PhD (Doctor of Philosophy) 2.

APA Accreditation: Clinical PhD (Doctor of Philosophy).

Student Applications/Admissions:

Student Applications

Clinical Psychology PhD (Doctor of Philosophy)—Applications 2007–2008, 92. Total applicants accepted 2007–2008, 4. Number full-time enrolled (new admits only) 2007–2008, 3. Number part-time enrolled (new admits only) 2007–2008, 0. Openings 2008–2009, 4. The median number of years required for completion of a degree in 2006–2007 were 6. The number of students enrolled full- and part-time who were dismissed or voluntarily withdrew from this program area in 2007–2008 were 0. *Cognitive Psychology PhD (Doctor of Philosophy)*—Applications 2007–2008, 65. Total applicants accepted 2007–2008, 1. Number full-time enrolled (new admits only) 2007–2008, 1. Number part-time enrolled (new admits only) 2007–2008, 0. Openings 2008–2009, 7. The median number of years required for completion of a degree in 2006–2007 were 5. The number of students enrolled full- and part-time who were dismissed or voluntarily withdrew from this program area in 2007–2008 were 0. *Personality Psychology PhD (Doctor of Philosophy)*—Applications 2007–2008, 12. Total applicants accepted 2007–2008, 0. Number full-time enrolled (new admits only) 2007–2008, 0. Number part-time enrolled (new admits only) 2007–2008, 0. The median number of years required for completion of a degree in 2006–2007 were 5. The number of students enrolled full- and part-time who were dismissed or voluntarily withdrew from this program area in 2007–2008 were 0. *Brain, Behavior, and Cognition PhD (Doctor of Philosophy)*—Applications 2007–2008, 45. Total applicants accepted 2007–2008, 4. Number full-time enrolled (new admits only) 2007–2008, 2. Number part-time enrolled (new admits only) 2007–2008, 0. Openings 2008–2009, 6. The median number of years required for completion of a degree in 2006–2007 were 5. The number of students enrolled full- and part-time who were dismissed or voluntarily withdrew from this program area in 2007–2008 were 1. *Social Psychology PhD (Doctor of Philosophy)*—Applications 2007–2008, 145. Total applicants accepted 2007–2008, 8. Number full-time enrolled (new admits only) 2007–2008, 2. Number part-time enrolled (new admits only) 2007–2008, 0. Openings 2008–2009, 7. The median number of years required for completion of a degree in 2006–2007 were 5. The number of students enrolled full- and part-time who were dismissed or voluntarily withdrew from this program area in 2007–2008 were 1.

Admissions Requirements:

Scores: Entries appear in this order: required test or GPA, minimum score (if required), median score of students entering in 2007–2008. Doctoral Programs: GRE-V no minimum stated, 685; GRE-Q no minimum stated, 741; overall undergraduate GPA no minimum stated. The Graduate School no longer calculates GPAs.

Other Criteria: (importance of criteria rated low, medium, or high): GRE/MAT scores—high, research experience—high, GPA—high, letters of recommendation—medium, interview—medium, statement of goals and objectives—medium.

Student Characteristics: The following represents characteristics of students in 2007–2008 in all graduate psychology programs in the department: Female—full-time 39, part-time 0; Male—full-time 23, part-time 0; African American/Black—full-time 0, part-time 0; Hispanic/Latino(a)—full-time 0, part-time 0; Asian/Pacific Islander—full-time 2, part-time 0; American Indian/Alaska Native—full-time 0, part-time 0; Caucasian/White—full-time 60, part-time 0; Multi-ethnic—full-time 0, part-time 0; students subject to the Americans With Disabilities Act—full-time 0, part-time 0; Unknown ethnicity—full-time 0, part-time 0; International students who hold an F-1 or J-1 Visa—full-time 1, part-time 0.

Financial Information/Assistance:

Tuition for Full-Time Study: *Doctoral:* State residents: per academic year $37,120; Nonstate residents: per academic year $37,120. Tuition is subject to change.

Financial Assistance:

First-Year Students: Fellowships and scholarships available for first year. Average amount paid per academic year: $19,140. Apply by December 31. Tuition remission given: full.

Advanced Students: Teaching assistantships available for advanced students. Average amount paid per academic year: $19,590. Average number of hours worked per week: 10. Tuition remission given: full. Research assistantships available for advanced students. Average amount paid per academic year: $19,590. Tuition remission given: partial. Fellowships and scholarships available for advanced students. Average amount paid per academic year: $19,140. Tuition remission given: full.

Additional Information: Of all students currently enrolled full time, 100% benefited from one or more of the listed financial assistance programs.

Internships/Practica: Doctoral Degree (PhD Clinical Psychology): For those doctoral students for whom a professional internship was required in this program prior to graduation, (2) students applied for an internship in 2006–2007, with (1) students obtaining an internship. Of those students who obtained an internship, (1) were paid internships. Of those students who obtained an internship, (1)students placed in APA/CPA-accredited internships, (0) students placed in internships not APA/CPA accredited, but listed with the Association of Psychology Postdoctoral and Internship Centers (APPIC), (0) students placed in internships conforming to guidelines of the Council of Directors of School Psychology Programs (CDSPP), (0) students placed in internships that were not APA/CPA-accredited, APPIC or CDSPP listed. A variety of internships in community settings is available.

Housing and Day Care: On-campus housing is available. There is a University-operated residence hall for graduate students, but no child care. See the following Web site for more information: http://www.stuaff.nwu.edu/grad_and_off/GOCH/Evanston_Incoming.html.

Employment of Department Graduates:

Master's Degree Graduates: Of those who graduated in the academic year 2006–2007, the following categories and numbers represent the postgraduate activities and employment of master's degree graduates: Enrolled in a postdoctoral residency/fellowship (n/a), employed in independent practice (n/a), total from the above (master's) (0).

Doctoral Degree Graduates: Of those who graduated in the academic year 2006–2007, the following categories and numbers represent the postgraduate activities and employment of doctoral degree graduates: Enrolled in a psychology doctoral program (n/a), enrolled in a postdoctoral residency/fellowship (0), employed in an academic position at a university (3), employed in an academic position at a 2-year/4-year college (2), employed in business or industry (1), total from the above (doctoral) (6).

Additional Information:

Orientation, Objectives, and Emphasis of Department: The faculty in each graduate area has designed programs tailored to the needs of students in that area. Whatever a student's field of interest, the department tries to produce doctoral students with a strong research orientation. Administrative barriers between areas are permeable; most faculty members take an active part in the instruction and research programs of more than one interest area. A significant population of postdoctoral fellows enhances the informal professional education of graduate students. In addition, all graduate students are given opportunities for teaching. Teaching is independent of type of financial aid.

Special Facilities or Resources: http://www.northwestern.edu/hr/eeo/?quicklinks.

Application Information:
Send to Florence Sales, Graduate Admissions Coordinator, 102 Swift Hall, Department of Psychology, Northwestern University, 2029 Sheridan Road, Evanston, IL 60208-2710; e-mail: f-sales@northwestern.edu. Application available online. URL of online application: https://www.app.applyyourself.com/?id=nwu-grad. Students are admitted in the Fall, application deadline December 31. *Fee:* $75.

Northwestern University, Feinberg School of Medicine

Department of Psychiatry and Behavioral Sciences, Division of Psychology
Abbott Hall, Suite 1205, 710 North Lake Shore Drive
Chicago, IL 60611
Telephone: (312) 908-8262
Fax: (312) 908-5070
E-mail: *m-reinecke@northwestern.edu*
Web: *http://www.clinpsych.northwestern.edu*

Department Information:
1970. Chief: Mark A. Reinecke, PhD. Number of faculty: total—full-time 15, part-time 10; women—full-time 6, part-time 6.

Programs and Degrees Offered:
Listed in the following order: Program area, degree type (T if terminal Master's), number awarded 7/06–6/07. Clinical PhD (Doctor of Philosophy) 1.

APA Accreditation: Clinical PhD (Doctor of Philosophy).

Student Applications/Admissions:
Student Applications
Clinical PhD (Doctor of Philosophy)—Applications 2007–2008, 231. Total applicants accepted 2007–2008, 12. Number full-time enrolled (new admits only) 2007–2008, 5. Number part-time enrolled (new admits only) 2007–2008, 0. Openings 2008–2009, 5. The median number of years required for completion of a degree in 2006–2007 were 6. The number of students enrolled full- and part-time who were dismissed or voluntarily withdrew from this program area in 2007–2008 were 0.

Admissions Requirements:
Scores: Entries appear in this order: required test or GPA, minimum score (if required), median score of students entering in 2007–2008. Doctoral Programs: GRE-V no minimum stated, 625; GRE-Q no minimum stated, 695; GRE-Subject (Psychology) no minimum stated, 710; overall undergraduate GPA 3.0, 3.6; Doctoral program GRE-Analytic no minimum stated.
Other Criteria: (importance of criteria rated low, medium, or high): GRE/MAT scores—medium, research experience—high, work experience—low, extracurricular activity—low, clinically related public service—medium, GPA—medium, letters of recommendation—high, interview—high, statement of goals and objectives—medium, undergraduate major in psychology—low. For additional information on admission requirements, go to http://www.clinpsych.northwestern.edu.

Student Characteristics: The following represents characteristics of students in 2007–2008 in all graduate psychology programs in the department: Female—full-time 30, part-time 0; Male—full-time 3, part-time 0; African American/Black—full-time 3, part-time 0; Hispanic/Latino(a)—full-time 2, part-time 0; Asian/Pacific Islander—full-time 1, part-time 0; American Indian/Alaska Native—full-time 0, part-time 0; Caucasian/White—full-time 26, part-time 0; Multi-ethnic—full-time 0, part-time 0; students subject to the Americans With Disabilities Act—full-time 0, part-time 0; Unknown ethnicity—full-time 1, part-time 0; International students who hold an F-1 or J-1 Visa—full-time 1, part-time 0.

Financial Information/Assistance:
Financial Assistance:
First-Year Students: Research assistantships available for first year. Average number of hours worked per week: 15. Tuition remission given: partial. Fellowships and scholarships available for first year. Tuition remission given: full and partial.
Advanced Students: Research assistantships available for advanced students. Average number of hours worked per week: 15. Tuition remission given: partial. Fellowships and scholarships available for advanced students. Tuition remission given: full and partial.
Additional Information: Of all students currently enrolled full time, 100% benefited from one or more of the listed financial assistance programs. Application and information available online at http://www.clinpsych.northwestern.edu.

Internships/Practica: Doctoral Degree (PhD Clinical): For those doctoral students for whom a professional internship was required in this program prior to graduation, (8) students applied for an internship in 2006–2007, with (5) students obtaining an internship. Of those students who obtained an internship, (5) were paid internships. Of those students who obtained an internship, (5) students placed in APA/CPA-accredited internships, (0) students placed in internships not APA/CPA-accredited, but listed with the Association of Psychology Postdoctoral and Internship Centers (APPIC), (0) students placed in internships conforming to guidelines of the Council of Directors of School Psychology Programs (CDSPP), (0) students placed in internships that were not APA/CPA-accredited, APPIC or CDSPP listed. Most practica are located at clinical sites affiliated with the Feinberg School of Medicine, Northwestern Memorial Hospital, or Children's Memorial Hospital. They include a university counseling center, an adult outpatient psychiatry clinic, several partial hospital programs, several neuropsychological sites, and programs at several child/adolescent sites. For additional information on education and training outcomes for our programs, see the following Web site: http://www.clinpsych.northwestern.edu.

Housing and Day Care: On-campus housing is available. Graduate and Off-campus Housing Office (312) 503-8514. On-campus day care facilities are available. Office of Child and Family Resources (847) 491-3612.

Employment of Department Graduates:

Master's Degree Graduates: Of those who graduated in the academic year 2006–2007, the following categories and numbers represent the postgraduate activities and employment of master's degree graduates: Enrolled in a postdoctoral residency/fellowship (n/a), employed in independent practice (n/a), total from the above (master's) (0).

Doctoral Degree Graduates: Of those who graduated in the academic year 2006–2007, the following categories and numbers represent the postgraduate activities and employment of doctoral degree graduates: Enrolled in a psychology doctoral program (n/a), enrolled in a postdoctoral residency/fellowship (1), total from the above (doctoral) (1).

Additional Information:

Orientation, Objectives, and Emphasis of Department: The goal of our doctoral program is to develop clinical psychologists well-trained in the scientist–practitioner model, skilled both in clinical practice and research. During tenure in this 5-year program, a student completes a curriculum of required courses, participates in at least 2 years of clinical practica, apprentices as a research assistant for 1 year, conducts an originally conceived small research project, completes a clinical internship, and writes a doctoral dissertation. Practica begin in the 2nd year. The program is committed to a training model in which intensive supervision in basic diagnostic, interviewing, and treatment skills acts as a basis for competent functioning in most clinical settings and with most patient populations. The division offers clinical subspecialties in neuropsychology, child psychology, as well as adult clinical psychology.

Application Information:

Send to Division of Psychology, Northwestern University Feinberg School of Medicine, Abbott Hall Suite 1205, 710 North Lake Shore Drive, Chicago, IL 60611-3078. Application available online. URL of online application: http://www.clinpsych.northwestern.edu; http://www.tgs.northwestern.edu. Students are admitted in the Fall, application deadline December 15. *Fee:* $50.

Roosevelt University

Department of Psychology
Arts and Sciences
430 South Michigan Avenue
Chicago, IL 60605-1394
Telephone: (312) 341-3760
Fax: (312) 341-6362
E-mail: *jchoca@roosevelt.edu*
Web: *http://www.roosevelt.edu*

Department Information:

1945. Chairperson: Dr. James Choca. Number of faculty: total—full-time 17, part-time 64; women—full-time 7, part-time 33; total—minority—full-time 4, part-time 11; women minority—full-time 2, part-time 3.

Programs and Degrees Offered:

Listed in the following order: Program area, degree type (T if terminal Master's), number awarded 7/06–6/07. Clinical Psychology MA/MS (Master of Arts/Science) (T) 28, Industrial/Organizational MA/MS (Master of Arts/Science) (T) 18, Clinical Professional Psychology MA/MS (Master of Arts/Science) (T) 43, Clinical Psychology PsyD (Doctor of Psychology) 4, Counseling Psychology MA/MS (Master of Arts/Science) (T).

APA Accreditation: Clinical PsyD (Doctor of Psychology).

Student Applications/Admissions:

Student Applications

Clinical Psychology MA/MS (Master of Arts/Science)—Applications 2007–2008, 130. Total applicants accepted 2007–2008, 77. Number full-time enrolled (new admits only) 2007–2008, 23. Number part-time enrolled (new admits only) 2007–2008, 4. Total enrolled 2007–2008 full-time, 37, part-time, 31. Openings 2008–2009, 40. The median number of years required for completion of a degree in 2006–2007 were 5. The number of students enrolled full- and part-time who were dismissed or voluntarily withdrew from this program area in 2007–2008 were 5. *Industrial/Organizational MA/MS (Master of Arts/Science)*—Applications 2007–2008, 77. Total applicants accepted 2007–2008, 41. Number full-time enrolled (new admits only) 2007–2008, 17. Number part-time enrolled (new admits only) 2007–2008, 9. Total enrolled 2007–2008 full-time, 43, part-time, 44. Openings 2008–2009, 50. The median number of years required for completion of a degree in 2006–2007 were 4. The number of students enrolled full- and part-time who were dismissed or voluntarily withdrew from this program area in 2007–2008 were 3. *Clinical Professional Psychology MA/MS (Master of Arts/Science)*—Applications 2007–2008, 117. Total applicants accepted 2007–2008, 73. Number full-time enrolled (new admits only) 2007–2008, 22. Number part-time enrolled (new admits only) 2007–2008, 13. Total enrolled 2007–2008 full-time, 85, part-time, 102. Openings 2008–2009, 75. The median number of years required for completion of a degree in 2006–2007 were 4. The number of students enrolled full- and part-time who were dismissed or voluntarily withdrew from this program area in 2007–2008 were 5. *Clinical Psychology PsyD (Doctor of Psychology)*—Applications 2007–2008, 144. Total applicants accepted 2007–2008, 17. Number full-time enrolled (new admits only) 2007–2008, 17. Number part-time enrolled (new admits only) 2007–2008, 0. Total enrolled 2007–2008 full-time, 57, part-time, 22. Openings 2008–2009, 20. The median number of years required for completion of a degree in 2006–2007 were 6. The number of students enrolled full- and part-time who were dismissed or voluntarily withdrew from this program area in 2007–2008 were 2. *Counseling Psychology MA/MS (Master of Arts/Science)*.

Admissions Requirements:

Scores: Entries appear in this order: required test or GPA, minimum score (if required), median score of students entering in 2007–2008. Master's Programs: overall undergraduate GPA 3.00; last 2 years GPA 3.00, 3.50; psychology GPA 3.00. Doctoral Programs: GRE-V 500; GRE-Q 500; overall undergraduate GPA 3.25; Doctoral program GRE-Analytic no minimum stated. GRE scores greater than the 50th percentile are considered over raw scores.

Other Criteria: (importance of criteria rated low, medium, or high): GRE/MAT scores—high, research experience—low, work experience—medium, extracurricular activity—low, clinically related public service—medium, GPA—high, letters of recommendation—medium, interview—high, statement of goals and objectives—medium. Ratings are shown for the PsyD program. For additional information on admission requirements, go to http://www.roosevelt.edu/cas/sp/psyd.htm.

Student Characteristics: The following represents characteristics of students in 2007–2008 in all graduate psychology programs in the department: Female—full-time 183, part-time 163; Male—full-time 39, part-time 36; African American/Black—full-time 34, part-time 46; Hispanic/Latino(a)—full-time 9, part-time 15; Asian/Pacific Islander—full-time 17, part-time 17; American Indian/Alaska Native—full-time 0, part-time 0; Caucasian/White—full-time 114, part-time 88; Multi-ethnic—full-time 0, part-time 0; students subject to the Americans With Disabilities Act—full-time 2, part-time 1; Unknown ethnicity—full-time 48, part-time 33; International students who hold an F-1 or J-1 Visa—full-time 4, part-time 5.

Financial Information/Assistance:

Tuition for Full-Time Study: *Master's:* State residents: $709 per credit hour; Nonstate residents: $709 per credit hour. *Doctoral:* State residents: $709 per credit hour; Nonstate residents: $709 per credit hour. Tuition is subject to change. See the following Web site for updates and changes in tuition costs: http://www.roosevelt.edu/financialaid/tuition.htm.

Financial Assistance:

First-Year Students: Research assistantships available for first year. Average amount paid per academic year: $5,200. Average number of hours worked per week: 17. Apply by March 31. Tuition remission given: full. Fellowships and scholarships available for first year. Average amount paid per academic year: $3,000. Average number of hours worked per week: 0. Apply by open.

Advanced Students: Research assistantships available for advanced students. Average amount paid per academic year: $5,200. Average number of hours worked per week: 17. Apply by March 31. Tuition remission given: full. Fellowships and scholarships available for advanced students. Apply by March 31.

Additional Information: Of all students currently enrolled full time, 15% benefited from one or more of the listed financial assistance programs. Application and information available online at http://www.roosevelt.edu/financialaid/default.htm.

Internships/Practica: Master's Degree (MA/MS Clinical Psychology): An internship experience such as a final research project or "capstone" experience is required of graduates. Master's Degree (MA/MS Industrial/Organizational): An internship experience such as a final research project or "capstone" experience is required of graduates. Master's Degree (MA/MS Clinical Professional Psychology): An internship experience such as a final research project or "capstone" experience is required of graduates. Doctoral Degree (PsyD Clinical Psychology): For those doctoral students for whom a professional internship was required in this program prior to graduation, (11) students applied for an internship in 2006–2007, with (9) students obtaining an internship. Of those students who obtained an internship, (8) were paid internships. Of those students who obtained an internship, (4) students placed in APA/CPA-accredited internships, (4) students placed in internships not APA/CPA-accredited, but listed with the Association of Psychology Postdoctoral and Internship Centers (APPIC), (0) students placed in internships conforming to guidelines of the Council of Directors of School Psychology Programs (CDSPP), (1) student placed in internships that were not APA/CPA accredited, APPIC or CDSPP listed. Students in our clinical programs have available over 250 sites in the greater Chicago area for practicum experience. We have a full-time Director of Training to assist students with this process. I/O, Clinical MA, and PsyD students have ample opportunities for training; I/O students nearly always obtain paid practicum experience.

Housing and Day Care: On-campus housing is available. See the following Web site for more information: http://www.roosevelt.edu/reslife/Buildings.htm. University Center (UC) is an 18-story, state-of-the-art, multiuniversity residence hall. Located just one block away from the Roosevelt University Auditorium Building, University Center houses students attending Roosevelt, Columbia, and DePaul. Further information is at: www.universitycenter.com. Roosevelt's newest residence hall combines contemporary apartments for upper class students in the historic loop Pittsfield Building. Located one block north of Roosevelt's Gage Building, Roosevelt on Washington (ROW) in Fornelli Hall is in the heart of downtown, just steps away from the Chicago Cultural Center and Millennium Park. Students can choose from fully furnished apartments with shared- or single-occupancy bedrooms. All units include a kitchen and living room. ROW will be available beginning Fall 2008. Students wanting to reside on an annual contract can live in UC for the summer and move to ROW in August. On-campus day care facilities are available. See the following Web site for more information: http://www.roosevelt.edu/current/child.htm. Licensed child care is available at the suburban campus in Schaumburg, IL.

Employment of Department Graduates:

Master's Degree Graduates: Of those who graduated in the academic year 2006–2007, the following categories and numbers represent the postgraduate activities and employment of master's degree graduates: Enrolled in a postdoctoral residency/fellowship (n/a), employed in independent practice (n/a), total from the above (master's) (0).

Doctoral Degree Graduates: Of those who graduated in the academic year 2006–2007, the following categories and numbers represent the postgraduate activities and employment of doctoral degree graduates: Enrolled in a psychology doctoral program (n/a), enrolled in a postdoctoral residency/fellowship (2), employed in independent practice (2), employed in an academic position at a university (0), employed in an academic position at a 2-year/4-year college (0), employed in other positions at a higher education institution (0), employed in a professional position in a school system (1), employed in business or industry (0), employed in government agency (0), employed in a community mental health/counseling center (0), employed in a hospital/medical center (0), still seeking employment (0), not seeking employment (0), other employment position (0), do not know (0), total from the above (doctoral) (5).

Additional Information:

Orientation, Objectives, and Emphasis of Department: Roosevelt University was founded over 60 years ago, in 1945, on the principles of social justice and equal educational access for all qualified students. We have a long history of inclusion and multicultural diversity. Our program's orientation reflects the diversity of contemporary psychology practice. A primary goal of the Department of Psychology is to prepare students to work effectively with diverse cultures in metropolitan settings. Master's degree programs in psychology have been offered since 1952, and the PsyD program, the first university-based clinical PsyD program in Illinois, was added in 1996. The PsyD program is designed to provide generalist training in all facets of clinical practice, in preparation for postdoctoral specialization of the student's choice. Three master's degree programs are offered: Our MA programs offer streamlined and personally tailored predoctoral training designed to help qualified students enter PhD and PsyD programs, including our own, or to prepare for MA-level licensure. Approximately 85% of our graduates who have applied to doctoral programs have been accepted. We prepare students for professional master's-level employment in mental health and I/O careers. Many of our students are several years beyond undergraduate graduation and continue to work full or part-time, while arranging their schedules around evening, daytime, and weekend courses offered at our downtown and suburban campuses.

Special Facilities or Resources: The Department of Psychology has an exceptional faculty who are actively involved in applied research and clinical practice, supplemented by a large and highly trained adjunct faculty who also are involved in clinical, forensic, and experimental work. In addition to the extensive Roosevelt library and other facilities, there is access to clinical, research, computer, and library facilities of major Chicago universities, hospitals, and clinics. Volunteer research assistantships are available to qualified students interested in doing publishable research. A major resource is the urban location with varied employment, educational, and cultural opportunities. The Stress Institute offers basic and advanced certificates in Stress Management, which incorporates a wide range of cognitive–behavioral courses for students and health professionals interested in enhancing their clinical stress management skills. The Children and Family Studies Initiative allows students to train for the clinical treatment of children and families. The Instructor Development Program prepares PsyD students to teach undergraduate courses during the last 2 years of their doctoral training.

Information for Students With Physical Disabilities: See the following Web site for more information: http://www.roosevelt.edu/dss/default.htm.

Application Information:

Send to Graduate Admission, Roosevelt University, 430 South Michigan Avenue, Chicago, IL 60605; http://www.roosevelt.edu/contact/default.htm. Application available online. URL of online application: http://www.roosevelt.edu/admission/graduate/howto-grad.htm. Students are admitted in the Fall, application deadline January 1—PsyD; programs have rolling admissions. MA programs have rolling admissions. *Fee:* $25.

Rosalind Franklin University of Medicine and Science

Department of Psychology
(formerly Finch University of Health Science, The Chicago Medical School)
3333 Green Bay Road
North Chicago, IL 60064
Telephone: (847) 578-8747
Fax: (847) 578-8758
E-mail: *john.calamari @rosalindfranklin.edu*
Web: *http://www.rosalindfranklin.edu/srhs/psychology*

Department Information:

1977. Associate Professor and Acting Chairman: John Calamari, PhD. Number of faculty: total—full-time 8; women—full-time 2; total—minority—full-time 1; women minority—full-time 1.

Programs and Degrees Offered:

Listed in the following order: Program area, degree type (T if terminal Master's), number awarded 7/06–6/07. Clinical PhD (Doctor of Philosophy) 14.

APA Accreditation: Clinical PhD (Doctor of Philosophy).

Student Applications/Admissions:

Student Applications

Clinical PhD (Doctor of Philosophy)—Applications 2007–2008, 63. Total applicants accepted 2007–2008, 21. Number full-time enrolled (new admits only) 2007–2008, 12. Total enrolled 2007–2008 full-time, 56. Openings 2008–2009, 7. The median number of years required for completion of a degree in 2006–2007 were 7. The number of students enrolled full- and part-time who were dismissed or voluntarily withdrew from this program area in 2007–2008 were 0.

Admissions Requirements:

Scores: Entries appear in this order: required test or GPA, minimum score (if required), median score of students entering in 2007–2008. Doctoral Programs: GRE-V 600, 700; GRE-Q 600, 620; GRE-Subject (Psychology) 600, 600; Doctoral program GRE-Analytic 4.5, 4.5. The Advanced Psychology GRE is required for those students who are not undergraduate Psychology majors or have a Master's degree in a non-Psychology discipline.

Other Criteria: (importance of criteria rated low, medium, or high): GRE/MAT scores—medium, research experience—high, work experience—low, extracurricular activity—medium, clinically related public service—medium, GPA—high, letters of recommendation—high, interview—high, statement of goals and objectives—high. These criteria are identical for all programs. Prospective applicants are invited to attend an Interview Day. For additional information on admission requirements, go to http://www.rosalindfranklin.edu/srhs/psychology/admissions.cfm.

Student Characteristics: The following represents characteristics of students in 2007–2008 in all graduate psychology programs in the department: Female—full-time 40, part-time 0; Male—full-time 16, part-time 0; African American/Black—full-time 2, part-time 0; Hispanic/Latino(a)—full-time 0, part-time 0; Asian/

Pacific Islander—full-time 6, part-time 0; American Indian/ Alaska Native—full-time 0, part-time 0; Caucasian/White—full-time 48, part-time 0; Unknown ethnicity—full-time 0, part-time 0.

Financial Information/Assistance:

Tuition for Full-Time Study: *Doctoral:* State residents: per academic year $21,500; Nonstate residents: per academic year $21,500. Tuition is subject to change.

Financial Assistance:

First-Year Students: Research assistantships available for first year. Average number of hours worked per week: 10. Tuition remission given: partial. Fellowships and scholarships available for first year. Tuition remission given: partial.

Advanced Students: Teaching assistantships available for advanced students. Average number of hours worked per week: 10. Tuition remission given: full and partial. Research assistantships available for advanced students. Average number of hours worked per week: 10. Tuition remission given: full and partial. Traineeships available for advanced students. Average number of hours worked per week: 10. Tuition remission given: full and partial. Fellowships and scholarships available for advanced students. Average number of hours worked per week: 10. Tuition remission given: full and partial.

Additional Information: Of all students currently enrolled full time, 52% benefited from one or more of the listed financial assistance programs. Application and information available online at http://www.rosalindfranklin.edu (go to Student Services and select link to financial aid).

Internships/Practica: Doctoral Degree (PhD clinical): For those doctoral students for whom a professional internship was required in this program prior to graduation, (17) students applied for an internship in 2006–2007, with (14) students obtaining an internship. Of those students who obtained an internship, (14) were paid internships. Of those students who obtained an internship, (13) students placed in APA/CPA-accredited internships, (1) student placed in internships not APA/CPA-accredited, but listed with the Association of Psychology Postdoctoral and Internship Centers (APPIC), (0) students placed in internships conforming to guidelines of the Council of Directors of School Psychology Programs (CDSPP), (0) students placed in internships that were not APA/CPA-accredited, APPIC or CDSPP listed. The Department enjoys formal relationships with many of the major clinical, health, and neuropsychology facilities in the catchment area from Chicago to the south and Milwaukee to the north. These include both inpatient and outpatient facilities. Thus, students have the opportunity to obtain experience and clinical training with a diverse range of clinical populations and socioeconomic strata.

Housing and Day Care: On-campus housing is available. The University currently has on-campus housing for students. For more infomation on housing, you may call (847) 578-8350 or e-mail campus.housing@rosalindfranklin.edu. No on-campus day care facilities are available.

Employment of Department Graduates:

Master's Degree Graduates: Of those who graduated in the academic year 2006–2007, the following categories and numbers represent the postgraduate activities and employment of master's degree graduates: Enrolled in a postdoctoral residency/fellowship (n/a), employed in independent practice (n/a), total from the above (master's) (0).

Doctoral Degree Graduates: Of those who graduated in the academic year 2006–2007, the following categories and numbers represent the postgraduate activities and employment of doctoral degree graduates: Enrolled in a psychology doctoral program (n/a), enrolled in a postdoctoral residency/fellowship (10), employed in independent practice (1), employed in business or industry (1), employed in a community mental health/counseling center (0), employed in a hospital/medical center (0), do not know (2), total from the above (doctoral) (14).

Additional Information:

Orientation, Objectives, and Emphasis of Department: The Department of Psychology offers an APA-approved program leading to the PhD degree in Clinical Psychology, with specialties in Health Psychology, Psychopathology, and Clinical Neuropsychology. Within the context of the general clinical training program, students select a specialty emphasis in either clinical neuropsychology, psychopathology, or health/behavioral medicine. The program provides students with intensive training in the methods and theories of clinical practice with emphasis in these specialty areas. Research is a vital part of the program and students work closely with professors throughout their training. Research topics include biopsychosocial issues associated with various medical illnesses (e.g., cancer, diabetes, heart disease, chronic pain), aging, psychopathology (e.g., schizophrenia, OCD, psychopathy), and neuropsychological features of various clinical populations (e.g., epilepsy, head injury, multiple sclerosis, AIDS, Alzheimer's disease, dementia, stroke). Subject populations range in age from childhood through adulthood and include those with physical and psychiatric disorders. The Department subscribes to the philosophy that a clinical psychologist is knowledgeable in formulating and solving scientific problems, and skilled in formulating clinical problems and applying empirically supported interventions. To this end, core courses are organized as integrated theory–research–practice units with a problem-solving orientation. Our goal is to graduate clinical psychologists who are highly trained, clinically effective, and able to contribute to the continuing development of the profession as practitioners, teachers, and researchers.

Special Facilities or Resources: Research facilities within the Department include an Experimental Neuropsychology Lab, Clinical Health Psychophysiology Lab, Neuroimaging Laboratory, and a Behavioral Therapy Lab. There are ongoing research programs in arthritis, oncology, diabetes, blood pressure regulation, pain and stress, epilepsy, anxiety disorders, schizophrenia, psychopathy, aging, and dementia. Collaborative research opportunities are also ongoing with a number of community and academic institutions in the area and include projects using MRI and fMRI to study higher order cognitive processes.

Application Information:

Send to Rosalind Franklin University of Medicine and Science, CHP Admissions Office, 3333 Green Bay Road, North Chicago, IL 60064. Application available online. URL of online application: http://www.rosalindfranklin.edu/srhs/psychology/admissions.cfm. Students are admitted in the Fall, application deadline December 1. *Fee:* $25.

Southern Illinois University Edwardsville

Department of Psychology
Box 1121
Edwardsville, IL 62026-1121
Telephone: (618) 650-2202
Fax: (618) 650-5087
E-mail: *bsulliv@siue.edu*
Web: *http://www.siue.edu/education/psychology/graduate/*

Department Information:

1964. Chairperson: Bryce F. Sullivan. Number of faculty: total—full-time 19, part-time 3; women—full-time 7, part-time 2.

Programs and Degrees Offered:

Listed in the following order: Program area, degree type (T if terminal Master's), number awarded 7/06–6/07. School Psychology EdS/MEd (School Psychology) 8, Clinical–Adult Psychology MA/MS (Master of Arts/Science) (T) 11, Industrial Organizational Psychology MA/MS (Master of Arts/Science) (T) 7, Clinical Child and School Psychology MA/MS (Master of Arts/Science) (T) 15.

Student Applications/Admissions:

Student Applications

School Psychology EdS/MEd (School Psychology)—Applications 2007–2008, 12. Total applicants accepted 2007–2008, 6. Number full-time enrolled (new admits only) 2007–2008, 6. Number part-time enrolled (new admits only) 2007–2008, 0. Openings 2008–2009, 10. The median number of years required for completion of a degree in 2006–2007 were 2. The number of students enrolled full- and part-time who were dismissed or voluntarily withdrew from this program area in 2007–2008 were 0. *Clinical–Adult Psychology MA/MS (Master of Arts/Science)*—Applications 2007–2008, 42. Total applicants accepted 2007–2008, 16. Number full-time enrolled (new admits only) 2007–2008, 10. Number part-time enrolled (new admits only) 2007–2008, 0. Openings 2008–2009, 10. The median number of years required for completion of a degree in 2006–2007 were 2. The number of students enrolled full- and part-time who were dismissed or voluntarily withdrew from this program area in 2007–2008 were 0. *Industrial Organizational Psychology MA/MS (Master of Arts/Science)*—Applications 2007–2008, 58. Total applicants accepted 2007–2008, 15. Number full-time enrolled (new admits only) 2007–2008, 9. Number part-time enrolled (new admits only) 2007–2008, 0. Openings 2008–2009, 10. The median number of years required for completion of a degree in 2006–2007 were 2. The number of students enrolled full- and part-time who were dismissed or voluntarily withdrew from this program area in 2007–2008 were 0. *Clinical Child and School Psychology MA/MS (Master of Arts/Science)*—Applications 2007–2008, 69. Total applicants accepted 2007–2008, 16. Number full-time enrolled (new admits only) 2007–2008, 10. Number part-time enrolled (new admits only) 2007–2008, 0. Openings 2008–2009, 10. The median number of years required for completion of a degree in 2006–2007 were 2. The number of students enrolled full- and part-time who were dismissed or voluntarily withdrew from this program area in 2007–2008 were 2.

Admissions Requirements:

Scores: Entries appear in this order: required test or GPA, minimum score (if required), median score of students entering in 2007–2008. Master's Programs: GRE-V 400, 445; GRE-Q 400, 555; overall undergraduate GPA 3.0, 3.69; psychology GPA 3.0, 3.7.

Other Criteria: (importance of criteria rated low, medium, or high): GRE/MAT scores—medium, research experience—high, work experience—medium, extracurricular activity—medium, clinically related public service—medium, GPA—high, letters of recommendation—high, interview—high, statement of goals and objectives—high. For additional information on admission requirements, go to http://www.siue.edu/education/psychology/graduate/apinfo.shtml.

Student Characteristics: The following represents characteristics of students in 2007–2008 in all graduate psychology programs in the department: Female—full-time 67, part-time 0; Male—full-time 11, part-time 0; African American/Black—full-time 4, part-time 0; Hispanic/Latino(a)—full-time 0, part-time 0; Asian/Pacific Islander—full-time 0, part-time 0; American Indian/Alaska Native—full-time 0, part-time 0; Caucasian/White—full-time 74, part-time 0; Multi-ethnic—full-time 0, part-time 0; students subject to the Americans With Disabilities Act—full-time 0, part-time 0; Unknown ethnicity—full-time 0, part-time 0; International students who hold an F-1 or J-1 Visa—full-time 0, part-time 0.

Financial Information/Assistance:

Tuition for Full-Time Study: *Master's:* State residents: per academic year $5,400, $225 per credit hour; Nonstate residents: per academic year $13,500, $563 per credit hour. See the following Web site for updates and changes in tuition costs: http://www.siue.edu/prospectivestudents/tuition_and_fees_2006-2007_graduate.htm.

Financial Assistance:

First-Year Students: Research assistantships available for first year. Average amount paid per academic year: $3,555. Average number of hours worked per week: 10. Apply by March 1. Tuition remission given: full. Fellowships and scholarships available for first year. Average amount paid per academic year: $7,425. Average number of hours worked per week: 0. Apply by January 15. Tuition remission given: full.

Advanced Students: Research assistantships available for advanced students. Average amount paid per academic year: $3,825. Average number of hours worked per week: 10. Apply by March 1. Tuition remission given: full.

Additional Information: Of all students currently enrolled full time, 75% benefited from one or more of the listed financial assistance programs. Application and information available online at: http://www.siue.edu/education/psychology/graduate/apinfo.shtml.

Internships/Practica: All graduate programs require at least four credit hours of supervised practicum experience in appropriate professional settings. The Specialist Degree Program also requires a 10-hour paid internship.

Housing and Day Care: On-campus housing is available. See the following Web site for more information: http://www.siue.edu/housing/index.shtml. On-campus day care facilities are available.

See the following Web site for more information: http://www.siue.edu/earlychildhood/about/faq.shtml.

Employment of Department Graduates:

Master's Degree Graduates: Of those who graduated in the academic year 2006–2007, the following categories and numbers represent the postgraduate activities and employment of master's degree graduates: Enrolled in a postdoctoral residency/fellowship (n/a), employed in independent practice (n/a), total from the above (master's) (0).

Doctoral Degree Graduates: Of those who graduated in the academic year 2006–2007, the following categories and numbers represent the postgraduate activities and employment of doctoral degree graduates: Enrolled in a psychology doctoral program (n/a), total from the above (doctoral) (0).

Additional Information:

Orientation, Objectives, and Emphasis of Department: The faculty comprises members whose skills span the entire field of psychology—clinical, experimental, social, industrial/organizational, school, community, and developmental. On the whole, the department is eclectic in orientation. Students in each specialization are provided with training that is balanced between scientific and applied orientations.

Special Facilities or Resources: The psychology department facilities house faculty offices, classrooms, and approximately 10,000 square feet of laboratory space. Sophisticated research and instructional equipment is available, including mini- and microcomputers, videotaping equipment, and computer terminals. Special laboratories are available for learning, motivation, information processing, developmental, clinical, and psychometric activities.

Information for Students With Physical Disabilities: See the following Web site for more information: http://www.siue.edu/dss/.

Application Information:

Send to Attention: Graduate Records Secretary, Psychology Department, Box 1121, Edwardsville, IL 62026. Application available online. URL of online application: http://www.siue.edu/education/psychology/graduate/. Students are admitted in the Fall, application deadline February 1. *Fee:* $30.

Southern Illinois University, at Carbondale

Department of Psychology
College of Liberal Arts
Life Science Building II, Room 281
Carbondale, IL 62901
Telephone: (618) 536-2301
Fax: (618) 453-3563
E-mail: *swanson@siu.edu*
Web: *http://www.psychology.siu.edu*

Department Information:

1948. Chairperson: Jane Swanson. Number of faculty: total—full-time 25, part-time 2; women—full-time 13, part-time 1; total—minority—full-time 5; women minority—full-time 4.

Programs and Degrees Offered:

Listed in the following order: Program area, degree type (T if terminal Master's), number awarded 7/06–6/07. Clinical PhD (Doctor of Philosophy) 7, Counseling PhD (Doctor of Philosophy) 11, Applied Psychology PhD (Doctor of Philosophy) 1, Brain and Cognitive Sciences PhD (Doctor of Philosophy) 4.

APA Accreditation: Clinical PhD (Doctor of Philosophy). Counseling PhD (Doctor of Philosophy).

Student Applications/Admissions:

Student Applications

Clinical PhD (Doctor of Philosophy)—Applications 2007–2008, 116. Total applicants accepted 2007–2008, 9. Number full-time enrolled (new admits only) 2007–2008, 5. Openings 2008–2009, 8. The median number of years required for completion of a degree in 2006–2007 were 5. The number of students enrolled full- and part-time who were dismissed or voluntarily withdrew from this program area in 2007–2008 were 1. *Counseling PhD (Doctor of Philosophy)*—Applications 2007–2008, 92. Total applicants accepted 2007–2008, 8. Number full-time enrolled (new admits only) 2007–2008, 4. Total enrolled 2007–2008 full-time, 31. Openings 2008–2009, 6. The median number of years required for completion of a degree in 2006–2007 were 5. The number of students enrolled full- and part-time who were dismissed or voluntarily withdrew from this program area in 2007–2008 were 1. *Applied Psychology PhD (Doctor of Philosophy)*—Applications 2007–2008, 12. Total applicants accepted 2007–2008, 4. Number full-time enrolled (new admits only) 2007–2008, 3. Number part-time enrolled (new admits only) 2007–2008, 0. Openings 2008–2009, 4. The median number of years required for completion of a degree in 2006–2007 were 6. The number of students enrolled full- and part-time who were dismissed or voluntarily withdrew from this program area in 2007–2008 were 0. *Brain and Cognitive Sciences PhD (Doctor of Philosophy)*—Applications 2007–2008, 23. Total applicants accepted 2007–2008, 7. Number full-time enrolled (new admits only) 2007–2008, 4. Total enrolled 2007–2008 full-time, 15. Openings 2008–2009, 5. The median number of years required for completion of a degree in 2006–2007 were 5. The number of students enrolled full- and part-time who were dismissed or voluntarily withdrew from this program area in 2007–2008 were 0.

Admissions Requirements:

Scores: Entries appear in this order: required test or GPA, minimum score (if required), median score of students entering in 2007–2008. Doctoral Programs: GRE-V no minimum stated, 620; GRE-Q no minimum stated, 700; overall undergraduate GPA no minimum stated, 3.76.

Other Criteria: (importance of criteria rated low, medium, or high): GRE/MAT scores—medium, research experience—high, work experience—medium, extracurricular activity—medium, clinically related public service—medium, GPA—medium, letters of recommendation—high, interview—medium, statement of goals and objectives—high. Some variation across programs. Clinical/work experiences relevant to programs are important. For additional information on admission requirements, go to http://www.psychology.siu.edu.

Student Characteristics: The following represents characteristics of students in 2007–2008 in all graduate psychology programs

in the department: Female—full-time 65, part-time 0; Male—full-time 31, part-time 0; African American/Black—full-time 11, part-time 0; Hispanic/Latino(a)—full-time 4, part-time 0; Asian/Pacific Islander—full-time 10, part-time 0; American Indian/Alaska Native—full-time 1, part-time 0; Caucasian/White—full-time 70, part-time 0; Multi-ethnic—full-time 0, part-time 0; students subject to the Americans With Disabilities Act—full-time 1, part-time 0; Unknown ethnicity—full-time 0, part-time 0; International students who hold an F-1 or J-1 Visa—full-time 7, part-time 0.

Financial Information/Assistance:

Tuition for Full-Time Study: *Master's:* State residents: per academic year $6,600, $275 per credit hour; Nonstate residents: per academic year $16,500, $687 per credit hour. *Doctoral:* State residents: per academic year $6,600, $275 per credit hour; Nonstate residents: per academic year $16,500, $687 per credit hour. Tuition is subject to change. Additional fees are assessed to students beyond the costs of tuition for the following: Health care and activity fees, approximately $1200 per semester. See the following Web site for updates and changes in tuition costs: http://www.siu.edu/gradschl/.

Financial Assistance:

First-Year Students: Teaching assistantships available for first year. Average amount paid per academic year: $11,592. Average number of hours worked per week: 20. Tuition remission given: full. Research assistantships available for first year. Average amount paid per academic year: $11,592. Average number of hours worked per week: 20. Tuition remission given: full. Traineeships available for first year. Average amount paid per academic year: $11,592. Average number of hours worked per week: 20. Tuition remission given: full. Fellowships and scholarships available for first year. Average amount paid per academic year: $11,592. Average number of hours worked per week: 20. Tuition remission given: full.

Advanced Students: Teaching assistantships available for advanced students. Average amount paid per academic year: $12,996. Average number of hours worked per week: 20. Tuition remission given: full. Research assistantships available for advanced students. Average amount paid per academic year: $12,996. Average number of hours worked per week: 20. Tuition remission given: full. Traineeships available for advanced students. Average amount paid per academic year: $12,996. Average number of hours worked per week: 20. Tuition remission given: full. Fellowships and scholarships available for advanced students. Average amount paid per academic year: $12,996. Average number of hours worked per week: 20. Tuition remission given: full.

Additional Information: Of all students currently enrolled full time, 100% benefited from one or more of the listed financial assistance programs. Application and information available online at http://www.gradapp.siu.edu/.

Internships/Practica: Doctoral Degree (PhD Clinical): For those doctoral students for whom a professional internship was required in this program prior to graduation, (4) students applied for an internship in 2006–2007, with (3) students obtaining an internship. Of those students who obtained an internship, (3) were paid internships. Of those students who obtained an internship, (3) students placed in APA/CPA-accredited internships, (0) students placed in internships not APA/CPA-accredited, but listed with the Association of Psychology Postdoctoral and Internship Centers (APPIC), (0) students placed in internships conforming to guidelines of the Council of Directors of School Psychology Programs (CDSPP), (0) students placed in internships that were not APA/CPA-accredited, APPIC or CDSPP listed. Doctoral Degree (PhD Counseling): For those doctoral students for whom a professional internship was required in this program prior to graduation, (5) students applied for an internship in 2006–2007, with (5) students obtaining an internship. Of those students who obtained an internship, (5) were paid internships. Of those students who obtained an internship, (5) students placed in APA/CPA accredited internships, (0) students placed in internships not APA/CPA-accredited, but listed with the Association of Psychology Postdoctoral and Internship Centers (APPIC), (0) students placed in internships conforming to guidelines of the Council of Directors of School Psychology Programs (CDSPP), (0) students placed in internships that were not APA/CPA-accredited, APPIC or CDSPP listed. A variety of practica and field experiences are available at a department Career Development and Resource Clinic, a university Clinical Center, campus Counseling Center, campus Health Service, Applied Research Consultants, and various local mental health centers, hospitals, and human service agencies. For additional information on education and training outcomes for our programs, see the following Web site: http://www.psychology.siu.edu.

Housing and Day Care: On-campus housing is available. See the following Web site for more information: http://www.housing.siu.edu/. On-campus day care facilities are available. See Rainbow's End Child Development Center Web site for more information: http://www.siu.edu/%7Estuddev/rainbow.html. Child Development Lab: (618) 536-4221.

Employment of Department Graduates:

Master's Degree Graduates: Of those who graduated in the academic year 2006–2007, the following categories and numbers represent the postgraduate activities and employment of master's degree graduates: Enrolled in a postdoctoral residency/fellowship (n/a), employed in independent practice (n/a), total from the above (master's) (0).

Doctoral Degree Graduates: Of those who graduated in the academic year 2006–2007, the following categories and numbers represent the postgraduate activities and employment of doctoral degree graduates: Enrolled in a psychology doctoral program (n/a), employed in independent practice (1), employed in an academic position at a university (5), employed in an academic position at a 2-year/4-year college (0), employed in other positions at a higher education institution (1), employed in a professional position in a school system (0), employed in business or industry (0), employed in government agency (1), employed in a community mental health/counseling center (12), employed in a hospital/medical center (1), still seeking employment (0), other employment position (0), do not know (2), total from the above (doctoral) (23).

Additional Information:

Orientation, Objectives, and Emphasis of Department: The department maintains a collaborative learning environment that is responsive to student needs, that promotes professional development, and that sustains high academic standards. In all programs the student selects courses from a rich curriculum that promotes mastery of core material while allowing the pursuit of particular interests. A favorable student–faculty ratio permits close supervision of students, whether in student research, clinical–applied practica, or training assignments that provide graduated experience in research, teaching, and service as a complement to formal coursework. Such training serves to expose students to many of the activities in which they will be engaged after receiving their degrees. Potential applicants should explore our Web site to learn more about the unique features of specific programs.

Special Facilities or Resources: The department is located in a building with extensive laboratory facilities for human and animal research available to all students. Additional facilities include a clinic and a counseling center for practicum and research experiences.

Information for Students With Physical Disabilities: See the following Web site for more information: http://www.siu.edu/~dss/.

Application Information:

Send to Psychology Graduate Admissions, SIUC, Mailcode 6502, Carbondale, IL 62901-6502. Application available online. URL of online application: http://www.psychology.siu.edu/apply.htm. Students are admitted in the Fall, application deadline varies. Application Deadline varies by program: Clinical: December 15; Counseling: December 15; Applied Psychology: February 1; Brain and Cognitive Sciences: February 1. *Fee:* $45. Students experiencing significant financial need may apply for waiver.

The Chicago School of Professional Psychology

Professional School
325 North Wells
Chicago, IL 60610
Telephone: (312) 329.6600
Fax: (312) 644.3333
E-mail: *hlabelle@thechicagoschool.edu*
Web: *http://www.thechicagoschool.edu*

Department Information:

1979. President: Michael Horowitz, PhD. Number of faculty: total—full-time 46, part-time 28; women—full-time 23, part-time 16; total—minority—full-time 8, part-time 5; women minority—full-time 6, part-time 3.

Programs and Degrees Offered:

Listed in the following order: Program area, degree type (T if terminal Master's), number awarded 7/06–6/07. Clinical Psychology PsyD (Doctor of Psychology) 57, Industrial & Organizational MA/MS (Master of Arts/Science) (T) 34, Forensic Psychology MA/MS (Master of Arts/Science) (T) 69, Clinical, Counseling Specialization MA/MS (Master of Arts/Science) (T) 37, Clinical, Applied Behavior Analysis Specialization MA/MS (Master of Arts/Science) (T) 0, Business Psychology PsyD (Doctor of Psychology) 0, School Psychology EdS/MEd (School Psychology) 0, Board Certified Behavior Analyst Respecialization Diploma 0.

APA Accreditation: Clinical PsyD (Doctor of Psychology).

Student Applications/Admissions:

Student Applications

Clinical Psychology PsyD (Doctor of Psychology)—Number full-time enrolled (new admits only) 2007–2008, 92. Number part-time enrolled (new admits only) 2007–2008, 1. Total enrolled 2007–2008 full-time, 368, part-time, 13. The median number of years required for completion of a degree in 2006–2007 were 6. *Industrial & Organizational MA/MS (Master of Arts/Science)*—Number full-time enrolled (new admits only) 2007–2008, 72. Number part-time enrolled (new admits only) 2007–2008, 12. Total enrolled 2007–2008 full-time, 114, part-time, 47. The median number of years required for completion of a degree in 2006–2007 were 2. *Forensic Psychology MA/MS (Master of Arts/Science)*—Number full-time enrolled (new admits only) 2007–2008, 105. Number part-time enrolled (new admits only) 2007–2008, 15. Total enrolled 2007–2008 full-time, 210, part-time, 84. The median number of years required for completion of a degree in 2006–2007 were 2. *Clinical, Counseling Specialization MA/MS (Master of Arts/Science)*—Number full-time enrolled (new admits only) 2007–2008, 139. Number part-time enrolled (new admits only) 2007–2008, 22. Total enrolled 2007–2008 full-time, 226, part-time, 47. The median number of years required for completion of a degree in 2006–2007 were 2. *Clinical, Applied Behavior Analysis Specialization MA/MS (Master of Arts/Science)*—Number full-time enrolled (new admits only) 2007–2008, 47. Number part-time enrolled (new admits only) 2007–2008, 2. Total enrolled 2007–2008 full-time, 87, part-time, 15. The median number of years required for completion of a degree in 2006–2007 were 2. *Business Psychology PsyD (Doctor of Psychology)*—Number full-time enrolled (new admits only) 2007–2008, 9. Number part-time enrolled (new admits only) 2007–2008, 1. Total enrolled 2007–2008 full-time, 26, part-time, 4. The median number of years required for completion of a degree in 2006–2007 were 5. *School Psychology EdS/MEd (School Psychology)*—Number full-time enrolled (new admits only) 2007–2008, 44. Number part-time enrolled (new admits only) 2007–2008, 2. Total enrolled 2007–2008 full-time, 70, part-time, 9. The median number of years required for completion of a degree in 2006–2007 were 3. *Board Certified Behavior Analyst Respecialization Diploma*—Number full-time enrolled (new admits only) 2007–2008, 0. Number part-time enrolled (new admits only) 2007–2008, 6.

Admissions Requirements:

Scores: Entries appear in this order: required test or GPA, minimum score (if required), median score of students entering in 2007–2008. Master's Programs: overall undergraduate GPA 3.0. Doctoral Programs: GRE-V no minimum stated; GRE-Q no minimum stated; overall undergraduate GPA 3.20; Doctoral program GRE-Analytic no minimum stated.

Other Criteria: (importance of criteria rated low, medium, or high): GRE/MAT scores—medium, research experience—low, work experience—high, extracurricular activity—low, clinically related public service—high, GPA—high, letters of recommendation—high, interview—high, statement of goals and objectives—medium. PsyD in Clinical and Business Psychology programs—interviews are required and by invitation. For additional information on admission requirements, go to http://www.thechicagoschool.edu/content.cfm/admission.

Student Characteristics: The following represents characteristics of students in 2007–2008 in all graduate psychology programs in the department: Female—full-time 882, part-time 180; Male—full-time 219, part-time 46; African American/Black—full-time 99, part-time 32; Hispanic/Latino(a)—full-time 62, part-time 21; Asian/Pacific Islander—full-time 53, part-time 6; American Indian/Alaska Native—full-time 4, part-time 2; Caucasian/White—full-time 727, part-time 138; Multi-ethnic—full-time 0, part-time 0; students subject to the Americans With Disabilities Act—full-time 0, part-time 0; Unknown ethnicity—full-time 101, part-time 24; International students who hold an F-1 or J-1 Visa—full-time 55, part-time 3.

Financial Information/Assistance:

Tuition for Full-Time Study: *Master's:* State residents: $710 per credit hour; Nonstate residents: $710 per credit hour. *Doctoral:* State residents: $855 per credit hour; Nonstate residents: $855 per credit hour. Tuition is subject to change. See the following Web site for updates and changes in tuition costs: http://www.thechicagoschool.edu/content.cfm/tuition_and_fees.

Financial Assistance:

First-Year Students: Teaching assistantships available for first year. Average amount paid per academic year: $1,000. Average number of hours worked per week: 8. Apply by March 1. Tuition remission given: partial. Research assistantships available for first year. Average amount paid per academic year: $2,000. Average number of hours worked per week: 8. Apply by March 1. Tuition remission given: partial. Fellowships and scholarships available for first year. Average amount paid per academic year: $5,000. Average number of hours worked per week: 10. Apply by March 1. Tuition remission given: partial.

Advanced Students: Teaching assistantships available for advanced students. Average amount paid per academic year: $1,000. Average number of hours worked per week: 8. Apply by N/A. Tuition remission given: partial. Research assistantships available for advanced students. Average amount paid per academic year: $2,000. Average number of hours worked per week: 8. Apply by N/A. Tuition remission given: partial. Fellowships and scholarships available for advanced students. Average amount paid per academic year: $5,000. Average number of hours worked per week: 10. Apply by April 15. Tuition remission given: partial.

Additional Information: Of all students currently enrolled full time, 20% benefited from one or more of the listed financial assistance programs. Application and information available online at http://www.thechicagoschool.edu/content.cfm/financing_your_education.

Internships/Practica: Master's Degree (MA/MS Forensic Psychology): An internship experience, such as, a final research project or "capstone" experience is required of graduates. Doctoral Degree (PsyD PsyD in Clinical Psychology): For those doctoral students for whom a professional internship was required in this program prior to graduation, (82) students applied for an internship in 2006–2007, with (77) students obtaining an internship. Of those students who obtained an internship, (72) were paid internships. Of those students who obtained an internship, (40) students placed in APA/CPA-accredited internships, (29) students placed in internships not APA/CPA accredited, but listed with the Association of Psychology Postdoctoral and Internship Centers (APPIC), (0) students placed in internships conforming to guidelines of the Council of Directors of School Psychology Programs (CDSPP), (8) students placed in internships that were not APA/CPA-accredited, APPIC or CDSPP listed. Currently there over 300 Assessment and Therapy Practicum sites in the city and surrounding area at which our students train.

Housing and Day Care: No on-campus housing is available. No on-campus day care facilities are available.

Employment of Department Graduates:

Master's Degree Graduates: Of those who graduated in the academic year 2006–2007, the following categories and numbers represent the postgraduate activities and employment of master's degree graduates: Enrolled in a postdoctoral residency/fellowship (n/a), employed in independent practice (n/a), total from the above (master's) (0).

Doctoral Degree Graduates: Of those who graduated in the academic year 2006–2007, the following categories and numbers represent the postgraduate activities and employment of doctoral degree graduates: Enrolled in a psychology doctoral program (n/a), total from the above (doctoral) (0).

Additional Information:

Orientation, Objectives, and Emphasis of Department: The Chicago School educates students to be competent practitioners by providing curricula that emphasize both a broad knowledge of the scientific and theoretical bases of psychology and the ability to apply that knowledge to specific employment situations. A student-centered environment, with personal advising and supervision provide opportunities for deepening awareness, knowledge, and skills. The programs are designed to integrate the study of cultural and individual differences and their impact in the clinical and work settings. The professional and ethical development of the student is of foremost concern throughout the educational program.

Special Facilities or Resources: The school has a Center for Multicultural and Diversity Studies that coordinates extracurricular learning activites and colloquia, sponsors a biannual Cultural Impact Conference and supports research opportunities with underserved populations in the community.

Application Information:

Send to Admission, Department Chicago School of Professional Psychology, 325 North Wells, Chicago, IL 60610. Application available online. URL of online application: https://www.app.applyyourself.com/?id=cspp. Students are admitted in the Fall, application deadline March 1; programs have rolling admissions. Early consideration deadline: PsyD in Clinical Psychology program—December 15; PsyD in Business Psychology, EdS in School Psychology, and MA programs—February 15. General consideration deadline: PsyD in Clinical Psychology program—February 15; PsyD in Business Psychology, EdS in School Psychology and MA programs—April 1. Space available: Contact the Admission Department after the above deadline for program availability. *Fee:* $50. McNair Scholars are eligible for an application fee waiver.

Western Illinois University

Department of Psychology
Arts and Sciences
Waggoner Hall
Macomb, IL 61455
Telephone: (309) 298-1919
Fax: (309) 298-2179
E-mail: *cj-kreps@wiu.edu.*
Web: *http://www.wiu.edu/users/psychology*

Department Information:

1960. Chairperson: Virginia A. Diehl. Number of faculty: total—full-time 23, part-time 2; women—full-time 13, part-time 2; total—minority—full-time 1; women minority—full-time 1.

Programs and Degrees Offered:

Listed in the following order: Program area, degree type (T if terminal Master's), number awarded 7/06–6/07. Clinical/Community Mental Health MA/MS (Master of Arts/Science) (T) 5, General Experimental MA/MS (Master of Arts/Science) (T) 6, School Specialist Degree Other 9.

Student Applications/Admissions:

Student Applications

Clinical/Community Mental Health MA/MS (Master of Arts/Science)—Applications 2007–2008, 29. Total applicants accepted 2007–2008, 9. Number full-time enrolled (new admits only) 2007–2008, 4. Total enrolled 2007–2008 full-time, 10. Openings 2008–2009, 8. The median number of years required for completion of a degree in 2006–2007 were 3. The number of students enrolled full- and part-time who were dismissed or voluntarily withdrew from this program area in 2007–2008 were 0. *General Experimental MA/MS (Master of Arts/Science)*—Applications 2007–2008, 35. Total applicants accepted 2007–2008, 7. Number full-time enrolled (new admits only) 2007–2008, 7. Number part-time enrolled (new admits only) 2007–2008, 0. Openings 2008–2009, 10. The median number of years required for completion of a degree in 2006–2007 were 2. The number of students enrolled full- and part-time who were dismissed or voluntarily withdrew from this program area in 2007–2008 were 1. *School Specialist Degree Other*—Applications 2007–2008, 35. Total applicants accepted 2007–2008, 20. Number full-time enrolled (new admits only) 2007–2008, 8. Number part-time enrolled (new admits only) 2007–2008, 0. Openings 2008–2009, 10. The median number of years required for completion of a degree in 2006–2007 were 3. The number of students enrolled full- and part-time who were dismissed or voluntarily withdrew from this program area in 2007–2008 were 0.

Admissions Requirements:

Scores: Entries appear in this order: required test or GPA, minimum score (if required), median score of students entering in 2007–2008. Master's Programs: GRE-V 498, 503; GRE-Q 538, 553; overall undergraduate GPA 3.13, 3.29; last 2 years GPA 3.25, 3.45; psychology GPA 3.38, 3.45. Doctoral Programs: We do not offer the Doctoral Program at Western Illinois University.

Other Criteria: (importance of criteria rated low, medium, or high): GRE/MAT scores—high, research experience—medium, work experience—medium, extracurricular activity—medium, clinically related public service—medium, GPA—high, letters of recommendation—high, statement of goals and objectives—high, specific undergraduate psychology courses taken—medium. There are certain undergraduate psychology courses required. These courses will have to be completed before the end of the 2nd year of the masters-level courses are completed. For additional information on admission requirements, go to http://www.wiu.edu/grad/catalog/psychology.php#Program.

Student Characteristics: The following represents characteristics of students in 2007–2008 in all graduate psychology programs in the department: Female—full-time 28, part-time 0; Male—full-time 18, part-time 0; African American/Black—full-time 0, part-time 0; Hispanic/Latino(a)—full-time 0, part-time 0; Asian/Pacific Islander—full-time 1, part-time 0; American Indian/Alaska Native—full-time 0, part-time 0; Caucasian/White—full-time 44, part-time 0; Multi-ethnic—full-time 1, part-time 0; students subject to the Americans With Disabilities Act—full-time 0, part-time 0; Unknown ethnicity—full-time 0, part-time 0; International students who hold an F-1 or J-1 Visa—full-time 2, part-time 0.

Financial Information/Assistance:

Tuition for Full-Time Study: *Master's:* State residents: per academic year $4,877, $216 per credit hour; Nonstate residents: per academic year $9,754, $433 per credit hour. Tuition is subject to change. See the following Web site for updates and changes in tuition costs: http://www.wiu.edu/grad/resources/fees.shtml.

Financial Assistance:

First-Year Students: Research assistantships available for first year. Average amount paid per academic year: $5,104. Average number of hours worked per week: 13. Apply by March 1. Tuition remission given: partial.

Advanced Students: Research assistantships available for advanced students. Average amount paid per academic year: $5,104. Average number of hours worked per week: 13. Apply by March 1. Tuition remission given: partial.

Additional Information: Of all students currently enrolled full time, 90% benefited from one or more of the listed financial assistance programs. Application and information available online at http://www.wiu.edu/grad/resources/fees.shtml.

Internships/Practica: Master's Degree (MA/MS Clinical/Community Mental Health): An internship experience such as a final research project or "capstone" experience is required of graduates. Master's Degree (MA/MS General Experimental): An internship experience such as a final research project or "capstone" experience is required of graduates. The Clinical/Community Mental Health program includes a four-semester practicum sequence of intensive, supervised work in the department's Psychology Clinic. A paid internship for which postgraduate credit is given prepares students for jobs in clinical psychology. Practicum work in community schools and the department's psychoeducational clinic under faculty supervision is required throughout both years of the School Psychology Program, and a paid internship for which postgraduate credit is given prepares students for certification in Illinois.

Housing and Day Care: On-campus housing is available. Contact Office of Graduate and Family Housing, Office of University

Housing and Dining Services in Seal Hall, (309) 298-3331. On-campus day care facilities are available. Contact WIU Preschool and Infant Center at Horrabin Hall.

Employment of Department Graduates:

Master's Degree Graduates: Of those who graduated in the academic year 2006–2007, the following categories and numbers represent the postgraduate activities and employment of master's degree graduates: Enrolled in a psychology doctoral program (6), enrolled in a postdoctoral residency/fellowship (n/a), employed in independent practice (n/a), employed in an academic position at a university (1), employed in an academic position at a 2-year/4-year college (4), employed in other positions at a higher education institution (1), employed in a professional position in a school system (50), employed in business or industry (0), employed in government agency (1), employed in a community mental health/counseling center (20), other employment position (3), total from the above (master's) (86).

Doctoral Degree Graduates: Of those who graduated in the academic year 2006–2007, the following categories and numbers represent the postgraduate activities and employment of doctoral degree graduates: Enrolled in a psychology doctoral program (n/a), total from the above (doctoral) (0).

Additional Information:

Orientation, Objectives, and Emphasis of Department: The psychology department offers master's degrees in clinical/community mental health (C/CMH), general experimental psychology, and a specialist degree in school psychology. C/CMH MS and school specialist degrees are 3-year programs with the 3rd year consisting of a paid internship. The emphasis in the CMH program is to prepare students to assume professional responsibilities in outpatient mental health settings. Central to the program is the practicum experience offered through the University Psychology Clinic. Graduates of the CMH program have found employment in a variety of mental health agencies, with over 90% of all graduates currently employed in mental health positions. Students in the general psychology program engage in 1 to 2 years of course work in psychology. The opportunity to specialize in industrial/organizational, social, developmental, or experimental psychology is available within the general psychology program. Many students completing the general program have been admitted to PhD programs in psychology. Students in the school psychology program acquire an academic background in psychology and a practical awareness of public school systems. During the 1st year of the program, students are placed in elementary schools for practical experience, and during their 2nd year, students work in the university psychoeducational clinic. Graduates of the program have had no difficulty finding employment as school psychologists following their internships. Many have also pursued doctoral training.

Special Facilities or Resources: The Department of Psychology is housed in a large modern structure providing facilities for teaching, clinical training, and human and animal research. The department has 55 rooms, including regular classrooms, seminar rooms, observation rooms, small experimental cubicles, and neuroscience labs. Computers are available throughout the department and campus. The department operates a psychology clinic for community referrals, which aids in clinical training, and a psychoeducational clinic for training in school psychology.

Information for Students With Physical Disabilities: See the following Web site for more information: http://www.student.services.wiu.edu/dss/DSS.asp.

Application Information:

Send to School of Graduate Studies, Western Illinois University, 1 University Circle, Macomb, IL 61455. Application available online. URL of online application: http://www.wiu.edu/grad/prospective/classification.shtml. Students are admitted in the Fall, application deadline March 1. Spring and Fall admission only pertains to the MS in General Experimental Program. The School Psychology and Clinical/Community Mental Health Programs only take Fall semester applicants and the application deadline is March 1. *Fee:* $30. Assistantships are available. Students must apply for an assistantship and be accepted to be awarded the assistantship after eligibility requirements are met. The assistantship consists of a tuition waiver and a monthly stipend.

Wheaton College

Department of Psychology
501 College Avenue
Wheaton, IL 60187-5593
Telephone: (630) 752-5762
Fax: (630) 752-7033
E-mail: *ted.kahn@wheaton.edu*
Web: *http://www.wheaton.edu*

Department Information:

1979. Chairperson: Robert J. Gregory, PhD. Number of faculty: total—full-time 14, part-time 5; women—full-time 5, part-time 4; total—minority—full-time 1, part-time 1; women minority—part-time 1.

Programs and Degrees Offered:

Listed in the following order: Program area, degree type (T if terminal Master's), number awarded 7/06–6/07. Clinical Psychology MA/MS (Master of Arts/Science) (T) 32, Clinical Psychology PsyD (Doctor of Psychology) 14, Counseling Ministries MA/MS (Master of Arts/Science) (T) 6.

APA Accreditation: Clinical PsyD (Doctor of Psychology).

Student Applications/Admissions:

Student Applications

Clinical Psychology MA/MS (Master of Arts/Science)—Applications 2007–2008, 80. Total applicants accepted 2007–2008, 42. Number full-time enrolled (new admits only) 2007–2008, 33. Number part-time enrolled (new admits only) 2007–2008, 1. Total enrolled 2007–2008 full-time, 60, part-time, 4. Openings 2008–2009, 30. The median number of years required for completion of a degree in 2006–2007 were 2. The number of students enrolled full- and part-time who were dismissed or voluntarily withdrew from this program area in 2007–2008 were 1. *Clinical Psychology PsyD (Doctor of Psychology)*—Applications 2007–2008, 65. Total applicants accepted 2007–2008, 31. Number full-time enrolled (new admits only) 2007–2008, 19. Number part-time enrolled (new admits only) 2007–2008, 0. Total enrolled 2007–2008 full-time, 98, part-time, 1. Openings 2008–2009, 20. The median number of years required for completion of a degree in 2006–2007 were 5. The number of students enrolled full- and part-time who were dismissed or voluntarily withdrew from this program area in 2007–2008 were 0. *Counseling Ministries MA/MS (Master of Arts/Science)*—Applications 2007–2008, 14. Total applicants accepted 2007–2008, 4. Number full-time enrolled (new admits only) 2007–2008, 1. Number part-time enrolled (new admits only) 2007–2008, 1. Total enrolled 2007–2008 full-time, 1, part-time, 2. Openings 2008–2009, 6. The median number of years required for completion of a degree in 2006–2007 was 1. The number of students enrolled full- and part-time who were dismissed or voluntarily withdrew from this program area in 2007–2008 were 0.

Admissions Requirements:

Scores: Entries appear in this order: required test or GPA, minimum score (if required), median score of students entering in 2007–2008. Master's Programs: GRE-V no minimum stated, 504; GRE-Q no minimum stated, 569; overall undergraduate GPA 3.0, 3.49. Doctoral Programs: GRE-V no minimum stated, 545; GRE-Q no minimum stated, 630; overall undergraduate GPA 3.0, 3.5; psychology GPA no minimum stated.

Other Criteria: (importance of criteria rated low, medium, or high): GRE/MAT scores—medium, research experience—medium, work experience—medium, extracurricular activity—medium, clinically related public service—medium, GPA—medium, letters of recommendation—high, interview—high, statement of goals and objectives—high, specific undergraduate psychology courses taken—medium.

Student Characteristics: The following represents characteristics of students in 2007–2008 in all graduate psychology programs in the department: Female—full-time 119, part-time 3; Male—full-time 40, part-time 4; African American/Black—full-time 6, part-time 0; Hispanic/Latino(a)—full-time 6, part-time 1; Asian/Pacific Islander—full-time 21, part-time 1; American Indian/Alaska Native—full-time 0, part-time 0; Caucasian/White—full-time 125, part-time 5; Multi-ethnic—full-time 1, part-time 0; students subject to the Americans With Disabilities Act—full-time 0, part-time 1; Unknown ethnicity—full-time 0, part-time 0.

Financial Information/Assistance:

Tuition for Full-Time Study: *Master's:* State residents: per academic year $13,920, $580 per credit hour; Nonstate residents: per academic year $13,920, $580 per credit hour. *Doctoral:* State residents: per academic year $22,800, $760 per credit hour; Nonstate residents: per academic year $22,800, $760 per credit hour. Tuition is subject to change. See the following Web site for updates and changes in tuition costs: http://www.wheaton.edu.

Financial Assistance:

First-Year Students: Teaching assistantships available for first year. Average amount paid per academic year: $5,000. Average number of hours worked per week: 10. Research assistantships available for first year. Average amount paid per academic year: $5,000. Average number of hours worked per week: 10. Fellowships and scholarships available for first year. Average amount paid per academic year: $5,000. Average number of hours worked per week: 0.

Advanced Students: Teaching assistantships available for advanced students. Average amount paid per academic year: $5,000. Average number of hours worked per week: 10. Research assistantships available for advanced students. Average amount paid per academic year: $5,000. Average number of hours worked per week: 10. Traineeships available for advanced students. Average amount paid per academic year: $5,000. Average number of hours worked per week: 15. Fellowships and scholarships available for advanced students. Average amount paid per academic year: $5,000. Average number of hours worked per week: 0.

Additional Information: Of all students currently enrolled full time, 80% benefited from one or more of the listed financial assistance programs.

Internships/Practica: Doctoral Degree (PsyD Clinical Psychology): For those doctoral students for whom a professional internship was required in this program prior to graduation, (17) students applied for an internship in 2006–2007, with (12) students obtaining an internship. Of those students who obtained an internship, (12) were paid internships. Of those students who obtained an internship, (9) students placed in APA/CPA-accredited internships, (1) student placed in internships not APA/CPA-accredited, but listed with the Association of Psychology Postdoctoral and Internship Centers (APPIC), (0) students placed in internships conforming to guidelines of the Council of Directors of School Psychology Programs (CDSPP), (2) students placed in internships that were not APA/CPA-accredited, APPIC or CDSPP listed. The Graduate Psychology Programs have liaisons with over 90 agencies in the Chicago and Suburban Area with facility types ranging from hospitals, clinics, community agencies, residential, and correctional facilities. The MA Program requires 500 on-site hours and the PsyD requires a minimum of 1,200 hours. Faculty are involved through professional development groups while students are placed in field assignments. For additional information on education and training outcomes for our programs, see the following Web site: http://www.wheaton.edu/psychology/graduate/overview/index.html.

Housing and Day Care: On-campus housing is available. See the following Web site for more information: http://www.housing@wheaton.edu. No on-campus day care facilities are available.

Employment of Department Graduates:

Master's Degree Graduates: Of those who graduated in the academic year 2006–2007, the following categories and numbers represent the postgraduate activities and employment of master's degree graduates: Enrolled in a postdoctoral residency/fellowship (n/a), employed in independent practice (n/a), total from the above (master's) (0).

Doctoral Degree Graduates: Of those who graduated in the academic year 2006–2007, the following categories and numbers represent the postgraduate activities and employment of doctoral degree graduates: Enrolled in a psychology doctoral program (n/a), enrolled in another graduate/professional program (0), enrolled in a postdoctoral residency/fellowship (1), employed in independent practice (2), employed in an academic position at a university (2), employed in an academic position at a 2-year/4-year college (0), employed in other positions at a higher education institution (0), employed in a professional position in a school system (0), employed in government agency (2), employed in a community mental health/counseling center (3), employed in a hospital/medical center (1), still seeking employment (1), other employment position (1), do not know (3), total from the above (doctoral) (16).

Additional Information:

Orientation, Objectives, and Emphasis of Department: The doctoral program aims to produce competent scholar–practitioners in clinical psychology who will understand professional practice as service. The primary emphasis of the MA program is the professional preparation of the master's level therapist for employment in clinical settings; a secondary objective is the preparation of selected students for doctoral studies. The departmental orientation is eclectic, with students exposed to the theory, research, and practical clinical skills of the major clinical models in use today. A preeminent concern of all faculty is the interface of psychological theory and practice with Christian faith. Thus, students also take coursework in the theory and practice of integrating psychology and Christian faith, and coursework in theology/biblical studies. Students are encouraged to participate in a growth-oriented group therapy experience or an individual therapy experience. The objectives of the department are to produce mature, capable master's- and doctoral-level clinicians who are well grounded in clinical theory and the essentials of professional practice, and who responsibly and capably relate their Christian faith and professional interests.

Personal Behavior Statement: http://www.wheatongrad.com/?p=71.

Special Facilities or Resources: The PsyD Program has its own computer laboratory and reading room for research and study. Many students work with faculty research projects. Opportunities exist for professional conference presentations and involvement in international projects.

Information for Students With Physical Disabilities: See the following Web site for more information: http://www.wheaton.edu.

Application Information:

Send to Graduate Admissions Office, Wheaton College, 501 College Avenue, Wheaton, IL, 60187. Application available online. URL of online application: http://www.wheatongrad.com/?p=21. Students are admitted in the Fall, application deadline January 15. January 15, deadline PsyD, March 1 deadline MA in Clinical Psychology, May 1 deadline MA in Counseling Ministries. *Fee:* $50.

Ball State University

Department of Counseling Psychology and Guidance Services
Teachers College, Room 622
Muncie, IN 47306-0585
Telephone: (765) 285-8040
Fax: (765) 285-2067
E-mail: *sbowman@bsu.edu*
Web: *http://www.bsu.edu/counselingpsych*

Department Information:

1967. Chairperson: Sharon L. Bowman. Number of faculty: total—full-time 9; women—full-time 7; women minority—full-time 2.

Programs and Degrees Offered:

Listed in the following order: Program area, degree type (T if terminal Master's), number awarded 7/06–6/07. Social Psychology MA/MS (Master of Arts/Science) (T) 7, Counseling MA/MS (Master of Arts/Science) (T) 35, Counseling Psychology PhD (Doctor of Philosophy) 7.

APA Accreditation: Counseling PhD (Doctor of Philosophy).

Student Applications/Admissions:

Student Applications

Social Psychology MA/MS (Master of Arts/Science)—Applications 2007–2008, 17. Total applicants accepted 2007–2008, 15. Number full-time enrolled (new admits only) 2007–2008, 9. Total enrolled 2007–2008 full-time, 17, part-time, 2. Openings 2008–2009, 10. The median number of years required for completion of a degree in 2006–2007 were 2. The number of students enrolled full- and part-time who were dismissed or voluntarily withdrew from this program area in 2007–2008 were 0. *Counseling MA/MS (Master of Arts/Science)*—Applications 2007–2008, 85. Total applicants accepted 2007–2008, 47. Number full-time enrolled (new admits only) 2007–2008, 35. Number part-time enrolled (new admits only) 2007–2008, 5. Total enrolled 2007–2008 full-time, 113, part-time, 22. Openings 2008–2009, 40. The median number of years required for completion of a degree in 2006–2007 were 2. The number of students enrolled full- and part-time who were dismissed or voluntarily withdrew from this program area in 2007–2008 were 2. *Counseling Psychology PhD (Doctor of Philosophy)*—Applications 2007–2008, 44. Total applicants accepted 2007–2008, 15. Number full-time enrolled (new admits only) 2007–2008, 10. Total enrolled 2007–2008 full-time, 35, part-time, 12. Openings 2008–2009, 10. The median number of years required for completion of a degree in 2006–2007 were 5. The number of students enrolled full- and part-time who were dismissed or voluntarily withdrew from this program area in 2007–2008 were 0.

Admissions Requirements:

Scores: Entries appear in this order: required test or GPA, minimum score (if required), median score of students entering in 2007–2008. Master's Programs: GRE-V no minimum stated; GRE-Q no minimum stated; overall undergraduate GPA 2.75, 3.33; psychology GPA 3.00. Doctoral Programs: GRE-V no minimum stated; GRE-Q no minimum stated; overall undergraduate GPA 3.20, 3.89. Applicants applying with only a BA degree must score at least 1100 on the GREs (V + Q), must have an undergraduate overall GPA of at least 3.2 on a 4.0 scale, and must have completed at least 15 semester or 24 quarter hours in undergraduate psychology classes with a GPA of 3.2 in such courses.

Other Criteria: (importance of criteria rated low, medium, or high): GRE/MAT scores—high, research experience—high, work experience—high, extracurricular activity—medium, clinically related public service—medium, GPA—high, letters of recommendation—high, interview—medium, statement of goals and objectives—high, multicultural experience—high. Interview is a requirement for the Doctoral Program, not the Master's programs. For additional information on admission requirements, go to http://www.bsu.edu/counselingpsych.

Student Characteristics: The following represents characteristics of students in 2007–2008 in all graduate psychology programs in the department: Female—full-time 140, part-time 26; Male—full-time 25, part-time 10; African American/Black—full-time 5, part-time 0; Hispanic/Latino(a)—full-time 2, part-time 0; Asian/Pacific Islander—full-time 5, part-time 0; American Indian/Alaska Native—full-time 0, part-time 0; Caucasian/White—full-time 140, part-time 36; Multi-ethnic—full-time 3, part-time 0; students subject to the Americans With Disabilities Act—full-time 3, part-time 0; Unknown ethnicity—full-time 0, part-time 0; International students who hold an F-1 or J-1 Visa—full-time 9, part-time 0.

Financial Information/Assistance:

Tuition for Full-Time Study: *Master's:* State residents: per academic year $6,650; Nonstate residents: per academic year $16,410. *Doctoral:* State residents: per academic year $6,650; Nonstate residents: per academic year $16,410. Tuition is subject to change. See the following Web site for updates and changes in tuition costs: http://www.bsu.edu/gradschool.

Financial Assistance:

First-Year Students: Teaching assistantships available for first year. Average amount paid per academic year: $9,250. Average number of hours worked per week: 20. Apply by December 15. Tuition remission given: full. Research assistantships available for first year. Average amount paid per academic year: $9,250. Average number of hours worked per week: 20. Apply by December 15. Tuition remission given: full. Fellowships and scholarships available for first year. Average amount paid per academic year: $14,000. Average number of hours worked per week: 0. Apply by February 1. Tuition remission given: full.

Advanced Students: Teaching assistantships available for advanced students. Average amount paid per academic year: $9,250. Average number of hours worked per week: 20. Apply by March 1. Tuition remission given: full. Research assistantships available for advanced students. Average amount paid per academic year: $9,250. Average number of hours worked per week: 20. Apply by March 1. Tuition remission given: full. Traineeships available for advanced students. Average amount paid per academic year: $9,250. Average number of hours worked per week: 20. Apply by March 1. Tuition remission given: full. Fellowships and scholarships available for advanced students. Average amount paid per academic year: $14,000. Average number of hours worked per week: 0. Apply by March 1. Tuition remission given: full.

Additional Information: Of all students currently enrolled full time, 80% benefited from one or more of the listed financial assistance programs.

Internships/Practica: Master's Degree (MA/MS counseling): An internship experience such as a final research project or "capstone" experience is required of graduates. Doctoral Degree (PhD Counseling Psychology): For those doctoral students for whom a professional internship was required in this program prior to graduation, (11) students applied for an internship in 2006–2007, with (7) students obtaining an internship. Of those students who obtained an internship, (7) were paid internships. Of those students who obtained an internship, (5) students placed in APA/CPA-accredited internships, (2) students placed in internships not APA/CPA-accredited, but listed with the Association of Psychology Postdoctoral and Internship Centers (APPIC), (0) students placed in internships conforming to guidelines of the Council of Directors of School Psychology Programs (CDSPP), (0) students placed in internships that were not APA/CPA accredited, APPIC or CDSPP listed. The department operates a practicum clinic that serves the surrounding community on a low-cost basis. All counseling master's students and doctoral students are required to complete at least one practicum in this clinic. Other practicum opportunities are available at the university counseling center, a local elementary school, and the nearby medical hospital. Master's students also are required to complete an internship prior to graduation. The Internship Director maintains a listing of available sites and assists students in identifying and securing such a site. Most of these sites are unpaid, although a few are paying sites. Doctoral students typically seek APA-approved predoctoral internship sites. There is one such site on campus, in the university's counseling center. Although that site does not guarantee a slot to students from this program, usually one student a year is placed there.

Housing and Day Care: On-campus housing is available. See the following Web site for more information: http://www.bsu.edu/housing. On-campus day care facilities are available. See the following Web site for more information: http://www.bsu.edu//fcs.

Employment of Department Graduates:

Master's Degree Graduates: Of those who graduated in the academic year 2006–2007, the following categories and numbers represent the postgraduate activities and employment of master's degree graduates: Enrolled in a psychology doctoral program (10), enrolled in another graduate/professional program (5), enrolled in a postdoctoral residency/fellowship (n/a), employed in independent practice (n/a), employed in an academic position at a university (0), employed in an academic position at a 2-year/4-year college (0), employed in other positions at a higher education institution (1), employed in a professional position in a school system (10), employed in business or industry (0), employed in government agency (0), employed in a community mental health/counseling center (3), employed in a hospital/medical center (1), other employment position (3), do not know (3), total from the above (master's) (36).

Doctoral Degree Graduates: Of those who graduated in the academic year 2006–2007, the following categories and numbers represent the postgraduate activities and employment of doctoral degree graduates: Enrolled in a psychology doctoral program (n/a), enrolled in a postdoctoral residency/fellowship (1), employed in independent practice (0), employed in an academic position at a 2-year/4-year college (0), employed in other positions at a higher education institution (3), employed in a professional position in a school system (0), employed in business or industry (0), employed in government agency (0), employed in a community mental health/counseling center (2), employed in a hospital/medical center (1), still seeking employment (0), not seeking employment (1), other employment position (0), total from the above (doctoral) (8).

Additional Information:

Orientation, Objectives, and Emphasis of Department: The objective of the master's counseling programs is to prepare persons to be effective counselors by providing students with a common professional core of courses and experiences. The faculty is committed to keeping abreast of trends, skills, and knowledge and to modifying the program to prepare students for their profession. Students will be able to practice in a variety of settings using therapeutic, preventive, or developmental counseling approaches. The counseling programs also prepare students for doctoral study in counseling psychology. The program goals are to develop an atmosphere conducive to inquiry, creativity, and learning and to the discovery of new knowledge through research, counseling, and interactive involvement between students and faculty. The master's program in social psychology provides a conceptual background for those pursuing careers in education, counseling, criminology, personnel work, and so forth. and prepares students for entry into doctoral programs in social psychology. The doctoral program is designed to broaden students' knowledge beyond the master's degree. The rigorous program includes a sound theoretical basis, a substantial experiential component, a research component, and a variety of assistantship assignments. A basic core of courses stresses competence in the social, psychological, biological, cognitive, and affective bases of behavior. The counseling psychology PhD program is structured within a scientist–professional model of training.

Special Facilities or Resources: Departmental instructional and research facilities are exceptional. The facilities of the department occupy the sixth floor of the Teachers College building and include 10 practicum rooms, an observation corridor, several group observation rooms, and computer access. Most of these facilities are linked to a control room for use of audio and video media. The computer terminals are connected to the university VAX computer cluster. The department operates an outpatient counseling clinic that serves as the training facility for all counseling graduate students. The clinic serves clients from Muncie and surrounding communities as well as Ball State faculty and staff. The university operates a separate state-of-the-art counseling center that serves as a training site for a select number of graduate students from the department.

Information for Students With Physical Disabilities: See the following Web site for more information: http://www.bsu.edu/dsd.

Application Information:

Send to Department of Counseling Psychology and Guidance Services, Teachers College, Ball State University, Muncie, IN 47306. Application available online. URL of online application: http://www.bsu.edu/counselingpsych. Students are admitted in the Winter, application deadline February 1; Summer, application deadline June 15. Doctoral program: December 15; Counseling (Rehabilitation track) has rolling admissions. The Summer deadline applies only to the Masters programs. *Fee:* $25 for BSU alumni; $35 for those who have not received a degree from Ball State University.

Ball State University (2007 data)

Department of Educational Psychology
Teachers College
Muncie, IN 47306
Telephone: (765) 285-8500
Fax: (765) 285-3653
E-mail: *lhuffman@bsu.edu*
Web: *http://www.bsu.edu/edpsych*

Department Information:

1967. Chairperson: Lisa F. Huffman. Number of faculty: total—full-time 18, part-time 15; women—full-time 9, part-time 9.

Programs and Degrees Offered:

Listed in the following order: Program area, degree type (T if terminal Master's), number awarded 7/06–6/07. School Psychology PhD (Doctor of Philosophy) 2, Educational Psychology MA/MS (Master of Arts/Science) (T) 11, School Psychology MA/MS (Master of Arts/Science) 8, School Psychology EdS/MEd (School Psychology) 5, Educational Psychology PhD (Doctor of Philosophy) 0.

APA Accreditation: School Psychology PhD (Doctor of Philosophy).

Student Applications/Admissions:

Student Applications

School Psychology PhD (Doctor of Philosophy)—Applications 2007–2008, 26. Total applicants accepted 2007–2008, 13. Number full-time enrolled (new admits only) 2007–2008, 13. Openings 2008–2009, 10. The median number of years required for completion of a degree in 2006–2007 were 4. The number of students enrolled full- and part-time who were dismissed or voluntarily withdrew from this program area in 2007–2008 were 0. *Educational Psychology MA/MS (Master of Arts/Science)*—Applications 2007–2008, 12. Total applicants accepted 2007–2008, 9. Number full-time enrolled (new admits only) 2007–2008, 9. Openings 2008–2009, 10. The median number of years required for completion of a degree in 2006–2007 were 2. The number of students enrolled full- and part-time who were dismissed or voluntarily withdrew from this program area in 2007–2008 were 0. *School Psychology MA/MS (Master of Arts/Science)*—Applications 2007–2008, 65. Total applicants accepted 2007–2008, 12. Number full-time enrolled (new admits only) 2007–2008, 12. Total enrolled 2007–2008 full-time, 12. Openings 2008–2009, 10. The median number of years required for completion of a degree in 2006–2007 was 1. The number of students enrolled full- and part-time who were dismissed or voluntarily withdrew from this program area in 2007–2008 were 0. *School Psychology EdS/MEd (School Psychology)*—Applications 2007–2008, 20. Total applicants accepted 2007–2008, 12. Number full-time enrolled (new admits only) 2007–2008, 12. Total enrolled 2007–2008 full-time, 19. Openings 2008–2009, 5. The median number of years required for completion of a degree in 2006–2007 were 3. The number of students enrolled full- and part-time who were dismissed or voluntarily withdrew from this program area in 2007–2008 were 0. *Educational Psychology PhD (Doctor of Philosophy)*—Applications 2007–2008, 10. Total applicants accepted 2007–2008, 6. Number full-time enrolled (new admits only) 2007–2008, 6. Number part-time enrolled (new admits only) 2007–2008, 0. Openings 2008–2009, 5. The number of students enrolled full- and part-time who were dismissed or voluntarily withdrew from this program area in 2007–2008 were 0.

Admissions Requirements:

Scores: Entries appear in this order: required test or GPA, minimum score (if required), median score of students entering in 2007–2008. Master's Programs: GRE-V no minimum stated, 426; GRE-Q no minimum stated, 546; overall undergraduate GPA 2.8, 3.4. Doctoral Programs: GRE-V no minimum stated, 575; GRE-Q no minimum stated, 623; overall undergraduate GPA 3.2, 3.6.

Other Criteria: (importance of criteria rated low, medium, or high): GRE/MAT scores—high, research experience—medium, work experience—medium, extracurricular activity—medium, clinically related public service—high, GPA—medium, letters of recommendation—high, statement of goals and objectives—medium, diversity—high. These do not apply to the MA in Educational Psychology. For additional information on admission requirements, go to http://www.bsu.edu/edpsych/.

Student Characteristics: The following represents characteristics of students in 2007–2008 in all graduate psychology programs in the department: Female—full-time 81, part-time 0; Male—full-time 20, part-time 0; African American/Black—full-time 2, part-time 0; Hispanic/Latino(a)—full-time 1, part-time 0; Asian/Pacific Islander—full-time 0, part-time 0; American Indian/Alaska Native—full-time 0, part-time 0; Caucasian/White—full-time 98, part-time 0; Multi-ethnic—full-time 0, part-time 0; students subject to the Americans With Disabilities Act—full-time 0, part-time 0; Unknown ethnicity—full-time 0, part-time 0.

Financial Information/Assistance:

Tuition for Full-Time Study: *Master's:* State residents: per academic year $6,030; Nonstate residents: per academic year $15,790. *Doctoral:* State residents: per academic year $6,030; Nonstate residents: per academic year $15,790. Tuition is subject to change. Tuition is waived with a graduate fellowship; majority of students receive funding.

Financial Assistance:

First-Year Students: Teaching assistantships available for first year. Average amount paid per academic year: $9,967. Average number of hours worked per week: 20. Apply by February 15. Tuition remission given: full. Research assistantships available for first year. Average amount paid per academic year: $9,967. Average number of hours worked per week: 20. Apply by February 15. Tuition remission given: full. Fellowships and scholarships available for first year. Average amount paid per academic year:

$9,967. Average number of hours worked per week: 0. Apply by February 15. Tuition remission given: full.

Advanced Students: Teaching assistantships available for advanced students. Average amount paid per academic year: $9,967. Average number of hours worked per week: 20. Apply by February 15. Tuition remission given: full. Research assistantships available for advanced students. Average amount paid per academic year: $9,967. Average number of hours worked per week: 20. Apply by February 15. Tuition remission given: full. Fellowships and scholarships available for advanced students. Average amount paid per academic year: $9,967. Average number of hours worked per week: 0. Apply by February 15. Tuition remission given: full.

Additional Information: Of all students currently enrolled full time, 100% benefited from one or more of the listed financial assistance programs. Application and information available online at http://www.bsu.edu/edpsych.

Internships/Practica: School psychology students are expected to be involved in practicum experiences from very early in their programs and to continue such experiences until they enroll in internships. (500 clock hours in practicum are expected.) A school-based internship of 1 academic year is required of School Psychology MA/EdS students. Internships are not required of graduate students in the Educational Psychology MA or PhD programs. No practicum or internship is required of the MA or PhD program in Educational Psychology.

Housing and Day Care: On-campus housing is available. See the following Web site for more information: http://www.bsu.edu/web/housing/. No on-campus day care facilities are available.

Employment of Department Graduates:

Master's Degree Graduates: Of those who graduated in the academic year 2006–2007, the following categories and numbers represent the postgraduate activities and employment of master's degree graduates: Enrolled in a postdoctoral residency/fellowship (n/a), employed in independent practice (n/a), total from the above (master's) (0).

Doctoral Degree Graduates: Of those who graduated in the academic year 2006–2007, the following categories and numbers represent the postgraduate activities and employment of doctoral degree graduates: Enrolled in a psychology doctoral program (n/a), enrolled in a postdoctoral residency/fellowship (6), employed in independent practice (3), employed in an academic position at a university (4), employed in an academic position at a 2-year/4-year college (2), employed in other positions at a higher education institution (3), employed in a professional position in a school system (7), employed in business or industry (0), employed in government agency (0), employed in a community mental health/counseling center (2), employed in a hospital/medical center (4), still seeking employment (0), other employment position (0), total from the above (doctoral) (31).

Additional Information:

Orientation, Objectives, and Emphasis of Department: The mission of the graduate programs is to train research scientists to make significant contributions in specialty areas and to address applied problems in educational settings. Our school psychology track further trains students to render diagnostic and remedial services and educational consultation. Specialty areas include neuropsychology, human development, learning, research methods/statistics, and gifted studies. Doctoral students are encouraged to become involved in ongoing research with faculty members. The MA/EdS program is designed to train students for the professional practice of School Psychology and to meet licensure requirements of Indiana and most states. The MA in Educational Psychology provides specialization options in human development, gifted and talented studies, and educational technology. Other specialization options can be tailored to meet the needs and interests of individual students.

Special Facilities or Resources: The department has an on-campus school psychology clinic, a neuropsychology laboratory, a computer laboratory, videotaping facilities, and adequate research facilities. The department is allied with the Office of Charter School Research and the Center for Gifted Studies and Talent Development.

Information for Students With Physical Disabilities: See the following Web site for more information: http://www.bsu.edu/dsd.

Application Information:

Send to Educational Psychology, TC 524, Ball State University, Muncie, IN 47306. Application available online. URL of online application: http://www.bsu.edu/edpsych/. Students are admitted in the Spring, application deadline February 15. Application for the new PhD in Educational Psychology: March 18. Application for MA/EdS and PhD in School Psychology: February 15. Currently there is rolling admissions for the MA in Educational Psychology. *Fee:* $35.

Ball State University

Department of Psychological Science
Sciences and Humanities
Muncie, IN 47306-0520
Telephone: (765) 285-1690
Fax: (765) 285-1702
E-mail: *kpickel@bsu.edu*
Web: *http://www.bsu.edu/psysc/masters/*

Department Information:

1968. Chairperson: Bernie Whitley. Number of faculty: total—full-time 20; women—full-time 8; total—minority—full-time 1; women minority—full-time 1.

Programs and Degrees Offered:

Listed in the following order: Program area, degree type (T if terminal Master's), number awarded 7/06–6/07. Clinical MA/MS (Master of Arts/Science) (T) 12, Cognitive and Social Processes MA/MS (Master of Arts/Science) (T) 8.

Student Applications/Admissions:

Student Applications

Clinical MA/MS (Master of Arts/Science)—Applications 2007–2008, 55. Total applicants accepted 2007–2008, 12. Number full-time enrolled (new admits only) 2007–2008, 12. Number part-time enrolled (new admits only) 2007–2008, 0. Openings 2008–2009, 12. The median number of years required for completion of a degree in 2006–2007 were 2. The number of students enrolled full- and part-time who were dismissed or voluntarily withdrew from this program area in 2007–2008 were 1. *Cognitive and Social Processes MA/MS (Master of Arts/Science)*—Applications 2007–2008, 19. Total applicants accepted 2007–2008, 7. Number full-time enrolled (new admits only) 2007–2008, 7. Number part-time enrolled (new admits only) 2007–2008, 0. Openings 2008–2009, 8. The median number of years required for completion of a degree in 2006–2007 were 2. The number of students enrolled full- and part-time who were dismissed or voluntarily withdrew from this program area in 2007–2008 were 0.

Admissions Requirements:

Scores: Entries appear in this order: required test or GPA, minimum score (if required), median score of students entering in 2007–2008. Master's Programs: GRE-V no minimum stated, 480; GRE-Q no minimum stated, 580; overall undergraduate GPA no minimum stated, 3.5; last 2 years GPA no minimum stated, 3.77; psychology GPA no minimum stated, 3.85; Masters GRE-Analytical no minimum stated, 4.6.

Other Criteria: (importance of criteria rated low, medium, or high): GRE/MAT scores—high, research experience—high, work experience—medium, extracurricular activity—low, clinically related public service—medium, GPA—high, letters of recommendation—high, statement of goals and objectives—high, interests fit with faculty research—high. Clinical service not important for Cognitive/Social Processes program. For additional information on admission requirements, go to http://www.bsu.edu/psysc/masters/.

Student Characteristics: The following represents characteristics of students in 2007–2008 in all graduate psychology programs in the department: Female—full-time 25, part-time 0; Male—full-time 14, part-time 0; African American/Black—full-time 2, part-time 0; Hispanic/Latino(a)—full-time 1, part-time 0; Asian/Pacific Islander—full-time 3, part-time 0; American Indian/Alaska Native—full-time 0, part-time 0; Caucasian/White—full-time 26, part-time 0; Multi-ethnic—full-time 1, part-time 0; students subject to the Americans With Disabilities Act—full-time 0, part-time 0; Unknown ethnicity—full-time 0, part-time 0; International students who hold an F-1 or J-1 Visa—full-time 6, part-time 0.

Financial Information/Assistance:

Tuition for Full-Time Study: *Master's:* State residents: per academic year $6,700; Nonstate residents: per academic year $18,000. Tuition is subject to change. See the following Web site for updates and changes in tuition costs: http://www.bsu.edu/bursar.

Financial Assistance:

First-Year Students: Teaching assistantships available for first year. Average amount paid per academic year: $7,957. Average number of hours worked per week: 20. Apply by March 1. Tuition remission given: partial. Research assistantships available for first year. Average amount paid per academic year: $7,957. Average number of hours worked per week: 20. Apply by March 1. Tuition remission given: partial. Fellowships and scholarships available for first year. Average number of hours worked per week: 0. Apply by March 1. Tuition remission given: partial.

Advanced Students: Teaching assistantships available for advanced students. Average amount paid per academic year: $7,957. Average number of hours worked per week: 20. Apply by March 1. Tuition remission given: partial. Research assistantships available for advanced students. Average amount paid per academic year: $7,957. Average number of hours worked per week: 20. Apply by March 1. Tuition remission given: partial. Fellowships and scholarships available for advanced students. Average amount paid per academic year: $8,000. Average number of hours worked per week: 0. Tuition remission given: partial.

Additional Information: Of all students currently enrolled full time, 90% benefited from one or more of the listed financial assistance programs. Application and information available online at http://www.bsu.edu/psysc/masters/.

Internships/Practica: Internships for clinical students are available at the University Counseling Center, Community Mental Health Centers, Youth Opportunity Center, a VA hospital, and many other locations.

Housing and Day Care: On-campus housing is available. See the following Web site for more information: http://www.bsu.edu/gradschool/housing/. On-campus day care facilities are available. See the following Web site for more information: http://www.bsu.edu/hrs/worklife/childcare/.

Employment of Department Graduates:

Master's Degree Graduates: Of those who graduated in the academic year 2006–2007, the following categories and numbers represent the postgraduate activities and employment of master's degree graduates: Enrolled in a psychology doctoral program (9), enrolled in a postdoctoral residency/fellowship (n/a), employed in independent practice (n/a), employed in a community mental health/counseling center (7), employed in a hospital/medical center (2), other employment position (3), total from the above (master's) (21).

Doctoral Degree Graduates: Of those who graduated in the academic year 2006–2007, the following categories and numbers represent the postgraduate activities and employment of doctoral degree graduates: Enrolled in a psychology doctoral program (n/a), total from the above (doctoral) (0).

Additional Information:

Orientation, Objectives, and Emphasis of Department: Our Clinical MA program is a 2-year, 48-credit hour program based on the scientist–practitioner model. Our Cognitive and Social program is a 2-year, 43-credit hour program that provides students with intensive training in cognitive and social psychology, research methods, and statistics. We admit a limited number of new students per year, which allows our faculty to work closely with students in terms of providing instruction and research opportunities. Our primary goal is to prepare students for doctoral study; during the past 3 years, 94% of our graduates who applied to a doctoral program and completed a thesis were accepted to a doctoral program. Our secondary mission is to serve those seeking employment upon completion of the master's degree. Faculty research interests include stereotyping and prejudice, industrial/organizational psychology, eyewitness memory, juror decision making, gender issues, multicultural issues/diversity, emotion, sexuality, problem solving/critical thinking, sexual behavior, community psychology, identity development, and interpersonal communication.

Special Facilities or Resources: Students have access to university and departmental computers and a wireless network. The department maintains space for faculty and student research. Internal grants are available for student research and travel.

Information for Students With Physical Disabilities: See the following Web site for more information: http://www.bsu.edu/dsd/.

Application Information:
Send to Kerri Pickel, PhD, Director of Graduate Studies, Department of Psychological Science, Ball State University, Muncie, IN 47306-0520. Application available online. URL of online application: http://www.bsu.edu/psysc/masters/. Students are admitted in the Fall, application deadline March 1. For Cognitive and Social Processes program, deadline is 5 weeks prior to either Fall or Spring semester if program is not full. *Fee:* $35. Waiver for McNair Scholars; fee is $25 for applicants who have ever received any degree from Ball State University.

Indiana State University

Department of Communication Disorders & Counseling, School, and Educational Psychology
Education
College of Education 1517
Terre Haute, IN 47809
Telephone: (812) 237-2870
Fax: (812) 237-2729
E-mail: *sedwards6@isugw.indstate.edu*
Web: *http://www.counseling.indstate.edu/dcp*

Department Information:
1968. Chairperson: Michele C. Boyer. Number of faculty: total—full-time 7, part-time 5; women—full-time 4, part-time 4; total—minority—full-time 1; women minority—full-time 1.

Programs and Degrees Offered:
Listed in the following order: Program area, degree type (T if terminal Master's), number awarded 7/06–6/07. Counseling Psychology PhD (Doctor of Philosophy) 8, Mental Health Counseling MA/MS (Master of Arts/Science) (T) 16.

APA Accreditation: Counseling PhD (Doctor of Philosophy).

Student Applications/Admissions:
Student Applications
Counseling Psychology PhD (Doctor of Philosophy)—Applications 2007–2008, 42. Total applicants accepted 2007–2008, 8. Number full-time enrolled (new admits only) 2007–2008, 8. Number part-time enrolled (new admits only) 2007–2008, 0. Openings 2008–2009, 8. The median number of years required for completion of a degree in 2006–2007 were 5. The number of students enrolled full- and part-time who were dismissed or voluntarily withdrew from this program area in 2007–2008 were 0. *Mental Health Counseling MA/MS (Master of Arts/Science)*—Applications 2007–2008, 30. Total applicants accepted 2007–2008, 12. Number full-time enrolled (new admits only) 2007–2008, 11. Number part-time enrolled (new admits only) 2007–2008, 1. Total enrolled 2007–2008 full-time, 24, part-time, 1. Openings 2008–2009, 20. The median number of years required for completion of a degree in 2006–2007 were 2. The number of students enrolled full- and part-time who were dismissed or voluntarily withdrew from this program area in 2007–2008 were 0.

Admissions Requirements:
Scores: Entries appear in this order: required test or GPA, minimum score (if required), median score of students entering in 2007–2008. Master's Programs: GRE-V 450; GRE-Q 450; MAT 40; overall undergraduate GPA 2.75. Doctoral Programs: GRE-V 500, 489; GRE-Q 500, 517; overall undergraduate GPA 2.5, 3.25.
Other Criteria: (importance of criteria rated low, medium, or high): GRE/MAT scores—medium, research experience—medium, work experience—high, extracurricular activity—medium, clinically related public service—high, GPA—medium, letters of recommendation—high, interview—high, statement of goals and objectives—high.

Student Characteristics: The following represents characteristics of students in 2007–2008 in all graduate psychology programs in the department: Female—full-time 51, part-time 1; Male—full-time 12, part-time 0; African American/Black—full-time 4, part-time 0; Hispanic/Latino(a)—full-time 3, part-time 0; Asian/Pacific Islander—full-time 3, part-time 0; American Indian/Alaska Native—full-time 1, part-time 0; Caucasian/White—full-time 52, part-time 1; Multi-ethnic—full-time 0, part-time 0; students subject to the Americans With Disabilities Act—full-time 0, part-time 0; Unknown ethnicity—full-time 0, part-time 0; International students who hold an F-1 or J-1 Visa—full-time 3, part-time 0.

Financial Information/Assistance:
Tuition for Full-Time Study: *Master's:* State residents: per academic year $5,562, $309 per credit hour; Nonstate residents: per academic year $11,052, $614 per credit hour. *Doctoral:* State residents: per academic year $7,415, $309 per credit hour; Nonstate residents: per academic year $14,736, $614 per credit hour. Tuition is subject to change. See the following Web site for updates and changes in tuition costs: http://www.indstate.edu/sogs/GradNewtemp/fee.html.

Financial Assistance:
First-Year Students: Teaching assistantships available for first year. Average amount paid per academic year: $7,500. Average number of hours worked per week: 15. Apply by March 1. Tuition remission given: partial. Research assistantships available for first year. Average amount paid per academic year: $7,500. Average number of hours worked per week: 15. Apply by March 1. Tuition remission given: partial. Fellowships and scholarships available for first year. Average amount paid per academic year: $7,500. Average number of hours worked per week: 15. Apply by March 1. Tuition remission given: partial.
Advanced Students: Teaching assistantships available for advanced students. Average amount paid per academic year: $7,500. Average number of hours worked per week: 15. Apply by March 1. Tuition remission given: partial. Research assistantships available for advanced students. Average amount paid per academic year: $7,500. Average number of hours worked per week: 15. Apply by March 1. Tuition remission given: partial. Fellowships and scholarships available for advanced students. Average amount paid per academic year: $7,500. Average number of hours worked per week: 15. Apply by March 1. Tuition remission given: partial.

Additional Information: Of all students currently enrolled full time, 50% benefited from one or more of the listed financial assistance programs. Application and information available online at http://web.indstate.edu/sogs/deptforms.html.

Internships/Practica: Master's Degree (MA/MS Mental Health Counseling): An internship experience such as a final research project or "capstone" experience is required of graduates. Doctoral Degree (PhD Counseling Psychology): For those doctoral students for whom a professional internship was required in this program prior to graduation, (8) students applied for an internship in 2006–2007, with (8) students obtaining an internship. Of those students who obtained an internship, (8) were paid internships. Of those students who obtained an internship, (7) students placed in APA/CPA-accredited internships, (1) students placed in internships not APA/CPA-accredited, but listed with the Association of Psychology Postdoctoral and Internship Centers (APPIC), (0) students placed in internships conforming to guidelines of the Council of Directors of School Psychology Programs (CDSPP), (0) students placed in internships that were not APA/CPA-accredited, APPIC or CDSPP listed. Doctoral practica are available on campus (Student Counseling Center) and in a variety of community settings (CMHC, schools, hospitals, prisons, VAMC, primary care medical settings), residential treatment facilities, and community college counseling centers.

Housing and Day Care: On-campus housing is available. See the following Web site for more information: http://www.indstate.edu/reslife/housing_policy.htm. On-campus day care facilities are available. See the following Web site for more information: http://www.indstate.edu/childcare/childcarecenter.htm.

Employment of Department Graduates:

Master's Degree Graduates: Of those who graduated in the academic year 2006–2007, the following categories and numbers represent the postgraduate activities and employment of master's degree graduates: Enrolled in a psychology doctoral program (1), enrolled in a postdoctoral residency/fellowship (n/a), employed in independent practice (n/a), employed in a community mental health/counseling center (14), total from the above (master's) (15).

Doctoral Degree Graduates: Of those who graduated in the academic year 2006–2007, the following categories and numbers represent the postgraduate activities and employment of doctoral degree graduates: Enrolled in a psychology doctoral program (n/a), enrolled in a postdoctoral residency/fellowship (2), employed in an academic position at a university (1), employed in a community mental health/counseling center (3), employed in a hospital/medical center (1), total from the above (doctoral) (7).

Additional Information:

Orientation, Objectives, and Emphasis of Department: The Counseling Psychology program is designed to prepare professional psychologists, through a scientist–professional model of training, for general practice in a variety of practice, service, and educational settings. These setting may include colleges and universities, mental health centers, medical care facilities, government agencies, private practice settings, and in the private corporate sector. The program is seen as an area of applied psychology that helps individuals solve problems by making more effective use of their resources. Toward this end, training and research focus on facilitating the personal, interpersonal, educational, and vocational development of individuals, as well as enhancing the environments in which they live. Attention is focused on individual clients' personal and social assets and strengths as well their sociopsychological liabilities and weaknesses. The program emphasizes human development, personalized assessment, and planned problem-solving, while deemphasizing dichotomies such as sick vs. well and abnormal versus normal. Our program allows flexibility for students to pursue personal career goals through focused electives, independent study, and specialized training experiences in practica, fieldwork, assistantship assignments, teaching, research, and community and university work experiences. Faculty members represent a broad range of professional and research interests, theoretical perspectives, and treatment modalities.

Special Facilities or Resources: The counseling psychology training area is housed in the College of Education, a 15-story structure. This area provides faculty and student offices, and a departmental clinic (individual and group therapy rooms, videotaping equipment with observation rooms, and a career and testing laboratory). Also available in the building are research stations, microcomputer labs, a statistics laboratory, a psychological evaluation library, testing rooms, and an instructional resource center.

Information for Students With Physical Disabilities: See the following Web site for more information: http://www.indstate.edu/sasc/dss/index.htm.

Application Information:

For the PhD program please send applications to Director of Training, ATTN: S. Edwards, COE 1517, Counseling Psychology, Indiana State University, Terre Haute, IN 47809. For the MS program please send applications to Director of Training, ATTN: S. Edwards, SE 1517, MS Program, Indiana State University, Terre Haute, IN 47809. Application available online. URL of online application: http://www.counseling.indstate.edu/dcp/app.htm. Students are admitted in the Fall, application deadline January 1. MS program deadline February 1; EdS program deadline January 15. *Fee:* $35.

Indiana State University

Department of Communication Disorders, Counseling, School, and Educational Psychology
College of Education
Terre Haute, IN 47809
Telephone: (812) 237-3588
Fax: (812) 237-7613
E-mail: *broberts@isugw.indstate.edu*
Web: *http://www.coe.indstate.edu/espy*

Department Information:

1981. Chairperson: Michele Boyer, PhD. Number of faculty: total—full-time 3; women—full-time 2.

Programs and Degrees Offered:

Listed in the following order: Program area, degree type (T if terminal Master's), number awarded 7/06–6/07. Guidance and Psychological Services PhD (Doctor of Philosophy) 4, Master's of Education in School Psychology Other 6, Educational Specialist in School Psychology EdS/MEd (School Psychology) 7.

APA Accreditation: School PhD (Doctor of Philosophy).

Student Applications/Admissions:

Student Applications

Guidance and Psychological Services PhD (Doctor of Philosophy)—Applications 2007–2008, 8. Total applicants accepted 2007–2008, 7. Number full-time enrolled (new admits only) 2007–2008, 5. Number part-time enrolled (new admits only) 2007–2008, 0. Openings 2008–2009, 8. The median number of years required for completion of a degree in 2006–2007 were 6. The number of students enrolled full- and part-time who were dismissed or voluntarily withdrew from this program area in 2007–2008 were 0. *Master's of Education in School Psychology Other*—Applications 2007–2008, 52. Total applicants accepted 2007–2008, 29. Number full-time enrolled (new admits only) 2007–2008, 12. Total enrolled 2007–2008 full-time, 12. Openings 2008–2009, 8. The median number of years required for completion of a degree in 2006–2007 was 1. The number of students enrolled full- and part-time who were dismissed or voluntarily withdrew from this program area in 2007–2008 were 0. *Educational Specialist in School Psychology EdS/MEd (School Psychology)*—Applications 2007–2008, 39. Total applicants accepted 2007–2008, 20. Number full-time enrolled (new admits only) 2007–2008, 6. Number part-time enrolled (new admits only) 2007–2008, 0. Openings 2008–2009, 8. The median number of years required for completion of a degree in 2006–2007 were 3. The number of students enrolled full- and part-time who were dismissed or voluntarily withdrew from this program area in 2007–2008 were 0.

Admissions Requirements:

Scores: Entries appear in this order: required test or GPA, minimum score (if required), median score of students entering in 2007–2008. Master's Programs: GRE-V 450, 480; GRE-Q 450, 590; overall undergraduate GPA 3.0, 3.21. The masters program is the first year of the EdS program; therefore the admission requirements for this program are the same as those for the EdS program. Doctoral Programs: GRE-V 450, 520; GRE-Q 450, 540; overall undergraduate GPA 3.0, 3.37.

Other Criteria: (importance of criteria rated low, medium, or high): GRE/MAT scores—medium, research experience—medium, work experience—medium, extracurricular activity—high, clinically related public service—high, GPA—high, letters of recommendation—high, interview—high, statement of goals and objectives—high, vita—high, undergraduate major in psychology—medium, specific undergraduate psychology courses taken—medium. For additional information on admission requirements, go to http://www.indstate.edu/sogs.

Student Characteristics: The following represents characteristics of students in 2007–2008 in all graduate psychology programs in the department: Female—full-time 10, part-time 0; Male—full-time 2, part-time 0; African American/Black—full-time 2, part-time 0; Hispanic/Latino(a)—full-time 1, part-time 0; Asian/Pacific Islander—full-time 1, part-time 0; American Indian/Alaska Native—full-time 0, part-time 0; Caucasian/White—full-time 48, part-time 0; Multi-ethnic—full-time 1, part-time 0; students subject to the Americans With Disabilities Act—full-time 0, part-time 0; Unknown ethnicity—full-time 0, part-time 0; International students who hold an F-1 or J-1 Visa—full-time 1, part-time 0.

Financial Information/Assistance:

Tuition for Full-Time Study: *Master's:* State residents: per academic year $5,562, $309 per credit hour; Nonstate residents: per academic year $11,052, $614 per credit hour. *Doctoral:* State residents: per academic year $7,415, $309 per credit hour; Nonstate residents: per academic year $14,736, $614 per credit hour. Tuition is subject to change. See the following Web site for updates and changes in tuition costs: http://www.web.indstate.edu/sogs.

Financial Assistance:

First-Year Students: Teaching assistantships available for first year. Average amount paid per academic year: $5,250. Average number of hours worked per week: 15. Apply by March 1. Tuition remission given: partial. Research assistantships available for first year. Average amount paid per academic year: $5,250. Average number of hours worked per week: 15. Apply by March 1. Tuition remission given: partial. Fellowships and scholarships available for first year. Average amount paid per academic year: $5,250. Average number of hours worked per week: 15. Apply by March 1. Tuition remission given: partial.

Advanced Students: Teaching assistantships available for advanced students. Average amount paid per academic year: $7,500. Average number of hours worked per week: 15. Apply by March 1. Tuition remission given: partial. Research assistantships available for advanced students. Average amount paid per academic year: $7,500. Average number of hours worked per week: 15. Apply by March 1. Tuition remission given: partial. Fellowships and scholarships available for advanced students. Average amount paid per academic year: $7,500. Average number of hours worked per week: 15. Apply by March 1. Tuition remission given: partial.

Additional Information: Of all students currently enrolled full time, 100% benefited from one or more of the listed financial assistance programs. Application and information available online at http://www.indstate.edu/finaid/.

Internships/Practica: Doctoral Degree (PhD Guidance and Psychological Services): For those doctoral students for whom a professional internship was required in this program prior to graduation, (7) students applied for an internship in 2006–2007, with (7) students obtaining an internship. Of those students who obtained an internship, (7) were paid internships. Of those students who obtained an internship, (7) students placed in APA/CPA-accredited internships, (0) students placed in internships not APA/CPA-accredited, but listed with the Association of Psychology Postdoctoral and Internship Centers (APPIC), (0) students placed in internships conforming to guidelines of the Council of Directors of School Psychology Programs (CDSPP), (0) students placed in internships that were not APA/CPA-accredited, APPIC or CDSPP listed. Students in all programs are required to complete a minimum of 160 direct contact hours each semester in which they are enrolled in the program. Practicum experiences include observation, consultation, assessment, counseling, and intervention with diverse populations ranging from preschool-aged to school-aged students, as well as with college students, parents, teachers, and other professionals. Practicum sites include the local Head Start, public school settings, the Porter School Psychology

Clinic, ISU ADHD Clinic, the READ Clinic as well as agencies such as Gibault, Inc., and Riley Children's Hospital. PhD students have the opportunity to complete advanced practicum requirements in school or clinical settings in order to gain additional experiences and to foster increasing autonomy. Final experiences include a 1,200-plus-hour school-based internship for EdS students and a 1,500-plus-hour predoctoral internship in clinic and/or school settings for PhD students. Predoctoral internship sites include public school settings, hospitals, and mental health agencies.

Housing and Day Care: On-campus housing is available. See the following Web site for more information: http://www.indstate.edu/reslife/. On-campus day care facilities are available. See the following Web site for more information: http://www.web.indstate.edu/childcare/.

Employment of Department Graduates:

Master's Degree Graduates: Of those who graduated in the academic year 2006–2007, the following categories and numbers represent the postgraduate activities and employment of master's degree graduates: Enrolled in a psychology doctoral program (4), enrolled in another graduate/professional program (0), enrolled in a postdoctoral residency/fellowship (n/a), employed in independent practice (n/a), employed in an academic position at a university (0), employed in an academic position at a 2-year/4-year college (0), employed in other positions at a higher education institution (0), employed in a professional position in a school system (0), employed in business or industry (0), employed in government agency (0), employed in a community mental health/counseling center (0), employed in a hospital/medical center (0), still seeking employment (0), other employment position (0), total from the above (master's) (4).

Doctoral Degree Graduates: Of those who graduated in the academic year 2006–2007, the following categories and numbers represent the postgraduate activities and employment of doctoral degree graduates: Enrolled in a psychology doctoral program (n/a), enrolled in another graduate/professional program (0), enrolled in a postdoctoral residency/fellowship (1), employed in independent practice (0), employed in an academic position at a university (1), employed in an academic position at a 2-year/4-year college (1), employed in other positions at a higher education institution (0), employed in a professional position in a school system (1), employed in business or industry (0), employed in government agency (0), employed in a community mental health/counseling center (0), employed in a hospital/medical center (0), still seeking employment (0), other employment position (0), total from the above (doctoral) (4).

Additional Information:

Orientation, Objectives, and Emphasis of Department: The PhD program in guidance and psychological services specialization in school psychology follows a scholar–practitioner model that serves as a foundation upon which program goals and objectives are based. The mission of the program is to prepare professional school psychologists as scholar–practitioners with a broad cognitive behavioral orientation through a program that is research based, theory driven, school focused, and experiential in nature.

Special Facilities or Resources: The program has a university-based clinic that provides psychological and educational services to children, youth, and families. The clinic includes programs specifically designed to serve children with autism spectrum disorders, children with reading disorders, and children with behavioral difficulties. The department partners with the Psychology Department to provide services through a university-based ADHD clinic. These clinics provide both clinical and research experiences. Community resources with which the department has established partnerships include a HeadStart facility, public and private schools, a residential facility for children and youth with behavioral disorders, and a local community center.

Information for Students With Physical Disabilities: See the following Web site for more information: http://www.indstate.edu/sasc.

Application Information:

Send to Bridget Roberts-Pittman, Director of School Psychology Training Program, College of Education, Room 1306, Indiana State University, Terrre Haute, IN 47809. Application available online. URL of online application: http://www.indstate.edu/sogs. Students are admitted in the Fall, application deadline January 15. *Fee:* $35. McNair scholar.

Indiana State University

Department of Psychology
Root Hall
Terre Haute, IN 47809
Telephone: (812) 237-4314
Fax: (812) 237-4378
E-mail: *pyriggs@isugw.indstate.edu*
Web: *http://www.web.indstate.edu/psych*

Department Information:

1968. Chairperson: Virgil Sheets. Number of faculty: total—full-time 13; women—full-time 7; total—minority—full-time 1; women minority—full-time 1; faculty subject to the Americans With Disabilities Act 13.

Programs and Degrees Offered:

Listed in the following order: Program area, degree type (T if terminal Master's), number awarded 7/06–6/07. General MA/MS (Master of Arts/Science) (T) 3, Clinical PsyD (Doctor of Psychology) 9.

APA Accreditation: Clinical PsyD (Doctor of Psychology).

Student Applications/Admissions:

Student Applications

General MA/MS (Master of Arts/Science)—Applications 2007–2008, 42. Total applicants accepted 2007–2008, 5. Number full-time enrolled (new admits only) 2007–2008, 5. Number part-time enrolled (new admits only) 2007–2008, 0. Openings 2008–2009, 4. The median number of years required for completion of a degree in 2006–2007 were 2. The number of students enrolled full- and part-time who were dismissed or voluntarily withdrew from this program area in 2007–2008 were 0. *Clinical PsyD (Doctor of Psychology)*—Applications 2007–2008, 127. Total applicants accepted 2007–2008, 8. Number full-time enrolled (new admits only) 2007–2008, 8.

Total enrolled 2007–2008 full-time, 40, part-time, 5. Openings 2008–2009, 8. The median number of years required for completion of a degree in 2006–2007 were 5. The number of students enrolled full- and part-time who were dismissed or voluntarily withdrew from this program area in 2007–2008 were 0.

Admissions Requirements:

Scores: Entries appear in this order: required test or GPA, minimum score (if required), median score of students entering in 2007–2008. Master's Programs: GRE-V 450, 555; GRE-Q 450, 520; overall undergraduate GPA 2.75, 3.64. GRE test criteria are not rigidly applied in all cases. Doctoral Programs: GRE-V 500, 565; GRE-Q 500, 591; overall undergraduate GPA 3.00, 3.38. GRE scores between 450 and 500 for GRE-V and 475 - 500 will be considered if other qualifications are strong. A master's degree is not required for admission, but a 3.50 GPA or above is needed if graduate work has been done.
Other Criteria: (importance of criteria rated low, medium, or high): GRE/MAT scores—high, research experience—high, work experience—medium, extracurricular activity—low, clinically related public service—high, GPA—high, letters of recommendation—high, interview—high, statement of goals and objectives—high. Formal interviews are not conducted for the Masters Program. Clinically related public service is low for the Master's Program. For additional information on admission requirements, go to http://web.indstate.edu/psych.

Student Characteristics: The following represents characteristics of students in 2007–2008 in all graduate psychology programs in the department: Female—full-time 30, part-time 4; Male—full-time 18, part-time 1; African American/Black—full-time 1, part-time 0; Hispanic/Latino(a)—full-time 2, part-time 1; Asian/Pacific Islander—full-time 2, part-time 0; American Indian/Alaska Native—full-time 0, part-time 0; Caucasian/White—full-time 43, part-time 4; Multi-ethnic—full-time 0, part-time 0; students subject to the Americans With Disabilities Act—full-time 0, part-time 0; Unknown ethnicity—full-time 0, part-time 0.

Financial Information/Assistance:

Tuition for Full-Time Study: *Master's:* State residents: per academic year $7,056, $294 per credit hour; Nonstate residents: per academic year $14,016, $584 per credit hour. *Doctoral:* State residents: per academic year $7,056, $294 per credit hour; Nonstate residents: per academic year $14,016, $584 per credit hour. Tuition is subject to change. Additional fees are assessed to students beyond the costs of tuition for the following: $60 Technology Fee, $100 recreation Fee, $15 Transportaiton Fee. See the following Web site for updates and changes in tuition costs: http://www.web.indstate.edu/sogs.

Financial Assistance:

First-Year Students: Teaching assistantships available for first year. Average amount paid per academic year: $7,000. Average number of hours worked per week: 20. Apply by March 15. Tuition remission given: partial. Research assistantships available for first year. Average amount paid per academic year: $7,000. Average number of hours worked per week: 20. Apply by March 15. Tuition remission given: partial. Fellowships and scholarships available for first year. Average amount paid per academic year: $7,000. Average number of hours worked per week: 15. Apply by March 15. Tuition remission given: partial.

Advanced Students: Teaching assistantships available for advanced students. Average amount paid per academic year: $7,000. Average number of hours worked per week: 20. Apply by March 15. Tuition remission given: partial. Research assistantships available for advanced students. Average amount paid per academic year: $7,000. Average number of hours worked per week: 20. Apply by March 15. Tuition remission given: partial. Fellowships and scholarships available for advanced students. Average amount paid per academic year: $7,000. Average number of hours worked per week: 15. Apply by March 15. Tuition remission given: partial.

Additional Information: Of all students currently enrolled full time, 100% benefited from one or more of the listed financial assistance programs. Application and information available online at http://www.web.indstate.edu.

Internships/Practica: Master's Degree (MA/MS General): An internship experience such as a final research project or "capstone" experience is required of graduates. Doctoral Degree (PsyD Clinical): For those doctoral students for whom a professional internship was required in this program prior to graduation, (8) students applied for an internship in 2006–2007, with (7) students obtaining an internship. Of those students who obtained an internship, (7) were paid internships. Of those students who obtained an internship, (7) students placed in APA/CPA-accredited internships, (0) students placed in internships not APA/CPA-accredited, but listed with the Association of Psychology Postdoctoral and Internship Centers (APPIC), (0) students placed in internships conforming to guidelines of the Council of Directors of School Psychology Programs (CDSPP), (0) students placed in internships that were not APA/CPA-accredited, APPIC or CDSPP listed. PsyD students are expected to participate in practicum experiences from the beginning of the program, with clinical responsibilities gradually increasing throughout enrollment. Second-year and third-year PsyD students see clients in the Psychology Clinic and are supervised by clinical faculty. Fourth-year students are placed in community mental health facilities under the supervision of a licensed psychologist.

Housing and Day Care: On-campus housing is available. Contact Residential Life: (812) 237-3993. On-campus day care facilities are available. Contact Early Childhood Education Center: (812) 237-2547.

Employment of Department Graduates:

Master's Degree Graduates: Of those who graduated in the academic year 2006–2007, the following categories and numbers represent the postgraduate activities and employment of master's degree graduates: Enrolled in a psychology doctoral program (1), enrolled in a postdoctoral residency/fellowship (n/a), employed in independent practice (n/a), total from the above (master's) (1).
Doctoral Degree Graduates: Of those who graduated in the academic year 2006–2007, the following categories and numbers represent the postgraduate activities and employment of doctoral degree graduates: Enrolled in a psychology doctoral program (n/a), enrolled in a postdoctoral residency/fellowship (2), employed in independent practice (1), employed in a community mental health/counseling center (10), other employment position (1), total from the above (doctoral) (14).

Additional Information:

Orientation, Objectives, and Emphasis of Department: The Doctor of Psychology program at Indiana State University follows a practitioner–scientist model of training in clinical psychology to guide the preparation and evaluation of its students. The primary goal is the training of skilled clinical psychologists in the assessment and treatment of psychological problems. The program seeks to develop a professional identity that values and pursues excellence in clinical practice, a spirit of active inquiry and critical thought, a commitment to the development and application of new knowledge in the field, an active sense of social responsibility combined with an appreciation and respect for cultural and individual differences, and an enduring commitment to personal and professional development. The program philosophy is to prepare all students as broad-based general clinicians, with encouragement to specialize through electives, research area, internship selection, and postdoctoral training. The Master's program, with an emphasis on basic psychology and research, is intended to serve as preparatory to entrance into doctoral-level study. Students are encouraged to become involved in research beginning with their first term in the program. Although the degree is in general psychology, some concentration is often possible. A main goal of the program is to have students leave with a sense of what it means to be a research psychologist.

Special Facilities or Resources: The department has a psychology clinic, mini- and microcomputers, and good laboratory facilities.

Information for Students With Physical Disabilities: See the following Web site for more information: http://www.web.indstate.edu/sasc/dss/index.htm.

Application Information:

Send to Department of Psychology, c/o Graduate Admissions, Root Hall, Indiana State University, Terre Haute, IN 47809. Application available online. URL of online application: http://www.web.indstate.edu/psych. Students are admitted in the Fall, application deadline January 1. Application deadline January 1 (PsyD); March 15 (Master's). *Fee:* $35.

Indiana University

Department of Counseling and Educational Psychology
School of Education
201 North Rose Avenue
Bloomington, IN 47405-1006
Telephone: (812) 856-8300
Fax: (812) 856-8333
E-mail: *joalexan@indiana.edu*
Web: *http://www.education.indiana.edu/cep*

Department Information:

1948. Chairperson: Joyce Alexander, PhD. Number of faculty: total—full-time 34, part-time 9; women—full-time 11, part-time 5; total—minority—full-time 6; women minority—full-time 2.

Programs and Degrees Offered:

Listed in the following order: Program area, degree type (T if terminal Master's), number awarded 7/06–6/07. Counseling Psychology PhD (Doctor of Philosophy) 9, Educational Psychology PhD (Doctor of Philosophy) 1, School Psychology, PhD (Doctor of Philosophy) 6, School Psychology, EdS/MEd (School Psychology) 7, Educational Psychology, MA/MS (Master of Arts/Science) 0.

APA Accreditation: Counseling PhD (Doctor of Philosophy). School Psychology PhD (Doctor of Philosophy).

Student Applications/Admissions:

Student Applications

Counseling Psychology PhD (Doctor of Philosophy)—Applications 2007–2008, 71. Total applicants accepted 2007–2008, 10. Number full-time enrolled (new admits only) 2007–2008, 6. Openings 2008–2009, 10. The median number of years required for completion of a degree in 2006–2007 were 6. The number of students enrolled full- and part-time who were dismissed or voluntarily withdrew from this program area in 2007–2008 were 0. *Educational Psychology PhD (Doctor of Philosophy)*—Applications 2007–2008, 47. Total applicants accepted 2007–2008, 24. Number full-time enrolled (new admits only) 2007–2008, 12. Openings 2008–2009, 12. The median number of years required for completion of a degree in 2006–2007 were 10. The number of students enrolled full- and part-time who were dismissed or voluntarily withdrew from this program area in 2007–2008 were 0. *School Psychology, PhD (Doctor of Philosophy)*—Applications 2007–2008, 30. Total applicants accepted 2007–2008, 9. Number full-time enrolled (new admits only) 2007–2008, 5. Openings 2008–2009, 7. The median number of years required for completion of a degree in 2006–2007 were 5. The number of students enrolled full- and part-time who were dismissed or voluntarily withdrew from this program area in 2007–2008 were 0. *School Psychology, EdS/MEd (School Psychology)*—Applications 2007–2008, 53. Total applicants accepted 2007–2008, 18. Number full-time enrolled (new admits only) 2007–2008, 9. Total enrolled 2007–2008 full-time, 26. Openings 2008–2009, 8. The median number of years required for completion of a degree in 2006–2007 were 3. The number of students enrolled full- and part-time who were dismissed or voluntarily withdrew from this program area in 2007–2008 were 0. *Educational Psychology, MA/MS (Master of Arts/Science)*—Applications 2007–2008, 14. Total applicants accepted 2007–2008, 4. Number full-time enrolled (new admits only) 2007–2008, 0. Total enrolled 2007–2008 full-time, 9. Openings 2008–2009, 8. The number of students enrolled full- and part-time who were dismissed or voluntarily withdrew from this program area in 2007–2008 were 0.

Admissions Requirements:

Scores: Entries appear in this order: required test or GPA, minimum score (if required), median score of students entering in 2007–2008. Master's Programs: GRE-V no minimum stated, 471; GRE-Q no minimum stated, 589; overall undergraduate GPA 3.0, 3.41; last 2 years GPA 3.0. Doctoral Programs: GRE-V no minimum stated, 520; GRE-Q no minimum stated, 629; overall undergraduate GPA 3.0, 3.57.

Other Criteria: (importance of criteria rated low, medium, or high): GRE/MAT scores—high, research experience—medium, work experience—medium, extracurricular activity—medium, clinically related public service—medium, GPA—high, letters of recommendation—medium, interview—high, statement of goals and objectives—medium. In both the PhD in Counseling Psychology and PhD in School Psychology programs personal interviews are required. GRE scores are interpreted differently for domestic and international applicants.

Student Characteristics: The following represents characteristics of students in 2007–2008 in all graduate psychology programs in the department: Female—full-time 133, part-time 0; Male—full-time 48, part-time 0; African American/Black—full-time 11, part-time 0; Hispanic/Latino(a)—full-time 13, part-time 0; Asian/Pacific Islander—full-time 28, part-time 0; American Indian/Alaska Native—full-time 0, part-time 0; Caucasian/White—full-time 111, part-time 0; Multi-ethnic—full-time 0, part-time 0; students subject to the Americans With Disabilities Act—full-time 0, part-time 0; Unknown ethnicity—full-time 18, part-time 0.

Financial Information/Assistance:

Tuition for Full-Time Study: *Master's:* State residents: $241 per credit hour; Nonstate residents: $703 per credit hour. *Doctoral:* State residents: $241 per credit hour; Nonstate residents: $703 per credit hour. Tuition is subject to change.

Financial Assistance:

First-Year Students: Teaching assistantships available for first year. Average amount paid per academic year: $14,000. Average number of hours worked per week: 18. Tuition remission given: partial. Research assistantships available for first year. Average amount paid per academic year: $11,750. Average number of hours worked per week: 18. Tuition remission given: partial. Fellowships and scholarships available for first year. Average amount paid per academic year: $17,000. Tuition remission given: full.

Advanced Students: Teaching assistantships available for advanced students. Average amount paid per academic year: $14,000. Average number of hours worked per week: 18. Tuition remission given: partial. Research assistantships available for advanced students. Average amount paid per academic year: $11,750. Average number of hours worked per week: 18. Tuition remission given: partial. Fellowships and scholarships available for advanced students. Average amount paid per academic year: $17,000. Tuition remission given: full.

Additional Information: Of all students currently enrolled full time, 80% benefited from one or more of the listed financial assistance programs. Application and information available online at http://www.indiana.edu/%7Ecepwp/finance.html.

Internships/Practica: Doctoral Degree (PhD Counseling Psychology): For those doctoral students for whom a professional internship was required in this program prior to graduation, (6) students applied for an internship in 2006–2007, with (6) students obtaining an internship. Of those students who obtained an internship, (6) were paid internships. Of those students who obtained an internship, (6) students placed in APA/CPA-accredited internships, (0) students placed in internships not APA/CPA accredited, but listed with the Association of Psychology Postdoctoral and Internship Centers (APPIC), (0) students placed in internships conforming to guidelines of the Council of Directors of School Psychology Programs (CDSPP), (0) students placed in internships that were not APA/CPA-accredited, APPIC or CDSPP listed. Doctoral Degree (PhD School Psychology): For those doctoral students for whom a professional internship was required in this program prior to graduation, (3) students applied for an internship in 2006–2007, with (3) students obtaining an internship. Of those students who obtained an internship, (3) were paid internships. Of those students who obtained an internship, (1) students placed in APA/CPA-accredited internships, (1) students placed in internships not APA/CPA-accredited, but listed with the Association of Psychology Postdoctoral and Internship Centers (APPIC), (0) students placed in internships conforming to guidelines of the Council of Directors of School Psychology Programs (CDSPP), (1) students placed in internships that were not APA/CPA-accredited, APPIC or CDSPP listed. All counseling and school psychology students must take both practica and internships.

Housing and Day Care: On-campus housing is available. See the following Web site for more information: http://www.rps.indiana.edu/housingrates.html. On-campus day care facilities are available. Campus Child Care Support, Poplars 734, Indiana University, Bloomington, IN 47405; (812) 855-5053.

Employment of Department Graduates:

Master's Degree Graduates: Of those who graduated in the academic year 2006–2007, the following categories and numbers represent the postgraduate activities and employment of master's degree graduates: Enrolled in a postdoctoral residency/fellowship (n/a), employed in independent practice (n/a), total from the above (master's) (0).

Doctoral Degree Graduates: Of those who graduated in the academic year 2006–2007, the following categories and numbers represent the postgraduate activities and employment of doctoral degree graduates: Enrolled in a psychology doctoral program (n/a), enrolled in another graduate/professional program (0), enrolled in a postdoctoral residency/fellowship (2), employed in independent practice (0), employed in an academic position at a university (2), employed in an academic position at a 2-year/4-year college (1), employed in other positions at a higher education institution (0), employed in a professional position in a school system (1), employed in business or industry (0), employed in government agency (1), employed in a community mental health/counseling center (2), employed in a hospital/medical center (0), still seeking employment (0), not seeking employment (0), other employment position (1), do not know (4), total from the above (doctoral) (14).

Additional Information:

Orientation, Objectives, and Emphasis of Department: The Department has multiple missions, but at the heart of our enterprise is a community of scholars working to contribute solutions to the problems faced by children, adolescents, and adults in the context of contemporary education. Additionally, the counseling psychology program promotes a broad range of interventions designed to facilitate the maximal adjustment of individuals. Faculty, staff, and students share a commitment to open-mindedness and to social justice. We recognize the complex and dynamic nature of the social fabric and welcome qualified students of all ethnic, racial, national, religious, gender, social class, sexual, political, and philosophic orientations. Faculty and students collaboratively investigate numerous facets of child and adolescent development, creativity, learning, metacognition, aging, semiotics, and inquiry methodologies. Our programs require an understanding of both quantitative and qualitative research paradigms. We ascribe to the scientist–practitioner model for preparing professional psychologists. Our graduates work in various research and practice settings; universities, public schools, state departments of education, mental health centers, hospitals, and corporations.

Special Facilities or Resources: Special facilities include the Institute for Child Study, Center for Human Growth, Center for Evaluation and Education Policy, Center for Adolescent and Family Studies, Center for Research on Learning and Technology, and the Indiana Institute on Disability and Community.

Information for Students With Physical Disabilities: (812) 855-7578.

Application Information:
Applications are accepted via the Web at http://www.indiana.edu/~educate/admiss.html. School Psychology EdS and PhD, and Counseling Psych PhD application deadline is December 1. Educational Psychology PhD application deadline is January 15. Educational Psychology MS deadline is January 15. Counseling/Counselor Education has deadlines of March 1 and November 1. Application available online. URL of online application: http://www.indiana.edu/%7Eeducate/appadvice.html. Students are admitted in the Fall, application deadline December 1. *Fee:* $65 for international students; $50 for domestic students.

Indiana University

Department of Psychological and Brain Sciences
Arts and Sciences
Psychology Building, 1101 East 10th Street
Bloomington, IN 47405
Telephone: (812) 855-2012
Fax: (812) 855-4691
E-mail: *psychgrd@indiana.edu*
Web: *http://www.psych.indiana.edu*

Department Information:
1919. Chairperson: Linda B. Smith. Number of faculty: total—full-time 49; women—full-time 12; total—minority—full-time 1; women minority—full-time 1; faculty subject to the Americans With Disabilities Act 1.

Programs and Degrees Offered:
Listed in the following order: Program area, degree type (T if terminal Master's), number awarded 7/06–6/07. Biology, Behavior, and Neuroscience PhD (Doctor of Philosophy) 3, Clinical Science PhD (Doctor of Philosophy) 3, Cognitive PhD (Doctor of Philosophy) 3, Developmental PhD (Doctor of Philosophy) 0, Social PhD (Doctor of Philosophy) 1, Cognitive Neuroscience PhD (Doctor of Philosophy) 0.

APA Accreditation: Clinical PhD (Doctor of Philosophy).

Student Applications/Admissions:
Student Applications
Biology, Behavior, and Neuroscience PhD (Doctor of Philosophy)—Applications 2007–2008, 33. Total applicants accepted 2007–2008, 4. Number full-time enrolled (new admits only) 2007–2008, 1. Number part-time enrolled (new admits only) 2007–2008, 0. Openings 2008–2009, 4. The median number of years required for completion of a degree in 2006–2007 were 5. The number of students enrolled full- and part-time who were dismissed or voluntarily withdrew from this program area in 2007–2008 were 0. *Clinical Science PhD (Doctor of Philosophy)*—Applications 2007–2008, 80. Total applicants accepted 2007–2008, 5. Number full-time enrolled (new admits only) 2007–2008, 5. Number part-time enrolled (new admits only) 2007–2008, 0. Openings 2008–2009, 7. The median number of years required for completion of a degree in 2006–2007 were 6. The number of students enrolled full- and part-time who were dismissed or voluntarily withdrew from this program area in 2007–2008 were 0. *Cognitive PhD (Doctor of Philosophy)*—Applications 2007–2008, 40. Total applicants accepted 2007–2008, 13. Number full-time enrolled (new admits only) 2007–2008, 9. Number part-time enrolled (new admits only) 2007–2008, 0. Openings 2008–2009, 8. The median number of years required for completion of a degree in 2006–2007 were 6. The number of students enrolled full- and part-time who were dismissed or voluntarily withdrew from this program area in 2007–2008 were 1. *Developmental PhD (Doctor of Philosophy)*—Applications 2007–2008, 6. Total applicants accepted 2007–2008, 2. Number full-time enrolled (new admits only) 2007–2008, 1. Number part-time enrolled (new admits only) 2007–2008, 0. Openings 2008–2009, 2. The median number of years required for completion of a degree in 2006–2007 were 6. The number of students enrolled full- and part-time who were dismissed or voluntarily withdrew from this program area in 2007–2008 were 0. *Social PhD (Doctor of Philosophy)*—Applications 2007–2008, 46. Total applicants accepted 2007–2008, 3. Number full-time enrolled (new admits only) 2007–2008, 3. Number part-time enrolled (new admits only) 2007–2008, 0. Openings 2008–2009, 3. The number of students enrolled full- and part-time who were dismissed or voluntarily withdrew from this program area in 2007–2008 were 0. *Cognitive Neuroscience PhD (Doctor of Philosophy)*—Applications 2007–2008, 0. Total applicants accepted 2007–2008, 0. Number full-time enrolled (new admits only) 2007–2008, 0. Number part-time enrolled (new admits only) 2007–2008, 0. Openings 2008–2009, 2. The number of students enrolled full- and part-time who were dismissed or voluntarily withdrew from this program area in 2007–2008 were 0.

Admissions Requirements:
Scores: Entries appear in this order: required test or GPA, minimum score (if required), median score of students entering in 2007–2008. Master's Programs: We do not offer admission into a master's program. Doctoral Programs: GRE-V no minimum stated, 608; GRE-Q no minimum stated, 714; overall undergraduate GPA no minimum stated, 3.68; Doctoral program GRE-Analytic no minimum stated, 5. Above scores are the means for accepted students.
Other Criteria: (importance of criteria rated low, medium, or high): GRE/MAT scores—high, research experience—high, GPA—high, letters of recommendation—high, interview—high, statement of goals and objectives—medium. For additional information on admission requirements, go to http://www.psych.indiana.edu.

Student Characteristics: The following represents characteristics of students in 2007–2008 in all graduate psychology programs in the department: Female—full-time 41, part-time 0; Male—full-time 41, part-time 0; African American/Black—full-time 3,

part-time 0; Hispanic/Latino(a)—full-time 4, part-time 0; Asian/Pacific Islander—full-time 14, part-time 0; American Indian/Alaska Native—full-time 0, part-time 0; Caucasian/White—full-time 60, part-time 0; Multi-ethnic—full-time 1, part-time 0; students subject to the Americans With Disabilities Act—full-time 1, part-time 0; Unknown ethnicity—full-time 0, part-time 0; International students who hold an F-1 or J-1 Visa—full-time 13, part-time 0.

Financial Information/Assistance:

Tuition for Full-Time Study: *Doctoral:* State residents: per academic year $7,950, $265 per credit hour; Nonstate residents: per academic year $23,190, $773 per credit hour. Tuition is subject to change. Additional fees are assessed to students beyond the costs of tuition for the following: activity fee, health fee, technology fee, transportation fee. See the following Web site for updates and changes in tuition costs: http://www.bursar.indiana.edu/body/rates/rates_and_policies.php.

Financial Assistance:

First-Year Students: Teaching assistantships available for first year. Average amount paid per academic year: $18,700. Average number of hours worked per week: 20. Apply by same. Tuition remission given: full. Research assistantships available for first year. Average amount paid per academic year: $18,700. Average number of hours worked per week: 20. Apply by same. Tuition remission given: full. Fellowships and scholarships available for first year. Average amount paid per academic year: $21,500. Average number of hours worked per week: 0. Apply by same. Tuition remission given: full.

Advanced Students: Teaching assistantships available for advanced students. Average amount paid per academic year: $18,700. Average number of hours worked per week: 20. Apply by none. Tuition remission given: full. Research assistantships available for advanced students. Average amount paid per academic year: $18,700. Average number of hours worked per week: 20. Apply by none. Tuition remission given: full. Fellowships and scholarships available for advanced students. Average amount paid per academic year: $21,500. Average number of hours worked per week: 20. Apply by none. Tuition remission given: full.

Additional Information: Of all students currently enrolled full time, 100% benefited from one or more of the listed financial assistance programs. Application and information available online at http://www.gradapp.indiana.edu.

Internships/Practica: Doctoral Degree (PhD Clinical Science): For those doctoral students for whom a professional internship was required in this program prior to graduation, (4) students applied for an internship in 2006–2007, with (4) students obtaining an internship. Of those students who obtained an internship, (4) were paid internships. Of those students who obtained an internship, (4) students placed in APA/CPA-accredited internships, (0) students placed in internships not APA/CPA accredited, but listed with the Association of Psychology Postdoctoral and Internship Centers (APPIC), (0) students placed in internships conforming to guidelines of the Council of Directors of School Psychology Programs (CDSPP), (0) students placed in internships that were not APA/CPA-accredited, APPIC or CDSPP listed. Internships are required for a clinical psychology major.

Housing and Day Care: On-campus housing is available. See the following Web site for more information: http://www.rps.indiana.edu/. On-campus day care facilities are available. See the following Web site for more information: http://www.childcare.indiana.edu/.

Employment of Department Graduates:

Master's Degree Graduates: Of those who graduated in the academic year 2006–2007, the following categories and numbers represent the postgraduate activities and employment of master's degree graduates: Enrolled in a postdoctoral residency/fellowship (n/a), employed in independent practice (n/a), total from the above (master's) (0).

Doctoral Degree Graduates: Of those who graduated in the academic year 2006–2007, the following categories and numbers represent the postgraduate activities and employment of doctoral degree graduates: Enrolled in a psychology doctoral program (n/a), enrolled in a postdoctoral residency/fellowship (3), employed in an academic position at a university (5), total from the above (doctoral) (8).

Additional Information:

Orientation, Objectives, and Emphasis of Department: Students acquire fundamental knowledge and are offered specialized training so that they may develop competence in research, teaching (college and university levels), and service. Close contact between faculty and students is made possible by a low ratio of graduate students to faculty. Extensive laboratory facilities are available for research in the major areas. A psychological clinic is maintained as a specialized unit of the department. The primary emphasis of the clinical training program is on the theoretical and scientific aspects of clinical psychology. However, in view of the diverse and changing nature of the field, the program's goal is to produce clinical psychologists who are well trained scientifically and clinically and who are capable of achieving excellence in their careers in either a clinical or an academic and research setting.

Special Facilities or Resources: Recently, the Department of Psychological and Brain Sciences became home to the IU Imaging Research Facility. The facility houses a 3T Siemens Magnetom Trio whole body system, used for magnetic resonance imaging (MRI) or functional MRI (fMRI), a noninvasive method for studying patterns of brain activity during mental operations. The facility gives our students the opportunity to be part of research labs doing MRI and fMRI studies and to take classes with the MRI scientists.

Information for Students With Physical Disabilities: See the following Web site for more information: http://www.129.79.17.23/dss/.

Application Information:

Send to Indiana University, Department of Psychological and Brain Scieces, Graduate Admissions, 1101 East 10th Street, Bloomington, IN 47405. Application available online. URL of online application: https://www.gradapp.indiana.edu/. Students are admitted in the Fall, application deadline December 15. December 1 is the application deadline for international graduate student candidates. *Fee:* $50. The department does not give application fee waivers or deferrals. However, certain fellowship programs for which our applicants can apply might offer such waivers of the application fee. The application fee is $60 for international students.

Indiana University–Purdue University Indianapolis (2007 data)

Department of Psychology
Science
402 North Blackford Street, Room LD 124
Indianapolis, IN 46202-3275
Telephone: (317) 274-6945
Fax: (317) 274-6756
E-mail: *gfetter@iupui.edu*
Web: *http://www.psych.iupui.edu*

Department Information:

1969. Chairperson: J. Gregor Fetterman, PhD. Number of faculty: total—full-time 24, part-time 13; women—full-time 9, part-time 10.

Programs and Degrees Offered:

Listed in the following order: Program area, degree type (T if terminal Master's), number awarded 7/06–6/07. Industrial/Organization MA/MS (Master of Arts/Science) (T) 5, Clinical Rehabilitation PhD (Doctor of Philosophy) 2, Psychobiology PhD (Doctor of Philosophy) 0.

APA Accreditation: Clinical PhD (Doctor of Philosophy).

Student Applications/Admissions:

Student Applications

Industrial/Organization MA/MS (Master of Arts/Science)—Applications 2007–2008, 50. Total applicants accepted 2007–2008, 6. Number full-time enrolled (new admits only) 2007–2008, 6. Number part-time enrolled (new admits only) 2007–2008, 0. Openings 2008–2009, 7. The median number of years required for completion of a degree in 2006–2007 were 4. The number of students enrolled full- and part-time who were dismissed or voluntarily withdrew from this program area in 2007–2008 were 0. *Clinical Rehabilitation PhD (Doctor of Philosophy)*—Applications 2007–2008, 42. Total applicants accepted 2007–2008, 4. Number full-time enrolled (new admits only) 2007–2008, 4. Number part-time enrolled (new admits only) 2007–2008, 0. Openings 2008–2009, 5. The median number of years required for completion of a degree in 2006–2007 were 5. The number of students enrolled full- and part-time who were dismissed or voluntarily withdrew from this program area in 2007–2008 were 1. *Psychobiology PhD (Doctor of Philosophy)*—Applications 2007–2008, 10. Total applicants accepted 2007–2008, 2. Number full-time enrolled (new admits only) 2007–2008, 2. Openings 2008–2009, 2. The median number of years required for completion of a degree in 2006–2007 were 6. The number of students enrolled full- and part-time who were dismissed or voluntarily withdrew from this program area in 2007–2008 were 0.

Admissions Requirements:

Scores: Entries appear in this order: required test or GPA, minimum score (if required), median score of students entering in 2007–2008. Master's Programs: GRE-V 550, 500; GRE-Q 550, 620; overall undergraduate GPA 3.0, 3.64. Note: Minimum GRE scores are neither necessary nor sufficient for admission. Doctoral Programs: GRE-V 600, 590; GRE-Q 600, 708; GRE-Subject (Psychology) 600, 690; overall undergraduate GPA 3.2, 3.65. Note: Minimum GRE scores are neither necessary nor sufficient for admission.

Other Criteria: (importance of criteria rated low, medium, or high): GRE/MAT scores—high, research experience—high, work experience—low, GPA—high, letters of recommendation—high, interview—medium, statement of goals and objectives—high. For additional information on admission requirements, go to http://psych.iupui.edu.

Student Characteristics: The following represents characteristics of students in 2007–2008 in all graduate psychology programs in the department: Female—full-time 44, part-time 0; Male—full-time 7, part-time 0; African American/Black—full-time 2, part-time 0; Hispanic/Latino(a)—full-time 2, part-time 0; Asian/Pacific Islander—full-time 1, part-time 0; American Indian/Alaska Native—full-time 0, part-time 0; Caucasian/White—full-time 46, part-time 0; Multi-ethnic—part-time 0; students subject to the Americans With Disabilities Act—full-time 0, part-time 0; Unknown ethnicity—full-time 0, part-time 0.

Financial Information/Assistance:

Tuition for Full-Time Study: *Master's:* State residents: per academic year $4,784, $199 per credit hour; Nonstate residents: per academic year $14,908, $621 per credit hour. *Doctoral:* State residents: per academic year $4,784, $199 per credit hour; Nonstate residents: per academic year $14,908, $621 per credit hour. Tuition is subject to change. See the following Web site for updates and changes in tuition costs: http://www.bursar.iupui.edu.

Financial Assistance:

First-Year Students: Research assistantships available for first year. Average amount paid per academic year: $11,000. Average number of hours worked per week: 20. Apply by January 1. Tuition remission given: partial. Fellowships and scholarships available for first year. Average amount paid per academic year: $22,000. Average number of hours worked per week: 0. Apply by January 1. Tuition remission given: partial.

Advanced Students: Teaching assistantships available for advanced students. Average amount paid per academic year: $11,000. Average number of hours worked per week: 20. Apply by January 1. Tuition remission given: partial. Research assistantships available for advanced students. Average amount paid per academic year: $11,000. Average number of hours worked per week: 20. Apply by January 1. Tuition remission given: partial. Fellowships and scholarships available for advanced students. Average amount paid per academic year: $22,000. Average number of hours worked per week: 0. Apply by January 1. Tuition remission given: partial.

Additional Information: Of all students currently enrolled full time, 100% benefited from one or more of the listed financial assistance programs. Application and information available online at http://psych.iupui.edu.

Internships/Practica: Clinical practica sites are located at IUPUI and within the Indianapolis area, and involve supervised clinical training individually tailored for each student. A practicum coordinator, the site supervisor, and the student develop specific contracts that emphasize education and the acquisition of clinical skills and knowledge, rather than experience per se. These contractual activities and goals are monitored and evaluated at the end of each placement. Practicum opportunities are varied and numerous and include many different types of clinical settings with different clinical populations. On-site supervisors are usually psychologists but also include psychiatrists, physiatrists, and other health professionals. Many sites in different settings are available. General practicum sites include a university counseling center and several psychiatric clinics. More advanced settings can be categorized as (a) Neuropsychology; (b) Behavioral Medicine or Health Psychology; (c) Severe Mental Illness/Psychiatric Rehabilitation. The I/O Master's Program offers opportunities to achieve applied experience in business settings. Students have the opportunity to sign up for practicum in the spring of their 2nd year. Students are typically placed in an organization for one 8-hour day each week of the semester. Paid summer internships (15–20 hours per week) in the community are also available.

Housing and Day Care: On-campus housing is available. See the following Web site for more information: http://www.housing.iupui.edu/. On-campus day care facilities are available. See the following Web site for more information: http://www.childcare.iupui.edu/.

Employment of Department Graduates:

Master's Degree Graduates: Of those who graduated in the academic year 2006–2007, the following categories and numbers represent the postgraduate activities and employment of master's degree graduates: Enrolled in a psychology doctoral program (4), enrolled in a postdoctoral residency/fellowship (n/a), employed in independent practice (n/a), total from the above (master's) (4). ***Doctoral Degree Graduates:*** Of those who graduated in the academic year 2006–2007, the following categories and numbers represent the postgraduate activities and employment of doctoral degree graduates: Enrolled in a psychology doctoral program (n/a), enrolled in a postdoctoral residency/fellowship (2), total from the above (doctoral) (2).

Additional Information:

Orientation, Objectives, and Emphasis of Department: Graduate education is offered at the PhD level in Clinical Rehabilitation Psychology and the Psychobiology of Addictions. The APA-Accredited Clinical program follows the scientist–practitioner model. A rigorous academic and research education is combined with supervised practical training. The clinical program provides specialization in behavioral medicine/health psychology, neuropsychology, and severe mental illness/psychiatric rehabilitation. The PhD program in the psychobiological bases of addictions emphasizes the core content areas of psychology along with specialization in psychobiology and animal models of addiction. Research, scholarship, and close faculty–student mentor relationships are viewed as integral training elements within both programs. Graduate training at the MS level is designed to provide students with theory and practice that will enable them to apply psychological techniques and findings to subsequent jobs. All students are required to take departmental methods courses and then specific area core courses and electives. The MS degree areas are applied in focus and science-based, and this reflects the interests and orientation of the faculty.

Special Facilities or Resources: IUPUI is a unique urban university campus with 27,000 students enrolled in 235 degree programs at the undergraduate and graduate level. The campus includes schools of law, dentistry, and medicine, among others, along with undergraduate programs in the arts, humanities, and science. In addition, there are over 75 research institutes, centers, laboratories and specialized programs. The Department of Psychology at IUPUI occupies teaching and research facilities in a modern science building in the heart of campus. Facilities include a 4,000-square foot space and self-contained area devoted to faculty and graduate student basic animal research in experimental psychology and psychobiology. Many of the research rooms are equipped for online computer recording to one of the faculty offices. Laboratories for human research, research rooms, and teaching laboratories are separately located on the first floor of the building. The Psychology Department maintains ties with the faculty and programs in other schools within IUPUI, including the School of Nursing, and the Departments of Psychiatry, Adolescent Medicine, and Neurology. The clinical program provides an unusually rich array of practicum opportunities in behavioral medicine, neuropsychology, and psychiatric rehabilitation.

Application Information:

Send to Breta J. Koester, IUPUI, Department of Psychology, LD124, 422 North Blackford Street, Indianapolis, IN 46202-3275. Application available online. URL of online application: http://www.psych.iupui.edu. Students are admitted in the Fall, application deadline January 1. Each program has a different application deadline. Clinical Rehabilitation and Psychobiology application deadline is January 1. Industrial/Organizational application deadline is February 1. *Fee:* $50. International $60.

Indianapolis, University of

Graduate Psychology Program
School of Psychological Sciences
1400 East Hanna Avenue, GH 109
Indianapolis, IN 46227
Telephone: (317) 788-3920
Fax: (317) 788-2120
E-mail: *psychology@uindy.edu*
Web: *http://www.psych.uindy.edu/*

Department Information:

1994. Dean: John McIlvried, PhD. Number of faculty: total—full-time 14, part-time 1; women—full-time 6, part-time 1; total—minority—full-time 2.

Programs and Degrees Offered:

Listed in the following order: Program area, degree type (T if terminal Master's), number awarded 7/06–6/07. Clinical MA/MS (Master of Arts/Science) 9, Clinical PsyD (Doctor of Psychology) 12.

APA Accreditation: Clinical PsyD (Doctor of Psychology).

Student Applications/Admissions:

Student Applications

Clinical MA/MS (Master of Arts/Science)—Applications 2007–2008, 75. Total applicants accepted 2007–2008, 33. Number full-time enrolled (new admits only) 2007–2008, 16. Number part-time enrolled (new admits only) 2007–2008, 0. Total enrolled 2007–2008 full-time, 29, part-time, 2. Openings 2008–2009, 16. The median number of years required for completion of a degree in 2006–2007 were 2. The number of students enrolled full- and part-time who were dismissed or voluntarily withdrew from this program area in 2007–2008 were 2. *Clinical PsyD (Doctor of Psychology)*—Applications 2007–2008, 117. Total applicants accepted 2007–2008, 46. Number full-time enrolled (new admits only) 2007–2008, 27. Number part-time enrolled (new admits only) 2007–2008, 0. Total enrolled 2007–2008 full-time, 120, part-time, 1. Openings 2008–2009, 23. The median number of years required for completion of a degree in 2006–2007 were 6. The number of students enrolled full- and part-time who were dismissed or voluntarily withdrew from this program area in 2007–2008 were 2.

Admissions Requirements:

Scores: Entries appear in this order: required test or GPA, minimum score (if required), median score of students entering in 2007–2008. Master's Programs: GRE-V no minimum stated, 550; GRE-Q no minimum stated, 575; overall undergraduate GPA no minimum stated, 3.57; psychology GPA no minimum stated, 3.6; Masters GRE-Analytical no minimum stated, 4. Doctoral Programs: GRE-V no minimum stated, 550; GRE-Q no minimum stated, 650; overall undergraduate GPA 3.0, 3.68; psychology GPA 3.0, 3.7; Doctoral program GRE-Analytic no minimum stated, 5.

Other Criteria: (importance of criteria rated low, medium, or high): GRE/MAT scores—high, research experience—medium, work experience—medium, extracurricular activity—low, clinically related public service—medium, GPA—high, letters of recommendation—high, interview—high, statement of goals and objectives—medium, 18 credit hours psychology—high. For additional information on admission requirements, go to http://psych.uindy.edu.

Student Characteristics: The following represents characteristics of students in 2007–2008 in all graduate psychology programs in the department: Female—full-time 123, part-time 2; Male—full-time 26, part-time 1; African American/Black—full-time 5, part-time 0; Hispanic/Latino(a)—full-time 0, part-time 0; Asian/Pacific Islander—full-time 2, part-time 0; American Indian/Alaska Native—full-time 0, part-time 0; Caucasian/White—full-time 112, part-time 2; Multi-ethnic—full-time 0, part-time 1; students subject to the Americans With Disabilities Act—full-time 1, part-time 0; Unknown ethnicity—full-time 30, part-time 0; International students who hold an F-1 or J-1 Visa—full-time 6, part-time 0.

Financial Information/Assistance:

Tuition for Full-Time Study: *Master's:* State residents: $630 per credit hour; Nonstate residents: $630 per credit hour. *Doctoral:* State residents: $630 per credit hour; Nonstate residents: $630 per credit hour. Tuition is subject to change. See the following Web site for updates and changes in tuition costs: http://www.psych.uindy.edu/psyd/finaid.php.

Financial Assistance:

First-Year Students: Teaching assistantships available for first year. Average amount paid per academic year: $0. Average number of hours worked per week: 11. Apply by January 10. Tuition remission given: partial. Research assistantships available for first year. Average amount paid per academic year: $0. Average number of hours worked per week: 11. Apply by January 10. Tuition remission given: partial. Fellowships and scholarships available for first year. Average amount paid per academic year: $0. Average number of hours worked per week: 0. Apply by January 10. Tuition remission given: full.

Advanced Students: Teaching assistantships available for advanced students. Average amount paid per academic year: $0. Average number of hours worked per week: 11. Apply by renewable. Tuition remission given: partial. Research assistantships available for advanced students. Average amount paid per academic year: $0. Average number of hours worked per week: 11. Apply by renewable. Tuition remission given: partial. Fellowships and scholarships available for advanced students. Average amount paid per academic year: $0. Average number of hours worked per week: 0. Apply by renewable. Tuition remission given: full.

Additional Information: Of all students currently enrolled full time, 30% benefited from one or more of the listed financial assistance programs. Application and information available online at http://finaid.uindy.edu.

Internships/Practica: Doctoral Degree (Clinical PsyD): For those doctoral students for whom a professional internship was required in this program prior to graduation, (14) students applied for an internship in 2006–2007, with (13) students obtaining an internship. Of those students who obtained an internship, (13) were paid internships. Of those students who obtained an internship, (10) students placed in APA/CPA-accredited internships, (3) students placed in internships not APA/CPA-accredited, but listed with the Association of Psychology Postdoctoral and Internship Centers (APPIC), (0) students placed in internships conforming to guidelines of the Council of Directors of School Psychology Programs (CDSPP), (0) students placed in internships that were not APA/CPA-accredited, APPIC or CDSPP listed. There are numerous clinical practica experiences available for both master's and doctoral students. Master's students obtain a minimum of 225 hours of supervised clinical practica experience (Mental Health Counseling requires 1,000 hours), and doctoral students receive a minimum of 1,200 hours of supervised clinical practica experience. Practica are available at numerous settings, including a major training medical center, local community hospitals, forensic settings, private practice placements, elementary schools, social service agencies, and mental health centers. At these placements, students gain supervised experience in clinical assessment and testing, psychotherapy, collaboration and consultation with interdisciplinary teams, program development and evaluation, treatment planning and case management, and participation in development and delivery of inservices to professional staff. In addition to mainstream psychological services, practicum students have opportunities to obtain specific training in forensics, psychodiagnostic assessment, neuropsychology, health psychology, pain, substance abuse/dependence, developmental disabilities, and HIV/AIDS. All doctoral practica are supervised by licensed, doctoral-level psychologists and all master's practica are supervised by licensed, master's-level mental health professionals. In conjunction with practica, students enroll in a professional practice seminar that addresses a wide variety of issues that confront mental health professionals and students. This professional practice seminar is taught by full-time University faculty. Doctoral students also must complete a 2,000-hour internship. The Director of Clinical Training provides assistance in locating training placements. For additional information on education and training outcomes for our programs, see the following Web site: http://www.psych.uindy.edu/psyd/education_and_training_outcomes.php.

Housing and Day Care: On-campus housing is available. See the following Web site for more information: http://www.uindy.edu/

reslife/. On-campus day care facilities are available. University Heights United Methodist Church, 4002 Otterbein Avenue, Indianapolis, IN 46227; Church office: (317) 787-5347.

Employment of Department Graduates:

Master's Degree Graduates: Of those who graduated in the academic year 2006–2007, the following categories and numbers represent the postgraduate activities and employment of master's degree graduates: Enrolled in a postdoctoral residency/fellowship (n/a), employed in independent practice (n/a), do not know (9), total from the above (master's) (9).

Doctoral Degree Graduates: Of those who graduated in the academic year 2006–2007, the following categories and numbers represent the postgraduate activities and employment of doctoral degree graduates: Enrolled in a psychology doctoral program (n/a), employed in independent practice (2), employed in an academic position at a university (3), employed in other positions at a higher education institution (1), employed in a community mental health/counseling center (2), employed in a hospital/medical center (1), not seeking employment (1), do not know (2), total from the above (doctoral) (12).

Additional Information:

Orientation, Objectives, and Emphasis of Department: The graduate program in clinical psychology at the University of Indianapolis is based on a practitioner–scholar model of training. As such, the program is committed to developing highly competent and qualified professionals. The focus of the program is on preparing individuals to aid in the prevention and treatment of human problems, as well as the enhancement of human functioning and potential. The program trains students in the general, integrative practice of professional psychology through a broad-based exposure to a variety of psychological approaches and modalities. In addition, the program offers specialized training in four clinical emphasis areas: health psychology/behavioral medicine, childhood and adolescent psychology, adult development and geropsychology, and a generalist track. The faculty believe that education is most effective when the relationship between students and faculty is characterized by mutual respect, responsibility, and dedication to excellence. The program is founded on a deep and abiding respect for diversity in individuals, the ethical practice of psychology, and a commitment to service to others. These core values are reflected in the selection of students, the coursework and training experiences offered, and the faculty who serve as role models and mentors.

Special Facilities or Resources: Specialized training facilities include several clinical therapy labs designed for supervised assessment, testing, and therapy, and for videotaping of clinical sessions utilized in feedback and instruction. The Large Groups Lab includes interconnected classrooms used for videotaping and monitoring of experiential group or class exercises, psychoeducational programs, and other large group activities. Individualized Study and Research Labs equipped with computers are available for research projects, classroom assignments, and personal study. Computer facilities in the School of Psychology and throughout the university allow access to word processing, spreadsheets, database operations, statistical packages, e-mail, wireless Internet, and online searching of library holdings. In addition, they offer the capability of conducting direct, online literature searches using a variety of different databases (e.g., PsycBOOKS, PsycINFO, PsycARTICLES, PsycEXTRA, MedLine, PEP CD). The library subscribes to the major psychology journals and contains the latest publications in the field of clinical psychology. The School has a graduate student lounge in which students meet to confer about class assignments, have group study sessions, practice presentations, or just relax between classes. The School also has an on-site Psychological Services Center, which offers treatment services to community residents on a sliding fee scale. Students receive applied training experience at the Center while conducting intake assessments or providing therapeutic services.

Information for Students With Physical Disabilities: See the following Web site for more information: http://www.uindy.edu/ssd/.

Application Information:

Send to Margie Keaton, PsyD, Director of Student Services, 1400 East Hanna Avenue, GH 109, Indianapolis, IN 46227. Application available online. URL of online application: https://www.applyweb.com/apply/uipsych/. Students are admitted in the Fall, application deadline January 10. Febraury 25 MA deadline. *Fee:* $55.

Notre Dame, University of

Department of Psychology
Arts and Letters
118 Haggar Hall
Notre Dame, IN 46556
Telephone: (574) 631-6650
Fax: (574) 631-8883
E-mail: *dlapsley@nd.edu*
Web: *http://www.nd.edu*

Department Information:

1965. Chairperson: Cindy Bergeman. Number of faculty: total—full-time 33; women—full-time 14; total—minority—full-time 6; women minority—full-time 3.

Programs and Degrees Offered:

Listed in the following order: Program area, degree type (T if terminal Master's), number awarded 7/06–6/07. Cognitive Psychology PhD (Doctor of Philosophy) 2, Counseling Psychology PhD (Doctor of Philosophy) 3, Developmental Psychology PhD (Doctor of Philosophy) 7, Quantitative Psychology PhD (Doctor of Philosophy) 3.

APA Accreditation: Counseling PhD (Doctor of Philosophy).

Student Applications/Admissions:

Student Applications

Cognitive Psychology PhD (Doctor of Philosophy)—Applications 2007–2008, 16. Total applicants accepted 2007–2008, 4. Number full-time enrolled (new admits only) 2007–2008, 1. Total enrolled 2007–2008 full-time, 8. Openings 2008–2009, 5. The median number of years required for completion of a degree in 2006–2007 were 6. The number of students enrolled full- and part-time who were dismissed or voluntarily withdrew from this program area in 2007–2008 were 1. *Counseling Psychology PhD (Doctor of Philosophy)*—Applications 2007–2008, 75. Total applicants accepted 2007–2008, 6. Number full-time enrolled (new admits only) 2007–2008, 3. Total enrolled 2007–2008 full-time, 25. Openings 2008–2009, 4. The median number of years required for completion of a degree in 2006–2007 were 7. The number of students enrolled full- and part-time who were dismissed or voluntarily withdrew from this program area in 2007–2008 were 0. *Developmental Psychology PhD (Doctor of Philosophy)*—Applications 2007–2008, 31. Total applicants accepted 2007–2008, 8. Number full-time enrolled (new admits only) 2007–2008, 2. Total enrolled 2007–2008 full-time, 17. Openings 2008–2009, 4. The median number of years required for completion of a degree in 2006–2007 were 5. The number of students enrolled full- and part-time who were dismissed or voluntarily withdrew from this program area in 2007–2008 were 0. *Quantitative Psychology PhD (Doctor of Philosophy)*—Applications 2007–2008, 21. Total applicants accepted 2007–2008, 5. Number full-time enrolled (new admits only) 2007–2008, 2. Number part-time enrolled (new admits only) 2007–2008, 0. Openings 2008–2009, 4. The median number of years required for completion of a degree in 2006–2007 were 7. The number of students enrolled full- and part-time who were dismissed or voluntarily withdrew from this program area in 2007–2008 were 2.

Admissions Requirements:

Scores: Entries appear in this order: required test or GPA, minimum score (if required), median score of students entering in 2007–2008. Doctoral Programs: GRE-V no minimum stated, 587; GRE-Q no minimum stated, 675; overall undergraduate GPA no minimum stated, 3.70.

Other Criteria: (importance of criteria rated low, medium, or high): GRE/MAT scores—high, research experience—high, work experience—low, extracurricular activity—low, clinically related public service—low, GPA—high, letters of recommendation—high, interview—medium, statement of goals and objectives—high, undergraduate major in psychology—high, specific undergraduate psychology courses taken—medium.

Student Characteristics: The following represents characteristics of students in 2007–2008 in all graduate psychology programs in the department: Female—full-time 44, part-time 0; Male—full-time 20, part-time 0; African American/Black—full-time 4, part-time 0; Hispanic/Latino(a)—full-time 6, part-time 0; Asian/Pacific Islander—full-time 11, part-time 0; American Indian/Alaska Native—full-time 0, part-time 0; Caucasian/White—full-time 43, part-time 0; students subject to the Americans With Disabilities Act—full-time 0, part-time 0; Unknown ethnicity—full-time 0, part-time 0.

Financial Information/Assistance:

Tuition for Full-Time Study: *Doctoral:* State residents: per academic year $31,000; Nonstate residents: per academic year $31,000.

Financial Assistance:

First-Year Students: Teaching assistantships available for first year. Average amount paid per academic year: $16,000. Tuition remission given: full. Research assistantships available for first year. Average amount paid per academic year: $16,000. Tuition remission given: full. Fellowships and scholarships available for first year. Average amount paid per academic year: $20,000. Tuition remission given: full.

Advanced Students: Teaching assistantships available for advanced students. Average amount paid per academic year: $16,000. Tuition remission given: full. Research assistantships available for advanced students. Average amount paid per academic year: $16,000. Tuition remission given: full. Fellowships and scholarships available for advanced students. Average amount paid per academic year: $20. Tuition remission given: full.

Additional Information: Of all students currently enrolled full time, 100% benefited from one or more of the listed financial assistance programs. Application and information available online at: http://www.nd.edu/~gradsch/.

Internships/Practica: Doctoral Degree (PhD Counseling Psychology): For those doctoral students for whom a professional internship was required in this program prior to graduation, (3) students applied for an internship in 2006–2007, with (3) students obtaining an internship. Of those students who obtained an internship, (3) were paid internships. Of those students who obtained an internship, (3) students placed in APA/CPA-accredited internships, (0) students placed in internships not APA/CPA accredited, but listed with the Association of Psychology Postdoctoral and Internship Centers (APPIC), (0) students placed in internships conforming to guidelines of the Council of Directors of School Psychology Programs (CDSPP), (0) students placed in internships that were not APA/CPA-accredited, APPIC or CDSPP listed. All students in the APA-accredited counseling program have an initial practicum of 13–17 hours per week at the University Counseling Center. These same students have opportunities for additional practicum placements in agencies in the community. The University Counseling Center also houses an APA-accredited internship. Advanced students in the accredited program are eligible to apply.

Housing and Day Care: On-campus housing is available. See the following Web site for more information: http://www.nd.edu/~orlh. On-campus day care facilities are available.

Employment of Department Graduates:

Master's Degree Graduates: Of those who graduated in the academic year 2006–2007, the following categories and numbers represent the postgraduate activities and employment of master's degree graduates: Enrolled in a postdoctoral residency/fellowship (n/a), employed in independent practice (n/a), total from the above (master's) (0).

Doctoral Degree Graduates: Of those who graduated in the academic year 2006–2007, the following categories and numbers represent the postgraduate activities and employment of doctoral degree graduates: Enrolled in a psychology doctoral program (n/a), enrolled in a postdoctoral residency/fellowship (5), employed in independent practice (3), employed in an academic position at a university (2), employed in other positions at a higher education institution (2), employed in business or industry (3), total from the above (doctoral) (15).

Additional Information:

Orientation, Objectives, and Emphasis of Department: The Department of Psychology at the University of Notre Dame is committed to excellence in psychological science and its applications. To realize this commitment a major focus is upon developing knowledge and expertise in the increasingly sophisticated methodology of the discipline. With this methodological core as its major emphasis and integrating link, the department has emphasized four content areas: cognitive, counseling, developmental, and quantitative psychology. In the context of the mores of the academy, the faculty of each content area organize and coordinate work in the three domains of research, graduate education, and undergraduate education. Using our methodological understandings as a base, we strive to find intellectual common ground among the content areas within our department and other disciplines throughout the social sciences and the academy.

Special Facilities or Resources: We are involved in the development of innovative science and practice experiences for undergraduate and graduate students in the local community. Currently, many faculty have excellent relationships with community groups (e.g., the local schools, hospitals, Madison Center, Logan center, Center for the Homeless, Head Start). Many faculty conduct research with undergraduate and graduate students in these settings. Over and above these research activities, many students volunteer in these agencies. Finally, counseling psychology graduate students receive supervision to work in Madison Center, Family and Children's Center, Michiana EAP, Oaklawn, St. Joseph Medical Center, and the Center for the Homeless and, in a new initiative, postdoctoral positions exist in the Multicultural Research Institute.

Information for Students With Physical Disabilities: See the following Web site for more information: http://www.nd.edu/~osd.

Application Information:

Send to Graduate Admissions, The Graduate School, University of Notre Dame, Notre Dame, IN 46556. Application available online. URL of online application: http://www.graduateschool.nd.edu/html/admissions/application-gateway.html. Students are admitted in the Fall, application deadline January 2. *Fee:* $50. In certain circumstances the Graduate School (at the address above) can approve the waiver of fees. Fee is $35 for applications received before December 1.

Purdue University

Department of Psychological Sciences
College of Liberal Arts
701 Third Street
West Lafayette, IN 47907-2884
Telephone: (765) 494-6067
Fax: (765) 496-1264
E-mail: *nobrien@psych.purdue.edu*
Web: *http://www.psych.purdue.edu*

Department Information:

1954. Professor and Head: Howard M. Weiss. Number of faculty: total—full-time 15, part-time 1; women—full-time 13, part-time 1; ; women minority—full-time 2.

Programs and Degrees Offered:

Listed in the following order: Program area, degree type (T if terminal Master's), number awarded 7/06–6/07. Clinical PhD (Doctor of Philosophy) 5, Cognitive PhD (Doctor of Philosophy) 3, Developmental PhD (Doctor of Philosophy) 3, Industrial/Organizational PhD (Doctor of Philosophy) 2, Learning and Memory PhD (Doctor of Philosophy) 0, Psychobiology PhD (Doctor of Philosophy) 1, Quantitative PhD (Doctor of Philosophy) 0, Social PhD (Doctor of Philosophy) 3, General PhD (Doctor of Philosophy) 1.

APA Accreditation: Clinical PhD (Doctor of Philosophy).

Student Applications/Admissions:

Student Applications

Clinical PhD (Doctor of Philosophy)—Applications 2007–2008, 127. Total applicants accepted 2007–2008, 6. Number full-time enrolled (new admits only) 2007–2008, 3. Number part-time enrolled (new admits only) 2007–2008, 0. Openings 2008–2009, 5. The median number of years required for completion of a degree in 2006–2007 were 5. The number of students enrolled full- and part-time who were dismissed or voluntarily withdrew from this program area in 2007–2008 were 0. *Cognitive PhD (Doctor of Philosophy)*—Applications 2007–2008, 11. Total applicants accepted 2007–2008, 1. Number full-time enrolled (new admits only) 2007–2008, 1. Number part-time enrolled (new admits only) 2007–2008, 0. Openings 2008–2009, 5. The median number of years required for completion of a degree in 2006–2007 were 5. The number of students enrolled full- and part-time who were dismissed or voluntarily withdrew from this program area in 2007–2008 were 0. *Developmental PhD (Doctor of Philosophy)*—Applications 2007–2008, 16. Total applicants accepted 2007–2008, 3. Number full-time enrolled (new admits only) 2007–2008, 2. Number part-time enrolled (new admits only) 2007–2008, 0. Openings 2008–2009, 2. The median number of years required for completion of a degree in 2006–2007 were 5. The number of students enrolled full- and part-time who were dismissed or voluntarily withdrew from this program area in 2007–2008 were 0. *Industrial/Organizational PhD (Doctor of Philosophy)*—Applications 2007–2008, 73. Total applicants accepted 2007–2008, 1. Number full-time enrolled (new admits only) 2007–2008, 0. Number part-time enrolled (new admits only) 2007–2008, 0. Openings 2008–2009, 2. The median number of years required for completion of a degree in 2006–2007 were 5. The number of students enrolled full- and part-time who were dismissed or voluntarily withdrew from this program area in 2007–2008 were 0. *Learning and Memory PhD (Doctor of Philosophy)*—Applications 2007–2008, 4. Total applicants accepted 2007–2008, 2. Number full-time enrolled (new admits only) 2007–2008, 1. Number part-time enrolled (new admits only) 2007–2008, 0. Openings 2008–2009, 2. The number of students enrolled full- and part-time who were dismissed or voluntarily withdrew from this program area in 2007–2008 were 0. *Psychobiology PhD (Doctor of Philosophy)*—Applications 2007–2008, 19. Total applicants accepted 2007–2008, 3. Number full-time enrolled (new admits only) 2007–2008, 2. Number part-time enrolled (new admits only) 2007–2008, 0. Openings 2008–2009, 5. The median number of years required for completion of a degree in 2006–2007 were 5. The number of students enrolled full- and part-time who were dismissed or voluntarily withdrew from this program area in 2007–2008 were 0. *Quantitative PhD (Doctor of Philosophy)*—Applications 2007–2008, 7. Total applicants accepted 2007–2008, 3. Number full-time enrolled (new admits only) 2007–2008, 0. Number part-time enrolled (new admits only) 2007–2008, 0. Openings 2008–2009, 3. The number of students enrolled full- and part-time who were dismissed or voluntarily withdrew from this program area in 2007–2008 were 0. *Social*

PhD (Doctor of Philosophy)—Applications 2007–2008, 87. Total applicants accepted 2007–2008, 4. Number full-time enrolled (new admits only) 2007–2008, 3. Number part-time enrolled (new admits only) 2007–2008, 0. Openings 2008–2009, 3. The median number of years required for completion of a degree in 2006–2007 were 5. The number of students enrolled full- and part-time who were dismissed or voluntarily withdrew from this program area in 2007–2008 were 0. *General PhD (Doctor of Philosophy)*—Applications 2007–2008, 0. Total applicants accepted 2007–2008, 0. Number full-time enrolled (new admits only) 2007–2008, 0. The median number of years required for completion of a degree in 2006–2007 were 5. The number of students enrolled full- and part-time who were dismissed or voluntarily withdrew from this program area in 2007–2008 were 0.

Admissions Requirements:

Scores: Entries appear in this order: required test or GPA, minimum score (if required), median score of students entering in 2007–2008. Doctoral Programs: GRE-V no minimum stated, 580; GRE-Q no minimum stated, 675; overall undergraduate GPA 3.0, 3.68; Doctoral program GRE-Analytic no minimum stated, 5.0.

Other Criteria: (importance of criteria rated low, medium, or high): GRE/MAT scores—high, research experience—medium, work experience—low, extracurricular activity—low, clinically related public service—high, GPA—high, letters of recommendation—high, interview—high, statement of goals and objectives—high. Not all areas hold formal interviews. Clinically related public service is important if you are applying to the clinical program. For additional information on admission requirements, go to http://www.psych.purdue.edu.

Student Characteristics: The following represents characteristics of students in 2007–2008 in all graduate psychology programs in the department: Female—full-time 72, part-time 0; Male—full-time 31, part-time 0; African American/Black—full-time 10, part-time 0; Hispanic/Latino(a)—full-time 4, part-time 0; Asian/Pacific Islander—full-time 7, part-time 0; American Indian/Alaska Native—full-time 0, part-time 0; Caucasian/White—full-time 62, part-time 0; Multi-ethnic—full-time 20, part-time 0; students subject to the Americans With Disabilities Act—full-time 1, part-time 0; Unknown ethnicity—full-time 0, part-time 0; International students who hold an F-1 or J-1 Visa—full-time 20, part-time 0.

Financial Information/Assistance:

Financial Assistance:

First-Year Students: Teaching assistantships available for first year. Average number of hours worked per week: 20. Apply by December 20. Tuition remission given: full. Research assistantships available for first year. Average number of hours worked per week: 20. Apply by December 20. Tuition remission given: full. Fellowships and scholarships available for first year. Apply by December 20. Tuition remission given: full.

Advanced Students: Teaching assistantships available for advanced students. Average number of hours worked per week: 20. Tuition remission given: full. Research assistantships available for advanced students. Average number of hours worked per week: 20. Tuition remission given: full. Fellowships and scholarships available for advanced students. Average number of hours worked per week: 20. Tuition remission given: full.

Additional Information: Of all students currently enrolled full time, 100% benefited from one or more of the listed financial assistance programs. Application and information available online at http://www.gradschool.purdue.edu/admissions/.

Internships/Practica: Doctoral Degree (PhD Clinical): For those doctoral students for whom a professional internship was required in this program prior to graduation, (5) students applied for an internship in 2006–2007, with (5) students obtaining an internship. Of those students who obtained an internship, (5) were paid internships. Of those students who obtained an internship, (5) students placed in APA/CPA-accredited internships, (0) students placed in internships not APA/CPA-accredited, but listed with the Association of Psychology Postdoctoral and Internship Centers (APPIC), (0) students placed in internships conforming to guidelines of the Council of Directors of School Psychology Programs (CDSPP), (0) students placed in internships that were not APA/CPA-accredited, APPIC or CDSPP listed. After the first-year requirements, clinical psychology students enroll in clinical practica carried out in the Purdue Psychology Treatment and Research Clinics. Practica include providing services for anxiety disorders, depression, personality disorders, Attention Deficit Hyperactivity Disorder, and oppositional disorders. Practicum training emphasizes use of empirically corroborated interventions for particular problems. A year-long clinical internship is required in order to complete training.

Housing and Day Care: On-campus housing is available. See the following Web site for more information: http://www.housing.purdue.edu. No on-campus day care facilities are available.

Employment of Department Graduates:

Master's Degree Graduates: Of those who graduated in the academic year 2006–2007, the following categories and numbers represent the postgraduate activities and employment of master's degree graduates: Enrolled in a postdoctoral residency/fellowship (n/a), employed in independent practice (n/a), total from the above (master's) (0).

Doctoral Degree Graduates: Of those who graduated in the academic year 2006–2007, the following categories and numbers represent the postgraduate activities and employment of doctoral degree graduates: Enrolled in a psychology doctoral program (n/a), total from the above (doctoral) (0).

Additional Information:

Orientation, Objectives, and Emphasis of Department: The dominant emphasis of the department is a commitment to research and scholarship as the major core of graduate education. All programs are structured so that students become involved in research activities almost immediately upon beginning their graduate education, and this involvement is expected to continue throughout an individual's entire graduate career.

Special Facilities or Resources: The department moved into the new psychological sciences building in 1980. Excellent research facilities are available in many areas, including more than 35 computer-controlled laboratories.

Information for Students With Physical Disabilities: See the following Web site for more information: http://www.psych.purdue.edu.

Application Information:
Send to Nancy O'Brien, Administrative Assistant, Psychological Sciences, 701 Third Street, Purdue University, West Lafayette, IN 47907-2004 USA. Application available online. URL of online application: http://www.gradschool.purdue.edu/admissions. Students are admitted in the Fall, application deadline December 20. *Fee:* $55.

Saint Francis, University of

Psychology and Counseling
School of Professional Studies
2701 Spring Street
Fort Wayne, IN 46808
Telephone: (260) 399-7700 ext 8422
Fax: (260) 399-8170
E-mail: *mfriedmeyer@sf.edu*
Web: *http://www.sf.edu*

Department Information:
1971. Chairperson: Mark H. Friedmeyer, MS. Number of faculty: total—full-time 5, part-time 4; women—full-time 1, part-time 3; minority—part-time 1; women minority—part-time 1.

Programs and Degrees Offered:
Listed in the following order: Program area, degree type (T if terminal Master's), number awarded 7/06–6/07. General Psychology MA/MS (Master of Arts/Science) (T) 6, Mental Health Counseling MA/MS (Master of Arts/Science) (T) 5, Pastoral Counseling MA/MS (Master of Arts/Science) 0, Advanced Certificate in Pastoral Counseling MA/MS (Master of Arts/Science) 2, School Counseling Other 4.

Student Applications/Admissions:
Student Applications
General Psychology MA/MS (Master of Arts/Science)—Applications 2007–2008, 9. Total applicants accepted 2007–2008, 8. Number full-time enrolled (new admits only) 2007–2008, 3. Number part-time enrolled (new admits only) 2007–2008, 5. Total enrolled 2007–2008 full-time, 4, part-time, 17. Openings 2008–2009, 8. The median number of years required for completion of a degree in 2006–2007 were 2. The number of students enrolled full- and part-time who were dismissed or voluntarily withdrew from this program area in 2007–2008 were 0. *Mental Health Counseling MA/MS (Master of Arts/Science)*—Applications 2007–2008, 9. Total applicants accepted 2007–2008, 7. Number full-time enrolled (new admits only) 2007–2008, 3. Number part-time enrolled (new admits only) 2007–2008, 4. Total enrolled 2007–2008 full-time, 16, part-time, 18. Openings 2008–2009, 8. The median number of years required for completion of a degree in 2006–2007 were 3. The number of students enrolled full- and part-time who were dismissed or voluntarily withdrew from this program area in 2007–2008 were 0. *Pastoral Counseling MA/MS (Master of Arts/Science)*—Applications 2007–2008, 0. Total applicants accepted 2007–2008, 0. Number full-time enrolled (new admits only) 2007–2008, 0. Number part-time enrolled (new admits only) 2007–2008, 0. Openings 2008–2009, 8. The median number of years required for completion of a degree in 2006–2007 was 1. The number of students enrolled full- and part-time who were dismissed or voluntarily withdrew from this program area in 2007–2008 were 0. *Advanced Certificate in Pastoral Counseling MA/MS (Master of Arts/Science)*—Applications 2007–2008, 0. Total applicants accepted 2007–2008, 0. Number full-time enrolled (new admits only) 2007–2008, 0. Number part-time enrolled (new admits only) 2007–2008, 0. Openings 2008–2009, 10. The median number of years required for completion of a degree in 2006–2007 was 1. The number of students enrolled full- and part-time who were dismissed or voluntarily withdrew from this program area in 2007–2008 were 0. *School Counseling Other*—Applications 2007–2008, 6. Total applicants accepted 2007–2008, 5. Number full-time enrolled (new admits only) 2007–2008, 2. Number part-time enrolled (new admits only) 2007–2008, 3. Total enrolled 2007–2008 full-time, 9, part-time, 16. Openings 2008–2009, 8. The median number of years required for completion of a degree in 2006–2007 were 2. The number of students enrolled full- and part-time who were dismissed or voluntarily withdrew from this program area in 2007–2008 were 0.

Admissions Requirements:
Scores: Entries appear in this order: required test or GPA, minimum score (if required), median score of students entering in 2007–2008. Master's Programs: overall undergraduate GPA 3.0, 3.3.
Other Criteria: (importance of criteria rated low, medium, or high): GRE/MAT scores—medium, research experience—medium, work experience—high, extracurricular activity—low, clinically related public service—high, GPA—high, letters of recommendation—high, interview—high, statement of goals and objectives—high, undergraduate major in psychology—high, specific undergraduate psychology courses taken—high.

Student Characteristics: The following represents characteristics of students in 2007–2008 in all graduate psychology programs in the department: Female—full-time 34, part-time 41; Male—full-time 5, part-time 4; African American/Black—full-time 1, part-time 4; Hispanic/Latino(a)—full-time 2, part-time 1; Asian/Pacific Islander—full-time 0, part-time 0; American Indian/Alaska Native—full-time 1, part-time 0; Caucasian/White—full-time 35, part-time 40; Multi-ethnic—full-time 0, part-time 0; students subject to the Americans With Disabilities Act—full-time 2, part-time 1; Unknown ethnicity—full-time 0, part-time 0.

Financial Information/Assistance:
Tuition for Full-Time Study: *Master's:* State residents: $660 per credit hour; Nonstate residents: $660 per credit hour.

Financial Assistance:
First-Year Students: Teaching assistantships available for first year. Average amount paid per academic year: $5,940. Average number of hours worked per week: 10. Apply by June 30.
Advanced Students: Teaching assistantships available for advanced students. Average amount paid per academic year: $5,940. Average number of hours worked per week: 10. Apply by June 30.

Additional Information: Of all students currently enrolled full time, 15% benefited from one or more of the listed financial assistance programs.

Internships/Practica: General Psychology Students can elect to do a practicum experience. This experience would be 150 clock hours (10 hours/week) of supervised practical field experience tailored to the individual needs and interests of the students. Students choosing to have a practicum experience have an "on-site" supervisor who helps define, mentor, and direct the student's activities. Students also have 15 hours of supervision on campus. This experience is designed to give students an opportunity to integrate formal education with work experience. Mental Health Counseling (MS) has required practicum and internship: Practicum: one semester of 100 hours/ 60 face-to-face client contact hours. Internship: one or two semesters of 600 hours/240 face-to-face client contact hours. Advanced Internship: one semester of 300 hours/120 face-to-face client contact hours.

Housing and Day Care: On-campus housing is available. See the following Web site for more information: http://www.sf.edu. No on-campus day care facilities are available.

Employment of Department Graduates:

Master's Degree Graduates: Of those who graduated in the academic year 2006–2007, the following categories and numbers represent the postgraduate activities and employment of master's degree graduates: Enrolled in a psychology doctoral program (3), enrolled in another graduate/professional program (0), enrolled in a postdoctoral residency/fellowship (n/a), employed in independent practice (n/a), employed in an academic position at a university (0), employed in an academic position at a 2-year/4-year college (0), employed in other positions at a higher education institution (0), employed in a professional position in a school system (4), employed in business or industry (0), employed in government agency (0), employed in a community mental health/counseling center (8), employed in a hospital/medical center (2), still seeking employment (0), other employment position (0), total from the above (master's) (17).

Doctoral Degree Graduates: Of those who graduated in the academic year 2006–2007, the following categories and numbers represent the postgraduate activities and employment of doctoral degree graduates: Enrolled in a psychology doctoral program (n/a), total from the above (doctoral) (0).

Additional Information:

Orientation, Objectives, and Emphasis of Department: The MS in Psychology Program is designed for people who are either interested in preparation for doctoral work or furthering their professional careers through a greater understanding of basic psychological principles. The primary goal of the program is to give students a solid, graduate-level grounding in psychology. This program emphasizes a mastery of psychological fundamentals, that is, theories and research methods, areas of specialization (development, social, abnormal behavior, physiological data, personality development, and behavior management techniques). Mental Health Counseling (MS): The program of study leading to the MS Degree in Mental Health Counseling is designed to prepare persons to function as Licensed Mental Health Counselors (LMHC) in health care residential, private practice, community agency, governmental, business, and industrial settings. The scope of practice for mental health counseling is defined in Section 24. IC 25-23.6-1-7.5 of the Indiana Code, which is available from the Psychology and Counseling Department. To successfully complete the MS in Mental Health Counseling, students will (a) Demonstrate ability to analyze, synthesize, and critique in a scholarly manner academic subject matter, professional journal articles, and other professional resources. Students will demonstrate ability to write coherently and professionally according to the Publication Manual of the American Psychological Association (4th edition) standards. (b) Promote and adhere to the standards/guidelines for ethical and professional conduct in all classroom and field experiences (i.e., American Counseling Association's Ethical Standards for Mental Health Professionals, and the American Psychological Association's Ethical Principles), as well as legal mandates regarding the practice of their profession. (c) Demonstrate an ability to synthesize, evaluate, and articulate broad knowledge of counseling theories and approaches. This will include an ability to apply scientific and measurement principles to the study of psychology. (d) Develop a capacity to communicate respect, empathy, and unconditional positive regard toward others, including demonstration of a tolerant, nonjudgmental attitude toward different ethnic/cultural heritage, value orientations, and lifestyles. (e) Recognize and effectively conceptualize the special needs of persons with varying mental, adjustment, developmental and/or chemical dependence disorders. Students will recognize the need for, request, and benefit from consultation and supervision when practicing in areas of insufficient competence. (f) Demonstrate competence to counsel/interview using basic listening and influencing skills in one-to-one, marital, family, and group counseling modalities. (g) Be prepared to seek employment as a Licensed Mental Health Counselor, enter a program of additional education/training, and/or seek other appropriate certifications. The MS in Pastoral Counseling program is designed for active members of the clergy with a minimum of a Bachelor's degree from an accredited college The program consists of three parts: a core of clinical courses (18 hours) in psychology, a foundation in Pastoral Counseling (27 hours), and elective courses (6 hours). Upon completion of nine additional credits, Master's degree students can quailfy to take the examination for licensure as a Licensed Professional Counselor. The Advanced Certificate in Pastroal Counseling is available for licensed mental health professionals, such as licensed clinical social workers, licensed mental health counselors, licensed marriage and family therapists, and licensed psychologists. The certificate program includes six courses (18 hours): Pastoral Theological Methods, History of Pastoral Care and Counseling, Pastoral Diagnosis, Franciscan Intellectual and Spiritual Tradition, Spirituality and Spiritual Formation, and Pastoral Care Specialist Training.

Application Information:

Send to Office of Admissions, Trinity Hall, Room 110A, University of Saint Francis, Fort Wayne, IN 46808. Application available online. URL of online application: http://www.sf.edu. Students are admitted in the Fall, application deadline; Winter, application deadline; Spring, application deadline; Summer, application deadline; Programs have rolling admissions. *Fee:* $20.

Valparaiso University

Department of Psychology
Arts and Sciences, Graduate Division
Dickmeyer Hall
Valparaiso, IN 46383
Telephone: (219) 464-5440
Fax: (219) 464-6878
E-mail: *daniel.arkkelin@valpo.edu*
Web: *http://www.valpo.edu/psych/graduate*

Department Information:

1958. Chairperson: Daniel Arkkelin. Number of faculty: total—full-time 9, part-time 4; women—full-time 3, part-time 3; total—minority—full-time 1; women minority—full-time 1.

Programs and Degrees Offered:

Listed in the following order: Program area, degree type (T if terminal Master's), number awarded 7/06–6/07. Counseling and Clinical Mental Health Counseling MA/MS (Master of Arts/Science) (T) 7, Psychology/Law MA/MS (Master of Arts/Science) 1.

Student Applications/Admissions:

Student Applications

Counseling and Clinical Mental Health Counseling MA/MS (Master of Arts/Science)—Applications 2007–2008, 88. Total applicants accepted 2007–2008, 17. Number full-time enrolled (new admits only) 2007–2008, 15. Number part-time enrolled (new admits only) 2007–2008, 4. Total enrolled 2007–2008 full-time, 39, part-time, 14. Openings 2008–2009, 25. The median number of years required for completion of a degree in 2006–2007 were 3. The number of students enrolled full- and part-time who were dismissed or voluntarily withdrew from this program area in 2007–2008 were 1. *Psychology/Law MA/MS (Master of Arts/Science)*—Applications 2007–2008, 30. Total applicants accepted 2007–2008, 9. Number full-time enrolled (new admits only) 2007–2008, 3. Number part-time enrolled (new admits only) 2007–2008, 1. Total enrolled 2007–2008 full-time, 3, part-time, 9. Openings 2008–2009, 5. The median number of years required for completion of a degree in 2006–2007 were 4. The number of students enrolled full- and part-time who were dismissed or voluntarily withdrew from this program area in 2007–2008 were 0.

Admissions Requirements:

Scores: Entries appear in this order: required test or GPA, minimum score (if required), median score of students entering in 2007–2008. Master's Programs: overall undergraduate GPA 3.0, 3.50.

Other Criteria: (importance of criteria rated low, medium, or high): research experience—medium, work experience—high, extracurricular activity—low, clinically related public service—medium, GPA—high, letters of recommendation—high, interview—medium, statement of goals and objectives—high, specific undergraduate psychology courses taken—low. Students applying for the joint programs in law and psychology must be admitted to both the Valparaiso University School of Law and the psychology or counseling graduate program. For additional information on admission requirements, go to http://www.valpo.edu/gce/graduate/admissions.php.

Student Characteristics: The following represents characteristics of students in 2007–2008 in all graduate psychology programs in the department: Female—full-time 32, part-time 14; Male—full-time 10, part-time 9; African American/Black—full-time 2, part-time 0; Hispanic/Latino(a)—full-time 1, part-time 0; Asian/Pacific Islander—full-time 0, part-time 0; American Indian/Alaska Native—full-time 0, part-time 0; Caucasian/White—full-time 42, part-time 12; Multi-ethnic—full-time 1, part-time 0; students subject to the Americans With Disabilities Act—full-time 1, part-time 0; Unknown ethnicity—full-time 0, part-time 1; International students who hold an F-1 or J-1 Visa—full-time 5, part-time 1.

Financial Information/Assistance:

Tuition for Full-Time Study: *Master's:* State residents: $420 per credit hour; Nonstate residents: $420 per credit hour. See the following Web site for updates and changes in tuition costs: http://www.valpo.edu/gce/graduate/costs.php. Higher tuition cost for this program: Students in the Psychology/Law program pay Law School tuition rate for law courses.

Financial Assistance:

First-Year Students: Teaching assistantships available for first year. Average amount paid per academic year: $1,000. Average number of hours worked per week: 10. Apply by March 1. Research assistantships available for first year. Average amount paid per academic year: $2,000. Average number of hours worked per week: 10. Apply by March 1. Traineeships available for first year. Average amount paid per academic year: $8,000. Average number of hours worked per week: 20. Apply by March 1. Tuition remission given: partial.

Advanced Students: Teaching assistantships available for advanced students. Average amount paid per academic year: $1,000. Average number of hours worked per week: 10. Apply by March 1. Research assistantships available for advanced students. Average amount paid per academic year: $2,000. Average number of hours worked per week: 10. Apply by March 1. Traineeships available for advanced students. Average amount paid per academic year: $8,000. Average number of hours worked per week: 20. Apply by March 1. Tuition remission given: partial.

Additional Information: Of all students currently enrolled full time, 30% benefited from one or more of the listed financial assistance programs. Application and information available online at http://www.valpo.edu/gce/graduate/.

Internships/Practica: Counseling and clinical mental health counseling students obtain practical training (practica and internships) in a variety of mental health settings in Northwest Indiana.

Housing and Day Care: No on-campus housing is available. No on-campus day care facilities are available.

Employment of Department Graduates:

Master's Degree Graduates: Of those who graduated in the academic year 2006–2007, the following categories and numbers represent the postgraduate activities and employment of master's degree graduates: Enrolled in a psychology doctoral program (1), enrolled in another graduate/professional program (1), enrolled in a postdoctoral residency/fellowship (n/a), employed in independent practice (n/a), employed in an academic position at a 2-year/4-year college (1), employed in a community mental health/

counseling center (4), still seeking employment (1), total from the above (master's) (8).

Doctoral Degree Graduates: Of those who graduated in the academic year 2006–2007, the following categories and numbers represent the postgraduate activities and employment of doctoral degree graduates: Enrolled in a psychology doctoral program (n/a), total from the above (doctoral) (0).

Additional Information:

Orientation, Objectives, and Emphasis of Department: The counseling program is designed to provide advanced training to persons planning or continuing in a counseling career. The program combines a strong theoretical background in counseling with applied work through both coursework and supervised practica. A thesis option is available. The clinical mental health counseling program is designed to lead toward licensure or certification in most of the 50 states. It involves additional coursework and experiential requirements. The JD/MA program provides traditional legal training, exposure to psychological theory and methods and integrated training in the application of psychological foundations to the practice of law. The program is offered jointly by the law school and psychology department. The JD/MA in clinical mental health counseling combines legal training and training in clinical mental health counseling, and is designed to lead to licensure or certification as a counselor in most of the 50 states.

Special Facilities or Resources: The Department maintains strong contacts with community and regional agencies involved in mental health and counseling as well as with the campus counseling center. In addition, an in-house clinical training lab utilizing audio- and videotaping may be used in student training of clinical skills. Extensive computer facilities and networks are available in the department and throughout campus.

Information for Students With Physical Disabilities: See the following Web site for more information: http://www.valpo.edu/cas/dss.

Application Information:

Send to Office of Graduate Studies, Kretzmann Hall, Valparaiso University, Valparaiso, IN 46383. Application available online. URL of online application: http://www.valpo.edu/gce/forms/main.htm. Students are admitted in the Fall, application deadline March 1. *Fee:* $30. Application fee for the dual programs in law and psychology is $20.

Iowa State University

Department of Psychology
Liberal Arts and Sciences
Lagomarcino Hall
Ames, IA 50011-3180
Telephone: (515) 294-1742
Fax: (515) 294-6424
E-mail: *dvogel@iastate.edu*
Web: *http://www.psychology.iastate.edu/*

Department Information:

1924. Chair: Doug G. Bonett. Number of faculty: total—full-time 25, part-time 6; women—full-time 9, part-time 3; total—minority—full-time 4; women minority—full-time 1.

Programs and Degrees Offered:

Listed in the following order: Program area, degree type (T if terminal Master's), number awarded 7/06–6/07. Counseling PhD (Doctor of Philosophy) 4, Social PhD (Doctor of Philosophy) 1, Cognitive PhD (Doctor of Philosophy) 1.

APA Accreditation: Counseling PhD (Doctor of Philosophy).

Student Applications/Admissions:

Student Applications

Counseling PhD (Doctor of Philosophy)—Applications 2007–2008, 57. Total applicants accepted 2007–2008, 7. Number full-time enrolled (new admits only) 2007–2008, 5. Number part-time enrolled (new admits only) 2007–2008, 0. Openings 2008–2009, 5. The median number of years required for completion of a degree in 2006–2007 were 5. The number of students enrolled full- and part-time who were dismissed or voluntarily withdrew from this program area in 2007–2008 were 0. *Social PhD (Doctor of Philosophy)*—Applications 2007–2008, 23. Total applicants accepted 2007–2008, 6. Number full-time enrolled (new admits only) 2007–2008, 4. Number part-time enrolled (new admits only) 2007–2008, 0. Openings 2008–2009, 2. The median number of years required for completion of a degree in 2006–2007 were 6. The number of students enrolled full- and part-time who were dismissed or voluntarily withdrew from this program area in 2007–2008 were 0. *Cognitive PhD (Doctor of Philosophy)*—Applications 2007–2008, 16. Total applicants accepted 2007–2008, 3. Number full-time enrolled (new admits only) 2007–2008, 2. Number part-time enrolled (new admits only) 2007–2008, 0. Openings 2008–2009, 4. The median number of years required for completion of a degree in 2006–2007 were 6. The number of students enrolled full- and part-time who were dismissed or voluntarily withdrew from this program area in 2007–2008 were 0.

Admissions Requirements:

Scores: Entries appear in this order: required test or GPA, minimum score (if required), median score of students entering in 2007–2008. Master's Programs: GRE-V no minimum stated; GRE-Q no minimum stated; GRE-Subject (Psychology) no minimum stated; overall undergraduate GPA no minimum stated; last 2 years GPA no minimum stated; psychology GPA no minimum stated. Doctoral Programs: GRE-V no minimum stated, 615; GRE-Q no minimum stated, 710; GRE-Subject (Psychology) no minimum stated, 630; overall undergraduate GPA no minimum stated, 3.79; psychology GPA no minimum stated, 3.83. TOEFL required for international applicants.

Other Criteria: (importance of criteria rated low, medium, or high): GRE/MAT scores—high, research experience—high, work experience—low, extracurricular activity—low, clinically related public service—low, GPA—high, letters of recommendation—high, interview—high, statement of goals and objectives—high, fit with faculty research—high, undergraduate major in psychology—medium, specific undergraduate psychology courses taken—medium. For additional information on admission requirements, go to http://www.psychology.iastate.edu.

Student Characteristics: The following represents characteristics of students in 2007–2008 in all graduate psychology programs in the department: Female—full-time 43, part-time 0; Male—full-time 21, part-time 0; African American/Black—full-time 4, part-time 0; Hispanic/Latino(a)—full-time 0, part-time 0; Asian/Pacific Islander—full-time 4, part-time 0; American Indian/Alaska Native—full-time 0, part-time 0; Caucasian/White—full-time 50, part-time 0; Multi-ethnic—full-time 0, part-time 0; students subject to the Americans With Disabilities Act—full-time 0, part-time 0; Unknown ethnicity—full-time 0, part-time 0; International students who hold an F-1 or J-1 Visa—full-time 6, part-time 0.

Financial Information/Assistance:

Tuition for Full-Time Study: *Doctoral:* State residents: per academic year $6,246, $345 per credit hour; Nonstate residents: per academic year $6,246, $345 per credit hour. Tuition is subject to change. See the following Web site for updates and changes in tuition costs: http://www.iastate.edu/~registrar/fees/.

Financial Assistance:

First-Year Students: Teaching assistantships available for first year. Average amount paid per academic year: $12,200. Average number of hours worked per week: 20. Apply by January 2. Tuition remission given: full. Research assistantships available for first year. Average amount paid per academic year: $12,200. Average number of hours worked per week: 20. Apply by January 2. Tuition remission given: full. Fellowships and scholarships available for first year. Average amount paid per academic year: $12,200. Average number of hours worked per week: 20. Apply by January 2. Tuition remission given: full.

Advanced Students: Teaching assistantships available for advanced students. Average amount paid per academic year: $12,200. Average number of hours worked per week: 20. Tuition remission given: full. Research assistantships available for advanced students. Average amount paid per academic year: $12,200. Average number of hours worked per week: 20. Tuition remission given: full.

Additional Information: Of all students currently enrolled full time, 100% benefited from one or more of the listed financial

assistance programs. Application and information available online at http://www.psychology.iastate.edu.

Internships/Practica: Doctoral Degree (PhD Counseling): For those doctoral students for whom a professional internship was required in this program prior to graduation, (6) students applied for an internship in 2006–2007, with (6) students obtaining an internship. Of those students who obtained an internship, (6) were paid internships. Of those students who obtained an internship, (6) students placed in APA/CPA-accredited internships, (0) students placed in internships not APA/CPA-accredited, but listed with the Association of Psychology Postdoctoral and Internship Centers (APPIC), (0) students placed in internships conforming to guidelines of the Council of Directors of School Psychology Programs (CDSPP), (0) students placed in internships that were not APA/CPA-accredited, APPIC or CDSPP listed. Sequential, progressive practica provide students in our professional programs with individually supervised applied training in their specialty area. All supervision is provided by appropriately certified/licensed faculty and adjuncts in a range of settings, including university counseling centers, major hospitals, outpatient clinics, child and adolescent treatment centers, correctional facilities, and the public school system. Based on such practica experience and their academic training, ISU students compete successfully for select predoctoral internships across the country.

Housing and Day Care: On-campus housing is available. See the following Web site for more information: http://www.iastate.edu/~dor/living.html. On-campus day care facilities are available. See the following Web site for more information: http://www.hrs.iastate.edu/childcare/homepage.shtml.

Employment of Department Graduates:

Master's Degree Graduates: Of those who graduated in the academic year 2006–2007, the following categories and numbers represent the postgraduate activities and employment of master's degree graduates: Enrolled in a psychology doctoral program (0), enrolled in another graduate/professional program (0), enrolled in a postdoctoral residency/fellowship (n/a), employed in independent practice (n/a), employed in an academic position at a university (0), employed in an academic position at a 2-year/4-year college (2), employed in other positions at a higher education institution (0), employed in a professional position in a school system (0), employed in business or industry (0), employed in government agency (0), employed in a community mental health/counseling center (0), employed in a hospital/medical center (0), still seeking employment (0), not seeking employment (0), other employment position (1), do not know (0), total from the above (master's) (3).

Doctoral Degree Graduates: Of those who graduated in the academic year 2006–2007, the following categories and numbers represent the postgraduate activities and employment of doctoral degree graduates: Enrolled in a psychology doctoral program (n/a), enrolled in another graduate/professional program (0), enrolled in a postdoctoral residency/fellowship (2), employed in independent practice (0), employed in an academic position at a university (0), employed in an academic position at a 2-year/4-year college (1), employed in other positions at a higher education institution (1), employed in a professional position in a school system (0), employed in business or industry (0), employed in government agency (0), employed in a community mental health/counseling center (0), employed in a hospital/medical center (0), still seeking employment (0), not seeking employment (0), other employment position (1), do not know (0), total from the above (doctoral) (5).

Additional Information:

Orientation, Objectives, and Emphasis of Department: Graduate programs emphasize the acquisition of a broad base of knowledge in psychology as well as concentration on the content and methodological skills requisite to performance in teaching, research, and applied activities. A strong research orientation is evident in all areas of the department, with involvement in research being required of all doctoral students throughout their graduate studies. Curriculum requirements for the degrees are based on a core course system, which is designed to enable students to tailor a program best suited to their particular objectives. Subsequent courses, seminars, research, and applied experiences are determined by the student and his or her graduate advisory committee. Additionally, teaching experience is available to all doctoral students, and extensive supervised practica experience is required of students in the applied programs.

Special Facilities or Resources: The department maintains the full array of physical facilities and equipment required for behavioral research. Observational and videotaping facilities are available for research and applied training. The department maintains a microcomputer lab, and the university maintains a superior computation center.

Application Information:

Send to Iowa State University, Graduate Admissions, Department of Psychology, W112 Lagomarcino, Ames, IA 50011. Application available online. URL of online application: http://www.psychology.iastate.edu. Students are admitted in the Fall, application deadline January 2. *Fee:* $30; $70 fee for international application (paper application).

Iowa, University of

Department of Psychology
Liberal Arts and Sciences
11 Seashore Hall East
Iowa City, IA 52242-1407
Telephone: (319) 335-2406
Fax: (319) 335-0191
E-mail: *alan-christensen@uiowa.edu*
Web: *http://www.psychology.uiowa.edu.*

Department Information:

1887. Chairperson: Alan J. Christensen. Number of faculty: total—full-time 35, part-time 5; women—full-time 10, part-time 2; total—minority—full-time 1, part-time 1; women minority—part-time 1.

Programs and Degrees Offered:

Listed in the following order: Program area, degree type (T if terminal Master's), number awarded 7/06–6/07. Behavioral and Cognitive Neuroscience PhD (Doctor of Philosophy) 0, Clinical PhD (Doctor of Philosophy) 2, Cognition and Perception PhD (Doctor of Philosophy) 2, Developmental Science PhD (Doctor of Philosophy) 0, Personality and Social PhD (Doctor of Philosophy) 2, Health PhD (Doctor of Philosophy) 0.

APA Accreditation: Clinical PhD (Doctor of Philosophy).

Student Applications/Admissions:

Student Applications

Behavioral and Cognitive Neuroscience PhD (Doctor of Philosophy)—Applications 2007–2008, 26. Total applicants accepted 2007–2008, 6. Number full-time enrolled (new admits only) 2007–2008, 2. Number part-time enrolled (new admits only) 2007–2008, 0. Openings 2008–2009, 3. The number of students enrolled full- and part-time who were dismissed or voluntarily withdrew from this program area in 2007–2008 were 0. *Clinical PhD (Doctor of Philosophy)*—Applications 2007–2008, 63. Total applicants accepted 2007–2008, 8. Number full-time enrolled (new admits only) 2007–2008, 3. Number part-time enrolled (new admits only) 2007–2008, 0. Openings 2008–2009, 4. The median number of years required for completion of a degree in 2006–2007 were 6. The number of students enrolled full- and part-time who were dismissed or voluntarily withdrew from this program area in 2007–2008 were 0. *Cognition and Perception PhD (Doctor of Philosophy)*—Applications 2007–2008, 25. Total applicants accepted 2007–2008, 4. Number full-time enrolled (new admits only) 2007–2008, 3. Number part-time enrolled (new admits only) 2007–2008, 0. Openings 2008–2009, 3. The median number of years required for completion of a degree in 2006–2007 were 6. The number of students enrolled full- and part-time who were dismissed or voluntarily withdrew from this program area in 2007–2008 were 0. *Developmental Science PhD (Doctor of Philosophy)*—Applications 2007–2008, 9. Total applicants accepted 2007–2008, 3. Number full-time enrolled (new admits only) 2007–2008, 1. Number part-time enrolled (new admits only) 2007–2008, 0. Openings 2008–2009, 3. The number of students enrolled full- and part-time who were dismissed or voluntarily withdrew from this program area in 2007–2008 were 0. *Personality and Social PhD (Doctor of Philosophy)*—Applications 2007–2008, 31. Total applicants accepted 2007–2008, 2. Number full-time enrolled (new admits only) 2007–2008, 2. Number part-time enrolled (new admits only) 2007–2008, 0. Openings 2008–2009, 3. The median number of years required for completion of a degree in 2006–2007 were 7. The number of students enrolled full- and part-time who were dismissed or voluntarily withdrew from this program area in 2007–2008 were 2. *Health PhD (Doctor of Philosophy)*—Applications 2007–2008, 14. Total applicants accepted 2007–2008, 1. Number full-time enrolled (new admits only) 2007–2008, 1. Number part-time enrolled (new admits only) 2007–2008, 0. Openings 2008–2009, 2. The number of students enrolled full- and part-time who were dismissed or voluntarily withdrew from this program area in 2007–2008 were 0.

Admissions Requirements:

Scores: Entries appear in this order: required test or GPA, minimum score (if required), median score of students entering in 2007–2008. Doctoral Programs: GRE-V no minimum stated, 620; GRE-Q no minimum stated, 670; overall undergraduate GPA no minimum stated; last 2 years GPA no minimum stated; psychology GPA no minimum stated.

Other Criteria: (importance of criteria rated low, medium, or high): GRE/MAT scores—high, research experience—high, work experience—low, extracurricular activity—low, clinically related public service—medium, GPA—high, letters of recommendation—high, interview—high, statement of goals and objectives—high. Formal interviews are required for most but not all areas (contact the department for more information). For additional information on admission requirements, go to http://www.psychology.uiowa.edu.

Student Characteristics: The following represents characteristics of students in 2007–2008 in all graduate psychology programs in the department: Female—full-time 62, part-time 0; Male—full-time 36, part-time 0; African American/Black—full-time 3, part-time 0; Hispanic/Latino(a)—full-time 10, part-time 0; Asian/Pacific Islander—full-time 8, part-time 0; American Indian/Alaska Native—full-time 0, part-time 0; Caucasian/White—full-time 77, part-time 0; Multi-ethnic—full-time 0, part-time 0; students subject to the Americans With Disabilities Act—full-time 1, part-time 0; Unknown ethnicity—full-time 0, part-time 0; International students who hold an F-1 or J-1 Visa—full-time 6, part-time 0.

Financial Information/Assistance:

Tuition for Full-Time Study: *Doctoral:* State residents: per academic year $6,819; Nonstate residents: per academic year $19,144. Tuition is subject to change. See the following Web site for updates and changes in tuition costs: http://www.registrar.uiowa.edu/tuition/.

Financial Assistance:

First-Year Students: Teaching assistantships available for first year. Average amount paid per academic year: $19,894. Average number of hours worked per week: 20. Tuition remission given: partial. Research assistantships available for first year. Average amount paid per academic year: $19,894. Average number of hours worked per week: 20. Tuition remission given: partial. Fellowships and scholarships available for first year. Average amount paid per academic year: $21,000. Average number of hours worked per week: 0. Tuition remission given: full.

Advanced Students: Teaching assistantships available for advanced students. Average amount paid per academic year: $20,016. Average number of hours worked per week: 20. Tuition remission given: partial. Research assistantships available for advanced students. Average amount paid per academic year: $20,016. Average number of hours worked per week: 20. Tuition remission given: partial. Fellowships and scholarships available for advanced students. Average amount paid per academic year: $25,000. Average number of hours worked per week: 0. Tuition remission given: full.

Additional Information: Of all students currently enrolled full time, 100% benefited from one or more of the listed financial assistance programs. Application and information available online at http://www.uiowa.edu/financial-aid/graduate/.

Internships/Practica: Doctoral Degree (PhD Clinical): For those doctoral students for whom a professional internship was required in this program prior to graduation, (7) students applied for an internship in 2006–2007, with (7) students obtaining an internship. Of those students who obtained an internship, (7) were paid internships. Of those students who obtained an internship, (7) students placed in APA/CPA-accredited internships, (0) students placed in internships not APA/CPA-accredited, but listed with the Association of Psychology Postdoctoral and Internship Centers (APPIC), (0) students placed in internships conforming to guidelines of the Council of Directors of School Psychology Programs (CDSPP), (0) students placed in internships that were not APA/CPA-accredited, APPIC or CDSPP listed. Students in our Clinical Psychology program participate in clinical assessment and treatment practica at our department-run clinic (the Carl E. Seashore Psychology Training Clinic) and in clinics run by departments such as Psychiatry and Neurology at the University of Iowa Hospitals and Clinics.

Housing and Day Care: On-campus housing is available. See the following Web site for more information: http://www.uiowa.edu/admissions/graduate/housing.html; http://www.uiowa.edu/hr/oe/worklife/famserv/. On-campus day care facilities are available. See the following Web site for more information: http://www.uiowa.edu/hr/oe/worklife/famserv/.

Employment of Department Graduates:

Master's Degree Graduates: Of those who graduated in the academic year 2006–2007, the following categories and numbers represent the postgraduate activities and employment of master's degree graduates: Enrolled in a postdoctoral residency/fellowship (n/a), employed in independent practice (n/a), total from the above (master's) (0).

Doctoral Degree Graduates: Of those who graduated in the academic year 2006–2007, the following categories and numbers represent the postgraduate activities and employment of doctoral degree graduates: Enrolled in a psychology doctoral program (n/a), enrolled in a postdoctoral residency/fellowship (3), employed in an academic position at a university (2), employed in business or industry (1), total from the above (doctoral) (6).

Additional Information:

Orientation, Objectives, and Emphasis of Department: The mission of the PhD program is to produce professional scholars who contribute significantly to the advancement of scientific psychological knowledge and who can effectively teach students about the science of psychology. Some of these scholars are also prepared to deliver psychological services. Our goal is to produce PhDs who have developed world-class programs of research, who have published extensively, and who have both broad and deep knowledge. Graduate training is organized into six broad training areas: Behavioral and Cognitive Neuroscience, Clinical Psychology, Cognition and Perception, Developmental Science, Health Psychology, and Personality and Social Psychology. The training programs are flexible, and there is considerable overlap and interaction among students and faculty in all areas, leading to an exciting intellectual environment. Students in good standing receive full support for at least 5 years. The student–faculty ratio remains quite low, usually less than 2 to 1. The department has been successful in establishing strong ties with other campus units such as Psychiatry, Neurology, the law school, and the business school. Through these associations, one may study such topics as the law and psychology, aging, consumer behavior, and neuroscience.

Special Facilities or Resources: The Kenneth W. Spence Laboratories of Psychology and adjoining space in Seashore Hall include automated data acquisition and analysis systems, extensive computing facilities, observation suites with remote audiovisual control and recording equipment, multiple animal facilities, several surgeries, a histology laboratory, soundproof chambers, closed-circuit TV systems, electrophysiological recording rooms, conditioning laboratories, the Carl E. Seashore Psychology Training Clinic, and well-equipped electronic, mechanical, woodworking, and computer shops. Well over half of the departmental laboratories have been extensively renovated or created anew within the past 5 years. In addition, many resources are available through collaboration with colleagues at the university hospital, the Iowa Veterans Administration Hospital, community service centers, and the Colleges of Medicine, Nursing, Dentistry, Engineering, Business, Education, and Law.

Information for Students With Physical Disabilities: See the following Web site for more information: http://www.uiowa.edu/~sds/.

Application Information:

Send to Graduate Admissions Office, 11 Seashore Hall E. Application available online. URL of online application: http://www.uiowa.edu/admissions/applications/graduate. Students are admitted in the Fall, application deadline December 15. *Fee:* $60; $85 for international applicants.

Iowa, University of

Division of Psychological and Quantitative Foundations
College of Education
361 Lindquist Center
Iowa City, IA 52242
Telephone: (319) 335-5577
Fax: (319) 335-6145
E-mail: *janet-ervin@uiowa.edu*
Web: *http://www.uiowa.edu*

Department Information:

Chairperson: Timothy Ansley. Number of faculty: total—full-time 10, part-time 9; women—full-time 4, part-time 5; total—minority—full-time 1; faculty subject to the Americans With Disabilities Act 19.

Programs and Degrees Offered:

Listed in the following order: Program area, degree type (T if terminal Master's), number awarded 7/06–6/07. Educational PhD (Doctor of Philosophy) 2, Educational Measurement and Statistics MA/MS (Master of Arts/Science) 6, Educational Measurement and Statistics PhD (Doctor of Philosophy) 6, School PhD (Doctor of Philosophy) 3, Counseling PhD (Doctor of Philosophy) 5.

APA Accreditation: School PhD (Doctor of Philosophy). Counseling PhD (Doctor of Philosophy).

Student Applications/Admissions:

Student Applications

Educational PhD (Doctor of Philosophy)—Applications 2007–2008, 13. Total applicants accepted 2007–2008, 10. Number full-time enrolled (new admits only) 2007–2008, 4. Total enrolled 2007–2008 full-time, 18. *Educational Measurement and Statistics MA/MS (Master of Arts/Science)*—Applications 2007–2008, 17. Total applicants accepted 2007–2008, 8. Number full-time enrolled (new admits only) 2007–2008, 7. Total enrolled 2007–2008 full-time, 20. The median number of years required for completion of a degree in 2006–2007 were 3. *Educational Measurement and Statistics PhD (Doctor of Philosophy)*—Applications 2007–2008, 33. Total applicants accepted 2007–2008, 17. Number full-time enrolled (new admits only) 2007–2008, 11. Total enrolled 2007–2008 full-time, 51. The median number of years required for completion of a degree in 2006–2007 were 4. *School PhD (Doctor of Philosophy)*—Applications 2007–2008, 26. Total applicants accepted 2007–2008, 10. Number full-time enrolled (new admits only) 2007–2008, 4. The median number of years required for completion of a degree in 2006–2007 were 5. *Counseling PhD (Doctor of Philosophy)*—Applications 2007–2008, 81. Total applicants accepted 2007–2008, 15. Number full-time enrolled (new admits only) 2007–2008, 7. Openings 2008–2009, 8. The median number of years required for completion of a degree in 2006–2007 were 5. The number of students enrolled full- and part-time who were dismissed or voluntarily withdrew from this program area in 2007–2008 were 0.

Admissions Requirements:

Scores: Entries appear in this order: required test or GPA, minimum score (if required), median score of students entering in 2007–2008. Doctoral Programs: overall undergraduate GPA 3.00.

Other Criteria: (importance of criteria rated low, medium, or high): GRE/MAT scores—high, research experience—high, work experience—medium, extracurricular activity—low, clinically related public service—high, GPA—high, letters of recommendation—high, interview—medium, statement of goals and objectives—high. School Psychology PhD/education specialist in school psychology: GRE/MAT scores—high, work experience—high, clinically related public service—high, GPA—high, letters of recommendation—high, interview—high, statement of goals and objectives—high, research experience—medium, extracurricular activity—low. For the Counseling Psychology Program: GPA—high, letters of recommendation—high, statement of goals and objectives—high, GRE/MAT scores—medium, research experience—medium, work experience—medium, clinically related public service—medium, interview—none.

Student Characteristics: The following represents characteristics of students in 2007–2008 in all graduate psychology programs in the department: Female—full-time 131, part-time 0; Male—full-time 47, part-time 0; African American/Black—full-time 12, part-time 0; Hispanic/Latino(a)—full-time 9, part-time 0; Asian/Pacific Islander—full-time 4, part-time 0; American Indian/Alaska Native—full-time 2, part-time 0; Caucasian/White—full-time 151, part-time 0; Unknown ethnicity—full-time 0, part-time 0.

Financial Information/Assistance:

Tuition for Full-Time Study: *Master's:* State residents: $346 per credit hour; Nonstate residents: $346 per credit hour. *Doctoral:* State residents: $346 per credit hour; Nonstate residents: $346 per credit hour. See the following Web site for updates and changes in tuition costs: http://www.uiowa.edu.

Financial Assistance:

First-Year Students: Research assistantships available for first year. Average amount paid per academic year: $16,277. Average number of hours worked per week: 20. Apply by April 1. Tuition remission given: partial.

Advanced Students: Research assistantships available for advanced students. Average amount paid per academic year: $16,277. Average number of hours worked per week: 20. Apply by April 1. Tuition remission given: partial. Fellowships and scholarships available for advanced students. Average amount paid per academic year: $16,277. Average number of hours worked per week: 20. Tuition remission given: partial.

Additional Information: Of all students currently enrolled full time, 5% benefited from one or more of the listed financial assistance programs.

Internships/Practica: Doctoral Degree (PhD School): For those doctoral students for whom a professional internship was required in this program prior to graduation, (6) students applied for an internship in 2006–2007, with (6) students obtaining an internship. Of those students who obtained an internship, (6) were paid internships. Of those students who obtained an internship, (5) students placed in APA/CPA-accredited internships, (0) students placed in internships not APA/CPA-accredited, but listed with the Association of Psychology Postdoctoral and Internship Centers (APPIC), (0) students placed in internships conforming to guidelines of the Council of Directors of School Psychology Programs (CDSPP), (1) student placed in internships that were not APA/CPA-accredited, APPIC or CDSPP listed. Doctoral Degree (PhD Counseling): For those doctoral students for whom a professional internship was required in this program prior to graduation, (8) students applied for an internship in 2006–2007, with (4) students obtaining an internship. Of those students who obtained an internship, (4) were paid internships. Of those students who obtained an internship, (4) students placed in APA/CPA accredited internships, (0) students placed in internships not APA/CPA-accredited, but listed with the Association of Psychology Postdoctoral and Internship Centers (APPIC), (0) students placed in internships conforming to guidelines of the Council of Directors of School Psychology Programs (CDSPP), (0) students placed in internships that were not APA/CPA-accredited, APPIC or CDSPP listed. There are multiple practicum sites at a variety of agencies, (e.g., university counseling centers, VA medical centers, community mental health centers). Educational Psychology Program: Formal internship and practica experiences are not available for MA students, although some students do find paid positions as teaching or research assistants in fields in which they have prior experience. At the PhD level, most students are supported by half-time fellowships or assistantships. In a research-oriented program, these paid positions serve the purpose of an internship or fellowship. School Psychology Program—Practica: Available in the public schools, The University of Iowa Hospitals and Clinics (Department of Pediatrics, Psychiatry, and Neurology), the Berlin–Blank National Center for Gifted, located in the College of Education, The Wendell Johnson Speech and Hearing Clinic at the University of Iowa, and in local mental health agencies.

Housing and Day Care: On-campus housing is available. See the following Web site for more information: http://www.uiowa.edu. On-campus day care facilities are available.

Employment of Department Graduates:

Master's Degree Graduates: Of those who graduated in the academic year 2006–2007, the following categories and numbers represent the postgraduate activities and employment of master's

degree graduates: Enrolled in a psychology doctoral program (4), enrolled in a postdoctoral residency/fellowship (n/a), employed in independent practice (n/a), do not know (2), total from the above (master's) (6).

Doctoral Degree Graduates: Of those who graduated in the academic year 2006–2007, the following categories and numbers represent the postgraduate activities and employment of doctoral degree graduates: Enrolled in a psychology doctoral program (n/a), enrolled in a postdoctoral residency/fellowship (1), employed in an academic position at a university (4), employed in a professional position in a school system (3), employed in business or industry (2), do not know (6), total from the above (doctoral) (16).

Additional Information:

Orientation, Objectives, and Emphasis of Department: The counseling psychology program endorses a scientist–practitioner model and expects students to be competent researchers and practitioners at the completion of their program. At the PhD level, the educational psychology program at the University of Iowa is designed to provide students with strong grounding in the psychology of learning and instruction. Students are encouraged to become proficient in both quantitative and qualitative research methods with an emphasis on the former. The study of individual differences is one program emphasis. At the MA level, the program provides a broad introduction to educational psychology and flexible accommodation of individual students' interest in diverse areas such as instructional technology, reading acquisition and program evaluation. The doctoral program in school psychology is committed to training professional psychologists who are knowledgeable about providing services to children in school, medical and mental health settings. The students will possess expertise in addressing children's social–emotional needs and learning processes. The program's curriculum has been developed to reflect consideration of multicultural issues within psychological theory, research, and professional development. The program strives to produce psychologists who are competent in working in a variety of settings with children and adolescents with a wide array of problems and be able to provide a wide range of psychological services to children and the adults in their lives.

Special Facilities or Resources: The University of Iowa Hospitals and Clinics provide multiple research opportunities. Outstanding computer facilities exist on the campus. Educational Psychology Program: Students in the educational psychology program frequently make use of two important resources of the University of Iowa College of Education. The Iowa Testing Programs, creator of the Iowa Tests of Basic Skills and the Iowa Tests of Educational Development, are housed here. Students have access to test databases for research and may work with faculty or research assistantships supported by the Iowa Measurement Research Foundation. The Berlin–Blank International Center for Gifted Education also provides opportunities for research, teaching, and counseling experiences as well as assistantship support. School Psychology Program: All of the above settings are open to applied research and have existing data available to students as do American College Testing and National Computer Systems, located in Iowa City, IA.

Application Information:

Send to Susan Cline, Student Services Admissions, College of Education, N310 Lindquist Center, Iowa City, IA 52242. For students admitted in the Fall, application deadlines are MA: May 1—MS, January 1—EP; PhD: January 1—EP, March 1—MS, January 1—CP, January 1—SP. For students admitted in the Spring, deadlines are MA: November 1—MS; PhD: September 1—MS. *Fee:* $50.

Northern Iowa, University of

Department of Psychology
Social and Behavioral Sciences
334 Baker Hall
Cedar Falls, IA 50614-0505
Telephone: (319) 273-2303
Fax: (319) 273-6188
E-mail: *harton@uni.edu*
Web: *http://www.uni.edu/psych/grad*

Department Information:

1968. Interim Head: Kim MacLin. Number of faculty: total—full-time 15, part-time 9; women—full-time 5, part-time 7.

Programs and Degrees Offered:

Listed in the following order: Program area, degree type (T if terminal Master's), number awarded 7/06–6/07. Social MA/MS (Master of Arts/Science) (T) 4, Industrial/Organizational MA/MS (Master of Arts/Science) (T) 4, Clinical Science MA/MS (Master of Arts/Science) (T) 6, Individualized Study MA/MS (Master of Arts/Science) 0.

Student Applications/Admissions:

Student Applications

Social MA/MS (Master of Arts/Science)—Applications 2007–2008, 15. Total applicants accepted 2007–2008, 9. Number full-time enrolled (new admits only) 2007–2008, 3. Number part-time enrolled (new admits only) 2007–2008, 0. Openings 2008–2009, 4. The median number of years required for completion of a degree in 2006–2007 were 2. The number of students enrolled full- and part-time who were dismissed or voluntarily withdrew from this program area in 2007–2008 were 0. *Industrial/Organizational MA/MS (Master of Arts/Science)*—Applications 2007–2008, 28. Total applicants accepted 2007–2008, 17. Number full-time enrolled (new admits only) 2007–2008, 9. Number part-time enrolled (new admits only) 2007–2008, 0. Openings 2008–2009, 7. The median number of years required for completion of a degree in 2006–2007 were 2. The number of students enrolled full- and part-time who were dismissed or voluntarily withdrew from this program area in 2007–2008 were 2. *Clinical Science MA/MS (Master of Arts/Science)*—Applications 2007–2008, 43. Total applicants accepted 2007–2008, 16. Number full-time enrolled (new admits only) 2007–2008, 7. Number part-time enrolled (new admits only) 2007–2008, 0. Openings 2008–2009, 7. The median number of years required for completion of a degree in 2006–2007 were 2. The number of students enrolled full- and part-time who were dismissed or voluntarily withdrew from this program area in 2007–2008 were 2. *Individualized Study MA/MS (Master of Arts/Science)*—Applications 2007–2008, 1. Total applicants accepted 2007–2008, 1. Number full-time enrolled (new admits only) 2007–2008, 1. Total enrolled 2007–2008 full-time, 1. Openings 2008–2009, 1. The median number of years required for completion of a degree in 2006–

2007 were 2. The number of students enrolled full- and part-time who were dismissed or voluntarily withdrew from this program area in 2007–2008 were 1.

Admissions Requirements:

Scores: Entries appear in this order: required test or GPA, minimum score (if required), median score of students entering in 2007–2008. Master's Programs: GRE-V 450, 507; GRE-Q 450, 615; overall undergraduate GPA 3.00, 3.44.

Other Criteria: (importance of criteria rated low, medium, or high): GRE/MAT scores—high, research experience—high, work experience—medium, extracurricular activity—low, clinically related public service—medium, GPA—high, letters of recommendation—high, interview—medium, statement of goals and objectives—high, undergraduate major in psychology—high, specific undergraduate psychology courses taken—medium. Clinically related public service is less important for the social and industrial/organizational emphases; work experience is less important for the social emphasis. For additional information on admission requirements, go to http://www.uni.edu/psych/grad.

Student Characteristics: The following represents characteristics of students in 2007–2008 in all graduate psychology programs in the department: Female—full-time 20, part-time 0; Male—full-time 12, part-time 0; African American/Black—full-time 3, part-time 0; Hispanic/Latino(a)—full-time 0, part-time 0; Asian/Pacific Islander—full-time 3, part-time 0; American Indian/Alaska Native—full-time 0, part-time 0; Caucasian/White—full-time 26, part-time 0; Multi-ethnic—full-time 0, part-time 0; students subject to the Americans With Disabilities Act—full-time 0, part-time 0; Unknown ethnicity—full-time 0, part-time 0; International students who hold an F-1 or J-1 Visa—full-time 0, part-time 0.

Financial Information/Assistance:

Tuition for Full-Time Study: *Master's:* State residents: per academic year $6,446; Nonstate residents: per academic year $14,874.

Financial Assistance:

First-Year Students: Teaching assistantships available for first year. Average amount paid per academic year: $4,196. Average number of hours worked per week: 10. Apply by February 1. Research assistantships available for first year. Average amount paid per academic year: $4,196. Average number of hours worked per week: 10. Apply by February 1. Traineeships available for first year. Average amount paid per academic year: $4,196. Average number of hours worked per week: 10. Apply by February 1. Fellowships and scholarships available for first year. Average amount paid per academic year: $3,223. Average number of hours worked per week: 0. Apply by February 1.

Advanced Students: Teaching assistantships available for advanced students. Average amount paid per academic year: $4,196. Average number of hours worked per week: 10. Apply by February 1. Research assistantships available for advanced students. Average amount paid per academic year: $4,196. Average number of hours worked per week: 10. Apply by February 1. Traineeships available for advanced students. Average amount paid per academic year: $4,196. Average number of hours worked per week: 10. Apply by February 1. Fellowships and scholarships available for advanced students. Average amount paid per academic year: $3,223. Average number of hours worked per week: 0. Apply by February 1.

Additional Information: Of all students currently enrolled full time, 100% benefited from one or more of the listed financial assistance programs. Application and information available online at http:/www.uni.edu/psych/grad.

Internships/Practica: Master's Degree (MA/MS Social): An internship experience such as a final research project or "capstone" experience is required of graduates. Master's Degree (MA/MS Industrial/Organizational): An internship experience such as a final research project or "capstone" experience is required of graduates. Master's Degree (MA/MS Clinical Science): An internship experience such as a final research project or "capstone" experience is required of graduates. A variety of practicum sites are available for 2nd-year students in the clinical science and industrial/organizational emphases. Clinical practicum sites have included the University Counseling Center, the State Psychiatric Hospital, correctional facilities, private hospitals, educational settings, and community-based agencies. I/O practicum sites have included the University's Human Resources Office, John Deere, Waterloo Industries, 3-M, and other local and out-of-state (during summer terms) businesses. Students in the social emphasis conduct independent first-year research projects under faculty supervision and present these research projects at regional and national professional conferences.

Housing and Day Care: On-campus housing is available. See the following Web site for more information: http://www.uni.edu/dor/ or contact Department of Residence, University of Northern Iowa, Cedar Falls, IA 50614-0252; On-campus day care facilities are available. See the following Web site for more information: http://www.uni.edu/cdc/ or contact Child Development Center, Price Laboratory School, Cedar Falls, IA 50614-0611.

Employment of Department Graduates:

Master's Degree Graduates: Of those who graduated in the academic year 2006–2007, the following categories and numbers represent the postgraduate activities and employment of master's degree graduates: Enrolled in a psychology doctoral program (8), enrolled in another graduate/professional program (0), enrolled in a postdoctoral residency/fellowship (n/a), employed in independent practice (n/a), employed in business or industry (5), do not know (1), total from the above (master's) (14).

Doctoral Degree Graduates: Of those who graduated in the academic year 2006–2007, the following categories and numbers represent the postgraduate activities and employment of doctoral degree graduates: Enrolled in a psychology doctoral program (n/a), total from the above (doctoral) (0).

Additional Information:

Orientation, Objectives, and Emphasis of Department: The MA program in General Psychology provides a strong empirical, research-based approach to the study of human behavior. Students may select one of three emphases: clinical science, social psychology, or industrial/organizational psychology. They may also choose to complete an individualized study program in conjunction with a faculty mentor. The objectives of the program are (a) to develop skills in research methodology; (b) to gain knowledge of basic areas of scientific psychology; and (c) to obtain competence in research, consulting, and/or clinical skills. The clinical science emphasis is designed for those who wish to either obtain doctoral degrees in clinical or counseling psychology or become master's-level providers of services operating in clinical settings under appropriate supervision. The social emphasis is designed for students who wish to pursue doctoral degrees in social psychology or master's-level research or teaching positions. The industrial/organizational emphasis is designed for those planning doctoral study in I/O psychology or a position in human resources or consulting.

Special Facilities or Resources: The department provides laboratory space for research with human participants; access to community facilities and populations for applied research; 24/7 access to computers for graduate students; and office space for graduate students. We are affiliated with two laboratory schools and a center for social research, and students have access to psychiatric, work, and community populations for research projects.

Information for Students With Physical Disabilities: See the following Web site for more information: http://www.uni.edu/disability/.

Application Information:

Send to Graduate Coordinator, Department of Psychology, University of Northern Iowa, Cedar Falls, IA 50614-0505. Application available online. URL of online application: http://www.uni.edu/psych/grad. Students are admitted in the Fall, application deadline April 30; Programs have rolling admissions. For full consideration, applications should be received by February 1, although applications will be considered if received by April 30 as space permits. *Fee:* $30. Application fee for international students is $50.

Emporia State University

Department of Psychology and Special Education
The Teachers College
1200 Commercial Street
Emporia, KS 66801-5087
Telephone: (620) 341-5317
Fax: (620) 341-5801
E-mail: *kweaver@emporia.edu*
Web: *http://www.emporia.edu/psyspe*

Department Information:

1932. Chairperson: Kenneth A. Weaver. Number of faculty: total—full-time 7, part-time 7; women—full-time 3, part-time 7.

Programs and Degrees Offered:

Listed in the following order: Program area, degree type (T if terminal Master's), number awarded 7/06–6/07. General Experimental MA/MS (Master of Arts/Science) (T) 3, School EdS/MEd (School Psychology) 6, Clinical Psychology MA/MS (Master of Arts/Science) (T) 9, Industrial/Organizational Psychology MA/MS (Master of Arts/Science) (T) 8.

Student Applications/Admissions:

Student Applications

General Experimental MA/MS (Master of Arts/Science)—Applications 2007–2008, 7. Total applicants accepted 2007–2008, 6. Number full-time enrolled (new admits only) 2007–2008, 4. Number part-time enrolled (new admits only) 2007–2008, 0. Openings 2008–2009, 15. The median number of years required for completion of a degree in 2006–2007 were 2. The number of students enrolled full- and part-time who were dismissed or voluntarily withdrew from this program area in 2007–2008 were 0. *School EdS/MEd (School Psychology)*—Applications 2007–2008, 12. Total applicants accepted 2007–2008, 10. Number full-time enrolled (new admits only) 2007–2008, 8. Number part-time enrolled (new admits only) 2007–2008, 0. Total enrolled 2007–2008 full-time, 15, part-time, 6. Openings 2008–2009, 15. The median number of years required for completion of a degree in 2006–2007 were 3. The number of students enrolled full- and part-time who were dismissed or voluntarily withdrew from this program area in 2007–2008 were 0. *Clinical Psychology MA/MS (Master of Arts/Science)*—Applications 2007–2008, 14. Total applicants accepted 2007–2008, 10. Number full-time enrolled (new admits only) 2007–2008, 7. Total enrolled 2007–2008 full-time, 18, part-time, 2. Openings 2008–2009, 15. The median number of years required for completion of a degree in 2006–2007 were 2. *Industrial/Organizational Psychology MA/MS (Master of Arts/Science)*—Applications 2007–2008, 14. Total applicants accepted 2007–2008, 12. Number full-time enrolled (new admits only) 2007–2008, 7. Number part-time enrolled (new admits only) 2007–2008, 0. Total enrolled 2007–2008 full-time, 27, part-time, 5. Openings 2008–2009, 15. The median number of years required for completion of a degree in 2006–2007 were 2. The number of students enrolled full- and part-time who were dismissed or voluntarily withdrew from this program area in 2007–2008 were 0.

Admissions Requirements:

Scores: Entries appear in this order: required test or GPA, minimum score (if required), median score of students entering in 2007–2008. Master's Programs: GRE-V no minimum stated; GRE-Q no minimum stated; MAT no minimum stated; overall undergraduate GPA 3.00; last 2 years GPA 3.25.

Other Criteria: (importance of criteria rated low, medium, or high): GRE/MAT scores—low, research experience—medium, work experience—medium, extracurricular activity—low, clinically related public service—low, GPA—high, letters of recommendation—high, statement of goals and objectives—high, undergraduate major in psychology—high, specific undergraduate psychology courses taken—high. For additional information on admission requirements, go to http://www.emporia.edu/psyspe.

Student Characteristics: The following represents characteristics of students in 2007–2008 in all graduate psychology programs in the department: Female—full-time 50, part-time 7; Male—full-time 28, part-time 3; African American/Black—full-time 0, part-time 0; Hispanic/Latino(a)—full-time 0, part-time 0; Asian/Pacific Islander—full-time 2, part-time 0; American Indian/Alaska Native—full-time 0, part-time 0; Caucasian/White—full-time 75, part-time 10; Multi-ethnic—full-time 1, part-time 0; students subject to the Americans With Disabilities Act—full-time 1, part-time 0; Unknown ethnicity—full-time 0, part-time 0; International students who hold an F-1 or J-1 Visa—full-time 2, part-time 0.

Financial Information/Assistance:

Tuition for Full-Time Study: *Master's:* State residents: per academic year $4,554, $204 per credit hour; Nonstate residents: per academic year $12,186, $522 per credit hour. Tuition is subject to change. See the following Web site for updates and changes in tuition costs: http://www.emporia.edu/busaff/tuitwaiv.htm.

Financial Assistance:

First-Year Students: Teaching assistantships available for first year. Average amount paid per academic year: $6,887. Average number of hours worked per week: 20. Apply by March 15. Tuition remission given: full. Research assistantships available for first year. Average amount paid per academic year: $6,887. Average number of hours worked per week: 20. Apply by March 15. Tuition remission given: full. Fellowships and scholarships available for first year. Average amount paid per academic year: $300. Apply by ongoing. Tuition remission given: partial.

Advanced Students: Teaching assistantships available for advanced students. Average amount paid per academic year: $6,887. Average number of hours worked per week: 20. Apply by March 15. Tuition remission given: full. Research assistantships available for advanced students. Average amount paid per academic year: $6,887. Average number of hours worked per week: 20. Apply by March 15. Tuition remission given: full. Fellowships and scholarships available for advanced students. Average amount paid per academic year: $300. Apply by ongoing. Tuition remission given: partial.

Additional Information: Of all students currently enrolled full time, 70% benefited from one or more of the listed financial assistance programs. Application and information available online at http://www.emporia.edu/grad/load.htm.

Internships/Practica: For Clinical students, internship is 750 clock hours in a mental health setting supervised by a PhD psychologist. For I/O students the internship is 350 clock hours in a business setting. For Experimental students, the internship is defined as experiences working in a laboratory setting. School Psychology and Special Education students do semester internships/practica in the schools. In addition, there is a 1-year, paid, post-EdS internship for School Psychology. For additional information on education and training outcomes for our programs, see the following Web site: http://www.emporia.edu/psyspe.

Housing and Day Care: On-campus housing is available. See the following Web site for more information: http://www.emporia.edu/reslife/index.htm. On-campus day care facilities are available. See the following Web site for more information: http://www.cece.emporia.edu/.

Employment of Department Graduates:

Master's Degree Graduates: Of those who graduated in the academic year 2006–2007, the following categories and numbers represent the postgraduate activities and employment of master's degree graduates: Enrolled in a psychology doctoral program (1), enrolled in a postdoctoral residency/fellowship (n/a), employed in independent practice (n/a), employed in an academic position at a 2-year/4-year college (1), employed in a professional position in a school system (6), employed in business or industry (8), employed in a community mental health/counseling center (7), still seeking employment (1), do not know (2), total from the above (master's) (26).

Doctoral Degree Graduates: Of those who graduated in the academic year 2006–2007, the following categories and numbers represent the postgraduate activities and employment of doctoral degree graduates: Enrolled in a psychology doctoral program (n/a), total from the above (doctoral) (0).

Additional Information:

Orientation, Objectives, and Emphasis of Department: Emporia State offers the Master of Science degree in general experimental psychology, clinical psychology, school psychology, and industrial/organizational psychology. Emporia State also offers a Specialist in Education degree in school psychology. Additionally, students may pursue the EdS degree in school psychology.

Special Facilities or Resources: In 1999, all classrooms in the Department of Psychology and Special Education were upgraded with multimedia technology. Facilities include cognitive and animal behavior, and physiological psychology laboratories; a complete animal vivarium; suites of rooms for administration of psychological tests and observation of testing or clinical and counseling sessions; and microprocessors and mainframe computer facilities.

Information for Students With Physical Disabilities: See the following Web site for more information: http://www.emporia.edu/disability/.

Application Information:

Send to Dean of Graduate Studies and Research, Campus Box 4003, Emporia State University, 1200 Commercial Street, Emporia, KS 66801. Application available online. URL of online application: http://www.emporia.edu/psyspe. Students are admitted in the Fall, application deadline October 1; Spring, application deadline March 1; Summer, application deadline June 1. School Psychology has continuous admission. *Fee:* $40.

Fort Hays State University

Department of Psychology
600 Park Street
Hays, KS 67601-4099
Telephone: (785) 628-4405
Fax: (785) 628-5861
E-mail: *hmarrs@fhsu.edu*
Web: *http://www.fhsu.edu/psych/*

Department Information:

1929. Chair: Heath Marrs. Number of faculty: total—full-time 7, part-time 1; women—full-time 4, part-time 1.

Programs and Degrees Offered:

Listed in the following order: Program area, degree type (T if terminal Master's), number awarded 7/06–6/07. Applied Clinical MA/MS (Master of Arts/Science) (T) 6, General MA/MS (Master of Arts/Science) (T) 1, School EdS/MEd (School Psychology) 5.

Student Applications/Admissions:

Student Applications

Applied Clinical MA/MS (Master of Arts/Science)—Applications 2007–2008, 15. Total applicants accepted 2007–2008, 11. Number full-time enrolled (new admits only) 2007–2008, 4. Number part-time enrolled (new admits only) 2007–2008, 0. Total enrolled 2007–2008 full-time, 11, part-time, 4. Openings 2008–2009, 7. The median number of years required for completion of a degree in 2006–2007 were 2. The number of students enrolled full- and part-time who were dismissed or voluntarily withdrew from this program area in 2007–2008 were 0. *General MA/MS (Master of Arts/Science)*—Applications 2007–2008, 3. Total applicants accepted 2007–2008, 3. Number full-time enrolled (new admits only) 2007–2008, 0. Number part-time enrolled (new admits only) 2007–2008, 1. Openings 2008–2009, 5. The median number of years required for completion of a degree in 2006–2007 were 2. The number of students enrolled full- and part-time who were dismissed or voluntarily withdrew from this program area in 2007–2008 were 0. *School EdS/MEd (School Psychology)*—Applications 2007–2008, 9. Total applicants accepted 2007–2008, 9. Number full-time enrolled (new admits only) 2007–2008, 7. Number part-time enrolled (new admits only) 2007–2008, 0. Total enrolled 2007–2008 full-time, 12, part-time, 2. Openings 2008–2009, 7. The median number of years required for completion of a degree in 2006–2007 were 2. The number of students enrolled full- and part-time who were dismissed or voluntarily withdrew from this program area in 2007–2008 were 1.

Admissions Requirements:

Scores: Entries appear in this order: required test or GPA, minimum score (if required), median score of students entering in 2007–2008. Master's Programs: GRE-V no minimum stated, 400; GRE-Q no minimum stated, 570; overall undergraduate GPA 3.00, 3.48; psychology GPA 3.00, 3.46.

Other Criteria: (importance of criteria rated low, medium, or high): GRE/MAT scores—medium, research experience—high, work experience—medium, extracurricular activity—medium, clinically related public service—medium, GPA—high, letters of recommendation—medium, interview—medium, statement of goals and objectives—medium.

Student Characteristics: The following represents characteristics of students in 2007–2008 in all graduate psychology programs in the department: Female—full-time 19, part-time 4; Male—full-time 7, part-time 2; African American/Black—full-time 0, part-time 0; Hispanic/Latino(a)—full-time 0, part-time 1; Asian/Pacific Islander—full-time 0, part-time 0; American Indian/Alaska Native—full-time 0, part-time 0; Caucasian/White—full-time 25, part-time 4; Multi-ethnic—full-time 1, part-time 1; students subject to the Americans With Disabilities Act—full-time 1, part-time 0; Unknown ethnicity—full-time 0, part-time 0.

Financial Information/Assistance:

Tuition for Full-Time Study: *Master's:* State residents: $155 per credit hour; Nonstate residents: $409 per credit hour. Tuition is subject to change. See the following Web site for updates and changes in tuition costs: http://www.fhsu.edu/gradschl/.

Financial Assistance:

First-Year Students: Teaching assistantships available for first year. Apply by March 1. Tuition remission given: partial.

Advanced Students: Teaching assistantships available for advanced students. Apply by March 1. Tuition remission given: partial. Fellowships and scholarships available for advanced students. Average amount paid per academic year: $600. Apply by March 15.

Additional Information: Of all students currently enrolled full time, 70% benefited from one or more of the listed financial assistance programs. Application and information available online at http://www.fhsu.edu/gradschl/.

Internships/Practica: Master's Degree (MA/MS Applied Clinical): An internship experience such as a final research project or "capstone" experience is required of graduates. Master's Degree (MA/MS General): An internship experience such as a final research project or "capstone" experience is required of graduates. All students in the applied psychology programs (clinical, school) are required to take a practicum in their specialty area. Students in the clinical psychology program receive initial practicum experience in the Kelly Center (an on-campus psychological services center), and then are required to complete an internship off-campus at a regional mental health agency or other approved agency. Students in the school psychology program receive initial practicum experience in a school district. School psychology graduates are also required to complete 1 year of paid, supervised post-EdS internship before being recommended for full licensure (certification). Students in the general psychology program have the opportunity to take apprenticeships concentrating on the teaching of psychology.

Housing and Day Care: On-campus housing is available. See the following Web site for more information: Graduate student housing: http://www.fhsu.edu/reslife/. On-campus day care facilities are available. See the following Web site for more information: Tiger Tots Nurturery Center, http://www.fhsu.edu/te/tig/index.html.

Employment of Department Graduates:

Master's Degree Graduates: Of those who graduated in the academic year 2006–2007, the following categories and numbers represent the postgraduate activities and employment of master's degree graduates: Enrolled in a postdoctoral residency/fellowship (n/a), employed in independent practice (n/a), total from the above (master's) (0).

Doctoral Degree Graduates: Of those who graduated in the academic year 2006–2007, the following categories and numbers represent the postgraduate activities and employment of doctoral degree graduates: Enrolled in a psychology doctoral program (n/a), total from the above (doctoral) (0).

Additional Information:

Orientation, Objectives, and Emphasis of Department: The department emphasizes a research approach to the understanding of behavior. We strive to provide basic empirical and theoretical foundations of psychology to prepare the student for doctoral study, for teaching, or for employment in a service or professional agency. The school program offers broad preparation for students in both psychology and education and includes training as a consultant to work with educators and parents as well as with children. The clinical program emphasizes the preparation of rural mental health workers, although many graduates go on to doctoral programs. The general program is intended to prepare the student for doctoral study.

Special Facilities or Resources: The department of psychology now occupies a newly remodeled building in the center of campus. Some of the new facilities in this building include: a 25-machine computer facility with separate spaces for individualized research and full Internet connections; testing and observation rooms for children, adults, and small groups; separate research and teaching labs for the major areas of psychology; an isolated small animal facility; and several seminar rooms. We are located adjacent to the student psychological services center. There is an active social organization for psychology graduate students. All students at the university have free remote Internet access.

Information for Students With Physical Disabilities: See the following Web site for more information: http://www.fhsu.edu/affirm/disabilities.php.

Application Information:

Send to Dean of the Graduate School, Fort Hays State University, 600 Park Street, Hays, KS 67601-4099. Application available online. URL of online application: http://www.fhsu.edu/gradschl/forms.shtml. Programs have rolling admissions. Deadline for financial aid is March 1. *Fee:* $35.

Kansas State University

Department of Psychology
College of Arts and Sciences
492 Bluemont Hall, 1100 Mid-Campus Drive
Manhattan, KS 66506-5302
Telephone: (785) 532-6850
Fax: (785) 532-5401
E-mail: *psych@ksu.edu*
Web: *http://www.ksu.edu/psych*

Department Information:

1951. Head: Jerome Frieman. Number of faculty: total—full-time 16, part-time 1; women—full-time 4, part-time 1.

Programs and Degrees Offered:

Listed in the following order: Program area, degree type (T if terminal Master's), number awarded 7/06–6/07. Animal Learning/Behavioral Neuroscience PhD (Doctor of Philosophy) 2, Cognitive and Human Factors PhD (Doctor of Philosophy) 3, Social/Personality Psychology PhD (Doctor of Philosophy) 3, Industrial/Organizational Psychology PhD (Doctor of Philosophy) 0, Industrial/Organizational (Distance) MA/MS (Master of Arts/Science) (T) 11, Occupational Health Psychology Other 3.

Student Applications/Admissions:

Student Applications

Animal Learning/Behavioral Neuroscience PhD (Doctor of Philosophy)—Applications 2007–2008, 10. Total applicants accepted 2007–2008, 1. Number full-time enrolled (new admits only) 2007–2008, 1. Total enrolled 2007–2008 full-time, 7. The median number of years required for completion of a degree in 2006–2007 were 5. The number of students enrolled full- and part-time who were dismissed or voluntarily withdrew from this program area in 2007–2008 were 0. *Cognitive and Human Factors PhD (Doctor of Philosophy)*—Applications 2007–2008, 17. Total applicants accepted 2007–2008, 9. Number full-time enrolled (new admits only) 2007–2008, 4. Number part-time enrolled (new admits only) 2007–2008, 0. Total enrolled 2007–2008 full-time, 10, part-time, 2. Openings 2008–2009, 3. The median number of years required for completion of a degree in 2006–2007 were 5. The number of students enrolled full- and part-time who were dismissed or voluntarily withdrew from this program area in 2007–2008 were 0. *Social/Personality Psychology PhD (Doctor of Philosophy)*—Applications 2007–2008, 38. Total applicants accepted 2007–2008, 2. Number full-time enrolled (new admits only) 2007–2008, 2. Total enrolled 2007–2008 full-time, 12. Openings 2008–2009, 3. The median number of years required for completion of a degree in 2006–2007 were 5. The number of students enrolled full- and part-time who were dismissed or voluntarily withdrew from this program area in 2007–2008 were 0. *Industrial/Organizational Psychology PhD (Doctor of Philosophy)*—Applications 2007–2008, 38. Total applicants accepted 2007–2008, 7. Number full-time enrolled (new admits only) 2007–2008, 2. Total enrolled 2007–2008 full-time, 14, part-time, 9. Openings 2008–2009, 2. The median number of years required for completion of a degree in 2006–2007 were 5. The number of students enrolled full- and part-time who were dismissed or voluntarily withdrew from this program area in 2007–2008 were 0. *Industrial/Organizational (Distance) MA/MS (Master of Arts/Science)*—Applications 2007–2008, 24. Total applicants accepted 2007–2008, 12. Number part-time enrolled (new admits only) 2007–2008, 12. Total enrolled 2007–2008 part-time, 25. Openings 2008–2009, 15. The median number of years required for completion of a degree in 2006–2007 were 2. The number of students enrolled full- and part-time who were dismissed or voluntarily withdrew from this program area in 2007–2008 were 0. *Occupational Health Psychology Other*—Applications 2007–2008, 5. Total applicants accepted 2007–2008, 4. Number part-time enrolled (new admits only) 2007–2008, 4. Total enrolled 2007–2008 part-time, 6. Openings 2008–2009, 10. The median number of years required for completion of a degree in 2006–2007 were 2. The number of students enrolled full- and part-time who were dismissed or voluntarily withdrew from this program area in 2007–2008 were 1.

Admissions Requirements:

Scores: Entries appear in this order: required test or GPA, minimum score (if required), median score of students entering in 2007–2008. Master's Programs: GRE-V no minimum stated; GRE-Q no minimum stated; overall undergraduate GPA no minimum stated; last 2 years GPA 3.0; Masters GRE-Analytical no minimum stated. Doctoral Programs: GRE-V no minimum stated, 499; GRE-Q no minimum stated, 591; overall undergraduate GPA no minimum stated, 3.81; Doctoral program GRE-Analytic no minimum stated. ***Other Criteria:*** (importance of criteria rated low, medium, or high): GRE/MAT scores—high, research experience—high, work experience—low, extracurricular activity—low, clinically related public service—low, GPA—high, letters of recommendation—high, statement of goals and objectives—high.

Student Characteristics: The following represents characteristics of students in 2007–2008 in all graduate psychology programs in the department: Female—full-time 32, part-time 0; Male—full-time 26, part-time 0; African American/Black—full-time 1, part-time 0; Hispanic/Latino(a)—full-time 1, part-time 0; Asian/Pacific Islander—full-time 5, part-time 0; American Indian/Alaska Native—full-time 0, part-time 0; Caucasian/White—full-time 51, part-time 0; students subject to the Americans With Disabilities Act—full-time 0, part-time 0; Unknown ethnicity—full-time 0, part-time 0; International students who hold an F-1 or J-1 Visa—full-time 5, part-time 0.

Financial Information/Assistance:

Tuition for Full-Time Study: *Master's:* State residents: $326 per credit hour; Nonstate residents: $657 per credit hour. *Doctoral:* State residents: $326 per credit hour; Nonstate residents: $657 per credit hour. Tuition is subject to change. See the following Web site for updates and changes in tuition costs: http://www.k-state.edu/controller/cashiers/fees/FY08/TuitionFeesScheduleGradFY08.pdf.

Financial Assistance:

First-Year Students: Teaching assistantships available for first year. Average amount paid per academic year: $10,327. Average number of hours worked per week: 20. Tuition remission given: full. Research assistantships available for first year. Average amount paid per academic year: $9,627. Average number of hours worked per week: 20. Tuition remission given: partial.

Advanced Students: Teaching assistantships available for advanced students. Average amount paid per academic year: $10,327. Average number of hours worked per week: 20. Tuition remission given: full. Research assistantships available for advanced students. Average amount paid per academic year: $9,627. Average number of hours worked per week: 20. Tuition remission given: partial.

Additional Information: Of all students currently enrolled full time, 85% benefited from one or more of the listed financial assistance programs.

Internships/Practica: Arrangements for internships in human factors/applied experimental and industrial/organizational psychology vary widely and are made on an individual basis.

Housing and Day Care: On-campus housing is available. See the following Web site for more information: http://www.ksu.edu/housing/family.html http://www.ksu.edu/ksucdc/. On-campus day care facilities are available.

Employment of Department Graduates:

Master's Degree Graduates: Of those who graduated in the academic year 2006–2007, the following categories and numbers represent the postgraduate activities and employment of master's degree graduates: Enrolled in a psychology doctoral program (4), enrolled in a postdoctoral residency/fellowship (n/a), employed in independent practice (n/a), employed in a professional position in a school system (1), total from the above (master's) (5).

Doctoral Degree Graduates: Of those who graduated in the academic year 2006–2007, the following categories and numbers represent the postgraduate activities and employment of doctoral degree graduates: Enrolled in a psychology doctoral program (n/a), employed in an academic position at a university (1), employed in an academic position at a 2-year/4-year college (3), employed in other positions at a higher education institution (2), employed in business or industry (1), total from the above (doctoral) (7).

Additional Information:

Orientation, Objectives, and Emphasis of Department: Both teaching and research are heavily emphasized. Training prepares students for a variety of positions, including teaching and research positions in colleges and universities. Students have also assumed research and evaluative positions in hospitals, clinics, governmental agencies, and industry.

Special Facilities or Resources: The department has rooms for individual and group research; several computer laboratories and remote terminal access to mainframe computers; a photographic darkroom; one-way observation facilities; an electrically shielded, light-tight, sound-deadened room for auditory and visual research; laboratories for behavioral research with animals; surgical and histological facilities; and colony rooms.

Information for Students With Physical Disabilities: See the following Web site for more information: http://www.ksu.edu/dss/.

Application Information:

Send to Graduate Admissions, Department of Psychology, 492 Bluemont Hall, 1100 Mid-Campus Drive, Kansas State University, Manhattan, KS 66506-5302. Application available online. URL of online application: http://www.k-state.edu/grad/. Students are admitted in the Fall, application deadline Feburary 15. Applicants for the Distance Master's Program in Industrial/Organizational Psychology should apply online at http://www.dce.ksu.edu/industrialpsych/. The deadline for applications is April 30. *Fee:* $30. International applicants must pay a $55 application fee in the form of an international cashier's check or money order.

Kansas, University of

Department of Applied Behavioral Science (formerly Human Development)
College of Arts and Sciences
1000 Sunnyside Avenue
Lawrence, KS 66045-7555
Telephone: (785) 864-4840
Fax: (785) 864-5202
E-mail: *absc@ku.edu*
Web: *http://www.absc.ku.edu*

Department Information:

1964. Chairperson: Edward K. Morris. Number of faculty: total—full-time 8; women—full-time 6; total—minority—full-time 1; women minority—full-time 1; faculty subject to the Americans With Disabilities Act 1.

Programs and Degrees Offered:

Listed in the following order: Program area, degree type (T if terminal Master's), number awarded 7/06–6/07. Behavioral Psychology PhD (Doctor of Philosophy) 8, Applied Behavioral Science MA/MS (Master of Arts/Science) 8.

Student Applications/Admissions:

Student Applications

Behavioral Psychology PhD (Doctor of Philosophy)—Applications 2007–2008, 30. Total applicants accepted 2007–2008, 10. Number full-time enrolled (new admits only) 2007–2008, 10. Total enrolled 2007–2008 full-time, 56. Openings 2008–2009, 10. The median number of years required for completion of a degree in 2006–2007 were 6. The number of students enrolled full- and part-time who were dismissed or voluntarily withdrew from this program area in 2007–2008 were 0. *Applied Behavioral Science MA/MS (Master of Arts/Science)*—Applications 2007–2008, 12. Total applicants accepted 2007–2008, 0. Number full-time enrolled (new admits only) 2007–2008, 0. Total enrolled 2007–2008 full-time, 3. Openings 2008–2009, 10. The median number of years required for completion of a degree in 2006–2007 were 3. The number of students enrolled full- and part-time who were dismissed or voluntarily withdrew from this program area in 2007–2008 were 0.

Admissions Requirements:

Scores: Entries appear in this order: required test or GPA, minimum score (if required), median score of students entering in 2007–2008. Doctoral Programs: GRE scores are not required for admission; however, several competitive fellowhship programs are available through the University which do require the GRE.

Other Criteria: (importance of criteria rated low, medium, or high): GRE/MAT scores—medium, research experience—high, work experience—high, extracurricular activity—low, clinically related public service—medium, GPA—high, letters of recommendation—high, interview—high, statement of goals and objectives—high. All admission decisions are made by individual faculty members, thus the admissions criteria vary by faculty members.. For additional information on admission requirements, go to http://www.absc.ku.edu/graduate/.

Student Characteristics: The following represents characteristics of students in 2007–2008 in all graduate psychology programs in the department: Female—full-time 46, part-time 0; Male—full-time 13, part-time 0; African American/Black—full-time 1, part-time 0; Hispanic/Latino(a)—full-time 2, part-time 0; Asian/Pacific Islander—full-time 2, part-time 0; Caucasian/White—full-time 54, part-time 0; students subject to the Americans With Disabilities Act—full-time 1, part-time 0; Unknown ethnicity—full-time 0, part-time 0.

Financial Information/Assistance:

Tuition for Full-Time Study: *Master's:* State residents: $241 per credit hour; Nonstate residents: $575 per credit hour. *Doctoral:* State residents: $241 per credit hour; Nonstate residents: $575 per credit hour. Tuition is subject to change. See the following Web site for updates and changes in tuition costs: http://www.registrar.ku.edu/.

Financial Assistance:

First-Year Students: Teaching assistantships available for first year. Apply by January 15. Tuition remission given: full. Research assistantships available for first year. Apply by January 15. Tuition remission given: full. Traineeships available for first year. Apply by January 15. Tuition remission given: full. Fellowships and scholarships available for first year. Apply by January 15. Tuition remission given: full.

Advanced Students: Teaching assistantships available for advanced students. Apply by vary. Tuition remission given: full. Research assistantships available for advanced students. Apply by vary. Tuition remission given: full. Traineeships available for advanced students. Apply by vary. Tuition remission given: full. Fellowships and scholarships available for advanced students. Apply by vary. Tuition remission given: full.

Additional Information: Of all students currently enrolled full time, 80% benefited from one or more of the listed financial assistance programs. Application and information available online at http://www.absc.ku.edu/.

Internships/Practica: A wide variety of research settings and practica sites are available to graduate students. They include: Behavioral Pediatrics; Center for Independent Living; Center for the Study of Mental Retardation and Related Problems; Child and Family Research Center; Community Programs for Adults with Mental Retardation; Edna A. Hill Child Development Center; Experimental Analysis of Behavior Laboratories; Family Enhancement Project; Gerontology Center; Juniper Gardens Project; Research on Children With Retardation; Schiefelbusch Institute for Life Span Studies; Work Group on Health Promotion and Community Development.

Housing and Day Care: On-campus housing is available. See the following Web site for more information: http://www.housing.ku.edu/. On-campus day care facilities are available. See the following Web site for more information: http://www.hilltop.ku.edu/; Edna A. Hill Child Development Center, ABS Department.

Employment of Department Graduates:

Master's Degree Graduates: Of those who graduated in the academic year 2006–2007, the following categories and numbers represent the postgraduate activities and employment of master's degree graduates: Enrolled in a psychology doctoral program (7), enrolled in a postdoctoral residency/fellowship (n/a), employed in independent practice (n/a), do not know (1), total from the above (master's) (8).

Doctoral Degree Graduates: Of those who graduated in the academic year 2006–2007, the following categories and numbers represent the postgraduate activities and employment of doctoral degree graduates: Enrolled in a psychology doctoral program (n/a), enrolled in a postdoctoral residency/fellowship (3), employed in an academic position at a university (2), employed in other positions at a higher education institution (1), employed in business or industry (1), do not know (1), total from the above (doctoral) (8).

Additional Information:

Orientation, Objectives, and Emphasis of Department: The primary purpose of the program is to train students in basic and applied research in behavior analysis. It features emphases in applied behavior analysis, early childhood, developmental disabilities, community health and development, the experimental analysis of human and animal behavior, conceptual issues in behavior analysis, independent living, and rehabilitation. Junior Colleague Model: Throughout the PhD training sequence, students work closely as junior colleagues with a faculty adviser and a research group. Although students typically work with one faculty adviser, they are free to select a different adviser if their interests change during the course of their training. Continuous Research Involvement: Students participate in research throughout their graduate careers in an individualized, intensive program. As a result, most students complete more research projects than those required for the degree.

Special Facilities or Resources: A wide range of research settings are available to graduate students. Populations and settings include both typically developing and disabled infants, toddlers, preschool children, elementary school settings, adolescents, adults, and elders. In addition the department has an animal laboratory facility.

Information for Students With Physical Disabilities: See the following Web site for more information: http://www.ku.edu/~ssdis/.

Application Information:

Send to Graduate School, 300 Strong Hall, Lawrence, KS 66045. For admissions information, to apply online, Graduate School catalog, Graduate Student Organizations, graduation and commencement information, graduate faculty appointments, and the Graduate School Handbook, go to http://www.ku.edu/~graduate/. Application available online. URL of online application: http://www.absc.ku.edu/graduate/. Students are admitted in the Fall, application deadline January 15. All admissions are based on selections by individual faculty members willing to serve as a mentor to the student; there is no centralized admission. There is no set number of students admitted in any year. Some admissions occur throughout the year. *Fee:* $55.

Kansas, University of
Department of Psychology
426 Fraser Hall
1415 Jayhawk Boulevard
Lawrence, KS 66045-7556
Telephone: (785) 864-4131
Fax: (785) 864-5696
E-mail: *gsimpson@ku.edu*
Web: *http://www.psych.ku.edu*

Department Information:

1916. Chairperson: Greg B. Simpson. Number of faculty: total—full-time 36; women—full-time 11; total—minority—full-time 2; women minority—full-time 1.

Programs and Degrees Offered:

Listed in the following order: Program area, degree type (T if terminal Master's), number awarded 7/06–6/07. Clinical PhD (Doctor of Philosophy) 4, Cognitive PhD (Doctor of Philosophy) 1, Quantitative PhD (Doctor of Philosophy) 0, Social PhD (Doctor of Philosophy) 1, Developmental PhD (Doctor of Philosophy) 0.

APA Accreditation: Clinical PhD (Doctor of Philosophy).

Student Applications/Admissions:

Student Applications

Clinical PhD (Doctor of Philosophy)—Applications 2007–2008, 110. Total applicants accepted 2007–2008, 8. Number full-time enrolled (new admits only) 2007–2008, 4. Number part-time enrolled (new admits only) 2007–2008, 0. Openings 2008–2009, 5. The median number of years required for completion of a degree in 2006–2007 were 6. The number of students enrolled full- and part-time who were dismissed or voluntarily withdrew from this program area in 2007–2008 were 1. *Cognitive PhD (Doctor of Philosophy)*—Applications 2007–2008, 20. Total applicants accepted 2007–2008, 2. Number full-time enrolled (new admits only) 2007–2008, 2. Openings 2008–2009, 4. The median number of years required for completion of a degree in 2006–2007 were 6. The number of students enrolled full- and part-time who were dismissed or voluntarily withdrew from this program area in 2007–2008 were 1. *Quantitative PhD (Doctor of Philosophy)*—Applications 2007–2008, 15. Total applicants accepted 2007–2008, 4. Number full-time enrolled (new admits only) 2007–2008, 2. Openings 2008–2009, 2. The median number of years required for completion of a degree in 2006–2007 were 5. The number of students enrolled full- and part-time who were dismissed or voluntarily withdrew from this program area in 2007–2008 were 0. *Social PhD (Doctor of Philosophy)*—Applications 2007–2008, 60. Total applicants accepted 2007–2008, 8. Number full-time enrolled (new admits only) 2007–2008, 3. Openings 2008–2009, 4. The median number of years required for completion of a degree in 2006–2007 were 6. The number of students enrolled full- and part-time who were dismissed or voluntarily withdrew from this program area in 2007–2008 were 0. *Developmental PhD (Doctor of Philosophy)*—Applications 2007–2008, 5. Total applicants accepted 2007–2008, 2. Number full-time enrolled (new admits only) 2007–2008, 1. Total enrolled 2007–2008 full-time, 3. Openings 2008–2009, 3. The median number of years required for completion of a degree in 2006–2007 were 5. The number of students enrolled full- and part-time who were dismissed or voluntarily withdrew from this program area in 2007–2008 were 0.

Admissions Requirements:

Scores: Entries appear in this order: required test or GPA, minimum score (if required), median score of students entering in 2007–2008. Doctoral Programs: GRE-V 420, 580; GRE-Q 510, 625; overall undergraduate GPA 3.0, 3.76; Doctoral program GRE-Analytic 3, 5.0.

Other Criteria: (importance of criteria rated low, medium, or high): GRE/MAT scores—high, research experience—high, work experience—low, extracurricular activity—low, clinically related public service—medium, GPA—high, letters of recommendation—high, interview—high, statement of goals and objectives—high, undergraduate major in psychology—medium, specific undergraduate psychology courses taken—medium. Writing sample for Clinical programs only. For additional information on admission requirements, go to http://www.psych.ku.edu/graduate_home.html.

Student Characteristics: The following represents characteristics of students in 2007–2008 in all graduate psychology programs in the department: Female—full-time 78, part-time 0; Male—full-time 29, part-time 0; African American/Black—full-time 3, part-time 0; Hispanic/Latino(a)—full-time 3, part-time 0; Asian/Pacific Islander—full-time 9, part-time 0; American Indian/Alaska Native—full-time 2, part-time 0; Caucasian/White—full-time 73, part-time 0; Multi-ethnic—full-time 0, part-time 0; students subject to the Americans With Disabilities Act—full-time 0, part-time 0; Unknown ethnicity—full-time 17, part-time 0; International students who hold an F-1 or J-1 Visa—full-time 9, part-time 0.

Financial Information/Assistance:

Tuition for Full-Time Study: *Master's:* State residents: $240 per credit hour; Nonstate residents: $575 per credit hour. *Doctoral:* State residents: $240 per credit hour; Nonstate residents: $575 per credit hour. Tuition is subject to change. See the following Web site for updates and changes in tuition costs: http://www.tuition.ku.edu/rates.shtml.

Financial Assistance:

First-Year Students: Teaching assistantships available for first year. Average amount paid per academic year: $12,000. Average number of hours worked per week: 20. Apply by December 1. Tuition remission given: full. Research assistantships available for first year. Average amount paid per academic year: $12,000. Average number of hours worked per week: 20. Apply by December 1. Tuition remission given: full. Fellowships and scholarships available for first year. Average amount paid per academic year: $15,000. Average number of hours worked per week: 40. Apply by December 1. Tuition remission given: full.

Advanced Students: Teaching assistantships available for advanced students. Average amount paid per academic year: $13,000. Average number of hours worked per week: 20. Apply by January 15. Tuition remission given: full. Research assistantships available for advanced students. Average amount paid per academic year: $13,000. Average number of hours worked per week: 20. Apply by January 15. Tuition remission given: full. Fellowships and scholarships available for advanced students. Average amount paid per academic year: $13,000. Average number of hours worked per week: 0. Apply by January 15. Tuition remission given: full.

Additional Information: Of all students currently enrolled full time, 65% benefited from one or more of the listed financial assistance programs. Application and information available online at http://www.psych.ku.edu.

Internships/Practica: No information provided.

Housing and Day Care: On-campus housing is available. See the following Web site for more information: http://www.housing.ku.edu/. On-campus day care facilities are available. See the following Web site for more information: http://www.hilltop.ku.edu/.

Employment of Department Graduates:

Master's Degree Graduates: Of those who graduated in the academic year 2006–2007, the following categories and numbers represent the postgraduate activities and employment of master's degree graduates: Enrolled in a postdoctoral residency/fellowship (n/a), employed in independent practice (n/a), total from the above (master's) (0).

Doctoral Degree Graduates: Of those who graduated in the academic year 2006–2007, the following categories and numbers represent the postgraduate activities and employment of doctoral degree graduates: Enrolled in a psychology doctoral program (n/a), enrolled in a postdoctoral residency/fellowship (4), employed in an academic position at a university (2), total from the above (doctoral) (6).

Additional Information:

Orientation, Objectives, and Emphasis of Department: With 36 full-time faculty, the department offers a wide range of opportunities for the study and treatment of human psychological and behavioral functioning. Students develop skills in statistics, research methods, and specific content areas with basic and applied emphases, with the flexibility to tailor programs to individual students' needs. Students in all programs (Clinical, Clinical Child, Developmental, Quantitative, Cognitive, or Social) may also complete coursework toward a minor in quantitative psychology. The Developmental Program is new in 2005, and began admitting students in 2006.

Special Facilities or Resources: The department has well-equipped computer labs, and access to university mainframe computers. The department maintains a computer and electronics shop for the construction of specialized equipment. Clinical and research support facilities include an on-site clinic with a test resource library, individual and group therapy rooms, and play and psychodrama rooms. Specialized research facilities include interview rooms with audio and video capacities, psychophysiological and stress laboratories, ERP facilities, eye-movement monitoring laboratories, and an anechoic chamber. The Kansas University Medical Center houses the Hoglund Brain Imaging Center, a state-of-the-art facility with fMRI and MEG laboratories.

Information for Students With Physical Disabilities: See the following Web site for more information: http://www.achievement.ku.edu/disability/.

Application Information:

Send to The University of Kansas Graduate School, 1450 Jayhawk Boulevard, Room 313, Lawrence, KS 66045-7535. Application available online. URL of online application: http://www.applyweb.com/apply/ukansg/majors/menu.html. Students are admitted in the Fall, application deadline December 1. *Fee:* $55.

Kansas, University of

Psychology and Research in Education
School of Education
Joseph R. Pearson Hall
1122 West Campus Road, Room 621
Lawrence, KS 66045-3101
Telephone: (785) 864-3931
Fax: (785) 864-3820
E-mail: *kmulton@ku.edu*
Web: *http://www.soe.ku.edu/pre/*

Department Information:

1955. Chairperson: Karen D. Multon, PhD. Number of faculty: total—full-time 13, part-time 5; women—full-time 3, part-time 3; total—minority—full-time 1, part-time 1; women minority—part-time 1.

Programs and Degrees Offered:

Listed in the following order: Program area, degree type (T if terminal Master's), number awarded 7/06–6/07. School Psychology PhD (Doctor of Philosophy) 3, Counseling Psychology MA/MS (Master of Arts/Science) (T) 13, Educational Psychology and Research PhD (Doctor of Philosophy) 4, Educational Psychology and Research Other 1, Counseling Psychology PhD (Doctor of Philosophy) 6, School Psychology EdS/MEd (School Psychology) 8.

APA Accreditation: School PhD (Doctor of Philosophy). Counseling PhD (Doctor of Philosophy).

Student Applications/Admissions:

Student Applications

School Psychology PhD (Doctor of Philosophy)—Applications 2007–2008, 14. Total applicants accepted 2007–2008, 5. Number full-time enrolled (new admits only) 2007–2008, 1. Number part-time enrolled (new admits only) 2007–2008, 0. Total enrolled 2007–2008 full-time, 7, part-time, 3. Openings 2008–2009, 4. The median number of years required for completion of a degree in 2006–2007 were 8. The number of students enrolled full- and part-time who were dismissed or voluntarily withdrew from this program area in 2007–2008 were 0. *Counseling Psychology MA/MS (Master of Arts/Science)*—Applications 2007–2008, 46. Total applicants accepted 2007–2008, 37. Number full-time enrolled (new admits only) 2007–2008, 15. Number part-time enrolled (new admits only) 2007–2008, 0. Total enrolled 2007–2008 full-time, 34, part-time, 12. Openings 2008–2009, 20. The median number of years required for completion of a degree in 2006–2007 were 4. The number of students enrolled full- and part-time who were dismissed or voluntarily withdrew from this program area in 2007–2008 were 0. *Educational Psychology and Research PhD (Doctor of Philosophy)*—Applications 2007–2008, 12. Total applicants accepted 2007–2008, 10. Number full-time enrolled (new admits only) 2007–2008, 4. Number part-time enrolled (new admits only) 2007–2008, 0. Total enrolled 2007–2008 full-time, 11, part-time, 6. Openings 2008–2009, 10. The median number of years required for completion of a degree in 2006–2007 were 8. The number of students enrolled full- and part-time who were dismissed or voluntarily withdrew from this program area in 2007–2008 were 0. *Educational Psychology and Research Other*—Applications 2007–2008, 7. Total applicants accepted 2007–2008, 3. Number full-time enrolled (new admits only) 2007–2008, 1. Number part-time enrolled (new admits only) 2007–2008, 1. Total enrolled 2007–2008 full-time, 2, part-time, 2. Openings 2008–2009, 5. The median number of years required for completion of a degree in 2006–2007 were 7. The number of students enrolled full- and part-time who were dismissed or voluntarily withdrew from this program area in 2007–2008 were 0. *Counseling Psychology PhD (Doctor of Philosophy)*—Applications 2007–2008, 73. Total applicants accepted 2007–2008, 13. Number full-time enrolled (new admits only) 2007–2008, 8. Number part-time enrolled (new admits only) 2007–2008, 0. Total enrolled 2007–2008 full-time, 33, part-time, 7. Openings 2008–2009, 8. The median number of years required for completion of a degree in 2006–2007 were 7. The number of students enrolled full- and part-time who were dismissed or voluntarily withdrew from this program area in 2007–2008 were 1. *School Psychology EdS/MEd (School Psychology)*—Applications 2007–2008, 41. Total applicants accepted 2007–2008, 22. Number full-time enrolled (new admits only) 2007–2008, 8. Number part-time enrolled (new admits only) 2007–2008, 0. Total enrolled 2007–2008 full-time, 16, part-time, 1. Openings 2008–2009, 10. The median number of years required for completion of a degree in 2006–2007 were 4. The number of students enrolled full- and part-time who were dismissed or voluntarily withdrew from this program area in 2007–2008 were 0.

Admissions Requirements:

Scores: Entries appear in this order: required test or GPA, minimum score (if required), median score of students entering in 2007–2008. Master's Programs: GRE-V 500, 460; GRE-Q 500, 525; overall undergraduate GPA 3.0, 3.4. The minimum requirements listed are for regular degree-seeking admission for the University of Kansas. However, there are instances when students are admitted under provisional or probationary status. The median scores listed above represent the group of students entering the Counseling Psychology MS program. The median scores for the Educational Psychology and Research MSEd program are GREV-478, GREQ-520, and UGPA-3.6. The median scores for the School Psychology EdS program are GREV-560, GREQ-610, and UGPA-3.3. The median scores represent data on incoming (currently enrolled) KU students in the Department of Psychology and Research in Education. Doctoral Programs: GRE-V 500, 528; GRE-Q 500, 600; overall undergraduate GPA 3.0, 3.7. The minimum requirements listed are for regular degree-seeking admission for the University of Kansas. However, there are instances when students are admitted under provisional or probationary status. The median scores listed above represent the group of students entering the Counseling Psychology PhD program. The median scores for the Educational Psychology and Research PhD program are GREV-415, GREQ-655, and UGPA-3.6. This program has a large percentage of international students. The median scores for the School Psychology PhD program are GREV-560, GREQ-610, and UGPA-3.3. The median scores represent data on incoming (currently enrolled) KU students in the Department of Psychology and Research in Education. The Counseling Psychology and School Psychology doctoral programs are APA accredited.

Other Criteria: (importance of criteria rated low, medium, or high): GRE/MAT scores—high, research experience—medium, work experience—medium, extracurricular activity—low, clinically related public service—low, GPA—high, letters of recommendation—high, interview—high, statement of goals and objectives—high. The admission criteria above are for applicants to the Counseling Psychology PhD program. The admission criteria for applicants to the School Psychology PhD program are GRE/MAT scores—high; research experience—high; work experience—medium; extracurricular activity—low; clinically related public service—high; UGPA—high; letters of recommendation—high; statement of goals and objectives—high. For additional information on admission requirements, go to http://soe.ku.edu/pre/.

Student Characteristics: The following represents characteristics of students in 2007–2008 in all graduate psychology programs in the department: Female—full-time 78, part-time 25; Male—full-time 25, part-time 6; African American/Black—full-time 5, part-time 1; Hispanic/Latino(a)—full-time 4, part-time 1; Asian/Pacific Islander—full-time 9, part-time 3; American Indian/Alaska Native—full-time 0, part-time 1; Caucasian/White—full-time 82, part-time 22; Multi-ethnic—full-time 0, part-time 0; students subject to the Americans With Disabilities Act—full-time 0, part-time 0; Unknown ethnicity—full-time 3, part-time 3; International students who hold an F-1 or J-1 Visa—full-time 7, part-time 3.

Financial Information/Assistance:

Tuition for Full-Time Study: *Master's:* State residents: $241 per credit hour; Nonstate residents: $575 per credit hour. *Doctoral:* State residents: $241 per credit hour; Nonstate residents: $575 per credit hour. Tuition is subject to change. See the following Web site for updates and changes in tuition costs: http://www.tuition.ku.edu/rates.shtml. Higher tuition cost for this program: The School of Education has a differential tuition fee of $17.15 per credit hour.

Financial Assistance:

First-Year Students: Teaching assistantships available for first year. Average amount paid per academic year: $6,900. Average number of hours worked per week: 12. Apply by February 15. Tuition remission given: full and partial. Research assistantships available for first year. Average amount paid per academic year: $7,000. Average number of hours worked per week: 12. Apply by varies. Tuition remission given: full and partial. Fellowships and scholarships available for first year. Apply by varies. Tuition remission given: full and partial.

Advanced Students: Teaching assistantships available for advanced students. Average amount paid per academic year: $6,900. Average number of hours worked per week: 12. Apply by February 15. Tuition remission given: full and partial. Research assistantships available for advanced students. Average amount paid per academic year: $7,000. Average number of hours worked per week: 12. Apply by varies. Tuition remission given: full and partial. Fellowships and scholarships available for advanced students. Apply by varies. Tuition remission given: full and partial.

Additional Information: Of all students currently enrolled full time, 70% benefited from one or more of the listed financial assistance programs. Application and information available online at http://www.financialaid.ku.edu; http://www.soe.ku.edu/students/scholarships; http://www.graduate.ku.edu/~graduate.

Internships/Practica: Doctoral Degree (PhD School Psychology): For those doctoral students for whom a professional internship was required in this program prior to graduation, (0) students applied for an internship in 2006–2007, with (0) students obtaining an internship. Of those students who obtained an internship, (0) were paid internships. Of those students who obtained an internship, (0) students placed in APA/CPA-accredited internships, (0) students placed in internships not APA/CPA accredited, but listed with the Association of Psychology Postdoctoral and Internship Centers (APPIC), (0) students placed in internships conforming to guidelines of the Council of Directors of School Psychology Programs (CDSPP), (0) students placed in internships that were not APA/CPA-accredited, APPIC or CDSPP listed. Doctoral Degree (PhD Counseling Psychology): For those doctoral students for whom a professional internship was required in this program prior to graduation, (4) students applied for an internship in 2006–2007, with (4) students obtaining an internship. Of those students who obtained an internship, (4) were paid internships. Of those students who obtained an internship, (4) students placed in APA/CPA-accredited internships, (0) students placed in internships not APA/CPA accredited, but listed with the Association of Psychology Postdoctoral and Internship Centers (APPIC), (0) students placed in internships conforming to guidelines of the Council of Directors of School Psychology Programs (CDSPP), (0) students placed in internships that were not APA/CPA-accredited, APPIC or CDSPP listed. The Counseling Psychology and School Psychology programs require practicum and/or internship courses as part of the degree requirements. Additionally, PRE graduate students enroll in field experience, seminars, and specific PRE courses to obtain additional training with special populations and/or psychological testing procedures (PRE 855, 865, 951, 995, and 998). Counseling Psychology doctoral students must participate in three semesters of practicum and 1 full year of internship (PRE 842, 948, 949, and 990). Both master's and doctoral students in the Counseling Psychology programs complete their practica in a variety of local applied settings. Our doctoral students in Counseling Psychology have been successful in obtaining APA-accredited internships in university counseling centers, veterans' administration medical centers, community mental health centers, and other human service agencies. Students in the School Psychology EdS program devote a full year to a school psychology internship (PRE 991). These students obtain internships in a variety of elementary, secondary, and special needs school settings throughout the country. Individuals obtaining their doctoral degree in School Psychology are required to participate in a second full year of internship (PRE 992). Course descriptions may be viewed at http://www.catalogs.ku.edu/graduate. Please see the section for the School of Education.

Housing and Day Care: On-campus housing is available. See the following Web site for more information: http://www.housing.ku.edu/. Residence halls, scholarship halls, and apartments are located on the KU—Lawrence campus. The Jayhawker Towers offers housing for single, nontraditional students, upperclass students and transfer students with more than 30 hours. Go to http:/www.housing.ku.edu/floorplans/floorplans_jayhawker.htm. Married students and students with families can apply for housing at Stouffer Place. Go to http://www.housing.ku.edu/floorplans/floorplans_stouffer.htm. The Sunflower Apartments offer housing opportunities for new faculty, unclassified staff, postdoctoral fellows, and visiting scholars. Go to http://www.housing.ku.edu/floorplans/floorplans_sunflower.htm. Graduate students may find employment opportunities serving as support staff and/or RAs with KU Student Housing. On-campus day care facilities are available. Individuals may utilize the Hilltop Child Development Center for childcare services at the University of Kansas. Priority placement is extended toward children of University of Kansas students, staff, and faculty. Limited non-KU enrollments may be possible. Hilltop has been in existence since 1972. Children may begin attending this facility at the age of 12 months. Hilltop provides high-quality care and education on the KU—Lawrence campus for toddlers, and preschoolers. After-school programs at certain elementary schools are also available in the city of Lawrence.

Employment of Department Graduates:

Master's Degree Graduates: Of those who graduated in the academic year 2006–2007, the following categories and numbers represent the postgraduate activities and employment of master's degree graduates: Enrolled in a postdoctoral residency/fellowship (n/a), employed in independent practice (n/a), total from the above (master's) (0).

Doctoral Degree Graduates: Of those who graduated in the academic year 2006–2007, the following categories and numbers represent the postgraduate activities and employment of doctoral degree graduates: Enrolled in a psychology doctoral program (n/a), employed in an academic position at a university (1), employed in other positions at a higher education institution (2), employed in a hospital/medical center (3), total from the above (doctoral) (6).

Additional Information:

Orientation, Objectives, and Emphasis of Department: Psychology and Research in Education offers graduate degrees in three distinct areas. The doctoral programs in Counseling Psychology and School Psychology are APA accredited. The EdS and PhD degrees in School Psychology are NASP accredited. Counseling Psychology trains professionals to possess the generalist skills to function in a wide array of work settings. This program is strongly committed to the training of scientist–practitioners focused on facilitating the personal, social, educational, and vocational development of individuals. School Psychology endorses the training model of the psychoeducational consultant with multifaceted skills drawn from psychology and education to assist children toward greater realization of their potential. The psychoeducational consultant is vitally concerned with enhancing teacher effectiveness, creating a positive classroom environment for children, and influencing educational thought within the school system. The Educational Psychology and Research Program offers instruction in five tracks. The objectives of the program are to prepare students to become faculty members, researchers, and measurement specialists. Students may focus on (a) growth and development, (b) learning and instruction, (c) measurement and assessment, (d) research and evaluation, or (e) statistics. Graduate study includes experiences in designing, conducting, and evaluating research and field experiences in a variety of settings.

Special Facilities or Resources: Students have employment and/or research opportunities with diverse populations in a variety of settings, including university-related facilities and public/private schools. KU's Multicultural Resource Center seeks to reshape notions of education, research, and public service to include a multicultural focus. The America Reads Challenge, Institute of Educational Research and Public Service, Center for Educational Testing and Evaluation, Center for Research on Learning, and the Center for Psychoeducational Services are under the umbrella of KU's School of Education; go to http://soe.ku.edu/research-services/. The Center for Psychoeducational Services serves the needs of local schools and community members while offering excellent training opportunities for School Psychology and Counseling Psychology students. Graduate students may work with preschool, school-age children and their families, and college students from the local area. KU's Life Span Institute, http://www.lsi.ku.edu/, has numerous programs such as the Juniper Gardens Children's Project, Beach Center on Disability, Research and Training Center on Independent Living, Gerontology Center, and the Work Group for Community Health and Development. The School of Education provides extensive media and Internet technology in its state-of-the-art facility, Joseph R. Pearson Hall. Students have access to mediated classrooms and laboratories, instructional and assessment libraries, audiovisual resources, and computer labs.

Information for Students With Physical Disabilities: See the following Web site for more information: http://www.achievement.ku.edu/disability or http://www.lsi.ku.edu/lsi.

Application Information:
The KU Graduate School application may be completed online at http://www.graduate.ku.edu/apply/. The PRE departmental application may be downloaded at http://www.soe.ku.edu/pre/. The departmental application should be sent to KU Psychology and Research in Education, Admissions Committee, 1122 West Campus Road, Room 621 JRP, Lawrence, KS 66045-3101. Additional PRE contact information: (785) 864-3931 phone; (785) 864-3820 fax; preadmit@ku.edu. Application available online. URL of online application: http://www.soe.ku.edu/pre. Students are admitted in the Fall, application deadline December 15, PhD; Summer, application deadline December 15, PhD. Doctoral Programs: November 15—Educational Psychology and Research, PhD, next Spring/Summer admission. December 15—Counseling Psychology, PhD program, next Summer/Fall admission. December 15—School Psychology, PhD program, next Summer/Fall admission. January 15—Educational Psychology and Research, PhD, next Summer/Fall admission. Master's Programs: November 15—Educational Psychology and Research, MSEd, next Spring/Summer admission. December 15—School Psychology, EdS program, next Summer/Fall admission. January 15—Counseling Psychology, MS program, next Summer/Fall admission. January 15—Educational Psychology and Research, MSEd, next Summer/Fall admission. *Fee:* $45. There is a fee of $45 for the online domestic application. Further application fee information may be viewed at http://www.graduate.ku.edu/apply. Individuals requesting an application fee waiver should send a letter directly to the chair of the Department of Psychology and Research in Education.

Pittsburg State University

Department of Psychology and Counseling
College of Education
207 Whitesitt Hall, 1701 South Broadway
Pittsburg, KS 66762-7551
Telephone: (620) 235-4523
Fax: (620) 235-6102
E-mail: *dhurford@pittstate.edu*
Web: *http://www.pittstate.edu/psych/*

Department Information:
1929. Chairperson: David P. Hurford. Number of faculty: total—full-time 7, part-time 5; women—full-time 7.

Programs and Degrees Offered:
Listed in the following order: Program area, degree type (T if terminal Master's), number awarded 7/06–6/07. Clinical Psychology MA/MS (Master of Arts/Science) (T) 6, Community Counseling MA/MS (Master of Arts/Science) (T) 6, General Psychology MA/MS (Master of Arts/Science) (T) 9, School Psychology EdS/MEd (School Psychology) 9, School Counseling MA/MS (Master of Arts/Science) (T) 3.

Student Applications/Admissions:
Student Applications
Clinical Psychology MA/MS (Master of Arts/Science)—Applications 2007–2008, 31. Total applicants accepted 2007–2008, 12. Number full-time enrolled (new admits only) 2007–2008, 10. Total enrolled 2007–2008 full-time, 12. Openings 2008–2009, 10. *Community Counseling MA/MS (Master of Arts/Science)*—Applications 2007–2008, 21. Total applicants accepted 2007–2008, 13. Number full-time enrolled (new admits only) 2007–2008, 13. Total enrolled 2007–2008 full-time, 22, part-time, 8. Openings 2008–2009, 15. The number of students enrolled full- and part-time who were dismissed or voluntarily withdrew from this program area in 2007–2008 were 2. *General Psychology MA/MS (Master of Arts/Science)*—Applications 2007–2008, 16. Total applicants accepted 2007–2008, 14. Number full-time enrolled (new admits only) 2007–2008, 10. Total enrolled 2007–2008 full-time, 11. Openings 2008–2009, 12. *School Psychology EdS/MEd (School Psychology)*—Applications 2007–2008, 7. Total applicants accepted 2007–2008, 7. Number full-time enrolled (new admits only) 2007–2008, 7. Total enrolled 2007–2008 full-time, 18, part-time, 4. Openings 2008–2009, 10. *School Counseling MA/MS (Master of Arts/Science)*—Applications 2007–2008, 14. Total applicants accepted 2007–2008, 14. Number full-time enrolled (new admits only) 2007–2008, 5. Number part-time enrolled (new admits only) 2007–2008, 3. Total enrolled 2007–2008 full-time, 14, part-time, 16. Openings 2008–2009, 10.

Admissions Requirements:
Scores: Entries appear in this order: required test or GPA, minimum score (if required), median score of students entering in 2007–2008. Master's Programs: GRE-V 400, 470; GRE-Q 400, 530; overall undergraduate GPA 3.00, 3.43; last 2 years GPA 3.00, 3.56; psychology GPA 3.00, 3.65; Masters GRE-Analytical 3.0. Same for all programs, but medians differ by program area.
Other Criteria: (importance of criteria rated low, medium, or high): GRE/MAT scores—high, research experience—me-

dium, work experience—high, extracurricular activity—low, clinically related public service—medium, GPA—high, letters of recommendation—high, interview—medium, statement of goals and objectives—high.

Student Characteristics: The following represents characteristics of students in 2007–2008 in all graduate psychology programs in the department: Female—full-time 60, part-time 23; Male—full-time 17, part-time 5; African American/Black—full-time 1, part-time 0; Hispanic/Latino(a)—full-time 0, part-time 1; Asian/Pacific Islander—full-time 2, part-time 0; American Indian/Alaska Native—full-time 0, part-time 0; Caucasian/White—full-time 75, part-time 27; Unknown ethnicity—full-time 0, part-time 0.

Financial Information/Assistance:

Tuition for Full-Time Study: *Master's:* State residents: per academic year $4,288, $181 per credit hour; Nonstate residents: per academic year $10,546, $442 per credit hour. Tuition is subject to change.

Financial Assistance:

First-Year Students: Teaching assistantships available for first year. Average amount paid per academic year: $4,660. Average number of hours worked per week: 20. Apply by March 1. Tuition remission given: full.

Advanced Students: Teaching assistantships available for advanced students. Average amount paid per academic year: $4,660. Average number of hours worked per week: 20. Apply by March 1. Tuition remission given: full.

Additional Information: Of all students currently enrolled full time, 5% benefited from one or more of the listed financial assistance programs.

Internships/Practica: All MS and EdS practitioner programs include a 3–8 semester hour (150–400 clock hour) practicum sequence and a 4–32 semester hour (600–1,200 clock hour) internship at a site appropriate to the specialty, and under the supervision of faculty and site supervisors. The internship in school psychology is postdegree, and is typically a paid internship. Some internships in other programs are also paid. All internships meet guidelines of the professional association or accrediting body of the specialty (i.e., CACREP, MPAC, NASP).

Housing and Day Care: On-campus housing is available. See the following Web site for more information: http://www.pittstate.edu/house/. No on-campus day care facilities are available.

Employment of Department Graduates:

Master's Degree Graduates: Of those who graduated in the academic year 2006–2007, the following categories and numbers represent the postgraduate activities and employment of master's degree graduates: Enrolled in a psychology doctoral program (2), enrolled in another graduate/professional program (3), enrolled in a postdoctoral residency/fellowship (n/a), employed in independent practice (n/a), employed in an academic position at a university (1), employed in an academic position at a 2-year/4-year college (2), employed in other positions at a higher education institution (0), employed in a professional position in a school system (20), employed in business or industry (0), employed in government agency (0), employed in a community mental health/counseling center (16), employed in a hospital/medical center (2), still seeking employment (2), other employment position (3), total from the above (master's) (51).

Doctoral Degree Graduates: Of those who graduated in the academic year 2006–2007, the following categories and numbers represent the postgraduate activities and employment of doctoral degree graduates: Enrolled in a psychology doctoral program (n/a), total from the above (doctoral) (0).

Additional Information:

Orientation, Objectives, and Emphasis of Department: The Department of Psychology and Counseling uses an interdisciplinary model to provide broad-based training, understanding, and appreciation of the specialties that we represent. The major objective of the department is to prepare graduates with knowledge in scientific foundations and practical applied skills to function as mental health service providers or to pursue study at the doctoral level. Faculty in the department represent a diverse collection of theoretical backgrounds in scientific and applied psychology. All faculty teach coursework in each program area, providing students with the opportunity to learn multidisciplinary approaches and models. The emphasis in the department is on integrated, cross-disciplinary studies within a close faculty–student colleague model that promotes frequent contact and close supervision, aimed at developing practitioner skills. The department is pleased to have the first accredited master's degree program in clinical psychology in the nation (MPAC accreditation received in May 1997), and enjoys CACREP accreditation of the master's degree program in community counseling. The department also enjoys NCATE accreditation of the MS degree program in school counseling and the EdS degree program in school psychology.

Personal Behavior Statement: Statement on department application above signature.

Special Facilities or Resources: The department has counseling and psychotherapy training facilities equipped with one-way mirrors and audio- and videotaping equipment. Microcomputer laboratories with network capacity, word processing, and SAS and SPSS software are available in the department. The university library, in addition to a large book collection, currently maintains over 150 periodical subscriptions in psychology. The department operates the Center for Human Services, an on-campus training, research, and service facility, which includes University Testing Services, a family counseling center, an adult assessment center, the Center for Assessment and Remediation of Reading Difficulties, the Attention Deficit/Hyperactivity Disorder Neurofeedback Diagnostic and Treatment Center, and the Welfare to Work Assessment Center. The department has a close working relationship with local hospitals and mental health facilities, and is a constituent member of the regional community service coalition.

Information for Students With Physical Disabilities: See the following Web site for more information: http://www.pittstate.edu/eoaa/.

Application Information:

Send to Chairperson, Department of Psychology and Counseling, Pittsburg State University, 1701 South Broadway, Pittsburg, KS 66762-7551. Students are admitted in the Fall, application deadline March 1; Spring, application deadline October 1; Summer, application deadline March 1. Applications for the MS in Clinical Psychology are normally accepted for Fall admission. Applications will be considered for Spring admission, but please note that this will extend the student's program of study by one semester. *Fee:* $30.

Washburn University

Department of Psychology
1700 College
Topeka, KS 66621
Telephone: (785) 670-1564
Fax: (785) 670-1004
E-mail: *dave.provorse@washburn.edu*
Web: *http://www.washburn.edu/cas/psychology/*

Department Information:

1940. Chairperson: Dave Provorse. Number of faculty: total—full-time 7, part-time 2; women—full-time 4, part-time 2.

Programs and Degrees Offered:

Listed in the following order: Program area, degree type (T if terminal Master's), number awarded 7/06–6/07. Clinical MA/MS (Master of Arts/Science) (T) 7.

Student Applications/Admissions:

Student Applications

Clinical MA/MS (Master of Arts/Science)—Applications 2007–2008, 40. Total applicants accepted 2007–2008, 10. Number full-time enrolled (new admits only) 2007–2008, 10. Openings 2008–2009, 12. The median number of years required for completion of a degree in 2006–2007 were 3. The number of students enrolled full- and part-time who were dismissed or voluntarily withdrew from this program area in 2007–2008 were 2.

Admissions Requirements:

Scores: Entries appear in this order: required test or GPA, minimum score (if required), median score of students entering in 2007–2008. Master's Programs: GRE-V no minimum stated, 500; GRE-Q no minimum stated, 610; overall undergraduate GPA no minimum stated, 3.3; last 2 years GPA no minimum stated, 3.4; psychology GPA no minimum stated, 3.5.

Other Criteria: (importance of criteria rated low, medium, or high): GRE/MAT scores—low, research experience—medium, work experience—medium, extracurricular activity—low, clinically related public service—medium, GPA—medium, letters of recommendation—high, statement of goals and objectives—medium, undergraduate major in psychology—medium, specific undergraduate psychology courses taken—medium. For additional information on admission requirements, go to http://www.washburn.edu/cas/psychology/ma_program.html#Admission.

Student Characteristics: The following represents characteristics of students in 2007–2008 in all graduate psychology programs in the department: Female—full-time 18, part-time 0; Male—full-time 11, part-time 0; African American/Black—full-time 1, part-time 0; Hispanic/Latino(a)—full-time 1, part-time 0; Asian/Pacific Islander—full-time 1, part-time 0; American Indian/Alaska Native—full-time 0, part-time 0; Caucasian/White—full-time 25, part-time 0; Multi-ethnic—full-time 1, part-time 0; Unknown ethnicity—full-time 0, part-time 0; International students who hold an F-1 or J-1 Visa—full-time 1, part-time 0.

Financial Information/Assistance:

Tuition for Full-Time Study: *Master's:* State residents: per academic year $4,590, $255 per credit hour; Nonstate residents: per academic year $9,360, $520 per credit hour. Tuition is subject to change. See the following Web site for updates and changes in tuition costs: http://www.washburn.edu/business-office/tuition.

Financial Assistance:

First-Year Students: Teaching assistantships available for first year. Average amount paid per academic year: $3,500. Average number of hours worked per week: 10. Apply by March 15. Research assistantships available for first year. Average amount paid per academic year: $750. Average number of hours worked per week: 3. Apply by August 15.

Advanced Students: Teaching assistantships available for advanced students. Average amount paid per academic year: $4,000. Average number of hours worked per week: 10. Apply by May 15. Research assistantships available for advanced students. Average amount paid per academic year: $1,500. Average number of hours worked per week: 5. Apply by August 15.

Additional Information: Of all students currently enrolled full time, 72% benefited from one or more of the listed financial assistance programs. Application and information available online at http://www.washburn.edu/cas/psychology.

Internships/Practica: Master's Degree (MA/MS Clinical): An internship experience such as a final research project or "capstone" experience is required of graduates. Psychological services are offered to the community through a clinic staffed by graduate students enrolled in practica. Services offered focus on remediation of anxiety and depression. Student therapists practice skills of diagnostic interviewing, and integrating interview information with personality and intelligence testing into the formulation of a DSM–IV–TR diagnosis. Under the close supervision of a faculty clinical psychologist, they use this information to conceptualize etiologies and develop and deliver therapeutic treatment options. The therapy processes implemented reflect several theoretical orientations, including Interpersonal Process, Cognitive–Behavioral, and Brief approaches. Issues of suicide, cross-cultural sensitivity, and individual therapist development are also addressed. An internship consisting of 750 supervised hours over an academic year is required of each student prior to graduation. This requirement is met by working 20 hours per week at an assigned site and meeting 3 hours weekly in a classroom setting. Both on-site and academic supervisors are available to the student throughout the internship. The types of experiences provided student interns include provision of individual adult and child therapy, cofacilitation of group therapy, psychological testing/assessment, and involvement in multidisciplinary treatment teams.

Housing and Day Care: On-campus housing is available. See the following Web site for more information: http://www.washburn.edu/services/studentlife/resliving/. No on-campus day care facilities are available.

Employment of Department Graduates:

Master's Degree Graduates: Of those who graduated in the academic year 2006–2007, the following categories and numbers represent the postgraduate activities and employment of master's degree graduates: Enrolled in a psychology doctoral program (0), enrolled in a postdoctoral residency/fellowship (n/a), employed in independent practice (n/a), employed in other positions at a higher education institution (1), employed in a community mental health/counseling center (4), employed in a hospital/medical center (0), other employment position (1), total from the above (master's) (6).

Doctoral Degree Graduates: Of those who graduated in the academic year 2006–2007, the following categories and numbers represent the postgraduate activities and employment of doctoral degree graduates: Enrolled in a psychology doctoral program (n/a), total from the above (doctoral) (0).

Additional Information:

Orientation, Objectives, and Emphasis of Department: Training is designed to establish a strong foundation in the content and methods of psychology. Students obtain experience and skills in research, psychological assessment, and individual and group therapy. Clinical training reflects an integrative blend of humanistic, cognitive–behavioral, interpersonal process, and brief therapies. The MA program is designed to prepare students for the pursuit of a doctoral degree in psychology, or for future employment as providers of psychological services in community mental health centers, hospitals, correctional settings, and other social service agencies and clinics that require master's-level training. Students with special interests in children, rural psychology, or correctional and prison settings have the opportunity to pursue these in their thesis research and internship placement.

Special Facilities or Resources: The psychology department, housed with other departments in a modern building, has well-equipped laboratories available for human experimentation. These facilities also include observation areas designed for the direct supervision of psychotherapy and psychological testing. The psychology department provides access to the University Academic Computer Center for computer hardware and software resources. Thesis research can be conducted by accessing participants from the undergraduate subject pool, or a wide array of community-based agencies.

Information for Students With Physical Disabilities: See the following Web site for more information: http://www.washburn.edu/services/studentaffairs/stuservices/disabilitiesguide.html.

Application Information:

Send to Department of Psychology, Washburn University, Topeka, KS 66621. Application available online. URL of online application: http://www.washburn.edu/cas/psychology/ma_application.html. Students are admitted in the Fall, application deadline March 15; Spring, application deadline December 1. *Fee:* $0.

Wichita State University

Department of Psychology
Fairmount College of Liberal Arts and Sciences
1845 Fairmount
Wichita, KS 67260-0034
Telephone: (316) 978-3170
Fax: (316) 978-3086
E-mail: *charles.burdsal@wichita.edu*
Web: *http://www.psychology.wichita.edu*

Department Information:

1948. Chairperson: Charles A. Burdsal. Number of faculty: total—full-time 14, part-time 1; women—full-time 11, part-time 1; total—minority—full-time 2; women minority—full-time 1.

Programs and Degrees Offered:

Listed in the following order: Program area, degree type (T if terminal Master's), number awarded 7/06–6/07. Clinical Psychology PhD (Doctor of Philosophy) 4, Human Factors PhD (Doctor of Philosophy) 3, Community PhD (Doctor of Philosophy) 2.

APA Accreditation: Clinical PhD (Doctor of Philosophy).

Student Applications/Admissions:

Student Applications

Clinical Psychology PhD (Doctor of Philosophy)—Applications 2007–2008, 40. Total applicants accepted 2007–2008, 4. Number full-time enrolled (new admits only) 2007–2008, 4. Openings 2008–2009, 3. The median number of years required for completion of a degree in 2006–2007 were 7. The number of students enrolled full- and part-time who were dismissed or voluntarily withdrew from this program area in 2007–2008 were 2. *Human Factors PhD (Doctor of Philosophy)*—Applications 2007–2008, 25. Total applicants accepted 2007–2008, 6. Number full-time enrolled (new admits only) 2007–2008, 6. Openings 2008–2009, 6. The median number of years required for completion of a degree in 2006–2007 were 5. The number of students enrolled full- and part-time who were dismissed or voluntarily withdrew from this program area in 2007–2008 were 0. *Community PhD (Doctor of Philosophy)*—Applications 2007–2008, 16. Total applicants accepted 2007–2008, 4. Number full-time enrolled (new admits only) 2007–2008, 4. Openings 2008–2009, 4. The median number of years required for completion of a degree in 2006–2007 were 5. The number of students enrolled full- and part-time who were dismissed or voluntarily withdrew from this program area in 2007–2008 were 0.

Admissions Requirements:

Scores: Entries appear in this order: required test or GPA, minimum score (if required), median score of students entering in 2007–2008. Doctoral Programs: GRE-V no minimum stated, 500; GRE-Q no minimum stated, 530; overall undergraduate GPA 3.00, 3.73; last 2 years GPA no minimum stated; psychology GPA no minimum stated, 3.82.

Other Criteria: (importance of criteria rated low, medium, or high): GRE/MAT scores—medium, research experience—high, work experience—medium, clinically related public service—medium, GPA—high, letters of recommendation—medium, interview—medium, statement of goals and objectives—high, undergraduate major in psychology—low, specific undergraduate psychology courses taken—low. For additional information on admission requirements, go to http://www.psychology.wichita.edu.

Student Characteristics: The following represents characteristics of students in 2007–2008 in all graduate psychology programs in the department: Female—full-time 42, part-time 0; Male—full-time 11, part-time 0; African American/Black—full-time 4, part-time 0; Hispanic/Latino(a)—full-time 5, part-time 0; Asian/Pacific Islander—full-time 2, part-time 0; American Indian/Alaska Native—part-time 0; Caucasian/White—full-time 41, part-time 0; Multi-ethnic—full-time 0, part-time 0; students subject to the Americans With Disabilities Act—full-time 0, part-time 0; Unknown ethnicity—full-time 1, part-time 0; International students who hold an F-1 or J-1 Visa—full-time 3, part-time 0.

Financial Information/Assistance:

Tuition for Full-Time Study: *Doctoral:* State residents: per academic year $4,989, $207 per credit hour; Nonstate residents: per academic year $13,387, $557 per credit hour. Tuition is subject to change. Additional fees are assessed to students beyond the costs of tuition for the following: student fees. See the following Web site for updates and changes in tuition costs: http://www.webs.wichita.edu/gradsch/.

Financial Assistance:

First-Year Students: Teaching assistantships available for first year. Average amount paid per academic year: $6,500. Average number of hours worked per week: 20. Tuition remission given: full and partial. Research assistantships available for first year. Average amount paid per academic year: $10,000. Average number of hours worked per week: 20.

Advanced Students: Teaching assistantships available for advanced students. Average amount paid per academic year: $7,500. Average number of hours worked per week: 20. Tuition remission given: full and partial. Research assistantships available for advanced students. Average amount paid per academic year: $10,000. Average number of hours worked per week: 20.

Additional Information: Of all students currently enrolled full time, 70% benefited from one or more of the listed financial assistance programs.

Internships/Practica: Doctoral Degree (PhD Clinical Psychology): For those doctoral students for whom a professional internship was required in this program prior to graduation, (2) students applied for an internship in 2006–2007, with (2) students obtaining an internship. Of those students who obtained an internship, (2) were paid internships. Of those students who obtained an internship, (2) students placed in APA/CPA-accredited internships, (0) students placed in internships not APA/CPA accredited, but listed with the Association of Psychology Postdoctoral and Internship Centers (APPIC), (0) students placed in internships conforming to guidelines of the Council of Directors of School Psychology Programs (CDSPP), (0) students placed in internships that were not APA/CPA-accredited, APPIC or CDSPP listed. An important aspect of the Human Factors Program is its requirement that all students complete an internship. The internship is designed to provide students with practical experience integrating their education in real-world situations. The internships have included positions with the FAA, Google, Bell Laboratories, IBM, Microsoft, and other similar settings. These placements have often led to post-PhD employment opportunities. In the Clinical and Community Programs, practicum opportunities, most of them funded, are available in on-campus training facilities and community agencies. Settings include the Psychology Clinic and the Counseling and Testing Center, both at Wichita State University; the Sedgwick County Department of Mental Health; Head Start; and various community-based projects. Students in the Clinical Program are required to complete 1 year of internship experience toward the end of their graduate studies.

Housing and Day Care: On-campus housing is available. See the following Web site for more information: http://www.wichita.edu. On-campus day care facilities are available.

Employment of Department Graduates:

Master's Degree Graduates: Of those who graduated in the academic year 2006–2007, the following categories and numbers represent the postgraduate activities and employment of master's degree graduates: Enrolled in a postdoctoral residency/fellowship (n/a), employed in independent practice (n/a), total from the above (master's) (0).

Doctoral Degree Graduates: Of those who graduated in the academic year 2006–2007, the following categories and numbers represent the postgraduate activities and employment of doctoral degree graduates: Enrolled in a psychology doctoral program (n/a), enrolled in a postdoctoral residency/fellowship (1), employed in independent practice (0), employed in an academic position at a university (1), employed in an academic position at a 2-year/4-year college (2), employed in business or industry (1), employed in government agency (2), employed in a community mental health/counseling center (1), total from the above (doctoral) (8).

Additional Information:

Orientation, Objectives, and Emphasis of Department: The Psychology Department, open to various theoretical orientations, emphasizes research in its three programs. The Human Factors Program is accredited by the Education Committee of the Human Factors and Ergonomics Society. This program provides students with wide exposure to research, training, practice, and literature in the field of Human Factors, as well as to issues in the wider context of basic and applied experimental psychology. Current human factors research involves cognitive functioning, aging, development, human–computer interactions, aerospace issues, perception, attention, vision, and driving-related issues, especially with the elderly. The APA-accredited Clinical Program seeks to integrate community and clinical psychology. The goal of the program is to educate and license students to be competent clinical psychologists who conceptualize, research, intervene, and treat problems at the individual, group, organizational, and societal levels. Special areas of interest and research include parent–child interaction, treatment and prevention of depression, treatment and prevention of delinquency, adolescent health and development, and assessment of personality and psychopathology. The Community Program seeks to educate students in community psychology with an emphasis on assessing and solving problems at the group, organizational, and societal levels. Special areas of research and practice include adolescent health and development, self-help groups, voluntary and paid helping relationships especially with the elderly, animal welfare, and treatment and prevention of delinquency. All three programs have an applied research focus.

Special Facilities or Resources: The department is located in Jabara Hall and maintains fully equipped laboratories. Currently active research groups include the Software Usability Research Lab, Perception and Attention Lab, Visual Psychophysics Lab, Decision Making Research Lab, Child and Family Research Center, Personality Research Lab, Quantitative Modeling Lab, and the Center for Community Support and Research. Our computer facilities are state-of-the-art and are available to students for coursework and research. The department also has access to the National Institute for Aviation Research, the Social Science Research Laboratory, and the University Computing Center. The Psychology Clinic, which is part of the psychology department, provides outpatient services via individual, group, and family modalities. The clinic has facilities for individual and group research. The statewide Center for Community Support and Research, with a computerized database and an 800 number, also operates out of the psychology department. Faculty maintain working relationships with a number of governmental and community agencies that facilitate student involvement in community practice and research. The agencies include the public school system, the Sedgwick County Department of Mental Health, and COMCARE, among others.

Information for Students With Physical Disabilities: See the following Web site for more information: http://www.webs.wichita.edu/disserv/.

Application Information:
Send to Graduate Coordinator, Psychology Department. Students are admitted in the Fall, application deadline January 15. *Fee:* $35. International students $50.

Eastern Kentucky University

Department of Psychology
Arts and Sciences
Cammack 127
Richmond, KY 40475
Telephone: (859) 622-1105
Fax: (859) 622-5871
E-mail: *robert.brubaker@eku.edu*
Web: *http://www.psychology.eku.edu*

Department Information:

1967. Chairperson: Robert G. Brubaker. Number of faculty: total—full-time 21, part-time 11; women—full-time 11, part-time 8; total—minority—full-time 1, part-time 1; women minority—full-time 1; faculty subject to the Americans With Disabilities Act 1.

Programs and Degrees Offered:

Listed in the following order: Program area, degree type (T if terminal Master's), number awarded 7/06–6/07. Clinical Psychology MA/MS (Master of Arts/Science) (T) 12, Industrial/Organizational MA/MS (Master of Arts/Science) (T) 4, School Psychology EdS/MEd (School Psychology) 9, General Psychology MA/MS (Master of Arts/Science) (T) 1.

Student Applications/Admissions:

Student Applications

Clinical Psychology MA/MS (Master of Arts/Science)—Applications 2007–2008, 57. Total applicants accepted 2007–2008, 24. Number full-time enrolled (new admits only) 2007–2008, 14. Total enrolled 2007–2008 full-time, 29. Openings 2008–2009, 15. The median number of years required for completion of a degree in 2006–2007 were 2. The number of students enrolled full- and part-time who were dismissed or voluntarily withdrew from this program area in 2007–2008 were 0. *Industrial/Organizational MA/MS (Master of Arts/Science)*—Applications 2007–2008, 29. Total applicants accepted 2007–2008, 15. Number full-time enrolled (new admits only) 2007–2008, 9. Number part-time enrolled (new admits only) 2007–2008, 0. Openings 2008–2009, 10. The median number of years required for completion of a degree in 2006–2007 were 2. The number of students enrolled full- and part-time who were dismissed or voluntarily withdrew from this program area in 2007–2008 were 0. *School Psychology EdS/MEd (School Psychology)*—Applications 2007–2008, 50. Total applicants accepted 2007–2008, 19. Number full-time enrolled (new admits only) 2007–2008, 9. Number part-time enrolled (new admits only) 2007–2008, 0. Openings 2008–2009, 10. The median number of years required for completion of a degree in 2006–2007 were 3. The number of students enrolled full- and part-time who were dismissed or voluntarily withdrew from this program area in 2007–2008 were 0. *General Psychology MA/MS (Master of Arts/Science)*—Applications 2007–2008, 5. Total applicants accepted 2007–2008, 2. Number full-time enrolled (new admits only) 2007–2008, 1. Total enrolled 2007–2008 full-time, 2. Openings 2008–2009, 4. The median number of years required for completion of a degree in 2006–2007 was 1. The number of students enrolled full- and part-time who were dismissed or voluntarily withdrew from this program area in 2007–2008 were 0.

Admissions Requirements:

Scores: Entries appear in this order: required test or GPA, minimum score (if required), median score of students entering in 2007–2008. Master's Programs: GRE-V no minimum stated, 450; GRE-Q no minimum stated, 510; overall undergraduate GPA 2.5, 3.4; last 2 years GPA no minimum stated; psychology GPA no minimum stated; Masters GRE-Analytical no minimum stated, 4.1.

Other Criteria: (importance of criteria rated low, medium, or high): GRE/MAT scores—medium, research experience—medium, work experience—medium, extracurricular activity—low, clinically related public service—high, GPA—medium, letters of recommendation—high, statement of goals and objectives—high, undergraduate major in psychology—medium, specific undergraduate psychology courses taken—medium.

Student Characteristics: The following represents characteristics of students in 2007–2008 in all graduate psychology programs in the department: Female—full-time 65, part-time 0; Male—full-time 11, part-time 0; African American/Black—full-time 3, part-time 0; Hispanic/Latino(a)—full-time 0, part-time 0; Asian/Pacific Islander—full-time 1, part-time 0; American Indian/Alaska Native—full-time 0, part-time 0; Caucasian/White—full-time 72, part-time 0; Unknown ethnicity—full-time 0, part-time 0.

Financial Information/Assistance:

Tuition for Full-Time Study: *Master's:* State residents: per academic year $5,610, $311 per credit hour; Nonstate residents: per academic year $15,610, $883 per credit hour. See the following Web site for updates and changes in tuition costs: http://www.billings.eku.edu/fees/regfee.php.

Financial Assistance:

First-Year Students: Research assistantships available for first year. Average amount paid per academic year: $5,000. Average number of hours worked per week: 20. Apply by March 15. Tuition remission given: partial.

Advanced Students: Research assistantships available for advanced students. Average amount paid per academic year: $5,000. Average number of hours worked per week: 20. Apply by May 1. Tuition remission given: partial.

Additional Information: Of all students currently enrolled full time, 80% benefited from one or more of the listed financial assistance programs. Application and information available online at http://www.finaid.eku.edu/.

Internships/Practica: Master's Degree (MA/MS Clinical Psychology): An internship experience such as a final research project or "capstone" experience is required of graduates. A variety of field placements are available within easy commuting distance from Richmond. Practicum sites have included private psychiatric and VA hospitals, the University counseling center, a residential treatment facility for children, alcohol and drug abuse treatment programs, and several adult and child outpatient mental health centers. School psychology students can choose from a variety of public and private elementary and secondary schools. Students have completed internships in Kentucky as well as many other states. Students in the I/O program work on practicum projects with various for-profit and nonprofit organizations in the region.

Housing and Day Care: On-campus housing is available. See the following Web site for more information: http://www.housing.eku.edu/. On-campus day care facilities are available.

Employment of Department Graduates:

Master's Degree Graduates: Of those who graduated in the academic year 2006–2007, the following categories and numbers represent the postgraduate activities and employment of master's degree graduates: Enrolled in a psychology doctoral program (4), enrolled in another graduate/professional program (1), enrolled in a postdoctoral residency/fellowship (n/a), employed in independent practice (n/a), employed in other positions at a higher education institution (1), employed in a professional position in a school system (7), employed in business or industry (9), employed in a community mental health/counseling center (9), total from the above (master's) (31).

Doctoral Degree Graduates: Of those who graduated in the academic year 2006–2007, the following categories and numbers represent the postgraduate activities and employment of doctoral degree graduates: Enrolled in a psychology doctoral program (n/a), total from the above (doctoral) (0).

Additional Information:

Orientation, Objectives, and Emphasis of Department: The MS program in clinical psychology is designed to train professional psychologists to work in clinics, hospitals, or other agencies. In the clinical program, approximately one third of the course hours are devoted to theory and research, one third to clinical skills training, and one third to practicum and internship placements in the community. The clinical program also offers specialized training and experience serving individuals with autism spectrum disorders and those who are deaf or hard of hearing. The PsyD program in school psychology is designed to train professional psychologists to work in schools and school-related agencies. The program involves 71 graduate hours including internship, is NASP approved, and meets Kentucky certification requirements. The certification program in school psychology is designed individually for the student with a degree in a related area who wishes to meet school psychology certification standards. Both programs meet the curriculum standards required for membership in the Council of Applied Master's Programs in Psychology and the North American Association for Master's Psychology, in which the department is an active participant. The clinical program is accredited nationally by the Master's Program Accreditation Council. The I/O program is designed to meet the education and training guidelines established by the Society for Industrial and Organizational Psychology. The scientist–practitioner I/O program prepares students to work in organizations and/or pursue a doctoral degree. Degree requirements include intensive required courses and electives, and practicum. Research opportunities are available in all programs, and all programs prepare students for doctoral study. The MS General Psychology program offers a flexible curriculum designed to prepare students for further graduate study in psychology or for a variety of nonapplied career options.

Special Facilities or Resources: Laboratories include several multipurpose rooms. The clinical training facility includes a group therapy room, individual therapy rooms, a testing room, and a play therapy room. All rooms have two-way mirror viewing and videotape facilities. The department operates a child and family clinic providing services to the community, with its primary mission the training of students.

Information for Students With Physical Disabilities: See the following Web site for more information: http://www.disabled.eku.edu/.

Application Information:

Send to Graduate School, Eastern Kentucky University, 521 Lancaster Avenue, Richmond, KY 40475; letters of recommendation should be sent to the Department Chair. Application available online. URL of online application: http://www.gradschool.eku.edu/. Students are admitted in the Fall, application deadline March 15. Applications after this date are considered on a space-available basis. *Fee:* $35.

Kentucky, University of

Department of Educational and Counseling Psychology
College of Education
Dickey Hall, Room 237
Lexington, KY 40506-0017
Telephone: (859) 257-7881
Fax: (859) 257-5662
E-mail: *lynda.brownwright@uky.edu*
Web: *http://www.uky.edu/education/edphead.html*

Department Information:

1968. Chairperson: Lynda Brown Wright. Number of faculty: total—full-time 13; women—full-time 8; total—minority—full-time 3; women minority—full-time 2.

Programs and Degrees Offered:

Listed in the following order: Program area, degree type (T if terminal Master's), number awarded 7/06–6/07. Counseling MA/MS (Master of Arts/Science) 6, Educational MA/MS (Master of Arts/Science) (T) 2, School MA/MS (Master of Arts/Science) 14, Counseling PhD (Doctor of Philosophy) 7, Educational PhD (Doctor of Philosophy) 7, School PhD (Doctor of Philosophy) 2.

APA Accreditation: Counseling PhD (Doctor of Philosophy). School PhD (Doctor of Philosophy).

Student Applications/Admissions:

Student Applications

Counseling MA/MS (Master of Arts/Science)—Applications 2007–2008, 48. Total applicants accepted 2007–2008, 15. Number full-time enrolled (new admits only) 2007–2008, 9. Number part-time enrolled (new admits only) 2007–2008, 0. Openings 2008–2009, 15. The median number of years required for completion of a degree in 2006–2007 were 2. The number of students enrolled full- and part-time who were dismissed or voluntarily withdrew from this program area in 2007–2008 were 0. *Educational MA/MS (Master of Arts/Science)*—Applications 2007–2008, 4. Total applicants accepted 2007–2008, 2. Number full-time enrolled (new admits only) 2007–2008, 2. Number part-time enrolled (new admits only) 2007–2008, 0. Total enrolled 2007–2008 full-time, 2, part-time, 2. Openings 2008–2009, 5. The median number of years required for completion of a degree in 2006–2007 were 2. The number of students enrolled full- and part-time who were dismissed or voluntarily withdrew from this program area in 2007–2008 were 0. *School MA/MS (Master of Arts/Science)*—Applications 2007–2008, 42. Total applicants accepted 2007–2008, 12. Number full-time enrolled (new admits only) 2007–2008, 10. Number part-time enrolled (new admits only) 2007–2008, 0. Openings 2008–2009, 12. The median number of years required for completion of a degree in 2006–2007 were 2. The number of students enrolled full- and part-time who were dismissed or voluntarily withdrew from this program area in 2007–2008 were 0. *Counseling PhD (Doctor of Philosophy)*—Applications 2007–2008, 55. Total applicants accepted 2007–2008, 4. Number full-time enrolled (new admits only) 2007–2008, 4. Number part-time enrolled (new admits only) 2007–2008, 0. Openings 2008–2009, 9. The median number of years required for completion of a degree in 2006–2007 were 5. The number of students enrolled full- and part-time who were dismissed or voluntarily withdrew from this program area in 2007–2008 were 0. *Educational PhD (Doctor of Philosophy)*—Applications 2007–2008, 0. Total applicants accepted 2007–2008, 0. Number full-time enrolled (new admits only) 2007–2008, 0. Number part-time enrolled (new admits only) 2007–2008, 0. Total enrolled 2007–2008 full-time, 9, part-time, 9. Openings 2008–2009, 5. The median number of years required for completion of a degree in 2006–2007 were 7. The number of students enrolled full- and part-time who were dismissed or voluntarily withdrew from this program area in 2007–2008 were 0. *School PhD (Doctor of Philosophy)*—Applications 2007–2008, 22. Total applicants accepted 2007–2008, 6. Number full-time enrolled (new admits only) 2007–2008, 0. Number part-time enrolled (new admits only) 2007–2008, 0. Total enrolled 2007–2008 full-time, 36, part-time, 9. Openings 2008–2009, 7. The median number of years required for completion of a degree in 2006–2007 were 6. The number of students enrolled full- and part-time who were dismissed or voluntarily withdrew from this program area in 2007–2008 were 0.

Admissions Requirements:

Scores: Entries appear in this order: required test or GPA, minimum score (if required), median score of students entering in 2007–2008. Master's Programs: GRE-V no minimum stated; GRE-Q no minimum stated; overall undergraduate GPA no minimum stated; last 2 years GPA no minimum stated. Doctoral Programs: GRE-V no minimum stated; GRE-Q no minimum stated; overall undergraduate GPA 3.00, 3.37.

Other Criteria: (importance of criteria rated low, medium, or high): GRE/MAT scores—medium, research experience—high, work experience—medium, extracurricular activity—medium, clinically related public service—high, GPA—medium, letters of recommendation—high, interview—high, statement of goals and objectives—high. Research experience and statement of goals are the highest priority for Educational Psychology programs. Work experiences and clinically related service are more important for School and Counseling programs. For additional information on admission requirements, go to http://www.uky.edu/Education/edphead.html.

Student Characteristics: The following represents characteristics of students in 2007–2008 in all graduate psychology programs in the department: Female—full-time 123, part-time 0; Male—full-time 31, part-time 0; African American/Black—full-time 19, part-time 1; Hispanic/Latino(a)—full-time 2, part-time 0; Asian/Pacific Islander—full-time 2, part-time 0; American Indian/Alaska Native—full-time 1, part-time 0; Caucasian/White—full-time 118, part-time 27; Multi-ethnic—full-time 0, part-time 0; students subject to the Americans With Disabilities Act—full-time 1, part-time 0; Unknown ethnicity—full-time 12, part-time 0; International students who hold an F-1 or J-1 Visa—full-time 4, part-time 0.

Financial Information/Assistance:

Tuition for Full-Time Study: *Master's:* State residents: per academic year $7,670, $401 per credit hour; Nonstate residents: per academic year $16,158, $843 per credit hour. *Doctoral:* State residents: per academic year $7,670, $401 per credit hour; Nonstate residents: per academic year $16,158, $843 per credit hour. Tuition is subject to change.

Financial Assistance:

First-Year Students: No information provided.

Advanced Students: No information provided.

Additional Information: Of all students currently enrolled full time, 60% benefited from one or more of the listed financial assistance programs. Application and information available online at http://www.coe.uky.edu/AcadServ/Text/ScholarshipInfo.pdf.

Internships/Practica: No information provided.

Housing and Day Care: On-campus housing is available. See the following Web site for more information: http://www.uky.edu/Housing/graduate_family/index.htm. On-campus day care facilities are available. See the following Web site for more information: http://www.research.uky.edu/gs/GradOrient.html.

Employment of Department Graduates:

Master's Degree Graduates: Of those who graduated in the academic year 2006–2007, the following categories and numbers represent the postgraduate activities and employment of master's degree graduates: Enrolled in a psychology doctoral program (6), enrolled in another graduate/professional program (2), enrolled in a postdoctoral residency/fellowship (n/a), employed in independent practice (n/a), employed in an academic position at a university (2), employed in an academic position at a 2-year/4-year college (1), employed in other positions at a higher education institution (3), employed in a professional position in a school system (5), employed in business or industry (0), employed in government agency (3), employed in a community mental health/counseling center (5), employed in a hospital/medical center (2), total from the above (master's) (29).

Doctoral Degree Graduates: Of those who graduated in the academic year 2006–2007, the following categories and numbers represent the postgraduate activities and employment of doctoral degree graduates: Enrolled in a psychology doctoral program (n/a), enrolled in another graduate/professional program (1), enrolled in a postdoctoral residency/fellowship (4), employed in independent practice (1), employed in an academic position at a university (2), employed in an academic position at a 2-year/4-year college (0), employed in other positions at a higher education institution (2), employed in a professional position in a school system (0), employed in business or industry (0), employed in government agency (0), employed in a community mental health/counseling center (0), total from the above (doctoral) (10).

Additional Information:

Orientation, Objectives, and Emphasis of Department: Three programs are housed within the department: counseling psychology, educational psychology, and school psychology. The program faculties in counseling psychology and in school psychology are committed to the scientist–practitioner model for professional training, whereas educational psychology faculty emphasize the researcher–teacher model. A strong emphasis has been placed upon the psychology core for all professional training. Counseling faculty research interests focus upon cultural diversity and social justice, counseling issues for sexual minorities, family processes, experiential therapies, and rape awareness. The school psychology faculty research interests focus upon evaluation and assessment, positive mental health outcomes, literacy and social development in young children, and direct interventions. The educational psychology faculty research interests include motivation in educational settings, cardiovascular stress in minority children, culture and socialization in relation to cognition, engagement in risky behaviors, and sleep deprivation. Students in each program are encouraged to establish mentoring relationships with their major professor by the beginning of their second semester. The counseling faculty intends to prepare professionals for diverse settings (e.g., colleges and universities, research facilities, hospitals, regional mental health centers, and private practice). The school psychology faculty aims to prepare scientist–practitioners who will function in school and university settings, in mental health consortia, and in private practice. The educational psychology faculty prepares graduates for research and teaching careers within higher education and applied research settings.

Special Facilities or Resources: The University of Kentucky is located on the western edge of Appalachia, which provides students with the opportunity to interact with a rich and varied American culture. The uniqueness of this potential client and research pool allows our students to examine attributes of the bridge between old, rural America and the future, more technological America. Microcomputer facilities are available within the department and within the college for student use in word processing, model development, simulation and evaluation, and data analysis. The university provides all the facilities and resources expected of a major research institution (e.g., extensive libraries, computer facilities, research environment, and medical center).

Application Information:

Send to Dr. Lynley Anderman, Director of Graduate Study, Department of Educational and Counseling Psychology, College of Education, University of Kentucky, 245 Dickey Hall, Lexington, KY 40506-0017. Application available online. URL of online application: http://www.uky.edu/Education/edphead.html. Students are admitted in the Fall, application deadline January 15. January15 deadline for PhD; March 1 deadline for Master's program. *Fee:* $40; $45 international.

Kentucky, University of

Department of Psychology
Arts and Sciences
Kastle Hall
Lexington, KY 40506-0044
Telephone: (859) 257-9640
Fax: (859) 323-1979
E-mail: *tdherr2@uky.edu*
Web: *http://www.uky.edu/ArtsSciences/Psychology*

Department Information:

1917. Chairperson: Charles R. Carlson, PhD, ABPP. Number of faculty: total—full-time 16; women—full-time 13; faculty subject to the Americans With Disabilities Act 1.

Programs and Degrees Offered:

Listed in the following order: Program area, degree type (T if terminal Master's), number awarded 7/06–6/07. Clinical PhD (Doctor of Philosophy) 5, Experimental PhD (Doctor of Philosophy) 4.

APA Accreditation: Clinical PhD (Doctor of Philosophy).

Student Applications/Admissions:

Student Applications

Clinical PhD (Doctor of Philosophy)—Applications 2007–2008, 177. Total applicants accepted 2007–2008, 9. Number full-time enrolled (new admits only) 2007–2008, 9. Openings 2008–2009, 6. The median number of years required for completion of a degree in 2006–2007 were 6. The number of students enrolled full- and part-time who were dismissed or voluntarily withdrew from this program area in 2007–2008 were 0. *Experimental PhD (Doctor of Philosophy)*—Applications 2007–2008, 69. Total applicants accepted 2007–2008, 8. Number full-time enrolled (new admits only) 2007–2008, 8. Openings 2008–2009, 8. The median number of years required for completion of a degree in 2006–2007 were 4. The number of students enrolled full- and part-time who were dismissed or voluntarily withdrew from this program area in 2007–2008 were 0.

Admissions Requirements:

Scores: Entries appear in this order: required test or GPA, minimum score (if required), median score of students entering in 2007–2008. Doctoral Programs: GRE-V no minimum stated; GRE-Q no minimum stated; overall undergraduate GPA 2.75; Doctoral program GRE-Analytic no minimum stated.

Other Criteria: (importance of criteria rated low, medium, or high): GRE/MAT scores—high, research experience—high, work experience—low, clinically related public service—medium, GPA—high, letters of recommendation—high, interview—high, statement of goals and objectives—high.

Student Characteristics: The following represents characteristics of students in 2007–2008 in all graduate psychology programs in the department: Female—full-time 59, part-time 0; Male—full-time 28, part-time 0; African American/Black—full-time 5, part-time 0; Hispanic/Latino(a)—full-time 2, part-time 0; Asian/Pacific Islander—full-time 3, part-time 0; American Indian/Alaska Native—full-time 1, part-time 0; Caucasian/White—

full-time 76, part-time 0; Multi-ethnic—full-time 0, part-time 0; students subject to the Americans With Disabilities Act—full-time 0, part-time 0; Unknown ethnicity—full-time 0, part-time 0.

Financial Information/Assistance:

Tuition for Full-Time Study: *Master's:* State residents: per academic year $7,670, $401 per credit hour; Nonstate residents: per academic year $16,158, $843 per credit hour. *Doctoral:* State residents: per academic year $7,670, $401 per credit hour; Nonstate residents: per academic year $16,158, $843 per credit hour. Tuition is subject to change.

Financial Assistance:

First-Year Students: Teaching assistantships available for first year. Average amount paid per academic year: $11,076. Average number of hours worked per week: 20. Apply by December 15. Tuition remission given: full. Research assistantships available for first year. Average amount paid per academic year: $11,076. Average number of hours worked per week: 20. Apply by December 15. Tuition remission given: full. Fellowships and scholarships available for first year. Average amount paid per academic year: $15,000. Average number of hours worked per week: 20. Apply by December 16. Tuition remission given: full.

Advanced Students: Teaching assistantships available for advanced students. Average amount paid per academic year: $11,076. Average number of hours worked per week: 20. Apply by December 15. Tuition remission given: full. Research assistantships available for advanced students. Average amount paid per academic year: $11,076. Average number of hours worked per week: 20. Apply by December 15. Tuition remission given: full. Fellowships and scholarships available for advanced students. Average amount paid per academic year: $15,000. Average number of hours worked per week: 20. Apply by December 15. Tuition remission given: full.

Additional Information: Of all students currently enrolled full time, 99% benefited from one or more of the listed financial assistance programs.

Internships/Practica: No information provided.

Housing and Day Care: On-campus housing is available. On-campus day care facilities are available.

Employment of Department Graduates:

Master's Degree Graduates: Of those who graduated in the academic year 2006–2007, the following categories and numbers represent the postgraduate activities and employment of master's degree graduates: Enrolled in a psychology doctoral program (0), enrolled in another graduate/professional program (0), enrolled in a postdoctoral residency/fellowship (n/a), employed in independent practice (n/a), employed in an academic position at a university (0), employed in an academic position at a 2-year/4-year college (0), employed in other positions at a higher education institution (0), employed in a professional position in a school system (0), employed in business or industry (0), employed in government agency (0), employed in a community mental health/counseling center (0), employed in a hospital/medical center (0), still seeking employment (0), other employment position (0), do not know (0), total from the above (master's) (0).

Doctoral Degree Graduates: Of those who graduated in the academic year 2006–2007, the following categories and numbers represent the postgraduate activities and employment of doctoral degree graduates: Enrolled in a psychology doctoral program (n/a), enrolled in a postdoctoral residency/fellowship (4), employed in independent practice (0), employed in an academic position at a university (2), employed in an academic position at a 2-year/4-year college (2), employed in other positions at a higher education institution (0), employed in a professional position in a school system (0), employed in business or industry (0), employed in government agency (0), employed in a community mental health/counseling center (0), employed in a hospital/medical center (0), still seeking employment (0), other employment position (0), do not know (0), total from the above (doctoral) (8).

Additional Information:

Orientation, Objectives, and Emphasis of Department: The goals of the doctoral program depend partly upon the specific program area in which a student enrolls. The program in Clinical Psychology follows the Boulder scientist–practitioner model. Students in the program receive broad exposure to the major theoretical perspectives influencing clinical psychology. All students are actively engaged in research throughout their graduate training. Beginning in the 2nd year of study, each student also receives extensive clinical experience via placements in mental or behavioral health settings. Graduates of the program are prepared to pursue an academic career or to be a practitioner. Students in the program in Experimental Psychology, Cognitive, Developmental, Social, Animal Learning, and Behavioral Neuroscience are trained as research scientists. They are exposed to the important theoretical perspectives and research paradigms of their respective areas. There is considerable latitude for individuals to define their specific programs of study. Graduates are prepared to pursue an academic career or a research position in an applied setting. Graduate study is based on a core curriculum model that would fulfill Graduate School requirements for the PhD degree. All students complete a Master's thesis, written and oral doctoral qualifying examinations, and a dissertation demonstrating accomplishment in independent research.

Special Facilities or Resources: The psychology department occupies its own three-story building located by the computer center and main campus library. Kastle Hall houses faculty and student offices, classrooms, and research space. Research facilities in the building include animal laboratories for behavioral and physiological research, observation rooms with one-way mirrors, extensive video equipment, and microcomputer equipped rooms for cognitive research. Two additional buildings on campus are available for behavioral research. Current faculty have collaborative arrangements with several facilities on campus, including the neuropsychology laboratories in the Department of Neurology, the Oro-Facial Pain Clinic in the College of Dentistry, the Central Animal Research Facility, and the Sanders-Brown Center on Aging. The department maintains a large undergraduate subject pool. Clinical training facilities are excellent and include a departmental clinic housed in a separate building and clinical placement arrangements with a variety of mental and behavioral health facilities in Lexington.

Application Information:

Send to 106 Kastle Hall, Department of Psychology, University of Kentucky, Lexington, KY 40506-0044. Application available online. URL of online application: http://www.uky.edu/AS/Psychology/

graduate/. Students are admitted in the Fall, application deadline January 3. *Fee:* $35.

Louisville, University of

Psychological and Brain Sciences
Arts and Sciences
317 Life Sciences Building
Louisville, KY 40292
Telephone: (502) 852-6775
Fax: (502) 852-8904
E-mail: *bburns@louisville.edu*
Web: *http://www.louisville.edu/a-s/psychology/*

Department Information:

1963. Chairperson: Barbara M. Burns. Number of faculty: total—full-time 31; women—full-time 14; total—minority—full-time 5; women minority—full-time 2.

Programs and Degrees Offered:

Listed in the following order: Program area, degree type (T if terminal Master's), number awarded 7/06–6/07. Clinical Psychology PhD (Doctor of Philosophy) 6, Experimental Psychology PhD (Doctor of Philosophy) 2.

APA Accreditation: Clinical PhD (Doctor of Philosophy).

Student Applications/Admissions:

Student Applications

Clinical Psychology PhD (Doctor of Philosophy)—Applications 2007–2008, 99. Total applicants accepted 2007–2008, 9. Number full-time enrolled (new admits only) 2007–2008, 9. Number part-time enrolled (new admits only) 2007–2008, 0. Openings 2008–2009, 7. The median number of years required for completion of a degree in 2006–2007 were 6. The number of students enrolled full- and part-time who were dismissed or voluntarily withdrew from this program area in 2007–2008 were 0. *Experimental Psychology PhD (Doctor of Philosophy)*—Applications 2007–2008, 16. Total applicants accepted 2007–2008, 7. Number full-time enrolled (new admits only) 2007–2008, 7. Number part-time enrolled (new admits only) 2007–2008, 0. Openings 2008–2009, 7. The median number of years required for completion of a degree in 2006–2007 were 6. The number of students enrolled full- and part-time who were dismissed or voluntarily withdrew from this program area in 2007–2008 were 0.

Admissions Requirements:

Scores: Entries appear in this order: required test or GPA, minimum score (if required), median score of students entering in 2007–2008. Doctoral Programs: GRE-V 550, 550; GRE-Q 550, 620; overall undergraduate GPA 3.0, 3.75; last 2 years GPA 3.0, 3.82; psychology GPA 3.0, 3.86; Doctoral program GRE-Analytic 3.00, 4.00. The above scores/GPAs reflect our Clinical Psychology PhD program. Experimental Psychology PhD program scores/GPAs are: GRE-V Minium 550 Median 600 GRE-Q Minimum 550 Median 620 GRE-Analytical Minimum 3.00 Median 4.00 Overall Undergraduate GPA Minimum 3.00 Median 3.56 Last two years GPA Minimum 3.00 Median 3.48 Psychology GPA Minimum 3.00 Median 3.62.

Other Criteria: (importance of criteria rated low, medium, or high): GRE/MAT scores—high, research experience—high, work experience—high, extracurricular activity—high, clinically related public service—high, GPA—high, letters of recommendation—high, interview—high, statement of goals and objectives—high, undergraduate major in psychology—medium, specific undergraduate psychology courses taken—medium. Experimental Psychology PhD does not require clinically related public service.

Student Characteristics: The following represents characteristics of students in 2007–2008 in all graduate psychology programs in the department: Female—full-time 58, part-time 0; Male—full-time 22, part-time 0; African American/Black—full-time 2, part-time 0; Hispanic/Latino(a)—full-time 1, part-time 0; Asian/Pacific Islander—full-time 6, part-time 0; American Indian/Alaska Native—full-time 0, part-time 0; Caucasian/White—full-time 71, part-time 0; Multi-ethnic—full-time 0, part-time 0; students subject to the Americans With Disabilities Act—full-time 0, part-time 0; Unknown ethnicity—full-time 0, part-time 0; International students who hold an F-1 or J-1 Visa—full-time 6, part-time 0.

Financial Information/Assistance:

Tuition for Full-Time Study: *Doctoral:* State residents: per academic year $10,042, $419 per credit hour; Nonstate residents: per academic year $24,120, $1,005 per credit hour. Tuition is subject to change. See the following Web site for updates and changes in tuition costs: http://www.louisville.edu/vpf/bursar/student/tuition.htm.

Financial Assistance:

First-Year Students: Teaching assistantships available for first year. Average amount paid per academic year: $20,000. Average number of hours worked per week: 20. Apply by December 1. Tuition remission given: full. Research assistantships available for first year. Average amount paid per academic year: $20,000. Average number of hours worked per week: 20. Apply by December 1. Tuition remission given: full. Fellowships and scholarships available for first year. Average amount paid per academic year: $20,000. Average number of hours worked per week: 0. Apply by December 1. Tuition remission given: full.

Advanced Students: Teaching assistantships available for advanced students. Average amount paid per academic year: $20,000. Average number of hours worked per week: 20. Apply by December 1. Tuition remission given: full. Research assistantships available for advanced students. Average amount paid per academic year: $20,000. Average number of hours worked per week: 20. Apply by December 1. Tuition remission given: full. Traineeships available for advanced students. Average amount paid per academic year: $0. Average number of hours worked per week: 0. Apply by varies. Fellowships and scholarships available for advanced students. Average amount paid per academic year: $20,000. Average number of hours worked per week: 0. Apply by December 1. Tuition remission given: full.

Additional Information: Of all students currently enrolled full time, 78% benefited from one or more of the listed financial assistance programs.

Internships/Practica: Doctoral Degree (PhD Clinical Psychology): For those doctoral students for whom a professional internship was required in this program prior to graduation, (9) students applied for an internship in 2006–2007, with (9) students obtaining an internship. Of those students who obtained an internship, (9) were paid internships. Of those students who obtained an internship, (9) students placed in APA/CPA-accredited internships, (0) students placed in internships not APA/CPA accredited, but listed with the Association of Psychology Postdoctoral and Internship Centers (APPIC), (0) students placed in internships conforming to guidelines of the Council of Directors of School Psychology Programs (CDSPP), (0) students placed in internships that were not APA/CPA-accredited, APPIC or CDSPP listed. Internship and practica are available in a number of community and government agencies. These include the Department of Psychiatry and Behavioral Sciences, Child Evaluation Center, Central State Hospital, Veterans Administration Medical Center, Seven Counties Services, and numerous other agencies.

Housing and Day Care: On-campus housing is available. See the following Web site for more information: http://www.louisville.edu/student/life/housing/. No on-campus day care facilities are available.

Employment of Department Graduates:

Master's Degree Graduates: Of those who graduated in the academic year 2006–2007, the following categories and numbers represent the postgraduate activities and employment of master's degree graduates: Enrolled in a postdoctoral residency/fellowship (n/a), employed in independent practice (n/a), total from the above (master's) (0).

Doctoral Degree Graduates: Of those who graduated in the academic year 2006–2007, the following categories and numbers represent the postgraduate activities and employment of doctoral degree graduates: Enrolled in a psychology doctoral program (n/a), enrolled in another graduate/professional program (1), employed in an academic position at a university (5), employed in a community mental health/counseling center (1), do not know (1), total from the above (doctoral) (8).

Additional Information:

Orientation, Objectives, and Emphasis of Department: The Clinical Psychology PhD Program adheres to a scientist–practitioner model and is designed to provide training in research, psychological assessment, psychological intervention, and legal and professional issues. Faculty research foci are in health psychology, geropsychology, and psychopathology. Clinical emphasis includes interpersonal and cognitive–behavioral approaches. This Experimental Psychology PhD program offers a flexible curriculum tailored to the individual student's interests while providing extensive training in the core processes of psychology, research methodology, and data analysis. Research is an integral component of the Experimental Psychology PhD, thus students begin working in their mentor's laboratory when they arrive on campus. Faculty research interests are varied, but fall into the following areas of strength: Cognitive Science, Developmental Science, Neuroscience, and Vision and Hearing Sciences. Recent graduates are pursuing their careers in academic and nonacademic fields in numerous settings, including universities and colleges, industry, government, and private consulting organizations.

Special Facilities or Resources: Departmental facilities include modern laboratories and a Psychological Services Center. The University Computing Center is available from departmental stations via a campuswide network. Additional training opportunities are available through such facilities as the Department of Psychiatry and Behavioral Sciences, the Child Evaluation Center, Central State Hospital, and numerous other community agencies.

Application Information:

Send to Graduate Admissions Office, University of Louisville, Houchens Room 6, Louisville, KY 40292-0001. Application available online. URL of online application: http://www.graduate.louisville.edu/students/application.html/. Students are admitted in the Fall, application deadline December 1. *Fee:* $50.

Morehead State University (Kentucky)

Department of Psychology
Science and Technology
601 Ginger Hall
Morehead, KY 40351
Telephone: (606) 783-2981
Fax: (606) 783-5077
E-mail: *l.couch@moreheadstate.edu*
Web: *http://www.moreheadstate.edu/psych*

Department Information:

1968. Interim Chair: Laurie L. Couch, PhD. Number of faculty: total—full-time 10; women—full-time 5; total—minority—full-time 1; women minority—full-time 1.

Programs and Degrees Offered:

Listed in the following order: Program area, degree type (T if terminal Master's), number awarded 7/06–6/07. Clinical/Counseling Psychology MA/MS (Master of Arts/Science) (T) 9, Experimental General MA/MS (Master of Arts/Science) (T) 2.

Student Applications/Admissions:

Student Applications

Clinical/Counseling Psychology MA/MS (Master of Arts/Science)—Applications 2007–2008, 34. Number full-time enrolled (new admits only) 2007–2008, 12. Number part-time enrolled (new admits only) 2007–2008, 1. Total enrolled 2007–2008 full-time, 28, part-time, 2. Openings 2008–2009, 14. The median number of years required for completion of a degree in 2006–2007 were 2. The number of students enrolled full- and part-time who were dismissed or voluntarily withdrew from this program area in 2007–2008 were 1. *Experimental General MA/MS (Master of Arts/Science)*—Applications 2007–2008, 4. Total applicants accepted 2007–2008, 3. Number full-time enrolled (new admits only) 2007–2008, 1. Number part-time enrolled (new admits only) 2007–2008, 0. The median number of years required for completion of a degree in 2006–2007 were 2. The number of students enrolled full- and part-time who were dismissed or voluntarily withdrew from this program area in 2007–2008 were 0.

Admissions Requirements:

Scores: Entries appear in this order: required test or GPA, minimum score (if required), median score of students entering in 2007–2008. Master's Programs: GRE-V 400, 500; overall undergraduate GPA 3.0, 3.45.

Other Criteria: (importance of criteria rated low, medium, or high): GRE/MAT scores—high, research experience—medium, work experience—low, extracurricular activity—low, clinically related public service—low, GPA—high, letters of recommendation—high, interview—high, statement of goals and objectives—medium, undergraduate major in psychology—low, specific undergraduate psychology courses taken—low. Research experience is highly valued for admission to experimental program.

Student Characteristics: The following represents characteristics of students in 2007–2008 in all graduate psychology programs in the department: Female—full-time 23, part-time 0; Male—full-time 5, part-time 2; African American/Black—full-time 2, part-time 0; Hispanic/Latino(a)—full-time 0, part-time 0; Asian/Pacific Islander—full-time 0, part-time 0; American Indian/Alaska Native—full-time 0, part-time 0; Caucasian/White—full-time 26, part-time 2; Multi-ethnic—full-time 0, part-time 0; students subject to the Americans With Disabilities Act—full-time 0, part-time 0; Unknown ethnicity—full-time 0, part-time 0; International students who hold an F-1 or J-1 Visa—full-time 0, part-time 0.

Financial Information/Assistance:

Tuition for Full-Time Study: *Master's:* State residents: per academic year $5,730, $320 per credit hour; Nonstate residents: per academic year $14,500, $810 per credit hour. Tuition is subject to change. See the following Web site for updates and changes in tuition costs: http://www.moreheadstate.edu/abc.

Financial Assistance:

First-Year Students: Teaching assistantships available for first year. Average amount paid per academic year: $3,000. Average number of hours worked per week: 10. Tuition remission given: partial. Research assistantships available for first year. Average amount paid per academic year: $3,000. Average number of hours worked per week: 10. Tuition remission given: partial.

Advanced Students: Teaching assistantships available for advanced students. Average amount paid per academic year: $6,000. Average number of hours worked per week: 20. Tuition remission given: partial. Research assistantships available for advanced students. Average amount paid per academic year: $6,000. Average number of hours worked per week: 20. Tuition remission given: partial.

Additional Information: Of all students currently enrolled full time, 81% benefited from one or more of the listed financial assistance programs.

Internships/Practica: Master's Degree (MA/MS Clinical/Counseling Psychology): An internship experience, such as, a final research project or "capstone" experience is required of graduates. Master's Degree (MA/MS Experimental General): An internship experience such as a final research project or "capstone" experience is required of graduates. Internships and practica placement sites are available in several different states.

Housing and Day Care: On-campus housing is available. See the following Web site for more information: http://www.moreheadstate.edu/housing/. On-campus day care facilities are available. See the following Web site for more information: http://www.moreheadstate.edu/cdc/.

Employment of Department Graduates:

Master's Degree Graduates: Of those who graduated in the academic year 2006–2007, the following categories and numbers represent the postgraduate activities and employment of master's degree graduates: Enrolled in a postdoctoral residency/fellowship (n/a), employed in independent practice (n/a), total from the above (master's) (0).

Doctoral Degree Graduates: Of those who graduated in the academic year 2006–2007, the following categories and numbers represent the postgraduate activities and employment of doctoral degree graduates: Enrolled in a psychology doctoral program (n/a), total from the above (doctoral) (0).

Additional Information:

Orientation, Objectives, and Emphasis of Department: The clinical and counseling programs are designed primarily to train master's-level psychologists to practice in a variety of settings, and lead to certification in states that provide for certification of master's level psychologists. However, approximately 25% of our students enter doctoral-level programs upon graduation. The practitioner model is emphasized in the program, with primary emphases on acquisition of applied clinical skills and knowledge of the general field of psychology. Consequently, competencies in critical analysis of theories, experimental design, and quantitative data analysis are expected. Clinical and counseling students are encouraged to participate in or conduct research ongoing in the department. Students interested in pursuing doctoral level training are encouraged to complete a thesis. The purpose of the experimental program is primarily to prepare students for entry into doctoral programs. Students and faculty are involved in research in several areas including cognitive, perception, animal learning and motivation, psychopharmacology, neurophysiology, developmental, social, and personality.

Special Facilities or Resources: The psychology program provides excellent laboratory facilities for the study of human and animal behavior. Faculty/student research programs are funded through both intra- and extramural grants. The department maintains two microcomputer laboratories, and offers training in the statistical package known as SPSS. Most accepted students are supported by graduate assistantships. Financial assistance for paper presentations at professional conferences is normally available.

Application Information:

Send to Graduate Office, Morehead State University, 701 Ginger Hall Morehead, KY 40351. Application available online. URL of online application: http://www.moreheadstate.edu/files/graduate_application.pdf. Students are admitted in the Spring, application deadline March 1; programs have rolling admissions. Preference will be given to applications received by March 1. Rolling admissions continue through June 15. *Fee:* $0.

Murray State University

Department of Psychology
Humanities and Fine Arts
212 Wells Hall
Murray, KY 42071-3318
Telephone: (270) 809-2851
Fax: (270) 809-2991
E-mail: *vickid.anderson@murraystate.edu*
Web: *http://www.murraystate.edu/chfa/psychology/graduate.htm*

Department Information:

1966. Chairperson: Dr. Renae D. Duncan. Number of faculty: total—full-time 9; women—full-time 5.

Programs and Degrees Offered:

Listed in the following order: Program area, degree type (T if terminal Master's), number awarded 7/06–6/07. Clinical MA/MS (Master of Arts/Science) (T) 10, General MA/MS (Master of Arts/Science) (T) 4.

Student Applications/Admissions:

Student Applications

Clinical MA/MS (Master of Arts/Science)—Applications 2007–2008, 30. Total applicants accepted 2007–2008, 9. Number full-time enrolled (new admits only) 2007–2008, 9. Number part-time enrolled (new admits only) 2007–2008, 0. Openings 2008–2009, 11. The median number of years required for completion of a degree in 2006–2007 were 2. The number of students enrolled full- and part-time who were dismissed or voluntarily withdrew from this program area in 2007–2008 were 2. *General MA/MS (Master of Arts/Science)*—Applications 2007–2008, 6. Total applicants accepted 2007–2008, 5. Number full-time enrolled (new admits only) 2007–2008, 3. Number part-time enrolled (new admits only) 2007–2008, 0. Openings 2008–2009, 5. The median number of years required for completion of a degree in 2006–2007 were 2. The number of students enrolled full- and part-time who were dismissed or voluntarily withdrew from this program area in 2007–2008 were 0.

Admissions Requirements:

Scores: Entries appear in this order: required test or GPA, minimum score (if required), median score of students entering in 2007–2008. Master's Programs: GRE-V no minimum stated; GRE-Q no minimum stated; overall undergraduate GPA 3.00, 3.33; psychology GPA 3.00, 3.47.

Other Criteria: (importance of criteria rated low, medium, or high): GRE/MAT scores—medium, research experience—medium, work experience—low, extracurricular activity—low, GPA—high, letters of recommendation—high, statement of goals and objectives—high, specific undergraduate psychology courses taken—medium.

Student Characteristics: The following represents characteristics of students in 2007–2008 in all graduate psychology programs in the department: Female—full-time 18, part-time 0; Male—full-time 3, part-time 0; African American/Black—full-time 0, part-time 0; Hispanic/Latino(a)—full-time 0, part-time 0; Asian/Pacific Islander—full-time 1, part-time 0; American Indian/Alaska Native—full-time 0, part-time 0; Caucasian/White—full-time 20, part-time 0; Multi-ethnic—full-time 0, part-time 0; students subject to the Americans With Disabilities Act—full-time 1, part-time 0; Unknown ethnicity—full-time 0, part-time 0; International students who hold an F-1 or J-1 Visa—full-time 2, part-time 0.

Financial Information/Assistance:

Tuition for Full-Time Study: *Master's:* State residents: per academic year $3,078, $260 per credit hour; Nonstate residents: per academic year $8,658, $722 per credit hour. Tuition is subject to change. See the following Web site for updates and changes in tuition costs: http://www.campus.murraystate.edu/administ/accounting/bursar/costs/index.cfm.

Financial Assistance:

First-Year Students: Research assistantships available for first year. Average amount paid per academic year: $4,200. Average number of hours worked per week: 10. Apply by March 15. Tuition remission given: partial.

Advanced Students: Research assistantships available for advanced students. Average amount paid per academic year: $4,200. Average number of hours worked per week: 10. Apply by March 15. Tuition remission given: partial.

Additional Information: Of all students currently enrolled full time, 50% benefited from one or more of the listed financial assistance programs.

Internships/Practica: Master's Degree (MA/MS Clinical): An internship experience such as a final research project or "capstone" experience is required of graduates. Master's Degree (MA/MS General): An internship experience such as a final research project or "capstone" experience is required of graduates. To gain experience conducting therapy and psychological evaluations, a supervised two-semester, 20 hour per week clinical practicum is required. Clinical psychology students serve their practica at the MSU Psychological Center, an on-campus treatment center, which provides therapy and assessments for children, adults, and families from the community as well as for university students and staff. In addition to gaining experience conducting therapy and assessments, our clinical graduate students receive 2½ hours per week of supervision with our PhD-level licensed clinical psychologists. This allows for a fine-tuning of clinical skills as well as an added assurance that the clinician is providing the best and most ethical services to the Center's clients.

Housing and Day Care: On-campus housing is available. See the following Web site for more information: http://www.mursuky.edu/secsv/hous/colcts.htm. On-campus day care facilities are available.

Employment of Department Graduates:

Master's Degree Graduates: Of those who graduated in the academic year 2006–2007, the following categories and numbers represent the postgraduate activities and employment of master's degree graduates: Enrolled in a psychology doctoral program (5), enrolled in another graduate/professional program (0), enrolled in a postdoctoral residency/fellowship (n/a), employed in independent practice (n/a), employed in an academic position at a university (0), employed in an academic position at a 2-year/4-year college (0), employed in other positions at a higher education institution (0), employed in a professional position in a school system (1), employed in business or industry (0), employed in government agency (0), employed in a community mental health/counseling center (5), employed in a hospital/medical center (0), still seeking employment (0), other employment position (4), total from the above (master's) (15).

Doctoral Degree Graduates: Of those who graduated in the academic year 2006–2007, the following categories and numbers represent the postgraduate activities and employment of doctoral degree graduates: Enrolled in a psychology doctoral program (n/a), total from the above (doctoral) (0).

Additional Information:

Orientation, Objectives, and Emphasis of Department: The clinical program is based on the philosophy that the master's degree is first and foremost a degree in psychology and that students should achieve a broad base of knowledge in the field. Thus, students are required to take five psychological foundations courses that prepare the graduate to enter the field of psychology and also provide the general psychology courses required by state licensing boards. Clinical students also receive intensive instruction in psychodiagnostics, which emphasizes the administration, scoring, and interpretation of a variety of intelligence and personality tests. The psychotherapy curriculum is primarily cognitive–behavioral in nature, though a variety of techniques and orientations are presented that teach the student how best to conduct psychotherapy with adults, children, families, and couples. Students are expected to participate in research and a master's thesis is required. The general program emphasizes psychological foundations and research methodology as preparation for doctoral studies, community college teaching, or applied research.

Special Facilities or Resources: The department has research laboratories, an on-site psychological clinic with testing and observation rooms, and complete facilities for practica in diagnostics and therapy. Students also share offices in the department. Each student is assigned a locking desk with personal computer.

Application Information:
Send to Graduate Admissions Committee. Application available online. URL of online application: http://www.murraystate.edu/main_entry/g_admissions.htm. Students are admitted in the Fall, application deadline March 15. Applications will be accepted after the deadline. However, late applications will be considered only if openings remain after review of applications received before the due date. *Fee:* $25.

Spalding University

School of Professional Psychology
College of Social Sciences and Humanities
851 South Fourth Street
Louisville, KY 40203
Telephone: (502) 585-7127
Fax: (502) 585-7159
E-mail: *esimpson@spalding.edu*
Web: *http://www.spalding.edu/psychology*

Department Information:
1952. Chairperson: Steven Katsikas, PhD. Number of faculty: total—full-time 12, part-time 14; women—full-time 7, part-time 5.

Programs and Degrees Offered:
Listed in the following order: Program area, degree type (T if terminal Master's), number awarded 7/06–6/07. Clinical Psychology PsyD (Doctor of Psychology) 24.

APA Accreditation: Clinical PsyD (Doctor of Psychology).

Student Applications/Admissions:
Student Applications
Clinical Psychology PsyD (Doctor of Psychology)—Applications 2007–2008, 106. Total applicants accepted 2007–2008, 41. Number full-time enrolled (new admits only) 2007–2008, 26. Number part-time enrolled (new admits only) 2007–2008, 0. Openings 2008–2009, 30. The median number of years required for completion of a degree in 2006–2007 were 7. The number of students enrolled full- and part-time who were dismissed or voluntarily withdrew from this program area in 2007–2008 were 3.

Admissions Requirements:
Scores: Entries appear in this order: required test or GPA, minimum score (if required), median score of students entering in 2007–2008. Doctoral Programs: GRE-V 500, 500; GRE-Q 500, 550; overall undergraduate GPA 3.0, 3.5; Doctoral program GRE-Analytic 4.5, 4.5.
Other Criteria: (importance of criteria rated low, medium, or high): GRE/MAT scores—medium, research experience—medium, work experience—medium, extracurricular activity—medium, clinically related public service—high, GPA—medium, letters of recommendation—high, interview—high, statement of goals and objectives—high.

Student Characteristics: The following represents characteristics of students in 2007–2008 in all graduate psychology programs in the department: Female—full-time 93, part-time 0; Male—full-time 29, part-time 0; African American/Black—full-time 5, part-time 0; Hispanic/Latino(a)—full-time 2, part-time 0; Asian/Pacific Islander—full-time 6, part-time 0; American Indian/Alaska Native—full-time 1, part-time 0; Caucasian/White—full-time 107, part-time 0; Multi-ethnic—full-time 1, part-time 0; students subject to the Americans With Disabilities Act—full-time 1, part-time 0; Unknown ethnicity—full-time 0, part-time 0; International students who hold an F-1 or J-1 Visa—full-time 4, part-time 0.

Financial Information/Assistance:
Tuition for Full-Time Study: *Doctoral:* State residents: $665 per credit hour; Nonstate residents: $665 per credit hour.

Financial Assistance:
First-Year Students: Research assistantships available for first year. Average amount paid per academic year: $5,800. Average number of hours worked per week: 15. Apply by March 1. Tuition remission given: partial.
Advanced Students: Teaching assistantships available for advanced students. Average amount paid per academic year: $7,980. Average number of hours worked per week: 15. Apply by March 1. Tuition remission given: partial. Research assistantships available for advanced students. Average amount paid per academic year: $5,800. Average number of hours worked per week: 15. Apply by March 1. Tuition remission given: partial.
Additional Information: Of all students currently enrolled full time, 47% benefited from one or more of the listed financial assistance programs. Application and information available online at http://www.spalding.edu/psychology.

Internships/Practica: Doctoral Degree (PsyD Doctor of Psychology in Clinical Psychology): For those doctoral students for whom a professional internship was required in this program prior to graduation, (20) students applied for an internship in 2006–2007, with (16) students obtaining an internship. Of those students who obtained an internship, (16) were paid internships. Of those students who obtained an internship, (15) students placed in APA/CPA-accredited internships, (0) students placed in internships not APA/CPA-accredited, but listed with the Association of Psychology Postdoctoral and Internship Centers (APPIC), (0) students placed in internships conforming to guidelines of the Council of Directors of School Psychology Programs (CDSPP),

(1) student placed in internships that were not APA/CPA accredited, APPIC or CDSPP listed. Often referred to as one of the School of Professional Psychology's "gems," our Graduate Practica Program prides itself on providing incredible opportunity to our students by creating avenues within our communities to take their classroom learning into real-world settings. It is within these venues that our students test their knowledge, gain experience, and contribute to the overall mental and physical health of humankind. Under the professional supervision of committed, licensed psychologists and professional staff, students find voice, presence, silence, and humility when serving those in need of quality mental health care, consultation, assessment, or other professional services best guided by those specifically trained in the science of human behavior. Practicum placements are carefully selected to best meet the training needs of our graduate students. Once partnered with a host site, these placements provide focused challenges and learning opportunities with diverse populations and across a variety of subspecialties, including health–behavioral medicine, forensics–corrections, pediatrics–child–adolescent–family, and adult/geriatrics. For a complete description of the School of Professional Psychology's Graduate Practica Program at Spalding University, we invite you to visit our Web site, http://www.spalding.edu/psychgradpractica.

Housing and Day Care: No on-campus housing is available. No on-campus day care facilities are available.

Employment of Department Graduates:

Master's Degree Graduates: Of those who graduated in the academic year 2006–2007, the following categories and numbers represent the postgraduate activities and employment of master's degree graduates: Enrolled in a postdoctoral residency/fellowship (n/a), employed in independent practice (n/a), total from the above (master's) (0).

Doctoral Degree Graduates: Of those who graduated in the academic year 2006–2007, the following categories and numbers represent the postgraduate activities and employment of doctoral degree graduates: Enrolled in a psychology doctoral program (n/a), employed in independent practice (4), employed in other positions at a higher education institution (3), employed in a professional position in a school system (1), employed in government agency (1), employed in a community mental health/counseling center (4), employed in a hospital/medical center (6), other employment position (3), do not know (2), total from the above (doctoral) (24).

Additional Information:

Orientation, Objectives, and Emphasis of Department: The training model of the Spalding School of Professional Psychology (SOPP) is a competency-based disciplined inquiry model. The SOPP focuses on six core competencies: relationship, assessment, intervention, research, supervision, and consultation. The professional brings all the relevant knowledge available to address the presenting problems of clients. Relevant knowledge includes scientific knowledge, training in the various competencies identified by NCSPP, and personal knowledge from professional experience. Thus, we educate and train students simultaneously in scientifically based knowledge relevant to the local situations encountered and in the professional competencies needed to address the specific issues raised by clients. The academic scientific core content specified by APA includes biological basis of behavior, cognitive–affective bases (learning), social bases of behavior, individual differences, history and systems of psychology, and research methods and statistics. These areas cover the theoretical and research basis for guiding conceptions relevant to situations that the professional encounters. The degree is a PsyD in clinical psychology, with a concentration in one of four emphasis areas: Adult Psychology, Health Psychology, Child–Adolescent–Family Psychology, and Forensic–Correctional Psychology.

Special Facilities or Resources: The faculty have various areas of expertise and interest and form research and discussion groups around these areas of interest. Current Research and Interest Groups include a Health Psychology Research Interest Group, a Violence Prevention Research Interest Group, and a Spirituality and Religion Research Interest Group. Because we are a professional training program, research is conducted in applied settings. Students who are active in the Health Psychology Research Interest Group are involved in all phases of research projects. Students and faculty collaborate with other universities, medical centers, and specialty medical clinics in conducting clinical research. Students also actively participate in State, regional, and national conferences in the presentation of these projects. Students are encouraged to select dissertation and other research projects based on their own desires as well as the interests of the faculty.

Application Information:

Send to Administrative Assistant, School of Professional Psychology. Application available online. URL of online application: http://www.spalding.edu/psychology. Students are admitted in the Fall, application deadline January 15. *Fee:* $30.

Western Kentucky University

Department of Psychology
College of Education and Behavioral Sciences
1906 College Heights Boulevard, 21030
Bowling Green, KY 42104-1030
Telephone: (270) 745-2695
Fax: (279) 745-6934
E-mail: *psych@wku.edu*
Web: *http://www.edtech.wku.edu/~psych/*

Department Information:

1931. Head: Steven J. Haggbloom. Number of faculty: total—full-time 21, part-time 9; women—full-time 14, part-time 2; women minority—full-time 5, part-time 1; faculty subject to the Americans With Disabilities Act 2.

Programs and Degrees Offered:

Listed in the following order: Program area, degree type (T if terminal Master's), number awarded 7/06–6/07. School Psychology EdS/MEd (School Psychology) 8, Clinical Psychology MA/MS (Master of Arts/Science) (T) 11, Experimental Psychology MA/MS (Master of Arts/Science) (T) 4, Industrial and Organizational Psychology MA/MS (Master of Arts/Science) (T) 9.

Student Applications/Admissions:

Student Applications

School Psychology EdS/MEd (School Psychology)—Applications 2007–2008, 29. Total applicants accepted 2007–2008, 14. Number full-time enrolled (new admits only) 2007–2008, 12.

Number part-time enrolled (new admits only) 2007–2008, 0. Openings 2008–2009, 10. The median number of years required for completion of a degree in 2006–2007 were 3. The number of students enrolled full- and part-time who were dismissed or voluntarily withdrew from this program area in 2007–2008 were 0. *Clinical Psychology MA/MS (Master of Arts/Science)*—Applications 2007–2008, 40. Total applicants accepted 2007–2008, 19. Number full-time enrolled (new admits only) 2007–2008, 12. Number part-time enrolled (new admits only) 2007–2008, 0. Openings 2008–2009, 10. The median number of years required for completion of a degree in 2006–2007 were 2. The number of students enrolled full- and part-time who were dismissed or voluntarily withdrew from this program area in 2007–2008 were 0. *Experimental Psychology MA/MS (Master of Arts/Science)*—Applications 2007–2008, 14. Total applicants accepted 2007–2008, 6. Number full-time enrolled (new admits only) 2007–2008, 5. Number part-time enrolled (new admits only) 2007–2008, 0. Openings 2008–2009, 10. The median number of years required for completion of a degree in 2006–2007 were 2. The number of students enrolled full- and part-time who were dismissed or voluntarily withdrew from this program area in 2007–2008 were 0. *Industrial and Organizational Psychology MA/MS (Master of Arts/Science)*—Applications 2007–2008, 22. Total applicants accepted 2007–2008, 14. Number full-time enrolled (new admits only) 2007–2008, 13. Number part-time enrolled (new admits only) 2007–2008, 0. Openings 2008–2009, 10. The median number of years required for completion of a degree in 2006–2007 were 2. The number of students enrolled full- and part-time who were dismissed or voluntarily withdrew from this program area in 2007–2008 were 1.

Admissions Requirements:

Scores: Entries appear in this order: required test or GPA, minimum score (if required), median score of students entering in 2007–2008. Master's Programs: GRE-V no minimum stated; GRE-Q no minimum stated; overall undergraduate GPA 2.75; psychology GPA 3.00. Minimum overall GPA of 3.00 for School Psychology program. Minimum quantitative GRE of 500 for I/O program. GRE Writing minimum score 3.5. Verbal + Quantitative GRE 750 minimum, GRE x GPA 2200 minimum.

Other Criteria: (importance of criteria rated low, medium, or high): GRE/MAT scores—high, research experience—medium, work experience—low, extracurricular activity—low, clinically related public service—medium, GPA—high, letters of recommendation—high, statement of goals and objectives—medium. Research experience is more important for the experimental program and clinically related public service is less important.

Student Characteristics: The following represents characteristics of students in 2007–2008 in all graduate psychology programs in the department: Female—full-time 50, part-time 0; Male—full-time 21, part-time 0; African American/Black—full-time 3, part-time 0; Hispanic/Latino(a)—full-time 0, part-time 0; Asian/Pacific Islander—full-time 0, part-time 0; American Indian/Alaska Native—full-time 0, part-time 0; Caucasian/White—full-time 65, part-time 0; Multi-ethnic—full-time 0, part-time 0; students subject to the Americans With Disabilities Act—full-time 1, part-time 0; Unknown ethnicity—full-time 0, part-time 0; International students who hold an F-1 or J-1 Visa—full-time 0, part-time 0.

Financial Information/Assistance:

Tuition for Full-Time Study: *Master's:* State residents: per academic year $7,014, $351 per credit hour; Nonstate residents: per academic year $7,678, $384 per credit hour. Tuition is subject to change. See the following Web site for updates and changes in tuition costs: http://www.wku.edu/bursar/.

Financial Assistance:

First-Year Students: Teaching assistantships available for first year. Average amount paid per academic year: $8,000. Average number of hours worked per week: 20. Apply by August 1. Tuition remission given: full and partial. Research assistantships available for first year. Average amount paid per academic year: $8,000. Average number of hours worked per week: 20. Apply by August 1. Tuition remission given: full and partial.

Advanced Students: Teaching assistantships available for advanced students. Average amount paid per academic year: $8,000. Average number of hours worked per week: 20. Apply by August 1. Tuition remission given: full and partial. Research assistantships available for advanced students. Average amount paid per academic year: $8,000. Average number of hours worked per week: 20. Apply by August 1. Tuition remission given: full and partial.

Additional Information: Of all students currently enrolled full time, 95% benefited from one or more of the listed financial assistance programs. Application and information available online at http://edtech.tph.wku.edu/~psych/programs/graduate/index.htm.

Internships/Practica: No information provided.

Housing and Day Care: On-campus housing is available. See the following Web site for more information: http://www.wku.edu/Dept/Support/Housing/HRL/HOME/. No on-campus day care facilities are available.

Employment of Department Graduates:

Master's Degree Graduates: Of those who graduated in the academic year 2006–2007, the following categories and numbers represent the postgraduate activities and employment of master's degree graduates: Enrolled in a postdoctoral residency/fellowship (n/a), employed in independent practice (n/a), total from the above (master's) (0).

Doctoral Degree Graduates: Of those who graduated in the academic year 2006–2007, the following categories and numbers represent the postgraduate activities and employment of doctoral degree graduates: Enrolled in a psychology doctoral program (n/a), total from the above (doctoral) (0).

Additional Information:

Special Facilities or Resources: The department has a training clinic for use by clinical and school psychology students, and laboratory space for experimental research in perception, cognition, motivation, and developmental psychology. Office space is available for most graduate students.

Information for Students With Physical Disabilities: See the following Web site for more information: http://www.wku.edu/Info/Student/disabil.htm.

Application Information:

Send to Office of Graduate Studies, Western Kentucky University, 1906 College Heights Boulevard, 11010 Bowling Green, KY 42101. Application available online. URL of online application: http://www.wku.edu/graduate/app.htm. Students are admitted in the Fall, application deadline March 1. *Fee:* $35.

Louisiana State University

Department of Psychology
Audubon Hall
Baton Rouge, LA 70803
Telephone: (225) 578-8745
Fax: (225) 578-4125
E-mail: *abaumei@lsu.edu*
Web: *http://www.lsu.edu/psychology/graduate/index.html*

Department Information:

1916. Chairperson: Alan Baumeister. Number of faculty: total—full-time 23; women—full-time 9.

Programs and Degrees Offered:

Listed in the following order: Program area, degree type (T if terminal Master's), number awarded 7/06–6/07. Biological PhD (Doctor of Philosophy) 0, Clinical PhD (Doctor of Philosophy) 6, Cognitive and Developmental PhD (Doctor of Philosophy) 1, Industrial/Organizational PhD (Doctor of Philosophy) 0, School PhD (Doctor of Philosophy) 4.

APA Accreditation: Clinical PhD (Doctor of Philosophy). School PhD (Doctor of Philosophy).

Student Applications/Admissions:

Student Applications

Biological PhD (Doctor of Philosophy)—Applications 2007–2008, 8. Total applicants accepted 2007–2008, 1. Number full-time enrolled (new admits only) 2007–2008, 1. Openings 2008–2009, 1. The number of students enrolled full- and part-time who were dismissed or voluntarily withdrew from this program area in 2007–2008 were 1. *Clinical PhD (Doctor of Philosophy)*—Applications 2007–2008, 135. Total applicants accepted 2007–2008, 15. Number full-time enrolled (new admits only) 2007–2008, 11. Openings 2008–2009, 16. The median number of years required for completion of a degree in 2006–2007 were 6. The number of students enrolled full- and part-time who were dismissed or voluntarily withdrew from this program area in 2007–2008 were 3. *Cognitive and Developmental PhD (Doctor of Philosophy)*—Applications 2007–2008, 9. Total applicants accepted 2007–2008, 7. Number full-time enrolled (new admits only) 2007–2008, 4. Openings 2008–2009, 4. The median number of years required for completion of a degree in 2006–2007 were 5. The number of students enrolled full- and part-time who were dismissed or voluntarily withdrew from this program area in 2007–2008 were 0. *Industrial/Organizational PhD (Doctor of Philosophy)*—Applications 2007–2008, 9. Total applicants accepted 2007–2008, 1. Number full-time enrolled (new admits only) 2007–2008, 1. Openings 2008–2009, 2. The number of students enrolled full- and part-time who were dismissed or voluntarily withdrew from this program area in 2007–2008 were 0. *School PhD (Doctor of Philosophy)*—Applications 2007–2008, 22. Total applicants accepted 2007–2008, 7. Number full-time enrolled (new admits only) 2007–2008, 6. Openings 2008–2009, 6. The median number of years required for completion of a degree in 2006–2007 were 5. The number of students enrolled full- and part-time who were dismissed or voluntarily withdrew from this program area in 2007–2008 were 1.

Admissions Requirements:

Scores: Entries appear in this order: required test or GPA, minimum score (if required), median score of students entering in 2007–2008. Doctoral Programs: GRE-V 500, 530; GRE-Q 500, 640; overall undergraduate GPA 3.0, 3.6.

Other Criteria: (importance of criteria rated low, medium, or high): GRE/MAT scores—high, research experience—high, work experience—medium, extracurricular activity—medium, clinically related public service—medium, GPA—high, letters of recommendation—high, interview—medium, statement of goals and objectives—high, undergraduate major in psychology—medium, specific undergraduate psychology courses taken—medium. Interview—clinical and school only. For additional information on admission requirements, go to http://www.lsu.edu/psychology/graduate/prospectivestudents.html.

Student Characteristics: The following represents characteristics of students in 2007–2008 in all graduate psychology programs in the department: Female—full-time 83, part-time 0; Male—full-time 31, part-time 0; African American/Black—full-time 6, part-time 0; Hispanic/Latino(a)—full-time 3, part-time 0; Asian/Pacific Islander—full-time 5, part-time 0; American Indian/Alaska Native—full-time 4, part-time 0; Caucasian/White—full-time 93, part-time 0; Multi-ethnic—full-time 2, part-time 0; students subject to the Americans With Disabilities Act—full-time 1, part-time 0; Unknown ethnicity—full-time 1, part-time 0; International students who hold an F-1 or J-1 Visa—full-time 3, part-time 0.

Financial Information/Assistance:

Tuition for Full-Time Study: *Doctoral:* State residents: per academic year $4,533; Nonstate residents: per academic year $12,833. Tuition is subject to change. See the following Web site for updates and changes in tuition costs: http://www.bgtplan.lsu.edu/fees/07-08/Grad.htm.

Financial Assistance:

First-Year Students: Teaching assistantships available for first year. Average amount paid per academic year: $10,500. Average number of hours worked per week: 20. Apply by January 15. Tuition remission given: full. Traineeships available for first year. Average amount paid per academic year: $12,000. Average number of hours worked per week: 20. Apply by January 15. Tuition remission given: full. Fellowships and scholarships available for first year. Average amount paid per academic year: $20,000. Apply by January 15. Tuition remission given: full.

Advanced Students: Teaching assistantships available for advanced students. Average amount paid per academic year: $13,500. Average number of hours worked per week: 20. Tuition remission given: full. Traineeships available for advanced students. Average amount paid per academic year: $12,000. Average number of hours worked per week: 20. Tuition remission given: full. Fellowships and scholarships available for advanced students.

Average amount paid per academic year: $20,000. Tuition remission given: full.

Additional Information: Of all students currently enrolled full time, 75% benefited from one or more of the listed financial assistance programs. Application and information available online. Admission application used for assistantship application.

Internships/Practica: Doctoral Degree (PhD Clinical): For those doctoral students for whom a professional internship was required in this program prior to graduation, (15) students applied for an internship in 2006–2007, with (15) students obtaining an internship. Of those students who obtained an internship, (14) were paid internships. Of those students who obtained an internship, (15) students placed in APA/CPA-accredited internships, (0) students placed in internships not APA/CPA-accredited, but listed with the Association of Psychology Postdoctoral and Internship Centers (APPIC), (0) students placed in internships conforming to guidelines of the Council of Directors of School Psychology Programs (CDSPP), (0) students placed in internships that were not APA/CPA-accredited, APPIC or CDSPP listed. Doctoral Degree (PhD School): For those doctoral students for whom a professional internship was required in this program prior to graduation, (5) students applied for an internship in 2006–2007, with (5) students obtaining an internship. Of those students who obtained an internship, (5) were paid internships. Of those students who obtained an internship, (4)students placed in APA/CPA-accredited internships, (0) students placed in internships not APA/CPA-accredited, but listed with the Association of Psychology Postdoctoral and Internship Centers (APPIC), (0) students placed in internships conforming to guidelines of the Council of Directors of School Psychology Programs (CDSPP), (1) students placed in internships that were not APA/CPA accredited, APPIC or CDSPP listed. See descriptions at http://www.lsu.edu/psychology/graduate/facilities.html.

Housing and Day Care: On-campus housing is available. See the following Web site for more information: http://appl003.lsu.edu/slas/reslifeweb.nsf/index. On-campus day care facilities are available. See the following Web site for more information: http://appl003.lsu.edu/slas/lsuchildcare.nsf/$Content/contact+us?opendocument.

Employment of Department Graduates:

Master's Degree Graduates: Of those who graduated in the academic year 2006–2007, the following categories and numbers represent the postgraduate activities and employment of master's degree graduates: Enrolled in a postdoctoral residency/fellowship (n/a), employed in independent practice (n/a), total from the above (master's) (0).

Doctoral Degree Graduates: Of those who graduated in the academic year 2006–2007, the following categories and numbers represent the postgraduate activities and employment of doctoral degree graduates: Enrolled in a psychology doctoral program (n/a), enrolled in a postdoctoral residency/fellowship (4), employed in an academic position at a university (4), employed in a hospital/medical center (2), do not know (1), total from the above (doctoral) (11).

Additional Information:

Orientation, Objectives, and Emphasis of Department: The Department of Psychology at Louisiana State University is committed to the view that psychology is both a science and a profession, and it regards all areas of specialization as interdependent. All graduate students, regardless of intended areas of specialization, receive broad training to develop the research skills needed to make scholarly contributions to the discipline of psychology throughout their subsequent careers. A student interested only in professional application of psychology without regard for research will not be comfortable in the graduate training program in this department. Both faculty and students in psychology recognize, however, that the model of the psychologist as a practitioner is a legitimate one. Those students whose main interest is in research are encouraged to develop familiarity with clinical, industrial, or developmental and educational settings as potential research environments. The sequence of graduate education reflects these emphases on research and on professional aspects of psychology.

Special Facilities or Resources: The department occupies a centrally located building, designed specifically to accommodate our program. Audubon Hall houses faculty offices, instructional space, desk space for graduate assistants, and research facilities for a wide array of human studies. A training clinic is located in Johnston Hall. Additional research and clinical training facilities are located at the Pennington Biomedical Research Center and Baton Rouge Clinic.

Information for Students With Physical Disabilities: See the following Web site for more information: http://www.appl003.lsu.edu/slas/ods.nsf/index.

Application Information:

Send to Admissions Committee, Graduate Secretary, 236 Audubon Hall, Department of Psychology, Louisiana State University, Baton Rouge, LA 70803-5501. Application available online. URL of online application: http://www.lsu.edu/psychology/graduate/2008 application.pdf. Students are admitted in the Fall, application deadline January 15. *Fee:* $0. There is no fee for the Department of Psychology application. There is a $25 fee for the Graduate School application.

Louisiana State University in Shreveport

Department of Psychology
College of Education and Human Development (CEHD)
One University Place
Shreveport, LA 71115
Telephone: (318) 797-5044
Fax: (318) 798-4171
E-mail: *Gary.Jones@lsus.edu*
Web: *http://www.lsus.edu/ehd/psyc/*

Department Information:

1967. Chairperson: Gary E. Jones, PhD. Number of faculty: total—full-time 11, part-time 5; women—full-time 5, part-time 2; total—minority—full-time 1.

Programs and Degrees Offered:

Listed in the following order: Program area, degree type (T if terminal Master's), number awarded 7/06–6/07. School Psychology (Specialist Degree) EdS/MEd (School Psychology) 7, Counseling Psychology MA/MS (Master of Arts/Science) (T) 20.

Student Applications/Admissions:

Student Applications

School Psychology (Specialist Degree) EdS/MEd (School Psychology)—Applications 2007–2008, 8. Total applicants accepted 2007–2008, 7. Number full-time enrolled (new admits only) 2007–2008, 3. Number part-time enrolled (new admits only) 2007–2008, 1. Total enrolled 2007–2008 full-time, 14, part-time, 2. Openings 2008–2009, 10. The median number of years required for completion of a degree in 2006–2007 were 3. The number of students enrolled full- and part-time who were dismissed or voluntarily withdrew from this program area in 2007–2008 were 2. *Counseling Psychology MA/MS (Master of Arts/Science)*—Applications 2007–2008, 60. Total applicants accepted 2007–2008, 48. Number full-time enrolled (new admits only) 2007–2008, 16. Number part-time enrolled (new admits only) 2007–2008, 5. Total enrolled 2007–2008 full-time, 55, part-time, 6. Openings 2008–2009, 20. The median number of years required for completion of a degree in 2006–2007 were 2. The number of students enrolled full- and part-time who were dismissed or voluntarily withdrew from this program area in 2007–2008 were 5.

Admissions Requirements:

Scores: Entries appear in this order: required test or GPA, minimum score (if required), median score of students entering in 2007–2008. Master's Programs: GRE-V 400; GRE-Q 400; overall undergraduate GPA 2.75. These requirements are for the psychology specialist in School Psychology and MS in Counseling Psychology degrees.

Other Criteria: (importance of criteria rated low, medium, or high): GRE/MAT scores—medium, research experience—low, work experience—low, extracurricular activity—low, clinically related public service—low, GPA—high, letters of recommendation—high, interview—medium, statement of goals and objectives—high, undergraduate major in psychology—medium, specific undergraduate psychology courses taken—low. The emphasis of these criteria is equally true for both SSP and MSCP programs. For additional information on admission requirements, go to http://www.lsus.edu/ehd/psyc/graduate.asp.

Student Characteristics: The following represents characteristics of students in 2007–2008 in all graduate psychology programs in the department: Female—full-time 56, part-time 6; Male—full-time 13, part-time 1; African American/Black—full-time 9, part-time 8; American Indian/Alaska Native—full-time 1, part-time 0; Caucasian/White—full-time 51, part-time 6; students subject to the Americans With Disabilities Act—full-time 0, part-time 0; Unknown ethnicity—full-time 1, part-time 0.

Financial Information/Assistance:

Tuition for Full-Time Study: *Master's:* State residents: per academic year $2,969, $164 per credit hour; Nonstate residents: per academic year $7,076, $393 per credit hour. See the following Web site for updates and changes in tuition costs: http://www.lsus.edu.

Financial Assistance:

First-Year Students: Research assistantships available for first year. Average amount paid per academic year: $3,200. Average number of hours worked per week: 20. Apply by June 1. Tuition remission given: partial.

Advanced Students: Teaching assistantships available for advanced students. Average amount paid per academic year: $3,200. Average number of hours worked per week: 20. Apply by June 1. Tuition remission given: partial.

Additional Information: Of all students currently enrolled full time, 5% benefited from one or more of the listed financial assistance programs.

Internships/Practica: Master's Degree (MA/MS Counseling Psychology): An internship experience such as a final research project or "capstone" experience is required of graduates. Practica for our Specialist degree students are carried out in surrounding parishes, which have cooperative agreements with the university for training purposes. There are two distinct practica experiences for our students. The first involves an observational practica required during the Introductory to School Psychology course. The second occurs during Psych 754—a formal 200-plus hour practica that is carried out in cooperating training parishes with supervisory field school psychologists. All students must complete an appropriate internship to qualify for State certification. These internships tend not to be APA approved but meet state certification requirements. Students in the MSCP program also are required to serve community-based supervised practicum experiences in addition to a two-semester internship experience supervised by an LPC or other appropriate mental health professional, which is acceptable to the program. These internships are not APA approved but meet LPC licensure requirements.

Housing and Day Care: On-campus housing is available. LSUS provides housing through University Court apartments. No on-campus day care facilities are available.

Employment of Department Graduates:

Master's Degree Graduates: Of those who graduated in the academic year 2006–2007, the following categories and numbers represent the postgraduate activities and employment of master's degree graduates: Enrolled in a psychology doctoral program (1), enrolled in another graduate/professional program (0), enrolled in a postdoctoral residency/fellowship (n/a), employed in independent practice (n/a), employed in an academic position at a university (0), employed in an academic position at a 2-year/4-year college (0), employed in other positions at a higher education institution (0), employed in a professional position in a school system (5), employed in business or industry (0), employed in government agency (0), employed in a community mental health/counseling center (8), employed in a hospital/medical center (0), still seeking employment (2), not seeking employment (2), other employment position (2), do not know (2), total from the above (master's) (22).

Doctoral Degree Graduates: Of those who graduated in the academic year 2006–2007, the following categories and numbers represent the postgraduate activities and employment of doctoral degree graduates: Enrolled in a psychology doctoral program (n/a), total from the above (doctoral) (0).

Additional Information:

Orientation, Objectives, and Emphasis of Department: The curriculum model upon which the program rests is based on the National Association of School Psychologists Training Standards (NASP) outlined for School Psychology: A Blueprint for Training and Practice II. The model to which the program adheres is the databased decision maker. It is important for school psychologists to establish accountability within the system by providing data that demonstrates their effectiveness. The School Psychology Training committee advocates a practitioner approach to fulfilling this goal. As a result, students are required to participate in two practica in the school system as well as a minimum 1,200-hour internship. In the MSCP program, students are trained in Counseling and courses and degree naturally lead to licensure as a Licensed Professional Counselor within the State of Louisiana. The program is a 48-hour program that is sufficient for Louisiana license, whereas some surrounding states require a 60-hour licensure. Additional courses to meet those expections are also offered. Students in this program generally do not pursue psychology careers, but instead seek employment as professional counselors.

Special Facilities or Resources: The Master's in Counseling Psychology and Specialist in School Psychology have state-of-the-art audio and video equipment for counseling and intervention techniques and skills, all housed in the psychology clinic and Department on campus.

Information for Students With Physical Disabilities: See the following Web site for more information: http://www.lsus.edu.

Application Information:
Send to Department Chair. Application available online. URL of online application: http://www.lsus.edu/admissions/forms.asp. Students are admitted in the Fall, application deadline check Web; Spring, application deadline check Web; Summer, application deadline check Web. The School Psychology Specialist Program and the MS in Counseling Psychology program only admits students who have completed a full application and submitted all required documents and requirements (including GRE scores) before the published deadlines indicated by the Gradaute Studies Office and the Program. Please consult the Department/Program or Graduate Studies Web pages for complete details and up-to-the-minute admissions procedures and policy. Applications will be considered only when all admissions materials have been received and the application is complete before the specified deadlines. *Fee:* $10.

Louisiana Tech University

Department of Psychology and Behavioral Sciences
College of Education
Box 10048, T.S.
Ruston, LA 71272
Telephone: (318) 257-4315
Fax: (318) 257-3442
E-mail: *tilman@latech.edu*
Web: *http://www.latech.edu/education/psych/*

Department Information:
1972. Department Head: Tilman Sheets, PhD. Number of faculty: total—full-time 16; women—full-time 7; total—minority—full-time 1; women minority—full-time 1.

Programs and Degrees Offered:
Listed in the following order: Program area, degree type (T if terminal Master's), number awarded 7/06–6/07. Counseling and Guidance MA/MS (Master of Arts/Science) (T) 26, Counseling Psychology PhD (Doctor of Philosophy) 5, Educational Psychology MA/MS (Master of Arts/Science) (T) 2, Industrial/Organizational MA/MS (Master of Arts/Science) (T) 22.

APA Accreditation: Counseling PhD (Doctor of Philosophy).

Student Applications/Admissions:
Student Applications
Counseling and Guidance MA/MS (Master of Arts/Science)—Applications 2007–2008, 30. Total applicants accepted 2007–2008, 22. Number full-time enrolled (new admits only) 2007–2008, 12. Number part-time enrolled (new admits only) 2007–2008, 10. Total enrolled 2007–2008 full-time, 22, part-time, 18. Openings 2008–2009, 24. The median number of years required for completion of a degree in 2006–2007 were 2. The number of students enrolled full- and part-time who were dismissed or voluntarily withdrew from this program area in 2007–2008 were 9. *Counseling Psychology PhD (Doctor of Philosophy)*—Applications 2007–2008, 27. Total applicants accepted 2007–2008, 7. Openings 2008–2009, 7. The median number of years required for completion of a degree in 2006–2007 were 6. The number of students enrolled full- and part-time who were dismissed or voluntarily withdrew from this program area in 2007–2008 were 0. *Educational Psychology MA/MS (Master of Arts/Science)*—Applications 2007–2008, 4. Total applicants accepted 2007–2008, 3. Number full-time enrolled (new admits only) 2007–2008, 3. Number part-time enrolled (new admits only) 2007–2008, 0. Openings 2008–2009, 4. The median number of years required for completion of a degree in 2006–2007 were 2. The number of students enrolled full- and part-time who were dismissed or voluntarily withdrew from this program area in 2007–2008 were 1. *Industrial/Organizational MA/MS (Master of Arts/Science)*—Applications 2007–2008, 32. Total applicants accepted 2007–2008, 26. Number full-time enrolled (new admits only) 2007–2008, 20. Number part-time enrolled (new admits only) 2007–2008, 6. Total enrolled 2007–2008 full-time, 20, part-time, 11. Openings 2008–2009, 26. The median number of years required for completion of a degree in 2006–2007 was 1. The number of students enrolled full- and part-time who were dismissed or voluntarily withdrew from this program area in 2007–2008 were 4.

Admissions Requirements:
Scores: Entries appear in this order: required test or GPA, minimum score (if required), median score of students entering in 2007–2008. Master's Programs: GRE-V no minimum stated; GRE-Q no minimum stated; overall undergraduate GPA no minimum stated; last 2 years GPA no minimum stated; psychology GPA no minimum stated. Admission requires a total score of at least 1200 for probationary admission or 1300 for full admission from the following equation: 200 x UGPA + VGRE + QGRE = 1300. Doctoral Programs: GRE-V no minimum stated, 550; GRE-Q no minimum stated, 610; overall undergraduate GPA no minimum stated, 3.50. Comment: Minimal composite GRE (V + Q) score for admission consideration is normally 1000.
Other Criteria: (importance of criteria rated low, medium, or high): GRE/MAT scores—high, research experience—high, work experience—medium, extracurricular activity—low, clinically related public service—medium, GPA—high, letters of recommendation—high, interview—high, statement of

goals and objectives—medium. These criteria apply to the PhD program.

Student Characteristics: The following represents characteristics of students in 2007–2008 in all graduate psychology programs in the department: Female—full-time 90, part-time 1; Male—full-time 56, part-time 0; African American/Black—full-time 40, part-time 0; Hispanic/Latino(a)—full-time 3, part-time 0; Asian/Pacific Islander—full-time 0, part-time 0; American Indian/Alaska Native—full-time 0, part-time 0; Caucasian/White—full-time 103, part-time 0; Unknown ethnicity—full-time 0, part-time 0.

Financial Information/Assistance:

Financial Assistance:

First-Year Students: Research assistantships available for first year. Average amount paid per academic year: $10,000. Average number of hours worked per week: 20.

Advanced Students: Teaching assistantships available for advanced students. Average amount paid per academic year: $10,000. Average number of hours worked per week: 20. Research assistantships available for advanced students. Average amount paid per academic year: $10,000. Average number of hours worked per week: 20.

Additional Information: Of all students currently enrolled full time, 20% benefited from one or more of the listed financial assistance programs.

Internships/Practica: Master's Degree (MA/MS Counseling and Guidance): An internship experience such as a final research project or "capstone" experience is required of graduates. Doctoral Degree (PhD Counseling Psychology): For those doctoral students for whom a professional internship was required in this program prior to graduation, (2) students applied for an internship in 2006–2007, with (1) student obtaining an internship. Of those students who obtained an internship, (1) were paid internships. Of those students who obtained an internship, (0) students placed in APA/CPA-accredited internships, (1) student placed in internships not APA/CPA-accredited, but listed with the Association of Psychology Postdoctoral and Internship Centers (APPIC), (0) students placed in internships conforming to guidelines of the Council of Directors of School Psychology Programs (CDSPP), (0) students placed in internships that were not APA/CPA accredited, APPIC or CDSPP listed. PhD Counseling Psychology students must complete a year-long internship. Practica are available throughout the region for PhD and MA students in their respective areas.

Housing and Day Care: On-campus housing is available. Contact Housing Office (318) 257-4917. On-campus day care facilities are available.

Employment of Department Graduates:

Master's Degree Graduates: Of those who graduated in the academic year 2006–2007, the following categories and numbers represent the postgraduate activities and employment of master's degree graduates: Enrolled in a postdoctoral residency/fellowship (n/a), employed in independent practice (n/a), total from the above (master's) (0).

Doctoral Degree Graduates: Of those who graduated in the academic year 2006–2007, the following categories and numbers represent the postgraduate activities and employment of doctoral degree graduates: Enrolled in a psychology doctoral program (n/a), total from the above (doctoral) (0).

Additional Information:

Orientation, Objectives, and Emphasis of Department: The Department of Psychology and Behavioral Sciences offers master's degree programs in counseling and guidance, educational psychology, and industrial/organizational psychology, in addition to the PhD in counseling psychology. The department strives to provide an eclectic and integrated approach to theory, research, and practice. The scientist–practitioner model provides the framework for most graduate programs. Successful degree candidates develop the knowledge and skills necessary for appropriate level positions in their respective fields in settings such as education, business, mental health, and government. The counseling psychology PhD includes training in assessment, career/vocational, and psychotherapy and is accredited by the American Psychological Association.

Application Information:

Send to Department Chair, Department of Psychology and Behavioral Sciences. Applications to the Doctoral Program should be sent to the Director of Training. Application available online. URL of online application: http://www.latech.edu/graduateschool/. Students are admitted in the Fall, application deadline September 1; Winter, application deadline November 30; Spring, application deadline March 2; Summer, application deadline May 31. PhD: full admissions in the Fall only, deadline December 15. *Fee:* $35.

Louisiana, University of, Lafayette

Department of Psychology
P.O. Box 43131 UL-Lafayette Station
Lafayette, LA 70504-3131
Telephone: (337) 482-6597
Fax: (337) 482-6587
E-mail: *csm5689@louisiana.edu*
Web: *http://www.louisiana.edu/Academic/LiberalArts/PSYC*

Department Information:

1970. Department Head: Cheryl S. Lynch. Number of faculty: total—full-time 7, part-time 1; women—full-time 5, part-time 3; women minority—full-time 1, part-time 1.

Programs and Degrees Offered:

Listed in the following order: Program area, degree type (T if terminal Master's), number awarded 7/06–6/07. Experimental, Applied MA/MS (Master of Arts/Science) (T) 4, Counselor Education MA/MS (Master of Arts/Science) (T) 20.

Student Applications/Admissions:

Student Applications

Experimental, Applied MA/MS (Master of Arts/Science)—Applications 2007–2008, 29. Total applicants accepted 2007–2008, 22. Number full-time enrolled (new admits only) 2007–2008, 15. Number part-time enrolled (new admits only) 2007–2008, 2. Total enrolled 2007–2008 full-time, 25, part-time, 18. Openings 2008–2009, 15. The median number of years required for completion of a degree in 2006–2007 were 2. The number of students enrolled full- and part-time who were dismissed or voluntarily withdrew from this program area in 2007–2008 were 3. *Counselor Education MA/MS (Master of Arts/Science)*—Applications 2007–2008, 40. Total applicants accepted 2007–2008, 30. Number full-time enrolled (new admits only) 2007–2008, 20. Number part-time enrolled (new admits only) 2007–2008, 10. Total enrolled 2007–2008 full-time, 22, part-time, 30. Openings 2008–2009, 25. The median number of years required for completion of a degree in 2006–2007 were 2. The number of students enrolled full- and part-time who were dismissed or voluntarily withdrew from this program area in 2007–2008 were 1.

Admissions Requirements:

Scores: Entries appear in this order: required test or GPA, minimum score (if required), median score of students entering in 2007–2008. Master's Programs: GRE-V 500, 455; GRE-Q 500, 540; last 2 years GPA 3.0. Exceptions to the minimum scores will be considered on a case-by-case basis if there is high strength/promise through another indicator. Also, scores in the right-hand column are for the Fall 2007 entering class.

Other Criteria: (importance of criteria rated low, medium, or high): GRE/MAT scores—medium, research experience—medium, work experience—medium, extracurricular activity—low, clinically related public service—medium, GPA—medium, letters of recommendation—high, statement of goals and objectives—medium.

Student Characteristics: The following represents characteristics of students in 2007–2008 in all graduate psychology programs in the department: Female—full-time 21, part-time 13; Male—full-time 4, part-time 5; African American/Black—full-time 2, part-time 4; Hispanic/Latino(a)—full-time 0, part-time 0; Asian/Pacific Islander—full-time 0, part-time 2; American Indian/Alaska Native—full-time 0, part-time 0; Caucasian/White—full-time 21, part-time 11; Multi-ethnic—full-time 0, part-time 0; students subject to the Americans With Disabilities Act—full-time 0, part-time 0; Unknown ethnicity—full-time 2, part-time 1; International students who hold an F-1 or J-1 Visa—full-time 2, part-time 1.

Financial Information/Assistance:

Tuition for Full-Time Study: *Master's:* State residents: per academic year $1,657; Nonstate residents: per academic year $4,747. Tuition is subject to change. Additional fees are assessed to students beyond the costs of tuition for the following: International Student Tuition (10-hour load): $1,725 and $4,815, respectively. See the following Web site for updates and changes in tuition costs: http://www.bursar.louisiana.edu/schedule-Spring2008.shtml#graduate.

Financial Assistance:

First-Year Students: Teaching assistantships available for first year. Average amount paid per academic year: $7,500. Average number of hours worked per week: 15. Apply by April 12. Tuition remission given: full.

Advanced Students: Teaching assistantships available for advanced students. Average amount paid per academic year: $7,500. Average number of hours worked per week: 15. Apply by April 12. Tuition remission given: full.

Additional Information: Of all students currently enrolled full time, 30% benefited from one or more of the listed financial assistance programs. Application and information available online at http://gradschool.louisiana.edu/.

Internships/Practica: Internships for master's students in the applied option are available at the Community Mental Health Center, local psychiatric and rehabilitation hospitals and facilities, private agencies and practices, and at the University Counseling and Testing Center.

Housing and Day Care: On-campus housing is available. See the following Web site for more information: http://www.louisiana.edu/Student/Housing/. On-campus day care facilities are available. See the following Web site for more information: http://www.louisiana.edu/Student/ChildDev/.

Employment of Department Graduates:

Master's Degree Graduates: Of those who graduated in the academic year 2006–2007, the following categories and numbers represent the postgraduate activities and employment of master's degree graduates: Enrolled in a psychology doctoral program (8), enrolled in a postdoctoral residency/fellowship (n/a), employed in independent practice (n/a), employed in other positions at a higher education institution (4), employed in a community mental health/counseling center (1), do not know (17), total from the above (master's) (30).

Doctoral Degree Graduates: Of those who graduated in the academic year 2006–2007, the following categories and numbers represent the postgraduate activities and employment of doctoral degree graduates: Enrolled in a psychology doctoral program (n/a), total from the above (doctoral) (0).

Additional Information:

Orientation, Objectives, and Emphasis of Department: The Department of Psychology at the University of Louisiana at Lafayette strives to promote the study of psychology as a science, as a profession, and as a means of promoting human welfare. A master's program is offered with options in general experimental or applied psychology. After obtaining their degree, general experimental students pursue the doctorate at other universities. Qualified students also have the option of applying to the university's doctoral program in Cognitive Science. Applied program students have found employment in the locality working for private and public agencies.

Special Facilities or Resources: The Psychology Department houses a computer laboratory for cognitive and social research. Computer-assisted instruction is available for several courses. Major physiological research is conducted at the nearby primate center, The New Iberia Research Center. An additional smaller physiological laboratory is housed in the Psychology Department. The University of Louisiana at Lafayette has excellent computer facilities. Many members of the department are also affiliated with the university's Institute for Cognitive Science, providing additional opportunities for research. There is also the possibility that students may be simultaneously enrolled in the Psychology MS program and the Cognitive Science PhD program.

Information for Students With Physical Disabilities: See the following Web site for more information: http://www.disability.louisiana.edu/.

Application Information:
Send to Graduate School Director, Martin Hall, University of Louisiana, Lafayette, LA 70504. Application available online. URL of online application: http://www.gradschool.louisiana.edu/. Students are admitted in the Fall, application deadline 30 days; Spring, application deadline 30 days; Summer, application deadline 30 days. Fellowships have a deadline of February 15; applicants seeking an assistantship ought to have all materials in by the start of April (for the Fall semester). *Fee:* $25. U.S. students' applications are due 30 days prior to start of semester. For international students, the fee is $30, and the deadline is 90 days prior to the semester.

Louisiana, University of, Monroe

Department of Psychology
University of Louisiana—Monroe
700 University Avenue
Monroe, LA 71209
Telephone: (318) 342-1330
Fax: (318) 342-1352
E-mail: *williamson@ulm.edu*
Web: *http://www.ulm.edu*

Department Information:
1965. Head: David Williamson. Number of faculty: total—full-time 4, part-time 3; women—full-time 3, part-time 2; women minority—full-time 1, part-time 1.

Programs and Degrees Offered:
Listed in the following order: Program area, degree type (T if terminal Master's), number awarded 7/06–6/07. Specialist in School Psychology EdS/MEd (School Psychology) 3, General MA/MS (Master of Arts/Science) (T) 1, Psychometric MA/MS (Master of Arts/Science) 11.

Student Applications/Admissions:
Student Applications
Specialist in School Psychology EdS/MEd (School Psychology)—Applications 2007–2008, 5. Total applicants accepted 2007–2008, 3. Number full-time enrolled (new admits only) 2007–2008, 1. Total enrolled 2007–2008 full-time, 13. Openings 2008–2009, 10. The median number of years required for completion of a degree in 2006–2007 were 2. The number of students enrolled full- and part-time who were dismissed or voluntarily withdrew from this program area in 2007–2008 were 0. *General MA/MS (Master of Arts/Science)*—Applications 2007–2008, 4. Total applicants accepted 2007–2008, 3. Number full-time enrolled (new admits only) 2007–2008, 3. Total enrolled 2007–2008 full-time, 4. Openings 2008–2009, 10. The median number of years required for completion of a degree in 2006–2007 were 2. *Psychometric MA/MS (Master of Arts/Science)*—Applications 2007–2008, 7. Total applicants accepted 2007–2008, 3. Number full-time enrolled (new admits only) 2007–2008, 3. Total enrolled 2007–2008 full-time, 12. Openings 2008–2009, 10. The median number of years required for completion of a degree in 2006–2007 were 2.

Admissions Requirements:
Scores: Entries appear in this order: required test or GPA, minimum score (if required), median score of students entering in 2007–2008. Master's Programs: GRE-V no minimum stated; GRE-Q no minimum stated; overall undergraduate GPA 2.75. For MS Program two of the three following are required: 900 Verbal/Quant GRE, 2.75 GPA, and 1900 when GPA 400 + GRE. For SSP Program two of the three following are required: 1000 Verbal/Quantitative GRE, 3.00 GPA, and 2000 when GPA 400 + GRE.
Other Criteria: (importance of criteria rated low, medium, or high): GRE/MAT scores—high, research experience—medium, work experience—medium, extracurricular activity—low, clinically related public service—medium, GPA—high, letters of recommendation—high.

Student Characteristics: The following represents characteristics of students in 2007–2008 in all graduate psychology programs in the department: Female—full-time 22, part-time 0; Male—full-time 7, part-time 0; African American/Black—full-time 6, part-time 0; Hispanic/Latino(a)—full-time 0, part-time 0; Asian/Pacific Islander—full-time 0, part-time 0; American Indian/Alaska Native—full-time 0, part-time 0; Caucasian/White—full-time 23, part-time 0; students subject to the Americans With Disabilities Act—full-time 0, part-time 0; Unknown ethnicity—full-time 0, part-time 0.

Financial Information/Assistance:
Tuition for Full-Time Study: *Master's:* State residents: per academic year $3,511; Nonstate residents: per academic year $9,470. See the following Web site for updates and changes in tuition costs: http://www.ulm.edu. Amount stated above includes tuition and fees.

Financial Assistance:
First-Year Students: Research assistantships available for first year. Average amount paid per academic year: $5,000. Average number of hours worked per week: 20. Tuition remission given: full.
Advanced Students: Research assistantships available for advanced students. Average amount paid per academic year: $5,000. Tuition remission given: full.
Additional Information: Of all students currently enrolled full time, 20% benefited from one or more of the listed financial assistance programs.

Internships/Practica: Master's Degree (MA/MS General): An internship experience such as a final research project or "capstone" experience is required of graduates. Practica and internships are required for the psychometric concentration of the MS program. Field, practica, and internships are included as an integral part of the specialist in school psychology program.

Housing and Day Care: On-campus housing is available. See the following Web site for more information: http://www.ulm.edu, search residential life. On-campus day care facilities are available. See the following Web site for more information: http://www.ulm.edu, search residential life.

Employment of Department Graduates:
Master's Degree Graduates: Of those who graduated in the academic year 2006–2007, the following categories and numbers represent the postgraduate activities and employment of master's degree graduates: Enrolled in a psychology doctoral program (3), enrolled in a postdoctoral residency/fellowship (n/a), employed

in independent practice (n/a), employed in a professional position in a school system (4), employed in a community mental health/ counseling center (3), total from the above (master's) (10).
Doctoral Degree Graduates: Of those who graduated in the academic year 2006–2007, the following categories and numbers represent the postgraduate activities and employment of doctoral degree graduates: Enrolled in a psychology doctoral program (n/a), total from the above (doctoral) (0).

Additional Information:
Orientation, Objectives, and Emphasis of Department: Two areas of concentration are available in the MS program. The general–experimental option focuses upon the basic science areas of psychology. The psychometric (preclinical) option is structured for those whose primary interest is employment in mental health or related settings. The specialist in school psychology program is designed so that a MS degree is awarded upon completion of the first phase of the program. All programs require a comprehensive examination and a thesis.

Special Facilities or Resources: A psychological services center includes a test library and special rooms. The department also has a computer room with 16 personal computers with printer for general student use.

Information for Students With Physical Disabilities: See the following Web site for more information: http://www.ulm.edu.

Application Information:
Send to Graduate School University of Louisiana—Monroe, 700 University Avenue, Monroe, LA 71209. Application available online. Students are admitted in the Fall, application deadline rolling; Winter, application deadline rolling; Spring, application deadline rolling; Summer, application deadline rolling. *Fee:* $20. Graduate Assistantships waiver all tuition (but not fees).

New Orleans, University of

Department of Psychology
College of Science
2001 Geology and Psychology Building
New Orleans, LA 70148
Telephone: (504) 280-6291
Fax: (504) 280-6049
E-mail: *lscarame@uno.edu*
Web: *http://www.uno.edu/~psyc/*

Department Information:
1982. Chairperson: Paul Frick. Number of faculty: total—full-time 9, part-time 1; women—full-time 3, part-time 1; faculty subject to the Americans With Disabilities Act 1.

Programs and Degrees Offered:
Listed in the following order: Program area, degree type (T if terminal Master's), number awarded 7/06–6/07. Applied Biopsychology PhD (Doctor of Philosophy) 0, Applied Developmental Psychology PhD (Doctor of Philosophy) 4.

Student Applications/Admissions:
Student Applications
Applied Biopsychology PhD (Doctor of Philosophy)—Applications 2007–2008, 12. Total applicants accepted 2007–2008, 0. Number full-time enrolled (new admits only) 2007–2008, 0. Number part-time enrolled (new admits only) 2007–2008, 0. Openings 2008–2009, 4. The median number of years required for completion of a degree in 2006–2007 were 6. The number of students enrolled full- and part-time who were dismissed or voluntarily withdrew from this program area in 2007–2008 were 0. *Applied Developmental Psychology PhD (Doctor of Philosophy)*—Applications 2007–2008, 25. Total applicants accepted 2007–2008, 3. Number full-time enrolled (new admits only) 2007–2008, 5. Number part-time enrolled (new admits only) 2007–2008, 0. Openings 2008–2009, 5. The median number of years required for completion of a degree in 2006–2007 were 4. The number of students enrolled full- and part-time who were dismissed or voluntarily withdrew from this program area in 2007–2008 were 1.

Admissions Requirements:
Scores: Entries appear in this order: required test or GPA, minimum score (if required), median score of students entering in 2007–2008. Doctoral Programs: GRE-V no minimum stated, 540; GRE-Q no minimum stated, 630; overall undergraduate GPA no minimum stated, 3.53.
Other Criteria: (importance of criteria rated low, medium, or high): GRE/MAT scores—high, research experience—high, work experience—low, extracurricular activity—low, clinically related public service—medium, GPA—high, letters of recommendation—high, statement of goals and objectives—high. For additional information on admission requirements, go to http://psyc.uno.edu/.

Student Characteristics: The following represents characteristics of students in 2007–2008 in all graduate psychology programs in the department: Female—full-time 14, part-time 0; Male—full-time 7, part-time 0; African American/Black—full-time 1, part-time 0; Hispanic/Latino(a)—full-time 2, part-time 0; Asian/ Pacific Islander—full-time 0, part-time 0; American Indian/ Alaska Native—full-time 0, part-time 0; Caucasian/White—full-time 18, part-time 0; Multi-ethnic—full-time 0, part-time 0; students subject to the Americans With Disabilities Act—full-time 0, part-time 0; Unknown ethnicity—full-time 0, part-time 0.

Financial Information/Assistance:
Tuition for Full-Time Study: *Doctoral:* State residents: per academic year $3,292; Nonstate residents: per academic year $10,336. Tuition is subject to change. See the following Web site for updates and changes in tuition costs: http://www.uno.edu.

Financial Assistance:
First-Year Students: Teaching assistantships available for first year. Average amount paid per academic year: $12,110. Average number of hours worked per week: 20. Tuition remission given: full. Research assistantships available for first year. Average amount paid per academic year: $15,421. Average number of hours worked per week: 20. Tuition remission given: full. Fellowships and scholarships available for first year. Average amount paid per academic year: $16,000. Tuition remission given: full.

Advanced Students: Teaching assistantships available for advanced students. Average amount paid per academic year: $12,110. Average number of hours worked per week: 20. Tuition remission given: partial. Research assistantships available for advanced students. Average amount paid per academic year: $15,421. Average number of hours worked per week: 20. Tuition remission given: full. Fellowships and scholarships available for advanced students. Average amount paid per academic year: $16,000. Tuition remission given: full.

Additional Information: Of all students currently enrolled full time, 100% benefited from one or more of the listed financial assistance programs. Application and information available online at http://psyc.uno.edu/index.htm.

Internships/Practica: Students in both applied specialties are required to complete 12 semester hours of practicum for the doctoral degree. There are a wide array of practicum experiences available and student's choice of practicum is based on his or her specific career objectives.

Housing and Day Care: On-campus housing is available. See the following Web site for more information: http://www.uno.edu. On-campus day care facilities are available.

Employment of Department Graduates:

Master's Degree Graduates: Of those who graduated in the academic year 2006–2007, the following categories and numbers represent the postgraduate activities and employment of master's degree graduates: Enrolled in a postdoctoral residency/fellowship (n/a), employed in independent practice (n/a), total from the above (master's) (0).

Doctoral Degree Graduates: Of those who graduated in the academic year 2006–2007, the following categories and numbers represent the postgraduate activities and employment of doctoral degree graduates: Enrolled in a psychology doctoral program (n/a), enrolled in a postdoctoral residency/fellowship (4), employed in an academic position at a university (0), employed in a community mental health/counseling center (0), employed in a hospital/medical center (0), total from the above (doctoral) (4).

Additional Information:

Orientation, Objectives, and Emphasis of Department: The University of New Orleans, Department of Psychology offers a PhD program with specializations in applied biopsychology and applied developmental psychology. The program was established in 1980 in response to a growing need for persons who are thoroughly trained in the basic content areas of human development or biopsychology, and who are able to translate that knowledge into practical applications. Both specialties emphasize research and service delivery in applied contexts. The applied developmental program has chosen to focus its training in the area of developmental psychopathology. Graduates are trained to work in a variety of settings where they can advance programmatic research focused on understanding psychopathological conditions from a developmental perspective and where they can make practical applications from this research (e.g., design and implement innovative prevention programs or develop assessments for at-risk children). Similarly, the applied biopsychology program has chosen to focus its training in the area of the biological bases of psychopathology. Graduates are trained to work in a variety of settings where they can advance programmatic research focused on understanding psychopathological conditions from a biological and neuroscience perspective and where they can make practical applications from this research (e.g., test pharmacological treatments for psychological disorders; development of neurological, psychophysiological, or other biological tests for psychological disorders).

Information for Students With Physical Disabilities: See the following Web site for more information: http://www.ods.uno.edu/.

Application Information:

Send to Graduate Coordinator, Department of Psychology, 2001 Geology and Psychology Building, New Orleans, LA 70148. Application available online. URL of online application: http://www.psyc.uno.edu/. Students are admitted in the Fall, application deadline February 15. *Fee:* $40.

Southeastern Louisiana University

Department of Psychology
Arts and Sciences
SLU 10831
Hammond, LA 70402
Telephone: (985) 549-2154
Fax: (985) 549-3892
E-mail: *jworthen@selu.edu*
Web: *http://www.selu.edu/Academic/Dept/Psyc*

Department Information:

Chairperson: Matt J. Rossano. Number of faculty: total—full-time 3, part-time 2; women—full-time 5, part-time 1.

Programs and Degrees Offered:

Listed in the following order: Program area, degree type (T if terminal Master's), number awarded 7/06–6/07. General Psychology MA/MS (Master of Arts/Science) (T) 4, Industrial/Organizational Concentration Other.

Student Applications/Admissions:

Student Applications

General Psychology MA/MS (Master of Arts/Science)—Applications 2007–2008, 30. Total applicants accepted 2007–2008, 8. Number full-time enrolled (new admits only) 2007–2008, 8. Number part-time enrolled (new admits only) 2007–2008, 0. Total enrolled 2007–2008 full-time, 25, part-time, 2. Openings 2008–2009, 12. The median number of years required for completion of a degree in 2006–2007 were 2. The number of students enrolled full- and part-time who were dismissed or voluntarily withdrew from this program area in 2007–2008 were 2. *Industrial/Organizational—No information provided.*

Admissions Requirements:

Scores: Entries appear in this order: required test or GPA, minimum score (if required), median score of students entering in 2007–2008. Master's Programs: GRE-V no minimum stated; GRE-Q no minimum stated; overall undergraduate GPA 3.0, 3.5; psychology GPA 3.0, 3.5. Minimum GPA of 2.5 and Minimum GRE (V+Q) of 850 required for conditional admittance.

Other Criteria: (importance of criteria rated low, medium, or high): GRE/MAT scores—high, research experience—high, work experience—low, extracurricular activity—low, clinically related public service—low, GPA—high, letters of recommendation—high, statement of goals and objectives—medium.

Student Characteristics: The following represents characteristics of students in 2007–2008 in all graduate psychology programs in the department: Female—full-time 19, part-time 1; Male—full-time 5, part-time 0; African American/Black—full-time 0, part-time 0; Hispanic/Latino(a)—full-time 1, part-time 0; Asian/Pacific Islander—full-time 0, part-time 0; American Indian/Alaska Native—full-time 0, part-time 0; Caucasian/White—full-time 22, part-time 1; Multi-ethnic—full-time 0, part-time 0; students subject to the Americans With Disabilities Act—full-time 1, part-time 0; Unknown ethnicity—full-time 0, part-time 0; International students who hold an F-1 or J-1 Visa—full-time 1, part-time 0.

Financial Information/Assistance:

Tuition for Full-Time Study: *Master's:* State residents: per academic year $2,318; Nonstate residents: per academic year $6,314. Tuition is subject to change.

Financial Assistance:

First-Year Students: Research assistantships available for first year. Average amount paid per academic year: $5,500. Average number of hours worked per week: 20. Apply by March 15. Tuition remission given: full. Fellowships and scholarships available for first year. Average amount paid per academic year: $3,500. Average number of hours worked per week: 0. Apply by March 15. Tuition remission given: full.

Advanced Students: Research assistantships available for advanced students. Average amount paid per academic year: $5,500. Average number of hours worked per week: 20. Apply by March 15. Tuition remission given: full.

Additional Information: Of all students currently enrolled full time, 40% benefited from one or more of the listed financial assistance programs.

Internships/Practica: Practica are available in clinical and counseling settings.

Housing and Day Care: On-campus housing is available. See the following Web site for more information: http://www.selu.edu/future_students/campus_life/housing/index.html. No on-campus day care facilities are available.

Employment of Department Graduates:

Master's Degree Graduates: Of those who graduated in the academic year 2006–2007, the following categories and numbers represent the postgraduate activities and employment of master's degree graduates: Enrolled in a psychology doctoral program (4), enrolled in another graduate/professional program (0), enrolled in a postdoctoral residency/fellowship (n/a), employed in independent practice (n/a), employed in an academic position at a university (0), employed in an academic position at a 2-year/4-year college (0), employed in other positions at a higher education institution (0), employed in a professional position in a school system (0), employed in business or industry (0), employed in government agency (0), employed in a community mental health/counseling center (0), employed in a hospital/medical center (0), still seeking employment (0), not seeking employment (0), other employment position (0), do not know (0), total from the above (master's) (4).

Doctoral Degree Graduates: Of those who graduated in the academic year 2006–2007, the following categories and numbers represent the postgraduate activities and employment of doctoral degree graduates: Enrolled in a psychology doctoral program (n/a), total from the above (doctoral) (0).

Additional Information:

Orientation, Objectives, and Emphasis of Department: The primary purpose of the MA in general psychology is to prepare the student for doctoral study. This goal is achieved by providing extensive research experience and advanced knowledge in several basic areas within psychology. In recent years, 90% of students who have successfully completed our Master's program in psychology have been placed into doctoral programs.

Special Facilities or Resources: The department has three 5-room laboratory suites for conducting research with humans. There are about 40 microcomputers and 7 printers in the department, about half of which are in a microcomputer laboratory. Statistical packages, such as SPSS, are available on the microcomputers and (via departmental terminal) on the university's mainframe computers.

Application Information:

Official transcripts, GRE scores, Application for Admission form, immunization form, and application fee should be sent to the following address: Enrollment Services, Graduate Admissions, SLU, 10752 Hammond, LA 70402-0752. Your letter of application and the letters from your three references should be sent directly to the Graduate Coordinator. In addition, send copies of everything sent to Enrollment Services (unofficial copies are acceptable). Send these to the following address: James B. Worthen, PhD, SLU, Box 10831, Hammond, LA 70402. Students are admitted in the Fall, application deadline March 15; Spring, application deadline November 15. *Fee:* $20.

Tulane University

Department of Psychology
School of Science and Engineering
2007 Stern Hall
New Orleans, LA 70118
Telephone: (504) 865-5331
Fax: (504) 862-8744
E-mail: *ruscher@tulane.edu*
Web: *http://www.psych.tulane.edu/*

Department Information:

1911. Chairperson: Janet B. Ruscher. Number of faculty: total—full-time 18; women—full-time 8; total—minority—full-time 3; women minority—full-time 1.

Programs and Degrees Offered:

Listed in the following order: Program area, degree type (T if terminal Master's), number awarded 7/06–6/07. Social PhD (Doctor of Philosophy) 1, School PhD (Doctor of Philosophy) 3,

Developmental PhD (Doctor of Philosophy) 2, Psychobiology/Cognitive Neuroscience PhD (Doctor of Philosophy) 1.

APA Accreditation: School PhD (Doctor of Philosophy).

Student Applications/Admissions:

Student Applications

Social PhD (Doctor of Philosophy)—Applications 2007–2008, 10. Total applicants accepted 2007–2008, 2. Number full-time enrolled (new admits only) 2007–2008, 2. Openings 2008–2009, 2. The median number of years required for completion of a degree in 2006–2007 were 5. The number of students enrolled full- and part-time who were dismissed or voluntarily withdrew from this program area in 2007–2008 were 0. *School PhD (Doctor of Philosophy)*—Applications 2007–2008, 23. Total applicants accepted 2007–2008, 7. Number full-time enrolled (new admits only) 2007–2008, 2. Openings 2008–2009, 4. The median number of years required for completion of a degree in 2006–2007 were 5. The number of students enrolled full- and part-time who were dismissed or voluntarily withdrew from this program area in 2007–2008 were 0. *Developmental PhD (Doctor of Philosophy)*—Applications 2007–2008, 8. Total applicants accepted 2007–2008, 2. Number full-time enrolled (new admits only) 2007–2008, 3. Openings 2008–2009, 2. The median number of years required for completion of a degree in 2006–2007 were 5. *Psychobiology/Cognitive Neuroscience PhD (Doctor of Philosophy)*—Applications 2007–2008, 12. Total applicants accepted 2007–2008, 3. Number full-time enrolled (new admits only) 2007–2008, 1. Total enrolled 2007–2008 full-time, 8, part-time, 1. Openings 2008–2009, 3. The median number of years required for completion of a degree in 2006–2007 were 6.

Admissions Requirements:

Scores: Entries appear in this order: required test or GPA, minimum score (if required), median score of students entering in 2007–2008. Master's Programs: GRE-V no minimum stated; GRE-Q no minimum stated; GRE-Subject (Psychology) no minimum stated; overall undergraduate GPA 3.2; Masters GRE-Analytical no minimum stated. Admission is made to PhD only Doctoral Programs: GRE-V 500, 620; GRE-Q 500, 620; overall undergraduate GPA 3.5, 3.5.

Other Criteria: (importance of criteria rated low, medium, or high): GRE/MAT scores—high, research experience—high, work experience—medium, extracurricular activity—low, clinically related public service—medium, GPA—high, letters of recommendation—high, interview—medium, statement of goals and objectives—medium, undergraduate major in psychology—low, specific undergraduate psychology courses taken—medium, Clinical experience and interview important for school psychology. Relevant work experience can be looked upon favorably in other programs (e.g., statistical consulting; market research).

Student Characteristics: The following represents characteristics of students in 2007–2008 in all graduate psychology programs in the department: Female—full-time 32, part-time 1; Male—full-time 6, part-time 0; African American/Black—full-time 4, part-time 0; Hispanic/Latino(a)—full-time 2, part-time 0; Asian/Pacific Islander—full-time 5, part-time 0; American Indian/Alaska Native—full-time 0, part-time 0; Caucasian/White—full-time 27, part-time 1; students subject to the Americans With Disabilities Act—full-time 0, part-time 0; Unknown ethnicity—full-time 0, part-time 0; International students who hold an F-1 or J-1 Visa—full-time 2, part-time 0.

Financial Information/Assistance:

Tuition for Full-Time Study: *Doctoral:* State residents: per academic year $35,100; Nonstate residents: per academic year $35,100. Tuition is subject to change. See the following Web site for updates and changes in tuition costs: http://www2.tulane.edu/main.cfm.

Financial Assistance:

First-Year Students: Teaching assistantships available for first year. Average amount paid per academic year: $16,300. Average number of hours worked per week: 12. Apply by February 1. Tuition remission given: full. Research assistantships available for first year. Average amount paid per academic year: $16,300. Average number of hours worked per week: 12. Apply by February 1. Tuition remission given: full. Fellowships and scholarships available for first year. Average amount paid per academic year: $16,300. Average number of hours worked per week: 12. Apply by February 1. Tuition remission given: full.

Advanced Students: Teaching assistantships available for advanced students. Average amount paid per academic year: $16,300. Average number of hours worked per week: 12. Tuition remission given: full. Research assistantships available for advanced students. Average amount paid per academic year: $16,300. Average number of hours worked per week: 12. Tuition remission given: full. Fellowships and scholarships available for advanced students. Average amount paid per academic year: $16,300. Average number of hours worked per week: 12. Tuition remission given: full.

Additional Information: Of all students currently enrolled full time, 100% benefited from one or more of the listed financial assistance programs. Application and information available online at http://www.tulane.edu/~gradprog/.

Internships/Practica: Doctoral Degree (PhD School): For those doctoral students for whom a professional internship was required in this program prior to graduation, (4) students applied for an internship in 2006–2007, with (4) students obtaining an internship. Of those students who obtained an internship, (4) were paid internships. Of those students who obtained an internship, (4) students placed in APA/CPA-accredited internships, (0) students placed in internships not APA/CPA-accredited, but listed with the Association of Psychology Postdoctoral and Internship Centers (APPIC), (0) students placed in internships conforming to guidelines of the Council of Directors of School Psychology Programs (CDSPP), (0) students placed in internships that were not APA/CPA-accredited, APPIC or CDSPP listed. Practice in Psychoeducational Assessment, School Consultation, Family–School Intervention, Cognitive–Behavioral Assessment/Intervention.

Housing and Day Care: On-campus housing is available. See the following Web site for more information: http://www2.tulane.edu/main.cfm. On-campus day care facilities are available.

Employment of Department Graduates:

Master's Degree Graduates: Of those who graduated in the academic year 2006–2007, the following categories and numbers represent the postgraduate activities and employment of master's

degree graduates: Enrolled in a postdoctoral residency/fellowship (n/a), employed in independent practice (n/a), total from the above (master's) (0).

Doctoral Degree Graduates: Of those who graduated in the academic year 2006–2007, the following categories and numbers represent the postgraduate activities and employment of doctoral degree graduates: Enrolled in a psychology doctoral program (n/a), enrolled in a postdoctoral residency/fellowship (3), employed in an academic position at a university (4), employed in an academic position at a 2-year/4-year college (2), employed in a hospital/medical center (2), total from the above (doctoral) (11).

Additional Information:

Orientation, Objectives, and Emphasis of Department: Tulane's Department of Psychology offers the PhD in the research areas listed above, as well as in applied areas of school psychology. The Department does not offer programs in clinical or counseling psychology. All students are expected to articulate an individualized plan of study by the end of the first year of training, a plan developed in consultation with an advisor and a committee of faculty members. Our two broad areas of substantive focus are development (e.g., infant, childhood, adolescence, cognitive aging, and neuroscience) and culture and context (e.g., minority youth, stereotyping, ecological systems). Students are required to complete empirical studies for the master's thesis and the dissertation, and are expected to carry out additional research while in training. The program in school psychology, which emphasizes normal developmental processes, will take a minimum of 4 years to complete, including a year's internship.

Special Facilities or Resources: The department has research laboratories and computer resources to facilitate research efforts requiring special equipment or space, including physiological, social, sensory, comparative, cognitive, and developmental psychology and human and animal learning. The Newcomb Children's Center, the Hebert facilities at Riverside for natural observation of animals, the laboratories of the Delta Primate Center, and the Audubon Zoological Gardens are available as research sites. There are also opportunities for research in the New Orleans area in organizations and industries, in public and private schools, and in hospitals and other settings serving children.

Information for Students With Physical Disabilities: See the following Web site for more information: http://www.tulane.edu/~erc/disability/index.html.

Application Information:

Send to Dean of the Graduate School, Tulane University, New Orleans, LA 70118. Application available online. URL of online application: http://www.tulane.edu/~gradprog/. Students are admitted in the Fall, application deadline January 15. *Fee:* $45.

Maine, University of
Department of Psychology
Liberal Arts and Sciences
5742 Little Hall
Orono, ME 04469-5742
Telephone: (207) 581-2030
Fax: (207) 581-6128
E-mail: *michael.robbins@umit.maine.edu*
Web: *http://www.umaine.edu/psych*

Department Information:

1926. Chairperson: Michael A. Robbins. Number of faculty: total—full-time 19, part-time 3; women—full-time 6.

Programs and Degrees Offered:

Listed in the following order: Program area, degree type (T if terminal Master's), number awarded 7/06–6/07. Clinical PhD (Doctor of Philosophy) 2, Development PhD (Doctor of Philosophy) 0, General MA/MS (Master of Arts/Science) 0, Psychological Sciences PhD (Doctor of Philosophy) 0.

APA Accreditation: Clinical PhD (Doctor of Philosophy).

Student Applications/Admissions:

Student Applications

Clinical PhD (Doctor of Philosophy)—Applications 2007–2008, 106. Total applicants accepted 2007–2008, 4. Number full-time enrolled (new admits only) 2007–2008, 4. Number part-time enrolled (new admits only) 2007–2008, 0. Openings 2008–2009, 4. The median number of years required for completion of a degree in 2006–2007 were 6. The number of students enrolled full- and part-time who were dismissed or voluntarily withdrew from this program area in 2007–2008 were 1. *Development PhD (Doctor of Philosophy)*—Applications 2007–2008, 6. Total applicants accepted 2007–2008, 0. Number full-time enrolled (new admits only) 2007–2008, 1. Openings 2008–2009, 2. The number of students enrolled full- and part-time who were dismissed or voluntarily withdrew from this program area in 2007–2008 were 0. *General MA/MS (Master of Arts/Science)*—Applications 2007–2008, 5. Total applicants accepted 2007–2008, 0. Openings 2008–2009, 3. The median number of years required for completion of a degree in 2006–2007 were 3. The number of students enrolled full- and part-time who were dismissed or voluntarily withdrew from this program area in 2007–2008 were 0. *Psychological Sciences PhD (Doctor of Philosophy)*—Applications 2007–2008, 18. Total applicants accepted 2007–2008, 2. Number full-time enrolled (new admits only) 2007–2008, 2. Total enrolled 2007–2008 full-time, 7. Openings 2008–2009, 4. The number of students enrolled full- and part-time who were dismissed or voluntarily withdrew from this program area in 2007–2008 were 0.

Admissions Requirements:

Scores: Entries appear in this order: required test or GPA, minimum score (if required), median score of students entering in 2007–2008. Master's Programs: GRE-V no minimum stated, 575; GRE-Q no minimum stated, 690; overall undergraduate GPA no minimum stated, 3.48. Doctoral Programs: GRE-V no minimum stated, 565; GRE-Q no minimum stated, 627; overall undergraduate GPA no minimum stated, 3.49.

Other Criteria: (importance of criteria rated low, medium, or high): GRE/MAT scores—medium, research experience—high, work experience—low, extracurricular activity—low, clinically related public service—medium, GPA—high, letters of recommendation—high, interview—high, statement of goals and objectives—high.

Student Characteristics: The following represents characteristics of students in 2007–2008 in all graduate psychology programs in the department: Female—full-time 24, part-time 0; Male—full-time 13, part-time 0; African American/Black—full-time 0, part-time 0; Hispanic/Latino(a)—full-time 0, part-time 0; Asian/Pacific Islander—full-time 0, part-time 0; American Indian/Alaska Native—full-time 0, part-time 0; Caucasian/White—full-time 36, part-time 0; Multi-ethnic—full-time 1, part-time 0; students subject to the Americans With Disabilities Act—full-time 1, part-time 0; Unknown ethnicity—full-time 0, part-time 0.

Financial Information/Assistance:

Tuition for Full-Time Study: *Master's:* State residents: $325 per credit hour; Nonstate residents: $926 per credit hour. *Doctoral:* State residents: $325 per credit hour; Nonstate residents: $926 per credit hour. Tuition is subject to change.

Financial Assistance:

First-Year Students: Teaching assistantships available for first year. Average number of hours worked per week: 12. Apply by no deadline. Tuition remission given: full. Research assistantships available for first year. Average number of hours worked per week: 20. Apply by no deadline. Tuition remission given: full.

Advanced Students: Teaching assistantships available for advanced students. Average number of hours worked per week: 12. Apply by no deadline. Tuition remission given: full. Research assistantships available for advanced students. Average number of hours worked per week: 12. Apply by no deadline. Tuition remission given: full. Traineeships available for advanced students. Average number of hours worked per week: 12. Apply by no deadline. Tuition remission given: full. Fellowships and scholarships available for advanced students. Average number of hours worked per week: 0. Apply by no deadline. Tuition remission given: full.

Additional Information: Of all students currently enrolled full time, 88% benefited from one or more of the listed financial assistance programs.

Internships/Practica: Doctoral Degree (PhD Clinical): For those doctoral students for whom a professional internship was required in this program prior to graduation, (3) students applied for an internship in 2006–2007, with (3) students obtaining an internship. Of those students who obtained an internship, (3) were paid internships. Of those students who obtained an internship, (3) students placed in APA/CPA-accredited internships, (0) students placed in internships not APA/CPA-accredited, but listed with the Association of Psychology Postdoctoral and Internship Centers (APPIC), (0) students placed in internships conforming to guidelines of the Council of Directors of School Psychology Programs (CDSPP), (0) students placed in internships that were not APA/CPA-accredited, APPIC or CDSPP listed. Several settings are used for practicum training: The Psychological Services Center housed within the department, Penobscot Job Corps, Kennebec Valley Mental Health Center, Penqis CAPS Head Start, School Administrative District 4, and 68, KidsPeace New England.

Housing and Day Care: On-campus housing is available. On-campus day care facilities are available.

Employment of Department Graduates:

Master's Degree Graduates: Of those who graduated in the academic year 2006–2007, the following categories and numbers represent the postgraduate activities and employment of master's degree graduates: Enrolled in a postdoctoral residency/fellowship (n/a), employed in independent practice (n/a), total from the above (master's) (0).

Doctoral Degree Graduates: Of those who graduated in the academic year 2006–2007, the following categories and numbers represent the postgraduate activities and employment of doctoral degree graduates: Enrolled in a psychology doctoral program (n/a), enrolled in a postdoctoral residency/fellowship (4), do not know (1), total from the above (doctoral) (5).

Additional Information:

Orientation, Objectives, and Emphasis of Department: The department believes that the best graduate education involves close working relationships between the faculty and the student. Thus, a high faculty-to-student ratio and small class sizes characterize the department. In addition, incoming students are selected to work with a faculty research mentor. There are also opportunities for individualized study and experience in directed readings, research, and teaching. A faculty committee, selected to represent the student's interests, will assist the student in planning an appropriate graduate program.

Special Facilities or Resources: Psychophysiological, perception, EEG laboratories; animal research laboratory; on-site practicum training center; department-run preschool.

Information for Students With Physical Disabilities: See the following Web site for more information: http://www.ume.maine.edu/onward/disable.htm.

Application Information:

Send to Graduate School, 5782 Winslow Hall, University of Maine, Orono, ME 04469-5782. Application available online. Students are admitted in the Spring, application deadline December 31. *Fee:* $50.

Baltimore, University of

Division of Applied Behavioral Sciences
Yale Gordon College of Liberal Arts
1420 North Charles Street
Baltimore, MD 21201-5779
Telephone: (410) 837-5310
Fax: (410) 837-4059
E-mail: *tmitchell@ubalt.edu*
Web: *http://www.ubalt.edu/cla_template.cfm?page=729*

Department Information:

1970. Graduate Program Director: Tom Mitchell, PhD. Number of faculty: total—full-time 7; women—full-time 5; ; women minority—full-time 1.

Programs and Degrees Offered:

Listed in the following order: Program area, degree type (T if terminal Master's), number awarded 7/06–6/07. Psychological Applications MA/MS (Master of Arts/Science) (T) 2, Counseling MA/MS (Master of Arts/Science) (T) 13, Industrial/Organizational MA/MS (Master of Arts/Science) (T) 19.

Student Applications/Admissions:

Student Applications

Psychological Applications MA/MS (Master of Arts/Science)—Applications 2007–2008, 16. Total applicants accepted 2007–2008, 12. Number full-time enrolled (new admits only) 2007–2008, 4. Number part-time enrolled (new admits only) 2007–2008, 10. Total enrolled 2007–2008 full-time, 7, part-time, 8. Openings 2008–2009, 10. The median number of years required for completion of a degree in 2006–2007 were 3. The number of students enrolled full- and part-time who were dismissed or voluntarily withdrew from this program area in 2007–2008 were 0. *Counseling MA/MS (Master of Arts/Science)*—Applications 2007–2008, 58. Total applicants accepted 2007–2008, 51. Number full-time enrolled (new admits only) 2007–2008, 10. Number part-time enrolled (new admits only) 2007–2008, 15. Total enrolled 2007–2008 full-time, 14, part-time, 32. Openings 2008–2009, 25. The median number of years required for completion of a degree in 2006–2007 were 4. The number of students enrolled full- and part-time who were dismissed or voluntarily withdrew from this program area in 2007–2008 were 2. *Industrial/Organizational MA/MS (Master of Arts/Science)*—Applications 2007–2008, 74. Total applicants accepted 2007–2008, 62. Number full-time enrolled (new admits only) 2007–2008, 20. Number part-time enrolled (new admits only) 2007–2008, 8. Total enrolled 2007–2008 full-time, 28, part-time, 33. Openings 2008–2009, 30. The median number of years required for completion of a degree in 2006–2007 were 3. The number of students enrolled full- and part-time who were dismissed or voluntarily withdrew from this program area in 2007–2008 were 1.

Admissions Requirements:

Scores: Entries appear in this order: required test or GPA, minimum score (if required), median score of students entering in 2007–2008. Master's Programs: GRE-V no minimum stated, 456; GRE-Q no minimum stated, 509; overall undergraduate GPA 3.0, 3.35.

Other Criteria: (importance of criteria rated low, medium, or high): GRE/MAT scores—medium, GPA—high, letters of recommendation—medium, statement of goals and objectives—medium.

Student Characteristics: The following represents characteristics of students in 2007–2008 in all graduate psychology programs in the department: Female—full-time 35, part-time 62; Male—full-time 14, part-time 11; African American/Black—full-time 12, part-time 25; Hispanic/Latino(a)—full-time 2, part-time 2; Asian/Pacific Islander—full-time 3, part-time 1; American Indian/Alaska Native—full-time 0, part-time 0; Caucasian/White—full-time 32, part-time 46; Multi-ethnic—full-time 0, part-time 0; students subject to the Americans With Disabilities Act—full-time 5, part-time 6; Unknown ethnicity—full-time 0, part-time 0.

Financial Information/Assistance:

Tuition for Full-Time Study: *Master's:* State residents: per academic year $10,544, $585 per credit hour; Nonstate residents: per academic year $14,738, $818 per credit hour. Tuition is subject to change.

Financial Assistance:

First-Year Students: Research assistantships available for first year. Average amount paid per academic year: $3,200. Average number of hours worked per week: 20. Apply by March 15. Tuition remission given: full.

Advanced Students: Research assistantships available for advanced students. Average amount paid per academic year: $3,200. Average number of hours worked per week: 20. Apply by March 15. Tuition remission given: full.

Additional Information: Of all students currently enrolled full time, 9% benefited from one or more of the listed financial assistance programs.

Internships/Practica: The Baltimore/Washington Metropolitan area provides a wide range of settings for paid practicum and internships. The academic and site supervisors work closely with the intern to insure a quaiity experience.

Housing and Day Care: No on-campus housing is available. No on-campus day care facilities are available.

Employment of Department Graduates:

Master's Degree Graduates: Of those who graduated in the academic year 2006–2007, the following categories and numbers represent the postgraduate activities and employment of master's degree graduates: Enrolled in a postdoctoral residency/fellowship (n/a), employed in independent practice (n/a), total from the above (master's) (0).

Doctoral Degree Graduates: Of those who graduated in the academic year 2006–2007, the following categories and numbers represent the postgraduate activities and employment of doctoral

degree graduates: Enrolled in a psychology doctoral program (n/a), total from the above (doctoral) (0).

Additional Information:

Orientation, Objectives, and Emphasis of Department: The Division of Applied Behavioral Sciences has a practitioner-oriented faculty of applied psychologists and researchers. For more information visit http://www.ubalt.edu/cla_template.cfm?page=729.

Special Facilities or Resources: Four different university labs and 100% of our classrooms provide Internet access, MS Office, and SPSS for students and faculty members. The Wagman Psychology Lab provides for computer-based testing and assessment.

Application Information:

Send to Office of Graduate Admissions, University of Baltimore, 1420 North Charles Street, Baltimore, MD 21201-5779. Application available online. URL of online application: http://www.ubalt.edu/admissions/graduate/dates.html. Students are admitted in the Fall, application deadline July 1; Spring, application deadline December 1. *Fee:* $30. $45 paper application; $30 online.

Frostburg State University

MS in Counseling Psychology Program
College of Liberal Arts and Sciences
Department of Psychology
101 Braddock Road
Frostburg, MD 21532
Telephone: (301) 687-4446
Fax: (301) 687-7418
E-mail: *mpmurtagh@frostburg.edu*
Web: *http://www.frostburg.edu/dept/psyc/graduate/coupsy.htm*

Department Information:

1977. Michael Murtagh, Graduate Program Coordinator: Kevin Peterson, Chair. Number of faculty: total—full-time 5, part-time 1; women—full-time 2; total—minority—full-time 1; women minority—full-time 1.

Programs and Degrees Offered:

Listed in the following order: Program area, degree type (T if terminal Master's), number awarded 7/06–6/07. Counseling Psychology MA/MS (Master of Arts/Science) (T) 19.

Student Applications/Admissions:

Student Applications

Counseling Psychology MA/MS (Master of Arts/Science)—Applications 2007–2008, 43. Total applicants accepted 2007–2008, 15. Number full-time enrolled (new admits only) 2007–2008, 12. Number part-time enrolled (new admits only) 2007–2008, 3. Total enrolled 2007–2008 full-time, 37, part-time, 6. Openings 2008–2009, 15. The median number of years required for completion of a degree in 2006–2007 were 3. The number of students enrolled full- and part-time who were dismissed or voluntarily withdrew from this program area in 2007–2008 were 3.

Admissions Requirements:

Scores: Entries appear in this order: required test or GPA, minimum score (if required), median score of students entering in 2007–2008. Master's Programs: overall undergraduate GPA 3.0. Minimum score on GRE (V + Q = 1000) or MAT (410) required only if the GPA is less than 3.0. Otherwise, scores do not need to be submitted.

Other Criteria: (importance of criteria rated low, medium, or high): GRE/MAT scores—low, research experience—low, work experience—high, extracurricular activity—low, clinically related public service—high, GPA—high, letters of recommendation—high, interview—high, statement of goals and objectives—high, undergrad. internship—high, undergraduate major in psychology—medium, specific undergraduate psychology courses taken—medium.

Student Characteristics: The following represents characteristics of students in 2007–2008 in all graduate psychology programs in the department: Female—full-time 29, part-time 5; Male—full-time 8, part-time 1; African American/Black—full-time 3, part-time 1; Hispanic/Latino(a)—full-time 1, part-time 0; Asian/Pacific Islander—full-time 1, part-time 0; American Indian/Alaska Native—full-time 0, part-time 0; Caucasian/White—full-time 27, part-time 5; Multi-ethnic—full-time 0, part-time 0; students subject to the Americans With Disabilities Act—full-time 0, part-time 0; Unknown ethnicity—full-time 5, part-time 0; International students who hold an F-1 or J-1 Visa—full-time 4, part-time 0.

Financial Information/Assistance:

Tuition for Full-Time Study: *Master's:* State residents: $305 per credit hour; Nonstate residents: $350 per credit hour. Tuition is subject to change. See the following Web site for updates and changes in tuition costs: http://www.frostburg.edu/admin/billing/.

Financial Assistance:

First-Year Students: Teaching assistantships available for first year. Average amount paid per academic year: $5,000. Average number of hours worked per week: 20. Apply by March 15. Tuition remission given: full. Research assistantships available for first year. Average amount paid per academic year: $5,000. Average number of hours worked per week: 20. Apply by March 15. Tuition remission given: full. Fellowships and scholarships available for first year. Average amount paid per academic year: $6,500. Average number of hours worked per week: 20. Apply by March 15. Tuition remission given: full.

Advanced Students: No information provided.

Additional Information: Of all students currently enrolled full time, 57% benefited from one or more of the listed financial assistance programs. Application and information available online at http://www.frostburg.edu/grad/pdf/ga_booklet.pdf.

Internships/Practica: Master's Degree (MA/MS counseling psychology): An internship experience such as a final research project or "capstone" experience is required of graduates. An extensive, two-semester internship experience is required that facilitates students' receptivity to supervisory feedback, enhances self-awareness, and provides a setting in which the transition from student to professional is accomplished. In addition to on-site supervision, students participate in individual and group supervision with FSU faculty. Past graduate internship sites for the MS Counseling Psychology program have included outpatient community mental health (the most frequent internship setting), college counseling, inpatient psychiatric, inpatient and outpatient addictions, family services, K–12 psychological assessment and alternative classroom and after school care programs, community health advocacy and counseling, criminal justice system, nursing homes, hospital-based crisis services, hospice, and domestic violence programs. Students construct their internship experiences in order to meet training goals they formulate. Students electing to complete graduate certificate programs in Addictions Counseling Psychology and Child and Family Counseling Psychology must complete at least 150 hours of direct services in settings consistent with the certificate program's focus. Internship experiences, in addition to at least four academic semesters of study, prepare graduates for positions as mental health counselors, marriage and family counselors, crisis counselors, drug and alcohol counselors, community health specialists, and in supervisory positions in a variety of settings.

Housing and Day Care: On-campus housing is available. See the following Web site for more information: http://www.frostburg.edu/clife/reslife.htm. On-campus day care facilities are available. See the following Web site for more information: http://www.frostburg.edu/about/vt/children.htm.

Employment of Department Graduates:

Master's Degree Graduates: Of those who graduated in the academic year 2006–2007, the following categories and numbers represent the postgraduate activities and employment of master's degree graduates: Enrolled in a postdoctoral residency/fellowship (n/a), employed in independent practice (n/a), total from the above (master's) (0).

Doctoral Degree Graduates: Of those who graduated in the academic year 2006–2007, the following categories and numbers represent the postgraduate activities and employment of doctoral degree graduates: Enrolled in a psychology doctoral program (n/a), total from the above (doctoral) (0).

Additional Information:

Orientation, Objectives, and Emphasis of Department: Providing training in professional psychology at the Master's level, FSU's program is designed for those pursuing further study in science-based counseling psychology. Our theoretical perspective is integrative, including cognitive–behavioral, family systems, developmental, feminist, multicultural, humanistic, and brief therapies. We emphasize training in empirically supported treatments for children, adolescents, families, and adults. Students develop counseling skills through learning about self, client, counselor–client relationships, and the importance of cultural contexts. Considerable attention is given not only to development of professional skills but also to personal development and multicultural awareness. These emphases reflect our belief that an effective counselor is one who is self-aware and receptive to consultation. For continuing study at the doctoral level, experience and knowledge gained in this program provide a firm foundation. Optional research opportunities prepare students for advanced graduate study in psychology. The Center for Children and Families offers unique research, educational, and service experiences. Two certificate programs provide specialized training in Addictions Counseling Psychology and Child and Family Counseling Psychology. These can be completed within the 3-year program of study, as well as courses required for licensure. All National Counselor Exam course areas are offered, and FSU offers this exam. The Master's in Psychology Accreditation Council accredits this program.

Special Facilities or Resources: Resources include specially designed counseling practice rooms for individual and group counseling. Two-way mirrors with adjacent observation rooms are available for supervision. Audiotaping and videotaping resources are available for faculty and student use. In addition, students' case conceptualization write-ups and all previous internship papers are available for restricted use by students.

Information for Students With Physical Disabilities: See the following Web site for more information: http://www.frostburg.edu/clife/studev.htm.

Application Information:

Send to Office of Graduate Services, 101 Braddock Road, Frostburg State University, Frostburg, MD 21532. Application available online. URL of online application: http://www.frostburg.edu/grad/application_instructions.htm. Students are admitted in the Fall, application deadline February 1; Programs have rolling admissions. March 15 for Graduate Assistantship applications. *Fee:* $30.

Johns Hopkins University

Department of Psychological and Brain Sciences
3400 North Charles Street
Baltimore, MD 21218
Telephone: (410) 516-6175
Fax: (410) 516-4478
E-mail: *hope.stein@jhu.edu*
Web: *http://www.psy.jhu.edu*

Department Information:

1881. Chairperson: Dr. Peter Holland. Number of faculty: total—full-time 13, part-time 13; women—full-time 4, part-time 4; faculty subject to the Americans With Disabilities Act 1.

Programs and Degrees Offered:

Listed in the following order: Program area, degree type (T if terminal Master's), number awarded 7/06–6/07. Biopsychology PhD (Doctor of Philosophy) 1, Cognitive PhD (Doctor of Philosophy) 2, Cognitive Neuroscience PhD (Doctor of Philosophy) 2, Developmental PhD (Doctor of Philosophy) 1.

Student Applications/Admissions:

Student Applications

Biopsychology PhD (Doctor of Philosophy)—Applications 2007–2008, 45. Total applicants accepted 2007–2008, 4. Number full-time enrolled (new admits only) 2007–2008, 1. Openings 2008–2009, 3. The median number of years required for completion of a degree in 2006–2007 were 5. The number of students enrolled full- and part-time who were dismissed or voluntarily withdrew from this program area in 2007–2008 were 0. *Cognitive PhD (Doctor of Philosophy)*—Applications 2007–2008, 21. Total applicants accepted 2007–2008, 2. Number full-time enrolled (new admits only) 2007–2008, 1. Total enrolled 2007–2008 full-time, 4. Openings 2008–2009, 2. The median number of years required for completion of a degree in 2006–2007 were 5. The number of students enrolled full- and part-time who were dismissed or voluntarily withdrew from this program area in 2007–2008 were 0. *Cognitive Neuroscience PhD (Doctor of Philosophy)*—Applications 2007–2008,

40. Total applicants accepted 2007–2008, 3. Number full-time enrolled (new admits only) 2007–2008, 3. Openings 2008–2009, 3. The median number of years required for completion of a degree in 2006–2007 were 5. The number of students enrolled full- and part-time who were dismissed or voluntarily withdrew from this program area in 2007–2008 were 0. *Developmental PhD (Doctor of Philosophy)*—Applications 2007–2008, 30. Total applicants accepted 2007–2008, 0. Number full-time enrolled (new admits only) 2007–2008, 0. Openings 2008–2009, 2. The median number of years required for completion of a degree in 2006–2007 were 5. The number of students enrolled full- and part-time who were dismissed or voluntarily withdrew from this program area in 2007–2008 were 1.

Admissions Requirements:

Scores: Entries appear in this order: required test or GPA, minimum score (if required), median score of students entering in 2007–2008. Master's Programs: GRE-V no minimum stated, 602; GRE-Q no minimum stated, 690. Doctoral Programs: GRE-V no minimum stated, 650; GRE-Q no minimum stated, 693; overall undergraduate GPA no minimum stated.

Other Criteria: (importance of criteria rated low, medium, or high): GRE/MAT scores—high, research experience—high, work experience—medium, extracurricular activity—low, clinically related public service—low, GPA—high, letters of recommendation—high, interview—high, statement of goals and objectives—high, sample of work—medium.

Student Characteristics: The following represents characteristics of students in 2007–2008 in all graduate psychology programs in the department: Female—full-time 10, part-time 0; Male—full-time 14, part-time 0; African American/Black—full-time 1, part-time 0; Hispanic/Latino(a)—full-time 1, part-time 0; Asian/Pacific Islander—full-time 3, part-time 0; American Indian/Alaska Native—full-time 0, part-time 0; Caucasian/White—full-time 19, part-time 0; Multi-ethnic—full-time 0, part-time 0; students subject to the Americans With Disabilities Act—full-time 0, part-time 0; Unknown ethnicity—full-time 0, part-time 0.

Financial Information/Assistance:

Financial Assistance:

First-Year Students: Teaching assistantships available for first year. Tuition remission given: full. Research assistantships available for first year.

Advanced Students: Teaching assistantships available for advanced students. Tuition remission given: full. Research assistantships available for advanced students.

Additional Information: Of all students currently enrolled full time, 100% benefited from one or more of the listed financial assistance programs. Application and information available online at http://www.psy.jhu.edu.

Internships/Practica: No information provided.

Housing and Day Care: No on-campus housing is available. No on-campus day care facilities are available.

Employment of Department Graduates:

Master's Degree Graduates: Of those who graduated in the academic year 2006–2007, the following categories and numbers represent the postgraduate activities and employment of master's degree graduates: Enrolled in a postdoctoral residency/fellowship (n/a), employed in independent practice (n/a), total from the above (master's) (0).

Doctoral Degree Graduates: Of those who graduated in the academic year 2006–2007, the following categories and numbers represent the postgraduate activities and employment of doctoral degree graduates: Enrolled in a psychology doctoral program (n/a), enrolled in a postdoctoral residency/fellowship (4), total from the above (doctoral) (4).

Additional Information:

Orientation, Objectives, and Emphasis of Department: The graduate program in psychology at The Johns Hopkins University emphasizes research training, stressing the application of basic research methodology to theoretical problems in psychology. Students are actively engaged in research projects within the first semester. There is a low student–faculty ratio; students work closely with their advisors. Courses, seminars, and research activities provide training so that students will emerge as independent investigators who can embark on successful research careers in psychology. Courses cover fundamental issues in experimental design and analysis, and provide a broad background in all the major areas of psychology. Advanced seminars deal with topics of current interest in various specific areas. The department has programs in cognitive psychology (including perceptual and cognitive development), cognitive neuroscience, quantitative psychology, and biopsychology. The evaluation of applications to our graduate program is based on many factors. They include both objective indicators, such as required GRE scores and undergraduate GPA, and more subjective information, such as a statement of purpose, a description of applicant's background and experience, and letters of recommendation. To select among the top candidates, we rely on letters of recommendation to provide a personal assessment of applicant's potential for graduate work by faculty mentors and advisors who know the applicant well. Students in good standing can expect to receive both tuition remission and salary.

Special Facilities or Resources: Each faculty member in the Department of Psychology maintains a laboratory for conducting research. The psychology building was recently renovated, and the research space is both excellent and plentiful. Every lab contains multiple microcomputer systems for experimentation, analysis, and word processing; most machines are connected via a local-area network to one another and to the Internet. In addition, individual laboratories contain special purpose equipment designed for the research carried out there. Laboratories in cognition, for example, include high-resolution display devices for experiments in visual. Quantitative psychology laboratories include UNIX work stations for computational analysis and simulation studies. Biopsychology laboratories have facilities for animal surgery, histology, electrophysiological recording of single units and evoked potentials, analysis of neurotransmitters through assays and high-pressure liquid chromatography, bioacoustics, and for general behavioral testing.

Application Information:

Send to Hope Stein, Academic Program Coordinator, JHU, Department of Psychological and Brain Sciences, 204 Ames Hall, Charles and 34th Streets, Baltimore, MD 21218. Application available online. URL of online application: http://www.psy.jhu.edu. Students are admitted in the Fall, application deadline December 15. Online Applications Only. *Fee:* $65.

Loyola College

Department of Psychology
4501 North Charles Street
Baltimore, MD 21210
Telephone: (410) 617-2696
Fax: (410) 617-5341
E-mail: *tpmartino@loyola.edu*
Web: *http://www.Loyola.edu/Psychology*

Department Information:

1968. Chairperson: Dr. Jen L. Lowry. Number of faculty: total—full-time 21, part-time 2; women—full-time 12; total—minority—full-time 3; women minority—full-time 3.

Programs and Degrees Offered:

Listed in the following order: Program area, degree type (T if terminal Master's), number awarded 7/06–6/07. Clinical MA/MS (Master of Arts/Science) (T) 43, Counseling MA/MS (Master of Arts/Science) (T) 27, Clinical PsyD (Doctor of Psychology) 12.

APA Accreditation: Clinical PsyD (Doctor of Psychology).

Student Applications/Admissions:

Student Applications

Clinical MA/MS (Master of Arts/Science)—Applications 2007–2008, 175. Total applicants accepted 2007–2008, 75. Number full-time enrolled (new admits only) 2007–2008, 27. Number part-time enrolled (new admits only) 2007–2008, 7. Total enrolled 2007–2008 full-time, 81, part-time, 20. Openings 2008–2009, 45. The median number of years required for completion of a degree in 2006–2007 were 2. The number of students enrolled full- and part-time who were dismissed or voluntarily withdrew from this program area in 2007–2008 were 0. *Counseling MA/MS (Master of Arts/Science)*—Applications 2007–2008, 117. Total applicants accepted 2007–2008, 61. Number full-time enrolled (new admits only) 2007–2008, 12. Number part-time enrolled (new admits only) 2007–2008, 5. Total enrolled 2007–2008 full-time, 49, part-time, 6. Openings 2008–2009, 35. The median number of years required for completion of a degree in 2006–2007 were 2. The number of students enrolled full- and part-time who were dismissed or voluntarily withdrew from this program area in 2007–2008 were 0. *Clinical PsyD (Doctor of Psychology)*—Applications 2007–2008, 344. Total applicants accepted 2007–2008, 34. Number full-time enrolled (new admits only) 2007–2008, 18. Total enrolled 2007–2008 full-time, 67. Openings 2008–2009, 15. The median number of years required for completion of a degree in 2006–2007 were 4. The number of students enrolled full- and part-time who were dismissed or voluntarily withdrew from this program area in 2007–2008 were 2.

Admissions Requirements:

Scores: Entries appear in this order: required test or GPA, minimum score (if required), median score of students entering in 2007–2008. Master's Programs: GRE-V no minimum stated, 540; GRE-Q no minimum stated, 580; overall undergraduate GPA 3.0, 3.4; psychology GPA 3.0; Masters GRE-Analytical no minimum stated, 5.0. Doctoral Programs: GRE-V no minimum stated, 580; GRE-Q no minimum stated, 620; overall undergraduate GPA 3.0, 3.5; Doctoral program GRE-Analytic no minimum stated, 5.0.

Other Criteria: (importance of criteria rated low, medium, or high): GRE/MAT scores—high, research experience—high, work experience—high, extracurricular activity—high, clinically related public service—high, GPA—high, letters of recommendation—high, interview—high, statement of goals and objectives—high, undergraduate major in psychology—low, specific undergraduate psychology courses taken—high. Interviews by invitation only for PsyD program. Interviews for Master's Program not applicable. For additional information on admission requirements, go to http://Graduate.loyola.edu.

Student Characteristics: The following represents characteristics of students in 2007–2008 in all graduate psychology programs in the department: Female—full-time 162, part-time 22; Male—full-time 35, part-time 4; African American/Black—full-time 18, part-time 2; Hispanic/Latino(a)—full-time 7, part-time 1; Asian/Pacific Islander—full-time 13, part-time 0; American Indian/Alaska Native—full-time 1, part-time 0; Caucasian/White—full-time 150, part-time 23; Multi-ethnic—full-time 5, part-time 0; students subject to the Americans With Disabilities Act—full-time 3, part-time 0; Unknown ethnicity—full-time 0, part-time 0; International students who hold an F-1 or J-1 Visa—full-time 3, part-time 0.

Financial Information/Assistance:

Tuition for Full-Time Study: *Master's:* State residents: $525 per credit hour; Nonstate residents: $525 per credit hour. *Doctoral:* State residents: per academic year $22,000; Nonstate residents: per academic year $22,000. Tuition is subject to change. Tuition costs vary by program.

Financial Assistance:

First-Year Students: No information provided.

Advanced Students: Teaching assistantships available for advanced students. Average amount paid per academic year: $1,500. Average number of hours worked per week: 10. Apply by May, November. Tuition remission given: partial. Research assistantships available for advanced students. Average amount paid per academic year: $1,500. Average number of hours worked per week: 10. Apply by May, November. Tuition remission given: partial. Fellowships and scholarships available for advanced students. Apply by varies. Tuition remission given: partial.

Additional Information: Of all students currently enrolled full time, 30% benefited from one or more of the listed financial assistance programs. Application and information available online at http://www.loyola.edu/HR/Student%20Employment/.

Internships/Practica: Master's Degree (MA/MS Clinical): An internship experience such as a final research project or "capstone" experience is required of graduates. Master's Degree (MA/MS Counseling): An internship experience such as a final research project or "capstone" experience is required of graduates. Doctoral Degree (PsyD Clinical): For those doctoral students for whom a professional internship was required in this program prior to graduation, (11) students applied for an internship in 2006–2007, with (11) students obtaining an internship. Of those students who obtained an internship, (11) were paid internships. Of those students who obtained an internship, (9) students placed in APA/CPA-accredited internships, (1) student placed in internships not APA/CPA-accredited, but listed with the Association of Psychology Postdoctoral and Internship Centers (APPIC), (0) students placed in internships conforming to guidelines of the Council of Directors of School Psychology Programs (CDSPP), (1) student placed in internships that were not APA/CPA accredited, APPIC or CDSPP listed. The MS program, Practitioner Track requires 300 hours of externship experience. The MS program, Thesis Track requires 150 hours of externship experience. Students are able to choose from a wide variety of sites approved by the Department. The PsyD program incorporates field placement training throughout the curriculum; a minimum total of 1,260 hours of field training is required. The final (5th) year of the PsyD program is a full-time internship.

Housing and Day Care: No on-campus housing is available. No on-campus day care facilities are available.

Employment of Department Graduates:

Master's Degree Graduates: Of those who graduated in the academic year 2006–2007, the following categories and numbers represent the postgraduate activities and employment of master's degree graduates: Enrolled in a psychology doctoral program (6), enrolled in another graduate/professional program (5), enrolled in a postdoctoral residency/fellowship (n/a), employed in independent practice (n/a), employed in a community mental health/counseling center (5), employed in a hospital/medical center (6), do not know (25), total from the above (master's) (47).

Doctoral Degree Graduates: Of those who graduated in the academic year 2006–2007, the following categories and numbers represent the postgraduate activities and employment of doctoral degree graduates: Enrolled in a psychology doctoral program (n/a), enrolled in a postdoctoral residency/fellowship (13), employed in independent practice (0), total from the above (doctoral) (13).

Additional Information:

Orientation, Objectives, and Emphasis of Department: The Master's programs in Clinical and Counseling Psychology at Loyola College provides training to individuals who wish to promote mental health in individuals, families, organizations, and communities though careers in direct service, leadership, research, and education. We strive to provide a learning environment that facilitates the development of skills in critical thinking, scholarship, assessment, and intervention, and that is grounded in an appreciation for both psychological science and human diversity. The goals of the PsyD program in Clinical Psychology are based on the scholar–professional model of training, designed to train autonomous practitioners of professional psychology who will deliver mental health services and lead others in service to the general public in diverse settings.

Special Facilities or Resources: Departmental facilities include the Loyola Clinic, a health psychology/behavioral medicine laboratory, audiovisual recording facilities, assessment and therapy training rooms, and a student lounge. Students have access to a campuswide computer system, including SPSS and SASS software. All graduate students have telephone voicemail and e-mail addresses. Advanced doctoral students are provided with individual workstations with computers.

Information for Students With Physical Disabilities: See the following Web site for more information: http://www.loyola.edu/dss.

Application Information:

Send to Office of Graduate Admissions, Loyola College in Maryland, 4501 North Charles Street, Baltimore, MD 21210. Application available online. URL of online application: http://www.graduate.loyola.edu/graduate/academics/psy/apply.asp. Students are admitted in the Fall, application deadline; Summer, application deadline. For Fall, deadlines are as follows: PsyD December 15; MS Thesis Track March 15; MS Practitioner Track March 15. For Summer (March 15), applications are accepted for MS, Practitioner Track only. *Fee:* $50.

Maryland, University of

Department of Psychology
College of Behavioral and Social Sciences
Biology and Psychology Building
College Park, MD 20742-4411
Telephone: (301) 405-5865
Fax: (301) 314-9566
E-mail: *psycgrad@psyc.umd.edu*
Web: *http://www.psychology.umd.edu*

Department Information:

1937. Chairperson: Thomas Wallsten. Number of faculty: total—full-time 32; women—full-time 11; total—minority—full-time 1.

Programs and Degrees Offered:

Listed in the following order: Program area, degree type (T if terminal Master's), number awarded 7/06–6/07. Clinical PhD (Doctor of Philosophy) 5, Developmental PhD (Doctor of Philosophy) 0, Counseling PhD (Doctor of Philosophy) 4, Cognitive and Neural Systems PhD (Doctor of Philosophy) 2, Social, Decision, and Organizational Sciences PhD (Doctor of Philosophy) 7.

APA Accreditation: Clinical PhD (Doctor of Philosophy). Counseling PhD (Doctor of Philosophy).

Student Applications/Admissions:

Student Applications

Clinical PhD (Doctor of Philosophy)—Applications 2007–2008, 266. Total applicants accepted 2007–2008, 11. Number full-time enrolled (new admits only) 2007–2008, 6. Openings 2008–2009, 6. The median number of years required for completion of a degree in 2006–2007 were 5. The number of students enrolled full- and part-time who were dismissed or voluntarily withdrew from this program area in 2007–2008 were 0. *Developmental PhD (Doctor of Philosophy)*—Applications 2007–2008, 19. Total applicants accepted 2007–2008, 1. Number full-time enrolled (new admits only) 2007–2008, 0. Openings 2008–2009, 3. The median number of years required for completion of a degree in 2006–2007 were 6. The number of students enrolled full- and part-time who were dismissed or voluntarily withdrew from this program area in 2007–2008 were 0. *Counseling PhD (Doctor of Philosophy)*—Applications 2007–2008, 120. Total applicants accepted 2007–2008, 6. Number full-time enrolled (new admits only) 2007–2008, 3. Total enrolled 2007–2008 full-time, 17. Openings 2008–2009, 4. The median number of years required for completion of a degree in 2006–2007 were 5. The number of students enrolled full- and part-time who were dismissed or voluntarily withdrew from this program area in 2007–2008 were 0. *Cognitive and Neural Systems PhD (Doctor of Philosophy)*—Applications 2007–2008, 7. Total applicants accepted 2007–2008, 0. Number full-time enrolled (new admits only) 2007–2008, 0. Total enrolled 2007–2008 full-time, 4. Openings 2008–2009, 3. The median number of years required for completion of a degree in 2006–2007 were 5. The number of students enrolled full- and part-time who were dismissed or voluntarily withdrew from this program area in 2007–2008 were 0. *Social, Decision, and Organizational Sciences PhD (Doctor of Philosophy)*—Applications 2007–2008, 191. Total applicants accepted 2007–2008, 12. Number full-time enrolled (new admits only) 2007–2008, 5. Total enrolled 2007–2008 full-time, 34. Openings 2008–2009, 6. The median number of years required for completion of a degree in 2006–2007 were 6. The number of students enrolled full- and part-time who were dismissed or voluntarily withdrew from this program area in 2007–2008 were 0.

Admissions Requirements:

Scores: Entries appear in this order: required test or GPA, minimum score (if required), median score of students entering in 2007–2008. Doctoral Programs: GRE-V no minimum stated, 610; GRE-Q no minimum stated, 730; overall undergraduate GPA no minimum stated, 3.7. Each area sets its own specific requirements.

Other Criteria: (importance of criteria rated low, medium, or high): GRE/MAT scores—high, research experience—high, work experience—low, extracurricular activity—low, clinically related public service—low, GPA—high, letters of recommendation—high, interview—high, statement of goals and objectives—high. The specific criteria vary across our five programs. Some require extracurricular activity, service, and interview, whereas others do not. Currently clinical holds a formal interview for applicants being considered for acceptance. For additional information on admission requirements, go to http://www.bsos.umd.edu/psyc/main/graduate/.

Student Characteristics: The following represents characteristics of students in 2007–2008 in all graduate psychology programs in the department: Female—full-time 70, part-time 0; Male—full-time 21, part-time 0; African American/Black—full-time 6, part-time 0; Hispanic/Latino(a)—full-time 4, part-time 0; Asian/Pacific Islander—full-time 5, part-time 0; American Indian/Alaska Native—full-time 2, part-time 0; Caucasian/White—full-time 56, part-time 0; Multi-ethnic—full-time 0, part-time 0; students subject to the Americans With Disabilities Act—full-time 0, part-time 0; Unknown ethnicity—full-time 5, part-time 0; International students who hold an F-1 or J-1 Visa—full-time 13, part-time 0.

Financial Information/Assistance:

Tuition for Full-Time Study: *Doctoral:* State residents: $427 per credit hour; Nonstate residents: $921 per credit hour. Tuition is subject to change. Additional fees are assessed to students beyond the costs of tuition for the following: technology, shuttle bus, athletic, recreation.

Financial Assistance:

First-Year Students: Teaching assistantships available for first year. Average amount paid per academic year: $14,385. Average number of hours worked per week: 20. Tuition remission given: full. Research assistantships available for first year. Average amount paid per academic year: $14,385. Average number of hours worked per week: 20. Tuition remission given: full. Fellowships and scholarships available for first year. Average amount paid per academic year: $14,385. Tuition remission given: full.

Advanced Students: Teaching assistantships available for advanced students. Average amount paid per academic year: $16,200. Tuition remission given: full. Research assistantships available for advanced students. Average amount paid per academic year: $16,200. Tuition remission given: full. Fellowships and scholarships available for advanced students. Average amount paid per academic year: $15,039. Tuition remission given: full.

Additional Information: Of all students currently enrolled full time, 100% benefited from one or more of the listed financial assistance programs. Application and information available online at http://www.gradschool.umd.edu/gss/admission.htm.

Internships/Practica: Doctoral Degree (PhD Clinical): For those doctoral students for whom a professional internship was required in this program prior to graduation, (5) students applied for an internship in 2006–2007, with (5) students obtaining an internship. Of those students who obtained an internship, (5) were paid internships. Of those students who obtained an internship, (5) students placed in APA/CPA-accredited internships, (0) students placed in internships not APA/CPA-accredited, but listed with the Association of Psychology Postdoctoral and Internship Centers (APPIC), (0) students placed in internships conforming to guidelines of the Council of Directors of School Psychology Programs (CDSPP), (0) students placed in internships that were not APA/CPA-accredited, APPIC or CDSPP listed. Doctoral Degree (PhD Counseling): For those doctoral students for whom a professional internship was required in this program prior to graduation, (4) students applied for an internship in 2006–2007, with (4) students obtaining an internship. Of those students who obtained an internship, (4) were paid internships. Of those students who obtained an internship, (4) students placed in APA/CPA accredited internships, (0) students placed in internships not APA/CPA-accredited, but listed with the Association of Psychology Postdoctoral and Internship Centers (APPIC), (0) students placed in internships conforming to guidelines of the Council of Directors of School Psychology Programs (CDSPP), (0) students placed in internships that were not APA/CPA-accredited, APPIC or CDSPP listed. The metropolitan area also has many psychologists who can provide students with excellent opportunities for collaboration and/or consultation. The specialty areas have established collaborative relationships with several federal and community agencies and hospitals as well as with businesses and consulting firms, where it is possible for students to arrange for research, practicum, and internship placement. These opportunities are available for Clinical and Counseling students at the National Institutes of Health, Veteran's Administration clinics and hospitals in Washington, DC, Baltimore Perry Point, Coatesville, Martinsburg, Kecoughton, and a number of others within a hundred mile radius of the University. Experiences include a wide range of research activities, as well as psychodiagnostic work, psychotherapy, and work within drug and alcohol abuse clinics. Various other hospitals, clinics, and research facilities in the Washington, DC, and Baltimore metropolitan area are also available. Industrial/

Organizational students also have opportunities for practitioner experiences in organizations such as the U.S. Office of Personnel Management, GEICO, Bell Atlantic, and various consulting firms.

Housing and Day Care: On-campus housing is available. Graduate Housing: (301) 422-0147. On-campus day care facilities are available. Center for Young Children: (301) 405-3168.

Employment of Department Graduates:

Master's Degree Graduates: Of those who graduated in the academic year 2006–2007, the following categories and numbers represent the postgraduate activities and employment of master's degree graduates: Enrolled in a postdoctoral residency/fellowship (n/a), employed in independent practice (n/a), total from the above (master's) (0).

Doctoral Degree Graduates: Of those who graduated in the academic year 2006–2007, the following categories and numbers represent the postgraduate activities and employment of doctoral degree graduates: Enrolled in a psychology doctoral program (n/a), enrolled in a postdoctoral residency/fellowship (7), employed in an academic position at a university (1), employed in an academic position at a 2-year/4-year college (1), employed in other positions at a higher education institution (4), employed in business or industry (4), other employment position (1), do not know (0), total from the above (doctoral) (18).

Additional Information:

Orientation, Objectives, and Emphasis of Department: The department offers a full-time graduate program with an emphasis on intensive individual training made possible by a 4-to-1 student/faculty ratio. All students are expected to participate in a variety of relevant experiences that, in addition to coursework and research training, can include practicum experiences, field training, and teaching. The department offers a variety of programs described in the admissions brochure as well as other emphases that cut across the various specialties. All programs have a strong research emphasis with programs in clinical, counseling, and industrial advocating the scientist–practitioner model. Please note that the Department of Psychology receives a large number of applications. As required by the Graduate School, we will consider any applicant who has all materials in by December 15. See our Web site: http://www.bsos.umd.edu/psyc.

Special Facilities or Resources: The Department of Psychology has all of the advantages of a large state university, and also has advantages offered by the many resources available in the metropolitan Washington–Baltimore area. The University is approximately 15 miles from the center of Washington, DC, and is in close proximity to a number of libraries, and state and federal agencies. Students are able to benefit from the excellent additional library resources of the community, such as the Library of Congress, National Library of Medicine, and the National Archives (which is located on the UMCP campus). The building in which the Department is housed was designed by the faculty to incorporate research and educational facilities for all specialty areas. The building contains special centers for research, with acoustical centers, observational units, video equipment, computer facilities, surgical facilities, and radio frequency shielding. Departmental laboratories are well equipped for research in animal behavior, audition, biopsychology, cognition, coordinated motor control, counseling, industrial/organizational psychology, learning, life-span development, psycholinguistics, psychotherapy, social psychology, and vision.

Information for Students With Physical Disabilities: See the following Web site for more information: http://www.counseling.umd.edu/DSS/.

Application Information:

Send to University of Maryland College Park, Enrollment Services Operations, Application for Graduate Admission, Room 0130 Mitchell Building, College Park, MD 20742. Application available online. URL of online application: http://www.gradschool.umd.edu/gss/admission.htm. Students are admitted in the Fall, application deadline December 15. *Fee:* $60.

Maryland, University of (2007 data)

Institute for Child Study/Department of Human Development
College of Education
College Park, MD 20742
Telephone: (301) 405-2827
Fax: (301) 405-2891
E-mail: *awigfiel@umd.edu*
Web: *http://www.inform.umd.edu/educ/depts/edhd*

Department Information:

1947. Chair: Allan Wigfield. Number of faculty: total—full-time 16, part-time 4; women—full-time 10, part-time 4.

Programs and Degrees Offered:

Listed in the following order: Program area, degree type (T if terminal Master's), number awarded 7/06–6/07. Developmental PhD (Doctor of Philosophy) 8, Educational Psychology PhD (Doctor of Philosophy) 4.

Student Applications/Admissions:

Student Applications

Developmental PhD (Doctor of Philosophy)—Applications 2007–2008, 40. Total applicants accepted 2007–2008, 11. Number full-time enrolled (new admits only) 2007–2008, 5. Total enrolled 2007–2008 full-time, 32. Openings 2008–2009, 10. The median number of years required for completion of a degree in 2006–2007 were 5. The number of students enrolled full- and part-time who were dismissed or voluntarily withdrew from this program area in 2007–2008 were 0. *Educational Psychology PhD (Doctor of Philosophy)*—Applications 2007–2008, 30. Total applicants accepted 2007–2008, 10. Number full-time enrolled (new admits only) 2007–2008, 5. Total enrolled 2007–2008 full-time, 32, part-time, 5. Openings 2008–2009, 10. The median number of years required for completion of a degree in 2006–2007 were 5. The number of students enrolled full- and part-time who were dismissed or voluntarily withdrew from this program area in 2007–2008 were 0.

Admissions Requirements:

Scores: Entries appear in this order: required test or GPA, minimum score (if required), median score of students entering in 2007–2008. Master's Programs: GRE-V 450, 560; GRE-Q 485, 600; overall undergraduate GPA 3.0, 3.25. Doctoral Programs: GRE-V 450, 580; GRE-Q 485, 620; overall undergraduate GPA 3.0, 3.32.

Other Criteria: (importance of criteria rated low, medium, or high): GRE/MAT scores—high, research experience—high, work experience—medium, clinically related public service—medium, GPA—medium, letters of recommendation—high, interview—medium, statement of goals and objectives—high.

Student Characteristics: The following represents characteristics of students in 2007–2008 in all graduate psychology programs in the department: Female—full-time 54, part-time 2; Male—full-time 10, part-time 3; African American/Black—full-time 5, part-time 0; Hispanic/Latino(a)—full-time 0, part-time 0; Asian/Pacific Islander—full-time 5, part-time 0; American Indian/Alaska Native—full-time 0, part-time 0; Caucasian/White—full-time 54, part-time 5; Multi-ethnic—full-time 0, part-time 0; students subject to the Americans With Disabilities Act—full-time 0, part-time 0; Unknown ethnicity—full-time 0, part-time 0.

Financial Information/Assistance:

Tuition for Full-Time Study: *Master's:* State residents: $411 per credit hour; Nonstate residents: $886 per credit hour. *Doctoral:* State residents: $411 per credit hour; Nonstate residents: $886 per credit hour. Tuition is subject to change. See the following Web site for updates and changes in tuition costs: http://www.umd.edu.

Financial Assistance:

First-Year Students: Research assistantships available for first year. Average amount paid per academic year: $15,000. Average number of hours worked per week: 20. Apply by December 1. Fellowships and scholarships available for first year. Average amount paid per academic year: $15,000. Average number of hours worked per week: 20. Apply by December 1. Tuition remission given: full.

Advanced Students: Teaching assistantships available for advanced students. Average amount paid per academic year: $15,000. Apply by December 1. Tuition remission given: full. Research assistantships available for advanced students. Average amount paid per academic year: $15,000. Traineeships available for advanced students. Average amount paid per academic year: $15,000. Tuition remission given: partial. Fellowships and scholarships available for advanced students. Average amount paid per academic year: $15,000. Tuition remission given: full.

Additional Information: Of all students currently enrolled full time, 90% benefited from one or more of the listed financial assistance programs. Application and information available online at http://www.gradschool.umd.edu/gss/admission.htm.

Internships/Practica: No information provided.

Housing and Day Care: On-campus housing is available. See the following Web site for more information: http://www.umd.edu. No on-campus day care facilities are available.

Employment of Department Graduates:

Master's Degree Graduates: Of those who graduated in the academic year 2006–2007, the following categories and numbers represent the postgraduate activities and employment of master's degree graduates: Enrolled in a postdoctoral residency/fellowship (n/a), employed in independent practice (n/a), employed in an academic position at a university (0), employed in an academic position at a 2-year/4-year college (0), employed in other positions at a higher education institution (2), employed in a professional position in a school system (15), employed in business or industry (0), employed in government agency (0), employed in a community mental health/counseling center (0), employed in a hospital/medical center (0), total from the above (master's) (19).

Doctoral Degree Graduates: Of those who graduated in the academic year 2006–2007, the following categories and numbers represent the postgraduate activities and employment of doctoral degree graduates: Enrolled in a psychology doctoral program (n/a), employed in an academic position at a university (5), employed in an academic position at a 2-year/4-year college (4), employed in other positions at a higher education institution (3), employed in a professional position in a school system (0), employed in business or industry (0), employed in government agency (3), employed in a community mental health/counseling center (0), employed in a hospital/medical center (0), total from the above (doctoral) (15).

Additional Information:

Orientation, Objectives, and Emphasis of Department: Human development courses are psychological in nature and are intended to increase the student's understanding of human behavior, including development, learning, and adjustment. Areas of concentration that relate to the institute's goals and interests include, but are not limited to, infancy and early childhood, adolescence, adult development and aging, development over the life span, cultural processes, neuropsychology, cognitive processes, personality, and learning. Information is drawn primarily from the major fields of psychology, sociology, and physiology. The graduate specialization in educational psychology program is intended to prepare educational psychologists for service in schools and other community agencies dealing with individuals of all ages, to prepare teachers of human development and educational psychology in higher education, and to prepare research-oriented individuals for service in public (state or federal) or private organizations. A graduate specialization in development science with the psychology department is also available. The research thrust of this specialization is primarily concerned with social and aspects of development. The developmental science specialization is designed to prepare researchers and teachers in higher education.

Special Facilities or Resources: Special facilities or resources include extensive research and computer facilities. Videotaping studios and observation rooms are located in the building. The Child Development Assessment Laboratory is associated with the department and is heavily used for neuropsychological assessments on children. Testing and observation rooms are available in the Center for Family Relationships and Culture. In addition, the Center for Young Children, a child care center for preschool children, is under the auspices of the unit and is a resource for students studying and researching this age group.

Application Information:

Send to Graduate Secretary EDHD, University of Maryland, College Park, MD 20742. Application available online. URL of online application: http://www.gradschool.umd.edu/gss/admission.htm. Students are admitted in the Fall, application deadline November 15; Spring, application deadline October 1; Summer, application deadline February 1. Deadline for financial aid consideration is November 15. *Fee:* $50.

Maryland, University of

School and Counseling Psychology Programs, Department of Counseling and Personnel Services
College of Education
3214 Benjamin Building
College Park, MD 20742
Telephone: (301) 405-2858
Fax: (301) 405-9995
E-mail: *caps@umd.edu*
Web: *http://www.education.umd.edu/EDCP/*

Department Information:

1967. Chairperson: Ruth Fassinger. Number of faculty: total—full-time 16, part-time 3; women—full-time 10, part-time 3; total—minority—full-time 4, part-time 1; women minority—full-time 2, part-time 1.

Programs and Degrees Offered:

Listed in the following order: Program area, degree type (T if terminal Master's), number awarded 7/06–6/07. Counseling Psychology PhD (Doctor of Philosophy) 8, School Psychology PhD (Doctor of Philosophy) 3.

APA Accreditation: School Psychology PhD (Doctor of Philosophy).

Student Applications/Admissions:

Student Applications

Counseling Psychology PhD (Doctor of Philosophy)—Applications 2007–2008, 204. Total applicants accepted 2007–2008, 8. Number full-time enrolled (new admits only) 2007–2008, 7. Number part-time enrolled (new admits only) 2007–2008, 0. Openings 2008–2009, 8. The median number of years required for completion of a degree in 2006–2007 were 6. The number of students enrolled full- and part-time who were dismissed or voluntarily withdrew from this program area in 2007–2008 were 0. *School Psychology PhD (Doctor of Philosophy)*—Applications 2007–2008, 70. Total applicants accepted 2007–2008, 17. Number full-time enrolled (new admits only) 2007–2008, 6. Number part-time enrolled (new admits only) 2007–2008, 0. Total enrolled 2007–2008 full-time, 23, part-time, 11. Openings 2008–2009, 8. The median number of years required for completion of a degree in 2006–2007 were 8. The number of students enrolled full- and part-time who were dismissed or voluntarily withdrew from this program area in 2007–2008 were 0.

Admissions Requirements:

Scores: Entries appear in this order: required test or GPA, minimum score (if required), median score of students entering in 2007–2008. Master's Programs: GRE-V no minimum stated; GRE-Q no minimum stated; overall undergraduate GPA no minimum stated; last 2 years GPA no minimum stated; psychology GPA no minimum stated. Doctoral Programs: GRE-V no minimum stated, 580; GRE-Q no minimum stated, 690; overall undergraduate GPA no minimum stated, 3.65; last 2 years GPA no minimum stated, 3.70; psychology GPA no minimum stated.

Other Criteria: (importance of criteria rated low, medium, or high): GRE/MAT scores—medium, research experience—high, work experience—medium, extracurricular activity—medium, clinically related public service—low, GPA—high, letters of recommendation—high, interview—medium, statement of goals and objectives—high. Criteria vary by program. Applicants should contact specific programs for detailed information. For additional information on admission requirements, go to http://www.education.umd.edu/edcp.

Student Characteristics: The following represents characteristics of students in 2007–2008 in all graduate psychology programs in the department: Female—full-time 35, part-time 13; Male—full-time 9, part-time 0; African American/Black—full-time 6, part-time 0; Hispanic/Latino(a)—full-time 4, part-time 0; Asian/Pacific Islander—full-time 4, part-time 2; Caucasian/White—full-time 27, part-time 13; Multi-ethnic—full-time 1, part-time 0; students subject to the Americans With Disabilities Act—full-time 0, part-time 0; Unknown ethnicity—full-time 0, part-time 0.

Financial Information/Assistance:

Tuition for Full-Time Study: *Doctoral:* State residents: per academic year $8,540, $427 per credit hour; Nonstate residents: per academic year $18,420, $921 per credit hour. Tuition is subject to change. Additional fees are assessed to students beyond the costs of tuition for the following: Various fees total $1,080 per year. See the following Web site for updates and changes in tuition costs: http://www.umd.edu/bursar/Tuitionfees.html.

Financial Assistance:

First-Year Students: Teaching assistantships available for first year. Average amount paid per academic year: $13,800. Average number of hours worked per week: 20. Apply by 12/15. Tuition remission given: full. Research assistantships available for first year. Average amount paid per academic year: $13,800. Average number of hours worked per week: 20. Apply by December 15. Tuition remission given: full. Fellowships and scholarships available for first year. Average amount paid per academic year: $13,900. Apply by December 15. Tuition remission given: full.

Advanced Students: Teaching assistantships available for advanced students. Average amount paid per academic year: $15,000. Average number of hours worked per week: 20. Apply by April 15. Tuition remission given: full. Research assistantships available for advanced students. Average amount paid per academic year: $15,000. Average number of hours worked per week: 20. Apply by April 15. Tuition remission given: full.

Additional Information: Of all students currently enrolled full time, 90% benefited from one or more of the listed financial assistance programs. Application and information available online at: http://www.education.umd.edu/studentinfo/graduate_info/admissionsreq.html.

Internships/Practica: Doctoral Degree (PhD School Psychology): For those doctoral students for whom a professional internship was required in this program prior to graduation, (4) students applied for an internship in 2006–2007, with (4) students obtaining an internship. Of those students who obtained an internship, (4) were paid internships. Of those students who obtained an internship, (4) students placed in APA/CPA-accredited internships, (0) students placed in internships not APA/CPA accredited, but listed with the Association of Psychology Postdoctoral and Internship Centers (APPIC), (0) students placed in internships conforming to guidelines of the Council of Directors of School Psychology Programs (CDSPP), (0) students placed in internships that were not APA/CPA-accredited, APPIC or CDSPP listed. The Washington, DC, area offers an abundance of training settings that supplement our on-campus training facilities. A number of practica are offered at the University of Maryland Counseling Center. In addition, other practica and externships are offered at schools, community agencies, hospitals, and other counseling centers. Counseling Psychology students all complete APA-approved intenrships. In order to maximize school-based training, students in the School Psychology program may complete internships that conform to CDSPP guidelines but that are not APA-approved.

Housing and Day Care: On-campus housing is available. See the following Web site for more information: http://www.union.umd.edu/GH/basic_needs/graduate_housing.html. No on-campus day care facilities are available.

Employment of Department Graduates:

Master's Degree Graduates: Of those who graduated in the academic year 2006–2007, the following categories and numbers represent the postgraduate activities and employment of master's degree graduates: Enrolled in a postdoctoral residency/fellowship (n/a), employed in independent practice (n/a), total from the above (master's) (0).

Doctoral Degree Graduates: Of those who graduated in the academic year 2006–2007, the following categories and numbers represent the postgraduate activities and employment of doctoral degree graduates: Enrolled in a psychology doctoral program (n/a), enrolled in a postdoctoral residency/fellowship (1), employed in an academic position at a university (1), employed in an academic position at a 2-year/4-year college (1), employed in other positions at a higher education institution (2), employed in a professional position in a school system (3), total from the above (doctoral) (8).

Additional Information:

Orientation, Objectives, and Emphasis of Department: Both the Counseling Psychology and School Psychology programs espouse the scientist–practitioner model of training. These programs enable students to become psychologists who are trained in general psychology, competent in providing effective assessment and intervention from a variety of theoretical perspectives, and in conducting research on a wide range of psychological topics. Note: The Counseling Psychology program is administered collaboratively by the departments of Counseling and Personnel Services and Psychology.

Special Facilities or Resources: Observation/training facilities and access to extensive library facilities both on and off campus (e.g., NIH Library of Medicine, Library of Congress).

Information for Students With Physical Disabilities: See the following Web site for more information: http://www.counseling.umd.edu/DSS/.

Application Information:

Send to Graduate Admissions, College of Education, 1210 Benjamin Building, University of Maryland, College Park, MD 20742. Application available online. URL of online application: http://www.gradschool.umd.edu/gss/admission.htm. Students are admitted in the Fall, application deadline December 15. *Fee:* $60.

Maryland, University of, Baltimore County

Department of Psychology
Arts and Sciences
1000 Hilltop Circle
Baltimore, MD 21250
Telephone: (410) 455-2567
Fax: (410) 455-1055
E-mail: *psycdept@umbc.edu*
Web: *http://www.umbc.edu/psyc/index.html*

Department Information:

1966. Chairperson: Linda Baker, PhD. Number of faculty: total—full-time 31; women—full-time 15, part-time 2; total—minority—full-time 3; women minority—full-time 1; faculty subject to the Americans With Disabilities Act 1.

Programs and Degrees Offered:

Listed in the following order: Program area, degree type (T if terminal Master's), number awarded 7/06–6/07. Applied Behavior Analysis MA/MS (Master of Arts/Science) (T) 17, Applied Developmental PhD (Doctor of Philosophy) 2, Human Services (Clinical, Behavioral Medicine, Community) PhD (Doctor of Philosophy) 11.

APA Accreditation: Clinical PhD (Doctor of Philosophy).

Student Applications/Admissions:

Student Applications

Applied Behavior Analysis MA/MS (Master of Arts/Science)—Applications 2007–2008, 56. Total applicants accepted 2007–2008, 26. Number full-time enrolled (new admits only) 2007–2008, 16. Number part-time enrolled (new admits only) 2007–2008, 0. Total enrolled 2007–2008 full-time, 20, part-time, 1. Openings 2008–2009, 12. The median number of years required for completion of a degree in 2006–2007 were 2. *Applied Developmental PhD (Doctor of Philosophy)*—Applications 2007–2008, 29. Total applicants accepted 2007–2008, 9. Number full-time enrolled (new admits only) 2007–2008, 3. Number part-time enrolled (new admits only) 2007–2008, 0. Total enrolled 2007–2008 full-time, 24, part-time, 9. Openings 2008–2009, 10. The median number of years required for completion of a degree in 2006–2007 were 9. *Human Services (Clinical, Behavioral Medicine, Community) PhD (Doctor of Philosophy)*—Applications 2007–2008, 116. Total applicants accepted 2007–2008, 13. Number full-time enrolled (new admits only) 2007–2008, 6. Number part-time enrolled (new admits only) 2007–2008, 0. Total enrolled 2007–2008 full-time, 55, part-time, 7. Openings 2008–2009, 12. The median number of years required for completion of a degree in 2006–2007 were 7.

Admissions Requirements:

Scores: Entries appear in this order: required test or GPA, minimum score (if required), median score of students entering in 2007–2008. Master's Programs: GRE-V no minimum stated; GRE-Q no minimum stated; overall undergraduate GPA 3.0. Doctoral Programs: GRE-V no minimum stated; GRE-Q no minimum stated; GRE-Subject (Psychology) no minimum stated; overall undergraduate GPA 3.0. GREs should be above the 50th percentile for HSP doctoral program.

Other Criteria: (importance of criteria rated low, medium, or high): GRE/MAT scores—high, research experience—high, work experience—medium, extracurricular activity—medium, clinically related public service—medium, GPA—high, letters of recommendation—high, interview—high, statement of goals and objectives—high. ADP puts less weight (low) on clinical service than does HSP. For additional information on admission requirements, go to http://www.umbc.edu/psyc/grad/hsp.html.

Student Characteristics: The following represents characteristics of students in 2007–2008 in all graduate psychology programs in the department: Female—full-time 85, part-time 16; Male—full-time 14, part-time 1; African American/Black—full-time 12, part-time 0; Hispanic/Latino(a)—full-time 6, part-time 1; Asian/Pacific Islander—full-time 6, part-time 1; American Indian/Alaska Native—full-time 0, part-time 0; Caucasian/White—full-time 63, part-time 13; Multi-ethnic—full-time 0, part-time 0; students subject to the Americans With Disabilities Act—full-time 0, part-time 0; Unknown ethnicity—full-time 12, part-time 2; International students who hold an F-1 or J-1 Visa—full-time 4, part-time 0.

Financial Information/Assistance:

Tuition for Full-Time Study: *Master's:* State residents: $412 per credit hour; Nonstate residents: $681 per credit hour. *Doctoral:* State residents: $412 per credit hour; Nonstate residents: $681 per credit hour. Tuition is subject to change.

Financial Assistance:

First-Year Students: Teaching assistantships available for first year. Average amount paid per academic year: $14,566. Average number of hours worked per week: 20. Tuition remission given: full. Research assistantships available for first year. Average amount paid per academic year: $14,566. Average number of hours worked per week: 20. Tuition remission given: full.

Advanced Students: Teaching assistantships available for advanced students. Average amount paid per academic year: $14,566. Average number of hours worked per week: 20. Tuition remission given: full. Research assistantships available for advanced students. Average amount paid per academic year: $14,566. Average number of hours worked per week: 20. Tuition remission given: full.

Additional Information: Of all students currently enrolled full time, 83% benefited from one or more of the listed financial assistance programs.

Internships/Practica: Doctoral Degree (PhD Human Services (Clinical, Behavioral Medicine, Community)): For those doctoral students for whom a professional internship was required in this program prior to graduation, (5) students applied for an internship in 2006–2007, with (4) students obtaining an internship. Of those students who obtained an internship, (4) were paid internships. Of those students who obtained an internship, (3) students placed in APA/CPA-accredited internships, (1) student placed in internships not APA/CPA-accredited, but listed with the Association of Psychology Postdoctoral and Internship Centers (APPIC), (0) students placed in internships conforming to guidelines of the Council of Directors of School Psychology Programs (CDSPP), (0) students placed in internships that were not APA/CPA accredited, APPIC or CDSPP listed. Course-linked practica provide students with a focused experience in the application of the skills and knowledge presented in the associated course. The course instructor is responsible for arranging these practica. Beyond the course-linked practica, students in the HSP and ADP programs are required to take a minimum of six additional credits of practicum, usually in their 2nd and 3rd years. These practica, in various clinical, research, and human services settings, are intended to give students a broader and more integrative experience in the application of the skills and knowledge that they have acquired in the various courses they have taken.

Housing and Day Care: On-campus housing is available. See the following Web site for more information: http://www.walkeravenueapts.com. On-campus day care facilities are available. Child Care Center: (410) 455-6830.

Employment of Department Graduates:

Master's Degree Graduates: Of those who graduated in the academic year 2006–2007, the following categories and numbers represent the postgraduate activities and employment of master's degree graduates: Enrolled in a postdoctoral residency/fellowship (n/a), employed in independent practice (n/a), total from the above (master's) (0).

Doctoral Degree Graduates: Of those who graduated in the academic year 2006–2007, the following categories and numbers represent the postgraduate activities and employment of doctoral degree graduates: Enrolled in a psychology doctoral program (n/a), total from the above (doctoral) (0).

Additional Information:

Orientation, Objectives, and Emphasis of Department: UMBC Psychology is committed to a scientist–practitioner model and emphasizes science with an applied psychological research focus. The department uses a biopsychosocial interactive framework as the foundation for exploring various problems and issues in psychology. Two doctoral graduate programs are housed in the department: Applied Developmental Psychology (ADP) and Human Services Psychology (HSP). The ADP program has three concentrations: Early Development/Early Intervention, Socioemotional Development of Children, and Educational Contexts of Development; students can affiliate flexibly with one or more concentrations. The ADP program is accredited by the ASPPB/National Register of Health Service Providers in Psychology. The HSP program consists of three subprograms: community–social, behavioral medicine, and an APA-approved clinical subprogram. Many HSP students take cross-area training in clinical–behavioral medicine or clinical–community areas. There is also a Master's program in Applied Behavior Analysis, housed at UMBC and in collaboration with the Kennedy Krieger Institute. Faculty represent a broad range of theoretical perspectives and maintain active research programs. The psychology department has many collaborative relationships for research and clinical and practical training opportunities with institutions in the Baltimore–Washington corridor.

Special Facilities or Resources: The Psychology Department at UMBC has numerous faculty research laboratories on campus in close proximity to faculty offices. Laboratories include equipment for psychological assessments, videotaping and coding, observation as well as an animal laboratory. The department has access to several large computer laboratories on campus and has a small computer laboratory for graduate students. Through collaborative arrangements with the medical school and other University of

Maryland System facilities, and Kennedy Krieger Institute, graduate students have access to different patient populations and opportunities for community based projects.

Application Information:
Send to Dean of Graduate School, 1000 Hilltop Circle, Baltimore, MD 21250. Application available online. URL of online application: http://www.umbc.edu/gradschool/admissions/. Students are admitted in the Fall, application deadline December 1. Applied Behavior Analysis Masters program deadline is March 1. Doctoral program in Applied Developmental Psychology is January 9. *Fee:* $50.

Towson University

Department of Psychology
8000 York Road
Towson, MD 21252
Telephone: (410) 704-3080
Fax: (410) 704-3800
E-mail: *cjohnson@towson.edu*
Web: *http://www.towson.edu/psychology/*

Department Information:
1965. Chairperson: Craig T. Johnson, PhD. Number of faculty: total—full-time 35, part-time 40; women—full-time 19, part-time 21; total—minority—full-time 4, part-time 2; women minority—full-time 4, part-time 2.

Programs and Degrees Offered:
Listed in the following order: Program area, degree type (T if terminal Master's), number awarded 7/06–6/07. Clinical MA/MS (Master of Arts/Science) (T) 12, Counseling MA/MS (Master of Arts/Science) (T) 17, Experimental MA/MS (Master of Arts/Science) (T) 11, School MA/MS (Master of Arts/Science) 15, Human Resource Development MA/MS (Master of Arts/Science) 35.

Student Applications/Admissions:
Student Applications
Clinical MA/MS (Master of Arts/Science)—Applications 2007–2008, 70. Total applicants accepted 2007–2008, 14. Number full-time enrolled (new admits only) 2007–2008, 16. Number part-time enrolled (new admits only) 2007–2008, 0. Openings 2008–2009, 16. The median number of years required for completion of a degree in 2006–2007 were 2. The number of students enrolled full- and part-time who were dismissed or voluntarily withdrew from this program area in 2007–2008 were 0. *Counseling MA/MS (Master of Arts/Science)*—Applications 2007–2008, 97. Total applicants accepted 2007–2008, 24. Number full-time enrolled (new admits only) 2007–2008, 16. Number part-time enrolled (new admits only) 2007–2008, 0. Total enrolled 2007–2008 full-time, 32, part-time, 4. Openings 2008–2009, 18. The median number of years required for completion of a degree in 2006–2007 were 2. The number of students enrolled full- and part-time who were dismissed or voluntarily withdrew from this program area in 2007–2008 were 2. *Experimental MA/MS (Master of Arts/Science)*—Applications 2007–2008, 41. Total applicants accepted 2007–2008, 21. Number full-time enrolled (new admits only) 2007–2008, 9. Number part-time enrolled (new admits only) 2007–2008, 3. Total enrolled 2007–2008 full-time, 24, part-time, 20. Openings 2008–2009, 15. The median number of years required for completion of a degree in 2006–2007 were 2. The number of students enrolled full- and part-time who were dismissed or voluntarily withdrew from this program area in 2007–2008 were 1. *School MA/MS (Master of Arts/Science)*—Applications 2007–2008, 81. Total applicants accepted 2007–2008, 14. Number full-time enrolled (new admits only) 2007–2008, 14. Number part-time enrolled (new admits only) 2007–2008, 0. Openings 2008–2009, 16. The median number of years required for completion of a degree in 2006–2007 were 3. The number of students enrolled full- and part-time who were dismissed or voluntarily withdrew from this program area in 2007–2008 were 0. *Human Resource Development MA/MS (Master of Arts/Science)*—Applications 2007–2008, 50. Total applicants accepted 2007–2008, 40. Number full-time enrolled (new admits only) 2007–2008, 0. Number part-time enrolled (new admits only) 2007–2008, 25. Openings 2008–2009, 40. The median number of years required for completion of a degree in 2006–2007 were 2. The number of students enrolled full- and part-time who were dismissed or voluntarily withdrew from this program area in 2007–2008 were 0.

Admissions Requirements:
Scores: Entries appear in this order: required test or GPA, minimum score (if required), median score of students entering in 2007–2008. Master's Programs: GRE-V no minimum stated, 510; GRE-Q no minimum stated, 520; last 2 years GPA 3.0, 3.25. The reported GRE statistics are an average across three of the four tracks of the Masters degree program; GRE is required for Clinical, Counseling, and School only. School Psychology has a minimum score of 400 in each section and a minimum score of 4.0 for the writing section. Clinical has a minimum cumulative GRE of 900. GPA statistics represent an average across all four tracks.
Other Criteria: (importance of criteria rated low, medium, or high): GRE/MAT scores—medium, research experience—medium, work experience—medium, clinically related public service—medium, GPA—high, letters of recommendation—high, interview—high, statement of goals and objectives—medium. Clinically related public service, letters of recommendation, and interview are all used by the clinical, counseling, and school psychology programs only. Research experience is very important for the experimental program. Counseling, experimental, and school psychology also use a letter of intent and consider it very important. For additional information on admission requirements, go to http://wwwnew.towson.edu/psychology/Graduate.htm.

Student Characteristics: The following represents characteristics of students in 2007–2008 in all graduate psychology programs in the department: Female—full-time 108, part-time 74; Male—full-time 18, part-time 20; African American/Black—full-time 11, part-time 3; Hispanic/Latino(a)—full-time 4, part-time 0; Asian/Pacific Islander—full-time 4, part-time 1; American Indian/Alaska Native—full-time 0, part-time 0; Caucasian/White—full-time 106, part-time 25; Multi-ethnic—full-time 1, part-time 0; students subject to the Americans With Disabilities Act—full-time 0, part-time 1; Unknown ethnicity—full-time 0, part-time 65; International students who hold an F-1 or J-1 Visa—full-time 0, part-time 0.

Financial Information/Assistance:

Tuition for Full-Time Study: *Master's:* State residents: $361 per credit hour; Nonstate residents: $675 per credit hour. Tuition is subject to change. Additional fees are assessed to students beyond the costs of tuition for the following: Technology fees: $6 per credit up to 12 credits. See the following Web site for updates and changes in tuition costs: http://wwwnew.towson.edu/adminfinance/fiscalplanning/bursar/.

Financial Assistance:

First-Year Students: Teaching assistantships available for first year. Average amount paid per academic year: $8,000. Average number of hours worked per week: 20. Apply by February 1. Tuition remission given: full and partial. Research assistantships available for first year. Average amount paid per academic year: $5,000. Average number of hours worked per week: 20. Apply by February 1. Tuition remission given: full and partial.

Advanced Students: Teaching assistantships available for advanced students. Average amount paid per academic year: $8,000. Average number of hours worked per week: 20. Apply by February 1. Tuition remission given: full and partial. Research assistantships available for advanced students. Average amount paid per academic year: $5,000. Average number of hours worked per week: 20. Apply by February 1. Tuition remission given: full and partial.

Additional Information: Of all students currently enrolled full time, 25% benefited from one or more of the listed financial assistance programs. Application and information available online at http://grad.towson.edu/finance/ga/index.asp.

Internships/Practica: Master's Degree (MA/MS Counseling): An internship experience such as a final research project or "capstone" experience is required of graduates. Master's Degree (MA/MS Experimental): An internship experience such as a final research project or "capstone" experience is required of graduates. School Psychology students are required to complete two 100-hour practica over two consecutive semesters in a local school system. The program culminates in a 1,200-hour internship that is to be completed full-time over 1 year or part-time over 2 consecutive years. At least 50% of the 1,200 hours must be completed in a public school system; however most students complete all hours in public schools. Students in clinical psychology can specialize by working in either an inpatient or outpatient facility. Among the internship placement sites for students in the clinical psychology program are community mental health centers and clinics, state psychiatric hospitals, and government agencies including the Department of Veteran Affairs and other specialized psychological service centers. Counseling students are required to complete a 240-hour practicum and a 300-hour internship over two semesters. Students are placed in community mental health centers, college counseling centers, drug and alcohol rehabilitation agencies, domestic violence centers, and other mental health service agencies. A limited number of graduate assistantships are available for students in the experimental psychology program.

Housing and Day Care: No on-campus housing is available. On-campus day care facilities are available. See the following Web site for more information: http://www.new.towson.edu/daycare/.

Employment of Department Graduates:

Master's Degree Graduates: Of those who graduated in the academic year 2006–2007, the following categories and numbers represent the postgraduate activities and employment of master's degree graduates: Enrolled in a psychology doctoral program (6), enrolled in a postdoctoral residency/fellowship (n/a), employed in independent practice (n/a), employed in an academic position at a 2-year/4-year college (2), employed in a professional position in a school system (15), employed in business or industry (23), employed in government agency (17), employed in a community mental health/counseling center (17), do not know (6), total from the above (master's) (86).

Doctoral Degree Graduates: Of those who graduated in the academic year 2006–2007, the following categories and numbers represent the postgraduate activities and employment of doctoral degree graduates: Enrolled in a psychology doctoral program (n/a), total from the above (doctoral) (0).

Additional Information:

Orientation, Objectives, and Emphasis of Department: The experimental psychology program is designed to prepare students for subsequent enrollment in PhD programs or for research jobs in industrial, government, private consulting, or hospital settings. Students receive comprehensive instruction in research design, statistical methods (both univariate and multivariate), computer applications (for both data collection and analysis), and take a series of courses in specialized areas of psychology (biological, cognitive, and social psychology). Students collaborate on research with faculty mentors and complete an empirical thesis. The Master of Arts in Clinical Psychology is designed for students seeking training and experience in the applied professional aspects of clinical psychology. Although approximately 50% of graduates go on to further graduate study in psychology, the primary focus of the program is the preparation of master's-level psychologists for employment in state and other nonprofit organizations. Because of the applied professional emphasis, the majority of required clinical courses address the theoretical and practical issues involved in providing direct clinical services. Students take courses in psychotherapy and behavior change, preparing them to practice individual, family, and group intervention techniques. Other courses in assessment prepare students to administer and interpret psychometric instruments used to conduct intellectual, neurological, and personality assessments. Advanced seminars in cognitive–behavior therapy are offered regularly. Practical supervised clinical experiences constitute a major portion of the program. Students complete a 9-month, half-time internship during which they provide supervised psychological services to clients in an off-campus mental health setting. The Counseling Psychology Program trains students to facilitate personal, educational, and vocational adjustment across the life span. The program offers a practioner track and a research track from which degree candidates choose. Graduates of the program may go on to meet the requirements of the Licensed Clinical Professional Counselor, pursue doctoral degree, and/or find employment in a wide variety of counseling agencies. The Towson University School Psychology Program is fully approved by the National Association of School Psychologists (NASP) and trains graduate students to become school psychologists. The program emphasizes consultation and early intervention. It is unique in its close relationship with its surrounding urban and suburban communities, which welcomes Towson's school psychology students in both practicum and internship settings. The Program offers a single 63-credit degree: the Master of Arts in Psychology with a concentration in School Psychology and the Certificate of Advanced Study (CAS) in School Psychology.

Special Facilities or Resources: The Psychology Building houses laboratories for histology and computer analysis as well as for the conduct of research in learning/motivation, physiological, comparative, cognitive, social, developmental, and general experimental psychology. Additionally, because of the popularity of the undergraduate Psychology major, there are many students willing to participate in research studies. In Fall, 2009, the department will begin a move to a new building with expanded facilities for training dyadic interactions as well as enhanced laboratory space.

Application Information:
Send to Graduate School, Towson University, Towson, MD 21252. Application available online. URL of online application: https://www.applyweb.com/apply/towson/menu.html. Students are admitted in the Fall, application deadline February 1; Spring, application deadline October 1. Clinical, Counseling, and School admit for the Fall with an application deadline of January 15. The Experimental program has deadlines of February 1 and March 1. Human Resource Development has rolling admission. *Fee:* $45 for online applications and $50 for hard copy applications.

Uniformed Services University of the Health Sciences

Medical and Clinical Psychology
F. Edward Hebert School of Medicine
4301 Jones Bridge Road
Bethesda, MD 20814
Telephone: (301) 295-9669
Fax: (301) 295-3034
E-mail: *csimmons@usuhs.mil*
Web: *http://www.usuhs.mil/mps*

Department Information:
1977. Chairperson: David S. Krantz, PhD. Number of faculty: total—full-time 7, part-time 1; women—full-time 3, part-time 1.

Programs and Degrees Offered:
Listed in the following order: Program area, degree type (T if terminal Master's), number awarded 7/06–6/07. Medical Psychology PhD (Doctor of Philosophy) 0, Clinical Psychology PhD (Doctor of Philosophy) 1, Medical Psychology Clinical Track PhD (Doctor of Philosophy) 0.

APA Accreditation: Clinical PhD (Doctor of Philosophy).

Student Applications/Admissions:
Student Applications
Medical Psychology PhD (Doctor of Philosophy)—Applications 2007–2008, 2. Total applicants accepted 2007–2008, 1. Number full-time enrolled (new admits only) 2007–2008, 1. Number part-time enrolled (new admits only) 2007–2008, 0. Openings 2008–2009, 3. The median number of years required for completion of a degree in 2006–2007 were 5. The number of students enrolled full- and part-time who were dismissed or voluntarily withdrew from this program area in 2007–2008 were 0. *Clinical Psychology PhD (Doctor of Philosophy)*—Total applicants accepted 2007–2008, 5. Number full-time enrolled (new admits only) 2007–2008, 5. Number part-time enrolled (new admits only) 2007–2008, 0. Openings 2008–2009, 5. The median number of years required for completion of a degree in 2006–2007 were 5. The number of students enrolled full- and part-time who were dismissed or voluntarily withdrew from this program area in 2007–2008 were 0. *Medical Psychology Clinical Track PhD (Doctor of Philosophy)*—Applications 2007–2008, 10. Total applicants accepted 2007–2008, 2. Number full-time enrolled (new admits only) 2007–2008, 2. Number part-time enrolled (new admits only) 2007–2008, 0. Openings 2008–2009, 2. The median number of years required for completion of a degree in 2006–2007 were 5. The number of students enrolled full- and part-time who were dismissed or voluntarily withdrew from this program area in 2007–2008 were 0.

Admissions Requirements:
Scores: Entries appear in this order: required test or GPA, minimum score (if required), median score of students entering in 2007–2008. Doctoral Programs: GRE-V 550; GRE-Q 550; overall undergraduate GPA 3.0.
Other Criteria: (importance of criteria rated low, medium, or high): GRE/MAT scores—high, research experience—high, work experience—low, extracurricular activity—low, clinically related public service—medium, GPA—high, letters of recommendation—high, interview—high, statement of goals and objectives—high, undergraduate major in psychology—low, specific undergraduate psychology courses taken—medium. For additional information on admission requirements, go to http://www.usuhs.mil/mps.

Student Characteristics: The following represents characteristics of students in 2007–2008 in all graduate psychology programs in the department: Female—full-time 23, part-time 0; Male—full-time 9, part-time 0; African American/Black—full-time 3, part-time 0; Hispanic/Latino(a)—full-time 1, part-time 0; Asian/Pacific Islander—full-time 2, part-time 0; American Indian/Alaska Native—full-time 1, part-time 0; Caucasian/White—full-time 25, part-time 0; Multi-ethnic—part-time 0; students subject to the Americans With Disabilities Act—full-time 0, part-time 0; Unknown ethnicity—full-time 0, part-time 0.

Financial Information/Assistance:
Tuition for Full-Time Study: *Master's:* State residents: per academic year $0; Nonstate residents: per academic year $0. *Doctoral:* State residents: per academic year $0; Nonstate residents: per academic year $0.

Financial Assistance:
First-Year Students: Traineeships available for first year. Average amount paid per academic year: $25,000. Average number of hours worked per week: 20. Fellowships and scholarships available for first year. Average amount paid per academic year: $25,000. Average number of hours worked per week: 20.
Advanced Students: Teaching assistantships available for advanced students. Average amount paid per academic year: $25,000. Average number of hours worked per week: 20. Research assistantships available for advanced students. Average amount paid per academic year: $25,000. Average number of hours worked per week: 20. Traineeships available for advanced students. Average amount paid per academic year: $25,000. Average number of hours worked per week: 20. Fellowships and scholarships available for advanced students. Average amount paid per academic year: $25,000. Average number of hours worked per week: 20.

Additional Information: Of all students currently enrolled full time, 90% benefited from one or more of the listed financial assistance programs. Application and information available online at http://www.usuhs.mil/mps.

Internships/Practica: Doctoral Degree (PhD Clinical Psychology): For those doctoral students for whom a professional internship was required in this program prior to graduation, (2) students applied for an internship in 2006–2007, with (2) students obtaining an internship. Of those students who obtained an internship, (2) were paid internships. Of those students who obtained an internship, (2) students placed in APA/CPA-accredited internships, (0) students placed in internships not APA/CPA accredited, but listed with the Association of Psychology Postdoctoral and Internship Centers (APPIC), (0) students placed in internships conforming to guidelines of the Council of Directors of School Psychology Programs (CDSPP), (0) students placed in internships that were not APA/CPA-accredited, APPIC or CDSPP listed. Doctoral Degree (PhD Medical Psychology Clinical Track): For those doctoral students for whom a professional internship was required in this program prior to graduation, (1) students applied for an internship in 2006–2007, with (1) students obtaining an internship. Of those students who obtained an internship, (1) were paid internships. Of those students who obtained an internship, (1) student placed in APA/CPA-accredited internships, (0) students placed in internships not APA/CPA-accredited, but listed with the Association of Psychology Postdoctoral and Internship Centers (APPIC), (0) students placed in internships conforming to guidelines of the Council of Directors of School Psychology Programs (CDSPP), (0) students placed in internships that were not APA/CPA-accredited, APPIC or CDSPP listed. Military Clinical Psychology and Clinical/Medical Psychology students complete the 12-month internship during the 5th and final year of the program within an APA-approved military or civilian clinical psychology training program. Practicum training occurs during the Fall, Winter, and Spring quarters of the 2nd, 3rd and 4th years. Students work at practica sites at local facilities for 6 to 10 hours per week.

Housing and Day Care: No on-campus housing is available. No on-campus day care facilities are available.

Employment of Department Graduates:

Master's Degree Graduates: Of those who graduated in the academic year 2006–2007, the following categories and numbers represent the postgraduate activities and employment of master's degree graduates: Enrolled in a postdoctoral residency/fellowship (n/a), employed in independent practice (n/a), total from the above (master's) (0).

Doctoral Degree Graduates: Of those who graduated in the academic year 2006–2007, the following categories and numbers represent the postgraduate activities and employment of doctoral degree graduates: Enrolled in a psychology doctoral program (n/a), employed in an academic position at a university (3), employed in government agency (1), employed in a hospital/medical center (1), total from the above (doctoral) (5).

Additional Information:

Orientation, Objectives, and Emphasis of Department: The Department's educational programs provide a background in general psychological principles. Two content areas are emphasized: Health Psychology and Clinical Psychology. Educational and research activities focus on the application of principles and methods of scientific psychology relevant to physical and mental health. The Department is set in a School of Medicine and has an interdisciplinary focus. A Clinical Psychology program for uniformed military personnel and a Medical Psychology clinical track for civilians are APA accredited and follow the scientist–practitioner model. A research/academic program in Medical Psychology encompasses the fields of Health Psychology and Behavioral Medicine. The Department provides many research opportunities for students in the graduate programs and opportunities for mentorship because of the active and varied research programs conducted by the full-time faculty. Research opportunities available for students all involve the study of behavioral, psychological, and biobehavioral factors in physical and mental health. In addition, several faculty in the Department participate in an NIH-funded predoctoral and postdoctoral training programs in cardiovascular behavioral medicine.

Special Facilities or Resources: The Department has office space, laboratory space for human and animal experimentation, multiple psychophysiology laboratories, and a biochemistry laboratory. There is access to classrooms, conference rooms, an excellent library, a computer center, audiovisual support, teaching hospitals, and a laboratory animal facility that is accredited by the Association for the Assessment and Accreditation of Laboratory Animal Care (AAALAC). The Bethesda campus of the National Institutes of Health, including the National Library of Medicine, is within walking distance from USUHS. The NIH is a resource for lecture series, specialized courses, funding information, and research collaborations. The major military training hospitals also are nearby, as are all the social and cultural offerings of Washington, DC.

Information for Students With Physical Disabilities: See the following Web site for more information: http://www.usuhs.mil/mps.

Application Information:

Send to Eleanor Metcalf, PhD, Associate Dean for Graduate Education, USUHS, 4301 Jones Bridge Road, Bethesda, MD 20814-4799. Application available online. URL of online application: http://www.cim.usuhs.mil/geo. Students are admitted in the Winter, application deadline January 15. *Fee:* $0.

Washington College

Department of Psychology
Washington Avenue
Chestertown, MD 21620-1197
Telephone: (410) 778-2800
Fax: (410) 778-7275
E-mail: *llittlefield2@washcoll.edu*
Web: *http://www.psychology.washcoll.edu*

Department Information:

1953. Chairperson: Lauren M. Littlefield, PhD. Number of faculty: total—full-time 6, part-time 6; women—full-time 2, part-time 2.

Programs and Degrees Offered:

Listed in the following order: Program area, degree type (T if terminal Master's), number awarded 7/06–6/07. General Experimental MA/MS (Master of Arts/Science) (T) 8.

Student Applications/Admissions:

Student Applications

General Experimental MA/MS (Master of Arts/Science)—Applications 2007–2008, 15. Total applicants accepted 2007–2008, 10. Number full-time enrolled (new admits only) 2007–2008, 3. Number part-time enrolled (new admits only) 2007–2008, 15. Total enrolled 2007–2008 full-time, 5, part-time, 25. Openings 2008–2009, 20. The median number of years required for completion of a degree in 2006–2007 were 3. The number of students enrolled full- and part-time who were dismissed or voluntarily withdrew from this program area in 2007–2008 were 0.

Admissions Requirements:

Scores: Entries appear in this order: required test or GPA, minimum score (if required), median score of students entering in 2007–2008. Master's Programs: GRE-V 500; GRE-Q 500; psychology GPA 3.0; Masters GRE-Analytical no minimum stated.

Other Criteria: (importance of criteria rated low, medium, or high): GRE/MAT scores—medium, research experience—medium, work experience—medium, extracurricular activity—low, clinically related public service—medium, GPA—high, letters of recommendation—high, statement of goals and objectives—medium, undergraduate major in psychology—medium, specific undergraduate psychology courses taken—medium. Applicants who do not have an undergraduate degree in psychology who earn a score at or above the 50th percentile on the Psychology GRE achievement test are given positive consideration. In unusual circumstances, individuals with degrees in areas other than psychology may receive provisional admission but need to earn a B or higher score in Statistics before full admission is granted. For additional information on admission requirements, go to http://grad.washcoll.edu/.

Student Characteristics: The following represents characteristics of students in 2007–2008 in all graduate psychology programs in the department: Female—full-time 4, part-time 20; Male—full-time 1, part-time 5; African American/Black—full-time 0, part-time 2; Hispanic/Latino(a)—full-time 0, part-time 0; Asian/Pacific Islander—full-time 0, part-time 0; American Indian/Alaska Native—full-time 0, part-time 1; Caucasian/White—full-time 5, part-time 19; Multi-ethnic—full-time 0, part-time 3; Unknown ethnicity—full-time 0, part-time 0.

Financial Information/Assistance:

Tuition for Full-Time Study: *Master's:* State residents: $292 per credit hour; Nonstate residents: $292 per credit hour. Tuition is subject to change. Additional fees are assessed to students beyond the costs of tuition for the following: $75 registration fee per course.

Financial Assistance:

First-Year Students: No information provided.

Advanced Students: No information provided.

Additional Information: No information provided.

Internships/Practica: The department enjoys excellent ties to local agencies such as the Upper Shore Community Mental Health Center (the regional residential facility located in Chestertown), Upper Shore Aging, both Kent and Queen Anne's counties school systems, residential facilities for developmentally disadvantaged individuals, troubled adolescents, etc. A variety of internships are available through the cooperation of these agencies.

Housing and Day Care: No on-campus housing is available. No on-campus day care facilities are available.

Employment of Department Graduates:

Master's Degree Graduates: Of those who graduated in the academic year 2006–2007, the following categories and numbers represent the postgraduate activities and employment of master's degree graduates: Enrolled in a postdoctoral residency/fellowship (n/a), employed in independent practice (n/a), total from the above (master's) (0).

Doctoral Degree Graduates: Of those who graduated in the academic year 2006–2007, the following categories and numbers represent the postgraduate activities and employment of doctoral degree graduates: Enrolled in a psychology doctoral program (n/a), total from the above (doctoral) (0).

Additional Information:

Orientation, Objectives, and Emphasis of Department: The goal of this program is to prepare graduate students for entry into a doctoral program of their choice and to generate master's-level professionals. The emphasis of the curriculum is on psychology as a scientific endeavor and the applications of that scientific discipline to real-world problems.

Special Facilities or Resources: The department has just moved into a newly renovated science center and has more than tripled its available classroom and laboratory space. Newly expanded resources include a computerize learning lab, preclinical behavioral pharmacology laboratory, digital video- and audiotaping facilities for clinical and social research, a biofeedback-based health psychology laboratory, a 64-channel EEG/ERP and a Transcranial Doppler facility, an eye movement lab, a small mammal surgery suite, and a computerized cognitive laboratory utilizing E-prime.

Application Information:

Send to Director of the Graduate Programs, 300 Washington Avenue, Chestertown, MD 21620-1197. Application available online. URL of online application: http://www.grad.washcoll.edu/. Students are admitted in the Fall, application deadline August 1; Spring, application deadline December 1; Summer, application deadline April 15. *Fee:* $45.

American International College (2007 data)

Department of Graduate Psychology
1000 State Street
Springfield, MA 01109
Telephone: (413) 737-7000
Fax: (413) 737-2803
E-mail: *rsprinth@acad.aic.edu*
Web: *http://www.aic.edu/web*

Department Information:

1979. Chairperson: Richard C. Sprinthall. Number of faculty: total—full-time 15, part-time 8; women—full-time 8, part-time 4.

Programs and Degrees Offered:

Listed in the following order: Program area, degree type (T if terminal Master's), number awarded 7/06–6/07. Clinical MA/MS (Master of Arts/Science) (T) 9, Educational MA/MS (Master of Arts/Science) 11, Educational Psychology EdD (Doctor of Education) 5, Forensic Psychology MA/MS (Master of Arts/Science) (T) 7.

Student Applications/Admissions:

Student Applications

Clinical MA/MS (Master of Arts/Science)—Applications 2007–2008, 29. Total applicants accepted 2007–2008, 15. Number full-time enrolled (new admits only) 2007–2008, 10. Number part-time enrolled (new admits only) 2007–2008, 11. Total enrolled 2007–2008 full-time, 18, part-time, 16. Openings 2008–2009, 15. The median number of years required for completion of a degree in 2006–2007 were 3. The number of students enrolled full- and part-time who were dismissed or voluntarily withdrew from this program area in 2007–2008 were 5. *Educational MA/MS (Master of Arts/Science)*—Applications 2007–2008, 15. Total applicants accepted 2007–2008, 10. Number full-time enrolled (new admits only) 2007–2008, 4. Number part-time enrolled (new admits only) 2007–2008, 7. Total enrolled 2007–2008 full-time, 8, part-time, 15. Openings 2008–2009, 15. The median number of years required for completion of a degree in 2006–2007 were 3. The number of students enrolled full- and part-time who were dismissed or voluntarily withdrew from this program area in 2007–2008 were 4. *Educational Psychology EdD (Doctor of Education)*—Applications 2007–2008, 31. Total applicants accepted 2007–2008, 10. Number full-time enrolled (new admits only) 2007–2008, 7. Number part-time enrolled (new admits only) 2007–2008, 3. Total enrolled 2007–2008 full-time, 22, part-time, 20. Openings 2008–2009, 10. The median number of years required for completion of a degree in 2006–2007 were 5. The number of students enrolled full- and part-time who were dismissed or voluntarily withdrew from this program area in 2007–2008 were 4. *Forensic Psychology MA/MS (Master of Arts/Science)*—Applications 2007–2008, 25. Total applicants accepted 2007–2008, 10. Number full-time enrolled (new admits only) 2007–2008, 4. Number part-time enrolled (new admits only) 2007–2008, 6. Total enrolled 2007–2008 full-time, 4, part-time, 6. Openings 2008–2009, 10. The median number of years required for completion of a degree in 2006–2007 were 3. The number of students enrolled full- and part-time who were dismissed or voluntarily withdrew from this program area in 2007–2008 were 0.

Admissions Requirements:

Scores: Entries appear in this order: required test or GPA, minimum score (if required), median score of students entering in 2007–2008. Master's Programs: overall undergraduate GPA no minimum stated, 3.00; last 2 years GPA no minimum stated, 3.15; psychology GPA no minimum stated, 3.40. Doctoral Programs: GRE-V no minimum stated, 570; GRE-Q no minimum stated, 500; overall undergraduate GPA no minimum stated, 3.00.

Other Criteria: (importance of criteria rated low, medium, or high): GRE/MAT scores—medium, research experience—high, work experience—high, extracurricular activity—medium, clinically related public service—medium, GPA—high, letters of recommendation—high, interview—high, statement of goals and objectives—high. GRE only for EdD.

Student Characteristics: The following represents characteristics of students in 2007–2008 in all graduate psychology programs in the department: Female—full-time 36, part-time 35; Male—full-time 26, part-time 22; African American/Black—full-time 5, part-time 3; Hispanic/Latino(a)—full-time 6, part-time 5; Asian/Pacific Islander—full-time 0, part-time 0; American Indian/Alaska Native—full-time 0, part-time 0; Caucasian/White—full-time 40, part-time 52; Multi-ethnic—full-time 0, part-time 0; students subject to the Americans With Disabilities Act—full-time 0, part-time 0; Unknown ethnicity—full-time 0, part-time 0.

Financial Information/Assistance:

Tuition for Full-Time Study: *Master's:* State residents: per academic year $10,530, $585 per credit hour; Nonstate residents: per academic year $10,530, $585 per credit hour. *Doctoral:* State residents: per academic year $10,530, $585 per credit hour; Nonstate residents: per academic year $10,530, $585 per credit hour.

Financial Assistance:

First-Year Students: Teaching assistantships available for first year. Average number of hours worked per week: 10. Apply by April 15. Tuition remission given: full. Research assistantships available for first year. Average number of hours worked per week: 10. Apply by April 15. Tuition remission given: full. Fellowships and scholarships available for first year. Average number of hours worked per week: 10. Apply by April 15. Tuition remission given: full.

Advanced Students: Teaching assistantships available for advanced students. Apply by April 15. Tuition remission given: full. Research assistantships available for advanced students. Apply by April 15. Tuition remission given: full. Fellowships and scholarships available for advanced students. Apply by April 15. Tuition remission given: full.

Additional Information: Of all students currently enrolled full time, 24% benefited from one or more of the listed financial assistance programs. Application and information available online at http://www.aic.edu.

Internships/Practica: Internships for doctoral candidates are available at the Curtis Blake Center for Learning Disabilities and at the college-operated Curtis Blake Day School for learning-disabled children.

Housing and Day Care: On-campus housing is available. Dean Blaine Stevens, American International College, 1000 State Street, Springfield, MA 01109. On-campus day care facilities are available.

Employment of Department Graduates:

Master's Degree Graduates: Of those who graduated in the academic year 2006–2007, the following categories and numbers represent the postgraduate activities and employment of master's degree graduates: Enrolled in a postdoctoral residency/fellowship (n/a), employed in independent practice (n/a), total from the above (master's) (0).

Doctoral Degree Graduates: Of those who graduated in the academic year 2006–2007, the following categories and numbers represent the postgraduate activities and employment of doctoral degree graduates: Enrolled in a psychology doctoral program (n/a), total from the above (doctoral) (0).

Additional Information:

Orientation, Objectives, and Emphasis of Department: All graduate programs are based on an integrated curriculum designed to produce psychologists trained in both theory and clinical skills. Solid courses in history, systems, learning theory, and research are included. Heavy emphasis is placed on experience in the context of a broad academic and research-oriented curriculum. The program includes an extensive practicum experience, affording opportunity for the student to gain familiarity with the field and to apply and sharpen skills developed previously. The school psychology program (60 hours) leads to certification by the Commonwealth of Massachusetts. The EdD program in educational psychology is focused primarily on the area of learning disabilities. Supervision is provided both on campus and at the practicum site.

Special Facilities or Resources: A wide range of supervised internship sites is available to MA and Ed.D. candidates in mental health centers, the college counseling center, and professional agencies.

Information for Students With Physical Disabilities: See the following Web site for more information: http://www.aic.edu.

Application Information:

Send to Department Chair. Students are admitted in the Fall, application deadline Mar 15. *Fee:* $25.

Assumption College

Division of Counseling Psychology
500 Salisbury Street
Worcester, MA 01609-1296
Telephone: (508) 767-7390
Fax: (508) 767-7263
E-mail: *doerfler@assumption.edu*
Web: *http://www.assumption.edu*

Department Information:

1962. Program Director: Leonard A. Doerfler. Number of faculty: total—full-time 3, part-time 7; women—full-time 1, part-time 4; ; women minority—part-time 2.

Programs and Degrees Offered:

Listed in the following order: Program area, degree type (T if terminal Master's), number awarded 7/06–6/07. Counseling MA/MS (Master of Arts/Science) (T) 40.

Student Applications/Admissions:

Student Applications

Counseling MA/MS (Master of Arts/Science)—Applications 2007–2008, 87. Total applicants accepted 2007–2008, 75. Number full-time enrolled (new admits only) 2007–2008, 30. Number part-time enrolled (new admits only) 2007–2008, 14. Total enrolled 2007–2008 full-time, 70, part-time, 30. Openings 2008–2009, 35. The median number of years required for completion of a degree in 2006–2007 were 2. The number of students enrolled full- and part-time who were dismissed or voluntarily withdrew from this program area in 2007–2008 were 5.

Admissions Requirements:

Scores: Entries appear in this order: required test or GPA, minimum score (if required), median score of students entering in 2007–2008. Master's Programs: overall undergraduate GPA 3.0, 3.4; psychology GPA 3.0, 3.4.

Other Criteria: (importance of criteria rated low, medium, or high): research experience—low, work experience—medium, extracurricular activity—low, clinically related public service—low, GPA—high, letters of recommendation—high, statement of goals and objectives—medium.

Student Characteristics: The following represents characteristics of students in 2007–2008 in all graduate psychology programs in the department: Female—full-time 68, part-time 21; Male—full-time 5, part-time 6; African American/Black—full-time 1, part-time 0; Hispanic/Latino(a)—full-time 3, part-time 0; Asian/Pacific Islander—full-time 0, part-time 0; American Indian/Alaska Native—full-time 0, part-time 0; Caucasian/White—full-time 59, part-time 17; students subject to the Americans With Disabilities Act—full-time 0, part-time 0; Unknown ethnicity—full-time 0, part-time 0; International students who hold an F-1 or J-1 Visa—full-time 4, part-time 0.

Financial Information/Assistance:

Tuition for Full-Time Study: *Master's:* State residents: $468 per credit hour; Nonstate residents: $468 per credit hour.

Financial Assistance:

First-Year Students: Fellowships and scholarships available for first year. Apply by March 1. Tuition remission given: partial.

Advanced Students: Fellowships and scholarships available for advanced students. Apply by March 1. Tuition remission given: partial.

Additional Information: Of all students currently enrolled full time, 15% benefited from one or more of the listed financial assistance programs. Application and information available online at http://www.assumption.edu.

Internships/Practica: Practicum and internship placements are available in a wide range of community settings. Students can elect to work in outpatient/community, college counseling centers, substance abuse, inpatient, residential, and correctional settings. Opportunities to work with children, adolescents, adults, and families are available. The department maintains a close working relationship with the University of Massachusetts Medical Center, McLean Hospital/Harvard Medical School, and other mental health training agencies; students attend clinical case conferences, workshops, and lectures at these agencies. Students often receive training in innovative treatment models like home-based, brief problem-focused, or cognitive–behavioral treatments.

Housing and Day Care: On-campus housing is available. Information can be obtained from the Graduate School office regarding the possibility of living on campus: (508) 767-7387. No on-campus day care facilities are available.

Employment of Department Graduates:

Master's Degree Graduates: Of those who graduated in the academic year 2006–2007, the following categories and numbers represent the postgraduate activities and employment of master's degree graduates: Enrolled in a psychology doctoral program (0), enrolled in a postdoctoral residency/fellowship (n/a), employed in independent practice (n/a), employed in other positions at a higher education institution (0), employed in a professional position in a school system (0), employed in government agency (0), employed in a community mental health/counseling center (0), total from the above (master's) (0).

Doctoral Degree Graduates: Of those who graduated in the academic year 2006–2007, the following categories and numbers represent the postgraduate activities and employment of doctoral degree graduates: Enrolled in a psychology doctoral program (n/a), total from the above (doctoral) (0).

Additional Information:

Orientation, Objectives, and Emphasis of Department: The program is organized to prepare students for entrance into doctoral programs in clinical and counseling psychology and for master's degree entry-level positions in a variety of mental health and related social service settings. Students are given conceptual preparation in a variety of theoretical positions in clinical and counseling psychology. A number of skill courses in counseling, testing, and research are an integral part of the program at both the entry and advanced levels. The goal of the program is to produce master's-level psychologists who show conceptual versatility in theory and practice and depth of preparation in one of several special areas of counseling work. The student takes classwork in areas such as personality theory, abnormal psychology, child development, counseling, advanced therapeutic procedure, measurement, and research. Outside of class the student gains applied experience in clinical practice in the one-semester practicum and two-semester internship.

Special Facilities or Resources: Special facilities on campus include a well-equipped media center and an observation laboratory. Students also have access to in-service training at a local medical school, agencies, and hospitals. The college is located within commuting distance of Boston training facilities. College libraries in Worcester operate on a consortium basis. Programs of study are available on campus in the summer.

Application Information:

Send to Dean of Graduate Studies, Graduate Office, Assumption College, 500 Salisbury Street, Worcester, MA 01609-1296. Students are admitted in the Fall, application deadline rolling; Spring, application deadline rolling; Summer, application deadline rolling. *Fee:* $30. Application fee waived for Assumption College alumni.

Boston College

Department of Counseling, Developmental, and Educational Psychology
309 Campion Hall, School of Education
Chestnut Hill, MA 02467
Telephone: (617) 552-4710
Fax: (617) 552-1981
E-mail: *lernerj@bc.edu*
Web: *http://www.bc.edu/schools/lsoe/about/departments/cdep.html*

Department Information:

1950. Interim Chairperson: Jacqueline Lerner, PhD. Number of faculty: total—full-time 17; women—full-time 12; total—minority—full-time 4; women minority—full-time 3.

Programs and Degrees Offered:

Listed in the following order: Program area, degree type (T if terminal Master's), number awarded 7/06–6/07. Counseling School MA/MS (Master of Arts/Science) (T) 16, Counseling Psychology PhD (Doctor of Philosophy) 8, Counseling Mental Health MA/MS (Master of Arts/Science) (T) 57, Developmental Educational Psychology MA/MS (Master of Arts/Science) (T) 13, Developmental Educational Psychology PhD (Doctor of Philosophy) 6.

APA Accreditation: Counseling PhD (Doctor of Philosophy).

Student Applications/Admissions:

Student Applications

Counseling School MA/MS (Master of Arts/Science)—Applications 2007–2008, 56. Total applicants accepted 2007–2008, 40. Number full-time enrolled (new admits only) 2007–2008, 15. Number part-time enrolled (new admits only) 2007–2008, 0. Openings 2008–2009, 30. The median number of years required for completion of a degree in 2006–2007 were 2. The number of students enrolled full- and part-time who were dismissed or voluntarily withdrew from this program area in 2007–2008 were 0. *Counseling Psychology PhD (Doctor of Philosophy)*—Applications 2007–2008, 271. Total applicants accepted 2007–2008, 7. Number full-time enrolled (new admits only) 2007–2008, 6. Number part-time enrolled (new admits only) 2007–2008, 0. Openings 2008–2009, 7. The median number of years required for completion of a degree in 2006–2007 were 7. The number of students enrolled full- and part-time who were dismissed or voluntarily withdrew from this program area in 2007–2008 were 1. *Counseling Mental Health MA/MS (Master of Arts/Science)*—Applications 2007–2008, 198. Total applicants accepted 2007–2008, 154. Number full-time enrolled (new admits only) 2007–2008, 57. Number part-time enrolled (new admits only) 2007–2008, 0. Openings 2008–2009, 60. The median number of years required for completion of a degree in 2006–2007 were 2. The number of students enrolled full- and part-time who were dismissed or voluntarily withdrew from this program area in 2007–2008 were 0. *Developmental Educational Psychology MA/MS (Master of Arts/Science)*—Applications 2007–2008, 67. Total applicants accepted 2007–2008, 31. Number full-time enrolled (new admits only) 2007–2008, 11. Number part-time enrolled (new admits only) 2007–2008, 0. Openings 2008–2009, 25. The median number of years required for completion of a degree in 2006–2007 were 2. The number of students enrolled full- and part-time who were dismissed or voluntarily withdrew from this program area in 2007–2008 were 0. *Developmental Educational Psychology PhD (Doctor of Philosophy)*—Applications 2007–2008, 43. Total applicants accepted 2007–2008, 6. Number full-time enrolled (new admits only) 2007–2008, 4. Number part-time enrolled (new admits only) 2007–2008, 0. Openings 2008–2009, 5. The median number of years required for completion of a degree in 2006–2007 were 5. The number of students enrolled full- and part-time who were dismissed or voluntarily withdrew from this program area in 2007–2008 were 0.

Admissions Requirements:

Scores: Entries appear in this order: required test or GPA, minimum score (if required), median score of students entering in 2007–2008. Master's Programs: GRE-V no minimum stated, 510; GRE-Q no minimum stated, 615; overall undergraduate GPA no minimum stated, 3.4. Doctoral Programs: GRE-V no minimum stated, 550; GRE-Q no minimum stated, 610; overall undergraduate GPA no minimum stated, 3.51.

Other Criteria: (importance of criteria rated low, medium, or high): GRE/MAT scores—medium, research experience—high, work experience—medium, extracurricular activity—low, clinically related public service—high, GPA—high, letters of recommendation—high, interview—high, statement of goals and objectives—high, social justice commitment—high. For developmental programs, clinically related public service is low. For counsleing programs, social justice commitment is high.

Student Characteristics: The following represents characteristics of students in 2007–2008 in all graduate psychology programs in the department: Female—full-time 185, part-time 16; Male—full-time 39, part-time 1; African American/Black—full-time 15, part-time 1; Hispanic/Latino(a)—full-time 12, part-time 1; Asian/Pacific Islander—full-time 15, part-time 1; American Indian/Alaska Native—full-time 1, part-time 0; Caucasian/White—full-time 140, part-time 12; Multi-ethnic—full-time 1, part-time 1; students subject to the Americans With Disabilities Act—full-time 0, part-time 0; Unknown ethnicity—full-time 12, part-time 2; International students who hold an F-1 or J-1 Visa—full-time 28, part-time 0.

Financial Information/Assistance:

Tuition for Full-Time Study: *Master's:* State residents: $922 per credit hour; Nonstate residents: $922 per credit hour. *Doctoral:* State residents: $922 per credit hour; Nonstate residents: $922 per credit hour. Tuition is subject to change.

Financial Assistance:

First-Year Students: Research assistantships available for first year. Average amount paid per academic year: $18,000. Average number of hours worked per week: 20. Apply by variable. Tuition remission given: partial.

Advanced Students: Teaching assistantships available for advanced students. Average amount paid per academic year: $18,000. Average number of hours worked per week: 20. Apply by variable. Tuition remission given: partial. Research assistantships available for advanced students. Average amount paid per academic year: $18,000. Average number of hours worked per week: 20. Apply by variable. Tuition remission given: partial.

Additional Information: Of all students currently enrolled full time, 50% benefited from one or more of the listed financial assistance programs. Application and information available online at http://www.bc.edu/schools/lsoe/gradadmission/.

Internships/Practica: Doctoral Degree (PhD Counseling Psychology): For those doctoral students for whom a professional internship was required in this program prior to graduation, (5) students applied for an internship in 2006–2007, with (4) students obtaining an internship. Of those students who obtained an internship, (4) were paid internships. Of those students who obtained an internship, (4) students placed in APA/CPA-accredited internships, (0) students placed in internships not APA/CPA-accredited, but listed with the Association of Psychology Postdoctoral and Internship Centers (APPIC), (0) students placed in internships conforming to guidelines of the Council of Directors of School Psychology Programs (CDSPP), (0) students placed in internships that were not APA/CPA-accredited, APPIC or CDSPP listed. Doctoral students in Counseling Psychology complete an advanced practicum in community mental health agencies, schools, clinics, hospitals, and college counseling centers. They also complete a 1-year predoctoral internship. Master's students in mental health and school counseling work with the Masters Program Coordinator to identify internships that meet requirements for mental health licensure or school counselor certification. Masters and Doctoral students in the Applied Developmental and Educational Psychology program can complete a non-required internship.

Housing and Day Care: On-campus housing is available. See the following Web site for more information: http://www.bc.edu/offices/reslife/. On-campus day care facilities are available. See the following Web site for more information: http://www.bc.edu/offices/hr/resources/docs/ccquickreference.html.

Employment of Department Graduates:

Master's Degree Graduates: Of those who graduated in the academic year 2006–2007, the following categories and numbers represent the postgraduate activities and employment of master's degree graduates: Enrolled in a postdoctoral residency/fellowship (n/a), employed in independent practice (n/a), total from the above (master's) (0).

Doctoral Degree Graduates: Of those who graduated in the academic year 2006–2007, the following categories and numbers represent the postgraduate activities and employment of doctoral degree graduates: Enrolled in a psychology doctoral program (n/a), total from the above (doctoral) (0).

Additional Information:

Orientation, Objectives, and Emphasis of Department: The Programs in Counseling, Developmental, and Educational Psychology emphasize a foundation in developmental theory, research skills, and a commitment to preparing professionals to work in public practice, public service, or academic or research institutions. The counseling psychology doctoral program espouses a scientist–practitioner model and provides broad-based training with special attention to group and individual counseling processes, theory and skill in research and assessment, and understanding individual development within a social context. Master's counseling students specialize in mental health counseling or school counseling. The program in Applied Developmental and Educational Psychology focuses on application and draws on psychology, educational and community programs, and engages public policies to enhance the development of individuals and their key institutional contexts—schools, families, and work settings—across the life span. Faculty research interests include psychotherapy, process and outcome, career and moral development, individual differences in cognitive and affective development including developmental disabilities, influence of gender role strain on the well-being of men, Asian American and Latino mental health, racial identity, marital and community violence, marital satisfaction, and prevention and intervention for promoting positive development among youth.

Special Facilities or Resources: Boston College offers ample student access to computing facilities (Alpha mainframe, Macintosh and PCs) at no charge to students. The Educational Resource Center houses current psychological assessment kits and computerized instructional software. The Thomas P. O'Neill Library is fully automated with all major computerized databases. Through the consortium, students may cross-register in courses in other greater Boston universities (Boston University, Brandeis, and Tufts). The career center provides comprehensive resources and information regarding career planning and placement.

Application Information:

Send to Boston College, LSOE Data Processing Center, P.O. Box 226, Randolph, MA 02368-9998. Application available online. URL of online application: http://www.bc.edu. Students are admitted in the Fall, application deadline December 15; Summer, application deadline June 15. Counseling MA programs, January 1; Counseling PhD, December 15. Developmental PhD, January 1. Developmental MA, June 15 and January 1. *Fee:* $60. All MA programs February 1; all PhD January 1.

Boston College (2007 data)

Department of Psychology
College of Arts and Sciences
140 Commonwealth Avenue, McGuinn 301
Chestnut Hill, MA 02467
Telephone: (617) 552-4100
Fax: (617) 552-0523
E-mail: *horvitjo@bc.edu*
Web: *http://www.bc.edu/schools/cas/psych/*

Department Information:

1950. Chairperson: James Russell. Number of faculty: total—full-time 19, part-time 7; women—full-time 9, part-time 6.

Programs and Degrees Offered:

Listed in the following order: Program area, degree type (T if terminal Master's), number awarded 7/06–6/07. Developmental PhD (Doctor of Philosophy) 2, Social and Cultural PhD (Doctor of Philosophy) 2, Cognitive, Affective, and Behavioral Neuroscience PhD (Doctor of Philosophy) 1.

Student Applications/Admissions:

Student Applications

Developmental PhD (Doctor of Philosophy)—Applications 2007–2008, 50. Total applicants accepted 2007–2008, 1. Number full-time enrolled (new admits only) 2007–2008, 0. Openings 2008–2009, 2. The median number of years required for completion of a degree in 2006–2007 were 4. *Social and Cultural PhD (Doctor of Philosophy)*—Applications 2007–2008, 90. Total applicants accepted 2007–2008, 2. Number full-time enrolled (new admits only) 2007–2008, 1. Openings 2008–2009, 1. The median number of years required for completion of a degree in 2006–2007 were 4. *Cognitive, Affective, and Behavioral Neuroscience PhD (Doctor of Philosophy)*—Applications 2007–2008, 45. Number full-time enrolled (new admits only) 2007–2008, 6. Total enrolled 2007–2008 full-time, 14. The median number of years required for completion of a degree in 2006–2007 were 4.

Admissions Requirements:

Scores: Entries appear in this order: required test or GPA, minimum score (if required), median score of students entering in 2007–2008. Master's Programs: GRE-V no minimum stated; GRE-Q no minimum stated; overall undergraduate GPA no minimum stated; psychology GPA no minimum stated. Doctoral Programs: GRE-V no minimum stated; GRE-Q no minimum stated; GRE-Subject (Psychology) no minimum stated; overall undergraduate GPA no minimum stated; psychology GPA no minimum stated; Doctoral program GRE-Analytic no minimum stated.

Other Criteria: (importance of criteria rated low, medium, or high): GRE/MAT scores—high, research experience—high, work experience—low, extracurricular activity—low, clinically related public service—low, GPA—high, letters of recommendation—high, interview—high, statement of goals and objectives—high. For additional information on admission requirements, go to http://www.bc.edu/schools/cas/psych/graduate.html.

Student Characteristics: The following represents characteristics of students in 2007–2008 in all graduate psychology programs in the department: Female—full-time 19, part-time 0; Male—full-time 3, part-time 0; African American/Black—full-time 0, part-time 0; Hispanic/Latino(a)—full-time 0, part-time 0; Asian/Pacific Islander—full-time 0, part-time 0; American Indian/Alaska Native—full-time 0, part-time 0; Caucasian/White—full-time 22, part-time 0; Multi-ethnic—full-time 0, part-time 0; students subject to the Americans With Disabilities Act—full-time 0, part-time 0; Unknown ethnicity—full-time 0, part-time 0.

Financial Information/Assistance:

Tuition for Full-Time Study: *Master's:* State residents: $1,040 per credit hour; Nonstate residents: $1,040 per credit hour. *Doctoral:* State residents: $1,040 per credit hour; Nonstate residents: $1,040 per credit hour. See the following Web site for updates and changes in tuition costs: http://www.gsas.bc.edu.

Financial Assistance:

First-Year Students: Research assistantships available for first year. Average amount paid per academic year: $18,500. Average number of hours worked per week: 20. Apply by January 2. Tuition remission given: full.

Advanced Students: Teaching assistantships available for advanced students. Average amount paid per academic year: $18,500. Average number of hours worked per week: 20. Apply by January 2. Tuition remission given: full. Fellowships and scholarships available for advanced students. Tuition remission given: partial.

Additional Information: Of all students currently enrolled full time, 100% benefited from one or more of the listed financial assistance programs.

Internships/Practica: No information provided.

Housing and Day Care: No on-campus housing is available. On-campus day care facilities are available.

Employment of Department Graduates:

Master's Degree Graduates: Of those who graduated in the academic year 2006–2007, the following categories and numbers represent the postgraduate activities and employment of master's degree graduates: Enrolled in a postdoctoral residency/fellowship (n/a), employed in independent practice (n/a), total from the above (master's) (0).

Doctoral Degree Graduates: Of those who graduated in the academic year 2006–2007, the following categories and numbers represent the postgraduate activities and employment of doctoral degree graduates: Enrolled in a psychology doctoral program (n/a), enrolled in a postdoctoral residency/fellowship (1), employed in an academic position at a university (4), employed in a hospital/medical center (1), total from the above (doctoral) (6).

Additional Information:

Orientation, Objectives, and Emphasis of Department: We emphasize rigorous research and a close working relationship between student and professor.

Special Facilities or Resources: The Psychology Department has a computer lab with 13 workstations. Individual faculty maintain research laboratories. The Biopsychology concentration has fully equipped new research laboratories. The new lab facility contains two components: An animal facility and research laboratory space. The animal facility includes state-of-the-art small animal housing and behavioral testing rooms, a surgery suite, and special procedure rooms that are equipped with hoods. The research laboratories consist of microscopy suite; dark room; data analysis room; and 3 research labs/wet labs equipped with hoods, sinks, and workspace.

Application Information:

Send to Boston College, Graduate School of Arts and Sciences, 140 Commonwealth Avenue, McGuinn 221, Chestnut Hill, MA 02467. Application available online. URL of online application: http://www.gsas.bc.edu. Students are admitted in the Fall, application deadline January 2nd. *Fee:* $70.

Boston University

Department of Psychology
64 Cummington Street
Boston, MA 02215
Telephone: (617) 353-2580
Fax: (617) 353-6933
E-mail: *mlyons@bu.edu*
Web: *http://www.bu.edu/psych*

Department Information:

1935. Chairperson: Michael Lyons. Number of faculty: total—full-time 27, part-time 1; women—full-time 14; minority—part-time 1.

Programs and Degrees Offered:

Listed in the following order: Program area, degree type (T if terminal Master's), number awarded 7/06–6/07. Brain, Behavior, and Cognition PhD (Doctor of Philosophy) 4, Clinical PhD (Doctor of Philosophy) 13, General MA/MS (Master of Arts/Science) (T) 29, Human Development PhD (Doctor of Philosophy) 2.

APA Accreditation: Clinical PhD (Doctor of Philosophy).

Student Applications/Admissions:

Student Applications

Brain, Behavior, and Cognition PhD (Doctor of Philosophy)—Applications 2007–2008, 94. Total applicants accepted 2007–2008, 5. Number full-time enrolled (new admits only) 2007–2008, 3. Openings 2008–2009, 4. The median number of years required for completion of a degree in 2006–2007 were 5. The number of students enrolled full- and part-time who were dismissed or voluntarily withdrew from this program area in 2007–2008 were 1. *Clinical PhD (Doctor of Philosophy)*—Applications 2007–2008, 580. Total applicants accepted 2007–2008, 17. Number full-time enrolled (new admits only) 2007–2008, 13. Number part-time enrolled (new admits only) 2007–2008, 0. Openings 2008–2009, 12. The median number of years required for completion of a degree in 2006–2007 were 6. The number of students enrolled full- and part-time who were dismissed or voluntarily withdrew from this program area in 2007–2008 were 0. *General MA/MS (Master of Arts/Science)*—Applications 2007–2008, 208. Total applicants accepted 2007–2008, 151. Number full-time enrolled (new admits only) 2007–2008, 40. Number part-time enrolled (new admits only) 2007–2008, 2. Total enrolled 2007–2008 full-time, 40, part-time, 10. Openings 2008–2009, 40. The median number of years required for completion of a degree in 2006–2007 was 1. The number of students enrolled full- and part-time who were dismissed or voluntarily withdrew from this program area in 2007–2008 were 1. *Human Development PhD (Doctor of Philosophy)*—Applications 2007–2008, 57. Total applicants accepted 2007–2008, 2. Number full-time enrolled (new admits only) 2007–2008, 1. Total enrolled 2007–2008 full-time, 11. Openings 2008–2009, 3. The median number of years required for completion of a degree in 2006–2007 were 5. The number of students enrolled full- and part-time who were dismissed or voluntarily withdrew from this program area in 2007–2008 were 0.

Admissions Requirements:

Scores: Entries appear in this order: required test or GPA, minimum score (if required), median score of students entering in 2007–2008. Master's Programs: GRE-V no minimum stated; GRE-Q no minimum stated; overall undergraduate GPA no minimum stated; last 2 years GPA no minimum stated; psychology GPA no minimum stated; Masters GRE-Analytical no minimum stated. Doctoral Programs: GRE-V no minimum stated; GRE-Q no minimum stated; overall undergraduate GPA no minimum stated; last 2 years GPA no minimum stated; psychology GPA no minimum stated; Doctoral program GRE-Analytic no minimum stated.

Other Criteria: (importance of criteria rated low, medium, or high): GRE/MAT scores—high, research experience—high, work experience—low, extracurricular activity—low, clinically related public service—high, GPA—high, letters of recommendation—high, interview—high, statement of goals and objectives—high.

Student Characteristics: The following represents characteristics of students in 2007–2008 in all graduate psychology programs in the department: Female—full-time 111, part-time 5; Male—full-time 35, part-time 5; African American/Black—full-time 8, part-time 0; Hispanic/Latino(a)—full-time 4, part-time 0; Asian/Pacific Islander—full-time 9, part-time 0; American Indian/Alaska Native—full-time 0, part-time 0; Caucasian/White—full-time 124, part-time 10; Multi-ethnic—full-time 1, part-time 0; students subject to the Americans With Disabilities Act—full-time 1, part-time 0; Unknown ethnicity—full-time 0, part-time 0; International students who hold an F-1 or J-1 Visa—full-time 13, part-time 5.

Financial Information/Assistance:

Tuition for Full-Time Study: *Master's:* State residents: per academic year $35,116, $1,185 per credit hour; Nonstate residents: per academic year $35,116, $1,185 per credit hour. *Doctoral:* State residents: per academic year $35,116, $1,185 per credit hour; Nonstate residents: per academic year $35,116, $1,185 per credit hour.

Financial Assistance:

First-Year Students: Teaching assistantships available for first year. Average amount paid per academic year: $17,500. Average number of hours worked per week: 20. Apply for 8 months. Tuition remission given: full. Research assistantships available for first year. Average amount paid per academic year: $26,250. Average number of hours worked per week: 20. Apply for 12 months. Tuition remission given: full. Fellowships and scholarships available for first year. Average amount paid per academic year: $18,000. Average number of hours worked per week: 0. Apply for 8 months. Tuition remission given: full.

Advanced Students: Teaching assistantships available for advanced students. Average amount paid per academic year: $17,500. Average number of hours worked per week: 20. Apply for 8 months. Tuition remission given: full. Research assistantships available for advanced students. Average amount paid per academic year: $26,250. Average number of hours worked per week: 20. Apply for 12 months. Tuition remission given: full. Traineeships available for advanced students. Average amount paid per academic year: $17,500. Average number of hours worked per week: 20. Apply for 12 months. Tuition remission given: full.

Additional Information: Of all students currently enrolled full time, 75% benefited from one or more of the listed financial assistance programs. Application and information available online at http://www.bu.edu/psych.

Internships/Practica: Doctoral Degree (PhD Clinical): For those doctoral students for whom a professional internship was required in this program prior to graduation, (17) students applied for an internship in 2006–2007, with (16) students obtaining an internship. Of those students who obtained an internship, (16) were paid internships. Of those students who obtained an internship, (16) students placed in APA/CPA-accredited internships, (0) students placed in internships not APA/CPA-accredited, but listed with the Association of Psychology Postdoctoral and Internship Centers (APPIC), (0) students placed in internships conforming to guidelines of the Council of Directors of School Psychology Programs (CDSPP), (0) students placed in internships that were not APA/CPA-accredited, APPIC or CDSPP listed. Students in the clinical doctoral program are involved in internships and practica as part of their degree requirements.

Housing and Day Care: No on-campus housing is available. No on-campus day care facilities are available.

Employment of Department Graduates:

Master's Degree Graduates: Of those who graduated in the academic year 2006–2007, the following categories and numbers represent the postgraduate activities and employment of master's degree graduates: Enrolled in a postdoctoral residency/fellowship (n/a), employed in independent practice (n/a), total from the above (master's) (0).

Doctoral Degree Graduates: Of those who graduated in the academic year 2006–2007, the following categories and numbers represent the postgraduate activities and employment of doctoral degree graduates: Enrolled in a psychology doctoral program (n/a), total from the above (doctoral) (0).

Additional Information:

Orientation, Objectives, and Emphasis of Department: The department offers specialized training leading to the PhD degree in three areas of concentration: clinical; brain, behavior, and cognition; and the program in human development with specializations in developmental, personality, social, and family. The PhD degree in psychology is awarded to students of scholarly competence as reflected by course achievement and by performance on written and oral examinations and of research competence as reflected by student's skillful application and communication of knowledge in the area of specialization. Breadth is encouraged within psychology and in related social, behavioral, and biological sciences, but it is also expected that the student will engage in intensive and penetrating study of a specialized area of the field.

Special Facilities or Resources: Laboratories for research pursuits in animal behavior, behavior disorders, child development, cognition, neurophysiology, molecular biology, and psychopharmacology add to the department's facilities. The Center for Anxiety and Related Disorders (CARD), a nationally recognized clinical research and treatment center, is a recent addition to the department, and allows students to engage in a variety of ongoing research projects and receive training in focused clinical interventions. In addition, the Boston area is fortunate to have a number of nationally known hospitals, counseling centers, and community mental health centers directly affiliated with our clinical program where students have opportunities to gain experience in a variety of clinical settings with different client populations. The New England Regional Primate Center, which is supported by the National Institutes of Health, is also available to Boston University faculty and students.

Application Information:
Send to Graduate School of Arts and Sciences, 705 Commonwealth Avenue, Boston, MA 02215. Application available online. URL of online application: http://www.bu.edu/cas/graduate. Students are admitted in the Fall, application deadline December 1. The deadline for applications to the Clinical PhD program is December 1. The deadline for applications to the Brain, Behavior, and Cognition PhD Program and the Human Development PhD Program is January 15. The application deadline for the MA only program is May 15. Applications will be reviewed beginning March 1. Please note that applications, as well as all credentials and supplementary materials, must be submitted in one packet by the deadline. Incomplete applications will not be reveiwed. *Fee:* $70.

Boston University

Divison of Graduate Medical Sciences, Program in Mental Health and Behavioral Medicine
School of Medicine
715 Albany Street, Robinson Building, Suite B-2903
Boston, MA 02118
Telephone: (617) 414-2320
Fax: (617) 414-2323
E-mail: *nicey@bu.edu*
Web: *http://www.bumc.bu.edu/mhbm*

Department Information:
2001. Chairperson: Stephen Brady, PhD. Number of faculty: total—full-time 5, part-time 3; women—full-time 4, part-time 2.

Programs and Degrees Offered:
Listed in the following order: Program area, degree type (T if terminal Master's), number awarded 7/06–6/07. Mental Health and Behavioral Medicine MA/MS (Master of Arts/Science) (T) 28.

Student Applications/Admissions:
Student Applications
Mental Health and Behavioral Medicine MA/MS (Master of Arts/Science)—Applications 2007–2008, 68. Total applicants accepted 2007–2008, 38. Number full-time enrolled (new admits only) 2007–2008, 31. Number part-time enrolled (new admits only) 2007–2008, 2. Total enrolled 2007–2008 full-time, 41, part-time, 2. Openings 2008–2009, 30. The median number of years required for completion of a degree in 2006–2007 were 2. The number of students enrolled full- and part-time who were dismissed or voluntarily withdrew from this program area in 2007–2008 were 1.

Admissions Requirements:
Scores: Entries appear in this order: required test or GPA, minimum score (if required), median score of students entering in 2007–2008. Master's Programs: GRE-V no minimum stated, 490; GRE-Q no minimum stated, 605; overall undergraduate GPA no minimum stated, 3.24.
Other Criteria: (importance of criteria rated low, medium, or high): GRE/MAT scores—medium, research experience—medium, work experience—medium, extracurricular activity—medium, clinically related public service—medium, GPA—medium, letters of recommendation—high, interview—high, statement of goals and objectives—high. For additional information on admission requirements, go to http://www.bumc.bu.edu/mhbm.

Student Characteristics: The following represents characteristics of students in 2007–2008 in all graduate psychology programs in the department: Female—full-time 39, part-time 1; Male—full-time 7, part-time 0; African American/Black—full-time 8, part-time 1; Hispanic/Latino(a)—full-time 1, part-time 0; Asian/Pacific Islander—full-time 2, part-time 0; American Indian/Alaska Native—full-time 0, part-time 0; Caucasian/White—full-time 35, part-time 0; Multi-ethnic—full-time 0, part-time 0; students subject to the Americans With Disabilities Act—full-time 0, part-time 0; Unknown ethnicity—full-time 0, part-time 0; International students who hold an F-1 or J-1 Visa—full-time 1, part-time 0.

Financial Information/Assistance:
Tuition for Full-Time Study: *Master's:* State residents: per academic year $36,540, $1,142 per credit hour; Nonstate residents: per academic year $36,540, $1,142 per credit hour.

Financial Assistance:
First-Year Students: No information provided.
Advanced Students: No information provided.
Additional Information: No information provided.

Internships/Practica: Completion of the Masters in Mental Health and Behavioral Medicine program prepares students for independent licensure as a Mental Health Counselor (LMHC). Our students are primarily trained to conduct clinical practice with urban multicultural underserved populations. Our clinical training program includes curricula in mental health, behavioral medicine, and neuroscience offered in an urban hospital and medical school environment. The coursework is intended to prepare students to provide clinical services to a range of individuals in diversified settings. More specifically, students are trained to perform brief forms of assessment and psychotherapeutic interventions in medical and behavioral health care settings. We offer clinical training opportunities in diverse settings such as psychiatric emergency department services, child, adolescent, and adult outpatient psychiatric clinics, medical and psychiatric inpatient services, adolescent substance abuse treatment centers, college counseling centers, and community mental health clinics. Our practicum program is a 16-hour a week commitment over the course of one semester, and our internship training is a 24-hour a week commitment over the course of an academic year. At the completion of the program students will have accumulated approximately 1,000 hours of clinical training.

Housing and Day Care: On-campus housing is available. For information on housing, send an e-mail to ohr@bu.edu. Office of Housing Resources. No on-campus day care facilities are available.

Employment of Department Graduates:

Master's Degree Graduates: Of those who graduated in the academic year 2006–2007, the following categories and numbers represent the postgraduate activities and employment of master's degree graduates: Enrolled in a psychology doctoral program (3), enrolled in another graduate/professional program (1), enrolled in a postdoctoral residency/fellowship (n/a), employed in independent practice (n/a), employed in a professional position in a school system (1), employed in government agency (1), employed in a community mental health/counseling center (3), other employment position (1), do not know (3), total from the above (master's) (13).

Doctoral Degree Graduates: Of those who graduated in the academic year 2006–2007, the following categories and numbers represent the postgraduate activities and employment of doctoral degree graduates: Enrolled in a psychology doctoral program (n/a), total from the above (doctoral) (0).

Additional Information:

Orientation, Objectives, and Emphasis of Department: The Mental Health and Behavioral Medicine Program is the first of its kind in the United States, as it is located within a School of Medicine. Our program curriculum blends scholarship, practical experience, and an appreciation of the scientific bases of assessment and treatments for behavioral and neurological disorders. Our objective is to provide Master's-level counselors with a strong foundation in psychopathology and psychotherapeutic intervention, as well as a background in behavioral medicine and neuroscience. Our primary focus is the development of professional counselors with the skills to develop as scholars, teachers, researchers, and clinicians. Our program fills a major gap in the delivery of mental health services in health care settings and to patients with health care concerns. Students have a unique opportunity to work with outstanding mentors in psychology, psychiatry, neuroscience, and medicine. Graduates of the Program assume positions in a variety of settings, including community mental health centers, college and university settings, clinical research settings, and government facilities. Approximately one half of our students pursue doctoral-level training either immediately upon graduation or soon thereafter. More specific information about course requirements, can be found on our Web site: http://www.bumc.bu.edu/mhbm.

Special Facilities or Resources: Because the program is housed within the Boston University School of Medicine and is part of Boston University, our students and faculty have access to a wide variety of academic and medical resources. Although not a required part of students' experiences in the program, many of our students collaborate in clinical research activities, which are always a part of our campus. Students also engage in a wide variety of clinical experiences, as described above in "Internships/Practica." Books, journals, and access to computerized literature searches currently are available in the Alumni Medical Library at BUSM. This full-service medical library contains most relevant publications for students in a mental health related program. On the Charles River Campus, the Charles Mugar Library is available for students who wish further supplementary readings in the behavioral and social sciences. As a member of the Boston Library Consortium, Boston University students have access to additional library collections through interlibrary loans. Overall, the library resources available to these students are excellent and do not require additional acquisitions. The current Mental Health and Behavioral Medicine Program occupies a newly renovated space with approximately 1,200 square feet for its administrative and core faculty office space.

Application Information:

Please see the Web site (below) for information regarding applications. Application available online. URL of online application: http://www.bumc.bu.edu/mhbm. Students are admitted in the Fall, application deadline rolling; Winter, application deadline rolling; Spring, application deadline rolling; Programs have rolling admissions. *Fee:* $50. All online applications are $60.

Brandeis University

Department of Psychology
415 South Street, Mail Stop 62
Waltham, MA 02454-9110
Telephone: (781) 736-3300
Fax: (781) 736-3291
E-mail: *gnat@brandeis.edu*
Web: *http://www.brandeis.edu/departments/psych*

Department Information:

1948. Chairperson: Margie E. Lachman, PhD. Number of faculty: total—full-time 4, part-time 3; women—full-time 3, part-time 1.

Programs and Degrees Offered:

Listed in the following order: Program area, degree type (T if terminal Master's), number awarded 7/06–6/07. Cognitive Neuroscience PhD (Doctor of Philosophy) 1, General MA/MS (Master of Arts/Science) (T) 4, Social/Developmental PhD (Doctor of Philosophy) 3.

Student Applications/Admissions:

Student Applications

Cognitive Neuroscience PhD (Doctor of Philosophy)—Applications 2007–2008, 12. Total applicants accepted 2007–2008, 2. Number full-time enrolled (new admits only) 2007–2008, 2. Number part-time enrolled (new admits only) 2007–2008, 0. Openings 2008–2009, 2. The median number of years required for completion of a degree in 2006–2007 were 5. The number of students enrolled full- and part-time who were dismissed or voluntarily withdrew from this program area in 2007–2008 were 0. *General MA/MS (Master of Arts/Science)*—Applications 2007–2008, 43. Total applicants accepted 2007–2008, 10. Number full-time enrolled (new admits only) 2007–2008, 6. Number part-time enrolled (new admits only) 2007–2008, 2. Total enrolled 2007–2008 full-time, 9, part-time, 1. Openings 2008–2009, 4. The median number of years required for completion of a degree in 2006–2007 was 1. The number of students enrolled full- and part-time who were dismissed or voluntarily withdrew from this program area in 2007–2008 were 0. *Social/Developmental PhD (Doctor of Philosophy)*—Applications 2007–2008, 32. Total applicants accepted 2007–2008, 7. Number full-time enrolled (new admits only) 2007–2008, 3. Number part-time enrolled (new admits only) 2007–2008, 1. Total enrolled 2007–2008 full-time, 19, part-time, 1. Openings 2008–2009, 4. The median number of years required for completion of a degree in 2006–2007 were 5. The number of students enrolled full- and part-time who were dismissed or voluntarily withdrew from this program area in 2007–2008 were 1.

Admissions Requirements:

Scores: Entries appear in this order: required test or GPA, minimum score (if required), median score of students entering in 2007–2008. Master's Programs: GRE-V no minimum stated; GRE-Q no minimum stated; overall undergraduate GPA no minimum stated; Masters GRE-Analytical no minimum stated. Doctoral Programs: GRE-V no minimum stated; GRE-Q no minimum stated; overall undergraduate GPA no minimum stated. GRE Subject strongly recommended.

Other Criteria: (importance of criteria rated low, medium, or high): GRE/MAT scores—high, research experience—high, work experience—medium, extracurricular activity—low, clinically related public service—low, GPA—high, letters of recommendation—high, interview—high, statement of goals and objectives—high. For additional information on admission requirements, go to http://www.brandeis.edu/departments/psych/grad.html.

Student Characteristics: The following represents characteristics of students in 2007–2008 in all graduate psychology programs in the department: Female—full-time 23, part-time 1; Male—full-time 7, part-time 2; African American/Black—full-time 0, part-time 0; Hispanic/Latino(a)—full-time 0, part-time 0; Asian/Pacific Islander—full-time 0, part-time 0; American Indian/Alaska Native—full-time 0, part-time 0; Caucasian/White—full-time 15, part-time 3; Multi-ethnic—full-time 0, part-time 0; students subject to the Americans With Disabilities Act—full-time 0, part-time 1; Unknown ethnicity—full-time 0, part-time 0; International students who hold an F-1 or J-1 Visa—full-time 12, part-time 0.

Financial Information/Assistance:

Tuition for Full-Time Study: *Master's:* State residents: per academic year $32,951; Nonstate residents: per academic year $32,951. *Doctoral:* State residents: per academic year $32,951; Nonstate residents: per academic year $32,951. Tuition is subject to change. See the following Web site for updates and changes in tuition costs: http://www.brandeis.edu/gsas/students/aid-handbook/costofattendance.html.

Financial Assistance:

First-Year Students: Research assistantships available for first year. Fellowships and scholarships available for first year. Average amount paid per academic year: $18,000. Apply by January 15. Tuition remission given: full.

Advanced Students: Teaching assistantships available for advanced students. Average amount paid per academic year: $6,000. Fellowships and scholarships available for advanced students. Average amount paid per academic year: $18,000. Tuition remission given: full.

Additional Information: Of all students currently enrolled full time, 80% benefited from one or more of the listed financial assistance programs. Application and information available online at http://www.brandeis.edu/gsas/prospectives/financial-assistance.html; http://www.brandeis.edu/gsas/ap.

Internships/Practica: No information provided.

Housing and Day Care: No on-campus housing is available. On-campus day care facilities are available. See the following Web site for more information: On-site day care available with cost based on sliding-fee scale. Web address: http://www.brandeis.edu/lemberg/.

Employment of Department Graduates:

Master's Degree Graduates: Of those who graduated in the academic year 2006–2007, the following categories and numbers represent the postgraduate activities and employment of master's degree graduates: Enrolled in a psychology doctoral program (3), enrolled in another graduate/professional program (0), enrolled in a postdoctoral residency/fellowship (n/a), employed in independent practice (n/a), employed in an academic position at a university (0), employed in an academic position at a 2-year/4-year college (0), employed in other positions at a higher education institution (0), employed in a professional position in a school system (0), employed in business or industry (0), employed in government agency (0), employed in a community mental health/counseling center (0), employed in a hospital/medical center (0), still seeking employment (0), other employment position (1), do not know (0), total from the above (master's) (4).

Doctoral Degree Graduates: Of those who graduated in the academic year 2006–2007, the following categories and numbers represent the postgraduate activities and employment of doctoral degree graduates: Enrolled in a psychology doctoral program (n/a), enrolled in another graduate/professional program (0), enrolled in a postdoctoral residency/fellowship (1), employed in independent practice (0), employed in an academic position at a university (1), employed in an academic position at a 2-year/4-year college (0), employed in other positions at a higher education institution (0), employed in a professional position in a school system (0), employed in business or industry (0), employed in government agency (1), employed in a community mental health/counseling center (0), employed in a hospital/medical center (0), still seeking employment (0), other employment position (0), total from the above (doctoral) (3).

Additional Information:

Orientation, Objectives, and Emphasis of Department: The goal of the PhD Program is to develop excellent researchers and teachers who will become leaders in psychological science. From the start of graduate study, research activity is emphasized. The program helps students develop an area of research specialization, and gives them opportunities to work in one of two general areas: social–developmental psychology or cognitive neuroscience. In both areas, dissertation supervisors are leaders in the following areas: motor control, visual perception, taste physiology and psychophysics, memory, learning, aggression, emotion, personality and cognition in adulthood and old age, social relations and health, stereotypes, and nonverbal communication.

Special Facilities or Resources: Laboratories in the Psychology Department are well-equipped for research on memory, speech recognition, psycholinguistics, visual psychophysics, visual perception, motor control, and spatial orientation, including a NASA-sponsored laboratory for research on human spatial orientation in unusual gravatational environments. Social and developmental psychology laboratories include one-way observation rooms, videorecording and eye-tracking apparatus. There are also opportunities for social neuroscience research through a collaborative grant with the MGH-NMR center. Child development research is facilitated by cooperative relations with the Lemberg Children's Center on the Brandeis campus; applied social research is facilitated by cooperative relations with the Brandeis University Florence Heller Graduate School for Advanced Studies in Social Welfare and the Graduate School of International Economics and Finance. Research on cognitive aging is supported by a training grant from the National Institute on Aging. A special feature of the aging program is an interest in the interaction of cognitive, social, and personality factors in healthy aging. The psychology department also participates in an interdisciplinary neuroscience program at the Volen National Center for Complex Systems located on the Brandeis Campus.

Information for Students With Physical Disabilities: See the following Web site for more information: http://www.brandeis.edu/as/dis/disabilities.html.

Application Information:
Send to Graduate School of Arts and Sciences, MS 31, Brandeis University, Waltham, MA 02454-9110. Application available online. URL of online application: http://www.brandeis.edu/gsas/apply/index.html. Students are admitted in the Fall, application deadline January 15. PhD: Fall deadline is January 15. Master's: Fall deadline is May 1. Brandeis offers three ways to obtain an application (a) Fill out our online application and submit electronically. (b) Download and print out an application from our Web site. (c) Request a hard copy application be sent to you by mail. Web site address: http://www.brandeis.edu/gsas/apply/index.html. *Fee:* $55.

Clark University (2007 data)

Frances L. Hiatt School of Psychology
950 Main Street
Worcester, MA 01610
Telephone: (508) 793-7274
Fax: (508) 793-7265
E-mail: *maddis@clarku.edu*
Web: *http://www.clarku.edu/~psydept/*

Department Information:
1889. Chairperson: Michael Addis, PhD. Number of faculty: total—full-time 18, part-time 8; women—full-time 7, part-time 5.

Programs and Degrees Offered:
Listed in the following order: Program area, degree type (T if terminal Master's), number awarded 7/06–6/07. Clinical PhD (Doctor of Philosophy) 6, Developmental PhD (Doctor of Philosophy) 6, Social, Cultural, and Evolutionary PhD (Doctor of Philosophy) 0.

APA Accreditation: Clinical PhD (Doctor of Philosophy).

Student Applications/Admissions:
Student Applications
Clinical PhD (Doctor of Philosophy)—Applications 2007–2008, 161. Total applicants accepted 2007–2008, 7. Number full-time enrolled (new admits only) 2007–2008, 4. Total enrolled 2007–2008 full-time, 31. Openings 2008–2009, 6. The median number of years required for completion of a degree in 2006–2007 were 7. The number of students enrolled full- and part-time who were dismissed or voluntarily withdrew from this program area in 2007–2008 were 0. *Developmental PhD (Doctor of Philosophy)*—Applications 2007–2008, 13. Total applicants accepted 2007–2008, 2. Number full-time enrolled (new admits only) 2007–2008, 1. Total enrolled 2007–2008 full-time, 14. Openings 2008–2009, 2. The median number of years required for completion of a degree in 2006–2007 were 6. The number of students enrolled full- and part-time who were dismissed or voluntarily withdrew from this program area in 2007–2008 were 0. *Social, Cultural, and Evolutionary PhD (Doctor of Philosophy)*—Applications 2007–2008, 23. Total applicants accepted 2007–2008, 2. Number full-time enrolled (new admits only) 2007–2008, 1. Total enrolled 2007–2008 full-time, 6. Openings 2008–2009, 2. The median number of years required for completion of a degree in 2006–2007 were 6. The number of students enrolled full- and part-time who were dismissed or voluntarily withdrew from this program area in 2007–2008 were 0.

Admissions Requirements:
Scores: Entries appear in this order: required test or GPA, minimum score (if required), median score of students entering in 2007–2008. Doctoral Programs: GRE-V no minimum stated, 675; GRE-Q no minimum stated, 660; overall undergraduate GPA no minimum stated, 3.80.
Other Criteria: (importance of criteria rated low, medium, or high): GRE/MAT scores—medium, research experience—high, work experience—medium, extracurricular activity—medium, clinically related public service—medium, GPA—medium, letters of recommendation—high, statement of goals and objectives—high.

Student Characteristics: The following represents characteristics of students in 2007–2008 in all graduate psychology programs in the department: Female—full-time 46, part-time 0; Male—full-time 6, part-time 0; African American/Black—full-time 2, part-time 0; Hispanic/Latino(a)—full-time 5, part-time 0; Asian/Pacific Islander—full-time 5, part-time 0; American Indian/Alaska Native—full-time 0, part-time 0; Caucasian/White—full-time 39, part-time 0; Multi-ethnic—full-time 1, part-time 0; students subject to the Americans With Disabilities Act—full-time 0, part-time 0; Unknown ethnicity—full-time 0, part-time 0.

Financial Information/Assistance:
Tuition for Full-Time Study: *Doctoral:* State residents: per academic year $31,200; Nonstate residents: per academic year $31,200.

Financial Assistance:
First-Year Students: Teaching assistantships available for first year. Average amount paid per academic year: $13,600. Average number of hours worked per week: 17. Tuition remission given: full. Research assistantships available for first year. Average amount paid per academic year: $13,600. Average number of hours worked per week: 17. Tuition remission given: full.

Advanced Students: Teaching assistantships available for advanced students. Average amount paid per academic year: $13,600. Average number of hours worked per week: 17. Tuition remission given: full. Research assistantships available for advanced students. Average amount paid per academic year: $13,600. Average number of hours worked per week: 17. Tuition remission given: full.

Additional Information: Of all students currently enrolled full time, 100% benefited from one or more of the listed financial assistance programs. Application and information available online at http://www.clarku.edu/departments/PSYCHOLOGY/grad/gradapp.cfm.

Internships/Practica: Doctoral students in clinical psychology enroll in a supervised practicum each year. These practica involve college students, children, couples, and families. In the 3rd year, practicum sites are individually arranged to provide experience in the student's special area of interest. These sites have included state mental institutions, VA neuropsychological units, residential child treatment facilities, etc. Doctoral clinical students also take one full-time year of internship training in APA-accredited agencies around the country.

Housing and Day Care: On-campus housing is available. See the following Web site for more information: http://www.clarku.edu/offices/housing/index.cfm. No on-campus day care facilities are available.

Employment of Department Graduates:

Master's Degree Graduates: Of those who graduated in the academic year 2006–2007, the following categories and numbers represent the postgraduate activities and employment of master's degree graduates: Enrolled in a psychology doctoral program (6), enrolled in a postdoctoral residency/fellowship (n/a), employed in independent practice (n/a), total from the above (master's) (6). ***Doctoral Degree Graduates:*** Of those who graduated in the academic year 2006–2007, the following categories and numbers represent the postgraduate activities and employment of doctoral degree graduates: Enrolled in a psychology doctoral program (n/a), employed in an academic position at a university (4), employed in an academic position at a 2-year/4-year college (2), employed in a hospital/medical center (5), still seeking employment (1), do not know (0), total from the above (doctoral) (12).

Additional Information:

Orientation, Objectives, and Emphasis of Department: The Department's philosophy affirms the unity of psychology as a subject matter and discourages rigid distinctions among kinds of psychologists and kinds of department programs. Nonetheless, the Department provides in-depth training in the student's area of specialization with a primary concern for theory development, conceptual analysis, and empirical investigation. A diversity of theoretical viewpoints is represented, including various developmental viewpoints. Students become acquainted with a variety of methods of investigation, not only with traditional experimental and naturalistic methods but also with phenomenological, structural, hermeneutic, and other qualitative methodologies. Each student's program is individualized to some degree, and education takes place through small seminars, one-to-one research and practicum training, individualized papers, and MA thesis and PhD dissertation work. Research and other scholarly work are strongly encouraged throughout the graduate experience.

Special Facilities or Resources: The Psychology Department possesses ample space, two entire floors and substantial parts of two others, most of it recently renovated, for offices, classes, laboratories, and clinical training. These include a child study area, facilities for studying family interactions, a human physiology laboratory, a personality–social research area, and dyadic and group clinical training facilities, all with one-way vision and recording facilities, as well as a chemosensory laboratory. The Heinz Werner Institute for Developmental Analysis functions in close connection with the Department. Additional opportunities for research exist in connection with the University of Massachusetts Medical School, the Worcester Foundation for Experimental Biology, schools, and other community settings. Clinical practicum settings include various area agencies.

Application Information:

Send to Graduate Admissions Secretary, Frances L. Hiatt School of Psychology, Clark University, 950 Main Street, Worcester, MA 01610. URL of online application: http://www.clarku.edu/departments/PSYCHOLOGY/grad/gradapp.cfm. Students are admitted in the Fall, application deadline January 5. *Fee:* $50. Fees waived in cases of financial need.

Harvard University

Department of Psychology
33 Kirkland Street
Cambridge, MA 02138
Telephone: (617) 495-3800
E-mail: *smkosslyn@wjh.harvard.edu*
Web: *http://www.wjh.harvard.edu/psych/grad_main.html*

Department Information:

1936. Chairperson: Stephen Kosslyn. Number of faculty: total—full-time 11, part-time 10; women—full-time 8, part-time 5; women minority—full-time 1, part-time 1.

Programs and Degrees Offered:

Listed in the following order: Program area, degree type (T if terminal Master's), number awarded 7/06–6/07. Clinical Psychology PhD (Doctor of Philosophy) 1, Cognition, Brain, and Behavior PhD (Doctor of Philosophy) 5, Developmental PhD (Doctor of Philosophy) 2, Experimental Psychopathology PhD (Doctor of Philosophy) 0, Organizational Behavior PhD (Doctor of Philosophy) 3, Social PhD (Doctor of Philosophy) 4.

Student Applications/Admissions:

Student Applications

Clinical Psychology PhD (Doctor of Philosophy)—Applications 2007–2008, 143. Total applicants accepted 2007–2008, 5. Number full-time enrolled (new admits only) 2007–2008, 4. Number part-time enrolled (new admits only) 2007–2008, 0. Openings 2008–2009, 4. The median number of years required for completion of a degree in 2006–2007 were 6. The number of students enrolled full- and part-time who were dismissed or voluntarily withdrew from this program area in 2007–2008 were 1. *Cognition, Brain, and Behavior PhD (Doctor of Philosophy)*—Applications 2007–2008, 107. Total applicants accepted 2007–2008, 7. Number full-time enrolled (new admits only) 2007–2008, 4. Number part-time enrolled (new admits only) 2007–2008, 0. Openings 2008–2009, 6. The median number of years required for completion of a degree in 2006–2007 were 6. The number of students enrolled full- and part-time who were dismissed or voluntarily withdrew from this program area in 2007–2008 were 1. *Developmental PhD (Doctor of Philosophy)*—Applications 2007–2008, 29. Total applicants accepted 2007–2008, 4. Number full-time enrolled (new admits only) 2007–2008, 2. Number part-time enrolled (new admits only) 2007–2008, 0. Openings 2008–2009, 4. The median number of years required for completion of a degree in 2006–2007 were 5. The number of students enrolled full- and part-time who were dismissed or voluntarily withdrew from this program area in 2007–2008 were 0. *Experimental Psychopathology PhD (Doctor of Philosophy)*—Applications 2007–2008, 143. Total applicants accepted 2007–2008, 0. Number full-time enrolled (new admits only) 2007–2008, 0. The number of students enrolled full- and part-time who were dismissed or voluntarily withdrew from this program area in 2007–2008 were 0. *Organizational Behavior PhD (Doctor of Philosophy)*—Number full-time enrolled (new admits only) 2007–2008, 2. Openings 2008–2009, 2. The median number of years required for completion of a degree in 2006–2007 were 5. The number of students enrolled full- and part-time who were dismissed or voluntarily withdrew from this program area in 2007–2008 were 0. *Social PhD (Doctor of Philosophy)*—Applications 2007–2008, 102. Total applicants accepted 2007–2008, 5. Number full-time enrolled (new admits only) 2007–2008, 1. Number part-time enrolled (new admits only) 2007–2008, 0. Openings 2008–2009, 7. The median number of years required for completion of a degree in 2006–2007 were 6. The number of students enrolled full- and part-time who were dismissed or voluntarily withdrew from this program area in 2007–2008 were 0.

Admissions Requirements:

Scores: Entries appear in this order: required test or GPA, minimum score (if required), median score of students entering in 2007–2008. Master's Programs: We have no terminal master's program. Doctoral Programs: GRE-V no minimum stated; GRE-Q no minimum stated; Doctoral program GRE-Analytic no minimum stated. Median V+Q = 1388. We don't track it separately, nor have we kept records of GPA. TOEFL exam with minimum score of 550 required for foreign applicants.

Other Criteria: (importance of criteria rated low, medium, or high): GRE/MAT scores—high, research experience—high, work experience—high, extracurricular activity—low, clinically related public service—medium, GPA—high, letters of recommendation—high, interview—high, statement of goals and objectives—high, undergraduate major in psychology—medium, specific undergraduate psychology courses taken—medium. For additional information on admission requirements, go to http://www.isites.harvard.edu/icb/icb.do?keyword=k3007&pageid=icb.page19815&pageContentId=icb.pageco.

Student Characteristics: The following represents characteristics of students in 2007–2008 in all graduate psychology programs in the department: Female—full-time 47, part-time 0; Male—full-time 38, part-time 0; African American/Black—full-time 2, part-time 0; Hispanic/Latino(a)—full-time 0, part-time 0; Asian/Pacific Islander—full-time 16, part-time 0; American Indian/Alaska Native—full-time 1, part-time 0; Caucasian/White—full-time 66, part-time 0; Multi-ethnic—full-time 0, part-time 0; students subject to the Americans With Disabilities Act—full-time 1, part-time 0; Unknown ethnicity—full-time 0, part-time 0.

Financial Information/Assistance:

Tuition for Full-Time Study: *Doctoral:* State residents: per academic year $34,264; Nonstate residents: per academic year $34,264. Tuition is subject to change. See the following Web site for updates and changes in tuition costs: http://www.gsas.harvard.edu/prospective_students/financial_aid.php.

Financial Assistance:

First-Year Students: Research assistantships available for first year. Fellowships and scholarships available for first year. Average amount paid per academic year: $23,640. Apply by December 15. Tuition remission given: full.

Advanced Students: Teaching assistantships available for advanced students. Average amount paid per academic year: $19,700. Average number of hours worked per week: 20. Apply by May 1. Research assistantships available for advanced students. Average amount paid per academic year: $19,700. Average number of hours worked per week: 20. Apply by varies. Fellowships and scholarships available for advanced students. Apply by varies.

Additional Information: Of all students currently enrolled full time, 95% benefited from one or more of the listed financial assistance programs. Application and information available online at http://apply.embark.com/grad/harvard/gsas/ for incoming students; dept. for continuing students.

Internships/Practica: Doctoral Degree (PhD Clinical Psychology): For those doctoral students for whom a professional internship was required in this program prior to graduation, (3) students applied for an internship in 2006–2007, with (3) students obtaining an internship. Of those students who obtained an internship, (3) were paid internships. Of those students who obtained an internship, (3) students placed in APA/CPA-accredited internships, (0) students placed in internships not APA/CPA accredited, but listed with the Association of Psychology Postdoctoral and Internship Centers (APPIC), (0) students placed in internships conforming to guidelines of the Council of Directors of School Psychology Programs (CDSPP), (0) students placed in internships that were not APA/CPA-accredited, APPIC or CDSPP listed. Students in the clinical program will have predoctoral practicum placements in a local Harvard-affiliated hospital. Students are required to have defended their thesis prospectus, and are strongly encouraged to collect most of the data prior to departing for internship, but the thesis project need not be completed before beginning the internship. Clinical internship applicants use the APPIC system.

Housing and Day Care: On-campus housing is available. See the following Web site for more information: Housing: http://www.gsas.harvard.edu/prospective_students/housing.php. On-campus day care facilities are available. See the following Web site for more information: http://www.employment.harvard.edu/benefits/pdf/ratecard.pdf.

Employment of Department Graduates:

Master's Degree Graduates: Of those who graduated in the academic year 2006–2007, the following categories and numbers represent the postgraduate activities and employment of master's degree graduates: Enrolled in a postdoctoral residency/fellowship (n/a), employed in independent practice (n/a), total from the above (master's) (0).

Doctoral Degree Graduates: Of those who graduated in the academic year 2006–2007, the following categories and numbers represent the postgraduate activities and employment of doctoral degree graduates: Enrolled in a psychology doctoral program (n/a), enrolled in a postdoctoral residency/fellowship (2), employed in an academic position at a university (6), employed in other positions at a higher education institution (0), employed in business or industry (2), still seeking employment (1), total from the above (doctoral) (11).

Additional Information:

Orientation, Objectives, and Emphasis of Department: The psychology department offers PhDs in psychology and social psychology. In conjunction with the Harvard Business School, there is also a PhD program in organizational behavior. The psychology department is divided into a social psychology program; a cognition, brain, and behavior program; and research and training groups in developmental psychology, experimental psychopathology, and clinical psychology. The aim of the program is to train students for careers in psychological research and teaching. These careers are mainly in academia. The emphasis of the program is heavily on research training; in addition to a small number of required courses, students do a 1st-year research project, a 2nd-year research project, and the doctoral dissertation. Students take a major examination or intense seminar(s) in their major specialty fields. Because most students prepare for academic careers, there is ample opportunity to serve as teaching fellows.

Special Facilities or Resources: The department is well equipped with facilities for conducting research. Faculty are the recipients of many grants in various areas of psychology, and graduate students play an essential role in the conduct of most of this research. William James Hall houses a well-staffed computer lab to serve faculty and students. The building also houses a psychology research library. Students are given offices, the use of laboratory space, and a sum of money for research support. The department encourages interdisciplinary study, and students have the benefit of taking courses and working with the faculty at other Harvard graduate schools (Education, Medical School, Public Health, etc.), and at Massachusetts Institute of Technology. The Cambridge and Boston areas are well endowed with research facilities and hospitals that offer resources, such as MRI equipment, to students.

Information for Students With Physical Disabilities: See the following Web site for more information: http://www.fas.harvard.edu/~aeo/.

Application Information:

Send to Harvard University, Office of Admissions, The Graduate School of Arts and Sciences, P.O. Box 9129, Cambridge, MA 02238-9129. Application available online. URL of online application: http://www.apply.embark.com/grad/harvard/gsas/. Students are admitted in the Fall, application deadline December 15. *Fee:* $90. Requests for waivers should be submitted in writing to the Graduate School of Arts and Sciences Admissions Office.

Lesley University

Division of Counseling and Psychology
29 Everett Street
Cambridge, MA 02138-2790
Telephone: (617) 349-8331
Fax: (617) 349-8333
E-mail: *sgere@mail.lesley.edu*
Web: *http://www.lesley.edu/gsass/30cpp.html*

Department Information:

1975. Division Director: Susan H. Gere, PhD. Number of faculty: total—full-time 8, part-time 35; women—full-time 6, part-time 31; total—minority—full-time 4, part-time 2; women minority—full-time 4, part-time 2.

Programs and Degrees Offered:

Listed in the following order: Program area, degree type (T if terminal Master's), number awarded 7/06–6/07. Clinical Mental Health Counsel MA/MS (Master of Arts/Science) (T) 22, Counseling and Psychology MA/MS (Master of Arts/Science) 10, Counseling Psychology–School MA/MS (Master of Arts/Science) 13, Counseling Psychology–Professional Counseling MA/MS (Master of Arts/Science) (T) 34, Counseling and Psychology Other 1, Advanced Professional Certificate–Other 1, Advanced Professional Certificate–Trauma Studies Respecialization Diploma 3, Clinical Mental Health Counseling–Holistic Studies MA/MS (Master of Arts/Science) (T) 5, Clinical Mental Health Counseling–Trauma Studies MA/MS (Master of Arts/Science) (T) 0, Clinical Mental Health Counseling–School Guidance MA/MS (Master of Arts/Science) (T) 4, Clinical Mental Health Counseling MA/MS (Master of Arts/Science) (T) 6, Advanced Professional Certificate Other 0.

Student Applications/Admissions:

Student Applications

Clinical Mental Health Counsel MA/MS (Master of Arts/Science)—Applications 2007–2008, 8. Total applicants accepted 2007–2008, 7. Number full-time enrolled (new admits only) 2007–2008, 6. Number part-time enrolled (new admits only) 2007–2008, 1. Total enrolled 2007–2008 full-time, 27, part-time, 16. Openings 2008–2009, 25. The median number of years required for completion of a degree in 2006–2007 were 3. The number of students enrolled full- and part-time who were dismissed or voluntarily withdrew from this program area in 2007–2008 were 0. *Counseling and Psychology MA/MS (Master of Arts/Science)*—Applications 2007–2008, 10. Total applicants accepted 2007–2008, 10. Number full-time enrolled (new admits only) 2007–2008, 8. Number part-time enrolled (new admits only) 2007–2008, 2. Total enrolled 2007–2008 full-time, 12, part-time, 7. Openings 2008–2009, 15. The median number of years required for completion of a degree in 2006–2007 were 2. The number of students enrolled full- and part-time who were dismissed or voluntarily withdrew from this program area in 2007–2008 were 0. *Counseling Psychology–School MA/MS (Master of Arts/Science)*—Applications 2007–2008, 3. Total applicants accepted 2007–2008, 3. Number full-time enrolled (new admits only) 2007–2008, 1. Number part-time enrolled (new admits only) 2007–2008, 2. Total enrolled 2007–2008 full-time, 13, part-time, 19. Openings 2008–2009, 15. The median number of years required for completion of a degree in 2006–2007 were 2. The number of students enrolled full- and part-time who were dismissed or voluntarily withdrew from this program area in 2007–2008 were 1. *Counseling Psychology–Professional Counseling MA/MS (Master of Arts/Science)*—Applications 2007–2008, 33. Total applicants accepted 2007–2008, 32. Number full-time enrolled (new admits only) 2007–2008, 5. Number part-time enrolled (new admits only) 2007–2008, 6. Total enrolled 2007–2008 full-time, 24, part-time, 62. Openings 2008–2009, 35. The median number of years required for completion of a degree in 2006–2007 were 3. The number of students enrolled full- and part-time who were dismissed or voluntarily withdrew from this program area in 2007–2008 were 4. *Counseling and Psychology Other*—Applications 2007–2008, 4. Total applicants accepted 2007–2008, 4. Number full-time enrolled (new admits only) 2007–2008, 1. Number part-time enrolled (new admits only) 2007–2008, 3. Total enrolled 2007–2008 full-time, 1, part-time, 5. Openings 2008–2009, 5. The median number of years required for completion of a degree in 2006–2007 were 2. The number of students enrolled full- and part-time who were dismissed or voluntarily withdrew from this program area in 2007–2008 were 0. *Advanced Professional Certificate Other*—Applications 2007–2008, 4. Total applicants accepted 2007–2008, 4. Number part-time enrolled (new admits only) 2007–2008, 4. Total enrolled 2007–2008 part-time, 5. Openings 2008–2009, 4. The median number of years required for completion of a degree in 2006–2007 was 1. The number of students enrolled full- and part-time who were dismissed or voluntarily withdrew from this program area in 2007–2008 were 0. *Advanced Professional Certificate–Trauma Studies Respecialization Diploma*—Applications 2007–2008, 13. Total applicants accepted 2007–2008, 13. Number part-time enrolled (new admits only) 2007–2008, 13. Total enrolled 2007–2008 part-time, 15. Openings 2008–2009, 10. The median number of years required for completion of a degree in 2006–2007 were 2. The number of students enrolled full- and part-time who were dismissed or voluntarily withdrew from this program area in 2007–2008 were 0. *Clinical Mental Health Counseling–Holistic Studies MA/MS (Master of Arts/Science)*—Applications 2007–2008, 19. Total applicants accepted 2007–2008, 18. Number full-time enrolled (new admits only) 2007–2008, 16. Number part-time enrolled (new admits only) 2007–2008, 2. Total enrolled 2007–2008 full-time, 34, part-time, 15. Openings 2008–2009, 20. The median number of years required for completion of a degree in 2006–2007 were 3. The number of students enrolled full- and part-time who were dismissed or voluntarily withdrew from this program area in 2007–2008 were 0. *Clinical Mental Health Counseling–Trauma Studies MA/MS (Master of Arts/Science)*—Applications 2007–2008, 4. Total applicants accepted 2007–2008, 4. Number full-time enrolled (new admits only) 2007–2008, 4. Number part-time enrolled (new admits only) 2007–2008, 0. Total enrolled 2007–2008 full-time, 10, part-time, 2. Openings 2008–2009, 15. The median number of years required for completion of a degree in 2006–2007 were 3. The number of students enrolled full- and part-time who were dismissed or voluntarily withdrew from this program area in 2007–2008 were 0. *Clinical Mental Health Counseling–School Guidance MA/MS (Master of Arts/Science)*—Applications 2007–2008, 11. Total applicants accepted 2007–2008, 10. Number full-time enrolled (new admits only) 2007–2008, 5. Number part-time enrolled (new admits only) 2007–2008, 5. Total enrolled 2007–2008 full-time, 20, part-time, 19. Openings 2008–2009, 15. The median number of years required for completion of a degree in 2006–2007 were 3. The number of students enrolled full- and part-time who were dismissed or voluntarily withdrew from this program area in 2007–2008 were 0. *Clinical Mental Health Counseling MA/MS (Master of Arts/Science)*—Applications 2007–2008, 2. Total applicants accepted 2007–2008, 2. Number full-time enrolled (new admits only) 2007–2008, 1. Number part-time enrolled (new admits only) 2007–2008, 1. Total enrolled 2007–2008 full-time, 5, part-time, 6. Openings 2008–2009, 15. The median number of years required for completion of a degree in 2006–2007 were 3. The number of students enrolled full- and part-time who were dismissed or voluntarily withdrew from this program area in 2007–2008 were 0. *Advanced Professional Certificate Other*—Applications 2007–2008, 3. Total applicants accepted 2007–2008, 3. Number part-time enrolled (new admits only) 2007–2008, 3. Total enrolled 2007–2008 part-time, 2. Openings 2008–2009, 4. The median number of years required for completion of a degree in 2006–2007 was 1. The number of students enrolled full- and part-time who were dismissed or voluntarily withdrew from this program area in 2007–2008 were 1.

Admissions Requirements:

Scores: Entries appear in this order: required test or GPA, minimum score (if required), median score of students entering in 2007–2008. Master's Programs: MAT 400, 417; overall undergraduate GPA 3.0, 3.2.

Other Criteria: (importance of criteria rated low, medium, or high): GRE/MAT scores—medium, research experience—low, work experience—medium, extracurricular activity—medium, clinically related public service—high, GPA—high, letters of recommendation—high, interview—high, statement of goals and objectives—high, undergraduate major in psychology—medium, specific undergraduate psychology courses taken—medium. Admissions review is holistically based. All elements are given full consideration. For additional information on admission requirements, go to http://www.lesley.edu/grad_admiss.html.

Student Characteristics: The following represents characteristics of students in 2007–2008 in all graduate psychology programs in the department: Female—full-time 160, part-time 174; Male—full-time 19, part-time 31; African American/Black—full-time 8, part-time 9; Hispanic/Latino(a)—full-time 3, part-time 5; Asian/Pacific Islander—full-time 3, part-time 1; American Indian/Alaska Native—full-time 3, part-time 1; Caucasian/White—full-time 126, part-time 119; Unknown ethnicity—full-time 2, part-time 3; International students who hold an F-1 or J-1 Visa—full-time 1, part-time 0.

Financial Information/Assistance:

Tuition for Full-Time Study: *Master's:* State residents: $765 per credit hour; Nonstate residents: $765 per credit hour. Tuition is subject to change. Tuition costs vary by program.

Financial Assistance:

First-Year Students: Research assistantships available for first year. Average amount paid per academic year: $3,400. Average number of hours worked per week: 10. Apply by June 23. Fellowships and scholarships available for first year. Average amount paid per academic year: $2,500. Apply by rolling.

Advanced Students: Research assistantships available for advanced students. Average amount paid per academic year: $3,400. Average number of hours worked per week: 10. Apply by June 23.

Additional Information: Of all students currently enrolled full time, 3% benefited from one or more of the listed financial assistance programs.

Internships/Practica: Field-based training is a vital component of the Counseling and Psychology programs. These experiences offer a way for students to verify, clarify, and challenge the theory acquired in the classroom as well as examine their own role as a clinician. The Field Training Office works closely with several hundred placement sites nationwide to ensure students diverse and personalized learning experiences that provide closely supervised opportunities to do counseling and consultative work with individuals, groups, and families. Students choose sites that fit their professional interests and their own schedules and locations. Students are required to complete 100 hours of practicum and 600 hours of internship. Some programs require additional 600 hours of internship. Students receive group supervision in the year-long seminar Clinical Practice and Supervision. Most placements are contracted with schools and agencies on a volunteer basis.

Housing and Day Care: No on-campus housing is available. No on-campus day care facilities are available.

Employment of Department Graduates:

Master's Degree Graduates: Of those who graduated in the academic year 2006–2007, the following categories and numbers represent the postgraduate activities and employment of master's degree graduates: Enrolled in a postdoctoral residency/fellowship (n/a), employed in independent practice (n/a), total from the above (master's) (0).

Doctoral Degree Graduates: Of those who graduated in the academic year 2006–2007, the following categories and numbers represent the postgraduate activities and employment of doctoral degree graduates: Enrolled in a psychology doctoral program (n/a), total from the above (doctoral) (0).

Additional Information:

Orientation, Objectives, and Emphasis of Department: The counseling and psychology degree programs prepare professionals in the fields of counseling and psychology at the Master's and CAGS levels. The Master of Arts in Clinical Mental Health Counseling program is a 60-credit option for those wishing the most comprehensive clinical training available at the master's level to support clinical mental health counseling practice and to pursue professional licensure in most states. Within the clinical mental health counseling program, a student has the option of specializing in holistic studies, nonspecialization, trauma studies, and school and community counseling (licensure options in either school guidance or school adjustment counseling). The Master of Arts in Counseling Psychology degree program is a 48-credit option. Within this program a school counseling specialization leads to guidance counselor licensure. The Master of Arts in Counseling Psychology, Professional Counseling Specialization program is a 60-credit option for those who wish to gain comprehensive clinical training at the master's level to support clinical mental health counseling practice and to pursue professional licensure in most states. All programs integrate theory and practice through course-based learning and field training. The self of the clinician as an instrument of change is a primary focus as is the understanding of the impact of power, privilege, and oppression in all our lives. Graduates are prepared for clinical positions in mental health and school settings. Graduates are prepared for clinical positions, or may elect to use the program to support further graduate work at the doctoral level.

Special Facilities or Resources: Counseling Psychology students have available to them all of the general resource facilities of Lesley University, such as the university library (including a testing center), computer facilities, the Kresge Student Center, and the Career Resource Center. In addition, the department has its own resource center, where bulletins announce area resources and opportunities for further professional study both locally and nationally. Additionally, audio- and videotape equipment is available to degree students for special projects.

Information for Students With Physical Disabilities: See the following Web site for more information: http://www.lesley.edu/services/student_affairs/disabilities.html.

Application Information:

Send to Office of Graduate Admissions, Lesley University, 29 Everett Street, Cambridge, MA 02138-2790. Application available online. URL of online application: http://www.lesley.edu/grad_admiss/printapp.html. Students are admitted in the Fall, application deadline rolling; Spring, application deadline rolling; Programs have rolling admissions. *Fee:* $50.

Massachusetts School of Professional Psychology

Professional School
221 Rivermoor Street
Boston, MA 02132
Telephone: (617) 327-6777
Fax: (617) 327-4447
E-mail: *mario_murga@mspp.edu*
Web: *http://www.mspp.edu*

Department Information:

1974. President: Nicholas A. Covino, PsyD. Number of faculty: total—part-time 22; women—full-time 11, part-time 13; ; women minority—full-time 3.

Programs and Degrees Offered:

Listed in the following order: Program area, degree type (T if terminal Master's), number awarded 7/06–6/07. Psychology PsyD (Doctor of Psychology) 41, Clinical Psychology Respecialization Diploma 2, School Psychology Specialist MA/MS (Master of Arts/Science) 0, Clinical Psychopharmacology Certificate MA/MS (Master of Arts/Science) (T) 14, Counseling Psychology MA/MS (Master of Arts/Science) (T) 0.

APA Accreditation: Clinical PsyD (Doctor of Psychology).

Student Applications/Admissions:

Student Applications

Psychology PsyD (Doctor of Psychology)—Applications 2007–2008, 333. Total applicants accepted 2007–2008, 112. Number full-time enrolled (new admits only) 2007–2008, 50. Number part-time enrolled (new admits only) 2007–2008, 2. Total enrolled 2007–2008 full-time, 200, part-time, 51. Openings 2008–2009, 60. The median number of years required for completion of a degree in 2006–2007 were 5. The number of students enrolled full- and part-time who were dismissed or voluntarily withdrew from this program area in 2007–2008 were 4. *Clinical Psychology Respecialization Diploma*—Applications 2007–2008, 1. Total applicants accepted 2007–2008, 1. Number full-time enrolled (new admits only) 2007–2008, 1. Number part-time enrolled (new admits only) 2007–2008, 0. Openings 2008–2009, 4. The median number of years required for completion of a degree in 2006–2007 were 3. The number of students enrolled full- and part-time who were dismissed or voluntarily withdrew from this program area in 2007–2008 were 0. *School Psychology Specialist Certificate MA/MS (Master of Arts/Science)*—Applications 2007–2008, 36. Total applicants accepted 2007–2008, 24. Number full-time enrolled (new admits only) 2007–2008, 9. Total enrolled 2007–2008 full-time, 21. Openings 2008–2009, 20. The median number of years required for completion of a degree in 2006–2007 were 3. The number of students enrolled full- and part-time who were dismissed or voluntarily withdrew from this program area in 2007–2008 were 0. *Clinical Psychopharmacology MA/MS (Master of Arts/Science)*—Applications 2007–2008, 0. Total applicants accepted 2007–2008, 0. Number full-time enrolled (new admits only) 2007–2008, 0. Number part-time enrolled (new admits only) 2007–2008, 0. Openings 2008–2009, 15. The median number of years required for completion of a degree in 2006–2007 were 2. The number of students enrolled full- and part-time who were dismissed or voluntarily withdrew from this program area in 2007–2008 were 0. *Counseling Psychology MA/MS (Master of Arts/Science)*—Applications 2007–2008, 46. Total applicants accepted 2007–2008, 27. Number full-time enrolled (new admits only) 2007–2008, 15. Number part-time enrolled (new admits only) 2007–2008, 0. Openings 2008–2009, 25. The median number of years required for completion of a degree in 2006–2007 were 2. The number of students enrolled full- and part-time who were dismissed or voluntarily withdrew from this program area in 2007–2008 were 1.

Admissions Requirements:

Scores: Entries appear in this order: required test or GPA, minimum score (if required), median score of students entering in 2007–2008. Master's Programs: GRE-V no minimum stated; GRE-Q no minimum stated; overall undergraduate GPA no minimum stated; psychology GPA no minimum stated; Masters GRE-Analytical no minimum stated. Doctoral Programs: GRE-V no minimum stated, 550; GRE-Q no minimum stated, 600; overall undergraduate GPA 3.00; psychology GPA 3.00.

Other Criteria: (importance of criteria rated low, medium, or high): GRE/MAT scores—medium, research experience—low, work experience—medium, extracurricular activity—high, clinically related public service—high, GPA—high, letters of recommendation—high, interview—high, statement of goals and objectives—high. For additional information on admission requirements, go to http://www.mspp.edu.

Student Characteristics: The following represents characteristics of students in 2007–2008 in all graduate psychology programs in the department: Female—full-time 174, part-time 65; Male—full-time 42, part-time 15; African American/Black—full-time 2, part-time 1; Hispanic/Latino(a)—full-time 10, part-time 1; Asian/Pacific Islander—full-time 7, part-time 1; American Indian/Alaska Native—full-time 0, part-time 0; Caucasian/White—full-time 164, part-time 32; Multi-ethnic—full-time 0, part-time 0; students subject to the Americans With Disabilities Act—full-time 1, part-time 0; Unknown ethnicity—full-time 27, part-time 31; International students who hold an F-1 or J-1 Visa—full-time 10, part-time 3.

Financial Information/Assistance:

Tuition for Full-Time Study: *Master's:* State residents: per academic year $20,616, $859 per credit hour; Nonstate residents: per academic year $20,616, $859 per credit hour. *Doctoral:* State residents: per academic year $20,616, $859 per credit hour; Nonstate residents: per academic year $20,616, $859 per credit hour. Tuition costs vary by program.

Financial Assistance:

First-Year Students: Fellowships and scholarships available for first year. Average amount paid per academic year: $2,000. Apply by February 14.

Advanced Students: Teaching assistantships available for advanced students. Research assistantships available for advanced students. Fellowships and scholarships available for advanced students. Average amount paid per academic year: $2,000. Apply by April 17.

Additional Information: Of all students currently enrolled full time, 43% benefited from one or more of the listed financial assistance programs.

Internships/Practica: Master's Degree (MA/MS Counseling Psychology): An internship experience such as a final research project or "capstone" experience is required of graduates. Doctoral Degree (PsyD Doctor of Psychology): For those doctoral students for whom a professional internship was required in this program prior to graduation, (99) students applied for an internship in 2006–2007, with (99) students obtaining an internship. Of those students who obtained an internship, (38) were paid internships. Of those students who obtained an internship, (4) students placed in APA/CPA-accredited internships, (0) students placed in internships not APA/CPA-accredited, but listed with the Association of Psychology Postdoctoral and Internship Centers (APPIC), (0) students placed in internships conforming to guidelines of the Council of Directors of School Psychology Programs (CDSPP), (95) students placed in internships that were not APA/CPA-accredited, APPIC or CDSPP listed. Field placements are an integral part of the program throughout the 4 years. The practica and internship experiences are integrated with the curriculum and individual's educational needs at each level of the program. Over 200 training sites are available in the greater Boston area including hospitals, mental health centers, court clinics, and other agencies offering mental health services. They provide students the opportunity to work with varied populations, life span issues, theoretical orientations, and treatment modalities in the context of supervised training. The large number of qualified agencies included in our training network enable students the option of applying for full- or half-time APA-approved internships or securing suitable, high-quality, local internships.

Housing and Day Care: No on-campus housing is available. No on-campus day care facilities are available.

Employment of Department Graduates:

Master's Degree Graduates: Of those who graduated in the academic year 2006–2007, the following categories and numbers represent the postgraduate activities and employment of master's degree graduates: Enrolled in a postdoctoral residency/fellowship (n/a), employed in independent practice (n/a), total from the above (master's) (0).

Doctoral Degree Graduates: Of those who graduated in the academic year 2006–2007, the following categories and numbers represent the postgraduate activities and employment of doctoral degree graduates: Enrolled in a psychology doctoral program (n/a), enrolled in a postdoctoral residency/fellowship (41), employed in other positions at a higher education institution (3), employed in a community mental health/counseling center (2), total from the above (doctoral) (46).

Additional Information:

Orientation, Objectives, and Emphasis of Department: The mission is to improve the quality of life by educating psychology practitioners to be capable of providing high-quality human services. Graduates should be able to help evaluate, ameliorate, and prevent psychosocial problems; help individuals, families, groups, organizations, and communities function effectively; exhibit competence in the practical application of existing psychosocial knowledge and an awareness of the possibility of extending this knowledge; and develop new professional roles, service models, and delivery systems capable of meeting the changing needs of society. The educational philosophy is evident in several characteristics that distinguish it from the traditional PhD program. Course content is presented as a foundation for professional practice rather than as scientific inquiry. This entails more of a difference in course objectives and emphasis than in content. Curriculum stresses seminars integrated with field placements, focusing on helping students to coordinate theory with skills and the development of insights useful in the practice of psychology. Courses are taught by psychologists experienced in the application of knowledge in their teaching areas. The first 2 years of the program provide students with a solid generic foundation for psychological practice; 3rd and 4th years allow for concentration in areas of individual interest.

Application Information:

Send to Admissions Office, MSPP 221, Rivermoor Street, Boston, MA 02132. Application available online. URL of online application: http://www.mspp.edu/apply. Students are admitted in the Fall, application deadline January. Respecialization Diploma—rolling admissions; School Psychology—rolling admissions; Counseling Psychology—rolling admissions on space-available basis; Organizational Psychology—rolling admissions; Forensic Psychology—rolling admisssions. *Fee:* $50.

Massachusetts, University of, Amherst

Department of Psychology
Tobin Hall
Amherst, MA 01003
Telephone: (413) 545-2383
Fax: (413) 545-0996
E-mail: *berthier@psych.umass.edu*
Web: *http://www.umass.edu/psychology*

Department Information:

1947. Chairperson: Melinda Novak. Number of faculty: total—full-time 50; women—full-time 22; total—minority—full-time 2, part-time 2; women minority—full-time 1, part-time 1.

Programs and Degrees Offered:

Listed in the following order: Program area, degree type (T if terminal Master's), number awarded 7/06–6/07. Clinical PhD (Doctor of Philosophy) 4, Cognitive PhD (Doctor of Philosophy) 3, Developmental PhD (Doctor of Philosophy) 0, Learning–Animal PhD (Doctor of Philosophy) 0, Neuroscience and Behavior MA/MS (Master of Arts/Science) (T) 0, Personality Social PhD (Doctor of Philosophy) 6, Psychology of Peace and the Prevention of Violence PhD (Doctor of Philosophy) 0.

APA Accreditation: Clinical PhD (Doctor of Philosophy).

Student Applications/Admissions:

Student Applications

Clinical PhD (Doctor of Philosophy)—Applications 2007–2008, 157. Total applicants accepted 2007–2008, 6. Number full-time enrolled (new admits only) 2007–2008, 6. Openings 2008–2009, 6. The median number of years required for completion of a degree in 2006–2007 were 5. *Cognitive PhD (Doctor of Philosophy)*—Applications 2007–2008, 30. Total applicants accepted 2007–2008, 2. Number full-time enrolled (new admits only) 2007–2008, 2. Openings 2008–2009, 3. The median number of years required for completion of a degree in 2006–2007 were 5. *Developmental PhD (Doctor of Philosophy)*—Applications 2007–2008, 31. Total applicants accepted 2007–2008, 2. Number full-time enrolled (new admits only) 2007–2008, 2. Openings 2008–2009, 3. The median number of years required for completion of a degree in 2006–2007 were 5. *Learning–Animal PhD (Doctor of Philosophy)*—Applications 2007–2008, 0. Total applicants accepted 2007–2008, 0. *Neuroscience and Behavior MA/MS (Master of Arts/Science)*—Applications 2007–2008, 0. Total applicants accepted 2007–2008, 0. *Personality Social PhD (Doctor of Philosophy)*—Applications 2007–2008, 68. Total applicants accepted 2007–2008, 0. Number full-time enrolled (new admits only) 2007–2008, 0. Openings 2008–2009, 3. The median number of years required for completion of a degree in 2006–2007 were 5. *Psychology of Peace and the Prevention of Violence PhD (Doctor of Philosophy)*—Applications 2007–2008, 17. Number full-time enrolled (new admits only) 2007–2008, 0. Total enrolled 2007–2008 full-time, 6. Openings 2008–2009, 3.

Admissions Requirements:

Scores: Entries appear in this order: required test or GPA, minimum score (if required), median score of students entering in 2007–2008. Doctoral Programs: GRE-V no minimum stated, 614; GRE-Q no minimum stated, 682; overall undergraduate GPA no minimum stated, 3.54.

Other Criteria: (importance of criteria rated low, medium, or high): GRE/MAT scores—high, research experience—high, work experience—low, GPA—high, letters of recommendation—high, interview—medium, statement of goals and objectives—medium. Only clinical requires an interview. Clinically related public service also is a criteria (low) in admission to clinical.

Student Characteristics: The following represents characteristics of students in 2007–2008 in all graduate psychology programs in the department: Female—full-time 54, part-time 0; Male—full-time 27, part-time 0; African American/Black—full-time 4, part-time 0; Hispanic/Latino(a)—full-time 2, part-time 0; Asian/Pacific Islander—full-time 2, part-time 0; American Indian/

Alaska Native—full-time 0, part-time 0; Caucasian/White—full-time 73, part-time 0; Multi-ethnic—full-time 0, part-time 0; students subject to the Americans With Disabilities Act—full-time 0, part-time 0; Unknown ethnicity—full-time 0, part-time 0.

Financial Information/Assistance:

Tuition for Full-Time Study: *Doctoral:* State residents: $110 per credit hour; Nonstate residents: $415 per credit hour. Tuition is subject to change. See the following Web site for updates and changes in tuition costs: http://www.umass.edu/gradschool/tuitfee/index.html.

Financial Assistance:

First-Year Students: Teaching assistantships available for first year. Average amount paid per academic year: $13,885. Average number of hours worked per week: 20. Tuition remission given: full. Research assistantships available for first year. Average amount paid per academic year: $13,885. Average number of hours worked per week: 20. Tuition remission given: full. Traineeships available for first year. Average amount paid per academic year: $13,885. Average number of hours worked per week: 20. Tuition remission given: full. Fellowships and scholarships available for first year. Average amount paid per academic year: $10,500. Average number of hours worked per week: 0. Tuition remission given: full.

Advanced Students: Teaching assistantships available for advanced students. Average amount paid per academic year: $13,885. Average number of hours worked per week: 20. Tuition remission given: full. Research assistantships available for advanced students. Average amount paid per academic year: $13,885. Average number of hours worked per week: 20. Tuition remission given: full. Traineeships available for advanced students. Average amount paid per academic year: $13,885. Average number of hours worked per week: 20. Tuition remission given: full. Fellowships and scholarships available for advanced students. Average amount paid per academic year: $10,500. Average number of hours worked per week: 0. Tuition remission given: full.

Additional Information: Of all students currently enrolled full time, 100% benefited from one or more of the listed financial assistance programs. Application and information available online at http://www.umass.edu/umfa.

Internships/Practica: Doctoral Degree (PhD Clinical): For those doctoral students for whom a professional internship was required in this program prior to graduation, (5) students applied for an internship in 2006–2007, with (5) students obtaining an internship. Of those students who obtained an internship, (5) were paid internships. Of those students who obtained an internship, (5) students placed in APA/CPA-accredited internships, (0) students placed in internships not APA/CPA-accredited, but listed with the Association of Psychology Postdoctoral and Internship Centers (APPIC), (0) students placed in internships conforming to guidelines of the Council of Directors of School Psychology Programs (CDSPP), (0) students placed in internships that were not APA/CPA-accredited, APPIC or CDSPP listed. Clinical students must complete an APA-approved clinical internship. None of these required internships are offered by our program.

Housing and Day Care: On-campus housing is available. See the following Web site for more information: http://www.umass.edu/grad_catalog/housing.html. On-campus day care facilities are available. See the following Web site for more information: http://www.home.oit.umass.edu/~cshrc/childcare/main.html.

Employment of Department Graduates:

Master's Degree Graduates: Of those who graduated in the academic year 2006–2007, the following categories and numbers represent the postgraduate activities and employment of master's degree graduates: Enrolled in a postdoctoral residency/fellowship (n/a), employed in independent practice (n/a), total from the above (master's) (0).

Doctoral Degree Graduates: Of those who graduated in the academic year 2006–2007, the following categories and numbers represent the postgraduate activities and employment of doctoral degree graduates: Enrolled in a psychology doctoral program (n/a), total from the above (doctoral) (0).

Additional Information:

Orientation, Objectives, and Emphasis of Department: The psychology program is designed to develop research scholars, college teachers, and scientific–professional psychologists in the six areas listed. Individual student programs combine basic courses and seminars in a variety of specialized areas, research experience, and practica in both on- and off-campus settings. Students may elect to minor in certain areas as well, including personality–social, quantitative methods, and applied social research. In addition, the social–personality area has begun a new specialization in the Psychology of Peace and Prevention of Violence. Students with applied interests, such as clinical and developmental, have ample opportunity for in-depth practical experience.

Special Facilities or Resources: The Department has specialized laboratory facilities, including biochemistry, eyetracking, video data analysis, and other laboratories. It maintains its own clinic for research, clinical training, and service to the community. It provides students with access to microcomputers and to the VAX mainframes at University Computing Services. Departmental facilities and faculty are supplemented by the University's participation in Five-College programs (with Amherst, Hampshire, Mount Holyoke, and Smith Colleges) and by cooperation with other University departments including Computer and Information Science, Industrial Engineering, Education, Linguistics, Sociology, and Biology. The University of Massachusetts also offers a separate PhD degree-granting program in neuroscience and behavior. Many of the students in this program receive the bulk of their training in the Psychology Department and work primarily with Psychology faculty. Students interested in training in neuroscience and behavior should apply for admission directly to that program.

Information for Students With Physical Disabilities: See the following Web site for more information: http://www.umass.edu/disability/.

Application Information:

Send to Graduate Admissions Office, Goodell Building, University of Massachusetts, Amherst, MA 01003. Application available online. URL of online application: http://www.umass.edu. Students are admitted in the Fall, application deadline see below. January 2 for Clinical; January 15 for Neuroscience and Behavior; February 1 for all other programs. *Fee:* $45. Application fee can be waived if GRE fees were waived.

Massachusetts, University of, Boston
Counseling and School Psychology
Graduate College of Education
100 Morrissey Boulevard
Boston, MA 02125-3393
Telephone: (617) 287-7631
Fax: (617) 287-7667
E-mail: *gonzalo.bacigalupe@umb.edu*
Web: *http://www.umb.edu/academics/departments/gce/programs/counseling/*

Department Information:

1982. Chairperson: Gonzalo Bacigalupe. Number of faculty: total—full-time 13, part-time 8; women—full-time 10, part-time 6; total—minority—full-time 3, part-time 2; women minority—full-time 1, part-time 1.

Programs and Degrees Offered:

Listed in the following order: Program area, degree type (T if terminal Master's), number awarded 7/06–6/07. School Psychology EdS/MEd (School Psychology) 25, Mental Health Counseling MA/MS (Master of Arts/Science) (T) 45, Rehabilitation Counseling MA/MS (Master of Arts/Science) (T) 7, School Counseling MA/MS (Master of Arts/Science) (T) 16, Family Therapy MA/MS (Master of Arts/Science) (T) 6.

Student Applications/Admissions:

Student Applications

School Psychology EdS/MEd (School Psychology)—Applications 2007–2008, 165. Total applicants accepted 2007–2008, 52. Number full-time enrolled (new admits only) 2007–2008, 17. Number part-time enrolled (new admits only) 2007–2008, 8. Total enrolled 2007–2008 full-time, 60, part-time, 34. Openings 2008–2009, 30. The median number of years required for completion of a degree in 2006–2007 were 3. *Mental Health Counseling MA/MS (Master of Arts/Science)*—Applications 2007–2008, 91. Total applicants accepted 2007–2008, 45. Number full-time enrolled (new admits only) 2007–2008, 13. Number part-time enrolled (new admits only) 2007–2008, 14. Total enrolled 2007–2008 full-time, 42, part-time, 42. Openings 2008–2009, 30. *Rehabilitation Counseling MA/MS (Master of Arts/Science)*—Applications 2007–2008, 12. Total applicants accepted 2007–2008, 10. Number full-time enrolled (new admits only) 2007–2008, 4. Number part-time enrolled (new admits only) 2007–2008, 3. Total enrolled 2007–2008 full-time, 12, part-time, 12. Openings 2008–2009, 15. *School Counseling MA/MS (Master of Arts/Science)*—Applications 2007–2008, 90. Total applicants accepted 2007–2008, 50. Number full-time enrolled (new admits only) 2007–2008, 10. Number part-time enrolled (new admits only) 2007–2008, 10. Total enrolled 2007–2008 full-time, 42, part-time, 42. Openings 2008–2009, 20. *Family Therapy MA/MS (Master of Arts/Science)*—Applications 2007–2008, 52. Total applicants accepted 2007–2008, 19. Number full-time enrolled (new admits only) 2007–2008, 4. Number part-time enrolled (new admits only) 2007–2008, 4. Total enrolled 2007–2008 full-time, 12, part-time, 13. Openings 2008–2009, 15.

Admissions Requirements:

Scores: Entries appear in this order: required test or GPA, minimum score (if required), median score of students entering in 2007–2008. Master's Programs: GRE-V no minimum stated, 500; GRE-Q no minimum stated, 500; MAT no minimum stated, 50th; overall undergraduate GPA no minimum stated, 3.0; last 2 years GPA no minimum stated, 3.0; psychology GPA no minimum stated, 3.0; Masters GRE-Analytical no minimum stated, 500. Either the GRE or the MAT is required for School Psychology, Family Therapy, Mental Health, and Rehabilitation Counseling. The Massachusetts Educator's Test of Literacy may be substituted for the GRE or MAT in School Counseling. The Massachusetts Educator's Test of Literacy is required for full admission to the School Psychology program. Recommended scores on all tests: 50th percentile. Recommended GPAs for all programs: 3.0

Other Criteria: (importance of criteria rated low, medium, or high): GRE/MAT scores—medium, research experience—low, work experience—high, extracurricular activity—high, clinically related public service—high, GPA—medium, letters of recommendation—high, interview—high, statement of goals and objectives—high.

Student Characteristics: The following represents characteristics of students in 2007–2008 in all graduate psychology programs in the department: Female—full-time 171, part-time 88; Male—full-time 29, part-time 23; African American/Black—full-time 14, part-time 10; Hispanic/Latino(a)—full-time 4, part-time 4; Asian/Pacific Islander—full-time 10, part-time 2; American Indian/Alaska Native—full-time 0, part-time 0; Caucasian/White—full-time 157, part-time 89; Multi-ethnic—full-time 0, part-time 0; Unknown ethnicity—full-time 5, part-time 2; International students who hold an F-1 or J-1 Visa—full-time 10, part-time 3.

Financial Information/Assistance:

Tuition for Full-Time Study: *Master's:* State residents: per academic year $11,574; Nonstate residents: per academic year $22,081. Tuition is subject to change. See the following Web site for updates and changes in tuition costs: http://www.umb.edu/administration_finance/bursar/tuition_fees.html.

Financial Assistance:

First-Year Students: Teaching assistantships available for first year. Average amount paid per academic year: $3,500. Average number of hours worked per week: 5. Apply by with acceptance. Tuition remission given: partial. Research assistantships available for first year. Average amount paid per academic year: $3,500. Average number of hours worked per week: 5. Apply by with acceptance. Tuition remission given: partial.

Advanced Students: Teaching assistantships available for advanced students. Average amount paid per academic year: $3,500. Average number of hours worked per week: 5. Apply by with acceptance. Tuition remission given: partial. Research assistantships available for advanced students. Average amount paid per academic year: $3,500. Average number of hours worked per week: 5. Apply by with acceptance. Tuition remission given: partial.

Additional Information: Of all students currently enrolled full time, 10% benefited from one or more of the listed financial assistance programs. Application and information available online at http://www.umb.edu/students/financial_aid/.

Internships/Practica: The department maintains collaborative partnerships with a number of Boston area schools, mental health clinics, rehabilitation centers, and other facilities which provide practicum and internship sites for students. For additional information on education and training outcomes for our programs, see the following Web site: http://www.umb.edu/academics/departments/gce/programs/counseling/Current_St.

Housing and Day Care: No on-campus housing is available. On-campus day care facilities are available.

Employment of Department Graduates:

Master's Degree Graduates: Of those who graduated in the academic year 2006–2007, the following categories and numbers represent the postgraduate activities and employment of master's degree graduates: Enrolled in a postdoctoral residency/fellowship (n/a), employed in independent practice (n/a), total from the above (master's) (0).

Doctoral Degree Graduates: Of those who graduated in the academic year 2006–2007, the following categories and numbers represent the postgraduate activities and employment of doctoral degree graduates: Enrolled in a psychology doctoral program (n/a), total from the above (doctoral) (0).

Additional Information:

Orientation, Objectives, and Emphasis of Department: The Department and our programs are committed to the preparation of highly qualified professionals who will seek to promote maximum growth and development of individuals (children, adolescents, and adults) with whom they work. This is accomplished through a carefully planned curricula that includes the following: interdisciplinary and multidisciplinary approaches; theory linked to practice; a practitioner–scientist approach; self-awareness and self-exploration activities; opportunities to learn and demonstrate respect for others; and socialization into the role of the profession. We value respect for the social foundations and cultural diversity of others and promote opportunities for students to learn how others construct their world. We emphasize to our students to focus on the assets and coping abilities of the people with whom they work rather than focusing on deficits. Additionally, we encourage the promotion of preventative services, which maximize individual functioning. Our programs are grounded in a systematic eclectic philosophical orientation, which includes systemic theory, social constructionism, social learning theory, and person-centered approaches.

Information for Students With Physical Disabilities: See the following Web site for more information: http://www.rosscenter.umb.edu/.

Application Information:

Send to Graduate Admissions, Quinn Adminstration Building, University of Massachusetts Boston, 100 Morrissey Boulevard, Boston, MA 02125. Application available online. URL of online application: http://www.umb.edu/admissions/graduate/apply/index.html. Students are admitted in the Fall, application deadline February 1. *Fee:* $40 application fee for Massachusetts residents, $60 for nonresidents.

Massachusetts, University of, Boston

Department of Psychology
College of Liberal Arts
Harbor Campus
Boston, MA 02125-3393
Telephone: (617) 287-6000
Fax: (617) 287-6336
E-mail: *celia.moore@umb.edu*
Web: *http://www.umb.edu/academics/graduate/clinical_psychology/*

Department Information:

1967. Department Chair: Celia Moore. Number of faculty: total—full-time 19, part-time 19; women—full-time 14, part-time 12; total—minority—full-time 5, part-time 4; women minority—full-time 4, part-time 3.

Programs and Degrees Offered:

Listed in the following order: Program area, degree type (T if terminal Master's), number awarded 7/06–6/07. Clinical PhD (Doctor of Philosophy) 10.

APA Accreditation: Clinical PhD (Doctor of Philosophy).

Student Applications/Admissions:

Student Applications

Clinical PhD (Doctor of Philosophy)—Applications 2007–2008, 256. Total applicants accepted 2007–2008, 12. Number full-time enrolled (new admits only) 2007–2008, 8. Openings 2008–2009, 8. The median number of years required for completion of a degree in 2006–2007 were 7. The number of students enrolled full- and part-time who were dismissed or voluntarily withdrew from this program area in 2007–2008 were 0.

Admissions Requirements:

Scores: Entries appear in this order: required test or GPA, minimum score (if required), median score of students entering in 2007–2008. Doctoral Programs: GRE-V no minimum stated, 640; GRE-Q no minimum stated, 665; GRE-Subject (Psychology) no minimum stated, 660; overall undergraduate GPA no minimum stated, 3.56; last 2 years GPA no minimum stated, 3.65; psychology GPA no minimum stated, 3.68; Doctoral program GRE-Analytic no minimum stated, 5.25.

Other Criteria: (importance of criteria rated low, medium, or high): GRE/MAT scores—medium, research experience—high, work experience—high, extracurricular activity—medium, clinically related public service—high, GPA—high, letters of recommendation—high, interview—high, statement of goals and objectives—high. For additional information on admission requirements, go to http://www.umb.edu/academics/cla/dept/psychology/gradprogram.html.

Student Characteristics: The following represents characteristics of students in 2007–2008 in all graduate psychology programs in the department: Female—full-time 49, part-time 0; Male—full-time 13, part-time 0; African American/Black—full-time 4, part-time 0; Hispanic/Latino(a)—full-time 3, part-time 0; Asian/Pacific Islander—full-time 9, part-time 0; American Indian/Alaska Native—full-time 0, part-time 0; Caucasian/White—

full-time 41, part-time 0; Multi-ethnic—full-time 5, part-time 0; students subject to the Americans With Disabilities Act—full-time 0, part-time 0; Unknown ethnicity—full-time 0, part-time 0.

Financial Information/Assistance:

Tuition for Full-Time Study: *Master's:* State residents: per academic year $0, $0 per credit hour; Nonstate residents: per academic year $0, $0 per credit hour. *Doctoral:* State residents: per academic year $0, $0 per credit hour; Nonstate residents: per academic year $0, $0 per credit hour. Tuition is subject to change.

Financial Assistance:

First-Year Students: Teaching assistantships available for first year. Average amount paid per academic year: $15,600. Average number of hours worked per week: 20. Apply by December 1. Tuition remission given: full. Research assistantships available for first year. Average amount paid per academic year: $15,600. Average number of hours worked per week: 20. Apply by December 1. Tuition remission given: full.

Advanced Students: Teaching assistantships available for advanced students. Average amount paid per academic year: $14,050. Average number of hours worked per week: 20. Tuition remission given: full. Research assistantships available for advanced students. Average amount paid per academic year: $13,600. Average number of hours worked per week: 20. Tuition remission given: full. Traineeships available for advanced students. Average amount paid per academic year: $23,044. Tuition remission given: full. Fellowships and scholarships available for advanced students. Average amount paid per academic year: $21,000. Tuition remission given: full.

Additional Information: Of all students currently enrolled full time, 79% benefited from one or more of the listed financial assistance programs. Application and information available online at http://www.umb.edu/academics/graduate/clinical_psychology/admission.html.

Internships/Practica: Doctoral Degree (PhD clinical): For those doctoral students for whom a professional internship was required in this program prior to graduation, (4) students applied for an internship in 2006–2007, with (3) students obtaining an internship. Of those students who obtained an internship, (3) were paid internships. Of those students who obtained an internship, (3) students placed in APA/CPA-accredited internships, (0) students placed in internships not APA/CPA-accredited, but listed with the Association of Psychology Postdoctoral and Internship Centers (APPIC), (0) students placed in internships conforming to guidelines of the Council of Directors of School Psychology Programs (CDSPP), (0) students placed in internships that were not APA/CPA-accredited, APPIC or CDSPP listed. Students do a 15 hour per week clinical practicum in the University Counseling Center in their 2nd year. They obtain supervised clinical experience doing intake evaluations, short-term dynamic and cognitive behavioral therapy, and some group and couples treatment. Students also do 20 hour per week clinical practica in a training hospital or community health center in their 3rd year. Examples of external practica include Cambridge Hospital, Children's Hospital, McLean Hospital, The Brookline Center, South Cove Health Center, and Chelsea Memorial Health Center. These agencies all serve a significant number of low-income and ethnic minority clients. Students get supervised clinical training in testing and assessment and a range of psychotherapeutic interventions with children, adolescents, and adults at their external practica. Students do a full-time, APA-approved clinical internship in their 5th year.

Housing and Day Care: No on-campus housing is available. No on-campus day care facilities are available.

Employment of Department Graduates:

Master's Degree Graduates: Of those who graduated in the academic year 2006–2007, the following categories and numbers represent the postgraduate activities and employment of master's degree graduates: Enrolled in a postdoctoral residency/fellowship (n/a), employed in independent practice (n/a), total from the above (master's) (0).

Doctoral Degree Graduates: Of those who graduated in the academic year 2006–2007, the following categories and numbers represent the postgraduate activities and employment of doctoral degree graduates: Enrolled in a psychology doctoral program (n/a), enrolled in a postdoctoral residency/fellowship (6), employed in an academic position at a university (1), still seeking employment (1), not seeking employment (1), do not know (1), total from the above (doctoral) (10).

Additional Information:

Orientation, Objectives, and Emphasis of Department: The Clinical Psychology PhD Program follows the scientist–practitioner model of clinical training. It provides a strong theoretical background in psychology and related social science disciplines as well as training in essential clinical skills and in conducting research. Its graduates function as professional psychologists who can translate their basic knowledge into practical applications and who can advance understanding of key problems through research or other scholarly activities. The programs primary goals and objects are to provide students with (a) a strong theoretical and empirical foundation in normal and abnormal development from early childhood through adolescence and adulthood; (b) a strong theoretical and empirical foundation in social and cultural perspectives on development especially as they affect students understanding of ethnic minority and low-income groups; (c) to provide students with solid grounding in the biopsychosocial approach to explaining and treating problems in living, symptomatic behavior, and mental illness, and with learning opportunities that foster interdisciplinary thinking; (d) a broad range of assessment and intervention skills that will help them treat problem behavior, promote healthy adaptation, and prevent individual and social problems from developing; (e) opportunities to develop competence in the basic research methodologies and data analytic techniques of psychology and their application to clinical issues. The program was one of three recipients of the 2001 APA Suinn Minority Achievement Award in recognition or our program's success in recruiting, educating, supporting, retaining, and graduating significant numbers of ethnic minority doctoral students.

Special Facilities or Resources: The Psychology Department's research laboratories support a wide range of research and teaching functions. There are several interaction rooms with one-way mirrors that can be used for clinical, social, and developmental research. These rooms are equipped with state-of-the-art audio and video recording equipment. The animal laboratories are fully equipped to conduct research in animal behavior, learning, and physiology. Other laboratories in the department support ongoing research in cognition, perception, and human electrophysiology.

The department maintains a network of microcomputers that can be used for research, data analysis, and other related functions. For larger projects, the University Computing Center operates a VAX cluster and a CDC Cyber 175 computer (housed at the University of Massachusetts at Amherst). The department's laboratory facilities also include woodworking and electronic shops, which are staffed by full-time experienced technicians. The technical staff provides programming, electronic, and other related support to the faculty and students in the department. Students in the clinical psychology program may also gain experience and have access to the facilities of other research centers and the university, including the Center for Survey Research, the Center for the Study of Social Acceptance, the William Monroe Trotter Institute for the Study of Black Culture, and the William Joiner Center for the Study of War and Social Consequences.

Information for Students With Physical Disabilities: See the following Web site for more information: http://www.rosscenter.umb.edu.

Application Information:

Send to Graduate Admissions, University of Massachusetts at Boston, 100 Morrissey Boulevard, Boston, MA 02125. Application available online. URL of online application: http://www.umb.edu/academics/graduate/clinical_psychology/admission.html. Students are admitted in the Fall, application deadline December 1. *Fee:* $50. Tuition and education operation fees are waived for the first four years for all the students accepted into the program.

Massachusetts, University of, Dartmouth

Psychology Department
College of Arts and Sciences
285 Old Westport Road
North Dartmouth, MA 02747-2300
Telephone: (508) 999-8380
Fax: (508) 999-9169
E-mail: *bhaimson@umassd.edu*
Web: *http://www.umassd.edu/cas/psychology/welcome.cfm*

Department Information:

1962. Chairperson: Barry Haimson. Number of faculty: total—full-time 17, part-time 7; women—full-time 6, part-time 2; faculty subject to the Americans With Disabilities Act 1.

Programs and Degrees Offered:

Listed in the following order: Program area, degree type (T if terminal Master's), number awarded 7/06–6/07. Clinical MA/MS (Master of Arts/Science) (T) 12, General/Research MA/MS (Master of Arts/Science) (T) 2.

Student Applications/Admissions:

Student Applications

Clinical MA/MS (Master of Arts/Science)—Applications 2007–2008, 70. Total applicants accepted 2007–2008, 21. Number full-time enrolled (new admits only) 2007–2008, 14. Total enrolled 2007–2008 full-time, 37. Openings 2008–2009, 12. The median number of years required for completion of a degree in 2006–2007 were 3. The number of students enrolled full- and part-time who were dismissed or voluntarily withdrew from this program area in 2007–2008 were 1. *General/Research MA/MS (Master of Arts/Science)*—Applications 2007–2008, 9. Total applicants accepted 2007–2008, 4. Number full-time enrolled (new admits only) 2007–2008, 4. Number part-time enrolled (new admits only) 2007–2008, 0. Openings 2008–2009, 5. The median number of years required for completion of a degree in 2006–2007 were 2. The number of students enrolled full- and part-time who were dismissed or voluntarily withdrew from this program area in 2007–2008 were 1.

Admissions Requirements:

Scores: Entries appear in this order: required test or GPA, minimum score (if required), median score of students entering in 2007–2008. Master's Programs: overall undergraduate GPA no minimum stated; last 2 years GPA no minimum stated; psychology GPA no minimum stated. Minimums are applied differently across options. Clinical Program does not require GRE. General Program requires GRE V, Q, and A. Subject also required if degree is in Psychology.

Other Criteria: (importance of criteria rated low, medium, or high): GRE/MAT scores—medium, research experience—high, work experience—high, clinically related public service—high, GPA—medium, letters of recommendation—high, interview—high, statement of goals and objectives—high. These criteria vary across options. The General Experimental program does not require work experience or clinical services.

Student Characteristics: The following represents characteristics of students in 2007–2008 in all graduate psychology programs in the department: Female—full-time 34, part-time 0; Male—full-time 11, part-time 0; African American/Black—full-time 1, part-time 0; Hispanic/Latino(a)—full-time 1, part-time 0; Asian/Pacific Islander—full-time 1, part-time 0; American Indian/Alaska Native—full-time 0, part-time 0; Caucasian/White—full-time 42, part-time 0; Multi-ethnic—part-time 0; students subject to the Americans With Disabilities Act—full-time 0, part-time 0; Unknown ethnicity—full-time 0, part-time 0.

Financial Information/Assistance:

Tuition for Full-Time Study: *Master's:* State residents: per academic year $1,553; Nonstate residents: per academic year $6,074. See the following Web site for updates and changes in tuition costs: http://www.umassd.edu/graduate/tuition/9credit.cfm.

Financial Assistance:

First-Year Students: Teaching assistantships available for first year. Average amount paid per academic year: $3,500. Average number of hours worked per week: 10. Tuition remission given: full. Research assistantships available for first year. Average amount paid per academic year: $7,000. Average number of hours worked per week: 20. Tuition remission given: full.

Advanced Students: Teaching assistantships available for advanced students. Average amount paid per academic year: $3,500. Average number of hours worked per week: 10. Tuition remission given: full. Research assistantships available for advanced students. Average amount paid per academic year: $7,000. Average number of hours worked per week: 20. Tuition remission given: full.

Additional Information: Of all students currently enrolled full time, 50% benefited from one or more of the listed financial assistance programs.

Internships/Practica: We have a wide variety of internship and practica experiences available for clinical students. Field experiences are tailored to specific student needs.

Housing and Day Care: No on-campus housing is available. On-campus day care facilities are available. See the following Web site for more information: http://www.umassd.edu/studentaffairs/student_services/children_resource.html.

Employment of Department Graduates:

Master's Degree Graduates: Of those who graduated in the academic year 2006–2007, the following categories and numbers represent the postgraduate activities and employment of master's degree graduates: Enrolled in a psychology doctoral program (1), enrolled in a postdoctoral residency/fellowship (n/a), employed in independent practice (n/a), employed in a community mental health/counseling center (11), total from the above (master's) (12).

Doctoral Degree Graduates: Of those who graduated in the academic year 2006–2007, the following categories and numbers represent the postgraduate activities and employment of doctoral degree graduates: Enrolled in a psychology doctoral program (n/a), total from the above (doctoral) (0).

Additional Information:

Orientation, Objectives, and Emphasis of Department: The general psychology option of the MA program in psychology is designed to prepare students for doctoral work in psychology and related fields, including cognitive science. The program combines coursework in basic areas of psychology with the opportunity to do collaborative research with faculty members. Students have considerable flexibility to tailor their programs to their individual needs. The outstanding feature of this program is the opportunity for close interaction between faculty and students, both in the classroom and in the laboratory, because of the low student–faculty ratio. The objectives of the Clinical–Behavioral Analysis option are to provide students with specific and applied research and problem-solving skills; to provide all clinical students with a broad exposure to a variety of therapy modalities; to provide students with extensive experiential learning opportunities, practica, internships and intensive supervision; and to prepare students for licensure as Certified Mental Health Counselors.

Personal Behavior Statement: All students in the Clinical program are required to read and approve a code of ethical behavior.

Application Information:

Send to Please send applications to Office of Graduate Studies. Application available online. URL of online application: http://www.umassd.edu/graduate/prospects/waystoapply.cfm. Students are admitted in the Fall, application deadline March 31 for Clinical only. Programs have rolling admissions. *Fee:* $55, $35 if resident of Massachusetts.

Massachusetts, University of, Lowell

Community Social Psychology Master's Program
Arts and Sciences
870 Broadway Street, Suite 1
Lowell, MA 01854-3043
Telephone: (978) 934-3950
Fax: (978) 934-3074
E-mail: *csp@uml.edu*
Web: *http://www.uml.edu/csp*

Department Information:

1980. Graduate Program Cordinator: Nina Coppens. Number of faculty: total—full-time 18; women—full-time 13; total—minority—full-time 3; women minority—full-time 2.

Programs and Degrees Offered:

Listed in the following order: Program area, degree type (T if terminal Master's), number awarded 7/06–6/07. Community Social Psychology MA/MS (Master of Arts/Science) (T) 9.

Student Applications/Admissions:

Student Applications

Community Social Psychology MA/MS (Master of Arts/Science)—Applications 2007–2008, 35. Total applicants accepted 2007–2008, 32. Number full-time enrolled (new admits only) 2007–2008, 12. Number part-time enrolled (new admits only) 2007–2008, 10. Total enrolled 2007–2008 full-time, 24, part-time, 21. Openings 2008–2009, 25. The median number of years required for completion of a degree in 2006–2007 were 2. The number of students enrolled full- and part-time who were dismissed or voluntarily withdrew from this program area in 2007–2008 were 0.

Admissions Requirements:

Scores: Entries appear in this order: required test or GPA, minimum score (if required), median score of students entering in 2007–2008. Master's Programs: GRE-V no minimum stated, 440; GRE-Q no minimum stated, 520; MAT no minimum stated, 38.3; overall undergraduate GPA 3.0, 3.32. Either the GRE V+Q or the MAT is required.

Other Criteria: (importance of criteria rated low, medium, or high): GRE/MAT scores—medium, research experience—medium, work experience—high, extracurricular activity—low, clinically related public service—medium, GPA—high, letters of recommendation—high, interview—low, statement of goals and objectives—high. For additional information on admission requirements, go to hhttp://www.uml.edu/college/arts_sciences/psychology/Prospective_Students/procedures.html.

Student Characteristics: The following represents characteristics of students in 2007–2008 in all graduate psychology programs in the department: Female—full-time 20, part-time 18; Male—full-time 4, part-time 3; African American/Black—full-time 1, part-time 2; Hispanic/Latino(a)—full-time 2, part-time 2; Asian/Pacific Islander—full-time 3, part-time 2; American Indian/Alaska Native—full-time 0, part-time 0; Caucasian/White—full-time 18, part-time 15; Multi-ethnic—full-time 0, part-time 0; students subject to the Americans With Disabilities Act—full-time 1, part-time 1; Unknown ethnicity—full-time 0, part-time 0.

Financial Information/Assistance:

Tuition for Full-Time Study: *Master's:* State residents: per academic year $8,240, $473 per credit hour; Nonstate residents: per academic year $16,462, $930 per credit hour. See the following Web site for updates and changes in tuition costs: http://www.uml.edu/grad/Financial_Information.html#Tuition%20and%20Fees.

Financial Assistance:

First-Year Students: Teaching assistantships available for first year. Average amount paid per academic year: $6,439. Average number of hours worked per week: 9. Apply by May 1. Tuition remission given: full.

Advanced Students: Teaching assistantships available for advanced students. Average amount paid per academic year: $6,439. Average number of hours worked per week: 9. Apply by May 1. Tuition remission given: full.

Additional Information: Of all students currently enrolled full time, 45% benefited from one or more of the listed financial assistance programs. Application and information available online at http://www.uml.edu/college/arts_sciences/psychology/Graduate/Forms_Manuals.html.

Internships/Practica: Master's Degree (MA/MS Community Social Psychology): An internship experience such as a final research project or "capstone" experience is required of graduates. There is a 1-year practicum requirement of 10 to 12 hours a week. Settings vary but much of the field work takes place directly in Lowell, MA, perhaps the most culturally diverse mid-size city in the United States, located just 25 miles from Boston.

Housing and Day Care: On-campus housing is available. See the following Web site for more information: http://www.uml.edu/student-services/. On-campus day care facilities are available.

Employment of Department Graduates:

Master's Degree Graduates: Of those who graduated in the academic year 2006–2007, the following categories and numbers represent the postgraduate activities and employment of master's degree graduates: Enrolled in a psychology doctoral program (2), enrolled in another graduate/professional program (1), enrolled in a postdoctoral residency/fellowship (n/a), employed in independent practice (n/a), employed in an academic position at a university (0), employed in an academic position at a 2-year/4-year college (0), employed in other positions at a higher education institution (0), employed in a professional position in a school system (1), employed in business or industry (0), employed in government agency (0), employed in a community mental health/counseling center (0), employed in a hospital/medical center (0), still seeking employment (1), other employment position (2), do not know (1), total from the above (master's) (8).

Doctoral Degree Graduates: Of those who graduated in the academic year 2006–2007, the following categories and numbers represent the postgraduate activities and employment of doctoral degree graduates: Enrolled in a psychology doctoral program (n/a), total from the above (doctoral) (0).

Additional Information:

Orientation, Objectives, and Emphasis of Department: The Community Social Psychology faculty and students share a commitment to social justice and the empowerment of all citizens. To those ends, our program is designed to help students understand the complex relationships between individual, family, and community well-being and the broader environment in which we live and work. Our mission is to provide students with the analytic, creative, organizational, and evaluative skills needed to design, implement, and assess programs that will facilitate positive changes within and across communities—changes that will empower all people to reach their full potential and empower social organizations, public and private, to be more responsive to human needs. CSP is a 36-credit master's degree program, providing opportunities for in-class learning experiences, field study, independent study, and interdisciplinary collaboration. Students admitted to our program will work with recognized faculty and talented students from diverse backgrounds. Our graduates are prepared for leadership positions in government, health and human services, and community and educational organizations in a variety of professional roles and capacities. Many also proceed on toward doctoral degrees.

Special Facilities or Resources: Special facilities and resources consist of a graduate student lounge/computer lab; grant-related technical services from the Office of Research Administration; numerous research centers such as the Center for Family, Work, and Community and the Center for Women and Work; and a unique multiethnic urban setting in a mid-sized city accessible to Boston.

Information for Students With Physical Disabilities: See the following Web site for more information: http://www.uml.edu/student-services/disability/default.html.

Application Information:

Send to Graduate School Admissions, 1 University Avenue, Lowell, MA 01854. Application available online. URL of online application: http://www.uml.edu/grad/req_app.htm. Students are admitted in the Fall. Programs have rolling admissions. We accept and act on applications year round. Most of our students start our program in the Fall semester. For students planning full-time study who wish to apply for TA support, that deadline is May 1 for Fall enrollment. Fee: $20 for Massachusettes residents, $35 all others.

Northeastern University

Department of Counseling and Applied Educational Psychology
Bouve College of Health Sciences
203 Lake Hall
Boston, MA 02115
Telephone: (617) 373-2485
Fax: (617) 373-8892
E-mail: *di.sheehan@neu.edu*
Web: *http://www.northeastern.edu/bouve/programs/graduate.html*

Department Information:

1983. Chair: William Sanchez, PhD. Number of faculty: total—full-time 19, part-time 16; women—full-time 13, part-time 14; total—minority—full-time 6, part-time 4; women minority—full-time 5, part-time 2.

Programs and Degrees Offered:

Listed in the following order: Program area, degree type (T if terminal Master's), number awarded 7/06–6/07. Combined PhD

(Doctor of Philosophy) 5, College Student Development MA/MS (Master of Arts/Science) (T) 26, Counseling Psychology MA/MS (Master of Arts/Science) (T) 28, Applied Behavioral Analysis MA/MS (Master of Arts/Science) (T) 13, School Psychology Certificate MA/MS (Master of Arts/Science) 30, School Counseling MA/MS (Master of Arts/Science) (T) 12, Early Intervention Other 4.

APA Accreditation: Combination PhD (Doctor of Philosophy).

Student Applications/Admissions:

Student Applications

Combined PhD (Doctor of Philosophy)—Applications 2007–2008, 93. Total applicants accepted 2007–2008, 10. Number full-time enrolled (new admits only) 2007–2008, 5. Number part-time enrolled (new admits only) 2007–2008, 0. Openings 2008–2009, 6. The median number of years required for completion of a degree in 2006–2007 were 6. The number of students enrolled full- and part-time who were dismissed or voluntarily withdrew from this program area in 2007–2008 were 2. *College Student Development MA/MS (Master of Arts/Science)*—Applications 2007–2008, 60. Total applicants accepted 2007–2008, 28. Number full-time enrolled (new admits only) 2007–2008, 16. Number part-time enrolled (new admits only) 2007–2008, 5. Total enrolled 2007–2008 full-time, 34, part-time, 10. Openings 2008–2009, 16. The median number of years required for completion of a degree in 2006–2007 were 2. The number of students enrolled full- and part-time who were dismissed or voluntarily withdrew from this program area in 2007–2008 were 0. *Counseling Psychology MA/MS (Master of Arts/Science)*—Applications 2007–2008, 60. Total applicants accepted 2007–2008, 28. Number full-time enrolled (new admits only) 2007–2008, 14. Number part-time enrolled (new admits only) 2007–2008, 0. Total enrolled 2007–2008 full-time, 38, part-time, 4. Openings 2008–2009, 28. The median number of years required for completion of a degree in 2006–2007 were 2. The number of students enrolled full- and part-time who were dismissed or voluntarily withdrew from this program area in 2007–2008 were 1. *Applied Behavioral Analysis MA/MS (Master of Arts/Science)*—Applications 2007–2008, 56. Total applicants accepted 2007–2008, 22. Number full-time enrolled (new admits only) 2007–2008, 0. Number part-time enrolled (new admits only) 2007–2008, 26. Total enrolled 2007–2008 full-time, 16, part-time, 44. Openings 2008–2009, 12. The median number of years required for completion of a degree in 2006–2007 were 2. The number of students enrolled full- and part-time who were dismissed or voluntarily withdrew from this program area in 2007–2008 were 0. *School Psychology Certificate MA/MS (Master of Arts/Science)*—Applications 2007–2008, 180. Total applicants accepted 2007–2008, 65. Number full-time enrolled (new admits only) 2007–2008, 24. Number part-time enrolled (new admits only) 2007–2008, 0. Total enrolled 2007–2008 full-time, 55, part-time, 2. Openings 2008–2009, 24. The median number of years required for completion of a degree in 2006–2007 were 3. The number of students enrolled full- and part-time who were dismissed or voluntarily withdrew from this program area in 2007–2008 were 0. *School Counseling MA/MS (Master of Arts/Science)*—Applications 2007–2008, 45. Total applicants accepted 2007–2008, 20. Number full-time enrolled (new admits only) 2007–2008, 14. Number part-time enrolled (new admits only) 2007–2008, 2. Total enrolled 2007–2008 full-time, 28, part-time, 6. Openings 2008–2009, 16. The median number of years required for completion of a degree in 2006–2007 were 2. The number of students enrolled full- and part-time who were dismissed or voluntarily withdrew from this program area in 2007–2008 were 0. *Early Intervention Other*—Applications 2007–2008, 20. Total applicants accepted 2007–2008, 10. Number full-time enrolled (new admits only) 2007–2008, 6. Number part-time enrolled (new admits only) 2007–2008, 2. Total enrolled 2007–2008 full-time, 7, part-time, 4. Openings 2008–2009, 6. The median number of years required for completion of a degree in 2006–2007 were 2. The number of students enrolled full- and part-time who were dismissed or voluntarily withdrew from this program area in 2007–2008 were 0.

Admissions Requirements:

Scores: Entries appear in this order: required test or GPA, minimum score (if required), median score of students entering in 2007–2008. Master's Programs: GRE-V 400, 470; GRE-Q 400, 540; overall undergraduate GPA 3.0, 3.28; psychology GPA no minimum stated. Programs scores are competitive. Department prefers 500 minimum in GRE Q and V. TOEFL scores for international applicants who do not hold undergraduate or graduate degrees from U.S. institutions, and whose native language is not English. Doctoral Programs: GRE-V 500, 560; GRE-Q 500, 560; overall undergraduate GPA 3.00, 3.47.

Other Criteria: (importance of criteria rated low, medium, or high): GRE/MAT scores—medium, research experience—medium, work experience—high, extracurricular activity—medium, clinically related public service—high, GPA—medium, letters of recommendation—high, interview—high, statement of goals and objectives—high.

Student Characteristics: The following represents characteristics of students in 2007–2008 in all graduate psychology programs in the department: Female—full-time 215, part-time 69; Male—full-time 15, part-time 6; African American/Black—full-time 8, part-time 1; Hispanic/Latino(a)—full-time 4, part-time 2; Asian/Pacific Islander—full-time 5, part-time 2; American Indian/Alaska Native—full-time 0, part-time 0; Caucasian/White—full-time 209, part-time 63; students subject to the Americans With Disabilities Act—part-time 1; Unknown ethnicity—full-time 0, part-time 0; International students who hold an F-1 or J-1 Visa—full-time 2, part-time 0.

Financial Information/Assistance:

Tuition for Full-Time Study: *Master's:* State residents: $980 per credit hour; Nonstate residents: $980 per credit hour. *Doctoral:* State residents: $980 per credit hour; Nonstate residents: $980 per credit hour. Tuition is subject to change.

Financial Assistance:

First-Year Students: No information provided.

Advanced Students: Teaching assistantships available for advanced students. Average amount paid per academic year: $14,125. Average number of hours worked per week: 20. Tuition remission given: full and partial. Fellowships and scholarships available for advanced students. Average number of hours worked per week: 0. Tuition remission given: partial.

Additional Information: Of all students currently enrolled full time, 10% benefited from one or more of the listed financial assistance programs.

Internships/Practica: Doctoral Degree (PhD combined): For those doctoral students for whom a professional internship was required in this program prior to graduation, (6) students applied for an internship in 2006–2007, with (5) students obtaining an internship. Of those students who obtained an internship, (5) were paid internships. Of those students who obtained an internship, (5) students placed in APA/CPA-accredited internships, (0) students placed in internships not APA/CPA-accredited, but listed with the Association of Psychology Postdoctoral and Internship Centers (APPIC), (0) students placed in internships conforming to guidelines of the Council of Directors of School Psychology Programs (CDSPP), (0) students placed in internships that were not APA/CPA-accredited, APPIC or CDSPP listed. Internship and field placement sites are varied depending on the program and specialization. Sites are in the Boston metropolitan area and include some of the most desirable and prestigious settings in the field.

Housing and Day Care: No on-campus housing is available. On-campus day care facilities are available. Child care services are available to campus personnel.

Employment of Department Graduates:

Master's Degree Graduates: Of those who graduated in the academic year 2006–2007, the following categories and numbers represent the postgraduate activities and employment of master's degree graduates: Enrolled in a postdoctoral residency/fellowship (n/a), employed in independent practice (n/a), total from the above (master's) (0).

Doctoral Degree Graduates: Of those who graduated in the academic year 2006–2007, the following categories and numbers represent the postgraduate activities and employment of doctoral degree graduates: Enrolled in a psychology doctoral program (n/a), total from the above (doctoral) (0).

Additional Information:

Orientation, Objectives, and Emphasis of Department: Philosophically, the combined school and counseling doctoral program is based on an ecological model. This model focuses on the contexts in which people and their environments intersect, including individuals' families, groups, cultures, and social, political, and economic institutions. Thus, the ecological model includes individual and interpersonal relationships along with their interactive physical and sociocultural environments. It employs a general systems perspective to understand the mutually reciprocal interactions of all of these elements. Central to this theoretical stance are assumptions of interdependence, circular and multilevel influence and causality, and interactive identities. Issues of gender, status, and culture are given special emphasis as well as the developmental stages of the individual, family, or group. The ecological model is large enough and sufficiently comprehensive to allow for teaching and using other models such as psychodynamic, behaviorist, and humanistic, as they help to explain behavior and phenomena in individuals, families, and groups. This allows faculty and students to teach, understand, and use many explanations of human activities. This ecological orientation provides the lenses through which students study psychological and counseling theory and research. In their varied fieldwork settings, students have the opportunity to translate this orientation into practice.

Special Facilities or Resources: Northeastern University, one of the largest private universities in the country, is located in Boston, a center of academic excellence and psychological research. There are numerous opportunities for diverse experiences, such as placements specializing in neuropsychology, early intervention, and sexual abuse. The campus is in the Back Bay, an area with a large student population and rich cultural opportunities. The Snell Library, one of the most advanced college libraries in the Boston area, provides access for students not only to its large psychology and education collections but also to media and microcomputer centers and an extensive global academic computer networking system. Northeastern students also have privileges at the other Boston area research libraries.

Information for Students With Physical Disabilities: See the following Web site for more information: http://www.access-disability-deaf.neu.edu/.

Application Information:

Send to Graduate Dean, Bouve College of Health Sciences, 123 Beharakis Health Science Building, Boston, MA 02115. Application available online. URL of online application: http://www.app.applyyourself.com/?=neu-grad. Students are admitted in the Fall, application deadline. Deadlines: combined School and Counseling Psychology PhD, December 15 for admission following Fall; MS Counseling Psychology, December 1 for admission following Fall; MS/CAGS School Psychology, suggested January 15 for admission following Fall. All other program have a suggested May 1 deadline. *Fee:* $50.

Northeastern University

Department of Psychology
Arts and Sciences
125 Nightingale Hall
Boston, MA 02115
Telephone: (617) 373-3076
Fax: (617) 373-8714
E-mail: *eskew@neu.edu*
Web: *http://www.psych.neu.edu*

Department Information:

1966. Chairperson: Rhea T. Eskew. Number of faculty: total—full-time 7, part-time 3; women—full-time 5; ; women minority—full-time 1.

Programs and Degrees Offered:

Listed in the following order: Program area, degree type (T if terminal Master's), number awarded 7/06–6/07. Language and Cognition PhD (Doctor of Philosophy) 0, Behavioral Neuroscience PhD (Doctor of Philosophy) 1, Social–Personality PhD (Doctor of Philosophy) 3, Perception PhD (Doctor of Philosophy) 0.

Student Applications/Admissions:

Student Applications

Language and Cognition PhD (Doctor of Philosophy)—Applications 2007–2008, 19. Total applicants accepted 2007–2008, 2. Number full-time enrolled (new admits only) 2007–2008, 2. Openings 2008–2009, 2. The median number of years required for completion of a degree in 2006–2007 were 5. The number of students enrolled full- and part-time who were dismissed or voluntarily withdrew from this program area in

2007–2008 were 1. *Behavioral Neuroscience PhD (Doctor of Philosophy)*—Applications 2007–2008, 38. Total applicants accepted 2007–2008, 1. Number full-time enrolled (new admits only) 2007–2008, 1. Openings 2008–2009, 2. The median number of years required for completion of a degree in 2006–2007 were 5. The number of students enrolled full- and part-time who were dismissed or voluntarily withdrew from this program area in 2007–2008 were 0. *Social–Personality PhD (Doctor of Philosophy)*—Applications 2007–2008, 63. Total applicants accepted 2007–2008, 1. Number full-time enrolled (new admits only) 2007–2008, 1. Openings 2008–2009, 3. The median number of years required for completion of a degree in 2006–2007 were 5. *Perception PhD (Doctor of Philosophy)*—Applications 2007–2008, 9. Total applicants accepted 2007–2008, 1. Number full-time enrolled (new admits only) 2007–2008, 0. Openings 2008–2009, 2. The median number of years required for completion of a degree in 2006–2007 were 5.

Admissions Requirements:

Scores: Entries appear in this order: required test or GPA, minimum score (if required), median score of students entering in 2007–2008. Master's Programs: GRE-V+Q is recommended strongly. Doctoral Programs: GRE-V no minimum stated, 580; GRE-Q no minimum stated, 660.

Other Criteria: (importance of criteria rated low, medium, or high): GRE/MAT scores—high, research experience—high, work experience—low, extracurricular activity—low, clinically related public service—low, GPA—high, letters of recommendation—high, interview—high, statement of goals and objectives—high.

Student Characteristics: The following represents characteristics of students in 2007–2008 in all graduate psychology programs in the department: Female—full-time 18, part-time 0; Male—full-time 7, part-time 0; African American/Black—full-time 1, part-time 0; Hispanic/Latino(a)—full-time 1, part-time 0; Asian/Pacific Islander—full-time 2, part-time 0; American Indian/Alaska Native—part-time 0; Caucasian/White—full-time 21, part-time 0; students subject to the Americans With Disabilities Act—full-time 0, part-time 0; Unknown ethnicity—full-time 0, part-time 0.

Financial Information/Assistance:

Tuition for Full-Time Study: *Doctoral:* State residents: $980 per credit hour; Nonstate residents: $980 per credit hour.

Financial Assistance:

First-Year Students: Teaching assistantships available for first year. Average amount paid per academic year: $22,920. Average number of hours worked per week: 20. Apply by January 15. Tuition remission given: full. Research assistantships available for first year. Average amount paid per academic year: $22,920. Average number of hours worked per week: 20. Apply by January 15. Tuition remission given: full.

Advanced Students: Teaching assistantships available for advanced students. Average amount paid per academic year: $22,920. Average number of hours worked per week: 20. Apply by January 15. Tuition remission given: full. Research assistantships available for advanced students. Average amount paid per academic year: $22,920. Average number of hours worked per week: 20. Apply by January 15. Tuition remission given: full.

Additional Information: Of all students currently enrolled full time, 100% benefited from one or more of the listed financial assistance programs. Application and information available online at http://marcom2.neu.edu/cas/graduate//admissions.html.

Internships/Practica: No information provided.

Housing and Day Care: No on-campus housing is available. On-campus day care facilities are available.

Employment of Department Graduates:

Master's Degree Graduates: Of those who graduated in the academic year 2006–2007, the following categories and numbers represent the postgraduate activities and employment of master's degree graduates: Enrolled in a postdoctoral residency/fellowship (n/a), employed in independent practice (n/a), total from the above (master's) (0).

Doctoral Degree Graduates: Of those who graduated in the academic year 2006–2007, the following categories and numbers represent the postgraduate activities and employment of doctoral degree graduates: Enrolled in a psychology doctoral program (n/a), enrolled in a postdoctoral residency/fellowship (3), employed in an academic position at a university (1), employed in other positions at a higher education institution (1), employed in business or industry (1), total from the above (doctoral) (6).

Additional Information:

Orientation, Objectives, and Emphasis of Department: The PhD program aims to train students to undertake basic research in the following areas: behavioral neuroscience; perception; language and cognition; and experimental, social, and personality. Students may expect to collaborate with faculty in conducting research in these areas using technically sophisticated research laboratories. The doctoral program also provides opportunities to gain teaching experience. It does not, however, provide clinical training.

Special Facilities or Resources: The department has a wide range of research laboratories containing state-of-the-art facilities in the following areas: behavioral neuroscience; perception; language and cognition; and experimental, social, and personality. These facilities include a large number of computers used for subject testing, data acquisition and analysis, graphics, and word processing. The facilities also house numerous special-purpose systems (e.g., eye trackers, histology facilities, multiple electrode EEG, fMRI, and speech-processing systems). In addition, laboratory resources outside the department are available to students through the collaborative network the department maintains with other institutions in the Boston/Cambridge area.

Application Information:

Send to Department of Psychology, 125 NI, Northeastern University, Boston, MA 02115. Students are admitted in the Fall, application deadline January 15. *Fee:* $50.

Springfield College (2007 data)
Department of Psychology
School of Arts and Sciences and Professional Studies
263 Alden Street
Springfield, MA 01109
Telephone: (413) 748-3322
Fax: (413) 748-3854
E-mail: *Amoriart@Spfldcol.edu*
Web: *http://www.spfldcol.edu*

Department Information:

1946. Chairperson: Ann Moriarty. Number of faculty: total—full-time 14, part-time 18; women—full-time 8, part-time 11.

Programs and Degrees Offered:

Listed in the following order: Program area, degree type (T if terminal Master's), number awarded 7/06–6/07. Athletic Counseling MA/MS (Master of Arts/Science) (T) 12, Industrial/Organizational MA/MS (Master of Arts/Science) (T) 18, Marriage and Family Therapy EdS/MEd (School Psychology) 11, Mental Health Counseling MA/MS (Master of Arts/Science) (T) 11, School Guidance Counseling Other 18, Students and Personnel Administration EdS/MEd (School Psychology) 17.

Student Applications/Admissions:

Student Applications

Athletic Counseling MA/MS (Master of Arts/Science)—Applications 2007–2008, 50. Total applicants accepted 2007–2008, 20. Number full-time enrolled (new admits only) 2007–2008, 12. Total enrolled 2007–2008 full-time, 25. Openings 2008–2009, 12. The median number of years required for completion of a degree in 2006–2007 were 2. The number of students enrolled full- and part-time who were dismissed or voluntarily withdrew from this program area in 2007–2008 were 1. *Industrial/Organizational MA/MS (Master of Arts/Science)*—Applications 2007–2008, 40. Total applicants accepted 2007–2008, 28. Number full-time enrolled (new admits only) 2007–2008, 16. Number part-time enrolled (new admits only) 2007–2008, 5. Total enrolled 2007–2008 full-time, 35, part-time, 5. Openings 2008–2009, 17. The median number of years required for completion of a degree in 2006–2007 were 2. The number of students enrolled full- and part-time who were dismissed or voluntarily withdrew from this program area in 2007–2008 were 1. *Marriage and Family Therapy EdS/MEd (School Psychology)*—Applications 2007–2008, 30. Total applicants accepted 2007–2008, 26. Number full-time enrolled (new admits only) 2007–2008, 14. Number part-time enrolled (new admits only) 2007–2008, 2. Total enrolled 2007–2008 full-time, 30, part-time, 2. Openings 2008–2009, 15. The median number of years required for completion of a degree in 2006–2007 were 2. The number of students enrolled full- and part-time who were dismissed or voluntarily withdrew from this program area in 2007–2008 were 1. *Mental Health Counseling MA/MS (Master of Arts/Science)*—Applications 2007–2008, 88. Total applicants accepted 2007–2008, 32. Number full-time enrolled (new admits only) 2007–2008, 32. Number part-time enrolled (new admits only) 2007–2008, 3. Total enrolled 2007–2008 full-time, 73, part-time, 2. Openings 2008–2009, 15. The median number of years required for completion of a degree in 2006–2007 were 2. The number of students enrolled full- and part-time who were dismissed or voluntarily withdrew from this program area in 2007–2008 were 0. *School Guidance Counseling Other*—Applications 2007–2008, 24. Total applicants accepted 2007–2008, 20. Number full-time enrolled (new admits only) 2007–2008, 8. Number part-time enrolled (new admits only) 2007–2008, 2. Total enrolled 2007–2008 full-time, 20, part-time, 16. Openings 2008–2009, 11. The median number of years required for completion of a degree in 2006–2007 were 2. The number of students enrolled full- and part-time who were dismissed or voluntarily withdrew from this program area in 2007–2008 were 2. *Students and Personnel Administration EdS/MEd (School Psychology)*—Applications 2007–2008, 47. Total applicants accepted 2007–2008, 40. Number full-time enrolled (new admits only) 2007–2008, 19. Number part-time enrolled (new admits only) 2007–2008, 4. Total enrolled 2007–2008 full-time, 34, part-time, 10. Openings 2008–2009, 12. The median number of years required for completion of a degree in 2006–2007 were 2.

Admissions Requirements:

Scores: Entries appear in this order: required test or GPA, minimum score (if required), median score of students entering in 2007–2008. Master's Programs: overall undergraduate GPA 2.6, 3.3; last 2 years GPA no minimum stated; psychology GPA no minimum stated. Different GPAs are required for different programs.

Other Criteria: (importance of criteria rated low, medium, or high): research experience—low, work experience—medium, extracurricular activity—medium, clinically related public service—high, GPA—medium, letters of recommendation—high, interview—medium, statement of goals and objectives—high. These criteria vary for different program areas.

Student Characteristics: The following represents characteristics of students in 2007–2008 in all graduate psychology programs in the department: Female—full-time 137, part-time 25; Male—full-time 80, part-time 10; African American/Black—full-time 14, part-time 7; Hispanic/Latino(a)—full-time 10, part-time 0; Asian/Pacific Islander—full-time 7, part-time 0; American Indian/Alaska Native—full-time 0, part-time 0; Caucasian/White—full-time 151, part-time 20; Multi-ethnic—full-time 35, part-time 8; students subject to the Americans With Disabilities Act—full-time 0, part-time 0; Unknown ethnicity—full-time 0, part-time 0.

Financial Information/Assistance:

Financial Assistance:

First-Year Students: Teaching assistantships available for first year. Apply by As needed. Tuition remission given: full and partial. Research assistantships available for first year. Apply by as needed. Fellowships and scholarships available for first year. Average amount paid per academic year: $2,000. Apply by March 1. Tuition remission given: full and partial.

Advanced Students: Teaching assistantships available for advanced students. Apply by As needed. Tuition remission given: full and partial. Research assistantships available for advanced students. Apply by as needed. Fellowships and scholarships available for advanced students. Average amount paid per academic year: $2,000. Apply by March 1. Tuition remission given: full and partial.

Additional Information: Of all students currently enrolled full time, 30% benefited from one or more of the listed financial assistance programs.

Internships/Practica: Numerous internships, paid and unpaid, exist for students in their field of study. Established affiliation agreements are in place with regional corporate, clinical, and counseling settings. A Cooperative Education Program provides students with opportunities for credited, paid internships.

Housing and Day Care: On-campus housing is available. Springfield College Student Affairs, 263 Alden Street, Sprigfield, MA 01109. On-campus day care facilities are available.

Employment of Department Graduates:

Master's Degree Graduates: Of those who graduated in the academic year 2006–2007, the following categories and numbers represent the postgraduate activities and employment of master's degree graduates: Enrolled in a postdoctoral residency/fellowship (n/a), employed in independent practice (n/a), total from the above (master's) (0).

Doctoral Degree Graduates: Of those who graduated in the academic year 2006–2007, the following categories and numbers represent the postgraduate activities and employment of doctoral degree graduates: Enrolled in a psychology doctoral program (n/a), total from the above (doctoral) (0).

Additional Information:

Orientation, Objectives, and Emphasis of Department: Understanding of personal values, attitudes, and needs is a primary characteristic of effective facilitators. The psychology and counseling programs, therefore, design many of the experiences to help students increase their awareness of self and the ways in which personal behavior affects others. Although mastery of content areas is expected, continual reference to personal relevance of that content is encouraged. Frequent opportunities are afforded for students to understand themselves better through participation in group and individual experiences. As a reflection of the value placed upon individual program development, the comprehensive examination requirement is not the traditional written and oral exercise. Some of the Psychology and Counseling programs use the portfolio system, which is an ongoing, active evaluation process. A more traditional thesis or research project is also offered and supported when chosen, and individual attention is readily available for both options.

Special Facilities or Resources: The department offers fully equipped counseling and research laboratories and audiovisual facility. Access to computers and excellent physiological and fitness laboratories are available. The Department also sponsors the Center for Performance Enhancement and Applied Research (CPEAR), which serves as a clearinghouse for information about grants and research opportunities.

Information for Students With Physical Disabilities: See the following Web site for more information: http://www.spfldcol.edu.

Application Information:

Send to Graduate Admissions, 263 Alden Street, Springfield, MA 01109. Application available online. URL of online application: http://www.spfldcol.edu. Students are admitted in the Fall, application deadline rolling; Winter, application deadline rolling; Spring, application deadline rolling; Summer, application deadline rolling; Programs have rolling admissions. *Fee:* $50.

Suffolk University

Department of Psychology
College of Arts and Sciences
41 Temple Street
Boston, MA 02114
Telephone: (617) 573-8293
Fax: (617) 367-2924
E-mail: *kbursik@suffolk.edu*
Web: *http://www.suffolk.edu/psychology*

Department Information:

1968. Chairperson: Krisanne Bursik. Number of faculty: total—full-time 16, part-time 12; women—full-time 10, part-time 5; total—minority—full-time 3; women minority—full-time 3; faculty subject to the Americans With Disabilities Act 1.

Programs and Degrees Offered:

Listed in the following order: Program area, degree type (T if terminal Master's), number awarded 7/06–6/07. Clinical Psychology PhD (Doctor of Philosophy) 4, Clinical Psychology Respecialization Respecialization Diploma 1.

APA Accreditation: Clinical PhD (Doctor of Philosophy).

Student Applications/Admissions:

Student Applications

Clinical Psychology PhD (Doctor of Philosophy)—Applications 2007–2008, 313. Total applicants accepted 2007–2008, 13. Number full-time enrolled (new admits only) 2007–2008, 12. Number part-time enrolled (new admits only) 2007–2008, 0. Total enrolled 2007–2008 full-time, 76, part-time, 6. Openings 2008–2009, 12. The median number of years required for completion of a degree in 2006–2007 were 6. The number of students enrolled full- and part-time who were dismissed or voluntarily withdrew from this program area in 2007–2008 were 1. *Clinical Psychology Respecialization Respecialization Diploma*—Applications 2007–2008, 1. Total applicants accepted 2007–2008, 1. Number full-time enrolled (new admits only) 2007–2008, 1. Number part-time enrolled (new admits only) 2007–2008, 0. Total enrolled 2007–2008 full-time, 1, part-time, 1. Openings 2008–2009, 1. The number of students enrolled full- and part-time who were dismissed or voluntarily withdrew from this program area in 2007–2008 were 0.

Admissions Requirements:

Scores: Entries appear in this order: required test or GPA, minimum score (if required), median score of students entering in 2007–2008. Doctoral Programs: GRE-V no minimum stated, 582; GRE-Q no minimum stated, 665; overall undergraduate GPA no minimum stated, 3.56; Doctoral program GRE-Analytic no minimum stated, 5.1.

Other Criteria: (importance of criteria rated low, medium, or high): GRE/MAT scores—medium, research experience—high, work experience—medium, extracurricular activity—low, clinically related public service—medium, GPA—high, letters of recommendation—high, interview—high, statement of goals and objectives—high, interest/program match—high, undergraduate major in psychology—medium, specific undergraduate psychology courses taken—medium. For additional information on admission requirements, go to http://www.suffolk.edu/psychology.

Student Characteristics: The following represents characteristics of students in 2007–2008 in all graduate psychology programs in the department: Female—full-time 66, part-time 6; Male—full-time 11, part-time 1; African American/Black—full-time 2, part-time 1; Hispanic/Latino(a)—full-time 1, part-time 0; Asian/Pacific Islander—full-time 5, part-time 0; American Indian/Alaska Native—full-time 0, part-time 0; Caucasian/White—full-time 60, part-time 5; Multi-ethnic—full-time 0, part-time 1; students subject to the Americans With Disabilities Act—full-time 0, part-time 0; Unknown ethnicity—full-time 9, part-time 0; International students who hold an F-1 or J-1 Visa—full-time 0, part-time 0.

Financial Information/Assistance:

Tuition for Full-Time Study: *Doctoral:* State residents: per academic year $26,400, $1,100 per credit hour; Nonstate residents: per academic year $26,400, $1,100 per credit hour. Tuition is subject to change. See the following Web site for updates and changes in tuition costs: http://www.suffolk.edu/admission/5199.html.

Financial Assistance:

First-Year Students: Fellowships and scholarships available for first year. Average amount paid per academic year: $13,200. Average number of hours worked per week: 7. Tuition remission given: partial.

Advanced Students: Teaching assistantships available for advanced students. Average number of hours worked per week: 7. Apply by April 1. Research assistantships available for advanced students. Average amount paid per academic year: $3,500. Average number of hours worked per week: 7. Apply by April 1. Fellowships and scholarships available for advanced students. Average amount paid per academic year: $13,200. Average number of hours worked per week: 7. Apply by April 1. Tuition remission given: partial.

Additional Information: Of all students currently enrolled full time, 100% benefited from one or more of the listed financial assistance programs. Application and information available online at https://www.applyweb.com/apply/suffcas.

Internships/Practica: Doctoral Degree (PhD Clinical Psychology): For those doctoral students for whom a professional internship was required in this program prior to graduation, (13) students applied for an internship in 2006–2007, with (12) students obtaining an internship. Of those students who obtained an internship, (12) were paid internships. Of those students who obtained an internship, (12) students placed in APA/CPA-accredited internships, (0) students placed in internships not APA/CPA accredited, but listed with the Association of Psychology Postdoctoral and Internship Centers (APPIC), (0) students placed in internships conforming to guidelines of the Council of Directors of School Psychology Programs (CDSPP), (0) students placed in internships that were not APA/CPA-accredited, APPIC or CDSPP listed. Suffolk University's clinical psychology doctoral program is committed to providing the highest quality program experiences available. Practicum sites have been chosen that provide students with supervision by appropriate professionals as well as offer training that is holistic and integrated in nature. Each practicum is designed to be consistent with the goal of the doctoral program, in the context of direct client service, consultation, and applied research. Internship/Practica: Two years of practicum experience are required of our doctoral students beginning in their 2nd academic year. A 3rd year is optional, but strongly recommended. Students receive weekly supervision by professionals at their practicum sites and attend a weekly practicum seminar at Suffolk University where they are able to integrate their practical experiences and educational training within the program. Students receive a total of 4 hours a week, on average, of individual and group supervision during each of their 3 years of practicum training. For additional information on education and training outcomes for our programs, see the following Web site: http://www.suffolk.edu/college/12140.html.

Housing and Day Care: No on-campus housing is available. No on-campus day care facilities are available.

Employment of Department Graduates:

Master's Degree Graduates: Of those who graduated in the academic year 2006–2007, the following categories and numbers represent the postgraduate activities and employment of master's degree graduates: Enrolled in a psychology doctoral program (15), enrolled in a postdoctoral residency/fellowship (n/a), employed in independent practice (n/a), do not know (2), total from the above (master's) (17).

Doctoral Degree Graduates: Of those who graduated in the academic year 2006–2007, the following categories and numbers represent the postgraduate activities and employment of doctoral degree graduates: Enrolled in a psychology doctoral program (n/a), enrolled in a postdoctoral residency/fellowship (5), employed in a community mental health/counseling center (1), not seeking employment (0), do not know (1), total from the above (doctoral) (7).

Additional Information:

Orientation, Objectives, and Emphasis of Department: Suffolk University's PhD program in Clinical Psychology is based on a balance and integration of the scientist and practitioner components of clinical training. The general orientation provides an understanding of the processes underlying adaptation and maladaptation across the life span and within a cultural frame. This approach also addresses methods for the prevention and intervention of pathology. Implications of this framework include the recognition that (a) knowledge of a breadth of psychological subdisciplines such as neuropsychology, developmental psychology, and cultural psychology is required to effectively work within the clinical developmental model; (b) professional psychologists can complement the roles of natural contexts such as families, relationships, schools, and workplaces in fostering development; and (c) psychological pain and conflict can be understood as indicative of a continuum of ongoing life span transformational processes, which include what is typically labeled normal development as well as the development or manifestation of psychopathology. Thus, the program emphasizes that clinical problems are best understood in the context of knowledge about normal and optimal development over the life span. The program strives to develop student competencies necessary for successfully working in a range of clinical, educational, research, organizational, and public policy settings. Throughout content and applied areas of training, the program encourages awareness of and respect for diversity of culture, language, national origin, race, gender, age, disability, religious beliefs, sexual orientation, lifestyle, and other individual differences. The program combines a strong theoretical and research background (in both quantitative and qualitative methodologies) with preparation to deliver high-quality psychological services to children, adolescents, and adults.

Special Facilities or Resources: The department has a variety of laboratory spaces available for general use by faculty and doctoral students. Special equipment includes one-way mirrors and video cameras. A great deal of research occurs off-site in the clinical, medical, and scholastic institutions of the Boston area. There is a computer lab for graduate student use within the department in addition to larger computer labs throughout the university. All computers provide access to SPSS, the Internet, and major academic search systems. Graduate students receive interlibrary loan and online document delivery privileges, and have access to most of the academic libraries in the Boston area.

Information for Students With Physical Disabilities: See the following Web site for more information: http://www.suffolk.edu/campuslife/3924.html.

Application Information:

Send to Office of Graduate Admissions, 8 Ashburton Place, Boston, MA 02108. Application available online. URL of online application: https://www.applyweb.com/apply/suffcas. Students are admitted in the Fall, application deadline December 1. Same deadline for all. *Fee:* $50.

Tufts University

Department of Education; School Psychology Program
Graduate School of Arts and Sciences
Paige Hall
Medford, MA 02155
Telephone: (617) 627-2393
Fax: (617) 627-3901
E-mail: *caroline.wandle@tufts.edu*
Web: *http://www.tufts.edu/as/ed*

Department Information:

1910. Program Director School Psychology: Caroline Wandle. Number of faculty: total—full-time 14, part-time 13; women—full-time 11, part-time 9; women minority—full-time 5.

Programs and Degrees Offered:

Listed in the following order: Program area, degree type (T if terminal Master's), number awarded 7/06–6/07. School MA/MS (Master of Arts/Science) 14.

Student Applications/Admissions:

Student Applications

School MA/MS (Master of Arts/Science)—Applications 2007–2008, 100. Total applicants accepted 2007–2008, 30. Number full-time enrolled (new admits only) 2007–2008, 18. Number part-time enrolled (new admits only) 2007–2008, 0. Openings 2008–2009, 18. The median number of years required for completion of a degree in 2006–2007 were 3. The number of students enrolled full- and part-time who were dismissed or voluntarily withdrew from this program area in 2007–2008 were 1.

Admissions Requirements:

Scores: Entries appear in this order: required test or GPA, minimum score (if required), median score of students entering in 2007–2008. Master's Programs: GRE-V no minimum stated, 550; GRE-Q no minimum stated, 600; overall undergraduate GPA 3.0, 3.6; last 2 years GPA no minimum stated. GRE writing score may be substituted for GRE analytic. Last 2 years GPA may be considered with more weight is some cases.

Other Criteria: (importance of criteria rated low, medium, or high): GRE/MAT scores—medium, research experience—medium, work experience—high, extracurricular activity—medium, clinically related public service—high, GPA—high, letters of recommendation—high, interview—high, statement of goals and objectives—high, multicultural interest—high, undergraduate major in psychology—low, specific undergraduate psychology courses taken—high.

Student Characteristics: The following represents characteristics of students in 2007–2008 in all graduate psychology programs in the department: Female—full-time 43, part-time 0; Male—full-time 7, part-time 0; African American/Black—full-time 2, part-time 0; Hispanic/Latino(a)—full-time 3, part-time 0; Asian/Pacific Islander—full-time 4, part-time 0; American Indian/Alaska Native—full-time 0, part-time 0; Caucasian/White—full-time 40, part-time 0; Multi-ethnic—full-time 1, part-time 0; students subject to the Americans With Disabilities Act—full-time 1, part-time 0; Unknown ethnicity—full-time 0, part-time 0; International students who hold an F-1 or J-1 Visa—full-time 0, part-time 0.

Financial Information/Assistance:

Tuition for Full-Time Study: *Master's:* State residents: per academic year $32,050; Nonstate residents: per academic year $32,050. Tuition is subject to change.

Financial Assistance:

First-Year Students: Teaching assistantships available for first year. Average amount paid per academic year: $1,300. Average number of hours worked per week: 4. Apply by September 1. Research assistantships available for first year. Average amount paid per academic year: $1,300. Average number of hours worked per week: 4. Apply by September 1. Fellowships and scholarships available for first year. Average amount paid per academic year: $10,000. Apply by February 1. Tuition remission given: partial.

Advanced Students: Teaching assistantships available for advanced students. Average amount paid per academic year: $1,300. Average number of hours worked per week: 4. Apply by September 1. Research assistantships available for advanced students. Average amount paid per academic year: $1,300. Average number of hours worked per week: 4. Apply by September 1. Fellowships and scholarships available for advanced students. Average amount paid per academic year: $10,000. Apply by February 1. Tuition remission given: partial.

Additional Information: Of all students currently enrolled full time, 90% benefited from one or more of the listed financial assistance programs. Application and information available online at http://www.ase.tufts.edu.

Internships/Practica: Students complete a school-based prepracticum experience of 150 hours during their first year and a school-based practicum of 600 hours during their 2nd year. Students complete a 1,200-hour internship during their 3rd year.

This may be completed through 600 hours in a school setting and 600 hours in a clinical setting, or all 1,200 hours in a school setting.

Housing and Day Care: On-campus housing is available. See the following Web site for more information: http://www.ase.tufts.edu. On-campus day care facilities are available.

Employment of Department Graduates:

Master's Degree Graduates: Of those who graduated in the academic year 2006–2007, the following categories and numbers represent the postgraduate activities and employment of master's degree graduates: Enrolled in a psychology doctoral program (0), enrolled in another graduate/professional program (0), enrolled in a postdoctoral residency/fellowship (n/a), employed in independent practice (n/a), employed in an academic position at a university (0), employed in an academic position at a 2-year/4-year college (0), employed in other positions at a higher education institution (0), employed in a professional position in a school system (15), employed in business or industry (0), employed in government agency (0), employed in a community mental health/counseling center (0), employed in a hospital/medical center (0), still seeking employment (0), other employment position (0), total from the above (master's) (15).

Doctoral Degree Graduates: Of those who graduated in the academic year 2006–2007, the following categories and numbers represent the postgraduate activities and employment of doctoral degree graduates: Enrolled in a psychology doctoral program (n/a), total from the above (doctoral) (0).

Additional Information:

Orientation, Objectives, and Emphasis of Department: Students are exposed to a broad spectrum of assessment and intervention techniques from various theoretical perspectives including psychodynamic, humanistic, cognitive–behavioral, and family systems. Assessment and intervention strategies are anchored in a developmental and sociocultural perspective that stresses the social, intellectual, and emotional growth of the individual from childhood through the early adult years. The school psychology program is approved by the Massachusetts Department of Education. Graduates who complete program requirements will be eligible for state licensure as a school psychologist. The program also is approved by the National Association of School Psychologists. The program is committed to preparing culturally competent school psychologists.

Special Facilities or Resources: Several courses of interest are offered through the Eliot-Pearson Department of Child Development. Tufts students may also cross-register for courses at several other Boston universities at no additional charge through a consortium arrangement.

Information for Students With Physical Disabilities: See the following Web site for more information: http://www.ase.tufts.edu.

Application Information:

Send to Office of Graduate and Professional Studies, Tufts University, Ballou Hall, Medford, MA 02155. Application available online. URL of online application: http://www.ase.tufts.edu. Students are admitted in the Fall, application deadline February 1. *Fee:* $50.

Tufts University

Department of Psychology
Psychology Building, 490 Boston Avenue
Medford, MA 02155
Telephone: (617) 627-3523
Fax: (617) 627-3181
E-mail: *lidia.bonaventura@tufts.edu*
Web: *http://www.ase.tufts.edu/psychology/*

Department Information:

Chairperson: Robert Cook. Number of faculty: total—full-time 9, part-time 10; women—full-time 10; women minority—full-time 2.

Programs and Degrees Offered:

Listed in the following order: Program area, degree type (T if terminal Master's), number awarded 7/06–6/07. General Experimental PhD (Doctor of Philosophy) 1.

Student Applications/Admissions:

Student Applications

General Experimental PhD (Doctor of Philosophy)—Applications 2007–2008, 121. Total applicants accepted 2007–2008, 15. Number full-time enrolled (new admits only) 2007–2008, 6. Total enrolled 2007–2008 full-time, 40. Openings 2008–2009, 8. The median number of years required for completion of a degree in 2006–2007 were 5. The number of students enrolled full- and part-time who were dismissed or voluntarily withdrew from this program area in 2007–2008 were 0.

Admissions Requirements:

Scores: Entries appear in this order: required test or GPA, minimum score (if required), median score of students entering in 2007–2008. Master's Programs: GRE-V no minimum stated; GRE-Q no minimum stated; MAT no minimum stated; overall undergraduate GPA no minimum stated; psychology GPA no minimum stated; GRE-Analytical no minimum stated. GRE-Subject is not required, but it is strongly recommended. Doctoral Programs: GRE-V no minimum stated; GRE-Q no minimum stated; overall undergraduate GPA no minimum stated; psychology GPA no minimum stated; GRE-Analytic no minimum stated. GRE-Subject is not required but is strongly recommended.

Other Criteria: (importance of criteria rated low, medium, or high): GRE/MAT scores—medium, research experience—high, work experience—medium, extracurricular activity—low, GPA—medium, letters of recommendation—high, interview—medium, statement of goals and objectives—high, research fit—high, undergraduate major in psychology—medium, specific undergraduate psychology courses taken—medium.

Student Characteristics: The following represents characteristics of students in 2007–2008 in all graduate psychology programs in the department: Female—full-time 25, part-time 0; Male—full-time 12, part-time 0; African American/Black—full-time 2, part-time 0; Hispanic/Latino(a)—full-time 0, part-time 0; Asian/Pacific Islander—full-time 3, part-time 0; American Indian/Alaska Native—full-time 0, part-time 0; Caucasian/White—full-time 31, part-time 0; Multi-ethnic—full-time 1, part-time 0;

students subject to the Americans With Disabilities Act—full-time 0, part-time 0; Unknown ethnicity—full-time 0, part-time 0; International students who hold an F-1 or J-1 Visa—full-time 4, part-time 0.

Financial Information/Assistance:

Tuition for Full-Time Study: *Doctoral:* State residents: per academic year $35,052; Nonstate residents: per academic year $35,052. See the following Web site for additional fees, updates, and changes in tuition costs: http://gradstudy.tufts.edu/.

Financial Assistance:

First-Year Students: Teaching assistantships available for first year. Average amount paid per academic year: $19,281. Average number of hours worked per week: 20. Tuition remission given: full. Research assistantships available for first year. Average amount paid per academic year: $19,281. Average number of hours worked per week: 20. Tuition remission given: full.

Advanced Students: Teaching assistantships available for advanced students. Average amount paid per academic year: $19,905. Average number of hours worked per week: 20. Tuition remission given: full. Research assistantships available for advanced students. Average amount paid per academic year: $19,905. Average number of hours worked per week: 20. Tuition remission given: full.

Additional Information: Of all students currently enrolled full time, 100% benefited from one or more of the listed financial assistance programs.

Internships/Practica: No information provided.

Housing and Day Care: No on-campus housing is available. On-campus day care facilities are available. See the following Web site for more information: http://www.ase.tufts.edu/tedcc/.

Employment of Department Graduates:

Master's Degree Graduates: Of those who graduated in the academic year 2006–2007, the following categories and numbers represent the postgraduate activities and employment of master's degree graduates: Enrolled in a postdoctoral residency/fellowship (n/a), employed in independent practice (n/a), total from the above (master's) (0).

Doctoral Degree Graduates: Of those who graduated in the academic year 2006–2007, the following categories and numbers represent the postgraduate activities and employment of doctoral degree graduates: Enrolled in a psychology doctoral program (n/a), total from the above (doctoral) (0).

Additional Information:

Orientation, Objectives, and Emphasis of Department: The Department of Psychology offers a graduate program in experimental psychology, with specializations in cognition, neuroscience, psychopathology, and developmental, and social psychology. The program is designed to produce broadly trained graduates who are prepared for careers in teaching, research, or applied psychology. The department does not offer clinical training. Accepted applicants generally possess a substantial college background in psychology, including familiarity with fundamental statistical concepts and research design. The university is a PhD track program, although completion of an MS is required as an integral part of the program. Students who already possess a master's degree may be admitted to the PhD program if a sufficient number of credits are acceptable for transfer and a thesis has been done. Areas of faculty research include infant perception, memory processes, animal cognition and learning, neural and hormonal control of animal sexual behavior, psychopharmacology, event-related brain potentials, neuropsychology of language processes, nutrition and behavior, experimental psychopathology, emotion, human factors, decision making, spatial cognition, psychology and law, and the social psychology of prejudicial attitudes. All graduate students participate in supervised research and/or teaching activities each semester. The department provides laboratory space and equipment for many kinds of research, and facilities are available for the behavioral and physiological study of humans and experimental animals.

Special Facilities or Resources: Department has relatively new research facilities for both human and animal research in areas of cognition, biopsychology, neuroscience, developmental, and social psychology.

Application Information:

Send to Graduate School, Tufts University, Ballou Hall, Medford, MA 02155. Application available online. URL of online application: http://www.ase.tufts.edu/gradstudy/admissions.htm. Students are admitted in the Fall, application deadline January 15. *Fee:* $50.

Tufts University (2007 data)

Eliot-Pearson Department of Child Development
Graduate School of Arts and Sciences
105 College Avenue
Medford, MA 02155
Telephone: (617) 627-3355
Fax: (617) 627-3503
E-mail: *Fred.Rothbaum@tufts.edu*
Web: *http://www.ase.tufts.edu/epcd*

Department Information:

1964. Chairperson: Fred Rothbaum. Number of faculty: total—full-time 21, part-time 12; women—full-time 14, part-time 11.

Programs and Degrees Offered:

Listed in the following order: Program area, degree type (T if terminal Master's), number awarded 7/06–6/07. MA/MS (Master of Arts/Science) 38, PhD (Doctor of Philosophy) 3, Certificate Other 1, MA Other 20.

Student Applications/Admissions:

Student Applications

MA/MS (Master of Arts/Science)—Applications 2007–2008, 102. Total applicants accepted 2007–2008, 75. Number full-time enrolled (new admits only) 2007–2008, 37. Number part-time enrolled (new admits only) 2007–2008, 2. Total enrolled 2007–2008 full-time, 66, part-time, 12. Openings 2008–2009, 60. The number of students enrolled full- and part-time who were dismissed or voluntarily withdrew from this program area in 2007–2008 were 1. *PhD (Doctor of Philosophy)*—Applications 2007–2008, 46. Total applicants accepted 2007–2008, 7. Number full-time enrolled (new admits only)

2007–2008, 6. Number part-time enrolled (new admits only) 2007–2008, 0. Openings 2008–2009, 5. The number of students enrolled full- and part-time who were dismissed or voluntarily withdrew from this program area in 2007–2008 were 0. *Certificate Other*—Applications 2007–2008, 1. Total applicants accepted 2007–2008, 1. Number full-time enrolled (new admits only) 2007–2008, 0. Number part-time enrolled (new admits only) 2007–2008, 0. Openings 2008–2009, 1. The number of students enrolled full- and part-time who were dismissed or voluntarily withdrew from this program area in 2007–2008 were 0. *MA Other*—Applications 2007–2008, 43. Total applicants accepted 2007–2008, 34. Number full-time enrolled (new admits only) 2007–2008, 13. Number part-time enrolled (new admits only) 2007–2008, 1. Total enrolled 2007–2008 full-time, 23, part-time, 3. Openings 2008–2009, 20. The number of students enrolled full- and part-time who were dismissed or voluntarily withdrew from this program area in 2007–2008 were 0.

Admissions Requirements:

Scores: Entries appear in this order: required test or GPA, minimum score (if required), median score of students entering in 2007–2008. Master's Programs: GRE-V no minimum stated; GRE-Q no minimum stated; overall undergraduate GPA no minimum stated; last 2 years GPA no minimum stated; Masters GRE-Analytical no minimum stated. Doctoral Programs: GRE-V no minimum stated; GRE-Q no minimum stated; overall undergraduate GPA no minimum stated; last 2 years GPA no minimum stated; Doctoral program GRE-Analytic no minimum stated.

Other Criteria: (importance of criteria rated low, medium, or high): GRE/MAT scores—high, research experience—medium, work experience—medium, extracurricular activity—low, clinically related public service—medium, GPA—medium, letters of recommendation—high, statement of goals and objectives—high. For additional information on admission requirements, go to http://ase.tufts.edu/GradStudy.

Student Characteristics: The following represents characteristics of students in 2007–2008 in all graduate psychology programs in the department: Female—full-time 104, part-time 15; Male—full-time 11, part-time 1; African American/Black—full-time 9, part-time 0; Hispanic/Latino(a)—full-time 9, part-time 0; Asian/Pacific Islander—full-time 10, part-time 0; American Indian/Alaska Native—full-time 0, part-time 0; Caucasian/White—full-time 63, part-time 13; Multi-ethnic—full-time 13, part-time 0; students subject to the Americans With Disabilities Act—full-time 0, part-time 0; Unknown ethnicity—full-time 11, part-time 3.

Financial Information/Assistance:

Tuition for Full-Time Study: *Master's:* State residents: per academic year $33,672, $3,367 per credit hour; Nonstate residents: per academic year $33,672, $3,367 per credit hour. *Doctoral:* State residents: per academic year $33,672, $3,367 per credit hour; Nonstate residents: per academic year $33,672, $3,367 per credit hour. See the following Web site for updates and changes in tuition costs: http://www.ase.tufts.edu/GradStudy.

Financial Assistance:

First-Year Students: Teaching assistantships available for first year. Average amount paid per academic year: $17,000. Average number of hours worked per week: 20. Apply by January 15. Tuition remission given: full. Research assistantships available for first year. Apply by varies. Fellowships and scholarships available for first year. Apply by January 15. Tuition remission given: full.

Advanced Students: Teaching assistantships available for advanced students. Average amount paid per academic year: $17,000. Average number of hours worked per week: 20. Apply by January 15. Tuition remission given: full. Research assistantships available for advanced students. Apply by varies. Fellowships and scholarships available for advanced students. Apply by January 15. Tuition remission given: full and partial.

Additional Information: Of all students currently enrolled full time, 80% benefited from one or more of the listed financial assistance programs. Application and information available online at http://ase.tufts.edu/GradStudy.

Internships/Practica: MA students engage in a semester-long internship in applied settings such as hospitals, mental health clinics, policy centers, museums. PhD students engage in full-time one-semester or half-time full-year applied internships in varied settings.

Housing and Day Care: On-campus housing is available. See the following Web site for more information: Please contact the Graduate and Professional Studies office at http://ase.tufts.edu/Gradstudy and the Residential Life office (ask for the off-campus housing) at (617) 627-3248 or at http://ase.tufts.edu/reslife/LEFT/Graduates/grad_students.html Off-campus listings, along with other information, can be found online at http://ase.tufts.edu/och. On-campus day care facilities are available at Tufts Educational Day Care Center. See the following Web site for more information: http://ase.tufts.edu/tedcc/policies.htm.

Employment of Department Graduates:

Master's Degree Graduates: Of those who graduated in the academic year 2006–2007, the following categories and numbers represent the postgraduate activities and employment of master's degree graduates: Enrolled in a postdoctoral residency/fellowship (n/a), employed in independent practice (n/a), total from the above (master's) (0).

Doctoral Degree Graduates: Of those who graduated in the academic year 2006–2007, the following categories and numbers represent the postgraduate activities and employment of doctoral degree graduates: Enrolled in a psychology doctoral program (n/a), total from the above (doctoral) (0).

Additional Information:

Orientation, Objectives, and Emphasis of Department: The department prepares students for a variety of careers that have, as their common prerequisite, a comprehensive understanding of children and their development. Students receive a foundation in psychological theory and research concerning the social, emotional, intellectual, linguistic, and physiological growth of children. Course material is complemented with progressively more involved practica encompassing observations and works with children in a wide variety of applied and research settings. The major aim of the program is to train people who can translate their knowledge about development into effective strategies for working with and on behalf of children. We believe that a background in child development is the best possible preparation for teaching and administrative careers in schools, children's advocacy and mental health agencies, hospitals, the media, government agencies concerned with the rights and welfare of children, and related fields. There is considerable room for flexibility in the program. For example, students with proficiency in one area, such as field experience, may concentrate on others, such as clinical theory and research. Also, students may choose from a rich variety of elective courses that touch upon such diverse topics as child advocacy, divorce and the family, and children's literature. The largest number of courses are in the area of developmental psychology, but there are also several courses in clinical and educational psychology and in the study of children and family policy.

Special Facilities or Resources: The department is housed in a complex of buildings on the Medford campus. The main building contains faculty, staff and TA offices, class meeting rooms, a library and a curriculum research lab. This building also includes the Eliot-Pearson Children's School, which serves normal and special-needs children aged 2 to 6. The school has observation booths for student use. Other buildings on campus house several faculty research projects, classrooms, and meeting rooms; Center for Reading and Language Research; and Institute for Applied Research in Youth Development. The department is also associated with the Tufts Educational Day Care Center. Students may work, as well as observe, in all of these settings. Both facilities are integrated into faculty research and research training for graduate students.

Information for Students With Physical Disabilities: See the following Web site for more information: http://www.studentservices.tufts.edu/DisabilityServices/information.htm.

Application Information:
Send to Tufts University, Graduate and Professional Studies, Ballou Hall, Medford, MA 02155. Application available online. URL of online application: http://www.ase.tufts.edu/gradstudy/admisApply.htm. Students are admitted in the Fall, application deadline January 15; Programs have rolling admissions. February 1 for joint-degree programs. *Fee:* $65.

Central Michigan University

Department of Psychology
Humanities and Social and Behavioral Sciences
Sloan Hall
Mount Pleasant, MI 48859
Telephone: (989) 774-3001
Fax: (989) 774-2553
E-mail: *hough1ba@cmich.edu*
Web: *http://www.chsbs.cmich.edu/psychology*

Department Information:

1965. Chairperson: Hajime Otani. Number of faculty: total—full-time 33, part-time 7; women—full-time 11, part-time 3; total—minority—full-time 4; women minority—full-time 2.

Programs and Degrees Offered:

Listed in the following order: Program area, degree type (T if terminal Master's), number awarded 7/06–6/07. Clinical PhD (Doctor of Philosophy) 9, Experimental PhD (Doctor of Philosophy) 5, General MA/MS (Master of Arts/Science) (T) 4, School PhD (Doctor of Philosophy) 4, Industrial/Organizational MA/MS (Master of Arts/Science) (T) 1, Industrial/Organizational PhD (Doctor of Philosophy) 6, School Master/Specialists Other 6, Accelerated Master's Experimental Program MA/MS (Master of Arts/Science).

APA Accreditation: Clinical PhD (Doctor of Philosophy). School PhD (Doctor of Philosophy).

Student Applications/Admissions:

Student Applications

Clinical PhD (Doctor of Philosophy)—Applications 2007–2008, 120. Total applicants accepted 2007–2008, 4. Number full-time enrolled (new admits only) 2007–2008, 4. Openings 2008–2009, 6. The median number of years required for completion of a degree in 2006–2007 were 6. The number of students enrolled full- and part-time who were dismissed or voluntarily withdrew from this program area in 2007–2008 were 0. *Experimental PhD (Doctor of Philosophy)*—Applications 2007–2008, 10. Total applicants accepted 2007–2008, 5. Number full-time enrolled (new admits only) 2007–2008, 5. Openings 2008–2009, 2. The median number of years required for completion of a degree in 2006–2007 were 5. *General MA/MS (Master of Arts/Science)*—Applications 2007–2008, 29. Total applicants accepted 2007–2008, 9. Number full-time enrolled (new admits only) 2007–2008, 9. Openings 2008–2009, 5. The median number of years required for completion of a degree in 2006–2007 were 4. The number of students enrolled full- and part-time who were dismissed or voluntarily withdrew from this program area in 2007–2008 were 0. *School PhD (Doctor of Philosophy)*—Applications 2007–2008, 46. Total applicants accepted 2007–2008, 9. Number full-time enrolled (new admits only) 2007–2008, 8. Total enrolled 2007–2008 full-time, 22. Openings 2008–2009, 3. The median number of years required for completion of a degree in 2006–2007 were 6. The number of students enrolled full- and part-time who were dismissed or voluntarily withdrew from this program area in 2007–2008 were 1. *Industrial/Organizational MA/MS (Master of Arts/Science)*—Applications 2007–2008, 24. Total applicants accepted 2007–2008, 3. Number full-time enrolled (new admits only) 2007–2008, 3. Total enrolled 2007–2008 full-time, 6. Openings 2008–2009, 1. The median number of years required for completion of a degree in 2006–2007 were 2. The number of students enrolled full- and part-time who were dismissed or voluntarily withdrew from this program area in 2007–2008 were 0. *Industrial/Organizational PhD (Doctor of Philosophy)*—Applications 2007–2008, 40. Total applicants accepted 2007–2008, 7. Number full-time enrolled (new admits only) 2007–2008, 7. Total enrolled 2007–2008 full-time, 31. The median number of years required for completion of a degree in 2006–2007 were 5. *School Master/Specialists Other*—Applications 2007–2008, 19. Total applicants accepted 2007–2008, 6. Number full-time enrolled (new admits only) 2007–2008, 6. Total enrolled 2007–2008 full-time, 17. The median number of years required for completion of a degree in 2006–2007 were 5. The number of students enrolled full- and part-time who were dismissed or voluntarily withdrew from this program area in 2007–2008 were 0. *Accelerated Master's Experimental Program MA/MS (Master of Arts/Science)*—Applications 2007–2008, 1. Total applicants accepted 2007–2008, 1. Number full-time enrolled (new admits only) 2007–2008, 1. Total enrolled 2007–2008 full-time, 2.

Admissions Requirements:

Scores: Entries appear in this order: required test or GPA, minimum score (if required), median score of students entering in 2007–2008. Master's Programs: GRE-V no minimum stated; GRE-Q no minimum stated; overall undergraduate GPA 3.00; psychology GPA 3.00. GRE-V and GRE-Q score requirements vary with each application pool. Doctoral Programs: GRE-V no minimum stated; GRE-Q no minimum stated; overall undergraduate GPA 3.00. GRE-V & GRE-Q requirements vary with each application pool.

Other Criteria: (importance of criteria rated low, medium, or high): GRE/MAT scores—medium, research experience—high, work experience—medium, extracurricular activity—low, clinically related public service—medium, GPA—high, letters of recommendation—high, statement of goals and objectives—high.

Student Characteristics: The following represents characteristics of students in 2007–2008 in all graduate psychology programs in the department: Female—full-time 90, part-time 0; Male—full-time 61, part-time 0; African American/Black—full-time 2, part-time 0; Asian/Pacific Islander—full-time 6, part-time 0; American Indian/Alaska Native—full-time 3, part-time 0; Caucasian/White—full-time 131, part-time 0; Multi-ethnic—full-time 1, part-time 0; Unknown ethnicity—full-time 8, part-time 0.

Financial Information/Assistance:

Tuition for Full-Time Study: *Master's:* State residents: $388 per credit hour; Nonstate residents: $719 per credit hour. *Doctoral:* State residents: $441 per credit hour; Nonstate residents: $798 per credit hour. Tuition is subject to change.

Financial Assistance:

First-Year Students: Research assistantships available for first year. Average amount paid per academic year: $10,000. Average number of hours worked per week: 20. Apply by February 6. Tuition remission given: partial. Fellowships and scholarships available for first year. Average amount paid per academic year: $10,000. Average number of hours worked per week: 24. Apply by February 6. Tuition remission given: partial.

Advanced Students: Teaching assistantships available for advanced students. Average amount paid per academic year: $13,250. Average number of hours worked per week: 20. Apply by February 6. Tuition remission given: partial. Research assistantships available for advanced students. Average amount paid per academic year: $12,250. Average number of hours worked per week: 20. Apply by February 6. Tuition remission given: partial. Fellowships and scholarships available for advanced students. Average amount paid per academic year: $12,250. Average number of hours worked per week: 24. Apply by February 6. Tuition remission given: partial.

Additional Information: Of all students currently enrolled full time, 68% benefited from one or more of the listed financial assistance programs. Application and information available online at http://www.chsbs.cmich.edu/psychology.

Internships/Practica: Master's Degree (MA/MS General): An internship experience such as a final research project or "capstone" experience is required of graduates. Master's Degree (MA/MS Industrial/Organizational): An internship experience such as a final research project or "capstone" experience is required of graduates. Doctoral Degree (PhD Clinical): For those doctoral students for whom a professional internship was required in this program prior to graduation, (7) students applied for an internship in 2006–2007, with (7) students obtaining an internship. Of those students who obtained an internship, (7) were paid internships. Of those students who obtained an internship, (7) students placed in APA/CPA-accredited internships, (0) students placed in internships not APA/CPA-accredited, but listed with the Association of Psychology Postdoctoral and Internship Centers (APPIC), (0) students placed in internships conforming to guidelines of the Council of Directors of School Psychology Programs (CDSPP), (0) students placed in internships that were not APA/CPA-accredited, APPIC or CDSPP listed. Doctoral Degree (PhD School): For those doctoral students for whom a professional internship was required in this program prior to graduation, (3) students applied for an internship in 2006–2007, with (3) students obtaining an internship. Of those students who obtained an internship, (3) were paid internships. Of those students who obtained an internship, (3) students placed in APA/CPA-accredited internships, (0) students placed in internships not APA/CPA-accredited, but listed with the Association of Psychology Postdoctoral and Internship Centers (APPIC), (0) students placed in internships conforming to guidelines of the Council of Directors of School Psychology Programs (CDSPP), (0) students placed in internships that were not APA/CPA-accredited, APPIC or CDSPP listed. Most practica and internships are arranged through agencies and schools outside the University. However, practica experiences are available through the Department's Psychological Training and Consultation Center. Second-year clinical students routinely have their first practicum at the Center.

Housing and Day Care: On-campus housing is available. Office of Residence Life, Bovee University Center, Room 201, Central Michigan University, Mount Pleasant, MI 48859-0001. No on-campus day care facilities are available.

Employment of Department Graduates:

Master's Degree Graduates: Of those who graduated in the academic year 2006–2007, the following categories and numbers represent the postgraduate activities and employment of master's degree graduates: Enrolled in a postdoctoral residency/fellowship (n/a), employed in independent practice (n/a), total from the above (master's) (0).

Doctoral Degree Graduates: Of those who graduated in the academic year 2006–2007, the following categories and numbers represent the postgraduate activities and employment of doctoral degree graduates: Enrolled in a psychology doctoral program (n/a), total from the above (doctoral) (0).

Additional Information:

Orientation, Objectives, and Emphasis of Department: Specialization is possible in the areas of clinical, applied experimental, industrial/organizational, and school psychology. There is also a general/experimental MS program with emphasis on foundations, statistics, methodology, and research, which is designed to prepare students for doctoral training or research positions in the public or private sectors. The clinical program follows a practitioner–scientist model, focusing on training for applied settings. The industrial/organizational program is oriented toward training students for careers in research, university, or business settings. The school program prepares school psychologists to provide consultation, intervention, and diagnostic services to schools and school children. The program meets Michigan requirements for certification.

Special Facilities or Resources: Space is reserved for student research with human subjects. Special equipment permits studies in learning, cognition, human factors, psychophysiology, neuropsychology, and perception. Computer laboratories are available, one specifically designated for clinical and school students. All computer labs have direct e-mail and Internet access, as well as statistical and research software. The Psychology Training and Consultation Center provides training, research, and service functions. In a separate building, space is devoted to animal research and teaching of behavioral neuroscience and experimental behavior analysis. The behavioral neuroscience laboratory contains a fully equipped surgical/historological suite, behavioral testing area and equipment, and a data analysis room including microscopes and an image analysis system. The experimental analysis laboratory is equipped with automated operant chambers for both birds and rodents. A Life-Span Development Research Center has been established in the Department.

Information for Students With Physical Disabilities: See the following Web site for more information: http://www.cmich.edu/student-disability/.

Application Information:

Send to Psychology Department, Sloan Hall, Central Michigan University, Mount Pleasant, MI 48859. Application available online. URL of online application: http://www.chsbs.cmich.edu/psychology. Students are admitted in the Fall, application deadline see comments. Industrial/Organizational deadline is January 1, Clinical and School deadline is January 15, and Experimental program deadline is February 1. *Fee:* $35.

Detroit–Mercy, University of (2007 data)

Department of Psychology
College of Liberal Arts and Education
4001 West McNichols
P.O. Box 19900
Detroit, MI 48219-0900
Telephone: (313) 578-0392
Fax: (313) 578-0507
E-mail: *abellsc@udmercy.edu*
Web: *http://www.udmercy.edu/catalog*

Department Information:

1946. Chairperson: Steven Abell, PhD. Number of faculty: total—full-time 16, part-time 20; women—full-time 11; faculty subject to the Americans With Disabilities Act 1.

Programs and Degrees Offered:

Listed in the following order: Program area, degree type (T if terminal Master's), number awarded 7/06–6/07. Industrial/Organizational MA/MS (Master of Arts/Science) (T) 7, Specialist in School Psychology Other 12, Clinical Psychology PhD (Doctor of Philosophy) 10, Clinical Psychology MA/MS (Master of Arts/Science) (T) 15.

APA Accreditation: Clinical PhD (Doctor of Philosophy).

Student Applications/Admissions:

Student Applications

Industrial/Organizational MA/MS (Master of Arts/Science)—Applications 2007–2008, 20. Total applicants accepted 2007–2008, 16. Total enrolled 2007–2008 full-time, 12, part-time, 10. Openings 2008–2009, 14. The median number of years required for completion of a degree in 2006–2007 were 2. *Specialist in School Psychology Other*—Applications 2007–2008, 40. Total applicants accepted 2007–2008, 12. Number full-time enrolled (new admits only) 2007–2008, 8. Number part-time enrolled (new admits only) 2007–2008, 4. Total enrolled 2007–2008 full-time, 16, part-time, 12. Openings 2008–2009, 12. The median number of years required for completion of a degree in 2006–2007 were 3. The number of students enrolled full- and part-time who were dismissed or voluntarily withdrew from this program area in 2007–2008 were 0. *Clinical Psychology PhD (Doctor of Philosophy)*—Applications 2007–2008, 75. Total applicants accepted 2007–2008, 10. Number full-time enrolled (new admits only) 2007–2008, 10. Number part-time enrolled (new admits only) 2007–2008, 0. Openings 2008–2009, 10. The median number of years required for completion of a degree in 2006–2007 were 6. The number of students enrolled full- and part-time who were dismissed or voluntarily withdrew from this program area in 2007–2008 were 0. *Clinical Psychology MA/MS (Master of Arts/Science)*—Applications 2007–2008, 60. Total applicants accepted 2007–2008, 15. Number full-time enrolled (new admits only) 2007–2008, 13. Number part-time enrolled (new admits only) 2007–2008, 2. Total enrolled 2007–2008 full-time, 30, part-time, 4. Openings 2008–2009, 15. The median number of years required for completion of a degree in 2006–2007 were 2. The number of students enrolled full- and part-time who were dismissed or voluntarily withdrew from this program area in 2007–2008 were 2.

Admissions Requirements:

Scores: Entries appear in this order: required test or GPA, minimum score (if required), median score of students entering in 2007–2008. Master's Programs: GRE-V 450, 550; GRE-Q 450, 500; overall undergraduate GPA 3.0, 3.3; last 2 years GPA 3.0, 3.4; psychology GPA 3.0, 3.5. Doctoral Programs: GRE-V 500, 550; GRE-Q 500, 630; GRE-Analytical 4.0, 4.5; overall undergraduate GPA 3.0, 3.7.

Other Criteria: (importance of criteria rated low, medium, or high): GRE/MAT scores—high, research experience—medium, work experience—medium, extracurricular activity—medium, clinically related public service—medium, GPA—high, letters of recommendation—high, interview—high, statement of goals and objectives—high. For the Clinical MA program, GRE scores are not given as much weight as GPA, letters of recommendation, and previous relevant work experience. For additional information on admission requirements, go to http://www.udmercy.edu/catalog.

Student Characteristics: The following represents characteristics of students in 2007–2008 in all graduate psychology programs in the department: Female—full-time 74, part-time 20; Male—full-time 30, part-time 10; African American/Black—full-time 5, part-time 0; Hispanic/Latino(a)—full-time 1, part-time 0; Asian/Pacific Islander—full-time 2, part-time 3; American Indian/Alaska Native—full-time 0, part-time 0; Caucasian/White—full-time 0, part-time 0; Unknown ethnicity—full-time 0, part-time 0.

Financial Information/Assistance:

Tuition for Full-Time Study: *Master's:* State residents: $810 per credit hour; Nonstate residents: $810 per credit hour. *Doctoral:* State residents: $760 per credit hour; Nonstate residents: $760 per credit hour. Tuition is subject to change. See the following Web site for updates and changes in tuition costs: http://www.udmercy.edu.

Financial Assistance:

First-Year Students: Teaching assistantships available for first year. Average number of hours worked per week: 15. Apply by January 1. Tuition remission given: partial. Research assistantships available for first year. Average number of hours worked per week: 15. Apply by January 1. Tuition remission given: partial.

Advanced Students: Teaching assistantships available for advanced students. Average number of hours worked per week: 15. Apply by January 1. Tuition remission given: partial. Research assistantships available for advanced students. Average number of hours worked per week: 15. Apply by January 1. Tuition remission given: partial.

Additional Information: Application and information available online at http://www.udmercy.edu.

Internships/Practica: Students have available for practicum and internship experiences a wide range of settings ranging from hospitals, inpatient and outpatient units, schools, community agencies, and businesses. Populations served can range from children, adolescents, and adults to prisoners and those requiring rehabilitation services. Assessments and interventions of various kinds are performed under the supervision of licensed or appropriately credentialed psychologists.

Housing and Day Care: On-campus housing is available. Although the University does not have on-campus housing specifically for graduate students, graduate students are eligible to live in the University's residence halls on the McNichols campus, which is also home to the Psychology Department. On-campus day care facilities are available. A licensed child care facility is currently located on the University's Outer Drive Campus, which has both a daytime and evening program.

Employment of Department Graduates:

Master's Degree Graduates: Of those who graduated in the academic year 2006–2007, the following categories and numbers represent the postgraduate activities and employment of master's degree graduates: Enrolled in a postdoctoral residency/fellowship (n/a), employed in independent practice (n/a), total from the above (master's) (0).

Doctoral Degree Graduates: Of those who graduated in the academic year 2006–2007, the following categories and numbers represent the postgraduate activities and employment of doctoral degree graduates: Enrolled in a psychology doctoral program (n/a), employed in independent practice (4), employed in a community mental health/counseling center (2), employed in a hospital/medical center (1), total from the above (doctoral) (7).

Additional Information:

Orientation, Objectives, and Emphasis of Department: The overall goal of graduate education in the Psychology Department is to train psychologists who are well-grounded in theory and research and who can function in a variety of settings. The theoretical emphasis of the doctoral program in clinical psychology is psychodynamic, whereas the orientations of the other programs are more eclectic. Regardless of orientation, however, students are exposed to different kinds of intervention techniques, each with its own theoretical rationale. The master's program in clinical psychology allows students to specialize in working with substance abuse or children. The specialist program in school psychology prepares students to function as psychologists in school settings, dealing with children and families. The master's program in industrial psychology focuses on human resource development and personnel management.

Special Facilities or Resources: The University of Detroit–Mercy runs the University Psychology Clinic, which serves the metropolitan area as a community mental health clinic. The clinic work is directed or supervised by faculty members and psychologists from the community. Students in the doctoral and masters programs in clinical and students in the specialist program in school psychology begin their clinical work in their 2nd year and continue with increasingly responsible supervised experiences.

Application Information:

Send to Mr. Steven Coddington, Admissions Office, University of Detroit–Mercy, 4001 West McNichols, Detroit, MI 48221. Online applications available at http://www.udmercy.edu. Students are admitted in the Fall, application deadline varies by program: PhD Clinical, January 1; School Psychology, February 1; Industrial/Organizational Psychology MA, March 1; Clinical MA, March 31. Application materials available online. *Fee:* $30 for the Clinical MA or Specialist program and $50 for the PhD program. The application fee is waived when students apply online at http://www.udmercy.edu.

Eastern Michigan University

Department of Psychology
College of Arts and Sciences
537 Mark Jefferson Hall
Ypsilanti, MI 48197
Telephone: (313) 487-1155
Fax: (313) 487-6553
E-mail: *psy_grad@emich.edu*
Web: *http://www.emich.edu/psychology*

Department Information:

1962. Interim Department Head: Carol Freedman-Doan. Number of faculty: total—full-time 23; women—full-time 12; total—minority—full-time 1.

Programs and Degrees Offered:

Listed in the following order: Program area, degree type (T if terminal Master's), number awarded 7/06–6/07. General Clinical Psychology MA/MS (Master of Arts/Science) (T) 17, Clinical Behavioral Psychology MA/MS (Master of Arts/Science) (T) 14, General Experimental Psychology. MA/MS (Master of Arts/Science) (T) 0, Clinical Psychology PhD (Doctor of Philosophy) 2.

APA Accreditation: Clinical PhD (Doctor of Philosophy).

Student Applications/Admissions:

Student Applications

General Clinical Psychology MA/MS (Master of Arts/Science)—Applications 2007–2008, 39. Total applicants accepted 2007–2008, 10. Number full-time enrolled (new admits only) 2007–2008, 9. Number part-time enrolled (new admits only) 2007–2008, 2. Total enrolled 2007–2008 full-time, 10, part-time, 4. Openings 2008–2009, 10. The median number of years required for completion of a degree in 2006–2007 were 2. The number of students enrolled full- and part-time who were dismissed or voluntarily withdrew from this program area in 2007–2008 were 0. *Clinical Behavioral Psychology MA/MS (Master of Arts/Science)*—Applications 2007–2008, 20. Total applicants accepted 2007–2008, 11. Number full-time enrolled (new admits only) 2007–2008, 8. Number part-time enrolled (new admits only) 2007–2008, 3. Total enrolled 2007–2008 full-time, 10, part-time, 10. Openings 2008–2009, 12. The median number of years required for completion of a degree in 2006–2007 were 3. The number of students enrolled full- and part-time who were dismissed or voluntarily withdrew from this program area in 2007–2008 were 0. *General Experimental Psychology. MA/MS (Master of Arts/Science)*—Applications 2007–2008, 6. Total applicants accepted 2007–2008, 1. Number full-time enrolled (new admits only) 2007–2008, 0. Number part-time enrolled (new admits only) 2007–2008, 1. Openings 2008–2009, 3. The number of students enrolled full- and part-time who were dismissed or voluntarily withdrew from this program area in 2007–2008 were 0. *Clinical Psychology PhD (Doctor of Philosophy)*—Applications 2007–2008, 95. Total applicants accepted 2007–2008, 8. Number full-time enrolled (new admits only) 2007–2008, 8. Number part-time enrolled (new admits only) 2007–2008, 0. Openings 2008–2009, 10. The median number of years required for completion of a degree in 2006–2007 were 5. The number of students enrolled full- and part-time who were dismissed or voluntarily withdrew from this program area in 2007–2008 were 1.

Admissions Requirements:

Scores: Entries appear in this order: required test or GPA, minimum score (if required), median score of students entering in 2007–2008. Master's Programs: GRE-V no minimum stated; GRE-Q no minimum stated; overall undergraduate GPA 3.0; Masters GRE-Analytical no minimum stated. A combined GRE score of 1000 is required and an analytical writing score of at least 4.5 is suggested. There is also a minimum GPA requirement of 3.0. Although the GRE Subject test is no longer required it is preferred. The mean GRE scores and GPA of those admitted to the PhD program can be found on the Psychology department Web page. Doctoral Programs: GRE-V no minimum stated; GRE-Q no minimum stated; overall undergraduate GPA 3.0; Doctoral program GRE-Analytic no minimum stated. A combined GRE score of 1000 is required and an analytical writing score of at least 4.5 is suggested. There is also a minimum GPA requirement of 3.0. Although the GRE Subject test is no longer required it is preferred.

Other Criteria: (importance of criteria rated low, medium, or high): GRE/MAT scores—high, research experience—medium, work experience—low, extracurricular activity—medium, clinically related public service—low, GPA—high, letters of recommendation—medium, interview—high, statement of goals and objectives—medium, fit with faculty research—high, undergraduate major in psychology—medium, specific undergraduate psychology courses taken—medium. Weight given to criteria vary among each of three programs but all programs require 20 undergraduate Psychology credit hours and a course in statistics and experimental psychology. For additional information on admission requirements, go to http://www.emich.edu/admissions/graduatestudents and http://www.emich.edu/psychology.

Student Characteristics: The following represents characteristics of students in 2007–2008 in all graduate psychology programs in the department: Female—full-time 52, part-time 11; Male—full-time 23, part-time 5; African American/Black—full-time 2, part-time 1; Hispanic/Latino(a)—full-time 0, part-time 1; Asian/Pacific Islander—full-time 4, part-time 1; American Indian/Alaska Native—full-time 0, part-time 0; Caucasian/White—full-time 64, part-time 11; Multi-ethnic—full-time 0, part-time 0; students subject to the Americans With Disabilities Act—full-time 1, part-time 0; Unknown ethnicity—full-time 5, part-time 2; International students who hold an F-1 or J-1 Visa—full-time 3, part-time 0.

Financial Information/Assistance:

Tuition for Full-Time Study: *Master's:* State residents: $373 per credit hour; Nonstate residents: $734 per credit hour. *Doctoral:* State residents: $429 per credit hour; Nonstate residents: $828 per credit hour. Tuition is subject to change. Additional fees are assessed to students beyond the costs of tuition for the following: Student and program fees are assessed by the university. Tuition costs vary by program. See the following Web site for updates and changes in tuition costs: http://www.emich.edu/controller/sbs/tuitionfeesoutline.html.

Financial Assistance:

First-Year Students: Research assistantships available for first year. Average amount paid per academic year: $7,800. Average number of hours worked per week: 20. Apply by February 15. Tuition remission given: partial. Fellowships and scholarships available for first year. Average amount paid per academic year: $15,000. Average number of hours worked per week: 20. Apply by December 15. Tuition remission given: full.

Advanced Students: Research assistantships available for advanced students. Average amount paid per academic year: $8,400. Average number of hours worked per week: 20. Apply by February 15. Tuition remission given: partial. Fellowships and scholarships available for advanced students. Average amount paid per academic year: $15,000. Average number of hours worked per week: 20. Apply by December 15. Tuition remission given: full.

Additional Information: Of all students currently enrolled full time, 37% benefited from one or more of the listed financial assistance programs. Application and information available online at http://www.gradschool.emich.edu/student/student_subdir/finasst_gradassist/finasst.html.

Internships/Practica: Master's Degree (MA/MS General Experimental Psychology): An internship experience such as a final research project or "capstone" experience is required of graduates. Doctoral Degree (PhD Clinical Psychology): For those doctoral students for whom a professional internship was required in this program prior to graduation, (6) students applied for an internship in 2006–2007, with (6) students obtaining an internship. Of those students who obtained an internship, (6) were paid internships. Of those students who obtained an internship, (6) students placed in APA/CPA-accredited internships, (0) students placed in internships not APA/CPA-accredited, but listed with the Association of Psychology Postdoctoral and Internship Centers (APPIC), (0) students placed in internships conforming to guidelines of the Council of Directors of School Psychology Programs (CDSPP), (0) students placed in internships that were not APA/CPA-accredited, APPIC or CDSPP listed. Practicum settings (unpaid) are available in the surrounding community for clinical and clinical behavioral students. In addition, the university offers mental health services involving practicum experiences at both the campus Snow Health Center and the EMU Psychology Clinic. Both terminal MS and PhD programs require sufficient practicum hours to meet the State of Michigan requirements for the Limited License in Psychology (LLP).

Housing and Day Care: On-campus housing is available. See the following Web site for more information: https://www.emich.edu/housing/. Contact Housing and Dining services: (734) 487-1300. The University offers married student/family housing as well as residence hall environments. On-campus day care facilities are available. See the following Web site for more information: http://www.emich.edu/uhs/childcare.html. Contact The Children's Institute, an on-campus facility at (734) 487-2348. Other private care facilities are located within a reasonable distance of campus.

Employment of Department Graduates:

Master's Degree Graduates: Of those who graduated in the academic year 2006–2007, the following categories and numbers represent the postgraduate activities and employment of master's degree graduates: Enrolled in a psychology doctoral program (2), enrolled in a postdoctoral residency/fellowship (n/a), employed in independent practice (n/a), total from the above (master's) (2).

Doctoral Degree Graduates: Of those who graduated in the academic year 2006–2007, the following categories and numbers represent the postgraduate activities and employment of doctoral

degree graduates: Enrolled in a psychology doctoral program (n/a), enrolled in a postdoctoral residency/fellowship (1), employed in an academic position at a university (1), employed in other positions at a higher education institution (1), employed in a hospital/medical center (1), total from the above (doctoral) (4).

Additional Information:

Orientation, Objectives, and Emphasis of Department: The Psychology Department offers three terminal Master's Degree programs and courses in several orientations, including behavioral, social, insight, developmental, and physiological. Within the two Master's clinical programs, the major emphases are on psychological assessment (Clinical Program) and behavioral treatment (Clinical Behavioral Program). Within each program there are a wide variety of theoretical, applied, and research interests. The goal of the Clinical and Clinical Behavioral programs is on giving students the background to immediately begin work in clinical treatment settings or to prepare them for entry into doctoral programs, as matches the student's educational objectives. The emphasis of the Master's in General Experimental Psychology is to prepare students for entry into higher level study in psychology or as researchers in applied/research settings. Because Psychology is considered a natural science at Eastern Michigan University, there is also an emphasis on basing clinical practice on research findings. Theses, although optional in the clinical programs, are expected to be research based. The PhD program in Clinical Psychology is designed to give advanced training in the supervision of mental health professionals in mental health care settings. The entry requirements for this program are somewhat more stringent than those of our Master's Program with a more competitive applicant pool. The PhD offers specializations in either general clinical or behavioral psychology, a terminal Master's Degree en route, a full 4-year doctoral fellowship that covers tuition and fees, plus an annual stipend. For more information on this program, please contact Graduate Secretary, 537 Mark Jefferson, Psychology Department, Eastern Michigan University, Ypsilanti, MI 48197; (734) 487-0047. Information is also available at on the EMU Psychology department Web page: http://www.emich.edu/psychology.

Special Facilities or Resources: The faculty, which consists of approximately 25 full-time members with PhDs and varying number of part-time lecturers, is eclectic in orientation with a wide variety of interests and professional backgrounds. Research interests and publication record of the faculty includes psychological test construction and validation, basic behavioral research with humans and nonhumans, the history of psychology, applied behavior analysis, physiological psychology, forensic psychology, personality, social psychology, and many more. Student enrollment is intentionally kept low in order to provide the students with ample opportunities to develop close working relationships with the faculty. Students regularly present at regional, national, and international conventions, as well as coauthor published papers with faculty. The facilities of the Psychology Department are located in the Mark Jefferson Science building and in the newly renovated Psychology Clinic at 611 West Cross. The department features a state-of-the-art computer laboratory, IEEE 802.11 (AirPort) wireless networking capabilities, human and animal research facilities, seminar rooms, a clinic with one-way observation capabilities, a new university library less than 3 minutes away on foot, and other equipment and supplies needed for advanced study.

Information for Students With Physical Disabilities: See the following Web site for more information: http://www.emich.edu/access_services/.

Application Information:

Send to Department of Psychology, Graduate Admissions Committee, 537 Mark Jefferson, Eastern Michigan University, Ypsilanti, MI 48197. Students are admitted in the Fall, application deadline See below. The deadline for PhD applications is December 15. The application deadline for the MS programs is February 15. Late applications will not be considered; all materials must be postmarked no later than the deadline date and meet all stated minimum requirements. Applicants who have not applied for graduate admission and paid the application fee will not be considered. All programs are Fall semester start only. All department admission requirements, procedures, and forms can be found at http://www.emich.edu/psychology. Please note that applying for Graduate Admission is a process that must be completed in addition to submitting the required department information. Do not arrange to have transcripts and GRE scores submitted to the department; this will delay the process. These materials should be sent to Admissions. Please note that there is no department applicaiton fee and the information that follows refers to the Graduate Admission application fee. *Fee:* $35. Graduate Admission applications that are submitted electronically via http://www.emich.edu/admissions/apply/index.html#gradm involve a fee of $25. If the applicant mails in a paper Graduate Admission application, the fee is $35.

Michigan School of Professional Psychology

26811 Orchard Lake Road
Farmington Hills, MI 48334-4512
Telephone: (248) 476-1122
Fax: (248) 476-1125
E-mail: *lpgallant@mispp.edu*
Web: *http://www.mispp.edu*

Department Information:

1980. President: Kerry Moustakas, PhD. Number of faculty: total—full-time 3, part-time 19; women—full-time 1, part-time 10; minority—part-time 1; women minority—part-time 1.

Programs and Degrees Offered:

Listed in the following order: Program area, degree type (T if terminal Master's), number awarded 7/06–6/07. PsyD (Doctor of Psychology) 11, MA/MS (Master of Arts/Science) (T) 31.

Student Applications/Admissions:

Student Applications

PsyD (Doctor of Psychology)—Applications 2007–2008, 46. Total applicants accepted 2007–2008, 26. Number full-time enrolled (new admits only) 2007–2008, 24. Number part-time enrolled (new admits only) 2007–2008, 0. Total enrolled 2007–2008 full-time, 64, part-time, 6. Openings 2008–2009, 24. The median number of years required for completion of a degree in 2006–2007 were 4. The number of students enrolled full- and part-time who were dismissed or voluntarily withdrew from this program area in 2007–2008 were 3. *MA/MS (Master of Arts/Science)*—Applications 2007–2008, 90. Total applicants accepted 2007–2008, 44. Number full-time enrolled (new admits only) 2007–2008, 40. Number part-time enrolled (new admits only) 2007–2008, 0. Openings 2008–2009, 40. The median number of years required for completion of a degree in 2006–2007 was 1. The number of students enrolled full- and part-time who were dismissed or voluntarily withdrew from this program area in 2007–2008 were 1.

Admissions Requirements:

Scores: Entries appear in this order: required test or GPA, minimum score (if required), median score of students entering in 2007–2008. Master's Programs: overall undergraduate GPA 3.0, 3.0; psychology GPA 3.0, 3.0. Doctoral Programs: overall undergraduate GPA 3.0, 3.0; psychology GPA 3.0, 3.0.

Other Criteria: (importance of criteria rated low, medium, or high): research experience—medium, work experience—high, extracurricular activity—medium, clinically related public service—high, GPA—medium, letters of recommendation—high, interview—high, statement of goals and objectives—high, scholarly writing sample—medium, undergraduate major in psychology—medium, specific undergraduate psychology courses taken—medium. Writing sample is needed for PsyD program only. For additional information on admission requirements, go to http://www.mispp.edu.

Student Characteristics: The following represents characteristics of students in 2007–2008 in all graduate psychology programs in the department: Female—full-time 78, part-time 3; Male—full-time 25, part-time 3; African American/Black—full-time 11, part-time 2; Hispanic/Latino(a)—full-time 5, part-time 1; Asian/Pacific Islander—full-time 3, part-time 0; American Indian/Alaska Native—full-time 0, part-time 0; Caucasian/White—full-time 76, part-time 3; Multi-ethnic—full-time 3, part-time 0; students subject to the Americans With Disabilities Act—full-time 0, part-time 0; Unknown ethnicity—full-time 5, part-time 0; International students who hold an F-1 or J-1 Visa—full-time 3, part-time 0.

Financial Information/Assistance:

Tuition for Full-Time Study: *Master's:* State residents: per academic year $21,255, $460 per credit hour; Nonstate residents: per academic year $21,255, $460 per credit hour. *Doctoral:* State residents: per academic year $18,930, $560 per credit hour; Nonstate residents: per academic year $18,930, $560 per credit hour. Tuition is subject to change. See the following Web site for updates and changes in tuition costs: http://www.mispp.edu.

Financial Assistance:

First-Year Students: No information provided.

Advanced Students: No information provided.

Additional Information: Of all students currently enrolled full time, 0% benefited from one or more of the listed financial assistance programs. Application and information available online at http://www.mispp.edu.

Internships/Practica: Master's Degree (MA/MS Masters): An internship experience such as a final research project or "capstone" experience is required of graduates. Doctoral Degree (PsyD): For those doctoral students for whom a professional internship was required in this program prior to graduation, (25) students applied for an internship in 2006–2007, with (25) students obtaining an internship. Of those students who obtained an internship, (1) were paid internships. Of those students who obtained an internship, (1) students placed in APA/CPA-accredited internships, (0) students placed in internships not APA/CPA-accredited, but listed with the Association of Psychology Postdoctoral and Internship Centers (APPIC), (0) students placed in internships conforming to guidelines of the Council of Directors of School Psychology Programs (CDSPP), (24) students placed in internships that were not APA/CPA-accredited, APPIC or CDSPP listed. There is a mandatory 500-hour practicum for master's students. A 500-hour practicum is required for doctoral students with a 2,000-hour internship in order to receive their PsyD degree and satisfy the state licensing board's requirements. For additional information on education and training outcomes for our programs, see the following Web site: http://www.mispp.ed.

Housing and Day Care: No on-campus housing is available. No on-campus day care facilities are available.

Employment of Department Graduates:

Master's Degree Graduates: Of those who graduated in the academic year 2006–2007, the following categories and numbers represent the postgraduate activities and employment of master's degree graduates: Enrolled in a psychology doctoral program (9), enrolled in another graduate/professional program (1), enrolled in a postdoctoral residency/fellowship (n/a), employed in independent practice (n/a), employed in an academic position at a university (0), employed in an academic position at a 2-year/4-year college (4), employed in a professional position in a school system (0), employed in business or industry (0), employed in government agency (1), employed in a community mental health/counseling center (9), employed in a hospital/medical center (3), still seeking employment (2), not seeking employment (0), do not know (2), total from the above (master's) (31).

Doctoral Degree Graduates: Of those who graduated in the academic year 2006–2007, the following categories and numbers represent the postgraduate activities and employment of doctoral degree graduates: Enrolled in a psychology doctoral program (n/a), enrolled in another graduate/professional program (0), enrolled in a postdoctoral residency/fellowship (0), employed in independent practice (5), employed in an academic position at a university (1), employed in an academic position at a 2-year/4-year college (1), employed in a professional position in a school system (0), employed in business or industry (1), employed in government agency (0), employed in a community mental health/counseling center (0), employed in a hospital/medical center (1), still seeking employment (0), do not know (2), total from the above (doctoral) (11).

Additional Information:

Orientation, Objectives, and Emphasis of Department: The mission of the Michigan School of Professional Psychology is to educate and train individuals to become reflective scholar–practitioners with the competencies necessary to serve diverse populations as professional Humanistic Psychologists and Psychotherapists.

Special Facilities or Resources: N/A.

Information for Students With Physical Disabilities: Our new facility is accessible to students with physical disabilities.

Application Information:

Send to Linda Potter-Gallant, MA Admissions Advisor, Michigan School of Professional Psychology, 26811 Orchard Lake Road, Farmington Hills, MI 48334-4512. Application available online. URL of online application: http://www.mispp.edu. Students are admitted in the Fall; Programs have rolling admissions. We accept applications all year round on a rolling basis. Our early admission deadline is January 15 and general admission deadline is March 1. We will continue to accept applications if there are spaces available. Students may be wait-listed. Enrollment is one time per year in September. *Fee:* $75.

Michigan State University

Department of Psychology
Social Science
202 Psychology Building
East Lansing, MI 48824-1116
Telephone: (517) 353-5258
Fax: (517) 432-2476
E-mail: *detwiler@msu.edu*
Web: *http://www.psychology.msu.edu*

Department Information:

1946. Chairperson: Neal Schmitt. Number of faculty: total—full-time 52; women—full-time 22; total—minority—full-time 7; women minority—full-time 1.

Programs and Degrees Offered:

Listed in the following order: Program area, degree type (T if terminal Master's), number awarded 7/06–6/07. Behavioral Neuroscience PhD (Doctor of Philosophy) 1, Clinical PhD (Doctor of Philosophy) 7, Ecological/Community PhD (Doctor of Philosophy), Industrial/Organizational PhD (Doctor of Philosophy) 6, Cognitive PhD (Doctor of Philosophy), Social/Personality PhD (Doctor of Philosophy).

APA Accreditation: Clinical PhD (Doctor of Philosophy).

Student Applications/Admissions:

Student Applications

Behavioral Neuroscience PhD (Doctor of Philosophy)—Applications 2007–2008, 7. Total applicants accepted 2007–2008, 5. Openings 2008–2009, 4. The median number of years required for completion of a degree in 2006–2007 were 6. The number of students enrolled full- and part-time who were dismissed or voluntarily withdrew from this program area in 2007–2008 were 0. *Clinical PhD (Doctor of Philosophy)*—Applications 2007–2008, 218. Total applicants accepted 2007–2008, 5. Openings 2008–2009, 5. The median number of years required for completion of a degree in 2006–2007 were 6. The number of students enrolled full- and part-time who were dismissed or voluntarily withdrew from this program area in 2007–2008 were 4. *Ecological/Community PhD (Doctor of Philosophy)*—Applications 2007–2008, 21. Total applicants accepted 2007–2008, 5. Openings 2008–2009, 5. The median number of years required for completion of a degree in 2006–2007 were 6. *Industrial/Organizational PhD (Doctor of Philosophy)*—Applications 2007–2008, 70. Total applicants accepted 2007–2008, 5. Openings 2008–2009, 5. The median number of years required for completion of a degree in 2006–2007 were 5. The number of students enrolled full- and part-time who were dismissed or voluntarily withdrew from this program area in 2007–2008 were 0. *Cognitive PhD (Doctor of Philosophy)*—Applications 2007–2008, 29. Total applicants accepted 2007–2008, 5. Openings 2008–2009, 5. The median number of years required for completion of a degree in 2006–2007 were 6. The number of students enrolled full- and part-time who were dismissed or voluntarily withdrew from this program area in 2007–2008 were 0. *Social/Personality PhD (Doctor of Philosophy)*—Applications 2007–2008, 42. Total applicants accepted 2007–2008, 5. Openings 2008–2009, 5. The median number of years required for completion of a degree in 2006–2007 were 6. The number of students enrolled full- and part-time who were dismissed or voluntarily withdrew from this program area in 2007–2008 were 0.

Admissions Requirements:

Scores: Entries appear in this order: required test or GPA, minimum score (if required), median score of students entering in 2007–2008. Master's Programs: GRE-V no minimum stated; GRE-Q no minimum stated; GRE-Subject (Psychology) no minimum stated; overall undergraduate GPA no minimum stated; last 2 years GPA no minimum stated; Masters GRE-Analytical no minimum stated. Doctoral Programs: GRE-V no minimum stated; GRE-Q no minimum stated; GRE-Subject (Psychology) no minimum stated; overall undergraduate GPA no minimum stated; last 2 years GPA no minimum stated; Doctoral program GRE-Analytic no minimum stated.

Other Criteria: (importance of criteria rated low, medium, or high): GRE/MAT scores—high, research experience—high, work experience—medium, extracurricular activity—medium, GPA—high, letters of recommendation—high, interview—high, statement of goals and objectives—high, undergraduate major in psychology—medium, specific undergraduate psychology courses taken—medium. Extra curricular, public service, and clinical activities are important for applicants to the clinical and ecological/community programs. For additional information on admission requirements, go to http://psychology.msu.edu.

Student Characteristics: The following represents characteristics of students in 2007–2008 in all graduate psychology programs in the department: Female—full-time 73, part-time 23; Male—full-time 30, part-time 12; African American/Black—full-time 5, part-time 0; Hispanic/Latino(a)—full-time 2, part-time 0; Asian/Pacific Islander—full-time 3, part-time 0; American Indian/Alaska Native—full-time 0, part-time 0; Caucasian/White—full-time 0, part-time 0; Unknown ethnicity—full-time 0, part-time 0.

Financial Information/Assistance:

Financial Assistance:

First-Year Students: Teaching assistantships available for first year. Average amount paid per academic year: $16,740. Average number of hours worked per week: 20. Apply by December 15. Tuition remission given: full. Research assistantships available for first year. Average amount paid per academic year: $16,740. Average number of hours worked per week: 20. Apply by December 15. Tuition remission given: full. Fellowships and scholarships available for first year. Average amount paid per academic year: $24,000. Average number of hours worked per week: 0. Apply by December 15. Tuition remission given: full.

Advanced Students: Teaching assistantships available for advanced students. Average amount paid per academic year: $18,408. Average number of hours worked per week: 20. Apply by none. Tuition remission given: full. Research assistantships available for advanced students. Average amount paid per academic year: $18,408. Average number of hours worked per week: 20. Apply by none. Tuition remission given: full. Fellowships and scholarships available for advanced students. Average amount paid per academic year: $24,000. Apply by none. Tuition remission given: full.

Additional Information: Of all students currently enrolled full time, 95% benefited from one or more of the listed financial assistance programs. Application and information available online at http://psychology.msu.edu.

Internships/Practica: Doctoral Degree (PhD Clinical): For those doctoral students for whom a professional internship was required in this program prior to graduation, (4) students applied for an internship in 2006–2007, with (4) students obtaining an internship. Of those students who obtained an internship, (4) were paid internships. Of those students who obtained an internship, (4) students placed in APA/CPA-accredited internships, (0) students placed in internships not APA/CPA-accredited, but listed with the Association of Psychology Postdoctoral and Internship Centers (APPIC), (0) students placed in internships conforming to guidelines of the Council of Directors of School Psychology Programs (CDSPP), (0) students placed in internships that were not APA/CPA-accredited, APPIC or CDSPP listed. Clinical practica provided by the clinical program at the department's Psychological Clinic.

Housing and Day Care: On-campus housing is available. See the following Web site for more information: http://www.hfs.msu.edu/uh/. On-campus day care facilities are available. See the following Web site for more information: http://www.vps.msu.edu/scdc/.

Employment of Department Graduates:

Master's Degree Graduates: Of those who graduated in the academic year 2006–2007, the following categories and numbers represent the postgraduate activities and employment of master's degree graduates: Enrolled in a postdoctoral residency/fellowship (n/a), employed in independent practice (n/a), total from the above (master's) (0).

Doctoral Degree Graduates: Of those who graduated in the academic year 2006–2007, the following categories and numbers represent the postgraduate activities and employment of doctoral degree graduates: Enrolled in a psychology doctoral program (n/a), total from the above (doctoral) (0).

Additional Information:

Orientation, Objectives, and Emphasis of Department: The main objective of our programs is to train researchers who will engage in the generation and application of knowledge in a wide range of areas in psychology.

Special Facilities or Resources: Facilities include the Psychological Clinic for the clinical program, which includes playrooms equipped for audio and video recording, testing equipment, computer-based record keeping system, and neuropsychological assessment lab. The Neuroscience–Biological Psychology Laboratories include research animal facilities, computers, light and electron-microscopy, and histology and endocrinology labs. The Vision Research Laboratory, Cognitive Processes Laboratories, Eye Movement Lab, and Speech Processing Lab provide automated facilities for conducting research in cognitive science. Additional observational labs equipped with video remote control equipment, one-way windows, and automated data recording equipment are available. Computer labs are available within the department and across campus.

Information for Students With Physical Disabilities: See the following Web site for more information: http://www2.rcpd.msu.edu/Home/.

Application Information:

Send to Graduate Secretary, Department of Psychology, 202 Psychology Building, Michigan State University, East Lansing, MI 48824. Application available online. URL of online application: http://www.psychology.msu.edu/. Students are admitted in the Fall, application deadline December 15. Department application and materials, as well as university application, is required by December 15. *Fee:* $50.

Michigan, University of

Combined Program in Education and Psychology
1406 School of Education, 610 East University Avenue
Ann Arbor, MI 48109-1259
Telephone: (734) 647-0626
Fax: (734) 615-2164
E-mail: *cpep@umich.edu*
Web: *http://www.soe.umich.edu/edpsych/index.html*

Department Information:

1956. Chairperson: Tabbye Chavous and Kevin Miller. Number of faculty: total—part-time 14; women—part-time 7; minority—part-time 4; women minority—part-time 3.

Programs and Degrees Offered:

Listed in the following order: Program area, degree type (T if terminal Master's), number awarded 7/06–6/07. Education and Psychology PhD (Doctor of Philosophy) 7.

Student Applications/Admissions:

Student Applications

Education and Psychology PhD (Doctor of Philosophy)—Applications 2007–2008, 77. Total applicants accepted 2007–2008, 0. Number full-time enrolled (new admits only) 2007–2008, 4. Total enrolled 2007–2008 full-time, 23. Openings 2008–2009, 5. The median number of years required for completion of a degree in 2006–2007 were 6. The number of students enrolled full- and part-time who were dismissed or voluntarily withdrew from this program area in 2007–2008 were 0.

Admissions Requirements:

Scores: Entries appear in this order: required test or GPA, minimum score (if required), median score of students entering in 2007–2008. Doctoral Programs: GRE-V no minimum stated, 620; GRE-Q no minimum stated, 723; overall undergraduate GPA no minimum stated, 3.6; Doctoral program GRE-Analytic no minimum stated, 740. We do require either the GRE-Analytic or GRE-Analytic Writing scores. Mean Analytic Writing scores are 5.0.

Other Criteria: (importance of criteria rated low, medium, or high): GRE/MAT scores—medium, research experience—high, work experience—medium, extracurricular activity—medium, clinically related public service—low, GPA—medium, letters of recommendation—high, interview—high, statement of goals and objectives—high, teaching/education—high. Other: Teaching/education-related experience. For additional information on admission requirements, go to http://www.soe.umich.edu/edpsych/admissions/index.html.

Student Characteristics: The following represents characteristics of students in 2007–2008 in all graduate psychology programs in the department: Female—full-time 16, part-time 0; Male—full-time 7, part-time 0; African American/Black—full-time 6, part-time 0; Hispanic/Latino(a)—full-time 2, part-time 0; Asian/Pacific Islander—full-time 1, part-time 0; American Indian/Alaska Native—full-time 0, part-time 0; Caucasian/White—full-time 12, part-time 0; Multi-ethnic—full-time 0, part-time 0; students subject to the Americans With Disabilities Act—full-time 0, part-time 0; Unknown ethnicity—full-time 2, part-time 0; International students who hold an F-1 or J-1 Visa—full-time 2, part-time 0.

Financial Information/Assistance:

Tuition for Full-Time Study: *Doctoral:* State residents: per academic year $15,558, $864 per credit hour; Nonstate residents: per academic year $31,468, $1,748 per credit hour. See the following Web site for updates and changes in tuition costs: http://www.umich.edu/~regoff/.

Financial Assistance:

First-Year Students: Research assistantships available for first year. Average amount paid per academic year: $22,704. Average number of hours worked per week: 20. Apply by December 15. Tuition remission given: full. Fellowships and scholarships available for first year. Average amount paid per academic year: $19,800. Average number of hours worked per week: 20. Apply by December 15. Tuition remission given: full.

Advanced Students: Teaching assistantships available for advanced students. Average amount paid per academic year: $22,797. Average number of hours worked per week: 20. Apply by varies. Tuition remission given: full. Research assistantships available for advanced students. Average amount paid per academic year: $22,704. Average number of hours worked per week: 20. Apply by varies. Tuition remission given: full. Fellowships and scholarships available for advanced students. Average amount paid per academic year: $19,800. Average number of hours worked per week: 20. Apply by varies. Tuition remission given: full.

Additional Information: Of all students currently enrolled full time, 100% benefited from one or more of the listed financial assistance programs.

Internships/Practica: No information provided.

Housing and Day Care: On-campus housing is available. See the following Web site for more information: http://www.housing.umich.edu or call the following phone number for more information: (734) 763-3164. On-campus day care facilities are available. See the following Web site for more information: http://www.umich.edu/~hraa/worklife/. For more childcare information call (734) 936-8677.

Employment of Department Graduates:

Master's Degree Graduates: Of those who graduated in the academic year 2006–2007, the following categories and numbers represent the postgraduate activities and employment of master's degree graduates: Enrolled in a postdoctoral residency/fellowship (n/a), employed in independent practice (n/a), total from the above (master's) (0).

Doctoral Degree Graduates: Of those who graduated in the academic year 2006–2007, the following categories and numbers represent the postgraduate activities and employment of doctoral degree graduates: Enrolled in a psychology doctoral program (n/a), enrolled in a postdoctoral residency/fellowship (3), employed in an academic position at a university (3), still seeking employment (1), total from the above (doctoral) (7).

Additional Information:

Orientation, Objectives, and Emphasis of Department: The Combined Program in Education and Psychology focuses on research training in instructional psychology, broadly defined. Students are trained to study educational issues and do research in educational settings, on significant educational problems related to learning. There are currently four main research foci: (a) human development in context of schools, families, and communities; (b) cognitive and learning sciences; (c) motivation and self-regulated learning; and (d) resilience and development. Faculty affiliated with the program have ongoing research programs on various important issues. These include projects on children's cognitive development and reading skills, children's achievement motivation, socialization in the schools, how computers are changing the ways in which children learn, and learning and achievement of ethnically diverse students. Students in the Program work with faculty on these projects and learn to design projects in their own areas of interest. They take courses taught by faculty members in the program, and also courses taught by faculty in the Psychology Department and the School of Education. Because the department is an independent interdepartmental unit, students have the unique opportunity to work with faculty in both the Psychology Department and the School of Education, in addition to the faculty directly affiliated with the program. Graduates are well prepared for teaching and research careers in academic and nonacademic settings. We are not a School Psychology or a Counseling Psychology program.

Special Facilities or Resources: The University of Michigan is blessed with an extensive scientific–scholarly community of psychologists that is virtually unique in breadth, diversity, and quality. Because of the close collaborative relationships that have evolved over the years, graduate and postgraduate students have the opportunity to learn and work in a wide variety of well-developed specialty centers. These include the Center for Human Growth and Development, the Center for Research on Learning and Teaching, the Center for Research on Women and Gender, the Human Performance Center, the Institute of Gerontology, the Institute for Social Research (i.e., Survey Research Center, Research Center for Group Dynamics, Center for Political Studies), the NASA Center of Excellence in Man–Systems Research, the Cognitive Science and Machine Intelligence Laboratory, the Human Factors Division of the University of Michigan Transportation Research Institute, the Kresge Hearing Research Institute, the Neuroscience Laboratory, the Evolution and Human Behavior Program, the Children's Center, the Vision Research Laboratory, and the Women's Studies Program.

In addition to these resources, the Michigan campus also offers an unusually diverse series of stimulating colloquium and seminar presentations, involving both local and visiting speakers, that contributes significantly to the available opportunities for professional growth and development.

Information for Students With Physical Disabilities: See the following Web site for more information: http://www.umich.edu/~sswd/.

Application Information:
Send to Department Chair. Application available online. URL of online application: http://www.rackham.umich.edu/Admis/index.html. Students are admitted in the Fall, application deadline December 15. *Fee:* $60 for U.S. citizens and permanent resident aliens; $75 for non-U.S. citizens.

Michigan, University of

Department of Psychology
Letters, Science, and Arts
530 Church Street, 1343 East Hall
Ann Arbor, MI 48109-1043
Telephone: (734) 764-2580
Fax: (734) 615-7584
E-mail: *psych.saa@umich.edu*
Web: *http://www.lsa.umich.edu/psych/grad/*

Department Information:
1929. Chair, Student Academic Affairs: John W. Hagen. Number of faculty: total—full-time 57, part-time 63; women—full-time 30, part-time 31; total—minority—full-time 15, part-time 11; women minority—full-time 8, part-time 4.

Programs and Degrees Offered:
Listed in the following order: Program area, degree type (T if terminal Master's), number awarded 7/06–6/07. Biopsychology PhD (Doctor of Philosophy) 2, Cognition and Perception PhD (Doctor of Philosophy) 3, Developmental PhD (Doctor of Philosophy) 6, Social PhD (Doctor of Philosophy) 3, Clinical PhD (Doctor of Philosophy) 7, Personality and Social Contexts PhD (Doctor of Philosophy) 4.

APA Accreditation: Clinical PhD (Doctor of Philosophy).

Student Applications/Admissions:
Student Applications
Biopsychology PhD (Doctor of Philosophy)—Applications 2007–2008, 68. Total applicants accepted 2007–2008, 8. Number full-time enrolled (new admits only) 2007–2008, 5. Total enrolled 2007–2008 full-time, 19. Openings 2008–2009, 3. The median number of years required for completion of a degree in 2006–2007 were 5. The number of students enrolled full- and part-time who were dismissed or voluntarily withdrew from this program area in 2007–2008 were 1. *Cognition and Perception PhD (Doctor of Philosophy)*—Applications 2007–2008, 110. Total applicants accepted 2007–2008, 10. Number full-time enrolled (new admits only) 2007–2008, 4. Total enrolled 2007–2008 full-time, 20. Openings 2008–2009, 3. The median number of years required for completion of a degree in 2006–2007 were 5. The number of students enrolled full- and part-time who were dismissed or voluntarily withdrew from this program area in 2007–2008 were 0. *Developmental PhD (Doctor of Philosophy)*—Applications 2007–2008, 87. Total applicants accepted 2007–2008, 10. Number full-time enrolled (new admits only) 2007–2008, 6. Total enrolled 2007–2008 full-time, 29. Openings 2008–2009, 5. The median number of years required for completion of a degree in 2006–2007 were 5. The number of students enrolled full- and part-time who were dismissed or voluntarily withdrew from this program area in 2007–2008 were 0. *Social PhD (Doctor of Philosophy)*—Applications 2007–2008, 143. Total applicants accepted 2007–2008, 10. Number full-time enrolled (new admits only) 2007–2008, 7. Total enrolled 2007–2008 full-time, 31. Openings 2008–2009, 4. The median number of years required for completion of a degree in 2006–2007 were 5. The number of students enrolled full- and part-time who were dismissed or voluntarily withdrew from this program area in 2007–2008 were 1. *Clinical PhD (Doctor of Philosophy)*—Applications 2007–2008, 327. Total applicants accepted 2007–2008, 7. Number full-time enrolled (new admits only) 2007–2008, 5. Total enrolled 2007–2008 full-time, 28. Openings 2008–2009, 3. The median number of years required for completion of a degree in 2006–2007 were 6. The number of students enrolled full- and part-time who were dismissed or voluntarily withdrew from this program area in 2007–2008 were 0. *Personality and Social Contexts PhD (Doctor of Philosophy)*—Applications 2007–2008, 81. Total applicants accepted 2007–2008, 5. Number full-time enrolled (new admits only) 2007–2008, 4. Number part-time enrolled (new admits only) 2007–2008, 0. Openings 2008–2009, 3. The median number of years required for completion of a degree in 2006–2007 were 5. The number of students enrolled full- and part-time who were dismissed or voluntarily withdrew from this program area in 2007–2008 were 0.

Admissions Requirements:
Scores: Entries appear in this order: required test or GPA, minimum score (if required), median score of students entering in 2007–2008. Master's Programs: GRE-V no minimum stated, 670; GRE-Q no minimum stated, 700; overall undergraduate GPA 3.7, 3.71; last 2 years GPA 3.5, 3.5; psychology GPA 3.5, 3.5. Doctoral Programs: GRE-V no minimum stated, 602; GRE-Q no minimum stated, 662; overall undergraduate GPA 3.0, 3.71.
Other Criteria: (importance of criteria rated low, medium, or high): GRE/MAT scores—medium, research experience—high, work experience—high, extracurricular activity—low, clinically related public service—low, GPA—medium, letters of recommendation—high, interview—high, statement of goals and objectives—high. For additional information on admission requirements, go to http://www.lsa.umich.edu/psych/grad/prospective/.

Student Characteristics: The following represents characteristics of students in 2007–2008 in all graduate psychology programs in the department: Female—full-time 101, part-time 0; Male—full-time 43, part-time 0; African American/Black—full-time 17, part-time 0; Hispanic/Latino(a)—full-time 9, part-time 0; Asian/Pacific Islander—full-time 19, part-time 0; American Indian/Alaska Native—full-time 1, part-time 0; Caucasian/White—

full-time 90, part-time 0; Multi-ethnic—full-time 4, part-time 0; students subject to the Americans With Disabilities Act—full-time 0, part-time 0; Unknown ethnicity—full-time 4, part-time 0; International students who hold an F-1 or J-1 Visa—full-time 27, part-time 0.

Financial Information/Assistance:

Tuition for Full-Time Study: *Doctoral:* State residents: per academic year $15,558, $1,172 per credit hour; Nonstate residents: per academic year $31,468, $2,056 per credit hour. Tuition is subject to change. See the following Web site for updates and changes in tuition costs: http://www.umich.edu/~regoff.

Financial Assistance:

First-Year Students: Fellowships and scholarships available for first year. Average amount paid per academic year: $20,700. Average number of hours worked per week: 22. Apply by December 5. Tuition remission given: full.

Advanced Students: Teaching assistantships available for advanced students. Average amount paid per academic year: $35,000. Average number of hours worked per week: 22. Apply by December 5. Tuition remission given: full. Research assistantships available for advanced students. Average amount paid per academic year: $35,000. Average number of hours worked per week: 22. Apply by December 5. Tuition remission given: full.

Additional Information: Of all students currently enrolled full time, 100% benefited from one or more of the listed financial assistance programs. Application and information available online at http://www.lsa.umich.edu/psych/grad/prospective/.

Internships/Practica: No information provided.

Housing and Day Care: On-campus housing is available. See the following Web site for more information: http://www.housing.umich.edu. On-campus day care facilities are available. For childcare info call (734) 936-8677.

Employment of Department Graduates:

Master's Degree Graduates: Of those who graduated in the academic year 2006–2007, the following categories and numbers represent the postgraduate activities and employment of master's degree graduates: Enrolled in a postdoctoral residency/fellowship (n/a), employed in independent practice (n/a), total from the above (master's) (0).

Doctoral Degree Graduates: Of those who graduated in the academic year 2006–2007, the following categories and numbers represent the postgraduate activities and employment of doctoral degree graduates: Enrolled in a psychology doctoral program (n/a), enrolled in a postdoctoral residency/fellowship (8), employed in an academic position at a university (6), employed in business or industry (2), still seeking employment (0), do not know (3), total from the above (doctoral) (19).

Additional Information:

Orientation, Objectives, and Emphasis of Department: The general objectives of the PhD program are to permit the student to achieve: (a) a general knowledge of the broad subject matter of psychology; (b) mastery of a specialized field; (c) competence in organizing, interpreting, and communicating effectively; (d) competence in research skills and creative work; and (e) professional skills relevant to their field of specialization. At its best, graduate education requires an intensive and intimate form of instruction. Psychology department faculty members are very accessible to students and research opportunities are available in a wide variety of labs and projects. Although the department is one of the largest in the country, we have developed procedures that not only allow each student freedom in planning an individualized program of study but also permit collaborative work with a small group of staff members.

Special Facilities or Resources: The University of Michigan provides a rich environment for graduate studies. The faculty in both education and psychology are internationally known for their scholarly productivity, and so students receive excellent training in how to conduct educational research. Faculty in the Psychology Department have ties to school officials in Ann Arbor and the greater Detroit area, which means students receive ample opportunities for working on many different kinds of educational projects. Students can take advantage of the university's excellent library and computer facilities, both of which are among the best in the country. A distinct advantage of the program is that it is interdepartmental in the graduate school with full resources and faculty available from both the Psychology Department and the School of Education. The department has close collaborative relationships with the Center for Human Growth and Development, the Center for Research on Learning and Teaching, the Center for Research on Women and Gender, the Human Performance Center, the Institute of Gerontology, the Institute for Social Research, the Cognitive Science and Machine Intelligence Laboratory, the Evolution and Human Behavior Program, and the Children's Center.

Application Information:

Send to Psychology Student Academic Affairs, 1343 East Hall, 530 Church Street, University of Michigan, Ann Arbor, MI 48109-1043. Application available online. URL of online application: http://www.lsa.umich.edu/psych/grad/prospective. Students are admitted in the Fall, application deadline December 5. May apply to up to three separate subplans within Psychology on the Rackham School of Graduate Studies with one fee payment. Read all application materials. *Fee:* $60; $75 for international applications.

Northern Michigan University

Department of Psychology
Arts and Sciences
1401 Presque Isle Avenue
Marquette, MI 49855
Telephone: (906) 227-2935
Fax: (906) 227-2954
E-mail: *sburns@nmu.edu*
Web: *http://www.nmu.edu/departments/psych.htm*

Department Information:

1950. Head and Professor: Sheila Burns. Number of faculty: total—full-time 5; women—full-time 5, part-time 1.

Programs and Degrees Offered:

Listed in the following order: Program area, degree type (T if terminal Master's), number awarded 7/06–6/07. Experimental Psychology MA/MS (Master of Arts/Science) 0, Training, Development, and Performance Improvement MA/MS (Master of Arts/ Science) (T) 12.

Student Applications/Admissions:

Student Applications

Experimental Psychology MA/MS (Master of Arts/Science)—Total applicants accepted 2007–2008, 0. The median number of years required for completion of a degree in 2006–2007 were 3. The number of students enrolled full- and part-time who were dismissed or voluntarily withdrew from this program area in 2007–2008 were 0. *Training, Development, and Performance Improvement MA/MS (Master of Arts/Science)*—Applications 2007–2008, 20. Total applicants accepted 2007–2008, 17. Openings 2008–2009, 25. The median number of years required for completion of a degree in 2006–2007 were 3.

Admissions Requirements:

Scores: Entries appear in this order: required test or GPA, minimum score (if required), median score of students entering in 2007–2008. Master's Programs: GRE-V no minimum stated; GRE-Q no minimum stated; GRE-Subject (Psychology) no minimum stated; overall undergraduate GPA 3.00; psychology GPA 3.00. Only the Experimental Psychology program asks for GRE scores. If other components of the application dossier warrant, an exception to the combined GRE V+Q of 1000 may be considered. Should have some psychology background for the Experimental Psychology program. The Training and Development program requires Introductory Psychology and Statistics.

Other Criteria: (importance of criteria rated low, medium, or high): GRE/MAT scores—medium, research experience—medium, work experience—medium, extracurricular activity—medium, clinically related public service—low, GPA—high, letters of recommendation—high, statement of goals and objectives—high, undergraduate major in psychology—low. Experimental Psychology program looks for a variety of psychology courses and expects students to have completed undergraduate statistics. The Training, Development, and Performance Improvement program requires the student take, if not already taken, Introductory Psychology and Statistics during the first year.

Student Characteristics: The following represents characteristics of students in 2007–2008 in all graduate psychology programs in the department: Female—full-time 7, part-time 7; Male—full-time 7, part-time 7; African American/Black—full-time 0, part-time 0; Hispanic/Latino(a)—full-time 0, part-time 0; Asian/Pacific Islander—full-time 1, part-time 0; American Indian/Alaska Native—full-time 0, part-time 0; Caucasian/White—full-time 0, part-time 0; Multi-ethnic—full-time 0, part-time 0; students subject to the Americans With Disabilities Act—full-time 1, part-time 0; Unknown ethnicity—full-time 0, part-time 0.

Financial Information/Assistance:

Financial Assistance:

First-Year Students: Teaching assistantships available for first year. Average amount paid per academic year: $7,000. Average number of hours worked per week: 20. Apply by May 1. Tuition remission given: full. Fellowships and scholarships available for first year. Average amount paid per academic year: $5,000. Average number of hours worked per week: 0. Apply by May 1.

Advanced Students: No information provided.

Additional Information: Of all students currently enrolled full time, 10% benefited from one or more of the listed financial assistance programs. Application and information available online at http://www.nmu.edu/graduate_studies/.

Internships/Practica: Training, Development, and Performance Improvement program may provide workplace placement in practica or internships for its students.

Housing and Day Care: On-campus housing is available. See the following Web site for more information: http://www.nmu.edu/. No on-campus day care facilities are available.

Employment of Department Graduates:

Master's Degree Graduates: Of those who graduated in the academic year 2006–2007, the following categories and numbers represent the postgraduate activities and employment of master's degree graduates: Enrolled in a psychology doctoral program (4), enrolled in another graduate/professional program (0), enrolled in a postdoctoral residency/fellowship (n/a), employed in independent practice (n/a), employed in an academic position at a university (0), employed in an academic position at a 2-year/4-year college (0), employed in other positions at a higher education institution (0), employed in a professional position in a school system (0), employed in business or industry (0), employed in government agency (0), employed in a community mental health/counseling center (0), employed in a hospital/medical center (0), still seeking employment (0), other employment position (0), total from the above (master's) (4).

Doctoral Degree Graduates: Of those who graduated in the academic year 2006–2007, the following categories and numbers represent the postgraduate activities and employment of doctoral degree graduates: Enrolled in a psychology doctoral program (n/a), enrolled in a postdoctoral residency/fellowship (0), employed in independent practice (0), employed in an academic position at a university (0), employed in an academic position at a 2-year/4-year college (0), employed in other positions at a higher education institution (0), employed in a professional position in a school system (0), employed in business or industry (0), employed in government agency (0), employed in a community mental health/counseling center (0), employed in a hospital/medical center (0), still seeking employment (0), other employment position (0), total from the above (doctoral) (0).

Additional Information:

Orientation, Objectives, and Emphasis of Department: The Experimental Psychology MS program is designed to prepare students for PhD programs and specialty jobs in the workplace. The Training, Development, and Performance Improvement MS program is designed for students who will be seeking related jobs upon graduation.

Special Facilities or Resources: Active research labs in the department: learning, perception, developmental, social, physiological (2), behavioral and historical. There is an up-to-date statistics lab. Graduate students are provided office and research space.

Information for Students With Physical Disabilities: See the following Web site for more information: http://www.nmu.edu/.

Application Information:
Send to Department Head Director of Graduate Studies, Department of Psychology, Northern Michigan University, Marquette, MI 49855. Application available online. URL of online application: http://www.nmu.edu/graduate_studies/. Students are admitted in the Fall, application deadline May 1; Winter, application deadline November 1. Graduate study applications are open until the semester begins. However, most decisions about graduate assistantships are made in May and if necessary, November. *Fee:* $50.

Wayne State University

Department of Psychology
Science
5057 Woodward Avenue, 7th Floor
Detroit, MI 48202
Telephone: (313) 577-2800
Fax: (313) 577-7636
E-mail: *aallen@wayne.edu*
Web: *http://www.psych.wayne.edu*

Department Information:
1923. Chairperson: R. Douglas Whitman. Number of faculty: total—full-time 35, part-time 10; women—full-time 12, part-time 5; total—minority—full-time 1; women minority—full-time 1; faculty subject to the Americans With Disabilities Act 1.

Programs and Degrees Offered:
Listed in the following order: Program area, degree type (T if terminal Master's), number awarded 7/06–6/07. Clinical Psychology PhD (Doctor of Philosophy) 8, Behavioral and Cognitive Neuroscience PhD (Doctor of Philosophy) 2, Industrial/Organizational Psychology PhD (Doctor of Philosophy) 4, Human Development MA/MS (Master of Arts/Science) (T) 1, Cognitive and Social Psychology Across the Lifespan PhD (Doctor of Philosophy) 5, Industrial/Organizational Psychology MA/MS (Master of Arts/Science) (T) 0.

APA Accreditation: Clinical PhD (Doctor of Philosophy).

Student Applications/Admissions:
Student Applications
Clinical Psychology PhD (Doctor of Philosophy)—Applications 2007–2008, 149. Total applicants accepted 2007–2008, 15. Number full-time enrolled (new admits only) 2007–2008, 9. Total enrolled 2007–2008 full-time, 67. Openings 2008–2009, 9. The median number of years required for completion of a degree in 2006–2007 were 7. The number of students enrolled full- and part-time who were dismissed or voluntarily withdrew from this program area in 2007–2008 were 0. *Behavioral and Cognitive Neuroscience PhD (Doctor of Philosophy)*—Applications 2007–2008, 18. Total applicants accepted 2007–2008, 6. Number full-time enrolled (new admits only) 2007–2008, 3. Total enrolled 2007–2008 full-time, 15. Openings 2008–2009, 5. The median number of years required for completion of a degree in 2006–2007 were 6. The number of students enrolled full- and part-time who were dismissed or voluntarily withdrew from this program area in 2007–2008 were 3. *Industrial/Organizational Psychology PhD (Doctor of Philosophy)*—Applications 2007–2008, 29. Total applicants accepted 2007–2008, 10. Number full-time enrolled (new admits only) 2007–2008, 5. Total enrolled 2007–2008 full-time, 27. Openings 2008–2009, 5. The median number of years required for completion of a degree in 2006–2007 were 6. The number of students enrolled full- and part-time who were dismissed or voluntarily withdrew from this program area in 2007–2008 were 0. *Human Development MA/MS (Master of Arts/Science)*—Applications 2007–2008, 10. Total applicants accepted 2007–2008, 4. Number part-time enrolled (new admits only) 2007–2008, 3. Openings 2008–2009, 10. The median number of years required for completion of a degree in 2006–2007 were 3. The number of students enrolled full- and part-time who were dismissed or voluntarily withdrew from this program area in 2007–2008 were 0. *Cognitive and Social Psychology Across the Lifespan PhD (Doctor of Philosophy)*—Applications 2007–2008, 35. Total applicants accepted 2007–2008, 10. Number full-time enrolled (new admits only) 2007–2008, 5. Total enrolled 2007–2008 full-time, 28. Openings 2008–2009, 5. The median number of years required for completion of a degree in 2006–2007 were 5. The number of students enrolled full- and part-time who were dismissed or voluntarily withdrew from this program area in 2007–2008 were 1. *Industrial/Organizational Psychology MA/MS (Master of Arts/Science)*—Applications 2007–2008, 42. Total applicants accepted 2007–2008, 26. Number full-time enrolled (new admits only) 2007–2008, 0. Number part-time enrolled (new admits only) 2007–2008, 15. Openings 2008–2009, 15. The number of students enrolled full- and part-time who were dismissed or voluntarily withdrew from this program area in 2007–2008 were 0.

Admissions Requirements:
Scores: Entries appear in this order: required test or GPA, minimum score (if required), median score of students entering in 2007–2008. Master's Programs: GRE-V no minimum stated, 500; GRE-Q no minimum stated, 480; overall undergraduate GPA 2.80; last 2 years GPA 3.00. Doctoral Programs: GRE-V no minimum stated, 610; GRE-Q no minimum stated, 620; overall undergraduate GPA 3.00, 3.50; last 2 years GPA 3.00.
Other Criteria: (importance of criteria rated low, medium, or high): GRE/MAT scores—high, research experience—high, work experience—low, extracurricular activity—low, clinically related public service—low, GPA—high, letters of recommendation—high, interview—high, statement of goals and objectives—high. For additional information on admission requirements, go to http://www.clas.wayne.edu/psychology/.

Student Characteristics: The following represents characteristics of students in 2007–2008 in all graduate psychology programs in the department: Female—full-time 104, part-time 22; Male—full-time 33, part-time 6; African American/Black—full-time 9, part-time 0; Hispanic/Latino(a)—full-time 3, part-time 0; Asian/Pacific Islander—full-time 15, part-time 0; American Indian/Alaska Native—full-time 0, part-time 0; Caucasian/White—full-time 110, part-time 0; Multi-ethnic—full-time 0, part-time 0; students subject to the Americans With Disabilities Act—full-time 0, part-time 0; Unknown ethnicity—full-time 0, part-time 28; International students who hold an F-1 or J-1 Visa—full-time 14, part-time 0.

Financial Information/Assistance:
Tuition for Full-Time Study: *Master's:* State residents: $402 per credit hour; Nonstate residents: $889 per credit hour. *Doctoral:*

State residents: $402 per credit hour; Nonstate residents: $889 per credit hour. Tuition is subject to change. Additional fees are assessed to students beyond the costs of tuition for the following: Omnibus Credits Hour Fee: $26.90; Registration Fee: $139.30; Fitness Center Fee: $25.00. See the following Web site for updates and changes in tuition costs: http://www.sdcl.wayne.edu/registrar/registrarhome.

Financial Assistance:

First-Year Students: Teaching assistantships available for first year. Average amount paid per academic year: $14,000. Average number of hours worked per week: 20. Tuition remission given: full. Research assistantships available for first year. Average amount paid per academic year: $14,000. Average number of hours worked per week: 20. Tuition remission given: full. Traineeships available for first year. Average amount paid per academic year: $14,000. Average number of hours worked per week: 20. Tuition remission given: full and partial. Fellowships and scholarships available for first year. Average amount paid per academic year: $14,000. Average number of hours worked per week: 20. Tuition remission given: full.

Advanced Students: Teaching assistantships available for advanced students. Average amount paid per academic year: $14,000. Average number of hours worked per week: 20. Tuition remission given: full. Research assistantships available for advanced students. Average amount paid per academic year: $14,000. Average number of hours worked per week: 20. Tuition remission given: full. Traineeships available for advanced students. Average amount paid per academic year: $14,000. Average number of hours worked per week: 20. Tuition remission given: full and partial. Fellowships and scholarships available for advanced students. Average amount paid per academic year: $14,000. Average number of hours worked per week: 20. Tuition remission given: full.

Additional Information: Application and information available online at http://www.gradschool.wayne.edu/Funding.html.

Internships/Practica: No information provided.

Housing and Day Care: On-campus housing is available. See the following Web site for more information: http://www.housing.wayne.edu; http://www.detroitmidtown.com; http://www.liveinwoodbridge.com. No on-campus day care facilities are available.

Employment of Department Graduates:

Master's Degree Graduates: Of those who graduated in the academic year 2006–2007, the following categories and numbers represent the postgraduate activities and employment of master's degree graduates: Enrolled in a postdoctoral residency/fellowship (n/a), employed in independent practice (n/a), total from the above (master's) (0).

Doctoral Degree Graduates: Of those who graduated in the academic year 2006–2007, the following categories and numbers represent the postgraduate activities and employment of doctoral degree graduates: Enrolled in a psychology doctoral program (n/a), total from the above (doctoral) (0).

Additional Information:

Orientation, Objectives, and Emphasis of Department: This department strives to select graduate students with a strong educational background and outstanding potential and to train them to be knowledgeable, ethical practitioners and research scholars in their chosen areas. Program admission is limited to persons planning to obtain the doctoral degree. Initial broad training is followed by specialized training.

Special Facilities or Resources: The behavioral and cognitive neuroscience area participates in the university neuroscience program. Excellent laboratory facilities are available in neurobiology, neuropharmacology, psychopharmacology, neuropsychology, and ethology. Several faculty in behavioral and cognitive neuroscience and other areas in the department work in the area of substance abuse. The clinical program emphasizes psychotherapy, community mental health, diagnostics, alcohol abuse issues, neuropsychology, and child and geropsychology. Clinical practice and research experience are obtained in a variety of clinical placements and in our own clinic. The cognitive program emphasizes cognition theory and its application to applied problems. The developmental area emphasizes life span studies and is affiliated with the Institute of Gerontology. The social psychology program has both basic and applied research emphases. Well-equipped laboratories in the department and at the Merrill-Palmer Institute, which is affiliated with the department, are available for cognitive, social, and developmental research. In addition, social psychology uses its urban setting to carry out field studies. The industrial/organizational area emphasizes organizational psychology, personnel research, and field placements. Excellent computer facilities and libraries support research in all areas.

Application Information:

Send to Graduate Office, Psychology Department, WSU, 5057 Woodward Avenue, 7th Floor, Detroit, MI 48202. Application available online. URL of online application: http://www.psych.wayne.edu/graduate/gradprostu2.htm. Students are admitted in the Fall, application deadline December 15. I/O and Human Development Master's Programs: Fall application deadline, June 15; Winter application deadline, October 15; Summer application deadline, March 15. *Fee:* $50.

Wayne State University

Division of Theoretical and Behavioral Foundations-Educational Psychology
College of Education
Detroit, MI 48202
Telephone: (313) 557-1614
Fax: (313) 577-5235
E-mail: *s.b.hillman@wayne.edu*
Web: *http://tbf.coe.wayne.edu*

Department Information:

1957. Chairperson: Stephen B. Hillman. Number of faculty: total—full-time 6, part-time 12; women—full-time 3, part-time 8; total—minority—full-time 1, part-time 1; women minority—full-time 1.

Programs and Degrees Offered:

Listed in the following order: Program area, degree type (T if terminal Master's), number awarded 7/06–6/07. Educational PhD (Doctor of Philosophy) 9, School MA/MS (Master of Arts/Science) 21.

Student Applications/Admissions:

Student Applications

Educational PhD (Doctor of Philosophy)—Applications 2007–2008, 9. Total applicants accepted 2007–2008, 6. Number part-time enrolled (new admits only) 2007–2008, 6. Openings 2008–2009, 10. The median number of years required for completion of a degree in 2006–2007 were 6. The number of students enrolled full- and part-time who were dismissed or voluntarily withdrew from this program area in 2007–2008 were 0. *School MA/MS (Master of Arts/Science)*—Applications 2007–2008, 44. Total applicants accepted 2007–2008, 22. Number full-time enrolled (new admits only) 2007–2008, 22. Total enrolled 2007–2008 full-time, 66. Openings 2008–2009, 32. The median number of years required for completion of a degree in 2006–2007 were 2. The number of students enrolled full- and part-time who were dismissed or voluntarily withdrew from this program area in 2007–2008 were 0.

Admissions Requirements:

Scores: Entries appear in this order: required test or GPA, minimum score (if required), median score of students entering in 2007–2008. Master's Programs: GRE-V no minimum stated; GRE-Q no minimum stated; overall undergraduate GPA no minimum stated. GRE for MA Program (School Psychology) only. Doctoral Programs: overall undergraduate GPA no minimum stated.

Other Criteria: (importance of criteria rated low, medium, or high): GRE/MAT scores—medium, research experience—medium, work experience—medium, extracurricular activity—medium, clinically related public service—medium, GPA—high, letters of recommendation—high, interview—high, statement of goals and objectives—high.

Student Characteristics: The following represents characteristics of students in 2007–2008 in all graduate psychology programs in the department: Female—full-time 47, part-time 28; Male—full-time 6, part-time 12; African American/Black—full-time 6, part-time 6; Hispanic/Latino(a)—full-time 0, part-time 0; Asian/Pacific Islander—full-time 1, part-time 1; American Indian/Alaska Native—part-time 0; Caucasian/White—full-time 46, part-time 20; students subject to the Americans With Disabilities Act—full-time 2, part-time 0; Unknown ethnicity—full-time 0, part-time 0.

Financial Information/Assistance:

Tuition for Full-Time Study: *Master's:* State residents: per academic year $4,800, $260 per credit hour; Nonstate residents: per academic year $9,600, $520 per credit hour. *Doctoral:* State residents: per academic year $4,800, $260 per credit hour; Nonstate residents: per academic year $9,600, $520 per credit hour. Tuition is subject to change. Additional fees are assessed to students beyond the costs of tuition for the following: Testing materials. See the following Web site for updates and changes in tuition costs: http://www.wayne.edu.

Financial Assistance:

First-Year Students: Fellowships and scholarships available for first year. Apply by March 1. Tuition remission given: full.

Advanced Students: Fellowships and scholarships available for advanced students. Apply by March 1. Tuition remission given: full.

Additional Information: Of all students currently enrolled full time, 15% benefited from one or more of the listed financial assistance programs.

Internships/Practica: No information provided.

Housing and Day Care: On-campus housing is available. On-campus day care facilities are available.

Employment of Department Graduates:

Master's Degree Graduates: Of those who graduated in the academic year 2006–2007, the following categories and numbers represent the postgraduate activities and employment of master's degree graduates: Enrolled in a psychology doctoral program (5), enrolled in a postdoctoral residency/fellowship (n/a), employed in independent practice (n/a), employed in a professional position in a school system (12), employed in a community mental health/counseling center (10), total from the above (master's) (27).

Doctoral Degree Graduates: Of those who graduated in the academic year 2006–2007, the following categories and numbers represent the postgraduate activities and employment of doctoral degree graduates: Enrolled in a psychology doctoral program (n/a), enrolled in a postdoctoral residency/fellowship (0), employed in independent practice (3), employed in an academic position at a university (0), employed in a professional position in a school system (6), do not know (2), total from the above (doctoral) (11).

Additional Information:

Orientation, Objectives, and Emphasis of Department: The department offers MA programs in school and community psychology, marriage and family psychology, and MEd and PhD programs in educational psychology. The program orientations are eclectic, using the scientist–practitioner model, with emphasis on application of theory at the master's degree level and on theoretical issues at the PhD level.

Application Information:

Send to Department Chair. Students are admitted in the Winter, application deadline February 15. MEd program rolling admissions throughout the year. *Fee:* $20.

Western Michigan University

Counselor Education and Counseling Psychology
College of Education
3102 Sangren Hall
1903 West Michigan Avenue
Kalamazoo, MI 49008-5226
Telephone: (269) 387-5100
Fax: (269) 387-5090
E-mail: *patrick.munley@wmich.edu*
Web: *http://www.wmich.edu/coe/cecp*

Department Information:

1970. Chairperson: Patrick H. Munley. Number of faculty: total—full-time 18, part-time 9; women—full-time 5, part-time 5; total—minority—full-time 4, part-time 3; women minority—full-time 1, part-time 2; faculty subject to the Americans With Disabilities Act 1.

Programs and Degrees Offered:

Listed in the following order: Program area, degree type (T if terminal Master's), number awarded 7/06–6/07. Counseling Psychology MA/MS (Master of Arts/Science) (T) 39, Counseling Psycholgy PhD (Doctor of Philosophy) 3.

APA Accreditation: Counseling PhD (Doctor of Philosophy).

Student Applications/Admissions:

Student Applications

Counseling Psychology MA/MS (Master of Arts/Science)—Applications 2007–2008, 76. Total applicants accepted 2007–2008, 71. Number full-time enrolled (new admits only) 2007–2008, 55. Number part-time enrolled (new admits only) 2007–2008, 16. Total enrolled 2007–2008 full-time, 223, part-time, 32. Openings 2008–2009, 55. The median number of years required for completion of a degree in 2006–2007 were 3. The number of students enrolled full- and part-time who were dismissed or voluntarily withdrew from this program area in 2007–2008 were 11. *Counseling Psycholgy PhD (Doctor of Philosophy)*—Applications 2007–2008, 52. Total applicants accepted 2007–2008, 9. Number full-time enrolled (new admits only) 2007–2008, 9. Number part-time enrolled (new admits only) 2007–2008, 0. Openings 2008–2009, 8. The median number of years required for completion of a degree in 2006–2007 were 6. The number of students enrolled full- and part-time who were dismissed or voluntarily withdrew from this program area in 2007–2008 were 0.

Admissions Requirements:

Scores: Entries appear in this order: required test or GPA, minimum score (if required), median score of students entering in 2007–2008. Master's Programs: overall undergraduate GPA 3.0; last 2 years GPA 3.0. Doctoral Programs: GRE-V no minimum stated; GRE-Q no minimum stated; overall undergraduate GPA 3.0; Doctoral program GRE-Analytic no minimum stated. GRE Subject (Psychology) scores are required for admission if applying upon virtue of a Bachelor's degree. GRE Subject (Psychology) scores are NOT required for those who hold a Master's degree.

Other Criteria: (importance of criteria rated low, medium, or high): GRE/MAT scores—high, research experience—high, work experience—medium, extracurricular activity—low, clinically related public service—low, GPA—high, letters of recommendation—high, interview—high, statement of goals and objectives—high, multicultural awareness—high, undergraduate major in psychology—low, specific undergraduate psychology courses taken—medium. For additional information on admission requirements, go to http://www.wmich.edu/coe/cecp/.

Student Characteristics: The following represents characteristics of students in 2007–2008 in all graduate psychology programs in the department: Female—full-time 222, part-time 25; Male—full-time 65, part-time 7; African American/Black—full-time 41, part-time 5; Hispanic/Latino(a)—full-time 5, part-time 2; Asian/Pacific Islander—full-time 9, part-time 1; American Indian/Alaska Native—full-time 3, part-time 0; Caucasian/White—full-time 215, part-time 22; Multi-ethnic—full-time 14, part-time 0; students subject to the Americans With Disabilities Act—full-time 0, part-time 0; Unknown ethnicity—full-time 0, part-time 2; International students who hold an F-1 or J-1 Visa—full-time 12, part-time 0.

Financial Information/Assistance:

Tuition for Full-Time Study: *Master's:* State residents: $345 per credit hour; Nonstate residents: $730 per credit hour. *Doctoral:* State residents: $345 per credit hour; Nonstate residents: $730 per credit hour. See the following Web site for updates and changes in tuition costs: http://www.wmich.edu/registrar/tuition.

Financial Assistance:

First-Year Students: Teaching assistantships available for first year. Average amount paid per academic year: $16,620. Average number of hours worked per week: 20. Apply by February 15. Tuition remission given: full. Research assistantships available for first year. Average amount paid per academic year: $16,620. Average number of hours worked per week: 20. Apply by February 15. Tuition remission given: full. Fellowships and scholarships available for first year. Average amount paid per academic year: $10,400. Average number of hours worked per week: 10. Apply by February 15. Tuition remission given: full and partial.

Advanced Students: Teaching assistantships available for advanced students. Average amount paid per academic year: $16,620. Average number of hours worked per week: 20. Apply by February 15. Tuition remission given: full. Research assistantships available for advanced students. Average amount paid per academic year: $16,620. Average number of hours worked per week: 20. Apply by February 15. Tuition remission given: full. Fellowships and scholarships available for advanced students. Apply by N/A.

Additional Information: Of all students currently enrolled full time, 95% benefited from one or more of the listed financial assistance programs. Application and information available online at http://www.wmich.edu/grad/funding/.

Internships/Practica: Master's Degree (MA/MS Counseling Psychology): An internship experience such as a final research project or "capstone" experience is required of graduates. Doctoral Degree (PhD Counseling Psycholgy): For those doctoral students for whom a professional internship was required in this program prior to graduation, (4) students applied for an internship in 2006–2007, with (4) students obtaining an internship. Of those students who obtained an internship, (3) were paid internships. Of those students who obtained an internship, (3) students placed in APA/CPA-accredited internships, (0) students placed in internships not APA/CPA-accredited, but listed with the Association of Psychology Postdoctoral and Internship Centers (APPIC), (0) students placed in internships conforming to guidelines of the Council of Directors of School Psychology Programs (CDSPP), (1) students placed in internships that were not APA/CPA accredited, APPIC or CDSPP listed. Master's level practica are available in a wide range of settings. Doctoral practica are also available in hospitals, clinics, university counseling centers, and so forth.

Housing and Day Care: On-campus housing is available. See the following Web site for more information: http://www.wmich.edu/housing/. On-campus day care facilities are available. See the following Web site for more information: http://www.wmich.edu/childrensplace/index.html.

Employment of Department Graduates:

Master's Degree Graduates: Of those who graduated in the academic year 2006–2007, the following categories and numbers represent the postgraduate activities and employment of master's degree graduates: Enrolled in a postdoctoral residency/fellowship (n/a), employed in independent practice (n/a), total from the above (master's) (0).

Doctoral Degree Graduates: Of those who graduated in the academic year 2006–2007, the following categories and numbers represent the postgraduate activities and employment of doctoral degree graduates: Enrolled in a psychology doctoral program (n/a), employed in a community mental health/counseling center (3), do not know (0), total from the above (doctoral) (3).

Additional Information:

Orientation, Objectives, and Emphasis of Department: The department prepares professional counseling psychologists at the master's and doctoral levels. The counseling psychology doctoral program's philosophy holds that theory, research, and practice are interdependent and complementary. The curriculum and practical experiences are designed to ensure professional competency in all three dimensions and facilitate their integration. Program graduates are typically employed in a variety of settings including academic departments, university counseling centers, community mental health agencies, hospitals, and independent practices. The curriculum was developed by the Counseling Psychology faculty and is based on guidelines and principles of the American Psychological Association (APA) for accreditation of professional psychology programs. Requirements include course work in the basic scientific core of psychology including research design and statistics, the biological bases of behavior, cognitive–affective bases of behavior, social bases of behavior, individual behavior and human development, and the history and systems of psychology. Requirements also involve course work in the specialization of Counseling Psychology including professional issues and ethics in counseling psychology, counseling theory and practice, consultation, supervision, vocational psychology, intellectual and personality assessment, supervised practica, and an emphasis in multicultural counseling psychology. Students are able to pursue specialty interests in Counseling Psychology through elective courses and other adjunctive experiences (e.g., involvement in faculty research, individual or group clinical supervision, etc.). In addition to course work and practica, students are required to successfully complete comprehensive examinations, a supervised APA approved predoctoral internship, and a dissertation that is psychologically focused. The student's doctoral chair and committee, along with the Counseling Psychology Training Committee, are responsible for helping the student develop a program of study and for monitoring the student's progress through the program.

Special Facilities or Resources: The department's primary training facility is the Center for Counseling and Psychological Services, which includes interview rooms, two group and family therapy rooms, and a seminar room; it is equipped with audio and video recording systems and provides for observation and telephone supervision. The department also maintains a comparable training clinic at the Graduate Center in Grand Rapids, Michigan. A wide variety of regional resources, including community clinics, schools, hospitals, and private clinics, are available to students.

Information for Students With Physical Disabilities: See the following Web site for more information: http://www.dsrs.wmich.edu.

Application Information:

Send to Department of Counselor Education and Counseling Psychology, 1903 West Michigan Avenue, WMU, Kalamazoo, MI 49008-5226. Application available online. URL of online application: http://www.wmich.edu/coe/cecp/admission/admincp.htm. Students are admitted in the Fall, application deadline January 10. The application deadline for PhD admissions is January 10. Application deadlines for MA admission are January 15, May 15 and September 15. See the department Web page for information on MA admissions, http://www.wmich.edu/coe/cecp/. *Fee:* $40.

Western Michigan University

Department of Psychology
Room 3740, Wood Hall
Kalamazoo, MI 49008
Telephone: (616) 387-4474
Fax: (616) 387-4550
E-mail: *r.wayne.fuqua@wmich.edu*
Web: *http://www.wmich.edu/psychology*

Department Information:

1952. Chairperson: R. Wayne Fuqua. Number of faculty: total—full-time 18, part-time 3; women—full-time 7, part-time 3; total—minority—full-time 1.

Programs and Degrees Offered:

Listed in the following order: Program area, degree type (T if terminal Master's), number awarded 7/06–6/07. Behavior Analysis MA/MS (Master of Arts/Science) (T) 18, Industrial/Organizational MA/MS (Master of Arts/Science) (T) 5, Behavior Analysis PhD (Doctor of Philosophy) 7, Clinical PhD (Doctor of Philosophy) 4.

APA Accreditation: Clinical PhD (Doctor of Philosophy).

Student Applications/Admissions:

Student Applications

Behavior Analysis MA/MS (Master of Arts/Science)—Applications 2007–2008, 61. Total applicants accepted 2007–2008, 18. Number full-time enrolled (new admits only) 2007–2008, 18. Openings 2008–2009, 18. The median number of years required for completion of a degree in 2006–2007 were 2. The number of students enrolled full- and part-time who were dismissed or voluntarily withdrew from this program area in 2007–2008 were 0. *Industrial/Organizational MA/MS (Master of Arts/Science)*—Applications 2007–2008, 26. Total applicants accepted 2007–2008, 10. Number full-time enrolled (new admits only) 2007–2008, 10. Openings 2008–2009, 8. The median number of years required for completion of a degree in 2006–2007 were 2. The number of students enrolled full- and part-time who were dismissed or voluntarily withdrew from this program area in 2007–2008 were 0. *Behavior Analysis PhD (Doctor of Philosophy)*—Applications 2007–2008, 50. Total applicants accepted 2007–2008, 7. Number full-time enrolled (new admits only) 2007–2008, 7. Openings 2008–2009,

8. The median number of years required for completion of a degree in 2006–2007 were 5. The number of students enrolled full- and part-time who were dismissed or voluntarily withdrew from this program area in 2007–2008 were 0. *Clinical PhD (Doctor of Philosophy)*—Applications 2007–2008, 112. Total applicants accepted 2007–2008, 5. Number full-time enrolled (new admits only) 2007–2008, 5. Openings 2008–2009, 5. The median number of years required for completion of a degree in 2006–2007 were 6. The number of students enrolled full- and part-time who were dismissed or voluntarily withdrew from this program area in 2007–2008 were 2.

Admissions Requirements:

Scores: Entries appear in this order: required test or GPA, minimum score (if required), median score of students entering in 2007–2008. Master's Programs: GRE-V 500, 556; GRE-Q 500, 547; overall undergraduate GPA 3.00, 3.70. Behavior Analysis Master's Minimum Score: No subscore below 400 and a minimum combined score of 900. Doctoral Programs: GRE-V 500, 569; GRE-Q 500, 575; overall undergraduate GPA 3.0, 3.66. Behavior Analysis GRE: no subscore below 400 and combined total minimum of 900.

Other Criteria: (importance of criteria rated low, medium, or high): GRE/MAT scores—high, research experience—high, work experience—medium, extracurricular activity—medium, clinically related public service—medium, GPA—medium, letters of recommendation—high, interview—high, statement of goals and objectives—high, behavioral analysis background—high. High importance placed on interpersonal skills. For additional information on admission requirements, go to http://www.wmich.edu/psychology.

Student Characteristics: The following represents characteristics of students in 2007–2008 in all graduate psychology programs in the department: Female—full-time 72, part-time 0; Male—full-time 41, part-time 0; African American/Black—full-time 3, part-time 0; Hispanic/Latino(a)—full-time 6, part-time 0; Asian/Pacific Islander—full-time 0, part-time 0; American Indian/Alaska Native—full-time 1, part-time 0; Caucasian/White—full-time 91, part-time 0; Multi-ethnic—full-time 1, part-time 0; students subject to the Americans With Disabilities Act—full-time 1, part-time 0; Unknown ethnicity—full-time 10, part-time 0.

Financial Information/Assistance:

Tuition for Full-Time Study: *Master's:* State residents: $324 per credit hour; Nonstate residents: $730 per credit hour. *Doctoral:* State residents: $324 per credit hour; Nonstate residents: $730 per credit hour. Tuition is subject to change. See the following Web site for updates and changes in tuition costs: http://www.wmich.edu/registrar/tuition/index.html.

Financial Assistance:

First-Year Students: Teaching assistantships available for first year. Average amount paid per academic year: $10,452. Average number of hours worked per week: 20. Tuition remission given: partial. Research assistantships available for first year. Average amount paid per academic year: $10,452. Average number of hours worked per week: 20. Tuition remission given: partial. Fellowships and scholarships available for first year. Average amount paid per academic year: $10,452. Average number of hours worked per week: 0. Tuition remission given: partial.

Advanced Students: Teaching assistantships available for advanced students. Average amount paid per academic year: $12,904. Average number of hours worked per week: 20. Tuition remission given: full. Research assistantships available for advanced students. Average amount paid per academic year: $12,904. Average number of hours worked per week: 20. Tuition remission given: full. Fellowships and scholarships available for advanced students. Average amount paid per academic year: $12,904. Average number of hours worked per week: 20. Tuition remission given: full.

Additional Information: Of all students currently enrolled full time, 80% benefited from one or more of the listed financial assistance programs. Application and information available online at http://www.wmich.edu/psychology.

Internships/Practica: No information provided.

Housing and Day Care: On-campus housing is available. See the following Web site for more information: http://www.wmich.edu/apartments; http://www.ocl.wmich.edu. On-campus day care facilities are available. See the following Web site for more information: http://www.wmich.edu/apartments; http://www.wmich.edu/childrensplace.

Employment of Department Graduates:

Master's Degree Graduates: Of those who graduated in the academic year 2006–2007, the following categories and numbers represent the postgraduate activities and employment of master's degree graduates: Enrolled in a postdoctoral residency/fellowship (n/a), employed in independent practice (n/a), total from the above (master's) (0).

Doctoral Degree Graduates: Of those who graduated in the academic year 2006–2007, the following categories and numbers represent the postgraduate activities and employment of doctoral degree graduates: Enrolled in a psychology doctoral program (n/a), total from the above (doctoral) (0).

Additional Information:

Orientation, Objectives, and Emphasis of Department: The Department of Psychology has a pervasive behavior analytic orientation, which is reflected in all of its graduate programs. Although the student may design a program of study to meet specific career goals, all programs require courses in behavior analysis. Applicants accepted into the program receive a personal appointment to an advisor and two faculty sponsors who serve as the thesis or dissertation committee and provide both academic and professional advising throughout the student's tenure at the University. The emphasis of the program is upon cooperation between student and faculty, and students are expected to assume positions of responsibility in teaching, research, and service within the department and in community-based programs. The faculty are involved in professional organizations and publish in a variety of scholarly journals. Students are also expected to become involved in these activities and contribute to research projects as coinvestigators, and to publications as coauthors.

Personal Behavior Statement: I have received a copy of the Department of Psychology Graduate Student Handbook and agree to abide by the program requirements and expectation described therein during the course of my training in the Department of Psychology. This included agreement to adhere to the Ethical Standards of the American Psychological Association, codes of ethics that are relevant to my area of specialization, the WMU Student Code, and the Student Academic Rights and Responsibilities as stipulated in the Graduate Catalog.

Special Facilities or Resources: Western Michigan University emphasizes computer usage and maintains several microcomputer laboratories for student use as well as a state-of-the-art mainframe computer system. The department research laboratories include microcomputer control systems, an animal colony for pigeons and rodents, and other support equipment for research with nonhuman participants. The Department has affiliations with a number of community-based schools and service organizations for children and adults diagnosed with autism spectrum disorders, developmental disabilities, and a range of mental illnesses. The clinical research laboratories include equipment for electrophysiological recording, fitness testing, and human operant research. The department also maintains an in-house clinic for training in therapeutic techniques under faculty supervision; the clinic includes facilities for adult, child, and family therapy.

Information for Students With Physical Disabilities: See the following Web site for more information: http://www.wmich.edu/psychology.

Application Information:
Send to Psychology Graduate Training, Department of Psychology, Western Michigan University, Kalamazoo, MI 49008. URL of online application: http://www.wmich.edu/psychology/grad/index.html. Students are admitted in the Fall, application deadline January 20. *Fee:* $40.

Argosy University/Twin Cities (2007 data)

Clinical Psychology
Minnesota School of Professional Psychology
1515 Central Parkway
Eagan, MN 55121
Telephone: (651) 846-2882
Fax: (651) 994-0144
E-mail: *jradke@argosyu.edu*
Web: *http://www.argosyu.edu*

Department Information:

1987. Program Chair: Kenneth B. Solberg. Number of faculty: total—full-time 15, part-time 19; women—full-time 8, part-time 9; faculty subject to the Americans With Disabilities Act 1.

Programs and Degrees Offered:

Listed in the following order: Program area, degree type (T if terminal Master's), number awarded 7/06–6/07. Clinical Psychology PsyD (Doctor of Psychology) 38, Marriage and Family Therapy MA/MS (Master of Arts/Science) (T) 53.

APA Accreditation: Clinical PsyD (Doctor of Psychology).

Student Applications/Admissions:

Student Applications

Clinical Psychology PsyD (Doctor of Psychology)—Applications 2007–2008, 175. Total applicants accepted 2007–2008, 105. Number full-time enrolled (new admits only) 2007–2008, 44. Number part-time enrolled (new admits only) 2007–2008, 8. Total enrolled 2007–2008 full-time, 200, part-time, 108. Openings 2008–2009, 50. The median number of years required for completion of a degree in 2006–2007 were 5. The number of students enrolled full- and part-time who were dismissed or voluntarily withdrew from this program area in 2007–2008 were 3. *Marriage and Family Therapy MA/MS (Master of Arts/Science)*—Applications 2007–2008, 77. Total applicants accepted 2007–2008, 50. Total enrolled 2007–2008 full-time, 117, part-time, 21. Openings 2008–2009, 50. The median number of years required for completion of a degree in 2006–2007 were 2. The number of students enrolled full- and part-time who were dismissed or voluntarily withdrew from this program area in 2007–2008 were 1.

Admissions Requirements:

Scores: Entries appear in this order: required test or GPA, minimum score (if required), median score of students entering in 2007–2008. Master's Programs: The GRE/MAT are not required, but may be requested.

Other Criteria: (importance of criteria rated low, medium, or high): GRE/MAT scores—low, research experience—low, work experience—medium, extracurricular activity—low, clinically related public service—medium, GPA—high, letters of recommendation—high, interview—high, statement of goals and objectives—medium.

Student Characteristics: The following represents characteristics of students in 2007–2008 in all graduate psychology programs in the department: Female—full-time 232, part-time 104; Male—full-time 85, part-time 25; African American/Black—full-time 8, part-time 4; Hispanic/Latino(a)—full-time 6, part-time 4; Asian/Pacific Islander—full-time 11, part-time 5; American Indian/Alaska Native—full-time 3, part-time 1; Caucasian/White—full-time 284, part-time 114; Multi-ethnic—full-time 5, part-time 1; students subject to the Americans With Disabilities Act—full-time 1, part-time 1; Unknown ethnicity—full-time 0, part-time 0.

Financial Information/Assistance:

Tuition for Full-Time Study: *Master's:* State residents: $525 per credit hour; Nonstate residents: $525 per credit hour. *Doctoral:* State residents: $850 per credit hour; Nonstate residents: $850 per credit hour. Tuition is subject to change. Tuition costs vary by program. See the following Web site for updates and changes in tuition costs: http://www.argosyu.edu.

Financial Assistance:

First-Year Students: Fellowships and scholarships available for first year. Average amount paid per academic year: $3,000. Average number of hours worked per week: 3. Apply by March. Tuition remission given: full and partial.

Advanced Students: Teaching assistantships available for advanced students. Average amount paid per academic year: $1,920. Average number of hours worked per week: 6. Apply by per term. Tuition remission given: full and partial. Fellowships and scholarships available for advanced students. Average amount paid per academic year: $3,000. Average number of hours worked per week: 3. Apply by March. Tuition remission given: full and partial.

Additional Information: No information provided.

Internships/Practica: Argosy University/Twin Cities places students in over 50 practicum sites. These training sites cover a wide range of training interests, including medical centers, clinics, counseling centers, prisons, state hospitals, schools, private practice, chemical dependency treatment centers, neuropsychological/rehabilitation centers, pain treatment centers, and managed care facilities. Students are placed in these sites based on their interests and training needs. Each practicum lasts 9 months and 600 hours. Students in the PsyD program focus on assessment skills during their first practicum and intervention skills during their second practicum, and are supervised by a licensed, doctoral-level psychologist.

Housing and Day Care: No on-campus housing is available. No on-campus day care facilities are available.

Employment of Department Graduates:

Master's Degree Graduates: Of those who graduated in the academic year 2006–2007, the following categories and numbers represent the postgraduate activities and employment of master's degree graduates: Enrolled in a psychology doctoral program (8), enrolled in a postdoctoral residency/fellowship (n/a), employed in independent practice (n/a), do not know (1), total from the above (master's) (9).

Doctoral Degree Graduates: Of those who graduated in the academic year 2006–2007, the following categories and numbers represent the postgraduate activities and employment of doctoral degree graduates: Enrolled in a psychology doctoral program (n/a), enrolled in a postdoctoral residency/fellowship (6), employed in independent practice (3), employed in business or industry (1), employed in a community mental health/counseling center (9), employed in a hospital/medical center (3), still seeking employment (1), do not know (11), total from the above (doctoral) (38).

Additional Information:

Orientation, Objectives, and Emphasis of Department: The APA-accredited PsyD program at Argosy University/Twin Cities requires 98 semester hours and is eclectic, experiential, and competency based. Faculty represent a range of orientations including psychodynamic, cognitive behavioral, systemic, interpersonal, narrative, and experiential. The program is committed to fostering the growth and development of each student's identity as a professional psychologist. The MA in Professional Counseling/Marriage and Family Therapy emphasizes development of a working theory and practice in interactional, systemic, and contextual therapy across interpersonal, intrapersonal, and social–cultural relationships. This MA program requires 45 semester credits, and includes a required portfolio process.

Special Facilities or Resources: Predoctoral foci in the PsyD program are available in Marriage and Family Therapy, Clinical Health Psychology, Forensic Psychology, Clinical Child Psychology, Industrial/Organizational Psychology, and Neuropsychology. We maintain both a university counseling clinic and a community-based clinic staffed by practicum students.

Application Information:

Send to Admissions Department, Argosy University/Twin Cities, 1515 Central Parkway, Eagan, MN 55121. Application available online. URL of online application: http://www.argosyu.edu. Students are admitted in the Fall, application deadline May 15; Winter, application deadline October 15. Programs have rolling admissions. Early application deadline is January 15. *Fee:* $50.

Metropolitan State University (2007 data)

Psychology/MA in Psychology Program
College of Professional Studies
1450 Energy Park Drive
St. Paul, MN 55108-5218
Telephone: (651) 999-5820
Fax: (651) 999-5803
E-mail: *mark.stasson@metrostate.edu*
Web: *http://www.metrostate.edu/cps/psych/grad*

Department Information:

1990. Chairperson: Deborah Bushway. Number of faculty: total—full-time 7, part-time 55; women—full-time 4, part-time 33.

Programs and Degrees Offered:

Listed in the following order: Program area, degree type (T if terminal Master's), number awarded 7/06–6/07. Psychology MA/MS (Master of Arts/Science) (T) 1.

Student Applications/Admissions:

Student Applications

Psychology MA/MS (Master of Arts/Science)—Applications 2007–2008, 24. Total applicants accepted 2007–2008, 11. Number full-time enrolled (new admits only) 2007–2008, 2. Number part-time enrolled (new admits only) 2007–2008, 5. Total enrolled 2007–2008 full-time, 8, part-time, 16. Openings 2008–2009, 15. The median number of years required for completion of a degree in 2006–2007 were 3. The number of students enrolled full- and part-time who were dismissed or voluntarily withdrew from this program area in 2007–2008 were 1.

Admissions Requirements:

Scores: Entries appear in this order: required test or GPA, minimum score (if required), median score of students entering in 2007–2008. Master's Programs: overall undergraduate GPA 3.0.

Other Criteria: (importance of criteria rated low, medium, or high): research experience—medium, work experience—high, extracurricular activity—medium, clinically related public service—low, GPA—high, letters of recommendation—medium, interview—high, statement of goals and objectives—high, Community-based work—high. For additional information on admission requirements, go to http://www.metrostate.edu/cps/psych/grad.

Student Characteristics: The following represents characteristics of students in 2007–2008 in all graduate psychology programs in the department: Female—full-time 6, part-time 14; Male—full-time 2, part-time 2; African American/Black—full-time 1, part-time 1; Hispanic/Latino(a)—full-time 0, part-time 1; Asian/Pacific Islander—full-time 0, part-time 1; American Indian/Alaska Native—full-time 1, part-time 1; Caucasian/White—full-time 6, part-time 12; Multi-ethnic—full-time 0, part-time 0; students subject to the Americans With Disabilities Act—full-time 1, part-time 1; Unknown ethnicity—full-time 0, part-time 0.

Financial Information/Assistance:

Tuition for Full-Time Study: *Master's:* State residents: $252 per credit hour; Nonstate residents: $496 per credit hour. Tuition is subject to change. See the following Web site for updates and changes in tuition costs: http://www.metrostate.edu/tuition/.

Financial Assistance:

First-Year Students: No information provided.

Advanced Students: No information provided.

Additional Information: Of all students currently enrolled full time, 0% benefited from one or more of the listed financial assistance programs. Application and information available online at: http://www.metrostate.edu/aid/index.html.

Internships/Practica: Community-based practica are arranged in consultation between the student and their faculty advisor. Practica are developed and implemented in cooperation with Metropolitan State University's Center for Community-Based Learning (http://www.metrostate.edu/ccbl).

Housing and Day Care: No on-campus housing is available. No on-campus day care facilities are available.

Employment of Department Graduates:

Master's Degree Graduates: Of those who graduated in the academic year 2006–2007, the following categories and numbers represent the postgraduate activities and employment of master's degree graduates: Enrolled in another graduate/professional program (2), enrolled in a postdoctoral residency/fellowship (n/a), employed in independent practice (n/a), employed in other positions at a higher education institution (1), not seeking employment (1), other employment position (4), total from the above (master's) (10).

Doctoral Degree Graduates: Of those who graduated in the academic year 2006–2007, the following categories and numbers represent the postgraduate activities and employment of doctoral degree graduates: Enrolled in a psychology doctoral program (n/a), total from the above (doctoral) (0).

Additional Information:

Orientation, Objectives, and Emphasis of Department: The Master of Arts in Psychology Program emphasizes the application of psychology in the form of community-based interventions that are rooted in the wisdom and work of members of each community. It is an innovative program, rooted in a community psychology model, in which students learn to combine theory, research, and practice to achieve positive social and community change. Prevention (rather than treatment) is a primary focus along with empowerment, health promotion, community organizing, and community development.

Information for Students With Physical Disabilities: See the following Web site for more information: http://www.metrostate.edu/studentaff/disability.html.

Application Information:

Send to MA Psychology Program Coordinator, 1450 Energy Park Drive, St. Paul, MN 55108-5218. Application available online. URL of online application: http://www.metrostate.edu/cps/psych/grad. Students are admitted in the Fall, application deadline March 1. If openings remain, applications might be considered in the order received until as late as June 1. *Fee:* $20. Metropolitan State University graduates are exempt from this fee.

Minnesota State University—Mankato

Department of Psychology
AH 23
Mankato, MN 56001
Telephone: (507) 389-2724
Fax: (507) 389-5831
E-mail: *carol.seifert@mnsu.edu*
Web: *http://www.mnsu.edu/psych/psych.html*

Department Information:

1964. Chairperson: Barry Ries. Number of faculty: total—full-time 16; women—full-time 7; total—minority—full-time 2; women minority—full-time 1; faculty subject to the Americans With Disabilities Act 1.

Programs and Degrees Offered:

Listed in the following order: Program area, degree type (T if terminal Master's), number awarded 7/06–6/07. Clinical MA/MS (Master of Arts/Science) 7, Industrial/Organizational MA/MS (Master of Arts/Science) (T) 5, School Psychology PsyD (Doctor of Psychology) 0.

Student Applications/Admissions:

Student Applications

Clinical MA/MS (Master of Arts/Science)—Applications 2007–2008, 42. Total applicants accepted 2007–2008, 20. Number full-time enrolled (new admits only) 2007–2008, 11. Total enrolled 2007–2008 full-time, 23. Openings 2008–2009, 10. The median number of years required for completion of a degree in 2006–2007 were 2. The number of students enrolled full- and part-time who were dismissed or voluntarily withdrew from this program area in 2007–2008 were 1. *Industrial/Organizational MA/MS (Master of Arts/Science)*—Applications 2007–2008, 57. Total applicants accepted 2007–2008, 18. Number full-time enrolled (new admits only) 2007–2008, 10. Total enrolled 2007–2008 full-time, 21. Openings 2008–2009, 10. The median number of years required for completion of a degree in 2006–2007 were 2. The number of students enrolled full- and part-time who were dismissed or voluntarily withdrew from this program area in 2007–2008 were 0. *School Psychology PsyD (Doctor of Psychology)*—Applications 2007–2008, 0. Total applicants accepted 2007–2008, 0. Number full-time enrolled (new admits only) 2007–2008, 0. Number part-time enrolled (new admits only) 2007–2008, 0. Openings 2008–2009, 7. The number of students enrolled full- and part-time who were dismissed or voluntarily withdrew from this program area in 2007–2008 were 0.

Admissions Requirements:

Scores: Entries appear in this order: required test or GPA, minimum score (if required), median score of students entering in 2007–2008. Master's Programs: GRE-V 500, 550; GRE-Q 500, 550; overall undergraduate GPA 3.0, 3.5. Doctoral Programs: GRE-V 500; GRE-Q 520; overall undergraduate GPA 3.4.

Other Criteria: (importance of criteria rated low, medium, or high): GRE/MAT scores—high, research experience—medium, work experience—low, extracurricular activity—low, clinically related public service—medium, GPA—medium, letters of recommendation—high, interview—medium, statement of goals and objectives—medium.

Student Characteristics: The following represents characteristics of students in 2007–2008 in all graduate psychology programs in the department: Female—full-time 27, part-time 0; Male—full-time 17, part-time 0; African American/Black—full-time 1, part-time 0; Asian/Pacific Islander—full-time 2, part-time 0; Caucasian/White—full-time 41, part-time 0; students subject to the Americans With Disabilities Act—full-time 0, part-time 0; Unknown ethnicity—full-time 0, part-time 0; International students who hold an F-1 or J-1 Visa—full-time 2, part-time 0.

Financial Information/Assistance:

Tuition for Full-Time Study: *Master's:* State residents: $275 per credit hour; Nonstate residents: $453 per credit hour. *Doctoral:* State residents: $400 per credit hour; Nonstate residents: $400 per credit hour. Tuition is subject to change. See the following Web site for updates and changes in tuition costs: http://www.mnsu.edu/busoff/acctsrec/tuition_fees/.

Financial Assistance:

First-Year Students: Teaching assistantships available for first year. Average amount paid per academic year: $4,000. Average number of hours worked per week: 10. Apply by March 15. Tuition remission given: partial.

Advanced Students: Teaching assistantships available for advanced students. Average amount paid per academic year: $4,000. Average number of hours worked per week: 10. Tuition remission given: partial.

Additional Information: Of all students currently enrolled full time, 50% benefited from one or more of the listed financial assistance programs.

Internships/Practica: A variety of clinical practica are available to our Clinical students. Sites have included the Mayo Clinic, the Munroe-Meyer Institute, Minneapolis VA Hospital, and local Riverview Clinic. I/O internship sites include Chiquita, ePredix, Minnesota Twins, Thrivent, 3M, and Army research labs.

Housing and Day Care: On-campus housing is available. See the following Web site for more information: http://www2.mnsu.edu/reslife/. On-campus day care facilities are available. See the following Web site for more information: http://www.coled.mnsu.edu/NewWeb/ChildrensHouse/tourtotheinsidehouse.html.

Employment of Department Graduates:

Master's Degree Graduates: Of those who graduated in the academic year 2006–2007, the following categories and numbers represent the postgraduate activities and employment of master's degree graduates: Enrolled in a psychology doctoral program (6), enrolled in another graduate/professional program (1), enrolled in a postdoctoral residency/fellowship (n/a), employed in independent practice (n/a), total from the above (master's) (7).

Doctoral Degree Graduates: Of those who graduated in the academic year 2006–2007, the following categories and numbers represent the postgraduate activities and employment of doctoral degree graduates: Enrolled in a psychology doctoral program (n/a), total from the above (doctoral) (0).

Additional Information:

Orientation, Objectives, and Emphasis of Department: The school psychology doctoral program is planned to begin in fall of 2008. It emphasizes data-based decision making, multiculturalism, mental health, and prevention. Graduates will be prepared to pursue certification and licensure at state and national levels. The clinical program is a research-based, predoctoral program with a strong behavioral emphasis. The goal of the I/O program is to provide broad theoretical and technical training for individuals who will function as human resource professionals or who will go on to doctoral programs in I/O psychology.

Special Facilities or Resources: I/O faculty have ongoing research partnerships with major organizations such as U.S. Airforce Department of Special Investigations, United Health group, 3M Corporation, Scholarship America, and the national Pork Board. Clinical faculty maintain professional relationships with Immanuel-St. Joseph Hospital, Mayo Health System, and area schools.

Information for Students With Physical Disabilities: See the following Web site for more information: http://www.mnsu.edu/dso/.

Application Information:

Send to Department of Psychology, AH 23, Minnesota State University, Mankato, Mankato, MN 56001. Students are admitted in the Fall, application deadline March 1. Anticipated application deadline for School Psychology PsyD program: January 15. *Fee:* $40.

Minnesota State University Moorhead

School Psychology Program
Social and Natural Sciences
1104 7th Avenue South
Moorhead, MN 56563
Telephone: (218) 477-2802
Fax: (218) 477-2602
E-mail: *schpsych@mnstate.edu*
Web: *http://www.mnstate.edu/gradpsyc*

Department Information:

1970. Program Director: Margaret L. Potter. Number of faculty: total—full-time 11; women—full-time 7; total—minority—full-time 1.

Programs and Degrees Offered:

Listed in the following order: Program area, degree type (T if terminal Master's), number awarded 7/06–6/07. School Psychology EdS/MEd (School Psychology) 10.

Student Applications/Admissions:

Student Applications

School Psychology EdS/MEd (School Psychology)—Applications 2007–2008, 34. Total applicants accepted 2007–2008, 17. Number full-time enrolled (new admits only) 2007–2008, 7. Number part-time enrolled (new admits only) 2007–2008, 0. Total enrolled 2007–2008 full-time, 20, part-time, 2. Openings 2008–2009, 9. The median number of years required for completion of a degree in 2006–2007 were 3. The number of students enrolled full- and part-time who were dismissed or voluntarily withdrew from this program area in 2007–2008 were 1.

Admissions Requirements:

Scores: Entries appear in this order: required test or GPA, minimum score (if required), median score of students entering in 2007–2008. Master's Programs: GRE-V no minimum stated, 440; GRE-Q no minimum stated, 630; overall undergraduate GPA 3.00, 3.7; last 2 years GPA 3.25.

Other Criteria: (importance of criteria rated low, medium, or high): GRE/MAT scores—high, research experience—medium, work experience—medium, extracurricular activity—medium, clinically related public service—low, GPA—high, letters of recommendation—high, interview—low, statement of goals and objectives—high, undergraduate major in psychology—medium, specific undergraduate psychology courses taken—medium.

Student Characteristics: The following represents characteristics of students in 2007–2008 in all graduate psychology programs in the department: Female—full-time 17, part-time 2; Male—full-time 3, part-time 0; African American/Black—full-time 0, part-time 0; Hispanic/Latino(a)—full-time 0, part-time 0; Asian/

Pacific Islander—full-time 0, part-time 0; American Indian/Alaska Native—full-time 0, part-time 0; Caucasian/White—full-time 20, part-time 2; Multi-ethnic—full-time 0, part-time 0; students subject to the Americans With Disabilities Act—full-time 0, part-time 0; Unknown ethnicity—full-time 0, part-time 0; International students who hold an F-1 or J-1 Visa—full-time 0, part-time 0.

Financial Information/Assistance:

Tuition for Full-Time Study: *Master's:* State residents: per academic year $6,200, $260 per credit hour; Nonstate residents: per academic year $6,200, $260 per credit hour. Tuition is subject to change. Additional fees are assessed to students beyond the costs of tuition for the following: basic university activity, health, and other fees. See the following Web site for updates and changes in tuition costs: http://www.mnstate.edu/busoff/tuitionfees.htm.

Financial Assistance:

First-Year Students: Research assistantships available for first year. Average amount paid per academic year: $1,700. Average number of hours worked per week: 5. Apply by May 15.

Advanced Students: Research assistantships available for advanced students. Average amount paid per academic year: $2,000. Average number of hours worked per week: 6. Apply by May 15.

Additional Information: Of all students currently enrolled full time, 90% benefited from one or more of the listed financial assistance programs.

Internships/Practica: Field-based practica in both 1st and 2nd years of study provide hands-on experience to students. Practica are supervised by local educators and school psychologists and are coordinated with on-campus course work so students can apply concepts and techniques learned in class. A 1,200-hour internship during the 3rd year of study serves as a capstone experience for student's training. Internships are usually positions within school districts or special education cooperatives in the tristate area, however students have completed internships in sites across the country.

Housing and Day Care: On-campus housing is available. See the following Web site for more information: http://www.mnstate.edu/housing. On-campus day care facilities are available. See the following Web site for more information: http://www.mnstate.edu/childcare.

Employment of Department Graduates:

Master's Degree Graduates: Of those who graduated in the academic year 2006–2007, the following categories and numbers represent the postgraduate activities and employment of master's degree graduates: Enrolled in a postdoctoral residency/fellowship (n/a), employed in independent practice (n/a), employed in a professional position in a school system (10), total from the above (master's) (10).

Doctoral Degree Graduates: Of those who graduated in the academic year 2006–2007, the following categories and numbers represent the postgraduate activities and employment of doctoral degree graduates: Enrolled in a psychology doctoral program (n/a), total from the above (doctoral) (0).

Additional Information:

Orientation, Objectives, and Emphasis of Department: Our goal is to provide the training necessary for our graduates to be skilled problem solvers in dealing with the needs of children, families, and others involved in the learning enterprise. Within a scientist–practitioner model and integrative perspective, the program's primary focus is on educating specialist-level professionals capable of working effectively in educational agencies and in collaboration with other human services providers. Our graduates are highly regarded by the schools and agencies within which they work because of their knowledge of current best practices in the field and because of their skills as team members.

Information for Students With Physical Disabilities: See the following Web site for more information: http://www.mnstate.edu/disability.

Application Information:

Send to Graduate Studies Office, Minnesota State University Moorhead, 1104 7th Avenue South, Moorhead, MN 56563. Application available online. URL of online application: http://www.mnstate.edu/graduate. Students are admitted in the Fall, application deadline February 15. Applications will be accepted after February 15 if space is available. *Fee:* $20.

Minnesota, University of

Department of Educational Psychology: Counseling and Student Personnel; School Psychology
Education and Human Development
178 Pillsbury Drive Southeast, 206 Burton Hall
Minneapolis, MN 55455
Telephone: (612) 624-1698
Fax: (612) 624-8241
E-mail: *shupp@umn.edu*
Web: *http://www.education.umn.edu/EdPsych*

Department Information:

1947. Chair: Susan Hupp. Number of faculty: total—full-time 36; women—full-time 14; total—minority—full-time 7; women minority—full-time 3; faculty subject to the Americans With Disabilities Act 1.

Programs and Degrees Offered:

Listed in the following order: Program area, degree type (T if terminal Master's), number awarded 7/06–6/07. Counseling and Student Personnel MA/MS (Master of Arts/Science) (T) 37, School Psychology PhD (Doctor of Philosophy) 5, Counseling and Student Personnel PhD (Doctor of Philosophy) 4, School Psychology EdS/MEd (School Psychology) 5.

APA Accreditation: School PhD (Doctor of Philosophy). Counseling PhD (Doctor of Philosophy).

Student Applications/Admissions:

Student Applications

Counseling and Student Personnel MA/MS (Master of Arts/Science)—Applications 2007–2008, 94. Total applicants accepted 2007–2008, 51. Number full-time enrolled (new admits only) 2007–2008, 33. Total enrolled 2007–2008 full-time, 77. Openings 2008–2009, 30. The median number of years required for completion of a degree in 2006–2007 were 2. The number of students enrolled full- and part-time who were dismissed or voluntarily withdrew from this program area in 2007–2008 were 0. *School Psychology PhD (Doctor of Philosophy)*—Applications 2007–2008, 26. Total applicants accepted 2007–2008, 9. Number full-time enrolled (new admits only) 2007–2008, 5. Total enrolled 2007–2008 full-time, 46. Openings 2008–2009, 8. The median number of years required for completion of a degree in 2006–2007 were 7. The number of students enrolled full- and part-time who were dismissed or voluntarily withdrew from this program area in 2007–2008 were 0. *Counseling and Student Personnel PhD (Doctor of Philosophy)*—Applications 2007–2008, 53. Total applicants accepted 2007–2008, 11. Number full-time enrolled (new admits only) 2007–2008, 6. Total enrolled 2007–2008 full-time, 48. Openings 2008–2009, 6. The median number of years required for completion of a degree in 2006–2007 were 7. The number of students enrolled full- and part-time who were dismissed or voluntarily withdrew from this program area in 2007–2008 were 0. *School Psychology EdS/MEd (School Psychology)*—Applications 2007–2008, 35. Total applicants accepted 2007–2008, 8. Number full-time enrolled (new admits only) 2007–2008, 7. Total enrolled 2007–2008 full-time, 23. Openings 2008–2009, 6. The median number of years required for completion of a degree in 2006–2007 were 3. The number of students enrolled full- and part-time who were dismissed or voluntarily withdrew from this program area in 2007–2008 were 0.

Admissions Requirements:

Scores: Entries appear in this order: required test or GPA, minimum score (if required), median score of students entering in 2007–2008. Master's Programs: GRE-V no minimum stated; GRE-Q no minimum stated; overall undergraduate GPA no minimum stated; last 2 years GPA no minimum stated; psychology GPA no minimum stated; Masters GRE-Analytical no minimum stated. Complete application is reviewed. Decision not based solely on GRE or GPA Doctoral Programs: GRE-V no minimum stated; GRE-Q no minimum stated; overall undergraduate GPA no minimum stated; last 2 years GPA no minimum stated; psychology GPA no minimum stated; Doctoral program GRE-Analytic no minimum stated. Decision is not solely based on GRE or GPA.

Other Criteria: (importance of criteria rated low, medium, or high): GRE/MAT scores—high, research experience—medium, work experience—medium, extracurricular activity—medium, clinically related public service—low, GPA—medium, letters of recommendation—high, interview—high, statement of goals and objectives—high. Counseling School Psychology Program (PhD): Research—high, work—high, extracurricular—high, public service—high, letters of recommendation—high, statement of goals—high, interview—none. For additional information on admission requirements, go to http://www.education.umn.edu/EdPsych.

Student Characteristics: The following represents characteristics of students in 2007–2008 in all graduate psychology programs in the department: Female—full-time 176, part-time 65; Male—full-time 60, part-time 13; African American/Black—full-time 5, part-time 2; Hispanic/Latino(a)—full-time 4, part-time 1; Asian/Pacific Islander—full-time 6, part-time 9; American Indian/Alaska Native—full-time 3, part-time 0; Caucasian/White—full-time 166, part-time 54; Multi-ethnic—full-time 0, part-time 0; Unknown ethnicity—full-time 9, part-time 2; International students who hold an F-1 or J-1 Visa—full-time 43, part-time 10.

Financial Information/Assistance:

Tuition for Full-Time Study: *Master's:* State residents: per academic year $9,740, $811 per credit hour; Nonstate residents: per academic year $16,838, $1,403 per credit hour. *Doctoral:* State residents: per academic year $9,740, $811 per credit hour; Nonstate residents: per academic year $16,838, $1,403 per credit hour. Tuition is subject to change. See the following Web site for updates and changes in tuition costs: http://www.onestop.umn.edu.

Financial Assistance:

First-Year Students: Teaching assistantships available for first year. Average amount paid per academic year: $6,326. Average number of hours worked per week: 10. Apply by 12/1. Tuition remission given: partial. Research assistantships available for first year. Average amount paid per academic year: $6,326. Average number of hours worked per week: 10. Apply by December 1. Tuition remission given: partial. Fellowships and scholarships available for first year. Average amount paid per academic year: $21,500. Average number of hours worked per week: 0. Apply by December 1. Tuition remission given: full.

Advanced Students: Teaching assistantships available for advanced students. Average amount paid per academic year: $6,326. Average number of hours worked per week: 10. Apply by December 1. Tuition remission given: partial. Research assistantships available for advanced students. Average amount paid per academic year: $6,326. Average number of hours worked per week: 10. Apply by December 1. Tuition remission given: partial. Fellowships and scholarships available for advanced students. Average amount paid per academic year: $21,500. Average number of hours worked per week: 0. Apply by December 1. Tuition remission given: full.

Additional Information: Of all students currently enrolled full time, 75% benefited from one or more of the listed financial assistance programs. Application and information available online; we use departmental application files for new students and knowledge of current students.

Internships/Practica: Doctoral Degree (PhD School Psychology): For those doctoral students for whom a professional internship was required in this program prior to graduation, (2) students applied for an internship in 2006–2007, with (2) students obtaining an internship. Of those students who obtained an internship, (2) were paid internships. Of those students who obtained an internship, (0) students placed in APA/CPA-accredited internships, (2) students placed in internships not APA/CPA accredited, but listed with the Association of Psychology Postdoctoral and Internship Centers (APPIC), (0) students placed in internships conforming to guidelines of the Council of Directors of School Psychology Programs (CDSPP), (0) students placed in internships that were not APA/CPA-accredited, APPIC or CDSPP listed. Doctoral Degree (PhD Counseling and Student Personnel): For those doctoral students for whom a professional internship was required in this program prior to graduation, (3) students applied for an internship in 2006–2007, with (3) students obtaining an internship. Of those students who obtained an internship, (3) were paid internships. Of those students who obtained an internship, (3) students placed in APA/CPA-accredited internships, (0) students placed in internships not APA/CPA-accredited, but listed with the Association of Psychology Postdoctoral and Internship Centers (APPIC), (0) students placed in internships conforming to guidelines of the Council of Directors of School Psychology Programs (CDSPP), (0) students placed in internships that were not APA/CPA-accredited, APPIC or CDSPP listed. Counseling and Student Personnel Psychology: MA students complete an academic year practicum in the 2nd year with a focus on community counseling, school counseling, or college student development. The practicum consists of direct work with clients/students, individual supervision on-site, and an academic seminar at the university. PhD students complete one or more practica and then a year-long internship. Some students stay in the Twin Cities for the internship; others go nationally. School Psychology: Doctoral students have three tiers of applied training. Tier 1: Year-long practica tied to assessment coursework followed by a 2nd year of practica tied to intervention coursework. Most of these experiences occur in metro area schools. Tier 2: Formal school practicum under the supervision of a school psychologist in Twin Cities area schools. In addition, doctoral students complete a community–clinical practica. These practica occur in a wide variety of settings including mental health and community agencies such as Indian Health Board, Washburn Child Guidance Center, Community University Health Care Center, and Fraser Family and Children Services. Tier 3: Internship. The majority completes their year-long internships in public schools settings, although some have found internships in settings that are a collaboration of community and educational settings. In one setting, interns work as part of a mental health and educational team providing school-based services to identified students with emotional and behavioral disorders.

Housing and Day Care: On-campus housing is available. See the following Web site for more information: http://www.umn.edu/housing. On-campus day care facilities are available. Contact University Child Care Center, 1600 Rollins Avenue Southeast, Minneapolis (a few blocks from campus); (612) 627-4014.

Employment of Department Graduates:

Master's Degree Graduates: Of those who graduated in the academic year 2006–2007, the following categories and numbers represent the postgraduate activities and employment of master's degree graduates: Enrolled in a psychology doctoral program (4), enrolled in a postdoctoral residency/fellowship (n/a), employed in independent practice (n/a), employed in an academic position at a 2-year/4-year college (2), employed in other positions at a higher education institution (2), employed in a professional position in a school system (5), employed in a hospital/medical center (1), still seeking employment (1), do not know (30), total from the above (master's) (45).

Doctoral Degree Graduates: Of those who graduated in the academic year 2006–2007, the following categories and numbers represent the postgraduate activities and employment of doctoral degree graduates: Enrolled in a psychology doctoral program (n/a), enrolled in a postdoctoral residency/fellowship (1), employed in independent practice (1), employed in an academic position at a university (1), employed in a professional position in a school system (3), employed in business or industry (1), not seeking employment (1), do not know (1), total from the above (doctoral) (9).

Additional Information:

Orientation, Objectives, and Emphasis of Department: Counseling and Student Personnel Psychology is intended to provide a fundamental body of knowledge and skills to prepare counselors and counseling psychologists for work in a variety of settings—counseling and human development, career development, staff development, and student personnel work. Although the focus is primarily on facilitating human development in educational settings, it is possible for individuals to prepare for community and agency settings as well. The faculty is committed to addressing current social issues such as diversity concerns and adolescent well-being. The CSPP program is designed for a select group of individuals with a demonstrated capacity for leadership and a commitment in the human services. School Psychology: The range of the school psychologist's impact includes, but is not limited to, the application of theory and research in the psychosocial development and learning of children and youth, social interaction processes, prevention and competence enhancement strategies, instructional intervention and program development, and delivery of mental health services. Our major training goal is to prepare school psychologists for roles within the educational enterprise. Competencies needed include knowledge in developmental psychology, personality and learning theory, and social psychology; assessing individual and systems needs; generating and implementing prevention programs and intervention strategies; collaborative consultation; diversity; and evaluating and redesigning programs. Training modalities include a variety of seminars and independent study projects. A wide range of community resources is available to facilitate goals of the program.

Special Facilities or Resources: Our graduate program is located within a major research university where many research projects are ongoing. The program is also located within a state—Minnesota—and major metropolitan area—the Twin Cities—that are known for innovations in human services. The result is that both the research climate and the practice climate are good ones for students. CSPP: The department has some flexibility in the design of student programs. Excellent facilities for research opportunities exist throughout the university. There is a time-shared instructional computing laboratory with batch and online computer facilities available for student use, and free access to the central university computer. Students may borrow laptops, video cameras, LCD projectors, audiorecorders, overheads, and VCRs. Students record counseling role-play sessions in a state-of-the-art digital counseling laboratory. School Psychology: Two job files (academic and professional service positions) exist. School Psychology Resources houses journals, books, and intervention and assessment materials. This collection supplements the Psychology Department Journal Seminar Room (for psychology majors) and the Florence Goodenough Reading Room (for child psychology majors), the University Psychology and Educational Library with its specialized computer search facilities, and the extensive university libraries system with holdings numbering approximately 3.5 million volumes. School psychology also maintains a collection of standardized, individual, and group psychometric tests, measures, and protocols that can be borrowed for coursework use.

Information for Students With Physical Disabilities: See the following Web site for more information: http://www.ds.umn.edu.

Application Information:

Send to School Psychology Program, 344 Elliott Hall, University of Minnesota, Minneapolis, MN 55455. Counseling and Student Personnel Psychology, 206 Burton Hall, University of Minnesota, Minneapolis, MN 55455. Application available online. URL of online application: http://www.education.umn.edu/EdPsych/default.html. Students are admitted in the Fall, application deadline December 1. *Fee:* $55.

Minnesota, University of

Department of Psychology
N218 Elliott Hall, 75 East River Road
Minneapolis, MN 55455
Telephone: (612) 625-4042
Fax: (612) 626-2079
E-mail: *psyapply@umn.edu*
Web: *http://www.psych.umn.edu*

Department Information:

1919. Chairperson: Gordon Legge. Number of faculty: total—full-time 44, part-time 36; women—full-time 10, part-time 16; total—minority—full-time 4, part-time 2; women minority—full-time 2, part-time 2; faculty subject to the Americans With Disabilities Act 1.

Programs and Degrees Offered:

Listed in the following order: Program area, degree type (T if terminal Master's), number awarded 7/06–6/07. Biological Psychopathology PhD (Doctor of Philosophy) 0, Clinical PhD (Doctor of Philosophy) 3, Cognitive and Biological PhD (Doctor of Philosophy) 6, Counseling PhD (Doctor of Philosophy) 5, Personality, Individual Differences and Behavioral Genetics PhD (Doctor of Philosophy) 1, Industrial/Organizational PhD (Doctor of Philosophy) 3, Quantitative/Psychometric Methods PhD (Doctor of Philosophy) 0, School PhD (Doctor of Philosophy) 0, Social PhD (Doctor of Philosophy) 1.

APA Accreditation: Clinical PhD (Doctor of Philosophy). Counseling PhD (Doctor of Philosophy).

Student Applications/Admissions:

Student Applications

Biological Psychopathology PhD (Doctor of Philosophy)—Applications 2007–2008, 6. Total applicants accepted 2007–2008, 0. Number full-time enrolled (new admits only) 2007–2008, 0. Openings 2008–2009, 1. The number of students enrolled full- and part-time who were dismissed or voluntarily withdrew from this program area in 2007–2008 were 0. *Clinical PhD (Doctor of Philosophy)*—Applications 2007–2008, 171. Total applicants accepted 2007–2008, 5. Number full-time enrolled (new admits only) 2007–2008, 2. Number part-time enrolled (new admits only) 2007–2008, 0. Openings 2008–2009, 5. The median number of years required for completion of a degree in 2006–2007 were 6. The number of students enrolled full- and part-time who were dismissed or voluntarily withdrew from this program area in 2007–2008 were 0. *Cognitive and Biological PhD (Doctor of Philosophy)*—Applications 2007–2008, 51. Total applicants accepted 2007–2008, 8. Number full-time enrolled (new admits only) 2007–2008, 6. Number part-time enrolled (new admits only) 2007–2008, 0. Openings 2008–2009, 5. The median number of years required for completion of a degree in 2006–2007 were 6. The number of students enrolled full- and part-time who were dismissed or voluntarily withdrew from this program area in 2007–2008 were 1. *Counseling PhD (Doctor of Philosophy)*—Applications 2007–2008, 79. Total applicants accepted 2007–2008, 7. Number full-time enrolled (new admits only) 2007–2008, 5. Number part-time enrolled (new admits only) 2007–2008, 0. Openings 2008–2009, 4. The median number of years required for completion of a degree in 2006–2007 were 7. The number of students enrolled full- and part-time who were dismissed or voluntarily withdrew from this program area in 2007–2008 were 0. *Personality, Individual Differences and Behavioral Genetics PhD (Doctor of Philosophy)*—Applications 2007–2008, 16. Total applicants accepted 2007–2008, 3. Number full-time enrolled (new admits only) 2007–2008, 2. Number part-time enrolled (new admits only) 2007–2008, 0. Openings 2008–2009, 2. The median number of years required for completion of a degree in 2006–2007 were 6. The number of students enrolled full- and part-time who were dismissed or voluntarily withdrew from this program area in 2007–2008 were 0. *Industrial/Organizational PhD (Doctor of Philosophy)*—Applications 2007–2008, 95. Total applicants accepted 2007–2008, 7. Number full-time enrolled (new admits only) 2007–2008, 3. Number part-time enrolled (new admits only) 2007–2008, 0. Openings 2008–2009, 4. The median number of years required for completion of a degree in 2006–2007 were 5. The number of students enrolled full- and part-time who were dismissed or voluntarily withdrew from this program area in 2007–2008 were 1. *Quantitative/Psychometric Methods PhD (Doctor of Philosophy)*—Applications 2007–2008, 17. Total applicants accepted 2007–2008, 3. Number full-time enrolled (new admits only) 2007–2008, 1. Number part-time enrolled (new admits only) 2007–2008, 0. Openings 2008–2009, 2. The number of students enrolled full- and part-time who were dismissed or voluntarily withdrew from this program area in 2007–2008 were 1. *School PhD (Doctor of Philosophy)*—Applications 2007–2008, 0. Total applicants accepted 2007–2008, 0. Number full-time enrolled (new admits only) 2007–2008, 0. Number part-time enrolled (new admits only) 2007–2008, 0. Openings 2008–2009, 1. The number of students enrolled full- and part-time who were dismissed or voluntarily withdrew from this program area in 2007–2008 were 0. *Social PhD (Doctor of Philosophy)*—Applications 2007–2008, 72. Total applicants accepted 2007–2008, 6. Number full-time enrolled (new admits only) 2007–2008, 5. Number part-time enrolled (new admits only) 2007–2008, 0. Openings 2008–2009, 4. The median number of years required for completion of a degree in 2006–2007 were 6. The number of students enrolled full- and part-time who were dismissed or voluntarily withdrew from this program area in 2007–2008 were 2.

Admissions Requirements:

Scores: Entries appear in this order: required test or GPA, minimum score (if required), median score of students entering in 2007–2008. Doctoral Programs: GRE-V no minimum stated, 658; GRE-Q no minimum stated, 743; overall undergraduate GPA no minimum stated, 3.70. Although we have no fixed requirements and admission decisions are based on an individual's complete record, it is desirable that applicants have either a GPA of 3.0 and GRE scores of at least 600 on both the verbal and quantitative sections or a GPA of 3.3 and scores of 500 or greater on the GRE verbal and quantitative sections. For the clinical program it is desirable that applicants have at least a 3.5 GPA and scores of at least 600 on the verbal and quantitative sections of the GRE. The GRE Subject Test in Psychology is recommended.

Other Criteria: (importance of criteria rated low, medium, or high): GRE/MAT scores—high, research experience—high, work experience—medium, extracurricular activity—medium, clinically related public service—medium, GPA—high, letters of recommendation—high, statement of goals and objectives—high. For additional information on admission requirements, go to http://www.psych.umn.edu.

Student Characteristics: The following represents characteristics of students in 2007–2008 in all graduate psychology programs in the department: Female—full-time 81, part-time 0; Male—full-time 66, part-time 0; African American/Black—full-time 0, part-time 0; Hispanic/Latino(a)—full-time 3, part-time 0; Asian/Pacific Islander—full-time 18, part-time 0; American Indian/Alaska Native—full-time 0, part-time 0; Caucasian/White—full-time 126, part-time 0; Multi-ethnic—full-time 0, part-time 0; students subject to the Americans With Disabilities Act—full-time 1, part-time 0; Unknown ethnicity—full-time 0, part-time 0; International students who hold an F-1 or J-1 Visa—full-time 20, part-time 0.

Financial Information/Assistance:

Tuition for Full-Time Study: *Doctoral:* State residents: per academic year $9,740, $812 per credit hour; Nonstate residents: per academic year $16,838, $1,403 per credit hour. Tuition is subject to change. See the following Web site for updates and changes in tuition costs: http://www.grad.umn.edu/prospective_students/.

Financial Assistance:

First-Year Students: Teaching assistantships available for first year. Average amount paid per academic year: $12,652. Average number of hours worked per week: 20. Apply by December 1. Tuition remission given: full. Research assistantships available for first year. Average amount paid per academic year: $12,652. Average number of hours worked per week: 20. Apply by December 1. Tuition remission given: full. Traineeships available for first year. Average amount paid per academic year: $0. Average number of hours worked per week: 0. Apply by December 1. Tuition remission given: full. Fellowships and scholarships available for first year. Average amount paid per academic year: $21,500. Average number of hours worked per week: 0. Apply by December 1. Tuition remission given: full.

Advanced Students: Teaching assistantships available for advanced students. Average amount paid per academic year: $12,652. Average number of hours worked per week: 20. Tuition remission given: full. Research assistantships available for advanced students. Average amount paid per academic year: $12,652. Average number of hours worked per week: 20. Tuition remission given: full. Traineeships available for advanced students. Average amount paid per academic year: $20,772. Average number of hours worked per week: 0. Tuition remission given: full. Fellowships and scholarships available for advanced students. Average amount paid per academic year: $18,126. Average number of hours worked per week: 0. Tuition remission given: full.

Additional Information: Of all students currently enrolled full time, 87% benefited from one or more of the listed financial assistance programs. Application and information available online at http://www.psych.umn.edu.

Internships/Practica: Doctoral Degree (PhD Clinical): For those doctoral students for whom a professional internship was required in this program prior to graduation, (9) students applied for an internship in 2006–2007, with (8) students obtaining an internship. Of those students who obtained an internship, (8) were paid internships. Of those students who obtained an internship, (8) students placed in APA/CPA-accredited internships, (0) students placed in internships not APA/CPA-accredited, but listed with the Association of Psychology Postdoctoral and Internship Centers (APPIC), (0) students placed in internships conforming to guidelines of the Council of Directors of School Psychology Programs (CDSPP), (0) students placed in internships that were not APA/CPA-accredited, APPIC or CDSPP listed. Doctoral Degree (PhD Counseling): For those doctoral students for whom a professional internship was required in this program prior to graduation, (2) students applied for an internship in 2006–2007, with (2) students obtaining an internship. Of those students who obtained an internship, (2) were paid internships. Of those students who obtained an internship, (2) students placed in APA/CPA accredited internships, (0) students placed in internships not APA/CPA-accredited, but listed with the Association of Psychology Postdoctoral and Internship Centers (APPIC), (0) students placed in internships conforming to guidelines of the Council of Directors of School Psychology Programs (CDSPP), (0) students placed in internships that were not APA/CPA-accredited, APPIC or CDSPP listed. Doctoral Degree (PhD School): For those doctoral students for whom a professional internship was required in this program prior to graduation, (0) students applied for an internship in 2006–2007, with (0) students obtaining an internship. Of those students who obtained an internship, (0) were paid internships. Of those students who obtained an internship, (0) students placed in APA/CPA-accredited internships, (0) students placed in internships not APA/CPA-accredited, but listed with the Association of Psychology Postdoctoral and Internship Centers (APPIC), (0) students placed in internships conforming to guidelines of the Council of Directors of School Psychology Programs (CDSPP), (0) students placed in internships that were not APA/CPA-accredited, APPIC or CDSPP listed. Internships are available at the university hospitals, the department's Vocational Assessment Clinic, the University Counseling and Consulting Services, the Veterans Administration, and several other governmental and private agencies throughout the area.

Housing and Day Care: On-campus housing is available. See the following Web site for more information: http://www.housing.umn.edu. On-campus day care facilities are available. See the following Web site for more information: http://www1.umn.edu/ohr/rap/childcare.html.

Employment of Department Graduates:

Master's Degree Graduates: Of those who graduated in the academic year 2006–2007, the following categories and numbers represent the postgraduate activities and employment of master's degree graduates: Enrolled in a psychology doctoral program (3), enrolled in another graduate/professional program (0), enrolled in a postdoctoral residency/fellowship (n/a), employed in independent practice (n/a), employed in an academic position at a university (0), employed in an academic position at a 2-year/4-year college (0), employed in other positions at a higher education institution (1), employed in a professional position in a school system (1), employed in business or industry (0), employed in government agency (0), employed in a community mental health/counseling center (0), employed in a hospital/medical center (0), still seeking employment (0), not seeking employment (0), other employment position (0), do not know (0), total from the above (master's) (5).

Doctoral Degree Graduates: Of those who graduated in the academic year 2006–2007, the following categories and numbers represent the postgraduate activities and employment of doctoral degree graduates: Enrolled in a psychology doctoral program (n/a), enrolled in another graduate/professional program (0), enrolled in a postdoctoral residency/fellowship (3), employed in independent practice (0), employed in an academic position at a university (9), employed in an academic position at a 2-year/4-year college (0), employed in other positions at a higher education institution (1), employed in a professional position in a school system (0), employed in business or industry (4), employed in government agency (0), employed in a community mental health/counseling center (0), employed in a hospital/medical center (2), still seeking employment (0), not seeking employment (0), other employment position (0), do not know (0), total from the above (doctoral) (19).

Additional Information:

Orientation, Objectives, and Emphasis of Department: Minnesota has a broad range of areas of specialization in the department, which cannot be described in detail here. The departmental application materials and program information available on the Web contain detailed relevant information on each program area. In general, the overall goal is to train the people who will become leaders in their chosen area of specialization. Consequently, the graduate training programs in the department are oriented first to the training of skilled researchers and teachers in psychology, and then to the training of specialists and practitioners. The PhD programs in Clinical, Counseling, and School Psychology are accredited by APA. Department faculty also participate in independent degree programs in neuroscience and cognitive science. The Department of Psychology and the Institute of Child Development offer a training program in child clinical psychology focused on the study of psychopathology in the context of development. The Developmental Psychopathology and Clinical Science (DPCS) Training Program is APA accredited as part of the Clinical Psychology Program. Admission to the DPCS program is coordinated by the Institute of Child Development, 51 East River Road, University of Minnesota, Minneapolis, MN 55455. The School Psychology PhD is offered jointly with the School Psychology Program. For information about this program, please write directly to the School Psychology Program, 250 Education Sciences, 56 East River Road, University of Minnesota, Minneapolis, MN 55455.

Special Facilities or Resources: The department offers extensive laboratory and computer facilities, a wide variety of resources and collaborative relationships both on and off campus, and several federally funded research projects. For example, three research centers are headquartered in the Department: Center for Cognitive Sciences, Center for the Study of Political Psychology, and Center for the Study of the Individual and Society. Other research centers with which the faculty are involved are located in Neuroscience, Radiology, Epidemiology, and Public Health. We have adjunct faculty at the University of Minnesota Counseling and Consulting Services, Carlson School of Management, Institute of Child Development, and Department of Educational Psychology; and in the VA Medical Center, Hennepin County Medical Center (Minneapolis), Ramsey County Medical Center (St. Paul), and Personnel Decisions International (Minneapolis).

Information for Students With Physical Disabilities: See the following Web site for more information: http://www.ds.umn.edu.

Application Information:

Send to Coordinator of Graduate Admissions, University of Minnesota, Department of Psychology, 249 Elliott Hall, 75 East River Road, Minneapolis, MN 55455. URL of online application: http://www.psych.umn.edu. Students are admitted in the Fall, application deadline December 1. Two applications are required to apply for graduate studies: the Department of Psychology Application for Graduate Work and the Graduate School Online Application for Admission available online at http://www.grad.umn.edu/prospective_students/apply_online.html. *Fee:* $55; $75 for international applicants. The application fee cannot be waived or deferred and is not refundable.

Minnesota, University of

Institute of Child Development
College of Education and Human Development
51 East River Road
Minneapolis, MN 55455
Telephone: (612) 624-0526
Fax: (612) 624-6373
E-mail: *icd@umn.edu*
Web: *http://www.education.umn.edu/icd/*

Department Information:

1925. Director: Nicki Crick. Number of faculty: total—full-time 22; women—full-time 9; total—minority—full-time 1; women minority—full-time 1.

Programs and Degrees Offered:

Listed in the following order: Program area, degree type (T if terminal Master's), number awarded 7/06–6/07. Child Psychology PhD (Doctor of Philosophy) 7, Child/Clinical Psychology PhD (Doctor of Philosophy) 1, Child/School Psychology PhD (Doctor of Philosophy) 0.

Student Applications/Admissions:

Student Applications

Child Psychology PhD (Doctor of Philosophy)—Applications 2007–2008, 19. Total applicants accepted 2007–2008, 10. Number full-time enrolled (new admits only) 2007–2008, 8. Total enrolled 2007–2008 full-time, 34. Openings 2008–2009, 8. The median number of years required for completion of a degree in 2006–2007 were 5. The number of students enrolled full- and part-time who were dismissed or voluntarily withdrew from this program area in 2007–2008 were 0. *Child/Clinical Psychology PhD (Doctor of Philosophy)*—Applications 2007–2008, 36. Total applicants accepted 2007–2008, 4. Number full-time enrolled (new admits only) 2007–2008, 4. Total enrolled 2007–2008 full-time, 18. Openings 2008–2009, 4. The median number of years required for completion of a degree in 2006–2007 were 6. The number of students enrolled full- and part-time who were dismissed or voluntarily withdrew from this program area in 2007–2008 were 0. *Child/School Psychology PhD (Doctor of Philosophy)*—Applications 2007–2008, 0. Total applicants accepted 2007–2008, 0. Number full-time enrolled (new admits only) 2007–2008, 0. Total enrolled 2007–2008 full-time, 1. Openings 2008–2009, 1. The number of students enrolled full- and part-time who were dismissed or voluntarily withdrew from this program area in 2007–2008 were 0.

Admissions Requirements:

Scores: Entries appear in this order: required test or GPA, minimum score (if required), median score of students entering in 2007–2008. Doctoral Programs: GRE-V no minimum stated; GRE-Q no minimum stated; overall undergraduate GPA no minimum stated; Doctoral program GRE-Analytic no minimum stated.

Other Criteria: (importance of criteria rated low, medium, or high): GRE/MAT scores—medium, research experience—high, work experience—low, extracurricular activity—low, clinically related public service—low, GPA—high, letters of recommendation—high, statement of goals and objectives—high. Clinically related public service rated low for joint Child/Clinical program. K–12 work/volunteer experience applies only to joint School Psychology program. For additional information on admission requirements, go to http://www.cehd.umn.edu/ICD/GradInfo/.

Student Characteristics: The following represents characteristics of students in 2007–2008 in all graduate psychology programs in the department: Female—full-time 46, part-time 0; Male—full-time 7, part-time 0; African American/Black—full-time 1, part-time 0; Hispanic/Latino(a)—full-time 3, part-time 0; Asian/Pacific Islander—full-time 3, part-time 0; American Indian/Alaska Native—full-time 1, part-time 0; Caucasian/White—full-time 45, part-time 0; Multi-ethnic—full-time 0, part-time 0; students subject to the Americans With Disabilities Act—full-time 2, part-time 0; Unknown ethnicity—full-time 0, part-time 0.

Financial Information/Assistance:

Tuition for Full-Time Study: *Doctoral:* State residents: per academic year $9,740, $811 per credit hour; Nonstate residents: per academic year $16,838, $1,403 per credit hour. Tuition is subject to change. See the following Web site for updates and changes in tuition costs: http://www.grad.umn.edu/Prospective_Students/Financing/index.html.

Financial Assistance:

First-Year Students: Teaching assistantships available for first year. Average amount paid per academic year: $12,650. Average number of hours worked per week: 20. Tuition remission given: full. Research assistantships available for first year. Average amount paid per academic year: $12,650. Average number of hours worked per week: 20. Tuition remission given: full. Fellowships and scholarships available for first year. Average amount paid per academic year: $22,500. Tuition remission given: full.

Advanced Students: Teaching assistantships available for advanced students. Average amount paid per academic year: $12,650. Average number of hours worked per week: 20. Tuition remission given: full. Research assistantships available for advanced students. Average amount paid per academic year: $12,650. Average number of hours worked per week: 20. Tuition remission given: full. Traineeships available for advanced students. Average amount paid per academic year: $15,579. Tuition remission given: full. Fellowships and scholarships available for advanced students. Average amount paid per academic year: $22,500. Tuition remission given: full.

Additional Information: Of all students currently enrolled full time, 100% benefited from one or more of the listed financial assistance programs.

Internships/Practica: Clinical and school psychology practica and internships are available within the local community to joint program students and are offered through our departmental affiliates. Field experiences are also offered to students in our Applied Developmental Psychology Certificate program.

Housing and Day Care: On-campus housing is available. On-campus housing for graduate students is limited to those with families. Off-campus student housing is available in the surrounding area. See the following Web sites for more information: http://www.grad.umn.edu/current_students/handbook/housing.html and http://www.housing.umn.edu/. On-campus day care facilities are available. Child-care is available at the University Child Care Center. See the following Web site for more information: http://www.cehd.umn.edu/ChildCareCenter/.

Employment of Department Graduates:

Master's Degree Graduates: Of those who graduated in the academic year 2006–2007, the following categories and numbers represent the postgraduate activities and employment of master's degree graduates: Enrolled in a postdoctoral residency/fellowship (n/a), employed in independent practice (n/a), total from the above (master's) (0).

Doctoral Degree Graduates: Of those who graduated in the academic year 2006–2007, the following categories and numbers represent the postgraduate activities and employment of doctoral degree graduates: Enrolled in a psychology doctoral program (n/a), enrolled in a postdoctoral residency/fellowship (3), employed in an academic position at a university (4), employed in other positions at a higher education institution (1), total from the above (doctoral) (8).

Additional Information:

Orientation, Objectives, and Emphasis of Department: The Institute program emphasizes training for research and academic careers and provides supplementary opportunities in areas of applied developmental psychology. The program offers a diversity of substantive and methodological approaches. In the core program, special strengths are in infancy, personality and social development, perception, cognitive processes, language development, biological bases of development, and developmental neuroscience. Formal applied training is available through the Developmental Psychopathology and Clinical Science (DPCS) and School Psychology joint programs. Formal minor programs are offered in Neuroscience, Cognitive Science, and Interpersonal Relationships Research. Students can complete an Applied Developmental Psychology Certificate program, focusing on such areas as educational programs and research, public policy, and policy-relevant research. Special training is also available through affiliations with the Center for Cognitive Sciences, the Center for Neurobehavioral Development, the Center for Early Education and Development, and the Consortium on Children, Youth, and Families.

Special Facilities or Resources: Physical and research facilities include an office for every student each equipped with an Ethernet connected computer and printer, a reference room with more than 4,500 volumes, 25 experiment rooms, a computer laboratory, a shop for construction of apparatus, and a laboratory nursery school. In addition, state-of-the-art research facilities and interdisciplinary collaborations facilitate cutting-edge neuroscience research in the areas of cognitive, behavioral, and social–emotional development. Onsite facilities include both high-density (128 channels) and low-density (32 channels) electrophysiological recording equipment and eyetracking equipment. Facilities at the Center for Neurobehavioral Development (opened in 2001) include autonomic and electrophysiological laboratories equipped with functional magnetic resonance imaging (fMRI) and event-related potential (ERP) equipment; audiovisual systems for online data collection, videotaping, presentations, and training; research suites, computer workroom, library and conference room; and subject exam rooms and family waiting and play rooms. At the Center for Magnetic Resonance Research, structural and functional MRI equipment is available.

Information for Students With Physical Disabilities: See the following Web site for more information: http://www.ds.umn.edu/.

Application Information:
Send to Chair of Admissions, Institute of Child Development, University of Minnesota, 51 East River Road, Minneapolis, MN 55455-0345. Application available online. URL of online application: http://www.cehd.umn.edu/icd/GradInfo/. Students are admitted in the Fall, application deadline December. *Fee:* $55; $75 for international applicants. Visa, Mastercard, Discover accepted.

Saint Mary's University of Minnesota

Counseling and Psychological Services
School of Graduate Studies
2500 Park Avenue
Minneapolis, MN 55404
Telephone: (612) 728-5113
Fax: (612) 728-5121
E-mail: *chuck@smumn.edu*
Web: *http://www.smumn.edu*

Department Information:
1983. Program Director: Christina Huck, PhD, LP. Number of faculty: total—full-time 2, part-time 64; women—full-time 2, part-time 30; minority—part-time 6; women minority—part-time 4.

Programs and Degrees Offered:
Listed in the following order: Program area, degree type (T if terminal Master's), number awarded 7/06–6/07. Counseling and Psychological Services MA/MS (Master of Arts/Science) (T) 45, Marriage and Family Therapy MA/MS (Master of Arts/Science) (T) 17, Graduate Certificate, Marriage and Family Therapy Other 13.

Student Applications/Admissions:
Student Applications
Counseling and Psychological Services MA/MS (Master of Arts/Science)—Applications 2007–2008, 127. Total applicants accepted 2007–2008, 113. Number full-time enrolled (new admits only) 2007–2008, 26. Number part-time enrolled (new admits only) 2007–2008, 38. Total enrolled 2007–2008 full-time, 88, part-time, 225. *Marriage and Family Therapy MA/MS (Master of Arts/Science)*—Applications 2007–2008, 51. Total applicants accepted 2007–2008, 42. Number full-time enrolled (new admits only) 2007–2008, 15. Number part-time enrolled (new admits only) 2007–2008, 18. Total enrolled 2007–2008 full-time, 69, part-time, 96. *Graduate Certificate, Marriage and Family Therapy Other*—Applications 2007–2008, 30. Total applicants accepted 2007–2008, 27. Number full-time enrolled (new admits only) 2007–2008, 3. Number part-time enrolled (new admits only) 2007–2008, 10. Total enrolled 2007–2008 full-time, 7, part-time, 48.

Admissions Requirements:
Scores: Entries appear in this order: required test or GPA, minimum score (if required), median score of students entering in 2007–2008. Master's Programs: overall undergraduate GPA 2.75.
Other Criteria: (importance of criteria rated low, medium, or high): research experience—medium, work experience—high, extracurricular activity—medium, clinically related public service—high, GPA—high, letters of recommendation—high, interview—high, statement of goals and objectives—high.

Student Characteristics: The following represents characteristics of students in 2007–2008 in all graduate psychology programs in the department: Female—full-time 137, part-time 303; Male—full-time 27, part-time 66; African American/Black—full-time 3, part-time 17; Hispanic/Latino(a)—full-time 3, part-time 6; Asian/Pacific Islander—full-time 6, part-time 13; American Indian/Alaska Native—full-time 0, part-time 0; Caucasian/White—full-time 130, part-time 286; Multi-ethnic—full-time 0, part-time 0; students subject to the Americans With Disabilities Act—part-time 3; Unknown ethnicity—full-time 22, part-time 47; International students who hold an F-1 or J-1 Visa—full-time 2, part-time 1.

Financial Information/Assistance:
Tuition for Full-Time Study: *Master's:* State residents: $340 per credit hour; Nonstate residents: $340 per credit hour.

Financial Assistance:
First-Year Students: Fellowships and scholarships available for first year. Average amount paid per academic year: $1,571. Apply by August 31.
Advanced Students: Fellowships and scholarships available for advanced students. Average amount paid per academic year: $1,835. Apply by August 1.
Additional Information: Of all students currently enrolled full time, 1% benefited from one or more of the listed financial assistance programs.

Internships/Practica: Master's Degree (MA/MS Counseling and Psychological Services): An internship experience such as a final research project or "capstone" experience is required of graduates. Master's Degree (MA/MS Marriage and Family Therapy): An internship experience such as a final research project or "capstone" experience is required of graduates. A wide variety of practicum sites are available for students.

Housing and Day Care: No on-campus housing is available. No on-campus day care facilities are available.

Employment of Department Graduates:

Master's Degree Graduates: Of those who graduated in the academic year 2006–2007, the following categories and numbers represent the postgraduate activities and employment of master's degree graduates: Enrolled in a postdoctoral residency/fellowship (n/a), employed in independent practice (n/a), total from the above (master's) (0).

Doctoral Degree Graduates: Of those who graduated in the academic year 2006–2007, the following categories and numbers represent the postgraduate activities and employment of doctoral degree graduates: Enrolled in a psychology doctoral program (n/a), total from the above (doctoral) (0).

Additional Information:

Orientation, Objectives, and Emphasis of Department: The Master of Arts Program in Counseling and Psychological Services prepares graduates for professional work in counseling, psychotherapy, and other psychological services. It is designed to enhance the student's understanding of the complex nature of human behavior and social interaction, and to develop tools for assessing human problems and assisting individuals in developing greater understanding and acceptance of themselves and their relationships with others. The program is designed to meet the educational requirements for Minnesota licensure for Licensed Professional Counselors. Students planning to seek licensure with the Minnesota Board of Psychology after earning a doctorate can work toward some of their educational requirements in the Master's program. The Counseling and Psychological Services Program is offered in Rochester, MN, as well as in Minneapolis.

Special Facilities or Resources: The majority of our faculty are adjunct (part-time) instructors who are practicing in the field. They bring a wealth of real-world experience to their teaching and possess strong academic credentials. Because our emphasis is on applied psychological competence, we consider the backgrounds of these practitioner–scholars to be a major strength of the program.

Application Information:

Send to Admissions, Saint Mary's University of MN, 2500 Park Avenue, Minneapolis, MN 55404. Application available online. URL of online application: http://www.smumn.edu. Students are admitted in the Fall, application deadline; Spring, application deadline; Summer, application deadline. Deadlines are somewhat flexible. Recommended applying 3 months before the start of the semester. *Fee:* $25.

St. Cloud State University (2007 data)

Counselor Education and Educational Psychology
College of Education
Education Building A-253, 720 South 4th Avenue
St. Cloud, MN 56301
Telephone: (320) 308-3131
Fax: (320) 308-4082
E-mail: *smhoover@stcloudstate.edu*
Web: *http://www.stcloudstate.edu/ceep*

Department Information:

2001. Chairperson: Jana Preble. Number of faculty: total—full-time 13, part-time 6; women—full-time 5, part-time 4.

Programs and Degrees Offered:

Listed in the following order: Program area, degree type (T if terminal Master's), number awarded 7/06–6/07. College Counseling and Student Development MA/MS (Master of Arts/Science) (T) 10, Rehabilitation Counseling Psychology MA/MS (Master of Arts/Science) (T) 7, School Counseling Psychology MA/MS (Master of Arts/Science) (T) 18.

Student Applications/Admissions:

Student Applications

College Counseling and Student Development MA/MS (Master of Arts/Science)—Applications 2007–2008, 17. Total applicants accepted 2007–2008, 16. Number full-time enrolled (new admits only) 2007–2008, 13. Number part-time enrolled (new admits only) 2007–2008, 7. Total enrolled 2007–2008 full-time, 23, part-time, 10. Openings 2008–2009, 20. The median number of years required for completion of a degree in 2006–2007 were 2. The number of students enrolled full- and part-time who were dismissed or voluntarily withdrew from this program area in 2007–2008 were 1. *Rehabilitation Counseling Psychology MA/MS (Master of Arts/Science)*—Applications 2007–2008, 13. Total applicants accepted 2007–2008, 12. Number full-time enrolled (new admits only) 2007–2008, 12. Number part-time enrolled (new admits only) 2007–2008, 5. Total enrolled 2007–2008 full-time, 18, part-time, 8. Openings 2008–2009, 15. The median number of years required for completion of a degree in 2006–2007 were 2. The number of students enrolled full- and part-time who were dismissed or voluntarily withdrew from this program area in 2007–2008 were 1. *School Counseling Psychology MA/MS (Master of Arts/Science)*—Applications 2007–2008, 28. Total applicants accepted 2007–2008, 23. Number full-time enrolled (new admits only) 2007–2008, 11. Number part-time enrolled (new admits only) 2007–2008, 10. Total enrolled 2007–2008 full-time, 22, part-time, 30. Openings 2008–2009, 20. The median number of years required for completion of a degree in 2006–2007 were 2. The number of students enrolled full- and part-time who were dismissed or voluntarily withdrew from this program area in 2007–2008 were 2.

Admissions Requirements:

Scores: Entries appear in this order: required test or GPA, minimum score (if required), median score of students entering in 2007–2008. Master's Programs: GRE-V no minimum stated; GRE-Q no minimum stated; overall undergraduate GPA no minimum stated; last 2 years GPA no minimum stated.

Other Criteria: (importance of criteria rated low, medium, or high): GRE/MAT scores—medium, research experience—medium, work experience—high, extracurricular activity—medium, clinically related public service—high, GPA—high, letters of recommendation—high, interview—high, statement of goals and objectives—high.

Student Characteristics: The following represents characteristics of students in 2007–2008 in all graduate psychology programs in the department: Female—full-time 54, part-time 40; Male—full-time 11, part-time 8; African American/Black—full-time 0, part-time 0; Hispanic/Latino(a)—full-time 2, part-time 0; Asian/Pacific Islander—full-time 2, part-time 0; American Indian/Alaska Native—full-time 2, part-time 0; Caucasian/White—full-time 42, part-time 69; students subject to the Americans With

Disabilities Act—full-time 6, part-time 3; Unknown ethnicity—full-time 0, part-time 0.

Financial Information/Assistance:

Tuition for Full-Time Study: *Master's:* State residents: $257 per credit hour; Nonstate residents: $401 per credit hour. Tuition is subject to change. See the following Web site for updates and changes in tuition costs: http://www.stcloudstate.edu.

Financial Assistance:

First-Year Students: Teaching assistantships available for first year. Average amount paid per academic year: $4,850. Average number of hours worked per week: 10. Tuition remission given: partial. Research assistantships available for first year. Average amount paid per academic year: $4,850. Average number of hours worked per week: 10. Tuition remission given: partial. Fellowships and scholarships available for first year. Average amount paid per academic year: $500.

Advanced Students: No information provided.

Additional Information: Of all students currently enrolled full time, 50% benefited from one or more of the listed financial assistance programs. Application and information available online at http://www.stcloudstate.edu.

Internships/Practica: Internship opportunities exist in mental health centers, university counseling centers, Veterans Administration hospitals, general hospitals, social service and welfare agencies, state rehabilitation offices, private rehabilitation companies, rehabilitation workshops and facilities, medical rehabilitation centers, and a number of human services agencies and school and college settings.

Housing and Day Care: On-campus housing is available. See the following Web site for more information: http://www.stcloudstate.edu. On-campus day care facilities are available.

Employment of Department Graduates:

Master's Degree Graduates: Of those who graduated in the academic year 2006–2007, the following categories and numbers represent the postgraduate activities and employment of master's degree graduates: Enrolled in a psychology doctoral program (3), enrolled in another graduate/professional program (3), enrolled in a postdoctoral residency/fellowship (n/a), employed in independent practice (n/a), employed in an academic position at a university (1), employed in other positions at a higher education institution (8), employed in a professional position in a school system (12), employed in business or industry (10), employed in a community mental health/counseling center (3), employed in a hospital/medical center (2), still seeking employment (2), other employment position (7), total from the above (master's) (56).

Doctoral Degree Graduates: Of those who graduated in the academic year 2006–2007, the following categories and numbers represent the postgraduate activities and employment of doctoral degree graduates: Enrolled in a psychology doctoral program (n/a), total from the above (doctoral) (0).

Additional Information:

Orientation, Objectives, and Emphasis of Department: The College Counseling and Student Development program prepares students to work in college counseling centers, career centers, and other student affairs positions in higher education. The Rehabilitation Counseling program is accredited by the Council on Rehabilitation Education and prepares students to work in a variety of public and private rehabilitation settings. The School Counseling program prepares students for licensure as elementary or secondary school counselors and is accredited by the Council for the Accreditation of Counseling and Related Educational Programs (CACREP).

Special Facilities or Resources: A counseling classroom surrounded by 10 counseling and observation suites allows for both individual and group counseling experiences. Audio and video equipment is available for taping and reviewing counseling sessions. A separate group room is also available for training and observation experiences. There is an animal laboratory containing pigeon and rat boxes with events controlled via a PDP-8.

Information for Students With Physical Disabilities: See the following Web site for more information: http://www.stcloudstate.edu/sds/.

Application Information:

Send to Department of Counselor and Educational Psychology. Application available online. Students are admitted in the Spring, application deadline March 1; Summer, application deadline June 15. Summer admissions occur only if there are vacancies remaining in the programs after the spring deadline and interviews. *Fee:* $35 (subject to change with revision of university graduate bulletin).

St. Cloud State University

Department of Psychology
Social Sciences
720 4th Avenue South
Saint Cloud, MN 56301
Telephone: (320) 308-4157
Fax: (320) 308-3098
E-mail: *dsprotolipac@stcloudstate.edu*
Web: *http://www.stcloudstate.edu/psychology/io/*

Department Information:

1963. Chairperson: Dr. Leslie Valdes. Number of faculty: total—full-time 12, part-time 9; women—full-time 7, part-time 5; total—minority—full-time 1; women minority—full-time 1.

Programs and Degrees Offered:

Listed in the following order: Program area, degree type (T if terminal Master's), number awarded 7/06–6/07. Industrial/Organizational Psychology MA/MS (Master of Arts/Science) (T) 5.

Student Applications/Admissions:

Student Applications

Industrial/Organizational Psychology MA/MS (Master of Arts/Science)—Applications 2007–2008, 28. Total applicants accepted 2007–2008, 15. Number full-time enrolled (new admits only) 2007–2008, 9. Openings 2008–2009, 10. The median number of years required for completion of a degree in 2006–2007 were 2. The number of students enrolled full- and part-time who were dismissed or voluntarily withdrew from this program area in 2007–2008 were 1.

Admissions Requirements:

Scores: Entries appear in this order: required test or GPA, minimum score (if required), median score of students entering in 2007–2008. Master's Programs: GRE-V no minimum stated; GRE-Q no minimum stated; overall undergraduate GPA 2.75; last 2 years GPA 2.75.

Other Criteria: (importance of criteria rated low, medium, or high): GRE/MAT scores—high, research experience—medium, work experience—medium, extracurricular activity—low, GPA—high, letters of recommendation—medium, statement of goals and objectives—medium, specific undergraduate psychology courses taken—low.

Student Characteristics: The following represents characteristics of students in 2007–2008 in all graduate psychology programs in the department: Female—full-time 9, part-time 0; Male—full-time 7, part-time 0; African American/Black—full-time 1, part-time 0; Hispanic/Latino(a)—full-time 0, part-time 0; Asian/Pacific Islander—full-time 0, part-time 0; American Indian/Alaska Native—full-time 0, part-time 0; Caucasian/White—full-time 15, part-time 0; Multi-ethnic—full-time 0, part-time 0; students subject to the Americans With Disabilities Act—full-time 0, part-time 0; Unknown ethnicity—full-time 0, part-time 0; International students who hold an F-1 or J-1 Visa—full-time 0, part-time 0.

Financial Information/Assistance:

Tuition for Full-Time Study: *Master's:* State residents: $267 per credit hour; Nonstate residents: $417 per credit hour. Tuition is subject to change. See the following Web site for updates and changes in tuition costs: http://www.stcloudstate.edu/graduatestudies.

Financial Assistance:

First-Year Students: Teaching assistantships available for first year. Average amount paid per academic year: $5,150. Average number of hours worked per week: 10. Tuition remission given: partial. Research assistantships available for first year. Average amount paid per academic year: $5,150. Average number of hours worked per week: 10. Tuition remission given: partial. Fellowships and scholarships available for first year.

Advanced Students: Teaching assistantships available for advanced students. Average amount paid per academic year: $5,150. Average number of hours worked per week: 10. Tuition remission given: partial. Research assistantships available for advanced students. Average amount paid per academic year: $5,150. Average number of hours worked per week: 10. Tuition remission given: partial. Fellowships and scholarships available for advanced students.

Additional Information: Of all students currently enrolled full time, 75% benefited from one or more of the listed financial assistance programs. Application and information available online at http://www.stcloudstate.edu/graduatestudies.

Internships/Practica: Students pursuing the Master's Degree in Industrial/Organizational Psychology have the option of completing either a practicum/internship or a thesis. The practicum/internship option is designed for students planning to seek employment upon completion of their degree. The thesis option is designed for students planning to seek a doctoral degree in Industrial/Organizational Psychology.

Housing and Day Care: On-campus housing is available. See the following Web site for more information: http://www.stcloudstate.edu/reslife/. On-campus day care facilities are available. See the following Web site for more information: http://www.stcloudstate.edu/childcare/. Contact Lindgren Child Care Center (320) 308-3296.

Employment of Department Graduates:

Master's Degree Graduates: Of those who graduated in the academic year 2006–2007, the following categories and numbers represent the postgraduate activities and employment of master's degree graduates: Enrolled in a postdoctoral residency/fellowship (n/a), employed in independent practice (n/a), employed in business or industry (4), total from the above (master's) (4).

Doctoral Degree Graduates: Of those who graduated in the academic year 2006–2007, the following categories and numbers represent the postgraduate activities and employment of doctoral degree graduates: Enrolled in a psychology doctoral program (n/a), total from the above (doctoral) (0).

Additional Information:

Orientation, Objectives, and Emphasis of Department: The St. Cloud State University Department of Psychology is dedicated to providing students with a quality graduate education. The Industrial/Organizational Psychology Master's Degree Program is designed to provide graduate students with the knowledge and skills that will prepare them for jobs in consulting, business, and government, or to continue their education. The curriculum reflects a commitment to the scientist–practitioner model of graduate education in psychology by including training in the theoretical and empirical bases of industrial/organizational psychology and in the application of these perspectives to work settings. Following the recommendations of the Society for Industrial/Organizational Psychology for master's level education, students' graduate experience will include (a) training in the core areas of industrial/organizational psychology, including personnel selection, training and organizational development, criterion development, and organizational theory; (b) a firm foundation in psychological theory, research methods, statistics, and psychometrics; and (c) the opportunity to obtain both research experience and applied experience while completing their education.

Special Facilities or Resources: The St. Cloud State University Psychology Department has a dedicated psychology laboratory facility (new space established in 1999). It has 10 rooms for individual and group testing. The lab has networked computers and a laser printer. Activities that take place in this lab include faculty and student research, meetings of student organizations, research seminars, and classroom demonstrations.

Information for Students With Physical Disabilities: See the following Web site for more information: http://www.stcloudstate.edu/sds/.

Application Information:

Send to School of Graduate Studies, 121 Administrative Services, St. Cloud State University, 720 4th Avenue South, St. Cloud, MN 56301. Application available online. URL of online application: http://www.stcloudstate.edu/graduatestudies/. Students are admitted in the Fall, application deadline March 1. *Fee:* $35.

St. Thomas, University of (2007 data)

Graduate School of Professional Psychology
1000 La Salle Avenue, TMH 451
Minneapolis, MN 55403-2005
Telephone: (651) 962-4650
Fax: (651) 962-4651
E-mail: *idwelch@stthomas.edu*
Web: *http://www.stthomas.edu/gradpsych*

Department Information:

1960. Dean: David Welch. Number of faculty: total—full-time 8, part-time 11; women—full-time 4, part-time 7.

Programs and Degrees Offered:

Listed in the following order: Program area, degree type (T if terminal Master's), number awarded 7/06–6/07. Counseling MA/MS (Master of Arts/Science) (T) 38, Counseling Psychology PsyD (Doctor of Psychology) 14.

APA Accreditation: Counseling PsyD (Doctor of Psychology).

Student Applications/Admissions:

Student Applications

Counseling MA/MS (Master of Arts/Science)—Applications 2007–2008, 99. Total applicants accepted 2007–2008, 39. Number full-time enrolled (new admits only) 2007–2008, 12. Number part-time enrolled (new admits only) 2007–2008, 27. Total enrolled 2007–2008 full-time, 23, part-time, 84. Openings 2008–2009, 42. The median number of years required for completion of a degree in 2006–2007 were 3. The number of students enrolled full- and part-time who were dismissed or voluntarily withdrew from this program area in 2007–2008 were 1. *Counseling Psychology PsyD (Doctor of Psychology)*—Applications 2007–2008, 37. Total applicants accepted 2007–2008, 15. Number full-time enrolled (new admits only) 2007–2008, 6. Number part-time enrolled (new admits only) 2007–2008, 9. Total enrolled 2007–2008 full-time, 25, part-time, 53. Openings 2008–2009, 12. The median number of years required for completion of a degree in 2006–2007 were 5. The number of students enrolled full- and part-time who were dismissed or voluntarily withdrew from this program area in 2007–2008 were 0.

Admissions Requirements:

Scores: Entries appear in this order: required test or GPA, minimum score (if required), median score of students entering in 2007–2008. Master's Programs: GRE-V no minimum stated; GRE-Q no minimum stated; MAT no minimum stated, 400; overall undergraduate GPA 2.75. Accept either the GRE or MAT. Doctoral Programs: GRE-V no minimum stated, 450; GRE-Q no minimum stated, 450; Doctoral program GRE-Analytic no minimum stated, 4. Require the GRE with a writing sample.

Other Criteria: (importance of criteria rated low, medium, or high): GRE/MAT scores—medium, research experience—low, work experience—high, extracurricular activity—low, clinically related public service—high, GPA—high, letters of recommendation—high, interview—high, statement of goals and objectives—high. The PsyD utilizes the practitioner–scholar model and emphasizes educating practitioners for direct service positions. For additional information on admission requirements, go to http://www.stthomas.edu/gradpsych.

Student Characteristics: The following represents characteristics of students in 2007–2008 in all graduate psychology programs in the department: Female—full-time 34, part-time 103; Male—full-time 14, part-time 34; African American/Black—full-time 0, part-time 3; Hispanic/Latino(a)—full-time 0, part-time 2; Asian/Pacific Islander—full-time 1, part-time 2; American Indian/Alaska Native—full-time 0, part-time 0; Caucasian/White—full-time 46, part-time 123; Multi-ethnic—full-time 1, part-time 7; students subject to the Americans With Disabilities Act—full-time 1, part-time 0; Unknown ethnicity—full-time 0, part-time 0.

Financial Information/Assistance:

Tuition for Full-Time Study: *Master's:* State residents: $549 per credit hour; Nonstate residents: $549 per credit hour. *Doctoral:* State residents: $733 per credit hour; Nonstate residents: $733 per credit hour. See the following Web site for updates and changes in tuition costs: http://www.stthomas.edu/gradpsych.

Financial Assistance:

First-Year Students: Fellowships and scholarships available for first year. Average amount paid per academic year: $2,500. Average number of hours worked per week: 0. Apply by August 1.

Advanced Students: Research assistantships available for advanced students. Average amount paid per academic year: $2,500. Average number of hours worked per week: 5. Apply by August 1.

Additional Information: Of all students currently enrolled full time, 1% benefited from one or more of the listed financial assistance programs. Application and information available online at http://www.stthomas.edu/financialservices.

Internships/Practica: Master's and doctoral students have available a wide variety of practica and internships in the surrounding community in the Twin Cities area. Application is competitive and supported by the practicum coordinator at UST. Students also participate in APPIC internships locally and across the country. Recent sites have included community mental health centers, regional hospitals, VA medical centers, residential chemical dependency centers, career and vocational services, college and university counseling and career centers, vocational rehabilitation programs, employee assistance counseling programs, health maintenance organizations, MN state hospitals, and the MN state prison system.

Housing and Day Care: No on-campus housing is available. On-campus day care facilities are available. See the following Web site for more information: http://www.ssthomas.edu/childdevelopment.

Employment of Department Graduates:

Master's Degree Graduates: Of those who graduated in the academic year 2006–2007, the following categories and numbers represent the postgraduate activities and employment of master's degree graduates: Enrolled in a psychology doctoral program (6), enrolled in a postdoctoral residency/fellowship (n/a), employed in independent practice (n/a), employed in other positions at a higher education institution (4), employed in a professional position in a school system (2), employed in business or industry (3), employed in a community mental health/counseling center (13), employed in a hospital/medical center (3), still seeking employment (2), other employment position (4), total from the above (master's) (37).

Doctoral Degree Graduates: Of those who graduated in the academic year 2006–2007, the following categories and numbers represent the postgraduate activities and employment of doctoral degree graduates: Enrolled in a psychology doctoral program (n/a), employed in independent practice (8), employed in a community mental health/counseling center (9), employed in a hospital/medical center (2), total from the above (doctoral) (19).

Additional Information:

Orientation, Objectives, and Emphasis of Department: The Graduate School of Professional Psychology is dedicated to the development of general practitioners who will make ethical, professional, creative contributions to their communities and their profession. The programs strive toward leadership in emphasizing a practitioner focus with adult learners. Teaching, scholarship, and service are responsive to diverse perspectives, a blend of practical and reflective inquiry, and social needs. The PsyD is accredited by the APA.

Personal Behavior Statement: The program has stated core values and personal competences that are a part of the training model. They may e-mail the school at gradpsych@stthomas.edu and request a copy of the Personal Characteristics that enrolled students sign when they enter the program.

Special Facilities or Resources: UST has developed the Center for Counseling Legal Services (IPC), which is an interprofessional clinic involving counseling psychology, social work, and law. This unique center provides free counseling and legal services to underserved populations in the Minneapolis/St. Paul vicinity.

Information for Students With Physical Disabilities: See the following Web site for more information: http://www.stthomas.edu/enhancementprog.

Application Information:

Send to Admissions, Graduate School of Professional Psychology, University of St. Thomas, 1000 La Salle Avenue, TMH451, Minneapolis, MN 55403. Application available online. URL of online application: http://www.stthomas.edu/gradpsych. Students are admitted in the Fall. Application March 1 for MA; February 1 for PsyD. *Fee:* $50.

Walden University

Psychology
School of Psychology
155 Fifth Avenue South
Minneapolis, MN 55401
Telephone: (800) 925-3368 X2431
Fax: (612) 338-5092
E-mail: *nina.nabors@waldenu.edu*
Web: *http://www.waldenu.edu*

Department Information:

1996. Associate Dean: Nina A. Nabors. Number of faculty: total—full-time 11, part-time 168; women—full-time 7, part-time 86; total—minority—full-time 4, part-time 24; women minority—full-time 3, part-time 10; faculty subject to the Americans With Disabilities Act 5.

Programs and Degrees Offered:

Listed in the following order: Program area, degree type (T if terminal Master's), number awarded 7/06–6/07. General Psychology MA/MS (Master of Arts/Science) (T) 165, Clinical Psychology PhD (Doctor of Philosophy) 18, Counseling Psychology PhD (Doctor of Philosophy) 5, Organizational Psychology PhD (Doctor of Philosophy) 3, Health Psychology PhD (Doctor of Philosophy) 5, School Psychology PhD (Doctor of Philosophy) 0, Industrial/Organizational MA/MS (Master of Arts/Science) 17, Organizational Psychology and Development MA/MS (Master of Arts/Science) (T) 0, General Psychology PhD (Doctor of Philosophy) 11.

Student Applications/Admissions:

Student Applications

General Psychology MA/MS (Master of Arts/Science)—Applications 2007–2008, 382. Total applicants accepted 2007–2008, 366. Number full-time enrolled (new admits only) 2007–2008, 298. Total enrolled 2007–2008 full-time, 1292. The median number of years required for completion of a degree in 2006–2007 were 3. *Clinical Psychology PhD (Doctor of Philosophy)*—Applications 2007–2008, 472. Total applicants accepted 2007–2008, 468. Number full-time enrolled (new admits only) 2007–2008, 468. Total enrolled 2007–2008 full-time, 904. The median number of years required for completion of a degree in 2006–2007 were 7. The number of students enrolled full- and part-time who were dismissed or voluntarily withdrew from this program area in 2007–2008 were 333. *Counseling Psychology PhD (Doctor of Philosophy)*—Applications 2007–2008, 247. Total applicants accepted 2007–2008, 245. Number full-time enrolled (new admits only) 2007–2008, 189. Total enrolled 2007–2008 full-time, 356. The median number of years required for completion of a degree in 2006–2007 were 6. *Organizational Psychology PhD (Doctor of Philosophy)*—Applications 2007–2008, 123. Total applicants accepted 2007–2008, 121. Number full-time enrolled (new admits only) 2007–2008, 100. Total enrolled 2007–2008 full-time, 353. The median number of years required for completion of a degree in 2006–2007 were 5. *Health Psychology PhD (Doctor of Philosophy)*—Applications 2007–2008, 107. Total applicants accepted 2007–2008, 107. Number full-time enrolled (new admits only) 2007–2008, 83. Total enrolled 2007–2008 full-time, 261. The median number of years required for completion of a degree in 2006–2007 were 6. *School Psychology PhD (Doctor of Philosophy)*—Applications 2007–2008, 89. Total applicants accepted 2007–2008, 84. Number full-time enrolled (new admits only) 2007–2008, 84. Total enrolled 2007–2008 full-time, 143. *Industrial/Organizational MA/MS (Master of Arts/Science)*—Applications 2007–2008, 118. Total applicants accepted 2007–2008, 116. Number full-time enrolled (new admits only) 2007–2008, 80. Total enrolled 2007–2008 full-time, 452. The median number of years required for completion of a degree in 2006–2007 were 2. *Organizational Psychology and Development MA/MS (Master of Arts/Science)*—Total enrolled 2007–2008 full-time, 45. *General Psychology PhD (Doctor of Philosophy)*—Total enrolled 2007–2008 full-time, 477. The median number of years required for completion of a degree in 2006–2007 were 4.

Admissions Requirements:

Scores: Entries appear in this order: required test or GPA, minimum score (if required), median score of students entering in 2007–2008. Master's Programs: overall undergraduate GPA 3.0, 3.5; last 2 years GPA 3.0, 3.5; psychology GPA 3.0, 3.5. Doctoral Programs: overall undergraduate GPA 3.0, 3.5; last 2 years GPA 3.0, 3.5; psychology GPA 3.0, 3.5.

Other Criteria: (importance of criteria rated low, medium, or high): research experience—low, extracurricular activity—low, clinically related public service—high, GPA—high, letters of recommendation—low, statement of goals and objectives—high, undergraduate major in psychology—low, specific undergraduate psychology courses taken—medium. For additional information on admission requirements, go to http://www.waldenu.edu/c/Student_Catalog/8898_9357.htm.

Student Characteristics: The following represents characteristics of students in 2007–2008 in all graduate psychology programs in the department: Female—full-time 3433, part-time 0; Male—full-time 920, part-time 0; African American/Black—full-time 904, part-time 0; Hispanic/Latino(a)—full-time 163, part-time 0; Asian/Pacific Islander—full-time 47, part-time 0; American Indian/Alaska Native—full-time 28, part-time 0; Caucasian/White—full-time 1593, part-time 0; Multi-ethnic—full-time 126, part-time 0; students subject to the Americans With Disabilities Act—full-time 9, part-time 0; Unknown ethnicity—full-time 1492, part-time 0.

Financial Information/Assistance:

Tuition for Full-Time Study: *Master's:* State residents: $345 per credit hour; Nonstate residents: $345 per credit hour. *Doctoral:* State residents: $420 per credit hour; Nonstate residents: $420 per credit hour. Tuition is subject to change. Tuition costs vary by program. See the following Web site for updates and changes in tuition costs: http://www.waldenu.edu/c/Student_Catalog/8900_9275.htm.

Financial Assistance:

First-Year Students: No information provided.

Advanced Students: Research assistantships available for advanced students. Average amount paid per academic year: $6,000. Average number of hours worked per week: 10. Apply by varies.

Additional Information: Of all students currently enrolled full time, 1% benefited from one or more of the listed financial assistance programs. Application and information available online at http://www.waldenu.edu/c/Student_Catalog/8900_9283.htm.

Internships/Practica: Master's Degree (MA/MS General Psychology): An internship experience such as a final research project or "capstone" experience is required of graduates. Our field placement coordinators work with students to arrange for practicum and internship sites. We do not at this time have available internship or practicum sites.

Housing and Day Care: No on-campus housing is available. No on-campus day care facilities are available.

Employment of Department Graduates:

Master's Degree Graduates: Of those who graduated in the academic year 2006–2007, the following categories and numbers represent the postgraduate activities and employment of master's degree graduates: Enrolled in a psychology doctoral program (49), enrolled in a postdoctoral residency/fellowship (n/a), employed in independent practice (n/a), do not know (75), total from the above (master's) (124).

Doctoral Degree Graduates: Of those who graduated in the academic year 2006–2007, the following categories and numbers represent the postgraduate activities and employment of doctoral degree graduates: Enrolled in a psychology doctoral program (n/a), do not know (34), total from the above (doctoral) (34).

Additional Information:

Orientation, Objectives, and Emphasis of Department: The program is based in a scholar–practitioner model and reflects the university mission of social change. Students have the opportunity to work with faculty with a diverse array of theoretical orientations.

Special Facilities or Resources: Our facilty has a testing site that is used in the assessment courses.

Information for Students With Physical Disabilities: See the following Web site for more information: http://www.waldenu.edu.

Application Information:

Send to Office of Student Enrollment, Walden University, 1001 Fleet Street, Baltimore, MD 21202 USA. Application available online. URL of online application: http://www.waldenu.edu/c/About/About_10168.htm. Students are admitted in the Fall, application deadline August 15; Winter, application deadline November 15; Spring, application deadline February 15; Summer, application deadline May 15. Programs have rolling admissions. *Fee:* $50.

Mississippi State University (2007 data)

Department of Counseling, Educational Psychology, and Special Education
College of Education
P.O. Box 9727
Mississippi State, MS 39762-5670
Telephone: (662) 325-3426
Fax: (662) 325-3263
E-mail: *hosie@colled.msstate.edu*
Web: *http://www.educ.msstate.edu/cepse/*

Department Information:
1954. Department Head: Thomas W. Hosie. Number of faculty: total—full-time 4; women—full-time 4.

Programs and Degrees Offered:
Listed in the following order: Program area, degree type (T if terminal Master's), number awarded 7/06–6/07. School PhD (Doctor of Philosophy) 4, Educational PhD (Doctor of Philosophy) 0.

APA Accreditation: School PhD (Doctor of Philosophy).

Student Applications/Admissions:

Student Applications

School PhD (Doctor of Philosophy)—Applications 2007–2008, 13. Total applicants accepted 2007–2008, 5. Number full-time enrolled (new admits only) 2007–2008, 5. Number part-time enrolled (new admits only) 2007–2008, 0. Openings 2008–2009, 6. The median number of years required for completion of a degree in 2006–2007 were 5. The number of students enrolled full- and part-time who were dismissed or voluntarily withdrew from this program area in 2007–2008 were 0. *Educational PhD (Doctor of Philosophy)*—Applications 2007–2008, 4. Total applicants accepted 2007–2008, 3. Number full-time enrolled (new admits only) 2007–2008, 3. Total enrolled 2007–2008 full-time, 11, part-time, 3. Openings 2008–2009, 5. The median number of years required for completion of a degree in 2006–2007 were 4. The number of students enrolled full- and part-time who were dismissed or voluntarily withdrew from this program area in 2007–2008 were 0.

Admissions Requirements:

Scores: Entries appear in this order: required test or GPA, minimum score (if required), median score of students entering in 2007–2008. Master's Programs: GRE-V no minimum stated; GRE-Q no minimum stated; overall undergraduate GPA 2.75, 3.00; last 2 years GPA 3.0, 3.2. Doctoral Programs: GRE-V no minimum stated; GRE-Q no minimum stated; overall undergraduate GPA no minimum stated, 3.00.

Other Criteria: (importance of criteria rated low, medium, or high): GRE/MAT scores—medium, research experience—medium, work experience—medium, extracurricular activity—low, clinically related public service—low, GPA—high, letters of recommendation—high, interview—high, statement of goals and objectives—high.

Student Characteristics: The following represents characteristics of students in 2007–2008 in all graduate psychology programs in the department: Female—full-time 35, part-time 0; Male—full-time 7, part-time 3; African American/Black—full-time 6, part-time 2; Hispanic/Latino(a)—full-time 1, part-time 1; Asian/Pacific Islander—full-time 2, part-time 0; American Indian/Alaska Native—full-time 0, part-time 0; Caucasian/White—full-time 32, part-time 0; Multi-ethnic—full-time 1, part-time 0; students subject to the Americans With Disabilities Act—full-time 0, part-time 0; Unknown ethnicity—full-time 0, part-time 0.

Financial Information/Assistance:

Tuition for Full-Time Study: *Master's:* State residents: per academic year $4,550, $253 per credit hour; Nonstate residents: per academic year $5,956, $331 per credit hour. *Doctoral:* State residents: per academic year $4,550, $253 per credit hour; Nonstate residents: per academic year $5,956, $331 per credit hour. See the following Web site for updates and changes in tuition costs: http://www.controller.msstate.edu/sas/account.htm.

Financial Assistance:

First-Year Students: Teaching assistantships available for first year. Average amount paid per academic year: $10,222. Average number of hours worked per week: 20. Tuition remission given: full. Research assistantships available for first year. Average amount paid per academic year: $10,222. Average number of hours worked per week: 20. Tuition remission given: full. Traineeships available for first year. Average amount paid per academic year: $7,987. Average number of hours worked per week: 20.

Advanced Students: Teaching assistantships available for advanced students. Average amount paid per academic year: $10,222. Average number of hours worked per week: 20. Tuition remission given: full. Research assistantships available for advanced students. Average amount paid per academic year: $10,222. Average number of hours worked per week: 20. Tuition remission given: full.

Additional Information: Of all students currently enrolled full time, 95% benefited from one or more of the listed financial assistance programs. Application and information available online or contact the Department.

Internships/Practica: The school psychology program offers students numerous practica and internship opportunities. Most practica are coordinated with school districts, medical centers and hospitals, community counseling centers, and the like. Internship and practica opportunities are tailored to meet the individual needs of students and a variety of options can be arranged. In general, students are encouraged to seek APA-approved internships.

Housing and Day Care: On-campus housing is available. See the following Web site for more information: http://www.msstate.edu/dept/housing/index.php. On-campus day care facilities are available.

Employment of Department Graduates:

Master's Degree Graduates: Of those who graduated in the academic year 2006–2007, the following categories and numbers

represent the postgraduate activities and employment of master's degree graduates: Enrolled in a psychology doctoral program (2), enrolled in another graduate/professional program (0), enrolled in a postdoctoral residency/fellowship (n/a), employed in independent practice (n/a), employed in an academic position at a university (0), employed in an academic position at a 2-year/4-year college (1), employed in other positions at a higher education institution (0), employed in a professional position in a school system (0), employed in business or industry (0), employed in government agency (0), employed in a community mental health/counseling center (0), employed in a hospital/medical center (0), still seeking employment (0), other employment position (0), do not know (0), total from the above (master's) (5).

Doctoral Degree Graduates: Of those who graduated in the academic year 2006–2007, the following categories and numbers represent the postgraduate activities and employment of doctoral degree graduates: Enrolled in a psychology doctoral program (n/a), enrolled in another graduate/professional program (0), enrolled in a postdoctoral residency/fellowship (0), employed in independent practice (0), employed in an academic position at a university (2), employed in an academic position at a 2-year/4-year college (0), employed in other positions at a higher education institution (0), employed in a professional position in a school system (1), employed in business or industry (0), employed in government agency (0), employed in a community mental health/counseling center (0), employed in a hospital/medical center (1), still seeking employment (0), other employment position (0), do not know (0), total from the above (doctoral) (4).

Additional Information:

Orientation, Objectives, and Emphasis of Department: Our graduate programs are designed primarily to help develop and train competent and ethical psychologists in several areas: school psychology and educational psychology. The programs are based on a scientist–practitioner model. The flexibility of these offerings gives the student the option of functioning as an educational psychologist in a variety of settings, thereby enhancing employment opportunities.

Special Facilities or Resources: The Educational Psychology faculty maintain close working relationships with the Department of Psychology, the Department of Counseling and Special Education, and others. Such relationships afford students the opportunity to work closely with diverse faculty members with various human services backgrounds. Moreover, students are encouraged to work closely with faculty on various creative projects and research. Additional opportunities exist at the Rehabilitation Research and Training Center on Blindness and Low Vision, the Bureau of Educational Research and Evaluation, and the Research and Curriculum Unit for Vocational–Technical Education, Social Science Research Center, all of which are connected with Mississippi State University.

Information for Students With Physical Disabilities: See the following Web site for more information: http://www.msstate.edu/dept/sss/.

Application Information:

Send to Mississippi State University, Office of Graduate Studies, P.O. Box G, Mississippi State, MS 39762-5507. Application available online. URL of online application: http://www.msstate.edu/dept/grad/admissions/. Students are admitted in the Fall, application deadline Feburary 1; programs have rolling admissions. Educational Psychology has a rolling admissions for Spring, Summer, and Fall admissions. Specialist program applications are due February 1 for School Psychology. *Fee:* $30.

Mississippi State University

Department of Psychology
Arts and Sciences
P.O. Drawer 6161
Mississippi State, MS 39762
Telephone: (662) 325-3202
Fax: (662) 325-7212
E-mail: *kja3@psychology.msstate.edu*
Web: *http://www.psychology.msstate.edu*

Department Information:

1966. Department Head: Stephen B. Klein. Number of faculty: total—full-time 14, part-time 9; women—full-time 6, part-time 3.

Programs and Degrees Offered:

Listed in the following order: Program area, degree type (T if terminal Master's), number awarded 7/06–6/07. Clinical Psychology MA/MS (Master of Arts/Science) (T) 7, Experimental Psychology MA/MS (Master of Arts/Science) (T) 1, Cognitive Science PhD (Doctor of Philosophy) 1.

Student Applications/Admissions:

Student Applications

Clinical Psychology MA/MS (Master of Arts/Science)—Applications 2007–2008, 31. Total applicants accepted 2007–2008, 14. Number full-time enrolled (new admits only) 2007–2008, 8. Number part-time enrolled (new admits only) 2007–2008, 0. Total enrolled 2007–2008 full-time, 19, part-time, 12. Openings 2008–2009, 10. The median number of years required for completion of a degree in 2006–2007 were 2. The number of students enrolled full- and part-time who were dismissed or voluntarily withdrew from this program area in 2007–2008 were 0. *Experimental Psychology MA/MS (Master of Arts/Science)*—Applications 2007–2008, 8. Total applicants accepted 2007–2008, 6. Number full-time enrolled (new admits only) 2007–2008, 2. Number part-time enrolled (new admits only) 2007–2008, 1. Total enrolled 2007–2008 full-time, 5, part-time, 3. Openings 2008–2009, 3. The median number of years required for completion of a degree in 2006–2007 were 3. The number of students enrolled full- and part-time who were dismissed or voluntarily withdrew from this program area in 2007–2008 were 0. *Cognitive Science PhD (Doctor of Philosophy)*—Applications 2007–2008, 10. Total applicants accepted 2007–2008, 5. Number full-time enrolled (new admits only) 2007–2008, 4. Number part-time enrolled (new admits only) 2007–2008, 0. Total enrolled 2007–2008 full-time, 8, part-time, 5. Openings 2008–2009, 3. The median number of years required for completion of a degree in 2006–2007 were 6. The number of students enrolled full- and part-time who were dismissed or voluntarily withdrew from this program area in 2007–2008 were 1.

Admissions Requirements:

Scores: Entries appear in this order: required test or GPA, minimum score (if required), median score of students entering in 2007–2008. Master's Programs: GRE-V 500, 500; GRE-Q 500, 605; last 2 years GPA 2.75, 3.66. The GPA of 2.75 is the minimum our Office of Graduate Admissions will accept for entry into the Graduate School. We look for a minimum GRE of 1000 (quantitative and verbal), but it's not an absolute requirement. The numbers under median are the figures for the latest group of applicants we accepted and who are actually enrolled in the clinical program. Doctoral Programs: GRE-V 500, 430; GRE-Q 500, 620. The numbers under median scores represent recent students enrolled into the program.

Other Criteria: (importance of criteria rated low, medium, or high): GRE/MAT scores—medium, research experience—high, work experience—medium, extracurricular activity—low, clinically related public service—medium, GPA—high, letters of recommendation—high, interview—low, statement of goals and objectives—high, specific undergraduate psychology courses taken—low. The clinically related public service would be relevant for applicants to the master's program, clinical concentration. Computer-related experience is relevant to the Cognitive PhD program. Interviews are not required. For additional information on admission requirements, go to http://www.psychology.msstate.edu.

Student Characteristics: The following represents characteristics of students in 2007–2008 in all graduate psychology programs in the department: Female—full-time 22, part-time 9; Male—full-time 10, part-time 5; African American/Black—full-time 3, part-time 0; Hispanic/Latino(a)—full-time 0, part-time 0; Asian/Pacific Islander—full-time 1, part-time 0; American Indian/Alaska Native—full-time 0, part-time 0; Caucasian/White—full-time 28, part-time 14; Multi-ethnic—full-time 0, part-time 0; students subject to the Americans With Disabilities Act—full-time 0, part-time 0; Unknown ethnicity—full-time 2, part-time 0; International students who hold an F-1 or J-1 Visa—full-time 1, part-time 0.

Financial Information/Assistance:

Tuition for Full-Time Study: *Master's:* State residents: per academic year $4,929, $274 per credit hour; Nonstate residents: per academic year $11,420, $634 per credit hour. *Doctoral:* State residents: per academic year $4,929, $274 per credit hour; Nonstate residents: per academic year $11,420, $634 per credit hour. Tuition is subject to change. See the following Web site for updates and changes in tuition costs: http://www.msstate.edu/dept/grad/Bulletin-fees.htm.

Financial Assistance:

First-Year Students: Teaching assistantships available for first year. Average amount paid per academic year: $6,940. Average number of hours worked per week: 20. Apply by NA. Tuition remission given: full.

Advanced Students: Teaching assistantships available for advanced students. Average amount paid per academic year: $11,950. Average number of hours worked per week: 20. Apply by NA. Tuition remission given: full. Research assistantships available for advanced students. Average amount paid per academic year: $11,950. Average number of hours worked per week: 20. Apply by NA. Tuition remission given: full. Traineeships available for advanced students. Average amount paid per academic year: $6,940. Average number of hours worked per week: 20. Apply by NA. Tuition remission given: full.

Additional Information: Of all students currently enrolled full time, 88% benefited from one or more of the listed financial assistance programs. No separate application for assistantships is required. Complete normal financial aid application.

Internships/Practica: Students in the clinical-emphasis program complete two 300 clock-hour practicum courses. These practica occur in a variety of settings, including public and private psychiatric hospitals and mental retardation facilities, community mental health centers, and so forth. Students are exposed to diverse client populations (e.g., in- and outpatient, children and adults with varied diagnoses and ethnic backgrounds).

Housing and Day Care: On-campus housing is available. See the following Web site for more information: http://www.housing.msstate.edu/grad/. No on-campus day care facilities are available.

Employment of Department Graduates:

Master's Degree Graduates: Of those who graduated in the academic year 2006–2007, the following categories and numbers represent the postgraduate activities and employment of master's degree graduates: Enrolled in a psychology doctoral program (3), enrolled in a postdoctoral residency/fellowship (n/a), employed in independent practice (n/a), employed in an academic position at a 2-year/4-year college (0), employed in a hospital/medical center (0), other employment position (4), do not know (1), total from the above (master's) (8).

Doctoral Degree Graduates: Of those who graduated in the academic year 2006–2007, the following categories and numbers represent the postgraduate activities and employment of doctoral degree graduates: Enrolled in a psychology doctoral program (n/a), other employment position (1), total from the above (doctoral) (1).

Additional Information:

Orientation, Objectives, and Emphasis of Department: Currently we offer both a MS and a PhD degree through different programs. Our master's degree programs offer concentrations in either experimental or clinical psychology. The Clinical master's program is accredited by the Master's in Psychology Accreditation Council (MPAC). Our PhD program awards a degree in Applied Cognitive Science through an interdisciplinary program housed in the Psychology Department but operated in cooperation with the Computer Science Department, the Industrial Engineering Department, and other units on campus. You can learn more about any of our programs by visiting the department's Web site at http://psychology.msstate.edu.

Special Facilities or Resources: The department houses a state-of-the-art computer lab for human subject data collection. Faculty laboratories include extensive computer labs for data collection, eye trackers, high-speed servers, and fast network access. Other research facilities, including a fMRI, are available through connections to other research facilities, both on-campus and off. Clinical students have research and training opportunities in the on-site Psychology Training Clinic and in several off-campus practicum placements.

Application Information:

Send to Graduate Admissions, Drawer 6305, Mississippi State, MS 39762. Application available online. URL of online application: http://www.msstate.edu/dept/grad/application.htm. Students are admitted in the Fall, application deadline January 15; Spring, application deadline November 1. The application deadline for the Cognitive Science PhD program is January 15. Although the deadline for full financial consideration is January 15, we will continue to review applications until May 1. Applications to the Master's Degree concentrations in Clinical and Experimental Psychology are reviewed continually beginning shortly after February 1. The masters programs have rolling admissions and encourage well-qualified applicants to apply up until May 1. However, earlier applicants receive earlier decisions and outstanding early applicants typically have a better chance of obtaining financial support. *Fee:* $30.

Mississippi, University of

Department of Psychology
Liberal Arts
205 Peabody Hall
University, MS 38677
Telephone: (662) 915-7383
Fax: (662) 915-5398
E-mail: *psych@olemiss.edu*
Web: *http://www.olemiss.edu/depts/psychology*

Department Information:

1932. Chairperson: Michael T. Allen. Number of faculty: total—full-time 7, part-time 3; women—full-time 7, part-time 3.

Programs and Degrees Offered:

Listed in the following order: Program area, degree type (T if terminal Master's), number awarded 7/06–6/07. Clinical PhD (Doctor of Philosophy) 9, Experimental PhD (Doctor of Philosophy) 2.

APA Accreditation: Clinical PhD (Doctor of Philosophy).

Student Applications/Admissions:

Student Applications

Clinical PhD (Doctor of Philosophy)—Applications 2007–2008, 117. Total applicants accepted 2007–2008, 8. Number full-time enrolled (new admits only) 2007–2008, 8. Openings 2008–2009, 8. The median number of years required for completion of a degree in 2006–2007 were 6. The number of students enrolled full- and part-time who were dismissed or voluntarily withdrew from this program area in 2007–2008 were 1. *Experimental PhD (Doctor of Philosophy)*—Applications 2007–2008, 10. Total applicants accepted 2007–2008, 2. Number full-time enrolled (new admits only) 2007–2008, 1. Number part-time enrolled (new admits only) 2007–2008, 0. Openings 2008–2009, 4. The median number of years required for completion of a degree in 2006–2007 were 5. The number of students enrolled full- and part-time who were dismissed or voluntarily withdrew from this program area in 2007–2008 were 1.

Admissions Requirements:

Scores: Entries appear in this order: required test or GPA, minimum score (if required), median score of students entering in 2007–2008. Master's Programs: No terminal Master's degree programs are offered. Doctoral Programs: GRE-V no minimum stated, 560; GRE-Q no minimum stated, 635; GRE-Subject (Psychology) no minimum stated, 640; overall undergraduate GPA no minimum stated, 3.5; last 2 years GPA 3.0. Master's GPA only applies to students entering with Master's degrees. The Graduate School requires a GPA of 3.0 or equivalent average on the last 60 hours of undergraduate course work in order to be admitted with full standing.

Other Criteria: (importance of criteria rated low, medium, or high): GRE/MAT scores—medium, research experience—high, work experience—medium, extracurricular activity—medium, clinically related public service—medium, GPA—medium, letters of recommendation—high, interview—high, statement of goals and objectives—high.

Student Characteristics: The following represents characteristics of students in 2007–2008 in all graduate psychology programs in the department: Female—full-time 40, part-time 0; Male—full-time 14, part-time 0; African American/Black—full-time 7, part-time 0; Hispanic/Latino(a)—full-time 2, part-time 0; Asian/Pacific Islander—full-time 0, part-time 0; American Indian/Alaska Native—full-time 1, part-time 0; Caucasian/White—full-time 43, part-time 0; Multi-ethnic—full-time 0, part-time 0; students subject to the Americans With Disabilities Act—full-time 0, part-time 0; Unknown ethnicity—full-time 1, part-time 0.

Financial Information/Assistance:

Tuition for Full-Time Study: *Master's:* State residents: per academic year $4,932, $274 per credit hour; Nonstate residents: per academic year $11,439, $635 per credit hour. *Doctoral:* State residents: per academic year $4,932, $274 per credit hour; Nonstate residents: per academic year $11,439, $635 per credit hour. Tuition is subject to change. See the following Web site for updates and changes in tuition costs: http://www.olemiss.edu.

Financial Assistance:

First-Year Students: Teaching assistantships available for first year. Average amount paid per academic year: $4,250. Average number of hours worked per week: 10. Apply by January 15. Tuition remission given: partial. Research assistantships available for first year. Average amount paid per academic year: $4,250. Average number of hours worked per week: 10. Apply by January 15. Tuition remission given: partial.

Advanced Students: Teaching assistantships available for advanced students. Average amount paid per academic year: $4,250. Average number of hours worked per week: 10. Apply by January 15. Tuition remission given: partial. Research assistantships available for advanced students. Average amount paid per academic year: $4,250. Average number of hours worked per week: 10. Apply by January 15. Tuition remission given: partial. Traineeships available for advanced students. Average amount paid per academic year: $8,000. Average number of hours worked per week: 20. Apply by January 15. Tuition remission given: partial. Fellowships and scholarships available for advanced students. Average amount paid per academic year: $3,000. Apply by January 15.

Additional Information: Of all students currently enrolled full time, 95% benefited from one or more of the listed financial assistance programs. Application and information available online at http://www.olemiss.edu/depts/graduate_school/apply.html.

Internships/Practica: Doctoral Degree (PhD Clinical): For those doctoral students for whom a professional internship was required

in this program prior to graduation, (9) students applied for an internship in 2006–2007, with (8) students obtaining an internship. Of those students who obtained an internship, (8) were paid internships. Of those students who obtained an internship, (8) students placed in APA/CPA-accredited internships, (0) students placed in internships not APA/CPA-accredited, but listed with the Association of Psychology Postdoctoral and Internship Centers (APPIC), (0) students placed in internships conforming to guidelines of the Council of Directors of School Psychology Programs (CDSPP), (0) students placed in internships that were not APA/CPA-accredited, APPIC or CDSPP listed. Practica or field placements are available for Clinical students beginning in the 2nd year of the program. Students serve as therapists on practicum teams in our in-house clinic for a minimum of 3 years under the direct supervision of the members of our clinical faculty, all of whom are licensed psychologists. After students have demonstrated a minimum level of competence in the clinic, they are allowed to apply for practicum positions at field placement agencies in the community where they are supervised by licensed practitioners who are employed by the field placement agency. In recent years, students have completed field placements at Community Mental Health Centers in Oxford and Tupelo, North Mississippi Regional Center in Oxford, North Mississippi Medical Center in Tupelo, St. Jude Children's Research Hospital in Memphis, and the DeSoto County (MS) School District. Students are assisted and advised by faculty in choosing field placements most appropriate to their individual career goals.

Housing and Day Care: On-campus housing is available. See the following Web site for more information: http://www.housing.olemiss.edu. On-campus day care facilities are available. The Willie Price University Nursery School is housed on campus and serves children ages 3–5 years. See the following Web site for more information: http://www.outreach.olemiss.edu/willieprice/.

Employment of Department Graduates:

Master's Degree Graduates: Of those who graduated in the academic year 2006–2007, the following categories and numbers represent the postgraduate activities and employment of master's degree graduates: Enrolled in a postdoctoral residency/fellowship (n/a), employed in independent practice (n/a), total from the above (master's) (0).

Doctoral Degree Graduates: Of those who graduated in the academic year 2006–2007, the following categories and numbers represent the postgraduate activities and employment of doctoral degree graduates: Enrolled in a psychology doctoral program (n/a), enrolled in another graduate/professional program (0), enrolled in a postdoctoral residency/fellowship (8), employed in independent practice (0), employed in an academic position at a university (1), employed in an academic position at a 2-year/4-year college (1), employed in a community mental health/counseling center (1), total from the above (doctoral) (11).

Additional Information:

Orientation, Objectives, and Emphasis of Department: The Department of Psychology offers programs of study in Clinical and Experimental Psychology leading to the Doctor of Philosophy degree. The Clinical program, which is fully accredited by the American Psychological Association, ordinarily requires 5 years beyond the bachelor's level to complete. Four of the 5 years are devoted to coursework and research, and the remaining year entails a clinical internship at an APA-approved training site. Requirements for the master's degree are also fulfilled during this period; however, the MA is considered to be a step in the doctoral training. The Clinical Program adheres to the scientist–practitioner model and emphasizes an empirical approach to clinical practice. A social learning or behavioral approach characterizes the clinical training offered. The Experimental Program is designed to prepare psychologists for careers in teaching and research. Specific programs include Behavioral Neuroscience, Cognitive Psychology, and Social Psychology. Students entering the Experimental Program are assigned a faculty mentor (major professor) whose research interests match their training goals. All students are required to engage in significant research projects.

Special Facilities or Resources: Most of the department's offices and laboratories are housed in the George Peabody Building. State-of-the-art facilities for animal research are available in a new centralized animal facility on campus. The psychology clinic has recently moved to a new location on campus, which provides for a more professional office environment and better client accessibility. The psychology clinic includes multipurpose rooms for evaluation, consultation, and therapy and observation rooms equipped with one-way mirrors and videotape equipment. The department offers computer-based laboratories for psychopharmacology, psychophysiology, operant conditioning, and behavioral toxicology. The department has close ties with the pharmacy and law schools (located on the Oxford campus) and with the medical school in Jackson.

Information for Students With Physical Disabilities: See the following Web site for more information: http://www.olemiss.edu.

Application Information:

Send to Admissions Chairperson for desired program. Application available online. URL of online application: https://www.secure.olemiss.edu/services/appl_index.html. Students are admitted in the Fall, application deadline January 15. *Fee:* $25. The application fee is $25 for Mississippi residents; $40 for out of state applicants. If an application is transmitted via an online application service, an additional charge may be required by the service.

Southern Mississippi, The University of

Department of Psychology
College of Education and Psychology
118 College Drive, 5025
Hattiesburg, MS 39406
Telephone: (601) 266-4177
Fax: (601) 266-5580
E-mail: *tammy.greer@usm.edu*
Web: *http://www.usm.edu/psy/*

Department Information:

1960. Chairperson: Tammy Greer. Number of faculty: total—full-time 32, part-time 2; women—full-time 11, part-time 2; total—minority—full-time 3; women minority—full-time 2.

Programs and Degrees Offered:

Listed in the following order: Program area, degree type (T if terminal Master's), number awarded 7/06–6/07. Counseling PhD (Doctor of Philosophy) 5, Clinical Psychology PhD (Doctor of

Philosophy) 5, Counseling MA/MS (Master of Arts/Science) (T) 2, Experimental PhD (Doctor of Philosophy) 1, School Psychology PhD (Doctor of Philosophy) 3.

APA Accreditation: Counseling PhD (Doctor of Philosophy). Clinical PhD (Doctor of Philosophy). School PhD (Doctor of Philosophy).

Student Applications/Admissions:

Student Applications

Counseling PhD (Doctor of Philosophy)—Applications 2007–2008, 45. Total applicants accepted 2007–2008, 14. Number full-time enrolled (new admits only) 2007–2008, 7. Number part-time enrolled (new admits only) 2007–2008, 0. Openings 2008–2009, 6. The median number of years required for completion of a degree in 2006–2007 were 6. The number of students enrolled full- and part-time who were dismissed or voluntarily withdrew from this program area in 2007–2008 were 0. *Clinical Psychology PhD (Doctor of Philosophy)*—Applications 2007–2008, 102. Total applicants accepted 2007–2008, 15. Number full-time enrolled (new admits only) 2007–2008, 9. Number part-time enrolled (new admits only) 2007–2008, 0. Openings 2008–2009, 9. The median number of years required for completion of a degree in 2006–2007 were 2. The number of students enrolled full- and part-time who were dismissed or voluntarily withdrew from this program area in 2007–2008 were 0. *Counseling MA/MS (Master of Arts/Science)*—Applications 2007–2008, 45. Total applicants accepted 2007–2008, 12. Number full-time enrolled (new admits only) 2007–2008, 12. Number part-time enrolled (new admits only) 2007–2008, 0. Openings 2008–2009, 10. The median number of years required for completion of a degree in 2006–2007 were 2. The number of students enrolled full- and part-time who were dismissed or voluntarily withdrew from this program area in 2007–2008 were 4. *Experimental PhD (Doctor of Philosophy)*—Applications 2007–2008, 19. Total applicants accepted 2007–2008, 4. Number full-time enrolled (new admits only) 2007–2008, 4. Number part-time enrolled (new admits only) 2007–2008, 0. Openings 2008–2009, 8. The median number of years required for completion of a degree in 2006–2007 were 4. The number of students enrolled full- and part-time who were dismissed or voluntarily withdrew from this program area in 2007–2008 were 0. *School Psychology PhD (Doctor of Philosophy)*—Applications 2007–2008, 18. Total applicants accepted 2007–2008, 14. Number full-time enrolled (new admits only) 2007–2008, 6. Number part-time enrolled (new admits only) 2007–2008, 0. Openings 2008–2009, 6. The median number of years required for completion of a degree in 2006–2007 were 6. The number of students enrolled full- and part-time who were dismissed or voluntarily withdrew from this program area in 2007–2008 were 1.

Admissions Requirements:

Scores: Entries appear in this order: required test or GPA, minimum score (if required), median score of students entering in 2007–2008. Master's Programs: GRE-V no minimum stated, 480; GRE-Q no minimum stated, 560. Doctoral Programs: GRE-V no minimum stated, 500; GRE-Q no minimum stated, 613; overall undergraduate GPA no minimum stated, 3.74. Check with program directors.

Other Criteria: (importance of criteria rated low, medium, or high): GRE/MAT scores—high, research experience—high, work experience—medium, extracurricular activity—low, clinically related public service—low, GPA—high, letters of recommendation—high, interview—high, statement of goals and objectives—high. Criteria vary by program. Check with program directors.

Student Characteristics: The following represents characteristics of students in 2007–2008 in all graduate psychology programs in the department: Female—full-time 103, part-time 0; Male—full-time 26, part-time 0; African American/Black—full-time 5, part-time 0; Hispanic/Latino(a)—full-time 4, part-time 0; Asian/Pacific Islander—full-time 6, part-time 0; American Indian/Alaska Native—full-time 0, part-time 0; Caucasian/White—full-time 113, part-time 0; Multi-ethnic—full-time 0, part-time 0; students subject to the Americans With Disabilities Act—full-time 0, part-time 0; Unknown ethnicity—full-time 1, part-time 0; International students who hold an F-1 or J-1 Visa—full-time 12, part-time 0.

Financial Information/Assistance:

Tuition for Full-Time Study: *Master's:* State residents: per academic year $7,371; . *Doctoral:* State residents: per academic year $7,371; Nonstate residents: per academic year $17,538. Tuition is subject to change. See the following Web site for updates and changes in tuition costs: http://www.usm.edu/graduatestudies/fees.php.

Financial Assistance:

First-Year Students: Teaching assistantships available for first year. Average amount paid per academic year: $6,000. Average number of hours worked per week: 20. Apply by January 15. Tuition remission given: full. Research assistantships available for first year. Average amount paid per academic year: $6,000. Average number of hours worked per week: 20. Apply by January 15. Tuition remission given: full.

Advanced Students: Teaching assistantships available for advanced students. Average amount paid per academic year: $6,000. Average number of hours worked per week: 20. Apply by January 15. Tuition remission given: full. Research assistantships available for advanced students. Average amount paid per academic year: $6,000. Average number of hours worked per week: 20. Apply by January 15. Tuition remission given: full.

Additional Information: Of all students currently enrolled full time, 99% benefited from one or more of the listed financial assistance programs. Application and information available online at http://www.usm.edu/financialaid/.

Internships/Practica: Doctoral Degree (PhD Counseling): For those doctoral students for whom a professional internship was required in this program prior to graduation, (7) students applied for an internship in 2006–2007, with (7) students obtaining an internship. Of those students who obtained an internship, (7) were paid internships. Of those students who obtained an internship, (6) students placed in APA/CPA-accredited internships, (1) students placed in internships not APA/CPA-accredited, but listed with the Association of Psychology Postdoctoral and Internship Centers (APPIC), (0) students placed in internships conforming to guidelines of the Council of Directors of School Psychology Programs (CDSPP), (0) students placed in internships that were not APA/CPA-accredited, APPIC or CDSPP listed. Doctoral Degree (PhD Clinical Psychology): For those doctoral students for whom a professional internship was required in this program prior to graduation, (4) students applied for an internship in 2006–2007, with (4) students obtaining an internship. Of those students who obtained an internship, (4) were paid internships. Of those students who obtained an internship, (4) students placed in APA/CPA-accredited internships, (0) students placed in internships not APA/CPA-accredited, but listed with the Association of Psychology Postdoctoral and Internship Centers (APPIC), (0) students placed in internships conforming to guidelines of the Council of Directors of School Psychology Programs (CDSPP), (0) students placed in internships that were not APA/CPA-accredited, APPIC or CDSPP listed. Doctoral Degree (PhD School Psychology): For those doctoral students for whom a professional internship was required in this program prior to graduation, (2) students applied for an internship in 2006–2007, with (2) students obtaining an internship. Of those students who obtained an internship, (2) were paid internships. Of those students who obtained an internship, (2) students placed in APA/CPA-accredited internships, (0) students placed in internships not APA/CPA-accredited, but listed with the Association of Psychology Postdoctoral and Internship Centers (APPIC), (0) students placed in internships conforming to guidelines of the Council of Directors of School Psychology Programs (CDSPP), (0) students placed in internships that were not APA/CPA-accredited, APPIC or CDSPP listed. Doctoral students from our three APA-approved programs (Clinical, Counseling, and School) begin practicum experiences in the on-campus clinics and progress to community externship placements as they gain experience and training. A student's final year is a full-time internship in an APA-accredited internship. Students have been placed throughout the United States, with the majority in health service settings such as Veterans Administration Medical Centers, medical schools, and comprehensive community mental health centers.

Housing and Day Care: On-campus housing is available. See the following Web site for more information: http://www.usm.edu/pinehaven. On-campus day care facilities are available. See the following Web site for more information: http://www.usm.edu/childandfamilystudies/child_development_center/index.htm.

Employment of Department Graduates:

Master's Degree Graduates: Of those who graduated in the academic year 2006–2007, the following categories and numbers represent the postgraduate activities and employment of master's degree graduates: Enrolled in a psychology doctoral program (1), enrolled in another graduate/professional program (0), enrolled in a postdoctoral residency/fellowship (n/a), employed in independent practice (n/a), employed in a community mental health/counseling center (7), total from the above (master's) (8).

Doctoral Degree Graduates: Of those who graduated in the academic year 2006–2007, the following categories and numbers represent the postgraduate activities and employment of doctoral degree graduates: Enrolled in a psychology doctoral program (n/a), enrolled in another graduate/professional program (0), enrolled in a postdoctoral residency/fellowship (1), employed in independent practice (0), employed in an academic position at a university (2), employed in an academic position at a 2-year/4-year college (2), employed in other positions at a higher education institution (0), employed in a professional position in a school system (1), employed in business or industry (0), employed in government agency (1), employed in a community mental health/counseling center (0), employed in a hospital/medical center (1), still seeking employment (0), not seeking employment (0), other employment position (0), do not know (0), total from the above (doctoral) (8).

Additional Information:

Orientation, Objectives, and Emphasis of Department: The department has four psychology doctoral programs (Clinical, Counseling, Experimental, and School), each with different emphases and orientations. Specific information about each program can be obtained from our Web site (http://www.usm.edu/psy). The departmental philosophy is built on the assumption that psychology is first and foremost a scientific discipline. Therefore, a common element of all the programs is a commitment to science and research, with exposure to the breadth and depth of the field of psychology. Students are challenged to develop critical thinking skills, and are taught to respect discovery and inquiry. The applied programs espouse the scientist–practitioner model of training and emphasize training in research as well as delivery of psychological services. The department offers opportunities for research and clinical training in several subareas, such as child clinical, multicultural issues, and child and family interventions.

Special Facilities or Resources: The department houses three psychology service training clinics. Research laboratories provide training in various areas such as sleep, behavioral neuroscience, and personality and experimental psychopathology. Off-campus facilities provide opportunities for research with marine mammals. Opportunities for research are also available at community facilities such as local hospitals and schools.

Information for Students With Physical Disabilities: See the following Web site for more information: http://www.usm.edu/ids/.

Application Information:

Send to the Admissions Coordinator; specify program. Students are admitted in the Fall, application deadline January 15. Counseling MS application deadline March 1. *Fee:* $25. Legal residents of Mississippi are exempt from the application fee.

Avila University

Graduate Psychology
School of Behavioral and Social Sciences
11901 Wornall Road
Kansas City, MO 64145-1698
Telephone: (816) 501-3665
Fax: (816) 501-2455
E-mail: *Maria.Hunt@avila.edu*
Web: *http://www.avila.edu/gradpsych*

Department Information:

1977. Director of Graduate Psychology: Regina Staves, PhD. Number of faculty: total—full-time 8, part-time 11; women—full-time 6, part-time 9; minority—part-time 5; women minority—part-time 2.

Programs and Degrees Offered:

Listed in the following order: Program area, degree type (T if terminal Master's), number awarded 7/06–6/07. Counseling Psychology MA/MS (Master of Arts/Science) (T) 19, General Psychology MA/MS (Master of Arts/Science) (T) 3, Organizational Development Psychology MA/MS (Master of Arts/Science) (T) 3, Counseling and Art Therapy MA/MS (Master of Arts/Science) (T) 0.

Student Applications/Admissions:

Student Applications

Counseling Psychology MA/MS (Master of Arts/Science)—Applications 2007–2008, 86. Total applicants accepted 2007–2008, 32. Number full-time enrolled (new admits only) 2007–2008, 15. Number part-time enrolled (new admits only) 2007–2008, 17. Total enrolled 2007–2008 full-time, 85, part-time, 20. Openings 2008–2009, 30. The median number of years required for completion of a degree in 2006–2007 were 3. The number of students enrolled full- and part-time who were dismissed or voluntarily withdrew from this program area in 2007–2008 were 3. *General Psychology MA/MS (Master of Arts/Science)*—Applications 2007–2008, 6. Total applicants accepted 2007–2008, 6. Openings 2008–2009, 10. The median number of years required for completion of a degree in 2006–2007 were 2. The number of students enrolled full- and part-time who were dismissed or voluntarily withdrew from this program area in 2007–2008 were 0. *Organizational Development Psychology MA/MS (Master of Arts/Science)*—Applications 2007–2008, 26. Total applicants accepted 2007–2008, 23. Number full-time enrolled (new admits only) 2007–2008, 14. Number part-time enrolled (new admits only) 2007–2008, 13. Total enrolled 2007–2008 full-time, 26, part-time, 38. Openings 2008–2009, 20. The median number of years required for completion of a degree in 2006–2007 were 2. The number of students enrolled full- and part-time who were dismissed or voluntarily withdrew from this program area in 2007–2008 were 3. *Counseling and Art Therapy MA/MS (Master of Arts/Science)*—Applications 2007–2008, 36. Total applicants accepted 2007–2008, 6. Number full-time enrolled (new admits only) 2007–2008, 6. Number part-time enrolled (new admits only) 2007–2008, 2. Total enrolled 2007–2008 full-time, 6, part-time, 2. Openings 2008–2009, 8. The number of students enrolled full- and part-time who were dismissed or voluntarily withdrew from this program area in 2007–2008 were 0.

Admissions Requirements:

Scores: Entries appear in this order: required test or GPA, minimum score (if required), median score of students entering in 2007–2008. Master's Programs: overall undergraduate GPA 3.0; last 2 years GPA 3.0, 3.25; psychology GPA 3.0, 3.25. General Psychology requires a GPA of 3.25. Organizational Development Psychology also requires a 3.25 GPA but does not require the Graduate Record Examination (GRE).

Other Criteria: (importance of criteria rated low, medium, or high): research experience—low, work experience—high, extracurricular activity—medium, clinically related public service—medium, GPA—high, letters of recommendation—high, interview—medium, statement of goals and objectives—high.

Student Characteristics: The following represents characteristics of students in 2007–2008 in all graduate psychology programs in the department: Female—full-time 90, part-time 29; Male—full-time 28, part-time 6; African American/Black—full-time 9, part-time 9; Hispanic/Latino(a)—full-time 5, part-time 0; Asian/Pacific Islander—full-time 1, part-time 0; American Indian/Alaska Native—full-time 0, part-time 0; Caucasian/White—full-time 92, part-time 26; students subject to the Americans With Disabilities Act—full-time 1, part-time 1; Unknown ethnicity—full-time 11, part-time 0.

Financial Information/Assistance:

Tuition for Full-Time Study: *Master's:* State residents: $415 per credit hour; Nonstate residents: $415 per credit hour. Tuition is subject to change. See the following Web site for updates and changes in tuition costs: http://www.avila.edu/gradpsych.

Financial Assistance:

First-Year Students: Teaching assistantships available for first year. Tuition remission given: partial. Fellowships and scholarships available for first year. Average amount paid per academic year: $500. Apply by July 1.

Advanced Students: Teaching assistantships available for advanced students. Average number of hours worked per week: 20. Apply by May 15. Tuition remission given: partial.

Additional Information: Of all students currently enrolled full time, 2% benefited from one or more of the listed financial assistance programs. Application and information available online at http://www.avila.edu/gradpsych.

Internships/Practica: There is a 750–1,000 contact hour internship (6 credit hours) at a site chosen by the student. There are a wide variety of internship sites—mental health agencies, psychiatric hospitals, and residential treatment programs, for example. Some students choose to work with specific populations, such as children and adolescents, the chronically mentally ill, in substance abuse treatment, to name a few. All interns have an approved on-site supervisor and meet once a week with the faculty internship advisor.

Housing and Day Care: On-campus housing is available. See the following Web site for more information: http://www.avila.edu. On-campus day care facilities are available. Contact Carol Frevert (816) 501-3668.

Employment of Department Graduates:

Master's Degree Graduates: Of those who graduated in the academic year 2006–2007, the following categories and numbers represent the postgraduate activities and employment of master's degree graduates: Enrolled in a psychology doctoral program (2), enrolled in another graduate/professional program (3), enrolled in a postdoctoral residency/fellowship (n/a), employed in independent practice (n/a), employed in an academic position at a university (1), employed in an academic position at a 2-year/4-year college (0), employed in other positions at a higher education institution (0), employed in a professional position in a school system (1), employed in business or industry (1), employed in government agency (0), employed in a community mental health/counseling center (6), employed in a hospital/medical center (1), still seeking employment (3), not seeking employment (2), other employment position (0), do not know (9), total from the above (master's) (29).

Doctoral Degree Graduates: Of those who graduated in the academic year 2006–2007, the following categories and numbers represent the postgraduate activities and employment of doctoral degree graduates: Enrolled in a psychology doctoral program (n/a), total from the above (doctoral) (0).

Additional Information:

Orientation, Objectives, and Emphasis of Department: The Master of Science in Psychology degree programs at Avila University are part of a values-based community of learning that respects the worth and dignity of all persons. Within this context, we are committed to the scientist–practitioner model. The Counseling Psychology and the Counseling and Art Therapy programs offer 60-credit degrees designed to train master's-level counseling psychologists and art therapists, respectively, for the delivery of mental health services in a variety of settings. Both programs meet the Missouri state educational requirements for licensure as a Licensed Professional Counselor. The Counseling and Art Therapy program also meets the American Art Therapy Association requirements to be a registered art therapist. The MSCP program also meets the Kansas state educational requirements for licensure as a Licensed Master's-level Psychologist. The 36-credit General Psychology degree offers students an in-depth survey of the theory, research and practices of psychology's many subdisciplines. The Organizational Development degree is a 37-credit degree designed to provide students with the practical, empirically tested principles, tools, and methodologies associated with effective change management. Avila University is a member of the Council of Applied Master's Programs in Psychology (CAMPP), the Council of Graduate Departments of Psychology (COGDOP), and is accredited by the Masters in Psychology Accreditation Council (MPAC).

Application Information:

Send to Director of Graduate Psychology, Avila University, 11901 Wornall Road, Kansas City, MO 64145. Application available online. URL of online application: http://www.avila.edu/gradpsych. Students are admitted in the Fall, application deadline August 1; Spring, application deadline December 31; Summer, application deadline May 1; Programs have rolling admissions. *Fee:* $0.

Forest Institute of Professional Psychology

Clinical Psychology
2885 West Battlefield Road
Springfield, MO 65807
Telephone: (417) 823-3477
Fax: (417) 823-3441
E-mail: *info@forest.edu*
Web: *http://www.forest.edu*

Department Information:

1979. President: Mark E. Skrade, PsyD. Number of faculty: total—full-time 15, part-time 32; women—full-time 7, part-time 17; total—minority—full-time 3; women minority—full-time 3; faculty subject to the Americans With Disabilities Act 1.

Programs and Degrees Offered:

Listed in the following order: Program area, degree type (T if terminal Master's), number awarded 7/06–6/07. Psychology MA/MS (Master of Arts/Science) (T) 46, Clinical Psychology PsyD (Doctor of Psychology) 36.

APA Accreditation: Clinical PsyD (Doctor of Psychology).

Student Applications/Admissions:

Student Applications

Psychology MA/MS (Master of Arts/Science)—Applications 2007–2008, 13. Total applicants accepted 2007–2008, 12. Number full-time enrolled (new admits only) 2007–2008, 10. Number part-time enrolled (new admits only) 2007–2008, 2. Total enrolled 2007–2008 full-time, 16, part-time, 9. Openings 2008–2009, 30. The median number of years required for completion of a degree in 2006–2007 were 2. The number of students enrolled full- and part-time who were dismissed or voluntarily withdrew from this program area in 2007–2008 were 2. *Clinical Psychology PsyD (Doctor of Psychology)*—Applications 2007–2008, 171. Total applicants accepted 2007–2008, 101. Number full-time enrolled (new admits only) 2007–2008, 55. Number part-time enrolled (new admits only) 2007–2008, 0. Total enrolled 2007–2008 full-time, 184, part-time, 34. Openings 2008–2009, 68. The median number of years required for completion of a degree in 2006–2007 were 5. The number of students enrolled full- and part-time who were dismissed or voluntarily withdrew from this program area in 2007–2008 were 10.

Admissions Requirements:

Scores: Entries appear in this order: required test or GPA, minimum score (if required), median score of students entering in 2007–2008. Master's Programs: GRE-V no minimum stated; GRE-Q no minimum stated; overall undergraduate GPA 3.0; last 2 years GPA 3.0; psychology GPA 3.0; Masters GRE-Analytical no minimum stated. Doctoral Programs: GRE-V no minimum stated; GRE-Q no minimum stated; overall undergraduate GPA 3.00; last 2 years GPA 3.00; psychology

GPA 3.00; Doctoral program GRE-Analytic no minimum stated.

Other Criteria: (importance of criteria rated low, medium, or high): GRE/MAT scores—medium, research experience—medium, work experience—medium, extracurricular activity—low, clinically related public service—medium, GPA—high, letters of recommendation—high, interview—high, statement of goals and objectives—high, specific undergraduate psychology courses taken—medium. For additional information on admission requirements, go to http://www.forest.edu/admissions.

Student Characteristics: The following represents characteristics of students in 2007–2008 in all graduate psychology programs in the department: African American/Black—part-time 0; Hispanic/Latino(a)—part-time 0; Caucasian/White—full-time 0, part-time 0; Unknown ethnicity—full-time 0, part-time 0.

Financial Information/Assistance:

Tuition for Full-Time Study: *Master's:* State residents: $565 per credit hour; Nonstate residents: $565 per credit hour. *Doctoral:* State residents: $565 per credit hour; Nonstate residents: $565 per credit hour. Tuition is subject to change. See the following Web site for updates and changes in tuition costs: http://www.forest.edu/academics/financial/tuition.asp.

Financial Assistance:

First-Year Students: Fellowships and scholarships available for first year. Apply by January 15. Tuition remission given: full and partial.

Advanced Students: Fellowships and scholarships available for advanced students. Apply by June 1.

Additional Information: No information provided.

Internships/Practica: Master's Degree (MA/MS Master of Arts in Psychology): An internship experience such as a final research project or "capstone" experience is required of graduates. Doctoral Degree (PsyD Doctorate in Clinical Psychology): For those doctoral students for whom a professional internship was required in this program prior to graduation, (36) students applied for an internship in 2006–2007, with (32) students obtaining an internship. Of those students who obtained an internship, (28) were paid internships. Of those students who obtained an internship, (11) students placed in APA/CPA-accredited internships, (21) students placed in internships not APA/CPA-accredited, but listed with the Association of Psychology Postdoctoral and Internship Centers (APPIC), (0) students placed in internships conforming to guidelines of the Council of Directors of School Psychology Programs (CDSPP), (0) students placed in internships that were not APA/CPA-accredited, APPIC or CDSPP listed. Forest Institute of Professional Psychology enjoys a close relationship with the major state and city mental health facilities in the metropolitan and rural areas. Currently, there are 60 practica experiences available to students. These opportunities provide a vast array of clinical experiences for a total of 1,200 practicum hours accumulated by the end of your required course work. During the 4th year of study, all students are required to complete a 2,000-hour internship. Forest Institute has several on-site internship opportunities ranging in a number of clinical experiences.

Housing and Day Care: On-campus housing is available. One and two-bedroom apartments are available. No on-campus day care facilities are available.

Employment of Department Graduates:

Master's Degree Graduates: Of those who graduated in the academic year 2006–2007, the following categories and numbers represent the postgraduate activities and employment of master's degree graduates: Enrolled in a postdoctoral residency/fellowship (n/a), employed in independent practice (n/a), total from the above (master's) (0).

Doctoral Degree Graduates: Of those who graduated in the academic year 2006–2007, the following categories and numbers represent the postgraduate activities and employment of doctoral degree graduates: Enrolled in a psychology doctoral program (n/a), enrolled in a postdoctoral residency/fellowship (36), total from the above (doctoral) (36).

Additional Information:

Orientation, Objectives, and Emphasis of Department: The design of the Clinical Psychology PsyD Program is based on the belief that a thorough understanding of the comprehensive body of psychological knowledge, skills, and attitudes is essential for professional practitioners. The acquisition of this broad-based understanding and these abilities requires that the curriculum cover a combination of didactic knowledge, skill training, and supervised clinical experience with faculty and supervisors who provide appropriate role models. The PsyD degree is designed for individuals seeking an educational and training program geared toward professional application. Students are prepared to offer professional services in diagnostic, therapeutic, consultative, and administrative settings. Research and investigation skills are complemented by an increased focus on the use of research findings and theoretical formulations. The field practicum and internship are supervised clinical experiences that are integrated with the academic coursework. The faculty represents a variety of theoretical orientations and is committed to the rigorous preparation of students to become competent providers of service as well as ethical contributing members of the professional community. The MA in psychology program is intended to provide a comprehensive exposure to the scientific foundations of psychology, including theories, concepts, and empirical knowledge of human development and behavior. The master's program is valuable to those who wish to increase their understanding of human behavior. These would include teachers, clergy, and training and personnel officers. The program also provides a solid foundation for eventual pursuit of a doctoral program. The MA program provides the necessary course work to obtain a counseling licensure at the master's level in most, if not all states.

Personal Behavior Statement: .

Special Facilities or Resources: Forest Institute is located in the heart of the Ozarks. The academic and administrative center sits on 58 acres of land and provides students with a modern facility and state-of-the-art equipment. Forest has both an on-site outpatient community mental health clinic and a rehabilitation–health psychology–neuropsychology clinic. Practicum involves a high degree of community services and resources. Students provide services in the rural Ozarks, are actively involved with the homeless organizations of the Ozarks, correctional facilities, and many other community-based opportunities.

Information for Students With Physical Disabilities: See the following Web site for more information: http://www.forest.edu.

Application Information:
Send to Forest Institute of Professional Psychology, Office of Admissions, 2885 West Battlefield Road, Springfield, MO 65807. Application available online. URL of online application: http://www.forest.edu. Students are admitted in the Fall, application deadline January 15; Winter, application deadline September 15; Summer, application deadline November 15; programs have rolling admissions. *Fee:* $50.

Missouri State University

Psychology Department
Health and Human Services
901 South National Avenue
Springfield, MO 65897
Telephone: (417) 836-5797
Fax: (417) 836-8330
E-mail: *robertjones@missouristate.edu*
Web: *http://www.psychology.missouristate.edu/graduateprograms.htm*

Department Information:
1967. Head: Robert G. Jones. Number of faculty: total—full-time 34, part-time 16; women—full-time 15, part-time 8; minority—part-time 2; women minority—part-time 2.

Programs and Degrees Offered:
Listed in the following order: Program area, degree type (T if terminal Master's), number awarded 7/06–6/07. Clinical MA/MS (Master of Arts/Science) (T) 15, Experimental MA/MS (Master of Arts/Science) (T) 1, Industrial/Organizational MA/MS (Master of Arts/Science) (T) 11.

Student Applications/Admissions:
Student Applications
Clinical MA/MS (Master of Arts/Science)—Applications 2007–2008, 24. Total applicants accepted 2007–2008, 8. Number full-time enrolled (new admits only) 2007–2008, 8. Number part-time enrolled (new admits only) 2007–2008, 0. Openings 2008–2009, 8. The median number of years required for completion of a degree in 2006–2007 were 2. The number of students enrolled full- and part-time who were dismissed or voluntarily withdrew from this program area in 2007–2008 were 0. *Experimental MA/MS (Master of Arts/Science)*—Applications 2007–2008, 12. Total applicants accepted 2007–2008, 3. Number full-time enrolled (new admits only) 2007–2008, 3. Number part-time enrolled (new admits only) 2007–2008, 0. Openings 2008–2009, 3. The median number of years required for completion of a degree in 2006–2007 were 2. The number of students enrolled full- and part-time who were dismissed or voluntarily withdrew from this program area in 2007–2008 were 1. *Industrial/Organizational MA/MS (Master of Arts/Science)*—Applications 2007–2008, 45. Total applicants accepted 2007–2008, 13. Number full-time enrolled (new admits only) 2007–2008, 13. Number part-time enrolled (new admits only) 2007–2008, 0. Openings 2008–2009, 10. The median number of years required for completion of a degree in 2006–2007 were 2. The number of students enrolled full- and part-time who were dismissed or voluntarily withdrew from this program area in 2007–2008 were 0.

Admissions Requirements:
Scores: Entries appear in this order: required test or GPA, minimum score (if required), median score of students entering in 2007–2008. Master's Programs: GRE-V 470, 542; GRE-Q 470, 550; overall undergraduate GPA 3.00, 3.72; psychology GPA 3.25, 3.88; Masters GRE-Analytical 4, 4.
Other Criteria: (importance of criteria rated low, medium, or high): GRE/MAT scores—medium, research experience—high, work experience—medium, extracurricular activity—medium, clinically related public service—high, GPA—high, letters of recommendation—high, statement of goals and objectives—high, undergraduate major in psychology—high, specific undergraduate psychology courses taken—high.

Student Characteristics: The following represents characteristics of students in 2007–2008 in all graduate psychology programs in the department: Female—full-time 28, part-time 0; Male—full-time 15, part-time 0; African American/Black—full-time 2, part-time 0; Hispanic/Latino(a)—full-time 1, part-time 0; Asian/Pacific Islander—full-time 3, part-time 0; American Indian/Alaska Native—full-time 0, part-time 0; Caucasian/White—full-time 34, part-time 0; Multi-ethnic—full-time 1, part-time 0; students subject to the Americans With Disabilities Act—full-time 0, part-time 0; Unknown ethnicity—full-time 0, part-time 0.

Financial Information/Assistance:
Tuition for Full-Time Study: *Master's:* State residents: per academic year $5,126, $206 per credit hour; Nonstate residents: per academic year $9,830, $402 per credit hour. Tuition is subject to change. Additional fees are assessed to students beyond the costs of tuition for the following: Student Services Fees. See the following Web site for updates and changes in tuition costs: http://www.graduate.missouristate.edu/39051.htm.

Financial Assistance:
First-Year Students: Research assistantships available for first year. Average amount paid per academic year: $7,050. Average number of hours worked per week: 20. Apply by July. Tuition remission given: full.
Advanced Students: Teaching assistantships available for advanced students. Average amount paid per academic year: $9,360. Average number of hours worked per week: 20. Apply by March. Tuition remission given: full. Research assistantships available for advanced students. Average amount paid per academic year: $7,050. Average number of hours worked per week: 20. Apply by July. Tuition remission given: full.
Additional Information: Of all students currently enrolled full time, 90% benefited from one or more of the listed financial assistance programs. Application and information available online at http://graduate.missouristate.edu/assistantship.htm.

Internships/Practica: Clinical students must complete two 175-contact hour practica. Placements are in a variety of mental health settings. Students who choose a nonthesis option must complete an additional 175-contact hour internship. Experimental practicum experience is acquired through basic laboratory research work tailored specifically to the graduate student's research area of interest. The goal of the practicum(s) is for the student to develop or acquire competence in various research methods and behavioral/cognitive measurement skills that will prepare the student for later doctoral work.

Housing and Day Care: On-campus housing is available. See the following Web site for more information: http://www.reslife.missouristate.edu/. On-campus day care facilities are available. See the following Web site for more information: http://www.education.missouristate.edu/cdc/.

Employment of Department Graduates:

Master's Degree Graduates: Of those who graduated in the academic year 2006–2007, the following categories and numbers represent the postgraduate activities and employment of master's degree graduates: Enrolled in a psychology doctoral program (7), enrolled in another graduate/professional program (0), enrolled in a postdoctoral residency/fellowship (n/a), employed in independent practice (n/a), employed in an academic position at a university (2), employed in an academic position at a 2-year/4-year college (3), employed in other positions at a higher education institution (2), employed in a professional position in a school system (0), employed in business or industry (2), employed in government agency (13), employed in a community mental health/counseling center (8), employed in a hospital/medical center (1), still seeking employment (2), not seeking employment (1), other employment position (0), do not know (0), total from the above (master's) (41).

Doctoral Degree Graduates: Of those who graduated in the academic year 2006–2007, the following categories and numbers represent the postgraduate activities and employment of doctoral degree graduates: Enrolled in a psychology doctoral program (n/a), total from the above (doctoral) (0).

Additional Information:

Orientation, Objectives, and Emphasis of Department: We are an eclectic department of 34 full-time faculty serving over 500 undergraduate majors. The faculty have diverse research interests including clinical, I/O, stress management, sport psychology, human learning, perception, motivation, animal learning, human skills, and memory. The department operates the Learning Diagnostic Clinic for diagnosis and remediation of special populations, as well as limited therapy for other psychological disorders.

Special Facilities or Resources: The Experimental track has five research labs that provide the means and opportunity for graduate students to conduct basic research. A brief description of each lab is as follows. The Infant Perception Laboratory houses basic computer hardware and software to accommodate basic research in visual scanning and psycho-physiological testing. The Music Perception and Cognition Lab houses computer hardware and software to generate a variety of auditory stimuli and has the facilities to conduct auditory learning and cognition research. The Implicit and Explicit Motivation Research Lab houses computer hardware and software to conduct research in automatic processing and to conduct Structural Equation Modeling and HLM analyses. The Animal Research Lab houses computer software, hardware, and small animal testing chamber designed to conduct research in visual discrimination learning. The Cognitive Strategies Research Lab provides the facility to test and design stimulus materials to conduct applied memory research. The department has 14 separate labs that serve the Experimental, Clinical, and Industrial/Organizational tracks. Research focusing on cognition, gender issues, lifespan development, motivation, body image, music, sports psychology, and animal behavior are available to all students regardless of their track. The department also has excellent computer support facilities in all labs. The department also oversees a clinic that primarily supports the University's desire to comply with the ADA. The clinic provides an excellent training facility for our clinical graduate students.

Information for Students With Physical Disabilities: See the following Web site for more information: http://www.missouristate.edu/disability/.

Application Information:

Send to Admissions Secretary. Students are admitted in the Spring, application deadline March 1. Will accept applications up to June 1 if all eight openings in each track are not filled. *Fee:* $35.

Missouri, University of, Columbia

Department of Educational, School, and Counseling Psychology
College of Education
16 Hill Hall
Columbia, MO 65211
Telephone: (573) 882-7731
Fax: (573) 884-5989
E-mail: *carrd@missouri.edu*
Web: *http://www.education.missouri.edu/ESCP/*

Department Information:

1953. Chairperson: Deborah Carr. Number of faculty: total—full-time 19, part-time 1; women—full-time 9, part-time 1; ; women minority—full-time 2.

Programs and Degrees Offered:

Listed in the following order: Program area, degree type (T if terminal Master's), number awarded 7/06–6/07. Counseling Psychology MA/MS (Master of Arts/Science) (T) 33, Educational Psychology MA/MS (Master of Arts/Science) (T) 1, School Psychology MA/MS (Master of Arts/Science) 4, Counseling Psychology Educational Specialist EdS/MEd (School Psychology) 7, Counseling Psychology PhD (Doctor of Philosophy) 7, Educational Psychology Educational Specialist EdS/MEd (School Psychology) 1, Educational Psychology PhD (Doctor of Philosophy) 3, School Psychology Educational Specialist EdS/MEd (School Psychology) 3, School Psychology PhD (Doctor of Philosophy) 1.

APA Accreditation: Counseling PhD (Doctor of Philosophy). School Psychology PhD (Doctor of Philosophy).

Student Applications/Admissions:

Student Applications

Counseling Psychology MA/MS (Master of Arts/Science)—Applications 2007–2008, 86. Total applicants accepted 2007–2008, 24. Number full-time enrolled (new admits only) 2007–2008, 24. Number part-time enrolled (new admits only) 2007–2008, 0. Openings 2008–2009, 28. The median number of years required for completion of a degree in 2006–2007 were 2. The number of students enrolled full- and part-time who were dismissed or voluntarily withdrew from this program area in 2007–2008 were 0. *Educational Psychology MA/MS (Master of Arts/Science)*—Applications 2007–2008, 8. Total applicants accepted 2007–2008, 2. Number full-time enrolled (new admits only) 2007–2008, 2. Number part-time enrolled (new admits only) 2007–2008, 0. Openings 2008–2009, 3. The median number of years required for completion of a degree in 2006–2007 were 2. The number of students enrolled full- and part-time who were dismissed or voluntarily withdrew from this program area in 2007–2008 were 0. *School Psychology MA/MS (Master of Arts/Science)*—Applications 2007–2008, 0. Total applicants accepted 2007–2008, 0. Number full-time enrolled (new admits only) 2007–2008, 0. Number part-time enrolled (new admits only) 2007–2008, 0. The median number of years required for completion of a degree in 2006–2007 were 3. The number of students enrolled full- and part-time who were dismissed or voluntarily withdrew from this program area in 2007–2008 were 0. *Counseling Psychology Educational Specialist EdS/MEd (School Psychology)*—Applications 2007–2008, 1. Total applicants accepted 2007–2008, 0. Number full-time enrolled (new admits only) 2007–2008, 0. Number part-time enrolled (new admits only) 2007–2008, 0. Total enrolled 2007–2008 full-time, 2, part-time, 1. Openings 2008–2009, 1. The median number of years required for completion of a degree in 2006–2007 were 2. The number of students enrolled full- and part-time who were dismissed or voluntarily withdrew from this program area in 2007–2008 were 0. *Counseling Psychology PhD (Doctor of Philosophy)*—Applications 2007–2008, 96. Total applicants accepted 2007–2008, 9. Number full-time enrolled (new admits only) 2007–2008, 9. Number part-time enrolled (new admits only) 2007–2008, 0. Openings 2008–2009, 8. The median number of years required for completion of a degree in 2006–2007 were 7. The number of students enrolled full- and part-time who were dismissed or voluntarily withdrew from this program area in 2007–2008 were 1. *Educational Psychology Educational Specialist EdS/MEd (School Psychology)*—Applications 2007–2008, 0. Total applicants accepted 2007–2008, 0. Number full-time enrolled (new admits only) 2007–2008, 1. Number part-time enrolled (new admits only) 2007–2008, 0. The median number of years required for completion of a degree in 2006–2007 were 2. The number of students enrolled full- and part-time who were dismissed or voluntarily withdrew from this program area in 2007–2008 were 0. *Educational Psychology PhD (Doctor of Philosophy)*—Applications 2007–2008, 15. Total applicants accepted 2007–2008, 6. Number full-time enrolled (new admits only) 2007–2008, 4. Number part-time enrolled (new admits only) 2007–2008, 0. Openings 2008–2009, 1. The median number of years required for completion of a degree in 2006–2007 were 3. The number of students enrolled full- and part-time who were dismissed or voluntarily withdrew from this program area in 2007–2008 were 0. *School Psychology Educational Specialist EdS/MEd (School Psychology)*—Applications 2007–2008, 6. Total applicants accepted 2007–2008, 5. Number full-time enrolled (new admits only) 2007–2008, 3. Number part-time enrolled (new admits only) 2007–2008, 0. Openings 2008–2009, 5. The number of students enrolled full- and part-time who were dismissed or voluntarily withdrew from this program area in 2007–2008 were 0. *School Psychology PhD (Doctor of Philosophy)*—Applications 2007–2008, 9. Total applicants accepted 2007–2008, 5. Number full-time enrolled (new admits only) 2007–2008, 2. Number part-time enrolled (new admits only) 2007–2008, 0. The median number of years required for completion of a degree in 2006–2007 were 6. The number of students enrolled full- and part-time who were dismissed or voluntarily withdrew from this program area in 2007–2008 were 0.

Admissions Requirements:

Scores: Entries appear in this order: required test or GPA, minimum score (if required), median score of students entering in 2007–2008. Master's Programs: GRE-V no minimum stated, 500; GRE-Q no minimum stated, 555; overall undergraduate GPA 3.00; last 2 years GPA 3.00. MAT not accepted for admission. Doctoral Programs: GRE-V no minimum stated, 530; GRE-Q no minimum stated, 600; overall undergraduate GPA 3.00; last 2 years GPA 3.00. MAT not accepted for admission.

Other Criteria: (importance of criteria rated low, medium, or high): GRE/MAT scores—medium, research experience—high, work experience—medium, extracurricular activity—medium, clinically related public service—medium, GPA—high, letters of recommendation—high, interview—high, statement of goals and objectives—high.

Student Characteristics: The following represents characteristics of students in 2007–2008 in all graduate psychology programs in the department: Female—full-time 120, part-time 1; Male—full-time 35, part-time 0; African American/Black—full-time 17, part-time 0; Hispanic/Latino(a)—full-time 8, part-time 0; Asian/Pacific Islander—full-time 3, part-time 0; American Indian/Alaska Native—full-time 2, part-time 0; Caucasian/White—full-time 125, part-time 1; students subject to the Americans With Disabilities Act—full-time 10, part-time 0; Unknown ethnicity—full-time 0, part-time 0; International students who hold an F-1 or J-1 Visa—full-time 30, part-time 0.

Financial Information/Assistance:

Tuition for Full-Time Study: *Master's:* State residents: $286 per credit hour; Nonstate residents: $453 per credit hour. *Doctoral:* State residents: $286 per credit hour; Nonstate residents: $453 per credit hour. Tuition is subject to change. See the following Web site for updates and changes in tuition costs: http://www.cashiers.missouri.edu/cost.htm.

Financial Assistance:

First-Year Students: Teaching assistantships available for first year. Average amount paid per academic year: $4,667. Average number of hours worked per week: 10. Apply by December 1. Tuition remission given: full. Research assistantships available for first year. Average amount paid per academic year: $4,667. Average number of hours worked per week: 10. Apply by December 1. Tuition remission given: full. Fellowships and scholarships available for first year. Average amount paid per academic year: $8,000. Apply by February 11. Tuition remission given: full.

Advanced Students: Teaching assistantships available for advanced students. Average amount paid per academic year: $4,667. Average number of hours worked per week: 10. Apply by April 1. Tuition remission given: full. Research assistantships available for advanced students. Tuition remission given: partial. Fellowships and scholarships available for advanced students. Tuition remission given: partial.

Additional Information: Of all students currently enrolled full time, 70% benefited from one or more of the listed financial assistance programs. Application and information available online at https://sfa.missouri.edu/.

Internships/Practica: Doctoral Degree (PhD Counseling Psychology): For those doctoral students for whom a professional internship was required in this program prior to graduation, (7) students applied for an internship in 2006–2007, with (7) students obtaining an internship. Of those students who obtained an internship, (7) were paid internships. Of those students who obtained an internship, (7) students placed in APA/CPA-accredited internships, (0) students placed in internships not APA/CPA accredited, but listed with the Association of Psychology Postdoctoral and Internship Centers (APPIC), (0) students placed in internships conforming to guidelines of the Council of Directors of School Psychology Programs (CDSPP), (0) students placed in internships that were not APA/CPA-accredited, APPIC or CDSPP listed. Doctoral Degree (PhD School Psychology): For those doctoral students for whom a professional internship was required in this program prior to graduation, (1) students applied for an internship in 2006–2007, with (1) students obtaining an internship. Of those students who obtained an internship, (1) were paid internships. Of those students who obtained an internship, (1) student placed in APA/CPA-accredited internships, (0) students placed in internships not APA/CPA-accredited, but listed with the Association of Psychology Postdoctoral and Internship Centers (APPIC), (0) students placed in internships conforming to guidelines of the Council of Directors of School Psychology Programs (CDSPP), (0) students placed in internships that were not APA/CPA-accredited, APPIC or CDSPP listed. Internships are available in counseling psychology: VA hospitals, rehabilitation centers, mental health centers, university student counseling services; in school psychology: public schools, schools of medicine; in school counseling: public schools; in rehabilitation counseling: rehabilitation centers, mental health centers, and drug and alcohol centers.

Housing and Day Care: On-campus housing is available. See the following Web site for more information: http://www.web.missouri.edu/~gradschl/studentlife/life.htm. No on-campus day care facilities are available.

Employment of Department Graduates:

Master's Degree Graduates: Of those who graduated in the academic year 2006–2007, the following categories and numbers represent the postgraduate activities and employment of master's degree graduates: Enrolled in a psychology doctoral program (7), enrolled in another graduate/professional program (3), enrolled in a postdoctoral residency/fellowship (n/a), employed in independent practice (n/a), employed in a professional position in a school system (2), employed in a community mental health/counseling center (3), employed in a hospital/medical center (2), still seeking employment (3), other employment position (2), do not know (16), total from the above (master's) (38).

Doctoral Degree Graduates: Of those who graduated in the academic year 2006–2007, the following categories and numbers represent the postgraduate activities and employment of doctoral degree graduates: Enrolled in a psychology doctoral program (n/a), enrolled in a postdoctoral residency/fellowship (1), employed in an academic position at a university (2), employed in an academic position at a 2-year/4-year college (3), employed in a professional position in a school system (2), still seeking employment (3), do not know (0), total from the above (doctoral) (11).

Additional Information:

Orientation, Objectives, and Emphasis of Department: The goals of the department include the preparation of students in the professional specialties of counseling, school and educational psychology, rehabilitation counseling, school counseling and student personnel work, and the conduct of research on the applications of psychological knowledge to counseling and educational settings. The department emphasizes general psychological foundations, assessment, career development, counselor training and supervision, group processes, and research on counseling processes and psychological measurement and assessment. The theoretical orientation of the faculty is eclectic.

Special Facilities or Resources: Individual and group counseling and psychological assessment training facilities are available in the department, the College of Education and the department's assessment and consultation clinic, and on campus in the Student Counseling Services. Supervised training opportunities also occur in the Career Planning and Placement Center and with the Vocational Assessment Program. A well-stocked library of references in the specialty areas is located in the department. Access to computer services is available across the campus.

Information for Students With Physical Disabilities: See the following Web site for more information: http://www.missouri.edu/services.htm#disability.

Application Information:

Send to Graduate Secretary, 16 Hill Hall, University of Missouri—Columbia, Educational, School, and Counseling Psychology, Columbia, MO 65211. Application available online. URL of online application: http://www.education.missouri.edu/ESCP/. Students are admitted in the Fall, application deadline December 1. *Fee:* $45. International applicants pay a $60 admissions fee. Fee is sent directly to the International Admissions Office, 210 Jesse Hall.

Missouri, University of, Columbia

Department of Psychological Sciences
College of Arts and Science
210 McAlester Hall
Columbia, MO 65211
Telephone: (573) 882-0838
Fax: (573) 882-7710
E-mail: *gradpsych@missouri.edu*
Web: *http://www.psychology.missouri.edu/*

Department Information:

1900. Chairperson: Ann Bettencourt. Number of faculty: total—full-time 38, part-time 10; women—full-time 11, part-time 7; total—minority—full-time 2, part-time 1; women minority—full-time 2, part-time 1.

Programs and Degrees Offered:

Listed in the following order: Program area, degree type (T if terminal Master's), number awarded 7/06–6/07. Clinical PhD (Doctor of Philosophy) 2, Cognition and Neuroscience PhD (Doctor of Philosophy) 2, Social and Personality PhD (Doctor of Philosophy) 3, Quantitative PhD (Doctor of Philosophy) 0, Developmental PhD (Doctor of Philosophy) 3, Joint Child Clinical and Developmental PhD (Doctor of Philosophy) 0, Joint Clinical and Quantitative PhD (Doctor of Philosophy).

APA Accreditation: Clinical PhD (Doctor of Philosophy).

Student Applications/Admissions:

Student Applications

Clinical PhD (Doctor of Philosophy)—Applications 2007–2008, 104. Total applicants accepted 2007–2008, 13. Number full-time enrolled (new admits only) 2007–2008, 6. Number part-time enrolled (new admits only) 2007–2008, 0. Openings 2008–2009, 5. The median number of years required for completion of a degree in 2006–2007 were 8. The number of students enrolled full- and part-time who were dismissed or voluntarily withdrew from this program area in 2007–2008 were 1. *Cognition and Neuroscience PhD (Doctor of Philosophy)*—Applications 2007–2008, 30. Total applicants accepted 2007–2008, 8. Number full-time enrolled (new admits only) 2007–2008, 4. Openings 2008–2009, 5. The median number of years required for completion of a degree in 2006–2007 were 6. The number of students enrolled full- and part-time who were dismissed or voluntarily withdrew from this program area in 2007–2008 were 0. *Social and Personality PhD (Doctor of Philosophy)*—Applications 2007–2008, 53. Total applicants accepted 2007–2008, 2. Number full-time enrolled (new admits only) 2007–2008, 1. Number part-time enrolled (new admits only) 2007–2008, 0. Openings 2008–2009, 7. The median number of years required for completion of a degree in 2006–2007 were 7. The number of students enrolled full- and part-time who were dismissed or voluntarily withdrew from this program area in 2007–2008 were 0. *Quantitative PhD (Doctor of Philosophy)*—Applications 2007–2008, 9. Total applicants accepted 2007–2008, 2. Number full-time enrolled (new admits only) 2007–2008, 1. Number part-time enrolled (new admits only) 2007–2008, 0. Openings 2008–2009, 2. The number of students enrolled full- and part-time who were dismissed or voluntarily withdrew from this program area in 2007–2008 were 0. *Developmental PhD (Doctor of Philosophy)*—Applications 2007–2008, 10. Total applicants accepted 2007–2008, 4. Number full-time enrolled (new admits only) 2007–2008, 3. Total enrolled 2007–2008 full-time, 5. Openings 2008–2009, 3. The median number of years required for completion of a degree in 2006–2007 were 6. The number of students enrolled full- and part-time who were dismissed or voluntarily withdrew from this program area in 2007–2008 were 0. *Joint Child Clinical and Developmental PhD (Doctor of Philosophy)*—Applications 2007–2008, 28. Total applicants accepted 2007–2008, 3. Number full-time enrolled (new admits only) 2007–2008, 2. Total enrolled 2007–2008 full-time, 7. Openings 2008–2009, 1. The number of students enrolled full- and part-time who were dismissed or voluntarily withdrew from this program area in 2007–2008 were 0. *Joint Clinical and Quantitative PhD (Doctor of Philosophy)—No information provided.*

Admissions Requirements:

Scores: Entries appear in this order: required test or GPA, minimum score (if required), median score of students entering in 2007–2008. Doctoral Programs: GRE-V no minimum stated, 584; GRE-Q no minimum stated, 705; overall undergraduate GPA 3.0, 3.68; last 2 years GPA no minimum stated, 3.78; psychology GPA no minimum stated, 3.81.

Other Criteria: (importance of criteria rated low, medium, or high): GRE/MAT scores—high, research experience—high, work experience—low, extracurricular activity—low, clinically related public service—low, GPA—medium, letters of recommendation—medium, interview—high, statement of goals and objectives—high. For additional information on admission requirements, go to http://psychology.missouri.edu/programs/grad.htm.

Student Characteristics: The following represents characteristics of students in 2007–2008 in all graduate psychology programs in the department: Female—full-time 53, part-time 0; Male—full-time 27, part-time 0; African American/Black—full-time 2, part-time 0; Hispanic/Latino(a)—full-time 6, part-time 0; Asian/Pacific Islander—full-time 12, part-time 0; American Indian/Alaska Native—full-time 0, part-time 0; Caucasian/White—full-time 57, part-time 0; Multi-ethnic—full-time 0, part-time 0; students subject to the Americans With Disabilities Act—full-time 0, part-time 0; Unknown ethnicity—full-time 3, part-time 0; International students who hold an F-1 or J-1 Visa—full-time 11, part-time 0.

Financial Information/Assistance:

Tuition for Full-Time Study: *Doctoral:* State residents: $286 per credit hour; Nonstate residents: $740 per credit hour. Tuition is subject to change. See the following Web site for updates and changes in tuition costs: http://www.cashiers.missouri.edu/cost.htm.

Financial Assistance:

First-Year Students: Teaching assistantships available for first year. Average amount paid per academic year: $11,923. Average number of hours worked per week: 20. Tuition remission given: full. Research assistantships available for first year. Average amount paid per academic year: $11,923. Average number of hours worked per week: 20. Tuition remission given: full. Fellowships and scholarships available for first year. Average amount paid per academic year: $13,500. Average number of hours worked per week: 20. Tuition remission given: full.

Advanced Students: Teaching assistantships available for advanced students. Average amount paid per academic year: $12,697. Average number of hours worked per week: 20. Tuition remission given: full. Research assistantships available for advanced students. Average amount paid per academic year: $12,697. Average number of hours worked per week: 20. Tuition remission given: full. Traineeships available for advanced students. Average amount paid per academic year: $12,697. Average number of hours worked per week: 20. Tuition remission given: full. Fellowships and scholarships available for advanced students. Average amount paid per academic year: $13,500. Average number of hours worked per week: 20. Tuition remission given: full.

Additional Information: Of all students currently enrolled full time, 100% benefited from one or more of the listed financial assistance programs. Departmental assistantships do not require a separate application.

Internships/Practica: Doctoral Degree (PhD Clinical): For those doctoral students for whom a professional internship was required in this program prior to graduation, (4) students applied for an internship in 2006–2007, with (4) students obtaining an internship. Of those students who obtained an internship, (4) were paid internships. Of those students who obtained an internship, (4) students placed in APA/CPA-accredited internships, (0) students placed in internships not APA/CPA-accredited, but listed with the Association of Psychology Postdoctoral and Internship Centers (APPIC), (0) students placed in internships conforming to guidelines of the Council of Directors of School Psychology Programs (CDSPP), (0) students placed in internships that were not

APA/CPA-accredited, APPIC or CDSPP listed. Doctoral Degree (PhD Joint Child Clinical and Developmental): For those doctoral students for whom a professional internship was required in this program prior to graduation, (1) students applied for an internship in 2006–2007, with (1) student obtaining an internship. Of those students who obtained an internship, (1) were paid internships. Of those students who obtained an internship, (1) student placed in APA/CPA-accredited internships, (0) students placed in internships not APA/CPA-accredited, but listed with the Association of Psychology Postdoctoral and Internship Centers (APPIC), (0) students placed in internships conforming to guidelines of the Council of Directors of School Psychology Programs (CDSPP), (0) students placed in internships that were not APA/CPA-accredited, APPIC or CDSPP listed. In clinical psychology, an APA-approved internship is required for the PhD degree.

Housing and Day Care: On-campus housing is available. See the following Web site for more information: http://www.reslife.missouri.edu/. On-campus day care facilities are available. See the following Web site for more information: http://www.cdl.missouri.edu.

Employment of Department Graduates:

Master's Degree Graduates: Of those who graduated in the academic year 2006–2007, the following categories and numbers represent the postgraduate activities and employment of master's degree graduates: Enrolled in a postdoctoral residency/fellowship (n/a), employed in independent practice (n/a), total from the above (master's) (0).

Doctoral Degree Graduates: Of those who graduated in the academic year 2006–2007, the following categories and numbers represent the postgraduate activities and employment of doctoral degree graduates: Enrolled in a psychology doctoral program (n/a), enrolled in a postdoctoral residency/fellowship (1), employed in an academic position at a university (3), employed in a community mental health/counseling center (1), do not know (2), total from the above (doctoral) (7).

Additional Information:

Orientation, Objectives, and Emphasis of Department: The clinical program is fully accredited by the American Psychological Association and is a charter member of the Academy of Psychological Clinical Science. All programs offer broad empirical and theoretical training with a research emphasis.

Special Facilities or Resources: The department has the following special facilities or resources: a psychology research facility, a psychological clinic, a medical school, a VA hospital, Mid-Missouri Mental Health Center, a counseling center, human experimental laboratories, a central computer system with extensive program library and remote terminal support, and departmental computers.

Information for Students With Physical Disabilities: See the following Web site for more information: http://www.disabilityservices.missouri.edu.

Application Information:

Send to Director of Graduate Admissions, Department of Psychological Sciences, University of Missouri, 210 McAlester Hall, Columbia, MO 65211. Application available online. URL of online application: http://www.psychology.missouri.edu/gradprogram.php. Students are admitted in the Fall, application deadline December 15. *Fee:* $45. There is a $60 application fee for nonresident international students.

Missouri, University of, Kansas City

Department of Psychology
4825 Troost, Suite 124
Kansas City, MO 64110
Telephone: (816) 235-1318
Fax: (816) 235-1062
E-mail: *psychology@umkc.edu*
Web: *http://www.cas.umkc.edu/psyc*

Department Information:

1940. Chairperson: Diane L. Filion, PhD. Number of faculty: total—full-time 12; women—full-time 8.

Programs and Degrees Offered:

Listed in the following order: Program area, degree type (T if terminal Master's), number awarded 7/06–6/07. Clinical Psychology PhD (Doctor of Philosophy) 1.

APA Accreditation: Clinical PhD (Doctor of Philosophy).

Student Applications/Admissions:

Student Applications

Clinical Psychology PhD (Doctor of Philosophy)—Applications 2007–2008, 83. Total applicants accepted 2007–2008, 5. Number full-time enrolled (new admits only) 2007–2008, 4. Number part-time enrolled (new admits only) 2007–2008, 0. Openings 2008–2009, 4. The median number of years required for completion of a degree in 2006–2007 were 6. The number of students enrolled full- and part-time who were dismissed or voluntarily withdrew from this program area in 2007–2008 were 1.

Admissions Requirements:

Scores: Entries appear in this order: required test or GPA, minimum score (if required), median score of students entering in 2007–2008. Doctoral Programs: GRE-V no minimum stated, 515; GRE-Q no minimum stated, 580; overall undergraduate GPA no minimum stated, 3.33; Doctoral program GRE-Analytic no minimum stated, 4.5. Please check the department Web site at http://cas.umkc.edu/psyc/grad/clinical.htm for program-specific admissions requirements.

Other Criteria: (importance of criteria rated low, medium, or high): GRE/MAT scores—high, research experience—high, work experience—medium, extracurricular activity—low, clinically related public service—medium, GPA—high, letters of recommendation—high, interview—high, statement of goals and objectives—high. For additional information on admission requirements, go to http://cas.umkc.edu/psyc/grad/clinical.htm.

Student Characteristics: The following represents characteristics of students in 2007–2008 in all graduate psychology programs in the department: Female—full-time 17, part-time 0; Male—full-time 5, part-time 0; African American/Black—full-time 1,

part-time 0; Hispanic/Latino(a)—full-time 1, part-time 0; Asian/Pacific Islander—full-time 0, part-time 0; American Indian/Alaska Native—full-time 0, part-time 0; Caucasian/White—full-time 20, part-time 0; Multi-ethnic—full-time 0, part-time 0; students subject to the Americans With Disabilities Act—full-time 0, part-time 0; Unknown ethnicity—full-time 0, part-time 0.

Financial Information/Assistance:

Tuition for Full-Time Study: *Doctoral:* State residents: $347 per credit hour; Nonstate residents: $801 per credit hour. Tuition is subject to change. See the following Web site for updates and changes in tuition costs: http://www.umkc.edu/adminfinance/finance/cashiers/feestructure.asp.

Financial Assistance:

First-Year Students: Teaching assistantships available for first year. Average amount paid per academic year: $9,000. Average number of hours worked per week: 20. Apply by 0. Tuition remission given: partial. Research assistantships available for first year. Average amount paid per academic year: $9,000. Average number of hours worked per week: 20. Apply by 0. Tuition remission given: partial. Fellowships and scholarships available for first year. Apply by varies. Tuition remission given: partial.

Advanced Students: Teaching assistantships available for advanced students. Average amount paid per academic year: $9,000. Average number of hours worked per week: 20. Tuition remission given: partial. Research assistantships available for advanced students. Average amount paid per academic year: $9,000. Average number of hours worked per week: 20. Tuition remission given: partial. Fellowships and scholarships available for advanced students. Apply by varies. Tuition remission given: partial.

Additional Information: Of all students currently enrolled full time, 100% benefited from one or more of the listed financial assistance programs. Application and information available online at http://sgs.umkc.edu/financial.asp.

Internships/Practica: Doctoral Degree (PhD Clinical Psychology): For those doctoral students for whom a professional internship was required in this program prior to graduation, (4) students applied for an internship in 2006–2007, with (3) students obtaining an internship. Of those students who obtained an internship, (2) were paid internships. Of those students who obtained an internship, (0) students placed in APA/CPA-accredited internships, (3) students placed in internships not APA/CPA accredited, but listed with the Association of Psychology Postdoctoral and Internship Centers (APPIC), (0) students placed in internships conforming to guidelines of the Council of Directors of School Psychology Programs (CDSPP), (0) students placed in internships that were not APA/CPA-accredited, APPIC or CDSPP listed. With a population of over 1.5 million, Kansas City offers numerous opportunities for practicum and research opportunities. A wide range of formal community practicum opportunities are offered to Clinical Psychology PhD students including placements at community agencies, medical centers, and other applied settings. Clinical psychology students are required to enroll in six semesters of practicum during which they are involved in many different types of clinical experiences ranging from supervised work in specialized health care programs to more general outpatient settings for psychotherapy and psychological assessment. Basic clinical practica include training in general mental health assessment and treatment areas such as crisis intervention, depression screening, personnel and disability evaluations, and treatment of adjustment problems, depression, and anxiety disorders. Advanced training opportunities in the assessment and treatment of obesity and eating disorders, smoking and other substance abuse, and chronic pain. In the 5th year of study, students are required to complete a 1-year clinical internship.

Housing and Day Care: On-campus housing is available. See the following Web site for more information: http://www.umkc.edu/housing/housingoptions.asp. On-campus day care facilities are available. See the following Web site for more information: http://www.education.umkc.edu/berkley/.

Employment of Department Graduates:

Master's Degree Graduates: Of those who graduated in the academic year 2006–2007, the following categories and numbers represent the postgraduate activities and employment of master's degree graduates: Enrolled in a postdoctoral residency/fellowship (n/a), employed in independent practice (n/a), total from the above (master's) (0).

Doctoral Degree Graduates: Of those who graduated in the academic year 2006–2007, the following categories and numbers represent the postgraduate activities and employment of doctoral degree graduates: Enrolled in a psychology doctoral program (n/a), employed in a hospital/medical center (1), total from the above (doctoral) (1).

Additional Information:

Orientation, Objectives, and Emphasis of Department: The psychology program integrates clinical and epidemiological research with the health and life sciences. The department seeks to enhance the public health, broadly defined, through rigorous training of students (education mission); provide an accessible resource for the integration of behavioral sciences and health research and healthcare (service mission); develop knowledge and enhance health outcomes through empirical research (research and evaluation mission); and incorporate integrity and respect for human and intellectual diversity in all our activities (human mission).

Information for Students With Physical Disabilities: See the following Web site for more information: http://www.umkc.edu/disability/.

Application Information:

For PhD degree, send University application and fee only to University of Missouri—Kansas City, Office of Admissions, Administrative Center, 5115 Oak, Kansas City, MO 64110. Send other PhD application materials to the department at UMKC Department of Psychology, Clinical PhD Program Admissions, 4825 Troost, Suite 124, Kansas City, MO 64110. See department Web site for application instructions: http://cas.umkc.edu/psyc/grad/clinical.htm. Application available online. URL of online application: http://www.umkc.edu/admissions/. Students are admitted in the Fall, application deadline January 15. *Fee:* $35.

Missouri, University of, Kansas City

Division of Counseling, Educational Psychology, and Exercise Science
School of Education
5100 Rockhill Road, 215
Kansas City, MO 64110
Telephone: (816) 235-2722
Fax: (816) 235-5270
E-mail: *Duanc@umkc.edu*
Web: *http://www.umkc.edu/education/divs/cpce/*

Department Information:

Chairperson: Changming Duan, PhD. Number of faculty: total—full-time 12; women—full-time 10; total—minority—full-time 4; women minority—full-time 3.

Programs and Degrees Offered:

Listed in the following order: Program area, degree type (T if terminal Master's), number awarded 7/06–6/07. Counseling Psychology PhD (Doctor of Philosophy) 4, Education Specialist Other, Counseling and Guidance MA/MS (Master of Arts/Science) (T) 27.

APA Accreditation: Counseling PhD (Doctor of Philosophy).

Student Applications/Admissions:

Student Applications

Counseling Psychology PhD (Doctor of Philosophy)—Applications 2007–2008, 84. Total applicants accepted 2007–2008, 6. Number full-time enrolled (new admits only) 2007–2008, 6. Openings 2008–2009, 6. The median number of years required for completion of a degree in 2006–2007 were 6. The number of students enrolled full- and part-time who were dismissed or voluntarily withdrew from this program area in 2007–2008 were 0. *Education Specialist Other*—Total enrolled 2007–2008 full-time, 11. *Counseling and Guidance MA/MS (Master of Arts/Science)*—Applications 2007–2008, 130. Total applicants accepted 2007–2008, 61. Number full-time enrolled (new admits only) 2007–2008, 47. Total enrolled 2007–2008 full-time, 133. Openings 2008–2009, 50. The median number of years required for completion of a degree in 2006–2007 were 3. The number of students enrolled full- and part-time who were dismissed or voluntarily withdrew from this program area in 2007–2008 were 0.

Admissions Requirements:

Scores: Entries appear in this order: required test or GPA, minimum score (if required), median score of students entering in 2007–2008. Master's Programs: GRE-V no minimum stated; GRE-Q no minimum stated; overall undergraduate GPA 2.75, last 2 years GPA 3.00. GRE required: minimum 900 combined verbal and quantitative scores, 4.0 writing score Doctoral Programs: GRE-V no minimum stated; GRE-Q no minimum stated; overall undergraduate GPA 3.00; last 2 years GPA 3.25. GRE required: minimum 1000 combined verbal and quantitative score, 4.5 writing score.

Other Criteria: (importance of criteria rated low, medium, or high): GRE/MAT scores—medium, research experience—high, work experience—medium, extracurricular activity—medium, clinically related public service—medium, GPA—high, letters of recommendation—high, interview—high, statement of goals and objectives—high, undergraduate major in psychology—medium.

Student Characteristics: The following represents characteristics of students in 2007–2008 in all graduate psychology programs in the department: Female—full-time 151, part-time 0; Male—full-time 28, part-time 0; African American/Black—full-time 7, part-time 0; Hispanic/Latino(a)—full-time 10, part-time 0; Asian/Pacific Islander—full-time 6, part-time 0; American Indian/Alaska Native—full-time 2, part-time 0; Caucasian/White—full-time 141, part-time 0; Multi-ethnic—full-time 1, part-time 0; students subject to the Americans With Disabilities Act—full-time 1, part-time 0; Unknown ethnicity—full-time 12, part-time 0; International students who hold an F-1 or J-1 Visa—full-time 3, part-time 0.

Financial Information/Assistance:

Tuition for Full-Time Study: *Master's:* State residents: $287 per credit hour; Nonstate residents: $454 per credit hour. *Doctoral:* State residents: per academic year $2,884, $287 per credit hour; Nonstate residents: per academic year $2,884, $287 per credit hour. Tuition is subject to change. See the following Web site for updates and changes in tuition costs: http://www.umkc.edu/umkc/catalog-grad/html/fees/9999.html.

Financial Assistance:

First-Year Students: Teaching assistantships available for first year. Average amount paid per academic year: $12,000. Average number of hours worked per week: 20. Apply by varies. Tuition remission given: partial. Research assistantships available for first year. Average amount paid per academic year: $12,000. Average number of hours worked per week: 20. Apply by varies. Tuition remission given: partial. Fellowships and scholarships available for first year. Apply by February 1. Tuition remission given: partial.

Advanced Students: No information provided.

Additional Information: Of all students currently enrolled full time, 80% benefited from one or more of the listed financial assistance programs. Application and information available online at http://www.umkc.edu/sgs/financial.

Internships/Practica: Master's Degree (MA/MS Counseling and Guidance): An internship experience such as a final research project or "capstone" experience is required of graduates. Doctoral Degree (PhD Counseling Psychology): For those doctoral students for whom a professional internship was required in this program prior to graduation, (5) students applied for an internship in 2006–2007, with (5) students obtaining an internship. Of those students who obtained an internship, (5) were paid internships. Of those students who obtained an internship, (5) students placed in APA/CPA-accredited internships, (0) students placed in internships not APA/CPA-accredited, but listed with the Association of Psychology Postdoctoral and Internship Centers (APPIC), (0) students placed in internships conforming to guidelines of the Council of Directors of School Psychology Programs (CDSPP), (0) students placed in internships that were not APA/CPA-accredited, APPIC or CDSPP listed. All programs offer a wide range of practicum and internship placements. The Division of Counseling Psychology and Counselor Education operates the Community Counseling Services, an in-house training facility serving individuals, couples, and families in the surrounding community. Advanced practica are also available in a variety of agencies including local community mental health centers, Veterans Affairs Hospitals, and other local service provision agencies.

Housing and Day Care: On-campus housing is available. See the following Web site for more information: http://www.umkc.edu/housing. No on-campus day care facilities are available.

Employment of Department Graduates:

Master's Degree Graduates: Of those who graduated in the academic year 2006–2007, the following categories and numbers represent the postgraduate activities and employment of master's degree graduates: Enrolled in a postdoctoral residency/fellowship (n/a), employed in independent practice (n/a), employed in an academic position at a university (0), employed in an academic position at a 2-year/4-year college (2), employed in other positions at a higher education institution (0), employed in a professional position in a school system (0), employed in business or industry (0), employed in government agency (0), employed in a community mental health/counseling center (3), employed in a hospital/medical center (1), still seeking employment (0), not seeking employment (0), other employment position (0), do not know (0), total from the above (master's) (6).

Doctoral Degree Graduates: Of those who graduated in the academic year 2006–2007, the following categories and numbers represent the postgraduate activities and employment of doctoral degree graduates: Enrolled in a psychology doctoral program (n/a), total from the above (doctoral) (0).

Additional Information:

Orientation, Objectives, and Emphasis of Department: Our Counseling Psychology program emphasizes the study of multicultural and individual diversity within a scientist–practitioner model. Consistent with the University of Missouri—Kansas City urban and metropolitan mission, the faculty is committed to educating future counseling psychologists to improve the welfare of individuals and communities through scholarship and applied interventions. The program faculty encourages students to develop primary identification with the core values of counseling psychology. These values emphasize (a) assets, strengths, and positive mental health; (b) respect for cultural and individual diversity; (c) scientific foundation for all activities; (d) developmental models of human growth; (e) relatively brief counseling interventions; (f) person-environment interaction; (g) education and prevention; (h) career/vocational development. Our commitment to cultural and individual diversity is reflected in (a) faculty composition, (b) student recruitment, (c) scholarship, (d) course content and offerings, (e) practicum opportunities, and (f) community service and consultation. Education in counseling psychology follows a developmental model in which science–practice integration is emphasized throughout the program. Early and progressive training is provided in research, culminating in professionals who can design, conduct, and evaluate research relevant for counseling psychologists. Similarly, early and progressive training in practice activity is emphasized. Program graduates will apply the values of counseling psychology to their work in a variety of employment settings, and as scientist–practitioners, their practice is informed by research and approached with a scientific attitude. Counseling psychologists abide by the American Psychological Association code of conduct. Students will understand the ethical, legal, and professional issues related to the science and practice of counseling psychology.

Information for Students With Physical Disabilities: See the following Web site for more information: http://www.umkc.edu/disability.

Application Information:

PhD in Counseling Psychology Program: Applications go to two places: Office of Admissions, University of Missouri—Kansas City, 5115 Oak, 5100 Rockhill Road, Kansas City, Missouri 64110; and Counseling Psychology Program, University of Missouri—Kansas City, ED 215, 5100 Rockhill Road, Kansas City, Missouri 64110. Students are admitted in the Fall, application deadline January 1. Please see program Web site for more details on application requirements and process (http://education.umkc.edu/CEP/). *Fee:* $25.

Missouri, University of, St. Louis

Department of Psychology
One University Boulevard
St. Louis, MO 63121
Telephone: (314) 516-5391
Fax: (314) 516-5392
E-mail: *robert_calsyn@UMSL.EDU*
Web: *http://www.umsl.edu/divisions/artscience/psychology*

Department Information:

1967. Chairperson: Robert J. Calsyn. Number of faculty: total—full-time 20; women—full-time 9; total—minority—full-time 2; women minority—full-time 1.

Programs and Degrees Offered:

Listed in the following order: Program area, degree type (T if terminal Master's), number awarded 7/06–6/07. Clinical PhD (Doctor of Philosophy) 4, Industrial/Organizational PhD (Doctor of Philosophy) 4, Behavioral Neuroscience PhD (Doctor of Philosophy) 0.

APA Accreditation: Clinical PhD (Doctor of Philosophy).

Student Applications/Admissions:

Student Applications

Clinical PhD (Doctor of Philosophy)—Applications 2007–2008, 115. Total applicants accepted 2007–2008, 16. Number full-time enrolled (new admits only) 2007–2008, 6. Number part-time enrolled (new admits only) 2007–2008, 0. Openings 2008–2009, 6. The median number of years required for completion of a degree in 2006–2007 were 6. The number of students enrolled full- and part-time who were dismissed or voluntarily withdrew from this program area in 2007–2008 were 1. *Industrial/Organizational PhD (Doctor of Philosophy)*—Applications 2007–2008, 55. Total applicants accepted 2007–2008, 10. Number full-time enrolled (new admits only) 2007–2008, 6. Number part-time enrolled (new admits only) 2007–2008, 0. Openings 2008–2009, 5. The median number of years required for completion of a degree in 2006–2007 were 7. The number of students enrolled full- and part-time who were dismissed or voluntarily withdrew from this program area in 2007–2008 were 1. *Behavioral Neuroscience PhD (Doctor of Philosophy)*—Applications 2007–2008, 8. Total applicants accepted 2007–2008, 2. Number full-time enrolled (new admits only) 2007–2008, 2. Number part-time enrolled (new admits only) 2007–2008, 0. Openings 2008–2009, 2. The median number of years required for completion of a degree in 2006–2007 were 5. The number of students enrolled full- and part-time who were dismissed or voluntarily withdrew from this program area in 2007–2008 were 0.

Admissions Requirements:

Scores: Entries appear in this order: required test or GPA, minimum score (if required), median score of students entering in 2007–2008. Master's Programs: GRE-V no minimum stated; GRE-Q no minimum stated; GRE-Subject (Psychology) no minimum stated; overall undergraduate GPA no minimum stated; psychology GPA no minimum stated; Masters GRE-Analytical no minimum stated. There are no minimum requirements. Median values vary by program. GRE-Subject not required for Clinical Doctoral Program. Doctoral Programs: GRE-V no minimum stated, 565; GRE-Q no minimum stated, 675; GRE-Subject (Psychology) no minimum stated, 700; overall undergraduate GPA no minimum stated, 3.8; psychology GPA no minimum stated, 3.6; Doctoral program GRE-Analytic no minimum stated, 4.5. There are no minimum requirements, but median scores vary by program.

Other Criteria: (importance of criteria rated low, medium, or high): GRE/MAT scores—high, research experience—high, work experience—medium, extracurricular activity—medium, clinically related public service—medium, GPA—high, letters of recommendation—high, interview—high, statement of goals and objectives—high. Only the clinical program has a formal interview procedure. Importance of criteria varies by program.

Student Characteristics: The following represents characteristics of students in 2007–2008 in all graduate psychology programs in the department: Female—full-time 55, part-time 0; Male—full-time 18, part-time 0; African American/Black—full-time 1, part-time 0; Hispanic/Latino(a)—full-time 1, part-time 0; Asian/Pacific Islander—full-time 1, part-time 0; American Indian/Alaska Native—full-time 0, part-time 0; Caucasian/White—full-time 70, part-time 0; Multi-ethnic—full-time 0, part-time 0; students subject to the Americans With Disabilities Act—full-time 0, part-time 0; Unknown ethnicity—full-time 0, part-time 0; International students who hold an F-1 or J-1 Visa—full-time 0, part-time 0.

Financial Information/Assistance:

Tuition for Full-Time Study: *Master's:* State residents: $276 per credit hour; Nonstate residents: $714 per credit hour. *Doctoral:* State residents: $276 per credit hour; Nonstate residents: $714 per credit hour. Tuition is subject to change. Additional fees are assessed to students beyond the costs of tuition for the following: parking and activities.

Financial Assistance:

First-Year Students: Teaching assistantships available for first year. Average amount paid per academic year: $11,500. Average number of hours worked per week: 20. Apply by January 15. Tuition remission given: full. Research assistantships available for first year. Average amount paid per academic year: $11,500. Average number of hours worked per week: 20. Apply by January 15. Tuition remission given: full.

Advanced Students: Teaching assistantships available for advanced students. Average amount paid per academic year: $11,500. Average number of hours worked per week: 20. Apply by January 15. Tuition remission given: full and partial. Research assistantships available for advanced students. Average amount paid per academic year: $11,500. Average number of hours worked per week: 20. Apply by January 15. Tuition remission given: full and partial.

Additional Information: Of all students currently enrolled full time, 65% benefited from one or more of the listed financial assistance programs.

Internships/Practica: Doctoral Degree (PhD Clinical): For those doctoral students for whom a professional internship was required in this program prior to graduation, (11) students applied for an internship in 2006–2007, with (8) students obtaining an internship. Of those students who obtained an internship, (8) were paid internships. Of those students who obtained an internship, (8) students placed in APA/CPA-accredited internships, (0) students placed in internships not APA/CPA-accredited, but listed with the Association of Psychology Postdoctoral and Internship Centers (APPIC), (0) students placed in internships conforming to guidelines of the Council of Directors of School Psychology Programs (CDSPP), (0) students placed in internships that were not APA/CPA-accredited, APPIC or CDSPP listed. Students (clinical) participate in practica in our Community Psychological Service (the psychology clinic) and a paid clinical clerkship, which may be in a community- or university-based program.

Housing and Day Care: On-campus housing is available. For information regarding on-campus housing, please call the Residence Hall at (314) 516-6877. Affordable housing for students is also available off campus. For example, a two-bedroom apartment is approximately $500–$600/month within a close commuting distance from campus. On-campus day care facilities are available. Contact Child Development Center at (314) 516-5658.

Employment of Department Graduates:

Master's Degree Graduates: Of those who graduated in the academic year 2006–2007, the following categories and numbers represent the postgraduate activities and employment of master's degree graduates: Enrolled in a psychology doctoral program (0), enrolled in another graduate/professional program (1), enrolled in a postdoctoral residency/fellowship (n/a), employed in independent practice (n/a), employed in an academic position at a university (0), employed in an academic position at a 2-year/4-year college (0), employed in other positions at a higher education institution (0), employed in a professional position in a school system (0), employed in business or industry (0), employed in government agency (0), employed in a community mental health/counseling center (0), employed in a hospital/medical center (2), still seeking employment (0), not seeking employment (0), other employment position (0), do not know (0), total from the above (master's) (3).

Doctoral Degree Graduates: Of those who graduated in the academic year 2006–2007, the following categories and numbers represent the postgraduate activities and employment of doctoral degree graduates: Enrolled in a psychology doctoral program (n/a), enrolled in a postdoctoral residency/fellowship (4), employed in independent practice (0), employed in an academic position at a university (0), employed in an academic position at a 2-year/4-year college (0), employed in other positions at a higher education institution (0), employed in a professional position in a school system (0), employed in business or industry (4), employed in government agency (0), employed in a community mental health/counseling center (0), employed in a hospital/medical center (0), still seeking employment (0), not seeking employment (0), other employment position (0), do not know (0), total from the above (doctoral) (8).

Additional Information:

Orientation, Objectives, and Emphasis of Department: The orientation of the department emphasizes psychology as science yet also recognizes the important social responsibilities of psychology, especially in the clinical and applied areas. Emphasis of behavioral neuroscience is in behavioral neuropharmacology/endocrinology with a secondary interest in neuroscience. The department offers a broad spectrum of high-quality programs at the undergraduate and graduate levels.

Special Facilities or Resources: The Department of Psychology is housed in Stadler Hall, and research laboratories and computers are conveniently located in the building. The psychological clinic (Community Psychological Service) is also contained within Stadler Hall. The Center for Trauma Recovery and Child Advocacy Center each have community clinics, which are housed on campus. Physical facilities include workshops and comparative, social, and human experimental laboratories. A wide range of research equipment is available, including videotaping facilities, computer terminals, and personal computers.

Information for Students With Physical Disabilities: See the following Web site for more information: http://www.umsl.edu/services/disabled/.

Application Information:

Send to Graduate Admissions, University of Missouri—St. Louis, 358 Millennium Student Center, 8001 Natural Bridge, St. Louis, MO 63121. Application available online. URL of online application: http://www.umsl.edu/divisions/graduate/pdf/gs-appl.pdf. Students are admitted in the Fall. Clinical deadline is January 15, I/O deadline is February 1, Behavioral Neuroscience is February 1. *Fee:* $25.

Saint Louis University

Department of Psychology
Arts and Sciences
221 North Grand Boulevard, 119 Shannon Hall
St. Louis, MO 63103-2010
Telephone: (314) 977-2300
Fax: (314) 977-1014
E-mail: *lavoiedj@slu.edu*
Web: *http://www.slu.edu/colleges/AS/PSY/*

Department Information:

1926. Chairperson: Donna J. LaVoie. Number of faculty: total—full-time 24; women—full-time 9.

Programs and Degrees Offered:

Listed in the following order: Program area, degree type (T if terminal Master's), number awarded 7/06–6/07. Cognitive Neuroscience PhD (Doctor of Philosophy) 1, Clinical PhD (Doctor of Philosophy) 7, Developmental PhD (Doctor of Philosophy) 0, Social PhD (Doctor of Philosophy) 0, Industrial/Organizational PhD (Doctor of Philosophy) 2.

APA Accreditation: Clinical PhD (Doctor of Philosophy).

Student Applications/Admissions:

Student Applications

Cognitive Neuroscience PhD (Doctor of Philosophy)—Applications 2007–2008, 14. Total applicants accepted 2007–2008, 2. Number full-time enrolled (new admits only) 2007–2008, 1. Number part-time enrolled (new admits only) 2007–2008, 0. Openings 2008–2009, 2. The median number of years required for completion of a degree in 2006–2007 were 5. The number of students enrolled full- and part-time who were dismissed or voluntarily withdrew from this program area in 2007–2008 were 1. *Clinical PhD (Doctor of Philosophy)*—Applications 2007–2008, 175. Total applicants accepted 2007–2008, 8. Number full-time enrolled (new admits only) 2007–2008, 8. Number part-time enrolled (new admits only) 2007–2008, 0. Openings 2008–2009, 8. The median number of years required for completion of a degree in 2006–2007 were 5. The number of students enrolled full- and part-time who were dismissed or voluntarily withdrew from this program area in 2007–2008 were 0. *Developmental PhD (Doctor of Philosophy)*—Applications 2007–2008, 10. Total applicants accepted 2007–2008, 2. Number full-time enrolled (new admits only) 2007–2008, 1. Number part-time enrolled (new admits only) 2007–2008, 0. Openings 2008–2009, 2. The median number of years required for completion of a degree in 2006–2007 were 5. The number of students enrolled full- and part-time who were dismissed or voluntarily withdrew from this program area in 2007–2008 were 1. *Social PhD (Doctor of Philosophy)*—Applications 2007–2008, 21. Total applicants accepted 2007–2008, 2. Number full-time enrolled (new admits only) 2007–2008, 2. Number part-time enrolled (new admits only) 2007–2008, 0. Openings 2008–2009, 2. The median number of years required for completion of a degree in 2006–2007 were 5. The number of students enrolled full- and part-time who were dismissed or voluntarily withdrew from this program area in 2007–2008 were 0. *Industrial/Organizational PhD (Doctor of Philosophy)*—Applications 2007–2008, 40. Total applicants accepted 2007–2008, 9. Number full-time enrolled (new admits only) 2007–2008, 8. Number part-time enrolled (new admits only) 2007–2008, 0. Openings 2008–2009, 5. The median number of years required for completion of a degree in 2006–2007 were 5. The number of students enrolled full- and part-time who were dismissed or voluntarily withdrew from this program area in 2007–2008 were 1.

Admissions Requirements:

Scores: Entries appear in this order: required test or GPA, minimum score (if required), median score of students entering in 2007–2008. Doctoral Programs: GRE-V no minimum stated, 535; GRE-Q no minimum stated, 615; overall undergraduate GPA no minimum stated, 3.65. Clinical prefers verbal (550), quantitative (550). Others prefer verbal + quantitative = 1000, but applicants with scores < 1000 will still be considered.

Other Criteria: (importance of criteria rated low, medium, or high): GRE/MAT scores—medium, research experience—high, work experience—medium, extracurricular activity—medium, clinically related public service—high, GPA—high, letters of recommendation—high, interview—high, statement of goals and objectives—high, fit with faculty expertise—high, undergraduate major in psychology—medium, specific undergraduate psychology courses taken—low. For nonclinical specialties, clinically related public service is low, and interview is medium. For all programs, applicant's fit with faculty research interests and expertise is high. For additional information on admission requirements, go to Psychology: http://www.slu.edu/x13053.xml; General: http://www.slu.edu/graduate/checklist.html.

Student Characteristics: The following represents characteristics of students in 2007–2008 in all graduate psychology programs in the department: Female—full-time 58, part-time 0; Male—full-time 27, part-time 0; African American/Black—full-time 12, part-time 0; Hispanic/Latino(a)—full-time 0, part-time 0; Asian/Pacific Islander—full-time 1, part-time 0; American Indian/Alaska Native—full-time 1, part-time 0; Caucasian/White—full-time 69, part-time 0; Multi-ethnic—full-time 0, part-time 0; students subject to the Americans With Disabilities Act—full-time 0, part-time 0; Unknown ethnicity—full-time 2, part-time 0.

Financial Information/Assistance:

Tuition for Full-Time Study: *Master's:* State residents: $845 per credit hour; Nonstate residents: $845 per credit hour. *Doctoral:* State residents: $845 per credit hour; Nonstate residents: $845 per credit hour. Tuition is subject to change. Additional fees are assessed to students beyond the costs of tuition for the following: graduation fees: MS, $75; PhD, $150. See the following Web site for updates and changes in tuition costs: http://www.slu.edu/graduate/forms/tuition_fees.pdf.

Financial Assistance:

First-Year Students: Teaching assistantships available for first year. Average amount paid per academic year: $12,000. Average number of hours worked per week: 20. Tuition remission given: full. Research assistantships available for first year. Average amount paid per academic year: $14,000. Average number of hours worked per week: 20. Tuition remission given: full. Fellowships and scholarships available for first year. Average amount paid per academic year: $19,000. Average number of hours worked per week: 20. Apply by February 1. Tuition remission given: full.

Advanced Students: Teaching assistantships available for advanced students. Average amount paid per academic year: $12,000. Average number of hours worked per week: 20. Tuition remission given: full. Research assistantships available for advanced students. Average amount paid per academic year: $14,000. Average number of hours worked per week: 20. Tuition remission given: full. Traineeships available for advanced students. Average amount paid per academic year: $14,000. Average number of hours worked per week: 20. Tuition remission given: partial. Fellowships and scholarships available for advanced students. Average amount paid per academic year: $19,000. Average number of hours worked per week: 20. Apply by February 1. Tuition remission given: full.

Additional Information: Of all students currently enrolled full time, 75% benefited from one or more of the listed financial assistance programs. Application and information available online at http://www.slu.edu/graduate/apply_now.html.

Internships/Practica: Doctoral Degree (PhD Clinical): For those doctoral students for whom a professional internship was required in this program prior to graduation, (10) students applied for an internship in 2006–2007, with (7) students obtaining an internship. Of those students who obtained an internship, (7) were paid internships. Of those students who obtained an internship, (7) students placed in APA/CPA-accredited internships, (0) students placed in internships not APA/CPA-accredited, but listed with the Association of Psychology Postdoctoral and Internship Centers (APPIC), (0) students placed in internships conforming to guidelines of the Council of Directors of School Psychology Programs (CDSPP), (0) students placed in internships that were not APA/CPA-accredited, APPIC or CDSPP listed. Opportunities for additional training and experience in clinical practice, research, and teaching are available through graduate assistantships and clerkships either within the university or at external placements in the community. These assistantships and clerkships provide financial support for students, as well as opportunities for supervised teaching, research, and clinical experience.

Housing and Day Care: No on-campus housing is available. No on-campus day care facilities are available.

Employment of Department Graduates:

Master's Degree Graduates: Of those who graduated in the academic year 2006–2007, the following categories and numbers represent the postgraduate activities and employment of master's degree graduates: Enrolled in a postdoctoral residency/fellowship (n/a), employed in independent practice (n/a), total from the above (master's) (0).

Doctoral Degree Graduates: Of those who graduated in the academic year 2006–2007, the following categories and numbers represent the postgraduate activities and employment of doctoral degree graduates: Enrolled in a psychology doctoral program (n/a), enrolled in a postdoctoral residency/fellowship (8), employed in an academic position at a university (1), employed in other positions at a higher education institution (1), employed in business or industry (3), employed in a hospital/medical center (4), total from the above (doctoral) (17).

Additional Information:

Orientation, Objectives, and Emphasis of Department: Our mission is to educate students in the discipline of psychology and its applications. We encourage intellectual curiosity, critical thinking, and ethical responsibility in our teaching, research, and practice. Our commitment to value-based, holistic education and our enthusiasm for psychology is realized in the products of our research, in our graduates, and in service to others. The Clinical Psychology Program offers broad-based education and training in both the science and practice of psychology to prepare its graduates to function as competent, ethical scientist–practitioners across a wide range of settings with diverse populations, problems and approaches. The Experimental Psychology program offers three concentrations of study: Developmental Psychology, Cognitive Neuroscience, and Social Psychology. The Developmental concentration emphasizes the development of children and adolescents with a focus on diversity, including gender, race, ethnicity, and culture. The Cognitive Neuroscience concentration reflects the interests of the faculty in the areas of memory, cognitive aging, language processing, and sleep. The Social Psychology concentration focuses on the study of attitudes and social influence, close relationships, victimization, prejudice, stigma and racial identity, and the social psychology of health. The Industrial/Organizational Psychology Program at Saint Louis University prepares doctoral-level professionals with the research, assessment and intervention skills to impact organizations, groups, and individuals at work.

Special Facilities or Resources: The Clinical Program operates an on-campus Psychological Services Center, which serves as a primary site for supervised clinical experiences with children, adolescents, adults, couples and families. The Clinical Program also has established collaborative relationships with various hospitals, agencies, institutions, and private practitioners throughout the community to provide advanced training and experience in the science and practice of psychology. Resources available to the Experimental students include animal housing; research suites for neuroscience and sleep research; and several laboratory suites for social, cognitive, and developmental research. In addition to space for laboratory research, the students in the Industrial/Organizational Program are involved with the Center for the Application of the Behavioral Science. Housed within the department, this Center provides opportunities for training in organizational consulting and program evaluation in field settings.

Information for Students With Physical Disabilities: See the following Web site for more information: http://www.slu.edu/services/daa/disabilities_services.html.

Application Information:
Send to The Graduate School, Saint Louis University, 3634 Lindell Boulevard, Suite 117, St. Louis, MO 63108, (314) 977-2240. Application available online. URL of online application: http://www.slu.edu/graduate/apply_now.html. Students are admitted in the Fall, application deadline January 1. *Fee:* $40.

Washington University in St. Louis

Department of Psychology
One Brookings Drive, Box 1125
St. Louis, MO 63130
Telephone: (314) 935-6520
Fax: (314) 935-7588
E-mail: *mcclelland@wustl.edu*
Web: *http://www.artsci.wustl.edu/~psych/index.html*

Department Information:
1924. Chairperson: Randy J. Larsen. Number of faculty: total—full-time 33, part-time 1; women—full-time 11; total—minority—full-time 3; women minority—full-time 1.

Programs and Degrees Offered:
Listed in the following order: Program area, degree type (T if terminal Master's), number awarded 7/06–6/07. Clinical PhD (Doctor of Philosophy) 2, Aging and Development PhD (Doctor of Philosophy) 0, Behavior, Brain, and Cognition PhD (Doctor of Philosophy) 2, Social and Personality PhD (Doctor of Philosophy) 1.

APA Accreditation: Clinical PhD (Doctor of Philosophy).

Student Applications/Admissions:
Student Applications
Clinical PhD (Doctor of Philosophy)—Applications 2007–2008, 131. Total applicants accepted 2007–2008, 12. Number full-time enrolled (new admits only) 2007–2008, 2. Number part-time enrolled (new admits only) 2007–2008, 0. Openings 2008–2009, 6. The median number of years required for completion of a degree in 2006–2007 were 6. The number of students enrolled full- and part-time who were dismissed or voluntarily withdrew from this program area in 2007–2008 were 0. *Aging and Development PhD (Doctor of Philosophy)*—Applications 2007–2008, 8. Total applicants accepted 2007–2008, 0. Number full-time enrolled (new admits only) 2007–2008, 2. Number part-time enrolled (new admits only) 2007–2008, 0. Openings 2008–2009, 2. The number of students enrolled full- and part-time who were dismissed or voluntarily withdrew from this program area in 2007–2008 were 0. *Behavior, Brain, and Cognition PhD (Doctor of Philosophy)*—Applications 2007–2008, 47. Total applicants accepted 2007–2008, 12. Number full-time enrolled (new admits only) 2007–2008, 7. Number part-time enrolled (new admits only) 2007–2008, 0. Openings 2008–2009, 10. The median number of years required for completion of a degree in 2006–2007 were 6. The number of students enrolled full- and part-time who were dismissed or voluntarily withdrew from this program area in 2007–2008 were 0. *Social and Personality PhD (Doctor of Philosophy)*—Applications 2007–2008, 27. Total applicants accepted 2007–2008, 3. Number full-time enrolled (new admits only) 2007–2008, 0. Number part-time enrolled (new admits only) 2007–2008, 0. Openings 2008–2009, 3. The median number of years required for completion of a degree in 2006–2007 were 6. The number of students enrolled full- and part-time who were dismissed or voluntarily withdrew from this program area in 2007–2008 were 0.

Admissions Requirements:
Scores: Entries appear in this order: required test or GPA, minimum score (if required), median score of students entering in 2007–2008. Doctoral Programs: GRE-V no minimum stated, 670; GRE-Q no minimum stated, 670; Doctoral program GRE-Analytic no minimum stated.
Other Criteria: (importance of criteria rated low, medium, or high): GRE/MAT scores—high, research experience—high, work experience—medium, clinically related public service—low, GPA—medium, letters of recommendation—high, interview—high, statement of goals and objectives—high, undergraduate major in psychology—medium, specific undergraduate psychology courses taken—medium. Interview is required for applicants prior to acceptance.

Student Characteristics: The following represents characteristics of students in 2007–2008 in all graduate psychology programs in the department: Female—full-time 50, part-time 0; Male—full-time 35, part-time 0; African American/Black—full-time 3, part-time 0; Hispanic/Latino(a)—full-time 2, part-time 0; Asian/Pacific Islander—full-time 9, part-time 0; American Indian/Alaska Native—full-time 0, part-time 0; Caucasian/White—full-time 57, part-time 0; Multi-ethnic—full-time 0, part-time 0; students subject to the Americans With Disabilities Act—full-time 0, part-time 0; Unknown ethnicity—full-time 14, part-time 0; International students who hold an F-1 or J-1 Visa—full-time 13, part-time 0.

Financial Information/Assistance:
Tuition for Full-Time Study: *Doctoral:* State residents: per academic year $36,200; Nonstate residents: per academic year $36,200.

Financial Assistance:

First-Year Students: Research assistantships available for first year. Average amount paid per academic year: $19,110. Average number of hours worked per week: 10. Tuition remission given: full. Traineeships available for first year. Average amount paid per academic year: $18,000. Average number of hours worked per week: 0. Tuition remission given: full. Fellowships and scholarships available for first year. Average amount paid per academic year: $20,000. Average number of hours worked per week: 0. Apply by January 25. Tuition remission given: full.

Advanced Students: Teaching assistantships available for advanced students. Average amount paid per academic year: $19,000. Average number of hours worked per week: 10. Tuition remission given: full. Research assistantships available for advanced students. Average amount paid per academic year: $19,000. Average number of hours worked per week: 15. Tuition remission given: full. Traineeships available for advanced students. Average amount paid per academic year: $20,772. Average number of hours worked per week: 0. Tuition remission given: full. Fellowships and scholarships available for advanced students. Average amount paid per academic year: $19,110. Average number of hours worked per week: 0. Tuition remission given: full.

Additional Information: Of all students currently enrolled full time, 100% benefited from one or more of the listed financial assistance programs.

Internships/Practica: No information provided.

Housing and Day Care: On-campus housing is available. Although on-campus housing is available, this is an option that is reserved to undergraduates. On-campus day care facilities are available.

Employment of Department Graduates:

Master's Degree Graduates: Of those who graduated in the academic year 2006–2007, the following categories and numbers represent the postgraduate activities and employment of master's degree graduates: Enrolled in a postdoctoral residency/fellowship (n/a), employed in independent practice (n/a), total from the above (master's) (0).

Doctoral Degree Graduates: Of those who graduated in the academic year 2006–2007, the following categories and numbers represent the postgraduate activities and employment of doctoral degree graduates: Enrolled in a psychology doctoral program (n/a), enrolled in a postdoctoral residency/fellowship (2), employed in an academic position at a university (3), total from the above (doctoral) (5).

Additional Information:

Orientation, Objectives, and Emphasis of Department: The emphasis within the clinical program is on training clinical scientists and promoting an integration of science and practice. Its goal is to train students who will lead the search for knowledge regarding the assessment, understanding, and treatment of psychological disorders. In the experimental programs, the development of generalists with one or more areas of specialization is the department's orientation.

Special Facilities or Resources: The department's extensive facilities include animal, human psychophysiological, psychoacoustic, and clinical training laboratories; computer labs; closed circuit TV; and Neuroimaging (fMRI) and Image Analysis Laboratory.

Application Information:

Send to Meg McClelland, Graduate Program Coordinator, Washington University, Department of Psychology, Campus Box 1125, St. Louis, MO 63130-4899. Application available online. URL of online application: https://www.apply.embark.com/grad/washu/gsas/. Students are admitted in the Fall, application deadline December 15. January 25 Chancellor's Fellowship (for candidates with undergraduate degrees from U.S. institutions who would enhance diversity at the university); February 1 Olin Women's Fellowship (for female candidates with undergraduate degrees from U.S. institutions). *Fee:* $35. Candidate must have attended an undergraduate institution within the United States and have received financial assistance. Fee wavier must be completed by a representative from the financial aid office at the undergraduate institution.

Montana State University

Department of Psychology
Letters and Science
304 Traphagen Hall, P.O. Box 173440
Bozeman, MT 59717-3440
Telephone: (406) 994-3801
Fax: (406) 994-3804
E-mail: *banderson@montana.edu*
Web: *http://www.montana.edu/wwwpy*

Department Information:

1950. Chairperson: Richard A. Block, PhD. Number of faculty: total—full-time 8, part-time 4; women—full-time 2, part-time 3.

Programs and Degrees Offered:

Listed in the following order: Program area, degree type (T if terminal Master's), number awarded 7/06–6/07. Psychological Science MA/MS (Master of Arts/Science) 6.

Student Applications/Admissions:

Student Applications

Psychological Science MA/MS (Master of Arts/Science)—Applications 2007–2008, 22. Total applicants accepted 2007–2008, 8. Number full-time enrolled (new admits only) 2007–2008, 7. Total enrolled 2007–2008 full-time, 14. Openings 2008–2009, 7. The median number of years required for completion of a degree in 2006–2007 were 2. The number of students enrolled full- and part-time who were dismissed or voluntarily withdrew from this program area in 2007–2008 were 1.

Admissions Requirements:

Scores: Entries appear in this order: required test or GPA, minimum score (if required), median score of students entering in 2007–2008. Master's Programs: GRE-V 500, 540; GRE-Q 500, 660; overall undergraduate GPA 3.00, 3.50; last 2 years GPA 3.00; psychology GPA 3.00, 3.70. GRE subject test in psychology required if not an undergrad psychology major.

Other Criteria: (importance of criteria rated low, medium, or high): GRE/MAT scores—medium, research experience—high, work experience—low, extracurricular activity—low, GPA—high, letters of recommendation—high, interview—low, statement of goals and objectives—high. For additional information on admission requirements, go to http://www.montana.edu/wwwpy.

Student Characteristics: The following represents characteristics of students in 2007–2008 in all graduate psychology programs in the department: Female—full-time 6, part-time 0; Male—full-time 6, part-time 0; African American/Black—full-time 0, part-time 0; Hispanic/Latino(a)—full-time 0, part-time 0; Asian/Pacific Islander—full-time 0, part-time 0; American Indian/Alaska Native—full-time 0, part-time 0; Caucasian/White—full-time 12, part-time 0; Multi-ethnic—full-time 0, part-time 0; students subject to the Americans With Disabilities Act—full-time 0, part-time 0; Unknown ethnicity—full-time 0, part-time 0.

Financial Information/Assistance:

Tuition for Full-Time Study: *Master's:* State residents: $320 per credit hour; Nonstate residents: $731 per credit hour. Tuition is subject to change. See the following Web site for updates and changes in tuition costs: http://www.montana.edu/wwwcat/expenses/FeeGrad.html.

Financial Assistance:

First-Year Students: Teaching assistantships available for first year. Average amount paid per academic year: $10,011. Average number of hours worked per week: 20. Apply by February 1. Tuition remission given: full. Fellowships and scholarships available for first year. Average amount paid per academic year: $1,000. Apply by February 1.

Advanced Students: Teaching assistantships available for advanced students. Average amount paid per academic year: $10,011. Average number of hours worked per week: 20. Apply by February 1. Tuition remission given: full.

Additional Information: Of all students currently enrolled full time, 100% benefited from one or more of the listed financial assistance programs. Application and information available online at http://www.montana.edu/wwwpy/msprogram.htm.

Internships/Practica: No information provided.

Housing and Day Care: On-campus housing is available. See the following Web site for more information: http://www.montana.edu/fgh/information/housing-options.php. On-campus day care facilities are available. See the following Web site for more information: http://www.montana.edu/wwwecp/network.html.

Employment of Department Graduates:

Master's Degree Graduates: Of those who graduated in the academic year 2006–2007, the following categories and numbers represent the postgraduate activities and employment of master's degree graduates: Enrolled in a psychology doctoral program (6), enrolled in another graduate/professional program (0), enrolled in a postdoctoral residency/fellowship (n/a), employed in independent practice (n/a), employed in an academic position at a university (0), employed in an academic position at a 2-year/4-year college (0), employed in other positions at a higher education institution (0), employed in a professional position in a school system (0), employed in business or industry (0), employed in government agency (0), employed in a community mental health/counseling center (0), employed in a hospital/medical center (0), still seeking employment (0), not seeking employment (0), other employment position (0), do not know (0), total from the above (master's) (6).

Doctoral Degree Graduates: Of those who graduated in the academic year 2006–2007, the following categories and numbers represent the postgraduate activities and employment of doctoral degree graduates: Enrolled in a psychology doctoral program (n/a), total from the above (doctoral) (0).

Additional Information:

Orientation, Objectives, and Emphasis of Department: Our 2-year, research-oriented MS program in psychological science is designed for students interested mainly in obtaining a PhD degree in areas such as cognitive psychology, social psychology, physiological psychology, and health psychology. Areas of faculty interest include cognitive psychology, social psychology, physiological psychology, and health psychology.

Special Facilities or Resources: Office space provided for graduate students, all of whom are graduate teaching assistants. Laboratory space for human and animal research is available.

Information for Students With Physical Disabilities: See the following Web site for more information: http://www.montana.edu/wwwres/disability/index.shtml.

Application Information:
Send to Graduate Admissions, Department of Psychology, 304 Traphagen Hall, Montana State University, P.O. Box 173440, Bozeman, MT 59717-3440. Application available online. URL of online application: http://www.montana.edu/gradstudies/apply.shtml. Students are admitted in the Fall, application deadline February 1. The Division of Graduate Education application form can be obtained and completed online at http://www.montana.edu/gradstudies/apply.shtml. However, you must also submit information using our department's supplemental form that can be obtained at http://www.montana.edu/wwwpy/gradprogram/supplemental.pdf. There is an essay requirement: In your application materials, you must include a one- to two-page letter of intent and personal statement that summarizes your academic background in psychology or related field, career plans, research experience, research interests, and why you are applying to Montana State University's MS program in psychological science. *Fee:* $50.

Montana, The University of

Department of Psychology
Arts and Sciences
143 Skaggs Building
Missoula, MT 59812-1584
Telephone: (406) 243-4521
Fax: (406) 243-6366
E-mail: *allen.szalda-petree@umontana.edu*
Web: *http://www.umt.edu/psych/*

Department Information:
1920. Chairperson: Allen Szalda-Petree. Number of faculty: total—full-time 18, part-time 1; women—full-time 7, part-time 1; total—minority—full-time 1; women minority—full-time 1.

Programs and Degrees Offered:
Listed in the following order: Program area, degree type (T if terminal Master's), number awarded 7/06–6/07. Clinical PhD (Doctor of Philosophy) 3, Developmental PhD (Doctor of Philosophy) 0, School MA/MS (Master of Arts/Science) (T) 6, School PhD (Doctor of Philosophy) 0, Animal Behavior–Cognition PhD (Doctor of Philosophy) 1.

APA Accreditation: Clinical PhD (Doctor of Philosophy).

Student Applications/Admissions:
Student Applications
Clinical PhD (Doctor of Philosophy)—Applications 2007–2008, 142. Total applicants accepted 2007–2008, 7. Number full-time enrolled (new admits only) 2007–2008, 7. Number part-time enrolled (new admits only) 2007–2008, 0. Total enrolled 2007–2008 full-time, 23, part-time, 17. Openings 2008–2009, 6. The median number of years required for completion of a degree in 2006–2007 were 6. The number of students enrolled full- and part-time who were dismissed or voluntarily withdrew from this program area in 2007–2008 were 0. *Developmental PhD (Doctor of Philosophy)*—Applications 2007–2008, 10. Total applicants accepted 2007–2008, 0. Number full-time enrolled (new admits only) 2007–2008, 0. Number part-time enrolled (new admits only) 2007–2008, 0. Total enrolled 2007–2008 full-time, 3, part-time, 1. Openings 2008–2009, 2. The number of students enrolled full- and part-time who were dismissed or voluntarily withdrew from this program area in 2007–2008 were 1. *School MA/MS (Master of Arts/Science)*—Applications 2007–2008, 14. Total applicants accepted 2007–2008, 6. Number full-time enrolled (new admits only) 2007–2008, 6. Number part-time enrolled (new admits only) 2007–2008, 0. Total enrolled 2007–2008 full-time, 14, part-time, 1. Openings 2008–2009, 4. The median number of years required for completion of a degree in 2006–2007 were 2. The number of students enrolled full- and part-time who were dismissed or voluntarily withdrew from this program area in 2007–2008 were 2. *School PhD (Doctor of Philosophy)*—Applications 2007–2008, 4. Total applicants accepted 2007–2008, 2. Number full-time enrolled (new admits only) 2007–2008, 2. Number part-time enrolled (new admits only) 2007–2008, 0. Openings 2008–2009, 1. The number of students enrolled full- and part-time who were dismissed or voluntarily withdrew from this program area in 2007–2008 were 0. *Animal Behavior–Cognition PhD (Doctor of Philosophy)*—Applications 2007–2008, 6. Total applicants accepted 2007–2008, 0. Number full-time enrolled (new admits only) 2007–2008, 0. Number part-time enrolled (new admits only) 2007–2008, 0. Openings 2008–2009, 2. The median number of years required for completion of a degree in 2006–2007 were 4. The number of students enrolled full- and part-time who were dismissed or voluntarily withdrew from this program area in 2007–2008 were 0.

Admissions Requirements:
Scores: Entries appear in this order: required test or GPA, minimum score (if required), median score of students entering in 2007–2008. Master's Programs: GRE-V 500, 410; GRE-Q 500, 460; GRE-Subject (Psychology) no minimum stated; last 2 years GPA 3.25, 3.30. Above (#11) information is for School Psychology terminal MA program. Doctoral Programs: GRE-V 525, 535; GRE-Q 525, 630; GRE-Subject (Psychology) no minimum stated; overall undergraduate GPA 3.25, 3.5. The Clinical program requires scores at 50th percentile or above for GRE Quantitative and Verbal.
Other Criteria: (importance of criteria rated low, medium, or high): GRE/MAT scores—high, research experience—medium, work experience—medium, extracurricular activity—low, clinically related public service—medium, GPA—high, letters of recommendation—high, interview—medium, statement of goals and objectives—medium. Clinical service is a criterion for clinical program only. For additional information on admission requirements, go to http://www2.umt.edu/psych/gradinfo.htm.

Student Characteristics: The following represents characteristics of students in 2007–2008 in all graduate psychology programs

in the department: Female—full-time 37, part-time 16; Male—full-time 9, part-time 3; African American/Black—full-time 1, part-time 1; Hispanic/Latino(a)—full-time 1, part-time 0; Asian/Pacific Islander—full-time 2, part-time 0; American Indian/Alaska Native—full-time 3, part-time 3; Caucasian/White—full-time 39, part-time 15; Multi-ethnic—full-time 0, part-time 0; students subject to the Americans With Disabilities Act—full-time 0, part-time 0; Unknown ethnicity—full-time 0, part-time 0; International students who hold an F-1 or J-1 Visa—full-time 0, part-time 0.

Financial Information/Assistance:

Tuition for Full-Time Study: *Master's:* State residents: per academic year $5,817, $288 per credit hour; Nonstate residents: per academic year $17,224, $763 per credit hour. *Doctoral:* State residents: per academic year $6,401, $312 per credit hour; Nonstate residents: per academic year $17,848, $789 per credit hour. Tuition is subject to change. See the following Web site for updates and changes in tuition costs: http://www.umt.edu/grad/money/.

Financial Assistance:

First-Year Students: Teaching assistantships available for first year. Average amount paid per academic year: $14,000. Average number of hours worked per week: 15. Apply by January 1. Tuition remission given: full. Research assistantships available for first year. Average amount paid per academic year: $12,000. Average number of hours worked per week: 15. Apply by open.

Advanced Students: Teaching assistantships available for advanced students. Average amount paid per academic year: $14,000. Average number of hours worked per week: 15. Apply by January 15. Tuition remission given: full. Research assistantships available for advanced students. Average amount paid per academic year: $12,000. Average number of hours worked per week: 15. Apply by open.

Additional Information: Of all students currently enrolled full time, 63% benefited from one or more of the listed financial assistance programs. Application and information available online at http://www.umt.edu/grad/.

Internships/Practica: No information provided.

Housing and Day Care: On-campus housing is available. Housing: University Villages, phone (406) 243-6030. On-campus day care facilities are available. Child Care: ASUM Office of Child Care, phone (406) 243-2542.

Employment of Department Graduates:

Master's Degree Graduates: Of those who graduated in the academic year 2006–2007, the following categories and numbers represent the postgraduate activities and employment of master's degree graduates: Enrolled in a postdoctoral residency/fellowship (n/a), employed in independent practice (n/a), employed in a professional position in a school system (6), total from the above (master's) (6).

Doctoral Degree Graduates: Of those who graduated in the academic year 2006–2007, the following categories and numbers represent the postgraduate activities and employment of doctoral degree graduates: Enrolled in a psychology doctoral program (n/a), enrolled in a postdoctoral residency/fellowship (1), employed in independent practice (1), employed in other positions at a higher education institution (1), still seeking employment (1), total from the above (doctoral) (4).

Additional Information:

Orientation, Objectives, and Emphasis of Department: The Clinical Psychology PhD program trains students in basic psychological science and clinical skills including assessment, diagnosis, and therapeutic interventions. The program is based on the scientist–practitioner model and a variety of theoretical orientations are represented and taught. The training is a balanced combination of coursework, practicum, and research. Upon completion of the program, graduates are well prepared for professional careers as clinical psychologists in institutional, academic, and private settings. In addition to generalist training, two specialty emphases are also offered: child and family, and neuropsychology. The Experimental Psychology PhD program offers major emphases in the fields of animal behavior–cognition and life span developmental psychology. Minor areas are offered in quantitative, program evaluation, and special areas of psychology (e.g., cognitive and social), as well as those fields in which majors are offered. Graduates have found placement in academic, research, and applied settings. The School Psychology program offers both doctoral (PhD) and specialist (EdS) level training based on the scientist–scholar–practitioner model and aimed at professional preparation of school psychologists who are grounded thoroughly in the principles of human development, behavior, and educational psychology. Doctoral candidates are trained to assume leadership roles in academia, research, and clinical and school practice. Specialist-level candidates are trained to provide psychoeducational services on a systems and individual basis.

Special Facilities or Resources: The Department of Psychology is housed in a modern building. It has classrooms; offices; research laboratories for social, developmental, and learning experimentation; and colony rooms for small animals. A clinical psychology center opened in the fall of 1983 and serves as a meeting place for clinical classes, seminars, research groups, and clinical services.

Information for Students With Physical Disabilities: See the following Web site for more information: http://www.umt.edu/dss/.

Application Information:

Send to Graduate Admissions, Department of Psychology, The University of Montana, Skaggs Building 143, Missoula, MT 59812-1584. Application available online. URL of online application: http://www.applyweb.com/apply/uomont/menu.html. Students are admitted in the Fall, application deadline January 1. The January 1 deadline is a firm date for the Clinical program. For Developmental and Animal Behavior–Cognition, October 15 is also acceptable. Late applications may be reviewed for the School Psychology programs. All deadlines are postmark dates. *Fee:* $45.

Nebraska, University of, Lincoln

Department of Educational Psychology
Teachers College
114 Teachers College Hall
Lincoln, NE 68588-0345
Telephone: (402) 472-2223
Fax: (402) 472-8319
E-mail: *rdeayala@unlserve.unl.edu*
Web: *http://www.edpsyc.unl.edu*

Department Information:

1908. Chairperson: R. J. De Ayala. Number of faculty: total—full-time 12; women—full-time 8.

Programs and Degrees Offered:

Listed in the following order: Program area, degree type (T if terminal Master's), number awarded 7/06–6/07. Cognition, Learning, Development PhD (Doctor of Philosophy) 3, Counseling PhD (Doctor of Philosophy) 6, Quantitative, Qualitative, and Psychometric Methods PhD (Doctor of Philosophy) 3, School PhD (Doctor of Philosophy) 7.

APA Accreditation: Counseling PhD (Doctor of Philosophy). School PhD (Doctor of Philosophy).

Student Applications/Admissions:

Student Applications

Cognition, Learning, Development PhD (Doctor of Philosophy)—Applications 2007–2008, 29. Total applicants accepted 2007–2008, 13. Number full-time enrolled (new admits only) 2007–2008, 9. Total enrolled 2007–2008 full-time, 30, part-time, 10. Openings 2008–2009, 5. *Counseling PhD (Doctor of Philosophy)*—Applications 2007–2008, 80. Total applicants accepted 2007–2008, 17. Number full-time enrolled (new admits only) 2007–2008, 9. Total enrolled 2007–2008 full-time, 49, part-time, 1. Openings 2008–2009, 9. *Quantitative, Qualitative, and Psychometric Methods PhD (Doctor of Philosophy)*—Applications 2007–2008, 23. Total applicants accepted 2007–2008, 16. Number full-time enrolled (new admits only) 2007–2008, 10. Total enrolled 2007–2008 full-time, 19, part-time, 10. Openings 2008–2009, 5. *School PhD (Doctor of Philosophy)*—Applications 2007–2008, 39. Total applicants accepted 2007–2008, 9. Number full-time enrolled (new admits only) 2007–2008, 6. Openings 2008–2009, 10.

Admissions Requirements:

Scores: Entries appear in this order: required test or GPA, minimum score (if required), median score of students entering in 2007–2008. Master's Programs: GRE-V no minimum stated, 500; GRE-Q no minimum stated, 575; overall undergraduate GPA no minimum stated, 3.00; psychology GPA no minimum stated. Doctoral Programs: GRE-V no minimum stated, 550; GRE-Q no minimum stated, 550; overall undergraduate GPA no minimum stated, 3.00.

Other Criteria: (importance of criteria rated low, medium, or high): GRE/MAT scores—high, research experience—high, work experience—high, extracurricular activity—medium, clinically related public service—high, GPA—high, letters of recommendation—high, interview—high, statement of goals and objectives—high. Minimum TOEFL score of 550.

Student Characteristics: The following represents characteristics of students in 2007–2008 in all graduate psychology programs in the department: Female—full-time 125, part-time 6; Male—full-time 18, part-time 15; African American/Black—full-time 5, part-time 0; Hispanic/Latino(a)—full-time 6, part-time 0; Asian/Pacific Islander—full-time 18, part-time 0; American Indian/Alaska Native—full-time 1, part-time 0; Caucasian/White—full-time 112, part-time 21; Multi-ethnic—full-time 0, part-time 0; students subject to the Americans With Disabilities Act—full-time 0, part-time 0; Unknown ethnicity—full-time 1, part-time 0; International students who hold an F-1 or J-1 Visa—full-time 11, part-time 0.

Financial Information/Assistance:

Tuition for Full-Time Study: *Master's:* State residents: $224 per credit hour; Nonstate residents: $604 per credit hour. *Doctoral:* State residents: $224 per credit hour; Nonstate residents: $604 per credit hour. Tuition is subject to change. See the following Web site for updates and changes in tuition costs: http://www.unl.edu/gradstudies/prospective/money.shtml.

Financial Assistance:

First-Year Students: Teaching assistantships available for first year. Average amount paid per academic year: $14,269. Average number of hours worked per week: 20. Tuition remission given: full. Research assistantships available for first year. Average amount paid per academic year: $14,269. Average number of hours worked per week: 20. Tuition remission given: full. Fellowships and scholarships available for first year. Average amount paid per academic year: $8,789. Average number of hours worked per week: 13. Tuition remission given: full.

Advanced Students: Teaching assistantships available for advanced students. Average number of hours worked per week: 20. Tuition remission given: full. Research assistantships available for advanced students. Average number of hours worked per week: 20. Tuition remission given: full. Fellowships and scholarships available for advanced students. Average amount paid per academic year: $8,789. Average number of hours worked per week: 13. Tuition remission given: full.

Additional Information: Of all students currently enrolled full time, 66% benefited from one or more of the listed financial assistance programs.

Internships/Practica: Doctoral Degree (PhD Counseling): For those doctoral students for whom a professional internship was required in this program prior to graduation, (3) students applied for an internship in 2006–2007, with (3) students obtaining an internship. Of those students who obtained an internship, (3) were paid internships. Of those students who obtained an internship, (3) students placed in APA/CPA-accredited internships, (0) students placed in internships not APA/CPA-accredited, but listed with the Association of Psychology Postdoctoral and Internship Centers (APPIC), (0) students placed in internships conforming to guidelines of the Council of Directors of School Psychology Programs (CDSPP), (0) students placed in internships that were not APA/CPA-accredited, APPIC or CDSPP listed. Doctoral Degree (PhD School): For those doctoral students for whom a professional internship was required in this program prior to graduation, (7) students applied for an internship in 2006–2007, with (7) students obtaining an internship. Of those students who obtained an internship, (7) were paid internships. Of those students who obtained an internship, (7) students placed in APA/CPA-accredited internships, (0) students placed in internships not APA/CPA-accredited, but listed with the Association of Psychology Postdoctoral and Internship Centers (APPIC), (0) students placed in internships conforming to guidelines of the Council of Directors of School Psychology Programs (CDSPP), (0) students placed in internships that were not APA/CPA accredited, APPIC or CDSPP listed. The Counseling Psychology and School Psychology programs both have sets of practicum courses wherein students provide direct and consultation services to students, staff and families in urban school settings. The Nebraska Internship Consortium in Professional Psychology is affiliated with the School Psychology Program. Doctoral students in the QQPM program are encouraged to obtain internships.

Housing and Day Care: On-campus housing is available. See the following Web site for more information: http://www.unl.edu/gradstudies/prospective/housing.shtml. On-campus day care facilities are available. See the following Web site for more information: http://www.hr.unl.edu/er/childcare.cfm and http://www.unl.edu/neunion/ChildCare/ChildFee.html.

Employment of Department Graduates:

Master's Degree Graduates: Of those who graduated in the academic year 2006–2007, the following categories and numbers represent the postgraduate activities and employment of master's degree graduates: Enrolled in a postdoctoral residency/fellowship (n/a), employed in independent practice (n/a), total from the above (master's) (0).

Doctoral Degree Graduates: Of those who graduated in the academic year 2006–2007, the following categories and numbers represent the postgraduate activities and employment of doctoral degree graduates: Enrolled in a psychology doctoral program (n/a), total from the above (doctoral) (0).

Additional Information:

Orientation, Objectives, and Emphasis of Department: The objective of the program is to develop applied behavioral scientists able to function in a variety of settings and roles ranging from educational settings to private practice. The broad base of the department offers a diversity of orientations and role models for students.

Special Facilities or Resources: The department operates the Counseling and School Psychology Clinic, which serves as a practicum site for School Psychology and Counseling Psychology programs. In addition, the department maintains excellent contact with the community, which promotes access to practical experiences and research subject pools. The department contains the Buros Center for Testing and its comprehensive reference library of assessment devices. The department also is home to the Center for Instructional Innovation, which conducts research on teaching and learning as well as the Nebraska Research Center on Children, Youth, Families, and Schools.

Information for Students With Physical Disabilities: See the following Web site for more information: http://www.unl.edu/equity/.

Application Information:

Send to Attention: Emily Burgess, Admissions Coordinator, Department of Educational Psychology, 114 Teachers College Hall, University of Nebraska—Lincoln, Lincoln, NE 68405. Application available online. URL of online application: http://www.edpsyc.unl.edu/graduate/apply.shtml. Students are admitted in the Fall, application deadline December 1–5, January 15; Spring, application deadline October 1. School Psychology program considers applications for admission December 1; Counseling Psychology program considers applications for admission December 5; Cognition, Learning, and Developmental consider applications for admissions at October 1, January 15, and May 15 deadlines. Quantitative, Qualitative, and Psychometric Methods (QQPM) considers applications for admissions at October 1 and January 15 deadline. *Fee:* $45. Written request for waiver of fee indicating need and justification for waiver or deferral of application fee.

Nebraska, University of, Lincoln

Department of Psychology
Arts and Sciences
238 Burnett Hall
Lincoln, NE 68588-0308
Telephone: (402) 472-3721
Fax: (402) 472-4637
E-mail: *jlongwell1@unl.edu*
Web: *http://www.unl.edu/psypage*

Department Information:

1889. Chairperson: David J. Hansen. Number of faculty: total—full-time 22; women—full-time 8; total—minority—full-time 4; women minority—full-time 1.

Programs and Degrees Offered:

Listed in the following order: Program area, degree type (T if terminal Master's), number awarded 7/06–6/07. Clinical PhD (Doctor of Philosophy) 7, Cognitive PhD (Doctor of Philosophy) 1, Law and Psychology, PhD (Doctor of Philosophy) 2, Comparative and Biopsychology PhD (Doctor of Philosophy) 1, Developmental PhD (Doctor of Philosophy) 2, Social–Personality PhD (Doctor of Philosophy) 1.

APA Accreditation: Clinical PhD (Doctor of Philosophy).

Student Applications/Admissions:

Student Applications

Clinical PhD (Doctor of Philosophy)—Applications 2007–2008, 200. Total applicants accepted 2007–2008, 10. Number full-time enrolled (new admits only) 2007–2008, 10. Total enrolled 2007–2008 full-time, 53. Openings 2008–2009, 10. The median number of years required for completion of a degree in 2006–2007 were 6. The number of students enrolled full- and part-time who were dismissed or voluntarily withdrew from this program area in 2007–2008 were 0. *Cognitive PhD (Doctor of Philosophy)*—Applications 2007–2008, 11. Total applicants accepted 2007–2008, 2. Number full-time enrolled (new admits only) 2007–2008, 1. Number part-time enrolled (new admits only) 2007–2008, 0. Openings 2008–2009, 1. The median number of years required for completion of a degree in 2006–2007 were 5. The number of students enrolled full- and part-time who were dismissed or voluntarily withdrew from this program area in 2007–2008 were 0. *Law and Psychology, PhD (Doctor of Philosophy)*—Applications 2007–2008, 25. Total applicants accepted 2007–2008, 1. Number full-time enrolled (new admits only) 2007–2008, 1. Number part-time enrolled (new admits only) 2007–2008, 0. Openings 2008–2009, 4. The median number of years required for completion of a degree in 2006–2007 were 5. The number of students enrolled full- and part-time who were dismissed or voluntarily withdrew from this program area in 2007–2008 were 0. *Comparative/ Biopsychology PhD (Doctor of Philosophy)*—Applications 2007–2008, 20. Total applicants accepted 2007–2008, 2. Number full-time enrolled (new admits only) 2007–2008, 1. Openings 2008–2009, 2. The median number of years required for completion of a degree in 2006–2007 were 5. The number of students enrolled full- and part-time who were dismissed or voluntarily withdrew from this program area in 2007–2008 were 0. *Developmental PhD (Doctor of Philosophy)*—Applications 2007–2008, 20. Total applicants accepted 2007–2008, 4. Number full-time enrolled (new admits only) 2007–2008, 4. Number part-time enrolled (new admits only) 2007–2008, 0. Openings 2008–2009, 3. The median number of years required for completion of a degree in 2006–2007 were 5. The number of students enrolled full- and part-time who were dismissed or voluntarily withdrew from this program area in 2007–2008 were 0. *Social–Personality PhD (Doctor of Philosophy)*—Applications 2007–2008, 39. Total applicants accepted 2007–2008, 1. Number full-time enrolled (new admits only) 2007–2008, 1. Number part-time enrolled (new admits only) 2007–2008, 0. Openings 2008–2009, 2. The median number of years required for completion of a degree in 2006–2007 were 5. The number of students enrolled full- and part-time who were dismissed or voluntarily withdrew from this program area in 2007–2008 were 0.

Admissions Requirements:

Scores: Entries appear in this order: required test or GPA, minimum score (if required), median score of students entering in 2007–2008. Doctoral Programs: GRE-V no minimum stated, 610; GRE-Q no minimum stated, 630; overall undergraduate GPA 3.0, 3.5; Doctoral program GRE-Analytic no minimum stated, 630.

Other Criteria: (importance of criteria rated low, medium, or high): GRE/MAT scores—medium, research experience—medium, work experience—medium, extracurricular activity—low, clinically related public service—medium, GPA—medium, letters of recommendation—high, interview—medium, statement of goals and objectives—medium, undergraduate major in psychology—low, specific undergraduate psychology courses taken—low. For additional information on admission requirements, go to http://www.unl.edu/psypage.

Student Characteristics: The following represents characteristics of students in 2007–2008 in all graduate psychology programs in the department: Female—full-time 78, part-time 0; Male—full-time 29, part-time 0; African American/Black—full-time 2, part-time 0; Hispanic/Latino(a)—full-time 9, part-time 0; Asian/ Pacific Islander—full-time 4, part-time 0; American Indian/ Alaska Native—full-time 1, part-time 0; Caucasian/White—full-time 91, part-time 0; Multi-ethnic—full-time 0, part-time 0; students subject to the Americans With Disabilities Act—full-time 2, part-time 0; Unknown ethnicity—full-time 0, part-time 0; International students who hold an F-1 or J-1 Visa—full-time 2, part-time 0.

Financial Information/Assistance:

Financial Assistance:

First-Year Students: Teaching assistantships available for first year. Average number of hours worked per week: 19. Tuition remission given: full. Research assistantships available for first year. Average number of hours worked per week: 19. Tuition remission given: full. Fellowships and scholarships available for first year. Average number of hours worked per week: 19.

Advanced Students: Teaching assistantships available for advanced students. Average number of hours worked per week: 19. Tuition remission given: full. Research assistantships available for advanced students. Average number of hours worked per week: 19. Tuition remission given: full. Fellowships and scholarships available for advanced students.

Additional Information: Of all students currently enrolled full time, 100% benefited from one or more of the listed financial assistance programs. Application and information available online at http://www.unl.edu/psypage.

Internships/Practica: Doctoral Degree (PhD Clinical): For those doctoral students for whom a professional internship was required in this program prior to graduation, (11) students applied for an internship in 2006–2007, with (11) students obtaining an internship. Of those students who obtained an internship, (11) were paid internships. Of those students who obtained an internship, (11) students placed in APA/CPA-accredited internships, (0) students placed in internships not APA/CPA-accredited, but listed with the Association of Psychology Postdoctoral and Internship Centers (APPIC), (0) students placed in internships conforming to guidelines of the Council of Directors of School Psychology Programs (CDSPP), (0) students placed in internships that were not APA/CPA-accredited, APPIC or CDSPP listed. The Clinical program offers numerous internship opportunities for students. We have an excellent record of placements for our students at high-quality internship sites throughout North America and participate in the APPIC internship process.

Housing and Day Care: On-campus housing is available. No on-campus day care facilities are available.

Employment of Department Graduates:

Master's Degree Graduates: Of those who graduated in the academic year 2006–2007, the following categories and numbers represent the postgraduate activities and employment of master's degree graduates: Enrolled in a postdoctoral residency/fellowship (n/a), employed in independent practice (n/a), total from the above (master's) (0).

Doctoral Degree Graduates: Of those who graduated in the academic year 2006–2007, the following categories and numbers represent the postgraduate activities and employment of doctoral degree graduates: Enrolled in a psychology doctoral program (n/a), total from the above (doctoral) (0).

Additional Information:

Orientation, Objectives, and Emphasis of Department: The Department of Psychology at the University of Nebraska—Lincoln offers PhD programs that emphasize the development of research and teaching excellence, collegial partnerships between students and faculty, and the cross-fertilization of ideas between specializations in the context of a rigorous, but flexible, training program. The goal of the clinical program is to produce broadly trained, scientifically oriented psychologists who have skills in both research and professional activities. The Cognitive, Biopsychology, Developmental, and Social–Personality programs all emphasize research training but also place equal importance upon training for college or university teaching and policy and applied careers. Students in the PhD/JD program take their first year in the Law College, and then concentrate on psychology plus law to graduate with a double doctorate.

Special Facilities or Resources: The department has a number of resources including the Ruth Staples Child Development Laboratory; the Center for Children, Families, and the Law; the BUROS Mental Measurement Institute; the NEAR Center; the UNL Public Policy Center; and the Lincoln Regional Mental Health Center.

Information for Students With Physical Disabilities: See the following Web site for more information: http://www.unl.edu/ssd/.

Application Information:

Send to Admissions Coordinator, Department of Psychology, UNL, 238 Burnett, Lincoln, NE 68588-0308. Application available online. URL of online application: http://www.unl.edu/psypage. Students are admitted in the Fall, application deadline January 2. The deadlines are January 2 for Clinical, January 15 for all others. *Fee:* $45.

Nebraska, University of, Omaha

Department of Psychology
Arts and Sciences
60th and Dodge Streets
Omaha, NE 68182-0274
Telephone: (402) 554-2592; Ext. 2313 Joseph Brown
Fax: (402) 554-2556
E-mail: *josephbrown@mail.unomaha.edu*
Web: *http://www.unomaha.edu/~psychweb/*

Department Information:

Chairperson: Kenneth A. Deffenbacher. Number of faculty: total—full-time 18; women—full-time 8; total—minority—full-time 3; women minority—full-time 2.

Programs and Degrees Offered:

Listed in the following order: Program area, degree type (T if terminal Master's), number awarded 7/06–6/07. Industrial/Organizational MA/MS (Master of Arts/Science) 0, School MA/MS (Master of Arts/Science) 5, Psychobiology PhD (Doctor of Philosophy) 0, Developmental MA/MS (Master of Arts/Science) 0, Experimental MA/MS (Master of Arts/Science) 1, Developmental PhD (Doctor of Philosophy) 1, School EdS/MEd (School Psychology) 4, Industrial/Organizational MA/MS (Master of Arts/Science) (T) 3, Industrial/Organizational PhD (Doctor of Philosophy) 1, Developmental MA/MS (Master of Arts/Science) (T) 0, Psychobiology MA/MS (Master of Arts/Science) 0.

Student Applications/Admissions:

Student Applications

Industrial/Organizational MA/MS (Master of Arts/Science)—Applications 2007–2008, 5. Total applicants accepted 2007–2008, 2. Number full-time enrolled (new admits only) 2007–2008, 1. Number part-time enrolled (new admits only) 2007–2008, 0. Openings 2008–2009, 5. The median number of years required for completion of a degree in 2006–2007 were 3. The number of students enrolled full- and part-time who were dismissed or voluntarily withdrew from this program area in 2007–2008 were 0. *School MA/MS (Master of Arts/Science)*—Applications 2007–2008, 27. Total applicants accepted 2007–2008, 15. Number full-time enrolled (new admits only) 2007–2008, 7. Openings 2008–2009, 6. The median number of years required for completion of a degree in 2006–2007 were 2. The number of students enrolled full- and part-time who were dismissed or voluntarily withdrew from this program area in 2007–2008 were 0. *Psychobiology PhD (Doctor of Philosophy)*—Applications 2007–2008, 1. Total applicants accepted 2007–2008, 1. Number full-time enrolled (new admits only) 2007–2008, 1. Number part-time enrolled (new admits only) 2007–2008, 0. Openings 2008–2009, 3. The number of students enrolled full- and part-time who were dismissed or voluntarily withdrew from this program area in 2007–2008 were 0. *Developmental MA/MS (Master of Arts/Science)*—Applications 2007–2008, 0. Total applicants accepted 2007–2008, 0. Number full-time enrolled (new admits only) 2007–2008, 0. Openings 2008–2009, 3. The median number of years required for completion of a degree in 2006–2007 were 3. The number of students enrolled full- and part-time who were dismissed or voluntarily withdrew from this program area in 2007–2008 were 0. *Experimental MA/MS (Master of Arts/Science)*—Applications 2007–2008, 3. Total applicants accepted 2007–2008, 3. Number full-time enrolled (new admits only) 2007–2008, 2. Number part-time enrolled (new admits only) 2007–2008, 0. Openings 2008–2009, 3. The number of students enrolled full- and part-time who were dismissed or voluntarily withdrew from this program area in 2007–2008 were 0. *Developmental PhD (Doctor of Philosophy)*—Applications 2007–2008, 2. Total applicants accepted 2007–2008, 1. Number full-time enrolled (new admits only) 2007–2008, 0. Number part-time enrolled (new admits only) 2007–2008, 0. Openings 2008–2009, 2. The median number of years required for completion of a degree in 2006–2007 were 6. The number of students enrolled full- and part-time who were dismissed or voluntarily withdrew from this program area in 2007–2008 were 0. *School EdS/MEd (School Psychology)*—Applications 2007–2008, 10. Total applicants accepted 2007–2008, 6. Number full-time enrolled (new admits only) 2007–2008, 6. Number part-time enrolled (new admits only) 2007–2008, 0. Openings 2008–2009, 5. The median number of years required for completion of a degree in 2006–2007 were 4. The number of students enrolled full- and part-time who were dismissed or voluntarily withdrew from this program area in 2007–2008 were 0. *Industrial/Organizational MA/MS (Master of Arts/Science)*—Applications 2007–2008, 7. Total applicants accepted 2007–2008, 1. Number full-time enrolled (new admits only) 2007–2008, 3. Number part-time enrolled (new admits only) 2007–2008, 0. Openings 2008–2009, 6. The median number of years required for completion of a degree in 2006–2007 were 2. The number of students enrolled full- and part-time who were dismissed or voluntarily withdrew from this program area in 2007–2008 were 1. *Industrial/Organizational PhD (Doctor of Philosophy)*—Applications 2007–2008, 8. Total applicants accepted 2007–2008, 4. Number full-time enrolled (new admits only) 2007–2008, 0. Total enrolled 2007–2008 full-time, 22. Openings 2008–2009, 3. The median number of years required for completion of a degree in 2006–2007 were 6. The number of students enrolled full- and part-time who were dismissed or voluntarily withdrew from this program area in 2007–2008 were 1. *Developmental MA/MS (Master of Arts/Science)*—Applications 2007–2008, 7. Total applicants accepted 2007–2008, 2. Number full-time enrolled (new admits only) 2007–2008, 2. Total enrolled 2007–2008 full-time, 3. Openings 2008–2009, 4. The median number of years required for completion of a degree in 2006–2007 were 3. The number of students enrolled full- and part-time who were dismissed or voluntarily withdrew from this program area in 2007–2008 were 0. *Psychobiology MA/MS (Master of Arts/Science)*—Applications 2007–2008, 6. Total applicants accepted 2007–2008, 2. Number full-time enrolled (new admits only) 2007–2008, 2. Total enrolled 2007–2008 full-time, 7. Openings 2008–2009, 3. The median number of years required for completion of a degree in 2006–2007 were 3. The number of students enrolled full- and part-time who were dismissed or voluntarily withdrew from this program area in 2007–2008 were 0.

Admissions Requirements:

Scores: Entries appear in this order: required test or GPA, minimum score (if required), median score of students entering in 2007–2008. Master's Programs: GRE-V no minimum stated, 590; GRE-Q no minimum stated, 588; overall undergraduate GPA no minimum stated, 3.54. Doctoral Programs: GRE-V no minimum stated, 517; GRE-Q no minimum stated, 653; GRE-Subject (Psychology) no minimum stated, 645; overall undergraduate GPA no minimum stated, 3.59.

Other Criteria: (importance of criteria rated low, medium, or high): GRE/MAT scores—high, research experience—high, work experience—medium, extracurricular activity—medium, clinically related public service—low, GPA—high, letters of recommendation—high, interview—medium, statement of goals and objectives—high.

Student Characteristics: The following represents characteristics of students in 2007–2008 in all graduate psychology programs in the department: Female—full-time 70, part-time 0; Male—full-time 27, part-time 0; African American/Black—full-time 2, part-time 0; Hispanic/Latino(a)—full-time 1, part-time 0; Asian/Pacific Islander—full-time 3, part-time 0; American Indian/Alaska Native—full-time 0, part-time 0; Caucasian/White—full-time 91, part-time 0; students subject to the Americans With Disabilities Act—full-time 0, part-time 0; Unknown ethnicity—full-time 0, part-time 0; International students who hold an F-1 or J-1 Visa—full-time 4, part-time 0.

Financial Information/Assistance:

Tuition for Full-Time Study: *Master's:* State residents: $193 per credit hour; Nonstate residents: $507 per credit hour. *Doctoral:* State residents: $193 per credit hour; Nonstate residents: $507 per credit hour. Tuition is subject to change.

Financial Assistance:

First-Year Students: Teaching assistantships available for first year. Average amount paid per academic year: $11,430. Average number of hours worked per week: 20. Apply by January 5. Tuition remission given: full. Research assistantships available for first year. Average amount paid per academic year: $11,430. Average number of hours worked per week: 20. Apply by January 5. Tuition remission given: full. Fellowships and scholarships available for first year. Average amount paid per academic year: $11,430. Average number of hours worked per week: 20. Apply by January 5. Tuition remission given: full and partial.

Advanced Students: Teaching assistantships available for advanced students. Average amount paid per academic year: $11,430. Average number of hours worked per week: 20. Apply by January 5. Tuition remission given: full. Research assistantships available for advanced students. Average amount paid per academic year: $11,430. Average number of hours worked per week: 20. Apply by January 5. Tuition remission given: full. Traineeships available for advanced students. Average number of hours worked per week: 20. Tuition remission given: full and partial. Fellowships and scholarships available for advanced students. Average amount paid per academic year: $11,430. Average number of hours worked per week: 20. Apply by January 5. Tuition remission given: full and partial.

Additional Information: Of all students currently enrolled full time, 50% benefited from one or more of the listed financial assistance programs.

Internships/Practica: An internship in school psychology is available and required within the EdS program leading to certification in the field of school psychology. Practica are also available (and for some degrees required) in industrial/organizational psychology and developmental psychology.

Housing and Day Care: On-campus housing is available. See the following Web site for more information: http://www.campushousing.com/uneb. On-campus day care facilities are available. See the following Web site for more information: http://www.mbsc.unomaha.edu/child.htm.

Employment of Department Graduates:

Master's Degree Graduates: Of those who graduated in the academic year 2006–2007, the following categories and numbers represent the postgraduate activities and employment of master's degree graduates: Enrolled in a postdoctoral residency/fellowship (n/a), employed in independent practice (n/a), total from the above (master's) (0).

Doctoral Degree Graduates: Of those who graduated in the academic year 2006–2007, the following categories and numbers represent the postgraduate activities and employment of doctoral degree graduates: Enrolled in a psychology doctoral program (n/a), total from the above (doctoral) (0).

Additional Information:

Orientation, Objectives, and Emphasis of Department: The department is broadly eclectic, placing emphasis on theory, research, and application. The MA program is primarily for students who anticipate continuing their education at the PhD level. The MA degree may be completed in eight areas of psychology. The MS program is primarily for students who view the master's degree as terminal and who wish to emphasize application in the fields of educational–school or industrial/organizational psychology. These two areas may be emphasized within the MA program as well.

Special Facilities or Resources: The department maintains extensive laboratory facilities in a variety of experimental areas, both human and animal. The animal colony consists of rats, gerbils, mice, and golden-lion tamarins. Up-to-date interactive computer facilities are readily available. The Center for Applied Psychological Services is a departmentally controlled, faculty–student consulting service that provides an opportunity to gain practical experience in industrial psychology and school psychology. The department maintains working relations with the Children's Rehabilitation Institute, the Department of Pediatrics, the Department of Physiology, and the University of Nebraska Medical Center. In addition, contact exists with the Boys Town Institute, Boys Town Home, Henry Doorly Zoo, Union Pacific Railroad, and Mutual of Omaha.

Application Information:
Send to Department Chair. Students are admitted in the Fall, application deadline January 5. *Fee:* $45.

Nevada, University of, Las Vegas

Department of Psychology
Liberal Arts
4505 Maryland Parkway
Las Vegas, NV 89154-5030
Telephone: (702) 895-3305
Fax: (702) 895-0195
E-mail: *psyunlv@unlv.nevada.edu*
Web: *http://www.psychology.unlv.edu*

Department Information:

1960. Chairperson: Mark H. Ashcraft. Number of faculty: total—full-time 24, part-time 13; women—full-time 9, part-time 6; total—minority—full-time 1; women minority—full-time 1.

Programs and Degrees Offered:

Listed in the following order: Program area, degree type (T if terminal Master's), number awarded 7/06–6/07. Clinical PhD (Doctor of Philosophy) 8, Experimental PhD (Doctor of Philosophy) 2.

APA Accreditation: Clinical PhD (Doctor of Philosophy).

Student Applications/Admissions:

Student Applications

Clinical PhD (Doctor of Philosophy)—Applications 2007–2008, 107. Total applicants accepted 2007–2008, 6. Number full-time enrolled (new admits only) 2007–2008, 6. Number part-time enrolled (new admits only) 2007–2008, 0. Openings 2008–2009, 10. The median number of years required for completion of a degree in 2006–2007 were 6. The number of students enrolled full- and part-time who were dismissed or voluntarily withdrew from this program area in 2007–2008 were 0. *Experimental PhD (Doctor of Philosophy)*—Applications 2007–2008, 35. Total applicants accepted 2007–2008, 6. Number full-time enrolled (new admits only) 2007–2008, 6. Number part-time enrolled (new admits only) 2007–2008, 0. Openings 2008–2009, 10. The median number of years required for completion of a degree in 2006–2007 were 7. The number of students enrolled full- and part-time who were dismissed or voluntarily withdrew from this program area in 2007–2008 were 0.

Admissions Requirements:

Scores: Entries appear in this order: required test or GPA, minimum score (if required), median score of students entering in 2007–2008. Doctoral Programs: GRE-V 550, 600; GRE-Q 550, 660; GRE-Subject (Psychology) 550, 650; overall undergraduate GPA 3.2, 3.7; psychology GPA 3.2, 3.7.

Other Criteria: (importance of criteria rated low, medium, or high): GRE/MAT scores—high, research experience—high, work experience—low, clinically related public service—medium, GPA—high, letters of recommendation—high, interview—high, statement of goals and objectives—high, specific undergraduate psychology courses taken—medium. Experimental Program ranks clinically related public services as low.

For additional information on admission requirements, go to http://psychology.unlv.edu/html/graduate_programs.html.

Student Characteristics: The following represents characteristics of students in 2007–2008 in all graduate psychology programs in the department: Female—full-time 63, part-time 0; Male—full-time 18, part-time 0; African American/Black—full-time 4, part-time 0; Hispanic/Latino(a)—full-time 6, part-time 0; Asian/Pacific Islander—full-time 1, part-time 0; American Indian/Alaska Native—full-time 0, part-time 0; Caucasian/White—full-time 62, part-time 0; Multi-ethnic—full-time 3, part-time 0; students subject to the Americans With Disabilities Act—full-time 0, part-time 0; Unknown ethnicity—full-time 5, part-time 0.

Financial Information/Assistance:

Tuition for Full-Time Study: *Doctoral:* State residents: $172 per credit hour; Nonstate residents: $272 per credit hour. Tuition is subject to change. Additional fees are assessed to students beyond the costs of tuition for the following: Lab assessment materials for some courses. See the following Web site for updates and changes in tuition costs: http://www.graduatecollege.unlv.edu/financing/cost_fees.htm.

Financial Assistance:

First-Year Students: Teaching assistantships available for first year. Average amount paid per academic year: $12,000. Average number of hours worked per week: 20. Apply by January 15. Tuition remission given: partial. Research assistantships available for first year. Average amount paid per academic year: $12,000. Average number of hours worked per week: 20. Apply by January 15. Tuition remission given: partial.

Advanced Students: Teaching assistantships available for advanced students. Average amount paid per academic year: $12,000. Average number of hours worked per week: 20. Apply by March 1. Tuition remission given: partial. Research assistantships available for advanced students. Average amount paid per academic year: $12,000. Average number of hours worked per week: 20. Apply by March 1. Tuition remission given: partial. Fellowships and scholarships available for advanced students. Average amount paid per academic year: $15,000. Average number of hours worked per week: 0. Apply by March 1. Tuition remission given: full.

Additional Information: Of all students currently enrolled full time, 94% benefited from one or more of the listed financial assistance programs. Application and information available online at http://graduatecollege.unlv.edu/financing/financing.htm.

Internships/Practica: Doctoral Degree (PhD Clinical): For those doctoral students for whom a professional internship was required in this program prior to graduation, (8) students applied for an internship in 2006–2007, with (8) students obtaining an internship. Of those students who obtained an internship, (8) were paid internships. Of those students who obtained an internship, (7) students placed in APA/CPA-accredited internships, (1) students placed in internships not APA/CPA-accredited, but listed with the Association of Psychology Postdoctoral and Internship Centers (APPIC), (0) students placed in internships conforming to guidelines of the Council of Directors of School Psychology Programs (CDSPP), (0) students placed in internships that were not APA/CPA-accredited, APPIC or CDSPP listed. Students work in various community practicum settings as part of their training experience. Additional information is available on the program Web site: http://psychology.unlv.edu. For additional information on education and training outcomes for our programs, see the following Web site: http://www.unlv.edu/studentlife/html/performance_and_outome_data.html.

Housing and Day Care: No on-campus housing is available. On-campus day care facilities are available. See the following Web site for more information: http://www.preschool.unlv.edu/Templates/index.html.

Employment of Department Graduates:

Master's Degree Graduates: Of those who graduated in the academic year 2006–2007, the following categories and numbers represent the postgraduate activities and employment of master's degree graduates: Enrolled in a postdoctoral residency/fellowship (n/a), employed in independent practice (n/a), total from the above (master's) (0).

Doctoral Degree Graduates: Of those who graduated in the academic year 2006–2007, the following categories and numbers represent the postgraduate activities and employment of doctoral degree graduates: Enrolled in a psychology doctoral program (n/a), employed in independent practice (2), employed in an academic position at a university (4), employed in other positions at a higher education institution (1), employed in a professional position in a school system (1), employed in business or industry (2), employed in government agency (1), employed in a community mental health/counseling center (2), employed in a hospital/medical center (2), other employment position (2), total from the above (doctoral) (17).

Additional Information:

Orientation, Objectives, and Emphasis of Department: Our programs combine a strong focus on major content areas of experimental psychology and methodology/statistics, while also providing opportunities to learn skills and conduct practicum and research that can be applied to real-world problems. In short, graduate training will produce experimental psychologists who can be employed in both academic and nonacademic settings. The department has the following goals: Generating new psychological knowledge through original scholarly research; disseminating psychological knowledge through scholarly articles, books, and other relevant media, and the development of professional conduct through mentorship and supervision of graduate and undergraduate students, and through effective teaching at the graduate and undergraduate levels; promoting self-exploration and self-awareness among students to develop an appreciation of diversity; creating a just, diverse, and humane working and learning environment; enhancing organizational climate, research, teaching/mentoring, and services related to multiculturalism and diversity; creating an effective and responsive administrative infrastructure to serve all stakeholders, including faculty, graduate and undergraduate students, other administrative units within the College and University, and the larger public; and serving the community by bringing faculty and student expertise to bear on important local and regional issues. The UNLV Experimental Psychology Doctoral Program is designed to prepare experimental psychologists for the rich opportunities that are presented by a changing employment picture. This program addresses the training needs of new psychologists in ways that traditional programs do not. Specifically, the program combines a strong focus on the major content areas of experimental psychology and methodology/statistics while also providing opportunities to learn skills and conduct research that can be applied to real-world problems. In short, graduate training will produce experimental psychologists who can be employed in both academic and nonacademic settings.

Special Facilities or Resources: The strongest resource of the UNLV Psychology Department is the many talents of its diverse faculty. Our graduate program is small enough to provide close personal interaction experiences for training, and yet we encourage students to demonstrate initiative and to undertake the major responsibility for their graduate learning experiences. Student research is encouraged within the department and throughout the university.

Information for Students With Physical Disabilities: See the following Web site for more information: http://www.unlv.edu/studentlife/disability/index.html.

Application Information:

All applicant materials, including applicant's Letter of Intent plus three letters of recommendation, are to be sent directly to UNLV Department of Psychology, Doctoral Program Admissions Committee, 4505 Maryland Parkway, Box 455030, Las Vegas, NV 89154-5030. Doctoral applicants must also send the required applicant materials to the UNLV Graduate College (minus the letter of intent and letters of recommend): http://graduatecollege.unlv.edu/admissions/admissions.htm. Application available online. URL of online application: http://www.psychology.unlv.edu/Psychology_Graduate_Program_Application.pdf. Students are admitted in the Fall, application deadline January 2. The application deadline for our Experimental Psychology Graduate Program is January 15, for matriculation the following Fall semester. *Fee:* $60. Waivers are obtained through the Graduate College office.

Nevada, University of, Reno

Department of Psychology/296
Liberal Arts
1664 North Virginia
Reno, NV 89557
Telephone: (775) 784-6828
Fax: (775) 784-1126
E-mail: *vmf@unr.edu*
Web: *http://www.unr.edu/psych/*

Department Information:

1920. Chairperson: Victoria M. Follette. Number of faculty: total—full-time 20; women—full-time 7; total—minority—full-time 2; women minority—full-time 2.

Programs and Degrees Offered:

Listed in the following order: Program area, degree type (T if terminal Master's), number awarded 7/06–6/07. Behavior Analysis PhD (Doctor of Philosophy) 6, Experimental PhD (Doctor of Philosophy) 4, Clinical PhD (Doctor of Philosophy) 8.

APA Accreditation: Clinical PhD (Doctor of Philosophy).

Student Applications/Admissions:

Student Applications

Behavior Analysis PhD (Doctor of Philosophy)—Applications 2007–2008, 40. Total applicants accepted 2007–2008, 6. Number full-time enrolled (new admits only) 2007–2008, 10. Number part-time enrolled (new admits only) 2007–2008, 30. Total enrolled 2007–2008 full-time, 51, part-time, 57. Openings 2008–2009, 6. The median number of years required for completion of a degree in 2006–2007 were 6. The number of students enrolled full- and part-time who were dismissed or voluntarily withdrew from this program area in 2007–2008 were 0. *Experimental PhD (Doctor of Philosophy)*—Applications 2007–2008, 12. Total applicants accepted 2007–2008, 6. Number full-time enrolled (new admits only) 2007–2008, 5. Number part-time enrolled (new admits only) 2007–2008, 0. Total enrolled 2007–2008 full-time, 12, part-time, 16. Openings 2008–2009, 5. The median number of years required for completion of a degree in 2006–2007 were 5. The number of students enrolled full- and part-time who were dismissed or voluntarily withdrew from this program area in 2007–2008 were 2. *Clinical PhD (Doctor of Philosophy)*—Applications 2007–2008, 110. Total applicants accepted 2007–2008, 8. Number full-time enrolled (new admits only) 2007–2008, 8. Number part-time enrolled (new admits only) 2007–2008, 0. Total enrolled 2007–2008 full-time, 44, part-time, 12. Openings 2008–2009, 8. The median number of years required for completion of a degree in 2006–2007 were 7. The number of students enrolled full- and part-time who were dismissed or voluntarily withdrew from this program area in 2007–2008 were 0.

Admissions Requirements:

Scores: Entries appear in this order: required test or GPA, minimum score (if required), median score of students entering in 2007–2008. Master's Programs: GRE-V no minimum stated, 470; GRE-Q no minimum stated, 510; GRE-Subject (Psychology) 550; overall undergraduate GPA 3.0. For the GRE-V+Q, the suggested score is 1200 for clinical. For the Undergraduate GPA, 3.5 is suggested for Clinical. Doctoral Programs: GRE-V no minimum stated, 550; GRE-Q no minimum stated, 545; GRE-Subject (Psychology) 550, 550; overall undergraduate GPA 3.0. 1200 for clinical for the GRE-V+Q. For the Undergraduate GPA, 3.5 suggested for clinical.

Other Criteria: (importance of criteria rated low, medium, or high): GRE/MAT scores—high, research experience—high, work experience—high, extracurricular activity—medium, clinically related public service—medium, GPA—high, letters of recommendation—high, interview—high, statement of goals and objectives—high. Interviews for admission into Behavior Analysis and Clinical is required.

Student Characteristics: The following represents characteristics of students in 2007–2008 in all graduate psychology programs in the department: Female—full-time 80, part-time 66; Male—full-time 28, part-time 26; African American/Black—full-time 0, part-time 2; Hispanic/Latino(a)—full-time 4, part-time 8; Asian/Pacific Islander—full-time 6, part-time 10; American Indian/Alaska Native—full-time 0, part-time 1; Caucasian/White—full-time 80, part-time 55; Multi-ethnic—full-time 0, part-time 0; students subject to the Americans With Disabilities Act—full-time 0, part-time 0; Unknown ethnicity—full-time 10, part-time 10.

Financial Information/Assistance:

Tuition for Full-Time Study: *Master's:* State residents: $176 per credit hour; Nonstate residents: per academic year $5,405, $189 per credit hour. *Doctoral:* State residents: $176 per credit hour; Nonstate residents: per academic year $5,405, $189 per credit hour. Tuition is subject to change. Additional fees are assessed to students beyond the costs of tuition for the following: Health Center (enrolled in six credits or more) $79. See the following Web site for updates and changes in tuition costs: http://www.unr.edu/vpaf/controller/cashier/fall.htm.

Financial Assistance:

First-Year Students: Teaching assistantships available for first year. Average amount paid per academic year: $15,000. Average number of hours worked per week: 20. Tuition remission given: full. Research assistantships available for first year. Average amount paid per academic year: $15,000. Average number of hours worked per week: 20. Tuition remission given: full.

Advanced Students: Teaching assistantships available for advanced students. Average amount paid per academic year: $15,000. Average number of hours worked per week: 20. Tuition remission given: full. Research assistantships available for advanced students. Average amount paid per academic year: $15,000. Average number of hours worked per week: 20. Tuition remission given: full.

Additional Information: Of all students currently enrolled full time, 90% benefited from one or more of the listed financial assistance programs. Application and information available online at http://www.unr.edu/content/students/financialaid.asp.

Internships/Practica: Doctoral Degree (PhD Clinical): For those doctoral students for whom a professional internship was required in this program prior to graduation, (11) students applied for an internship in 2006–2007, with (9) students obtaining an internship. Of those students who obtained an internship, (9) were paid internships. Of those students who obtained an internship, (9) students placed in APA/CPA-accredited internships, (0) students placed in internships not APA/CPA-accredited, but listed with the Association of Psychology Postdoctoral and Internship Centers (APPIC), (0) students placed in internships conforming to guidelines of the Council of Directors of School Psychology Programs (CDSPP), (0) students placed in internships that were not APA/CPA-accredited, APPIC or CDSPP listed. The department offers several teaching and research assistantships. Experimental—Some students receive support as research assistants through individual faculty grants. Behavior Analysis—All doctoral students and most master's students receive full support from assistantships or consultation services. Clinical—Participation in clinical practica is required for students. From the last half of the 1st year through the 3rd year students see clients at the Psychological Service Center, an in-house clinic. During the 4th year, students are required to complete a 1,000-hour practicum (externship) on campus or at agencies in the area. Finally, students are required to complete a 2,000-hour, APA-approved internship during their final year. For additional information on education and training outcomes for our programs, see the following Web site: http://www.unr.edu/psych/clinical/index.html.

Housing and Day Care: On-campus housing is available. See the following Web site for more information: http://www.unr.edu/reslife/html/oncampus.html. On-campus day care facilities are available.

Employment of Department Graduates:

Master's Degree Graduates: Of those who graduated in the academic year 2006–2007, the following categories and numbers represent the postgraduate activities and employment of master's degree graduates: Enrolled in a psychology doctoral program (0), enrolled in another graduate/professional program (0), enrolled in a postdoctoral residency/fellowship (n/a), employed in independent practice (n/a), employed in an academic position at a university (0), employed in an academic position at a 2-year/4-year college (0), employed in business or industry (0), employed in government agency (0), still seeking employment (0), not seeking employment (0), other employment position (0), do not know (0), total from the above (master's) (0).

Doctoral Degree Graduates: Of those who graduated in the academic year 2006–2007, the following categories and numbers represent the postgraduate activities and employment of doctoral degree graduates: Enrolled in a psychology doctoral program (n/a), enrolled in another graduate/professional program (0), employed in an academic position at a 2-year/4-year college (0), employed in government agency (0), employed in a community mental health/counseling center (0), still seeking employment (0), not seeking employment (0), other employment position (0), do not know (0), total from the above (doctoral) (0).

Additional Information:

Orientation, Objectives, and Emphasis of Department: The Cognitive and Brain Science (previously Experimental) program in psychology is research oriented. The division offers specialized work in human cognition and cognitive neuroscience; learning, perception, and psychophysics; and animal communication. The clinical program has a scientist–practitioner emphasis and offers skills in psychotherapy, assessment, evaluation, and community psychology. The behavior analysis program emphasizes applied behavior analysis, especially in institutional settings, and examines both the theoretical and applied ramifications of the behavioral programs.

Special Facilities or Resources: Experimental—the program has active labs with facilities for research in visual perception, memory, cognition, and animal behavior and communication (including opportunities for research at the primate center at Central Washington University). Behavior Analysis—the program has a lab where they work with autistic children and developmentally disabled clients. Clinical—the primary academic and research facility of the program is the Psychological Service Center, an in-house training clinic that serves the community by offering services on a sliding fee basis.

Information for Students With Physical Disabilities: See the following Web site for more information: http://www.unr.edu/stsv/slservices/drc/.

Application Information:

Send to Specify Clinical, Behavioral Analysis, or Experimental Admissions, Psychology Department/296, University of Nevada, Reno, NV 89557. URL of online application: http://www.unr.edu/psych/gradappl.html. Students are admitted in the Fall, application deadline. For the Fall semester, the deadline for Clinical is January 1, January 1 for Behavior Analysis, and March 1 for Experimental. For the Spring semester, the deadline is November 1 for Experimental only. *Fee:* $60; $40 if previously enrolled in UNR. International students pay nonrefundable application fee: $95 U.S. dollars. If applying to more than one graduate program, a fee for each additional application is $40 for all applicants.

Antioch University New England

Clinical Psychology
40 Avon Street
Keene, NH 03431-3552
Telephone: (603) 357-3122
Fax: (603) 357-1679
E-mail: *rpeterson@antiochne.edu*
Web: *http://www.antiochne.edu*

Department Information:

1982. Professor and Chair: Roger L. Peterson, PhD ABPP. Number of faculty: total—full-time 11, part-time 15; women—full-time 5, part-time 4; total—minority—full-time 1; women minority—full-time 1.

Programs and Degrees Offered:

Listed in the following order: Program area, degree type (T if terminal Master's), number awarded 7/06–6/07. Clinical Psychology PsyD (Doctor of Psychology) 25.

APA Accreditation: Clinical PsyD (Doctor of Psychology).

Student Applications/Admissions:

Student Applications

Clinical Psychology PsyD (Doctor of Psychology)—Applications 2007–2008, 81. Total applicants accepted 2007–2008, 51. Number full-time enrolled (new admits only) 2007–2008, 35. Number part-time enrolled (new admits only) 2007–2008, 0. Openings 2008–2009, 27. The median number of years required for completion of a degree in 2006–2007 were 6. The number of students enrolled full- and part-time who were dismissed or voluntarily withdrew from this program area in 2007–2008 were 4.

Admissions Requirements:

Scores: Entries appear in this order: required test or GPA, minimum score (if required), median score of students entering in 2007–2008. Master's Programs: No terminal masters degree, so this is not applicable. Doctoral Programs: GRE-V 340, 530; GRE-Q 420, 610; GRE-Subject (Psychology) 410, 600; overall undergraduate GPA 2.44, 3.55; Doctoral program GRE-Analytic 350, 450. NB: The 340 verbal GRE was for an international student.

Other Criteria: (importance of criteria rated low, medium, or high): GRE/MAT scores—high, research experience—medium, work experience—medium, extracurricular activity—low, clinically related public service—medium, GPA—high, letters of recommendation—high, interview—high, statement of goals and objectives—high, undergraduate major in psychology—medium, specific undergraduate psychology courses taken—medium.

Student Characteristics: The following represents characteristics of students in 2007–2008 in all graduate psychology programs in the department: Female—full-time 129, part-time 0; Male—full-time 33, part-time 0; African American/Black—full-time 1, part-time 0; Hispanic/Latino(a)—full-time 5, part-time 0; Asian/Pacific Islander—full-time 1, part-time 0; American Indian/Alaska Native—full-time 0, part-time 0; Caucasian/White—full-time 149, part-time 0; Multi-ethnic—full-time 3, part-time 0; students subject to the Americans With Disabilities Act—full-time 3, part-time 0; Unknown ethnicity—full-time 3, part-time 0; International students who hold an F-1 or J-1 Visa—full-time 0, part-time 0.

Financial Information/Assistance:

Tuition for Full-Time Study: *Doctoral:* State residents: per academic year $26,150; Nonstate residents: per academic year $26,150. Tuition is subject to change.

Financial Assistance:

First-Year Students: Teaching assistantships available for first year. Research assistantships available for first year. Average amount paid per academic year: $1,500. Average number of hours worked per week: 6.

Advanced Students: Teaching assistantships available for advanced students. Average amount paid per academic year: $1,550. Average number of hours worked per week: 6. Research assistantships available for advanced students. Average amount paid per academic year: $2,150. Average number of hours worked per week: 5.

Additional Information: Of all students currently enrolled full time, 14% benefited from one or more of the listed financial assistance programs. Application and information available online at http://www.antiochne.edu/cp/.

Internships/Practica: Doctoral Degree (PsyD Clinical Psychology): For those doctoral students for whom a professional internship was required in this program prior to graduation, (22) students applied for an internship in 2006–2007, with (20) students obtaining an internship. Of those students who obtained an internship, (19) were paid internships. Of those students who obtained an internship, (12) students placed in APA/CPA-accredited internships, (6) students placed in internships not APA/CPA accredited, but listed with the Association of Psychology Postdoctoral and Internship Centers (APPIC), (0) students placed in internships conforming to guidelines of the Council of Directors of School Psychology Programs (CDSPP), (2) students placed in internships that were not APA/CPA-accredited, APPIC or CDSPP listed. Students complete practica at agencies within driving distance around New England. About 12 students per year do practicum at the Antioch Psychological Services Center (PSC), within the Department of Clinical Psychology. It functions as a mental health clinic providing a range of psychological services to residents from Keene and surrounding communities, and to Antioch New England students in departments other than Clinical Psychology. These services include individual psychotherapy, couple and family therapy, individual and family assessment, and various problem-specific psychoeducational groups and seminars. In addition, the PSC is actively involved in community outreach services; clinicians are encouraged to develop public psychoeducation and consultation activities, and to work in collaboration with other social service agencies for the purpose of ongoing community needs assessment and program development.

A practicum at the PSC offers the student a unique opportunity for more concentrated interaction with core faculty—through supervision, training, and involvement in applied clinical and research projects of mutual interest. Specialized training opportunities exist for students interested in health psychology, family therapy, and assessment.

Housing and Day Care: No on-campus housing is available. No on-campus day care facilities are available.

Employment of Department Graduates:

Master's Degree Graduates: Of those who graduated in the academic year 2006–2007, the following categories and numbers represent the postgraduate activities and employment of master's degree graduates: Enrolled in a postdoctoral residency/fellowship (n/a), employed in independent practice (n/a), total from the above (master's) (0).

Doctoral Degree Graduates: Of those who graduated in the academic year 2006–2007, the following categories and numbers represent the postgraduate activities and employment of doctoral degree graduates: Enrolled in a psychology doctoral program (n/a), enrolled in a postdoctoral residency/fellowship (10), employed in a community mental health/counseling center (5), employed in a hospital/medical center (5), still seeking employment (2), other employment position (2), do not know (4), total from the above (doctoral) (28).

Additional Information:

Orientation, Objectives, and Emphasis of Department: Our practitioner–scholar program prepares professional psychologists for multiple roles for the expanded world of 21st century clinical psychology, including not only intervention, assessment, and research but also supervision, management, administration, consultation, and public policy. With a commitment to social responsibility, social justice, and diversity, we emphasize a social vision of clinical psychology, responsive to the needs of the larger society. The program includes broad training with a range of theoretical perspectives, a sound psychological knowledge base, and supervised practice. It follows the educational model developed by the National Council of Schools and Programs of Professional Psychology (NCSPP). This model specifies seven core professional competency areas: relationship, assessment, intervention, research and evaluation, consultation and education, management and supervision, and diversity (we have required courses in each) and, of course, includes basic psychological science. Research for clinical psychology is rooted in solving professional and social problems, where science and practice are integrated and complementary in the required dissertation. Preparation as "local clinical scientists" includes opportunities for training in program evaluation, as well as a range of other psychological topics and methodologies. Our pedagogy brings together theory, practice, and research through integrative, reflective learning experiences that help students develop their professional "voice."

Special Facilities or Resources: The Center for Research on Psychological Practice (CROPP) in the Department of Clinical Psychology serves both the department and the community. This center is designed to address particular emerging educational aspects of doctoral training in clinical psychology that are not regularly included within the usual professional psychology curriculum—those relevant to applied clinical research skills and the associated administrative, consultative, and policy-creation roles of doctoral-level psychologists. Several specific areas of research are priorities for CROPP. These include program evaluation and quality assurance issues, such as needs assessment, outcome and satisfaction research, cost-benefit analysis, policy analysis, and other topics relevant to mental health service management: public welfare issues such as treatment access, utilization, and outcome for underserved, rural, low socioeconomic, and minority populations; development of novel treatment and delivery systems; and methodological issues including the assessment and development of methods and measures appropriate for practice research. The research is done primarily in community service settings and entails collaboration with agencies and caregivers throughout the region. The development of this kind of research center, particularly within the context of a doctoral program in clinical psychology, has not, to our knowledge, been done elsewhere in the country. The Antioch University New England Multicultural Center for Research and Practice addresses the diverse array of emerging multicultural information which represents an enormous and unique opportunity to revolutionize and improve education, training, research, and human services, while addressing concerns of social justice. The Center has a particular focus on racial and ethnic minority and immigrant youth, adults, and families. It provides an excellent model of how the combination of research and practice can have a positive impact on communities across New England and beyond. The services of the Multicultural Center include social support for racial and ethnic minority people; individual and group multicultural interactions; workshops on multicultural awareness and acceptance; workshops on racism and stereotypes; consultation with professionals, educators, and businesses on multicultural applications and services; and coalition-building among disenfranchised groups. Its Web-based services include access to multicultural tests housed in the Center, resources of multicultural test titles and reviews, multicultural lecture notes, awareness exercises, documentation of process and outcome of multicultural service delivery, and a national multicultural course syllabus archive.

Application Information:

Send to Office of Doctoral Admissions, Antioch University New England, 40 Avon Street, Keene, NH, 03431-3552. Application available online. URL of online application: http://www.antiochne.edu/admissions/download.cfm. Students are admitted in the Fall, application deadline January 9. *Fee:* $75.

Dartmouth College (2007 data)

Psychological and Brain Sciences
6207 Moore Hall
Hanover, NH 03755-3578
Telephone: (603) 646-3181
Fax: (603) 646-1419
E-mail: *Ann.S.Clark@Dartmouth.EDU*
Web: *http://www.dartmouth.edu/artsci/psych/grad.html*

Department Information:

1894. Chairperson: Ann S. Clark. Number of faculty: total—full-time 20, part-time 10; women—full-time 5, part-time 4.

Programs and Degrees Offered:

Listed in the following order: Program area, degree type (T if terminal Master's), number awarded 7/06–6/07. General Experimental PhD (Doctor of Philosophy) 4.

Student Applications/Admissions:

Student Applications

General Experimental PhD (Doctor of Philosophy)—Applications 2007–2008, 96. Total applicants accepted 2007–2008, 12. Number full-time enrolled (new admits only) 2007–2008, 4. Openings 2008–2009, 4. The median number of years required for completion of a degree in 2006–2007 were 4. The number of students enrolled full- and part-time who were dismissed or voluntarily withdrew from this program area in 2007–2008 were 0.

Admissions Requirements:

Scores: Entries appear in this order: required test or GPA, minimum score (if required), median score of students entering in 2007–2008. Doctoral Programs: GRE-V no minimum stated; GRE-Q no minimum stated; overall undergraduate GPA no minimum stated; Doctoral program GRE-Analytic no minimum stated.

Other Criteria: (importance of criteria rated low, medium, or high): GRE/MAT scores—high, research experience—high, work experience—medium, extracurricular activity—low, GPA—high, letters of recommendation—high, interview—medium, statement of goals and objectives—high.

Student Characteristics: The following represents characteristics of students in 2007–2008 in all graduate psychology programs in the department: Female—full-time 15, part-time 0; Male—full-time 12, part-time 0; African American/Black—full-time 0, part-time 0; Hispanic/Latino(a)—full-time 1, part-time 0; Asian/Pacific Islander—full-time 0, part-time 0; American Indian/Alaska Native—full-time 1, part-time 0; Caucasian/White—full-time 25, part-time 0; Unknown ethnicity—full-time 0, part-time 0.

Financial Information/Assistance:

Tuition for Full-Time Study: *Doctoral:* State residents: per academic year $0, $0 per credit hour.

Financial Assistance:

First-Year Students: Fellowships and scholarships available for first year. Average amount paid per academic year: $17,386. Apply by none. Tuition remission given: full.

Advanced Students: Fellowships and scholarships available for advanced students. Average amount paid per academic year: $19,020. Tuition remission given: full.

Additional Information: Of all students currently enrolled full time, 100% benefited from one or more of the listed financial assistance programs.

Internships/Practica: No information provided.

Housing and Day Care: On-campus housing is available. No on-campus day care facilities are available.

Employment of Department Graduates:

Master's Degree Graduates: Of those who graduated in the academic year 2006–2007, the following categories and numbers represent the postgraduate activities and employment of master's degree graduates: Enrolled in a postdoctoral residency/fellowship (n/a), employed in independent practice (n/a), total from the above (master's) (0).

Doctoral Degree Graduates: Of those who graduated in the academic year 2006–2007, the following categories and numbers represent the postgraduate activities and employment of doctoral degree graduates: Enrolled in a psychology doctoral program (n/a), enrolled in a postdoctoral residency/fellowship (5), total from the above (doctoral) (5).

Additional Information:

Orientation, Objectives, and Emphasis of Department: The graduate program offers training in social psychology, cognition–perception, cognitive neuroscience, and behavioral neuroscience. Many of our students pursue research that bridges these areas. Because of its moderate size, the program emphasizes a close working relationship between faculty and students. The program has a strong experimental orientation in which students serve research and teaching apprenticeships with faculty. The emphasis is on professional development for academic careers.

Special Facilities or Resources: The department has excellent laboratories with ample equipment and superior computer facilities.

Application Information:

Send to Chair, Graduate Committee, 6207 Moore Hall, Hanover, NH 03755-3578. Students are admitted in the Fall, application deadline December 15. *Fee:* $50.

New Hampshire, University of

Department of Psychology
Conant Hall
Durham, NH 03824
Telephone: (603) 862-2360
Fax: (603) 862-4986
E-mail: *janicec@unh.edu*
Web: *http://www.unh.edu/psychology/*

Department Information:

1923. Chairperson: Robert G. Mair. Number of faculty: total—full-time 22, part-time 1; women—full-time 6; total—minority—full-time 1.

Programs and Degrees Offered:

Listed in the following order: Program area, degree type (T if terminal Master's), number awarded 7/06–6/07. Developmental PhD (Doctor of Philosophy), Sensation–Perception PhD (Doctor of Philosophy), Social–Personality PhD (Doctor of Philosophy), Cognitive Neuroscience PhD (Doctor of Philosophy), Behavioral Neuroscience PhD (Doctor of Philosophy).

Student Applications/Admissions:

Student Applications

Developmental PhD (Doctor of Philosophy)—Total enrolled 2007–2008 full-time, 6. *Sensation–Perception PhD (Doctor of*

Philosophy)—Total enrolled 2007–2008 full-time, 2. *Social–Personality PhD (Doctor of Philosophy)*—Total enrolled 2007–2008 full-time, 14. *Cognitive Neuroscience PhD (Doctor of Philosophy)*—Total enrolled 2007–2008 full-time, 3. *Behavioral Neuroscience PhD (Doctor of Philosophy)*—Total enrolled 2007–2008 full-time, 4.

Admissions Requirements:

Scores: Entries appear in this order: required test or GPA, minimum score (if required), median score of students entering in 2007–2008. Doctoral Programs: GRE-V no minimum stated; GRE-Q no minimum stated; overall undergraduate GPA no minimum stated; psychology GPA no minimum stated; Doctoral program GRE-Analytic no minimum stated. GRE-subject (Psychology) recommended.

Other Criteria: (importance of criteria rated low, medium, or high): GRE/MAT scores—high, research experience—high, work experience—low, extracurricular activity—low, GPA—high, letters of recommendation—high, interview—low, statement of goals and objectives—high, interests match program—high, undergraduate major in psychology—medium, specific undergraduate psychology courses taken—medium. For additional information on admission requirements, go to http://www.unh.edu/psychology/grad_pro.htm.

Student Characteristics: The following represents characteristics of students in 2007–2008 in all graduate psychology programs in the department: Female—full-time 17, part-time 0; Male—full-time 12, part-time 0; African American/Black—full-time 0, part-time 0; Hispanic/Latino(a)—full-time 0, part-time 0; Asian/Pacific Islander—full-time 0, part-time 0; American Indian/Alaska Native—full-time 0, part-time 0; Caucasian/White—full-time 28, part-time 0; Multi-ethnic—full-time 1, part-time 0; students subject to the Americans With Disabilities Act—full-time 0, part-time 0; Unknown ethnicity—full-time 0, part-time 0; International students who hold an F-1 or J-1 Visa—full-time 2, part-time 0.

Financial Information/Assistance:

Financial Assistance:

First-Year Students: Teaching assistantships available for first year. Average amount paid per academic year: $14,100. Average number of hours worked per week: 20. Apply by January 15. Tuition remission given: full.

Advanced Students: Teaching assistantships available for advanced students. Average amount paid per academic year: $15,050. Average number of hours worked per week: 20. Tuition remission given: full. Fellowships and scholarships available for advanced students. Average amount paid per academic year: $16,000. Tuition remission given: full.

Additional Information: Of all students currently enrolled full time, 100% benefited from one or more of the listed financial assistance programs. Application and information available online at http://www.unh.edu/psychology/grad_pro.htm.

Internships/Practica: No information provided.

Housing and Day Care: On-campus housing is available. See the following Web site for more information: http://www.unhinfo.unh.edu/housing/gradhousing/gradhousing.html and http://www.unh.edu/housing/famhousing/index.html. On-campus day care facilities are available. See the following Web site for more information: http://www.csdc.unh.edu/.

Employment of Department Graduates:

Master's Degree Graduates: Of those who graduated in the academic year 2006–2007, the following categories and numbers represent the postgraduate activities and employment of master's degree graduates: Enrolled in a postdoctoral residency/fellowship (n/a), employed in independent practice (n/a), total from the above (master's) (0).

Doctoral Degree Graduates: Of those who graduated in the academic year 2006–2007, the following categories and numbers represent the postgraduate activities and employment of doctoral degree graduates: Enrolled in a psychology doctoral program (n/a), employed in business or industry (1), not seeking employment (1), do not know (1), total from the above (doctoral) (3).

Additional Information:

Orientation, Objectives, and Emphasis of Department: The program's basic goal is the preparation of doctoral students for academic careers. We focus on the development of psychologists who have a broad knowledge of psychology, who can teach and communicate effectively, and who can carry out sound research. Specialties are offered in the following areas: Brain, Behavior, and Cognition (behavioral and cognitive neuroscience, cognition, vision); Developmental Psychology; and Social Psychology–Personality. Besides completing academic courses, our program places a distinctive emphasis on preparing graduate students for future roles as faculty members in college or university settings. Students complete a year-long seminar and practicum in the teaching of psychology, which introduces them to the theory and practice of teaching, while they concurrently teach under the supervision of master–teachers. Students also gain experience in other faculty roles such as sponsoring undergraduate students' research and serving on committees. Students are involved in research activities throughout the program. After graduation, most students secure academic positions. All students receive tuition waivers and stipends for at least 4 years, in exchange for serving as teaching or research assistants in their early years and as teachers in their later years. Students can apply for research and summer funding.

Special Facilities or Resources: The department occupies several buildings and offers research facilities, equipment, and resources in all of its areas of specialization. In addition, the department has up-to-date computing and related resources.

Application Information:

Send to Dean of the Graduate School, University of New Hampshire, Thompson Hall, Durham, NH 03824. Application available online. URL of online application: http://www.unh.edu/psychology/grad_pro.htm. Students are admitted in the Fall, no deadline. Review of applications begins January 15 and continues until the incoming class is filled. *Fee:* $60. Financial aid applications are available.

Fairleigh Dickinson University, Madison
Department of Psychology M-AB2-01
College at Florham
285 Madison Avenue
Madison, NJ 07940
Telephone: (973) 443-8547
Fax: (973) 443-8562
E-mail: *diane_wentworth@fdu.edu*
Web: *http://www.fdu.edu*

Department Information:

1962. Chairperson: Dr. Diane Keyser Wentworth. Number of faculty: total—full-time 9, part-time 15; women—full-time 7, part-time 8; total—minority—full-time 2; women minority—full-time 2.

Programs and Degrees Offered:

Listed in the following order: Program area, degree type (T if terminal Master's), number awarded 7/06–6/07. Counseling MA/MS (Master of Arts/Science) (T) 49, Industrial/Organizational MA/MS (Master of Arts/Science) (T) 10, Organizational Behavior MA/MS (Master of Arts/Science) (T) 6.

Student Applications/Admissions:

Student Applications

Counseling MA/MS (Master of Arts/Science)—Applications 2007–2008, 87. Total applicants accepted 2007–2008, 70. Number full-time enrolled (new admits only) 2007–2008, 16. Number part-time enrolled (new admits only) 2007–2008, 14. Total enrolled 2007–2008 full-time, 58, part-time, 54. Openings 2008–2009, 30. The median number of years required for completion of a degree in 2006–2007 were 3. The number of students enrolled full- and part-time who were dismissed or voluntarily withdrew from this program area in 2007–2008 were 1. *Industrial/Organizational MA/MS (Master of Arts/Science)*—Applications 2007–2008, 20. Total applicants accepted 2007–2008, 14. Number full-time enrolled (new admits only) 2007–2008, 7. Number part-time enrolled (new admits only) 2007–2008, 5. Total enrolled 2007–2008 full-time, 15, part-time, 13. Openings 2008–2009, 20. The median number of years required for completion of a degree in 2006–2007 were 3. The number of students enrolled full- and part-time who were dismissed or voluntarily withdrew from this program area in 2007–2008 were 0. *Organizational Behavior MA/MS (Master of Arts/Science)*—Applications 2007–2008, 5. Total applicants accepted 2007–2008, 4. Number full-time enrolled (new admits only) 2007–2008, 0. Number part-time enrolled (new admits only) 2007–2008, 4. Openings 2008–2009, 15. The median number of years required for completion of a degree in 2006–2007 were 3. The number of students enrolled full- and part-time who were dismissed or voluntarily withdrew from this program area in 2007–2008 were 0.

Admissions Requirements:

Scores: Entries appear in this order: required test or GPA, minimum score (if required), median score of students entering in 2007–2008. Master's Programs: GRE-V 500, 530; GRE-Q 500, 520; overall undergraduate GPA 3.0, 3.4; psychology GPA 3.0, 3.5; Masters GRE-Analytical 500, 500.

Other Criteria: (importance of criteria rated low, medium, or high): GRE/MAT scores—medium, research experience—medium, work experience—medium, extracurricular activity—medium, clinically related public service—low, GPA—high, letters of recommendation—high, interview—medium, statement of goals and objectives—high, undergraduate major in psychology—medium, specific undergraduate psychology courses taken—medium. Organizational program has a minimum work experience requirement. For additional information on admission requirements, go to http://www.fdu.edu.

Student Characteristics: The following represents characteristics of students in 2007–2008 in all graduate psychology programs in the department: Female—full-time 57, part-time 62; Male—full-time 16, part-time 20; African American/Black—full-time 7, part-time 7; Hispanic/Latino(a)—full-time 7, part-time 9; Asian/Pacific Islander—full-time 4, part-time 4; American Indian/Alaska Native—full-time 0, part-time 1; Caucasian/White—full-time 40, part-time 46; Multi-ethnic—full-time 0, part-time 1; students subject to the Americans With Disabilities Act—full-time 0, part-time 0; Unknown ethnicity—full-time 15, part-time 14; International students who hold an F-1 or J-1 Visa—full-time 2, part-time 2.

Financial Information/Assistance:

Tuition for Full-Time Study: *Master's:* State residents: $869 per credit hour; Nonstate residents: $869 per credit hour. Tuition is subject to change. See the following Web site for updates and changes in tuition costs: http://www.fdu.edu.

Financial Assistance:

First-Year Students: Teaching assistantships available for first year. Average amount paid per academic year: $1,000. Average number of hours worked per week: 20. Apply by March 31. Tuition remission given: full and partial.

Advanced Students: Teaching assistantships available for advanced students. Average amount paid per academic year: $1,000. Average number of hours worked per week: 20. Apply by March 31. Tuition remission given: full and partial.

Additional Information: Of all students currently enrolled full time, 7% benefited from one or more of the listed financial assistance programs. Application and information available online at http://www.fdu.edu.

Internships/Practica: Master's Degree (MA/MS Counseling): An internship experience such as a final research project or "capstone" experience is required of graduates. Master's Degree (MA/MS Industrial/Organizational): An internship experience such as a final research project or "capstone" experience is required of graduates. Both the Masters in Counseling and Industrial/Organizational Psychology have numerous practica and/or internship opportunities available in a variety of program-related settings. Counseling students complete their required practica/internships, supervised hours, and an additional 12 credits of graduate work and can become eligible to sit for the New Jersey Licensed Professional Counselor designation if so desired.

Housing and Day Care: On-campus housing is available. See the following Web site for more information: http://www.fdu.edu. No on-campus day care facilities are available.

Employment of Department Graduates:

Master's Degree Graduates: Of those who graduated in the academic year 2006–2007, the following categories and numbers represent the postgraduate activities and employment of master's degree graduates: Enrolled in a psychology doctoral program (4), enrolled in another graduate/professional program (2), enrolled in a postdoctoral residency/fellowship (n/a), employed in independent practice (n/a), total from the above (master's) (6).

Doctoral Degree Graduates: Of those who graduated in the academic year 2006–2007, the following categories and numbers represent the postgraduate activities and employment of doctoral degree graduates: Enrolled in a psychology doctoral program (n/a), total from the above (doctoral) (0).

Additional Information:

Orientation, Objectives, and Emphasis of Department: The programs and courses offered by the psychology department are designed to meet the needs of students who wish to prepare for careers in various scientific and professional areas of psychology such as research, teaching, and practice in a variety of settings (e.g., treatment centers, school settings, private practice, counseling centers, human resource departments, consulting organizations). In addition, programs and courses also meet the needs of students who wish to develop a background for subsequent work leading to a doctoral degree.

Personal Behavior Statement: Graduate Code of Conduct at http://www.fdu.edu.

Special Facilities or Resources: The department provides facilities for research in both counseling practices and industrial/organizational behavior. Most faculty members are practicing psychologists as well as researchers and provide intern-type experiences for students. The department publishes *The Journal of Psychology and the Behavioral Sciences* that is an outlet for student research. Students are highly involved in the publication process.

Information for Students With Physical Disabilities: See the following Web site for more information: http://www.fdu.edu.

Application Information:

Send to Office of Graduate Admissions, Fairleigh Dickinson University, 285 Madison Avenue, Madison, NJ 07940. See the FDU Web site to apply, http://www.fdu.edu. Application available online. Students are admitted in the Fall. Programs have rolling admissions. *Fee:* $40.

Fairleigh Dickinson University, Metropolitan Campus

School of Psychology
University College: Arts-Sciences-Professional Studies
1000 River Road
Teaneck, NJ 07666
Telephone: (201) 692-2300
Fax: (201) 692-2304
E-mail: *capuano@fdu.edu*
Web: *http://www.fdu.edu*

Department Information:

1960. Director: Christopher A. Capuano, PhD. Number of faculty: total—full-time 18, part-time 11; women—full-time 9, part-time 4.

Programs and Degrees Offered:

Listed in the following order: Program area, degree type (T if terminal Master's), number awarded 7/06–6/07. General/Theoretical MA/MS (Master of Arts/Science) (T) 14, Clinical PhD (Doctor of Philosophy) 11, School PsyD (Doctor of Psychology) 16, Psychopharmacology MA/MS (Master of Arts/Science) (T) 11, School MA/MS (Master of Arts/Science) (T) 4, Forensic MA/MS (Master of Arts/Science) (T) 0.

APA Accreditation: Clinical PhD (Doctor of Philosophy).

Student Applications/Admissions:

Student Applications

General/Theoretical MA/MS (Master of Arts/Science)—Applications 2007–2008, 32. Total applicants accepted 2007–2008, 12. Number full-time enrolled (new admits only) 2007–2008, 6. Number part-time enrolled (new admits only) 2007–2008, 6. Total enrolled 2007–2008 full-time, 32, part-time, 24. Openings 2008–2009, 12. The median number of years required for completion of a degree in 2006–2007 were 3. The number of students enrolled full- and part-time who were dismissed or voluntarily withdrew from this program area in 2007–2008 were 2. *Clinical PhD (Doctor of Philosophy)*—Applications 2007–2008, 225. Total applicants accepted 2007–2008, 32. Number full-time enrolled (new admits only) 2007–2008, 11. Number part-time enrolled (new admits only) 2007–2008, 0. Openings 2008–2009, 14. The median number of years required for completion of a degree in 2006–2007 were 5. The number of students enrolled full- and part-time who were dismissed or voluntarily withdrew from this program area in 2007–2008 were 2. *School PsyD (Doctor of Psychology)*—Applications 2007–2008, 40. Total applicants accepted 2007–2008, 12. Number full-time enrolled (new admits only) 2007–2008, 10. Openings 2008–2009, 15. The median number of years required for completion of a degree in 2006–2007 were 3. The number of students enrolled full- and part-time who were dismissed or voluntarily withdrew from this program area in 2007–2008 were 1. *Psychopharmacology MA/MS (Master of Arts/Science)*—Applications 2007–2008, 27. Total applicants accepted 2007–2008, 27. Number part-time enrolled (new admits only) 2007–2008, 27. Total enrolled 2007–2008 part-time, 47. Openings 2008–2009, 20. The median number of years required for completion of a degree in 2006–2007 were 2. The number of students enrolled full- and part-time who were dismissed or voluntarily withdrew from this program area in 2007–2008 were 8. *School MA/MS (Master of Arts/Science)*—Total applicants accepted 2007–2008, 18. Number full-time enrolled (new admits only) 2007–2008, 10. Number part-time enrolled (new admits only) 2007–2008, 8. Total enrolled 2007–2008 full-time, 29, part-time, 10. Openings 2008–2009, 20. The median number of years required for completion of a degree in 2006–2007 were 3. The number of students enrolled full- and part-time who were dismissed or voluntarily withdrew from this program area in 2007–2008 were 7. *Forensic MA/MS (Master of Arts/Science)*—Number full-time enrolled (new admits only) 2007–2008, 0. Number part-time enrolled (new admits only) 2007–2008, 0. Openings 2008–2009, 12.

Admissions Requirements:

Scores: Entries appear in this order: required test or GPA, minimum score (if required), median score of students entering in 2007–2008. Master's Programs: GRE-V 500, 560; GRE-Q 500, 580; GRE-Subject (Psychology) 500, 570; overall undergraduate GPA 3.00, 3.20; psychology GPA 3.25, 3.40. Minimum scores/GPAs indicated are preferred, not required. Doctoral Programs: GRE-V 550, 590; GRE-Q 550, 610; GRE-Subject (Psychology) 600, 640; overall undergraduate GPA 3.25, 3.50. Minimum scores/GPAs indicated are preferred, not required.

Other Criteria: (importance of criteria rated low, medium, or high): research experience—high, work experience—medium, extracurricular activity—medium, clinically related public service—high, letters of recommendation—high, interview—high, statement of goals and objectives—high. These criteria are used for admission to PhD and PsyD programs. For PsyD program, research experience would be low and work experience would be medium-high. For additional information on admission requirements, go to http://www.fdu.edu/schoolofpsychology.

Student Characteristics: The following represents characteristics of students in 2007–2008 in all graduate psychology programs in the department: Female—full-time 117, part-time 70; Male—full-time 84, part-time 11; Caucasian/White—full-time 0, part-time 0; Unknown ethnicity—full-time 0, part-time 0.

Financial Information/Assistance:

Tuition for Full-Time Study: *Master's:* State residents: $869 per credit hour; Nonstate residents: $869 per credit hour. *Doctoral:* State residents: per academic year $27,628; Nonstate residents: per academic year $22,774.

Financial Assistance:

First-Year Students: Research assistantships available for first year. Average amount paid per academic year: $15,814. Average number of hours worked per week: 20. Apply by PhD students.

Advanced Students: Research assistantships available for advanced students. Average amount paid per academic year: $13,814. Average number of hours worked per week: 20. Apply by PhD students.

Additional Information: Of all students currently enrolled full time, 33% benefited from one or more of the listed financial assistance programs. Application and information available online at http://www.fdu.edu/schoolofpsychology.

Internships/Practica: Master's Degree (MA/MS Psychopharmacology): An internship experience such as a final research project or "capstone" experience is required of graduates. Master's Degree (MA/MS School): An internship experience such as a final research project or "capstone" experience is required of graduates. Master's Degree (MA/MS Forensic): An internship experience, such as, a final research project or "capstone" experience is required of graduates. Doctoral Degree (PhD Clinical): For those doctoral students for whom a professional internship was required in this program prior to graduation, (23) students applied for an internship in 2006–2007, with (21) students obtaining an internship. Of those students who obtained an internship, (21) were paid internships. Of those students who obtained an internship, (20) students placed in APA/CPA-accredited internships, (1) students placed in internships not APA/CPA-accredited, but listed with the Association of Psychology Postdoctoral and Internship Centers (APPIC), (0) students placed in internships conforming to guidelines of the Council of Directors of School Psychology Programs (CDSPP), (0) students placed in internships that were not APA/CPA-accredited, APPIC or CDSPP listed. Doctoral Degree (PsyD School): For those doctoral students for whom a professional internship was required in this program prior to graduation, (13) students applied for an internship in 2006–2007, with (13) students obtaining an internship. Of those students who obtained an internship, (13) were paid internships. Of those students who obtained an internship, (0) students placed in APA/CPA-accredited internships, (0) students placed in internships not APA/CPA-accredited, but listed with the Association of Psychology Postdoctoral and Internship Centers (APPIC), (0) students placed in internships conforming to guidelines of the Council of Directors of School Psychology Programs (CDSPP), (13) students placed in internships that were not APA/CPA-accredited, APPIC or CDSPP listed. All PhD students are required to complete research and clinical practica during their first 3 years. Clinical practica may be completed on-campus at the University's Center for Psychological Services.

Housing and Day Care: No on-campus housing is available. No on-campus day care facilities are available.

Employment of Department Graduates:

Master's Degree Graduates: Of those who graduated in the academic year 2006–2007, the following categories and numbers represent the postgraduate activities and employment of master's degree graduates: Enrolled in a postdoctoral residency/fellowship (n/a), employed in independent practice (n/a), total from the above (master's) (0).

Doctoral Degree Graduates: Of those who graduated in the academic year 2006–2007, the following categories and numbers represent the postgraduate activities and employment of doctoral degree graduates: Enrolled in a psychology doctoral program (n/a), total from the above (doctoral) (0).

Additional Information:

Orientation, Objectives, and Emphasis of Department: The orientation of the department is essentially based on the scientist–practitioner model. In terms of theoretical orientations, some faculty are dynamicists, some behaviorists, and some humanists, though there is a sense of eclecticism that pervades those who are practitioners. There is a considerable emphasis on empirical research as the preferred basis for developing a theoretical orientation.

Special Facilities or Resources: The department operates the Center for Psychological Services, which provides students in the PhD and PsyD programs opportunities in therapy and assessment with adults, children, families, and couples. The department has research laboratories equipped for experiments with humans as well as with small animals. Equipment includes computer facilities, both micro- and mainframe, a four-channel physiograph, electrophysiological stimulating and recording equipment, operant equipment for programming and recording behavior, two- and four-channel tachistoscopes, various other sensory apparatus, standard and computer-based EEG recorders, and equipment and supplies for psychopharmacological studies.

Application Information:

Send to School of Psychology (T-WH1-01), Fairleigh Dickinson University, 1000 River Road, Teaneck, NJ 07666. Students are admitted in the Fall. Application deadline for Fall: January 15, PhD; March 1, PsyD; March 15, MA School; March 15, MA Forensic. Spring admission is only for applicants to the BA/MA and MA programs in general/theoretical psychology. *Fee:* $40. The application fee is waived or deferred for Fairleigh Dickinson graduates; $40 for doctoral programs and $35 for MA programs.

Georgian Court University

Psychology Department/Counseling Psychology
900 Lakewood Avenue
Lakewood, NJ 08701-2697
Telephone: (732) 987-2619
Fax: (732) 987-2090
E-mail: *dasilvam@georgian.edu*
Web: *http://www.georgian.edu/psychgy/ps-wwd.htm*

Department Information:

1972. Director of Graduate Programs in Counseling Psychology: Mimi da Silva, PhD. Number of faculty: total—full-time 11, part-time 6; women—full-time 7, part-time 4.

Programs and Degrees Offered:

Listed in the following order: Program area, degree type (T if terminal Master's), number awarded 7/06–6/07. Counseling MA/MS (Master of Arts/Science) (T) 15, Substance Abuse Counseling MA/MS (Master of Arts/Science) (T) 0.

Student Applications/Admissions:

Student Applications

Counseling MA/MS (Master of Arts/Science)—Applications 2007–2008, 43. Total applicants accepted 2007–2008, 20. Number full-time enrolled (new admits only) 2007–2008, 10. Number part-time enrolled (new admits only) 2007–2008, 10. Total enrolled 2007–2008 full-time, 20, part-time, 71. Openings 2008–2009, 20. The median number of years required for completion of a degree in 2006–2007 were 3. The number of students enrolled full- and part-time who were dismissed or voluntarily withdrew from this program area in 2007–2008 were 1. *Substance Abuse Counseling MA/MS (Master of Arts/Science)*—Applications 2007–2008, 5. Total applicants accepted 2007–2008, 3. Number full-time enrolled (new admits only) 2007–2008, 1. Total enrolled 2007–2008 full-time, 1. Openings 2008–2009, 8. The number of students enrolled full- and part-time who were dismissed or voluntarily withdrew from this program area in 2007–2008 were 0.

Admissions Requirements:

Scores: Entries appear in this order: required test or GPA, minimum score (if required), median score of students entering in 2007–2008. Master's Programs: GRE-V no minimum stated, 450; GRE-Q no minimum stated, 510; overall undergraduate GPA 3.00.

Other Criteria: (importance of criteria rated low, medium, or high): GRE/MAT scores—low, research experience—medium, work experience—high, extracurricular activity—medium, clinically related public service—high, GPA—high, letters of recommendation—high, interview—high, statement of goals and objectives—high, undergraduate major in psychology—low, specific undergraduate psychology courses taken—high.

Student Characteristics: The following represents characteristics of students in 2007–2008 in all graduate psychology programs in the department: Female—full-time 26, part-time 76; Male—full-time 4, part-time 5; African American/Black—full-time 0, part-time 2; Hispanic/Latino(a)—full-time 0, part-time 5; Asian/Pacific Islander—full-time 0, part-time 2; American Indian/Alaska Native—full-time 0, part-time 0; Caucasian/White—full-time 21, part-time 72; students subject to the Americans With Disabilities Act—full-time 1, part-time 3; Unknown ethnicity—full-time 0, part-time 0; International students who hold an F-1 or J-1 Visa—part-time 1.

Financial Information/Assistance:

Tuition for Full-Time Study: *Master's:* State residents: $682 per credit hour; Nonstate residents: $682 per credit hour.

Financial Assistance:

First-Year Students: No information provided.

Advanced Students: Research assistantships available for advanced students. Average number of hours worked per week: 9. Apply by April 30. Tuition remission given: partial.

Additional Information: Of all students currently enrolled full time, 8% benefited from one or more of the listed financial assistance programs.

Internships/Practica: Master's Degree (MA/MS Counseling): An internship experience such as a final research project or "capstone" experience is required of graduates. Practicum experiences take place in college counseling centers, mental health outpatient facilities, inpatient state and private hospitals, and schools.

Housing and Day Care: No on-campus housing is available. No on-campus day care facilities are available.

Employment of Department Graduates:

Master's Degree Graduates: Of those who graduated in the academic year 2006–2007, the following categories and numbers represent the postgraduate activities and employment of master's degree graduates: Enrolled in a postdoctoral residency/fellowship (n/a), employed in independent practice (n/a), employed in a professional position in a school system (8), employed in a community mental health/counseling center (6), total from the above (master's) (14).

Doctoral Degree Graduates: Of those who graduated in the academic year 2006–2007, the following categories and numbers represent the postgraduate activities and employment of doctoral degree graduates: Enrolled in a psychology doctoral program (n/a), total from the above (doctoral) (0).

Additional Information:

Orientation, Objectives, and Emphasis of Department: Course work for both the Master's and School Psychology Certificate program is designed to provide sound clinical training based in theory. The Professional Counselor Certificate Program is for students who have an MA degree who wish to pursue additional coursework necessary to academically qualify for the Licensed Professional Counselor designation through the State of New Jersey. The majority of the faculty is full-time with experience in clinical and school settings. Four full-time faculty and three adjuncts are licensed to practice psychology in NJ and bring a wealth of diverse clinical experience. Four of the full-time faculty and one adjunct are certified school psychologists with many years of experience in the public and parochial schools. Course work will prepare the students to work in diverse settings, to make assessments of children and adults, to develop clinical skills with strong theoretical underpinnings, and to become competent professionals. Practica experiences are provided in a variety of settings in the surrounding community, with supervision provided on-site and within the classroom. School psychology externships meet NJ state requirements. Courses meet in the late afternoon and evening. Students may attend either part-time or full-time. Georgian Court University is a private Catholic institution.

Special Facilities or Resources: There are four computer labs available on campus and an interactive television lab.

Application Information:

Send to Uta McQuade, Dpeartment of Psychology, Georgian Court University, Lakewood, NJ 08701. Students are admitted in the Fall, application deadline March 30. *Fee:* $40.

Kean University

Department of Psychology
Morris Avenue
Union, NJ 07083
Telephone: (908) 737-4000
Fax: (908) 737-4004
E-mail: *sbousque@kean.edu*
Web: *http://www.kean.edu*

Department Information:

1969. Chairperson: Dr. Suzanne Bousquet. Number of faculty: total—full-time 19, part-time 40; women—full-time 12, part-time 20; total—minority—full-time 3, part-time 20; women minority—full-time 3, part-time 10; faculty subject to the Americans With Disabilities Act 1.

Programs and Degrees Offered:

Listed in the following order: Program area, degree type (T if terminal Master's), number awarded 7/06–6/07. Marriage and Family Therapy Other 4, Human Behavior and Organizational Psychology MA/MS (Master of Arts/Science) (T) 14, Psychological Services MA/MS (Master of Arts/Science) (T) 11, School Psychology MA/MS (Master of Arts/Science) (T) 8, Educational Psychology MA/MS (Master of Arts/Science) 5.

Student Applications/Admissions:

Student Applications

Marriage and Family Therapy Other—Applications 2007–2008, 20. Total applicants accepted 2007–2008, 17. Total enrolled 2007–2008 full-time, 9, part-time, 10. Openings 2008–2009, 12. The median number of years required for completion of a degree in 2006–2007 were 3. The number of students enrolled full- and part-time who were dismissed or voluntarily withdrew from this program area in 2007–2008 were 0. *Human Behavior and Organizational Psychology MA/MS (Master of Arts/Science)*—Applications 2007–2008, 23. Total applicants accepted 2007–2008, 21. Total enrolled 2007–2008 full-time, 11, part-time, 28. Openings 2008–2009, 20. The number of students enrolled full- and part-time who were dismissed or voluntarily withdrew from this program area in 2007–2008 were 0. *Psychological Services MA/MS (Master of Arts/Science)*—Applications 2007–2008, 20. Total applicants accepted 2007–2008, 17. Total enrolled 2007–2008 full-time, 7, part-time, 30. Openings 2008–2009, 15. The median number of years required for completion of a degree in 2006–2007 were 3. The number of students enrolled full- and part-time who were dismissed or voluntarily withdrew from this program area in 2007–2008 were 0. *School Psychology MA/MS (Master of Arts/Science)*—Applications 2007–2008, 61. Total applicants accepted 2007–2008, 13. Total enrolled 2007–2008 full-time, 10, part-time, 23. Openings 2008–2009, 12. The number of students enrolled full- and part-time who were dismissed or voluntarily withdrew from this program area in 2007–2008 were 0. *Educational Psychology MA/MS (Master of Arts/Science)*—Applications 2007–2008, 6. Total applicants accepted 2007–2008, 3. Total enrolled 2007–2008 part-time, 3. Openings 2008–2009, 12. The median number of years required for completion of a degree in 2006–2007 were 3. The number of students enrolled full- and part-time who were dismissed or voluntarily withdrew from this program area in 2007–2008 were 0.

Admissions Requirements:

Scores: Entries appear in this order: required test or GPA, minimum score (if required), median score of students entering in 2007–2008. Master's Programs: GRE-V no minimum stated; GRE-Q no minimum stated; overall undergraduate GPA 3.0; last 2 years GPA 3.0; psychology GPA 3.0.

Other Criteria: (importance of criteria rated low, medium, or high): GRE/MAT scores—high, research experience—medium, work experience—medium, extracurricular activity—low, clinically related public service—high, GPA—high, letters of recommendation—high, interview—medium, statement of goals and objectives—medium.

Student Characteristics: The following represents characteristics of students in 2007–2008 in all graduate psychology programs in the department: Female—full-time 19, part-time 88; Male—full-time 5, part-time 23; Caucasian/White—full-time 0, part-time 0; Unknown ethnicity—full-time 24, part-time 111.

Financial Information/Assistance:

Tuition for Full-Time Study: *Master's:* State residents: per academic year $5,883, $462 per credit hour; Nonstate residents: per

academic year $7,551, $562 per credit hour. Tuition is subject to change. See the following Web site for updates and changes in tuition costs: http://www.kean.edu.

Financial Assistance:

First-Year Students: Teaching assistantships available for first year. Average amount paid per academic year: $3,217. Average number of hours worked per week: 15. Apply by June 1. Tuition remission given: full.

Advanced Students: Teaching assistantships available for advanced students. Average amount paid per academic year: $3,217. Average number of hours worked per week: 15. Apply by June 1. Tuition remission given: full.

Additional Information: Of all students currently enrolled full time, 20% benefited from one or more of the listed financial assistance programs. Application and information available online at http://www.kean.edu.

Internships/Practica: Internships are available for school psychology, marriage and family therapy, and behavioral science students in a variety of settings.

Housing and Day Care: No on-campus housing is available. On-campus day care facilities are available. See the following Web site for more information: http://www.kean.edu.

Employment of Department Graduates:

Master's Degree Graduates: Of those who graduated in the academic year 2006–2007, the following categories and numbers represent the postgraduate activities and employment of master's degree graduates: Enrolled in a postdoctoral residency/fellowship (n/a), employed in independent practice (n/a), total from the above (master's) (0).

Doctoral Degree Graduates: Of those who graduated in the academic year 2006–2007, the following categories and numbers represent the postgraduate activities and employment of doctoral degree graduates: Enrolled in a psychology doctoral program (n/a), total from the above (doctoral) (0).

Additional Information:

Orientation, Objectives, and Emphasis of Department: Our academic emphasis is eclectic. All classes are small, which facilitates the opportunity for personal growth.

Special Facilities or Resources: Special resources include two complete computer facilities. One is integrated with statistics, tests and measurement, and experimental psychology courses; the other is used in conjunction with professional psychology testing courses and general instruction.

Information for Students With Physical Disabilities: See the following Web site for more information: http://www.kean.edu.

Application Information:

Send to Office of Graduate Admissions, Kean University, Union, NJ 07083. Application available online. URL of online application: http://www.kean.edu. Students are admitted in the Fall, application deadline May 1; Spring, application deadline November 1. For School Psychology, deadline is March 15. Spring admits for all programs except School Psychology and Educational Psychology. *Fee:* $60 for U.S. residents and $150 for international students.

Rowan University

Department of Psychology
College of Liberal Arts and Sciences
201 Mullica Hill Road
Glassboro, NJ 08028-1701
Telephone: (856) 256-4500 ext 3780
Fax: (856) 256-4892
E-mail: *Angeloned@rowan.edu*
Web: *http://www.rowan.edu/colleges/las/departments/psychology/*

Department Information:

1969. Program Coordinator: D. J. Angelone, PhD. Number of faculty: total—full-time 18; women—full-time 12; total—minority—full-time 3; women minority—full-time 3.

Programs and Degrees Offered:

Listed in the following order: Program area, degree type (T if terminal Master's), number awarded 7/06–6/07. Clinical Mental Health Counseling MA/MS (Master of Arts/Science) 12.

Student Applications/Admissions:

Student Applications

Clinical Mental Health Counseling MA/MS (Master of Arts/Science)—Applications 2007–2008, 50. Total applicants accepted 2007–2008, 15. Number full-time enrolled (new admits only) 2007–2008, 12. Number part-time enrolled (new admits only) 2007–2008, 3. Total enrolled 2007–2008 full-time, 24, part-time, 11. Openings 2008–2009, 15. The median number of years required for completion of a degree in 2006–2007 were 2. The number of students enrolled full- and part-time who were dismissed or voluntarily withdrew from this program area in 2007–2008 were 2.

Admissions Requirements:

Scores: Entries appear in this order: required test or GPA, minimum score (if required), median score of students entering in 2007–2008. Master's Programs: GRE-V no minimum stated; GRE-Q no minimum stated; overall undergraduate GPA 3.0; psychology GPA no minimum stated; Masters GRE-Analytical no minimum stated.

Other Criteria: (importance of criteria rated low, medium, or high): GRE/MAT scores—medium, research experience—medium, work experience—medium, extracurricular activity—low, clinically related public service—high, GPA—high, letters of recommendation—high, interview—high, statement of goals and objectives—high, specific undergraduate psychology courses taken—medium.

Student Characteristics: The following represents characteristics of students in 2007–2008 in all graduate psychology programs in the department: Female—full-time 19, part-time 10; Male—full-time 5, part-time 1; African American/Black—full-time 0, part-time 2; Hispanic/Latino(a)—full-time 0, part-time 0; Asian/Pacific Islander—full-time 2, part-time 0; American Indian/Alaska Native—full-time 1, part-time 0; Caucasian/White—full-time 21, part-time 9; Multi-ethnic—full-time 0, part-time 0; students subject to the Americans With Disabilities Act—full-time 0, part-time 0; Unknown ethnicity—full-time 0, part-time 0; International students who hold an F-1 or J-1 Visa—full-time 0, part-time 0.

Financial Information/Assistance:

Tuition for Full-Time Study: *Master's:* State residents: per academic year $5,312, $590 per credit hour; Nonstate residents: per academic year $5,312, $590 per credit hour. Tuition is subject to change. See the following Web site for updates and changes in tuition costs: http://www.rowan.edu/adminfinance/bursar/tuitionfeesandrates.html.

Financial Assistance:

First-Year Students: Research assistantships available for first year. Average amount paid per academic year: $4,000. Average number of hours worked per week: 20. Tuition remission given: partial. Fellowships and scholarships available for first year. Average amount paid per academic year: $4,000. Average number of hours worked per week: 20. Tuition remission given: partial.

Advanced Students: Research assistantships available for advanced students. Average amount paid per academic year: $4,000. Tuition remission given: partial. Fellowships and scholarships available for advanced students. Average amount paid per academic year: $4,000. Tuition remission given: partial.

Additional Information: Of all students currently enrolled full time, 20% benefited from one or more of the listed financial assistance programs. Application and information available online at http://www.rowan.edu/graduateschool/financial_aid/graduate_assistantships.htm#compensation.

Internships/Practica: Practica are available in a wide range of mental health settings.

Housing and Day Care: On-campus housing is available. See the following Web site for more information: http://www.rowan.edu/studentaffairs/reslife/assignment/. On-campus day care facilities are available. See the following Web site for more information: http://www.rowan.edu/colleges/education/childcare/.

Employment of Department Graduates:

Master's Degree Graduates: Of those who graduated in the academic year 2006–2007, the following categories and numbers represent the postgraduate activities and employment of master's degree graduates: Enrolled in a postdoctoral residency/fellowship (n/a), employed in independent practice (n/a), total from the above (master's) (0).

Doctoral Degree Graduates: Of those who graduated in the academic year 2006–2007, the following categories and numbers represent the postgraduate activities and employment of doctoral degree graduates: Enrolled in a psychology doctoral program (n/a), total from the above (doctoral) (0).

Additional Information:

Orientation, Objectives, and Emphasis of Department: The program is designed to be consistent with an evidence-based practice model. This 60-credit Master's program prepares students to become mental health counselors and is designed to meet the coursework and practicum requirements of the National Board of Certified Counselors. Students completing this program and additional supervised hours will be eligible to apply for the New Jersey Licensed Professional Counseling Certification. Graduates may also qualify for licensure in other states as well dependant upon specific state criteria and guidelines.

Special Facilities or Resources: Rowan's Child and Family Assessment Clinic provides opportunities for both clinical assessment and research. The clinic uses a broad range of assessment tools and techniques to evaluate the functioning and needs of children and families involved in the child welfare system.

Application Information:
Send to The Graduate School, Rowan University, 201 Mullica Hill Road, Glassboro, NJ 08028-1701. Application available online. URL of online application: http://www.rowan.edu/graduateschool/prospective_students/grad_application/index.htm. Students are admitted in the Fall, application deadline February 15. *Fee:* $50.

Rutgers University—New Brunswick

Graduate Program in Psychology
Faculty of Arts and Sciences
152 Frelinghuysen Road
Piscataway, NJ 08854-8020
Telephone: (732) 445-2556
Fax: (732) 445-2263
E-mail: *gradvc@rci.rutgers.edu*
Web: *http://www.psych.rutgers.edu/graduate/*

Department Information:
1942. Chair and Graduate Director: Gretchen Chapman. Number of faculty: total—full-time 47; women—full-time 15; total—minority—full-time 3; faculty subject to the Americans With Disabilities Act 1.

Programs and Degrees Offered:
Listed in the following order: Program area, degree type (T if terminal Master's), number awarded 7/06–6/07. Clinical PhD (Doctor of Philosophy) 5, Behavioral Neuroscience PhD (Doctor of Philosophy) 4, Cognitive PhD (Doctor of Philosophy) 1, Social PhD (Doctor of Philosophy) 2.

APA Accreditation: Clinical PhD (Doctor of Philosophy).

Student Applications/Admissions:

Student Applications

Clinical PhD (Doctor of Philosophy)—Applications 2007–2008, 263. Total applicants accepted 2007–2008, 8. Number full-time enrolled (new admits only) 2007–2008, 4. Total enrolled 2007–2008 full-time, 35. Openings 2008–2009, 8. The median number of years required for completion of a degree in 2006–2007 were 6. The number of students enrolled full- and part-time who were dismissed or voluntarily withdrew from this program area in 2007–2008 were 0. *Behavioral Neuroscience PhD (Doctor of Philosophy)*—Applications 2007–2008, 34. Total applicants accepted 2007–2008, 4. Number full-time enrolled (new admits only) 2007–2008, 3. Total enrolled 2007–2008 full-time, 16. Openings 2008–2009, 4. The median number of years required for completion of a degree in 2006–2007 were 6. The number of students enrolled full- and part-time who were dismissed or voluntarily withdrew from this program area in 2007–2008 were 1. *Cognitive PhD (Doctor of Philosophy)*—Applications 2007–2008, 53. Total applicants accepted 2007–2008, 15. Number full-time enrolled (new admits only) 2007–2008, 5. Total enrolled 2007–2008 full-time, 22. Openings 2008–2009, 6. The median number of years required for completion of a degree in 2006–2007 were 5. The number of students enrolled full- and part-time who were dismissed or voluntarily withdrew from this program area in 2007–2008 were 0. *Social PhD (Doctor of Philosophy)*—Applications 2007–2008, 86. Total applicants accepted 2007–2008, 8. Number full-time enrolled (new admits only) 2007–2008, 5. Total enrolled 2007–2008 full-time, 22. Openings 2008–2009, 5. The median number of years required for completion of a degree in 2006–2007 were 5. The number of students enrolled full- and part-time who were dismissed or voluntarily withdrew from this program area in 2007–2008 were 0.

Admissions Requirements:

Scores: Entries appear in this order: required test or GPA, minimum score (if required), median score of students entering in 2007–2008. Doctoral Programs: GRE-V no minimum stated, 617; GRE-Q no minimum stated, 696; overall undergraduate GPA no minimum stated, 3.60. GRE Subject test in Psychology is highly recommended.

Other Criteria: (importance of criteria rated low, medium, or high): GRE/MAT scores—high, research experience—high, clinically related public service—low, GPA—high, letters of recommendation—high, interview—medium, statement of goals and objectives—high. For additional information on admission requirements, go to http://www.psychology.rutgers.edu/graduate/.

Student Characteristics: The following represents characteristics of students in 2007–2008 in all graduate psychology programs in the department: Female—full-time 69, part-time 0; Male—full-time 30, part-time 0; African American/Black—full-time 5, part-time 0; Hispanic/Latino(a)—full-time 4, part-time 0; Asian/Pacific Islander—full-time 15, part-time 0; American Indian/Alaska Native—full-time 0, part-time 0; Caucasian/White—full-time 75, part-time 0; Multi-ethnic—full-time 0, part-time 0; students subject to the Americans With Disabilities Act—full-time 1, part-time 0; Unknown ethnicity—full-time 0, part-time 0; International students who hold an F-1 or J-1 Visa—full-time 11, part-time 0.

Financial Information/Assistance:

Tuition for Full-Time Study: *Doctoral:* State residents: per academic year $14,134, $587 per credit hour; Nonstate residents: per academic year $20,948, $873 per credit hour. Tuition is subject to change. See the following Web site for updates and changes in tuition costs: http://www.gradstudy.rutgers.edu/costs.html.

Financial Assistance:

First-Year Students: Teaching assistantships available for first year. Average number of hours worked per week: 15. Apply by January 1. Tuition remission given: full. Research assistantships available for first year. Average number of hours worked per week: 15. Apply by January 1. Tuition remission given: full. Traineeships available for first year. Apply by January 1. Tuition remission given: full. Fellowships and scholarships available for first year. Apply by January 1. Tuition remission given: full.

Advanced Students: Teaching assistantships available for advanced students. Average number of hours worked per week: 15. Apply by January 1. Tuition remission given: full. Research assistantships available for advanced students. Average number of hours worked per week: 15. Apply by January 1. Tuition remission given: full. Traineeships available for advanced students. Apply by January 1. Tuition remission given: full. Fellowships and scholarships available for advanced students. Apply by January 1. Tuition remission given: full.

Additional Information: Of all students currently enrolled full time, 98% benefited from one or more of the listed financial assistance programs. Application and information available online at http://studentaid.rutgers.edu/.

Internships/Practica: Doctoral Degree (PhD Clinical): For those doctoral students for whom a professional internship was required in this program prior to graduation, (11) students applied for an internship in 2006–2007, with (11) students obtaining an internship. Of those students who obtained an internship, (11) were paid internships. Of those students who obtained an internship, (11) students placed in APA/CPA-accredited internships, (0) students placed in internships not APA/CPA-accredited, but listed with the Association of Psychology Postdoctoral and Internship Centers (APPIC), (0) students placed in internships conforming to guidelines of the Council of Directors of School Psychology Programs (CDSPP), (0) students placed in internships that were not APA/CPA-accredited, APPIC or CDSPP listed. Clinical students must complete an APA-approved clinical internship. None of these required internships are offered by our program. There are several university-based practica, including both general and specialty outpatient clinics, however, where clinical students do training before their internships.

Housing and Day Care: On-campus housing is available. See the following Web site for more information: http://www.housing.rutgers.edu/ns/. On-campus day care facilities are available. See the following Web site for more information: http://www.nbweb.rutgers.edu/menus/childcare.shtml.

Employment of Department Graduates:

Master's Degree Graduates: Of those who graduated in the academic year 2006–2007, the following categories and numbers represent the postgraduate activities and employment of master's degree graduates: Enrolled in a psychology doctoral program (0), enrolled in another graduate/professional program (0), enrolled in a postdoctoral residency/fellowship (n/a), employed in independent practice (n/a), employed in an academic position at a university (0), employed in an academic position at a 2-year/4-year college (0), employed in other positions at a higher education institution (0), employed in a professional position in a school system (0), employed in business or industry (0), employed in government agency (0), employed in a community mental health/counseling center (0), employed in a hospital/medical center (0), still seeking employment (0), other employment position (0), total from the above (master's) (0).

Doctoral Degree Graduates: Of those who graduated in the academic year 2006–2007, the following categories and numbers represent the postgraduate activities and employment of doctoral degree graduates: Enrolled in a psychology doctoral program (n/a), enrolled in a postdoctoral residency/fellowship (8), employed in independent practice (0), employed in an academic position at a university (0), employed in an academic position at a 2-year/4-year college (1), employed in other positions at a higher education institution (0), employed in a professional position in a school system (0), employed in business or industry (0), employed in government agency (0), employed in a community mental health/counseling center (1), employed in a hospital/medical center (1), still seeking employment (0), other employment position (1), total from the above (doctoral) (12).

Additional Information:

Orientation, Objectives, and Emphasis of Department: The Rutgers University Graduate Program in Psychology has one of the country's largest faculties, including 50 full-time professors of psychology. The graduate program trains students for careers as professors; researchers in government, corporate, and nonprofit settings; and clinical researchers. There are four main areas (Behavioral Neuroscience, Cognitive Psychology, Clinical Psychology, and Social Psychology) and two intradisciplinary programs: Health Psychology and Developmental Psychology (students with intradisciplinary interest must apply to one of the four main areas). Faculty advisors closely mentor students through a series of progressively more sophisticated research experiences. Basic courses and more advanced specialty seminars are available within each area of psychology. The clinical program is designed to develop clinical scientists.

Information for Students With Physical Disabilities: See the following Web site for more information: http://www.rci.rutgers.edu/~polcomp/disab.shtml.

Application Information:

Send to Office of Graduate and Professional Admissions, Rutgers, The State University of New Jersey, 18 Bishop Place, New Brunswick, NJ 08901-8530. Students are admitted in the Fall, application deadline January 1. *Fee:* $50. Fee waived for McNair Scholars.

Rutgers University—Newark Campus (2007 data)

Department of Psychology
101 Warren Street
Newark, NJ 07102
Telephone: (973) 353-5440 Ext. 221
Fax: (973) 353-1171
E-mail: *kkressel@andromeda.rutgers.edu*
Web: *http://www.psych.rutgers.edu*

Department Information:

1946. Chairperson: Maggie Shiffrar. Number of faculty: total—full-time 15, part-time 2; women—full-time 5, part-time 1.

Programs and Degrees Offered:

Listed in the following order: Program area, degree type (T if terminal Master's), number awarded 7/06–6/07. Experimental Psychology PhD (Doctor of Philosophy) 4.

Student Applications/Admissions:

Student Applications

Experimental Psychology PhD (Doctor of Philosophy)—Applications 2007–2008, 29. Total applicants accepted 2007–2008, 1. Number full-time enrolled (new admits only) 2007–2008, 1. Openings 2008–2009, 4. The median number of years required for completion of a degree in 2006–2007 were 5. The number of students enrolled full- and part-time who were dismissed or voluntarily withdrew from this program area in 2007–2008 were 1.

Admissions Requirements:

Scores: Entries appear in this order: required test or GPA, minimum score (if required), median score of students entering in 2007–2008. Doctoral Programs: GRE-V 500, 570; GRE-Q 500, 638; overall undergraduate GPA 3.0, 3.5.

Other Criteria: (importance of criteria rated low, medium, or high): GRE/MAT scores—medium, research experience—high, work experience—low, extracurricular activity—low, clinically related public service—low, GPA—medium, letters of recommendation—high, interview—high, statement of goals and objectives—high.

Student Characteristics: The following represents characteristics of students in 2007–2008 in all graduate psychology programs in the department: Female—full-time 17, part-time 0; Male—full-time 7, part-time 0; African American/Black—full-time 1, part-time 0; Hispanic/Latino(a)—full-time 2, part-time 0; Asian/Pacific Islander—full-time 2, part-time 0; American Indian/Alaska Native—full-time 0, part-time 0; Caucasian/White—full-time 0, part-time 0; Multi-ethnic—full-time 0, part-time 0; students subject to the Americans With Disabilities Act—full-time 1, part-time 0; Unknown ethnicity—full-time 0, part-time 0.

Financial Information/Assistance:

Tuition for Full-Time Study: *Doctoral:* State residents: per academic year $9,668; Nonstate residents: per academic year $14,370. Tuition is subject to change. See the following Web site for updates and changes in tuition costs: http://www.gradstudy.rutgers.edu/costs.html.

Financial Assistance:

First-Year Students: Teaching assistantships available for first year. Average amount paid per academic year: $18,000. Average number of hours worked per week: 15. Tuition remission given: full. Research assistantships available for first year. Average amount paid per academic year: $18,000. Average number of hours worked per week: 15. Tuition remission given: full. Fellowships and scholarships available for first year. Average amount paid per academic year: $18,000. Average number of hours worked per week: 15. Tuition remission given: full.

Advanced Students: Teaching assistantships available for advanced students. Average amount paid per academic year: $18,000. Average number of hours worked per week: 15. Tuition remission given: full. Research assistantships available for advanced students. Average amount paid per academic year: $18,000. Average number of hours worked per week: 15. Tuition remission given: full. Fellowships and scholarships available for advanced students. Average amount paid per academic year: $16,000. Average number of hours worked per week: 15. Tuition remission given: full.

Additional Information: Of all students currently enrolled full time, 90% benefited from one or more of the listed financial assistance programs.

Internships/Practica: None.

Housing and Day Care: On-campus housing is available. See the following Web site for more information: http://www.newark.rutgers.edu/~reslife/. No on-campus day care facilities are available.

Employment of Department Graduates:

Master's Degree Graduates: Of those who graduated in the academic year 2006–2007, the following categories and numbers represent the postgraduate activities and employment of master's degree graduates: Enrolled in a postdoctoral residency/fellowship (n/a), employed in independent practice (n/a), total from the above (master's) (0).

Doctoral Degree Graduates: Of those who graduated in the academic year 2006–2007, the following categories and numbers represent the postgraduate activities and employment of doctoral degree graduates: Enrolled in a psychology doctoral program (n/a), enrolled in a postdoctoral residency/fellowship (4), employed in business or industry (1), do not know (1), total from the above (doctoral) (6).

Additional Information:

Orientation, Objectives, and Emphasis of Department: Our doctoral program emphasizes research in five areas: Cognitive Science, Perception, Cognitive Neuroscience, Social Psychology, and the Biopsychology of Emotion and Adaptive Behavior. Specific research areas include visual perception, categorization, perceptual development and learning, computational modeling, conflict mediation, social cognition, attachment, parental behavior, attention, language, analgesia, brain imaging (fMRI and EEG), cognitive and social cognitive neuroscience, and the neuroendocrine system. With a faculty to graduate student ratio of 1:2, we emphasize hands-on, integrative research training in state-of-the-art research facilities. Generally, graduate students take classes and conduct research during their first 2 years. A comprehensive exam is given at the beginning of the 3rd year. After this, students focus on their dissertation research. After graduating, our doctoral students successfully obtain postdoctoral research positions, faculty positions, and/or research and development positions in industrial and government settings. You can learn more about our program at http://psychology.rutgers.edu/.

Special Facilities or Resources: The Psychology Department occupies about 42,000 square feet on the first, third, and fourth floors of Smith Hall and has its own servers (psychology.rutgers.edu), computing laboratory, and individual laboratories for behavioral, neurophysiological, neuroanatomical, and neuropharmacological research. There are 16,400 square feet available for animal holding, animal testing, and animal support areas. In the Cognitive Science and Perception areas, research is conducted using one-way observation rooms, video equipment, high-speed graphics computers (SGI, SUN, P6s, Macs, etc.), cutting-edge driving simulators, and an active optical motion tracking system as well as access to a newly acquired high-performance parallel supercomputer (IBM-SP). The Psychology Department with UMDNJ also supports an ERP and a fMRI brain imaging facility for general usage throughout the various programs of study. Students have the use of the John Cotton Dana Library, with a collection of over 550,000 volumes as well as rapid and easy access to the Rutgers University libraries in New Brunswick and to the University of Medicine and Dentistry of New Jersey library in Newark.

Information for Students With Physical Disabilities: See the following Web site for more information: http://www.lrc.rutgers.edu/disabilities.html.

Application Information:

Send to Office of Graduate Admissions, Rutgers, The State University of New Jersey, 249 University Avenue, Newark, NJ 07102-1896; (973) 353-5205. Application available online. URL of online application: http://www.gradstudy.rutgers.edu. Students are admitted in the Fall, application deadline January 15; Spring, application deadline November 1. For additional information about this doctoral Psychology program, consult http://www.psych.rutgers.edu. *Fee:* $50.

Rutgers—The State University of New Jersey

Department of Clinical Psychology
Graduate School of Applied and Professional Psychology
152 Frelinghuysen Road
Piscataway, NJ 08854
Telephone: (732) 445-2000 Ext. 117
Fax: (732) 445-4888
E-mail: *bbry@rci.rutgers.edu*
Web: *http://www.gsappweb.rutgers.edu*

Department Information:

1974. Chair: Brenna H. Bry. Number of faculty: total—full-time 9, part-time 5; women—full-time 7, part-time 7; women minority—full-time 2, part-time 1; faculty subject to the Americans With Disabilities Act 1.

Programs and Degrees Offered:

Listed in the following order: Program area, degree type (T if terminal Master's), number awarded 7/06–6/07. Clinical PsyD (Doctor of Psychology) 17.

APA Accreditation: Clinical PsyD (Doctor of Psychology).

Student Applications/Admissions:

Student Applications

Clinical PsyD (Doctor of Psychology)—Applications 2007–2008, 467. Total applicants accepted 2007–2008, 20. Number full-time enrolled (new admits only) 2007–2008, 15. Number part-time enrolled (new admits only) 2007–2008, 0. Openings 2008–2009, 15. The median number of years required for completion of a degree in 2006–2007 were 6. The number of students enrolled full- and part-time who were dismissed or voluntarily withdrew from this program area in 2007–2008 were 2.

Admissions Requirements:

Scores: Entries appear in this order: required test or GPA, minimum score (if required), median score of students entering in 2007–2008. Doctoral Programs: GRE-V N/A, 650; GRE-Q N/A, 670; GRE-Subject (Psychology) N/A, 710; overall undergraduate GPA N/A, 3.70. Median scores are calculated on students admitted for academic year 2007-08.

Other Criteria: (importance of criteria rated low, medium, or high): GRE/MAT scores—medium, research experience—medium, work experience—high, extracurricular activity—high, clinically related public service—high, GPA—high, letters of recommendation—high, interview—high, statement of goals and objectives—high. MAT not required for admission to PsyD program. For additional information on admission requirements, go to http://gsappweb.rutgers.edu.

Student Characteristics: The following represents characteristics of students in 2007–2008 in all graduate psychology programs

in the department: Female—full-time 72, part-time 0; Male—full-time 26, part-time 0; African American/Black—full-time 11, part-time 0; Hispanic/Latino(a)—full-time 10, part-time 0; Asian/Pacific Islander—full-time 8, part-time 0; American Indian/Alaska Native—full-time 0, part-time 0; Caucasian/White—full-time 68, part-time 0; Multi-ethnic—full-time 0, part-time 0; students subject to the Americans With Disabilities Act—full-time 2, part-time 0; Unknown ethnicity—full-time 5, part-time 0; International students who hold an F-1 or J-1 Visa—full-time 5, part-time 0.

Financial Information/Assistance:

Tuition for Full-Time Study: *Doctoral:* State residents: per academic year $14,098, $587 per credit hour; Nonstate residents: per academic year $20,948, $873 per credit hour. Tuition is subject to change. Additional fees are assessed to students beyond the costs of tuition for the following: college fees and computer fees. See the following Web site for updates and changes in tuition costs: http://www.rci.rutgers.edu/~sfs/index.html.

Financial Assistance:

First-Year Students: Fellowships and scholarships available for first year. Average amount paid per academic year: $10,000. Tuition remission given: partial.

Advanced Students: Teaching assistantships available for advanced students. Average amount paid per academic year: $16,988. Tuition remission given: full. Research assistantships available for advanced students. Average amount paid per academic year: $16,988. Tuition remission given: full. Traineeships available for advanced students. Average amount paid per academic year: $20,772. Tuition remission given: full. Fellowships and scholarships available for advanced students. Average amount paid per academic year: $10,000. Tuition remission given: partial.

Additional Information: Of all students currently enrolled full time, 25% benefited from one or more of the listed financial assistance programs. Application and information available online at http://gsappweb.rutgers.edu.

Internships/Practica: Doctoral Degree (PsyD Clinical): For those doctoral students for whom a professional internship was required in this program prior to graduation, (17) students applied for an internship in 2006–2007, with (17) students obtaining an internship. Of those students who obtained an internship, (17) were paid internships. Of those students who obtained an internship, (13) students placed in APA/CPA-accredited internships, (2) students placed in internships not APA/CPA-accredited, but listed with the Association of Psychology Postdoctoral and Internship Centers (APPIC), (0) students placed in internships conforming to guidelines of the Council of Directors of School Psychology Programs (CDSPP), (2) students placed in internships that were not APA/CPA-accredited, APPIC or CDSPP listed. The PsyD program provides a broadly based practicum program that is structured around the needs and interests of our students. Students can choose placements in hospitals, which include a hospice program, neuropsychological testing and long- and short-term inpatient treatment programs for both adolescents and adults. They can choose to be placed in university-based specialty clinics, traditional community mental health centers, college counseling centers or specialized schools for children (autism, learning disabled, emotionally disturbed). Students can be placed in public school based mental health clinics, in programs that provide service to at-risk youth, those with serious mental illness, and those with addictive disorders. Our programs are selected for their attention to supervision but also for their balance regarding gender, race, and socioeconomic levels. For additional information on education and training outcomes for our programs, see the following Web site: http://www.gsappweb.rutgers.edu.

Housing and Day Care: On-campus housing is available. On-campus housing may be available in the form of Resident Hall advisors. Students should e-mail rockaway@rci.rutgers.edu after admission to obtain on-campus housing information. On-campus day care facilities are available. See the following Web site for more information: http://www.ruinfo.rutgers.edu/.

Employment of Department Graduates:

Master's Degree Graduates: Of those who graduated in the academic year 2006–2007, the following categories and numbers represent the postgraduate activities and employment of master's degree graduates: Enrolled in a postdoctoral residency/fellowship (n/a), employed in independent practice (n/a), total from the above (master's) (0).

Doctoral Degree Graduates: Of those who graduated in the academic year 2006–2007, the following categories and numbers represent the postgraduate activities and employment of doctoral degree graduates: Enrolled in a psychology doctoral program (n/a), enrolled in another graduate/professional program (0), enrolled in a postdoctoral residency/fellowship (0), employed in independent practice (1), employed in an academic position at a university (0), employed in an academic position at a 2-year/4-year college (0), employed in other positions at a higher education institution (0), employed in a professional position in a school system (0), employed in business or industry (0), employed in government agency (0), employed in a community mental health/counseling center (2), employed in a hospital/medical center (7), not seeking employment (0), other employment position (1), do not know (6), total from the above (doctoral) (17).

Additional Information:

Orientation, Objectives, and Emphasis of Department: The PsyD program emphasizes pragmatic training in problem-solving and planned change techniques. Didactic training in basic psychological principles is coupled with practical, graduate instruction in a range of assessment and intervention modes. The level of involvement becomes progressively more intense during the student's course of training. Most courses include (a) a seminar component oriented around case discussions and substantive theoretical issues of clinical import, (b) a practicum component during which students see clients in the intervention mode or problem area under study, and (c) a supervision component by which the student receives guidance from an experienced clinical instructor in a wide range of applied clinical settings. All three components are coordinated around a central conceptual issue, such as a mode of intervention or a clinical problem area. Instruction and supervision are offered by full-time faculty and senior psychologists whose primary professional involvement is in applied clinical settings throughout the state. In addition to required general core courses, students may emphasize training within any of three perspectives: psychodynamic, behavioral, or systems approaches. This last perspective focuses on family, organizational and community services.

Special Facilities or Resources: The Center for Applied Psychology at GSAPP is the focal point for the field experiences that are critical in the development of professional psychologists. The projects overseen by the Center are cornerstones of training for our students; the GSAPP Psychological Clinic, the Foster Care Counseling project, the Natural Setting Therapeutic Management program, the Anxiety Disorders Clinic, and our extensive network of practicum placements are all available to our students. Students are placed in community-based organizations where the recipients of the services we provide are often underserved. These placements include community mental health centers, hospitals, special schools, and other programs. All students are placed in a practicum setting for at least 1 full day per week during their years at GSAPP. All students see clients through our Clinic and receive 1 hour of individual supervision for each hour of therapy. The Clinic has specialty subclinics, which will allow students to gain experience and supervision in specific treatment approaches working with faculty experts.

Information for Students With Physical Disabilities: See the following Web site for more information: http://www.rcstudentservice.rutgers.edu/disability.html.

Application Information:
Send to Graduate and Professional Admissions, Rutgers, The State University of New Jersey, 18 Bishop Place, New Brunswick, NJ 08901-8530. Application available online. URL of online application: http://www.gradstudy.rutgers.edu. Students are admitted in the Fall, application deadline January 5. *Fee:* $60. Project 1000: fee waived.

Rutgers—The State University of New Jersey, Graduate School of Applied and Professional Psychology

Department of Applied Psychology
152 Frelinghuysen Road
Busch Campus, Psychology Building Addition
Piscataway, NJ 08854
Telephone: (732) 445-2000 Ext. 104
Fax: (732) 445-4888
E-mail: *sgforman@rci.rutgers.edu*
Web: *http://www.gsappweb.rutgers.edu*

Department Information:
1974. Chairperson: Susan G. Forman, PhD. Number of faculty: total—full-time 6, part-time 7; women—full-time 4, part-time 6; total—minority—full-time 1; women minority—full-time 1.

Programs and Degrees Offered:
Listed in the following order: Program area, degree type (T if terminal Master's), number awarded 7/06–6/07. Organizational PsyD (Doctor of Psychology) 10, School PsyD (Doctor of Psychology) 11.

APA Accreditation: School PsyD (Doctor of Psychology).

Student Applications/Admissions:
Student Applications
Organizational PsyD (Doctor of Psychology)—Applications 2007–2008, 0. Total applicants accepted 2007–2008, 0. Number full-time enrolled (new admits only) 2007–2008, 0. Number part-time enrolled (new admits only) 2007–2008, 0. The median number of years required for completion of a degree in 2006–2007 were 6. The number of students enrolled full- and part-time who were dismissed or voluntarily withdrew from this program area in 2007–2008 were 1. *School PsyD (Doctor of Psychology)*—Applications 2007–2008, 78. Total applicants accepted 2007–2008, 21. Number full-time enrolled (new admits only) 2007–2008, 15. Number part-time enrolled (new admits only) 2007–2008, 0. Total enrolled 2007–2008 full-time, 63. Openings 2008–2009, 15. The median number of years required for completion of a degree in 2006–2007 were 4. The number of students enrolled full- and part-time who were dismissed or voluntarily withdrew from this program area in 2007–2008 were 2.

Admissions Requirements:
Scores: Entries appear in this order: required test or GPA, minimum score (if required), median score of students entering in 2007–2008. Doctoral Programs: GRE-V no minimum stated, 560; GRE-Q no minimum stated, 620; GRE-Subject (Psychology) no minimum stated, 620; overall undergraduate GPA no minimum stated, 3.48; Doctoral program GRE-Analytic no minimum stated, 5.0. Masters GPA required if student has completed a masters program. All applicants are presumed to have the equivalent of an undergraduate degree in psychology.
Other Criteria: (importance of criteria rated low, medium, or high): GRE/MAT scores—high, research experience—medium, work experience—high, extracurricular activity—medium, clinically related public service—high, GPA—high, letters of recommendation—high, interview—high, statement of goals and objectives—high, undergraduate major in psychology—medium, specific undergraduate psychology courses taken—high. MAT not required for admission into the PsyD programs. For additional information on admission requirements, go to http://gsappweb.rutgers.edu.

Student Characteristics: The following represents characteristics of students in 2007–2008 in all graduate psychology programs in the department: Female—full-time 70, part-time 0; Male—full-time 18, part-time 0; African American/Black—full-time 12, part-time 0; Hispanic/Latino(a)—full-time 1, part-time 0; Asian/Pacific Islander—full-time 5, part-time 0; American Indian/Alaska Native—full-time 0, part-time 0; Caucasian/White—full-time 70, part-time 0; Multi-ethnic—full-time 0, part-time 0; students subject to the Americans With Disabilities Act—full-time 0, part-time 0; Unknown ethnicity—full-time 0, part-time 0.

Financial Information/Assistance:
Tuition for Full-Time Study: *Doctoral:* State residents: per academic year $14,098, $587 per credit hour; Nonstate residents: per academic year $20,948, $873 per credit hour. Tuition is subject to change. Additional fees are assessed to students beyond the costs of tuition for the following: college fee and computer fee. See the following Web site for updates and changes in tuition costs: http://www.studentabc.rutgers.edu/tuition/tuitionpdf.html.

Financial Assistance:
First-Year Students: Traineeships available for first year. Average amount paid per academic year: $12,000. Tuition remission given: full. Fellowships and scholarships available for first year. Average amount paid per academic year: $12,500. Tuition remission given: partial.

Advanced Students: Teaching assistantships available for advanced students. Average amount paid per academic year: $16,988. Tuition remission given: full. Traineeships available for advanced students. Average amount paid per academic year: $12,000. Tuition remission given: full. Fellowships and scholarships available for advanced students. Average amount paid per academic year: $12,500. Tuition remission given: partial.

Additional Information: Of all students currently enrolled full time, 25% benefited from one or more of the listed financial assistance programs. Application and information available online at http://studentaid.rutgers.edu.

Internships/Practica: Doctoral Degree (PsyD Organizational): For those doctoral students for whom a professional internship was required in this program prior to graduation, (6) students applied for an internship in 2006–2007, with (6) students obtaining an internship. Of those students who obtained an internship, (6) were paid internships. Of those students who obtained an internship, (0) students placed in APA/CPA-accredited internships, (0) students placed in internships not APA/CPA accredited, but listed with the Association of Psychology Postdoctoral and Internship Centers (APPIC), (0) students placed in internships conforming to guidelines of the Council of Directors of School Psychology Programs (CDSPP), (6) students placed in internships that were not APA/CPA-accredited, APPIC or CDSPP listed. Doctoral Degree (PsyD School): For those doctoral students for whom a professional internship was required in this program prior to graduation, (8) students applied for an internship in 2006–2007, with (8) students obtaining an internship. Of those students who obtained an internship, (8) were paid internships. Of those students who obtained an internship, (2) students placed in APA/CPA-accredited internships, (0) students placed in internships not APA/CPA-accredited, but listed with the Association of Psychology Postdoctoral and Internship Centers (APPIC), (6) students placed in internships conforming to guidelines of the Council of Directors of School Psychology Programs (CDSPP), (0) students placed in internships that were not APA/CPA-accredited, APPIC or CDSPP listed. A special component of the student's training is the integration of practica experiences with didactic courses from the second semester of the 1st year throughout the remaining semesters of training. These experiences begin by introducing the student to the roles and functions of a school psychologist, the functioning of child study teams, and a variety of schooling issues. For three consecutive semesters, students spend a minimum of 1 day per week in a public school with a doctoral-level school psychologist supervisor/mentor. During the fifth and sixth semester, students may elect a different practicum experience from their first based upon their interests. These practica experiences are supervised by on-site doctoral school psychologists and by on-campus faculty. The courses, the practica, and the supervision comprise the planned scaffold for educating students. In addition, there are numerous opportunities for learning and practice through colloquia, symposia, informal discussions, faculty projects, the psychological clinic, and the Center for Applied Psychology.

Housing and Day Care: On-campus housing is available. See the following Web site for more information: http://www.housing.rutgers.edu or http://www.rutgers.edu, click on Search Rutgers and type in "on-campus housing." On-campus day care facilities are available. See the following Web site for more information: http://www.nbweb.rutgers.edu/menus/childcare.shtml at http://www.rutgers.edu, click on Search Rutgers and type in "child care."

Employment of Department Graduates:

Master's Degree Graduates: Of those who graduated in the academic year 2006–2007, the following categories and numbers represent the postgraduate activities and employment of master's degree graduates: Enrolled in a postdoctoral residency/fellowship (n/a), employed in independent practice (n/a), total from the above (master's) (0).

Doctoral Degree Graduates: Of those who graduated in the academic year 2006–2007, the following categories and numbers represent the postgraduate activities and employment of doctoral degree graduates: Enrolled in a psychology doctoral program (n/a), enrolled in another graduate/professional program (0), enrolled in a postdoctoral residency/fellowship (0), employed in independent practice (0), employed in an academic position at a university (0), employed in an academic position at a 2-year/4-year college (0), employed in other positions at a higher education institution (0), employed in a professional position in a school system (11), employed in business or industry (10), employed in government agency (0), employed in a community mental health/counseling center (0), employed in a hospital/medical center (0), still seeking employment (0), other employment position (0), total from the above (doctoral) (21).

Additional Information:

Orientation, Objectives, and Emphasis of Department: The department of applied psychology is a unit dedicated (a) to enhancement of mental health and learning of children, adolescents, and adults in schools and related educational settings, and (b) to development of organizations that allow schooling to occur in effective and efficient ways. Three interrelated dimensions serve to structure the department. An applied research dimension signifies the important weight placed on generating new knowledge; an education and training dimension reflects concern for development of high-level practitioners and leaders of school psychology; an organizational and community services dimension is targeted at providing schools and related educational settings with consultation and technical assistance in areas of instruction and learning. A continuum of instruction ranges from observation and assessment through intervention models that include supervised experience as an essential component of didactic instruction. Core faculty are augmented by senior psychologists whose major professional involvement is in the schools or organizational and community settings.

Special Facilities or Resources: There are two special facilities that are an integrated part of the training program. One is an on-site psychological clinic that serves the university and state communities. Assessment and intervention programs are offered. The other is the Center for Applied Psychology, a division of GSAPP, that develops, implements, and evaluates projects involving faculty, students, and others from the community. Included in these projects are the Eating Disorders Clinic, Foster Care Counseling, and a home-based intervention program for developmentally disabled individuals.

Information for Students With Physical Disabilities: See the following Web site for more information: http://www.gsappweb.rutgers.edu.

Application Information:

Send to Rutgers University, Graduate Admissions, 18 Bishop Place, New Brunswick, NJ 08901, or request application and catalog online at http://gradstudy.rutgers.edu. Application available online. URL of online application: http://www.gradstudy.rutgers.edu. Students are admitted in the Fall, application deadline January 5. *Fee:* $60. Project 1000 application fee is waived. Contact Graduate Admissions at (732) 932-7711 to find out about other application fee waivers.

Rutgers—The State University of New Jersey, New Brunswick

Department of Educational Psychology
Graduate School of Education
10 Seminary Place
New Brunswick, NJ 08901-1183
Telephone: (732) 932-7496 Ext. 8327
Fax: (732) 932-6829
E-mail: *mccune@rci.rutgers.edu*
Web: *http://www.gse.rutgers.edu*

Department Information:

1923. Chairperson: Lorraine McCune. Number of faculty: total—full-time 15; women—full-time 8.

Programs and Degrees Offered:

Listed in the following order: Program area, degree type (T if terminal Master's), number awarded 7/06–6/07. Learning, Cognition, and Development Other 4, Special Education Other 41, Counseling Psychology EdD (Doctor of Education) 0, Educational Psychology PhD (Doctor of Philosophy) 3, Educational Statistics and Measurement Other 2, Educational Statistics and Measurement EdD (Doctor of Education) 0, Special Education EdD (Doctor of Education) 2, Counseling Psychology Other 23.

Student Applications/Admissions:

Student Applications

Learning, Cognition, and Development Other—Applications 2007–2008, 21. Total applicants accepted 2007–2008, 12. Openings 2008–2009, 10. The median number of years required for completion of a degree in 2006–2007 was 1. The number of students enrolled full- and part-time who were dismissed or voluntarily withdrew from this program area in 2007–2008 were 0. *Special Education Other*—Applications 2007–2008, 45. Total applicants accepted 2007–2008, 24. Openings 2008–2009, 35. The median number of years required for completion of a degree in 2006–2007 was 1. The number of students enrolled full- and part-time who were dismissed or voluntarily withdrew from this program area in 2007–2008 were 0. *Counseling Psychology EdD (Doctor of Education)*—Applications 2007–2008, 0. Total applicants accepted 2007–2008, 0. Number full-time enrolled (new admits only) 2007–2008, 0. Number part-time enrolled (new admits only) 2007–2008, 0. The median number of years required for completion of a degree in 2006–2007 were 6. The number of students enrolled full- and part-time who were dismissed or voluntarily withdrew from this program area in 2007–2008 were 0. *Educational Psychology PhD (Doctor of Philosophy)*—Applications 2007–2008, 20. The median number of years required for completion of a degree in 2006–2007 were 5. *Educational Statistics and Measurement Other*—Applications 2007–2008, 10. Total applicants accepted 2007–2008, 9. Openings 2008–2009, 10. The median number of years required for completion of a degree in 2006–2007 was 1. The number of students enrolled full- and part-time who were dismissed or voluntarily withdrew from this program area in 2007–2008 were 0. *Educational Statistics and Measurement EdD (Doctor of Education)*—Applications 2007–2008, 0. Total applicants accepted 2007–2008, 0. Number full-time enrolled (new admits only) 2007–2008, 0. Number part-time enrolled (new admits only) 2007–2008, 0. The number of students enrolled full- and part-time who were dismissed or voluntarily withdrew from this program area in 2007–2008 were 0. *Special Education EdD (Doctor of Education)*—Applications 2007–2008, 14. Total applicants accepted 2007–2008, 3. Openings 2008–2009, 5. *Counseling Psychology Other*—Applications 2007–2008, 76. Total applicants accepted 2007–2008, 52. Openings 2008–2009, 50. The median number of years required for completion of a degree in 2006–2007 were 2.

Admissions Requirements:

Scores: Entries appear in this order: required test or GPA, minimum score (if required), median score of students entering in 2007–2008. Master's Programs: GRE-V no minimum stated; GRE-Q no minimum stated; overall undergraduate GPA 3.00. For Ed.M. applicants the GRE V+Q minimum score is 1000. For international students TOEFL is required with a minimum score of computerized 213 / paper 550 / or internet based: writing 22, speaking 23, reading 21, listening 17. Doctoral Programs: GRE-V no minimum stated; GRE-Q no minimum stated; overall undergraduate GPA 3.00. For Ed.D. candidates the GREV+Q minimum score is 1100. For PhD candidates the GRE V+Q average is 1250. For international students TOEFL is required with a minimum score of computerized 213 / paper 550 / or internet based: writing 22, speaking 23, reading 21, listening 17.

Other Criteria: (importance of criteria rated low, medium, or high): GRE/MAT scores—high, research experience—high, work experience—medium, GPA—high, letters of recommendation—high, statement of goals and objectives—high. For additional information on admission requirements, go to http://www.gradstudy.rutgers.edu.

Student Characteristics: The following represents characteristics of students in 2007–2008 in all graduate psychology programs in the department: Caucasian/White—full-time 0, part-time 0; Unknown ethnicity—full-time 0, part-time 0.

Financial Information/Assistance:

Tuition for Full-Time Study: *Master's:* State residents: per academic year $12,381, $516 per credit hour; Nonstate residents: per academic year $18,406, $767 per credit hour. *Doctoral:* State residents: per academic year $12,381, $516 per credit hour; Nonstate residents: per academic year $18,406, $767 per credit hour. Tuition is subject to change. See the following Web site for updates and changes in tuition costs: http://www.studentabc.rutgers.edu.

Financial Assistance:

First-Year Students: Teaching assistantships available for first year. Average amount paid per academic year: $18,347. Average number of hours worked per week: 15. Apply by February 1.

Tuition remission given: full. Research assistantships available for first year. Average amount paid per academic year: $18,347. Average number of hours worked per week: 15. Apply by February 1. Tuition remission given: full. Fellowships and scholarships available for first year. Average number of hours worked per week: 0. Apply by March 1.

Advanced Students: Teaching assistantships available for advanced students. Average amount paid per academic year: $18,347. Average number of hours worked per week: 15. Apply by February 1. Tuition remission given: full. Research assistantships available for advanced students. Average amount paid per academic year: $18,347. Average number of hours worked per week: 15. Apply by February 1. Tuition remission given: full. Fellowships and scholarships available for advanced students. Apply by March 1.

Additional Information: Application and information available online at http://studentaid.rutgers.edu/.

Internships/Practica: No information provided.

Housing and Day Care: On-campus housing is available. See the following Web site for more information: For on-campus housing, http://www.housing.rutgers.edu/ie; for off-campus housing, http:/ruoffcampus.rutgers.edu. On-campus day care facilities are available. See the following Web site for more information: http://www.nbpweb.rutgers.edu/menus/childcare.shtml.

Employment of Department Graduates:

Master's Degree Graduates: Of those who graduated in the academic year 2006–2007, the following categories and numbers represent the postgraduate activities and employment of master's degree graduates: Enrolled in a postdoctoral residency/fellowship (n/a), employed in independent practice (n/a), total from the above (master's) (0).

Doctoral Degree Graduates: Of those who graduated in the academic year 2006–2007, the following categories and numbers represent the postgraduate activities and employment of doctoral degree graduates: Enrolled in a psychology doctoral program (n/a), total from the above (doctoral) (0).

Additional Information:

Orientation, Objectives, and Emphasis of Department: The Department of Educational Psychology offers a PhD in Educational Psychology that seeks to prepare scholarly researchers in areas that include theory and methods of statistical analysis, evaluation, and measurement as applied to educational issues; and the psychology of human learning, cognition, and development in schools, families, and communities. An EdD in Special Education, which prepares individuals seeking professional positions in the field, is also offered. At the master's level, the Department offers graduate Master's in Education (EdM) degree programs of study in (a) counseling psychology; (b) educational statistics, measurement and evaluation; (c) learning, cognition, and development; and (d) special education. Completion of these master's degree programs can also result in various professional credentials including certification as Learning Disabilities Teacher Consultant and School Counselor. The Department also offers a certificate program in Interdisciplinary Infant Studies. All programs in the Department include research training and pertain to the description, explanation, and optimization of human development in various contexts.

Special Facilities or Resources: We have all the resources normally associated with a major research university.

Information for Students With Physical Disabilities: See the following Web site for more information: http://www.rci.rutgers.edu/~divcoaff/.

Application Information:
Send to Office of Graduate and Professional Admissions, Rutgers, The State University of New Jersey, 18 Bishop Place, New Brunswick, NJ 08901-8530; phone: (732) 932-7711 fax: (732) 932-8231. Application available online. URL of online application: http://www.gradstudy.rutgers.edu. Students are admitted in the Fall, application deadline November 1; Spring, application deadline February 1. PhD program has Fall admission only: February 1 deadline. EdD admissions is temporarily suspended in Counseling Psychology. Students interested in EdD in Learning, Cognition, and Development, or Educational Statistics and Measurement should refer to PhD in Educational Psychology. Admissions to EdD in Learning, Cognition, and Development, and Educational Statistics and Measurement suspended. *Fee:* $60. Contact the Office of Graduate and Professional Admissions about fee waivers or deferrals.

Seton Hall University

Professional Psychology and Family Therapy
Education and Human Services
400 South Orange Avenue
South Orange, NJ 07079
Telephone: (973) 761-9451
Fax: (973) 275-2188
E-mail: *palmerla@shu.edu*
Web: *http://www.shu.edu*

Department Information:
1965. Chairperson: Laura Palmer, PhD. Number of faculty: total—full-time 10; women—full-time 5; total—minority—full-time 3; women minority—full-time 1.

Programs and Degrees Offered:
Listed in the following order: Program area, degree type (T if terminal Master's), number awarded 7/06–6/07. Counseling Psychology PhD (Doctor of Philosophy) 7, Counseling (Online) MA/MS (Master of Arts/Science) (T) 21.

APA Accreditation: Counseling PhD (Doctor of Philosophy).

Student Applications/Admissions:

Student Applications

Counseling Psychology PhD (Doctor of Philosophy)—Applications 2007–2008, 96. Total applicants accepted 2007–2008, 8. Number full-time enrolled (new admits only) 2007–2008, 6. Total enrolled 2007–2008 full-time, 26. Openings 2008–2009, 6. The median number of years required for completion of a degree in 2006–2007 were 6. The number of students enrolled full- and part-time who were dismissed or voluntarily withdrew from this program area in 2007–2008 were 0. *Counseling (Online) MA/MS (Master of Arts/Science)*—Applications 2007–2008, 127. Total applicants accepted 2007–2008, 94.

Number part-time enrolled (new admits only) 2007–2008, 80. Total enrolled 2007–2008 part-time, 133. Openings 2008–2009, 36. The median number of years required for completion of a degree in 2006–2007 were 3. The number of students enrolled full- and part-time who were dismissed or voluntarily withdrew from this program area in 2007–2008 were 7.

Admissions Requirements:

Scores: Entries appear in this order: required test or GPA, minimum score (if required), median score of students entering in 2007–2008. Master's Programs: GRE-V no minimum stated; GRE-Q no minimum stated. Doctoral Programs: GRE-V 350, 482; GRE-Q 390, 521; overall undergraduate GPA 2.0, 3.24; Doctoral program GRE-Analytic 390, 551.

Other Criteria: (importance of criteria rated low, medium, or high): GRE/MAT scores—medium, research experience—high, work experience—medium, extracurricular activity—medium, clinically related public service—medium, GPA—medium, letters of recommendation—high, interview—high, statement of goals and objectives—high. PhD program scientist–practitioner model of training; Master's and EdS programs clinically focused. For additional information on admission requirements, go to http://www.shu.edu.

Student Characteristics: The following represents characteristics of students in 2007–2008 in all graduate psychology programs in the department: Caucasian/White—full-time 0, part-time 0; Multi-ethnic—full-time 0, part-time 0; students subject to the Americans With Disabilities Act—full-time 0, part-time 0; Unknown ethnicity—full-time 0, part-time 0.

Financial Information/Assistance:

Tuition for Full-Time Study: *Master's:* State residents: $780 per credit hour; Nonstate residents: $780 per credit hour. *Doctoral:* State residents: $780 per credit hour; Nonstate residents: $780 per credit hour. Tuition is subject to change. See the following Web site for updates and changes in tuition costs: http://www.shu.edu.

Financial Assistance:

First-Year Students: Research assistantships available for first year. Average amount paid per academic year: $4,500. Average number of hours worked per week: 20. Apply by Spring. Tuition remission given: full.

Advanced Students: Research assistantships available for advanced students. Average amount paid per academic year: $4,500. Average number of hours worked per week: 20. Apply by Spring. Tuition remission given: full.

Additional Information: Of all students currently enrolled full time, 90% benefited from one or more of the listed financial assistance programs. Application and information available online at http://www.shu.edu.

Internships/Practica: Doctoral Degree (PhD Counseling Psychology PhD): For those doctoral students for whom a professional internship was required in this program prior to graduation, (4) students applied for an internship in 2006–2007, with (4) students obtaining an internship. Of those students who obtained an internship, (3) were paid internships. Of those students who obtained an internship, (1) student placed in APA/CPA-accredited internships, (2) students placed in internships not APA/CPA-accredited, but listed with the Association of Psychology Postdoctoral and Internship Centers (APPIC), (0) students placed in internships conforming to guidelines of the Council of Directors of School Psychology Programs (CDSPP), (1) student placed in internships that were not APA/CPA-accredited, APPIC or CDSPP listed. The Marriage and Family students follow the standards of the Commission on Accreditation for Marriage and Family Therapy Education. The doctoral students adhere to Psychology guidelines.

Housing and Day Care: No on-campus housing is available. No on-campus day care facilities are available.

Employment of Department Graduates:

Master's Degree Graduates: Of those who graduated in the academic year 2006–2007, the following categories and numbers represent the postgraduate activities and employment of master's degree graduates: Enrolled in a psychology doctoral program (0), enrolled in another graduate/professional program (0), enrolled in a postdoctoral residency/fellowship (n/a), employed in independent practice (n/a), employed in an academic position at a university (0), employed in an academic position at a 2-year/4-year college (0), employed in other positions at a higher education institution (0), employed in a professional position in a school system (0), employed in business or industry (0), employed in government agency (0), employed in a community mental health/counseling center (0), employed in a hospital/medical center (0), still seeking employment (0), other employment position (0), total from the above (master's) (0).

Doctoral Degree Graduates: Of those who graduated in the academic year 2006–2007, the following categories and numbers represent the postgraduate activities and employment of doctoral degree graduates: Enrolled in a psychology doctoral program (n/a), enrolled in a postdoctoral residency/fellowship (0), employed in independent practice (0), employed in an academic position at a university (0), employed in an academic position at a 2-year/4-year college (0), employed in other positions at a higher education institution (0), employed in a professional position in a school system (0), employed in business or industry (0), employed in government agency (0), employed in a community mental health/counseling center (0), employed in a hospital/medical center (0), still seeking employment (0), other employment position (0), total from the above (doctoral) (0).

Additional Information:

Orientation, Objectives, and Emphasis of Department: The Marriage and Family program is based on a systemic orientation to family psychology and family therapy. The goals of Counseling Psychology encompass knowledge of the science of psychology and counseling psychology as a specialty, integration of research and practice, and commitment to ongoing professional development. Professional counselors are mental health practitioners trained to help individual clients and groups address common developmental challenges and transitions as well as more severe emotional difficulties. School psychology students learn to specialize in assessment and evaluations in schools. Programs listed as MA/EdS are combined programs in which students are afforded the opportunity to continue their studies without applying for the advanced degree.

Special Facilities or Resources: The department has individual counseling and assessment rooms, family and couple laboratories, and group therapy rooms, all of which are wired with state-of-the-art audiovisual equipment with centralized viewing in a control room. There are rooms for data analyses as well.

Information for Students With Physical Disabilities: See the following Web site for more information: http://www.shu.edu.

Application Information:
Send to Graduate Admissions, College of Education and Human Services, Seton Hall University, South Orange, NJ 07079. Application available online. URL of online application: http://www.education.shu.edu/admissions/applyonline.html. Students are admitted in the Fall, application deadline none; Winter, application deadline none; Spring, application deadline none; Summer, application deadline none. Counseling Psychology PhD (January 15), all other programs rolling admissions. *Fee:* $50.

Seton Hall University

Psychology/Experimental Psychology
Arts and Sciences
400 South Orange Avenue
South Orange, NJ 07079
Telephone: (973) 761-9484
Fax: (973) 275-5829
E-mail: *levyjeff@shu.edu*
Web: *http://www.shu.edu/academics/artsci/psychology/*

Department Information:
1952. Chairperson: Jeffrey C. Levy, PhD. Number of faculty: total—full-time 12, part-time 5; women—full-time 7, part-time 3; minority—part-time 1; women minority—part-time 1; faculty subject to the Americans With Disabilities Act 1.

Programs and Degrees Offered:
Listed in the following order: Program area, degree type (T if terminal Master's), number awarded 7/06–6/07. Experimental Psychology MA/MS (Master of Arts/Science) (T) 4.

Student Applications/Admissions:
Student Applications
Experimental Psychology MA/MS (Master of Arts/Science)—Applications 2007–2008, 17. Total applicants accepted 2007–2008, 10. Number full-time enrolled (new admits only) 2007–2008, 6. Number part-time enrolled (new admits only) 2007–2008, 0. Total enrolled 2007–2008 full-time, 9. Openings 2008–2009, 8. The median number of years required for completion of a degree in 2006–2007 were 2. The number of students enrolled full- and part-time who were dismissed or voluntarily withdrew from this program area in 2007–2008 were 1.

Admissions Requirements:
Scores: Entries appear in this order: required test or GPA, minimum score (if required), median score of students entering in 2007–2008. Master's Programs: GRE-V 450, 491; GRE-Q 500, 613; overall undergraduate GPA 3.00, 3.64.
Other Criteria: (importance of criteria rated low, medium, or high): GRE/MAT scores—medium, research experience—medium, extracurricular activity—medium, GPA—high, letters of recommendation—high, statement of goals and objectives—high.

Student Characteristics: The following represents characteristics of students in 2007–2008 in all graduate psychology programs in the department: Female—full-time 7, part-time 0; Male—full-time 2, part-time 0; African American/Black—full-time 1, part-time 0; Caucasian/White—full-time 8, part-time 0; Unknown ethnicity—full-time 0, part-time 0.

Financial Information/Assistance:
Tuition for Full-Time Study: *Master's:* State residents: per academic year $14,868, $826 per credit hour; . Tuition is subject to change. Additional fees are assessed to students beyond the costs of tuition for the following: University and Technology Fees, $305 per semester. See the following Web site for updates and changes in tuition costs: http://www.shu.edu/applying/graduate/tuition-costs.cfm.

Financial Assistance:
First-Year Students: Teaching assistantships available for first year. Average amount paid per academic year: $8,500. Average number of hours worked per week: 20. Tuition remission given: full and partial. Research assistantships available for first year. Average amount paid per academic year: $5,200. Average number of hours worked per week: 20. Tuition remission given: full and partial.
Advanced Students: Teaching assistantships available for advanced students. Average amount paid per academic year: $8,500. Average number of hours worked per week: 20. Tuition remission given: full and partial. Research assistantships available for advanced students. Average amount paid per academic year: $5,200. Average number of hours worked per week: 20. Tuition remission given: full and partial.
Additional Information: Of all students currently enrolled full time, 44% benefited from one or more of the listed financial assistance programs. Application and information available online at http://artsci.shu.edu/psychology/graduate.htm.

Internships/Practica: No information provided.

Housing and Day Care: No on-campus housing is available. No on-campus day care facilities are available.

Employment of Department Graduates:
Master's Degree Graduates: Of those who graduated in the academic year 2006–2007, the following categories and numbers represent the postgraduate activities and employment of master's degree graduates: Enrolled in a psychology doctoral program (3), enrolled in a postdoctoral residency/fellowship (n/a), employed in independent practice (n/a), employed in an academic position at a 2-year/4-year college (1), employed in business or industry (2), total from the above (master's) (6).
Doctoral Degree Graduates: Of those who graduated in the academic year 2006–2007, the following categories and numbers represent the postgraduate activities and employment of doctoral degree graduates: Enrolled in a psychology doctoral program (n/a), total from the above (doctoral) (0).

Additional Information:
Orientation, Objectives, and Emphasis of Department: The MS degree in experimental psychology is designed specifically for

students seeking to gain a solid foundation in empirical research for eventual entry into PhD programs in scientific psychology or for students desiring to explore the field. The Experimental Psychology program consists of 36 credits to be completed in 2 years. All incoming students are required to participate in research each semester. The courses offered (including a research thesis) comprise traditional areas in experimental psychology with optional concentrations in General Psychology and Behavioral Neuroscience. The Behavioral Neuroscience concentration represents courses that are most directly relevant to behavioral studies of brain functioning.

Special Facilities or Resources: Faculty have private offices of approximately 150 square feet each. A suite of nine 8' X 8' cubicles are available for graduate student use. An animal conditioning laboratory consists of eight test cubicles, each equipped with an operant chamber interfaced to an IBM desktop computer. A five-room physiological psychology suite of approximately 400 square feet is used for surgical preparations, histology, and behavioral testing of rodents. Several mazes are also available for the study of learning and memory in rodents. The laboratories share access to two animal colony rooms for housing rodents. Research space for human experimental psychology investigations includes a corridor lined by 11 research cubicles each one approximately 90 square feet and a research participant reception area of approximately 200 square feet. Equipment for these cubicles includes desktop computers and associated equipment that allows them to function as laboratory control devices. Three of these machines have video capture cards permitting still frame capture and video-conferencing with Sony video camcorders. In addition, the department's perceptual laboratory consists of a three-room suite totaling 650 square feet. A one-way vision room is also available.

Application Information:

Send to Office of the Dean, College of Arts and Sciences, Fahy Hall, Room 128, Seton Hall University, South Orange, NJ 07079. Application available online. URL of online application: https://www.apply.embark.com/grad/setonhall/cas/17/. Students are admitted in the Fall, application deadline July 1; Spring, application deadline November 1. Strong applications submitted before April 1 have a greater chance of admittance and of receiving graduate assistantships. *Fee:* $50.

William Paterson University

Psychology/MA in Clinical and Counseling Psychology
Humanities and Social Sciences
300 Pompton Road
Wayne, NJ 07470
Telephone: (973) 720-3400
Fax: (973) 720-3392
E-mail: *diamondb@wpunj.edu*
Web: *http://www.wpunj.edu/cohss/psychology/Masters.htm*

Department Information:

1999. Graduate Director: Bruce J. Diamond, PhD. Number of faculty: total—full-time 7; women—full-time 5; total—minority—full-time 1; women minority—full-time 1.

Programs and Degrees Offered:

Listed in the following order: Program area, degree type (T if terminal Master's), number awarded 7/06–6/07. Clinical and Counseling Psychology MA/MS (Master of Arts/Science) (T) 15.

Student Applications/Admissions:

Student Applications

Clinical and Counseling Psychology MA/MS (Master of Arts/Science)—Applications 2007–2008, 64. Total applicants accepted 2007–2008, 42. Number full-time enrolled (new admits only) 2007–2008, 11. Number part-time enrolled (new admits only) 2007–2008, 9. Total enrolled 2007–2008 full-time, 23, part-time, 27. Openings 2008–2009, 20. The median number of years required for completion of a degree in 2006–2007 were 3. The number of students enrolled full- and part-time who were dismissed or voluntarily withdrew from this program area in 2007–2008 were 2.

Admissions Requirements:

Scores: Entries appear in this order: required test or GPA, minimum score (if required), median score of students entering in 2007–2008. Master's Programs: GRE-V 500; overall undergraduate GPA 3.0. We require a minimum score of 5.0 out of 6.0 on the Analytical Section (essay).

Other Criteria: (importance of criteria rated low, medium, or high): GRE/MAT scores—high, research experience—medium, work experience—medium, extracurricular activity—medium, clinically related public service—medium, GPA—high, letters of recommendation—high, interview—medium, statement of goals and objectives—high. Also required undergraduate background including the following courses: General Psychology, Abnormal or Personality Psychology, Statistics or Experimental Design, and Developmental or Child Psychology. For additional information on admission requirements, go to http://www.wpunj.edu/cohss/psychology/masters.htm.

Student Characteristics: The following represents characteristics of students in 2007–2008 in all graduate psychology programs in the department: Female—full-time 19, part-time 23; Male—full-time 4, part-time 4; African American/Black—full-time 2, part-time 4; Hispanic/Latino(a)—full-time 2, part-time 2; Asian/Pacific Islander—full-time 0, part-time 1; American Indian/Alaska Native—full-time 0, part-time 0; Caucasian/White—full-time 19, part-time 20; Multi-ethnic—full-time 0, part-time 0; students subject to the Americans With Disabilities Act—full-time 0, part-time 0; Unknown ethnicity—full-time 0, part-time 0.

Financial Information/Assistance:

Tuition for Full-Time Study: *Master's:* State residents: per academic year $13,550, $542 per credit hour; Nonstate residents: per academic year $21,025, $841 per credit hour.

Financial Assistance:

First-Year Students: Traineeships available for first year. Average amount paid per academic year: $6,000. Average number of hours worked per week: 20. Apply by April 1. Tuition remission given: full.

Advanced Students: Traineeships available for advanced students. Average amount paid per academic year: $6,000. Average number of hours worked per week: 20. Apply by April 1. Tuition remission given: full.

Additional Information: Of all students currently enrolled full time, 27% benefited from one or more of the listed financial assistance programs. Application and information available online at http://ww2.wpunj.edu/admissn/gradf/graduate/grad_gainfo.htm.

Internships/Practica: Master's Degree (MA/MS Clinical and Counseling Psychology): An internship experience such as a final research project or "capstone" experience is required of graduates. Interns have served in a wide variety of inpatient and outpatient settings including hospitals, community mental health clinics, group homes, drug treatment facilities, rehabilitation centers, correctional facilities, and gerontology programs. Interns can generally structure the internship around individual scheduling needs. Students can arrange their own internships or can use the program's database of internship sites. All sites must satisfy programmatic, state and accrediting body statutes and regulations. After licensure or under proper supervision, graduates are able to conduct assessments; counsel individuals, groups, and families using appropriate interview and intervention techniques; participate in institutional and organizational research projects; and work on an elective basis with a variety of populations (e.g., children, adolescents, the elderly, the severely mentally ill, the neurologically impaired, substance abusers, and others).

Housing and Day Care: On-campus housing is available. See the following Web site for more information: http://ww2.wpunj.edu/admissn/gradf/graduate/grad_quickfacts.htm. On-campus day care facilities are available. See the following Web site for more information: http://www.wpunj.edu.

Employment of Department Graduates:

Master's Degree Graduates: Of those who graduated in the academic year 2006–2007, the following categories and numbers represent the postgraduate activities and employment of master's degree graduates: Enrolled in a psychology doctoral program (2), enrolled in another graduate/professional program (0), enrolled in a postdoctoral residency/fellowship (n/a), employed in independent practice (n/a), employed in an academic position at a university (2), employed in an academic position at a 2-year/4-year college (0), employed in other positions at a higher education institution (0), employed in a professional position in a school system (0), employed in business or industry (0), employed in government agency (0), employed in a community mental health/counseling center (15), employed in a hospital/medical center (3), still seeking employment (0), not seeking employment (0), other employment position (0), do not know (0), total from the above (master's) (22).

Doctoral Degree Graduates: Of those who graduated in the academic year 2006–2007, the following categories and numbers represent the postgraduate activities and employment of doctoral degree graduates: Enrolled in a psychology doctoral program (n/a), total from the above (doctoral) (0).

Additional Information:

Orientation, Objectives, and Emphasis of Department: Master's Level Tracks in Clinical and Counseling Psychology Track 1 Professional Practice of Counseling This track prepares students for positions in non-school settings. The curriculum is designed to help students meet the following academic and clinical experience requirements mandated for licensure as a Licensed Professional Counselor (LPC) in New Jersey: 60 credits of work in specified areas that provide a foundation for taking the National Counselor Examination and 4,500 hours of supervised clinical experience (at least 3,000 hours of which have to be Post-Master's degree). The track provides core and elective courses in the theoretical, empirical, ethical and cross-cultural foundations of counseling in addition to supervised clinical fieldwork. Track 2 Clinical Health Psychology This track prepares students in preventing and treating and researching disorders and dysfunctions in mental and physical health by fostering a knowledge and understanding of the biopsychosocial factors that contribute to the onset and progression of these disorders and dysfunctions at the individual and group level. Graduates work in a variety of settings including primary care, clinical psychology, community-based clinics and agencies, for profit and not-for-profit sites, local, state, regional, federal and international health research and treatment facilities as well as in academia. Track 3 International and Online E-Clinical Track For information see our website (http://www.wpunj.edu).

Special Facilities or Resources: The University has a modern library with numerous online databases, media, and study areas. The new University Commons provides a food mall, recreation area, ballrooms, and informal leisure spaces and lounges. The campus is wired and includes numerous labs equipped with a variety of software applications for teaching and research. The campus also has an active Instructional Research Technology Lab that helps support IT-related activities. The Psychology Department contains a wide array of assessments, tests, videos, and equipment that are available to faculty and students. Research facilities will be significantly enhanced in our soon-to-be renovated academic building. The graduate faculty have ongoing research in a variety of areas including clinical health psychology; mind–body approaches to well-being; life span issues; trauma; substance abuse and addiction; coping with chronic illness in pediatric populations; relationships between personality, career choice, and substance abuse; gerontology; serious and persistent psychiatric disorders; and the neuropsychology and cognitive neuroscience underlying memory, information processing, executive function and peripheral and central neurophysiology. The 370-acre campus is 30 minutes from New York City, 45 minutes from scenic northern New Jersey and 90 minutes from the Pocono Mountains.

Information for Students With Physical Disabilities: See the following Web site for more information: http://www.wpunj.edu.

Application Information:

Send to Office of Graduate Studies, Raubinger Hall, Room 139, William Paterson University, 300 Pompton Road, Wayne, NJ 07470. Application available online. URL of online application: http://ww2.wpunj.edu/admissn/gradf/graduate/grad_apply_now.htm. Students are admitted in the Fall, application deadline March 1. *Fee:* $50.

New Mexico Highlands University
Division of Psychology
Department of Behavioral Sciences
Hewett Hall
Las Vegas, NM 87701-4073
Telephone: (505) 454-3343
Fax: (505) 454-3331
E-mail: *jlhill@nmhu.edu*
Web: *http://www.nmhu.edu/psychology/*

Department Information:

1946. Psychology Program Coordinator: Jean L. Hill. Number of faculty: total—full-time 5, part-time 1; women—full-time 3, part-time 1; total—minority—full-time 1.

Programs and Degrees Offered:

Listed in the following order: Program area, degree type (T if terminal Master's), number awarded 7/06–6/07. General–Clinical–Counseling MA/MS (Master of Arts/Science) (T) 1.

Student Applications/Admissions:

Student Applications

General–Clinical–Counseling MA/MS (Master of Arts/Science)—Applications 2007–2008, 25. Total applicants accepted 2007–2008, 18. Number full-time enrolled (new admits only) 2007–2008, 10. Number part-time enrolled (new admits only) 2007–2008, 0. Total enrolled 2007–2008 full-time, 18, part-time, 6. Openings 2008–2009, 15. The median number of years required for completion of a degree in 2006–2007 were 7. The number of students enrolled full- and part-time who were dismissed or voluntarily withdrew from this program area in 2007–2008 were 1.

Admissions Requirements:

Scores: Entries appear in this order: required test or GPA, minimum score (if required), median score of students entering in 2007–2008. Master's Programs: overall undergraduate GPA no minimum stated; psychology GPA 3.00, 3.45.

Other Criteria: (importance of criteria rated low, medium, or high): research experience—medium, work experience—medium, extracurricular activity—low, clinically related public service—medium, letters of recommendation—medium, statement of goals and objectives—high.

Student Characteristics: The following represents characteristics of students in 2007–2008 in all graduate psychology programs in the department: Female—full-time 12, part-time 3; Male—full-time 6, part-time 3; African American/Black—full-time 1, part-time 0; Hispanic/Latino(a)—full-time 5, part-time 1; Asian/Pacific Islander—full-time 0, part-time 0; American Indian/Alaska Native—full-time 0, part-time 0; Caucasian/White—full-time 12, part-time 5; Multi-ethnic—full-time 0, part-time 0; students subject to the Americans With Disabilities Act—full-time 0, part-time 0; Unknown ethnicity—full-time 0, part-time 0; International students who hold an F-1 or J-1 Visa—full-time 1, part-time 0.

Financial Information/Assistance:

Tuition for Full-Time Study: *Master's:* State residents: per academic year $2,424, $101 per credit hour; Nonstate residents: per academic year $10,248, $427 per credit hour. Tuition is subject to change.

Financial Assistance:

First-Year Students: Teaching assistantships available for first year. Average amount paid per academic year: $6,500. Average number of hours worked per week: 20. Tuition remission given: full and partial. Research assistantships available for first year. Average amount paid per academic year: $6,500. Average number of hours worked per week: 20. Tuition remission given: full and partial. Fellowships and scholarships available for first year. Average amount paid per academic year: $6,500. Average number of hours worked per week: 20. Tuition remission given: full and partial.

Advanced Students: Teaching assistantships available for advanced students. Average amount paid per academic year: $6,500. Average number of hours worked per week: 20. Tuition remission given: full and partial. Research assistantships available for advanced students. Average amount paid per academic year: $6,500. Average number of hours worked per week: 20. Tuition remission given: full and partial. Fellowships and scholarships available for advanced students. Average amount paid per academic year: $6,500. Average number of hours worked per week: 20. Tuition remission given: full and partial.

Additional Information: Of all students currently enrolled full time, 80% benefited from one or more of the listed financial assistance programs.

Internships/Practica: Students in the Clinical Psychology/Counseling track must complete 12 credit hours of field experience. Completion of the 12 credit hours ensures that each student in this track gains 720 hours of direct clinical experience while completing the program. Field experience placements are arranged through cooperative planning by the student, the program, and the agency. Students from our program have been placed with the following agencies: the forensic, adolescent, and adult units of the state psychiatric hospital; the local community mental health center; the state juvenile correctional facility; local schools; an equine therapy program; and many others.

Housing and Day Care: On-campus housing is available. On-campus day care facilities are available.

Employment of Department Graduates:

Master's Degree Graduates: Of those who graduated in the academic year 2006–2007, the following categories and numbers represent the postgraduate activities and employment of master's degree graduates: Enrolled in a postdoctoral residency/fellowship (n/a), employed in independent practice (n/a), employed in a community mental health/counseling center (1), total from the above (master's) (1).

Doctoral Degree Graduates: Of those who graduated in the academic year 2006–2007, the following categories and numbers represent the postgraduate activities and employment of doctoral

degree graduates: Enrolled in a psychology doctoral program (n/a), total from the above (doctoral) (0).

Additional Information:

Orientation, Objectives, and Emphasis of Department: The department offers two tracks that lead to a Master of Science degree in psychology. The General Psychology track requires 36 credit hours and is intended to provide a background similar to that given in many PhD programs. This track is organized around a general core of courses designed to educate the student in all areas of psychology with the opportunity to further pursue an area of interest such as physiological experimental, neuropsychological, or social psychology. This track is especially useful for those students whose goals include either entering a doctoral program or working in a nonclinical position (research, etc.) upon completing the master's degree. The Clinical Psychology/Counseling track is a 67-credit hour emphasis area that is unique because it is one of the only programs in the United States that provides comprehensive training in psychological training and assessment in four areas: neuropsychological, behavioral, intelligence, and personality. This track is designed to prepare students to continue their education at the doctoral level or to work as a master's-level clinician. The student successfully completing this track will qualify for licensure as a master's-level clincian in approximately 40 states.

Special Facilities or Resources: The department offers excellent animal laboratory facilities for experimental–physiological research, as well as laboratories for human subjects research. In addition, the department has an extensive computer laboratory. We also have a close relationship with the state psychiatric hospital, which is located in the community.

Application Information:

Send to Psychology Program Coordinator. Students are admitted in the Fall, application deadline June 1. Earlier applications receive preferential treatment for financial aid. *Fee:* $15.

New Mexico State University

Counseling and Educational Psychology
College of Education
Box 30001 MSC 3CEP
Las Cruces, NM 88003-8001
Telephone: (505) 646-2121
Fax: (505) 646-8035
E-mail: *eadams@nmsu.edu*
Web: *http://www.education.nmsu.edu/cep/*

Department Information:

1905. Department Head: Eve M. Adams. Number of faculty: total—full-time 10; women—full-time 6; total—minority—full-time 3, part-time 2; women minority—full-time 3, part-time 1.

Programs and Degrees Offered:

Listed in the following order: Program area, degree type (T if terminal Master's), number awarded 7/06–6/07. Counseling and Guidance MA/MS (Master of Arts/Science) (T) 10, School Psychology EdS/MEd (School Psychology) 5, Counseling Psychology PhD (Doctor of Philosophy) 6.

APA Accreditation: Counseling PhD (Doctor of Philosophy).

Student Applications/Admissions:

Student Applications

Counseling and Guidance MA/MS (Master of Arts/Science)—Applications 2007–2008, 28. Total applicants accepted 2007–2008, 13. Number full-time enrolled (new admits only) 2007–2008, 6. Number part-time enrolled (new admits only) 2007–2008, 7. Total enrolled 2007–2008 full-time, 15, part-time, 15. Openings 2008–2009, 13. The median number of years required for completion of a degree in 2006–2007 were 2. The number of students enrolled full- and part-time who were dismissed or voluntarily withdrew from this program area in 2007–2008 were 1. *School Psychology EdS/MEd (School Psychology)*—Applications 2007–2008, 18. Total applicants accepted 2007–2008, 10. Number full-time enrolled (new admits only) 2007–2008, 5. Number part-time enrolled (new admits only) 2007–2008, 4. Total enrolled 2007–2008 full-time, 31, part-time, 11. Openings 2008–2009, 12. The median number of years required for completion of a degree in 2006–2007 were 3. The number of students enrolled full- and part-time who were dismissed or voluntarily withdrew from this program area in 2007–2008 were 4. *Counseling Psychology PhD (Doctor of Philosophy)*—Applications 2007–2008, 51. Total applicants accepted 2007–2008, 7. Number full-time enrolled (new admits only) 2007–2008, 7. Number part-time enrolled (new admits only) 2007–2008, 0. Openings 2008–2009, 6. The median number of years required for completion of a degree in 2006–2007 were 4. The number of students enrolled full- and part-time who were dismissed or voluntarily withdrew from this program area in 2007–2008 were 1.

Admissions Requirements:

Scores: Entries appear in this order: required test or GPA, minimum score (if required), median score of students entering in 2007–2008. Master's Programs: GRE-V no minimum stated, 456; GRE-Q no minimum stated, 464; overall undergraduate GPA 3.0, 3.5; last 2 years GPA no minimum stated. Doctoral Programs: GRE-V no minimum stated, 500; GRE-Q no minimum stated, 530; overall undergraduate GPA 3.0, 3.4; Doctoral program GRE-Analytic no minimum stated, 5. Median scores for EdS Program are: GRE Verbal 430, Quantitative 430, and MA GPA 3.35.

Other Criteria: (importance of criteria rated low, medium, or high): GRE/MAT scores—medium, research experience—high, work experience—medium, extracurricular activity—medium, clinically related public service—high, GPA—high, letters of recommendation—high, interview—high, statement of goals and objectives—high, writing sample—medium, undergraduate major in psychology—low, specific undergraduate psychology courses taken—low. Criteria do vary for different programs. Please go to Web site for program-specific information.. For additional information on admission requirements, go to http://education.nmsu.edu/cep/.

Student Characteristics: The following represents characteristics of students in 2007–2008 in all graduate psychology programs in the department: Female—full-time 57, part-time 15; Male—full-time 20, part-time 11; African American/Black—full-time

5, part-time 1; Hispanic/Latino(a)—full-time 32, part-time 16; Asian/Pacific Islander—full-time 2, part-time 0; American Indian/Alaska Native—full-time 1, part-time 1; Caucasian/White—full-time 32, part-time 8; Multi-ethnic—full-time 2, part-time 0; students subject to the Americans With Disabilities Act—full-time 2, part-time 0; Unknown ethnicity—full-time 3, part-time 0; International students who hold an F-1 or J-1 Visa—full-time 1, part-time 0.

Financial Information/Assistance:

Tuition for Full-Time Study: *Master's:* State residents: per academic year $6,308, $200 per credit hour; Nonstate residents: per academic year $16,334, $625 per credit hour. *Doctoral:* State residents: per academic year $6,308, $200 per credit hour; Nonstate residents: per academic year $16,334, $625 per credit hour. Tuition is subject to change. See the following Web site for updates and changes in tuition costs: http://www.gradschool.nmsu.edu/.

Financial Assistance:

First-Year Students: Teaching assistantships available for first year. Average amount paid per academic year: $7,800. Average number of hours worked per week: 10. Apply by varies. Tuition remission given: partial. Research assistantships available for first year. Average amount paid per academic year: $7,800. Average number of hours worked per week: 10. Apply by varies. Tuition remission given: partial. Fellowships and scholarships available for first year. Average amount paid per academic year: $4,500. Apply by varies. Tuition remission given: full.

Advanced Students: Teaching assistantships available for advanced students. Average amount paid per academic year: $7,800. Average number of hours worked per week: 10. Apply by varies. Tuition remission given: partial. Research assistantships available for advanced students. Average amount paid per academic year: $7,800. Average number of hours worked per week: 10. Apply by varies. Tuition remission given: partial. Fellowships and scholarships available for advanced students. Average amount paid per academic year: $4,500. Apply by varies. Tuition remission given: full.

Additional Information: Of all students currently enrolled full time, 60% benefited from one or more of the listed financial assistance programs. Application and information available online at http://education.nmsu.edu/departments/academic/cep/phd/assistantships.html.

Internships/Practica: Master's Degree (MA/MS Counseling and Guidance): An internship experience such as a final research project or "capstone" experience is required of graduates. Doctoral Degree (PhD Counseling Psychology): For those doctoral students for whom a professional internship was required in this program prior to graduation, (8) students applied for an internship in 2006–2007, with (8) students obtaining an internship. Of those students who obtained an internship, (8) were paid internships. Of those students who obtained an internship, (7) students placed in APA/CPA-accredited internships, (0) students placed in internships not APA/CPA-accredited, but listed with the Association of Psychology Postdoctoral and Internship Centers (APPIC), (0) students placed in internships conforming to guidelines of the Council of Directors of School Psychology Programs (CDSPP), (1) students placed in internships that were not APA/CPA-accredited, APPIC or CDSPP listed. Practicum placements include the NMSU Counseling Center, the Las Cruces Public Schools, a primary care setting, community mental health centers, hospitals, adolescent residential centers, the Department of Vocational Rehabilitation, military bases, and nursing homes.

Housing and Day Care: On-campus housing is available. See the following Web site for more information: http://www.nmsu.edu/~housing/. On-campus day care facilities are available. Call (505) 646-3206 for university childcare. Call (505) 527-1149 for community resources.

Employment of Department Graduates:

Master's Degree Graduates: Of those who graduated in the academic year 2006–2007, the following categories and numbers represent the postgraduate activities and employment of master's degree graduates: Enrolled in a psychology doctoral program (2), enrolled in another graduate/professional program (0), enrolled in a postdoctoral residency/fellowship (n/a), employed in independent practice (n/a), employed in an academic position at a university (0), employed in an academic position at a 2-year/4-year college (0), employed in other positions at a higher education institution (0), employed in a professional position in a school system (3), employed in business or industry (0), employed in government agency (0), employed in a community mental health/counseling center (6), employed in a hospital/medical center (0), still seeking employment (0), not seeking employment (0), other employment position (0), do not know (0), total from the above (master's) (11).

Doctoral Degree Graduates: Of those who graduated in the academic year 2006–2007, the following categories and numbers represent the postgraduate activities and employment of doctoral degree graduates: Enrolled in a psychology doctoral program (n/a), enrolled in another graduate/professional program (0), enrolled in a postdoctoral residency/fellowship (0), employed in independent practice (0), employed in an academic position at a university (1), employed in an academic position at a 2-year/4-year college (0), employed in other positions at a higher education institution (3), employed in a professional position in a school system (0), employed in business or industry (0), employed in government agency (0), employed in a community mental health/counseling center (1), employed in a hospital/medical center (1), still seeking employment (0), not seeking employment (0), other employment position (0), do not know (0), total from the above (doctoral) (6).

Additional Information:

Orientation, Objectives, and Emphasis of Department: The major thrust of the department is the preparation of professionals for licensure and positions in counseling psychology, mental health and school counseling, school psychology, and related areas. Three graduate degrees are available: Doctor of Philosophy, Masters of Arts, and Specialist in Education. The PhD in Counseling Psychology, which is accredited by the American Psychological Association, is based on the scientist–practitioner model through which both research and service delivery skills are acquired. Graduates of the program are prepared to conduct research, provide service, teach, and supervise. Emphases in the Counseling Psychology program include cultural diversity, generalist training in a variety of modalities, supervision, and consultation. The Master of Arts in Counseling and Guidance prepares professional counselors to offer individual, family, and group counseling in schools, agencies, hospitals, and private practice. The curriculum covers human development, appraisal, diagnosis, treatment planning, and individual and professional issues. The School Psychology Program (EdS) prepares professionals for positions in public schools and other organizations that require advanced assessment, counseling, consultation, and supervision skills. A major research project (thesis) is a degree requirement.

Special Facilities or Resources: The Counseling and School Psychology Training and Research Center is a training and service facility sponsored by the Department of Counseling and Educational Psychology that provides excellent opportunities for supervised counseling and supervision-of-supervision. Four rooms are available for videotaping and have one-way mirrors, telephones, and microphone and speakers for live supervision of counseling and live supervision of supervision. A portable video camera is available for use in other rooms. The facility has a state-of-the-art bug in the ear system that helps facilitate live supervision for immediate feedback to the counselor in training. We also have extensive training with similar supervisory capabilities at the Family Medicine Center, a primary care center staffed by Family Medicine residents and Counseling Psychology students.

Information for Students With Physical Disabilities: See the following Web site for more information: http://www.nmsu.edu/~ssd/.

Application Information:
Application to the department should be mailed to Training Director (of specific program to which you are applying), Department of Counseling and Educational Psychology, MSC 3CEP/Box 30001, Las Cruces, NM 88003-8001 Applications to the Graduate School should be mailed to The Graduate School, MSC 3G/Box 30001, Las Cruces, NM 88003-8001. Application available online. URL of online application: http://www.nmsu.edu/~gradcolg/app.html. Students are admitted in the Fall, application deadline March 1; Summer, application deadline December 15. The PhD Program deadline is December 15; the EdS Program deadline is January 15; the MA Program deadline is March 1. The Graduate School does not have any deadlines, but Graduate School materials should be sent approximately 1 month in advance of the department deadlines. *Fee:* $30. McNair scholars can have their fees waived.

New Mexico State University (2007 data)

Department of Psychology
Department 3452, P.O. Box 30001
Las Cruces, NM 88003
Telephone: (505) 646-2502
Fax: (505) 646-6212
E-mail: *jemcdon@nmsu.edu*
Web: *http://www-psych.nmsu.edu*

Department Information:
1950. Head: James E. McDonald. Number of faculty: total—full-time 13; women—full-time 4.

Programs and Degrees Offered:
Listed in the following order: Program area, degree type (T if terminal Master's), number awarded 7/06–6/07. Cognitive MA/MS (Master of Arts/Science) (T) 5, Engineering MA/MS (Master of Arts/Science) (T) 3, Social MA/MS (Master of Arts/Science) (T) 4, Cognitive PhD (Doctor of Philosophy) 2, Engineering PhD (Doctor of Philosophy) 0, Social PhD (Doctor of Philosophy) 3.

Student Applications/Admissions:

Student Applications

Cognitive MA/MS (Master of Arts/Science)—Applications 2007–2008, 8. Total applicants accepted 2007–2008, 4. Number full-time enrolled (new admits only) 2007–2008, 3. Total enrolled 2007–2008 full-time, 8, part-time, 2. Openings 2008–2009, 3. The median number of years required for completion of a degree in 2006–2007 were 3. The number of students enrolled full- and part-time who were dismissed or voluntarily withdrew from this program area in 2007–2008 were 0. *Engineering MA/MS (Master of Arts/Science)*—Applications 2007–2008, 10. Total applicants accepted 2007–2008, 5. Number full-time enrolled (new admits only) 2007–2008, 3. Number part-time enrolled (new admits only) 2007–2008, 0. Total enrolled 2007–2008 full-time, 9, part-time, 7. Openings 2008–2009, 3. The median number of years required for completion of a degree in 2006–2007 were 3. The number of students enrolled full- and part-time who were dismissed or voluntarily withdrew from this program area in 2007–2008 were 0. *Social MA/MS (Master of Arts/Science)*—Applications 2007–2008, 15. Total applicants accepted 2007–2008, 8. Number full-time enrolled (new admits only) 2007–2008, 5. Number part-time enrolled (new admits only) 2007–2008, 0. Total enrolled 2007–2008 full-time, 9, part-time, 2. Openings 2008–2009, 3. The median number of years required for completion of a degree in 2006–2007 were 3. The number of students enrolled full- and part-time who were dismissed or voluntarily withdrew from this program area in 2007–2008 were 0. *Cognitive PhD (Doctor of Philosophy)*—Applications 2007–2008, 3. Total applicants accepted 2007–2008, 1. Number full-time enrolled (new admits only) 2007–2008, 0. Number part-time enrolled (new admits only) 2007–2008, 0. Total enrolled 2007–2008 full-time, 4, part-time, 2. Openings 2008–2009, 2. The median number of years required for completion of a degree in 2006–2007 were 4. The number of students enrolled full- and part-time who were dismissed or voluntarily withdrew from this program area in 2007–2008 were 0. *Engineering PhD (Doctor of Philosophy)*—Applications 2007–2008, 3. Total applicants accepted 2007–2008, 0. Number full-time enrolled (new admits only) 2007–2008, 0. Number part-time enrolled (new admits only) 2007–2008, 0. Total enrolled 2007–2008 full-time, 4, part-time, 1. Openings 2008–2009, 2. The number of students enrolled full- and part-time who were dismissed or voluntarily withdrew from this program area in 2007–2008 were 0. *Social PhD (Doctor of Philosophy)*—Applications 2007–2008, 5. Total applicants accepted 2007–2008, 3. Number full-time enrolled (new admits only) 2007–2008, 2. Number part-time enrolled (new admits only) 2007–2008, 0. Total enrolled 2007–2008 full-time, 7, part-time, 1. Openings 2008–2009, 2. The median number of years required for completion of a degree in 2006–2007 were 4. The number of students enrolled full- and part-time who were dismissed or voluntarily withdrew from this program area in 2007–2008 were 0.

Admissions Requirements:

Scores: Entries appear in this order: required test or GPA, minimum score (if required), median score of students entering in 2007–2008. Master's Programs: GRE-V no minimum stated, 545; GRE-Q no minimum stated, 572; overall undergraduate

GPA no minimum stated, 3.56. Doctoral Programs: GRE-V no minimum stated, 587; GRE-Q no minimum stated, 593; overall undergraduate GPA no minimum stated, 3.35.

Other Criteria: (importance of criteria rated low, medium, or high): GRE/MAT scores—high, research experience—medium, work experience—low, GPA—high, letters of recommendation—high, statement of goals and objectives—medium.

Student Characteristics: The following represents characteristics of students in 2007–2008 in all graduate psychology programs in the department: Female—full-time 25, part-time 8; Male—full-time 15, part-time 7; African American/Black—full-time 0, part-time 0; Hispanic/Latino(a)—full-time 10, part-time 2; Asian/Pacific Islander—full-time 2, part-time 0; American Indian/Alaska Native—full-time 0, part-time 0; Caucasian/White—full-time 29, part-time 13; Multi-ethnic—full-time 0, part-time 0; students subject to the Americans With Disabilities Act—full-time 0, part-time 0; Unknown ethnicity—full-time 0, part-time 0.

Financial Information/Assistance:

Tuition for Full-Time Study: *Master's:* State residents: per academic year $4,543, $189 per credit hour; Nonstate residents: per academic year $14,173, $590 per credit hour. *Doctoral:* State residents: per academic year $4,543, $189 per credit hour; Nonstate residents: per academic year $14,173, $590 per credit hour. Tuition is subject to change. See the following Web site for updates and changes in tuition costs: http://www.nmsu.edu/~uar/schecosts/schcosts.htm.

Financial Assistance:

First-Year Students: Teaching assistantships available for first year. Average amount paid per academic year: $15,000. Average number of hours worked per week: 20. Apply by March 1. Tuition remission given: partial. Research assistantships available for first year. Average amount paid per academic year: $15,000. Average number of hours worked per week: 20. Apply by March 1. Tuition remission given: partial. Fellowships and scholarships available for first year. Apply by March 1.

Advanced Students: Teaching assistantships available for advanced students. Average amount paid per academic year: $15,000. Average number of hours worked per week: 20. Apply by March 1. Tuition remission given: partial. Research assistantships available for advanced students. Average amount paid per academic year: $15,000. Average number of hours worked per week: 20. Apply by March 1. Tuition remission given: partial. Fellowships and scholarships available for advanced students. Average amount paid per academic year: $15,000. Apply by March 1.

Additional Information: Of all students currently enrolled full time, 100% benefited from one or more of the listed financial assistance programs. Application and information available online at http://gradschool.nmsu.edu/fellowships/.

Internships/Practica: For the PhD degree in Engineering Psychology, students must complete an internship in an industrial, government, or other laboratory setting of at least 3 months in duration. Many master's students in Engineering Psychology and Cognitive Psychology spend a summer or half year as an intern in industry, but it is not required for the MA degree.

Housing and Day Care: On-campus housing is available. Housing Information: Department of Housing and Dining Services, MSC 3BB, New Mexico State University, P.O. Box 30001, Las Cruces, NM 88003-8001. On-campus day care facilities are available.

Employment of Department Graduates:

Master's Degree Graduates: Of those who graduated in the academic year 2006–2007, the following categories and numbers represent the postgraduate activities and employment of master's degree graduates: Enrolled in a psychology doctoral program (8), enrolled in a postdoctoral residency/fellowship (n/a), employed in independent practice (n/a), employed in business or industry (4), total from the above (master's) (12).

Doctoral Degree Graduates: Of those who graduated in the academic year 2006–2007, the following categories and numbers represent the postgraduate activities and employment of doctoral degree graduates: Enrolled in a psychology doctoral program (n/a), employed in an academic position at a 2-year/4-year college (3), employed in business or industry (3), total from the above (doctoral) (6).

Additional Information:

Orientation, Objectives, and Emphasis of Department: The department offers an MA degree in general experimental psychology that allows an emphasis in cognitive, engineering, or social psychology. The PhD is offered in the major areas of cognitive, engineering, and social psychology. Within these areas there is special emphasis on language processing, human–computer interaction, and cross-cultural psychology, respectively. Students must earn an MA degree before being admitted to the doctoral program. All programs are experimentally oriented and have the distinctive characteristic of pursuing and extending basic research questions in applied settings.

Special Facilities or Resources: All faculty members have specialized laboratories with a wide variety of computer hardware and software. These include a teamwork lab that is used to conduct research on team cognition in complex task environments, an eye-tracking lab used to study perceptual and cognitive issues, a biopsychology lab equipped to measure ERPs, and a developmental laboratory equipped with sophisticated equipment for recording, analyzing, and editing mother–infant interactions.

Information for Students With Physical Disabilities: See the following Web site for more information: http://www.nmsu.edu/~ssd/.

Application Information:

Send to Chair of Graduate Committee, Department of Psychology, MSC 3452, New Mexico State University, Las Cruces, NM 88003-8001. Application available online. URL of online application: http://www.gradschool.nmsu.edu/admit-form.html. Students are admitted in the Fall, application deadline March 1. *Fee:* $30. Online application is for NMSU graduate school only. Separate application materials (including forms for letters of reference) must be requested from the Psychology Department.

New Mexico, University of
Department of Psychology
Arts and Science
Logan Hall, MSC03 2220
Albuquerque, NM 87131-1161
Telephone: (505) 277-5009
Fax: (505) 277-1394
E-mail: *ryeo@unm.edu*
Web: *http://www.psych.unm.edu*

Department Information:

1960. Chairperson: Ron Yeo. Number of faculty: total—full-time 26, part-time 8; women—full-time 11, part-time 4; total—minority—full-time 3; women minority—full-time 2.

Programs and Degrees Offered:

Listed in the following order: Program area, degree type (T if terminal Master's), number awarded 7/06–6/07. Clinical PhD (Doctor of Philosophy) 4, Developmental PhD (Doctor of Philosophy) 0, Quantitative PhD (Doctor of Philosophy) 0, Evolutionary PhD (Doctor of Philosophy) 0, Cognition Brain and Behavior PhD (Doctor of Philosophy) 1.

APA Accreditation: Clinical PhD (Doctor of Philosophy).

Student Applications/Admissions:

Student Applications

Clinical PhD (Doctor of Philosophy)—Applications 2007–2008, 123. Total applicants accepted 2007–2008, 9. Number full-time enrolled (new admits only) 2007–2008, 5. Number part-time enrolled (new admits only) 2007–2008, 0. Openings 2008–2009, 5. The median number of years required for completion of a degree in 2006–2007 were 6. The number of students enrolled full- and part-time who were dismissed or voluntarily withdrew from this program area in 2007–2008 were 1. *Developmental PhD (Doctor of Philosophy)*—Applications 2007–2008, 3. Total applicants accepted 2007–2008, 1. Number full-time enrolled (new admits only) 2007–2008, 1. Number part-time enrolled (new admits only) 2007–2008, 0. Openings 2008–2009, 1. The number of students enrolled full- and part-time who were dismissed or voluntarily withdrew from this program area in 2007–2008 were 0. *Quantitative PhD (Doctor of Philosophy)*—Applications 2007–2008, 2. Total applicants accepted 2007–2008, 0. Number full-time enrolled (new admits only) 2007–2008, 0. Number part-time enrolled (new admits only) 2007–2008, 0. The number of students enrolled full- and part-time who were dismissed or voluntarily withdrew from this program area in 2007–2008 were 0. *Evolutionary PhD (Doctor of Philosophy)*—Applications 2007–2008, 21. Total applicants accepted 2007–2008, 0. Number full-time enrolled (new admits only) 2007–2008, 2. Number part-time enrolled (new admits only) 2007–2008, 0. Openings 2008–2009, 1. The median number of years required for completion of a degree in 2006–2007 were 5. The number of students enrolled full- and part-time who were dismissed or voluntarily withdrew from this program area in 2007–2008 were 0. *Cognition Brain and Behavior PhD (Doctor of Philosophy)*—Applications 2007–2008, 17. Total applicants accepted 2007–2008, 4. Number full-time enrolled (new admits only) 2007–2008, 4. Number part-time enrolled (new admits only) 2007–2008, 0. Openings 2008–2009, 3. The median number of years required for completion of a degree in 2006–2007 were 5. The number of students enrolled full- and part-time who were dismissed or voluntarily withdrew from this program area in 2007–2008 were 1.

Admissions Requirements:

Scores: Entries appear in this order: required test or GPA, minimum score (if required), median score of students entering in 2007–2008. Doctoral Programs: GRE-V no minimum stated, 561; GRE-Q no minimum stated, 630; GRE-Subject (Psychology) no minimum stated, 644; overall undergraduate GPA 3.0, 3.58; Doctoral program GRE-Analytic no minimum stated, 5.
Other Criteria: (importance of criteria rated low, medium, or high): GRE/MAT scores—high, research experience—high, work experience—medium, extracurricular activity—medium, clinically related public service—medium, GPA—high, letters of recommendation—high, interview—high, statement of goals and objectives—high, specific undergraduate psychology courses taken—medium. The importance for the interview and special skills varies. For additional information on admission requirements, go to http://psych.unm.edu/grad_apply.html.

Student Characteristics: The following represents characteristics of students in 2007–2008 in all graduate psychology programs in the department: Female—full-time 61, part-time 0; Male—full-time 24, part-time 0; African American/Black—full-time 1, part-time 0; Hispanic/Latino(a)—full-time 12, part-time 0; Asian/Pacific Islander—full-time 3, part-time 0; American Indian/Alaska Native—full-time 0, part-time 0; Caucasian/White—full-time 66, part-time 0; Multi-ethnic—full-time 1, part-time 0; Unknown ethnicity—full-time 2, part-time 0.

Financial Information/Assistance:

Tuition for Full-Time Study: *Master's:* State residents: per academic year $4,973, $209 per credit hour; Nonstate residents: per academic year $14,942. *Doctoral:* State residents: per academic year $4,973, $209 per credit hour; Nonstate residents: per academic year $14,942. Tuition is subject to change. See the following Web site for updates and changes in tuition costs: http://www.unm.edu/~bursar/tuitionrates.html.

Financial Assistance:

First-Year Students: Teaching assistantships available for first year. Average amount paid per academic year: $12,223. Average number of hours worked per week: 20. Apply by January 15. Tuition remission given: full. Research assistantships available for first year. Average amount paid per academic year: $14,000. Average number of hours worked per week: 20. Apply by January 15. Tuition remission given: full. Fellowships and scholarships available for first year. Average amount paid per academic year: $3,000. Apply by March 1.

Advanced Students: Teaching assistantships available for advanced students. Average amount paid per academic year: $13,445. Average number of hours worked per week: 20. Apply by January 15. Tuition remission given: full. Research assistantships available for advanced students. Average amount paid per academic year: $14,500. Average number of hours worked per week: 20. Apply by January 15. Tuition remission given: full. Fellowships and scholarships available for advanced students. Average amount paid per academic year: $8,000. Apply by March 1.

Additional Information: Of all students currently enrolled full time, 75% benefited from one or more of the listed financial assistance programs. Application and information available online at http://www.unm.edu/~grad/funding/funding.html.

Internships/Practica: No information provided.

Housing and Day Care: On-campus housing is available. See the following Web site for more information: Residence housing: http://www.unm.edu/~reshalls/; off-campus housing: http://och.unm.edu. On-campus day care facilities are available. See the following Web site for more information: http://www.unm.edu/~weecare.

Employment of Department Graduates:

Master's Degree Graduates: Of those who graduated in the academic year 2006–2007, the following categories and numbers represent the postgraduate activities and employment of master's degree graduates: Enrolled in a postdoctoral residency/fellowship (n/a), employed in independent practice (n/a), total from the above (master's) (0).

Doctoral Degree Graduates: Of those who graduated in the academic year 2006–2007, the following categories and numbers represent the postgraduate activities and employment of doctoral degree graduates: Enrolled in a psychology doctoral program (n/a), total from the above (doctoral) (0).

Additional Information:

Orientation, Objectives, and Emphasis of Department: Founded in 1960, the doctoral training program in psychology is based on the premise that psychology, in all of its areas, is fundamentally an experimental discipline. For all students, the PhD degree is awarded in general experimental psychology, and students acquire a solid foundation in both scientific methodology and general psychology. Within this framework, students specialize in any of several competency areas. The well-trained psychologist, within this perspective, is one who combines competence in the general discipline of psychology with excellence in his or her chosen specialization.

Special Facilities or Resources: The department is housed in a building on the central campus. In addition to faculty and administrative offices and seminar rooms, the building is equipped for sophisticated research. There are soundproof chambers for conducting experiments, a variety of timing devices, computer terminals, and electromechanical measuring equipment. Laboratory facilities exist for research in human memory, learning, cognitive psychology, perception, information processing, attention, decision making, developmental, social, personality, neuropsychology, psychophysiology, and clinical psychology. The building also has a large animal research facility with primates and rodents. The campus animal research facility is equipped for surgery and for delicate measurements of brain activities as well as for tests of physical, cognitive, and emotional responses. Microcomputers are widely used in individual faculty laboratories and in a graduate student computer room. The Department of Psychology Clinic opened in 1982 and offers diagnostic and therapeutic services to the Albuquerque community while providing an excellent training facility for clinical students.

Application Information:

Send application, fee, and transcripts to University of New Mexico, Office of Graduate Admissions, MSC06 3720, Albuquerque, NM 87131. Letters of recomendation, letter of intent, GRE scores, transcripts, and department application should be sent directly to University of New Mexico, Department of Psychology, MSC03 2220 Albuquerque, NM 87131. Application available online. URL of online application: http://www.unm.edu/~grad/admissions/admissions.html. Students are admitted in the Fall, application deadline January 15. The deadline for full financial consideration is January 15; we accept applications through May 1 if positions remain. *Fee:* $50.

Adelphi University
The Derner Institute of Advanced Psychological Studies, School of Professional Psychology
Adelphi University
158 Cambridge Avenue
Garden City, NY 11530
Telephone: (516) 877-4185
Fax: (516) 877-4805
E-mail: *chin@adelphi.edu*
Web: *http://www.adelphi.edu*

Department Information:
1952. Dean: Jean Lau Chin. Number of faculty: total—full-time 25, part-time 172; women—full-time 11, part-time 95; total—minority—full-time 3, part-time 12; women minority—full-time 3, part-time 10.

Programs and Degrees Offered:
Listed in the following order: Program area, degree type (T if terminal Master's), number awarded 7/06–6/07. Clinical PhD (Doctor of Philosophy) 23, Psychoanalysis Other 28, Respecialization Diploma PhD (Doctor of Philosophy) 0, General Psychology MA/MS (Master of Arts/Science) (T) 44, School Psychology MA/MS (Master of Arts/Science) (T) 17, Mental Health Counseling MA/MS (Master of Arts/Science) (T) 17.

APA Accreditation: Clinical PhD (Doctor of Philosophy).

Student Applications/Admissions:
Student Applications
Clinical PhD (Doctor of Philosophy)—Applications 2007–2008, 240. Total applicants accepted 2007–2008, 48. Number full-time enrolled (new admits only) 2007–2008, 24. Openings 2008–2009, 20. The median number of years required for completion of a degree in 2006–2007 were 6. The number of students enrolled full- and part-time who were dismissed or voluntarily withdrew from this program area in 2007–2008 were 1. *Psychoanalysis Other*—Applications 2007–2008, 50. Total applicants accepted 2007–2008, 48. Number full-time enrolled (new admits only) 2007–2008, 0. Number part-time enrolled (new admits only) 2007–2008, 47. Openings 2008–2009, 45. The median number of years required for completion of a degree in 2006–2007 were 3. The number of students enrolled full- and part-time who were dismissed or voluntarily withdrew from this program area in 2007–2008 were 8. *Respecialization Diploma PhD (Doctor of Philosophy)*—Applications 2007–2008, 2. Total applicants accepted 2007–2008, 1. Number part-time enrolled (new admits only) 2007–2008, 1. Openings 2008–2009, 2. The number of students enrolled full- and part-time who were dismissed or voluntarily withdrew from this program area in 2007–2008 were 0. *General Psychology MA/MS (Master of Arts/Science)*—Applications 2007–2008, 128. Total applicants accepted 2007–2008, 60. Number full-time enrolled (new admits only) 2007–2008, 40. Number part-time enrolled (new admits only) 2007–2008, 20. Total enrolled 2007–2008 full-time, 75, part-time, 50. Openings 2008–2009, 60. The median number of years required for completion of a degree in 2006–2007 was 1. The number of students enrolled full- and part-time who were dismissed or voluntarily withdrew from this program area in 2007–2008 were 6. *School Psychology MA/MS (Master of Arts/Science)*—Applications 2007–2008, 120. Total applicants accepted 2007–2008, 60. Number full-time enrolled (new admits only) 2007–2008, 31. Number part-time enrolled (new admits only) 2007–2008, 0. Openings 2008–2009, 30. The median number of years required for completion of a degree in 2006–2007 were 3. The number of students enrolled full- and part-time who were dismissed or voluntarily withdrew from this program area in 2007–2008 were 1. *Mental Health Counseling MA/MS (Master of Arts/Science)*—Applications 2007–2008, 43. Total applicants accepted 2007–2008, 22. Number full-time enrolled (new admits only) 2007–2008, 20. Total enrolled 2007–2008 full-time, 55. Openings 2008–2009, 20. The median number of years required for completion of a degree in 2006–2007 were 2. The number of students enrolled full- and part-time who were dismissed or voluntarily withdrew from this program area in 2007–2008 were 3.

Admissions Requirements:
Scores: Entries appear in this order: required test or GPA, minimum score (if required), median score of students entering in 2007–2008. Master's Programs: overall undergraduate GPA 3.00; last 2 years GPA no minimum stated. For the General Program, and for the School Psychology program, a mimimum GPA of 3.0 is required; for the MA program in Mental Health Counseling, a minimum GPA of 3.1 is required Doctoral Programs: GRE-V 550, 600; GRE-Q 550, 650; GRE-Subject (Psychology) 550, 640; overall undergraduate GPA 3.00, 3.40. We consider all applications, and will admit students below 550 GRE's if there are compensatory situations. But, applicants with scores below the listed minima are infrequently accepted.
Other Criteria: (importance of criteria rated low, medium, or high): GRE/MAT scores—high, research experience—high, work experience—high, extracurricular activity—low, clinically related public service—high, GPA—high, letters of recommendation—high, interview—high, statement of goals and objectives—high, specific undergraduate psychology courses taken—high.

Student Characteristics: The following represents characteristics of students in 2007–2008 in all graduate psychology programs in the department: Female—full-time 306, part-time 25; Male—full-time 68, part-time 105; African American/Black—full-time 29, part-time 11; Hispanic/Latino(a)—full-time 13, part-time 3; Asian/Pacific Islander—full-time 14, part-time 1; American Indian/Alaska Native—full-time 0, part-time 0; Caucasian/White—full-time 318, part-time 115; Multi-ethnic—full-time 0, part-time 0; students subject to the Americans With Disabilities Act—full-time 0, part-time 0; Unknown ethnicity—full-time 0, part-time 0; International students who hold an F-1 or J-1 Visa—full-time 10, part-time 2.

Financial Information/Assistance:
Tuition for Full-Time Study: *Master's:* State residents: $755 per credit hour; Nonstate residents: $755 per credit hour. *Doctoral:*

State residents: per academic year $30,000; Nonstate residents: per academic year $30,000. See the following Web site for updates and changes in tuition costs: http://www.adelphi.edu.

Financial Assistance:

First-Year Students: Teaching assistantships available for first year. Average amount paid per academic year: $7,500. Average number of hours worked per week: 7. Apply by April 15. Tuition remission given: partial. Research assistantships available for first year. Average amount paid per academic year: $7,500. Average number of hours worked per week: 7. Apply by April 15. Tuition remission given: partial.

Advanced Students: Teaching assistantships available for advanced students. Average amount paid per academic year: $7,500. Average number of hours worked per week: 7. Apply by April 15. Tuition remission given: partial. Research assistantships available for advanced students. Average amount paid per academic year: $7,500. Average number of hours worked per week: 7. Apply by April 15. Tuition remission given: partial.

Additional Information: Of all students currently enrolled full time, 85% benefited from one or more of the listed financial assistance programs.

Internships/Practica: Doctoral Degree (PhD Clinical): For those doctoral students for whom a professional internship was required in this program prior to graduation, (18) students applied for an internship in 2006–2007, with (17) students obtaining an internship. Of those students who obtained an internship, (17) were paid internships. Of those students who obtained an internship, (15) students placed in APA/CPA-accredited internships, (1) student placed in internships not APA/CPA-accredited, but listed with the Association of Psychology Postdoctoral and Internship Centers (APPIC), (0) students placed in internships conforming to guidelines of the Council of Directors of School Psychology Programs (CDSPP), (1) student placed in internships that were not APA/CPA-accredited, APPIC or CDSPP listed. Doctoral Degree (PhD Respecialization Diploma): For those doctoral students for whom a professional internship was required in this program prior to graduation, (0) students applied for an internship in 2006–2007, with (0) students obtaining an internship. Of those students who obtained an internship, (0) were paid internships. Of those students who obtained an internship, (0) students placed in APA/CPA-accredited internships, (0) students placed in internships not APA/CPA-accredited, but listed with the Association of Psychology Postdoctoral and Internship Centers (APPIC), (0) students placed in internships conforming to guidelines of the Council of Directors of School Psychology Programs (CDSPP), (0) students placed in internships that were not APA/CPA-accredited, APPIC or CDSPP listed. For the doctoral program, students are assigned to the Psychological Services Clinic, the training facility of the PhD Program. Beginning in the 1st year of the doctoral program, students are trained to perform intake evaluations. In the following years, students are to perform psychodiagnostic evaluations and psychotherapy. Students are also assigned to externships at full-service mental health centers during their 2nd year of training. During their 5th year, students complete a 1-year internship in clinical psychology. For the Postdoctoral Program, students are assigned to the Postdoctoral Psychotherapy Center, the training facility of the Postdoctoral Program.

Housing and Day Care: On-campus housing is available. There is little on-campus housing for graduate students, but one to two students in the PhD program each year elect to live in the undergraduate student dormitories. On-campus day care facilities are available. There is a Child Activity Center available to faculty and students.

Employment of Department Graduates:

Master's Degree Graduates: Of those who graduated in the academic year 2006–2007, the following categories and numbers represent the postgraduate activities and employment of master's degree graduates: Enrolled in a psychology doctoral program (24), enrolled in another graduate/professional program (14), enrolled in a postdoctoral residency/fellowship (n/a), employed in independent practice (n/a), employed in a professional position in a school system (15), employed in business or industry (6), employed in a community mental health/counseling center (7), employed in a hospital/medical center (7), do not know (5), total from the above (master's) (78).

Doctoral Degree Graduates: Of those who graduated in the academic year 2006–2007, the following categories and numbers represent the postgraduate activities and employment of doctoral degree graduates: Enrolled in a psychology doctoral program (n/a), enrolled in a postdoctoral residency/fellowship (3), employed in independent practice (2), employed in an academic position at a university (2), employed in other positions at a higher education institution (2), employed in a community mental health/counseling center (5), employed in a hospital/medical center (9), total from the above (doctoral) (23).

Additional Information:

Orientation, Objectives, and Emphasis of Department: The Derner Institute of Advanced Psychological Studies is the first university-based professional school of psychology. The orientation is psychodynamic and scholar–professional. The doctoral program in clinical and the respecialization program are oriented toward community service and prepare the students for careers in clinical service; the postdoctoral programs prepare graduates for the practice of psychoanalysis and psychotherapy. All doctoral programs offer supervised experience in research and theory. The clinical program consists of 4 years of coursework, which includes at least 1 day a week of supervised practice each year and a 5th-year full-time internship; the respecialization program consists of 2 years of coursework, including at least 1 day a week of supervised practice each year and a 3rd-year full-time internship; the postdoctoral programs consist of 4 years of seminars, case conferences, personal therapy, and supervised practice; the master's program consists of 2 years of course work, which includes a thesis or project. A new MA program in School Psychology was begun in Spring 2003; it is a 3-year program, with a joint emphasis on didactic instruction and supervised practice. A new MA program in Mental Health Counseling, also with a joint emphasis on didactic instruction and supervised practice, was begun in Fall 2004.

Special Facilities or Resources: Facilities include a videotape recording studio and perception, learning, developmental, cognition, and applied research laboratories. The Institute has close interaction with two health-related professional schools, the Adelphi School of Nursing and the Adelphi School of Social Work, and with affiliated community school and clinical facilities. The Institute maintains two major clinical facilities, the Adelphi University Psychological Services Center and the Postdoctoral Psychotherapy Center. An APA-accredited continuing education program brings a series of distinguished workshops to the campus.

Application Information:
Send to Graduate Admissions. Application available online. URL of online application: https://www.applyweb.com/apply/adelphi/menu.html. Students are admitted in the Fall, application deadline January 15; Spring, application deadline. Applicants for the PhD program have a January 15 deadline. MA applicants may begin in either Fall or Spring semester. There is no application deadline for the MA in General Psychology. For School Psychology the application deadline is March 1. For the MA program in Mental health Counseling the deadline is April 1. Postdoctoral applicants begin in Fall only, but no application deadline. *Fee:* $50. Graduate admissions will waive application fee if a request for waiver is completed.

Alfred University

Division of School Psychology
Graduate School
Saxon Drive
Alfred, NY 14802-1205
Telephone: (607) 871-2212
Fax: (607) 871-3422
E-mail: *fevangel@alfred.edu*
Web: *http://www.alfred.edu*

Department Information:
1953. Chairperson: Nancy J. Evangelista. Number of faculty: total—full-time 7, part-time 6; women—full-time 3, part-time 3; faculty subject to the Americans With Disabilities Act 1.

Programs and Degrees Offered:
Listed in the following order: Program area, degree type (T if terminal Master's), number awarded 7/06–6/07. MA/CAS Program in School Psychology EdS/MEd (School Psychology) 26, Doctoral Program in School Psychology PsyD (Doctor of Psychology) 0.

APA Accreditation: School PsyD (Doctor of Psychology).

Student Applications/Admissions:
Student Applications
MA/CAS Program in School Psychology EdS/MEd (School Psychology)—Applications 2007–2008, 49. Total applicants accepted 2007–2008, 30. Number full-time enrolled (new admits only) 2007–2008, 14. Number part-time enrolled (new admits only) 2007–2008, 0. Openings 2008–2009, 15. The median number of years required for completion of a degree in 2006–2007 were 3. The number of students enrolled full- and part-time who were dismissed or voluntarily withdrew from this program area in 2007–2008 were 0. *Doctoral Program in School Psychology PsyD (Doctor of Psychology)*—Applications 2007–2008, 39. Total applicants accepted 2007–2008, 16. Number full-time enrolled (new admits only) 2007–2008, 5. Number part-time enrolled (new admits only) 2007–2008, 0. Total enrolled 2007–2008 full-time, 30, part-time, 23. Openings 2008–2009, 7. The median number of years required for completion of a degree in 2006–2007 were 6. The number of students enrolled full- and part-time who were dismissed or voluntarily withdrew from this program area in 2007–2008 were 1.

Admissions Requirements:
Scores: Entries appear in this order: required test or GPA, minimum score (if required), median score of students entering in 2007–2008. Master's Programs: GRE-V no minimum stated, 480; GRE-Q no minimum stated, 555; overall undergraduate GPA 2.70, 3.51; Masters GRE-Analytical no minimum stated, 4.5. Doctoral Programs: GRE-V no minimum stated, 525; GRE-Q no minimum stated, 640; overall undergraduate GPA 2.70, 3.64.
Other Criteria: (importance of criteria rated low, medium, or high): GRE/MAT scores—medium, research experience—medium, work experience—medium, extracurricular activity—medium, clinically related public service—low, GPA—high, letters of recommendation—medium, interview—high, statement of goals and objectives—high, undergraduate major in psychology—medium. The PsyD program places a higher emphasis on research experience. For additional information on admission requirements, go to http://www.alfred.edu/gradschool/school_psychology/applying.html.

Student Characteristics: The following represents characteristics of students in 2007–2008 in all graduate psychology programs in the department: Female—full-time 60, part-time 17; Male—full-time 10, part-time 6; African American/Black—full-time 2, part-time 1; Hispanic/Latino(a)—full-time 1, part-time 1; Asian/Pacific Islander—full-time 0, part-time 0; American Indian/Alaska Native—full-time 1, part-time 0; Caucasian/White—full-time 63, part-time 21; Multi-ethnic—full-time 0, part-time 0; students subject to the Americans With Disabilities Act—full-time 0, part-time 0; Unknown ethnicity—full-time 3, part-time 0; International students who hold an F-1 or J-1 Visa—full-time 0, part-time 0.

Financial Information/Assistance:
Tuition for Full-Time Study: *Master's:* State residents: per academic year $30,016, $680 per credit hour; Nonstate residents: per academic year $30,016, $680 per credit hour. *Doctoral:* State residents: per academic year $30,016, $680 per credit hour; Nonstate residents: per academic year $30,016, $680 per credit hour. Tuition is subject to change. See the following Web site for updates and changes in tuition costs: http://www.alfred.edu/finaid/graduate/cost.html.

Financial Assistance:
First-Year Students: Research assistantships available for first year. Average amount paid per academic year: $16,008. Average number of hours worked per week: 7. Apply by none. Tuition remission given: partial. Fellowships and scholarships available for first year. Average amount paid per academic year: $10,000. Average number of hours worked per week: 0. Apply by January 15. Tuition remission given: full and partial.
Advanced Students: Teaching assistantships available for advanced students. Average amount paid per academic year: $16,008. Average number of hours worked per week: 7. Apply by none. Tuition remission given: partial. Research assistantships available for advanced students. Average amount paid per academic year: $8,000. Average number of hours worked per week: 5. Apply by none. Tuition remission given: partial. Traineeships available for advanced students. Average amount paid per aca-

demic year: $32,016. Average number of hours worked per week: 15. Apply by variable. Tuition remission given: full.

Additional Information: Of all students currently enrolled full time, 100% benefited from one or more of the listed financial assistance programs.

Internships/Practica: Doctoral Degree (PsyD Doctoral Program in School Psychology): For those doctoral students for whom a professional internship was required in this program prior to graduation, (10) students applied for an internship in 2006–2007, with (10) students obtaining an internship. Of those students who obtained an internship, (10) were paid internships. Of those students who obtained an internship, (0) students placed in APA/CPA-accredited internships, (0) students placed in internships not APA/CPA-accredited, but listed with the Association of Psychology Postdoctoral and Internship Centers (APPIC), (10) students placed in internships conforming to guidelines of the Council of Directors of School Psychology Programs (CDSPP), (0) students placed in internships that were not APA/CPA accredited, APPIC or CDSPP listed. Master's and doctoral students may pursue internships anyplace in the United States. Most master's students choose sites at public schools across New York State and northern Pennsylvania. Doctoral students are required to complete a portion of their internship in a school setting, but many also choose sites and internship experiences in both school and clinical settings. A portion of doctoral students each year choose to intern at APPIC and APA accredited sites. For additional information on education and training outcomes for our programs, see the following Web site: http://www.alfred.edu/gradschool/school_psychology/psyd_specialization.html.

Housing and Day Care: On-campus housing is available. Limited on-campus dormitory housing is available for graduate students. Most graduate students live off campus. For information contact: Residence Life Office, Alfred University, Saxon Drive, Alfred, NY 14802. See the following Web site for more information: http://www.alfred.edu. On-campus day care facilities are available. A private Montessori school is located close to campus. For information, contact: Alfred Montessori School, 8 1/2 South Main Street, Alfred, NY 14802. (607) 871-2233.

Employment of Department Graduates:

Master's Degree Graduates: Of those who graduated in the academic year 2006–2007, the following categories and numbers represent the postgraduate activities and employment of master's degree graduates: Enrolled in a psychology doctoral program (2), enrolled in another graduate/professional program (0), enrolled in a postdoctoral residency/fellowship (n/a), employed in independent practice (n/a), employed in an academic position at a university (1), employed in an academic position at a 2-year/4-year college (0), employed in other positions at a higher education institution (1), employed in a professional position in a school system (19), employed in business or industry (0), employed in government agency (0), employed in a community mental health/counseling center (2), employed in a hospital/medical center (0), still seeking employment (0), not seeking employment (1), other employment position (0), do not know (0), total from the above (master's) (26).

Doctoral Degree Graduates: Of those who graduated in the academic year 2006–2007, the following categories and numbers represent the postgraduate activities and employment of doctoral degree graduates: Enrolled in a psychology doctoral program (n/a), enrolled in another graduate/professional program (0), enrolled in a postdoctoral residency/fellowship (0), employed in independent practice (0), employed in an academic position at a university (1), employed in an academic position at a 2-year/4-year college (0), employed in other positions at a higher education institution (1), employed in a professional position in a school system (3), employed in business or industry (0), employed in government agency (0), employed in a community mental health/counseling center (0), employed in a hospital/medical center (0), still seeking employment (0), not seeking employment (0), other employment position (0), do not know (0), total from the above (doctoral) (5).

Additional Information:

Orientation, Objectives, and Emphasis of Department: The Alfred School Psychology program emphasizes a field-centered, systems-oriented, practitioner–scientist approach. The primary goal of the program is the preparation of problem-solving psychologists with special concern for the application of psychological knowledge in a variety of child- and family-related settings. Students acquire knowledge in a wide variety of psychological theories and practices; skills are learned and then demonstrated in a number of different applied settings. They develop the personal characteristics and academic competencies necessary to work effectively with others in the identification, prevention, and remediation of psychological and educational problems with children and adults. Training in school psychology at Alfred University offers extensive one-to-one contact between students and faculty members to encourage the personalized learning process. PsyD students are involved in field experience and research orientation from the first semester on. Training in the following areas is provided: knowledge base in psychology and education; assessment, intervention, and remediation including counseling, play therapy, and family work; consulting and training with teachers, administrators, and parents; research methodology; program evaluation; and professional identification and functioning. Training at the doctoral level emphasizes applied research and the development of an area of specialization.

Special Facilities or Resources: Departmental resources include an extensive library of psychological and educational assessment materials, an audio- and videotape library, and library of counseling and intervention materials. All students gain practicum experience in the on-campus Child and Family Services Center, operated by the Division of School Psychology. The Center provides consultation, assessment, and counseling services to children and families of the region. The Center is a state-of-the-art facility with all therapy and consultation rooms equipped with observation mirrors and remote audio- and videorecording equipment. The Center serves training, service, and research functions for faculty and students. Graduate students have a work and computer room and a spacious lounge. Additionally, all graduate students have access to the mainframe computer and numerous PCs at no cost.

Information for Students With Physical Disabilities: See the following Web site for more information: http://www.alfred.edu/academics/disabled.html.

Application Information:

Send to Graduate Admissions, Alfred University, Saxon Drive, Alfred, NY 14802. Application available online. URL of online application: http://www.alfred.edu. Students are admitted in the Fall, application deadline January 15. Deadline for Fall admission to the PsyD program is January 15; for the MA/CAS program the deadline is February 15. Late applications may be considered if places in the class still exist for qualified applicants. *Fee:* $50. Waiver of fee available for students who meet with admissions personnel on-campus prior to application.

City University of New York (2007 data)

Department of Psychology/Biopsychology and Behavioral Neuroscience PhD Subprogram
Hunter College (all data for PhD subprogram)
695 Park Avenue, Room 611 North Building
New York, NY 10021
Telephone: (212) 772-5550 Psych; (212) 772-5621 Bio
Fax: (212) 772-5620
E-mail: *vanya.quinones@hunter.cuny.edu*
Web: *http://www.maxweber.hunter.cuny.edu/psych/biopsych.htm*

Department Information:

1962. Program Head for Biopsychology and Behavioral Neurosciene: Vanya Quinones. Number of faculty: total—full-time 23; women—full-time 7.

Programs and Degrees Offered:

Listed in the following order: Program area, degree type (T if terminal Master's), number awarded 7/06–6/07. Biopsychology and Behavioral Neuroscience PhD (Doctor of Philosophy) 9.

Student Applications/Admissions:

Student Applications

Biopsychology and Behavioral Neuroscience PhD (Doctor of Philosophy)—Applications 2007–2008, 25. Total applicants accepted 2007–2008, 11. Number full-time enrolled (new admits only) 2007–2008, 11. Openings 2008–2009, 5. The median number of years required for completion of a degree in 2006–2007 were 5. The number of students enrolled full- and part-time who were dismissed or voluntarily withdrew from this program area in 2007–2008 were 0.

Admissions Requirements:

Scores: Entries appear in this order: required test or GPA, minimum score (if required), median score of students entering in 2007–2008. Master's Programs: GRE-V no minimum stated; GRE-Q no minimum stated; GRE-Subject (Psychology) no minimum stated; overall undergraduate GPA no minimum stated; psychology GPA no minimum stated. Doctoral Programs: GRE-V 600; GRE-Q 600; overall undergraduate GPA 3.00. GRE in Subject area by end of first year of program.

Other Criteria: (importance of criteria rated low, medium, or high): GRE/MAT scores—low, research experience—high, extracurricular activity—low, GPA—high, letters of recommendation—high, interview—medium, statement of goals and objectives—high.

Student Characteristics: The following represents characteristics of students in 2007–2008 in all graduate psychology programs in the department: Female—full-time 24, part-time 0; Male—full-time 9, part-time 0; African American/Black—full-time 2, part-time 0; Hispanic/Latino(a)—full-time 7, part-time 0; Asian/Pacific Islander—full-time 1, part-time 0; American Indian/Alaska Native—full-time 0, part-time 0; Caucasian/White—full-time 23, part-time 0; students subject to the Americans With Disabilities Act—full-time 0, part-time 0; Unknown ethnicity—full-time 0, part-time 0.

Financial Information/Assistance:

Tuition for Full-Time Study: *Doctoral:* State residents: per academic year $5,270; Nonstate residents: $475 per credit hour. Tuition is subject to change.

Financial Assistance:

First-Year Students: Teaching assistantships available for first year. Average amount paid per academic year: $18,025. Tuition remission given: full. Research assistantships available for first year. Average amount paid per academic year: $18,025. Tuition remission given: full. Fellowships and scholarships available for first year. Average amount paid per academic year: $24,000. Tuition remission given: full.

Advanced Students: Teaching assistantships available for advanced students. Average amount paid per academic year: $18,025. Tuition remission given: full. Fellowships and scholarships available for advanced students. Average amount paid per academic year: $24,000. Tuition remission given: full.

Additional Information: Of all students currently enrolled full time, 100% benefited from one or more of the listed financial assistance programs.

Internships/Practica: No information provided.

Housing and Day Care: On-campus housing is available. We have a limited number of dorm rooms available. On-campus day care facilities are available. The Graduate Center has child care facilities.

Employment of Department Graduates:

Master's Degree Graduates: Of those who graduated in the academic year 2006–2007, the following categories and numbers represent the postgraduate activities and employment of master's degree graduates: Enrolled in a postdoctoral residency/fellowship (n/a), employed in independent practice (n/a), total from the above (master's) (0).

Doctoral Degree Graduates: Of those who graduated in the academic year 2006–2007, the following categories and numbers represent the postgraduate activities and employment of doctoral degree graduates: Enrolled in a psychology doctoral program (n/a), enrolled in a postdoctoral residency/fellowship (6), employed in other positions at a higher education institution (4), employed in government agency (1), employed in a hospital/medical center (1), total from the above (doctoral) (12).

Additional Information:

Orientation, Objectives, and Emphasis of Department: The doctoral program in biopsychology and behavioral neuroscience interrelates the concepts and methods of neuroscience, cognitive science, the biological disciplines, and behavior analysis to offer a comparative and ontogenetic perspective on species-typical behavior and behavior acquired and modified during the individual's life cycle. Basic psychological processes are studied in conjunction with contributions from neurobiology, ethology, ecology, evolutionary biology, genetics, endocrinology, pharmacology, and other sciences to illuminate the many ways in which all species adapt, survive, reproduce, and evolve. Through diversified laboratory experiences plus core courses, electives, seminars, colloquia, and field studies, students develop an interdisciplinary perspective. Neuroscience and animal behavior are taught jointly with the biology faculty. Electives address a wide range of topics in basic and applied areas of traditional psychology, neuroscience, and cognitive science. The biopsychology program provides unique training for basic research and teaching in the field of animal and human behavior, and in the application of biobehavioral knowledge to problems in industrial, business, institutional, health, and environmental settings. Students in the MA program may take courses in social, developmental, cognitive, and other areas of psychology as well as in biopsychology. We try to arrange individualized programs for two populations of students: those oriented toward the PhD for whom research training is a prime concern, and those with diverse career aspirations who are oriented toward a general graduate background in psychology.

Special Facilities or Resources: Laboratories for research with human subjects and with a variety of animal species are located at Hunter College. The College has a modern animal-care facility. Facilities for field research in animal behavior are available at the Southwest Field Station of the American Museum of Natural History in the Chiricahua Mountains of Arizona. Additional research opportunities are available through minority programs such as RCMI, MBRS, MIDARP, and through the Center for the Study of Gene Structure and Function. There is also collaboration with programs such as Biology, Chemistry, and Physiology and faculty affiliations with many other academic and research institutes in New York City. Hunter College lab facilities include equipment for electrophysiology, phase-fluorescence, and transmission microscopy, electron- and scanning-electron microscopy, radio immunoassay, high-performance liquid chromatography, autoradiography and other radioreceptor techniques, human and animal psychophysiology, histology, operant and classical conditioning, and video and cinematographic analysis. Computer facilities include a variety of micro- and minicomputers as well as access to the University computer center. Doctoral students may register for specialized courses at any CUNY campus and have privileges at all CUNY libraries.

Application Information:

Send to Graduate Admissions, 695 Park Avenue, Hunter College, CUNY, New York, NY 10021 for the Master's Program. Office of Admissions, Graduate School-CUNY, 365 Fifth Avenue, New York, NY 10016-4309 for the Psychology PhD Program; a copy should be sent to the Biopsychology Program here at Hunter College, Room 611 North Building as well. Students are admitted in the Fall, application deadline February 1. Fall deadline; November 7 for MA, February 1 for PhD. Applications for Biospsychology PhD are sent to Admissions Office, City University Graduate Center, 365 Fifth Avenue, New York, NY 10016-4309, (212) 817-7000. *Fee:* $125.

City University of New York: Brooklyn College

School Psychologist Graduate Program, School of Education
Brooklyn College
2900 Bedford Avenue, Room 1205 James
Brooklyn, NY 11210
Telephone: (718) 951-5876
Fax: (718) 951-4232
E-mail: *rubinson@brooklyn.cuny.edu*
Web: *http://www.depthome.brooklyn.cuny.edu/schooled*

Department Information:

1968. Program Head: Florence Rubinson. Number of faculty: total—full-time 6, part-time 3; women—full-time 4, part-time 2; ; women minority—full-time 1.

Programs and Degrees Offered:

Listed in the following order: Program area, degree type (T if terminal Master's), number awarded 7/06–6/07. School Psychologist Program MA/MS (Master of Arts/Science) 20, Bilingual School Psychologist Graduate Program MA/MS (Master of Arts/Science) 8.

Student Applications/Admissions:

Student Applications

School Psychologist Program MA/MS (Master of Arts/Science)—Applications 2007–2008, 125. Total applicants accepted 2007–2008, 27. Number full-time enrolled (new admits only) 2007–2008, 20. Number part-time enrolled (new admits only) 2007–2008, 7. Total enrolled 2007–2008 full-time, 43, part-time, 48. The median number of years required for completion of a degree in 2006–2007 were 3. The number of students enrolled full- and part-time who were dismissed or voluntarily withdrew from this program area in 2007–2008 were 9. *Bilingual School Psychologist Graduate Program MA/MS (Master of Arts/Science)*—Applications 2007–2008, 25. Total applicants accepted 2007–2008, 2. Number full-time enrolled (new admits only) 2007–2008, 0. Number part-time enrolled (new admits only) 2007–2008, 2. Total enrolled 2007–2008 full-time, 2, part-time, 8. Openings 2008–2009, 15. The median number of years required for completion of a degree in 2006–2007 were 3. The number of students enrolled full- and part-time who were dismissed or voluntarily withdrew from this program area in 2007–2008 were 2.

Admissions Requirements:

Scores: Entries appear in this order: required test or GPA, minimum score (if required), median score of students entering in 2007–2008. Master's Programs: overall undergraduate GPA 3.0, 3.5; psychology GPA 3.0, 3.5.

Other Criteria: (importance of criteria rated low, medium, or high): GRE/MAT scores—low, research experience—high, work experience—high, extracurricular activity—medium, clinically related public service—high, GPA—high, letters of recommendation—high, interview—high, statement of goals and objectives—high, writing sample—high.

Student Characteristics: The following represents characteristics of students in 2007–2008 in all graduate psychology programs in the department: Female—full-time 36, part-time 50; Male—full-time 9, part-time 6; African American/Black—full-time 3,

part-time 10; Hispanic/Latino(a)—full-time 6, part-time 12; Asian/Pacific Islander—full-time 0, part-time 2; American Indian/Alaska Native—full-time 0, part-time 0; Caucasian/White—full-time 35, part-time 32; students subject to the Americans With Disabilities Act—full-time 0, part-time 0; Unknown ethnicity—full-time 0, part-time 0.

Financial Information/Assistance:

Financial Assistance:

First-Year Students: Fellowships and scholarships available for first year. Apply by March 15.

Advanced Students: Fellowships and scholarships available for advanced students. Apply by March 15.

Additional Information: Of all students currently enrolled full time, 10% benefited from one or more of the listed financial assistance programs. Application and information available online at http://www.brooklyn.cuny.edu.

Internships/Practica: Internships are available and coordinated through our program with various schools, both public and private, working with both the mainstream population, as well as special populations. In addition, internships are available in mental health clinics, agencies, and hospitals. Practica in assessment, intervention, consultation, and counseling are designed to reinforce students' course work. For additional information on education and training outcomes for our programs, see the following Web site: http://wwwdepthome.brooklyn.cuny.edu/education/.

Housing and Day Care: No on-campus housing is available. On-campus day care facilities are available. Early Childhood Center for children ages 0–5.

Employment of Department Graduates:

Master's Degree Graduates: Of those who graduated in the academic year 2006–2007, the following categories and numbers represent the postgraduate activities and employment of master's degree graduates: Enrolled in a psychology doctoral program (5), enrolled in another graduate/professional program (0), enrolled in a postdoctoral residency/fellowship (n/a), employed in independent practice (n/a), employed in a professional position in a school system (22), employed in a hospital/medical center (2), total from the above (master's) (29).

Doctoral Degree Graduates: Of those who graduated in the academic year 2006–2007, the following categories and numbers represent the postgraduate activities and employment of doctoral degree graduates: Enrolled in a psychology doctoral program (n/a), total from the above (doctoral) (0).

Additional Information:

Orientation, Objectives, and Emphasis of Department: The aim of the school psychologists' training program is to meet the community needs for professionally competent personnel to function in the schools as consultants on psychological aspects of learning and mental health. Students are prepared to make assessments of situations involving children, parents, and school personnel to achieve the more optimal functioning of children in the school setting. Coursework will prepare students in the areas of measurement and evaluation, personality understanding, educational objectives and procedures, curriculum development, and research. Students will also be trained to achieve greater integration between school and community. Elements of the program will provide students with opportunities for self-reflection, collaboration with other professionals and families, and engagement in issues of diversity and social justice.

Special Facilities or Resources: In addition to the use of the Brooklyn College library, students are welcome to use all the libraries at other colleges within the CUNY system. The School Psychology Program also has a small library of texts and journals for the students' use.

Information for Students With Physical Disabilities: See the following Web site for more information: http://www.brooklyn.cuny.edu.

Application Information:

Send to Department Chair. Application available online. Students are admitted in the Fall, application deadline March 1. There are two admissions applications—one program application and one general graduate admissions application. Both are available through the department Web page. *Fee:* $125.

City University of New York: Brooklyn College

Department of Psychology
Brooklyn
2900 Bedford Avenue
Brooklyn, NY 11210
Telephone: (718) 951-5601
Fax: (718) 951-4814
E-mail: *AaronK@brooklyn.cuny.edu*
Web: *http://www.depthome.brooklyn.cuny.edu/psych*

Department Information:

1935. PhD Program Head or MA Program Head: Aaron Kozbelt or Benzion Chanowitz. Number of faculty: total—full-time 10, part-time 11; women—full-time 7.

Programs and Degrees Offered:

Listed in the following order: Program area, degree type (T if terminal Master's), number awarded 7/06–6/07. Psychology: Cognition, Brain, and Behavior PhD (Doctor of Philosophy) 7, Experimental Psychology MA/MS (Master of Arts/Science) (T) 6, Industrial and Organizational Psychology MA/MS (Master of Arts/Science) (T) 31, Mental Health Counseling MA/MS (Master of Arts/Science) (T) 0.

Student Applications/Admissions:

Student Applications

Psychology: Cognition, Brain, and Behavior PhD (Doctor of Philosophy)—Applications 2007–2008, 35. Total applicants accepted 2007–2008, 7. Number full-time enrolled (new admits only) 2007–2008, 6. Number part-time enrolled (new admits only) 2007–2008, 0. Openings 2008–2009, 6. The median number of years required for completion of a degree in 2006–2007 were 5. The number of students enrolled full- and part-time who were dismissed or voluntarily withdrew from this program area in 2007–2008 were 1. *Experimental Psychology MA/MS (Master of Arts/Science)*—Applications 2007–2008, 32. Total applicants accepted 2007–2008, 22. Number full-time enrolled (new admits only) 2007–2008, 0. Number part-time enrolled (new admits only) 2007–2008, 17. Openings 2008–2009, 15. The median number of years required for completion of a degree in 2006–2007 were 3. The number of students enrolled full- and part-time who were dismissed or voluntarily withdrew from this program area in 2007–2008 were 0. *Industrial and Organizational Psychology MA/MS (Master of Arts/Science)*—Applications 2007–2008, 113. Total applicants accepted 2007–2008, 54. Number full-time enrolled (new admits only) 2007–2008, 6. Number part-time enrolled (new admits only) 2007–2008, 32. Total enrolled 2007–2008 full-time, 8, part-time, 61. Openings 2008–2009, 35. The median number of years required for completion of a degree in 2006–2007 were 3. The number of students enrolled full- and part-time who were dismissed or voluntarily withdrew from this program area in 2007–2008 were 0. *Mental Health Counseling MA/MS (Master of Arts/Science)*—Applications 2007–2008, 115. Total applicants accepted 2007–2008, 35. Number full-time enrolled (new admits only) 2007–2008, 32. Number part-time enrolled (new admits only) 2007–2008, 0. Openings 2008–2009, 40. The median number of years required for completion of a degree in 2006–2007 were 2. The number of students enrolled full- and part-time who were dismissed or voluntarily withdrew from this program area in 2007–2008 were 3.

Admissions Requirements:

Scores: Entries appear in this order: required test or GPA, minimum score (if required), median score of students entering in 2007–2008. Master's Programs: overall undergraduate GPA 3.0. Courses in statistics and research methods are required. Doctoral Programs: GRE-V no minimum stated; GRE-Q no minimum stated; overall undergraduate GPA 3.5; last 2 years GPA 3.5; psychology GPA 3.6; Doctoral program GRE-Analytic no minimum stated.

Other Criteria: (importance of criteria rated low, medium, or high): GRE/MAT scores—medium, research experience—high, work experience—medium, extracurricular activity—low, clinically related public service—low, GPA—medium, letters of recommendation—high, interview—medium, statement of goals and objectives—high, psychology coursework—high, undergraduate major in psychology—medium, specific undergraduate psychology courses taken—high. The MA program in Industrial and Organizational have a greater emphasis on applications of psychology. The MA in Experimental Psychology and the PhD program in Cognition, Brain, and Behavior focus on a strong background in research. All programs require courses in statistics and research methods (except MHC). For additional information on admission requirements, go to http://depthome.brooklyn.cuny.edu/psych/doctoral/PHDApply.htm.

Student Characteristics: The following represents characteristics of students in 2007–2008 in all graduate psychology programs in the department: Female—full-time 65, part-time 68; Male—full-time 27, part-time 25; African American/Black—full-time 15, part-time 26; Hispanic/Latino(a)—full-time 4, part-time 19; Asian/Pacific Islander—full-time 6, part-time 5; American Indian/Alaska Native—full-time 0, part-time 0; Caucasian/White—full-time 66, part-time 40; Multi-ethnic—full-time 0, part-time 0; students subject to the Americans With Disabilities Act—full-time 1, part-time 0; Unknown ethnicity—full-time 1, part-time 3; International students who hold an F-1 or J-1 Visa—full-time 4, part-time 0.

Financial Information/Assistance:

Tuition for Full-Time Study: *Master's:* State residents: per academic year $3,200, $270 per credit hour; Nonstate residents: per academic year $6,000, $500 per credit hour. *Doctoral:* State residents: per academic year $2,860, $325 per credit hour; Nonstate residents: per academic year $3,920, $510 per credit hour. Tuition is subject to change. Additional fees are assessed to students beyond the costs of tuition for the following: student technology fee, student activity fee, CUNY consolidation fee. Tuition costs vary by program. See the following Web site for updates and changes in tuition costs: http://www.gc.cuny.edu/current_students/tuition_curnt_stdnts.htm or www.brooklyn.cuny.edu.

Financial Assistance:

First-Year Students: Teaching assistantships available for first year. Average amount paid per academic year: $12,000. Average number of hours worked per week: 20. Apply by January 15. Tuition remission given: full. Research assistantships available for first year. Average amount paid per academic year: $14,000. Average number of hours worked per week: 20. Apply by January 15. Tuition remission given: partial. Fellowships and scholarships available for first year. Average amount paid per academic year: $2,000. Apply by January 1. Tuition remission given: partial.

Advanced Students: Teaching assistantships available for advanced students. Average amount paid per academic year: $12,000. Average number of hours worked per week: 20. Apply by January 1. Tuition remission given: full. Research assistantships available for advanced students. Average amount paid per academic year: $14,000. Average number of hours worked per week: 20. Apply by January 1. Tuition remission given: partial. Fellowships and scholarships available for advanced students. Average amount paid per academic year: $2,000. Apply by February 1. Tuition remission given: partial.

Additional Information: Application and information available online at http://depthome.brooklyn.cuny.edu/psych/doctoral/PHDApply.htm.

Internships/Practica: Master's Degree (MA/MS Mental Health Counseling): An internship experience such as a final research project or "capstone" experience is required of graduates. The MA program in Industrial/Organizational psychology has an internship component that most students avail themselves of. It functions as both training and as an opportunity to experience the hands-on application of principles in a work setting. The MA program in Mental Health Counseling requires two semesters of predegree supervised internships. An additional 6,000 hours or postdegree supervised internship is required for licensure. For additional information on education and training outcomes for our programs, see the following Web site: http://www.depthome.brooklyn.cuny.edu/psych/graduate.htm.

Housing and Day Care: No on-campus housing is available. On-campus day care facilities are available. See the following Web site for more information: http://www.depthome.brooklyn.cuny.edu/ecc.

Employment of Department Graduates:

Master's Degree Graduates: Of those who graduated in the academic year 2006–2007, the following categories and numbers

represent the postgraduate activities and employment of master's degree graduates: Enrolled in a psychology doctoral program (6), enrolled in another graduate/professional program (3), enrolled in a postdoctoral residency/fellowship (n/a), employed in independent practice (n/a), employed in an academic position at a university (0), employed in an academic position at a 2-year/4-year college (0), employed in other positions at a higher education institution (1), employed in a professional position in a school system (1), employed in business or industry (6), employed in government agency (0), employed in a community mental health/ counseling center (4), do not know (1), total from the above (master's) (22).

Doctoral Degree Graduates: Of those who graduated in the academic year 2006–2007, the following categories and numbers represent the postgraduate activities and employment of doctoral degree graduates: Enrolled in a psychology doctoral program (n/a), enrolled in a postdoctoral residency/fellowship (2), employed in an academic position at a university (2), employed in an academic position at a 2-year/4-year college (2), employed in a professional position in a school system (1), employed in business or industry (1), other employment position (1), do not know (1), total from the above (doctoral) (10).

Additional Information:

Orientation, Objectives, and Emphasis of Department: The PhD program is broadly based, with concentrations in cognitive neuroscience, cognition, learning, social, and developmental psychology. These diverse areas are bound by a commitment to empirical methods and theory development; we train research scientists in basic and applied approaches using the apprenticeship mode. The CUNY consortium allows students to collaborate with faculty at other CUNY campuses and research universities in New York. Students work with faculty in chosen areas of specialization and are encouraged to collaborate with other faculty and students. Historically, graduates have started careers in teaching and research as well as in applied fields. The MA program in Experimental Psychology mirrors the first 2 years of the PhD program. The Industrial/Organizational Psychology MA program offers training in two tracks: Human Relations, with focus on the group, and Organizational Behavior, with focus on the organization. Graduates from both tracks are prepared for entry-level, executive positions in Human Resources and Personnel. The MA program in Mental Health Counseling provides experiential learning with counseling practicum experience in mental health settings, along with comprehensive course work that prepares students for practice in mental health counseling. Graduates are eligible to take the NYS licensing exam, which permits private and independent practice of counseling.

Special Facilities or Resources: There are over a dozen active laboratories in the department focusing on topics such as the physiology of taste and preference formation; children's acquisition of spatial knowledge; transactive knowledge in organizations; implicit learning in cognitive disorders; visual functions in Down syndrome; creativity and cognition in the arts; comparative psychology in cephalopods, amphibians, and crustaceans; hippocampal atrophy in early Alzheimer's disease; implicit impression formation; Darwinian models of mate selection; biomemetic robotics; neurodegeneration in the aged; and parent–child communication. All labs are well equipped and some supported by grants from NSF, NIH, NASA, DARPA, and other organizations. Several faculty have appointments and working collaborations with research labs in city hospitals and medical schools with access to technologies such as fMRI.

Information for Students With Physical Disabilities: See the following Web site for more information: http://www.gc.cuny.edu/current_students/handbook/studentServices.htm#12.

Application Information:

For PhD Program in Psychology: Cognition, Brain, and Behavior apply to Office of Admissions, Graduate Center of CUNY, 365 Fifth Avenue, New York, NY 10016-4309. MA Programs apply to Office of Graduate Admissions, Brooklyn College, 2900 Bedford Avenue, Brooklyn, NY 11210. Application available online. URL of online application: http://www.depthome.brooklyn.cuny.edu/psych/doctoral/PHDApply.htm or http://www.brooklyn.cuny.edu. Students are admitted in the Fall, application deadline see below; Spring, application deadline November 1 (MA). MA application for Mental Health Counseling is February 1. All other MA applications deadline for Fall is March 1. Spring admissions are for the Experimental MA program only. PhD applications deadline is January 15. PhD Minority applicants should apply by January 1 to secure chance to apply for minority fellowships. Other Financial Aid deadline is February 1 for all students. For PhD applicants interested in working with faculty in the program at Brooklyn College, it is crucial that you select the 'Cognition, Brain, and Behavior' subprogram on the list of Graduate Center psychology programs. Check respective box in application materials. Please contact the Head of the Subprogram, Aaron Kozbelt, by e-mail when sending in your application (AaronK@brooklyn.cuny.edu). *Fee:* $125. Requests for waivers can be made to Office of Admissions and contact the Head of the PhD program.

City University of New York: Graduate Center

Learning Processes and Behavior Analysis Doctoral Subprogram
Queens College
65-30 Kissena Boulevard
Flushing, NY 11367
Telephone: (718) 997-3630
Fax: (718) 997-3257
E-mail: *bruce.brown@qc.cuny.edu*
Web: *http://www.qcpages.qc.cuny.edu/Psychology/graduate/phd/learnprocess/index.html*

Department Information:

1967. Program Head: Bruce L. Brown. Number of faculty: total—full-time 8; women—full-time 2; total—minority—full-time 1; women minority—full-time 1.

Programs and Degrees Offered:

Listed in the following order: Program area, degree type (T if terminal Master's), number awarded 7/06–6/07. Learning Processes and Behavior Analysis PhD (Doctor of Philosophy) 7.

Student Applications/Admissions:

Student Applications

Learning Processes and Behavior Analysis PhD (Doctor of Philosophy)—Applications 2007–2008, 26. Total applicants accepted 2007–2008, 9. Number full-time enrolled (new admits only) 2007–2008, 4. Openings 2008–2009, 5. The median number of years required for completion of a degree in 2006–2007 were 8. The number of students enrolled full- and part-time who were dismissed or voluntarily withdrew from this program area in 2007–2008 were 1.

Admissions Requirements:

Scores: Entries appear in this order: required test or GPA, minimum score (if required), median score of students entering in 2007–2008. Doctoral Programs: GRE-V no minimum stated; GRE-Q no minimum stated; overall undergraduate GPA no minimum stated; Doctoral program GRE-Analytic no minimum stated. Complete transcripts are required for applications to the Learning Processes program.

Other Criteria: (importance of criteria rated low, medium, or high): GRE/MAT scores—medium, research experience—high, work experience—low, extracurricular activity—low, clinically related public service—low, GPA—high, letters of recommendation—high, interview—low, statement of goals and objectives—high, undergraduate major in psychology—medium, specific undergraduate psychology courses taken—high.

Student Characteristics: The following represents characteristics of students in 2007–2008 in all graduate psychology programs in the department: Female—full-time 25, part-time 0; Male—full-time 16, part-time 0; African American/Black—full-time 0, part-time 0; Hispanic/Latino(a)—full-time 1, part-time 0; Asian/Pacific Islander—full-time 0, part-time 0; American Indian/Alaska Native—full-time 0, part-time 0; Caucasian/White—full-time 39, part-time 0; Multi-ethnic—full-time 0, part-time 0; students subject to the Americans With Disabilities Act—full-time 0, part-time 0; Unknown ethnicity—full-time 1, part-time 0.

Financial Information/Assistance:

Tuition for Full-Time Study: *Doctoral:* State residents: per academic year $5,720, $325 per credit hour; Nonstate residents: $560 per credit hour. Tuition is subject to change.

Financial Assistance:

First-Year Students: Fellowships and scholarships available for first year. Average amount paid per academic year: $15,000. Average number of hours worked per week: 20. Apply by January 1. Tuition remission given: full.

Advanced Students: Teaching assistantships available for advanced students. Average amount paid per academic year: $10,000. Average number of hours worked per week: 6. Tuition remission given: full. Fellowships and scholarships available for advanced students. Average amount paid per academic year: $2,250. Average number of hours worked per week: 0.

Additional Information: Of all students currently enrolled full time, 49% benefited from one or more of the listed financial assistance programs. Application and information available online at http://www.gc.cuny.edu/prospective_students/prospective_index.htm.

Internships/Practica: Information concerning practica and internships is available on request. Internships are available, but not required.

Housing and Day Care: No on-campus housing is available. No on-campus day care facilities are available.

Employment of Department Graduates:

Master's Degree Graduates: Of those who graduated in the academic year 2006–2007, the following categories and numbers represent the postgraduate activities and employment of master's degree graduates: Enrolled in a psychology doctoral program (0), enrolled in another graduate/professional program (0), enrolled in a postdoctoral residency/fellowship (n/a), employed in independent practice (n/a), employed in an academic position at a university (0), employed in an academic position at a 2-year/4-year college (0), employed in other positions at a higher education institution (0), employed in a professional position in a school system (0), employed in business or industry (0), employed in government agency (0), employed in a community mental health/counseling center (0), employed in a hospital/medical center (0), still seeking employment (0), other employment position (0), total from the above (master's) (0).

Doctoral Degree Graduates: Of those who graduated in the academic year 2006–2007, the following categories and numbers represent the postgraduate activities and employment of doctoral degree graduates: Enrolled in a psychology doctoral program (n/a), enrolled in a postdoctoral residency/fellowship (0), employed in independent practice (0), employed in an academic position at a university (0), employed in an academic position at a 2-year/4-year college (0), employed in other positions at a higher education institution (1), employed in a professional position in a school system (4), employed in business or industry (0), employed in government agency (0), employed in a community mental health/counseling center (2), employed in a hospital/medical center (0), still seeking employment (0), not seeking employment (0), other employment position (0), total from the above (doctoral) (7).

Additional Information:

Orientation, Objectives, and Emphasis of Department: The Learning Processes program offers doctoral students in Psychology training in the experimental analysis of human and animal behavior and in applied behavior analysis. Students and faculty investigate a wide spectrum of behavioral processes through lectures and experimental laboratory course work, advanced seminars, informal student–faculty discussions, practica, internships, and individual research projects. Faculty and students publish regularly in peer-reviewed journals and are strongly represented at major national and international conferences. Their current research interests include such topics as categorization and concept formation, language acquisition, affective behavior, behavioral assessment, human and animal timing, pattern recognition, stimulus control, behavioral community psychology, education and training of children with autism, and staff training in organizational settings. The Learning Processes program is accredited in behavior analysis by the Association for Behavior Analysis, and its curriculum is licensure-qualifying in New York State. In addition, the Behavior Analyst Certification Board, Inc., has approved a subset of the curriculum as a course sequence that meets the coursework requirements for eligibility to take the Board Certified Behavior Analyst Examination. Applicants will have to meet additional requirements to qualify.

Special Facilities or Resources: A full description of the program can be found on our Web site: http://qcpages.qc.cuny.edu/Psychology/graduate/phd/learnprocess/index.html.

Application Information:
Send to Office of Admissions, The Graduate School and University Center of the City University of New York, 365 Fifth Avenue, New York, NY 10016-4309. Application available online. URL of online application: http://www.gc.cuny.edu/prospective_students/admissions_index.htm. Students are admitted in the Fall, application deadline January 1. March 1 deadline for nonfinancial aid applications. *Fee:* $125.

City University of New York: Graduate Center

Neuropsychology Doctoral Program
Queens College
65-30 Kissena Boulevard
Flushing, NY 11367
Telephone: (718) 997-3630
Fax: (718) 997-3257
E-mail: *joshua.brumberg@qc.cuny.edu*
Web: *http://www.qcneuropsychology.org/*

Department Information:
1968. Program head: Joshua C. Brumberg, PhD. Number of faculty: total—full-time 27, part-time 3; women—full-time 11, part-time 2.

Programs and Degrees Offered:
Listed in the following order: Program area, degree type (T if terminal Master's), number awarded 7/06–6/07. Clinical Neuropsychology PhD (Doctor of Philosophy) 8, Basic Neuropsychology PhD (Doctor of Philosophy) 3.

Student Applications/Admissions:
Student Applications
Clinical Neuropsychology PhD (Doctor of Philosophy)—Applications 2007–2008, 75. Total applicants accepted 2007–2008, 18. Number full-time enrolled (new admits only) 2007–2008, 8. Total enrolled 2007–2008 full-time, 53. The median number of years required for completion of a degree in 2006–2007 were 7. The number of students enrolled full- and part-time who were dismissed or voluntarily withdrew from this program area in 2007–2008 were 1. *Basic Neuropsychology PhD (Doctor of Philosophy)*—Applications 2007–2008, 20. Total applicants accepted 2007–2008, 5. Number full-time enrolled (new admits only) 2007–2008, 3. Total enrolled 2007–2008 full-time, 15. The median number of years required for completion of a degree in 2006–2007 were 4. The number of students enrolled full- and part-time who were dismissed or voluntarily withdrew from this program area in 2007–2008 were 1.

Admissions Requirements:
Scores: Entries appear in this order: required test or GPA, minimum score (if required), median score of students entering in 2007–2008. Master's Programs: GRE-V no minimum stated; GRE-Q no minimum stated; overall undergraduate GPA no minimum stated; psychology GPA no minimum stated; Masters GRE-Analytical no minimum stated. Doctoral Programs: GRE-V no minimum stated; GRE-Q no minimum stated; overall undergraduate GPA no minimum stated; psychology GPA no minimum stated; Doctoral program GRE-Analytic no minimum stated.

Other Criteria: (importance of criteria rated low, medium, or high): GRE/MAT scores—medium, research experience—high, work experience—low, extracurricular activity—low, clinically related public service—low, GPA—high, letters of recommendation—high, interview—high, statement of goals and objectives—high, undergraduate major in psychology—low, Interviews will be carried out for the clinical track only. For additional information on admission requirements, go to http://www.qcneuropsychology.org/prospective_students.

Student Characteristics: The following represents characteristics of students in 2007–2008 in all graduate psychology programs in the department: Female—full-time 50, part-time 0; Male—full-time 18, part-time 0; African American/Black—full-time 2, part-time 0; Hispanic/Latino(a)—full-time 3, part-time 0; Asian/Pacific Islander—full-time 5, part-time 0; American Indian/Alaska Native—full-time 0, part-time 0; Caucasian/White—full-time 58, part-time 0; Multi-ethnic—full-time 0, part-time 0; students subject to the Americans With Disabilities Act—full-time 0, part-time 0; Unknown ethnicity—full-time 0, part-time 0; International students who hold an F-1 or J-1 Visa—full-time 5, part-time 0.

Financial Information/Assistance:
Tuition for Full-Time Study: *Doctoral:* State residents: per academic year $5,710; Nonstate residents: $560 per credit hour. Tuition is subject to change. See the following Web site for updates and changes in tuition costs: http://www.gc.cuny.edu/prospective_students/viewbook/master_finance.htm.

Financial Assistance:
First-Year Students: Teaching assistantships available for first year. Average amount paid per academic year: $0. Average number of hours worked per week: 0. Tuition remission given: full and partial. Research assistantships available for first year. Average amount paid per academic year: $0. Average number of hours worked per week: 0. Tuition remission given: full and partial. Traineeships available for first year. Average amount paid per academic year: $0. Average number of hours worked per week: 0. Tuition remission given: full and partial. Fellowships and scholarships available for first year. Average amount paid per academic year: $0. Average number of hours worked per week: 0. Tuition remission given: full and partial.
Advanced Students: Teaching assistantships available for advanced students. Average number of hours worked per week: 0. Tuition remission given: full and partial. Research assistantships available for advanced students. Average number of hours worked per week: 0. Tuition remission given: full and partial. Fellowships and scholarships available for advanced students. Average number of hours worked per week: 0. Tuition remission given: full and partial.
Additional Information: Of all students currently enrolled full time, 60% benefited from one or more of the listed financial assistance programs. Application and information available online at http://www.gc.cuny.edu/prospective_students/viewbook/master_finance.htm.

Internships/Practica: Doctoral Degree (PhD Clinical Neuropsychology): For those doctoral students for whom a professional internship was required in this program prior to graduation, (9) students applied for an internship in 2006–2007, with (7) students obtaining an internship. Of those students who obtained an internship, (7) were paid internships. Of those students who obtained an internship, (6) students placed in APA/CPA-accredited internships, (1) student placed in internships not APA/CPA accredited, but listed with the Association of Psychology Postdoctoral and Internship Centers (APPIC), (0) students placed in internships conforming to guidelines of the Council of Directors of School Psychology Programs (CDSPP), (0) students placed in internships that were not APA/CPA-accredited, APPIC or CDSPP listed. Clinical track students expereince at least three different clinical practicums. For additional information on education and training outcomes for our programs, see the following Web site: http://www.qcneuropsychology.org/current_students.

Housing and Day Care: No on-campus housing is available. On-campus day care facilities are available. See the following Web site for more information: http://www.qcpages.qc.cuny.edu/qcchild/.

Employment of Department Graduates:

Master's Degree Graduates: Of those who graduated in the academic year 2006–2007, the following categories and numbers represent the postgraduate activities and employment of master's degree graduates: Enrolled in a psychology doctoral program (0), enrolled in another graduate/professional program (0), enrolled in a postdoctoral residency/fellowship (n/a), employed in independent practice (n/a), employed in an academic position at a university (0), employed in an academic position at a 2-year/4-year college (0), employed in other positions at a higher education institution (0), employed in a professional position in a school system (0), employed in business or industry (0), employed in government agency (0), employed in a community mental health/counseling center (0), employed in a hospital/medical center (0), still seeking employment (0), other employment position (0), total from the above (master's) (0).

Doctoral Degree Graduates: Of those who graduated in the academic year 2006–2007, the following categories and numbers represent the postgraduate activities and employment of doctoral degree graduates: Enrolled in a psychology doctoral program (n/a), enrolled in a postdoctoral residency/fellowship (6), employed in independent practice (0), employed in an academic position at a university (0), employed in an academic position at a 2-year/4-year college (0), employed in other positions at a higher education institution (0), employed in a professional position in a school system (0), employed in business or industry (0), employed in government agency (0), employed in a community mental health/counseling center (0), employed in a hospital/medical center (2), still seeking employment (0), other employment position (0), total from the above (doctoral) (8).

Additional Information:

Orientation, Objectives, and Emphasis of Department: The Neuropsychology subprogram is an academically oriented PhD program with a core philosophy based on two premises. The first of these is that productive research, effective teaching, and responsible clinical practice are integrally interdependent. That is, effective teaching must include critical analysis of current research data, and clinical assessment and treatment procedures must be empirically validated. The second premise is that the understanding of impaired or disordered brain function in humans requires rigorous training in the neurosciences as well as in the traditional clinical topics. The subprogram was designed to train professionals with competence in research and/or teaching in the area of brain–behavior relationships, and in the application of these competencies in clinical settings. There are two tracks within the program: the basic track requires 60 course credits; the clinical track requires 82 credits including at least 2 years of practicum training. Both tracks focus heavily on neuroscience topics, and provides intensive experience in human and animal experimentation. The clinical track also provides students the opportunity to acquire and apply the skills appropriate to the practice of clinical neuropsychology. Students in the clinical track thus receive training in the evaluation of psychological and neuropsychological function in various clinical populations, which may include children or adults, neurological, neurosurgical, rehabilitation medicine and psychiatric patients, as well as in the use of rehabilitative, psychotherapeutic, and remediative techniques. A full-year internship is required for graduation from the clinical track.

Special Facilities or Resources: The Neuropsychology program has well-equipped laboratories for clinical and basic neuropsychology research. Equipment include evoked potential recording setups, microscopy, and histology and imaging cores.

Information for Students With Physical Disabilities: See the following Web site for more information: http://www.qc.cuny.edu/student_affairs/special_services.php.

Application Information:

Send to Office of Admissions, The Graduate School and University Center of the City University of New York, 365 Fifth Avenue, New York, NY 10016-4309. Application available online. URL of online application: http://www.gc.cuny.edu/admin_offices/admissions/index.htm. Students are admitted in the Fall, application deadline December 15. *Fee:* $125.

City University of New York: Graduate School and University Center

PhD Program in Educational Psychology
365 Fifth Avenue
New York, NY 10016-4309
Telephone: (212) 817-8285
Fax: (212) 817-1516
E-mail: *mkopala@gc.cuny.edu*
Web: *http://www.gc.cuny.edu*

Department Information:

1969. Executive Officer: Mary Kopala. Number of faculty: total—full-time 35, part-time 1; women—full-time 14; total—minority—full-time 4; women minority—full-time 1.

Programs and Degrees Offered:

Listed in the following order: Program area, degree type (T if terminal Master's), number awarded 7/06–6/07. Educational Psychology PhD (Doctor of Philosophy) 6.

APA Accreditation: School PhD (Doctor of Philosophy).

Student Applications/Admissions:

Student Applications

Educational Psychology PhD (Doctor of Philosophy)—Applications 2007–2008, 99. Total applicants accepted 2007–2008,

33. Number full-time enrolled (new admits only) 2007–2008, 13. Number part-time enrolled (new admits only) 2007–2008, 5. Total enrolled 2007–2008 full-time, 122, part-time, 12. Openings 2008–2009, 18. The median number of years required for completion of a degree in 2006–2007 were 8. The number of students enrolled full- and part-time who were dismissed or voluntarily withdrew from this program area in 2007–2008 were 3.

Admissions Requirements:

Scores: Entries appear in this order: required test or GPA, minimum score (if required), median score of students entering in 2007–2008. Master's Programs: GRE-V no minimum stated; GRE-Q no minimum stated. Doctoral Programs: GRE-V no minimum stated; GRE-Q no minimum stated; overall undergraduate GPA no minimum stated; psychology GPA no minimum stated.

Other Criteria: (importance of criteria rated low, medium, or high): GRE/MAT scores—high, research experience—medium, work experience—medium, extracurricular activity—low, clinically related public service—low, GPA—medium, letters of recommendation—high, interview—high, statement of goals and objectives—high, undergraduate major in psychology—low, specific undergraduate psychology courses taken—low. For additional information on admission requirements, go to http://www.gc.cuny.edu.

Student Characteristics: The following represents characteristics of students in 2007–2008 in all graduate psychology programs in the department: Female—full-time 98, part-time 10; Male—full-time 24, part-time 2; African American/Black—full-time 5, part-time 1; Hispanic/Latino(a)—full-time 5, part-time 0; Asian/Pacific Islander—full-time 5, part-time 2; American Indian/Alaska Native—full-time 0, part-time 0; Caucasian/White—full-time 69, part-time 6; Multi-ethnic—full-time 0, part-time 0; students subject to the Americans With Disabilities Act—full-time 3, part-time 0; Unknown ethnicity—full-time 38, part-time 3; International students who hold an F-1 or J-1 Visa—full-time 8, part-time 1.

Financial Information/Assistance:

Tuition for Full-Time Study: *Doctoral:* State residents: per academic year $5,720; Nonstate residents: per academic year $13,440, $560 per credit hour. Additional fees are assessed to students beyond the costs of tuition for the following: Student activities fee, $41.60/semester; technology fee, $37.50/semester. See the following Web site for updates and changes in tuition costs: http://www.gc.cuny.edu; tuition fees are reduced as students progress through the program.

Financial Assistance:

First-Year Students: Teaching assistantships available for first year. Average amount paid per academic year: $18,000. Average number of hours worked per week: 5. Apply by February 1. Tuition remission given: full. Research assistantships available for first year. Average amount paid per academic year: $5,000. Average number of hours worked per week: 5. Apply by February 1. Fellowships and scholarships available for first year. Average amount paid per academic year: $5,000. Average number of hours worked per week: 5. Apply by February 1.

Advanced Students: Teaching assistantships available for advanced students. Average amount paid per academic year: $18,000. Average number of hours worked per week: 10. Apply by February 1. Tuition remission given: full. Research assistantships available for advanced students. Average amount paid per academic year: $4,000. Average number of hours worked per week: 4. Apply by February 1. Fellowships and scholarships available for advanced students. Average amount paid per academic year: $5,000. Average number of hours worked per week: 5. Apply by February 1.

Additional Information: Of all students currently enrolled full time, 50% benefited from one or more of the listed financial assistance programs. Application and information available online at http://www.gc.cuny.edu.

Internships/Practica: Doctoral Degree (PhD Educational Psychology): For those doctoral students for whom a professional internship was required in this program prior to graduation, (9) students applied for an internship in 2006–2007, with (7) students obtaining an internship. Of those students who obtained an internship, (7) were paid internships. Of those students who obtained an internship, (0) students placed in APA/CPA-accredited internships, (0) students placed in internships not APA/CPA-accredited, but listed with the Association of Psychology Postdoctoral and Internship Centers (APPIC), (7) students placed in internships conforming to guidelines of the Council of Directors of School Psychology Programs (CDSPP), (0) students placed in internships that were not APA/CPA-accredited, APPIC or CDSPP listed. Details concerning internship or practica can be found on our Web site: http://www.gc.cuny.edu under 'Student Brochures,' for the School Psychology specialization.

Housing and Day Care: No on-campus housing is available. On-campus day care facilities are available. There is a Child Development and Learning Center (Room 3201) under the direction of Linda Perrotta.

Employment of Department Graduates:

Master's Degree Graduates: Of those who graduated in the academic year 2006–2007, the following categories and numbers represent the postgraduate activities and employment of master's degree graduates: Enrolled in a psychology doctoral program (0), enrolled in another graduate/professional program (0), enrolled in a postdoctoral residency/fellowship (n/a), employed in independent practice (n/a), employed in an academic position at a university (0), employed in an academic position at a 2-year/4-year college (0), employed in other positions at a higher education institution (0), employed in a professional position in a school system (0), employed in business or industry (0), employed in government agency (0), employed in a community mental health/counseling center (0), employed in a hospital/medical center (0), still seeking employment (0), not seeking employment (0), other employment position (0), do not know (0), total from the above (master's) (0).

Doctoral Degree Graduates: Of those who graduated in the academic year 2006–2007, the following categories and numbers represent the postgraduate activities and employment of doctoral degree graduates: Enrolled in a psychology doctoral program (n/a), enrolled in another graduate/professional program (0), enrolled in a postdoctoral residency/fellowship (0), employed in independent practice (0), employed in an academic position at a university (0), employed in an academic position at a 2-year/4-year college (0), employed in other positions at a higher education institution (0), employed in a professional position in a school system (6), employed in business or industry (0), employed in government agency (0), employed in a community mental health/counseling center (0), employed in a hospital/medical center (0), still seeking employment (0), not seeking employment (0), other employment position (0), do not know (0), total from the above (doctoral) (6).

Additional Information:

Orientation, Objectives, and Emphasis of Department: The PhD program in Educational Psychology is research oriented, preparing students for teaching, research, and program development in various educational settings such as universities, school systems, research institutions, community agencies, as well as in educational publishing, television, and in other agencies with training programs. Four areas of concentration are offered: quantitative methods in educational and psychological research, learning development and instruction, school psychology, and educational policy analysis.

Special Facilities or Resources: The Educational Psychology program is affiliated with a university-based research institute, CASE (Center for Advanced Study in Education). CASE is heavily involved in the evaluation and implementation of various applied educational programs. Our faculty and students have worked as principle investigators and research assistants on CASE projects.

Information for Students With Physical Disabilities: See the following Web site for more information: http://www.gc.cuny.edu.

Application Information:

Send to Admissions Office, CUNY Graduate Center, 365 Fifth Avenue, New York City, NY 10016-4309. Application available online. URL of online application: http://www.gc.cuny.edu. Students are admitted in the Fall, application deadline January 15. Deadline for financial aid applicants is February 1. *Fee:* $125.

City University of New York: Graduate School and University Center

PhD Program in Psychology
365 Fifth Avenue
New York, NY 10016-4309
Telephone: (212) 817-8705/8753/8706
Fax: (212) 817-1533
E-mail: *jglick@gc.cuny.edu*
Web: *http://www.gc.cuny.edu*

Department Information:

1961. Executive Officer: Joseph Glick. Number of faculty: total—full-time 170, part-time 18; women—full-time 75, part-time 7; total—minority—full-time 18; women minority—full-time 8.

Programs and Degrees Offered:

Listed in the following order: Program area, degree type (T if terminal Master's), number awarded 7/06–6/07. Biopsychology and Behavioral Neuroscience PhD (Doctor of Philosophy) 4, Clinical PhD (Doctor of Philosophy) 17, Developmental PhD (Doctor of Philosophy) 4, Cognition, Brain, and Behavior PhD (Doctor of Philosophy) 7, Cognitive Neuroscience PhD (Doctor of Philosophy) 1, Environmental PhD (Doctor of Philosophy) 4, Industrial/Organizational PhD (Doctor of Philosophy) 5, Learning Processes and Behavior Analysis PhD (Doctor of Philosophy) 2, Neuropsychology PhD (Doctor of Philosophy) 4, Social/Personality PhD (Doctor of Philosophy) 4, Forensic Psychology PhD (Doctor of Philosophy).

Student Applications/Admissions:

Student Applications

Biopsychology and Behavioral Neuroscience PhD (Doctor of Philosophy)—Applications 2007–2008, 27. Total applicants accepted 2007–2008, 6. Openings 2008–2009, 8. The median number of years required for completion of a degree in 2006–2007 were 6. *Clinical PhD (Doctor of Philosophy)*—Applications 2007–2008, 274. Total applicants accepted 2007–2008, 12. Openings 2008–2009, 12. The median number of years required for completion of a degree in 2006–2007 were 6. *Developmental PhD (Doctor of Philosophy)*—Applications 2007–2008, 38. Total applicants accepted 2007–2008, 12. Number full-time enrolled (new admits only) 2007–2008, 8. Openings 2008–2009, 8. The median number of years required for completion of a degree in 2006–2007 were 6. *Cognition, Brain, and Behavior PhD (Doctor of Philosophy)*—Applications 2007–2008, 35. Total applicants accepted 2007–2008, 7. Number full-time enrolled (new admits only) 2007–2008, 6. Number part-time enrolled (new admits only) 2007–2008, 0. Openings 2008–2009, 6. The median number of years required for completion of a degree in 2006–2007 were 5. The number of students enrolled full- and part-time who were dismissed or voluntarily withdrew from this program area in 2007–2008 were 1. *Cognitive Neuroscience PhD (Doctor of Philosophy)*—Applications 2007–2008, 25. Total applicants accepted 2007–2008, 7. Openings 2008–2009, 5. The median number of years required for completion of a degree in 2006–2007 were 8. *Environmental PhD (Doctor of Philosophy)*—Applications 2007–2008, 22. Total applicants accepted 2007–2008, 10. Openings 2008–2009, 10. The median number of years required for completion of a degree in 2006–2007 were 7. *Industrial/Organizational PhD (Doctor of Philosophy)*—Applications 2007–2008, 25. Total applicants accepted 2007–2008, 5. Openings 2008–2009, 7. The median number of years required for completion of a degree in 2006–2007 were 7. *Learning Processes and Behavior Analysis PhD (Doctor of Philosophy)*—Applications 2007–2008, 38. Total applicants accepted 2007–2008, 7. Openings 2008–2009, 10. The median number of years required for completion of a degree in 2006–2007 were 6. *Neuropsychology PhD (Doctor of Philosophy)*—Applications 2007–2008, 68. Total applicants accepted 2007–2008, 9. Openings 2008–2009, 8. *Social/Personality PhD (Doctor of Philosophy)*—Applications 2007–2008, 62. Total applicants accepted 2007–2008, 8. Number full-time enrolled (new admits only) 2007–2008, 6. Openings 2008–2009, 79. *Forensic Psychology PhD (Doctor of Philosophy)*—Applications 2007–2008, 166. Total applicants accepted 2007–2008, 12. Number full-time enrolled (new admits only) 2007–2008, 10. Openings 2008–2009, 10.

Admissions Requirements:

Scores: Entries appear in this order: required test or GPA, minimum score (if required), median score of students entering in 2007–2008. Master's Programs: GRE-V no minimum stated; GRE-Q no minimum stated. Clinical requires the Psychology subject test Doctoral Programs: GRE-V 550; GRE-Q 550; GRE-Subject (Psychology) 550; overall undergraduate GPA

3.0. "Minimum scores" are flexible depending on the complete application package, and any special circumstances that may apply.

Other Criteria: (importance of criteria rated low, medium, or high): GRE/MAT scores—medium, research experience—medium, work experience—low, extracurricular activity—low, clinically related public service—medium, GPA—medium, letters of recommendation—high, interview—high, statement of goals and objectives—high, depending on program Subject test of GRE may be or not be required. Check each subprogram's Web site. Similarly, GRE and GPA requirements may vary.

Student Characteristics: The following represents characteristics of students in 2007–2008 in all graduate psychology programs in the department: Female—full-time 340, part-time 2; Male—full-time 128, part-time 2; African American/Black—full-time 39, part-time 0; Hispanic/Latino(a)—full-time 72, part-time 0; Asian/Pacific Islander—full-time 20, part-time 0; American Indian/Alaska Native—full-time 1, part-time 0; Caucasian/White—full-time 0, part-time 0; Unknown ethnicity—full-time 0, part-time 0.

Financial Information/Assistance:

Financial Assistance:

First-Year Students: Teaching assistantships available for first year. Average amount paid per academic year: $5,000. Average number of hours worked per week: 5. Tuition remission given: partial. Research assistantships available for first year. Average amount paid per academic year: $9,000. Average number of hours worked per week: 15. Fellowships and scholarships available for first year. Average amount paid per academic year: $18,000. Average number of hours worked per week: 10. Tuition remission given: full.

Advanced Students: Teaching assistantships available for advanced students. Average amount paid per academic year: $11,000. Average number of hours worked per week: 12. Tuition remission given: full. Research assistantships available for advanced students. Fellowships and scholarships available for advanced students. Average amount paid per academic year: $18,000. Average number of hours worked per week: 15. Tuition remission given: full.

Additional Information: Of all students currently enrolled full time, 90% benefited from one or more of the listed financial assistance programs.

Internships/Practica: Clinical students ar placed at agencies or hosptials; Neuropsychology students are placed at hospitals or clinics; Learning Processes students are placed in service agencies and treatment facilities. Forensic students find placement in various justice system related positions.

Housing and Day Care: No on-campus housing is available. On-campus day care facilities are available. At each campus.

Employment of Department Graduates:

Master's Degree Graduates: Of those who graduated in the academic year 2006–2007, the following categories and numbers represent the postgraduate activities and employment of master's degree graduates: Enrolled in a postdoctoral residency/fellowship (n/a), employed in independent practice (n/a), total from the above (master's) (0).

Doctoral Degree Graduates: Of those who graduated in the academic year 2006–2007, the following categories and numbers represent the postgraduate activities and employment of doctoral degree graduates: Enrolled in a psychology doctoral program (n/a), enrolled in a postdoctoral residency/fellowship (4), employed in an academic position at a university (16), employed in an academic position at a 2-year/4-year college (9), employed in a professional position in a school system (13), employed in business or industry (2), total from the above (doctoral) (44).

Additional Information:

Orientation, Objectives, and Emphasis of Department: The Developmental subprogram offers training in all areas of developmental research, with emphasis on social, cognitive, and language development. The Environmental subprogram provides interdisciplinary training with relationships between the physical environment and behavior. Concepts and approaches of fields such as urban planning, psychology, architecture, geography, anthropology, landscape architecture, and sociology are learned in a context that emphasizes the integration of systematic research and applied work with the development of theory. The Social/Personality subprogram trains students in the theory and research methods of both social and personality psychology. A health psychology concentration is available to students in all subprograms. Through courses, research projects, and practica, the concentration seeks to train psychologists to be able to work in a variety of health-related settings. Industrial/Organizational Psychology trains people to do research in organizations and in personnel issues. Neuropsychology trains students in both basic and clinical neuroscience. Learning Processes offers training in applied behavior analysis. Clinical offers training in psychodynamic approaches to mental health with particular attention paid to minority populations. Experimental Psychology and Experimental Cognition focus on the experimental approach to a wide variety of phenomena. Forensic Psychology has two tracks, clinical (90 credits) and experimental (60 credits); the clinical track prepares people to work within the criminal justice system in a variety of clinical roles. The experimental track prepares people in basic research dealing with the interface of psychology and the law.

Special Facilities or Resources: Computers for student use are available in the library; at computer hubs, on most academic floors; and at student carrel spaces in the academic program offices. An assortment of programming languages and statistical, graphical, wordprocessing, and specialty software applications are provided. Also available are laser printers, file format translation, image scanning, and optical character recognition facilities. Adaptive technology for students with disabilities is available and includes screen-access software and such peripheral devices as reading machines, a computer-linked closed-circuit TV, and a Braille printer. Most computers designated for students are 400Mhz Celeron processor systems with 6GB hard drives, 64 MB Ram, and 15-inch flat-screen monitors. Five special-purpose classrooms, with a total of more than 100 computers, are furnished with 450 Mhz Pentium III computers and 15-inch flat-screen monitors. Students may access UNIX-based academic software from home or via a telnet session upon request. The UNIX accounts provide access to statistical or other academic software but not e-mail support. Information Resources maintains an ongoing program of equipment, computer hardware, and software modernization and provides such client services as documentation, training, and lab consulting. Workshops are held throughout the year on a wide range of topics and include many hands-on training programs.

Information for Students With Physical Disabilities: See the following Web site for more information: http://www.gc.cuny.edu.

Application Information:
Send to Admissions Office, City University Graduate Center, 365 Fifth Avenue, New York, NY 10016-4309; Phone: (212) 817-7470; E-mail: admissions@gc.cuny.edu. URL of online application: http://www.gc.cuny.edu/prospective_students/index.htm. Students are admitted in the Fall, application deadline is January 1 for Clinical and Neuropsychology; December 15 for Social Personality; January 15 for Developmental, Environmental, Forensic; February 1 for Cognitive Neuroscience, Industrial/Organizational; March 1 for Biopsychology and Behavioral Neuroscience; March 15 for Learning Processes and Behavior Analysis, and Cognition, Brain, and Behavior. *Fee:* $125.

City University of New York: John Jay College of Criminal Justice

Department of Psychology, MA Program in Forensic Psychology
John Jay College of Criminal Justice, CUNY
445 West 59th Street
New York, NY 10019
Telephone: (212) 237-8782
Fax: (212) 237-8742
E-mail: *Jwulach@jjay.cuny.edu*
Web: *http://www.jjay.cuny.edu*

Department Information:
1976. Director: James S. Wulach, PhD, JD. Number of faculty: total—full-time 32, part-time 12; women—full-time 25, part-time 8; total—minority—full-time 8, part-time 1; women minority—full-time 3; faculty subject to the Americans With Disabilities Act 9.

Programs and Degrees Offered:
Listed in the following order: Program area, degree type (T if terminal Master's), number awarded 7/06–6/07. Forensic Psychology MA/MS (Master of Arts/Science) (T) 148, Forensic Mental Health Counseling MA/MS (Master of Arts/Science) 0.

Student Applications/Admissions:
Student Applications
Forensic Psychology MA/MS (Master of Arts/Science)—Applications 2007–2008, 486. Total applicants accepted 2007–2008, 389. Number full-time enrolled (new admits only) 2007–2008, 134. Number part-time enrolled (new admits only) 2007–2008, 123. Total enrolled 2007–2008 full-time, 216, part-time, 208. Openings 2008–2009, 175. The median number of years required for completion of a degree in 2006–2007 were 2. The number of students enrolled full- and part-time who were dismissed or voluntarily withdrew from this program area in 2007–2008 were 26. *Forensic Mental Health Counseling MA/MS (Master of Arts/Science)*—Applications 2007–2008, 0. Total applicants accepted 2007–2008, 0. Number full-time enrolled (new admits only) 2007–2008, 30. Number part-time enrolled (new admits only) 2007–2008, 10. Total enrolled 2007–2008 full-time, 30, part-time, 10. Openings 2008–2009, 35. The number of students enrolled full- and part-time who were dismissed or voluntarily withdrew from this program area in 2007–2008 were 0.

Admissions Requirements:
Scores: Entries appear in this order: required test or GPA, minimum score (if required), median score of students entering in 2007–2008. Master's Programs: GRE-V 500, 500; GRE-Q 500, 520; overall undergraduate GPA 3.0, 3.2. Doctoral Programs: No REQUIRED minimum scores. Each candidate is evaluated individually.
Other Criteria: (importance of criteria rated low, medium, or high): GRE/MAT scores—high, research experience—low, work experience—low, GPA—high, letters of recommendation—low, statement of goals and objectives—low. MA Program: GPA and GRE scores weighted most heavily. For additional information on admission requirements, go to http://www.jjay.cuny.edu.

Student Characteristics: The following represents characteristics of students in 2007–2008 in all graduate psychology programs in the department: Female—full-time 163, part-time 153; Male—full-time 53, part-time 55; African American/Black—full-time 14, part-time 12; Hispanic/Latino(a)—full-time 21, part-time 16; Asian/Pacific Islander—full-time 14, part-time 10; American Indian/Alaska Native—full-time 1, part-time 0; Caucasian/White—full-time 133, part-time 129; Multi-ethnic—full-time 19, part-time 23; students subject to the Americans With Disabilities Act—full-time 6, part-time 4; Unknown ethnicity—full-time 14, part-time 18.

Financial Information/Assistance:
Tuition for Full-Time Study: *Master's:* State residents: per academic year $6,400, $270 per credit hour; Nonstate residents: $500 per credit hour. Tuition is subject to change. See the following Web site for updates and changes in tuition costs: http://www.jjay.cuny.edu.

Financial Assistance:
First-Year Students: No information provided.
Advanced Students: No information provided.
Additional Information: No information provided.

Internships/Practica: MA Program in Forensic Psychology: Most students complete a 300-hour externship in local forensic psychology settings such as hospitals or prisons. MA Program in Forensic Mental Health Counseling: Most students complete a 600-hour externship in local forensic psychology settings such as hospitals or prisons. For additional information on education and training outcomes for our programs, see the following Web site: http://www.jjay.cuny.edu.

Housing and Day Care: No on-campus housing is available. On-campus day care facilities are available. See the following Web site for more information: http://www.jjay.cuny.edu. Alphabetical index, go to Children's Center.

Employment of Department Graduates:
Master's Degree Graduates: Of those who graduated in the academic year 2006–2007, the following categories and numbers represent the postgraduate activities and employment of master's

degree graduates: Enrolled in a postdoctoral residency/fellowship (n/a), employed in independent practice (n/a), total from the above (master's) (0).

Doctoral Degree Graduates: Of those who graduated in the academic year 2006–2007, the following categories and numbers represent the postgraduate activities and employment of doctoral degree graduates: Enrolled in a psychology doctoral program (n/a), total from the above (doctoral) (0).

Additional Information:

Orientation, Objectives, and Emphasis of Department: (MA Program in Forensic Psychology): This 42-credit program is designed to train students to provide professional MA-level psychological services to, and within, the legal system—especially the criminal justice system. Thus, in addition to offering (and requiring) traditional master's-level clinical psychology courses, we offer specialized courses in psychology and the law; the psychology and treatment of juvenile and adult offenders and the victims of crime; forensic evaluation and testimony; jury research; eyewitness research; psychological profiles of homicidal offenders; psychology of terrorism; and forensic psychological research. There is a research track for advanced students to work on MA theses with professors. Courses are primarily offered in the afternoon and evening. Many of our full-time faculty members have postdoctoral psychological certifications; six are lawyers as well as psychologists; and many have extensive forensic experience as practitioners and/or researchers. In addition, the full educational resources of the John Jay College of Criminal Justice are available to our students. Some of our graduates become MA psychologists within the criminal justice system, working with offenders, delinquents, and victims. Other graduates enhance their present careers in law enforcement, probation, or parole by completing the program. Many of our graduates continue their education in psychology doctoral programs or in law. (MA Program in Forensic Mental Health Counseling): This is a new 60-credit program, sponsored by the Psychology Department, that has been approved by NY State as a "license eligible" program for NY Mental Health Counselors, with a forensic spcialization. Coursework is similar to the MA Program in Forensic Psychology, with less emphasis on research, and more courses oriented toward becoming a NY-licensed mental health counselor.

Special Facilities or Resources: The department maintains affiliations with the major forensic psychology institutions in the New York metropolitan area. The Program is endowed for student psychology research in the Forensic Psychology Research Institute. In addition, the full academic resources and educational milieu of John Jay College of Criminal Justice, CUNY, are available to our students.

Information for Students With Physical Disabilities: See the following Web site for more information: http://www.jjay.cuny.edu.

Application Information:

Send to MA Program: Graduate Admissions, John Jay College of Criminal Justice, CUNY, Room 4205N, 445 West 59th Street, New York, NY 10019; phone number: (212) 237-8863. Application available online. URL of online application: http://www.jjay.cuny.edu. Students are admitted in the Fall, application deadline June 30; Spring, application deadline December 1; Summer, application deadline December 1. *Fee:* $125.

City University of New York: John Jay College of Criminal Justice (2007 data)

Doctoral Program in Forensic Psychology (Clinical and Experimental tracks)
John Jay College of Criminal Justice, CUNY
445 West 59th Street
New York, NY 10019
Telephone: (212) 237-8252
E-mail: *forensicpsychphd@jjay.cuny.edu*
Web: *http://www.gc.cuny.edu*

Department Information:

2002. Program Director: Barbara Stanley, PhD. Number of faculty: total—full-time 28; women—full-time 14.

Programs and Degrees Offered:

Listed in the following order: Program area, degree type (T if terminal Master's), number awarded 7/06–6/07. Forensic Psychology Clinical Track PhD (Doctor of Philosophy) 0, Forensic Psychology Experimental Track PhD (Doctor of Philosophy) 0.

Student Applications/Admissions:

Student Applications

Forensic Psychology Clinical Track PhD (Doctor of Philosophy)—The number of students enrolled full- and part-time who were dismissed or voluntarily withdrew from this program area in 2007–2008 were 1. *Forensic Psychology Experimental Track PhD (Doctor of Philosophy)*.

Admissions Requirements:

Scores: Entries appear in this order: required test or GPA, minimum score (if required), median score of students entering in 2007–2008. Doctoral Programs: GRE-V no minimum stated; GRE-Q no minimum stated; GRE-Subject (Psychology) no minimum stated; overall undergraduate GPA no minimum stated; Doctoral program GRE-Analytic no minimum stated.

Other Criteria: (importance of criteria rated low, medium, or high): GRE/MAT scores—high, research experience—medium, work experience—medium, extracurricular activity—low, clinically related public service—medium, GPA—high, letters of recommendation—high, interview—high, statement of goals and objectives—high.

Student Characteristics: The following represents characteristics of students in 2007–2008 in all graduate psychology programs in the department: Female—full-time 18, part-time 0; Male—full-time 2, part-time 0; Hispanic/Latino(a)—full-time 3, part-time 0; Caucasian/White—full-time 17, part-time 0; students subject to the Americans With Disabilities Act—full-time 0, part-time 0; Unknown ethnicity—full-time 0, part-time 0.

Financial Information/Assistance:

Tuition for Full-Time Study: *Doctoral:* State residents: per academic year $5,720; Nonstate residents: $560 per credit hour.

Financial Assistance:

First-Year Students: Teaching assistantships available for first year. Average amount paid per academic year: $13,000. Tuition remission given: full. Research assistantships available for first year. Average amount paid per academic year: $13,000. Tuition remission given: full. Fellowships and scholarships available for first year. Average amount paid per academic year: $15,000. Tuition remission given: full.

Advanced Students: Teaching assistantships available for advanced students. Average amount paid per academic year: $13,000. Tuition remission given: full. Research assistantships available for advanced students. Average amount paid per academic year: $13,000. Tuition remission given: full.

Additional Information: Of all students currently enrolled full time, 100% benefited from one or more of the listed financial assistance programs.

Internships/Practica: No information provided.

Housing and Day Care: No on-campus housing is available. No on-campus day care facilities are available.

Employment of Department Graduates:

Master's Degree Graduates: Of those who graduated in the academic year 2006–2007, the following categories and numbers represent the postgraduate activities and employment of master's degree graduates: Enrolled in a postdoctoral residency/fellowship (n/a), employed in independent practice (n/a), total from the above (master's) (0).

Doctoral Degree Graduates: Of those who graduated in the academic year 2006–2007, the following categories and numbers represent the postgraduate activities and employment of doctoral degree graduates: Enrolled in a psychology doctoral program (n/a), total from the above (doctoral) (0).

Application Information:

Send to Admissions Office, The Graduate Center, City University of New York. Students are admitted in the Fall, application deadline December 15. *Fee:* $125.

Columbia University

Health and Behavior Studies/School Psychology
Teachers College
525 West 120th Street, Box 120
New York, NY 10027
Telephone: (212) 678-3942
Fax: (212) 678-4034
E-mail: *peverly@tc.edu*
Web: *http://www.tc.columbia.edu/hbs/schoolpsych/*

Department Information:

1996. Chairperson: John Allegrante. Number of faculty: total—full-time 3, part-time 11; women—full-time 1, part-time 7.

Programs and Degrees Offered:

Listed in the following order: Program area, degree type (T if terminal Master's), number awarded 7/06–6/07. School Psychology PhD (Doctor of Philosophy) 8, School Psychology EdS/MEd (School Psychology) 22.

APA Accreditation: School PhD (Doctor of Philosophy).

Student Applications/Admissions:

Student Applications

School Psychology PhD (Doctor of Philosophy)—Applications 2007–2008, 67. Total applicants accepted 2007–2008, 4. Number full-time enrolled (new admits only) 2007–2008, 4. Number part-time enrolled (new admits only) 2007–2008, 0. Total enrolled 2007–2008 full-time, 19, part-time, 10. Openings 2008–2009, 4. The median number of years required for completion of a degree in 2006–2007 were 8. The number of students enrolled full- and part-time who were dismissed or voluntarily withdrew from this program area in 2007–2008 were 2. *School Psychology EdS/MEd (School Psychology)*—Applications 2007–2008, 142. Total applicants accepted 2007–2008, 57. Number full-time enrolled (new admits only) 2007–2008, 24. Number part-time enrolled (new admits only) 2007–2008, 0. Openings 2008–2009, 20. The median number of years required for completion of a degree in 2006–2007 were 3. The number of students enrolled full- and part-time who were dismissed or voluntarily withdrew from this program area in 2007–2008 were 2.

Admissions Requirements:

Scores: Entries appear in this order: required test or GPA, minimum score (if required), median score of students entering in 2007–2008. Master's Programs: GRE-V no minimum stated, 510; GRE-Q no minimum stated, 675; overall undergraduate GPA no minimum stated, 3.60. Doctoral Programs: GRE-V no minimum stated, 580; GRE-Q no minimum stated, 770; overall undergraduate GPA no minimum stated, 3.42.

Other Criteria: (importance of criteria rated low, medium, or high): GRE/MAT scores—medium, research experience—high, work experience—medium, extracurricular activity—medium, clinically related public service—medium, GPA—high, letters of recommendation—high, interview—high, statement of goals and objectives—high.

Student Characteristics: The following represents characteristics of students in 2007–2008 in all graduate psychology programs in the department: Female—full-time 76, part-time 10; Male—full-time 6, part-time 0; African American/Black—full-time 4, part-time 3; Hispanic/Latino(a)—full-time 2, part-time 1; Asian/Pacific Islander—full-time 8, part-time 2; American Indian/Alaska Native—full-time 0, part-time 0; Caucasian/White—full-time 68, part-time 4; Multi-ethnic—full-time 0, part-time 0; students subject to the Americans With Disabilities Act—full-time 2, part-time 0; Unknown ethnicity—full-time 0, part-time 0; International students who hold an F-1 or J-1 Visa—full-time 1, part-time 0.

Financial Information/Assistance:

Tuition for Full-Time Study: *Master's:* State residents: $1,030 per credit hour; Nonstate residents: $1,030 per credit hour. *Doctoral:* State residents: $1,030 per credit hour; Nonstate residents: $1,030 per credit hour. Additional fees are assessed to students beyond the costs of tuition for the following: College fee, Medical fee, application fee, research fee. See the following Web site for updates and changes in tuition costs: http://www.tc.columbia.edu.

Financial Assistance:

First-Year Students: Fellowships and scholarships available for first year. Average amount paid per academic year: $12,360. Apply by none. Tuition remission given: partial.

Advanced Students: Teaching assistantships available for advanced students. Average amount paid per academic year: $1,775. Average number of hours worked per week: 5. Apply by none. Tuition remission given: partial. Fellowships and scholarships available for advanced students. Average amount paid per academic year: $12,360. Apply by none. Tuition remission given: partial.

Additional Information: Of all students currently enrolled full time, 25% benefited from one or more of the listed financial assistance programs. Application and information available online at http://www.tc.columbia.edu.

Internships/Practica: Doctoral Degree (PhD School Psychology): For those doctoral students for whom a professional internship was required in this program prior to graduation, (3) students applied for an internship in 2006–2007, with (3) students obtaining an internship. Of those students who obtained an internship, (3) were paid internships. Of those students who obtained an internship, (2) students placed in APA/CPA-accredited internships, (0) students placed in internships not APA/CPA accredited, but listed with the Association of Psychology Postdoctoral and Internship Centers (APPIC), (1) student placed in internships conforming to guidelines of the Council of Directors of School Psychology Programs (CDSPP), (0) students placed in internships that were not APA/CPA-accredited, APPIC or CDSPP listed. First year—Two practica in our Center for Educational and Psychological Services: (a) Practicum in Assessment of Reading and School Subject Difficulties (Fall); (b) Practicum in Psychoeducational Assessment with Culturally Diverse Students (Spring); Second year—Students engage in (a) Fieldwork (2 days/week over the academic year in one of our cooperating inner-city schools) (b) a practicum in psychoeducational groups (the groups are run within students' fieldwork sites); Third year—Externship (2 days/week over an academic year; most students are required to do two externships: one in a school and one in a hospital or clinic); Fourth or Fifth year—Internship (full calendar year; students must have an approved dissertation proposal before they begin to do the internship after completing most or all of their dissertation).

Housing and Day Care: On-campus housing is available. See the following Web site for more information: http://www.tc.columbia.edu. On-campus day care facilities are available.

Employment of Department Graduates:

Master's Degree Graduates: Of those who graduated in the academic year 2006–2007, the following categories and numbers represent the postgraduate activities and employment of master's degree graduates: Enrolled in another graduate/professional program (1), enrolled in a postdoctoral residency/fellowship (n/a), employed in independent practice (n/a), employed in a professional position in a school system (21), total from the above (master's) (22).

Doctoral Degree Graduates: Of those who graduated in the academic year 2006–2007, the following categories and numbers represent the postgraduate activities and employment of doctoral degree graduates: Enrolled in a psychology doctoral program (n/a), enrolled in a postdoctoral residency/fellowship (1), employed in a professional position in a school system (3), employed in business or industry (1), employed in a hospital/medical center (1), total from the above (doctoral) (6).

Additional Information:

Orientation, Objectives, and Emphasis of Department: The primary theoretical orientation of our program is cognitive and developmental with strong applications to instruction and mental health. We place a particularly strong emphasis on prevention and intervention in these areas. Throughout the curriculum, there is a balance between science and practice, and we ensure that all students are well grounded in the theory and methods of psychological science. Most students opt to go through the general curriculum. However, some have adopted a specialization in the deaf and hearing impaired.

Special Facilities or Resources: The School Psychology program has strong collaborative relationships with four inner-city schools that serve as fieldwork and sites for our master's and doctoral students.

Information for Students With Physical Disabilities: See the following Web site for more information: http://www.tc.columbia.edu.

Application Information:

Send to Office of Admissions, Box 302, Teachers College, Columbia University, 525 West 120th Street, New York, NY 10027; (212) 678-3710. Application available online. URL of online application: http://www.tc.columbia.edu/admissions. Students are admitted in the Fall, application deadline December 15. January 15 for the EdM Program. *Fee:* $65. Reapplicants—$35.

Cornell University

Department of Human Development
The New York State College of Human Ecology
G77 Martha Van Rensselaer Hall
Ithaca, NY 14853-4401
Telephone: (607) 255-7620
Fax: (607) 255-9856
E-mail: *blb5@cornell.edu*
Web: *http://www.human.cornell.edu/che/HD/graduate/index.cfm*

Department Information:

1925. Chairperson: Ritch Savin-Williams. Number of faculty: total—full-time 21; women—full-time 8; total—minority—full-time 3; women minority—full-time 2.

Programs and Degrees Offered:

Listed in the following order: Program area, degree type (T if terminal Master's), number awarded 7/06–6/07. Developmental PhD (Doctor of Philosophy) 2, Human Development Family Studies PhD (Doctor of Philosophy) 0.

Student Applications/Admissions:

Student Applications

Developmental PhD (Doctor of Philosophy)—Applications 2007–2008, 60. Total applicants accepted 2007–2008, 13. Number full-time enrolled (new admits only) 2007–2008, 5. Number part-time enrolled (new admits only) 2007–2008, 0. Openings 2008–2009, 4. The median number of years required for completion of a degree in 2006–2007 were 5. The number of students enrolled full- and part-time who were dismissed or voluntarily withdrew from this program area in 2007–2008 were 0. *Human Development Family Studies PhD (Doctor of Philosophy)*—Applications 2007–2008, 6. Total applicants accepted 2007–2008, 0. Number full-time enrolled (new admits only) 2007–2008, 0. Number part-time enrolled (new admits only) 2007–2008, 0. Openings 2008–2009, 1. The number of students enrolled full- and part-time who were dismissed or voluntarily withdrew from this program area in 2007–2008 were 0.

Admissions Requirements:

Scores: Entries appear in this order: required test or GPA, minimum score (if required), median score of students entering in 2007–2008. Doctoral Programs: GRE-V 600, 620; GRE-Q 600, 750; overall undergraduate GPA no minimum stated, 3.8.

Other Criteria: (importance of criteria rated low, medium, or high): GRE/MAT scores—high, research experience—high, work experience—low, extracurricular activity—low, clinically related public service—low, GPA—high, letters of recommendation—high, statement of goals and objectives—high, specific undergraduate psychology courses taken—medium.

Student Characteristics: The following represents characteristics of students in 2007–2008 in all graduate psychology programs in the department: Female—full-time 24, part-time 0; Male—full-time 7, part-time 0; African American/Black—full-time 1, part-time 0; Hispanic/Latino(a)—full-time 2, part-time 0; Asian/Pacific Islander—full-time 2, part-time 0; American Indian/Alaska Native—full-time 0, part-time 0; Caucasian/White—full-time 16, part-time 0; Multi-ethnic—full-time 0, part-time 0; students subject to the Americans With Disabilities Act—full-time 0, part-time 0; Unknown ethnicity—full-time 10, part-time 0; International students who hold an F-1 or J-1 Visa—full-time 10, part-time 0.

Financial Information/Assistance:

Tuition for Full-Time Study: *Doctoral:* State residents: per academic year $20,800; Nonstate residents: per academic year $20,800. Tuition is subject to change.

Financial Assistance:

First-Year Students: Teaching assistantships available for first year. Average amount paid per academic year: $20,710. Average number of hours worked per week: 15. Apply by January 1. Tuition remission given: full. Research assistantships available for first year. Average amount paid per academic year: $20,710. Average number of hours worked per week: 15. Apply by January 1. Tuition remission given: full. Traineeships available for first year. Average amount paid per academic year: $20,710. Average number of hours worked per week: 15. Apply by January 1. Tuition remission given: full. Fellowships and scholarships available for first year. Average amount paid per academic year: $20,710. Average number of hours worked per week: 0. Apply by January 1. Tuition remission given: full.

Advanced Students: Teaching assistantships available for advanced students. Average amount paid per academic year: $20,710. Average number of hours worked per week: 15. Apply by January 1. Tuition remission given: full. Research assistantships available for advanced students. Average amount paid per academic year: $20,710. Average number of hours worked per week: 15. Apply by January 1. Tuition remission given: full. Traineeships available for advanced students. Average amount paid per academic year: $20,710. Average number of hours worked per week: 15. Apply by January 1. Tuition remission given: full. Fellowships and scholarships available for advanced students. Average amount paid per academic year: $20,710. Average number of hours worked per week: 0. Apply by January 1. Tuition remission given: full.

Additional Information: Of all students currently enrolled full time, 100% benefited from one or more of the listed financial assistance programs.

Internships/Practica: No information provided.

Housing and Day Care: On-campus housing is available. See the following Web site for more information: http://www.campuslife.cornell.edu/graduate_housing/. On-campus day care facilities are available. See the following Web site for more information: http://www.ohr.cornell.edu/benefits/lifeEvents/childcare.html.

Employment of Department Graduates:

Master's Degree Graduates: Of those who graduated in the academic year 2006–2007, the following categories and numbers represent the postgraduate activities and employment of master's degree graduates: Enrolled in a postdoctoral residency/fellowship (n/a), employed in independent practice (n/a), total from the above (master's) (0).

Doctoral Degree Graduates: Of those who graduated in the academic year 2006–2007, the following categories and numbers represent the postgraduate activities and employment of doctoral degree graduates: Enrolled in a psychology doctoral program (n/a), employed in an academic position at a university (1), employed in a professional position in a school system (1), total from the above (doctoral) (2).

Additional Information:

Orientation, Objectives, and Emphasis of Department: The field offers two general majors. The major in Developmental Psychology focuses on individual development and the effects of various intrinsic and extrinsic factors. The major in Human Development and Family Studies focuses on the interrelationships among the individual, the family, and the larger society. The major in Developmental Psychology provides focused training in the subareas of cognition, social–personality, and biological bases of behavior. The major in Human Development and Family Studies bridges basic and applied research, especially from a life course perspective. Both majors place heavy emphasis on research training. Students are prepared for careers in academic life (in departments of psychology, sociology, or human development); in government agencies; and in a range of programs situated in community agencies, health centers, and private enterprise. We do not offer training in clinical or counseling psychology, marriage counseling, or family therapy.

Special Facilities or Resources: The department houses a number of laboratories dedicated to individual projects as well as several nondedicated laboratories, including rooms with audio and visual recording capability. The department operates a day care center that provides numerous opportunities for research, and opportunities for research also exist in area public schools, nursery schools and day care centers, and youth service agencies. The department also maintains graduate student computer facilities with statistical software and various programs such as E-prime and Noldus. In addition, the department has ties with several centers in the

College including the Bronfenbrenner Life Course Institute (with its concentration on life course studies), the Family Life Development Center (which concentrates on families under stress), the Institute for Research on Children, and the Institute for Translational Research on Aging.

Information for Students With Physical Disabilities: See the following Web site for more information: http://www.sas.cornell.edu/CLT/campus/sds/index.html.

Application Information:
Send to Bonnie Biata, Human Development, G77 Martha VanRensselaer Hall, Cornell Universtiy, Ithaca, NY 14853. Application available online. URL of online application: http://www.gradschool.edu/index.php?p=1. Students are admitted in the Fall, application deadline January 1. *Fee:* $70. In cases of extreme financial need, a fee waiver will be considered. A letter of request for a waiver and documentation of need such as a letter from the college financial aid office needs to be submitted.

Cornell University

Graduate Field of Psychology
Arts
211 Uris Hall
Ithaca, NY 14853-7601
Telephone: (607) 255-3834
Fax: (607) 255-8433
E-mail: *pac34@cornell.edu*
Web: *http://www.psych.cornell.edu*

Department Information:
1885. Director of Graduate Studies: David J. Field. Number of faculty: total—full-time 25, part-time 2; women—full-time 8, part-time 1; ; women minority—full-time 1.

Programs and Degrees Offered:
Listed in the following order: Program area, degree type (T if terminal Master's), number awarded 7/06–6/07. Behavioral and Evolutionary Neuroscience (BEN) PhD (Doctor of Philosophy) 1, Perception, Cognition, and Development (PCD) PhD (Doctor of Philosophy) 1, Social–Personality Psychology PhD (Doctor of Philosophy) 2.

Student Applications/Admissions:
Student Applications
Behavioral and Evolutionary Neuroscience (BEN) PhD (Doctor of Philosophy)—Applications 2007–2008, 28. Total applicants accepted 2007–2008, 4. Number full-time enrolled (new admits only) 2007–2008, 2. Openings 2008–2009, 2. The median number of years required for completion of a degree in 2006–2007 were 5. The number of students enrolled full- and part-time who were dismissed or voluntarily withdrew from this program area in 2007–2008 were 1. *Perception, Cognition and Development (PCD) PhD (Doctor of Philosophy)*—Applications 2007–2008, 43. Total applicants accepted 2007–2008, 4. Number full-time enrolled (new admits only) 2007–2008, 2. Openings 2008–2009, 2. The median number of years required for completion of a degree in 2006–2007 were 5. The number of students enrolled full- and part-time who were dismissed or voluntarily withdrew from this program area in 2007–2008 were 1. *Social–Personality Psychology PhD (Doctor of Philosophy)*—Applications 2007–2008, 103. Total applicants accepted 2007–2008, 5. Number full-time enrolled (new admits only) 2007–2008, 3. Openings 2008–2009, 3. The median number of years required for completion of a degree in 2006–2007 were 4.

Admissions Requirements:
Scores: Entries appear in this order: required test or GPA, minimum score (if required), median score of students entering in 2007–2008. Doctoral Programs: GRE-V no minimum stated, 562; GRE-Q no minimum stated, 685; GRE-Subject (Psychology) no minimum stated, 720; overall undergraduate GPA no minimum stated.
Other Criteria: (importance of criteria rated low, medium, or high): GRE/MAT scores—high, research experience—high, work experience—low, extracurricular activity—low, GPA—high, letters of recommendation—high, statement of goals and objectives—high.

Student Characteristics: The following represents characteristics of students in 2007–2008 in all graduate psychology programs in the department: Female—full-time 24, part-time 0; Male—full-time 16, part-time 0; African American/Black—full-time 2, part-time 0; Hispanic/Latino(a)—full-time 1, part-time 0; Asian/Pacific Islander—full-time 9, part-time 0; American Indian/Alaska Native—full-time 0, part-time 0; Caucasian/White—full-time 28, part-time 0; Unknown ethnicity—full-time 0, part-time 0.

Financial Information/Assistance:
Financial Assistance:
First-Year Students: Teaching assistantships available for first year. Average amount paid per academic year: $20,000. Average number of hours worked per week: 20. Fellowships and scholarships available for first year. Average amount paid per academic year: $20,000.
Advanced Students: No information provided.
Additional Information: Of all students currently enrolled full time, 100% benefited from one or more of the listed financial assistance programs.

Internships/Practica: No information provided.

Housing and Day Care: On-campus housing is available. On-campus day care facilities are available.

Employment of Department Graduates:
Master's Degree Graduates: Of those who graduated in the academic year 2006–2007, the following categories and numbers represent the postgraduate activities and employment of master's degree graduates: Enrolled in a postdoctoral residency/fellowship (n/a), employed in independent practice (n/a), total from the above (master's) (0).
Doctoral Degree Graduates: Of those who graduated in the academic year 2006–2007, the following categories and numbers represent the postgraduate activities and employment of doctoral degree graduates: Enrolled in a psychology doctoral program (n/a), enrolled in a postdoctoral residency/fellowship (3), other employment position (1), total from the above (doctoral) (4).

Additional Information:

Orientation, Objectives, and Emphasis of Department: The Psychology Department of the College of Arts and Sciences at Cornell has a faculty of 27 psychologists and is divided into three areas—perception, cognition, and development (encompassing cognition, language, perception, and its developmental perspectives); behavioral and evolutionary neuroscience (focusing on hormones and behavior, neural development, and sensory systems); and social–personality psychology (social cognition, judgment, and decision making). We do not have clinical, community, or counseling programs. We have a strong research orientation, training our students to become professional academics or researchers. Our 40 students design their graduate programs under the supervision of their special committees. These committees consist of at least four members of the graduate faculty at Cornell; at least three are from within the department. The chair of the committee is a member of the Graduate Field of Psychology, which consists of the 27 members of our department plus 20 researchers in allied fields (human development, education, industrial and labor relations, and neurobiology and behavior). Two other committee members serve as minor members, one of whom can be outside the Graduate Field of Psychology, and the fourth member oversees breadth requirements.

Special Facilities or Resources: The three areas of our program each have laboratories associated with them. Each of the members of the Perception, Cognition, and Development program has a separate laboratory, fully equipped with state-of-the-art computer equipment. In addition, the program has several computer-based teaching laboratories. The Behavioral Evolutionary Neuroscience group each have separate labs and computers, and animal housing facilities where relevant, but they share much of equipment and lab space. There is also a teaching lab associated with BEN's group labs. The social–personality psychologists share a large lab space with the sociology department. The department also has a small research library and machine, wood, and electronic shops.

Application Information:

Send to Graduate School, Caldwell Hall, Cornell University, Ithaca, NY 14853. Application available online. URL of online application: http://www.gradschool.cornell.edu. Students are admitted in the Fall, application deadline December 15. *Fee:* $70.

Fordham University

Department of Psychology
Arts and Sciences
441 East Fordham Road
Bronx, NY 10458
Telephone: (718) 817-3775
Fax: (718) 817-3785
E-mail: *schiaffino@fordham.edu*
Web: *http://www.fordham.edu/faculty/Undergraduate/Psych*

Department Information:

1933. Chairperson: Kathleen M. Schiaffino. Number of faculty: total—full-time 16, part-time 2; women—full-time 9; ; women minority—full-time 2.

Programs and Degrees Offered:

Listed in the following order: Program area, degree type (T if terminal Master's), number awarded 7/06–6/07. Clinical PhD (Doctor of Philosophy) 7, Psychometric PhD (Doctor of Philosophy) 5, Applied Developmental Psychology PhD (Doctor of Philosophy) 1.

APA Accreditation: Clinical PhD (Doctor of Philosophy).

Student Applications/Admissions:

Student Applications

Clinical PhD (Doctor of Philosophy)—Applications 2007–2008, 400. Total applicants accepted 2007–2008, 19. Number full-time enrolled (new admits only) 2007–2008, 11. Number part-time enrolled (new admits only) 2007–2008, 0. Openings 2008–2009, 12. The median number of years required for completion of a degree in 2006–2007 were 6. The number of students enrolled full- and part-time who were dismissed or voluntarily withdrew from this program area in 2007–2008 were 1. *Psychometric PhD (Doctor of Philosophy)*—Applications 2007–2008, 10. Total applicants accepted 2007–2008, 9. Number full-time enrolled (new admits only) 2007–2008, 4. Number part-time enrolled (new admits only) 2007–2008, 0. Openings 2008–2009, 4. The median number of years required for completion of a degree in 2006–2007 were 6. The number of students enrolled full- and part-time who were dismissed or voluntarily withdrew from this program area in 2007–2008 were 1. *Applied Developmental Psychology PhD (Doctor of Philosophy)*—Applications 2007–2008, 27. Total applicants accepted 2007–2008, 13. Number full-time enrolled (new admits only) 2007–2008, 6. Number part-time enrolled (new admits only) 2007–2008, 0. Openings 2008–2009, 6. The median number of years required for completion of a degree in 2006–2007 were 5. The number of students enrolled full- and part-time who were dismissed or voluntarily withdrew from this program area in 2007–2008 were 1.

Admissions Requirements:

Scores: Entries appear in this order: required test or GPA, minimum score (if required), median score of students entering in 2007–2008. Master's Programs: GRE-V no minimum stated; GRE-Q no minimum stated; GRE-Subject (Psychology) no minimum stated; MAT no minimum stated; overall undergraduate GPA no minimum stated; last 2 years GPA no minimum stated; psychology GPA no minimum stated. Doctoral Programs: GRE-V no minimum stated; GRE-Q no minimum stated; GRE-Subject (Psychology) no minimum stated; MAT no minimum stated; overall undergraduate GPA 3.5; last 2 years GPA no minimum stated; psychology GPA no minimum stated.

Other Criteria: (importance of criteria rated low, medium, or high): GRE/MAT scores—high, research experience—high, work experience—medium, extracurricular activity—medium, clinically related public service—medium, GPA—high, letters of recommendation—high, interview—high, statement of goals and objectives—high, undergraduate major in psychology—medium, specific undergraduate psychology courses taken—high.

Student Characteristics: The following represents characteristics of students in 2007–2008 in all graduate psychology programs in the department: Female—full-time 88, part-time 0; Male—

full-time 58, part-time 0; African American/Black—full-time 13, part-time 0; Hispanic/Latino(a)—full-time 9, part-time 0; Asian/Pacific Islander—full-time 18, part-time 0; Caucasian/White—full-time 106, part-time 0; Unknown ethnicity—full-time 0, part-time 0.

Financial Information/Assistance:

Tuition for Full-Time Study: *Doctoral:* State residents: $995 per credit hour; Nonstate residents: $995 per credit hour. Tuition is subject to change. See the following Web site for updates and changes in tuition costs: http://www.fordham.edu/faculty/Graduate_Schools/GSAS_Fees_for_2002206632.html.

Financial Assistance:

First-Year Students: Teaching assistantships available for first year. Average amount paid per academic year: $17,900. Average number of hours worked per week: 15. Apply by January 8. Tuition remission given: full. Research assistantships available for first year. Average amount paid per academic year: $17,900. Average number of hours worked per week: 15. Apply by January 8. Tuition remission given: full. Fellowships and scholarships available for first year. Average amount paid per academic year: $20,000. Average number of hours worked per week: 8. Apply by January 8. Tuition remission given: full.

Advanced Students: Teaching assistantships available for advanced students. Average amount paid per academic year: $19,200. Average number of hours worked per week: 15. Apply by February 15. Tuition remission given: full. Research assistantships available for advanced students. Average amount paid per academic year: $19,200. Average number of hours worked per week: 15. Apply by February 15. Tuition remission given: full. Fellowships and scholarships available for advanced students. Average amount paid per academic year: $20,000. Average number of hours worked per week: 15. Apply by February 15. Tuition remission given: full.

Additional Information: Of all students currently enrolled full time, 90% benefited from one or more of the listed financial assistance programs. Application and information available online at http://www.fordham.edu/faculty/Graduate_Schools/Financial_Aid6667.html.

Internships/Practica: Doctoral Degree (PhD Clinical): For those doctoral students for whom a professional internship was required in this program prior to graduation, (7) students applied for an internship in 2006–2007, with (6) students obtaining an internship. Of those students who obtained an internship, (6) were paid internships. Of those students who obtained an internship, (6) students placed in APA/CPA-accredited internships, (0) students placed in internships not APA/CPA-accredited, but listed with the Association of Psychology Postdoctoral and Internship Centers (APPIC), (0) students placed in internships conforming to guidelines of the Council of Directors of School Psychology Programs (CDSPP), (0) students placed in internships that were not APA/CPA-accredited, APPIC or CDSPP listed. Internships in a variety of public and private facilities are available for students after they have completed their coursework in the program.

Housing and Day Care: No on-campus housing is available. No on-campus day care facilities are available.

Employment of Department Graduates:

Master's Degree Graduates: Of those who graduated in the academic year 2006–2007, the following categories and numbers represent the postgraduate activities and employment of master's degree graduates: Enrolled in a postdoctoral residency/fellowship (n/a), employed in independent practice (n/a), total from the above (master's) (0).

Doctoral Degree Graduates: Of those who graduated in the academic year 2006–2007, the following categories and numbers represent the postgraduate activities and employment of doctoral degree graduates: Enrolled in a psychology doctoral program (n/a), enrolled in another graduate/professional program (0), do not know (13), total from the above (doctoral) (13).

Additional Information:

Orientation, Objectives, and Emphasis of Department: Clinical psychology prepares students for practice, research, and teaching in the clinical field as both professionals and scientists. Courses can be grouped under four major areas: clinical theory and methodology, research topics and methods, behavioral classification and assessment, and treatment approaches. Specializations include Family and Child, Health/Neuropsychology, and Forensics. There is a full-time, 1-year internship. Applied Developmental Psychology (ADP) trains professionals who can conduct both basic and applied research in developmental processes across the life span and who can share their knowledge in academic and community-based setting. ADP focuses on the interplay between developmental processes and social contexts including design and evaluation of programs; consultation to courts, lawyers, and public policy makers; development and evaluation of programs and materials directed at children and families; and parent and family education. The Psychometrics program focuses on the quantitative and research-oriented commonalities relevant to most of the behavioral sciences, and their applications in industry, education, and the health services. Students in Psychometrics become familiar with statistics, psychological testing, use of computer systems, and other research techniques, as well as with the psychology of individual differences.

Application Information:

Send to Graduate Admissions Office, Keating 216. Students are admitted in the Fall, application deadline December 13. *Fee:* $70. Paper application fee is $85; electronic application fee is $70.

Fordham University

Division of Psychological and Educational Services
Graduate School of Education
113 West 60th Street, Room 1008
New York, NY 10023
Telephone: (212) 636-6460
Fax: (212) 636-6461
E-mail: *pes@fordham.edu*
Web: *http://www.fordham.edu/gse*

Department Information:

1927. Chairperson: Mitchell Rabinowitz. Number of faculty: total—full-time 14, part-time 8; women—full-time 10, part-time 8.

Programs and Degrees Offered:

Listed in the following order: Program area, degree type (T if terminal Master's), number awarded 7/06–6/07. Counseling Psychology PhD (Doctor of Philosophy) 7, Educational Psychology

PhD (Doctor of Philosophy) 0, School Psychology PhD (Doctor of Philosophy) 8, Professional Diploma in School Psychology Other 30, Professional Diploma in Bilingual School Psychology Other 5.

APA Accreditation: Counseling PhD (Doctor of Philosophy). School PhD (Doctor of Philosophy).

Student Applications/Admissions:

Student Applications

Counseling Psychology PhD (Doctor of Philosophy)—Applications 2007–2008, 121. Total applicants accepted 2007–2008, 12. Number full-time enrolled (new admits only) 2007–2008, 12. Total enrolled 2007–2008 full-time, 36, part-time, 38. Openings 2008–2009, 12. The median number of years required for completion of a degree in 2006–2007 were 8. The number of students enrolled full- and part-time who were dismissed or voluntarily withdrew from this program area in 2007–2008 were 2. *Educational Psychology PhD (Doctor of Philosophy)*—Applications 2007–2008, 11. Total applicants accepted 2007–2008, 5. Number full-time enrolled (new admits only) 2007–2008, 6. Total enrolled 2007–2008 full-time, 16, part-time, 12. Openings 2008–2009, 8. The number of students enrolled full- and part-time who were dismissed or voluntarily withdrew from this program area in 2007–2008 were 0. *School Psychology PhD (Doctor of Philosophy)*—Applications 2007–2008, 90. Total applicants accepted 2007–2008, 20. Number full-time enrolled (new admits only) 2007–2008, 10. Total enrolled 2007–2008 full-time, 50, part-time, 30. Openings 2008–2009, 10. The median number of years required for completion of a degree in 2006–2007 were 7. The number of students enrolled full- and part-time who were dismissed or voluntarily withdrew from this program area in 2007–2008 were 2. *Professional Diploma in School Psychology Other*—Applications 2007–2008, 90. Total applicants accepted 2007–2008, 40. Number full-time enrolled (new admits only) 2007–2008, 19. Number part-time enrolled (new admits only) 2007–2008, 6. Total enrolled 2007–2008 full-time, 50, part-time, 25. Openings 2008–2009, 30. The median number of years required for completion of a degree in 2006–2007 were 3. The number of students enrolled full- and part-time who were dismissed or voluntarily withdrew from this program area in 2007–2008 were 0. *Professional Diploma in Bilingual School Psychology Other*—Applications 2007–2008, 8. Total applicants accepted 2007–2008, 6. Number full-time enrolled (new admits only) 2007–2008, 5. Total enrolled 2007–2008 full-time, 22. Openings 2008–2009, 8. The median number of years required for completion of a degree in 2006–2007 were 3. The number of students enrolled full- and part-time who were dismissed or voluntarily withdrew from this program area in 2007–2008 were 0.

Admissions Requirements:

Scores: Entries appear in this order: required test or GPA, minimum score (if required), median score of students entering in 2007–2008. Master's Programs: overall undergraduate GPA no minimum stated. Doctoral Programs: GRE-V no minimum stated; GRE-Q no minimum stated; overall undergraduate GPA no minimum stated.

Other Criteria: (importance of criteria rated low, medium, or high): GRE/MAT scores—high, research experience—medium, work experience—medium, extracurricular activity—medium, clinically related public service—medium, GPA—high, letters of recommendation—high, interview—low, statement of goals and objectives—high.

Student Characteristics: The following represents characteristics of students in 2007–2008 in all graduate psychology programs in the department: Female—full-time 155, part-time 86; Male—full-time 19, part-time 19; African American/Black—full-time 8, part-time 6; Hispanic/Latino(a)—full-time 16, part-time 6; Asian/Pacific Islander—full-time 12, part-time 4; American Indian/Alaska Native—full-time 0, part-time 0; Caucasian/White—full-time 132, part-time 88; Multi-ethnic—full-time 0, part-time 1; students subject to the Americans With Disabilities Act—full-time 5, part-time 0; Unknown ethnicity—full-time 6, part-time 0.

Financial Information/Assistance:

Financial Assistance:

First-Year Students: Research assistantships available for first year. Average number of hours worked per week: 7. Apply by March. Tuition remission given: partial.

Advanced Students: Research assistantships available for advanced students. Average number of hours worked per week: 12. Apply by March. Tuition remission given: full and partial.

Additional Information: Of all students currently enrolled full time, 60% benefited from one or more of the listed financial assistance programs.

Internships/Practica: No information provided.

Housing and Day Care: No on-campus housing is available. No on-campus day care facilities are available.

Employment of Department Graduates:

Master's Degree Graduates: Of those who graduated in the academic year 2006–2007, the following categories and numbers represent the postgraduate activities and employment of master's degree graduates: Enrolled in a postdoctoral residency/fellowship (n/a), employed in independent practice (n/a), total from the above (master's) (0).

Doctoral Degree Graduates: Of those who graduated in the academic year 2006–2007, the following categories and numbers represent the postgraduate activities and employment of doctoral degree graduates: Enrolled in a psychology doctoral program (n/a), enrolled in a postdoctoral residency/fellowship (1), employed in other positions at a higher education institution (1), employed in government agency (1), employed in a community mental health/counseling center (1), employed in a hospital/medical center (3), total from the above (doctoral) (7).

Application Information:

Send to Office of Admissions, Room 1115, Fordham University at Lincoln Center, 113 West 60th Street, New York, NY 10023. Application available online. URL of online application: http://www.fordham.edu/gse. Students are admitted in the Fall, application deadline see Web site. Counseling Psychology PhD, December 15; School Psychology PhD and PD, January 15; Counseling MSE, March 1; Educational Psychology programs have rolling admissions. *Fee:* $50; $100 for paper application.

Hofstra University

Department of Psychology
Hofstra College of Liberal Arts and Sciences
135 Hofstra University
Hempstead, NY 11549
Telephone: (516) 463-5624
Fax: (516) 463-6052
E-mail: *Charles.F.Levinthal@hofstra.edu*
Web: *http://www.hofstra.edu/Academics/HCLAS/Psychology/*

Department Information:

1948. Chairperson: Charles F. Levinthal, PhD. Number of faculty: total—full-time 34, part-time 19; women—full-time 12, part-time 8; total—minority—full-time 2, part-time 1; women minority—full-time 1; faculty subject to the Americans With Disabilities Act 1.

Programs and Degrees Offered:

Listed in the following order: Program area, degree type (T if terminal Master's), number awarded 7/06–6/07. Clinical PhD (Doctor of Philosophy) 16, Industrial-Organizational MA/MS (Master of Arts/Science) (T) 19, School-Community PsyD (Doctor of Psychology) 15, Applied Organizational Psychology PhD (Doctor of Philosophy) 2.

APA Accreditation: Clinical PhD (Doctor of Philosophy). Clinical PsyD (Doctor of Psychology).

Student Applications/Admissions:

Student Applications

Clinical PhD (Doctor of Philosophy)—Applications 2007–2008, 221. Total applicants accepted 2007–2008, 23. Number full-time enrolled (new admits only) 2007–2008, 14. Openings 2008–2009, 15. The median number of years required for completion of a degree in 2006–2007 were 5. The number of students enrolled full- and part-time who were dismissed or voluntarily withdrew from this program area in 2007–2008 were 1. *Industrial-Organizational MA/MS (Master of Arts/Science)*—Applications 2007–2008, 94. Total applicants accepted 2007–2008, 55. Number full-time enrolled (new admits only) 2007–2008, 23. Number part-time enrolled (new admits only) 2007–2008, 4. Total enrolled 2007–2008 full-time, 49, part-time, 7. Openings 2008–2009, 24. The median number of years required for completion of a degree in 2006–2007 were 2. The number of students enrolled full- and part-time who were dismissed or voluntarily withdrew from this program area in 2007–2008 were 2. *School-Community PsyD (Doctor of Psychology)*—Applications 2007–2008, 100. Total applicants accepted 2007–2008, 18. Number full-time enrolled (new admits only) 2007–2008, 10. Number part-time enrolled (new admits only) 2007–2008, 2. Total enrolled 2007–2008 full-time, 54, part-time, 3. Openings 2008–2009, 12. The median number of years required for completion of a degree in 2006–2007 were 5. *Applied Organizational Psychology PhD (Doctor of Philosophy)*—Applications 2007–2008, 20. Total applicants accepted 2007–2008, 10. Number full-time enrolled (new admits only) 2007–2008, 6. Number part-time enrolled (new admits only) 2007–2008, 2. Total enrolled 2007–2008 full-time, 28, part-time, 2. Openings 2008–2009, 8. The median number of years required for completion of a degree in 2006–2007 were 3. The number of students enrolled full- and part-time who were dismissed or voluntarily withdrew from this program area in 2007–2008 were 0.

Admissions Requirements:

Scores: Entries appear in this order: required test or GPA, minimum score (if required), median score of students entering in 2007–2008. Master's Programs: GRE-V 500, 510; GRE-Q 500, 600; overall undergraduate GPA 3.0, 3.5. Applications are accepted from students with undergraduate preparation in Psychology or Business. Doctoral Programs: GRE-V 500; GRE-Q 500; GRE-Subject (Psychology) no minimum stated; overall undergraduate GPA 3.0; psychology GPA no minimum stated. For PhD in Clinical Psychology in 2005 - GRE Mean scores: V-603 Q-683 Psych-654 GPA-3.44 see program information and admissions data go to: http://www.hofstra.edu/ClinicalPsy For PhD in Applied Organizational Psychology, the minimum score for the GRE-Q is 600, and the subject test in Psychology is not required.

Other Criteria: (importance of criteria rated low, medium, or high): GRE/MAT scores—high, research experience—high, work experience—medium, extracurricular activity—medium, clinically related public service—medium, GPA—high, letters of recommendation—medium, interview—high, statement of goals and objectives—medium. For Clinical PhD program: research experience—high, especially professional presentations and publications; clinically related public service—high, statement of goals and objectives—high. For PsyD program: research experience—low, clinically related public service—medium, statement of goals and objectives—medium. For PhD in Applied Organizational Psychology, a master's degree in one of the social sciences or in business is required.

Student Characteristics: The following represents characteristics of students in 2007–2008 in all graduate psychology programs in the department: Female—full-time 141, part-time 7; Male—full-time 77, part-time 5; African American/Black—full-time 9, part-time 2; Hispanic/Latino(a)—full-time 6, part-time 2; Asian/Pacific Islander—full-time 7, part-time 2; American Indian/Alaska Native—full-time 0, part-time 0; Caucasian/White—full-time 196, part-time 6; Multi-ethnic—full-time 0, part-time 0; students subject to the Americans With Disabilities Act—full-time 1, part-time 0; Unknown ethnicity—full-time 0, part-time 0; International students who hold an F-1 or J-1 Visa—full-time 0, part-time 0.

Financial Information/Assistance:

Tuition for Full-Time Study: *Master's:* State residents: $790 per credit hour; Nonstate residents: $790 per credit hour. *Doctoral:* State residents: $790 per credit hour; Nonstate residents: $790 per credit hour. Tuition is subject to change.

Financial Assistance:

First-Year Students: Teaching assistantships available for first year. Average number of hours worked per week: 6. Apply by variable. Research assistantships available for first year. Average number of hours worked per week: 5. Apply by variable. Tuition remission given: partial. Fellowships and scholarships available for first year. Apply by variable. Tuition remission given: partial.

Advanced Students: Teaching assistantships available for advanced students. Average number of hours worked per week: 6. Apply by variable. Research assistantships available for advanced students. Average number of hours worked per week: 5. Apply by variable. Tuition remission given: partial. Fellowships and scholarships available for advanced students. Apply by varable. Tuition remission given: partial.

Additional Information: Of all students currently enrolled full time, 33% benefited from one or more of the listed financial assistance programs.

Internships/Practica: Doctoral Degree (PsyD School/Community): For those doctoral students for whom a professional internship was required in this program prior to graduation, (18) students applied for an internship in 2006–2007, with (18) students obtaining an internship. Of those students who obtained an internship, (9) were paid internships. Of those students who obtained an internship, (0) students placed in APA/CPA-accredited internships, (0) students placed in internships not APA/CPA accredited, but listed with the Association of Psychology Postdoctoral and Internship Centers (APPIC), (0) students placed in internships conforming to guidelines of the Council of Directors of School Psychology Programs (CDSPP), (18) students placed in internships that were not APA/CPA-accredited, APPIC or CDSPP listed. In the Clinical PhD and PsyD programs, students complete a series of practica in which assessment, testing, and interviewing skills are developed. PhD students complete various courses and role-playing experiences in adult psychotherapy. PhD students are required to apply for internships using the APPIC national match process following the completion of all coursework and the defense of a dissertation proposal. Please see the Clinical program Web site for internship data. PsyD students complete a diversified and extended internship over a 2-year period. The students are first placed in a school (3 days per week) and then in a community agency (3 days per week). In the PhD program in Applied Organizational Psychology, a major part of the student's training, including a paid internship, research courses, and doctoral dissertation, will involve projects in organizations. The internship provides practical experience working for an organization for approximately 20 hours per week, under the supervision of a manager designated by the organization and approved by the program faculty. All research projects, including the dissertation, must serve the educational needs of the students and advance scientific knowledge in the field of organizational psychology; they cannot only serve the interests of the organization. Dissertation research may be conducted in the laboratory, the organization, or both. In addition to sound scientific methodology, the dissertation must have both practical and theoretical significance. This integration of science and practice is a major objective of the program. MA students in Industrial/Organizational Psychology, during their 2nd year of training, complete an internship in a business setting.

Housing and Day Care: On-campus housing is available. On-campus day care facilities are available. Child care is available in the Saltzman Community Services Center.

Employment of Department Graduates:

Master's Degree Graduates: Of those who graduated in the academic year 2006–2007, the following categories and numbers represent the postgraduate activities and employment of master's degree graduates: Enrolled in a psychology doctoral program (11), enrolled in a postdoctoral residency/fellowship (n/a), employed in independent practice (n/a), employed in business or industry (13), total from the above (master's) (24).

Doctoral Degree Graduates: Of those who graduated in the academic year 2006–2007, the following categories and numbers represent the postgraduate activities and employment of doctoral degree graduates: Enrolled in a psychology doctoral program (n/a), employed in an academic position at a university (2), employed in an academic position at a 2-year/4-year college (3), employed in other positions at a higher education institution (1), employed in a professional position in a school system (12), employed in business or industry (1), employed in a community mental health/counseling center (3), employed in a hospital/medical center (2), total from the above (doctoral) (24).

Additional Information:

Orientation, Objectives, and Emphasis of Department: The PhD Program in Clinical Psychology is designed to provide doctoral students with assessment and therapeutic skill competence along with a solid scientific foundation in order to have careers working with the wide variety of psychopathology found among the mentally ill. The program employs a scientist–practitioner model of education. Program graduates have readily found employment in a wide variety of mental health clinics, group practices, public and private agencies, as well as hospitals and medical centers. Many have chosen academic paths by becoming college and university faculty members, medical school faculty, research scientists, expert consultants, or editors for psychological publishers. The clinical psychology program is based upon cognitive–behavioral theory and represents the full psychotherapeutic spectrum of this orientation. The APA-accredited PsyD program in School/Community Psychology trains practitioners who are skilled in providing psychological services to children, families, and schools. Schools are viewed as being part of the larger community. Thus, in addition to being trained in a school-based, direct service model, emphasis is placed upon training students whose subject of study is the educational or community system in which children develop. PsyD students are trained as consultants who may be involved in educational and mental health program implementation and evaluation in settings such as the judicial system, the schools, personnel agencies, police departments, immigration centers, etc. Most graduates of the PsyD program are employed in schools. The PhD Program in Applied Organizational Psychology prepares students for careers as psychologists in business, industry, government, and other private and public organizations. Graduates of this program are trained to apply scientific methods to the solutions of problems related to individual and group behavior in organizations. They are also capable of teaching and researching these topics in higher education settings. The program's overall approach is based on a scientist–practitioner model in which students are exposed to research methodology, factual content, theory, and the application of these skills and knowledge to the solution of practical problems in organizations. The MA Program in Industrial/Organizational Psychology prepares students for careers in human resources, training, management, and organizational development. It provides a background in statistics, research design, social psychology, cognition and perception, and learning. The courses in I/O Psychology include selection, training, performance appraisal, worker motivation, and organization development. The curriculum is strengthened by an internship sequence that provides on-site supervised experience working on applied projects in business. The types of work that graduates perform include employee selection, management development, survey research, training, organizational development, performance appraisal, career development, and program evaluation.

Special Facilities or Resources: A community services center, the Psychological Evaluation, Research, and Counseling Clinic (PERCC), provides practicum experiences for students in the areas of assessment, intervention, and research. A laboratory, instrumented for videotaping, is equipped to handle research in areas of interviewing, communication, problem solving, psychotherapy, and team building. An outstanding library and a computer center are also available, as are many department microcomputers and videotape equipment. The student workroom has six computers for exclusive doctoral student use and all major software programs are available for student use.

Information for Students With Physical Disabilities: See the following Web site for more information: http://www.hofstra.edu/StudentServ/Advise/adv_phed.cfm.

Application Information:
Send to Graduate Admissions, Bernon Hall, Hofstra University, Hempstead, NY 11549. Application available online. URL of online application: http://www.hofstra.edu/Academics/Graduate/GS_Admissions/gs_admissions_applying.cfm. Students are admitted in the Fall, application deadline January 15. Deadline for the PhD in Clinical Psychology is January 15. Deadline for the PsyD in School/Community Psychology is January 15. Applications for the MA in Industrial/Organizational Psychology are accepted on a rolling basis until the class is filled. Deadline for the PhD in Applied Organizational Psychology is February 1. *Fee:* $60.

Iona College (2007 data)

Department of Psychology/Masters of Arts in Psychology
715 North Avenue
New Rochelle, NY 10801
Telephone: (914) 637-7788
Fax: (914) 633-2528
E-mail: *pjirik-babb@iona.edu*
Web: *http://www.iona.edu/academic/arts_sci/departments/*

Department Information:
1963. Chairperson: Pauline Jirik-Babb, PhD. Number of faculty: total—full-time 10, part-time 23; women—full-time 5, part-time 19.

Programs and Degrees Offered:
Listed in the following order: Program area, degree type (T if terminal Master's), number awarded 7/06–6/07. School MA/MS (Master of Arts/Science) (T) 11, Industrial/Organizational MA/MS (Master of Arts/Science) (T) 6, Mental Health Counseling MA/MS (Master of Arts/Science) (T) 2, Experimental MA/MS (Master of Arts/Science) (T) 2.

Student Applications/Admissions:
Student Applications
School MA/MS (Master of Arts/Science)—Applications 2007–2008, 38. Total applicants accepted 2007–2008, 24. Number full-time enrolled (new admits only) 2007–2008, 7. Number part-time enrolled (new admits only) 2007–2008, 3. Total enrolled 2007–2008 full-time, 23, part-time, 10. Openings 2008–2009, 17. The median number of years required for completion of a degree in 2006–2007 were 3. The number of students enrolled full- and part-time who were dismissed or voluntarily withdrew from this program area in 2007–2008 were 3. *Industrial/Organizational MA/MS (Master of Arts/Science)*—Applications 2007–2008, 25. Total applicants accepted 2007–2008, 15. Number full-time enrolled (new admits only) 2007–2008, 5. Number part-time enrolled (new admits only) 2007–2008, 5. Total enrolled 2007–2008 full-time, 12, part-time, 12. Openings 2008–2009, 15. The median number of years required for completion of a degree in 2006–2007 were 3. *Mental Health Counseling MA/MS (Master of Arts/Science)*—Applications 2007–2008, 25. Total applicants accepted 2007–2008, 14. Number full-time enrolled (new admits only) 2007–2008, 9. Number part-time enrolled (new admits only) 2007–2008, 5. Total enrolled 2007–2008 full-time, 22, part-time, 10. Openings 2008–2009, 15. The median number of years required for completion of a degree in 2006–2007 were 3. The number of students enrolled full- and part-time who were dismissed or voluntarily withdrew from this program area in 2007–2008 were 2. *Experimental MA/MS (Master of Arts/Science)*—Number full-time enrolled (new admits only) 2007–2008, 8. Total enrolled 2007–2008 full-time, 11, part-time, 1. Openings 2008–2009, 6. The median number of years required for completion of a degree in 2006–2007 were 3.

Admissions Requirements:
Scores: Entries appear in this order: required test or GPA, minimum score (if required), median score of students entering in 2007–2008. Master's Programs: overall undergraduate GPA 3.0. The Chair may grant exceptions to the minimum requrements for admission as a non-matriculated student.
Other Criteria: (importance of criteria rated low, medium, or high): research experience—high, work experience—medium, extracurricular activity—medium, clinically related public service—medium, GPA—high, letters of recommendation—high, interview—low.

Student Characteristics: The following represents characteristics of students in 2007–2008 in all graduate psychology programs in the department: Caucasian/White—full-time 0, part-time 0; Unknown ethnicity—full-time 0, part-time 0.

Financial Information/Assistance:
Tuition for Full-Time Study: *Master's:* State residents: $665 per credit hour; Nonstate residents: $665 per credit hour.

Financial Assistance:
First-Year Students: Fellowships and scholarships available for first year. Average amount paid per academic year: $14,600. Average number of hours worked per week: 20. Tuition remission given: partial.
Advanced Students: Fellowships and scholarships available for advanced students. Average amount paid per academic year: $14,600. Average number of hours worked per week: 20. Tuition remission given: partial.
Additional Information: Of all students currently enrolled full time, 15% benefited from one or more of the listed financial assistance programs.

Internships/Practica: Students specializing in areas that may meet New York State requirements for employment, certification, or licensure are required to take appropriate internship courses. Although there is no guarantee that the student will get accepted by a site, the department fully assists its students by providing instruction and personal guidance.

Housing and Day Care: On-campus housing is available. See the following Web site for more information: http://www.iona.edu. No on-campus day care facilities are available.

Employment of Department Graduates:

Master's Degree Graduates: Of those who graduated in the academic year 2006–2007, the following categories and numbers represent the postgraduate activities and employment of master's degree graduates: Enrolled in a postdoctoral residency/fellowship (n/a), employed in independent practice (n/a), total from the above (master's) (0).

Doctoral Degree Graduates: Of those who graduated in the academic year 2006–2007, the following categories and numbers represent the postgraduate activities and employment of doctoral degree graduates: Enrolled in a psychology doctoral program (n/a), total from the above (doctoral) (0).

Additional Information:

Orientation, Objectives, and Emphasis of Department: The MA in Psychology degree, with areas of specialization in Experimental Psychology, School Psychology, Industrial/Organizational Psychology, and Applied Mental Health Counseling, has been designed for persons who are considering a career in psychology or who are en route to doctoral study in psychology, or are already employed in the field. The program provides a balance of theoretical, methodological, and practical expertise, as well as extensive training in written and oral expression. It is designed to provide pertinent new experiences, to enhance knowledge in substantive areas, and to facilitate maximum development of essential professional competencies and attitudes. The masters program in Psychology has several goals. Students gain an understanding of the scientific method and training in how to frame, test, and evaluate hypotheses; an appreciation of how human problems can be resolved through the application of psychological knowledge, scientific skills, and problem-solving strategies; expertise in utilizing the scientific database of psychology to advance the welfare of their fellow citizens; an opportunity to address quality of life issues and complex social problems with techniques of cooperation, social facilitation, listening, and self-improvement.

Personal Behavior Statement: Students are informed of how we expect graduate students to act and are asked to sign a document agreeing to uphold appropriate, ethical standards of behavior.

Special Facilities or Resources: The Department contains 2,000 square feet of research space and supports research projects in specialties of psychology including social, perception, developmental, learning, treatment, and cognition. Extensive computer and software capabilities are available.

Application Information:

Send to Office of Graduate Admissions, School of Arts and Sciences. Students are admitted in the Fall. Programs have rolling admissions. *Fee:* $50.

Long Island University

Department of Psychology
C. W. Post
720 Northern Boulevard
Brookville, NY 11548
Telephone: (516) 299-2377
Fax: (516) 299-3105
E-mail: *gerald.lachter@liu.edu*
Web: *http://www.cwpost.liu.edu/cwis/cwp/clas/psych/*

Department Information:

1954. Chairperson: Gerald D. Lachter. Number of faculty: total—full-time 21, part-time 5; women—full-time 8, part-time 4; total—minority—full-time 1.

Programs and Degrees Offered:

Listed in the following order: Program area, degree type (T if terminal Master's), number awarded 7/06–6/07. Experimental MA/MS (Master of Arts/Science) (T) 2, Clinical PsyD (Doctor of Psychology) 10, Advanced Certificate Applied Behavior Analysis Other 10.

APA Accreditation: Clinical PsyD (Doctor of Psychology).

Student Applications/Admissions:

Student Applications

Experimental MA/MS (Master of Arts/Science)—Applications 2007–2008, 35. Total applicants accepted 2007–2008, 13. Number full-time enrolled (new admits only) 2007–2008, 1. Number part-time enrolled (new admits only) 2007–2008, 0. Openings 2008–2009, 10. The median number of years required for completion of a degree in 2006–2007 were 2. The number of students enrolled full- and part-time who were dismissed or voluntarily withdrew from this program area in 2007–2008 were 0. *Clinical PsyD (Doctor of Psychology)*—Applications 2007–2008, 237. Total applicants accepted 2007–2008, 45. Number full-time enrolled (new admits only) 2007–2008, 15. Total enrolled 2007–2008 full-time, 66. Openings 2008–2009, 16. The median number of years required for completion of a degree in 2006–2007 were 5. *Advanced Certificate Applied Behavior Analysis Other*—Applications 2007–2008, 35. Total applicants accepted 2007–2008, 20. Number part-time enrolled (new admits only) 2007–2008, 21. Total enrolled 2007–2008 part-time, 21. Openings 2008–2009, 20. The median number of years required for completion of a degree in 2006–2007 was 1. The number of students enrolled full- and part-time who were dismissed or voluntarily withdrew from this program area in 2007–2008 were 0.

Admissions Requirements:

Scores: Entries appear in this order: required test or GPA, minimum score (if required), median score of students entering in 2007–2008. Master's Programs: GRE-V 500, 573; GRE-Q 500, 573; overall undergraduate GPA 3.2, 3.33. GRE's are not required for admission to the Advanced Certificate Program Doctoral Programs: GRE-V 550, 580; GRE-Q 550, 650; GRE-Subject (Psychology) 610, 650; overall undergraduate GPA 3.5, 3.80.

Other Criteria: (importance of criteria rated low, medium, or high): GRE/MAT scores—medium, research experience—

high, work experience—high, extracurricular activity—low, clinically related public service—high, GPA—high, letters of recommendation—high, interview—high, statement of goals and objectives—medium, undergraduate major in psychology—medium, specific undergraduate psychology courses taken—medium. For additional information on admission requirements, go to http://www.cwpost.liunet.edu/cwis/cwp/clas/psych/doctoral/.

Student Characteristics: The following represents characteristics of students in 2007–2008 in all graduate psychology programs in the department: Female—full-time 56, part-time 19; Male—full-time 38, part-time 2; African American/Black—full-time 2, part-time 2; Hispanic/Latino(a)—full-time 5, part-time 2; Asian/Pacific Islander—full-time 4, part-time 0; American Indian/Alaska Native—full-time 1, part-time 0; Caucasian/White—full-time 82, part-time 17; Multi-ethnic—full-time 0, part-time 0; students subject to the Americans With Disabilities Act—full-time 5, part-time 0; Unknown ethnicity—full-time 0, part-time 0.

Financial Information/Assistance:

Tuition for Full-Time Study: *Master's:* State residents: $882 per credit hour; Nonstate residents: $882 per credit hour. *Doctoral:* State residents: per academic year $28,800; Nonstate residents: per academic year $28,800. Tuition is subject to change.

Financial Assistance:

First-Year Students: Teaching assistantships available for first year. Tuition remission given: partial. Research assistantships available for first year. Tuition remission given: partial.

Advanced Students: Teaching assistantships available for advanced students. Tuition remission given: partial. Research assistantships available for advanced students. Tuition remission given: partial.

Additional Information: Of all students currently enrolled full time, 75% benefited from one or more of the listed financial assistance programs. Application and information available online at http://www.cwpost.liu.edu.

Internships/Practica: A wide range of internship and practicum placements are available.

Housing and Day Care: On-campus housing is available. See the following Web site for more information: http://www.cwpost.liu.edu/cwis/cwp/stuact/housing/housing.html. No on-campus day care facilities are available.

Employment of Department Graduates:

Master's Degree Graduates: Of those who graduated in the academic year 2006–2007, the following categories and numbers represent the postgraduate activities and employment of master's degree graduates: Enrolled in a psychology doctoral program (1), enrolled in another graduate/professional program (0), enrolled in a postdoctoral residency/fellowship (n/a), employed in independent practice (n/a), total from the above (master's) (1).

Doctoral Degree Graduates: Of those who graduated in the academic year 2006–2007, the following categories and numbers represent the postgraduate activities and employment of doctoral degree graduates: Enrolled in a psychology doctoral program (n/a), employed in a community mental health/counseling center (12), employed in a hospital/medical center (2), total from the above (doctoral) (14).

Additional Information:

Orientation, Objectives, and Emphasis of Department: The Master's degree program gives students a broad background in Experimental Psychology. Faculty interests include Behavior Analysis, Cognition and Perception, and Neuroscience. The program is designed to prepare students for admission to doctoral programs, or to give them the skills necessary to obtain employment. The Clinical Psychology doctoral program is distinctive in three ways. First, the mission of the program is to teach scholar–practitioners to provide clinical psychology services in the public sector. Second, in addition to developing clinical psychologists with the basic knowledge, skills, and values necessary for competent and ethical practice, students receive advanced training in one of three areas of concentration: family violence, developmental disabilities, or serious and persistent mental illness. These concentrations represent an attempt to provide underserved populations with highly trained clinical psychologists motivated and able to offer helpful services. Third, the program offers students a focus on two theoretical orientations: psychodynamic and cognitive–behavioral. Each year students receive supervised training in clinical practice at various area mental health facilities. Students also receive considerable individual attention throughout the educational experience.

Special Facilities or Resources: Laboratories exist for the study of animal and human learning, cognition and perception, and neuroscience. The PsyD program has its own Psychological Services Center that provides mental health services to the community as well as serving as a site for training students.

Application Information:
Send to Graduate Admissions, C. W. Post Campus of Long Island University, Brookville, NY 11548. Application available online. URL of online application: http://www.cwpost.liu.edu/cwis/cwp/admissions/graduate/howtoapplyg.html. Students are admitted in the Fall. Programs have rolling admissions. Fall deadlines — February 1 for PsyD; June 1 for MA; August 1 for Advanced Certificate Program. *Fee:* $30.

Long Island University

Psychology/Clinical Psychology
Richard L. Conolly College
1 University Plaza
Brooklyn, NY 11201
Telephone: (718) 488-1164
Fax: (718) 488-1179
E-mail: *nicholas.papouchis@liu.edu*

Department Information:

1967. Director, PhD Program in Clinical Psychology: Nicholas Papouchis. Number of faculty: total—full-time 16, part-time 6; women—full-time 5, part-time 3; total—minority—full-time 6, part-time 2; women minority—full-time 2, part-time 2; faculty subject to the Americans With Disabilities Act 1.

Programs and Degrees Offered:

Listed in the following order: Program area, degree type (T if terminal Master's), number awarded 7/06–6/07. Clinical PhD

(Doctor of Philosophy) 8, General MA/MS (Master of Arts/Science) (T) 8.

APA Accreditation: Clinical PhD (Doctor of Philosophy).

Student Applications/Admissions:

Student Applications

Clinical PhD (Doctor of Philosophy)—Applications 2007–2008, 210. Total applicants accepted 2007–2008, 28. Number full-time enrolled (new admits only) 2007–2008, 16. Number part-time enrolled (new admits only) 2007–2008, 0. Total enrolled 2007–2008 full-time, 106, part-time, 14. Openings 2008–2009, 17. The median number of years required for completion of a degree in 2006–2007 were 6. The number of students enrolled full- and part-time who were dismissed or voluntarily withdrew from this program area in 2007–2008 were 2. *General MA/MS (Master of Arts/Science)*—Applications 2007–2008, 15. Total applicants accepted 2007–2008, 9. Number full-time enrolled (new admits only) 2007–2008, 0. Number part-time enrolled (new admits only) 2007–2008, 9. Total enrolled 2007–2008 full-time, 10, part-time, 32. Openings 2008–2009, 20. The median number of years required for completion of a degree in 2006–2007 were 4. The number of students enrolled full- and part-time who were dismissed or voluntarily withdrew from this program area in 2007–2008 were 0.

Admissions Requirements:

Scores: Entries appear in this order: required test or GPA, minimum score (if required), median score of students entering in 2007–2008. Master's Programs: overall undergraduate GPA 2.75, 3.0; psychology GPA 3.0, 3.2. Doctoral Programs: GRE-V 550, 650; GRE-Q 550, 650; GRE-Subject (Psychology) 600, 625; overall undergraduate GPA 3.2, 3.6; Doctoral program GRE-Analytic 4.5, 5.0.

Other Criteria: (importance of criteria rated low, medium, or high): GRE/MAT scores—high, research experience—medium, work experience—medium, extracurricular activity—low, clinically related public service—medium, GPA—high, letters of recommendation—high, interview—high, statement of goals and objectives—medium, undergraduate major in psychology—low, specific undergraduate psychology courses taken—low. For additional information on admission requirements, go to http://www.liu.edu.

Student Characteristics: The following represents characteristics of students in 2007–2008 in all graduate psychology programs in the department: Female—full-time 88, part-time 34; Male—full-time 28, part-time 12; African American/Black—full-time 11, part-time 20; Hispanic/Latino(a)—full-time 15, part-time 6; Asian/Pacific Islander—full-time 4, part-time 0; American Indian/Alaska Native—full-time 1, part-time 0; Caucasian/White—full-time 85, part-time 18; Multi-ethnic—part-time 2; students subject to the Americans With Disabilities Act—full-time 0, part-time 0; Unknown ethnicity—full-time 0, part-time 0; International students who hold an F-1 or J-1 Visa—full-time 2, part-time 0.

Financial Information/Assistance:

Tuition for Full-Time Study: *Master's*: State residents: $835 per credit hour; Nonstate residents: $835 per credit hour. *Doctoral:* State residents: per academic year $34,126, $1,091 per credit hour; Nonstate residents: per academic year $34,126, $1,091 per credit hour. Tuition is subject to change. See the following Web site for updates and changes in tuition costs: http://www.liu.edu click on Brooklyn Campus.

Financial Assistance:

First-Year Students: Research assistantships available for first year. Average number of hours worked per week: 10. Apply by April. Tuition remission given: partial. Fellowships and scholarships available for first year. Average amount paid per academic year: $4,000. Average number of hours worked per week: 10. Apply by April 15. Tuition remission given: full.

Advanced Students: Teaching assistantships available for advanced students. Average amount paid per academic year: $4,800. Average number of hours worked per week: 10. Apply by April 15. Tuition remission given: partial. Research assistantships available for advanced students. Average amount paid per academic year: $1,400. Average number of hours worked per week: 10. Apply by April 15. Tuition remission given: partial. Fellowships and scholarships available for advanced students. Average amount paid per academic year: $4,000. Average number of hours worked per week: 10. Apply by April 15. Tuition remission given: full.

Additional Information: Of all students currently enrolled full time, 100% benefited from one or more of the listed financial assistance programs.

Internships/Practica: Doctoral Degree (PhD clinical): For those doctoral students for whom a professional internship was required in this program prior to graduation, (19) students applied for an internship in 2006–2007, with (19) students obtaining an internship. Of those students who obtained an internship, (19) were paid internships. Of those students who obtained an internship, (18) students placed in APA/CPA-accredited internships, (1) student placed in internships not APA/CPA-accredited, but listed with the Association of Psychology Postdoctoral and Internship Centers (APPIC), (0) students placed in internships conforming to guidelines of the Council of Directors of School Psychology Programs (CDSPP), (0) students placed in internships that were not APA/CPA-accredited, APPIC or CDSPP listed. Students in the master's program have a variety of practica available to them. Doctoral practicum settings and internships in the New York City Metropolitan area are among the best in the country and offer training with a wide range of clinical patients and a number of specializations. Among these are child training, family training, neuropsychology, and forensic training. Students in the PhD program regularly train in the best of these externship and practicum settings, and over the 3 years from 2002 to 2005 doctoral students matched 100% with their internship choices. For 2005–2006 the percentage of doctoral students matching was 90%, for 2006–2007 students matched 100%, and for 2007–2008, 95% of the students matched.

Housing and Day Care: On-campus housing is available. See the following Web site for more information: http://www.liu.edu Brooklyn Campus. On-campus day care facilities are available. See the following Web site for more information: http://www.liu.edu Brooklyn Campus.

Employment of Department Graduates:

Master's Degree Graduates: Of those who graduated in the academic year 2006–2007, the following categories and numbers

represent the postgraduate activities and employment of master's degree graduates: Enrolled in a psychology doctoral program (2), enrolled in a postdoctoral residency/fellowship (n/a), employed in independent practice (n/a), employed in a professional position in a school system (3), employed in a community mental health/counseling center (1), employed in a hospital/medical center (2), total from the above (master's) (8).

Doctoral Degree Graduates: Of those who graduated in the academic year 2006–2007, the following categories and numbers represent the postgraduate activities and employment of doctoral degree graduates: Enrolled in a psychology doctoral program (n/a), employed in an academic position at a university (1), employed in a professional position in a school system (1), employed in government agency (1), employed in a community mental health/counseling center (2), employed in a hospital/medical center (3), total from the above (doctoral) (8).

Additional Information:

Orientation, Objectives, and Emphasis of Department: The PhD and master's programs are housed in an urban institution with a multicultural undergraduate student body. This diversity enriches the students' appreciation of the complexity of the clinical and theoretical issues relevant to work in psychology. The theoretical orientation of the clinical training sequence reflects the spectrum of psychodynamic approaches to treatment and familiarizes students with cognitive–behavioral and family systems approaches as well. Clinical students are exposed, in a graded series of practicum experiences, to both short-term and longer term approaches to psychotherapy with the New York area's culturally diverse clinical populations. Students are also trained in a range of psychological assessment procedures including cognitive, projective, and neuropsychological testing. The program also seeks to train clinical psychologists who are competent in research and carefully grounded in the science of psychology. To this end doctoral students receive extensive training in research design and statistics early in their coursework and complete a 2nd-year research project preparatory to beginning their dissertation. The final goal and emphasis of the department and the PhD program is to enable students to develop a broad base of knowledge in clinical psychology. Doctoral students are provided with opportunities for clinical training with adults, children, and adolescents; training in family therapy, group therapy, and research; and training in a range of topics relevant to psychology.

Special Facilities or Resources: The Department of Psychology has the following facilities and resources: An on-site Psychological Services Center where clinical students' clinical work is carefully supervised by the doctoral faculty; an ongoing psychotherapy research group; research labs for the study of unconscious cognitive processes and personality and mood/anxiety disorders; training in child and adolescent clinical work at a number of New York area clinical training facilities; opportunity for specialized electives in neuropsychology; free access to computer training and computer facilities; full-tuition, minority research fellowships for selected minority doctoral candidates. Finally, students in the PhD program have the spectrum of New York City's clinical and educational facilities available for them to be trained in. The PhD program has also sponsored the development of the Center for Studies in Ethnicity and Human Development under the leadership of Dr. Carol Magai. This center is devoted to research with diverse ethnic groups and minorities.

Application Information:

Send to Admissions Office, Long Island University, Brooklyn Campus, 1 University Plaza, Brooklyn, NY 11201. Application available online. URL of online application: http://www.liu.edu, click on the Brooklyn Campus Web site. Students are admitted in the Fall, application deadline January 15. For MA program, deadline is 1 month before the beginning of the semester. *Fee:* $30.

Marist College

Department of Psychology
Poughkeepsie, NY 12601
Telephone: (845) 575-3000
Fax: (845) 575-3965
E-mail: *james.regan@marist.edu*
Web: *http://www.marist.edu/graduate*

Department Information:

1972. Graduate Program Director: James Regan PhD. Number of faculty: total—full-time 16, part-time 10; women—full-time 6, part-time 8; total—minority—full-time 4, part-time 3; women minority—full-time 2, part-time 3; faculty subject to the Americans With Disabilities Act 4.

Programs and Degrees Offered:

Listed in the following order: Program area, degree type (T if terminal Master's), number awarded 7/06–6/07. General MA/MS (Master of Arts/Science) (T) 12, School MA/MS (Master of Arts/Science) (T) 22, Mental Health Counseling MA/MS (Master of Arts/Science) 15.

Student Applications/Admissions:

Student Applications

General MA/MS (Master of Arts/Science)—Applications 2007–2008, 40. Total applicants accepted 2007–2008, 10. Number full-time enrolled (new admits only) 2007–2008, 10. Number part-time enrolled (new admits only) 2007–2008, 0. Openings 2008–2009, 10. The median number of years required for completion of a degree in 2006–2007 were 2. The number of students enrolled full- and part-time who were dismissed or voluntarily withdrew from this program area in 2007–2008 were 2. *School MA/MS (Master of Arts/Science)*—Applications 2007–2008, 96. Total applicants accepted 2007–2008, 77. Number full-time enrolled (new admits only) 2007–2008, 11. Number part-time enrolled (new admits only) 2007–2008, 5. Total enrolled 2007–2008 full-time, 26, part-time, 25. Openings 2008–2009, 30. The median number of years required for completion of a degree in 2006–2007 were 3. The number of students enrolled full- and part-time who were dismissed or voluntarily withdrew from this program area in 2007–2008 were 2. *Mental Health Counseling MA/MS (Master of Arts/Science)*—Applications 2007–2008, 30. Total applicants accepted 2007–2008, 18. Number full-time enrolled (new admits only) 2007–2008, 15. Number part-time enrolled (new admits only) 2007–2008, 3. Total enrolled 2007–2008 full-time, 50, part-time, 15. Openings 2008–2009, 18. The median number of years required for completion of a degree in 2006–2007 were 2. The number of students enrolled full- and part-time who were dismissed or voluntarily withdrew from this program area in 2007–2008 were 2.

Admissions Requirements:

Scores: Entries appear in this order: required test or GPA, minimum score (if required), median score of students entering in 2007–2008. Master's Programs: GRE-V no minimum stated; GRE-Q no minimum stated; overall undergraduate GPA 3.00, 3.30.

Other Criteria: (importance of criteria rated low, medium, or high): GRE/MAT scores—medium, research experience—medium, work experience—medium, extracurricular activity—low, clinically related public service—medium, GPA—high, letters of recommendation—medium, interview—medium, statement of goals and objectives—medium.

Student Characteristics: The following represents characteristics of students in 2007–2008 in all graduate psychology programs in the department: Female—full-time 83, part-time 33; Male—full-time 13, part-time 7; African American/Black—full-time 5, part-time 4; Hispanic/Latino(a)—full-time 4, part-time 3; Asian/Pacific Islander—full-time 1, part-time 1; American Indian/Alaska Native—full-time 0, part-time 0; Caucasian/White—full-time 80, part-time 32; Multi-ethnic—full-time 3, part-time 0; students subject to the Americans With Disabilities Act—full-time 1, part-time 2; Unknown ethnicity—full-time 3, part-time 0.

Financial Information/Assistance:

Tuition for Full-Time Study: *Master's:* State residents: per academic year $15,600, $650 per credit hour; Nonstate residents: per academic year $15,600, $650 per credit hour. Tuition is subject to change. See the following Web site for updates and changes in tuition costs: http://www.marist.edu/graduate.

Financial Assistance:

First-Year Students: Research assistantships available for first year. Average amount paid per academic year: $4,500. Average number of hours worked per week: 10. Apply by August 1. Tuition remission given: partial.

Advanced Students: Research assistantships available for advanced students. Average amount paid per academic year: $4,500. Average number of hours worked per week: 10. Apply by August 1. Tuition remission given: partial.

Additional Information: Of all students currently enrolled full time, 80% benefited from one or more of the listed financial assistance programs. Application and information available online at http://www.marist.edu.

Internships/Practica: Master's Degree (MA/MS General): An internship experience such as a final research project or "capstone" experience is required of graduates. The Mid-Hudson area has many public and private agencies dealing with mental health, developmental disabilities, criminal justice, and social services. In addition, numerous school districts particpate with the school psychology program. Students choose their own placement site in consultation with faculty supervisor.

Housing and Day Care: No on-campus housing is available. On-campus day care facilities are available.

Employment of Department Graduates:

Master's Degree Graduates: Of those who graduated in the academic year 2006–2007, the following categories and numbers represent the postgraduate activities and employment of master's degree graduates: Enrolled in a psychology doctoral program (10), enrolled in another graduate/professional program (5), enrolled in a postdoctoral residency/fellowship (n/a), employed in independent practice (n/a), employed in an academic position at a 2-year/4-year college (3), employed in other positions at a higher education institution (3), employed in a professional position in a school system (22), employed in business or industry (2), employed in government agency (2), employed in a community mental health/counseling center (8), employed in a hospital/medical center (2), still seeking employment (2), total from the above (master's) (59).

Doctoral Degree Graduates: Of those who graduated in the academic year 2006–2007, the following categories and numbers represent the postgraduate activities and employment of doctoral degree graduates: Enrolled in a psychology doctoral program (n/a), total from the above (doctoral) (0).

Additional Information:

Orientation, Objectives, and Emphasis of Department: The Master of Arts programs focuses on either mental health counseling or school psychology. The program goals include providing students with the relevant theory, skills, and practical experience that will enable them to perform competently in assessing individual differences in counseling and in planning and implementing effective individual, group, and system-level interventions. Students interested in working in community settings will find a variety of opportunities for hands-on experience. The mental health counseling program fulfills the academic component for students who want to be licensed in New York State as Mental Health Counselors and the school psychology program leads to New York certification as a school psychologist.

Special Facilities or Resources: Interested students can assist in research at facilities such as the Nathan Kline Research Institute, The Center for Advanced Brain Imaging, The Marist Institute for Community Research, Hudson River Psychiatric Center, Dutchess Country Department of Mental Hygiene and Public Health, and the Montrose and Castlepoint Veterans Hospitals.

Information for Students With Physical Disabilities: See the following Web site for more information: http://www.Marist.edu.

Application Information:

Send to Director of Graduate Admissions, Marist College, Poughkeepsie, NY 12601. Application available online. URL of online application: http://www.marist.edu/graduate. Students are admitted in the Fall, application deadline July 1; Spring, application deadline December 1; Summer, application deadline April 15. Students considered after deadlines as space allows. *Fee:* $50.

New York University

Department of Applied Psychology
The Steinhardt School of Education
239 Greene Street, Room 400 and Room 500
New York, NY 10003
Telephone: (212) 998-5555
Fax: (212) 995-3654
E-mail: *bfb3@nyu.edu*
Web: *http://www.steinhardt.nyu.edu/appsych*

Department Information:

1990. Chairperson: Dr. Carola Suárez-Orozco. Number of faculty: total—full-time 30, part-time 33; women—full-time 22, part-time

21; women minority—full-time 6, part-time 7; faculty subject to the Americans With Disabilities Act 5.

Programs and Degrees Offered:

Listed in the following order: Program area, degree type (T if terminal Master's), number awarded 7/06–6/07. Counseling and Guidance MA/MS (Master of Arts/Science) (T) 75, Counseling PhD (Doctor of Philosophy) 5, Psychological Development PhD (Doctor of Philosophy) 3, Educational Psychology MA/MS (Master of Arts/Science) (T) 28, School Psychologist PhD (Doctor of Philosophy) 2, School PsyD (Doctor of Psychology) 3, Psychology and Social Intervention PhD (Doctor of Philosophy).

APA Accreditation: Counseling PhD (Doctor of Philosophy). School PhD (Doctor of Philosophy). School PsyD (Doctor of Psychology).

Student Applications/Admissions:

Student Applications

Counseling and Guidance MA/MS (Master of Arts/Science)—Applications 2007–2008, 600. Total applicants accepted 2007–2008, 190. Number full-time enrolled (new admits only) 2007–2008, 89. Total enrolled 2007–2008 full-time, 202. Openings 2008–2009, 90. The median number of years required for completion of a degree in 2006–2007 were 2. The number of students enrolled full- and part-time who were dismissed or voluntarily withdrew from this program area in 2007–2008 were 1. *Counseling PhD (Doctor of Philosophy)*—Applications 2007–2008, 175. Total applicants accepted 2007–2008, 3. Number full-time enrolled (new admits only) 2007–2008, 3. Total enrolled 2007–2008 full-time, 22, part-time, 21. Openings 2008–2009, 4. *Psychological Development PhD (Doctor of Philosophy)*—Applications 2007–2008, 58. Total applicants accepted 2007–2008, 3. Number full-time enrolled (new admits only) 2007–2008, 3. Total enrolled 2007–2008 full-time, 5, part-time, 19. Openings 2008–2009, 4. The number of students enrolled full- and part-time who were dismissed or voluntarily withdrew from this program area in 2007–2008 were 0. *Educational Psychology MA/MS (Master of Arts/Science)*—Applications 2007–2008, 130. Total applicants accepted 2007–2008, 101. Number full-time enrolled (new admits only) 2007–2008, 52. Total enrolled 2007–2008 full-time, 39, part-time, 48. Openings 2008–2009, 45. *School Psychologist PhD (Doctor of Philosophy)*—Applications 2007–2008, 68. Total applicants accepted 2007–2008, 4. Number full-time enrolled (new admits only) 2007–2008, 4. Total enrolled 2007–2008 full-time, 24. Openings 2008–2009, 4. The median number of years required for completion of a degree in 2006–2007 were 7. *School PsyD (Doctor of Psychology)*—Applications 2007–2008, 0. Total applicants accepted 2007–2008, 0. Total enrolled 2007–2008 full-time, 16. The median number of years required for completion of a degree in 2006–2007 were 7. *Psychology and Social Intervention PhD (Doctor of Philosophy)*—Number full-time enrolled (new admits only) 2007–2008, 0. Number part-time enrolled (new admits only) 2007–2008, 0. Openings 2008–2009, 4.

Admissions Requirements:

Scores: Entries appear in this order: required test or GPA, minimum score (if required), median score of students entering in 2007–2008. Master's Programs: overall undergraduate GPA no minimum stated, 3.20. Master's programs do not require GRE scores. Doctoral Programs: GRE-V 500, 520; GRE-Q 500, 600; overall undergraduate GPA no minimum stated, 3.20.

Other Criteria: (importance of criteria rated low, medium, or high): GRE/MAT scores—medium, research experience—high, work experience—medium, extracurricular activity—low, clinically related public service—medium, GPA—medium, letters of recommendation—high, interview—high, statement of goals and objectives—high. The above criteria range from "medium" to "high" for admission into the doctoral programs. Masters programs primarily consider GPA, statement of goals and obectives, and letters of recommendation; interviews sometimes required for master's applicants. For additional information on admission requirements, go to http://www.nyu.edu/education/graduate.admissions.

Student Characteristics: The following represents characteristics of students in 2007–2008 in all graduate psychology programs in the department: Female—full-time 237, part-time 68; Male—full-time 71, part-time 20; African American/Black—full-time 21, part-time 15; Hispanic/Latino(a)—full-time 11, part-time 3; Asian/Pacific Islander—full-time 13, part-time 6; American Indian/Alaska Native—full-time 0, part-time 0; Caucasian/White—full-time 263, part-time 64; Unknown ethnicity—full-time 0, part-time 0.

Financial Information/Assistance:

Financial Assistance:

First-Year Students: Fellowships and scholarships available for first year. Average number of hours worked per week: 20. Apply by March 1.

Advanced Students: Teaching assistantships available for advanced students. Average number of hours worked per week: 20. Apply by March 1. Tuition remission given: full. Research assistantships available for advanced students. Average number of hours worked per week: 20. Tuition remission given: full. Traineeships available for advanced students. Fellowships and scholarships available for advanced students. Apply by March 1.

Additional Information: Of all students currently enrolled full time, 50% benefited from one or more of the listed financial assistance programs. Application and information available online at http://steinhardt.nyu.edu/financial_aid/.

Internships/Practica: Master's Degree (MA/MS Counseling and Guidance): An internship experience such as a final research project or "capstone" experience is required of graduates. Available in the following areas: school and university counseling; counseling in community agencies, hospitals, and business; school psychology; psychological development; measurement and evaluation.

Housing and Day Care: On-campus housing is available. See the following Web site for more information: http://www.nyu.edu/housing/. No on-campus day care facilities are available.

Employment of Department Graduates:

Master's Degree Graduates: Of those who graduated in the academic year 2006–2007, the following categories and numbers represent the postgraduate activities and employment of master's degree graduates: Enrolled in a postdoctoral residency/fellowship (n/a), employed in independent practice (n/a), total from the above (master's) (0).

Doctoral Degree Graduates: Of those who graduated in the academic year 2006–2007, the following categories and numbers represent the postgraduate activities and employment of doctoral degree graduates: Enrolled in a psychology doctoral program (n/a), total from the above (doctoral) (0).

Additional Information:

Orientation, Objectives, and Emphasis of Department: The cornerstone of our department is the marriage of theory and practice driven by the University's commitment to being a private university in the public service. To this end, the department's programs reflect both a concern for excellence in teaching and the opportunity to learn from involvement in community-based data collection. Emphasis and specific core requirements differ somewhat from program to program, but include a solid foundation in the basic psychological disciplines. Departmental faculty have research projects in several areas, and students have the opportunity to participate in community-based data collection. Departmental faculty have ongoing research projects in many areas, including cognition; language; social and emotional development; health and human development; applied measurement and research methods; working people's lives; spirituality; multicultural assessment; group and organizational dynamics; psychopathology and personality; sexual and gender identity; communication and creative expression; trauma and resilience; parenting; immigration.

Special Facilities or Resources: The Infancy Studies Laboratory conducts research in infant temperament, perceptual development, learning and attention, parenting views and child rearing styles. The Measurement Laboratory contains educational and psychological tests and reference books. PC computers are available for data analysis and word processing. The Psychoeducational Center assigns school psychologists-in-training to schools, settlement houses, clinics, and day care centers and is a clearinghouse of scholarly papers resulting from collaborative activities of doctoral students and faculty. The Center for Research on Culture, Development, and Education conducts longitudinal research on the pathways to educational success in early childhood and early adolescence, among New York City families of five ethnic groups. Center for Health, Identity, Behavior, and Prevention Studies (CHIBPS) conducts formative and intervention research on social and psychological factors that contribute to HIV transmission and the synergy between drug use, mental health, and HIV transmission. The Child and Family Policy Center conducts research, offers technical assistance, and works to disseminate state-of-the field knowledge to bring children's healthy development and school success to the forefront of policymaking, program design, and practice. The Arnold and Rosalie Weiss Resource Center in Applied Psychology provides a departmental library to assist students and researchers within the department.

Information for Students With Physical Disabilities: See the following Web site for more information: http://www.nyu.edu/osl/csd/.

Application Information:

Send to Office of Graduate Admissions, The Steinhardt School of Education, New York University, 82 Washington Square East, Floor 3, New York, NY 10003. Application available online. URL of online application: http://www.steinhardt.nyu.edu/graduate_admissions/application. Students are admitted in the Fall, application deadline February 1 (MA); Spring, application deadline December 1 (MA). Fall deadline: doctoral January 15; Educational Psychology Master's has rolling admissions. *Fee:* $50; $60 for international students.

New York University, Graduate School of Arts and Science

Department of Psychology
6 Washington Place, Room 550
New York, NY 10003
Telephone: (212) 998-7900
Fax: (212) 995-4018
E-mail: *s.zoubok@nyu.edu*
Web: *http://www.psych.nyu.edu*

Department Information:

1950. Chairperson: Marisa Carrasco. Number of faculty: total—full-time 32; women—full-time 10; total—minority—full-time 1; women minority—full-time 1.

Programs and Degrees Offered:

Listed in the following order: Program area, degree type (T if terminal Master's), number awarded 7/06–6/07. General Psychology MA/MS (Master of Arts/Science) (T) 40, Industrial/Organizational MA/MS (Master of Arts/Science) (T) 14, Cognition and Perception PhD (Doctor of Philosophy) 5, Social PhD (Doctor of Philosophy) 6.

Student Applications/Admissions:

Student Applications

General Psychology MA/MS (Master of Arts/Science)—Applications 2007–2008, 393. Total applicants accepted 2007–2008, 242. Number part-time enrolled (new admits only) 2007–2008, 74. Total enrolled 2007–2008 part-time, 144. *Industrial/Organizational MA/MS (Master of Arts/Science)*—Applications 2007–2008, 243. Total applicants accepted 2007–2008, 100. Number part-time enrolled (new admits only) 2007–2008, 29. Total enrolled 2007–2008 part-time, 67. *Cognition and Perception PhD (Doctor of Philosophy)*—Applications 2007–2008, 181. Total applicants accepted 2007–2008, 24. Number full-time enrolled (new admits only) 2007–2008, 12. Total enrolled 2007–2008 full-time, 44. *Social PhD (Doctor of Philosophy)*—Applications 2007–2008, 236. Total applicants accepted 2007–2008, 10. Number full-time enrolled (new admits only) 2007–2008, 5. Total enrolled 2007–2008 full-time, 35.

Admissions Requirements:

Scores: Entries appear in this order: required test or GPA, minimum score (if required), median score of students entering in 2007–2008. Master's Programs: GRE-V 530, 550; GRE-Q 530, 630; overall undergraduate GPA 3.0; Masters GRE-Analytical 4.5, 5. The Master's program expects a minimum score of 4.5 on the GRE Analytical Writing test. The median score of enrolled master's students is 5.0. Doctoral Programs: GRE-V no minimum stated; GRE-Q no minimum stated.

Other Criteria: (importance of criteria rated low, medium, or high): GRE/MAT scores—medium, research experience—high, work experience—low, extracurricular activity—low, clinically related public service—low, GPA—medium, letters of recommendation—high, statement of goals and objectives—high. These rankings are for the PhD only. For master's program, letters of recommendation and statement of goals and objectives have high importance; other criteria are low; no interviews are given. GRE/GPA varies by program.

Student Characteristics: The following represents characteristics of students in 2007–2008 in all graduate psychology programs in the department: Female—full-time 51, part-time 156; Male—full-time 32, part-time 55; African American/Black—full-time 4, part-time 12; Hispanic/Latino(a)—full-time 2, part-time 6; Asian/Pacific Islander—full-time 11, part-time 25; American Indian/Alaska Native—full-time 0, part-time 0; Caucasian/White—full-time 55, part-time 107; Multi-ethnic—full-time 4, part-time 5; Unknown ethnicity—full-time 7, part-time 56.

Financial Information/Assistance:

Financial Assistance:

First-Year Students: Teaching assistantships available for first year. Average amount paid per academic year: $22,000. Average number of hours worked per week: 20. Apply by December 18. Tuition remission given: full. Research assistantships available for first year. Average amount paid per academic year: $22,000. Average number of hours worked per week: 20. Apply by December 18. Tuition remission given: full. Traineeships available for first year. Tuition remission given: full. Fellowships and scholarships available for first year. Average amount paid per academic year: $22,000. Apply by December 18. Tuition remission given: full.

Advanced Students: Teaching assistantships available for advanced students. Average amount paid per academic year: $22,000. Average number of hours worked per week: 20. Apply by December 18. Tuition remission given: full. Research assistantships available for advanced students. Average amount paid per academic year: $22,000. Average number of hours worked per week: 20. Apply by December 18. Tuition remission given: full. Traineeships available for advanced students. Tuition remission given: full. Fellowships and scholarships available for advanced students. Average amount paid per academic year: $22,000. Apply by December 18. Tuition remission given: full.

Additional Information: Of all students currently enrolled full time, 100% benefited from one or more of the listed financial assistance programs. Application and information available online at http://www.nyu.edu/gsas/Admissions/ObtainApp.html.

Internships/Practica: Master's students may opt to take Fieldwork, which would enable them to obtain supervised experience in selected agencies, clinics, and industrial and nonprofit organizations relevant to the career or academic objectives of the student.

Housing and Day Care: On-campus housing is available. See the following Web site for more information: http://www.nyu.edu/housing/. No on-campus day care facilities are available.

Employment of Department Graduates:

Master's Degree Graduates: Of those who graduated in the academic year 2006–2007, the following categories and numbers represent the postgraduate activities and employment of master's degree graduates: Enrolled in a postdoctoral residency/fellowship (n/a), employed in independent practice (n/a), total from the above (master's) (0).

Doctoral Degree Graduates: Of those who graduated in the academic year 2006–2007, the following categories and numbers represent the postgraduate activities and employment of doctoral degree graduates: Enrolled in a psychology doctoral program (n/a), total from the above (doctoral) (0).

Additional Information:

Orientation, Objectives, and Emphasis of Department: The doctoral programs all emphasize research. The Cognition Perception program has faculty whose research focuses on memory, emotion, psycholinguistics, categorization, cognitive neuroscience, visual perception, and attention. The Social program trains researchers in theory and methods for understanding individuals and groups in social and organizational contexts. Training is provided in subareas ranging from social cognition to motivation, personality, close relationships, groups, and organizations. A doctoral concentration in Developmental Psychology emphasizes research training cutting across the traditional areas of psychology. Students may minor in quantitative psychology or in any of the above programs. The Master's Program in General Psychology has the flexibility to suit students who wish to explore several areas of psychology to find the area that interests them most, as well as students who wish to shape their course of study to fit special interests and needs, including preparation for admission to a doctoral program. The Master's Program in Industrial/Organizational Psychology is designed to prepare graduates to apply research and principles of human behavior to a variety of organizational settings, such as human resources departments and management consulting firms. The program can also be modified for students who are preparing for admission to doctoral programs in Industrial/Organizational and related fields. Students in the master's programs may opt for either full- or part-time status.

Special Facilities or Resources: The Department of Psychology maintains laboratories, classrooms, project rooms, and a magnetic resonance (MR) neuroimaging facility. Modern laboratories are continually improved through grants from foundations and federal agencies. The Center for Brain Imaging houses a research-dedicated 3 Tesla Seimens MR system for the use of faculty and students interested in research using function brain imaging. The Center includes faculty members from both the Department of Psychology and the Center for Neural Science, as well as individuals whose expertise is in MR physics and statistical methods for analysis. The department maintains several computer classrooms and laboratories, and the University offers technical courses on emerging computational tools. Faculty laboratories are equipped with specialized computer equipment within each of the graduate programs. The department collaborates closely with the Center for Neural Science in maintaining a technical shop.

Application Information:

Send to New York University, Graduate School of Arts and Sciences, Graduate Enrollment Services, P.O. Box 907, New York, NY 10276-0907. Application available online. URL of online application: http://www.gsas.nyu.edu/object/grad.admissions.onlineapp. Students are admitted in the Fall, Spring, and Summer. PhD students admitted only in the Fall (application deadline December 18). Master's in General Psychology: Fall deadline June 1; Spring deadline November 1; Summer deadline April 1. Master's in Industrial/Organizational Psychology: Fall deadline March 1; Spring deadline October 1; Summer deadline March 1. *Fee:* $75. The Graduate School of Arts and Sciences does not waive application fees.

Pace University
Department of Psychology
Dyson College of Arts and Sciences
One Pace Plaza
New York, NY 10038
Telephone: (212) 346-1506
Fax: (212) 346-1618
E-mail: *HKrauss@pace.edu*
Web: *http://www.pace.edu/dyson/psychology*

Department Information:

1961. Chairperson: Herbert H. Krauss. Number of faculty: total—full-time 12, part-time 12; women—full-time 7, part-time 6; total—minority—full-time 4, part-time 1; women minority—full-time 3.

Programs and Degrees Offered:

Listed in the following order: Program area, degree type (T if terminal Master's), number awarded 7/06–6/07. General MA/MS (Master of Arts/Science) (T) 16, School-Clinical Child Psychology PsyD (Doctor of Psychology) 17, School Psychology EdS/MEd (School Psychology) 20.

APA Accreditation: Combination PsyD (Doctor of Psychology).

Student Applications/Admissions:

Student Applications

General MA/MS (Master of Arts/Science)—Applications 2007–2008, 100. Total applicants accepted 2007–2008, 72. Openings 2008–2009, 25. The median number of years required for completion of a degree in 2006–2007 were 2. The number of students enrolled full- and part-time who were dismissed or voluntarily withdrew from this program area in 2007–2008 were 1. *School-Clinical Child Psychology PsyD (Doctor of Psychology)*—Applications 2007–2008, 291. Total applicants accepted 2007–2008, 69. Number full-time enrolled (new admits only) 2007–2008, 27. Number part-time enrolled (new admits only) 2007–2008, 0. Total enrolled 2007–2008 full-time, 121, part-time, 10. Openings 2008–2009, 20. The median number of years required for completion of a degree in 2006–2007 were 7. The number of students enrolled full- and part-time who were dismissed or voluntarily withdrew from this program area in 2007–2008 were 0. *School Psychology EdS/MEd (School Psychology)*—Applications 2007–2008, 8. Total applicants accepted 2007–2008, 3. Total enrolled 2007–2008 full-time, 6. Openings 2008–2009, 5. The median number of years required for completion of a degree in 2006–2007 were 3. The number of students enrolled full- and part-time who were dismissed or voluntarily withdrew from this program area in 2007–2008 were 0.

Admissions Requirements:

Scores: Entries appear in this order: required test or GPA, minimum score (if required), median score of students entering in 2007–2008. Master's Programs: GRE-V no minimum stated, 520; GRE-Q no minimum stated, 520; overall undergraduate GPA no minimum stated; last 2 years GPA no minimum stated; psychology GPA no minimum stated. The admissions indices for the MA and MSEd programs vary somewhat. The figures cited above are approximations based on admissions data from the past several years. Doctoral Programs: GRE-V 500, 640; GRE-Q 500, 640; GRE-Subject (Psychology) 500, 640; overall undergraduate GPA no minimum stated, 3.60. The figures provided are approximations based on admissions data from the past several years.

Other Criteria: (importance of criteria rated low, medium, or high): GRE/MAT scores—high, research experience—medium, work experience—medium, extracurricular activity—low, clinically related public service—medium, GPA—high, letters of recommendation—high, interview—high, statement of goals and objectives—high, undergraduate major in psychology—medium, specific undergraduate psychology courses taken—low. These criteria are used for the MSEd and PsyD programs only. For additional information on admission requirements, go to http://www.pace.edu.

Student Characteristics: The following represents characteristics of students in 2007–2008 in all graduate psychology programs in the department: Female—full-time 127, part-time 30; Male—full-time 16, part-time 5; African American/Black—full-time 6, part-time 2; Hispanic/Latino(a)—full-time 20, part-time 5; Asian/Pacific Islander—full-time 10, part-time 2; American Indian/Alaska Native—full-time 0, part-time 0; Caucasian/White—full-time 94, part-time 22; Multi-ethnic—full-time 2, part-time 2; students subject to the Americans With Disabilities Act—full-time 0, part-time 0; Unknown ethnicity—full-time 11, part-time 2.

Financial Information/Assistance:

Financial Assistance:

First-Year Students: Research assistantships available for first year. Average amount paid per academic year: $2,500. Average number of hours worked per week: 10. Apply by February 1. Tuition remission given: partial. Fellowships and scholarships available for first year. Average amount paid per academic year: $5,000. Apply by February 1.

Advanced Students: Teaching assistantships available for advanced students. Apply by February 1. Research assistantships available for advanced students. Average amount paid per academic year: $2,500. Average number of hours worked per week: 10. Apply by February 1. Tuition remission given: partial. Fellowships and scholarships available for advanced students. Average amount paid per academic year: $5,000. Apply by February 1.

Additional Information: Of all students currently enrolled full time, 50% benefited from one or more of the listed financial assistance programs. Application and information available online at http://www.pace.edu.

Internships/Practica: Doctoral Degree (PsyD School-Clinical Child Psychology): For those doctoral students for whom a professional internship was required in this program prior to graduation, (25) students applied for an internship in 2006–2007, with (25) students obtaining an internship. Of those students who obtained an internship, (24) were paid internships. Of those students who obtained an internship, (15) students placed in APA/CPA accredited internships, (5) students placed in internships not APA/CPA-accredited, but listed with the Association of Psychology Postdoctoral and Internship Centers (APPIC), (5) students placed in internships conforming to guidelines of the Council of Directors of School Psychology Programs (CDSPP), (0) students placed in internships that were not APA/CPA-accredited, APPIC or CDSPP listed. Most school psychology and bilingual school psychology internships occur in the New York metropolitan region, including Long Island, Westchester County, and school districts throughout northern and central New Jersey. Doctoral internships are typically secured through the APPIC system. Doctoral students typically secure internships in the New York metropolitan region. For additional information on education and training outcomes for our programs, see the following Web site: http://www.pace.edu/PsyD.

Housing and Day Care: On-campus housing is available. There is some on-campus housing available. No on-campus day care facilities are available.

Employment of Department Graduates:

Master's Degree Graduates: Of those who graduated in the academic year 2006–2007, the following categories and numbers represent the postgraduate activities and employment of master's degree graduates: Enrolled in a postdoctoral residency/fellowship (n/a), employed in independent practice (n/a), total from the above (master's) (0).

Doctoral Degree Graduates: Of those who graduated in the academic year 2006–2007, the following categories and numbers represent the postgraduate activities and employment of doctoral degree graduates: Enrolled in a psychology doctoral program (n/a), enrolled in a postdoctoral residency/fellowship (2), employed in an academic position at a 2-year/4-year college (0), employed in other positions at a higher education institution (0), employed in a professional position in a school system (8), employed in a community mental health/counseling center (5), employed in a hospital/medical center (3), total from the above (doctoral) (18).

Additional Information:

Orientation, Objectives, and Emphasis of Department: The PsyD program in School/Clinical Child Psychology at Pace University is a professional practice training program that is dedicated to the training model of school/clinical child psychologists as practitioner–scholars. The focus is on developing individuals whose theoretical and research knowledge, and professional skills enable them to deliver a broad array of direct and indirect psychological services to infants, children, adolescents, and families, and the personnel, organizations, and institutions that serve them. The purpose of the program is to train school/clinical child psychology practitioners to possess broad knowledge about general psychological theoretical foundations, as well as more specific knowledge pertaining to the scientific foundations of psychological practice and professional School/Clinical Child Psychology practice competencies. School psychologists in training receive instruction and supervision related to following ethical guidelines and being sensitive to diversity and multicultural issues. The program coordinates placement in University-based and field-based supervised training experiences, which are carefully integrated with theoretical coursework and a seminar, enabling practitioners in training to compare key aspects of professional functioning across a wide variety of settings. There are 16 specific training goals of the School/Clinical Child Psychology program. The goals include the following: 1. Psychoeducational assessment related to school difficulties and learning disorders. 2. Psychological assessment related to personality and mental disorders. 3. Delivery of psychological interventions aimed at ameliorating adjustment and personal difficulties experienced by children, adolescents, and families. 4. Delivery of psychoeducational interventions aimed at ameliorating learning difficulties experienced by children, adolescents, and families. 5. Providing psychological services with an awareness of and sensitivity to ethnic and cultural diversity. 6. Development and/or implementation of programmatic/preventive interventions. 7. Development and/or implementation of a broad range of consultation services. 8. Enlisting the aid of community agencies to secure services or prevent circumstances contributing to unsatisfactory adjustment or behavior problems. 9. Initiating and/or directing group interventions. 10. Initiating and/or directing family interventions. 11. Conducting in-service training sessions for parents and/or school personnel. 12. Coordinating interdisciplinary assessment and intervention strategies. 13. Providing psychotherapy to children, adolescents, and families. 14. Providing diagnoses related to mental disorders. 15. Carrying out applied research. 16. Supervising the provision of direct psychological services.

Special Facilities or Resources: The Psychology Department maintains the McShane Center for Psychological Services. This on-site training facility provides practicum training for students in the MS Ed, MSEd Bilingual, and PsyD programs. For example, training opportunties include biofeedback, interviewing, parent–infant observations, psychodiagnostics, and psychotherapy.

Information for Students With Physical Disabilities: See the following Web site for more information: http://www.pace.edu.

Application Information:

Send to Graduate Admissions, Pace University, 1 Pace Plaza, New York, NY 10038. Application available online. URL of online application: http://www.pace.edu. Students are admitted in the Fall, application deadline February 1; Winter, application deadline August 1; Spring, application deadline December 1; Summer, application deadline May 1. February 1 deadline for MSEd and PsyD programs; this is the only application date for these two programs. Fall deadline for MA is August 1, Spring deadline for MA is December 1, and Summer deadline for MA is May 1. *Fee:* $65. Check with graduate admissions for current application fee (212) 346-1531.

Rensselaer Polytechnic Institute

Cognitive Science
110 8th Street, Carnegie Building, Room 305
Troy, NY 12180-3590
Telephone: (518) 276-6473
Fax: (518) 276-8268
E-mail: *osgane@rpi.edu*
Web: *http://www.cogsci.rpi.edu*

Department Information:

2000. Chairperson: Selmer Bringsjord. Number of faculty: total—full-time 21, part-time 5; women—full-time 2; total—minority—full-time 2; women minority—full-time 1.

Programs and Degrees Offered:

Listed in the following order: Program area, degree type (T if terminal Master's), number awarded 7/06–6/07. Cognitive Science PhD (Doctor of Philosophy).

Student Applications/Admissions:

Student Applications

Cognitive Science PhD (Doctor of Philosophy)—Applications 2007–2008, 26. Total applicants accepted 2007–2008, 4. Number full-time enrolled (new admits only) 2007–2008, 3. Total enrolled 2007–2008 full-time, 16. Openings 2008–2009, 4.

Admissions Requirements:

Scores: Entries appear in this order: required test or GPA, minimum score (if required), median score of students entering in 2007–2008. Doctoral Programs: GRE-V 600, 620; GRE-Q 600, 780; Doctoral program GRE-Analytic 4, 4.5.

Other Criteria: (importance of criteria rated low, medium, or high): GRE/MAT scores—high, research experience—high, work experience—low, extracurricular activity—low, GPA—medium, letters of recommendation—high, interview—medium, statement of goals and objectives—high.

Student Characteristics: The following represents characteristics of students in 2007–2008 in all graduate psychology programs in the department: Female—full-time 5, part-time 0; Male—full-time 11, part-time 0; African American/Black—full-time 0, part-time 0; Hispanic/Latino(a)—full-time 1, part-time 0; Asian/Pacific Islander—full-time 3, part-time 0; American Indian/Alaska Native—full-time 0, part-time 0; Caucasian/White—full-time 12, part-time 0; Unknown ethnicity—full-time 0, part-time 0.

Financial Information/Assistance:

Tuition for Full-Time Study: *Doctoral:* State residents: per academic year $36,950, $1,540 per credit hour; Nonstate residents: per academic year $36,950, $1,540 per credit hour.

Financial Assistance:

First-Year Students: Teaching assistantships available for first year. Average amount paid per academic year: $16,000. Average number of hours worked per week: 20. Apply by January 15. Tuition remission given: full. Research assistantships available for first year. Average amount paid per academic year: $16,000. Average number of hours worked per week: 20. Apply by January 15. Tuition remission given: full. Fellowships and scholarships available for first year. Average amount paid per academic year: $20,000. Apply by January 15. Tuition remission given: full.

Advanced Students: No information provided.

Additional Information: Of all students currently enrolled full time, 100% benefited from one or more of the listed financial assistance programs. Application and information available online at http://gradadmissions.rpi.edu/application.

Internships/Practica: No information provided.

Housing and Day Care: On-campus housing is available. On-campus day care facilities are available.

Employment of Department Graduates:

Master's Degree Graduates: Of those who graduated in the academic year 2006–2007, the following categories and numbers represent the postgraduate activities and employment of master's degree graduates: Enrolled in a postdoctoral residency/fellowship (n/a), employed in independent practice (n/a), total from the above (master's) (0).

Doctoral Degree Graduates: Of those who graduated in the academic year 2006–2007, the following categories and numbers represent the postgraduate activities and employment of doctoral degree graduates: Enrolled in a psychology doctoral program (n/a), total from the above (doctoral) (0).

Additional Information:

Orientation, Objectives, and Emphasis of Department: The department is committed to the concept of integrated cognitive systems. Specifically, research and teaching falls into areas that together cover low- to high-level cognition, whether in minds or machines: reasoning (human and machine); computational cognitive modeling; cognitive engineering; perception and action.

Special Facilities or Resources: Modern research facilities, including the CogWorks Laboratory, Interactive and Distance Education Assessment (IDEA) Laboratory, Rensselaer Artificial Intelligence and Reasoning Laboratory (RAIR Lab), Perception and Action Lab (PandA Lab), Human-Level Intelligence Laboratory, the Cogntiive Architecture Laboratory (CogArch Lab), and dedicated space in the Institute's new Social and Behavioral Research Laboratory provide a new expression of the Department's interests in cognitive science that integrates the diverse research activities of the faculty in the Department.

Information for Students With Physical Disabilities: See the following Web site for more information: http://www.rpi.edu/dept/student-life/www/.

Application Information:

Send to Admissions, Rensselaer Polytechnic Institute, Troy, NY 12180. Application available online. URL of online application: https://www.apply.embark.com/grad/rpi/66/. Students are admitted in the Fall, application deadline January 15. *Fee:* $75.

Roberts Wesleyan College

Social Science Division/Graduate Psychology Program
2301 Westside Drive
Rochester, NY 14624
Telephone: (585) 594-6011
Fax: (585) 594-6124
E-mail: *repass_cheryl@roberts.edu*
Web: *http://www.roberts.edu/gradpsych*

Department Information:

2001. Department Chairperson: Cheryl L. Repass. Number of faculty: total—full-time 8; women—full-time 5.

Programs and Degrees Offered:

Listed in the following order: Program area, degree type (T if terminal Master's), number awarded 7/06–6/07. School Psychology MA/MS (Master of Arts/Science) (T) 17, School Counseling MA/MS (Master of Arts/Science) (T) 7.

Student Applications/Admissions:

Student Applications

School Psychology MA/MS (Master of Arts/Science)—Applications 2007–2008, 46. Total applicants accepted 2007–2008,

26. Number full-time enrolled (new admits only) 2007–2008, 17. Number part-time enrolled (new admits only) 2007–2008, 0. Total enrolled 2007–2008 full-time, 57, part-time, 2. Openings 2008–2009, 20. The median number of years required for completion of a degree in 2006–2007 were 3. The number of students enrolled full- and part-time who were dismissed or voluntarily withdrew from this program area in 2007–2008 were 2. *School Counseling MA/MS (Master of Arts/Science)*—Applications 2007–2008, 27. Total applicants accepted 2007–2008, 16. Number full-time enrolled (new admits only) 2007–2008, 13. Number part-time enrolled (new admits only) 2007–2008, 1. Total enrolled 2007–2008 full-time, 20, part-time, 4. Openings 2008–2009, 15. The median number of years required for completion of a degree in 2006–2007 were 2. The number of students enrolled full- and part-time who were dismissed or voluntarily withdrew from this program area in 2007–2008 were 1.

Admissions Requirements:

Scores: Entries appear in this order: required test or GPA, minimum score (if required), median score of students entering in 2007–2008. Master's Programs: GRE-V None, 480; GRE-Q None, 520; overall undergraduate GPA 3.00, 3.30; last 2 years GPA None, 3.40; psychology GPA none, 3.20.

Other Criteria: (importance of criteria rated low, medium, or high): GRE/MAT scores—medium, work experience—medium, extracurricular activity—low, clinically related public service—low, GPA—high, letters of recommendation—high, interview—high, statement of goals and objectives—high, Personal Statement—high. For additional information on admission requirements, go to http://www.roberts.edu/gradpsych.

Student Characteristics: The following represents characteristics of students in 2007–2008 in all graduate psychology programs in the department: Female—full-time 68, part-time 6; Male—full-time 9, part-time 0; African American/Black—full-time 5, part-time 0; Hispanic/Latino(a)—full-time 1, part-time 0; Asian/Pacific Islander—full-time 0, part-time 0; American Indian/Alaska Native—full-time 0, part-time 0; Caucasian/White—full-time 71, part-time 6; Multi-ethnic—part-time 0; students subject to the Americans With Disabilities Act—full-time 0, part-time 0; Unknown ethnicity—full-time 0, part-time 0.

Financial Information/Assistance:

Tuition for Full-Time Study: *Master's:* State residents: per academic year $15,000, $560 per credit hour. See the following Web site for updates and changes in tuition costs: http://www.roberts.edu/gradpsych.

Financial Assistance:

First-Year Students: No information provided.

Advanced Students: Teaching assistantships available for advanced students. Average amount paid per academic year: $500. Average number of hours worked per week: 8. Apply by none.

Additional Information: Of all students currently enrolled full time, 5% benefited from one or more of the listed financial assistance programs.

Internships/Practica: Master's Degree (MA/MS School Psychology): An internship experience such as a final research project or "capstone" experience is required of graduates. Master's Degree (MA/MS School Counseling): An internship experience such as a final research project or "capstone" experience is required of graduates. Students in School Psychology complete a 1,200-hour internship their 3rd year which is typically paid by the school district in the form of a stipend. Out-of-state internships are also a possiblity. These internships pay any wheres from $28,000 to $37,000 and are also contracted for 1,200 hours. Students in School Counseling secure local unpaid internships for 600 hours.

Housing and Day Care: No on-campus housing is available. No on-campus day care facilities are available.

Employment of Department Graduates:

Master's Degree Graduates: Of those who graduated in the academic year 2006–2007, the following categories and numbers represent the postgraduate activities and employment of master's degree graduates: Enrolled in a psychology doctoral program (1), enrolled in another graduate/professional program (0), enrolled in a postdoctoral residency/fellowship (n/a), employed in independent practice (n/a), employed in an academic position at a university (0), employed in an academic position at a 2-year/4-year college (0), employed in other positions at a higher education institution (0), employed in a professional position in a school system (21), employed in business or industry (0), employed in government agency (1), employed in a community mental health/counseling center (0), employed in a hospital/medical center (0), still seeking employment (0), not seeking employment (1), other employment position (0), total from the above (master's) (24).

Doctoral Degree Graduates: Of those who graduated in the academic year 2006–2007, the following categories and numbers represent the postgraduate activities and employment of doctoral degree graduates: Enrolled in a psychology doctoral program (n/a), total from the above (doctoral) (0).

Additional Information:

Orientation, Objectives, and Emphasis of Department: The Mission of the School Psychology and School Counseling Programs is to prepare students, in a Christian context, for effective, compassionate, professional practice. The programs aim to prepare students for exemplary service and leadership in private and public agencies and educational institutions, utilizing a scientist–practitioner approach, with special attention given to the Christian community, locally, nationally, and internationally.

Personal Behavior Statement: The full text of the statement is included in our application. The application is available online at http://www.roberts.edu/gradpsych or by requesting an application at (585) 594-6011 or (800) 777-4792 (ext. 6011).

Information for Students With Physical Disabilities: Contact the Learning Center at (585) 594-6270 or (800) 777-4792 (ext. 6270).

Application Information:

Send to Division of Social Sciences, Graduate Admissions Office, Roberts Wesleyan College, 2301 Westside Drive, Rochester, NY 14624-1997. Application available online. URL of online application: http://www.roberts.edu/gradpsych. Students are admitted in the Fall, application deadline March 1. After March 1, admissions will be handled on a rolling basis, as space in the program permits. *Fee:* $35. Application fee is waived for online applicants.

Rochester, University of (2007 data)

Department of Clinical and Social Sciences in Psychology
Arts, Sciences, and Engineering
Meliora Hall 355, RC Box 270266
Rochester, NY 14627-0266
Telephone: (585) 273-3264
Fax: (585) 273-1100
E-mail: *loretta.pratt@rochester.edu*
Web: *http://www.psych.rochester.edu/csp/*

Department Information:

1935. Chairperson: Miron Zuckerman. Number of faculty: total—full-time 14, part-time 12; women—full-time 4, part-time 4.

Programs and Degrees Offered:

Listed in the following order: Program area, degree type (T if terminal Master's), number awarded 7/06–6/07. Clinical PhD (Doctor of Philosophy) 2, Developmental PhD (Doctor of Philosophy) 2, Social-Personality PhD (Doctor of Philosophy) 0.

APA Accreditation: Clinical PhD (Doctor of Philosophy).

Student Applications/Admissions:

Student Applications

Clinical PhD (Doctor of Philosophy)—Applications 2007–2008, 115. Total applicants accepted 2007–2008, 3. Number full-time enrolled (new admits only) 2007–2008, 3. Number part-time enrolled (new admits only) 2007–2008, 0. Openings 2008–2009, 4. The median number of years required for completion of a degree in 2006–2007 were 7. The number of students enrolled full- and part-time who were dismissed or voluntarily withdrew from this program area in 2007–2008 were 0. *Developmental PhD (Doctor of Philosophy)*—Applications 2007–2008, 22. Total applicants accepted 2007–2008, 2. Number full-time enrolled (new admits only) 2007–2008, 2. Number part-time enrolled (new admits only) 2007–2008, 0. Openings 2008–2009, 5. The median number of years required for completion of a degree in 2006–2007 were 6. The number of students enrolled full- and part-time who were dismissed or voluntarily withdrew from this program area in 2007–2008 were 2. *Social-Personality PhD (Doctor of Philosophy)*—Applications 2007–2008, 73. Total applicants accepted 2007–2008, 3. Number full-time enrolled (new admits only) 2007–2008, 3. Number part-time enrolled (new admits only) 2007–2008, 0. Openings 2008–2009, 4. The median number of years required for completion of a degree in 2006–2007 were 6. The number of students enrolled full- and part-time who were dismissed or voluntarily withdrew from this program area in 2007–2008 were 0.

Admissions Requirements:

Scores: Entries appear in this order: required test or GPA, minimum score (if required), median score of students entering in 2007–2008. Doctoral Programs: GRE-V no minimum stated; GRE-Q no minimum stated; Doctoral program GRE-Analytic no minimum stated. Please Note: Scores reflected above are only for Clinical program.

Other Criteria: (importance of criteria rated low, medium, or high): GRE/MAT scores—medium, research experience—high, work experience—high, extracurricular activity—medium, clinically related public service—medium, GPA—high, letters of recommendation—high, interview—high, statement of goals and objectives—high.

Student Characteristics: The following represents characteristics of students in 2007–2008 in all graduate psychology programs in the department: Female—full-time 35, part-time 0; Male—full-time 17, part-time 0; African American/Black—full-time 2, part-time 0; Hispanic/Latino(a)—full-time 5, part-time 0; Asian/Pacific Islander—full-time 2, part-time 0; American Indian/Alaska Native—full-time 1, part-time 0; Caucasian/White—full-time 41, part-time 0; Multi-ethnic—full-time 1, part-time 0; students subject to the Americans With Disabilities Act—full-time 0, part-time 0; Unknown ethnicity—full-time 0, part-time 0.

Financial Information/Assistance:

Tuition for Full-Time Study: *Doctoral:* State residents: $1,020 per credit hour; Nonstate residents: $1,020 per credit hour.

Financial Assistance:

First-Year Students: Teaching assistantships available for first year. Average amount paid per academic year: $14,000. Tuition remission given: full. Research assistantships available for first year. Average amount paid per academic year: $14,000. Tuition remission given: full. Fellowships and scholarships available for first year. Average amount paid per academic year: $15,000. Tuition remission given: full.

Advanced Students: Teaching assistantships available for advanced students. Average amount paid per academic year: $13,000. Tuition remission given: full. Research assistantships available for advanced students. Average amount paid per academic year: $13,000. Tuition remission given: full. Fellowships and scholarships available for advanced students. Average amount paid per academic year: $14,000. Tuition remission given: full.

Additional Information: Of all students currently enrolled full time, 64% benefited from one or more of the listed financial assistance programs. Application and information available online at http://www.psych.rochester.edu/graduate/.

Internships/Practica: Some students are supported via teaching and research assistantships as well as part-time assignments at several local agencies including Mt. Hope Family Center, Childrens' Institute, University of Rochester Medical Center, and the University of Rochester Counseling Center. Suitable clinical practica and a 1-year clinical internship ensure continuity of clinical training throughout the student's stay in the program.

Housing and Day Care: On-campus housing is available. See the following Web site for more information: http://www.reslife.rochester.edu/graduate/topics.php. No on-campus day care facilities are available.

Employment of Department Graduates:

Master's Degree Graduates: Of those who graduated in the academic year 2006–2007, the following categories and numbers represent the postgraduate activities and employment of master's degree graduates: Enrolled in a postdoctoral residency/fellowship (n/a), employed in independent practice (n/a), total from the above (master's) (0).

Doctoral Degree Graduates: Of those who graduated in the academic year 2006–2007, the following categories and numbers

represent the postgraduate activities and employment of doctoral degree graduates: Enrolled in a psychology doctoral program (n/a), enrolled in another graduate/professional program (0), enrolled in a postdoctoral residency/fellowship (0), employed in independent practice (0), employed in an academic position at a university (2), employed in an academic position at a 2-year/4-year college (0), employed in other positions at a higher education institution (0), employed in a professional position in a school system (0), employed in business or industry (0), employed in government agency (0), employed in a community mental health/counseling center (1), employed in a hospital/medical center (1), still seeking employment (0), not seeking employment (0), other employment position (0), total from the above (doctoral) (4).

Additional Information:

Orientation, Objectives, and Emphasis of Department: The primary goal of the graduate program in the Department of Clinical and Social Sciences in Psychology is to provide highly qualified applicants a broad range of coursework, research experience, and practical training that will equip them to make independent contributions to psychology. Our department offers PhD training in three areas of psychology: Clinical, Developmental, and Social–Personality. A program in Human Motivation cuts across the clinical and social areas. Two additional research units are affiliated with the department—the Mt. Hope Family Center and the Childrens' Institute. The Mt. Hope Family Center provides opportunities for training and research in developmental psychopathology. The Childrens' Institute provides similar opportunities for work on the detection and prevention of young children's adjustment problems. Graduate training emphasizes research skills. We make no distinction between basic and applied research, recognizing that training in basic research is a prerequisite for applied work, and that applied research often illuminates fundamental psychological processes. To excel in any discipline, students need outstanding facilities, distinguished faculty, and an environment promoting their full integration in the research endeavor. We feel that our Department combines all of these characteristics.

Special Facilities or Resources: The Mt. Hope Family Center offers a unique combination of service, training, and research. The service component focuses on the assessment and treatment of families experiencing severe familial dysfunction and of children at risk of foster care placement and/or emotional difficulties. Treatment programs include (a) a full-time preschool program with psychoeducational treatment for families and a parent–child attachment intervention for children ages 3 to 5 and their caregivers, and (b) an after-school program for at-risk school-aged children. The Childrens' Institute aims to develop, implement, and evaluate programs to maximize adjustment of individuals (particularly young children) to their environments; and apply psychological methods and knowledge to the solution of community problems in mental health. The Institute develops programs to address longstanding mental health problems from a preventive standpoint (a) by analyzing and modifying social environments (such as schools); (b) by training young children in age-appropriate, adaptive social competencies; (c) by identifying ways to reduce stress and training children to cope with it; and (d) developing programs for early identification and prevention of school adjustment problems and enhancing wellness.

Information for Students With Physical Disabilities: See the following Web site for more information: http://www.rochester.edu/ada/.

Application Information:

Send to Maryann Gilbert, Academic Coordinator, Department of Clinical and Social Sciences in Psychology, University of Rochester, Meliora Hall 451, RC Box 270266, Rochester, NY 14627-0266. Application available online. URL of online application: https://www.its-w2ks08.acs.rochester.edu/admgrad/. Students are admitted in the Fall, application deadline December 15. December 15 is the deadline for our Clinical and Developmental programs. January 20 is the application deadline for our Social–Personality program. *Fee:* $0.

Sage Colleges, The

Department of Psychology
45 Ferry Street
Troy, NY 12180
Telephone: (518) 244-2221
Fax: (518) 244-4564
E-mail: *poppej@sage.edu*
Web: *http://www.sage.edu*

Department Information:

Department Chair: Dr. Jean E. Poppei. Number of faculty: total—full-time 11, part-time 9; women—full-time 10, part-time 4; total—minority—full-time 1; women minority—full-time 1.

Programs and Degrees Offered:

Listed in the following order: Program area, degree type (T if terminal Master's), number awarded 7/06–6/07. Community MA/MS (Master of Arts/Science) (T) 10, Counseling and Community Psychology MA/MS (Master of Arts/Science) (T) 19, Certificate in Forensic Mental Health Other 1.

Student Applications/Admissions:

Student Applications

Community MA/MS (Master of Arts/Science)—Applications 2007–2008, 12. Total applicants accepted 2007–2008, 8. Number full-time enrolled (new admits only) 2007–2008, 0. Number part-time enrolled (new admits only) 2007–2008, 7. Openings 2008–2009, 20. The median number of years required for completion of a degree in 2006–2007 were 3. The number of students enrolled full- and part-time who were dismissed or voluntarily withdrew from this program area in 2007–2008 were 1. *Counseling and Community Psychology MA/MS (Master of Arts/Science)*—Applications 2007–2008, 51. Total applicants accepted 2007–2008, 34. Number part-time enrolled (new admits only) 2007–2008, 30. Total enrolled 2007–2008 part-time, 96. Openings 2008–2009, 30. The median number of years required for completion of a degree in 2006–2007 were 4. The number of students enrolled full- and part-time who were dismissed or voluntarily withdrew from this program area in 2007–2008 were 6. *Certificate in Forensic Mental Health Other*—Applications 2007–2008, 7. Total applicants accepted 2007–2008, 7. Number part-time enrolled (new admits only) 2007–2008, 7. Total enrolled 2007–2008 part-time, 24. Openings 2008–2009, 10. The median number of years required for completion of a degree in 2006–2007 were 3. The number of students enrolled full- and part-time who were dismissed or voluntarily withdrew from this program area in 2007–2008 were 1.

Admissions Requirements:

Scores: Entries appear in this order: required test or GPA, minimum score (if required), median score of students entering in 2007–2008. Master's Programs: overall undergraduate GPA no minimum stated. Community Psychology: 2.7 Counseling/Community Psychology: 3.00 Certificate in Forensic Mental Health 3.00

Other Criteria: (importance of criteria rated low, medium, or high): research experience—low, work experience—high, clinically related public service—medium, GPA—high, letters of recommendation—high, interview—high, statement of goals and objectives—high, undergraduate major in psychology—medium, specific undergraduate psychology courses taken—medium. Certificate in Forensic Mental Health: undergraduate degree in social sciences. For additional information on admission requirements, go to http://www.sage.edu/sgs.

Student Characteristics: The following represents characteristics of students in 2007–2008 in all graduate psychology programs in the department: Female—part-time 118; Male—full-time 0, part-time 9; African American/Black—full-time 0, part-time 9; Hispanic/Latino(a)—full-time 0, part-time 4; Asian/Pacific Islander—full-time 0, part-time 0; American Indian/Alaska Native—full-time 0, part-time 1; Caucasian/White—full-time 0, part-time 113; Multi-ethnic—part-time 0; students subject to the Americans With Disabilities Act—part-time 0; Unknown ethnicity—full-time 0, part-time 0.

Financial Information/Assistance:

Tuition for Full-Time Study: *Master's:* State residents: $515 per credit hour; Nonstate residents: $515 per credit hour. Tuition is subject to change.

Financial Assistance:

First-Year Students: Research assistantships available for first year. Average number of hours worked per week: 10. Apply by June 1. Tuition remission given: partial.

Advanced Students: Research assistantships available for advanced students. Average number of hours worked per week: 10. Tuition remission given: partial.

Additional Information: Of all students currently enrolled full time, 25% benefited from one or more of the listed financial assistance programs. Application and information available online at http://www.sage.edu/sgs.

Internships/Practica: Master's Degree (MA/MS Counseling and Community Psychology): An internship experience such as a final research project or "capstone" experience is required of graduates. As part of each degree, all students are required to complete an internship (direct services) and/or externship (not direct services) placement, depending upon the selected area of concentration. Internships comprise 1-year counseling placements in a setting appropriate to the student's interests; externships are one-semester projects in a setting of the student's choice.

Housing and Day Care: On-campus housing is available. See the following Web site for more information: http://www.sage.edu/sgs. No on-campus day care facilities are available.

Employment of Department Graduates:

Master's Degree Graduates: Of those who graduated in the academic year 2006–2007, the following categories and numbers represent the postgraduate activities and employment of master's degree graduates: Enrolled in a psychology doctoral program (0), enrolled in another graduate/professional program (0), enrolled in a postdoctoral residency/fellowship (n/a), employed in independent practice (n/a), employed in an academic position at a university (0), employed in an academic position at a 2-year/4-year college (0), employed in government agency (1), employed in a community mental health/counseling center (6), other employment position (2), do not know (16), total from the above (master's) (25).

Doctoral Degree Graduates: Of those who graduated in the academic year 2006–2007, the following categories and numbers represent the postgraduate activities and employment of doctoral degree graduates: Enrolled in a psychology doctoral program (n/a), total from the above (doctoral) (0).

Additional Information:

Orientation, Objectives, and Emphasis of Department: Our two degrees (MA in Community Psychology, and MA in Counseling/Community Psychology) provide students with the academic and skills training to become practitioners at the master's level. The programs range in credits from 39 to 60, depending on degree and, for Community Psychology, track. The emphasis is on developing and strengthening student skills for application (whether individual or systems level) in the context of strong theoretical foundations. Graduates of MA in Counseling/Community Psychology are eligible to sit for licensure as a mental health counselor in New York State.

Special Facilities or Resources: In addition to the faculty resources one would assume at the master's level, a particular advantage for psychology programs at Sage Graduate School is our prime location in the Capital District area of New York State. The geographic size, population density, and availability of widely varied populations make possible a wide variety of experiences.

Information for Students With Physical Disabilities: See the following Web site for more information: http://www.sage.edu.

Application Information:

Send to Graduate Admissions, The Sage Colleges, 45 Ferry Street, Troy, NY 12180. Application available online. URL of online application: http://www.sage.edu/sgs. Students are admitted in the Fall, application deadline April 1; Spring, application deadline November 1; Summer, application deadline April 1. Community Psychology: rolling admissions; Counseling/Community Psychology: November 1 for Spring, April 1 for Summer and Fall; Forensic Mental Health Certificate: November 1 for Spring; April 1 for Fall. *Fee:* $40. Fee waived for graduates of The Sage Colleges.

Saint Bonaventure University (2007 data)

Department of Counselor Education
St. Bonaventure University
P.O. Box AV
St. Bonaventure, NY 14778
Telephone: (716) 375-2374
Fax: (716) 375-2360
E-mail: *czuck@sbu.edu*
Web: *http://www.schoolofed.sbu.edu/*

Department Information:

1950. Chairperson: Craig Zuckerman. Number of faculty: total—full-time 6, part-time 1; women—full-time 2.

Programs and Degrees Offered:

Listed in the following order: Program area, degree type (T if terminal Master's), number awarded 7/06–6/07. School Counseling Other 40, Agency Counseling Other 10, Advanced Certificate in School Other 15, Advanced Certificate in Agency Other 5.

Student Applications/Admissions:

Student Applications

School Counseling Other—Applications 2007–2008, 60. Total applicants accepted 2007–2008, 45. Number full-time enrolled (new admits only) 2007–2008, 30. Number part-time enrolled (new admits only) 2007–2008, 10. Total enrolled 2007–2008 full-time, 80, part-time, 25. Openings 2008–2009, 40. The median number of years required for completion of a degree in 2006–2007 were 2. The number of students enrolled full- and part-time who were dismissed or voluntarily withdrew from this program area in 2007–2008 were 5. *Agency Counseling Other*—Applications 2007–2008, 15. Total applicants accepted 2007–2008, 13. Number full-time enrolled (new admits only) 2007–2008, 7. Number part-time enrolled (new admits only) 2007–2008, 3. Total enrolled 2007–2008 full-time, 20, part-time, 5. Openings 2008–2009, 15. The median number of years required for completion of a degree in 2006–2007 were 2. The number of students enrolled full- and part-time who were dismissed or voluntarily withdrew from this program area in 2007–2008 were 2. *Advanced Certificate in School Other*—Applications 2007–2008, 10. Total applicants accepted 2007–2008, 10. Number full-time enrolled (new admits only) 2007–2008, 0. Number part-time enrolled (new admits only) 2007–2008, 8. Openings 2008–2009, 15. The median number of years required for completion of a degree in 2006–2007 were 3. The number of students enrolled full- and part-time who were dismissed or voluntarily withdrew from this program area in 2007–2008 were 2. *Advanced Certificate in Agency Other*—Applications 2007–2008, 7. Total applicants accepted 2007–2008, 5. Number full-time enrolled (new admits only) 2007–2008, 0. Number part-time enrolled (new admits only) 2007–2008, 4. Openings 2008–2009, 10. The median number of years required for completion of a degree in 2006–2007 were 3. The number of students enrolled full- and part-time who were dismissed or voluntarily withdrew from this program area in 2007–2008 were 2.

Admissions Requirements:

Scores: Entries appear in this order: required test or GPA, minimum score (if required), median score of students entering in 2007–2008. Master's Programs: MAT no minimum stated; overall undergraduate GPA 3.0. Students may submit either the GRE or MAT

Other Criteria: (importance of criteria rated low, medium, or high): GRE/MAT scores—medium, extracurricular activity—low, GPA—high, letters of recommendation—medium, interview—high, statement of goals and objectives—medium.

Student Characteristics: The following represents characteristics of students in 2007–2008 in all graduate psychology programs in the department: Female—full-time 85, part-time 60; Male—full-time 15, part-time 10; African American/Black—full-time 3, part-time 2; Hispanic/Latino(a)—full-time 2, part-time 1; Asian/Pacific Islander—full-time 0, part-time 0; American Indian/Alaska Native—full-time 1, part-time 1; Caucasian/White—full-time 94, part-time 66; Multi-ethnic—full-time 0, part-time 0; students subject to the Americans With Disabilities Act—full-time 2, part-time 1; Unknown ethnicity—full-time 0, part-time 0.

Financial Information/Assistance:

Tuition for Full-Time Study: *Master's:* State residents: $650 per credit hour; Nonstate residents: $650 per credit hour.

Financial Assistance:

First-Year Students: No information provided.

Advanced Students: No information provided.

Additional Information: Application and information available online at http://www.sbu.edu.

Internships/Practica: Many local opportunities exist for internships in both school counseling programs and at agency counseling sites. We have also started an on-site, outpatient, mental health and academic counseling clinic on the main campus of St. Bonaventure University, which offers practical experiences.

Housing and Day Care: On-campus housing is available. No on-campus day care facilities are available.

Employment of Department Graduates:

Master's Degree Graduates: Of those who graduated in the academic year 2006–2007, the following categories and numbers represent the postgraduate activities and employment of master's degree graduates: Enrolled in a postdoctoral residency/fellowship (n/a), employed in independent practice (n/a), total from the above (master's) (0).

Doctoral Degree Graduates: Of those who graduated in the academic year 2006–2007, the following categories and numbers represent the postgraduate activities and employment of doctoral degree graduates: Enrolled in a psychology doctoral program (n/a), total from the above (doctoral) (0).

Additional Information:

Orientation, Objectives, and Emphasis of Department: The mission of the Department of Counselor Education is to prepare students for the professional practice of counseling in a multicultural and diverse society. Specific program goals are (a) support for the mission of St. Bonaventure University; and (b) adherence to the highest standards of counselor education.

Special Facilities or Resources: St. Bonaventure University's School of Education Outpatient Counseling Clinic opened in

2004 offering academic, behavioral, and mental health services to children, their families, and adults in the community. The clinic serves both the college community and the surrounding underserved communities in four New York counties as well as neighboring communities in Pennsylvania. The clinic offers group and individual counseling.

Application Information:
Send to School of Graduate Studies. Students are admitted in the Fall, application deadline August 1; Spring, application deadline December 1; Summer, application deadline April 1. *Fee:* $30. If applying online, the fee is waived.

St. John's University

Department of Psychology
St. John's College of Arts and Sciences
8000 Utopia Parkway
Jamaica, NY 11439
Telephone: (718) 990-6368
Fax: (718) 990-6705
E-mail: *digiuser@stjohns.edu*
Web: *http://www.new.stjohns.edu*

Department Information:
1958. Chairperson: Raymond DiGiuseppe. Number of faculty: total—full-time 30, part-time 27; women—full-time 12, part-time 15; total—minority—full-time 6, part-time 4; women minority—full-time 4, part-time 3; faculty subject to the Americans With Disabilities Act 1.

Programs and Degrees Offered:
Listed in the following order: Program area, degree type (T if terminal Master's), number awarded 7/06–6/07. Clinical Psychology PhD (Doctor of Philosophy) 15, General-Experimental Psychology MA/MS (Master of Arts/Science) (T) 4, School Psychology MA/MS (Master of Arts/Science) (T) 17, School Psychology PsyD (Doctor of Psychology) 19.

APA Accreditation: Clinical PhD (Doctor of Philosophy).

Student Applications/Admissions:
Student Applications
Clinical Psychology PhD (Doctor of Philosophy)—Applications 2007–2008, 280. Total applicants accepted 2007–2008, 12. Number full-time enrolled (new admits only) 2007–2008, 12. Number part-time enrolled (new admits only) 2007–2008, 0. Openings 2008–2009, 12. The median number of years required for completion of a degree in 2006–2007 were 6. The number of students enrolled full- and part-time who were dismissed or voluntarily withdrew from this program area in 2007–2008 were 2. *General-Experimental Psychology MA/MS (Master of Arts/Science)*—Applications 2007–2008, 15. Total applicants accepted 2007–2008, 5. Number full-time enrolled (new admits only) 2007–2008, 0. Number part-time enrolled (new admits only) 2007–2008, 4. Total enrolled 2007–2008 full-time, 2, part-time, 10. Openings 2008–2009, 12. The median number of years required for completion of a degree in 2006–2007 were 2. The number of students enrolled full- and part-time who were dismissed or voluntarily withdrew from this program area in 2007–2008 were 0. *School Psychology MA/MS (Master of Arts/Science)*—Applications 2007–2008, 37. Total applicants accepted 2007–2008, 16. Number full-time enrolled (new admits only) 2007–2008, 14. Number part-time enrolled (new admits only) 2007–2008, 2. Total enrolled 2007–2008 full-time, 35, part-time, 10. Openings 2008–2009, 16. The median number of years required for completion of a degree in 2006–2007 were 3. The number of students enrolled full- and part-time who were dismissed or voluntarily withdrew from this program area in 2007–2008 were 0. *School Psychology PsyD (Doctor of Psychology)*—Applications 2007–2008, 89. Total applicants accepted 2007–2008, 20. Number full-time enrolled (new admits only) 2007–2008, 15. Number part-time enrolled (new admits only) 2007–2008, 0. Total enrolled 2007–2008 full-time, 60, part-time, 59. Openings 2008–2009, 16. The median number of years required for completion of a degree in 2006–2007 were 6. The number of students enrolled full- and part-time who were dismissed or voluntarily withdrew from this program area in 2007–2008 were 1.

Admissions Requirements:
Scores: Entries appear in this order: required test or GPA, minimum score (if required), median score of students entering in 2007–2008. Master's Programs: GRE-V no minimum stated, 500; GRE-Q no minimum stated, 500; GRE-Subject (Psychology) no minimum stated, 520; overall undergraduate GPA no minimum stated, 3.0; psychology GPA no minimum stated, 3.0; Masters GRE-Analytical no minimum stated. The scores mentioned above are the minimum scores required for admissions to the Graduate Programs in the College of Arts and Sciences. The scores of admitted students are higher in the doctoral programs. The GRE scores are required for the doctoral programs and the MS program in School Psychology. GRE scores are not required for MA in General Experimental Psychology. Doctoral Programs: GRE-V no minimum stated, 630; GRE-Q no minimum stated, 650; GRE-Subject (Psychology) no minimum stated, 640; overall undergraduate GPA no minimum stated, 3.61; Doctoral program GRE-Analytic no minimum stated, 4.5.
Other Criteria: (importance of criteria rated low, medium, or high): GRE/MAT scores—high, research experience—high, work experience—medium, extracurricular activity—medium, clinically related public service—high, GPA—high, letters of recommendation—high, interview—high, statement of goals and objectives—high. Interviews are required for PhD, PsyD, and MS programs. Clinically related public service is not applicable to MA program in General-Experimental Psychology.

Student Characteristics: The following represents characteristics of students in 2007–2008 in all graduate psychology programs in the department: Female—full-time 216, part-time 18; Male—full-time 27, part-time 6; African American/Black—full-time 25, part-time 2; Hispanic/Latino(a)—full-time 26, part-time 6; Asian/Pacific Islander—full-time 25, part-time 4; American Indian/Alaska Native—full-time 0, part-time 0; Caucasian/White—full-time 165, part-time 12; students subject to the Americans With Disabilities Act—full-time 0, part-time 0; Unknown ethnicity—full-time 0, part-time 0.

Financial Information/Assistance:
Tuition for Full-Time Study: Nonstate residents: $845 per credit hour. *Doctoral:* Nonstate residents: $945 per credit hour. Tuition

is subject to change. Tuition costs vary by program. Higher tuition cost for this program: The tuition costs are Clinical Psychology $945; School Psychology $845; and General Psychology $770.

Financial Assistance:

First-Year Students: Teaching assistantships available for first year. Average amount paid per academic year: $6,000. Average number of hours worked per week: 18. Apply by January 15. Tuition remission given: full. Research assistantships available for first year. Average amount paid per academic year: $8,000. Average number of hours worked per week: 18. Apply by January 15. Tuition remission given: full.

Advanced Students: Teaching assistantships available for advanced students. Average amount paid per academic year: $6,000. Average number of hours worked per week: 18. Apply by January 15. Tuition remission given: full. Research assistantships available for advanced students. Average amount paid per academic year: $8,000. Average number of hours worked per week: 18. Apply by January 15. Tuition remission given: full. Fellowships and scholarships available for advanced students. Average amount paid per academic year: $8,000. Average number of hours worked per week: 0. Apply by January 15. Tuition remission given: full.

Additional Information: Of all students currently enrolled full time, 25% benefited from one or more of the listed financial assistance programs.

Internships/Practica: Doctoral Degree (PhD Clinical Psychology): For those doctoral students for whom a professional internship was required in this program prior to graduation, (12) students applied for an internship in 2006–2007, with (12) students obtaining an internship. Of those students who obtained an internship, (12) were paid internships. Of those students who obtained an internship, (10) students placed in APA/CPA-accredited internships, (0) students placed in internships not APA/CPA accredited, but listed with the Association of Psychology Postdoctoral and Internship Centers (APPIC), (0) students placed in internships conforming to guidelines of the Council of Directors of School Psychology Programs (CDSPP), (2) students placed in internships that were not APA/CPA-accredited, APPIC or CDSPP listed. Doctoral Degree (PsyD School Psychology): For those doctoral students for whom a professional internship was required in this program prior to graduation, (24) students applied for an internship in 2006–2007, with (24) students obtaining an internship. Of those students who obtained an internship, (24) were paid internships. Of those students who obtained an internship, (0) students placed in APA/CPA-accredited internships, (0) students placed in internships not APA/CPA-accredited, but listed with the Association of Psychology Postdoctoral and Internship Centers (APPIC), (24) students placed in internships conforming to guidelines of the Council of Directors of School Psychology Programs (CDSPP), (0) students placed in internships that were not APA/CPA-accredited, APPIC or CDSPP listed. Students in the PhD program in Clinical Psychology complete practica in our Center for Psychological Services during all 4 full-time years of study. They compete a 2-day per week externship in a clinical facility during their 3rd and 4th years. A full-time internship is required in the 5th year. Students in the MS program in school psychology complete an assessment practica in the 2nd year at our Center for Psychological Services. This includes work in the clinic and in one or more local schools. A full-time internship is required in the 3rd year in either in a public school setting or at an agency serving children or adolescents. Students in the PsyD program in School Psychology complete an assessment practica in the 2nd year and a psychotherapy practica (Summer, Fall, and Spring semesters) in the 4th year at our Center for Psychological Services. Students complete a 3-day per week internship in a public school in the 3rd year, and a 3-day per week externship in a school, clinic, or facility for exceptional children in the 4th year. A full-time internship is required in the 5th year.

Housing and Day Care: On-campus housing is available. E-mail: reslife@stjohns.edu or Call: (718) 990-2417. No on-campus day care facilities are available.

Employment of Department Graduates:

Master's Degree Graduates: Of those who graduated in the academic year 2006–2007, the following categories and numbers represent the postgraduate activities and employment of master's degree graduates: Enrolled in a psychology doctoral program (8), enrolled in another graduate/professional program (0), enrolled in a postdoctoral residency/fellowship (n/a), employed in independent practice (n/a), employed in an academic position at a university (0), employed in an academic position at a 2-year/4-year college (0), employed in other positions at a higher education institution (0), employed in a professional position in a school system (16), employed in business or industry (4), employed in government agency (2), total from the above (master's) (30).

Doctoral Degree Graduates: Of those who graduated in the academic year 2006–2007, the following categories and numbers represent the postgraduate activities and employment of doctoral degree graduates: Enrolled in a psychology doctoral program (n/a), total from the above (doctoral) (0).

Additional Information:

Orientation, Objectives, and Emphasis of Department: The department emphasizes preparation in the science of psychology by integrating theory and practice. The MA program offers a thesis and a nonthesis track. Training at the doctoral level is provided in Clinical Psychology (PhD) and School Psychology (PsyD). The Clinical Psychology program has a child track and a general track. Both school psychology programs have a track to serve bilingual children. Students in the doctoral program in Clinical Psychology are exposed to diverse theoretical approaches in contemporary clinical practice, particularly psychoanalytic, cognitive–behavioral, and family systems models. Students follow either a general track of study in clinical psychology or a track in clinical child psychology. The doctoral program in School Psychology is anchored within the scholar–practitioner model. Students receive a firm foundation in the basic science of psychology upon which training in the practice of psychology is built. Students are trained to be scholars who can use their scientific background in psychology to assess and intervene with children, adolescents, and their families, and to consult with parents, teachers, and organizations on the development of programs to enhance children's educational and mental health needs. A strong emphasis is placed on using empirically supported assessment instruments and interventions. The MS and PsyD programs in school psychology lead to certification as a school psychologist. The PsyD prgram also leads to admissions to the licensing exam in psychology. Students who are bilingual may select a track of study leading to certification as a bilingual school psychologist.

Special Facilities or Resources: The Center for Psychological Services is a university-based training site for students in our

Clinical and School Psychology programs. The Center provides comprehensive psychological services to the community at a modest cost. The Center also serves as a site for student and faculty research.

Application Information:
Send to Graduate Admissions, Newman Hall Room 106, St. John's University, 8000 Utopia Parkway, Jamaica, NY 11439. Application available online. URL of online application: http://www.new.stjohns.edu/admission/undergraduate/apply.sju. Students are admitted in the Fall, application deadline January 15; Spring, application deadline rolling; Summer, application deadline rolling. Doctoral programs have Fall admission only with a deadline of January 15. For the MS in School Psychology: Fall admission only with a deadline of May 1. For the MA in General Experimental: rolling admissions. *Fee:* $45.

State University of New York at Buffalo

Department of Counseling, School and Educational Psychology
409 Baldy Hall
Buffalo, NY 14260-1000
Telephone: (716) 645-2484
Fax: (716) 645-6616
E-mail: *nmyers@buffalo.edu*
Web: *http://www.gse.buffalo.edu*

Department Information:
1949. Chairperson: Scott T. Meier. Number of faculty: total—full-time 18, part-time 1; women—full-time 9; total—minority—full-time 4; women minority—full-time 3.

Programs and Degrees Offered:
Listed in the following order: Program area, degree type (T if terminal Master's), number awarded 7/06–6/07. Counselor Education PhD (Doctor of Philosophy) 8, Educational Psychology PhD (Doctor of Philosophy) 2, Rehabilitation Counseling MA/MS (Master of Arts/Science) (T) 11, School Counseling Other 33, Educational Psychology MA/MS (Master of Arts/Science) (T) 3, School Psychology MA/MS (Master of Arts/Science) (T) 11, Counseling/School Psychology PhD (Doctor of Philosophy) 14, Mental Health Counseling MA/MS (Master of Arts/Science) (T) 4.

APA Accreditation: Combination PhD (Doctor of Philosophy).

Student Applications/Admissions:
Student Applications
Counselor Education PhD (Doctor of Philosophy)—Applications 2007–2008, 9. Total applicants accepted 2007–2008, 4. Number full-time enrolled (new admits only) 2007–2008, 0. Number part-time enrolled (new admits only) 2007–2008, 4. Total enrolled 2007–2008 full-time, 11, part-time, 10. Openings 2008–2009, 4. The median number of years required for completion of a degree in 2006–2007 were 6. The number of students enrolled full- and part-time who were dismissed or voluntarily withdrew from this program area in 2007–2008 were 1. *Educational Psychology PhD (Doctor of Philosophy)*—Applications 2007–2008, 25. Total applicants accepted 2007–2008, 7. Number full-time enrolled (new admits only) 2007–2008, 3. Number part-time enrolled (new admits only) 2007–2008, 0. Total enrolled 2007–2008 full-time, 7, part-time, 6. Openings 2008–2009, 5. The median number of years required for completion of a degree in 2006–2007 were 5. The number of students enrolled full- and part-time who were dismissed or voluntarily withdrew from this program area in 2007–2008 were 0. *Rehabilitation Counseling MA/MS (Master of Arts/Science)*—Applications 2007–2008, 20. Total applicants accepted 2007–2008, 11. Number full-time enrolled (new admits only) 2007–2008, 8. Number part-time enrolled (new admits only) 2007–2008, 3. Total enrolled 2007–2008 full-time, 13, part-time, 5. Openings 2008–2009, 10. The median number of years required for completion of a degree in 2006–2007 were 2. The number of students enrolled full- and part-time who were dismissed or voluntarily withdrew from this program area in 2007–2008 were 0. *School Counseling Other*—Applications 2007–2008, 82. Total applicants accepted 2007–2008, 40. Number full-time enrolled (new admits only) 2007–2008, 30. Number part-time enrolled (new admits only) 2007–2008, 2. Total enrolled 2007–2008 full-time, 37, part-time, 16. Openings 2008–2009, 25. The median number of years required for completion of a degree in 2006–2007 was 1. The number of students enrolled full- and part-time who were dismissed or voluntarily withdrew from this program area in 2007–2008 were 1. *Educational Psychology MA/MS (Master of Arts/Science)*—Applications 2007–2008, 30. Total applicants accepted 2007–2008, 13. Number full-time enrolled (new admits only) 2007–2008, 5. Number part-time enrolled (new admits only) 2007–2008, 2. Total enrolled 2007–2008 full-time, 13, part-time, 6. Openings 2008–2009, 5. The median number of years required for completion of a degree in 2006–2007 were 2. The number of students enrolled full- and part-time who were dismissed or voluntarily withdrew from this program area in 2007–2008 were 0. *School Psychology MA/MS (Master of Arts/Science)*—Applications 2007–2008, 90. Total applicants accepted 2007–2008, 12. Number full-time enrolled (new admits only) 2007–2008, 10. Number part-time enrolled (new admits only) 2007–2008, 0. Openings 2008–2009, 12. The median number of years required for completion of a degree in 2006–2007 were 3. The number of students enrolled full- and part-time who were dismissed or voluntarily withdrew from this program area in 2007–2008 were 0. *Counseling/School Psychology PhD (Doctor of Philosophy)*—Applications 2007–2008, 98. Total applicants accepted 2007–2008, 16. Number full-time enrolled (new admits only) 2007–2008, 16. Number part-time enrolled (new admits only) 2007–2008, 0. Openings 2008–2009, 12. The median number of years required for completion of a degree in 2006–2007 were 4. The number of students enrolled full- and part-time who were dismissed or voluntarily withdrew from this program area in 2007–2008 were 0. *Mental Health Counseling MA/MS (Master of Arts/Science)*—Applications 2007–2008, 40. Total applicants accepted 2007–2008, 13. Number full-time enrolled (new admits only) 2007–2008, 11. Number part-time enrolled (new admits only) 2007–2008, 2. Total enrolled 2007–2008 full-time, 24, part-time, 4. Openings 2008–2009, 10. The median number of years required for completion of a degree in 2006–2007 were 2. The number of students enrolled full- and part-time who were dismissed or voluntarily withdrew from this program area in 2007–2008 were 0.

Admissions Requirements:

Scores: Entries appear in this order: required test or GPA, minimum score (if required), median score of students entering in 2007–2008. Master's Programs: GRE-V no minimum stated, 505; GRE-Q no minimum stated, 565; overall undergraduate GPA no minimum stated, 3.3. Doctoral Programs: GRE-V no minimum stated, 545; GRE-Q no minimum stated, 612; overall undergraduate GPA no minimum stated, 3.3.

Other Criteria: (importance of criteria rated low, medium, or high): GRE/MAT scores—high, research experience—medium, work experience—low, extracurricular activity—low, clinically related public service—medium, GPA—high, letters of recommendation—medium, interview—high, statement of goals and objectives—high, undergraduate major in psychology—low, specific undergraduate psychology courses taken—low. Not all programs conduct personal interviews.

Student Characteristics: The following represents characteristics of students in 2007–2008 in all graduate psychology programs in the department: Female—full-time 160, part-time 36; Male—full-time 36, part-time 11; African American/Black—full-time 17, part-time 1; Hispanic/Latino(a)—full-time 3, part-time 1; Asian/Pacific Islander—full-time 13, part-time 0; American Indian/Alaska Native—full-time 0, part-time 1; Caucasian/White—full-time 163, part-time 44; Multi-ethnic—full-time 0, part-time 0; students subject to the Americans With Disabilities Act—full-time 0, part-time 0; Unknown ethnicity—full-time 0, part-time 0; International students who hold an F-1 or J-1 Visa—full-time 13, part-time 0.

Financial Information/Assistance:

Tuition for Full-Time Study: *Master's:* State residents: per academic year $6,900, $288 per credit hour; Nonstate residents: per academic year $10,920, $455 per credit hour. *Doctoral:* State residents: per academic year $6,900, $288 per credit hour; Nonstate residents: per academic year $10,920, $455 per credit hour. Tuition is subject to change. See the following Web site for updates and changes in tuition costs: http://www.gse.buffalo.edu.

Financial Assistance:

First-Year Students: Research assistantships available for first year. Average amount paid per academic year: $9,000. Average number of hours worked per week: 20. Apply by April 15. Tuition remission given: full and partial.

Advanced Students: Research assistantships available for advanced students. Average amount paid per academic year: $9,000. Average number of hours worked per week: 20. Apply by April 15. Tuition remission given: full and partial.

Additional Information: Of all students currently enrolled full time, 10% benefited from one or more of the listed financial assistance programs. Application and information available online at http://www.buffalo.gse.edu.

Internships/Practica: Master's Degree (MA/MS Educational Psychology): An internship experience such as a final research project or "capstone" experience is required of graduates. Master's Degree (MA/MS School Psychology): An internship experience such as a final research project or "capstone" experience is required of graduates. Master's Degree (MA/MS Mental Health Counseling): An internship experience such as a final research project or "capstone" experience is required of graduates. Doctoral Degree (PhD Counseling/School Psychology): For those doctoral students for whom a professional internship was required in this program prior to graduation, (12) students applied for an internship in 2006–2007, with (11) students obtaining an internship. Of those students who obtained an internship, (11) were paid internships. Of those students who obtained an internship, (6) students placed in APA/CPA-accredited internships, (0) students placed in internships not APA/CPA-accredited, but listed with the Association of Psychology Postdoctoral and Internship Centers (APPIC), (3) students placed in internships conforming to guidelines of the Council of Directors of School Psychology Programs (CDSPP), (2) students placed in internships that were not APA/CPA-accredited, APPIC or CDSPP listed. Practicum and internships avaliable at area schools, community agencies, and hospitals. Experience with death and end-of-life issues, forensics, persons with disabilities, and assessment is available. The Web address below giving information on education and training outcomes for our programs is for the Counseling/School Psychology doctoral program only. For additional information on education and training outcomes for our programs, see the following Web site: http://www.gse.buffalo.edu/programs/csep/1/outcomes.asp.

Housing and Day Care: On-campus housing is available. See the following Web site for more information: http://www.wings.buffalo.edu. On-campus day care facilities are available. See the following Web site for more information: http://www.gse.buffalo.edu or http://src.buffalo.edu/news/newgradstudents.shtml.

Employment of Department Graduates:

Master's Degree Graduates: Of those who graduated in the academic year 2006–2007, the following categories and numbers represent the postgraduate activities and employment of master's degree graduates: Enrolled in a psychology doctoral program (3), enrolled in another graduate/professional program (0), enrolled in a postdoctoral residency/fellowship (n/a), employed in independent practice (n/a), employed in an academic position at a university (0), employed in an academic position at a 2-year/4-year college (0), employed in other positions at a higher education institution (0), employed in a professional position in a school system (26), employed in business or industry (0), employed in government agency (3), employed in a community mental health/counseling center (5), employed in a hospital/medical center (1), still seeking employment (7), not seeking employment (3), other employment position (5), do not know (8), total from the above (master's) (61).

Doctoral Degree Graduates: Of those who graduated in the academic year 2006–2007, the following categories and numbers represent the postgraduate activities and employment of doctoral degree graduates: Enrolled in a psychology doctoral program (n/a), enrolled in another graduate/professional program (0), enrolled in a postdoctoral residency/fellowship (1), employed in independent practice (1), employed in an academic position at a university (3), employed in an academic position at a 2-year/4-year college (1), employed in other positions at a higher education institution (3), employed in a professional position in a school system (7), employed in business or industry (0), employed in government agency (0), employed in a community mental health/counseling center (5), employed in a hospital/medical center (1), still seeking employment (2), not seeking employment (0), other employment position (0), do not know (4), total from the above (doctoral) (28).

Additional Information:

Orientation, Objectives, and Emphasis of Department: Departmental emphasis is on research based counseling with adults, college students, adolescents, children, and persons with disabilities. Doctoral programs follow the scientist–practitioner model. Some focus on preparing college faculty. Increased integration of counseling, school, and educational psychology programs is developing. Field experience and research experience are continuous through the programs.

Special Facilities or Resources: Department offers training experiences in a wide variety of schools, agencies, and college in both urban and suburban settings.

Application Information:

Send to Office of Graduate Admissions, Graduate School of Education, 366 Baldy Hall, University at Buffalo, The State University of New York, Buffalo, NY 14260-1000. Application available online. URL of online application: http://www.buffalo.gse.edu. Students are admitted in the Fall, application deadline February 1. Counselor Education, Mental Health Counseling, and Rehabilitation Counseling have a March 1 application deadline for fall admission. Educational Psychology has rolling admissions and applications are considered for both Fall and Spring admission. *Fee:* $50.

State University of New York at Buffalo

Department of Psychology
College of Arts and Sciences
210 Park Hall
Buffalo, NY 14260-4110
Telephone: (716) 645-3650
Fax: (716) 645-3801
E-mail: *ccolder@buffalo.edu*
Web: *http://www.psychology.buffalo.edu*

Department Information:

1921. Chair: Paul A. Luce. Number of faculty: total—full-time 32; women—full-time 12; women minority—full-time 2.

Programs and Degrees Offered:

Listed in the following order: Program area, degree type (T if terminal Master's), number awarded 7/06–6/07. Behavioral Neuroscience PhD (Doctor of Philosophy) 3, Clinical PhD (Doctor of Philosophy) 2, Cognitive PhD (Doctor of Philosophy) 0, Social-Personality PhD (Doctor of Philosophy) 0, General MA/MS (Master of Arts/Science) (T) 6.

APA Accreditation: Clinical PhD (Doctor of Philosophy).

Student Applications/Admissions:

Student Applications

Behavioral Neuroscience PhD (Doctor of Philosophy)—Applications 2007–2008, 21. Total applicants accepted 2007–2008, 8. Number full-time enrolled (new admits only) 2007–2008, 4. Total enrolled 2007–2008 full-time, 10. Openings 2008–2009, 3. The median number of years required for completion of a degree in 2006–2007 were 7. The number of students enrolled fuli- and part-time who were dismissed or voluntarily withdrew from this program area in 2007–2008 were 1. *Clinical PhD (Doctor of Philosophy)*—Applications 2007–2008, 181. Total applicants accepted 2007–2008, 25. Number full-time enrolled (new admits only) 2007–2008, 14. Total enrolled 2007–2008 full-time, 35. Openings 2008–2009, 6. The median number of years required for completion of a degree in 2006–2007 were 8. The number of students enrolled full- and part-time who were dismissed or voluntarily withdrew from this program area in 2007–2008 were 0. *Cognitive PhD (Doctor of Philosophy)*—Applications 2007–2008, 17. Total applicants accepted 2007–2008, 9. Number full-time enrolled (new admits only) 2007–2008, 4. Total enrolled 2007–2008 full-time, 15. Openings 2008–2009, 3. The median number of years required for completion of a degree in 2006–2007 were 4. The number of students enrolled full- and part-time who were dismissed or voluntarily withdrew from this program area in 2007–2008 were 0. *Social-Personality PhD (Doctor of Philosophy)*—Applications 2007–2008, 49. Total applicants accepted 2007–2008, 5. Number full-time enrolled (new admits only) 2007–2008, 3. Total enrolled 2007–2008 full-time, 8. Openings 2008–2009, 3. The median number of years required for completion of a degree in 2006–2007 were 5. The number of students enrolled full- and part-time who were dismissed or voluntarily withdrew from this program area in 2007–2008 were 0. *General MA/MS (Master of Arts/Science)*—Applications 2007–2008, 81. Total applicants accepted 2007–2008, 11. Number full-time enrolled (new admits only) 2007–2008, 9. Total enrolled 2007–2008 full-time, 12. Openings 2008–2009, 20. The median number of years required for completion of a degree in 2006–2007 were 2. The number of students enrolled full- and part-time who were dismissed or voluntarily withdrew from this program area in 2007–2008 were 1.

Admissions Requirements:

Scores: Entries appear in this order: required test or GPA, minimum score (if required), median score of students entering in 2007–2008. Master's Programs: GRE-V no minimum stated; GRE-Q no minimum stated; Masters GRE-Analytical no minimum stated. Doctoral Programs: GRE-V no minimum stated; GRE-Q no minimum stated; Doctoral program GRE-Analytic no minimum stated.

Other Criteria: (importance of criteria rated low, medium, or high): GRE/MAT scores—medium, research experience—high, work experience—low, extracurricular activity—low, clinically related public service—medium, GPA—high, letters of recommendation—high, interview—medium, statement of goals and objectives—high. Interview for Clinical only. For additional information on admission requirements, go to http://www.psychology.buffalo.edu.

Student Characteristics: The following represents characteristics of students in 2007–2008 in all graduate psychology programs in the department: Female—full-time 50, part-time 0; Male—full-time 30, part-time 0; African American/Black—full-time 3, part-time 0; Hispanic/Latino(a)—full-time 4, part-time 0; Asian/Pacific Islander—full-time 8, part-time 0; American Indian/Alaska Native—full-time 0, part-time 0; Caucasian/White—full-time 65, part-time 0; Multi-ethnic—full-time 0, part-time 0; students subject to the Americans With Disabilities Act—full-time 0, part-time 0; Unknown ethnicity—full-time 0, part-time 0.

Financial Information/Assistance:

Tuition for Full-Time Study: *Master's:* State residents: per academic year $8,288, $288 per credit hour; Nonstate residents: per academic year $12,308, $455 per credit hour. *Doctoral:* State residents: per academic year $8,288, $288 per credit hour; Nonstate residents: per academic year $12,308, $455 per credit hour. Tuition is subject to change. See the following Web site for updates and changes in tuition costs: http://www.src.buffalo.edu.

Financial Assistance:

First-Year Students: Teaching assistantships available for first year. Average amount paid per academic year: $13,585. Average number of hours worked per week: 20. Tuition remission given: full. Research assistantships available for first year. Average amount paid per academic year: $13,585. Average number of hours worked per week: 20. Tuition remission given: full. Fellowships and scholarships available for first year. Average amount paid per academic year: $6,000. Tuition remission given: full.

Advanced Students: Teaching assistantships available for advanced students. Average amount paid per academic year: $13,585. Average number of hours worked per week: 20. Tuition remission given: full. Research assistantships available for advanced students. Average amount paid per academic year: $13,585. Average number of hours worked per week: 20. Tuition remission given: full. Fellowships and scholarships available for advanced students. Average amount paid per academic year: $6,000. Tuition remission given: full.

Additional Information: Of all students currently enrolled full time, 79% benefited from one or more of the listed financial assistance programs. Application and information available online at http:/www.psychology.buffalo.edu.

Internships/Practica: Doctoral Degree (PhD Clinical): For those doctoral students for whom a professional internship was required in this program prior to graduation, (4) students applied for an internship in 2006–2007, with (3) students obtaining an internship. Of those students who obtained an internship, (3) were paid internships. Of those students who obtained an internship, (3)students placed in APA/CPA-accredited internships, (0) students placed in internships not APA/CPA-accredited, but listed with the Association of Psychology Postdoctoral and Internship Centers (APPIC), (0) students placed in internships conforming to guidelines of the Council of Directors of School Psychology Programs (CDSPP), (0) students placed in internships that were not APA/CPA-accredited, APPIC or CDSPP listed. Several clinical practica are offered each year for students in the doctoral program in Clinical Psychology and for other doctoral students with permission of the instructor. In addition, there is a summer practicum focused on treatment of children with attention-deficit/hyperactivity disorder.

Housing and Day Care: On-campus housing is available. See the following Web site for more information: http://www.grad.buffalo.edu/. On-campus day care facilities are available. See the following Web site for more information: http://wings.buffalo.edu/services/ccc.

Employment of Department Graduates:

Master's Degree Graduates: Of those who graduated in the academic year 2006–2007, the following categories and numbers represent the postgraduate activities and employment of master's degree graduates: Enrolled in a postdoctoral residency/fellowship (n/a), employed in independent practice (n/a), total from the above (master's) (0).

Doctoral Degree Graduates: Of those who graduated in the academic year 2006–2007, the following categories and numbers represent the postgraduate activities and employment of doctoral degree graduates: Enrolled in a psychology doctoral program (n/a), total from the above (doctoral) (0).

Additional Information:

Orientation, Objectives, and Emphasis of Department: The Department of Psychology offers doctoral degrees in Behavioral Neuroscience, Clinical Psychology, Cognitive Psychology, and Social/Personality Psychology and a Master's degree in psychology with several specializations. The department has as its defining characteristic and distinguishing mission the conduct and communication of research and scholarship that contributes to the scientific understanding of psychology and the provision of high-quality graduate education and training. The department is dedicated to offering state-of-the-art education and training to its graduate students to prepare them to become leading researchers and to assume important positions in academic institutions or professional practice. We offer students a learning environment that is exciting and challenging, one that will allow them to follow their interests and fully develop their research skills. The research emphasis in the doctoral program in Behavioral Neuroscience is on the neural, endocrine, and molecular bases of behavior. Areas of specialization in Clinical Psychology include adult mood and anxiety disorders, relationship dysfunction, behavioral medicine, attention-deficit/hyperactivity disorder, and child and adolescent aggression and substance abuse. The program in Cognitive Psychology focuses on the processes underlying perception, attention, memory, spoken and written language comprehension, language acquisition, categorization, problem solving, and thinking. Faculty research interests in the Social-Personality program include close relationships, social cognition, self-concept, and self-esteem. Complete information is available on the department's Web site at http://wings.buffalo.edu/psychology.

Special Facilities or Resources: The Department of Psychology has specialized research facilities for the study of language comprehension, auditory and speech perception, memory, categorization, animal cognition, visual perception, attention, social interaction, small group processes, animal surgery research, behavior therapy, human psychophysiology and biofeedback, and neurochemical and electrophysiological investigations into the physiological bases of behavior. Many of these laboratories are computer based. The department also has ample facilities for individual and group therapy, marriage counseling, and therapeutic work with children. One-way vision screens and videotape equipment are available for observation and supervision. Internships are available through the department's Psychological Services Center. Excellent facilities are available for working with animals. Students have liberal access to the University's computing services on the North Campus.

Application Information:

Send to Director of Graduate Admissions, Department of Psychology, University at Buffalo—The State University of New York, Park Hall Room 210, Buffalo, NY 14260-4110. Application available online. URL of online application: http://www.psychology.buffalo.edu. Students are admitted in the Fall, application deadline for PhD is December 1. MA Application deadline for Fall enrollment is May 1. *Fee:* $50.

State University of New York at New Paltz

Department of Psychology/Graduate Program
JFT 314, 600 Hawk Drive
New Paltz, NY 12561-2440
Telephone: (845) 257-3467
Fax: (845) 257-3474
E-mail: *gradpsych@newpaltz.edu*
Web: *http://www.newpaltz.edu/psychology/graduate*

Department Information:

1969. Chairperson: Douglas Maynard. Number of faculty: total—full-time 15, part-time 4; women—full-time 8, part-time 3; total—minority—full-time 3, part-time 1; women minority—full-time 1, part-time 1.

Programs and Degrees Offered:

Listed in the following order: Program area, degree type (T if terminal Master's), number awarded 7/06–6/07. Psychology MA/MS (Master of Arts/Science) (T) 9, Mental Health Counseling MA/MS (Master of Arts/Science) (T).

Student Applications/Admissions:

Student Applications

Psychology MA/MS (Master of Arts/Science)—Applications 2007–2008, 38. Total applicants accepted 2007–2008, 26. Number full-time enrolled (new admits only) 2007–2008, 14. Number part-time enrolled (new admits only) 2007–2008, 1. Openings 2008–2009, 6. The number of students enrolled full- and part-time who were dismissed or voluntarily withdrew from this program area in 2007–2008 were 0. *Mental Health Counseling MA/MS (Master of Arts/Science)*—Total enrolled 2007–2008 full-time, 39. Openings 2008–2009, 12.

Admissions Requirements:

Scores: Entries appear in this order: required test or GPA, minimum score (if required), median score of students entering in 2007–2008. Master's Programs: GRE-V no minimum stated, 500; GRE-Q no minimum stated, 550; overall undergraduate GPA 3.0, 3.5; psychology GPA 3.0, 3.5. Students must take the General GRE (Verbal, Quantitative, and Analytical Writing sections) and have a 3.0 undergraduate GPA (overall and in psychology classes). Other admissions requirements are as follows: Baccalaureate degree from a regionally accredited institution; successful completion of undergraduate General Psychology, Statistics, Experimental Methods, or Research Methods in Psychology; Psychology subject GRE scores optional; completed application for admission to the Master of Arts Program in Psychology; two official transcripts of all undergraduate and graduate work; three letters of recommendation. International students must meet additional university-wide requirements for admission. For details see http://www.newpaltz.edu/admissions/intern_academic.html

Other Criteria: (importance of criteria rated low, medium, or high): GRE/MAT scores—medium, research experience—high, work experience—high, extracurricular activity—high, clinically related public service—medium, GPA—high, letters of recommendation—high, interview—medium, statement of goals and objectives—high, writing ability—high. The Psychology and Mental Health Counseling programs may weigh criteria differently. Interviews may not always be part of the process. For additional information on admission requirements, go to http://www.newpaltz.edu/psychology.

Student Characteristics: The following represents characteristics of students in 2007–2008 in all graduate psychology programs in the department: Female—full-time 30, part-time 8; Male—full-time 8, part-time 3; Caucasian/White—full-time 0, part-time 0; Unknown ethnicity—full-time 0, part-time 0.

Financial Information/Assistance:

Tuition for Full-Time Study: *Master's:* State residents: per academic year $6,900, $288 per credit hour; Nonstate residents: per academic year $10,500, $438 per credit hour. Tuition is subject to change. See the following Web site for updates and changes in tuition costs: http://www.newpaltz.edu/financialaid/tuition.html.

Financial Assistance:

First-Year Students: Teaching assistantships available for first year. Average amount paid per academic year: $5,000. Average number of hours worked per week: 20. Apply by varies. Tuition remission given: partial. Research assistantships available for first year. Apply by varies. Traineeships available for first year. Apply by varies. Fellowships and scholarships available for first year. Average number of hours worked per week: 10. Apply by varies. Tuition remission given: partial.

Advanced Students: Teaching assistantships available for advanced students. Average amount paid per academic year: $5,000. Average number of hours worked per week: 20. Tuition remission given: partial. Research assistantships available for advanced students. Apply by varies. Fellowships and scholarships available for advanced students. Apply by varies. Tuition remission given: partial.

Additional Information: Of all students currently enrolled full time, 30% benefited from one or more of the listed financial assistance programs. Application and information available online at http://www.newpaltz.edu/financialaid.

Internships/Practica: All students in the Mental Health Counseling program complete a practicum at the college counseling center and the career advising center. Additional internship opportunities are available with regional public and private mental health agencies. In addition to practicum and internship requirements, mental health counseling students complete a curriculum of mental health counseling coursework. The program is registered with New York State as a program meeting the educational requirements for mental health counseling licensure.

Housing and Day Care: On-campus housing is available. See the following Web site for more information: http://www.newpaltz.edu/reslife/ or contact Residence Life: (845) 257-4444. On-campus day care facilities are available. See the following Web site for more information: http://www.newpaltz.edu/services/children.html. Contact The Children's Center: (845) 257-2910.

Employment of Department Graduates:

Master's Degree Graduates: Of those who graduated in the academic year 2006–2007, the following categories and numbers represent the postgraduate activities and employment of master's degree graduates: Enrolled in a postdoctoral residency/fellowship (n/a), employed in independent practice (n/a), total from the above (master's) (0).

Doctoral Degree Graduates: Of those who graduated in the academic year 2006–2007, the following categories and numbers represent the postgraduate activities and employment of doctoral degree graduates: Enrolled in a psychology doctoral program (n/a), total from the above (doctoral) (0).

Additional Information:

Orientation, Objectives, and Emphasis of Department: Founded in 1828, America's 99th oldest university is an exciting blend of tradition and vision, providing students with the skills and knowledge needed to meet the challenges of the 21st century. SUNY New Paltz offers graduate training in psychology and mental health counseling. The 36-credit MA in Psychology program offers general graduate training in psychology. The program provides students with the opportunity to select electives in a variety of fields including social, experimental, and organizational psychology as well as counseling. The program may serve as preparation for those training for entry into a doctoral program or as additional training for those who plan to enter or are already involved in applied areas of psychology. The 48-credit MS in Mental Health Counseling program serves both students looking to become licensed as mental health counselors and those seeking to eventually proceed into doctoral training programs. Degree requirements cover a core curriculum and specialization courses. Three fieldwork courses provide hands-on mental health counseling training experiences under supervision of licensed professionals. The program is registered with the State Education Department as meeting the educational requirements necessary for mental health counseling licensure in New York, making this a very marketable degree.

Special Facilities or Resources: Laboratory facilities and equipment (computers, videotaping equipment) are available to support student and faculty research in a variety of research areas (see department Web site for research details: http://www.newpaltz.edu/psychology). The department also maintains links to local and community organizations for research opportunities. In addition the department has a computer lab for research and instruction with Internet access. All graduate students have access to word processing, SPSS, and the Web through the campus computer network.

Information for Students With Physical Disabilities: See the following Web site for more information: http://www.newpaltz.edu/drc.

Application Information:

Applications and instructions for submission are available online (http://www.newpaltz.edu/graduate/applications.cfm). Some materials can be submitted online, whereas others must be mailed to the following address: The Graduate School, SUNY New Paltz, 1 Hawk Drive, New Paltz, NY 12561-2443. Application available online. URL of online application: http://www.newpaltz.edu/graduate/apply.html. Students are admitted in the Fall, application deadline February 15; Spring, application deadline November 15. For the MA in Psychology: For Fall admission, application review begins February 15 and continues until the Fall class is filled. For Spring admission, applications must be received by November 15. The vast majority of admissions are done for Fall semester. For the MS in Mental Health Counseling: All admissions for the MS in Mental Health Counseling program are done for the Fall semester. Application review begins February 15 and continues until the class is filled. Graduate assistantships are available to selected students each year. Current stipends are $2,500 per semester ($5,000 per academic year) plus a six-credit tuition waiver per semester. Assistantship duties involve assisting faculty in teaching and research. Contact the program at (845) 257-3467 for further information about assistantships. *Fee:* $50.

State University of New York, Binghamton University

Psychology
Arts and Sciences
P.O. Box 6000
Binghamton, NY 13902-6000
Telephone: (607) 777-2334
Fax: (607) 777-4890
E-mail: *rmiller@binghamton.edu*
Web: *http://www.psychology.binghamton.edu*

Department Information:

1965. Chairperson: Peter Gerhardstein. Number of faculty: total—full-time 28, part-time 6; women—full-time 10, part-time 2; total—minority—full-time 2; women minority—full-time 2.

Programs and Degrees Offered:

Listed in the following order: Program area, degree type (T if terminal Master's), number awarded 7/06–6/07. Behavioral Neuroscience PhD (Doctor of Philosophy) 1, Clinical PhD (Doctor of Philosophy) 5, Cognitive PhD (Doctor of Philosophy) 1.

APA Accreditation: Clinical PhD (Doctor of Philosophy).

Student Applications/Admissions:

Student Applications

Behavioral Neuroscience PhD (Doctor of Philosophy)—Applications 2007–2008, 32. Total applicants accepted 2007–2008, 11. Number full-time enrolled (new admits only) 2007–2008, 7. Number part-time enrolled (new admits only) 2007–2008, 0. Openings 2008–2009, 5. The median number of years required for completion of a degree in 2006–2007 were 6. The number of students enrolled full- and part-time who were dismissed or voluntarily withdrew from this program area in 2007–2008 were 0. *Clinical PhD (Doctor of Philosophy)*—Applications 2007–2008, 211. Total applicants accepted 2007–2008, 15. Number full-time enrolled (new admits only) 2007–2008, 8. Number part-time enrolled (new admits only) 2007–2008, 0. Openings 2008–2009, 7. The median number of years required for completion of a degree in 2006–2007 were 6. The number of students enrolled full- and part-time who were dismissed or voluntarily withdrew from this program area in 2007–2008 were 0. *Cognitive PhD (Doctor of Philosophy)*—Applications 2007–2008, 24. Total applicants accepted 2007–2008, 8. Number full-time enrolled (new admits only) 2007–2008, 4. Number part-time enrolled (new admits only) 2007–2008, 0. Openings 2008–2009, 5. The median number of years required for completion of a degree in 2006–2007 were 5. The number of students enrolled full- and part-time who were dismissed or voluntarily withdrew from this program area in 2007–2008 were 1.

Admissions Requirements:

Scores: Entries appear in this order: required test or GPA, minimum score (if required), median score of students entering in 2007–2008. Doctoral Programs: GRE-V no minimum stated, 570; GRE-Q no minimum stated, 640; overall undergraduate GPA no minimum stated, 3.5; Doctoral program GRE-Analytic no minimum stated. Although we don't require a minimum GRE in all areas we look at each applicant on an individual basis.

Other Criteria: (importance of criteria rated low, medium, or high): GRE/MAT scores—high, research experience—high, work experience—medium, extracurricular activity—low, clinically related public service—low, GPA—high, letters of recommendation—high, interview—high, statement of goals and objectives—high, undergraduate major in psychology—low, specific undergraduate psychology courses taken—medium.

Student Characteristics: The following represents characteristics of students in 2007–2008 in all graduate psychology programs in the department: Female—full-time 54, part-time 0; Male—full-time 39, part-time 0; African American/Black—full-time 3, part-time 0; Hispanic/Latino(a)—full-time 4, part-time 0; Asian/Pacific Islander—full-time 4, part-time 0; American Indian/Alaska Native—full-time 0, part-time 0; Caucasian/White—full-time 81, part-time 0; Multi-ethnic—full-time 0, part-time 0; students subject to the Americans With Disabilities Act—full-time 1, part-time 0; Unknown ethnicity—full-time 0, part-time 0; International students who hold an F-1 or J-1 Visa—full-time 5, part-time 0.

Financial Information/Assistance:

Tuition for Full-Time Study: *Doctoral:* State residents: per academic year $6,300; Nonstate residents: per academic year $10,900. Tuition is subject to change. Additional fees are assessed to students beyond the costs of tuition for the following: Assorted: About $1,000 per year.

Financial Assistance:

First-Year Students: Teaching assistantships available for first year. Average amount paid per academic year: $16,500. Average number of hours worked per week: 10. Tuition remission given: full. Research assistantships available for first year. Average amount paid per academic year: $16,500. Tuition remission given: full. Fellowships and scholarships available for first year. Average amount paid per academic year: $16,500. Tuition remission given: full.

Advanced Students: Teaching assistantships available for advanced students. Average amount paid per academic year: $16,500. Average number of hours worked per week: 10. Tuition remission given: full. Research assistantships available for advanced students. Average amount paid per academic year: $16,500. Tuition remission given: full. Fellowships and scholarships available for advanced students. Average amount paid per academic year: $16,500. Tuition remission given: full.

Additional Information: Of all students currently enrolled full time, 98% benefited from one or more of the listed financial assistance programs.

Internships/Practica: Doctoral Degree (PhD Clinical): For those doctoral students for whom a professional internship was required in this program prior to graduation, (8) students applied for an internship in 2006–2007, with (8) students obtaining an internship. Of those students who obtained an internship, (8) were paid internships. Of those students who obtained an internship, (7) students placed in APA/CPA-accredited internships, (1) student placed in internships not APA/CPA-accredited, but listed with the Association of Psychology Postdoctoral and Internship Centers (APPIC), (0) students placed in internships conforming to guidelines of the Council of Directors of School Psychology Programs (CDSPP), (0) students placed in internships that were not APA/CPA-accredited, APPIC or CDSPP listed. Students in the clinical area are required to complete two practica, a psychotherapy practicum and a community practicum. The psychotherapy practicum is conducted in the department clinic under the supervision of a faculty member and generally involves the joint treatment of a variety of problems across a broad range of ages and diagnoses. The community practicum consists of supervised clinical activity and/or research at one of a wide range of local agencies, hospitals, or clinics. Students in cognitive psychology are invited—but not required—to complete a research-related practicum in industry. Past internships included training at GE, IBM, Microsoft, Lockheed Martin, and others.

Housing and Day Care: No on-campus housing is available. On-campus day care facilities are available.

Employment of Department Graduates:

Master's Degree Graduates: Of those who graduated in the academic year 2006–2007, the following categories and numbers represent the postgraduate activities and employment of master's degree graduates: Enrolled in a postdoctoral residency/fellowship (n/a), employed in independent practice (n/a), total from the above (master's) (0).

Doctoral Degree Graduates: Of those who graduated in the academic year 2006–2007, the following categories and numbers represent the postgraduate activities and employment of doctoral degree graduates: Enrolled in a psychology doctoral program (n/a), enrolled in a postdoctoral residency/fellowship (7), employed in independent practice (0), employed in an academic position at a university (0), employed in an academic position at a 2-year/4-year college (0), employed in other positions at a higher education institution (0), employed in a professional position in a school system (0), employed in business or industry (0), employed in government agency (0), employed in a community mental health/counseling center (0), employed in a hospital/medical center (0), still seeking employment (0), other employment position (0), total from the above (doctoral) (7).

Additional Information:

Orientation, Objectives, and Emphasis of Department: The Psychology Department emphasizes basic and applied research in its three areas of specialization, clinical psychology, cognitive psychology, and behavioral neuroscience. The goal of our APA-accredited Clinical program is to develop scientists and practitioners. By virtue of ongoing research involvement, students are expected to contribute to knowledge about psychopathology, assessment, and treatment. Our Cognitive program has two major research emphases, one focused on learning and memory, and the other focused on perception and language (both in the visual and auditory domains). Researchers in this area also work in industrial settings and collaborate with local industry. Our Behavioral Neuroscience program emphasizes the study of neural and hormonal bases of normal and abnormal behavior and their developmental antecedents in preclinical animal models.

Special Facilities or Resources: All faculty have state-of-the-art, spacious laboratories. The Clinical program supports an active in-house mental health clinic. Members of the cognitive area have access to sophisticated systems for the manipulation of auditory and visual stimuli and the online measurement of cognitive processes, and members of the behavioral neurosciences area share multiuser histology, microneuroimaging, and neurochemistry laboratories.

Application Information:
Send to Graduate Admissions Office. Application available online. URL of online application: http://www.gradschool.binghamton.edu/. Students are admitted in the Fall, application deadline January 1. *Fee:* $55.

State University of New York, College at Brockport

Department of Psychology
350 New Campus Drive
Brockport, NY 14420
Telephone: (585) 395-2488
Fax: (585) 395-2116
E-mail: *psychdpt@brockport.edu*
Web: *http://www.brockport.edu/psh/grad/*

Department Information:
1965. Chairperson: Melissa M. Brown. Number of faculty: total—full-time 14, part-time 5; women—full-time 11, part-time 2.

Programs and Degrees Offered:
Listed in the following order: Program area, degree type (T if terminal Master's), number awarded 7/06–6/07. Clinical MA/MS (Master of Arts/Science) (T) 6.

Student Applications/Admissions:
Student Applications
Clinical MA/MS (Master of Arts/Science)—Applications 2007–2008, 16. Total applicants accepted 2007–2008, 5. Number full-time enrolled (new admits only) 2007–2008, 4. Number part-time enrolled (new admits only) 2007–2008, 1. Total enrolled 2007–2008 full-time, 19, part-time, 4. Openings 2008–2009, 15. The median number of years required for completion of a degree in 2006–2007 were 2. The number of students enrolled full- and part-time who were dismissed or voluntarily withdrew from this program area in 2007–2008 were 0.

Admissions Requirements:
Scores: Entries appear in this order: required test or GPA, minimum score (if required), median score of students entering in 2007–2008. Master's Programs: GRE-V 400, 500; GRE-Q 400, 560; overall undergraduate GPA 3.00, 3.25; last 2 years GPA 3.00, 3.25; psychology GPA 3.00, 3.50.
Other Criteria: (importance of criteria rated low, medium, or high): GRE/MAT scores—medium, research experience—medium, work experience—medium, clinically related public service—medium, GPA—high, letters of recommendation—high, interview—high, statement of goals and objectives—high, Psychology GPA—high, undergraduate major in psychology—medium, specific undergraduate psychology courses taken—low, TOEFL if appropriate 550. For additional information on admission requirements, go to http://www.brockport.edu/psh/grad/.

Student Characteristics: The following represents characteristics of students in 2007–2008 in all graduate psychology programs in the department: Female—full-time 11, part-time 3; Male—full-time 4, part-time 1; African American/Black—full-time 0, part-time 0; Hispanic/Latino(a)—full-time 1, part-time 0; Asian/Pacific Islander—full-time 1, part-time 0; American Indian/Alaska Native—full-time 0, part-time 0; Caucasian/White—full-time 13, part-time 4; Multi-ethnic—full-time 2, part-time 0; students subject to the Americans With Disabilities Act—full-time 0, part-time 0; Unknown ethnicity—full-time 0, part-time 0.

Financial Information/Assistance:
Tuition for Full-Time Study: *Master's:* State residents: per academic year $6,912, $288 per credit hour; Nonstate residents: $455 per credit hour. Tuition is subject to change.

Financial Assistance:
First-Year Students: Teaching assistantships available for first year. Average amount paid per academic year: $6,000. Average number of hours worked per week: 20. Apply by May 15. Tuition remission given: full.
Advanced Students: Teaching assistantships available for advanced students. Average amount paid per academic year: $6,000. Average number of hours worked per week: 20. Apply by May 15. Tuition remission given: full.
Additional Information: Of all students currently enrolled full time, 10% benefited from one or more of the listed financial assistance programs. Application and information available online at http://www.brockport.edu/psh/grad/.

Internships/Practica: Master's Degree (MA/MS Clinical): An internship experience such as a final research project or "capstone" experience is required of graduates. Practical experience is in one of nearly 50 human service agencies in western New York, including the college counseling center, VA and academic medical centers, and state and local mental health, developmental disability and autism centers, and other community service agencies. Each practicum placement is developed individually, based on the specific student and agency involved. Each practicum is supervised by an agency staff member as well as a faculty member from the Department of Psychology. Students must successfully complete all required coursework before beginning the practicum.

Housing and Day Care: No on-campus housing is available. On-campus day care facilities are available.

Employment of Department Graduates:
Master's Degree Graduates: Of those who graduated in the academic year 2006–2007, the following categories and numbers represent the postgraduate activities and employment of master's degree graduates: Enrolled in a psychology doctoral program (0), enrolled in another graduate/professional program (0), enrolled in a postdoctoral residency/fellowship (n/a), employed in indepen-

dent practice (n/a), employed in an academic position at a university (0), employed in an academic position at a 2-year/4-year college (0), employed in other positions at a higher education institution (0), employed in a professional position in a school system (0), employed in business or industry (0), employed in government agency (0), employed in a community mental health/counseling center (5), employed in a hospital/medical center (1), still seeking employment (0), other employment position (0), total from the above (master's) (6).

Doctoral Degree Graduates: Of those who graduated in the academic year 2006–2007, the following categories and numbers represent the postgraduate activities and employment of doctoral degree graduates: Enrolled in a psychology doctoral program (n/a), total from the above (doctoral) (0).

Additional Information:

Orientation, Objectives, and Emphasis of Department: The MA in psychology program is designed to prepare students for both doctoral work and also careers in applied psychology and the helping professions. Students are trained as scientists and practitioners, concerned with the application of psychological principles to the treatment and prevention of behavior disorders. Courses provide theoretical and practical training in contemporary methods of assessment, behavioral and cognitive–behavioral clinical intervention, and program evaluation applicable to child, adolescent, and adult populations. Faculty includes board-certified applied behavior analysts and licensed psychologists.

Special Facilities or Resources: The department has facilities for research in the biobehavioral sciences, as well as sensory–perceptual, clinical, developmental, and personality psychology topics and assessment/intervention training. Laboratory space, computer equipment, and an extensive file of psychological assessment instruments are also available.

Information for Students With Physical Disabilities: See the following Web site for more information: http://www.brockport.edu.

Application Information:

Send to Office of Graduate Studies, SUNY College at Brockport, 350 New Campus Drive, Brockport, NY 14420-2914; e-mail gradadmit@brockport.edu. Students are admitted in the Fall, application deadline May 15. *Fee:* $50.

State University of New York, College at Plattsburgh

Psychology Department
Beaumont Hall, 101 Broad Street
Plattsburgh, NY 12901
Telephone: (518) 564-3076
Fax: (518) 564-3397
E-mail: *william.gaeddert@plattsburgh.edu*
Web: *http://www.plattsburgh.edu/academics/psychology*

Department Information:

1970. Chairperson: Drs. Wendy Braje and William Gaeddert, Co-Chairs. Number of faculty: total—full-time 13, part-time 5; women—full-time 6, part-time 4; total—minority—full-time 1.

Programs and Degrees Offered:

Listed in the following order: Program area, degree type (T if terminal Master's), number awarded 7/06–6/07. School Psychology MA/MS (Master of Arts/Science) (T) 6.

Student Applications/Admissions:

Student Applications

School Psychology MA/MS (Master of Arts/Science)—Applications 2007–2008, 30. Total applicants accepted 2007–2008, 15. Number full-time enrolled (new admits only) 2007–2008, 10. Number part-time enrolled (new admits only) 2007–2008, 0. Openings 2008–2009, 10. The median number of years required for completion of a degree in 2006–2007 were 4. The number of students enrolled full- and part-time who were dismissed or voluntarily withdrew from this program area in 2007–2008 were 1.

Admissions Requirements:

Scores: Entries appear in this order: required test or GPA, minimum score (if required), median score of students entering in 2007–2008. Master's Programs: overall undergraduate GPA 3.00, 3.20.

Other Criteria: (importance of criteria rated low, medium, or high): GRE/MAT scores—low, research experience—medium, work experience—high, extracurricular activity—low, clinically related public service—medium, GPA—high, letters of recommendation—medium, statement of goals and objectives—high, undergraduate major in psychology—low, specific undergraduate psychology courses taken—medium. For additional information on admission requirements, go to http://www.plattsburgh.edu/academics/psychology/graduateprogram/.

Student Characteristics: The following represents characteristics of students in 2007–2008 in all graduate psychology programs in the department: Female—full-time 25, part-time 1; Male—full-time 5, part-time 0; African American/Black—full-time 0, part-time 0; Hispanic/Latino(a)—full-time 3, part-time 0; Asian/Pacific Islander—full-time 0, part-time 0; American Indian/Alaska Native—full-time 0, part-time 0; Caucasian/White—full-time 27, part-time 0; Multi-ethnic—full-time 0, part-time 0; students subject to the Americans With Disabilities Act—full-time 0, part-time 0; Unknown ethnicity—full-time 0, part-time 0.

Financial Information/Assistance:

Tuition for Full-Time Study: *Master's:* State residents: per academic year $6,900, $288 per credit hour; Nonstate residents: per academic year $10,920, $455 per credit hour. Tuition is subject to change.

Financial Assistance:

First-Year Students: Research assistantships available for first year. Average amount paid per academic year: $4,600. Average number of hours worked per week: 10. Apply by February 1. Tuition remission given: partial. Traineeships available for first year. Average amount paid per academic year: $5,000. Average number of hours worked per week: 15. Apply by February 1. Tuition remission given: partial.

Advanced Students: Research assistantships available for advanced students. Average amount paid per academic year: $4,600. Average number of hours worked per week: 10. Apply by February 1. Tuition remission given: partial. Traineeships available for advanced students. Average amount paid per academic year: $5,000. Average number of hours worked per week: 15. Apply by February 1. Tuition remission given: full.

Additional Information: Of all students currently enrolled full time, 40% benefited from one or more of the listed financial assistance programs.

Internships/Practica: During the third and final year of graduate study, students are placed within school districts on a full-time basis. School districts sometimes offer a stipend under contractual agreement with the graduate student and the University. Stipends range from $7,000 to $14,000. Relocating to a school district in order to receive a stipend might be necessary.

Housing and Day Care: On-campus housing is available. Graduate Admissions, Kehoe Building, Plattsburgh State University of New York, 101 Broad Street, Plattsburgh, NY 12901. On-campus day care facilities are available.

Employment of Department Graduates:

Master's Degree Graduates: Of those who graduated in the academic year 2006–2007, the following categories and numbers represent the postgraduate activities and employment of master's degree graduates: Enrolled in a psychology doctoral program (0), enrolled in a postdoctoral residency/fellowship (n/a), employed in independent practice (n/a), employed in a professional position in a school system (9), still seeking employment (0), total from the above (master's) (9).

Doctoral Degree Graduates: Of those who graduated in the academic year 2006–2007, the following categories and numbers represent the postgraduate activities and employment of doctoral degree graduates: Enrolled in a psychology doctoral program (n/a), total from the above (doctoral) (0).

Additional Information:

Orientation, Objectives, and Emphasis of Department: The curriculum is a 3-year, 70-hour MA program in psychology. The program offers coursework in psychological theories and skill development and applied experiences in area schools and community agencies. The goal of the program is to enable students to work effectively with individuals and groups and to act as psychological resources in schools and the community. A unique feature of the program is that many courses, beginning in the first semester, combine theory and research with practicum experiences in school and clinical work. Students develop competencies in personality, research methods, psychological assessment, behavior modification, individual and group psychotherapy, and community mental health. An important aspect of graduate training is the internship served the 3rd year of graduate study at area schools. The Psychology Department and the agencies involved provide extensive supervision of students' work.

Special Facilities or Resources: All students participate in off-site practicum experiences in local schools. The Neuropsychology Clinic and Psychoeducational Services center provide some graduate students with on-site practicum experiences. The Nexus Program (an after-school program for children diagnosed on the autism spectrum) provides some graduate students with on-site practicum experiences.

Information for Students With Physical Disabilities: See the following Web site for more information: http://www.plattsburgh.edu.

Application Information:

Send to Graduate Admissions, Kehoe Hall, SUNY Plattsburgh, 101 Broad Street, Plattsburgh, NY 12901. Application available online. URL of online application: http://www.plattsburgh.edu/admissions/forms.php. Students are admitted in the Fall, application deadline February 1. *Fee:* $75.

State University of New York, University at Albany

Department of Psychology
College of Arts and Sciences
1400 Washington Avenue
Albany, NY 12222
Telephone: (518) 442-4820
Fax: (518) 442-4867
E-mail: *cm949@albany.edu*
Web: *http://www.albany.edu/psy/*

Department Information:

1950. Chairperson: Kevin J. Williams. Number of faculty: total—full-time 29; women—full-time 12; total—minority—full-time 5; women minority—full-time 4.

Programs and Degrees Offered:

Listed in the following order: Program area, degree type (T if terminal Master's), number awarded 7/06–6/07: Biopsychology PhD (Doctor of Philosophy) 2, Clinical PhD (Doctor of Philosophy) 9, Cognitive PhD (Doctor of Philosophy) 1, Industrial/Organizational PhD (Doctor of Philosophy) 3, Social/Personality PhD (Doctor of Philosophy) 0, Industrial/Organizational MA/MS (Master of Arts/Science) (T) 0.

APA Accreditation: Clinical PhD (Doctor of Philosophy).

Student Applications/Admissions:

Student Applications

Biopsychology PhD (Doctor of Philosophy)—Applications 2007–2008, 21. Total applicants accepted 2007–2008, 7. Number full-time enrolled (new admits only) 2007–2008, 3. Number part-time enrolled (new admits only) 2007–2008, 0. Total enrolled 2007–2008 full-time, 17, part-time, 1. Openings 2008–2009, 3. The median number of years required for completion of a degree in 2006–2007 were 8. The number of students enrolled full- and part-time who were dismissed or voluntarily withdrew from this program area in 2007–2008 were 2. *Clinical PhD (Doctor of Philosophy)*—Applications 2007–2008, 205. Total applicants accepted 2007–2008, 10. Number full-time enrolled (new admits only) 2007–2008, 8. Number part-time enrolled (new admits only) 2007–2008, 0. Openings 2008–2009, 6. The median number of years required for completion of a degree in 2006–2007 were 8. The number of students enrolled full- and part-time who were dismissed or voluntarily withdrew from this program area in 2007–2008 were 0. *Cognitive PhD (Doctor of Philosophy)*—Applications 2007–2008, 7. Total applicants accepted 2007–2008, 5. Number full-time enrolled (new admits only) 2007–2008, 3. Number part-time enrolled (new admits only) 2007–2008, 0. Openings 2008–2009, 3. The median number of years required for completion of a degree in 2006–2007 were 5. The number of students enrolled full- and part-time who were dismissed or voluntarily withdrew from this program area in 2007–2008 were 1. *Industrial/Organizational PhD (Doctor of Philosophy)*—Applications 2007–2008, 22. Total applicants accepted 2007–2008, 10. Number full-time enrolled (new admits only) 2007–2008, 3. Number part-time enrolled (new admits only) 2007–2008, 0. Total enrolled 2007–2008 full-time, 11, part-time, 3. Openings 2008–2009, 3. The median number of years required for completion of a degree in 2006–2007 were 5. The number of students enrolled full- and part-time who were dismissed or voluntarily withdrew from this program area in 2007–2008 were 0. *Social/Personality PhD (Doctor of Philosophy)*—Applications 2007–2008, 10. Total applicants accepted 2007–2008, 6. Number full-time enrolled (new admits only) 2007–2008, 2. Number part-time enrolled (new admits only) 2007–2008, 0. Total enrolled 2007–2008 full-time, 7, part-time, 3. Openings 2008–2009, 3. The number of students enrolled full- and part-time who were dismissed or voluntarily withdrew from this program area in 2007–2008 were 2. *Industrial/Organizational MA/MS (Master of Arts/Science)*—Applications 2007–2008, 6. Total applicants accepted 2007–2008, 3. Number full-time enrolled (new admits only) 2007–2008, 2. Number part-time enrolled (new admits only) 2007–2008, 0. Openings 2008–2009, 3. The number of students enrolled full- and part-time who were dismissed or voluntarily withdrew from this program area in 2007–2008 were 0.

Admissions Requirements:

Scores: Entries appear in this order: required test or GPA, minimum score (if required), median score of students entering in 2007–2008. Master's Programs: GRE-V 500; GRE-Q 600; overall undergraduate GPA 3.0; psychology GPA 3.25. Master's degree offered only in the Industrial/Organizational program. Doctoral Programs: GRE-V 500, 585; GRE-Q 600, 661; GRE-Subject (Psychology) 600, 653; overall undergraduate GPA 3.0, 3.58; psychology GPA 3.25, 3.71.

Other Criteria: (importance of criteria rated low, medium, or high): GRE/MAT scores—high, research experience—high, work experience—low, extracurricular activity—low, clinically related public service—medium, GPA—high, letters of recommendation—high, interview—high, statement of goals and objectives—high, undergraduate major in psychology—medium, specific undergraduate psychology courses taken—medium. The interview process and clinically related service are relevant for the Clinical Psychology program only. For additional information on admission requirements, go to http://www.albany.edu/psy.

Student Characteristics: The following represents characteristics of students in 2007–2008 in all graduate psychology programs in the department: Female—full-time 76, part-time 7; Male—full-time 24, part-time 0; African American/Black—full-time 6, part-time 0; Hispanic/Latino(a)—full-time 5, part-time 0; Asian/Pacific Islander—full-time 11, part-time 1; American Indian/Alaska Native—full-time 0, part-time 0; Caucasian/White—full-time 76, part-time 6; Multi-ethnic—full-time 2, part-time 0; students subject to the Americans With Disabilities Act—full-time 0, part-time 0; Unknown ethnicity—full-time 0, part-time 0; International students who hold an F-1 or J-1 Visa—full-time 10, part-time 0.

Financial Information/Assistance:

Tuition for Full-Time Study: *Master's:* State residents: per academic year $6,900, $288 per credit hour; Nonstate residents: per academic year $10,920, $455 per credit hour. *Doctoral:* State residents: per academic year $6,900, $288 per credit hour; Nonstate residents: per academic year $10,920, $455 per credit hour. Tuition is subject to change. Additional fees are assessed to students beyond the costs of tuition for the following: university fee, comprehensive service fee, and graduate student organization fee. See the following Web site for updates and changes in tuition costs: http://www.albany.edu/studentaccounts/charges.htm.

Financial Assistance:

First-Year Students: Teaching assistantships available for first year. Average amount paid per academic year: $14,000. Average number of hours worked per week: 20. Apply by January 15. Tuition remission given: full. Research assistantships available for first year. Average amount paid per academic year: $14,000. Average number of hours worked per week: 20. Apply by January 15. Tuition remission given: full.

Advanced Students: Teaching assistantships available for advanced students. Average amount paid per academic year: $14,000. Average number of hours worked per week: 20. Apply by None. Tuition remission given: full and partial. Research assistantships available for advanced students. Average amount paid per academic year: $14,000. Average number of hours worked per week: 20. Apply by None. Tuition remission given: full and partial.

Additional Information: Of all students currently enrolled full time, 94% benefited from one or more of the listed financial assistance programs. Application and information available online at http://www.albany.edu/graduate/.

Internships/Practica: Doctoral Degree (PhD Clinical): For those doctoral students for whom a professional internship was required in this program prior to graduation, (8) students applied for an internship in 2006–2007, with (4) students obtaining an internship. Of those students who obtained an internship, (4) were paid internships. Of those students who obtained an internship, (4) students placed in APA/CPA-accredited internships, (0) students placed in internships not APA/CPA-accredited, but listed with the Association of Psychology Postdoctoral and Internship Centers (APPIC), (0) students placed in internships conforming to guidelines of the Council of Directors of School Psychology Programs (CDSPP), (0) students placed in internships that were not APA/CPA-accredited, APPIC or CDSPP listed. During the 2nd year of our doctoral program in Clinical Psychology, students are placed at the Psychological Services Center, a University-operated center that serves the general population of the city of Albany. During this placement students are supervised by members of the Clinical faculty. In their 3rd year, students are required to participate in a community-based practicum. These practica include community mental health centers, VA inpatient and outpatient centers, inpatient and outpatient clinics in community hospitals and rehabilitation centers, residential facilities for youth, and the University's counseling center. Students may also elect to participate in an additional community-based practicum experience during their 4th year of training. Students are encouraged to attend APA-accredited internships during their 5th year of study. Our students have attended internships in a variety of settings including children's hospitals, psychiatric hospitals, VA hospitals, university-affiliated medical centers, general hospitals, and rehabilitation centers. Practicum and internship placements for doctoral students in the Industrial/Organizational Psychology specialization are possible with a number of local and national corporations and government agencies.

Housing and Day Care: On-campus housing is available. See the following Web site for more information: http://www.albany.edu/housing. On-campus day care facilities are available. See the following Web site for more information: http://www.albany.edu; contact U-Kids Child Care (518) 442-2660.

Employment of Department Graduates:

Master's Degree Graduates: Of those who graduated in the academic year 2006–2007, the following categories and numbers represent the postgraduate activities and employment of master's degree graduates: Enrolled in a postdoctoral residency/fellowship (n/a), employed in independent practice (n/a), total from the above (master's) (0).

Doctoral Degree Graduates: Of those who graduated in the academic year 2006–2007, the following categories and numbers represent the postgraduate activities and employment of doctoral degree graduates: Enrolled in a psychology doctoral program (n/a), enrolled in another graduate/professional program (0), enrolled in a postdoctoral residency/fellowship (1), employed in independent practice (1), employed in an academic position at a university (2), employed in an academic position at a 2-year/4-year college (0), employed in other positions at a higher education institution (0), employed in a professional position in a school system (0), employed in business or industry (4), employed in government agency (1), employed in a community mental health/counseling center (0), employed in a hospital/medical center (3), still seeking employment (1), not seeking employment (0), other employment position (0), do not know (2), total from the above (doctoral) (15).

Additional Information:

Orientation, Objectives, and Emphasis of Department: All facets of the graduate program reflect a commitment to the empirical tradition in psychology. Thus, involvement in research is stressed in all areas of study. Students begin an apprentice relationship with faculty members upon entry into the department and are expected to remain actively involved in research throughout their graduate careers. A major goal of the department is to train individuals who will make research contributions to the field. All areas of concentration train students for careers as teachers and research scientists. In addition, the social, clinical, and, industrial/organizational areas prepare students for careers in applied settings. The orientation of the Clinical program emphasizes cognitive and behavioral approaches. Admission is offered in five areas: Biopsychology, Clinical, Cognitive, Industrial/Organizational, and Social/Personality.

Special Facilities or Resources: Resources and facilities include university- and grant-funded student stipends, plus stipends from other campus sources; a state-of-the-art animal facility and research laboratories in the Life Sciences Building; several human research laboratories; grant-supported research and treatment clinics; the Psychological Services Center for practicum training; and a variety of research equipment.

Information for Students With Physical Disabilities: See the following Web site for more information: http://www.albany.edu/studentlife.

Application Information:

Send to Office of Graduate Admissions, University Administration Building 121, 1400 Washington Avenue, Albany, NY 12222. Application available online. URL of online application: http://www.albany.edu/graduate/applyonline.shtml. Students are admitted in the Fall, application deadline see below. PhD programs: January 1 for Clinical Psychology; January 15 for all other areas. I/O MA program: March 15. *Fee:* $75.

State University of New York, University at Albany

Department of Educational and Counseling Psychology
School of Education
1400 Washington Avenue
Albany, NY 12222
Telephone: (518) 442-5050
Fax: (518) 442-4953
E-mail: *kquinn@uamail.albany.edu*
Web: *http://www.albany.edu/education/contact_us.html*

Department Information:

1963. Directors (Counseling Psychology, School Psychology, Educational Psychology): Myrna Friedlander, David Miller, Joan Newman. Number of faculty: total—full-time 13, part-time 7; women—full-time 15, part-time 10; women minority—full-time 1, part-time 20.

Programs and Degrees Offered:

Listed in the following order: Program area, degree type (T if terminal Master's), number awarded 7/06–6/07. Counseling Psychology PhD (Doctor of Philosophy) 5, School Psychology PsyD (Doctor of Psychology) 3, Educational Psychology MA/MS (Master of Arts/Science) 10, Educational Psychology PhD (Doctor of Philosophy) 8, School Psychology Other 3, School Counseling Other 9, Mental Health Counseling MA/MS (Master of Arts/Science) 10.

APA Accreditation: Counseling PhD (Doctor of Philosophy). School PsyD (Doctor of Psychology).

Student Applications/Admissions:

Student Applications

Counseling Psychology PhD (Doctor of Philosophy)—Applications 2007–2008, 85. Total applicants accepted 2007–2008, 10. Number full-time enrolled (new admits only) 2007–2008, 7. Number part-time enrolled (new admits only) 2007–2008, 0. Total enrolled 2007–2008 full-time, 48, part-time, 3. Openings 2008–2009, 8. The median number of years required for completion of a degree in 2006–2007 were 7. The number of students enrolled full- and part-time who were dismissed or voluntarily withdrew from this program area in 2007–2008 were 2. *School Psychology PsyD (Doctor of Psychology)*—Applications 2007–2008, 55. Total applicants accepted 2007–2008, 6. Number full-time enrolled (new admits only) 2007–2008, 6. Number part-time enrolled (new admits only) 2007–2008, 0. Openings 2008–2009, 5. The median number of years required for completion of a degree in 2006–2007 were 5. The number of students enrolled full- and part-time who were dismissed or voluntarily withdrew from this program area in 2007–2008 were 1. *Educational Psychology MA/MS (Master of*

Arts/Science)—Applications 2007–2008, 12. Total applicants accepted 2007–2008, 9. Number full-time enrolled (new admits only) 2007–2008, 5. Number part-time enrolled (new admits only) 2007–2008, 2. Total enrolled 2007–2008 full-time, 6, part-time, 14. Openings 2008–2009, 30. The median number of years required for completion of a degree in 2006–2007 were 2. The number of students enrolled full- and part-time who were dismissed or voluntarily withdrew from this program area in 2007–2008 were 0. *Educational Psychology PhD (Doctor of Philosophy)*—Applications 2007–2008, 20. Total applicants accepted 2007–2008, 11. Number full-time enrolled (new admits only) 2007–2008, 6. Number part-time enrolled (new admits only) 2007–2008, 2. Total enrolled 2007–2008 full-time, 25, part-time, 14. Openings 2008–2009, 8. The median number of years required for completion of a degree in 2006–2007 were 6. The number of students enrolled full- and part-time who were dismissed or voluntarily withdrew from this program area in 2007–2008 were 2. *School Psychology Other*—Applications 2007–2008, 27. Total applicants accepted 2007–2008, 10. Number full-time enrolled (new admits only) 2007–2008, 10. Number part-time enrolled (new admits only) 2007–2008, 0. Openings 2008–2009, 10. The median number of years required for completion of a degree in 2006–2007 were 3. The number of students enrolled full- and part-time who were dismissed or voluntarily withdrew from this program area in 2007–2008 were 0. *School Counseling Other*—Applications 2007–2008, 30. Total applicants accepted 2007–2008, 12. Number full-time enrolled (new admits only) 2007–2008, 10. Openings 2008–2009, 10. The median number of years required for completion of a degree in 2006–2007 were 2. The number of students enrolled full- and part-time who were dismissed or voluntarily withdrew from this program area in 2007–2008 were 1. *Mental Health Counseling MA/MS (Master of Arts/Science)*—Applications 2007–2008, 68. Total applicants accepted 2007–2008, 15. Number full-time enrolled (new admits only) 2007–2008, 16. Number part-time enrolled (new admits only) 2007–2008, 0. Openings 2008–2009, 15. The median number of years required for completion of a degree in 2006–2007 were 2. The number of students enrolled full- and part-time who were dismissed or voluntarily withdrew from this program area in 2007–2008 were 0.

Admissions Requirements:

Scores: Entries appear in this order: required test or GPA, minimum score (if required), median score of students entering in 2007–2008. Master's Programs: GRE-V no minimum stated; GRE-Q no minimum stated; overall undergraduate GPA no minimum stated; psychology GPA no minimum stated. The GRE-Analytical is required for school psychology but not counseling psychology Doctoral Programs: GRE-V no minimum stated; GRE-Q no minimum stated; overall undergraduate GPA no minimum stated; psychology GPA no minimum stated. Typically the scores for the master's and Certificate of Advanced Study programs are lower than those for the doctoral programs.

Other Criteria: (importance of criteria rated low, medium, or high): GRE/MAT scores—high, research experience—high, work experience—medium, extracurricular activity—medium, clinically related public service—medium, GPA—high, letters of recommendation—high, interview—high, statement of goals and objectives—high. In Counseling Psychology, research experience is rated more highly for PhD applicants than for master's and CAS applicants. For additional information on admission requirements, go to http://www.albany.edu/counseling_psych; http://www.albany.edu/schoolpsych; http://www.albany.edu/educational_psychology.

Student Characteristics: The following represents characteristics of students in 2007–2008 in all graduate psychology programs in the department: Female—full-time 140, part-time 23; Male—full-time 32, part-time 6; African American/Black—full-time 10, part-time 3; Hispanic/Latino(a)—full-time 6, part-time 1; Asian/Pacific Islander—full-time 14, part-time 0; American Indian/Alaska Native—full-time 0, part-time 0; Caucasian/White—full-time 159, part-time 21; Multi-ethnic—full-time 1, part-time 0; students subject to the Americans With Disabilities Act—full-time 1, part-time 2; Unknown ethnicity—full-time 0, part-time 0; International students who hold an F-1 or J-1 Visa—full-time 22, part-time 1.

Financial Information/Assistance:

Tuition for Full-Time Study: *Master's:* State residents: per academic year $6,900, $288 per credit hour; Nonstate residents: per academic year $10,920, $455 per credit hour. *Doctoral:* State residents: per academic year $6,900, $288 per credit hour; Nonstate residents: per academic year $10,920, $455 per credit hour. Tuition is subject to change. Additional fees are assessed to students beyond the costs of tuition for the following: university, comprehensive, graduate student organization fees, insurance for international students. See the following Web site for updates and changes in tuition costs: http://www.albany.edu/studentaccounts/charges2008spring.htm.

Financial Assistance:

First-Year Students: Research assistantships available for first year. Average amount paid per academic year: $12,000. Average number of hours worked per week: 20. Apply by December 15. Tuition remission given: full. Fellowships and scholarships available for first year. Average amount paid per academic year: $12,000. Apply by December 15. Tuition remission given: full.

Advanced Students: Teaching assistantships available for advanced students. Average amount paid per academic year: $11,000. Average number of hours worked per week: 20. Apply by April 1. Tuition remission given: full. Research assistantships available for advanced students. Average amount paid per academic year: $11,000. Average number of hours worked per week: 20. Apply by April 1. Tuition remission given: full. Traineeships available for advanced students. Average amount paid per academic year: $9,000. Average number of hours worked per week: 22. Apply by April 1. Tuition remission given: full. Fellowships and scholarships available for advanced students. Average amount paid per academic year: $11,000. Apply by April 1. Tuition remission given: full.

Additional Information: Of all students currently enrolled full time, 60% benefited from one or more of the listed financial assistance programs. Application and information available online at http://www.albany.educ/financial_aid/.

Internships/Practica: Doctoral Degree (PhD Counseling Psychology): For those doctoral students for whom a professional internship was required in this program prior to graduation, (9) students applied for an internship in 2006–2007, with (9) students obtaining an internship. Of those students who obtained an internship, (9) were paid internships. Of those students who obtained an internship, (8) students placed in APA/CPA-accredited internships, (0) students placed in internships not APA/CPA-accredited, but listed with the Association of Psychology Postdoctoral and Internship Centers (APPIC), (0) students placed in internships conforming to guidelines of the Council of Directors of School Psychology Programs (CDSPP), (1) student placed in internships that were not APA/CPA-accredited, APPIC or CDSPP listed. In Counseling Psychology, PhD students take beginning and advanced practica in specialized procedures. The initial year-long practicum is taken at the university-operated Psychological Services Center, a training facility for graduate students in the Counseling and Clinical Psychology programs. Opportunities for practica in specialized procedures are typically community based, and have included inpatient and outpatient assessment in college and university counseling centers; private, state, and general hospitals; community mental health agencies; and residential treatment settings for youth. Our doctoral students have been highly successful in obtaining their preferred APA-accredited internships. Master's students in counseling take practica and internships in public schools, hospitals, and community agencies. Both PsyD and CAS students in School Psychology complete a two-semester, school-based practicum under the supervision of the University clinical supervisor. Experiences that the students complete include assessments, individual and group counseling, classroom interventions, tutoring, and consultation. Doctoral students in school psychology complete additional field training experiences in local schools and agencies to reinforce basic skills and to develop additional skills in consultation, prevention, and systems issues. Certificate students complete a 1-year, full-time internship in a public school system to develop and reinforce basic skill competencies needed for future employment. For additional information on education and training outcomes for our programs, see the following Web site (for the PhD in counseling psychology): http://www.albany.edu/counseling_psy.

Housing and Day Care: On-campus housing is available. See the following Web site for more information: http://www.albany.edu/housing/ or http://www.albany.edu/opsoca/off_campus_housing/. On-campus day care facilities are available. See the following Web site for more information: http://www.albany.edu/cpsp/sites/u/u1.html. Phone: (518) 442-2660 (U-Kids Child Care).

Employment of Department Graduates:

Master's Degree Graduates: Of those who graduated in the academic year 2006–2007, the following categories and numbers represent the postgraduate activities and employment of master's degree graduates: Enrolled in another graduate/professional program (1), enrolled in a postdoctoral residency/fellowship (n/a), employed in independent practice (n/a), employed in a professional position in a school system (3), other employment position (1), do not know (36), total from the above (master's) (41).

Doctoral Degree Graduates: Of those who graduated in the academic year 2006–2007, the following categories and numbers represent the postgraduate activities and employment of doctoral degree graduates: Enrolled in a psychology doctoral program (n/a), enrolled in a postdoctoral residency/fellowship (2), employed in an academic position at a university (1), employed in an academic position at a 2-year/4-year college (2), employed in other positions at a higher education institution (1), employed in a professional position in a school system (2), employed in a community mental health/counseling center (1), employed in a hospital/medical center (1), other employment position (4), total from the above (doctoral) (14).

Additional Information:

Orientation, Objectives, and Emphasis of Department: The master's programs in School Psychology and in Mental Health and School Counseling are practitioner focused. In the School and Counseling psychology doctoral programs, practice and science are viewed as complementary and interdependent, implemented thorough coursework in psychological foundations, research methods, intervention theory and assessment, and by research and practice opportunities via assistantships, professional development activities, practica, specialized coursework, and independent study. Our generalist training emphasizes normal development and theory and methods relating to prevention and remediation of intra- and interpersonal human concerns. We have many opportunities to explore issues of individual and cultural diversity, to learn a variety of theoretical orientations, to pursue a range of research topics and methods, to study with a multicultural array of colleagues, to work with diverse client populations in multiple work settings, and to engage in varied professional roles. The master's program in educational psychology and statistics focuses on research-based knowledge of human development, learning and individual differences, and the development of skills and understanding of research methodology. The program serves two main groups of students: those students seeking professional teaching certification in New York state, and students desiring introductory graduate work in psychology.

Special Facilities or Resources: Fee-for-service training clinic, the Psychological Services Center, is directed by a licensed psychologist. Second-year doctoral students are supervised by licensed faculty using one-way mirrors and live video monitoring. Advanced doctoral students may have assistantships at the Center, where they gain additional experience in psychodiagnostic testing and psychotherapy. Assistants also provide assessment and intervention services for outside agencies that contract with the Center for services (e.g., private schools, Family Court, etc.). One unique aspect of the program in Counseling Psychology is the opportunity for PhD students who are reasonably fluent in Spanish to participate in an exchange program with a family therapy training program in northwestern Spain. The Division of School Psychology maintans ongoing training partnerships with a number of local school districts and community agencies. Faculty in the Educational Psychology and Methodology Division are associated with two centers that provide students with opportunities to gain experience to supplement their coursework. The Child Research and Study Center undertakes research into the acquisition and remediation of reading skill, and consultation with schools and parents regarding children's school related difficulties. The Evaluation Consortium contracts to evaluate a wide variety of programs provided by schools and agencies.

Information for Students With Physical Disabilities: See the following Web site for more information: http://www.albany.edu/studentlife/dss/dss.html.

Application Information:

Send to Office of Graduate Studies, University of Albany, State University of New York, 1400 Washington Avenue, Albany, NY 12222. Application available online. URL of online application: http://www.albany.edu/graduate/applyonline.shtml. Students are admitted in the

Fall, application deadline see below; Summer, application deadline February 15. MS and CAS applications for Mental Health and School Counseling are due February 15 for Summer admission. MS and CAS applicants for Educational Psychology are suggested for March 1 and October 15. PhD applications for Counseling Psychology are due December 15. PhD applications for Educational Psychology are due January 15. CAS and PsyD applications for School Psychology are due January 2. *Fee:* $75.

Stony Brook University

Department of Psychology
Stony Brook, NY 11794-2500
Telephone: (631) 632-7855
Fax: (631) 632-7876
E-mail: *mwollmuth@notes.cc.sunysb.edu*
Web: *http://www.psychology.sunysb.edu*

Department Information:

1961. Chair: Nancy Squires. Number of faculty: total—full-time 31; women—full-time 15; total—minority—full-time 3; women minority—full-time 2.

Programs and Degrees Offered:

Listed in the following order: Program area, degree type (T if terminal Master's), number awarded 7/06–6/07. Biopsychology PhD (Doctor of Philosophy) 3, Clinical PhD (Doctor of Philosophy) 6, Cognitive/Experimental PhD (Doctor of Philosophy) 4, Social/Health PhD (Doctor of Philosophy) 6.

APA Accreditation: Clinical PhD (Doctor of Philosophy).

Student Applications/Admissions:

Student Applications

Biopsychology PhD (Doctor of Philosophy)—Total applicants accepted 2007–2008, 4. Number full-time enrolled (new admits only) 2007–2008, 4. Total enrolled 2007–2008 full-time, 15. Openings 2008–2009, 5. The median number of years required for completion of a degree in 2006–2007 were 5. The number of students enrolled full- and part-time who were dismissed or voluntarily withdrew from this program area in 2007–2008 were 1. *Clinical PhD (Doctor of Philosophy)*—Applications 2007–2008, 335. Total applicants accepted 2007–2008, 11. Number full-time enrolled (new admits only) 2007–2008, 6. Total enrolled 2007–2008 full-time, 38. Openings 2008–2009, 6. The median number of years required for completion of a degree in 2006–2007 were 6. The number of students enrolled full- and part-time who were dismissed or voluntarily withdrew from this program area in 2007–2008 were 2. *Cognitive/Experimental PhD (Doctor of Philosophy)*—Applications 2007–2008, 34. Total applicants accepted 2007–2008, 9. Number full-time enrolled (new admits only) 2007–2008, 5. Total enrolled 2007–2008 full-time, 17. Openings 2008–2009, 5. The median number of years required for completion of a degree in 2006–2007 were 5. The number of students enrolled full- and part-time who were dismissed or voluntarily withdrew from this program area in 2007–2008 were 2. *Social/Health PhD (Doctor of Philosophy)*—Applications 2007–2008, 78. Total applicants accepted 2007–2008, 5. Number full-time enrolled (new admits only) 2007–2008, 1. Total enrolled 2007–2008 full-time, 25. Openings 2008–2009, 6. The median number of years required for completion of a degree in 2006–2007 were 5. The number of students enrolled full- and part-time who were dismissed or voluntarily withdrew from this program area in 2007–2008 were 0.

Admissions Requirements:

Scores: Entries appear in this order: required test or GPA, minimum score (if required), median score of students entering in 2007–2008. Master's Programs: We do not offer a Master's program. Doctoral programs: GRE-V 600, 625; GRE-Q 600, 695; overall undergraduate GPA 3.5, 3.7; Doctoral program GRE-Analytic 600, 5.

Other Criteria: (importance of criteria rated low, medium, or high): GRE/MAT scores—high, research experience—high, work experience—low, extracurricular activity—low, clinically related public service—low, GPA—medium, letters of recommendation—high, interview—medium, statement of goals and objectives—high. These critera vary for different program areas.

Student Characteristics: The following represents characteristics of students in 2007–2008 in all graduate psychology programs in the department: Female—full-time 70, part-time 0; Male—full-time 25, part-time 0; African American/Black—full-time 1, part-time 0; Hispanic/Latino(a)—full-time 7, part-time 0; Asian/Pacific Islander—full-time 9, part-time 0; American Indian/Alaska Native—full-time 0, part-time 0; Caucasian/White—full-time 78, part-time 0; students subject to the Americans With Disabilities Act—full-time 0, part-time 0; Unknown ethnicity—full-time 0, part-time 0; International students who hold an F-1 or J-1 Visa—full-time 10, part-time 0.

Financial Information/Assistance:

Tuition for Full-Time Study: *Doctoral:* State residents: per academic year $5,184, $288 per credit hour; Nonstate residents: per academic year $8,190, $455 per credit hour. Tuition is subject to change.

Financial Assistance:

First-Year Students: Teaching assistantships available for first year. Average amount paid per academic year: $17,145. Average number of hours worked per week: 20. Apply by December 15. Tuition remission given: full. Research assistantships available for first year. Average amount paid per academic year: $17,145. Average number of hours worked per week: 20. Apply by December 15. Tuition remission given: full.

Advanced Students: No information provided.

Additional Information: Of all students currently enrolled full time, 99% benefited from one or more of the listed financial assistance programs. Application and information available online at http://www.grad.sunysb.edu/prospective/applying/index.shtml.

Internships/Practica: No information provided.

Housing and Day Care: On-campus housing is available. See the following Web site for more information: http://www.studentaffairs.stonybrook.edu/residence. On-campus day care facilities are available. See the following Web site for more information: http://www.ws.cc.stonybrook.edu/sb/childcare/.

Employment of Department Graduates:

Master's Degree Graduates: Of those who graduated in the academic year 2006–2007, the following categories and numbers represent the postgraduate activities and employment of master's degree graduates: Enrolled in a postdoctoral residency/fellowship (n/a), employed in independent practice (n/a), total from the above (master's) (0).

Doctoral Degree Graduates: Of those who graduated in the academic year 2006–2007, the following categories and numbers represent the postgraduate activities and employment of doctoral degree graduates: Enrolled in a psychology doctoral program (n/a), enrolled in a postdoctoral residency/fellowship (7), employed in an academic position at a university (7), employed in other positions at a higher education institution (1), still seeking employment (1), total from the above (doctoral) (16).

Additional Information:

Orientation, Objectives, and Emphasis of Department: In all areas, the primary emphasis is on research training through research advisement and apprenticeship. Students are encouraged to become involved in ongoing research immediately and to engage in independent research when sufficient skills and knowledge permit, with the goal of becoming active and original contributors. As the first behavioral clinical curriculum in the country, Stony Brook has served as a model for a number of other behaviorally oriented clinical programs and continues to be a leader in that field. Research in the experimental area focuses on human perception and cognition and now includes visual cognition, psycholinguistics, memory, attention, and perception. The biopsychology research of core faculty spans the fields of behavioral neuroscience, molecular biology, cognitive neuroscience, and affective neuroscience. Students obtain a broad foundation in neuroscience while developing expertise in a focused research program. Research in social and health psychology includes the study of close relationships in adults and children; prejudice, racism, and stereotyping; and the representation and processing of social experience, motivation, and self-regulation.

Special Facilities or Resources: Besides faculty laboratories for human, animal, and physiological research, and electronics and machine shops, other campus facilities for research and graduate training include Psychological Center, the training, research, and service unit for clinical psychology; Point of Woods Laboratory School with a special education class for elementary students; University Preschool with children from 18 months to 5 years of age; University Marital Therapy Clinic; and Suffolk Child Development Center, a private school for autistic, retarded, aphasic, and developmentally delayed children. Clinical neuropsychology uses affiliations with the University Health Sciences Center, local schools, an agency for the mentally retarded, and a Veterans Administration hospital. Departmental CRT terminals and 12 additional terminals and two printers in the division's Social Science Data Laboratory are used with campus computers.

Application Information:

Send to Graduate Office, Department of Psychology, Stony Brook University, Stony Brook, NY 11794-2500. Application available on-line. URL of online application: http://www.psychology.sunysb.edu/psychology/grad/gradapply.htm. Students are admitted in the Fall, application deadline December 15. *Fee:* $60.

Syracuse University

Department of Psychology
Arts and Sciences
430 Huntington Hall, 150 Marshall Street
Syracuse, NY 13244-2340
Telephone: (315) 443-2354
Fax: (315) 443-4085
E-mail: *bhfiese@syr.edu*
Web: *http://www.psychweb.syr.edu*

Department Information:

1952. Chairperson: Barbara H. Fiese. Number of faculty: total—full-time 29, part-time 2; women—full-time 11, part-time 2; total—minority—full-time 5, part-time 2; women minority—full-time 3, part-time 2.

Programs and Degrees Offered:

Listed in the following order: Program area, degree type (T if terminal Master's), number awarded 7/06–6/07. Clinical PhD (Doctor of Philosophy) 3, Experimental PhD (Doctor of Philosophy) 1, School PhD (Doctor of Philosophy) 3, Social PhD (Doctor of Philosophy) 0.

APA Accreditation: Clinical PhD (Doctor of Philosophy). School PhD (Doctor of Philosophy).

Student Applications/Admissions:

Student Applications

Clinical PhD (Doctor of Philosophy)—Applications 2007–2008, 108. Total applicants accepted 2007–2008, 10. Number full-time enrolled (new admits only) 2007–2008, 6. Openings 2008–2009, 4. The median number of years required for completion of a degree in 2006–2007 were 7. The number of students enrolled full- and part-time who were dismissed or voluntarily withdrew from this program area in 2007–2008 were 1. *Experimental PhD (Doctor of Philosophy)*—Applications 2007–2008, 13. Total applicants accepted 2007–2008, 3. Number full-time enrolled (new admits only) 2007–2008, 1. Openings 2008–2009, 4. The median number of years required for completion of a degree in 2006–2007 were 7. The number of students enrolled full- and part-time who were dismissed or voluntarily withdrew from this program area in 2007–2008 were 0. *School PhD (Doctor of Philosophy)*—Applications 2007–2008, 29. Total applicants accepted 2007–2008, 4. Number full-time enrolled (new admits only) 2007–2008, 3. Number part-time enrolled (new admits only) 2007–2008, 0. Openings 2008–2009, 5. The median number of years required for completion of a degree in 2006–2007 were 6. The number of students enrolled full- and part-time who were dismissed or voluntarily withdrew from this program area in 2007–2008 were 1. *Social PhD (Doctor of Philosophy)*—Applications 2007–2008, 49. Total applicants accepted 2007–2008, 6. Number full-time enrolled (new admits only) 2007–2008, 1. Number part-time enrolled (new admits only) 2007–2008, 0. Openings 2008–2009, 2. The number of students enrolled full- and part-time who were dismissed or voluntarily withdrew from this program area in 2007–2008 were 1.

Admissions Requirements:

Scores: Entries appear in this order: required test or GPA, minimum score (if required), median score of students entering in 2007–2008. Doctoral Programs: GRE-V 500; GRE-Q 600; overall undergraduate GPA 3.0. GRE required by all programs. Subject required for Clinical Psychology Program only. Subject minimum score is 500.

Other Criteria: (importance of criteria rated low, medium, or high): GRE/MAT scores—high, research experience—high, work experience—medium, extracurricular activity—low, clinically related public service—medium, GPA—high, letters of recommendation—high, interview—high, statement of goals and objectives—high. Interview requirements vary from program to program. For additional information on admission requirements, go to http://psychweb.syr.edu.

Student Characteristics: The following represents characteristics of students in 2007–2008 in all graduate psychology programs in the department: Female—full-time 51, part-time 0; Male—full-time 12, part-time 0; African American/Black—full-time 1, part-time 0; Hispanic/Latino(a)—full-time 1, part-time 0; Asian/Pacific Islander—full-time 1, part-time 0; American Indian/Alaska Native—full-time 0, part-time 0; Caucasian/White—full-time 52, part-time 0; Multi-ethnic—full-time 1, part-time 0; students subject to the Americans With Disabilities Act—full-time 0, part-time 0; Unknown ethnicity—full-time 0, part-time 0; International students who hold an F-1 or J-1 Visa—full-time 7, part-time 0.

Financial Information/Assistance:

Tuition for Full-Time Study: *Doctoral:* State residents: per academic year $18,216, $1,012 per credit hour; Nonstate residents: per academic year $18,216, $1,012 per credit hour. Tuition is subject to change. See the following Web site for updates and changes in tuition costs: http://www.financialaid.syr.edu.

Financial Assistance:

First-Year Students: Teaching assistantships available for first year. Average amount paid per academic year: $11,974. Average number of hours worked per week: 20. Apply by January 1. Tuition remission given: full. Research assistantships available for first year. Average amount paid per academic year: $11,974. Average number of hours worked per week: 20. Apply by January 1. Tuition remission given: full and partial. Fellowships and scholarships available for first year. Average amount paid per academic year: $19,570. Average number of hours worked per week: 0. Apply by January 1. Tuition remission given: full.

Advanced Students: Teaching assistantships available for advanced students. Average amount paid per academic year: $11,974. Average number of hours worked per week: 20. Apply by n/a. Tuition remission given: full. Research assistantships available for advanced students. Average amount paid per academic year: $11,974. Average number of hours worked per week: 20. Apply by n/a. Tuition remission given: full and partial. Fellowships and scholarships available for advanced students. Average amount paid per academic year: $19,570. Average number of hours worked per week: 0. Apply by n/a. Tuition remission given: full.

Additional Information: Of all students currently enrolled full time, 61% benefited from one or more of the listed financial assistance programs.

Internships/Practica: Doctoral Degree (PhD Clinical): For those doctoral students for whom a professional internship was required in this program prior to graduation, (1) student applied for an internship in 2006–2007, with (1) student obtaining an internship. Of those students who obtained an internship, (1) were paid internships. Of those students who obtained an internship, (0) students placed in APA/CPA-accredited internships, (1) students placed in internships not APA/CPA-accredited, but listed with the Association of Psychology Postdoctoral and Internship Centers (APPIC), (0) students placed in internships conforming to guidelines of the Council of Directors of School Psychology Programs (CDSPP), (0) students placed in internships that were not APA/CPA-accredited, APPIC or CDSPP listed. Doctoral Degree (PhD School): For those doctoral students for whom a professional internship was required in this program prior to graduation, (3) students applied for an internship in 2006–2007, with (3) students obtaining an internship. Of those students who obtained an internship, (3) were paid internships. Of those students who obtained an internship, (0) students placed in APA/CPA-accredited internships, (0) students placed in internships not APA/CPA-accredited, but listed with the Association of Psychology Postdoctoral and Internship Centers (APPIC), (3) students placed in internships conforming to guidelines of the Council of Directors of School Psychology Programs (CDSPP), (0) students placed in internships that were not APA/CPA-accredited, APPIC or CDSPP listed. Students in the Clinical and School Psychology training programs have appropriate internship and practica experiences available in hospitals, schools, and other community and university settings. Following completion of their coursework, clinical students complete APA-approved internships as part of their required program of study.

Housing and Day Care: On-campus housing is available. See the following Web site for more information: http://www.housingmealplans.syr.edu. On-campus day care facilities are available.

Employment of Department Graduates:

Master's Degree Graduates: Of those who graduated in the academic year 2006–2007, the following categories and numbers represent the postgraduate activities and employment of master's degree graduates: Enrolled in a psychology doctoral program (0), enrolled in a postdoctoral residency/fellowship (n/a), employed in independent practice (n/a), total from the above (master's) (0).

Doctoral Degree Graduates: Of those who graduated in the academic year 2006–2007, the following categories and numbers represent the postgraduate activities and employment of doctoral degree graduates: Enrolled in a psychology doctoral program (n/a), enrolled in a postdoctoral residency/fellowship (2), employed in an academic position at a university (2), employed in a professional position in a school system (1), employed in a community mental health/counseling center (1), other employment position (1), total from the above (doctoral) (7).

Additional Information:

Orientation, Objectives, and Emphasis of Department: Our goal is to train high-caliber scientists in psychology. Students work closely with a faculty advisor whose research interests are similar to the student's (one can change to a new advisor, however, if one's research interests change). Our APA-approved programs in clinical and school psychology are based on the Boulder scientist–practitioner model. There are four thematic foci in the department: Cognitive Aging; Health and Behavior; the Scholarship of the Causes, Consequences, and Remediation of Social Challenges; and the Psychology of Children in Home and School. Students can gain exposure to research in coping with chronic illness, HIV prevention, memory processes in older adults, school-based intervention, substance abuse, stigma and group process, to name a few. A second goal is training future teachers of psychology. Students typically engage in several semesters of teaching, beginning with sections of introductory psychology and moving on to teach more specialized courses. Entering students participate in the University's "Future Professoriate Program," a teaching practicum nationally known for helping new graduate students enter the profession. Other teaching opportunities are available in the Department's Allport Project, which involves undergraduates in faculty research activities. As part of this program, graduate students may offer supervised but essentially independent seminars for undergraduates in their specialty area. Students enrolled in the clinical and school psychology programs gain clinical experience through our university-based psychological services center and placement in area schools and hospitals.

Special Facilities or Resources: The Department of Psychology is housed in Huntington Hall, an historic building that has been remodeled to provide offices and seminar rooms, as well as laboratories for the study of cognition, social psychology, behavioral medicine, family interaction, and group processes. Labs and offices are equipped with microcomputers for data collection and analysis. A separate wing houses the Department's Psychological Services Center, which offers facilities for clinical and school psychology practicum training and research. In addition, the Department has two facilities on campus and two facilities off campus that provide additional lab space. Other facilities are available through faculty collaborations with researchers at the Upstate Medical University, which is adjacent to Huntington Hall. The Department and its Center for Health and Behavior support two full-time computer technicians.

Information for Students With Physical Disabilities: See the following Web site for more information: http://www.sumweb.syr.edu/ss/dserv/.

Application Information:
Send to Graduate School, Suite 303, Bowne Hall, Syracuse University, Syracuse, NY 13244-1200. Application available online. URL of online application: http://www.apply.embark.com/grad/Syracuse/37. Students are admitted in the Fall, application deadline January 1. To be considered for a University Fellowship, completed applications must be received by January 1. Due to APA requirements, all applications (fellowship and nonfellowship) for the School and Clinical Psychology Programs are due by January 1. *Fee:* $65.

Teachers College, Columbia University (2007 data)

Department of Counseling and Clinical Psychology
Box 102, 525 West 120th Street
New York, NY 10027-6696
Telephone: (212) 678-3257
Fax: (212) 678-3275
E-mail: *edavis@tc.edu*
Web: *http://www.tc.columbia.edu*

Department Information:
1996. Co-Chairs: Elizabeth Midlarsky and Marie Miville. Number of faculty: total—full-time 16, part-time 20; women—full-time 10, part-time 13; faculty subject to the Americans With Disabilities Act 1.

Programs and Degrees Offered:
Listed in the following order: Program area, degree type (T if terminal Master's), number awarded 7/06–6/07. Clinical PhD (Doctor of Philosophy) 21, Counseling PhD (Doctor of Philosophy) 14, Psychological Counseling Other 89, Personality and Psychopathology MA/MS (Master of Arts/Science) (T) 70.

APA Accreditation: Clinical PhD (Doctor of Philosophy). Counseling PhD (Doctor of Philosophy).

Student Applications/Admissions:
Student Applications
Clinical PhD (Doctor of Philosophy)—Applications 2007–2008, 341. Total applicants accepted 2007–2008, 7. Number full-time enrolled (new admits only) 2007–2008, 7. Total enrolled 2007–2008 full-time, 40, part-time, 12. Openings 2008–2009, 8. The median number of years required for completion of a degree in 2006–2007 were 5. The number of students enrolled full- and part-time who were dismissed or voluntarily withdrew from this program area in 2007–2008 were 0. *Counseling PhD (Doctor of Philosophy)*—Applications 2007–2008, 242. Total applicants accepted 2007–2008, 8. Number full-time enrolled (new admits only) 2007–2008, 8. Total enrolled 2007–2008 full-time, 39, part-time, 11. Openings 2008–2009, 8. The median number of years required for completion of a degree in 2006–2007 were 8. The number of students enrolled full- and part-time who were dismissed or voluntarily withdrew from this program area in 2007–2008 were 0. *Psychological Counseling Other*—Applications 2007–2008, 189. Total applicants accepted 2007–2008, 98. Number full-time enrolled (new admits only) 2007–2008, 75. Number part-time enrolled (new admits only) 2007–2008, 9. Total enrolled 2007–2008 full-time, 152, part-time, 68. Openings 2008–2009, 80. The median number of years required for completion of a degree in 2006–2007 were 2. The number of students enrolled full- and part-time who were dismissed or voluntarily withdrew from this program area in 2007–2008 were 2. *Personality and Psychopathology MA/MS (Master of Arts/Science)*—Applications 2007–2008, 130. Total applicants accepted 2007–2008, 107. Number full-time enrolled (new admits only) 2007–2008, 92. Number part-time enrolled (new admits only) 2007–2008, 15. Total enrolled 2007–2008 full-time, 127, part-time, 55. Openings 2008–2009, 95. The median number of years required for completion of a degree in 2006–2007 was 1. The number of students enrolled full- and part-time who were dismissed or voluntarily withdrew from this program area in 2007–2008 were 2.

Admissions Requirements:
Scores: Entries appear in this order: required test or GPA, minimum score (if required), median score of students entering in 2007–2008. Master's Programs: GRE-V no minimum stated; GRE-Q no minimum stated; GRE-Subject (Psychology) no minimum stated; overall undergraduate GPA no minimum stated, 3.5; last 2 years GPA no minimum stated; Masters GRE-Analytical no minimum stated. GRE scores are not required for MEd. For MA, GRE scores are strongly recommended but not required. Doctoral Programs: GRE-V no minimum stated; GRE-Q no minimum stated; GRE-Subject

(Psychology) no minimum stated; overall undergraduate GPA no minimum stated; last 2 years GPA no minimum stated; Doctoral program GRE-Analytic no minimum stated. The criteria varies across program. For more specific informaton please contact the Director of Training for each program area. Subject GREs are required only for the Clinical doctoral program.

Other Criteria: (importance of criteria rated low, medium, or high): The criteria varies across programs. For more specific informaton, please contact the Director of Training for each program area. For additional information on admission requirements, go to http://www.tc.edu/ccp.

Student Characteristics: The following represents characteristics of students in 2007–2008 in all graduate psychology programs in the department: Female—full-time 291, part-time 124; Male—full-time 67, part-time 22; African American/Black—full-time 40, part-time 20; Hispanic/Latino(a)—full-time 21, part-time 6; Asian/Pacific Islander—full-time 37, part-time 12; American Indian/Alaska Native—full-time 0, part-time 1; Caucasian/White—full-time 151, part-time 61; Multi-ethnic—full-time 1, part-time 0; students subject to the Americans With Disabilities Act—full-time 8, part-time 14; Unknown ethnicity—full-time 108, part-time 46.

Financial Information/Assistance:

Tuition for Full-Time Study: *Master's:* State residents: per academic year $32,960, $1,030 per credit hour; Nonstate residents: per academic year $32,960, $1,030 per credit hour. *Doctoral:* State residents: $1,030 per credit hour; Nonstate residents: $1,030 per credit hour. Tuition is subject to change.

Financial Assistance:

First-Year Students: Fellowships and scholarships available for first year. Average amount paid per academic year: $12,000. Apply by December 15. Tuition remission given: partial.

Advanced Students: Teaching assistantships available for advanced students. Tuition remission given: partial. Research assistantships available for advanced students. Tuition remission given: partial. Fellowships and scholarships available for advanced students. Average amount paid per academic year: $6,600. Tuition remission given: partial.

Additional Information: Of all students currently enrolled full time, 40% benefited from one or more of the listed financial assistance programs. Application and information available online at http://www.tc.edu/admissions/finaid.htm.

Internships/Practica: Master's students in the Department of Counseling and Clinical Psychology complete fieldwork appropriate to their track or area of interest in a variety of settings including schools, hospitals, diverse mental health clinics, and rehabilitation centers. Doctoral students do externships in settings similar to the ones indicated above, in preparation for their required APA-approved internships. In addition, all PhD students as well as the MEd students engage in practicum experiences at the Center for Educational and Psychological Services at the College. The Center is a community resource that provides low-cost services for the public utilizing graduate students from several departments within the College. All students receive supervision provided by full-time and adjunct faculty.

Housing and Day Care: On-campus housing is available. See the following Web site for more information: http://www.tc.columbia.edu/housing/. On-campus day care facilities are available. See the following Web site for more information: http://www.tc.edu/centers/hollingworth/; http://www.tc.edu/centers/citp/.

Employment of Department Graduates:

Master's Degree Graduates: Of those who graduated in the academic year 2006–2007, the following categories and numbers represent the postgraduate activities and employment of master's degree graduates: Enrolled in a psychology doctoral program (22), enrolled in a postdoctoral residency/fellowship (n/a), employed in independent practice (n/a), total from the above (master's) (22).

Doctoral Degree Graduates: Of those who graduated in the academic year 2006–2007, the following categories and numbers represent the postgraduate activities and employment of doctoral degree graduates: Enrolled in a psychology doctoral program (n/a), enrolled in another graduate/professional program (0), enrolled in a postdoctoral residency/fellowship (6), employed in an academic position at a university (2), employed in other positions at a higher education institution (1), employed in a community mental health/counseling center (2), employed in a hospital/medical center (2), still seeking employment (1), total from the above (doctoral) (15).

Additional Information:

Orientation, Objectives, and Emphasis of Department: This department prepares students to investigate and address the psychological needs of individuals, families, groups, organizations and institutions, and communities. Counseling Psychology focuses on normal and optimal development across the life span, with particular attention to expanding knowledge and skills in occupational choice and transitions, and multicultural and group counseling. Clinical Psychology primarily uses a broad-based psychodynamic perspective to study and treat a variety of psychological and psychoeducational problems. In addition to sharing an interest and appreciation for the critical role of culture in development and adaptation, both programs highly value the teaching of clinical and research skills. Thus, students in this department are trained to become knowledgeable and proficient researchers, to provide psychological and educational leadership, and to be effective practitioners. Specifically, graduates from these programs seek positions in teaching, research, policy, administration, psychotherapy, and counseling.

Special Facilities or Resources: The College provides academic and research support in several ways. Students of the college have access to all the libraries of Columbia University. Of particular interest, in addition to the Milbank Memorial Library here at Teachers College, are the Psychology Library on the main Columbia campus and the library at the School of Social Work. Technology has transformed most libraries to computer-oriented environments with immediate access to information. The Library not only provides the access but instruction to students so they may avail themselves of the new technology. The ERIC system as well as Interlibrary Loan are also available. The Microcomputer Center provides students with access to PC and Mac computers, which allow for sharing disk, file, and printer resources as well as e-mail services to Columbia University and to the Internet. Other hardware includes CD-ROMs, zip drives, a color scanner, and a sound and video digitizer.

Information for Students With Physical Disabilities: See the following Web site for more information: http://www.tc.columbia.edu/administration/ossd/.

Application Information:
Send to Admissions Office, Box 302, Teachers College, Columbia University, 525 West 120th Street, New York, NY 10027-6696. Application available online. URL of online application: https://www.app.applyyourself.com/?id=col-tc. Students are admitted in the Fall, application deadline (see below). The Doctoral application deadline is December 15. For Master's applications, all admissions materials must be received by January 15 for priority consideration or by April 15 for final consideration. *Fee:* $60. Waiver is available. Hardship verification is done via a letter from Financial Aid Officer at the applicant's previous academic institution.

The New School for Social Research

Department of Psychology
65 Fifth Avenue, F-330
New York, NY 10003
Telephone: (212) 229-5727
Fax: (212) 989-0846
E-mail: *gfpsych@newschool.edu*
Web: *http://www.newschool.edu/gf/psy/*

Department Information:
1936. Chairperson: Joan Miller, PhD. Number of faculty: total—full-time 18, part-time 1; women—full-time 8, part-time 1; total—minority—full-time 3; women minority—full-time 1.

Programs and Degrees Offered:
Listed in the following order: Program area, degree type (T if terminal Master's), number awarded 7/06–6/07. Mental Health Substance Abuse MA/MS (Master of Arts/Science) (T) 8, Clinical Psychology PhD (Doctor of Philosophy) 9, Cognitive, Social, Developmental Psychology (CSD) PhD (Doctor of Philosophy) 4, General Psychology Masters Program MA/MS (Master of Arts/Science) (T) 46.

APA Accreditation: Clinical PhD (Doctor of Philosophy).

Student Applications/Admissions:
Student Applications
Mental Health Substance Abuse MA/MS (Master of Arts/Science)—Applications 2007–2008, 39. Total applicants accepted 2007–2008, 26. Number full-time enrolled (new admits only) 2007–2008, 5. Number part-time enrolled (new admits only) 2007–2008, 1. Total enrolled 2007–2008 full-time, 5, part-time, 8. Openings 2008–2009, 8. The median number of years required for completion of a degree in 2006–2007 were 2. The number of students enrolled full- and part-time who were dismissed or voluntarily withdrew from this program area in 2007–2008 were 0. *Clinical Psychology PhD (Doctor of Philosophy)*—Applications 2007–2008, 24. Total applicants accepted 2007–2008, 16. Number full-time enrolled (new admits only) 2007–2008, 15. Number part-time enrolled (new admits only) 2007–2008, 0. Openings 2008–2009, 16. The median number of years required for completion of a degree in 2006–2007 were 5. The number of students enrolled full- and part-time who were dismissed or voluntarily withdrew from this program area in 2007–2008 were 1. *Cognitive, Social, Developmental Psychology (CSD) PhD (Doctor of Philosophy)*—Applications 2007–2008, 6. Total applicants accepted 2007–2008, 4. Number full-time enrolled (new admits only) 2007–2008, 3. Total enrolled 2007–2008 full-time, 21. Openings 2008–2009, 10. The median number of years required for completion of a degree in 2006–2007 were 5. The number of students enrolled full- and part-time who were dismissed or voluntarily withdrew from this program area in 2007–2008 were 0. *General Psychology Masters Program MA/MS (Master of Arts/Science)*—Applications 2007–2008, 237. Total applicants accepted 2007–2008, 185. Number full-time enrolled (new admits only) 2007–2008, 44. Number part-time enrolled (new admits only) 2007–2008, 8. Total enrolled 2007–2008 full-time, 96, part-time, 52. Openings 2008–2009, 75. The median number of years required for completion of a degree in 2006–2007 were 2. The number of students enrolled full- and part-time who were dismissed or voluntarily withdrew from this program area in 2007–2008 were 17.

Admissions Requirements:
Scores: Entries appear in this order: required test or GPA, minimum score (if required), median score of students entering in 2007–2008. Master's Programs: GRE-V 400, 530; GRE-Q 400, 610; overall undergraduate GPA 3.2, 3.43. Doctoral Programs: overall undergraduate GPA 3.2. GRE scores are included in applications to our Master's Programs only. Because all applicants to our PhD programs are New School Master's students, and considering that the GRE is not a consideration for admission into the PhD programs, there is no need for GRE scores to be reported a second time.
Other Criteria: (importance of criteria rated low, medium, or high): GRE/MAT scores—medium, research experience—medium, work experience—high, extracurricular activity—medium, clinically related public service—medium, GPA—high, letters of recommendation—high, interview—medium, statement of goals and objectives—high, writing sample—high. Only Master's students at The New School for Social Research are eligible to apply to our PhD Programs. Outside applicants with previous graduate credit must apply first to the MA program at The New School for Social Research, then once they complete 12 credits of course work here, they may transfer credits from a previous degree. Often, students with previous graduate credit are able to enter the PhD Program after only 1 year of study here. Only Clinical PhD applicants are interviewed; all PhD applicants submit a detailed statement and research plan. All PhD applicants must have a 3.30 GPA in their master's-level courses, and must successfully complete the MA comprehensive examinations. For additional information on admission requirements, go to http://www.socialresearch.newschool.edu/admissions/index.htm.

Student Characteristics: The following represents characteristics of students in 2007–2008 in all graduate psychology programs in the department: Female—full-time 146, part-time 48; Male—full-time 56, part-time 12; African American/Black—full-time 8, part-time 7; Hispanic/Latino(a)—full-time 14, part-time 5; Asian/Pacific Islander—full-time 6, part-time 6; American Indian/Alaska Native—full-time 1, part-time 2; Caucasian/White—full-time 136, part-time 27; Multi-ethnic—full-time 19, part-time 1; students subject to the Americans With Disabilities Act—full-time 5, part-time 0; Unknown ethnicity—full-time 18, part-time 12.

Financial Information/Assistance:

Tuition for Full-Time Study: *Master's:* State residents: $1,508 per credit hour; Nonstate residents: $1,508 per credit hour. *Doctoral:* State residents: $1,508 per credit hour; Nonstate residents: $1,508 per credit hour. Tuition is subject to change. See the following Web site for updates and changes in tuition costs: http://www.newschool.edu/gf.

Financial Assistance:

First-Year Students: Fellowships and scholarships available for first year. Average amount paid per academic year: $7,800. Apply by December 15. Tuition remission given: partial.

Advanced Students: Teaching assistantships available for advanced students. Average amount paid per academic year: $6,000. Average number of hours worked per week: 10. Apply by March 1. Research assistantships available for advanced students. Average amount paid per academic year: $6,000. Average number of hours worked per week: 15. Apply by March 1. Traineeships available for advanced students. Average amount paid per academic year: $3,000. Average number of hours worked per week: 10. Apply by January 22. Fellowships and scholarships available for advanced students. Average amount paid per academic year: $9,660. Apply by March 1. Tuition remission given: partial.

Additional Information: Of all students currently enrolled full time, 56% benefited from one or more of the listed financial assistance programs. Application and information available online at http://www.newschool.edu/gf/students/continuning.htm.

Internships/Practica: Doctoral Degree (PhD Clinical Psychology): For those doctoral students for whom a professional internship was required in this program prior to graduation, (20) students applied for an internship in 2006–2007, with (20) students obtaining an internship. Of those students who obtained an internship, (20) were paid internships. Of those students who obtained an internship, (20) students placed in APA/CPA-accredited internships, (0) students placed in internships not APA/CPA accredited, but listed with the Association of Psychology Postdoctoral and Internship Centers (APPIC), (0) students placed in internships conforming to guidelines of the Council of Directors of School Psychology Programs (CDSPP), (0) students placed in internships that were not APA/CPA-accredited, APPIC or CDSPP listed. Depending on their research areas, students pursuing general psychology can gain internship and work experience in a range of applied settings, including industry research labs and nonprofit organizations. Master's-level psychology students who are interested in applying to the Clinical PhD program are strongly encouraged to pursue volunteer clinical positions available at local hospitals or institutes. First-year doctoral students in the Clinical program participate in an integrated program designed to help students develop as scientist–practitioners. The practicum is based at Beth Israel Medical Center and involves supervised psychotherapy and Structured Clinical Interview for *DSM–IV–TR* (SCID) training within the Brief Psychotherapy Research Program established at Beth Israel. Students also spend 4 hours per week on an inpatient rotation, co-leading groups, and attending relevant unit meetings. Clinical supervision is provided by The New School faculty and by Beth Israel staff psychologists and psychiatrists. This experience provides strong preparation for the 16–20 hour per week externships in their 2nd and 3rd years of PhD-level study at approved, affiliated sites. After completing their dissertation proposals, all Clinical PhD students are required to complete an APA-accredited predoctoral internship. During the internship application process, students receive administrative and academic support services from the Director of Clinical Training, Assistant Director of Clinical Training, and the Clinical Program Coordinator. For additional information on education and training outcomes for our programs, see the following Web site: http://www.newschool.edu/gf/psy/phd_clinical_psychology.htm.

Housing and Day Care: On-campus housing is available. See the following for more information: The New School Office of Housing, 8 East 16th Street, 5th Floor, New York, NY 10003; http://www.newschool.edu/studentaffairs/housing/. No on-campus day care facilities are available.

Employment of Department Graduates:

Master's Degree Graduates: Of those who graduated in the academic year 2006–2007, the following categories and numbers represent the postgraduate activities and employment of master's degree graduates: Enrolled in a postdoctoral residency/fellowship (n/a), employed in independent practice (n/a), total from the above (master's) (0).

Doctoral Degree Graduates: Of those who graduated in the academic year 2006–2007, the following categories and numbers represent the postgraduate activities and employment of doctoral degree graduates: Enrolled in a psychology doctoral program (n/a), enrolled in a postdoctoral residency/fellowship (2), employed in independent practice (1), employed in a hospital/medical center (4), not seeking employment (1), do not know (1), total from the above (doctoral) (9).

Additional Information:

Orientation, Objectives, and Emphasis of Department: The Psychology Department provides a broad theoretical background emphasizing the scientific study of human behavior. The master's program accommodates both full- and part-time students, with courses in cognitive, developmental, social, and clinical psychology. All MA students design and carry out original individual research projects. At the PhD level, students may specialize either in research psychology or in clinical psychology. The doctoral program reflects an apprenticeship model in which students work closely with individual faculty on collaborative research. Admission to doctoral candidacy is based on students' academic performance in our master's program, interviews with faculty, a personal essay, and passing the psychology comprehensive examination. There is a strong emphasis on cultural psychology as a framework for understanding basic psychological theories, and on approaching psychology in ways that are sensitive to sociocultural diversity. Students enrolled in the PhD Program in Cognitive, Development, and Social Psychology (CSD) are prepared for careers in academics as well as in applied settings. Within the Clinical Psychology doctoral program, there is a strong emphasis on both theory and research. Clinical students have opportunities to gain clinical experience and are prepared as scientist–practitioners equally at home in clinical, research, and teaching settings.

Special Facilities or Resources: All students may participate in collaborative research projects with faculty in labs that feature equipment and software dedicated to the particular research carried out by department members (see http://www.newschool.edu/gf/psy). Students have library access not only at New School social science libraries but also at NYU's Bobst library, the Cooper Union Library, and other libraries within a New York consortium.

Various state-of-the-art computing facilities are also available. For Clinical PhD students, the New School–Beth Israel Center for Clinical Training and Research provides unusually broad training in outpatient clinics, inpatient units, and clinical research programs. First-year Clinical PhD students have access to the Psychology library at Beth Israel Medical Center, perform intake evaluations on Beth Israel's psychiatry outpatient clinic, and provide group therapy on adult inpatient units. They also attend psychiatry grand rounds and training seminars on child abuse and assault prevention. Second- and 3rd-year Clinical students may continue work at Beth Israel Medical Center conducting therapy through the Brief Psychotherapy Research Project. Psychotherapy sessions are videotaped with patients' consent, and students review these sessions in supervision with Beth Israel supervising psychologists. Cases are also discussed in externship seminars with New School University faculty.

Information for Students With Physical Disabilities: See the following Web site for more information: http://www.newschool.edu/studentaffairs/st_disability_over.html.

Application Information:
Send to Office of Admisisons, New School for Social Research, 65 Fifth Avenue, Room 101, New York, NY 10003. Application available online. URL of online application: http://www.socialresearch.newschool.edu/admissions/apply.htm. Students are admitted in the Fall, application deadline August 1; Spring, application deadline December 15. Programs have rolling admissions. Applications for Fall admission completed by January 15 may be considered for full-funding fellowships. *Fee:* $50.

Yeshiva University

Ferkauf Graduate School of Psychology
Albert Einstein College of Medicine
1300 Morris Park Avenue
Bronx, NY 10461-1602
Telephone: (718) 430-3850
Fax: (718) 430-3960
E-mail: *gill@aecom.yu.edu*
Web: *http://www.yu.edu/ferkauf*

Department Information:
1957. Dean: Lawrence J. Siegel, PhD, ABPP. Number of faculty: total—full-time 29, part-time 28; women—full-time 13, part-time 17; total—minority—full-time 5, part-time 6; women minority—full-time 3, part-time 4; faculty subject to the Americans With Disabilities Act 1.

Programs and Degrees Offered:
Listed in the following order: Program area, degree type (T if terminal Master's), number awarded 7/06–6/07. Clinical PsyD (Doctor of Psychology) 21, Clinical Health PhD (Doctor of Philosophy) 15, School/Clinical Child PsyD (Doctor of Psychology) 21, Mental Health Counseling MA/MS (Master of Arts/Science) (T) 10.

APA Accreditation: Clinical PsyD (Doctor of Psychology). Clinical PhD (Doctor of Philosophy). Combination PsyD (Doctor of Psychology).

Student Applications/Admissions:
Student Applications
Clinical PsyD (Doctor of Psychology)—Applications 2007–2008, 300. Total applicants accepted 2007–2008, 79. Number full-time enrolled (new admits only) 2007–2008, 23. Total enrolled 2007–2008 full-time, 118, part-time, 11. Openings 2008–2009, 21. The median number of years required for completion of a degree in 2006–2007 were 5. The number of students enrolled full- and part-time who were dismissed or voluntarily withdrew from this program area in 2007–2008 were 2. *Clinical Health PhD (Doctor of Philosophy)*—Applications 2007–2008, 100. Total applicants accepted 2007–2008, 41. Number full-time enrolled (new admits only) 2007–2008, 14. Total enrolled 2007–2008 full-time, 81, part-time, 3. Openings 2008–2009, 15. The median number of years required for completion of a degree in 2006–2007 were 5. The number of students enrolled full- and part-time who were dismissed or voluntarily withdrew from this program area in 2007–2008 were 1. *School/Clinical Child PsyD (Doctor of Psychology)*—Applications 2007–2008, 200. Total applicants accepted 2007–2008, 43. Number full-time enrolled (new admits only) 2007–2008, 24. Total enrolled 2007–2008 full-time, 101, part-time, 9. Openings 2008–2009, 20. The median number of years required for completion of a degree in 2006–2007 were 5. The number of students enrolled full- and part-time who were dismissed or voluntarily withdrew from this program area in 2007–2008 were 1. *Mental Health Counseling MA/MS (Master of Arts/Science)*—Applications 2007–2008, 300. Total applicants accepted 2007–2008, 111. Number full-time enrolled (new admits only) 2007–2008, 25. Number part-time enrolled (new admits only) 2007–2008, 5. Total enrolled 2007–2008 full-time, 44, part-time, 6. Openings 2008–2009, 25. The median number of years required for completion of a degree in 2006–2007 were 2. The number of students enrolled full- and part-time who were dismissed or voluntarily withdrew from this program area in 2007–2008 were 1.

Admissions Requirements:
Scores: Entries appear in this order: required test or GPA, minimum score (if required), median score of students entering in 2007–2008. Master's Programs: GRE-V no minimum stated; GRE-Q no minimum stated; overall undergraduate GPA 3.0, 3.5; psychology GPA 3.0, 3.5. Doctoral Programs: GRE-V no minimum stated; GRE-Q no minimum stated; overall undergraduate GPA 3.0, 3.5.
Other Criteria: (importance of criteria rated low, medium, or high): GRE/MAT scores—high, research experience—high, work experience—high, extracurricular activity—high, clinically related public service—high, GPA—high, letters of recommendation—high, interview—high, statement of goals and objectives—high.

Student Characteristics: The following represents characteristics of students in 2007–2008 in all graduate psychology programs in the department: Female—full-time 249, part-time 15; Male—full-time 95, part-time 14; African American/Black—full-time 9, part-time 0; Hispanic/Latino(a)—full-time 21, part-time 1; Asian/Pacific Islander—full-time 9, part-time 1; American Indian/Alaska Native—full-time 0, part-time 0; Caucasian/White—full-time 0, part-time 0; Multi-ethnic—full-time 4, part-time 1; students subject to the Americans With Disabilities Act—

full-time 1, part-time 1; Unknown ethnicity—full-time 0, part-time 0.

Financial Information/Assistance:

Tuition for Full-Time Study: *Master's:* State residents: per academic year $14,500, $1,140 per credit hour; Nonstate residents: per academic year $14,500, $1,140 per credit hour. *Doctoral:* State residents: per academic year $14,500, $1,175 per credit hour; Nonstate residents: per academic year $14,500, $1,175 per credit hour. Tuition is not available at this time. Tuition is subject to change. See the following Web site for updates and changes in tuition costs: http://www.yu.edu/student_aid/.

Financial Assistance:

First-Year Students: Teaching assistantships available for first year. Average amount paid per academic year: $4,000. Average number of hours worked per week: 10. Research assistantships available for first year. Average amount paid per academic year: $1,000. Average number of hours worked per week: 20. Traineeships available for first year. Average amount paid per academic year: $15,000. Average number of hours worked per week: 20. Fellowships and scholarships available for first year. Average amount paid per academic year: $20,000. Average number of hours worked per week: 0.

Advanced Students: Teaching assistantships available for advanced students. Average amount paid per academic year: $4,000. Average number of hours worked per week: 10. Research assistantships available for advanced students. Average amount paid per academic year: $10,000. Average number of hours worked per week: 20. Traineeships available for advanced students. Average amount paid per academic year: $15,000. Average number of hours worked per week: 20. Fellowships and scholarships available for advanced students. Average amount paid per academic year: $20,000. Average number of hours worked per week: 0.

Additional Information: Of all students currently enrolled full time, 70% benefited from one or more of the listed financial assistance programs. Application and information available online at http://www.yu.edu/student_aid/.

Internships/Practica: Master's Degree (MA/MS Mental Health Counseling): An internship experience such as a final research project or "capstone" experience is required of graduates. Doctoral Degree (PsyD Clinical): For those doctoral students for whom a professional internship was required in this program prior to graduation, (29) students applied for an internship in 2006–2007, with (29) students obtaining an internship. Of those students who obtained an internship, (27) were paid internships. Of those students who obtained an internship, (23) students placed in APA/CPA-accredited internships, (4) students placed in internships not APA/CPA-accredited, but listed with the Association of Psychology Postdoctoral and Internship Centers (APPIC), (0) students placed in internships conforming to guidelines of the Council of Directors of School Psychology Programs (CDSPP), (2) students placed in internships that were not APA/CPA accredited, APPIC or CDSPP listed. Doctoral Degree (PhD Clinical Health): For those doctoral students for whom a professional internship was required in this program prior to graduation, (11) students applied for an internship in 2006–2007, with (11) students obtaining an internship. Of those students who obtained an internship, (11) were paid internships. Of those students who obtained an internship, (10) students placed in APA/CPA accredited internships, (1) student placed in internships not APA/CPA-accredited, but listed with the Association of Psychology Postdoctoral and Internship Centers (APPIC), (0) students placed in internships conforming to guidelines of the Council of Directors of School Psychology Programs (CDSPP), (0) students placed in internships that were not APA/CPA-accredited, APPIC or CDSPP listed. Doctoral Degree (PsyD School/Clinical Child): For those doctoral students for whom a professional internship was required in this program prior to graduation, (10) students applied for an internship in 2006–2007, with (10) students obtaining an internship. Of those students who obtained an internship, (10) were paid internships. Of those students who obtained an internship, (9) students placed in APA/CPA-accredited internships, (0) students placed in internships not APA/CPA accredited, but listed with the Association of Psychology Postdoctoral and Internship Centers (APPIC), (1) student placed in internships conforming to guidelines of the Council of Directors of School Psychology Programs (CDSPP), (0) students placed in internships that were not APA/CPA-accredited, APPIC or CDSPP listed. Examples listed in catalog and on Web site at http://www.yu.edu/ferkauf.

Housing and Day Care: No on-campus housing is available. No on-campus day care facilities are available.

Employment of Department Graduates:

Master's Degree Graduates: Of those who graduated in the academic year 2006–2007, the following categories and numbers represent the postgraduate activities and employment of master's degree graduates: Enrolled in a psychology doctoral program (65), enrolled in another graduate/professional program (5), enrolled in a postdoctoral residency/fellowship (n/a), employed in independent practice (n/a), total from the above (master's) (70).

Doctoral Degree Graduates: Of those who graduated in the academic year 2006–2007, the following categories and numbers represent the postgraduate activities and employment of doctoral degree graduates: Enrolled in a psychology doctoral program (n/a), enrolled in a postdoctoral residency/fellowship (3), employed in independent practice (7), employed in an academic position at a university (2), employed in an academic position at a 2-year/4-year college (2), employed in other positions at a higher education institution (1), employed in a professional position in a school system (15), employed in business or industry (3), employed in a community mental health/counseling center (11), employed in a hospital/medical center (20), still seeking employment (1), other employment position (2), do not know (1), total from the above (doctoral) (68).

Additional Information:

Orientation, Objectives, and Emphasis of Department: The objective of the Ferkauf Graduate School of Psychology is to promote a balance between the scientific research orientation and the practitioner model. Clinical Psychology (Health emphasis) program places greater emphasis upon applied and basic research, whereas the Clinical and School/Clinical Child Psychology programs focus on the scientist–practitioner model with integrated clinical research and supervised practicum experiences. Further, Ferkauf offers PhD and PsyD degrees placing emphasis on research in the former and on application in the latter. A comprehensive theoretical orientation is offered with a psychodynamic focus and an applied behavioral emphasis. In all specialty areas, and at all levels of training, there is a strong commitment to the foundations of psychology, and a core of basic courses is required in all programs. Collaborations with the major New York City health and hospital institutions and schools are well established for all programs.

Special Facilities or Resources: All psychology programs offer practicum experience through Ferkauf's Center for Psychological and Psychoeducational Services. The Center provides a wide range of evaluation, remediation, and therapeutic services for children, adolescents, and adults in the neighboring communities, in addition to consultation services directly to the local schools. Ferkauf is located on Yeshiva University's campus of the Albert Einstein College of Medicine, which has led to the development of cooperative programs and activities with various disciplines in medicine as well as added training opportunities for students at the various service delivery agencies affiliated with the medical college.

Application Information:
Send to Director of Admissions, Ferkauf Graduate School of Psychology, 1300 Morris Park Avenue, Bronx, NY 10461. Application available online. URL of online application: http://www.yu.edu/ferkauf/FGS03APP.pdf. Students are admitted in the Fall, application deadline January 1. Mental Health Counseling Psychology MA deadline is February 15. *Fee:* $50.

Appalachian State University

Department of Psychology
Arts and Science
Smith-Wright Hall
Boone, NC 28608
Telephone: (828) 262-2272
Fax: (828) 262-2974
E-mail: *foxpa@appstate.edu*
Web: *http://www.als.appstate.edu/dept/psych*

Department Information:

1966. Chairperson: Paul A. Fox. Number of faculty: total—full-time 13, part-time 3; women—full-time 13, part-time 1.

Programs and Degrees Offered:

Listed in the following order: Program area, degree type (T if terminal Master's), number awarded 7/06–6/07. General MA/MS (Master of Arts/Science) (T) 2, Industrial/Organizational MA/MS (Master of Arts/Science) (T) 4, Clinical Health Psychology MA/MS (Master of Arts/Science) (T) 10, Specialist in School Psychology Other 6.

Student Applications/Admissions:

Student Applications

General MA/MS (Master of Arts/Science)—Applications 2007–2008, 22. Total applicants accepted 2007–2008, 7. Number full-time enrolled (new admits only) 2007–2008, 4. Number part-time enrolled (new admits only) 2007–2008, 0. Openings 2008–2009, 5. The median number of years required for completion of a degree in 2006–2007 were 3. *Industrial/Organizational MA/MS (Master of Arts/Science)*—Applications 2007–2008, 57. Total applicants accepted 2007–2008, 20. Number full-time enrolled (new admits only) 2007–2008, 9. Number part-time enrolled (new admits only) 2007–2008, 0. Openings 2008–2009, 10. The median number of years required for completion of a degree in 2006–2007 were 2. *Clinical Health Psychology MA/MS (Master of Arts/Science)*—Applications 2007–2008, 67. Total applicants accepted 2007–2008, 14. Number full-time enrolled (new admits only) 2007–2008, 10. Total enrolled 2007–2008 full-time, 25. Openings 2008–2009, 10. The median number of years required for completion of a degree in 2006–2007 were 3. The number of students enrolled full- and part-time who were dismissed or voluntarily withdrew from this program area in 2007–2008 were 2. *Specialist in School Psychology Other*—Applications 2007–2008, 55. Total applicants accepted 2007–2008, 18. Number full-time enrolled (new admits only) 2007–2008, 11. Number part-time enrolled (new admits only) 2007–2008, 0. Openings 2008–2009, 10. The median number of years required for completion of a degree in 2006–2007 were 3. The number of students enrolled full- and part-time who were dismissed or voluntarily withdrew from this program area in 2007–2008 were 1.

Admissions Requirements:

Scores: Entries appear in this order: required test or GPA, minimum score (if required), median score of students entering in 2007–2008. Master's Programs: GRE-V no minimum stated, 510; GRE-Q no minimum stated, 590; overall undergraduate GPA 3.0, 3.4.

Other Criteria: (importance of criteria rated low, medium, or high): GRE/MAT scores—high, research experience—medium, work experience—low, extracurricular activity—low, clinically related public service—low, GPA—high, letters of recommendation—medium, interview—high, statement of goals and objectives—high. An interview is not required for Industrial/Organizational or Experimental Psychology.

Student Characteristics: The following represents characteristics of students in 2007–2008 in all graduate psychology programs in the department: Female—full-time 56, part-time 0; Male—full-time 22, part-time 0; African American/Black—full-time 3, part-time 0; Hispanic/Latino(a)—full-time 1, part-time 0; Asian/Pacific Islander—full-time 1, part-time 0; American Indian/Alaska Native—full-time 0, part-time 0; Caucasian/White—full-time 74, part-time 0; students subject to the Americans With Disabilities Act—full-time 1, part-time 0; Unknown ethnicity—full-time 0, part-time 0.

Financial Information/Assistance:

Tuition for Full-Time Study: *Master's:* State residents: per academic year $4,424; Nonstate residents: per academic year $14,007. Tuition is subject to change.

Financial Assistance:

First-Year Students: Research assistantships available for first year. Average amount paid per academic year: $5,000. Average number of hours worked per week: 10. Fellowships and scholarships available for first year. Average amount paid per academic year: $1,025. Average number of hours worked per week: 10. Apply by January.

Advanced Students: Teaching assistantships available for advanced students. Average amount paid per academic year: $7,500. Average number of hours worked per week: 15. Research assistantships available for advanced students. Average amount paid per academic year: $5,000. Average number of hours worked per week: 10.

Additional Information: Of all students currently enrolled full time, 90% benefited from one or more of the listed financial assistance programs. Application and information available online at http://www.appstate.edu.

Internships/Practica: Clinical Health—Students complete two semester-long practica. These are often at the Unversity Counseling Center, the Psychology AD/HD Clinic, or at two other regional mental health institutes. Students complete a 1,000-hour internship at a medical or mental health setting. School—Students complete two semester-long practica in public schools and a 1,200-hour internship, half of which must be in a public school setting. Industrial/Organizational-Human Resources Management—Students have the option of completing a 450-hour internship in human resources or organizational development.

Housing and Day Care: No on-campus housing is available. No on-campus day care facilities are available.

Employment of Department Graduates:

Master's Degree Graduates: Of those who graduated in the academic year 2006–2007, the following categories and numbers represent the postgraduate activities and employment of master's degree graduates: Enrolled in a psychology doctoral program (4), enrolled in a postdoctoral residency/fellowship (n/a), employed in independent practice (n/a), employed in an academic position at a 2-year/4-year college (1), employed in a professional position in a school system (7), employed in business or industry (10), employed in a community mental health/counseling center (2), employed in a hospital/medical center (1), still seeking employment (1), total from the above (master's) (26).

Doctoral Degree Graduates: Of those who graduated in the academic year 2006–2007, the following categories and numbers represent the postgraduate activities and employment of doctoral degree graduates: Enrolled in a psychology doctoral program (n/a), total from the above (doctoral) (0).

Additional Information:

Orientation, Objectives, and Emphasis of Department: The department is student oriented, with a director for each graduate program. The General Experimental program is primarily predoctoral, but one can structure an applied orientation. The Clinical Health and School programs stress professional training, and the majority of graduates obtain positions in the area of preparation after finishing their master's degree. The Industrial/Organizational and Human Resource Management program is a cooperative program with the Department of Management in the College of Business.

Special Facilities or Resources: Biofeedback facilities, student computer laboratory, neuroscience laboratory, and an animal operant conditioning laboratory, and a shared Psychology Clinic/Research House are available. Beginning in the Fall, an Institute for Health and Human Services will be operating.

Application Information:

Send to Dean, Cratis D. Williams Graduate School, John E. Thomas Building, Appalachian State University, Boone, NC 28608. Application available online. URL of online application: http://www.appstate.edu. Students are admitted in the Fall, application deadline February 15. We begin reviewing applications and setting up interviews on February 15. We look at later arriving applications as needed to fill program goals. *Fee:* $35.

Duke University

Department of Psychology and Neuroscience
229 Psychology/Sociology Building
P.O. Box 90085
9 Flowers Drive
Durham, NC 27708
Telephone: (919) 660-5715
Fax: (919) 660-5726
E-mail: *morrell@duke.edu*
Web: *http://www.pn.aas.duke.edu*

Department Information:

1948. Chairman: Dr. Timothy Strauman. Number of faculty: total—full-time 27, part-time 14; women—full-time 12, part-time 4; total—minority—full-time 4; women minority—full-time 2.

Programs and Degrees Offered:

Listed in the following order: Program area, degree type (T if terminal Master's), number awarded 7/06–6/07. Clinical Psychology PhD (Doctor of Philosophy) 3, Developmental Psychology PhD (Doctor of Philosophy) 2, Social Psychology PhD (Doctor of Philosophy) 1, Systems and Integrative Neuroscience PhD (Doctor of Philosophy) 1, Cognition and Cognitive Neuroscience PhD (Doctor of Philosophy) 2.

APA Accreditation: Clinical PhD (Doctor of Philosophy).

Student Applications/Admissions:

Student Applications

Clinical Psychology PhD (Doctor of Philosophy)—Applications 2007–2008, 269. Total applicants accepted 2007–2008, 9. Number full-time enrolled (new admits only) 2007–2008, 7. Number part-time enrolled (new admits only) 2007–2008, 0. Openings 2008–2009, 4. The median number of years required for completion of a degree in 2006–2007 were 7. The number of students enrolled full- and part-time who were dismissed or voluntarily withdrew from this program area in 2007–2008 were 1. *Developmental Psychology PhD (Doctor of Philosophy)*—Applications 2007–2008, 44. Total applicants accepted 2007–2008, 6. Number full-time enrolled (new admits only) 2007–2008, 6. Number part-time enrolled (new admits only) 2007–2008, 0. Openings 2008–2009, 3. The median number of years required for completion of a degree in 2006–2007 were 5. The number of students enrolled full- and part-time who were dismissed or voluntarily withdrew from this program area in 2007–2008 were 1. *Social Psychology PhD (Doctor of Philosophy)*—Applications 2007–2008, 79. Total applicants accepted 2007–2008, 3. Number full-time enrolled (new admits only) 2007–2008, 2. Number part-time enrolled (new admits only) 2007–2008, 0. Openings 2008–2009, 3. The median number of years required for completion of a degree in 2006–2007 were 5. The number of students enrolled full- and part-time who were dismissed or voluntarily withdrew from this program area in 2007–2008 were 1. *Systems and Integrative Neuroscience PhD (Doctor of Philosophy)*—Applications 2007–2008, 6. Total applicants accepted 2007–2008, 2. Number full-time enrolled (new admits only) 2007–2008, 0. Number part-time enrolled (new admits only) 2007–2008, 0. Openings 2008–2009, 3. The median number of years required for completion of a degree in 2006–2007 were 5. The number of students enrolled full- and part-time who were dismissed or voluntarily withdrew from this program area in 2007–2008 were 0. *Cognition and Cognitive Neuroscience PhD (Doctor of Philosophy)*—Applications 2007–2008, 67. Total applicants accepted 2007–2008, 5. Number full-time enrolled (new admits only) 2007–2008, 2. Number part-time enrolled (new admits only) 2007–2008, 0. Openings 2008–2009, 1. The median number of years required for completion of a degree in 2006–2007 were 5. The number of students enrolled full- and part-time who were dismissed or voluntarily withdrew from this program area in 2007–2008 were 0.

Admissions Requirements:

Scores: Entries appear in this order: required test or GPA, minimum score (if required), median score of students entering in 2007–2008. Doctoral Programs: GRE-V no minimum stated, 587; GRE-Q no minimum stated, 676; GRE-Subject (Psychology) no minimum stated, 689; overall undergraduate GPA no minimum stated, 3.6. The GRE Subject test is required for the Clinical program only. Please see our website for mean scores for applicants admitted. Median score for Writing Assessment is 4.7.

Other Criteria: (importance of criteria rated low, medium, or high): GRE/MAT scores—high, research experience—high, work experience—medium, extracurricular activity—low, clinically related public service—medium, GPA—high, letters of recommendation—high, interview—high, statement of goals and objectives—high. For additional information on admission requirements, go to http://pn.aas.duke.edu.

Student Characteristics: The following represents characteristics of students in 2007–2008 in all graduate psychology programs in the department: Female—full-time 67, part-time 0; Male—full-time 20, part-time 0; African American/Black—full-time 6, part-time 0; Hispanic/Latino(a)—full-time 4, part-time 0; Asian/Pacific Islander—full-time 4, part-time 0; American Indian/Alaska Native—full-time 1, part-time 0; Caucasian/White—full-time 72, part-time 0; Multi-ethnic—full-time 0, part-time 0; students subject to the Americans With Disabilities Act—full-time 0, part-time 0; Unknown ethnicity—full-time 0, part-time 0; International students who hold an F-1 or J-1 Visa—full-time 5, part-time 0.

Financial Information/Assistance:

Tuition for Full-Time Study: *Doctoral:* State residents: per academic year $31,100; Nonstate residents: per academic year $31,100. Tuition is subject to change. See the following Web site for updates and changes in tuition costs: http://www.gradschool.duke.edu/. Tuition and registration fees are waived for all admitted students.

Financial Assistance:

First-Year Students: Teaching assistantships available for first year. Average amount paid per academic year: $18,980. Average number of hours worked per week: 19. Apply by December 1. Tuition remission given: full. Research assistantships available for first year. Average amount paid per academic year: $18,980. Average number of hours worked per week: 19. Apply by December 1. Tuition remission given: full. Fellowships and scholarships available for first year. Average amount paid per academic year: $18,980. Apply by December 1. Tuition remission given: full.

Advanced Students: Teaching assistantships available for advanced students. Average amount paid per academic year: $18,980. Average number of hours worked per week: 19. Apply by December 1. Tuition remission given: full. Research assistantships available for advanced students. Average amount paid per academic year: $18,980. Average number of hours worked per week: 19. Apply by December 1. Tuition remission given: full. Fellowships and scholarships available for advanced students. Average amount paid per academic year: $18,980. Apply by December 1. Tuition remission given: full.

Additional Information: Of all students currently enrolled full time, 100% benefited from one or more of the listed financial assistance programs. Application and information available online at http://www.gradschool.duke.edu/. No application needed for TA or RA financial assistance.

Internships/Practica: Doctoral Degree (PhD Clinical Psychology): For those doctoral students for whom a professional internship was required in this program prior to graduation, (3) students applied for an internship in 2006–2007, with (3) students obtaining an internship. Of those students who obtained an internship, (3) were paid internships. Of those students who obtained an internship, (3) students placed in APA/CPA-accredited internships, (0) students placed in internships not APA/CPA accredited, but listed with the Association of Psychology Postdoctoral and Internship Centers (APPIC), (0) students placed in internships conforming to guidelines of the Council of Directors of School Psychology Programs (CDSPP), (0) students placed in internships that were not APA/CPA-accredited, APPIC or CDSPP listed. Doctoral students in our clinical program receive experience in our own departmental clinic as well as a great number of local institutions and medical center facilities.

Housing and Day Care: On-campus housing is available. See the following Web site for more information: http://community housing.duke.edu. On-campus day care facilities are available. See the following Web site for more information: http://www.hr.duke.edu/dcc/.

Employment of Department Graduates:

Master's Degree Graduates: Of those who graduated in the academic year 2006–2007, the following categories and numbers represent the postgraduate activities and employment of master's degree graduates: Enrolled in a postdoctoral residency/fellowship (n/a), employed in independent practice (n/a), total from the above (master's) (0).

Doctoral Degree Graduates: Of those who graduated in the academic year 2006–2007, the following categories and numbers represent the postgraduate activities and employment of doctoral degree graduates: Enrolled in a psychology doctoral program (n/a), enrolled in a postdoctoral residency/fellowship (6), employed in an academic position at a university (2), do not know (1), total from the above (doctoral) (9).

Additional Information:

Orientation, Objectives, and Emphasis of Department: The department features a strong mentor-oriented training program with areas of specialization in clinical health and adult and child psychology. Also, programs in developmental and social psychology. Emphasis is placed on informal interaction among faculty and students; seminars and small groups of faculty and graduate students meet regularly.

Special Facilities or Resources: The department features a strong mentor-oriented training program with areas of specialization in clinical health and adult and child psychology. Also, programs in developmental and social psychology. Emphasis is placed on informal interaction among faculty and students; seminars and small groups of faculty and graduate students meet regularly. Collaborations are available with faculty in the Center for Cognitive Neuroscience, the Center for the Study of Aging and Human Development, and the Fuqua School of Business. Training in developmental psychology focuses on cognitive, linguistic, personality, and social development. Additional collaborations are available with faculty in Medical Psychology, the Center for Aging and Human Development, the Center for Child and Family Policy, and the Carolina Consortium on Human Development and UNC–Duke Collaborative Graduate Certificate Program in Developmental Psychology. This is a joint effort between Duke's Psychology, Social and Health Sciences, and the University of North Carolina at Chapel Hill Developmental Program. The

Clinical Training Program is conducted jointly with the Division of Medical Psychology at Duke University Medical Center. This program has three major foci: child psychopathology and intervention, adult disorders and treatment, and health psychology. State-of-the-art facilities including specially equipped laboratories and clinics are available for student use. These include computational facilities for word processing, data analysis, and experimental programming. Collaborative ties also exist with the Center for Child and Family Policy.

Information for Students With Physical Disabilities: See the following Web site for more information: http://www.access.duke.edu/studentIssues.asp.

Application Information:
Send to Graduate School, 127 Allen Building, Box 90066, Durham, NC 27708. Application available online. URL of online application: http://www.gradschool.duke.edu/onlineapp.htm. Students are admitted in the Fall, application deadline December 1. Due to the high volume of Clinical applications we receive, we require that Clinical applications be submitted by December 1. We encourage a December 1 deadline for all other programs as well but will review these applications until December 15. *Fee:* $75. There is a discount of $10 for applications received by the December 1 deadline.

East Carolina University

Department of Psychology
Arts and Sciences
104 Rawl
Greenville, NC 27858-4353
Telephone: (252) 328-6800
Fax: (252) 328-6283
E-mail: *ericsonj@ecu.edu*
Web: *http://www.ecu.edu/psyc*

Department Information:
1959. Chair: Kathleen A. Lawler Row. Number of faculty: total—full-time 33; women—full-time 16; total—minority—full-time 2; women minority—full-time 2; faculty subject to the Americans With Disabilities Act 1.

Programs and Degrees Offered:
Listed in the following order: Program area, degree type (T if terminal Master's), number awarded 7/06–6/07. School Psychology MA/MS (Master of Arts/Science) (T) 8, General MA/MS (Master of Arts/Science) (T) 7, Health Psychology PhD (Doctor of Philosophy) 0.

Student Applications/Admissions:
Student Applications
School Psychology MA/MS (Master of Arts/Science)—Applications 2007–2008, 45. Total applicants accepted 2007–2008, 14. Number full-time enrolled (new admits only) 2007–2008, 7. Number part-time enrolled (new admits only) 2007–2008, 0. Openings 2008–2009, 8. The median number of years required for completion of a degree in 2006–2007 were 3. The number of students enrolled full- and part-time who were dismissed or voluntarily withdrew from this program area in 2007–2008 were 1. *General MA/MS (Master of Arts/Science)*—Applications 2007–2008, 67. Total applicants accepted 2007–2008, 42. Number full-time enrolled (new admits only) 2007–2008, 10. Number part-time enrolled (new admits only) 2007–2008, 0. Total enrolled 2007–2008 full-time, 18. Openings 2008–2009, 8. The median number of years required for completion of a degree in 2006–2007 were 2. The number of students enrolled full- and part-time who were dismissed or voluntarily withdrew from this program area in 2007–2008 were 0. *Health Psychology PhD (Doctor of Philosophy)*—Applications 2007–2008, 45. Total applicants accepted 2007–2008, 10. Number full-time enrolled (new admits only) 2007–2008, 7. Number part-time enrolled (new admits only) 2007–2008, 0. Openings 2008–2009, 9. The median number of years required for completion of a degree in 2006–2007 were 5. The number of students enrolled full- and part-time who were dismissed or voluntarily withdrew from this program area in 2007–2008 were 0.

Admissions Requirements:
Scores: Entries appear in this order: required test or GPA, minimum score (if required), median score of students entering in 2007–2008. Master's Programs: GRE-V 500, 540; GRE-Q 500, 630; overall undergraduate GPA 3.0, 3.45; last 2 years GPA 3.00, 3.65. Doctoral Programs: GRE-V 550, 600; GRE-Q 550, 600; GRE-Subject (Psychology) no minimum stated; overall undergraduate GPA 3.5; last 2 years GPA no minimum stated; psychology GPA no minimum stated; Doctoral program GRE-Analytic 550, 600.
Other Criteria: (importance of criteria rated low, medium, or high): GRE/MAT scores—high, research experience—high, work experience—medium, extracurricular activity—low, clinically related public service—medium, GPA—high, letters of recommendation—high, interview—high, statement of goals and objectives—high, undergraduate major in psychology—medium, specific undergraduate psychology courses taken—medium. Doctoral programs strongly recommend interview. For additional information on admission requirements, go to http://www.ecu.edu/psyc or http://www.ecu.edu/gradschool.

Student Characteristics: The following represents characteristics of students in 2007–2008 in all graduate psychology programs in the department: Female—full-time 35, part-time 0; Male—full-time 9, part-time 0; African American/Black—full-time 2, part-time 0; Hispanic/Latino(a)—full-time 0, part-time 0; Asian/Pacific Islander—full-time 1, part-time 0; American Indian/Alaska Native—full-time 0, part-time 0; Caucasian/White—full-time 41, part-time 0; Multi-ethnic—full-time 0, part-time 0; students subject to the Americans With Disabilities Act—full-time 1, part-time 0; Unknown ethnicity—full-time 0, part-time 0.

Financial Information/Assistance:
Tuition for Full-Time Study: *Master's:* State residents: per academic year $4,484, $238 per credit hour; Nonstate residents: per academic year $14,800, $811 per credit hour. *Doctoral:* State residents: per academic year $4,484, $238 per credit hour; Nonstate residents: per academic year $14,800, $811 per credit hour. Tuition is subject to change. See the following Web site for updates and changes in tuition costs: http://www.ecu.edu/gradschool/.

Financial Assistance:

First-Year Students: Teaching assistantships available for first year. Average amount paid per academic year: $3,750. Average number of hours worked per week: 10. Apply by March 1. Research assistantships available for first year. Average amount paid per academic year: $3,750. Average number of hours worked per week: 10. Apply by March 1. Tuition remission given: partial. Fellowships and scholarships available for first year. Average amount paid per academic year: $7,500. Average number of hours worked per week: 20. Apply by March 1. Tuition remission given: partial.

Advanced Students: Teaching assistantships available for advanced students. Average amount paid per academic year: $15,000. Average number of hours worked per week: 20. Apply by February 15. Tuition remission given: full. Research assistantships available for advanced students. Average amount paid per academic year: $15,000. Average number of hours worked per week: 20. Apply by February 15. Tuition remission given: full. Fellowships and scholarships available for advanced students. Average amount paid per academic year: $3,000. Average number of hours worked per week: 0. Apply by February 15.

Additional Information: Of all students currently enrolled full time, 80% benefited from one or more of the listed financial assistance programs.

Internships/Practica: Master's Degree (MA/MS General): An internship experience such as a final research project or "capstone" experience is required of graduates. School internships in area school systems offer stipends of up to $2,450 per month for 10 months. Paid I/O internships are usually available during the summer. Predoctoral internships are completed during the 5th year of the PhD Health Psychology program. We admitted our first doctoral class Fall semester 2007.

Housing and Day Care: On-campus housing is available. Some limited housing for graduate students is available. See the following Web site for more information: http://www.ecu.edu/campusliving/. No on-campus day care facilities are available.

Employment of Department Graduates:

Master's Degree Graduates: Of those who graduated in the academic year 2006–2007, the following categories and numbers represent the postgraduate activities and employment of master's degree graduates: Enrolled in a psychology doctoral program (6), enrolled in another graduate/professional program (1), enrolled in a postdoctoral residency/fellowship (n/a), employed in independent practice (n/a), employed in an academic position at a university (0), employed in an academic position at a 2-year/4-year college (0), employed in other positions at a higher education institution (0), employed in a professional position in a school system (7), employed in business or industry (6), employed in government agency (0), employed in a community mental health/counseling center (0), employed in a hospital/medical center (5), still seeking employment (0), other employment position (3), do not know (1), total from the above (master's) (29).

Doctoral Degree Graduates: Of those who graduated in the academic year 2006–2007, the following categories and numbers represent the postgraduate activities and employment of doctoral degree graduates: Enrolled in a psychology doctoral program (n/a), total from the above (doctoral) (0).

Additional Information:

Orientation, Objectives, and Emphasis of Department: The School Psychology MA/CAS program is approved by the National Association of School Psychologists and the NC Department of Public Instruction. The program provides training and experience in assessment, consultation, and intervention. The General Psychology program offers students the opportunity to specialize in two concentrations. The Academic concentration prepares students to teach psychology at the Community/Junior College level. The Industrial/Organizational concentration prepares students for careers involving the application of psychology and human resources in organizations. Students who complete the PhD in Health Psychology will be prepared for a number of practitioner, faculty, and research roles within various health care and academic settings. The clinical health concentration trains students to become members of primary health care teams in hospitals, health maintenance organizations, community mental health agencies, and private practice. The pediatric school psychology concentration prepares psychologists for practice within settings that serve children and adolescents with health-related problems. Clinical health graduates are eligible to apply for licensure as a Licensed Psychologist and Health Services Provider-Psychologist (HSP-P) and pediatric school psychology graduates are eligible to apply for licensures as a school psychologist as well as for licensure as a Licensed Psychologist and Health Services Provider-Psychologist (HSP-P) by the NC State Board of Psychology. The program will be eligible to seek accreditation by the American Psychological Association and the doctoral program requirements of the National Association of School Psychologists in 2012.

Special Facilities or Resources: The department has student computer facilities, interview and testing facilities, and animal laboratory. The Clinical and School programs work closely with community schools and mental health agencies. The doctoral health psychology program works closely with the Brody School of Medicine, family care practices, state health agencies, as well as with the Sleep Disorders Center and psychiatric medicine.

Information for Students With Physical Disabilities: See the following Web site for more information: http://www.ecu.edu/dss.

Application Information:

Send to East Carolina University Graduate School, Greenville, NC 27858-4353. Application available online. URL of online application: http://www.ecu.edu/psyc/grad/index.htm. Students are admitted in the Fall, application deadline February 15. March 1 deadline for all MA programs. February 15 deadline for PhD Health Psychology Program. *Fee:* $50.

Fayetteville State University

Department of Psychology
College of Arts and Sciences
1200 Murchison Road
Fayetteville, NC 28301
Telephone: (910) 672-1413
Fax: (910) 672-1043
E-mail: *sfranzblau@uncfsu.edu*
Web: *http://www.uncfsu.edu/psychology/*

Department Information:

1998. Chairperson: Susan Franzblau, PhD Interim. Number of faculty: total—full-time 12, part-time 18; women—full-time 6, part-time 11; women minority—full-time 5.

Programs and Degrees Offered:

Listed in the following order: Program area, degree type (T if terminal Master's), number awarded 7/06–6/07. Masters Program Track in Counseling MA/MS (Master of Arts/Science) (T) 9, Masters Program Track in Experimental Psychology MA/MS (Master of Arts/Science) (T) 0.

Student Applications/Admissions:

Student Applications

Masters Program Track in Counseling MA/MS (Master of Arts/Science)—Applications 2007–2008, 35. Total applicants accepted 2007–2008, 23. Number full-time enrolled (new admits only) 2007–2008, 13. Number part-time enrolled (new admits only) 2007–2008, 3. Total enrolled 2007–2008 full-time, 34, part-time, 9. Openings 2008–2009, 12. The median number of years required for completion of a degree in 2006–2007 were 4. The number of students enrolled full- and part-time who were dismissed or voluntarily withdrew from this program area in 2007–2008 were 2. *Masters Program Track in Experimental Psychology MA/MS (Master of Arts/Science)*—Applications 2007–2008, 4. Total applicants accepted 2007–2008, 3. Number full-time enrolled (new admits only) 2007–2008, 2. Number part-time enrolled (new admits only) 2007–2008, 0. Openings 2008–2009, 6. The number of students enrolled full- and part-time who were dismissed or voluntarily withdrew from this program area in 2007–2008 were 0.

Admissions Requirements:

Scores: Entries appear in this order: required test or GPA, minimum score (if required), median score of students entering in 2007–2008. Master's Programs: GRE-V no minimum stated, 400; GRE-Q no minimum stated, 400; last 2 years GPA no minimum stated, 3.5; psychology GPA no minimum stated, 3.5.

Other Criteria: (importance of criteria rated low, medium, or high): GRE/MAT scores—medium, research experience—medium, work experience—low, extracurricular activity—low, clinically related public service—low, GPA—high, letters of recommendation—medium, interview—medium, statement of goals and objectives—medium. Research experience is weighted more heavily for the Experimental Program. For additional information on admission requirements, go to http://www.uncfsu.edu/psychology/gradstudents/Admissions/Admit.htm.

Student Characteristics: The following represents characteristics of students in 2007–2008 in all graduate psychology programs in the department: Female—full-time 32, part-time 7; Male—full-time 4, part-time 2; African American/Black—full-time 16, part-time 2; Hispanic/Latino(a)—full-time 1, part-time 1; Asian/Pacific Islander—full-time 0, part-time 0; American Indian/Alaska Native—full-time 2, part-time 0; Caucasian/White—full-time 17, part-time 5; Multi-ethnic—full-time 0, part-time 1; students subject to the Americans With Disabilities Act—full-time 1, part-time 0; Unknown ethnicity—full-time 0, part-time 0.

Financial Information/Assistance:

Tuition for Full-Time Study: *Master's:* State residents: per academic year $3,336, $417 per credit hour; Nonstate residents: per academic year $12,926, $1,615 per credit hour. Tuition is subject to change. See the following Web site for updates and changes in tuition costs: http://www.uncfsu.edu/bursar/fees.htm.

Financial Assistance:

First-Year Students: No information provided.

Advanced Students: Fellowships and scholarships available for advanced students. Average amount paid per academic year: $5,000. Average number of hours worked per week: 10. Tuition remission given: partial.

Additional Information: Of all students currently enrolled full time, 3% benefited from one or more of the listed financial assistance programs. Application and information available online at http://www.uncfsu.edu/cbas/grad.htm.

Internships/Practica: Practica and internships are provided through supervised off-site or on-site placements. Counseling graduate students may choose placement in our training facility, which provides counseling services to students presenting with a variety of life adjustment issues. Alternatively, counseling graduate students may choose placement at a variety of other sites in the surrounding community. These include placements that provide academic, career–vocational, mental health counseling services in surrounding area college counseling centers, community mental health centers, or correctional facilities.

Housing and Day Care: On-campus housing is available. See the following Web site for more information: http://www.uncfsu.edu/ResLife/. No on-campus day care facilities are available.

Employment of Department Graduates:

Master's Degree Graduates: Of those who graduated in the academic year 2006–2007, the following categories and numbers represent the postgraduate activities and employment of master's degree graduates: Enrolled in a psychology doctoral program (0), enrolled in another graduate/professional program (0), enrolled in a postdoctoral residency/fellowship (n/a), employed in independent practice (n/a), employed in an academic position at a 2-year/4-year college (2), employed in other positions at a higher education institution (0), employed in a community mental health/counseling center (1), still seeking employment (1), do not know (1), total from the above (master's) (5).

Doctoral Degree Graduates: Of those who graduated in the academic year 2006–2007, the following categories and numbers represent the postgraduate activities and employment of doctoral degree graduates: Enrolled in a psychology doctoral program (n/a), total from the above (doctoral) (0).

Additional Information:

Orientation, Objectives, and Emphasis of Department: The Department of Psychology offers graduate programs for individuals with either applied or research interests. The Department offers a Masters of Arts degree in Psychology with two tracks. Individuals may pursue the 48-unit counseling program track, or the 36-unit experimental program track. The mission of the counseling program track is to produce highly skilled, license eligible graduates who reflect the state-of-art in counseling; to increase the knowledge and skills of students in the area of multicultural counseling; and to provide field experiences that reflect the community counseling needs of an increasingly pluralistic society. The mission of the experimental program track is to provide an opportunity for advanced study of psychological theory and research techniques; prepare students for employment in business, government, and research settings; prepare individuals to be psychology teachers in community or junior colleges; and to prepare students for advanced study leading to the doctoral degree.

Special Facilities or Resources: The General Experimental Psychology track is new and will be accepting students for the first time in fall 2006. There are increasing opportunities for academic and research collaboration with the universities in the Raleigh/Durham/Chapel Hill area, which is approximately an hour and half drive north of the main campus. Department facilities are currently undergoing a major renovation and construction, which is projected to be finished in 2007.

Information for Students With Physical Disabilities: See the following Web site for more information: http://www.uncfsu.edu/studentaffairs/CFPD/cfpddss.htm.

Application Information:
Send to originals to Director of Admissions, Fayetteville State University, 1200 Murchison Road, Fayetteville, NC 28301-4298; and one set of copies to Coordinator, Graduate Program, Department of Psychology, Fayetteville State University, 1200 Murchison Road, Fayetteville, NC 28301-4298. Application available online. URL of online application: http://www.uncfsu.edu/psychology/gradstudents/Admissions/Admit.htm. Students are admitted in the Fall, application deadline March 15. Please make copies of all application materials and send them to Department of Psychology, Graduate Committee, Fayetteville State University, 1200 Murchison Road, Fayetteville, NC 28301. *Fee:* $25.

North Carolina State University

Department of Psychology
College of Humanities and Social Sciences
640 Poe Hall, Box 7650
Raleigh, NC 27695-7650
Telephone: (919) 515-2251
Fax: (919) 515-1716
E-mail: *don_mershon@ncsu.edu*
Web: *http://www.psychology.chass.ncsu.edu/*

Department Information:
1938. Department Head: Douglas J. Gillan. Number of faculty: total—full-time 14, part-time 4; women—full-time 13; ; women minority—full-time 1.

Programs and Degrees Offered:
Listed in the following order: Program area, degree type (T if terminal Master's), number awarded 7/06–6/07. Human Factors and Ergonomics PhD (Doctor of Philosophy), Developmental PhD (Doctor of Philosophy), Industrial/Organizational PhD (Doctor of Philosophy), Public Interest PhD (Doctor of Philosophy), School Psychology PhD (Doctor of Philosophy).

APA Accreditation: School PhD (Doctor of Philosophy).

Student Applications/Admissions:
Student Applications
Human Factors and Ergonomics PhD (Doctor of Philosophy)—Applications 2007–2008, 30. Number full-time enrolled (new admits only) 2007–2008, 3. Total enrolled 2007–2008 full-time, 12, part-time, 7. Openings 2008–2009, 4. *Developmental PhD (Doctor of Philosophy)*—Applications 2007–2008, 26. Number full-time enrolled (new admits only) 2007–2008, 2. Total enrolled 2007–2008 full-time, 13, part-time, 4. Openings 2008–2009, 4. *Industrial/Organizational PhD (Doctor of Philosophy)*—Applications 2007–2008, 102. Number full-time enrolled (new admits only) 2007–2008, 8. Total enrolled 2007–2008 full-time, 18, part-time, 8. Openings 2008–2009, 5. *Public Interest PhD (Doctor of Philosophy)*—Applications 2007–2008, 31. Number full-time enrolled (new admits only) 2007–2008, 3. Total enrolled 2007–2008 full-time, 19, part-time, 12. Openings 2008–2009, 5. *School Psychology PhD (Doctor of Philosophy)*—Applications 2007–2008, 50. Number full-time enrolled (new admits only) 2007–2008, 3. Total enrolled 2007–2008 full-time, 16, part-time, 10. Openings 2008–2009, 4.

Admissions Requirements:
Scores: Entries appear in this order: required test or GPA, minimum score (if required), median score of students entering in 2007–2008. Master's Programs: GRE-V no minimum stated, 550; GRE-Q no minimum stated, 640; overall undergraduate GPA 3.0, 3.6. GRE Subject test in psychology is strongly recommended for students with nonpsychology undergraduate majors as a demonstration of their preparedness for graduate study in the field. With respect to the General GRE, although no absolute minima are listed, applicants to most programs are expected to have scores at or above the 50th percentiles. Doctoral Programs: GRE-V no minimum stated, 550; GRE-Q no minimum stated, 640; overall undergraduate GPA 3.0, 3.6. GRE Subject test in psychology is strongly recommended for students with nonpsychology undergraduate majors as a demonstration of their preparedness for graduate study in the field. With respect to the General GRE, although no absolute minima are listed, applicants to most programs are expected to have scores at or above the 50th percentiles.
Other Criteria: (importance of criteria rated low, medium, or high): GRE/MAT scores—high, research experience—high, work experience—medium, extracurricular activity—low, GPA—high, letters of recommendation—high, interview—medium, statement of goals and objectives—high, research interests—high. Psychology in the Public Interest gives greater weight to work experience and public service than do other program areas. The School Psychology program operates a by-invitation Interview Day for those applicants who pass an initial selection process. (Developmental Psychology and I/O Psychology also offer a Program Visitation Day for applicants already recommended for acceptance.). For additional information on admission requirements, go to Information Sheet and Program Brochures (and FAQ) available at http://www4.ncsu.edu/~mershon/FDF/.

Student Characteristics: The following represents characteristics of students in 2007–2008 in all graduate psychology programs in the department: Female—full-time 64, part-time 32; Male—full-time 14, part-time 9; African American/Black—full-time 12, part-time 7; Hispanic/Latino(a)—full-time 7, part-time 4; Asian/Pacific Islander—full-time 5, part-time 2; American Indian/Alaska Native—full-time 0, part-time 0; Caucasian/White—full-time 54, part-time 28; students subject to the Americans With Disabilities Act—full-time 1, part-time 0; Unknown ethnicity—

full-time 0, part-time 0; International students who hold an F-1 or J-1 Visa—full-time 5, part-time 0.

Financial Information/Assistance:

Tuition for Full-Time Study: *Master's:* State residents: per academic year $4,268; Nonstate residents: per academic year $16,316. *Doctoral:* State residents: per academic year $4,268; Nonstate residents: per academic year $16,316. Tuition is subject to change. Additional fees are assessed to students beyond the costs of tuition for the following: As of 2007–2008, fees of $1,368 per year were also required. See the following Web site for updates and changes in tuition costs: http://www.fis.ncsu.edu/cashier/tuition/gradtuition.asp.

Financial Assistance:

First-Year Students: Teaching assistantships available for first year. Average amount paid per academic year: $12,500. Average number of hours worked per week: 20. Apply by same as application. Tuition remission given: full. Research assistantships available for first year. Average amount paid per academic year: $14,500. Average number of hours worked per week: 20. Apply by same as application. Tuition remission given: full.

Advanced Students: Teaching assistantships available for advanced students. Average amount paid per academic year: $12,500. Average number of hours worked per week: 20. Tuition remission given: full. Research assistantships available for advanced students. Average amount paid per academic year: $14,500. Average number of hours worked per week: 20. Tuition remission given: full.

Additional Information: Of all students currently enrolled full time, 50% benefited from one or more of the listed financial assistance programs. No separate application; indicate interest on regular application and/or in Personal Statement.

Internships/Practica: Doctoral Degree (PhD School Psychology): For those doctoral students for whom a professional internship was required in this program prior to graduation, (3) students applied for an internship in 2006–2007, with (3) students obtaining an internship. Of those students who obtained an internship, (1) were paid internships. Of those students who obtained an internship, (0) students placed in APA/CPA-accredited internships, (0) students placed in internships not APA/CPA accredited, but listed with the Association of Psychology Postdoctoral and Internship Centers (APPIC), (3) students placed in internships conforming to guidelines of the Council of Directors of School Psychology Programs (CDSPP), (0) students placed in internships that were not APA/CPA-accredited, APPIC or CDSPP listed. Practica and internships are required for both master's and doctoral students in the School Psychology program. These include supervised experiences in assessment, consultation, intervention, research, and professional school psychology in a wide variety of school-related settings. Students in Human Factors and Ergonomics are also expected to obtain employment for at least one summer/semester in one of the many suitable companies located in the Research Triangle area.

Housing and Day Care: On-campus housing is available. See the following Web site for more information: http://www.ncsu.edu/housing/. No on-campus day care facilities are available.

Employment of Department Graduates:

Master's Degree Graduates: Of those who graduated in the academic year 2006–2007, the following categories and numbers represent the postgraduate activities and employment of master's degree graduates: Enrolled in a postdoctoral residency/fellowship (n/a), employed in independent practice (n/a), total from the above (master's) (0).

Doctoral Degree Graduates: Of those who graduated in the academic year 2006–2007, the following categories and numbers represent the postgraduate activities and employment of doctoral degree graduates: Enrolled in a psychology doctoral program (n/a), total from the above (doctoral) (0).

Additional Information:

Orientation, Objectives, and Emphasis of Department: The department trains in the scientist–practitioner model. Students are expected to become knowledgeable about both research and application within their area of study. There are five specialty areas with different emphases. Developmental Psychology stresses a balance of conceptual, research–analytical, and application skills and encompasses social and cognitive development from infancy to old age. Human Factors and Ergonomics emphasizes the cognitive–perceptual aspects of human factors, including research on visual displays, visual and auditory spatial judgments, ergonomics for older adults and the effective information transfer for complex systems. This track has a cooperative relationship with the Biomechanics Program in Industrial and Systems Engineering. The Psychology in the Public Interest program (formerly known as Human Resource Development and Community Psychology) is a problem-oriented program dealing with research and professional issues in communities and social systems. Industrial/Organizational (I/O) students may concentrate in areas such as performance appraisal, selection, training, job analysis, work motivation, organizational theory, and development. School Psychology develops behavioral scientists who apply psychological knowledge and techniques in school and family settings to help students, parents, and teachers.

Special Facilities or Resources: The department is housed on two floors of a modern building. Students with assistantships share offices. All programs have appropriate laboratory space and facilities. These include specialized lab facilities: Audition Laboratory, Cognitive–Development Laboratory, Ergonomics Laboratory, Human–Computer Interaction Laboratory, Social Development Laboratory, and Visual Performance Laboratory. Ergonomics, Public Interest, I/O, and School students may have opportunities to work in state government, industry, schools, and community agencies to gain practical and research experience. As this area is developing rapidly, more opportunities appear each year. Students are, however, required to maintain continuous registration and carry an adequate course load each semester. Students are permitted to enroll in courses at the University of North Carolina—Chapel Hill and at Duke University, as if the courses were offered on their home campus. Once basic research, statistics, and program course requirements are satisfied, students have considerable flexibility in developing individually tailored plans of study.

Information for Students With Physical Disabilities: See the following Web site for more information: http://www.ncsu.edu/provost/offices/affirm_action/dss/.

Application Information:

Send application, fees, and letters of recommendation through an online application system at http://www2.acs.ncsu.edu/grad/apply

grad.htm. Personal Statements (on departmental forms available at http://www4.ncsu.edu/~mershon/application_statements): submit as .doc email attachment to addresses indicated on form. Transcripts and other communications may be sent to Director of Graduate Programs, Psychology Department, Box 7650, NCSU, Raleigh, NC 27695-7650. Questions/problems concerning the application system itself should be addressed to: The Graduate School, Box 7102, NCSU, Raleigh, NC 27695-7102 or contact Web master indicated within the ApplyYourself system. Application available online. URL of online application: http://www2.acs.ncsu.edu/grad/applygrad.htm. Students are admitted in the Fall, application deadline January 15. The program in School Psychology sets its deadline at December 15. The full department is considering a similar shift from the current mid-January date. Please check with department during Fall 2008 to be sure of actual application deadline for Fall 2009. Information will also be available on the university's Web site. *Fee:* $65 for U.S. citizens and permanent residents; $75 for non-resident (international) applicants. McNair Scholars, or other U.S. citizens with significant financial restrictions, may request waiver of the application fee; contact Graduate School, NCSU (Campus Box 7102), Raleigh, NC 27695-7102 for details. Waivers are not available for international applicants.

North Carolina, University of, at Greensboro (2007 data)

Department of Psychology
College of Arts and Sciences
296 Eberhart Building, P.O. Box 26170
Greensboro, NC 27402-6170
Telephone: (336) 334-5013
Fax: (336) 334-5066
E-mail: *gfmichel@uncg.edu*
Web: *http://www.uncg.edu/psy/*

Department Information:

1925. Department Head: George F. Michel. Number of faculty: total—full-time 25, part-time 2; women—full-time 9.

Programs and Degrees Offered:

Listed in the following order: Program area, degree type (T if terminal Master's), number awarded 7/06–6/07. Clinical PhD (Doctor of Philosophy) 5, Cognitive PhD (Doctor of Philosophy) 0, Developmental PhD (Doctor of Philosophy) 0, Social PhD (Doctor of Philosophy) 3.

APA Accreditation: Clinical PhD (Doctor of Philosophy).

Student Applications/Admissions:

Student Applications

Clinical PhD (Doctor of Philosophy)—Applications 2007–2008, 143. Total applicants accepted 2007–2008, 8. Number full-time enrolled (new admits only) 2007–2008, 8. Number part-time enrolled (new admits only) 2007–2008, 0. Openings 2008–2009, 9. The median number of years required for completion of a degree in 2006–2007 were 6. The number of students enrolled full- and part-time who were dismissed or voluntarily withdrew from this program area in 2007–2008 were 0. *Cognitive PhD (Doctor of Philosophy)*—Applications 2007–2008, 12. Total applicants accepted 2007–2008, 1. Number full-time enrolled (new admits only) 2007–2008, 1. Number part-time enrolled (new admits only) 2007–2008, 0. Openings 2008–2009, 2. The median number of years required for completion of a degree in 2006–2007 were 5. The number of students enrolled full- and part-time who were dismissed or voluntarily withdrew from this program area in 2007–2008 were 0. *Developmental PhD (Doctor of Philosophy)*—Applications 2007–2008, 14. Total applicants accepted 2007–2008, 2. Number full-time enrolled (new admits only) 2007–2008, 2. Number part-time enrolled (new admits only) 2007–2008, 0. Openings 2008–2009, 3. The median number of years required for completion of a degree in 2006–2007 were 5. The number of students enrolled full- and part-time who were dismissed or voluntarily withdrew from this program area in 2007–2008 were 0. *Social PhD (Doctor of Philosophy)*—Applications 2007–2008, 27. Total applicants accepted 2007–2008, 0. Number full-time enrolled (new admits only) 2007–2008, 0. Number part-time enrolled (new admits only) 2007–2008, 0. The median number of years required for completion of a degree in 2006–2007 were 6. The number of students enrolled full- and part-time who were dismissed or voluntarily withdrew from this program area in 2007–2008 were 0.

Admissions Requirements:

Scores: Entries appear in this order: required test or GPA, minimum score (if required), median score of students entering in 2007–2008. Master's Programs: GRE-V 590, 680; GRE-Q 640, 780; GRE-Subject (Psychology) 660, 700; overall undergraduate GPA 3.4, 3.8. Doctoral Programs: GRE-V no minimum stated, 590; GRE-Q no minimum stated, 640; GRE-Subject (Psychology) no minimum stated; overall undergraduate GPA no minimum stated, 3.6.

Other Criteria: (importance of criteria rated low, medium, or high): GRE/MAT scores—high, research experience—high, work experience—low, extracurricular activity—low, clinically related public service—medium, GPA—high, letters of recommendation—high, interview—high, statement of goals and objectives—high.

Student Characteristics: The following represents characteristics of students in 2007–2008 in all graduate psychology programs in the department: Female—full-time 34, part-time 0; Male—full-time 15, part-time 0; African American/Black—full-time 3, part-time 0; Hispanic/Latino(a)—full-time 2, part-time 0; Asian/Pacific Islander—full-time 0, part-time 0; American Indian/Alaska Native—full-time 0, part-time 0; Caucasian/White—full-time 38, part-time 0; Multi-ethnic—full-time 0, part-time 0; students subject to the Americans With Disabilities Act—full-time 1, part-time 0; Unknown ethnicity—full-time 0, part-time 0.

Financial Information/Assistance:

Tuition for Full-Time Study: *Doctoral:* State residents: per academic year $2,842, $336 per credit hour; Nonstate residents: per academic year $13,892. Tuition is subject to change.

Financial Assistance:

First-Year Students: Research assistantships available for first year. Average amount paid per academic year: $10,000. Average number of hours worked per week: 12. Apply by December 15. Tuition remission given: partial.

Advanced Students: Research assistantships available for advanced students. Average amount paid per academic year:

$10,000. Average number of hours worked per week: 12. Apply by December 15.

Additional Information: Of all students currently enrolled full time, 90% benefited from one or more of the listed financial assistance programs. Application and information available online at http://www.uncg.edu/grs.

Internships/Practica: No information provided.

Housing and Day Care: On-campus housing is available. Housing and Residence Life, 1st floor, Mendenhall-Ragsdale Building. (336) 334-5636. On-campus day care facilities are available.

Employment of Department Graduates:

Master's Degree Graduates: Of those who graduated in the academic year 2006–2007, the following categories and numbers represent the postgraduate activities and employment of master's degree graduates: Enrolled in a postdoctoral residency/fellowship (n/a), employed in independent practice (n/a), total from the above (master's) (0).

Doctoral Degree Graduates: Of those who graduated in the academic year 2006–2007, the following categories and numbers represent the postgraduate activities and employment of doctoral degree graduates: Enrolled in a psychology doctoral program (n/a), employed in an academic position at a 2-year/4-year college (3), employed in other positions at a higher education institution (4), employed in business or industry (2), employed in a community mental health/counseling center (2), employed in a hospital/medical center (2), total from the above (doctoral) (13).

Additional Information:

Orientation, Objectives, and Emphasis of Department: The objective is to provide scholarship and methodological and practical skills to enable the student to function in a variety of academic, research, and service settings. The program has an experimental orientation, with four major areas of concentration: clinical, which includes applied training and clinical research training in a variety of service settings; developmental, which includes basic research in behavioral, cognitive, language, and social development in infant, child, adolescent, and adult humans and in animals; cognitive, which includes basic research in human memory, cognition, and language; and social, designed to introduce students to theoretical issues and to applied, biological, and developmental perspectives in social psychology. Although the program is oriented toward the PhD as the terminal degree, an applicant with a bachelor's degree is admitted into the master's program. Upon successful completion of the requirements for the master's degree, the student's work is reviewed for admission into the PhD program.

Special Facilities or Resources: The Department of Psychology is located in the Life Sciences Building. Space is devoted to classrooms; research laboratories; vivaria; the Psychology Clinic; faculty, student, and secretarial offices; a computer terminal room; a library; and a lounge. Graduate students share offices with one or two other students. Active research laboratories in each of the specialty areas contain an assortment of items: animal test chambers with supporting apparatus for research in perception, learning, and the development of social behavior; automated equipment for studying concept formation and problem-solving behavior in humans, signal-averaging computers with XY plotters for analyses of electrophysical correlates of behavior; soundproof chambers; electronic psychoacoustic equipment for stimulus control in auditory research with humans and animals; videotape studio; polygraphs for psychological recording; and observation rooms with one-way mirrors. The university computer center is available to faculty members and graduate students involved in research. Facilities include interactive and batch access to the large-sized computer on campus. Virtually all computer languages and standard software packages are available. The university library has an exceptional collection of journals and books. The department also has its own library located in the Life Sciences Building.

Information for Students With Physical Disabilities: See the following Web site for more information: http://www.uncg.edu/psy/.

Application Information:

Send to UNCG, Graduate School, P.O. Box 26176, Greensboro, NC 27402-6176. Application available online. URL of online application: http://www.uncg.edu/grs. Students are admitted in the Fall, application deadline December 15. December 15 for all areas, Clinical, Cognitive, Developmental, and Social. *Fee:* $45.

North Carolina, University of, Chapel Hill

Department of Psychology
Arts and Sciences
Campus Box 3270
Chapel Hill, NC 27599-3270
Telephone: (919) 962-4155
Fax: (919) 962-2537
E-mail: *k_hill@unc.edu*
Web: *http://www.psych.unc.edu*

Department Information:

1921. Chairperson: Donald T. Lysle. Number of faculty: total—full-time 56, part-time 4; women—full-time 27, part-time 2; total—minority—full-time 4; women minority—full-time 3.

Programs and Degrees Offered:

Listed in the following order: Program area, degree type (T if terminal Master's), number awarded 7/06–6/07. Clinical PhD (Doctor of Philosophy) 16, Cognitive PhD (Doctor of Philosophy) 6, Developmental PhD (Doctor of Philosophy) 1, Behavioral Neuroscience PhD (Doctor of Philosophy) 5, Quantitative PhD (Doctor of Philosophy) 1, Social PhD (Doctor of Philosophy) 3.

APA Accreditation: Clinical PhD (Doctor of Philosophy).

Student Applications/Admissions:

Student Applications

Clinical PhD (Doctor of Philosophy)—Applications 2007–2008, 389. Total applicants accepted 2007–2008, 16. Number full-time enrolled (new admits only) 2007–2008, 9. Openings 2008–2009, 8. The median number of years required for completion of a degree in 2006–2007 were 5. *Cognitive PhD (Doctor of Philosophy)*—Applications 2007–2008, 36. Total applicants accepted 2007–2008, 7. Number full-time enrolled (new admits only) 2007–2008, 1. Total enrolled 2007–2008 full-time, 16. Openings 2008–2009, 3. The median number of years required for completion of a degree in 2006–2007 were 5. The number of students enrolled full- and part-time who were dismissed or voluntarily withdrew from this program area in 2007–2008 were 1. *Developmental PhD (Doctor of Philosophy)*—Applications 2007–2008, 32. Total applicants accepted 2007–2008, 3. Number full-time enrolled (new admits only) 2007–2008, 2. Openings 2008–2009, 4. The median number of years required for completion of a degree in 2006–2007 were 5. *Behavioral Neuroscience PhD (Doctor of Philosophy)*—Applications 2007–2008, 22. Total applicants accepted 2007–2008, 2. Number full-time enrolled (new admits only) 2007–2008, 1. Openings 2008–2009, 3. The median number of years required for completion of a degree in 2006–2007 were 5. *Quantitative PhD (Doctor of Philosophy)*—Applications 2007–2008, 17. Total applicants accepted 2007–2008, 4. Number full-time enrolled (new admits only) 2007–2008, 1. Openings 2008–2009, 3. The median number of years required for completion of a degree in 2006–2007 were 5. *Social PhD (Doctor of Philosophy)*—Applications 2007–2008, 65. Total applicants accepted 2007–2008, 7. Number full-time enrolled (new admits only) 2007–2008, 5. Openings 2008–2009, 3. The median number of years required for completion of a degree in 2006–2007 were 5.

Admissions Requirements:

Scores: Entries appear in this order: required test or GPA, minimum score (if required), median score of students entering in 2007–2008. Doctoral Programs: GRE-V 50%, 627; GRE-Q 50%, 701; last 2 years GPA 3.0, 3.68.

Other Criteria: (importance of criteria rated low, medium, or high): GRE/MAT scores—high, research experience—high, work experience—medium, clinically related public service—medium, GPA—high, letters of recommendation—high, interview—medium, statement of goals and objectives—high.

Student Characteristics: The following represents characteristics of students in 2007–2008 in all graduate psychology programs in the department: Female—full-time 86, part-time 0; Male—full-time 49, part-time 0; African American/Black—full-time 14, part-time 0; Hispanic/Latino(a)—full-time 2, part-time 0; Asian/Pacific Islander—full-time 10, part-time 0; American Indian/Alaska Native—part-time 0; Caucasian/White—full-time 109, part-time 0; Unknown ethnicity—full-time 0, part-time 0.

Financial Information/Assistance:

Tuition for Full-Time Study: *Doctoral:* State residents: per academic year $6,236; Nonstate residents: per academic year $20,234.

Financial Assistance:

First-Year Students: Research assistantships available for first year. Average amount paid per academic year: $15,000. Average number of hours worked per week: 15. Tuition remission given: full and partial. Traineeships available for first year. Average amount paid per academic year: $20,772. Tuition remission given: full and partial. Fellowships and scholarships available for first year. Average amount paid per academic year: $20,000. Tuition remission given: full and partial.

Advanced Students: Teaching assistantships available for advanced students. Average amount paid per academic year: $16,400. Average number of hours worked per week: 15. Tuition remission given: full and partial. Research assistantships available for advanced students. Average amount paid per academic year: $15,000. Average number of hours worked per week: 15. Tuition remission given: full and partial. Traineeships available for advanced students. Average amount paid per academic year: $20,772. Tuition remission given: full. Fellowships and scholarships available for advanced students. Average amount paid per academic year: $20,000. Tuition remission given: full.

Additional Information: Of all students currently enrolled full time, 75% benefited from one or more of the listed financial assistance programs.

Internships/Practica: Doctoral Degree (PhD Clinical): For those doctoral students for whom a professional internship was required in this program prior to graduation, (13) students applied for an internship in 2006–2007, with (12) students obtaining an internship. Of those students who obtained an internship, (12) were paid internships. Of those students who obtained an internship, (10) students placed in APA/CPA-accredited internships, (2) students placed in internships not APA/CPA-accredited, but listed with the Association of Psychology Postdoctoral and Internship Centers (APPIC), (0) students placed in internships conforming to guidelines of the Council of Directors of School Psychology Programs (CDSPP), (0) students placed in internships that were not APA/CPA-accredited, APPIC or CDSPP listed. Students within the doctoral program in clinical psychology engage in a wide range of clinical practica activities beginning in the 1st year of doctoral study. A variety of sites are included in our practicum arrangements. One of these sites is the University of North Carolina Medical School, which includes opportunities in a number of areas including child, family, adolescent, and adults. There are also specialized opportunities at that site to work with children with developmental disabilities and college students in a university counseling setting. Students also receive training at John Umstead Hospital, a state psychiatric hospital; opportunities there range from child, adolescent, adult, and geriatric patients. Overall Umstead Hospital emphasizes treatment of more disturbed individuals, but opportunities are available as well for outpatient treatment. Students are involved in our Psychology Department Psychological Services Center, our in-house outpatient treatment facility. Students work with a wide variety of clients within that context, with specialized opportunities in the anxiety disorders and marital therapy. Among other sites, students provide consultation to the local school system, to the Orange-Person-Chatham Mental Health Center, and a variety of other sites that are arranged on an as-needed basis.

Housing and Day Care: No on-campus housing is available. No on-campus day care facilities are available.

Employment of Department Graduates:

Master's Degree Graduates: Of those who graduated in the academic year 2006–2007, the following categories and numbers represent the postgraduate activities and employment of master's degree graduates: Enrolled in a postdoctoral residency/fellowship (n/a), employed in independent practice (n/a), total from the above (master's) (0).

Doctoral Degree Graduates: Of those who graduated in the academic year 2006–2007, the following categories and numbers represent the postgraduate activities and employment of doctoral degree graduates: Enrolled in a psychology doctoral program (n/a), total from the above (doctoral) (0).

Additional Information:

Orientation, Objectives, and Emphasis of Department: Each graduate training program is designed to acquaint students with the theoretical and research content of their specialty and to train them in the research and teaching skills needed to make contributions to science and society. In addition, certain programs (for example, the Clinical program) include an emphasis on the development of competence in appropriate professional skills. Faculty members maintain a balance of commitment to research, teaching, and service.

Special Facilities or Resources: Affiliated clinical and research facilities are: the Psychological Services Center, Psychology Department; John Umstead State Hospital, Butner, NC; North Carolina Memorial Hospital, Chapel Hill; Murdoch Center for the Retarded, Butner; Division for Disorders of Development and Learning, Chapel Hill; VA Hospital, Durham; Frank Porter Graham Child Development Center, Chapel Hill; Carolina Population Center, Chapel Hill; Alcoholic Rehabilitation Center, Butner; North Carolina Highway Safety Research Center, Chapel Hill; L. L. Thurstone Psychometric Laboratory, Chapel Hill; Human Psychophysiology Laboratory, Chapel Hill; Institute for Research in Social Sciences, Chapel Hill; Laboratory for Computing and Cognition, Chapel Hill; Neurobiology Curriculum, University of North Carolina; Research Laboratories of the U.S. Environmental Protection Agency, Research Triangle Park; and TEACCH Division, North Carolina Memorial Hospital, specializing in the treatment and education of individuals with autism and related disorders of communication.

Application Information:

Send to Graduate Admissions, CB 3270, 203 Davie Hall, Department of Psychology, UNC—Chapel Hill, Chapel Hill, NC 27599-3270. Application available online. Students are admitted in the Fall, application deadline January 1. *Fee:* $73.

North Carolina, University of, Charlotte

Department of Psychology
Arts and Sciences
9201 University City Boulevard
Charlotte, NC 28223-0001
Telephone: (704) 687-4731
Fax: (704) 687-3096
E-mail: *rtedesch@email.uncc.edu*
Web: *http://www.uncc.edu/psychology/*

Department Information:

1960. Graduate Coordinator: Dr. Richard Tedeschi. Number of faculty: total—full-time 19, part-time 6; women—full-time 14, part-time 5; total—minority—full-time 3; women minority—full-time 2.

Programs and Degrees Offered:

Listed in the following order: Program area, degree type (T if terminal Master's), number awarded 7/06–6/07. Clinical/Community MA/MS (Master of Arts/Science) (T) 3, Industrial/Organizational MA/MS (Master of Arts/Science) (T) 7, Organizational Science PhD (Doctor of Philosophy) 0, Health Psychology PhD (Doctor of Philosophy) 0.

APA Accreditation: School PhD (Doctor of Philosophy).

Student Applications/Admissions:

Student Applications

Clinical/Community MA/MS (Master of Arts/Science)—Applications 2007–2008, 75. Total applicants accepted 2007–2008, 10. Number full-time enrolled (new admits only) 2007–2008, 10. Number part-time enrolled (new admits only) 2007–2008, 0. Total enrolled 2007–2008 full-time, 17, part-time, 20. Openings 2008–2009, 12. The median number of years required for completion of a degree in 2006–2007 were 2. The number of students enrolled full- and part-time who were dismissed or voluntarily withdrew from this program area in 2007–2008 were 2. *Industrial/Organizational MA/MS (Master of Arts/Science)*—Applications 2007–2008, 103. Total applicants accepted 2007–2008, 12. Total enrolled 2007–2008 full-time, 21, part-time, 3. Openings 2008–2009, 12. The median number of years required for completion of a degree in 2006–2007 were 2. The number of students enrolled full- and part-time who were dismissed or voluntarily withdrew from this program area in 2007–2008 were 1. *Organizational Science PhD (Doctor of Philosophy)*—Applications 2007–2008, 50. Total applicants accepted 2007–2008, 8. Number full-time enrolled (new admits only) 2007–2008, 8. Total enrolled 2007–2008 full-time, 8. Openings 2008–2009, 4. The median number of years required for completion of a degree in 2006–2007 were 2. The number of students enrolled full- and part-time who were dismissed or voluntarily withdrew from this program area in 2007–2008 were 0. *Health Psychology PhD (Doctor of Philosophy)*—Applications 2007–2008, 35. Total applicants accepted 2007–2008, 6. Number full-time enrolled (new admits only) 2007–2008, 6. Total enrolled 2007–2008 full-time, 14. The median number of years required for completion of a degree in 2006–2007 were 2. The number of students enrolled full- and part-time who were dismissed or voluntarily withdrew from this program area in 2007–2008 were 0.

Admissions Requirements:

Scores: Entries appear in this order: required test or GPA, minimum score (if required), median score of students entering in 2007–2008. Master's Programs: GRE-V 500, 554; GRE-Q 500, 600; GRE-Subject (Psychology) no minimum stated, 570; overall undergraduate GPA 3.0, 3.4. GRE Subject (Psychology) is not required

Other Criteria: (importance of criteria rated low, medium, or high): GRE/MAT scores—high, research experience—high, work experience—medium, extracurricular activity—low, clinically related public service—medium, GPA—high, letters of recommendation—high, interview—low, statement of goals and objectives—high for Clinical/Community only.

Student Characteristics: The following represents characteristics of students in 2007–2008 in all graduate psychology programs in the department: Female—full-time 63, part-time 18; Male—full-time 13, part-time 2; African American/Black—full-time 2, part-time 0; Hispanic/Latino(a)—full-time 1, part-time 0; Asian/Pacific Islander—full-time 0, part-time 0; American Indian/Alaska Native—full-time 0, part-time 0; Caucasian/White—full-time 36, part-time 0; Multi-ethnic—full-time 0, part-time 0;

students subject to the Americans With Disabilities Act—full-time 0, part-time 0; Unknown ethnicity—full-time 0, part-time 0; International students who hold an F-1 or J-1 Visa—full-time 1, part-time 0.

Financial Information/Assistance:

Tuition for Full-Time Study: *Master's:* State residents: per academic year $3,552, $476 per credit hour; Nonstate residents: per academic year $13,759, $1,752 per credit hour. Tuition is subject to change.

Financial Assistance:

First-Year Students: Teaching assistantships available for first year. Average amount paid per academic year: $9,000. Average number of hours worked per week: 20. Apply by March 1. Research assistantships available for first year. Average amount paid per academic year: $8,500. Average number of hours worked per week: 20. Apply by March 1. Fellowships and scholarships available for first year. Average amount paid per academic year: $2,150. Apply by March 1.

Advanced Students: Teaching assistantships available for advanced students. Average amount paid per academic year: $9,000. Average number of hours worked per week: 20. Research assistantships available for advanced students. Average amount paid per academic year: $8,500. Average number of hours worked per week: 20.

Additional Information: Of all students currently enrolled full time, 60% benefited from one or more of the listed financial assistance programs. Application and information available online at http://www.uncc.edu/finaid.

Internships/Practica: Clinical/Community: Students are required to enroll in two semesters of practicum, working 22 hours per week in community agencies such as mental health centers, prisons, hospitals, and nonprofit organizations. Industrial/Organizational: An extensive practicum component utilizes the Charlotte area as setting for applied experience. All students must complete 3 hours of projects in I/O pscychology and they are strongly encouraged to take 6 hours.

Housing and Day Care: On-campus housing is available. No on-campus day care facilities are available.

Employment of Department Graduates:

Master's Degree Graduates: Of those who graduated in the academic year 2006–2007, the following categories and numbers represent the postgraduate activities and employment of master's degree graduates: Enrolled in a postdoctoral residency/fellowship (n/a), employed in independent practice (n/a), employed in other positions at a higher education institution (1), employed in business or industry (4), total from the above (master's) (5).

Doctoral Degree Graduates: Of those who graduated in the academic year 2006–2007, the following categories and numbers represent the postgraduate activities and employment of doctoral degree graduates: Enrolled in a psychology doctoral program (n/a), total from the above (doctoral) (0).

Additional Information:

Orientation, Objectives, and Emphasis of Department: The objective of the master's degree program is to train psychologists in the knowledge and skills necessary to address problems encountered in industry, organizations, and the community. The program has an applied emphasis. Graduates of the program are eligible to apply for licensing in North Carolina as psychological associates. Although our goals emphasize application of psychological principles in organizational, clinical, and community settings, the rigorous program allows students to prepare themselves well for further education in psychology.

Special Facilities or Resources: The psychology department is housed in a modern classroom office building that provides offices, demonstration rooms, a workshop, and specialty laboratories for research. Facilities include a computerized laboratory with 37 microcomputers; many small testing, training, and interview rooms with one-way mirrors for direct observation; audio intercommunications; and closed circuit television. There is extensive audio and video equipment available as well as a research trailer, tachistoscopes, programming and timing equipment, and microcomputers. The psychometric laboratory contains an extensive inventory of current tests of intelligence, personality, and interest, as well as calculators and microcomputers for testing, test score evaluation, and data analysis. A well-equipped physiological laboratory is available for work including human electrophysiology.

Application Information:

Send to Graduate Admissions, UNC—Charlotte, 9201 University City Boulevard, Charlotte, NC 28223. Students are admitted in the Fall, application deadline March 1. February 1 is the deadline for Industrial/Organizational program. March 1 is the deadline for Clinical/Community MA program. December 1 is the deadline for Health PhD program. *Fee:* $35.

North Carolina, University of, Wilmington

Psychology
Arts and Sciences
601 South College Road
Wilmington, NC 28403-5612
Telephone: (910) 962-3370
Fax: (910) 962-7010
E-mail: *mackains@uncw.edu*
Web: *http://www.uncw.edu/psy/*

Department Information:

1972. Chairperson: J. Mark Galizio, PhD. Number of faculty: total—full-time 28; women—full-time 13; total—minority—full-time 4; women minority—full-time 2; faculty subject to the Americans With Disabilities Act 1.

Programs and Degrees Offered:

Listed in the following order: Program area, degree type (T if terminal Master's), number awarded 7/06–6/07. General Psychology MA/MS (Master of Arts/Science) (T) 9, Applied Behavior Analysis (Clinical) MA/MS (Master of Arts/Science) (T) 1, Substance Abuse Treatment (Clinical) MA/MS (Master of Arts/Science) (T) 6.

Student Applications/Admissions:

Student Applications

General Psychology MA/MS (Master of Arts/Science)—Applications 2007–2008, 50. Total applicants accepted 2007–2008, 15. Number full-time enrolled (new admits only) 2007–2008,

10. Number part-time enrolled (new admits only) 2007–2008, 0. Total enrolled 2007–2008 full-time, 15, part-time, 7. Openings 2008–2009, 14. The median number of years required for completion of a degree in 2006–2007 were 2. The number of students enrolled full- and part-time who were dismissed or voluntarily withdrew from this program area in 2007–2008 were 0. *Applied Behavior Analysis (Clinical) MA/MS (Master of Arts/Science)*—Applications 2007–2008, 22. Total applicants accepted 2007–2008, 6. Number full-time enrolled (new admits only) 2007–2008, 4. Number part-time enrolled (new admits only) 2007–2008, 0. Openings 2008–2009, 6. The median number of years required for completion of a degree in 2006–2007 were 3. The number of students enrolled full- and part-time who were dismissed or voluntarily withdrew from this program area in 2007–2008 were 1. *Substance Abuse Treatment (Clinical) MA/MS (Master of Arts/Science)*—Applications 2007–2008, 35. Total applicants accepted 2007–2008, 9. Number full-time enrolled (new admits only) 2007–2008, 7. Number part-time enrolled (new admits only) 2007–2008, 0. Openings 2008–2009, 7. The median number of years required for completion of a degree in 2006–2007 were 3. The number of students enrolled full- and part-time who were dismissed or voluntarily withdrew from this program area in 2007–2008 were 0.

Admissions Requirements:

Scores: Entries appear in this order: required test or GPA, minimum score (if required), median score of students entering in 2007–2008. Master's Programs: GRE-V no minimum stated, 530; GRE-Q no minimum stated, 530; overall undergraduate GPA no minimum stated, 3.5; last 2 years GPA no minimum stated, 3.5. Applicants without an undergraduate major in psychology must have a minimum 21 semester hours of psychology courses, including courses in statistics and psychology research methods, and also an acceptable score on the (Psychology) GRE Subject test.

Other Criteria: (importance of criteria rated low, medium, or high): GRE/MAT scores—high, research experience—high, work experience—low, extracurricular activity—low, clinically related public service—medium, GPA—high, letters of recommendation—high, interview—high, statement of goals and objectives—high. In the Substance Abuse Treatment Psychology concentration, clinically related public service may be given more weight because this concentration emphasizes the development of clinical as well as research skills. In the Applied Behavior Analysis concentration, previous experience—volunteer or paid— with people with disabilities is very important. Coursework in learning and principles of behavior change are also highly desirable. For additional information on admission requirements, go to http://www.uncw.edu/psy/.

Student Characteristics: The following represents characteristics of students in 2007–2008 in all graduate psychology programs in the department: Female—full-time 27, part-time 4; Male—full-time 15, part-time 3; African American/Black—full-time 4, part-time 1; Hispanic/Latino(a)—full-time 2, part-time 0; Asian/Pacific Islander—full-time 1, part-time 1; American Indian/Alaska Native—full-time 0, part-time 0; Caucasian/White—full-time 33, part-time 4; Multi-ethnic—full-time 2, part-time 1; students subject to the Americans With Disabilities Act—full-time 2, part-time 0; Unknown ethnicity—full-time 0, part-time 0; International students who hold an F-1 or J-1 Visa—full-time 2, part-time 0.

Financial Information/Assistance:

Tuition for Full-Time Study: *Master's:* State residents: per academic year $4,460; Nonstate residents: per academic year $14,296. Tuition is subject to change. Tuition costs vary by program. See the following Web site for updates and changes in tuition costs: http://www.uncw.edu/grad_info/grad_support.html.

Financial Assistance:

First-Year Students: Teaching assistantships available for first year. Average amount paid per academic year: $9,500. Average number of hours worked per week: 20. Apply by January 15. Tuition remission given: partial. Research assistantships available for first year. Average amount paid per academic year: $9,500. Average number of hours worked per week: 20. Apply by January 15. Tuition remission given: partial. Traineeships available for first year. Apply by January 15.

Advanced Students: Teaching assistantships available for advanced students. Average amount paid per academic year: $9,500. Average number of hours worked per week: 20. Apply by January 15. Research assistantships available for advanced students. Average amount paid per academic year: $9,500. Average number of hours worked per week: 20. Apply by January 15.

Additional Information: Of all students currently enrolled full time, 83% benefited from one or more of the listed financial assistance programs.

Internships/Practica: Master's Degree (MA/MS Applied Behavior Analysis (clinical)): An internship experience such as a final research project or "capstone" experience is required of graduates. Master's Degree (MA/MS Substance Abuse Treatment (clinical)): An internship experience such as a final research project or "capstone" experience is required of graduates. In the Substance Abuse Treatment Psychology concentration and our new Applied Behavior Analysis concentration, students are prepared for work with dual diagnosis clients or with developmentally disabled clients through the completion of a required practicum and internship. The required internship and practicum consist of at least 1,500 hours total of supervised experience working with substance abuse, autism, mental retardation, and other psychological and behavioral problems. Training sites include community mental health centers, correctional institutions, university counseling centers, inpatient and outpatient substance abuse treatment centers, and residential centers for autistic and mentally retarded individuals.

Housing and Day Care: On-campus housing is available. See the following Web site for more information: http://www.uncwil.edu/grad_info/housing.htm. No on-campus day care facilities are available.

Employment of Department Graduates:

Master's Degree Graduates: Of those who graduated in the academic year 2006–2007, the following categories and numbers represent the postgraduate activities and employment of master's degree graduates: Enrolled in a psychology doctoral program (4), enrolled in another graduate/professional program (1), enrolled in a postdoctoral residency/fellowship (n/a), employed in independent practice (n/a), employed in an academic position at a university (0), employed in an academic position at a 2-year/4-year college (2), employed in other positions at a higher education institution (1), employed in a professional position in a school system (0), employed in business or industry (2), employed in government agency (1), employed in a community mental health/counseling center (4), employed in a hospital/medical center (0), still seeking employment (0), not seeking employment (1), other employment position (2), total from the above (master's) (18).

Doctoral Degree Graduates: Of those who graduated in the academic year 2006–2007, the following categories and numbers represent the postgraduate activities and employment of doctoral degree graduates: Enrolled in a psychology doctoral program (n/a), total from the above (doctoral) (0).

Additional Information:

Orientation, Objectives, and Emphasis of Department: The department is committed to fostering an understanding of psychological research and stresses the relationship between students and professors in this process. Research methodology and application are emphasized for all students. Students in the General Psychology concentration are prepared to continue to the PhD in a variety of content areas. Students completing the clinical concentration in Substance Abuse Treatment are prepared to work with dual diagnosis clients in mental health clinics and other public service agencies. The clinical Applied Behavior Analysis concentration prepares students for work primarily with autistic and mentally retarded individuals. The SATP and ABA graduates meet all academic requirements to apply for North Carolina state licensure as a Psychological Associate and either North Carolina state certification as a Licensed Clinical Addictions Specialist (SATP concentration) or national Board Certification as a Behavior Analyst (BCBA concentration).

Special Facilities or Resources: Special facilities or resources include research laboratories (behavioral pharmacology, human, and animal) and videotape and digital recording equipment. All students have access to word processing, SAS, and SPSS on the university computer system.

Information for Students With Physical Disabilities: See the following Web site for more information: http://www.uncw.edu/stuaff/disability/students_transition.htm.

Application Information:

Send to Graduate School, University of North Carolina—Wilmington, 601 South College Road, Wilmington, NC 28403-5955. Application available online. URL of online application: http://www.uncw.edu/grad%5Finfo/prospectivestudents.htm. Students are admitted in the Fall, application deadline January 15. *Fee:* $45. Fee waived for McNair scholars.

Wake Forest University

Department of Psychology
Arts and Sciences
P.O. Box 7778
Winston-Salem, NC 27109
Telephone: (336) 758-5424
Fax: (336) 758-4733
E-mail: *seta@wfu.edu*
Web: *http://www.wfu.edu/psychology*

Department Information:

1958. Director of Graduate Studies: Catherine E. Seta. Number of faculty: total—full-time 11, part-time 2; women—full-time 7, part-time 1; ; women minority—full-time 1.

Programs and Degrees Offered:

Listed in the following order: Program area, degree type (T if terminal Master's), number awarded 7/06–6/07. General MA/MS (Master of Arts/Science) (T) 11.

Student Applications/Admissions:

Student Applications

General MA/MS (Master of Arts/Science)—Applications 2007–2008, 115. Total applicants accepted 2007–2008, 14. Number full-time enrolled (new admits only) 2007–2008, 9. Number part-time enrolled (new admits only) 2007–2008, 0. Openings 2008–2009, 12. The median number of years required for completion of a degree in 2006–2007 were 2. The number of students enrolled full- and part-time who were dismissed or voluntarily withdrew from this program area in 2007–2008 were 1.

Admissions Requirements:

Scores: Entries appear in this order: required test or GPA, minimum score (if required), median score of students entering in 2007–2008. Master's Programs: GRE-V no minimum stated, 590; GRE-Q no minimum stated, 690; overall undergraduate GPA 3.00, 3.6; psychology GPA 3.00, 3.6; Masters GRE-Analytical no minimum stated, 5.00.

Other Criteria: (importance of criteria rated low, medium, or high): GRE/MAT scores—medium, research experience—high, work experience—low, extracurricular activity—low, clinically related public service—low, GPA—medium, letters of recommendation—high, interview—medium, statement of goals and objectives—high.

Student Characteristics: The following represents characteristics of students in 2007–2008 in all graduate psychology programs in the department: Female—full-time 14, part-time 0; Male—full-time 5, part-time 0; African American/Black—full-time 0, part-time 0; Hispanic/Latino(a)—full-time 0, part-time 0; Asian/Pacific Islander—full-time 1, part-time 0; American Indian/Alaska Native—full-time 0, part-time 0; Caucasian/White—full-time 16, part-time 0; Multi-ethnic—full-time 2, part-time 0; students subject to the Americans With Disabilities Act—full-time 1, part-time 0; Unknown ethnicity—full-time 0, part-time 0.

Financial Information/Assistance:

Tuition for Full-Time Study: *Master's:* State residents: per academic year $26,985, $970 per credit hour; Nonstate residents: per academic year $26,985, $970 per credit hour. Tuition is subject to change. See the following Web site for updates and changes in tuition costs: http://www2.wfubmc.edu/graduate/.

Financial Assistance:

First-Year Students: Teaching assistantships available for first year. Average amount paid per academic year: $8,500. Average number of hours worked per week: 12. Apply by January 15. Tuition remission given: full. Research assistantships available for first year. Average amount paid per academic year: $8,500. Average number of hours worked per week: 12. Apply by January 15. Tuition remission given: full.

Advanced Students: Teaching assistantships available for advanced students. Average amount paid per academic year: $8,500. Average number of hours worked per week: 12. Apply by January 15. Tuition remission given: full. Research assistantships available for advanced students. Average amount paid per academic year: $8,500. Average number of hours worked per week: 12. Apply by January 15. Tuition remission given: full.

Additional Information: Of all students currently enrolled full time, 100% benefited from one or more of the listed financial assistance programs. Application and information available online at http://www2.wfubmc.edu/graduate/application.html.

Internships/Practica: No information provided.

Housing and Day Care: No on-campus housing is available. No on-campus day care facilities are available.

Employment of Department Graduates:

Master's Degree Graduates: Of those who graduated in the academic year 2006–2007, the following categories and numbers represent the postgraduate activities and employment of master's degree graduates: Enrolled in a psychology doctoral program (3), enrolled in a postdoctoral residency/fellowship (n/a), employed in independent practice (n/a), total from the above (master's) (3). ***Doctoral Degree Graduates:*** Of those who graduated in the academic year 2006–2007, the following categories and numbers represent the postgraduate activities and employment of doctoral degree graduates: Enrolled in a psychology doctoral program (n/a), total from the above (doctoral) (0).

Additional Information:

Orientation, Objectives, and Emphasis of Department: The department aims to provide rigorous master's-level training, with an emphasis on mastery of theory, research methodology, and content in the basic areas of psychology. This is a general, research-oriented MA program for capable students, most of whom will continue to the PhD.

Special Facilities or Resources: The Department of Psychology occupies a beautiful and spacious new building that is equipped with state-of-the art teaching and laboratory facilities. Learning resources include in-class multimedia instruction equipment, departmental mini- and microcomputers, departmental and university libraries, and information technology centers. Ample research space is available, including social, developmental, cognitive, perception, physiological, and animal behavior laboratories. Office space is available for graduate students. The department has links with the Wake Forest University School of Medicine (e.g., Neuroscience), which can provide opportunities for students. All students work closely with individual faculty on research during both years (2:1 student–faculty ratio). Wake Forest University offers the academic and technological resources, facilities, and Division I athletic programs, music, theater, and art associated with a larger university with the individual attention that a smaller university can provide.

Information for Students With Physical Disabilities: See the following Web site for more information: http://www2.wfubmc.edu/graduate/currentstudent.html.

Application Information:

Send to Dean of Graduate School, Wake Forest University, P.O. Box 7487, Winston-Salem, NC 27109. Application available online. URL of online application: http://www2.wfubmc.edu/graduate/AppProcedures.html. Students are admitted in the Spring, application deadline January 15. *Fee:* $45.

Western Carolina University

Department of Psychology
College of Education and Allied Professions
301 Killian Building
Cullowhee, NC 28723
Telephone: (828) 227-7361
Fax: (828) 227-7005
E-mail: *mccord@wcu.edu*
Web: *http://www.wcu.edu/ceap/psychology/psyhome.htm*

Department Information:

1919. Department Head: David M. McCord, PhD. Number of faculty: total—full-time 17, part-time 5; women—full-time 7, part-time 4; minority—part-time 1.

Programs and Degrees Offered:

Listed in the following order: Program area, degree type (T if terminal Master's), number awarded 7/06–6/07. Clinical Psychology MA/MS (Master of Arts/Science) (T) 5, School Psychology MA/MS (Master of Arts/Science) (T) 8, General-Experimental Psychology MA/MS (Master of Arts/Science) (T) 1.

Student Applications/Admissions:

Student Applications

Clinical Psychology MA/MS (Master of Arts/Science)—Applications 2007–2008, 45. Total applicants accepted 2007–2008, 6. Number full-time enrolled (new admits only) 2007–2008, 5. Number part-time enrolled (new admits only) 2007–2008, 0. Openings 2008–2009, 8. The median number of years required for completion of a degree in 2006–2007 were 2. The number of students enrolled full- and part-time who were dismissed or voluntarily withdrew from this program area in 2007–2008 were 1. *School Psychology MA/MS (Master of Arts/Science)*—Applications 2007–2008, 35. Total applicants accepted 2007–2008, 9. Number full-time enrolled (new admits only) 2007–2008, 8. Number part-time enrolled (new admits only) 2007–2008, 0. Openings 2008–2009, 9. The median number of years required for completion of a degree in 2006–2007 were 3. The number of students enrolled full- and part-time who were dismissed or voluntarily withdrew from this program area in 2007–2008 were 1. *General-Experimental Psychology MA/MS (Master of Arts/Science)*—Applications 2007–2008, 16. Total applicants accepted 2007–2008, 8. Number full-time enrolled (new admits only) 2007–2008, 8. Number part-time enrolled (new admits only) 2007–2008, 1. Total enrolled 2007–2008 full-time, 8, part-time, 1. Openings 2008–2009, 8. The median number of years required for completion of a degree in 2006–2007 were 2. The number of students enrolled full- and part-time who were dismissed or voluntarily withdrew from this program area in 2007–2008 were 0.

Admissions Requirements:

Scores: Entries appear in this order: required test or GPA, minimum score (if required), median score of students entering in 2007–2008. Master's Programs: GRE-V 500, 500; GRE-Q 500, 600; last 2 years GPA 3.00, 3.40; psychology GPA 3.00, 3.40. Doctoral Programs: GRE-V no minimum stated; GRE-Q no minimum stated; overall undergraduate GPA no minimum stated; last 2 years GPA no minimum stated; psychology GPA no minimum stated.

Other Criteria: (importance of criteria rated low, medium, or high): GRE/MAT scores—high, research experience—high, work experience—medium, extracurricular activity—medium, clinically related public service—medium, GPA—high, letters of recommendation—high, interview—high, statement of goals and objectives—high.

Student Characteristics: The following represents characteristics of students in 2007–2008 in all graduate psychology programs in the department: Female—full-time 27, part-time 0; Male—full-time 10, part-time 1; African American/Black—full-time 2, part-time 0; Hispanic/Latino(a)—full-time 0, part-time 0; Asian/Pacific Islander—full-time 1, part-time 0; American Indian/Alaska Native—full-time 0, part-time 0; Caucasian/White—full-time 32, part-time 0; Multi-ethnic—full-time 0, part-time 0; students subject to the Americans With Disabilities Act—full-time 0, part-time 0; Unknown ethnicity—full-time 0, part-time 0.

Financial Information/Assistance:

Tuition for Full-Time Study: *Master's:* State residents: per academic year $4,943; Nonstate residents: per academic year $14,528.

Financial Assistance:

First-Year Students: Teaching assistantships available for first year. Average amount paid per academic year: $7,000. Average number of hours worked per week: 15. Apply by February 1. Tuition remission given: partial.

Advanced Students: Teaching assistantships available for advanced students. Average amount paid per academic year: $7,000. Average number of hours worked per week: 15. Apply by February 1. Tuition remission given: partial. Research assistantships available for advanced students. Average amount paid per academic year: $7,000. Average number of hours worked per week: 15. Apply by February 1. Tuition remission given: partial.

Additional Information: Of all students currently enrolled full time, 100% benefited from one or more of the listed financial assistance programs.

Internships/Practica: Public schools, mental health centers, private hospitals, psychological services center, private schools, and alternative schools.

Housing and Day Care: No on-campus housing is available. No on-campus day care facilities are available.

Employment of Department Graduates:

Master's Degree Graduates: Of those who graduated in the academic year 2006–2007, the following categories and numbers represent the postgraduate activities and employment of master's degree graduates: Enrolled in a postdoctoral residency/fellowship (n/a), employed in independent practice (n/a), total from the above (master's) (0).

Doctoral Degree Graduates: Of those who graduated in the academic year 2006–2007, the following categories and numbers represent the postgraduate activities and employment of doctoral degree graduates: Enrolled in a psychology doctoral program (n/a), total from the above (doctoral) (0).

Additional Information:

Orientation, Objectives, and Emphasis of Department: The Master or Arts in Psychology program has three concentrations, Clinical, School, and General Experimental. All three concentrations focus on empirically validated methods with a research emphasis. Both the Clinical Psychology and School Psychology programs emphasize a scientist–practitioner model. Master of Arts in Psychology—Clinical (2 years). Purpose: (a) To provide students with professional training in the practice of clinical psychology including skills in diagnosis, assessment, therapy and research. (b) To prepare the student for doctoral training in clinical psychology. Master of Arts in Psychology—School (3 years). Purpose: The school psychology curriculum is organized to accomplish several goals: to gain an understanding of psychological theories, concepts, and research regarding human behavior, and apply that knowledge to promote human welfare in the school setting. They will have a basic background in both psychology and education designed to provide a general theoretical applied orientation in order to function effectively as a psychologist in an educational setting. They will have sufficient academic training to interpret and apply educational and psychological research in a critical manner. They will develop at least one area of expertise to make a distinct contribution as a school psychologist in a school system. They will gain an understanding of the educational system. They will have an understanding of professional problems and issues as well as how to follow approved ethical practices. Purpose and general description of General Experimental track: This track is a part of a master's program in psychology that was established in 1970. The purpose of the track is to prepare students for entry into doctoral programs in areas of experimental psychology such as cognitive, developmental, social, and neuropsychology. To achieve this objective, advanced coursework is offered in research methodology and content areas of experimental psychology, and students engage in research through a thesis requirement, as well as through elective directed study courses that provide opportunities for involvement in faculty research.

Special Facilities or Resources: The department includes shared offices for most graduate students, with space for research and for our psychological services clinic, which provides assessment and intervention to individuals within and outside of the university.

Application Information:

Send to School of Research and Graduate Studies: WCU, Cullowhee, NC 28723. Application available online. URL of online application: http://www.wcu.edu/200.asp. Students are admitted in the Fall, application deadline February 1. *Fee:* $35.

Minot State University

Minot State University School Psychology Program
Education and Health Sciences
500 University Avenue West
Minot, ND 58707
Telephone: (701) 858-4262
Fax: (701) 858-4260
E-mail: *casey.coleman@minotstateu.edu*
Web: *http://www.misu.nodak.edu/*

Department Information:

1991. Chairperson: Donald Burke. Number of faculty: total—full-time 9; women—full-time 7.

Programs and Degrees Offered:

Listed in the following order: Program area, degree type (T if terminal Master's), number awarded 7/06–6/07. Education Specialist in School Psychology EdS/MEd (School Psychology) 6.

Student Applications/Admissions:

Student Applications

Education Specialist in School Psychology EdS/MEd (School Psychology)—Applications 2007–2008, 12. Total applicants accepted 2007–2008, 5. Number full-time enrolled (new admits only) 2007–2008, 5. Total enrolled 2007–2008 full-time, 13, part-time, 1. Openings 2008–2009, 10. The median number of years required for completion of a degree in 2006–2007 were 3. The number of students enrolled full- and part-time who were dismissed or voluntarily withdrew from this program area in 2007–2008 were 0.

Admissions Requirements:

Scores: Entries appear in this order: required test or GPA, minimum score (if required), median score of students entering in 2007–2008. Master's Programs: GRE-V 450, 550; GRE-Q 450, 500; overall undergraduate GPA 2.75, 3.25. Students without the overall GPA must appeal to the chairperson and receive special written permission to be considered for admission.

Other Criteria: (importance of criteria rated low, medium, or high): GRE/MAT scores—high, research experience—low, work experience—high, extracurricular activity—medium, clinically related public service—medium, GPA—medium, letters of recommendation—low, interview—medium, statement of goals and objectives—medium.

Student Characteristics: The following represents characteristics of students in 2007–2008 in all graduate psychology programs in the department: Female—full-time 8, part-time 1; Male—full-time 5, part-time 0; African American/Black—full-time 0, part-time 0; Hispanic/Latino(a)—full-time 0, part-time 0; Asian/Pacific Islander—full-time 0, part-time 0; American Indian/Alaska Native—full-time 0, part-time 0; Caucasian/White—full-time 13, part-time 1; Multi-ethnic—full-time 0, part-time 0; students subject to the Americans With Disabilities Act—full-time 0, part-time 0; Unknown ethnicity—full-time 0, part-time 0.

Financial Information/Assistance:

Tuition for Full-Time Study: *Master's:* State residents: per academic year $3,273; Nonstate residents: per academic year $8,223.

Financial Assistance:

First-Year Students: Teaching assistantships available for first year. Average number of hours worked per week: 10. Research assistantships available for first year. Average number of hours worked per week: 10. Tuition remission given: partial.

Advanced Students: Research assistantships available for advanced students. Average number of hours worked per week: 10. Tuition remission given: partial.

Additional Information: Of all students currently enrolled full time, 45% benefited from one or more of the listed financial assistance programs.

Internships/Practica: School Psychology Practicum I: This practicum provides students an opportunity to apply their learning from content courses to elementary and secondary students who are failing to find success in school. The assessment of processing problems that sometimes underlie learning disabilities will be examined. School Psychology Practicum II: This is a capstone course wherein the students apply information learned and skills acquired in previous courses in diagnosis and remediation planning of actual school-based cases. Theory and techniques are applied to assisting school children with challenging learning and behavior problems. Emphasis will be placed on deciding whether a diagnostic or consultative role will best meet a particular child's needs. Internship: The internship will involve spending 1,200 hours in schools or a similar setting. It will also involve an integrative experience where the individual will demonstrate competencies in assessment, programming, consultation, and counseling.

Housing and Day Care: On-campus housing is available. See the following Web site for more information: http://www.minotstateu.edu/admin/housing.html. No on-campus day care facilities are available.

Employment of Department Graduates:

Master's Degree Graduates: Of those who graduated in the academic year 2006–2007, the following categories and numbers represent the postgraduate activities and employment of master's degree graduates: Enrolled in a psychology doctoral program (1), enrolled in another graduate/professional program (0), enrolled in a postdoctoral residency/fellowship (n/a), employed in independent practice (n/a), employed in an academic position at a university (0), employed in an academic position at a 2-year/4-year college (0), employed in other positions at a higher education institution (0), employed in a professional position in a school system (5), employed in business or industry (0), employed in government agency (0), employed in a community mental health/counseling center (0), employed in a hospital/medical center (0), still seeking employment (0), not seeking employment (0), other employment position (0), total from the above (master's) (6).

Doctoral Degree Graduates: Of those who graduated in the academic year 2006–2007, the following categories and numbers represent the postgraduate activities and employment of doctoral degree graduates: Enrolled in a psychology doctoral program (n/a), total from the above (doctoral) (0).

Additional Information:

Orientation, Objectives, and Emphasis of Department: The Education Specialist degree in school psychology is designed to prepare students for certification by the National Association of School Psychology (NASP) and as a School Psychologist in the State of North Dakota. Graduate students participate in a rigorous 3-year program. The program emphasizes hands-on experience culminating in a 1-year, 1,200-hour internship. The emphasis of the program is to provide the student with the theoretical and practical skills to be an effective school psychologist. The curriculum stresses teaching assessment skills, intervention techniques, and consultative strategies through numerous practicum opportunities. The program trains practitioners who are culturally competent service providers. The school psychology program at Minot State University trains practitioners who are prepared to work under a Response-to-Intervention (RTI) framework in rurally based schools that typify a state like North Dakota. The ideal practitioner in a rural setting is a generalist who combines appropriate educational and behavioral assessments with a knowledge of educational curriculum and instruction to develop appropriate interventions for a broad range of student concerns.

Special Facilities or Resources: The Minot State University School Psychology program is pleased to announce the creation of an ongoing clinic as part of the activities of our 2nd-year students. The clinic opened its doors in Fall of 2007.

Application Information:

Send to Graduate School, Minot State University, 500 University Avenue West, Minot, ND 58707. Application available online. Students are admitted in the Fall, application deadline March 15. *Fee:* $35.

North Dakota State University

Department of Psychology
Science and Mathematics
115 Minard Hall
Fargo, ND 58105
Telephone: (701) 231-8622
Fax: (701) 231-8426
E-mail: *NDSU.psych@ndsu.edu*
Web: *http://www.psych.ndsu.nodak.edu/*

Department Information:

1965. Chairperson: Paul D. Rokke. Number of faculty: total—full-time 17, part-time 7; women—full-time 4, part-time 5.

Programs and Degrees Offered:

Listed in the following order: Program area, degree type (T if terminal Master's), number awarded 7/06–6/07. Clinical MA/MS (Master of Arts/Science) (T) 4, Cognitive and Visual Neuroscience PhD (Doctor of Philosophy) 0, Health/Social PhD (Doctor of Philosophy) 2.

Student Applications/Admissions:

Student Applications

Clinical MA/MS (Master of Arts/Science)—Applications 2007–2008, 13. Total applicants accepted 2007–2008, 4. Number full-time enrolled (new admits only) 2007–2008, 4. Openings 2008–2009, 6. The median number of years required for completion of a degree in 2006–2007 were 2. The number of students enrolled full- and part-time who were dismissed or voluntarily withdrew from this program area in 2007–2008 were 0. *Cognitive and Visual Neuroscience PhD (Doctor of Philosophy)*—Applications 2007–2008, 3. Total applicants accepted 2007–2008, 1. Number full-time enrolled (new admits only) 2007–2008, 1. Total enrolled 2007–2008 full-time, 8. Openings 2008–2009, 3. The median number of years required for completion of a degree in 2006–2007 were 4. The number of students enrolled full- and part-time who were dismissed or voluntarily withdrew from this program area in 2007–2008 were 1. *Health/Social PhD (Doctor of Philosophy)*—Applications 2007–2008, 6. Total applicants accepted 2007–2008, 2. Number full-time enrolled (new admits only) 2007–2008, 2. Total enrolled 2007–2008 full-time, 13. Openings 2008–2009, 3. The median number of years required for completion of a degree in 2006–2007 were 4. The number of students enrolled full- and part-time who were dismissed or voluntarily withdrew from this program area in 2007–2008 were 1.

Admissions Requirements:

Scores: Entries appear in this order: required test or GPA, minimum score (if required), median score of students entering in 2007–2008. Master's Programs: GRE-V no minimum stated, 510; GRE-Q no minimum stated, 592; overall undergraduate GPA no minimum stated, 3.80; Masters GRE-Analytical no minimum stated, 5.0. Doctoral Programs: GRE-V no minimum stated, 612; GRE-Q no minimum stated, 650; overall undergraduate GPA no minimum stated, 3.58; Doctoral program GRE-Analytic no minimum stated, 4.5.

Other Criteria: (importance of criteria rated low, medium, or high): GRE/MAT scores—high, research experience—high, extracurricular activity—low, GPA—high, letters of recommendation—high, statement of goals and objectives—high, undergraduate major in psychology—low, specific undergraduate psychology courses taken—medium.

Student Characteristics: The following represents characteristics of students in 2007–2008 in all graduate psychology programs in the department: Female—full-time 22, part-time 0; Male—full-time 10, part-time 0; African American/Black—full-time 1, part-time 0; Hispanic/Latino(a)—full-time 0, part-time 0; Asian/Pacific Islander—full-time 1, part-time 0; American Indian/Alaska Native—full-time 0, part-time 0; Caucasian/White—full-time 30, part-time 0; students subject to the Americans With Disabilities Act—full-time 0, part-time 0; Unknown ethnicity—full-time 0, part-time 0.

Financial Information/Assistance:

Tuition for Full-Time Study: *Master's:* State residents: per academic year $5,995, $224 per credit hour; Nonstate residents: per academic year $14,354, $598 per credit hour. *Doctoral:* State residents: per academic year $5,995, $224 per credit hour; Nonstate residents: per academic year $14,354, $598 per credit hour. Additional fees are assessed to students beyond the costs of tuition for the following: Student fees cover cost of wellness center, technology access, and athletic events.

Financial Assistance:

First-Year Students: Teaching assistantships available for first year. Average amount paid per academic year: $5,800. Average number of hours worked per week: 10. Apply by March 1. Tuition remission given: full. Research assistantships available for first year. Average amount paid per academic year: $5,800. Average number of hours worked per week: 10. Apply by March 1. Tuition remission given: full.

Advanced Students: Teaching assistantships available for advanced students. Average amount paid per academic year: $16,000. Average number of hours worked per week: 20. Apply by March 1. Tuition remission given: full. Research assistantships available for advanced students. Average amount paid per academic year: $16,000. Average number of hours worked per week: 20. Apply by March 1. Tuition remission given: full. Fellowships and scholarships available for advanced students. Average amount paid per academic year: $16,000. Average number of hours worked per week: 20. Apply by March 1. Tuition remission given: full.

Additional Information: Of all students currently enrolled full time, 100% benefited from one or more of the listed financial assistance programs.

Internships/Practica: Our Master's program in Clinical Psychology has a number of clinical practica that provide a variety of experiences. These include work with traditional one-on-one counseling, chronic pain, eating disorders, behavior analysis, developmental disabilities, child and adolescent pscyhotherapy, community mental health, and clinical neuropsychology. Research practica are available for doctoral students who wish to develop applied research skills and experiences. Sites include a private foundation for reseach on addictions and eating disorders, a nationally prominent organization for clinical drug trials, a chronic pain treatment program, a community mental health center, and several sites devoted to survey research.

Housing and Day Care: On-campus housing is available. See the following Web site for more information: http://www.ndsu.edu/reslife/. On-campus day care facilities are available. See the following Web site for more information: http://www.ndsu.edu/cdfs/center_childdev.htm.

Employment of Department Graduates:

Master's Degree Graduates: Of those who graduated in the academic year 2006–2007, the following categories and numbers represent the postgraduate activities and employment of master's degree graduates: Enrolled in a psychology doctoral program (4), enrolled in a postdoctoral residency/fellowship (n/a), employed in independent practice (n/a), employed in other positions at a higher education institution (1), employed in business or industry (1), employed in a community mental health/counseling center (1), total from the above (master's) (7).

Doctoral Degree Graduates: Of those who graduated in the academic year 2006–2007, the following categories and numbers represent the postgraduate activities and employment of doctoral degree graduates: Enrolled in a psychology doctoral program (n/a), enrolled in a postdoctoral residency/fellowship (2), employed in an academic position at a university (2), employed in a community mental health/counseling center (1), total from the above (doctoral) (5).

Additional Information:

Orientation, Objectives, and Emphasis of Department: Our strong research tradition has earned us a reputation as one of the best small psychology departments in the nation. Our clinical master's program is over 30 years old, and many of our alumni have gone on to earn PhDs at top institutions. Our doctoral program emphasizes our strengths in health psychology and neuroscience. PhD training is designed to produce graduates with records in research and teaching, which will make them highly competitive for employment in both traditional academic and nontraditional government and private sector settings. Our programs are based on a mentoring model in which students work closely with specific faculty members who match their research interests. Potential applicants should visit our Web site (http://www.psych.ndsu.nodak.edu/) to learn about specific faculty interests and accomplishments.

Special Facilities or Resources: The department has state-of-the-art facilities for research in electrophysiology (including EEG), vision, and cognition, as well as ample space for other research projects. A center for research on virtual reality, multisensory integration, driving simulation is very active. As the largest population center in the region, Fargo-Moorhead serves as a center for medical services for a large geographic area. There are three major hospitals (including a VA), a medical school Department of Neuroscience, a psychiatric hospital, a neuroscience research institute, and a private pharmaceutical research institute, which offer opportunities for collaboration. NDSU also has a Research and Technology Park, which may offer research experiences involving advanced technology.

Information for Students With Physical Disabilities: See the following Web site for more information: http://www.ndsu.edu/counseling/.

Application Information:

Send to Office of Graduate Studies, P.O. Box 5790, NDSU, Fargo, ND 58105-5790. Materials available online at http://www.ndsu.nodak.edu/gradschool/. Application available online. URL of online application: http://www.ndsu.edu/gradschool/. Students are admitted in the Fall, application deadline February 15. Applications arriving after deadlines will be considered until positions are filled. *Fee:* $35.

North Dakota, University of

Department of Counseling Psychology and Community Services/PhD in Counseling Psychology; MA in Counseling
Education and Human Development
290 Centennial Drive, Stop 8255
Grand Forks, ND 58202-8255
Telephone: (701) 777-2729
Fax: (701) 777-3184
E-mail: *cl.juntunen@und.edu*
Web: *http://www.counseling.und.edu*

Department Information:

1963. Chairperson: Dr. Michael Loewy. Number of faculty: total—full-time 10, part-time 1; women—full-time 4; total—minority—full-time 1; women minority—full-time 1.

Programs and Degrees Offered:

Listed in the following order: Program area, degree type (T if terminal Master's), number awarded 7/06–6/07. Counseling Psychology PhD (Doctor of Philosophy) 6, Counseling MA/MS (Master of Arts/Science) (T) 15.

APA Accreditation: Counseling PhD (Doctor of Philosophy).

Student Applications/Admissions:

Student Applications

Counseling Psychology PhD (Doctor of Philosophy)—Applications 2007–2008, 45. Total applicants accepted 2007–2008, 7. Number full-time enrolled (new admits only) 2007–2008, 8. Number part-time enrolled (new admits only) 2007–2008, 0. Total enrolled 2007–2008 full-time, 34. Openings 2008–2009, 6. The median number of years required for completion of a degree in 2006–2007 were 5. The number of students enrolled full- and part-time who were dismissed or voluntarily withdrew from this program area in 2007–2008 were 1. *Counseling MA/MS (Master of Arts/Science)*—Applications 2007–2008, 31. Total applicants accepted 2007–2008, 18. Number full-time enrolled (new admits only) 2007–2008, 13. Number part-time enrolled (new admits only) 2007–2008, 2. Total enrolled 2007–2008 full-time, 31, part-time, 24. Openings 2008–2009, 20. The median number of years required for completion of a degree in 2006–2007 were 2. The number of students enrolled full- and part-time who were dismissed or voluntarily withdrew from this program area in 2007–2008 were 1.

Admissions Requirements:

Scores: Entries appear in this order: required test or GPA, minimum score (if required), median score of students entering in 2007–2008. Master's Programs: overall undergraduate GPA 2.75; last 2 years GPA 3.00. MA program requires either GRE or MAT. Doctoral Programs: GRE-V no minimum stated, 561; GRE-Q no minimum stated, 574; Doctoral program GRE-Analytic no minimum stated. GRE-Writing required for PhD program.

Other Criteria: (importance of criteria rated low, medium, or high): GRE/MAT scores—medium, research experience—high, work experience—medium, extracurricular activity—medium, clinically related public service—medium, GPA—medium, letters of recommendation—high, interview—high, statement of goals and objectives—high, prerequisites—medium, undergraduate major in psychology—low, specific undergraduate psychology courses taken—medium. For additional information on admission requirements, go to http://www.und.edu/dept/grad/pdf/PDF/04%20Supplemental%20Application%20Form.pdf.

Student Characteristics: The following represents characteristics of students in 2007–2008 in all graduate psychology programs in the department: Female—full-time 55, part-time 21; Male—full-time 10, part-time 3; African American/Black—full-time 2, part-time 0; Hispanic/Latino(a)—full-time 0, part-time 1; Asian/Pacific Islander—full-time 1, part-time 0; American Indian/Alaska Native—full-time 3, part-time 3; Caucasian/White—full-time 59, part-time 20; Multi-ethnic—full-time 0, part-time 0; students subject to the Americans With Disabilities Act—full-time 2, part-time 0; Unknown ethnicity—full-time 0, part-time 0; International students who hold an F-1 or J-1 Visa—full-time 4, part-time 0.

Financial Information/Assistance:

Tuition for Full-Time Study: *Master's:* State residents: per academic year $6,510; Nonstate residents: per academic year $15,537. *Doctoral:* State residents: per academic year $6,510; Nonstate residents: per academic year $15,537. Tuition is subject to change. Additional fees are assessed to students beyond the costs of tuition for the following: MA—cost of comprehensive exam ($30); PhD—cost of supplies for assessment courses (approximately $50). See the following Web site for updates and changes in tuition costs: http://www.und.edu/dept/busoff/tuitionrates.html.

Financial Assistance:

First-Year Students: Teaching assistantships available for first year. Average amount paid per academic year: $5,901. Average number of hours worked per week: 10. Tuition remission given: full. Research assistantships available for first year. Average amount paid per academic year: $11,803. Average number of hours worked per week: 10. Tuition remission given: full.

Advanced Students: Teaching assistantships available for advanced students. Average amount paid per academic year: $7,133. Average number of hours worked per week: 10. Tuition remission given: full. Research assistantships available for advanced students. Average amount paid per academic year: $14,266. Average number of hours worked per week: 10. Tuition remission given: full. Traineeships available for advanced students. Tuition remission given: full. Fellowships and scholarships available for advanced students. Tuition remission given: full.

Additional Information: Of all students currently enrolled full time, 50% benefited from one or more of the listed financial assistance programs. Application and information available online at http://www.und.edu/dept/finaid/ or contact P.O. Box 8371, Grand Forks, ND 58202-8371; phone: (701) 777-3121.

Internships/Practica: Master's Degree (MA/MS Counseling): An internship experience such as a final research project or "capstone" experience is required of graduates. Doctoral Degree (PhD Counseling Psychology): For those doctoral students for whom a professional internship was required in this program prior to graduation, (4) students applied for an internship in 2006–2007, with (3) students obtaining an internship. Of those students who obtained an internship, (3) were paid internships. Of those students who obtained an internship, (3) students placed in APA/CPA-accredited internships, (0) students placed in internships not APA/CPA-accredited, but listed with the Association of Psychology Postdoctoral and Internship Centers (APPIC), (0) students placed in internships conforming to guidelines of the Council of Directors of School Psychology Programs (CDSPP), (0) students placed in internships that were not APA/CPA accredited, APPIC or CDSPP listed. The first practicum for MA students provides live supervision from peers, doctoral supervisors, and faculty. Practicum is an introduction to counseling practice with an emphasis on development, improvement, and evaluation of counseling relationships. Students use counseling skills in practice with real clients and live supervision. School counseling students' practicum experience is based in the schools of Grand Forks, ND. MA students complete a two-semester, half-time, supervised counseling experience at an external site, typically completed during the 2nd year in the program. Group, individual, couples and family counseling, individual supervision, case conferencing, administrative activities, outreach services, and professional consultations are some of the possible opportunities. Placements are in community agencies, university counseling centers, schools, and other sites to fit the career goals of the student. All MA students are supervised weekly by a supervisor at the site. The supervisor must have an MA in Counseling or equivalent preparation. Doctoral students are required to complete three semesters of field placement in a community agency, in addition to the equivalent of the MA-level practicum and internship, for a total of six semesters of practica. The doctoral-level field placements focus on developing advanced skills, integrating theory and evidence-based practice decision-making, and increasing treatment planning abilities. Many doctoral students also complete optional semesters of practica with emphases in assessment or another area of particular interest to them. In recent years predoctoral interns have been placed at university counseling centers, mental health agencies, and VA and other medical centers. The training director and program faculty assist students with this process. All doctoral students are supervised by licensed psychologists. For additional information on education and training outcomes for our programs, see the following Web site: (http://www.und.edu/dept/coun/doctoral/dataoutcomephd.pdf.

Housing and Day Care: On-campus housing is available. See the following Web site for more information: http://www.housing.und.edu/; e-mail: housing@mail.und.edu; 525 Stanford Road, Stop 9029, Grand Forks, ND 58202-9029. Phone (701) 777-4251. On-campus day care facilities are available. See the following Web site for more information: http://www.housing.und.edu/ucc; University Children' Center, 525 Stanford Road, Stop 9026, Grand Forks, ND 58202-9026. Phone: (701) 777-3947.

Employment of Department Graduates:

Master's Degree Graduates: Of those who graduated in the academic year 2006–2007, the following categories and numbers represent the postgraduate activities and employment of master's degree graduates: Enrolled in a psychology doctoral program (1), enrolled in another graduate/professional program (1), enrolled in a postdoctoral residency/fellowship (n/a), employed in independent practice (n/a), employed in an academic position at a university (0), employed in an academic position at a 2-year/4-year college (0), employed in other positions at a higher education institution (1), employed in a professional position in a school system (2), employed in business or industry (0), employed in government agency (0), employed in a community mental health/counseling center (5), employed in a hospital/medical center (0), still seeking employment (0), not seeking employment (0), other employment position (0), do not know (3), total from the above (master's) (13).

Doctoral Degree Graduates: Of those who graduated in the academic year 2006–2007, the following categories and numbers represent the postgraduate activities and employment of doctoral degree graduates: Enrolled in a psychology doctoral program (n/a), enrolled in another graduate/professional program (0), enrolled in a postdoctoral residency/fellowship (0), employed in independent practice (0), employed in an academic position at a university (0), employed in an academic position at a 2-year/4-year college (0), employed in other positions at a higher education institution (1), employed in a professional position in a school system (0), employed in business or industry (0), employed in government agency (0), employed in a community mental health/counseling center (3), employed in a hospital/medical center (0), still seeking employment (0), other employment position (0), total from the above (doctoral) (4).

Additional Information:

Orientation, Objectives, and Emphasis of Department: The Department of Counseling at the University of North Dakota affirms as a primary value the integration of practice and science throughout the professional life span, from training through career-long participation in the profession. Whether a counselor's or counseling psychologist's career is primarily involved with direct services to clients, or with educational services to students in academia, or with consultative services to organizations, we view science and practice as necessary and complementary aspects of our professional identity. There is no relative importance implied by the order of the words; they are mutual, reciprocal components, best depicted in a circular fashion, not a linear one. An equally important value is best captured by the word diversity, which is to be sought, valued, and respected. We use the word in a very broad sense. Included in diversity is the variety of cultures, backgrounds, values, religions, and experiences among our faculty and students; we seek such diversity actively. Also included, though, is the diversity of our professional ways of practice across many theoretical models, the diversity of our ways of learning, our ways of doing science, the diversity of our strengths, our needs, and the diversity of our goals and ways of achieving them.

Special Facilities or Resources: Our Practicum Clinic is in a new counseling facility that we share with the University Counseling Center and with Northeast Human Services in downtown Grand Forks, North Dakota. The facility has an observation area wherein we can view sessions live or through video monitors. We also are able to communicate with the counselor-in-training through a walkie–talkie system (bug in the ear).

Information for Students With Physical Disabilities: See the following Web site for more information: http://www.und.edu/dept/dss/.

Application Information:

Applicants are encouraged to apply online. URL of online application: http://www.apply.embark.com/grad/northdakota. Students are admitted in the Fall, application deadline January 3. February 1 for the Master's program. *Fee:* $35. The application fee is waived if you have received a master's or doctoral degree from UND or if you are a McNair Scholar.

North Dakota, University of

Department of Psychology
Arts and Science
P.O. Box 8380
Grand Forks, ND 58202-8380
Telephone: (701) 777-3451
Fax: (701) 777-3454
E-mail: *alan_king@und.nodak.edu*
Web: *http://www.ndwild.psych.und.nodak.edu/dept/clinical.html*

Department Information:

1921. Chairperson: Jeffrey Weatherly. Number of faculty: total—full-time 17; women—full-time 4; total—minority—full-time 1; faculty subject to the Americans With Disabilities Act 1.

Programs and Degrees Offered:

Listed in the following order: Program area, degree type (T if terminal Master's), number awarded 7/06–6/07. Clinical PhD (Doctor of Philosophy) 7, General Experimental PhD (Doctor of Philosophy) 1.

APA Accreditation: Clinical PhD (Doctor of Philosophy).

Student Applications/Admissions:

Student Applications

Clinical PhD (Doctor of Philosophy)—Applications 2007–2008, 85. Total applicants accepted 2007–2008, 7. Number full-time enrolled (new admits only) 2007–2008, 8. Number part-time enrolled (new admits only) 2007–2008, 0. Openings 2008–2009, 7. The median number of years required for completion of a degree in 2006–2007 were 5. The number of students enrolled full- and part-time who were dismissed or voluntarily withdrew from this program area in 2007–2008 were 0. *General Experimental PhD (Doctor of Philosophy)*—Applications 2007–2008, 12. Total applicants accepted 2007–2008, 2. Number full-time enrolled (new admits only) 2007–2008, 2. Number part-time enrolled (new admits only) 2007–2008, 0. Openings 2008–2009, 3. The median number of years required for completion of a degree in 2006–2007 were 5. The number of students enrolled full- and part-time who were dismissed or voluntarily withdrew from this program area in 2007–2008 were 0.

Admissions Requirements:

Scores: Entries appear in this order: required test or GPA, minimum score (if required), median score of students entering in 2007–2008. Master's Programs: GRE-V no minimum stated, 525; GRE-Q no minimum stated, 605; GRE-Subject (Psychology) no minimum stated, 640; overall undergraduate GPA 3.2, 3.59; last 2 years GPA no minimum stated, 3.7. Clinical graduate program requires a minimum of 30th percentile scores for both the Verbal and Quantitative sections of the GRE as well as an Analytic Writing test score exceeding 2.5. Doctoral Programs: GRE-V no minimum stated, 525; GRE-Q no minimum stated, 605; GRE-Subject (Psychology) no minimum stated, 640; last 2 years GPA no minimum stated, 3.70; Doctoral program GRE-Analytic no minimum stated.

Other Criteria: (importance of criteria rated low, medium, or high): GRE/MAT scores—medium, research experience—high, work experience—medium, extracurricular activity—low, clinically related public service—medium, GPA—high, letters of recommendation—medium, interview—low, statement of goals and objectives—medium. For additional information on admission requirements, go to http://ndwild.psych.und.nodak.edu/dept/clinicaladmission.html.

Student Characteristics: The following represents characteristics of students in 2007–2008 in all graduate psychology programs in the department: Female—full-time 32, part-time 0; Male—full-time 15, part-time 0; African American/Black—full-time 1, part-time 0; Hispanic/Latino(a)—full-time 0, part-time 0; Asian/Pacific Islander—full-time 0, part-time 0; American Indian/Alaska Native—full-time 15, part-time 0; Caucasian/White—full-time 38, part-time 0; students subject to the Americans With Disabilities Act—full-time 0, part-time 0; Unknown ethnicity—full-time 0, part-time 0.

Financial Information/Assistance:

Financial Assistance:

First-Year Students: Teaching assistantships available for first year. Average amount paid per academic year: $11,241. Average number of hours worked per week: 15. Apply by January 15. Tuition remission given: full.

Advanced Students: Traineeships available for advanced students. Tuition remission given: full.

Additional Information: Of all students currently enrolled full time, 100% benefited from one or more of the listed financial assistance programs.

Internships/Practica: Doctoral Degree (PhD Clinical): For those doctoral students for whom a professional internship was required in this program prior to graduation, (11) students applied for an internship in 2006–2007, with (6) students obtaining an internship. Of those students who obtained an internship, (6) were paid internships. Of those students who obtained an internship, (6) students placed in APA/CPA-accredited internships, (0) students placed in internships not APA/CPA-accredited, but listed with the Association of Psychology Postdoctoral and Internship Centers (APPIC), (0) students placed in internships conforming to guidelines of the Council of Directors of School Psychology Programs (CDSPP), (0) students placed in internships that were not APA/CPA-accredited, APPIC or CDSPP listed. Psychological Services Center (PSC): Each year you will be assigned to one of the four PSC supervision teams. These teams are primarily supervised by program faculty, and students typically plan to work with as many different PSC supervisors as possible during their time in the program. You will be assigned to a team during your first year, but in subsequent years your preferences will be taken into consideration during team assignments. This process usually occurs late in the Spring semester. PSC teams typically consist of one or two students from each class. Student responsibilities, duties, and opportunities will vary from team to team. The Clinical curriculum provides requirements regarding the number of Clinical Practice (PSY 580) credit hours in which you should enroll each semester. External Placements: The Clinical program also maintains agreements with a variety of institutions within and beyond the Grand Forks community to provide more extensive training opportunities. Upper-level students compete for these positions in April and May of each year. Clinical students are required to complete at least seven PSYC 587 credits (1 full year at 16–20 hrs/wk) placement prior to internship with most students completing 2 years to enhance their internship competitiveness. Our rate of success in attaining accredited internships on APPIC match day has been 40/47 over the past 7 years (85%).

Housing and Day Care: On-campus housing is available. On-campus day care facilities are available.

Employment of Department Graduates:

Master's Degree Graduates: Of those who graduated in the academic year 2006–2007, the following categories and numbers represent the postgraduate activities and employment of master's degree graduates: Enrolled in a postdoctoral residency/fellowship (n/a), employed in independent practice (n/a), total from the above (master's) (0).

Doctoral Degree Graduates: Of those who graduated in the academic year 2006–2007, the following categories and numbers represent the postgraduate activities and employment of doctoral degree graduates: Enrolled in a psychology doctoral program (n/a),

enrolled in a postdoctoral residency/fellowship (1), employed in a community mental health/counseling center (3), employed in a hospital/medical center (4), total from the above (doctoral) (8).

Additional Information:

Orientation, Objectives, and Emphasis of Department: The Psychology Department at the University of North Dakota offers doctoral programs in Experimental and Clinical Psychology. Experimental students work out individualized programs of study and research with their advisory committees and are encouraged to develop research productivity early in the program. Course work and research opportunities are strongest in the cognitive, social, and behavioral areas. Because the Clinical program leads to a PhD rather than a professional PsyD degree, the emphasis is on the understanding of general psychological theory and the application of the scientific method to research issues. Clinical students work on developing interpersonal skills, and applying both analytic thought and intuitive judgment to problems of individuals, families, and communities. A variety of ongoing research programs help train students in the scientist–practitioner model. The Clinical program works closely with the Indians in Psychology Doctoral Education (INPSYDE) program to facilitate entry of Native Americans into clinical psychology and to improve services available to rural, Native American communities. Finally, all students, with specific encouragement for the Experimental students, have opportunities to develop expertise in teaching.

Special Facilities or Resources: The department has practicum placements for training in rural community mental health, a low faculty–student ratio, a campus-based psychological services center, and a faculty with active research programs. The Department also has dedicated laboratories capable of computer-assisted monitoring and recording of various physiological and psychological measures in humans (e.g., eye movements, reaction time, sexual response, autonomic nervous system function) as well as in animals (e.g., operant behavior). The University's library has a wide range of holdings in psychology and is tied into an interlibrary loan network. The Department's computers are available for research and provide access to UND's main computer system. Medline, PSYCLIT, and ERIC computer literature searches are available to students. Additional research facilities have been developed in conjunction with the adjacent USDA Grand Forks Human Nutrition Research Center and include a computerized neuropsychological laboratory, sleep EEG rooms, and animal behavior laboratories.

Information for Students With Physical Disabilities: See the following Web site for more information: http://www.ndwild.psych.und.nodak.edu/dept/clinical.html.

Application Information:

Send to Graduate School, University of North Dakota, Box 8178, Grand Forks, ND 58202. Application available online. URL of online application: http://www.ndwild.psych.und.nodak.edu/dept/clinical.html. Students are admitted in the Fall, application deadline January 15. *Fee:* $35.

Akron, University of

Department of Counseling, Collaborative Program in Counseling Psychology
The College of Education
27 Fir Hill
Akron, OH 44325-5007
Telephone: (330) 972- 7777
Fax: (330) 972-5292
E-mail: *sz@uakron.edu*
Web: *http://www.uakron.edu/colleges/educ/Counseling/index.php*

Department Information:
1968. Chairperson: Dr. Karin Jordan. Number of faculty: total—full-time 12, part-time 4; women—full-time 7, part-time 1; total—minority—full-time 1.

Programs and Degrees Offered:
Listed in the following order: Program area, degree type (T if terminal Master's), number awarded 7/06–6/07. Collaborative Program in Counseling Psychology PhD (Doctor of Philosophy) 2.

APA Accreditation: Counseling PhD (Doctor of Philosophy).

Student Applications/Admissions:

Student Applications

Collaborative Program in Counseling Psychology PhD (Doctor of Philosophy)—Applications 2007–2008, 35. Total applicants accepted 2007–2008, 4. Number full-time enrolled (new admits only) 2007–2008, 3. Number part-time enrolled (new admits only) 2007–2008, 0. Total enrolled 2007–2008 full-time, 12, part-time, 15. Openings 2008–2009, 4. The median number of years required for completion of a degree in 2006–2007 were 6. The number of students enrolled full- and part-time who were dismissed or voluntarily withdrew from this program area in 2007–2008 were 0.

Admissions Requirements:

Scores: Entries appear in this order: required test or GPA, minimum score (if required), median score of students entering in 2007–2008. Doctoral Programs: GRE-V no minimum stated, 590; GRE-Q no minimum stated, 680; GRE-Subject (Psychology) no minimum stated, 710; overall undergraduate GPA 2.75, 3.80.

Other Criteria: (importance of criteria rated low, medium, or high): GRE/MAT scores—high, research experience—high, work experience—medium, extracurricular activity—low, clinically related public service—low, GPA—high, letters of recommendation—high, interview—high, statement of goals and objectives—high. For additional information on admission requirements, go to http://www3.uakron.edu/psychology/counseling/.

Student Characteristics: The following represents characteristics of students in 2007–2008 in all graduate psychology programs in the department: Female—full-time 9, part-time 15; Male—full-time 3, part-time 2; African American/Black—full-time 0, part-time 1; Hispanic/Latino(a)—full-time 0, part-time 0; Asian/Pacific Islander—full-time 0, part-time 1; American Indian/Alaska Native—full-time 0, part-time 0; Caucasian/White—full-time 12, part-time 15; Multi-ethnic—full-time 0, part-time 0; students subject to the Americans With Disabilities Act—full-time 0, part-time 1; Unknown ethnicity—full-time 0, part-time 0; International students who hold an F-1 or J-1 Visa—full-time 0, part-time 0.

Financial Information/Assistance:

Tuition for Full-Time Study: *Doctoral:* State residents: $342 per credit hour; Nonstate residents: $587 per credit hour. Tuition is subject to change. See the following Web site for updates and changes in tuition costs: http://www.uakron.edu/busfin/studentfin/tuition.php.

Financial Assistance:

First-Year Students: Teaching assistantships available for first year. Average amount paid per academic year: $10,500. Average number of hours worked per week: 20. Apply by April 15. Tuition remission given: full. Research assistantships available for first year. Average amount paid per academic year: $10,500. Average number of hours worked per week: 20. Apply by April 15. Tuition remission given: full.

Advanced Students: Teaching assistantships available for advanced students. Average amount paid per academic year: $10,500. Average number of hours worked per week: 20. Apply by April 15. Tuition remission given: full. Research assistantships available for advanced students. Average amount paid per academic year: $10,500. Average number of hours worked per week: 20. Apply by April 15. Tuition remission given: full.

Additional Information: Of all students currently enrolled full time, 76% benefited from one or more of the listed financial assistance programs. Application and information available online at http://www.uakron.edu/grdsch/gradAsst.php.

Internships/Practica: Doctoral Degree (PhD Collaborative Program in Counseling Psychology): For those doctoral students for whom a professional internship was required in this program prior to graduation, (4) students applied for an internship in 2006–2007, with (4) students obtaining an internship. Of those students who obtained an internship, (4) were paid internships. Of those students who obtained an internship, (4) students placed in APA/CPA-accredited internships, (0) students placed in internships not APA/CPA-accredited, but listed with the Association of Psychology Postdoctoral and Internship Centers (APPIC), (0) students placed in internships conforming to guidelines of the Council of Directors of School Psychology Programs (CDSPP), (0) students placed in internships that were not APA/CPA accredited, APPIC or CDSPP listed. Practica are offered in the department's clinic, the counseling center on campus, and a broad range of settings in the community.

Housing and Day Care: Limited on-campus housing is available. See the following Web site for more information: http://www.uakron.edu/studentaff/reslife/. On-campus day care facilities are available. Childcare is available on campus for a fee at the Center for Child Development. See the following Web site for more information: http://www3.uakron.edu/hefe/ccd.htm.

Employment of Department Graduates:

Master's Degree Graduates: Of those who graduated in the academic year 2006–2007, the following categories and numbers represent the postgraduate activities and employment of master's degree graduates: Enrolled in a postdoctoral residency/fellowship (n/a), employed in independent practice (n/a), total from the above (master's) (0).

Doctoral Degree Graduates: Of those who graduated in the academic year 2006–2007, the following categories and numbers represent the postgraduate activities and employment of doctoral degree graduates: Enrolled in a psychology doctoral program (n/a), enrolled in another graduate/professional program (0), employed in independent practice (1), employed in an academic position at a university (0), employed in an academic position at a 2-year/4-year college (1), employed in other positions at a higher education institution (0), employed in a professional position in a school system (0), employed in business or industry (0), employed in government agency (0), employed in a community mental health/counseling center (2), employed in a hospital/medical center (1), still seeking employment (0), not seeking employment (0), other employment position (0), total from the above (doctoral) (5).

Additional Information:

Orientation, Objectives, and Emphasis of Department: The department subscribes to a scientist–practitioner model of training. Its objective is to provide a core of courses in general psychology and courses in the specialty of counseling psychology. The emphasis is on preparation for teaching, research, and practice career paths.

Personal Behavior Statement: See Appendix F, Informed Consent Regarding CPCP Student Competence, in the Handbook for Graduate Students in the Collaborative Program, available at http://www3.uakron.edu/psychology/counseling/.

Special Facilities or Resources: The department has its own computer lab and houses the College of Education Clinic for Individual and Family Counseling.

Information for Students With Physical Disabilities: See the following Web site for more information: http://www3.uakron.edu/access/.

Application Information:

Send to Graduate School, Polsky Building, Room 469, The University of Akron, Akron, OH 44325-2101. Application available online. URL of online application: http://www.uakron.edu/gradsch/. Students are admitted in the Fall, application deadline January 15. All applications go to the Graduate School; online applications are strongly preferred. Prospective students with Master's degrees in a related field should indicate that they are applying to the Collaborative Program in Counseling Psychology (PhD) through the Department of Counseling. Prospective students with Bachelor's degrees should indicate that they are applying to the Collaborative Program in Counseling Psychology (MA/PhD) through the Department of Psychology. Note that the program information and data in this entry reflect only the half of the Collaborative Program located in the Department of Counseling. *Fee:* $30. Contact Graduate School.

Akron, University of

Department of Psychology
Buchtel College of Arts and Sciences
Arts and Sciences Building
290 East Buchtel Avenue
Akron, OH 44325-4301
Telephone: (330) 972-7280
Fax: (330) 972-5174
E-mail: *plevy@uakron.edu*
Web: *http://www.uakron.edu/psychology*

Department Information:

1921. Chairperson: Paul E. Levy. Number of faculty: total—full-time 19, part-time 1; women—full-time 7, part-time 1.

Programs and Degrees Offered:

Listed in the following order: Program area, degree type (T if terminal Master's), number awarded 7/06–6/07. Counseling PhD (Doctor of Philosophy) 2, Applied Cognitive Aging PhD (Doctor of Philosophy) 2, Applied Cognitive Aging (Thesis) MA/MS (Master of Arts/Science) 0, Industrial/Organizational (Thesis) MA/MS (Master of Arts/Science) (T) 7, Industrial/Organizational (Personnel, Nonthesis) MA/MS (Master of Arts/Science) (T) 2, Industrial/Organizational PhD (Doctor of Philosophy) 7, Industrial/Gerontological PhD (Doctor of Philosophy) 0.

APA Accreditation: Counseling PhD (Doctor of Philosophy).

Student Applications/Admissions:

Student Applications

Counseling PhD (Doctor of Philosophy)—Applications 2007–2008, 58. Total applicants accepted 2007–2008, 8. Number full-time enrolled (new admits only) 2007–2008, 4. Number part-time enrolled (new admits only) 2007–2008, 0. Total enrolled 2007–2008 full-time, 21, part-time, 12. Openings 2008–2009, 5. The median number of years required for completion of a degree in 2006–2007 were 6. The number of students enrolled full- and part-time who were dismissed or voluntarily withdrew from this program area in 2007–2008 were 0. *Applied Cognitive Aging PhD (Doctor of Philosophy)*—Applications 2007–2008, 0. Total applicants accepted 2007–2008, 0. Number full-time enrolled (new admits only) 2007–2008, 0. Number part-time enrolled (new admits only) 2007–2008, 0. The median number of years required for completion of a degree in 2006–2007 were 5. The number of students enrolled full- and part-time who were dismissed or voluntarily withdrew from this program area in 2007–2008 were 0. *Applied Cognitive Aging (Thesis) MA/MS (Master of Arts/Science)*—Applications 2007–2008, 0. Total applicants accepted 2007–2008, 0. Number full-time enrolled (new admits only) 2007–2008, 0. Number part-time enrolled (new admits only) 2007–2008, 0. The number of students enrolled full- and part-time who were dismissed or voluntarily withdrew from this program area in 2007–2008 were 0. *Industrial/Organizational (Thesis) MA/MS (Master of Arts/Science)*—Applications 2007–2008, 33. Total applicants accepted 2007–2008, 15. Number full-time enrolled (new admits only) 2007–2008, 7. Number part-time enrolled (new admits only) 2007–2008, 0. Openings 2008–2009, 6. The median number of years required for completion of a degree in 2006–2007 were 2. The number of students enrolled full- and part-time who were dismissed or voluntarily withdrew from this program area in 2007–2008 were 0. *Industrial/Organizational (Personnel, Nonthesis) MA/MS (Master of Arts/Science)*—Applications 2007–2008, 12. Total applicants accepted 2007–2008, 0. Number full-time enrolled (new admits only) 2007–2008, 0. Number part-time enrolled (new admits only) 2007–2008, 0. Openings 2008–2009, 5. The median number of years required for completion of a degree in 2006–2007 were 2. The number of students enrolled full- and part-time who were dismissed or voluntarily withdrew from this program area in 2007–2008 were 0. *Industrial/Organizational PhD (Doctor of Philosophy)*—Applications 2007–2008, 8. Total applicants accepted 2007–2008, 1. Number full-time enrolled (new admits only) 2007–2008, 0. Number part-time enrolled (new admits only) 2007–2008, 0. Total enrolled 2007–2008 full-time, 14, part-time, 8. Openings 2008–2009, 6. The median number of years required for completion of a degree in 2006–2007 were 6. The number of students enrolled full- and part-time who were dismissed or voluntarily withdrew from this program area in 2007–2008 were 0. *Industrial/Gerontological PhD (Doctor of Philosophy)*—Applications 2007–2008, 1. Total applicants accepted 2007–2008, 0. Number full-time enrolled (new admits only) 2007–2008, 1. Number part-time enrolled (new admits only) 2007–2008, 0. Total enrolled 2007–2008 full-time, 2, part-time, 3. Openings 2008–2009, 1. The number of students enrolled full- and part-time who were dismissed or voluntarily withdrew from this program area in 2007–2008 were 0.

Admissions Requirements:

Scores: Entries appear in this order: required test or GPA, minimum score (if required), median score of students entering in 2007–2008. Master's Programs: GRE-V 500, 520; GRE-Q 500, 640; GRE-Subject (Psychology) 500, 610; overall undergraduate GPA 2.75, 3.54; psychology GPA 3.00, 3.70. These minimum GRE scores and GPA values are guidelines rather than absolute thresholds. Exceptions may be made given other evidence of high potential. These scores are for the terminal MA degree. Doctoral Programs: GRE-V 550, 570; GRE-Q 550, 640; GRE-Subject (Psychology) 550, 670; overall undergraduate GPA 3.00, 3.71; psychology GPA 3.25, 3.82. These minimum GRE scores and GPA values are guidelines rather than absolute thresholds. Exceptions may be made given other evidence of high potential. The MA GPA is relevant only to programs admitting directly to the PhD

Other Criteria: (importance of criteria rated low, medium, or high): GRE/MAT scores—high, research experience—high, work experience—low, extracurricular activity—low, clinically related public service—low, GPA—high, letters of recommendation—medium, interview—medium, statement of goals and objectives—high. Telephone interviews are used as a selection criterion only in the Counseling Psychology program. Clinical service may be considered more heavily for admissions to the Counseling Psychology MA/PhD program. I/O program does telephone screening of those whom it intends to accept. Both programs have visit days when those offered admission are invited to spend a day or two meeting with students and faculty. For additional information on admission requirements, go to http://www3.uakron.edu/psychology/gradschool/minreq.html.

Student Characteristics: The following represents characteristics of students in 2007–2008 in all graduate psychology programs in the department: Female—full-time 42, part-time 18; Male—full-time 15, part-time 9; African American/Black—full-time 4, part-time 3; Hispanic/Latino(a)—full-time 2, part-time 0; Asian/Pacific Islander—full-time 4, part-time 2; American Indian/Alaska Native—full-time 0, part-time 0; Caucasian/White—full-time 47, part-time 22; Multi-ethnic—full-time 0, part-time 0; students subject to the Americans With Disabilities Act—full-time 0, part-time 0; Unknown ethnicity—full-time 0, part-time 0; International students who hold an F-1 or J-1 Visa—full-time 6, part-time 2.

Financial Information/Assistance:

Tuition for Full-Time Study: *Master's:* State residents: per academic year $10,756, $343 per credit hour; Nonstate residents: per academic year $18,246, $588 per credit hour. *Doctoral:* State residents: per academic year $10,756, $343 per credit hour; Nonstate residents: per academic year $18,246, $588 per credit hour. Tuition is subject to change. See the following Web site for updates and changes in tuition costs: http://www.uakron.edu/busfin/studentfin/grad.php.

Financial Assistance:

First-Year Students: Teaching assistantships available for first year. Average amount paid per academic year: $12,500. Average number of hours worked per week: 20. Apply by January 15. Tuition remission given: full. Fellowships and scholarships available for first year. Average amount paid per academic year: $0. Average number of hours worked per week: 0. Apply by January 15. Tuition remission given: full.

Advanced Students: Teaching assistantships available for advanced students. Average amount paid per academic year: $12,200. Average number of hours worked per week: 20. Apply by April 15. Tuition remission given: full. Research assistantships available for advanced students. Average amount paid per academic year: $12,200. Average number of hours worked per week: 20. Apply by April 15. Tuition remission given: full.

Additional Information: Of all students currently enrolled full time, 95% benefited from one or more of the listed financial assistance programs. Application and information available online at http://www3.uakron.edu/psychology/gradschool/.

Internships/Practica: Doctoral Degree (PhD Counseling): For those doctoral students for whom a professional internship was required in this program prior to graduation, (9) students applied for an internship in 2006–2007, with (8) students obtaining an internship. Of those students who obtained an internship, (8) were paid internships. Of those students who obtained an internship, (8) students placed in APA/CPA-accredited internships, (0) students placed in internships not APA/CPA-accredited, but listed with the Association of Psychology Postdoctoral and Internship Centers (APPIC), (0) students placed in internships conforming to guidelines of the Council of Directors of School Psychology Programs (CDSPP), (0) students placed in internships that were not APA/CPA-accredited, APPIC or CDSPP listed. Practica are offered in the department's own Counseling Training Clinic and Center for Organizational Research. Students also have access to a wide variety of community-based practica in industrial and public settings, hospitals, the University's Counseling Testing and Careers Center, and community mental health centers.

Housing and Day Care: Limited on-campus housing is available. See the following Web site for more information: http://www.

uakron.edu/studentaff/reslife/housingmain.php. On-campus day care facilities are available. Child care is available on campus for a fee at the Center for Child Development, a center run by the College of Education and College of Fine and Applied Arts. See the following Web site for more information: http://www3.uakron.edu/hefe/ccd/ccd.htm.

Employment of Department Graduates:

Master's Degree Graduates: Of those who graduated in the academic year 2006–2007, the following categories and numbers represent the postgraduate activities and employment of master's degree graduates: Enrolled in a psychology doctoral program (13), enrolled in another graduate/professional program (0), enrolled in a postdoctoral residency/fellowship (n/a), employed in independent practice (n/a), employed in an academic position at a university (0), employed in an academic position at a 2-year/4-year college (0), employed in other positions at a higher education institution (0), employed in a professional position in a school system (0), employed in business or industry (2), employed in government agency (0), employed in a community mental health/counseling center (0), employed in a hospital/medical center (0), still seeking employment (0), not seeking employment (0), other employment position (0), do not know (0), total from the above (master's) (15).

Doctoral Degree Graduates: Of those who graduated in the academic year 2006–2007, the following categories and numbers represent the postgraduate activities and employment of doctoral degree graduates: Enrolled in a psychology doctoral program (n/a), enrolled in another graduate/professional program (0), enrolled in a postdoctoral residency/fellowship (0), employed in independent practice (0), employed in an academic position at a university (5), employed in an academic position at a 2-year/4-year college (0), employed in other positions at a higher education institution (0), employed in a professional position in a school system (0), employed in business or industry (4), employed in government agency (0), employed in a community mental health/counseling center (0), employed in a hospital/medical center (0), still seeking employment (0), not seeking employment (0), other employment position (0), do not know (0), total from the above (doctoral) (9).

Additional Information:

Orientation, Objectives, and Emphasis of Department: The department's goals are to (a) increase and diffuse psychological knowledge by advancing the discipline both as a science and as a means of promoting human welfare; (b) promote psychology in all its branches in the broadest and most liberal manner; (c) encourage research in psychology; and (d) advance high standards of education, achievement, professional ethics, and conduct. The department subscribes to a scientist–practitioner model of training. Graduate students take a common set of courses in foundational areas of psychology in addition to their specialty coursework, with study in the specialty area beginning early in graduate training. The emphasis is on preparation for teaching as well as for research, industrial, or mental health services career paths. Industrial/organizational, industrial gerontological, and counseling psychology are the specialty emphases at the MA and PhD level.

Special Facilities or Resources: To enhance research and instruction, we maintain a number of psychological research laboratories designed for individual and group studies, and equipped with computers, one-way viewing mirrors, video equipment, etc. Over 60 computers are available to faculty and students for word processing, statistical analysis, classroom instruction, e-mail correspondence, and Web access. A programmer/technician provides full-time support for the hardware and software for the department and writes custom software for experimental control, stimulus display, and data collection. We maintain an in-house library of teaching resources for graduate teaching assistants, as well as a test library with over 100 tests and manuals for assessment of a broad range of constructs. We are affiliated with the university's Institute for Life Span Development and Gerontology and the Archives of the History of American Psychology.

Information for Students With Physical Disabilities: See the following Web site for more information: http://www3.uakron.edu/access/.

Application Information:

Send to Graduate School, The University of Akron, Polsky Building Room 469, Akron, OH 44325-2101. Application available online. URL of online application: http://www.uakron.edu/gradsch/admissions/applProc.php. Students are admitted in the Fall, application deadline January 15. We require the full application package be submitted at one time to the Department of Psychology per instructions on our Web page at http://www3.uakron.edu/psychology/gradschool/checklist.html. *Fee:* $30 domestic student; an international student's fee is $40.

Bowling Green State University (2007 data)

Department of Psychology
Bowling Green, OH 43403
Telephone: (419) 372-2301
Fax: (419) 372-6013
E-mail: *pwatson@bgnet.bgsu.edu*
Web: *http://www.bgsu.edu/departments/psych/*

Department Information:

1947. Chairperson: Dale S. Klopfer. Number of faculty: total—full-time 28, part-time 4; women—full-time 10, part-time 1.

Programs and Degrees Offered:

Listed in the following order: Program area, degree type (T if terminal Master's), number awarded 7/06–6/07. Clinical PhD (Doctor of Philosophy) 7, Developmental PhD (Doctor of Philosophy) 1, Neural and Cognitive PhD (Doctor of Philosophy) 3, Industrial/Organizational PhD (Doctor of Philosophy) 6.

APA Accreditation: Clinical PhD (Doctor of Philosophy).

Student Applications/Admissions:

Student Applications

Clinical PhD (Doctor of Philosophy)—Applications 2007–2008, 116. Total applicants accepted 2007–2008, 14. Number full-time enrolled (new admits only) 2007–2008, 8. Openings 2008–2009, 10. The median number of years required for completion of a degree in 2006–2007 were 6. The number of students enrolled full- and part-time who were dismissed or voluntarily withdrew from this program area in 2007–2008 were 0. *Developmental PhD (Doctor of Philosophy)*—Applications 2007–2008, 4. Total applicants accepted 2007–2008, 3. Number full-time enrolled (new admits only) 2007–2008, 2. Total enrolled 2007–2008 full-time, 7. Openings 2008–2009, 3. The median number of years required for completion of a degree in 2006–2007 were 5. The number of students enrolled full- and part-time who were dismissed or voluntarily withdrew from this program area in 2007–2008 were 0. *Neural and Cognitive PhD (Doctor of Philosophy)*—Applications 2007–2008, 19. Total applicants accepted 2007–2008, 10. Number full-time enrolled (new admits only) 2007–2008, 3. Total enrolled 2007–2008 full-time, 29. Openings 2008–2009, 6. The median number of years required for completion of a degree in 2006–2007 were 6. The number of students enrolled full- and part-time who were dismissed or voluntarily withdrew from this program area in 2007–2008 were 0. *Industrial/Organizational PhD (Doctor of Philosophy)*—Applications 2007–2008, 68. Total applicants accepted 2007–2008, 16. Number full-time enrolled (new admits only) 2007–2008, 4. Total enrolled 2007–2008 full-time, 29. Openings 2008–2009, 6. The median number of years required for completion of a degree in 2006–2007 were 5. The number of students enrolled full- and part-time who were dismissed or voluntarily withdrew from this program area in 2007–2008 were 0.

Admissions Requirements:

Scores: Entries appear in this order: required test or GPA, minimum score (if required), median score of students entering in 2007–2008. Doctoral Programs: GRE-V no minimum stated, 555; GRE-Q no minimum stated, 640; GRE-Subject (Psychology) no minimum stated, 600; overall undergraduate GPA no minimum stated, 3.79.

Other Criteria: (importance of criteria rated low, medium, or high): GRE/MAT scores—high, research experience—high, work experience—medium, extracurricular activity—medium, clinically related public service—high, GPA—high, letters of recommendation—high, interview—high, statement of goals and objectives—high. Clinically related public service and interview are high for Clinical program only. For additional information on admission requirements, go to http://www.bgsu.edu/departments/psych.

Student Characteristics: The following represents characteristics of students in 2007–2008 in all graduate psychology programs in the department: Female—full-time 98, part-time 0; Male—full-time 40, part-time 0; African American/Black—full-time 0, part-time 0; Hispanic/Latino(a)—full-time 4, part-time 0; Asian/Pacific Islander—full-time 4, part-time 0; American Indian/Alaska Native—full-time 0, part-time 0; Caucasian/White—full-time 130, part-time 0; Multi-ethnic—full-time 0, part-time 0; students subject to the Americans With Disabilities Act—full-time 0, part-time 0; Unknown ethnicity—full-time 0, part-time 0.

Financial Information/Assistance:

Tuition for Full-Time Study: *Doctoral:* State residents: per academic year $16,518; Nonstate residents: per academic year $27,480. Tuition is subject to change.

Financial Assistance:

First-Year Students: Teaching assistantships available for first year. Average amount paid per academic year: $12,615. Average number of hours worked per week: 20. Apply by December 15. Tuition remission given: full. Research assistantships available for first year. Average amount paid per academic year: $12,615. Average number of hours worked per week: 20. Apply by December 15. Tuition remission given: full.

Advanced Students: Teaching assistantships available for advanced students. Average amount paid per academic year: $15,111. Average number of hours worked per week: 20. Apply by December 15. Tuition remission given: full. Research assistantships available for advanced students. Average amount paid per academic year: $15,111. Average number of hours worked per week: 20. Apply by December 15. Tuition remission given: full. Traineeships available for advanced students. Average amount paid per academic year: $15,111. Average number of hours worked per week: 20. Apply by December 15. Tuition remission given: full. Fellowships and scholarships available for advanced students. Average amount paid per academic year: $16,598. Average number of hours worked per week: 0. Apply by March. Tuition remission given: full.

Additional Information: Of all students currently enrolled full time, 100% benefited from one or more of the listed financial assistance programs. Application and information available online at http://www.bgsu.edu/departments/psych/application.pdf.

Internships/Practica: In their beginning years, Clinical students are placed on Basic Clinical Skills practicum teams through the Department's Psychological Services Center (PSC) that provide experience with a broad range of clients and clinical problems. Students focus on the application of such basic clinical skills as psychological assessment and interventions, the integration of science and practice, case conceptualization, clinical judgement, and decision-making report writing. In their 2nd year students begin receiving in-house training in psychotherapy through the PSC. As Clinical students progress through the program, they are placed on Advanced Clinical Skills teams that involve them in current projects providing "hands-on" experience with the integration of research and practice as it applies to individuals, health and behavioral medicine, the community, or special populations (e.g., children; problem drinkers). More advanced Clinical students are provided practicum opportunities consistent with their interest through a number of outside placements, such as community mental health centers, a nearby medical college, the university counseling center and health service, an inpatient child and adolescent facility, hospital-based rehabilitation centers, treatment centers for children and families, and programs for individuals with severe mental disabilities and emotional disorders. Industrial/Organizational students are strongly encouraged to apply for a formal internship after completion of their Master's project. Although such experiences are encouraged and typically followed, internships are not required of I/O students for completion of the doctoral degree. Other experiences through coursework activities and Institute for Psychological Research and Application (IPRA) projects can collectively serve the same function as an internship.

Housing and Day Care: No on-campus housing is available. No on-campus day care facilities are available.

Employment of Department Graduates:

Master's Degree Graduates: Of those who graduated in the academic year 2006–2007, the following categories and numbers represent the postgraduate activities and employment of master's degree graduates: Enrolled in a postdoctoral residency/fellowship

(n/a), employed in independent practice (n/a), total from the above (master's) (0).

Doctoral Degree Graduates: Of those who graduated in the academic year 2006–2007, the following categories and numbers represent the postgraduate activities and employment of doctoral degree graduates: Enrolled in a psychology doctoral program (n/a), total from the above (doctoral) (0).

Additional Information:

Orientation, Objectives, and Emphasis of Department: The primary goal of the PhD program is the development of scientists capable of advancing psychological knowledge. The program is characterized by both an emphasis on extensive academic training in general psychology and an early and continuing commitment to research. Although each graduate student will seek an area in which to develop his or her own expertise, students will be expected to be knowledgeable about many areas and will be encouraged to pursue interests that cross conventional specialty lines. The program is research oriented. Each student normally works in close association with a sponsor or chairperson whose special competence matches the student's interest, but students are free to pursue research interests with any faculty member and in any area(s) they choose. Both basic and applied research are well represented within the department. The Clinical program has concentrations in clinical child, behavioral medicine, and community, as well as general clinical.

Special Facilities or Resources: The department is located in the psychology building with excellent facilities for all forms of research. The building houses all faculty and graduate students. The department operates a community-oriented Psychological Services Center and the Institute for Psychological Research and Application. The department operates its own computer facility with terminals to the mainframe computer available in the building, as well as a microcomputer facility.

Application Information:

Send to Graduate Secretary. Application available online. URL of online application: http://www.bgsu.edu/departments/psych/application.pdf. Students are admitted in the Fall, application deadline December 15. December 15 deadline for Clinical and January 1 deadline for Industrial/Organizational, Developmental, and Neural and Cognitive. *Fee:* $30. Application fee may be deferred for members of minority groups.

Case Western Reserve University

Department of Psychology
Arts and Sciences
Mather Memorial Building, 11220 Bellflower Road, Room 103
Cleveland, OH 44106-7123
Telephone: (216) 368-2686
Fax: (216) 368-4891
E-mail: *rlg2@case.edu*
Web: *http://www.cwru.edu/artsci/pscl/*

Department Information:

1928. Chairperson: Robert L. Greene. Number of faculty: total—full-time 15; women—full-time 7; total—minority—full-time 1.

Programs and Degrees Offered:

Listed in the following order: Program area, degree type (T if terminal Master's), number awarded 7/06–6/07. Clinical PhD (Doctor of Philosophy) 2, Experimental PhD (Doctor of Philosophy) 2.

APA Accreditation: Clinical PhD (Doctor of Philosophy).

Student Applications/Admissions:

Student Applications

Clinical PhD (Doctor of Philosophy)—Applications 2007–2008, 155. Total applicants accepted 2007–2008, 5. Number full-time enrolled (new admits only) 2007–2008, 5. Number part-time enrolled (new admits only) 2007–2008, 0. Openings 2008–2009, 6. The median number of years required for completion of a degree in 2006–2007 were 6. The number of students enrolled full- and part-time who were dismissed or voluntarily withdrew from this program area in 2007–2008 were 0. *Experimental PhD (Doctor of Philosophy)*—Applications 2007–2008, 15. Total applicants accepted 2007–2008, 3. Number full-time enrolled (new admits only) 2007–2008, 2. Number part-time enrolled (new admits only) 2007–2008, 0. Openings 2008–2009, 2. The median number of years required for completion of a degree in 2006–2007 were 4. The number of students enrolled full- and part-time who were dismissed or voluntarily withdrew from this program area in 2007–2008 were 0.

Admissions Requirements:

Scores: Entries appear in this order: required test or GPA, minimum score (if required), median score of students entering in 2007–2008. Master's Programs: The department doesn't accept applications for a master's degree. Doctoral Programs: These scores are only preferred. Each application is evaluated on an individual basis and takes into consideration transcripts, statement of purpose and recommendation letters as well as specific test scores.

Other Criteria: (importance of criteria rated low, medium, or high): GRE/MAT scores—high, research experience—high, work experience—low, extracurricular activity—low, clinically related public service—medium, GPA—high, letters of recommendation—medium, interview—medium, statement of goals and objectives—medium.

Student Characteristics: The following represents characteristics of students in 2007–2008 in all graduate psychology programs in the department: Female—full-time 31, part-time 0; Male—full-time 5, part-time 0; African American/Black—full-time 1, part-time 0; Hispanic/Latino(a)—full-time 2, part-time 0; Asian/Pacific Islander—full-time 2, part-time 0; American Indian/Alaska Native—full-time 0, part-time 0; Caucasian/White—full-time 31, part-time 0; Multi-ethnic—full-time 0, part-time 0; students subject to the Americans With Disabilities Act—full-time 0, part-time 0; Unknown ethnicity—full-time 0, part-time 0.

Financial Information/Assistance:

Tuition for Full-Time Study: *Master's:* State residents: per academic year $29,800, $1,242 per credit hour; Nonstate residents: per academic year $29,800, $1,242 per credit hour. *Doctoral:* State residents: per academic year $29,800, $1,242 per credit hour;

Nonstate residents: per academic year $29,800, $1,242 per credit hour. Tuition is subject to change.

Financial Assistance:

First-Year Students: Research assistantships available for first year. Average amount paid per academic year: $19,000. Tuition remission given: full. Traineeships available for first year. Average amount paid per academic year: $20,772. Tuition remission given: full.

Advanced Students: Research assistantships available for advanced students. Average amount paid per academic year: $19,000. Tuition remission given: full. Traineeships available for advanced students. Average amount paid per academic year: $20,722. Tuition remission given: full. Fellowships and scholarships available for advanced students. Average amount paid per academic year: $19,000. Tuition remission given: full.

Additional Information: Of all students currently enrolled full time, 73% benefited from one or more of the listed financial assistance programs. Application and information available online at http://www.case.edu/artsci/pscl.

Internships/Practica: Doctoral Degree (PhD Clinical): For those doctoral students for whom a professional internship was required in this program prior to graduation, (2) students applied for an internship in 2006–2007, with (2) students obtaining an internship. Of those students who obtained an internship, (2) were paid internships. Of those students who obtained an internship, (2) students placed in APA/CPA-accredited internships, (0) students placed in internships not APA/CPA-accredited, but listed with the Association of Psychology Postdoctoral and Internship Centers (APPIC), (0) students placed in internships conforming to guidelines of the Council of Directors of School Psychology Programs (CDSPP), (0) students placed in internships that were not APA/CPA-accredited, APPIC or CDSPP listed. The Clinical Psychology graduate program has a number of practica placements in the Cleveland area. Students spend time in different settings during their 2nd, 3rd, and 4th years. In addition, the department requires two in-house practica in different types of psychotherapy.

Housing and Day Care: On-campus housing is available. No on-campus day care facilities are available.

Employment of Department Graduates:

Master's Degree Graduates: Of those who graduated in the academic year 2006–2007, the following categories and numbers represent the postgraduate activities and employment of master's degree graduates: Enrolled in a postdoctoral residency/fellowship (n/a), employed in independent practice (n/a), total from the above (master's) (0).

Doctoral Degree Graduates: Of those who graduated in the academic year 2006–2007, the following categories and numbers represent the postgraduate activities and employment of doctoral degree graduates: Enrolled in a psychology doctoral program (n/a), enrolled in another graduate/professional program (0), enrolled in a postdoctoral residency/fellowship (0), employed in independent practice (0), employed in an academic position at a university (0), employed in an academic position at a 2-year/4-year college (0), employed in other positions at a higher education institution (2), employed in a professional position in a school system (0), employed in business or industry (0), employed in government agency (0), employed in a community mental health/counseling center (0), employed in a hospital/medical center (2), still seeking employment (0), other employment position (0), do not know (0), total from the above (doctoral) (4).

Additional Information:

Orientation, Objectives, and Emphasis of Department: The graduate program seeks to give students a thorough grounding in basic areas of fact and theory in psychology, to train them in research methods by which knowledge in the behavioral sciences is advanced, and to prepare them for careers as teachers and researchers. During the 1st year, students begin a research clerkship under the tutelage of a faculty member. A variety of facilities and subject populations are available for the study of developmental processes, and a number of well-equipped laboratories are used for research in perception, memory, cognition, learning, physiological psychology, and individual differences. The department offers programs in Experimental and Clinical Psychology. Within each of these major areas of concentration, a number of subspecializations are available. For Clinical Psychology, these include adult, child, and pediatric psychology. For Experimental Psychology, the areas of specialization are determined by the faculty member with whom the student works. These include, but are not limited to, cognition, human intelligence, aging, social, and physiological psychology.

Special Facilities or Resources: A number of excellent facilities for clinical training and research are available on campus and in the surrounding community, such as the Student Counseling Center of Case Western Reserve, University Hospitals, the Cleveland Veterans Administration Hospital, and MetroHealth Medical Center. The department also maintains an extensive perceptual development laboratory to study the developmental aspects of learning, cognition, and language acquisition, and several experimental laboratories for the study of learning, perception, cognition, and physiological psychology, and social psychology.

Application Information:

Send to Department of Psychology, Case Western Reserve University, 10900 Euclid Avenue, Cleveland, OH 44106-7123. Students are admitted in the Fall, application deadline is January 8 for Clinical and February 15 for Experimental and Mental Retardation. *Fee:* $50.

Cincinnati, University of

Department of Psychology
Arts and Sciences
429 Dyer Hall
Cincinnati, OH 45221-0376
Telephone: (513) 556-5539
Fax: (513) 556-1904
E-mail: *steven.howe@uc.edu*
Web: *http://www.ucaswww.mcm.uc.edu/psychology*

Department Information:

1901. Head: Steven R. Howe, PhD. Number of faculty: total—full-time 26; women—full-time 12; total—minority—full-time 6; women minority—full-time 4.

Programs and Degrees Offered:

Listed in the following order: Program area, degree type (T if terminal Master's), number awarded 7/06–6/07. Clinical PhD

(Doctor of Philosophy) 13, Human Factors/Experimental Psychology PhD (Doctor of Philosophy) 3.

APA Accreditation: Clinical PhD (Doctor of Philosophy).

Student Applications/Admissions:

Student Applications

Clinical PhD (Doctor of Philosophy)—Applications 2007–2008, 225. Total applicants accepted 2007–2008, 6. Number full-time enrolled (new admits only) 2007–2008, 6. Number part-time enrolled (new admits only) 2007–2008, 0. Openings 2008–2009, 7. The median number of years required for completion of a degree in 2006–2007 were 6. The number of students enrolled full- and part-time who were dismissed or voluntarily withdrew from this program area in 2007–2008 were 0. *Human Factors/Experimental Psychology PhD (Doctor of Philosophy)*—Applications 2007–2008, 27. Total applicants accepted 2007–2008, 5. Number full-time enrolled (new admits only) 2007–2008, 5. Number part-time enrolled (new admits only) 2007–2008, 0. Total enrolled 2007–2008 full-time, 22, part-time, 6. Openings 2008–2009, 8. The median number of years required for completion of a degree in 2006–2007 were 9. The number of students enrolled full- and part-time who were dismissed or voluntarily withdrew from this program area in 2007–2008 were 0.

Admissions Requirements:

Scores: Entries appear in this order: required test or GPA, minimum score (if required), median score of students entering in 2007–2008. Doctoral Programs: GRE-V no minimum stated, 540; GRE-Q no minimum stated, 665; overall undergraduate GPA no minimum stated, 3.74; Doctoral program GRE-Analytic no minimum stated, 4.5.

Other Criteria: (importance of criteria rated low, medium, or high): GRE/MAT scores—medium, research experience—high, work experience—high, extracurricular activity—medium, clinically related public service—high, GPA—high, letters of recommendation—high, interview—high, statement of goals and objectives—high, See below—high, undergraduate major in psychology—medium, specific undergraduate psychology courses taken—high. In addition to background, experience, and academic record, it is important that an applicant's research interests correspond with the interests of one or more of the faculty who are recruiting students. Clinically related public service is only relevant to students applying to Clinical. For additional information on admission requirements, go to http://asweb.artsci.uc.edu/psychology.

Student Characteristics: The following represents characteristics of students in 2007–2008 in all graduate psychology programs in the department: Female—full-time 47, part-time 3; Male—full-time 21, part-time 1; African American/Black—full-time 8, part-time 0; Hispanic/Latino(a)—full-time 6, part-time 0; Asian/Pacific Islander—full-time 6, part-time 0; American Indian/Alaska Native—full-time 0, part-time 0; Caucasian/White—full-time 48, part-time 4; Multi-ethnic—full-time 0, part-time 0; students subject to the Americans With Disabilities Act—full-time 3, part-time 0; Unknown ethnicity—full-time 0, part-time 0; International students who hold an F-1 or J-1 Visa—full-time 5, part-time 0.

Financial Information/Assistance:

Tuition for Full-Time Study: *Doctoral:* State residents: per academic year $15,728, $404 per credit hour; Nonstate residents: per academic year $28,840, $732 per credit hour.

Financial Assistance:

First-Year Students: Teaching assistantships available for first year. Tuition remission given: full. Research assistantships available for first year. Tuition remission given: full. Fellowships and scholarships available for first year. Tuition remission given: full.

Advanced Students: Teaching assistantships available for advanced students. Tuition remission given: full. Research assistantships available for advanced students. Tuition remission given: full. Traineeships available for advanced students. Tuition remission given: full. Fellowships and scholarships available for advanced students. Tuition remission given: full.

Additional Information: Of all students currently enrolled full time, 99% benefited from one or more of the listed financial assistance programs. Application and information available online at http://asweb.artsci.uc.edu/psychology.

Internships/Practica: Doctoral Degree (PhD Clinical): For those doctoral students for whom a professional internship was required in this program prior to graduation, (7) students applied for an internship in 2006–2007, with (6) students obtaining an internship. Of those students who obtained an internship, (6) were paid internships. Of those students who obtained an internship, (6) students placed in APA/CPA-accredited internships, (0) students placed in internships not APA/CPA-accredited, but listed with the Association of Psychology Postdoctoral and Internship Centers (APPIC), (0) students placed in internships conforming to guidelines of the Council of Directors of School Psychology Programs (CDSPP), (0) students placed in internships that were not APA/CPA-accredited, APPIC or CDSPP listed. All clinical students in years 3 and 4 typically perform a paid, 20-hour/week clinical (or clinical research) training placement at an external site in the Greater Cincinnati area. Often these placements are at the University of Cincinnati Medical Center, the Cincinnati Children's Hospital Medical Center, or a variety of community agencies. If students need a 5th year of support prior to beginning an APA-accredited clinical internship, we can generally arrange a clinical training opportunity, although priority for placements goes to students in years 1 through 4. Although most of our nonclinical students do their paid training assignments within the department, there are also paid external training slots available for some of our students in private industry or with the federal government.

Housing and Day Care: On-campus housing is available. On-campus day care facilities are available.

Employment of Department Graduates:

Master's Degree Graduates: Of those who graduated in the academic year 2006–2007, the following categories and numbers represent the postgraduate activities and employment of master's degree graduates: Enrolled in a postdoctoral residency/fellowship (n/a), employed in independent practice (n/a), total from the above (master's) (0).

Doctoral Degree Graduates: Of those who graduated in the academic year 2006–2007, the following categories and numbers represent the postgraduate activities and employment of doctoral

degree graduates: Enrolled in a psychology doctoral program (n/a), enrolled in a postdoctoral residency/fellowship (8), employed in independent practice (0), employed in an academic position at a university (2), employed in an academic position at a 2-year/4-year college (1), employed in business or industry (0), employed in government agency (1), employed in a community mental health/counseling center (0), employed in a hospital/medical center (1), not seeking employment (1), do not know (2), total from the above (doctoral) (16).

Additional Information:

Orientation, Objectives, and Emphasis of Department: The University of Cincinnati offers the PhD in psychology, including an APA-accredited training program in Clinical Psychology. Clinical students must specify a specialty training area, which may include health, neuropsychology, or general training. For students who are not seeking clinical training, we offer training primarily in human factors, ecological psychology, and experimental neuropsychology. The doctoral program is limited to full-time students who show outstanding promise. Students are admitted to the doctoral program to work with a faculty research mentor. Faculty mentors are responsible for ensuring that students are actively engaged in doing research from the very start of their graduate school career, and that this work leads successfully to a Master's thesis and a dissertation.

Special Facilities or Resources: The department's Clinical program has close ties to the UC College of Medicine, Cincinnati Children's Hospital Medical Center, and a wide range of community agencies. The Human Factors faculty at UC are involved in the Southwest Ohio Human Factors/Ergonomics Consortium. Through this consortium, students have access to courses offered at nearby universities and to training sites at the Wright Patterson Air Force Base.

Application Information:

Send to Graduate Secretary, Department of Psychology, University of Cincinnati, P.O. Box 210376, Cincinnati, OH 45221-0376. Application available online. URL of online application: http://www.asweb.artsci.uc.edu/psychology. Students are admitted in the Fall, application deadline January 3, 2009. *Fee:* $45.

Cincinnati, University of

Human Services/School Psychology
Education, Criminal Justice, and Human Services
P.O. Box 210068
Cincinnati, OH 45221-0068
Telephone: (513) 556-3335
Fax: (513) 556-3898
E-mail: *janet.graden@uc.edu*
Web: *http://www.uc.edu/schoolpsychology/*

Department Information:

1992. Division Head: Janet Graden. Number of faculty: total—full-time 5, part-time 2; women—full-time 3, part-time 1.

Programs and Degrees Offered:

Listed in the following order: Program area, degree type (T if terminal Master's), number awarded 7/06–6/07. School Psychology PhD (Doctor of Philosophy) 2, School Psychology EdS/MEd (School Psychology) 10.

Student Applications/Admissions:

Student Applications

School Psychology PhD (Doctor of Philosophy)—Applications 2007–2008, 14. Total applicants accepted 2007–2008, 6. Number full-time enrolled (new admits only) 2007–2008, 3. Number part-time enrolled (new admits only) 2007–2008, 0. Total enrolled 2007–2008 full-time, 9, part-time, 8. Openings 2008–2009, 4. The median number of years required for completion of a degree in 2006–2007 were 8. The number of students enrolled full- and part-time who were dismissed or voluntarily withdrew from this program area in 2007–2008 were 0. *School Psychology EdS/MEd (School Psychology)*—Applications 2007–2008, 67. Total applicants accepted 2007–2008, 17. Number full-time enrolled (new admits only) 2007–2008, 12. Number part-time enrolled (new admits only) 2007–2008, 0. Openings 2008–2009, 12. The median number of years required for completion of a degree in 2006–2007 were 3. The number of students enrolled full- and part-time who were dismissed or voluntarily withdrew from this program area in 2007–2008 were 0.

Admissions Requirements:

Scores: Entries appear in this order: required test or GPA, minimum score (if required), median score of students entering in 2007–2008. Master's Programs: GRE-V no minimum stated, 530; GRE-Q no minimum stated, 630; overall undergraduate GPA 3.0, 3.8; last 2 years GPA no minimum stated, 3.9; psychology GPA no minimum stated, 3.9. Doctoral Programs: GRE-V no minimum stated, 520; GRE-Q no minimum stated, 550; GRE-Subject (Psychology) no minimum stated, 600; overall undergraduate GPA 3.25, 3.6; last 2 years GPA no minimum stated, 3.8; psychology GPA no minimum stated, 3.9.

Other Criteria: (importance of criteria rated low, medium, or high): GRE/MAT scores—high, research experience—medium, work experience—medium, extracurricular activity—medium, clinically related public service—high, GPA—high, letters of recommendation—high, interview—high, statement of goals and objectives—high. Specific, focused goals aligned with doctoral study (including research) are expected for doctoral study. For additional information on admission requirements, go to http://www.uc.edu/schoolpsychology/.

Student Characteristics: The following represents characteristics of students in 2007–2008 in all graduate psychology programs in the department: Female—full-time 40, part-time 8; Male—full-time 4, part-time 0; African American/Black—full-time 1, part-time 0; Hispanic/Latino(a)—full-time 0, part-time 1; Asian/Pacific Islander—full-time 0, part-time 0; American Indian/Alaska Native—full-time 1, part-time 0; Caucasian/White—full-time 42, part-time 7; Multi-ethnic—full-time 0, part-time 0; students subject to the Americans With Disabilities Act—full-time 0, part-time 0; Unknown ethnicity—full-time 0, part-time 0.

Financial Information/Assistance:

Tuition for Full-Time Study: *Master's:* State residents: per academic year $11,661, $389 per credit hour; Nonstate residents: per academic year $21,495, $717 per credit hour. *Doctoral:* State residents: per academic year $11,661, $389 per credit hour; Nonstate residents: per academic year $21,495, $717 per credit hour. Tuition is subject to change. See the following Web site for updates and changes in tuition costs: http://www.uc.edu.

Financial Assistance:

First-Year Students: Research assistantships available for first year. Average amount paid per academic year: $10,000. Average number of hours worked per week: 20. Tuition remission given: full. Fellowships and scholarships available for first year. Average amount paid per academic year: $15,000. Average number of hours worked per week: 20. Tuition remission given: full.

Advanced Students: Teaching assistantships available for advanced students. Average number of hours worked per week: 20. Tuition remission given: full. Research assistantships available for advanced students. Average amount paid per academic year: $10,200. Average number of hours worked per week: 20. Tuition remission given: full. Traineeships available for advanced students. Average amount paid per academic year: $25,000. Average number of hours worked per week: 40. Tuition remission given: partial. Fellowships and scholarships available for advanced students. Average amount paid per academic year: $15,000. Average number of hours worked per week: 20. Tuition remission given: full and partial.

Additional Information: Of all students currently enrolled full time, 100% benefited from one or more of the listed financial assistance programs. Application and information available online at http://www.grad.uc.edu.

Internships/Practica: All students, specialist and doctoral level, complete extensive practica experiences prior to internship in field settings that include local school districts and educational agencies. In the first year, students are enrolled in externship, in which they are placed in schools (urban settings, K–12) to learn about schooling, educational issues, effective instruction, and roles and responsibilities of various personnel. Field experiences also occur to support foundation skills in applied behavior analysis and academic and behavioral intervention. Doctoral students also participate as research team members in schools in years 1 through 3. Throughout the 2nd year, students are enrolled each quarter in an integrated practicum experience in which students obtain extensive supervised experience in delivery of services from a consultative, intervention-based tiered services delivery model. Students collaborate to design, implement, and evaluate prevention and intervention plans in the practicum, incorporating elements of their learning from across course work. In addition, they complete field experiences in behavioral counseling and functional assessment. Third-year doctoral students completed advanced field-based work in research and facilitating systems change. Specialist-level students complete a 10-month, 1,500-hour school-based internship. These internships are arranged through the program and are paid. In the internship, students provide a full range of comprehensive school psychological services, with supervision from a licensed school psychologist and from university faculty. Doctoral students complete an Advanced School Experience in year 3, participating in leadership, staff development, supervision, and research activities. Doctoral students complete a 1,500-hour internship consistent with CDSPP, APA, and NASP internship requirements.

Housing and Day Care: On-campus housing is available. See the following Web site for more information: http://www.uc.edu/housing/. On-campus day care facilities are available. See the following Web site for more information: http://www.ucchildcare.org.

Employment of Department Graduates:

Master's Degree Graduates: Of those who graduated in the academic year 2006–2007, the following categories and numbers represent the postgraduate activities and employment of master's degree graduates: Enrolled in a postdoctoral residency/fellowship (n/a), employed in independent practice (n/a), employed in a professional position in a school system (10), total from the above (master's) (10).

Doctoral Degree Graduates: Of those who graduated in the academic year 2006–2007, the following categories and numbers represent the postgraduate activities and employment of doctoral degree graduates: Enrolled in a psychology doctoral program (n/a), employed in an academic position at a university (0), employed in a professional position in a school system (2), total from the above (doctoral) (2).

Additional Information:

Orientation, Objectives, and Emphasis of Department: The School Psychology program at the University of Cincinnati is dedicated to preparing highly competent professional school psychologists, at the specialist (EdS) and doctoral (PhD) levels, according to the scientist–practitioner model. The program builds on foundations in psychology and education, and fosters a special sensitivity to cultural diversity of all people and respect for the uniqueness and human dignity of each person. The program emphasizes the delivery of school psychological services within a tiered services delivery model (prevention to targeted intervention) using a collaborative consultation model from an ecological/behavioral orientation. Students learn to view problems from an ecological/systems perspective focusing on child, family, school and community and to provide comprehensive intervention-based services utilizing databased decision making to design, implement, and evaluate strategies for preventing and resolving learning and adjustment problem situations across a tiered service delivery model. A child advocacy perspective, built on a scientist–practitioner foundation, provides a framework for guiding decisions and practices to support positive outcomes for all children. Both theoretical and empirical bases of professional practice are emphasized and a diverse range of practical experiences are provided throughout all preparation (preschool to high school, in urban, suburban, and rural settings). The program is noted for its intervention emphasis, focusing on databased decision making across all tiers of service delivery (prevention and schoolwide intervention, target and supplemental intervention, and intensive, individualized intervention). In addition to these program themes, training at the doctoral level emphasizes advanced research and evaluation training, leadership supervision, and systems-level change facilitation. Doctoral students participate as research team members in schools in years 1 through 3.

Special Facilities or Resources: The program has access to excellent field-based training and research partnerships through collaborative relationships with several local school districts, educational agencies, and Head Start programs. Research facilities include statistical consultation for students, a college evaluation services center, and support for student research through college-sponsored mentoring grants.

Information for Students With Physical Disabilities: See the following Web site for more information: http://www.uc.edu/sas/disability.

Application Information:

Send to Admission Coordinator, School Psychology Program, University of Cincinnati, P.O. Box 210068, Cincinnati, OH 45221-0068. Application available online. URL of online application: http://www.grad.uc.edu. Students are admitted in the Fall, application deadline January 15. *Fee:* $40.

Cleveland State University

Department of Psychology
College of Science
2121 Euclid Avenue
Cleveland, OH 44115
Telephone: (216) 687-2544
Fax: (216) 687-9294
E-mail: *d.grilly@csuohio.edu*
Web: *http://www.sciences.csuohio.edu/departments/psychology/*

Department Information:

1964. Chairperson: David M. Grilly. Number of faculty: total—full-time 22, part-time 16; women—full-time 6, part-time 8; total—minority—full-time 2, part-time 2; women minority—full-time 1, part-time 2.

Programs and Degrees Offered:

Listed in the following order: Program area, degree type (T if terminal Master's), number awarded 7/06–6/07. Clinical Psychology MA/MS (Master of Arts/Science) (T) 7, Consumer–Industrial MA/MS (Master of Arts/Science) (T) 8, Diversity Management MA/MS (Master of Arts/Science) (T) 10, Experimental Research MA/MS (Master of Arts/Science) (T) 2, School Psychology Other 8, Adult Development and Aging PhD (Doctor of Philosophy) 0.

Student Applications/Admissions:

Student Applications

Clinical Psychology MA/MS (Master of Arts/Science)—Applications 2007–2008, 73. Total applicants accepted 2007–2008, 12. Number full-time enrolled (new admits only) 2007–2008, 12. Number part-time enrolled (new admits only) 2007–2008, 0. Openings 2008–2009, 12. The median number of years required for completion of a degree in 2006–2007 were 2. The number of students enrolled full- and part-time who were dismissed or voluntarily withdrew from this program area in 2007–2008 were 1. *Consumer–Industrial MA/MS (Master of Arts/Science)*—Applications 2007–2008, 30. Total applicants accepted 2007–2008, 10. Number full-time enrolled (new admits only) 2007–2008, 5. Total enrolled 2007–2008 full-time, 15. Openings 2008–2009, 10. The median number of years required for completion of a degree in 2006–2007 were 3. The number of students enrolled full- and part-time who were dismissed or voluntarily withdrew from this program area in 2007–2008 were 2. *Diversity Management MA/MS (Master of Arts/Science)*—Applications 2007–2008, 20. Total applicants accepted 2007–2008, 16. Number full-time enrolled (new admits only) 2007–2008, 17. Number part-time enrolled (new admits only) 2007–2008, 0. Openings 2008–2009, 20. The median number of years required for completion of a degree in 2006–2007 were 2. The number of students enrolled full- and part-time who were dismissed or voluntarily withdrew from this program area in 2007–2008 were 6. *Experimental Research MA/MS (Master of Arts/Science)*—Applications 2007–2008, 11. Total applicants accepted 2007–2008, 4. Number full-time enrolled (new admits only) 2007–2008, 4. Total enrolled 2007–2008 full-time, 10. Openings 2008–2009, 10. The median number of years required for completion of a degree in 2006–2007 were 3. The number of students enrolled full- and part-time who were dismissed or voluntarily withdrew from this program area in 2007–2008 were 0. *School Psychology Other*—Applications 2007–2008, 40. Total applicants accepted 2007–2008, 12. Number full-time enrolled (new admits only) 2007–2008, 12. Number part-time enrolled (new admits only) 2007–2008, 0. Openings 2008–2009, 14. The median number of years required for completion of a degree in 2006–2007 were 3. The number of students enrolled full- and part-time who were dismissed or voluntarily withdrew from this program area in 2007–2008 were 2. *Adult Development and Aging PhD (Doctor of Philosophy)*—Applications 2007–2008, 0. Total applicants accepted 2007–2008, 0. Number full-time enrolled (new admits only) 2007–2008, 0. Number part-time enrolled (new admits only) 2007–2008, 0. Openings 2008–2009, 2. The number of students enrolled full- and part-time who were dismissed or voluntarily withdrew from this program area in 2007–2008 were 0.

Admissions Requirements:

Scores: Entries appear in this order: required test or GPA, minimum score (if required), median score of students entering in 2007–2008. Master's Programs: GRE-V no minimum stated, 493; GRE-Q no minimum stated, 608; overall undergraduate GPA no minimum stated, 3.5. Requirements vary per program. All programs look for GREs at about the 50th percentile level; the Diversity program does not require GRE.

Other Criteria: (importance of criteria rated low, medium, or high): GRE/MAT scores—high, research experience—medium, work experience—low, clinically related public service—low, GPA—medium, letters of recommendation—medium, interview—high, statement of goals and objectives—high, undergraduate major in psychology—medium, specific undergraduate psychology courses taken—medium. Only the Clinical, School, and Diversity programs require an interview. For additional information on admission requirements, go to http://sciences.csuohio.edu/departments/psychology/.

Student Characteristics: The following represents characteristics of students in 2007–2008 in all graduate psychology programs in the department: Female—full-time 82, part-time 0; Male—full-time 30, part-time 0; African American/Black—full-time 23, part-time 0; Hispanic/Latino(a)—full-time 3, part-time 0; Asian/Pacific Islander—full-time 2, part-time 0; American Indian/Alaska Native—full-time 0, part-time 0; Caucasian/White—full-time 82, part-time 0; Multi-ethnic—full-time 1, part-time 0; students subject to the Americans With Disabilities Act—full-time 0, part-time 0; Unknown ethnicity—full-time 1, part-time 0; International students who hold an F-1 or J-1 Visa—full-time 2, part-time 0.

Financial Information/Assistance:

Tuition for Full-Time Study: *Master's:* State residents: per academic year $11,420, $440 per credit hour; Nonstate residents: per academic year $21,690, $835 per credit hour. Tuition is subject to change. See the following Web site for updates and changes in tuition costs: http://www.csuohio.edu/tuition/. Higher tuition cost for this program: Diversity Management Program.

Financial Assistance:

First-Year Students: Teaching assistantships available for first year. Average number of hours worked per week: 10. Apply by February 15. Tuition remission given: partial.

Advanced Students: Teaching assistantships available for advanced students. Average number of hours worked per week: 10. Apply by March 15. Tuition remission given: partial.

Additional Information: Of all students currently enrolled full time, 34% benefited from one or more of the listed financial assistance programs.

Internships/Practica: Master's Degree (MA/MS Clinical Psychology): An internship experience such as a final research project or "capstone" experience is required of graduates. Clinical students and 3rd-year School Psychology students complete a 20-hour/40-hour per week internship, respectively, as part of the degree requirements. Consumer and Industrial Research Program students are encouraged to apply for paid internships in the business settings to earn hands-on consulting or research experiences. Practicum during the 2-year curriculum are integrated into coursework.

Housing and Day Care: On-campus housing is available. See the following Web site for more information: http://www.csuohio.edu/housing/. On-campus day care facilities are available. See the following Web site for more information: http://www.csuohio.edu/childcare/.

Employment of Department Graduates:

Master's Degree Graduates: Of those who graduated in the academic year 2006–2007, the following categories and numbers represent the postgraduate activities and employment of master's degree graduates: Enrolled in a psychology doctoral program (1), enrolled in another graduate/professional program (0), enrolled in a postdoctoral residency/fellowship (n/a), employed in independent practice (n/a), employed in a professional position in a school system (7), employed in business or industry (13), employed in a community mental health/counseling center (3), other employment position (5), do not know (9), total from the above (master's) (38).

Doctoral Degree Graduates: Of those who graduated in the academic year 2006–2007, the following categories and numbers represent the postgraduate activities and employment of doctoral degree graduates: Enrolled in a psychology doctoral program (n/a), total from the above (doctoral) (0).

Additional Information:

Orientation, Objectives, and Emphasis of Department: Departmental faculty provide significant breadth across the entire discipline as well as considerable depth in professional and applied areas. The Clinical program is a CAMPP-approved program. It emphasizes theory, principles, and application, which prepares students for more advanced training (PhD, PsyD, EdD) or for jobs requiring psychological service in clinical, community, and educational settings. Orientations include psychodynamic, cognitive, and behavioral viewpoints in assessment and individual, group, family, and community intervention. The School program is NASP accredited. A post-MA year fulfills requirements for Psychology Specialist degree in Ohio. The primary goals of the Experimental Research Program are to train students to conduct scientific research in a chosen area of psychology, and to prepare students for further graduate work in psychology or for employment in research settings and institutions. The Consumer–Industrial Research Program prepares students to apply psychological concepts and research techniques in business and in institutional settings. It combines advanced quantitative research with hands-on experience involving problems and issues encountered in industrial and service organizations. The Diversity Management Program is designed for professionals and people who want to work in the field of diversity, either as scholars or as practitioners. It provides an opportunity to develop the leadership skills and cultural competence necessary to work effectively in today's organizations.

Information for Students With Physical Disabilities: See the following Web site for more information: http://www.csuohio.edu/clc/disability/index.htm.

Application Information:

Send to Graduate Secretary, Department of Psychology, Cleveland State University, 2121 Euclid Avenue, Cleveland, OH 44115-2440. Application available online. URL of online application: http://www.csuohio.edu/admissions/gradForm.html. Students are admitted in the Fall, application deadline February 15. January 15 for Clinical program, March 1 for Experimental Research program, March 15 for Consumer and Industrial Research program. Applications received after February 15 may be considered. Rolling deadline for Diversity Management program. *Fee:* $30.

Dayton, University of

Department of Psychology
300 College Park Avenue
Dayton, OH 45469-1430
Telephone: (937) 229-2713
Fax: (937) 229-3900
E-mail: *biers@udayton.edu*
Web: *http://www.udayton.edu/~psych*

Department Information:

1937. Chairperson: David W. Biers. Number of faculty: total—full-time 16, part-time 13; women—full-time 5, part-time 8.

Programs and Degrees Offered:

Listed in the following order: Program area, degree type (T if terminal Master's), number awarded 7/06–6/07. Clinical MA/MS (Master of Arts/Science) (T) 5, General MA/MS (Master of Arts/Science) (T) 0.

Student Applications/Admissions:

Student Applications

Clinical MA/MS (Master of Arts/Science)—Applications 2007–2008, 79. Total applicants accepted 2007–2008, 24. Number full-time enrolled (new admits only) 2007–2008, 13. Number part-time enrolled (new admits only) 2007–2008, 0. Openings 2008–2009, 12. *General MA/MS (Master of Arts/Science)*—Applications 2007–2008, 19. Total applicants accepted 2007–2008, 10. Number full-time enrolled (new admits only) 2007–2008, 7. Number part-time enrolled (new admits only) 2007–2008, 0. Openings 2008–2009, 8.

Admissions Requirements:

Scores: Entries appear in this order: required test or GPA, minimum score (if required), median score of students entering in 2007–2008. Master's Programs: GRE-V no minimum stated; GRE-Q no minimum stated; overall undergraduate GPA 3.0.

Other Criteria: (importance of criteria rated low, medium, or high): GRE/MAT scores—high, research experience—high, work experience—medium, extracurricular activity—low, clinically related public service—medium, GPA—high, letters of recommendation—high, interview—low, statement of goals and objectives—high, undergraduate major in psychology—medium, specific undergraduate psychology courses taken—high.

Student Characteristics: The following represents characteristics of students in 2007–2008 in all graduate psychology programs in the department: Female—full-time 21, part-time 0; Male—full-time 10, part-time 0; African American/Black—full-time 1, part-time 0; Hispanic/Latino(a)—full-time 0, part-time 0; Asian/Pacific Islander—full-time 1, part-time 0; American Indian/Alaska Native—full-time 0, part-time 0; Caucasian/White—full-time 29, part-time 0; Multi-ethnic—full-time 0, part-time 0; students subject to the Americans With Disabilities Act—full-time 0, part-time 0; Unknown ethnicity—full-time 0, part-time 0; International students who hold an F-1 or J-1 Visa—full-time 0, part-time 0.

Financial Information/Assistance:

Tuition for Full-Time Study: *Master's:* State residents: $668 per credit hour; Nonstate residents: $668 per credit hour.

Financial Assistance:

First-Year Students: Teaching assistantships available for first year. Average amount paid per academic year: $9,896. Average number of hours worked per week: 20. Apply by March 1. Tuition remission given: full. Research assistantships available for first year. Average amount paid per academic year: $9,896. Average number of hours worked per week: 20. Apply by March 1. Tuition remission given: full. Traineeships available for first year. Average amount paid per academic year: $6,000. Average number of hours worked per week: 17. Apply by March 1. Tuition remission given: partial.

Advanced Students: Teaching assistantships available for advanced students. Average amount paid per academic year: $10,194. Average number of hours worked per week: 20. Apply by March 1. Tuition remission given: full. Research assistantships available for advanced students. Average amount paid per academic year: $10,194. Average number of hours worked per week: 20. Apply by March 1. Tuition remission given: full.

Additional Information: Of all students currently enrolled full time, 85% benefited from one or more of the listed financial assistance programs.

Internships/Practica: A limited mumber of paid traineeship placements at local mental health agencies are available for both 1st and 2nd year Clinical students. These traineeships satisfy the programs's practica requirements and include partial tuition remission. The human factors practicum is required of all program students and enables the student to gain practical experience working for governmental agencies or industrial firms during the summer between their 1st and 2nd years.

Housing and Day Care: No on-campus housing is available. On-campus day care facilities are available.

Employment of Department Graduates:

Master's Degree Graduates: Of those who graduated in the academic year 2006–2007, the following categories and numbers represent the postgraduate activities and employment of master's degree graduates: Enrolled in a psychology doctoral program (2), enrolled in a postdoctoral residency/fellowship (n/a), employed in independent practice (n/a), employed in a community mental health/counseling center (2), employed in a hospital/medical center (1), total from the above (master's) (5).

Doctoral Degree Graduates: Of those who graduated in the academic year 2006–2007, the following categories and numbers represent the postgraduate activities and employment of doctoral degree graduates: Enrolled in a psychology doctoral program (n/a), total from the above (doctoral) (0).

Additional Information:

Orientation, Objectives, and Emphasis of Department: The Department of Psychology offers graduate programs leading to the MA degree in clinical and general psychology. Emphasis is placed on integrating theory and literature with appropriate applied experience and on competence in the development of relevant research. This is the product of individual supervision and a low student-to-faculty ratio. The aim of the department is to prepare the student for doctoral training or employment at the MA level in an applied/community setting, in research, or in teaching. A recent survey has shown that over 86% of our MA graduates who applied for doctoral programs in the last 6 years were accepted. Also, 98% of our MA graduates seeking employment have found jobs in psychologically related areas.

Special Facilities or Resources: Laboratory and computer facilities are available to support student and faculty research. These include microlaboratory facilities for research in cognitive science, human factors, social psychology, and clinical psychology as well as a state-of-the-art Information Science Research Laboratory for multidisciplinary research in human–computer interaction. In additon, research opportunities are available through the university's Research Institute, the Center for Family and Community Research, and local community agencies.

Application Information:

Application available online. URL of online application: http://www.gradadmission.udayton.edu. Students are admitted in the Fall, application deadline March 1. *Fee:* $30. Fee waived if apply online.

Kent State University

Department of Psychology
Arts and Sciences
Kent, OH 44242
Telephone: (330) 672-2166
Fax: (330) 672-3786
E-mail: *gradpsych@kent.edu*
Web: *http://www.dept.kent.edu/psychology/*

Department Information:
1936. Chairperson: Mary Ann Stephens. Number of faculty: total—full-time 30; women—full-time 12; total—minority—full-time 4; women minority—full-time 3; faculty subject to the Americans With Disabilities Act 2.

Programs and Degrees Offered:
Listed in the following order: Program area, degree type (T if terminal Master's), number awarded 7/06–6/07. Clinical PhD (Doctor of Philosophy) 15, Experimental PhD (Doctor of Philosophy) 7.

APA Accreditation: Clinical PhD (Doctor of Philosophy).

Student Applications/Admissions:

Student Applications

Clinical PhD (Doctor of Philosophy)—Applications 2007–2008, 245. Total applicants accepted 2007–2008, 15. Number full-time enrolled (new admits only) 2007–2008, 15. Number part-time enrolled (new admits only) 2007–2008, 0. Openings 2008–2009, 12. The median number of years required for completion of a degree in 2006–2007 were 6. The number of students enrolled full- and part-time who were dismissed or voluntarily withdrew from this program area in 2007–2008 were 2. *Experimental PhD (Doctor of Philosophy)*—Applications 2007–2008, 52. Total applicants accepted 2007–2008, 9. Number full-time enrolled (new admits only) 2007–2008, 9. Number part-time enrolled (new admits only) 2007–2008, 0. Openings 2008–2009, 12. The median number of years required for completion of a degree in 2006–2007 were 4. The number of students enrolled full- and part-time who were dismissed or voluntarily withdrew from this program area in 2007–2008 were 1.

Admissions Requirements:

Scores: Entries appear in this order: required test or GPA, minimum score (if required), median score of students entering in 2007–2008. Doctoral Programs: GRE-V no minimum stated, 540; GRE-Q no minimum stated, 645; overall undergraduate GPA 3.00, 3.77. The above median scores are for applicants who were admitted to our clinical program (and accepted) in spring 2006. The median scores for students who accepted admission into our experimental program that year are: GRE-V: 520; GRE-Q: 630; Overall undergrad GPA: 3.62.

Other Criteria: (importance of criteria rated low, medium, or high): GRE/MAT scores—high, research experience—high, work experience—low, extracurricular activity—low, clinically related public service—low, GPA—high, letters of recommendation—high, interview—high, statement of goals and objectives—high, specific undergraduate psychology courses taken—medium. For additional information on admission requirements, go to http://dept.kent.edu/psychology/.

Student Characteristics: The following represents characteristics of students in 2007–2008 in all graduate psychology programs in the department: Female—full-time 91, part-time 0; Male—full-time 27, part-time 0; African American/Black—full-time 4, part-time 0; Hispanic/Latino(a)—full-time 6, part-time 0; Asian/Pacific Islander—full-time 4, part-time 0; American Indian/Alaska Native—full-time 1, part-time 0; Caucasian/White—full-time 90, part-time 0; Multi-ethnic—full-time 0, part-time 0; students subject to the Americans With Disabilities Act—full-time 1, part-time 0; Unknown ethnicity—full-time 13, part-time 0; International students who hold an F-1 or J-1 Visa—full-time 11, part-time 0.

Financial Information/Assistance:

Tuition for Full-Time Study: *Master's:* State residents: per academic year $8,968, $408 per credit hour; . *Doctoral:* State residents: per academic year $8,968, $408 per credit hour; . Tuition is subject to change.

Financial Assistance:

First-Year Students: Teaching assistantships available for first year. Average amount paid per academic year: $12,863. Average number of hours worked per week: 20. Apply by January 1. Tuition remission given: full. Research assistantships available for first year. Average amount paid per academic year: $12,863. Average number of hours worked per week: 20. Apply by January 1. Tuition remission given: full.

Advanced Students: Teaching assistantships available for advanced students. Average amount paid per academic year: $12,863. Average number of hours worked per week: 20. Apply by January 1. Tuition remission given: full. Research assistantships available for advanced students. Average amount paid per academic year: $12,863. Average number of hours worked per week: 20. Apply by January 1. Tuition remission given: full. Traineeships available for advanced students. Average amount paid per academic year: $12,863. Average number of hours worked per week: 20. Apply by January 1. Tuition remission given: full. Fellowships and scholarships available for advanced students. Average amount paid per academic year: $6,000. Average number of hours worked per week: 10. Apply by January 1. Tuition remission given: full.

Additional Information: Of all students currently enrolled full time, 100% benefited from one or more of the listed financial assistance programs. Application and information available online at http://dept.kent.edu/psychology/gradprograms/how_to_apply.htm.

Internships/Practica: Doctoral Degree (PhD Clinical): For those doctoral students for whom a professional internship was required in this program prior to graduation, (7) students applied for an internship in 2006–2007, with (6) students obtaining an internship. Of those students who obtained an internship, (6) were paid internships. Of those students who obtained an internship, (6) students placed in APA/CPA-accredited internships, (0) students placed in internships not APA/CPA-accredited, but listed with the Association of Psychology Postdoctoral and Internship Centers (APPIC), (0) students placed in internships conforming to guidelines of the Council of Directors of School Psychology Programs (CDSPP), (0) students placed in internships that were not APA/CPA-accredited, APPIC or CDSPP listed. Seven semesters of clinical practica are required through the department's Psychological Clinic; 1,000 hours of supervised clinical experience at local field placement sites are provided with additional hours sometimes available; 2,000 hours of supervised internship experience in a program accredited by the American Psychological Association (these are competitive internships) are required.

Housing and Day Care: On-campus housing is available. Contact Residence Services, Korb Hall, Kent State University, P.O. Box 5190, Kent, OH 44242-0001 Phone number: (330) 672-7000. On-campus day care facilities are available. Contact Child Development Center: (330) 672-2559.

Employment of Department Graduates:

Master's Degree Graduates: Of those who graduated in the academic year 2006–2007, the following categories and numbers represent the postgraduate activities and employment of master's degree graduates: Enrolled in a psychology doctoral program (15), enrolled in another graduate/professional program (0), enrolled in a postdoctoral residency/fellowship (n/a), employed in independent practice (n/a), employed in an academic position at a university (0), employed in an academic position at a 2-year/4-year college (0), employed in other positions at a higher education institution (0), employed in a professional position in a school system (0), employed in business or industry (0), employed in government agency (0), employed in a community mental health/counseling center (0), employed in a hospital/medical center (0), still seeking employment (0), not seeking employment (0), other employment position (0), do not know (0), total from the above (master's) (15).

Doctoral Degree Graduates: Of those who graduated in the academic year 2006–2007, the following categories and numbers represent the postgraduate activities and employment of doctoral degree graduates: Enrolled in a psychology doctoral program (n/a), enrolled in a postdoctoral residency/fellowship (14), employed in independent practice (0), employed in an academic position at a university (1), employed in an academic position at a 2-year/4-year college (2), employed in other positions at a higher education institution (0), employed in a professional position in a school system (0), employed in business or industry (0), employed in government agency (0), employed in a community mental health/counseling center (1), employed in a hospital/medical center (1), other employment position (1), do not know (2), total from the above (doctoral) (22).

Additional Information:

Orientation, Objectives, and Emphasis of Department: Doctoral training is provided in clinical and in various experimental areas. The doctoral program requires full-time, continuous enrollment and is strongly research oriented. Students in Clinical may specialize in adult psychopathology, assessment, child, or health. Students in Experimental may specialize in biopsychology, child, cognitive, health, or social psychology. Students in both programs can obtain a Minor in Quantitative Methods. A common program of basic core courses is required of all students. Training facilities and laboratories are freely available to graduate students. The program's objective is to train those who can contribute through research, teaching, service, innovation, and administration.

Special Facilities or Resources: The department has well-equipped laboratories available for human and animal experimentation. Research opportunities are also available in various mental health and hospital settings in the area and at the SUMMA/KSU Center for the Treatment and Study of Traumatic Stress. Clinical training opportunities are available in the Psychological Clinic, which is staffed by clinical faculty and graduate students. The Applied Psychology Center supports research focused on psychological problems of social significance.

Information for Students With Physical Disabilities: See the following Web site for more information: http://www.kent.edu/sas.

Application Information:

Send to Chair, Graduate Admissions, Department of Psychology, Kent State University, Kent, OH 44242. Application available online. URL of online application: http://www.admissions.kent.edu/apply/Graduate/. Students are admitted in the Fall, application deadline January 1. *Fee:* $30.

Kent State University

School Psychology Program
College and Graduate School of Education, Health, and Human
405 White Hall
Kent, OH 44242
Telephone: (330) 672-2294
Fax: (330) 672-2512
E-mail: *kanhalt@kent.edu*
Web: *http://www.ehhs.kent.edu/spsy/index.cfm*

Department Information:

1964. Department Chair: Awilda Hamilton. Number of faculty: total—full-time 4, part-time 2; women—full-time 1, part-time 2; total—minority—full-time 1; women minority—full-time 1.

Programs and Degrees Offered:

Listed in the following order: Program area, degree type (T if terminal Master's), number awarded 7/06–6/07. School Psychology PhD (Doctor of Philosophy) 2, School Psychology EdS/MEd (School Psychology) 13.

APA Accreditation: School PhD (Doctor of Philosophy).

Student Applications/Admissions:

Student Applications

School Psychology PhD (Doctor of Philosophy)—Applications 2007–2008, 6. Total applicants accepted 2007–2008, 3. Number full-time enrolled (new admits only) 2007–2008, 3. Number part-time enrolled (new admits only) 2007–2008, 0. Total enrolled 2007–2008 full-time, 9, part-time, 14. Openings 2008–2009, 4. The number of students enrolled full- and part-time who were dismissed or voluntarily withdrew from this program area in 2007–2008 were 2. *School Psychology EdS/MEd (School Psychology)*—Applications 2007–2008, 36. Total applicants accepted 2007–2008, 26. Number full-time enrolled (new admits only) 2007–2008, 26. Number part-time enrolled (new admits only) 2007–2008, 0. Total enrolled 2007–2008 full-time, 55, part-time, 1. Openings 2008–2009, 15. The median number of years required for completion of a degree in 2006–2007 were 3. The number of students enrolled full- and part-time who were dismissed or voluntarily withdrew from this program area in 2007–2008 were 0.

Admissions Requirements:

Scores: Entries appear in this order: required test or GPA, minimum score (if required), median score of students entering in 2007–2008. Master's Programs: GRE-V none, 491; GRE-Q none, 572; overall undergraduate GPA 3.5, 3.6; Masters GRE-Analytical none, 4.6. Doctoral Programs: GRE-V 550, 550; GRE-Q none, 580; overall undergraduate GPA 3.5, 3.2.

Other Criteria: (importance of criteria rated low, medium, or high): GRE/MAT scores—medium, research experience—medium, work experience—high, extracurricular activity—medium, clinically related public service—medium, GPA—medium, letters of recommendation—high, interview—high, statement of goals and objectives—high, interview—high. For additional information on admission requirements, go to http://www.ehhs.kent.edu/spsy/index.cfm.

Student Characteristics: The following represents characteristics of students in 2007–2008 in all graduate psychology programs in the department: Female—full-time 50, part-time 7; Male—full-time 5, part-time 3; African American/Black—full-time 1, part-time 0; Hispanic/Latino(a)—full-time 1, part-time 0; Asian/Pacific Islander—full-time 0, part-time 0; American Indian/Alaska Native—full-time 0, part-time 0; Caucasian/White—full-time 53, part-time 10; Multi-ethnic—full-time 0, part-time 0; students subject to the Americans With Disabilities Act—full-time 0, part-time 0; Unknown ethnicity—full-time 0, part-time 0; International students who hold an F-1 or J-1 Visa—full-time 0, part-time 0.

Financial Information/Assistance:

Tuition for Full-Time Study: *Master's:* State residents: per academic year $8,968, $408 per credit hour; Nonstate residents: per academic year $15,980, $728 per credit hour. *Doctoral:* State residents: per academic year $8,968, $408 per credit hour; Nonstate residents: per academic year $15,980, $728 per credit hour. Tuition is subject to change. See the following Web site for updates and changes in tuition costs: http://www.kent.edu.

Financial Assistance:

First-Year Students: Teaching assistantships available for first year. Average amount paid per academic year: $7,000. Average number of hours worked per week: 20. Apply by May 1. Tuition remission given: full. Research assistantships available for first year. Average amount paid per academic year: $7,000. Average number of hours worked per week: 20. Apply by May 1. Tuition remission given: full.

Advanced Students: Teaching assistantships available for advanced students. Average amount paid per academic year: $9,500. Average number of hours worked per week: 20. Apply by May 1. Tuition remission given: full. Research assistantships available for advanced students. Average amount paid per academic year: $9,500. Average number of hours worked per week: 20. Apply by May 1. Tuition remission given: full.

Additional Information: Of all students currently enrolled full time, 54% benefited from one or more of the listed financial assistance programs.

Internships/Practica: Doctoral Degree (PhD School Psychology): For those doctoral students for whom a professional internship was required in this program prior to graduation, (2) students applied for an internship in 2006–2007, with (2) students obtaining an internship. Of those students who obtained an internship, (2) were paid internships. Of those students who obtained an internship, (1) student placed in APA/CPA-accredited internships, (0) students placed in internships not APA/CPA accredited, but listed with the Association of Psychology Postdoctoral and Internship Centers (APPIC), (0) students placed in internships conforming to guidelines of the Council of Directors of School Psychology Programs (CDSPP), (1) student placed in internships that were not APA/CPA-accredited, APPIC or CDSPP listed. Practica occur in educational and mental health settings that are chosen to provide (a) comprehensive experiences that complement previous and current preparation, (b) appropriate supervision and mentorship, and (c) applied experiences to address individual and program objectives. EdS students take 2 years of practica prior to internship. Doctoral students who enter without specialist-level training in school psychology participate in 3 years of practica. Both the specialist level and doctoral internships in School Psychology follow the completion of all course work and practica. Specialist-level internships are fulltime for an academic year, and must occur in school settings. If completed in Ohio, the internship must conform to the Ohio Internship in School Psychology Guidelines. These internships have historically been state supported, and students receive a generous training stipend. A variety of approved settings may be appropriate for the doctoral internship, including educational settings, hospitals, and mental health centers. Students without a previous, specialist-level internship of fewer than 9 months, full time, in a school setting, must complete at least 1,350 hours (600 hours of the internship in an approved school setting). For students completing these requirements in Ohio, the internship must conform to the Ohio Internship in School Psychology Guidelines.

Housing and Day Care: On-campus housing is available. See the following Web site for more information: http://www.res.kent.edu/main.htm. On-campus day care facilities are available. See the following Web site for more information: http://www.kent.edu/childdevelopmentcenter/.

Employment of Department Graduates:

Master's Degree Graduates: Of those who graduated in the academic year 2006–2007, the following categories and numbers represent the postgraduate activities and employment of master's degree graduates: Enrolled in a psychology doctoral program (0), enrolled in another graduate/professional program (0), enrolled in a postdoctoral residency/fellowship (n/a), employed in independent practice (n/a), employed in a professional position in a school system (13), total from the above (master's) (13).

Doctoral Degree Graduates: Of those who graduated in the academic year 2006–2007, the following categories and numbers represent the postgraduate activities and employment of doctoral degree graduates: Enrolled in a psychology doctoral program (n/a), total from the above (doctoral) (0).

Additional Information:

Orientation, Objectives, and Emphasis of Department: The KSU School Psychology program embraces a preventive mental health model as a context for the study of psychological and educational principles that influence the adjustment of individuals and systems. A commitment to using the science of psychology to promote human welfare is emphasized. In addition, recognizing the pluralistic nature of our society, the program is committed to fostering in its students sensitivity to, appreciation for, and understanding of all individual differences. A scientist–practitioner model of training, which conceptualizes school psychologists as data-oriented problem solvers and transmitters of psychological knowledge and skill, provides another organizing theme of training. The program emphasizes the provision of services to individual schools and children, in addition to attaining a functional understanding of systems–consultation and the ability to promote and implement primary and secondary prevention programs to optimize adjustment. Because the program's emphasis is on the application of psychology in applied educational and mental health settings, students are required to demonstrate competence in the substantive content areas of psychological and educational theory and practice. Other related areas outside the school psychology core include coursework in the biological, cognitive–perceptual, social, and developmental bases of behavior, as well as in the areas of curriculum and instruction, educational foundations, and research.

Special Facilities or Resources: The Center for Disability studies provides interdisciplinary research support for faculty and graduate students engaged in research on disability issues. The Child Development Center, an early childhood model laboratory school, provides opportunities for faculty and student research and practice. The Family Child Learning Center, which offers early intervention services to infants and toddlers with disabilities and their families, offers a training location for grant-funded school psychology students and for faculty research. The Counseling and Human Development Center (CHDC) provides students with a practicum experience through the supervised provision of assessment services to university students and the local community. The CHDC is equipped with one-way mirrors, split-screen videotaping facilities, and in-room telephones based around seven recently refurbished counseling cubicles. This permits observation by our students at the time of assessment and counseling and allows for videotaping for viewing at a later time. The Bureau of Educational Research provides a source of support for students who are engaged in research activities, including data entry and analysis.

Information for Students With Physical Disabilities: See the following Web site for more information: http://www.registrars.kent.edu/disability/default.htm.

Application Information:

Send to Office of Graduate Student Services, 418 White Hall, Kent State University, Kent, OH 44242. Application available online. URL of online application: http://www.ehhs.kent.edu/spsy/index.cfm. Students are admitted in the Fall, application deadline October 15; Spring, application deadline January 10; Summer, application deadline June 15. *Fee:* $30.

Marietta College

Department of Psychology
215 Fifth Street
Marietta, OH 45750
Telephone: (740) 376-4762
Fax: (740) 376-4459
E-mail: *sibickym@marietta.edu*
Web: *http://www.marietta.edu/*

Department Information:

1930. Director of the Masters of Psychology Program: Mark E. Sibicky. Number of faculty: total—full-time 5, part-time 1; women—full-time 3, part-time 1.

Programs and Degrees Offered:

Listed in the following order: Program area, degree type (T if terminal Master's), number awarded 7/06–6/07. General Psychology MA/MS (Master of Arts/Science) (T) 4.

Student Applications/Admissions:

Student Applications

General Psychology MA/MS (Master of Arts/Science)—Applications 2007–2008, 24. Total applicants accepted 2007–2008, 7. Number full-time enrolled (new admits only) 2007–2008, 7. Number part-time enrolled (new admits only) 2007–2008, 0. Openings 2008–2009, 8. The median number of years required for completion of a degree in 2006–2007 were 2.

Admissions Requirements:

Scores: Entries appear in this order: required test or GPA, minimum score (if required), median score of students entering in 2007–2008. Master's Programs: GRE-V 500; GRE-Q 500; overall undergraduate GPA 2.8; psychology GPA 3.0.

Other Criteria: (importance of criteria rated low, medium, or high): GRE/MAT scores—medium, research experience—medium, work experience—low, extracurricular activity—medium, GPA—high, letters of recommendation—high, statement of goals and objectives—high, Course work in psychology—high, undergraduate major in psychology—medium, specific undergraduate psychology courses taken—high. For additional information on admission requirements, go to http://www.marietta.edu/.

Student Characteristics: The following represents characteristics of students in 2007–2008 in all graduate psychology programs in the department: Female—full-time 17, part-time 0; Male—full-time 3, part-time 0; Caucasian/White—full-time 20, part-time 0; students subject to the Americans With Disabilities Act—full-time 0, part-time 0; Unknown ethnicity—full-time 0, part-time 0.

Financial Information/Assistance:

Tuition for Full-Time Study: *Master's:* State residents: $565 per credit hour; Nonstate residents: $565 per credit hour. Tuition is subject to change. See the following Web site for updates and changes in tuition costs: http://www.marietta.edu/.

Financial Assistance:

First-Year Students: Research assistantships available for first year. Average amount paid per academic year: $7,000. Average number of hours worked per week: 20. Apply by April 1. Tuition remission given: full. Traineeships available for first year. Average amount paid per academic year: $4,000. Average number of hours worked per week: 30. Apply by April 1.

Advanced Students: Research assistantships available for advanced students. Average amount paid per academic year: $7,000. Average number of hours worked per week: 20. Apply by April 1. Tuition remission given: full. Traineeships available for advanced students. Average amount paid per academic year: $4,000. Average number of hours worked per week: 25. Apply by April 1.

Additional Information: Of all students currently enrolled full time, 2% benefited from one or more of the listed financial assistance programs.

Internships/Practica: Master's Degree (MA/MS General Psychology): An internship experience such as a final research project or "capstone" experience is required of graduates. Students select two three-credit electives in an applied professional practica experience. The practica is designed to provide students with an applied experience relating to their career interests in psychology. Students choose electives from the following areas: The Teaching of Psychology, designed to train students to be effective instructors of psychology; Supervised Internship in the area of clinical, developmental, or the college's residence life program; Directed Independent Research in which students pursue their own research interests under the direction of a faculty member. For additional information on education and training outcomes for our programs, see the following Web site: http://www.marietta.edu/.

Housing and Day Care: No on-campus housing is available. No on-campus day care facilities are available.

Employment of Department Graduates:

Master's Degree Graduates: Of those who graduated in the academic year 2006–2007, the following categories and numbers represent the postgraduate activities and employment of master's degree graduates: Enrolled in a psychology doctoral program (2), enrolled in another graduate/professional program (1), enrolled in a postdoctoral residency/fellowship (n/a), employed in independent practice (n/a), employed in an academic position at a 2-year/4-year college (2), employed in a community mental health/counseling center (2), total from the above (master's) (7).

Doctoral Degree Graduates: Of those who graduated in the academic year 2006–2007, the following categories and numbers represent the postgraduate activities and employment of doctoral degree graduates: Enrolled in a psychology doctoral program (n/a), total from the above (doctoral) (0).

Additional Information:

Orientation, Objectives, and Emphasis of Department: The Psychology Department at Marietta College offers a 2-year Master of Arts Degree in General Psychology. The program is designed to give students a strong graduate-level foundation in psychology so students may pursue further education in psychology at the PhD level or to aid students in securing employment in a field related to psychology. The orientation of the department faculty is that psychology is a science, and that psychological research and knowledge can be applied to improving people's lives. The 2-year program consists of 24 core content courses in psychology, 6 hours of applied practicum electives in an area of professional psychology (e.g., clinical internship, developmental internship, teaching of psychology), and 6 hours of supervised thesis research. The program offers the opportunity for students to focus their interest in the area of clinical, social, developmental, cognitive, physiological or applied psychology. Students are taught in small seminars by outstanding teachers, with exceptional research and professional experience. Faculty have high expectations in terms of student's academic performance yet are committed to helping students achieve their educational and professional goals.

Special Facilities or Resources: The Psychology Department at Marietta College has a newly remodeled human research laboratory equipped with several research cubicles, videorecording equipment, one-way observational windows, and specialized cognitive and physiological research equipment and software. Students interested in children and families have internship and research opportunities at the Marietta College Center for Families and Children. This on-campus facility is maintained by the psychology and education departments to provide services to children and families in the community. The department also maintains its own separate student computer lab equipped with SPSS and other software. Students have access to graduate research and conference travel funds. There is also a designated graduate seminar room and student lounge area.

Information for Students With Physical Disabilities: See the following Web site for more information: http://www.marietta.edu/~arc/.

Application Information:

Send to Cathy Brown, Director of Graduate Programs, Marietta College, 215 Fifth Street, Marietta, OH, 45750-4005. Students are admitted in the Fall, application deadline April 1. *Fee:* $25.

Miami University (Ohio)

Department of Psychology
Oxford, OH 45056
Telephone: (513) 529-2400
Fax: (513) 529-2420
E-mail: *markls@muohio.edu*
Web: *http://www.units.muohio.edu/psychology/*

Department Information:

1888. Chairperson: Carl E. Paternite. Number of faculty: total—full-time 31, part-time 1; women—full-time 15, part-time 1; total—minority—full-time 3; women minority—full-time 2.

Programs and Degrees Offered:

Listed in the following order: Program area, degree type (T if terminal Master's), number awarded 7/06–6/07. Clinical PhD (Doctor of Philosophy) 3, Brain and Cognitive Science PhD (Doctor of Philosophy) 0, Social PhD (Doctor of Philosophy) 1.

APA Accreditation: Clinical PhD (Doctor of Philosophy).

Student Applications/Admissions:

Student Applications

Clinical PhD (Doctor of Philosophy)—Applications 2007–2008, 173. Total applicants accepted 2007–2008, 6. Number full-time enrolled (new admits only) 2007–2008, 6. Number part-time enrolled (new admits only) 2007–2008, 0. Openings 2008–2009, 6. The median number of years required for completion of a degree in 2006–2007 were 6. The number of students enrolled full- and part-time who were dismissed or voluntarily withdrew from this program area in 2007–2008 were 2. *Brain and Cognitive Science PhD (Doctor of Philosophy)*—Applications 2007–2008, 17. Total applicants accepted 2007–2008, 4. Number full-time enrolled (new admits only) 2007–2008, 4. Number part-time enrolled (new admits only) 2007–2008, 0. Openings 2008–2009, 4. The median number of years required for completion of a degree in 2006–2007 were 5. The number of students enrolled full- and part-time who were dismissed or voluntarily withdrew from this program area in 2007–2008 were 0. *Social PhD (Doctor of Philosophy)*—Applications 2007–2008, 44. Total applicants accepted 2007–2008, 2. Number full-time enrolled (new admits only) 2007–2008,

2. Number part-time enrolled (new admits only) 2007–2008, 0. Openings 2008–2009, 3. The median number of years required for completion of a degree in 2006–2007 were 5. The number of students enrolled full- and part-time who were dismissed or voluntarily withdrew from this program area in 2007–2008 were 0.

Admissions Requirements:

Scores: Entries appear in this order: required test or GPA, minimum score (if required), median score of students entering in 2007–2008. Doctoral Programs: GRE-V no minimum stated, 610; GRE-Q no minimum stated, 650; GRE-Subject (Psychology) no minimum stated, 690; overall undergraduate GPA 3.0, 3.7; Doctoral program GRE-Analytic no minimum stated, 5.0.

Other Criteria: (importance of criteria rated low, medium, or high): GRE/MAT scores—medium, research experience—high, work experience—low, extracurricular activity—medium, clinically related public service—medium, GPA—high, letters of recommendation—high, interview—medium, statement of goals and objectives—high.

Student Characteristics: The following represents characteristics of students in 2007–2008 in all graduate psychology programs in the department: Female—full-time 41, part-time 8; Male—full-time 32, part-time 4; African American/Black—full-time 2, part-time 0; Hispanic/Latino(a)—full-time 1, part-time 1; Asian/Pacific Islander—full-time 2, part-time 0; American Indian/Alaska Native—full-time 1, part-time 0; Caucasian/White—full-time 67, part-time 11; Multi-ethnic—full-time 0, part-time 0; students subject to the Americans With Disabilities Act—full-time 0, part-time 0; Unknown ethnicity—full-time 0, part-time 0.

Financial Information/Assistance:

Tuition for Full-Time Study: *Doctoral:* State residents: per academic year $11,765, $435 per credit hour; Nonstate residents: per academic year $24,624, $970 per credit hour. Tuition is subject to change. See the following Web site for updates and changes in tuition costs: http://www.miamiu.muohio.edu/graduate/fees.

Financial Assistance:

First-Year Students: Teaching assistantships available for first year. Average amount paid per academic year: $13,101. Average number of hours worked per week: 20. Apply by January 1. Tuition remission given: full. Research assistantships available for first year. Average amount paid per academic year: $13,101. Average number of hours worked per week: 20. Apply by January 1. Tuition remission given: full.

Advanced Students: Teaching assistantships available for advanced students. Average amount paid per academic year: $17,595. Average number of hours worked per week: 20. Tuition remission given: full. Research assistantships available for advanced students. Average amount paid per academic year: $13,101. Average number of hours worked per week: 20. Tuition remission given: full. Fellowships and scholarships available for advanced students. Average amount paid per academic year: $17,678. Average number of hours worked per week: 20. Tuition remission given: full.

Additional Information: Of all students currently enrolled full time, 100% benefited from one or more of the listed financial assistance programs. Application and information available online at http://www.units.muohio.edu/psychology/.

Internships/Practica: Doctoral Degree (PhD Clinical): For those doctoral students for whom a professional internship was required in this program prior to graduation, (6) students applied for an internship in 2006–2007, with (6) students obtaining an internship. Of those students who obtained an internship, (6) were paid internships. Of those students who obtained an internship, (6) students placed in APA/CPA-accredited internships, (0) students placed in internships not APA/CPA-accredited, but listed with the Association of Psychology Postdoctoral and Internship Centers (APPIC), (0) students placed in internships conforming to guidelines of the Council of Directors of School Psychology Programs (CDSPP), (0) students placed in internships that were not APA/CPA-accredited, APPIC or CDSPP listed. There are opportunities for students to engage in practica and internships as well as conduct applied research. Traineeships for advanced Clinical students are available in a wide range of settings including community mental health centers, hospitals, and school systems. For additional information on education and training outcomes for our programs, see the following Web site: http://www.units.muohio.edu/psychology/.

Housing and Day Care: On-campus housing is available. See the following Web site for more information: http://www.miami.muohio.edu/housing/. On-campus day care facilities are available. See the following Web site for more information: http://www.childcare.muohio.edu/.

Employment of Department Graduates:

Master's Degree Graduates: Of those who graduated in the academic year 2006–2007, the following categories and numbers represent the postgraduate activities and employment of master's degree graduates: Enrolled in a postdoctoral residency/fellowship (n/a), employed in independent practice (n/a), total from the above (master's) (0).

Doctoral Degree Graduates: Of those who graduated in the academic year 2006–2007, the following categories and numbers represent the postgraduate activities and employment of doctoral degree graduates: Enrolled in a psychology doctoral program (n/a), enrolled in a postdoctoral residency/fellowship (1), employed in independent practice (0), employed in an academic position at a university (0), employed in other positions at a higher education institution (1), other employment position (1), total from the above (doctoral) (3).

Additional Information:

Orientation, Objectives, and Emphasis of Department: The goal of the department is to provide an environment in which students thrive intellectually. We strive for a balance between enough structure to gauge student progress and provide grounding in the breadth of psychology and enough freedom for students to design programs optimal to their own professional goals. The department provides training and experience in research, teaching, and application of psychology. The department offers basic and applied research orientations in all programs. The Clinical program emphasizes a theory–research–practicum combination, so that graduates will be able to function in a variety of academic and service settings. The objective of the department is to produce skilled, informed, and enthusiastic psychologists, capable of contributing to their field in a variety of ways.

Special Facilities or Resources: The department has laboratories dedicated to the study of social cognition, group processes, and social interaction as well as fundamental cognitive process of perception, categorization, decision making and choice, spatial cognition, and motor control. Two laboratories use virtual environments to study spatial cognition and posture. One of these laboratories has created one of the largest virtual environments in the world. Two psychobiology laboratories offer advanced facilities for neurological recording, drug delivery, and pharmacological and histological analyses. The Psychology Clinic includes group and child therapy rooms, individual assessment and therapy rooms, a test library, conference room, and offices for the clinic director and a full-time secretary. Clinical services are offered in a training or research context to university students and the Oxford community, including a school-based mental health program. Research with children is facilitated by a good relationship with local public school systems and child-care facilities. Access to clinical populations is available through the Psychology Clinic and through cooperative arrangements with mental health centers in nearby communities. Several clinical faculty are engaged in community action projects related to mental health needs in local communities.

Information for Students With Physical Disabilities: See the following Web site for more information: http://www.units.muohio.edu/oeeo/odr/.

Application Information:
Send to Graduate School, 102 Roudebush, Miami University, Oxford, OH 45056. Application available online. URL of online application: http://www.miami.muohio.edu/graduate/. Students are admitted in the Fall, application deadline January 1. *Fee:* $35.

Ohio State University

School of Physical Activity and Educational Services
Education
100A PAES Building, 305 West 17th Avenue
Columbus, OH 43210
Telephone: (614) 292-5909
Fax: (614) 292-4255
E-mail: *miranda.2@osu.edu*
Web: *http://www.coe.ohio-state.edu-paes*

Department Information:
1996. Director: Donna Pastore. Number of faculty: total—full-time 5; women—full-time 3; women minority—full-time 2.

Programs and Degrees Offered:
Listed in the following order: Program area, degree type (T if terminal Master's), number awarded 7/06–6/07. School MA/MS (Master of Arts/Science) (T) 16, School PhD (Doctor of Philosophy) 2.

Student Applications/Admissions:
Student Applications
School MA/MS (Master of Arts/Science)—Applications 2007–2008, 89. Total applicants accepted 2007–2008, 12. Number full-time enrolled (new admits only) 2007–2008, 11. Openings 2008–2009, 10. The median number of years required for completion of a degree in 2006–2007 were 3. The number of students enrolled full- and part-time who were dismissed or voluntarily withdrew from this program area in 2007–2008 were 1. *School PhD (Doctor of Philosophy)*—Applications 2007–2008, 15. Total applicants accepted 2007–2008, 5. Number full-time enrolled (new admits only) 2007–2008, 2. Total enrolled 2007–2008 full-time, 19. Openings 2008–2009, 5. The median number of years required for completion of a degree in 2006–2007 were 5. The number of students enrolled full- and part-time who were dismissed or voluntarily withdrew from this program area in 2007–2008 were 0.

Admissions Requirements:
Scores: Entries appear in this order: required test or GPA, minimum score (if required), median score of students entering in 2007–2008. Master's Programs: GRE-V 500, 628; GRE-Q 500, 589; overall undergraduate GPA 3.0, 3.5. Doctoral Programs: GRE-V 500, 670; GRE-Q 500, 648; overall undergraduate GPA 3.0, 3.6.
Other Criteria: (importance of criteria rated low, medium, or high): GRE/MAT scores—high, research experience—medium, work experience—medium, extracurricular activity—low, clinically related public service—medium, GPA—high, letters of recommendation—high, interview—high, statement of goals and objectives—high.

Student Characteristics: The following represents characteristics of students in 2007–2008 in all graduate psychology programs in the department: Female—full-time 22, part-time 2; Male—full-time 7, part-time 0; African American/Black—full-time 6, part-time 0; Hispanic/Latino(a)—full-time 1, part-time 0; Asian/Pacific Islander—full-time 0, part-time 0; American Indian/Alaska Native—full-time 0, part-time 0; Caucasian/White—full-time 24, part-time 2; Multi-ethnic—full-time 0, part-time 0; students subject to the Americans With Disabilities Act—full-time 0, part-time 0; Unknown ethnicity—full-time 0, part-time 0; International students who hold an F-1 or J-1 Visa—full-time 0, part-time 0.

Financial Information/Assistance:
Tuition for Full-Time Study: *Master's:* State residents: per academic year $9,000; Nonstate residents: per academic year $21,000. *Doctoral:* State residents: per academic year $9,000; Nonstate residents: per academic year $21,000. Tuition is subject to change.

Financial Assistance:
First-Year Students: Fellowships and scholarships available for first year. Average amount paid per academic year: $10,000. Apply by January 1. Tuition remission given: full.
Advanced Students: Fellowships and scholarships available for advanced students. Average amount paid per academic year: $10,000. Apply by January 1. Tuition remission given: full.
Additional Information: Of all students currently enrolled full time, 40% benefited from one or more of the listed financial assistance programs.

Internships/Practica: Master's Degree (MA/MS school): An internship experience such as a final research project or "capstone" experience is required of graduates. Doctoral Degree (PhD School): For those doctoral students for whom a professional internship was required in this program prior to graduation, (1) student applied for an internship in 2006–2007, with (1) student obtaining an internship. Of those students who obtained an internship, (1) were paid internships. Of those students who obtained an internship, (0) students placed in APA/CPA-accredited internships, (0) students placed in internships not APA/CPA-accredited, but listed with the Association of Psychology Postdoctoral and Internship Centers (APPIC), (0) students placed in internships conforming to guidelines of the Council of Directors of School Psychology Programs (CDSPP), (1) student placed in internships that were not APA/CPA-accredited, APPIC or CDSPP listed. Master's students are engaged in practica during their 2 years of study. All students gain experience in an urban school district as well as either a rural or suburban setting. Students are involved in a 9-month school-based internship in the Central Ohio area. Internships are paid.

Housing and Day Care: On-campus housing is available. See the following Web site for more information: http://www.osuhousing.com/. On-campus day care facilities are available. See the following Web site for more information: http://www.hr.osu.edu/ccc/home.htm.

Employment of Department Graduates:

Master's Degree Graduates: Of those who graduated in the academic year 2006–2007, the following categories and numbers represent the postgraduate activities and employment of master's degree graduates: Enrolled in a postdoctoral residency/fellowship (n/a), employed in independent practice (n/a), employed in a professional position in a school system (10), total from the above (master's) (10).

Doctoral Degree Graduates: Of those who graduated in the academic year 2006–2007, the following categories and numbers represent the postgraduate activities and employment of doctoral degree graduates: Enrolled in a psychology doctoral program (n/a), total from the above (doctoral) (0).

Additional Information:

Orientation, Objectives, and Emphasis of Department: The Counselor Education, Rehabilitation Services, and School Psychology Section in the School of Physical Activity and Educational Services emphasizes the preparation of individuals who can function in human services settings such as public and private schools and universities, social agencies, state and federal government agencies, business and industry, hospitals and health care facilities, and rehabilitation agencies. Emphasizing primary prevention, the program will help students, learners, and clients achieve optimal levels of human functioning and advocate for organizations and systems that promote optimal levels of human functioning. Students in the program may undertake course work to emphasize one or more of the three areas: (a) counselor education, (b) rehabilitation services, or (c) school psychology.

Special Facilities or Resources: The School of Physical Activities and Educational Services moved into a new building Spring of 2007. The Counselor Education and School Psychology programs have a state-of-the-art clinic facility. The clinic is scheduled to open in Fall 2008.

Application Information:

Send to School of Physical Activity and Educational Services, Student Services and Academic Programs, 100A PAES Building, 305 West 17th Avenue, Columbus, OH 43210. Students are admitted in the Fall, application deadline January 15. *Fee:* $40.

Ohio State University, The

Department of Psychology
College of Social and Behavioral Sciences
225 Psychology Building, 1835 Neil Avenue
Columbus, OH 43210
Telephone: (614) 292-4112
Fax: (614) 292-4537
E-mail: *sexton.3@osu.edu*
Web: *http://www.psy.ohio-state.edu*

Department Information:

1907. Chairperson: Gifford Weary, PhD. Number of faculty: total—full-time 45, part-time 15; women—full-time 11, part-time 6; total—minority—full-time 3, part-time 1; women minority—part-time 1.

Programs and Degrees Offered:

Listed in the following order: Program area, degree type (T if terminal Master's), number awarded 7/06–6/07. Clinical PhD (Doctor of Philosophy) 6, Cognitive PhD (Doctor of Philosophy) 2, Counseling Psychology PhD (Doctor of Philosophy) 7, Developmental PhD (Doctor of Philosophy) 1, Industrial/Organizational PhD (Doctor of Philosophy) 1, Mental Retardation/Development PhD (Doctor of Philosophy) 0, Behavioral Neuroscience PhD (Doctor of Philosophy) 2, Quantitative PhD (Doctor of Philosophy) 3, Social PhD (Doctor of Philosophy) 3.

APA Accreditation: Clinical PhD (Doctor of Philosophy). Counseling PhD (Doctor of Philosophy).

Student Applications/Admissions:

Student Applications

Clinical PhD (Doctor of Philosophy)—Applications 2007–2008, 252. Total applicants accepted 2007–2008, 23. Number full-time enrolled (new admits only) 2007–2008, 14. Number part-time enrolled (new admits only) 2007–2008, 0. Total enrolled 2007–2008 full-time, 38, part-time, 2. Openings 2008–2009, 8. The median number of years required for completion of a degree in 2006–2007 were 6. The number of students enrolled full- and part-time who were dismissed or voluntarily withdrew from this program area in 2007–2008 were 0. *Cognitive PhD (Doctor of Philosophy)*—Applications 2007–2008, 41. Total applicants accepted 2007–2008, 9. Number full-time enrolled (new admits only) 2007–2008, 3. Number part-time enrolled (new admits only) 2007–2008, 0. Openings 2008–2009, 5. The median number of years required for completion of a degree in 2006–2007 were 7. The number of students enrolled full- and part-time who were dismissed or voluntarily withdrew from this program area in 2007–2008 were 0. *Counseling Psychology PhD (Doctor of Philosophy)*—Applications 2007–2008, 0. Total applicants accepted 2007–2008, 0. Number full-time enrolled (new admits only) 2007–2008, 0. Number part-time enrolled (new admits only) 2007–2008, 0. The median number of years required for completion of a degree in 2006–2007 were 5. The number of students enrolled full- and part-time who were dismissed or voluntarily withdrew from this program area in 2007–2008 were 0. *Developmental PhD (Doctor of Philosophy)*—Applications 2007–2008, 15. Total applicants accepted 2007–2008, 4. Number full-time enrolled (new admits only) 2007–2008, 0. Number part-time enrolled (new admits only) 2007–2008, 0. Openings 2008–2009, 3. The median number of years required for completion of a degree in 2006–2007 were 3. The number of students enrolled full- and part-time who were dismissed or voluntarily withdrew from this program area in 2007–2008 were 1. *Industrial/Organizational PhD (Doctor of Philosophy)*—Applications 2007–2008, 0. Total applicants accepted 2007–2008, 0. The median number of years required for completion of a degree in 2006–2007 were 8. The number of students enrolled full- and part-time who were dismissed or voluntarily withdrew from this program area in 2007–2008 were 0. *Mental Retardation/Development PhD (Doctor of Philosophy)*—Applications 2007–2008, 25. Total applicants accepted 2007–2008, 3. Number full-time enrolled (new admits only) 2007–2008, 2. Number part-time enrolled (new admits only) 2007–2008, 0. Openings 2008–2009, 2. The number of students enrolled full- and part-time who were dismissed or voluntarily withdrew from this program area in 2007–2008 were 0. *Behavioral Neuroscience PhD (Doctor of Philosophy)*—Applications 2007–2008, 50. Total applicants accepted 2007–2008, 3. Number full-time enrolled (new admits only) 2007–2008, 2. Number part-time enrolled (new admits only) 2007–2008, 0. Openings 2008–2009, 5. The median number of years required for completion of a degree in 2006–2007 were 6. The number of students enrolled full- and part-time who were dismissed or voluntarily withdrew from this program area in 2007–2008 were 0. *Quantitative PhD (Doctor of Philosophy)*—Applications 2007–2008, 30. Total applicants accepted 2007–2008, 13. Number full-time enrolled (new admits only) 2007–2008, 4. Number part-time enrolled (new admits only) 2007–2008, 0. Openings 2008–2009, 3. The median number of years required for completion of a degree in 2006–2007 were 7. The number of students enrolled full- and part-time who were dismissed or voluntarily withdrew from this program area in 2007–2008 were 1. *Social PhD (Doctor of Philosophy)*—Applications 2007–2008, 113. Total applicants accepted 2007–2008, 9. Number full-time enrolled (new admits only) 2007–2008, 3. Number part-time enrolled (new admits only) 2007–2008, 0. Total enrolled 2007–2008 full-time, 25, part-time, 2. Openings 2008–2009, 5. The median number of years required for completion of a degree in 2006–2007 were 6. The number of students enrolled full- and part-time who were dismissed or voluntarily withdrew from this program area in 2007–2008 were 1.

Admissions Requirements:

Scores: Entries appear in this order: required test or GPA, minimum score (if required), median score of students entering in 2007–2008. Doctoral Programs: GRE-V 600, 625; GRE-Q 600, 730; overall undergraduate GPA 3.2, 3.69. GRE exceptions can be made when there is other evidence of high potential. Please note that to qualify for University Fellowships, the above required scores must be met.

Other Criteria: (importance of criteria rated low, medium, or high): research experience—high, work experience—low, extracurricular activity—low, clinically related public service—low, letters of recommendation—high, statement of goals and objectives—high. Clinical area ranks interview as high.

Student Characteristics: The following represents characteristics of students in 2007–2008 in all graduate psychology programs in the department: Female—full-time 76, part-time 2; Male—full-time 34, part-time 3; African American/Black—full-time 5, part-time 0; Hispanic/Latino(a)—full-time 6, part-time 1; Asian/Pacific Islander—full-time 13, part-time 2; American Indian/Alaska Native—full-time 1, part-time 0; Caucasian/White—full-time 84, part-time 2; Multi-ethnic—full-time 1, part-time 0; students subject to the Americans With Disabilities Act—full-time 0, part-time 0; Unknown ethnicity—full-time 0, part-time 0.

Financial Information/Assistance:

Tuition for Full-Time Study: *Doctoral:* State residents: per academic year $13,296, $414 per credit hour; Nonstate residents: per academic year $32,168, $886 per credit hour. Tuition is subject to change. See the following Web site for updates and changes in tuition costs: http://www.gradapply.osu.edu/BufferCosts.htm.

Financial Assistance:

First-Year Students: Teaching assistantships available for first year. Average amount paid per academic year: $11,025. Average number of hours worked per week: 20. Apply by December 15. Tuition remission given: full. Research assistantships available for first year. Average amount paid per academic year: $11,025. Average number of hours worked per week: 20. Apply by December 15. Tuition remission given: full. Fellowships and scholarships available for first year. Average amount paid per academic year: $15,072. Average number of hours worked per week: 0. Apply by December 15. Tuition remission given: full.

Advanced Students: Teaching assistantships available for advanced students. Average amount paid per academic year: $12,555. Average number of hours worked per week: 20. Apply by December 15. Tuition remission given: full. Research assistantships available for advanced students. Average amount paid per academic year: $12,555. Average number of hours worked per week: 20. Apply by December 15. Tuition remission given: full. Traineeships available for advanced students. Average amount paid per academic year: $12,555. Average number of hours worked per week: 20. Apply by December 15. Tuition remission given: full.

Additional Information: Of all students currently enrolled full time, 100% benefited from one or more of the listed financial assistance programs. Application and information available online at http://www.psy.ohio-state.edu.

Internships/Practica: Doctoral Degree (PhD Clinical): For those doctoral students for whom a professional internship was required in this program prior to graduation, (8) students applied for an internship in 2006–2007, with (5) students obtaining an internship. Of those students who obtained an internship, (5) were paid internships. Of those students who obtained an internship, (5) students placed in APA/CPA-accredited internships, (0) students placed in internships not APA/CPA-accredited, but listed with the Association of Psychology Postdoctoral and Internship Centers (APPIC), (0) students placed in internships conforming to guidelines of the Council of Directors of School Psychology Programs (CDSPP), (0) students placed in internships that were not APA/CPA-accredited, APPIC or CDSPP listed. Doctoral Degree (PhD Counseling Psychology): For those doctoral students for whom a professional internship was required in this program prior to graduation, (8) students applied for an internship in 2006–2007, with (7) students obtaining an internship. Of those students who obtained an internship, (7) were paid internships. Of those students who obtained an internship, (7) students placed in APA/CPA-accredited internships, (0) students placed in internships not APA/CPA-accredited, but listed with the Association of Psychology Postdoctoral and Internship Centers (APPIC), (0) students placed in internships conforming to guidelines of the Council of Directors of School Psychology Programs (CDSPP), (0) students placed in internships that were not APA/CPA accredited, APPIC or CDSPP listed. Doctoral Degree (PhD Mental Retardation/Development): For those doctoral students for whom a professional internship was required in this program prior to graduation, (1) student applied for an internship in 2006–2007, with (1) student obtaining an internship. Of those students who obtained an internship, (1) were paid internships. Of those students who obtained an internship, (1) student placed in APA/CPA-accredited internships, (0) students placed in internships not APA/CPA-accredited, but listed with the Association of Psychology Postdoctoral and Internship Centers (APPIC), (0) students placed in internships conforming to guidelines of the Council of Directors of School Psychology Programs (CDSPP), (0) students placed in internships that were not APA/CPA accredited, APPIC or CDSPP listed. For students in the Clinical training program, initial practica are conducted at the in-house Psychological Services Center (PSC), supervised by core clinical faculty. Following 1 year of in-house training, students progress to advanced clinical experiences at program-approved externship sites throughout the community where students gain clinical assessment and treatment experiences in a variety of settings consistent with the program's three training tracks: Adult Psychopathology, Health Psychology, and Child–Clinical Psychology. Advanced students also have the opportunity to continue treating clients in the in-house PSC while receiving supervision from adjunct faculty in the community. Additionally, all students must complete a 1-year, full-time internship in clinical psychology prior to the award of the doctoral degree. Counseling psychology students complete three in-house practica where each counseling session is observed by a supervisor followed by 1 hour of individual supervision. External practicum sites include a variety of sites in the central Ohio area including university counseling centers, departments of rehabilitation psychology, VA medical centers, psychiatric hospitals, community mental health centers, forensic psychology at state correctional facilities, OPA psychology advocacy program, and pain management and sport psychology clinics.

Housing and Day Care: On-campus housing is available. See the following Web site for more information: http://www.osuhousing.com/gradhouse.html. For off-campus information: http://www.osuoffcampus.com. On-campus day care facilities are available. See the following Web site for more information: http://www.hr.osu.edu/ccc/home.htm.

Employment of Department Graduates:

Master's Degree Graduates: Of those who graduated in the academic year 2006–2007, the following categories and numbers represent the postgraduate activities and employment of master's degree graduates: Enrolled in a psychology doctoral program (23), enrolled in another graduate/professional program (0), enrolled in a postdoctoral residency/fellowship (n/a), employed in independent practice (n/a), total from the above (master's) (23).

Doctoral Degree Graduates: Of those who graduated in the academic year 2006–2007, the following categories and numbers represent the postgraduate activities and employment of doctoral degree graduates: Enrolled in a psychology doctoral program (n/a), enrolled in a postdoctoral residency/fellowship (11), employed in an academic position at a university (8), employed in business or industry (4), employed in a hospital/medical center (1), do not know (2), total from the above (doctoral) (26).

Additional Information:

Orientation, Objectives, and Emphasis of Department: The department is comprehensive in nature, with PhD programs in nearly all the major fields of study in psychology. The programs all strive to educate psychological scientists, and there is consequently a strong emphasis on research training in the doctoral programs, even in the applied areas. Our objective is to prepare theoretically sophisticated psychologists who leave us with effective skills to build upon in their later careers and with the ability to grow as psychology develops as a science and profession.

Special Facilities or Resources: There are several research labs specializing in the various programs of the OSU psychology department. Please visit http://www.psy.ohio-state.edu and click on "Labs" in the header for more detailed information. In addition, because The Ohio State University is a well-known and well-established research institution, there are several nondepartment labs located throughout the campus that would be of possible interest to psychology graduate students.

Information for Students With Physical Disabilities: See the following Web site for more information: http://www.ods.ohio-state.edu/.

Application Information:

Application must be submitted online. The online application is available at http://www.psy.ohio-state.edu, then click on "Graduate application" for further instructions. URL of online application: http://www.psy.ohio-state.edu/gradadv/app.htm. Students are admitted in the Fall, application deadline December 15. Deadline for all international applicants—December 1. *Fee:* $40. International applications $50.

Ohio University

Department of Psychology
Arts and Sciences
200 Porter Hall
Athens, OH 45701-2979
Telephone: (740) 593-1707
Fax: (740) 593-0579
E-mail: *carlsonb@ohiou.edu*
Web: *http://www.psych.ohiou.edu*

Department Information:

1922. Chairperson: Bruce Carlson, PhD. Number of faculty: total—full-time 27, part-time 5; women—full-time 12, part-time 4; total—minority—full-time 3, part-time 1; women minority—full-time 2.

Programs and Degrees Offered:

Listed in the following order: Program area, degree type (T if terminal Master's), number awarded 7/06–6/07. Clinical PhD (Doctor of Philosophy) 6, Industrial/Organizational PhD (Doctor of Philosophy) 0, Social PhD (Doctor of Philosophy) 1, Cognitive

PhD (Doctor of Philosophy) 1, Health PhD (Doctor of Philosophy) 1, Applied Quantitative PhD (Doctor of Philosophy) 0.

APA Accreditation: Clinical PhD (Doctor of Philosophy).

Student Applications/Admissions:

Student Applications

Clinical PhD (Doctor of Philosophy)—Applications 2007–2008, 135. Total applicants accepted 2007–2008, 8. Number full-time enrolled (new admits only) 2007–2008, 10. Total enrolled 2007–2008 full-time, 50. Openings 2008–2009, 10. The median number of years required for completion of a degree in 2006–2007 were 6. The number of students enrolled full- and part-time who were dismissed or voluntarily withdrew from this program area in 2007–2008 were 1. *Industrial/Organizational PhD (Doctor of Philosophy)*—Applications 2007–2008, 22. Total applicants accepted 2007–2008, 4. Number full-time enrolled (new admits only) 2007–2008, 3. Openings 2008–2009, 3. The number of students enrolled full- and part-time who were dismissed or voluntarily withdrew from this program area in 2007–2008 were 0. *Social PhD (Doctor of Philosophy)*—Applications 2007–2008, 14. Total applicants accepted 2007–2008, 2. Number full-time enrolled (new admits only) 2007–2008, 5. Total enrolled 2007–2008 full-time, 14. Openings 2008–2009, 3. The number of students enrolled full- and part-time who were dismissed or voluntarily withdrew from this program area in 2007–2008 were 0. *Cognitive PhD (Doctor of Philosophy)*—Applications 2007–2008, 6. Total applicants accepted 2007–2008, 3. Number full-time enrolled (new admits only) 2007–2008, 0. Total enrolled 2007–2008 full-time, 3. Openings 2008–2009, 2. The number of students enrolled full- and part-time who were dismissed or voluntarily withdrew from this program area in 2007–2008 were 0. *Health PhD (Doctor of Philosophy)*—Applications 2007–2008, 9. Total applicants accepted 2007–2008, 2. Number full-time enrolled (new admits only) 2007–2008, 2. Total enrolled 2007–2008 full-time, 8. Openings 2008–2009, 2. The number of students enrolled full- and part-time who were dismissed or voluntarily withdrew from this program area in 2007–2008 were 1. *Applied Quantitative PhD (Doctor of Philosophy)*—Applications 2007–2008, 4. Total applicants accepted 2007–2008, 3. Number full-time enrolled (new admits only) 2007–2008, 0. Total enrolled 2007–2008 full-time, 5. Openings 2008–2009, 2.

Admissions Requirements:

Scores: Entries appear in this order: required test or GPA, minimum score (if required), median score of students entering in 2007–2008. Doctoral Programs: GRE-V no minimum stated, 577; GRE-Q no minimum stated, 671; GRE-Subject (Psychology) no minimum stated, 650; overall undergraduate GPA no minimum stated, 3.60.

Other Criteria: (importance of criteria rated low, medium, or high): GRE/MAT scores—high, research experience—high, work experience—low, extracurricular activity—low, clinically related public service—medium, GPA—high, letters of recommendation—high, interview—medium, statement of goals and objectives—medium, undergraduate major in psychology—low, specific undergraduate psychology courses taken—low. For additional information on admission requirements, go to http://www.psych.ohiou.edu/academics/grad_studies/grad_studies.html.

Student Characteristics: The following represents characteristics of students in 2007–2008 in all graduate psychology programs in the department: Female—full-time 53, part-time 0; Male—full-time 30, part-time 0; African American/Black—full-time 3, part-time 0; Hispanic/Latino(a)—full-time 2, part-time 0; Asian/Pacific Islander—full-time 7, part-time 0; American Indian/Alaska Native—full-time 0, part-time 0; Caucasian/White—full-time 71, part-time 0; Multi-ethnic—full-time 0, part-time 0; students subject to the Americans With Disabilities Act—full-time 0, part-time 0; Unknown ethnicity—full-time 0, part-time 0.

Financial Information/Assistance:

Tuition for Full-Time Study: *Master's:* State residents: per academic year $7,605; Nonstate residents: per academic year $15,597. *Doctoral:* State residents: per academic year $7,605; Nonstate residents: per academic year $15,597. Tuition is subject to change. Additional fees are assessed to students beyond the costs of tuition for the following: general, technology, medical (optional), and legal (optional) fees. See the following Web site for updates and changes in tuition costs: http://www.ohio.edu/graduate/index.cfm.

Financial Assistance:

First-Year Students: Teaching assistantships available for first year. Average amount paid per academic year: $13,300. Average number of hours worked per week: 15. Tuition remission given: full. Research assistantships available for first year. Average amount paid per academic year: $13,300. Average number of hours worked per week: 15. Tuition remission given: full. Fellowships and scholarships available for first year. Average amount paid per academic year: $17,300. Average number of hours worked per week: 8. Tuition remission given: full.

Advanced Students: Teaching assistantships available for advanced students. Average amount paid per academic year: $13,300. Average number of hours worked per week: 15. Tuition remission given: full. Research assistantships available for advanced students. Average amount paid per academic year: $13,300. Average number of hours worked per week: 15. Tuition remission given: full. Traineeships available for advanced students. Average amount paid per academic year: $13,300. Average number of hours worked per week: 15. Tuition remission given: full. Fellowships and scholarships available for advanced students. Average amount paid per academic year: $17,300. Average number of hours worked per week: 8. Tuition remission given: full.

Additional Information: Of all students currently enrolled full time, 100% benefited from one or more of the listed financial assistance programs. Application and information available online at http://www.psych.ohiou.edu/.

Internships/Practica: Doctoral Degree (PhD Clinical): For those doctoral students for whom a professional internship was required in this program prior to graduation, (6) students applied for an internship in 2006–2007, with (5) students obtaining an internship. Of those students who obtained an internship, (5) were paid internships. Of those students who obtained an internship, (5) students placed in APA/CPA-accredited internships, (0) students placed in internships not APA/CPA-accredited, but listed with the Association of Psychology Postdoctoral and Internship Centers (APPIC), (0) students placed in internships conforming to guidelines of the Council of Directors of School Psychology Programs (CDSPP), (0) students placed in internships that were not APA/CPA-accredited, APPIC or CDSPP listed. Clinical doctoral interns are placed in APA-approved, 1-year internships throughout the country. Supervised training in clinical skills is provided for all clinical students in area mental health agencies, clinics, and the departmental psychology clinic. Such training is in addition to traineeships and internships. Supervised practicum experience is provided for organizational students in area industries and organizations. For additional information on education and training outcomes for our programs, see the following Web site: http://www.psych.ohiou.edu/academics/grad_studies/clinical.html.

Housing and Day Care: On-campus housing is available. See the following Web site for more information: http://www.ohio.edu/graduate/index.cfm. On-campus day care facilities are available. See the following Web site for more information: http://www.ohiou.edu/childdevcenter/index.htm.

Employment of Department Graduates:

Master's Degree Graduates: Of those who graduated in the academic year 2006–2007, the following categories and numbers represent the postgraduate activities and employment of master's degree graduates: Enrolled in a postdoctoral residency/fellowship (n/a), employed in independent practice (n/a), total from the above (master's) (0).

Doctoral Degree Graduates: Of those who graduated in the academic year 2006–2007, the following categories and numbers represent the postgraduate activities and employment of doctoral degree graduates: Enrolled in a psychology doctoral program (n/a), enrolled in a postdoctoral residency/fellowship (4), employed in an academic position at a university (1), employed in an academic position at a 2-year/4-year college (1), employed in business or industry (1), employed in a community mental health/counseling center (1), employed in a hospital/medical center (1), total from the above (doctoral) (9).

Additional Information:

Orientation, Objectives, and Emphasis of Department: The Clinical doctoral program is a scientist–practitioner program, offering balanced training in research and clinical skills. Practicum training is offered in intellectual and personality assessment. Therapy sequences are offered in health psychology, individual and group psychotherapy, behavior modification, and child psychology. Traineeships are available at the university counseling center and area mental health agencies and clinics. The department has a psychology training clinic. The doctoral program in Experimental Psychology provides intensive training in scholarly and research activities, preparing the student for positions in academic and research settings. The department offers an applied quantitative psychology track. This track offers advanced training in quantitative methods to graduate students who are concurrently studying in one of the other Experimental or Clinical Psychology programs. Besides the usual coursework in psychology, students who select this track receive extensive training in mathematics, computer science, and statistics.

Special Facilities or Resources: A new addition to Porter Hall, where the Department of Psychology is housed, will be completed during the Summer of 2008. This addition will contain numerous research labs equipped for a wide variety of human research activities, including psychophysiology, cognitive, social, and health. The department has its own clinic, which is used to train clinical doctoral students. Two computer laboratories in the Psychology Department, one with 30 computers and one with 4 computers, are also available for student research. All computer services are free of charge. Ohio University recently awarded the Psychology Department selective investment funds, which represent a major increase in funding for the department.

Information for Students With Physical Disabilities: See the following Web site for more information: http://www.ohio.edu/equity/disabilityservices/.

Application Information:
Send to Graduate Studies, Ohio University, 44 University Terrace, McKee House, Athens, OH 45701-2979. Application available online. URL of online application: http://www.ohio.edu/graduate/prospective_student_forms.cfm. Students are admitted in the Fall, application deadline January 1. *Fee:* $50. The fee is waived or deferred with a statement of need from the financial aid office of the applicant's college.

Toledo, University of

Department of Psychology
Arts and Science
Department of Psychology, The University of Toledo, MS#948
Toledo, OH 43606
Telephone: (419) 530-2717
Fax: (419) 530-8479
E-mail: *joseph.hovey@utoledo.edu*
Web: *http://www.utoledo.edu/psychology/*

Department Information:

1913. Chairperson: Joseph D. Hovey. Number of faculty: total—full-time 18; women—full-time 8; total—minority—full-time 3; women minority—full-time 1.

Programs and Degrees Offered:

Listed in the following order: Program area, degree type (T if terminal Master's), number awarded 7/06–6/07. Behavioral Science PhD (Doctor of Philosophy) 4, Clinical PhD (Doctor of Philosophy) 8.

APA Accreditation: Clinical PhD (Doctor of Philosophy).

Student Applications/Admissions:

Student Applications

Behavioral Science PhD (Doctor of Philosophy)—Applications 2007–2008, 45. Total applicants accepted 2007–2008, 6. Number full-time enrolled (new admits only) 2007–2008, 6. Number part-time enrolled (new admits only) 2007–2008, 0. Openings 2008–2009, 6. The median number of years required for completion of a degree in 2006–2007 were 5. The number of students enrolled full- and part-time who were dismissed or voluntarily withdrew from this program area in 2007–2008 were 1. *Clinical PhD (Doctor of Philosophy)*—Applications 2007–2008, 88. Total applicants accepted 2007–2008, 12. Number full-time enrolled (new admits only) 2007–2008, 9. Number part-time enrolled (new admits only) 2007–2008, 0. Openings 2008–2009, 6. The median number of years required for completion of a degree in 2006–2007 were 6. The number of students enrolled full- and part-time who were dismissed or voluntarily withdrew from this program area in 2007–2008 were 0.

Admissions Requirements:

Scores: Entries appear in this order: required test or GPA, minimum score (if required), median score of students entering in 2007–2008. Master's Programs: GRE-V no minimum stated; GRE-Q no minimum stated; GRE-Subject (Psychology) no minimum stated; overall undergraduate GPA no minimum stated; last 2 years GPA no minimum stated; psychology GPA no minimum stated; Masters GRE-Analytical no minimum stated. Doctoral Programs: GRE-V no minimum stated; GRE-Q no minimum stated; GRE-Subject (Psychology) no minimum stated; overall undergraduate GPA no minimum stated; last 2 years GPA no minimum stated; psychology GPA no minimum stated; Doctoral program GRE-Analytic no minimum stated.

Other Criteria: (importance of criteria rated low, medium, or high): GRE/MAT scores—high, research experience—high, work experience—medium, extracurricular activity—medium, clinically related public service—low, GPA—high, letters of recommendation—high, interview—medium, statement of goals and objectives—high, undergraduate major in psychology—medium. For additional information on admission requirements, go to http://www.utoledo.edu/psychology.

Student Characteristics: The following represents characteristics of students in 2007–2008 in all graduate psychology programs in the department: Female—full-time 39, part-time 0; Male—full-time 17, part-time 0; African American/Black—full-time 0, part-time 0; Hispanic/Latino(a)—full-time 1, part-time 0; Asian/Pacific Islander—full-time 4, part-time 0; American Indian/Alaska Native—full-time 0, part-time 0; Caucasian/White—full-time 51, part-time 0; Multi-ethnic—full-time 0, part-time 0; students subject to the Americans With Disabilities Act—full-time 0, part-time 0; Unknown ethnicity—full-time 0, part-time 0; International students who hold an F-1 or J-1 Visa—full-time 2, part-time 0.

Financial Information/Assistance:

Financial Assistance:

First-Year Students: Research assistantships available for first year. Average amount paid per academic year: $11,000. Average number of hours worked per week: 20. Tuition remission given: full.

Advanced Students: Teaching assistantships available for advanced students. Average amount paid per academic year: $11,000. Average number of hours worked per week: 20. Tuition remission given: full. Research assistantships available for advanced students. Average amount paid per academic year: $11,000. Average number of hours worked per week: 20. Tuition remission given: full. Traineeships available for advanced students. Average amount paid per academic year: $11,000. Average number of hours worked per week: 20. Tuition remission given: full.

Additional Information: Of all students currently enrolled full time, 100% benefited from one or more of the listed financial assistance programs. Application and information available online at http://www.utoledo.edu/psychology.

Internships/Practica: No information provided.

Housing and Day Care: On-campus housing is available. See the following Web site for more information: http://www.utoledo.edu. On-campus day care facilities are available.

Employment of Department Graduates:

Master's Degree Graduates: Of those who graduated in the academic year 2006–2007, the following categories and numbers represent the postgraduate activities and employment of master's degree graduates: Enrolled in a postdoctoral residency/fellowship (n/a), employed in independent practice (n/a), total from the above (master's) (0).

Doctoral Degree Graduates: Of those who graduated in the academic year 2006–2007, the following categories and numbers represent the postgraduate activities and employment of doctoral degree graduates: Enrolled in a psychology doctoral program (n/a), total from the above (doctoral) (0).

Additional Information:

Orientation, Objectives, and Emphasis of Department: Our department features an APA-accredited Clinical Psychology PhD program as well as a Behavioral Science PhD program, offering specializations in either Social Psychology, Developmental Psychology, Cognitive Psychology, and Behavioral Neuroscience and Learning. Although these programs differ in many respects, the purpose of both programs is to provide superior training in psychological research methods, statistical procedures, clinical practice, and theoretical comprehension. Our doctoral training emphasizes the inculcation of scientific attitudes with regard to (a) the gathering and evaluation of information, (b) the solving of basic and applied research problems, and in the clinical area, (c) clinical assessment and psychotherapy.

Special Facilities or Resources: http://www.utoledo.edu/psychology.

Information for Students With Physical Disabilities: See the following Web site for more information: http://www.student-services.utoledo.edu/accessibility/index.html.

Application Information:

Send to Graduate School, University of Toledo, Toledo, OH 43606. Application available online. URL of online application: http://www.utoledo.edu/psychology. Students are admitted in the Fall, application deadline January 15. *Fee:* $35.

Wright State University

Department of Psychology
College of Science and Mathematics
335 Fawcett Hall
3640 Colonel Glenn Highway
Dayton, OH 45435-0001
Telephone: (937) 775-3348
Fax: (937) 775-3347
E-mail: *john.flach@wright.edu*
Web: *http://www.psych.wright.edu*

Department Information:

1979. Chairperson: John M. Flach. Number of faculty: total—full-time 11, part-time 12; women—full-time 9, part-time 4; women minority—full-time 1; faculty subject to the Americans With Disabilities Act 1.

Programs and Degrees Offered:

Listed in the following order: Program area, degree type (T if terminal Master's), number awarded 7/06–6/07. Industrial/Organizational PhD (Doctor of Philosophy) 1, Human Factors PhD (Doctor of Philosophy) 0.

Student Applications/Admissions:

Student Applications

Industrial/Organizational PhD (Doctor of Philosophy)—Applications 2007–2008, 39. Total applicants accepted 2007–2008, 8. Number full-time enrolled (new admits only) 2007–2008, 4. Number part-time enrolled (new admits only) 2007–2008, 0. Openings 2008–2009, 5. The median number of years required for completion of a degree in 2006–2007 were 5. The number of students enrolled full- and part-time who were dismissed or voluntarily withdrew from this program area in 2007–2008 were 0. *Human Factors PhD (Doctor of Philosophy)*—Applications 2007–2008, 15. Total applicants accepted 2007–2008, 8. Number full-time enrolled (new admits only) 2007–2008, 3. Number part-time enrolled (new admits only) 2007–2008, 0. Total enrolled 2007–2008 full-time, 23, part-time, 6. Openings 2008–2009, 5. The number of students enrolled full- and part-time who were dismissed or voluntarily withdrew from this program area in 2007–2008 were 1.

Admissions Requirements:

Scores: Entries appear in this order: required test or GPA, minimum score (if required), median score of students entering in 2007–2008. Master's Programs: GRE-V 550; GRE-Q 550; overall undergraduate GPA 3.0, 3.29. To be competitive, V + Q GRE scores combined should be above 1100. Doctoral Programs: GRE-V 550; GRE-Q 550; overall undergraduate GPA 3.15, 3.49. To be competitive, V + Q GRE scores combined should be above 1100.

Other Criteria: (importance of criteria rated low, medium, or high): GRE/MAT scores—high, research experience—high, work experience—medium, extracurricular activity—low, GPA—high, letters of recommendation—high, interview—medium, statement of goals and objectives—high. For additional information on admission requirements, go to http://www.psych.wright.edu.

Student Characteristics: The following represents characteristics of students in 2007–2008 in all graduate psychology programs in the department: Female—full-time 18, part-time 3; Male—full-time 21, part-time 3; African American/Black—full-time 1, part-time 0; Hispanic/Latino(a)—full-time 3, part-time 0; Asian/Pacific Islander—full-time 6, part-time 0; American Indian/Alaska Native—full-time 1, part-time 0; Caucasian/White—full-time 28, part-time 6; Multi-ethnic—full-time 0, part-time 0; students subject to the Americans With Disabilities Act—full-time 1, part-time 0; Unknown ethnicity—full-time 0, part-time 0.

Financial Information/Assistance:

Tuition for Full-Time Study: *Master's:* State residents: per academic year $3,240, $298 per credit hour; Nonstate residents: per academic year $5,482, $507 per credit hour. *Doctoral:* State residents: per academic year $3,240, $298 per credit hour; Nonstate residents: per academic year $5,482, $507 per credit hour. Tuition is subject to change.

Financial Assistance:

First-Year Students: Teaching assistantships available for first year. Average amount paid per academic year: $12,648. Average number of hours worked per week: 20. Apply by January 1. Tuition remission given: full. Research assistantships available for first year. Average amount paid per academic year: $12,648. Average number of hours worked per week: 20. Apply by January 1. Tuition remission given: full. Fellowships and scholarships available for first year. Average amount paid per academic year: $13,000. Average number of hours worked per week: 20. Apply by January 1. Tuition remission given: full.

Advanced Students: Teaching assistantships available for advanced students. Average amount paid per academic year: $12,648. Average number of hours worked per week: 20. Apply by January 1. Tuition remission given: full. Research assistantships available for advanced students. Average amount paid per academic year: $12,648. Average number of hours worked per week: 20. Apply by January 1. Tuition remission given: full.

Additional Information: Of all students currently enrolled full time, 100% benefited from one or more of the listed financial assistance programs.

Internships/Practica: Students participate in internships and practice with local businesses and Wright Patterson Air Force Base. Students working at the Base can receive support.

Housing and Day Care: No on-campus housing is available. On-campus day care facilities are available. Contact Mini University, Inc., (937) 775-4070.

Employment of Department Graduates:

Master's Degree Graduates: Of those who graduated in the academic year 2006–2007, the following categories and numbers represent the postgraduate activities and employment of master's degree graduates: Enrolled in a psychology doctoral program (7), enrolled in another graduate/professional program (0), enrolled in a postdoctoral residency/fellowship (n/a), employed in independent practice (n/a), employed in an academic position at a university (0), employed in an academic position at a 2-year/4-year college (0), employed in other positions at a higher education institution (0), employed in a professional position in a school system (0), employed in business or industry (0), employed in government agency (0), employed in a community mental health/counseling center (0), employed in a hospital/medical center (0), still seeking employment (0), other employment position (0), total from the above (master's) (7).

Doctoral Degree Graduates: Of those who graduated in the academic year 2006–2007, the following categories and numbers represent the postgraduate activities and employment of doctoral degree graduates: Enrolled in a psychology doctoral program (n/a), enrolled in a postdoctoral residency/fellowship (0), employed in independent practice (0), employed in an academic position at a university (0), employed in an academic position at a 2-year/4-year college (0), employed in other positions at a higher education institution (0), employed in a professional position in a school system (0), employed in business or industry (1), employed in government agency (0), employed in a community mental health/counseling center (0), employed in a hospital/medical center (0), still seeking employment (0), other employment position (0), total from the above (doctoral) (1).

Additional Information:

Orientation, Objectives, and Emphasis of Department: The department offers MS and PhD degrees in Human Factors and Industrial/Organizational Psychology. Students specialize in one of these areas, but the program is designed to foster an understanding of both areas and the importance of considering both aspects in the design of industrial, aerospace, health care, or other systems. The program prepares students for careers in research, teaching, design and practice in government, consulting, business, or industry. It includes course work, research training, and experience with system design and applications. Students work closely with faculty beginning early in the program. Human Factors, including cognitive engineering, deals with the characteristics of human beings that are applicable to the design of systems and devices of all kinds, whereas Industrial/Organizational deals with individual or group behaviors in work settings (macrosystem variables). The department has a critical mass of students and faculty in these areas and is unique because its focus on applied psychology does not include students in Clinical Psychology. Both majors are strengthened by being located in the Dayton, Ohio metropolitan region, which is a rapidly developing high-technology sector, a major human factors and cognitive engineering research and development center, and a region of considerable industrial and corporate strength.

Special Facilities or Resources: The Department of Psychology has modern state-of-the-art research laboratories, well-equipped teaching laboratories, and office space for faculty and graduate assistants. Specialized equipment in dedicated research laboratories supports research on sensory processes, motor control, spatial orientation, human computer interaction and display design, flight simulation, cultural cognition, naturalistic decision making, memory, aging, expertise, teamwork, assessment, training, and stress in the workplace. In addition, faculty and student share a number of individual and group testing rooms. Computer facilities include over 350 UNIX workstations, PCs, and Macintoshes. The department works cooperatively with research laboratories, research and development organizations, and corporations in the region. These include facilities for virtual environment generation, including 3D visual displays, 3D auditory displays, and tactile–haptic displays. The Virtual Environment Research, Interactive Technology, and Simulation (VERITAS) facility, which is owned and operated by Wright State University but housed at Wright Patterson Air Force Base, is unique in the world. The facility includes a room-size display that surrounds the user with interactive 3D auditory and visual images. The Department of Psychology has a Memorandum of Agreement with the U.S. Air Force Research Laboratory that facilitates utilization of its sophisticated behavioral laboratories such as flight simulators and the Auditory Localization Facility. The Air Force Research Laboratory supports multination research on complex cognition. The department has two well-equipped laboratories for the study of the performance and training for complex team tasks.

Information for Students With Physical Disabilities: Contact the Director of Office of Disability Services for more information: jeff.vernooy@wright.edu.

Application Information:

Send to School of Graduate Studies, Wright State University, E344 Student Union, 3640 Colonel Glenn Highway, Dayton, OH 45435-0001. Application available online. URL of online application: http://www.sogs.wright.edu. Students are admitted in the Fall, application deadline January 1. Send three letters of recommendation on letterhead (no form required) to the School of Graduate Studies at the address listed above. *Fee:* $25.

Wright State University

School of Professional Psychology
3640 Colonel Glenn Highway
Dayton, OH 45435
Telephone: (937) 775-3490
Fax: (937) 775-3434
E-mail: *eve.wolf@wright.edu*
Web: *http://www.wright.edu/sopp/*

Department Information:

1979. Interim Dean: La Pearl Logan Winfrey, PhD. Number of faculty: total—full-time 17, part-time 8; women—full-time 9, part-time 6; total—minority—full-time 4; women minority—full-time 2; faculty subject to the Americans With Disabilities Act 1.

Programs and Degrees Offered:

Listed in the following order: Program area, degree type (T if terminal Master's), number awarded 7/06–6/07. Clinical PsyD (Doctor of Psychology) 29.

APA Accreditation: Clinical PsyD (Doctor of Psychology).

Student Applications/Admissions:

Student Applications

Clinical PsyD (Doctor of Psychology)—Applications 2007–2008, 155. Total applicants accepted 2007–2008, 31. Number full-time enrolled (new admits only) 2007–2008, 29. Number part-time enrolled (new admits only) 2007–2008, 0. Openings 2008–2009, 29. The median number of years required for completion of a degree in 2006–2007 were 5. The number of students enrolled full- and part-time who were dismissed or voluntarily withdrew from this program area in 2007–2008 were 4.

Admissions Requirements:

Scores: Entries appear in this order: required test or GPA, minimum score (if required), median score of students entering in 2007–2008. Doctoral Programs: GRE-V 500, 498; GRE-Q 500, 553; GRE-Subject (Psychology) 500, 600; overall undergraduate GPA 3.0, 3.6.

Other Criteria: (importance of criteria rated low, medium, or high): GRE/MAT scores—medium, research experience—low, work experience—medium, extracurricular activity—medium, clinically related public service—high, GPA—high, letters of recommendation—high, interview—high, statement of goals and objectives—high, Resume—high, undergraduate major in psychology—medium. For additional information on admission requirements, go to http://www.wright.edu/sopp.

Student Characteristics: The following represents characteristics of students in 2007–2008 in all graduate psychology programs in the department: Female—full-time 93, part-time 0; Male—

full-time 31, part-time 0; African American/Black—full-time 20, part-time 0; Hispanic/Latino(a)—full-time 7, part-time 0; Asian/ Pacific Islander—full-time 8, part-time 0; American Indian/ Alaska Native—full-time 0, part-time 0; Caucasian/White—full-time 87, part-time 0; Multi-ethnic—full-time 2, part-time 0; students subject to the Americans With Disabilities Act—full-time 4, part-time 0; Unknown ethnicity—full-time 0, part-time 0; International students who hold an F-1 or J-1 Visa—full-time 7, part-time 0.

Financial Information/Assistance:

Tuition for Full-Time Study: *Doctoral:* State residents: per academic year $15,746, $379 per credit hour; Nonstate residents: per academic year $25,072, $591 per credit hour. Tuition is subject to change.

Financial Assistance:

First-Year Students: Fellowships and scholarships available for first year. Average amount paid per academic year: $9,540. Tuition remission given: full and partial.

Advanced Students: Traineeships available for advanced students. Average amount paid per academic year: $7,000. Average number of hours worked per week: 16. Fellowships and scholarships available for advanced students. Average amount paid per academic year: $11,996. Average number of hours worked per week: 0. Tuition remission given: partial.

Additional Information: Of all students currently enrolled full time, 100% benefited from one or more of the listed financial assistance programs.

Internships/Practica: Doctoral Degree (PsyD clinical): For those doctoral students for whom a professional internship was required in this program prior to graduation, (22) students applied for an internship in 2006–2007, with (21) students obtaining an internship. Of those students who obtained an internship, (21) were paid internships. Of those students who obtained an internship, (18) students placed in APA/CPA-accredited internships, (2) students placed in internships not APA/CPA-accredited, but listed with the Association of Psychology Postdoctoral and Internship Centers (APPIC), (0) students placed in internships conforming to guidelines of the Council of Directors of School Psychology Programs (CDSPP), (1) students placed in internships that were not APA/CPA-accredited, APPIC or CDSPP listed. During years 2, 3, and 4 of the doctoral program, students are assigned to year-long practicum placements for 2 days (16–20 hours) per week. Most practicum placements are paid positions, at an average rate of $7,000 per year. Approximately half the practicum placements are in the two clinical–teaching facilities operated by the school. These include the Center for Psychological Services on WSU's campus, which provides psychological services for the university's student body, and the Ellis Institute, which is located in an urban, predominately African American section of the city and which provides a broad range of psychological services and special treatment programs developed in response to the needs of the Dayton community. The remaining practicum placements are located in a broad array of service settings located primarily in the Dayton and Cincinnati areas. These practicum settings include public agencies, correctional settings, hospitals, health and mental health clinics, and a number of private practices of area psychologists. For additional information on education and training outcomes for our programs, see the following Web site: http://www.wright.edu/sopp.

Housing and Day Care: On-campus housing is available. See the following Web site for more information: http://www.wright.edu/ students/housing. On-campus day care facilities are available. See the following Web site for more information: http://www. miniuniversity.net/Wright-State-University.asp.

Employment of Department Graduates:

Master's Degree Graduates: Of those who graduated in the academic year 2006–2007, the following categories and numbers represent the postgraduate activities and employment of master's degree graduates: Enrolled in a postdoctoral residency/fellowship (n/a), employed in independent practice (n/a), total from the above (master's) (0).

Doctoral Degree Graduates: Of those who graduated in the academic year 2006–2007, the following categories and numbers represent the postgraduate activities and employment of doctoral degree graduates: Enrolled in a psychology doctoral program (n/a), enrolled in another graduate/professional program (0), enrolled in a postdoctoral residency/fellowship (10), employed in independent practice (7), employed in an academic position at a university (0), employed in an academic position at a 2-year/4-year college (0), employed in other positions at a higher education institution (3), employed in a professional position in a school system (0), employed in business or industry (0), employed in government agency (3), employed in a community mental health/counseling center (2), employed in a hospital/medical center (2), still seeking employment (2), other employment position (0), do not know (0), total from the above (doctoral) (29).

Additional Information:

Orientation, Objectives, and Emphasis of Department: The School of Professional Psychology is committed to a practitioner model of professional education that educates students at the doctoral level for the eclectic, general practice of psychology. As a part of its educational mission, the school emphasizes cultural and other aspects of diversity in the composition of its student body, faculty, and curriculum. The curriculum is organized around six core competency areas that are fundamental to the practice of psychology currently and in the future, including research and evaluation, assessment, intervention, management and supervision, and consultation and education. In years 1 and 2 the curriculum is designed around foundation coursework and the development of basic competencies. Years 3 and 4 are devoted to the development of advanced competency levels.

Special Facilities or Resources: The program operates two large clinical service centers that are designed to accommodate academic teaching, clinical training, clinical program development, and research. The Psychology Service Center is located in an outpatient health care facility on the university's campus. This service center provides assessment and group and individual therapy services to the university student body, which numbers approximately 15,000. Opportunities are available for trainees to participate in crisis intervention, prevention programs, outreach to residence halls, and multidisciplinary training with medical and nursing students. The second service center, the Ellis Institute, is located in an urban, primarily African American section of Dayton. The Ellis Institute provides assessment and group and individual therapy to children, adolescents, and adults form the Dayton community. Several special treatment programs provide unique opportunities for trainees. These include violence prevention programs for minority adolescents, treatment programs addressing perpetrators and victims of domestic violence, anxiety and depression in children, mental health needs of deaf individuals, and the needs of clients and families of people with HIV/AIDS and herpes. Both service centers house classrooms, trainee and faculty offices, and computers for student use in research and training activities, and both facilities are equipped with state-of-the-art equipment for videotaped and live clinical supervision.

Information for Students With Physical Disabilities: See the following Web site for more information: http://www.wright.edu/students/dis_services/.

Application Information:
Send to Office of Admissions/Alumni Relations, 110 Health Sciences Building, Wright State University, Dayton, OH 45435. Application available online. URL of online application: http://www.wright.edu/sopp. Students are admitted in the Fall, application deadline January 15. *Fee:* $50. Application fee can be waived if applicant provides data of financial hardship.

Xavier University

Department of Psychology
College of Social Sciences, Health and Education
Elet Hall
Cincinnati, OH 45207-6511
Telephone: (513) 745-3533
Fax: (513) 745-3327
E-mail: *dacey@xavier.edu*
Web: *http://www.xu.edu*

Department Information:
1962. Chairperson: Christine M. Dacey, PhD, ABPP. Number of faculty: total—full-time 16, part-time 10; women—full-time 8, part-time 5; total—minority—full-time 2, part-time 1; women minority—full-time 2, part-time 1.

Programs and Degrees Offered:
Listed in the following order: Program area, degree type (T if terminal Master's), number awarded 7/06–6/07. Clinical PsyD (Doctor of Psychology) 15, Experimental MA/MS (Master of Arts/Science) (T) 0, Industrial/Organizational MA/MS (Master of Arts/Science) (T) 15.

APA Accreditation: Clinical PsyD (Doctor of Psychology).

Student Applications/Admissions:
Student Applications
Clinical PsyD (Doctor of Psychology)—Applications 2007–2008, 187. Total applicants accepted 2007–2008, 35. Number full-time enrolled (new admits only) 2007–2008, 17. Number part-time enrolled (new admits only) 2007–2008, 0. Total enrolled 2007–2008 full-time, 79, part-time, 13. Openings 2008–2009, 16. The median number of years required for completion of a degree in 2006–2007 were 5. The number of students enrolled full- and part-time who were dismissed or voluntarily withdrew from this program area in 2007–2008 were 5. *Experimental MA/MS (Master of Arts/Science)*—Applications 2007–2008, 11. Total applicants accepted 2007–2008, 1. Number full-time enrolled (new admits only) 2007–2008, 1. Number part-time enrolled (new admits only) 2007–2008, 0. The number of students enrolled full- and part-time who were dismissed or voluntarily withdrew from this program area in 2007–2008 were 0. *Industrial/Organizational MA/MS (Master of Arts/Science)*—Applications 2007–2008, 46. Total applicants accepted 2007–2008, 31. Number full-time enrolled (new admits only) 2007–2008, 10. Number part-time enrolled (new admits only) 2007–2008, 0. Total enrolled 2007–2008 full-time, 16, part-time, 1. Openings 2008–2009, 10. The median number of years required for completion of a degree in 2006–2007 were 4. The number of students enrolled full- and part-time who were dismissed or voluntarily withdrew from this program area in 2007–2008 were 0.

Admissions Requirements:
Scores: Entries appear in this order: required test or GPA, minimum score (if required), median score of students entering in 2007–2008. Master's Programs: GRE-V no minimum stated; GRE-Q no minimum stated; GRE-Subject (Psychology) no minimum stated; overall undergraduate GPA 3.0; psychology GPA 3.0; Masters GRE-Analytical no minimum stated. GRE-Subject (Psychology) is required of those without psychology as their undergraduate major or minor; 18 hours of psychology courses with statistics and research methods required of those without psychology as major/degree. A Test and Measurement course is required for PsyD and MA program. An Industrial/Organizational psychology course is required for the MA in I/O program. Doctoral Programs: GRE-V no minimum stated; GRE-Q no minimum stated; overall undergraduate GPA 3.0; psychology GPA 3.0; Doctoral program GRE-Analytic no minimum stated. The GRE-Subject is required of those without psychology as their undergraduate major or minor; 18 semester hours of psychology courses with statistics and research methods required of those without psychology as major/degree. A Test and Measurement course is required for PsyD program.
Other Criteria: (importance of criteria rated low, medium, or high): GRE/MAT scores—high, research experience—medium, work experience—medium, extracurricular activity—low, clinically related public service—medium, GPA—high, letters of recommendation—high, interview—low, statement of goals and objectives—high. For additional information on admission requirements, go to http://www.xu.edu/psychology.

Student Characteristics: The following represents characteristics of students in 2007–2008 in all graduate psychology programs in the department: Female—full-time 70, part-time 12; Male—full-time 26, part-time 2; African American/Black—full-time 4, part-time 0; Hispanic/Latino(a)—full-time 0, part-time 0; Asian/Pacific Islander—full-time 4, part-time 0; American Indian/Alaska Native—full-time 0, part-time 0; Caucasian/White—full-time 87, part-time 14; Multi-ethnic—full-time 0, part-time 0; students subject to the Americans With Disabilities Act—full-time 1, part-time 0; Unknown ethnicity—full-time 1, part-time 0; International students who hold an F-1 or J-1 Visa—full-time 2, part-time 0.

Financial Information/Assistance:
Tuition for Full-Time Study: *Master's:* State residents: $555 per credit hour; Nonstate residents: $555 per credit hour. *Doctoral:* State residents: $690 per credit hour; Nonstate residents: $690

per credit hour. Additional fees are assessed to students beyond the costs of tuition for the following: assessment course materials, diversity course fee, APAGS dues. Tuition costs vary by program.

Financial Assistance:

First-Year Students: Teaching assistantships available for first year. Average number of hours worked per week: 20. Apply by January 15. Tuition remission given: partial. Research assistantships available for first year. Average number of hours worked per week: 10. Apply by January 15. Tuition remission given: partial. Fellowships and scholarships available for first year. Apply by January 15. Tuition remission given: partial.

Advanced Students: Teaching assistantships available for advanced students. Average number of hours worked per week: 10. Apply by March 1. Tuition remission given: partial. Traineeships available for advanced students. Apply by March 1. Tuition remission given: partial. Fellowships and scholarships available for advanced students. Apply by March 1. Tuition remission given: partial.

Additional Information: Of all students currently enrolled full time, 56% benefited from one or more of the listed financial assistance programs. Application and information available online at http://www.xu.edu/psychology.

Internships/Practica: Doctoral Degree (PsyD Clinical): For those doctoral students for whom a professional internship was required in this program prior to graduation, (16) students applied for an internship in 2006–2007, with (14) students obtaining an internship. Of those students who obtained an internship, (14) were paid internships. Of those students who obtained an internship, (10) students placed in APA/CPA-accredited internships, (0) students placed in internships not APA/CPA-accredited, but listed with the Association of Psychology Postdoctoral and Internship Centers (APPIC), (0) students placed in internships conforming to guidelines of the Council of Directors of School Psychology Programs (CDSPP), (4) students placed in internships that were not APA/CPA-accredited, APPIC or CDSPP listed. In an urban setting, the university has established relationships with a number of private and public agencies, businesses, hospitals, and mental health care centers. PsyD students are given the opportunity to work with underserved populations within the three areas of interest in our PsyD program—child/adolescent, older adults, and severe mental illness.

Housing and Day Care: No on-campus housing is available. No on-campus day care facilities are available.

Employment of Department Graduates:

Master's Degree Graduates: Of those who graduated in the academic year 2006–2007, the following categories and numbers represent the postgraduate activities and employment of master's degree graduates: Enrolled in a postdoctoral residency/fellowship (n/a), employed in independent practice (n/a), total from the above (master's) (0).

Doctoral Degree Graduates: Of those who graduated in the academic year 2006–2007, the following categories and numbers represent the postgraduate activities and employment of doctoral degree graduates: Enrolled in a psychology doctoral program (n/a), enrolled in a postdoctoral residency/fellowship (8), employed in independent practice (0), employed in an academic position at a university (0), employed in an academic position at a 2-year/4-year college (0), employed in other positions at a higher education institution (2), employed in a professional position in a school system (0), employed in business or industry (0), employed in government agency (0), employed in a community mental health/counseling center (0), employed in a hospital/medical center (4), still seeking employment (0), not seeking employment (0), other employment position (1), do not know (0), total from the above (doctoral) (15).

Additional Information:

Orientation, Objectives, and Emphasis of Department: Both the master's and doctoral programs provide students with the knowledge and range of skills necessary to provide psychological services in today's changing professional climate. Our objective for master's students is to prepare them for immediate employment or entry into a doctoral program in their field. Our objective for the doctoral program is to prepare students to serve as clinical psychologists in their communities. The basic philosophy of the PsyD program is to educate skilled practitioners who have a solid appreciation of the role of science in all aspects of professional activity. It is based on a practitioner–scientist model of training.

Special Facilities or Resources: The department has affiliation with the Psychological Services Center on campus, which provides psychological services to both the university population and the Greater Cincinnati community. The Center provides the opportunity for training, service, and research. There are opportunities to work in various other areas (e.g., student development) in the university. The department also has established contact with care providers in the community, which provides the opportunity to learn the delivery of service and research that occurs in such organizations.

Information for Students With Physical Disabilities: See the following Web site for more information: http://www.xu.edu/lac.

Application Information:

Send to Margaret Maybury, Assistant Director, Enrollment and Student Services, Psychology Department, Xavier University, 3800 Victory Parkway, Cincinnati, OH 45207-6511. Application available online. URL of online application: http://www.xu.edu/psychology. Students are admitted in the Fall, application deadline January 15 for PsyD. Febraury 1 deadline for master's applicants. *Fee:* $35.

Central Oklahoma, University of

Department of Psychology
100 North University Drive
Edmond, OK 73034
Telephone: (405) 974-5707
Fax: (405) 974-3822
E-mail: *mknight@ucok.edu*

Department Information:

1968. Chairperson: Mike Knight. Number of faculty: total—full-time 13, part-time 5; women—full-time 7, part-time 4; total—minority—full-time 1; women minority—full-time 1; faculty subject to the Americans With Disabilities Act 13.

Programs and Degrees Offered:

Listed in the following order: Program area, degree type (T if terminal Master's), number awarded 7/06–6/07. Counseling Psychology MA/MS (Master of Arts/Science) (T) 38, General Psychology MA/MS (Master of Arts/Science) (T) 12, Experimental Psychology MA/MS (Master of Arts/Science) 6.

Student Applications/Admissions:

Student Applications

Counseling Psychology MA/MS (Master of Arts/Science)—Applications 2007–2008, 88. Total applicants accepted 2007–2008, 85. Total enrolled 2007–2008 full-time, 88, part-time, 23. Openings 2008–2009, 25. The median number of years required for completion of a degree in 2006–2007 were 2. The number of students enrolled full- and part-time who were dismissed or voluntarily withdrew from this program area in 2007–2008 were 22. *General Psychology MA/MS (Master of Arts/Science)*—Applications 2007–2008, 30. Total applicants accepted 2007–2008, 30. Total enrolled 2007–2008 full-time, 20, part-time, 10. Openings 2008–2009, 25. The median number of years required for completion of a degree in 2006–2007 were 2. The number of students enrolled full- and part-time who were dismissed or voluntarily withdrew from this program area in 2007–2008 were 0. *Experimental Psychology MA/MS (Master of Arts/Science)*—Applications 2007–2008, 28. Total applicants accepted 2007–2008, 22. Total enrolled 2007–2008 full-time, 20, part-time, 10. Openings 2008–2009, 10. The median number of years required for completion of a degree in 2006–2007 were 2. The number of students enrolled full- and part-time who were dismissed or voluntarily withdrew from this program area in 2007–2008 were 5.

Admissions Requirements:

Scores: Entries appear in this order: required test or GPA, minimum score (if required), median score of students entering in 2007–2008. Master's Programs: GRE-V no minimum stated; GRE-Q no minimum stated; overall undergraduate GPA 2.5; last 2 years GPA 2.75. Attain a combined score of 900 on Verbal + Quantitative, or a 3.5 on the GRE Written Test.

Other Criteria: (importance of criteria rated low, medium, or high): GRE/MAT scores—medium, research experience—high, work experience—medium, extracurricular activity—medium, clinically related public service—high, letters of recommendation—high.

Student Characteristics: The following represents characteristics of students in 2007–2008 in all graduate psychology programs in the department: Female—full-time 54, part-time 10; Male—full-time 24, part-time 6; African American/Black—full-time 18, part-time 4; Hispanic/Latino(a)—full-time 9, part-time 1; Asian/Pacific Islander—full-time 7, part-time 0; American Indian/Alaska Native—full-time 6, part-time 0; Caucasian/White—full-time 81, part-time 0; Multi-ethnic—part-time 36; students subject to the Americans With Disabilities Act—full-time 7, part-time 3; Unknown ethnicity—full-time 0, part-time 0.

Financial Information/Assistance:

Tuition for Full-Time Study: *Master's:* State residents: $88 per credit hour; Nonstate residents: $207 per credit hour.

Financial Assistance:

First-Year Students: No information provided.

Advanced Students: No information provided.

Additional Information: Of all students currently enrolled full time, 0% benefited from one or more of the listed financial assistance programs.

Internships/Practica: Practicum and internships are available through our program in Counseling Psychology. Students initially work in our departmental clinic and then are placed off-campus in community mental health clinics in our area.

Housing and Day Care: No on-campus housing is available. No on-campus day care facilities are available.

Employment of Department Graduates:

Master's Degree Graduates: Of those who graduated in the academic year 2006–2007, the following categories and numbers represent the postgraduate activities and employment of master's degree graduates: Enrolled in a postdoctoral residency/fellowship (n/a), employed in independent practice (n/a), total from the above (master's) (0).

Doctoral Degree Graduates: Of those who graduated in the academic year 2006–2007, the following categories and numbers represent the postgraduate activities and employment of doctoral degree graduates: Enrolled in a psychology doctoral program (n/a), total from the above (doctoral) (0).

Additional Information:

Orientation, Objectives, and Emphasis of Department: Excellent training to pursue doctoral work. General Experimental option or Licensed Professional Counselor (LPC), or Licensed Behavioral Practitioner (LPB) Counseling Psychology option.

Special Facilities or Resources: The department has excellent computer facilities. It also has excellent clinic facilities with audio and visual equipment to train students in community counseling.

Application Information:

Send to Dean of the Graduate College, 100 North University Drive, University of Central Oklahoma, Edmund, OK 73034. Students are admitted in the Fall, application deadline November 1; Spring, application deadline March 1. These deadlines are for the Counseling option only. Experimental and General are open enrollment. *Fee:* $0.

East Central University (2007 data)

Department of Psychology
1100 East 14th Street
Ada, OK 74820-6999
Telephone: (580) 332-8000
Fax: (580) 310-5317
E-mail: *chart@mailclerk.ecok.edu*
Web: *http://www.ecok.edu*

Department Information:

1965. Chairperson: Chris Hart. Number of faculty: total—full-time 6, part-time 5; women—full-time 1, part-time 3.

Programs and Degrees Offered:

Listed in the following order: Program area, degree type (T if terminal Master's), number awarded 7/06–6/07. Psychological Services MA/MS (Master of Arts/Science) (T).

Student Applications/Admissions:

Student Applications

Psychological Services MA/MS (Master of Arts/Science)

Other Criteria: (importance of criteria rated low, medium, or high): GRE/MAT scores—medium, research experience—medium, work experience—medium, extracurricular activity—medium, clinically related public service—medium, GPA—medium, letters of recommendation—medium, interview—medium, statement of goals and objectives—medium.

Student Characteristics: The following represents characteristics of students in 2007–2008 in all graduate psychology programs in the department: Female—full-time 10, part-time 3; Male—full-time 7, part-time 2; Asian/Pacific Islander—full-time 1, part-time 0; American Indian/Alaska Native—full-time 1, part-time 1; Caucasian/White—full-time 7, part-time 6; Unknown ethnicity—full-time 0, part-time 0.

Financial Information/Assistance:

Tuition for Full-Time Study: *Master's:* State residents: per academic year $2,010, $85 per credit hour; Nonstate residents: per academic year $3,370, $155 per credit hour. Tuition is subject to change. See the following Web site for updates and changes in tuition costs: http://www.ecok.edu.

Financial Assistance:

First-Year Students: Teaching assistantships available for first year. Average number of hours worked per week: 20. Traineeships available for first year.

Advanced Students: Teaching assistantships available for advanced students. Average amount paid per academic year: $2,700. Average number of hours worked per week: 10. Traineeships available for advanced students. Average amount paid per academic year: $2,700. Average number of hours worked per week: 10. Fellowships and scholarships available for advanced students.

Additional Information: Of all students currently enrolled full time, 7% benefited from one or more of the listed financial assistance programs.

Internships/Practica: Students are assisted in obtaining practicum sites. They also have the option of locating their own sites. Several local sites are available at community mental health centers, counseling centers, and private psychiatric hospitals.

Housing and Day Care: On-campus housing is available. See the following Web site for more information: http://www.ecok.edu. On-campus day care facilities are available.

Employment of Department Graduates:

Master's Degree Graduates: Of those who graduated in the academic year 2006–2007, the following categories and numbers represent the postgraduate activities and employment of master's degree graduates: Enrolled in a psychology doctoral program (1), enrolled in a postdoctoral residency/fellowship (n/a), employed in independent practice (n/a), employed in a professional position in a school system (1), employed in business or industry (2), employed in a community mental health/counseling center (2), do not know (2), total from the above (master's) (9).

Doctoral Degree Graduates: Of those who graduated in the academic year 2006–2007, the following categories and numbers represent the postgraduate activities and employment of doctoral degree graduates: Enrolled in a psychology doctoral program (n/a), total from the above (doctoral) (0).

Additional Information:

Orientation, Objectives, and Emphasis of Department: Emphasis is on graduate training designed for individuals interested in acquiring or upgrading their skills and providing psychological services to a variety of client populations. This program has been designated as a Master of Science in psychological services. This is an innovative program covering areas of study traditionally included in master's-level programs in clinical psychology, mental health specialist, and community psychology. The program of study includes a balanced combination of required academic work and supervised practical experience to prepare the student to provide the psychological services of counseling, consulting, and testing. This graduate program in psychological services is being expanded to 60 semester hours, 12 of which are for practicum experience. A student also has an option of writing a thesis in lieu of 6 hours of practicum. Training is provided in psycholgical assessment and evaluation, theory and research, techniques of counseling and behavior change, and community consultation. The 60-hour program will allow students to meet all the core course requirements for Oklahoma licensing as either a Licensed Professional Counselor or a Licensed Behavioral Practitioner.

Special Facilities or Resources: Practicum students are expected to locate their own practicum sites, however, there are several local mental health facilities that accommodate students including a community mental health center, a psychiatric hospital, and several counseling centers. Classes are held in a central location adjacent to faculty offices and training facilities. Small classes ensure close interaction between students and faculty.

Application Information:

Send to Dr. Alvin Turner, Dean, School fo Graduate Studies, 1100 East 14th Street, East Central University, Ada, OK 74820-6999. Students are admitted in the Fall. Programs have rolling admissions. *Fee:* $0.

Oklahoma State University

Department of Psychology
Arts and Sciences
116 North Murray Hall
Stillwater, OK 74078-3064
Telephone: (405) 744-6027
Fax: (405) 744-8067
E-mail: *maureen.sullivan@okstate.edu*
Web: *http://www.psychology.okstate.edu*

Department Information:

1920. Head: Maureen A. Sullivan. Number of faculty: total—full-time 18, part-time 1; women—full-time 8, part-time 1; total—minority—full-time 3, part-time 1; women minority—full-time 1, part-time 1.

Programs and Degrees Offered:

Listed in the following order: Program area, degree type (T if terminal Master's), number awarded 7/06–6/07. Clinical PhD (Doctor of Philosophy) 8, Life-Span Developmental PhD (Doctor of Philosophy) 1.

APA Accreditation: Clinical PhD (Doctor of Philosophy).

Student Applications/Admissions:

Student Applications

Clinical PhD (Doctor of Philosophy)—Applications 2007–2008, 118. Total applicants accepted 2007–2008, 5. Number full-time enrolled (new admits only) 2007–2008, 5. Number part-time enrolled (new admits only) 2007–2008, 0. Openings 2008–2009, 5. The median number of years required for completion of a degree in 2006–2007 were 5. The number of students enrolled full- and part-time who were dismissed or voluntarily withdrew from this program area in 2007–2008 were 2. *Life-Span Developmental PhD (Doctor of Philosophy)*—Applications 2007–2008, 25. Total applicants accepted 2007–2008, 6. Number full-time enrolled (new admits only) 2007–2008, 6. Number part-time enrolled (new admits only) 2007–2008, 0. Openings 2008–2009, 5. The median number of years required for completion of a degree in 2006–2007 were 5. The number of students enrolled full- and part-time who were dismissed or voluntarily withdrew from this program area in 2007–2008 were 3.

Admissions Requirements:

Scores: Entries appear in this order: required test or GPA, minimum score (if required), median score of students entering in 2007–2008. Master's Programs: GRE-V no minimum stated; GRE-Q no minimum stated; overall undergraduate GPA no minimum stated; last 2 years GPA no minimum stated; psychology GPA no minimum stated. No terminal masters program. Doctoral Programs: GRE-V no minimum stated, 500; GRE-Q no minimum stated, 600; overall undergraduate GPA no minimum stated, 3.5; last 2 years GPA no minimum stated, 3.73; psychology GPA no minimum stated, 3.7.

Other Criteria: (importance of criteria rated low, medium, or high): GRE/MAT scores—high, research experience—high, work experience—low, extracurricular activity—low, clinically related public service—low, GPA—high, letters of recommendation—high, interview—high, statement of goals and objectives—high. For additional information on admission requirements, go to http://psychology.okstate.edu/grad/index.html#app.

Student Characteristics: The following represents characteristics of students in 2007–2008 in all graduate psychology programs in the department: Female—full-time 43, part-time 0; Male—full-time 20, part-time 0; African American/Black—full-time 2, part-time 0; Hispanic/Latino(a)—full-time 8, part-time 0; Asian/Pacific Islander—full-time 3, part-time 0; American Indian/Alaska Native—full-time 8, part-time 0; Caucasian/White—full-time 41, part-time 0; Multi-ethnic—full-time 0, part-time 0; students subject to the Americans With Disabilities Act—full-time 1, part-time 0; Unknown ethnicity—full-time 1, part-time 0; International students who hold an F-1 or J-1 Visa—full-time 2, part-time 0.

Financial Information/Assistance:

Tuition for Full-Time Study: *Master's:* State residents: $148 per credit hour; Nonstate residents: $554 per credit hour. *Doctoral:* State residents: $148 per credit hour; Nonstate residents: $554 per credit hour. Tuition is subject to change. See the following Web site for updates and changes in tuition costs: http://www.bursar.okstate.edu/tuitionestimate.asp.

Financial Assistance:

First-Year Students: Teaching assistantships available for first year. Average amount paid per academic year: $9,801. Average number of hours worked per week: 20. Tuition remission given: partial. Traineeships available for first year. Average amount paid per academic year: $12,540. Average number of hours worked per week: 20. Tuition remission given: full. Fellowships and scholarships available for first year. Average amount paid per academic year: $2,500. Average number of hours worked per week: 0.

Advanced Students: Teaching assistantships available for advanced students. Average amount paid per academic year: $11,276. Average number of hours worked per week: 20. Tuition remission given: partial. Research assistantships available for advanced students. Tuition remission given: partial. Traineeships available for advanced students. Average amount paid per academic year: $12,540. Average number of hours worked per week: 20. Tuition remission given: full. Fellowships and scholarships available for advanced students. Average amount paid per academic year: $2,500. Average number of hours worked per week: 0.

Additional Information: Of all students currently enrolled full time, 100% benefited from one or more of the listed financial assistance programs. Application and information available online at http://psychology.okstate.edu/grad/index.html#app.

Internships/Practica: Doctoral Degree (PhD clinical): For those doctoral students for whom a professional internship was required in this program prior to graduation, (4) students applied for an internship in 2006–2007, with (2) students obtaining an internship. Of those students who obtained an internship, (2) were paid internships. Of those students who obtained an internship, (2) students placed in APA/CPA-accredited internships, (0) students placed in internships not APA/CPA-accredited, but listed with the Association of Psychology Postdoctoral and Internship Centers (APPIC), (0) students placed in internships conforming to guidelines of the Council of Directors of School Psychology Programs (CDSPP), (0) students placed in internships that were not APA/CPA-accredited, APPIC or CDSPP listed. For Clinical students, the first 2 years of practicum experience are through our on-site clinic. Advanced students are eligible to participate in external supervised practica at affiliated agencies.

Housing and Day Care: On-campus housing is available. See the following Web site for more information: http://www.reslife.okstate.edu. No on-campus day care facilities are available.

Employment of Department Graduates:

Master's Degree Graduates: Of those who graduated in the academic year 2006–2007, the following categories and numbers represent the postgraduate activities and employment of master's degree graduates: Enrolled in a postdoctoral residency/fellowship (n/a), employed in independent practice (n/a), total from the above (master's) (0).

Doctoral Degree Graduates: Of those who graduated in the academic year 2006–2007, the following categories and numbers represent the postgraduate activities and employment of doctoral degree graduates: Enrolled in a psychology doctoral program (n/a), enrolled in a postdoctoral residency/fellowship (6), employed in independent practice (0), employed in an academic position at a university (1), employed in a community mental health/counseling center (1), employed in a hospital/medical center (3), total from the above (doctoral) (11).

Additional Information:

Orientation, Objectives, and Emphasis of Department: The doctoral program in clinical psychology is based on the scientist–practitioner model. The program emphasizes the development of knowledge and skills in basic psychology, clinical theory, assessment and treatment procedures, and research. Practica, coursework, and internships are selected to enhance the student's interests. Students are expected, through additional coursework, specialized practica, and research, to develop a subspecialty in general clinical, clinical child, or health psychology. The program in Life Span Developmental Psychology is a true life span program that has three primary goals: instruction in content areas of developmental psychology, training in research methodology and quantitative analysis, and preparation for teaching and/or research on applied topics. Students with interests in animal behavior, personality, psycholinguistics, social psychology, and quantitative methods are also encouraged to apply.

Special Facilities or Resources: The Department of Psychology is located in North Murray Hall near the center of the OSU campus. All students are provided office space that they share with two to four others. Each graduate student office is equipped with one or two personal computers with server access to SPSS, MS Office, the Internet, and printers. Wireless Internet access is available in North Murray Hall. Every student is also provided a free e-mail account. Graduate students also share a common room with a refrigerator, microwave oven, two additional computers, and a printer. In addition, the Department of Psychology maintains a 24-station computer lab for student research, teaching, and other endeavors. The department operates the Psychological Services Center, an on-campus facility for clinical work and research. The center has equipment and facilities to accommodate a number of specialized services and functions, including videotaping, direct observation of clinical work using one-way mirrors, and direct supervision through telephones placed in therapy rooms. The department maintains liaison with many off-campus organizations and agencies that provide the student with access to special populations for research as well as clinical activities. The department offers a variety of support services through the Psychology Diversified Students Program and the Psychology Graduate Students Association. Students are provided preadmission and postadmission assistance.

Information for Students With Physical Disabilities: See the following Web site for more information: http://www.okstate.edu/ucs/stdis.

Application Information:

Send to Maureen A. Sullivan, Department of Psychology, OSU, 116 North Murray Hall, Stillwater, OK 74078-3064. Application available online. URL of online application: http://www.psychology.okstate.edu/grad/index.html#app. Students are admitted in the Fall, application deadline January 1 for Clinical; February 1 for Life Span Developmental. *Fee:* $40.

Oklahoma State University

School of Applied Health and Educational Psychology
College of Education
434 Willard Hall
Stillwater, OK 74078
Telephone: (405) 744-6040
Fax: (405) 744-6756
E-mail: *john.romans@okstate.edu*
Web: *http://www.okstate.edu/education/sahepcore.html*

Department Information:

1997. School Head: Dr. John S. C. Romans, PhD. Number of faculty: total—full-time 34, part-time 23; women—full-time 15, part-time 15; total—minority—full-time 3; women minority—full-time 3.

Programs and Degrees Offered:

Listed in the following order: Program area, degree type (T if terminal Master's), number awarded 7/06–6/07. Counseling Psychology PhD (Doctor of Philosophy) 6, School Psychology PhD (Doctor of Philosophy) 5, School Psychology EdS/MEd (School Psychology) 0, Educational Psychology PhD (Doctor of Philosophy) 6.

APA Accreditation: Counseling PhD (Doctor of Philosophy). School PhD (Doctor of Philosophy).

Student Applications/Admissions:

Student Applications

Counseling Psychology PhD (Doctor of Philosophy)—Applications 2007–2008, 64. Total applicants accepted 2007–2008, 8. Number full-time enrolled (new admits only) 2007–2008, 8. Number part-time enrolled (new admits only) 2007–2008,

0. Total enrolled 2007–2008 full-time, 26, part-time, 20. Openings 2008–2009, 8. The median number of years required for completion of a degree in 2006–2007 were 6. The number of students enrolled full- and part-time who were dismissed or voluntarily withdrew from this program area in 2007–2008 were 0. *School Psychology PhD (Doctor of Philosophy)*—Applications 2007–2008, 16. Total applicants accepted 2007–2008, 8. Number full-time enrolled (new admits only) 2007–2008, 8. Number part-time enrolled (new admits only) 2007–2008, 0. Total enrolled 2007–2008 full-time, 34, part-time, 6. Openings 2008–2009, 8. The median number of years required for completion of a degree in 2006–2007 were 5. The number of students enrolled full- and part-time who were dismissed or voluntarily withdrew from this program area in 2007–2008 were 0. *School Psychology EdS/MEd (School Psychology)*—Applications 2007–2008, 11. Total applicants accepted 2007–2008, 6. Number full-time enrolled (new admits only) 2007–2008, 6. Number part-time enrolled (new admits only) 2007–2008, 0. Openings 2008–2009, 8. The median number of years required for completion of a degree in 2006–2007 were 4. The number of students enrolled full- and part-time who were dismissed or voluntarily withdrew from this program area in 2007–2008 were 1. *Educational Psychology PhD (Doctor of Philosophy)*—Applications 2007–2008, 14. Total applicants accepted 2007–2008, 8. Number full-time enrolled (new admits only) 2007–2008, 8. Total enrolled 2007–2008 full-time, 20, part-time, 9. Openings 2008–2009, 8. The median number of years required for completion of a degree in 2006–2007 were 5. The number of students enrolled full- and part-time who were dismissed or voluntarily withdrew from this program area in 2007–2008 were 0.

Admissions Requirements:

Scores: Entries appear in this order: required test or GPA, minimum score (if required), median score of students entering in 2007–2008. Master's Programs: MAT no minimum stated, 47; overall undergraduate GPA no minimum stated, 3.88. School Psychology Ed.S Program Median Score GRE-V 465, GRE-Q 500, GRE-A 4, Overall GPA 3.2 Doctoral Programs: School Psychology PhD Program median score GRE-V 500, GRE-Q 560, GRE-A 4.5, GPA 3.5.

Other Criteria: (importance of criteria rated low, medium, or high): GRE/MAT scores—medium, research experience—medium, work experience—medium, extracurricular activity—medium, clinically related public service—medium, GPA—medium, letters of recommendation—high, interview—high, statement of goals and objectives—high. School Psychology: work experience and clinically related public service—low, letters and interview—high, statement of goals—high. For additional information on admission requirements, go to http://gradcollege.okstate.edu/default.htm.

Student Characteristics: The following represents characteristics of students in 2007–2008 in all graduate psychology programs in the department: Female—full-time 73, part-time 18; Male—full-time 24, part-time 17; African American/Black—full-time 9, part-time 3; Hispanic/Latino(a)—full-time 8, part-time 2; Asian/Pacific Islander—full-time 7, part-time 2; American Indian/Alaska Native—full-time 4, part-time 4; Caucasian/White—full-time 66, part-time 22; Multi-ethnic—full-time 3, part-time 2; students subject to the Americans With Disabilities Act—full-time 0, part-time 0; Unknown ethnicity—full-time 0, part-time 0; International students who hold an F-1 or J-1 Visa—full-time 3, part-time 0.

Financial Information/Assistance:

Tuition for Full-Time Study: *Master's:* State residents: per academic year $2,664, $148 per credit hour; Nonstate residents: per academic year $9,985, $554 per credit hour. *Doctoral:* State residents: per academic year $2,664, $148 per credit hour; Nonstate residents: per academic year $9,985, $5,554 per credit hour. Tuition is subject to change. Tuition costs vary by program. See the following Web site for updates and changes in tuition costs: http://www.bursar.okstate.edu/tuition.html.

Financial Assistance:

First-Year Students: Teaching assistantships available for first year. Average amount paid per academic year: $4,005. Average number of hours worked per week: 10. Apply by April 15. Tuition remission given: full and partial. Research assistantships available for first year. Average amount paid per academic year: $8,010. Average number of hours worked per week: 20. Apply by April 15. Tuition remission given: full and partial. Traineeships available for first year. Apply by n/a. Tuition remission given: partial.

Advanced Students: Teaching assistantships available for advanced students. Average amount paid per academic year: $4,635. Average number of hours worked per week: 10. Apply by April 15. Tuition remission given: full and partial. Research assistantships available for advanced students. Average amount paid per academic year: $4,635. Average number of hours worked per week: 10. Apply by April 15. Tuition remission given: full and partial. Traineeships available for advanced students. Average amount paid per academic year: $9,270. Average number of hours worked per week: 20. Apply by n/a. Tuition remission given: partial. Fellowships and scholarships available for advanced students. Average amount paid per academic year: $250. Apply by n/a. Tuition remission given: partial.

Additional Information: Of all students currently enrolled full time, 87% benefited from one or more of the listed financial assistance programs. Application and information available online at http://www.okstate.edu/education/prospectivestudentsflash.html.

Internships/Practica: Doctoral Degree (PhD Counseling Psychology): For those doctoral students for whom a professional internship was required in this program prior to graduation, (8) students applied for an internship in 2006–2007, with (7) students obtaining an internship. Of those students who obtained an internship, (7) were paid internships. Of those students who obtained an internship, (7) students placed in APA/CPA-accredited internships, (0) students placed in internships not APA/CPA accredited, but listed with the Association of Psychology Postdoctoral and Internship Centers (APPIC), (0) students placed in internships conforming to guidelines of the Council of Directors of School Psychology Programs (CDSPP), (0) students placed in internships that were not APA/CPA-accredited, APPIC or CDSPP listed. Doctoral Degree (PhD School Psychology): For those doctoral students for whom a professional internship was required in this program prior to graduation, (7) students applied for an internship in 2006–2007, with (7) students obtaining an internship. Of those students who obtained an internship, (7) were paid internships. Of those students who obtained an internship, (7) students placed in APA/CPA-accredited internships,

(0) students placed in internships not APA/CPA-accredited, but listed with the Association of Psychology Postdoctoral and Internship Centers (APPIC), (0) students placed in internships conforming to guidelines of the Council of Directors of School Psychology Programs (CDSPP), (0) students placed in internships that were not APA/CPA-accredited, APPIC or CDSPP listed. Multiple settings for internship experiences are available nationally on a competitive basis; faculty must approve site selection. Students have obtained internships in a wide variety of settings (i.e., health centers, hospital settings). Internships must meet established standards for predoctoral internships in counseling psychology. Practica are available at on-campus agencies, including a university counseling service, a mental health clinic at the student hospital, a career information center, and a marriage and family counseling service. Several off-campus placements are within a 75-mile radius of Stillwater, particularly in and around Tulsa and Oklahoma City, and sites include a stipend and public school settings. School Psychology PhD students are required to compete for internship through APPIC. There has been 100% match for school psychology students. School Psychology EdS students complete the internship in approved public school settings. Practica are completed in public school settings and in the School Psychology Center.

Housing and Day Care: On-campus housing is available. See the following Web site for more information: http://www.reslife.okstate.edu. OSU Residential Life, 1st Floor IBA Hall, Stillwater, OK 74078-0636; Phone: (405) 744-5592, Fax: (405) 744-6775. No on-campus day care facilities are available.

Employment of Department Graduates:

Master's Degree Graduates: Of those who graduated in the academic year 2006–2007, the following categories and numbers represent the postgraduate activities and employment of master's degree graduates: Enrolled in a psychology doctoral program (0), enrolled in a postdoctoral residency/fellowship (n/a), employed in independent practice (n/a), total from the above (master's) (0). ***Doctoral Degree Graduates:*** Of those who graduated in the academic year 2006–2007, the following categories and numbers represent the postgraduate activities and employment of doctoral degree graduates: Enrolled in a psychology doctoral program (n/a), enrolled in a postdoctoral residency/fellowship (3), employed in independent practice (1), employed in an academic position at a university (1), employed in other positions at a higher education institution (1), still seeking employment (1), total from the above (doctoral) (7).

Additional Information:

Orientation, Objectives, and Emphasis of Department: Counseling Psychology—The orientation of the Counseling Psychology program is consistent both with the historical development of counseling psychology and with the current roles and functions of counseling psychology. We give major emphasis to prevention/developmental/educational interventions, and to remediation of problems that arise in the normal development of relatively well-functioning people. The focus on prevention and developmental change brings us to seek knowledge and skills related to facilitation of growth, such as training in education, consultation, environmental change, and self-help. It is the focus upon the assets, skills and strengths, and possibilities for further development of persons that is most reflective of the general philosophical orientation, of counseling psychology and of this program. School Psychology—The School Psychology program is based on the scientist–practitioner model, which emphasizes the application of the scientific knowledge base and methodological rigor in the delivery of school psychology services and in conducting research. Training in the scientist–practitioner model at OSU is for the purpose of developing a Science-Based Learner Success (SBLS) orientation in our students. Our philosophy is that all children and youth have the right to be successful and school psychologists are important agents who assist children, families, and others to be successful. Success refers not only to accomplishment of immediate goals but also to long-range goals of adulthood such as contributing to society, social integration, meaningful work, and maximizing personal potentials. The SBLS orientation focuses on prevention and intervention services related to children's psychoeducational and mental health and wellness. School Specialist and Doctoral programs are also approved by the National Association of School Psychologists. Educational Psychology is concerned with all aspects of psychology that are relevant to education, in particular, focal areas in the professions of human development, education of the gifted and talented, and instructional psychology. Educational Psychology—The Educational Psychology program is to bring together theory and research from psychology and related disciplines in order to facilitate healthy human development and effective learning and teaching in any educational setting. The program is designed to prepare graduates to teach in college or university settings, public education, and/or to do research in university, business, and government settings.

Special Facilities or Resources: Community/School Services, Counseling Psychology Clinic, and the School Psychology Clinic.

Information for Students With Physical Disabilities: See the following Web site for more information: http://www.okstate.edu/ucs/stdis/index.html.

Application Information:

Send to OSU Graduate College, Oklahoma State University, 202 Whitehurst, Stillwater, OK 74078-1019; Phone: (405) 744-6368; Fax: (405) 744-0355. Please send program admission criteria to College of Education, Graduate Studies Records, Oklahoma State University, 325 Willard, Stillwater, OK 74078. Application available online. URL of online application: http://www.gradcollege.okstate.edu/apply/default.htm. Students are admitted in the Spring, application deadline see below. Counseling Psychology application deadlines: PhD, January 15; Master's, March 15 and October 15. School Psychology application deadline: PhD, February 1. Educational Psychology application deadline: PhD, February 1; Master's, rolling. Educational Specalist application deadline: PhD: March 1. Applications completed after these deadlines might prevent your acceptance. You should contact your department and ask about their deadline. A complete application must be submitted at least 30 days prior to the departmental deadline if it is prior to the Fall or Spring deadline listed above. Applications not received by the deadlines may not receive admissions decisions in time to enter the country. *Fee:* $40. The application fee is nonrefundable. The international application fee is $75.

Oklahoma, University of
Department of Educational Psychology
College of Education
820 Van Vleet Oval, Room 321
Norman, OK 73019-2041
Telephone: (405) 325-5974
Fax: (405) 325-6655
E-mail: *edpsych@ou.edu*
Web: *http://www.ou.edu/education/edpsy/epsy.htm*

Department Information:

1986. Chairperson: Dr. Teresa K. DeBacker. Number of faculty: total—full-time 23, part-time 2; women—full-time 15, part-time 2; total—minority—full-time 4; women minority—full-time 3.

Programs and Degrees Offered:

Listed in the following order: Program area, degree type (T if terminal Master's), number awarded 7/06–6/07. Counseling Psychology PhD (Doctor of Philosophy) 8, Community Counseling MEd Other 15, Instructional Psychology and Technology MEd Other 5, Instructional Psychology and Technology PhD (Doctor of Philosophy) 5, School Counseling MEd Other 7, Special Education MEd Other 10, Special Education PhD (Doctor of Philosophy) 1.

APA Accreditation: Counseling PhD (Doctor of Philosophy).

Student Applications/Admissions:

Student Applications

Counseling Psychology PhD (Doctor of Philosophy)—Applications 2007–2008, 69. Total applicants accepted 2007–2008, 8. Number full-time enrolled (new admits only) 2007–2008, 8. Number part-time enrolled (new admits only) 2007–2008, 0. Total enrolled 2007–2008 full-time, 22, part-time, 27. Openings 2008–2009, 6. The median number of years required for completion of a degree in 2006–2007 were 4. The number of students enrolled full- and part-time who were dismissed or voluntarily withdrew from this program area in 2007–2008 were 2. *Community Counseling MEd Other*—Applications 2007–2008, 42. Total applicants accepted 2007–2008, 17. Number full-time enrolled (new admits only) 2007–2008, 16. Number part-time enrolled (new admits only) 2007–2008, 1. Total enrolled 2007–2008 full-time, 29, part-time, 2. Openings 2008–2009, 20. The median number of years required for completion of a degree in 2006–2007 were 2. The number of students enrolled full- and part-time who were dismissed or voluntarily withdrew from this program area in 2007–2008 were 1. *Instructional Psychology and Technology MEd Other*—Applications 2007–2008, 19. Total applicants accepted 2007–2008, 12. Number full-time enrolled (new admits only) 2007–2008, 6. Number part-time enrolled (new admits only) 2007–2008, 5. Total enrolled 2007–2008 full-time, 9, part-time, 25. Openings 2008–2009, 15. The median number of years required for completion of a degree in 2006–2007 were 4. The number of students enrolled full- and part-time who were dismissed or voluntarily withdrew from this program area in 2007–2008 were 5. *Instructional Psychology and Technology PhD (Doctor of Philosophy)*—Applications 2007–2008, 4. Total applicants accepted 2007–2008, 3. Number full-time enrolled (new admits only) 2007–2008, 0. Number part-time enrolled (new admits only) 2007–2008, 3. Total enrolled 2007–2008 full-time, 2, part-time, 20. Openings 2008–2009, 10. The median number of years required for completion of a degree in 2006–2007 were 5. The number of students enrolled full- and part-time who were dismissed or voluntarily withdrew from this program area in 2007–2008 were 1. *School Counseling MEd Other*—Applications 2007–2008, 16. Total applicants accepted 2007–2008, 5. Number full-time enrolled (new admits only) 2007–2008, 5. Number part-time enrolled (new admits only) 2007–2008, 0. Openings 2008–2009, 5. The median number of years required for completion of a degree in 2006–2007 were 2. The number of students enrolled full- and part-time who were dismissed or voluntarily withdrew from this program area in 2007–2008 were 1. *Special Education MEd Other*—Applications 2007–2008, 21. Total applicants accepted 2007–2008, 17. Number full-time enrolled (new admits only) 2007–2008, 8. Number part-time enrolled (new admits only) 2007–2008, 7. Total enrolled 2007–2008 full-time, 14, part-time, 17. Openings 2008–2009, 20. The median number of years required for completion of a degree in 2006–2007 were 2. The number of students enrolled full- and part-time who were dismissed or voluntarily withdrew from this program area in 2007–2008 were 4. *Special Education PhD (Doctor of Philosophy)*—Applications 2007–2008, 8. Total applicants accepted 2007–2008, 4. Number full-time enrolled (new admits only) 2007–2008, 2. Number part-time enrolled (new admits only) 2007–2008, 2. Total enrolled 2007–2008 full-time, 14, part-time, 17. Openings 2008–2009, 10. The median number of years required for completion of a degree in 2006–2007 were 6. The number of students enrolled full- and part-time who were dismissed or voluntarily withdrew from this program area in 2007–2008 were 1.

Admissions Requirements:

Scores: Entries appear in this order: required test or GPA, minimum score (if required), median score of students entering in 2007–2008. Master's Programs: GRE-V no minimum stated, 510; GRE-Q no minimum stated, 510; last 2 years GPA 2.75, 3.40. Community Counseling and School Counseling require the GRE. Special Education and Instructional Psychology and Technology do not require it for admission at the master's level. Doctoral Programs: GRE-V no minimum stated, 560; GRE-Q no minimum stated, 630; overall undergraduate GPA 3.00, 3.80; last 2 years GPA 3.0, 3.80. GPA of 3.0 for a minimum of 18 hours coursework in psychology or a related field is required for entrance into the Counseling Psychology PhD program. Applicants to the Counseling Psychology PhD program must also have completed English Composition I and II with a grade of A or B in addition to college algebra or a more advanced form of mathematics with a grade of A or B.

Other Criteria: (importance of criteria rated low, medium, or high): GRE/MAT scores—medium, research experience—medium, work experience—medium, extracurricular activity—medium, clinically related public service—medium, GPA—medium, letters of recommendation—medium, interview—high, statement of goals and objectives—medium. The Instructional Psychology and Technology programs do not require interviews for all applicants. However, the Admissions Committee may require some students to interview in order to make final decisions regarding admission. For additional information on admission requirements, go to http://www.ou.edu/education/edpsy.

Student Characteristics: The following represents characteristics of students in 2007–2008 in all graduate psychology programs in the department: Female—full-time 75, part-time 75; Male—full-time 20, part-time 32; African American/Black—full-time 5, part-time 12; Hispanic/Latino(a)—full-time 4, part-time 6; Asian/Pacific Islander—full-time 2, part-time 3; American Indian/Alaska Native—full-time 12, part-time 5; Caucasian/White—full-time 63, part-time 75; Multi-ethnic—full-time 1, part-time 0; students subject to the Americans With Disabilities Act—full-time 0, part-time 2; Unknown ethnicity—full-time 8, part-time 6; International students who hold an F-1 or J-1 Visa—full-time 8, part-time 9.

Financial Information/Assistance:

Tuition for Full-Time Study: *Master's:* State residents: per academic year $3,882, $143 per credit hour; Nonstate residents: per academic year $13,986, $518 per credit hour. *Doctoral:* State residents: per academic year $3,882, $143 per credit hour; Nonstate residents: per academic year $13,986, $518 per credit hour. Tuition is subject to change. Additional fees are assessed to students beyond the costs of tuition for the following: university services, course materials, and technology. Tuition costs vary by program. See the following Web site for updates and changes in tuition costs: http://www.ou.edu/bursar.

Financial Assistance:

First-Year Students: Teaching assistantships available for first year. Average amount paid per academic year: $9,900. Average number of hours worked per week: 20. Apply by see program. Tuition remission given: full and partial. Research assistantships available for first year. Average amount paid per academic year: $9,900. Average number of hours worked per week: 20. Apply by see program. Tuition remission given: full and partial. Fellowships and scholarships available for first year. Average amount paid per academic year: $9,900. Apply by see program. Tuition remission given: full and partial.

Advanced Students: Teaching assistantships available for advanced students. Average amount paid per academic year: $9,900. Average number of hours worked per week: 20. Apply by see program. Tuition remission given: full and partial. Research assistantships available for advanced students. Average amount paid per academic year: $9,900. Average number of hours worked per week: 20. Apply by see program. Tuition remission given: full and partial. Fellowships and scholarships available for advanced students. Average amount paid per academic year: $5,000. Apply by see program. Tuition remission given: full.

Additional Information: Of all students currently enrolled full time, 26% benefited from one or more of the listed financial assistance programs. Application and information available online at http://www.ou.edu/education/edpsy.

Internships/Practica: Doctoral Degree (PhD Counseling Psychology): For those doctoral students for whom a professional internship was required in this program prior to graduation, (9) students applied for an internship in 2006–2007, with (8) students obtaining an internship. Of those students who obtained an internship, (8) were paid internships. Of those students who obtained an internship, (8) students placed in APA/CPA-accredited internships, (0) students placed in internships not APA/CPA accredited, but listed with the Association of Psychology Postdoctoral and Internship Centers (APPIC), (0) students placed in internships conforming to guidelines of the Council of Directors of School Psychology Programs (CDSPP), (0) students placed in internships that were not APA/CPA-accredited, APPIC or CDSPP listed. Master's: Numerous hospitals and clinics in the local area. Doctoral: Students choose from APA-accredited sites (two in the local area, and others across the nation).

Housing and Day Care: On-campus housing is available. See the following Web site for more information: http://www.housing.ou.edu. On-campus day care facilities are available. See the following Web site for more information: http://www.childrensworld.com/.

Employment of Department Graduates:

Master's Degree Graduates: Of those who graduated in the academic year 2006–2007, the following categories and numbers represent the postgraduate activities and employment of master's degree graduates: Enrolled in a psychology doctoral program (6), enrolled in another graduate/professional program (0), enrolled in a postdoctoral residency/fellowship (n/a), employed in independent practice (n/a), employed in an academic position at a university (0), employed in an academic position at a 2-year/4-year college (0), employed in other positions at a higher education institution (0), employed in a professional position in a school system (0), employed in business or industry (0), employed in government agency (1), employed in a community mental health/counseling center (0), employed in a hospital/medical center (0), still seeking employment (0), not seeking employment (0), other employment position (0), do not know (30), total from the above (master's) (37).

Doctoral Degree Graduates: Of those who graduated in the academic year 2006–2007, the following categories and numbers represent the postgraduate activities and employment of doctoral degree graduates: Enrolled in a psychology doctoral program (n/a), enrolled in another graduate/professional program (0), enrolled in a postdoctoral residency/fellowship (0), employed in independent practice (1), employed in an academic position at a university (2), employed in an academic position at a 2-year/4-year college (2), employed in other positions at a higher education institution (5), employed in a professional position in a school system (0), employed in business or industry (0), employed in government agency (3), employed in a community mental health/counseling center (0), employed in a hospital/medical center (0), still seeking employment (0), not seeking employment (0), other employment position (0), do not know (1), total from the above (doctoral) (14).

Additional Information:

Orientation, Objectives, and Emphasis of Department: The Counseling Psychology program emphasizes training in working with couples and families with children. The program has a scientist–practitioner orientation designed to encourage the professional development of the students. Minority applications are encouraged for all of our programs.

Personal Behavior Statement: We require students to sign an agreement to behave in accordance with APA ethical guidelines.

Special Facilities or Resources: The Counseling Psychology Clinic is a community-based training site for our students. The clientele reflects diverse diagnostic classifications with some cultural diversity. Couples, children, and families make up a large proportion of the population served by the clinic.

Information for Students With Physical Disabilities: See the following Web site for more information: http://www.sa.ou.edu/ods/.

Application Information:
Send to Graduate Programs Officer, Department of Educational Psychology, University of Oklahoma, 820 Van Vleet Oval, Room 321, Norman, OK 73019-2041. Application available online. URL of online application: http://www.ou.edu/education/edpsy. Students are admitted in the Fall, application deadline see below; Spring, application deadline see below; Summer, application deadline see below. Deadline for Counseling PhD is January 10 (begins in Fall semester). Deadline for Community Counseling MEd is January 31 (begins in Summer semester). Deadline for School Counseling MEd is January 31 (begins in Summer semester). Deadlines for Instructional Psychology and Technology MEd: Spring, October 15; Fall, March 15 and July 1. Deadline for Instructional Psychology and Technology PhD: Fall only, February 1. Special Education PhD: March 1, Fall admission only. Special Education MEd: Spring, November 1; Fall, April 1. *Fee:* $0. The University of Oklahoma Office of Admissions charges an application fee: $40 for U.S. students, $90 for international. The Department of Educational Psychology does not have an application fee.

Oklahoma, University of

Department of Psychology
Arts and Sciences
455 West Lindsey
Norman, OK 73019-2007
Telephone: (405) 325-4511, (800) 522-0772, ext 4512
Fax: (405) 325-4737
E-mail: *KPaine@ou.edu*
Web: *http://www.ou.edu/cas/psychology/*

Department Information:
1928. Chairperson: Jorge Mendoza. Number of faculty: total—full-time 21, part-time 1; women—full-time 9, part-time 1; total—minority—full-time 2; women minority—full-time 1.

Programs and Degrees Offered:
Listed in the following order: Program area, degree type (T if terminal Master's), number awarded 7/06–6/07. Industrial/Organizational MA/MS (Master of Arts/Science) (T) 0, Social PhD (Doctor of Philosophy) 1, Animal Cognition PhD (Doctor of Philosophy) 0, Cognitive PhD (Doctor of Philosophy) 0, Development PhD (Doctor of Philosophy) 0, Experimental Personality PhD (Doctor of Philosophy) 0, Industrial/Organizational PhD (Doctor of Philosophy), Quantitative/Measurement PhD (Doctor of Philosophy) 0.

Student Applications/Admissions:
Student Applications
Industrial/Organizational MA/MS (Master of Arts/Science)—Applications 2007–2008, 6. Total applicants accepted 2007–2008, 0. Number full-time enrolled (new admits only) 2007–2008, 0. Number part-time enrolled (new admits only) 2007–2008, 0. Openings 2008–2009, 2. *Social PhD (Doctor of Philosophy)*—Applications 2007–2008, 14. Total applicants accepted 2007–2008, 3. Number full-time enrolled (new admits only) 2007–2008, 1. Number part-time enrolled (new admits only) 2007–2008, 0. Openings 2008–2009, 3. The median number of years required for completion of a degree in 2006–2007 were 5. *Animal Cognition PhD (Doctor of Philosophy)*—Applications 2007–2008, 0. Total applicants accepted 2007–2008, 0. Number full-time enrolled (new admits only) 2007–2008, 0. Number part-time enrolled (new admits only) 2007–2008, 0. Openings 2008–2009, 1. *Cognitive PhD (Doctor of Philosophy)*—Applications 2007–2008, 5. Total applicants accepted 2007–2008, 4. Number full-time enrolled (new admits only) 2007–2008, 3. Number part-time enrolled (new admits only) 2007–2008, 0. Total enrolled 2007–2008 full-time, 8, part-time, 1. Openings 2008–2009, 4. *Development PhD (Doctor of Philosophy)*—Applications 2007–2008, 7. Total applicants accepted 2007–2008, 0. Number full-time enrolled (new admits only) 2007–2008, 0. Number part-time enrolled (new admits only) 2007–2008, 0. Openings 2008–2009, 3. *Experimental Personality PhD (Doctor of Philosophy)*—Applications 2007–2008, 1. Total applicants accepted 2007–2008, 1. Number full-time enrolled (new admits only) 2007–2008, 1. Number part-time enrolled (new admits only) 2007–2008, 0. Openings 2008–2009, 2. *Industrial/Organizational PhD (Doctor of Philosophy)*—Applications 2007–2008, 46. Total applicants accepted 2007–2008, 10. Number full-time enrolled (new admits only) 2007–2008, 4. Number part-time enrolled (new admits only) 2007–2008, 0. Total enrolled 2007–2008 full-time, 27. Openings 2008–2009, 6. The median number of years required for completion of a degree in 2006–2007 were 5. *Quantitative/Measurement PhD (Doctor of Philosophy)*—Applications 2007–2008, 9. Total applicants accepted 2007–2008, 4. Number full-time enrolled (new admits only) 2007–2008, 1. Total enrolled 2007–2008 full-time, 5, part-time, 2. Openings 2008–2009, 3. The number of students enrolled full- and part-time who were dismissed or voluntarily withdrew from this program area in 2007–2008 were 1.

Admissions Requirements:
Scores: Entries appear in this order: required test or GPA, minimum score (if required), median score of students entering in 2007–2008. Master's Programs: GRE-V no minimum stated; GRE-Q no minimum stated; overall undergraduate GPA no minimum stated; last 2 years GPA no minimum stated; psychology GPA no minimum stated. Doctoral Programs: GRE-V no minimum stated, 545; GRE-Q no minimum stated, 630; overall undergraduate GPA no minimum stated, 3.75; last 2 years GPA no minimum stated; psychology GPA no minimum stated.
Other Criteria: (importance of criteria rated low, medium, or high): GRE/MAT scores—high, research experience—high, work experience—low, extracurricular activity—low, GPA—high, letters of recommendation—high, interview—medium, statement of goals and objectives—high, undergraduate major in psychology—low, specific undergraduate psychology courses taken—medium. Work experience is more important to I/O.

Student Characteristics: The following represents characteristics of students in 2007–2008 in all graduate psychology programs in the department: Female—full-time 32, part-time 2; Male—full-time 24, part-time 1; African American/Black—full-time 1, part-time 0; Hispanic/Latino(a)—full-time 1, part-time 0; Asian/Pacific Islander—full-time 2, part-time 1; American Indian/Alaska Native—full-time 0, part-time 0; Caucasian/White—full-time 48, part-time 2; students subject to the Americans With

Disabilities Act—full-time 0, part-time 1; Unknown ethnicity—full-time 4, part-time 0.

Financial Information/Assistance:

Tuition for Full-Time Study: *Master's:* State residents: $144 per credit hour; Nonstate residents: $518 per credit hour. *Doctoral:* State residents: $144 per credit hour; Nonstate residents: $518 per credit hour. Tuition is subject to change. See the following Web site for updates and changes in tuition costs: http://www.ou.edu/bursar/fees.htm. Higher tuition cost for this program: Note: all areas have additional fees that cannot be waived.

Financial Assistance:

First-Year Students: Teaching assistantships available for first year. Average amount paid per academic year: $12,430. Average number of hours worked per week: 20. Tuition remission given: partial. Research assistantships available for first year. Average amount paid per academic year: $12,430. Average number of hours worked per week: 20. Tuition remission given: partial. Fellowships and scholarships available for first year. Average amount paid per academic year: $19,430. Average number of hours worked per week: 20. Tuition remission given: full.

Advanced Students: Teaching assistantships available for advanced students. Average amount paid per academic year: $13,260. Average number of hours worked per week: 20. Tuition remission given: partial. Research assistantships available for advanced students. Average amount paid per academic year: $13,260. Average number of hours worked per week: 20. Tuition remission given: partial.

Additional Information: Of all students currently enrolled full time, 95% benefited from one or more of the listed financial assistance programs. Application and information available online at http://www.ou.edu/cas/psychology/grad/application.htm.

Internships/Practica: No information provided.

Housing and Day Care: On-campus housing is available. See the following Web site for more information: http://www.housing.ou.edu/. On-campus day care facilities are available. See the following Web site for more information: http://www.gradweb.ou.edu/docs/archives/Gb2001/generalinfo.htm.

Employment of Department Graduates:

Master's Degree Graduates: Of those who graduated in the academic year 2006–2007, the following categories and numbers represent the postgraduate activities and employment of master's degree graduates: Enrolled in a postdoctoral residency/fellowship (n/a), employed in independent practice (n/a), total from the above (master's) (0).

Doctoral Degree Graduates: Of those who graduated in the academic year 2006–2007, the following categories and numbers represent the postgraduate activities and employment of doctoral degree graduates: Enrolled in a psychology doctoral program (n/a), employed in an academic position at a university (1), employed in an academic position at a 2-year/4-year college (1), employed in business or industry (5), total from the above (doctoral) (7).

Additional Information:

Orientation, Objectives, and Emphasis of Department: All programs are highly research oriented within the broad framework of experimental psychology. The department aims to produce creative and productive psychologists to function in academic and research settings, and toward this end emphasizes early and continuing involvement in research. Achievement of orientation and objectives is demonstrated by the excellent placement record of doctoral graduates, and by the department's recent rating as ninth in the nation in percentage of publishing faculty. An excellent program in Quantitative Methods in Psychology is an especially attractive feature of the quality graduate training offered.

Special Facilities or Resources: The department offers modern research facilities with microprocessor-controlled laboratories, instrumentation shops with a full-time engineer, a small animal colony, a university computing center, a departmental computing center for graduate students, and graduate offices located near faculty and departmental offices.

Application Information:

Send to Graduate Admissions Committee, Department of Psychology, University of Oklahoma, 455 West Lindsey, Room 705, Norman, OK 73019-2007. Application available online. URL of online application: http://www.ou.edu/cas/psychology/grad/application.htm. Students are admitted in the Fall, application deadline January 1. *Fee:* $40; $90 for international students.

Tulsa, University of

Department of Psychology
800 South Tucker Drive
Tulsa, OK 74104-3189
Telephone: (918) 631-2248
Fax: (918) 631-2833
E-mail: *sandra-barney@utulsa.edu*
Web: *http://www.cas.utulsa.edu/psych/*

Department Information:

1926. Chairperson: Dr. Judy Berry. Number of faculty: total—full-time 11, part-time 6; women—full-time 5, part-time 3.

Programs and Degrees Offered:

Listed in the following order: Program area, degree type (T if terminal Master's), number awarded 7/06–6/07. Industrial/Organizational PhD (Doctor of Philosophy) 3, Industrial/Organizational MA/MS (Master of Arts/Science) (T) 11, Clinical Psychology MA/MS (Master of Arts/Science) (T) 4, Clinical Psychology PhD (Doctor of Philosophy) 6, Clinical MA/JD MA/MS (Master of Arts/Science) (T) 0, Industrial/Organizational MA/JD Other 0.

APA Accreditation: Clinical PhD (Doctor of Philosophy).

Student Applications/Admissions:

Student Applications

Industrial/Organizational PhD (Doctor of Philosophy)—Applications 2007–2008, 20. Total applicants accepted 2007–2008, 3. Number full-time enrolled (new admits only) 2007–2008, 2. Number part-time enrolled (new admits only) 2007–2008, 0. Openings 2008–2009, 3. The median number of years required for completion of a degree in 2006–2007 were 6. The number of students enrolled full- and part-time who were dismissed or voluntarily withdrew from this program area in 2007–2008 were 0. *Industrial/Organizational MA/MS (Master of*

Arts/Science)—Applications 2007–2008, 24. Total applicants accepted 2007–2008, 12. Number full-time enrolled (new admits only) 2007–2008, 5. Number part-time enrolled (new admits only) 2007–2008, 0. Openings 2008–2009, 6. The median number of years required for completion of a degree in 2006–2007 were 2. The number of students enrolled full- and part-time who were dismissed or voluntarily withdrew from this program area in 2007–2008 were 0. *Clinical Psychology MA/MS (Master of Arts/Science)*—Applications 2007–2008, 15. Total applicants accepted 2007–2008, 4. Number full-time enrolled (new admits only) 2007–2008, 1. Openings 2008–2009, 5. The median number of years required for completion of a degree in 2006–2007 were 2. The number of students enrolled full- and part-time who were dismissed or voluntarily withdrew from this program area in 2007–2008 were 0. *Clinical Psychology PhD (Doctor of Philosophy)*—Applications 2007–2008, 47. Total applicants accepted 2007–2008, 9. Number full-time enrolled (new admits only) 2007–2008, 5. Number part-time enrolled (new admits only) 2007–2008, 0. Openings 2008–2009, 5. The median number of years required for completion of a degree in 2006–2007 were 5. The number of students enrolled full- and part-time who were dismissed or voluntarily withdrew from this program area in 2007–2008 were 0. *Clinical MA/JD MA/MS (Master of Arts/Science)*—Applications 2007–2008, 2. Total applicants accepted 2007–2008, 0. Number full-time enrolled (new admits only) 2007–2008, 0. Number part-time enrolled (new admits only) 2007–2008, 0. Openings 2008–2009, 1. The median number of years required for completion of a degree in 2006–2007 were 5. The number of students enrolled full- and part-time who were dismissed or voluntarily withdrew from this program area in 2007–2008 were 0. *Industrial/Organizational MA/JD Other*—Applications 2007–2008, 1. Total applicants accepted 2007–2008, 0. Number full-time enrolled (new admits only) 2007–2008, 0. Number part-time enrolled (new admits only) 2007–2008, 0. Openings 2008–2009, 1. The median number of years required for completion of a degree in 2006–2007 were 5. The number of students enrolled full- and part-time who were dismissed or voluntarily withdrew from this program area in 2007–2008 were 0.

Admissions Requirements:

Scores: Entries appear in this order: required test or GPA, minimum score (if required), median score of students entering in 2007–2008. Master's Programs: GRE-V no minimum stated, 560; GRE-Q no minimum stated, 590; overall undergraduate GPA 3.00, 3.68; Masters GRE-Analytical no minimum stated, 4.5. Minimum undergraduate GPA of 3.0 required for admission. No minimum GRE scores. Acceptable GRE scores in comparison to current applicant pool. Medians are reported for Clinical. Admissions are based on total scores and other factors. Doctoral Programs: GRE-V no minimum stated, 590; GRE-Q no minimum stated, 660; overall undergraduate GPA 3.00, 3.76; Doctoral program GRE-Analytic no minimum stated, 5.5. Minimum undergraduate GPA of 3.0 required for admission. GRE scores are assessed in comparison to current applicant pool. Medians are reported for Clinical. Admissions are based on total scores and other factors.

Other Criteria: (importance of criteria rated low, medium, or high): GRE/MAT scores—high, research experience—high, work experience—low, extracurricular activity—low, clinically related public service—medium, GPA—high, letters of recommendation—high, interview—high, statement of goals and objectives—high, quality of undergrad inst—medium, undergraduate major in psychology—medium, specific undergraduate psychology courses taken—medium, interview for clinical only. For additional information on admission requirements, go to http://www.cas.utulsa.edu/psych.

Student Characteristics: The following represents characteristics of students in 2007–2008 in all graduate psychology programs in the department: Female—full-time 57, part-time 0; Male—full-time 23, part-time 0; African American/Black—full-time 3, part-time 0; Hispanic/Latino(a)—full-time 3, part-time 0; Asian/Pacific Islander—full-time 3, part-time 0; American Indian/Alaska Native—full-time 6, part-time 0; Caucasian/White—full-time 63, part-time 0; Multi-ethnic—full-time 0, part-time 0; students subject to the Americans With Disabilities Act—full-time 0, part-time 0; Unknown ethnicity—full-time 2, part-time 0; International students who hold an F-1 or J-1 Visa—full-time 2, part-time 0.

Financial Information/Assistance:

Tuition for Full-Time Study: *Master's:* State residents: $864 per credit hour; Nonstate residents: $864 per credit hour. *Doctoral:* State residents: $864 per credit hour; Nonstate residents: $864 per credit hour. Tuition is subject to change. See the following Web site for updates and changes in tuition costs: http://www.utulsa.edu/graduate/Files/Expenses/COSTEST.HTM.

Financial Assistance:

First-Year Students: Teaching assistantships available for first year. Average amount paid per academic year: $11,594. Average number of hours worked per week: 20. Apply by February 1. Tuition remission given: full. Research assistantships available for first year. Average amount paid per academic year: $11,594. Average number of hours worked per week: 20. Apply by February 1. Tuition remission given: full. Fellowships and scholarships available for first year. Average number of hours worked per week: 20. Apply by varies. Tuition remission given: full and partial.

Advanced Students: Teaching assistantships available for advanced students. Average amount paid per academic year: $12,020. Average number of hours worked per week: 20. Apply by February 1. Tuition remission given: full. Research assistantships available for advanced students. Average amount paid per academic year: $12,020. Average number of hours worked per week: 20. Apply by February 1. Tuition remission given: full. Fellowships and scholarships available for advanced students. Average number of hours worked per week: 20. Apply by varies. Tuition remission given: full and partial.

Additional Information: Of all students currently enrolled full time, 50% benefited from one or more of the listed financial assistance programs. Application and information available online at http://www.utulsa.edu/Financial/Aid.html.

Internships/Practica: Master's Degree (MA/MS Industrial/Organizational): An internship experience such as a final research project or "capstone" experience is required of graduates. Doctoral Degree (PhD Clinical Psychology): For those doctoral students for whom a professional internship was required in this program prior to graduation, (9) students applied for an internship in 2006–2007, with (7) students obtaining an internship. Of those students who obtained an internship, (7) were paid internships. Of those students who obtained an internship, (7) students placed in APA/CPA-accredited internships, (0) students placed in internships not APA/CPA-accredited, but listed with the Association of Psychology Postdoctoral and Internship Centers (APPIC), (0) students placed in internships conforming to guidelines of the Council of Directors of School Psychology Programs (CDSPP), (0) students placed in internships that were not APA/CPA-accredited, APPIC or CDSPP listed. In the Clinical program, supervised applied training begins early in the program. Practicum experiences occur primarily in community settings, utilizing the wide variety of agencies with which the department has relationships and allowing the student to interact with various mental health professionals. Placements include the university health center, community mental health centers, hospitals, community service agencies, and private practice groups. Attempts are made to allow students to choose practicum activities that are most consistent with their professional goals, although it is recognized that a diversity of experiences can provide a strong foundation for professional development. Practicum activities are supervised by an on-site professional, and the practicum experience is organized and monitored by the Coordinator of Practicum Training in conjunction with the Clinical Program Committee.

Housing and Day Care: On-campus housing is available. See the following Web site for more information: http://www.utulsa.edu/housing/index.html. On-campus day care facilities are available. The University of Tulsa Child Development Center offers on-campus child care for the children of TU students, staff and faculty, and the public. The Center, which opened in January 1994, is operated by Children's World Learning Center. The facility features 7,900 square feet of interior space with a capacity for 148 children between the ages of 6 weeks and 12 years, and offers all-day care, before and after school programs, and transportation to and from nearby Tulsa schools.

Employment of Department Graduates:

Master's Degree Graduates: Of those who graduated in the academic year 2006–2007, the following categories and numbers represent the postgraduate activities and employment of master's degree graduates: Enrolled in a psychology doctoral program (6), enrolled in a postdoctoral residency/fellowship (n/a), employed in independent practice (n/a), employed in business or industry (4), employed in government agency (1), employed in a community mental health/counseling center (1), other employment position (1), do not know (1), total from the above (master's) (14). ***Doctoral Degree Graduates:*** Of those who graduated in the academic year 2006–2007, the following categories and numbers represent the postgraduate activities and employment of doctoral degree graduates: Enrolled in a psychology doctoral program (n/a), enrolled in a postdoctoral residency/fellowship (2), employed in independent practice (1), employed in an academic position at a university (2), employed in business or industry (2), employed in government agency (1), employed in a community mental health/counseling center (1), total from the above (doctoral) (9).

Additional Information:

Orientation, Objectives, and Emphasis of Department: Our graduate programs in applied psychology are central to the departmental mission, which is to generate new psychological knowledge to help individuals, organizations, and communities make decisions and solve problems; to offer a future-oriented, intellectually challenging, and socially relevant curriculum; and to equip students to make a difference through their work by providing them with an extensive knowledge base as well as the analytical and practical skills needed to apply knowledge wisely. Our programs train students to do what applied psychologists actually do in today's society. The programs in I/O psychology emphasize personnel psychology and organizational development, theory and behavior, with a special focus on individual assessment. The doctoral program in Clinical Psychology develops scientist–practitioners using the following training components. First, coursework is distributed across clinical core, general psychology, methodology core, and elective offerings. Second, research mentoring is experienced in the precandidacy and dissertation projects. Third, procedural knowledge is developed in clinical practicum and internship training. Fourth, declarative knowledge is developed through comprehensive written and oral examinations covering general psychological knowledge and methods, and clinical psychology.

Special Facilities or Resources: The Department of Psychology is located in Lorton Hall, a building located near the center of the TU campus. The building contains faculty offices, classrooms, offices for graduate students on assistantships, research space, and clinical training space. McFarlin Library, a 2-minute walk from Lorton Hall, contains more than 3 million items and more than 6,000 periodical subscriptions. The library's catalog is computerized and is accessible from terminals across campus. Computer searches of the major information databases in psychology are available to students at no charge. Major computer application suites and statistical packages (e.g., SPSS) are available for word processing, data analyses, test interpretation, and other tasks. The university has several computer labs with a variety of hardware configurations and software packages for student use. Visiting scholars and professionals often join the graduate faculty in presenting special courses, workshops, and seminars. Each year, colloquium speakers offer opinions, ideas, and research on topics of current interest in psychology.

Information for Students With Physical Disabilities: See the following Web site for more information: http://www.utulsa.edu/academicsupport/DisabilityServices.htm.

Application Information:

Send to Graduate School, University of Tulsa, 800 South Tucker Drive, Tulsa, OK 74104. Application available online. URL of online application: http://www.utulsa.edu/graduate/. Students are admitted in the Fall, application deadline December 1. Applications are reviewed once a year for a Fall entering semester. For the Clinical Psychology program, the application due date for the Fall 2009 entering semester is December 1, 2008. For the Industrial/Organizational psychology program, the application due date for the Fall 2009 entering semester is January 15, 2009. *Fee:* $40.

George Fox University
Graduate Department of Clinical Psychology
School of Behavioral and Health Sciences
414 North Meridian Street, V104
Newberg, OR 97132-2697
Telephone: (800) 631-0921, ext. 2263
Fax: (503) 554 2371
E-mail: *psyd@georgefox.edu*
Web: *http://www.psyd.georgefox.edu*

Department Information:
1981. Chairperson: Wayne Adams. Number of faculty: total—full-time 8, part-time 6; women—full-time 3, part-time 3; minority—part-time 2; women minority—part-time 1.

Programs and Degrees Offered:
Listed in the following order: Program area, degree type (T if terminal Master's), number awarded 7/06–6/07. Clinical Psychology PsyD (Doctor of Psychology) 15.

APA Accreditation: Clinical PsyD (Doctor of Psychology).

Student Applications/Admissions:
Student Applications
Clinical Psychology PsyD (Doctor of Psychology)—Applications 2007–2008, 84. Total applicants accepted 2007–2008, 28. Number full-time enrolled (new admits only) 2007–2008, 21. Number part-time enrolled (new admits only) 2007–2008, 0. Openings 2008–2009, 20. The median number of years required for completion of a degree in 2006–2007 were 5. The number of students enrolled full- and part-time who were dismissed or voluntarily withdrew from this program area in 2007–2008 were 2.

Admissions Requirements:
Scores: Entries appear in this order: required test or GPA, minimum score (if required), median score of students entering in 2007–2008. Master's Programs: A master's degree is earned by students as they progress through the program. However, application and acceptance is made only to the PsyD program (i.e., there is no terminal master's program). Doctoral Programs: GRE-V no minimum stated, 505; GRE-Q no minimum stated, 576; GRE-Subject (Psychology) none, 498; overall undergraduate GPA 3.0, 3.52; last 2 years GPA no minimum stated; psychology GPA no minimum stated, 3.74. No rigid acceptance formula is used but each application is evaluated based upon overall individual strengths, and the potential to benefit from and contribute to the program, as well as potential to become a competent licensed psychologist. However, evidence must exist to document strong likelihood of academic and clinical success.
Other Criteria: (importance of criteria rated low, medium, or high): GRE/MAT scores—medium, research experience—medium, work experience—medium, extracurricular activity—low, clinically related public service—medium, GPA—high, letters of recommendation—high, interview—high, statement of goals and objectives—high, Christian worldview—high, undergraduate major in psychology—medium, specific undergraduate psychology courses taken—medium. For additional information on admission requirements, go to http://psyd.georgefox.edu.

Student Characteristics: The following represents characteristics of students in 2007–2008 in all graduate psychology programs in the department: Female—full-time 56, part-time 0; Male—full-time 41, part-time 0; African American/Black—full-time 2, part-time 0; Hispanic/Latino(a)—full-time 3, part-time 0; Asian/Pacific Islander—full-time 4, part-time 0; American Indian/Alaska Native—full-time 1, part-time 0; Caucasian/White—full-time 81, part-time 0; Multi-ethnic—full-time 1, part-time 0; students subject to the Americans With Disabilities Act—full-time 1, part-time 0; Unknown ethnicity—full-time 5, part-time 0.

Financial Information/Assistance:
Tuition for Full-Time Study: *Master's:* State residents: $690 per credit hour; Nonstate residents: $690 per credit hour. *Doctoral:* State residents: $690 per credit hour; Nonstate residents: $690 per credit hour. Tuition is subject to change. Additional fees are assessed to students beyond the costs of tuition for the following: $70 per semester student fee. See the following Web site for updates and changes in tuition costs: http://www.georgefox.edu/offices/stu_fin_srv/cost_psyd.html.

Financial Assistance:
First-Year Students: Fellowships and scholarships available for first year. Average amount paid per academic year: $4,000. Average number of hours worked per week: 0. Apply by March 30. Tuition remission given: partial.
Advanced Students: Teaching assistantships available for advanced students. Average amount paid per academic year: $3,000. Average number of hours worked per week: 5. Apply by variable. Research assistantships available for advanced students. Average amount paid per academic year: $2,100. Average number of hours worked per week: 5. Apply by variable. Fellowships and scholarships available for advanced students. Average amount paid per academic year: $4,000. Average number of hours worked per week: 0. Apply by March 30. Tuition remission given: partial.
Additional Information: Of all students currently enrolled full time, 40% benefited from one or more of the listed financial assistance programs. Application and information available online at http://psyd.georgefox.edu.

Internships/Practica: Doctoral Degree (PsyD Clinical Psychology): For those doctoral students for whom a professional internship was required in this program prior to graduation, (12) students applied for an internship in 2006–2007, with (12) students obtaining an internship. Of those students who obtained an internship, (12) were paid internships. Of those students who obtained an internship, (8) students placed in APA/CPA-accredited internships, (4) students placed in internships not APA/CPA accredited, but listed with the Association of Psychology Postdoctoral and Internship Centers (APPIC), (0) students placed in internships conforming to guidelines of the Council of Directors of School Psychology Programs (CDSPP), (0) students placed in internships that were not APA/CPA-accredited, APPIC or CDSPP listed. Students are required to complete 4 years of practicum (minimum of 1,500 hours) in a variety of settings in the greater Portland metropolitan area. Practicum settings include hospitals, community mental health agencies, drug and alcohol programs, behavioral medicine clinics, schools, and prisons. Inpatient and outpatient experiences are available. All practicum experience is gained under the careful supervision of licensed psychologists at the practicum sites. Additionally, students receive weekly clinical oversight on campus by core faculty. Students apply for internships within the system developed by the Association of Psychology Postdoctoral and Internship Centers (APPIC). Students complete a 1-year full-time internship (2,000 hours) at an approved internship site during their 5th year in the program. Usually, 90% of applicants obtain an APA- and/or APPIC-approved internship sites.

Housing and Day Care: No on-campus housing is available. No on-campus day care facilities are available.

Employment of Department Graduates:

Master's Degree Graduates: Of those who graduated in the academic year 2006–2007, the following categories and numbers represent the postgraduate activities and employment of master's degree graduates: Enrolled in another graduate/professional program (0), enrolled in a postdoctoral residency/fellowship (n/a), employed in independent practice (n/a), still seeking employment (0), total from the above (master's) (0).

Doctoral Degree Graduates: Of those who graduated in the academic year 2006–2007, the following categories and numbers represent the postgraduate activities and employment of doctoral degree graduates: Enrolled in a psychology doctoral program (n/a), enrolled in another graduate/professional program (0), enrolled in a postdoctoral residency/fellowship (8), employed in independent practice (0), employed in an academic position at a university (0), employed in an academic position at a 2-year/4-year college (0), employed in other positions at a higher education institution (0), employed in a professional position in a school system (0), employed in business or industry (0), employed in government agency (1), employed in a community mental health/counseling center (2), employed in a hospital/medical center (0), still seeking employment (0), other employment position (0), do not know (1), total from the above (doctoral) (12).

Additional Information:

Orientation, Objectives, and Emphasis of Department: The goal of the Graduate Department of Clinical Psychology (GDCP) is to prepare professional psychologists who are competent to provide psychological services in a wide variety of clinical settings, who are knowledgeable in critical evaluation and application of psychological research, and who are committed to the highest standards of professional ethics. The central distinctive feature of the program is the integration of a Christian worldview and the science of psychology at philosophical, practical, and personal levels. Graduates are trained broadly but also as specialists in meeting the unique psychological needs of the Christian community and others who wish a spiritual dimension to be included in their treatment. Other distinctives of the program include close mentoring using clinical and research team models, and an option for training emphases in Assessment, Rural, and Health Psychology. Graduates are prepared for licensure as clinical psychologists. Alumni of the GDCP are licensed in numerous states throughout the United States. They engage in practice in a variety of settings, including independent and group practice, hospitals, community mental health clinics, government, corrections, public health agencies, and church and para-church organizations. Graduates also teach in a variety of settings, including colleges and seminaries.

Personal Behavior Statement: The statement appears both on the University's Web site, the program's Web site as well as in the application for admission.

Special Facilities or Resources: High-speed microcomputers, laser printers, and complete statistical (SPSS PC+) and graphics software are provided in a computer lab. The Murdock Learning Resource Center provides library support for the psychology program. The library has excellent access to materials important to contemporary clinical and empirical work in most areas of clinical psychology. In addition, the library receives more than 140 periodicals in psychology and related disciplines, most available electronically. Students also have online access to major computerized databases through library services, including PsycInfo, DIALOG, ERIC, and many others. In addition to full-text access to many psychology journals, George Fox University maintains cooperative arrangements with other local educational institutions providing psychology students with a full range of user services, including interlibrary loans and direct borrowing privileges. A full range of traditional campus facilities are also available such as athletic, arts outlets, student lounge, and meal service. A newly remodeled building is the campus location for the PsyD program. The new quarters include all PsyD classrooms, faculty offices, student lounge area, computer lab, cafe, conference rooms, clinical demonstration and videotaping rooms, and student parking.

Information for Students With Physical Disabilities: See the following Web site for more information: http://www.psyd.georgefox.edu.

Application Information:

Send to Adina McConaughey, Graduate Admission Officer, Graduate School of Clinical Psychology, George Fox University, Box 6089, 414 North Meridian Street, Newberg, OR 97132; Phone: (503) 554-2263. Application available online. URL of online application: https://www.applyweb.com/apply/gfu/menu.html. Students are admitted in the Winter, application deadline January 15. Special circumstances for delayed or late applications will be considered. Especially strong applicants will be considered after deadline, on a space-available basis. *Fee:* $40.

Lewis & Clark College, Graduate School of Education and Counseling

Counseling Psychology Department
Graduate School of Education and Counseling
0615 Southwest Palatine Hill Road, Box 86
Portland, OR 97219-7899
Telephone: (503) 768-6060
Fax: (503) 768-6065
E-mail: *cpsy@lclark.edu*
Web: *http://www.education.lclark.edu/dept/cpsy/*

Department Information:

1972. Department Chair: Tod Sloan, PhD. Number of faculty: total—full-time 11, part-time 1; women—full-time 7, part-time 1; total—minority—full-time 1; women minority—full-time 1.

Programs and Degrees Offered:

Listed in the following order: Program area, degree type (T if terminal Master's), number awarded 7/06–6/07. School Psychology EdS/MEd (School Psychology) 12, Addictions Treatment MA/MS (Master of Arts/Science) (T) 11, Community Counseling MA/MS (Master of Arts/Science) (T) 37, Marriage, Couple, and Family Therapy MA/MS (Master of Arts/Science) (T) 9, Psychological and Cultural Studies MA/MS (Master of Arts/Science) (T) 0.

Student Applications/Admissions:

Student Applications

School Psychology EdS/MEd (School Psychology)—Applications 2007–2008, 38. Total applicants accepted 2007–2008, 26. Number full-time enrolled (new admits only) 2007–2008, 12. Number part-time enrolled (new admits only) 2007–2008, 2. Total enrolled 2007–2008 full-time, 31, part-time, 18. Openings 2008–2009, 20. The median number of years required for completion of a degree in 2006–2007 were 3. The number of students enrolled full- and part-time who were dismissed or voluntarily withdrew from this program area in 2007–2008 were 0. *Addictions Treatment MA/MS (Master of Arts/Science)*—Applications 2007–2008, 25. Total applicants accepted 2007–2008, 21. Number full-time enrolled (new admits only) 2007–2008, 13. Number part-time enrolled (new admits only) 2007–2008, 0. Total enrolled 2007–2008 full-time, 38, part-time, 4. Openings 2008–2009, 20. The median number of years required for completion of a degree in 2006–2007 were 3. The number of students enrolled full- and part-time who were dismissed or voluntarily withdrew from this program area in 2007–2008 were 1. *Community Counseling MA/MS (Master of Arts/Science)*—Applications 2007–2008, 81. Total applicants accepted 2007–2008, 69. Number full-time enrolled (new admits only) 2007–2008, 32. Number part-time enrolled (new admits only) 2007–2008, 4. Total enrolled 2007–2008 full-time, 85, part-time, 21. Openings 2008–2009, 60. The median number of years required for completion of a degree in 2006–2007 were 3. The number of students enrolled full- and part-time who were dismissed or voluntarily withdrew from this program area in 2007–2008 were 2. *Marriage, Couple, and Family Therapy MA/MS (Master of Arts/Science)*—Applications 2007–2008, 59. Total applicants accepted 2007–2008, 34. Number full-time enrolled (new admits only) 2007–2008, 21. Number part-time enrolled (new admits only) 2007–2008, 1. Total enrolled 2007–2008 full-time, 41, part-time, 4. Openings 2008–2009, 20. The median number of years required for completion of a degree in 2006–2007 were 3. The number of students enrolled full- and part-time who were dismissed or voluntarily withdrew from this program area in 2007–2008 were 2. *Psychological and Cultural Studies MA/MS (Master of Arts/Science)*—Applications 2007–2008, 3. Total applicants accepted 2007–2008, 2. Number full-time enrolled (new admits only) 2007–2008, 1. Number part-time enrolled (new admits only) 2007–2008, 0. Openings 2008–2009, 10. The median number of years required for completion of a degree in 2006–2007 were 2. The number of students enrolled full- and part-time who were dismissed or voluntarily withdrew from this program area in 2007–2008 were 0.

Admissions Requirements:

Scores: Entries appear in this order: required test or GPA, minimum score (if required), median score of students entering in 2007–2008. Master's Programs: GRE-Subject (Psychology) 550; overall undergraduate GPA 2.75, 3.3. No minimum is required for GRE V + Q + Analytical.

Other Criteria: (importance of criteria rated low, medium, or high): GRE/MAT scores—low, research experience—medium, work experience—medium, extracurricular activity—medium, clinically related public service—low, GPA—medium, letters of recommendation—high, interview—low, statement of goals and objectives—high. All programs sometimes require an interview. For additional information on admission requirements, go to http://education.lclark.edu/dept/gseadmit/.

Student Characteristics: The following represents characteristics of students in 2007–2008 in all graduate psychology programs in the department: Female—full-time 157, part-time 44; Male—full-time 41, part-time 6; African American/Black—full-time 3, part-time 1; Hispanic/Latino(a)—full-time 10, part-time 1; Asian/Pacific Islander—full-time 3, part-time 2; American Indian/Alaska Native—full-time 0, part-time 0; Caucasian/White—full-time 146, part-time 36; Multi-ethnic—full-time 14, part-time 3; Unknown ethnicity—full-time 22, part-time 7; International students who hold an F-1 or J-1 Visa—full-time 0, part-time 0.

Financial Information/Assistance:

Tuition for Full-Time Study: *Master's:* State residents: $645 per credit hour; Nonstate residents: $645 per credit hour. Tuition is subject to change.

Financial Assistance:

First-Year Students: Fellowships and scholarships available for first year. Apply by TBA.

Advanced Students: Fellowships and scholarships available for advanced students. Apply by TBA.

Additional Information: Application and information available online at http://www.lclark.edu/dept/sfs/.

Internships/Practica: Master's Degree (MA/MS Addictions Treatment): An internship experience such as a final research project or "capstone" experience is required of graduates. Master's Degree (MA/MS Community Counseling): An internship experience such as a final research project or "capstone" experience is required of graduates. Master's Degree (MA/MS Marriage, Couple and Family Therapy): An internship experience such as a final research project or "capstone" experience is required of graduates. Internship and practicum placements in community agencies and schools provide students with opportunities for supervised professional practice. As part of each placement, students receive supervision from qualified professionals in their community or school setting. Students also receive weekly instruction and supervision from on-campus instructors throughout their internship and practicum placements. Required hours, supervision, and activities meet standards set by licensing bodies for students in their respective specialty areas. This ensures that students will be qualified to pursue licensing after completing their degree program. Internships in marriage and family therapy, community counseling, and addictions counseling involve part-time placements. Internships in school psychology are full-time for 1 academic year and usually involve a stipend to the student.

Housing and Day Care: On-campus housing is available. Only the undergraduate campus has housing. Most graduate students find apartments and houses in the immediate area. No on-campus day care facilities are available.

Employment of Department Graduates:

Master's Degree Graduates: Of those who graduated in the academic year 2006–2007, the following categories and numbers represent the postgraduate activities and employment of master's degree graduates: Enrolled in a postdoctoral residency/fellowship (n/a), employed in independent practice (n/a), total from the above (master's) (0).

Doctoral Degree Graduates: Of those who graduated in the academic year 2006–2007, the following categories and numbers represent the postgraduate activities and employment of doctoral degree graduates: Enrolled in a psychology doctoral program (n/a), total from the above (doctoral) (0).

Additional Information:

Orientation, Objectives, and Emphasis of Department: Lewis and Clark College's Department of Counseling Psychology prepares professional counselors, therapists, and school psychologists to lead, serve, and work for social justice in community and school settings. Faculty and students are committed to disseminating and expanding the knowledge base relevant to this mission, promoting the use of evidence-based treatment and prevention procedures, and adhering to the highest ethical standards as practitioners and researchers. The programs in counseling psychology prepare highly qualified mental health professionals for employment in public agencies, community-based programs, and schools. Curricular options also exist for those who would like to concentrate on research and establish a foundation in pursuit of doctoral training. We are especially interested in preparing students for multicultural competence and social justice advocacy.

Personal Behavior Statement: http://www.lclark.edu/dept/cpsy/objects/EthicalGuidelines.pdf.

Special Facilities or Resources: The program has established collaborative relationships with community schools and agencies, which provide students opportunities to participate in ongoing research and program evaluation. These opportunities are open to students planning to complete a thesis and also to students who wish to secure increased training and experience without doing a full thesis.

Information for Students With Physical Disabilities: See the following Web site for more information: http://www.lclark.edu/~access.

Application Information:

Send to Counseling Psychology Department, Lewis & Clark College, Graduate School of Education and Counseling Admissions, MSC 87, 0615 Southwest Palatine Hill Road, Portland, OR 97219-7899. Application available online. URL of online application: http://www.lclark.edu/dept/gseadmit/. Students are admitted in the Fall, application deadline February 1; Spring, application deadline October 1; Summer, application deadline February 1; Programs have rolling admissions. Special Students (not fully admitted to a program who may take 9 semester hours within 1 year) should consult admissions office for application deadlines. *Fee:* $50. Fee waived for online application.

Oregon, University of

Counseling Psychology
College of Education
5251 University of Oregon
Eugene, OR 97403-5251
Telephone: (541) 346-2456
Fax: (541) 346-6778
E-mail: *cpsy@uoregon.edu*
Web: *http://www.counpsych.uoregon.edu*

Department Information:

1954. Area Head: Linda Forrest. Number of faculty: total—full-time 4, part-time 2; women—full-time 3, part-time 2; ; women minority—full-time 1; faculty subject to the Americans With Disabilities Act 1.

Programs and Degrees Offered:

Listed in the following order: Program area, degree type (T if terminal Master's), number awarded 7/06–6/07. Counseling Psychology PhD (Doctor of Philosophy) 6.

APA Accreditation: Counseling PhD (Doctor of Philosophy).

Student Applications/Admissions:

Student Applications

Counseling Psychology PhD (Doctor of Philosophy)—Applications 2007–2008, 183. Total applicants accepted 2007–2008, 10. Number full-time enrolled (new admits only) 2007–2008, 8. Number part-time enrolled (new admits only) 2007–2008, 0. Openings 2008–2009, 8. The median number of years required for completion of a degree in 2006–2007 were 6. The number of students enrolled full- and part-time who were dismissed or voluntarily withdrew from this program area in 2007–2008 were 1.

Admissions Requirements:

Scores: Entries appear in this order: required test or GPA, minimum score (if required), median score of students entering in 2007–2008. Master's Programs: GRE-V no minimum stated; GRE-Q no minimum stated; overall undergraduate GPA no minimum stated; Masters GRE-Analytical no minimum stated. Major GPA Doctoral Programs: GRE-V 380, 557; GRE-Q 410, 624; overall undergraduate GPA 2.4, 3.54; Doctoral program GRE-Analytic 3.5, 4.7.

Other Criteria: (importance of criteria rated low, medium, or high): GRE/MAT scores—medium, research experience—high, work experience—medium, extracurricular activity—medium, clinically related public service—medium, GPA—high, letters of recommendation—high, interview—high, statement of goals and objectives—high, second language skills—medium, undergraduate major in psychology—medium, specific undergraduate psychology courses taken—medium. For additional information on admission requirements, go to http://counpsych.uoregon.edu.

Student Characteristics: The following represents characteristics of students in 2007–2008 in all graduate psychology programs in the department: Female—full-time 41, part-time 0; Male—full-time 9, part-time 0; African American/Black—full-time 5, part-time 0; Hispanic/Latino(a)—full-time 11, part-time 0; Asian/

Pacific Islander—full-time 9, part-time 0; American Indian/ Alaska Native—full-time 0, part-time 0; Caucasian/White—full-time 21, part-time 0; Multi-ethnic—full-time 0, part-time 0; students subject to the Americans With Disabilities Act—full-time 3, part-time 0; Unknown ethnicity—full-time 4, part-time 0; International students who hold an F-1 or J-1 Visa—full-time 0, part-time 0.

Financial Information/Assistance:

Tuition for Full-Time Study: *Doctoral:* State residents: per academic year $10,035, $372 per credit hour; Nonstate residents: per academic year $14,799, $548 per credit hour. Tuition is subject to change. See the following Web site for updates and changes in tuition costs: http://www.registrar.uoregon.edu/common/tuition/tuitionrates.php. Note: There are additional fees.

Financial Assistance:

First-Year Students: Teaching assistantships available for first year. Average amount paid per academic year: $9,501. Average number of hours worked per week: 16. Apply by March. Tuition remission given: full. Fellowships and scholarships available for first year. Average amount paid per academic year: $9,501. Average number of hours worked per week: 16. Apply by March. Tuition remission given: full.

Advanced Students: Teaching assistantships available for advanced students. Average amount paid per academic year: $9,501. Average number of hours worked per week: 16. Apply by March. Tuition remission given: full. Research assistantships available for advanced students. Average amount paid per academic year: $9,501. Average number of hours worked per week: 16. Apply by March. Tuition remission given: full. Fellowships and scholarships available for advanced students. Average amount paid per academic year: $9,501. Average number of hours worked per week: 16. Apply by March. Tuition remission given: full.

Additional Information: Of all students currently enrolled full time, 100% benefited from one or more of the listed financial assistance programs. Application and information available online at http://financialaid.uoregon.edu/.

Internships/Practica: Doctoral Degree (PhD Counseling Psychology): For those doctoral students for whom a professional internship was required in this program prior to graduation, (3) students applied for an internship in 2006–2007, with (3) students obtaining an internship. Of those students who obtained an internship, (3) were paid internships. Of those students who obtained an internship, (3) students placed in APA/CPA-accredited internships, (0) students placed in internships not APA/CPA accredited, but listed with the Association of Psychology Postdoctoral and Internship Centers (APPIC), (0) students placed in internships conforming to guidelines of the Council of Directors of School Psychology Programs (CDSPP), (0) students placed in internships that were not APA/CPA-accredited, APPIC or CDSPP listed. All students are required to participate in both adult and child/family practica. Numerous externship opportunities exist throughout the community.

Housing and Day Care: On-campus housing is available. See the following Web site for more information: http://www.housing.uoregon.edu/. On-campus day care facilities are available.

Employment of Department Graduates:

Master's Degree Graduates: Of those who graduated in the academic year 2006–2007, the following categories and numbers represent the postgraduate activities and employment of master's degree graduates: Enrolled in a psychology doctoral program (0), enrolled in another graduate/professional program (0), enrolled in a postdoctoral residency/fellowship (n/a), employed in independent practice (n/a), employed in an academic position at a university (0), employed in an academic position at a 2-year/4-year college (0), employed in other positions at a higher education institution (0), employed in a professional position in a school system (0), employed in business or industry (0), employed in government agency (0), employed in a community mental health/counseling center (0), employed in a hospital/medical center (0), still seeking employment (0), not seeking employment (0), other employment position (0), do not know (0), total from the above (master's) (0).

Doctoral Degree Graduates: Of those who graduated in the academic year 2006–2007, the following categories and numbers represent the postgraduate activities and employment of doctoral degree graduates: Enrolled in a psychology doctoral program (n/a), enrolled in another graduate/professional program (0), enrolled in a postdoctoral residency/fellowship (0), employed in independent practice (0), employed in an academic position at a university (0), employed in an academic position at a 2-year/4-year college (0), employed in other positions at a higher education institution (0), employed in a professional position in a school system (0), employed in business or industry (0), employed in government agency (0), employed in a community mental health/counseling center (0), employed in a hospital/medical center (0), still seeking employment (0), not seeking employment (0), other employment position (0), do not know (0), total from the above (doctoral) (0).

Additional Information:

Orientation, Objectives, and Emphasis of Department: Accredited by the American Psychological Association (APA) since 1955, the UO doctoral program in Counseling Psychology emphasizes an ecological model of training, research, and practice. Students focus research and training in prevention and treatment relevant to work with children, adolescents, families, and adults. The ecological model holds that human behavior occurs within a context of multiple interacting systems, influenced by unique social, historical, political, and cultural factors. Students in the CPSY program are trained to view assessment, intervention, and research within the contexts of these systems. Development of multicultural competencies is emphasized throughout the curriculum.

Special Facilities or Resources: Students work cooperatively in research areas at Oregon Social Learning Center, the Oregon Research Institute, and the Child and Family Center.

Information for Students With Physical Disabilities: See the following Web site for more information: http://www.ds.uoregon.edu/.

Application Information:

Send to Academic Secretary, Counseling Psychology, 5251 University of Oregon, Eugene, OR 97403-5251. Application available online. URL of online application: http://www.counpsych.uoregon.edu/admissions.htm. Students are admitted in the Fall, application deadline approximately December 15. Please see Web site for specific deadline each year. *Fee:* $50. Contact UO Admissions regarding conditions for waiver or deferral of fee.

Oregon, University of

Department of Psychology
College of Arts and Sciences
1227 University of Oregon
Eugene, OR 97403-1227
Telephone: (541) 346-5060
Fax: (541) 346-4911
E-mail: *gradsec@psych.uoregon.edu*
Web: *http://www.psychweb.uoregon.edu*

Department Information:

1895. Department Head: Louis J. Moses, PhD. Number of faculty: total—full-time 24, part-time 4; women—full-time 8, part-time 1; total—minority—full-time 5; women minority—full-time 1.

Programs and Degrees Offered:

Listed in the following order: Program area, degree type (T if terminal Master's), number awarded 7/06–6/07. Clinical PhD (Doctor of Philosophy) 3, Cognitive/Neuroscience PhD (Doctor of Philosophy) 2, Developmental PhD (Doctor of Philosophy) 2, Individualized Master's MA/MS (Master of Arts/Science) (T) 8, Social/Personality PhD (Doctor of Philosophy) 1.

APA Accreditation: Clinical PhD (Doctor of Philosophy).

Student Applications/Admissions:

Student Applications

Clinical PhD (Doctor of Philosophy)—Applications 2007–2008, 216. Total applicants accepted 2007–2008, 4. Number full-time enrolled (new admits only) 2007–2008, 4. Total enrolled 2007–2008 full-time, 25, part-time, 4. Openings 2008–2009, 4. *Cognitive/Neuroscience PhD (Doctor of Philosophy)*—Applications 2007–2008, 60. Total applicants accepted 2007–2008, 6. Number full-time enrolled (new admits only) 2007–2008, 6. Total enrolled 2007–2008 full-time, 16. Openings 2008–2009, 2. The number of students enrolled full- and part-time who were dismissed or voluntarily withdrew from this program area in 2007–2008 were 1. *Developmental PhD (Doctor of Philosophy)*—Applications 2007–2008, 25. Total applicants accepted 2007–2008, 1. Number full-time enrolled (new admits only) 2007–2008, 1. Total enrolled 2007–2008 full-time, 7. Openings 2008–2009, 2. *Individualized Master's MA/MS (Master of Arts/Science)*—Applications 2007–2008, 19. Total applicants accepted 2007–2008, 9. Number full-time enrolled (new admits only) 2007–2008, 8. Total enrolled 2007–2008 full-time, 21. Openings 2008–2009, 10. *Social/Personality PhD (Doctor of Philosophy)*—Applications 2007–2008, 55. Total applicants accepted 2007–2008, 4. Number full-time enrolled (new admits only) 2007–2008, 4. Total enrolled 2007–2008 full-time, 17. Openings 2008–2009, 2.

Admissions Requirements:

Scores: Entries appear in this order: required test or GPA, minimum score (if required), median score of students entering in 2007–2008. Master's Programs: overall undergraduate GPA no minimum stated, 3.44; psychology GPA no minimum stated. The GRE is recommended (not required) for admission to the Individualized Master's Program. Doctoral Programs: GRE-V no minimum stated, 619; GRE-Q no minimum stated, 714; overall undergraduate GPA no minimum stated, 3.72; Doctoral program GRE-Analytic no minimum stated, 723.

Other Criteria: (importance of criteria rated low, medium, or high): GRE/MAT scores—high, research experience—high, work experience—low, extracurricular activity—low, clinically related public service—medium, GPA—high, letters of recommendation—high, interview—high, statement of goals and objectives—high. Please check with department regarding interviews. For additional information on admission requirements, go to http://psychweb.uoregon.edu.

Student Characteristics: The following represents characteristics of students in 2007–2008 in all graduate psychology programs in the department: Female—full-time 55, part-time 3; Male—full-time 31, part-time 1; African American/Black—full-time 1, part-time 0; Hispanic/Latino(a)—full-time 2, part-time 1; Asian/Pacific Islander—full-time 6, part-time 2; American Indian/Alaska Native—full-time 0, part-time 0; Caucasian/White—full-time 47, part-time 1; Multi-ethnic—full-time 5, part-time 0; students subject to the Americans With Disabilities Act—full-time 0, part-time 0; Unknown ethnicity—full-time 25, part-time 0; International students who hold an F-1 or J-1 Visa—full-time 13, part-time 0.

Financial Information/Assistance:

Financial Assistance:

First-Year Students: Teaching assistantships available for first year. Tuition remission given: full. Research assistantships available for first year. Tuition remission given: full. Fellowships and scholarships available for first year. Tuition remission given: partial.

Advanced Students: Teaching assistantships available for advanced students. Tuition remission given: full. Research assistantships available for advanced students. Tuition remission given: full. Fellowships and scholarships available for advanced students. Tuition remission given: partial.

Additional Information: Of all students currently enrolled full time, 95% benefited from one or more of the listed financial assistance programs.

Internships/Practica: Master's Degree (MA/MS Individualized Master's): An internship experience such as a final research project or "capstone" experience is required of graduates. Doctoral Degree (PhD Clinical): For those doctoral students for whom a professional internship was required in this program prior to graduation, (5) students applied for an internship in 2006–2007, with (5) students obtaining an internship. Of those students who obtained an internship, (5) were paid internships. Of those students who obtained an internship, (5) students placed in APA/CPA-accredited internships, (0) students placed in internships not APA/CPA-accredited, but listed with the Association of Psychology Postdoctoral and Internship Centers (APPIC), (0) students placed in internships conforming to guidelines of the Council of Directors of School Psychology Programs (CDSPP), (0) students placed in internships that were not APA/CPA accredited, APPIC or CDSPP listed. See http://psychweb.uoregon.edu/gradprog/uopsy_clinhandbook_F07.pdf.

Housing and Day Care: On-campus housing is available. See the following Web site for more information: http://www.housing.uoregon.edu. On-campus day care facilities are available. See the following Web site for more information: http://www.housing.uoregon.edu/FHA/child.html.

Employment of Department Graduates:

Master's Degree Graduates: Of those who graduated in the academic year 2006–2007, the following categories and numbers represent the postgraduate activities and employment of master's degree graduates: Enrolled in a postdoctoral residency/fellowship (n/a), employed in independent practice (n/a), total from the above (master's) (0).

Doctoral Degree Graduates: Of those who graduated in the academic year 2006–2007, the following categories and numbers represent the postgraduate activities and employment of doctoral degree graduates: Enrolled in a psychology doctoral program (n/a), total from the above (doctoral) (0).

Additional Information:

Orientation, Objectives, and Emphasis of Department: The course of study is tailored largely to the student's particular needs. There are minimal formal requirements for the doctorate, which include three course sequences (contemporary issues in psychology, statistics, and a first-year research practicum); a supporting area requirement, consisting of at least two graduate-level graded courses, and a major project, such as a paper or teaching an original course; a major preliminary examination; and, of course, the doctoral dissertation. Clinical students engage in several practica beginning in the first year. All programs require and are organized to facilitate student research from the first year.

Special Facilities or Resources: Straub Hall houses the psychology clinic, equipment for psychophysiological research, specialized facilities for research in child and social psychology, and experimental laboratories for human research. Numerous microcomputers are available for research and teaching. A short distance from the main psychology building are well-equipped animal labs for research in physiological psychology. Graduate students and faculty participate in interdisciplinary programs in cognitive science, neuroscience, and developmental psychopathology. Local nonprofit research groups including Oregon Research Institute, Oregon Social Learning Center, and Decision Research provide unusual auspices and opportunities for students.

Information for Students With Physical Disabilities: See the following Web site for more information: http://www.ds.uoregon.edu/.

Application Information:

Send to Graduate Secretary, Department of Psychology, 1227 University of Oregon, Eugene, OR 97403-1227. Application available online. URL of online application: http://www.psychweb.uoregon.edu. Students are admitted in the Fall, application deadline December 15. Individualized master's deadline for Fall admission is May 15. *Fee:* $50.

Pacific University

School of Professional Psychology
HPC/Pacific University, 222 Southeast 8th Avenue, Suite 563
Hillsboro, OR 97123-4218
Telephone: (503) 352-7277
Fax: (503) 352-7320
E-mail: *waldronk@pacificu.edu*
Web: *http://www.pacificu.edu*

Department Information:

1979. Dean: Michel Hersen. Number of faculty: total—full-time 18, part-time 19; women—full-time 14, part-time 15; women minority—full-time 4, part-time 1; faculty subject to the Americans With Disabilities Act 2.

Programs and Degrees Offered:

Listed in the following order: Program area, degree type (T if terminal Master's), number awarded 7/06–6/07. Clinical PsyD (Doctor of Psychology) 25, Counseling MA/MS (Master of Arts/Science) (T) 33.

APA Accreditation: Clinical PsyD (Doctor of Psychology).

Student Applications/Admissions:

Student Applications

Clinical PsyD (Doctor of Psychology)—Applications 2007–2008, 225. Total applicants accepted 2007–2008, 98. Number full-time enrolled (new admits only) 2007–2008, 55. Number part-time enrolled (new admits only) 2007–2008, 0. Total enrolled 2007–2008 full-time, 184, part-time, 64. Openings 2008–2009, 50. The median number of years required for completion of a degree in 2006–2007 were 5. The number of students enrolled full- and part-time who were dismissed or voluntarily withdrew from this program area in 2007–2008 were 6. *Counseling MA/MS (Master of Arts/Science)*—Applications 2007–2008, 111. Total applicants accepted 2007–2008, 68. Number full-time enrolled (new admits only) 2007–2008, 35. Number part-time enrolled (new admits only) 2007–2008, 4. Total enrolled 2007–2008 full-time, 76, part-time, 7. Openings 2008–2009, 45. The median number of years required for completion of a degree in 2006–2007 were 2. The number of students enrolled full- and part-time who were dismissed or voluntarily withdrew from this program area in 2007–2008 were 1.

Admissions Requirements:

Scores: Entries appear in this order: required test or GPA, minimum score (if required), median score of students entering in 2007–2008. Doctoral Programs: GRE-V no minimum stated; GRE-Q no minimum stated; overall undergraduate GPA no minimum stated, 3.1; last 2 years GPA no minimum stated, 3.4; Doctoral program GRE-Analytic no minimum stated. Desirable minimum scores: Total of 1100 for the Verbal and Quantitative portions. Analytic Writing, at least the 50th percentile. Master's GPA is required for advanced standing applicants. TOEFL is required for those for whom English is not the native language. Minimum score for paper test is 600; computer test, 105.

Other Criteria: (importance of criteria rated low, medium, or high): GRE/MAT scores—medium, research experience—

medium, work experience—medium, extracurricular activity—low, clinically related public service—low, GPA—medium, letters of recommendation—high, interview—high, statement of goals and objectives—medium, undergraduate major in psychology—low, specific undergraduate psychology courses taken—medium. GRE scores required for PsyD program only. (GRE is not required for Respecialization applicants.) For additional information on admission requirements, go to http://www.pacificu.edu/spp/admissions/index.cfm.

Student Characteristics: The following represents characteristics of students in 2007–2008 in all graduate psychology programs in the department: Female—full-time 180, part-time 55; Male—full-time 80, part-time 16; African American/Black—full-time 2, part-time 1; Hispanic/Latino(a)—full-time 4, part-time 1; Asian/Pacific Islander—full-time 17, part-time 4; American Indian/Alaska Native—full-time 3, part-time 1; Caucasian/White—full-time 198, part-time 52; Multi-ethnic—full-time 0, part-time 0; students subject to the Americans With Disabilities Act—full-time 6, part-time 5; Unknown ethnicity—full-time 36, part-time 12; International students who hold an F-1 or J-1 Visa—full-time 1, part-time 0.

Financial Information/Assistance:

Tuition for Full-Time Study: *Master's:* State residents: per academic year $18,240, $742 per credit hour; Nonstate residents: per academic year $18,240, $742 per credit hour. *Doctoral:* State residents: per academic year $25,410, $770 per credit hour; Nonstate residents: per academic year $25,410, $770 per credit hour. Tuition is subject to change. See the following Web sites for updates and changes in tuition costs: http://www.pacificu.edu/spp/admissions/clinical/financialaid.cfm; http://www.pacificu.edu/spp/admiss.

Financial Assistance:

First-Year Students: Research assistantships available for first year. Average amount paid per academic year: $3,000. Average number of hours worked per week: 7. Fellowships and scholarships available for first year. Average amount paid per academic year: $3,000. Apply by January 10.

Advanced Students: Teaching assistantships available for advanced students. Average amount paid per academic year: $3,600. Average number of hours worked per week: 7. Apply by April 1. Research assistantships available for advanced students. Average amount paid per academic year: $3,000. Average number of hours worked per week: 7. Apply by April 1. Fellowships and scholarships available for advanced students. Average amount paid per academic year: $3,000. Apply by April 1. Tuition remission given: partial.

Additional Information: Of all students currently enrolled full time, 30% benefited from one or more of the listed financial assistance programs.

Internships/Practica: Doctoral Degree (PsyD Clinical): For those doctoral students for whom a professional internship was required in this program prior to graduation, (39) students applied for an internship in 2006–2007, with (36) students obtaining an internship. Of those students who obtained an internship, (36) were paid internships. Of those students who obtained an internship, (24) students placed in APA/CPA-accredited internships, (10) students placed in internships not APA/CPA-accredited, but listed with the Association of Psychology Postdoctoral and Internship Centers (APPIC), (0) students placed in internships conforming to guidelines of the Council of Directors of School Psychology Programs (CDSPP), (2) students placed in internships that were not APA/CPA-accredited, APPIC or CDSPP listed. Each PsyD student is required to complete six terms (24 credits, 2 years) of practica. The practicum experience includes a minimum of 500 training hours per year, approximately one third to one half of which are in direct service, one fourth in supervisory and training activities, and the remainder in administrative and clerical duties related to the above. Training entails the integration of theoretical knowledge through its application in clinical practice. The experience shall include supervised practice in the application of professional psychological competencies with a range of client populations, age groups, problems, and service settings. The initial year of practicum is typically served at the Psychological Service Center. Later experiences are usually taken at community placements. Upon successful completion of practicum training, required coursework, and Candidacy Examination, the student is ready to begin an internship. Internship requires one calendar year of full-time experience, or 2 years half time, at an approved site. MA Counseling Psychology students complete 15 credits (3 terms) of practicum in their 2nd year.

Housing and Day Care: No on-campus housing is available. No on-campus day care facilities are available.

Employment of Department Graduates:

Master's Degree Graduates: Of those who graduated in the academic year 2006–2007, the following categories and numbers represent the postgraduate activities and employment of master's degree graduates: Enrolled in a postdoctoral residency/fellowship (n/a), employed in independent practice (n/a), total from the above (master's) (0).

Doctoral Degree Graduates: Of those who graduated in the academic year 2006–2007, the following categories and numbers represent the postgraduate activities and employment of doctoral degree graduates: Enrolled in a psychology doctoral program (n/a), enrolled in another graduate/professional program (0), enrolled in a postdoctoral residency/fellowship (7), employed in independent practice (2), employed in an academic position at a 2-year/4-year college (1), employed in other positions at a higher education institution (2), employed in a professional position in a school system (0), employed in business or industry (0), employed in government agency (6), employed in a community mental health/counseling center (0), employed in a hospital/medical center (1), still seeking employment (0), not seeking employment (1), other employment position (0), do not know (5), total from the above (doctoral) (25).

Additional Information:

Orientation, Objectives, and Emphasis of Department: The School of Professional Psychology at Pacific University educates informed practitioners of scientifically based professional psychology who are responsive to the latest empirical findings in the field. We strive to maintain a facilitative academic community based on collaborative inquiry. Faculty and students work together in multiple roles in program develoment, clinical research, and governance. We underscore provision of services to diverse populations at the individual, family, group, and community levels.

Special Facilities or Resources: The Psychological Service Center of the Pacific University School of Professional Psychology provides a full range of quality outpatient psychological services to residents of the Portland Metropolitan area while providing intensive training for doctoral-level clinical psychology students and providing a setting for ongoing clinical research. The full range of psychodiagnostic and treatment services is provided to a variety of client populations, including intellectual, personality, and neuropsychological assessment; individual therapy; family therapy; group therapy; and consultation. The Iris Clinic in Hillsboro provides the opportunity to provide services in Spanish.

Information for Students With Physical Disabilities: See the following Web site for more information: http://www.pacificu.edu/studentlife/department/lss.cfm.

Application Information:

Send to Office of Admissions, Pacific University, 222 Southeast 8th Avenue, Suite 212, Hillsboro, OR 97123; E-mail: admissions@pacificu.edu; Phone: (503) 352-2218; (877) 722-8648 ext. 2218. URL of online application: http://www.pacificu.edu/spp/admissions/howtoapply.cfm. Students are admitted in the Fall, application deadline January 10. MA Counseling Psychology, March 5. *Fee:* $40.

Portland State University

Psychology Department
College of Liberal Arts and Sciences
P.O. Box 751
Portland, OR 97207-0751
Telephone: (503) 725-3923
Fax: (503) 725-3904
E-mail: *mankowskie@pdx.edu*
Web: *http://www.psy.pdx.edu/*

Department Information:

1955. Chairperson: Sherwin Davidson, PhD. Number of faculty: total—full-time 12, part-time 1; women—full-time 8; faculty subject to the Americans With Disabilities Act 17.

Programs and Degrees Offered:

Listed in the following order: Program area, degree type (T if terminal Master's), number awarded 7/06–6/07. Applied Developmental PhD (Doctor of Philosophy) 2, Applied Social and Community PhD (Doctor of Philosophy) 2, Industrial/Organizational PhD (Doctor of Philosophy) 5.

Student Applications/Admissions:

Student Applications

Applied Developmental PhD (Doctor of Philosophy)—Applications 2007–2008, 15. Total applicants accepted 2007–2008, 4. Number full-time enrolled (new admits only) 2007–2008, 4. Openings 2008–2009, 4. The median number of years required for completion of a degree in 2006–2007 were 6. The number of students enrolled full- and part-time who were dismissed or voluntarily withdrew from this program area in 2007–2008 were 0. *Applied Social and Community PhD (Doctor of Philosophy)*—Applications 2007–2008, 60. Total applicants accepted 2007–2008, 6. Number full-time enrolled (new admits only) 2007–2008, 5. Number part-time enrolled (new admits only) 2007–2008, 0. Openings 2008–2009, 5. The median number of years required for completion of a degree in 2006–2007 were 6. The number of students enrolled full- and part-time who were dismissed or voluntarily withdrew from this program area in 2007–2008 were 0. *Industrial/Organizational PhD (Doctor of Philosophy)*—Applications 2007–2008, 80. Total applicants accepted 2007–2008, 6. Number full-time enrolled (new admits only) 2007–2008, 6. Number part-time enrolled (new admits only) 2007–2008, 0. Openings 2008–2009, 6. The median number of years required for completion of a degree in 2006–2007 were 6. The number of students enrolled full- and part-time who were dismissed or voluntarily withdrew from this program area in 2007–2008 were 0.

Admissions Requirements:

Scores: Entries appear in this order: required test or GPA, minimum score (if required), median score of students entering in 2007–2008. Master's Programs: GRE-V no minimum stated; GRE-Q no minimum stated; overall undergraduate GPA 3.00; last 2 years GPA no minimum stated; psychology GPA no minimum stated; Masters GRE-Analytical no minimum stated. Doctoral Programs: GRE-V no minimum stated; GRE-Q no minimum stated; overall undergraduate GPA 3.00; last 2 years GPA no minimum stated; psychology GPA no minimum stated; Doctoral program GRE-Analytic no minimum stated. Verbal + Quantitative score must be at least 1100.

Other Criteria: (importance of criteria rated low, medium, or high): GRE/MAT scores—high, research experience—high, work experience—medium, extracurricular activity—medium, clinically related public service—low, GPA—high, letters of recommendation—high, statement of goals and objectives—high.

Student Characteristics: The following represents characteristics of students in 2007–2008 in all graduate psychology programs in the department: Female—full-time 41, part-time 0; Male—full-time 13, part-time 0; African American/Black—full-time 1, part-time 0; Hispanic/Latino(a)—full-time 4, part-time 0; Asian/Pacific Islander—full-time 4, part-time 0; American Indian/Alaska Native—part-time 0; Caucasian/White—full-time 45, part-time 0; Unknown ethnicity—full-time 0, part-time 0.

Financial Information/Assistance:

Tuition for Full-Time Study: *Master's:* State residents: per academic year $7,651; Nonstate residents: per academic year $12,241. *Doctoral:* State residents: per academic year $7,651; Nonstate residents: per academic year $12,241. Tuition is subject to change. See the following Web site for updates and changes in tuition costs: http://www.pdx.edu/registration/tuition.html.

Financial Assistance:

First-Year Students: Teaching assistantships available for first year. Average amount paid per academic year: $6,300. Average number of hours worked per week: 12. Tuition remission given: full. Research assistantships available for first year. Average amount paid per academic year: $6,300. Average number of hours worked per week: 12. Tuition remission given: full. Fellowships and scholarships available for first year. Average amount paid per academic year: $6,300. Average number of hours worked per week: 12. Tuition remission given: full.

Advanced Students: Teaching assistantships available for advanced students. Average amount paid per academic year: $6,300. Average number of hours worked per week: 12. Tuition remission given: full. Research assistantships available for advanced students. Average amount paid per academic year: $6,300. Average number of hours worked per week: 12. Tuition remission given: full. Fellowships and scholarships available for advanced students. Average amount paid per academic year: $6,300. Average number of hours worked per week: 12. Tuition remission given: full.

Additional Information: Of all students currently enrolled full time, 100% benefited from one or more of the listed financial assistance programs.

Internships/Practica: The university is located in downtown Portland, the major metropolitan area in the state of Oregon. Consequently, internships are readily available in a variety of applied settings. Placements are also available through the ongoing research activities of the faculty. The program is structured to provide everyone with (a) training in the basics of applied psychology and research methods, and (b) expertise in the psychological theories and research methods in their area of specialty. The basic training is provided by three advanced applied courses in the three areas we consider central to the understanding of social issues: social and group processes (referred to as Applied Social); organizational and institutional processes (referred to as Industrial/Organizational); and process of change (referred to as Applied Developmental). Training in research methods is provided via a sequence of quantitative methods courses, two of which are required. The department offers a number of additional quantitative offerings that include Factor Analysis, Structural Equation Modeling, and Psychometrics and Scale Construction. Because the program emphasizes applied psychology, students receive training in their area of specialty not only through close work with faculty but also through structured participation in community organizations. Graduate students work in close collaboration with their faculty advisors and other members of the faculty who serve in a mentor role. Student experiences include seminars on special topics, individual reading and conference arrangements, research practica, and collaboration on joint projects. The primary vehicles for interactions with community organizations are practica and internships. To ensure relevant learning, these are supervised by departmental faculty. The program culminates for students in their own independent research (i.e., thesis and/or dissertation). For further information, see http://www.psy.pdx.edu/community/community.htm.

Housing and Day Care: On-campus housing is available. See the following Web site for more information: http://www.pdx.edu/housing/. On-campus day care facilities are available. See the following Web site for more information: http://www.tcc.pdx.edu/welcome.php or http://www.hgcdc.pdx.edu/.

Employment of Department Graduates:

Master's Degree Graduates: Of those who graduated in the academic year 2006–2007, the following categories and numbers represent the postgraduate activities and employment of master's degree graduates: Enrolled in a postdoctoral residency/fellowship (n/a), employed in independent practice (n/a), total from the above (master's) (0).

Doctoral Degree Graduates: Of those who graduated in the academic year 2006–2007, the following categories and numbers represent the postgraduate activities and employment of doctoral degree graduates: Enrolled in a psychology doctoral program (n/a), total from the above (doctoral) (0).

Additional Information:

Orientation, Objectives, and Emphasis of Department: The department accepts applicants to both the MA/MS (initiated Fall 1969) and PhD (initiated fall 1986) programs. The master's program is fully integrated into the doctoral program. Those who are admitted to the master's program may later apply for admission to the doctoral program, conditional upon demonstrated competence at the master's level. The aim of the program is to prepare graduates for a university career and/or a research/service career in a variety of settings, such as governmental agencies, manufacturing and service industries, health organizations, and labor organizations. Students are given a broad background in applied psychology. Doctoral students major in one of the following three specialty areas and select a minor in a second. Applied Developmental focuses on educational settings, family studies, and aging processes, providing training in family development (i.e., the processes of change that families as systems of member relationships experience), family and work (i.e., the interactive relationships between the two domains of family and work life), family and school, family processes in adult life, as well as cultural issues. Industrial/Organizational covers areas of theory, research methods, and social issues relevant to organizational and occupational life. Areas of study include leadership, work motivation, job stress, and organizational development. Applied Social/Community deals with how social–psychological research methods, findings, and theories are applied to (a) social issues (e.g., prejudice, violence, AIDS, disabilities, problem behavior, child safety, and energy conservation); (b) professions and institutions (e.g., health and law); and (c) the design and evaluation of social interventions.

Special Facilities or Resources: The Department of Psychology's location in the heart of downtown Portland offers unique academic and research opportunities in the service of the department's applied mission. Strong collaborative relationships with local industry, organizations, and community agencies offer venues for course-related projects, faculty research initiatives, practicum placements, and required student research. A number of University-based resources also enhance our students' skills and experiences. For example, the University's writing center allows faculty and students to hone technical writing skills. The Instructional Development Center provides training in computer and media-based applications to foster improved teaching and more sophisticated research approaches.

Information for Students With Physical Disabilities: See the following Web site for more information: http://www.pdx.edu/uasc/drc.html.

Application Information:

Send to Portland State University, Department of Psychology, P.O. Box 751, Portland, OR 97207-0751. Application available online. URL of online application: http://www.psy.pdx.edu/graduate. Students are admitted in the Fall, application deadline January 15. *Fee:* $50.

Southern Oregon University

Master in Mental Health Counseling
1250 Siskiyou Boulevard
Ashland, OR 97520
Telephone: (541) 552-6947
Fax: (541) 552-6988
E-mail: *MAP@sou.edu*
Web: *http://www.sou.edu/psych/map*

Department Information:

2000. Chairperson: Mary Russell- Miller PhD. Number of faculty: total—full-time 5; women—full-time 3; total—minority—full-time 1; women minority—full-time 1.

Programs and Degrees Offered:

Listed in the following order: Program area, degree type (T if terminal Master's), number awarded 7/06–6/07. Mental Health Counseling MA/MS (Master of Arts/Science) 20.

Student Applications/Admissions:

Student Applications

Mental Health Counseling MA/MS (Master of Arts/Science)—Applications 2007–2008, 50. Total applicants accepted 2007–2008, 24. Number full-time enrolled (new admits only) 2007–2008, 24. Number part-time enrolled (new admits only) 2007–2008, 0. Openings 2008–2009, 21. The median number of years required for completion of a degree in 2006–2007 were 2. The number of students enrolled full- and part-time who were dismissed or voluntarily withdrew from this program area in 2007–2008 were 0.

Admissions Requirements:

Scores: Entries appear in this order: required test or GPA, minimum score (if required), median score of students entering in 2007–2008. Master's Programs: GRE-V 400, 500; GRE-Q 400, 500; overall undergraduate GPA 3.00; last 2 years GPA 3.00; psychology GPA 3.00; Masters GRE-Analytical 3.0, 4.5.

Other Criteria: (importance of criteria rated low, medium, or high): GRE/MAT scores—high, research experience—low, work experience—low, extracurricular activity—low, clinically related public service—low, GPA—high, letters of recommendation—high, statement of goals and objectives—high, specific undergraduate psychology courses taken—high. For additional information on admission requirements, go to www.sou.edu/psych/map.

Student Characteristics: The following represents characteristics of students in 2007–2008 in all graduate psychology programs in the department: Female—full-time 16, part-time 0; Male—full-time 8, part-time 0; African American/Black—full-time 1, part-time 0; Hispanic/Latino(a)—full-time 2, part-time 0; Asian/Pacific Islander—full-time 2, part-time 0; American Indian/Alaska Native—full-time 1, part-time 0; Caucasian/White—full-time 36, part-time 0; Multi-ethnic—full-time 1, part-time 0; students subject to the Americans With Disabilities Act—full-time 0, part-time 0; Unknown ethnicity—full-time 1, part-time 0; International students who hold an F-1 or J-1 Visa—full-time 2, part-time 0.

Financial Information/Assistance:

Tuition for Full-Time Study: *Master's:* State residents: per academic year $13,000; Nonstate residents: per academic year $18,000. Tuition is subject to change. See the following Web site for updates and changes in tuition costs: http://www.sou.edu/bus_serv/Student_Fin_Info/student_fin_info.html.

Financial Assistance:

First-Year Students: Teaching assistantships available for first year. Average amount paid per academic year: $2,400. Average number of hours worked per week: 12. Tuition remission given: partial.

Advanced Students: Teaching assistantships available for advanced students. Average amount paid per academic year: $2,400. Average number of hours worked per week: 12. Tuition remission given: partial.

Additional Information: Of all students currently enrolled full time, 99% benefited from one or more of the listed financial assistance programs. Application and information available online at http://www.sou.edu/psych/map.

Internships/Practica: The Mental Health Counseling program requires practicum during the 1st year of courses. Internship placement in the community for students in the 2nd year is required to help fulfill state license requirements. MHC students are trained to become Licensed Professional Counselors in the state of Oregon.

Housing and Day Care: On-campus housing is available. See the following Web site for more information: http://www.sou.edu/housing/. On-campus day care facilities are available. See the following Web site for more information: http://www.sou.edu/scc/.

Employment of Department Graduates:

Master's Degree Graduates: Of those who graduated in the academic year 2006–2007, the following categories and numbers represent the postgraduate activities and employment of master's degree graduates: Enrolled in a psychology doctoral program (0), enrolled in another graduate/professional program (0), enrolled in a postdoctoral residency/fellowship (n/a), employed in independent practice (n/a), total from the above (master's) (0).

Doctoral Degree Graduates: Of those who graduated in the academic year 2006–2007, the following categories and numbers represent the postgraduate activities and employment of doctoral degree graduates: Enrolled in a psychology doctoral program (n/a), total from the above (doctoral) (0).

Additional Information:

Orientation, Objectives, and Emphasis of Department: The principle objective of the Master's Degree in Mental Health Counseling is to provide professional training in the application of psychological principles and methodologies in order to increase functioning and service delivery in public and private agencies, organizations, and communities. The Mental Health Counseling program is based on a common integrated core of courses. The central goal of this core is to train master's-level practitioners who are grounded in professional ethics and values, well-versed in the empirical nature of their professions, and sensitive to and supportive of the increasing multicultural diversity of our communities.

Personal Behavior Statement: Application packet available at http://www.sou.edu/psych/map then Application Questions, page 11 of the application packet.

Special Facilities or Resources: The Mental Health Counseling track is accredited by the Council for Accreditation of Counseling and Related Educational Programs (CACREP). This track is also recognized by the Oregon Board of Licensed Professional Counselors and Therapists (OBLPCT) as meeting the education requirements for application for licensure at a Licensed Professional Counselor in Oregon. The MHC track is also designed to meet the majority of requirement for licensure as a marriage and family therapist in California.

Application Information:
Send to Master in Mental Health Counseling, Southern Oregon University, 1250 Siskiyou Boulevard, Ashland, OR 97520. Application available online. URL of online application: http://www.sou.edu/psych/map. Students are admitted in the Fall, application deadline February 15; programs have rolling admissions. Contact Graduate Office Coordinator for admission specifics (541) 552-6947. *Fee:* $50. Application fee for University Application only (http://www.sou.edu/admissions/graduate), not MHC application. Both applications required.

Arcadia University
Department of Psychology
450 South Easton Road
Glenside, PA 19038-3295
Telephone: (267) 620-4130
Fax: (215) 881-8758
E-mail: *bartolie@arcadia.edu*
Web: *http://www.arcadia.edu*

Department Information:
1986. Eleonora Bartoli, PhD, Director; MACP: Les Sdorow, PhD, Department Chair. Number of faculty: total—full-time 8, part-time 9; women—full-time 3, part-time 5; total—minority—full-time 2, part-time 1; women minority—full-time 2, part-time 1.

Programs and Degrees Offered:
Listed in the following order: Program area, degree type (T if terminal Master's), number awarded 7/06–6/07. Elementary School Counseling MA/MS (Master of Arts/Science) (T), Secondary School Counseling MA/MS (Master of Arts/Science) (T), Community Counseling: Child and Family Therapy MA/MS (Master of Arts/Science) (T), Community Counseling: Trauma MA/MS (Master of Arts/Science) (T), Community Counseling: General MA/MS (Master of Arts/Science) (T).

Student Applications/Admissions:
Student Applications
Elementary School Counseling MA/MS (Master of Arts/Science)—Secondary School Counseling MA/MS (Master of Arts/Science)—Community Counseling: Child and Family Therapy MA/MS (Master of Arts/Science)—Community Counseling: Trauma MA/MS (Master of Arts/Science)—Community Counseling: General MA/MS (Master of Arts/Science).

Admissions Requirements:
Scores: Entries appear in this order: required test or GPA, minimum score (if required), median score of students entering in 2007–2008. Master's Programs: GRE-V no minimum stated; GRE-Q no minimum stated; MAT no minimum stated; overall undergraduate GPA no minimum stated; psychology GPA no minimum stated. Either GRE or MAT is required.
Other Criteria: (importance of criteria rated low, medium, or high): GRE/MAT scores—medium, research experience—medium, work experience—medium, extracurricular activity—medium, clinically related public service—medium, GPA—high, letters of recommendation—high, interview—high, statement of goals and objectives—high.

Student Characteristics: The following represents characteristics of students in 2007–2008 in all graduate psychology programs in the department: Female—full-time 20, part-time 25; Male—full-time 6, part-time 10; Caucasian/White—full-time 0, part-time 0; Unknown ethnicity—full-time 0, part-time 0.

Financial Information/Assistance:
Tuition for Full-Time Study: *Master's:* State residents: $580 per credit hour; Nonstate residents: $580 per credit hour.

Financial Assistance:
First-Year Students: No information provided.
Advanced Students: No information provided.
Additional Information: Application and information available online at http://www.arcadia.edu/prospective/default.aspx?id=606.

Internships/Practica: Master's Degree (MA/MS Elementary School Counseling): An internship experience such as a final research project or "capstone" experience is required of graduates. Master's Degree (MA/MS Secondary School Counseling): An internship experience such as a final research project or "capstone" experience is required of graduates. Master's Degree (MA/MS Community Counseling: Child and Family Therapy): An internship experience such as a final research project or "capstone" experience is required of graduates. Master's Degree (MA/MS Community Counseling: Trauma): An internship experience such as a final research project or "capstone" experience is required of graduates. Master's Degree (MA/MS Community Counseling: General): An internship experience such as a final research project or "capstone" experience is required of graduates. A practicum and an internship are required. Students have access to a variety of mental health agencies throughout the Philadelphia area.

Housing and Day Care: No on-campus housing is available. No on-campus day care facilities are available.

Employment of Department Graduates:
Master's Degree Graduates: Of those who graduated in the academic year 2006–2007, the following categories and numbers represent the postgraduate activities and employment of master's degree graduates: Enrolled in a postdoctoral residency/fellowship (n/a), employed in independent practice (n/a), total from the above (master's) (0).
Doctoral Degree Graduates: Of those who graduated in the academic year 2006–2007, the following categories and numbers represent the postgraduate activities and employment of doctoral degree graduates: Enrolled in a psychology doctoral program (n/a), total from the above (doctoral) (0).

Additional Information:
Orientation, Objectives, and Emphasis of Department: The Graduate Programs in Counseling Psychology prepares master's-level students for professional positions in schools, social service, rehabilitation, industrial, health, and mental health settings. Graduates will be able to work as community mental health specialists, mental health counselors, crisis counselors, drug and alcohol counselors, illness and wellness counselors, geriatric counselors, employee-assistance counselors, school counselors, and staff developers or trainers. The program is designed on a part-time basis for the working professional. The orientation of the program is integrative with a strong emphasis on multicultural and evidence-based practices. Pennsylvania now licenses master's-level counselors as Licensed Professional Counselors (LPC). Arcadia University's Master of Arts in Counseling Psychology provides the academic background to apply for licensure once 3,600 hours of mandated experience are acquired and the National Counselors Exam is taken.

Application Information:
Send to Office of Enrollment Management, Arcadia University, Glenside, PA 19038-3295; admiss@arcadia.edu. Application available online. URL of online application: http://www.arcadia.edu/admission. Students are admitted in the Fall, application deadline rolling. Programs have rolling admissions. *Fee:* $40. The fee for online applications is only $20; the fee is waived for applications submitted by indivduals who attended one of the Graduate Open House programs organized by the Office of Graduate and Professional Studies.

Bryn Mawr College
Department of Psychology
101 North Merion Avenue
Bryn Mawr, PA 19010-2899
Telephone: (610) 526-5010
Fax: (610) 526-7476
E-mail: *aogle@brynmawr.edu*
Web: *http://www.brynmawr.edu/psychology/cdpp/*

Department Information:
1890. Chairperson: Earl Thomas. Number of faculty: total—full-time 4, part-time 5; women—full-time 3, part-time 5; women minority—full-time 1.

Programs and Degrees Offered:
Listed in the following order: Program area, degree type (T if terminal Master's), number awarded 7/06–6/07. Clinical Developmental Psychology Program PhD (Doctor of Philosophy) 3.

Student Applications/Admissions:
Student Applications
Clinical Developmental Psychology Program PhD (Doctor of Philosophy)—Applications 2007–2008, 55. Total applicants accepted 2007–2008, 7. Number full-time enrolled (new admits only) 2007–2008, 4. Total enrolled 2007–2008 full-time, 34. Openings 2008–2009, 3. The median number of years required for completion of a degree in 2006–2007 were 7. The number of students enrolled full- and part-time who were dismissed or voluntarily withdrew from this program area in 2007–2008 were 0.

Admissions Requirements:
Scores: Entries appear in this order: required test or GPA, minimum score (if required), median score of students entering in 2007–2008. Doctoral Programs: GRE-V no minimum stated, 510; GRE-Q no minimum stated, 710; overall undergraduate GPA no minimum stated, 3.62; Doctoral program GRE-Analytic no minimum stated, 5.5.
Other Criteria: (importance of criteria rated low, medium, or high): GRE/MAT scores—medium, research experience—high, work experience—medium, extracurricular activity—low, clinically related public service—medium, GPA—high, letters of recommendation—high, interview—high, statement of goals and objectives—high. For additional information on admission requirements, go to http://www.brynmawr.edu/psychology/BMCPsychology-CDPPapplication.shtml.

Student Characteristics: The following represents characteristics of students in 2007–2008 in all graduate psychology programs in the department: Female—full-time 33, part-time 0; Male—full-time 1, part-time 0; African American/Black—full-time 1, part-time 0; Hispanic/Latino(a)—full-time 1, part-time 0; Asian/Pacific Islander—full-time 3, part-time 0; American Indian/Alaska Native—full-time 0, part-time 0; Caucasian/White—full-time 29, part-time 0; Multi-ethnic—full-time 0, part-time 0; students subject to the Americans With Disabilities Act—full-time 0, part-time 0; Unknown ethnicity—full-time 0, part-time 0; International students who hold an F-1 or J-1 Visa—full-time 2, part-time 0.

Financial Information/Assistance:
Tuition for Full-Time Study: *Doctoral:* State residents: per academic year $4,079, $1,632 per credit hour; Nonstate residents: per academic year $4,079, $1,632 per credit hour. Tuition is subject to change. See the following Web site for updates and changes in tuition costs: http://www.brynmawr.edu/psychology/financial_aid.shtml.

Financial Assistance:
First-Year Students: Teaching assistantships available for first year. Average amount paid per academic year: $12,000. Average number of hours worked per week: 17. Tuition remission given: partial. Research assistantships available for first year. Average amount paid per academic year: $13,000. Average number of hours worked per week: 17. Tuition remission given: partial.
Advanced Students: Teaching assistantships available for advanced students. Average amount paid per academic year: $14,000. Average number of hours worked per week: 17. Tuition remission given: partial. Research assistantships available for advanced students. Average amount paid per academic year: $14,000. Average number of hours worked per week: 17. Tuition remission given: partial.
Additional Information: Of all students currently enrolled full time, 100% benefited from one or more of the listed financial assistance programs. Application and information available online at http://www.brynmawr.edu/psychology/financial_aid.shtml.

Internships/Practica: Doctoral Degree (PhD Clinical Developmental Psychology Program): For those doctoral students for whom a professional internship was required in this program prior to graduation, (4) students applied for an internship in 2006–2007, with (4) students obtaining an internship. Of those students who obtained an internship, (4) were paid internships. Of those students who obtained an internship, (3) students placed in APA/CPA-accredited internships, (1) student placed in internships not APA/CPA-accredited, but listed with the Association of Psychology Postdoctoral and Internship Centers (APPIC), (0) students placed in internships conforming to guidelines of the Council of Directors of School Psychology Programs (CDSPP), (0) students placed in internships that were not APA/CPA accredited, APPIC or CDSPP listed. All students complete a sequence of clincial practica. During the 3rd year of the program students comple a half-time assessment/clinical practicum, typically in a school setting. In their 4th year, they complete a half-time clinical placement in local community mental health settings, university counseling centers, residential treatment facilities, university-affilliated training specialty clinics (e.g., specializing in anxiety disorders or eating disorders) or other clinically intensive settings. Many students complete additional part-time practica, and all students complete a year-long clinical internship (6th year).

Housing and Day Care: No on-campus housing is available. No on-campus day care facilities are available.

Employment of Department Graduates:

Master's Degree Graduates: Of those who graduated in the academic year 2006–2007, the following categories and numbers represent the postgraduate activities and employment of master's degree graduates: Enrolled in a postdoctoral residency/fellowship (n/a), employed in independent practice (n/a), total from the above (master's) (0).

Doctoral Degree Graduates: Of those who graduated in the academic year 2006–2007, the following categories and numbers represent the postgraduate activities and employment of doctoral degree graduates: Enrolled in a psychology doctoral program (n/a), enrolled in another graduate/professional program (0), enrolled in a postdoctoral residency/fellowship (0), employed in independent practice (0), employed in an academic position at a university (0), employed in an academic position at a 2-year/4-year college (0), employed in other positions at a higher education institution (0), employed in a professional position in a school system (0), employed in business or industry (0), employed in government agency (0), employed in a community mental health/counseling center (1), employed in a hospital/medical center (1), still seeking employment (0), not seeking employment (1), other employment position (0), do not know (0), total from the above (doctoral) (3).

Additional Information:

Orientation, Objectives, and Emphasis of Department: The program integrates research and practice within a framework that views the developing individual in changing family, school, and societal contexts. Students enrolled in the Clinical Developmental Psychology doctoral program obtain an understanding of basic psychological processes across the life span and acquire the requisite skills to conduct effective research on these processes. The Clinical Developmental Psychology program adheres to the scientist–practitioner model and offers clinical training that is informed by research. The focus of the program is on children and families within the larger social contexts of school and community.

Special Facilities or Resources: Each faculty member has a state-of-the-art lab with space and computers for students. The Child Study Institute (CSI) is the clinical training facility of the Department of Psychology. Staffed by licensed psychologists (including members of the department faculty), reading and math specialists, and predoctoral trainees in the clinical developmental program, CSI offers diagnostic assessment, school admission testing, individual, family, and group psychotherapy, and reading, math, and study skills tutoring. All students in the program receive family therapy training with live supervision at CSI. The Phebe Anna Thorne School is a nursery school and preschool research laboratory for the Department of Psychology and includes programs for both normally developing children and language-delayed preschoolers. Two first-year doctoral students in the Department of Psychology serve as teaching assistants in the Thorne School each year. The greater Philadelphia area features a very large and diverse community of psychologists, as well as many medical schools, teaching hospitals, mental health facilities, and research settings.

Application Information:

Send to Graduate School of Arts and Sciences, Bryn Mawr College, 101 North Merion Avenue, Bryn Mawr, PA 19010. Application available online. URL of online application: http://www.brynmawr.edu/gsas/prospective_students/howtoapply.shtml. Students are admitted in the Fall, application deadline January 7. *Fee:* $30.

Bucknell University

Department of Psychology
Arts and Sciences
O'Leary Center for Psychology and Geology
Lewisburg, PA 17837
Telephone: (570) 577-1200
Fax: (570) 577-7007
E-mail: *ahalpern@bucknell.edu*
Web: *http://www.bucknell.edu/Psychology.xml*

Department Information:

1927. Chairperson: Dr. T. Joel Wade. Number of faculty: total—full-time 3; women—full-time 2.

Programs and Degrees Offered:

Listed in the following order: Program area, degree type (T if terminal Master's), number awarded 7/06–6/07. General Experimental Psychology MA/MS (Master of Arts/Science) (T) 3.

Student Applications/Admissions:

Student Applications

General Experimental Psychology MA/MS (Master of Arts/Science)—Applications 2007–2008, 15. Total applicants accepted 2007–2008, 3. Number full-time enrolled (new admits only) 2007–2008, 3. Total enrolled 2007–2008 full-time, 5. Openings 2008–2009, 2. The median number of years required for completion of a degree in 2006–2007 were 2. The number of students enrolled full- and part-time who were dismissed or voluntarily withdrew from this program area in 2007–2008 were 0.

Admissions Requirements:

Scores: Entries appear in this order: required test or GPA, minimum score (if required), median score of students entering in 2007–2008. Master's Programs: GRE-V no minimum stated; GRE-Q no minimum stated; GRE-Subject (Psychology) no minimum stated; overall undergraduate GPA no minimum stated; Masters GRE-Analytical no minimum stated.

Other Criteria: (importance of criteria rated low, medium, or high): GRE/MAT scores—medium, research experience—high, work experience—low, extracurricular activity—low, GPA—medium, letters of recommendation—high, interview—medium, statement of goals and objectives—high, match with faculty—high. The primary criterion for acceptance for acceptance into the Master's program at Bucknell is that the candidate demonstrates that there is a clear match between the research and academic interests of the propsective student and at least one faculty member who would serve as the advisor and mentor to that student. Please write about potential mentors in your statement. Although interviews are not required they are strongly recommended.

Student Characteristics: The following represents characteristics of students in 2007–2008 in all graduate psychology programs in the department: Female—full-time 5, part-time 0; Male—

full-time 0, part-time 0; African American/Black—full-time 0, part-time 0; Hispanic/Latino(a)—full-time 0, part-time 0; Asian/Pacific Islander—full-time 0, part-time 0; American Indian/Alaska Native—full-time 0, part-time 0; Caucasian/White—full-time 5, part-time 0; Multi-ethnic—full-time 0, part-time 0; students subject to the Americans With Disabilities Act—full-time 0, part-time 0; Unknown ethnicity—full-time 0, part-time 0; International students who hold an F-1 or J-1 Visa—full-time 0, part-time 0.

Financial Information/Assistance:

Financial Assistance:

First-Year Students: Teaching assistantships available for first year. Average amount paid per academic year: $8,800. Average number of hours worked per week: 20. Apply by March 1. Tuition remission given: full.

Advanced Students: Teaching assistantships available for advanced students. Average amount paid per academic year: $8,800. Average number of hours worked per week: 20. Apply by April 1. Tuition remission given: full.

Additional Information: Of all students currently enrolled full time, 100% benefited from one or more of the listed financial assistance programs.

Internships/Practica: Master's Degree (MA/MS General Experimental Psychology): An internship experience such as a final research project or "capstone" experience is required of graduates. Although we offer no formal internship placements, there is ample opportunity for students to gain practical experience during their graduate studies at Bucknell. Bucknell University is located near Geisinger Medical Center and Danville State Psychiatric Hospital. These settings afford some potential research and training opportunities for students outside of the classroom. Occasionally, the University Psychological Services and Counseling Center offers a graduate assistantship that gives students training in counseling, mainly with undergradautes. Field work opportunities also exist for students interested in animal behavior and comparative psychology. Recently, we have had students initiate field opportunities leading to research on chimpanzees in Uganda and macaques in Indonesia.

Housing and Day Care: No on-campus housing is available. On-campus day care facilities are available. Sunflower Child Care Center is on campus.

Employment of Department Graduates:

Master's Degree Graduates: Of those who graduated in the academic year 2006–2007, the following categories and numbers represent the postgraduate activities and employment of master's degree graduates: Enrolled in a psychology doctoral program (2), enrolled in another graduate/professional program (1), enrolled in a postdoctoral residency/fellowship (n/a), employed in independent practice (n/a), total from the above (master's) (3).

Doctoral Degree Graduates: Of those who graduated in the academic year 2006–2007, the following categories and numbers represent the postgraduate activities and employment of doctoral degree graduates: Enrolled in a psychology doctoral program (n/a), total from the above (doctoral) (0).

Additional Information:

Orientation, Objectives, and Emphasis of Department: The department is committed to providing training to students in general experimental psychology. The Master's program is a full-time, 2-year program that leads to either the MA or MS. The program is small, with an average of four or five students in psychology. The small size means that students work closely with faculty. Students typically take two seminars per semester, as well as a monthly proseminar. The main focus of the program, however, is on conducting high-quality empirical research under the supervision of a faculty mentor. These research experiences typically form the basis for the master's thesis, which is a requirement of the program. The great majority of our students intend to continue on to PhD programs, and thus our goal is to give the kind of background and experience that will prepare the students for more advanced study. All of our graduate students become heavily involved in research in one of several well-equipped laboratories in comparative, physiological, learning, cognitive, social, abnormal, developmental psychopathology, personality, or developmental psychology. Several of our faculty form a Neuroscience core. We do not offer a program in Clinical Psychology and do not provide clinical training. Our program does, however, provide an excellent background in research and coursework for students who hope to continue in doctoral programs in clinical psychology. We have had great success in recent years in placing students in PhD programs in psychology and related fields.

Special Facilities or Resources: In the autumn of 2002 the Psychology Department opened its doors to a new, state-of-the-art psychology building, The O'Leary Center. The O'Leary Center completes Bucknell's science quadrangle and is adjacent to the Biology and Chemistry buildings. The O'Leary Center offers abundant laboratory space that allows faculty to involve their students in research. These labs are equipped with computer facilities and cutting-edge research equipment used for training graduates and undergraduates in the latest research methods. Some examples of our lab facilities include EEG technology for noninvasive brain-imaging research (Event-Related Potential) in typically and atypically developing children; observation and testing rooms complete with two-way mirrors and video-monitoring equipment; child observation and testing rooms for behavioral and neuropsychological assessment of children; psychophysiological feedback of heart rate, blood pressure, and skin response for research on emotions and social interaction; eye-tracking, color vision, and sensory adaptation equipment; research tools for studying human cognition and memory; resources for studying nonhuman learning as well as stereotaxic equipment for studying brain–behavior associations. The department's primate facility includes four species of seminaturally housed primates: Hamadryas baboons, Capuchin and squirrel monkeys, and lion-tailed macaques. These extraordinary facilities distinguish Bucknell's Psychology department from other universities of its kind.

Application Information:

Send to Graduate Admissions Office, Bucknell University, Lewisburg, PA 17837. Students are admitted in the Spring, application deadline March 1; programs have rolling admissions. Fall admission only, deadline for admission and financial aid applications, March 1. Applications may still be considered after March 1 if spaces remain available. Prospective applicants are encouraged to contact the department in advance of March 1 for advice. *Fee:* $25.

Carnegie Mellon University
Department of Psychology
Humanities and Social Sciences
Baker Hall 342E
Pittsburgh, PA 15213
Telephone: (412) 268-6026
Fax: (412) 268-2798
E-mail: *donahoe@andrew.cmu.edu*
Web: *http://www.psy.cmu.edu/*

Department Information:

1948. Head: Michael Scheier. Number of faculty: total—full-time 25, part-time 4; women—full-time 10, part-time 2; total—minority—full-time 1; women minority—full-time 1.

Programs and Degrees Offered:

Listed in the following order: Program area, degree type (T if terminal Master's), number awarded 7/06–6/07. Cognitive/Cognitive Neuroscience PhD (Doctor of Philosophy) 2, Developmental PhD (Doctor of Philosophy) 0, Social/Health/Personality PhD (Doctor of Philosophy) 0, Psychology and Behavioral Decision Research PhD (Doctor of Philosophy) 0.

Student Applications/Admissions:

Student Applications

Cognitive/Cognitive Neuroscience PhD (Doctor of Philosophy)—Applications 2007–2008, 95. Total applicants accepted 2007–2008, 8. Number full-time enrolled (new admits only) 2007–2008, 8. Number part-time enrolled (new admits only) 2007–2008, 0. Openings 2008–2009, 3. The median number of years required for completion of a degree in 2006–2007 were 5. The number of students enrolled full- and part-time who were dismissed or voluntarily withdrew from this program area in 2007–2008 were 0. *Developmental PhD (Doctor of Philosophy)*—Applications 2007–2008, 15. Total applicants accepted 2007–2008, 1. Number full-time enrolled (new admits only) 2007–2008, 1. Number part-time enrolled (new admits only) 2007–2008, 0. Openings 2008–2009, 1. The median number of years required for completion of a degree in 2006–2007 were 5. The number of students enrolled full- and part-time who were dismissed or voluntarily withdrew from this program area in 2007–2008 were 0. *Social/Health/Personality PhD (Doctor of Philosophy)*—Applications 2007–2008, 46. Total applicants accepted 2007–2008, 2. Number full-time enrolled (new admits only) 2007–2008, 0. Number part-time enrolled (new admits only) 2007–2008, 0. Openings 2008–2009, 2. The median number of years required for completion of a degree in 2006–2007 were 5. The number of students enrolled full- and part-time who were dismissed or voluntarily withdrew from this program area in 2007–2008 were 1. *Psychology and Behavioral Decision Research PhD (Doctor of Philosophy)*—Applications 2007–2008, 0. Total applicants accepted 2007–2008, 0. Number full-time enrolled (new admits only) 2007–2008, 0. Number part-time enrolled (new admits only) 2007–2008, 0. The number of students enrolled full- and part-time who were dismissed or voluntarily withdrew from this program area in 2007–2008 were 0.

Admissions Requirements:

Scores: Entries appear in this order: required test or GPA, minimum score (if required), median score of students entering in 2007–2008. Doctoral Programs: GRE-V no minimum stated, 600; GRE-Q no minimum stated, 710; overall undergraduate GPA no minimum stated, 3.4. No specific scores—nothing weighted more than other requirements.

Other Criteria: (importance of criteria rated low, medium, or high): GRE/MAT scores—high, research experience—high, work experience—low, GPA—high, letters of recommendation—high, interview—high, statement of goals and objectives—high. GPA, GRE, Statement of Purpose, Undergraduate Academic and Research Experience, Letter of Recommendation. For additional information on admission requirements, go to http://www.psy.cmu.edu/home/programs/applying.html.

Student Characteristics: The following represents characteristics of students in 2007–2008 in all graduate psychology programs in the department: Female—full-time 21, part-time 0; Male—full-time 12, part-time 0; African American/Black—full-time 0, part-time 0; Hispanic/Latino(a)—full-time 2, part-time 0; Asian/Pacific Islander—full-time 8, part-time 0; American Indian/Alaska Native—full-time 0, part-time 0; Caucasian/White—full-time 23, part-time 0; Multi-ethnic—full-time 0, part-time 0; students subject to the Americans With Disabilities Act—full-time 0, part-time 0; Unknown ethnicity—full-time 0, part-time 0; International students who hold an F-1 or J-1 Visa—full-time 11, part-time 0.

Financial Information/Assistance:

Tuition for Full-Time Study: *Doctoral:* State residents: per academic year $32,594; Nonstate residents: per academic year $32,594. Tuition is subject to change. See the following Web site for updates and changes in tuition costs: http://www.cmu.edu.

Financial Assistance:

First-Year Students: Fellowships and scholarships available for first year. Average amount paid per academic year: $20,772. Tuition remission given: full.

Advanced Students: Fellowships and scholarships available for advanced students. Average amount paid per academic year: $20,772. Tuition remission given: full.

Additional Information: Of all students currently enrolled full time, 100% benefited from one or more of the listed financial assistance programs. Application and information available online at http://www.psy.cmu.edu/home/programs/applying.html.

Internships/Practica: No information provided.

Housing and Day Care: On-campus housing is available. See the following Web site for more information: http://www.housing.cmu.edu. On-campus day care facilities are available. See the following Web site for more information: http:/hr.web.cmu.edu/current/work-life/childcare.

Employment of Department Graduates:

Master's Degree Graduates: Of those who graduated in the academic year 2006–2007, the following categories and numbers represent the postgraduate activities and employment of master's degree graduates: Enrolled in a postdoctoral residency/fellowship (n/a), employed in independent practice (n/a), total from the above (master's) (0).

Doctoral Degree Graduates: Of those who graduated in the academic year 2006–2007, the following categories and numbers

represent the postgraduate activities and employment of doctoral degree graduates: Enrolled in a psychology doctoral program (n/a), employed in an academic position at a university (1), employed in government agency (1), total from the above (doctoral) (2).

Additional Information:

Orientation, Objectives, and Emphasis of Department: The department offers doctoral programs in the areas of Cognitive Psychology, Cognitive Neuroscience, Social–Personality Psychology, and Developmental Psychology. Because the graduate program is small, the student's course of study can be tailored to meet individual needs and interests. Further, students have many opportunities to work closely with faculty members on research projects of mutual interest. Carnegie Mellon University has a strong tradition of interdisciplinary research, and it is easy for students to interact with faculty and students from other graduate programs on campus. Many of our students take courses or engage in research with people from the departments of Computer Science, Statistics, Social Science, English, Philosophy, and the Graduate School of Industrial Administration.

Special Facilities or Resources: Please see Web site (http://www.psy.cmu.edu).

Application Information:

Send to Graduate Program Coordinator, Department of Psychology, Carnegie Mellon University, Pittsburgh, PA 15213. Application available online. URL of online application: http://www.psy.cmu.edu/home/programs/applyonline.html. Students are admitted in the Fall, application deadline December 15. *Fee:* $45. Financial hardship.

Carnegie Mellon University

Tepper School of Business at Carnegie Mellon
Schenley Park
Pittsburgh, PA 15213
Telephone: (412) 268-1319
Fax: (412) 268-7064
E-mail: *pg14+@andrew.cmu.edu*
Web: *http://www.wpweb2k.tepper.cmu.edu/obt/index.html*

Department Information:

OB PhD Coordinator: Paul S. Goodman. Number of faculty: total—full-time 7; women—full-time 3; total—minority—full-time 1.

Programs and Degrees Offered:

Listed in the following order: Program area, degree type (T if terminal Master's), number awarded 7/06–6/07. Organizational Behavior and Theory PhD (Doctor of Philosophy) 1.

Student Applications/Admissions:

Student Applications

Organizational Behavior and Theory PhD (Doctor of Philosophy)—Total applicants accepted 2007–2008, 7. Number full-time enrolled (new admits only) 2007–2008, 3. Total enrolled 2007–2008 full-time, 13. Openings 2008–2009, 3.

Admissions Requirements:

Scores: Entries appear in this order: required test or GPA, minimum score (if required), median score of students entering in 2007–2008. Doctoral Programs: GRE-V no minimum stated; GRE-Q no minimum stated; overall undergraduate GPA no minimum stated.

Other Criteria: (importance of criteria rated low, medium, or high): GRE/MAT scores—high, GPA—high, letters of recommendation—high, statement of goals and objectives—high.

Student Characteristics: The following represents characteristics of students in 2007–2008 in all graduate psychology programs in the department: Female—full-time 5, part-time 0; Male—full-time 8, part-time 0; African American/Black—full-time 0, part-time 0; Hispanic/Latino(a)—full-time 0, part-time 0; Asian/Pacific Islander—full-time 6, part-time 0; American Indian/Alaska Native—full-time 0, part-time 0; Caucasian/White—full-time 7, part-time 0; students subject to the Americans With Disabilities Act—full-time 0, part-time 0; Unknown ethnicity—full-time 0, part-time 0; International students who hold an F-1 or J-1 Visa—full-time 5, part-time 0.

Financial Information/Assistance:

Financial Assistance:

First-Year Students: Fellowships and scholarships available for first year. Apply by January 2. Tuition remission given: full.

Advanced Students: Fellowships and scholarships available for advanced students. Apply by January 2. Tuition remission given: full.

Additional Information: Of all students currently enrolled full time, 100% benefited from one or more of the listed financial assistance programs.

Internships/Practica: No information provided.

Housing and Day Care: No on-campus housing is available. No on-campus day care facilities are available.

Employment of Department Graduates:

Master's Degree Graduates: Of those who graduated in the academic year 2006–2007, the following categories and numbers represent the postgraduate activities and employment of master's degree graduates: Enrolled in a postdoctoral residency/fellowship (n/a), employed in independent practice (n/a), total from the above (master's) (0).

Doctoral Degree Graduates: Of those who graduated in the academic year 2006–2007, the following categories and numbers represent the postgraduate activities and employment of doctoral degree graduates: Enrolled in a psychology doctoral program (n/a), employed in an academic position at a 2-year/4-year college (1), total from the above (doctoral) (1).

Additional Information:

Orientation, Objectives, and Emphasis of Department: The goal of the doctoral program in Organizational Psychology and Theory at the Tepper School of Business is to produce scientists who will make significant research contributions to our understanding of the structure and functioning of organizations. To achieve this goal, the student is placed in a learning environment where a unique set of quantitative and discipline-based skills can be acquired. The opportunities for interdisciplinary work at Tepper provide new avenues for approaching organizational problems. The program attempts to combine structure and flexibility. Structure is achieved by identifying a set of core areas in which the student should become competent. These are quantitative methods, design and measurement, organization theory, and a selected specialty area. Flexibility in the program is achieved by having students and their advisers work out a combination of learning activities consistent with the students' interests and needs. Courses, participation in research projects, summer papers, and special tutorials with individual faculty are some of these learning activities.

Application Information:
Send to Tepper School of Business at Carnegie Mellon, PhD Program, Carnegie Mellon University, Pittsburgh, PA 15213. Application available online. URL of online application: http://www.business.tepper.cmu.edu/default.aspx?id=141049. Students are admitted in the Fall, application deadline January 2. *Fee:* $50.

Chestnut Hill College

Department of Professional Psychology
9601 Germantown Avenue
Philadelphia, PA 19118-2693
Telephone: (215) 248-7077
Fax: (215) 248-7155
E-mail: *profpsyc@chc.edu*
Web: *http://www.chc.edu*

Department Information:
1987. Chairperson: Joseph A. Micucci, PhD, ABPP. Number of faculty: total—full-time 10, part-time 29; women—full-time 4, part-time 12; total—minority—full-time 2, part-time 2; women minority—full-time 2, part-time 1.

Programs and Degrees Offered:
Listed in the following order: Program area, degree type (T if terminal Master's), number awarded 7/06–6/07. Clinical Psychology PsyD (Doctor of Psychology) 8, Clinical and Counseling Psychology MA/MS (Master of Arts/Science) (T) 65.

APA Accreditation: Clinical PsyD (Doctor of Psychology).

Student Applications/Admissions:

Student Applications

Clinical Psychology PsyD (Doctor of Psychology)—Applications 2007–2008, 138. Total applicants accepted 2007–2008, 42. Number full-time enrolled (new admits only) 2007–2008, 11. Number part-time enrolled (new admits only) 2007–2008, 14. Total enrolled 2007–2008 full-time, 42, part-time, 68. Openings 2008–2009, 20. The median number of years required for completion of a degree in 2006–2007 were 6. The number of students enrolled full- and part-time who were dismissed or voluntarily withdrew from this program area in 2007–2008 were 2. *Clinical and Counseling Psychology MA/MS (Master of Arts/Science)*—Applications 2007–2008, 191. Total applicants accepted 2007–2008, 92. Number full-time enrolled (new admits only) 2007–2008, 21. Number part-time enrolled (new admits only) 2007–2008, 35. Total enrolled 2007–2008 full-time, 80, part-time, 150. The median number of years required for completion of a degree in 2006–2007 were 3.

Admissions Requirements:

Scores: Entries appear in this order: required test or GPA, minimum score (if required), median score of students entering in 2007–2008. Master's Programs: Master's programs require either the Miller Analogies Test (MAT) or the GRE (general test; subject test not required). Minimum scores are not specified. All factors are weighted in considering applications. Doctoral Programs: GRE (general test) is required for applicants with bachelor's degrees. Applicants with a master's degree in Clinical or Counseling Psychology or a closely related field may submit either GRE or MAT scores. The program does not specify a cutoff score. All factors are weighted in considering applications.

Other Criteria: (importance of criteria rated low, medium, or high): GRE/MAT scores—high, research experience—low, work experience—low, extracurricular activity—low, clinically related public service—low, GPA—high, letters of recommendation—high, interview—high, statement of goals and objectives—high, writing ability—high, undergraduate major in psychology—medium, specific undergraduate psychology courses taken—high. Writing ability is a criterion for the PsyD program. Applicants to the PsyD program must have completed at least four undergraduate courses in psychology including General Psychology, Abnormal Psychology, and Statistics. For additional information on admission requirements, go to http://www.chc.edu/page_template.asp?section=3&file=351_admissions.

Student Characteristics: The following represents characteristics of students in 2007–2008 in all graduate psychology programs in the department: Female—full-time 104, part-time 181; Male—full-time 18, part-time 37; African American/Black—full-time 18, part-time 26; Hispanic/Latino(a)—full-time 2, part-time 4; Asian/Pacific Islander—full-time 1, part-time 4; American Indian/Alaska Native—full-time 0, part-time 0; Caucasian/White—full-time 99, part-time 184; Unknown ethnicity—full-time 2, part-time 0; International students who hold an F-1 or J-1 Visa—full-time 2, part-time 0.

Financial Information/Assistance:

Tuition for Full-Time Study: *Master's:* State residents: $515 per credit hour; Nonstate residents: $515 per credit hour. *Doctoral:* State residents: $750 per credit hour; Nonstate residents: $750 per credit hour. Tuition is subject to change. See the following Web site for updates and changes in tuition costs: http://www.chc.edu/page_template.asp?section=3&file=369_tuition.

Financial Assistance:

First-Year Students: Teaching assistantships available for first year. Average number of hours worked per week: 12. Tuition remission given: partial. Research assistantships available for first year. Average number of hours worked per week: 12. Tuition remission given: partial.

Advanced Students: Teaching assistantships available for advanced students. Average number of hours worked per week: 12. Tuition remission given: partial. Research assistantships available for advanced students. Average number of hours worked per week: 12. Tuition remission given: partial.

Additional Information: No information provided.

Internships/Practica: Master's Degree (MA/MS Clinical and Counseling Psychology): An internship experience such as a final research project or "capstone" experience is required of graduates. Doctoral Degree (PsyD Clinical Psychology): For those doctoral students for whom a professional internship was required in this program prior to graduation, (9) students applied for an internship in 2006–2007, with (9) students obtaining an internship. Of those students who obtained an internship, (8) were paid internships. Of those students who obtained an internship, (3) students placed in APA/CPA-accredited internships, (3) students placed in internships not APA/CPA-accredited, but listed with the Association of Psychology Postdoctoral and Internship Centers (APPIC), (0) students placed in internships conforming to guidelines of the Council of Directors of School Psychology Programs (CDSPP), (3) students placed in internships that were not APA/CPA-accredited, APPIC or CDSPP listed. Every student who attends either the master's program or the doctoral program at Chestnut Hill College in the Department of Professional Psychology must complete a practicum and internship. We have a two faculty members dedicated to assisting students in securing the most appropriate site for their experiential training. At the present time the College has 50 mental health facilities that have been approved as sites for doctoral practicums or internships. Doctoral students complete an assessment practicum as well as a clinical practicum. Students have the option of completing an APA, APPIC, or other program-approved internship. Doctoral students are required to apply for APA/APPIC internships. For additional information on education and training outcomes for our programs, see the following Web site: http://www.chc.edu/page_template.asp?section=3&file=507_Program_Data_and_Co.

Housing and Day Care: No on-campus housing is available. No on-campus day care facilities are available.

Employment of Department Graduates:

Master's Degree Graduates: Of those who graduated in the academic year 2006–2007, the following categories and numbers represent the postgraduate activities and employment of master's degree graduates: Enrolled in a postdoctoral residency/fellowship (n/a), employed in independent practice (n/a), total from the above (master's) (0).

Doctoral Degree Graduates: Of those who graduated in the academic year 2006–2007, the following categories and numbers represent the postgraduate activities and employment of doctoral degree graduates: Enrolled in a psychology doctoral program (n/a), enrolled in a postdoctoral residency/fellowship (2), employed in independent practice (0), employed in an academic position at a university (1), employed in a professional position in a school system (1), employed in a community mental health/counseling center (4), employed in a hospital/medical center (0), do not know (0), total from the above (doctoral) (8).

Additional Information:

Orientation, Objectives, and Emphasis of Department: The theoretical base of the Department of Professional Psychology at Chestnut Hill College is a complementary blend of psychodynamic and systems theories. The insights of psychodynamic theory, including modern object relations theory, serve as a method for understanding the individual. Likewise, the perspective of systems theory addresses ways individuals, families, and communities influence one another. This synergistic blend of psychodynamic and systems theories promotes a holistic understanding of human behavior within family and social contexts.

Special Facilities or Resources: Chestnut Hill College is located in Philadelphia, Pennsylvania. Because of our location we have numerous contacts with local academic and research facilities. We are part of a library consortium that increases the available lending privileges offered to each student.

Application Information:
Send to Director of Graduate Admissions, Chestnut Hill College, 9601 Germantown Avenue, Philadelphia, PA 19118-2693. Application available online. URL of online application: http://www.chc.edu/page_template.asp?section=3&file=331_admissions. Students are admitted in the Fall. All students in the PsyD Program begin classes in the Fall semester. Students in the terminal master's program may begin classes in the Fall, Spring, or Summer semester. Master's program has rolling admissions. *Fee:* $75. PsyD application fee is $75. Master's application fee is $50.

Drexel University

Department of Psychology
College of Arts and Sciences
MS 626, 245 North 15th Street
Philadelphia, PA 19102
Telephone: (215) 762-7249
Fax: (215) 762-8625
E-mail: *kirk.heilbrun@drexel.edu*
Web: *http://www.psychology.drexel.edu*

Department Information:

2002. Chairperson: Kirk Heilbrun. Number of faculty: total—full-time 24, part-time 7; women—full-time 12, part-time 7; total—minority—full-time 2, part-time 2; women minority—full-time 1, part-time 2.

Programs and Degrees Offered:

Listed in the following order: Program area, degree type (T if terminal Master's), number awarded 7/06–6/07. Clinical PhD (Doctor of Philosophy) 12, Psychology (Nonclinical) MA/MS (Master of Arts/Science) (T) 7, Law Psychology PhD (Doctor of Philosophy) 2.

APA Accreditation: Clinical PhD (Doctor of Philosophy).

Student Applications/Admissions:

Student Applications

Clinical PhD (Doctor of Philosophy)—Applications 2007–2008, 420. Total applicants accepted 2007–2008, 10. Number full-time enrolled (new admits only) 2007–2008, 9. Openings 2008–2009, 10. The median number of years required for completion of a degree in 2006–2007 were 5. The number of students enrolled full- and part-time who were dismissed or voluntarily withdrew from this program area in 2007–2008 were 0. *Psychology (Nonclinical) MA/MS (Master of Arts/Science)*—Applications 2007–2008, 25. Total applicants accepted 2007–2008, 10. Number full-time enrolled (new admits only) 2007–2008, 9. Total enrolled 2007–2008 full-time, 18. Openings 2008–2009, 10. The median number of years required for completion of a degree in 2006–2007 were 2. The number of students enrolled full- and part-time who were dismissed or voluntarily withdrew from this program area in 2007–2008 were 0. *Law Psychology PhD (Doctor of Philosophy)*—Applications 2007–2008, 18. Total applicants accepted 2007–2008, 2. Number full-time enrolled (new admits only) 2007–2008,

2. Total enrolled 2007–2008 full-time, 15. Openings 2008–2009, 1. The median number of years required for completion of a degree in 2006–2007 were 7. The number of students enrolled full- and part-time who were dismissed or voluntarily withdrew from this program area in 2007–2008 were 1.

Admissions Requirements:

Scores: Entries appear in this order: required test or GPA, minimum score (if required), median score of students entering in 2007–2008. Master's Programs: GRE-V no minimum stated, 570; GRE-Q no minimum stated, 590; overall undergraduate GPA no minimum stated, 3.5. Doctoral Programs: GRE-V no minimum stated, 645; GRE-Q no minimum stated, 690; GRE-Subject (Psychology) no minimum stated, 650; overall undergraduate GPA no minimum stated, 3.6. Higher scores and GPA are expected for applicants to the doctoral programs.

Other Criteria: (importance of criteria rated low, medium, or high): GRE/MAT scores—high, research experience—high, work experience—low, extracurricular activity—low, clinically related public service—medium, GPA—high, letters of recommendation—high, interview—high, statement of goals and objectives—high, fit with faculty mentor—high.

Student Characteristics: The following represents characteristics of students in 2007–2008 in all graduate psychology programs in the department: Female—full-time 62, part-time 0; Male—full-time 11, part-time 0; African American/Black—full-time 5, part-time 0; Hispanic/Latino(a)—full-time 6, part-time 0; Asian/Pacific Islander—full-time 1, part-time 0; American Indian/Alaska Native—full-time 0, part-time 0; Caucasian/White—full-time 66, part-time 0; Multi-ethnic—full-time 2, part-time 0; students subject to the Americans With Disabilities Act—full-time 2, part-time 0; Unknown ethnicity—full-time 0, part-time 0.

Financial Information/Assistance:

Tuition for Full-Time Study: *Master's:* State residents: $800 per credit hour; Nonstate residents: $800 per credit hour. *Doctoral:* State residents: $800 per credit hour; Nonstate residents: $800 per credit hour. Tuition is subject to change.

Financial Assistance:

First-Year Students: Teaching assistantships available for first year. Average amount paid per academic year: $9. Average number of hours worked per week: 15. Tuition remission given: full. Research assistantships available for first year. Average amount paid per academic year: $10. Tuition remission given: full.

Advanced Students: Research assistantships available for advanced students. Average amount paid per academic year: $9. Average number of hours worked per week: 10. Tuition remission given: full. Traineeships available for advanced students. Average amount paid per academic year: $9. Average number of hours worked per week: 20. Tuition remission given: full. Fellowships and scholarships available for advanced students. Average amount paid per academic year: $5. Tuition remission given: full.

Additional Information: Of all students currently enrolled full time, 80% benefited from one or more of the listed financial assistance programs.

Internships/Practica: Doctoral Degree (PhD Clinical): For those doctoral students for whom a professional internship was required in this program prior to graduation, (13) students applied for an internship in 2006–2007, with (13) students obtaining an internship. Of those students who obtained an internship, (13) were paid internships. Of those students who obtained an internship, (13) students placed in APA/CPA-accredited internships, (0) students placed in internships not APA/CPA-accredited, but listed with the Association of Psychology Postdoctoral and Internship Centers (APPIC), (0) students placed in internships conforming to guidelines of the Council of Directors of School Psychology Programs (CDSPP), (0) students placed in internships that were not APA/CPA-accredited, APPIC or CDSPP listed. Doctoral Degree (PhD Law Psychology): For those doctoral students for whom a professional internship was required in this program prior to graduation, (3) students applied for an internship in 2006–2007, with (3) students obtaining an internship. Of those students who obtained an internship, (3) were paid internships. Of those students who obtained an internship, (3) students placed in APA/CPA-accredited internships, (0) students placed in internships not APA/CPA-accredited, but listed with the Association of Psychology Postdoctoral and Internship Centers (APPIC), (0) students placed in internships conforming to guidelines of the Council of Directors of School Psychology Programs (CDSPP), (0) students placed in internships that were not APA/CPA-accredited, APPIC or CDSPP listed. On-campus practicum sites include the Student Counseling and Development Center, the Forensic Clinic, and the Heart Failure/Cardiac Transplant Center. Off-campus practicum sites include a variety of in- and outpatient psychiatric units, Children's Hospital of Philadelphia, and approximately 60 other practicum sites.

Housing and Day Care: On-campus housing is available. Center City Campus on Campus Housing: Stiles Alumni Hall houses up to 315 undergraduate and graduate students from the Center City Campus and Queen Lane campuses. The Hall contains one-, two-, and three-bedroom unfurnished apartments. Each student is given their own bedroom, but will share a kitchen, bathroom, and living space. The bedrooms are carpeted and each room has temperature control, cable, local phone service, and Internet access. Main campus: Drexel main campus has seven residence halls and is home to approximately 2,600 residents. Graduate students, upperclassmen, and some transfer students are assigned to Van Rensselaer and North Hall. No on-campus day care facilities are available.

Employment of Department Graduates:

Master's Degree Graduates: Of those who graduated in the academic year 2006–2007, the following categories and numbers represent the postgraduate activities and employment of master's degree graduates: Enrolled in a psychology doctoral program (2), enrolled in a postdoctoral residency/fellowship (n/a), employed in independent practice (n/a), employed in business or industry (2), employed in government agency (1), employed in a hospital/medical center (1), total from the above (master's) (6).

Doctoral Degree Graduates: Of those who graduated in the academic year 2006–2007, the following categories and numbers represent the postgraduate activities and employment of doctoral degree graduates: Enrolled in a psychology doctoral program (n/a), enrolled in a postdoctoral residency/fellowship (5), employed in an academic position at a university (1), employed in an academic position at a 2-year/4-year college (1), employed in government agency (1), employed in a community mental health/counseling center (1), employed in a hospital/medical center (4), other employment position (2), total from the above (doctoral) (15).

Additional Information:

Orientation, Objectives, and Emphasis of Department: The Drexel University Department of Psychology has doctoral programs based heavily upon a scientist–practitioner model of training in clinical psychology and has been designed to place emphasis on both components, but somewhat greater emphasis on research. The theoretical orientation is based largely on Social Learning Theory, in which students gain proficiency in the theory and practice of broad-spectrum behavioral approaches to assessment and intervention. The PhD program offers concentrations in health psychology, neuropsychology, and forensic psychology. The MS program (nonclinical) is designed to provide students with research skills in preparation for application for doctoral training or employment with researchers in academia, industry, or public sector settings.

Special Facilities or Resources: The graduate psychology programs at Drexel University have space on both the Drexel Main Campus in West Philadelphia and the center city campus. Drexel has a major tertiary care medical center that provides exceptional opportunities in health related areas for psychology. In addition, a Division of Behavioral Neurobiology and the University Neurobiology program, as well as the University Neurosciences program, provide opportunities for learning and collaboration on research at neuropharmacologic and neurophysiologic levels to complement our neuropsychological training.

Application Information:

Send to Graduate Admission, Drexel University, 3141 Chestnut Street, Suite 212, Philadelphia, PA 19104. Telephone: (215) 895-2000. http://www.drexel.edu. Application available online. URL of online application: http://www.psychology.drexel.edu. Students are admitted in the Fall, application deadline December 1. MS deadline February 15. *Fee:* $50.

Duquesne University

Department of Counseling, Psychology and Special Education, School Psychology Program
School of Education
102C Canevin Hall
Pittsburgh, PA 15282
Telephone: (412) 396-1058
Fax: (412) 396-1340
E-mail: *czwalgaa@duq.edu*
Web: *http://www.schoolpsych.duq.edu*

Department Information:

1969. Program Director: Kara McGoey, PhD. Number of faculty: total—full-time 6, part-time 3; women—full-time 4, part-time 2.

Programs and Degrees Offered:

Listed in the following order: Program area, degree type (T if terminal Master's), number awarded 7/06–6/07. Master's in Child Psychology Other 19, Certificate of Advanced Graduate Study School Other 5, School Psychology PhD (Doctor of Philosophy) 5.

Student Applications/Admissions:

Student Applications

Master's in Child Psychology Other—Applications 2007–2008, 15. Total applicants accepted 2007–2008, 13. Number full-time enrolled (new admits only) 2007–2008, 4. Number part-time enrolled (new admits only) 2007–2008, 0. Openings 2008–2009, 15. The median number of years required for completion of a degree in 2006–2007 were 2. The number of students enrolled full- and part-time who were dismissed or voluntarily withdrew from this program area in 2007–2008 were 0. *Certificate of Advanced Graduate Study School Other*—Applications 2007–2008, 60. Total applicants accepted 2007–2008, 15. Number full-time enrolled (new admits only) 2007–2008, 8. Number part-time enrolled (new admits only) 2007–2008, 0. Openings 2008–2009, 10. The median number of years required for completion of a degree in 2006–2007 were 3. The number of students enrolled full- and part-time who were dismissed or voluntarily withdrew from this program area in 2007–2008 were 0. *School Psychology PhD (Doctor of Philosophy)*—Applications 2007–2008, 22. Total applicants accepted 2007–2008, 7. Number full-time enrolled (new admits only) 2007–2008, 6. Number part-time enrolled (new admits only) 2007–2008, 0. Openings 2008–2009, 6. The median number of years required for completion of a degree in 2006–2007 were 5. The number of students enrolled full- and part-time who were dismissed or voluntarily withdrew from this program area in 2007–2008 were 1.

Admissions Requirements:

Scores: Entries appear in this order: required test or GPA, minimum score (if required), median score of students entering in 2007–2008. Master's Programs: GRE-V no minimum stated; GRE-Q no minimum stated; overall undergraduate GPA 3.0; last 2 years GPA 3.0; Masters GRE-Analytical no minimum stated. GRE scores are required for the Certificate of Advanced Graduate Study Program. GRE scores are not required for the MSEd Child Psychology Program. Doctoral Programs: GRE-V no minimum stated; GRE-Q no minimum stated; overall undergraduate GPA 3.0; last 2 years GPA 3.0; Doctoral program GRE-Analytic no minimum stated.

Other Criteria: (importance of criteria rated low, medium, or high): GRE/MAT scores—high, research experience—medium, work experience—medium, extracurricular activity—low, clinically related public service—low, GPA—high, letters of recommendation—medium, interview—high, statement of goals and objectives—high, undergraduate major in psychology—low, specific undergraduate psychology courses taken—low. For additional information on admission requirements, go to http://www.schoolpsych.duq.edu.

Student Characteristics: The following represents characteristics of students in 2007–2008 in all graduate psychology programs in the department: Female—full-time 72, part-time 0; Male—full-time 20, part-time 0; African American/Black—full-time 5, part-time 0; Hispanic/Latino(a)—full-time 1, part-time 0; Asian/Pacific Islander—full-time 2, part-time 0; American Indian/Alaska Native—full-time 0, part-time 0; Caucasian/White—full-time 82, part-time 0; Multi-ethnic—full-time 1, part-time 0;

students subject to the Americans With Disabilities Act—full-time 0, part-time 0; Unknown ethnicity—full-time 0, part-time 0; International students who hold an F-1 or J-1 Visa—full-time 1, part-time 0.

Financial Information/Assistance:

Tuition for Full-Time Study: *Master's:* State residents: per academic year $12,720, $848 per credit hour; Nonstate residents: per academic year $12,720, $848 per credit hour. *Doctoral:* State residents: per academic year $19,504, $848 per credit hour; Nonstate residents: per academic year $19,504, $848 per credit hour. Tuition is subject to change. Tuition costs vary by program. See the following Web site for updates and changes in tuition costs: http://www.schoolpsych.duq.edu.

Financial Assistance:

First-Year Students: Research assistantships available for first year. Average number of hours worked per week: 20. Apply by March 1. Tuition remission given: full.

Advanced Students: Research assistantships available for advanced students. Average number of hours worked per week: 20. Apply by March 1. Tuition remission given: full.

Additional Information: Of all students currently enrolled full time, 5% benefited from one or more of the listed financial assistance programs. Application and information available online at http://www.schoolpsych.duq.edu.

Internships/Practica: Doctoral Degree (PhD in School Psychology): For those doctoral students for whom a professional internship was required in this program prior to graduation, (6) students applied for an internship in 2006–2007, with (6) students obtaining an internship. Of those students who obtained an internship, (6) were paid internships. Of those students who obtained an internship, (0) students placed in APA/CPA-accredited internships, (0) students placed in internships not APA/CPA-accredited, but listed with the Association of Psychology Postdoctoral and Internship Centers (APPIC), (6) students placed in internships conforming to guidelines of the Council of Directors of School Psychology Programs (CDSPP), (0) students placed in internships that were not APA/CPA-accredited, APPIC or CDSPP listed. Certification program requires two practica and one internship; doctoral program requires two practica, one doctoral practica, and one internship. Please refer to http://www.schoolpsych.duq.edu for more information (we are anticipating APA accreditation April 2008). For additional information on education and training outcomes for our programs, see the following Web site: http://www.schoolpsych.duq.edu.

Housing and Day Care: On-campus housing is available. See the following Web site for more information: http://www.residencelife.duq.edu. On-campus day care facilities are available. See the following Web site for more information: http://www.hr.duq.edu/employment/universityprograms.

Employment of Department Graduates:

Master's Degree Graduates: Of those who graduated in the academic year 2006–2007, the following categories and numbers represent the postgraduate activities and employment of master's degree graduates: Enrolled in a psychology doctoral program (0), enrolled in another graduate/professional program (0), enrolled in a postdoctoral residency/fellowship (n/a), employed in independent practice (n/a), employed in an academic position at a university (0), employed in an academic position at a 2-year/4-year college (0), employed in other positions at a higher education institution (0), employed in a professional position in a school system (11), employed in business or industry (0), employed in government agency (0), employed in a community mental health/counseling center (0), employed in a hospital/medical center (0), still seeking employment (0), not seeking employment (0), other employment position (0), do not know (0), total from the above (master's) (11).

Doctoral Degree Graduates: Of those who graduated in the academic year 2006–2007, the following categories and numbers represent the postgraduate activities and employment of doctoral degree graduates: Enrolled in a psychology doctoral program (n/a), enrolled in another graduate/professional program (0), enrolled in a postdoctoral residency/fellowship (0), employed in independent practice (1), employed in an academic position at a university (0), employed in an academic position at a 2-year/4-year college (0), employed in other positions at a higher education institution (0), employed in a professional position in a school system (4), employed in business or industry (0), employed in government agency (0), employed in a community mental health/counseling center (0), employed in a hospital/medical center (0), still seeking employment (0), not seeking employment (0), other employment position (1), do not know (0), total from the above (doctoral) (6).

Additional Information:

Orientation, Objectives, and Emphasis of Department: The Duquesne University School Psychology program, guided by the belief that all children can learn, is dedicated to providing both breadth and depth of professional training in a theoretically integrated, research-based learning environment. The program prepares ethical practitioners, scientists, and scholars who are life-long learners committed to enhancing the well-being of youth, their families, and the systems that serve them. The program achieves this by engaging in scholarly activities that advance the field of school psychology, maintaining a modern curriculum that employs aspects of multiculturalism and diversity, examining emerging trends in the profession, conducting continuous outcome assessment for program improvement, and providing support to our graduates.

Special Facilities or Resources: The program has a curriculum library of current psychological and educational tests for training and research purposes.

Information for Students With Physical Disabilities: See the following Web site for more information: http://www.duq.edu.

Application Information:

Send to Dr. Kara McGoey, School Psychology Program, 102C Canevin Hall, Pittsburgh, PA 15282. Students are admitted in the Winter, application deadline February 1. Master's in School Psychology has rolling admissions. *Fee:* $50. The $50 application fee is waived if application inquiry is completed online. The three-page hard copy of the application is still required to be mailed in.

Duquesne University
Department of Psychology
McAnulty College and Graduate School of Liberal Arts
600 Forbes Avenue
Pittsburgh, PA 15282
Telephone: (412) 396-6520
Fax: (412) 396-5197
E-mail: *psychology@duq.edu*
Web: *http://www.gradpsych.duq.edu/*

Department Information:

1959. Chairperson: Daniel Burston, PhD. Number of faculty: total—full-time 16; women—full-time 4; total—minority—full-time 2.

Programs and Degrees Offered:

Listed in the following order: Program area, degree type (T if terminal Master's), number awarded 7/06–6/07. Clinical PhD (Doctor of Philosophy) 7.

APA Accreditation: Clinical PhD (Doctor of Philosophy).

Student Applications/Admissions:

Student Applications

Clinical PhD (Doctor of Philosophy)—Applications 2007–2008, 82. Total applicants accepted 2007–2008, 7. Number full-time enrolled (new admits only) 2007–2008, 7. Number part-time enrolled (new admits only) 2007–2008, 0. Openings 2008–2009, 7. The median number of years required for completion of a degree in 2006–2007 were 8. The number of students enrolled full- and part-time who were dismissed or voluntarily withdrew from this program area in 2007–2008 were 1.

Admissions Requirements:

Scores: Entries appear in this order: required test or GPA, minimum score (if required), median score of students entering in 2007–2008. Master's Programs: MA no longer offered. Doctoral Programs: GRE-V no minimum stated; GRE-Q no minimum stated; overall undergraduate GPA no minimum stated; Doctoral program GRE-Analytic no minimum stated.

Other Criteria: (importance of criteria rated low, medium, or high): GRE/MAT scores—medium, research experience—medium, work experience—medium, extracurricular activity—medium, clinically related public service—medium, GPA—medium, letters of recommendation—high, interview—high, statement of goals and objectives—high.

Student Characteristics: The following represents characteristics of students in 2007–2008 in all graduate psychology programs in the department: Female—full-time 31, part-time 0; Male—full-time 33, part-time 0; African American/Black—full-time 2, part-time 0; Hispanic/Latino(a)—full-time 3, part-time 0; Asian/Pacific Islander—full-time 2, part-time 0; American Indian/Alaska Native—full-time 1, part-time 0; Caucasian/White—full-time 50, part-time 0; Multi-ethnic—full-time 2, part-time 0; students subject to the Americans With Disabilities Act—full-time 0, part-time 0; Unknown ethnicity—full-time 4, part-time 0; International students who hold an F-1 or J-1 Visa—full-time 11, part-time 0.

Financial Information/Assistance:

Financial Assistance:

First-Year Students: Research assistantships available for first year. Average amount paid per academic year: $13,000. Average number of hours worked per week: 15. Apply by December 15. Tuition remission given: full.

Advanced Students: Teaching assistantships available for advanced students. Average amount paid per academic year: $13,000. Average number of hours worked per week: 15. Apply by December 15. Tuition remission given: full. Research assistantships available for advanced students. Average amount paid per academic year: $13,000. Average number of hours worked per week: 15. Apply by December 15. Tuition remission given: full.

Additional Information: Of all students currently enrolled full time, 100% benefited from one or more of the listed financial assistance programs. Application and information available online at http://www.gradpsych.duq.edu.

Internships/Practica: Doctoral Degree (PhD Clinical): For those doctoral students for whom a professional internship was required in this program prior to graduation, (5) students applied for an internship in 2006–2007, with (5) students obtaining an internship. Of those students who obtained an internship, (5) were paid internships. Of those students who obtained an internship, (5) students placed in APA/CPA-accredited internships, (0) students placed in internships not APA/CPA-accredited, but listed with the Association of Psychology Postdoctoral and Internship Centers (APPIC), (0) students placed in internships conforming to guidelines of the Council of Directors of School Psychology Programs (CDSPP), (0) students placed in internships that were not APA/CPA-accredited, APPIC or CDSPP listed. The Duquesne University Psychology Clinic, which serves more than 70 clients weekly, is the primary training facility for the doctoral students. All services, including assessment and psychotherapy for Duquesne University students, employees, and members of the greater Pittsburgh communities, are provided by the doctoral students. Licensed clinical faculty members and selected licensed adjunct faculty psychologists in the community are involved in the supervision of all doctoral students. The first 4 years of the doctoral program typically involve case work at the clinic. Additionally, students attend at least 1 academic year of external practicum placement in settings such as hospitals, university counseling centers, and VA centers. External practica are typically completed during the 3rd year of the program. A 2nd year of external practicum training, taken in the 4th year, is strongly recommended. For additional information on education and training outcomes for our programs, see the following Web site: http://www.gradpsych.duq.edu/DUeducationandtrainingoutcomes.htm.

Housing and Day Care: On-campus housing is available. See the following Web site for more information: http://www.duq.edu. On-campus day care facilities are available. See the following Web site for more information: http://www.duq.edu.

Employment of Department Graduates:

Master's Degree Graduates: Of those who graduated in the academic year 2006–2007, the following categories and numbers represent the postgraduate activities and employment of master's degree graduates: Enrolled in a postdoctoral residency/fellowship (n/a), employed in independent practice (n/a), total from the above (master's) (0).

Doctoral Degree Graduates: Of those who graduated in the academic year 2006–2007, the following categories and numbers represent the postgraduate activities and employment of doctoral degree graduates: Enrolled in a psychology doctoral program (n/a), total from the above (doctoral) (0).

Additional Information:

Orientation, Objectives, and Emphasis of Department: Internationally recognized for over three decades, the Psychology Department at Duquesne University engages in the systematic and rigorous articulation of psychology as a human science. The department understands psychology as a positive response to the challenges of the 21st century—one which includes existentialism, phenomenology, hermeneutics, psychoanalylsis and depth psychology, feminism, critical theory, post-structuralism, and a sensitivity to the diverse cultural contexts within which this response may find expression. Psychology as a human science pursues collaborative, qualitative research methods that pay special attention to what is particular to human beings and their worlds. Accordingly, the department educates psychologists who are sensitive to the multiple meanings of human life and who work toward the liberation and well-being of persons individually as well as in the community.

Special Facilities or Resources: The psychology clinic provides the opportunity for supervised training in personal counseling and for research in the field of counseling and psychotherapy. Field placements are available in Clinical. The Silverman Center is a research center containing a comprehensive collection of world literature in phenomenology.

Information for Students With Physical Disabilities: See the following Web site for more information: http://www.fdss.duq.edu/Text/text_sss.html.

Application Information:

Send to Duquesne University, McAnulty College and Graduate School of Liberals Arts, Graduate Office, 600 Forbes Avenue, Pittsburgh, PA 15282. Application available online. URL of online application: http://www.gradpsych.duq.edu/applications.html. Students are admitted in the Fall, application deadline December 15. January 15 is the absolute deadline for documents to support the application. *Fee:* $50. No fee for applications filed online.

Edinboro University of Pennsylvania

Department of Psychology
Liberal Arts
106 Compton Hall
Edinboro, PA 16444
Telephone: (814) 732-2774
Fax: (814) 732-2005
E-mail: *leginbucell@edinboro.edu*
Web: *http://www.psychology.edinboro.edu/*

Department Information:

1963. Chairperson: Cynthia Legin-Bucell, PhD. Number of faculty: total—full-time 15; women—full-time 6; faculty subject to the Americans With Disabilities Act 1.

Programs and Degrees Offered:

Listed in the following order: Program area, degree type (T if terminal Master's), number awarded 7/06–6/07. Clinical Psychology MA/MS (Master of Arts/Science) (T) 16.

Student Applications/Admissions:

Student Applications

Clinical Psychology MA/MS (Master of Arts/Science)—Applications 2007–2008, 40. Total applicants accepted 2007–2008, 20. Number full-time enrolled (new admits only) 2007–2008, 6. Number part-time enrolled (new admits only) 2007–2008, 6. Total enrolled 2007–2008 full-time, 18, part-time, 8. Openings 2008–2009, 15. The median number of years required for completion of a degree in 2006–2007 were 2. The number of students enrolled full- and part-time who were dismissed or voluntarily withdrew from this program area in 2007–2008 were 0.

Admissions Requirements:

Scores: Entries appear in this order: required test or GPA, minimum score (if required), median score of students entering in 2007–2008. Master's Programs: GRE-V no minimum stated, 540; GRE-Q no minimum stated, 450; overall undergraduate GPA 3.0, 3.4. GRE Scores are preferred. MAT scores are accepted. It is not necessary to take both.

Other Criteria: (importance of criteria rated low, medium, or high): GRE/MAT scores—high, research experience—medium, work experience—medium, extracurricular activity—low, clinically related public service—medium, GPA—high, letters of recommendation—high, statement of goals and objectives—medium, undergraduate major in psychology—low, specific undergraduate psychology courses taken—medium. For additional information on admission requirements, go to http://psychology.edinboro.edu/MA/MA_Contents.htm.

Student Characteristics: The following represents characteristics of students in 2007–2008 in all graduate psychology programs in the department: Female—full-time 10, part-time 7; Male—full-time 8, part-time 1; African American/Black—full-time 0, part-time 0; Hispanic/Latino(a)—full-time 0, part-time 0; Asian/Pacific Islander—full-time 0, part-time 0; American Indian/Alaska Native—full-time 0, part-time 0; Caucasian/White—full-time 18, part-time 8; Multi-ethnic—full-time 0, part-time 0; students subject to the Americans With Disabilities Act—full-time 0, part-time 0; Unknown ethnicity—full-time 0, part-time 0.

Financial Information/Assistance:

Tuition for Full-Time Study: *Master's:* State residents: per academic year $6,214, $345 per credit hour; Nonstate residents: per academic year $9,944, $552 per credit hour. Tuition is subject to change. See the following Web site for updates and changes in tuition costs: http://www.departments.edinboro.edu/graduatestudies/admissions/tuition.html.

Financial Assistance:

First-Year Students: Research assistantships available for first year. Average amount paid per academic year: $4,050. Average number of hours worked per week: 18. Apply by February 15. Tuition remission given: full and partial.

Advanced Students: Research assistantships available for advanced students. Average amount paid per academic year:

$4,050. Average number of hours worked per week: 18. Apply by February 15. Tuition remission given: full and partial.

Additional Information: Of all students currently enrolled full time, 75% benefited from one or more of the listed financial assistance programs. Application and information available online at http://departments.edinboro.edu/graduatestudies/financial_aid/financial_aid.html.

Internships/Practica: Master's Degree (MA/MS Master of Arts in Clinical Psychology): An internship experience such as a final research project or "capstone" experience is required of graduates. Students are required to take a one-semester, full-time clinical internship. During the internship, internship sites are expected to provide students with the following experiences: (a) individual and group psychotherapy, (b) administration and interpretation of psychometric techniques, and (c) supervision by a licensed psychologist. Internships are available in various sites including community mental health centers, state psychiatric hospitals, residential facilities for children and adolescents, VA outpatient clinics, local hospitals, correctional institutions, and counseling centers. We attempt to help each student find an internship that closely matches his or her interests. Students can also negotiate new internship sites (within our geographic area) as long as an approved, licensed supervisor is available. An optional summer practicum experience is available for students seeking licensure as a professional counselor license in Pennsylvania. Internship placement rate has been 100%.

Housing and Day Care: On-campus housing is available. Information about on- and off-campus housing can be obtained from the Office or Residence Life and Housing via the Internet: http://www.edinboro.edu/cwis/studaff/housing/index.html. By mail: Office of Residence Life and Housing, Edinboro University of Pennsylvania, 150 Perry Lane, Edinboro, PA 16444. By e-mail: boroliving@edinboro.edu; telephone: (814) 732-2818. No on-campus day care facilities are available.

Employment of Department Graduates:

Master's Degree Graduates: Of those who graduated in the academic year 2006–2007, the following categories and numbers represent the postgraduate activities and employment of master's degree graduates: Enrolled in a psychology doctoral program (0), enrolled in another graduate/professional program (0), enrolled in a postdoctoral residency/fellowship (n/a), employed in independent practice (n/a), employed in an academic position at a university (0), employed in an academic position at a 2-year/4-year college (0), employed in other positions at a higher education institution (0), employed in a professional position in a school system (0), employed in business or industry (0), employed in government agency (0), employed in a community mental health/counseling center (0), employed in a hospital/medical center (0), still seeking employment (0), not seeking employment (0), other employment position (0), do not know (0), total from the above (master's) (0).

Doctoral Degree Graduates: Of those who graduated in the academic year 2006–2007, the following categories and numbers represent the postgraduate activities and employment of doctoral degree graduates: Enrolled in a psychology doctoral program (n/a), total from the above (doctoral) (0).

Additional Information:

Orientation, Objectives, and Emphasis of Department: The MA program in Clinical Psychology adheres to the scientist–practitioner model for preparation of practitioners who have the requisite foundation of clinical and empirical knowledge. This orientation prepares students for the lifelong practice of professional psychology. Graduates of our program are prepared to perform clinical services, at the highest levels of competence, in accordance with the ethical principles of psychologists. Past graduates have gained employment at a professional level in a wide variety of human service organizations and agencies. The training program offers intensive coursework in psychological assessment, therapy, psychopathology, neuropsychology, psychopharmacology, ethics, and research. Some students will immediately use these skills in clinical settings. Other students, recognizing their interest in pursuing a terminal degree in psychology, will use this training experience as a springboard to doctoral training.

Special Facilities or Resources: Part-time study is available. All courses (except the internship) can be taken in the evening for part-time study.

Information for Students With Physical Disabilities: See the following Web site for more information: http://www.edinboro.edu/cwis/tac/dis_serv/eupds.htm.

Application Information:

Send to School of Graduate Studies and Research, Edinboro University of Pennsylvania, Bigger's House, 148 Meadville Street, Edinboro, PA 16444. Application available online. URL of online application: https://www.applyweb.com/apply/edingrad/menu.html. Students are admitted in the Fall, application deadline February 15. Applications for Fall 2009 admission will be accepted and reviewed until April 15, 2009. However, application prior to February 15 is required for consideration in assigning graduate assistantships. *Fee:* $30. The full application fee of $30 is required for students who have not previously attended Edinboro University of Pennsylvania. There is a reduced application fee ($7) for students who have graduated from Edinboro University.

Geneva College

Graduate Counseling
MA in Counseling, 3200 College Avenue
Beaver Falls, PA 15010
Telephone: (724) 847-6697
Fax: (724) 847-6101
E-mail: *counseling@geneva.edu*
Web: *http://www.geneva.edu*

Department Information:

1987. MA in Counseling Program Director: Carol Luce, PhD. Number of faculty: total—full-time 4; women—full-time 1; faculty subject to the Americans With Disabilities Act 1.

Programs and Degrees Offered:

Listed in the following order: Program area, degree type (T if terminal Master's), number awarded 7/06–6/07. Marriage and Family Counseling MA/MS (Master of Arts/Science) 6, Mental

Health Counseling MA/MS (Master of Arts/Science) 5, School Counseling MA/MS (Master of Arts/Science) 6.

Student Applications/Admissions:

Student Applications

Marriage and Family Counseling MA/MS (Master of Arts/Science)—Applications 2007–2008, 11. Total applicants accepted 2007–2008, 9. Number full-time enrolled (new admits only) 2007–2008, 6. Number part-time enrolled (new admits only) 2007–2008, 1. Total enrolled 2007–2008 full-time, 11, part-time, 5. Openings 2008–2009, 6. The median number of years required for completion of a degree in 2006–2007 were 3. The number of students enrolled full- and part-time who were dismissed or voluntarily withdrew from this program area in 2007–2008 were 1. *Mental Health Counseling MA/MS (Master of Arts/Science)*—Applications 2007–2008, 20. Total applicants accepted 2007–2008, 11. Number full-time enrolled (new admits only) 2007–2008, 7. Number part-time enrolled (new admits only) 2007–2008, 3. Total enrolled 2007–2008 full-time, 10, part-time, 6. Openings 2008–2009, 6. The median number of years required for completion of a degree in 2006–2007 were 2. The number of students enrolled full- and part-time who were dismissed or voluntarily withdrew from this program area in 2007–2008 were 2. *School Counseling MA/MS (Master of Arts/Science)*—Applications 2007–2008, 9. Total applicants accepted 2007–2008, 3. Number full-time enrolled (new admits only) 2007–2008, 2. Number part-time enrolled (new admits only) 2007–2008, 1. Total enrolled 2007–2008 full-time, 8, part-time, 7. Openings 2008–2009, 6. The median number of years required for completion of a degree in 2006–2007 were 3. The number of students enrolled full- and part-time who were dismissed or voluntarily withdrew from this program area in 2007–2008 were 1.

Admissions Requirements:

Scores: Entries appear in this order: required test or GPA, minimum score (if required), median score of students entering in 2007–2008. Master's Programs: GRE-V no minimum stated; GRE-Q no minimum stated; MAT no minimum stated; overall undergraduate GPA no minimum stated; Masters GRE-Analytical no minimum stated. GRE General Test or MAT required but not both. Suggested scores—50th percentile for acceptance.

Other Criteria: (importance of criteria rated low, medium, or high): GRE/MAT scores—medium, research experience—low, work experience—medium, extracurricular activity—medium, clinically related public service—medium, GPA—medium, letters of recommendation—high, interview—low, statement of goals and objectives—high, specific undergraduate psychology courses taken—medium. Undergraduate courses should include 12 credits in psychology, counseling, or sociology. Undergraduate statistics is highly recommended. For additional information on admission requirements, go to http://www.geneva.edu.

Student Characteristics: The following represents characteristics of students in 2007–2008 in all graduate psychology programs in the department: Female—full-time 21, part-time 16; Male—full-time 8, part-time 2; African American/Black—full-time 3, part-time 3; Hispanic/Latino(a)—full-time 0, part-time 0; Asian/Pacific Islander—full-time 0, part-time 0; American Indian/Alaska Native—full-time 0, part-time 0; Caucasian/White—full-time 25, part-time 15; Multi-ethnic—full-time 1, part-time 0; students subject to the Americans With Disabilities Act—full-time 0, part-time 0; Unknown ethnicity—full-time 0, part-time 0; International students who hold an F-1 or J-1 Visa—full-time 0, part-time 0.

Financial Information/Assistance:

Tuition for Full-Time Study: *Master's:* State residents: $595 per credit hour; Nonstate residents: $595 per credit hour. Tuition is subject to change.

Financial Assistance:

First-Year Students: No information provided.

Advanced Students: No information provided.

Additional Information: Application and information available online.Graduate assistant applications are available through the MA in Counseling Program office.

Internships/Practica: A practicum and internship program is in place. This practicum and internship experience is in line with the CACREP standards for master's level counseling programs. Details are as follows: practica are 100 hours in length with individual and group supervision and direct client contact; marriage and family internships are 600 hours in length with direct client contact included; mental health internships are 900 hours in length with direct client contact hours included; school internships are 600 hours in length with 300 hours being on the elementary level and 300 hours on the secondary level. All internships will involve site placements typically in the Beaver County and Pittsburgh area, supervision via qualified master's and/or doctoral prepared practitioners, and onsite as well as college supervision. Practica and internship experiences are arranged by the faculty coordinators. For additional information on education and training outcomes for our programs, see the following Web site: http://www.geneva.edu.

Housing and Day Care: No on-campus housing is available. No on-campus day care facilities are available.

Employment of Department Graduates:

Master's Degree Graduates: Of those who graduated in the academic year 2006–2007, the following categories and numbers represent the postgraduate activities and employment of master's degree graduates: Enrolled in a psychology doctoral program (0), enrolled in another graduate/professional program (0), enrolled in a postdoctoral residency/fellowship (n/a), employed in independent practice (n/a), employed in an academic position at a university (0), employed in an academic position at a 2-year/4-year college (0), employed in other positions at a higher education institution (0), employed in a professional position in a school system (2), employed in business or industry (0), employed in government agency (0), employed in a community mental health/counseling center (12), employed in a hospital/medical center (0), other employment position (1), do not know (2), total from the above (master's) (17).

Doctoral Degree Graduates: Of those who graduated in the academic year 2006–2007, the following categories and numbers represent the postgraduate activities and employment of doctoral degree graduates: Enrolled in a psychology doctoral program (n/a), total from the above (doctoral) (0).

Additional Information:

Orientation, Objectives, and Emphasis of Department: The philosophies of counseling in the MA in Counseling program at Geneva College are embedded in a Christian view of human nature and God's created world. A growing body of research literature affirms that Christian faith establishes a basis for healthy personality development, interpersonal relations, and mental health. A multidimensional holistic view of persons examines the interweaving of physical, emotional, social, cognitive, behavioral, and spiritual aspects of life. Integrative psychotherapeutic conceptualizations based on this multidimensionality promote healing and change. Counseling students and faculty engage in Christian spiritual growth thus modeling adherence to the faith and values they profess and facilitating academic learning, counseling, effectiveness, and ability to consult in the larger church community and beyond. The MA in Counseling program at Geneva College provides academic training in the development of knowledge, skills, and personal awareness pertinent to the counseling profession, and encourages students to integrate Christian faith and Biblical knowledge with the training and practice of counseling. The program is designed so that postbaccalaureate students who complete this degree and acquire the required postgraduate supervised experience in the practice of counseling will be eligible to become licensed professional counselors.

Personal Behavior Statement: Adherence to ACA and ASCA Ethical Guidelines are expected.

Special Facilities or Resources: Department facilities include a computer lab and a modern clinical counseling facility. The computer lab is equipped with WordPerfect for Windows, SPSS for Windows, and various experimental and clinical software resources. The lab is also connected to Internet and Netscape on the World Wide Web.

Information for Students With Physical Disabilities: See the following Web site for more information: http://www.geneva.edu.

Application Information:

Send to MA in Counseling Program Manager, Geneva College, 3200 College Avenue, Beaver Falls, PA 15010. Application available online. URL of online application: http://www.geneva.edu/page/counseling. Students are admitted in the Fall, application deadline open; Spring, application deadline open; Summer, application deadline open; programs have rolling admissions. *Fee:* $50. Application fee will be waived for online application.

Immaculata University

Department of Graduate Psychology
College of Graduate Studies
Box 500, Loyola Hall
Immaculata, PA 19345-0500
Telephone: (215) 647-4400 Exts. 3211, 3212, 3213
Fax: (610) 993-8550
E-mail: *jyalof@immaculata.edu*
Web: *http://www.immaculata.edu*

Department Information:

1983. Chairperson: Jed Yalof. Number of faculty: total—full-time 10, part-time 15; women—full-time 7, part-time 7; total—minority—full-time 1; women minority—full-time 1.

Programs and Degrees Offered:

Listed in the following order: Program area, degree type (T if terminal Master's), number awarded 7/06–6/07. Clinical PsyD (Doctor of Psychology) 6, Counseling MA/MS (Master of Arts/Science) (T) 38, Elementary School Certification (T), School Certification (T), School Secondary Certification, School Psychology PsyD (Doctor of Psychology) 4.

APA Accreditation: Clinical PsyD (Doctor of Psychology).

Student Applications/Admissions:

Student Applications

Clinical PsyD (Doctor of Psychology)—Applications 2007–2008, 106. Total applicants accepted 2007–2008, 48. Number full-time enrolled (new admits only) 2007–2008, 22. Number part-time enrolled (new admits only) 2007–2008, 0. Total enrolled 2007–2008 full-time, 65, part-time, 47. Openings 2008–2009, 25. The median number of years required for completion of a degree in 2006–2007 were 6. The number of students enrolled full- and part-time who were dismissed or voluntarily withdrew from this program area in 2007–2008 were 1. *Counseling MA/MS (Master of Arts/Science)*—Applications 2007–2008, 104. Total applicants accepted 2007–2008, 83. Total enrolled 2007–2008 full-time, 15, part-time, 106. The number of students enrolled full- and part-time who were dismissed or voluntarily withdrew from this program area in 2007–2008 were 2. *Elementary School Certification MA/MS* — Total enrolled 2007–2008 full-time, 2, part-time, 13. *School Certification* —Total enrolled 2007–2008 full-time, 13, part-time, 17. *School Secondary Certification*—Total enrolled 2007–2008 full-time, 8, part-time, 13. *School Psychology PsyD (Doctor of Psychology)*—Total enrolled 2007–2008 full-time, 2, part-time, 8.

Admissions Requirements:

Scores: Entries appear in this order: required test or GPA, minimum score (if required), median score of students entering in 2007–2008. Master's Programs: MAT no minimum stated; overall undergraduate GPA 3.0. Test scores not required for MA if GPA is above 3.0 Doctoral Programs: GRE-V no minimum stated; GRE-Q no minimum stated; MAT no minimum stated; overall undergraduate GPA no minimum stated. Applicants applying to the PsyD program with BA only, 3.3 minimum GPA required.

Other Criteria: (importance of criteria rated low, medium, or high): GRE/MAT scores—medium, GPA—medium, letters of recommendation—medium, interview—high, statement of goals and objectives—medium. PsyD Clinical Psychology accepts BA, MA, or equivalency in psychology or MA in another field; PsyD School Psychology accepts BA, MA, or equivalency in psychology or MA in another field and students already certified in school psychology. Admissions criteria differ for applicants to MA Counseling versus PsyD Clinical and School programs. For additional information on admission requirements, go to http://www.immaculata.edu.

Student Characteristics: The following represents characteristics of students in 2007–2008 in all graduate psychology programs in the department: Female—full-time 90, part-time 164; Male—full-time 15, part-time 40; African American/Black—full-time 12, part-time 10; Hispanic/Latino(a)—full-time 3, part-time 2; Asian/Pacific Islander—full-time 5, part-time 1; American Indian/Alaska Native—full-time 0, part-time 0; Caucasian/White—full-time 83, part-time 184; Multi-ethnic—full-time 0, part-time 0; Unknown ethnicity—full-time 2, part-time 7.

Financial Information/Assistance:

Tuition for Full-Time Study: *Master's:* State residents: $515 per credit hour. *Doctoral:* State residents: $725 per credit hour. Tuition is subject to change.

Financial Assistance:

First-Year Students: No information provided.

Advanced Students: No information provided.

Additional Information: Application and information available online at http://www.immaculata.edu.

Internships/Practica: Master's Degree (MA/MS Counseling): An internship experience such as a final research project or "capstone" experience is required of graduates. Master's Degree (MA/MS Elementary School Certification): An internship experience such as a final research project or "capstone" experience is required of graduates. Master's Degree (MA/MS School Certification): An internship experience such as a final research project or "capstone" experience is required of graduates. Doctoral Degree (PsyD Clinical): For those doctoral students for whom a professional internship was required in this program prior to graduation, (17) students applied for an internship in 2006–2007, with (16) students obtaining an internship. Of those students who obtained an internship, (16) were paid internships. Of those students who obtained an internship, (3) students placed in APA/CPA accredited internships, (13) students placed in internships not APA/CPA-accredited, but listed with the Association of Psychology Postdoctoral and Internship Centers (APPIC), (0) students placed in internships conforming to guidelines of the Council of Directors of School Psychology Programs (CDSPP), (0) students placed in internships that were not APA/CPA-accredited, APPIC or CDSPP listed. Doctoral Degree (PsyD School Psychology): For those doctoral students for whom a professional internship was required in this program prior to graduation, (2) students applied for an internship in 2006–2007, with (2) students obtaining an internship. Of those students who obtained an internship, (2) were paid internships. Of those students who obtained an internship, (0) students placed in APA/CPA-accredited internships, (2) students placed in internships not APA/CPA-accredited, but listed with the Association of Psychology Postdoctoral and Internship Centers (APPIC), (0) students placed in internships conforming to guidelines of the Council of Directors of School Psychology Programs (CDSPP), (0) students placed in internships that were not APA/CPA-accredited, APPIC or CDSPP listed. The department has an APPIC consortium for predoctoral internship training to which its students are encouraged to apply, in addition to applying to APA-accredited sites and other APPIC internships both locally and nationally. Clinical doctoral students complete diagnostic and therapy placements prior to internship. Elective field placements are available and encouraged for Clinical Psychology doctoral students. Students entering the PsyD program with BA or equivalent are required to complete a field placement early in their program of study as one of their electives. School doctoral students complete a practicum prior to internship. Students apply for work with either the master's field site coordinator or doctoral field site and predoctoral internship coordinator to identify prospective field placements for their different programs of study. The Graduate Psychology Department places counseling psychology, school psychology, and clinical psychology students at sites throughout the Philadelphia and tricounty area and with supervisors with qualifications specific to student and program requirements.

Housing and Day Care: No on-campus housing is available. No on-campus day care facilities are available.

Employment of Department Graduates:

Master's Degree Graduates: Of those who graduated in the academic year 2006–2007, the following categories and numbers represent the postgraduate activities and employment of master's degree graduates: Enrolled in a postdoctoral residency/fellowship (n/a), employed in independent practice (n/a), total from the above (master's) (0).

Doctoral Degree Graduates: Of those who graduated in the academic year 2006–2007, the following categories and numbers represent the postgraduate activities and employment of doctoral degree graduates: Enrolled in a psychology doctoral program (n/a), employed in independent practice (1), employed in a professional position in a school system (5), employed in government agency (1), employed in a community mental health/counseling center (2), other employment position (1), total from the above (doctoral) (10).

Additional Information:

Orientation, Objectives, and Emphasis of Department: At the master's level, the department's orientation is the professional preparation of the master's counselor in relation to counselor licensure in PA. The department also prepares students for elementary school counseling, secondary school counseling, and school psychology certification. Program information for the combined MA with certification in one of these three areas is reported. There are also certification-only programs for students with the MA degree; these programs have lower enrollment. In all cases, training emphasizes knowledge, skill, and competency through classroom, practicum, and internship. The department's orientation is the preparation of doctoral-level clinical psychologists within the practitioner–scholar model of professional psychology. This preparation entails a generalist curriculum emphasizing theory, therapy, diagnostics, and clinical training, with doctoral dissertation research aligned with a practitioner model. The department's preparation of doctoral-level school psychologists is practitioner oriented, focusing on advanced assessment and intervention, human diversity, biological bases, school–neuropsychological application, research, and consultation within the context of school settings.

Special Facilities or Resources: The college has a comprehensive center for academic computing and modern technology available for student computer needs and utilization. The Gabrielle Library was opened in 1993 and houses journals and texts, and has online search available to students.

Information for Students With Physical Disabilities: See the following Web site for more information: http://www.immaculata.edu.

Application Information:

Send to Director of Graduate Admission, Immaculata University, 1145 King Road, Box 500, Immaculata, PA 19345. Students are admitted in the Fall, application deadline rolling; Winter, application deadline rolling; Spring, application deadline rolling; Summer, application deadline rolling. PsyD: January 15 application deadline for May admissions; February 1 for Fall. Application fee is $35 for master's, $50 for doctoral programs.

Indiana University of Pennsylvania

Department of Psychology
Natural Sciences and Mathematics
201 Uhler Hall
Indiana, PA 15705
Telephone: (724) 357-4519
Fax: (724) 357-4087
E-mail: *goodwin@iup.edu*
Web: *http://www.iup.edu*

Department Information:

1984. Chairperson: Mary Lou Zanich, PhD. Number of faculty: total—full-time 22, part-time 6; women—full-time 12, part-time 6; total—minority—full-time 2; women minority—full-time 1.

Programs and Degrees Offered:

Listed in the following order: Program area, degree type (T if terminal Master's), number awarded 7/06–6/07. Clinical Psychology PsyD (Doctor of Psychology) 8.

APA Accreditation: Clinical PsyD (Doctor of Psychology).

Student Applications/Admissions:

Student Applications

Clinical Psychology PsyD (Doctor of Psychology)—Applications 2007–2008, 83. Total applicants accepted 2007–2008, 14. Number full-time enrolled (new admits only) 2007–2008, 13. Total enrolled 2007–2008 full-time, 63, part-time, 5. Openings 2008–2009, 12. The median number of years required for completion of a degree in 2006–2007 were 6. The number of students enrolled full- and part-time who were dismissed or voluntarily withdrew from this program area in 2007–2008 were 1.

Admissions Requirements:

Scores: Entries appear in this order: required test or GPA, minimum score (if required), median score of students entering in 2007–2008. Doctoral Programs: GRE-V 500, 550; GRE-Q 500, 650; GRE-Subject (Psychology) 500, 650; overall undergraduate GPA 3.0, 3.5.

Other Criteria: (importance of criteria rated low, medium, or high): GRE/MAT scores—high, research experience—medium, work experience—medium, clinically related public service—high, GPA—high, letters of recommendation—high, interview—high, statement of goals and objectives—high. For additional information on admission requirements, go to http://www.iup.edu/psychology.

Student Characteristics: The following represents characteristics of students in 2007–2008 in all graduate psychology programs in the department: Female—full-time 54, part-time 4; Male—full-time 9, part-time 1; African American/Black—full-time 1, part-time 0; Hispanic/Latino(a)—full-time 2, part-time 0; Asian/Pacific Islander—full-time 1, part-time 0; American Indian/Alaska Native—full-time 1, part-time 0; Caucasian/White—full-time 58, part-time 5; Multi-ethnic—full-time 0, part-time 0; students subject to the Americans With Disabilities Act—full-time 0, part-time 0; Unknown ethnicity—full-time 0, part-time 0; International students who hold an F-1 or J-1 Visa—full-time 1, part-time 0.

Financial Information/Assistance:

Tuition for Full-Time Study: *Doctoral:* State residents: per academic year $6,214, $345 per credit hour; Nonstate residents: per academic year $9,944, $552 per credit hour. Tuition is subject to change. Additional fees are assessed to students beyond the costs of tuition for the following: technology fee, activity fee, instructional fee, registration fee.

Financial Assistance:

First-Year Students: Research assistantships available for first year. Average amount paid per academic year: $3,040. Average number of hours worked per week: 10. Apply by March 15. Tuition remission given: partial. Fellowships and scholarships available for first year. Average amount paid per academic year: $5,000. Average number of hours worked per week: 0. Apply by March 15.

Advanced Students: Teaching assistantships available for advanced students. Average amount paid per academic year: $20,299. Average number of hours worked per week: 15. Apply by March 15. Research assistantships available for advanced students. Average amount paid per academic year: $3,040. Average number of hours worked per week: 10. Apply by March 15. Tuition remission given: partial. Fellowships and scholarships available for advanced students. Average amount paid per academic year: $1,000. Apply by April 15.

Additional Information: Of all students currently enrolled full time, 100% benefited from one or more of the listed financial assistance programs. Application and information available online at http://www.iup.edu/psychology.

Internships/Practica: Doctoral Degree (PsyD Clinical Psychology): For those doctoral students for whom a professional internship was required in this program prior to graduation, (11) students applied for an internship in 2006–2007, with (10) students obtaining an internship. Of those students who obtained an internship, (10) were paid internships. Of those students who obtained an internship, (7) students placed in APA/CPA-accredited internships, (3) students placed in internships not APA/CPA accredited, but listed with the Association of Psychology Postdoctoral and Internship Centers (APPIC), (0) students placed in internships conforming to guidelines of the Council of Directors of School Psychology Programs (CDSPP), (0) students placed in internships that were not APA/CPA-accredited, APPIC or CDSPP listed. Students begin clinical experiences in the 1st year through course-based practica. During the 2nd and later years, students enroll in the department-sponsored Center for Applied Psychology (CAP) training clinics. These clinics employ a live supervision model. Training in the CAP clinics is supplemented with required external practica, currently available at approximately 23 different sites.

Housing and Day Care: No on-campus housing is available. On-campus day care facilities are available. There is a day care center on campus, however, it is not managed by IUP. They do offer some subsidized day care.

Employment of Department Graduates:

Master's Degree Graduates: Of those who graduated in the academic year 2006–2007, the following categories and numbers represent the postgraduate activities and employment of master's degree graduates: Enrolled in a postdoctoral residency/fellowship (n/a), employed in independent practice (n/a), total from the above (master's) (0).

Doctoral Degree Graduates: Of those who graduated in the academic year 2006–2007, the following categories and numbers represent the postgraduate activities and employment of doctoral degree graduates: Enrolled in a psychology doctoral program (n/a), enrolled in a postdoctoral residency/fellowship (1), employed in government agency (1), employed in a community mental health/counseling center (5), not seeking employment (1), total from the above (doctoral) (8).

Additional Information:

Orientation, Objectives, and Emphasis of Department: The Psychology Department offers a Doctor of Psychology degree in Clinical Psychology (PsyD) that places emphasis upon professional applications of psychology based on a solid grounding in the scientific knowledge base of psychology. Training follows a generalist model with opportunities to develop advanced competencies during the last 2 years through courses and special practica. The core curriculum consists of seven areas including elective coursework. Heavy emphasis is placed on integrating psychological knowledge with treatment, evaluation, consultation, and service delivery program design. The program is designed to meet the academic requirements of licensure and provide the background to assume responsibilities in appropriate professional settings.

Special Facilities or Resources: The Department of Psychology includes two 16-computer laboratories, individual research space with audio and DVD capabilities, seminar rooms, and a graduate student lounge. Each graduate student office is provided with computer access to the department server and the Internet. The facilities for the CAP include 12 treatment rooms as well as one seminar room, all connected with a master DVD system. The CAP also houses computer facilities for test administration and scoring.

Information for Students With Physical Disabilities: See the following Web site for more information: http://www.iup.edu/advising/dss.html.

Application Information:

Send to Graduate School Admissions, Indiana University of Pennsylvania, Stright Hall, Indiana, PA 15705. Application available online. URL of online application: http://www.iup.edu/graduate. Students are admitted in the Fall, application deadline December 15; Summer, application deadline December 15. *Fee:* $30.

LaSalle University

Clinical–Counseling Psychology Program
1900 West Olney Avenue
Philadelphia, PA 19141
Telephone: (215) 951-1767
Fax: (215) 991-3585
E-mail: *rooney@lasalle.edu*
Web: *http://www.lasalle.edu*

Department Information:

1948. Director: John J. Rooney, PhD. Number of faculty: total—full-time 9, part-time 19; women—full-time 6, part-time 8; minority—part-time 4; women minority—part-time 1.

Programs and Degrees Offered:

Listed in the following order: Program area, degree type (T if terminal Master's), number awarded 7/06–6/07. Clinical Counseling Psychology MA/MS (Master of Arts/Science) 50.

Student Applications/Admissions:

Student Applications

Clinical Counseling Psychology MA/MS (Master of Arts/Science)—Applications 2007–2008, 396. Total applicants accepted 2007–2008, 184. Number full-time enrolled (new admits only) 2007–2008, 70. Number part-time enrolled (new admits only) 2007–2008, 12. Total enrolled 2007–2008 full-time, 125, part-time, 265. Openings 2008–2009, 100. The median number of years required for completion of a degree in 2006–2007 were 3. The number of students enrolled full- and part-time who were dismissed or voluntarily withdrew from this program area in 2007–2008 were 6.

Admissions Requirements:

Scores: Entries appear in this order: required test or GPA, minimum score (if required), median score of students entering in 2007–2008. Master's Programs: GRE-V 450, 550; GRE-Q 550, 650; MAT 50; overall undergraduate GPA 3.0; psychology GPA 3.3; Masters GRE-Analytical 4, 5. Either the GRE or MAT is required, not both.

Other Criteria: (importance of criteria rated low, medium, or high): GRE/MAT scores—medium, research experience—medium, work experience—medium, extracurricular activity—medium, clinically related public service—medium, GPA—high, letters of recommendation—high, statement of goals and objectives—medium. For additional information on admission requirements, go to http://www.lasalle.edu/admiss/grad/psych/.

Student Characteristics: The following represents characteristics of students in 2007–2008 in all graduate psychology programs in the department: Female—full-time 100, part-time 200; Male—full-time 25, part-time 65; African American/Black—full-time 9, part-time 45; Hispanic/Latino(a)—full-time 3, part-time 12; Asian/Pacific Islander—full-time 2, part-time 10; American Indian/Alaska Native—full-time 0, part-time 0; Caucasian/White—full-time 107, part-time 196; Multi-ethnic—full-time 4, part-time 2; students subject to the Americans With Disabilities Act—full-time 0, part-time 0; Unknown ethnicity—full-time 0, part-time 0; International students who hold an F-1 or J-1 Visa—full-time 3, part-time 0.

Financial Information/Assistance:

Tuition for Full-Time Study: *Master's:* State residents: $550 per credit hour; Nonstate residents: $550 per credit hour. Tuition is subject to change.

Financial Assistance:

First-Year Students: Fellowships and scholarships available for first year. Average amount paid per academic year: $1,250. Apply by July/November.

Advanced Students: Teaching assistantships available for advanced students. Average amount paid per academic year: $4,500. Average number of hours worked per week: 10. Apply by July/December. Research assistantships available for advanced students. Average amount paid per academic year: $4,500. Average number of hours worked per week: 10. Apply by July/December. Traineeships available for advanced students. Fellowships and scholarships available for advanced students. Average amount paid per academic year: $2,500. Apply by July/November.

Additional Information: Of all students currently enrolled full time, 25% benefited from one or more of the listed financial assistance programs. Application and information available online at http://www.lasalle.edu.

Internships/Practica: 125 Students are placed in sites, located throughout the tristate area. The internship placements are specific to the areas of concentrations and supervised by professionals highly qualified in particular realms of expertise.

Housing and Day Care: On-campus housing is available. See the following Web site for more information: http://www.lasalle.edu/students/dean/admin/housing/gradhousing.htm. On-campus day care facilities are available. Building Blocks Child Development Center.

Employment of Department Graduates:

Master's Degree Graduates: Of those who graduated in the academic year 2006–2007, the following categories and numbers represent the postgraduate activities and employment of master's degree graduates: Enrolled in a postdoctoral residency/fellowship (n/a), employed in independent practice (n/a), total from the above (master's) (0).

Doctoral Degree Graduates: Of those who graduated in the academic year 2006–2007, the following categories and numbers represent the postgraduate activities and employment of doctoral degree graduates: Enrolled in a psychology doctoral program (n/a), total from the above (doctoral) (0).

Additional Information:

Orientation, Objectives, and Emphasis of Department: Four areas of concentration are available within the program: psychological counseling, marriage and family therapy, addictions counseling, and industrial organizational psychology. The program stresses skills training and clinical preparation for these concentrations, including preparation for licensed professional counselor or licensed marriage and family therapist. It also prepares students for doctoral studies. The program is based on a holistic view of the person, which stresses the integration of the psychological, systemic, cultural, and spiritual dimensions of experience.

Special Facilities or Resources: Counselor training facilities include room and equipment for videotaping counseling sessions with individuals and families. A clinic for supervised training of students was opened in 1985. It has all the resources, equipment, and staff needed in such a facility.

Application Information:

Send to Dr. John Rooney, La Salle University, MA Clinical Counseling Psychology, Box 268, 1900 West Olney Avenue, Philadelphia, PA 19141. Application available online. URL of online application: http://www.lasalle.edu/admiss/grad/apply_nowgrad.php. Students are admitted in the Fall, Spring, and Summer programs have rolling admissions. Although there are no formal application deadlines, we recommend that all information necessary be received by August 1, December 1, and April 1, for the Fall, Spring, and Summer terms, respectively. International student applications should be completed at least 2 months prior to the dates listed above. *Fee:* $35. Fee waived for online application, which is recommended.

Lehigh University (2007 data)

Department of Education and Human Services
Education
Mountain Top Campus, 111 Research Drive
Bethlehem, PA 18015
Telephone: (610) 758-3241
Fax: (610) 758-6223
E-mail: *nil3@lehigh.edu*
Web: *http://www.lehigh.edu/collegeofeducation/flashpage*

Department Information:

1995. Chairperson: Nicholas Ladany. Number of faculty: total—full-time 31, part-time 12; women—full-time 12, part-time 7.

Programs and Degrees Offered:

Listed in the following order: Program area, degree type (T if terminal Master's), number awarded 7/06–6/07. Counseling Psychology PhD (Doctor of Philosophy) 2, Counseling and Human Services Other 12, Elementary School Counseling Other 2, School PhD (Doctor of Philosophy) 1, Secondary School Counseling Other 1, School (Education Specialist) EdS/MEd (School Psychology) 5, International Counseling (MEd) Other 0.

APA Accreditation: Counseling PhD (Doctor of Philosophy). School PhD (Doctor of Philosophy).

Student Applications/Admissions:

Student Applications

Counseling Psychology PhD (Doctor of Philosophy)—Applications 2007–2008, 70. Total applicants accepted 2007–2008, 7. Number full-time enrolled (new admits only) 2007–2008, 5. Number part-time enrolled (new admits only) 2007–2008, 0. Total enrolled 2007–2008 full-time, 23, part-time, 11. Openings 2008–2009, 7. The median number of years required for completion of a degree in 2006–2007 were 6. The number of students enrolled full- and part-time who were dismissed or voluntarily withdrew from this program area in 2007–2008 were 0. *Counseling and Human Services Other*—Applications 2007–2008, 41. Total applicants accepted 2007–2008, 24. Number full-time enrolled (new admits only) 2007–2008, 9. Number part-time enrolled (new admits only) 2007–2008, 4. Total enrolled 2007–2008 full-time, 22, part-time, 14. Openings 2008–2009, 40. The median number of years required for completion of a degree in 2006–2007 were 2. The number of students enrolled full- and part-time who were dismissed or voluntarily withdrew from this program area in 2007–2008 were 0. *Elementary School Counseling Other*—Applications 2007–2008, 13. Total applicants accepted 2007–2008, 11. Number full-time enrolled (new admits only) 2007–2008, 7. Number part-time enrolled (new admits only) 2007–2008, 2. Total enrolled 2007–2008 full-time, 5, part-time, 5. Openings 2008–2009, 10. The median number of years required for completion of a degree in 2006–2007 were 2. The number of students enrolled full- and part-time who were dismissed or voluntarily withdrew from this program area in 2007–2008 were 0. *School PhD (Doctor of Philosophy)*—Applications 2007–2008, 57. Total applicants accepted 2007–2008, 3. Number full-time enrolled (new admits only) 2007–2008, 3. Number part-time enrolled (new admits only) 2007–2008, 0. Total enrolled 2007–2008 full-time, 18, part-time, 19. Openings 2008–2009, 9. The median number of years required for completion of a degree in 2006–2007 were 6. The number of students enrolled full- and part-time who were dismissed or voluntarily withdrew from this program area in 2007–2008 were 0. *Secondary School Counseling Other*—Applications 2007–2008, 16. Total applicants accepted 2007–2008, 10. Number full-time enrolled (new admits only) 2007–2008, 9. Number part-time enrolled (new admits only) 2007–2008, 3. Total enrolled 2007–2008 full-time, 6, part-time, 9. Openings 2008–2009, 10. The median number of years required for completion of a degree in 2006–2007 were 2. The number of students enrolled full- and part-time who were dismissed or voluntarily withdrew from this program area in 2007–2008 were 0. *School (Education Specialist) EdS/MEd (School Psychology)*—Applications 2007–2008, 37. Total applicants accepted 2007–2008, 8. Number full-time enrolled (new admits only) 2007–2008, 8. Number part-time enrolled (new admits only) 2007–2008, 0. Total enrolled 2007–2008 full-time, 20, part-time, 1. Openings 2008–2009, 11. The median number of years required for completion of a degree in 2006–2007 were 3. The number of students enrolled full- and part-time who were dismissed or voluntarily withdrew from this program area in 2007–2008 were 0. *International Counseling (MEd) Other*—Applications 2007–2008, 2. Total applicants accepted 2007–2008, 2. Number full-time enrolled (new admits only) 2007–2008, 0. Number part-time enrolled (new admits only) 2007–2008, 2. Openings 2008–2009, 10. The median number of years required for completion of a degree in 2006–2007 were 2. The number of students enrolled full- and part-time who were dismissed or voluntarily withdrew from this program area in 2007–2008 were 0.

Admissions Requirements:

Scores: Entries appear in this order: required test or GPA, minimum score (if required), median score of students entering in 2007–2008. Master's Programs: overall undergraduate GPA 3.00; last 2 years GPA no minimum stated; psychology GPA no minimum stated. No minimums are set by the programs. Writing subtest of GRE also required if taken in past two years. Doctoral Programs: GRE-V no minimum stated; GRE-Q no minimum stated; overall undergraduate GPA 3.00. Varies per program.

Other Criteria: (importance of criteria rated low, medium, or high): GRE/MAT scores—medium, research experience—high, work experience—medium, extracurricular activity—medium, clinically related public service—medium, GPA—high, letters of recommendation—medium, interview—medium, statement of goals and objectives—high. Criteria vary by program.

Student Characteristics: The following represents characteristics of students in 2007–2008 in all graduate psychology programs in the department: Female—full-time 79, part-time 55; Male—full-time 15, part-time 13; African American/Black—full-time 10, part-time 3; Hispanic/Latino(a)—full-time 3, part-time 2; Asian/Pacific Islander—full-time 5, part-time 4; American Indian/Alaska Native—full-time 1, part-time 0; Caucasian/White—full-time 66, part-time 49; Multi-ethnic—full-time 2, part-time 1; Unknown ethnicity—full-time 5, part-time 2.

Financial Information/Assistance:

Tuition for Full-Time Study: *Master's:* State residents: $510 per credit hour; Nonstate residents: $510 per credit hour. *Doctoral:* State residents: $510 per credit hour; Nonstate residents: $510 per credit hour.

Financial Assistance:

First-Year Students: Research assistantships available for first year. Average amount paid per academic year: $12,000. Average number of hours worked per week: 20. Apply by January 1. Tuition remission given: full and partial. Traineeships available for first year. Average amount paid per academic year: $12,000. Average number of hours worked per week: 20. Apply by January 1. Tuition remission given: full and partial. Fellowships and scholarships available for first year. Average amount paid per academic year: $12,000. Average number of hours worked per week: 20. Apply by January 1. Tuition remission given: full and partial.

Advanced Students: Research assistantships available for advanced students. Average amount paid per academic year: $12,000. Average number of hours worked per week: 20. Tuition remission given: full and partial. Traineeships available for advanced students. Average amount paid per academic year: $12,000. Average number of hours worked per week: 20. Tuition remission given: full and partial. Fellowships and scholarships available for advanced students. Average amount paid per academic year: $12,000. Average number of hours worked per week: 20. Tuition remission given: full and partial.

Additional Information: Of all students currently enrolled full time, 80% benefited from one or more of the listed financial assistance programs.

Internships/Practica: The Counseling Psychology program maintains contracts with a variety of practicum settings. Training in individual, group, couples, and family counseling are readily available. Students receive at least 2 hours of individual and 2 hours of group supervision per week. Many sites provide additional training on specific issues in counseling. The Counseling Psychology programs have established a partnership with a local urban school district to provide enhanced in-school psychological services in elementary and middle schools. The School Psychology program, in cooperation with Centennial School, the University-affiliated school for students with emotional and behavioral disorders, supports a predoctoral internship opportunity in school psychology.

Housing and Day Care: On-campus housing is available. See the following Web site for more information: http://www3.lehigh.edu/

studentlife/slgraduatetransfer.asp. On-campus day care facilities are available. See the following Web site for more information: http://www.lehigh.edu/~inluccc/cc.html.

Employment of Department Graduates:

Master's Degree Graduates: Of those who graduated in the academic year 2006–2007, the following categories and numbers represent the postgraduate activities and employment of master's degree graduates: Enrolled in a postdoctoral residency/fellowship (n/a), employed in independent practice (n/a), total from the above (master's) (0).

Doctoral Degree Graduates: Of those who graduated in the academic year 2006–2007, the following categories and numbers represent the postgraduate activities and employment of doctoral degree graduates: Enrolled in a psychology doctoral program (n/a), total from the above (doctoral) (0).

Additional Information:

Orientation, Objectives, and Emphasis of Department: The College of Education offers degree programs in Counseling and School Psychology. The program in School Psychology offers training at both educational specialist (NASP-approved) and doctoral (PhD) levels (NASP-approved and APA-accredited). Within the PhD program, subspecializations in Health/Pediatric School Psychology and in Counseling Psychology/Special Education are offered. The program at all levels is behaviorally oriented, emphasizing problem-solving based research, consultation, behavioral assessment, and intervention in the implementation of school psychology services. The program in Counseling Psychology emphasizes a scientist–practitioner model and trains professional psychologists for employment in educational, industrial, and community settings. The Counseling Psychology program also offers training at the master's level.

Special Facilities or Resources: The School Psychology program has a number of research and training projects that are focused on students with behavior and cognitive disabilities. The department has recently established the Center for Promoting Research to Practice, a unit that houses several major research grants involved in bringing known research findings into school and community settings. The department also has university-affiliated training and research programs that provide living arrangements and day treatment programs for adults with developmental disabilities. The department also operates a laboratory school for children and adolescents with emotional disturbance. All facilities are integrated into the training of students primarily in the School Psychology programs. The Counseling Psychology program has a lab for video taping and editing. Both programs have established partnerships with urban school districts. School Psychology has recently established a national internship in the University laboratory school for students with emotional and behavior disorders.

Application Information:

Send to Ms. Donna Johnson, College of Education, Lehigh University, 111 Research Drive, Bethlehem, PA 18015. Application available online. URL of online application: https://www.lewisweb.cc.lehigh.edu:448/pls/prod/bwskalog.P_DispLoginNon. Students are admitted in the Fall, application deadline January 1. Counseling Psychology (master's), March 1. Fall admission for Counseling Psychology and School Psychology. *Fee:* $65.

Lehigh University

Department of Psychology
Arts and Sciences
17 Memorial Drive East
Bethlehem, PA 18015
Telephone: (610) 758-3630
Fax: (610) 758-6277
E-mail: *agn3@lehigh.edu*
Web: *http://www.lehigh.edu/~inpsy/gradprogram.html*

Department Information:

1931. Chairperson: Diane Hyland. Number of faculty: total—full-time 11, part-time 2; women—full-time 7, part-time 1.

Programs and Degrees Offered:

Listed in the following order: Program area, degree type (T if terminal Master's), number awarded 7/06–6/07. Human Cognition and Development PhD (Doctor of Philosophy) 1.

Student Applications/Admissions:

Student Applications

Human Cognition and Development PhD (Doctor of Philosophy)—Applications 2007–2008, 50. Total applicants accepted 2007–2008, 2. Number full-time enrolled (new admits only) 2007–2008, 3. Number part-time enrolled (new admits only) 2007–2008, 0. Openings 2008–2009, 2. The median number of years required for completion of a degree in 2006–2007 were 9. The number of students enrolled full- and part-time who were dismissed or voluntarily withdrew from this program area in 2007–2008 were 2.

Admissions Requirements:

Scores: Entries appear in this order: required test or GPA, minimum score (if required), median score of students entering in 2007–2008. Master's Programs: GRE-V no minimum stated, 600; GRE-Q no minimum stated, 600; overall undergraduate GPA no minimum stated, 3.5. Doctoral Programs: GRE-V no minimum stated, 625; GRE-Q no minimum stated, 630; overall undergraduate GPA no minimum stated, 3.7.

Other Criteria: (importance of criteria rated low, medium, or high): GRE/MAT scores—medium, research experience—high, work experience—low, GPA—medium, letters of recommendation—high, interview—medium, statement of goals and objectives—high. For additional information on admission requirements, go to http://www.lehigh.edu/~inpsy/requirements.html.

Student Characteristics: The following represents characteristics of students in 2007–2008 in all graduate psychology programs in the department: Female—full-time 12, part-time 0; Male—full-time 5, part-time 0; African American/Black—full-time 0, part-time 0; Hispanic/Latino(a)—full-time 1, part-time 0; Asian/Pacific Islander—full-time 1, part-time 0; American Indian/Alaska Native—full-time 0, part-time 0; Caucasian/White—full-time 14, part-time 0; Multi-ethnic—full-time 1, part-time 0; students subject to the Americans With Disabilities Act—full-time 0, part-time 0; Unknown ethnicity—full-time 0, part-time 0.

Financial Information/Assistance:

Tuition for Full-Time Study: *Master's:* State residents: $1,100 per credit hour. *Doctoral:* State residents: $1,100 per credit hour. Tuition is subject to change. See the following Web site for updates and changes in tuition costs: http://www.cas.lehigh.edu/casweb/Content/default.aspx?pageid=57.

Financial Assistance:

First-Year Students: Teaching assistantships available for first year. Average amount paid per academic year: $15,700. Average number of hours worked per week: 15. Apply by January 15. Tuition remission given: full. Research assistantships available for first year. Average amount paid per academic year: $15,700. Average number of hours worked per week: 15. Apply by January 15. Tuition remission given: full. Fellowships and scholarships available for first year. Average amount paid per academic year: $20,000. Average number of hours worked per week: 0. Apply by January 15. Tuition remission given: full.

Advanced Students: Teaching assistantships available for advanced students. Average amount paid per academic year: $16,200. Average number of hours worked per week: 15. Apply by n/a. Tuition remission given: full. Research assistantships available for advanced students. Average amount paid per academic year: $16,200. Average number of hours worked per week: 15. Apply by n/a. Tuition remission given: full. Fellowships and scholarships available for advanced students. Average amount paid per academic year: $2,200. Average number of hours worked per week: 0. Apply by n/a. Tuition remission given: full.

Additional Information: Of all students currently enrolled full time, 100% benefited from one or more of the listed financial assistance programs. Application and information available online at http://www.lehigh.edu/~inpsy/applying.html.

Internships/Practica: No information provided.

Housing and Day Care: On-campus housing is available. See the following Web site for more information: http://www3.lehigh.edu/studentlife/housing/graduatetransfer.asp. On-campus day care facilities are available. See the following Web site for more information: http://www.lehigh.edu/~inluccc/.

Employment of Department Graduates:

Master's Degree Graduates: Of those who graduated in the academic year 2006–2007, the following categories and numbers represent the postgraduate activities and employment of master's degree graduates: Enrolled in a psychology doctoral program (0), enrolled in another graduate/professional program (1), enrolled in a postdoctoral residency/fellowship (n/a), employed in independent practice (n/a), total from the above (master's) (1).

Doctoral Degree Graduates: Of those who graduated in the academic year 2006–2007, the following categories and numbers represent the postgraduate activities and employment of doctoral degree graduates: Enrolled in a psychology doctoral program (n/a), employed in an academic position at a university (1), employed in an academic position at a 2-year/4-year college (0), total from the above (doctoral) (1).

Additional Information:

Orientation, Objectives, and Emphasis of Department: The doctoral program in Psychology is a research-intensive program that combines focus with flexibility. Focus is provided by the program emphasis on Human Cognition and Development and by a core curriculum. Flexibility is provided by the ability to tailor a research specialization in an area of Cognition and Language, Developmental Psychology, or Social Cognition and Personality. Graduate students define an area of specialization through their selection of graduate seminars and through their research experiences. All students are actively engaged in research throughout their residence in the program, and they work in collaboration with faculty members and student colleagues. Departmental faculty conduct research on basic cognitive, linguistic, and social–cognitive processes, and the development of these processes across the life span. See Web pages to obtain a more detailed sense of the range of our current research activity. In addition to research within the psychology department, the psychology faculty and students partake in interdisciplinary endeavors with researchers from other university departments and programs, including the Cognitive Science program.

Special Facilities or Resources: The department's well-equipped laboratories provide an excellent setting for research. The department has extensive facilities available for graduate student research, including a child study center, and cognitive, developmental, and social laboratories. Lehigh has a sophisticated network system that connects all campus computers and servers together and provides easy access to the Internet and the World Wide Web.

Information for Students With Physical Disabilities: See the following Web site for more information: http://www.lehigh.edu/~inacsup/disabilities/faqs_4b.html.

Application Information:

Send to Graduate Programs Office, Lehigh University, 9 West Packer Avenue, Bethlehem, PA 18015-3075. Application available online. URL of online application: http://www.lehigh.edu/~inpsy/applying.html. Students are admitted in the Fall, application deadline January 15. *Fee:* $65.

Marywood University

Department of Psychology and Counseling
McGowan Center for Graduate and Professional Studies, 2300 Adams Avenue
Scranton, PA 18509
Telephone: (570) 348-6226
Fax: (570) 340-6040
E-mail: *OBrien@ES.Marywood.Edu*
Web: *http://www.marywood.edu/Departments/psychology/index.html*

Department Information:

1940. Chairperson: Edward J. O'Brien, PhD. Number of faculty: total—full-time 14, part-time 27; women—full-time 5, part-time 17; total—minority—full-time 1, part-time 2; women minority—full-time 1, part-time 1.

Programs and Degrees Offered:

Listed in the following order: Program area, degree type (T if terminal Master's), number awarded 7/06–6/07. Elementary School Counseling MA/MS (Master of Arts/Science) (T) 4, Mental Health Counseling MA/MS (Master of Arts/Science) (T) 5,

Secondary School Counseling MA/MS (Master of Arts/Science) (T) 11, General Theoretical MA/MS (Master of Arts/Science) (T) 15, School Psychology EdS/MEd (School Psychology) 6, Clinical Psychology PsyD (Doctor of Psychology) 2, Clinical Services MA/MS (Master of Arts/Science) (T) 8, Child Clinical Services MA/MS (Master of Arts/Science) (T) 1.

APA Accreditation: Clinical PsyD (Doctor of Psychology).

Student Applications/Admissions:

Student Applications

Elementary School Counseling MA/MS (Master of Arts/Science)—Applications 2007–2008, 11. Total applicants accepted 2007–2008, 10. Number full-time enrolled (new admits only) 2007–2008, 3. Number part-time enrolled (new admits only) 2007–2008, 4. Total enrolled 2007–2008 full-time, 5, part-time, 7. Openings 2008–2009, 10. The median number of years required for completion of a degree in 2006–2007 were 3. The number of students enrolled full- and part-time who were dismissed or voluntarily withdrew from this program area in 2007–2008 were 1. *Mental Health Counseling MA/MS (Master of Arts/Science)*—Applications 2007–2008, 22. Total applicants accepted 2007–2008, 15. Number full-time enrolled (new admits only) 2007–2008, 8. Number part-time enrolled (new admits only) 2007–2008, 1. Total enrolled 2007–2008 full-time, 10, part-time, 10. Openings 2008–2009, 10. The median number of years required for completion of a degree in 2006–2007 were 3. The number of students enrolled full- and part-time who were dismissed or voluntarily withdrew from this program area in 2007–2008 were 2. *Secondary School Counseling MA/MS (Master of Arts/Science)*—Applications 2007–2008, 11. Total applicants accepted 2007–2008, 8. Number full-time enrolled (new admits only) 2007–2008, 4. Number part-time enrolled (new admits only) 2007–2008, 2. Total enrolled 2007–2008 full-time, 8, part-time, 10. Openings 2008–2009, 10. The median number of years required for completion of a degree in 2006–2007 were 3. The number of students enrolled full- and part-time who were dismissed or voluntarily withdrew from this program area in 2007–2008 were 1. *General Theoretical MA/MS (Master of Arts/Science)*—Applications 2007–2008, 59. Total applicants accepted 2007–2008, 42. Number full-time enrolled (new admits only) 2007–2008, 22. Number part-time enrolled (new admits only) 2007–2008, 2. Total enrolled 2007–2008 full-time, 32, part-time, 11. Openings 2008–2009, 15. The median number of years required for completion of a degree in 2006–2007 were 3. The number of students enrolled full- and part-time who were dismissed or voluntarily withdrew from this program area in 2007–2008 were 1. *School Psychology EdS/MEd (School Psychology)*—Applications 2007–2008, 23. Total applicants accepted 2007–2008, 17. Number full-time enrolled (new admits only) 2007–2008, 6. Number part-time enrolled (new admits only) 2007–2008, 2. Total enrolled 2007–2008 full-time, 8, part-time, 17. Openings 2008–2009, 15. The median number of years required for completion of a degree in 2006–2007 were 3. The number of students enrolled full- and part-time who were dismissed or voluntarily withdrew from this program area in 2007–2008 were 0. *Clinical Psychology PsyD (Doctor of Psychology)*—Applications 2007–2008, 66. Total applicants accepted 2007–2008, 8. Number full-time enrolled (new admits only) 2007–2008, 8. Total enrolled 2007–2008 full-time, 32, part-time, 6. Openings 2008–2009, 8. The median number of years required for completion of a degree in 2006–2007 were 5. The number of students enrolled full- and part-time who were dismissed or voluntarily withdrew from this program area in 2007–2008 were 0. *Clinical Services MA/MS (Master of Arts/Science)*—Applications 2007–2008, 2. Total applicants accepted 2007–2008, 2. Number full-time enrolled (new admits only) 2007–2008, 1. Number part-time enrolled (new admits only) 2007–2008, 0. Total enrolled 2007–2008 full-time, 6, part-time, 3. Openings 2008–2009, 10. The median number of years required for completion of a degree in 2006–2007 were 3. The number of students enrolled full- and part-time who were dismissed or voluntarily withdrew from this program area in 2007–2008 were 1. *Child Clinical Services MA/MS (Master of Arts/Science)*—Applications 2007–2008, 1. Total applicants accepted 2007–2008, 1. Number full-time enrolled (new admits only) 2007–2008, 1. Number part-time enrolled (new admits only) 2007–2008, 0. Total enrolled 2007–2008 full-time, 2, part-time, 1. Openings 2008–2009, 8. The median number of years required for completion of a degree in 2006–2007 were 3. The number of students enrolled full- and part-time who were dismissed or voluntarily withdrew from this program area in 2007–2008 were 0.

Admissions Requirements:

Scores: Entries appear in this order: required test or GPA, minimum score (if required), median score of students entering in 2007–2008. Master's Programs: GRE-V 500; GRE-Q 500; overall undergraduate GPA 3.0; psychology GPA 3.0. Students applying for master's programs may take either the GRE or the MAT. Scores listed above are preferred. Individuals with scores lower than preferred will be considered. Doctoral Programs: GRE-V 500; GRE-Q 500; overall undergraduate GPA 3.3; psychology GPA 3.3.

Other Criteria: (importance of criteria rated low, medium, or high): GRE/MAT scores—medium, research experience—medium, work experience—medium, extracurricular activity—low, clinically related public service—medium, GPA—high, letters of recommendation—high, interview—low, statement of goals and objectives—medium, undergraduate major in psychology—medium, specific undergraduate psychology courses taken—medium. PsyD program requires an interview. For additional information on admission requirements, go to http://www.marywood.edu/Admissions/Graduate/index.stm.

Student Characteristics: The following represents characteristics of students in 2007–2008 in all graduate psychology programs in the department: Female—full-time 83, part-time 50; Male—full-time 20, part-time 15; African American/Black—full-time 4, part-time 1; Hispanic/Latino(a)—full-time 1, part-time 1; Asian/Pacific Islander—full-time 2, part-time 1; American Indian/Alaska Native—full-time 0, part-time 1; Caucasian/White—full-time 74, part-time 52; Multi-ethnic—full-time 0, part-time 0; students subject to the Americans With Disabilities Act—full-time 0, part-time 1; Unknown ethnicity—full-time 22, part-time 9; International students who hold an F-1 or J-1 Visa—full-time 2, part-time 0.

Financial Information/Assistance:

Tuition for Full-Time Study: *Master's:* State residents: $695 per credit hour; Nonstate residents: $695 per credit hour. *Doctoral:* State residents: $785 per credit hour; Nonstate residents: $785 per credit hour. See the following Web site for updates and changes in tuition costs: http://www.marywood.edu/fin_aid/index.stm.

Financial Assistance:

First-Year Students: Research assistantships available for first year. Average amount paid per academic year: $5,405. Average number of hours worked per week: 20. Apply by February 15. Tuition remission given: full. Fellowships and scholarships available for first year. Average amount paid per academic year: $4,830. Average number of hours worked per week: 0. Apply by February 15.

Advanced Students: Research assistantships available for advanced students. Average amount paid per academic year: $5,405. Average number of hours worked per week: 20. Apply by February 15. Tuition remission given: full. Fellowships and scholarships available for advanced students. Average amount paid per academic year: $4,830. Average number of hours worked per week: 0. Apply by February 15.

Additional Information: Of all students currently enrolled full time, 60% benefited from one or more of the listed financial assistance programs. Application and information available online at http://www.marywood.edu/grad_finaid/finance.stm.

Internships/Practica: Master's Degree (MA/MS Elementary School Counseling): An internship experience such as a final research project or "capstone" experience is required of graduates. Master's Degree (MA/MS Mental Health Counseling): An internship experience such as a final research project or "capstone" experience is required of graduates. Master's Degree (MA/MS Secondary School Counseling): An internship experience such as a final research project or "capstone" experience is required of graduates. Master's Degree (MA/MS General Theoretical): An internship experience such as a final research project or "capstone" experience is required of graduates. Doctoral Degree (PsyD Clinical Psychology): For those doctoral students for whom a professional internship was required in this program prior to graduation, (8) students applied for an internship in 2006–2007, with (8) students obtaining an internship. Of those students who obtained an internship, (8) were paid internships. Of those students who obtained an internship, (2) students placed in APA/CPA-accredited internships, (6) students placed in internships not APA/CPA-accredited, but listed with the Association of Psychology Postdoctoral and Internship Centers (APPIC), (0) students placed in internships conforming to guidelines of the Council of Directors of School Psychology Programs (CDSPP), (0) students placed in internships that were not APA/CPA-accredited, APPIC or CDSPP listed. Students have access to training at many schools, psychiatric hospitals, rehabilitation programs, community mental health programs, and prisons in the region of Northeastern Pennsylvania. The long history (we have been providing graduate-level training for over 60 years) and size of our programs has provided us with the opportunity to develop close working relationships with most schools, social services, and mental health agencies in the region. The PsyD program (initiated in 2001) places students in both internal and external practicum sites and regional and national placements in internship sites. The department houses a community-based mental health clinic, the Psychological Services Center, which provides training opportunities for master's and doctoral students in the program while providing significant clinical and school psychology services to children, adolescents, and adults in the area. For additional information on education and training outcomes for our programs, see the following Web site: http://www.marywood.edu/Departments/psychology/index.html.

Housing and Day Care: No on-campus housing is available. On-campus day care facilities are available. Contact Graduate Admissions Office for details.

Employment of Department Graduates:

Master's Degree Graduates: Of those who graduated in the academic year 2006–2007, the following categories and numbers represent the postgraduate activities and employment of master's degree graduates: Enrolled in a postdoctoral residency/fellowship (n/a), employed in independent practice (n/a), total from the above (master's) (0).

Doctoral Degree Graduates: Of those who graduated in the academic year 2006–2007, the following categories and numbers represent the postgraduate activities and employment of doctoral degree graduates: Enrolled in a psychology doctoral program (n/a), total from the above (doctoral) (0).

Additional Information:

Orientation, Objectives, and Emphasis of Department: The department provides students with a variety of coherent training experiences that lead to diverse career paths in school counseling, agency mental health work, school psychology, and doctoral-level training in clinical psychology. Masters students in psychology all enter initially in the General Theoretical program and then apply for the clinical services of child clinical services after completing 12 credits (candidacy). Ethical and professional practice issues are considered extensively. Professional guidelines are emphasized that increase students' awareness of their developing expertise and the limits of this expertise. Professional standards for practice, certification, and licensing guidelines are integrated into courses and advisement. Licensing of master's graduates in Counseling and Psychology in Pennsylvania is now possible with the implementation of the Professional Counseling Act. The Counseling Programs are accredited by the Council for the Accreditation of Counseling and Related Educational Programs (CACREP). The PsyD program follows the Vail model, training students to be scholar–practitioners and is a designee of the Association of State and Provincial Psychology Boards (ASPPB) and accredited by the American Psychological Association. The PsyD program includes both foundation courses in psychology and applied training. The use of empirically supported assessments and intervention techniques is emphasized along with a focus on outcomes assessment. There are opportunities for work with children, adolescents, and adults. The PsyD program primarily is cognitive–behavioral in focus, with additional training provided in interpersonal and other approaches to psychotherapy.

Special Facilities or Resources: The department moved into the McGowan Center for Graduate and Professional Studies in the Fall, 1998, semester. This building more than doubled the research and clinical training facilities available to students and faculty in the department. Research facilities include three state-of-the-art computer laboratories that provide for group and individual instruction, computer-equipped research cubicles that provide for online data collection, psychophysiological monitoring equipment, videotaping and editing facilities, digital video and CD-ROM/DVD creation capabilities, and an extensive testing laboratory. The department operates a clinic, the Psychological Services Center, which provides treatment and observation rooms for practicum training, individual therapy, play therapy, family, and group therapy.

Information for Students With Physical Disabilities: See the following Web site for more information: http://www.marywood.edu/Disabilities/disabilityservices.html.

Application Information:
Send to Graduate Admissions Office, Marywood University. Application available online. URL of online application: http://www.marywood.edu/admissions/graduate/apply.stm. Students are admitted in the Fall, application deadline April 1; Spring, application deadline November 15; Summer, application deadline April 1. Applications for the PsyD program are due January 15. Contact Graduate Admissions for application deadline for School Psychology (will be changed for 2009). Only the Counseling Programs have applications in the Fall for first enrollment in the Spring. *Fee:* $35.

Millersville University

Department of Psychology
Byerly Hall
Millersville, PA 17551
Telephone: (717) 872-3093
Fax: (717) 871-2480
E-mail: *claudia.haferkamp@millersville.edu*
Web: *http://www.millersville.edu*

Department Information:
1967. Claudia Haferkamp, PhD. Graduate Program Coordinator: Helena Tuleya-Payne. Number of faculty: total—full-time 19, part-time 11; women—full-time 14, part-time 8; total—minority—full-time 4; women minority—full-time 4.

Programs and Degrees Offered:
Listed in the following order: Program area, degree type (T if terminal Master's), number awarded 7/06–6/07. Clinical Psychology MA/MS (Master of Arts/Science) (T) 10, School Counseling Other 8, School Psychology MA/MS (Master of Arts/Science) 4, Supervision of School Guidance Other, Supervision of School Psychology MA/MS (Master of Arts/Science) 0.

Student Applications/Admissions:
Student Applications
Clinical Psychology MA/MS (Master of Arts/Science)—Applications 2007–2008, 35. Total applicants accepted 2007–2008, 24. Number full-time enrolled (new admits only) 2007–2008, 16. Number part-time enrolled (new admits only) 2007–2008, 8. Total enrolled 2007–2008 full-time, 19, part-time, 28. Openings 2008–2009, 25. The median number of years required for completion of a degree in 2006–2007 were 2. *School Counseling Other*—Applications 2007–2008, 44. Total applicants accepted 2007–2008, 24. Number full-time enrolled (new admits only) 2007–2008, 9. Number part-time enrolled (new admits only) 2007–2008, 39. Total enrolled 2007–2008 full-time, 9, part-time, 39. Openings 2008–2009, 25. *School Psychology MA/MS (Master of Arts/Science)*—Applications 2007–2008, 39. Total applicants accepted 2007–2008, 28. Number full-time enrolled (new admits only) 2007–2008, 28. Number part-time enrolled (new admits only) 2007–2008, 16. Total enrolled 2007–2008 full-time, 28, part-time, 16. Openings 2008–2009, 25. *Supervision of School Guidance Other*—Applications 2007–2008, 24. Total applicants accepted 2007–2008, 21. Number full-time enrolled (new admits only) 2007–2008, 8. Number part-time enrolled (new admits only) 2007–2008, 13. Total enrolled 2007–2008 full-time, 8, part-time, 13. Openings 2008–2009, 5. *Supervision of School Psychology MA/MS (Master of Arts/Science)*—Applications 2007–2008, 24. Total applicants accepted 2007–2008, 21. Number full-time enrolled (new admits only) 2007–2008, 6. Number part-time enrolled (new admits only) 2007–2008, 18. Total enrolled 2007–2008 full-time, 6, part-time, 18. Openings 2008–2009, 5.

Admissions Requirements:
Scores: Entries appear in this order: required test or GPA, minimum score (if required), median score of students entering in 2007–2008. Master's Programs: GRE-V 450; GRE-Q 450; overall undergraduate GPA 2.75. The scoring of the Analytical Writing Section of the GRE General Test was changed to a 0 to 6 scale. Millersville has established a score of 3.5 on the Analytical Writing Section of the GRE General Test as equivalent to a score of 450 in the other sections.
Other Criteria: (importance of criteria rated low, medium, or high): GRE/MAT scores—medium, research experience—low, work experience—high, extracurricular activity—low, clinically related public service—high, GPA—medium, letters of recommendation—high, interview—high, statement of goals and objectives—medium, undergraduate major in psychology—medium, specific undergraduate psychology courses taken—medium. All psychology graduate programs seek to prepare practitioners for work in either school or mental health settings. Therefore, practical experience outside the classroom is highly valued and may include undergraduate practica or internships, volunteer work experience, and a wide range of pre- and postbaccalaureate-level jobs in schools and/or mental health settings. See specific program descriptions for further details.

Student Characteristics: The following represents characteristics of students in 2007–2008 in all graduate psychology programs in the department: Female—full-time 53, part-time 84; Male—full-time 12, part-time 20; African American/Black—full-time 5, part-time 2; Hispanic/Latino(a)—full-time 1, part-time 1; Asian/Pacific Islander—full-time 1, part-time 0; Caucasian/White—full-time 51, part-time 83; Unknown ethnicity—full-time 6, part-time 18.

Financial Information/Assistance:
Tuition for Full-Time Study: *Master's:* State residents: per academic year $3,107; Nonstate residents: per academic year $4,972. Tuition is subject to change. See the following Web site for updates and changes in tuition costs: Full-time tuition costs are based on 9–15 credit hours, plus $345 for every credit over 15 hours.

Financial Assistance:
First-Year Students: No information provided.
Advanced Students: No information provided.
Additional Information: Application and information available online at: Graduate assistantships offer $5,000 stipend (1st year) and $5,400 (2nd year) and tuition waiver.

Internships/Practica: Master's Degree (MA/MS Clinical Psychology): An internship experience such as a final research project or "capstone" experience is required of graduates. Field experiences/ practica are required of all students in the Clinical, School Counseling, and School Psychology programs. Students in the Certification Program in School Psychology are required to complete a full-time internship over 1 academic year (minimum 1,200 hours) or on a half-time basis over 2 consecutive academic years.

Housing and Day Care: No on-campus housing is available. No on-campus day care facilities are available.

Employment of Department Graduates:

Master's Degree Graduates: Of those who graduated in the academic year 2006–2007, the following categories and numbers represent the postgraduate activities and employment of master's degree graduates: Enrolled in a postdoctoral residency/fellowship (n/a), employed in independent practice (n/a), total from the above (master's) (0).

Doctoral Degree Graduates: Of those who graduated in the academic year 2006–2007, the following categories and numbers represent the postgraduate activities and employment of doctoral degree graduates: Enrolled in a psychology doctoral program (n/a), total from the above (doctoral) (0).

Additional Information:

Orientation, Objectives, and Emphasis of Department: All programs emphasize academic training in theory, research skills and ability to evaluate research, practical experience, and a high degree of self-awareness and interpersonal relationship skills. The MS program in Clinical Psychology prepares clinicians with skills in psychological assessment and diagnosis, and an eclectic cognitive–behavioral repertoire of skills in individual, group, and family therapies. Graduates may obtain PA licensure as "professional counselors" and work in a wide range of inpatient and outpatient mental health settings with children and adults. The Certification Program in School Psychology is approved by the National Association of School Psychologists and prepares students for entry-level positions as school psychologists. Knowledge about the educational process, psychological and emotional growth, and databased decision-making are central to the training program and enable students as problem solvers to promote effective learning in children. The MEd and Certification in School Counseling programs prepare students for the profession of school counseling in grades K–12. Operating under a prevention–intervention model, students develop into professionals who are responsive to the needs of the school setting.

Special Facilities or Resources: A microcomputer lab and terminal access to the university's mainframe computer are available in the department. Millersville's campus is wireless-enabled. There is a psychoeducational clinic with one-way observation capability and videotape facilities. Ganser Library houses approximately a half million books and provides access to nearly 3,500 periodical titles. Electronic resources available via the World Wide Web, as well as the Millersville University library catalog, are accessible from the University home page. The research and information needs of faculty, staff, and students are met by subject specialists who provide extensive reference service within the library, at off-site locations, and electronically. Scholarly research is supported by a comprehensive and well-developed library collection that is continually being augmented by the most current and up-to-date resources available, both in print and electronic format. The library belongs to several statewide and regional library consortia that allows for resource sharing, reciprocal borrowing, and collaborative purchasing.

Information for Students With Physical Disabilities: See the following Web site for more information: http://www.millersville.edu.

Application Information:

Send to Graduate Studies Office, Millersville University, P.O. Box 1002, Millersville, PA 17551-0302. URL of online application: http://www.muweb.millersvill.edu/~graduate/pdf/GradStudiesAppweb07.pdf. Students are admitted in the Fall, application deadline October 1; Winter, application deadline October 1; Spring, application deadline February 1; Summer, application deadline June 1. Applicants whose graduate applications are not fully complete by the deadline may apply for "nondegree status" from Graduate Studies. Nondegree status will permit the student enroll in a graduate class with permission from the Graduate Program Coordinator. When/if the nondegree applicant is accepted into a graduate program, a maximum of nine nondegree credits can be applied to the graduate program. *Fee:* $25.

Penn State Harrisburg

Psychology Program
777 West Harrisburg Pike
Middletown, PA 17057-4898
Telephone: (717) 948-6059
Fax: (717) 948-6519
E-mail: *dvo@psu.edu*
Web: *http://www.hbg.psu.edu*

Department Information:

1992. Coordinator: Thomas Bowers. Number of faculty: total—full-time 10; women—full-time 6.

Programs and Degrees Offered:

Listed in the following order: Program area, degree type (T if terminal Master's), number awarded 7/06–6/07. Applied Clinical Psychology MA/MS (Master of Arts/Science) (T) 9, Applied Psychological Research MA/MS (Master of Arts/Science) (T) 0.

Student Applications/Admissions:

Student Applications

Applied Clinical Psychology MA/MS (Master of Arts/Science)—Applications 2007–2008, 42. Total applicants accepted 2007–2008, 22. Number full-time enrolled (new admits only) 2007–2008, 13. Number part-time enrolled (new admits only) 2007–2008, 3. Total enrolled 2007–2008 full-time, 20, part-time, 19. Openings 2008–2009, 15. The median number of years required for completion of a degree in 2006–2007 were 4. The number of students enrolled full- and part-time who were dismissed or voluntarily withdrew from this program area in 2007–2008 were 0. *Applied Psychological Research MA/MS (Master of Arts/Science)*—Applications 2007–2008, 6. Total applicants accepted 2007–2008, 5. Number full-time enrolled (new admits only) 2007–2008, 3. Number part-time enrolled (new admits only) 2007–2008, 0. Total enrolled 2007–2008 full-time, 3, part-time, 3. Openings 2008–2009, 5. The number of students enrolled full- and part-time who were dismissed or voluntarily withdrew from this program area in 2007–2008 were 0.

Admissions Requirements:

Scores: Entries appear in this order: required test or GPA, minimum score (if required), median score of students entering in 2007–2008. Master's Programs: GRE-V no minimum stated, 480; GRE-Q no minimum stated, 530; last 2 years GPA 3.00, 3.78; Masters GRE-Analytical no minimum stated, 4.0.

Other Criteria: (importance of criteria rated low, medium, or high): GRE/MAT scores—high, research experience—medium, work experience—low, extracurricular activity—low, clinically related public service—low, GPA—high, letters of recommendation—high, interview—high, statement of goals and objectives—high, undergraduate major in psychology—low, specific undergraduate psychology courses taken—high. For additional information on admission requirements, go to php.scripts.psu.edu/dept/iit/hbg/Programs/Graduate/MastersDegrees.php.

Student Characteristics: The following represents characteristics of students in 2007–2008 in all graduate psychology programs in the department: Female—full-time 18, part-time 18; Male—full-time 5, part-time 4; African American/Black—full-time 1, part-time 1; Hispanic/Latino(a)—full-time 1, part-time 1; Asian/Pacific Islander—full-time 2, part-time 0; American Indian/Alaska Native—full-time 0, part-time 0; Caucasian/White—full-time 17, part-time 18; Multi-ethnic—full-time 0, part-time 0; students subject to the Americans With Disabilities Act—full-time 0, part-time 0; Unknown ethnicity—full-time 2, part-time 2; International students who hold an F-1 or J-1 Visa—full-time 1, part-time 0.

Financial Information/Assistance:

Tuition for Full-Time Study: *Master's:* State residents: per academic year $14,738, $614 per credit hour; Nonstate residents: per academic year $20,340, $848 per credit hour. Tuition is subject to change. See the following Web site for updates and changes in tuition costs: http://www.tuition.psu.edu/.

Financial Assistance:

First-Year Students: Research assistantships available for first year. Average amount paid per academic year: $13,600. Average number of hours worked per week: 20. Apply by February 1. Tuition remission given: full. Fellowships and scholarships available for first year. Average amount paid per academic year: $13,365. Average number of hours worked per week: 20. Apply by February 1. Tuition remission given: full.

Advanced Students: Fellowships and scholarships available for advanced students. Apply by varies. Tuition remission given: full.

Additional Information: Of all students currently enrolled full time, 10% benefited from one or more of the listed financial assistance programs. Application and information available online at http://www.hbg.psu.edu.

Internships/Practica: Master's Degree (MA/MS Applied Clinical Psychology): An internship experience such as a final research project or "capstone" experience is required of graduates. Master's Degree (MA/MS Applied Psychological Research): An internship experience such as a final research project or "capstone" experience is required of graduates. Students in the Applied Clinical Psychology program are required to complete seven credits of supervised clinical internships. Students in the Applied Psychological Research program are required to complete six credits of research in collaboration with the program faculty.

Housing and Day Care: On-campus housing is available. See the following Web site for more information: http://www.hfs.psu.edu/harrisburg/housing. On-campus day care facilities are available. See http://www.php.scripts.psu.edu/dept/iit/hbg/facultystaff/childcare.php.

Employment of Department Graduates:

Master's Degree Graduates: Of those who graduated in the academic year 2006–2007, the following categories and numbers represent the postgraduate activities and employment of master's degree graduates: Enrolled in a postdoctoral residency/fellowship (n/a), employed in independent practice (n/a), total from the above (master's) (0).

Doctoral Degree Graduates: Of those who graduated in the academic year 2006–2007, the following categories and numbers represent the postgraduate activities and employment of doctoral degree graduates: Enrolled in a psychology doctoral program (n/a), total from the above (doctoral) (0).

Additional Information:

Orientation, Objectives, and Emphasis of Department: The Applied Clinical Psychology program prepares students to work as mental health professionals in a variety of settings and is intended to provide the academic training necessary for graduates to apply for master's-level licensing for mental health professionals in the Commonwealth of Pennsylvania. The overall model emphasizes the scientific bases of behavior, including biological, social, and individual difference factors. The training model is health oriented rather than pathology oriented and emphasizes the development of helping skills, including both assessment and intervention. The Applied Psychological Research program focuses on the development of research skills within the context of scientific training in psychology. The program is designed to meet the needs of students who plan careers in research or administration within human services or similar organizations, who plan to conduct research in other settings, or who plan to pursue doctoral study. Students can select electives and research experiences to reflect their individual interests in consultation with their advisor.

Special Facilities or Resources: The Psychology program maintains a small on-site clinic for the assessment of specific learning disorders in college students. This clinic provides advanced Applied Clinical Psychology students the opportunity to assist with psychological testing, report writing, diagnosis, and treatment recommendations under the supervision of the program faculty. Most students avail themselves of the resources in community hospitals, residential, and outpatient insitiutions for hands-on clinical and research experience. The department maintains an on-campus research facility, which is available for use by graduate students working with faculty on research projects.

Information for Students With Physical Disabilities: Contact Alan Babcock, Disability Services Coordinator: (717) 948-6025.

Application Information:

Send to Graduate Admissions, Penn State Harrisburg, 777 West Harrisburg Pike, Middletown, PA 17057-4898. Application available online.

URL of online application: http://www.php.scripts.psu.edu/dept/iit/hbg/admissions/gradapp.php. Students are admitted in the Fall, application deadline April 30. January 10 application deadline for University fellowships and assistantships. We review applications on a rolling basis. Early applications are encouraged. *Fee:* $45.

Pennsylvania State University

Counseling Psychology Program
Education
327 Cedar Building
University Park, PA 16802
Telephone: (814) 865-8304
Fax: (814) 863-7750
E-mail: *eas14@psu.edu*
Web: *http://www.ed.psu.edu/cnpsy/index.asp*

Department Information:
1982. Head of Department: Dr. Spencer G. Niles. Number of faculty: total—full-time 4; women—full-time 3.

Programs and Degrees Offered:
Listed in the following order: Program area, degree type (T if terminal Master's), number awarded 7/06–6/07. Counseling Psychology PhD (Doctor of Philosophy) 6.

APA Accreditation: Counseling PhD (Doctor of Philosophy).

Student Applications/Admissions:
Student Applications
Counseling Psychology PhD (Doctor of Philosophy)—Applications 2007–2008, 74. Total applicants accepted 2007–2008, 8. Number full-time enrolled (new admits only) 2007–2008, 5. Number part-time enrolled (new admits only) 2007–2008, 0. Total enrolled 2007–2008 full-time, 30, part-time, 2. Openings 2008–2009, 6. The median number of years required for completion of a degree in 2006–2007 were 4. The number of students enrolled full- and part-time who were dismissed or voluntarily withdrew from this program area in 2007–2008 were 0.

Admissions Requirements:
Scores: Entries appear in this order: required test or GPA, minimum score (if required), median score of students entering in 2007–2008. Doctoral Programs: GRE-V no minimum stated; GRE-Q no minimum stated; overall undergraduate GPA no minimum stated; Doctoral program GRE-Analytic no minimum stated.
Other Criteria: (importance of criteria rated low, medium, or high): GRE/MAT scores—high, research experience—high, work experience—medium, extracurricular activity—low, clinically related public service—medium, GPA—high, letters of recommendation—high, interview—high, statement of goals and objectives—high, Masters degree—high. For additional information on admission requirements, go to http://www.ed.psu.edu/cnpsy/.

Student Characteristics: The following represents characteristics of students in 2007–2008 in all graduate psychology programs in the department: Female—full-time 23, part-time 2; Male—full-time 7, part-time 0; African American/Black—full-time 4, part-time 0; Hispanic/Latino(a)—full-time 4, part-time 0; Asian/Pacific Islander—full-time 1, part-time 1; American Indian/Alaska Native—full-time 0, part-time 0; Caucasian/White—full-time 18, part-time 1; Multi-ethnic—full-time 0, part-time 0; students subject to the Americans With Disabilities Act—full-time 0, part-time 0; Unknown ethnicity—full-time 3, part-time 0; International students who hold an F-1 or J-1 Visa—full-time 3, part-time 0.

Financial Information/Assistance:
Tuition for Full-Time Study: *Doctoral:* State residents: per academic year $13,948, $581 per credit hour; Nonstate residents: per academic year $25,150, $1,048 per credit hour. Tuition is subject to change. See the following Web site for updates and changes in tuition costs: http://www.tuition.psu.edu.

Financial Assistance:
First-Year Students: Teaching assistantships available for first year. Average amount paid per academic year: $12,600. Average number of hours worked per week: 20. Tuition remission given: full. Research assistantships available for first year. Average amount paid per academic year: $12,600. Average number of hours worked per week: 20. Tuition remission given: full. Fellowships and scholarships available for first year. Average amount paid per academic year: $16,100. Tuition remission given: full.
Advanced Students: Teaching assistantships available for advanced students. Average amount paid per academic year: $12,600. Average number of hours worked per week: 20. Tuition remission given: full. Research assistantships available for advanced students. Average amount paid per academic year: $12,600. Average number of hours worked per week: 20. Tuition remission given: full.
Additional Information: Of all students currently enrolled full time, 73% benefited from one or more of the listed financial assistance programs.

Internships/Practica: Doctoral Degree (PhD Counseling Psychology): For those doctoral students for whom a professional internship was required in this program prior to graduation, (6) students applied for an internship in 2006–2007, with (6) students obtaining an internship. Of those students who obtained an internship, (6) were paid internships. Of those students who obtained an internship, (6) students placed in APA/CPA-accredited internships, (0) students placed in internships not APA/CPA-accredited, but listed with the Association of Psychology Postdoctoral and Internship Centers (APPIC), (0) students placed in internships conforming to guidelines of the Council of Directors of School Psychology Programs (CDSPP), (0) students placed in internships that were not APA/CPA-accredited, APPIC or CDSPP listed. Students are placed in practicum in the College of Education Counseling Service in their first semester. Supervision consists of 1 and 1/2 hours of individual supervision and a 2-hour seminar. The same supervision and seminar arrangements are provided for the second practicum at Penn State's Career Services. A counseling psychology faculty member conducts the seminar and coordinates the interaction of students with the staff at Career Services. Although the program does not require students to be on campus during the summer, most students continue their practicum work at Penn State's Counseling and Psychological Services (CAPS) during the summer of their 1st year and for Fall and Spring of their 2nd year. At CAPS, in addition to a 2-hour seminar for case discussion and presentation, individual supervision is provided by the members of the CAPS staff and interns from their APA-approved internship program. Students must also take an additional one-semester practicum in their 3rd year at either at Centre Volunteers in Medicine or an inpatient psychiatric hospital, both in town. Students typically apply for internships in their 3rd or 4th year and go on internship in their 4th or 5th year. The program specifies that students apply to and accept only APA-approved internship positions.

Housing and Day Care: On-campus housing is available. See the following Web site for more information: http://www.hfs.psu.edu/universitypark/. On-campus day care facilities are available. See the following Web site for more information: http://www.ohr.psu.edu/WorkLife/childsub.cfm.

Employment of Department Graduates:

Master's Degree Graduates: Of those who graduated in the academic year 2006–2007, the following categories and numbers represent the postgraduate activities and employment of master's degree graduates: Enrolled in a postdoctoral residency/fellowship (n/a), employed in independent practice (n/a), total from the above (master's) (0).

Doctoral Degree Graduates: Of those who graduated in the academic year 2006–2007, the following categories and numbers represent the postgraduate activities and employment of doctoral degree graduates: Enrolled in a psychology doctoral program (n/a), employed in an academic position at a university (1), employed in other positions at a higher education institution (1), employed in government agency (1), employed in a community mental health/counseling center (1), do not know (2), total from the above (doctoral) (6).

Additional Information:

Orientation, Objectives, and Emphasis of Department: The Counseling Psychology program at The Pennsylvania State University endorses the scientist–practitioner model of training. Psychological training is provided within this model with equal emphasis and value placed on both scholarly and clinical work as well as their integration. A primary goal of the program is the preparation of counseling psychologists for professional roles as academics, researchers, or practitioners who are concerned with interventions involving individual behavior and institutional settings that are focused on relational, multicultural, career, and psychosocial issues. More specifically, the primary objective of Penn State's Counseling Psychology program is to train carefully selected and promising graduate students to function as thoughtful, ethical, caring, and competent professional psychologists. Whereas the Counseling Psychology program is fully accredited by the American Psychological Association, our faculty and students strive to exceed the standards required for accreditation. One particular area in which we attempt to do so is in engendering a multicultural perspective in our students. At Penn State, we do not merely recognize the diversity represented in our faculty, students, and clients, we actively affirm the richness of our cultures and we embrace the continual challenge of examining ourselves to determine how to more effectively serve a pluralistic society.

Special Facilities or Resources: The department maintains a Resource Center that includes many of the professional journals, reference, and testing materials pertinent to the curriculum. Doctoral students are provided offices, when available, with access to personal computers. The university provides each student with an e-mail account. The College of Education Counseling Service is located in the building and provides practicum experiences for graduate students. The Service is coordinated by a licensed psychologist and serves clients from the campus, providing personal, academic, and vocational counseling. The Service has individual counseling rooms equipped for video recording and live observation through one-way mirrors.

Information for Students With Physical Disabilities: See the following Web site for more information: http://www.equity.psu.edu.ods/.

Application Information:

Send to Counseling Psychology Doctoral Program, 327 Cedar Building, Penn State, University Park, PA 16802. Application available online. URL of online application: http://www.ed.psu.edu/cnpsy/. Students are admitted in the Fall, application deadline December 15. *Fee:* $45.

Pennsylvania State University

Department of Psychology
111 Bruce V. Moore Building
University Park, PA 16802-3104
Telephone: (814) 863-1721
Fax: (814) 863-7002
E-mail: *bjc2@psu.edu*
Web: *http://www.psych.la.psu.edu*

Department Information:

1933. Department of Psychology: Melvin M. Mark. Number of faculty: total—full-time 52, part-time 1; women—full-time 23; total—minority—full-time 5; women minority—full-time 2.

Programs and Degrees Offered:

Listed in the following order: Program area, degree type (T if terminal Master's), number awarded 7/06–6/07. Clinical PhD (Doctor of Philosophy) 8, Clinical/Child PhD (Doctor of Philosophy) 2, Cognitive PhD (Doctor of Philosophy) 3, Developmental PhD (Doctor of Philosophy) 0, Industrial/Organizational PhD (Doctor of Philosophy) 4, Social PhD (Doctor of Philosophy) 4.

APA Accreditation: Clinical PhD (Doctor of Philosophy).

Student Applications/Admissions:

Student Applications

Clinical PhD (Doctor of Philosophy)—Applications 2007–2008, 163. Total applicants accepted 2007–2008, 5. Number full-time enrolled (new admits only) 2007–2008, 5. Total enrolled 2007–2008 full-time, 54, part-time, 5. Openings 2008–2009, 6. The median number of years required for completion of a degree in 2006–2007 were 7. The number of students enrolled full- and part-time who were dismissed or voluntarily withdrew from this program area in 2007–2008 were 0. *Clinical/Child PhD (Doctor of Philosophy)*—Applications 2007–2008, 146. Total applicants accepted 2007–2008, 4. Number full-time enrolled (new admits only) 2007–2008, 4. Total enrolled 2007–2008 full-time, 52, part-time, 3. Openings 2008–

2009, 5. The median number of years required for completion of a degree in 2006–2007 were 6. The number of students enrolled full- and part-time who were dismissed or voluntarily withdrew from this program area in 2007–2008 were 1. *Cognitive PhD (Doctor of Philosophy)*—Applications 2007–2008, 58. Total applicants accepted 2007–2008, 4. Number full-time enrolled (new admits only) 2007–2008, 4. Total enrolled 2007–2008 full-time, 30, part-time, 1. Openings 2008–2009, 3. The median number of years required for completion of a degree in 2006–2007 were 5. The number of students enrolled full- and part-time who were dismissed or voluntarily withdrew from this program area in 2007–2008 were 1. *Developmental PhD (Doctor of Philosophy)*—Applications 2007–2008, 33. Total applicants accepted 2007–2008, 3. Number full-time enrolled (new admits only) 2007–2008, 3. Total enrolled 2007–2008 full-time, 18, part-time, 1. Openings 2008–2009, 2. The number of students enrolled full- and part-time who were dismissed or voluntarily withdrew from this program area in 2007–2008 were 0. *Industrial/Organizational PhD (Doctor of Philosophy)*—Applications 2007–2008, 78. Total applicants accepted 2007–2008, 4. Number full-time enrolled (new admits only) 2007–2008, 4. Total enrolled 2007–2008 full-time, 54, part-time, 3. Openings 2008–2009, 4. The median number of years required for completion of a degree in 2006–2007 were 5. The number of students enrolled full- and part-time who were dismissed or voluntarily withdrew from this program area in 2007–2008 were 0. *Social PhD (Doctor of Philosophy)*—Applications 2007–2008, 70. Total applicants accepted 2007–2008, 4. Number full-time enrolled (new admits only) 2007–2008, 4. Total enrolled 2007–2008 full-time, 29, part-time, 1. Openings 2008–2009, 3. The median number of years required for completion of a degree in 2006–2007 were 5. The number of students enrolled full- and part-time who were dismissed or voluntarily withdrew from this program area in 2007–2008 were 0.

Admissions Requirements:

Scores: Entries appear in this order: required test or GPA, minimum score (if required), median score of students entering in 2007–2008. Doctoral Programs: GRE-V no minimum stated; GRE-Q no minimum stated; last 2 years GPA no minimum stated, 3.84; Doctoral program GRE-Analytic no minimum stated. We do not have a formal cut-off score. GRE Subject exam not required.

Other Criteria: (importance of criteria rated low, medium, or high): GRE/MAT scores—high, research experience—high, work experience—medium, extracurricular activity—low, clinically related public service—medium, GPA—high, letters of recommendation—high, interview—high, statement of goals and objectives—high, undergraduate major in psychology—medium, specific undergraduate psychology courses taken—medium. Clinical weighs work, clinical experience, and interviews heavily; other areas do not weight these factors strongly. For additional information on admission requirements, go to http://psych.la.psu.edu.

Student Characteristics: The following represents characteristics of students in 2007–2008 in all graduate psychology programs in the department: Female—full-time 161, part-time 14; Male—full-time 76, part-time 0; African American/Black—full-time 13, part-time 0; Hispanic/Latino(a)—full-time 10, part-time 0; Asian/Pacific Islander—full-time 20, part-time 2; American Indian/Alaska Native—full-time 0, part-time 0; Caucasian/White—full-time 194, part-time 12; Multi-ethnic—full-time 0, part-time 0; students subject to the Americans With Disabilities Act—full-time 0, part-time 0; Unknown ethnicity—full-time 0, part-time 0; International students who hold an F-1 or J-1 Visa—full-time 30, part-time 0.

Financial Information/Assistance:

Tuition for Full-Time Study: *Doctoral:* State residents: per academic year $13,948, $581 per credit hour; Nonstate residents: per academic year $25,150, $1,048 per credit hour. Tuition is subject to change. See the following Web site for updates and changes in tuition costs: http://www.psu.edu.

Financial Assistance:

First-Year Students: Teaching assistantships available for first year. Average amount paid per academic year: $15,165. Average number of hours worked per week: 20. Apply by December 1. Tuition remission given: full. Research assistantships available for first year. Average amount paid per academic year: $15,165. Average number of hours worked per week: 20. Apply by December 1. Tuition remission given: full. Fellowships and scholarships available for first year. Average amount paid per academic year: $20,000. Average number of hours worked per week: 0. Apply by December 1. Tuition remission given: full.

Advanced Students: Teaching assistantships available for advanced students. Average amount paid per academic year: $15,165. Average number of hours worked per week: 20. Apply by none. Tuition remission given: full. Research assistantships available for advanced students. Average amount paid per academic year: $15,165. Average number of hours worked per week: 20. Apply by none. Tuition remission given: full. Fellowships and scholarships available for advanced students. Average amount paid per academic year: $20,000. Average number of hours worked per week: 0. Apply by none. Tuition remission given: full.

Additional Information: Of all students currently enrolled full time, 85% benefited from one or more of the listed financial assistance programs.

Internships/Practica: Doctoral Degree (PhD Clinical): For those doctoral students for whom a professional internship was required in this program prior to graduation, (9) students applied for an internship in 2006–2007, with (8) students obtaining an internship. Of those students who obtained an internship, (8) were paid internships. Of those students who obtained an internship, (8) students placed in APA/CPA-accredited internships, (0) students placed in internships not APA/CPA-accredited, but listed with the Association of Psychology Postdoctoral and Internship Centers (APPIC), (0) students placed in internships conforming to guidelines of the Council of Directors of School Psychology Programs (CDSPP), (0) students placed in internships that were not APA/CPA-accredited, APPIC or CDSPP listed. Doctoral Degree (PhD Clinical/Child): For those doctoral students for whom a professional internship was required in this program prior to graduation, (2) students applied for an internship in 2006–2007, with (2) students obtaining an internship. Of those students who obtained an internship, (2) were paid internships. Of those students who obtained an internship, (2) students placed in APA/CPA-accredited internships, (0) students placed in internships not APA/CPA-accredited, but listed with the Association of Psychology Postdoctoral and Internship Centers (APPIC), (0) students placed in internships conforming to guidelines of the Council of

Directors of School Psychology Programs (CDSPP), (0) students placed in internships that were not APA/CPA accredited, APPIC or CDSPP listed. No information is provided.

Housing and Day Care: On-campus housing is available. See the following Web site for more information: http://www.psu.edu. On-campus day care facilities are available.

Employment of Department Graduates:

Master's Degree Graduates: Of those who graduated in the academic year 2006–2007, the following categories and numbers represent the postgraduate activities and employment of master's degree graduates: Enrolled in a postdoctoral residency/fellowship (n/a), employed in independent practice (n/a), total from the above (master's) (0).

Doctoral Degree Graduates: Of those who graduated in the academic year 2006–2007, the following categories and numbers represent the postgraduate activities and employment of doctoral degree graduates: Enrolled in a psychology doctoral program (n/a), enrolled in a postdoctoral residency/fellowship (9), employed in an academic position at a university (5), employed in an academic position at a 2-year/4-year college (2), employed in business or industry (3), employed in a community mental health/counseling center (2), total from the above (doctoral) (21).

Additional Information:

Orientation, Objectives, and Emphasis of Department: Graduate study in psychology at Penn State is characterized by highly flexible, individualized programs leading to the PhD in Psychology. Each student is associated with one of the five program areas offered in the department: clinical (including child clinical); cognitive; developmental; industrial/organizational; and social. (Specialization in behavioral neuroscience is possible in any program area). Students in any program area may combine their program of study with a specialization in behavioral neuroscience by choosing appropriate courses and seminars. Students choosing this specialization may pursue the integration of neuroscience methods and theories by applying these approaches to research topics within their program areas. Within each area, certain courses are usually suggested for all students. The details of a student's program, however, are worked out on an individual basis with a faculty advisor. A major specialization and breadth outside the major are required. The major is selected from among the six specialty areas of the department listed above; breadth requirements are flexible and individualized to career goals. Depending upon the individual student's particular program of study, graduates may be employed in academic departments, research institutes, industry, governmental agencies, or various service delivery settings.

Special Facilities or Resources: The department has clinical, learning–cognition, perception, physiological, psychophysiology, developmental, and social laboratories; microcomputer laboratories; access to the University's mainframe and electronic communication system (e-mail and Internet) and computer laboratories; clinical practica in local mental health centers and hospitals in addition to the department's Psychological Clinic, which functions as a mental health center for the catchment area of central Pennsylvania; industrial/organizational practica in industrial and government organizations; and developmental practica and research opportunities in day care and preschool settings. A number of centers or institutes are housed within or affiliated with the department, including a new Child Study Center.

Application Information:

Send to Graduate Admissions, Department of Psychology, Penn State University, 109 Moore Building, University Park, PA 16802. Application available online. URL of online application: http://www.psych.la.psu.edu. Students are admitted in the Fall, application deadline December 1. December 1 is the deadline for all areas. *Fee:* $45.

Pennsylvania State University

Educational Psychology
Education
125 Cedar Building
University Park, PA 16802
Telephone: (814) 863-2286
Fax: (814) 863-1002
E-mail: *rsd7@psu.edu*
Web: *http://www.espse.ed.psu.edu/edpsy2/edpsyhome.html*

Department Information:

1968. Professor in Charge: Rayne A. Sperling. Number of faculty: total—full-time 8, part-time 1; women—full-time 6; total—minority—full-time 1; women minority—full-time 1; faculty subject to the Americans With Disabilities Act 1.

Programs and Degrees Offered:

Listed in the following order: Program area, degree type (T if terminal Master's), number awarded 7/06–6/07. Educational PhD (Doctor of Philosophy) 5.

Student Applications/Admissions:

Student Applications

Educational PhD (Doctor of Philosophy)—Applications 2007–2008, 23. Total applicants accepted 2007–2008, 9. Number full-time enrolled (new admits only) 2007–2008, 3. Number part-time enrolled (new admits only) 2007–2008, 0. Total enrolled 2007–2008 full-time, 27, part-time, 2. Openings 2008–2009, 8. The median number of years required for completion of a degree in 2006–2007 were 6. The number of students enrolled full- and part-time who were dismissed or voluntarily withdrew from this program area in 2007–2008 were 2.

Admissions Requirements:

Scores: Entries appear in this order: required test or GPA, minimum score (if required), median score of students entering in 2007–2008. Master's Programs: GRE-V no minimum stated, 550; GRE-Q no minimum stated, 600; overall undergraduate GPA no minimum stated, 3.50; last 2 years GPA no minimum stated, 3.62. Doctoral Programs: GRE-V no minimum stated, 550; GRE-Q no minimum stated, 600; overall undergraduate GPA no minimum stated, 3.50; last 2 years GPA no minimum stated, 3.62; psychology GPA no minimum stated.

Other Criteria: (importance of criteria rated low, medium, or high): GRE/MAT scores—medium, research experience—medium, work experience—medium, extracurricular activity—low, GPA—medium, letters of recommendation—high, statement of goals and objectives—high, teaching experience—medium, undergraduate major in psychology—medium, specific undergraduate psychology courses taken—medium. Interview optional. For additional information on admission requirements, go to http://espse.ed.psu.edu/edpsych/35.

Student Characteristics: The following represents characteristics of students in 2007–2008 in all graduate psychology programs in the department: Female—full-time 20, part-time 1; Male—full-time 7, part-time 1; African American/Black—full-time 0, part-time 0; Hispanic/Latino(a)—full-time 1, part-time 0; Asian/Pacific Islander—full-time 8, part-time 0; American Indian/Alaska Native—full-time 0, part-time 0; Caucasian/White—full-time 18, part-time 0; Multi-ethnic—full-time 0, part-time 0; students subject to the Americans With Disabilities Act—full-time 0, part-time 0; Unknown ethnicity—full-time 0, part-time 0; International students who hold an F-1 or J-1 Visa—full-time 8, part-time 0.

Financial Information/Assistance:

Financial Assistance:

First-Year Students: Teaching assistantships available for first year. Average amount paid per academic year: $14,200. Average number of hours worked per week: 20. Apply by January 15. Tuition remission given: full. Research assistantships available for first year. Average amount paid per academic year: $14,200. Average number of hours worked per week: 20. Apply by January 15. Tuition remission given: full. Fellowships and scholarships available for first year. Average amount paid per academic year: $15,696. Average number of hours worked per week: 0. Apply by January 15. Tuition remission given: full.

Advanced Students: Teaching assistantships available for advanced students. Average amount paid per academic year: $14,200. Average number of hours worked per week: 20. Tuition remission given: full. Research assistantships available for advanced students. Average amount paid per academic year: $14,200. Average number of hours worked per week: 20. Tuition remission given: full. Fellowships and scholarships available for advanced students. Average amount paid per academic year: $15,696. Tuition remission given: full.

Additional Information: Of all students currently enrolled full time, 80% benefited from one or more of the listed financial assistance programs. Application and information available online at http://espse.ed.psu.edu/edpsych/index.php.

Internships/Practica: No information provided.

Housing and Day Care: On-campus housing is available. See the following Web site for more information: http://www.gradsch.psu.edu/ http://www.hfs.psu.edu/. On-campus day care facilities are available. See the following Web site for more information: http://www.hhdev.psu.edu/hdfs/cp/cdl/index.html.

Employment of Department Graduates:

Master's Degree Graduates: Of those who graduated in the academic year 2006–2007, the following categories and numbers represent the postgraduate activities and employment of master's degree graduates: Enrolled in a psychology doctoral program (3), enrolled in another graduate/professional program (0), enrolled in a postdoctoral residency/fellowship (n/a), employed in independent practice (n/a), total from the above (master's) (3).

Doctoral Degree Graduates: Of those who graduated in the academic year 2006–2007, the following categories and numbers represent the postgraduate activities and employment of doctoral degree graduates: Enrolled in a psychology doctoral program (n/a), employed in an academic position at a university (1), employed in an academic position at a 2-year/4-year college (2), employed in other positions at a higher education institution (1), total from the above (doctoral) (4).

Additional Information:

Orientation, Objectives, and Emphasis of Department: Students may specialize and do research in one of the following areas: (a) human learning and memory as applied to instruction and education or (b) educational and psychological measurement. There are two options in the master's program. A thesis option is available in either of the two areas. The learning faculty primarily focus on research related to text processing and problem solving, which includes learning to read, learning from text, and knowledge application such as problem solving and decision making. There is also some emphasis on instruction for students who are at risk. The role of epistemic beliefs as well as motivational variables are also studied by program faculty. The measurement faculty focus on applied measurement issues particularly validity, generalizabilty theory, and latent variable modeling. Faculty collaborate across the learning and measurement strands and foster such collaboration among students and graduates as well.

Special Facilities or Resources: Penn State has an exceptional library and is on the leading edge of use in instructional and research technologies.

Application Information:

Send to Admissions Committee, Educational Pyschology Program, 227 Cedar Building, Penn State University, University Park, PA 16802. Application available online. URL of online application: http://www.espse.ed.psu.edu/edpsy2/edpsyhome.html. Students are admitted in the Fall, application deadline January 15. Programs have rolling admissions. Fall admission open but application must be received by January 15 for fellowship or graduate asssistantship consideration. Financial aid decisions made starting January 15. *Fee:* $45.

Pennsylvania State University (2007 data)

Program in School Psychology
College of Education
125 Cedar Building
University Park, PA 16802
Telephone: (814) 865-1881
Fax: (814) 865-7066
E-mail: *jcd12@psu.edu*
Web: *http://www.espse.ed.psu.edu/schoolpsych/index.php*

Department Information:

1965. Professor in Charge: James C. DiPerna. Number of faculty: total—full-time 5, part-time 5; women—full-time 2, part-time 3.

Programs and Degrees Offered:

Listed in the following order: Program area, degree type (T if terminal Master's), number awarded 7/06–6/07. School PhD (Doctor of Philosophy) 7.

APA Accreditation: School PhD (Doctor of Philosophy).

Student Applications/Admissions:

Student Applications

School PhD (Doctor of Philosophy)—Applications 2007–2008, 87. Total applicants accepted 2007–2008, 22. Number full-time enrolled (new admits only) 2007–2008, 8. Number part-time enrolled (new admits only) 2007–2008, 0. Openings 2008–2009, 6. The median number of years required for completion of a degree in 2006–2007 were 8. The number of students enrolled full- and part-time who were dismissed or voluntarily withdrew from this program area in 2007–2008 were 0.

Admissions Requirements:

Scores: Entries appear in this order: required test or GPA, minimum score (if required), median score of students entering in 2007–2008. Doctoral Programs: GRE-V 480, 550; GRE-Q 470, 620; last 2 years GPA 3.0, 3.75.

Other Criteria: (importance of criteria rated low, medium, or high): GRE/MAT scores—medium, research experience—medium, work experience—medium, clinically related public service—low, GPA—medium, letters of recommendation—high, interview—high, statement of goals and objectives—high.

Student Characteristics: The following represents characteristics of students in 2007–2008 in all graduate psychology programs in the department: Female—full-time 24, part-time 0; Male—full-time 2, part-time 0; African American/Black—full-time 3, part-time 0; Hispanic/Latino(a)—full-time 0, part-time 0; Asian/Pacific Islander—part-time 0; American Indian/Alaska Native—full-time 0, part-time 0; Caucasian/White—full-time 22, part-time 0; Multi-ethnic—full-time 1, part-time 0; students subject to the Americans With Disabilities Act—full-time 0, part-time 0; Unknown ethnicity—full-time 0, part-time 0.

Financial Information/Assistance:

Tuition for Full-Time Study: *Doctoral:* State residents: per academic year $13,224; Nonstate residents: per academic year $24,060. Tuition is subject to change. See the following Web site for updates and changes in tuition costs: http://www.bursar.psu.edu/.

Financial Assistance:

First-Year Students: Teaching assistantships available for first year. Average amount paid per academic year: $12,500. Average number of hours worked per week: 20. Apply by January 1. Tuition remission given: full. Research assistantships available for first year. Average amount paid per academic year: $12,500. Average number of hours worked per week: 20. Apply by January 1. Tuition remission given: full. Fellowships and scholarships available for first year. Average amount paid per academic year: $15,500. Average number of hours worked per week: 0. Apply by January 1. Tuition remission given: full.

Advanced Students: Teaching assistantships available for advanced students. Average amount paid per academic year: $12,500. Average number of hours worked per week: 20. Tuition remission given: full. Research assistantships available for advanced students. Average amount paid per academic year: $12,500. Average number of hours worked per week: 20. Tuition remission given: full. Fellowships and scholarships available for advanced students. Average amount paid per academic year: $13,000. Apply by April 1. Tuition remission given: full.

Additional Information: Of all students currently enrolled full time, 95% benefited from one or more of the listed financial assistance programs. Application and information available online at http://www.gradsch.psu.edu/.

Internships/Practica: All students engage in 1,000 hours of practica devoted to assessment, intervention, consultation, and supervision activities. Students also complete a 1,500-hour internship in schools under the supervision of a psychologist licensed for professional practice and certified as a school psychologist. All students obtain paid internships in schools.

Housing and Day Care: On-campus housing is available. See the following Web site for more information: http://www.hfs.psu.edu/housing/graduates/lease.shtml. On-campus day care facilities are available. See the following Web site for more information: http://www.hhdev.psu.edu/hdfs/cp/.

Employment of Department Graduates:

Master's Degree Graduates: Of those who graduated in the academic year 2006–2007, the following categories and numbers represent the postgraduate activities and employment of master's degree graduates: Enrolled in a psychology doctoral program (0), enrolled in another graduate/professional program (0), enrolled in a postdoctoral residency/fellowship (n/a), employed in independent practice (n/a), employed in an academic position at a university (0), employed in an academic position at a 2-year/4-year college (0), employed in other positions at a higher education institution (0), employed in a professional position in a school system (0), employed in business or industry (0), employed in government agency (0), employed in a community mental health/counseling center (0), employed in a hospital/medical center (0), still seeking employment (0), not seeking employment (0), other employment position (0), do not know (0), total from the above (master's) (0).

Doctoral Degree Graduates: Of those who graduated in the academic year 2006–2007, the following categories and numbers represent the postgraduate activities and employment of doctoral degree graduates: Enrolled in a psychology doctoral program (n/a), enrolled in another graduate/professional program (0), enrolled in a postdoctoral residency/fellowship (0), employed in independent practice (0), employed in an academic position at a university (0), employed in an academic position at a 2-year/4-year college (0), employed in other positions at a higher education institution (0), employed in a professional position in a school system (7), employed in business or industry (0), employed in government agency (0), employed in a community mental health/counseling center (0), employed in a hospital/medical center (0), still seeking employment (0), other employment position (0), do not know (0), total from the above (doctoral) (7).

Additional Information:

Orientation, Objectives, and Emphasis of Department: School psychologists from Penn State are exemplary scientist–practitioners, firmly grounded in both psychology and education. Our graduates are professional school psychologists who provide solutions for the many problems facing children. They contribute to the practice and knowledge base of psychology as it relates to education. Penn State school psychologists become leaders in the field as well as in academia. In conjunction with providing psychological services, school psychologists will be lifelong learners who sustain an interest in maintaining and developing sound practices, which derive from up-to-date, research-based information. Psychologists will thoughtfully and critically evaluate their practices and remain informed consumers of available literature, assessment tools, and intervention strategies. School psychologists will help to provide a bridge to integrate research with professional practice along with other educators, systems, and institutions.

Special Facilities or Resources: The School Psychology program operates the CEDAR School Psychology Clinic. The CEDAR Clinic contains well-appointed clinic rooms with direct observation facilities and a closed-circuit video system, which facilitate practicum supervision. Computers are available to students within the program, department, and university. Access to e-mail and the Internet are provided to all students and use of technology is encouraged by faculty. The Pattee and Paterno Libraries house an impressive array of scholarly resources. As a major research university, Penn State sponsors a number of research institutes and centers in education, psychology, and human development.

Information for Students With Physical Disabilities: See the following Web site for more information: http://www.equity.psu.edu/ods/index.html.

Application Information:

Send to Graduate Programs in School Psychology, Admissions Committee, 125 Cedar Building, Pennsylvania State University, University Park, PA 16802. Application available online. URL of online application: http://www.espse.ed.psu.edu/schoolpsych/53. Students are admitted in the Fall, application deadline January 15. January 1 for consideration for assistantship and fellowship. *Fee:* $60.

Pennsylvania State University, The

Department of Human Development and Family Studies, Graduate Program in Human Development and Family Studies
College of Health and Human Development
S-110 Henderson Building
University Park, PA 16802
Telephone: (814) 863-8000
Fax: (814) 863-7963
E-mail: *dmt16@psu.edu*
Web: *http://www.hhdev.psu.edu/hdfs/grad/index.html*

Department Information:

1974. Professor in Charge of Graduate Program: Douglas Teti. Number of faculty: total—full-time 33; women—full-time 15; total—minority—full-time 4; women minority—full-time 4.

Programs and Degrees Offered:

Listed in the following order: Program area, degree type (T if terminal Master's), number awarded 7/06–6/07. Human Development and Family Studies PhD (Doctor of Philosophy) 10.

Student Applications/Admissions:

Student Applications

Human Development and Family Studies PhD (Doctor of Philosophy)—Applications 2007–2008, 72. Total applicants accepted 2007–2008, 26. Number full-time enrolled (new admits only) 2007–2008, 18. Number part-time enrolled (new admits only) 2007–2008, 0. Openings 2008–2009, 18. The median number of years required for completion of a degree in 2006–2007 were 5. The number of students enrolled full- and part-time who were dismissed or voluntarily withdrew from this program area in 2007–2008 were 0.

Admissions Requirements:

Scores: Entries appear in this order: required test or GPA, minimum score (if required), median score of students entering in 2007–2008. Doctoral Programs: GRE-V no minimum stated, 600; GRE-Q no minimum stated, 700; overall undergraduate GPA ——, 3.79; Doctoral program GRE-Analytic no minimum stated.

Other Criteria: (importance of criteria rated low, medium, or high): GRE/MAT scores—high, research experience—high, work experience—low, extracurricular activity—low, GPA—high, letters of recommendation—high, interview—low, statement of goals and objectives—high, writing sample—high.

Student Characteristics: The following represents characteristics of students in 2007–2008 in all graduate psychology programs in the department: Female—full-time 71, part-time 0; Male—full-time 8, part-time 0; African American/Black—full-time 6, part-time 0; Hispanic/Latino(a)—full-time 1, part-time 0; Asian/Pacific Islander—full-time 6, part-time 0; American Indian/Alaska Native—full-time 0, part-time 0; Caucasian/White—full-time 57, part-time 0; Multi-ethnic—full-time 0, part-time 0; students subject to the Americans With Disabilities Act—full-time 0, part-time 0; Unknown ethnicity—full-time 0, part-time 0; International students who hold an F-1 or J-1 Visa—full-time 9, part-time 0.

Financial Information/Assistance:

Tuition for Full-Time Study: *Doctoral:* State residents: per academic year $19,937, $581 per credit hour; Nonstate residents: per academic year $25,430, $810 per credit hour. Tuition is subject to change. See the following Web site for updates and changes in tuition costs: http://www.tuition.psu.edu.

Financial Assistance:

First-Year Students: Teaching assistantships available for first year. Average amount paid per academic year: $15,165. Average number of hours worked per week: 20. Apply by January 5. Tuition remission given: full. Research assistantships available for first year. Average amount paid per academic year: $15,165. Average number of hours worked per week: 20. Apply by January 5. Tuition remission given: full. Fellowships and scholarships available for first year. Average amount paid per academic year: $15,800. Average number of hours worked per week: 10. Apply by January 5. Tuition remission given: full.

Advanced Students: Teaching assistantships available for advanced students. Average amount paid per academic year: $15,165. Average number of hours worked per week: 20. Apply by September. Tuition remission given: full. Research assistantships available for advanced students. Average amount paid per academic year: $15,165. Average number of hours worked per week: 20. Apply by September. Tuition remission given: full.

Additional Information: Of all students currently enrolled full time, 100% benefited from one or more of the listed financial assistance programs.

Internships/Practica: No information provided.

Housing and Day Care: On-campus housing is available. See the following Web site for more information: http://www.personal.psu.edu/HDFS_CDL/. On-campus day care facilities are available.

Employment of Department Graduates:

Master's Degree Graduates: Of those who graduated in the academic year 2006–2007, the following categories and numbers represent the postgraduate activities and employment of master's degree graduates: Enrolled in a postdoctoral residency/fellowship (n/a), employed in independent practice (n/a), total from the above (master's) (0).

Doctoral Degree Graduates: Of those who graduated in the academic year 2006–2007, the following categories and numbers represent the postgraduate activities and employment of doctoral degree graduates: Enrolled in a psychology doctoral program (n/a), enrolled in another graduate/professional program (0), enrolled in a postdoctoral residency/fellowship (9), employed in independent practice (0), employed in an academic position at a university (1), employed in an academic position at a 2-year/4-year college (0), employed in other positions at a higher education institution (0), employed in a professional position in a school system (0), employed in business or industry (0), employed in government agency (0), employed in a community mental health/counseling center (0), employed in a hospital/medical center (0), still seeking employment (0), not seeking employment (0), other employment position (0), do not know (0), total from the above (doctoral) (10).

Additional Information:

Orientation, Objectives, and Emphasis of Department: The basic objectives of the human development and family studies (HDFS) program are the following: to expand knowledge about the development and functioning of individuals, small groups, and families; to improve methods for studying processes of human development and change; and to create and disseminate improved techniques and strategies for enhancing individual and family functioning, helping people learn to cope more effectively with problems of living, and preventing normal life problems from becoming serious difficulties. The program takes a life span perspective, recognizing that the most important aspects of development and types of life tasks and situations vary from infancy and childhood through maturity and old age, as well as through the life cycle of the family, and that each phase of development is a precursor to the next. There is a firm commitment to an interdisciplinary and multiprofessional approach to these objectives and to the development of competence in applying rigorous methods of empirical inquiry. All students are expected to acquire a broad interdisciplinary base of knowledge and to develop competence in depth in one of four primary program areas: family development, individual development, human development intervention, or methodology.

Special Facilities or Resources: Several additional facilities are associated with the College of Health and Human Development that provide significant resources to our Department, in terms of graduate training opportunities and student funding. These include the Child Development Laboratory and Bennett Family Center, which are high-quality early child care programs providing care to children from early infancy through kindergarten. Each unit has observational rooms for the study of individual and group behavior of children and adults. Our students also avail themselves of the resources provided by several College-based centers, including the Prevention Research Center for the Promotion of Human Development (Mark Greenberg, PhD, Director), the Methodology Center (Linda Collins, PhD, Director), the Methodology Consulting Center (Michael Rovine, PhD, Director), the Center for Childhood Obesity (Leann Birch, PhD, Director), the Center for Human Development and Family Research in Diverse Contexts (Emilie Smith, PhD, Director), and the Gerontology Center (Melissa Hardy, PhD, Director). All of these centers are directed by HDFS faculty and provide a variety of funding and training opportunities for our graduate students. The Centers are direct outgrowths of our program's four core areas: Individual Development, Prevention/Intervention, Methodology, and Family Development.

Application Information:

Send to Graduate Admissions, c/o Mary Jo Spicer, Penn State University, Department of Human Development and Family Studies, S211 Henderson Building, University Park, PA 16802. Application available online. URL of online application: http://www.psu.edu/dept/HDFS/. Students are admitted in the Winter, application deadline January 5. Must take GRE Exams no later than November to be considered for admission. *Fee:* $45 for online application fee and $60 fee for paper application.

Pennsylvania, University of

Applied Psychology—Human Development Division
Graduate School of Education
3700 Walnut Street
Philadelphia, PA 19104-6216
Telephone: (215) 898-4176
Fax: (215) 573-2115
E-mail: *evelynj@gse.upenn.edu*
Web: *http://www.gse.upenn.edu/aphd/*

Department Information:

1975. Chair, Applied Psychology—Human Development Division: Howard C. Stevenson, PhD. Number of faculty: total—full-time 7, part-time 3; women—full-time 3, part-time 3; total—minority—full-time 5; women minority—full-time 3.

Programs and Degrees Offered:

Listed in the following order: Program area, degree type (T if terminal Master's), number awarded 7/06–6/07. Psychological Services MA/MS (Master of Arts/Science) (T) 27, Inderdisciplinary Studies in Human Development MA/MS (Master of Arts/Science) 2, Inderdisciplinary Studies in Human Development PhD (Doctor of Philosophy) 2, Professional Counseling and Psychology 4, Professional School Counseling Certification 0, Professional School Counseling MA/MS (Master of Arts/Science).

Student Applications/Admissions:

Student Applications

Psychological Services MA/MS (Master of Arts/Science)—Applications 2007–2008, 59. Total applicants accepted 2007–2008,

49. Number full-time enrolled (new admits only) 2007–2008, 49. Number part-time enrolled (new admits only) 2007–2008, 3. Total enrolled 2007–2008 full-time, 63, part-time, 6. Openings 2008–2009, 35. The median number of years required for completion of a degree in 2006–2007 was 1. The number of students enrolled full- and part-time who were dismissed or voluntarily withdrew from this program area in 2007–2008 were 0. *Inderdisciplinary Studies in Human Development MA/MS (Master of Arts/Science)*—Applications 2007–2008, 25. Total applicants accepted 2007–2008, 20. Number full-time enrolled (new admits only) 2007–2008, 7. Number part-time enrolled (new admits only) 2007–2008, 0. Total enrolled 2007–2008 full-time, 16, part-time, 4. Openings 2008–2009, 20. The median number of years required for completion of a degree in 2006–2007 was 1. *Inderdisciplinary Studies in Human Development PhD (Doctor of Philosophy)*—Applications 2007–2008, 34. Total applicants accepted 2007–2008, 3. Number full-time enrolled (new admits only) 2007–2008, 2. Number part-time enrolled (new admits only) 2007–2008, 0. Openings 2008–2009, 3. The median number of years required for completion of a degree in 2006–2007 were 5. *Professional Counseling and Psychology MA/MS (Master of Arts/Science)*—Applications 2007–2008, 13. Total applicants accepted 2007–2008, 10. Number full-time enrolled (new admits only) 2007–2008, 10. Number part-time enrolled (new admits only) 2007–2008, 0. Total enrolled 2007–2008 full-time, 9, part-time, 1. Openings 2008–2009, 20. The median number of years required for completion of a degree in 2006–2007 were 2. The number of students enrolled full- and part-time who were dismissed or voluntarily withdrew from this program area in 2007–2008 were 0. *Professional School Counseling Certification*—Applications 2007–2008, 13. Total applicants accepted 2007–2008, 12. Number full-time enrolled (new admits only) 2007–2008, 11. Number part-time enrolled (new admits only) 2007–2008, 0. Openings 2008–2009, 20. The median number of years required for completion of a degree in 2006–2007 were 2. *Professional School Counseling MA/MS (Master of Arts/Science)*—Applications 2007–2008, 25. Total applicants accepted 2007–2008, 23. Number full-time enrolled (new admits only) 2007–2008, 20. Number part-time enrolled (new admits only) 2007–2008, 0. Openings 2008–2009, 25. The median number of years required for completion of a degree in 2006–2007 were 2.

Admissions Requirements:

Scores: Entries appear in this order: required test or GPA, minimum score (if required), median score of students entering in 2007–2008. Master's Programs: GRE-V no minimum stated; GRE-Q no minimum stated; overall undergraduate GPA no minimum stated; psychology GPA no minimum stated. Note: The Executive Program in Professional School Counseling does not require the GRE exam. Doctoral Programs: GRE-V no minimum stated; GRE-Q no minimum stated; overall undergraduate GPA 3.25, 3.41.

Other Criteria: (importance of criteria rated low, medium, or high): GRE/MAT scores—high, research experience—medium, work experience—medium, extracurricular activity—low, clinically related public service—medium, GPA—high, letters of recommendation—high, interview—high, statement of goals and objectives—high, undergraduate major in psychology—low, specific undergraduate psychology courses taken—low. For additional information on admission requirements, go to http://www.gse.upenn.edu/admissions_financial/.

Student Characteristics: The following represents characteristics of students in 2007–2008 in all graduate psychology programs in the department: Female—full-time 126, part-time 8; Male—full-time 11, part-time 3; African American/Black—full-time 21, part-time 2; Hispanic/Latino(a)—full-time 0, part-time 0; Asian/Pacific Islander—full-time 14, part-time 3; American Indian/Alaska Native—full-time 0, part-time 0; Caucasian/White—full-time 77, part-time 6; Multi-ethnic—full-time 10, part-time 0; students subject to the Americans With Disabilities Act—full-time 0, part-time 0; Unknown ethnicity—full-time 15, part-time 0; International students who hold an F-1 or J-1 Visa—full-time 15, part-time 4.

Financial Information/Assistance:

Financial Assistance:

First-Year Students: Teaching assistantships available for first year. Average number of hours worked per week: 20. Apply by December 15. Tuition remission given: full. Research assistantships available for first year. Average number of hours worked per week: 20. Apply by December 15. Tuition remission given: full. Fellowships and scholarships available for first year. Average number of hours worked per week: 20. Apply by December 15. Tuition remission given: full.

Advanced Students: Teaching assistantships available for advanced students. Average number of hours worked per week: 20. Apply by ongoing. Research assistantships available for advanced students. Average number of hours worked per week: 20. Apply by ongoing. Fellowships and scholarships available for advanced students. Average number of hours worked per week: 20. Apply by ongoing.

Additional Information: Of all students currently enrolled full time, 60% benefited from one or more of the listed financial assistance programs.

Internships/Practica: MSEd students in Psychological Services engage in supervised practica for 8 hours a week for two semesters. Placements include schools, community colleges, career services, clinics, and community agencies. MPhil students are required to complete a supervised two-semester, 20-hour per week internship. The Professional School Counseling MSEd is an executive-style master's-degree program for working educators and professionals interested in working as school counselors. The program has been created in partnership with the American School Counselor Association (ASCA). The Professional School Counseling (PSC) master's program uses an executive-learning format that enables students to earn their degree without giving up their current employment. The degree can be earned in 2 years of monthly weekend classes and 1 week of intensive study each summer. Students who successfully complete this program may apply to the Pennsylvania Department of Education-approved Certification Program in School Counseling and receive the Educational Specialist School Counselor certificate.

Housing and Day Care: On-campus housing is available. See the following Web site for more information: http://www.business-services.upenn.edu/housing/. On-campus day care facilities are available. See the following Web site for more information: http://www.business-services.upenn.edu/childcare/.

Employment of Department Graduates:

Master's Degree Graduates: Of those who graduated in the academic year 2006–2007, the following categories and numbers represent the postgraduate activities and employment of master's degree graduates: Enrolled in a postdoctoral residency/fellowship (n/a), employed in independent practice (n/a), total from the above (master's) (0).

Doctoral Degree Graduates: Of those who graduated in the academic year 2006–2007, the following categories and numbers represent the postgraduate activities and employment of doctoral degree graduates: Enrolled in a psychology doctoral program (n/a), total from the above (doctoral) (0).

Additional Information:

Orientation, Objectives, and Emphasis of Department: The Applied Psychology Human Development Division at Penn GSE provides students with a foundation in the core concepts of psychology: intervention, prevention, assessment, learning and development, and field practice or research. Students engage in the challenge of framing major psychological, educational, and social questions, of identifying and developing evidence bearing on those questions, and of working productively at the level of the individual, the community, the nation, and the world. Our orientation in psychological practice and research is toward discovery of what works best and why, advancing our understanding of ways to characterize and resolve psychological and social problems, and promoting the use of that knowledge in professional practice and in educational and public policy contexts. Students are prepared for careers in teaching, research, and practice in schools and universities, in clinical settings and mental health agencies, in government and the corporate world. Our objectives are to provide students with the richest possible opportunities to develop productive careers. The MSEd in Psychological Services prepares students for practice in diverse community agencies; graduates also may obtain certification in guidance counseling. Our MPhil program in Professional Counseling and Psychology is for students who have already earned a 48 credit master's degree in clinical or counseling psychology (or related mental health field) and wish to pursue licensure as a professional counselor (LPC). The Professional School Counselor Program is a new executive-style master's degree program for working educators and professionals interested in working as school counselors. The program has been created in partnership with the American School Counselor Association (ASCA). The new master's program uses an executive-learning format that enables students to earn their degree without giving up their current employment. The degree can be earned in 2 years of monthly weekend classes and 1 week of intensive study each summer. Students who successfully complete this program may apply to the Pennsylvania Department of Education-approved Certification Program in School Counseling and receive the Educational Specialist School Counselor certificate. The program also meets the educational requirements for Professional Counseling licensure, which involves extra supervised experience beyond the basic degree completion process. The Interdisciplinary Studies in Human Development PhD, and MSEd programs combine the study of social, emotional, cognitive, and physical aspects of human development that are focused on urban populations, considered within ecocultural contexts, and relevant to social policies. Given Penn GSE's commitment to urban education and our West Philadelphia setting, students are encouraged to create a specialized program of study that leads to an enriched understanding of the diverse perspectives of human development across the life span. Specialized options may represent one of the following career interests: traditional academic appointment; youth programming and services; urban and ethnic studies; adult development and learning; corporate human resources development; international programming (e.g., work with NGOs); foundation administration and program development; and collaborative efforts in health care facilities. Conceptually and methodologically, ISHD students are expected to integrate established psychological approaches with perspectives from other social and biological sciences. Students are encouraged to select courses from such disciplines as anthropology, psychology, sociology, philosophy, linguistics, communications, nursing, medicine, social work, and business.

Special Facilities or Resources: The Division houses the Center for Health Achievement, Neighborhood Growth and Ethnic Studies (CHANGES) providing students with research mentorship and opportunities. The Division maintains ongoing research programs on early numeracy development, examination of the protective roles of racial identity and racial socialization for African American youth in schools, and understanding the role of various risk and protective factors on the health and well-being of youth. Our building was recently renovated and houses state-of-the-art computer labs and renovated classrooms, as well as wireless access.

Information for Students With Physical Disabilities: See the following Web site for more information: http://www.vpul.upenn.edu/lrc/sds/index.html.

Application Information:

Send to Admissions Office, Graduate School of Education, University of Pennsylvania, 3700 Walnut Street, Philadelphia, PA 19104-6216. Application available online. URL of online application: http://www.gse.upenn.edu. Students are admitted in the Fall, application deadline for PhD is December 15; Winter, application deadline see below; Spring, application deadline see below; Summer, application deadline see below; programs have rolling admissions. This deadline is for applications to the PhD program in Interdisciplinary Studies in Human Development only. Applications may be accepted the next business day. Executive Program in Professional School Counseling MSEd deadline is June 1. Applications for Psychological Services, Interdisciplinary Studies in Human Development MSEd and Professional Counseling and Psychology MPhil programs are accepted on a rolling admissions basis. *Fee:* $65. Fee is usually waived upon request.

Pennsylvania, University of

Department of Psychology
3720 Walnut Street
Philadelphia, PA 19104
Telephone: (215) 898-7300
Fax: (215) 898-7301
E-mail: *greermb@psych.upenn.edu*
Web: *http://www.psych.upenn.edu/grad.html*

Department Information:

1887. Chairperson: Dr. David Brainard. Number of faculty: total—full-time 10; women—full-time 10; women minority—full-time 2.

Programs and Degrees Offered:

Listed in the following order: Program area, degree type (T if terminal Master's), number awarded 7/06–6/07. Psychology PhD (Doctor of Philosophy) 6, Clinical Psychology PhD (Doctor of Philosophy) 3.

APA Accreditation: Clinical PhD (Doctor of Philosophy).

Student Applications/Admissions:

Student Applications

Psychology PhD (Doctor of Philosophy)—Applications 2007–2008, 193. Total applicants accepted 2007–2008, 15. Number full-time enrolled (new admits only) 2007–2008, 5. Total enrolled 2007–2008 full-time, 26. Openings 2008–2009, 6. The median number of years required for completion of a degree in 2006–2007 were 5. The number of students enrolled full- and part-time who were dismissed or voluntarily withdrew from this program area in 2007–2008 were 2. *Clinical Psychology PhD (Doctor of Philosophy)*—Applications 2007–2008, 242. Total applicants accepted 2007–2008, 10. Number full-time enrolled (new admits only) 2007–2008, 4. Total enrolled 2007–2008 full-time, 19. Openings 2008–2009, 4. The median number of years required for completion of a degree in 2006–2007 were 6. The number of students enrolled full- and part-time who were dismissed or voluntarily withdrew from this program area in 2007–2008 were 1.

Admissions Requirements:

Scores: Entries appear in this order: required test or GPA, minimum score (if required), median score of students entering in 2007–2008. Doctoral Programs: GRE-V no minimum stated, 680; GRE-Q no minimum stated, 740; overall undergraduate GPA no minimum stated, 3.8.

Other Criteria: (importance of criteria rated low, medium, or high): GRE/MAT scores—medium, research experience—high, work experience—low, clinically related public service—low, GPA—medium, letters of recommendation—medium, interview—low, statement of goals and objectives—high. For additional information on admission requirements, go to http://www.psych.upenn.edu.

Student Characteristics: The following represents characteristics of students in 2007–2008 in all graduate psychology programs in the department: Female—full-time 24, part-time 0; Male—full-time 21, part-time 0; African American/Black—full-time 0, part-time 0; Hispanic/Latino(a)—full-time 1, part-time 0; Asian/Pacific Islander—full-time 4, part-time 0; American Indian/Alaska Native—full-time 0, part-time 0; Caucasian/White—full-time 40, part-time 0; students subject to the Americans With Disabilities Act—full-time 0, part-time 0; Unknown ethnicity—full-time 0, part-time 0.

Financial Information/Assistance:

Financial Assistance:

First-Year Students: Traineeships available for first year. Average amount paid per academic year: $21,000. Average number of hours worked per week: 12. Apply by December 15. Tuition remission given: full. Fellowships and scholarships available for first year. Average amount paid per academic year: $21,000. Average number of hours worked per week: 12. Apply by December 15. Tuition remission given: full.

Advanced Students: Teaching assistantships available for advanced students. Average amount paid per academic year: $21,000. Average number of hours worked per week: 12. Apply by December 15. Tuition remission given: full. Research assistantships available for advanced students. Average amount paid per academic year: $21,000. Average number of hours worked per week: 12. Apply by December 15. Tuition remission given: full. Traineeships available for advanced students. Average amount paid per academic year: $21,000. Average number of hours worked per week: 12. Apply by December 15. Tuition remission given: full. Fellowships and scholarships available for advanced students. Average amount paid per academic year: $21,000. Average number of hours worked per week: 12. Apply by December 15. Tuition remission given: full.

Additional Information: Of all students currently enrolled full time, 100% benefited from one or more of the listed financial assistance programs.

Internships/Practica: Doctoral Degree (PhD Clinical Psychology): For those doctoral students for whom a professional internship was required in this program prior to graduation, (4) students applied for an internship in 2006–2007, with (3) students obtaining an internship. Of those students who obtained an internship, (3) were paid internships. Of those students who obtained an internship, (3) students placed in APA/CPA-accredited internships, (0) students placed in internships not APA/CPA accredited, but listed with the Association of Psychology Postdoctoral and Internship Centers (APPIC), (0) students placed in internships conforming to guidelines of the Council of Directors of School Psychology Programs (CDSPP), (0) students placed in internships that were not APA/CPA-accredited, APPIC or CDSPP listed. Because of the wealth of opportunities for clinical training in the Philadelphia area, Penn does not run an in-house psychological services clinic. Rather, Penn's Clinical students have the opportunity to participate in practica at local hospitals, clinics, and research facilities staffed and run by world-renowned clinical scientists. The Associate Director of Clinical Training helps students decide which practicum experiences best suit the student's needs and interests, and arranges for placements at the appropriate sites. For additional information on education and training outcomes for our programs, see the following Web site: http://www.psych.upenn.edu/grad/clinprog.htm.

Housing and Day Care: On-campus housing is available. See the following Web site for more information: http://www.upenn.edu/campus/housing.php. No on-campus day care facilities are available.

Employment of Department Graduates:

Master's Degree Graduates: Of those who graduated in the academic year 2006–2007, the following categories and numbers represent the postgraduate activities and employment of master's degree graduates: Enrolled in a postdoctoral residency/fellowship (n/a), employed in independent practice (n/a), total from the above (master's) (0).

Doctoral Degree Graduates: Of those who graduated in the academic year 2006–2007, the following categories and numbers represent the postgraduate activities and employment of doctoral degree graduates: Enrolled in a psychology doctoral program (n/a), total from the above (doctoral) (0).

Additional Information:

Orientation, Objectives, and Emphasis of Department: The Department of Psychology at the University of Pennsylvania offers curricular and research opportunities for the study of sensation, perception, cognition, cognitive neuroscience, decision making, language, learning, motivation, emotion, motor control, psychopathology, and social processes. Biological, cultural, developmental, comparative, experimental, and mathematical approaches to these areas are used in ongoing teaching and research. The department has an APA-accredited clinical program that is designed to prepare students for research careers in inteventions, psychopathology and personality. The interests of the faculty and students in the department cover the entire field of research-oriented psychology. Still, the Department of Psychology at Pennsylvania functions as a single unit whose guiding principle is scientific excellence. Students are admitted to the department. The primary determinant of acceptance is academic promise rather than specific area of interest. Faculty join together from different subdisciplines for teaching and research purposes so that students become conversant with issues in a number of different areas. Most graduate students and faculty attend the weekly departmental colloquia. A high level of interaction among department members (students and faculty), within and across disciplines, helps generate both a shared set of interests in the theoretical, historical, and philosophical foundations of psychology and active collaboration in research projects. This level of intellectual interaction is made possible, in part, by the small size of the department; there are 28 full-time faculty members and approximately 40 graduate students in residence. The first-year program is divided between courses that introduce various areas of psychology and a focused research experience. A deep involvement in research continues throughout the graduate program and is supplemented by participation in seminars, the weekly departmental colloquium, teaching, and general intellectual give and take.

Special Facilities or Resources: The department has a fully equipped wood, metal, and electronics shop. In addition, the department has a well-equipped laboratory building, a microvax connected to Internet (used extensively), and many accessible microcomputers. Also readily available for research in the near environs of the department are four major University-affiliated hospitals, and urban public and private schools.

Information for Students With Physical Disabilities: See the following Web site for more information: http://www.vpul.upenn.edu/lrc/sds/index.html.

Application Information:

Send to Graduate School of Arts and Sciences, Suite 322A, 3401 Walnut Street, Philadelphia, PA 19104. Application available online. URL of online application: https://www.galaxy.isc-seo.upenn.edu:7778/pls/gaadmin/gapk0101.bf00?P_SRS_DIV=GAS&P_SRS_MAJOR=PSYC. Students are admitted in the Fall, application deadline December 15. *Fee:* $70.

Philadelphia College of Osteopathic Medicine

Psychology Department
4190 City Avenue
Philadelphia, PA 19131-1693
Telephone: (215) 871-6442
Fax: (215) 871-6458
E-mail: *RobertD@pcom.edu*
Web: *http://www.pcom.edu*

Department Information:

1995. Chairperson: Robert A. DiTomasso, PhD, ABPP. Number of faculty: total—full-time 22, part-time 50; women—full-time 11, part-time 33; total—minority—full-time 3, part-time 10; women minority—full-time 2, part-time 7; faculty subject to the Americans With Disabilities Act 1.

Programs and Degrees Offered:

Listed in the following order: Program area, degree type (T if terminal Master's), number awarded 7/06–6/07. Certificate of Advanced Graduate Study Other 5, Counseling and Clinical Health Psychology MA/MS (Master of Arts/Science) (T) 28, Clinical Psychology Respecialization Diploma 0, Clinical Psychology PsyD (Doctor of Psychology) 34, Organizational Development and Leadership MA/MS (Master of Arts/Science) (T) 14, School Psychology PsyD (Doctor of Psychology) 7, School Psychology MA/MS (Master of Arts/Science) (T) 19, Educational Specialist in School Psychology EdS/MEd (School Psychology) 9, School Psychology Respecialization Diploma 1.

APA Accreditation: Clinical PsyD (Doctor of Psychology).

Student Applications/Admissions:

Student Applications

Certificate of Advanced Graduate Study Other—Applications 2007–2008, 39. Total applicants accepted 2007–2008, 20. Number full-time enrolled (new admits only) 2007–2008, 0. Number part-time enrolled (new admits only) 2007–2008, 15. Openings 2008–2009, 15. The median number of years required for completion of a degree in 2006–2007 was 1. The number of students enrolled full- and part-time who were dismissed or voluntarily withdrew from this program area in 2007–2008 were 0. *Counseling and Clinical Health Psychology MA/MS (Master of Arts/Science)*—Applications 2007–2008, 116. Total applicants accepted 2007–2008, 53. Number full-time enrolled (new admits only) 2007–2008, 33. Number part-time enrolled (new admits only) 2007–2008, 0. Total enrolled 2007–2008 full-time, 55, part-time, 8. Openings 2008–2009, 33. The median number of years required for completion of a degree in 2006–2007 were 2. The number of students enrolled full- and part-time who were dismissed or voluntarily withdrew from this program area in 2007–2008 were 2. *Clinical Psychology Respecialization Diploma*—Applications 2007–2008, 1. Total applicants accepted 2007–2008, 1. Number full-time enrolled (new admits only) 2007–2008, 1. Number part-time enrolled (new admits only) 2007–2008, 0. Openings 2008–2009, 2. The number of students enrolled full- and part-time who were dismissed or voluntarily withdrew from this program area in 2007–2008 were 0. *Clinical Psychology PsyD (Doctor of Psychology)*—Applications 2007–2008, 153. Total applicants accepted 2007–2008, 42. Number full-time enrolled (new admits only) 2007–2008, 28. Number part-time enrolled (new admits only) 2007–2008, 0. Openings 2008–2009, 28. The median number of years required for completion of a degree in 2006–2007 were 6. The number of students enrolled full- and part-time who were dismissed or voluntarily withdrew from this program area in 2007–2008 were 5. *Organizational Development and Leadership MA/MS (Master of Arts/ Science)*—Applications 2007–2008, 41. Total applicants accepted 2007–2008, 24. Number full-time enrolled (new admits only) 2007–2008, 19. Total enrolled 2007–2008 full-time, 39. Openings 2008–2009, 25. The median number of years required for completion of a degree in 2006–2007 were 2. The number of students enrolled full- and part-time who were dismissed or voluntarily withdrew from this program area in 2007–2008 were 1. *School Psychology PsyD (Doctor of Psychology)*—Applications 2007–2008, 28. Total applicants accepted 2007–2008, 22. Number full-time enrolled (new admits only) 2007–2008, 16. Number part-time enrolled (new admits only) 2007–2008, 0. Openings 2008–2009, 15. The median number of years required for completion of a degree in 2006–2007 were 4. The number of students enrolled full- and part-time who were dismissed or voluntarily withdrew from this program area in 2007–2008 were 2. *School Psychology MA/MS (Master of Arts/Science)*—Applications 2007–2008, 62. Total applicants accepted 2007–2008, 37. Number full-time enrolled (new admits only) 2007–2008, 19. Number part-time enrolled (new admits only) 2007–2008, 0. Openings 2008–2009, 20. The median number of years required for completion of a degree in 2006–2007 was 1. The number of students enrolled full- and part-time who were dismissed or voluntarily withdrew from this program area in 2007–2008 were 0. *Educational Specialist in School Psychology EdS/MEd (School Psychology)*—Applications 2007–2008, 36. Total applicants accepted 2007–2008, 26. Number full-time enrolled (new admits only) 2007–2008, 20. Number part-time enrolled (new admits only) 2007–2008, 0. Openings 2008–2009, 20. The median number of years required for completion of a degree in 2006–2007 were 3. The number of students enrolled full- and part-time who were dismissed or voluntarily withdrew from this program area in 2007–2008 were 0. *School Psychology Respecialization Diploma*—Applications 2007–2008, 0. Total applicants accepted 2007–2008, 0. Number full-time enrolled (new admits only) 2007–2008, 0. Number part-time enrolled (new admits only) 2007–2008, 0. Openings 2008–2009, 3. The median number of years required for completion of a degree in 2006–2007 were 2. The number of students enrolled full- and part-time who were dismissed or voluntarily withdrew from this program area in 2007–2008 were 0.

Admissions Requirements:

Scores: Entries appear in this order: required test or GPA, minimum score (if required), median score of students entering in 2007–2008. Master's Programs: GRE-V no minimum stated; GRE-Q no minimum stated; MAT no minimum stated; overall undergraduate GPA 3.0, 3.4; Masters GRE-Analytical no minimum stated. The EdS program requires the GRE-81 (subject area psychology exam) and Praxis I. MS in Counseling and Clinical Health Psychology and MS in School Psychology programs require either the MAT or GRE. The MS in Organizational Development and Leadership program does not require either the MAT or GRE. Doctoral Programs: overall undergraduate GPA 3.0, 3.5. The PsyD in School Psychology program requires the Praxis II.

Other Criteria: (importance of criteria rated low, medium, or high): GRE/MAT scores—medium, research experience—low, work experience—high, extracurricular activity—medium, clinically related public service—high, GPA—high, letters of recommendation—high, interview—high, statement of goals and objectives—high, graded writing sample—high, undergraduate major in psychology—medium, specific undergraduate psychology courses taken—medium. Work experience is weighted medium as admission criteria for the MS in School Psychology, MS in Counseling and Clinical Health Psychology, and certificate programs. Work experience is weighted high as admission criteria for the MS in ODL, EdS and PsyD programs. In addition, a master's degree in psychology or a related field is required for admissions to the Clinical PsyD program. Master's and EdS degrees are admissions requirements for the PsyD in School Psychology program. For additional information on admission requirements, go to http://www.pcom.edu.

Student Characteristics: The following represents characteristics of students in 2007–2008 in all graduate psychology programs in the department: Female—full-time 290, part-time 13; Male—full-time 92, part-time 11; African American/Black—full-time 56, part-time 7; Hispanic/Latino(a)—full-time 10, part-time 2; Asian/Pacific Islander—full-time 11, part-time 0; American Indian/Alaska Native—full-time 3, part-time 0; Caucasian/White—full-time 290, part-time 14; Multi-ethnic—full-time 2, part-time 0; students subject to the Americans With Disabilities Act—full-time 8, part-time 1; Unknown ethnicity—full-time 10, part-time 1; International students who hold an F-1 or J-1 Visa—full-time 1, part-time 0.

Financial Information/Assistance:

Tuition for Full-Time Study: *Master's:* State residents: $628 per credit hour; Nonstate residents: $628 per credit hour. *Doctoral:* State residents: $867 per credit hour; Nonstate residents: $867 per credit hour. Tuition is subject to change. Additional fees are assessed to students beyond the costs of tuition for the following: Comprehensive fee (each term): $117; Graduation fee (only charged to those graduating): $250. Tuition costs vary by program. See the following Web site for updates and changes in tuition costs: http://www.pcom.edu/Administration/Administrative_Departments/Bursar_s_Office/Bursar_s_Office.html. Higher tuition cost for EdS: $700/credit hour.

Financial Assistance:

First-Year Students: Research assistantships available for first year. Average amount paid per academic year: $6,000. Average number of hours worked per week: 12. Apply by late summer. Fellowships and scholarships available for first year. Average amount paid per academic year: $1,000. Apply by award. Tuition remission given: partial.

Advanced Students: Teaching assistantships available for advanced students. Average amount paid per academic year: $1,500. Average number of hours worked per week: 24. Apply by assignment. Research assistantships available for advanced students. Average amount paid per academic year: $7,200. Average number of hours worked per week: 12. Apply by late summer.

Additional Information: Of all students currently enrolled full time, 2% benefited from one or more of the listed financial

assistance programs. Application and information available online at http://www.pcom.edu.

Internships/Practica: Master's Degree (MA/MS in Organizational Development and Leadership): An internship experience such as a final research project or "capstone" experience is required of graduates. Doctoral Degree (PsyD Doctor of Psychology in Clinical Psychology): For those doctoral students for whom a professional internship was required in this program prior to graduation, (19) students applied for an internship in 2006–2007, with (18) students obtaining an internship. Of those students who obtained an internship, (18) were paid internships. Of those students who obtained an internship, (5) students placed in APA/CPA-accredited internships, (12) students placed in internships not APA/CPA-accredited, but listed with the Association of Psychology Postdoctoral and Internship Centers (APPIC), (0) students placed in internships conforming to guidelines of the Council of Directors of School Psychology Programs (CDSPP), (1) student placed in internships that were not APA/CPA accredited, APPIC or CDSPP listed. Doctoral Degree (PsyD Doctor of Psychology in School Psychology): For those doctoral students for whom a professional internship was required in this program prior to graduation, (16) students applied for an internship in 2006–2007, with (16) students obtaining an internship. Of those students who obtained an internship, (11) were paid internships. Of those students who obtained an internship, (0) students placed in APA/CPA-accredited internships, (0) students placed in internships not APA/CPA-accredited, but listed with the Association of Psychology Postdoctoral and Internship Centers (APPIC), (16) students placed in internships conforming to guidelines of the Council of Directors of School Psychology Programs (CDSPP), (0) students placed in internships that were not APA/CPA-accredited, APPIC or CDSPP listed. Practica are fieldwork experiences completed by master's-level and doctoral students at a PCOM-approved clinical training site. The minimum weekly hour requirements vary from program to program. Practicum sites are committed to excellence in the training of professionals and provide extensive supervision and formative clinical experiences. They offer a wide range of training, including the use of empirically supported interventions, brief treatment models, cognitive behavioral therapy, and treatment of psychological and medical problems. Students engage in evaluation, psychological testing (PsyD only), psychotherapy, and professional clinical work. Practica include seminars taught by faculty that provide a place for students to discuss their experiences and help them integrate coursework with on-site training. Students participate in pratica at the Psychology Department's Center for Brief Therapy, a multifaceted clinical training center, as well as sites including community agencies, hospitals, university counseling centers, prisons, and specialized treatment centers. The department has a broad network of practicum sites in Pennsylvania, New Jersey, Maryland, and Delaware. Students apply for internships through the APPIC matching program. For additional information on education and training outcomes for our programs, see the following Web site: http://www.pcom.edu/Academic_Programs/aca_psych/aca_psych.html.

Housing and Day Care: No on-campus housing is available. No on-campus day care facilities are available.

Employment of Department Graduates:

Master's Degree Graduates: Of those who graduated in the academic year 2006–2007, the following categories and numbers represent the postgraduate activities and employment of master's degree graduates: Enrolled in a psychology doctoral program (8), enrolled in another graduate/professional program (14), enrolled in a postdoctoral residency/fellowship (n/a), employed in independent practice (n/a), employed in a professional position in a school system (5), employed in business or industry (14), employed in a community mental health/counseling center (13), employed in a hospital/medical center (5), other employment position (2), total from the above (master's) (61).

Doctoral Degree Graduates: Of those who graduated in the academic year 2006–2007, the following categories and numbers represent the postgraduate activities and employment of doctoral degree graduates: Enrolled in a psychology doctoral program (n/a), enrolled in another graduate/professional program (0), enrolled in a postdoctoral residency/fellowship (3), employed in other positions at a higher education institution (1), employed in a professional position in a school system (7), employed in business or industry (1), employed in government agency (4), employed in a community mental health/counseling center (18), employed in a hospital/medical center (7), total from the above (doctoral) (41).

Additional Information:

Orientation, Objectives, and Emphasis of Department: The mission of the Department of Psychology at PCOM is to prepare highly skilled, compassionate doctoral level psychologists and master's-level psychological specialists to provide empirically based, active, focused, and collaborative assessments and treatments with sensitivity to cultural and ethnic diversity and the underserved. Grounded in the cognitive behavioral tradition, the graduate programs in psychology train practitioner–scholars to offer assessment, therapeutic interventions, consultation, and follow-up services, and to engage in scholarly activities in the fields of clinical and school psychology. The PCOM Department of Psychology offers graduate programs in psychology at several levels to suit a variety of professional needs and interests.

Special Facilities or Resources: The academic facilities in Philadelphia include state-of-the-art amphitheaters and classroom facilities, computer laboratories with extensive software including PsycLIT and SPSS, a recently renovated library that includes sophisticated online resources, and the HealthNet teleconferencing system. The Center for Brief Therapy, a mental health clinic housed in the Department of Psychology, provides multifaceted clinical training and research opportunities for students. PCOM also has three neighborhood health care centers in Philadelphia and one in LaPorte, Pennsylvania.

Information for Students With Physical Disabilities: See the following Web site for more information: http://www.pcom.edu/Student_Life/Student_Affairs_Main/Academic_Personal.htm.

Application Information:

Send to Philadelphia College of Osteopathic Medicine, Department of Admissions, 4170 City Avenue, Philadelphia, PA 19131. Application available online. URL of online application: http://www.pcom.edu/General_Information/apply_now.html. Students are admitted in the Fall, application deadline rolling; Winter, application deadline rolling; Spring, application deadline rolling; Summer, application deadline rolling; Programs have rolling admissions. The PsyD in Clinical Psychology, PsyD in School Psychology, EdS in School Psychology, MS in Counseling and Clinical Health Psychology, and CAGS programs admit students in the Fall term only. The MS in School Psychology program admits students in the Summer term only. The MS in ODL program admits during all terms. *Fee:* $50. Attendance at any PCOM Open House or submission of online application will qualify applicant for fee waiver.

Pittsburgh, University of

Department of Psychology in Education
School of Education
5930 Posvar Hall
Pittsburgh, PA 15260
Telephone: (412) 624-7230
Fax: (412) 624-7231
E-mail: *johnson@pitt.edu*
Web: *http://www.education.pitt.edu*

Department Information:

1986. Chairman: Carl Johnson. Number of faculty: total—full-time 7, part-time 5; women—full-time 4, part-time 5; total—minority—full-time 1; women minority—full-time 1.

Programs and Degrees Offered:

Listed in the following order: Program area, degree type (T if terminal Master's), number awarded 7/06–6/07. Applied Developmental Psychology MA/MS (Master of Arts/Science) 35, Applied Developmental Psycholology PhD (Doctor of Philosophy) 6.

Student Applications/Admissions:

Student Applications

Applied Developmental Psychology MA/MS (Master of Arts/Science)—Applications 2007–2008, 67. Total applicants accepted 2007–2008, 49. Number full-time enrolled (new admits only) 2007–2008, 19. Number part-time enrolled (new admits only) 2007–2008, 19. Total enrolled 2007–2008 full-time, 29, part-time, 36. Openings 2008–2009, 40. The median number of years required for completion of a degree in 2006–2007 were 2. *Applied Developmental Psycholology PhD (Doctor of Philosophy)*—Applications 2007–2008, 26. Total applicants accepted 2007–2008, 6. Number full-time enrolled (new admits only) 2007–2008, 3. Number part-time enrolled (new admits only) 2007–2008, 1. Total enrolled 2007–2008 full-time, 13, part-time, 9. Openings 2008–2009, 6.

Admissions Requirements:

Scores: Entries appear in this order: required test or GPA, minimum score (if required), median score of students entering in 2007–2008. Master's Programs: overall undergraduate GPA no minimum stated, 3.00. GRE is not required for any of the master's programs. International students are not required to take GRE but must take TOEFL. Doctoral Programs: GRE-V no minimum stated; GRE-Q no minimum stated; overall undergraduate GPA 3.00. International students are not required to take GRE but must take TOEFL.

Other Criteria: (importance of criteria rated low, medium, or high): GRE/MAT scores—medium, research experience—medium, work experience—medium, extracurricular activity—low, clinically related public service—medium, GPA—medium, letters of recommendation—medium, statement of goals and objectives—high, specific undergraduate psychology courses taken—high. For additional information on admission requirements, go to http://www.education.pitt.edu/.

Student Characteristics: The following represents characteristics of students in 2007–2008 in all graduate psychology programs in the department: Female—full-time 35, part-time 55; Male—full-time 4, part-time 4; African American/Black—full-time 4, part-time 4; Hispanic/Latino(a)—full-time 0, part-time 0; Asian/Pacific Islander—full-time 7, part-time 3; American Indian/Alaska Native—full-time 0, part-time 0; Caucasian/White—full-time 27, part-time 51; Unknown ethnicity—full-time 1, part-time 1.

Financial Information/Assistance:

Tuition for Full-Time Study: *Master's:* State residents: per academic year $15,530, $604 per credit hour; Nonstate residents: per academic year $27,570, $1,103 per credit hour. *Doctoral:* State residents: per academic year $15,530, $604 per credit hour; Nonstate residents: per academic year $27,570, $1,103 per credit hour. See the following Web site for updates and changes in tuition costs: http://www.education.pitt.edu/.

Financial Assistance:

First-Year Students: Teaching assistantships available for first year. Average amount paid per academic year: $3,768. Average number of hours worked per week: 10. Tuition remission given: partial. Research assistantships available for first year. Average amount paid per academic year: $11,830. Average number of hours worked per week: 20. Tuition remission given: full.

Advanced Students: Teaching assistantships available for advanced students. Average amount paid per academic year: $3,768. Average number of hours worked per week: 10. Tuition remission given: partial. Research assistantships available for advanced students. Average amount paid per academic year: $11,830. Average number of hours worked per week: 20. Tuition remission given: full. Fellowships and scholarships available for advanced students. Average amount paid per academic year: $5,915. Average number of hours worked per week: 10. Tuition remission given: partial.

Additional Information: Of all students currently enrolled full time, 20% benefited from one or more of the listed financial assistance programs. Application and information available online at http://www.education.pitt.edu/.

Internships/Practica: The Applied Developmental program maintains extensive connections with community organizations that provide opportunities for internships in programs that serve children, youth and families in many different capacities.

Housing and Day Care: No on-campus housing is available. On-campus day care facilities are available. Contact University Child Development Center, 635 Clyde Street; (412) 383-2100.

Employment of Department Graduates:

Master's Degree Graduates: Of those who graduated in the academic year 2006–2007, the following categories and numbers represent the postgraduate activities and employment of master's degree graduates: Enrolled in a postdoctoral residency/fellowship (n/a), employed in independent practice (n/a), total from the above (master's) (0).

Doctoral Degree Graduates: Of those who graduated in the academic year 2006–2007, the following categories and numbers

represent the postgraduate activities and employment of doctoral degree graduates: Enrolled in a psychology doctoral program (n/a), total from the above (doctoral) (0).

Additional Information:

Orientation, Objectives, and Emphasis of Department: The Master of Science Degree in Applied Developmental Psychology emphasizes the integration of knowledge of human development with the skills and expertise essential for developing, implementing, and evaluating effective programs for children, youth and families. Graduates of the program pursue professional careers as program administrators and child development specialists in areas such as teaching, research, and professional practice.

Special Facilities or Resources: The Applied Developmental program is closely allied with several leading research, policy, and service organizations in the University including the Learning Policy Center (http://www.education.pitt.edu/research/pclp.aspx); the Office of Child Development (http://www.education.pitt.edu/ocd); and the University, Community, Leaders, and Individuals with Disabilities (UCLID) Center (http://www.uclid.org).

Information for Students With Physical Disabilities: See the following Web site for more information: http://www.drs.pitt.edu/.

Application Information:

Send to University of Pittsburgh School of Education, Student Service Center, 5930 Wesley West Posvar Hall, Pittsburgh, PA 15260. Application available online. URL of online application: http://www.education.pitt.edu/. Students are admitted in the Fall, application deadline March 1; Spring, application deadline November 1; Summer, application deadline March 1. Applications after the deadlines are seriously considered if all the places are not filled. *Fee:* $50.

Pittsburgh, University of

Psychology
Arts and Sciences
3129 Sennott Square, 210 South Bouquet Street
Pittsburgh, PA 15260
Telephone: (412) 624-4502
Fax: (412) 624-4428
E-mail: *psygrad@pitt.edu*
Web: *http://www.psychology.pitt.edu*

Department Information:

1904. Chairperson: Anthony R. Caggiula. Number of faculty: total—full-time 40, part-time 4; women—full-time 17, part-time 2; total—minority—full-time 5; women minority—full-time 4.

Programs and Degrees Offered:

Listed in the following order: Program area, degree type (T if terminal Master's), number awarded 7/06–6/07. Clinical PhD (Doctor of Philosophy) 7, Cognitive PhD (Doctor of Philosophy) 3, Developmental PhD (Doctor of Philosophy) 0, Biological and Health PhD (Doctor of Philosophy) 0, Individualized PhD (Doctor of Philosophy) 0, Social PhD (Doctor of Philosophy) 1.

APA Accreditation: Clinical PhD (Doctor of Philosophy).

Student Applications/Admissions:

Student Applications

Clinical PhD (Doctor of Philosophy)—Applications 2007–2008, 337. Total applicants accepted 2007–2008, 12. Number full-time enrolled (new admits only) 2007–2008, 4. Openings 2008–2009, 5. The median number of years required for completion of a degree in 2006–2007 were 7. The number of students enrolled full- and part-time who were dismissed or voluntarily withdrew from this program area in 2007–2008 were 1. *Cognitive PhD (Doctor of Philosophy)*—Applications 2007–2008, 134. Total applicants accepted 2007–2008, 10. Number full-time enrolled (new admits only) 2007–2008, 4. Openings 2008–2009, 4. The median number of years required for completion of a degree in 2006–2007 were 7. The number of students enrolled full- and part-time who were dismissed or voluntarily withdrew from this program area in 2007–2008 were 2. *Developmental PhD (Doctor of Philosophy)*—Applications 2007–2008, 39. Total applicants accepted 2007–2008, 3. Number full-time enrolled (new admits only) 2007–2008, 2. Openings 2008–2009, 2. The number of students enrolled full- and part-time who were dismissed or voluntarily withdrew from this program area in 2007–2008 were 0. *Biological and Health PhD (Doctor of Philosophy)*—Applications 2007–2008, 21. Total applicants accepted 2007–2008, 0. Number full-time enrolled (new admits only) 2007–2008, 0. Total enrolled 2007–2008 full-time, 3. Openings 2008–2009, 4. The number of students enrolled full- and part-time who were dismissed or voluntarily withdrew from this program area in 2007–2008 were 0. *Individualized PhD (Doctor of Philosophy)*—Applications 2007–2008, 3. Total applicants accepted 2007–2008, 0. Number full-time enrolled (new admits only) 2007–2008, 0. Openings 2008–2009, 1. The number of students enrolled full- and part-time who were dismissed or voluntarily withdrew from this program area in 2007–2008 were 1. *Social PhD (Doctor of Philosophy)*—Applications 2007–2008, 25. Total applicants accepted 2007–2008, 1. Number full-time enrolled (new admits only) 2007–2008, 0. Openings 2008–2009, 2. The median number of years required for completion of a degree in 2006–2007 were 7. The number of students enrolled full- and part-time who were dismissed or voluntarily withdrew from this program area in 2007–2008 were 1.

Admissions Requirements:

Scores: Entries appear in this order: required test or GPA, minimum score (if required), median score of students entering in 2007–2008. Doctoral Programs: GRE-V no minimum stated, 660; GRE-Q no minimum stated, 710; overall undergraduate GPA 3.0, 3.74; Doctoral program GRE-Analytic no minimum stated, 5. GRE Psychology subject test is required for applicants to Clinical programs.

Other Criteria: (importance of criteria rated low, medium, or high): GRE/MAT scores—high, research experience—high, work experience—medium, extracurricular activity—low, clinically related public service—low, GPA—high, letters of recommendation—high, interview—high, statement of goals and objectives—medium. For additional information on admission requirements, go to http://www.psychology.pitt.edu.

Student Characteristics: The following represents characteristics of students in 2007–2008 in all graduate psychology programs in the department: Female—full-time 81, part-time 0; Male—full-time 21, part-time 0; African American/Black—full-time 7,

part-time 0; Hispanic/Latino(a)—full-time 4, part-time 0; Asian/Pacific Islander—full-time 4, part-time 0; American Indian/Alaska Native—full-time 0, part-time 0; Caucasian/White—full-time 87, part-time 0; students subject to the Americans With Disabilities Act—full-time 0, part-time 0; Unknown ethnicity—full-time 0, part-time 0; International students who hold an F-1 or J-1 Visa—full-time 11, part-time 0.

Financial Information/Assistance:

Tuition for Full-Time Study: *Doctoral:* State residents: per academic year $14,880, $604 per credit hour; Nonstate residents: per academic year $26,920, $1,103 per credit hour. Tuition is subject to change. See the following Web site for updates and changes in tuition costs: http://www.bc.pitt.edu/students/tuition.html.

Financial Assistance:

First-Year Students: Teaching assistantships available for first year. Average amount paid per academic year: $14,485. Average number of hours worked per week: 20. Apply by December 1. Tuition remission given: full. Research assistantships available for first year. Average amount paid per academic year: $13,040. Average number of hours worked per week: 20. Apply by December 1. Tuition remission given: full. Traineeships available for first year. Average amount paid per academic year: $20,000. Apply by December 1. Tuition remission given: full. Fellowships and scholarships available for first year. Average amount paid per academic year: $17,162. Average number of hours worked per week: 0. Apply by December 1. Tuition remission given: full.

Advanced Students: Teaching assistantships available for advanced students. Average amount paid per academic year: $15,070. Average number of hours worked per week: 20. Tuition remission given: full. Research assistantships available for advanced students. Average amount paid per academic year: $13,500. Average number of hours worked per week: 20. Tuition remission given: full. Traineeships available for advanced students. Average amount paid per academic year: $20,000. Tuition remission given: full. Fellowships and scholarships available for advanced students. Average amount paid per academic year: $17,500. Average number of hours worked per week: 0. Tuition remission given: full.

Additional Information: Of all students currently enrolled full time, 100% benefited from one or more of the listed financial assistance programs. Application and information available online at http://www.psychology.pitt.edu.

Internships/Practica: Doctoral Degree (PhD Clinical): For those doctoral students for whom a professional internship was required in this program prior to graduation, (5) students applied for an internship in 2006–2007, with (5) students obtaining an internship. Of those students who obtained an internship, (5) were paid internships. Of those students who obtained an internship, (5) students placed in APA/CPA-accredited internships, (0) students placed in internships not APA/CPA-accredited, but listed with the Association of Psychology Postdoctoral and Internship Centers (APPIC), (0) students placed in internships conforming to guidelines of the Council of Directors of School Psychology Programs (CDSPP), (0) students placed in internships that were not APA/CPA-accredited, APPIC or CDSPP listed.

Housing and Day Care: No on-campus housing is available. On-campus day care facilities are available. See the following Web site for more information: http://www.hr.pitt.edu/ucdc/.

Employment of Department Graduates:

Master's Degree Graduates: Of those who graduated in the academic year 2006–2007, the following categories and numbers represent the postgraduate activities and employment of master's degree graduates: Enrolled in a postdoctoral residency/fellowship (n/a), employed in independent practice (n/a), total from the above (master's) (0).

Doctoral Degree Graduates: Of those who graduated in the academic year 2006–2007, the following categories and numbers represent the postgraduate activities and employment of doctoral degree graduates: Enrolled in a psychology doctoral program (n/a), enrolled in a postdoctoral residency/fellowship (9), employed in an academic position at a university (1), employed in an academic position at a 2-year/4-year college (1), total from the above (doctoral) (11).

Additional Information:

Orientation, Objectives, and Emphasis of Department: Basic research training is emphasized, and most projects carry out research with important practical implications. The graduate programs include Clinical Psychology, Cognitive Psychology and Cognitive Neuroscience, Developmental Psychology, Biological and Health Psychology, Social Psychology, and joint programs in Clinical Developmental and Clinical Health Psychology. Some examples of training opportunities are projects on infant socialization, cognitive, language and social development of children, psychological stress on the cardiovascular and immune systems, nicotine and alcohol use, decision making in groups, stereotyping, reading processes, school and nonschool learning, and brain models of attention and reading. Seminars are small (5–12 students), and close working relationships are encouraged with faculty, especially the student's advisor. Excellent relationships with other departments and schools offer unusually flexible opportunities to carry out interdisciplinary work and gain access to scholars in the Pittsburgh community. All students are expected to teach at least one course and carry out an original research dissertation. Financial support is available for students through teaching, research, and fellowships.

Special Facilities or Resources: The facilities of the department include experimental laboratories, extensive computer facilities, a small-groups laboratory, the Clinical Psychology Center, and the laboratories of the Learning Research and Development Center. These services offer the advanced graduate student opportunities for supervised practicum and research experiences. The department also maintains cooperative arrangements with many organizations in Pittsburgh engaged in various kinds of psychological work. These include Children's Hospital, Pittsburgh Cancer Institute, the Western Psychiatric Institute and Clinic, and several local agencies of the Veterans Administration Medical Centers. Collaboration with these organizations consists of part-time instruction by the staffs of these agencies, the sharing of laboratory and clinical facilities, and the appointment in those organizations of graduate students in psychology as clinical assistants, research assistants, or as part-time employees.

Information for Students With Physical Disabilities: See the following Web site for more information: http://www.drs.pitt.edu/.

Application Information:

All applications must be submitted online. Application available online. URL of online application: http://www.psychology.pitt.edu. Students are admitted in the Fall, application deadline December 1. *Fee:* $50. Fees deferred for McNair Scholars.

Saint Joseph's University

Department of Psychology
5600 City Avenue
Philadelphia, PA 19131-1395
Telephone: (610) 660-1800
Fax: (610) 660-1819
E-mail: *jmindell@sju.edu*
Web: *http://www.sju.edu/psychology*

Department Information:

1960. Director, Graduate Psychology Program: Jodi A. Mindell, PhD. Number of faculty: total—full-time 5, part-time 1; women—full-time 5, part-time 1; women minority—full-time 1.

Programs and Degrees Offered:

Listed in the following order: Program area, degree type (T if terminal Master's), number awarded 7/06–6/07. Experimental MA/MS (Master of Arts/Science) (T) 16.

Student Applications/Admissions:

Student Applications

Experimental MA/MS (Master of Arts/Science)—Applications 2007–2008, 35. Total applicants accepted 2007–2008, 15. Number full-time enrolled (new admits only) 2007–2008, 14. Openings 2008–2009, 16. The median number of years required for completion of a degree in 2006–2007 were 2. The number of students enrolled full- and part-time who were dismissed or voluntarily withdrew from this program area in 2007–2008 were 2.

Admissions Requirements:

Scores: Entries appear in this order: required test or GPA, minimum score (if required), median score of students entering in 2007–2008. Master's Programs: GRE-V 500, 520; GRE-Q 500, 560; overall undergraduate GPA 3.2, 3.5; last 2 years GPA 3.2, 3.6; psychology GPA 3.2, 3.65.

Other Criteria: (importance of criteria rated low, medium, or high): GRE/MAT scores—medium, research experience—high, work experience—low, extracurricular activity—medium, clinically related public service—low, GPA—high, letters of recommendation—high, interview—medium, statement of goals and objectives—medium.

Student Characteristics: The following represents characteristics of students in 2007–2008 in all graduate psychology programs in the department: Female—full-time 20, part-time 0; Male—full-time 6, part-time 0; African American/Black—full-time 1, part-time 0; Hispanic/Latino(a)—full-time 0, part-time 0; Asian/Pacific Islander—full-time 0, part-time 0; American Indian/Alaska Native—full-time 0, part-time 0; Caucasian/White—full-time 25, part-time 0; students subject to the Americans With Disabilities Act—full-time 0, part-time 0; Unknown ethnicity—full-time 0, part-time 0; International students who hold an F-1 or J-1 Visa—full-time 1, part-time 0.

Financial Information/Assistance:

Tuition for Full-Time Study: *Master's:* State residents: $722 per credit hour; Nonstate residents: $722 per credit hour.

Financial Assistance:

First-Year Students: No information provided.

Advanced Students: Teaching assistantships available for advanced students. Average amount paid per academic year: $7,200. Average number of hours worked per week: 20. Tuition remission given: full. Research assistantships available for advanced students. Average amount paid per academic year: $7,200. Average number of hours worked per week: 20. Tuition remission given: full.

Additional Information: Of all students currently enrolled full time, 23% benefited from one or more of the listed financial assistance programs.

Internships/Practica: No information provided.

Housing and Day Care: No on-campus housing is available. On-campus day care facilities are available at Children's School at St. John's. See the following Web site for more information: http://www.stjohnlm.org/address.html.

Employment of Department Graduates:

Master's Degree Graduates: Of those who graduated in the academic year 2006–2007, the following categories and numbers represent the postgraduate activities and employment of master's degree graduates: Enrolled in a postdoctoral residency/fellowship (n/a), employed in independent practice (n/a), total from the above (master's) (0).

Doctoral Degree Graduates: Of those who graduated in the academic year 2006–2007, the following categories and numbers represent the postgraduate activities and employment of doctoral degree graduates: Enrolled in a psychology doctoral program (n/a), total from the above (doctoral) (0).

Additional Information:

Orientation, Objectives, and Emphasis of Department: The Saint Joseph's University graduate program in Experimental Psychology is designed to provide students with a solid grounding in the scientific study of psychology. Graduates of the program will have a firm foundation in the scientific method and the skills with which to pursue the scientific study of psychological questions. The program offers a traditional and academically oriented 36-credit curriculum, which requires a qualifying comprehensive examination and an empirical thesis project. The program is designed for successful completion over 2 academic years. Additionally, a 5-year combined Bachelor/Master of Science degree in psychology is offered. The Saint Joseph's University psychology graduate program has been constructed to complement the strengths and interests of the present psychology faculty and facilities and to reflect the current state of the discipline of psychology. The curriculum is composed of three major components: an 8-credit common core required of all students; 24 credits of content-based courses; and a 16-credit research component in which students complete the comprehensive examination and research thesis.

Special Facilities or Resources: All psychology faculty have equipped and active research laboratories in which graduate students pursue independent research projects for completion of their thesis requirement. Support facilities for graduate-level research and education are impressive. A vivarium, certifiable by the United States Public Health Service, for the housing of animal subjects is in operation and is fully staffed. For research involving human subjects, the department coordinates a subject pool consisting of approximately 300 subjects per semester. Additionally, the Psychology Department at Saint Joseph's operates PsyNet, a state-of-the-art Macintosh AppleShare local area network that is attached to a campuswide computer network through an EtherNet connection. PsyNet consists of 35 Macintosh computers and peripherals for all faculty and staff plus fileservers and laser printers. Two student computer classrooms/laboratories that include an additional 20 computers are also available within the department. PsyNet software includes various word processing, statistical, spreadsheet, database, graphics, and simulation packages.

Application Information:
Send to Graduate Admissions Office, Saint Joseph's University, 5600 City Avenue, Philadelphia, PA 19131-1395. Students are admitted in the Fall, application deadline March 1. *Fee:* $35.

Shippensburg University (2007 data)

Department of Psychology
Arts and Sciences
114 Franklin Science Center
Shippensburg, PA 17257
Telephone: (717) 477-1657
Fax: (717) 477-4057
E-mail: *rlhale@ship.edu*
Web: *http://www.ship.edu/gradschool/deptpsy.html*

Department Information:
1970. Chair Graduate Program in Psychology: Robert L. Hale, PhD. Number of faculty: total—full-time 21, part-time 3; women—full-time 6, part-time 3.

Programs and Degrees Offered:
Listed in the following order: Program area, degree type (T if terminal Master's), number awarded 7/06–6/07. General MA/MS (Master of Arts/Science) (T) 11.

Student Applications/Admissions:
Student Applications
General MA/MS (Master of Arts/Science)—Applications 2007–2008, 34. Total applicants accepted 2007–2008, 15. Number full-time enrolled (new admits only) 2007–2008, 8. Number part-time enrolled (new admits only) 2007–2008, 0. Total enrolled 2007–2008 full-time, 26, part-time, 5. Openings 2008–2009, 12. The median number of years required for completion of a degree in 2006–2007 were 2. The number of students enrolled full- and part-time who were dismissed or voluntarily withdrew from this program area in 2007–2008 were 0.

Admissions Requirements:
Scores: Entries appear in this order: required test or GPA, minimum score (if required), median score of students entering in 2007–2008. Master's Programs: overall undergraduate GPA 2.75, 3.21.

Other Criteria: (importance of criteria rated low, medium, or high): research experience—medium, work experience—low, extracurricular activity—low, GPA—medium, letters of recommendation—medium, statement of goals and objectives—medium.

Student Characteristics: The following represents characteristics of students in 2007–2008 in all graduate psychology programs in the department: Female—full-time 15, part-time 5; Male—full-time 11, part-time 0; African American/Black—full-time 1, part-time 0; Hispanic/Latino(a)—full-time 0, part-time 0; Asian/Pacific Islander—full-time 0, part-time 0; American Indian/Alaska Native—full-time 0, part-time 0; Caucasian/White—full-time 25, part-time 5; Multi-ethnic—full-time 0, part-time 0; students subject to the Americans With Disabilities Act—full-time 0, part-time 0; Unknown ethnicity—full-time 0, part-time 0.

Financial Information/Assistance:
Tuition for Full-Time Study: *Master's:* State residents: per academic year $2,944, $327 per credit hour; Nonstate residents: per academic year $4,711, $523 per credit hour. Tuition is subject to change. See the following Web site for updates and changes in tuition costs: http://www.ship.edu.

Financial Assistance:
First-Year Students: Research assistantships available for first year. Average amount paid per academic year: $2,163. Average number of hours worked per week: 14. Apply by April 1. Tuition remission given: full.
Advanced Students: Research assistantships available for advanced students. Average amount paid per academic year: $2,163. Average number of hours worked per week: 14. Apply by April 1. Tuition remission given: full.
Additional Information: Of all students currently enrolled full time, 20% benefited from one or more of the listed financial assistance programs. Application and information available online at http://www.ship.edu.

Internships/Practica: No internships are available at the master's level.

Housing and Day Care: No on-campus housing is available. No on-campus day care facilities are available.

Employment of Department Graduates:
Master's Degree Graduates: Of those who graduated in the academic year 2006–2007, the following categories and numbers represent the postgraduate activities and employment of master's degree graduates: Enrolled in a postdoctoral residency/fellowship (n/a), employed in independent practice (n/a), total from the above (master's) (0).
Doctoral Degree Graduates: Of those who graduated in the academic year 2006–2007, the following categories and numbers represent the postgraduate activities and employment of doctoral degree graduates: Enrolled in a psychology doctoral program (n/a), total from the above (doctoral) (0).

Additional Information:
Orientation, Objectives, and Emphasis of Department: The Master's program in psychology is designed to provide advanced general knowledge of the field and the opportunity to develop

more specific research skills. In conference with faculty advisors, each candidate develops a personal program designed to meet his or her own specific needs and interests. This program serves as an effective stepping stone program for those desiring further graduate training at the doctoral level. No training is provided in applied areas of psychology.

Special Facilities or Resources: The psychology department at Shippensburg University is housed in Franklin Science Center. Animal colonies and research facilities (wet labs and testing rooms) are located in this building, as are human research facilities, a microcomputer laboratory, research cubicles, videotaping equipment, and two-way mirrored rooms.

Information for Students With Physical Disabilities: Franklin Science Center is wheelchair accessible.

Application Information:
Send to Office of Graduate Admissions, Shippensburg University, 1871 Old Main Drive, Shippensburg, PA 17257. Application available online. URL of online application: http://www.ship.edu. Students are admitted in the Fall, application deadline April 1; Spring, application deadline November 4; Summer, application deadline April 1. *Fee:* $30.

Temple University (2007 data)

Department of Psychological Studies in Education
Ritter Hall Annex, 2nd Floor
1301 Cecil B. Moore Avenue
Philadelphia, PA 19122
Telephone: (215) 204-6009
Fax: (215) 204-6013
E-mail: *jrosenfe@temple.edu*
Web: *http://www.temple.edu*

Department Information:
1984. Chairperson, Psychological studies in Education: Joseph G. Rosenfeld. Number of faculty: total—full-time 21, part-time 30; women—full-time 7, part-time 12.

Programs and Degrees Offered:
Listed in the following order: Program area, degree type (T if terminal Master's), number awarded 7/06–6/07. School Psychology PhD (Doctor of Philosophy) 8, Counseling Psychology PhD (Doctor of Philosophy) 10, Educational Psychology PhD (Doctor of Philosophy) 9, Educational Psychology MA/MS (Master of Arts/Science) (T) 20, Adult and Organizational Development MA/MS (Master of Arts/Science) (T) 10, Counseling Psychology MA/MS (Master of Arts/Science) (T) 30, School Psychology, MA/MS (Master of Arts/Science) 3.

APA Accreditation: School PhD (Doctor of Philosophy). Counseling PhD (Doctor of Philosophy).

Student Applications/Admissions:
Student Applications
School Psychology PhD (Doctor of Philosophy)—Applications 2007–2008, 40. Total applicants accepted 2007–2008, 6. Number full-time enrolled (new admits only) 2007–2008, 3. Total enrolled 2007–2008 full-time, 56, part-time, 7. Openings 2008–2009, 4. The median number of years required for completion of a degree in 2006–2007 were 7. The number of students enrolled full- and part-time who were dismissed or voluntarily withdrew from this program area in 2007–2008 were 2. *Counseling Psychology PhD (Doctor of Philosophy)*—Applications 2007–2008, 0. Total applicants accepted 2007–2008, 0. Number full-time enrolled (new admits only) 2007–2008, 0. Number part-time enrolled (new admits only) 2007–2008, 0. The median number of years required for completion of a degree in 2006–2007 were 5. *Educational Psychology PhD (Doctor of Philosophy)*—Applications 2007–2008, 23. Total applicants accepted 2007–2008, 10. Number full-time enrolled (new admits only) 2007–2008, 3. Number part-time enrolled (new admits only) 2007–2008, 3. Total enrolled 2007–2008 full-time, 20, part-time, 34. Openings 2008–2009, 8. The median number of years required for completion of a degree in 2006–2007 were 7. The number of students enrolled full- and part-time who were dismissed or voluntarily withdrew from this program area in 2007–2008 were 3. *Educational Psychology MA/MS (Master of Arts/Science)*—Applications 2007–2008, 35. Total applicants accepted 2007–2008, 21. Number full-time enrolled (new admits only) 2007–2008, 2. Number part-time enrolled (new admits only) 2007–2008, 14. Total enrolled 2007–2008 full-time, 3, part-time, 39. Openings 2008–2009, 15. The median number of years required for completion of a degree in 2006–2007 were 3. The number of students enrolled full- and part-time who were dismissed or voluntarily withdrew from this program area in 2007–2008 were 2. *Adult and Organizational Development MA/MS (Master of Arts/Science)*—Applications 2007–2008, 30. Total applicants accepted 2007–2008, 20. Number full-time enrolled (new admits only) 2007–2008, 10. Number part-time enrolled (new admits only) 2007–2008, 2. Total enrolled 2007–2008 full-time, 20, part-time, 8. Openings 2008–2009, 15. The median number of years required for completion of a degree in 2006–2007 were 2. The number of students enrolled full- and part-time who were dismissed or voluntarily withdrew from this program area in 2007–2008 were 1. *Counseling Psychology MA/MS (Master of Arts/Science)*—Applications 2007–2008, 60. Total applicants accepted 2007–2008, 30. Number full-time enrolled (new admits only) 2007–2008, 20. Number part-time enrolled (new admits only) 2007–2008, 10. Total enrolled 2007–2008 full-time, 40, part-time, 20. Openings 2008–2009, 30. The median number of years required for completion of a degree in 2006–2007 were 2. The number of students enrolled full- and part-time who were dismissed or voluntarily withdrew from this program area in 2007–2008 were 3. *School Psychology, MA/MS (Master of Arts/Science)*—Applications 2007–2008, 25. Number full-time enrolled (new admits only) 2007–2008, 5. Number part-time enrolled (new admits only) 2007–2008, 2. Total enrolled 2007–2008 full-time, 7, part-time, 4. Openings 2008–2009, 10. The median number of years required for completion of a degree in 2006–2007 were 3. The number of students enrolled full- and part-time who were dismissed or voluntarily withdrew from this program area in 2007–2008 were 0.

Admissions Requirements:
Scores: Entries appear in this order: required test or GPA, minimum score (if required), median score of students entering in 2007–2008. Master's Programs: overall undergraduate GPA

3.0, 3.3. Different Scores are required by different programs. The Graduate School requires a minimum GPA of 3.0 or admission test (GRE or MAT depending on the program) at the 65th percentile. The Psychology GRE is required for school psychology and counseling psychology. GRE or MAT for otheres Doctoral Programs: GRE-V 500, 625; GRE-Q 500, 630; GRE-Subject (Psychology) no minimum stated; overall undergraduate GPA 3.0, 3.38; last 2 years GPA 3.0, 3.5. Different scores and GPAs are required for different programs. Contact the program. Most programs require a GPA of 3.25 in both graduate and undergraduate courses and GRE V+Q of 1100. For the programs that require a Psychology GRE the score should be at least 500.

Other Criteria: (importance of criteria rated low, medium, or high): GRE/MAT scores—medium, research experience—medium, work experience—medium, extracurricular activity—medium, clinically related public service—low, GPA—high, letters of recommendation—high, interview—high, statement of goals and objectives—high.

Student Characteristics: The following represents characteristics of students in 2007–2008 in all graduate psychology programs in the department: Female—full-time 130, part-time 75; Male—full-time 46, part-time 37; American Indian/Alaska Native—part-time 0; Caucasian/White—full-time 0, part-time 0; students subject to the Americans With Disabilities Act—full-time 3, part-time 2; Unknown ethnicity—full-time 0, part-time 0.

Financial Information/Assistance:

Tuition for Full-Time Study: *Master's:* State residents: $465 per credit hour; Nonstate residents: $634 per credit hour. *Doctoral:* State residents: $465 per credit hour; Nonstate residents: $634 per credit hour. Tuition is subject to change. See the following Web site for updates and changes in tuition costs: http://www.temple.edu.

Financial Assistance:

First-Year Students: Fellowships and scholarships available for first year. Average amount paid per academic year: $18,000. Average number of hours worked per week: 0. Apply by January 2. Tuition remission given: full.

Advanced Students: Teaching assistantships available for advanced students. Average amount paid per academic year: $18,000. Average number of hours worked per week: 20. Apply by March 15. Tuition remission given: full. Research assistantships available for advanced students. Average amount paid per academic year: $18,000. Average number of hours worked per week: 20. Apply by March 15. Tuition remission given: full. Fellowships and scholarships available for advanced students. Average amount paid per academic year: $18,000. Average number of hours worked per week: 0. Apply by January 2. Tuition remission given: full.

Additional Information: Of all students currently enrolled full time, 30% benefited from one or more of the listed financial assistance programs.

Internships/Practica: For a master's degree and certification as a school psychologist, students are placed in an internship for 1 academic year. The average renumeration is $12,000. Practicum sites include public, private, and parochial schools and community mental health centers. Internships are supervised by department faculty and doctoral-level school psychologists. For the doctoral program, 1-year internships are available. Renumeration is highly variable for $8,750 to $22,000. Counseling internships are also paid. Practica experiences are part of coursework and are not paid.

Housing and Day Care: On-campus housing is available. Child care is available in the community. Contact the University Housing Office, (215) 204-7184. No on-campus day care facilities are available.

Employment of Department Graduates:

Master's Degree Graduates: Of those who graduated in the academic year 2006–2007, the following categories and numbers represent the postgraduate activities and employment of master's degree graduates: Enrolled in a psychology doctoral program (8), enrolled in a postdoctoral residency/fellowship (n/a), employed in independent practice (n/a), employed in a professional position in a school system (15), employed in a community mental health/counseling center (20), employed in a hospital/medical center (4), do not know (23), total from the above (master's) (70).

Doctoral Degree Graduates: Of those who graduated in the academic year 2006–2007, the following categories and numbers represent the postgraduate activities and employment of doctoral degree graduates: Enrolled in a psychology doctoral program (n/a), employed in an academic position at a university (4), employed in an academic position at a 2-year/4-year college (2), employed in other positions at a higher education institution (1), employed in a professional position in a school system (8), employed in a community mental health/counseling center (8), do not know (3), total from the above (doctoral) (29).

Additional Information:

Orientation, Objectives, and Emphasis of Department: PSE is a graduate-level department offering master's and doctoral programs in four areas: Adult and Organizational Development, Counseling Psychology, Educational Psychology and Educational Psychology Instructional Learning Technology, and School Psychology. Certification is also offered in School Psychology and Counseling Psychology. Counseling Psychology and the School Psychology doctoral programs are APA accredited. The AOD program offers only the master's degree at this time. There are a variety of objectives and emphases. The student should write to the separate program within the department.

Special Facilities or Resources: The department conducts a psychoeducational clinic with observation and recording facilities. Counseling Psychology runs clinics in Family and Community Counseling and Vocational and Educational Guidance School Psychology also has a low-incidence disabilities practicum.

Information for Students With Physical Disabilities: See the following Web site for more information: http://www.temple.edu. Contact Disabilities Resources and Services (215) 204-1280.

Application Information:

Send to Office of Student Services (R-A 238), 1301 Cecil B. Moore, Philadelphia, PA 19122. URL of online application: http://www.temple.edu. Students are admitted in the Fall, application deadline January 2; Spring, application deadline October 2. Counseling Psychology and School Psychology: January 2. AOD and Educational Psychology have rolling admissions and will admit for each session. *Fee:* $40.

Temple University
Department of Psychology
College of Liberal Arts
1701 North 13th Street, Room 668
Philadelphia, PA 19122-6085
Telephone: (215) 204-7321
Fax: (215) 204-5539
E-mail: *marsha.weinraub@temple.edu*
Web: *http://www.temple.edu/psychology*

Department Information:

1924. Chairperson: Willis F. Overton. Number of faculty: total—full-time 32; women—full-time 12; total—minority—full-time 4; women minority—full-time 2.

Programs and Degrees Offered:

Listed in the following order: Program area, degree type (T if terminal Master's), number awarded 7/06–6/07. Clinical PhD (Doctor of Philosophy) 7, Developmental PhD (Doctor of Philosophy) 2, Brain, Behavior, and Cognition PhD (Doctor of Philosophy) 5, Social PhD (Doctor of Philosophy) 3, Developmental Psychopathology PhD (Doctor of Philosophy) 0.

APA Accreditation: Clinical PhD (Doctor of Philosophy).

Student Applications/Admissions:

Student Applications

Clinical PhD (Doctor of Philosophy)—Applications 2007–2008, 222. Total applicants accepted 2007–2008, 11. Number full-time enrolled (new admits only) 2007–2008, 12. Openings 2008–2009, 12. The median number of years required for completion of a degree in 2006–2007 were 6. The number of students enrolled full- and part-time who were dismissed or voluntarily withdrew from this program area in 2007–2008 were 0. *Developmental PhD (Doctor of Philosophy)*—Applications 2007–2008, 55. Total applicants accepted 2007–2008, 10. Number full-time enrolled (new admits only) 2007–2008, 5. Openings 2008–2009, 5. The median number of years required for completion of a degree in 2006–2007 were 5. The number of students enrolled full- and part-time who were dismissed or voluntarily withdrew from this program area in 2007–2008 were 1. *Brain, Behavior, and Cognition PhD (Doctor of Philosophy)*—Applications 2007–2008, 52. Total applicants accepted 2007–2008, 5. Number full-time enrolled (new admits only) 2007–2008, 5. Openings 2008–2009, 5. The median number of years required for completion of a degree in 2006–2007 were 5. The number of students enrolled full- and part-time who were dismissed or voluntarily withdrew from this program area in 2007–2008 were 2. *Social PhD (Doctor of Philosophy)*—Applications 2007–2008, 47. Total applicants accepted 2007–2008, 2. Number full-time enrolled (new admits only) 2007–2008, 2. Openings 2008–2009, 2. The median number of years required for completion of a degree in 2006–2007 were 5. The number of students enrolled full- and part-time who were dismissed or voluntarily withdrew from this program area in 2007–2008 were 0. *Developmental Psychopathology PhD (Doctor of Philosophy)*—Applications 2007–2008, 25. Total applicants accepted 2007–2008, 4. Number full-time enrolled (new admits only) 2007–2008, 2. Openings 2008–2009, 2.

Admissions Requirements:

Scores: Entries appear in this order: required test or GPA, minimum score (if required), median score of students entering in 2007–2008. Master's Programs: overall undergraduate GPA no minimum stated. Doctoral Programs: GRE-V 550, 630; GRE-Q 550, 670; overall undergraduate GPA 3.5, 3.65.

Other Criteria: (importance of criteria rated low, medium, or high): GRE/MAT scores—high, research experience—high, work experience—low, extracurricular activity—low, clinically related public service—low, GPA—high, letters of recommendation—high, interview—high, statement of goals and objectives—high.

Student Characteristics: The following represents characteristics of students in 2007–2008 in all graduate psychology programs in the department: Female—full-time 56, part-time 0; Male—full-time 33, part-time 0; African American/Black—full-time 5, part-time 0; Hispanic/Latino(a)—full-time 0, part-time 0; Asian/Pacific Islander—full-time 5, part-time 0; American Indian/Alaska Native—full-time 0, part-time 0; Caucasian/White—full-time 0, part-time 0; Unknown ethnicity—full-time 0, part-time 0.

Financial Information/Assistance:

Tuition for Full-Time Study: *Doctoral:* State residents: $256 per credit hour; Nonstate residents: $532 per credit hour. Tuition is subject to change. See the following Web site for updates and changes in tuition costs: http://www.temple.edu/psychology.

Financial Assistance:

First-Year Students: Teaching assistantships available for first year. Average amount paid per academic year: $14,455. Average number of hours worked per week: 20. Tuition remission given: full. Research assistantships available for first year. Average amount paid per academic year: $14,455. Average number of hours worked per week: 20. Tuition remission given: full. Fellowships and scholarships available for first year. Average amount paid per academic year: $20,000. Average number of hours worked per week: 0. Tuition remission given: full.

Advanced Students: Teaching assistantships available for advanced students. Average amount paid per academic year: $14,455. Average number of hours worked per week: 20. Tuition remission given: full. Research assistantships available for advanced students. Average amount paid per academic year: $14,455. Average number of hours worked per week: 20. Tuition remission given: full. Fellowships and scholarships available for advanced students. Average amount paid per academic year: $20,000. Average number of hours worked per week: 0. Tuition remission given: full.

Additional Information: Of all students currently enrolled full time, 100% benefited from one or more of the listed financial assistance programs. Application and information available online at http://www.temple.edu/psychology.

Internships/Practica: Clinical students complete a 2,000-hour predoctoral internship at an agency or hospital typically in the Philadelphia metropolitan area.

Housing and Day Care: On-campus housing is available. See the following Web site for more information: http://www.temple.edu. No on-campus day care facilities are available.

Employment of Department Graduates:

Master's Degree Graduates: Of those who graduated in the academic year 2006–2007, the following categories and numbers represent the postgraduate activities and employment of master's degree graduates: Enrolled in a postdoctoral residency/fellowship (n/a), employed in independent practice (n/a), total from the above (master's) (0).

Doctoral Degree Graduates: Of those who graduated in the academic year 2006–2007, the following categories and numbers represent the postgraduate activities and employment of doctoral degree graduates: Enrolled in a psychology doctoral program (n/a), total from the above (doctoral) (0).

Additional Information:

Orientation, Objectives, and Emphasis of Department: The Psychology Department offers graduate training in: brain, behavior, and cognition; clinical; developmental; developmental psychopathology; and social decision making and emotions. All doctoral programs are designed to prepare students for teaching in universities and colleges, conducting research in field and laboratory settings, and providing consultation in applied settings. The Clinical program trains scientist–practitioners and provides students with research and clinical experience.

Special Facilities or Resources: The Psychology Department occupies eight floors of a high-rise building. The physical resources housed in the building include the Psychological Services Center (an in-house mental health facility where Clinical students obtain practicum experience in psychotherapy), extensive laboratory space for human research, a human electrophysiology lab, an infant behavior lab, numerous observation rooms with one-way mirrors, audiovisual equipment (including mobile video equipment), and excellent computer facilities including numerous micro- and minicomputers.

Information for Students With Physical Disabilities: See the following Web site for more information: http://www.temple.edu.

Application Information:

Send to Graduate Admissions Secretary. Application available online. URL of online application: http://www.temple.edu/psychology. Students are admitted in the Fall, application deadline December 15. *Fee:* $40.

Villanova University

Department of Psychology
800 Lancaster Avenue
Villanova, PA 19085
Telephone: (610) 519-4720
Fax: (610) 519-4269
E-mail: *psychologyinformation@villanova.edu*
Web: *http://www.villanova.edu/artsci/psychology/*

Department Information:

1962. Chairperson: Thomas Toppino. Number of faculty: total—full-time 16, part-time 6; women—full-time 5, part-time 3; total—minority—full-time 2, part-time 1; women minority—full-time 1, part-time 1.

Programs and Degrees Offered:

Listed in the following order: Program area, degree type (T if terminal Master's), number awarded 7/06–6/07. General MA/MS (Master of Arts/Science) (T) 18.

Student Applications/Admissions:

Student Applications

General MA/MS (Master of Arts/Science)—Applications 2007–2008, 122. Total applicants accepted 2007–2008, 29. Number full-time enrolled (new admits only) 2007–2008, 16. Openings 2008–2009, 21. The median number of years required for completion of a degree in 2006–2007 were 2. The number of students enrolled full- and part-time who were dismissed or voluntarily withdrew from this program area in 2007–2008 were 0.

Admissions Requirements:

Scores: Entries appear in this order: required test or GPA, minimum score (if required), median score of students entering in 2007–2008. Master's Programs: GRE-V no minimum stated, 550; GRE-Q no minimum stated, 640; overall undergraduate GPA no minimum stated, 3.7; psychology GPA no minimum stated, 3.8; Masters GRE-Analytical no minimum stated, 5.0.

Other Criteria: (importance of criteria rated low, medium, or high): GRE/MAT scores—high, research experience—medium, work experience—low, extracurricular activity—low, clinically related public service—low, GPA—high, letters of recommendation—high, interview—medium, statement of goals and objectives—medium, undergraduate major in psychology—medium, specific undergraduate psychology courses taken—high. For additional information on admission requirements, go to http://www.villanova.edu/artsci/psychology/graduate/admission/.

Student Characteristics: The following represents characteristics of students in 2007–2008 in all graduate psychology programs in the department: Female—full-time 23, part-time 0; Male—full-time 14, part-time 0; African American/Black—full-time 2, part-time 0; Hispanic/Latino(a)—full-time 0, part-time 0; Asian/Pacific Islander—full-time 1, part-time 0; American Indian/Alaska Native—full-time 0, part-time 0; Caucasian/White—full-time 34, part-time 0; Multi-ethnic—full-time 0, part-time 0; students subject to the Americans With Disabilities Act—full-time 0, part-time 0; Unknown ethnicity—full-time 0, part-time 0; International students who hold an F-1 or J-1 Visa—full-time 1, part-time 0.

Financial Information/Assistance:

Tuition for Full-Time Study: *Master's:* State residents: $585 per credit hour; Nonstate residents: $585 per credit hour. Tuition is subject to change. See the following Web site for updates and changes in tuition costs: http://www.villanova.edu/artsci/psychology/graduate/admission/cost.htm.

Financial Assistance:

First-Year Students: Research assistantships available for first year. Average amount paid per academic year: $12,656. Average number of hours worked per week: 20. Apply by March 15. Tuition remission given: full. Traineeships available for first year. Average amount paid per academic year: $6,328. Average number of hours worked per week: 14. Apply by March 15. Tuition remission given: full. Fellowships and scholarships available for first year. Average amount paid per academic year: $0. Average number of hours worked per week: 7. Apply by March 15. Tuition remission given: full.

Advanced Students: Research assistantships available for advanced students. Average amount paid per academic year: $126,565. Average number of hours worked per week: 20. Apply by March 15. Tuition remission given: full. Traineeships available for advanced students. Average amount paid per academic year: $6,328. Average number of hours worked per week: 14. Apply by March 15. Tuition remission given: full. Fellowships and scholarships available for advanced students. Average amount paid per academic year: $0. Average number of hours worked per week: 7. Apply by March 15. Tuition remission given: full.

Additional Information: Of all students currently enrolled full time, 55% benefited from one or more of the listed financial assistance programs. Application and information available online at http://www.villanova.edu/artsci/college/academics/graduate/policies/index.htm?page=gradasst.htm.

Internships/Practica: No information provided.

Housing and Day Care: No on-campus housing is available. No on-campus day care facilities are available.

Employment of Department Graduates:

Master's Degree Graduates: Of those who graduated in the academic year 2006–2007, the following categories and numbers represent the postgraduate activities and employment of master's degree graduates: Enrolled in a psychology doctoral program (7), enrolled in another graduate/professional program (2), enrolled in a postdoctoral residency/fellowship (n/a), employed in independent practice (n/a), employed in business or industry (2), employed in a community mental health/counseling center (1), still seeking employment (3), total from the above (master's) (15).

Doctoral Degree Graduates: Of those who graduated in the academic year 2006–2007, the following categories and numbers represent the postgraduate activities and employment of doctoral degree graduates: Enrolled in a psychology doctoral program (n/a), total from the above (doctoral) (0).

Additional Information:

Orientation, Objectives, and Emphasis of Department: The department offers a program of study leading to the Master of Science in psychology. Individually tailored to meet each student's career interests and needs, the program provides a solid foundation in psychology with special emphasis on preparation for doctoral work. All incoming students are required to take a seminar in the foundations of research and a statistics course. All students also take laboratory courses in cognition and learning and biopsychology. Depending upon the student's interest, he or she selects four elective courses from a reasonably broad range of course offerings such as psychopathology, psychological testing, developmental psychology, social psychology, personality, theories of psychotherapy, behavior modification, special topics, and individual research. During the 2nd year, student efforts are concentrated on the thesis project, which is an intensive empirically based project, done under the supervision of a faculty mentor. The Student–faculty ratio approaches 2:1, allowing close interaction, careful advisement, and individual attention. The department has an active, research-oriented faculty.

Special Facilities or Resources: In addition to office space for faculty and all graduate assistants, the department has approximately 5,800 square feet available for research. Equipment of particular interest to the graduate student includes electronic, and computer-controlled tachistoscopes; animal conditioning chambers; cognitive and computer labs; complete facilities for surgery and histology, including stereotaxic equipment for brain implantation; environmental chambers and rooms equipped for observation and automated recording of animal behavior; radial mazes; well-equipped vision labs; one-way vision rooms; audio and video recording and playback facilities; facilities for the design and development of experiments; and computer-based teaching labs. University computing facilities are all networked, with hundreds of remote terminals available.

Application Information:

Send to Dean, Graduate School, Villanova University, 800 Lancaster Avenue, Villanova, PA 19085. Application available online. URL of online application: http://www.gradartsci.villanova.edu/. Students are admitted in the Fall, application deadline none; programs have rolling admissions. Strong applications received by March 15 have a better chance of acceptance. Completed applications must be received by March 15 to ensure full consideration for financial aid. *Fee:* $50.

West Chester University of Pennsylvania

Department of Psychology
West Chester, PA 19383
Telephone: (610) 436-2945
Fax: (610) 436-2846
E-mail: *LRieserdan@wcupa.edu*
Web: *http://www.wcupa.edu/_academics/sch_cas.psy/*

Department Information:

1967. Chairperson: Sandra Kerr. Number of faculty: total—full-time 20, part-time 8; women—full-time 13, part-time 6; total—minority—full-time 3; women minority—full-time 1.

Programs and Degrees Offered:

Listed in the following order: Program area, degree type (T if terminal Master's), number awarded 7/06–6/07. Clinical MA/MS (Master of Arts/Science) (T) 13, General MA/MS (Master of Arts/Science) (T) 2, Industrial/Organizational MA/MS (Master of Arts/Science) (T) 7.

Student Applications/Admissions:

Student Applications

Clinical MA/MS (Master of Arts/Science)—Applications 2007–2008, 104. Total applicants accepted 2007–2008, 72. Number full-time enrolled (new admits only) 2007–2008, 21. Number part-time enrolled (new admits only) 2007–2008, 2. Total enrolled 2007–2008 full-time, 59, part-time, 15. Openings 2008–2009, 25. The median number of years required for completion of a degree in 2006–2007 were 2. The number of students enrolled full- and part-time who were dismissed or voluntarily withdrew from this program area in 2007–2008 were 0. *General MA/MS (Master of Arts/Science)*—Applications 2007–2008, 12. Total applicants accepted 2007–2008, 3. Number full-time enrolled (new admits only) 2007–2008, 2. Number part-time enrolled (new admits only) 2007–2008, 1. Total enrolled 2007–2008 full-time, 5, part-time, 4. Openings 2008–2009, 4. The median number of years required for completion of a degree in 2006–2007 were 2. The number of students enrolled full- and part-time who were dismissed or voluntarily withdrew from this program area in 2007–2008 were 1. *Industrial/Organizational MA/MS (Master of Arts/Science)*—Applications 2007–2008, 48. Total applicants accepted 2007–2008, 33. Number full-time enrolled (new admits only) 2007–2008, 5. Number part-time enrolled (new admits only) 2007–2008, 2. Total enrolled 2007–2008 full-time, 20, part-time, 15. Openings 2008–2009, 12. The median number of years required for completion of a degree in 2006–2007 were 2.

Admissions Requirements:

Scores: Entries appear in this order: required test or GPA, minimum score (if required), median score of students entering in 2007–2008. Master's Programs: GRE-V 500, 500; GRE-Q 500, 555; overall undergraduate GPA 3.00, 3.3; psychology GPA 3.20, 3.4.

Other Criteria: (importance of criteria rated low, medium, or high): GRE/MAT scores—high, research experience—medium, work experience—medium, extracurricular activity—medium, clinically related public service—medium, GPA—high, letters of recommendation—high, statement of goals and objectives—high.

Student Characteristics: The following represents characteristics of students in 2007–2008 in all graduate psychology programs in the department: Female—full-time 42, part-time 32; Male—full-time 24, part-time 15; African American/Black—full-time 2, part-time 3; Hispanic/Latino(a)—full-time 0, part-time 0; Asian/Pacific Islander—full-time 0, part-time 0; American Indian/Alaska Native—full-time 0, part-time 0; Caucasian/White—full-time 0, part-time 0; students subject to the Americans With Disabilities Act—part-time 2; Unknown ethnicity—full-time 0, part-time 0.

Financial Information/Assistance:

Tuition for Full-Time Study: *Master's:* State residents: per academic year $3,024, $336 per credit hour; Nonstate residents: per academic year $4,839, $538 per credit hour. Tuition is subject to change.

Financial Assistance:

First-Year Students: Research assistantships available for first year. Average amount paid per academic year: $2,500. Average number of hours worked per week: 10. Apply by March 1. Tuition remission given: partial.

Advanced Students: Research assistantships available for advanced students. Average amount paid per academic year: $2,500. Average number of hours worked per week: 10. Apply by March 1. Tuition remission given: partial.

Additional Information: Of all students currently enrolled full time, 40% benefited from one or more of the listed financial assistance programs.

Internships/Practica: Master's Degree (MA/MS Clinical): An internship experience such as a final research project or "capstone" experience is required of graduates. Master's Degree (MA/MS General): An internship experience such as a final research project or "capstone" experience is required of graduates. Master's Degree (MA/MS Industrial/ Organizational): An internship experience such as a final research project or "capstone" experience is required of graduates. Clinical students are required to complete 6 credit hours of practicum and internship in a mental health setting. I/O students are required to complete a 3-credit-hour internship in business or industry.

Housing and Day Care: No on-campus housing is available. On-campus day care facilities are available. See the following Web site for more information: http://www.wcupa.edu/_services/stu.chi/.

Employment of Department Graduates:

Master's Degree Graduates: Of those who graduated in the academic year 2006–2007, the following categories and numbers represent the postgraduate activities and employment of master's degree graduates: Enrolled in a postdoctoral residency/fellowship (n/a), employed in independent practice (n/a), total from the above (master's) (0).

Doctoral Degree Graduates: Of those who graduated in the academic year 2006–2007, the following categories and numbers represent the postgraduate activities and employment of doctoral degree graduates: Enrolled in a psychology doctoral program (n/a), total from the above (doctoral) (0).

Additional Information:

Orientation, Objectives, and Emphasis of Department: The concentration in clinical psychology is designed for students who wish to work in applied settings such as community mental health facilities, hospitals, counseling centers, and other social and rehabilitation agencies, or who wish to continue their education at the doctoral level. Students with the latter goal in mind are strongly encouraged to engage in research in the course of their master's degree training by participating in faculty members' ongoing research programs or conducting their own research under faculty supervision for research report or thesis credit. The industrial/organizational concentration is appropriate for students interested in employment in business or industry, or for those who wish to continue their education at the doctoral level in a related area. A three-credit internship and three- to six-credit research report or thesis are required. With careful selection of electives, internship placement, and research focus, students are able to develop specialization in human factors, personnel evaluation and placement, or group and organizational processes. The concentration in general psychology, in addition to exposing students to the major traditional subject matter of psychology, also provides the opportunity to explore particular areas of psychology in depth through the appropriate selection of elective coursework and research. The general concentration is appropriate for students interested in continuing their education at the doctoral level, as well as those interested in employment, particularly in research positions, upon the receipt of their master's degree.

Special Facilities or Resources: The department has laboratory space and equipment to support a variety of animal and human research.

Application Information:

Send to Office of Graduate Studies and Sponsored Research, West Chester University, West Chester, PA 19383. Application available online. URL of online application: http://www.wcupa.edu/_ADMISSIONS/SCH_DGR/application.html. Students are admitted in the Fall, application deadline March 1. Late applications will be reviewed if space remains in the program. *Fee:* $35.

Widener University (2007 data)

Institute for Graduate Clinical Psychology
One University Place
Chester, PA 19013
Telephone: (610) 499-1206
Fax: (610) 499-4625
E-mail: *VMBrabender@widener.edu*
Web: *http://www.widener.edu*

Department Information:

1970. Associate Dean and Director: Virginia Brabender. Number of faculty: total—full-time 14, part-time 45; women—full-time 5, part-time 25.

Programs and Degrees Offered:

Listed in the following order: Program area, degree type (T if terminal Master's), number awarded 7/06–6/07. Clinical Psychology (Doctor of Psychology) 28, Law Psychology Other 2.

APA Accreditation: Clinical PsyD (Doctor of Psychology).

Student Applications/Admissions:

Student Applications

Clinical Psychology (Doctor of Psychology)—Applications 2007–2008, 352. Total applicants accepted 2007–2008, 55. Number full-time enrolled (new admits only) 2007–2008, 32. Number part-time enrolled (new admits only) 2007–2008, 0. Openings 2008–2009, 33. The median number of years required for completion of a degree in 2006–2007 were 5. The number of students enrolled full- and part-time who were dismissed or voluntarily withdrew from this program area in 2007–2008 were 1. *Law Psychology Other*—Applications 2007–2008, 16. Total applicants accepted 2007–2008, 5. Number full-time enrolled (new admits only) 2007–2008, 3. Number part-time enrolled (new admits only) 2007–2008, 0. Openings 2008–2009, 3. The median number of years required for completion of a degree in 2006–2007 were 6. The number of students enrolled full- and part-time who were dismissed or voluntarily withdrew from this program area in 2007–2008 were 0.

Admissions Requirements:

Scores: Entries appear in this order: required test or GPA, minimum score (if required), median score of students entering in 2007–2008. Doctoral Programs: GRE-V 600; GRE-Q 600; overall undergraduate GPA 3.20. GRE-V, GRE-Q are required; GRE Psychology subject scores are highly recommended. MAT scores are not required. A minimum GPA of 3.2 for the highest degreee earned is strongly recommended. LSAT scores are required for the JD/PsyD program.

Other Criteria: (importance of criteria rated low, medium, or high): GRE/MAT scores—high, work experience—medium, extracurricular activity—medium, clinically related public service—medium, GPA—high, letters of recommendation—high, interview—high, statement of goals and objectives—high. An undergraduate major is not required. We encourage applications from individuals from various disciplines and with a wide range of experiences.

Student Characteristics: The following represents characteristics of students in 2007–2008 in all graduate psychology programs in the department: Female—full-time 131, part-time 0; Male—full-time 43, part-time 0; African American/Black—full-time 9, part-time 0; Hispanic/Latino(a)—full-time 3, part-time 0; Asian/Pacific Islander—full-time 13, part-time 0; American Indian/Alaska Native—full-time 2, part-time 0; Caucasian/White—full-time 144, part-time 0; Multi-ethnic—full-time 1, part-time 0; students subject to the Americans With Disabilities Act—full-time 0, part-time 0; Unknown ethnicity—full-time 2, part-time 0.

Financial Information/Assistance:

Tuition for Full-Time Study: *Doctoral:* State residents: per academic year $20,400; Nonstate residents: per academic year $20,400. Tuition is subject to change.

Financial Assistance:

First-Year Students: Fellowships and scholarships available for first year. Tuition remission given: partial.

Advanced Students: Fellowships and scholarships available for advanced students. Tuition remission given: partial.

Additional Information: Of all students currently enrolled full time, 32% benefited from one or more of the listed financial assistance programs.

Internships/Practica: The program has an exclusively affiliated internship that is a half-time over a 2-year period. The APA-accredited internship is housed at Widener University, but placements are within a 40-mile radius of the campus. 100% of 4th- and 5th-year students are placed.

Housing and Day Care: On-campus housing is available. A small amout of graduate housing is available through the university; however, there is ample housing in the immediate area surrounding Widener. On-campus day care facilities are available.

Employment of Department Graduates:

Master's Degree Graduates: Of those who graduated in the academic year 2006–2007, the following categories and numbers represent the postgraduate activities and employment of master's degree graduates: Enrolled in a postdoctoral residency/fellowship (n/a), employed in independent practice (n/a), total from the above (master's) (0).

Doctoral Degree Graduates: Of those who graduated in the academic year 2006–2007, the following categories and numbers represent the postgraduate activities and employment of doctoral degree graduates: Enrolled in a psychology doctoral program (n/a), total from the above (doctoral) (0).

Additional Information:

Orientation, Objectives, and Emphasis of Department: The PsyD program retains the basic skills and knowledge traditional to clinical psychology, such as psychodiagnostic testing and psychotherapy, while simultaneously exposing the individual to new ideas and practices in the field. The Law Psychology (JD/PsyD) program presumes that every law and court decision is in part based upon psychological assumptions about how people act and how their actions can be controlled. It is designed to train lawyer–clinical psychologists to identify and evaluate these assumptions and apply their psychological knowledge to improve the law, legal process, and legal system. Students earn a law degree from the Widener University School of Law, and a doctorate in psychology from Widener's Institute for Graduate Clinical Psychology. The

PsyD/MBA program is based on the premise that health care organizations as well as the mental health and health care fields at large are in need of well-trained leaders and advocates who integrate psychological and business–organizational knowledge.

Special Facilities or Resources: One of the hallmarks of our program is the variety of internship and practica opportunities available to students, all of which are within driving distance of the university. A corollary resource is the availability of practicing clinicians to teach in the program, a factor that provides breadth, relevance, and enrichment to the curriculum. Widener University is situated near Philadelphia and in the middle of the Eastern corridor between New York and Washington, DC. As a result, our students enjoy a rich diversity of educational resources, field experiences, and employment opportunities. Here is a place where you can enjoy big cities or the beauty of the countryside, a vast array of cultural events and historical opportunities, and all forms of sports, arts, and entertainment. It is a wonderful place to live, learn, and work.

Information for Students With Physical Disabilities: See the following Web site for more information: http://www.widener.edu/sss/sssmain.html.

Application Information:
Send to Director of Admissions, The Institute for Graduate Clinical Psychology, Widener University, One University Place, Chester, PA 19013. Application available online. URL of online application: http://www.widener.edu. Students are admitted in the Fall, application deadline December 31. *Fee:* $75.

Widener University

Law Psychology (JD/PsyD) Graduate Training Program
Institute for Graduate Clinical Psychology and School of Law
One University Place
Chester, PA 19013-5792
Telephone: (610) 499-1206
Fax: (610) 499-4625
E-mail: *aelwork@widener.edu*
Web: *http://www.widener.edu/jdpsyd*

Department Information:
1989. Director (within Institute for Graduate Clinical Psychology): Amiram Elwork, PhD. Number of faculty: total—full-time 13, part-time 15; women—full-time 5, part-time 10; total—minority—full-time 2, part-time 4; women minority—full-time 1, part-time 2.

Programs and Degrees Offered:
Listed in the following order: Program area, degree type (T if terminal Master's), number awarded 7/06–6/07. Law Psychology (JD/PsyD) Other 2.

Student Applications/Admissions:
Student Applications
Law Psychology (JD/PsyD) Other—Applications 2007–2008, 20. Total applicants accepted 2007–2008, 2. Number full-time enrolled (new admits only) 2007–2008, 2. Openings 2008–2009, 3. The median number of years required for completion of a degree in 2006–2007 were 6. The number of students enrolled full- and part-time who were dismissed or voluntarily withdrew from this program area in 2007–2008 were 0.

Admissions Requirements:
Scores: Entries appear in this order: required test or GPA, minimum score (if required), median score of students entering in 2007–2008. Doctoral Programs: GRE-V no minimum stated, 70%; GRE-Q no minimum stated, 70%; GRE-Subject (Psychology) no minimum stated, 70%; overall undergraduate GPA no minimum stated, 3.5; Doctoral program GRE-Analytic no minimum stated, 70%. LSAT required median score 70%.
Other Criteria: (importance of criteria rated low, medium, or high): GRE/MAT scores—high, research experience—low, work experience—medium, extracurricular activity—low, clinically related public service—medium, GPA—high, letters of recommendation—medium, interview—high, statement of goals and objectives—high, LSAT—high.

Student Characteristics: The following represents characteristics of students in 2007–2008 in all graduate psychology programs in the department: Female—full-time 6, part-time 0; Male—full-time 13, part-time 0; Asian/Pacific Islander—full-time 1, part-time 0; Caucasian/White—full-time 18, part-time 0; Unknown ethnicity—full-time 0, part-time 0.

Financial Information/Assistance:
Tuition for Full-Time Study: *Doctoral:* State residents: per academic year $22,500; Nonstate residents: per academic year $22,500. Tuition is subject to change.

Financial Assistance:
First-Year Students: Fellowships and scholarships available for first year. Average amount paid per academic year: $0. Average number of hours worked per week: 0. Tuition remission given: partial.
Advanced Students: Traineeships available for advanced students. Average amount paid per academic year: $0. Average number of hours worked per week: 0. Tuition remission given: partial. Fellowships and scholarships available for advanced students. Average amount paid per academic year: $0. Average number of hours worked per week: 0. Tuition remission given: partial.
Additional Information: Of all students currently enrolled full time, 80% benefited from one or more of the listed financial assistance programs.

Internships/Practica: Students are in field placements during 5 of the 6 years of training. During 2 of the first 3 years, students are assigned to clinical psychology practica. These are introductory experiences designed to acquaint the students with a variety of settings in which they can develop fundamental psychological skills in testing and assessment and psychotherapy and intervention. Fourth-year field experiences are in a legal setting (law firm, court, legal agency), where they are given an opportunity to practice their legal skills. Fifth- and 6th-year experiences are internship rotations that allow students the opportunity to sharpen their clinical and forensic psychology skills. Widener's APA-accredited integrated clinical internship with its various rotations (including forensic rotations) is highly unusual. In most programs, students participate in internships that are independent of their graduate programs. Our internship is embedded in the program. While continuing to take their coursework, students complete their internship rotations over a 2-year period at various clinical sites affiliated with Widener. This allows for better integration between coursework and practical experience and relieves the student of the inconveniences associated with finding a separate internship and/or relocating.

Housing and Day Care: On-campus housing is available. See the following Web site for more information: http://www.widener.edu. On-campus day care facilities are available.

Employment of Department Graduates:

Master's Degree Graduates: Of those who graduated in the academic year 2006–2007, the following categories and numbers represent the postgraduate activities and employment of master's degree graduates: Enrolled in a psychology doctoral program (0), enrolled in another graduate/professional program (0), enrolled in a postdoctoral residency/fellowship (n/a), employed in independent practice (n/a), employed in an academic position at a university (0), employed in an academic position at a 2-year/4-year college (0), employed in other positions at a higher education institution (0), employed in a professional position in a school system (0), employed in business or industry (0), employed in government agency (0), employed in a community mental health/counseling center (0), employed in a hospital/medical center (0), still seeking employment (0), other employment position (0), total from the above (master's) (0).

Doctoral Degree Graduates: Of those who graduated in the academic year 2006–2007, the following categories and numbers represent the postgraduate activities and employment of doctoral degree graduates: Enrolled in a psychology doctoral program (n/a), enrolled in a postdoctoral residency/fellowship (0), employed in independent practice (0), employed in an academic position at a university (0), employed in an academic position at a 2-year/4-year college (0), employed in other positions at a higher education institution (0), employed in a professional position in a school system (0), employed in business or industry (0), employed in government agency (0), employed in a community mental health/counseling center (0), employed in a hospital/medical center (0), still seeking employment (0), other employment position (0), total from the above (doctoral) (0).

Additional Information:

Orientation, Objectives, and Emphasis of Department: Widener University's Law Psychology graduate program is based on the idea that many legal issues involve underlying psychological questions. It trains graduates to combine their knowledge of psychology and law and bring fresh insights to the process of understanding, evaluating and correcting important psycholegal problems. Although a large portion of the curriculum is similar to that required of all students in the PsyD and JD programs, it includes a number of courses and requirements (e.g., dissertation) designed specifically to help students acquire an integration of psychology and law and to develop specialized skills. In addition, students are given opportunities to put their integrated skills into practice within their field placements. Students develop special expertise on many issues at the interface of law and clinical psychology and are prepared to play diverse roles in society, including lawyer, forensic psychologist, professor, consultant, administrator, policy maker, judge, legislator, etc. This 6-year program offers several benefits: (a) It allows students to pursue clinical psychology and law simultaneously; (b) it saves students the equivalent of 2 years of tuition and time; (c) it trains graduates to integrate the two fields conceptually and offers them a significant way of differentiating themselves in the job market.

Special Facilities or Resources: Widener University is situated near Philadelphia and in the middle of the eastern corridor between New York and Washington, DC. As a result, our students enjoy a rich diversity of educational resources, field experiences, and employment opportunities. Whether you enjoy big cities or beautiful scenery, cultural events and history, all forms of entertainment and sports, our location is an ideal place to live, learn, and work.

Information for Students With Physical Disabilities: See the following Web site for more information: http://www.widener.edu/.

Application Information:

Send to Law Psychology Graduate Program—Admissions, Institute for Graduate Clinical Psychology, One University Place, Chester, PA 19013-5792. Application available online. URL of online application: https://www.applyweb.com/apply/widener/indexa.html. Students are admitted in the Fall, application deadline February 1. *Fee:* $60.

Carlos Albizu University (2007 data)

San Juan Campus
Box 9023711
Old San Juan, PR 00902-3711
Telephone: (787) 725-6500
Fax: (787) 721-7187
E-mail: *galtieri@albizu.edu*
Web: *http://www.albizu.edu*

Department Information:

1972. Chancellor: Lourdes R. Garcia. EdD. Number of faculty: total—full-time 18, part-time 24; women—full-time 8, part-time 11.

Programs and Degrees Offered:

Listed in the following order: Program area, degree type (T if terminal Master's), number awarded 7/06–6/07. PsyD Program (Doctor of Psychology) 57, Clinical PhD (Doctor of Philosophy) 7, General Psychology PhD (Doctor of Philosophy) 3.

APA Accreditation: Clinical PsyD (Doctor of Psychology). Clinical PhD (Doctor of Philosophy).

Student Applications/Admissions:

Student Applications

PsyD Program (Doctor of Psychology)—Applications 2007–2008, 55. Total applicants accepted 2007–2008, 42. Number full-time enrolled (new admits only) 2007–2008, 42. Total enrolled 2007–2008 full-time, 306, part-time, 40. Openings 2008–2009, 45. The number of students enrolled full- and part-time who were dismissed or voluntarily withdrew from this program area in 2007–2008 were 2. *Clinical PhD (Doctor of Philosophy)*—Applications 2007–2008, 30. Total applicants accepted 2007–2008, 26. Number full-time enrolled (new admits only) 2007–2008, 26. Number part-time enrolled (new admits only) 2007–2008, 0. Total enrolled 2007–2008 full-time, 140, part-time, 21. Openings 2008–2009, 30. The median number of years required for completion of a degree in 2006–2007 were 8. The number of students enrolled full- and part-time who were dismissed or voluntarily withdrew from this program area in 2007–2008 were 4. *General Psychology PhD (Doctor of Philosophy)*—Applications 2007–2008, 6. Total applicants accepted 2007–2008, 2. Number full-time enrolled (new admits only) 2007–2008, 2. Number part-time enrolled (new admits only) 2007–2008, 0. Openings 2008–2009, 8. The median number of years required for completion of a degree in 2006–2007 were 7. The number of students enrolled full- and part-time who were dismissed or voluntarily withdrew from this program area in 2007–2008 were 0.

Admissions Requirements:

Scores: Entries appear in this order: required test or GPA, minimum score (if required), median score of students entering in 2007–2008. Master's Programs: overall undergraduate GPA no minimum stated. EXADEP Admissions Test for Graduate Studies in Puerto Rico. (For data collection purposes only.) Doctoral Programs: overall undergraduate GPA 3.25, 3.87. EXADEP Admissions Test for Graduate Studies in Puerto Rico. (For data collection purposes only.)

Other Criteria: (importance of criteria rated low, medium, or high): research experience—low, work experience—low, extracurricular activity—low, clinically related public service—medium, GPA—high, letters of recommendation—medium, interview—high, statement of goals and objectives—high, EXADEP Admissions Test for Graduate Studies in Puerto Rico. (For data collection purposes only.) For additional information on admission requirements, go to http://www.sju.albizu.edu.

Student Characteristics: The following represents characteristics of students in 2007–2008 in all graduate psychology programs in the department: Female—full-time 366, part-time 53; Male—full-time 80, part-time 8; African American/Black—full-time 0, part-time 0; Hispanic/Latino(a)—full-time 441, part-time 61; Asian/Pacific Islander—full-time 0, part-time 0; American Indian/Alaska Native—full-time 0, part-time 0; Caucasian/White—full-time 2, part-time 0; Multi-ethnic—full-time 3, part-time 0; Unknown ethnicity—full-time 0, part-time 0.

Financial Information/Assistance:

Tuition for Full-Time Study: *Master's:* State residents: per academic year $3,046, $250 per credit hour. *Doctoral:* State residents: per academic year $3,274, $288 per credit hour. Tuition costs vary by program. See the following Web site for updates and changes in tuition costs: http://www.sju.albizu.edu.

Financial Assistance:

First-Year Students: Fellowships and scholarships available for first year. Apply by varies.

Advanced Students: Teaching assistantships available for advanced students. Average number of hours worked per week: 10. Apply by March. Research assistantships available for advanced students. Average number of hours worked per week: 20. Apply by varies. Fellowships and scholarships available for advanced students. Apply by varies.

Additional Information: Of all students currently enrolled full time, 85% benefited from one or more of the listed financial assistance programs. Application and information available online at http://www.sju.albizu.edu.

Internships/Practica: Clinical Practicums: Complete 780 hours at the Community Mental Clinic and/or other agencies. For doctoral students: Residency requirement: Full-time residency of years is required of all doctoral students. Clinical Practicums: All students in a clinical degree program are required complete the clinical practicum at the Mental Health Services Clinic and/or designated agency. The content and sequence of practicum experiences ensure the integration of science and practice in our program. The first four sessions of practice combine clinical and research activities, and the last two sessions include solely research activities. During the first 2 years of training students dedicate 6 hours weekly to the clinical practicum and 2 hours weekly to the research practicum, spending an average of 8 hours weekly in these activities. Research practicum competencies and clinical practicum competencies are organized sequentially. The PhD in General Psychology program includes three supervised practica (for a total of 400 hours) in the areas of consulting, research, and teaching.

Housing and Day Care: No on-campus housing is available. No on-campus day care facilities are available.

Employment of Department Graduates:

Master's Degree Graduates: Of those who graduated in the academic year 2006–2007, the following categories and numbers represent the postgraduate activities and employment of master's degree graduates: Enrolled in a postdoctoral residency/fellowship (n/a), employed in independent practice (n/a), total from the above (master's) (0).

Doctoral Degree Graduates: Of those who graduated in the academic year 2006–2007, the following categories and numbers represent the postgraduate activities and employment of doctoral degree graduates: Enrolled in a psychology doctoral program (n/a), employed in independent practice (24), employed in an academic position at a university (1), employed in an academic position at a 2-year/4-year college (2), employed in other positions at a higher education institution (0), employed in a professional position in a school system (0), employed in business or industry (0), employed in government agency (0), employed in a community mental health/counseling center (11), employed in a hospital/medical center (0), still seeking employment (3), not seeking employment (2), other employment position (19), do not know (10), total from the above (doctoral) (75).

Additional Information:

Orientation, Objectives, and Emphasis of Department: The Clinical Psychology (PsyD) doctoral program is designed to train clinical psychologists with the necessary competencies to provide services to clients, families, and groups in the social system. It focalizes in a holistic perspective, dynamic and integrated that puts emphasis in sensibility toward cultural diversity. It offers a clinical training that is sequential, didactic, and experiential throughout the course work and the clinical practices offered to the community. The program is designed to prepare clinical psychologists with skills pertaining to the following areas: psychotherapy, psychodiagnosis, administration and evaluation of mental health programs, as well as to occupy job positions as supervisors, and to provide direct psychotherapeutic services and professional consulting. General objectives of the program: Develop skills in clinical interventions taking into consideration norms, values, and beliefs in the social and cultural context where the services are being provided. Develop skills in assessment taking into consideration the individual, social, cultural, group, and gender needs as well as any other needs. Develop the critical capacity of the student so that he or she can use the clinical intervention findings in an effective manner. Familiarize the student with the philosophic theoric background of the psychotherapeutic models. Develop sensibility in the students so that they take into considerations sociocultural values and the belief system of their clients when providing services. Develop skills in the clinical application of psychological assessment instruments, taking into consideration the cultural context. Provide clinical experience under the supervision of a competent supervisor with license and a doctorate degree in clinical psychology. The PhD program offers doctoral education and training in clinical psychology, having as one of its major goals the preparation of students for research scholarship and clinical practice. The program's mission emphasizes a holistic, dynamic, and integrated perspective, which is realized through a balanced and interconnected sequence of didactic offerings, research opportunities, and experiential clinical training placements where services are provided to the community. These activities are developed within a context of awareness and sensitivity toward culturally diverse constituencies, with special attention to the Puerto Rican society. The PhD Clinical psychology follows an Adapted Scholar–Practitioner Model (ASPM). The purpose of the Doctoral of Philosophy in General Psychology program is to train doctoral-level students, already licensed as psychologists in Puerto Rico, in the areas of consulting, teaching, and scientific research. The curricular sequence of the PhD in General Psychology program includes 69 credits of course work, three supervised practica (for a total of 400 hours), Qualifying Exam, and a dissertation. The program is offered only at the Puerto Rico campus. The training model is based on the development of the following specialized skills: Development of needs assessment for educational and social services organizations, program development and evaluation, preparation of remedial strategies to promote quality of programs and services, curriculum development and evaluation, research project, article presentation and publication, consultation models and strategies application, teaching strategies and styles. Training objectives upon competition of academic requirements the students must be able to develop assessment methods for educational and social services, construct and evaluate program designs, construct and evaluate a curriculum, serve as professional consultants for private and governmental organization, develop and conduct research projects, and serve as professors considering different learning styles.

Special Facilities or Resources: Community Mental Health Clinic: The purpose of the Community Mental Health Clinic (CMHC) of the San Juan Campus is to offer mental health services to the Puerto Rican community. Service offerings are designed for the specific needs of target populations and address the psychological needs that can be attended in a community clinic center. The Community Mental Health Clinic offers students a unique opportunity to receive high-quality multicultural–multilingual professional training in the areas of psychotherapy, clinical assessment, community consultation, and preventive mental health. The Carlos Albizu University is able to offer a sliding-fee scale to those clients that qualify. The Carlos Albizu University serves the mental health needs of children, adolescents, adults, elderly, and families and offers specialized services to victims of sexual abuse under the Sexual Abuse Program. Continuing Education Program: The Continuing Education Program of the PRIP is a significant resource for the fulfillment of continuing education requirements for psychologists and other mental health professionals and health service providers. The program is accredited by the American Psychological Association since 1984. The Continuing Education program is a qualified provider of continuing education credits as recognized by the Puerto Rico Licensing Boards for Psychologists, Occupational and Physical Therapists, Physicians, Nurses, and Mental Health Educators. Scientific Research Institute: The Scientific Research Institute (SRI) is a specialized research center established for the purpose of advancing the role of science in the understanding of human behavior and society. SRI is designed to provide training experiences for students, foment faculty involvement in research, develop data banks for present and future projects, and provide specialized services to the academic community and community at large. Depending upon availability of funds, scholarships are offered for students to work in research projects sponsored by SRI. SRI is committed to multidisciplinary studies and to collaborative efforts with Puerto Rican, United States, and international research centers.

Information for Students With Physical Disabilities: See the following Web site for more information: http://www.sju.albizu.edu.

Application Information:
Send to Student Affairs Office, Box 9023711, Old San Juan, San Juan, PR 00902-3711. Application available online. URL of online application: http://www.sju.albizu.edu. Students are admitted in the Fall, application deadline July 15; Winter, application deadline December 15; Summer, application deadline May 15. *Fee:* $75.

Puerto Rico, University of

Department of Psychology
College of Social Sciences
P.O. Box 23345
San Juan, PR 00931-3345
Telephone: (787) 764-0000 ext 3164, 4170
Fax: (787) 763-4599
E-mail: *psic@uprrp.edu*
Web: *http://www.psic.uprrp.edu*

Department Information:
1963. Chairperson: Dolores Miranda-Gierbolini, PhD. Number of faculty: total—full-time 25, part-time 2; women—full-time 19, part-time 1; total—minority—full-time 25, part-time 2; women minority—full-time 19, part-time 1.

Programs and Degrees Offered:
Listed in the following order: Program area, degree type (T if terminal Master's), number awarded 7/06–6/07. Clinical MA/MS (Master of Arts/Science) 3, Clinical PhD (Doctor of Philosophy) 6, Academic Research MA/MS (Master of Arts/Science) (T) 1, Academic Research PhD (Doctor of Philosophy) 3, Industrial/Organizational MA/MS (Master of Arts/Science) (T) 8, Industrial/Organizational PhD (Doctor of Philosophy) 1, Social/Community MA/MS (Master of Arts/Science) (T) 4, Social/Community PhD (Doctor of Philosophy) 7.

Student Applications/Admissions:
Student Applications
Clinical MA/MS (Master of Arts/Science)—Applications 2007–2008, 68. Total applicants accepted 2007–2008, 15. Number full-time enrolled (new admits only) 2007–2008, 14. Number part-time enrolled (new admits only) 2007–2008, 0. Openings 2008–2009, 16. The median number of years required for completion of a degree in 2006–2007 were 4. The number of students enrolled full- and part-time who were dismissed or voluntarily withdrew from this program area in 2007–2008 were 5. *Clinical PhD (Doctor of Philosophy)*—Applications 2007–2008, 0. Total applicants accepted 2007–2008, 0. Number full-time enrolled (new admits only) 2007–2008, 0. Number part-time enrolled (new admits only) 2007–2008, 0. Total enrolled 2007–2008 full-time, 53, part-time, 2. The median number of years required for completion of a degree in 2006–2007 were 9. The number of students enrolled full- and part-time who were dismissed or voluntarily withdrew from this program area in 2007–2008 were 1. *Academic Research MA/MS (Master of Arts/Science)*—Applications 2007–2008, 16. Total applicants accepted 2007–2008, 8. Number full-time enrolled (new admits only) 2007–2008, 7. Number part-time enrolled (new admits only) 2007–2008, 0. Total enrolled 2007–2008 full-time, 10, part-time, 6. Openings 2008–2009, 6. The median number of years required for completion of a degree in 2006–2007 were 5. The number of students enrolled full- and part-time who were dismissed or voluntarily withdrew from this program area in 2007–2008 were 2. *Academic Research PhD (Doctor of Philosophy)*—Applications 2007–2008, 0. Total applicants accepted 2007–2008, 0. Number full-time enrolled (new admits only) 2007–2008, 0. Number part-time enrolled (new admits only) 2007–2008, 0. Total enrolled 2007–2008 full-time, 16, part-time, 1. The median number of years required for completion of a degree in 2006–2007 were 11. The number of students enrolled full- and part-time who were dismissed or voluntarily withdrew from this program area in 2007–2008 were 2. *Industrial/Organizational MA/MS (Master of Arts/Science)*—Applications 2007–2008, 32. Total applicants accepted 2007–2008, 8. Number full-time enrolled (new admits only) 2007–2008, 7. Number part-time enrolled (new admits only) 2007–2008, 0. Total enrolled 2007–2008 full-time, 28, part-time, 2. Openings 2008–2009, 8. The median number of years required for completion of a degree in 2006–2007 were 6. The number of students enrolled full- and part-time who were dismissed or voluntarily withdrew from this program area in 2007–2008 were 2. *Industrial/Organizational PhD (Doctor of Philosophy)*—Applications 2007–2008, 0. Total applicants accepted 2007–2008, 0. Number full-time enrolled (new admits only) 2007–2008, 0. Number part-time enrolled (new admits only) 2007–2008, 0. Total enrolled 2007–2008 full-time, 11, part-time, 1. The median number of years required for completion of a degree in 2006–2007 were 14. The number of students enrolled full- and part-time who were dismissed or voluntarily withdrew from this program area in 2007–2008 were 0. *Social/Community MA/MS (Master of Arts/Science)*—Applications 2007–2008, 13. Total applicants accepted 2007–2008, 8. Number full-time enrolled (new admits only) 2007–2008, 4. Number part-time enrolled (new admits only) 2007–2008, 1. Total enrolled 2007–2008 full-time, 20, part-time, 4. Openings 2008–2009, 9. The median number of years required for completion of a degree in 2006–2007 were 6. The number of students enrolled full- and part-time who were dismissed or voluntarily withdrew from this program area in 2007–2008 were 4. *Social/Community PhD (Doctor of Philosophy)*—Applications 2007–2008, 0. Total applicants accepted 2007–2008, 0. Number full-time enrolled (new admits only) 2007–2008, 0. Number part-time enrolled (new admits only) 2007–2008, 0. Total enrolled 2007–2008 full-time, 20, part-time, 3. The median number of years required for completion of a degree in 2006–2007 were 10. The number of students enrolled full- and part-time who were dismissed or voluntarily withdrew from this program area in 2007–2008 were 2.

Admissions Requirements:
Scores: Entries appear in this order: required test or GPA, minimum score (if required), median score of students entering in 2007–2008. Master's Programs: overall undergraduate GPA

3.00, 3.70; psychology GPA 3.00, 4.00. Doctoral Programs: overall undergraduate GPA 3.00, 3.70; psychology GPA 3.00, 4.00.

Other Criteria: (importance of criteria rated low, medium, or high): research experience—medium, work experience—low, extracurricular activity—low, clinically related public service—medium, GPA—high, interview—high, statement of goals and objectives—high, EXADEP score Spanish GRE—high, undergraduate major in psychology—medium, specific undergraduate psychology courses taken—medium. Students may present GRE scores instead of the Spanish version known as EXADEP for all graduate programs. For additional information on admission requirements, go to http://psic.uprrp.edu/aplicargradu.htm.

Student Characteristics: The following represents characteristics of students in 2007–2008 in all graduate psychology programs in the department: Female—full-time 150, part-time 15; Male—full-time 44, part-time 4; Hispanic/Latino(a)—full-time 194, part-time 19; Caucasian/White—full-time 0, part-time 0; students subject to the Americans With Disabilities Act—full-time 5, part-time 0; Unknown ethnicity—full-time 0, part-time 0; International students who hold an F-1 or J-1 Visa—full-time 1, part-time 0.

Financial Information/Assistance:

Tuition for Full-Time Study: *Master's:* State residents: per academic year $1,952, $122 per credit hour; Nonstate residents: per academic year $5,664, $354 per credit hour. *Doctoral:* State residents: per academic year $1,952, $122 per credit hour; Nonstate residents: per academic year $5,664, $354 per credit hour. Tuition is subject to change. See the following Web site for updates and changes in tuition costs: http://www.graduados.uprrp.edu/admisiones/#.

Financial Assistance:

First-Year Students: Teaching assistantships available for first year. Average amount paid per academic year: $8,000. Average number of hours worked per week: 18. Tuition remission given: full. Research assistantships available for first year. Average amount paid per academic year: $12,000. Average number of hours worked per week: 18. Tuition remission given: full. Fellowships and scholarships available for first year. Average amount paid per academic year: $1,000. Average number of hours worked per week: 0. Tuition remission given: full.

Advanced Students: Teaching assistantships available for advanced students. Average amount paid per academic year: $10,000. Average number of hours worked per week: 18. Tuition remission given: full. Research assistantships available for advanced students. Average amount paid per academic year: $12,000. Average number of hours worked per week: 18. Tuition remission given: full. Fellowships and scholarships available for advanced students. Average amount paid per academic year: $10,000. Average number of hours worked per week: 0. Apply by March 31.

Additional Information: Of all students currently enrolled full time, 20% benefited from one or more of the listed financial assistance programs. Application and information available online at http://graduados.uprrp.edu/asuntos_estudiantiles/becas.htm.

Internships/Practica: Doctoral Degree (PhD Clinical): For those doctoral students for whom a professional internship was required in this program prior to graduation, (10) students applied for an internship in 2006–2007, with (10) students obtaining an internship. Of those students who obtained an internship, (10) were paid internships. Of those students who obtained an internship, (0) students placed in APA/CPA-accredited internships, (0) students placed in internships not APA/CPA-accredited, but listed with the Association of Psychology Postdoctoral and Internship Centers (APPIC), (0) students placed in internships conforming to guidelines of the Council of Directors of School Psychology Programs (CDSPP), (10) students placed in internships that were not APA/CPA-accredited, APPIC or CDSPP listed. All programs require at least two semesters of practica; a 2,000-hour internship is also required to complete the clinical psychology specialty. The settings for practica and internships include the University Center for Psychological Services and Research, public and private mental health clinics and hospitals, community-based organizations, government agencies, private businesses, educational institutions, and other settings according to the specialty. Some internship sites are located outside of Puerto Rico, in Florida, New York, and other continetal U.S. locations. In their practica, students perform tasks that include clinical, organizational, and community services—teaching undergraduate psychology courses, coordinating community interventions, researching problems such as learning disabilities, eating disorders, violence, and depression; promoting tolerance in ethnically diverse communities; computer-based teaching; behavioral effects of brain damage; ecological issues of urban areas, homelessness, and social problems in Caribbean nations; standardizing and developing culturally relevant testing instruments, public policy issues, and others.

Housing and Day Care: On-campus housing is available. See the following Web site for more information: http://www.graduados.uprrp.edu/asuntos_estudiantiles/vivienda.htm. On-campus day care facilities are available. See the following Web site for more information: http://www.graduados.uprrp.edu/asuntos_estudiantiles/cuido_hijos.htm.

Employment of Department Graduates:

Master's Degree Graduates: Of those who graduated in the academic year 2006–2007, the following categories and numbers represent the postgraduate activities and employment of master's degree graduates: Enrolled in a psychology doctoral program (8), enrolled in another graduate/professional program (1), enrolled in a postdoctoral residency/fellowship (n/a), employed in independent practice (n/a), do not know (7), total from the above (master's) (16).

Doctoral Degree Graduates: Of those who graduated in the academic year 2006–2007, the following categories and numbers represent the postgraduate activities and employment of doctoral degree graduates: Enrolled in a psychology doctoral program (n/a), employed in independent practice (1), employed in an academic position at a university (6), employed in a professional position in a school system (1), employed in a hospital/medical center (1), still seeking employment (2), do not know (7), total from the above (doctoral) (18).

Additional Information:

Orientation, Objectives, and Emphasis of Department: The Psychology Graduate Program of the University of Puerto Rico was established in 1963, when the Master's degree in Psychology was offered for the first time in Puerto Rico. In 1986, the doctoral program was established, with four specialties: Clinical, Social/ Community, Academic Research and Industrial/Organizational. The program adheres to the scientist–practitioner model and its vision is to be the foremost graduate program in psychology in the Caribbean. The program's objectives are (a) to develop a critical approach to the study of psychology and the capacity to contribute to the understanding of Puerto Ricans and others; (b) to develop psychologists who are competent researchers, with profound knowledge of Puerto Rican reality, who may increase knowledge, for the psychological understanding of behavior in general and Puerto Rican society in particular; (c) to prepare competent professionals who respond conscientiously and with social responsibility to the needs of psychological services for individuals, families, groups, organizations, and communities; (d) to reinforce the development of undergraduate programs through a constant exchange of ideas and activities with graduate students; (e) to provide the opportunity to prepare and improve professional competencies in psychology professors. The program's curriculum provides opportunities to learn and apply diverse theoretical orientations and research modalities.

Special Facilities or Resources: Founded in 1986 as part of the Department of Psychology Graduate Program, the University Center for Psychological Services and Research (CUSEP, for its Spanish acronym) is intended to facilitate student and faculty research as well as training and psychological services. CUSEP offers a unique context in which faculty and students can integrate professional practice, theory, and research. The research unit, one of the principal components of the Center, promotes, supports, and develops quality biopsychosocial studies by training students and developing the faculty members' research skills. In this way, this unit aims to generate and extend knowledge, and form responsible researchers who will help satisfy the needs of the Puerto Rican population. The Center for Urban Action, Community and Economical Development (CAUCE, for its initials in Spanish) was established by the University of Puerto Rico to promote revitalization of the urban communities of Rio Piedras, which surround the UPR Campus. Psychology Department faculty and students share projects and interventions with other departments, such as Social Work and Rehabilitation Counseling. Social and community workshops are carried out to support grassroots organizations in communities in the San Juan Metropolitan area.

Information for Students With Physical Disabilities: See the following Web site for more information: http://www.graduados.uprrp.edu/asuntos_estudiantiles/personas_con_impedimentos.

Application Information:

Send to Department of Psychology, University of Puerto Rico, Río Piedras Campus, P.O. Box 23345, San Juan, PR 00931-3345. Application available online. URL of online application: https://www.app.applyyourself.com/?id=upr-grad. Students are admitted in the Fall, application deadline January 17. *Fee:* $20.

Brown University
Psychology
Graduate School
89 Waterman Street
Providence, RI 02912
Telephone: (401) 863-2727
Fax: (401) 863-1300
E-mail: *rebecca_burwell@brown.edu*
Web: *http://www.brown.edu/Departments/Psychology/*

Department Information:

1892. Chairperson: William Heindel. Number of faculty: total—full-time 4, part-time 1; women—full-time 4, part-time 1; women minority—part-time 1.

Programs and Degrees Offered:

Listed in the following order: Program area, degree type (T if terminal Master's), number awarded 7/06–6/07. Experimental Psychology PhD (Doctor of Philosophy) 4, Track: Behavioral Neuroscience PhD (Doctor of Philosophy), Track: Cognitive Processes PhD (Doctor of Philosophy), Track: Sensation and Perception PhD (Doctor of Philosophy), Track: Social Psychology PhD (Doctor of Philosophy).

Student Applications/Admissions:

Student Applications

Experimental Psychology PhD (Doctor of Philosophy)—Applications 2007–2008, 76. Total applicants accepted 2007–2008, 6. Number full-time enrolled (new admits only) 2007–2008, 4. Total enrolled 2007–2008 full-time, 14. Openings 2008–2009, 6. The median number of years required for completion of a degree in 2006–2007 were 5. The number of students enrolled full- and part-time who were dismissed or voluntarily withdrew from this program area in 2007–2008 were 0. *Track: Behavioral Neuroscience PhD (Doctor of Philosophy); Track: Cognitive Processes PhD (Doctor of Philosophy); Track: Sensation and Perception PhD (Doctor of Philosophy); Track: Social Psychology PhD (Doctor of Philosophy).*

Admissions Requirements:

Scores: Entries appear in this order: required test or GPA, minimum score (if required), median score of students entering in 2007–2008. Master's Programs: Brown University does not have a terminal master's program in psychology. Doctoral Programs: GRE-V no minimum stated; GRE-Q no minimum stated; overall undergraduate GPA no minimum stated; last 2 years GPA no minimum stated; psychology GPA no minimum stated.

Other Criteria: (importance of criteria rated low, medium, or high): GRE/MAT scores—medium, research experience—high, work experience—low, extracurricular activity—low, GPA—high, letters of recommendation—high, interview—medium, statement of goals and objectives—high. For additional information on admission requirements, go to http://www.brown.edu/Departments/Psychology/.

Student Characteristics: The following represents characteristics of students in 2007–2008 in all graduate psychology programs in the department: Female—full-time 8, part-time 0; Male—full-time 6, part-time 0; African American/Black—full-time 0, part-time 0; Hispanic/Latino(a)—full-time 1, part-time 0; Asian/Pacific Islander—full-time 1, part-time 0; American Indian/Alaska Native—full-time 0, part-time 0; Caucasian/White—full-time 10, part-time 0; Multi-ethnic—full-time 0, part-time 0; students subject to the Americans With Disabilities Act—full-time 0, part-time 0; Unknown ethnicity—full-time 0, part-time 0; International students who hold an F-1 or J-1 Visa—full-time 2, part-time 0.

Financial Information/Assistance:

Tuition for Full-Time Study: *Doctoral:* State residents: per academic year $33,888; Nonstate residents: per academic year $33,888. Tuition is subject to change.

Financial Assistance:

First-Year Students: Teaching assistantships available for first year. Average amount paid per academic year: $21,500. Apply by January 15. Tuition remission given: full. Research assistantships available for first year. Average amount paid per academic year: $21,500. Apply by January 15. Tuition remission given: full. Fellowships and scholarships available for first year. Average amount paid per academic year: $21,500. Apply by January 15. Tuition remission given: full.

Advanced Students: Teaching assistantships available for advanced students. Average amount paid per academic year: $20,500. Apply by January 15. Tuition remission given: full. Research assistantships available for advanced students. Average amount paid per academic year: $20,500. Apply by January 15. Tuition remission given: full. Fellowships and scholarships available for advanced students. Average amount paid per academic year: $20,500. Apply by January 15. Tuition remission given: full.

Additional Information: Of all students currently enrolled full time, 100% benefited from one or more of the listed financial assistance programs. Application and information included in graduate application form.

Internships/Practica: No information provided.

Housing and Day Care: On-campus housing is available. See the following Web site for more information: http://www.brown.edu/Administration/ResLife/. On-campus day care facilities are available. See the following Web site for more information: http://www.brown.edu/Administration/George_Street_Journal/vol24/24GSJ05f.html.

Employment of Department Graduates:

Master's Degree Graduates: Of those who graduated in the academic year 2006–2007, the following categories and numbers represent the postgraduate activities and employment of master's degree graduates: Enrolled in another graduate/professional program (0), enrolled in a postdoctoral residency/fellowship (n/a), employed in independent practice (n/a), total from the above (master's) (0).

Doctoral Degree Graduates: Of those who graduated in the academic year 2006–2007, the following categories and numbers represent the postgraduate activities and employment of doctoral degree graduates: Enrolled in a psychology doctoral program (n/a), total from the above (doctoral) (0).

Additional Information:

Orientation, Objectives, and Emphasis of Department: The graduate program in the Department of Psychology is designed to educate and train scientists and scholars who will make contributions to society through their research and teaching. Students generally complete the PhD in 5 years. Financial support including a stipend and tuition is guaranteed for 5 years. Funding is also available after the 5th year for students in good standing. PhDs in Psychology from Brown are prepared for a range of scientific careers in both academic and applied settings. The graduate program in Psychology is designed for candidates seeking the PhD degree. Some students also elect to take a master's degree as a step toward the PhD, but students are not accepted for master's-level work only. Graduate training in Psychology is part of a close, collaborative relationship between the student, the faculty advisor, and the student's graduate committee. Decisions about specific course work, research training, and teaching responsibilities are based more on the student's research interests and goals than on rigid, predefined programs of study. In this way, students can develop interdisciplinary curricula that take advantage of the collective strengths of Brown in the study of brain, mind, and behavior. Although students have considerable flexibility in designing their program of study, students should be aware of the major substantive areas within the department. Degrees in psychology are currently offered with specializations in behavioral neuroscience, sensation and perception, cognitive processes, and social and personality.

Special Facilities or Resources: The Walter S. Hunter Laboratory houses most facilities for research and teaching in psychology. It includes laboratory facilitities for research in behavioral and cognitive neuroscience, sensation and perception, behavior and cognition, and social psychology. There are also teaching laboratories for introductory and advanced courses that have computers and specialized equipment. The Hunter Laboratory is conveniently located near the center of the Brown campus, and it is close to the buildings housing the Department of Cognitive and Linguistic Sciences, the Department of Neuroscience, and the Department of Ecology and Evolutionary Biology. Graduate students in psychology often enroll in courses in other life sciences, and also in courses in Applied Mathematics and Computer Science.

Information for Students With Physical Disabilities: See the following Web site for more information: http://www.brown.edu/Student_Services/Office_of_Student_Life/dss/.

Application Information:

Preferred method of application is online. If not possible, applications can be sent to Brown University, Graduate School, 47 George Street, Box 1867, Providence, RI 02912; (401) 863-2600. Application available online. URL of online application: http://www.brown.edu/Divisions/Graduate_School/admissions/. Students are admitted in the Winter, application deadline January 6. *Fee:* $70.

Rhode Island College

Psychology
Rhode Island College
600 Mount Pleasant Avenue
Providence, RI 02908
Telephone: (401) 456-8015
Fax: (401) 456-8751
E-mail: *psychgradprgm@ric.edu*
Web: *http://www.ric.edu/academics/grad_gen.html*

Department Information:

Director, Graduate Studies in Psychology: Christine A. Marco, PhD. Number of faculty: total—full-time 17, part-time 1; women—full-time 8, part-time 1; total—minority—full-time 1; women minority—full-time 1; faculty subject to the Americans With Disabilities Act 3.

Programs and Degrees Offered:

Listed in the following order: Program area, degree type (T if terminal Master's), number awarded 7/06–6/07. Psychology MA/MS (Master of Arts/Science) (T) 6.

Student Applications/Admissions:

Student Applications

Psychology MA/MS (Master of Arts/Science)—Applications 2007–2008, 13. Total applicants accepted 2007–2008, 11. Number full-time enrolled (new admits only) 2007–2008, 2. Number part-time enrolled (new admits only) 2007–2008, 4. Total enrolled 2007–2008 full-time, 3, part-time, 11. The median number of years required for completion of a degree in 2006–2007 were 3.

Admissions Requirements:

Scores: Entries appear in this order: required test or GPA, minimum score (if required), median score of students entering in 2007–2008. Master's Programs: GRE-V no minimum stated; GRE-Q no minimum stated; MAT no minimum stated; overall undergraduate GPA 3.0; psychology GPA 3.0. Scores are required from either the GRE or MAT.

Other Criteria: (importance of criteria rated low, medium, or high): GRE/MAT scores—high, research experience—high, GPA—high, letters of recommendation—high, statement of goals and objectives—high, undergraduate major in psychology—high, specific undergraduate psychology courses taken—high. An interview may be required. For additional information on admission requirements, go to http://www.ric.edu/facultyArtsSciences/graduate_requirements.php.

Student Characteristics: The following represents characteristics of students in 2007–2008 in all graduate psychology programs in the department: Female—full-time 1, part-time 10; Male—full-time 2, part-time 1; Caucasian/White—full-time 0, part-time 0; Unknown ethnicity—full-time 0, part-time 0.

Financial Information/Assistance:

Tuition for Full-Time Study: *Master's:* State residents: $276 per credit hour; Nonstate residents: $580 per credit hour. Tuition is subject to change. Additional fees are assessed to students beyond the costs of tuition. See the following Web site for updates and changes in tuition costs: http://www.ric.edu/facultyArtsSciences/graduate_requirements.php.

Financial Assistance:

First-Year Students: Teaching assistantships available for first year. Average amount paid per academic year: $3,500. Apply by April 1. Tuition remission given: full. Fellowships and scholarships available for first year. Average amount paid per academic year: $1,000. Apply by April 1.

Advanced Students: Teaching assistantships available for advanced students. Average amount paid per academic year: $3,500. Apply by April 1. Tuition remission given: full.

Additional Information: Of all students currently enrolled full time, 5% benefited from one or more of the listed financial assistance programs. Application and information available online at http://www.ric.edu/facultyArtsSciences/graduate_requirements.php.

Internships/Practica: No information provided.

Housing and Day Care: No on-campus housing is available. On-campus day care facilities are available. A cooperative preschool is available. Contact Dr. Laupa at mlaupa@ric.edu.

Employment of Department Graduates:

Master's Degree Graduates: Of those who graduated in the academic year 2006–2007, the following categories and numbers represent the postgraduate activities and employment of master's degree graduates: Enrolled in a postdoctoral residency/fellowship (n/a), employed in independent practice (n/a), total from the above (master's) (0).

Doctoral Degree Graduates: Of those who graduated in the academic year 2006–2007, the following categories and numbers represent the postgraduate activities and employment of doctoral degree graduates: Enrolled in a psychology doctoral program (n/a), total from the above (doctoral) (0).

Additional Information:

Orientation, Objectives, and Emphasis of Department: The MA program in psychology at Rhode Island College provides a basic graduate education in psychology with a core curriculum in research methods and statistics, and the main content areas of personality, cognitive, developmental, and social psychology. The MA in psychology prepares students for doctoral study and has applications for careers in such areas as business, education, and human services.

Information for Students With Physical Disabilities: See the following Web site for more information: http://www.ric.edu/disabilityservices/.

Application Information:

Send to Graduate Program Admissions, c/o Dean of the Faculty of Arts and Sciences, 150 Gaige Hall, Rhode Island College, 600 Mount Pleasant Avenue, Providence, RI 02908. Application available online. URL of online application: http://www.ric.edu/facultyArtsSciences/graduate_requirements.php. Students are admitted in the Fall, application deadline April 1; Spring, application deadline November 1; programs have rolling admissions. Rolling admissions are available on a space-available basis. *Fee:* $50.

Rhode Island, University of, Chafee Social Sciences Center

Department of Psychology
Arts and Sciences
Room 313 Chafee Building
10 Chafee Road
Kingston, RI 02881
Telephone: (401) 874-2193
Fax: (401) 874-2157
E-mail: *morokoff@uri.edu*
Web: *http://www.uri.edu/artsci/psy*

Department Information:

1961. Chairperson: Patricia J. Morokoff. Number of faculty: total—full-time 13; women—full-time 13; ; women minority—full-time 1.

Programs and Degrees Offered:

Listed in the following order: Program area, degree type (T if terminal Master's), number awarded 7/06–6/07. School Psychology MA/MS (Master of Arts/Science) (T) 2, Clinical Psychology PhD (Doctor of Philosophy) 14, School Psychology PhD (Doctor of Philosophy) 7, Behavioral Science PhD (Doctor of Philosophy) 3.

APA Accreditation: Clinical PhD (Doctor of Philosophy). On Probation PhD (Doctor of Philosophy).

Student Applications/Admissions:

Student Applications

School Psychology MA/MS (Master of Arts/Science)—Applications 2007–2008, 33. Total applicants accepted 2007–2008, 9. Number full-time enrolled (new admits only) 2007–2008, 6. Number part-time enrolled (new admits only) 2007–2008, 0. Openings 2008–2009, 5. The median number of years required for completion of a degree in 2006–2007 were 3. The number of students enrolled full- and part-time who were dismissed or voluntarily withdrew from this program area in 2007–2008 were 0. *Clinical Psychology PhD (Doctor of Philosophy)*—Applications 2007–2008, 248. Total applicants accepted 2007–2008, 8. Number full-time enrolled (new admits only) 2007–2008, 7. Number part-time enrolled (new admits only) 2007–2008, 0. Openings 2008–2009, 7. The median number of years required for completion of a degree in 2006–2007 were 6. The number of students enrolled full- and part-time who were dismissed or voluntarily withdrew from this program area in 2007–2008 were 1. *School Psychology PhD (Doctor of Philosophy)*—Applications 2007–2008, 27. Total applicants accepted 2007–2008, 11. Number full-time enrolled (new admits only) 2007–2008, 4. Number part-time enrolled (new admits only) 2007–2008, 0. Openings 2008–2009, 7. The median number of years required for completion of a degree in 2006–2007 were 5. The number of students enrolled full- and part-time who were dismissed or voluntarily withdrew from this program area in 2007–2008 were 0. *Behavioral Science PhD (Doctor of Philosophy)*—Applications 2007–2008, 24. Total applicants accepted 2007–2008, 12. Number full-time enrolled (new admits only) 2007–2008, 5. Number part-time enrolled (new admits only) 2007–2008, 0. Openings 2008–2009, 6. The median number of years required for completion of a degree in 2006–2007 were 5. The number of students enrolled full- and part-time who were dismissed or voluntarily withdrew from this program area in 2007–2008 were 1.

Admissions Requirements:

Scores: Entries appear in this order: required test or GPA, minimum score (if required), median score of students entering in 2007–2008. Doctoral Programs: GRE-V no minimum stated; GRE-Q no minimum stated; overall undergraduate GPA 3.0. Behavioral Science Program: We recommend a minimum V+Q of 1100. Clinical Program: For GRE we look at V and Q scores only and there is no minimum. There is no required minimum GPA. School Program: We recommend a minimum of 1100 (MS) and 1200 (PhD) for two best GRE scores.

Other Criteria: (importance of criteria rated low, medium, or high): GRE/MAT scores—medium, research experience—medium, work experience—medium, extracurricular activity—low, clinically related public service—medium, GPA—medium, letters of recommendation—high, interview—high, statement of goals and objectives—high. Importance of criteria varies by program. Behavioral Science: High emphasis on research interest and experience; no required interview; we also look at GPA, GRE, focus and quality of personal statement, teaching experience, multicultural interests, reference letters, and program–applicant fit. Clinical Program: Factors we look at are GRE, GPA, program–applicant match, research experience, clinical experience, life experience, letters of recommendation, and overall evaluation. Interview required. School Program: Academic aptitude (GRE+ GPA), quality of personal statement, research and applied experience, letters of recommendation, fit between applicant goals and program offerings. For additional information on admission requirements, go to http://www.uri.edu/artsci/psy.

Student Characteristics: The following represents characteristics of students in 2007–2008 in all graduate psychology programs in the department: Female—full-time 80, part-time 0; Male—full-time 33, part-time 0; African American/Black—full-time 5, part-time 0; Hispanic/Latino(a)—full-time 7, part-time 0; Asian/Pacific Islander—full-time 11, part-time 0; American Indian/Alaska Native—full-time 2, part-time 0; Caucasian/White—full-time 88, part-time 0; Multi-ethnic—full-time 0, part-time 0; students subject to the Americans With Disabilities Act—full-time 1, part-time 0; Unknown ethnicity—full-time 0, part-time 0; International students who hold an F-1 or J-1 Visa—full-time 3, part-time 0.

Financial Information/Assistance:

Tuition for Full-Time Study: *Master's:* State residents: per academic year $8,678, $420 per credit hour; Nonstate residents: per academic year $24,776, $1,270 per credit hour. *Doctoral:* State residents: per academic year $8,678, $420 per credit hour; Nonstate residents: per academic year $24,776, $1,270 per credit hour. Tuition is subject to change. Additional fees are assessed to students beyond the costs of tuition for the following: health, student services, accident/sick insurance, one-time registration. See the following Web site for updates and changes in tuition costs: http://www.uri.edu/es/acadinfo/acadyear/tuition.html.

Financial Assistance:

First-Year Students: Teaching assistantships available for first year. Average amount paid per academic year: $12,544. Average number of hours worked per week: 20. Apply by March 16. Tuition remission given: full. Research assistantships available for first year. Average amount paid per academic year: $12,544. Average number of hours worked per week: 20. Apply by varies. Tuition remission given: full. Fellowships and scholarships available for first year. Average amount paid per academic year: $12,544. Average number of hours worked per week: 0. Apply by February 21. Tuition remission given: full.

Advanced Students: Teaching assistantships available for advanced students. Average amount paid per academic year: $13,000. Average number of hours worked per week: 20. Apply by March 16. Tuition remission given: full. Research assistantships available for advanced students. Average amount paid per academic year: $13,000. Average number of hours worked per week: 20. Apply by varies. Tuition remission given: full. Fellowships and scholarships available for advanced students. Average amount paid per academic year: $13,000. Average number of hours worked per week: 0. Apply by February 21. Tuition remission given: full.

Additional Information: Of all students currently enrolled full time, 60% benefited from one or more of the listed financial assistance programs. Application and information available online at http://www.uri.edu/artsci/psy.

Internships/Practica: Master's Degree (MA/MS School Psychology (specialist level, MS)): An internship experience such as a final research project or "capstone" experience is required of graduates. Doctoral Degree (PhD Clinical Psychology): For those doctoral students for whom a professional internship was required in this program prior to graduation, (4) students applied for an internship in 2006–2007, with (4) students obtaining an internship. Of those students who obtained an internship, (4) were paid internships. Of those students who obtained an internship, (4) students placed in APA/CPA-accredited internships, (0) students placed in internships not APA/CPA-accredited, but listed with the Association of Psychology Postdoctoral and Internship Centers (APPIC), (0) students placed in internships conforming to guidelines of the Council of Directors of School Psychology Programs (CDSPP), (0) students placed in internships that were not APA/CPA-accredited, APPIC or CDSPP listed. Doctoral Degree (PhD School Psychology): For those doctoral students for whom a professional internship was required in this program prior to graduation, (3) students applied for an internship in 2006–2007, with (3) students obtaining an internship. Of those students who obtained an internship, (3) were paid internships. Of those students who obtained an internship, (1) student placed in APA/CPA-accredited internships, (0) students placed in internships not APA/CPA-accredited, but listed with the Association of Psychology Postdoctoral and Internship Centers (APPIC), (2) students placed in internships conforming to guidelines of the Council of Directors of School Psychology Programs (CDSPP), (0) students placed in internships that were not APA/CPA-accredited, APPIC or CDSPP listed. The Department has an excellent record of placing Clinical and School students in high-quality approved internships for the later stages of doctoral training. Many graduates are invited to postdoctoral positions. The department's rich network of contacts in southern New England also provides placement opportunities for externship practicum experience earlier in a student's program, and there are off-campus research practicum opportunities as well.

Housing and Day Care: On-campus housing for graduate students is available at the Graduate Student Village, an apartment complex adjacent to the campus. Contact (401) 874-5390 or (401) 874-2232 or at the University Web site: http://www.uri.edu (see link for housing). On-campus day care facilities are available. Child care is available through a cooperative day care in the complex or with the University Child Development Center (space is limited). Please call (401) 874-2758 or see the following Web site for more information: http://www.uri.edu.

Employment of Department Graduates:

Master's Degree Graduates: Of those who graduated in the academic year 2006–2007, the following categories and numbers represent the postgraduate activities and employment of master's degree graduates: Enrolled in a psychology doctoral program (0), enrolled in another graduate/professional program (0), enrolled in a postdoctoral residency/fellowship (n/a), employed in independent practice (n/a), employed in an academic position at a university (0), employed in an academic position at a 2-year/4-year college (0), employed in other positions at a higher education institution (0), employed in a professional position in a school system (2), employed in business or industry (0), employed in government agency (0), employed in a community mental health/counseling center (0), employed in a hospital/medical center (0), still seeking employment (0), not seeking employment (0), other employment position (0), do not know (0), total from the above (master's) (2).

Doctoral Degree Graduates: Of those who graduated in the academic year 2006–2007, the following categories and numbers represent the postgraduate activities and employment of doctoral degree graduates: Enrolled in a psychology doctoral program (n/a), enrolled in another graduate/professional program (0), enrolled in a postdoctoral residency/fellowship (8), employed in independent practice (3), employed in an academic position at a university (2), employed in an academic position at a 2-year/4-year college (0), employed in other positions at a higher education institution (1), employed in a professional position in a school system (5), employed in business or industry (0), employed in government agency (0), employed in a community mental health/counseling center (1), employed in a hospital/medical center (2), still seeking employment (0), not seeking employment (0), other employment position (0), do not know (1), total from the above (doctoral) (23).

Additional Information:

Orientation, Objectives, and Emphasis of Department: The URI Psychology Department has a strong scientist–practitioner orientation in its Clinical and School Psychology programs, and an applied quantitative emphasis in its Behavioral Science program. There is a lively interaction among the programs, which is an especially attractive feature of the department. The research and professional interests of the faculty fall into these interest areas: (a) health psychology; (b) research methodology; (c) gender, diversity, and multicultural research; (d) family, child, and community research; (e) neuropsychology; (f) clinical psychology practice; and (g) child and school psychology practice. Graduates of our programs have developed diverse careers in academia, government service, private industry, the nonprofit sector, and private consulting and practice.

Special Facilities or Resources: The department operates an on-campus training facility, the Psychological Consultation Center, where students train under direct faculty supervision for professional practice service roles with individual clients, families, and children. The department is closely allied with the Cancer Prevention Research Center, one of the nation's leading centers for behavioral health promotion and disease prevention. Students also participate in research and training activities with the department's Community Research and Services Team, the URI Family Resource Partnership, the Feinstein Hunger Center, as well as with several training partnerships with medical centers and community mental health service agencies.

Information for Students With Physical Disabilities: See the following Web site for more information: http://www.uri.edu/disability/services/.

Application Information:

Send to Admissions/Clinical, Admissions/School, or Admissions/Behavioral Science, Department of Psychology, 10 Chafee Road, 313 Chafee Building, Kingston, RI 02881. Application available online. URL of online application: http://www.uri.edu/artsci/psy. Students are admitted in the Fall, application deadline see below. Deadlines: Clinical, December 15; School, January 15; Behavioral, Science January 20. *Fee:* $50.

Roger Williams University

Department of Psychology
Arts and Sciences
One Old Ferry Road
Bristol, RI 02809-2921
Telephone: (401) 254-3509
Fax: (401) 254-3286
E-mail: *dwhitworth@rwu.edu*
Web: *http://www.rwu.edu*

Department Information:

1969. Chairperson: Don Whitworth, PhD. Number of faculty: total—full-time 12, part-time 11; women—full-time 6, part-time 7; total—minority—full-time 3, part-time 2; women minority—full-time 1, part-time 1.

Programs and Degrees Offered:

Listed in the following order: Program area, degree type (T if terminal Master's), number awarded 7/06–6/07. Forensic Psychology MA/MS (Master of Arts/Science) (T).

Student Applications/Admissions:

Student Applications

Forensic Psychology MA/MS (Master of Arts/Science)—Applications 2007–2008, 46. Total applicants accepted 2007–2008, 18. Number full-time enrolled (new admits only) 2007–2008, 16. Number part-time enrolled (new admits only) 2007–2008, 0. Openings 2008–2009, 20. The number of students enrolled full- and part-time who were dismissed or voluntarily withdrew from this program area in 2007–2008 were 0.

Admissions Requirements:

Scores: Entries appear in this order: required test or GPA, minimum score (if required), median score of students entering in 2007–2008. Master's Programs: GRE-V 500; GRE-Q 500; overall undergraduate GPA 3.0; last 2 years GPA 3.2; psychology GPA 3.0.

Other Criteria: (importance of criteria rated low, medium, or high): GRE/MAT scores—high, research experience—high, work experience—medium, extracurricular activity—low, clinically related public service—medium, GPA—high, letters of recommendation—high, statement of goals and objectives—high, specific undergraduate psychology courses taken—high.

Student Characteristics: The following represents characteristics of students in 2007–2008 in all graduate psychology programs in the department: Female—full-time 20, part-time 0; Male—full-time 10, part-time 0; Hispanic/Latino(a)—full-time 1, part-time 0; Caucasian/White—full-time 26, part-time 0; Unknown ethnicity—full-time 3, part-time 0.

Financial Information/Assistance:

Tuition for Full-Time Study: *Master's:* State residents: per academic year $14,400, $600 per credit hour; Nonstate residents: per academic year $14,400, $600 per credit hour. Tuition is subject to change. See the following Web site for updates and changes in tuition costs: http://www.rwu.edu/Administration/Bursar/Graduate+Tuition+and+Fees.htm.

Financial Assistance:

First-Year Students: Research assistantships available for first year. Average amount paid per academic year: $1,000. Apply by March 15. Fellowships and scholarships available for first year. Average amount paid per academic year: $1,500. Apply by March 15.

Advanced Students: Research assistantships available for advanced students. Average amount paid per academic year: $1,000. Fellowships and scholarships available for advanced students. Average amount paid per academic year: $1,500.

Additional Information: Of all students currently enrolled full time, 70% benefited from one or more of the listed financial assistance programs. Application and information available online at http://www.rwu.edu/admission/financialaid/.

Internships/Practica: The clincial training program for the Master's of Arts in Forensic Psychology at Roger Williams University offers a wide range of practicum placement sites in Massachusetts and Rhode Island with opportunities to clinically work with a diversity of forensic populations. We currently have practicum placements within adult and juvenile correctional settings, adult inpatient forensic hospitals and state hospitals, juvenile court clinics, juvenile treatment programs, state and federal correctional programs for the evaluation and treatment of adult sex offenders, community mental health programs, and outpatient substance abuse programs. There are also a few research practicum placements available. Students receive comprehensive training and clinical supervision onsite from practicing forensic psychologists and forensic mental health practitioners in the assessment and treatment of forensic mental health patients and clients. The focus of the clinical practicum placements is to provide the student with an opportunity to apply clinical skills and techniques learned in clinical course work. Students are encouraged to examine case studies, training issues, ethical dilemmas, and conflicts within their continued course work on campus. The practicum placements function as a vital place for students to form professional relationships in the field and to network with allied forensic mental health professionals, a key to later opportunities for employment in the forensic mental health field. Practicum placements also provide a valueable enhancement of a student's application for continued graduate education toward a doctorate in psychology.

Housing and Day Care: On-campus housing is available. See the following Web site for more information: http://www.rwu.edu/studentlife/residencelife/universityhousing/communities/anchorage apartments.htm. No on-campus day care facilities are available.

Employment of Department Graduates:

Master's Degree Graduates: Of those who graduated in the academic year 2006–2007, the following categories and numbers represent the postgraduate activities and employment of master's degree graduates: Enrolled in a psychology doctoral program (5), enrolled in a postdoctoral residency/fellowship (n/a), employed in independent practice (n/a), employed in a community mental health/counseling center (3), employed in a hospital/medical center (1), total from the above (master's) (9).

Doctoral Degree Graduates: Of those who graduated in the academic year 2006–2007, the following categories and numbers represent the postgraduate activities and employment of doctoral degree graduates: Enrolled in a psychology doctoral program (n/a), total from the above (doctoral) (0).

Additional Information:

Orientation, Objectives, and Emphasis of Department: The Psychology Department strives to provide assessment and treatment skills for students interested in employment in a forensic setting or further training at the doctoral level. Faculty members work closely with students to help them develop an understanding and appreciation of the role of psychologists in legal proceedings and the law. Students are prepared to apply these skills to the problems of community and of the larger society. The department stresses tolerance for the views of others and an appreciation of the value of diversity. Other departmental objectives include preparing students to evaluate published research and think critically about their own ideas and the ideas of others.

Information for Students With Physical Disabilities: See the following Web site for more information: http://www.rwu.edu.

Application Information:

Send to Suzanne Faubl, Director of Graduate Admission, Office of Graduate Admission, One Old Ferry Road, Bristol, RI 02809. Application available online. URL of online application: http://www.rwu.edu/admission/graduate/. Students are admitted in the Fall, application deadline March 15. *Fee:* $50.

Citadel, The

Department of Psychology
171 Moultrie Street
Charleston, SC 29409
Telephone: (843) 953-5320
Fax: (843) 953-6797
E-mail: *steve.nida@citadel.edu*
Web: *http://www.citadel.edu*

Department Information:

1976. Department Head: Steve A. Nida. Number of faculty: total—full-time 11, part-time 6; women—full-time 3, part-time 3; total—minority—full-time 1; faculty subject to the Americans With Disabilities Act 1.

Programs and Degrees Offered:

Listed in the following order: Program area, degree type (T if terminal Master's), number awarded 7/06–6/07. School Psychology EdS/MEd (School Psychology) 13, Clinical Counseling MA/MS (Master of Arts/Science) (T) 18.

Student Applications/Admissions:

Student Applications

School Psychology EdS/MEd (School Psychology)—Applications 2007–2008, 36. Total applicants accepted 2007–2008, 30. Number full-time enrolled (new admits only) 2007–2008, 20. Number part-time enrolled (new admits only) 2007–2008, 0. Total enrolled 2007–2008 full-time, 49, part-time, 3. Openings 2008–2009, 20. The median number of years required for completion of a degree in 2006–2007 were 3. The number of students enrolled full- and part-time who were dismissed or voluntarily withdrew from this program area in 2007–2008 were 3. *Clinical Counseling MA/MS (Master of Arts/Science)*—Applications 2007–2008, 45. Total applicants accepted 2007–2008, 29. Number full-time enrolled (new admits only) 2007–2008, 16. Number part-time enrolled (new admits only) 2007–2008, 9. Total enrolled 2007–2008 full-time, 23, part-time, 44. Openings 2008–2009, 30. The median number of years required for completion of a degree in 2006–2007 were 3. The number of students enrolled full- and part-time who were dismissed or voluntarily withdrew from this program area in 2007–2008 were 15.

Admissions Requirements:

Scores: Entries appear in this order: required test or GPA, minimum score (if required), median score of students entering in 2007–2008. Master's Programs: Applicants must submit a score for either the GRE or the MAT. Numbers appearing above are for the School Psychology program. Minimum GRE scores are 500 (each section) for Clinical Counseling program; minimum GPA for Clinical Counseling program is 2.75.

Other Criteria: (importance of criteria rated low, medium, or high): GRE/MAT scores—high, research experience—medium, work experience—medium, extracurricular activity—low, clinically related public service—medium, GPA—high, letters of recommendation—high, statement of goals and objectives—high.

Student Characteristics: The following represents characteristics of students in 2007–2008 in all graduate psychology programs in the department: Female—full-time 65, part-time 44; Male—full-time 7, part-time 3; African American/Black—full-time 9, part-time 10; Hispanic/Latino(a)—full-time 2, part-time 0; Asian/Pacific Islander—full-time 0, part-time 0; American Indian/Alaska Native—full-time 2, part-time 0; Caucasian/White—full-time 58, part-time 37; Multi-ethnic—full-time 1, part-time 0; students subject to the Americans With Disabilities Act—full-time 5, part-time 1; Unknown ethnicity—full-time 0, part-time 0; International students who hold an F-1 or J-1 Visa—full-time 0, part-time 0.

Financial Information/Assistance:

Tuition for Full-Time Study: *Master's:* State residents: $280 per credit hour; Nonstate residents: $503 per credit hour. See the following Web site for updates and changes in tuition costs: http://www.citadel.edu/cgps/index.shtml.

Financial Assistance:

First-Year Students: Teaching assistantships available for first year. Average amount paid per academic year: $7,000. Average number of hours worked per week: 20. Apply by open. Research assistantships available for first year. Average amount paid per academic year: $7,000. Average number of hours worked per week: 20. Apply by open.

Advanced Students: Teaching assistantships available for advanced students. Average amount paid per academic year: $7,000. Average number of hours worked per week: 20. Apply by open. Research assistantships available for advanced students. Average amount paid per academic year: $7,000. Average number of hours worked per week: 20. Apply by open.

Additional Information: Of all students currently enrolled full time, 25% benefited from one or more of the listed financial assistance programs. Application and information available online at http://citadel.edu/cgps.

Internships/Practica: EdS in School Psychology: two practica courses where students provide services in the public school systems (40 and 125 hours, respectively); 1,200-hour internship (paid), at least 600 of which involve direct services within the public school system. MA in Psychology: Clinical Counseling: one practicum (150 hours) and one internship (600 hours) where students provide clinical/counseling services in public mental health/substance abuse treatment facilities. These are unpaid field experiences.

Housing and Day Care: No on-campus housing is available. No on-campus day care facilities are available.

Employment of Department Graduates:

Master's Degree Graduates: Of those who graduated in the academic year 2006–2007, the following categories and numbers represent the postgraduate activities and employment of master's degree graduates: Enrolled in a psychology doctoral program (1), enrolled in another graduate/professional program (0), enrolled in a postdoctoral residency/fellowship (n/a), employed in independent practice (n/a), employed in an academic position at a university (0), employed in an academic position at a 2-year/4-year college (0), employed in other positions at a higher education institution (0), employed in a professional position in a school system (12), employed in business or industry (0), employed in government agency (0), employed in a community mental health/counseling center (12), employed in a hospital/medical center (2), still seeking employment (0), not seeking employment (0), other employment position (0), do not know (4), total from the above (master's) (31).

Doctoral Degree Graduates: Of those who graduated in the academic year 2006–2007, the following categories and numbers represent the postgraduate activities and employment of doctoral degree graduates: Enrolled in a psychology doctoral program (n/a), total from the above (doctoral) (0).

Additional Information:

Orientation, Objectives, and Emphasis of Department: The School Psychology program is based on the scientist–practitioner model and emphasizes the school psychologist as a data-based problem solver who applies psychological principles, knowledge, and skill to processes and problems of education and schooling. Students are trained to provide a range of psychological assessment, consultation, intervention, prevention, program development and evaluation services with the goal of maximizing student learning and development. The School Psychology program has been accredited by the National Association of School Psychologists (NASP) since 1988. Students in the Master of Arts in Psychology: Clinical Counseling program are prepared to become scholarly practitioners of psychosocial counseling in community agencies, including college counseling centers, hospitals, mental health centers, and social services agencies. The program's model blends didactic and experience-based training to facilitate students' ability to utilize an empirical approach to assessment, goal development, intervention, and evaluation of services for a wide range of individuals and families experiencing a variety of psychosocial difficulties. The program is accredited by the Master's in Psychology Accreditation Council and is a member of the Council of Applied Master's Programs in Psychology.

Special Facilities or Resources: The Citadel's Department of Psychology enjoys a strong working relationship with the area school districts and agencies that provide mental health and substance abuse services. In addition, the nearby Medical University of South Carolina provides internship opportunities.

Information for Students With Physical Disabilities: See the following Web site for more information: http://www.citadel.edu/academics/psyc.

Application Information:

Send to College of Graduate and Professional Studies, The Citadel, 171 Moultrie Street, Charleston, SC 29409. Application available online. URL of online application: http://www.coldprd.citadel.edu/appprod/app0105_inp.cfm. Students are admitted in the Fall, application deadline March 15. *Fee:* $25.

Clemson University

Department of Psychology
418 Brackett Hall
Clemson, SC 29634-1355
Telephone: (864) 656-3210
Fax: (864) 656-0358
E-mail: *cpagano@clemson.edu*
Web: *http://www.clemson.edu/psych/*

Department Information:

1976. Graduate Program Coordinator: Chris Pagano. Number of faculty: total—full-time 20, part-time 2; women—full-time 8, part-time 2; total—minority—full-time 3.

Programs and Degrees Offered:

Listed in the following order: Program area, degree type (T if terminal Master's), number awarded 7/06–6/07. Human Factors PhD (Doctor of Philosophy) 7, Industrial/Organizational PhD (Doctor of Philosophy) 9.

Student Applications/Admissions:

Student Applications

Human Factors PhD (Doctor of Philosophy)—Applications 2007–2008, 35. Total applicants accepted 2007–2008, 7. Number full-time enrolled (new admits only) 2007–2008, 6. Number part-time enrolled (new admits only) 2007–2008, 0. Openings 2008–2009, 6. The median number of years required for completion of a degree in 2006–2007 were 4. The number of students enrolled full- and part-time who were dismissed or voluntarily withdrew from this program area in 2007–2008 were 1. *Industrial/Organizational PhD (Doctor of Philosophy)*—Applications 2007–2008, 150. Total applicants accepted 2007–2008, 8. Number full-time enrolled (new admits only) 2007–2008, 7. Total enrolled 2007–2008 full-time, 21, part-time, 6. Openings 2008–2009, 8. The median number of years required for completion of a degree in 2006–2007 were 4. The number of students enrolled full- and part-time who were dismissed or voluntarily withdrew from this program area in 2007–2008 were 1.

Admissions Requirements:

Scores: Entries appear in this order: required test or GPA, minimum score (if required), median score of students entering in 2007–2008. Master's Programs: GRE-V no minimum stated, 520; GRE-Q no minimum stated, 630; overall undergraduate GPA no minimum stated, 3.40; Master's GRE-Analytical no minimum stated, 5.0. Doctoral Programs: GRE-V no minimum stated, 570; GRE-Q no minimum stated, 650; overall undergraduate GPA no minimum stated, 3.60; Doctoral program GRE-Analytic no minimum stated, 5.0.

Other Criteria: (importance of criteria rated low, medium, or high): GRE/MAT scores—high, research experience—high, work experience—medium, extracurricular activity—low, GPA—high, letters of recommendation—high, interview—medium, statement of goals and objectives—high, undergraduate major in psychology—medium, specific undergraduate psychology courses taken—low. For additional information on admission requirements, go to http://www.clemson.edu/psych/.

Student Characteristics: The following represents characteristics of students in 2007–2008 in all graduate psychology programs in the department: Female—full-time 21, part-time 4; Male—full-time 14, part-time 2; African American/Black—full-time 2, part-time 1; Hispanic/Latino(a)—full-time 0, part-time 0; Asian/Pacific Islander—full-time 0, part-time 0; American Indian/Alaska Native—full-time 0, part-time 0; Caucasian/White—full-time 32, part-time 5; Multi-ethnic—full-time 1, part-time 0; students subject to the Americans With Disabilities Act—full-time 0, part-time 0; Unknown ethnicity—full-time 0, part-time 0.

Financial Information/Assistance:

Tuition for Full-Time Study: *Master's:* State residents: per academic year $1,900; Nonstate residents: per academic year $1,900. *Doctoral:* State residents: per academic year $1,900; Nonstate residents: per academic year $1,900. Tuition is subject to change.

Financial Assistance:

First-Year Students: Teaching assistantships available for first year. Average amount paid per academic year: $15,000. Average number of hours worked per week: 20. Apply by December 31. Tuition remission given: full and partial. Research assistantships available for first year. Average amount paid per academic year: $16,000. Average number of hours worked per week: 20. Apply by December 31. Tuition remission given: full and partial. Fellowships and scholarships available for first year. Average amount paid per academic year: $10,000. Average number of hours worked per week: 0. Apply by December 31.

Advanced Students: Teaching assistantships available for advanced students. Average amount paid per academic year: $16,000. Average number of hours worked per week: 20. Apply by December 31. Tuition remission given: full and partial. Research assistantships available for advanced students. Average amount paid per academic year: $18,000. Average number of hours worked per week: 20. Apply by December 31. Tuition remission given: full and partial. Fellowships and scholarships available for advanced students. Average amount paid per academic year: $10,000. Average number of hours worked per week: 0. Apply by December 31.

Additional Information: Of all students currently enrolled full time, 95% benefited from one or more of the listed financial assistance programs. Application and information available online at http://citadel.edu/cgps.

Internships/Practica: Doctoral Degree (PhD Human Factors): For those doctoral students for whom a professional internship was required in this program prior to graduation, (5) students applied for an internship in 2006–2007, with (5) students obtaining an internship. Of those students who obtained an internship, (5) were paid internships. Of those students who obtained an internship, (0) students placed in APA/CPA-accredited internships, (0) students placed in internships not APA/CPA accredited, but listed with the Association of Psychology Postdoctoral and Internship Centers (APPIC), (0) students placed in internships conforming to guidelines of the Council of Directors of School Psychology Programs (CDSPP), (5) students placed in internships that were not APA/CPA-accredited, APPIC or CDSPP listed. Doctoral Degree (PhD Industrial/Organizational): For those doctoral students for whom a professional internship was required in this program prior to graduation, (6) students applied for an internship in 2006–2007, with (6) students obtaining an internship. Of those students who obtained an internship, (6) were paid internships. Of those students who obtained an internship, (0) students placed in APA/CPA-accredited internships, (0) students placed in internships not APA/CPA accredited, but listed with the Association of Psychology Postdoctoral and Internship Centers (APPIC), (0) students placed in internships conforming to guidelines of the Council of Directors of School Psychology Programs (CDSPP), (6) students placed in internships that were not APA/CPA-accredited, APPIC or CDSPP listed. Students complete a summer intership as part of the requirements for the MS degree.

Housing and Day Care: On-campus housing is available. See the following Web site for more information: http://www.housing.clemson.edu/. No on-campus day care facilities are available.

Employment of Department Graduates:

Master's Degree Graduates: Of those who graduated in the academic year 2006–2007, the following categories and numbers represent the postgraduate activities and employment of master's degree graduates: Enrolled in a psychology doctoral program (4), enrolled in a postdoctoral residency/fellowship (n/a), employed in independent practice (n/a), employed in business or industry (2), employed in government agency (1), total from the above (master's) (7).

Doctoral Degree Graduates: Of those who graduated in the academic year 2006–2007, the following categories and numbers represent the postgraduate activities and employment of doctoral degree graduates: Enrolled in a psychology doctoral program (n/a), employed in an academic position at a university (0), employed in business or industry (2), total from the above (doctoral) (2).

Additional Information:

Orientation, Objectives, and Emphasis of Department: The faculty of the Psychology Department are committed to excellence in teaching and research. The primary goals of the Master of Science degree program are to provide students with an essential core of knowledge in applied psychology and to develop applied research skills. The program is specifically designed to provide the student with the requisite theoretical foundations, skills in quantitative techniques and experimental design, and the practical problem-solving skills necessary to address real world problems in industry, business, and government. The emphasis is on the direct application of acquired training upon completion of the program. All of our graduate programs have a heavy out-of-the-classroom research component with a required empirical thesis. The PhD programs prepare the student to generate and use knowledge in accordance with the scientist–practitioner model. In addition to the traditional areas of study in Industrial/Organizational Psychology and Human Factors (Engineering) Psychology, a new emphasis area in Occupational Health Psychology has been added to both the MS and PhD degree programs.

Special Facilities or Resources: The Psychology Department is housed on four floors of Brackett Hall. Students have access to several laboratories, including a Process Control Simulator Lab, Task Performance Lab, Psychophysiology Research Lab, Sleep Research Lab, Perception and Action Lab, Motion Sciences Lab, Un-coupled motion simulation Lab, Human Memory and Perception Lab, Visual Performance Lab, Driving Simulator Lab, Usability Testing Lab, Advanced Reading Technologies Lab, Personnel Selection and Performance Appraisal Lab, Workplace Training Research Lab, I/O Research Lab, Social Psychology Lab, Cognitive Aging Lab, Residential Research Lab, as well as Virtual Reality and Robotics and Teleoperation facilities.

Information for Students With Physical Disabilities: See the following Web site for more information: http://www.stuaff.clemson.edu/redfern/sds/.

Application Information:
The online application is very strongly recommended. Office of Graduate Admissions, 103 Sikes Hall, Clemson University, Clemson, SC 29634. Before applying, all applicants should contact cpagano@clemson.edu for more information. Application available online. URL of online application: http://www.grad.clemson.edu/Admission.php. Students are admitted in the Fall, application deadline December 31. *Fee:* $55.

Francis Marion University

Master's of Science in Applied Psychology
P.O. Box 100547
Florence, SC 29501-0547
Telephone: (843) 661-1641
Fax: (843) 661-1628
E-mail: *jhester@fmarion.edu*
Web: *http://www.fmarion.edu/academics/psychology*

Department Information:
1970. Chair: John R. Hester, PhD. Number of faculty: total—full-time 11, part-time 8; women—full-time 4, part-time 5.

Programs and Degrees Offered:
Listed in the following order: Program area, degree type (T if terminal Master's), number awarded 7/06–6/07. Clinical/Counseling MA/MS (Master of Arts/Science) (T) 4, School MA/MS (Master of Arts/Science) (T) 5.

Student Applications/Admissions:
Student Applications
Clinical/Counseling MA/MS (Master of Arts/Science)—Applications 2007–2008, 27. Total applicants accepted 2007–2008, 11. Number full-time enrolled (new admits only) 2007–2008, 6. Number part-time enrolled (new admits only) 2007–2008, 0. Openings 2008–2009, 10. The median number of years required for completion of a degree in 2006–2007 were 3. The number of students enrolled full- and part-time who were dismissed or voluntarily withdrew from this program area in 2007–2008 were 0. *School MA/MS (Master of Arts/Science)*—Applications 2007–2008, 17. Total applicants accepted 2007–2008, 8. Number full-time enrolled (new admits only) 2007–2008, 5. Number part-time enrolled (new admits only) 2007–2008, 0. Total enrolled 2007–2008 full-time, 26, part-time, 1. Openings 2008–2009, 10. The median number of years required for completion of a degree in 2006–2007 were 3.

Admissions Requirements:
Scores: Entries appear in this order: required test or GPA, minimum score (if required), median score of students entering in 2007–2008. Master's Programs: GRE-V no minimum stated, 480; GRE-Q no minimum stated, 530; overall undergraduate GPA 3.00, 3.45; psychology GPA 3.00, 3.41. An overall General GRE score of 950 or higher is the minimum required.
Other Criteria: (importance of criteria rated low, medium, or high): GRE/MAT scores—high, research experience—medium, work experience—medium, extracurricular activity—low, clinically related public service—medium, GPA—high, letters of recommendation—high, statement of goals and objectives—medium, specific undergraduate psychology courses taken—medium.

Student Characteristics: The following represents characteristics of students in 2007–2008 in all graduate psychology programs in the department: Female—full-time 48, part-time 1; Male—full-time 3, part-time 0; African American/Black—full-time 5, part-time 0; Hispanic/Latino(a)—full-time 0, part-time 0; Asian/Pacific Islander—full-time 2, part-time 0; American Indian/Alaska Native—full-time 0, part-time 0; Caucasian/White—full-time 42, part-time 1; Multi-ethnic—full-time 0, part-time 0; students subject to the Americans With Disabilities Act—full-time 0, part-time 0; Unknown ethnicity—full-time 2, part-time 0; International students who hold an F-1 or J-1 Visa—full-time 1, part-time 0.

Financial Information/Assistance:
Tuition for Full-Time Study: *Master's:* State residents: per academic year $7,003, $350 per credit hour; Nonstate residents: per academic year $14,006, $700 per credit hour. Tuition is subject to change. See the following Web site for updates and changes in tuition costs: http://www.fmarion.edu.

Financial Assistance:
First-Year Students: Teaching assistantships available for first year. Average amount paid per academic year: $8,000. Average number of hours worked per week: 20. Research assistantships available for first year. Average amount paid per academic year: $7,000. Average number of hours worked per week: 20. Fellowships and scholarships available for first year. Average amount paid per academic year: $500.
Advanced Students: Teaching assistantships available for advanced students. Average amount paid per academic year: $8,000. Average number of hours worked per week: 20. Research assistantships available for advanced students. Average amount paid per academic year: $7,000. Average number of hours worked per week: 20. Fellowships and scholarships available for advanced students. Average amount paid per academic year: $500.
Additional Information: Of all students currently enrolled full time, 35% benefited from one or more of the listed financial assistance programs.

Internships/Practica: Master's Degree (MA/MS Clinical/Counseling): An internship experience such as a final research project or "capstone" experience is required of graduates. Master's Degree (MA/MS School): An internship experience such as a final research project or "capstone" experience is required of graduates. Internships occur in a variety of community settings. Typically Clinical/Counseling students complete a full-time, 6-month internship in state human service agencies. The School Psychology internship is a full-time experience as a school psychologist during a Fall and Spring semester. All interns develop a broad array of skills under supervision.

Housing and Day Care: On-campus housing is available. Francis Marion University has housing available in the form of dorms and apartments on campus. Also, there are a number of apartments located off campus not far from the university. See the following Web site for more information: http://www.fmarion.edu or contact Housing and Residence Life: (843) 661-1330. On-campus day care facilities are available. The Child Care Center will open in August 2008.

Employment of Department Graduates:

Master's Degree Graduates: Of those who graduated in the academic year 2006–2007, the following categories and numbers represent the postgraduate activities and employment of master's degree graduates: Enrolled in a postdoctoral residency/fellowship (n/a), employed in independent practice (n/a), do not know (9), total from the above (master's) (9).

Doctoral Degree Graduates: Of those who graduated in the academic year 2006–2007, the following categories and numbers represent the postgraduate activities and employment of doctoral degree graduates: Enrolled in a psychology doctoral program (n/a), do not know (9), total from the above (doctoral) (9).

Additional Information:

Orientation, Objectives, and Emphasis of Department: The primary purpose of the program is to prepare professionals for employment in human services agencies, schools, or similar settings. The program also provides for the continuing education of those individuals currently employed in the helping professions and prepares students for further graduate study.

Special Facilities or Resources: The department has excellent laboratory facilities on campus including a computer laboratory. Regional human services facilities, community agencies, and school districts are accessible off campus.

Information for Students With Physical Disabilities: See the following Web site for more information: http://www.fmarion.edu/students.

Application Information:

Send to Graduate Office, Francis Marion University, P.O. Box 100547, Florence, SC 29501-0547. Application available online. URL of online application: http://www.fmarion.edu/academics/GraduatePrograms. Students are admitted in the Fall, application deadline March 15; Spring, application deadline October 15; programs have rolling admissions. *Fee:* $30.

South Carolina, University of

Department of Psychology
College of Arts and Sciences
1512 Pendleton Street
Columbia, SC 29208
Telephone: (803) 777-4137
Fax: (803) 777-9558
E-mail: *Mactutus@sc.edu*
Web: *http://www.psych.sc.edu*

Department Information:

1912. Department Chair: Charles F. Mactutus. Number of faculty: total—full-time 35, part-time 12; women—full-time 13, part-time 8; total—minority—full-time 4; women minority—full-time 4.

Programs and Degrees Offered:

Listed in the following order: Program area, degree type (T if terminal Master's), number awarded 7/06–6/07. Clinical/Community PhD (Doctor of Philosophy) 13, Experimental PhD (Doctor of Philosophy) 2, School Psychology PhD (Doctor of Philosophy) 11.

APA Accreditation: Clinical PhD (Doctor of Philosophy). School PhD (Doctor of Philosophy).

Student Applications/Admissions:

Student Applications

Clinical/Community PhD (Doctor of Philosophy)—Applications 2007–2008, 121. Total applicants accepted 2007–2008, 11. Number full-time enrolled (new admits only) 2007–2008, 9. Number part-time enrolled (new admits only) 2007–2008, 0. Total enrolled 2007–2008 full-time, 31, part-time, 18. Openings 2008–2009, 8. The median number of years required for completion of a degree in 2006–2007 were 7. The number of students enrolled full- and part-time who were dismissed or voluntarily withdrew from this program area in 2007–2008 were 0. *Experimental PhD (Doctor of Philosophy)*—Applications 2007–2008, 29. Total applicants accepted 2007–2008, 8. Number full-time enrolled (new admits only) 2007–2008, 7. Number part-time enrolled (new admits only) 2007–2008, 0. Total enrolled 2007–2008 full-time, 19, part-time, 2. Openings 2008–2009, 7. The median number of years required for completion of a degree in 2006–2007 were 5. The number of students enrolled full- and part-time who were dismissed or voluntarily withdrew from this program area in 2007–2008 were 0. *School Psychology PhD (Doctor of Philosophy)*—Applications 2007–2008, 44. Total applicants accepted 2007–2008, 0. Number full-time enrolled (new admits only) 2007–2008, 5. Number part-time enrolled (new admits only) 2007–2008, 0. Total enrolled 2007–2008 full-time, 25, part-time, 11. The median number of years required for completion of a degree in 2006–2007 were 5. The number of students enrolled full- and part-time who were dismissed or voluntarily withdrew from this program area in 2007–2008 were 1.

Admissions Requirements:

Scores: Entries appear in this order: required test or GPA, minimum score (if required), median score of students entering in 2007–2008. Doctoral Programs: GRE-V no minimum stated, 550; GRE-Q no minimum stated, 630; GRE-Subject (Psychology) no minimum stated, 600; overall undergraduate GPA no minimum stated, 3.4; last 2 years GPA no minimum stated, 3.8; psychology GPA no minimum stated, 3.65. Median scores vary for different programs. Psychology Subject GRE is only required for the Clinical/Community doctoral program, although the Experimental and School Psychology programs will accept the Subject GRE score.

Other Criteria: (importance of criteria rated low, medium, or high): GRE/MAT scores—medium, research experience—high, work experience—medium, extracurricular activity—medium, clinically related public service—medium, GPA—high, letters of recommendation—high, interview—high, statement of goals and objectives—high. Criteria vary for different programs.

Student Characteristics: The following represents characteristics of students in 2007–2008 in all graduate psychology programs

in the department: Female—full-time 56, part-time 23; Male—full-time 19, part-time 8; African American/Black—full-time 3, part-time 6; Hispanic/Latino(a)—full-time 3, part-time 0; Asian/Pacific Islander—full-time 4, part-time 2; American Indian/Alaska Native—full-time 0, part-time 0; Caucasian/White—full-time 58, part-time 19; Multi-ethnic—full-time 0, part-time 0; students subject to the Americans With Disabilities Act—full-time 1, part-time 0; Unknown ethnicity—full-time 7, part-time 4; International students who hold an F-1 or J-1 Visa—full-time 3, part-time 3.

Financial Information/Assistance:

Tuition for Full-Time Study: *Doctoral:* State residents: per academic year $8,888, $440 per credit hour; Nonstate residents: per academic year $19,180, $936 per credit hour. Tuition is subject to change. Additional fees are assessed to students beyond the costs of tuition for the following: one time matriculation fee, technology and lab fees, international student fees and taxes, health insurance. See the following Web site for updates and changes in tuition costs: http://www.sc.edu/bursar/schedule.html.

Financial Assistance:

First-Year Students: Teaching assistantships available for first year. Average amount paid per academic year: $14,000. Average number of hours worked per week: 20. Tuition remission given: full. Research assistantships available for first year. Average amount paid per academic year: $14,000. Average number of hours worked per week: 20. Tuition remission given: full.

Advanced Students: Teaching assistantships available for advanced students. Average amount paid per academic year: $14,000. Average number of hours worked per week: 20. Tuition remission given: full. Research assistantships available for advanced students. Average amount paid per academic year: $14,000. Average number of hours worked per week: 20. Tuition remission given: full.

Additional Information: Of all students currently enrolled full time, 100% benefited from one or more of the listed financial assistance programs. All students offered admission are considered for financial assistance by the admissions committee.

Internships/Practica: Doctoral Degree (PhD Clinical/Community): For those doctoral students for whom a professional internship was required in this program prior to graduation, (6) students applied for an internship in 2006–2007, with (6) students obtaining an internship. Of those students who obtained an internship, (6) were paid internships. Of those students who obtained an internship, (6) students placed in APA/CPA-accredited internships, (0) students placed in internships not APA/CPA-accredited, but listed with the Association of Psychology Postdoctoral and Internship Centers (APPIC), (0) students placed in internships conforming to guidelines of the Council of Directors of School Psychology Programs (CDSPP), (0) students placed in internships that were not APA/CPA-accredited, APPIC or CDSPP listed. Doctoral Degree (PhD School Psychology): For those doctoral students for whom a professional internship was required in this program prior to graduation, (4) students applied for an internship in 2006–2007, with (4) students obtaining an internship. Of those students who obtained an internship, (4) were paid internships. Of those students who obtained an internship, (2) students placed in APA/CPA-accredited internships, (2) students placed in internships not APA/CPA-accredited, but listed with the Association of Psychology Postdoctoral and Internship Centers (APPIC), (0) students placed in internships conforming to guidelines of the Council of Directors of School Psychology Programs (CDSPP), (0) students placed in internships that were not APA/CPA-accredited, APPIC or CDSPP listed. Students in School Psychology and Clinical/Community psychology complete at least 1 year of half-time placement in a community service agency expanding their experience with a diverse client population and multidisciplinary service providers. For additional information on education and training outcomes for our programs, see the following Web site: http://www.psych.sc.edu/.

Housing and Day Care: On-campus housing is available. See the following Web site for more information: http://www.housing.sc.edu/famgrad.asp. On-campus day care facilities are available. See the following Web site for more information: http://www.sc.edu/childrenscenter/history.shtml.

Employment of Department Graduates:

Master's Degree Graduates: Of those who graduated in the academic year 2006–2007, the following categories and numbers represent the postgraduate activities and employment of master's degree graduates: Enrolled in a psychology doctoral program (4), enrolled in another graduate/professional program (1), enrolled in a postdoctoral residency/fellowship (n/a), employed in independent practice (n/a), total from the above (master's) (5).

Doctoral Degree Graduates: Of those who graduated in the academic year 2006–2007, the following categories and numbers represent the postgraduate activities and employment of doctoral degree graduates: Enrolled in a psychology doctoral program (n/a), enrolled in a postdoctoral residency/fellowship (4), employed in an academic position at a university (2), employed in other positions at a higher education institution (1), employed in a professional position in a school system (6), employed in business or industry (1), employed in a community mental health/counseling center (5), employed in a hospital/medical center (2), total from the above (doctoral) (21).

Additional Information:

Orientation, Objectives, and Emphasis of Department: The department has interdisciplinary research emphases in developmental cognitive neuroscience/neurodevelopmental disorders, prevention science, reading and language, and ethnic minority health and mental health. The experimental program offers concentrations in cognitive, developmental, and behavioral neuroscience, built on broad scientific training in experimental psychology. The School Psychology program includes emphasis in child assessment, individual and group consultation, educational research, and professional roles. In Clinical/Community, there is a wide latitude of choices: assessment, psychotherapy and behavioral interventions, community psychology, and consultation. Regular clinical/community training includes both adults and children, with an option of special emphasis on children or community settings.

Special Facilities or Resources: The special facilities and resources of the department include the university-directed psychological service center, the medical school, the VA hospital, the department-directed outpatient psychological services center, mental health centers, and other educational and mental health service settings. Other laboratories include Behavioral Pharmacology Lab; Behavioral Neuroscience Lab with high-density EEG and MRI; Developmental Sensory Neuroscience Lab; Experimental and Cognitive Processes Lab; Infant Attention Lab; Judgment and Decision Making Lab; and Attention and Perception Lab. We are actively involved in community agencies, the psychiatric training institution, and the psychopharmacology laboratory.

Information for Students With Physical Disabilities: See the following Web site for more information: http://www.sa.sc.edu/sds/.

Application Information:
Send to Graduate Admissions Coordinator, Department of Psychology, University of South Carolina, Columbia, SC 29208. Application available online. URL of online application: http://www.gradschool.sc.edu/login. Students are admitted in the Fall, application deadline December 1. Application deadline for Fall admission in Clinical/Community Psychology is December 1, Experimental Psychology and School Psychology, January 1. Applications for admissions should be sumbitted electronically. *Fee:* $40.

Winthrop University

Department of Psychology
Arts and Sciences
135 Kinard
Rock Hill, SC 29733
Telephone: (803) 323-2117
Fax: (803) 323-2371
E-mail: *prusj@winthrop.edu*
Web: *http://www.winthrop.edu/psychology*

Department Information:
1923. Chairperson: Dr. Joe Prus. Number of faculty: total—full-time 14, part-time 6; women—full-time 7, part-time 4; women minority—full-time 1, part-time 1.

Programs and Degrees Offered:
Listed in the following order: Program area, degree type (T if terminal Master's), number awarded 7/06–6/07. School Psychology Other 10.

Student Applications/Admissions:
Student Applications
School Psychology Other—Applications 2007–2008, 75. Total applicants accepted 2007–2008, 10. Number full-time enrolled (new admits only) 2007–2008, 10. Number part-time enrolled (new admits only) 2007–2008, 0. Openings 2008–2009, 10. The median number of years required for completion of a degree in 2006–2007 were 3. The number of students enrolled full- and part-time who were dismissed or voluntarily withdrew from this program area in 2007–2008 were 0.

Admissions Requirements:
Scores: Entries appear in this order: required test or GPA, minimum score (if required), median score of students entering in 2007–2008. Master's Programs: GRE-V no minimum stated, 540; GRE-Q no minimum stated, 560; overall undergraduate GPA no minimum stated, 3.60; last 2 years GPA no minimum stated, 3.70; psychology GPA no minimum stated, 3.70; Master's GRE-Analytical no minimum stated.

Other Criteria: (importance of criteria rated low, medium, or high): GRE/MAT scores—low, research experience—low, work experience—medium, extracurricular activity—low, clinically related public service—medium, GPA—high, letters of recommendation—high, interview—high, statement of goals and objectives—medium, experience with children—high. For additional information on admission requirements, go to http://www.winthrop.edu/psychology.

Student Characteristics: The following represents characteristics of students in 2007–2008 in all graduate psychology programs in the department: Female—full-time 29, part-time 0; Male—full-time 1, part-time 0; African American/Black—full-time 4, part-time 0; Hispanic/Latino(a)—full-time 2, part-time 0; Asian/Pacific Islander—full-time 0, part-time 0; American Indian/Alaska Native—full-time 0, part-time 0; Caucasian/White—full-time 24, part-time 0; students subject to the Americans With Disabilities Act—full-time 0, part-time 0; Unknown ethnicity—full-time 0, part-time 0.

Financial Information/Assistance:
Tuition for Full-Time Study: *Master's:* State residents: per academic year $9,834, $412 per credit hour; Nonstate residents: per academic year $14,330, $596 per credit hour. Tuition is subject to change. See the following Web site for updates and changes in tuition costs: http://www.winthrop.edu.

Financial Assistance:
First-Year Students: Teaching assistantships available for first year. Average amount paid per academic year: $3,600. Average number of hours worked per week: 20. Apply by April 15. Tuition remission given: partial. Research assistantships available for first year. Average amount paid per academic year: $3,600. Average number of hours worked per week: 20. Apply by April 15. Tuition remission given: partial. Traineeships available for first year. Fellowships and scholarships available for first year. Average amount paid per academic year: $1,000. Apply by April 15. Tuition remission given: partial.

Advanced Students: Traineeships available for advanced students. Average amount paid per academic year: $4,500. Average number of hours worked per week: 15. Apply by n/a. Tuition remission given: full and partial.

Additional Information: Of all students currently enrolled full time, 90% benefited from one or more of the listed financial assistance programs.

Internships/Practica: The program provides paid traineeships during the 2nd year and internships during the 3rd year in area school districts and agencies. Rural, suburban, and urban field settings include diverse student–client populations. A limited number of nonschool internship placements are available for up to 600 clock hours of the 1,200–hour internship. The internship includes a full range of school psychological services. Each intern receives weekly supervision from both a faculty and field-based credentialed supervisor.

Housing and Day Care: On-campus housing is available. See the following Web site for more information: http://www.winthrop.edu. On-campus day care facilities are available.

Employment of Department Graduates:
Master's Degree Graduates: Of those who graduated in the academic year 2006–2007, the following categories and numbers

represent the postgraduate activities and employment of master's degree graduates: Enrolled in a postdoctoral residency/fellowship (n/a), employed in independent practice (n/a), employed in a professional position in a school system (10), total from the above (master's) (10).

Doctoral Degree Graduates: Of those who graduated in the academic year 2006–2007, the following categories and numbers represent the postgraduate activities and employment of doctoral degree graduates: Enrolled in a psychology doctoral program (n/a), total from the above (doctoral) (0).

Additional Information:

Orientation, Objectives, and Emphasis of Department: The Winthrop School Psychology program is designed to prepare practitioners who are competent to provide a full range of school psychological services, including consultation, behavioral intervention, psychoeducational assessment, research and evaluation, and counseling. The 3-year, full-time program leading to both MS and Specialist in School Psychology degrees qualifies graduates for state and national certification as a school psychologist pending attainment of a passing score on the Praxis II specialty exam in school psychology. Program emphasis is placed on evidenced-based psychological and psychoeducational methods. Students are prepared to work with diverse clients from birth to adulthood, including those with low-incidence disabilities, and with families, teachers, and others in the schools and community. The program provides an applied, competency-based approach to training that progresses sequentially from foundations and practica courses to a 450-hour traineeship to a 1,200-hour internship, and affords maximum individualized supervision. Comprehensive assessment of student learning and development, from entry into the program to acquisition of professional positions or admissions into doctoral programs, is conducted through multiple methods. Program faculty represent considerable ethnic and experiential diversity. All have advanced degrees in school psychology; are active in the profession at local, state, and national levels; and view teaching and supervision as their primary roles. A collaborative approach to learning, and cooperation among students, are emphasized in the program.

Special Facilities or Resources: Winthrop University is a state-supported institution of about 6,500 students that provides students with access to an academic computer center, state-of-the-art health center, university library with nearly 500,000 volumes and 4,000 periodicals and serials, and a variety of other resources. Access to such department resources as a computer workroom and school psychology mini-library and assessment resource center are available. Winthrop's 418-acre campus is located in the greater Charlotte, NC area, which includes a great variety of school districts, human service agencies, libraries, and other resources that may be of personal or professional interest to graduate students in school psychology.

Information for Students With Physical Disabilities: See the following Web site for more information: http://www.winthrop.edu.

Application Information:

Send to Office of Graduate Studies, Winthrop University, Rock Hill, SC 29733. Application available online. URL of online application: http://www.winthrop.edu/graduate_studies. Students are admitted in the Fall, application deadline February 1. *Fee:* $50. Application fee may be waived by program director in cases of financial hardship.

South Dakota, University of
Department of Psychology
414 East Clark Street
Vermillion, SD 57069
Telephone: (605) 677-5351
Fax: (605) 677-3195
E-mail: *rquevill@usd.edu*
Web: *http://www.usd.edu/psyc*

Department Information:

1926. Chairperson: Randal Quevillon. Number of faculty: total—full-time 15, part-time 1; women—full-time 7; total—minority—full-time 3; women minority—full-time 2.

Programs and Degrees Offered:

Listed in the following order: Program area, degree type (T if terminal Master's), number awarded 7/06–6/07. Clinical PhD (Doctor of Philosophy) 7, Human Factors PhD (Doctor of Philosophy) 4.

APA Accreditation: Clinical PhD (Doctor of Philosophy).

Student Applications/Admissions:

Student Applications

Clinical PhD (Doctor of Philosophy)—Applications 2007–2008, 95. Total applicants accepted 2007–2008, 11. Number full-time enrolled (new admits only) 2007–2008, 6. Openings 2008–2009, 6. The median number of years required for completion of a degree in 2006–2007 were 7. The number of students enrolled full- and part-time who were dismissed or voluntarily withdrew from this program area in 2007–2008 were 1. *Human Factors PhD (Doctor of Philosophy)*—Applications 2007–2008, 12. Total applicants accepted 2007–2008, 5. Number full-time enrolled (new admits only) 2007–2008, 2. Openings 2008–2009, 2. The median number of years required for completion of a degree in 2006–2007 were 7. The number of students enrolled full- and part-time who were dismissed or voluntarily withdrew from this program area in 2007–2008 were 0.

Admissions Requirements:

Scores: Entries appear in this order: required test or GPA, minimum score (if required), median score of students entering in 2007–2008. Doctoral Programs: GRE-V no minimum stated, 536; GRE-Q no minimum stated, 665; GRE-Subject (Psychology) no minimum stated, 660; overall undergraduate GPA 3.00, 3.88; Doctoral program GRE-Analytic no minimum stated, 4.9.

Other Criteria: (importance of criteria rated low, medium, or high): GRE/MAT scores—medium, research experience—high, work experience—medium, extracurricular activity—medium, clinically related public service—medium, GPA—medium, letters of recommendation—high, interview—high, statement of goals and objectives—medium, match with program—high. GRE and GPA weightings vary by program, as do service, extracurricular, and goals and objectives criteria. Applicant's responses to the Supplemental Application questions are highly weighted in the Clinical program admissions process. The Clinical program requires an interview and the Human Factors program does not. For additional information on admission requirements, go to http://www.usd.edu/psyc/.

Student Characteristics: The following represents characteristics of students in 2007–2008 in all graduate psychology programs in the department: Female—full-time 38, part-time 0; Male—full-time 22, part-time 0; African American/Black—full-time 2, part-time 0; Hispanic/Latino(a)—full-time 1, part-time 0; Asian/Pacific Islander—full-time 2, part-time 0; American Indian/Alaska Native—full-time 4, part-time 0; Caucasian/White—full-time 51, part-time 0; Multi-ethnic—full-time 0, part-time 0; students subject to the Americans With Disabilities Act—full-time 4, part-time 0; Unknown ethnicity—full-time 0, part-time 0; International students who hold an F-1 or J-1 Visa—full-time 1, part-time 0.

Financial Information/Assistance:

Tuition for Full-Time Study: *Doctoral:* State residents: $125 per credit hour; Nonstate residents: $369 per credit hour. Tuition is subject to change. See the following Web site for updates and changes in tuition costs: http://www.usd.edu/gradsch/financialinfo.cfm.

Financial Assistance:

First-Year Students: Teaching assistantships available for first year. Average amount paid per academic year: $5,500. Average number of hours worked per week: 16. Tuition remission given: partial. Research assistantships available for first year. Average amount paid per academic year: $5,500. Average number of hours worked per week: 16. Tuition remission given: partial. Fellowships and scholarships available for first year. Average amount paid per academic year: $9,000. Average number of hours worked per week: 16. Tuition remission given: partial.

Advanced Students: Teaching assistantships available for advanced students. Average amount paid per academic year: $6,000. Average number of hours worked per week: 16. Tuition remission given: partial. Research assistantships available for advanced students. Average amount paid per academic year: $10,000. Average number of hours worked per week: 16. Tuition remission given: partial. Traineeships available for advanced students. Average amount paid per academic year: $10,000. Average number of hours worked per week: 16. Tuition remission given: partial. Fellowships and scholarships available for advanced students. Average amount paid per academic year: $10,000. Average number of hours worked per week: 16. Tuition remission given: partial.

Additional Information: Of all students currently enrolled full time, 100% benefited from one or more of the listed financial assistance programs.

Internships/Practica: Doctoral Degree (PhD Clinical): For those doctoral students for whom a professional internship was required in this program prior to graduation, (9) students applied for an internship in 2006–2007, with (9) students obtaining an internship. Of those students who obtained an internship, (9) were paid internships. Of those students who obtained an internship, (6) students placed in APA/CPA-accredited internships, (1) student placed in internships not APA/CPA-accredited, but listed with the Association of Psychology Postdoctoral and Internship Centers (APPIC), (0) students placed in internships conforming to guidelines of the Council of Directors of School Psychology Programs (CDSPP), (2) students placed in internships that were not APA/CPA-accredited, APPIC or CDSPP listed. Several internships are available in Human Factors: placements with IBM, Lockheed, Hewlett-Packard, and Intel have been recent examples. In Clinical, a 12-month internship is required in the final year, and we are proud of the record our students have achieved in obtaining top placements. We also have available a series of paid clinical placements (see community resources). In addition, many graduate courses include practicum components, and Clinical students are placed on practicum teams through the Psychological Services Center each semester.

Housing and Day Care: On-campus housing is available. See the following Web site for more information: http://www.usd.edu/reslife/ also available on the student services menu at http://www.usd.edu/studentserv/. On-campus day care facilities are available. See the following Web site for more information: http://www.usd.edu/childcare/ also available on the student services menu at http://www.usd.edu/studentserv/.

Employment of Department Graduates:

Master's Degree Graduates: Of those who graduated in the academic year 2006–2007, the following categories and numbers represent the postgraduate activities and employment of master's degree graduates: Enrolled in a psychology doctoral program (19), enrolled in a postdoctoral residency/fellowship (n/a), employed in independent practice (n/a), total from the above (master's) (19). ***Doctoral Degree Graduates:*** Of those who graduated in the academic year 2006–2007, the following categories and numbers represent the postgraduate activities and employment of doctoral degree graduates: Enrolled in a psychology doctoral program (n/a), employed in independent practice (0), employed in an academic position at a university (1), employed in an academic position at a 2-year/4-year college (0), employed in business or industry (0), employed in government agency (2), employed in a community mental health/counseling center (1), employed in a hospital/medical center (1), not seeking employment (0), other employment position (2), do not know (1), total from the above (doctoral) (8).

Additional Information:

Orientation, Objectives, and Emphasis of Department: The department seeks to develop scholars who can contribute to the expansion of psychological information. The major goals of the theoretically eclectic program in Clinical Psychology are to increase students' knowledge of and identification with psychology as a method of inquiry about human behavior and to provide students with the theory, skills, and experience to function in a professional, research, or academic capacity. Training is provided in traditional areas as well as disaster psychology, rural community psychology, cross-cultural issues (particularly work with American Indian populations), program evaluation, neuropsychology, family therapy, and women's issues. The experience thus provided serves to broaden professional competencies and increase the versatility of the program's graduates. The overall mission of Human Factors Psychology is to improve living and working through knowledge of the abilities and limitations of the person part of human–machine or sociotechnical systems. The program's goal is to train doctoral-level professionals qualified to do research in industry, government, and universities. As an element of their training, all graduate students conduct empirical investigations. In recent years, the Human Factors Laboratory has supported studies of information processing, human–computer interfaces, motor performance, program evaluation and testing, traffic safety, transportation systems, and the effects of chemical agents and stress on human efficiency.

Special Facilities or Resources: Available to all psychology graduate students are computer lab facilities including word processing and statistical analysis software. Microcomputers are also easily accessible within the department for personal computing and research purposes. Much general purpose, highly adaptable research equipment is available to both Clinical and Human Factors students. The Human Factors Laboratory is particularly well-equipped for experimentation within the specialty areas of current interest to associated faculty. The department houses the Disaster Mental Health Institute, a South Dakota Board of Regents Center of Exellence, which provides unique research and service opportunities for graduate students as well as specialized coursework and assistantships. The Psychological Services Center, which supplies clinical services for both University students and the general public, accepts referrals from physicians, schools, and other community and state agencies. The Center has offices equipped for a variety of diagnostic and therapeutic activities, including neuropsychological work. The department's students take full advantage of training and experience available at local, state, and regional mental health facilities.

Information for Students With Physical Disabilities: See the following Web site for more information: http://www.usd.edu/disabrs/.

Application Information:

Send to Dean, Graduate School, University of South Dakota, 414 East Clark Street, Vermilion, SD 57069-2390. Application available online. URL of online application: http://www.usd.edu/gradsch/gradapp.cfm. Students are admitted in the Fall, application deadline January 5. Clinical program due January 5, Human Factors program due February 15. *Fee:* $35.

Austin Peay State University

Department of Psychology
601 College Street
Clarksville, TN 37044
Telephone: (931) 221-7233
Fax: (931) 221-6267
E-mail: *Fungs@apsu.edu*
Web: *http://www.apsu.edu/psychology*

Department Information:

1968. Chairperson: Dr. Samuel Fung. Number of faculty: total—full-time 13; women—full-time 5; total—minority—full-time 2; women minority—full-time 1; faculty subject to the Americans With Disabilities Act 1.

Programs and Degrees Offered:

Listed in the following order: Program area, degree type (T if terminal Master's), number awarded 7/06–6/07. Community Counseling MA/MS (Master of Arts/Science) (T) 3, Industrial/Organizational Psychology MA/MS (Master of Arts/Science) (T) 4, School Counseling MA/MS (Master of Arts/Science) (T) 3, School Counseling EdS/MEd (School Psychology) 1.

Student Applications/Admissions:

Student Applications

Community Counseling MA/MS (Master of Arts/Science)—Applications 2007–2008, 5. Total applicants accepted 2007–2008, 4. Number full-time enrolled (new admits only) 2007–2008, 5. Number part-time enrolled (new admits only) 2007–2008, 1. Total enrolled 2007–2008 full-time, 14. Openings 2008–2009, 10. The median number of years required for completion of a degree in 2006–2007 were 2. *Industrial/Organizational Psychology MA/MS (Master of Arts/Science)*—Applications 2007–2008, 30. Total applicants accepted 2007–2008, 13. Number full-time enrolled (new admits only) 2007–2008, 4. Total enrolled 2007–2008 full-time, 7. Openings 2008–2009, 15. The median number of years required for completion of a degree in 2006–2007 were 2. The number of students enrolled full- and part-time who were dismissed or voluntarily withdrew from this program area in 2007–2008 were 0. *School Counseling MA/MS (Master of Arts/Science)*—Applications 2007–2008, 15. Total applicants accepted 2007–2008, 8. Number full-time enrolled (new admits only) 2007–2008, 8. Number part-time enrolled (new admits only) 2007–2008, 3. Total enrolled 2007–2008 full-time, 16. Openings 2008–2009, 10. The median number of years required for completion of a degree in 2006–2007 were 2. *School Counseling EdS/MEd (School Psychology)*—Applications 2007–2008, 3. Total applicants accepted 2007–2008, 3. Number full-time enrolled (new admits only) 2007–2008, 0. Number part-time enrolled (new admits only) 2007–2008, 3. Openings 2008–2009, 5. The median number of years required for completion of a degree in 2006–2007 were 2.

Admissions Requirements:

Scores: Entries appear in this order: required test or GPA, minimum score (if required), median score of students entering in 2007–2008. Master's Programs: GRE-V 400, 455; GRE-Q 400, 470; overall undergraduate GPA 3.0, 3.22. We employ a compensatory admissions model such that weakness in one area may be compensated for by strength in another.

Other Criteria: (importance of criteria rated low, medium, or high): GRE/MAT scores—high, research experience—low, GPA—high, letters of recommendation—medium.

Student Characteristics: The following represents characteristics of students in 2007–2008 in all graduate psychology programs in the department: Female—full-time 28, part-time 0; Male—full-time 9, part-time 0; African American/Black—full-time 4, part-time 0; Hispanic/Latino(a)—full-time 2, part-time 0; Asian/Pacific Islander—full-time 0, part-time 0; American Indian/Alaska Native—full-time 1, part-time 0; Caucasian/White—full-time 30, part-time 0; students subject to the Americans With Disabilities Act—full-time 0, part-time 0; Unknown ethnicity—full-time 0, part-time 0.

Financial Information/Assistance:

Tuition for Full-Time Study: *Master's:* State residents: per academic year $5,285, $315 per credit hour; Nonstate residents: per academic year $12,645, $683 per credit hour. Tuition is subject to change. See the following Web site for updates and changes in tuition costs: http://www.apsu.edu/businessoffice/acctrec/tuition_fees.htm.

Financial Assistance:

First-Year Students: Teaching assistantships available for first year. Average amount paid per academic year: $9,265. Average number of hours worked per week: 20. Apply by March 1. Tuition remission given: partial.

Advanced Students: Teaching assistantships available for advanced students. Average amount paid per academic year: $9,265. Average number of hours worked per week: 20. Apply by March 1. Tuition remission given: partial.

Additional Information: Of all students currently enrolled full time, 15% benefited from one or more of the listed financial assistance programs. Application and information available online at http://www.apsu.edu/cogs.

Internships/Practica: There are some paid internships available at the present. A variety of unpaid internships are available in mental health agencies, schools, or community agencies.

Housing and Day Care: On-campus housing is available. See the following Web site for more information: http://www.apsu.edu/housing. On-campus day care facilities are available. See the following Web site for more information: http://www.apsu.edu/clc.

Employment of Department Graduates:

Master's Degree Graduates: Of those who graduated in the academic year 2006–2007, the following categories and numbers represent the postgraduate activities and employment of master's degree graduates: Enrolled in a postdoctoral residency/fellowship (n/a), employed in independent practice (n/a), total from the above (master's) (0).

Doctoral Degree Graduates: Of those who graduated in the academic year 2006–2007, the following categories and numbers represent the postgraduate activities and employment of doctoral degree graduates: Enrolled in a psychology doctoral program (n/a), total from the above (doctoral) (0).

Additional Information:

Orientation, Objectives, and Emphasis of Department: The programs in the department are based on the concept that both a strong foundation in theoretical principles and the development of skills in the application of these principles and techniques is necessary in the training of psychologists or counselors. The Master of Arts with a major in psychology offers three options. The Industrial/Organizational program educates students to design, develop, implement, and evaluate psychologically based human resources interventions in organizations. The School Counseling program is designed to meet the competencies required by the state of Tennessee and to provide students with the necessary knowledge and skills to perform efficiently in the elementary and secondary school settings. The objective of the Community Counseling program is to meet the needs of employment, human services, or other agency counselors requiring a master's degree related to their particular vocational needs.

Special Facilities or Resources: The Department of Psychology has a variety of facilities to provide learning and research opportunities. Rooms equipped with one-way observation windows, video, and other monitoring equipment are available for counseling, testing, and human research. The department has arranged for intern and practicum experiences with a variety of community agencies. Laboratories for vision, infant development, animal learning, and behavioral physiology are available for faculty and student research. The department has numerous microcomputers connected to the University's high-speed fiber-optic network for data collection, analysis, and the preparation of manuscripts.

Application Information:

Send to Office of Graduate Studies, Austin Peay State University, Clarksville, TN 37044. Application available online. URL of online application: http://www.apsu.edu. Students are admitted in the Fall, application deadline March 1; Spring, application deadline November 1. We begin to review applications beginning March 1, but continue to accept applications and admit students until program capacity is reached. *Fee:* $25.

East Tennessee State University

Department of Psychology
College of Arts and Sciences
Box 70649 (Psychology)
Johnson City, TN 37614-0649
Telephone: (423) 439-4424
Fax: (423) 439-5695
E-mail: *dixonw@mail.etsu.edu*
Web: *http://www.etsu.edu/psychology/*

Department Information:

1966. Chairperson: Wallace E. Dixon, Jr. Number of faculty: total—full-time 12, part-time 7; women—full-time 5, part-time 5; minority—part-time 1.

Programs and Degrees Offered:

Listed in the following order: Program area, degree type (T if terminal Master's), number awarded 7/06–6/07. General Psychology MA/MS (Master of Arts/Science) (T) 1, Clinical Psychology PhD (Doctor of Philosophy).

Student Applications/Admissions:

Student Applications

General Psychology MA/MS (Master of Arts/Science)—Applications 2007–2008, 10. Total applicants accepted 2007–2008, 3. Number full-time enrolled (new admits only) 2007–2008, 3. Total enrolled 2007–2008 full-time, 5, part-time, 3. Openings 2008–2009, 4. The median number of years required for completion of a degree in 2006–2007 were 2. The number of students enrolled full- and part-time who were dismissed or voluntarily withdrew from this program area in 2007–2008 were 0. *Clinical Psychology PhD (Doctor of Philosophy)*—Applications 2007–2008, 41. Total applicants accepted 2007–2008, 8. Number full-time enrolled (new admits only) 2007–2008, 8. Total enrolled 2007–2008 full-time, 8. Openings 2008–2009, 8. The number of students enrolled full- and part-time who were dismissed or voluntarily withdrew from this program area in 2007–2008 were 1.

Admissions Requirements:

Scores: Entries appear in this order: required test or GPA, minimum score (if required), median score of students entering in 2007–2008. Master's Programs: GRE-V 500, 511; GRE-Q 500, 560; GRE-Subject (Psychology) no minimum stated; overall undergraduate GPA 3.00, 3.40; last 2 years GPA 3.50; psychology GPA 3.3, 3.4. Doctoral Programs: GRE-V 430, 510; GRE-Q 440, 560; overall undergraduate GPA 3.25, 3.63; psychology GPA 3.50, 3.65; Doctoral program GRE-Analytic 4.0, 4.5. The GRE-Analytic subtest is replaced with the writing subtest.

Other Criteria: (importance of criteria rated low, medium, or high): GRE/MAT scores—high, research experience—high, work experience—medium, extracurricular activity—low, clinically related public service—low, GPA—high, letters of recommendation—high, interview—medium, statement of goals and objectives—high. Interview is none to low for the general program. For additional information on admission requirements, go to http://www.etsu.edu/psychology/.

Student Characteristics: The following represents characteristics of students in 2007–2008 in all graduate psychology programs in the department: Female—full-time 12, part-time 6; Male—full-time 5, part-time 2; African American/Black—full-time 0, part-time 1; Hispanic/Latino(a)—full-time 0, part-time 0; Asian/Pacific Islander—full-time 1, part-time 0; American Indian/Alaska Native—full-time 0, part-time 0; Caucasian/White—full-time 16, part-time 7; Multi-ethnic—full-time 0, part-time 0; students subject to the Americans With Disabilities Act—full-time 1, part-time 0; Unknown ethnicity—full-time 0, part-time 0; International students who hold an F-1 or J-1 Visa—full-time 0, part-time 0.

Financial Information/Assistance:

Tuition for Full-Time Study: *Master's:* State residents: per academic year $5,446, $288 per credit hour; Nonstate residents: per academic year $10,276, $446 per credit hour. *Doctoral:* State residents: per academic year $5,446, $288 per credit hour; Nonstate residents: per academic year $10,276, $446 per credit hour. Tuition is subject to change. See the following Web site for updates and changes in tuition costs: http://www.etsu.edu/reg/.

Financial Assistance:

First-Year Students: Research assistantships available for first year. Average amount paid per academic year: $12,000. Average number of hours worked per week: 20. Apply by February 1. Tuition remission given: full and partial.

Advanced Students: Traineeships available for advanced students. Average amount paid per academic year: $12,000. Average number of hours worked per week: 20. Apply by February 1. Tuition remission given: partial.

Additional Information: Application and information available online at http://www.etsu.edu/finaid/financial.htm.

Internships/Practica: Internships and practica in assessment and therapy are available to students enrolled in the Clinical Psychology program. They are conducted in the area mental health, behavioral health- and primary care facilities under the joint supervision of departmental faculty and adjunct faculty located in the facilities. Students also participate in intensive clinical training in the department's training clinic.

Housing and Day Care: On-campus housing is available. See the following Web site for more information: http://www.etsu.edu/students/housing/housing.htm. On-campus day care facilities are available. See the following Web site for more information: http://www.etsu.edu/students/caps/Childcare.htm.

Employment of Department Graduates:

Master's Degree Graduates: Of those who graduated in the academic year 2006–2007, the following categories and numbers represent the postgraduate activities and employment of master's degree graduates: Enrolled in a psychology doctoral program (2), enrolled in a postdoctoral residency/fellowship (n/a), employed in independent practice (n/a), total from the above (master's) (2).

Doctoral Degree Graduates: Of those who graduated in the academic year 2006–2007, the following categories and numbers represent the postgraduate activities and employment of doctoral degree graduates: Enrolled in a psychology doctoral program (n/a), total from the above (doctoral) (0).

Additional Information:

Orientation, Objectives, and Emphasis of Department: The Department of Psychology, College of Arts and Sciences, offers a Master's of Arts Degree in general psychology and a new Doctor of Philosophy in clinical psychology. The general psychology option prepares students for various endeavors, such as teaching at the community college level and doctoral study in psychology. The clinical psychology option provides students with training in clinical psychology with an emphasis in integrated rural primary care psychology.

Special Facilities or Resources: The psychology department maintains general experimental psychology, physiological psychology, and clinical psychology laboratory facilities. All laboratories are used for undergraduate and graduate instructional research and for student and faculty research. Assistantships and employment are available outside of the department, including the medical school.

Application Information:

Send to School of Graduate Studies, East Tennessee State University, P.O. Box 70720, Johnson City, TN 37614-1710. Application available online. URL of online application: http://www.etsu.edu/gradstud/. Students are admitted in the Fall, application deadline February 1. The Clinical program deadline is February 1; the General program is March 1. Students are normally admitted only in the Fall term, although exceptions for students in the General option can sometimes be made. All applications are reviewed by a departmental admissions committee, and a telephone interview may be conducted. *Fee:* $25.

Memphis, University of

Department of Counseling, Educational Psychology and Research, Program in Counseling Psychology
Education
100 Ball Building
Memphis, TN 38152
Telephone: (901) 678-2841
Fax: (901) 678-5114
E-mail: *slease@memphis.edu*
Web: *http://www.cpsy.memphis.edu*

Department Information:

1972. Chairperson: Douglas Strohmer. Number of faculty: total—full-time 21, part-time 5; women—full-time 12, part-time 2; women minority—full-time 4, part-time 1; faculty subject to the Americans With Disabilities Act 2.

Programs and Degrees Offered:

Listed in the following order: Program area, degree type (T if terminal Master's), number awarded 7/06–6/07. Counseling Psychology PhD (Doctor of Philosophy) 10.

APA Accreditation: Counseling PhD (Doctor of Philosophy).

Student Applications/Admissions:

Student Applications

Counseling Psychology PhD (Doctor of Philosophy)—Applications 2007–2008, 36. Total applicants accepted 2007–2008, 16. Number full-time enrolled (new admits only) 2007–2008, 8. Number part-time enrolled (new admits only) 2007–2008, 0. Total enrolled 2007–2008 full-time, 36, part-time, 5. Openings 2008–2009, 8. The median number of years required for completion of a degree in 2006–2007 were 4. The number of students enrolled full- and part-time who were dismissed or voluntarily withdrew from this program area in 2007–2008 were 0.

Admissions Requirements:

Scores: Entries appear in this order: required test or GPA, minimum score (if required), median score of students entering in 2007–2008. Doctoral Programs: GRE-V 500, 530; GRE-Q 500, 600. GRE score information is for PhD in Counseling Psychology only.

Other Criteria: (importance of criteria rated low, medium, or high): GRE/MAT scores—high, research experience—medium, work experience—medium, clinically related public service—low, GPA—high, letters of recommendation—high, interview—medium, statement of goals and objectives—high, fit with program philosophy—high. Criteria for PhD in Counseling Psychology only. For additional information on admission requirements, go to http://cpsy.memphis.edu.

Student Characteristics: The following represents characteristics of students in 2007–2008 in all graduate psychology programs in the department: Female—full-time 24, part-time 4; Male—full-time 12, part-time 1; African American/Black—full-time 4, part-time 1; Hispanic/Latino(a)—full-time 0, part-time 0; Asian/Pacific Islander—full-time 3, part-time 0; American Indian/Alaska Native—full-time 0, part-time 0; Caucasian/White—full-time 29, part-time 4; students subject to the Americans With Disabilities Act—full-time 1, part-time 0; Unknown ethnicity—full-time 0, part-time 0; International students who hold an F-1 or J-1 Visa—full-time 5, part-time 0.

Financial Information/Assistance:

Tuition for Full-Time Study: *Master's:* State residents: per academic year $11,118, $405 per credit hour; Nonstate residents: per academic year $27,366, $899 per credit hour. *Doctoral:* State residents: per academic year $11,118, $405 per credit hour; Nonstate residents: per academic year $27,366, $899 per credit hour. Tuition is subject to change. See the following Web site for updates and changes in tuition costs: http://www.bf.memphis.edu/finance/bursar/feepayment.php.

Financial Assistance:

First-Year Students: Research assistantships available for first year. Average amount paid per academic year: $8,000. Average number of hours worked per week: 20. Apply by April 1. Tuition remission given: full and partial. Fellowships and scholarships available for first year. Apply by varies.

Advanced Students: Teaching assistantships available for advanced students. Average amount paid per academic year: $8,000. Average number of hours worked per week: 20. Apply by April 1. Tuition remission given: full and partial. Research assistantships available for advanced students. Average amount paid per academic year: $8,000. Average number of hours worked per week: 20. Apply by April 1. Tuition remission given: full and partial. Traineeships available for advanced students. Average amount paid per academic year: $10,000. Average number of hours worked per week: 20. Apply by varies. Tuition remission given: partial. Fellowships and scholarships available for advanced students. Apply by varies. Tuition remission given: full.

Additional Information: Of all students currently enrolled full time, 92% benefited from one or more of the listed financial assistance programs. Application and information available online at http://academics.memphis.edu/gradschool/gainfo.html or http://coe.memphis.edu/cepr.

Internships/Practica: Doctoral Degree (PhD Counseling Psychology): For those doctoral students for whom a professional internship was required in this program prior to graduation, (12) students applied for an internship in 2006–2007, with (12) students obtaining an internship. Of those students who obtained an internship, (12) were paid internships. Of those students who obtained an internship, (9) students placed in APA/CPA accredited internships, (3) students placed in internships not APA/CPA-accredited, but listed with the Association of Psychology Postdoctoral and Internship Centers (APPIC), (0) students placed in internships conforming to guidelines of the Council of Directors of School Psychology Programs (CDSPP), (0) students placed in internships that were not APA/CPA-accredited, APPIC or CDSPP listed. Doctoral students complete a minimum of two practica during their 3 years of coursework; many students complete up to four practica. The department has an extensive network of relationships with community agencies for providing practicum placements for students. These placements include university and college counseling centers, VAs and hospitals, community mental health centers, private practice, pediatric neuroassessment, and correctional services. For additional information on education and training outcomes for our programs, see the following Web site: http://www.coe.memphis.edu/cepr/CPSY_Graduate_Information.htm.

Housing and Day Care: On-campus housing is available. See the following Web site for more information: http://www.people.memphis.edu/~reslife/. On-campus day care facilities are available. See the following Web site for more information: http://www.reslifeweb.memphis.edu/reslife/childcareweb/index.html.

Employment of Department Graduates:

Master's Degree Graduates: Of those who graduated in the academic year 2006–2007, the following categories and numbers represent the postgraduate activities and employment of master's degree graduates: Enrolled in a postdoctoral residency/fellowship (n/a), employed in independent practice (n/a), total from the above (master's) (0).

Doctoral Degree Graduates: Of those who graduated in the academic year 2006–2007, the following categories and numbers represent the postgraduate activities and employment of doctoral degree graduates: Enrolled in a psychology doctoral program (n/a), enrolled in a postdoctoral residency/fellowship (0), employed in independent practice (2), employed in an academic position at a university (1), employed in an academic position at a 2-year/4-year college (0), employed in other positions at a higher education institution (2), employed in a professional position in a school system (0), employed in business or industry (0), employed in government agency (1), employed in a community mental health/counseling center (2), employed in a hospital/medical center (2), total from the above (doctoral) (10).

Additional Information:

Orientation, Objectives, and Emphasis of Department: The PhD in Counseling Psychology at the University of Memphis is designed to train psychologists who promote human development in the areas of mental health, career development, emotional and social learning, and decision making in a rapidly changing global environment. Training is organized around the scientist–practitioner model of critical thinking and emphasizes multicultural competency and responsibility and commitment to human welfare. Didactic and experiential activities are designed to anchor persons firmly within the discipline of psychology. The program emphasizes research, development, prevention, and remediation as vehicles for helping individuals, families, and groups achieve competence and a sense of well-being. The department has a strong commitment to training professionals to work with diverse populations in urban settings. Within the context of the University mission, students are expected to develop the critical thinking skills necessary for lifelong learning and to contribute to the global community. Students are expected to acquire (a) an identity as a counseling psychologist; (b) a knowledge foundation in psychology, research, counseling, psychological evaluation, and professional standards; and (c) skills in research, practice, and teaching.

The program is individualized to meet the student's goals. Graduates are prepared for positions in various settings, including counseling centers, mental health centers, hospitals, private practice, or academia.

Special Facilities or Resources: Department faculty have research teams that provide opportunities for faculty and students to collaborate on research and consultation products. Many students are also involved in cross-disciplinary research with Psychology and Women's Studies faculty.

Information for Students With Physical Disabilities: See the following Web site for more information: http://www.people.memphis.edu/~sds/.

Application Information:

Send to Suzanne Lease, Counseling Psychology Admissions, 100 Ball Building, The University of Memphis Memphis, TN 38152. Application available online. URL of online application: http://www.cpsy.memphis.edu. Students are admitted in the Fall, application deadline January 15. The application for the Counseling Psychology program can be obtained online from the program Web page. Applications for programs other than Counseling Psychology go to the Admissions Secretary, department office address. For all programs, there are separate applications to the Graduate School and to the specific programs in the department. *Fee:* $35. This is the Graduate School application fee for domestic students. The fee is $60 for international students. Application to the Graduate School may be made at: http://academics.memphis.edu/gradschool/admproc.html.

Memphis, University of (2007 data)

Department of Psychology
College of Arts and Sciences
202 Psychology Building
Memphis, TN 38152-3230
Telephone: (901) 678-2145
Fax: (901) 678-2579
E-mail: *a-graesser@memphis.edu*
Web: *http://www.psyc.memphis.edu/*

Department Information:

1957. Chairperson: Arthur C. Graesser. Number of faculty: total—full-time 35, part-time 3; women—full-time 8, part-time 1; faculty subject to the Americans With Disabilities Act 1.

Programs and Degrees Offered:

Listed in the following order: Program area, degree type (T if terminal Master's), number awarded 7/06–6/07. Clinical Psychology PhD (Doctor of Philosophy) 4, School MA/EDS MA/MS (Master of Arts/Science) (T) 9, General Psychology MA/MS (Master of Arts/Science) (T) 7, School Psychology PhD (Doctor of Philosophy) 2, Experimental Psychology PhD (Doctor of Philosophy) 6.

APA Accreditation: Clinical PhD (Doctor of Philosophy).

Student Applications/Admissions:

Student Applications

Clinical Psychology PhD (Doctor of Philosophy)—Applications 2007–2008, 118. Total applicants accepted 2007–2008, 9. Number full-time enrolled (new admits only) 2007–2008, 7. Number part-time enrolled (new admits only) 2007–2008, 0. Openings 2008–2009, 8. The median number of years required for completion of a degree in 2006–2007 were 6. The number of students enrolled full- and part-time who were dismissed or voluntarily withdrew from this program area in 2007–2008 were 1. *School MA/EDS MA/MS (Master of Arts/Science)*—Applications 2007–2008, 17. Total applicants accepted 2007–2008, 12. Number full-time enrolled (new admits only) 2007–2008, 9. Number part-time enrolled (new admits only) 2007–2008, 2. Total enrolled 2007–2008 full-time, 27, part-time, 2. Openings 2008–2009, 12. The median number of years required for completion of a degree in 2006–2007 were 3. The number of students enrolled full- and part-time who were dismissed or voluntarily withdrew from this program area in 2007–2008 were 1. *General Psychology MA/MS (Master of Arts/Science)*—Applications 2007–2008, 37. Total applicants accepted 2007–2008, 24. Number full-time enrolled (new admits only) 2007–2008, 10. Number part-time enrolled (new admits only) 2007–2008, 4. Total enrolled 2007–2008 full-time, 22, part-time, 11. Openings 2008–2009, 15. The median number of years required for completion of a degree in 2006–2007 were 3. The number of students enrolled full- and part-time who were dismissed or voluntarily withdrew from this program area in 2007–2008 were 0. *School Psychology PhD (Doctor of Philosophy)*—Applications 2007–2008, 6. Total applicants accepted 2007–2008, 0. Number full-time enrolled (new admits only) 2007–2008, 0. Number part-time enrolled (new admits only) 2007–2008, 0. Openings 2008–2009, 3. The median number of years required for completion of a degree in 2006–2007 were 5. The number of students enrolled full- and part-time who were dismissed or voluntarily withdrew from this program area in 2007–2008 were 0. *Experimental Psychology PhD (Doctor of Philosophy)*—Applications 2007–2008, 41. Total applicants accepted 2007–2008, 17. Number full-time enrolled (new admits only) 2007–2008, 15. Number part-time enrolled (new admits only) 2007–2008, 0. Openings 2008–2009, 6. The median number of years required for completion of a degree in 2006–2007 were 5. The number of students enrolled full- and part-time who were dismissed or voluntarily withdrew from this program area in 2007–2008 were 2.

Admissions Requirements:

Scores: Entries appear in this order: required test or GPA, minimum score (if required), median score of students entering in 2007–2008. Master's Programs: GRE-V 450, 520; GRE-Q 450, 630; overall undergraduate GPA 2.5, 3.5. The minimum undergraduate GPA required for the MA/EdS is 3.0/4.0. For the MSGP, the minimum undergraduate GPA required is 2.5/40. A minimum combined verbal and quantitative score of 900 is required for both master's program. Doctoral Programs: GRE-V 550, 530; GRE-Q 550, 650; overall undergraduate GPA 2.75, 3.5. A minimum combined verbal and quantitative score of 1100 is required for the PhD programs in Clinical, Experimental, and School programs.

Other Criteria: (importance of criteria rated low, medium, or high): GRE/MAT scores—high, research experience—high, work experience—medium, extracurricular activity—low, clinically related public service—low, GPA—high, letters of recommendation—high, interview—low, statement of goals and objectives—high.

Student Characteristics: The following represents characteristics of students in 2007–2008 in all graduate psychology programs in the department: Female—full-time 92, part-time 9; Male—full-time 47, part-time 4; African American/Black—full-time 12, part-time 1; Hispanic/Latino(a)—full-time 4, part-time 1; Asian/Pacific Islander—full-time 12, part-time 0; American Indian/Alaska Native—full-time 0, part-time 0; Caucasian/White—full-time 110, part-time 11; Multi-ethnic—full-time 0, part-time 0; students subject to the Americans With Disabilities Act—full-time 0, part-time 0; Unknown ethnicity—full-time 1, part-time 0.

Financial Information/Assistance:

Tuition for Full-Time Study: *Master's:* State residents: per academic year $8,376, $349 per credit hour; Nonstate residents: per academic year $19,128, $797 per credit hour. *Doctoral:* State residents: per academic year $8,376, $349 per credit hour; Nonstate residents: per academic year $19,128, $797 per credit hour. Tuition is subject to change. See the following Web site for updates and changes in tuition costs: http://www.bf.memphis.edu/ebursar/.

Financial Assistance:

First-Year Students: Teaching assistantships available for first year. Average amount paid per academic year: $11,000. Average number of hours worked per week: 20. Tuition remission given: full. Research assistantships available for first year. Average amount paid per academic year: $11,000. Average number of hours worked per week: 20. Tuition remission given: full.

Advanced Students: Teaching assistantships available for advanced students. Average amount paid per academic year: $12,000. Average number of hours worked per week: 20. Tuition remission given: full. Research assistantships available for advanced students. Average amount paid per academic year: $12,000. Average number of hours worked per week: 20. Tuition remission given: full.

Additional Information: Of all students currently enrolled full time, 65% benefited from one or more of the listed financial assistance programs. Application and information available online at http://www.psyc.memphis.edu/.

Internships/Practica: The department has an extensive network of relationships with local agencies for providing practicum experiences for students. PhD clinical students work 20 hours per week at several of these practicum sites for a minimum of 1 year. All students can use these sites for other forms of practicum experience and research as the need arises. The department has no in-house internships. Students complete internships during the 4th or 5th year at sites nationwide.

Housing and Day Care: On-campus housing is available. See the following Web site for more information: http://www.www.people.memphis.edu/~reslife/. On-campus day care facilities are available. See the following Web site for more information: http://www.reslifeweb.memphis.edu/reslife/childcareweb/index.html.

Employment of Department Graduates:

Master's Degree Graduates: Of those who graduated in the academic year 2006–2007, the following categories and numbers represent the postgraduate activities and employment of master's degree graduates: Enrolled in another graduate/professional program (0), enrolled in a postdoctoral residency/fellowship (n/a), employed in independent practice (n/a), employed in an academic position at a university (0), employed in an academic position at a 2-year/4-year college (0), employed in other positions at a higher education institution (1), employed in a professional position in a school system (9), employed in business or industry (0), employed in government agency (0), employed in a community mental health/counseling center (0), employed in a hospital/medical center (0), still seeking employment (0), other employment position (0), do not know (10), total from the above (master's) (20).

Doctoral Degree Graduates: Of those who graduated in the academic year 2006–2007, the following categories and numbers represent the postgraduate activities and employment of doctoral degree graduates: Enrolled in a psychology doctoral program (n/a), enrolled in another graduate/professional program (0), enrolled in a postdoctoral residency/fellowship (5), employed in independent practice (0), employed in an academic position at a university (0), employed in an academic position at a 2-year/4-year college (1), employed in other positions at a higher education institution (0), employed in a professional position in a school system (0), employed in business or industry (2), employed in government agency (1), employed in a hospital/medical center (0), still seeking employment (0), other employment position (0), do not know (8), total from the above (doctoral) (17).

Additional Information:

Orientation, Objectives, and Emphasis of Department: The department philosophy emphasizes the training of experimentally sophisticated research scientists and practitioners. All programs have a strong research emphasis. Professional training is based upon a research foundation and students are exposed to a broad range of theoretical perspectives. Diversity of professional training activities and collaborative research activities is emphasized. Students are afforded maximum freedom to pursue their own interests and tailor programs to their needs. All PhD and master's programs are serviced by six research areas within the department: Behavioral Medicine, Behavioral Neuroscience, Child and Family Studies, Cognitive and Social Processes, Industrial/Organizational and Applied Psychology, and Psychopathology/Psychotherapy.

Special Facilities or Resources: The department as a whole has a strong research orientation, and an NSF study published in 2003 found the Psychology Department at The University of Memphis to rank sixth among psychology departments across the nation in total research and development expenditures. The department is housed in a modern, well-equipped barrier-free building, providing offices and laboratory space for all students. The department includes the Center for Applied Psychological Research (CAPR), the Institute for Intelligent Systems (IIS), the Universities Prevention Center, and the Psychological Services Center (PSC). The CAPR is the state-sponsored center of excellence that has provided the department with approximately $1 million per year for the past 20 years. The IIS is an interdisciplinary enterprise comprised of researchers and students from the fields of cognitive psychology, computer science, mathematics, physics, neuroscience, education, linguistics, philosophy, anthropology, engineering, and business. The Prevention Center is a joint venture of The University of Memphis and the University of Tennessee, Memphis. Researchers and staff are dedicated to developing ways of preventing cancer and cardiovascular diseases. The Psychological Services Center is a fee-for-service outpatient mental health clinic located in the psychology building. In this clinic doctoral students receive intensive supervision as they learn to provide a wide range of assessment and intervention services. In addition, the PSC provides an invaluable resource for the conduct of a variety of research projects. The clients are referred from the greater Memphis area.

Information for Students With Physical Disabilities: See the following Web site for more information: http://www.people.memphis.edu/~sds/.

Application Information:

There are two applications (see Web site for directions). One is sent to the Graduate School of the University of Memphis at the following address: The University of Memphis, Graduate School Admissions Office, Wilder Tower 101, Memphis, TN 38152. The other is sent to the Department of Psychology at the following address: Graduate Admissions, Department of Psychology, 202 Psychology Building, University of Memphis, Memphis, TN 38152. Application available on-line. URL of online application: http://www.psyc.memphis.edu/application/. Students are admitted in the Fall, application deadline see below. The application deadline for all PhD programs is January 15. The application deadline for the master's program in General Psychology is May 15. The application deadline for the MA/EdS in School Psychology is June 15. *Fee:* $50. The application fee for the graduate school is $35 for domestic students and $60 for international students. There is an additional fee of $15 for the Department of Psychology application.

Middle Tennessee State University

Department of Psychology
Education and Behavioral Science
Box 87
Murfreesboro, TN 37132
Telephone: (615) 898-2706
Fax: (615) 898-5027
E-mail: *alittlep@mtsu.edu*
Web: *http://www.mtsu.edu/~psych*

Department Information:

1967. Chairperson: Dennis R. Papini. Number of faculty: total—full-time 47, part-time 13; women—full-time 20, part-time 8; total—minority—full-time 2, part-time 1.

Programs and Degrees Offered:

Listed in the following order: Program area, degree type (T if terminal Master's), number awarded 7/06–6/07. Clinical MA/MS (Master of Arts/Science) (T) 6, Experimental MA/MS (Master of Arts/Science) (T) 2, Industrial/Organizational MA/MS (Master of Arts/Science) (T) 12, Quantitative MA/MS (Master of Arts/Science) (T) 4, School Psychology EdS/MEd (School Psychology) 13, School Psychology EdS/MEd (School Psychology) 12, Professional Counseling Other 12.

Student Applications/Admissions:

Student Applications

Clinical MA/MS (Master of Arts/Science)—Applications 2007–2008, 28. Total applicants accepted 2007–2008, 24. Number full-time enrolled (new admits only) 2007–2008, 6. Number part-time enrolled (new admits only) 2007–2008, 0. Total enrolled 2007–2008 full-time, 23, part-time, 4. Openings 2008–2009, 15. The median number of years required for completion of a degree in 2006–2007 were 2. The number of students enrolled full- and part-time who were dismissed or voluntarily withdrew from this program area in 2007–2008 were 0. *Experimental MA/MS (Master of Arts/Science)*—Applications 2007–2008, 8. Total applicants accepted 2007–2008, 4. Openings 2008–2009, 20. The number of students enrolled full- and part-time who were dismissed or voluntarily withdrew from this program area in 2007–2008 were 4. *Industrial/Organizational MA/MS (Master of Arts/Science)*—Applications 2007–2008, 80. Total applicants accepted 2007–2008, 17. Number full-time enrolled (new admits only) 2007–2008, 11. Total enrolled 2007–2008 full-time, 24, part-time, 2. Openings 2008–2009, 12. The median number of years required for completion of a degree in 2006–2007 were 2. *Quantitative MA/MS (Master of Arts/Science)*—Applications 2007–2008, 9. Total applicants accepted 2007–2008, 7. Number full-time enrolled (new admits only) 2007–2008, 6. Total enrolled 2007–2008 full-time, 12, part-time, 1. Openings 2008–2009, 6. The median number of years required for completion of a degree in 2006–2007 were 2. The number of students enrolled full- and part-time who were dismissed or voluntarily withdrew from this program area in 2007–2008 were 1. *School Psychology EdS/MEd (School Psychology)*—Applications 2007–2008, 32. Total applicants accepted 2007–2008, 22. Number full-time enrolled (new admits only) 2007–2008, 11. Number part-time enrolled (new admits only) 2007–2008, 1. Total enrolled 2007–2008 full-time, 28, part-time, 2. Openings 2008–2009, 12. The median number of years required for completion of a degree in 2006–2007 were 3. The number of students enrolled full- and part-time who were dismissed or voluntarily withdrew from this program area in 2007–2008 were 1. *School Psychology EdS/MEd (School Psychology)*—Applications 2007–2008, 32. Total applicants accepted 2007–2008, 20. Number full-time enrolled (new admits only) 2007–2008, 12. Number part-time enrolled (new admits only) 2007–2008, 1. Total enrolled 2007–2008 full-time, 30, part-time, 3. Openings 2008–2009, 13. The median number of years required for completion of a degree in 2006–2007 were 3. The number of students enrolled full- and part-time who were dismissed or voluntarily withdrew from this program area in 2007–2008 were 1. *Professional Counseling Other*—Applications 2007–2008, 40. Total applicants accepted 2007–2008, 18. Number full-time enrolled (new admits only) 2007–2008, 12. Number part-time enrolled (new admits only) 2007–2008, 6. Total enrolled 2007–2008 full-time, 30, part-time, 16. Openings 2008–2009, 25. The median number of years required for completion of a degree in 2006–2007 were 3. The number of students enrolled full- and part-time who were dismissed or voluntarily withdrew from this program area in 2007–2008 were 4.

Admissions Requirements:

Scores: Entries appear in this order: required test or GPA, minimum score (if required), median score of students entering in 2007–2008. Master's Programs: GRE-V 450, 550; GRE-Q 450, 500; overall undergraduate GPA 3.00, 3.4. Professional Counseling/Mental Health—1000 on GRE (with scores no lower than 400 on either the Verbal or Quantitative portion of the exam).

Other Criteria: (importance of criteria rated low, medium, or high): GRE/MAT scores—high, research experience—high, work experience—low, extracurricular activity—low, clinically related public service—medium, GPA—high, letters of recommendation—high, interview—high, statement of goals and objectives—high. Interview: School Counseling only. Statement of goals and objectives for Experimental and School Psychology only.

Student Characteristics: The following represents characteristics of students in 2007–2008 in all graduate psychology programs in the department: Female—full-time 89, part-time 0; Male—full-time 30, part-time 0; African American/Black—full-time 10, part-time 0; Hispanic/Latino(a)—part-time 0; Asian/Pacific Islander—full-time 1, part-time 0; American Indian/Alaska Native—part-time 0; Caucasian/White—full-time 100, part-time 0; Multi-ethnic—full-time 8, part-time 0; Unknown ethnicity—full-time 0, part-time 0.

Financial Information/Assistance:

Tuition for Full-Time Study: *Master's:* State residents: per academic year $5,138, $337 per credit hour; Nonstate residents: per academic year $15,070, $741 per credit hour. See the following Web site for updates and changes in tuition costs: http://www.mtsu.edu/~bursarmt.

Financial Assistance:

First-Year Students: Research assistantships available for first year. Average amount paid per academic year: $4,550. Average number of hours worked per week: 20. Apply by March/October 1. Tuition remission given: full and partial.

Advanced Students: Research assistantships available for advanced students. Average amount paid per academic year: $7,000. Average number of hours worked per week: 20. Apply by March 1. Tuition remission given: full.

Additional Information: Of all students currently enrolled full time, 50% benefited from one or more of the listed financial assistance programs. Application and information available online at http://www.mtsu.edu/~graduate.

Internships/Practica: Master's Degree (MA/MS Clinical): An internship experience such as a final research project or "capstone" experience is required of graduates. Master's Degree (MA/MS Experimental): An internship experience such as a final research project or "capstone" experience is required of graduates. Field placements are available in a variety of mental health facilities, inpatient facilities, the VA hospital, drug abuse facilities, K–12 school settings, and industrial sites.

Housing and Day Care: On-campus housing is available. See the following Web site for more information: http://www.mtsu.edu/~housing/; http://www.mtsu.edu/info/dcl.html. On-campus day care facilities are available.

Employment of Department Graduates:

Master's Degree Graduates: Of those who graduated in the academic year 2006–2007, the following categories and numbers represent the postgraduate activities and employment of master's degree graduates: Enrolled in a psychology doctoral program (2), enrolled in a postdoctoral residency/fellowship (n/a), employed in independent practice (n/a), employed in a professional position in a school system (13), employed in business or industry (3), still seeking employment (0), total from the above (master's) (18).

Doctoral Degree Graduates: Of those who graduated in the academic year 2006–2007, the following categories and numbers represent the postgraduate activities and employment of doctoral degree graduates: Enrolled in a psychology doctoral program (n/a), total from the above (doctoral) (0).

Additional Information:

Orientation, Objectives, and Emphasis of Department: We have an applied department with research and service priorities. A strong academic program is available for students seeking to improve their backgrounds in core areas of psychology for admission to doctoral programs. Applied programs lead to certification and/or licensure in school psychology, school counseling, and clinical (http://www.mtsu.edu/~psych). Industrial/Organizational program nationally acclaimed (for more about the I/O program, see http://www.mtsu.edu/~iopsych).

Information for Students With Physical Disabilities: See the following Web site for more information: http://www.mtsu.edu/~dssemail.

Application Information:

Send to Office of Graduate Studies, Cope Administration Building, 114 Middle, Tennessee State University, Murfreesboro, TN 37132. Application available online. URL of online application: http://www.mtsu.edu/~graduate. Students are admitted in the Fall, application deadline October 1; Spring, application deadline March 1. Applicants to the Clinical and School Psychology programs must submit a supplemental applications and three letters of recommendation on supplied forms. Professional Counseling applicants require special recommendation forms and typed essay (500 words or less). Industrial/Organizational, Experimental, and School Psychology require a Personal Statement. Forms can be obtained from the Department of Psychology or online through the psychology department Web site. *Fee:* $30.

Tennessee, University of, Chattanooga

Department of Psychology
350 Holt Hall
Chattanooga, TN 37403
Telephone: (423) 425-4262
Fax: (423) 425-4284
E-mail: *michael-biderman@utc.edu*
Web: *http://www.utc.edu/ioprog*

Department Information:

1969. Head: Paul J. Watson. Number of faculty: total—full-time 13, part-time 8; women—full-time 4, part-time 4; total—minority—full-time 1, part-time 1; women minority—full-time 1, part-time 1.

Programs and Degrees Offered:

Listed in the following order: Program area, degree type (T if terminal Master's), number awarded 7/06–6/07. Industrial/Organizational MA/MS (Master of Arts/Science) (T) 21, Research MA/MS (Master of Arts/Science) (T) 6.

Student Applications/Admissions:

Student Applications

Industrial/Organizational MA/MS (Master of Arts/Science)—Applications 2007–2008, 54. Total applicants accepted 2007–

2008, 50. Number full-time enrolled (new admits only) 2007–2008, 19. Openings 2008–2009, 20. The median number of years required for completion of a degree in 2006–2007 were 2. The number of students enrolled full- and part-time who were dismissed or voluntarily withdrew from this program area in 2007–2008 were 0. *Research MA/MS (Master of Arts/Science)*—Applications 2007–2008, 8. Total applicants accepted 2007–2008, 6. Number full-time enrolled (new admits only) 2007–2008, 4. Openings 2008–2009, 8. The median number of years required for completion of a degree in 2006–2007 were 2. The number of students enrolled full- and part-time who were dismissed or voluntarily withdrew from this program area in 2007–2008 were 0.

Admissions Requirements:

Scores: Entries appear in this order: required test or GPA, minimum score (if required), median score of students entering in 2007–2008. Master's Programs: GRE-V no minimum stated, 460; GRE-Q no minimum stated, 530; overall undergraduate GPA no minimum stated, 3.40. We use a formula: 200 x UGPA + (GREV+GREQ)/2. We generally admit those whose formula score exceeds 1150. We take letters or reference and a personal statement into account.

Other Criteria: (importance of criteria rated low, medium, or high): GRE/MAT scores—high, research experience—medium, work experience—medium, extracurricular activity—low, clinically related public service—low, GPA—high, letters of recommendation—medium, interview—low, statement of goals and objectives—medium. Admission to the Research program requires sponsorship of a faculty member. For additional information on admission requirements, go to http://www.utc.edu/ioprog.

Student Characteristics: The following represents characteristics of students in 2007–2008 in all graduate psychology programs in the department: Female—full-time 30, part-time 0; Male—full-time 12, part-time 0; African American/Black—full-time 2, part-time 0; Hispanic/Latino(a)—full-time 1, part-time 0; Asian/Pacific Islander—full-time 2, part-time 0; American Indian/Alaska Native—full-time 0, part-time 0; Caucasian/White—full-time 37, part-time 0; students subject to the Americans With Disabilities Act—full-time 0, part-time 0; Unknown ethnicity—full-time 0, part-time 0; International students who hold an F-1 or J-1 Visa—full-time 2, part-time 0.

Financial Information/Assistance:

Tuition for Full-Time Study: *Master's:* State residents: per academic year $5,854; Nonstate residents: per academic year $15,818. Tuition is subject to change. See the following Web site for updates and changes in tuition costs: http://www.utc.edu.

Financial Assistance:

First-Year Students: Teaching assistantships available for first year. Average amount paid per academic year: $1,600. Average number of hours worked per week: 5. Apply by August 20. Research assistantships available for first year. Average amount paid per academic year: $2,750. Average number of hours worked per week: 10. Apply by July 1. Tuition remission given: partial.

Advanced Students: Teaching assistantships available for advanced students. Average amount paid per academic year: $1,600. Average number of hours worked per week: 5. Apply by August 20. Research assistantships available for advanced students. Average amount paid per academic year: $2,750. Average number of hours worked per week: 10. Apply by July 1. Tuition remission given: partial.

Additional Information: Of all students currently enrolled full time, 50% benefited from one or more of the listed financial assistance programs. Application and information available online at http://www.utc.edu/gradstudies.

Internships/Practica: The integration of course work and practice throughout the students' graduate academic program is essential to prepare I/O students for applied professional careers. To achieve this end, I/O students become involved in a variety of real life work organization activities through completion of a practicum program. They are encouraged to start this practicum after their second semester of academic work. Six semester hours of practicum credit are required (involving at least 300 hours of actual work time), and an additional three semester hours may be taken as a part of the elective portion of the program. The practicum is carried out in private and public work organizations in which the students engage in a wide variety of projects under the guidance of field supervisors, coordinated by the I/O faculty.

Housing and Day Care: On-campus housing is available. See the following Web site for more information: http://www.utc.edu. On-campus day care facilities are available.

Employment of Department Graduates:

Master's Degree Graduates: Of those who graduated in the academic year 2006–2007, the following categories and numbers represent the postgraduate activities and employment of master's degree graduates: Enrolled in a psychology doctoral program (2), enrolled in a postdoctoral residency/fellowship (n/a), employed in independent practice (n/a), employed in business or industry (20), employed in government agency (1), do not know (10), total from the above (master's) (33).

Doctoral Degree Graduates: Of those who graduated in the academic year 2006–2007, the following categories and numbers represent the postgraduate activities and employment of doctoral degree graduates: Enrolled in a psychology doctoral program (n/a), total from the above (doctoral) (0).

Additional Information:

Orientation, Objectives, and Emphasis of Department: The goal of the I/O program is to provide students with the training necessary to pursue a variety of I/O related fields. These include, but are not limited to, positions in human resources, industrial/organizational consulting, training, and organization development. The I/O program can be used as a preparation for the pursuit of doctoral training in I/O related fields of study. The curriculum is organized around specific core knowledge domains particular to I/O psychology. The industrial domain includes content such as job analysis, selection, and training. The organizational domain includes content such as work motivation, attitudes, leadership, organizational development, and group processes. The third domain, research methodology, includes experimental design and univariate and multivariate statistical analysis. The research program is designed primarily to prepare students to pursue doctoral-level training. Students work in an apprenticeship model with faculty to develop strong design and analysis skills.

Special Facilities or Resources: Center for Applied Social Research conducts surveys and other applied research in the community. We have a close relationship with SHRM Chattanooga, the local SHRM chapter, and with several local work organizations.

Information for Students With Physical Disabilities: See the following Web site for more information: http://www.utc.edu/Units/OfficeForStudentsWithDisabilities.

Application Information:
Send to Graduate School, 5305 University of Tennessee—Chattanooga, Chattanooga, TN 37403. Application available online. URL of online application: http://www.utc.edu/ioprog. Students are admitted in the Fall, application deadline March 15; Winter, application deadline March 15; Spring, application deadline see comments; Summer, application deadline see comments; programs have rolling admissions. Students may be admitted after the March deadline if space permits. Programs are designed to begin in the Fall semester. Spring and Summer admissions are possible although students admitted in Spring or Summer will likely require more than 2 years to complete the program. *Fee:* $25.

Tennessee, University of, Knoxville

Department of Educational Psychology and Counseling
Education, Health, and Human Sciences
525 Jane and David Bailey Education Complex
Knoxville, TN 37996-3452
Telephone: (865) 974-8145
Fax: (865) 974-0135
E-mail: *mccallum@utk.edu*
Web: *http://www.coe.utk.edu/programs/graduate.html*

Department Information:
1956. Head: R. Steve McCallum. Number of faculty: total—full-time 30, part-time 2; women—full-time 13; total—minority—full-time 1; faculty subject to the Americans With Disabilities Act 1.

Programs and Degrees Offered:
Listed in the following order: Program area, degree type (T if terminal Master's), number awarded 7/06–6/07. School Psychology PhD (Doctor of Philosophy) 8, Educational Psychology PhD (Doctor of Philosophy) 4, Assessment and Evaluation PhD (Doctor of Philosophy) 2, Instructional Technology PhD (Doctor of Philosophy).

APA Accreditation: School PhD (Doctor of Philosophy).

Student Applications/Admissions:
Student Applications
School Psychology PhD (Doctor of Philosophy)—Applications 2007–2008, 40. Total applicants accepted 2007–2008, 7. Number full-time enrolled (new admits only) 2007–2008, 7. Openings 2008–2009, 7. The median number of years required for completion of a degree in 2006–2007 were 5. The number of students enrolled full- and part-time who were dismissed or voluntarily withdrew from this program area in 2007–2008 were 1. *Educational Psychology PhD (Doctor of Philosophy)*—Applications 2007–2008, 20. Total applicants accepted 2007–2008, 8. Number full-time enrolled (new admits only) 2007–2008, 8. Number part-time enrolled (new admits only) 2007–2008, 0. Total enrolled 2007–2008 full-time, 33, part-time, 2. Openings 2008–2009, 1. The median number of years required for completion of a degree in 2006–2007 were 4. The number of students enrolled full- and part-time who were dismissed or voluntarily withdrew from this program area in 2007–2008 were 1. *Assessment and Evaluation PhD (Doctor of Philosophy)*—Applications 2007–2008, 10. Total applicants accepted 2007–2008, 3. Number full-time enrolled (new admits only) 2007–2008, 1. Number part-time enrolled (new admits only) 2007–2008, 2. Total enrolled 2007–2008 full-time, 6, part-time, 6. Openings 2008–2009, 4. The median number of years required for completion of a degree in 2006–2007 were 4. The number of students enrolled full- and part-time who were dismissed or voluntarily withdrew from this program area in 2007–2008 were 0. *Instructional Technology PhD (Doctor of Philosophy)*—Applications 2007–2008, 10. Total enrolled 2007–2008 full-time, 25. Openings 2008–2009, 8. The median number of years required for completion of a degree in 2006–2007 were 4. The number of students enrolled full- and part-time who were dismissed or voluntarily withdrew from this program area in 2007–2008 were 0.

Admissions Requirements:
Scores: Entries appear in this order: required test or GPA, minimum score (if required), median score of students entering in 2007–2008. Master's Programs: GRE-V no minimum stated; GRE-Q no minimum stated; overall undergraduate GPA 3.0, 3.4; Masters GRE-Analytical no minimum stated. Doctoral Programs: GRE-V no minimum stated; GRE-Q no minimum stated; overall undergraduate GPA 3.0, 3.55; Doctoral program GRE-Analytic no minimum stated. At least 50th percentile on V and 40th percentile on other scale for a total of 1070 this year, plus a 4.5 on Writing scale. Foreign students must take the TOEFL for Educational Psychology.
Other Criteria: (importance of criteria rated low, medium, or high): GRE/MAT scores—medium, research experience—low, work experience—low, extracurricular activity—medium, clinically related public service—medium, GPA—high, letters of recommendation—medium, interview—low, statement of goals and objectives—medium.

Student Characteristics: The following represents characteristics of students in 2007–2008 in all graduate psychology programs in the department: Female—full-time 110, part-time 5; Male—full-time 70, part-time 9; African American/Black—full-time 10, part-time 0; Hispanic/Latino(a)—full-time 1, part-time 0; Asian/Pacific Islander—full-time 2, part-time 0; American Indian/Alaska Native—full-time 0, part-time 0; Caucasian/White—full-time 165, part-time 14; Multi-ethnic—full-time 2, part-time 0; students subject to the Americans With Disabilities Act—full-time 2, part-time 0; Unknown ethnicity—full-time 0, part-time 0.

Financial Information/Assistance:
Tuition for Full-Time Study: *Master's:* State residents: per academic year $5,032, $272 per credit hour; Nonstate residents: per academic year $14,114, $777 per credit hour. *Doctoral:* State residents: per academic year $5,032, $272 per credit hour; Nonstate residents: per academic year $14,114, $777 per credit hour. Tuition is subject to change.

Financial Assistance:

First-Year Students: Teaching assistantships available for first year. Average amount paid per academic year: $6,000. Average number of hours worked per week: 10. Apply by January 31. Tuition remission given: full. Research assistantships available for first year. Average amount paid per academic year: $4,000. Average number of hours worked per week: 10. Apply by January 31. Tuition remission given: full.

Advanced Students: Teaching assistantships available for advanced students. Average amount paid per academic year: $6,000. Average number of hours worked per week: 10. Apply by January 31. Tuition remission given: full. Research assistantships available for advanced students. Average amount paid per academic year: $5,000. Average number of hours worked per week: 10. Apply by January 31. Tuition remission given: full.

Additional Information: Of all students currently enrolled full time, 25% benefited from one or more of the listed financial assistance programs.

Internships/Practica: Doctoral Degree (PhD School Psychology): For those doctoral students for whom a professional internship was required in this program prior to graduation, (5) students applied for an internship in 2006–2007, with (5) students obtaining an internship. Of those students who obtained an internship, (5) were paid internships. Of those students who obtained an internship, (5) students placed in APA/CPA-accredited internships, (0) students placed in internships not APA/CPA accredited, but listed with the Association of Psychology Postdoctoral and Internship Centers (APPIC), (0) students placed in internships conforming to guidelines of the Council of Directors of School Psychology Programs (CDSPP), (0) students placed in internships that were not APA/CPA-accredited, APPIC- or CDSPP-listed. Assessment, counseling, and consultation practica are required of all School Psychology and Counseling students. In addition, a 1,500-hour internship is required for EdS students and a 2,000-hour internship is required for PhD students. The department is a member of an APA-approved internship consortium.

Housing and Day Care: On-campus housing is available. On-campus day care facilities are available.

Employment of Department Graduates:

Master's Degree Graduates: Of those who graduated in the academic year 2006–2007, the following categories and numbers represent the postgraduate activities and employment of master's degree graduates: Enrolled in a psychology doctoral program (15), enrolled in another graduate/professional program (12), enrolled in a postdoctoral residency/fellowship (n/a), employed in independent practice (n/a), employed in an academic position at a university (5), employed in an academic position at a 2-year/4-year college (2), employed in other positions at a higher education institution (2), employed in a professional position in a school system (6), employed in business or industry (5), total from the above (master's) (47).

Doctoral Degree Graduates: Of those who graduated in the academic year 2006–2007, the following categories and numbers represent the postgraduate activities and employment of doctoral degree graduates: Enrolled in a psychology doctoral program (n/a), enrolled in a postdoctoral residency/fellowship (2), total from the above (doctoral) (2).

Additional Information:

Orientation, Objectives, and Emphasis of Department: Members of the Educational Psychology and Counseling Department envision playing an instrumental role in the creation of contextually linked learning environments that promote and enhance success for all learners. We expect these environments to exemplify a spirit of collaboration and cooperation, respect for diversity, concern for mental and physical health, positive attitudes toward constructive and meaningful change, and a commitment to lifelong learning. Faculty and students in the Psychoeducational Studies Unit are expected to model the behaviors and reflect the values that are necessary to achieve this vision. The Psychoeducational Studies Unit will provide national leadership in creating learning environments that (a) foster psychological health, (b) address authentic educational needs, and (c) promote lifelong learning. Unit faculty and students will draw upon a growing body of knowledge about the psychology, biology, and social and cultural contexts of learning in promoting systematic change that leads to the enhancement of the learner. Specifically, the Unit will seek opportunities in a diversity of contexts for learners to apply information-based problem solving, engage in critical thinking, provide counseling services, and implement the structures and processes necessary for effective collaboration.

Application Information:

Send Department Application to Julie Harden, Educational Psychology and Counseling, 453 Claxton Complex, The University of Tennessee, Knoxville, TN 37996-3452; send Graduate School Application to Graduate/International Admissions, 201 Student Services, The University of Tennessee, Knoxville, TN 37996. Application available online. URL of online application: http://www.web.utk.edu/~edpsych/perspective_students.html. Students are admitted in the Winter, January 15 deadline for PhD and EdS in School Psychology and PhD in Educational Psychology. No deadlines for MS in Educational Psychology. *Fee:* $35.

Tennessee, University of, Knoxville (2007 data)

Department of Psychology
Arts and Sciences
312 Austin Peay Building
Knoxville, TN 37996-0900
Telephone: (865) 974-3328
Fax: (865) 974-3330
E-mail: *cjogle@utk.edu*
Web: *http://www.psychology.utk.edu/*

Department Information:

1957. Department Head: James E. Lawler. Number of faculty: total—full-time 26, part-time 22; women—full-time 9, part-time 6.

Programs and Degrees Offered:

Listed in the following order: Program area, degree type (T if terminal Master's), number awarded 7/06–6/07. Clinical PhD (Doctor of Philosophy) 5, Experimental MA/MS (Master of Arts/Science) (T) 1, Counseling PhD (Doctor of Philosophy) 2, Experimental PhD (Doctor of Philosophy) 9.

APA Accreditation: Clinical PhD (Doctor of Philosophy). Counseling PhD (Doctor of Philosophy).

Student Applications/Admissions:

Student Applications

Clinical PhD (Doctor of Philosophy)—Applications 2007–2008, 80. Total applicants accepted 2007–2008, 7. Number full-time enrolled (new admits only) 2007–2008, 7. Openings 2008–2009, 8. The number of students enrolled full- and part-time who were dismissed or voluntarily withdrew from this program area in 2007–2008 were 0. *Experimental MA/MS (Master of Arts/Science)*—Applications 2007–2008, 11. Total applicants accepted 2007–2008, 2. Number full-time enrolled (new admits only) 2007–2008, 2. Openings 2008–2009, 4. The median number of years required for completion of a degree in 2006–2007 were 2. The number of students enrolled full- and part-time who were dismissed or voluntarily withdrew from this program area in 2007–2008 were 0. *Counseling PhD (Doctor of Philosophy)*—Applications 2007–2008, 49. Total applicants accepted 2007–2008, 5. Number full-time enrolled (new admits only) 2007–2008, 5. Total enrolled 2007–2008 full-time, 28. Openings 2008–2009, 6. The median number of years required for completion of a degree in 2006–2007 were 5. The number of students enrolled full- and part-time who were dismissed or voluntarily withdrew from this program area in 2007–2008 were 0. *Experimental PhD (Doctor of Philosophy)*—Applications 2007–2008, 24. Total applicants accepted 2007–2008, 7. Number full-time enrolled (new admits only) 2007–2008, 6. Total enrolled 2007–2008 full-time, 29. Openings 2008–2009, 7. The median number of years required for completion of a degree in 2006–2007 were 4. The number of students enrolled full- and part-time who were dismissed or voluntarily withdrew from this program area in 2007–2008 were 1.

Admissions Requirements:

Scores: Entries appear in this order: required test or GPA, minimum score (if required), median score of students entering in 2007–2008. Master's Programs: GRE-V no minimum stated, 470; GRE-Q no minimum stated, 460; GRE-Subject (Psychology) no minimum stated, 580; overall undergraduate GPA no minimum stated, 3.48. The GRE General Exam is required for all programs. Doctoral Programs: GRE-Subject (Psychology) no minimum stated, 690; overall undergraduate GPA 3.0, 3.84.

Other Criteria: (importance of criteria rated low, medium, or high): GRE/MAT scores—high, research experience—high, work experience—low, extracurricular activity—low, clinically related public service—low, GPA—high, letters of recommendation—high, interview—high, statement of goals and objectives—high.

Student Characteristics: The following represents characteristics of students in 2007–2008 in all graduate psychology programs in the department: Female—full-time 74, part-time 0; Male—full-time 36, part-time 0; African American/Black—full-time 3, part-time 0; Hispanic/Latino(a)—full-time 4, part-time 0; Asian/Pacific Islander—full-time 4, part-time 0; American Indian/Alaska Native—full-time 0, part-time 0; Caucasian/White—full-time 98, part-time 0; Multi-ethnic—full-time 1, part-time 0; students subject to the Americans With Disabilities Act—full-time 0, part-time 0; Unknown ethnicity—full-time 0, part-time 0.

Financial Information/Assistance:

Tuition for Full-Time Study: *Master's:* State residents: per academic year $6,366, $310 per credit hour; Nonstate residents: per academic year $17,932, $937 per credit hour. *Doctoral:* State residents: per academic year $6,366, $310 per credit hour; Nonstate residents: per academic year $17,932, $937 per credit hour. Tuition is subject to change. See the following Web site for updates and changes in tuition costs: http://www.web.utk.edu/~bursar/.

Financial Assistance:

First-Year Students: Research assistantships available for first year. Tuition remission given: full. Fellowships and scholarships available for first year.

Advanced Students: Teaching assistantships available for advanced students. Tuition remission given: full. Research assistantships available for advanced students. Tuition remission given: full. Fellowships and scholarships available for advanced students.

Additional Information: Of all students currently enrolled full time, 100% benefited from one or more of the listed financial assistance programs.

Internships/Practica: All Clinical students are required to participate in two 12-month practica, one in our Departmental Psychological Clinic and the other in a community mental health facility. Both practica are supervised by doctoral degreed clinical psychologists, and the clientele are children, adolescents, and adults who seek help for their emotional and behavioral problems. In addition, Clinical and Counseling students are required to serve a 1-year internship.

Housing and Day Care: On-campus housing is available. See the following Web site for more information: http://www.uthousing.utk.edu. On-campus day care facilities are available. See the following Web site for more information: http://www.web.utk.edu/~utkchl.

Employment of Department Graduates:

Master's Degree Graduates: Of those who graduated in the academic year 2006–2007, the following categories and numbers represent the postgraduate activities and employment of master's degree graduates: Enrolled in a postdoctoral residency/fellowship (n/a), employed in independent practice (n/a), total from the above (master's) (0).

Doctoral Degree Graduates: Of those who graduated in the academic year 2006–2007, the following categories and numbers represent the postgraduate activities and employment of doctoral degree graduates: Enrolled in a psychology doctoral program (n/a), total from the above (doctoral) (0).

Additional Information:

Orientation, Objectives, and Emphasis of Department: The graduate faculty maintain active research programs in cognition, developmental, ethology, gender, health, organizational, personality, phenomenology, psychobiology, psychometrics, sensation/perception, and social psychology. The MA program is appropriate for students wanting a master's degree as part of progress toward a doctorate, or for those who wish to complement a degree in a different field. The Experimental PhD program prepares students for academic and research careers, and for careers involving the application of psychological principles as practitioners in industrial, forensic, organizational, and community settings. Areas of concentration include applied psychology, child development, cognition, and consciousness, health psychology, phenomenology, and social/personality. The Clinical PhD program combines psychodynamic and research components, requiring exposure to a wide range of theoretical views and technical practices. Minors available are child development, health psychology, and social psychology. In order to foster appropriate breadth and interdisciplinary training, some cognate work outside the department of psychology is required of all doctoral students. The Counseling program is designed to enable students to become behavioral scientists, skilled in psychological research and its application. Students are trained to provide services to a wide variety of clients in numerous settings. Program objectives are to train doctoral-level counseling psychologists who have knowledge of, and competence in, (a) the foundation and discipline of psychology, (b) social science research and methodology, and (c) specific therapeutic and intervention skills related to being a counseling psychologist.

Special Facilities or Resources: Facilities include computer support in equipment and staff, human and animal laboratories, a psychology clinic for training and research, and a new university library with expanded serials holdings.

Information for Students With Physical Disabilities: See the following Web site for more information: http://www.ods.utk.edu/.

Application Information:

Send to Ms. Connie J. Ogle, 312C Austin Peay Building, University of Tennessee, Knoxville, TN 37996-0900. Students are admitted in the Fall. In Fall 2007, the Department may change some application deadlines for Fall 2008. Please contact Connie Ogle at cjogle@utk.edu in August 2007 for specific 2008 program application deadlines. *Fee:* $35. Applicants must submit two separate applications: (a) the Graduate School application together with the $35 application fee, and official transcripts and GRE scores; (b) the Psychology Department application together with unofficial transcripts, GRE scores, and other material as indicated on the Departmental application. Forms are to be submitted separately to the offices indicated on the Psychology Department application, and all Departmental application material must be received by the respective program deadlines.

Tennessee, University of, Knoxville

Industrial and Organizational Psychology Program
Business Administration
408 Stokely Management Center
Knoxville, TN 37996-0545
Telephone: (865) 974-4843
Fax: (865) 974-2048
E-mail: *ghurst@utk.edu*
Web: *http://www.bus.utk.edu/iopsyc*

Department Information:

1964. Director: Joan R. Rentsch. Number of faculty: total—full-time 4; women—full-time 1.

Programs and Degrees Offered:

Listed in the following order: Program area, degree type (T if terminal Master's), number awarded 7/06–6/07. Industrial/Organizational PhD (Doctor of Philosophy) 4.

Student Applications/Admissions:

Student Applications

Industrial/Organizational PhD (Doctor of Philosophy)—Applications 2007–2008, 60. Total applicants accepted 2007–2008, 3. Number full-time enrolled (new admits only) 2007–2008, 3. Number part-time enrolled (new admits only) 2007–2008, 0. Openings 2008–2009, 3. The median number of years required for completion of a degree in 2006–2007 were 5. The number of students enrolled full- and part-time who were dismissed or voluntarily withdrew from this program area in 2007–2008 were 0.

Admissions Requirements:

Scores: Entries appear in this order: required test or GPA, minimum score (if required), median score of students entering in 2007–2008. Doctoral Programs: GRE-V no minimum stated, 570; GRE-Q no minimum stated, 675; overall undergraduate GPA 3.5, 3.65; last 2 years GPA no minimum stated, 3.85; psychology GPA no minimum stated.

Other Criteria: (importance of criteria rated low, medium, or high): GRE/MAT scores—high, research experience—high, work experience—medium, extracurricular activity—low, GPA—high, letters of recommendation—high, statement of goals and objectives—high.

Student Characteristics: The following represents characteristics of students in 2007–2008 in all graduate psychology programs in the department: Female—full-time 16, part-time 0; Male—full-time 9, part-time 0; African American/Black—full-time 1, part-time 0; Hispanic/Latino(a)—full-time 1, part-time 0; Asian/Pacific Islander—full-time 0, part-time 0; American Indian/Alaska Native—full-time 0, part-time 0; Caucasian/White—full-time 0, part-time 0; Multi-ethnic—full-time 0, part-time 0; students subject to the Americans With Disabilities Act—full-time 0, part-time 0; Unknown ethnicity—full-time 23, part-time 0.

Financial Information/Assistance:

Tuition for Full-Time Study: *Doctoral:* State residents: per academic year $6,366, $310 per credit hour; Nonstate residents: per academic year $10,770, $937 per credit hour. Tuition is subject to change.

Financial Assistance:

First-Year Students: Teaching assistantships available for first year. Average amount paid per academic year: $10,779. Average number of hours worked per week: 15. Tuition remission given: full. Research assistantships available for first year. Average amount paid per academic year: $10,779. Average number of hours worked per week: 15. Tuition remission given: full. Fellowships and scholarships available for first year. Average amount paid per academic year: $10,779. Average number of hours worked per week: 15.

Advanced Students: Teaching assistantships available for advanced students. Average amount paid per academic year: $10,779. Average number of hours worked per week: 15. Tuition remission given: full. Research assistantships available for advanced students. Average amount paid per academic year: $10,779. Average number of hours worked per week: 15. Tuition remission given: full. Traineeships available for advanced students. Fellowships and scholarships available for advanced students. Tuition remission given: full.

Additional Information: Of all students currently enrolled full time, 100% benefited from one or more of the listed financial assistance programs.

Internships/Practica: An internship or practicum is required but these vary considerably.

Housing and Day Care: On-campus housing is available. No on-campus day care facilities are available.

Employment of Department Graduates:

Master's Degree Graduates: Of those who graduated in the academic year 2006–2007, the following categories and numbers represent the postgraduate activities and employment of master's degree graduates: Enrolled in a postdoctoral residency/fellowship (n/a), employed in independent practice (n/a), total from the above (master's) (0).

Doctoral Degree Graduates: Of those who graduated in the academic year 2006–2007, the following categories and numbers represent the postgraduate activities and employment of doctoral degree graduates: Enrolled in a psychology doctoral program (n/a), employed in an academic position at a university (2), employed in business or industry (2), total from the above (doctoral) (4).

Additional Information:

Orientation, Objectives, and Emphasis of Department: The Industrial/Organizational program is designed to prepare students for personnel, managerial, and organizational research; for university teaching; and for consulting relationships with industry. The program emphasizes a scientist–practitioner model in applying and conducting research based on accepted theory found in classical and modern organization theory, organizational behavior, psychology, management, and statistics.

Special Facilities or Resources: Computing and Academic Services (CAS) provides computing facilities, services, and support for the university's teaching, research, public service, and administrative activities. Individual UNIX and Lotus Notes accounts are provided for students, faculty, and staff for the duration of their affiliation with UTK at no charge. CAS maintains 6 staffed computing labs, 15 unstaffed labs, and supports computing installations in all residence halls. Training and documentation are also available through CAS. Statistical and mathematical consulting is available to all students, faculty, and staff. CAS operates the core mainframe and large-scale servers; equipment includes multiple systems from SUN, SGI, and IBM systems. In addition to university computing services and facilities, the Department of Management and the College of Business Administration provide students with microcomputers in student offices, which are networked to departmental printers and the Internet. The University Libraries own approximately 2 million volumes and subscribe to more than 11,000 periodicals and other serial titles. The Libraries' membership in the Association of Research Libraries reflects the University's emphasis on graduate instruction and research and the support of comprehensive collections of library materials on a permanent basis.

Application Information:

Application available online. URL of online application: http://www.bus.utk.edu/iopsyc. Students are admitted in the Fall, application deadline February 1. *Fee:* $35.

Vanderbilt University

Human and Organizational Development
Peabody College of Education and Human Development
Peabody 90, 230 Appleton Place
Nashville, TN 37203-5721
Telephone: (615) 322-8484
Fax: (615) 343-2661
E-mail: *joe.cunningham@vanderbilt.edu*
Web: *http://www.peabody.vanderbilt.edu/hod/index.htm*

Department Information:

1999. Chairperson: Joseph Cunningham, EdD. Number of faculty: total—full-time 17, part-time 12; women—full-time 7, part-time 9; total—minority—full-time 2; women minority—full-time 1.

Programs and Degrees Offered:

Listed in the following order: Program area, degree type (T if terminal Master's), number awarded 7/06–6/07. Human Development Counseling Other 23, Community Research and Action PhD (Doctor of Philosophy) 3, Community Development Action Other 7.

Student Applications/Admissions:

Student Applications

Human Development Counseling Other—Applications 2007–2008, 110. Total applicants accepted 2007–2008, 47. Number full-time enrolled (new admits only) 2007–2008, 25. Number part-time enrolled (new admits only) 2007–2008, 0. Total enrolled 2007–2008 full-time, 44, part-time, 1. Openings 2008–2009, 24. The median number of years required for completion of a degree in 2006–2007 was 1. The number of students enrolled full- and part-time who were dismissed or voluntarily withdrew from this program area in 2007–2008 were 0. *Community Research and Action PhD (Doctor of Philosophy)*—Applications 2007–2008, 93. Total applicants accepted 2007–2008, 6. Number full-time enrolled (new admits only) 2007–2008, 4. Number part-time enrolled (new admits only) 2007–2008, 0. Openings 2008–2009, 10. The median number of years required for completion of a degree in 2006–2007 were 3. The number of students enrolled full- and part-time who were dismissed or voluntarily withdrew from this program area in 2007–2008 were 0. *Community Development Action Other*—Applications 2007–2008, 60. Total applicants accepted 2007–2008, 15. Number full-time enrolled (new admits only) 2007–2008, 9. Number part-time enrolled (new admits only) 2007–2008, 1. Total enrolled 2007–2008 full-time, 12, part-time, 3. Openings 2008–2009, 15. The median number of years required for completion of a degree in 2006–2007 was 1. The number of students enrolled full- and part-time who were dismissed or voluntarily withdrew from this program area in 2007–2008 were 1.

Admissions Requirements:

Scores: Entries appear in this order: required test or GPA, minimum score (if required), median score of students entering

in 2007–2008. Master's Programs: GRE-V 500, 600; GRE-Q 500, 600; MAT 410, 430; overall undergraduate GPA 3.0, 3.5; last 2 years GPA 3.0, 3.5; Master's GRE-Analytical 3.5, 3.5. The MEd in CDA will only accept the GRE scores. A GPA of 3.0 is essential. The MEd in HDC will take either the MAT or GRE scores. A GPA of 3.0 is essential. Doctoral Programs: GRE-V 600, 650; GRE-Q 600, 660; overall undergraduate GPA 3.3, 3.6; last 2 years GPA 3.6, 3.6; psychology GPA 3.5, 3.6; Doctoral program GRE-Analytic 4.5, 4.5.

Other Criteria: (importance of criteria rated low, medium, or high): GRE/MAT scores—high, research experience—medium, work experience—medium, extracurricular activity—low, clinically related public service—medium, GPA—high, letters of recommendation—high, interview—high, statement of goals and objectives—high, writing samples—high, undergraduate major in psychology—low, specific undergraduate psychology courses taken—low. Research experience less important for Master's programs than for PhD program. Clinically related public service helpful for all programs. For additional information on admission requirements, go to http://peabody.vanderbilt.edu/admissions/graduate.htm.

Student Characteristics: The following represents characteristics of students in 2007–2008 in all graduate psychology programs in the department: Female—full-time 64, part-time 4; Male—full-time 20, part-time 0; African American/Black—full-time 18, part-time 0; Hispanic/Latino(a)—full-time 5, part-time 0; Asian/Pacific Islander—full-time 0, part-time 0; American Indian/Alaska Native—full-time 0, part-time 0; Caucasian/White—full-time 57, part-time 4; Multi-ethnic—full-time 4, part-time 0; students subject to the Americans With Disabilities Act—full-time 1, part-time 0; Unknown ethnicity—full-time 0, part-time 0; International students who hold an F-1 or J-1 Visa—full-time 4, part-time 0.

Financial Information/Assistance:

Tuition for Full-Time Study: *Master's:* State residents: per academic year $18,360, $18,360 per credit hour; Nonstate residents: per academic year $18,360, $18,360 per credit hour. *Doctoral:* State residents: per academic year $25,812, $1,434 per credit hour; Nonstate residents: per academic year $25,812, $25,812 per credit hour. Tuition is subject to change. Additional fees are assessed to students beyond the costs of tuition for the following: Student health insurance, student activities and recreation fees, transcript fee (one time only). See the following Web site for updates and changes in tuition costs: http://www.vanderbilt.edu/catalogs/.

Financial Assistance:

First-Year Students: Teaching assistantships available for first year. Average amount paid per academic year: $14,000. Average number of hours worked per week: 20. Apply by February 1. Tuition remission given: full. Research assistantships available for first year. Average amount paid per academic year: $14,000. Average number of hours worked per week: 20. Apply by February 1. Tuition remission given: full. Traineeships available for first year. Average amount paid per academic year: $20,772. Average number of hours worked per week: 20. Apply by February 1. Tuition remission given: full. Fellowships and scholarships available for first year. Average amount paid per academic year: $24,000. Average number of hours worked per week: 20. Apply by February 1. Tuition remission given: full.

Advanced Students: Teaching assistantships available for advanced students. Average amount paid per academic year: $14,000. Average number of hours worked per week: 20. Apply by February 1. Tuition remission given: full. Research assistantships available for advanced students. Average amount paid per academic year: $14,000. Average number of hours worked per week: 20. Apply by February 1. Tuition remission given: full. Traineeships available for advanced students. Average amount paid per academic year: $20,772. Average number of hours worked per week: 20. Apply by February 1. Tuition remission given: full. Fellowships and scholarships available for advanced students. Average amount paid per academic year: $24,000. Average number of hours worked per week: 20. Apply by February 1. Tuition remission given: full.

Additional Information: Of all students currently enrolled full time, 100% benefited from one or more of the listed financial assistance programs. Application and information available online at http://peabody.vanderbilt.edu.

Internships/Practica: The CDA and CRA programs require a 15-week internship. Possible sites: Mayor's Office/Metro Council/Planning Commission, local or international community development organization, regional planning or civic design center, youth development center, healthcare corporation, neighborhood health clinic, alcohol and drug treatment center, welfare or housing agency, State health and human service agencies, Vanderbilt Institute for Public Policy Studies (Centers for Mental Health Policy, Evaluation Research and Methodology, Child and Family Policy, Crime and Justice Policy, Environmental Management Studies, Health Policy, Psychotherapy Research and Policy, State and Local Policy). The HDC program requires a 1-year internship that provides opportunities to apply knowledge and skills primarily in the areas of social service agencies, mental health centers, schools (K–12), employee assistance programs, other human services delivery programs.

Housing and Day Care: On-campus housing is available. See the following Web site for more information: http://www.vanderbilt.edu/ResEd/main/index.php. On-campus day care facilities are available. See the following Web site for more information: http://www.vanderbilt.edu/HRS/wellness/childcare.htm.

Employment of Department Graduates:

Master's Degree Graduates: Of those who graduated in the academic year 2006–2007, the following categories and numbers represent the postgraduate activities and employment of master's degree graduates: Enrolled in a psychology doctoral program (0), enrolled in another graduate/professional program (2), enrolled in a postdoctoral residency/fellowship (n/a), employed in independent practice (n/a), employed in an academic position at a university (0), employed in an academic position at a 2-year/4-year college (0), employed in other positions at a higher education institution (1), employed in a professional position in a school system (5), employed in business or industry (2), employed in government agency (0), employed in a community mental health/counseling center (14), employed in a hospital/medical center (1), still seeking employment (0), other employment position (5), do not know (0), total from the above (master's) (30).

Doctoral Degree Graduates: Of those who graduated in the academic year 2006–2007, the following categories and numbers represent the postgraduate activities and employment of doctoral degree graduates: Enrolled in a psychology doctoral program (n/a),

employed in an academic position at a university (3), total from the above (doctoral) (3).

Additional Information:

Orientation, Objectives, and Emphasis of Department: Although the vast majority of faculty in the department are psychologists, our orientation is interdisciplinary. There are three graduate programs, all oriented to helping diverse communities and individuals identify and develop their strengths: a long-standing Master's in Human Development Counseling (HDC), a Master's in Community Development Action (CDA), and a PhD in Community Research and Action (CRA). The latter two started in 2001. The HDC program prepares students to meet the psychological needs of the normally developing population, who sometimes require professional help. Through a humanistic training model and a 2-year curriculum, students develop a strong theoretical grounding in life span human development, and school or community counseling. The CDA program is for those who desire training for program administration and evaluation work in either public or private, international or domestic, community service, planning, or development organizations. The doctoral degree in Community Research and Action is designed to train action researchers for academic or program/policy-related careers in applied community studies (i.e., community psychology, community development, prevention, community health, mental health, organizational change, and ethics). Coursework in qualitative and quantitative methods and evaluation research is required. The program builds on the one in Community Psychology previously in the Department of Psychology and Human Development and reflects the move in the field to become interdisciplinary.

Special Facilities or Resources: Peabody College has its own library, several computer centers, and nationally known research centers, including the Learning Sciences Institute and the Kennedy Center for Research on human development, mental retardation, and other disabilities. Also on the beautiful and historic Peabody campus is the Vanderbilt Institute for Public Policy Studies (Centers for Mental Health Policy, Evaluation Research and Methodology, Child and Family Policy, Crime and Justice Policy, Environmental Management Studies, Health Policy, Psychotherapy Research and Policy, State and Local Policy). In our own department, we now have a new center, the Center for Community Studies. Located in Nashville, the Tennessee state capital, opportunities abound for research and internships in state and local health and human service agencies and schools.

Information for Students With Physical Disabilities: See the following Web site for more information: http://www.vanderbilt.edu/odc/.

Application Information:

For PhD and MEd programs send to Office of Graduate Admissions, Peabody College of Vanderbilt University, 230 Appleton Place, MSC 327, Peabody Station, Nashville, TN 37203-5721; (866) PC ADMIT (toll free); (615) 322-8410 (in Nashville); e-mail peabody.admissions-@vanderbilt.edu. For further information on application procedures, write, call, or e-mail Sherrie Lane, Graduate Secretary and Graduate Admissions Coordinator, Department of Human and Organizational Development, Peabody College of Vanderbilt University, Box 90, Peabody Station, 230 Appleton Place, Nashville, TN 37203-5721; (615) 322-8484; Fax (615) 343-2661; e-mail sherrie.a.lane@vanderbilt.edu. Application available online. URL of online application: http://www.peabody.vanderbilt.edu/x3006.xml. Students are admitted in the Fall, application deadline December 31; Spring, application deadline November 1; Summer, application deadline February 1. November 1 for CDA program for Spring admission and February 1 for CDA Summer admission. *Fee:* $40. Application fee is waived when applying online.

Vanderbilt University

Psychological Sciences
111 21st Avenue South or Peabody College 512
230 Appleton Place
Nashville, TN 37203
Telephone: (615) 322-2874
Fax: (615) 343-8449
E-mail: *vay.welch@vanderbilt.edu or sharone.k.hall@vanderbilt.edu*
Web: *http://www.vanderbilt.edu/psychological_sciences/home*

Department Information:

1925. Chairs: Andrew J. Tomarken and David Cole. Number of faculty: total—full-time 64, part-time 6; women—full-time 32, part-time 3; total—minority—full-time 3; women minority—full-time 2.

Programs and Degrees Offered:

Listed in the following order: Program area, degree type (T if terminal Master's), number awarded 7/06–6/07. Neuroscience PhD (Doctor of Philosophy) 1, Clinical Science PhD (Doctor of Philosophy) 9, Cognition and Cognitive Neuroscience PhD (Doctor of Philosophy) 1, Developmental Science PhD (Doctor of Philosophy) 0, Quantitative Methods and Evaluation PhD (Doctor of Philosophy) 1.

APA Accreditation: Clinical PhD (Doctor of Philosophy).

Student Applications/Admissions:

Student Applications

Neuroscience PhD (Doctor of Philosophy)—Applications 2007–2008, 48. Total applicants accepted 2007–2008, 3. Number full-time enrolled (new admits only) 2007–2008, 0. Number part-time enrolled (new admits only) 2007–2008, 0. Openings 2008–2009, 3. The median number of years required for completion of a degree in 2006–2007 were 5. The number of students enrolled full- and part-time who were dismissed or voluntarily withdrew from this program area in 2007–2008 were 1. *Clinical Science PhD (Doctor of Philosophy)*—Applications 2007–2008, 407. Total applicants accepted 2007–2008, 11. Number full-time enrolled (new admits only) 2007–2008, 5. Number part-time enrolled (new admits only) 2007–2008, 0. Openings 2008–2009, 10. The median number of years required for completion of a degree in 2006–2007 were 6. The number of students enrolled full- and part-time who were dismissed or voluntarily withdrew from this program area in 2007–2008 were 0. *Cognition and Cognitive Neuroscience PhD (Doctor of Philosophy)*—Applications 2007–2008, 134. Total applicants accepted 2007–2008, 9. Number full-time enrolled (new admits only) 2007–2008, 5. Total enrolled 2007–2008 full-time, 24. Openings 2008–2009, 6. The median number of years required for completion of a degree in 2006–2007 were 3. The number of students enrolled full- and part-time who were dismissed or voluntarily withdrew from this program area in 2007–2008 were 2. *Developmental Science PhD (Doctor of Philosophy)*—Applications 2007–2008, 51. Total applicants accepted 2007–2008, 5. Number full-time enrolled (new admits only) 2007–2008, 3. Total enrolled 2007–2008 full-time, 12. Openings 2008–2009, 3. The number of students enrolled full- and part-time who were dismissed or voluntarily withdrew from this program area in 2007–2008 were 0. *Quantitative Methods and Evaluation PhD (Doctor of Philosophy)*—Applications 2007–2008, 28. Total applicants accepted 2007–2008, 1. Number full-time enrolled (new admits only) 2007–2008, 0. Total enrolled 2007–2008 full-time, 6. Openings 2008–2009, 4. The median number of years required for completion of a degree in 2006–2007 were 6. The number of students enrolled full- and part-time who were dismissed or voluntarily withdrew from this program area in 2007–2008 were 0.

Admissions Requirements:

Scores: Entries appear in this order: required test or GPA, minimum score (if required), median score of students entering in 2007–2008. Master's Programs: not applicable. Doctoral Programs: GRE-V 550, 650; GRE-Q 550, 690. All requirements are the same for all program areas.

Other Criteria: (importance of criteria rated low, medium, or high): GRE/MAT scores—high, research experience—high, work experience—low, extracurricular activity—low, clinically related public service—low, GPA—high, letters of recommendation—high, interview—high, statement of goals and objectives—high, undergraduate major in psychology—low. For additional information on admission requirements, go to http://www.vanderbilt.edu/psychological_sciences/home.

Student Characteristics: The following represents characteristics of students in 2007–2008 in all graduate psychology programs in the department: Female—full-time 69, part-time 0; Male—full-time 27, part-time 0; African American/Black—full-time 9, part-time 0; Hispanic/Latino(a)—full-time 5, part-time 0; Asian/Pacific Islander—full-time 15, part-time 0; American Indian/Alaska Native—full-time 0, part-time 0; Caucasian/White—full-time 67, part-time 0; Multi-ethnic—full-time 0, part-time 0; students subject to the Americans With Disabilities Act—full-time 0, part-time 0; Unknown ethnicity—full-time 0, part-time 0.

Financial Information/Assistance:

Tuition for Full-Time Study: *Doctoral:* State residents: per academic year $34,416, $1,434 per credit hour; Nonstate residents: per academic year $34,416, $1,434 per credit hour. Tuition is subject to change.

Financial Assistance:

First-Year Students: Teaching assistantships available for first year. Average amount paid per academic year: $20,000. Average number of hours worked per week: 20. Apply by December 15. Tuition remission given: full. Research assistantships available for first year. Average amount paid per academic year: $20,000. Average number of hours worked per week: 20. Apply by December 15. Tuition remission given: full. Fellowships and scholarships available for first year. Average amount paid per academic year: $20,000. Average number of hours worked per week: 20. Apply by December 15. Tuition remission given: full.

Advanced Students: Teaching assistantships available for advanced students. Average amount paid per academic year: $20,000. Average number of hours worked per week: 20. Apply by December 15. Tuition remission given: full. Research assistantships available for advanced students. Average amount paid per academic year: $20,000. Average number of hours worked per week: 20. Apply by December 15. Tuition remission given: full. Traineeships available for advanced students. Average amount paid per academic year: $20,272. Average number of hours worked per week: 20. Apply by December 15. Tuition remission given: full. Fellowships and scholarships available for advanced students. Average amount paid per academic year: $20,000. Average number of hours worked per week: 20. Apply by December 15. Tuition remission given: full.

Additional Information: Of all students currently enrolled full time, 100% benefited from one or more of the listed financial assistance programs. Application and information available online at https://graduateapplications.vanderbilt.edu/.

Internships/Practica: Doctoral Degree (PhD Clinical Science): For those doctoral students for whom a professional internship was required in this program prior to graduation, (5) students applied for an internship in 2006–2007, with (5) students obtaining an internship. Of those students who obtained an internship, (5) were paid internships. Of those students who obtained an internship, (5) students placed in APA/CPA-accredited internships, (0) students placed in internships not APA/CPA accredited, but listed with the Association of Psychology Postdoctoral and Internship Centers (APPIC), (0) students placed in internships conforming to guidelines of the Council of Directors of School Psychology Programs (CDSPP), (0) students placed in internships that were not APA/CPA-accredited, APPIC or CDSPP listed. We offer up to two dozen different placements for students to do their practica. These include two VA Medical Centers, VU Child and Adolescent Psychiatric Hospital, VU Diabetes Center, VU Psychological and Counseling Center, Mobile Crisis Response Service, public school systems, state prison, and mental health facilities for both children and adults.

Housing and Day Care: No on-campus housing is available. On-campus day care facilities are available. See the following Web site for more information: http://www.vanderbilt.edu/HRS/wellness/childcare.htm.

Employment of Department Graduates:

Master's Degree Graduates: Of those who graduated in the academic year 2006–2007, the following categories and numbers represent the postgraduate activities and employment of master's degree graduates: Enrolled in a postdoctoral residency/fellowship (n/a), employed in independent practice (n/a), total from the above (master's) (0).

Doctoral Degree Graduates: Of those who graduated in the academic year 2006–2007, the following categories and numbers represent the postgraduate activities and employment of doctoral degree graduates: Enrolled in a psychology doctoral program (n/a), enrolled in a postdoctoral residency/fellowship (8), employed in an academic position at a university (2), employed in other positions at a higher education institution (1), employed in a hospital/medical center (1), total from the above (doctoral) (12).

Additional Information:

Orientation, Objectives, and Emphasis of Department: The doctoral program in Psychological Sciences is offered jointly by the

Department of Psychology in the College of Arts and Science and the Department of Psychology and Human Development in the Peabody College at Vanderbilt University. The program focuses on psychological theory and the development of original empirical research. Students are admitted to work toward the PhD in these areas: Clinical Science, Cognition and Cognitive Neuroscience, Developmental Science, Neuroscience, or Quantitative Methods and Evaluation. A major goal is the placement of students in academic settings. The curriculum is designed to (a) familiarize students with major areas of psychology, (b) provide specialized training in at least one of the five specific areas, and (c) provide students flexibility to enroll in classes consistent with their research interests. Students take core courses in quantitative methods and substantive area, enroll in advanced seminars, and attend weekly area group colloquia. In addition to coursework, we expect students to be continually involved in research throughout their tenure in our program. We use a one-on-one mentoring model as a primary though not exclusive means of advisement for the acquisition of scientific skills by students.

Special Facilities or Resources: Psychological Sciences is housed in Wilson Hall, Jesup Psychological Laboratory, and Hobbs Laboratory of Human Development. We have state-of-the-art laboratories for carrying out basic research with humans and animals that include computer stimulus presentation and response collection capabilities, computers for data analysis and computational modeling, and specialized research equipment (including eyetracking environments, virtual reality, and custom experimental hardware and electronics). Research with humans, including both adults and children, and including those with brain damage and mental illness, is conducted in laboratories at Wilson, Hobbs, and at laboratories in the Kennedy Center and the Vanderbilt Medical Center. Wilson Hall contains an AAALAC-accredited animal care facility with dedicated and experienced staff to support husbandry, enrichment, and surgery for species used in basic research. Faculty members have their own dedicated laboratory space for conducting clinical, cognition and cognitive neuroscience, developmental, neuroscience, and quantitative research. Research in psychological sciences is enhanced by a number of research centers that support a variety of shared research equipment and services: Advanced Computing Center for Research and Education, Center for Integrative and Cognitive Neuroscience, Institute for Imaging Science, Kennedy Center, Learning Sciences Institute, and Vanderbilt Vision Research Center.

Information for Students With Physical Disabilities: See the following Web site for more information: http://www.vanderbilt.edu/odc/.

Application Information:
Materials that need to be mailed go to the following address: Psychological Sciences Program, Vanderbilt University, GPC 324, 230 Appleton Place, Nashville, TN 37203-5721. Application available online. URL of online application: https://www.graduateapplications.vanderbilt.edu/. Students are admitted in the Fall, application deadline December 15. *Fee:* $0.

Vanderbilt University, Peabody College

Department of Psychology and Human Development
Peabody 0552
230 Appleton Place
Nashville, TN 37203-5701
Telephone: (615) 322-8141
Fax: (615) 343-9494
E-mail: *sharone.k.hall@vanderbilt.edu*
Web: *http://www.peabody.vanderbilt.edu/psychology*

Department Information:
1915. Chairperson: John J. Rieser. Number of faculty: total—full-time 36, part-time 5; women—full-time 23, part-time 2; total—minority—full-time 1; women minority—full-time 1.

Programs and Degrees Offered:
Listed in the following order: Program area, degree type (T if terminal Master's), number awarded 7/06–6/07. Clinical PhD (Doctor of Philosophy) 7, Cognitive PhD (Doctor of Philosophy) 1, Developmental PhD (Doctor of Philosophy) 0, Quantitative Methods PhD (Doctor of Philosophy) 1, Community PhD (Doctor of Philosophy) 2.

APA Accreditation: Clinical PhD (Doctor of Philosophy).

Student Applications/Admissions:
Student Applications
Clinical PhD (Doctor of Philosophy)—Applications 2007–2008, 228. Total applicants accepted 2007–2008, 6. Number full-time enrolled (new admits only) 2007–2008, 3. Number part-time enrolled (new admits only) 2007–2008, 0. Openings 2008–2009, 8. The median number of years required for completion of a degree in 2006–2007 were 7. The number of students enrolled full- and part-time who were dismissed or voluntarily withdrew from this program area in 2007–2008 were 0. *Cognitive PhD (Doctor of Philosophy)*—Applications 2007–2008, 61. Total applicants accepted 2007–2008, 0. Number full-time enrolled (new admits only) 2007–2008, 0. Number part-time enrolled (new admits only) 2007–2008, 0. Openings 2008–2009, 3. The median number of years required for completion of a degree in 2006–2007 were 3. The number of students enrolled full- and part-time who were dismissed or voluntarily withdrew from this program area in 2007–2008 were 0. *Developmental PhD (Doctor of Philosophy)*—Applications 2007–2008, 51. Total applicants accepted 2007–2008, 5. Number full-time enrolled (new admits only) 2007–2008, 3. Number part-time enrolled (new admits only) 2007–2008, 0. Openings 2008–2009, 3. The number of students enrolled full- and part-time who were dismissed or voluntarily withdrew from this program area in 2007–2008 were 0. *Quantitative Methods PhD (Doctor of Philosophy)*—Applications 2007–2008, 28. Total applicants accepted 2007–2008, 1. Number full-time enrolled (new admits only) 2007–2008, 0. Number part-time enrolled (new admits only) 2007–2008, 0. Openings 2008–2009, 4. The median number of years required for completion of a degree in 2006–2007 were 6. The number of students enrolled full- and part-time who were dismissed or voluntarily

withdrew from this program area in 2007–2008 were 0. *Community PhD (Doctor of Philosophy)*—Applications 2007–2008, 0. Total applicants accepted 2007–2008, 0. Number full-time enrolled (new admits only) 2007–2008, 0. Number part-time enrolled (new admits only) 2007–2008, 0. The median number of years required for completion of a degree in 2006–2007 were 11. The number of students enrolled full- and part-time who were dismissed or voluntarily withdrew from this program area in 2007–2008 were 1.

Admissions Requirements:

Scores: Entries appear in this order: required test or GPA, minimum score (if required), median score of students entering in 2007–2008. Doctoral Programs: GRE-V no minimum stated, 690; GRE-Q no minimum stated, 720; overall undergraduate GPA no minimum stated, 3.6.

Other Criteria: (importance of criteria rated low, medium, or high): GRE/MAT scores—medium, research experience—high, work experience—low, extracurricular activity—low, clinically related public service—low, GPA—medium, letters of recommendation—high, interview—medium, statement of goals and objectives—high. Interview is required for Clinical only.

Student Characteristics: The following represents characteristics of students in 2007–2008 in all graduate psychology programs in the department: Female—full-time 44, part-time 0; Male—full-time 11, part-time 0; African American/Black—full-time 6, part-time 0; Hispanic/Latino(a)—full-time 4, part-time 0; Asian/Pacific Islander—full-time 4, part-time 0; American Indian/Alaska Native—full-time 0, part-time 0; Caucasian/White—full-time 41, part-time 0; Multi-ethnic—full-time 0, part-time 0; students subject to the Americans With Disabilities Act—full-time 0, part-time 0; Unknown ethnicity—full-time 0, part-time 0; International students who hold an F-1 or J-1 Visa—full-time 4, part-time 0.

Financial Information/Assistance:

Financial Assistance:

First-Year Students: Research assistantships available for first year. Apply by December 15. Traineeships available for first year. Apply by December 15. Fellowships and scholarships available for first year. Apply by December 15.

Advanced Students: Teaching assistantships available for advanced students. Apply by December 15. Research assistantships available for advanced students. Apply by December 15. Traineeships available for advanced students. Apply by December 15. Fellowships and scholarships available for advanced students. Apply by December 15.

Additional Information: Of all students currently enrolled full time, 85% benefited from one or more of the listed financial assistance programs. Application and information available online at https://graduateapplications.vanderbilt.edu/.

Internships/Practica: No information provided.

Housing and Day Care: No on-campus housing is available. No on-campus day care facilities are available.

Employment of Department Graduates:

Master's Degree Graduates: Of those who graduated in the academic year 2006–2007, the following categories and numbers represent the postgraduate activities and employment of master's degree graduates: Enrolled in a postdoctoral residency/fellowship (n/a), employed in independent practice (n/a), total from the above (master's) (0).

Doctoral Degree Graduates: Of those who graduated in the academic year 2006–2007, the following categories and numbers represent the postgraduate activities and employment of doctoral degree graduates: Enrolled in a psychology doctoral program (n/a), enrolled in a postdoctoral residency/fellowship (7), employed in an academic position at a university (1), employed in other positions at a higher education institution (2), other employment position (1), total from the above (doctoral) (11).

Additional Information:

Orientation, Objectives, and Emphasis of Department: The Department of Psychology and Human Development offers a rigorous program of academic and research training. Students become involved immediately in scholarly inquiry under the mentorship of a faculty advisor. The department has a clear focus on child and adolescent development, and on the persons and social systems (particularly families and schools) that influence this development. Major areas of inquiry concentrate in the following: cognitive and social development, including information processing, language development, problem solving, motivation, memory development, social referencing, motor skill development, and perceptual and spatial development in both mentally retarded and nonretarded children; developmental psychopathology, including such issues as social–cognitive factors in childhood depression and antisocial behavior in children and adolescents; and behavioral pediatrics, one major focus of which is on coping with chronic childhood illness. Another major research focus is in basic and applied social psychology, including program evaluation, victimization, health psychology, and the relationships between individuals and organizations. Other areas of interest include the philosophical foundations of psychology and mental health policy, with particular interest on the ethical dimensions of intervention. Clearly, all of these research areas are integrated among clinical, developmental, cognitive, and social domains, and we attempt to recruit students who will take advantage of the unique resources available here. There is extensive scholarly collaboration between the Peabody program and the program in Vanderbilt's College of Arts and Science. Students may work with faculty and take courses in both departments.

Special Facilities or Resources: There are exceptional resources available in the Peabody and Vanderbilt community. Members of the faculty are housed in two modern buildings with laboratory and computer facilities. The University has a state-of-the-art VAX 8800 mainframe, available to students. The library system contains over 1.7 million volumes, with particular strength in education- and psychology-related publications. In addition, most members of the department's faculty are also research scholars in the John F. Kennedy Center for Research on Education and Human Development, a major national behavioral research center located on the Peabody campus. Facilities within the Kennedy Center include the Family and Child Study Center and the Susan Gray

School, which serves developmentally delayed and at-risk children. There are opportunities for research collaboration with the Vanderbilt Institute for Public Policy Studies (particularly its Center for the Study of Children and Families and its Health Policy Center), as well as with such Medical Center departments as adolescent medicine, child and adolescent psychiatry, and the comprehensive developmental evaluation center. There is a university counseling center and an ample array of community agencies available for practicum experiences.

Application Information:
Send to Psychology and Human Development, c/o The Graduate School, 411 Kirkland Hall, Vanderbilt University, Nashville, TN 37240. Application available online. URL of online application: https://www.graduateapplications.vanderbilt.edu/. Students are admitted in the Fall, application deadline December 15. *Fee:* $40. Apply online at no cost.

Abilene Christian University

Department of Psychology
College of Arts and Sciences
ACU Box 28011
Abilene, TX 79699
Telephone: (325) 674-2310
Fax: (325) 674-6968
E-mail: *beckr@acu.edu*
Web: *http://www.acu.edu/psychology*

Department Information:

1968. Chair: Richard Beck. Number of faculty: total—full-time 9, part-time 4; women—full-time 2, part-time 2; total—minority—full-time 1.

Programs and Degrees Offered:

Listed in the following order: Program area, degree type (T if terminal Master's), number awarded 7/06–6/07. School Psychology MA/MS (Master of Arts/Science) (T) 3, Clinical Psychology MA/MS (Master of Arts/Science) (T) 9, Counseling Psychology MA/MS (Master of Arts/Science) (T) 5, General Psychology MA/MS (Master of Arts/Science) 5.

Student Applications/Admissions:

Student Applications

School Psychology MA/MS (Master of Arts/Science)—Applications 2007–2008, 8. Total applicants accepted 2007–2008, 7. Openings 2008–2009, 10. The median number of years required for completion of a degree in 2006–2007 were 3. The number of students enrolled full- and part-time who were dismissed or voluntarily withdrew from this program area in 2007–2008 were 0. *Clinical Psychology MA/MS (Master of Arts/Science)*—Applications 2007–2008, 24. Total applicants accepted 2007–2008, 21. Openings 2008–2009, 15. The median number of years required for completion of a degree in 2006–2007 were 2. The number of students enrolled full- and part-time who were dismissed or voluntarily withdrew from this program area in 2007–2008 were 0. *Counseling Psychology MA/MS (Master of Arts/Science)*—Applications 2007–2008, 0. Total applicants accepted 2007–2008, 0. The median number of years required for completion of a degree in 2006–2007 were 2. The number of students enrolled full- and part-time who were dismissed or voluntarily withdrew from this program area in 2007–2008 were 0. *General Psychology MA/MS (Master of Arts/Science)*—Applications 2007–2008, 10. Total applicants accepted 2007–2008, 5. Number full-time enrolled (new admits only) 2007–2008, 5. Total enrolled 2007–2008 full-time, 5. Openings 2008–2009, 5. The median number of years required for completion of a degree in 2006–2007 were 2.

Admissions Requirements:

Scores: Entries appear in this order: required test or GPA, minimum score (if required), median score of students entering in 2007–2008. Master's Programs: GRE-V 500; GRE-Q 500; overall undergraduate GPA 3.00.

Other Criteria: (importance of criteria rated low, medium, or high): GRE/MAT scores—high, research experience—high, work experience—medium, extracurricular activity—medium, clinically related public service—medium, GPA—high, letters of recommendation—high, statement of goals and objectives—high.

Student Characteristics: The following represents characteristics of students in 2007–2008 in all graduate psychology programs in the department: Female—full-time 21, part-time 1; Male—full-time 14, part-time 1; African American/Black—full-time 0, part-time 0; Hispanic/Latino(a)—full-time 3, part-time 0; Asian/Pacific Islander—part-time 0; American Indian/Alaska Native—full-time 0, part-time 0; Caucasian/White—full-time 32, part-time 0; students subject to the Americans With Disabilities Act—full-time 0, part-time 0; Unknown ethnicity—full-time 0, part-time 0.

Financial Information/Assistance:

Tuition for Full-Time Study: *Master's:* State residents: $596 per credit hour; Nonstate residents: $596 per credit hour. See the following Web site for updates and changes in tuition costs: http://www.acu.edu/academics/grad/academicprograms/financialinfo.html.

Financial Assistance:

First-Year Students: Teaching assistantships available for first year. Average amount paid per academic year: $2,900. Average number of hours worked per week: 10. Apply by April 15. Tuition remission given: partial. Research assistantships available for first year. Average amount paid per academic year: $2,900. Average number of hours worked per week: 10. Apply by April 15. Tuition remission given: partial. Fellowships and scholarships available for first year. Average amount paid per academic year: $1,000. Average number of hours worked per week: 0.

Advanced Students: Teaching assistantships available for advanced students. Average amount paid per academic year: $2,900. Average number of hours worked per week: 10. Apply by April 15. Tuition remission given: partial. Research assistantships available for advanced students. Average amount paid per academic year: $2,900. Average number of hours worked per week: 10. Apply by April 15. Tuition remission given: partial.

Additional Information: Of all students currently enrolled full time, 80% benefited from one or more of the listed financial assistance programs.

Internships/Practica: Full-time paid internships are available for students in the MS in School Psychology. Students in the Counseling and Clinical programs do practica in a variety of community agencies, health care, and school settings.

Housing and Day Care: On-campus housing is available. No on-campus day care facilities are available.

Employment of Department Graduates:

Master's Degree Graduates: Of those who graduated in the academic year 2006–2007, the following categories and numbers represent the postgraduate activities and employment of master's degree graduates: Enrolled in a postdoctoral residency/fellowship

(n/a), employed in independent practice (n/a), total from the above (master's) (0).

Doctoral Degree Graduates: Of those who graduated in the academic year 2006–2007, the following categories and numbers represent the postgraduate activities and employment of doctoral degree graduates: Enrolled in a psychology doctoral program (n/a), total from the above (doctoral) (0).

Additional Information:

Orientation, Objectives, and Emphasis of Department: The MS in School Psychology is approved by the National Association of School Psychologists. The department has two objectives for its graduate programs: (a) prepare capable students for doctoral study in psychology, and (b) prepare students to be effective in psychological assessment and intervention. Programs emphasize short-term cognitive–behavioral strategies with sound empirical support and thorough training in both cognitive and personality assessment. Students may focus on either adult or child and adolescent clients. Within the master's degree students may also pursue a "Graduate Certificate in Conflict Resolution." Faculty share and challenge students to explore the implications and application of a Christian world view.

Special Facilities or Resources: An explicit goal of the program is to prepare students with research tools and experience for the pursuit of doctoral study in psychology through research classes and the master's thesis. Ongoing collaboration with the University Counseling Center provides clinical and counseling research opportunities.

Application Information:

Send to ACU Graduate School, ACU Box 29140, Abilene, TX 79699. URL of online application: http://www.acu.edu/admissions/graduate/info.html. Students are admitted in the Fall, application deadline March 31; Spring, application deadline October 31; Summer, application deadline February 15. *Fee:* $40.

Angelo State University

Department of Psychology, Sociology, and Social Work
College of Liberal and Fine Arts
2601 West Avenue N
San Angelo, TX 76909
Telephone: (325) 942-2068
Fax: (325) 942-2290
E-mail: *Bill.Davidson@angelo.edu*
Web: *http://www.angelo.edu/dept/psychology_sociology/*

Department Information:

1983. Department Head: William B. Davidson. Number of faculty: total—full-time 13, part-time 8; women—full-time 3, part-time 5; total—minority—full-time 2, part-time 1; women minority—full-time 1, part-time 1.

Programs and Degrees Offered:

Listed in the following order: Program area, degree type (T if terminal Master's), number awarded 7/06–6/07. Counseling MA/MS (Master of Arts/Science) (T) 7, General MA/MS (Master of Arts/Science) (T) 7, Industrial/Organizational MA/MS (Master of Arts/Science) (T) 10.

Student Applications/Admissions:

Student Applications

Counseling MA/MS (Master of Arts/Science)—Applications 2007–2008, 25. Total applicants accepted 2007–2008, 13. Number full-time enrolled (new admits only) 2007–2008, 11. Number part-time enrolled (new admits only) 2007–2008, 2. Total enrolled 2007–2008 full-time, 15, part-time, 13. Openings 2008–2009, 10. The median number of years required for completion of a degree in 2006–2007 were 2. The number of students enrolled full- and part-time who were dismissed or voluntarily withdrew from this program area in 2007–2008 were 0. *General MA/MS (Master of Arts/Science)*—Applications 2007–2008, 6. Total applicants accepted 2007–2008, 5. Number full-time enrolled (new admits only) 2007–2008, 2. Number part-time enrolled (new admits only) 2007–2008, 0. Total enrolled 2007–2008 full-time, 10, part-time, 4. Openings 2008–2009, 8. The median number of years required for completion of a degree in 2006–2007 were 2. The number of students enrolled full- and part-time who were dismissed or voluntarily withdrew from this program area in 2007–2008 were 0. *Industrial/Organizational MA/MS (Master of Arts/Science)*—Applications 2007–2008, 11. Total applicants accepted 2007–2008, 11. Number full-time enrolled (new admits only) 2007–2008, 5. Number part-time enrolled (new admits only) 2007–2008, 0. Total enrolled 2007–2008 full-time, 11, part-time, 1. Openings 2008–2009, 10. The median number of years required for completion of a degree in 2006–2007 were 2. The number of students enrolled full- and part-time who were dismissed or voluntarily withdrew from this program area in 2007–2008 were 0.

Admissions Requirements:

Scores: Entries appear in this order: required test or GPA, minimum score (if required), median score of students entering in 2007–2008. Master's Programs: GRE-V 450; GRE-Q 450; overall undergraduate GPA 3.0; Masters GRE-Analytical 4.0.

Other Criteria: (importance of criteria rated low, medium, or high): GRE/MAT scores—high, research experience—low, work experience—low, GPA—high, letters of recommendation—medium, statement of goals and objectives—medium, undergraduate major in psychology—low, specific undergraduate psychology courses taken—low. The criteria do vary for different programs. For additional information on admission requirements, go to http://www.angelo.edu/dept/psychology_sociology/graduate_programs.htm.

Student Characteristics: The following represents characteristics of students in 2007–2008 in all graduate psychology programs in the department: Female—full-time 23, part-time 11; Male—full-time 13, part-time 7; African American/Black—full-time 1, part-time 1; Hispanic/Latino(a)—full-time 2, part-time 3; Asian/Pacific Islander—full-time 0, part-time 0; American Indian/Alaska Native—full-time 2, part-time 0; Caucasian/White—full-time 31, part-time 14; Multi-ethnic—full-time 0, part-time 0; students subject to the Americans With Disabilities Act—full-time 0, part-time 0; Unknown ethnicity—full-time 0, part-time 0; International students who hold an F-1 or J-1 Visa—full-time 1, part-time 1.

Financial Information/Assistance:

Tuition for Full-Time Study: *Master's:* State residents: per academic year $3,826, $273 per credit hour; Nonstate residents: per

academic year $8,830, $548 per credit hour. Tuition is subject to change. See the following Web site for updates and changes in tuition costs: http://www.angelo.edu/dept/grad_school.

Financial Assistance:

First-Year Students: Research assistantships available for first year. Average amount paid per academic year: $5,414. Average number of hours worked per week: 17. Apply by April 15. Fellowships and scholarships available for first year. Average amount paid per academic year: $2,300. Apply by March 1.

Advanced Students: Teaching assistantships available for advanced students. Average amount paid per academic year: $10,877. Average number of hours worked per week: 20. Apply by March 1. Research assistantships available for advanced students. Average amount paid per academic year: $5,414. Average number of hours worked per week: 17. Apply by April 15. Fellowships and scholarships available for advanced students. Average amount paid per academic year: $2,300. Apply by March 1.

Additional Information: Of all students currently enrolled full time, 36% benefited from one or more of the listed financial assistance programs. Application and information available online at http://www.angelo.edu/forms/pdf/applgradasstTA.pdf.

Internships/Practica: Practicum opportunities are available in many local public and private mental health facilities and also in local corporate entities.

Housing and Day Care: On-campus housing is available. See the following Web site for more information: http://www.angelo.edu. No on-campus day care facilities are available.

Employment of Department Graduates:

Master's Degree Graduates: Of those who graduated in the academic year 2006–2007, the following categories and numbers represent the postgraduate activities and employment of master's degree graduates: Enrolled in a postdoctoral residency/fellowship (n/a), employed in independent practice (n/a), total from the above (master's) (0).

Doctoral Degree Graduates: Of those who graduated in the academic year 2006–2007, the following categories and numbers represent the postgraduate activities and employment of doctoral degree graduates: Enrolled in a psychology doctoral program (n/a), total from the above (doctoral) (0).

Additional Information:

Orientation, Objectives, and Emphasis of Department: The department emphasizes personalized training, small class sizes, and a balance between research skills and practitioner skills.

Special Facilities or Resources: The department is equipped with a state-of-the-art psychology laboratory and a microcomputer laboratory.

Information for Students With Physical Disabilities: See the following Web site for more information: http://www.angelo.edu/dept/grad_school.

Application Information:

Send to Office of the Graduate Dean, Angelo State University, ASU Station #11025, San Angelo, TX 76909-1025. Application available online. URL of online application: http://www.angelo.edu/grad_school. Students are admitted in the Fall, application deadline July 15; Spring, application deadline December 1; Summer, application deadline April 30. Summer I application deadline is April 30; Summer II application deadline is May 31. *Fee:* $40.

Argosy University/Dallas Campus

Clinical Psychology
8080 Park Lane, Suite 400A
Dallas, TX 75231
Telephone: (214) 459-2222
Fax: (214) 459-2225
E-mail: *brwall@argosy.edu*
Web: *http://www.argosy.edu (see campuses)*

Department Information:

2002. Chairperson: Brenda Wall, PhD. Number of faculty: total—full-time 11, part-time 1; women—full-time 7; total—minority—full-time 4; women minority—full-time 4.

Programs and Degrees Offered:

Listed in the following order: Program area, degree type (T if terminal Master's), number awarded 7/06–6/07. Clinical Psychology PsyD (Doctor of Psychology) 6, Clinical Psychology MA/MS (Master of Arts/Science) (T) 14, Community Counseling MA/MS (Master of Arts/Science) (T).

Student Applications/Admissions:

Student Applications

Clinical Psychology PsyD (Doctor of Psychology)—Applications 2007–2008, 95. Total applicants accepted 2007–2008, 42. Number full-time enrolled (new admits only) 2007–2008, 24. Total enrolled 2007–2008 full-time, 92, part-time, 104. Openings 2008–2009, 25. The median number of years required for completion of a degree in 2006–2007 were 5. The number of students enrolled full- and part-time who were dismissed or voluntarily withdrew from this program area in 2007–2008 were 5. *Clinical Psychology MA/MS (Master of Arts/Science)*—Applications 2007–2008, 37. Total applicants accepted 2007–2008, 10. Number full-time enrolled (new admits only) 2007–2008, 5. Number part-time enrolled (new admits only) 2007–2008, 2. Total enrolled 2007–2008 full-time, 6, part-time, 4. Openings 2008–2009, 10. The median number of years required for completion of a degree in 2006–2007 were 3. The number of students enrolled full- and part-time who were dismissed or voluntarily withdrew from this program area in 2007–2008 were 4. *Community Counseling MA/MS (Master of Arts/Science)*—Total enrolled 2007–2008 full-time, 200. Openings 2008–2009, 90.

Admissions Requirements:

Scores: Entries appear in this order: required test or GPA, minimum score (if required), median score of students entering in 2007–2008. Master's Programs: overall undergraduate GPA 3.00; last 2 years GPA 3.00; psychology GPA 3.00. Master of Arts in Community Counseling: 3.00 Doctoral Programs: overall undergraduate GPA 3.25; last 2 years GPA 3.25.

Other Criteria: (importance of criteria rated low, medium, or high): research experience—low, work experience—low, extracurricular activity—low, clinically related public service—medium, GPA—high, letters of recommendation—

high, interview—high, statement of goals and objectives—high, Resume—high, undergraduate major in psychology—medium, specific undergraduate psychology courses taken—high.

Student Characteristics: The following represents characteristics of students in 2007–2008 in all graduate psychology programs in the department: Female—full-time 195, part-time 86; Male—full-time 36, part-time 18; African American/Black—full-time 71, part-time 48; Hispanic/Latino(a)—full-time 44, part-time 12; Asian/Pacific Islander—full-time 5, part-time 4; American Indian/Alaska Native—full-time 1, part-time 3; Caucasian/White—full-time 110, part-time 37; Multi-ethnic—full-time 0, part-time 0; students subject to the Americans With Disabilities Act—full-time 1, part-time 0; Unknown ethnicity—full-time 0, part-time 0.

Financial Information/Assistance:

Tuition for Full-Time Study: *Master's:* State residents: $895 per credit hour; Nonstate residents: $895 per credit hour. *Doctoral:* State residents: $895 per credit hour; Nonstate residents: $895 per credit hour. Tuition is subject to change. Tuition costs vary by program. See the following Web site for updates and changes in tuition costs: http://www.argosy.edu.

Financial Assistance:

First-Year Students: Fellowships and scholarships available for first year. Average amount paid per academic year: $1,000. Apply by May 31.

Advanced Students: Teaching assistantships available for advanced students. Apply by May 31. Fellowships and scholarships available for advanced students. Average amount paid per academic year: $1,000. Apply by May 31.

Additional Information: Of all students currently enrolled full time, 25% benefited from one or more of the listed financial assistance programs. Application and information available online at http://www.argosy.edu.

Internships/Practica: Master's Degree (MA/MS Community Counseling): An internship experience such as a final research project or "capstone" experience is required of graduates. Doctoral Degree (PsyD Clinical Psychology): For those doctoral students for whom a professional internship was required in this program prior to graduation, (18) students applied for an internship in 2006–2007, with (12) students obtaining an internship. Of those students who obtained an internship, (8) were paid internships. Of those students who obtained an internship, (3) students placed in APA/CPA-accredited internships, (9) students placed in internships not APA/CPA-accredited, but listed with the Association of Psychology Postdoctoral and Internship Centers (APPIC), (0) students placed in internships conforming to guidelines of the Council of Directors of School Psychology Programs (CDSPP), (0) students placed in internships that were not APA/CPA-accredited, APPIC or CDSPP listed. The variety of practicum and internship sites is increasing as our program grows and now includes several hospitals, counseling centers, county juvenile programs, rehabilitation centers, pain management centers, university counseling centers, and homeless programs. Opportunities for students range from neuropsychology, adolescent assessment, offender intervention, low birth weight programs, mental retardation, attention deficit programs, adult incarceration, and bilingual clinical support.

Housing and Day Care: No on-campus housing is available. No on-campus day care facilities are available.

Employment of Department Graduates:

Master's Degree Graduates: Of those who graduated in the academic year 2006–2007, the following categories and numbers represent the postgraduate activities and employment of master's degree graduates: Enrolled in a postdoctoral residency/fellowship (n/a), employed in independent practice (n/a), other employment position (9), total from the above (master's) (9).

Doctoral Degree Graduates: Of those who graduated in the academic year 2006–2007, the following categories and numbers represent the postgraduate activities and employment of doctoral degree graduates: Enrolled in a psychology doctoral program (n/a), total from the above (doctoral) (0).

Additional Information:

Orientation, Objectives, and Emphasis of Department: Current emphasis in all our graduate programs is a practitioner–scholar model with diversity integrated within all coursework and practical experience. Most teaching faculty have more than 10 years of teaching and/or clinical years of experience provided in a very student-centered program of study. All faculty have doctoral-level education, with specialities in diversity, testing and assessment, psychodynamic psychotherapy, health psychology, art therapy, exceptional children, substance abuse, and forensics. Theoretical orientations range from faith-based, client-centered, to psychoanalytic and cognitive–behavioral.

Information for Students With Physical Disabilities: See the following Web site for more information: http://www.argosy.edu select Dallas Campus.

Application Information:

Send to Admissions Office, Argosy University, Dallas Campus, 8080 Park Lane, Suite 500, Dallas, Texas 75231. Application available online. URL of online application: http://www.argosy.edu. Students are admitted in the Fall, application deadline January 15; Spring, application deadline October 15. PsyD admissions are in Fall and Spring only. *Fee:* $50.

Baylor University

Department of Psychology and Neuroscience, PhD Program in Psychology
Arts and Sciences
One Bear Place 97334
Waco, TX 76798-7334
Telephone: (254) 710-2961
Fax: (254) 710-3033
E-mail: *Matthew_Stanford@baylor.edu*
Web: *http://www.baylor.edu/psychologyneuroscience*

Department Information:

1950. Chairperson: J.L. Diaz-Granados, PhD. Number of faculty: total—full-time 19; women—full-time 5; total—minority—full-time 2; women minority—full-time 1.

Programs and Degrees Offered:

Listed in the following order: Program area, degree type (T if terminal Master's), number awarded 7/06–6/07. Clinical Psychology PsyD (Doctor of Psychology) 12, Psychology PhD (Doctor of Philosophy) 2.

APA Accreditation: Clinical PsyD (Doctor of Psychology).

Student Applications/Admissions:

Student Applications

Clinical Psychology PsyD (Doctor of Psychology)—Applications 2007–2008, 156. Total applicants accepted 2007–2008, 7. Number full-time enrolled (new admits only) 2007–2008, 7. Openings 2008–2009, 7. The median number of years required for completion of a degree in 2006–2007 were 5. The number of students enrolled full- and part-time who were dismissed or voluntarily withdrew from this program area in 2007–2008 were 1. *Psychology PhD (Doctor of Philosophy)*—Applications 2007–2008, 38. Total applicants accepted 2007–2008, 1. Number full-time enrolled (new admits only) 2007–2008, 1. Total enrolled 2007–2008 full-time, 11. Openings 2008–2009, 4. The median number of years required for completion of a degree in 2006–2007 were 5. The number of students enrolled full- and part-time who were dismissed or voluntarily withdrew from this program area in 2007–2008 were 0.

Admissions Requirements:

Scores: Entries appear in this order: required test or GPA, minimum score (if required), median score of students entering in 2007–2008. Doctoral Programs: GRE-V no minimum stated; GRE-Q no minimum stated; overall undergraduate GPA 2.80.

Other Criteria: (importance of criteria rated low, medium, or high): GRE/MAT scores—high, research experience—high, work experience—medium, extracurricular activity—medium, clinically related public service—medium, GPA—high, letters of recommendation—high, interview—high, statement of goals and objectives—medium.

Student Characteristics: The following represents characteristics of students in 2007–2008 in all graduate psychology programs in the department: Female—full-time 26, part-time 0; Male—full-time 9, part-time 0; African American/Black—full-time 0, part-time 0; Hispanic/Latino(a)—full-time 3, part-time 0; Asian/Pacific Islander—full-time 3, part-time 0; American Indian/Alaska Native—full-time 0, part-time 0; Caucasian/White—full-time 28, part-time 0; Multi-ethnic—full-time 1, part-time 0; students subject to the Americans With Disabilities Act—full-time 0, part-time 0; Unknown ethnicity—full-time 0, part-time 0.

Financial Information/Assistance:

Tuition for Full-Time Study: *Doctoral:* State residents: $925 per credit hour; Nonstate residents: $925 per credit hour. Tuition is subject to change. See the following Web site for updates and changes in tuition costs: http://www.baylor.edu/graduate/index.php?id=2847.

Financial Assistance:

First-Year Students: Teaching assistantships available for first year. Average amount paid per academic year: $16,000. Average number of hours worked per week: 20. Apply by January 2. Tuition remission given: full and partial. Research assistantships available for first year. Average amount paid per academic year: $16,000. Average number of hours worked per week: 20. Apply by January 2. Tuition remission given: full and partial. Traineeships available for first year. Average amount paid per academic year: $16,000. Average number of hours worked per week: 20. Apply by January 2. Tuition remission given: full and partial. Fellowships and scholarships available for first year. Tuition remission given: partial.

Advanced Students: Teaching assistantships available for advanced students. Average amount paid per academic year: $16,000. Average number of hours worked per week: 20. Apply by January 2. Tuition remission given: full and partial. Research assistantships available for advanced students. Average amount paid per academic year: $16,000. Average number of hours worked per week: 20. Apply by January 2. Tuition remission given: full and partial. Traineeships available for advanced students. Average amount paid per academic year: $16,000. Average number of hours worked per week: 20. Apply by January 2. Tuition remission given: full and partial. Fellowships and scholarships available for advanced students. Tuition remission given: partial.

Additional Information: Of all students currently enrolled full time, 100% benefited from one or more of the listed financial assistance programs. Application and information available online at http://www.baylor.edu/psychologyneuroscience.

Internships/Practica: The PsyD Program incorporates an extensive practicum program with placements available in 16 community agencies and treatment facilities. Of our graduates over the last 11 years, 105 of 107 have obtained APA-accredited internships.

Housing and Day Care: No on-campus housing is available. On-campus day care facilities are available. Contact Piper Child Development Center, 315 Washington Avenue, Waco, Texas 76701.

Employment of Department Graduates:

Master's Degree Graduates: Of those who graduated in the academic year 2006–2007, the following categories and numbers represent the postgraduate activities and employment of master's degree graduates: Enrolled in a postdoctoral residency/fellowship (n/a), employed in independent practice (n/a), total from the above (master's) (0).

Doctoral Degree Graduates: Of those who graduated in the academic year 2006–2007, the following categories and numbers represent the postgraduate activities and employment of doctoral degree graduates: Enrolled in a psychology doctoral program (n/a), enrolled in a postdoctoral residency/fellowship (2), employed in independent practice (6), employed in an academic position at a university (0), employed in a community mental health/counseling center (2), employed in a hospital/medical center (2), still seeking employment (0), total from the above (doctoral) (12).

Additional Information:

Orientation, Objectives, and Emphasis of Department: The department offers a broad range of courses in the areas of clinical psychology, behavioral neuroscience, and social psychology. The Doctor of Psychology (PsyD) program has the longest history of accreditation by the American Psychological Association. The PsyD program emphasizes a professional–scholar model with a goal of developing competencies based on current research and scholarship in clinical psychology. Extensive practicum experience is integrated with concurrent coursework . A formal dissertation involving applied clinical research is also required. The goal of Baylor's PsyD program is to develop professional psychologists with the conceptual and clinical competencies necessary to deliver psychological services in a manner that is effective and responsive to individual and societal needs both now and in the future. The doctoral program in Psychology (PhD) has two training tracks; Behavioral Neuroscience and Social Psychology. Doctoral students are expected to acquire sufficient knowledge and expertise to permit them to work as independent scholars at the frontier of their field upon graduation. Extensive training is provided in laboratory research and experimental design for social psychology and behavioral neuroscience students. The Doctor of Philosophy (PhD) degree is ultimately awarded to those individuals who have attained a high level of scholarship in a selected field through independent study, research, and creative thought.

Special Facilities or Resources: The department has a number of well-equipped research laboratories. PhD program: Computer-controlled programmable laboratory in memory and cognition; complete facilities for research on animal learning and behavior (including animal colony); developmental psychobiology laboratory, with facilities for behavioral and pharmacological research, including teratological studies; inhalation chambers for administration of ethanol (and other substances). Single-subject brain-recording (EEG) and electron microscopy facilities available. The department also houses a community clinic that facilitates the clinical training and related research activities for PsyD students.

Application Information:

Send to Baylor University, Graduate Admissions, One Bear Place 97264, Waco, TX 76798. Application available online. URL of online application: http://www.baylor.edu/graduate/home.php. Students are admitted in the Fall, application deadline February 15; Summer, application deadline January 2. Psychology (PhD), February 15; only accept applications for Fall admission Clinical Psychology (PsyD), January 2; only accept applications for Summer admission. *Fee:* $40.

Houston Baptist University (2007 data)

Psychology Department
College of Education and Behavioral Sciences
7502 Fondren Road
Houston, TX 77074
Telephone: (281) 649-3000 ext. 2316
Fax: (281) 649-3361
E-mail: *bking@hbu.edu*
Web: *http://www.hbu.edu*

Department Information:

1985. Chairperson: Renata Nero, PhD. Number of faculty: total—full-time 5, part-time 7; women—full-time 3, part-time 6.

Programs and Degrees Offered:

Listed in the following order: Program area, degree type (T if terminal Master's), number awarded 7/06–6/07. Psychology MA/MS (Master of Arts/Science) (T) 18, Christian Counseling MA/MS (Master of Arts/Science) (T) 8.

Student Applications/Admissions:

Student Applications

Psychology MA/MS (Master of Arts/Science)—Applications 2007–2008, 61. Total applicants accepted 2007–2008, 28. Number full-time enrolled (new admits only) 2007–2008, 18. Number part-time enrolled (new admits only) 2007–2008, 3. Total enrolled 2007–2008 full-time, 50, part-time, 26. Openings 2008–2009, 45. The median number of years required for completion of a degree in 2006–2007 were 2. The number of students enrolled full- and part-time who were dismissed or voluntarily withdrew from this program area in 2007–2008 were 1. *Christian Counseling MA/MS (Master of Arts/Science)*—Applications 2007–2008, 17. Total applicants accepted 2007–2008, 7. Number full-time enrolled (new admits only) 2007–2008, 5. Number part-time enrolled (new admits only) 2007–2008, 1. Total enrolled 2007–2008 full-time, 20, part-time, 3. Openings 2008–2009, 30. The median number of years required for completion of a degree in 2006–2007 were 2. The number of students enrolled full- and part-time who were dismissed or voluntarily withdrew from this program area in 2007–2008 were 0.

Admissions Requirements:

Scores: Entries appear in this order: required test or GPA, minimum score (if required), median score of students entering in 2007–2008. Master's Programs: GRE-V 400, 460; GRE-Q no minimum stated, 540; overall undergraduate GPA 2.8.

Other Criteria: (importance of criteria rated low, medium, or high): GRE/MAT scores—high, clinically related public service—low, GPA—high, letters of recommendation—medium, interview—medium, statement of goals and objectives—medium. For additional information on admission requirements, go to http://www.hbu.edu.

Student Characteristics: The following represents characteristics of students in 2007–2008 in all graduate psychology programs in the department: Female—full-time 59, part-time 26; Male—full-time 11, part-time 3; African American/Black—full-time 12, part-time 10; Hispanic/Latino(a)—full-time 12, part-time 2; Asian/Pacific Islander—full-time 3, part-time 1; American Indian/Alaska Native—full-time 1, part-time 0; Caucasian/White—full-time 41, part-time 16; Multi-ethnic—full-time 1, part-time 0; students subject to the Americans With Disabilities Act—full-time 0, part-time 0; Unknown ethnicity—full-time 0, part-time 0.

Financial Information/Assistance:

Tuition for Full-Time Study: *Master's:* State residents: $450 per credit hour; Nonstate residents: $450 per credit hour. Tuition is subject to change. See the following Web site for updates and changes in tuition costs: http://www.hbu.edu.

Financial Assistance:

First-Year Students: No information provided.

Advanced Students: No information provided.

Additional Information: Of all students currently enrolled full time, 0% benefited from one or more of the listed financial assistance programs. Application and information available online at http://www.hbu.edu.

Internships/Practica: Students complete their practicum requirements (450 clock hours supervised by a licensed psychologist or licensed professional counselor-supervisor) in area hospitals, social service agencies, schools and counseling centers. MACC students complete their practica in church or Christian counseling centers.

LSSP students complete a 1,200 hour internship in a school setting.

Housing and Day Care: On-campus housing is available. Contact Husky Village (281) 649-3100. No on-campus day care facilities are available.

Employment of Department Graduates:

Master's Degree Graduates: Of those who graduated in the academic year 2006–2007, the following categories and numbers represent the postgraduate activities and employment of master's degree graduates: Enrolled in a postdoctoral residency/fellowship (n/a), employed in independent practice (n/a), total from the above (master's) (0).

Doctoral Degree Graduates: Of those who graduated in the academic year 2006–2007, the following categories and numbers represent the postgraduate activities and employment of doctoral degree graduates: Enrolled in a psychology doctoral program (n/a), total from the above (doctoral) (0).

Additional Information:

Orientation, Objectives, and Emphasis of Department: The master's program follows the scientist–practitioner model of training. Some students become psychological associates, some seek doctoral training, and a large number add the 12 hours required to become licensed specialists in school psychology. The majority pursue licensure as professional counselors.

Special Facilities or Resources: The department has a full-time faculty of dedicated, teaching professionals. All graduate faculty hold terminal degrees. Two are licensed psychologists, one is a licensed professional counselor–supervisor, and two are social psychologists. All adjuncts have terminal degrees and are practicing clinicians. Computer facilities are available for use in research and statistical analyses.

Information for Students With Physical Disabilities: See the following Web site for more information: http://www.hbu.edu/hbu/Academic_Accommodations_for_students_with_Learning.asp.

Application Information:

Send to Master of Arts in Psychology, Houston Baptist University, 7502 Fondren, Houston, TX 77074. Master of Arts in Christian Counseling, Houston Baptist University, 7502 Fondren, Houston, TX 77074. Application available online. URL of online application: http://www.hbu.edu. Students are admitted in the Fall, application deadline August 1; Winter, application deadline November 1; Spring, application deadline February 1; Summer, application deadline May 1; programs have rolling admissions. Deadlines are flexible. *Fee:* $25.

Houston, University of

Department of Educational Psychology
College of Education
491 Farish Hall
Houston, TX 77204-5029
Telephone: (713) 743-5019
Fax: (713) 743-4996
E-mail: *dprater@uh.edu*
Web: *http://www.coe.uh.edu/mycoe/epsy/*

Department Information:

1980. Chairperson: Dr. Doris Prater. Number of faculty: total—full-time 22, part-time 6; women—full-time 10, part-time 4; total—minority—full-time 8, part-time 2; women minority—full-time 6.

Programs and Degrees Offered:

Listed in the following order: Program area, degree type (T if terminal Master's), number awarded 7/06–6/07. Counseling Psychology PhD (Doctor of Philosophy) 10, Educational Psychology and Individual Differences PhD (Doctor of Philosophy) 6, Counseling MEd Other 30, Educational Psychology MEd Other 4, Special Education MEd Other 17, School Psychology PhD (Doctor of Philosophy) 0.

APA Accreditation: Counseling PhD (Doctor of Philosophy).

Student Applications/Admissions:

Student Applications

Counseling Psychology PhD (Doctor of Philosophy)—Applications 2007–2008, 60. Total applicants accepted 2007–2008, 16. Number full-time enrolled (new admits only) 2007–2008, 9. Total enrolled 2007–2008 full-time, 51. Openings 2008–2009, 10. The median number of years required for completion of a degree in 2006–2007 were 7. The number of students enrolled full- and part-time who were dismissed or voluntarily withdrew from this program area in 2007–2008 were 0. *Educational Psychology and Individual Differences PhD (Doctor of Philosophy)*—Applications 2007–2008, 18. Total applicants accepted 2007–2008, 6. Number full-time enrolled (new admits only) 2007–2008, 4. Total enrolled 2007–2008 full-time, 26. Openings 2008–2009, 6. The median number of years required for completion of a degree in 2006–2007 were 4. The number of students enrolled full- and part-time who were dismissed or voluntarily withdrew from this program area in 2007–2008 were 1. *Counseling MEd Other*—Applications 2007–2008, 72. Total applicants accepted 2007–2008, 44. Number full-time enrolled (new admits only) 2007–2008, 15. Number part-time enrolled (new admits only) 2007–2008, 29. Total enrolled 2007–2008 full-time, 20, part-time, 50. Openings 2008–2009, 40. The median number of years required for completion of a degree in 2006–2007 were 2. The number of students enrolled full- and part-time who were dismissed or voluntarily withdrew from this program area in 2007–2008 were 0. *Educational Psychology MEd Other*—Applications 2007–2008, 11. Total applicants accepted 2007–2008, 5. Number full-time enrolled (new admits only) 2007–2008, 5. Total enrolled 2007–2008 full-time, 14, part-time, 10. Openings 2008–2009, 8. The median number of years required for completion of a degree in 2006–2007 were 3. The number of students enrolled full- and part-time who were dismissed or voluntarily withdrew from this program area in 2007–2008 were 3. *Special Education MEd Other*—Applications 2007–2008, 24. Total applicants accepted 2007–2008, 11. Number full-time enrolled (new admits only) 2007–2008, 2. Number part-time enrolled (new admits only) 2007–2008, 8. Total enrolled 2007–2008 full-time, 4, part-time, 16. *School Psychology PhD (Doctor of Philosophy)*—Applications 2007–2008, 11. Total applicants accepted 2007–2008, 5. Number full-time enrolled (new admits only) 2007–2008, 4. Total enrolled 2007–2008 full-time, 17. Openings 2008–2009, 7. The number of students enrolled full- and part-time who were dismissed or voluntarily withdrew from this program area in 2007–2008 were 0.

Admissions Requirements:

Scores: Entries appear in this order: required test or GPA, minimum score (if required), median score of students entering in 2007–2008. Master's Programs: GRE-V 30%; GRE-Q 30%; MAT 400; last 2 years GPA 3.0. May take either MAT or GRE Doctoral Programs: GRE-V 35%; GRE-Q 35%; last 2 years GPA 3.0.

Other Criteria: (importance of criteria rated low, medium, or high): GRE/MAT scores—high, research experience—high, work experience—high, extracurricular activity—high, clinically related public service—high, GPA—high, letters of recommendation—high, interview—high, statement of goals and objectives—high. PhD programs emphasize research experience and research interests more than do the master's programs. For additional information on admission requirements, go to http://www.coe.uh.edu/psgrad.cfm.

Student Characteristics: The following represents characteristics of students in 2007–2008 in all graduate psychology programs in the department: Female—full-time 110, part-time 63; Male—full-time 22, part-time 13; African American/Black—full-time 8, part-time 12; Hispanic/Latino(a)—full-time 11, part-time 8; Asian/Pacific Islander—full-time 8, part-time 11; American Indian/Alaska Native—full-time 0, part-time 1; Caucasian/White—full-time 92, part-time 42; Multi-ethnic—full-time 0, part-time 0; students subject to the Americans With Disabilities Act—full-time 0, part-time 0; Unknown ethnicity—full-time 4, part-time 2; International students who hold an F-1 or J-1 Visa—full-time 1, part-time 0.

Financial Information/Assistance:

Tuition for Full-Time Study: *Master's:* State residents: per academic year $6,288, $262 per credit hour; Nonstate residents: per academic year $12,984, $541 per credit hour. *Doctoral:* State residents: per academic year $6,288, $1,262 per credit hour; Nonstate residents: per academic year $12,984, $541 per credit hour. Tuition is subject to change. Additional fees are assessed to students beyond the costs of tuition for the following: room, board, books, supplies, miscellaneous expenses are about $10,745. See the following Web site for updates and changes in tuition costs: http://www.uh.edu/admissions/pages/gFinanInfo.htm.

Financial Assistance:

First-Year Students: Teaching assistantships available for first year. Average amount paid per academic year: $12,732. Average number of hours worked per week: 20. Tuition remission given: full. Research assistantships available for first year. Average amount paid per academic year: $12,732. Average number of hours worked per week: 20. Tuition remission given: full. Fellowships and scholarships available for first year. Tuition remission given: full and partial.

Advanced Students: Teaching assistantships available for advanced students. Average amount paid per academic year: $15,132. Average number of hours worked per week: 20. Tuition remission given: full. Research assistantships available for advanced students. Average amount paid per academic year: $15,132. Average number of hours worked per week: 20. Tuition remission given: full. Fellowships and scholarships available for advanced students. Tuition remission given: full and partial.

Additional Information: Of all students currently enrolled full time, 33% benefited from one or more of the listed financial assistance programs. Application and information available online at http://www.uh.edu/admissions/financial/graduate/.

Internships/Practica: Doctoral Degree (PhD Counseling Psychology): For those doctoral students for whom a professional internship was required in this program prior to graduation, (4) students applied for an internship in 2006–2007, with (3) students obtaining an internship. Of those students who obtained an internship, (3) were paid internships. Of those students who obtained an internship, (3)students placed in APA/CPA-accredited internships, (0) students placed in internships not APA/CPA-accredited, but listed with the Association of Psychology Postdoctoral and Internship Centers (APPIC), (0) students placed in internships conforming to guidelines of the Council of Directors of School Psychology Programs (CDSPP), (0) students placed in internships that were not APA/CPA-accredited, APPIC or CDSPP listed. Doctoral Degree (PhD School Psychology): For those doctoral students for whom a professional internship was required in this program prior to graduation, (3) students applied for an internship in 2006–2007, with (3) students obtaining an internship. Of those students who obtained an internship, (3) were paid internships. Of those students who obtained an internship, (2)students placed in APA/CPA-accredited internships, (0) students placed in internships not APA/CPA-accredited, but listed with the Association of Psychology Postdoctoral and Internship Centers (APPIC), (1) students placed in internships conforming to guidelines of the Council of Directors of School Psychology Programs (CDSPP), (0) students placed in internships that were not APA/CPA-accredited, APPIC or CDSPP listed. All counseling psychology doctoral students and counseling master's students participate in supervised practica at numerous sites throughout the Houston area. Examples of the types of sites at which students have completed practica include veteran's and children's hospitals, counseling centers and school districts. In addition, doctoral counseling psychology students are required to complete a one year full time internship approved by the faculty. These sites range widely in orientation, focus and geographic location. All school psychology doctoral students must complete one to two years of advanced practicum (depending on experience) as well as a one year, full-time predoctoral internship. A supervised school psychology practicum may also be required (waived for those in possession of the Texas Licensed Specialist in School Psychology [LSSP] credential, or its equivalent). Most practica are arranged for students, and are available at various sites around the Houston area, including school districts, Texas Children's Hospital, M.D. Anderson Children's Cancer Hospital, and other health care and community settings. Internship sites are available in a variety of settings in the Houston area and around the country. Five of six intern applicants have obtained internships at APA accredited sites.

Housing and Day Care: On-campus housing is available. See the following Web site for more information: http://www.uh.edu/housing/. On-campus day care facilities are available. See the following Web site for more information: http://www.uh.edu/ccc/.

Employment of Department Graduates:

Master's Degree Graduates: Of those who graduated in the academic year 2006–2007, the following categories and numbers represent the postgraduate activities and employment of master's

degree graduates: Enrolled in a postdoctoral residency/fellowship (n/a), employed in independent practice (n/a), total from the above (master's) (0).

Doctoral Degree Graduates: Of those who graduated in the academic year 2006–2007, the following categories and numbers represent the postgraduate activities and employment of doctoral degree graduates: Enrolled in a psychology doctoral program (n/a), enrolled in a postdoctoral residency/fellowship (1), employed in independent practice (2), employed in other positions at a higher education institution (1), employed in a professional position in a school system (1), employed in a community mental health/counseling center (1), employed in a hospital/medical center (2), total from the above (doctoral) (8).

Additional Information:

Orientation, Objectives, and Emphasis of Department: The primary intent of the doctoral program in Counseling Psychology is to prepare highly skilled psychologists in the scientist–practitioner model of counseling. Counseling psychologists may assume several roles in a variety of settings in the professional community. These may include supervision and training of counselors and other "helping" personnel; providing personal, educational, and career counseling services; college and university teaching; research; and consultation to public systems, schools, and other community organizations concerned with psychological and interpersonal development. The Educational Psychology and Individual Differences program is dedicated to the advancement and application of knowledge relevant to human learning, development, and psychological functioning and to the meaningful application of such knowledge, especially within academic contexts. To achieve this goal, the program produces high-quality, innovative research and scholarship designed to advance the knowledge and understanding within these areas. Graduates pursue careers as faculty members, researchers, and other leadership positions within institutions of higher education, research organizations, government agencies, and in school districts. The mission of the PhD program in School Psychology is the preparation of professional psychologists in the scientist–practitioner tradition. We prepare psychologists for leadership roles in public and private PK–12 schools and health and mental health related settings. We expect our first graduate in August 2008, and we expect to have approximately 23–25 doctoral students enrolled for the 2008–2009 academic year. Our APA accreditation self-study was submitted in February 2008 and we anticipate an accreditation site visit in Fall 2008. The Master's of Education (MEd) degree program in Counseling is offered through the Department of Educational Psychology. The major objective of this program is to prepare counselors to assume positions in education and mental health settings, such as public schools, junior colleges, university counseling and advisement centers, and community mental health agencies. The major objective of the Master's of Education (MEd) degree program in Educational Psychology is to offer students preparation in (a) psychological theories and their application (i.e., human learning, development, the individual differences that exist within these areas, and their application to teaching and learning in school and other educational settings) and (b) research, measurement, and evaluation. The Master's of Education (MEd) degree program in Special Education is offered through the Department of Educational Psychology. The Master's degree in Special Education provides students the option of meeting Texas Education Agency requirements for certification in one of three areas: Generic Special Education, Educational Diagnostician, or Severely Handicapped Education.

Special Facilities or Resources: Located in the heart of a highly diverse metropolitan area with almost 5 million inhabitants, the department has access to a wealth of community resources (e.g., 56 school districts, a range of community-based mental health and specialty clinics and agencies, a large VA Hospital, 20 hospitals within the Texas Medical Center). Within the College of Education, the Center for Information Technology in Education (CITE) Laboratory, with a full-time staff of 10, provides faculty, staff, and students with computing and multimedia environments, technology resources, and timely service-oriented user support. The CITE Lab gives students broad access to computers, grayscale and color laser printers, scanners, digital still and video cameras, CD and DVD writing software; 300 MB of Web space; and off-campus access to the terminal server. Students also have access to the facilities of the University of Houston Human Development Laboratory School (HDL). The Lab School is a unique and exciting model educational program that promotes a child's reasoning, autonomous self-regulation, interpersonal understanding, and social collaboration (including conflict resolution), and provides opportunities for observation, consultation, and research with the preschool population.

Information for Students With Physical Disabilities: See the following Web site for more information: http://www.uh.edu/csd/.

Application Information:

Send to Ms. Mary Bess Kelley, University of Houston, Room 160, Farish Hall, Houston, TX 77204-5871. Application available online. URL of online application: http://www.coe.uh.edu/psgrad.cfm. Students are admitted in the Fall, application deadline varies; Spring, application deadline varies. Our programs' application deadlines are on different dates during the year: Counseling Psychology PhD and School Psychology PhD: first Monday in December; Counseling MEd: January 10; Educational Psychology and Individual Differences PhD: February 15; Educational Psychology MEd and Special Education MEd: March 15 (Fall), October 15 (Spring). *Fee:* $45.

Houston, University of

Department of Psychology
College of Liberal Arts and Social Sciences
126 Heyne Building
Houston, TX 77204-5022
Telephone: (713) 743-8508
Fax: (713) 743-8588
E-mail: *ptolar@uh.edu*
Web: *http://www.psychology.uh.edu*

Department Information:

1939. Chairperson: David J. Francis. Number of faculty: total—full-time 30, part-time 2; women—full-time 11, part-time 2; total—minority—full-time 5; women minority—full-time 3.

Programs and Degrees Offered:

Listed in the following order: Program area, degree type (T if terminal Master's), number awarded 7/06–6/07. Clinical PhD (Doctor of Philosophy) 5, Industrial/Organizational PhD (Doctor of Philosophy) 0, Social PhD (Doctor of Philosophy) 2, Developmental PhD (Doctor of Philosophy) 1.

APA Accreditation: Clinical PhD (Doctor of Philosophy).

Student Applications/Admissions:

Student Applications

Clinical PhD (Doctor of Philosophy)—Applications 2007–2008, 224. Total applicants accepted 2007–2008, 18. Number full-time enrolled (new admits only) 2007–2008, 14. Number part-time enrolled (new admits only) 2007–2008, 0. Openings 2008–2009, 12. The median number of years required for completion of a degree in 2006–2007 were 8. The number of students enrolled full- and part-time who were dismissed or voluntarily withdrew from this program area in 2007–2008 were 0. *Industrial/Organizational PhD (Doctor of Philosophy)*—Applications 2007–2008, 77. Total applicants accepted 2007–2008, 16. Number full-time enrolled (new admits only) 2007–2008, 5. Number part-time enrolled (new admits only) 2007–2008, 0. Openings 2008–2009, 6. The number of students enrolled full- and part-time who were dismissed or voluntarily withdrew from this program area in 2007–2008 were 0. *Social PhD (Doctor of Philosophy)*—Applications 2007–2008, 20. Total applicants accepted 2007–2008, 1. Number full-time enrolled (new admits only) 2007–2008, 0. Number part-time enrolled (new admits only) 2007–2008, 0. Openings 2008–2009, 4. The median number of years required for completion of a degree in 2006–2007 were 6. The number of students enrolled full- and part-time who were dismissed or voluntarily withdrew from this program area in 2007–2008 were 0. *Developmental PhD (Doctor of Philosophy)*—Applications 2007–2008, 15. Total applicants accepted 2007–2008, 5. Number full-time enrolled (new admits only) 2007–2008, 4. Total enrolled 2007–2008 full-time, 8. Openings 2008–2009, 4. The median number of years required for completion of a degree in 2006–2007 were 5. The number of students enrolled full- and part-time who were dismissed or voluntarily withdrew from this program area in 2007–2008 were 0.

Admissions Requirements:

Scores: Entries appear in this order: required test or GPA, minimum score (if required), median score of students entering in 2007–2008. Doctoral Programs: GRE-V no minimum stated; GRE-Q no minimum stated; overall undergraduate GPA no minimum stated; Doctoral program GRE-Analytic no minimum stated. Specific minimums are not required.

Other Criteria: (importance of criteria rated low, medium, or high): GRE/MAT scores—medium, research experience—high, work experience—medium, extracurricular activity—medium, clinically related public service—medium, GPA—medium, letters of recommendation—high, interview—high, statement of goals and objectives—high. The Clinical program requires an interview. For additional information on admission requirements, go to http://www.psych.uh.edu/GraduatePrograms/ApplicationInformation/.

Student Characteristics: The following represents characteristics of students in 2007–2008 in all graduate psychology programs in the department: Female—full-time 97, part-time 0; Male—full-time 31, part-time 0; African American/Black—full-time 6, part-time 0; Hispanic/Latino(a)—full-time 13, part-time 0; Asian/Pacific Islander—full-time 6, part-time 0; American Indian/Alaska Native—full-time 0, part-time 0; Caucasian/White—full-time 103, part-time 0; Multi-ethnic—full-time 0, part-time 0; students subject to the Americans With Disabilities Act—full-time 1, part-time 0; Unknown ethnicity—full-time 0, part-time 0.

Financial Information/Assistance:

Tuition for Full-Time Study: *Doctoral:* State residents: per academic year $6,337, $211 per credit hour; Nonstate residents: per academic year $14,677, $489 per credit hour. Tuition is subject to change. See the following Web site for updates and changes in tuition costs: http://www.uh.edu/financial/graduate/.

Financial Assistance:

First-Year Students: Teaching assistantships available for first year. Average amount paid per academic year: $11,580. Average number of hours worked per week: 20. Apply by appointment. Tuition remission given: full. Research assistantships available for first year. Average amount paid per academic year: $14,400. Average number of hours worked per week: 20. Apply by appointment. Tuition remission given: full. Fellowships and scholarships available for first year. Average amount paid per academic year: $3,000. Apply by appointment. Tuition remission given: full.

Advanced Students: Teaching assistantships available for advanced students. Average amount paid per academic year: $13,200. Average number of hours worked per week: 20. Apply by appointment. Tuition remission given: full. Research assistantships available for advanced students. Average amount paid per academic year: $16,800. Average number of hours worked per week: 20. Apply by appointment. Tuition remission given: full. Fellowships and scholarships available for advanced students. Average amount paid per academic year: $3,000. Apply by appointment. Tuition remission given: full.

Additional Information: Of all students currently enrolled full time, 85% benefited from one or more of the listed financial assistance programs. Application and information available online at http://www.uh.edu/gs/new/comp_fellow.htm and http://www.uh.edu/admissions/financial/.

Internships/Practica: Doctoral Degree (PhD Clinical): For those doctoral students for whom a professional internship was required in this program prior to graduation, (13) students applied for an internship in 2006–2007, with (13) students obtaining an internship. Of those students who obtained an internship, (13) were paid internships. Of those students who obtained an internship, (13) students placed in APA/CPA-accredited internships, (0) students placed in internships not APA/CPA-accredited, but listed with the Association of Psychology Postdoctoral and Internship Centers (APPIC), (0) students placed in internships conforming to guidelines of the Council of Directors of School Psychology Programs (CDSPP), (0) students placed in internships that were not APA/CPA-accredited, APPIC or CDSPP listed. Internships are available for advanced students at a number of sites that include private industry, medical centers, state hospitals, and private practices. For additional information on education and training outcomes for our programs, see the following Web site: http://www.psychology.uh.edu/GraduatePrograms/Clinical/PublicDisclosure2007.

Housing and Day Care: On-campus housing is available. See the following Web site for more information: http://www.uh.edu/housing/. On-campus day care facilities are available. See the following Web site for more information: http://www.uh.edu/admin/ccce/.

Employment of Department Graduates:

Master's Degree Graduates: Of those who graduated in the academic year 2006–2007, the following categories and numbers represent the postgraduate activities and employment of master's degree graduates: Enrolled in a postdoctoral residency/fellowship (n/a), employed in independent practice (n/a), total from the above (master's) (0).

Doctoral Degree Graduates: Of those who graduated in the academic year 2006–2007, the following categories and numbers represent the postgraduate activities and employment of doctoral degree graduates: Enrolled in a psychology doctoral program (n/a), total from the above (doctoral) (0).

Additional Information:

Orientation, Objectives, and Emphasis of Department: Clinical offers APA-approved training in research, assessment, intervention, and consultation related to complex human problems, including behavioral problems having a neurological basis. Industrial/Organizational offers broad training in industrial/organizational psychology with options for specialization in either the personnel or organizational subfields. Social emphasizes research careers in behavioral and preventive medicine; interpersonal interaction processes, with an emphasis on close relationships and motivation; and social cognition. Developmental focuses on experimental research in developmental cognitive neuroscience, including perception, speech, language, reading, attention, decision making, memory, and emotion using imaging, electrophysiological, and neurochemical techniques in human and animal models.

Special Facilities or Resources: The facilities of the department are comparable to those of any major department in a large university. A variety of community settings are available for applied research in all areas of specialization. Specialized laboratories have modern equipment for research in family and couple interaction, biofeedback, personnel interviewing, and electrophysiology, as well as access to an fMRI scanner. Several research and clinical practica are available within the community and at several hospitals (the Texas Medical Center is one of the largest in the world). The department has over 150 computer work stations.

Information for Students With Physical Disabilities: See the following Web site for more information: http://www.uh.edu/csd/.

Application Information:

Send to Academic Affairs Office, Department of Psychology, 126 Heyne Building, University of Houston, Houston, TX 77204-5022. Application available online. URL of online application: http://www.uh.edu/admissions/. Students are admitted in the Fall, application deadline see below. Deadline for Clinical is December 15. Deadline for Developmental, I/O, and Social is January 15. If students apply online, please also send hard copy of application to Academic Affairs Office listed above. *Fee:* $40. In cases of financial hardship, a waiver of the application fee may be requested by writing to Dr. Roy Lachman, Director of Graduate Education, University of Houston, Department of Psychology, 126 Heyne Building, Houston, TX 77204-5022.

Lamar University—Beaumont

Department of Psychology
Arts and Sciences
P.O. Box 10036
Beaumont, TX 77710
Telephone: (409) 880-8285
Fax: (409) 880-1779
E-mail: *randolph.smith@lamar.edu*
Web: *http://www.Lamar.edu*

Department Information:

1964. Chairperson: Randolph A. Smith. Number of faculty: total—full-time 10, part-time 3; women—full-time 7, part-time 2; ; women minority—full-time 1.

Programs and Degrees Offered:

Listed in the following order: Program area, degree type (T if terminal Master's), number awarded 7/06–6/07. Community/Clinical MA/MS (Master of Arts/Science) (T) 4, Industrial/Organizational MA/MS (Master of Arts/Science) (T) 3.

Student Applications/Admissions:

Student Applications

Community/Clinical MA/MS (Master of Arts/Science)—Applications 2007–2008, 10. Total applicants accepted 2007–2008, 4. Number full-time enrolled (new admits only) 2007–2008, 3. Number part-time enrolled (new admits only) 2007–2008, 0. Total enrolled 2007–2008 full-time, 9, part-time, 4. Openings 2008–2009, 5. The median number of years required for completion of a degree in 2006–2007 were 2. The number of students enrolled full- and part-time who were dismissed or voluntarily withdrew from this program area in 2007–2008 were 1. *Industrial/Organizational MA/MS (Master of Arts/Science)*—Applications 2007–2008, 12. Total applicants accepted 2007–2008, 7. Number full-time enrolled (new admits only) 2007–2008, 5. Number part-time enrolled (new admits only) 2007–2008, 1. Total enrolled 2007–2008 full-time, 9, part-time, 3. Openings 2008–2009, 5. The median number of years required for completion of a degree in 2006–2007 were 2. The number of students enrolled full- and part-time who were dismissed or voluntarily withdrew from this program area in 2007–2008 were 2.

Admissions Requirements:

Scores: Entries appear in this order: required test or GPA, minimum score (if required), median score of students entering in 2007–2008. Master's Programs: GRE-V 500, 500; GRE-Q 500, 535; overall undergraduate GPA 2.75, 3.15; last 2 years GPA 2.75, 3.30.

Other Criteria: (importance of criteria rated low, medium, or high): GRE/MAT scores—high, research experience—medium, work experience—low, extracurricular activity—low, clinically related public service—low, GPA—medium, letters of recommendation—low, statement of goals and objectives—low, undergraduate major in psychology—low, specific undergraduate psychology courses taken—high.

Student Characteristics: The following represents characteristics of students in 2007–2008 in all graduate psychology programs in the department: Female—full-time 12, part-time 6; Male—

full-time 6, part-time 1; African American/Black—full-time 1, part-time 0; Hispanic/Latino(a)—full-time 1, part-time 0; Asian/ Pacific Islander—full-time 0, part-time 0; American Indian/ Alaska Native—full-time 0, part-time 0; Caucasian/White—full-time 16, part-time 7; students subject to the Americans With Disabilities Act—full-time 0, part-time 0; Unknown ethnicity—full-time 0, part-time 0.

Financial Information/Assistance:

Tuition for Full-Time Study: *Master's:* State residents: $120 per credit hour; Nonstate residents: $336 per credit hour. Tuition is subject to change. Additional fees are assessed to students beyond the costs of tuition for the following: Health center, technology, library, student services. See the following Web site for updates and changes in tuition costs: http://www.lamar.edu.

Financial Assistance:

First-Year Students: Teaching assistantships available for first year. Average amount paid per academic year: $4,500. Average number of hours worked per week: 20. Tuition remission given: partial. Fellowships and scholarships available for first year. Average amount paid per academic year: $1,000. Tuition remission given: partial.

Advanced Students: Teaching assistantships available for advanced students. Average amount paid per academic year: $4,500. Average number of hours worked per week: 20. Tuition remission given: partial. Fellowships and scholarships available for advanced students. Average amount paid per academic year: $1,000. Tuition remission given: partial.

Additional Information: Of all students currently enrolled full time, 100% benefited from one or more of the listed financial assistance programs.

Internships/Practica: Master's Degree (MA/MS Community/ Clinical): An internship experience such as a final research project or "capstone" experience is required of graduates. Master's Degree (MA/MS Industrial/Organizational): An internship experience such as a final research project or "capstone" experience is required of graduates. A variety of community health settings provide useful practicum experiences for Community/Clinical students in child, adolescent, and adult counseling and assessment. There is also a clinic in the Psychology Department where students practice counseling under supervision. Practicum experiences for the Industrial/Organizational students place them in a variety of organizational and industrial work environments.

Housing and Day Care: On-campus housing is available. Lamar University, Office of Residence Life, Box 10041, Beaumont, TX 77710. On-campus day care facilities are available.

Employment of Department Graduates:

Master's Degree Graduates: Of those who graduated in the academic year 2006–2007, the following categories and numbers represent the postgraduate activities and employment of master's degree graduates: Enrolled in a psychology doctoral program (1), enrolled in a postdoctoral residency/fellowship (n/a), employed in independent practice (n/a), do not know (3), total from the above (master's) (4).

Doctoral Degree Graduates: Of those who graduated in the academic year 2006–2007, the following categories and numbers represent the postgraduate activities and employment of doctoral degree graduates: Enrolled in a psychology doctoral program (n/a), total from the above (doctoral) (0).

Additional Information:

Orientation, Objectives, and Emphasis of Department: The Department of Psychology offers a program of study leading to the Master of Science degree in applied psychology. It is designed to prepare professional personnel for employment in business, industry, or community mental health agencies. The MS in Community/Clinical Psychology includes training in therapy techniques for individuals, groups, and families. The MS in Industrial/ Organizational Psychology integrates the traditional areas of industrial psychology with the more contemporary areas of organizational development and analysis. Both programs also prepare graduates for entry to doctoral programs.

Special Facilities or Resources: The department currently maintains a psychological clinic that is used for training and research. It is available to both the student population as well as those in the surrounding community. The department also has a computer lab and research space.

Application Information:

Send to Graduate Admissions, Lamar University, Box 10078, Beaumont, TX 77710. Application available online. URL of online application: http://www.lamar.edu. Students are admitted in the Fall, application deadline March 15. *Fee:* $30.

Midwestern State University

Department of Psychology
Prothro-Yeager College of Humanities and Social Sciences
3410 Taft Boulevard
Wichita Falls, TX 76308
Telephone: (940) 397-4340
Fax: (940) 397-4682
E-mail: *george.diekhoff@mwsu.edu*
Web: *http://www.libarts.mwsu.edu/psychology/index.asp*

Department Information:

1975. Chairperson: George M. Diekhoff. Number of faculty: total—full-time 5; women—full-time 1; total—minority—full-time 1; women minority—full-time 1.

Programs and Degrees Offered:

Listed in the following order: Program area, degree type (T if terminal Master's), number awarded 7/06–6/07. Clinical and Counseling Psychology MA/MS (Master of Arts/Science) (T) 8.

Student Applications/Admissions:

Student Applications

Clinical and Counseling Psychology MA/MS (Master of Arts/ Science)—Applications 2007–2008, 22. Total applicants accepted 2007–2008, 9. Number full-time enrolled (new admits only) 2007–2008, 7. Number part-time enrolled (new admits only) 2007–2008, 0. Openings 2008–2009, 10. The median number of years required for completion of a degree in 2006–2007 were 2. The number of students enrolled full- and part-time who were dismissed or voluntarily withdrew from this program area in 2007–2008 were 1.

Admissions Requirements:

Scores: Entries appear in this order: required test or GPA, minimum score (if required), median score of students entering in 2007–2008. Master's Programs: GRE-V 500, 500; GRE-Q 500, 540; overall undergraduate GPA 3.0, 3.4; psychology GPA 3.0, 3.5; Master's GRE-Analytical 4.5, 5.

Other Criteria: (importance of criteria rated low, medium, or high): GRE/MAT scores—high, research experience—low, work experience—low, extracurricular activity—low, clinically related public service—low, GPA—high, letters of recommendation—medium, statement of goals and objectives—medium, undergraduate major in psychology—medium, specific undergraduate psychology courses taken—medium.

Student Characteristics: The following represents characteristics of students in 2007–2008 in all graduate psychology programs in the department: Female—full-time 15, part-time 0; Male—full-time 3, part-time 0; African American/Black—full-time 1, part-time 0; Hispanic/Latino(a)—full-time 1, part-time 0; Asian/Pacific Islander—full-time 1, part-time 0; American Indian/Alaska Native—full-time 0, part-time 0; Caucasian/White—full-time 14, part-time 0; Multi-ethnic—full-time 0, part-time 0; students subject to the Americans With Disabilities Act—full-time 0, part-time 0; Unknown ethnicity—full-time 0, part-time 0; International students who hold an F-1 or J-1 Visa—full-time 1, part-time 0.

Financial Information/Assistance:

Financial Assistance:

First-Year Students: Research assistantships available for first year. Average amount paid per academic year: $3,750. Average number of hours worked per week: 5. Apply by July 1. Fellowships and scholarships available for first year. Average amount paid per academic year: $1,000. Average number of hours worked per week: 0. Apply by July 1. Tuition remission given: partial.

Advanced Students: Teaching assistantships available for advanced students. Average amount paid per academic year: $3,750. Average number of hours worked per week: 5. Apply by July 1. Tuition remission given: partial. Research assistantships available for advanced students. Average amount paid per academic year: $3,750. Average number of hours worked per week: 5. Apply by July 1. Tuition remission given: partial. Fellowships and scholarships available for advanced students. Average amount paid per academic year: $1,000. Average number of hours worked per week: 0. Apply by July 1. Tuition remission given: partial.

Additional Information: Of all students currently enrolled full time, 100% benefited from one or more of the listed financial assistance programs. Application and information included with departmental application for admission.

Internships/Practica: Students completing the Clinical/Counseling program complete 9 credit hours of practicum for a total of 450 clock hours of work and study in an applied clinical/counseling setting.

Housing and Day Care: On-campus housing is available. See the following Web site for more information: http://www.mwsu.edu. No on-campus day care facilities are available.

Employment of Department Graduates:

Master's Degree Graduates: Of those who graduated in the academic year 2006–2007, the following categories and numbers represent the postgraduate activities and employment of master's degree graduates: Enrolled in a postdoctoral residency/fellowship (n/a), employed in independent practice (n/a), total from the above (master's) (0).

Doctoral Degree Graduates: Of those who graduated in the academic year 2006–2007, the following categories and numbers represent the postgraduate activities and employment of doctoral degree graduates: Enrolled in a psychology doctoral program (n/a), total from the above (doctoral) (0).

Additional Information:

Orientation, Objectives, and Emphasis of Department: The Clinical/Counseling Psychology graduate program is available in either a 50-hour or 60-hour curriculum option and is designed to lead to certification as a Licensed Professional Counselor (LPC) or Licensed Psychological Associate (LPA). Students may pursue thesis or nonthesis options. Although our emphasis is on training the master's-level practitioner, we actively encourage our students to pursue doctoral training, and we see the training we provide as a first step toward that goal.

Personal Behavior Statement: No personal statement is required. However, all students must pass a criminal background check prior to enrolling in the first of three required clinical practicum courses.

Special Facilities or Resources: Midwestern State University is located near two state hospitals, a regional community mental health and mental retardation center, and two private psychiatric hospitals. A newly remodeled clinic and computer lab are available for student use, and graduate research and teaching assistants are provided with office space. Financial assistance to Texas nonresidents includes waiver of the nonresident tuition differential.

Information for Students With Physical Disabilities: See the following Web site for more information: http://www.mwsu.edu.

Application Information:

Send to George M. Diekhoff, Chair, Department of Psychology, Midwestern State University, 3410 Taft, Wichita Falls, TX 76308. Application available online. URL of online application: http://www.libarts.mwsu.edu/psychology/ma/. Students are admitted in the Fall, application deadline July 1; Spring, application deadline November 15. Separate application must be made to the University. This can be done online at http://admissions.mwsu.edu/apply.asp. *Fee:* $35.

North Texas, University of

Department of Psychology
College of Arts and Sciences
P.O. Box 311280
Denton, TX 76203-1280
Telephone: (940) 565-2671
Fax: (940) 565-4682
E-mail: *amym@unt.edu*
Web: *http://www.psyc.unt.edu*

Department Information:

1968. Chairperson: Linda L. Marshall. Number of faculty: total—full-time 26, part-time 4; women—full-time 8, part-time 3; total—

minority—full-time 2; faculty subject to the Americans With Disabilities Act 2.

Programs and Degrees Offered:

Listed in the following order: Program area, degree type (T if terminal Master's), number awarded 7/06–6/07. Clinical Psychology: Health and Behavioral Medicine PhD (Doctor of Philosophy) 8, Experimental Psychology PhD (Doctor of Philosophy) 0, Counseling Psychology PhD (Doctor of Philosophy) 7, Clinical Psychology PhD (Doctor of Philosophy) 7.

APA Accreditation: Clinical PhD (Doctor of Philosophy). Counseling PhD (Doctor of Philosophy). Clinical PhD (Doctor of Philosophy).

Student Applications/Admissions:

Student Applications

Clinical Psychology: Health and Behavioral Medicine PhD (Doctor of Philosophy)—Applications 2007–2008, 27. Total applicants accepted 2007–2008, 8. Number full-time enrolled (new admits only) 2007–2008, 8. Number part-time enrolled (new admits only) 2007–2008, 0. Openings 2008–2009, 8. The median number of years required for completion of a degree in 2006–2007 were 6. The number of students enrolled full- and part-time who were dismissed or voluntarily withdrew from this program area in 2007–2008 were 1. *Experimental Psychology PhD (Doctor of Philosophy)*—Applications 2007–2008, 20. Total applicants accepted 2007–2008, 3. Number full-time enrolled (new admits only) 2007–2008, 3. Number part-time enrolled (new admits only) 2007–2008, 0. Openings 2008–2009, 5. The median number of years required for completion of a degree in 2006–2007 were 6. The number of students enrolled full- and part-time who were dismissed or voluntarily withdrew from this program area in 2007–2008 were 0. *Counseling Psychology PhD (Doctor of Philosophy)*—Applications 2007–2008, 101. Total applicants accepted 2007–2008, 8. Number full-time enrolled (new admits only) 2007–2008, 8. Number part-time enrolled (new admits only) 2007–2008, 0. Openings 2008–2009, 8. The median number of years required for completion of a degree in 2006–2007 were 6. The number of students enrolled full- and part-time who were dismissed or voluntarily withdrew from this program area in 2007–2008 were 1. *Clinical Psychology PhD (Doctor of Philosophy)*—Applications 2007–2008, 157. Total applicants accepted 2007–2008, 8. Number full-time enrolled (new admits only) 2007–2008, 8. Number part-time enrolled (new admits only) 2007–2008, 0. Openings 2008–2009, 8. The median number of years required for completion of a degree in 2006–2007 were 6. The number of students enrolled full- and part-time who were dismissed or voluntarily withdrew from this program area in 2007–2008 were 2.

Admissions Requirements:

Scores: Entries appear in this order: required test or GPA, minimum score (if required), median score of students entering in 2007–2008. Master's Programs: GRE-V no minimum stated; GRE-Q no minimum stated; overall undergraduate GPA no minimum stated; last 2 years GPA no minimum stated; psychology GPA no minimum stated. The minimum criteria for consideration for admission are 24 hours of psychology, 12 advanced, plus: MA minimum criteria for application requires one of these four: Applicant must submit their GRE verbal and quantitative scores and have (a) 2.8 overall on the BA or 3.0 on the last 60 hours of the BA, (b) 3.0 in psychology coursework, (c) Master's degree in another field, or (d) first or second author in a peer-reviewed scientific or professional journal. Doctoral Programs: GRE-V no minimum stated; GRE-Q no minimum stated; overall undergraduate GPA no minimum stated, 3.60; last 2 years GPA no minimum stated, 3.70; psychology GPA no minimum stated, 3.83. The minimum criteria for consideration for admission are 24 hours of psychology, 12 advanced, plus PhD minimum criteria for application requires one of these six: Applicants must submit their GRE verbal and quantitative scores, and have (a) 3.0 overall on the BA, (b) 3.5 on the last 60 hours of the BA, (c) 3.5 in undergraduate psychology coursework, (d) 3.5 on a completed Master's degree (exclusive of practicum and thesis), (e) completed doctoral degree in another field, or (f) first or second author on an article in a peer-reviewed scientific or professional journal.

Other Criteria: (importance of criteria rated low, medium, or high): GRE/MAT scores—medium, research experience—high, work experience—medium, extracurricular activity—medium, clinically related public service—high, GPA—medium, letters of recommendation—medium, interview—medium, statement of goals and objectives—high, undergraduate major in psychology—medium, specific undergraduate psychology courses taken—high. Applying to more than one program is not encouraged. If you do elect to apply to more than one program, submit a separate application packet for each program. Each application submitted must be in packet form and mailed under separate cover for each program to which you are applying. Each packet must include a completed Psychology department application, photocopies of transcripts, photocopies of GRE score reports, personal résumé, and a statement of goals. The statement of goals is an essay in which you describe your interest in seeking a graduate degree in psychology. The statement can include descriptions of the ways you can enrich diversity of the program, including language fluency, life experiences, and commitment to working with diverse populations; reasons for applying to the program and to UNT; academic goals; research interests; applied practice goals; and so forth. You should convey a fuller picture beyond the scope of a review of past academic records, test scores, and reference letters. Separate letters of recommendation for each program to which you are applying are required and letters must have a program specified. We prefer that letters of recommendation accompany the application packet, however, they may be submitted under separate cover directly from the recommender. If they accompany the application packet, these letters must be sealed and signed across the back flap by the referee. Materials submitted to the School of Graduate Studies do not need to be duplicated for each program to which you are applying.

Student Characteristics: The following represents characteristics of students in 2007–2008 in all graduate psychology programs in the department: Female—full-time 155, part-time 0; Male—full-time 55, part-time 0; African American/Black—full-time 8, part-time 0; Hispanic/Latino(a)—full-time 13, part-time 0; Asian/Pacific Islander—full-time 9, part-time 0; American Indian/Alaska Native—full-time 0, part-time 0; Caucasian/White—full-time 180, part-time 0; Multi-ethnic—full-time 0, part-time 0; students subject to the Americans With Disabilities Act—full-time 4, part-time 0; Unknown ethnicity—full-time 0, part-time 0; International students who hold an F-1 or J-1 Visa—full-time 3, part-time 0.

Financial Information/Assistance:

Tuition for Full-Time Study: *Master's:* State residents: per academic year $6,622, $473 per credit hour; Nonstate residents: per academic year $13,294, $752 per credit hour. *Doctoral:* State residents: per academic year $6,622, $473 per credit hour; Nonstate residents: per academic year $13,294, $752 per credit hour. Tuition is subject to change. Additional fees are assessed to students beyond the costs of tuition for the following: please go to following link for list of additional fees http://essc.unt.edu/saucs/tuition.htm. See the following Web site for updates and changes in tuition costs: http://www.essc.unt.edu/saucs/tuition.htm.

Financial Assistance:

First-Year Students: Teaching assistantships available for first year. Average amount paid per academic year: $6,500. Average number of hours worked per week: 20. Apply by April 15. Tuition remission given: partial. Research assistantships available for first year. Average amount paid per academic year: $6,800. Average number of hours worked per week: 20. Tuition remission given: partial. Traineeships available for first year. Average amount paid per academic year: $5,000. Average number of hours worked per week: 10. Fellowships and scholarships available for first year. Average amount paid per academic year: $1,000. Apply by April 15. Tuition remission given: partial.

Advanced Students: Teaching assistantships available for advanced students. Average amount paid per academic year: $7,200. Average number of hours worked per week: 20. Apply by April 15. Tuition remission given: partial. Research assistantships available for advanced students. Average amount paid per academic year: $6,800. Average number of hours worked per week: 20. Tuition remission given: partial. Traineeships available for advanced students. Average amount paid per academic year: $12,000. Average number of hours worked per week: 20. Tuition remission given: partial. Fellowships and scholarships available for advanced students. Average amount paid per academic year: $12,000. Apply by January 15. Tuition remission given: partial.

Additional Information: Of all students currently enrolled full time, 73% benefited from one or more of the listed financial assistance programs.

Internships/Practica: For additional information on education and training outcomes for our programs, see the following Web site: (Counseling Psychology/Clinical Psychology Student Outcomes) http://www.psyc.unt.edu.

Housing and Day Care: On-campus housing is available. See the following Web site for more information: http://www.unt.edu/housing/. No on-campus day care facilities are available.

Employment of Department Graduates:

Master's Degree Graduates: Of those who graduated in the academic year 2006–2007, the following categories and numbers represent the postgraduate activities and employment of master's degree graduates: Enrolled in a psychology doctoral program (4), enrolled in a postdoctoral residency/fellowship (n/a), employed in independent practice (n/a), employed in a community mental health/counseling center (1), total from the above (master's) (5). ***Doctoral Degree Graduates:*** Of those who graduated in the academic year 2006–2007, the following categories and numbers represent the postgraduate activities and employment of doctoral degree graduates: Enrolled in a psychology doctoral program (n/a), enrolled in a postdoctoral residency/fellowship (5), employed in independent practice (1), employed in an academic position at a university (2), employed in other positions at a higher education institution (2), employed in business or industry (1), employed in government agency (1), employed in a community mental health/counseling center (2), employed in a hospital/medical center (6), other employment position (1), total from the above (doctoral) (21).

Additional Information:

Orientation, Objectives, and Emphasis of Department: Our department adopts the scientist–practitioner model, fostering an appreciation of psychology as a science and as a profession. We embrace a multiplicity of theoretical viewpoints and research interests. Students are involved in graded research and/or clinical practicum experiences by integrating experiential with didactic instruction. Experimental Psychology provides a highly individualized program for the student interested in study and research in one of several specialized areas. Clinical and Counseling Psychology programs support the development of a well-rounded professional psychologist. These purposes include a thorough grounding in scientific methodology and an orientation to the profession, development of competency in psychological assessment and evaluation, and training in various psychotherapeutic and counseling techniques and skills. Clinical Psychology: Health and Behavioral Medicine involves a joint program with UNT Health Science Center, which emphasizes mind–body interaction as students focus on the matrix of biopsychosocial and environmental processes in understanding etiological and diagnostic factors of illness, prevention, and recovery in order to meet the holistic needs of the individual.

Special Facilities or Resources: Centers: The Psychology Clinic at the University of North Texas was founded in 1972 with the purpose of providing professional training, scientific research, and community service. Professional, competent training in clinical services and research is offered to graduate students in the APA-accredited Clinical, Counseling, and Clinical Health and Behavior Medicine Psychology PhD programs in the Department of Psychology. The Clinic staff is comprised of teams of licensed psychologists and doctoral-level psychology students who provide therapy and psychological testing to adults, adolescents, children, couples, and families. All clients receive the benefits of a licensed psychologist's supervisory expertise and oversight. As a nonprofit training clinic, we can provide clients with professional, confidential psychological services based on a reduced-cost sliding scale. We provide services to a wide range of people, with problems ranging from everyday stress and relationship issues to more serious problems like depression, anxiety, bi-polar disorder, ADHD, and chronic medical conditions. The research and service activities of the Clinic involve members of the entire Psychology Department and are directed toward prevention, evaluation, and intervention (http://www.psyc.unt.edu/clinic). The Center for Sport Psychology and Performance Excellence (CSPPE) provides interdisciplinary training for students in psychology and kinesiology who are interested in specializing in sport psychology. Through the Center, students work with Psychology and KHPR faculty in coursework, research, and applied experiences (http://www.sportpsych.unt.edu). The Center for Psychosocial Health Research is an interdisciplinary center that conducts research on wellness in a chronic illness context. Our research focuses on exploring stigma and forgiveness as a stressor and coping strategy for people living with HIV/AIDS and for the LGBT community (http://www.unt.edu/cph). The Sleep and Health research lab focuses on the epidemiology of sleep and health and explores the role insomnia plays as a risk factor for psychological and medical disorders in various populations. Practicum and research experiences are available through the University of North Texas Health Science Center in departments of pediatrics, family medicine, internal medicine, gerontology, and rehabilitation medicine. Labs: Brain-Mapping Facility, Applied Psychophysiology and Biofeedback Lab, Neurofeedback Lab, Psychoneuroimmunology Lab, Computer and Statistics Lab, Neuropsychology Lab.

Information for Students With Physical Disabilities: See the following Web site for more information: http://www.unt.edu/oda/.

Application Information:

Send to Psychology Department, Graduate Admissions, University of North Texas, Box 311280, Denton, TX 76203-1280. Application available online. URL of online application: http://www.psyc.unt.edu. Students are admitted in the Fall, application deadline December 1. PLEASE BE AWARE: There are two separate application processes: (a)You must apply and be accepted to the Robert B. Toulouse School of Graduate Studies. The graduate school application can be completed using the Texas Common Application available at http://www.applytexas.org. For this application there is a $50 fee. The Robert B. Toulouse School of Graduate Studies will need the following documents in addition to your completed online application: official transcripts from prior universities and your official GRE scores sent in electronically from ETS. Our Institution Code is 6481. Department and major field codes are as follows: 2001 Clinical; 2005 Counseling; 2007 Experimental; 2016 Psychology; 2099 Psychology Other. If more information regarding the GRE is needed please refer to the GRE Web site at http://www.ets.org/gre. The graduate school deadline is 2 weeks prior to the department deadline. (b) The other application you must complete is available on our Psychology Web site at http://www.psyc.unt.edu/forms/Appform.09.pdf.

Our Lady of the Lake University

Psychology
School of Professional Studies
411 Southwest 24th Street
San Antonio, TX 78207
Telephone: (210) 431-3914
Fax: (210) 431-3927
E-mail: *Andek@lake.ollusa.edu*
Web: *http://www.ollusa.edu*

Department Information:

1983. Chairperson: Kathryn Anderson. Number of faculty: total—full-time 13, part-time 22; women—full-time 10, part-time 15; total—minority—full-time 5, part-time 8; women minority—full-time 4, part-time 6.

Programs and Degrees Offered:

Listed in the following order: Program area, degree type (T if terminal Master's), number awarded 7/06–6/07. Counseling Psychology PsyD (Doctor of Psychology) 4, School MA/MS (Master of Arts/Science) (T) 11, Marriage and Family Therapy MA/MS (Master of Arts/Science) (T) 11, Counseling Pyschology MA/MS (Master of Arts/Science) (T) 10.

APA Accreditation: Counseling PsyD (Doctor of Psychology).

Student Applications/Admissions:

Student Applications

Counseling Psychology PsyD (Doctor of Psychology)—Applications 2007–2008, 23. Total applicants accepted 2007–2008, 9. Number full-time enrolled (new admits only) 2007–2008, 5. Number part-time enrolled (new admits only) 2007–2008, 0. Total enrolled 2007–2008 full-time, 15, part-time, 15. Openings 2008–2009, 8. The median number of years required for completion of a degree in 2006–2007 were 6. The number of students enrolled full- and part-time who were dismissed or voluntarily withdrew from this program area in 2007–2008 were 2. *School MA/MS (Master of Arts/Science)*—Applications 2007–2008, 19. Total applicants accepted 2007–2008, 11. Number full-time enrolled (new admits only) 2007–2008, 8. Number part-time enrolled (new admits only) 2007–2008, 0. Total enrolled 2007–2008 full-time, 48, part-time, 10. Openings 2008–2009, 10. The median number of years required for completion of a degree in 2006–2007 were 2. The number of students enrolled full- and part-time who were dismissed or voluntarily withdrew from this program area in 2007–2008 were 0. *Marriage and Family Therapy MA/MS (Master of Arts/Science)*—Applications 2007–2008, 17. Total applicants accepted 2007–2008, 13. Number full-time enrolled (new admits only) 2007–2008, 9. Number part-time enrolled (new admits only) 2007–2008, 0. Total enrolled 2007–2008 full-time, 41, part-time, 10. Openings 2008–2009, 10. The median number of years required for completion of a degree in 2006–2007 were 2. The number of students enrolled full- and part-time who were dismissed or voluntarily withdrew from this program area in 2007–2008 were 2. *Counseling Pyschology MA/MS (Master of Arts/Science)*—Applications 2007–2008, 42. Total applicants accepted 2007–2008, 31. Number full-time enrolled (new admits only) 2007–2008, 20. Number part-time enrolled (new admits only) 2007–2008, 0. Total enrolled 2007–2008 full-time, 60, part-time, 15. Openings 2008–2009, 10. The median number of years required for completion of a degree in 2006–2007 were 2. The number of students enrolled full- and part-time who were dismissed or voluntarily withdrew from this program area in 2007–2008 were 1.

Admissions Requirements:

Scores: Entries appear in this order: required test or GPA, minimum score (if required), median score of students entering in 2007–2008. Master's Programs: overall undergraduate GPA 2.5; last 2 years GPA 3.0, 3.22. May take either the GRE or the MAT with no minimum score required. Doctoral Programs: GRE-V none, 500; GRE-Q none, 520; GRE-Subject (Psychology) 520; overall undergraduate GPA no minimum stated. Doctoral applicants must take the GRE psychogy subject exam in addition to the standard GRE.

Other Criteria: (importance of criteria rated low, medium, or high): GRE/MAT scores—medium, research experience—low, work experience—high, extracurricular activity—low, clinically related public service—medium, GPA—high, letters of recommendation—high, interview—high, statement of goals and objectives—high.

Student Characteristics: The following represents characteristics of students in 2007–2008 in all graduate psychology programs in the department: Female—full-time 176, part-time 25; Male—full-time 13, part-time 0; African American/Black—full-time 8, part-time 8; Hispanic/Latino(a)—full-time 82, part-time 25; Asian/Pacific Islander—full-time 1, part-time 0; American Indian/Alaska Native—full-time 0, part-time 0; Caucasian/White—full-time 61, part-time 17; Multi-ethnic—full-time 0, part-time 0; students subject to the Americans With Disabilities Act—full-time 0, part-time 0; Unknown ethnicity—full-time 12, part-time 0.

Financial Information/Assistance:

Tuition for Full-Time Study: *Master's:* State residents: $628 per credit hour; Nonstate residents: $628 per credit hour. *Doctoral:* State residents: $728 per credit hour; Nonstate residents: $728 per credit hour. Tuition is subject to change. See the following Web site for updates and changes in tuition costs: http://www.ollusa.edu/s/346/ollu.aspx?sid=346&gid=1&pgid=909.

Financial Assistance:

First-Year Students: Teaching assistantships available for first year. Average amount paid per academic year: $5,000. Average number of hours worked per week: 12. Apply by not specific. Research assistantships available for first year. Average amount paid per academic year: $5,000. Average number of hours worked per week: 12. Apply by not specific. Fellowships and scholarships available for first year. Average amount paid per academic year: $11,000. Average number of hours worked per week: 0. Apply by after admission.

Advanced Students: Teaching assistantships available for advanced students. Average amount paid per academic year: $5,000. Average number of hours worked per week: 12. Research assistantships available for advanced students. Average amount paid per academic year: $7,000. Average number of hours worked per week: 12. Fellowships and scholarships available for advanced students. Average amount paid per academic year: $11,000.

Additional Information: Of all students currently enrolled full time, 20% benefited from one or more of the listed financial assistance programs.

Internships/Practica: Doctoral Degree (PsyD Counseling Psychology): For those doctoral students for whom a professional internship was required in this program prior to graduation, (3) students applied for an internship in 2006–2007, with (3) students obtaining an internship. Of those students who obtained an internship, (3) were paid internships. Of those students who obtained an internship, (3) students placed in APA/CPA-accredited internships, (0) students placed in internships not APA/CPA-accredited, but listed with the Association of Psychology Postdoctoral and Internship Centers (APPIC), (0) students placed in internships conforming to guidelines of the Council of Directors of School Psychology Programs (CDSPP), (0) students placed in internships that were not APA/CPA-accredited, APPIC or CDSPP listed. The Psychology Department operates a training clinic, the Community Counseling Service (CCS), which serves as the initial practical site for all master's and doctoral students. At the CCS, practica students work in teams of up to six students under the live supervision of psychology faculty. The CCS is located in and serves a low-income, predominantly Mexican American community. Supervision of Spanish-language psychotherapy is available. A variety of off-campus sites are available to students in their second and subsequent semesters of practica. Students are placed at off-campus sites according to their career interests and training needs. Available practica sites include public and private schools, hospitals, and community agencies.

Housing and Day Care: On-campus housing is available. See the following Web site for more information: http://www.ollusa.edu/s/346/ollu.aspx?sid=346&gid=1&pgid=885. On-campus day care facilities are available. There is a Child Development Center on campus for small children. There is also an elementary school on campus. Both services charge a fee.

Employment of Department Graduates:

Master's Degree Graduates: Of those who graduated in the academic year 2006–2007, the following categories and numbers represent the postgraduate activities and employment of master's degree graduates: Enrolled in a postdoctoral residency/fellowship (n/a), employed in independent practice (n/a), total from the above (master's) (0).

Doctoral Degree Graduates: Of those who graduated in the academic year 2006–2007, the following categories and numbers represent the postgraduate activities and employment of doctoral degree graduates: Enrolled in a psychology doctoral program (n/a), enrolled in a postdoctoral residency/fellowship (2), employed in independent practice (0), employed in an academic position at a university (0), employed in an academic position at a 2-year/4-year college (0), employed in a hospital/medical center (1), total from the above (doctoral) (3).

Additional Information:

Orientation, Objectives, and Emphasis of Department: Graduate psychology programs at OLLU adhere to the practitioner–scholar model of training and emphasize brief, systemic approaches to psychotherapy. Postmodern and multicultural perspectives are infused throughout the curriculum, including practica. A certificate in psychological services for Spanish-speaking populations is available.

Personal Behavior Statement: Our PsyD Handbook (p. 6) provides information about our Comprehensive Evaluation of Student Competence. New students sign a copy to acknowledge receipt of the policy: http://www.ollusa.edu/s/346/images/editor_documents/Psych/PsyD%20Handbook%202007-Final.pdf.

Special Facilities or Resources: The department's training clinic serves as both a training and research facility. Research facilities are also available in the building, which houses the Psychology Department.

Application Information:

Send to Graduate Admissions Office, Our Lady of the Lake University, 411 Southwest 24th Street, San Antonio, TX 78207. Application available online. URL of online application: http://www.admissions.ollusa.edu/. Students are admitted in the Fall, application deadline January 15; Spring, application deadline; Summer, application deadline. January 15 for PsyD program, Fall admission; March 1 for MS programs, Fall admission; early decision July 1 for MS, Fall admission, extended deadline. *Fee:* $25. If accepted, the fee is applied to the first semester's tuition.

Rice University

Department of Psychology
6100 Main Street MS 25
Houston, TX 77005-1892
Telephone: (713) 348-4856
Fax: (713) 348-5221
E-mail: *motowidlo@rice.edu*
Web: *http://www.ruf.rice.edu/~psyc/*

Department Information:

1966. Chairperson: Steve Motowidlo. Number of faculty: women—full-time 8; women minority—full-time 1.

Programs and Degrees Offered:

Listed in the following order: Program area, degree type (T if terminal Master's), number awarded 7/06–6/07. Industrial/Organizational PhD (Doctor of Philosophy) 2, Cognitive PhD (Doctor of Philosophy) 3, Human–Computer Interaction and Human Factors PhD (Doctor of Philosophy) 2, Training PhD (Doctor of Philosophy) 0.

Student Applications/Admissions:

Student Applications

Industrial/Organizational PhD (Doctor of Philosophy)—Applications 2007–2008, 84. Total applicants accepted 2007–2008, 6. Number full-time enrolled (new admits only) 2007–2008, 5. Total enrolled 2007–2008 full-time, 18. Openings 2008–2009, 3. The median number of years required for completion of a degree in 2006–2007 were 5. The number of students enrolled full- and part-time who were dismissed or voluntarily withdrew from this program area in 2007–2008 were 0. *Cognitive PhD (Doctor of Philosophy)*—Applications 2007–2008, 34. Total applicants accepted 2007–2008, 5. Number full-time enrolled (new admits only) 2007–2008, 2. Number part-time enrolled (new admits only) 2007–2008, 0. Openings 2008–2009, 4. The median number of years required for completion of a degree in 2006–2007 were 5. The number of students enrolled full- and part-time who were dismissed or voluntarily withdrew from this program area in 2007–2008 were 0. *Human–Computer Interaction and Human Factors PhD (Doctor of Philosophy)*—Applications 2007–2008, 18. Total applicants accepted 2007–2008, 1. Number full-time enrolled (new admits only) 2007–2008, 2. Number part-time enrolled (new admits only) 2007–2008, 0. Openings 2008–2009, 3. The median number of years required for completion of a degree in 2006–2007 were 5. The number of students enrolled full- and part-time who were dismissed or voluntarily withdrew from this program area in 2007–2008 were 0. *Training PhD (Doctor of Philosophy)*—Applications 2007–2008, 2. Total applicants accepted 2007–2008, 0. Number full-time enrolled (new admits only) 2007–2008, 0. Number part-time enrolled (new admits only) 2007–2008, 0. Openings 2008–2009, 2. The number of students enrolled full- and part-time who were dismissed or voluntarily withdrew from this program area in 2007–2008 were 0.

Admissions Requirements:

Scores: Entries appear in this order: required test or GPA, minimum score (if required), median score of students entering in 2007–2008. Master's Programs: GRE-V no minimum stated; GRE-Q no minimum stated; overall undergraduate GPA no minimum stated; Master's GRE-Analytical no minimum stated. There is no specific score requirement for test scores. Doctoral Programs: GRE-V no minimum stated, 579; GRE-Q no minimum stated, 687; overall undergraduate GPA 3.0, 3.67; Doctoral program GRE-Analytic no minimum stated. There is no specific score requirement for test scores.

Other Criteria: (importance of criteria rated low, medium, or high): GRE/MAT scores—high, research experience—high, work experience—low, extracurricular activity—low, clinically related public service—low, GPA—high, letters of recommendation—high, statement of goals and objectives—high. For additional information on admission requirements, go to http://www.ruf.rice.edu/~psyc.

Student Characteristics: The following represents characteristics of students in 2007–2008 in all graduate psychology programs in the department: Female—full-time 29, part-time 0; Male—full-time 15, part-time 0; African American/Black—full-time 3, part-time 0; Hispanic/Latino(a)—full-time 3, part-time 0; Asian/Pacific Islander—full-time 8, part-time 0; American Indian/Alaska Native—full-time 0, part-time 0; Caucasian/White—full-time 25, part-time 0; Multi-ethnic—full-time 0, part-time 0; students subject to the Americans With Disabilities Act—full-time 1, part-time 0; Unknown ethnicity—full-time 0, part-time 0.

Financial Information/Assistance:

Tuition for Full-Time Study: *Master's:* State residents: per academic year $28,400; Nonstate residents: per academic year $28,400. *Doctoral:* State residents: per academic year $28,400; Nonstate residents: per academic year $28,400. Tuition is subject to change. See the following Web site for updates and changes in tuition costs: http://www.rgs.rice.edu/Grad/Admissions/overview.cfm.

Financial Assistance:

First-Year Students: Fellowships and scholarships available for first year. Average amount paid per academic year: $18,500. Apply by January 15. Tuition remission given: full.

Advanced Students: Research assistantships available for advanced students. Average amount paid per academic year: $18,500. Apply by January 15. Tuition remission given: full. Fellowships and scholarships available for advanced students. Average amount paid per academic year: $18,500. Apply by January 15. Tuition remission given: full.

Additional Information: Of all students currently enrolled full time, 100% benefited from one or more of the listed financial assistance programs. Application and information available online at http://www.ruf.rice.edu/~psyc/graduate/.

Internships/Practica: Graduate students beyond their 3rd year have the opportunity to work in internships in the Houston area. Although not required, many of our students work part-time in local organizations including NASA, the Texas Medical Center, Hewlett Packard, and a variety of consulting firms. Other students work in summer internships around the country.

Housing and Day Care: On-campus housing is available. See the following Web site for more information: University Graduate Apartments http://riceinfo.rice.edu/maps/space/gra/. No on-campus day care facilities are available.

Employment of Department Graduates:

Master's Degree Graduates: Of those who graduated in the academic year 2006–2007, the following categories and numbers represent the postgraduate activities and employment of master's degree graduates: Enrolled in a psychology doctoral program (1), enrolled in another graduate/professional program (0), enrolled in a postdoctoral residency/fellowship (n/a), employed in independent practice (n/a), total from the above (master's) (1).

Doctoral Degree Graduates: Of those who graduated in the academic year 2006–2007, the following categories and numbers represent the postgraduate activities and employment of doctoral degree graduates: Enrolled in a psychology doctoral program (n/a), enrolled in another graduate/professional program (0), enrolled in a postdoctoral residency/fellowship (1), employed in independent practice (0), employed in an academic position at a university (0), employed in an academic position at a 2-year/4-year college (0), employed in other positions at a higher education institution (0), employed in a professional position in a school system (0), employed in business or industry (5), employed in government agency (2), employed in a community mental health/counseling center (0), employed in a hospital/medical center (0), still seeking employment (0), not seeking employment (0), other employment position (0), do not know (0), total from the above (doctoral) (8).

Additional Information:

Orientation, Objectives, and Emphasis of Department: The Rice program emphasizes training in basic and applied research and in the skills necessary to conduct research. The content areas to which this emphasis is applied are cognitive psychology (including cognitive neuroscience), industrial/organizational, and human–computer interaction. We believe that training in research and research skills generalizes very broadly to the kinds of tasks that professional psychologists will be asked to perform both in the university laboratory and in addressing such diverse applied questions as organizational management, system design, or program evaluation. Students in the Cognitive Neuroscience program are encouraged to participate in courses and research opportunities available from our joint program in Neuroscience with Baylor College of Medicine. Students in the other areas are encouraged to develop research interests that combine content areas across the department. Industrial/organizational and human factors psychologists, for example, might collaborate on research dealing with organizational communication via electronic mail. Cognitive and industrial/organizational psychologists might, for instance, investigate cognitive processes underlying performance appraisal; and human factors and cognitive psychologists might collaborate on studies of risk perception and the perceptual and attentional properties of computer displays. Although some of our students prefer to devote their energies to laboratory research in preparation for academic positions in basic areas, many students take advantage of the opportunities we provide for "real world" experience. The department arranges internships or practica in a wide variety of settings for interested advanced students.

Special Facilities or Resources: Graduate students in the Rice Psychology programs benefit from their access to a large and vital Houston business community, NASA, and over 40 teaching and research centers in the Texas Medical Center. Within the department, graduate students in all programs have ready access to a variety of powerful Macintosh (G-4 and iMac) and Windows-based computers that more than meet the needs of students for data collection, simulation, instruction, word processing, and computation. The department contains facilities for the study of dyadic and small group interaction, social judgment, decision making, and computer interface design. In addition to the facilities physicially located in the Psychology Department, Rice University has a state-of-the-art computer laboratory for research in the social sciences that has been constructed with support from the National Science Foundation. The cognitive neuroscience area has benefitted from the recent acquisition of a transcranial magnetic stimulation (TMS) device for investigating brain function, two eye-tracking devices, a Silicon Graphics workstation for neuroimaging data analysis and 3D rendering of brains from MRI scans, and a dense-sensor array (128 channel) event-related potential (ERP) recording system that allows the detailed description of neural systems. Collaborations with institutions in the nearby Texas Medical Center provide access to functional neuroimaging facilties, which include the new Houston Neuroimaging Laboratory at Baylor College of Medicine that has two 3T research-dedicated scanners.

Information for Students With Physical Disabilities: See the following Web site for more information: http://www.dss.rice.edu/primary.cfm?doc_id=1267.

Application Information:

Send to Graduate Chair, Psychology Department, Rice University, MS 25, 6100 Main Street, Houston, TX 77005. Application available online. URL of online application: http://www.ruf.rice.edu/~psyc/graduate/. Students are admitted in the Fall, application deadline January 15. *Fee:* $40. Conditions for waiver of fee: Hardship.

Sam Houston State University

Department of Psychology
Humanities and Social Sciences
Box 2447
Huntsville, TX 77341-2447
Telephone: (936) 294-1174
Fax: (936) 294-3798
E-mail: *psychology@shsu.edu*
Web: *http://www.shsu.edu/~psy_www/*

Department Information:

1970. Chairperson: Donna Desforges. Number of faculty: total—full-time 17, part-time 8; women—full-time 8, part-time 2; total—minority—full-time 1; faculty subject to the Americans With Disabilities Act 1.

Programs and Degrees Offered:

Listed in the following order: Program area, degree type (T if terminal Master's), number awarded 7/06–6/07. Clinical MA/MS (Master of Arts/Science) (T) 15, General MA/MS (Master of Arts/Science) (T) 2, School MA/MS (Master of Arts/Science) (T) 9, Clinical (Forensic Emphasis) PhD (Doctor of Philosophy) 6.

APA Accreditation: Clinical PhD (Doctor of Philosophy).

Student Applications/Admissions:

Student Applications

Clinical MA/MS (Master of Arts/Science)—Applications 2007–2008, 40. Total applicants accepted 2007–2008, 25. Number full-time enrolled (new admits only) 2007–2008, 20. Number part-time enrolled (new admits only) 2007–2008, 2. Total enrolled 2007–2008 full-time, 42, part-time, 2. Openings 2008–2009, 20. The median number of years required for completion of a degree in 2006–2007 were 2. The number of students enrolled full- and part-time who were dismissed or voluntarily withdrew from this program area in 2007–2008 were 1. *General MA/MS (Master of Arts/Science)*—Applications 2007–2008, 12. Total applicants accepted 2007–2008, 7. Number full-time enrolled (new admits only) 2007–2008, 6. Total enrolled 2007–2008 full-time, 11, part-time, 1. Openings 2008–2009, 10. The median number of years required for completion of a degree in 2006–2007 were 2. The number of students enrolled full- and part-time who were dismissed or voluntarily withdrew from this program area in 2007–2008 were 1. *School MA/MS (Master of Arts/Science)*—Applications 2007–2008, 11. Total applicants accepted 2007–2008, 7. Number full-time enrolled (new admits only) 2007–2008, 6. Number part-time enrolled (new admits only) 2007–2008, 0. Total enrolled 2007–2008 full-time, 17, part-time, 3. Openings 2008–2009, 10. The median number of years required for completion of a degree in 2006–2007 were 3. The number of students enrolled full- and part-time who were dismissed or voluntarily withdrew from this program area in 2007–2008 were 0. *Clinical (Forensic Emphasis) PhD (Doctor of Philosophy)*—Applications 2007–2008, 94. Total applicants accepted 2007–2008, 8. Number full-time enrolled (new admits only) 2007–2008, 7. Number part-time enrolled (new admits only) 2007–2008, 0. Openings 2008–2009, 8. The median number of years required for completion of a degree in 2006–2007 were 7. The number of students enrolled full- and part-time who were dismissed or voluntarily withdrew from this program area in 2007–2008 were 1.

Admissions Requirements:

Scores: Entries appear in this order: required test or GPA, minimum score (if required), median score of students entering in 2007–2008. Master's Programs: GRE-V no minimum stated, 480; GRE-Q no minimum stated, 590; overall undergraduate GPA no minimum stated, 3.4. Doctoral Programs: GRE-V no minimum stated, 560; GRE-Q no minimum stated, 660; GRE-Subject (Psychology) no minimum stated; overall undergraduate GPA no minimum stated, 3.40.

Other Criteria: (importance of criteria rated low, medium, or high): GRE/MAT scores—high, research experience—high, work experience—low, extracurricular activity—low, clinically related public service—medium, GPA—high, letters of recommendation—high, interview—high, statement of goals and objectives—high, fit with the program—high, specific undergraduate psychology courses taken—medium. No interview is required for admission to our Master's program. For additional information on admission requirements, go to http://www.shsu.edu/~psy_www/phd.htm.

Student Characteristics: The following represents characteristics of students in 2007–2008 in all graduate psychology programs in the department: Female—full-time 98, part-time 4; Male—full-time 15, part-time 2; African American/Black—full-time 6, part-time 1; Hispanic/Latino(a)—full-time 8, part-time 0; Asian/Pacific Islander—full-time 4, part-time 0; American Indian/Alaska Native—full-time 0, part-time 0; Caucasian/White—full-time 94, part-time 5; Multi-ethnic—full-time 1, part-time 0; students subject to the Americans With Disabilities Act—full-time 1, part-time 0; Unknown ethnicity—full-time 0, part-time 0; International students who hold an F-1 or J-1 Visa—full-time 2, part-time 0.

Financial Information/Assistance:

Tuition for Full-Time Study: *Master's:* State residents: per academic year $9,056, $184 per credit hour; Nonstate residents: per academic year $14,208, $417 per credit hour. *Doctoral:* State residents: per academic year $9,056, $184 per credit hour; . Tuition is subject to change. Additional fees are assessed to students beyond the costs of tuition for the following: student service, student center, computer use, library, recreational sports, advisement, and records. See the following Web site for updates and changes in tuition costs: http://www.shsu.edu/schedule/.

Financial Assistance:

First-Year Students: Teaching assistantships available for first year. Average amount paid per academic year: $10,000. Average number of hours worked per week: 20. Research assistantships available for first year. Average amount paid per academic year: $10,000. Average number of hours worked per week: 20. Fellowships and scholarships available for first year. Average amount paid per academic year: $10,000.

Advanced Students: Teaching assistantships available for advanced students. Average amount paid per academic year: $10,000. Average number of hours worked per week: 20. Research assistantships available for advanced students. Average amount paid per academic year: $10,000. Average number of hours worked per week: 20. Traineeships available for advanced students. Average amount paid per academic year: $10,000. Average number of hours worked per week: 20. Fellowships and scholarships available for advanced students. Average amount paid per academic year: $10,000.

Additional Information: Of all students currently enrolled full time, 75% benefited from one or more of the listed financial assistance programs. Application and information available online at http://www.shsu.edu/~grs_www/application/index.html.

Internships/Practica: Master's Degree (MA/MS School): An internship experience such as a final research project or "capstone" experience is required of graduates. Doctoral Degree (PhD Clinical [Forensic Emphasis]): For those doctoral students for whom a professional internship was required in this program prior to graduation, (3) students applied for an internship in 2006–2007, with (3) students obtaining an internship. Of those students who obtained an internship, (3) were paid internships. Of those students who obtained an internship, (3) students placed in APA/CPA-accredited internships, (0) students placed in internships not APA/CPA-accredited, but listed with the Association of Psychology Postdoctoral and Internship Centers (APPIC), (0) students placed in internships conforming to guidelines of the Council of Directors of School Psychology Programs (CDSPP), (0) students placed in internships that were not APA/CPA accredited, APPIC or CDSPP listed. We offer a variety of internships and practica for each of the applied tracks. Students in the School Psychology program complete a 1-year internship in schools. There are a variety of practica placements for students in the Clinical Psychology master's program, including the University Counseling Center, area community mental health centers, and the psychological services centers of the Texas Department of Criminal Justice (TDCJ). Students in the Clinical doctoral program may be assigned to any of the aforementioned clinical sites, as well as to a variety of other practica, including Ben Taub General Hospital in Houston, ADAPT Counseling, various private facilities and practices, and The Institute for Rehabilitation and Research (neuropsychology). These students also work at our on-campus Psychological Services Center, which provides both general mental health services (e.g., individual psychotherapy, couples counseling, psychological assessment), and forensic services (e.g., treatment programs for offender populations and evaluations for the courts).

Housing and Day Care: On-campus housing is available. See the following Web site for more information: http://www.shsu.edu/~hou_www/. No on-campus day care facilities are available.

Employment of Department Graduates:

Master's Degree Graduates: Of those who graduated in the academic year 2006–2007, the following categories and numbers represent the postgraduate activities and employment of master's degree graduates: Enrolled in a psychology doctoral program (4), enrolled in a postdoctoral residency/fellowship (n/a), employed in independent practice (n/a), employed in an academic position at a university (1), employed in other positions at a higher education institution (2), employed in a professional position in a school system (9), employed in a community mental health/counseling center (4), do not know (4), total from the above (master's) (24).
Doctoral Degree Graduates: Of those who graduated in the academic year 2006–2007, the following categories and numbers represent the postgraduate activities and employment of doctoral degree graduates: Enrolled in a psychology doctoral program (n/a), employed in government agency (2), employed in a hospital/medical center (3), do not know (1), total from the above (doctoral) (6).

Additional Information:

Orientation, Objectives, and Emphasis of Department: The Clinical and School Master's programs are applied training programs that develop effective Master's-level practitioners. Students in these programs receive extensive and eclectic training in both psychotherapy and psychometrics, and conclude their training with extensive supervised practicum experience. Graduates can seek licensure as psychological associates through Texas State Board of Examiners of Psychologists. Graduates of the School program can seek national certification from National Association of School Psychologists and licensure as specialists in school psychology in Texas. Other licensures within the state of Texas such as professional counselors licensure may be available with additional course work. The General track involves broader exposure to psychology's core disciplines and allows the student more elective flexibility to craft an individual specialty. The focus within the General program is on developing research skills. Graduates of all three programs often progress to doctoral training here or elsewhere. Our Clinical doctoral program is a scientist–practitioner program that provides broad and general training in clinical psychology with an emphasis on forensic psychology and the training of legally informed clinicians. In addition to extensive training in general psychological assessment and treatment, students participate in conducting a variety of forensic evaluations for the courts (e.g., risk assessment, competence, and sanity evaluations). Students will have the basic preparation they need to pursue postdoctoral specialty training and conduct legally relevant clinical psychology research.

Special Facilities or Resources: The department enjoys ample testing and observation space, including a live animal facility. The university's computing facilities offer extensive access to personal comuters complete with the latest software. The area provides access to a wide variety of clinical and research populations. These include persons housed in medical and mental health facilities located in the Texas Medical Center, as well as juvenile and auldt offender populations. The town of Huntsville (population 35,078) is located in southeastern Texas with Houston only 1 hour away.

Information for Students With Physical Disabilities: See the following Web site for more information: http://www.shsu.edu/~counsel/sswd.html.

Application Information:
Send Master's applications to A. Jerry Bruce. Send applications to PhD program to Mary Alice Conroy. Master's degree applications should all be sent to Office of Graduate Studies, Sam Houston State University, P.O. Box 2478, Huntsville, TX 77341-2478. Doctoral applications should be sent to Department of Psychology, Sam Houston State University, P.O. Box 2447, Huntsville, TX 77341-2447. Application available online. URL of online application: http://www.shsu.edu/~grs_www/application/index.html. Students are admitted in the Fall, application deadline July 1; Spring, application deadline November 1; Summer, application deadline April 1. These deadlines are for our Master's programs, but we encourage early applications; all three Master's have rolling admissions, and admission into those programs becomes more competitive as the deadlines approach. December 15 is the deadline for the doctoral program; that program admits students only in the Fall. *Fee:* $20. The fee for the Master's program is $20. $40 is the application fee for the doctoral program (includes $20 Graduate School application fee and $20 doctoral program application fee).

Southern Methodist University

Department of Psychology
Dedman College
6424 Hilltop Lane
Dallas, TX 75275-0442
Telephone: (214) 768-4924
Fax: (214) 768-3910
E-mail: *aconner@smu.edu*
Web: *http://www.smu.edu/psychology/*

Department Information:
1925. Chairperson: Ernest Jouriles, PhD. Number of faculty: total—full-time 14; women—full-time 6; total—minority—full-time 1; women minority—full-time 1.

Programs and Degrees Offered:
Listed in the following order: Program area, degree type (T if terminal Master's), number awarded 7/06–6/07. Clinical Psychology PhD (Doctor of Philosophy) 0.

Student Applications/Admissions:

Student Applications

Clinical Psychology PhD (Doctor of Philosophy)—Applications 2007–2008, 92. Total applicants accepted 2007–2008, 6. Number full-time enrolled (new admits only) 2007–2008, 5. Total enrolled 2007–2008 full-time, 21. Openings 2008–2009, 5. The number of students enrolled full- and part-time who were dismissed or voluntarily withdrew from this program area in 2007–2008 were 0.

Admissions Requirements:

Scores: Entries appear in this order: required test or GPA, minimum score (if required), median score of students entering in 2007–2008. Master's Programs: No longer admitting students to the MA progam. Doctoral Programs: GRE-V no minimum stated, 678; GRE-Q no minimum stated, 648; overall undergraduate GPA 3.0; Doctoral program GRE-Analytic no minimum stated.

Other Criteria: (importance of criteria rated low, medium, or high): GRE/MAT scores—high, research experience—high, work experience—low, extracurricular activity—medium, clinically related public service—medium, GPA—high, letters of recommendation—high, interview—high, statement of goals and objectives—high, research interests—high, undergraduate major in psychology—low, specific undergraduate psychology courses taken—low. Match of research interests with those of faculty is important for graduate programs. For additional information on admission requirements, go to http://www.smu.edu/psychology/graduate.

Student Characteristics: The following represents characteristics of students in 2007–2008 in all graduate psychology programs in the department: Female—full-time 18, part-time 0; Male—full-time 3, part-time 0; African American/Black—full-time 1, part-time 0; Hispanic/Latino(a)—full-time 2, part-time 0; Asian/Pacific Islander—full-time 2, part-time 0; American Indian/Alaska Native—full-time 1, part-time 0; Caucasian/White—full-time 15, part-time 0; Multi-ethnic—full-time 0, part-time 0; students subject to the Americans With Disabilities Act—full-time 0, part-time 0; Unknown ethnicity—full-time 0, part-time 0; International students who hold an F-1 or J-1 Visa—full-time 0, part-time 0.

Financial Information/Assistance:

Tuition for Full-Time Study: *Doctoral:* State residents: per academic year $22,140, $1,230 per credit hour; Nonstate residents: per academic year $22,140, $1,230 per credit hour.

Financial Assistance:

First-Year Students: Research assistantships available for first year. Average amount paid per academic year: $14,000. Average number of hours worked per week: 20. Apply by January 1. Tuition remission given: full.

Advanced Students: Research assistantships available for advanced students. Average amount paid per academic year: $14,000. Average number of hours worked per week: 20. Apply by January 1. Tuition remission given: full.

Additional Information: Of all students currently enrolled full time, 100% benefited from one or more of the listed financial assistance programs. Application and information available online at http://www.smu.edu/psychology/gradprograms.htm.

Internships/Practica: Doctoral Degree (PhD Clinical Psychology): For those doctoral students for whom a professional internship was required in this program prior to graduation, (1) students applied for an internship in 2006–2007, with (1) students obtaining an internship. Of those students who obtained an internship, (1) were paid internships. Of those students who obtained an internship, (1) students placed in APA/CPA-accredited internships, (0) students placed in internships not APA/CPA accredited, but listed with the Association of Psychology Postdoctoral and Internship Centers (APPIC), (0) students placed in internships conforming to guidelines of the Council of Directors of School Psychology Programs (CDSPP), (0) students placed in internships that were not APA/CPA-accredited, APPIC or CDSPP listed. Practicum placements are available for students in the Clinical PhD program in the 2nd, 3rd, and 4th years. For additional information on education and training outcomes for our programs, see the following Web site: http://www.smu.edu/psychology/graduate/gradphdprogram.html.

Housing and Day Care: On-campus housing is available. See the following Web site for more information: http://www.smu.edu/housing. On-campus day care facilities are available. See the following Web site for more information: http://www.smu.edu/catalogs/graduate/services.asp.

Employment of Department Graduates:

Master's Degree Graduates: Of those who graduated in the academic year 2006–2007, the following categories and numbers represent the postgraduate activities and employment of master's degree graduates: Enrolled in a psychology doctoral program (1), enrolled in a postdoctoral residency/fellowship (n/a), employed in independent practice (n/a), employed in a community mental health/counseling center (2), do not know (1), total from the above (master's) (4).

Doctoral Degree Graduates: Of those who graduated in the academic year 2006–2007, the following categories and numbers represent the postgraduate activities and employment of doctoral degree graduates: Enrolled in a psychology doctoral program (n/a), total from the above (doctoral) (0).

Additional Information:

Orientation, Objectives, and Emphasis of Department: The mission of SMU's 70-hour doctoral program in Clinical Psychology is to train psychologists whose professional activities are based on scientific knowledge and methods. The program integrates rigorous research training with state-of the-art, evidence-based clinical training. Thus, our program emphasizes the development of conceptual and research skills as well as scientifically based clinical practice skills. The overarching goal is for our graduates to use empirical methods to advance psychological knowledge and whose approach to clinical phenomena is consistent with scientific evidence. We will no longer be admitting students to the MA program.

Special Facilities or Resources: The department houses a Family Research Center and has a number of well-equipped laboratories for research on various topics in clinical psychology.

Information for Students With Physical Disabilities: See the following Web site for more information: http://www.smu.edu/studentlife/OSSD_Facts.asp.

Application Information:

Send to Office of Graduate Studies, Southern Methodist University, P.O. Box 750240, Dallas, TX 75275-0240. Application available online. URL of online application: http://www.smu.edu/graduate/

ToApply.htm. Students are admitted in the Fall, application deadline See below. January 1 for PhD students. No longer admitting students to the MA program. *Fee:* $75.

St. Mary's University

Department of Psychology
Humanities and Social Sciences
One Camino Santa Maria
San Antonio, TX 78228-8573
Telephone: (210) 436-3314
Fax: (210) 431-4301
E-mail: *powen@stamrytx.edu, gpool@stmarytx.edu*
Web: *http://www.stmarytx.edu/grad/psychology*

Department Information:

1965. Chairperson: Patricia Owen. Number of faculty: total—full-time 6, part-time 6; women—full-time 4, part-time 2.

Programs and Degrees Offered:

Listed in the following order: Program area, degree type (T if terminal Master's), number awarded 7/06–6/07. Clinical MA/MS (Master of Arts/Science) (T) 8, Industrial/Organizational MA/MS (Master of Arts/Science) (T) 5.

Student Applications/Admissions:

Student Applications

Clinical MA/MS (Master of Arts/Science)—Applications 2007–2008, 41. Total applicants accepted 2007–2008, 11. Number full-time enrolled (new admits only) 2007–2008, 13. Number part-time enrolled (new admits only) 2007–2008, 2. Total enrolled 2007–2008 full-time, 22, part-time, 3. Openings 2008–2009, 20. The median number of years required for completion of a degree in 2006–2007 were 2. The number of students enrolled full- and part-time who were dismissed or voluntarily withdrew from this program area in 2007–2008 were 2. *Industrial/Organizational MA/MS (Master of Arts/Science)*—Applications 2007–2008, 39. Total applicants accepted 2007–2008, 15. Number full-time enrolled (new admits only) 2007–2008, 6. Number part-time enrolled (new admits only) 2007–2008, 1. Total enrolled 2007–2008 full-time, 15, part-time, 6. Openings 2008–2009, 20. The median number of years required for completion of a degree in 2006–2007 were 2. The number of students enrolled full- and part-time who were dismissed or voluntarily withdrew from this program area in 2007–2008 were 0.

Admissions Requirements:

Scores: Entries appear in this order: required test or GPA, minimum score (if required), median score of students entering in 2007–2008. Master's Programs: GRE-V 400, 500; GRE-Q 400, 500; overall undergraduate GPA no minimum stated, 3.0; last 2 years GPA no minimum stated, 3.2; psychology GPA 3.0, 3.0. Regular enrollment status is recommended for students who have a combined verbal and quantitative GRE score of 1000 (each section is at least 400), an undergraduate cumulative and psychology grade point average of 3.0 or greater, and final course grades of B or better in Research Methods and Statistics.

Other Criteria: (importance of criteria rated low, medium, or high): GRE/MAT scores—high, research experience—high, work experience—medium, extracurricular activity—medium, clinically related public service—medium, GPA—high, letters of recommendation—high, interview—low, statement of goals and objectives—high. Clinically related public service for Clinical MA/MS; work-related experience for Industrial/Organizational MA/MS.

Student Characteristics: The following represents characteristics of students in 2007–2008 in all graduate psychology programs in the department: Female—full-time 40, part-time 6; Male—full-time 6, part-time 4; African American/Black—full-time 2, part-time 0; Hispanic/Latino(a)—full-time 17, part-time 1; Asian/Pacific Islander—full-time 2, part-time 0; American Indian/Alaska Native—full-time 0, part-time 0; Caucasian/White—full-time 25, part-time 9; Multi-ethnic—full-time 0, part-time 0; students subject to the Americans With Disabilities Act—full-time 0, part-time 0; Unknown ethnicity—full-time 0, part-time 0.

Financial Information/Assistance:

Tuition for Full-Time Study: *Master's:* State residents: per academic year $11,430, $635 per credit hour; Nonstate residents: per academic year $11,430, $635 per credit hour. Tuition is subject to change. See the following Web site for updates and changes in tuition costs: http://www.stmarytx.edu/businessoffice/?go=tuit_07.

Financial Assistance:

First-Year Students: Teaching assistantships available for first year. Average amount paid per academic year: $4,000. Average number of hours worked per week: 15. Apply by March 1. Fellowships and scholarships available for first year. Average amount paid per academic year: $4,000. Average number of hours worked per week: 15. Apply by March 15.

Advanced Students: Teaching assistantships available for advanced students. Average amount paid per academic year: $4,000. Average number of hours worked per week: 15. Apply by March 1. Fellowships and scholarships available for advanced students. Average amount paid per academic year: $4,000. Average number of hours worked per week: 15. Apply by March 15.

Additional Information: Of all students currently enrolled full time, 4% benefited from one or more of the listed financial assistance programs. Application and information available online at http://www.stmarytx.edu/finaid/.

Internships/Practica: Master's Degree (MA/MS Industrial/Organizational): An internship experience such as a final research project or "capstone" experience is required of graduates. Clinical students are required to complete two practica under the supervision of a psychologist licensed in the state of Texas (450 total hours). Industrial/Organizational students are required to complete one practicum (225 total hours).

Housing and Day Care: On-campus housing is available. See the following Web site for more information: http://www.stmarytx.edu/reslife/. No on-campus day care facilities are available.

Employment of Department Graduates:

Master's Degree Graduates: Of those who graduated in the academic year 2006–2007, the following categories and numbers

represent the postgraduate activities and employment of master's degree graduates: Enrolled in a psychology doctoral program (1), enrolled in another graduate/professional program (1), enrolled in a postdoctoral residency/fellowship (n/a), employed in independent practice (n/a), employed in an academic position at a university (0), employed in an academic position at a 2-year/4-year college (0), employed in other positions at a higher education institution (0), employed in a professional position in a school system (0), employed in business or industry (1), employed in government agency (2), employed in a community mental health/counseling center (2), employed in a hospital/medical center (0), still seeking employment (0), other employment position (0), do not know (1), total from the above (master's) (8).

Doctoral Degree Graduates: Of those who graduated in the academic year 2006–2007, the following categories and numbers represent the postgraduate activities and employment of doctoral degree graduates: Enrolled in a psychology doctoral program (n/a), total from the above (doctoral) (0).

Additional Information:

Orientation, Objectives, and Emphasis of Department: Clinical Psychology graduates are trained to be proficient in assessment, diagnosis, and intervention. Their education prepares them for entry to a PhD or PsyD program in Clinical Psychology and positions in a variety of clinical settings ranging from school districts to psychiatric hospitals to university counseling centers. Industrial/Organizational Psychology graduates are trained to be proficient in job analysis, performance appraisal, personnel selection, survey development, and training, and other related areas in the field. Their education prepares them for entry to a PhD program in Industrial/Organizational Psychology or a career in business and industry. Those interested in a career in business and industry are prepared for job opportunities in positions emphasizing the quantification of human behavior.

Special Facilities or Resources: Students have access to university services such as the Service Learning Center, the Center for Legal and Social Justice, and the 21st Century Leadership Center. Graduate students may choose to study abroad in Innsbruck, Austria for summer courses. Annual activities include the President's Peace Commission, the Lin Great Speaker Series, Oysterbake, and the Annual Research Exhibition. Students are able to join the San Antonio Area I/O Psychology organization.

Information for Students With Physical Disabilities: See the following Web site for more information: http://www.stmarytx.edu/disability/.

Application Information:

Send to Graduate Admissions, St. Mary's University, One Camino Santa Maria, San Antonio, TX 78228. Application available online. URL of online application: http://www.stmarytx.edu/grad/graduate_application/main_menu.php. Students are admitted in the Fall, application deadline May 30; Summer, application deadline March 30; Programs have rolling admissions. The deadline for students who wish to be considered for Fall assistantships is March 1. *Fee:* $35. No fee if online application is submitted.

Stephen F. Austin State University

Department of Psychology
Liberal and Applied Arts and Sciences
Box 13046, SFA Station
Nacogdoches, TX 75962
Telephone: (936) 468-4402
Fax: (936) 468-4015
E-mail: *heiderj@sfasu.edu*
Web: *http://www.sfasu.edu/sfapsych/front.html*

Department Information:

1962. Chairperson: Dr. Kandy Stahl. Number of faculty: total—full-time 9, part-time 4; women—full-time 5, part-time 3; total—minority—full-time 1.

Programs and Degrees Offered:

Listed in the following order: Program area, degree type (T if terminal Master's), number awarded 7/06–6/07. General Psychology MA/MS (Master of Arts/Science) (T).

Student Applications/Admissions:

Student Applications

General Psychology MA/MS (Master of Arts/Science)—Total applicants accepted 2007–2008, 13. Number full-time enrolled (new admits only) 2007–2008, 12. Number part-time enrolled (new admits only) 2007–2008, 1. Openings 2008–2009, 20.

Admissions Requirements:

Scores: Entries appear in this order: required test or GPA, minimum score (if required), median score of students entering in 2007–2008. Master's Programs: GRE-V no minimum stated; GRE-Q no minimum stated; overall undergraduate GPA 3.00; last 2 years GPA 3.00; psychology GPA 3.00. Applicants must achieve a Factor Score of 1300. Factor Score = (GRE V + Q) + (GPA x 100)

Other Criteria: (importance of criteria rated low, medium, or high): GRE/MAT scores—high, research experience—low, work experience—low, extracurricular activity—low, clinically related public service—low, GPA—high, letters of recommendation—medium, statement of goals and objectives—medium, undergraduate major in psychology—low, specific undergraduate psychology courses taken—high. For additional information on admission requirements, go to http://www.sfasu.edu/sfapsych/front.html.

Student Characteristics: The following represents characteristics of students in 2007–2008 in all graduate psychology programs in the department: Female—full-time 27, part-time 1; Male—full-time 14, part-time 1; African American/Black—full-time 1, part-time 1; Hispanic/Latino(a)—full-time 0, part-time 1; Asian/Pacific Islander—full-time 2, part-time 0; American Indian/Alaska Native—full-time 0, part-time 0; Caucasian/White—full-time 38, part-time 0; Multi-ethnic—full-time 0, part-time 0; students subject to the Americans With Disabilities Act—full-time 1, part-time 1; Unknown ethnicity—full-time 0, part-time 0.

Financial Information/Assistance:

Tuition for Full-Time Study: *Master's:* State residents: per academic year $4,536, $126 per credit hour; Nonstate residents: per

academic year $14,472, $402 per credit hour. Tuition is subject to change. Additional fees are assessed to students beyond the costs of tuition for the following: student service, student center, computer use, library use, publication, recreation center use. Students awarded assistantships pay tuition at in-state rate. All tuitions based on 36-hour degree.

Financial Assistance:

First-Year Students: Teaching assistantships available for first year. Average amount paid per academic year: $9,225. Average number of hours worked per week: 20. Apply by May 15. Research assistantships available for first year. Average amount paid per academic year: $9,225. Average number of hours worked per week: 20. Apply by May 15.

Advanced Students: Teaching assistantships available for advanced students. Average amount paid per academic year: $9,225. Average number of hours worked per week: 20. Research assistantships available for advanced students. Average amount paid per academic year: $9,225. Average number of hours worked per week: 20.

Additional Information: Of all students currently enrolled full time, 49% benefited from one or more of the listed financial assistance programs. Application and information available online at http://www.sfasu.edu/sfapsych/front.html.

Internships/Practica: N/A.

Housing and Day Care: On-campus housing is available. See the following Web site for more information: http://www.sfasu.edu/housing/. On-campus day care facilities are available. See the following Web site for more information: http://www.education.sfasu.edu/ele/CENTERS/ECLAB.HTM.

Employment of Department Graduates:

Master's Degree Graduates: Of those who graduated in the academic year 2006–2007, the following categories and numbers represent the postgraduate activities and employment of master's degree graduates: Enrolled in a postdoctoral residency/fellowship (n/a), employed in independent practice (n/a), total from the above (master's) (0).

Doctoral Degree Graduates: Of those who graduated in the academic year 2006–2007, the following categories and numbers represent the postgraduate activities and employment of doctoral degree graduates: Enrolled in a psychology doctoral program (n/a), total from the above (doctoral) (0).

Additional Information:

Orientation, Objectives, and Emphasis of Department: The primary goal of this 1-year, 36-hour, General Psychology MA program is to prepare students for admission to doctoral training programs in psychology by enabling them to earn graduate course credit and gain valuable research and teaching experience. Our degree program would also be of interest to persons who would like to earn an MA in psychology as a means of furthering their professional goals (e.g., by augmenting their research skills), even if those goals have no explicit connection to psychology. This is a nonthesis master's program. However, students can elect to continue for a 2nd year in order to conduct a formal thesis research project. Students interested in a career in teaching psychology have the option of enrolling in a teaching seminar; excellent performance in this course could lead to an opportunity to teach a freshman-level course, should the student elect to remain in the program for a 2nd year. Applications for Spring admission will be considered; however, students entering in Spring should recognize that, due to course prerequisites, they will not be able to complete the program in 1 year. Completion of the program would require an additional Spring semester.

Special Facilities or Resources: The department's facilities occupy more than 20,000 square feet. An extensive Research Suite and other research spaces permit data collection either with individual participants or groups. The spaces include 50 PC microcomputers for various programs in the department. There are also laboratories for human research in sensory psychophysics, learning, cognition, social, developmental, personality, and industrial/organizational psychology. Supplemental technical assistance from facilities in other departments on campus is available. All department classrooms are supplied with multimedia equipment. The department has an instructional computing laboratory consisting of 21 networked PC microcomputers and extensive supporting hardware and software for computing across the psychology curriculum. Most laboratory areas, classrooms, and graduate assistant offices contain both PC and Macintosh microcomputers, many of which are networked and support research and instruction.

Information for Students With Physical Disabilities: See the following Web site for more information: http://www.sfasu.edu/disabilityservices/index.htm.

Application Information:

Send general graduate school application, GRE scores, official transcripts to Graduate School, SFASU, Box 13024, Nacogdoches, TX 75962; send all other materials (see forms on department graduate program Web site) and letters of recommendation to Dr. Gary G. Ford, Graduate Program Coordinator, Department of Psychology, Stephen F. Austin State University, Box 13046, SFA Station, Nacogdoches, TX 75962. Application available online. URL of online application: http://www.sfasu.edu/sfapsych/front.html. Students are admitted in the Fall, application deadline August 1; Summer, application deadline May 1. The earlier the submission, the greater the likelihood of receiving an assistantship. We recommend applications be received by September 15 and April 15, although we will accept them later. *Fee:* $25.

Texas A&M International University

Department of Behavioral, Applied Sciences, and Criminal Justice
College of Arts and Sciences
5201 University Boulevard
Laredo, TX 78041-1900
Telephone: (956) 326-2475
Fax: (956) 326-2474
E-mail: *brudolph@tamiu.edu*
Web: *http://www.tamiu.edu/coas/psy*

Department Information:

1994. Director of Master's Program in Counseling Psychology: Bonnie A. Rudolph. Number of faculty: total—full-time 18, part-time 11; women—full-time 2, part-time 3; women minority—full-time 1, part-time 3.

Programs and Degrees Offered:

Listed in the following order: Program area, degree type (T if terminal Master's), number awarded 7/06–6/07. Counseling Psychology MA/MS (Master of Arts/Science) (T) 15, Psychology MA/MS (Master of Arts/Science) (T) 0.

Student Applications/Admissions:

Student Applications

Counseling Psychology MA/MS (Master of Arts/Science)—Applications 2007–2008, 14. Total applicants accepted 2007–2008, 14. Number full-time enrolled (new admits only) 2007–2008, 1. Number part-time enrolled (new admits only) 2007–2008, 13. Total enrolled 2007–2008 full-time, 3, part-time, 18. Openings 2008–2009, 15. The median number of years required for completion of a degree in 2006–2007 were 2. The number of students enrolled full- and part-time who were dismissed or voluntarily withdrew from this program area in 2007–2008 were 1. *Psychology MA/MS (Master of Arts/Science)*—Applications 2007–2008, 6. Total applicants accepted 2007–2008, 6. Number part-time enrolled (new admits only) 2007–2008, 6. Total enrolled 2007–2008 part-time, 6. Openings 2008–2009, 6. The median number of years required for completion of a degree in 2006–2007 were 2. The number of students enrolled full- and part-time who were dismissed or voluntarily withdrew from this program area in 2007–2008 were 0.

Admissions Requirements:

Scores: Entries appear in this order: required test or GPA, minimum score (if required), median score of students entering in 2007–2008. Master's Programs: GRE-V no minimum stated; GRE-Q no minimum stated; overall undergraduate GPA no minimum stated; last 2 years GPA no minimum stated; psychology GPA no minimum stated.

Other Criteria: (importance of criteria rated low, medium, or high): GRE/MAT scores—medium, research experience—medium, work experience—medium, extracurricular activity—medium, clinically related public service—high, GPA—medium, letters of recommendation—medium, interview—high, statement of goals and objectives—medium, specific undergraduate psychology courses taken—high, The Master's in Counseling Psychology requriers four undergraduate courses be completed with a B average across them. They are abnormal, personality, research methods, and theories and principles of testing.

Student Characteristics: The following represents characteristics of students in 2007–2008 in all graduate psychology programs in the department: Female—full-time 4, part-time 24; Male—full-time 0, part-time 2; African American/Black—full-time 0, part-time 0; Hispanic/Latino(a)—full-time 3, part-time 26; Asian/Pacific Islander—full-time 0, part-time 0; American Indian/Alaska Native—full-time 0, part-time 0; Caucasian/White—full-time 1, part-time 0; Multi-ethnic—full-time 0, part-time 0; students subject to the Americans With Disabilities Act—part-time 0; Unknown ethnicity—full-time 0, part-time 0.

Financial Information/Assistance:

Tuition for Full-Time Study: *Master's:* State residents: per academic year $1,781, $178 per credit hour; Nonstate residents: per academic year $4,561, $456 per credit hour. See the following Web site for updates and changes in tuition costs: http://www.tamiu.edu/graduatestudies.edu.

Financial Assistance:

First-Year Students: Teaching assistantships available for first year. Average number of hours worked per week: 20. Apply by May 1. Research assistantships available for first year. Average amount paid per academic year: $9,000. Average number of hours worked per week: 20. Apply by May 1. Fellowships and scholarships available for first year. Average amount paid per academic year: $1,500. Average number of hours worked per week: 0. Apply by May 1.

Advanced Students: Teaching assistantships available for advanced students. Average amount paid per academic year: $9,000. Average number of hours worked per week: 20. Apply by May 1. Research assistantships available for advanced students. Average amount paid per academic year: $9,000. Average number of hours worked per week: 20. Apply by May 1.

Additional Information: Of all students currently enrolled full time, 15% benefited from one or more of the listed financial assistance programs.

Internships/Practica: Master's Degree (MA/MS Counseling Psychology): An internship experience such as a final research project or "capstone" experience is required of graduates. Master's Degree (MA/MS Masters of Science in Psychology): An internship experience such as a final research project or "capstone" experience is required of graduates. The practicum and internships offer unique training opportunities to prepare competent counselors. Competence exercises include alliance and outcome measurement as well as session process analyses, in addition to more conventional training in documentation and treatment planning. Practicum and internships consist of working at settings such as college counseling centers, forensic settings, drug and alcohol counseling and prevention agencies, domestic violence–battered women shelters, child advocacy centers, and professional counseling clinics. On-site supervisors provide 30-minute supervision sessions. Psychologists on campus provide an additional 2.5 hours of supervision in individual, triadic, and group formats. Peer feedback and group cohesiveness are also vital parts of training. All graduates complete Practicum and Counseling Internship I. Students who choose the nonthesis (clinical) track also complete Internship II. The clinical track provides a total of three semesters of practical experience in counseling (600 hours), a minimum of which is 240 hours of face-to-face counseling activities.

Housing and Day Care: On-campus housing is available. See the following Web site for more information: http://www.tamiu.edu. No on-campus day care facilities are available.

Employment of Department Graduates:

Master's Degree Graduates: Of those who graduated in the academic year 2006–2007, the following categories and numbers represent the postgraduate activities and employment of master's degree graduates: Enrolled in a psychology doctoral program (1), enrolled in a postdoctoral residency/fellowship (n/a), employed in independent practice (n/a), employed in an academic position at a university (4), employed in an academic position at a 2-year/4-year college (2), employed in other positions at a higher education institution (2), employed in a professional position in a school system (2), employed in government agency (5), employed in a community mental health/counseling center (6), employed in a hospital/medical center (1), total from the above (master's) (23). ***Doctoral Degree Graduates:*** Of those who graduated in the academic year 2006–2007, the following categories and numbers represent the postgraduate activities and employment of doctoral degree graduates: Enrolled in a psychology doctoral program (n/a), total from the above (doctoral) (0).

Additional Information:

Orientation, Objectives, and Emphasis of Department: The Master of Arts in Counseling Psychology provides training for counselors with strong foundations in eclectic, humanistic, multicultural and community perspectives. Students in our international campus and community are self-reflective active learners. The excellent student–faculty ratio (average class = 11) provides extra attention for its students to identify and achieve their own individual goals. There is an advisory board composed of student and faculty representatives as well as community leaders, which strives to expand the counseling program to improve the quality of life in South Texas. Students complete courses in counseling theories, techniques, and attitudes, multicultural counseling, human development, psychopathology, ethical and legal issues, group counseling, career counseling, assessment, and statistical research design. Electives include coursework in crisis counseling, brief collaborative therapy, community interventions, play therapy, elderly mental health, Latino mental health, alcohol and drug counseling, and bilingualism. Faculty are specialists in brief collaborative therapy, crisis intervention, psycholinguistics, memory, multicultural counseling, psychotherapy research, and counselor professional development. Graduates are eligible to sit for the Licensed Professional Counselor (LPC-Texas) Examination. Students can select a thesis track if they are interested in research and further study at the doctoral level. Our program meets every recommendation of the Multicultural Competency Checklist. The new MS in Psychology is designed to prepare the student for PhD work. The focus of preparation is methodology and research.

Special Facilities or Resources: The international flavor of the University and Texas–Mexico border community provide a rich milieu for multicultural and community counseling exploration and education. This is one of the program's greatest resources. Texas A&M International is one of the fastest growing university communities in the United States. Additionally, an off-campus community counseling center, The Texas A&M International University Community Stress Center, offers free bilingual counseling and psychoeducational services. At this center student counselors complete practicums and internships in direct and indirect community and client interventions with faculty supervision. The Master's of Arts in Counseling Psychology (MACP) program works closely with Career Services, Student Counseling, and Academic Support and Enrichment to provide training and employment opportunities for student counselors. A departmental computer lab exists that is currently used for cognitive and language research. It is equipped for detailed analysis of research in memory, cognition, psycholinguistics, bilingualism, as well as other research. A Counseling and Research lab is equipped with digital and video recording, internet video conferencing and standard computer programs. It is available for student use in recording counseling sessions and conducting research.

Application Information:

Send to Texas A&M International University, Office of Graduate Studies and Research, 5201 University Boulevard, Laredo, TX 78041-1900. Application available online. URL of online application: http://www.tamiu.edu/gradschool/. Students are admitted in the Fall, application deadline April 30; Spring, application deadline November 30; Summer, application deadline April 30. *Fee:* $25. $10.00 late fee if submitted after he dealine.

Texas A&M University

Department of Psychology
Liberal Arts
Psychology Department
College Station, TX 77843-4235
Telephone: (979) 845-2581
Fax: (979) 845-4727
E-mail: *sstarr@psych.tamu.edu*
Web: *http://www.psychology.tamu.edu*

Department Information:

1968. Department Head: Les Morey. Number of faculty: total—full-time 39, part-time 2; women—full-time 14, part-time 1; total—minority—full-time 6; women minority—full-time 3.

Programs and Degrees Offered:

Listed in the following order: Program area, degree type (T if terminal Master's), number awarded 7/06–6/07. Developmental PhD (Doctor of Philosophy) 1, Industrial/Organizational PhD (Doctor of Philosophy) 1, Social PhD (Doctor of Philosophy) 2, Behavioral and Cellular Neuroscience PhD (Doctor of Philosophy) 2, Clinical PhD (Doctor of Philosophy) 8, Cognitive PhD (Doctor of Philosophy) 3.

APA Accreditation: Clinical PhD (Doctor of Philosophy).

CPA Accreditation: Clinical PhD (Doctor of Philosophy).

Student Applications/Admissions:

Student Applications

Developmental PhD (Doctor of Philosophy)—Applications 2007–2008, 9. Total applicants accepted 2007–2008, 0. Number full-time enrolled (new admits only) 2007–2008, 0. Total enrolled 2007–2008 full-time, 2. Openings 2008–2009, 1. The number of students enrolled full- and part-time who were dismissed or voluntarily withdrew from this program area in 2007–2008 were 0. *Industrial/Organizational PhD (Doctor of Philosophy)*—Applications 2007–2008, 75. Total applicants accepted 2007–2008, 11. Number full-time enrolled (new admits only) 2007–2008, 3. Total enrolled 2007–2008 full-time, 14, part-time, 8. Openings 2008–2009, 4. The median number of years required for completion of a degree in 2006–2007 were 5. The number of students enrolled full- and part-time who were dismissed or voluntarily withdrew from this program area in 2007–2008 were 0. *Social PhD (Doctor of Philosophy)*—Applications 2007–2008, 30. Total applicants accepted 2007–2008, 5. Number full-time enrolled (new admits only) 2007–2008, 2. Total enrolled 2007–2008 full-time, 5, part-time, 2. Openings 2008–2009, 6. The number of students enrolled full- and part-time who were dismissed or voluntarily withdrew from this program area in 2007–2008 were 0. *Behavioral and Cellular Neuroscience PhD (Doctor of Philosophy)*—Applications 2007–2008, 17. Total applicants accepted 2007–2008, 5. Number full-time enrolled (new admits only) 2007–2008, 3. Number part-time enrolled (new admits only) 2007–2008, 0. Total enrolled 2007–2008 full-time, 14, part-time, 1. Openings 2008–2009, 5. The median number of years required for completion of a degree in 2006–2007 were 5. *Clinical PhD (Doctor of Philosophy)*—Applications 2007–2008, 159. Total applicants accepted 2007–2008, 10. Number full-time enrolled (new admits only) 2007–2008, 7. Total enrolled 2007–2008 full-time, 20, part-time, 8. Openings 2008–2009, 5. The number of students enrolled full- and part-time who were dismissed or voluntarily withdrew from this program area in 2007–2008 were 0. *Cognitive PhD (Doctor of Philosophy)*—Applications 2007–2008, 16. Total applicants accepted 2007–2008, 1. Number full-time enrolled (new admits only) 2007–2008, 0. Openings 2008–2009, 4. The median number of years required for completion of a degree in 2006–2007 were 5. The number of students enrolled full- and part-time who were dismissed or voluntarily withdrew from this program area in 2007–2008 were 0.

Admissions Requirements:

Scores: Entries appear in this order: required test or GPA, minimum score (if required), median score of students entering in 2007–2008. Doctoral Programs: GRE-V no minimum stated, 570; GRE-Q no minimum stated, 700; overall undergraduate GPA no minimum stated; last 2 years GPA 3.0, 3.71.

Other Criteria: (importance of criteria rated low, medium, or high): GRE/MAT scores—high, research experience—high, work experience—high, extracurricular activity—high, clinically related public service—high, GPA—high, letters of recommendation—high, interview—high, statement of goals and objectives—high.

Student Characteristics: The following represents characteristics of students in 2007–2008 in all graduate psychology programs in the department: Female—full-time 41, part-time 14; Male—full-time 22, part-time 5; African American/Black—full-time 6, part-time 1; Hispanic/Latino(a)—full-time 13, part-time 1; Asian/Pacific Islander—full-time 7, part-time 5; American Indian/Alaska Native—full-time 0, part-time 0; Caucasian/White—full-time 37, part-time 12; Multi-ethnic—full-time 0, part-time 0; students subject to the Americans With Disabilities Act—full-time 0, part-time 0; Unknown ethnicity—full-time 0, part-time 0; International students who hold an F-1 or J-1 Visa—full-time 4, part-time 1.

Financial Information/Assistance:

Tuition for Full-Time Study: *Doctoral:* State residents: $206 per credit hour; Nonstate residents: $484 per credit hour. Tuition is subject to change.

Financial Assistance:

First-Year Students: Teaching assistantships available for first year. Average amount paid per academic year: $10,867. Average number of hours worked per week: 20. Apply by December 15. Tuition remission given: full. Research assistantships available for first year. Average amount paid per academic year: $10,867. Average number of hours worked per week: 20. Apply by December 15. Tuition remission given: full. Fellowships and scholarships available for first year. Average amount paid per academic year: $25,000. Apply by December 15. Tuition remission given: full.

Advanced Students: Teaching assistantships available for advanced students. Average amount paid per academic year: $10,867. Average number of hours worked per week: 20. Tuition remission given: full. Research assistantships available for advanced students. Average amount paid per academic year: $10,867. Average number of hours worked per week: 20. Tuition remission given: full.

Additional Information: Of all students currently enrolled full time, 95% benefited from one or more of the listed financial assistance programs. Application and information available online at http://www.tamu.edu/admissions and/or http://www.psychology.tamu.edu.

Internships/Practica: No information provided.

Housing and Day Care: On-campus housing is available. On-campus day care facilities are available.

Employment of Department Graduates:

Master's Degree Graduates: Of those who graduated in the academic year 2006–2007, the following categories and numbers represent the postgraduate activities and employment of master's degree graduates: Enrolled in a postdoctoral residency/fellowship (n/a), employed in independent practice (n/a), total from the above (master's) (0).

Doctoral Degree Graduates: Of those who graduated in the academic year 2006–2007, the following categories and numbers represent the postgraduate activities and employment of doctoral degree graduates: Enrolled in a psychology doctoral program (n/a), enrolled in a postdoctoral residency/fellowship (7), employed in an academic position at a university (5), employed in other positions at a higher education institution (1), employed in a hospital/medical center (2), total from the above (doctoral) (15).

Additional Information:

Orientation, Objectives, and Emphasis of Department: The goals of the PhD program in Psychology are to prepare students for careers as researchers and teachers at colleges and universities, and to prepare students for careers as scientist–practitioners in Clinical Psychology and Industrial/Organizational Psychology. The department offers a PhD in six areas of specialization: Behavioral Neuroscience, Clinical (accredited by the APA), Cognitive, Developmental, Social, and Industrial/Organizational Psychology. The department enrolls approximately 100 graduate students and offers numerous opportunities for student collaboration with faculty. The student–faculty ratio is approximately 3:1, which allows individualized attention to develop research and/or professional skills. Over the last decade, all graduates have obtained full-time employment as researchers, teachers, or practitioners. Faculty members are heavily involved in the placement of graduate students.

Special Facilities or Resources: The department is housed in an attractive four-story building that contains faculty and graduate student offices, research laboratories, administrative offices, and classrooms. Laboratory facilities are excellent, including labs designated for faculty and student research in behavioral neuroscience, cognitive, developmental, industrial/organizational, and social psychology. The department also maintains a Psychology Clinic in which Clinical students are trained to provide a range of psychological services and conduct applied research under supervision from the Clinical faculty.

Information for Students With Physical Disabilities: See the following Web site for more information: http://www.studentlife.tamu.edu/ssd.

Application Information:
Send to Texas A&M University, Graduate Admissions Supervisor, Department of Psychology, College Station, TX 77843-4235. Application available online. Students are admitted in the Fall, application deadline December 15. *Fee:* $50.

Texas A&M University
Educational Psychology
College of Education and Human Development
704 Harrington Tower, MS 4225
College Station, TX 77843-4225
Telephone: (979) 845-1831
Fax: (979) 862-1256
E-mail: *mbenz@tamu.edu*
Web: *http://www.epsy.tamu.edu*

Department Information:
Department Head: Mike Benz. Number of faculty: total—full-time 50, part-time 3; women—full-time 29, part-time 2; total—minority—full-time 18; women minority—full-time 11.

Programs and Degrees Offered:
Listed in the following order: Program area, degree type (T if terminal Master's), number awarded 7/06–6/07. School Psychology PhD (Doctor of Philosophy) 4, Counseling Psychology PhD (Doctor of Philosophy) 5.

APA Accreditation: School PhD (Doctor of Philosophy). Counseling PhD (Doctor of Philosophy).

Student Applications/Admissions:
Student Applications
School Psychology PhD (Doctor of Philosophy)—Applications 2007–2008, 39. Total applicants accepted 2007–2008, 16. Number full-time enrolled (new admits only) 2007–2008, 8. Number part-time enrolled (new admits only) 2007–2008, 0. Openings 2008–2009, 10. The median number of years required for completion of a degree in 2006–2007 were 5. The number of students enrolled full- and part-time who were dismissed or voluntarily withdrew from this program area in 2007–2008 were 0. *Counseling Psychology PhD (Doctor of Philosophy)*—Applications 2007–2008, 83. Total applicants accepted 2007–2008, 10. Number full-time enrolled (new admits only) 2007–2008, 11. Total enrolled 2007–2008 full-time, 46. Openings 2008–2009, 10. The median number of years required for completion of a degree in 2006–2007 were 5. The number of students enrolled full- and part-time who were dismissed or voluntarily withdrew from this program area in 2007–2008 were 0.

Admissions Requirements:
Scores: Entries appear in this order: required test or GPA, minimum score (if required), median score of students entering in 2007–2008. Master's Programs: GRE-V no minimum stated, 510; GRE-Q no minimum stated, 620; overall undergraduate GPA no minimum stated, 3.64; last 2 years GPA no minimum stated. Doctoral Programs: GRE-V no minimum stated, 510; GRE-Q no minimum stated, 620; overall undergraduate GPA no minimum stated, 3.64; last 2 years GPA no minimum stated.
Other Criteria: (importance of criteria rated low, medium, or high): GRE/MAT scores—medium, research experience—high, work experience—medium, extracurricular activity—medium, clinically related public service—high, GPA—medium, letters of recommendation—high, interview—high, statement of goals and objectives—high, fit with program—high, undergraduate major in psychology—low, specific undergraduate psychology courses taken—low. For additional information on admission requirements, go to http://epsy.tamu.edu/articles/graduate_admissions.

Student Characteristics: The following represents characteristics of students in 2007–2008 in all graduate psychology programs in the department: Female—full-time 55, part-time 20; Male—full-time 19, part-time 7; African American/Black—full-time 11, part-time 5; Hispanic/Latino(a)—full-time 16, part-time 7; Asian/Pacific Islander—full-time 6, part-time 2; American Indian/Alaska Native—full-time 0, part-time 0; Caucasian/White—full-time 41, part-time 13; Multi-ethnic—full-time 0, part-time 0; students subject to the Americans With Disabilities Act—full-time 0, part-time 0; Unknown ethnicity—full-time 0, part-time 0; International students who hold an F-1 or J-1 Visa—full-time 0, part-time 0.

Financial Information/Assistance:
Tuition for Full-Time Study: *Master's:* State residents: $206 per credit hour; Nonstate residents: $484 per credit hour. *Doctoral:* State residents: $206 per credit hour; Nonstate residents: $484 per credit hour. Tuition is subject to change. See the following Web site for updates and changes in tuition costs: http://www.finance.tamu.edu/sbs/tuition/fee_information.asp#tuition_fees.

Financial Assistance:
First-Year Students: Research assistantships available for first year. Average amount paid per academic year: $14,400. Average number of hours worked per week: 20. Apply by vary. Fellowships and scholarships available for first year. Average amount paid per academic year: $20,000. Average number of hours worked per week: 20. Apply by January 18 & February 9.
Advanced Students: Teaching assistantships available for advanced students. Average amount paid per academic year: $7,500. Average number of hours worked per week: 10. Apply by vary. Research assistantships available for advanced students. Average amount paid per academic year: $14,400. Average number of hours worked per week: 20. Apply by vary. Fellowships and scholarships available for advanced students. Average amount paid per academic year: $12,000. Apply by vary.
Additional Information: Of all students currently enrolled full time, 60% benefited from one or more of the listed financial assistance programs. Application and information available online at http://www.epsy.tamu.edu.

Internships/Practica: Doctoral Degree (PhD School Psychology): For those doctoral students for whom a professional internship was required in this program prior to graduation, (12) students applied for an internship in 2006–2007, with (12) students obtaining an internship. Of those students who obtained an internship, (12) were paid internships. Of those students who obtained an internship, (9) students placed in APA/CPA-accredited internships, (0) students placed in internships not APA/CPA accredited, but listed with the Association of Psychology Postdoctoral and Internship Centers (APPIC), (3) students placed in internships conforming to guidelines of the Council of Directors of School Psychology Programs (CDSPP), (0) students placed in internships that were not APA/CPA-accredited, APPIC or CDSPP listed. Doctoral Degree (PhD Counseling Psychology): For those doctoral students for whom a professional internship was required in this program prior to graduation, (13) students applied for an internship in 2006–2007, with (13) students obtaining an internship. Of those students who obtained an internship, (13) were paid internships. Of those students who obtained an internship, (13) students placed in APA/CPA-accredited internships, (0) students placed in internships not APA/CPA accredited, but listed with the Association of Psychology Postdoctoral and Internship Centers (APPIC), (0) students placed in internships conforming to guidelines of the Council of Directors of School Psychology Programs (CDSPP), (0) students placed in internships that were not APA/CPA-accredited, APPIC or CDSPP listed. Students in SPSY and CPSY participate in APPIC match program.

Housing and Day Care: On-campus housing is available. See the following Web site for more information: http://www.reslife.tamu.edu/. No on-campus day care facilities are available.

Employment of Department Graduates:

Master's Degree Graduates: Of those who graduated in the academic year 2006–2007, the following categories and numbers represent the postgraduate activities and employment of master's degree graduates: Enrolled in a postdoctoral residency/fellowship (n/a), employed in independent practice (n/a), total from the above (master's) (0).

Doctoral Degree Graduates: Of those who graduated in the academic year 2006–2007, the following categories and numbers represent the postgraduate activities and employment of doctoral degree graduates: Enrolled in a psychology doctoral program (n/a), total from the above (doctoral) (0).

Additional Information:

Orientation, Objectives, and Emphasis of Department: We are among the top-ranked Educational Psychology departments in the nation. We are committed to making a difference through excellence in our research, education, and community outreach activities.

Personal Behavior Statement: http://www.tamu.edu/aggiehonor/.

Special Facilities or Resources: EREL CAC.

Information for Students With Physical Disabilities: See the following Web site for more information: http://www.disability.tamu.edu/.

Application Information:

Application available online. URL of online application: http://www.epsy.tamu.edu/articles/graduate_admissions. Students are admitted in the Fall, application deadline December 1; Spring, application deadline March 15, December 1. All doctoral (PhD) programs October 15. All Master's programs for Spring admission (except School Counseling which does not admit for Spring) March 15. All Master's programs for Summer and Fall admission April 1 and July 1. Hispanic Bilingual Education PhD and Special Education PhD alternative deadlines, priority is given those students who apply by December 1. *Fee:* $50, $75 for international applicants.

Texas A&M University—Commerce

Department of Psychology and Special Education
College of Education and Human Services
Henderson Hall
Commerce, TX 75429
Telephone: (903) 886-5594
Fax: (903) 886-5510
E-mail: *thenley@tamu-commerce.edu*
Web: *http://www.tamu-commerce.edu/psychology/*

Department Information:

1962. Department Head: Dr. Tracy Henley. Number of faculty: total—full-time 14, part-time 4; women—full-time 7, part-time 2; total—minority—full-time 3; women minority—full-time 3.

Programs and Degrees Offered:

Listed in the following order: Program area, degree type (T if terminal Master's), number awarded 7/06–6/07. Educational Psychology PhD (Doctor of Philosophy) 3, School MA/MS (Master of Arts/Science) (T) 12, Applied MA/MS (Master of Arts/Science) (T) 6, General Experimental MA/MS (Master of Arts/Science) (T) 2.

Student Applications/Admissions:

Student Applications

Educational Psychology PhD (Doctor of Philosophy)—Applications 2007–2008, 34. Total applicants accepted 2007–2008, 12. Number full-time enrolled (new admits only) 2007–2008, 8. Number part-time enrolled (new admits only) 2007–2008, 4. Total enrolled 2007–2008 full-time, 39, part-time, 20. Openings 2008–2009, 10. The median number of years required for completion of a degree in 2006–2007 were 6. The number of students enrolled full- and part-time who were dismissed or voluntarily withdrew from this program area in 2007–2008 were 6. *School MA/MS (Master of Arts/Science)*—Applications 2007–2008, 20. Total applicants accepted 2007–2008, 17. Number full-time enrolled (new admits only) 2007–2008, 9. Number part-time enrolled (new admits only) 2007–2008, 8. Total enrolled 2007–2008 full-time, 50, part-time, 10. Openings 2008–2009, 10. The median number of years required for completion of a degree in 2006–2007 were 2. The number of students enrolled full- and part-time who were dismissed or voluntarily withdrew from this program area in 2007–2008 were 1. *Applied MA/MS (Master of Arts/Science)*—Applications 2007–2008, 6. Total applicants accepted 2007–2008, 4. Number full-time enrolled (new admits only) 2007–2008, 4. Total enrolled 2007–2008 full-time, 6, part-time, 2. Openings 2008–2009, 10. The median number of years required for completion of a degree in 2006–2007 were 2. The number of students enrolled full- and part-time who were dismissed or voluntarily withdrew from this program area in 2007–2008 were 0. *General Experimental MA/MS (Master of Arts/Science)*—Applications 2007–2008, 3. Total applicants accepted 2007–2008, 3. Number full-time enrolled (new admits only) 2007–2008, 3. Number part-time enrolled (new admits only) 2007–2008, 0. Openings 2008–2009, 10. The median number of years required for completion of a degree in 2006–2007 were 3. The number of students enrolled full- and part-time who were dismissed or voluntarily withdrew from this program area in 2007–2008 were 0.

Admissions Requirements:

Scores: Entries appear in this order: required test or GPA, minimum score (if required), median score of students entering in 2007–2008. Master's Programs: GRE-V no minimum stated, 450; GRE-Q no minimum stated, 450; overall undergraduate GPA 2.75, 3.0; last 2 years GPA 3.0, 3.2. Doctoral Programs: GRE-V no minimum stated, 500; GRE-Q no minimum stated, 540; overall undergraduate GPA 3.0, 3.0; last 2 years GPA 3.00, 3.4; psychology GPA 3.00, 3.5.

Other Criteria: (importance of criteria rated low, medium, or high): GRE/MAT scores—medium, research experience—medium, work experience—medium, GPA—medium, letters of recommendation—medium, statement of goals and objectives—high, undergraduate major in psychology—low. Greater importance would be assigned to prior research experience, graduate education, and publications and scholarly activity for the doctoral program. For additional information on admission requirements, go to http://www.tamu-commerce.edu/psychology/doctoral.htm.

Student Characteristics: The following represents characteristics of students in 2007–2008 in all graduate psychology programs in the department: Female—full-time 68, part-time 25; Male—full-time 30, part-time 7; African American/Black—full-time 7, part-time 1; Hispanic/Latino(a)—full-time 3, part-time 0; Asian/Pacific Islander—full-time 9, part-time 4; American Indian/Alaska Native—full-time 0, part-time 0; Caucasian/White—full-time 79, part-time 27; students subject to the Americans With Disabilities Act—full-time 0, part-time 0; Unknown ethnicity—full-time 0, part-time 0.

Financial Information/Assistance:

Tuition for Full-Time Study: *Master's:* State residents: $244 per credit hour; Nonstate residents: $522 per credit hour. *Doctoral:* State residents: $244 per credit hour; Nonstate residents: $522 per credit hour. Tuition is subject to change. See the following Web site for updates and changes in tuition costs: http://www.tamu-commerce.edu/fiscal/PaymentInfo/Tuition_Fees/studentfees2007.html.

Financial Assistance:

First-Year Students: Teaching assistantships available for first year. Average amount paid per academic year: $10,000. Average number of hours worked per week: 20. Apply by Fall/Spring. Tuition remission given: partial. Research assistantships available for first year. Average amount paid per academic year: $10,000. Average number of hours worked per week: 20. Apply by Fall/Spring. Tuition remission given: partial. Fellowships and scholarships available for first year. Average amount paid per academic year: $1,000. Apply by Fall. Tuition remission given: partial.

Advanced Students: Teaching assistantships available for advanced students. Average amount paid per academic year: $11,800. Average number of hours worked per week: 20. Apply by Fall/Spring. Tuition remission given: partial. Research assistantships available for advanced students. Average amount paid per academic year: $11,800. Average number of hours worked per week: 20. Apply by Fall/Spring. Tuition remission given: partial. Fellowships and scholarships available for advanced students. Average amount paid per academic year: $1,000. Apply by Fall. Tuition remission given: partial.

Additional Information: Of all students currently enrolled full time, 10% benefited from one or more of the listed financial assistance programs. Application and information available online at http://www.tamu-commerce.edu/psychology/doctoral.htm.

Internships/Practica: There are on-site university clinic practica for School and Applied programs. The School Psychology program requires a 1,200-hour internship in the public schools.

Housing and Day Care: On-campus housing is available. See the following Web site for more information: http://www.tamu-commerce.edu/housing/. On-campus day care facilities are available.

Employment of Department Graduates:

Master's Degree Graduates: Of those who graduated in the academic year 2006–2007, the following categories and numbers represent the postgraduate activities and employment of master's degree graduates: Enrolled in a psychology doctoral program (2), enrolled in another graduate/professional program (1), enrolled in a postdoctoral residency/fellowship (n/a), employed in independent practice (n/a), employed in an academic position at a university (0), employed in an academic position at a 2-year/4-year college (0), employed in other positions at a higher education institution (0), employed in a professional position in a school system (11), employed in business or industry (0), employed in government agency (0), employed in a community mental health/counseling center (3), employed in a hospital/medical center (0), still seeking employment (0), other employment position (0), total from the above (master's) (17).

Doctoral Degree Graduates: Of those who graduated in the academic year 2006–2007, the following categories and numbers represent the postgraduate activities and employment of doctoral degree graduates: Enrolled in a psychology doctoral program (n/a), enrolled in a postdoctoral residency/fellowship (0), employed in independent practice (0), employed in an academic position at a university (1), employed in an academic position at a 2-year/4-year college (0), employed in other positions at a higher education institution (1), employed in a professional position in a school system (1), employed in business or industry (0), employed in government agency (0), employed in a community mental health/counseling center (0), employed in a hospital/medical center (0), still seeking employment (0), other employment position (0), total from the above (doctoral) (3).

Additional Information:

Orientation, Objectives, and Emphasis of Department: The focus of the Educational Psychology program is human cognition and instruction. Students will acquire an in-depth knowledge of human learning and cognition, instructional strategies, and research and evaluation. This emphasis will prepare students to integrate knowledge of human cognition and instructional practice across a variety of occupational, educational and content matter domains, with emphasis on applications of learning technologies. The applied master's program is fully accredited by the Interorganizational Board of Accreditation for Master's in Psychology Programs (IBAMPP). The applied master's program is designed to prepare students to meet the requirements for certification as an associate psychologist in the State of Texas. Associate psychologists are employed in a variety of governmental and private organizations, such as mental health centers, clinics, and hospitals. The School Psychology program has been conditionally approved by the National Association of School Psychologists (NASP) and includes coursework in psychological foundations, educational foundations, assessment, interventions (direct and indirect), statistics and research design, professional school psychology, and practica and internship.

Special Facilities or Resources: Multimedia Instructional Lab, multimedia classrooms, on-site Integrated University Clinic, research partnerships with business industry, Center for Excellence learning technologies, support for online learning, Cogitive Developmental Lab, Cognitive Science Lab, Cognition Lab, Health Psychology Lab, Social Cognition Lab, and School Psychology Resource Center.

Information for Students With Physical Disabilities: See the following Web site for more information: http://www.tamu-commerce.edu/administration/president/procedures/A1301.htm.

Application Information:
Send to Graduate School, P.O. Box 3011, Texas A&M—Commerce, Commerce, TX 75429-3011. Application available online. URL of online application: http://www.tamu-commerce.edu/gradschool/. Students are admitted in the Fall, application deadline April; Spring, application deadline November; Summer, application deadline July; Programs have rolling admissions. *Fee:* $35.

Texas A&M University—Kingsville

Department of Psychology
Arts and Sciences
700 University Blvd.
Kingsville, TX 78363-8202
Telephone: (361) 593-4181
Fax: (361) 593-2707
E-mail: *jmchen@tamuk.edu*
Web: *http://www.tamuk.edu/psycsoci*

Department Information:
Chairperson: Jieming Chen. Number of faculty: total—full-time 1; women—full-time 2, part-time 2; women minority—full-time 1, part-time 1; faculty subject to the Americans With Disabilities Act 1.

Programs and Degrees Offered:
Listed in the following order: Program area, degree type (T if terminal Master's), number awarded 7/06–6/07. Psychology MA/MS (Master of Arts/Science) (T) 8.

Student Applications/Admissions:
Student Applications
Psychology MA/MS (Master of Arts/Science)—Total enrolled 2007–2008 full-time, 24, part-time, 20.

Admissions Requirements:
Scores: Entries appear in this order: required test or GPA, minimum score (if required), median score of students entering in 2007–2008. Master's Programs: overall undergraduate GPA 2.6.
Other Criteria: (importance of criteria rated low, medium, or high): GRE/MAT scores—low, GPA—high. For additional information on admission requirements, go to http://www.tamuk.edu/grad/.

Student Characteristics: The following represents characteristics of students in 2007–2008 in all graduate psychology programs in the department: Female—full-time 15, part-time 16; Male—full-time 3, part-time 4; African American/Black—full-time 1, part-time 1; Hispanic/Latino(a)—full-time 12, part-time 14; Asian/Pacific Islander—full-time 1, part-time 1; American Indian/Alaska Native—full-time 1, part-time 0; Caucasian/White—full-time 3, part-time 4; Unknown ethnicity—full-time 0, part-time 0.

Financial Information/Assistance:
Financial Assistance:
First-Year Students: No information provided.
Advanced Students: No information provided.
Additional Information: Of all students currently enrolled full time, 0% benefited from one or more of the listed financial assistance programs. Application and information available online at http://www.tamuk.edu/finaid/.

Internships/Practica: A number of placement sites are available for masters students enrolled in the practicum course.

Housing and Day Care: On-campus housing is available. See the following Web site for more information: http://www.tamuk.edu/intpro/Housing.htm. On-campus day care facilities are available. See the following Web site for more information: http://www.tamuk.edu/aghs/departments/cyc/main.html.

Employment of Department Graduates:
Master's Degree Graduates: Of those who graduated in the academic year 2006–2007, the following categories and numbers represent the postgraduate activities and employment of master's degree graduates: Enrolled in a postdoctoral residency/fellowship (n/a), employed in independent practice (n/a), total from the above (master's) (0).
Doctoral Degree Graduates: Of those who graduated in the academic year 2006–2007, the following categories and numbers represent the postgraduate activities and employment of doctoral degree graduates: Enrolled in a psychology doctoral program (n/a), total from the above (doctoral) (0).

Additional Information:

Information for Students With Physical Disabilities: See the following Web site for more information: http://www.tamuk.edu/sass/LifeServices/ssd_main.htm.

Application Information:
Send to Dean, College of Graduate Studies Texas A&M University—Kingsville MSC 118 Kingsville, TX 78363. Students are admitted

in the Fall, application deadline June; Spring, application deadline December; Summer, application deadline April; Programs have rolling admissions. Applications received and decisions made on a rolling basis. *Fee:* $35.

Texas Christian University

Department of Psychology
College of Science and Engineering
TCU Box 298920
Fort Worth, TX 76129
Telephone: (817) 257-7410
Fax: (817) 257-7681
E-mail: *m.eudaly@tcu.edu*
Web: *http://www.psy.tcu.edu/*

Department Information:

1959. Chairperson: Timothy Barth. Number of faculty: total—full-time 16, part-time 2; women—full-time 5, part-time 1; total—minority—full-time 3; women minority—full-time 1.

Programs and Degrees Offered:

Listed in the following order: Program area, degree type (T if terminal Master's), number awarded 7/06–6/07. Experimental PhD (Doctor of Philosophy) 3.

Student Applications/Admissions:

Student Applications

Experimental PhD (Doctor of Philosophy)—Applications 2007–2008, 19. Total applicants accepted 2007–2008, 15. Number full-time enrolled (new admits only) 2007–2008, 6. Number part-time enrolled (new admits only) 2007–2008, 0. Openings 2008–2009, 6. The median number of years required for completion of a degree in 2006–2007 were 4. The number of students enrolled full- and part-time who were dismissed or voluntarily withdrew from this program area in 2007–2008 were 0.

Admissions Requirements:

Scores: Entries appear in this order: required test or GPA, minimum score (if required), median score of students entering in 2007–2008. Doctoral Programs: GRE-V no minimum stated, 520; GRE-Q no minimum stated, 640; overall undergraduate GPA 3.2, 3.39; last 2 years GPA 3.2, 3.60; psychology GPA 3.2, 3.60.

Other Criteria: (importance of criteria rated low, medium, or high): GRE/MAT scores—low, research experience—high, GPA—medium, letters of recommendation—high, statement of goals and objectives—high. For additional information on admission requirements, go to http://www.psy.tcu.edu.

Student Characteristics: The following represents characteristics of students in 2007–2008 in all graduate psychology programs in the department: Female—full-time 21, part-time 0; Male—full-time 7, part-time 0; African American/Black—full-time 0, part-time 0; Hispanic/Latino(a)—full-time 1, part-time 0; Asian/Pacific Islander—full-time 2, part-time 0; American Indian/Alaska Native—full-time 0, part-time 0; Caucasian/White—full-time 25, part-time 0; Multi-ethnic—full-time 0, part-time 0; students subject to the Americans With Disabilities Act—full-time 30, part-time 0; Unknown ethnicity—full-time 0, part-time 0; International students who hold an F-1 or J-1 Visa—full-time 2, part-time 0.

Financial Information/Assistance:

Tuition for Full-Time Study: *Master's:* State residents: $935 per credit hour; Nonstate residents: $935 per credit hour. *Doctoral:* State residents: $935 per credit hour; Nonstate residents: $935 per credit hour. See the following Web site for updates and changes in tuition costs: http://www.tcu.edu.

Financial Assistance:

First-Year Students: Fellowships and scholarships available for first year. Average amount paid per academic year: $17,000. Average number of hours worked per week: 0. Apply by none. Tuition remission given: full.

Advanced Students: Teaching assistantships available for advanced students. Average amount paid per academic year: $14,000. Average number of hours worked per week: 10. Apply by February 1. Tuition remission given: full.

Additional Information: Of all students currently enrolled full time, 96% benefited from one or more of the listed financial assistance programs. Application and information available online at http://www.psy.tcu.edu/gradpro.html.

Internships/Practica: No information provided.

Housing and Day Care: On-campus housing is available. See the following Web site for more information: http://www.rlh.tcu.edu/GSA.HTM. No on-campus day care facilities are available.

Employment of Department Graduates:

Master's Degree Graduates: Of those who graduated in the academic year 2006–2007, the following categories and numbers represent the postgraduate activities and employment of master's degree graduates: Enrolled in a psychology doctoral program (6), enrolled in another graduate/professional program (0), enrolled in a postdoctoral residency/fellowship (n/a), employed in independent practice (n/a), employed in an academic position at a university (0), employed in an academic position at a 2-year/4-year college (0), employed in other positions at a higher education institution (0), employed in a professional position in a school system (0), employed in business or industry (0), employed in government agency (0), employed in a community mental health/counseling center (0), employed in a hospital/medical center (0), still seeking employment (0), not seeking employment (1), other employment position (0), do not know (0), total from the above (master's) (7).

Doctoral Degree Graduates: Of those who graduated in the academic year 2006–2007, the following categories and numbers represent the postgraduate activities and employment of doctoral degree graduates: Enrolled in a psychology doctoral program (n/a), enrolled in another graduate/professional program (0), enrolled in a postdoctoral residency/fellowship (0), employed in independent practice (0), employed in an academic position at a university (2), employed in an academic position at a 2-year/4-year college (0), employed in other positions at a higher education institution (0), employed in a professional position in a school system (0), employed in business or industry (1), employed in government agency (1), employed in a community mental health/counseling center (0), employed in a hospital/medical center (0), still seeking employment (0), other employment position (0), total from the above (doctoral) (4).

Additional Information:

Orientation, Objectives, and Emphasis of Department: The psychology graduate program at Texas Christian University leads to a predoctoral master's in experimental psychology and a PhD in general experimental psychology. The PhD is awarded in general experimental psychology. The program is not limited to traditional experimental psychology, nor is it committed solely to laboratory-based methods. The department has long held that a measure of specialized knowledge—built upon a firm but broad base of psychological principles and methods—constitutes the best plan for most of its students. Within this plan the student may study diverse areas of interest with emphasis possible in the following: learning-comparative, perception–cognition, social, personality, applied quantitative methods, and behavioral neuroscience. All graduate students receive training in both teaching and research. The environment is stimulating, informal, and conducive to close student–faculty relations.

Special Facilities or Resources: Assuming that physical proximity is conducive to more interdisciplinary work of substance, TCU has located all its science-related activities in or near the Science Research Center, dedicated in 1971. The Department of Psychology occupies two floors of the center's Winton-Scott Hall. The university library, containing over 1 million volumes, is located next to the science facilities. About 140 periodicals of psychological interest are available. Full-time personnel skilled in electronics, glass blowing, woodworking, and metal working aid in construction and maintenance of special equipment or instruments. TCU has 10 open computer labs equipped with Windows-based PCs and Macintosh computers (over 100 Windows-based machines and 39 Mac-based machines). All of the labs provide full Internet access and laser printing. Additionally, some of the labs have scanners, zip drives, CD burners, and Web cams. The Psychology Department also has a computer lab with six Windows-based PCs, all of which are connected to the Internet, and a networked laser printer. Additionally, all of the research laboratories in the department have networked computers. From the various labs, students have access to a variety of software including SPSS, SAS, SYSTAT, and Microsoft Office. Also, the University provides e-mail accounts and storage space on the University server.

Information for Students With Physical Disabilities: See the following Web site for more information: http://www.acs.tcu.edu/disability.htm.

Application Information:

Send to Charles G. Lord, Coordinator of Graduate Studies, TCU Box 298920, Fort Worth, TX 76129. Application available online. URL of online application: http://www.psy.tcu.edu. Students are admitted in the Fall, no application deadline. Students are admitted in the Fall. No deadline for admission; however, February 15 is recommended to be considered for funding. *Fee:* $50. Fees can be waived for exceptional or needy applicants. Contact the Graduate Director.

Texas of the Permian Basin, The University of

Psychology Department
College of Arts and Sciences
4901 East University Boulevard
Odessa, TX 79762
Telephone: (432) 552-2325
Fax: (432) 552-3325
E-mail: *montgomery_L@utpb.edu*
Web: *http://www.utpb.edu*

Department Information:

1973. Chairperson: Linda Montgomery. Number of faculty: total—full-time 3, part-time 1; women—full-time 2, part-time 1.

Programs and Degrees Offered:

Listed in the following order: Program area, degree type (T if terminal Master's), number awarded 7/06–6/07. Clinical Psychology MA/MS (Master of Arts/Science) (T) 6, Applied Research and Human Development MA/MS (Master of Arts/Science) (T) 3.

Student Applications/Admissions:

Student Applications

Clinical Psychology MA/MS (Master of Arts/Science)—Applications 2007–2008, 12. Total applicants accepted 2007–2008, 10. Number full-time enrolled (new admits only) 2007–2008, 10. Total enrolled 2007–2008 full-time, 10, part-time, 20. Openings 2008–2009, 10. The median number of years required for completion of a degree in 2006–2007 were 3. The number of students enrolled full- and part-time who were dismissed or voluntarily withdrew from this program area in 2007–2008 were 1. *Applied Research and Human Development MA/MS (Master of Arts/Science)*—Applications 2007–2008, 5. Total applicants accepted 2007–2008, 5. Number full-time enrolled (new admits only) 2007–2008, 5. Total enrolled 2007–2008 full-time, 5, part-time, 5. Openings 2008–2009, 5. The median number of years required for completion of a degree in 2006–2007 were 3. The number of students enrolled full- and part-time who were dismissed or voluntarily withdrew from this program area in 2007–2008 were 0.

Admissions Requirements:

Scores: Entries appear in this order: required test or GPA, minimum score (if required), median score of students entering in 2007–2008. Master's Programs: GRE-V 400; GRE-Q 400; overall undergraduate GPA 3.0; last 2 years GPA 3.0; psychology GPA 3.0. GRE scores are informational and not limits. Current formulas for regular status: Add (GPA for last 60 undergraduate hours times 200) + (Total GRE). This must equal 1600 to qualify for admission with regular status. Students are evaluated on a case-by-case basis and may be admitted at a provisional status.

Other Criteria: (importance of criteria rated low, medium, or high): GRE/MAT scores—high, research experience—low, work experience—low, extracurricular activity—low, clinically related public service—low, GPA—high, letters of recommendation—high, statement of goals and objectives—high, undergraduate major in psychology—low, specific undergraduate psychology courses taken—low.

Student Characteristics: The following represents characteristics of students in 2007–2008 in all graduate psychology programs in the department: Female—full-time 20, part-time 15; Male—full-time 15, part-time 10; African American/Black—full-time 1, part-time 1; Hispanic/Latino(a)—full-time 10, part-time 8; Asian/Pacific Islander—full-time 2, part-time 0; American Indian/Alaska Native—full-time 0, part-time 0; Caucasian/White—full-time 22, part-time 16; students subject to the Americans With Disabilities Act—full-time 1, part-time 1; Unknown ethnicity—full-time 0, part-time 0.

Financial Information/Assistance:

Tuition for Full-Time Study: *Master's:* State residents: per academic year $2,200, $122 per credit hour; Nonstate residents: per academic year $6,200, $342 per credit hour. Tuition is subject to change.

Financial Assistance:

First-Year Students: Research assistantships available for first year. Average amount paid per academic year: $8,000. Average number of hours worked per week: 19. Apply by April 15. Fellowships and scholarships available for first year. Average amount paid per academic year: $500. Apply by July 15.

Advanced Students: Teaching assistantships available for advanced students. Average amount paid per academic year: $9,000. Apply by April 15. Fellowships and scholarships available for advanced students. Average amount paid per academic year: $500.

Additional Information: Of all students currently enrolled full time, 20% benefited from one or more of the listed financial assistance programs. Application and information available online at http://www.utpb.edu.

Internships/Practica: Master's Degree (MA/MS Clinical Psychology): An internship experience such as a final research project or "capstone" experience is required of graduates. Master's Degree (MA/MS Applied Research and Human Development): An internship experience such as a final research project or "capstone" experience is required of graduates. The University Counseling Center has opportunities for supervised clinical practicum. Other practicums are available in the community. Most students accumulate hours leading to Licensed Professional Counselor (LPC) certification in the State of Texas. Students also qualify for certification as Psychology Associates in the State of Texas.

Housing and Day Care: On-campus housing is available. See the following Web site for more information: Campus housing is new and in excellent condition. See housing at http://www.utpb.edu. No on-campus day care facilities are available.

Employment of Department Graduates:

Master's Degree Graduates: Of those who graduated in the academic year 2006–2007, the following categories and numbers represent the postgraduate activities and employment of master's degree graduates: Enrolled in a postdoctoral residency/fellowship (n/a), employed in independent practice (n/a), employed in a community mental health/counseling center (3), employed in a hospital/medical center (1), total from the above (master's) (4).

Doctoral Degree Graduates: Of those who graduated in the academic year 2006–2007, the following categories and numbers represent the postgraduate activities and employment of doctoral degree graduates: Enrolled in a psychology doctoral program (n/a), total from the above (doctoral) (0).

Additional Information:

Orientation, Objectives, and Emphasis of Department: The Master of Arts program in Psychology offers concentrations in both Clinical and Applied Research. The program offers students the opportunity to prepare themselves to work in mental health centers, juvenile detention centers, child service agencies, specialized school services, residential treatment facilities, and family counseling agencies, and to teach in community colleges or study at the doctoral level (PhD). The Clinical Psychology concentration is aimed at training students in the assessment and treatment of mental disorders, through individual, family, and group therapies. The program offers instruction in child, adolescent, and adult disorders. Successful completion of the Clinical Psychology concentration is designed to provide students with the opportunity to become eligible to take the state examinations for certification as a Psychological Associate (45 hours) or Licensed Professional Counselor (51 hours). The Licensed Professional Counselor certification requires an additional 2,000 supervised hours after the MA degree. The Applied Research concentration focuses on advanced psychological theory (i.e., developmental, personality, social, etc.), research methods, statistics, and manuscript preparation. The Applied Research concentration offers students the opportunity to prepare themselves to serve in governmental and community college or to pursue additional graduate study at the doctoral level. All students in the Applied Research concentration are expected to be involved in research activities throughout their graduate program.

Special Facilities or Resources: We have a newly remodeled on-campus center that has a counseling area for clinical practicums and research space for applied research and thesis projects. In addition cooperative arrangements are made with community health centers, schools, governmental agencies, and mental health practitioners for research and practicum opportunities.

Information for Students With Physical Disabilities: See the following Web site for more information: http://www.utpb.edu.

Application Information:

Send to Graduate Studies, The University of Texas of the Permian Basin, 4901 East University, Odessa, TX 79762. Application available online. URL of online application: http://www.utpb.edu/utpb_adm/academicaffairs/graduatestudiesresearch/studentinfo/graduateapplications.htm. Students are admitted in the Fall, application deadline May 1; Spring, application deadline November 1. Students may enter the program at any time as provisional before gaining full admission. *Fee:* $0.

Texas Southwestern Medical Center at Dallas, University of

Division of Psychology, Graduate Program in Clinical Psychology
5323 Harry Hines Boulevard
Dallas, TX 75390-9044
Telephone: (214) 648-5277
Fax: (214) 648-5297
E-mail: *hm.evans@utsouthwestern.edu*
Web: *http://www.utsouthwestern.edu/utsw/home/education/psychology/index.html*

Department Information:

1956. Chairperson: C. Munro Cullum, PhD. Number of faculty: total—full-time 17, part-time 24; women—full-time 12, part-time 18; total—minority—full-time 7, part-time 2; women minority—full-time 3, part-time 2; faculty subject to the Americans With Disabilities Act 7.

Programs and Degrees Offered:

Listed in the following order: Program area, degree type (T if terminal Master's), number awarded 7/06–6/07. Clinical Psychology PhD (Doctor of Philosophy) 10.

APA Accreditation: Clinical PhD (Doctor of Philosophy).

Student Applications/Admissions:

Student Applications

Clinical Psychology PhD (Doctor of Philosophy)—Applications 2007–2008, 139. Total applicants accepted 2007–2008, 10. Number full-time enrolled (new admits only) 2007–2008, 10. Openings 2008–2009, 10. The median number of years required for completion of a degree in 2006–2007 were 5. The number of students enrolled full- and part-time who were dismissed or voluntarily withdrew from this program area in 2007–2008 were 2.

Admissions Requirements:

Scores: Entries appear in this order: required test or GPA, minimum score (if required), median score of students entering in 2007–2008. Doctoral Programs: GRE-V 500, 625; GRE-Q 500, 625; overall undergraduate GPA 3.0, 3.5; Doctoral program GRE-Analytic no minimum stated.

Other Criteria: (importance of criteria rated low, medium, or high): GRE/MAT scores—high, research experience—high, work experience—high, extracurricular activity—low, clinically related public service—medium, GPA—high, letters of recommendation—high, interview—high, statement of goals and objectives—high, undergraduate major in psychology—medium, specific undergraduate psychology courses taken—medium. For additional information on admission requirements, go to http://www8.utsouthwestern.edu/utsw/cda/dept23139/files/83598.html.

Student Characteristics: The following represents characteristics of students in 2007–2008 in all graduate psychology programs in the department: Female—full-time 32, part-time 0; Male—full-time 13, part-time 0; African American/Black—full-time 1, part-time 0; Hispanic/Latino(a)—full-time 5, part-time 0; Asian/Pacific Islander—full-time 5, part-time 0; American Indian/Alaska Native—full-time 0, part-time 0; Caucasian/White—full-time 34, part-time 0; Multi-ethnic—full-time 0, part-time 0; students subject to the Americans With Disabilities Act—full-time 0, part-time 0; Unknown ethnicity—full-time 0, part-time 0; International students who hold an F-1 or J-1 Visa—full-time 1, part-time 0.

Financial Information/Assistance:

Tuition for Full-Time Study: *Doctoral:* State residents: per academic year $6,530, $50 per credit hour; Nonstate residents: per academic year $17,928, $328 per credit hour. Tuition is subject to change. See the following Web site for updates and changes in tuition costs: http://www8.utsouthwestern.edu/utsw/cda/dept20424/files/81518.html.

Financial Assistance:

First-Year Students: Teaching assistantships available for first year. Apply by January 1, 2009. Research assistantships available for first year. Apply by January 1.

Advanced Students: Teaching assistantships available for advanced students. Research assistantships available for advanced students. Average amount paid per academic year: $7,200. Traineeships available for advanced students. Average amount paid per academic year: $14,400. Average number of hours worked per week: 36.

Additional Information: Of all students currently enrolled full time, 77% benefited from one or more of the listed financial assistance programs. Application and information available online at http://www.utsouthwestern.edu/utsw/home/financialaid/index.html.

Internships/Practica: Doctoral Degree (PhD Clincal Psychology): For those doctoral students for whom a professional internship was required in this program prior to graduation, (18) students applied for an internship in 2006–2007, with (18) students obtaining an internship. Of those students who obtained an internship, (18) were paid internships. Of those students who obtained an internship, (18) students placed in APA/CPA-accredited internships, (0) students placed in internships not APA/CPA accredited, but listed with the Association of Psychology Postdoctoral and Internship Centers (APPIC), (0) students placed in internships conforming to guidelines of the Council of Directors of School Psychology Programs (CDSPP), (0) students placed in internships that were not APA/CPA-accredited, APPIC or CDSPP listed. The program provides more than 1,000 hours of clinical practica, followed by an APA-accredited captive internship. These clinical experiences are closely supervised. In order to achieve the goal of broad professional preparation, students will have a number of different clinical placements over the course of their practicum and internship assignments. These assignments are carried out at UT Southwestern facilities, agencies, regional medical centers, area schools, university counseling centers, and rehabilitation institutes. These clinical training sites include the following: Parkland Memorial Hospital (PMH); Parkland Community Oriented Care Clinic (PMH); Neuropsychology Service (UTSWMC); McDermott Pain Management Center (UTSWMC); University Rehabilitation Center (UTSWMC); Children's Medical Center (CMC); Cystic Fibrosis Center (CMC); Episcopal School of Dallas (CMC); Sleep Disorder Center (CMC); the Mental Health Service of Southern Methodist University, Student Counseling Center at the University of Texas at Arlington, Terrell State Hospital, Dallas County Juvenile Department, Baylor University Medical Center, Baylor Institute for Rehabilitation; Presbyterian Hospital of Dallas, Shelton School, and Fairhill School.

Housing and Day Care: On-campus housing is available. See the following Web site for more information: http://www3.utsouthwestern.edu/campushousing/. On-campus day care facilities are available. See the following Web site for more information: http://www.utsouthwestern.edu/utsw/cda/dept264142/files/264181.html#campus.

Employment of Department Graduates:

Master's Degree Graduates: Of those who graduated in the academic year 2006–2007, the following categories and numbers represent the postgraduate activities and employment of master's degree graduates: Enrolled in a postdoctoral residency/fellowship (n/a), employed in independent practice (n/a), total from the above (master's) (0).

Doctoral Degree Graduates: Of those who graduated in the academic year 2006–2007, the following categories and numbers represent the postgraduate activities and employment of doctoral degree graduates: Enrolled in a psychology doctoral program (n/a), enrolled in a postdoctoral residency/fellowship (8), total from the above (doctoral) (8).

Additional Information:

Orientation, Objectives, and Emphasis of Department: The Graduate Program in Clinical Psychology is a 4-year doctoral program with an affiliated predoctoral internship program in Clinical Psychology, which is separately accredited by the APA. The program provides a combination of experiences in both clinical and research settings reflecting our basic training philosophy, which is a clinician–researcher model. Our specific objectives include offering the student the opportunity to acquire, experience, or develop the following: (a) a closely knit integration between basic psychological knowledge (both theoretical and empirical) and responsible professional services; (b) a wide variety of supervised and broadly conceived clinical and consulting experiences; (c) a sensitivity to professional responsibilities in the context of significant social needs; (d) an understanding of research principles, methodology, and skill in formulating, designing, and implementing psychological research; and (e) a competence and confidence in the role of psychology in multidisciplinary settings.

Special Facilities or Resources: UT Southwestern has a number of laboratories and clinical settings investigating brain–behavior relationship, as well as many projects focusing on the psychosocial aspects of various medical and psychiatric disorders. Disorders studied include affective illness, anxiety, schizophrenia, sleep–wake dysfunctions, and medical conditions such as Alzheimer's Disease, epilepsy, temporomandibular disorder, cystic fibrosis, and organ transplantation. Notable examples of comprehensive clinical research programs at UT Southwestern include the following: an affective disorders research program, a sleep disorders research laboratory, an Alzheimer's Disease Center, a neuropsychology laboratory, a pain management program, a schizophrenia research program that includes translational research, and research programs in basic neuroscience.

Information for Students With Physical Disabilities: See the following Web site for more information: http://www.utsouthwestern.edu/utsw/cda/dept26446/files/70472.html.

Application Information:

Applications accepted only through Internet address. Application available online. URL of online application: http://www.utsouthwestern.edu/gradapp. Students are admitted in the Fall, application deadline January 1. Applications accepted only through Internet address above. *Fee:* $0.

Texas State University—San Marcos

Psychology Department/Master of Arts in Health Psychology Program
College of Liberal Arts
601 University Drive
San Marcos, TX 78666-4616
Telephone: (512) 245-2526
Fax: (512) 245-3153
E-mail: *fb12@txstate.edu*
Web: *http://www.psych.txstate.edu*

Department Information:

1969. Chairperson: Frank Barrios, PhD. Number of faculty: total—full-time 26, part-time 3; women—full-time 11, part-time 1; total—minority—full-time 2.

Programs and Degrees Offered:

Listed in the following order: Program area, degree type (T if terminal Master's), number awarded 7/06–6/07. Health Psychology MA/MS (Master of Arts/Science) (T) 10.

Student Applications/Admissions:

Student Applications

Health Psychology MA/MS (Master of Arts/Science)—Applications 2007–2008, 45. Total applicants accepted 2007–2008, 24. Number full-time enrolled (new admits only) 2007–2008, 23. Number part-time enrolled (new admits only) 2007–2008, 1. Total enrolled 2007–2008 full-time, 32, part-time, 2. Openings 2008–2009, 18. The median number of years required for completion of a degree in 2006–2007 were 2. The number of students enrolled full- and part-time who were dismissed or voluntarily withdrew from this program area in 2007–2008 were 1.

Admissions Requirements:

Scores: Entries appear in this order: required test or GPA, minimum score (if required), median score of students entering in 2007–2008. Master's Programs: GRE-V no minimum stated; GRE-Q no minimum stated; last 2 years GPA 3.0, 3.0; psychology GPA 3.0, 3.25. Combined GRE-V and GRE-Q minimum score preference is 1000.

Other Criteria: (importance of criteria rated low, medium, or high): GRE/MAT scores—medium, research experience—high, work experience—medium, extracurricular activity—low, clinically related public service—medium, GPA—medium, letters of recommendation—high, interview—medium, statement of goals and objectives—high, undergraduate major in psychology—high, specific undergraduate psychology courses taken—high. For additional information on admission requirements, go to http://www.psych.txstate.edu/graduate/gradreq.php.

Student Characteristics: The following represents characteristics of students in 2007–2008 in all graduate psychology programs in the department: Female—full-time 24, part-time 1; Male—full-time 8, part-time 1; African American/Black—full-time 3, part-time 0; Hispanic/Latino(a)—full-time 7, part-time 0; Asian/Pacific Islander—full-time 0, part-time 0; American Indian/Alaska Native—full-time 0, part-time 0; Caucasian/White—full-time 20, part-time 2; Multi-ethnic—full-time 2, part-time 0; Unknown ethnicity—full-time 0, part-time 0; International students who hold an F-1 or J-1 Visa—full-time 3, part-time 0.

Financial Information/Assistance:

Tuition for Full-Time Study: *Master's:* State residents: per academic year $5,506, $367 per credit hour; Nonstate residents: per academic year $11,066, $738 per credit hour. Tuition is subject to change. See the following Web site for updates and changes in tuition costs: http://www.finaid.txstate.edu/graduate/cost.html.

Financial Assistance:

First-Year Students: Teaching assistantships available for first year. Average amount paid per academic year: $4,900. Average number of hours worked per week: 10. Apply by March 1. Research assistantships available for first year. Average amount paid per academic year: $4,900. Average number of hours worked per week: 10. Apply by March 1. Fellowships and scholarships available for first year. Average amount paid per academic year: $5,000. Average number of hours worked per week: 0. Apply by variable. Tuition remission given: partial.

Advanced Students: Teaching assistantships available for advanced students. Average amount paid per academic year: $4,900. Average number of hours worked per week: 10. Apply by March 1. Research assistantships available for advanced students. Average amount paid per academic year: $4,900. Average number of hours worked per week: 10. Apply by March 1. Fellowships and scholarships available for advanced students. Average amount paid per academic year: $5,000. Average number of hours worked per week: 0. Apply by variable. Tuition remission given: partial.

Additional Information: Of all students currently enrolled full time, 55% benefited from one or more of the listed financial assistance programs. Application and information available online at http://www.gradcollege.txstate.edu.

Internships/Practica: Multiple practicum sites are avaliable and students in the clinical track must complete two semesters of practicum. Practicum sites include rehabilitation centers, behavioral health clinics, medical centers, pain clinics, juvenile forensic sites, state hospitals and facililites for persons with developmental disabilities, and offices of private practitioners.

Housing and Day Care: On-campus housing is available. See the following Web site for more information: http://www.reslife.txstate.edu. On-campus day care facilities are available. See the following Web site for more information: http://www.fcs.txstate.edu/cdc.htm.

Employment of Department Graduates:

Master's Degree Graduates: Of those who graduated in the academic year 2006–2007, the following categories and numbers represent the postgraduate activities and employment of master's degree graduates: Enrolled in a psychology doctoral program (6), enrolled in another graduate/professional program (3), enrolled in a postdoctoral residency/fellowship (n/a), employed in independent practice (n/a), employed in a professional position in a school system (2), employed in business or industry (1), employed in government agency (4), employed in a community mental health/counseling center (4), employed in a hospital/medical center (2), still seeking employment (2), other employment position (2), do not know (9), total from the above (master's) (35).

Doctoral Degree Graduates: Of those who graduated in the academic year 2006–2007, the following categories and numbers represent the postgraduate activities and employment of doctoral degree graduates: Enrolled in a psychology doctoral program (n/a), total from the above (doctoral) (0).

Additional Information:

Orientation, Objectives, and Emphasis of Department: The master's program is intended to provide master's-level students with specific clinical skills, cognitive behavioral intervention techniques, and research skills for entry into PhD programs and direct employment in a variety of medical and health care settings. The program has been revised to offer two tracks, clinical and research.

Special Facilities or Resources: The Psychology Department at Texas State University is currently developing relationships with the surrounding area's medical communities such as San Antonio's and Austin's major medical centers. We are also in the process of developing relationships with the community health centers and private clinics.

Information for Students With Physical Disabilities: See the following Web site for more information: http://www.ods.txstate.edu/.

Application Information:

Send to Graduate College, Texas State University, 601 University Drive, San Marcos, TX 78666-4605. Students are admitted in the Fall, application deadline March 15. It should be noted that the deadline for many scholarships (including those administered by the Graduate College and Liberal Arts Graduate Scholarships) is March 1, and students who have complete application packets by February 1 will be given priority for departmental assistantships. *Fee:* $40. This is the Graduate College fee, not a departmental fee.

Texas Tech University

Department of Psychology
Arts and Sciences
Box 42051
Lubbock, TX 79409-2051
Telephone: (806) 742-3711, ext. 222
Fax: (806) 742-0818
E-mail: *david.rudd@ttu.edu or kay.hill@ttu.edu*
Web: *http://www.psychology.ttu.edu*

Department Information:

1950. Chairperson: M. David Rudd, PhD, ABPP. Number of faculty: total—full-time 28, part-time 8; women—full-time 12, part-time 5; total—minority—full-time 1, part-time 2; women minority—part-time 1; faculty subject to the Americans With Disabilities Act 1.

Programs and Degrees Offered:

Listed in the following order: Program area, degree type (T if terminal Master's), number awarded 7/06–6/07. Clinical Psychology PhD (Doctor of Philosophy) 7, Cognitive/Applied Cognitive PhD (Doctor of Philosophy) 2, Counseling Psychology PhD (Doctor of Philosophy) 5, General Experimental PhD (Doctor of Philosophy) 0, Human Factors PhD (Doctor of Philosophy) 2, Social Psychology PhD (Doctor of Philosophy) 2.

APA Accreditation: Clinical PhD (Doctor of Philosophy). Counseling PhD (Doctor of Philosophy).

Student Applications/Admissions:

Student Applications

Clinical Psychology PhD (Doctor of Philosophy)—Applications 2007–2008, 160. Total applicants accepted 2007–2008, 7. Number full-time enrolled (new admits only) 2007–2008, 7. Number part-time enrolled (new admits only) 2007–2008, 0. Openings 2008–2009, 6. The median number of years required for completion of a degree in 2006–2007 were 5. The number of students enrolled full- and part-time who were dismissed or voluntarily withdrew from this program area in 2007–2008 were 1. *Cognitive/Applied Cognitive PhD (Doctor of Philosophy)*—Applications 2007–2008, 7. Total applicants accepted 2007–2008, 2. Number full-time enrolled (new admits only) 2007–2008, 2. Number part-time enrolled (new admits only) 2007–2008, 0. Openings 2008–2009, 3. The median number of years required for completion of a degree in 2006–2007 were 5. The number of students enrolled full- and part-time who were dismissed or voluntarily withdrew from this program area in 2007–2008 were 0. *Counseling Psychology PhD (Doctor of Philosophy)*—Applications 2007–2008, 81. Total applicants accepted 2007–2008, 6. Number full-time enrolled (new admits only) 2007–2008, 6. Number part-time enrolled (new admits only) 2007–2008, 0. Openings 2008–2009, 6. The median number of years required for completion of a degree in 2006–2007 were 5. The number of students enrolled full- and part-time who were dismissed or voluntarily withdrew from this program area in 2007–2008 were 1. *General Experimental PhD (Doctor of Philosophy)*—Applications 2007–2008, 1. Total applicants accepted 2007–2008, 1. Number full-time enrolled (new admits only) 2007–2008, 1. Number part-time enrolled (new admits only) 2007–2008, 0. Openings 2008–2009, 1. The median number of years required for completion of a degree in 2006–2007 were 5. The number of students enrolled full- and part-time who were dismissed or voluntarily withdrew from this program area in 2007–2008 were 0. *Human Factors PhD (Doctor of Philosophy)*—Applications 2007–2008, 31. Total applicants accepted 2007–2008, 2. Number full-time enrolled (new admits only) 2007–2008, 2. Number part-time enrolled (new admits only) 2007–2008, 0. Openings 2008–2009, 3. The median number of years required for completion of a degree in 2006–2007 were 5. The number of students enrolled full- and part-time who were dismissed or voluntarily withdrew from this program area in 2007–2008 were 1. *Social Psychology PhD (Doctor of Philosophy)*—Applications 2007–2008, 14. Total applicants accepted 2007–2008, 2. Number full-time enrolled (new admits only) 2007–2008, 2. Number part-time enrolled (new admits only) 2007–2008, 0. Openings 2008–2009, 3. The median number of years required for completion of a degree in 2006–2007 were 5. The number of students enrolled full- and part-time who were dismissed or voluntarily withdrew from this program area in 2007–2008 were 0.

Admissions Requirements:

Scores: Entries appear in this order: required test or GPA, minimum score (if required), median score of students entering in 2007–2008. Master's Programs: The above scores are for the terminal MA program in Experimental Psychology. Doctoral Programs: The above scores are for the doctoral (PhD) programs in Clinical, Counseling, and Experimental Psychology. Slight variations in the median scores occur from program to program.

Other Criteria: (importance of criteria rated low, medium, or high): GRE/MAT scores—medium, research experience—high, work experience—medium, extracurricular activity—low, clinically related public service—medium, GPA—medium, letters of recommendation—high, interview—medium, statement of goals and objectives—high, undergraduate major in psychology—low. Work experience for Experimental—low, Counseling—medium, Clinical—high; extracurricular activity for Experimental—low, Counseling—low, Clinical—medium; clinically related public service for Counseling—medium, Clinical—medium; interview for Clinical—medium, Counseling—medium, Experimental—low. For additional information on admission requirements, go to http://www.psychology.ttu.edu.

Student Characteristics: The following represents characteristics of students in 2007–2008 in all graduate psychology programs in the department: Female—full-time 68, part-time 0; Male—full-time 41, part-time 0; African American/Black—full-time 7, part-time 0; Hispanic/Latino(a)—full-time 16, part-time 0; Asian/Pacific Islander—full-time 4, part-time 0; American Indian/Alaska Native—full-time 0, part-time 0; Caucasian/White—full-time 77, part-time 0; Multi-ethnic—full-time 2, part-time 0; students subject to the Americans With Disabilities Act—full-time 1, part-time 0; Unknown ethnicity—full-time 3, part-time 0.

Financial Information/Assistance:

Tuition for Full-Time Study: *Master's:* State residents: per academic year $4,440, $185 per credit hour; Nonstate residents: per academic year $11,040, $460 per credit hour. *Doctoral:* State residents: per academic year $4,440, $185 per credit hour; Nonstate residents: per academic year $11,040, $460 per credit hour. Tuition is subject to change. See the following Web site for updates and changes in tuition costs: http://www.depts.ttu.edu/studentbusinessservices.

Financial Assistance:

First-Year Students: Teaching assistantships available for first year. Average amount paid per academic year: $11,000. Average number of hours worked per week: 20. Tuition remission given: partial. Research assistantships available for first year. Average amount paid per academic year: $11,000. Average number of hours worked per week: 20. Tuition remission given: partial. Fellowships and scholarships available for first year. Average amount paid per academic year: $1,000. Average number of hours worked per week: 0. Tuition remission given: partial.

Advanced Students: Teaching assistantships available for advanced students. Average amount paid per academic year: $12,000. Average number of hours worked per week: 20. Tuition remission given: partial. Research assistantships available for advanced students. Average amount paid per academic year: $12,000. Average number of hours worked per week: 20. Tuition remission given: partial. Fellowships and scholarships available for advanced students. Average amount paid per academic year: $1,000. Average number of hours worked per week: 0. Tuition remission given: partial.

Additional Information: Of all students currently enrolled full time, 90% benefited from one or more of the listed financial assistance programs. Application and information available online at https://www.depts.ttu.edu/psy/psy.php?page=graduate/application/checkapply.

Internships/Practica: Doctoral Degree (PhD Clinical Psychology): For those doctoral students for whom a professional internship was required in this program prior to graduation, (5) students applied for an internship in 2006–2007, with (4) students obtaining an internship. Of those students who obtained an internship, (4) were paid internships. Of those students who obtained an internship, (4) students placed in APA/CPA-accredited internships, (0) students placed in internships not APA/CPA accredited, but listed with the Association of Psychology Postdoctoral and Internship Centers (APPIC), (0) students placed in internships conforming to guidelines of the Council of Directors of School Psychology Programs (CDSPP), (0) students placed in internships that were not APA/CPA-accredited, APPIC or CDSPP listed. Doctoral Degree (PhD Counseling Psychology): For those doctoral students for whom a professional internship was required in this program prior to graduation, (4) students applied for an internship in 2006–2007, with (3) students obtaining an internship. Of those students who obtained an internship, (3) were paid internships. Of those students who obtained an internship, (3) students placed in APA/CPA-accredited internships, (0) students placed in internships not APA/CPA accredited, but listed with the Association of Psychology Postdoctoral and Internship Centers (APPIC), (0) students placed in internships conforming to guidelines of the Council of Directors of School Psychology Programs (CDSPP), (0) students placed in internships that were not APA/CPA-accredited, APPIC or CDSPP listed. Doctoral Degree (PhD Human Factors): For those doctoral students for whom a professional internship was required in this program prior to graduation, (2) students applied for an internship in 2006–2007, with (2) students obtaining an internship. Of those students who obtained an internship, (2) were paid internships. Of those students who obtained an internship, (0) students placed in APA/CPA-accredited internships, (0) students placed in internships not APA/CPA-accredited, but listed with the Association of Psychology Postdoctoral and Internship Centers (APPIC), (0) students placed in internships conforming to guidelines of the Council of Directors of School Psychology Programs (CDSPP), (2) students placed in internships that were not APA/CPA-accredited, APPIC or CDSPP listed. Practica available in our Psychology Clinic and the Texas Tech University Counseling Center. Paid practica are available in the community. Such placements include a psychiatric prison, the pain clinic and Neuropsychiatry Department in the TTU Health Sciences Center, the local school district, a community mental health center, and conducting assessments at the state school and with local psychologists. For additional information on education and training outcomes for our programs, see the following Web site: http://www.psychology.ttu.edu.

Housing and Day Care: On-campus housing is available. Graduate students can live in dormatories. See the following Web site for more information: http://www.hous.ttu.edu/studenthousing/livingoptions.htm. On-campus day care facilities are available. Day care is available through the College of Human Development, TTU, on a limited basis.

Employment of Department Graduates:

Master's Degree Graduates: Of those who graduated in the academic year 2006–2007, the following categories and numbers represent the postgraduate activities and employment of master's degree graduates: Enrolled in a psychology doctoral program (1), enrolled in another graduate/professional program (1), enrolled in a postdoctoral residency/fellowship (n/a), employed in independent practice (n/a), total from the above (master's) (2).

Doctoral Degree Graduates: Of those who graduated in the academic year 2006–2007, the following categories and numbers represent the postgraduate activities and employment of doctoral degree graduates: Enrolled in a psychology doctoral program (n/a), enrolled in a postdoctoral residency/fellowship (3), employed in an academic position at a university (2), employed in an academic position at a 2-year/4-year college (2), employed in other positions at a higher education institution (1), employed in a professional position in a school system (1), employed in government agency (1), employed in a community mental health/counseling center (3), employed in a hospital/medical center (4), other employment position (1), total from the above (doctoral) (18).

Additional Information:

Orientation, Objectives, and Emphasis of Department: The Clinical program adheres to a basic scientist–practitioner model with equal emphasis given to these components of clinical training. The program strives to develop student competencies in the following areas: psychotherapy and other major patterns of psychological treatment, clinical research, psychodiagnostic assessment, psychopathology, personality, and general psychology. The doctoral specialization in counseling psychology is also firmly committed to a concept of balanced scientist–practitioner training and is designed to foster the development of competence in basic psychology, counseling and psychotherapy, psychological assessment, psychological research, and professional ethics. Programs in experimental psychology (cognitive/applied cognitive, social, human factors) encompass a variety of research interests, both basic and applied. Students in these programs are exposed to the data, methods, and theories and a wide variety of basic areas of psychology while at the same time developing a commitment to an area of special interest through research with a faculty mentor. Collaborative work across departmental programs is encouraged, and the department also collaborates with colleagues in management, industrial engineering, neuroscience, neuropsychiatry, and the Health Sciences Center.

Special Facilities or Resources: The department is housed in its own four-story building, which includes a large, well-equipped psychology clinic for practicum training, numerous laboratories equipped for human research activities, and sufficient student workspace and offices. The university maintains constantly expanding computing support systems that can be accessed from computers in the psychology building. The Psychology Department has a number of microcomputers and software available for student use. The university enjoys an unusually good relationship with the local metropolitan community of over 200,000 residents.

Major medical facilities, a private psychiatric hospital, a psychiatric prison and a state school for the developmentally disabled are located within the city, and APA-accredited internship training is available in the University Counseling Center. The cost of living is quite low and the climate is excellent. Texas Tech University (and the Lubbock region) was recently identifed as having the most inexpensive housing market of surveyed university towns in the United States.

Information for Students With Physical Disabilities: See the following Web site for more information: http://www.studentaffairs.ttu.edu/accesstech/.

Application Information:
Send to Texas Tech University, Admissions, Psychology Department, Box 42051, Lubbock, TX 79409-2051. Application available online. URL of online application: https://www.depts.ttu.edu/psy/psy.php?page=graduate/application/checkapply. Students are admitted in the Fall. Deadlines for application: Counseling: January 2, Clinical: January 2, Experimental: February 1. All materials must be received by February 1 for consideration into the University's prestigious Chancellor's Fellowships. Presently, this is an additional $3,000/year for 3 years. *Fee:* $50. There is one application fee required to apply to all Texas State Universities, using the Texas Common Application.

Texas Tech University (2007 data)

Educational Psychology and Leadership/Educational Psychology
College of Education
Box 41071
Lubbock, TX 79409-1071
Telephone: (806) 742-2393
Fax: (806) 742-2179
E-mail: *patsy.mountz@ttu.edu*
Web: *http://www.educ.ttu.edu*

Department Information:
1963. Program Coordinator: Hansel Burley, PhD. Number of faculty: total—full-time 7, part-time 2; women—full-time 3, part-time 1.

Programs and Degrees Offered:
Listed in the following order: Program area, degree type (T if terminal Master's), number awarded 7/06–6/07. Educational Psychology PhD (Doctor of Philosophy) 2.

Student Applications/Admissions:
Student Applications
Educational Psychology PhD (Doctor of Philosophy)—Applications 2007–2008, 10. Total applicants accepted 2007–2008, 9. Number full-time enrolled (new admits only) 2007–2008, 5. Total enrolled 2007–2008 full-time, 20, part-time, 2. Openings 2008–2009, 15. The median number of years required for completion of a degree in 2006–2007 were 4. The number of students enrolled full- and part-time who were dismissed or voluntarily withdrew from this program area in 2007–2008 were 1.

Admissions Requirements:
Scores: Entries appear in this order: required test or GPA, minimum score (if required), median score of students entering in 2007–2008. Master's Programs: GRE-V 400, 400; GRE-Q 400, 400; overall undergraduate GPA 3.00, 3.00; last 2 years GPA 3.00, 3.00. We have a holistic admissions process. The scores provided above are desired scores, but students can still be admitted if other data are excellent. Doctoral Programs: GRE-V 550, 550; GRE-Q 550, 550; overall undergraduate GPA 3.25, 3.25; last 2 years GPA 3.25, 3.25. Our admission's system allows us to include information from these standardized tests, but no weights are assigned because our decision is made based on a holistic method that includes a variety of other material (letters of recommendation, interviews, etc.) that the student is required to submit.
Other Criteria: (importance of criteria rated low, medium, or high): research experience—medium, work experience—high, extracurricular activity—medium, clinically related public service—low, GPA—medium, letters of recommendation—high, interview—medium, statement of goals and objectives—high.

Student Characteristics: The following represents characteristics of students in 2007–2008 in all graduate psychology programs in the department: Female—full-time 12, part-time 1; Male—full-time 8, part-time 1; African American/Black—full-time 3, part-time 0; Hispanic/Latino(a)—full-time 2, part-time 0; Asian/Pacific Islander—full-time 7, part-time 0; American Indian/Alaska Native—full-time 0, part-time 0; Caucasian/White—full-time 8, part-time 2; Multi-ethnic—full-time 0, part-time 0; students subject to the Americans With Disabilities Act—full-time 0, part-time 0; Unknown ethnicity—full-time 0, part-time 0.

Financial Information/Assistance:
Tuition for Full-Time Study: *Master's:* State residents: per academic year $2,976, $124 per credit hour; Nonstate residents: per academic year $9,168, $382 per credit hour. *Doctoral:* State residents: per academic year $2,976, $124 per credit hour; Nonstate residents: per academic year $9,168, $382 per credit hour.

Financial Assistance:
First-Year Students: Teaching assistantships available for first year. Average amount paid per academic year: $9,450. Average number of hours worked per week: 20. Apply by March 15. Tuition remission given: partial. Research assistantships available for first year. Average amount paid per academic year: $9,450. Average number of hours worked per week: 20. Apply by March 15. Tuition remission given: partial. Fellowships and scholarships available for first year. Tuition remission given: partial.
Advanced Students: Teaching assistantships available for advanced students. Average amount paid per academic year: $9,450. Average number of hours worked per week: 20. Apply by March 15. Tuition remission given: partial. Research assistantships available for advanced students. Average amount paid per academic year: $9,450. Average number of hours worked per week: 20. Apply by March 15. Tuition remission given: partial.
Additional Information: Of all students currently enrolled full time, 80% benefited from one or more of the listed financial assistance programs. Application and information available online at http://www.educ.ttu.edu.

Internships/Practica: Our doctoral students typically will be allowed to team teach with faculty who have graduate status. They may also teach an undergraduate course in educational psychology.

Housing and Day Care: On-campus housing is available. See the following Web site for more information: http://www.hous.ttu.edu/HOC/housing_on_campus.asp. On-campus day care facilities are available. See the following Web site for more information: http://www.hs.ttu.edu/cdrc/default.htm.

Employment of Department Graduates:

Master's Degree Graduates: Of those who graduated in the academic year 2006–2007, the following categories and numbers represent the postgraduate activities and employment of master's degree graduates: Enrolled in a postdoctoral residency/fellowship (n/a), employed in independent practice (n/a), employed in an academic position at a university (0), total from the above (master's) (0).

Doctoral Degree Graduates: Of those who graduated in the academic year 2006–2007, the following categories and numbers represent the postgraduate activities and employment of doctoral degree graduates: Enrolled in a psychology doctoral program (n/a), enrolled in a postdoctoral residency/fellowship (1), employed in independent practice (1), employed in an academic position at a university (8), employed in other positions at a higher education institution (1), employed in a professional position in a school system (1), still seeking employment (2), total from the above (doctoral) (14).

Additional Information:

Orientation, Objectives, and Emphasis of Department: The objectives of the Educational Psychology program are to impart the following: (a) understanding of philosophical, historical, cultural, and psychological influences on educational theory; (b) understanding of measurement processes and their relationship to educational theory and practice; (c) understanding of research processes, including the component parts of methodology and statistics and their relationship to educational theory and practice; (d) appreciation for the importance of research in graduate study and professional life; (e) ability to conduct rigorous independent research; (f) ability to add knowledge to instructional programs; and (g) ability to be a critical and reflective thinker. The doctoral program emphasizes a broad concept of professional development that focuses on knowledge of the foundations of education (history, philosophy, cultural); research (research methodology, statistics, measurement); essential areas of knowledge in educational psychology (human development, motivation and learning, etc.); and practice (internships in college teaching, research and program development in schools, individual and collaborative research). Graduates of the doctoral program are prepared to assume roles as college teachers of educational psychology, as research and development specialists in schools, and in service centers, measurement agencies (i.e., ACT and ETS), and other agencies and organizations where the knowledge and skills of educational psychology are required.

Special Facilities or Resources: Our college has a computer lab reserved for graduate students and faculty with laser printers, VAX terminals, MacIntosh and IBM computers, and an array of graphing, word processing, and statistical software. We also have a research lab with equipment and staff to support both quantitative and qualitative research agendas. In addition, travel money is available for students with accepted proposals to professional meetings. All students have free access to their own computer accounts for access to library services, many other databases for research, and the Internet.

Information for Students With Physical Disabilities: See the following Web site for more information: http://www.ttu.edu.

Application Information:

Send to Office of Graduate Admissions, Texas Tech University, P.O. Box 41030, Lubbock, TX 79409-1070; Phone: (806) 742-2787. Application available online. URL of online application: http://www.educ.ttu.edu. Students are admitted in the Fall, application deadline May 1; Spring, application deadline October 1; programs have rolling admissions. Application should be complete at least 3 months prior to the date of intended enrollment. *Fee:* $25. Fee waived or deferred for full-time Texas Tech employees, spouses, and dependents less than 25 years.

Texas Woman's University

Department of Psychology and Philosophy
Arts and Sciences
P.O. Box 425470
Denton, TX 76204
Telephone: (940) 898-2303
Fax: (940) 898-2301
E-mail: *dmiller@mail.twu.edu*
Web: *http://www.twu.edu/as/psyphil/index.htm*

Department Information:

1942. Chairperson: Daniel C. Miller, PhD, ABPP. Number of faculty: total—full-time 14; women—full-time 8; total—minority—full-time 3; women minority—full-time 2.

Programs and Degrees Offered:

Listed in the following order: Program area, degree type (T if terminal Master's), number awarded 7/06–6/07. Counseling Psychology PhD (Doctor of Philosophy) 6, School Psychology PhD (Doctor of Philosophy) 3.

APA Accreditation: Counseling PhD (Doctor of Philosophy).

Student Applications/Admissions:

Student Applications

Counseling Psychology PhD (Doctor of Philosophy)—Applications 2007–2008, 82. Total applicants accepted 2007–2008, 10. Number full-time enrolled (new admits only) 2007–2008, 10. Number part-time enrolled (new admits only) 2007–2008, 0. Openings 2008–2009, 10. The median number of years required for completion of a degree in 2006–2007 were 6. The number of students enrolled full- and part-time who were dismissed or voluntarily withdrew from this program area in 2007–2008 were 2. *School Psychology PhD (Doctor of Philosophy)*—Applications 2007–2008, 25. Total applicants accepted 2007–2008, 8. Number full-time enrolled (new admits only) 2007–2008, 8. Number part-time enrolled (new admits only) 2007–2008, 0. Total enrolled 2007–2008 full-time, 28, part-time, 6. Openings 2008–2009, 8. The median number of years required for completion of a degree in 2006–2007 were

5. The number of students enrolled full- and part-time who were dismissed or voluntarily withdrew from this program area in 2007–2008 were 2.

Admissions Requirements:

Scores: Entries appear in this order: required test or GPA, minimum score (if required), median score of students entering in 2007–2008. Master's Programs: GRE-V 500, 580; GRE-Q 500, 570; overall undergraduate GPA 3.00, 3.50; last 2 years GPA 3.50, 3.60; psychology GPA 3.50, 3.75. Doctoral Programs: GRE-V 500, 585; GRE-Q 500, 585; overall undergraduate GPA 3.0, 3.60; last 2 years GPA 3.5, 3.65; psychology GPA 3.5, 3.70. Counseling Psychology program requires the GRE-Writing Sample.

Other Criteria: (importance of criteria rated low, medium, or high): GRE/MAT scores—medium, research experience—medium, work experience—high, extracurricular activity—medium, clinically related public service—medium, GPA—high, letters of recommendation—high, interview—high, statement of goals and objectives—high, writing skills—high.

Student Characteristics: The following represents characteristics of students in 2007–2008 in all graduate psychology programs in the department: Female—full-time 53, part-time 4; Male—full-time 9, part-time 2; African American/Black—full-time 5, part-time 0; Hispanic/Latino(a)—full-time 7, part-time 0; Asian/Pacific Islander—full-time 8, part-time 1; American Indian/Alaska Native—full-time 0, part-time 0; Caucasian/White—full-time 61, part-time 5; Multi-ethnic—full-time 1, part-time 0; students subject to the Americans With Disabilities Act—full-time 0, part-time 0; Unknown ethnicity—full-time 0, part-time 0; International students who hold an F-1 or J-1 Visa—full-time 1, part-time 0.

Financial Information/Assistance:

Tuition for Full-Time Study: *Master's:* State residents: $464 per credit hour; Nonstate residents: $745 per credit hour. *Doctoral:* State residents: $464 per credit hour; Nonstate residents: $745 per credit hour. Tuition is subject to change. Additional fees are assessed to students beyond the costs of tuition for the following: extra fees including library fee, student union fee, etc. See the following Web site for updates and changes in tuition costs: http://www.twu.edu/o-controller/cashiers/Tuition%20Chart%20FALL-SPRING-SUMIII.htm.

Financial Assistance:

First-Year Students: Teaching assistantships available for first year. Average amount paid per academic year: $11,808. Average number of hours worked per week: 20. Apply by April. Research assistantships available for first year. Apply by varies.

Advanced Students: Teaching assistantships available for advanced students. Average amount paid per academic year: $11,808. Average number of hours worked per week: 20. Apply by April. Research assistantships available for advanced students. Apply by varies.

Additional Information: Of all students currently enrolled full time, 20% benefited from one or more of the listed financial assistance programs. Application and information available online at http://www.twu.edu/admissions/graduate.

Internships/Practica: Doctoral Degree (PhD Counseling Psychology): For those doctoral students for whom a professional internship was required in this program prior to graduation, (3) students applied for an internship in 2006–2007, with (2) students obtaining an internship. Of those students who obtained an internship, (2) were paid internships. Of those students who obtained an internship, (2) students placed in APA/CPA-accredited internships, (0) students placed in internships not APA/CPA-accredited, but listed with the Association of Psychology Postdoctoral and Internship Centers (APPIC), (0) students placed in internships conforming to guidelines of the Council of Directors of School Psychology Programs (CDSPP), (0) students placed in internships that were not APA/CPA-accredited, APPIC or CDSPP listed. Doctoral Degree (PhD School Psychology): For those doctoral students for whom a professional internship was required in this program prior to graduation, (5) students applied for an internship in 2006–2007, with (5) students obtaining an internship. Of those students who obtained an internship, (5) were paid internships. Of those students who obtained an internship, (3) students placed in APA/CPA-accredited internships, (0) students placed in internships not APA/CPA-accredited, but listed with the Association of Psychology Postdoctoral and Internship Centers (APPIC), (0) students placed in internships conforming to guidelines of the Council of Directors of School Psychology Programs (CDSPP), (2) students placed in internships that were not APA/CPA-accredited, APPIC or CDSPP listed. There are numerous placements in the Dallas–Fort Worth metropolitan area. Doctoral students are expected to use the APPIC Directory for internship placement.

Housing and Day Care: On-campus housing is available. Contact University Housing, (940) 898-3676. No on-campus day care facilities are available.

Employment of Department Graduates:

Master's Degree Graduates: Of those who graduated in the academic year 2006–2007, the following categories and numbers represent the postgraduate activities and employment of master's degree graduates: Enrolled in a psychology doctoral program (6), enrolled in a postdoctoral residency/fellowship (n/a), employed in independent practice (n/a), employed in a professional position in a school system (10), total from the above (master's) (16).

Doctoral Degree Graduates: Of those who graduated in the academic year 2006–2007, the following categories and numbers represent the postgraduate activities and employment of doctoral degree graduates: Enrolled in a psychology doctoral program (n/a), enrolled in a postdoctoral residency/fellowship (3), employed in a professional position in a school system (3), employed in business or industry (1), employed in a community mental health/counseling center (3), employed in a hospital/medical center (1), total from the above (doctoral) (11).

Additional Information:

Orientation, Objectives, and Emphasis of Department: Both the APA-accredited Counseling Psychology doctoral program and the Counseling Psychology master's program prepare students in the practitioner–scientist model for counseling practice with particular emphasis on family systems, gender issues, assessment, and psychotherapeutic work with individuals and families in their contextual systems. The model provides clear training in both practice and science, but emphasizes practice, practice that is informed by science. The programs' philosophy, curricula, faculty, and students, situated within the unique context of the TWU mission, attempt to create an atmosphere that is supportive, open, and flexible. Graduate training in school psychology at the master's level provides a program emphasizing direct service to school settings. Specific competencies and areas of specialization stressed in coursework and field-based training include child development, psychopathology, theories and principles of learning, behavioral intervention and prevention strategies, diagnostic assessment, and evaluation techniques. Doctoral-level training in school psychology focuses on applied preparation and training experiences in professional school psychology. This program prepares students in skills required in direct-to-client services (for example, diagnostic assessment and evaluation skills, therapeutic and intervention techniques, and competencies in the application of learning principles). This program also provides training and supervised experiences in the consultation model, emphasizing such competencies as systems and organizational analysis, supervision of programs and services, diagnostic team leadership, grant proposal writing, in-service education, and general coordination of school-based services in a consultative capacity.

Special Facilities or Resources: The University Counseling Center is an APA-approved internship site.

Information for Students With Physical Disabilities: See the following Web site for more information: http://www.twu.edu/dss/.

Application Information:

Send to Admissions Coordinator, Department of Psychology and Philosophy, Texas Woman's University, P.O. Box 425470, Denton, TX 76204-5470. Application available online. URL of online application: http://www.twu.edu/admissions/apply.htm. Students are admitted in the Fall, application deadline February 1. March 1 for MA counseling psychology program. December 15 for PhD Counseling Program. *Fee:* $30.

Texas, University of, Arlington

Department of Psychology
College of Science
Department of Psychology, UTA Box 19528
Arlington, TX 76019-0528
Telephone: (817) 272-2281
Fax: (817) 272-2364
E-mail: *gatchel@uta.edu*
Web: *http://www.uta.edu/psychology*

Department Information:

1959. Chairperson: Robert J. Gatchel. Number of faculty: total—full-time 20, part-time 1; women—full-time 6, part-time 1; total—minority—full-time 3; women minority—full-time 2.

Programs and Degrees Offered:

Listed in the following order: Program area, degree type (T if terminal Master's), number awarded 7/06–6/07. Experimental General PhD (Doctor of Philosophy) 13, Industrial/Organizational PhD (Doctor of Philosophy) 1, Health General PhD (Doctor of Philosophy) 0.

Student Applications/Admissions:

Student Applications

Experimental General PhD (Doctor of Philosophy)—Applications 2007–2008, 26. Total applicants accepted 2007–2008, 3. Number full-time enrolled (new admits only) 2007–2008, 3. Number part-time enrolled (new admits only) 2007–2008, 0. Openings 2008–2009, 7. The median number of years required for completion of a degree in 2006–2007 were 6. The number of students enrolled full- and part-time who were dismissed or voluntarily withdrew from this program area in 2007–2008 were 2. *Industrial/Organizational PhD (Doctor of Philosophy)*—Applications 2007–2008, 33. Total applicants accepted 2007–2008, 2. Number full-time enrolled (new admits only) 2007–2008, 2. Number part-time enrolled (new admits only) 2007–2008, 0. Openings 2008–2009, 5. The median number of years required for completion of a degree in 2006–2007 were 2. The number of students enrolled full- and part-time who were dismissed or voluntarily withdrew from this program area in 2007–2008 were 1. *Health General PhD (Doctor of Philosophy)*—Applications 2007–2008, 9. Total applicants accepted 2007–2008, 8. Number full-time enrolled (new admits only) 2007–2008, 8. Number part-time enrolled (new admits only) 2007–2008, 0. Openings 2008–2009, 7. The number of students enrolled full- and part-time who were dismissed or voluntarily withdrew from this program area in 2007–2008 were 0.

Admissions Requirements:

Scores: Entries appear in this order: required test or GPA, minimum score (if required), median score of students entering in 2007–2008. Master's Programs: GRE-V no minimum stated, 500; GRE-Q no minimum stated, 561; overall undergraduate GPA 3.0, 3.5; Master's GRE-Analytical no minimum stated, 4.4. Doctoral Programs: GRE-V no minimum stated, 500; GRE-Q no minimum stated, 616; overall undergraduate GPA 3.0, 3.9; Doctoral program GRE-Analytic no minimum stated, 4.3.

Other Criteria: (importance of criteria rated low, medium, or high): GRE/MAT scores—medium, research experience—high, extracurricular activity—low, clinically related public service—low, GPA—medium, letters of recommendation—high, statement of goals and objectives—high, undergraduate major in psychology—low, specific undergraduate psychology courses taken—medium. For additional information on admission requirements, go to http://www.uta.edu/psychology.

Student Characteristics: The following represents characteristics of students in 2007–2008 in all graduate psychology programs in the department: Female—full-time 47, part-time 0; Male—full-time 17, part-time 0; African American/Black—full-time 3, part-time 0; Hispanic/Latino(a)—full-time 6, part-time 0; Asian/Pacific Islander—full-time 0, part-time 0; American Indian/Alaska Native—full-time 0, part-time 0; Caucasian/White—full-time 47, part-time 0; Multi-ethnic—full-time 8, part-time 0; students subject to the Americans With Disabilities Act—full-time 0, part-time 0; Unknown ethnicity—full-time 0, part-time 0; International students who hold an F-1 or J-1 Visa—full-time 8, part-time 0.

Financial Information/Assistance:

Tuition for Full-Time Study: *Master's:* State residents: per academic year $5,528, $307 per credit hour; Nonstate residents: per academic year $10,478, $582 per credit hour. *Doctoral:* State residents: per academic year $5,528, $307 per credit hour; Nonstate residents: per academic year $10,478, $582 per credit hour. Tuition is subject to change. See the following Web site for updates and changes in tuition costs: http://www.policy.uta.edu/UtaSfs/Application?cmd=feedescr.

Financial Assistance:

First-Year Students: Teaching assistantships available for first year. Average amount paid per academic year: $15,000. Average number of hours worked per week: 20. Tuition remission given: partial. Research assistantships available for first year. Average amount paid per academic year: $15,000. Average number of hours worked per week: 20. Tuition remission given: partial.

Advanced Students: Teaching assistantships available for advanced students. Average amount paid per academic year: $17,400. Average number of hours worked per week: 20. Tuition remission given: partial. Research assistantships available for advanced students. Average amount paid per academic year: $17,400. Average number of hours worked per week: 20. Tuition remission given: partial.

Additional Information: Of all students currently enrolled full time, 75% benefited from one or more of the listed financial assistance programs.

Internships/Practica: Master's Degree (PhD Industrial/Organizational): An internship experience such as a final research project or "capstone" experience is required of graduates. The Arlington–Dallas–Fort Worth area is a major center of business and industrial growth in Texas and offers diverse practical opportunities in consulting firms, corporations, government and private agencies, as well as health and health care agencies, social agencies, and the like.

Housing and Day Care: On-campus housing is available. See the following Web site for more information: See http://www2.uta.edu/housing/ for information about local housing. No on-campus day care facilities are available.

Employment of Department Graduates:

Master's Degree Graduates: Of those who graduated in the academic year 2006–2007, the following categories and numbers represent the postgraduate activities and employment of master's degree graduates: Enrolled in a psychology doctoral program (7), enrolled in another graduate/professional program (1), enrolled in a postdoctoral residency/fellowship (n/a), employed in independent practice (n/a), employed in an academic position at a university (0), employed in an academic position at a 2-year/4-year college (1), employed in other positions at a higher education institution (0), employed in a professional position in a school system (0), employed in business or industry (1), employed in government agency (0), employed in a community mental health/counseling center (0), employed in a hospital/medical center (0), still seeking employment (0), not seeking employment (0), other employment position (0), do not know (0), total from the above (master's) (10).

Doctoral Degree Graduates: Of those who graduated in the academic year 2006–2007, the following categories and numbers represent the postgraduate activities and employment of doctoral degree graduates: Enrolled in a psychology doctoral program (n/a), enrolled in another graduate/professional program (0), enrolled in a postdoctoral residency/fellowship (0), employed in independent practice (0), employed in an academic position at a university (1), employed in an academic position at a 2-year/4-year college (0), employed in other positions at a higher education institution (0), employed in a professional position in a school system (0), employed in business or industry (1), employed in government agency (0), employed in a community mental health/counseling center (0), employed in a hospital/medical center (1), still seeking employment (0), not seeking employment (1), other employment position (0), do not know (0), total from the above (doctoral) (4).

Additional Information:

Orientation, Objectives, and Emphasis of Department: The objective of graduate work in psychology is to educate the student in the methods and basic content of the discipline and to provide an apprenticeship in the execution of creative research in laboratory and/or field settings. The graduate programs provide comprehensive interdisciplinary training in Experimental Psychology, Health Psychology, and Industrial/Organizational Psychology. All students in the graduate program are broadly trained in statistical and experimental design. The concentration in Experimental Psychology is designed to form a basis for the doctoral program but is open to those seeking a terminal master's degree. The Experimental program trains students to be research scientists in areas of interest that include animal behavior, animal learning, cognitive, developmental, evolutionary, neuroscience, quantitative, and social/personality psychology. The concentration in Health Psychology is designed to train researchers in health and behavior, working at the cutting edge of interdisciplinary, biomedical, and biobehavioral investigation in areas such as pain, stress, psychoimmunology, cancer, and aging. The Master's of Science in Industrial/Organizational Psychology combines rigorous course work in experimental design, quantitative methods, and management with practicum experience enabling students to perform effectively in the workplace.

Personal Behavior Statement: Statement of Ethics, Professionalism, and Conduct found on page 27 in the Psychology Graduate Student Handbook http://www.uta.edu/psychology/grad_students/GraduateHandbook2007.pdf.

Special Facilities or Resources: Each faculty member who is active in research in the Psychology Department is fortunate to have ample space. The department has approximately 18,000 total square feet of research space; 7,000 square feet for human subject research and 11,000 square feet for animal research. Graduate students work in faculty labs and use their research facilities. The department is able to utilize modern audiovisual technology in the classroom and is equipped with computer facilities for graduate research. Graduate students have in-office network connections as well as computer access in research laboratories and departmental computer labs. In addition to the departmental computer labs, the university academic computing services operate seven on-campus computing facilities and serves the academic and research needs of the university. The University Libraries include the Central Library, the Architecture and Fine Arts Library, and the Science and Engineering Library. Library resources include a full array of modern technological access to print electronic information, Internet access, and an extensive interlibrary loan network in addition to the 2,430,000 books, periodicals, documents, technical reports, on hand.

Information for Students With Physical Disabilities: See the following Web site for more information: http://www.uta.edu/disability/.

Application Information:
Send to Department of Psychology, Box 19528, The University of Texas at Arlington, Arlington, TX 76019-0528. Application available online. URL of online application: https://www.applytexas.org/adappc/gen/c_start.WBX. Students are admitted in the Fall, application deadline February 1; Spring, application deadline October 17; programs have rolling admissions. These deadlines are for U.S. student applications. International student application deadlines are in April and September. Please review http://grad.uta.edu/leftmenupages/admissions_deadlines.asp. *Fee:* $30. Application fee for international students is $60.

Texas, University of, Austin

Department of Educational Psychology
College of Education
1 University Station, D5800
Austin, TX 78712-1296
Telephone: (512) 471-4155
Fax: (512) 471-1288
E-mail: *emmer@mail.utexas.edu*
Web: *http://www.edpsych.edb.utexas.edu*

Department Information:
1923. Chairperson: Edmund T. Emmer. Number of faculty: total—full-time 29, part-time 13; women—full-time 16, part-time 7; total—minority—full-time 4, part-time 2; women minority—full-time 1, part-time 2; faculty subject to the Americans With Disabilities Act 1.

Programs and Degrees Offered:
Listed in the following order: Program area, degree type (T if terminal Master's), number awarded 7/06–6/07. Counseling Psychology PhD (Doctor of Philosophy) 11, Counselor Education (Med) Other 13, Human Development and Education PhD (Doctor of Philosophy) 5, Learning, Cognition, and Instruction PhD (Doctor of Philosophy) 3, Quantitative Methods PhD (Doctor of Philosophy) 2, School Psychology PhD (Doctor of Philosophy) 12, Academic Educational Psychology (Med) Other 5, Academic Educational Psychology MA/MS (Master of Arts/Science) (T) 3.

APA Accreditation: Counseling PhD (Doctor of Philosophy). School PhD (Doctor of Philosophy).

Student Applications/Admissions:
Student Applications
Counseling Psychology PhD (Doctor of Philosophy)—Applications 2007–2008, 153. Total applicants accepted 2007–2008, 16. Number full-time enrolled (new admits only) 2007–2008, 9. Number part-time enrolled (new admits only) 2007–2008, 0. Total enrolled 2007–2008 full-time, 42, part-time, 17. Openings 2008–2009, 12. The median number of years required for completion of a degree in 2006–2007 were 7. The number of students enrolled full- and part-time who were dismissed or voluntarily withdrew from this program area in 2007–2008 were 2. *Counselor Education (Med) Other*—Applications 2007–2008, 49. Total applicants accepted 2007–2008, 26. Number full-time enrolled (new admits only) 2007–2008, 12. Number part-time enrolled (new admits only) 2007–2008, 1. Total enrolled 2007–2008 full-time, 21, part-time, 6. Openings 2008–2009, 20. The median number of years required for completion of a degree in 2006–2007 were 2. The number of students enrolled full- and part-time who were dismissed or voluntarily withdrew from this program area in 2007–2008 were 2. *Human Development and Education PhD (Doctor of Philosophy)*—Applications 2007–2008, 16. Total applicants accepted 2007–2008, 8. Number full-time enrolled (new admits only) 2007–2008, 3. Number part-time enrolled (new admits only) 2007–2008, 0. Total enrolled 2007–2008 full-time, 14, part-time, 4. Openings 2008–2009, 6. The median number of years required for completion of a degree in 2006–2007 were 6. The number of students enrolled full- and part-time who were dismissed or voluntarily withdrew from this program area in 2007–2008 were 0. *Learning, Cognition, and Instruction PhD (Doctor of Philosophy)*—Applications 2007–2008, 11. Total applicants accepted 2007–2008, 10. Number full-time enrolled (new admits only) 2007–2008, 5. Number part-time enrolled (new admits only) 2007–2008, 0. Total enrolled 2007–2008 full-time, 32, part-time, 6. Openings 2008–2009, 6. The median number of years required for completion of a degree in 2006–2007 were 5. The number of students enrolled full- and part-time who were dismissed or voluntarily withdrew from this program area in 2007–2008 were 0. *Quantitative Methods PhD (Doctor of Philosophy)*—Applications 2007–2008, 25. Total applicants accepted 2007–2008, 20. Number full-time enrolled (new admits only) 2007–2008, 5. Number part-time enrolled (new admits only) 2007–2008, 0. Total enrolled 2007–2008 full-time, 18, part-time, 10. Openings 2008–2009, 6. The median number of years required for completion of a degree in 2006–2007 were 4. The number of students enrolled full- and part-time who were dismissed or voluntarily withdrew from this program area in 2007–2008 were 2. *School Psychology PhD (Doctor of Philosophy)*—Applications 2007–2008, 53. Total applicants accepted 2007–2008, 22. Number full-time enrolled (new admits only) 2007–2008, 12. Number part-time enrolled (new admits only) 2007–2008, 0. Total enrolled 2007–2008 full-time, 51, part-time, 14. Openings 2008–2009, 12. The median number of years required for completion of a degree in 2006–2007 were 6. The number of students enrolled full- and part-time who were dismissed or voluntarily withdrew from this program area in 2007–2008 were 1. *Academic Educational Psychology (Med) Other*—Applications 2007–2008, 10. Total applicants accepted 2007–2008, 5. Number full-time enrolled (new admits only) 2007–2008, 3. Number part-time enrolled (new admits only) 2007–2008, 1. Total enrolled 2007–2008 full-time, 7, part-time, 4. Openings 2008–2009, 5. The median number of years required for completion of a degree in 2006–2007 were 2. The number of students enrolled full- and part-time who were dismissed or voluntarily withdrew from this program area in 2007–2008 were 0. *Academic Educational Psychology MA/MS (Master of Arts/Science)*—Applications 2007–2008, 19. Total applicants accepted 2007–2008, 9. Number full-time enrolled (new admits only) 2007–2008, 5. Number part-time enrolled (new admits only) 2007–2008, 1. Total enrolled 2007–2008 full-time, 6, part-time, 4. Openings 2008–2009, 5. The median number of years required for completion of a degree in 2006–2007 were 2. The number of students enrolled full- and part-time who were dismissed or voluntarily withdrew from this program area in 2007–2008 were 2.

Admissions Requirements:

Scores: Entries appear in this order: required test or GPA, minimum score (if required), median score of students entering in 2007–2008. Master's Programs: GRE-V no minimum stated, 510; GRE-Q no minimum stated, 630. The median upper-division and graduate coursework GPA was 3.73. Doctoral Programs: GRE-V no minimum stated, 610; GRE-Q no minimum stated, 625.

Other Criteria: (importance of criteria rated low, medium, or high): GRE/MAT scores—high, research experience—medium, work experience—medium, extracurricular activity—medium, clinically related public service—medium, GPA—high, letters of recommendation—high, interview—medium, statement of goals and objectives—high. Different areas may consider criteria somewhat differently upon occasion. For additional information on admission requirements, go to http://edpsych.edb.utexas.edu.

Student Characteristics: The following represents characteristics of students in 2007–2008 in all graduate psychology programs in the department: Female—full-time 130, part-time 49; Male—full-time 61, part-time 16; African American/Black—full-time 5, part-time 3; Hispanic/Latino(a)—full-time 26, part-time 8; Asian/Pacific Islander—full-time 36, part-time 15; American Indian/Alaska Native—full-time 1, part-time 0; Caucasian/White—full-time 123, part-time 39; Multi-ethnic—full-time 0, part-time 0; students subject to the Americans With Disabilities Act—full-time 1, part-time 0; Unknown ethnicity—full-time 0, part-time 0; International students who hold an F-1 or J-1 Visa—full-time 22, part-time 11.

Financial Information/Assistance:

Tuition for Full-Time Study: *Master's:* State residents: $334 per credit hour; Nonstate residents: $704 per credit hour. *Doctoral:* State residents: $334 per credit hour; Nonstate residents: $704 per credit hour. Tuition is subject to change. Tuition costs vary by program. See the following Web site for updates and changes in tuition costs: http://www.utexas.edu/business/accounting/pubs/tf_gradsem.pdf.

Financial Assistance:

First-Year Students: Teaching assistantships available for first year. Average amount paid per academic year: $12,475. Average number of hours worked per week: 20. Apply by April 1. Tuition remission given: partial. Fellowships and scholarships available for first year. Average amount paid per academic year: $1,000. Average number of hours worked per week: 0. Apply by December 1.

Advanced Students: Teaching assistantships available for advanced students. Average amount paid per academic year: $12,475. Average number of hours worked per week: 20. Apply by April 1. Tuition remission given: partial. Research assistantships available for advanced students. Average amount paid per academic year: $10,872. Average number of hours worked per week: 20. Apply by April 1. Tuition remission given: partial. Fellowships and scholarships available for advanced students. Average amount paid per academic year: $1,000. Average number of hours worked per week: 0. Apply by December 1.

Additional Information: Of all students currently enrolled full time, 40% benefited from one or more of the listed financial assistance programs. Application and information available online at http://edpsych.edb.utexas.edu/admissions.

Internships/Practica: Master's Degree (MA/MS Academic Educational Psychology (MA)): An internship experience such as a final research project or "capstone" experience is required of graduates. Doctoral Degree (PhD Counseling Psychology): For those doctoral students for whom a professional internship was required in this program prior to graduation, (11) students applied for an internship in 2006–2007, with (11) students obtaining an internship. Of those students who obtained an internship, (11) were paid internships. Of those students who obtained an internship, (11) students placed in APA/CPA-accredited internships, (0) students placed in internships not APA/CPA-accredited, but listed with the Association of Psychology Postdoctoral and Internship Centers (APPIC), (0) students placed in internships conforming to guidelines of the Council of Directors of School Psychology Programs (CDSPP), (0) students placed in internships that were not APA/CPA-accredited, APPIC or CDSPP listed. Doctoral Degree (PhD School Psychology): For those doctoral students for whom a professional internship was required in this program prior to graduation, (11) students applied for an internship in 2006–2007, with (11) students obtaining an internship. Of those students who obtained an internship, (11) were paid internships. Of those students who obtained an internship, (9) students placed in APA/CPA-accredited internships, (0) students placed in internships not APA/CPA-accredited, but listed with the Association of Psychology Postdoctoral and Internship Centers (APPIC), (2) students placed in internships conforming to guidelines of the Council of Directors of School Psychology Programs (CDSPP), (0) students placed in internships that were not APA/CPA-accredited, APPIC or CDSPP listed. In the Counseling Psychology program, internships are generally available in APA-approved counseling and mental health centers, other university counseling centers, and community and hospital settings that provide in-depth supervision. In the School Psychology program, internship sites are often in APA-approved, school systems, and hospital and community settings that have an educational component. Other programs coordinate a variety of practicum settings to provide both research and applied experiences.

Housing and Day Care: On-campus housing is available. See the following Web site for more information: http://www.utexas.edu/student/housing. On-campus day care facilities are available. See the following Web site for more information: http://www.utexas.edu/services/childcare.

Employment of Department Graduates:

Master's Degree Graduates: Of those who graduated in the academic year 2006–2007, the following categories and numbers represent the postgraduate activities and employment of master's degree graduates: Enrolled in a psychology doctoral program (0), enrolled in another graduate/professional program (0), enrolled in a postdoctoral residency/fellowship (n/a), employed in independent practice (n/a), employed in an academic position at a university (1), employed in an academic position at a 2-year/4-year college (0), employed in other positions at a higher education institution (2), employed in a professional position in a school system (6), employed in business or industry (0), employed in government agency (1), employed in a community mental health/counseling center (1), employed in a hospital/medical center (0), still seeking employment (3), other employment position (0), do not know (7), total from the above (master's) (21).

Doctoral Degree Graduates: Of those who graduated in the academic year 2006–2007, the following categories and numbers

represent the postgraduate activities and employment of doctoral degree graduates: Enrolled in a psychology doctoral program (n/a), enrolled in another graduate/professional program (0), enrolled in a postdoctoral residency/fellowship (10), employed in independent practice (2), employed in an academic position at a university (3), employed in an academic position at a 2-year/4-year college (1), employed in other positions at a higher education institution (3), employed in a professional position in a school system (1), employed in business or industry (4), employed in government agency (1), employed in a community mental health/counseling center (2), employed in a hospital/medical center (1), still seeking employment (2), other employment position (3), do not know (0), total from the above (doctoral) (33).

Additional Information:

Orientation, Objectives, and Emphasis of Department: Training in educational psychology relates human behavior to the educational process as it occurs in the home, in peer groups, in nursery school through graduate school, in business and industry, in the military, in institutions for persons with physical or mental disabilities, and in a myriad of other settings. In so doing, it includes study in the following areas: the biological bases of behavior; history and systems of psychology and of education; the psychology of learning, motivation, cognition, and instruction; developmental, social, and personality psychology; psychological and educational measurement, statistics, evaluation, and research methodology; the professional areas of school psychology and counseling psychology; and general academic educational psychology.

Special Facilities or Resources: The University of Texas at Austin has the fifth largest academic library in the United States and also provides online access to hundreds of electronic databases. Our department also has access, through our college's Learning Technology Center, to several microcomputer and multimedia laboratories, technical assistance, resource materials, and audiovisual equipment and services. Academic computing facilities are extensive, ranging from mainframes to microcomputers. Additional resources include several university-wide centers with which our faculty are associated, including UT's Counseling and Mental Health Center.

Information for Students With Physical Disabilities: See the following Web site for more information: http://www.utexas.edu/depts/dos/ssd.

Application Information:

Send official transcripts and GRE scores to GIAC, UT-Austin, P.O. Box 7608, Austin, TX 78713-7608. Send letters of recommendation and personal statement to Graduate Adviser Educational Psychology, 1 University Station, D5800 Austin, TX 78712-1296. Application available online. URL of online application: http://www.utexas.edu/student/admissions/grad. Students are admitted in the Fall, application deadline see below; Summer, application deadline March 1. The deadline for Counseling Psychology and School Psychology is December 1. The priority deadline for other PhD areas is February 1. PhD applicants are admitted for the Fall semester only. The priority deadline for the master's areas is March 1 for Summer and Fall. *Fee:* $50. Fee may be waived, at the discretion of Graduate Admissions, in cases of demonstrated financial need.

Texas, University of, Austin (2007 data)

Department of Human Ecology, Division of Human Development and Family Sciences
Natural Science
Department of Human Ecology, 1 University Station A2700
Austin, TX 78712-0141
Telephone: (512) 475-8800
Fax: (512) 475-8662
E-mail: *surra@mail.utexas.edu*
Web: *http://www.he.utexas.edu/hdfs/hdfsgrad.php*

Department Information:

1910. Chairperson: Catherine Surra, PhD. Number of faculty: total—full-time 13; women—full-time 9.

Programs and Degrees Offered:

Listed in the following order: Program area, degree type (T if terminal Master's), number awarded 7/06–6/07. Human Development and Family Sciences PhD (Doctor of Philosophy) 5.

Student Applications/Admissions:

Student Applications

Human Development and Family Sciences PhD (Doctor of Philosophy)—Applications 2007–2008, 32. Total applicants accepted 2007–2008, 9. Number full-time enrolled (new admits only) 2007–2008, 6. Openings 2008–2009, 8. The median number of years required for completion of a degree in 2006–2007 were 5. The number of students enrolled full- and part-time who were dismissed or voluntarily withdrew from this program area in 2007–2008 were 0.

Admissions Requirements:

Scores: Entries appear in this order: required test or GPA, minimum score (if required), median score of students entering in 2007–2008. Master's Programs: GRE-V no minimum stated, 590; GRE-Q no minimum stated, 630; overall undergraduate GPA no minimum stated; last 2 years GPA no minimum stated. Doctoral Programs: GRE-V no minimum stated, 590; GRE-Q no minimum stated, 630; overall undergraduate GPA no minimum stated; last 2 years GPA no minimum stated.

Other Criteria: (importance of criteria rated low, medium, or high): GRE/MAT scores—medium, research experience—high, work experience—low, extracurricular activity—low, clinically related public service—low, GPA—medium, letters of recommendation—high, statement of goals and objectives—high.

Student Characteristics: The following represents characteristics of students in 2007–2008 in all graduate psychology programs in the department: Female—full-time 30, part-time 0; Male—full-time 6, part-time 0; African American/Black—full-time 1, part-time 0; Hispanic/Latino(a)—full-time 0, part-time 0; Asian/Pacific Islander—full-time 6, part-time 0; American Indian/Alaska Native—full-time 0, part-time 0; Caucasian/White—full-time 29, part-time 0; students subject to the Americans With Disabilities Act—full-time 0, part-time 0; Unknown ethnicity—full-time 0, part-time 0.

Financial Information/Assistance:

Tuition for Full-Time Study: *Master's:* State residents: per academic year $2,781; Nonstate residents: per academic year $5,898. *Doctoral:* State residents: per academic year $2,781; Nonstate residents: per academic year $5,898. Tuition is subject to change. See the following Web site for updates and changes in tuition costs: http://www.utexas.edu/student/admissions/gradus/usgradcost.html.

Financial Assistance:

First-Year Students: Teaching assistantships available for first year. Average amount paid per academic year: $15,600. Average number of hours worked per week: 20. Apply by January 15. Tuition remission given: full. Research assistantships available for first year. Average amount paid per academic year: $15,600. Average number of hours worked per week: 20. Apply by January 15. Tuition remission given: full. Fellowships and scholarships available for first year. Average amount paid per academic year: $15,600. Apply by January 15. Tuition remission given: full.

Advanced Students: Teaching assistantships available for advanced students. Average amount paid per academic year: $16,140. Average number of hours worked per week: 20. Apply by January 15. Tuition remission given: full. Research assistantships available for advanced students. Average amount paid per academic year: $16,140. Average number of hours worked per week: 20. Apply by January 15. Tuition remission given: full. Fellowships and scholarships available for advanced students. Average amount paid per academic year: $16,000. Apply by January 15. Tuition remission given: full.

Additional Information: Of all students currently enrolled full time, 92% benefited from one or more of the listed financial assistance programs.

Internships/Practica: A variety of practicum experiences may be arranged to meet students' individual needs.

Housing and Day Care: On-campus housing is available. See the following Web site for more information: http://www.utexas.edu/student/housing/. On-campus day care facilities are available. See the following Web site for more information: http://www.utexas.edu/services/childcare/.

Employment of Department Graduates:

Master's Degree Graduates: Of those who graduated in the academic year 2006–2007, the following categories and numbers represent the postgraduate activities and employment of master's degree graduates: Enrolled in a postdoctoral residency/fellowship (n/a), employed in independent practice (n/a), total from the above (master's) (0).

Doctoral Degree Graduates: Of those who graduated in the academic year 2006–2007, the following categories and numbers represent the postgraduate activities and employment of doctoral degree graduates: Enrolled in a psychology doctoral program (n/a), enrolled in a postdoctoral residency/fellowship (1), employed in an academic position at a university (2), employed in business or industry (2), total from the above (doctoral) (5).

Additional Information:

Orientation, Objectives, and Emphasis of Department: The program leading to the PhD in Human Development and Family Sciences is designed to prepare individuals for research, teaching, and administrative positions in colleges and universities and for positions in research, government, and other public and private settings. The focus of the program is research concerning the interplay between individual development and family relationships. Development of the individual is considered within the context of the family, peer group, community, and culture. The family is studied as a system of relationships, with attention given to roles, communication, conflict resolution and negotiation, socialization, and family members' perceptions and emotions during interactions with one another. The program emphasizes the investigation of the family and other social processes that contribute to competence and optimal development in individuals from birth to maturity and on how such competencies, once developed, are reflected in interpersonal relationships and family interactions. The MA program in Human Development and Family Sciences is designed to deepen the student's knowledge of normal development within the context of the family, peer group, community, and culture, and to develop the student's skill in generating new knowledge in the field through basic or applied research.

Special Facilities or Resources: The graduate program is housed in the Sarah and Charles Seay building, supporting wireless Internet service with access to the university's extensive library collection and statistical software packages, and a computer lab reserved for graduate student research. The Seay building contains a number of facilities for data collection, including five rooms in which children, couples, or families can be observed unobtrusively behind a one-way mirror in an observation booth. Students in the program may become involved in the university child and family laboratory, a laboratory preschool with about 80 3- to 5-year-old children enrolled each semester. The school contains research rooms and observation facilities. In addition to the departmental resources, the multicultural population of Austin constitutes a rich resource for both research and practicum experiences. The library, computation center, and support services of the University of Texas at Austin are among the best in the nation. Free services available to students include the Learning Skills Center, Career Choice Information Center, and Counseling Center.

Information for Students With Physical Disabilities: See the following Web site for more information: http://www.deanofstudents.utexas.edu/ssd/index.php.

Application Information:

Send to Graduate Coordinator, Human Development and Family Sciences, The University of Texas at Austin, Department of Human Ecology, 1 University Station, A2700 Seay Building, Room 2.412 Austin, TX 78712-0141. Application available online. URL of online application: http://www.utexas.edu/student/admissions/grad/. Students are admitted in the Fall, application deadline December 15. *Fee:* $50.

Texas, University of, Austin

Department of Psychology
College of Liberal Arts
1 University Station A8000
Austin, TX 78712
Telephone: (512) 471-6398
Fax: (512) 471-5935
E-mail: *mazzucco@psy.utexas.edu*
Web: *http://www.psy.utexas.edu*

Department Information:

1910. Chairperson: James Pennebaker. Number of faculty: total—full-time 55, part-time 8; women—full-time 16, part-time 7; total—minority—full-time 4, part-time 1; women minority—full-time 1.

Programs and Degrees Offered:

Listed in the following order: Program area, degree type (T if terminal Master's), number awarded 7/06–6/07. Behavioral Neuroscience PhD (Doctor of Philosophy) 0, Clinical PhD (Doctor of Philosophy) 1, Cognition and Perception PhD (Doctor of Philosophy) 2, Developmental PhD (Doctor of Philosophy) 4, Individual Differences and Evolutionary Psychology PhD (Doctor of Philosophy) 4, Sensory Neuroscience PhD (Doctor of Philosophy) 0, Social and Personality PhD (Doctor of Philosophy) 3.

APA Accreditation: Clinical PhD (Doctor of Philosophy).

Student Applications/Admissions:

Student Applications

Behavioral Neuroscience PhD (Doctor of Philosophy)—Applications 2007–2008, 30. Total applicants accepted 2007–2008, 1. Number full-time enrolled (new admits only) 2007–2008, 1. Openings 2008–2009, 2. The median number of years required for completion of a degree in 2006–2007 were 7. The number of students enrolled full- and part-time who were dismissed or voluntarily withdrew from this program area in 2007–2008 were 0. *Clinical PhD (Doctor of Philosophy)*—Applications 2007–2008, 277. Total applicants accepted 2007–2008, 8. Number full-time enrolled (new admits only) 2007–2008, 5. Openings 2008–2009, 5. The median number of years required for completion of a degree in 2006–2007 were 7. The number of students enrolled full- and part-time who were dismissed or voluntarily withdrew from this program area in 2007–2008 were 1. *Cognition and Perception PhD (Doctor of Philosophy)*—Applications 2007–2008, 36. Total applicants accepted 2007–2008, 3. Number full-time enrolled (new admits only) 2007–2008, 2. Openings 2008–2009, 3. The median number of years required for completion of a degree in 2006–2007 were 6. The number of students enrolled full- and part-time who were dismissed or voluntarily withdrew from this program area in 2007–2008 were 2. *Developmental PhD (Doctor of Philosophy)*—Applications 2007–2008, 32. Total applicants accepted 2007–2008, 6. Number full-time enrolled (new admits only) 2007–2008, 4. Openings 2008–2009, 4. The median number of years required for completion of a degree in 2006–2007 were 5. The number of students enrolled full- and part-time who were dismissed or voluntarily withdrew from this program area in 2007–2008 were 0. *Individual Differences and Evolutionary Psychology PhD (Doctor of Philosophy)*—Applications 2007–2008, 41. Total applicants accepted 2007–2008, 0. Number full-time enrolled (new admits only) 2007–2008, 0. The median number of years required for completion of a degree in 2006–2007 were 5. The number of students enrolled full- and part-time who were dismissed or voluntarily withdrew from this program area in 2007–2008 were 0. *Sensory Neuroscience PhD (Doctor of Philosophy)*—Applications 2007–2008, 4. Total applicants accepted 2007–2008, 1. Number full-time enrolled (new admits only) 2007–2008, 1. Total enrolled 2007–2008 full-time, 4, part-time, 1. Openings 2008–2009, 1. The median number of years required for completion of a degree in 2006–2007 were 6. The number of students enrolled full- and part-time who were dismissed or voluntarily withdrew from this program area in 2007–2008 were 0. *Social and Personality PhD (Doctor of Philosophy)*—Applications 2007–2008, 118. Total applicants accepted 2007–2008, 5. Number full-time enrolled (new admits only) 2007–2008, 4. Openings 2008–2009, 5. The median number of years required for completion of a degree in 2006–2007 were 5. The number of students enrolled full- and part-time who were dismissed or voluntarily withdrew from this program area in 2007–2008 were 0.

Admissions Requirements:

Scores: Entries appear in this order: required test or GPA, minimum score (if required), median score of students entering in 2007–2008. Doctoral Programs: GRE-V no minimum stated, 660; GRE-Q no minimum stated, 720.

Other Criteria: (importance of criteria rated low, medium, or high): GRE/MAT scores—high, research experience—high, work experience—low, clinically related public service—low, GPA—high, letters of recommendation—high, interview—high, statement of goals and objectives—high, undergraduate major in psychology—medium, specific undergraduate psychology courses taken—medium. For additional information on admission requirements, go to http://www.psy.utexas.edu/psy/GradProgram/application.html.

Student Characteristics: The following represents characteristics of students in 2007–2008 in all graduate psychology programs in the department: Female—full-time 71, part-time 0; Male—full-time 44, part-time 0; African American/Black—full-time 2, part-time 0; Hispanic/Latino(a)—full-time 7, part-time 0; Asian/Pacific Islander—full-time 8, part-time 0; American Indian/Alaska Native—full-time 0, part-time 0; Caucasian/White—full-time 75, part-time 0; students subject to the Americans With Disabilities Act—full-time 1, part-time 0; Unknown ethnicity—full-time 22, part-time 0; International students who hold an F-1 or J-1 Visa—full-time 9, part-time 0.

Financial Information/Assistance:

Tuition for Full-Time Study: *Doctoral:* State residents: $492 per credit hour; Nonstate residents: $885 per credit hour. Tuition is subject to change. Additional fees are assessed to students beyond the costs of tuition for the following: All students pay $200/credit hour in fees plus some courses have lab fees. See the following Web site for updates and changes in tuition costs: http://www.utexas.edu/business/accounting/sar/t_f_rates.html.

Financial Assistance:

First-Year Students: Teaching assistantships available for first year. Average amount paid per academic year: $14,518. Average number of hours worked per week: 20. Tuition remission given: full. Research assistantships available for first year. Average amount paid per academic year: $14,518. Average number of hours worked per week: 20. Tuition remission given: full. Fellowships and scholarships available for first year. Average amount paid per academic year: $5,200. Tuition remission given: full.

Advanced Students: Teaching assistantships available for advanced students. Average amount paid per academic year: $15,790. Average number of hours worked per week: 20. Tuition remission given: full. Research assistantships available for advanced students. Average amount paid per academic year: $15,790. Average number of hours worked per week: 20. Tuition remission given: full. Fellowships and scholarships available for advanced students. Average amount paid per academic year: $18,000. Tuition remission given: full.

Additional Information: Of all students currently enrolled full time, 100% benefited from one or more of the listed financial assistance programs. Application and information available online at http://www.psy.utexas.edu/psy/GradProgram/financial.html.

Internships/Practica: Doctoral Degree (PhD Clinical): For those doctoral students for whom a professional internship was required in this program prior to graduation, (5) students applied for an internship in 2006–2007, with (5) students obtaining an internship. Of those students who obtained an internship, (5) were paid internships. Of those students who obtained an internship, (5) students placed in APA/CPA-accredited internships, (0) students placed in internships not APA/CPA-accredited, but listed with the Association of Psychology Postdoctoral and Internship Centers (APPIC), (0) students placed in internships conforming to guidelines of the Council of Directors of School Psychology Programs (CDSPP), (0) students placed in internships that were not APA/CPA-accredited, APPIC or CDSPP listed. Clinical students participate in practica at agencies in the Austin area, including the Austin State Hospital, Austin Child Guidance Center, Brown Schools, and the UT Counseling–Psychological Services Center. Most students select an internship at nationally recognized clinical settings such as the Langley Porter Neuropsychiatric Institute, or the University of California at San Diego Psychological Internship Consortium. Local settings are also available. For additional information on education and training outcomes for our programs, see the following Web site: http://www.psy.utexas.edu/psy/clinical/index.html.

Housing and Day Care: On-campus housing is available. See the following Web site for more information: http://www.utexas.edu/student/housing/. University Apartments (primarily for married students) not physically located on campus. See the following Web site for more information: http://www.utexas.edu/student/housing/index.php?site=0&scode=2&id=639&is_main=1. On-campus day care facilities are available. See the following Web site for more information: http://www.utexas.edu/childcenter/.

Employment of Department Graduates:

Master's Degree Graduates: Of those who graduated in the academic year 2006–2007, the following categories and numbers represent the postgraduate activities and employment of master's degree graduates: Enrolled in another graduate/professional program (1), enrolled in a postdoctoral residency/fellowship (n/a), employed in independent practice (n/a), total from the above (master's) (1).

Doctoral Degree Graduates: Of those who graduated in the academic year 2006–2007, the following categories and numbers represent the postgraduate activities and employment of doctoral degree graduates: Enrolled in a psychology doctoral program (n/a), enrolled in another graduate/professional program (1), enrolled in a postdoctoral residency/fellowship (1), employed in an academic position at a university (4), employed in an academic position at a 2-year/4-year college (1), employed in other positions at a higher education institution (2), employed in a professional position in a school system (1), employed in business or industry (1), other employment position (0), total from the above (doctoral) (11).

Additional Information:

Orientation, Objectives, and Emphasis of Department: The major goal of graduate training in the Department of Psychology is to aid in developing the competence and professional commitment that are essential to scholarly contributions in the field of psychology. All students, upon completing the program, are expected to be well informed about general psychology, well qualified to conduct independent research, and prepared to teach in their area of interest. Within certain specialized areas, they will be prepared for professional practice. The program culminates in the PhD degree, and it is designed for the person committed to psychological research and an academic career. All of the graduate study areas have a strong academic research emphasis. All of the areas also recognize the necessity of developing knowledge and skills for applied research positions and, in the clinical area, for professional competence. Specific information about the emphases of the graduate program areas may be obtained from the department. If you request this information, please indicate the program areas in which you are interested.

Special Facilities or Resources: The Department of Psychology moved into the Seay Building in May of 2002. This building houses seminar rooms, offices, and research laboratories. The research space includes small rooms for individual testing and larger rooms for group experiments. Some rooms have adjacent observation rooms. An anechoic testing chamber is available for auditory research. All of the departmental laboratories have computers associated with them. Departmental computers are available for student use. Facilities for research with children include the Children's Research Laboratory with numerous experimental suites. The facilities of the Animal Resource Center support research with animals. The support resources of the department include two well-equipped shops with full-time technicians and staff for computer assistance. The support resources of the university include the Computation Center, one of the finest academic computation facilities in the United States, and the Perry-Castaneda Library, one of the largest academic libraries in the country. Faculty members in the Department of Psychology are affiliated with the Center for Perceptual Systems, the Institute for Cognitive Science, and the Institute for Neuroscience.

Information for Students With Physical Disabilities: See the following Web site for more information: http://www.deanofstudents.utexas.edu/ssd/.

Application Information:

Send to The University of Texas at Austin, Graduate and International Admissions Center, P.O. Box 7608, Austin, TX 78713-7608. Application available online. URL of online application: http://www.applytexas.org. Students are admitted in the Fall, application deadline

January 1; programs have rolling admissions. The new deadline for the Clinical Area only is December 1. *Fee:* $50. McNair Scholars will have a waived fee.

Texas, University of, El Paso (2007 data)

Department of Psychology
500 West University
El Paso, TX 79968-0553
Telephone: (915) 747-5551
Fax: (915) 747-6553
E-mail: *ecastaneda9@utep.edu*
Web: *http://www.academics.utep.edu/Default.aspx?tabid=6423*

Department Information:

1965. Chairperson: Harmon Hosch. Number of faculty: total—full-time 16, part-time 1; women—full-time 4, part-time 1.

Programs and Degrees Offered:

Listed in the following order: Program area, degree type (T if terminal Master's), number awarded 7/06–6/07. Psychology MA/MS (Master of Arts/Science) (T) 4, Psychology PhD (Doctor of Philosophy) 6.

Student Applications/Admissions:

Student Applications

Psychology MA/MS (Master of Arts/Science)—Applications 2007–2008, 19. Total applicants accepted 2007–2008, 4. Number full-time enrolled (new admits only) 2007–2008, 10. Openings 2008–2009, 4. The median number of years required for completion of a degree in 2006–2007 were 3. The number of students enrolled full- and part-time who were dismissed or voluntarily withdrew from this program area in 2007–2008 were 1. *Psychology PhD (Doctor of Philosophy)*—Applications 2007–2008, 44. Total applicants accepted 2007–2008, 19. Number full-time enrolled (new admits only) 2007–2008, 8. Number part-time enrolled (new admits only) 2007–2008, 0. Openings 2008–2009, 4. The median number of years required for completion of a degree in 2006–2007 were 5. The number of students enrolled full- and part-time who were dismissed or voluntarily withdrew from this program area in 2007–2008 were 0.

Admissions Requirements:

Scores: Entries appear in this order: required test or GPA, minimum score (if required), median score of students entering in 2007–2008. Master's Programs: GRE-V no minimum stated, 470; GRE-Q no minimum stated, 490; overall undergraduate GPA no minimum stated, 3.4. Doctoral Programs: GRE-V no minimum stated, 515; GRE-Q no minimum stated, 625; overall undergraduate GPA no minimum stated, 3.6.

Other Criteria: (importance of criteria rated low, medium, or high): GRE/MAT scores—high, research experience—high, work experience—low, extracurricular activity—low, clinically related public service—low, GPA—high, letters of recommendation—high, statement of goals and objectives—high.

Student Characteristics: The following represents characteristics of students in 2007–2008 in all graduate psychology programs in the department: Female—full-time 37, part-time 0; Male—full-time 21, part-time 0; African American/Black—full-time 1, part-time 0; Hispanic/Latino(a)—full-time 25, part-time 0; Asian/Pacific Islander—full-time 3, part-time 0; American Indian/Alaska Native—full-time 2, part-time 0; Caucasian/White—full-time 27, part-time 0; Multi-ethnic—full-time 0, part-time 0; students subject to the Americans With Disabilities Act—full-time 0, part-time 0; Unknown ethnicity—full-time 0, part-time 0.

Financial Information/Assistance:

Tuition for Full-Time Study: *Master's:* State residents: per academic year $2,943, $163 per credit hour; Nonstate residents: per academic year $7,893, $438 per credit hour. *Doctoral:* State residents: per academic year $2,943, $163 per credit hour; Nonstate residents: per academic year $7,893, $438 per credit hour. Tuition is subject to change.

Financial Assistance:

First-Year Students: Teaching assistantships available for first year. Average amount paid per academic year: $15,000. Average number of hours worked per week: 20. Apply by January 15. Tuition remission given: full. Research assistantships available for first year. Average amount paid per academic year: $15,000. Average number of hours worked per week: 20. Apply by January 15. Tuition remission given: full.

Advanced Students: Teaching assistantships available for advanced students. Average amount paid per academic year: $15,000. Average number of hours worked per week: 20. Apply by January 15. Tuition remission given: full. Research assistantships available for advanced students. Average amount paid per academic year: $15,000. Average number of hours worked per week: 20. Apply by January 15. Tuition remission given: full.

Additional Information: Of all students currently enrolled full time, 100% benefited from one or more of the listed financial assistance programs.

Internships/Practica: The Clinical MA program requires 3 hours of internship.

Housing and Day Care: On-campus housing is available. On-campus day care facilities are available.

Employment of Department Graduates:

Master's Degree Graduates: Of those who graduated in the academic year 2006–2007, the following categories and numbers represent the postgraduate activities and employment of master's degree graduates: Enrolled in a psychology doctoral program (1), enrolled in another graduate/professional program (0), enrolled in a postdoctoral residency/fellowship (n/a), employed in independent practice (n/a), employed in an academic position at a university (0), employed in an academic position at a 2-year/4-year college (1), employed in other positions at a higher education institution (1), employed in a professional position in a school system (0), employed in business or industry (1), employed in government agency (0), employed in a community mental health/counseling center (0), employed in a hospital/medical center (0), still seeking employment (0), not seeking employment (0), other employment position (0), do not know (1), total from the above (master's) (5).

Doctoral Degree Graduates: Of those who graduated in the academic year 2006–2007, the following categories and numbers represent the postgraduate activities and employment of doctoral

degree graduates: Enrolled in a psychology doctoral program (n/a), enrolled in a postdoctoral residency/fellowship (0), employed in independent practice (0), employed in an academic position at a university (0), employed in an academic position at a 2-year/4-year college (0), employed in other positions at a higher education institution (0), employed in a professional position in a school system (0), employed in business or industry (2), employed in government agency (0), employed in a community mental health/counseling center (0), employed in a hospital/medical center (0), still seeking employment (0), not seeking employment (0), other employment position (0), do not know (0), total from the above (doctoral) (2).

Additional Information:

Orientation, Objectives, and Emphasis of Department: The PhD program is designed to train research psychologists and offers three areas of focus: (a) health, (b) legal, and (c) social, cognitive, and neuroscience. The General Experimental MA program, intended for students who will pursue a PhD degree, emphasizes research methodology and experimental design, and focuses on a variety of substantive areas in psychology. The Clinical MA program is designed as a terminal master's degree and emphasizes all applied skills in psychological assessment. A special focus is directed toward bilingual, bicultural research issues.

Information for Students With Physical Disabilities: See the following Web site for more information: http://www.utep.edu/prospectivestudents/.

Application Information:

Send to UTEP, Graduate School, Academic Service Building, Room 223, El Paso, TX 79968-0566. Application available online. URL of online application: http://www.academics.utep.edu/Default.aspx?tabid=25001. Students are admitted in the Fall, application deadline January 15. *Fee:* $15.

Texas, University of, Pan American

Department of Psychology and Anthropology, MA in Psychology
College of Social and Behavioral Sciences
1201 West University Drive, SBSC 358
Edinburg, TX 78541
Telephone: (956) 381-3329
Fax: (956) 381-3333
E-mail: *pgasquoine@panam.edu*
Web: *http://www.utpa.edu/dept/psych-anth*

Department Information:

1972. Graduate Program Director: Philip Gasquoine, PhD. Number of faculty: total—full-time 11; women—full-time 2; total—minority—full-time 2; women minority—full-time 1.

Programs and Degrees Offered:

Listed in the following order: Program area, degree type (T if terminal Master's), number awarded 7/06–6/07. Clinical MA/MS (Master of Arts/Science) (T) 3, Experimental MA/MS (Master of Arts/Science) (T) 1.

Student Applications/Admissions:

Student Applications

Clinical MA/MS (Master of Arts/Science)—Applications 2007–2008, 15. Total applicants accepted 2007–2008, 11. Number full-time enrolled (new admits only) 2007–2008, 8. Number part-time enrolled (new admits only) 2007–2008, 3. Total enrolled 2007–2008 full-time, 23, part-time, 18. Openings 2008–2009, 18. The median number of years required for completion of a degree in 2006–2007 were 3. The number of students enrolled full- and part-time who were dismissed or voluntarily withdrew from this program area in 2007–2008 were 0. *Experimental MA/MS (Master of Arts/Science)*—Applications 2007–2008, 1. Total applicants accepted 2007–2008, 1. Total enrolled 2007–2008 full-time, 1, part-time, 1. Openings 2008–2009, 3. The median number of years required for completion of a degree in 2006–2007 were 3. The number of students enrolled full- and part-time who were dismissed or voluntarily withdrew from this program area in 2007–2008 were 0.

Admissions Requirements:

Scores: Entries appear in this order: required test or GPA, minimum score (if required), median score of students entering in 2007–2008. Master's Programs: GRE-V no minimum stated, 400; GRE-Q no minimum stated, 450; overall undergraduate GPA 3.0, 3.2; last 2 years GPA 3.0, 3.3; psychology GPA 3.0, 3.4.

Other Criteria: (importance of criteria rated low, medium, or high): GRE/MAT scores—low, research experience—high, work experience—high, extracurricular activity—low, clinically related public service—medium, GPA—high, letters of recommendation—high, statement of goals and objectives—medium, undergraduate major in psychology—medium, specific undergraduate psychology courses taken—medium.

Student Characteristics: The following represents characteristics of students in 2007–2008 in all graduate psychology programs in the department: Female—full-time 21, part-time 10; Male—full-time 3, part-time 9; African American/Black—full-time 0, part-time 0; Hispanic/Latino(a)—full-time 19, part-time 16; Asian/Pacific Islander—full-time 0, part-time 0; American Indian/Alaska Native—full-time 0, part-time 0; Caucasian/White—full-time 5, part-time 3; students subject to the Americans With Disabilities Act—full-time 0, part-time 0; Unknown ethnicity—full-time 0, part-time 0; International students who hold an F-1 or J-1 Visa—full-time 1, part-time 0.

Financial Information/Assistance:

Tuition for Full-Time Study: *Master's:* State residents: per academic year $2,864, $159 per credit hour; Nonstate residents: per academic year $7,868, $437 per credit hour. Tuition is subject to change. Additional fees are assessed to students beyond the costs of tuition for the following: $75. Tuition increases each year are mandated by the state legislature. Fees are charged in addition.

Financial Assistance:

First-Year Students: Teaching assistantships available for first year. Average amount paid per academic year: $7,000. Average number of hours worked per week: 19. Research assistantships available for first year. Average amount paid per academic year: $10,000. Average number of hours worked per week: 19.

Advanced Students: Teaching assistantships available for advanced students. Average amount paid per academic year: $7,000. Average number of hours worked per week: 19. Research assistantships available for advanced students. Average amount paid per academic year: $10,000. Average number of hours worked per week: 19.

Additional Information: Of all students currently enrolled full time, 17% benefited from one or more of the listed financial assistance programs.

Internships/Practica: Internships are for 480 clock hours, at least 100 of which must involve direct patient contact. Internship sites include independent licensed psychologists, and public and private mental health clinics and hospitals.

Housing and Day Care: On-campus housing is available. See the following Web site for more information: http://www.utpa.edu/reslife; Residence Life, phone: (956) 381-3439; e-mail: home@panam.edu. On-campus day care facilities are available. Contact Child Care Center, phone (956) 316-7989.

Employment of Department Graduates:

Master's Degree Graduates: Of those who graduated in the academic year 2006–2007, the following categories and numbers represent the postgraduate activities and employment of master's degree graduates: Enrolled in a postdoctoral residency/fellowship (n/a), employed in independent practice (n/a), total from the above (master's) (0).

Doctoral Degree Graduates: Of those who graduated in the academic year 2006–2007, the following categories and numbers represent the postgraduate activities and employment of doctoral degree graduates: Enrolled in a psychology doctoral program (n/a), total from the above (doctoral) (0).

Additional Information:

Orientation, Objectives, and Emphasis of Department: The Master's in Clinical Psychology is designed to provide theory, research-based assessment and intervention strategies, skills training, practical knowledge, *DSM*-based diagnostic assessment skills, clinical experience, and supervision of professional practices in the field of applied psychology. Multicultural professional practices are emphasized as the community service base is largely bilingual (English/Spanish) and of Hispanic origin. The program is designed to fulfill prerequisite and academic requirements for taking the Texas State Board of Examiners of Psychologists Exam as a Psychological Associate. By careful choice of two graduate course electives, MA candidates fulfill the academic requirements for license as a Licensed Professional Counselor (LPC).

Special Facilities or Resources: Graduate psychology clinic has six consultation rooms, including monitoring equipment (A/V) for individual and group sessions and supervision. The department also has equipment and computers to conduct research on perception, cognition, stress management, and other areas of faculty interest.

Application Information:

Send to Office of Graduate Studies, Administration Building Room 116, University of Texas—Pan American, 1201 West University Drive, Edinburg, TX 78541. Application available online. URL of online application: http://www.utpa.edu/gradschool. Students are admitted in the Fall, application deadline July 1; Spring, application deadline November 1; Summer, application deadline Apr 1. *Fee:* $35.

Texas, University of, Tyler

Department of Psychology
3900 University Boulevard
Tyler, TX 75799
Telephone: (903) 566-7130
Fax: (903) 565-5560
E-mail: *rmcclure@mail.uttyl.edu*
Web: *http://www.uttyler.edu*

Department Information:

1973. Chairperson: Charles Barke. Number of faculty: total—full-time 11, part-time 6; women—full-time 3, part-time 6.

Programs and Degrees Offered:

Listed in the following order: Program area, degree type (T if terminal Master's), number awarded 7/06–6/07. Counseling Psychology MA/MS (Master of Arts/Science) (T) 4, School Counseling MA/MS (Master of Arts/Science) (T) 10, Clinical MA/MS (Master of Arts/Science) (T) 10.

Student Applications/Admissions:

Student Applications

Counseling Psychology MA/MS (Master of Arts/Science)—Applications 2007–2008, 22. Total applicants accepted 2007–2008, 15. Number full-time enrolled (new admits only) 2007–2008, 9. Number part-time enrolled (new admits only) 2007–2008, 6. Total enrolled 2007–2008 full-time, 25, part-time, 22. Openings 2008–2009, 20. The median number of years required for completion of a degree in 2006–2007 were 2. The number of students enrolled full- and part-time who were dismissed or voluntarily withdrew from this program area in 2007–2008 were 5. *School Counseling MA/MS (Master of Arts/Science)*—Applications 2007–2008, 18. Total applicants accepted 2007–2008, 14. Number full-time enrolled (new admits only) 2007–2008, 2. Number part-time enrolled (new admits only) 2007–2008, 12. Total enrolled 2007–2008 full-time, 18, part-time, 32. Openings 2008–2009, 15. The median number of years required for completion of a degree in 2006–2007 were 2. The number of students enrolled full- and part-time who were dismissed or voluntarily withdrew from this program area in 2007–2008 were 3. *Clinical MA/MS (Master of Arts/Science)*—Applications 2007–2008, 30. Total applicants accepted 2007–2008, 14. Number full-time enrolled (new admits only) 2007–2008, 8. Number part-time enrolled (new admits only) 2007–2008, 6. Total enrolled 2007–2008 full-time, 30, part-time, 10. Openings 2008–2009, 15. The median number of years required for completion of a degree in 2006–2007 were 2. The number of students enrolled full- and part-time who were dismissed or voluntarily withdrew from this program area in 2007–2008 were 4.

Admissions Requirements:

Scores: Entries appear in this order: required test or GPA, minimum score (if required), median score of students entering in 2007–2008. Master's Programs: GRE-V 450, 550; GRE-Q 450, 540; GRE-Subject (Psychology) 550, 610; overall undergraduate GPA 3.0, 3.3; last 2 years GPA 3.0, 3.4. School Counseling only requires 870 total GRE V & Q added together. ***Other Criteria:*** (importance of criteria rated low, medium, or high): GRE/MAT scores—high, research experience—low, work experience—low, extracurricular activity—low, clinically related public service—low, GPA—high, letters of recommendation—high, interview—low, statement of goals and objectives—medium.

Student Characteristics: The following represents characteristics of students in 2007–2008 in all graduate psychology programs in the department: Female—full-time 59, part-time 52; Male—full-time 14, part-time 12; African American/Black—full-time 5, part-time 0; Hispanic/Latino(a)—full-time 12, part-time 6; Asian/Pacific Islander—full-time 3, part-time 0; American Indian/Alaska Native—full-time 1, part-time 0; Caucasian/White—full-time 53, part-time 58; students subject to the Americans With Disabilities Act—full-time 3, part-time 0; Unknown ethnicity—full-time 0, part-time 0.

Financial Information/Assistance:

Tuition for Full-Time Study: *Master's:* State residents: per academic year $4,476, $50 per credit hour; Nonstate residents: per academic year $11,076, $325 per credit hour. Tuition is subject to change. See the following Web site for updates and changes in tuition costs: http://www.uttyler.edu.

Financial Assistance:

First-Year Students: Fellowships and scholarships available for first year. Average amount paid per academic year: $1,000. Apply by February 1. Tuition remission given: partial.

Advanced Students: Research assistantships available for advanced students. Average amount paid per academic year: $5,000. Average number of hours worked per week: 20. Apply by February 1. Tuition remission given: partial. Fellowships and scholarships available for advanced students. Average amount paid per academic year: $1,000. Apply by February 1. Tuition remission given: partial.

Additional Information: Of all students currently enrolled full time, 20% benefited from one or more of the listed financial assistance programs. Application and information available online at http://www.uttyler.edu.

Internships/Practica: Practica available include nearby private psychiatric hospitals, MHMR facilities, children's therapy facilities, crisis centers and safe houses for abused women, neuropsychology rehabilitation hospitals, prisons, and schools.

Housing and Day Care: On-campus housing is available. See the following Web site for more information: http://www.uttyler.edu. University Pines Housing: (903) 566-7082; UTT Dorms: (903) 566-7008. No on-campus day care facilities are available.

Employment of Department Graduates:

Master's Degree Graduates: Of those who graduated in the academic year 2006–2007, the following categories and numbers represent the postgraduate activities and employment of master's degree graduates: Enrolled in a psychology doctoral program (3), enrolled in a postdoctoral residency/fellowship (n/a), employed in independent practice (n/a), employed in an academic position at a 2-year/4-year college (1), employed in a professional position in a school system (8), employed in a community mental health/counseling center (5), employed in a hospital/medical center (2), still seeking employment (2), total from the above (master's) (21). ***Doctoral Degree Graduates:*** Of those who graduated in the academic year 2006–2007, the following categories and numbers represent the postgraduate activities and employment of doctoral degree graduates: Enrolled in a psychology doctoral program (n/a), total from the above (doctoral) (0).

Additional Information:

Orientation, Objectives, and Emphasis of Department: The purpose of our program is to prepare competent, applied practitioners at the master's level. The curriculum is very practical, stressing clinical assessment and intervention, and hands-on experience in relevant areas. Our students have been very successful in finding employment in mental health settings and in gaining admission to clinical and counseling doctoral programs. Special opportunities are provided for training in clinical neuropsychological assessment and psychopharmacology, for training in marital and family counseling and school counseling, or for training to become a licensed specialist in school psychology.

Information for Students With Physical Disabilities: See the following Web site for more information: http://www.uttyler.edu.

Application Information:

Send to Robert F. McClure, PhD, Psychology Graduate Coordinator, Department of Psychology, University of Texas at Tyler, Tyler, TX 75799. Application available online. URL of online application: http://www.uttyler.edu. Students are admitted in the Fall, application deadline February 1; Spring, application deadline October 1. *Fee:* $25. Fee for university application.

Trinity University (2007 data)

Department of Education
One Trinity Place
San Antonio, TX 78212
Telephone: (210) 999-7501
Fax: (210) 999-7592
E-mail: *Terry.Robertson@trinity.edu*

Department Information:

1976. Director of School Psychology Program: Terry Robertson. Number of faculty: total—full-time 2, part-time 11; women—full-time 1, part-time 5.

Programs and Degrees Offered:

Listed in the following order: Program area, degree type (T if terminal Master's), number awarded 7/06–6/07. School Psychology MA/MS (Master of Arts/Science) (T) 10.

Student Applications/Admissions:

Student Applications

School Psychology MA/MS (Master of Arts/Science)—Applications 2007–2008, 23. Total applicants accepted 2007–2008, 15. Number full-time enrolled (new admits only) 2007–2008, 12. Number part-time enrolled (new admits only) 2007–2008, 0. Openings 2008–2009, 15. The median number of years required for completion of a degree in 2006–2007 were 2. The number of students enrolled full- and part-time who were dismissed or voluntarily withdrew from this program area in 2007–2008 were 2.

Admissions Requirements:

Scores: Entries appear in this order: required test or GPA, minimum score (if required), median score of students entering in 2007–2008. Master's Programs: overall undergraduate GPA 3.0; last 2 years GPA 3.0; psychology GPA 3.0.

Other Criteria: (importance of criteria rated low, medium, or high): GRE/MAT scores—medium, research experience—medium, work experience—medium, extracurricular activity—medium, clinically related public service—medium, GPA—medium, letters of recommendation—medium, interview—medium, statement of goals and objectives—medium.

Student Characteristics: The following represents characteristics of students in 2007–2008 in all graduate psychology programs in the department: Female—full-time 34, part-time 0; Male—full-time 6, part-time 0; African American/Black—full-time 1, part-time 0; Hispanic/Latino(a)—full-time 10, part-time 0; Asian/Pacific Islander—full-time 1, part-time 0; American Indian/Alaska Native—full-time 0, part-time 0; Caucasian/White—full-time 28, part-time 0; Multi-ethnic—full-time 0, part-time 0; students subject to the Americans With Disabilities Act—full-time 0, part-time 0; Unknown ethnicity—full-time 0, part-time 0.

Financial Information/Assistance:

Financial Assistance:

First-Year Students: No information provided.

Advanced Students: No information provided.

Additional Information: Of all students currently enrolled full time, 100% benefited from one or more of the listed financial assistance programs.

Internships/Practica: All students have graduate assistantships in career-related work. The average award per student is $14,000 per year for the 2 years of academic work ($28,000). The required 3rd year internship is funded at $28,000 for each student. Students may apply directly to school districts, which may offer a higher salary.

Housing and Day Care: No on-campus housing is available. No on-campus day care facilities are available.

Employment of Department Graduates:

Master's Degree Graduates: Of those who graduated in the academic year 2006–2007, the following categories and numbers represent the postgraduate activities and employment of master's degree graduates: Enrolled in a postdoctoral residency/fellowship (n/a), employed in independent practice (n/a), total from the above (master's) (0).

Doctoral Degree Graduates: Of those who graduated in the academic year 2006–2007, the following categories and numbers represent the postgraduate activities and employment of doctoral degree graduates: Enrolled in a psychology doctoral program (n/a), total from the above (doctoral) (0).

Additional Information:

Orientation, Objectives, and Emphasis of Department: The Trinity University Department of Education offers the 60 semester-hour master of arts in school psychology. The purpose of this program is to prepare graduates to provide psychological services in school settings. The courses and practicum experiences offer the theory and skills necessary for assessment, consultation, and counseling functions. Specific application of assessment and consultation skills to classroom instruction is stressed in Trinity's program. All graduates will be eligible to take the examination for Licensed Specialist in School Psychology and to apply for Nationally Certified School Psychologist. The program has full approval by the National Association of School Psychologists.

Special Facilities or Resources: Part-time faculty are either psychologists or consultants with local school districts, or work at the Psychological Corporation, a major developer of assessment instruments used in schools and clinics.

Application Information:

Send to Dr. Terry Robertson, Trinity University, Education Department, One Trinity Place, San Antonio, TX 78212. Students are admitted in the Fall, application deadline February 1. *Fee:* $30.

West Texas A&M University (2007 data)

Department of Behavioral Sciences
P.O. Box 60296
Canyon, TX 79016
Telephone: (806) 651-2590
Fax: (806) 651-2728
E-mail: *gbyrd@mail.wtamu.edu*
Web: *http://www.wtamu.edu*

Department Information:

1971. Chairperson: Gary R. Byrd. Number of faculty: total—full-time 5, part-time 2; women—full-time 2, part-time 1.

Programs and Degrees Offered:

Listed in the following order: Program area, degree type (T if terminal Master's), number awarded 7/06–6/07. Psychology MA/MS (Master of Arts/Science) (T) 4.

Student Applications/Admissions:

Student Applications

Psychology MA/MS (Master of Arts/Science)—Applications 2007–2008, 15. Total applicants accepted 2007–2008, 9. Number full-time enrolled (new admits only) 2007–2008, 2. Number part-time enrolled (new admits only) 2007–2008, 7. Total enrolled 2007–2008 full-time, 6, part-time, 20. Openings 2008–2009, 11. The median number of years required for completion of a degree in 2006–2007 were 3. The number of students enrolled full- and part-time who were dismissed or voluntarily withdrew from this program area in 2007–2008 were 2.

Admissions Requirements:

Scores: Entries appear in this order: required test or GPA, minimum score (if required), median score of students entering in 2007–2008. Master's Programs: GRE-V 440, 530; GRE-Q 360, 590; overall undergraduate GPA 3.10, 3.52; Master's GRE-Analytical 3.5, 5.0.

Other Criteria: (importance of criteria rated low, medium, or high): GRE/MAT scores—high, research experience—medium, work experience—low, extracurricular activity—low, clinically related public service—low, GPA—high, letters of recommendation—high, statement of goals and objectives—medium.

Student Characteristics: The following represents characteristics of students in 2007–2008 in all graduate psychology programs in the department: Female—full-time 2, part-time 10; Male—full-time 4, part-time 10; African American/Black—full-time 0, part-time 1; Hispanic/Latino(a)—full-time 0, part-time 2; Asian/Pacific Islander—full-time 0, part-time 1; American Indian/Alaska Native—full-time 0, part-time 0; Caucasian/White—full-time 6, part-time 16; Multi-ethnic—full-time 0, part-time 0; students subject to the Americans With Disabilities Act—full-time 0, part-time 0; Unknown ethnicity—full-time 0, part-time 0.

Financial Information/Assistance:

Tuition for Full-Time Study: *Master's:* State residents: per academic year $3,717, $177 per credit hour; Nonstate residents: per academic year $8,022, $382 per credit hour. Tuition is subject to change. See the following Web site for updates and changes in tuition costs: http://www.wtamu.edu.

Financial Assistance:

First-Year Students: Traineeships available for first year. Average amount paid per academic year: $3,400. Average number of hours worked per week: 10. Apply by August 15. Tuition remission given: partial. Fellowships and scholarships available for first year. Average amount paid per academic year: $700. Apply by August 1. Tuition remission given: partial.

Advanced Students: Teaching assistantships available for advanced students. Average amount paid per academic year: $3,400. Average number of hours worked per week: 15. Apply by August 15. Tuition remission given: partial. Research assistantships available for advanced students. Average amount paid per academic year: $3,300. Average number of hours worked per week: 15. Apply by August 15. Tuition remission given: partial. Fellowships and scholarships available for advanced students. Average amount paid per academic year: $600. Apply by August 1. Tuition remission given: partial.

Additional Information: Of all students currently enrolled full time, 33% benefited from one or more of the listed financial assistance programs. Application and information available online at http://wtamu.edu.

Internships/Practica: In addition to clinical and counseling practica, the program offers service-learning opportunities in the community.

Housing and Day Care: On-campus housing is available. See the following Web site for more information: http://www.wtamu.edu; Office of Student Services, WTAMU, Canyon, TX 79016; phone: (806) 651-2050. On-campus day care facilities are available.

Employment of Department Graduates:

Master's Degree Graduates: Of those who graduated in the academic year 2006–2007, the following categories and numbers represent the postgraduate activities and employment of master's degree graduates: Enrolled in a psychology doctoral program (1), enrolled in another graduate/professional program (0), enrolled in a postdoctoral residency/fellowship (n/a), employed in independent practice (n/a), employed in an academic position at a university (0), employed in an academic position at a 2-year/4-year college (0), employed in other positions at a higher education institution (0), employed in a professional position in a school system (0), employed in business or industry (0), employed in government agency (0), employed in a community mental health/counseling center (0), employed in a hospital/medical center (0), still seeking employment (0), not seeking employment (0), other employment position (0), do not know (2), total from the above (master's) (4).

Doctoral Degree Graduates: Of those who graduated in the academic year 2006–2007, the following categories and numbers represent the postgraduate activities and employment of doctoral degree graduates: Enrolled in a psychology doctoral program (n/a), total from the above (doctoral) (0).

Additional Information:

Orientation, Objectives, and Emphasis of Department: The primary purpose of the program is to create opportunities for students that have strong qualifications for graduate work and have a bachelor's degree in psychology but need clarification as to which specialization they should seek in their doctoral studies, have a weak dimension in their application qualifications for graduate studies and wish to enhance their potential for admission to a doctoral program, do not have a bachelor's degree in psychology but are promising students who now wish to become competitive for psychology doctoral programs, or seek employment at the master's level of professional psychology.

Special Facilities or Resources: The department has a variety of facilities that can be viewed in five functional subdivisions. First, there are several large experimental research laboratories that contain equipment for electrophysiological measures (EEG, EMG, EOG, and hemisphereric electronic equipment), is highly versatile, and can be controlled by lab computers. Second, there are facilities to record data for field studies such as the behavior of children in their home setting or animals in their natural settings. Third, a psychometric lab provides storage and space for administering psychological tests. Fourth, a large community foundation has a partnership with the department to provide a setting for training a limited number of students in program evaluation for community grants and projects. And, finally, there are eight community mental health facilities (two are residential) that provide practicum settings for students interested in clinical or counseling training.

Application Information:

Send to Dr. Richard Harland, Psychology Graduate Coordinator, P.O. Box 60296, WTAMU, Canyon, TX 79016. Students are admitted in the Fall, application deadline August 1; Spring, application deadline December 1; Summer, application deadline May 1. *Fee:* $0.

Brigham Young University

Department of Counseling Psychology and Special Education
David O. McKay School of Education
340 MCKB
Provo, UT 84602
Telephone: (801) 422-3857
Fax: (801) 422-0198
E-mail: *aaron_jackson@byu.edu*
Web: *http://www.education.byu.edu/cpse/index.html*

Department Information:

1969. Department Chair: Mary Anne Prater. Number of faculty: total—full-time 3, part-time 2; women—full-time 3, part-time 1.

Programs and Degrees Offered:

Listed in the following order: Program area, degree type (T if terminal Master's), number awarded 7/06–6/07. School Psychology EdS/MEd (School Psychology) 12, Counseling Psychology PhD (Doctor of Philosophy) 6.

APA Accreditation: Counseling PhD (Doctor of Philosophy).

Student Applications/Admissions:

Student Applications

School Psychology EdS/MEd (School Psychology)—Applications 2007–2008, 34. Total applicants accepted 2007–2008, 12. Number full-time enrolled (new admits only) 2007–2008, 12. Total enrolled 2007–2008 full-time, 34. Openings 2008–2009, 12. The median number of years required for completion of a degree in 2006–2007 were 3. The number of students enrolled full- and part-time who were dismissed or voluntarily withdrew from this program area in 2007–2008 were 1. *Counseling Psychology PhD (Doctor of Philosophy)*—Applications 2007–2008, 34. Total applicants accepted 2007–2008, 8. Number full-time enrolled (new admits only) 2007–2008, 6. Number part-time enrolled (new admits only) 2007–2008, 0. Total enrolled 2007–2008 full-time, 40. Openings 2008–2009, 6. The median number of years required for completion of a degree in 2006–2007 were 5. The number of students enrolled full- and part-time who were dismissed or voluntarily withdrew from this program area in 2007–2008 were 2.

Admissions Requirements:

Scores: Entries appear in this order: required test or GPA, minimum score (if required), median score of students entering in 2007–2008. Doctoral Programs: last 2 years GPA 3.0, 3.75.

Other Criteria: (importance of criteria rated low, medium, or high): GRE/MAT scores—medium, research experience—medium, work experience—medium, extracurricular activity—low, clinically related public service—medium, GPA—high, letters of recommendation—medium, interview—high, statement of goals and objectives—high, undergraduate major in psychology—low, specific undergraduate psychology courses taken—medium.

Student Characteristics: The following represents characteristics of students in 2007–2008 in all graduate psychology programs in the department: Female—full-time 59, part-time 0; Male—full-time 34, part-time 0; African American/Black—full-time 0, part-time 0; Hispanic/Latino(a)—full-time 4, part-time 0; Asian/Pacific Islander—full-time 4, part-time 0; American Indian/Alaska Native—full-time 4, part-time 0; Caucasian/White—full-time 76, part-time 0; Multi-ethnic—full-time 0, part-time 0; students subject to the Americans With Disabilities Act—full-time 0, part-time 0; Unknown ethnicity—full-time 0, part-time 0; International students who hold an F-1 or J-1 Visa—full-time 1, part-time 0.

Financial Information/Assistance:

Tuition for Full-Time Study: *Master's:* State residents: per academic year $4,580, $254 per credit hour; Nonstate residents: per academic year $9,160, $455 per credit hour. *Doctoral:* State residents: per academic year $4,580, $254 per credit hour; Nonstate residents: per academic year $9,160, $455 per credit hour. Tuition is subject to change. See the following Web site for updates and changes in tuition costs: http://www.saas.byu.edu/tuition/.

Financial Assistance:

First-Year Students: Teaching assistantships available for first year. Average amount paid per academic year: $7,800. Average number of hours worked per week: 15. Apply by varies. Tuition remission given: partial. Research assistantships available for first year. Average amount paid per academic year: $7,800. Average number of hours worked per week: 15. Apply by varies. Tuition remission given: partial.

Advanced Students: Teaching assistantships available for advanced students. Average amount paid per academic year: $8,600. Average number of hours worked per week: 15. Apply by varies. Tuition remission given: partial. Research assistantships available for advanced students. Average amount paid per academic year: $8,600. Average number of hours worked per week: 15. Apply by varies. Tuition remission given: partial.

Additional Information: Of all students currently enrolled full time, 100% benefited from one or more of the listed financial assistance programs.

Internships/Practica: Doctoral Degree (PhD Counseling Psychology): For those doctoral students for whom a professional internship was required in this program prior to graduation, (9) students applied for an internship in 2006–2007, with (8) students obtaining an internship. Of those students who obtained an internship, (8) were paid internships. Of those students who obtained an internship, (8) students placed in APA/CPA-accredited internships, (0) students placed in internships not APA/CPA-accredited, but listed with the Association of Psychology Postdoctoral and Internship Centers (APPIC), (0) students placed in internships conforming to guidelines of the Council of Directors of School Psychology Programs (CDSPP), (0) students placed in internships that were not APA/CPA-accredited, APPIC or CDSPP listed. Master's students complete practica for 5 hours per week during the 1st and 2nd years of study and a full-time internship (five eighths of teacher pay) the 3rd year. Doctoral students admitted at the bachelor's level complete two semesters of introductory practicum. All doctoral students complete four semesters of practicum in BYU's counseling center. They also complete one teaching practicum, and two community-based practica. A full-year internship is required. Assistance is given for placements.

Housing and Day Care: On-campus housing is available. See the following Web site for more information: http://www.byu.edu/housing/. No on-campus day care facilities are available.

Employment of Department Graduates:

Master's Degree Graduates: Of those who graduated in the academic year 2006–2007, the following categories and numbers represent the postgraduate activities and employment of master's degree graduates: Enrolled in a postdoctoral residency/fellowship (n/a), employed in independent practice (n/a), total from the above (master's) (0).

Doctoral Degree Graduates: Of those who graduated in the academic year 2006–2007, the following categories and numbers represent the postgraduate activities and employment of doctoral degree graduates: Enrolled in a psychology doctoral program (n/a), employed in independent practice (1), employed in other positions at a higher education institution (4), employed in a professional position in a school system (1), employed in a community mental health/counseling center (1), total from the above (doctoral) (7).

Additional Information:

Orientation, Objectives, and Emphasis of Department: The Department of Counseling Psychology and Special Education offers master's programs in Special Education, EdS degree in School Psychology, and a PhD program in Counseling Psychology. The School Psychology program prepares students for certification as school psychologists. The Counseling Psychology program prepares individuals for licensure as psychologists. The program is both broad-based and specific in nature; that is, one is expected to take certain courses that could be required for licensure or for certification and graduation, but the program encourages students to take coursework in varied disciplines such as marriage and family therapy, organizational behavior, and other fields allied with psychology and education. The focus of the School Psychology EdS program is to prepare graduates for K–12 school settings. The doctoral program prepares counseling psychologists to work in counseling centers, academic positions, and other mental health settings.

Personal Behavior Statement: http://campuslife.byu.edu/HONORCODE/index.htm.

Special Facilities or Resources: The department has a Counseling Psychology Center (clinic) with five individual counseling rooms and one large group room available for the observation and videotaping of students in counseling and assessment. These are assigned specifically to the department, whereas an abundance of other media-related facilities for the teaching and learning experience are available on campus as well as off campus. The department also provides spacious study and work carrels. The Counseling and Career Center has eight offices for practicum students. All of these offices have videotaping capabilities and are equipped for live supervision.

Information for Students With Physical Disabilities: See the following Web site for more information: http://www.campuslife.byu.edu/uac/.

Application Information:

Send to Office of Graduate Studies, B-356 ASB, BYU, Provo, UT 84602. On-line applications are preferred. Application available on-line. URL of online application: http://www.byu.edu/gradstudies/. Students are admitted in the Fall, application deadline January 15. Counseling Psychology and School Psychology admit Fall only. *Fee:* $50.

Brigham Young University

Department of Psychology
Family, Home, and Social Sciences
1001 SWKT
Provo, UT 84602-5543
Telephone: (801) 422-4287
Fax: (801) 422-0602
E-mail: *lisa_norton@byu.edu*
Web: *http://www.psychology.byu.edu*

Department Information:

1921. Chairperson: Ramona O. Hopkins. Number of faculty: total—full-time 29, part-time 2; women—full-time 6; total—minority—full-time 1; women minority—full-time 1.

Programs and Degrees Offered:

Listed in the following order: Program area, degree type (T if terminal Master's), number awarded 7/06–6/07. General PhD (Doctor of Philosophy) 2, Clinical PhD (Doctor of Philosophy) 9, General MA/MS (Master of Arts/Science) (T) 10.

APA Accreditation: Clinical PhD (Doctor of Philosophy).

Student Applications/Admissions:

Student Applications

General PhD (Doctor of Philosophy)—Applications 2007–2008, 19. Total applicants accepted 2007–2008, 4. Number full-time enrolled (new admits only) 2007–2008, 4. Total enrolled 2007–2008 full-time, 22. Openings 2008–2009, 5. The median number of years required for completion of a degree in 2006–2007 were 6. The number of students enrolled full- and part-time who were dismissed or voluntarily withdrew from this program area in 2007–2008 were 0. *Clinical PhD (Doctor of Philosophy)*—Applications 2007–2008, 60. Total applicants accepted 2007–2008, 10. Number full-time enrolled (new admits only) 2007–2008, 10. Total enrolled 2007–2008 full-time, 54. Openings 2008–2009, 10. The median number of years required for completion of a degree in 2006–2007 were 5. The number of students enrolled full- and part-time who were dismissed or voluntarily withdrew from this program area in 2007–2008 were 5. *General MA/MS (Master of Arts/Science)*—Applications 2007–2008, 26. Total applicants accepted 2007–2008, 11. Number full-time enrolled (new admits only) 2007–2008, 9. Total enrolled 2007–2008 full-time, 31. Openings 2008–2009, 10. The median number of years required for completion of a degree in 2006–2007 were 3. The number of students enrolled full- and part-time who were dismissed or voluntarily withdrew from this program area in 2007–2008 were 0.

Admissions Requirements:

Scores: Entries appear in this order: required test or GPA, minimum score (if required), median score of students entering in 2007–2008. Master's Programs: GRE-V no minimum stated, 550; GRE-Q no minimum stated, 630; overall undergraduate GPA no minimum stated; last 2 years GPA no minimum stated, 3.77. Doctoral Programs: GRE-V no minimum stated, 610; GRE-Q no minimum stated, 710; overall undergraduate GPA no minimum stated; last 2 years GPA no minimum stated, 3.89.

Other Criteria: (importance of criteria rated low, medium, or high): GRE/MAT scores—high, research experience—high, work experience—medium, extracurricular activity—low, clinically related public service—medium, GPA—high, letters of recommendation—high, interview—high, statement of goals and objectives—high. The clinically related public service refers to Clinical PhD applicants only.

Student Characteristics: The following represents characteristics of students in 2007–2008 in all graduate psychology programs in the department: Female—full-time 32, part-time 0; Male—full-time 75, part-time 0; African American/Black—full-time 3, part-time 0; Hispanic/Latino(a)—full-time 4, part-time 0; Asian/Pacific Islander—full-time 6, part-time 0; American Indian/Alaska Native—full-time 0, part-time 0; Caucasian/White—full-time 0, part-time 0; Multi-ethnic—full-time 1, part-time 0; students subject to the Americans With Disabilities Act—full-time 1, part-time 0; Unknown ethnicity—full-time 93, part-time 0; International students who hold an F-1 or J-1 Visa—full-time 9, part-time 0.

Financial Information/Assistance:

Tuition for Full-Time Study: *Master's:* State residents: per academic year $5,160, $287 per credit hour; Nonstate residents: per academic year $10,320, $573 per credit hour. *Doctoral:* State residents: per academic year $5,160, $287 per credit hour; Nonstate residents: per academic year $10,320, $573 per credit hour. Tuition is subject to change. See the following Web site for updates and changes in tuition costs: Resident tuition given to members of the sponsoring institution regardless of state of origin.

Financial Assistance:

First-Year Students: Teaching assistantships available for first year. Average amount paid per academic year: $8,500. Average number of hours worked per week: 13. Tuition remission given: partial. Research assistantships available for first year. Average amount paid per academic year: $8,500. Average number of hours worked per week: 13. Tuition remission given: partial.

Advanced Students: Teaching assistantships available for advanced students. Average amount paid per academic year: $9,000. Average number of hours worked per week: 13. Tuition remission given: partial. Research assistantships available for advanced students. Average amount paid per academic year: $9,000. Average number of hours worked per week: 13. Tuition remission given: partial. Traineeships available for advanced students. Average amount paid per academic year: $15,000. Average number of hours worked per week: 20. Tuition remission given: partial.

Additional Information: Of all students currently enrolled full time, 98% benefited from one or more of the listed financial assistance programs.

Internships/Practica: Doctoral Degree (PhD Clinical): For those doctoral students for whom a professional internship was required in this program prior to graduation, (10) students applied for an internship in 2006–2007, with (9) students obtaining an internship. Of those students who obtained an internship, (9) were paid internships. Of those students who obtained an internship, (9) students placed in APA/CPA-accredited internships, (0) students placed in internships not APA/CPA-accredited, but listed with the Association of Psychology Postdoctoral and Internship Centers (APPIC), (0) students placed in internships conforming to guidelines of the Council of Directors of School Psychology Programs (CDSPP), (0) students placed in internships that were not APA/CPA-accredited, APPIC or CDSPP listed. Clinical PhD students complete 3 types of practica: (a) BYU Comprehensive Clinic Integrative Practicum: Students see clients from the community in their first 3 years under the supervision of full-time clinical faculty. The clinic is a unique interdisciplinary training and research facility housing state-of-the-art audiovisual and computer resources for BYU's Clinical Psychology, Marriage and Family Therapy, Social Work, and Communication Disorders programs. (b) Clerkships: Students are required to complete two unpaid clerkships of 60 hours each. The clerkships allow students to work with different service agencies dealing with different focus groups: examples include prison, state hospital, residential treatment centers, private practice with a variety of age groups and presenting problems, developmentally disabled/autistic classrooms, and rehabilitation centers. (c) Externships: The Clinical program arranges reimbursed training placements for students in over 25 community agencies where students are supervised by onsite licensed professionals, who typically hold adjunct appointments in the Psychology Department. These opportunities provide an excellent foundation for the integration of classroom experiences with practical work applications. For additional information on education and training outcomes for our programs, see the following Web site: http://www.psychology.byu.edu.

Housing and Day Care: On-campus housing is available. See the following Web site for more information: http://www.byu.edu/housing/ or contact the BYU Campus Accommodations Office at (801) 422-2611, toll-free (877) 403-0040. No on-campus day care facilities are available.

Employment of Department Graduates:

Master's Degree Graduates: Of those who graduated in the academic year 2006–2007, the following categories and numbers represent the postgraduate activities and employment of master's degree graduates: Enrolled in a psychology doctoral program (4), enrolled in another graduate/professional program (2), enrolled in a postdoctoral residency/fellowship (n/a), employed in independent practice (n/a), employed in other positions at a higher education institution (1), not seeking employment (1), total from the above (master's) (8).

Doctoral Degree Graduates: Of those who graduated in the academic year 2006–2007, the following categories and numbers represent the postgraduate activities and employment of doctoral degree graduates: Enrolled in a psychology doctoral program (n/a), enrolled in a postdoctoral residency/fellowship (4), employed in independent practice (2), employed in an academic position at a university (3), employed in business or industry (2), employed in a hospital/medical center (2), total from the above (doctoral) (13).

Additional Information:

Orientation, Objectives, and Emphasis of Department: The mission of the Psychology Department is to discover, disseminate, and apply principles of psychology within a scholarly framework that is compatible with the values and purposes of Brigham Young University and its sponsor. Three degrees are offered: Clinical Psychology PhD, General Psychology PhD (emphasis areas in Applied Social Psychology, Behavioral Neurobiology, and Theoretical/Philosophical Psychology), and General MS. For the General PhD, students complete a common core of course work during the first three semesters. By the end of the 2nd year students complete the requirements for an MS degree, including a master's thesis, if the degree has not been previously received. For the Clinical PhD, students do not complete a master's thesis. The philosophy of the Clinical Psychology program adheres to the scientist–professional model. Training focuses on academic and research competence as well as on theory and practicum experiences necessary to develop strong clinical skills. The program is eclectic in its theoretical approach, drawing from a wide range of orientations in an attempt to give broad exposure to a diversity of traditional and innovative approaches. If they wish, students may elect to complete an emphasis in Child, Adolescent, and Family; Clinical Neuropsychology; or Clinical Research.

Personal Behavior Statement: Although the university is sponsored by the LDS (Mormon) Church, non-LDS students are welcome and considered without bias. The university does expect that all students, regardless of religion, maintain the behavioral standards of the university. These include high standards of honor, integrity, and morality; graciousness in personal behavior; and abstinence from such things as tobacco, alcohol, and the nonmedical use of drugs. The text of this agreement can be viewed at http://campuslife.byu.edu/honorcode/.

Special Facilities or Resources: Family, Home, and Social Sciences Computing Center: The center assists faculty and students with data processing and other computing needs on mainframe and personal computers. Technical support and consultation services for both statistics and graphics are available to students working on research projects, theses, and dissertations. Special computer facilities in the department support research in psycholinguistics, neuroimaging, neurophysiology, social psychology, and experimental analysis of human and animal behavior. Psychobiology Research Laboratories: These laboratories are equipped with facilities for brain–behavior analysis. Full histology and electrophysiology laboratories, along with the necessary surgical facilities, are available. Neuroimaging and Behavior Laboratory: Research and training in the area of neuroimaging and cognitive neuroscience are supported by a laboratory consisting of multiple computers, video, data storage, and printer workstations. These are supported by software that allows for the capture, processing, isolation, and imaging output of specific areas of the brain from MRI and CT images and from metabolic imaging studies. Multivariate Data Visualization Laboratory: Faculty and students interested in multivariate visualization of data and large-scale data analysis are supported by a mathematical psychology laboratory consisting of a network of NT workstations and laboratories for behavior analysis. Three laboratories feature online control of experimental procedures and data recording.

Information for Students With Physical Disabilities: See the following Web site for more information: http://www.campuslife.byu.edu/uac/.

Application Information:

Send to Graduate Studies Office, B-356 ASB, Brigham Young University, Provo, UT 84602. Application available online. URL of online application: https://www.app.applyyourself.com/?id=byugrad. Students are admitted in the Fall, application deadline January 1. Online applications are required. See www.byu.edu/gradstudies. (Please contact Graduate Studies if you are unable to complete an application online.) *Fee:* $50.

Utah State University

Department of Psychology
Education
2810 Old Main Hill
Logan, UT 84322-2810
Telephone: (435) 797-1460
Fax: (435) 797-1448
E-mail: *david.stein@usu.edu*
Web: *http://www.usu.edu/psychology/*

Department Information:

1938. Chairperson: David M. Stein, PhD. Number of faculty: total—full-time 20, part-time 8; women—full-time 10, part-time 4; total—minority—full-time 2; women minority—full-time 2.

Programs and Degrees Offered:

Listed in the following order: Program area, degree type (T if terminal Master's), number awarded 7/06–6/07. Combined Clinical/Counseling/School PhD (Doctor of Philosophy) 5, Experimental and Applied Psychological Science PhD (Doctor of Philosophy) 2, School Psychology MA/MS (Master of Arts/Science) (T) 6, School Counseling MA/MS (Master of Arts/Science) (T) 38.

APA Accreditation: Combination PhD (Doctor of Philosophy).

Student Applications/Admissions:

Student Applications

Combined Clinical/Counseling/School PhD (Doctor of Philosophy)—Applications 2007–2008, 78. Total applicants accepted 2007–2008, 10. Number full-time enrolled (new admits only) 2007–2008, 8. Number part-time enrolled (new admits only) 2007–2008, 0. Openings 2008–2009, 8. The median number of years required for completion of a degree in 2006–2007 were 7. The number of students enrolled full- and part-time who were dismissed or voluntarily withdrew from this program area in 2007–2008 were 0. *Experimental and Applied Psychological Science PhD (Doctor of Philosophy)*—Applications 2007–2008, 9. Total applicants accepted 2007–2008, 4. Number full-time enrolled (new admits only) 2007–2008, 3. Number part-time enrolled (new admits only) 2007–2008, 0. Openings 2008–2009, 5. The number of students enrolled full- and part-time who were dismissed or voluntarily withdrew from this program area in 2007–2008 were 1. *School Psychology MA/MS (Master of Arts/Science)*—Applications 2007–2008, 20. Total applicants accepted 2007–2008, 6. Number full-time enrolled (new admits only) 2007–2008, 4. Total enrolled 2007–2008 full-time, 15. Openings 2008–2009, 5. The median number of years required for completion of a degree in 2006–2007 were 3. The number of students enrolled full- and part-time who were dismissed or voluntarily withdrew from this program area in 2007–2008 were 0. *School Counseling MA/MS (Master of Arts/Science)*—Applications 2007–2008, 89. Total applicants accepted 2007–2008, 78. Total enrolled 2007–2008 full-time, 62, part-time, 6. Openings 2008–2009, 45. The median number of years required for completion of a degree in 2006–2007 were 2.

Admissions Requirements:

Scores: Entries appear in this order: required test or GPA, minimum score (if required), median score of students entering in 2007–2008. Master's Programs: GRE-V 550, 525; GRE-Q 550, 590; last 2 years GPA 3.25, 3.58. MAT is accepted in lieu of GRE for School Counseling. Doctoral Programs: GRE-V 550, 530; GRE-Q 550, 640; last 2 years GPA 3.25, 3.76. Median scores are for the combined Clinical/Counseling/School PhD program. Scores for the REM PhD program are similar. Scores for MS programs tends to be slightly lower.

Other Criteria: (importance of criteria rated low, medium, or high): GRE/MAT scores—high, research experience—medium, work experience—medium, extracurricular activity—low, clinically related public service—medium, GPA—high, letters of recommendation—high, interview—high, statement of goals and objectives—high. Some programs (Clinical/Counseling/School PhD) use the above criteria in a formula, whereas others (REM) rely primarily on GPA, GRE, and letters.. For additional information on admission requirements, go to http://www.coe.usu.edu/psyc/index.html.

Student Characteristics: The following represents characteristics of students in 2007–2008 in all graduate psychology programs in the department: Female—full-time 118, part-time 11; Male—full-time 58, part-time 10; African American/Black—full-time 2, part-time 0; Hispanic/Latino(a)—full-time 3, part-time 1; Asian/Pacific Islander—full-time 3, part-time 1; American Indian/Alaska Native—full-time 5, part-time 1; Caucasian/White—full-time 153, part-time 18; students subject to the Americans With Disabilities Act—full-time 0, part-time 0; Unknown ethnicity—full-time 0, part-time 0.

Financial Information/Assistance:

Tuition for Full-Time Study: *Master's:* State residents: per academic year $3,712, $349 per credit hour; Nonstate residents: per academic year $9,281, $874 per credit hour. *Doctoral:* State residents: per academic year $3,712, $349 per credit hour; Nonstate residents: per academic year $9,281, $874 per credit hour. Tuition is subject to change. See the following Web site for updates and changes in tuition costs: http://www.usu.edu/registrar/payment/pdf/2006_07_tuition.pdf.

Financial Assistance:

First-Year Students: Teaching assistantships available for first year. Average amount paid per academic year: $7,000. Average number of hours worked per week: 20. Apply by January 15. Tuition remission given: full and partial. Research assistantships available for first year. Average amount paid per academic year: $11,000. Average number of hours worked per week: 20. Apply by varies. Tuition remission given: full and partial. Fellowships and scholarships available for first year. Average amount paid per academic year: $13,500. Apply by January 15. Tuition remission given: full and partial.

Advanced Students: Teaching assistantships available for advanced students. Average amount paid per academic year: $8,000. Average number of hours worked per week: 20. Apply by February 15. Tuition remission given: full and partial. Research assistantships available for advanced students. Average amount paid per academic year: $11,000. Average number of hours worked per week: 20. Apply by varies. Tuition remission given: full and partial.

Additional Information: Of all students currently enrolled full time, 100% benefited from one or more of the listed financial assistance programs.

Internships/Practica: Doctoral Degree (PhD Combined Clinical/Counseling/School): For those doctoral students for whom a professional internship was required in this program prior to graduation, (6) students applied for an internship in 2006–2007, with (5) students obtaining an internship. Of those students who obtained an internship, (5) were paid internships. Of those students who obtained an internship, (5) students placed in APA/CPA-accredited internships, (0) students placed in internships not APA/CPA-accredited, but listed with the Association of Psychology Postdoctoral and Internship Centers (APPIC), (0) students placed in internships conforming to guidelines of the Council of Directors of School Psychology Programs (CDSPP), (0) students placed in internships that were not APA/CPA-accredited, APPIC or CDSPP listed. Practica are available for master's and doctoral students. Students are place in a variety of sites including community mental health centers, the USU Counseling Center, the Center for Persons with Disabilities (a University Center for Excellence), residential eating disorders treatment facility, and medical facilities in the area. Students from the Combined program accept internships across the country. Internships for students in the REM program are generally with local or regional consulting firms.

Housing and Day Care: On-campus housing is available. See the following Web site for more information: http://www.housing.usu.edu. On-campus day care facilities are available. See the following Web site for more information: http://www.usuchild.usu.edu.

Employment of Department Graduates:

Master's Degree Graduates: Of those who graduated in the academic year 2006–2007, the following categories and numbers represent the postgraduate activities and employment of master's degree graduates: Enrolled in a psychology doctoral program (0), enrolled in another graduate/professional program (0), enrolled in a postdoctoral residency/fellowship (n/a), employed in independent practice (n/a), employed in an academic position at a university (0), employed in an academic position at a 2-year/4-year college (0), employed in other positions at a higher education institution (0), employed in a professional position in a school system (6), employed in business or industry (0), employed in government agency (0), employed in a community mental health/counseling center (0), employed in a hospital/medical center (0), still seeking employment (0), other employment position (0), do not know (38), total from the above (master's) (44).

Doctoral Degree Graduates: Of those who graduated in the academic year 2006–2007, the following categories and numbers represent the postgraduate activities and employment of doctoral degree graduates: Enrolled in a psychology doctoral program (n/a), enrolled in a postdoctoral residency/fellowship (2), employed in independent practice (0), employed in an academic position at a university (0), employed in an academic position at a 2-year/4-year college (0), employed in other positions at a higher education institution (0), employed in a professional position in a school system (0), employed in government agency (0), employed in a community mental health/counseling center (1), employed in a hospital/medical center (0), still seeking employment (0), other employment position (0), total from the above (doctoral) (3).

Additional Information:

Orientation, Objectives, and Emphasis of Department: The Utah State University Department of Psychology offers two graduate PhD programs. Research and evaluation methodology offers training emphasizing methods and techniques for conducting research and evaluation studies in psychology or education settings. The combined Clinical/Counseling/School Psychology offers professional and scientific training in a combination of clinical, counseling, and school psychology (accredited by the American Psychological Association since 1975) and two master's degrees in School Psychology and School Counseling. The two graduate PhD programs share a common core of doctoral courses intended to provide an advanced overview of several major areas of psychology. All doctoral programs offer extensive training within their specific areas; however, the common core is designed to ensure that no student will complete the PhD without being exposed to the diverse theoretical and methodological perspectives in the field of psychology. The common core also provides students the opportunity to become aware of the scholarly interests of faculty members in all programs, thus broadening students' choices of faculty advisors and dissertation chairpersons. Full tuition waivers are available to PhD students for 70 semester hours of academic credit.

Special Facilities or Resources: Students in all graduate programs benefit from the following departmental facilities: the Basic Behavior Laboratory for nonhuman research, the Human Behavior Laboratory for analysis of human behavior, the Counseling Laboratory for research and training in counseling and clinical practice, and the Community Clinic for supervised experience in actual therapy. In addition, the department has cooperative relations with other campus and off-campus facilities that provide excellent settings for student assistantships, research, and training, including the Bear River Mental Health Center, the USU Center for Persons with Disabilities, the USU Counseling Center and the Logan Regional Hospital Behavioral Medicine Unit.

Application Information:

Send to Utah State University, School of Graduate Studies, Logan, UT 84322-0900. Application available online. URL of online application: http://www.usu.edu/gradsch. Students are admitted in the Fall, application deadline January 15; Spring, application deadline March 1; Summer, application deadline June 1. Research and Evaluation Methodology PhD will accept applications if the alloted openings are not filled as of February 1. Combined Clinical/Counseling/School Psychology program deadline is January 15, School Psychology is March 1, and School Counseling is June 1. *Fee:* $55.

Utah, University of

Department of Educational Psychology, Counseling Psychology and School Psychology Programs
College of Education
1705 East Campus Center Drive, Room 327
Salt Lake City, UT 84112-9255
Telephone: (801) 581-7148
Fax: (801) 581-5566
E-mail: *clark@ed.utah.edu*
Web: *http://www.ed.utah.edu/psych*

Department Information:

1949. Chairperson: Elaine Clark. Number of faculty: total—full-time 16, part-time 4; women—full-time 7, part-time 3; total—minority—full-time 5, part-time 1; women minority—full-time 2, part-time 1.

Programs and Degrees Offered:

Listed in the following order: Program area, degree type (T if terminal Master's), number awarded 7/06–6/07. Counseling Psychology PhD (Doctor of Philosophy) 8, School Psychology PhD (Doctor of Philosophy) 11, Learning Sciences PhD (Doctor of Philosophy) 0, Instructional Design and Educational Technology Other 11, Professional Counseling MA/MS (Master of Arts/Science) (T) 7, School Counseling EdS/MEd (School Psychology) 11, Statistics MA/MS (Master of Arts/Science) (T) 0.

APA Accreditation: Counseling PhD (Doctor of Philosophy). School PhD (Doctor of Philosophy).

Student Applications/Admissions:

Student Applications

Counseling Psychology PhD (Doctor of Philosophy)—Applications 2007–2008, 66. Total applicants accepted 2007–2008, 6. Number full-time enrolled (new admits only) 2007–2008, 6. Total enrolled 2007–2008 full-time, 42. Openings 2008–2009, 6. The median number of years required for completion of a degree in 2006–2007 were 6. The number of students enrolled full- and part-time who were dismissed or voluntarily withdrew from this program area in 2007–2008 were 0. *School Psychology PhD (Doctor of Philosophy)*—Applications 2007–2008, 47. Total applicants accepted 2007–2008, 14. Number full-time enrolled (new admits only) 2007–2008, 9. Total enrolled 2007–2008 full-time, 42. Openings 2008–2009, 8. The median number of years required for completion of a degree in 2006–2007 were 6. The number of students enrolled full- and part-time who were dismissed or voluntarily withdrew from this program area in 2007–2008 were 1. *Learning Sciences PhD (Doctor of Philosophy)*—Applications 2007–2008, 7. Total applicants accepted 2007–2008, 3. Number full-time enrolled (new admits only) 2007–2008, 3. Total enrolled 2007–2008 full-time, 6. Openings 2008–2009, 5. The median number of years required for completion of a degree in 2006–2007 were 5. The number of students enrolled full- and part-time who were dismissed or voluntarily withdrew from this program area in 2007–2008 were 0. *Instructional Design and Educational Technology Other*—Applications 2007–2008, 15. Total applicants accepted 2007–2008, 13. Number full-time enrolled (new admits only) 2007–2008, 13. Total enrolled 2007–2008 full-time, 30. Openings 2008–2009, 20. The median number of years required for completion of a degree in 2006–2007 were 2. The number of students enrolled full- and part-time who were dismissed or voluntarily withdrew from this program area in 2007–2008 were 0. *Professional Counseling MA/MS (Master of Arts/Science)*—Applications 2007–2008, 33. Total applicants accepted 2007–2008, 11. Number full-time enrolled (new admits only) 2007–2008, 11. Total enrolled 2007–2008 full-time, 32. Openings 2008–2009, 10. The median number of years required for completion of a degree in 2006–2007 were 3. The number of students enrolled full- and part-time who were dismissed or voluntarily withdrew from this program area in 2007–2008 were 0. *School Counseling EdS/MEd (School Psychology)*—Applications 2007–2008, 25. Total applicants accepted 2007–2008, 14. Number full-time enrolled (new admits only) 2007–2008, 12. Number part-time enrolled (new admits only) 2007–2008, 0. Openings 2008–2009, 11. The median number of years required for completion of a degree in 2006–2007 were 2. The number of students enrolled full- and part-time who were dismissed or voluntarily withdrew from this program area in 2007–2008 were 0. *Statistics MA/MS (Master of Arts/Science)*—Applications 2007–2008, 1. Total applicants accepted 2007–2008, 1. Number full-time enrolled (new admits only) 2007–2008, 1. Total enrolled 2007–2008 full-time, 2.

Admissions Requirements:

Scores: Entries appear in this order: required test or GPA, minimum score (if required), median score of students entering in 2007–2008. Master's Programs: GRE-V no minimum stated, 572; GRE-Q no minimum stated, 620; overall undergraduate GPA 3.00, 3.47; Master's GRE-Analytical no minimum stated. Doctoral Programs: GRE-V no minimum stated, 545; GRE-Q no minimum stated, 600; overall undergraduate GPA no minimum stated, 3.56.

Other Criteria: (importance of criteria rated low, medium, or high): GRE/MAT scores—high, research experience—high, work experience—high, extracurricular activity—medium, clinically related public service—medium, GPA—high, letters of recommendation—high, statement of goals and objectives—high. Each program reviews and rates its own applicants.

Student Characteristics: The following represents characteristics of students in 2007–2008 in all graduate psychology programs in the department: Female—full-time 55, part-time 59; Male—full-time 28, part-time 31; African American/Black—full-time 2, part-time 1; Hispanic/Latino(a)—full-time 4, part-time 8; Asian/Pacific Islander—full-time 1, part-time 2; American Indian/Alaska Native—full-time 6, part-time 0; Caucasian/White—full-time 65, part-time 74; Multi-ethnic—full-time 0, part-time 0; students subject to the Americans With Disabilities Act—full-time 0, part-time 0; Unknown ethnicity—full-time 3, part-time 3; International students who hold an F-1 or J-1 Visa—full-time 2, part-time 2.

Financial Information/Assistance:

Tuition for Full-Time Study: *Master's:* State residents: per academic year $3,200; Nonstate residents: per academic year $10,000. *Doctoral:* State residents: per academic year $3,200; Nonstate residents: per academic year $10,000. Tuition is subject to change. See the following Web site for updates and changes in tuition costs: http://www.ed.utah.edu.

Financial Assistance:

First-Year Students: Teaching assistantships available for first year. Average amount paid per academic year: $5,500. Average number of hours worked per week: 10. Apply by April. Tuition remission given: partial. Research assistantships available for first year. Average amount paid per academic year: $5,500. Average number of hours worked per week: 10. Apply by flexible. Tuition remission given: partial.

Advanced Students: Teaching assistantships available for advanced students. Average amount paid per academic year: $5,500. Average number of hours worked per week: 10. Apply by April. Tuition remission given: partial. Research assistantships available for advanced students. Average amount paid per academic year: $5,500. Average number of hours worked per week: 10. Apply by flexible. Tuition remission given: partial. Traineeships available for advanced students. Apply by varies. Fellowships and scholarships available for advanced students. Average number of hours worked per week: 0. Apply by varies.

Additional Information: Of all students currently enrolled full time, 50% benefited from one or more of the listed financial assistance programs.

Internships/Practica: Doctoral Degree (PhD Counseling Psychology): For those doctoral students for whom a professional internship was required in this program prior to graduation, (3) students applied for an internship in 2006–2007, with (2) students obtaining an internship. Of those students who obtained an internship, (2) were paid internships. Of those students who obtained an internship, (2) students placed in APA/CPA-accredited internships, (0) students placed in internships not APA/CPA-accredited, but listed with the Association of Psychology Postdoctoral and Internship Centers (APPIC), (0) students placed in internships conforming to guidelines of the Council of Directors of School Psychology Programs (CDSPP), (0) students placed in internships that were not APA/CPA-accredited, APPIC or CDSPP listed. Doctoral Degree (PhD School Psychology): For those doctoral students for whom a professional internship was required in this program prior to graduation, (6) students applied for an internship in 2006–2007, with (6) students obtaining an internship. Of those students who obtained an internship, (6) were paid internships. Of those students who obtained an internship, (1) student placed in APA/CPA-accredited internships, (1) student placed in internships not APA/CPA-accredited, but listed with the Association of Psychology Postdoctoral and Internship Centers (APPIC), (0) students placed in internships conforming to guidelines of the Council of Directors of School Psychology Programs (CDSPP), (4) students placed in internships that were not APA/CPA-accredited, APPIC or CDSPP listed. Practica for Counseling Psychology doctoral students vary and include such settings as University of Utah counseling center and other campus services, community mental health settings, hospital settings, and private practice. Predoctoral internships are typically taken nationally in university counseling centers, community mental health settings, veterans hospitals, and specialty settings.

Housing and Day Care: On-campus housing is available. See the following Web site for more information: http://www.orl.utah.edu/. On-campus day care facilities are available. See the following Web site for more information: http://www.childcare.utah.edu/.

Employment of Department Graduates:

Master's Degree Graduates: Of those who graduated in the academic year 2006–2007, the following categories and numbers

represent the postgraduate activities and employment of master's degree graduates: Enrolled in a postdoctoral residency/fellowship (n/a), employed in independent practice (n/a), employed in an academic position at a 2-year/4-year college (0), employed in a professional position in a school system (20), employed in a community mental health/counseling center (12), employed in a hospital/medical center (0), total from the above (master's) (32). ***Doctoral Degree Graduates:*** Of those who graduated in the academic year 2006–2007, the following categories and numbers represent the postgraduate activities and employment of doctoral degree graduates: Enrolled in a psychology doctoral program (n/a), employed in an academic position at a university (5), employed in an academic position at a 2-year/4-year college (0), employed in other positions at a higher education institution (2), employed in a professional position in a school system (2), employed in business or industry (1), employed in government agency (0), still seeking employment (0), other employment position (0), do not know (0), total from the above (doctoral) (10).

Additional Information:

Orientation, Objectives, and Emphasis of Department: The department of educational psychology at the University of Utah is characterized by an emphasis on the application of behavioral sciences to educational and psychological processes. The department is organized into three program areas: Counseling and Counseling Psychology (MS, MEd, PhD), School Psychology (MS, PhD), and Learning Sciences with three subprograms: Learning and Cognition (PhD), a master's-level program in Instructional Design and Educational Technology (IDET; MEd), and an interdepartmental program that leads to a Master's in Statistics (MSTAT). The basic master's-level programming includes 1 to 2 years of academic work (and in some cases an additional year of internship). Doctoral programs include Counseling Psychology (APA accredited since 1957), School Psychology (APA accredited since 1986), and Learning Sciences Learning and Cognition area. The emphasis of the department is on the application of psychological principles in educational and human service settings. In addition, doctoral programs represent a scientist–practitioner model with considerable emphasis on the development of research as well as professional skills. Information describing the objectives and emphases of specific program areas within the department is available on request.

Special Facilities or Resources: A variety of research and training opportunities are available to students through relationships the department has developed with various university and community facilities. Included are the university counseling center, medical center, computer center, and the adjacent regional Veterans Administration Medical Center. Community facilities include local school districts, community mental health centers, children's hospital, general hospitals, child guidance clinics, and various state social service agencies. The department maintains its own statistics laboratory. Students have access to computer stations and use of college computer network.

Information for Students With Physical Disabilities: See the following Web site for more information: http://www.hr.utah.edu/oeo/disab/.

Application Information:

Send to Admission, University of Utah, Department of Educational Psychology, 1705 East Campus Center Drive, Room 327, Salt Lake City, Utah 84112-9255. Application available online. URL of online application: http://www.edps.ed.utah.edu/. Students are admitted in the Fall, application deadline December 15. *Fee:* $45.

Utah, University of

Department of Psychology
Social and Behavioral Science
380 South 1530 East, Room 502
Salt Lake City, UT 84112
Telephone: (801) 581-6124
Fax: (801) 581-5841
E-mail: *nancy.seegmiller@psych.utah.edu*
Web: *http://www.psych.utah.edu*

Department Information:

1925. Chairperson: Frances J. Friedrich. Number of faculty: total—full-time 28, part-time 4; women—full-time 12, part-time 2; total—minority—full-time 5; women minority—full-time 2.

Programs and Degrees Offered:

Listed in the following order: Program area, degree type (T if terminal Master's), number awarded 7/06–6/07. Clinical Psychology PhD (Doctor of Philosophy) 3, Cognition and Neuralscience PhD (Doctor of Philosophy) 0, Developmental Psychology PhD (Doctor of Philosophy) 1, Social Psychology PhD (Doctor of Philosophy) 1.

APA Accreditation: Clinical PhD (Doctor of Philosophy).

Student Applications/Admissions:

Student Applications

Clinical Psychology PhD (Doctor of Philosophy)—Applications 2007–2008, 128. Total applicants accepted 2007–2008, 9. Number full-time enrolled (new admits only) 2007–2008, 5. Number part-time enrolled (new admits only) 2007–2008, 0. Openings 2008–2009, 6. The median number of years required for completion of a degree in 2006–2007 were 7. The number of students enrolled full- and part-time who were dismissed or voluntarily withdrew from this program area in 2007–2008 were 2. *Cognition and Neuralscience PhD (Doctor of Philosophy)*—Applications 2007–2008, 26. Total applicants accepted 2007–2008, 6. Number full-time enrolled (new admits only) 2007–2008, 5. Number part-time enrolled (new admits only) 2007–2008, 0. Openings 2008–2009, 3. The number of students enrolled full- and part-time who were dismissed or voluntarily withdrew from this program area in 2007–2008 were 1. *Developmental Psychology PhD (Doctor of Philosophy)*—Applications 2007–2008, 12. Total applicants accepted 2007–2008, 1. Number full-time enrolled (new admits only) 2007–2008, 0. Number part-time enrolled (new admits only) 2007–2008, 0. Openings 2008–2009, 4. The median number of years required for completion of a degree in 2006–2007 were 7. The number of students enrolled full- and part-time who were dismissed or voluntarily withdrew from this program area in 2007–2008 were 1. *Social Psychology PhD (Doctor of Philosophy)*—Applications 2007–2008, 28. Total applicants accepted 2007–2008, 3. Number full-time enrolled (new admits only) 2007–2008, 0. Number part-time enrolled (new admits only) 2007–2008, 0. Openings 2008–2009, 3. The median number of years required for completion of a degree in 2006–2007 were 4. The number of students enrolled full- and part-time who were dismissed or voluntarily withdrew from this program area in 2007–2008 were 1.

Admissions Requirements:

Scores: Entries appear in this order: required test or GPA, minimum score (if required), median score of students entering in 2007–2008. Master's Programs: GRE-V no minimum stated; GRE-Q no minimum stated; GRE-Subject (Psychology) no minimum stated; Master's GRE-Analytical no minimum stated. The subject test is required for the Clinical program. Doctoral Programs: GRE-V no minimum stated, 555; GRE-Q no minimum stated, 638; GRE-Subject (Psychology) no minimum stated, 633; overall undergraduate GPA 3.0, 3.53; Doctoral program GRE-Analytic no minimum stated, 4.8. The subject test is required for the Clinical program.

Other Criteria: (importance of criteria rated low, medium, or high): GRE/MAT scores—medium, research experience—high, work experience—medium, extracurricular activity—medium, clinically related public service—medium, GPA—medium, letters of recommendation—high, interview—high, statement of goals and objectives—high.

Student Characteristics: The following represents characteristics of students in 2007–2008 in all graduate psychology programs in the department: Female—full-time 38, part-time 0; Male—full-time 21, part-time 0; African American/Black—full-time 0, part-time 0; Hispanic/Latino(a)—full-time 3, part-time 0; Asian/Pacific Islander—full-time 5, part-time 0; American Indian/Alaska Native—full-time 0, part-time 0; Caucasian/White—full-time 50, part-time 0; Multi-ethnic—full-time 1, part-time 0; students subject to the Americans With Disabilities Act—full-time 0, part-time 0; Unknown ethnicity—full-time 0, part-time 0; International students who hold an F-1 or J-1 Visa—full-time 3, part-time 0.

Financial Information/Assistance:

Tuition for Full-Time Study: *Master's:* State residents: per academic year $4,990, $455 per credit hour; Nonstate residents: per academic year $15,850, $1,622 per credit hour. *Doctoral:* State residents: per academic year $4,990, $455 per credit hour; Nonstate residents: per academic year $15,850, $1,622 per credit hour. Tuition is subject to change. See the following Web site for updates and changes in tuition costs: http://www.utah.edu.

Financial Assistance:

First-Year Students: Teaching assistantships available for first year. Average amount paid per academic year: $11,000. Average number of hours worked per week: 20. Apply by TBA. Tuition remission given: full. Research assistantships available for first year. Average amount paid per academic year: $11,000. Average number of hours worked per week: 20. Apply by TBA. Tuition remission given: full. Fellowships and scholarships available for first year. Average amount paid per academic year: $11,000. Apply by TBA. Tuition remission given: full.

Advanced Students: Teaching assistantships available for advanced students. Average amount paid per academic year: $11,000. Average number of hours worked per week: 20. Apply by TBA. Tuition remission given: full. Research assistantships available for advanced students. Average amount paid per academic year: $11,000. Average number of hours worked per week: 20. Apply by TBA. Tuition remission given: full. Fellowships and scholarships available for advanced students. Average amount paid per academic year: $11,000. Apply by TBA. Tuition remission given: full.

Additional Information: Of all students currently enrolled full time, 92% benefited from one or more of the listed financial assistance programs. Application and information available online at http://www.psych.utah.edu.

Internships/Practica: Doctoral Degree (PhD Clinical Psychology): For those doctoral students for whom a professional internship was required in this program prior to graduation, (3) students applied for an internship in 2006–2007, with (2) students obtaining an internship. Of those students who obtained an internship, (2) were paid internships. Of those students who obtained an internship, (2) students placed in APA/CPA-accredited internships, (0) students placed in internships not APA/CPA accredited, but listed with the Association of Psychology Postdoctoral and Internship Centers (APPIC), (0) students placed in internships conforming to guidelines of the Council of Directors of School Psychology Programs (CDSPP), (0) students placed in internships that were not APA/CPA-accredited, APPIC or CDSPP listed. Extensive clinical training experiences are available through close ties with facilities in the community. A sample of these include the Veteran's Administration Hospital, the University Medical Center, Primary Children's Hospital, the Children's Behavioral Therapy Unit, the Juvenile Detention Center, the University Neuropsychiatric Institute, the University Counseling Center, and local community health centers. There are four APA-approved internships in the local community.

Housing and Day Care: On-campus housing is available. See the following Web site for more information: http://www.utah.edu. On-campus day care facilities are available.

Employment of Department Graduates:

Master's Degree Graduates: Of those who graduated in the academic year 2006–2007, the following categories and numbers represent the postgraduate activities and employment of master's degree graduates: Enrolled in a postdoctoral residency/fellowship (n/a), employed in independent practice (n/a), total from the above (master's) (0).

Doctoral Degree Graduates: Of those who graduated in the academic year 2006–2007, the following categories and numbers represent the postgraduate activities and employment of doctoral degree graduates: Enrolled in a psychology doctoral program (n/a), enrolled in another graduate/professional program (0), enrolled in a postdoctoral residency/fellowship (0), employed in independent practice (0), employed in an academic position at a university (2), employed in an academic position at a 2-year/4-year college (0), employed in other positions at a higher education institution (0), employed in a professional position in a school system (1), employed in business or industry (1), employed in government agency (0), employed in a community mental health/counseling center (0), employed in a hospital/medical center (1), still seeking employment (0), not seeking employment (0), other employment position (0), do not know (0), total from the above (doctoral) (5).

Additional Information:

Orientation, Objectives, and Emphasis of Department: We offer comprehensive training in psychology, including Clinical (general, child–family, health, and neuropsychology emphases), Developmental, Experimental-Physiological, and Social. Students generally receive support throughout their training. Students are selected for area programs with individual faculty advisers. They do research in their areas, and Clinical students also receive applied training. Graduates accept jobs in academic departments, research centers, and applied settings.

Special Facilities or Resources: Special facilities include the Early Childhood Education Center and three on-campus hospitals.

Application Information:

Send to Graduate Admissions Secretary, Psychology Department, 380 South 1530 East, Room 502, Salt Lake City, UT 84112. Application available online. URL of online application: http://www.psych.utah.edu/graduate/index.html. Students are admitted in the Fall, application deadline December 15. *Fee:* $45.

Goddard College (2007 data)

MA Psychology and Counseling Program
123 Pitkin Road
Plainfield, VT 05667
Telephone: (802) 454-8311, (800) 468-4888
Fax: (802) 454-1029
E-mail: *Steven.James@goddard.edu*
Web: *http://www.goddard.edu*

Department Information:

1988. Chairperson: Steven E. James, PhD. Number of faculty: total—full-time 1, part-time 6; women—part-time 4.

Programs and Degrees Offered:

Listed in the following order: Program area, degree type (T if terminal Master's), number awarded 7/06–6/07. Organizational Development MA/MS (Master of Arts/Science) (T) 1, Sexual Orientation MA/MS (Master of Arts/Science) (T) 2, Counseling MA/MS (Master of Arts/Science) (T) 12, Psychology MA/MS (Master of Arts/Science) (T) 0.

Student Applications/Admissions:

Student Applications

Organizational Development MA/MS (Master of Arts/Science)—Applications 2007–2008, 2. Total applicants accepted 2007–2008, 2. Openings 2008–2009, 2. The median number of years required for completion of a degree in 2006–2007 were 2. The number of students enrolled full- and part-time who were dismissed or voluntarily withdrew from this program area in 2007–2008 were 0. *Sexual Orientation MA/MS (Master of Arts/Science)*—Applications 2007–2008, 7. Total applicants accepted 2007–2008, 6. Number full-time enrolled (new admits only) 2007–2008, 6. Number part-time enrolled (new admits only) 2007–2008, 0. Openings 2008–2009, 10. The median number of years required for completion of a degree in 2006–2007 were 2. The number of students enrolled full- and part-time who were dismissed or voluntarily withdrew from this program area in 2007–2008 were 0. *Counseling MA/MS (Master of Arts/Science)*—Applications 2007–2008, 25. Total applicants accepted 2007–2008, 20. Number full-time enrolled (new admits only) 2007–2008, 20. Number part-time enrolled (new admits only) 2007–2008, 5. Total enrolled 2007–2008 full-time, 44, part-time, 7. Openings 2008–2009, 20. The median number of years required for completion of a degree in 2006–2007 were 2. The number of students enrolled full- and part-time who were dismissed or voluntarily withdrew from this program area in 2007–2008 were 2. *Psychology MA/MS (Master of Arts/Science)*—Applications 2007–2008, 0. Total applicants accepted 2007–2008, 0. Number full-time enrolled (new admits only) 2007–2008, 0. Number part-time enrolled (new admits only) 2007–2008, 0. Openings 2008–2009, 1. The number of students enrolled full- and part-time who were dismissed or voluntarily withdrew from this program area in 2007–2008 were 0.

Admissions Requirements:

Scores: Entries appear in this order: required test or GPA, minimum score (if required), median score of students entering in 2007–2008. Master's Programs: overall undergraduate GPA no minimum stated; psychology GPA no minimum stated.

Other Criteria: (importance of criteria rated low, medium, or high): research experience—low, work experience—high, extracurricular activity—medium, clinically related public service—high, GPA—medium, letters of recommendation—high, interview—low, statement of goals and objectives—high. For additional information on admission requirements, go to http://www.goddard.edu.

Student Characteristics: The following represents characteristics of students in 2007–2008 in all graduate psychology programs in the department: Female—full-time 38, part-time 0; Male—full-time 16, part-time 0; African American/Black—full-time 4, part-time 0; Hispanic/Latino(a)—full-time 0, part-time 0; Asian/Pacific Islander—full-time 1, part-time 0; American Indian/Alaska Native—full-time 2, part-time 0; Caucasian/White—full-time 45, part-time 0; Multi-ethnic—full-time 2, part-time 0; students subject to the Americans With Disabilities Act—full-time 6, part-time 0; Unknown ethnicity—full-time 0, part-time 0.

Financial Information/Assistance:

Tuition for Full-Time Study: *Master's:* State residents: per academic year $11,500; Nonstate residents: per academic year $11,500. Tuition is subject to change. See the following Web site for updates and changes in tuition costs: http://www.goddard.edu.

Financial Assistance:

First-Year Students: Fellowships and scholarships available for first year. Average amount paid per academic year: $1,445. Average number of hours worked per week: 0. Apply by rolling. Tuition remission given: partial.

Advanced Students: Fellowships and scholarships available for advanced students. Average amount paid per academic year: $1,445. Average number of hours worked per week: 0. Apply by rolling. Tuition remission given: partial.

Additional Information: Of all students currently enrolled full time, 0% benefited from one or more of the listed financial assistance programs. Application and information available online at http://www.goddard.edu.

Internships/Practica: Students are required to complete a minimum of 300 hours of supervised practicum during the program. This practicum takes place at a location convenient to the student that has been reviewed and evaluated by the program faculty as appropriate to the student's plan of study, providing appropriated licensed supervision and offering direct counseling experience. Students propose sites at which they would like to work to the faculty for review and approval.

Housing and Day Care: On-campus housing is available. See the following Web site for more information: Contact: http://www.@ goddard.edu. No on-campus day care facilities are available.

Employment of Department Graduates:

Master's Degree Graduates: Of those who graduated in the academic year 2006–2007, the following categories and numbers represent the postgraduate activities and employment of master's degree graduates: Enrolled in a psychology doctoral program (6), enrolled in another graduate/professional program (0), enrolled in a postdoctoral residency/fellowship (n/a), employed in independent practice (n/a), employed in an academic position at a university (2), employed in an academic position at a 2-year/4-year college (0), employed in other positions at a higher education institution (1), employed in a professional position in a school system (1), employed in business or industry (3), employed in government agency (0), employed in a community mental health/counseling center (13), employed in a hospital/medical center (1), still seeking employment (1), other employment position (2), total from the above (master's) (30).

Doctoral Degree Graduates: Of those who graduated in the academic year 2006–2007, the following categories and numbers represent the postgraduate activities and employment of doctoral degree graduates: Enrolled in a psychology doctoral program (n/a), total from the above (doctoral) (0).

Additional Information:

Orientation, Objectives, and Emphasis of Department: Graduate study in Psychology and Counseling consists of a unique combination of intensive campus residencies and directed, independent study off campus. Students design their own emphasis of study or enter into the defined concentrations in organizational development or sexual orientation studies. The primary goal of the program is to develop skills in individual, family, and/or community psychology, grounded in theory and research, personal experience and self-knowledge, and relevant to current social complexities. While pursuing their own specialized interests, students gain mastery in the broad range of subjects necessary for the effective and ethical practice of counseling. Study begins each semester with a week-long residency at the college, a time of planning for the ensuing semester and attending seminars. Returning home, the student begins implementation of the detailed study plan based upon the student's particular interests and needs, and mastery of relevant theory and research and completion of a supervised practicum with a minimum of 300 hours. Through appropriate design of their study plan, students may meet the educational requirements for master's level licensure or certification in their state. The program is approved by the Council of Applied Master's Programs in Psychology.

Application Information:

Send to Admissions Office. Application available online. URL of online application: http://www.goddard.edu/admissions/applyonline.html. Students are admitted in the Fall, application deadline August 15; Spring, application deadline February 15. *Fee:* $40. Waiver by written petition.

Saint Michael's College

Psychology Department/Graduate Program in Clinical Psychology
Saint Michael's College
One Winooski Park
Colchester, VT 05439
Telephone: (802) 654-2206
Fax: (802) 654-2697
E-mail: *rmiller@smcvt.edu*
Web: *http://www.smcvt.edu/graduate*

Department Information:

1984. Director: Ronald B. Miller. Number of faculty: total—full-time 5, part-time 6; women—full-time 1, part-time 4.

Programs and Degrees Offered:

Listed in the following order: Program area, degree type (T if terminal Master's), number awarded 7/06–6/07. Graduate Clinical Psychology MA/MS (Master of Arts/Science) (T) 10.

Student Applications/Admissions:

Student Applications

Graduate Clinical Psychology MA/MS (Master of Arts/Science)—Applications 2007–2008, 32. Total applicants accepted 2007–2008, 22. Number full-time enrolled (new admits only) 2007–2008, 8. Number part-time enrolled (new admits only) 2007–2008, 9. Total enrolled 2007–2008 full-time, 14, part-time, 52. Openings 2008–2009, 17. The median number of years required for completion of a degree in 2006–2007 were 3. The number of students enrolled full- and part-time who were dismissed or voluntarily withdrew from this program area in 2007–2008 were 0.

Admissions Requirements:

Scores: Entries appear in this order: required test or GPA, minimum score (if required), median score of students entering in 2007–2008. Master's Programs: overall undergraduate GPA 3.00, 3.35; last 2 years GPA 3.25, 3.40; psychology GPA 3.25, 3.50.

Other Criteria: (importance of criteria rated low, medium, or high): research experience—low, work experience—high, extracurricular activity—medium, clinically related public service—high, GPA—high, letters of recommendation—medium, interview—high, statement of goals and objectives—medium.

Student Characteristics: The following represents characteristics of students in 2007–2008 in all graduate psychology programs in the department: Female—full-time 12, part-time 35; Male—full-time 8, part-time 10; African American/Black—full-time 1, part-time 1; Hispanic/Latino(a)—full-time 1, part-time 0; Asian/Pacific Islander—full-time 0, part-time 0; American Indian/Alaska Native—full-time 0, part-time 1; Caucasian/White—full-time 16, part-time 35; Multi-ethnic—full-time 1, part-time 1; students subject to the Americans With Disabilities Act—full-time 1, part-time 1; Unknown ethnicity—full-time 0, part-time 0; International students who hold an F-1 or J-1 Visa—full-time 1, part-time 0.

Financial Information/Assistance:

Tuition for Full-Time Study: *Master's:* State residents: $485 per credit hour; Nonstate residents: $485 per credit hour. Tuition is subject to change. See the following Web site for updates and changes in tuition costs: http://www.smcvt.edu/graduate/courses/tuition.asp.

Financial Assistance:

First-Year Students: Teaching assistantships available for first year. Average number of hours worked per week: 20. Apply by July 1. Tuition remission given: full and partial.

Advanced Students: No information provided.

Additional Information: Of all students currently enrolled full time, 5% benefited from one or more of the listed financial assistance programs. Application and information available online at http://www.smcvt.edu/graduate/admission/finaid.asp.

Internships/Practica: Master's Degree (MA/MS Graduate Clinical Psychology): An internship experience such as a final research project or "capstone" experience is required of graduates. We have practice and internship sites in the following settings: schools, college counseling centers, teaching hospitals, correctional centers, Visiting Nurses Association, community mental health outpatient and residential offices, drug and alcohol treatment center, adolescent day treatment program.

Housing and Day Care: No on-campus housing is available. On-campus day care facilities are available. See the following Web site for more information: http://www.smcvt.edu/gradprograms.

Employment of Department Graduates:

Master's Degree Graduates: Of those who graduated in the academic year 2006–2007, the following categories and numbers represent the postgraduate activities and employment of master's degree graduates: Enrolled in a psychology doctoral program (0), enrolled in another graduate/professional program (0), enrolled in a postdoctoral residency/fellowship (n/a), employed in independent practice (n/a), employed in an academic position at a university (0), employed in an academic position at a 2-year/4-year college (0), employed in other positions at a higher education institution (0), employed in a professional position in a school system (1), employed in business or industry (0), employed in government agency (0), employed in a community mental health/counseling center (11), employed in a hospital/medical center (0), still seeking employment (0), other employment position (2), do not know (1), total from the above (master's) (15).

Doctoral Degree Graduates: Of those who graduated in the academic year 2006–2007, the following categories and numbers represent the postgraduate activities and employment of doctoral degree graduates: Enrolled in a psychology doctoral program (n/a), total from the above (doctoral) (0).

Additional Information:

Orientation, Objectives, and Emphasis of Department: The focus of the MA program in Clinical Psychology is on the integration of theory, research, and practice in the preparation of professional psychologists. Our goal is to provide an educational milieu that respects the individual educational goals of the student, and fosters intellectual, personal, and professional development. The program is eclectic in orientation and the faculty offer a diversity of interests, orientations, and experiences within the framework of our curriculum. We see ourselves as preparing students for professional practice in community agencies, schools, hospitals, and public and private clinics. Cross-registration in the courses offered by the college's other master's degree programs in education, administration, and theology is available for those wishing an interdisciplinary emphasis. The curriculum is also designed with two further objectives in mind: (a) the preparation of students for state licensing examinations, and (b) further doctoral study in professional psychology at another institution. All classes are held in the evening, permitting full- or part-time study. The program seeks to integrate a psychodynamic understanding of the therapeutic relationship with humanistic values, and a social systems perspective.

Special Facilities or Resources: St. Michael's College offers the graduate student a faculty committed to teaching and professional training in a nonbureaucratic learning environment. All clinical courses are taught by highly experienced clinical practitioners who serve as part-time faculty. The full-time faculty teach core courses in general, developmental, and social psychology, as well as research methods. The college has excellent computing facilities for the support of social science research.

Application Information:

Send to Graduate Admission, Saint Michael's College, One Winooski Park, Box 286, Colchester, VT 05439. Application available online. URL of online application: http://www.smcvt.edu/graduate. Programs have rolling admissions. Fall enrollment is recommended, and applications for Fall are encouraged by July 1, in order to be eligible for TA positions. *Fee:* $35.

Vermont, University of

Department of Psychology
Arts and Sciences
2 Colchester Avenue; John Dewey Hall
Burlington, VT 05405-0134
Telephone: (802) 656-2670
Fax: (802) 656-8783
E-mail: *psychology@uvm.edu*
Web: *http://www.uvm.edu/psychology*

Department Information:

1937. Chairperson: William Falls, PhD. Number of faculty: total—full-time 23, part-time 6; women—full-time 12, part-time 4; faculty subject to the Americans With Disabilities Act 1.

Programs and Degrees Offered:

Listed in the following order: Program area, degree type (T if terminal Master's), number awarded 7/06–6/07. Experimental General PhD (Doctor of Philosophy) 2, Clinical PhD (Doctor of Philosophy) 3.

APA Accreditation: Clinical PhD (Doctor of Philosophy).

Student Applications/Admissions:

Student Applications

Experimental General PhD (Doctor of Philosophy)—Applications 2007–2008, 43. Total applicants accepted 2007–2008, 2. Number full-time enrolled (new admits only) 2007–2008, 2. Number part-time enrolled (new admits only) 2007–2008, 0. Openings 2008–2009, 2. The median number of years required for completion of a degree in 2006–2007 were 6. The number of students enrolled full- and part-time who were dismissed or voluntarily withdrew from this program area in 2007–2008 were 1. *Clinical PhD (Doctor of Philosophy)*—Applications 2007–2008, 176. Total applicants accepted 2007–2008, 6. Number full-time enrolled (new admits only) 2007–2008, 6. Number part-time enrolled (new admits only) 2007–2008, 0. Openings 2008–2009, 6. The median number of years required for completion of a degree in 2006–2007 were 7. The number of students enrolled full- and part-time who were dismissed or voluntarily withdrew from this program area in 2007–2008 were 1.

Admissions Requirements:

Scores: Entries appear in this order: required test or GPA, minimum score (if required), median score of students entering in 2007–2008. Doctoral Programs: GRE-V 580, 640; GRE-Q 450, 650; GRE-Subject (Psychology) 660, 710; overall undergraduate GPA 3.42, 3.68.

Other Criteria: (importance of criteria rated low, medium, or high): GRE/MAT scores—high, research experience—high, work experience—medium, extracurricular activity—low, clinically related public service—medium, GPA—high, letters of recommendation—high, interview—medium, statement of goals and objectives—high. Clinically related public service is of importance for Clinical program only.

Student Characteristics: The following represents characteristics of students in 2007–2008 in all graduate psychology programs in the department: Female—full-time 45, part-time 0; Male—full-time 9, part-time 0; African American/Black—full-time 1, part-time 0; Hispanic/Latino(a)—full-time 5, part-time 0; Asian/Pacific Islander—full-time 0, part-time 0; American Indian/Alaska Native—full-time 0, part-time 0; Caucasian/White—full-time 48, part-time 0; Multi-ethnic—full-time 0, part-time 0; students subject to the Americans With Disabilities Act—full-time 0, part-time 0; Unknown ethnicity—full-time 0, part-time 0; International students who hold an F-1 or J-1 Visa—full-time 6, part-time 0.

Financial Information/Assistance:

Tuition for Full-Time Study: *Doctoral:* State residents: $434 per credit hour; Nonstate residents: $434 per credit hour. Tuition is subject to change.

Financial Assistance:

First-Year Students: Teaching assistantships available for first year. Average amount paid per academic year: $15,000. Average number of hours worked per week: 20. Tuition remission given: full. Research assistantships available for first year. Average amount paid per academic year: $23,000. Average number of hours worked per week: 20. Traineeships available for first year. Average amount paid per academic year: $15,000. Average number of hours worked per week: 20.

Advanced Students: Teaching assistantships available for advanced students. Average amount paid per academic year: $15,000. Average number of hours worked per week: 20. Tuition remission given: full. Research assistantships available for advanced students. Average amount paid per academic year: $23,000. Average number of hours worked per week: 20. Traineeships available for advanced students. Average amount paid per academic year: $15,000. Average number of hours worked per week: 20.

Additional Information: Of all students currently enrolled full time, 100% benefited from one or more of the listed financial assistance programs. Application and information available online at http://www.uvm.edu/psychology/.

Internships/Practica: Doctoral Degree (PhD Clinical): For those doctoral students for whom a professional internship was required in this program prior to graduation, (3) students applied for an internship in 2006–2007, with (3) students obtaining an internship. Of those students who obtained an internship, (3) were paid internships. Of those students who obtained an internship, (3) students placed in APA/CPA-accredited internships, (0) students placed in internships not APA/CPA-accredited, but listed with the Association of Psychology Postdoctoral and Internship Centers (APPIC), (0) students placed in internships conforming to guidelines of the Council of Directors of School Psychology Programs (CDSPP), (0) students placed in internships that were not APA/CPA-accredited, APPIC or CDSPP listed. Multiple clinical practica are available, including outpatient and inpatient adult assessment and psychotherapy, outpatient child and adolescent assessment and psychotherapy, community mental health centers, and medical center hospital. All practica are funded for 20 hours per week.

Housing and Day Care: On-campus housing is available. See the following Web site for more information: http://www.reslife.uvm.edu/~rlweb/graduate_students/. On-campus day care facilities are available. See the following Web site for more information: http://www.uvm.edu/~ips1/ccc/.

Employment of Department Graduates:

Master's Degree Graduates: Of those who graduated in the academic year 2006–2007, the following categories and numbers represent the postgraduate activities and employment of master's degree graduates: Enrolled in a psychology doctoral program (0), enrolled in another graduate/professional program (0), enrolled in a postdoctoral residency/fellowship (n/a), employed in independent practice (n/a), employed in an academic position at a university (0), employed in an academic position at a 2-year/4-year college (0), employed in other positions at a higher education institution (0), employed in a professional position in a school system (0), employed in business or industry (0), employed in government agency (0), employed in a community mental health/counseling center (0), employed in a hospital/medical center (0), still seeking employment (0), other employment position (0), total from the above (master's) (0).

Doctoral Degree Graduates: Of those who graduated in the academic year 2006–2007, the following categories and numbers represent the postgraduate activities and employment of doctoral degree graduates: Enrolled in a psychology doctoral program (n/a), enrolled in a postdoctoral residency/fellowship (1), employed in independent practice (0), employed in an academic position at a university (0), employed in an academic position at a 2-year/4-year college (0), employed in other positions at a higher education institution (2), employed in a professional position in a school system (0), employed in business or industry (0), employed in government agency (0), employed in a community mental health/counseling center (0), employed in a hospital/medical center (1), still seeking employment (0), other employment position (0), do not know (1), total from the above (doctoral) (5).

Additional Information:

Orientation, Objectives, and Emphasis of Department: Orientation, Objectives, and Emphasis of Department: The Clinical Psychology program is based upon a scientist–practitioner model and is designed to develop competent professional psychologists who can function in applied academic or research positions. Training stresses early placement in a variety of nearby clinical facilities and simultaneous research training relevant to clinical problems. Clinical orientations are primarily cognitive–behavioral. The General Experimental program admits students in three broad specialty areas: (a) basic and applied developmental and social psychology that includes research on ways in which people simultaneously influence and are influenced by social situations and cultural contexts; (b) biobehavioral psychology that focuses on behavioral and neurobiological approaches to learning, memory, emotion, and drug abuse; and (c) human behavioral pharmacology and substance abuse treatment. Students must fulfill General Experimental program requirements as well as requirements for the specialty area in which they are accepted. Applicants should be as specific as possible about their program interest areas.

Special Facilities or Resources: The department has excellent laboratories in behavioral neuroscience, group dynamics, developmental, human psychophysiology, and general human testing. Excellent computer facilities, and an in-house psychology clinic with clinical research equipment are available.

Information for Students With Physical Disabilities: See the following Web site for more information: http://www.uvm.edu/~dosa/sss/.

Application Information:

Send to Graduate College, Admissions Office, Waterman Building, University of Vermont, Burlington, VT 05405. Application available online. URL of online application: http://www.uvm.edu/~gradcoll/?Page=admissions.html. Students are admitted in the Fall, application deadline December 1; Winter, application deadline January 15. *Fee:* $40. Possibility of waiver for minority applicants.

Argosy University/Washington, DC

Clinical Psychology
American School of Professional Psychology
1550 Wilson Boulevard, Suite 600
Arlington, VA 22209
Telephone: (703) 526-5800
Fax: (703) 243-8973
E-mail: *rbarrett@argosy.edu*
Web: *http://www.argosy.edu*

Department Information:

1994. Chair, Clinical Psychology Programs: Robert F. Barrett, PhD. Number of faculty: total—full-time 26, part-time 2; women—full-time 15, part-time 1; total—minority—full-time 7, part-time 1; women minority—full-time 5, part-time 1.

Programs and Degrees Offered:

Listed in the following order: Program area, degree type (T if terminal Master's), number awarded 7/06–6/07. Clinical Psychology MA/MS (Master of Arts/Science) (T) 14, Clinical Psychology PsyD (Doctor of Psychology) 65.

APA Accreditation: Clinical PsyD (Doctor of Psychology).

Student Applications/Admissions:

Student Applications

Clinical Psychology MA/MS (Master of Arts/Science)—Applications 2007–2008, 99. Total applicants accepted 2007–2008, 35. Number full-time enrolled (new admits only) 2007–2008, 27. Number part-time enrolled (new admits only) 2007–2008, 1. Total enrolled 2007–2008 full-time, 46, part-time, 8. Openings 2008–2009, 20. The median number of years required for completion of a degree in 2006–2007 were 2. The number of students enrolled full- and part-time who were dismissed or voluntarily withdrew from this program area in 2007–2008 were 8. *Clinical Psychology PsyD (Doctor of Psychology)*—Applications 2007–2008, 336. Total applicants accepted 2007–2008, 86. Number full-time enrolled (new admits only) 2007–2008, 68. Number part-time enrolled (new admits only) 2007–2008, 4. Total enrolled 2007–2008 full-time, 250, part-time, 170. Openings 2008–2009, 90. The median number of years required for completion of a degree in 2006–2007 were 5. The number of students enrolled full- and part-time who were dismissed or voluntarily withdrew from this program area in 2007–2008 were 18.

Admissions Requirements:

Scores: Entries appear in this order: required test or GPA, minimum score (if required), median score of students entering in 2007–2008. Master's Programs: overall undergraduate GPA 3.0, 3.17; last 2 years GPA 3.0, 3.38; psychology GPA 3.0, 3.43. MA applicants should have minimum of 3.0 in highest degree earned. GRE scores are optional. Doctoral Programs: overall undergraduate GPA 3.25, 3.37; last 2 years GPA 3.25, 3.39; psychology GPA 3.25, 3.6. Applicants should have a minimum of 3.25 for highest degree earned. Program will review overall GPA, last 2 years GPA and psychology GPA for 3.25 GPA. GRE scores are optional.

Other Criteria: (importance of criteria rated low, medium, or high): research experience—low, work experience—high, extracurricular activity—low, clinically related public service—high, GPA—high, letters of recommendation—high, interview—high, statement of goals and objectives—high. Clinical experience is less important for applicants to MA program.

Student Characteristics: The following represents characteristics of students in 2007–2008 in all graduate psychology programs in the department: Female—full-time 245, part-time 150; Male—full-time 51, part-time 28; African American/Black—full-time 56, part-time 58; Hispanic/Latino(a)—full-time 15, part-time 6; Asian/Pacific Islander—full-time 9, part-time 9; American Indian/Alaska Native—full-time 1, part-time 0; Caucasian/White—full-time 195, part-time 102; students subject to the Americans With Disabilities Act—full-time 17, part-time 4; Unknown ethnicity—full-time 19, part-time 4; International students who hold an F-1 or J-1 Visa—full-time 7, part-time 1.

Financial Information/Assistance:

Tuition for Full-Time Study: *Master's:* State residents: per academic year $21,675, $895 per credit hour; Nonstate residents: per academic year $21,675, $895 per credit hour. *Doctoral:* State residents: per academic year $21,675, $895 per credit hour; Nonstate residents: per academic year $21,675, $895 per credit hour. Tuition is subject to change. See the following Web site for updates and changes in tuition costs: http://www.argosy.edu.

Financial Assistance:

First-Year Students: Fellowships and scholarships available for first year. Average amount paid per academic year: $2,250. Average number of hours worked per week: 6. Apply by September 8. Tuition remission given: full and partial.

Advanced Students: Teaching assistantships available for advanced students. Average amount paid per academic year: $2,685. Average number of hours worked per week: 8. Apply by variable. Tuition remission given: full and partial. Research assistantships available for advanced students. Average amount paid per academic year: $850. Average number of hours worked per week: 4. Apply by variable. Tuition remission given: full and partial. Fellowships and scholarships available for advanced students. Average amount paid per academic year: $1,700. Average number of hours worked per week: 8. Apply by variable. Tuition remission given: full and partial.

Additional Information: Of all students currently enrolled full time, 18% benefited from one or more of the listed financial assistance programs.

Internships/Practica: Master's Degree (MA/MS Clinical Psychology): An internship experience such as a final research project or "capstone" experience is required of graduates. Doctoral Degree (PsyD Clinical Psychology): For those doctoral students for whom a professional internship was required in this program prior to graduation, (71) students applied for an internship in 2006–2007, with (69) students obtaining an internship. Of those students who obtained an internship, (66) were paid internships. Of those students who obtained an internship, (41) students placed in APA/CPA-accredited internships, (24) students placed in internships not APA/CPA-accredited, but listed with the Association of Psychology Postdoctoral and Internship Centers (APPIC), (0) students placed in internships conforming to guidelines of the Council of Directors of School Psychology Programs (CDSPP), (4) students placed in internships that were not APA/CPA accredited, APPIC or CDSPP listed. Practicum: Practicum training is designed to give students the opportunity to work under supervision with a clinical population within a mental health delivery system. Students learn to apply their theoretical knowledge; implement, develop, and assess the efficacy of clinical techniques; and develop the professional attitudes important for the identity of a professional psychologist. Doctoral students complete two training practica sequences (600 hours each) focusing on assessment or psychotherapy skills or integrating the two. Master's students are required to complete one practicum (600 hours). Internship: All doctoral students are required to complete a 1-year (12-month) internship as a condition for graduation. This intensive and supervised contact with clients is essential for giving greater breadth and depth to the student's overall academic experience. Typically, students will begin the internship during their 4th or 5th year, depending on the student's progress through the curriculum.

Housing and Day Care: No on-campus housing is available. No on-campus day care facilities are available.

Employment of Department Graduates:

Master's Degree Graduates: Of those who graduated in the academic year 2006–2007, the following categories and numbers represent the postgraduate activities and employment of master's degree graduates: Enrolled in a psychology doctoral program (83), enrolled in another graduate/professional program (2), enrolled in a postdoctoral residency/fellowship (n/a), employed in independent practice (n/a), employed in a community mental health/counseling center (1), other employment position (1), do not know (4), total from the above (master's) (91).

Doctoral Degree Graduates: Of those who graduated in the academic year 2006–2007, the following categories and numbers represent the postgraduate activities and employment of doctoral degree graduates: Enrolled in a psychology doctoral program (n/a), enrolled in another graduate/professional program (0), enrolled in a postdoctoral residency/fellowship (8), employed in independent practice (7), employed in an academic position at a university (0), employed in an academic position at a 2-year/4-year college (0), employed in other positions at a higher education institution (1), employed in a professional position in a school system (1), employed in business or industry (0), employed in government agency (3), employed in a community mental health/counseling center (3), employed in a hospital/medical center (9), still seeking employment (0), other employment position (3), do not know (12), total from the above (doctoral) (47).

Additional Information:

Orientation, Objectives, and Emphasis of Department: Department of Clinical Psychology. The doctoral program in Clinical Psychology (PsyD) is designed to educate and train students to function effectively in diverse professional roles. The program emphasizes the development of attitudes, knowledge, and skills essential in the formation of professional psychologists who are committed to the ethical provision of quality services. The school offers a broad-based curriculum, providing a meaningful integration of diverse theoretical perspectives, scholarship, and practice. The program offers concentrations in forensic psychology, health and neuropsychology, child and family, and diversity. Opportunities are available for students to develop expertise in a number of areas including the provision of services to specific populations such as children and families; theoretical perspectives such as cognitive–behavioral, family systems, psychodynamic, and client centered; and areas of application such as forensics and health psychology. The Master's degree (MA) in Clinical Psychology is designed to meet the needs of both those students seeking a terminal degree for work in the mental health field and those who eventually plan to pursue a doctoral degree. The program provides a solid core of basic psychology, as well as a strong clinical orientation with an emphasis in psychological assessment.

Special Facilities or Resources: Argosy University is conveniently located minutes from downtown Washington, DC. The on-site library has developed a focused psychology collection consisting of reference titles and books, journals, diagnostic assessment instruments, and audiovisual equipment. There are two computer labs and students have full access to both computerized literature searches and electronic text of most journals. In addition, students have access to the rich library resources of the Washington, DC, area including the National Library of Medicine and the Library of Congress.

Information for Students With Physical Disabilities: ADA Contact Person: Chayla Haynes, chhaynes@argosy.edu.

Application Information:

Send to Admissions Department, Argosy University/Washington, DC, 1550 Wilson Boulevard, Suite 600, Arlington, VA 22209. Students are admitted in the Fall, application deadline January 15. Fall application deadline: application must be completed by January 15 to qualify for the April 1 decision. *Fee:* $50.

Argosy University/Washington, DC (2007 data)

Counselor Education
American School of Professional Psychology
1550 Wilson Boulevard, Suite 600
Arlington, VA 22209
Telephone: (703) 526-5800
Fax: (703) 243-8973
E-mail: *clogan@argosyu.edu*
Web: *http://www.argosyu.edu*

Department Information:

1998. Program Chair: Colleen R. Logan, PhD. Number of faculty: total—full-time 5, part-time 15; women—full-time 4, part-time 9.

Programs and Degrees Offered:

Listed in the following order: Program area, degree type (T if terminal Master's), number awarded 7/06–6/07. Community Counseling MA/MS (Master of Arts/Science) (T) 27, Counseling Psychology EdD (Doctor of Education) 0.

Student Applications/Admissions:

Student Applications

Community Counseling MA/MS (Master of Arts/Science)—Applications 2007–2008, 129. Total applicants accepted 2007–2008, 75. Number full-time enrolled (new admits only) 2007–2008, 59. Total enrolled 2007–2008 full-time, 105, part-time, 55. Openings 2008–2009, 79. The median number of years required for completion of a degree in 2006–2007 were 2. The number of students enrolled full- and part-time who were dismissed or voluntarily withdrew from this program area in 2007–2008 were 1. *Counseling Psychology EdD (Doctor of Education)*—Applications 2007–2008, 37. Total applicants accepted 2007–2008, 25. Number full-time enrolled (new admits only) 2007–2008, 18. Total enrolled 2007–2008 full-time, 48, part-time, 27. Openings 2008–2009, 26. The median number of years required for completion of a degree in 2006–2007 were 3. The number of students enrolled full- and part-time who were dismissed or voluntarily withdrew from this program area in 2007–2008 were 1.

Admissions Requirements:

Scores: Entries appear in this order: required test or GPA, minimum score (if required), median score of students entering in 2007–2008. Master's Programs: overall undergraduate GPA 3.0; last 2 years GPA 3.0; psychology GPA 3.0.

Other Criteria: (importance of criteria rated low, medium, or high): research experience—low, work experience—medium, extracurricular activity—medium, clinically related public service—medium, GPA—high, letters of recommendation—high, interview—low, statement of goals and objectives—high. For additional information on admission requirements, go to http://www.argosyu.edu.

Student Characteristics: The following represents characteristics of students in 2007–2008 in all graduate psychology programs in the department: Female—full-time 129, part-time 67; Male—full-time 24, part-time 15; African American/Black—full-time 75, part-time 28; Hispanic/Latino(a)—full-time 7, part-time 3; Asian/Pacific Islander—full-time 8, part-time 5; American Indian/Alaska Native—full-time 1, part-time 1; Caucasian/White—full-time 46, part-time 38; students subject to the Americans With Disabilities Act—full-time 4, part-time 0; Unknown ethnicity—full-time 16, part-time 7.

Financial Information/Assistance:

Tuition for Full-Time Study: *Master's:* State residents: $560 per credit hour; Nonstate residents: $560 per credit hour. *Doctoral:* State residents: $780 per credit hour; Nonstate residents: $780 per credit hour. Tuition is subject to change. See the following Web site for updates and changes in tuition costs: http://www.argosyu.edu.

Financial Assistance:

First-Year Students: No information provided.

Advanced Students: Teaching assistantships available for advanced students.

Additional Information: No information provided.

Internships/Practica: The Counseling Department maintains training relationships with 70–90 local and out-of-area treatment providers and agencies. Master's level students must complete a mandatory three-semester training experience (6 credit hours) once they have completed prerequisite course work. Students apply for and secure placements in a variety of settings including Community Service Board facilities (outpatient and residential mental health, substance abuse, and psychosocial rehabilitation programs), hospital-based treatment facilities, school systems, private residential treatment facilities, nonprofit social services and mental health agencies, and correctional institutions. Students are expected to work 8–10 hours per week at a training site as a practicum student. Students are expected to work 16–20 hours per week at the training site in order to complete a 600-hour internship that includes 240 hours of direct client contact. Students perform individual and group counseling and psychoeducational services under supervision by licensed mental health treatment providers as required by local jurisdictional regulations. The practicum aims to provide a training experience that replicates the professional environment in which students will eventually be employed. The emphasis is on professional development of the counselor trainee in core therapeutic skill areas, as well as in use of supervision, case reporting, record keeping, and development of collegial relationships with other mental health practitioners.

Housing and Day Care: No on-campus housing is available. No on-campus day care facilities are available.

Employment of Department Graduates:

Master's Degree Graduates: Of those who graduated in the academic year 2006–2007, the following categories and numbers represent the postgraduate activities and employment of master's degree graduates: Enrolled in a postdoctoral residency/fellowship (n/a), employed in independent practice (n/a), do not know (0), total from the above (master's) (0).

Doctoral Degree Graduates: Of those who graduated in the academic year 2006–2007, the following categories and numbers represent the postgraduate activities and employment of doctoral degree graduates: Enrolled in a psychology doctoral program (n/a), do not know (0), total from the above (doctoral) (0).

Additional Information:

Orientation, Objectives, and Emphasis of Department: The Argosy DC Community Counseling program mission is to create a learning environment that promotes academic excellence, professional competence, and personal integrity. We serve a diverse, metropolitan student body who are intrinsically motivated to help others. The program actively engages faculty and students in the preparation of counselors who meet the needs of a dynamic and diverse community. The purpose of the Community Counseling program is to deliver those core learning experiences established by academic program accrediting and state licensure boards to assure that students completing our program are competent, ethical counselors prepared for postgraduate positions on the path to Professional Counseling licensure.

Application Information:

Send to Admissions Department, AU/Washington DC, 1550 Wilson Boulevard, Suite 600, Arlington, VA 22209. Application available online. Students are admitted in the Fall, application deadline June 15; Spring, application deadline November 15; Summer, application deadline March 1. *Fee:* $50.

Argosy University/Washington, DC

Forensic Psychology
American School of Professional Psychology
1550 Wilson Blvd., Suite 600
Arlington, VA 22209
Telephone: (703) 526-5800
Fax: (703) 243-8973
E-mail: *wberger@argosy.edu*
Web: *http://www.argosyu.edu*

Department Information:

2002. Program Chair: Wendy B. Berger, PhD. Number of faculty: total—full-time 3; women—full-time 2; total—minority—full-time 1; women minority—full-time 1.

Programs and Degrees Offered:

Listed in the following order: Program area, degree type (T if terminal Master's), number awarded 7/06–6/07. Forensic Psychology MA/MS (Master of Arts/Science) (T) 53.

Student Applications/Admissions:

Student Applications

Forensic Psychology MA/MS (Master of Arts/Science)—Applications 2007–2008, 149. Total applicants accepted 2007–2008, 102. Number full-time enrolled (new admits only) 2007–2008, 89. Total enrolled 2007–2008 full-time, 196. The median number of years required for completion of a degree in 2006–2007 were 2. The number of students enrolled full- and part-time who were dismissed or voluntarily withdrew from this program area in 2007–2008 were 30.

Admissions Requirements:

Scores: Entries appear in this order: required test or GPA, minimum score (if required), median score of students entering in 2007–2008. Master's Programs: overall undergraduate GPA 3.0; psychology GPA 3.0.

Other Criteria: (importance of criteria rated low, medium, or high): GRE/MAT scores—low, research experience—low, work experience—medium, clinically related public service—low, GPA—high, letters of recommendation—medium, interview—medium, statement of goals and objectives—high.

Student Characteristics: The following represents characteristics of students in 2007–2008 in all graduate psychology programs in the department: Female—full-time 165, part-time 0; Male—full-time 31, part-time 0; African American/Black—full-time 61, part-time 0; Hispanic/Latino(a)—full-time 8, part-time 0; Caucasian/White—full-time 102, part-time 0; students subject to the Americans With Disabilities Act—full-time 1, part-time 1; Unknown ethnicity—full-time 25, part-time 0; International students who hold an F-1 or J-1 Visa—full-time 4, part-time 0.

Financial Information/Assistance:

Tuition for Full-Time Study: *Master's:* State residents: $560 per credit hour; Nonstate residents: $560 per credit hour. Tuition is subject to change.

Financial Assistance:

First-Year Students: Fellowships and scholarships available for first year. Average amount paid per academic year: $1,000. Apply by same as application.

Advanced Students: No information provided.

Additional Information: Of all students currently enrolled full time, 90% benefited from one or more of the listed financial assistance programs. Application and information available online at http://www.argosy.edu.

Internships/Practica: Master's Degree (MA/MS Forensic Psychology): An internship experience such as a final research project or "capstone" experience is required of graduates. The field placement option of the Forensic Psychology Seminar is a supervised out-of-class experience in a forensic setting designed for students to gain experience and exposure to forensic practice within professional settings. The training provides students with the opportunity to apply theoretical knowledge and the principles of research, and to develop the professional and personal attitudes important to their professional identity. For additional information on education and training outcomes for our programs, see the following Web site: http://www.argosydc.net/academicprog/forensic.

Housing and Day Care: No on-campus housing is available. No on-campus day care facilities are available.

Employment of Department Graduates:

Master's Degree Graduates: Of those who graduated in the academic year 2006–2007, the following categories and numbers represent the postgraduate activities and employment of master's degree graduates: Enrolled in a postdoctoral residency/fellowship (n/a), employed in independent practice (n/a), total from the above (master's) (0).

Doctoral Degree Graduates: Of those who graduated in the academic year 2006–2007, the following categories and numbers represent the postgraduate activities and employment of doctoral degree graduates: Enrolled in a psychology doctoral program (n/a), total from the above (doctoral) (0).

Additional Information:

Orientation, Objectives, and Emphasis of Department: The master's program in Forensic Psychology at Argosy University, Washington, DC is designed to educate and train individuals who are currently employed or wish to be trained to work in fields that utilize the study and practice of forensic psychology. The curriculum provides for an understanding of theory, training, and practice of forensic psychology. The program emphasizes the development of students who are committed to the ethical provision of quality services to diverse clients and organizations. The program maintains policies and delivery formats suitable for working adults.

Special Facilities or Resources: The field placement is designed to provide the student with practical experience integrating course work with experience. Students will have the opportunity to work with staff and/or court-mandated clients, law enforcement, or other legal systems. Examples of field placement sites include juvenile, adult, and domestic relations court programs; court-assigned mentoring or advocacy programs; probation and parole departments; correctional facilities; police departments; and victim or offender treatment programs.

Information for Students With Physical Disabilities: See the following Web site for more information: http://www.argosydc.net/stuaffairs.

Application Information:
Send to Admissions Department, 1550 Wilson Boulevard, Suite 600, Arlington, VA 22209. Application available online. URL of online application: http://www.argosy.edu. Students are admitted in the Fall, application deadline May 15; Spring, application deadline October 15; Summer, application deadline April 1; programs have rolling admissions. *Fee:* $50.

College of William and Mary

Department of Psychology/Predoctoral MA Program
P.O. Box 8795
Williamsburg, VA 23187-8795
Telephone: (757) 221-3872
Fax: (757) 221-3896
E-mail: *bbpumi@wm.edu*
Web: *https://www.wm.edu/psychology/ma.php*

Department Information:
1946. Chairperson: Constance J. Pilkington, PhD. Number of faculty: total—full-time 19, part-time 8; women—full-time 7, part-time 3.

Programs and Degrees Offered:
Listed in the following order: Program area, degree type (T if terminal Master's), number awarded 7/06–6/07. General MA/MS (Master of Arts/Science) (T) 6.

Student Applications/Admissions:
Student Applications
General MA/MS (Master of Arts/Science)—Applications 2007–2008, 96. Total applicants accepted 2007–2008, 11. Number full-time enrolled (new admits only) 2007–2008, 7. Number part-time enrolled (new admits only) 2007–2008, 0. Openings 2008–2009, 7. The median number of years required for completion of a degree in 2006–2007 were 2. The number of students enrolled full- and part-time who were dismissed or voluntarily withdrew from this program area in 2007–2008 were 0.

Admissions Requirements:
Scores: Entries appear in this order: required test or GPA, minimum score (if required), median score of students entering in 2007–2008. Master's Programs: GRE-V no minimum stated, 547; GRE-Q no minimum stated, 644; overall undergraduate GPA no minimum stated, 3.65; psychology GPA no minimum stated, 3.68. Note: No minimums required for the above.
Other Criteria: (importance of criteria rated low, medium, or high): GRE/MAT scores—medium, research experience—high, work experience—medium, extracurricular activity—low, clinically related public service—low, GPA—medium, letters of recommendation—high, statement of goals and objectives—high. For additional information on admission requirements, go to http://web.wm.edu/psyc/ma.php.

Student Characteristics: The following represents characteristics of students in 2007–2008 in all graduate psychology programs in the department: Female—full-time 13, part-time 0; Male—full-time 1, part-time 0; African American/Black—full-time 1, part-time 0; Hispanic/Latino(a)—full-time 0, part-time 0; Asian/Pacific Islander—full-time 0, part-time 0; American Indian/Alaska Native—full-time 0, part-time 0; Caucasian/White—full-time 12, part-time 0; Multi-ethnic—full-time 1, part-time 0; students subject to the Americans With Disabilities Act—full-time 0, part-time 0; Unknown ethnicity—full-time 0, part-time 0.

Financial Information/Assistance:
Tuition for Full-Time Study: *Master's:* State residents: per academic year $9,800, $275 per credit hour; Nonstate residents: per academic year $23,014, $760 per credit hour. Tuition is subject to change.

Financial Assistance:
First-Year Students: Teaching assistantships available for first year. Average amount paid per academic year: $9,000. Average number of hours worked per week: 20. Apply by February 15. Tuition remission given: full. Research assistantships available for first year. Average amount paid per academic year: $9,000. Average number of hours worked per week: 20. Apply by February 15. Tuition remission given: full. Fellowships and scholarships available for first year. Average amount paid per academic year: $9,000. Average number of hours worked per week: 20. Apply by February 15. Tuition remission given: full.
Advanced Students: Teaching assistantships available for advanced students. Average amount paid per academic year: $9,000. Average number of hours worked per week: 20. Apply by February 15. Tuition remission given: full. Research assistantships available for advanced students. Average amount paid per academic year: $9,000. Average number of hours worked per week: 20. Apply by February 15. Tuition remission given: full. Fellowships and scholarships available for advanced students. Average amount paid per academic year: $9,000. Average number of hours worked per week: 20. Apply by February 15. Tuition remission given: full.
Additional Information: Of all students currently enrolled full time, 100% benefited from one or more of the listed financial assistance programs. Application and information available online at http://www.wm.edu/psychology/ma.php.

Internships/Practica: No information provided.

Housing and Day Care: On-campus housing is available. Office of Residence Life, College of William and Mary, P.O. Box 8795, Williamsburg, VA 23187-8795. See the following Web site for more information: http://www.wm.edu/reslife/forms/graduate/Housing. On-campus day care facilities are available. Office of Residence Life, College of William and Mary, P.O. Box 8795, Williamsburg, VA 23187-8795.

Employment of Department Graduates:
Master's Degree Graduates: Of those who graduated in the academic year 2006–2007, the following categories and numbers represent the postgraduate activities and employment of master's degree graduates: Enrolled in a psychology doctoral program (5), enrolled in a postdoctoral residency/fellowship (n/a), employed in independent practice (n/a), employed in other positions at a higher education institution (1), do not know (1), total from the above (master's) (7).
Doctoral Degree Graduates: Of those who graduated in the academic year 2006–2007, the following categories and numbers represent the postgraduate activities and employment of doctoral

degree graduates: Enrolled in a psychology doctoral program (n/a), total from the above (doctoral) (0).

Additional Information:

Orientation, Objectives, and Emphasis of Department: The General Psychology MA program is designed to prepare students for admission to PhD programs. Students are not admitted if they are not planning to further their education. There is a heavy research emphasis throughout both years of the program.

Special Facilities or Resources: Faculty members develop and work with the MA students to design, conduct, and analyze research data, These studies are often published in professional journals. Subjects accessible for research include college students and rats. Computer facilities are available in the department that are strictly for MA students.

Application Information:

Application and application fee must be sent to the A&S Graduate Office, The College of William and Mary, P.O. Box 8795, Williamsburg, VA 23187-8795. All supporting material should be sent in one package to Director of Graduate Admissions, Psychology Department, The College of William and Mary, P.O. Box 8795, Williamsburg, VA 23187-8795. Application, application fee, and all supporting material must be postmarked by February 15. GRE scores are sent directly from ETS. Application available online. URL of online application: http://www.applyweb.com/apply/wmgrad/. Students are admitted in the Fall, application deadline February 15. There is the option of applying online (see above URL address) or sending in the paper copy of the application to the A&S Graduate Office (see address above). *Fee:* $45.

George Mason University

Department of Psychology
Humanities and Social Sciences
4400 University Drive, MSN 3F5
Fairfax, VA 22030-4444
Telephone: (703) 993-1342
Fax: (703) 993-1359
E-mail: *jshort@gmu.edu*
Web: *http://www.gmu.edu/departments/psychology*

Department Information:

1966. Chairperson: Deborah Boehm-Davis. Number of faculty: total—full-time 48, part-time 11; women—full-time 20, part-time 6; total—minority—full-time 3, part-time 2; women minority—full-time 1, part-time 1.

Programs and Degrees Offered:

Listed in the following order: Program area, degree type (T if terminal Master's), number awarded 7/06–6/07. Clinical PhD (Doctor of Philosophy) 11, Industrial/Organizational PhD (Doctor of Philosophy) 6, Human Factors/Applied Cognition PhD (Doctor of Philosophy) 0, Applied Developmental PhD (Doctor of Philosophy) 4, Biopsychology PhD (Doctor of Philosophy) 2, School/Certificate MA/MS (Master of Arts/Science) (T) 9, Industrial/Organizational MA/MS (Master of Arts/Science) (T) 16, Human Factors/Applied Cognition MA/MS (Master of Arts/Science) (T) 6, Biopsychology MA/MS (Master of Arts/Science) (T) 4, Applied Developmental MA/MS (Master of Arts/Science) (T) 7.

APA Accreditation: Clinical PhD (Doctor of Philosophy).

Student Applications/Admissions:

Student Applications

Clinical PhD (Doctor of Philosophy)—Applications 2007–2008, 212. Total applicants accepted 2007–2008, 15. Number full-time enrolled (new admits only) 2007–2008, 7. Number part-time enrolled (new admits only) 2007–2008, 0. Total enrolled 2007–2008 full-time, 40, part-time, 5. Openings 2008–2009, 8. The median number of years required for completion of a degree in 2006–2007 were 5. The number of students enrolled full- and part-time who were dismissed or voluntarily withdrew from this program area in 2007–2008 were 0. *Industrial/Organizational PhD (Doctor of Philosophy)*—Applications 2007–2008, 143. Total applicants accepted 2007–2008, 16. Number full-time enrolled (new admits only) 2007–2008, 7. Number part-time enrolled (new admits only) 2007–2008, 0. Total enrolled 2007–2008 full-time, 23, part-time, 11. Openings 2008–2009, 5. The median number of years required for completion of a degree in 2006–2007 were 7. The number of students enrolled full- and part-time who were dismissed or voluntarily withdrew from this program area in 2007–2008 were 0. *Human Factors/Applied Cognition PhD (Doctor of Philosophy)*—Applications 2007–2008, 13. Total applicants accepted 2007–2008, 5. Number full-time enrolled (new admits only) 2007–2008, 2. Number part-time enrolled (new admits only) 2007–2008, 0. Total enrolled 2007–2008 full-time, 16, part-time, 1. Openings 2008–2009, 3. The number of students enrolled full- and part-time who were dismissed or voluntarily withdrew from this program area in 2007–2008 were 0. *Applied Developmental PhD (Doctor of Philosophy)*—Applications 2007–2008, 34. Total applicants accepted 2007–2008, 10. Number full-time enrolled (new admits only) 2007–2008, 5. Number part-time enrolled (new admits only) 2007–2008, 0. Total enrolled 2007–2008 full-time, 19, part-time, 9. Openings 2008–2009, 5. The median number of years required for completion of a degree in 2006–2007 were 7. The number of students enrolled full- and part-time who were dismissed or voluntarily withdrew from this program area in 2007–2008 were 0. *Biopsychology PhD (Doctor of Philosophy)*—Applications 2007–2008, 19. Total applicants accepted 2007–2008, 6. Number full-time enrolled (new admits only) 2007–2008, 2. Number part-time enrolled (new admits only) 2007–2008, 0. Total enrolled 2007–2008 full-time, 12, part-time, 3. Openings 2008–2009, 2. The median number of years required for completion of a degree in 2006–2007 were 8. The number of students enrolled full- and part-time who were dismissed or voluntarily withdrew from this program area in 2007–2008 were 0. *School/Certificate MA/MS (Master of Arts/Science)*—Applications 2007–2008, 70. Total applicants accepted 2007–2008, 17. Number full-time enrolled (new admits only) 2007–2008, 9. Number part-time enrolled (new admits only) 2007–2008, 0. Openings 2008–2009, 8. The median number of years required for completion of a degree in 2006–2007 were 3. The number of students enrolled full- and part-time who were dismissed or voluntarily withdrew from this program area in 2007–2008 were 0. *Industrial/Organizational MA/MS (Master of Arts/Science)*—Applications 2007–2008, 132. Total applicants accepted 2007–2008, 38. Number full-time enrolled (new admits only) 2007–2008, 16. Number part-time enrolled (new admits only) 2007–2008, 0. Total enrolled 2007–2008 full-time, 17, part-time, 13. Openings 2008–2009, 13. The median number of years required for completion of a degree in 2006–2007 were 2. The number of students enrolled full- and part-time who were dismissed or voluntarily withdrew from this program area in 2007–2008 were 0. *Human Factors/Applied Cognition MA/MS (Master of Arts/Science)*—Applications 2007–2008, 34. Total applicants accepted 2007–2008, 12. Number full-time enrolled (new admits only) 2007–2008, 9. Number part-time enrolled (new admits only) 2007–2008, 0. Total enrolled 2007–2008 full-time, 19, part-time, 7. Openings 2008–2009, 10. The median number of years required for completion of a degree in 2006–2007 were 3. The number of students enrolled full- and part-time who were dismissed or voluntarily withdrew from this program area in 2007–2008 were 3. *Biopsychology MA/MS (Master of Arts/Science)*—Applications 2007–2008, 19. Total applicants accepted 2007–2008, 5. Number full-time enrolled (new admits only) 2007–2008, 3. Number part-time enrolled (new admits only) 2007–2008, 0. Total enrolled 2007–2008 full-time, 7, part-time, 9. Openings 2008–2009, 4. The median number of years required for completion of a degree in 2006–2007 were 3. The number of students enrolled full- and part-time who were dismissed or voluntarily withdrew from this program area in 2007–2008 were 0. *Applied Developmental MA/MS (Master of Arts/Science)*—Applications 2007–2008, 47. Total applicants accepted 2007–2008, 23. Number full-time enrolled (new admits only) 2007–2008, 18. Number part-time enrolled (new admits only) 2007–2008, 0. Total enrolled 2007–2008 full-time, 14, part-time, 3. Openings 2008–2009, 13. The median number of years required for completion of a degree in 2006–2007 were 2. The number of students enrolled full- and part-time who were dismissed or voluntarily withdrew from this program area in 2007–2008 were 0.

Admissions Requirements:

Scores: Entries appear in this order: required test or GPA, minimum score (if required), median score of students entering in 2007–2008. Master's Programs: GRE-V no minimum stated, 581; GRE-Q no minimum stated, 634; overall undergraduate GPA no minimum stated, 3.44; last 2 years GPA 3.0, 3.71; psychology GPA 3.33. Doctoral Programs: GRE-V 500, 647; GRE-Q 600, 703; overall undergraduate GPA 3.0, 3.72; last 2 years GPA 3.25, 3.64; psychology GPA 3.33. Clinical program has minimum V+Q GRE scores in the 70th percentile. Clinical applicants are strongly recommended to take the GRE Psychology Subject Test. Other programs prefer at least 1100 combined but will consider other applicants.

Other Criteria: (importance of criteria rated low, medium, or high): GRE/MAT scores—high, research experience—high, work experience—high, extracurricular activity—low, clinically related public service—medium, GPA—high, letters of recommendation—high, interview—high, statement of goals and objectives—high, completed by deadline—high. The Clinical and School programs interview a select group by invitation only. The Biopsychology, Develpmental, Human Factors/Applied Cognition, and Industrial/Organizational programs do not require an interview but hold an open house for selected students to attend. For additional information on admission requirements, go to http://www.gmu.edu/departments/psychology.

Student Characteristics: The following represents characteristics of students in 2007–2008 in all graduate psychology programs in the department: Female—full-time 134, part-time 39; Male—full-time 54, part-time 22; African American/Black—full-time 7, part-time 0; Hispanic/Latino(a)—full-time 9, part-time 3; Asian/Pacific Islander—full-time 15, part-time 1; American Indian/Alaska Native—full-time 0, part-time 0; Caucasian/White—full-time 139, part-time 53; Multi-ethnic—full-time 4, part-time 2; students subject to the Americans With Disabilities Act—full-time 0, part-time 0; Unknown ethnicity—full-time 14, part-time 2; International students who hold an F-1 or J-1 Visa—full-time 2, part-time 0.

Financial Information/Assistance:

Tuition for Full-Time Study: *Master's:* State residents: per academic year $8,425, $337 per credit hour; Nonstate residents: per academic year $20,280, $845 per credit hour. *Doctoral:* State residents: per academic year $8,425, $337 per credit hour; Nonstate residents: per academic year $20,280, $845 per credit hour. Tuition is subject to change. See the following Web site for updates and changes in tuition costs: http://www.studentaccounts.gmu.edu/index.html.

Financial Assistance:

First-Year Students: Teaching assistantships available for first year. Average amount paid per academic year: $11,900. Apply by January 1. Tuition remission given: full. Research assistantships available for first year. Average amount paid per academic year: $11,900. Apply by January 1. Tuition remission given: full.

Advanced Students: Teaching assistantships available for advanced students. Average amount paid per academic year: $11,000. Apply by February 15. Tuition remission given: full and partial. Research assistantships available for advanced students. Average amount paid per academic year: $11,000. Apply by February 15. Tuition remission given: full and partial.

Additional Information: Of all students currently enrolled full time, 40% benefited from one or more of the listed financial assistance programs. Application and information available online at http://www.gmu.edu/departments/psychology.

Internships/Practica: Master's Degree (MA/MS School/Certificate): An internship experience such as a final research project or "capstone" experience is required of graduates. Master's Degree (MA/MS Biopsychology): An internship experience such as a final research project or "capstone" experience is required of graduates. Doctoral Degree (PhD Clinical): For those doctoral students for whom a professional internship was required in this program prior to graduation, (7) students applied for an internship in 2006–2007, with (6) students obtaining an internship. Of those students who obtained an internship, (5) were paid internships. Of those students who obtained an internship, (4) students placed in APA/CPA-accredited internships, (2) students placed in internships not APA/CPA-accredited, but listed with the Association of Psychology Postdoctoral and Internship Centers (APPIC), (0) students placed in internships conforming to guidelines of the Council of Directors of School Psychology Programs (CDSPP), (0) students placed in internships that were not APA/CPA-accredited, APPIC or CDSPP listed. All programs either require or offer practicum placements in a wide variety of settings, including mental health treatment facilities, medical facilities, schools, government agencies, the military, and businesses and organizations. (Please see our Web site for more information.)

Housing and Day Care: On-campus housing is available. See the following Web site for more information: http://www.housing.gmu.edu/ Limited amount of graduate housing is available. On-campus day care facilities are available. See the following Web site for more information: http://www.gmu.edu/service.ccc.

Employment of Department Graduates:

Master's Degree Graduates: Of those who graduated in the academic year 2006–2007, the following categories and numbers represent the postgraduate activities and employment of master's degree graduates: Enrolled in a postdoctoral residency/fellowship (n/a), employed in independent practice (n/a), total from the above (master's) (0).

Doctoral Degree Graduates: Of those who graduated in the academic year 2006–2007, the following categories and numbers represent the postgraduate activities and employment of doctoral degree graduates: Enrolled in a psychology doctoral program (n/a), total from the above (doctoral) (0).

Additional Information:

Orientation, Objectives, and Emphasis of Department: All graduate programs emphasize both basic research and the application of research to solving problems in families, schools, industry, government, and health care settings.

Personal Behavior Statement: The university has an Honor Code.

Special Facilities or Resources: The Developmental research area includes individual test rooms, a family interaction room, and a number of faculty research areas; some of the test rooms are equipped with video and computers. Biopsychology includes a rodent colony, modern facilities for behavior testing (including drug self-administration), a Neurolucida system for neuroanatomical evaluation, and extensive histological capability. Biopsychology also has collaborative relationships with the Center for Biomedical Genomics and Informatics for gene microarray work, and the Krasnow Institute for Advanced Study for neuroanatomy, neurophysiology, and neural modeling work. The Human Factors/Applied Cognitive labs include numerous workstations for computer display and data collection, several eyetrackers, several simulators (including a cockpit simulator) and human electrophysiology; a Near Infrared Imaging System is planned for the very near future. Industrial/Organizational research space includes laboratory space for work on groups, teamwork, and leadership. Clinical facilities include a professional Clinic, and research and interview space in faculty labs. The Center for Cognitive Development, housed in the same building as the Clinic, works with local school systems and the School and Clinical programs on issues related to child development. Some students use nearby resources for research, such as the National Institutes of Health.

Information for Students With Physical Disabilities: See the following Web site for more information: http://www.gmu.edu/student/drc/.

Application Information:

Send to College of Humanities and Social Sciences, Graduate Admissions, George Mason University, 4400 University Drive, MSN 2D2, Fairfax, VA 22030-4444. Application available online. URL of online application: http://www.admissions.gmu.edu. Students are admitted in the Fall, application deadline December 1. December 1 for Clinical PhD, Applied Developmental PhD; December 15 for Industrial/Organizational PhD; January 1 for Biopsychology PhD, Human Factors/Applied Cognition PhD; January 15 for School MA; February 1 for Applied Developmental MA, Biopsychology MA, Industrial/Organizational MA, and Human Factors/Applied Cognition MA. *Fee:* $60.

Institute for the Psychological Sciences

Department of Psychology
2001 Jefferson Davis Highway Suite 511
Arlington, VA 22202
Telephone: (703) 416-1441
E-mail: *wnordling@ipsciences.edu*
Web: *http://www.ipsciences.edu*

Department Information:

1999. Chairperson: William Nordling, PhD. Number of faculty: total—full-time 8, part-time 1; women—full-time 2.

Programs and Degrees Offered:

Listed in the following order: Program area, degree type (T if terminal Master's), number awarded 7/06–6/07. Clinical M.S., General MS MA/MS (Master of Arts/Science) (T) 8.

Student Applications/Admissions:

Student Applications

Clinical M.S., General MS MA/MS (Master of Arts/Science)—Applications 2007–2008, 34. Total applicants accepted 2007–2008, 19. Number full-time enrolled (new admits only) 2007–2008, 15. Number part-time enrolled (new admits only) 2007–2008, 6. Total enrolled 2007–2008 full-time, 41, part-time, 6. Openings 2008–2009, 25. The median number of years required for completion of a degree in 2006–2007 were 2. The number of students enrolled full- and part-time who were dismissed or voluntarily withdrew from this program area in 2007–2008 were 4.

Admissions Requirements:

Scores: Entries appear in this order: required test or GPA, minimum score (if required), median score of students entering in 2007–2008. Master's Programs: overall undergraduate GPA 3.0; psychology GPA 3.0. Doctoral Programs: overall undergraduate GPA 3.0; psychology GPA 3.0.

Other Criteria: (importance of criteria rated low, medium, or high): GRE/MAT scores—low, research experience—low, work experience—low, extracurricular activity—low, clinically related public service—low, GPA—high, letters of recommendation—high, interview—high, statement of goals and objectives—high, essays on application—high.

Student Characteristics: The following represents characteristics of students in 2007–2008 in all graduate psychology programs in the department: Female—full-time 20, part-time 7; Male—full-time 11, part-time 1; Hispanic/Latino(a)—full-time 3, part-time 0; Asian/Pacific Islander—full-time 2, part-time 0; Caucasian/White—full-time 26, part-time 0; students subject to the Americans With Disabilities Act—full-time 0, part-time 0; Unknown ethnicity—full-time 0, part-time 0; International students who hold an F-1 or J-1 Visa—full-time 5, part-time 0.

Financial Information/Assistance:

Tuition for Full-Time Study: *Master's:* State residents: per academic year $18,356, $706 per credit hour; Nonstate residents: per academic year $18,356, $706 per credit hour. *Doctoral:* State residents: per academic year $18,616, $716 per credit hour; Nonstate residents: per academic year $18,616, $716 per credit hour. Tuition is subject to change. Additional fees are assessed to students beyond the costs of tuition for the following: library, student activities, graduation, transcript requests, practicum fee, application fee. Tuition costs vary by program. See the following Web site for updates and changes in tuition costs: http://www.ipsciences.edu. Higher tuition cost for this program: PsyD.

Financial Assistance:

First-Year Students: Fellowships and scholarships available for first year. Average number of hours worked per week: 0. Apply by March 15. Tuition remission given: full and partial.

Advanced Students: Teaching assistantships available for advanced students. Average number of hours worked per week: 10. Apply by March 15. Tuition remission given: full and partial. Research assistantships available for advanced students. Average number of hours worked per week: 10. Apply by March 15. Tuition remission given: full and partial. Traineeships available for advanced students. Average number of hours worked per week: 10. Apply by March 15. Tuition remission given: full and partial. Fellowships and scholarships available for advanced students. Apply by March 15. Tuition remission given: full and partial.

Additional Information: Of all students currently enrolled full time, 78% benefited from one or more of the listed financial assistance programs. Application and information available online at http://www.ipsciences.edu/www/docs/227.39/.

Internships/Practica: In their 3rd year of training PsyD students participate in a year-long practicum in the IPS training clinic. PsyD students in their 4th year of training and MS students in an optional 3rd year of training have access to a wide variety of externship/practica sites given that the Institute is located in the Washington, DC metro area.

Housing and Day Care: No on-campus housing is available. No on-campus day care facilities are available.

Employment of Department Graduates:

Master's Degree Graduates: Of those who graduated in the academic year 2006–2007, the following categories and numbers represent the postgraduate activities and employment of master's degree graduates: Enrolled in a psychology doctoral program (14), enrolled in another graduate/professional program (1), enrolled in a postdoctoral residency/fellowship (n/a), employed in independent practice (n/a), employed in an academic position at a university (0), employed in an academic position at a 2-year/4-year college (0), employed in other positions at a higher education institution (1), employed in a professional position in a school system (2), employed in business or industry (4), employed in government agency (0), employed in a community mental health/counseling center (8), employed in a hospital/medical center (0), still seeking employment (1), not seeking employment (6), other employment position (3), do not know (5), total from the above (master's) (45).

Doctoral Degree Graduates: Of those who graduated in the academic year 2006–2007, the following categories and numbers represent the postgraduate activities and employment of doctoral degree graduates: Enrolled in a psychology doctoral program (n/a), enrolled in another graduate/professional program (1), enrolled in a postdoctoral residency/fellowship (4), employed in independent practice (0), employed in an academic position at a university (0), employed in an academic position at a 2-year/4-year college (0), employed in other positions at a higher education institution (2), employed in a professional position in a school system (0), employed in business or industry (0), employed in government agency (0), employed in a community mental health/counseling center (4), employed in a hospital/medical center (1), still seeking employment (0), not seeking employment (0), other employment position (0), do not know (0), total from the above (doctoral) (12).

Additional Information:

Orientation, Objectives, and Emphasis of Department: The department adopts a practioner–scholar model of training and education of psychologists. In doing so the degree programs form the students who can practice scientific psychology integrated with a Catholic worldview.

Special Facilities or Resources: The Washington, DC metro area is an enviornment rich in educational and cultural resources for students. In addition to the IPS Library, students have access to the libraries of other universities and centers of learning within the area. The IPS also has a chapel and a chaplain who provide students with opportunities for spiritual development.

Application Information:

Send to Institute for the Psychological Sciences, Admissions, 2001 Jefferson Davis Highway, Suite 511, Arlington, VA 22202. Application available online. URL of online application: http://www.ipsciences.edu. Programs have rolling admissions. Early enrollment deadline March 31; Fall admission deadline June 1. *Fee:* $50.

James Madison University (2007 data)

Department of Graduate Psychology
MSC 7401
Harrisonburg, VA 22807
Telephone: (540) 568-2556
Fax: (540) 568-3322
E-mail: *rogerssj@jmu.edu*
Web: *http://www.psyc.jmu.edu*

Department Information:

1967. Head, Department of Graduate Psychology: Sheena Rogers, PhD. Number of faculty: total—full-time 28, part-time 5; women—full-time 13, part-time 5.

Programs and Degrees Offered:

Listed in the following order: Program area, degree type (T if terminal Master's), number awarded 7/06–6/07. Psychological Sciences MA/MS (Master of Arts/Science) (T) 11, Community Counseling Other 11, School Psychology EdS/MEd (School Psychology) 16, School Counseling EdS/MEd (School Psychology) 3, College Student Personnel Administration MA/MS (Master of

Arts/Science) (T) 13, Combined Integrated Clinical and School Psychology PsyD (Doctor of Psychology) 2, Assessment and Measurement PhD (Doctor of Philosophy) 3.

APA Accreditation: Combination PsyD (Doctor of Psychology).

Student Applications/Admissions:

Student Applications

Psychological Sciences MA/MS (Master of Arts/Science)—Applications 2007–2008, 41. Total applicants accepted 2007–2008, 10. Number full-time enrolled (new admits only) 2007–2008, 10. Number part-time enrolled (new admits only) 2007–2008, 0. Total enrolled 2007–2008 full-time, 20, part-time, 2. Openings 2008–2009, 10. The median number of years required for completion of a degree in 2006–2007 were 2. The number of students enrolled full- and part-time who were dismissed or voluntarily withdrew from this program area in 2007–2008 were 0. *Community Counseling Other*—Applications 2007–2008, 72. Total applicants accepted 2007–2008, 9. Number full-time enrolled (new admits only) 2007–2008, 8. Number part-time enrolled (new admits only) 2007–2008, 1. Total enrolled 2007–2008 full-time, 36, part-time, 5. Openings 2008–2009, 10. The median number of years required for completion of a degree in 2006–2007 were 3. The number of students enrolled full- and part-time who were dismissed or voluntarily withdrew from this program area in 2007–2008 were 0. *School Psychology EdS/MEd (School Psychology)*—Applications 2007–2008, 80. Total applicants accepted 2007–2008, 10. Number full-time enrolled (new admits only) 2007–2008, 8. Total enrolled 2007–2008 full-time, 31, part-time, 1. Openings 2008–2009, 10. The median number of years required for completion of a degree in 2006–2007 were 3. The number of students enrolled full- and part-time who were dismissed or voluntarily withdrew from this program area in 2007–2008 were 0. *School Counseling EdS/MEd (School Psychology)*—Applications 2007–2008, 35. Total applicants accepted 2007–2008, 9. Number full-time enrolled (new admits only) 2007–2008, 7. Number part-time enrolled (new admits only) 2007–2008, 2. Total enrolled 2007–2008 full-time, 26, part-time, 5. Openings 2008–2009, 10. The median number of years required for completion of a degree in 2006–2007 were 3. The number of students enrolled full- and part-time who were dismissed or voluntarily withdrew from this program area in 2007–2008 were 0. *College Student Personnel Administration MA/MS (Master of Arts/Science)*—Applications 2007–2008, 44. Total applicants accepted 2007–2008, 15. Number full-time enrolled (new admits only) 2007–2008, 13. Number part-time enrolled (new admits only) 2007–2008, 2. Total enrolled 2007–2008 full-time, 25, part-time, 2. Openings 2008–2009, 14. The median number of years required for completion of a degree in 2006–2007 were 2. The number of students enrolled full- and part-time who were dismissed or voluntarily withdrew from this program area in 2007–2008 were 0. *Combined Integrated Clinical and School Psychology PsyD (Doctor of Psychology)*—Applications 2007–2008, 48. Total applicants accepted 2007–2008, 7. Number full-time enrolled (new admits only) 2007–2008, 7. Openings 2008–2009, 6. The median number of years required for completion of a degree in 2006–2007 were 4. The number of students enrolled full- and part-time who were dismissed or voluntarily withdrew from this program area in 2007–2008 were 0. *Assessment and Measurement PhD (Doctor of Philosophy)*—Applications 2007–2008, 15. Total applicants accepted 2007–2008, 8. Number full-time enrolled (new admits only) 2007–2008, 7. Number part-time enrolled (new admits only) 2007–2008, 1. Total enrolled 2007–2008 full-time, 15, part-time, 4. Openings 2008–2009, 4. The median number of years required for completion of a degree in 2006–2007 were 4. The number of students enrolled full- and part-time who were dismissed or voluntarily withdrew from this program area in 2007–2008 were 0.

Admissions Requirements:

Scores: Entries appear in this order: required test or GPA, minimum score (if required), median score of students entering in 2007–2008. Master's Programs: overall undergraduate GPA no minimum stated; last 2 years GPA no minimum stated; psychology GPA no minimum stated. Psychological Sciences—GRE-V 544; GRE-Q 614; GRE-A 624; GRE-S 650; Overall GPA 3.47; Jr/Sr GPA 3.70; Psych GPA 3.84. Community Counseling—GRE-V 525; GRE-Q 473; GRE-A546; Overall GPA 328; Jr/Sr GPA 3.53; Psych GPA 3.58. School Counseling—GRE-V 525; GRE-Q 587; GRE-A 620; Overall GPA 3.08; Jr/Sr GPA 3.22; Psych GPA 3.23. School Psychology—GRE-V 471; GRE-Q 570; GRE-A 607; Overall GPA 3.24; Jr/Sr GPA 3.59; Psych GPA 3.44. College Student Personnel Administration—GRE-V 459; GRE-Q 520; GRE-A 567; Overall GPA 3.17. GRE Subject exam recommended for Psychological Sciences program only. Doctoral Programs: Assessment and Measurement (PhD)—GRE-V 540; GRE-Q 570; GRE+Analytical 630. Although the Combined Integrated Doctoral Program in Clinical and School Psychology does require GRE V, Q, A, and Subject scores, applicants are reviewed on the basis of a wide range of admission criteria (please see http://cep.jmu.edu/clinicalpsyd for additional information).

Other Criteria: (importance of criteria rated low, medium, or high): Psychological Sciences—GRE/MAT scores—high, research experience—medium, work experience—low, clinically related public service—medium, letters of recommendation—high. CSPA—research experience—medium, work experience—high, clinically related public service—medium, GPA—high, letters of recommendation—high. School Psychology—GRE/MAT scores—low, research experience—medium, work experience—medium, extracurricular activity—medium, clinically related public service—high, GPA—high, letters of recommendation—high. Community Counseling—GRE/MAT scores—low, research experience—high, work experience—low, extracurricular activity—high, clinically related public service—medium, GPA—high, letters of recommendation—medium. School Counseling—GRE/MAT scores—low, research experience—high, work experience—low, extracurricular activity—high, clinically related public service—medium, GPA—high, letters of recommendation—medium. PhD Assessment and Management—GRE/MAT scores—medium, research experience—medium, work experience—low, clinically related public service—high, GPA—high, letters of recommendation—high. PsyD Clinical and School—GRE/MAT scores—medium, research experience—high, work experience—high, extracurricular activity—high, clinically related public service—high, GPA—high, letters of recommendation—high.

Student Characteristics: The following represents characteristics of students in 2007–2008 in all graduate psychology programs in the department: Female—full-time 142, part-time 15; Male—full-time 36, part-time 4; African American/Black—full-time 3, part-time 1; Hispanic/Latino(a)—full-time 2, part-time 0; Asian/Pacific Islander—full-time 5, part-time 3; American Indian/Alaska Native—full-time 0, part-time 0; Caucasian/White—full-time 168, part-time 15; students subject to the Americans With Disabilities Act—full-time 0, part-time 0; Unknown ethnicity—full-time 0, part-time 0.

Financial Information/Assistance:

Tuition for Full-Time Study: *Master's:* State residents: $246 per credit hour; Nonstate residents: $701 per credit hour.

Financial Assistance:

First-Year Students: Teaching assistantships available for first year. Average amount paid per academic year: $8,167. Average number of hours worked per week: 20. Apply by Fall. Tuition remission given: full. Research assistantships available for first year. Average amount paid per academic year: $6,959. Average number of hours worked per week: 20. Apply by Fall. Tuition remission given: full. Traineeships available for first year. Tuition remission given: partial. Fellowships and scholarships available for first year. Tuition remission given: partial.

Advanced Students: Teaching assistantships available for advanced students. Average amount paid per academic year: $8,167. Average number of hours worked per week: 20. Apply by Fall. Tuition remission given: full. Research assistantships available for advanced students. Average amount paid per academic year: $6,959. Average number of hours worked per week: 20. Apply by Fall. Tuition remission given: full. Traineeships available for advanced students. Tuition remission given: partial. Fellowships and scholarships available for advanced students. Tuition remission given: partial.

Additional Information: Of all students currently enrolled full time, 90% benefited from one or more of the listed financial assistance programs. Application and information available online at http://www.jmu.edu/cgapp.

Internships/Practica: The department maintains a large network of internship sites for specialists for EdS and PsyD students. These sites are housed in public school settings, community mental health agencies, hospitals, and other human service facilities. In addition, the department maintains two doctoral-level internships in the Human Development Center (an on-campus comprehensive mental health clinic for children and families). The department provides practicum training through the University's Human Development Center and the Counseling and Student Development Center.

Housing and Day Care: No on-campus housing is available. No on-campus day care facilities are available.

Employment of Department Graduates:

Master's Degree Graduates: Of those who graduated in the academic year 2006–2007, the following categories and numbers represent the postgraduate activities and employment of master's degree graduates: Enrolled in a postdoctoral residency/fellowship (n/a), employed in independent practice (n/a), total from the above (master's) (0).

Doctoral Degree Graduates: Of those who graduated in the academic year 2006–2007, the following categories and numbers represent the postgraduate activities and employment of doctoral degree graduates: Enrolled in a psychology doctoral program (n/a), total from the above (doctoral) (0).

Additional Information:

Orientation, Objectives, and Emphasis of Department: All specialist and doctoral programs provide the necessary academic requirements in training for certification by the State Department of Education and licensure by the State Board of Psychology in Virginia. The Counseling program meets the requirements for licensure as a professional counselor (LPC) in the Commonwealth of Virginia. The Psychological Sciences program prepares students for further study at the doctoral level or for employment. The program (MA) is research based; in addition to coursework a research apprenticeship, comprehensive examination, and thesis is required. The Combined Integrated Doctoral Program in Clinical and School Psychology prepares students for licensure as clinical psychologists. Our program is fully accredited by the American Psychological Association, and is designed for students possessing advanced graduate degrees and professional experience in applied mental health fields. Depending upon their background, students are able to complete the course work portion of the program in either 2 or 3 years. We have an excellent track record of placing student in APA-accredited internships; our graduates assume professional positions in a range of contexts including, but not limited to, mental health clinics, child and family agencies, public schools, administrative and leadership positions, training and supervisory roles, and private practice. Please see http://cep.jmu.edu/clinicalpsyd for additional information about our innovative program.

Special Facilities or Resources: Students have access to a state-of-the-art university computer network, microcomputers, animal laboratory, test library, and videotape equipment.

Application Information:

Send to Department of Graduate Psychology, Graduate Admissions, MSC 7401, James Madison University, Harrisonburg, VA 22807. Application available online. URL of online application: http://www.psyc.jmu.edu. Students are admitted in the Fall. Application deadline for PhD in Assessment and Measurement, and College Student Personnel Administration March 1; Community Counseling, School Counseling, Psychological Sciences February 1; School Psychology February 15; Combined Interated Doctoral Program in Clinical, and School Psychology February 1. *Fee:* $55.

Marymount University

Department of Forensic Psychology
School of Education and Human Services
2807 North Glebe Road
Arlington, VA 22207
Telephone: (703) 284-5705
Fax: (703) 284-5708
E-mail: *mary.lindahl@marymount.edu*
Web: *http://www.marymount.edu/academic/sehs/fp/fphome.htm*

Department Information:

2000. Chairperson: Dr. Mary Lindahl. Number of faculty: total—full-time 3, part-time 10; women—full-time 2, part-time 6; minority—part-time 2; women minority—part-time 2.

Programs and Degrees Offered:

Listed in the following order: Program area, degree type (T if terminal Master's), number awarded 7/06–6/07. Forensic Psychology MA/MS (Master of Arts/Science) (T) 95.

Student Applications/Admissions:

Student Applications

Forensic Psychology MA/MS (Master of Arts/Science)—Applications 2007–2008, 236. Total applicants accepted 2007–2008, 120. Number full-time enrolled (new admits only) 2007–2008, 87. Total enrolled 2007–2008 full-time, 134, part-time, 43. Openings 2008–2009, 90. The median number of years required for completion of a degree in 2006–2007 were 2. The number of students enrolled full- and part-time who were dismissed or voluntarily withdrew from this program area in 2007–2008 were 3.

Admissions Requirements:

Scores: Entries appear in this order: required test or GPA, minimum score (if required), median score of students entering in 2007–2008. Master's Programs: GRE-V 250, 470; GRE-Q 280, 550; overall undergraduate GPA 2.00, 3.36. The GRE-Writing Assessment, which is now part of the GRE, is required of all students.

Other Criteria: (importance of criteria rated low, medium, or high): GRE/MAT scores—medium, research experience—low, work experience—medium, extracurricular activity—medium, clinically related public service—low, GPA—high, letters of recommendation—medium, statement of goals and objectives—medium, undergraduate major in psychology—low, specific undergraduate psychology courses taken—low. For additional information on admission requirements, go to http://www.marymount.edu/academic/sehs/fp/fpadmiss.htm.

Student Characteristics: The following represents characteristics of students in 2007–2008 in all graduate psychology programs in the department: Female—full-time 117, part-time 36; Male—full-time 17, part-time 7; African American/Black—full-time 12, part-time 6; Hispanic/Latino(a)—full-time 2, part-time 2; Asian/Pacific Islander—full-time 5, part-time 0; American Indian/Alaska Native—full-time 1, part-time 0; Caucasian/White—full-time 100, part-time 31; Multi-ethnic—full-time 1, part-time 2; students subject to the Americans With Disabilities Act—full-time 2, part-time 0; Unknown ethnicity—full-time 10, part-time 2; International students who hold an F-1 or J-1 Visa—full-time 3, part-time 0.

Financial Information/Assistance:

Tuition for Full-Time Study: *Master's:* State residents: $655 per credit hour; Nonstate residents: $655 per credit hour. Tuition is subject to change. Additional fees are assessed to students beyond the costs of tuition for the following: $6.70 per credit hour technology fee, new student fee $30 (one-time), $55 internship application fee. See the following Web site for updates and changes in tuition costs: http://www.marymount.edu/financialinfo/current.html#graduate.

Financial Assistance:

First-Year Students: Research assistantships available for first year. Average amount paid per academic year: $2,500. Average number of hours worked per week: 20. Apply by Summer. Tuition remission given: full.

Advanced Students: Research assistantships available for advanced students. Average amount paid per academic year: $2,500. Average number of hours worked per week: 20. Apply by Summer. Tuition remission given: full.

Additional Information: Application and information available online at http://www.marymount.edu/financialaid/graduate.html.

Internships/Practica: Master's Degree (MA/MS Forensic Psychology): An internship experience such as a final research project or "capstone" experience is required of graduates. Forensic psychology students may choose an internship in a wide variety of settings, including local and state correctional facilities, local community mental health treatment centers, victim witness programs, domestic violence programs and shelters, national and local mental health advocacy organizations, child welfare agencies and advocacy organizations, adult services agencies (serving incapacitated and incompetent adult), juvenile court services, state and local law enforcement, federal law enforcement and justice agencies, and any and all areas in which psychological expertise and psychological services (including counseling) would be applied in a legal setting (criminal, civil, and juvenile justice).

Housing and Day Care: No on-campus housing is available. No on-campus day care facilities are available.

Employment of Department Graduates:

Master's Degree Graduates: Of those who graduated in the academic year 2006–2007, the following categories and numbers represent the postgraduate activities and employment of master's degree graduates: Enrolled in a postdoctoral residency/fellowship (n/a), employed in independent practice (n/a), total from the above (master's) (0).

Doctoral Degree Graduates: Of those who graduated in the academic year 2006–2007, the following categories and numbers represent the postgraduate activities and employment of doctoral degree graduates: Enrolled in a psychology doctoral program (n/a), total from the above (doctoral) (0).

Additional Information:

Orientation, Objectives, and Emphasis of Department: The Department of Forensic Psychology offers a Master of Arts in Forensic Psychology. This degree provides graduates with the skills and knowledge they need to provide effective, high-quality services in a variety of forensic settings. These settings include probation and parole, victim assistance, law enforcement, and other arenas within the juvenile, civil, and criminal justice systems. To accomplish this goal, the program balances the acquisition of traditional psychological knowledge and skills with a specialized understanding of the justice system.

Special Facilities or Resources: The location of Marymount in suburban Washington provides our students with a large number of opportunities for internships and employment in the area, especially with federal agencies. The university is a member of the Washington Consortium of College and Universities, which gives the students access to the library facilities and classes of most of the major universities in the area. In addition, the Department of Forensic Psychology has a joint research project with the FBI's Behavioral Science Unit. Selected students have the opportunity to work on research projects with faculty using closed criminal case files provided by the FBI. Also, approximately every other summer, students have the opportunity to learn about and experience forensic psychology in the English justice system via a collaborative relationship with the Forensic Psychology Program at London Metropolitan University.

Application Information:

Send to Office of Graduate Admissions, Marymount University, 2807 North Glebe Road, Arlington, VA 22207. Application available on-line. URL of online application: https://www.applyweb.com/apply/marymu/menu.html. Students are admitted in the Fall, application deadline February 15. *Fee:* $40. Admitted students can defer for up to 1 year. Deposit is required to reserve space.

Old Dominion University

Department of Psychology
College of Sciences
Mills Godwin Building—Room 250
Norfolk, VA 23529-0267
Telephone: (757) 683-4439
Fax: (757) 683-5087
E-mail: *jsanchez@odu.edu*
Web: *http://www.sci.odu.edu/psychology/*

Department Information:

1954. Chairperson: Janis Sanchez. Number of faculty: total—full-time 26, part-time 9; women—full-time 13, part-time 6; total—minority—full-time 1; women minority—full-time 1.

Programs and Degrees Offered:

Listed in the following order: Program area, degree type (T if terminal Master's), number awarded 7/06–6/07. General MA/MS (Master of Arts/Science) (T) 4, Industrial/Organizational PhD (Doctor of Philosophy) 3, Human Factors PhD (Doctor of Philosophy) 1, Applied Experimental PhD (Doctor of Philosophy) 0, Clinical Psychology PsyD (Doctor of Psychology) 12.

Student Applications/Admissions:

Student Applications

General MA/MS (Master of Arts/Science)—Applications 2007–2008, 51. Total applicants accepted 2007–2008, 9. Number full-time enrolled (new admits only) 2007–2008, 9. Total enrolled 2007–2008 full-time, 22. Openings 2008–2009, 10. The median number of years required for completion of a degree in 2006–2007 were 2. The number of students enrolled full- and part-time who were dismissed or voluntarily withdrew from this program area in 2007–2008 were 2. *Industrial/Organizational PhD (Doctor of Philosophy)*—Applications 2007–2008, 20. Total applicants accepted 2007–2008, 4. Number full-time enrolled (new admits only) 2007–2008, 2. Total enrolled 2007–2008 full-time, 7, part-time, 11. Openings 2008–2009, 3. The median number of years required for completion of a degree in 2006–2007 were 5. The number of students enrolled full- and part-time who were dismissed or voluntarily withdrew from this program area in 2007–2008 were 1. *Human Factors PhD (Doctor of Philosophy)*—Applications 2007–2008, 13. Total applicants accepted 2007–2008, 4. Number full-time enrolled (new admits only) 2007–2008, 4. Total enrolled 2007–2008 full-time, 11, part-time, 3. Openings 2008–2009, 3. The median number of years required for completion of a degree in 2006–2007 were 5. The number of students enrolled full- and part-time who were dismissed or voluntarily withdrew from this program area in 2007–2008 were 0. *Applied Experimental PhD (Doctor of Philosophy)*—Applications 2007–2008, 7. Total applicants accepted 2007–2008, 5. Number full-time enrolled (new admits only) 2007–2008, 3. Total enrolled 2007–2008 full-time, 5, part-time, 2. Openings 2008–2009, 3. The median number of years required for completion of a degree in 2006–2007 were 5. The number of students enrolled full- and part-time who were dismissed or voluntarily withdrew from this program area in 2007–2008 were 0. *Clinical Psychology PsyD (Doctor of Psychology)*—Applications 2007–2008, 167. Total applicants accepted 2007–2008, 19. Number full-time enrolled (new admits only) 2007–2008, 10. Total enrolled 2007–2008 full-time, 10. Openings 2008–2009, 10. The median number of years required for completion of a degree in 2006–2007 were 5. The number of students enrolled full- and part-time who were dismissed or voluntarily withdrew from this program area in 2007–2008 were 1.

Admissions Requirements:

Scores: Entries appear in this order: required test or GPA, minimum score (if required), median score of students entering in 2007–2008. Master's Programs: GRE-V no minimum stated, 540; GRE-Q no minimum stated, 637; GRE-Subject (Psychology) no minimum stated, 643; overall undergraduate GPA no minimum stated, 3.49; Master's GRE-Analytical no minimum stated, 4.5. Doctoral Programs: GRE-V no minimum stated, 570; GRE-Q no minimum stated, 625; GRE-Subject (Psychology) no minimum stated, 650; overall undergraduate GPA no minimum stated, 3.44; Doctoral program GRE-Analytic no minimum stated, 5.0.

Other Criteria: (importance of criteria rated low, medium, or high): GRE/MAT scores—high, research experience—high, work experience—medium, extracurricular activity—medium, clinically related public service—low, GPA—high, letters of recommendation—medium, interview—medium, statement of goals and objectives—medium.

Student Characteristics: The following represents characteristics of students in 2007–2008 in all graduate psychology programs in the department: Female—full-time 43, part-time 0; Male—full-time 17, part-time 0; African American/Black—full-time 6, part-time 0; Hispanic/Latino(a)—full-time 1, part-time 0; Asian/Pacific Islander—full-time 1, part-time 0; American Indian/Alaska Native—full-time 0, part-time 0; Caucasian/White—full-time 48, part-time 0; Multi-ethnic—full-time 1, part-time 0; students subject to the Americans With Disabilities Act—full-time 0, part-time 0; Unknown ethnicity—full-time 3, part-time 0; International students who hold an F-1 or J-1 Visa—full-time 61, part-time 0.

Financial Information/Assistance:

Tuition for Full-Time Study: *Master's:* State residents: $304 per credit hour; Nonstate residents: $761 per credit hour. *Doctoral:* State residents: $304 per credit hour; Nonstate residents: $761 per credit hour. Tuition is subject to change.

Financial Assistance:

First-Year Students: Teaching assistantships available for first year. Average amount paid per academic year: $12,000. Average number of hours worked per week: 20. Apply by January

15. Tuition remission given: full. Fellowships and scholarships available for first year. Average amount paid per academic year: $15,000. Apply by January 15. Tuition remission given: full.

Advanced Students: Teaching assistantships available for advanced students. Average amount paid per academic year: $12,000. Average number of hours worked per week: 20. Tuition remission given: full. Research assistantships available for advanced students. Average amount paid per academic year: $12,000. Average number of hours worked per week: 20. Tuition remission given: full. Fellowships and scholarships available for advanced students. Average amount paid per academic year: $15,000. Tuition remission given: full.

Additional Information: Of all students currently enrolled full time, 75% benefited from one or more of the listed financial assistance programs.

Internships/Practica: Doctoral Degree (PsyD Clinical Psychology): For those doctoral students for whom a professional internship was required in this program prior to graduation, (9) students applied for an internship in 2006–2007, with (8) students obtaining an internship. Of those students who obtained an internship, (7) were paid internships. Of those students who obtained an internship, (8) students placed in APA/CPA-accredited internships, (0) students placed in internships not APA/CPA accredited, but listed with the Association of Psychology Postdoctoral and Internship Centers (APPIC), (0) students placed in internships conforming to guidelines of the Council of Directors of School Psychology Programs (CDSPP), (0) students placed in internships that were not APA/CPA-accredited, APPIC or CDSPP listed. Internships are highly encouraged for all three PhD programs and are available at local businesses, hospitals, and military and government agencies, as well as out of state. Practicum and internship experiences are also available for all graduate students.

Housing and Day Care: On-campus housing is available. On-campus day care facilities are available.

Employment of Department Graduates:

Master's Degree Graduates: Of those who graduated in the academic year 2006–2007, the following categories and numbers represent the postgraduate activities and employment of master's degree graduates: Enrolled in a psychology doctoral program (0), enrolled in another graduate/professional program (0), enrolled in a postdoctoral residency/fellowship (n/a), employed in independent practice (n/a), employed in an academic position at a university (1), employed in business or industry (4), do not know (2), total from the above (master's) (7).

Doctoral Degree Graduates: Of those who graduated in the academic year 2006–2007, the following categories and numbers represent the postgraduate activities and employment of doctoral degree graduates: Enrolled in a psychology doctoral program (n/a), total from the above (doctoral) (0).

Additional Information:

Orientation, Objectives, and Emphasis of Department: The department offers PhD programs in Applied Experimental, Human Factors, and Industrial/Organizational Psychology. Concentrations within Applied Experimental include community, developmental, health, and psychophysiology. Concentrations within Human Factors include aviation, cognitive processes, neuroergonomics, and modeling and simulation. Concentrations within Industrial/Organizational include organizational and personnel. The programs are designed to provide in-depth training in applied experimental, human factors, or industrial/organizational psychology and specialized training in an area of concentration. A program of graduate study leading to the degree of Master of Science with a concentration in general psychology is also offered by the department. The department participates in the Virginia Consortium Program in Clinical Psychology, which in collaboration with the College of William and Mary, Eastern Virginia Medical School, and Norfolk State University, offers the PsyD in Clinical Psychology. For information regarding the PsyD program see Virginia Consortium Program in Clinical Psychology.

Special Facilities or Resources: The department has a new Human Computer Interaction and Usability Analysis lab, a state-of-the art driving simulator, psychophysiological recording equipment, an animal lab, and other research facilities. A close collaboration with the Virginia Modeling, Analysis, and Simulation Center provides students with opportunities to engage in command and control simulation, surgical simulation, and virtual reality research. The psychology faculty and graduate students also maintain active collaborations with NASA Langley Research Center, Eastern Virginia Medical School, the Center for Pediatric Research, Children's Hospital of the King's Daughters, and community and government groups such as Virginia Department of Motor Vehicles, Department of Public Health, and Tidewater AIDS Crisis Taskforce.

Information for Students With Physical Disabilities: See the following Web site for more information: http://www.odu.edu/webroot/orgs/stu/stuserv.nsf/pages/dswebpage.

Application Information:

Send to Old Dominion University, Office of Graduate Admissions, 105 Rollins Hall, Norfolk, VA 23529-0050. Application available online. URL of online application: http://www.admissions.odu.edu/graduate.php?page=apply. Students are admitted in the Winter, application deadline January 15. January 15 for PhD, May 15 for MS. *Fee:* $30. The fee is waived or deferred if the applicant is an ODU graduate.

Radford University

Department of Psychology
Arts and Sciences
P.O. Box 6946
Radford, VA 24142-6946
Telephone: (540) 831-5361
Fax: (540) 831-6113
E-mail: *hlips@radford.edu*
Web: *http://www.radford.edu/psyc-web*

Department Information:

1937. Chairperson: Hilary M. Lips. Number of faculty: total—full-time 24, part-time 4; women—full-time 10, part-time 3; faculty subject to the Americans With Disabilities Act 1.

Programs and Degrees Offered:

Listed in the following order: Program area, degree type (T if terminal Master's), number awarded 7/06–6/07. Counseling PsyD (Doctor of Psychology) 0, Clinical MA/MS (Master of Arts/Science) (T) 6, Experimental MA/MS (Master of Arts/Science) (T) 3, Industrial/Organizational MA/MS (Master of Arts/Science) (T) 13, School EdS/MEd (School Psychology) 8.

Student Applications/Admissions:

Student Applications

Counseling PsyD (Doctor of Psychology)—Number full-time enrolled (new admits only) 2007–2008, 0. The number of students enrolled full- and part-time who were dismissed or voluntarily withdrew from this program area in 2007–2008 were 0. *Clinical MA/MS (Master of Arts/Science)*—Applications 2007–2008, 38. Total applicants accepted 2007–2008, 15. Number full-time enrolled (new admits only) 2007–2008, 10. Number part-time enrolled (new admits only) 2007–2008, 0. Openings 2008–2009, 10. The median number of years required for completion of a degree in 2006–2007 were 2. The number of students enrolled full- and part-time who were dismissed or voluntarily withdrew from this program area in 2007–2008 were 0. *Experimental MA/MS (Master of Arts/Science)*—Applications 2007–2008, 11. Total applicants accepted 2007–2008, 11. Number full-time enrolled (new admits only) 2007–2008, 7. Openings 2008–2009, 8. The median number of years required for completion of a degree in 2006–2007 were 2. The number of students enrolled full- and part-time who were dismissed or voluntarily withdrew from this program area in 2007–2008 were 0. *Industrial/Organizational MA/MS (Master of Arts/Science)*—Applications 2007–2008, 56. Total applicants accepted 2007–2008, 31. Number full-time enrolled (new admits only) 2007–2008, 13. Openings 2008–2009, 13. The median number of years required for completion of a degree in 2006–2007 were 2. The number of students enrolled full- and part-time who were dismissed or voluntarily withdrew from this program area in 2007–2008 were 0. *School EdS/MEd (School Psychology)*—Applications 2007–2008, 22. Total applicants accepted 2007–2008, 19. Number full-time enrolled (new admits only) 2007–2008, 11. Openings 2008–2009, 12. The median number of years required for completion of a degree in 2006–2007 were 3. The number of students enrolled full- and part-time who were dismissed or voluntarily withdrew from this program area in 2007–2008 were 0.

Admissions Requirements:

Scores: Entries appear in this order: required test or GPA, minimum score (if required), median score of students entering in 2007–2008. Master's Programs: GRE-V 480, 523; GRE-Q 480, 560; overall undergraduate GPA 3.0, 3.5; last 2 years GPA 3.00, 3.70; psychology GPA 3.0, 3.6. The Psychology Subject GRE is not required for admission. However, it is recommended that students take this examination and submit the score along with their application. For students who may wish to enhance their chances of acceptance into a competitive program, the Psychology GRE score may be helpful for the committee's consideration of their credentials. Doctoral Programs: GRE-V no minimum stated; GRE-Q no minimum stated; Doctoral program GRE-Analytic no minimum stated.

Other Criteria: (importance of criteria rated low, medium, or high): GRE/MAT scores—medium, research experience—high, work experience—high, extracurricular activity—medium, clinically related public service—high, GPA—high, letters of recommendation—high, interview—high, statement of goals and objectives—medium, undergraduate major in psychology—medium, specific undergraduate psychology courses taken—low. Interview required for doctoral program but not for masters' programs. For additional information on admission requirements, go to http://www.radford.edu/~psyc-web/.

Student Characteristics: The following represents characteristics of students in 2007–2008 in all graduate psychology programs in the department: Female—full-time 73, part-time 0; Male—full-time 17, part-time 0; African American/Black—full-time 2, part-time 0; Hispanic/Latino(a)—full-time 1, part-time 0; Asian/Pacific Islander—full-time 2, part-time 0; American Indian/Alaska Native—full-time 0, part-time 0; Caucasian/White—full-time 85, part-time 0; Multi-ethnic—full-time 0, part-time 0; students subject to the Americans With Disabilities Act—full-time 0, part-time 0; Unknown ethnicity—full-time 0, part-time 0; International students who hold an F-1 or J-1 Visa—full-time 1, part-time 0.

Financial Information/Assistance:

Tuition for Full-Time Study: *Master's:* State residents: per academic year $6,686, $279 per credit hour; Nonstate residents: per academic year $12,466, $519 per credit hour. Tuition is subject to change. See the following Web site for updates and changes in tuition costs: http://www.stuacct.asp.radford.edu/acad_fees/costs.aspx.

Financial Assistance:

First-Year Students: Teaching assistantships available for first year. Average amount paid per academic year: $8,000. Average number of hours worked per week: 20. Apply by March 1. Tuition remission given: partial. Research assistantships available for first year. Average amount paid per academic year: $4,000. Average number of hours worked per week: 10. Apply by March 1. Traineeships available for first year. Average amount paid per academic year: $13,500. Average number of hours worked per week: 20. Apply by January 15. Tuition remission given: full.

Advanced Students: Teaching assistantships available for advanced students. Average amount paid per academic year: $8,700. Average number of hours worked per week: 20. Apply by February 15. Tuition remission given: partial. Research assistantships available for advanced students. Average amount paid per academic year: $3,100. Average number of hours worked per week: 10. Traineeships available for advanced students. Average amount paid per academic year: $13,500. Average number of hours worked per week: 20. Apply by PsyD only. Tuition remission given: full.

Additional Information: Of all students currently enrolled full time, 90% benefited from one or more of the listed financial assistance programs. Application and information available online at http://finaid.asp.radford.edu/grprog.html.

Internships/Practica: Master's Degree (MA/MS Clinical): An internship experience such as a final research project or "capstone" experience is required of graduates. Internships and/or practica are required for all programs.

Housing and Day Care: On-campus housing is available. See the following Web site for more information: http://www.radford.edu/~res-life/. No on-campus day care facilities are available.

Employment of Department Graduates:

Master's Degree Graduates: Of those who graduated in the academic year 2006–2007, the following categories and numbers

represent the postgraduate activities and employment of master's degree graduates: Enrolled in a psychology doctoral program (2), enrolled in a postdoctoral residency/fellowship (n/a), employed in independent practice (n/a), employed in a professional position in a school system (8), employed in business or industry (12), employed in a community mental health/counseling center (4), other employment position (2), total from the above (master's) (28).

Doctoral Degree Graduates: Of those who graduated in the academic year 2006–2007, the following categories and numbers represent the postgraduate activities and employment of doctoral degree graduates: Enrolled in a psychology doctoral program (n/a), total from the above (doctoral) (0).

Additional Information:

Orientation, Objectives, and Emphasis of Department: The department aims to train psychologists who are well versed in both the theoretical and applied aspects of the discipline. The emphasis of the department is eclectic: school, clinical, experimental, industrial/organizational, and counseling options are available. The School program is an EdS program that also provides preparation for certification and licensing as a school psychologist in Virginia. We are starting a PsyD program in Counseling Psychology, with an emphasis on rural mental health, in the Fall of 2008.

Special Facilities or Resources: We have computer laboratories and some research space for use by graduate students. We have good animal lab facilities. The department has established a center for gender studies and laboratory for brain research.

Information for Students With Physical Disabilities: See the following Web site for more information: http://www.radford.edu/~dro/.

Application Information:

Send to College of Graduate and Professional Studies, P.O. Box 6928, Radford University, Radford, VA 24142. Application available online. URL of online application: http://www.radford.edu/gradcollege/apply/index.html. Students are admitted in the Fall, application deadline March 1. Applications for the PsyD program in Counseling Psychology are due (and must be complete) by January 15. *Fee:* $40.

Regent University

Doctoral Program in Clinical Psychology
School of Psychology and Counseling
1000 Regent University Drive
Virginia Beach, VA 23464
Telephone: (757) 226-4366
Fax: (757) 226-4304
E-mail: *willhat@regent.edu*
Web: *http://www.regent.edu/psyd*

Department Information:

1996. Chairperson: William L. Hathaway, PhD. Number of faculty: total—full-time 10, part-time 8; women—full-time 6, part-time 6; total—minority—full-time 2, part-time 3; women minority—full-time 2, part-time 3; faculty subject to the Americans With Disabilities Act 1.

Programs and Degrees Offered:

Listed in the following order: Program area, degree type (T if terminal Master's), number awarded 7/06–6/07. Clinical Psychology PsyD (Doctor of Psychology) 15.

APA Accreditation: Clinical PsyD (Doctor of Psychology).

Student Applications/Admissions:

Student Applications

Clinical Psychology PsyD (Doctor of Psychology)—Applications 2007–2008, 87. Total applicants accepted 2007–2008, 33. Number full-time enrolled (new admits only) 2007–2008, 18. Number part-time enrolled (new admits only) 2007–2008, 0. Total enrolled 2007–2008 full-time, 118, part-time, 1. Openings 2008–2009, 20. The median number of years required for completion of a degree in 2006–2007 were 5. The number of students enrolled full- and part-time who were dismissed or voluntarily withdrew from this program area in 2007–2008 were 3.

Admissions Requirements:

Scores: Entries appear in this order: required test or GPA, minimum score (if required), median score of students entering in 2007–2008. Doctoral Programs: GRE-V no minimum stated; GRE-Q no minimum stated; overall undergraduate GPA 3.0, 3.7; Doctoral program GRE-Analytic no minimum stated. The GRE Writing exam is required for all applicants. This exam is included in the GRE General Exam as of October 2002.

Other Criteria: (importance of criteria rated low, medium, or high): GRE/MAT scores—high, research experience—medium, work experience—medium, extracurricular activity—medium, clinically related public service—medium, GPA—high, letters of recommendation—medium, interview—medium, statement of goals and objectives—medium, leadership experiences—medium, undergraduate major in psychology—medium, specific undergraduate psychology courses taken—medium.

Student Characteristics: The following represents characteristics of students in 2007–2008 in all graduate psychology programs in the department: Female—full-time 87, part-time 3; Male—full-time 29, part-time 0; African American/Black—full-time 21, part-time 1; Hispanic/Latino(a)—full-time 6, part-time 0; Asian/Pacific Islander—full-time 3, part-time 1; American Indian/Alaska Native—full-time 0, part-time 0; Caucasian/White—full-time 80, part-time 1; Multi-ethnic—full-time 5, part-time 0; students subject to the Americans With Disabilities Act—full-time 5, part-time 1; Unknown ethnicity—full-time 1, part-time 0; International students who hold an F-1 or J-1 Visa—full-time 3, part-time 0.

Financial Information/Assistance:

Tuition for Full-Time Study: *Doctoral:* State residents: $695 per credit hour; Nonstate residents: $695 per credit hour. Tuition is subject to change.

Financial Assistance:

First-Year Students: Fellowships and scholarships available for first year. Average amount paid per academic year: $3,000. Apply by August 1. Tuition remission given: partial.

Advanced Students: Teaching assistantships available for advanced students. Average amount paid per academic year:

$7,500. Average number of hours worked per week: 12. Apply by April 1. Research assistantships available for advanced students. Average amount paid per academic year: $7,500. Average number of hours worked per week: 12. Apply by April 1. Fellowships and scholarships available for advanced students. Average amount paid per academic year: $3,250. Apply by April 1. Tuition remission given: partial.

Additional Information: Of all students currently enrolled full time, 98% benefited from one or more of the listed financial assistance programs.

Internships/Practica: Doctoral Degree (PsyD Clinical Psychology): For those doctoral students for whom a professional internship was required in this program prior to graduation, (21) students applied for an internship in 2006–2007, with (18) students obtaining an internship. Of those students who obtained an internship, (18) were paid internships. Of those students who obtained an internship, (10) students placed in APA/CPA-accredited internships, (8) students placed in internships not APA/CPA accredited, but listed with the Association of Psychology Postdoctoral and Internship Centers (APPIC), (0) students placed in internships conforming to guidelines of the Council of Directors of School Psychology Programs (CDSPP), (0) students placed in internships that were not APA/CPA-accredited, APPIC or CDSPP listed. All PsyD students complete a three-semester placement in the campus training clinica, the Psychological Services Center, during their 2nd year. A three-semester practica placement is completed during the 3rd year at any of a wide variety of community practica sites such as military and VA clinics, inpatient brain injury units, psychiatric hospitals, group practices, community mental health agencies, Christian outpatient practices, or correctional settings.

Housing and Day Care: On-campus housing is available. See the following Web site for more information: http://www.regent.edu/campuses/vb/village/. No on-campus day care facilities are available.

Employment of Department Graduates:

Master's Degree Graduates: Of those who graduated in the academic year 2006–2007, the following categories and numbers represent the postgraduate activities and employment of master's degree graduates: Enrolled in a postdoctoral residency/fellowship (n/a), employed in independent practice (n/a), total from the above (master's) (0).

Doctoral Degree Graduates: Of those who graduated in the academic year 2006–2007, the following categories and numbers represent the postgraduate activities and employment of doctoral degree graduates: Enrolled in a psychology doctoral program (n/a), enrolled in a postdoctoral residency/fellowship (3), employed in independent practice (2), employed in government agency (5), employed in a community mental health/counseling center (3), employed in a hospital/medical center (2), total from the above (doctoral) (15).

Additional Information:

Orientation, Objectives, and Emphasis of Department: The Doctoral Program in Clinical Psychology adopts a practitioner–scholar model of clinical training within an educational context committed to the integration of scientific psychology and a Christian worldview. The clinical training is broad and general, however marital and family therapy, consulting psychology, clinical child psychology, and health psychology are emphases among the faculty and in the curriculum.

Personal Behavior Statement: The Community Life form is contained in the application.

Special Facilities or Resources: Regent is located in Virginia Beach, Virginia, which is part of Tidewater, the largest urban area in Virginia. There are numerous community resources for practica. The campus also houses the Psychological Services Center, our doctoral training clinic that provides services to the campus and surrounding community. The PSC includes state-of-the-art technology for videotaping and observation of clinical activities.

Application Information:

Send to Central Enrollment, SC218, 1000 Regent University Drive, Virginia Beach, Virginia 23464; e-mail: psycoun@regent.edu. Application available online. URL of online application: http://www.regent.edu/psychology/apply. Students are admitted in the Fall, application deadline January 15. *Fee:* $50.

Richmond, University of (2007 data)

Department of Psychology
Arts and Sciences
Richmond Hall
Richmond, VA 23173
Telephone: (804) 289-8123
Fax: (804) 287-1905
E-mail: *pli@richmond.edu*
Web: *http://www.psychology.richmond.edu/*

Department Information:

1913. Chairperson: Scott Allison, Professor of Psychology. Number of faculty: total—full-time 10, part-time 3; women—full-time 5, part-time 2.

Programs and Degrees Offered:

Listed in the following order: Program area, degree type (T if terminal Master's), number awarded 7/06–6/07. General MA/MS (Master of Arts/Science) (T) 4.

Student Applications/Admissions:

Student Applications

General MA/MS (Master of Arts/Science)—Applications 2007–2008, 77. Total applicants accepted 2007–2008, 4. Openings 2008–2009, 4. The median number of years required for completion of a degree in 2006–2007 were 2. The number of students enrolled full- and part-time who were dismissed or voluntarily withdrew from this program area in 2007–2008 were 0.

Admissions Requirements:

Scores: Entries appear in this order: required test or GPA, minimum score (if required), median score of students entering in 2007–2008. Master's Programs: GRE-V 600, 610; GRE-Q 600, 620; overall undergraduate GPA 3.3, 3.3; last 2 years GPA 3.0; psychology GPA 3.5, 3.5.

Other Criteria: (importance of criteria rated low, medium, or high): GRE/MAT scores—high, research experience—high, work experience—medium, extracurricular activity—medium, clinically related public service—medium, GPA—high, letters of recommendation—high, interview—medium, statement of goals and objectives—high.

Student Characteristics: The following represents characteristics of students in 2007–2008 in all graduate psychology programs in the department: Female—full-time 5, part-time 0; Male—full-time 4, part-time 0; African American/Black—full-time 1, part-time 0; Hispanic/Latino(a)—full-time 0, part-time 0; Asian/Pacific Islander—full-time 1, part-time 0; American Indian/Alaska Native—full-time 0, part-time 0; Caucasian/White—full-time 7, part-time 0; Unknown ethnicity—full-time 0, part-time 0.

Financial Information/Assistance:

Tuition for Full-Time Study: *Master's:* State residents: per academic year $34,850; Nonstate residents: per academic year $34,850. See the following Web site for updates and changes in tuition costs: http://www.asgraduate.richmond.edu/.

Financial Assistance:

First-Year Students: Teaching assistantships available for first year. Average amount paid per academic year: $34,850. Tuition remission given: full. Fellowships and scholarships available for first year. Average amount paid per academic year: $2,000. Tuition remission given: partial.

Advanced Students: Teaching assistantships available for advanced students. Average amount paid per academic year: $34,850. Tuition remission given: full. Fellowships and scholarships available for advanced students. Average amount paid per academic year: $2,000. Tuition remission given: partial.

Additional Information: Of all students currently enrolled full time, 100% benefited from one or more of the listed financial assistance programs.

Internships/Practica: Our department has many solid relationships with placement sites around Richmond. For example, we regularly place students in the Medical College of Virginia; Psychological Consultants; Virginia Treatment Center; and social services center.

Housing and Day Care: No on-campus housing is available. No on-campus day care facilities are available.

Employment of Department Graduates:

Master's Degree Graduates: Of those who graduated in the academic year 2006–2007, the following categories and numbers represent the postgraduate activities and employment of master's degree graduates: Enrolled in a psychology doctoral program (3), enrolled in another graduate/professional program (1), enrolled in a postdoctoral residency/fellowship (n/a), employed in independent practice (n/a), employed in government agency (1), total from the above (master's) (5).

Doctoral Degree Graduates: Of those who graduated in the academic year 2006–2007, the following categories and numbers represent the postgraduate activities and employment of doctoral degree graduates: Enrolled in a psychology doctoral program (n/a), total from the above (doctoral) (0).

Additional Information:

Orientation, Objectives, and Emphasis of Department: The graduate program in psychology at the University of Richmond offers an MA in General Psychology. The program is built around a core curriculum with a strong emphasis on research. Scholarship and research competence are expected of persons trained at the master's level. Provision is made for each student to carry out an appropriate program of individual research in a particular area of interest. Although the present program does not prepare students as specialists in any particular field, it trains the students with a depth and breadth of research experience in specific areas of psychology. The program also provides a strong foundation for advanced training at the PhD level. For more information about the program, please visit http://cogsci.richmond.edu/grad/.

Special Facilities or Resources: The Department of Psychology occupies three floors of Richmond Hall on the beautiful University of Richmond campus. The hall was renovated in 1979, and again in 1990. Currently it houses state-of-the-art laboratory facilities for neuroscience research, including image analysis and computerized microscopy; excellent laboratory facilities for performing cognitive and child development research; exceptional laboratory space and equipment for performing cognitive and aging-related research in psychology; and outstanding computer resources in general, in the form of laboratories and work-stations available to students. Moreover, there is ample money available for graduate student research and research-related travel to scientific conferences, and a supportive environment for hardworking students in the area of psychology.

Information for Students With Physical Disabilities: See the following Web site for more information: http://www.richmond.edu.

Application Information:

Send to Graduate School, Boatwright Administrative Wing, University of Richmond, VA 23173. Application available online. URL of online application: http://www.asgraduate.richmond.edu/. Students are admitted in the Fall, application deadline February 10. *Fee:* $30. Financial need must be documented to receive a waiver for the application fee.

Virginia Commonwealth University

Department of Psychology
Humanities and Sciences
806 West Franklin Street, Box 842018
Richmond, VA 23284-2018
Telephone: (804) 828-1193
Fax: (804) 828-2237
E-mail: *srvrana@vcu.edu*
Web: *http://www.has.vcu.edu/psy/*

Department Information:

1969. Chairperson: Scott Vrana. Number of faculty: total—full-time 33; women—full-time 15; total—minority—full-time 4; women minority—full-time 2; faculty subject to the Americans With Disabilities Act 1.

Programs and Degrees Offered:

Listed in the following order: Program area, degree type (T if terminal Master's), number awarded 7/06–6/07. Clinical Psychology PhD (Doctor of Philosophy) 1, Counseling Psychology PhD (Doctor of Philosophy) 3, Experimental Psychology: Social PhD (Doctor of Philosophy) 1, Experimental Psychology: Biopsychology PhD (Doctor of Philosophy) 0, Experimental Psychology: Developmental PhD (Doctor of Philosophy) 1.

APA Accreditation: Clinical PhD (Doctor of Philosophy). Counseling PhD (Doctor of Philosophy).

Student Applications/Admissions:

Student Applications

Clinical Psychology PhD (Doctor of Philosophy)—Applications 2007–2008, 201. Total applicants accepted 2007–2008, 16. Number full-time enrolled (new admits only) 2007–2008, 12. Total enrolled 2007–2008 full-time, 45, part-time, 4. Openings 2008–2009, 9. The median number of years required for completion of a degree in 2006–2007 were 6. The number of students enrolled full- and part-time who were dismissed or voluntarily withdrew from this program area in 2007–2008 were 1. *Counseling Psychology PhD (Doctor of Philosophy)*—Applications 2007–2008, 180. Total applicants accepted 2007–2008, 13. Number full-time enrolled (new admits only) 2007–2008, 7. Total enrolled 2007–2008 full-time, 42, part-time, 3. Openings 2008–2009, 7. The median number of years required for completion of a degree in 2006–2007 were 6. The number of students enrolled full- and part-time who were dismissed or voluntarily withdrew from this program area in 2007–2008 were 1. *Experimental Psychology: Social PhD (Doctor of Philosophy)*—Applications 2007–2008, 24. Total applicants accepted 2007–2008, 4. Number full-time enrolled (new admits only) 2007–2008, 4. Number part-time enrolled (new admits only) 2007–2008, 0. Total enrolled 2007–2008 full-time, 11, part-time, 2. Openings 2008–2009, 3. The median number of years required for completion of a degree in 2006–2007 were 5. The number of students enrolled full- and part-time who were dismissed or voluntarily withdrew from this program area in 2007–2008 were 0. *Experimental Psychology: Biopsychology PhD (Doctor of Philosophy)*—Applications 2007–2008, 22. Total applicants accepted 2007–2008, 3. Number full-time enrolled (new admits only) 2007–2008, 3. Number part-time enrolled (new admits only) 2007–2008, 0. Total enrolled 2007–2008 full-time, 9, part-time, 2. Openings 2008–2009, 2. The median number of years required for completion of a degree in 2006–2007 were 4. The number of students enrolled full- and part-time who were dismissed or voluntarily withdrew from this program area in 2007–2008 were 0. *Experimental Psychology: Developmental PhD (Doctor of Philosophy)*—Applications 2007–2008, 15. Total applicants accepted 2007–2008, 4. Number full-time enrolled (new admits only) 2007–2008, 1. Number part-time enrolled (new admits only) 2007–2008, 0. Total enrolled 2007–2008 full-time, 6, part-time, 3. Openings 2008–2009, 3. The median number of years required for completion of a degree in 2006–2007 were 4. The number of students enrolled full- and part-time who were dismissed or voluntarily withdrew from this program area in 2007–2008 were 1.

Admissions Requirements:

Scores: Entries appear in this order: required test or GPA, minimum score (if required), median score of students entering in 2007–2008. Master's Programs: GRE-V 500, 571; GRE-Q 500, 601; overall undergraduate GPA 3.0, 3.23. Students are accepted for PhD degree only. Programs vary in their emphasis on scores and their requirements. For funding, all require a minumum of 1000 on GRE V+Q. Doctoral Programs: GRE-V 500, 571; GRE-Q 500, 601; overall undergraduate GPA 3.0, 3.5.

Other Criteria: (importance of criteria rated low, medium, or high): GRE/MAT scores—high, research experience—high, work experience—high, extracurricular activity—medium, clinically related public service—medium, GPA—high, letters of recommendation—high, interview—medium, statement of goals and objectives—medium. The Experimental programs stress research experience, GPA, letters of recommendation, and GREs more than the Clinical and Counseling programs. The Clinical and Counseling programs stress match between student interests and faculty interests. This match is important, but not as highly stressed by the Experimental programs. Clinical and Counseling programs stress importance of clinically related public service, interviews, and statement of goals and objectives. For additional information on admission requirements, go to http://www.has.vcu.edu/psy/index.html.

Student Characteristics: The following represents characteristics of students in 2007–2008 in all graduate psychology programs in the department: Female—full-time 88, part-time 19; Male—full-time 16, part-time 9; African American/Black—full-time 9, part-time 4; Hispanic/Latino(a)—full-time 5, part-time 0; Asian/Pacific Islander—full-time 5, part-time 0; American Indian/Alaska Native—full-time 1, part-time 0; Caucasian/White—full-time 79, part-time 24; Multi-ethnic—full-time 0, part-time 0; students subject to the Americans With Disabilities Act—full-time 4, part-time 0; Unknown ethnicity—full-time 5, part-time 0; International students who hold an F-1 or J-1 Visa—full-time 1, part-time 0.

Financial Information/Assistance:

Tuition for Full-Time Study: *Master's:* State residents: per academic year $7,224; Nonstate residents: per academic year $15,904. *Doctoral:* State residents: per academic year $7,224; Nonstate residents: per academic year $15,904. Tuition is subject to change. See the following Web site for updates and changes in tuition costs: Costs for the entire 2006-07 year, see http://www.pubinfo.vcu.edu/sa/taf.asp for more information.

Financial Assistance:

First-Year Students: Teaching assistantships available for first year. Average amount paid per academic year: $13,520. Average number of hours worked per week: 20. Tuition remission given: full. Research assistantships available for first year. Average amount paid per academic year: $13,520. Average number of hours worked per week: 20. Tuition remission given: full and partial. Fellowships and scholarships available for first year. Tuition remission given: full.

Advanced Students: Teaching assistantships available for advanced students. Average amount paid per academic year:

$13,520. Average number of hours worked per week: 20. Tuition remission given: full and partial. Research assistantships available for advanced students. Average amount paid per academic year: $13,520. Average number of hours worked per week: 20. Tuition remission given: full and partial. Fellowships and scholarships available for advanced students. Tuition remission given: full.

Additional Information: Of all students currently enrolled full time, 90% benefited from one or more of the listed financial assistance programs.

Internships/Practica: Doctoral Degree (PhD Clinical Psychology): For those doctoral students for whom a professional internship was required in this program prior to graduation, (6) students applied for an internship in 2006–2007, with (6) students obtaining an internship. Of those students who obtained an internship, (6) were paid internships. Of those students who obtained an internship, (6) students placed in APA/CPA-accredited internships, (0) students placed in internships not APA/CPA accredited, but listed with the Association of Psychology Postdoctoral and Internship Centers (APPIC), (0) students placed in internships conforming to guidelines of the Council of Directors of School Psychology Programs (CDSPP), (0) students placed in internships that were not APA/CPA-accredited, APPIC or CDSPP listed. Doctoral Degree (PhD Counseling Psychology): For those doctoral students for whom a professional internship was required in this program prior to graduation, (9) students applied for an internship in 2006–2007, with (9) students obtaining an internship. Of those students who obtained an internship, (8) were paid internships. Of those students who obtained an internship, (8) students placed in APA/CPA-accredited internships, (1) student placed in internships not APA/CPA accredited, but listed with the Association of Psychology Postdoctoral and Internship Centers (APPIC), (0) students placed in internships conforming to guidelines of the Council of Directors of School Psychology Programs (CDSPP), (0) students placed in internships that were not APA/CPA-accredited, APPIC or CDSPP listed. Practicum (external) and internship required for Clinical and Counseling programs. Sites range from the following: VA hospitals, federal prisons, counseling centers, medical campus opportunities, children's hospitals, and juvenile facilities.

Housing and Day Care: On-campus housing is available. See the following Web site for more information: http://www.students.vcu.edu/housing. On-campus day care facilities are available. See the following Web site for more information: http://www.vcu.edu/maps/mcvmap/childcar/childcar.htm or www.vcu.edu/maps/acmap/vcuccc/vcuccc.htm.

Employment of Department Graduates:

Master's Degree Graduates: Of those who graduated in the academic year 2006–2007, the following categories and numbers represent the postgraduate activities and employment of master's degree graduates: Enrolled in a postdoctoral residency/fellowship (n/a), employed in independent practice (n/a), total from the above (master's) (0).

Doctoral Degree Graduates: Of those who graduated in the academic year 2006–2007, the following categories and numbers represent the postgraduate activities and employment of doctoral degree graduates: Enrolled in a psychology doctoral program (n/a), enrolled in another graduate/professional program (0), do not know (9), total from the above (doctoral) (9).

Additional Information:

Orientation, Objectives, and Emphasis of Department: The graduate programs in psychology are designed to provide a core education in the basic science of psychology and to enable students to develop skills specific to their area of interest. Students are educated first as psychologists, and are then helped to develop competence in a more specialized area relevant to their scholarly and professional objectives. In addition to formal research requirements for the thesis and dissertation, students in the graduate programs are encouraged to conduct independent research, participate in research teams, or collaborate with faculty conducting research on an ongoing basis. The Clinical and Counseling psychology programs strongly emphasize the scientist–practitioner model. Students in the Clinical program may elect to develop specialized competency in one of several different tracks, including behavior therapy–cognitive behavior therapy, behavioral medicine, clinical child, and adult psychotherapy process. The Counseling Psychology program prepares students to function in a variety of research and applied settings and to work with people experiencing a broad range of emotional, social, or behavioral problems. The Experimental program stresses the acquisition of experimental skills as well as advanced training in one of three specialty areas: biopsychology, developmental psychology, and social psychology. We currently are developing an experimentally oriented doctoral program in health psychology.

Personal Behavior Statement: The university requires all students sign a standard honor code.

Special Facilities or Resources: The department maintains laboratories for research in the areas of biopsychology, developmental, social, psychophysiology, behavioral assessment, and psychotherapy process. The department also operates the Center for Psychological Services and Development, which provides mental health services for clients referred from throughout the Richmond metropolitan area. Students in the Clinical and Counseling programs complete practica in the Center and in a variety of off-campus practicum facilities located in the community. Cooperation with a variety of programs and departments on the University's medical campus, the Medical College of Virginia, is extensive for both research and training.

Information for Students With Physical Disabilities: See the following Web site for more information: http://www.students.vcu.edu/dss/.

Application Information:

Send to School of Graduate Studies, VCU, Box 843051, Richmond, VA 23284; the forms needed for application are to be downloaded from http://www.vcu.edu/graduate/ps/admission.html. Application available online. URL of online application: http://www.vcu.edu/graduate/ps/admission.html. Students are admitted in the Fall, application deadlines December 1 for Counseling Psychology, December 10 for Clinical Psychology, January 10 for Developmental Psychology, Social Psychology, and Biopsychology. Students applying to the Experimental program should clearly indicate the division to which they are seeking admission. *Fee:* $50.

Virginia Consortium Program in Clinical Psychology

Program in Clinical Psychology
W&M, EVMS, NSU, & ODU
Virginia Beach Higher Education Center
1881 University Drive, Suite 239
Virginia Beach, VA 23453
Telephone: (757) 368-1820
Fax: (757) 368-1823
E-mail: *exoneill@odu.edu*
Web: *http://www.sci.odu.edu/vcpcp/*

Department Information:

1978. Chairperson: Robin Lewis. Number of faculty: total—full-time 34; women—full-time 16; total—minority—full-time 9; women minority—full-time 7.

Programs and Degrees Offered:

Listed in the following order: Program area, degree type (T if terminal Master's), number awarded 7/06–6/07. Clinical Psychology PsyD (Doctor of Psychology) 8.

APA Accreditation: Clinical PsyD (Doctor of Psychology).

Student Applications/Admissions:

Student Applications

Clinical Psychology PsyD (Doctor of Psychology)—Applications 2007–2008, 207. Total applicants accepted 2007–2008, 17. Number full-time enrolled (new admits only) 2007–2008, 10. Number part-time enrolled (new admits only) 2007–2008, 0. Openings 2008–2009, 10. The median number of years required for completion of a degree in 2006–2007 were 5. The number of students enrolled full- and part-time who were dismissed or voluntarily withdrew from this program area in 2007–2008 were 1.

Admissions Requirements:

Scores: Entries appear in this order: required test or GPA, minimum score (if required), median score of students entering in 2007–2008. Doctoral Programs: GRE-V no minimum stated, 575; GRE-Q no minimum stated, 630; overall undergraduate GPA 2.5, 3.76; Doctoral program GRE-Analytic no minimum stated, 5.0.

Other Criteria: (importance of criteria rated low, medium, or high): GRE/MAT scores—medium, research experience—medium, work experience—medium, extracurricular activity—low, clinically related public service—medium, GPA—medium, letters of recommendation—medium, interview—high, statement of goals and objectives—high, undergraduate major in psychology—medium, specific undergraduate psychology courses taken—medium. For additional information on admission requirements, go to http://www.sci.odu.edu/vcpcp/ at Application Info, Admission Requirements.

Student Characteristics: The following represents characteristics of students in 2007–2008 in all graduate psychology programs in the department: Female—full-time 37, part-time 0; Male—full-time 10, part-time 0; African American/Black—full-time 7, part-time 0; Hispanic/Latino(a)—full-time 2, part-time 0; Asian/Pacific Islander—full-time 5, part-time 0; American Indian/Alaska Native—full-time 0, part-time 0; Caucasian/White—full-time 33, part-time 0; Multi-ethnic—full-time 0, part-time 0; students subject to the Americans With Disabilities Act—full-time 0, part-time 0; Unknown ethnicity—full-time 0, part-time 0; International students who hold an F-1 or J-1 Visa—full-time 0, part-time 0.

Financial Information/Assistance:

Tuition for Full-Time Study: *Doctoral:* State residents: per academic year $2,475; Nonstate residents: per academic year $2,475. Tuition is subject to change. Additional fees are assessed to students beyond the costs of tuition for the following: dissertation binding and microfilming; graduation fee. See the following Web site for updates and changes in tuition costs: All applicants: see http://www.sci.odu.edu/vcpcp, at Application Info to learn about tuition reductions.

Financial Assistance:

First-Year Students: Teaching assistantships available for first year. Average amount paid per academic year: $8,000. Average number of hours worked per week: 10. Apply by January 2. Tuition remission given: partial. Research assistantships available for first year. Average amount paid per academic year: $7,000. Average number of hours worked per week: 8. Apply by January 2. Tuition remission given: partial.

Advanced Students: Teaching assistantships available for advanced students. Average amount paid per academic year: $8,250. Average number of hours worked per week: 10. Apply by March 15. Tuition remission given: partial. Research assistantships available for advanced students. Average amount paid per academic year: $7,500. Average number of hours worked per week: 8. Apply by March 15. Tuition remission given: partial. Traineeships available for advanced students. Average amount paid per academic year: $8,000. Average number of hours worked per week: 20. Apply by March 15. Tuition remission given: partial.

Additional Information: Of all students currently enrolled full time, 100% benefited from one or more of the listed financial assistance programs. Application and information available online at http://www.sci.odu.edu/vcpcp/ at Application Info.

Internships/Practica: Doctoral Degree (PsyD Clinical Psychology): For those doctoral students for whom a professional internship was required in this program prior to graduation, (9) students applied for an internship in 2006–2007, with (7) students obtaining an internship. Of those students who obtained an internship, (6) were paid internships. Of those students who obtained an internship, (7) students placed in APA/CPA-accredited internships, (0) students placed in internships not APA/CPA accredited, but listed with the Association of Psychology Postdoctoral and Internship Centers (APPIC), (0) students placed in internships conforming to guidelines of the Council of Directors of School Psychology Programs (CDSPP), (0) students placed in internships that were not APA/CPA-accredited, APPIC or CDSPP listed. Practicum training is offered in a variety of diverse settings such as mental health centers, medical hospitals, children's residential treatment facilities, public school systems, university counseling centers, social services clinics, private practices, and neuropsychology rehabilitation units. Settings include inpatient, partial hospitalization, residential, and outpatient. Populations include infants, children, adolescents, adults, and elderly from most socioeconomic levels and ethnic groups. Services include most forms of assessment; individual, group, and family intervention modalities; and consultative and other indirect services. Placements are arranged to assure that each student is exposed to several settings and populations. For additional information on education and training outcomes for our programs, see the following Web site: http://www.sci.odu.edu/vcpcp, at Our Program, at Outcome Data.

Housing and Day Care: On-campus housing is available. Graduate housing is available at some of the sponsoring schools. However, the program operates on a calendar year and the schools on an academic year, so students must vacate graduate housing at the end of the Spring semester while still in classes. This leaves them looking for housing during the summer semester. No on-campus day care facilities are available.

Employment of Department Graduates:

Master's Degree Graduates: Of those who graduated in the academic year 2006–2007, the following categories and numbers represent the postgraduate activities and employment of master's degree graduates: Enrolled in a postdoctoral residency/fellowship (n/a), employed in independent practice (n/a), total from the above (master's) (0).

Doctoral Degree Graduates: Of those who graduated in the academic year 2006–2007, the following categories and numbers represent the postgraduate activities and employment of doctoral degree graduates: Enrolled in a psychology doctoral program (n/a), enrolled in a postdoctoral residency/fellowship (1), employed in other positions at a higher education institution (0), employed in a professional position in a school system (0), employed in government agency (2), employed in a community mental health/counseling center (3), employed in a hospital/medical center (1), not seeking employment (1), total from the above (doctoral) (8).

Additional Information:

Orientation, Objectives, and Emphasis of Department: The Virginia Consortium is a single, unified program cosponsored by four institutions: The College of William and Mary, Eastern Virginia Medical School, Norfolk State University, and Old Dominion University. Its mission is to produce practicing clinical psychologists who are competent in individual and cultural diversity, educated in the basic subjects and methods of psychological science, capable of critically assimilating and generating new knowledge, proficient in the delivery and evaluation of clinical services, and able to assume leadership positions in health service delivery organizations. The curriculum is generalist in content and in theoretical orientation. It includes education in the major theoretical and technical models: psychodynamic, behavioral, phenomenological, and family systems. Training is provided in intervention at the individual, group, family, and community and organizational levels. Knowledge acquired in the classroom is applied in an orderly sequence of supervised practica providing exposure to multiple settings, populations, and intervention modalities. Practicum objectives are integrated with the goals of classroom education to facilitate systematic and cumulative acquisition of clinical skills. In the 3rd year, the student pursues individual interests by integrating individualized coursework with advanced practica and a clinical dissertation. In the 4th year, the student receives intensive training in a full-time clinical internship.

Special Facilities or Resources: Students are considered full-time in all four sponsoring schools. This permits access to four libraries with several computerized literature search databases and 400 periodicals in psychology; four computing centers; multiple health services; and a variety of athletic facilities. Research includes a social psychology laboratory with observational capabilities and facilities: 54 laboratory rooms; and 10 research rooms with various specialized capabilities. Research may also be conducted at practicum placement facilities.

Information for Students With Physical Disabilities: See the following Web site for more information: http://www.sci.odu.edu/vcpcp/ at Our Schools.

Application Information:

Send to Program Office, Virginia Consortium Program in Clinical Psychology, Virginia Beach Higher Education Center, 1881 University Drive, Suite 239, Virginia Beach, VA 23453. Application available online. URL of online application: http://www.sci.odu.edu/vcpcp, at Application Info, at Application Process. Students are admitted in the Fall, application deadline January 2. January 2 is an application and credential deadline including transcripts and GRE scores. Applicants should plan to take an October or November GRE exam, and submit an early request for transcripts. *Fee:* $40. No fee waiver available.

Virginia Polytechnic Institute and State University

Department of Psychology
College of Science
109 Williams Hall
Blacksburg, VA 24061
Telephone: (540) 231-6581
Fax: (540) 231-3652
E-mail: *kirbydd@vt.edu*
Web: *http://www.psyc.vt.edu/*

Department Information:

1965. Chairperson: Robert S. Stephens. Number of faculty: total—full-time 8; women—full-time 6; women minority—full-time 1.

Programs and Degrees Offered:

Listed in the following order: Program area, degree type (T if terminal Master's), number awarded 7/06–6/07. Clinical PhD (Doctor of Philosophy) 7, Industrial/ Organizational PhD (Doctor of Philosophy) 1, Developmental and Biological Psychology PhD (Doctor of Philosophy) 2.

APA Accreditation: Clinical PhD (Doctor of Philosophy).

Student Applications/Admissions:

Student Applications

Clinical PhD (Doctor of Philosophy)—Applications 2007–2008, 150. Total applicants accepted 2007–2008, 14. Number full-time enrolled (new admits only) 2007–2008, 9. Number part-time enrolled (new admits only) 2007–2008, 0. Total enrolled 2007–2008 full-time, 38, part-time, 1. Openings 2008–2009, 10. The median number of years required for completion of a degree in 2006–2007 were 5. The number of students enrolled full- and part-time who were dismissed or voluntarily withdrew from this program area in 2007–2008 were 0. *Industrial/Organizational PhD (Doctor of Philosophy)*—Applications 2007–2008, 45. Total applicants accepted 2007–2008, 1. Number full-time enrolled (new admits only) 2007–2008, 1. Number part-time enrolled (new admits only) 2007–2008, 0. Total enrolled 2007–2008 full-time, 17, part-time, 1. Openings 2008–2009, 2. The median number of years required for completion of a degree in 2006–2007 were 4. The number of students enrolled full- and part-time who were dismissed or voluntarily withdrew from this program area in 2007–2008 were 0. *Developmental and Biological Psychology PhD (Doctor of Philosophy)*—Applications 2007–2008, 26. Total applicants accepted 2007–2008, 9. Number full-time enrolled (new admits only) 2007–2008, 5. Number part-time enrolled (new admits only) 2007–2008, 0. Total enrolled 2007–2008 full-time, 13, part-time, 1. Openings 2008–2009, 6. The median number of years required for completion of a degree in 2006–2007 were 4. The number of students enrolled full- and part-time who were dismissed or voluntarily withdrew from this program area in 2007–2008 were 0.

Admissions Requirements:

Scores: Entries appear in this order: required test or GPA, minimum score (if required), median score of students entering in 2007–2008. Doctoral Programs: GRE-V no minimum stated, 570; GRE-Q no minimum stated, 651; overall undergraduate GPA 3.0, 3.7.

Other Criteria: (importance of criteria rated low, medium, or high): GRE/MAT scores—high, research experience—high, work experience—low, clinically related public service—medium, GPA—high, letters of recommendation—high, interview—medium, statement of goals and objectives—medium, undergraduate major in psychology—low, specific undergraduate psychology courses taken—low, congruence of applicant's goals with program objectives and faculty research—high. For additional information on admission requirements, go to http://www.psyc.vt.edu/graduate/.

Student Characteristics: The following represents characteristics of students in 2007–2008 in all graduate psychology programs in the department: Female—full-time 41, part-time 3; Male—full-time 27, part-time 0; African American/Black—full-time 7, part-time 0; Hispanic/Latino(a)—full-time 6, part-time 0; Asian/Pacific Islander—full-time 4, part-time 0; American Indian/Alaska Native—full-time 0, part-time 0; Caucasian/White—full-time 43, part-time 2; Multi-ethnic—full-time 3, part-time 0; students subject to the Americans With Disabilities Act—full-time 0, part-time 0; Unknown ethnicity—full-time 5, part-time 1.

Financial Information/Assistance:

Tuition for Full-Time Study: *Doctoral:* State residents: per academic year $8,986; Nonstate residents: per academic year $15,350. Tuition is subject to change. See the following Web site for updates and changes in tuition costs: http://www.bursar.vt.edu/.

Financial Assistance:

First-Year Students: Teaching assistantships available for first year. Average amount paid per academic year: $13,716. Average number of hours worked per week: 20. Tuition remission given: full. Research assistantships available for first year. Average amount paid per academic year: $14,544. Average number of hours worked per week: 20. Tuition remission given: full.

Advanced Students: Teaching assistantships available for advanced students. Average amount paid per academic year: $14,544. Average number of hours worked per week: 20. Tuition remission given: full. Research assistantships available for advanced students. Average amount paid per academic year: $15,795. Average number of hours worked per week: 20. Tuition remission given: full.

Additional Information: Of all students currently enrolled full time, 95% benefited from one or more of the listed financial assistance programs. Application and information available online at http://www.psyc.vt.edu/graduate.

Internships/Practica: Doctoral Degree (PhD Clinical): For those doctoral students for whom a professional internship was required in this program prior to graduation, (6) students applied for an internship in 2006–2007, with (6) students obtaining an internship. Of those students who obtained an internship, (6) were paid internships. Of those students who obtained an internship, (6) students placed in APA/CPA-accredited internships, (0) students placed in internships not APA/CPA-accredited, but listed with the Association of Psychology Postdoctoral and Internship Centers (APPIC), (0) students placed in internships conforming to guidelines of the Council of Directors of School Psychology Programs (CDSPP), (0) students placed in internships that were not APA/CPA-accredited, APPIC or CDSPP listed. Students in Clinical Psychology complete practica in department-run, off-campus clinics serving adults and children from the community. They also complete an externship in one of a variety of local agency and hospital settings. They also are required to complete a predoctoral clinical internship as part of the PhD. Students in Industrial/Organizational psychology are encouraged to pursue Summer internships.

Housing and Day Care: On-campus housing is available. See the following Web site for more information: http://www.grads.vt.edu/student_life/student_handbook/housing.html. No on-campus day care facilities are available.

Employment of Department Graduates:

Master's Degree Graduates: Of those who graduated in the academic year 2006–2007, the following categories and numbers represent the postgraduate activities and employment of master's degree graduates: Enrolled in a postdoctoral residency/fellowship (n/a), employed in independent practice (n/a), total from the above (master's) (0).

Doctoral Degree Graduates: Of those who graduated in the academic year 2006–2007, the following categories and numbers represent the postgraduate activities and employment of doctoral degree graduates: Enrolled in a psychology doctoral program (n/a), enrolled in a postdoctoral residency/fellowship (6), employed in an academic position at a university (2), employed in other positions at a higher education institution (2), total from the above (doctoral) (10).

Additional Information:

Orientation, Objectives, and Emphasis of Department: The graduate programs are designed to ensure that students receive excellent preparation in research methods and psychological theory in order to be successful in either academic or applied settings. Training and experience in the teaching of psychology is available. The Clinical Psychology program is based on the clinical–scientist model and emphasizes research methods and theory in understanding, preventing, and treating health and mental health problems in adults and children. Clinical concentrations include child, adult, and health psychology. The Industrial/Organizational Psychology program prepares students for research and teaching positions as well as for the solution of individual, group, and organizational problems in applied work settings. Psychometrics, research design, and statistics are emphasized. The Developmental and Biological Psychology program trains students in experimental psychology with a focus on preparing psychologists for teaching and research settings. Students may concentrate their studies in developmental or psychobiological research areas or both.

Special Facilities or Resources: The Psychological Services Center and Child Study Center are located off-campus and provide the foundation for practicum and research training in Clinical Psychology. The Center for Research in Health Behavior is also located off-campus and is primarily involved in prevention research supported by the National Institutes of Health. Virginia Tech Community Partners is another off-campus research facility, located in downtown Roanoke. Faculty, students, and staff benefit from Virginia Tech's state-of-the-art communications system that links every dormitory room, laboratory, office, and classroom to computing capabilities, audio and video data, and the World Wide Web. The entire campus has easy access to supercomputers across the country, worldwide libraries, and data systems. Department resources also include two state-of-the-art laboratories that are dedicated to undergraduate and graduate teaching and research. The psychophysiological laboratory includes eight computer workstations, five EEG/Evoked Potential work stations (32-channel Neuroscan; Neurosearch-24), eye-tracker equipment, Coulbourn physiological units, and extensive perception equipment. The other computer laboratory includes 25 computer workstations with cognitive and neurophysiological experiments, SAS and SPSS statistical packages, Bilog and Multilog programs. Graduate students also have ready access to PC and Macintosh computers for word processing and Internet access.

Information for Students With Physical Disabilities: See the following Web site for more information: http://www.ssd.vt.edu/.

Application Information:

Send to Graduate School Admissions, Graduate Life Center (Mail code 0325), Virginia Polytechnic Institute and State University, Blacksburg, VA 24061 and Graduate Admissions Coordinator, 109 Williams Hall, Department of Psychology, 0436 Virginia Tech, Blacksburg, VA 24061. Application available online. URL of online application: https://www.applyweb.com/apply/vtechg/index.html. Students are admitted in the Fall, application deadline December 15. Application deadline for Clinical is December 15. Application deadline for Developmental and Biological Psychology is January 5. Application deadline for Industrial/Organizational Psychology is January 15. *Fee:* $45.

Virginia State University

Department of Psychology
School of Engineering, Science, and Technology
1 Hayden Drive, Box 9079 Hunter-McDaniel 102S
Petersburg, VA 23806
Telephone: (804) 524-5938
Fax: (804) 524-5460
E-mail: *ohill@vsu.edu*
Web: *http://www.vsu.edu/pages/783.asp*

Department Information:

1883. Chairperson: Oliver W. Hill, Jr., PhD. Number of faculty: total—full-time 14, part-time 5; women—full-time 9, part-time 2; total—minority—full-time 13, part-time 2; women minority—full-time 9, part-time 1.

Programs and Degrees Offered:

Listed in the following order: Program area, degree type (T if terminal Master's), number awarded 7/06–6/07. Psychology MA/MS (Master of Arts/Science) (T) 25.

Student Applications/Admissions:

Student Applications

Psychology MA/MS (Master of Arts/Science)—Total applicants accepted 2007–2008, 24. Number full-time enrolled (new admits only) 2007–2008, 22. Number part-time enrolled (new admits only) 2007–2008, 2. Total enrolled 2007–2008 full-time, 54, part-time, 8. Openings 2008–2009, 15. The number of students enrolled full- and part-time who were dismissed or voluntarily withdrew from this program area in 2007–2008 were 8.

Admissions Requirements:

Scores: Entries appear in this order: required test or GPA, minimum score (if required), median score of students entering in 2007–2008. Master's Programs: GRE-V 400; GRE-Q 400; overall undergraduate GPA 2.80; psychology GPA 3.00. Requirements are currently in revision. Please check our Web site for updated information.

Other Criteria: (importance of criteria rated low, medium, or high): GRE/MAT scores—medium, research experience—medium, work experience—low, extracurricular activity—low, clinically related public service—low, GPA—high, letters of recommendation—high, interview—medium, statement of goals and objectives—medium, undergraduate major in psychology—medium, specific undergraduate psychology courses taken—high.

Student Characteristics: The following represents characteristics of students in 2007–2008 in all graduate psychology programs in the department: Female—full-time 48, part-time 7; Male—full-time 6, part-time 1; African American/Black—full-time 52, part-time 8; Caucasian/White—full-time 2, part-time 0; students subject to the Americans With Disabilities Act—full-time 0, part-time 0; Unknown ethnicity—full-time 0, part-time 0.

Financial Information/Assistance:

Tuition for Full-Time Study: *Master's:* State residents: per academic year $5,677; Nonstate residents: per academic year $12,142. Tuition is subject to change.

Financial Assistance:

First-Year Students: Research assistantships available for first year. Average amount paid per academic year: $6,000. Average number of hours worked per week: 20. Apply by March 31.

Advanced Students: Fellowships and scholarships available for advanced students. Average number of hours worked per week: 0. Apply by March 31.

Additional Information: Of all students currently enrolled full time, 75% benefited from one or more of the listed financial assistance programs. Application and information available online at http://www.vsu.edu/include/grad-cat04.pdf.

Internships/Practica: Clinical students must complete three sections of practicum. Placements usually match the student's career goals and the characteristics of the practicum site.

Housing and Day Care: On-campus housing is available. On-campus housing is available for single students. Average cost of on-campus housing per semester is $1,732 and costs for board is $1,272 per semester. No on-campus day care facilities are available.

Employment of Department Graduates:

Master's Degree Graduates: Of those who graduated in the academic year 2006–2007, the following categories and numbers represent the postgraduate activities and employment of master's degree graduates: Enrolled in a psychology doctoral program (8), enrolled in another graduate/professional program (5), enrolled in a postdoctoral residency/fellowship (n/a), employed in independent practice (n/a), employed in a professional position in a school system (2), employed in business or industry (15), employed in government agency (12), employed in a community mental health/counseling center (2), employed in a hospital/medical center (4), total from the above (master's) (48).

Doctoral Degree Graduates: Of those who graduated in the academic year 2006–2007, the following categories and numbers represent the postgraduate activities and employment of doctoral degree graduates: Enrolled in a psychology doctoral program (n/a), total from the above (doctoral) (0).

Additional Information:

Orientation, Objectives, and Emphasis of Department: Students who select the General Psychology master's program usually plan to apply to doctoral programs. Students who select the Clinical program either have aspirations to attend a doctoral program or have a goal to obtain state licensure and practice with their master's degree in private or public agencies. Students who have been admitted to doctoral programs after completion of any concentration—General or Clinical—of our master's program usually matriculated successfully. Students in the Clinical master's programs learn diagnostic and evaluation skills, and are placed in practicum sites. All students must complete a thesis.

Special Facilities or Resources: The psychology department recently renovated its Clinical lab to expand its test library, add videotaping capability, and provide electronic report writing capability. The psychology experimental computer lab was updated in Fall 2006. Current faculty research projects include studies of cardiovascular response to stress in African Americans, STD/HIV prevention and health care seeking behavior in African Americans, religiosity and health, stress and burnout among healthcare workers, psychoepistemology.

Information for Students With Physical Disabilities: See the following Web site for more information: http://www.vsu.edu/pages/323.asp.

Application Information:

Send to School of Graduate Studies, Research and Outreach, 1 Hayden Drive, Box 9080, VSU, Petersburg, VA 23806-0001. Application available online. URL of online application: http://www.vsu.edu/pages/252.asp. Students are admitted in the Fall, application deadline April 1; Spring, application deadline November 1; programs have rolling admissions. Clinical graduate students are only admitted in the Fall term. *Fee:* $25.

Virginia, University of

Curry Programs in Clinical and School Psychology
Curry School of Education
P.O. Box 400270
Charlottesville, VA 22904-4270
Telephone: (434) 924-7472
Fax: (434) 924-1433
E-mail: *abl2x@Virginia.EDU*
Web: *http://www.curry.edschool.virginia.edu/go/clinpsych*

Department Information:

1976. Director: Ann Loper. Number of faculty: total—full-time 8, part-time 1; women—full-time 5, part-time 1; total—minority—full-time 1; women minority—full-time 1.

Programs and Degrees Offered:

Listed in the following order: Program area, degree type (T if terminal Master's), number awarded 7/06–6/07. Clinical PhD (Doctor of Philosophy) 9.

APA Accreditation: Clinical PhD (Doctor of Philosophy).

Student Applications/Admissions:

Student Applications

Clinical PhD (Doctor of Philosophy)—Applications 2007–2008, 146. Total applicants accepted 2007–2008, 12. Number full-time enrolled (new admits only) 2007–2008, 7. Total enrolled 2007–2008 full-time, 35. Openings 2008–2009, 7. The median number of years required for completion of a degree in 2006–2007 were 5. The number of students enrolled full- and part-time who were dismissed or voluntarily withdrew from this program area in 2007–2008 were 0.

Admissions Requirements:

Scores: Entries appear in this order: required test or GPA, minimum score (if required), median score of students entering in 2007–2008. Doctoral Programs: GRE-V none, 600; GRE-Q none, 676; overall undergraduate GPA none, 3.6; last 2 years GPA no minimum stated.

Other Criteria: (importance of criteria rated low, medium, or high): GRE/MAT scores—medium, research experience—medium, work experience—medium, extracurricular activity—low, clinically related public service—medium, GPA—high, letters of recommendation—high, interview—high, statement of goals and objectives—high. For additional information on admission requirements, go to http://www.curry.edschool.virginia.edu/clinpsych/.

Student Characteristics: The following represents characteristics of students in 2007–2008 in all graduate psychology programs in the department: Female—full-time 28, part-time 0; Male—full-time 7, part-time 0; African American/Black—full-time 5, part-time 0; Hispanic/Latino(a)—full-time 0, part-time 0; Asian/Pacific Islander—full-time 3, part-time 0; American Indian/Alaska Native—full-time 0, part-time 0; Caucasian/White—full-time 27, part-time 0; Multi-ethnic—full-time 0, part-time 0; students subject to the Americans With Disabilities Act—full-time 0, part-time 0; Unknown ethnicity—full-time 0, part-time 0.

Financial Information/Assistance:

Tuition for Full-Time Study: *Doctoral:* State residents: per academic year $11,240; Nonstate residents: per academic year $21,240.

Financial Assistance:

First-Year Students: Teaching assistantships available for first year. Average amount paid per academic year: $2,000. Average number of hours worked per week: 10. Apply by March 1. Tuition remission given: partial. Research assistantships available for first year. Average amount paid per academic year: $5,000. Average number of hours worked per week: 10. Apply by March 1. Tuition remission given: partial. Fellowships and scholarships available for first year. Average amount paid per academic year: $5,000. Average number of hours worked per week: 10. Apply by March 1. Tuition remission given: full.

Advanced Students: Teaching assistantships available for advanced students. Average amount paid per academic year: $2,000. Average number of hours worked per week: 10. Apply by March 1. Tuition remission given: partial. Research assistantships available for advanced students. Average amount paid per academic year: $5,000. Average number of hours worked per week: 10. Tuition remission given: partial. Fellowships and scholarships available for advanced students. Average amount paid per academic year: $5,000. Average number of hours worked per week: 10. Apply by March 1. Tuition remission given: full.

Additional Information: Of all students currently enrolled full time, 100% benefited from one or more of the listed financial assistance programs.

Internships/Practica: Doctoral Degree (PhD Clinical): For those doctoral students for whom a professional internship was required in this program prior to graduation, (7) students applied for an internship in 2006–2007, with (6) students obtaining an internship. Of those students who obtained an internship, (6) were paid internships. Of those students who obtained an internship, (6) students placed in APA/CPA-accredited internships, (0) students placed in internships not APA/CPA-accredited, but listed with the Association of Psychology Postdoctoral and Internship Centers (APPIC), (0) students placed in internships conforming to guidelines of the Council of Directors of School Psychology Programs (CDSPP), (0) students placed in internships that were not APA/CPA-accredited, APPIC or CDSPP listed. Students undertake external clinical practica and school internships in area public and private schools, state mental hospitals and residential treatment centers for children or adults, a regional medically affiliated children's rehabilitation center, a family stress clinic, and other mental health settings in the university and community. During the 5th year of training, students complete a full-time 1-year internship in clinical psychology.

Housing and Day Care: On-campus housing is available. See the following Web site for more information: http://www.virginia.edu/housing/housing.htm. On-campus day care facilities are available. See the following Web site for more information: http://www.virginia.edu/childdevelopmentcenter/enrollment.htm.

Employment of Department Graduates:

Master's Degree Graduates: Of those who graduated in the academic year 2006–2007, the following categories and numbers represent the postgraduate activities and employment of master's degree graduates: Enrolled in a postdoctoral residency/fellowship (n/a), employed in independent practice (n/a), total from the above (master's) (0).

Doctoral Degree Graduates: Of those who graduated in the academic year 2006–2007, the following categories and numbers represent the postgraduate activities and employment of doctoral degree graduates: Enrolled in a psychology doctoral program (n/a), enrolled in a postdoctoral residency/fellowship (4), employed in a professional position in a school system (1), employed in a hospital/medical center (2), total from the above (doctoral) (7).

Additional Information:

Orientation, Objectives, and Emphasis of Department: The primary goal of the training program in the Curry Programs in Clinical and School Psychology is to produce clinical and school psychologists who will make substantial contributions to the field in a variety of professional and scientific roles. The majority of graduates seek leadership positions in settings such as medical centers, schools, and mental health agencies, whereas others pursue academic and research careers. All students complete a common core of coursework and practica in both basic science and professional skills. Students have the opportunity for specialized training and research in concentration areas such as family therapy, forensic psychology, and school interventions, among others. The predominant theoretical and practice orientations of the faculty are cognitive behavioral, psychodynamic, and family systems. All students are expected to develop clinical and research skills, and the integration of clinical, classroom, and research experiences is emphasized. Many students in the PhD program pursue training in both clinical and school psychology through the clinical–school track. A separate EdD program in school psychology admits experienced school psychologists who are prepared for leadership positions in school and university settings.

Special Facilities or Resources: The Curry Program operates its own comprehensive psychological clinic, the Center for Clinical Psychology Services, serving families, couples, and individuals of all ages and diverse backgrounds. The Center is well equipped for live and videotaped supervision and conveniently located in Ruffner Hall, along with student and faculty offices. In addition, the Program has close working relationships with numerous community agencies, schools, clinics, and hospitals that permit training and research in many different mental health and educational settings. Our students have research and consultation opportunities with numerous projects, including the Adolescent Parenting Stress Project, Family Empowerment Project, Project on Equity and Schooling, Teaching Stress Project, Education for Incarcerated Parents Project, Young Women Leaders Program, and the

Virginia Youth Violence Project. The Curry School of Education is a national leader in instructional technology, with outstanding computing facilities and technology support, smart classrooms, and its own library. Students enjoy easy access to the extensive University of Virginia Library system, which includes a collection of nearly 5 million volumes and has state-of-the-art electronic library resources.

Information for Students With Physical Disabilities: See the following Web site for more information: http://www.virginia.edu/eop/disability.html.

Application Information:
Send to Admissions Office, Curry School of Education, P.O. Box 400261, University of Virginia, Charlottesville, VA 22904-4261. Application available online. URL of online application: http://www.curry.edschool.virginia.edu/admissions/. Students are admitted in the Fall, application deadline January 5. *Fee:* $60. If fee imposes economic hardship, it may be waived. Request information from Curry School Admissions office at address above.

Virginia, University of

Department of Psychology
102 Gilmer Hall, P.O. Box 400400
Charlottesville, VA 22904-4400
Telephone: (434) 982-4750
Fax: (434) 982-4766
E-mail: *psychology@virginia.edu*
Web: *http://www.virginia.edu/~psych*

Department Information:
1929. Chairperson: David L. Hill. Number of faculty: total—full-time 33; women—full-time 10; total—minority—full-time 5; women minority—full-time 1.

Programs and Degrees Offered:
Listed in the following order: Program area, degree type (T if terminal Master's), number awarded 7/06–6/07. Clinical PhD (Doctor of Philosophy) 5, Cognitive PhD (Doctor of Philosophy) 4, Community PhD (Doctor of Philosophy) 1, Developmental PhD (Doctor of Philosophy) 2, Quantitative PhD (Doctor of Philosophy) 3, Social PhD (Doctor of Philosophy) 4, Sensory Systems and Neuroscience PhD (Doctor of Philosophy) 2.

APA Accreditation: Clinical PhD (Doctor of Philosophy).

Student Applications/Admissions:
Student Applications
Clinical PhD (Doctor of Philosophy)—Applications 2007–2008, 245. Total applicants accepted 2007–2008, 7. Number full-time enrolled (new admits only) 2007–2008, 4. Openings 2008–2009, 5. The median number of years required for completion of a degree in 2006–2007 were 7. The number of students enrolled full- and part-time who were dismissed or voluntarily withdrew from this program area in 2007–2008 were 0. *Cognitive PhD (Doctor of Philosophy)*—Applications 2007–2008, 24. Total applicants accepted 2007–2008, 3. Number full-time enrolled (new admits only) 2007–2008, 2. Number part-time enrolled (new admits only) 2007–2008, 0. Openings 2008–2009, 3. The median number of years required for completion of a degree in 2006–2007 were 6. The number of students enrolled full- and part-time who were dismissed or voluntarily withdrew from this program area in 2007–2008 were 0. *Community PhD (Doctor of Philosophy)*—Applications 2007–2008, 30. Total applicants accepted 2007–2008, 3. Number full-time enrolled (new admits only) 2007–2008, 0. Number part-time enrolled (new admits only) 2007–2008, 0. Openings 2008–2009, 2. The median number of years required for completion of a degree in 2006–2007 were 7. *Developmental PhD (Doctor of Philosophy)*—Applications 2007–2008, 42. Total applicants accepted 2007–2008, 4. Number full-time enrolled (new admits only) 2007–2008, 1. Openings 2008–2009, 4. The median number of years required for completion of a degree in 2006–2007 were 6. *Quantitative PhD (Doctor of Philosophy)*—Applications 2007–2008, 10. Total applicants accepted 2007–2008, 3. Number full-time enrolled (new admits only) 2007–2008, 3. Number part-time enrolled (new admits only) 2007–2008, 0. Openings 2008–2009, 2. The median number of years required for completion of a degree in 2006–2007 were 6. *Social PhD (Doctor of Philosophy)*—Applications 2007–2008, 132. Total applicants accepted 2007–2008, 6. Number full-time enrolled (new admits only) 2007–2008, 2. Number part-time enrolled (new admits only) 2007–2008, 0. Openings 2008–2009, 3. The median number of years required for completion of a degree in 2006–2007 were 6. *Sensory Systems and Neuroscience PhD (Doctor of Philosophy)*—Applications 2007–2008, 7. Total applicants accepted 2007–2008, 0. Number full-time enrolled (new admits only) 2007–2008, 0. Number part-time enrolled (new admits only) 2007–2008, 0. Openings 2008–2009, 1. The median number of years required for completion of a degree in 2006–2007 were 6. The number of students enrolled full- and part-time who were dismissed or voluntarily withdrew from this program area in 2007–2008 were 1.

Admissions Requirements:
Scores: Entries appear in this order: required test or GPA, minimum score (if required), median score of students entering in 2007–2008. Doctoral Programs: GRE-V no minimum stated; GRE-Q no minimum stated; overall undergraduate GPA no minimum stated; last 2 years GPA no minimum stated; psychology GPA no minimum stated; Doctoral program GRE-Analytic no minimum stated.
Other Criteria: (importance of criteria rated low, medium, or high): GRE/MAT scores—medium, research experience—high, work experience—medium, extracurricular activity—low, clinically related public service—low, GPA—high, letters of recommendation—high, interview—medium, statement of goals and objectives—high. Publications and presentations at conferences are valued as actual work experience in an area related to the degree sought.

Student Characteristics: The following represents characteristics of students in 2007–2008 in all graduate psychology programs in the department: Female—full-time 63, part-time 0; Male—full-time 28, part-time 0; African American/Black—full-time 6, part-time 0; Hispanic/Latino(a)—full-time 5, part-time 0; Asian/Pacific Islander—full-time 10, part-time 0; American Indian/Alaska Native—full-time 1, part-time 0; Caucasian/White—full-time 69, part-time 0; Multi-ethnic—full-time 0, part-time 0;

students subject to the Americans With Disabilities Act—full-time 0, part-time 0; Unknown ethnicity—full-time 0, part-time 0.

Financial Information/Assistance:

Tuition for Full-Time Study: *Doctoral:* State residents: per academic year $10,596; Nonstate residents: per academic year $21,193. Tuition is subject to change.

Financial Assistance:

First-Year Students: Teaching assistantships available for first year. Tuition remission given: full. Research assistantships available for first year. Tuition remission given: full. Fellowships and scholarships available for first year.

Advanced Students: Teaching assistantships available for advanced students. Tuition remission given: full. Research assistantships available for advanced students. Tuition remission given: full. Fellowships and scholarships available for advanced students.

Additional Information: Of all students currently enrolled full time, 100% benefited from one or more of the listed financial assistance programs.

Internships/Practica: Doctoral Degree (PhD Clinical): For those doctoral students for whom a professional internship was required in this program prior to graduation, (4) students applied for an internship in 2006–2007, with (4) students obtaining an internship. Of those students who obtained an internship, (3) were paid internships. Of those students who obtained an internship, (3) students placed in APA/CPA-accredited internships, (1) student placed in internships not APA/CPA-accredited, but listed with the Association of Psychology Postdoctoral and Internship Centers (APPIC), (0) students placed in internships conforming to guidelines of the Council of Directors of School Psychology Programs (CDSPP), (0) students placed in internships that were not APA/CPA-accredited, APPIC or CDSPP listed. For Clinical program: Multiple practica at University Hospital, State Mental Hospital for children and adults, Kluge Children's Center, Community Mental Health Center, Law and Psychiatry Unit, Department Clinic, and other places as connections and student interest suggest.

Housing and Day Care: On-campus housing is available. See the following Web site for more information: http://www.virginia.edu/housing/. On-campus day care facilities are available. See the following Web site for more information: http://www.virginia.edu/childdevelopmentcenter/enrollment.htm.

Employment of Department Graduates:

Master's Degree Graduates: Of those who graduated in the academic year 2006–2007, the following categories and numbers represent the postgraduate activities and employment of master's degree graduates: Enrolled in a postdoctoral residency/fellowship (n/a), employed in independent practice (n/a), employed in an academic position at a university (8), total from the above (master's) (8).

Doctoral Degree Graduates: Of those who graduated in the academic year 2006–2007, the following categories and numbers represent the postgraduate activities and employment of doctoral degree graduates: Enrolled in a psychology doctoral program (n/a), total from the above (doctoral) (0).

Additional Information:

Orientation, Objectives, and Emphasis of Department: The department emphasizes research on a wide spectrum of psychological issues with clinical, developmental, social, cognitive, sensory systems and neuroscience, quantitative, and community specialties. In addition, new tracks are being developed, such as social ecology and development, law and psychology, family, and minority issues.

Special Facilities or Resources: The department has in excess of 50,000 square feet for offices, laboratories, seminar rooms, and classrooms. Special facilities include rooms for psychophysical investigations, a suite of rooms devoted to developmental, clinical, and social laboratories, and specialized research facilities for the study of animal behavior and psychobiology. Sound-attenuated rooms, electrically shielded rooms, numerous one-way vision rooms, surgery and vivarium rooms, and a darkroom are all available. There is also a library for psychology and biology housed in the same building. There are ample computer facilities. All labs are connected to a local area network and a university-wide local area network. This allows the labs to connect to other available University machines such as IBM RS/6000 UNIX machines.

Information for Students With Physical Disabilities: See the following Web site for more information: http://www.virginia.edu/studenthealth/lnec.html.

Application Information:

Send to Dean of the Graduate School, University of Virginia, P.O. Box 400775, 437 Cabell Hall, Charlottesville, VA 22904-4775. Application available online. URL of online application: http://www.virginia.edu/psychology/graduate/. Students are admitted in the Fall, application deadline December 1. *Fee:* $40.

Argosy University/Seattle (2007 data)

Clinical Psychology (MA and PsyD); Counseling Psychology (MA and EdD)
Washington School of Professional Psychology
2601-A Elliott Avenue
Seattle, WA 98121
Telephone: (206) 283-4500
Fax: (206) 283-5777
E-mail: *fparks@argosy.edu*
Web: *http://www.argosyu.edu*

Department Information:

1997. Chair, Clinical; Chair, Counseling: Frances M. Parks, PhD, ABPP/ Diedra L. Clay, PsyD. Number of faculty: total—full-time 9; women—full-time 6.

Programs and Degrees Offered:

Listed in the following order: Program area, degree type (T if terminal Master's), number awarded 7/06–6/07. Clinical Psychology MA/MS (Master of Arts/Science) (T) 48, Counseling Psychology MA/MS (Master of Arts/Science) (T) 46.

Student Applications/Admissions:

Student Applications

Clinical Psychology MA/MS (Master of Arts/Science)—Number full-time enrolled (new admits only) 2007–2008, 15. Total enrolled 2007–2008 full-time, 40. Openings 2008–2009, 20. The median number of years required for completion of a degree in 2006–2007 were 2. *Counseling Psychology MA/MS (Master of Arts/Science)*—Openings 2008–2009, 20. The median number of years required for completion of a degree in 2006–2007 were 2.

Admissions Requirements:

Scores: Entries appear in this order: required test or GPA, minimum score (if required), median score of students entering in 2007–2008. Master's Programs: overall undergraduate GPA 3.0; last 2 years GPA 3.0; psychology GPA 3.0. Minimum GPA for MA clinical psychology program is 3.00 from an accredited undergraduate/graduate program. If you do not meet the required GPA, you may submit GRE scores. Doctoral Programs: overall undergraduate GPA 3.25; last 2 years GPA 3.25; psychology GPA 3.25. Minimum GPA for PsyD Psychology program is 3.25 from an accredited undergraduate/graduate program.

Other Criteria: (importance of criteria rated low, medium, or high): research experience—low, work experience—medium, extracurricular activity—medium, clinically related public service—high, GPA—high, letters of recommendation—high, interview—high, statement of goals and objectives—high. For entry into master's-level programs, work experience is not expected. For additional information on admission requirements, go to http://www.argosyu.edu/admissions/.

Student Characteristics: The following represents characteristics of students in 2007–2008 in all graduate psychology programs in the department: Female—full-time 165, part-time 130; Male—full-time 63, part-time 39; African American/Black—full-time 11, part-time 5; Hispanic/Latino(a)—full-time 7, part-time 2; Asian/Pacific Islander—full-time 17, part-time 15; American Indian/Alaska Native—full-time 6, part-time 2; Caucasian/White—full-time 176, part-time 134; Multi-ethnic—full-time 4, part-time 0; students subject to the Americans With Disabilities Act—full-time 16, part-time 0; Unknown ethnicity—full-time 11, part-time 11.

Financial Information/Assistance:

Financial Assistance:

First-Year Students: Fellowships and scholarships available for first year. Average amount paid per academic year: $3,000. Tuition remission given: partial.

Advanced Students: Teaching assistantships available for advanced students. Research assistantships available for advanced students. Fellowships and scholarships available for advanced students.

Additional Information: No information provided.

Internships/Practica: WSPP's current list of approved practicum sites for master's- and doctoral-level students includes state and community mental health facilities, state correctional facilities from minimum to maximum security, juvenile detention centers, outpatient clinics, private psychiatric hospitals, psychiatric units and community hospitals, treatment centers for developmentally disabled and behavior disordered, and chemical dependence treatment programs. We also have practicum placements in multicultural or diverse practicum settings, including mental health agencies serving Native Americans, Asian Americans, and African Americans. Local internships may involve the above sites. We are in the process of developing an onsite clinic.

Housing and Day Care: No on-campus housing is available. No on-campus day care facilities are available.

Employment of Department Graduates:

Master's Degree Graduates: Of those who graduated in the academic year 2006–2007, the following categories and numbers represent the postgraduate activities and employment of master's degree graduates: Enrolled in a postdoctoral residency/fellowship (n/a), employed in independent practice (n/a), total from the above (master's) (0).

Doctoral Degree Graduates: Of those who graduated in the academic year 2006–2007, the following categories and numbers represent the postgraduate activities and employment of doctoral degree graduates: Enrolled in a psychology doctoral program (n/a), total from the above (doctoral) (0).

Additional Information:

Orientation, Objectives, and Emphasis of Department: The primary purpose of the program is to educate and train students in the major aspects of clinical or counseling practice. To ensure that students are prepared adequately, the curriculum integrates theory, training, research and practice, preparing students to work with a wide range of populations in need of psychological services and in a broad range of roles.

Application Information:
Send to Admissions Office, Argosy University/Seattle, 2601-A Elliott Avenue, Seattle, WA 98121; phone: (800) 377-0617. Application available online. URL of online application: http://www.argosyu.edu/admissions/. Students are admitted in the Fall, application deadline April 15; Spring, application deadline November 1; Summer, application deadline March 1. Rolling admissions. The above deadline dates are recommended dates. *Fee:* $50.

Central Washington University

Department of Psychology
College of the Sciences
400 East University Way
Ellensburg, WA 98926-7575
Telephone: (509) 963-2381
Fax: (509) 963-2307
E-mail: *steins@cwu.edu*
Web: *http://www.cwu.edu/~psych/*

Department Information:
1965. Chairperson: Stephanie Stein. Number of faculty: total—full-time 25, part-time 9; women—full-time 9, part-time 4.

Programs and Degrees Offered:
Listed in the following order: Program area, degree type (T if terminal Master's), number awarded 7/06–6/07. Mental Health Counseling MA/MS (Master of Arts/Science) (T) 2, School Counseling Other 3, Experimental MA/MS (Master of Arts/Science) (T) 5, School Psychology EdS/MEd (School Psychology) 8.

Student Applications/Admissions:
Student Applications
Mental Health Counseling MA/MS (Master of Arts/Science)—Applications 2007–2008, 28. Total applicants accepted 2007–2008, 6. Number full-time enrolled (new admits only) 2007–2008, 5. Number part-time enrolled (new admits only) 2007–2008, 0. Total enrolled 2007–2008 full-time, 16, part-time, 3. Openings 2008–2009, 8. The median number of years required for completion of a degree in 2006–2007 were 2. The number of students enrolled full- and part-time who were dismissed or voluntarily withdrew from this program area in 2007–2008 were 1. *School Counseling Other*—Applications 2007–2008, 12. Total applicants accepted 2007–2008, 4. Number full-time enrolled (new admits only) 2007–2008, 4. Number part-time enrolled (new admits only) 2007–2008, 0. Total enrolled 2007–2008 full-time, 4, part-time, 1. Openings 2008–2009, 4. The median number of years required for completion of a degree in 2006–2007 were 2. The number of students enrolled full- and part-time who were dismissed or voluntarily withdrew from this program area in 2007–2008 were 0. *Experimental MA/MS (Master of Arts/Science)*—Applications 2007–2008, 9. Total applicants accepted 2007–2008, 4. Number full-time enrolled (new admits only) 2007–2008, 4. Number part-time enrolled (new admits only) 2007–2008, 0. Total enrolled 2007–2008 full-time, 8, part-time, 7. Openings 2008–2009, 12. The median number of years required for completion of a degree in 2006–2007 were 2. The number of students enrolled full- and part-time who were dismissed or voluntarily withdrew from this program area in 2007–2008 were 0. *School Psychology EdS/MEd (School Psychology)*—Applications 2007–2008, 16. Total applicants accepted 2007–2008, 5. Number full-time enrolled (new admits only) 2007–2008, 5. Number part-time enrolled (new admits only) 2007–2008, 0. Total enrolled 2007–2008 full-time, 12, part-time, 4. Openings 2008–2009, 8. The median number of years required for completion of a degree in 2006–2007 were 3. The number of students enrolled full- and part-time who were dismissed or voluntarily withdrew from this program area in 2007–2008 were 0.

Admissions Requirements:
Scores: Entries appear in this order: required test or GPA, minimum score (if required), median score of students entering in 2007–2008. Master's Programs: GRE-V 450; GRE-Q 450; last 2 years GPA 3.00.
Other Criteria: (importance of criteria rated low, medium, or high): GRE/MAT scores—high, research experience—medium, work experience—medium, extracurricular activity—low, clinically related public service—medium, GPA—high, letters of recommendation—high, statement of goals and objectives—high, undergraduate major in psychology—medium, specific undergraduate psychology courses taken—medium. For additional information on admission requirements, go to http://www.cwu.edu/~masters/graduateStudies/index.html.

Student Characteristics: The following represents characteristics of students in 2007–2008 in all graduate psychology programs in the department: Female—full-time 29, part-time 13; Male—full-time 11, part-time 2; African American/Black—full-time 1, part-time 0; Hispanic/Latino(a)—full-time 3, part-time 2; Asian/Pacific Islander—full-time 0, part-time 1; American Indian/Alaska Native—full-time 0, part-time 0; Caucasian/White—full-time 35, part-time 12; Multi-ethnic—full-time 0, part-time 0; students subject to the Americans With Disabilities Act—full-time 0, part-time 0; Unknown ethnicity—full-time 1, part-time 0; International students who hold an F-1 or J-1 Visa—full-time 1, part-time 0.

Financial Information/Assistance:
Tuition for Full-Time Study: *Master's:* State residents: per academic year $6,627; Nonstate residents: per academic year $14,817. Tuition is subject to change. See the following Web site for updates and changes in tuition costs: http://www.cwu.edu/~regi/tuition.html.

Financial Assistance:
First-Year Students: Teaching assistantships available for first year. Average amount paid per academic year: $15,685. Average number of hours worked per week: 20. Apply by February 1. Tuition remission given: full. Research assistantships available for first year. Average amount paid per academic year: $15,685. Average number of hours worked per week: 20. Apply by February 1. Tuition remission given: full.
Advanced Students: Teaching assistantships available for advanced students. Average amount paid per academic year: $15,685. Average number of hours worked per week: 20. Apply by February 1. Tuition remission given: full. Research assistantships available for advanced students. Average amount paid per academic year: $15,685. Average number of hours worked per week: 20. Apply by February 1. Tuition remission given: full.
Additional Information: Of all students currently enrolled full time, 45% benefited from one or more of the listed financial

assistance programs. Application and information available online at http://www.cwu.edu/~masters/graduateStudies/assistant.html.

Internships/Practica: Master's Degree (MA/MS Mental Health Counseling): An internship experience such as a final research project or "capstone" experience is required of graduates. Master's Degree (MA/MS Experimental): An internship experience such as a final research project or "capstone" experience is required of graduates. Mental Health Counseling Psychology program requires four quarters of practica and 900-hour internship. School Counseling program requires four quarters of practica and 400-hour internship. School Psychology program requires two quarters of practica and 1-year internship. Recent school psychology internships have been paid positions. Practica in applied experimental psychology are offered.

Housing and Day Care: On-campus housing is available. See the following Web site for more information: http://www.cwu.edu/~housing/. On-campus day care facilities are available. See the following Web site for more information: http://www.cwu.edu/~ecenter/eclc.html.

Employment of Department Graduates:

Master's Degree Graduates: Of those who graduated in the academic year 2006–2007, the following categories and numbers represent the postgraduate activities and employment of master's degree graduates: Enrolled in a postdoctoral residency/fellowship (n/a), employed in independent practice (n/a), employed in an academic position at a 2-year/4-year college (1), employed in other positions at a higher education institution (1), employed in a professional position in a school system (8), employed in business or industry (1), employed in government agency (3), employed in a community mental health/counseling center (2), other employment position (2), total from the above (master's) (18).

Doctoral Degree Graduates: Of those who graduated in the academic year 2006–2007, the following categories and numbers represent the postgraduate activities and employment of doctoral degree graduates: Enrolled in a psychology doctoral program (n/a), total from the above (doctoral) (0).

Additional Information:

Orientation, Objectives, and Emphasis of Department: Central Washington University's graduate program in psychology prepares students for professional employment in a variety of settings including mental health agencies, public schools, community colleges, and business or industry. We also prepare students for successful completion of doctoral degree programs in psychology. The programs include extensive supervision in practicum and internship settings and research partnerships with faculty mentors. School Psychology program is NASP approved. Mental Health Counseling program is CACREP accredited. The educational requirements of the Animal Behavior Society's Associate Applied Animal Behaviorist Certificate can be met by completing the MS Experimental degree program with an appropriate selection of core and elective courses.

Special Facilities or Resources: Our facilities include an on-site community counseling and psychological assessment center for training in counseling and testing; animal research laboratories, including a laboratory for the study of language learning in chimpanzees; a human behavior laboratory; a computer lab; and a complete mechanical and electrical instrumentation services center.

Information for Students With Physical Disabilities: See the following Web site for more information: http://www.cwu.edu/~dss/.

Application Information:

Send to Office of Graduate Studies, Central Washington University, 400 East University Way, Ellensburg, WA 98926-7510. Application available online. URL of online application: http://www.cwu.edu/~masters/forms/formsGraduate.html. Students are admitted in the Fall, application deadline April 1; Winter, application deadline April 1. Winter and Spring admission possible for Experimental Psychology program only. Admissions may close earlier depending on available space. *Fee:* $50. Application fee may be waived by demonstration of financial need.

Gonzaga University

Department of Counselor Education
School of Education
East 501 Boone Avenue
Spokane, WA 99258-0025
Telephone: (509) 323-3512
Fax: (509) 323-5964
E-mail: *ebennett@soe.gonzaga.edu*
Web: *http://www.gonzaga.edu/Academics/Colleges+and+Schools/School+of+Education/Counselor+Education/default.asp*

Department Information:

1960. Chairperson: Elisabeth Bennett. Number of faculty: total—full-time 3, part-time 9; women—full-time 1, part-time 6; minority—part-time 2; women minority—part-time 1.

Programs and Degrees Offered:

Listed in the following order: Program area, degree type (T if terminal Master's), number awarded 7/06–6/07. School Counseling MA/MS (Master of Arts/Science) (T) 10, Community Counseling MA/MS (Master of Arts/Science) (T) 18.

Student Applications/Admissions:

Student Applications

School Counseling MA/MS (Master of Arts/Science)—Applications 2007–2008, 44. Total applicants accepted 2007–2008, 9. Number full-time enrolled (new admits only) 2007–2008, 8. Number part-time enrolled (new admits only) 2007–2008, 1. Total enrolled 2007–2008 full-time, 18, part-time, 2. Openings 2008–2009, 10. The median number of years required for completion of a degree in 2006–2007 were 2. The number of students enrolled full- and part-time who were dismissed or voluntarily withdrew from this program area in 2007–2008 were 1. *Community Counseling MA/MS (Master of Arts/Science)*—Applications 2007–2008, 90. Total applicants accepted 2007–2008, 23. Number full-time enrolled (new admits only) 2007–2008, 20. Number part-time enrolled (new admits only) 2007–2008, 3. Total enrolled 2007–2008 full-time, 38, part-time, 5. Openings 2008–2009, 20. The median number of years required for completion of a degree in 2006–2007 were 2. The number of students enrolled full- and part-time who were dismissed or voluntarily withdrew from this program area in 2007–2008 were 2.

Admissions Requirements:

Scores: Entries appear in this order: required test or GPA, minimum score (if required), median score of students entering in 2007–2008. Master's Programs: GRE-V no minimum stated; GRE-Q no minimum stated; MAT no minimum stated; overall undergraduate GPA 3.0; Master's GRE-Analytical no minimum stated. Students may submit either the GRE or MAT. It is preferential that test scores fall around the 50th percentile and that GPAs are 3.0 or above. Students with lower scores should make explanation in their personal statements.

Other Criteria: (importance of criteria rated low, medium, or high): GRE/MAT scores—low, work experience—medium, extracurricular activity—medium, clinically related public service—medium, GPA—medium, letters of recommendation—high, interview—high, statement of goals and objectives—high, emotional intelligence—high, undergraduate major in psychology—low, specific undergraduate psychology courses taken—low. For additional information on admission requirements, go to http://www.gonzaga.edu/Academics/Colleges+and+Schools/School+of+Education/Counselor+Education/defaul.

Student Characteristics: The following represents characteristics of students in 2007–2008 in all graduate psychology programs in the department: Female—full-time 84, part-time 5; Male—full-time 12, part-time 2; African American/Black—full-time 2, part-time 0; Hispanic/Latino(a)—full-time 3, part-time 1; Asian/Pacific Islander—full-time 1, part-time 0; American Indian/Alaska Native—full-time 3, part-time 2; Caucasian/White—full-time 84, part-time 4; Multi-ethnic—full-time 1, part-time 0; students subject to the Americans With Disabilities Act—full-time 3, part-time 0; Unknown ethnicity—full-time 1, part-time 0; International students who hold an F-1 or J-1 Visa—full-time 1, part-time 0.

Financial Information/Assistance:

Tuition for Full-Time Study: *Master's:* State residents: $710 per credit hour; Nonstate residents: $710 per credit hour. Tuition is subject to change. See the following Web site for updates and changes in tuition costs: http://www.gonzaga.edu.

Financial Assistance:

First-Year Students: Teaching assistantships available for first year. Average amount paid per academic year: $2,700. Average number of hours worked per week: 6. Apply by April 15. Research assistantships available for first year. Average amount paid per academic year: $2,700. Average number of hours worked per week: 6. Apply by April 15.

Advanced Students: Teaching assistantships available for advanced students. Average amount paid per academic year: $2,800. Average number of hours worked per week: 6. Apply by April 15. Research assistantships available for advanced students. Average amount paid per academic year: $2,800. Average number of hours worked per week: 6. Apply by April 15.

Additional Information: Of all students currently enrolled full time, 20% benefited from one or more of the listed financial assistance programs. Application and information available online; see the department.

Internships/Practica: Master's Degree (MA/MS School Counseling): An internship experience such as a final research project or "capstone" experience is required of graduates. Master's Degree (MA/MS Community Counseling): An internship experience such as a final research project or "capstone" experience is required of graduates. Students complete a 100-hour practicum and a 600-hour internship at a site chosen by the student to meet his or her professional interests. School track students currently are placed in schools at elementary, junior high, high school, and alternative settings. Agency track students are placed at sites including but not limited to geriatric, hospital, community mental health, adolescent, marriage and family, child, community college, career, and life-skills settings. A strong reputation within our community has afforded students to select quality placements.

Housing and Day Care: On-campus housing is available. See the following Web site for more information: http://www.gonzaga.edu. No on-campus day care facilities are available.

Employment of Department Graduates:

Master's Degree Graduates: Of those who graduated in the academic year 2006–2007, the following categories and numbers represent the postgraduate activities and employment of master's degree graduates: Enrolled in a psychology doctoral program (3), enrolled in another graduate/professional program (2), enrolled in a postdoctoral residency/fellowship (n/a), employed in independent practice (n/a), employed in an academic position at a 2-year/4-year college (1), employed in other positions at a higher education institution (3), employed in a professional position in a school system (10), employed in business or industry (1), employed in government agency (1), employed in a community mental health/counseling center (5), other employment position (2), total from the above (master's) (28).

Doctoral Degree Graduates: Of those who graduated in the academic year 2006–2007, the following categories and numbers represent the postgraduate activities and employment of doctoral degree graduates: Enrolled in a psychology doctoral program (n/a), total from the above (doctoral) (0).

Additional Information:

Orientation, Objectives, and Emphasis of Department: The philosophical theme running throughout the university is humanism. A realistic, balanced attitude is a necessary prerequisite for assisting others professionally. Careful selection of students helps to ensure the inclusion of healthy individuals with the highest potential for success, as does faculty modeling, encouragement of trust, and communication of clear expectations. Indicators of counselor success are demonstration of skills and conflict resolution, consistent interpersonal behaviors, recognition of strengths and weaknesses, a clear grasp of goals, and self-knowledge of one's impact on others, as well as a strong academic performance. Acquisition of counseling competence comes through both personal and professional growth. Immersion in an intensive course of study with a closely linked group of peers encourages open and honest processing, which, in turn, contributes to personal growth. The department believes that students must possess insight and awareness, and clarity about the boundaries between their personal issues and those of the client. Students training to become professionals must be treated as professionals. Faculty practice collegiality with students, maintain high standards of performance, and furnish an atmosphere of professionalism. Students share cases, exchanging professional advice and input. In addition to the presentation of major theories of counseling, students must develop a personal theory of counseling and demonstrate competence in its use. Faculty are humanistic, but eclectic, disseminating information about effective techniques without imposing any one approach on the students. Students are closely observed in the classroom, practicum, and internship and receive critical monitoring and evaluation from faculty, field supervisor, and peers. School and Community programs are CACREP accredited.

Special Facilities or Resources: The Department of Counselor Education is proud to offer a modern and complete clinic training center, with four practicum rooms, a departmental library, and conference room. The clinic has two-way glass, and is equipped with audio–video technological equipment that can be operated in the clinic room by either the student (for taping and reviewing personal work) or by any department faculty member from faculty offices (for viewing and/or taping).

Information for Students With Physical Disabilities: See the following Web site for more information: http://www.gonzaga.edu.

Application Information:
Send to Graduate Admissions, School of Education, Gonzaga University, 502 East Boone, Spokane, WA 99258-0025. Application available online. URL of online application: http://www.gonzaga.edu/Academics/Colleges-and-Schools/School-of-Education/Graduate-Admissions/GraduateAdmissionsForms/Requirements.asp. Students are admitted in the Fall, application deadline January 15 and March 1. We have two applications deadlines. The first in January is for early admittance. This has allowed students early preparations for attending Gonzaga. The second is regular admittance. Students may also seek admission on a part-time basis at these times. Students may gain permission to enroll as nonmatriculated in order to begin part-time courses before official admission. *Fee:* $45.

Puget Sound, University of

School of Education
1500 North Warner 1051
Tacoma, WA 98416
Telephone: (253) 879-3344
Fax: (253) 879-3926
E-mail: *kirchner@ups.edu*
Web: *http://www.ups.edu*

Department Information:
Director: Grace L. Kirchner. Number of faculty: total—full-time 2, part-time 3; women—full-time 2, part-time 1.

Programs and Degrees Offered:
Listed in the following order: Program area, degree type (T if terminal Master's), number awarded 7/06–6/07. School Counseling Other 11, Agency Counseling Other 5, Pastoral Counseling Other.

Student Applications/Admissions:
Student Applications
School Counseling Other—Applications 2007–2008, 26. Total applicants accepted 2007–2008, 17. Number full-time enrolled (new admits only) 2007–2008, 5. Number part-time enrolled (new admits only) 2007–2008, 3. Total enrolled 2007–2008 full-time, 5, part-time, 16. Openings 2008–2009, 12. The median number of years required for completion of a degree in 2006–2007 were 3. The number of students enrolled full- and part-time who were dismissed or voluntarily withdrew from this program area in 2007–2008 were 0. *Agency Counseling Other*—Applications 2007–2008, 5. Total applicants accepted 2007–2008, 4. Number full-time enrolled (new admits only) 2007–2008, 1. Number part-time enrolled (new admits only) 2007–2008, 2. Total enrolled 2007–2008 full-time, 3, part-time, 3. Openings 2008–2009, 5. The median number of years required for completion of a degree in 2006–2007 were 3. The number of students enrolled full- and part-time who were dismissed or voluntarily withdrew from this program area in 2007–2008 were 0. *Pastoral Counseling Other*—Applications 2007–2008, 2. Total enrolled 2007–2008 part-time, 1.

Admissions Requirements:
Scores: Entries appear in this order: required test or GPA, minimum score (if required), median score of students entering in 2007–2008. Master's Programs: GRE-V no minimum stated; GRE-Q no minimum stated; overall undergraduate GPA no minimum stated; Master's GRE-Analytical no minimum stated.
Other Criteria: (importance of criteria rated low, medium, or high): GRE/MAT scores—medium, work experience—medium, extracurricular activity—low, clinically related public service—medium, GPA—medium, letters of recommendation—medium, interview—medium, statement of goals and objectives—medium.

Student Characteristics: The following represents characteristics of students in 2007–2008 in all graduate psychology programs in the department: Female—full-time 4, part-time 19; Male—full-time 4, part-time 1; African American/Black—full-time 1, part-time 3; Asian/Pacific Islander—part-time 1; American Indian/Alaska Native—part-time 1; Caucasian/White—full-time 6, part-time 10; Unknown ethnicity—full-time 1, part-time 5; International students who hold an F-1 or J-1 Visa—part-time 1.

Financial Information/Assistance:
Tuition for Full-Time Study: *Master's:* State residents: $650 per credit hour; Nonstate residents: $650 per credit hour. Tuition is subject to change. See the following Web site for updates and changes in tuition costs: http://www.ups.edu/x3884.xml.

Financial Assistance:
First-Year Students: No information provided.
Advanced Students: No information provided.
Additional Information: No information provided.

Internships/Practica: We require a 400-hour internship in a school or agency setting. These 400 hours are in addition to an on-campus practicum that meets once per week for the academic year.

Housing and Day Care: On-campus housing is available. Students must carry 2 units per semester to qualify for on campus housing. No on-campus day care facilities are available.

Employment of Department Graduates:

Master's Degree Graduates: Of those who graduated in the academic year 2006–2007, the following categories and numbers represent the postgraduate activities and employment of master's degree graduates: Enrolled in a psychology doctoral program (0), enrolled in another graduate/professional program (0), enrolled in a postdoctoral residency/fellowship (n/a), employed in independent practice (n/a), employed in an academic position at a university (0), employed in an academic position at a 2-year/4-year college (0), employed in other positions at a higher education institution (1), employed in a professional position in a school system (10), employed in business or industry (0), employed in government agency (0), employed in a community mental health/counseling center (5), employed in a hospital/medical center (0), other employment position (0), total from the above (master's) (16).

Doctoral Degree Graduates: Of those who graduated in the academic year 2006–2007, the following categories and numbers represent the postgraduate activities and employment of doctoral degree graduates: Enrolled in a psychology doctoral program (n/a), total from the above (doctoral) (0).

Additional Information:

Orientation, Objectives, and Emphasis of Department: We are housed in the School of Education and our primary mission is to train school counselors; however, many of our graduates find employment in social service settings.

Application Information:

Send to Office of Admission. Application available online. URL of online application: http://www.ups.edu/x482.xml. Students are admitted in the Spring, application deadline March 1. *Fee:* $65; $25 if previously admitted to University.

Seattle Pacific University

Clinical Psychology Department
School of Psychology, Family and Community
3307 Third Avenue, West
Seattle, WA 98119
Telephone: (206) 281-2916
Fax: (206) 281-2695
E-mail: *skidmore@spu.edu*
Web: *http://www.spu.edu/depts/spfc/clinicalpsych*

Department Information:

1995. Chairperson: Jay R. Skidmore, PhD. Number of faculty: total—full-time 6, part-time 6; women—full-time 3, part-time 4; total—minority—full-time 1, part-time 1.

Programs and Degrees Offered:

Listed in the following order: Program area, degree type (T if terminal Master's), number awarded 7/06–6/07. Clinical Psychology PhD (Doctor of Philosophy) 15.

APA Accreditation: Clinical PhD (Doctor of Philosophy).

Student Applications/Admissions:

Student Applications

Clinical Psychology PhD (Doctor of Philosophy)—Applications 2007–2008, 110. Total applicants accepted 2007–2008, 16. Number full-time enrolled (new admits only) 2007–2008, 14. Number part-time enrolled (new admits only) 2007–2008, 0. Total enrolled 2007–2008 full-time, 70, part-time, 20. Openings 2008–2009, 15. The median number of years required for completion of a degree in 2006–2007 were 6. The number of students enrolled full- and part-time who were dismissed or voluntarily withdrew from this program area in 2007–2008 were 1.

Admissions Requirements:

Scores: Entries appear in this order: required test or GPA, minimum score (if required), median score of students entering in 2007–2008. Doctoral Programs: GRE-V no minimum stated, 630; GRE-Q no minimum stated, 620; overall undergraduate GPA 3.00, 3.70.

Other Criteria: (importance of criteria rated low, medium, or high): GRE/MAT scores—high, research experience—medium, work experience—low, extracurricular activity—low, clinically related public service—medium, GPA—high, letters of recommendation—high, interview—high, statement of goals and objectives—high, match with program—high. For additional information on admission requirements, go to http://www.spu.edu/depts/pfc/clinicalpsych/.

Student Characteristics: The following represents characteristics of students in 2007–2008 in all graduate psychology programs in the department: Female—full-time 60, part-time 16; Male—full-time 10, part-time 4; African American/Black—full-time 2, part-time 1; Hispanic/Latino(a)—full-time 4, part-time 1; Asian/Pacific Islander—full-time 3, part-time 1; American Indian/Alaska Native—full-time 1, part-time 1; Caucasian/White—full-time 60, part-time 16; Multi-ethnic—full-time 0, part-time 0; students subject to the Americans With Disabilities Act—full-time 0, part-time 0; Unknown ethnicity—full-time 0, part-time 0.

Financial Information/Assistance:

Tuition for Full-Time Study: *Doctoral:* State residents: $611 per credit hour; Nonstate residents: $611 per credit hour. Tuition is subject to change.

Financial Assistance:

First-Year Students: No information provided.

Advanced Students: Teaching assistantships available for advanced students. Average amount paid per academic year: $8,000. Average number of hours worked per week: 15. Research assistantships available for advanced students. Average amount paid per academic year: $4,000. Average number of hours worked per week: 8. Fellowships and scholarships available for advanced students. Average amount paid per academic year: $8,000. Average number of hours worked per week: 15.

Additional Information: Of all students currently enrolled full time, 20% benefited from one or more of the listed financial assistance programs.

Internships/Practica: Doctoral Degree (PhD Clinical psychology): For those doctoral students for whom a professional internship was required in this program prior to graduation, (16) students applied for an internship in 2006–2007, with (13) students obtaining an internship. Of those students who obtained an internship, (13) were paid internships. Of those students who obtained an internship, (9) students placed in APA/CPA-accredited internships, (3) students placed in internships not APA/CPA accredited, but listed with the Association of Psychology Postdoctoral and Internship Centers (APPIC), (0) students placed in internships conforming to guidelines of the Council of Directors of School Psychology Programs (CDSPP), (1) student placed in internships that were not APA/CPA-accredited, APPIC or CDSPP listed. Clinical training requirements include two 1-year practicum placements during the 3rd and 4th years of the program (part-time, averaging 16 hours per week, resulting in average total practicum experience of approximately 1,200 hours), as well as a full-time 1-year (2,000 hours) clinical psychology internship during the 5th year of the PhD program. Practicum placements are external to the university in a variety of mental health centers, hospitals, medical and dental clinics, and rehabilitation facilities in the greater Puget Sound area. Students apply for their internship in the APPIC Match and each year most obtain placements at competitive mental health and medical centers around the country. Theoretical models and orientations among the faculty include cognitive behavioral, psychodynamic, interpersonal, family systems, and humanistic approaches. Faculty tend to integrate more than one perspective in theories, teaching, and professional practices. We incorporate and contribute to evidence-based research, and expect our students to utilize clinical science as well as theory in their clinical work.

Housing and Day Care: No on-campus housing is available. On-campus day care facilities are available at First Free Methodist Church, across the street from SPU campus.

Employment of Department Graduates:

Master's Degree Graduates: Of those who graduated in the academic year 2006–2007, the following categories and numbers represent the postgraduate activities and employment of master's degree graduates: Enrolled in a postdoctoral residency/fellowship (n/a), employed in independent practice (n/a), total from the above (master's) (0).

Doctoral Degree Graduates: Of those who graduated in the academic year 2006–2007, the following categories and numbers represent the postgraduate activities and employment of doctoral degree graduates: Enrolled in a psychology doctoral program (n/a), enrolled in a postdoctoral residency/fellowship (3), employed in independent practice (4), employed in an academic position at a university (1), employed in an academic position at a 2-year/4-year college (1), employed in other positions at a higher education institution (1), employed in a community mental health/counseling center (2), employed in a hospital/medical center (1), do not know (2), total from the above (doctoral) (15).

Additional Information:

Orientation, Objectives, and Emphasis of Department: The Clinical Psychology PhD program at SPU is designed to provide training in professional psychology in accordance with the Local Clinical Scientist (LCS) model of doctoral education, described in the article, "The Local Clinical Scientist: A Bridge Between Science and Practice," published in *American Psychologist* (Stricker & Trierweiler, 1995). The Local Clinical Scientist extends the scientific and professional ideals in the original Boulder scientist–practitioner (BSP) model of clinical psychology (Raimy, 1950). At the same time, we try to encompass broader concepts of science and more explicitly integrate the art of clinical practice. We also endorse the core competencies outlined by the National Council of Schools and Programs of Professional Psychology (NCSPP), and are committed to helping students achieve mastery of the core competencies of clinical skills. Our doctoral program typically requires 4 years of graduate coursework, during which clinical practicum training as well as dissertation research are also completed, followed by a 1-year full-time internship (elsewhere) in the fifth year. We are an an APA-accredited program in Clinical Psychology, and also a "designated doctoral program" with ASPPB/NR, which verifies our curriculum meets the educational requirements for licensing psychologists in the United States.

Personal Behavior Statement: Refer to the student application.

Special Facilities or Resources: The school maintains a fully-equipped suite of psychology research laboratories, including a psychophysiological lab, child developmental lab, and social psychology lab. The University's newly opened Science Building has wet labs, animal learning facilities, and a psychophysiological demonstration classroom. The department is housed in Marston Hall, which was completely renovated for us in 2001. The University Library is a four-story structure with conference rooms, private study rooms and group meeting rooms. The library contains approximately 10,000 volumes relevant to the field of psychology, including books, media, a test file, and over 500 journals available either in paper, microfilm, or full-text online. In addition to traditional interlibrary loan services, Seattle Pacific University is a member of the Orbis Cascade Alliance, a consortium of 26 public and private academic libraries in Washington and Oregon, which provides access to a combined collection of over 22 million volumes of books and other materials. Students have access to several computer labs on campus, which have SPSS installed. Student are given an SPU e-mail account and have 24/7 access to our online Blackboard where program forms, syllabi, schedules, and so forth are posted for students to download.

Information for Students With Physical Disabilities: See the following Web site for more information: http://www.spu.edu/depts/cfl/dss/index.asp.

Application Information:

Send to Graduate Center, Seattle Pacific University. Application available online. URL of online application: https://www.app.applyyourself.com/?id=spu-grad. Students are admitted in the Fall, application deadline December 15. *Fee:* $75.

Seattle University

Graduate Psychology Program
Arts and Sciences
901 12th Avenue, P.O. Box 222000
Seattle, WA 98122-1090
Telephone: (206) 296-5400
Fax: (206) 296-2141
E-mail: *eppsych@seattleu.edu*
Web: *http://www.seattleu.edu/artsci/gradpsy/*

Department Information:

1981. Director, Graduate Program: Kevin Krycka, PsyD. Number of faculty: total—full-time 4, part-time 5; women—full-time 1, part-time 2.

Programs and Degrees Offered:

Listed in the following order: Program area, degree type (T if terminal Master's), number awarded 7/06–6/07. Existential Phenomenological MA/MS (Master of Arts/Science) (T) 18.

Student Applications/Admissions:

Student Applications

Existential Phenomenological MA/MS (Master of Arts/Science)—Applications 2007–2008, 55. Total applicants accepted 2007–2008, 20. Number full-time enrolled (new admits only) 2007–2008, 13. Number part-time enrolled (new admits only) 2007–2008, 1. Total enrolled 2007–2008 full-time, 31, part-time, 5. Openings 2008–2009, 20. The median number of years required for completion of a degree in 2006–2007 were 2. The number of students enrolled full- and part-time who were dismissed or voluntarily withdrew from this program area in 2007–2008 were 0.

Admissions Requirements:

Scores: Entries appear in this order: required test or GPA, minimum score (if required), median score of students entering in 2007–2008. Master's Programs: overall undergraduate GPA 3.00. Overall Undergraduate GPA 3.0

Other Criteria: (importance of criteria rated low, medium, or high): research experience—medium, work experience—medium, extracurricular activity—medium, clinically related public service—high, GPA—medium, letters of recommendation—medium, interview—high, Bio/writing sample—high, undergraduate major in psychology—low, specific undergraduate psychology courses taken—medium. Other: Some awareness of existential phenomenological perspective in psychology and philoosophy. For additional information on admission requirements, go to http://www.seattleu.edu/artsci/gradpsy/.

Student Characteristics: The following represents characteristics of students in 2007–2008 in all graduate psychology programs in the department: Female—full-time 18, part-time 2; Male—full-time 13, part-time 3; African American/Black—full-time 0, part-time 1; Hispanic/Latino(a)—full-time 4, part-time 1; Asian/Pacific Islander—full-time 1, part-time 0; American Indian/Alaska Native—full-time 0, part-time 0; Caucasian/White—full-time 25, part-time 3; Multi-ethnic—full-time 1, part-time 0; students subject to the Americans With Disabilities Act—full-time 0, part-time 0; Unknown ethnicity—full-time 31, part-time 5; International students who hold an F-1 or J-1 Visa—full-time 0, part-time 0.

Financial Information/Assistance:

Tuition for Full-Time Study: *Master's:* State residents: per academic year $14,580, $540 per credit hour; Nonstate residents: per academic year $14,580, $540 per credit hour. Tuition is subject to change. See the following Web site for updates and changes in tuition costs: http://www.seattleu.edu/sfs/.

Financial Assistance:

First-Year Students: No information provided.

Advanced Students: No information provided.

Additional Information: Of all students currently enrolled full time, 12% benefited from one or more of the listed financial assistance programs.

Internships/Practica: Master's Degree (MA/MS Existential Phenomenological): An internship experience, such as, a final research project or "capstone" experience is required of graduates. A variety of supervised internships (typically about 20 hours per week during 2nd year) in a wide variety of community agencies, hospitals, shelters, and clinics.

Housing and Day Care: On-campus housing is available. See the following Web site for more information: http://www.seattleu.edu/housing; Seattle University, P.O. Box 222000, Seattle, Washington 98122-1090 attention Housing and Residential Life. No on-campus day care facilities are available.

Employment of Department Graduates:

Master's Degree Graduates: Of those who graduated in the academic year 2006–2007, the following categories and numbers represent the postgraduate activities and employment of master's degree graduates: Enrolled in a psychology doctoral program (1), enrolled in another graduate/professional program (1), enrolled in a postdoctoral residency/fellowship (n/a), employed in independent practice (n/a), employed in an academic position at a university (0), employed in an academic position at a 2-year/4-year college (0), employed in other positions at a higher education institution (0), employed in a professional position in a school system (1), employed in business or industry (0), employed in government agency (0), employed in a community mental health/counseling center (11), employed in a hospital/medical center (0), still seeking employment (1), other employment position (4), total from the above (master's) (19).

Doctoral Degree Graduates: Of those who graduated in the academic year 2006–2007, the following categories and numbers represent the postgraduate activities and employment of doctoral degree graduates: Enrolled in a psychology doctoral program (n/a), total from the above (doctoral) (0).

Additional Information:

Orientation, Objectives, and Emphasis of Department: With an emphasis on existential phenomenological psychology, this master's degree is designed to offer an interdisciplinary program focusing on the qualitative, experiential study of psychological events in the context of the person's life. By laying the foundations for a therapeutic attitude, the program prepares students for entrance into the helping professions or for further study of the psychological world. It is humanistic in that it intends to deepen the appreciation for the human condition by rigorous reflection on immediate psychological experiences and on the wisdom accumulated by the long tradition of the humanities. It is phenomenological in that it develops an attitude of openness and wonder toward psychological reality without holding theoretical prejudgments. It is therapeutic in that it focuses on the psychological conditions that help people deal with the difficulties of life.

Special Facilities or Resources: The program has a tradition of involving selected students in qualitative research projects.

Application Information:

Send to Graduate Admissions Office, Seattle University, P.O. Box 222000, Seattle, WA 98122-1090; some material goes to Graduate Psychology, Seattle University, P.O. Box 222000, Seattle, WA 98122-1090. Application available online. URL of online application: http://www.seattleu.edu/home/prospective_students/graduate_students/how_to_apply/. Students are admitted in the Fall, application deadline January 25. *Fee:* $55.

Walla Walla University
School of Education and Psychology
204 South College Avenue
College Place, WA 99324
Telephone: (509) 527-2211, (800) 541-8900
Fax: (509) 527-2248
E-mail: *lee.stough@wallawalla.edu*
Web: *http://www.wallawalla.edu/counseling*

Department Information:

1965. Dean: Julian Melgosa. Number of faculty: total—full-time 5; women—full-time 2; total—minority—full-time 1.

Programs and Degrees Offered:

Listed in the following order: Program area, degree type (T if terminal Master's), number awarded 7/06–6/07. Counseling Psychology MA/MS (Master of Arts/Science) (T) 4.

Student Applications/Admissions:

Student Applications

Counseling Psychology MA/MS (Master of Arts/Science)—Applications 2007–2008, 19. Total applicants accepted 2007–2008, 15. Number full-time enrolled (new admits only) 2007–2008, 12. Total enrolled 2007–2008 full-time, 16, part-time, 1. Openings 2008–2009, 12. The median number of years required for completion of a degree in 2006–2007 were 2. The number of students enrolled full- and part-time who were dismissed or voluntarily withdrew from this program area in 2007–2008 were 1.

Admissions Requirements:

Scores: Entries appear in this order: required test or GPA, minimum score (if required), median score of students entering in 2007–2008. Master's Programs: GRE-V no minimum stated, 470; GRE-Q no minimum stated, 550; overall undergraduate GPA 2.75, 3.27; Master's GRE-Analytical no minimum stated, 4.5.

Other Criteria: (importance of criteria rated low, medium, or high): GRE/MAT scores—medium, research experience—low, work experience—medium, extracurricular activity—low, clinically related public service—medium, GPA—high, letters of recommendation—high, interview—high, statement of goals and objectives—high, undergraduate major in psychology—medium.

Student Characteristics: The following represents characteristics of students in 2007–2008 in all graduate psychology programs in the department: Female—full-time 11, part-time 1; Male—full-time 5, part-time 0; Hispanic/Latino(a)—full-time 1, part-time 0; Asian/Pacific Islander—full-time 1, part-time 0; Caucasian/White—full-time 14, part-time 1; Unknown ethnicity—full-time 0, part-time 0.

Financial Information/Assistance:

Tuition for Full-Time Study: *Master's:* State residents: $492 per credit hour; Nonstate residents: $492 per credit hour. Tuition is subject to change.

Financial Assistance:

First-Year Students: Fellowships and scholarships available for first year. Average amount paid per academic year: $2,340. Average number of hours worked per week: 0.

Advanced Students: Fellowships and scholarships available for advanced students. Average amount paid per academic year: $2,340. Average number of hours worked per week: 0.

Additional Information: Of all students currently enrolled full time, 100% benefited from one or more of the listed financial assistance programs. Application and information available online at http://www.wallawalla.edu/student-financial-services.html.

Internships/Practica: Master's Degree (MA/MS Counseling Psychology): An internship experience such as a final research project or "capstone" experience is required of graduates. The School of Education and Psychology operates a free counseling center for the community on site. The counseling center comprises four private counseling rooms and a group room that are equipped with one-way mirrors and videocameras. During the 2nd year of their program, students begin working in the center and have the opportunity to develop their clinical skills counseling individuals, couples, and families presenting with a variety of concerns. Program faculty provide individual and group supervision in either live or videotaped formats on a regular basis. After successfully completing the supervised practica, students complete a 400–600 hour internship at an approved site in the community. The School has developed relationships with various agencies where students will receive quality internship experiences that fit their interests.

Housing and Day Care: On-campus housing is available. Contact Student Administration, Walla Walla University, 204 South College Avenue, College Place, WA 99324. On-campus day care facilities are available. Contact Child Development Center, Walla Walla University, 204 South College Avenue, College Place, WA 99324.

Employment of Department Graduates:

Master's Degree Graduates: Of those who graduated in the academic year 2006–2007, the following categories and numbers represent the postgraduate activities and employment of master's degree graduates: Enrolled in a psychology doctoral program (1), enrolled in a postdoctoral residency/fellowship (n/a), employed in independent practice (n/a), employed in a community mental health/counseling center (2), other employment position (1), total from the above (master's) (4).

Doctoral Degree Graduates: Of those who graduated in the academic year 2006–2007, the following categories and numbers represent the postgraduate activities and employment of doctoral degree graduates: Enrolled in a psychology doctoral program (n/a), total from the above (doctoral) (0).

Additional Information:

Orientation, Objectives, and Emphasis of Department: The School of Education and Psychology offers thesis and nonthesis Master of Arts degrees in Counseling Psychology. Our program is designed to promote clinical, theoretical, academic, and personal growth through study, supervision, and service. Students are expected to attain a broad range of competence in the core areas in counseling psychology including human development and learning, individual and group counseling, career development, assessment, ethics, research, and statistics. Faculty present an integrative approach to treatment that focuses on the core principles, core processes, and a variety of strategies for working with emotion, cognition, and interpersonal and systemic factors. Students acquire a range of clinical skills they can use in working with diverse clients and learn to apply theory to practice through supervised practica and internship experiences. In a supportive, yet challenging environment, students are encouraged to build upon life experiences and personal strengths, and take advantage of the opportunities to expand their awareness of self and others. If students desire, faculty assist them in the development and application of a philosophy of Christian service. All graduates are prepared to take the National Counselor's Exam and to become licensed Mental Health Counselors, or to continue their training in doctoral programs.

Special Facilities or Resources: The School of Education and Psychology operates a free counseling center for the community where ongoing outcome research is being conducted. An enriched preschool program for children ages 3–5 is located in the on-site child development center.

Application Information:
Send to Graduate Studies, Walla Walla University, 204 South College Avenue, College Place, WA 99324. Application available online. URL of online application: http://www.wallawalla.edu/academics/graduate/checklist.html. Students are admitted in the Fall. *Fee:* $50.

Washington State University

Department of Psychology
Liberal Arts
P.O. Box 644820
Pullman, WA 99164-4820
Telephone: (509) 335-2631
Fax: (509) 335-5043
E-mail: *psych@wsu.edu*
Web: *http://www.wsu.edu/psychology*

Department Information:
1946. Chairperson: John Hinson. Number of faculty: total—full-time 17, part-time 1; women—full-time 7, part-time 1; total—minority—full-time 2; women minority—full-time 1.

Programs and Degrees Offered:
Listed in the following order: Program area, degree type (T if terminal Master's), number awarded 7/06–6/07. Clinical PhD (Doctor of Philosophy) 6, Experimental PhD (Doctor of Philosophy) 2.

APA Accreditation: Clinical PhD (Doctor of Philosophy).

Student Applications/Admissions:
Student Applications
Clinical PhD (Doctor of Philosophy)—Applications 2007–2008, 180. Total applicants accepted 2007–2008, 6. Number full-time enrolled (new admits only) 2007–2008, 6. Number part-time enrolled (new admits only) 2007–2008, 0. Openings 2008–2009, 6. The median number of years required for completion of a degree in 2006–2007 were 6. The number of students enrolled full- and part-time who were dismissed or voluntarily withdrew from this program area in 2007–2008 were 0. *Experimental PhD (Doctor of Philosophy)*—Applications 2007–2008, 48. Total applicants accepted 2007–2008, 5. Number full-time enrolled (new admits only) 2007–2008, 5. Number part-time enrolled (new admits only) 2007–2008, 0. Openings 2008–2009, 6. The median number of years required for completion of a degree in 2006–2007 were 5. The number of students enrolled full- and part-time who were dismissed or voluntarily withdrew from this program area in 2007–2008 were 0.

Admissions Requirements:
Scores: Entries appear in this order: required test or GPA, minimum score (if required), median score of students entering in 2007–2008. Doctoral Programs: GRE-V no minimum stated, 625; GRE-Q no minimum stated, 645; overall undergraduate GPA no minimum stated, 3.6; psychology GPA no minimum stated, 3.7.
Other Criteria: (importance of criteria rated low, medium, or high): GRE/MAT scores—high, research experience—high, work experience—medium, extracurricular activity—low, clinically related public service—high, GPA—high, letters of recommendation—high, interview—high, statement of goals and objectives—high. Applicants to the Experimental Psychology program are not expected to demonstrate any clinically related public service. Applicants to the Experimental Psychology program are not required to have an interview, but a visit is encouraged.

Student Characteristics: The following represents characteristics of students in 2007–2008 in all graduate psychology programs in the department: Female—full-time 36, part-time 0; Male—full-time 15, part-time 0; African American/Black—full-time 2, part-time 0; Hispanic/Latino(a)—full-time 5, part-time 0; Asian/Pacific Islander—full-time 3, part-time 0; American Indian/Alaska Native—full-time 0, part-time 0; Caucasian/White—full-time 41, part-time 0; Multi-ethnic—full-time 0, part-time 0; students subject to the Americans With Disabilities Act—full-time 0, part-time 0; Unknown ethnicity—full-time 0, part-time 0; International students who hold an F-1 or J-1 Visa—full-time 6, part-time 0.

Financial Information/Assistance:
Tuition for Full-Time Study: *Doctoral:* State residents: per academic year $7,550, $354 per credit hour; Nonstate residents: per academic year $18,398, $896 per credit hour. Tuition is subject to change. See the following Web site for updates and changes in tuition costs: http://www.gradsch.wsu.edu/finances.html.

Financial Assistance:
First-Year Students: Teaching assistantships available for first year. Average amount paid per academic year: $12,371. Average number of hours worked per week: 20. Apply by December 31. Tuition remission given: full.
Advanced Students: Teaching assistantships available for advanced students. Average amount paid per academic year: $13,126. Average number of hours worked per week: 20. Apply by December 31. Tuition remission given: full.
Additional Information: Of all students currently enrolled full time, 95% benefited from one or more of the listed financial assistance programs.

Internships/Practica: Doctoral Degree (PhD Clinical): For those doctoral students for whom a professional internship was required in this program prior to graduation, (5) students applied for an internship in 2006–2007, with (4) students obtaining an internship. Of those students who obtained an internship, (4) were paid internships. Of those students who obtained an internship, (4) students placed in APA/CPA-accredited internships, (0) students placed in internships not APA/CPA-accredited, but listed with the Association of Psychology Postdoctoral and Internship Centers (APPIC), (0) students placed in internships conforming to guidelines of the Council of Directors of School Psychology Programs (CDSPP), (0) students placed in internships that were not APA/CPA-accredited, APPIC or CDSPP listed. Psychology Clinic Practicum, Counseling Services Practicum, and Medical Psychology Practicum at University Hospital.

Housing and Day Care: On-campus housing is available. See the following Web site for more information: http://www.livingat.wsu.edu/hdrl/FutureStudents/FS_Main.htm. On-campus day care facilities are available. See the following Web site for more information: http://www.gradsch.wsu.edu/future-students.

Employment of Department Graduates:

Master's Degree Graduates: Of those who graduated in the academic year 2006–2007, the following categories and numbers represent the postgraduate activities and employment of master's degree graduates: Enrolled in a postdoctoral residency/fellowship (n/a), employed in independent practice (n/a), total from the above (master's) (0).

Doctoral Degree Graduates: Of those who graduated in the academic year 2006–2007, the following categories and numbers represent the postgraduate activities and employment of doctoral degree graduates: Enrolled in a psychology doctoral program (n/a), enrolled in a postdoctoral residency/fellowship (4), employed in independent practice (0), employed in an academic position at a university (0), employed in an academic position at a 2-year/4-year college (0), employed in business or industry (1), employed in government agency (2), employed in a community mental health/counseling center (0), not seeking employment (1), total from the above (doctoral) (8).

Additional Information:

Orientation, Objectives, and Emphasis of Department: The objectives of the graduate programs are to prepare individuals to make contributions and hold leadership positions in basic and applied research, teaching, clinical psychology, public service, or some combination of these areas. The Clinical program is a broad, general one requiring student commitment to both research and clinical work. The emphases within the Experimental program are cognitive, behavior analysis, physiological psychology, social, and visual perception.

Special Facilities or Resources: The Department of Psychology is located in Johnson Tower, near the center of campus. Fully equipped laboratories and shop facilities are available for research in social behavior, cognition, perception, human and animal learning, the experimental and applied analysis of behavior, and physiological and sensory psychology. The Psychology Clinic is operated as a training facility within the department.

Information for Students With Physical Disabilities: See the following Web site for more information: http://www.drc.wsu.edu.

Application Information:

Send to WSU Graduate School and the Psychology Department at the following address: Graduate Admissions, Attn: Chair, Graduate Admissions Committee, Psychology Department, Washington State University, P.O. Box 644820, Pullman, WA 99164-4820. Application available online. URL of online application: http://www.gradsch.wsu.edu. Students are admitted in the Fall, application deadline December 31. *Fee:* $50.

Washington State University

Educational Leadership and Counseling Psychology Education
P.O. Box 642136
Pullman, WA 99164-2136
Telephone: (509) 335-7016
Fax: (509) 335-2097
E-mail: *gradstudies@wsu.edu*
Web: *http://www.education.wsu.edu/graduate/specializations/counselingpsych*

Department Information:

Chairperson: Dr. Phyllis Erdman. Number of faculty: total—full-time 9; women—full-time 5; total—minority—full-time 3; women minority—full-time 2.

Programs and Degrees Offered:

Listed in the following order: Program area, degree type (T if terminal Master's), number awarded 7/06–6/07. Counseling Psychology PhD (Doctor of Philosophy) 7, Educational Psychology PhD (Doctor of Philosophy) 2, MA or EdM With a Specialization in Counseling Other 12, MA or EdM Educational Psychology Other 0.

APA Accreditation: Counseling PhD (Doctor of Philosophy).

Student Applications/Admissions:

Student Applications

Counseling Psychology PhD (Doctor of Philosophy)—Applications 2007–2008, 57. Total applicants accepted 2007–2008, 13. Number full-time enrolled (new admits only) 2007–2008, 6. Total enrolled 2007–2008 full-time, 31, part-time, 8. Openings 2008–2009, 7. The median number of years required for completion of a degree in 2006–2007 were 6. The number of students enrolled full- and part-time who were dismissed or voluntarily withdrew from this program area in 2007–2008 were 0. *Educational Psychology PhD (Doctor of Philosophy)*—Applications 2007–2008, 4. Total applicants accepted 2007–2008, 3. Number full-time enrolled (new admits only) 2007–2008, 1. Number part-time enrolled (new admits only) 2007–2008, 0. Openings 2008–2009, 4. The median number of years required for completion of a degree in 2006–2007 were 4. The number of students enrolled full- and part-time who were dismissed or voluntarily withdrew from this program area in 2007–2008 were 0. *MA or EdM With a Specialization in Counseling Other*—Applications 2007–2008, 39. Total applicants accepted 2007–2008, 31. Number full-time enrolled (new admits only) 2007–2008, 13. Number part-time enrolled (new admits only) 2007–2008, 10. Total enrolled 2007–2008 full-time, 21, part-time, 23. Openings 2008–2009, 25. The median number of years required for completion of a degree in 2006–2007 were 2. The number of students enrolled full- and part-time who were dismissed or voluntarily withdrew from this program area in 2007–2008 were 0. *MA or EdM Educational Psychology Other*—Applications 2007–2008, 5. Total applicants accepted 2007–2008, 2. Number full-time enrolled (new admits only) 2007–2008, 1. Number part-time enrolled (new admits only) 2007–2008, 0. Openings 2008–2009, 3. The median number of years required for completion of a degree in 2006–2007 were 2. The number of students enrolled full- and part-time who were dismissed or voluntarily withdrew from this program area in 2007–2008 were 0.

Admissions Requirements:

Scores: Entries appear in this order: required test or GPA, minimum score (if required), median score of students entering in 2007–2008. Master's Programs: GRE-V no minimum stated; GRE-Q no minimum stated; overall undergraduate GPA no minimum stated; last 2 years GPA no minimum stated. Doctoral Programs: GRE-V no minimum stated; GRE-Q no minimum stated; overall undergraduate GPA no minimum stated; last 2 years GPA no minimum stated.

Other Criteria: (importance of criteria rated low, medium, or high): GRE/MAT scores—medium, research experience—medium, work experience—medium, extracurricular activity—low, GPA—high, letters of recommendation—medium, statement of goals and objectives—high. These criteria do differ for different program areas. Program review criteria include previous academic record (GPA); GRE scores, which are required by the program; appropriateness of interests and goals for the program; previous counseling, research, volunteer work, or other experience relevant to the program; and current letters of recommendation. No single factor is weighted so heavily as to preculde admission to the program. For additional information on admission requirements, go to http://education.wsu.edu/graduate/specializations/counselingpsych.

Student Characteristics: The following represents characteristics of students in 2007–2008 in all graduate psychology programs in the department: Female—full-time 49, part-time 26; Male—full-time 10, part-time 5; African American/Black—full-time 3, part-time 2; Hispanic/Latino(a)—full-time 12, part-time 2; Asian/Pacific Islander—full-time 8, part-time 1; American Indian/Alaska Native—full-time 1, part-time 2; Caucasian/White—full-time 25, part-time 21; Multi-ethnic—full-time 0, part-time 0; students subject to the Americans With Disabilities Act—full-time 1, part-time 0; Unknown ethnicity—full-time 10, part-time 3; International students who hold an F-1 or J-1 Visa—full-time 8, part-time 1.

Financial Information/Assistance:

Tuition for Full-Time Study: *Master's:* State residents: per academic year $7,550, $378 per credit hour; Nonstate residents: per academic year $18,398, $920 per credit hour. *Doctoral:* State residents: per academic year $7,550, $378 per credit hour; Nonstate residents: per academic year $18,398, $920 per credit hour. See the following Web site for updates and changes in tuition costs: http://www.wsu.edu/studacct/tutionFees.htm.

Financial Assistance:

First-Year Students: Teaching assistantships available for first year. Average amount paid per academic year: $12,370. Average number of hours worked per week: 20. Tuition remission given: full. Research assistantships available for first year. Average amount paid per academic year: $12,370. Average number of hours worked per week: 20. Tuition remission given: full. Fellowships and scholarships available for first year.

Advanced Students: Teaching assistantships available for advanced students. Average amount paid per academic year: $13,126. Average number of hours worked per week: 20. Tuition remission given: full. Research assistantships available for advanced students. Average amount paid per academic year: $13,126. Average number of hours worked per week: 20. Tuition remission given: full. Fellowships and scholarships available for advanced students.

Additional Information: Of all students currently enrolled full time, 75% benefited from one or more of the listed financial assistance programs. Application and information available online at http://education.wsu.edu/graduate/specializations/counselingpsych.

Internships/Practica: Doctoral Degree (PhD PhD in Counseling Psychology): For those doctoral students for whom a professional internship was required in this program prior to graduation, (3) students applied for an internship in 2006–2007, with (2) students obtaining an internship. Of those students who obtained an internship, (2) were paid internships. Of those students who obtained an internship, (2)students placed in APA/CPA-accredited internships, (0) students placed in internships not APA/CPA-accredited, but listed with the Association of Psychology Postdoctoral and Internship Centers (APPIC), (0) students placed in internships conforming to guidelines of the Council of Directors of School Psychology Programs (CDSPP), (0) students placed in internships that were not APA/CPA-accredited, APPIC or CDSPP listed. See Web sites http://education.wsu.edu/graduate/specializations/counselingpsych or http://education.wsu.edu/graduate/specializations/edpsychology.

Housing and Day Care: On-campus housing is available. See the following Web site for more information: http://www.wsu.edu/future-students/housing/index.html. On-campus day care facilities are available. See the following Web site for more information: http://www.childrenscenter.wsu.edu.

Employment of Department Graduates:

Master's Degree Graduates: Of those who graduated in the academic year 2006–2007, the following categories and numbers represent the postgraduate activities and employment of master's degree graduates: Enrolled in a psychology doctoral program (0), enrolled in another graduate/professional program (1), enrolled in a postdoctoral residency/fellowship (n/a), employed in independent practice (n/a), employed in an academic position at a university (0), employed in an academic position at a 2-year/4-year college (0), employed in other positions at a higher education institution (0), employed in a professional position in a school system (2), employed in business or industry (1), employed in government agency (0), employed in a community mental health/counseling center (2), employed in a hospital/medical center (0), still seeking employment (0), not seeking employment (0), other employment position (0), do not know (3), total from the above (master's) (9).

Doctoral Degree Graduates: Of those who graduated in the academic year 2006–2007, the following categories and numbers represent the postgraduate activities and employment of doctoral degree graduates: Enrolled in a psychology doctoral program (n/a),

enrolled in a postdoctoral residency/fellowship (3), employed in independent practice (0), employed in an academic position at a university (1), employed in an academic position at a 2-year/4-year college (0), employed in other positions at a higher education institution (2), employed in a professional position in a school system (0), employed in business or industry (1), employed in government agency (0), employed in a community mental health/counseling center (0), employed in a hospital/medical center (0), still seeking employment (0), not seeking employment (0), other employment position (0), do not know (1), total from the above (doctoral) (8).

Additional Information:

Orientation, Objectives, and Emphasis of Department: http://education.wsu.edu/graduate/specializations/counselingpsych or http://education.wsu.edu/graduate/specializations/edpsychology.

Special Facilities or Resources: See Web sites http://education.wsu.edu/graduate/specializations/counselingpsych or http://education.wsu.edu/graduate/specializations/edpsychology.

Information for Students With Physical Disabilities: See the following Web site for more information: http://www.drc.wsu.edu/.

Application Information:

Send to College of Education, Office of Graduate Studies, 252 Cleveland Hall, P.O. Box 642114, Pullman, WA 99164-2114. Students are admitted in the Fall, application deadline January 10. Applicants must also apply to the WSU graduate school. *Fee:* $50.

Washington, University of

Department of Psychology
Arts and Sciences
Box 351525
Seattle, WA 98195-1525
Telephone: (206) 543-8687
Fax: (206) 685-3157
E-mail: *sbuck@u.washington.edu*
Web: *http://www.web.psych.washington.edu/*

Department Information:

1917. Chairperson: Steven L. Buck, PhD. Number of faculty: total—full-time 45, part-time 5; women—full-time 17, part-time 4; total—minority—full-time 11; women minority—full-time 4.

Programs and Degrees Offered:

Listed in the following order: Program area, degree type (T if terminal Master's), number awarded 7/06–6/07. Animal Behavior PhD (Doctor of Philosophy) 0, Clinical PhD (Doctor of Philosophy) 2, Child Clinical PhD (Doctor of Philosophy) 4, Cognition and Perception PhD (Doctor of Philosophy) 3, Developmental PhD (Doctor of Philosophy) 4, Behavioral Neuroscience PhD (Doctor of Philosophy) 2, Social and Personality PhD (Doctor of Philosophy) 0.

APA Accreditation: Clinical PhD (Doctor of Philosophy).

Student Applications/Admissions:

Student Applications

Animal Behavior PhD (Doctor of Philosophy)—Applications 2007–2008, 36. Total applicants accepted 2007–2008, 1. Number full-time enrolled (new admits only) 2007–2008, 0. Number part-time enrolled (new admits only) 2007–2008, 0. Total enrolled 2007–2008 full-time, 8, part-time, 2. Openings 2008–2009, 3. The number of students enrolled full- and part-time who were dismissed or voluntarily withdrew from this program area in 2007–2008 were 1. *Clinical PhD (Doctor of Philosophy)*—Applications 2007–2008, 203. Total applicants accepted 2007–2008, 5. Number full-time enrolled (new admits only) 2007–2008, 5. Number part-time enrolled (new admits only) 2007–2008, 0. Total enrolled 2007–2008 full-time, 35, part-time, 4. Openings 2008–2009, 4. The median number of years required for completion of a degree in 2006–2007 were 6. The number of students enrolled full- and part-time who were dismissed or voluntarily withdrew from this program area in 2007–2008 were 0. *Child Clinical PhD (Doctor of Philosophy)*—Applications 2007–2008, 202. Total applicants accepted 2007–2008, 5. Number full-time enrolled (new admits only) 2007–2008, 4. Number part-time enrolled (new admits only) 2007–2008, 0. Total enrolled 2007–2008 full-time, 25, part-time, 7. Openings 2008–2009, 4. The median number of years required for completion of a degree in 2006–2007 were 7. The number of students enrolled full- and part-time who were dismissed or voluntarily withdrew from this program area in 2007–2008 were 1. *Cognition and Perception PhD (Doctor of Philosophy)*—Applications 2007–2008, 40. Total applicants accepted 2007–2008, 3. Number full-time enrolled (new admits only) 2007–2008, 3. Number part-time enrolled (new admits only) 2007–2008, 0. Total enrolled 2007–2008 full-time, 15, part-time, 2. Openings 2008–2009, 8. The median number of years required for completion of a degree in 2006–2007 were 6. The number of students enrolled full- and part-time who were dismissed or voluntarily withdrew from this program area in 2007–2008 were 0. *Developmental PhD (Doctor of Philosophy)*—Applications 2007–2008, 47. Total applicants accepted 2007–2008, 0. Number full-time enrolled (new admits only) 2007–2008, 0. Number part-time enrolled (new admits only) 2007–2008, 0. Total enrolled 2007–2008 full-time, 10, part-time, 3. Openings 2008–2009, 4. The median number of years required for completion of a degree in 2006–2007 were 6. The number of students enrolled full- and part-time who were dismissed or voluntarily withdrew from this program area in 2007–2008 were 1. *Behavioral Neuroscience PhD (Doctor of Philosophy)*—Applications 2007–2008, 30. Total applicants accepted 2007–2008, 3. Number full-time enrolled (new admits only) 2007–2008, 1. Number part-time enrolled (new admits only) 2007–2008, 0. Total enrolled 2007–2008 full-time, 13, part-time, 5. Openings 2008–2009, 3. The median number of years required for completion of a degree in 2006–2007 were 6. The number of students enrolled full- and part-time who were dismissed or voluntarily withdrew from this program area in 2007–2008 were 1. *Social and Personality PhD (Doctor of Philosophy)*—Applications 2007–2008, 83. Total applicants accepted 2007–2008, 6. Number full-time enrolled (new admits only) 2007–2008, 4. Number part-time enrolled (new admits only) 2007–2008, 0. Total enrolled 2007–2008 full-time, 13, part-time, 2. Openings 2008–2009, 3. The number of students enrolled full- and part-time who were dismissed or voluntarily withdrew from this program area in 2007–2008 were 0.

Admissions Requirements:

Scores: Entries appear in this order: required test or GPA, minimum score (if required), median score of students entering in 2007–2008. Master's Programs: Not Applicable Doctoral Programs: GRE-V no minimum stated, 580; GRE-Q no minimum stated, 710; last 2 years GPA no minimum stated, 3.72. Clinical area scores/GPAs are generally higher. Please refer to link for admissions brochure on Web site for figures of most recent admissions: http://web.psych.washington.edu/graduate/apply.html.

Other Criteria: (importance of criteria rated low, medium, or high): GRE/MAT scores—high, research experience—high, work experience—medium, extracurricular activity—low, clinically related public service—low, GPA—medium, letters of recommendation—high, interview—high, statement of goals and objectives—high. Individual areas evaluate applications differently, but all require a strong background in research experience and/or statistics. For additional information on admission requirements, go to http://web.psych.washington.edu/graduate/.

Student Characteristics: The following represents characteristics of students in 2007–2008 in all graduate psychology programs in the department: Female—full-time 85, part-time 18; Male—full-time 34, part-time 7; African American/Black—full-time 5, part-time 1; Hispanic/Latino(a)—full-time 11, part-time 3; Asian/Pacific Islander—full-time 13, part-time 1; American Indian/Alaska Native—full-time 0, part-time 0; Caucasian/White—full-time 88, part-time 19; Multi-ethnic—full-time 2, part-time 1; students subject to the Americans With Disabilities Act—full-time 1, part-time 0; Unknown ethnicity—full-time 0, part-time 0; International students who hold an F-1 or J-1 Visa—full-time 8, part-time 0.

Financial Information/Assistance:

Tuition for Full-Time Study: *Doctoral:* State residents: per academic year $9,417; Nonstate residents: per academic year $21,464. Tuition is subject to change. Additional fees are assessed to students beyond the costs of tuition for the following: The tuition waiver provided for Teaching or Research Assistant appointments cover most fees. See the following Web site for updates and changes in tuition costs: http://www.washington.edu/students/sfs/sao/tuition/ttn_grad1.html.

Financial Assistance:

First-Year Students: Teaching assistantships available for first year. Average amount paid per academic year: $14,904. Average number of hours worked per week: 20. Tuition remission given: full. Research assistantships available for first year. Average amount paid per academic year: $14,904. Average number of hours worked per week: 20. Tuition remission given: full. Traineeships available for first year. Average amount paid per academic year: $14,904. Average number of hours worked per week: 20. Tuition remission given: full.

Advanced Students: Teaching assistantships available for advanced students. Average amount paid per academic year: $16,020. Average number of hours worked per week: 20. Tuition remission given: full. Research assistantships available for advanced students. Average amount paid per academic year: $16,020. Average number of hours worked per week: 20. Tuition remission given: full. Traineeships available for advanced students. Average amount paid per academic year: $16,020. Average number of hours worked per week: 20. Tuition remission given: full.

Additional Information: Of all students currently enrolled full time, 95% benefited from one or more of the listed financial assistance programs. Assistantships and tuition/fee waivers are provided with the offer of admission.

Internships/Practica: Doctoral Degree (PhD Clinical): For those doctoral students for whom a professional internship was required in this program prior to graduation, (3) students applied for an internship in 2006–2007, with (3) students obtaining an internship. Of those students who obtained an internship, (3) were paid internships. Of those students who obtained an internship, (3) students placed in APA/CPA-accredited internships, (0) students placed in internships not APA/CPA-accredited, but listed with the Association of Psychology Postdoctoral and Internship Centers (APPIC), (0) students placed in internships conforming to guidelines of the Council of Directors of School Psychology Programs (CDSPP), (0) students placed in internships that were not APA/CPA-accredited, APPIC or CDSPP listed. Doctoral Degree (PhD Child Clinical): For those doctoral students for whom a professional internship was required in this program prior to graduation, (6) students applied for an internship in 2006–2007, with (6) students obtaining an internship. Of those students who obtained an internship, (6) were paid internships. Of those students who obtained an internship, (6) students placed in APA/CPA-accredited internships, (0) students placed in internships not APA/CPA-accredited, but listed with the Association of Psychology Postdoctoral and Internship Centers (APPIC), (0) students placed in internships conforming to guidelines of the Council of Directors of School Psychology Programs (CDSPP), (0) students placed in internships that were not APA/CPA accredited, APPIC or CDSPP listed. A variety of local and national predoctoral internships are available in clinical psychology.

Housing and Day Care: On-campus housing is available. See the following Web site for more information: http://www.hfs.washington.edu/. On-campus day care facilities are available. See the following Web site for more information: http://www.depts.washington.edu/ovpsl/childcare/.

Employment of Department Graduates:

Master's Degree Graduates: Of those who graduated in the academic year 2006–2007, the following categories and numbers represent the postgraduate activities and employment of master's degree graduates: Enrolled in a postdoctoral residency/fellowship (n/a), employed in independent practice (n/a), total from the above (master's) (0).

Doctoral Degree Graduates: Of those who graduated in the academic year 2006–2007, the following categories and numbers represent the postgraduate activities and employment of doctoral degree graduates: Enrolled in a psychology doctoral program (n/a), enrolled in a postdoctoral residency/fellowship (5), employed in an academic position at a university (3), employed in an academic position at a 2-year/4-year college (1), employed in other positions at a higher education institution (1), employed in a professional position in a school system (1), employed in business or industry (1), do not know (3), total from the above (doctoral) (15).

Additional Information:

Orientation, Objectives, and Emphasis of Department: The program is committed to research-oriented scientific psychology. No degree programs are available in Counseling or Humanistic Psychology. The Clinical program emphasizes both clinical and research competencies and has areas of specialization in child clinical, and subspecialties in behavioral medicine, health psychology, and community psychology. Diversity science and quantitative psychology minors are now available.

Special Facilities or Resources: University and urban settings provide many resources, including the University of Washington Medical Center, UW Autism Center, Addictive Behaviors Research Center, Psychological Services and Training Center, Behavioral Research and Therapy Clinics, Institute for Learning and Brain Sciences, UW Center for Anxiety and Traumatic Stress, Washington National Primate Research Center, Children's Hospital and Regional Medical Center; nearby Veterans Administration facilities, and Sound Mental Health.

Information for Students With Physical Disabilities: See the following Web site for more information: http://www.washington.edu/admin/dso/.

Application Information:

Send to Graduate Selections Committee, Department of Psychology, Box 351525, University of Washington, Seattle, WA 98195-1525. Application available online. URL of online application: http://www.web.psych.washington.edu/graduate/apply.html. Students are admitted in the Fall, application deadline December 15. November 1 for international applicants to UW Graduate School. December 15 for international applicants to Psychology Department. *Fee:* $50. Note that in order to use the online application, you must pay the fee online using a MasterCard or Visa card (both credit and debit cards are accepted), or electronic personal check (for those with U.S. bank accounts). The Fee Waiver Application is only available to U.S. citizens and those holding permanent resident status. These applicants may be qualified to apply for an application fee waiver, based upon their financial profiles.

Washington, University of

Educational Psychology Area in College of Education
312 Miller Hall, Box 353600
Seattle, WA 98195-3600
Telephone: (206) 543-1846 or (206) 543-1139
Fax: (206) 543-8439
E-mail: *abbottr@u.washington.edu*
Web: *http://www.depts.washington.edu/coe/programs/ep/index.html*

Department Information:

1965. Chairperson: Robert D. Abbott. Number of faculty: total—full-time 18, part-time 5; women—full-time 12, part-time 3; total—minority—full-time 2, part-time 2; women minority—full-time 2, part-time 1.

Programs and Degrees Offered:

Listed in the following order: Program area, degree type (T if terminal Master's), number awarded 7/06–6/07. School Psychology EdS/MEd (School Psychology) 8, Cognitive Studies in Education MEd and PhD Other 6, School Psychology PhD (Doctor of Philosophy) 4, Human Development and Cognition PhD (Doctor of Philosophy) 2, Measurement, Statistics, and Research Design PhD (Doctor of Philosophy) 2.

APA Accreditation: School PhD (Doctor of Philosophy).

Student Applications/Admissions:

Student Applications

School Psychology EdS/MEd (School Psychology)—Applications 2007–2008, 65. Total applicants accepted 2007–2008, 18. Number full-time enrolled (new admits only) 2007–2008, 7. Number part-time enrolled (new admits only) 2007–2008, 0. Openings 2008–2009, 12. The median number of years required for completion of a degree in 2006–2007 were 3. The number of students enrolled full- and part-time who were dismissed or voluntarily withdrew from this program area in 2007–2008 were 0. *Cognitive Studies in Education MEd and PhD Other*—Applications 2007–2008, 50. Total applicants accepted 2007–2008, 15. Total enrolled 2007–2008 full-time, 29. Openings 2008–2009, 12. The median number of years required for completion of a degree in 2006–2007 were 6. The number of students enrolled full- and part-time who were dismissed or voluntarily withdrew from this program area in 2007–2008 were 0. *School Psychology PhD (Doctor of Philosophy)*—Applications 2007–2008, 50. Total applicants accepted 2007–2008, 12. Number full-time enrolled (new admits only) 2007–2008, 12. Total enrolled 2007–2008 full-time, 34. Openings 2008–2009, 12. The median number of years required for completion of a degree in 2006–2007 were 6. The number of students enrolled full- and part-time who were dismissed or voluntarily withdrew from this program area in 2007–2008 were 0. *Human Development and Cognition PhD (Doctor of Philosophy)*—Applications 2007–2008, 20. Total applicants accepted 2007–2008, 5. Total enrolled 2007–2008 full-time, 14, part-time, 10. Openings 2008–2009, 8. The median number of years required for completion of a degree in 2006–2007 were 6. The number of students enrolled full- and part-time who were dismissed or voluntarily withdrew from this program area in 2007–2008 were 0. *Measurement, Statistics, and Research Design PhD (Doctor of Philosophy)*—Applications 2007–2008, 12. Total applicants accepted 2007–2008, 4. Number full-time enrolled (new admits only) 2007–2008, 3. Total enrolled 2007–2008 full-time, 7, part-time, 3. Openings 2008–2009, 6. The median number of years required for completion of a degree in 2006–2007 were 5. The number of students enrolled full- and part-time who were dismissed or voluntarily withdrew from this program area in 2007–2008 were 0.

Admissions Requirements:

Scores: Entries appear in this order: required test or GPA, minimum score (if required), median score of students entering in 2007–2008. Master's Programs: GRE-V 500, 530; GRE-Q 500, 600; last 2 years GPA 3.0, 3.6. School Psychology: GRE V+Q=1000, minimum of 500 each in V+Q or 50th %tile which ever is higher. Doctoral Programs: GRE-V 500, 590; GRE-Q 500, 620.

Other Criteria: (importance of criteria rated low, medium, or high): GRE/MAT scores—high, research experience—medium, work experience—high, clinically related public service—medium, GPA—high, letters of recommendation—

high, interview—medium, statement of goals and objectives—high.

Student Characteristics: The following represents characteristics of students in 2007–2008 in all graduate psychology programs in the department: Female—full-time 50, part-time 12; Male—full-time 25, part-time 7; African American/Black—full-time 3, part-time 0; Hispanic/Latino(a)—full-time 3, part-time 0; Asian/Pacific Islander—full-time 10, part-time 0; American Indian/Alaska Native—full-time 0, part-time 0; Caucasian/White—full-time 59, part-time 0; Multi-ethnic—full-time 0, part-time 0; students subject to the Americans With Disabilities Act—full-time 0, part-time 0; Unknown ethnicity—full-time 0, part-time 0; International students who hold an F-1 or J-1 Visa—full-time 5, part-time 0.

Financial Information/Assistance:

Financial Assistance:

First-Year Students: Teaching assistantships available for first year. Average amount paid per academic year: $11,340. Average number of hours worked per week: 20. Apply by April/filled. Tuition remission given: full. Research assistantships available for first year. Average amount paid per academic year: $11,340. Average number of hours worked per week: 20. Apply by open. Tuition remission given: full. Fellowships and scholarships available for first year. Apply by open/Spring. Tuition remission given: full and partial.

Advanced Students: Teaching assistantships available for advanced students. Average amount paid per academic year: $15,000. Average number of hours worked per week: 20. Apply by April/filled. Tuition remission given: full. Research assistantships available for advanced students. Average amount paid per academic year: $15,000. Average number of hours worked per week: 20. Apply by Open. Tuition remission given: full. Traineeships available for advanced students. Average amount paid per academic year: $25,000. Average number of hours worked per week: 40. Apply by Winter. Fellowships and scholarships available for advanced students. Apply by open/Spring. Tuition remission given: full and partial.

Additional Information: Of all students currently enrolled full time, 40% benefited from one or more of the listed financial assistance programs.

Internships/Practica: Doctoral Degree (PhD School Psychology): For those doctoral students for whom a professional internship was required in this program prior to graduation, (5) students applied for an internship in 2006–2007, with (5) students obtaining an internship. Of those students who obtained an internship, (5) were paid internships. Of those students who obtained an internship, (2) students placed in APA/CPA-accredited internships, (0) students placed in internships not APA/CPA accredited, but listed with the Association of Psychology Postdoctoral and Internship Centers (APPIC), (3) students placed in internships conforming to guidelines of the Council of Directors of School Psychology Programs (CDSPP), (0) students placed in internships that were not APA/CPA-accredited, APPIC or CDSPP listed. During the 3rd year, master's students complete a 1,500-hour internship in the public schools, which is often paid.

Housing and Day Care: On-campus housing is available. See the following Web site for more information: http://www.washington.edu/hfs/; http://www.washington.edu/hfs/famhous.html; http://depts.washington.edu/asuwsha/. On-campus day care facilities are available through Childcare Assistance Program for Students. See the following Web site for more information: http://www.washington.edu/students/ovpsa/cc/ and "Resources for Graduate Students" with more information on childcare: http://www.grad.washington.edu/area/area_stud.htm.

Employment of Department Graduates:

Master's Degree Graduates: Of those who graduated in the academic year 2006–2007, the following categories and numbers represent the postgraduate activities and employment of master's degree graduates: Enrolled in a psychology doctoral program (15), enrolled in a postdoctoral residency/fellowship (n/a), employed in independent practice (n/a), employed in a professional position in a school system (10), total from the above (master's) (25).

Doctoral Degree Graduates: Of those who graduated in the academic year 2006–2007, the following categories and numbers represent the postgraduate activities and employment of doctoral degree graduates: Enrolled in a psychology doctoral program (n/a), enrolled in a postdoctoral residency/fellowship (2), employed in an academic position at a university (5), employed in other positions at a higher education institution (1), employed in a professional position in a school system (5); total from the above (doctoral) (13).

Additional Information:

Orientation, Objectives, and Emphasis of Department: The emphasis is on the application of psychology to educational processes. The doctoral programs require extensive research preparation and involvement in research projects during a doctoral student's entire program. The master's degree program in School Psychology leads to national Certification as a School Psychologist (NCSP). The doctoral program in School Psychology also includes internship experience and coursework necessary for licensure as a psychologist.

Special Facilities or Resources: Library and computer facilities are of high quality and accessibility. A well-staffed Clinical Training Laboratory, located in the same building as classrooms and faculty offices, provides psychological services supervised by program faculty to infants, toddlers, school-aged children, and their parents. This clinic has video and audio recording, observation rooms, and microcomputers to support clinical services and research efforts, as well as an extensive library of psychological tests. There are within the University of Washington several other departments and programs with behavioral science emphases, including a health sciences complex that offers resources for coursework, clinical experience, and supervision.

Information for Students With Physical Disabilities: See the following Web site for more information: http://www.washington.edu/admin/eoo/dso/.

Application Information:

Send to Office of Admissions and Academic Support, College of Education, 206 Miller, Box 353600, University of Washington, Seattle, WA 98195-3600. Students are admitted in the Fall, application deadline December 1; Winter, application deadline November 1; Spring, application deadline February 1; Summer, application deadline December 15. Deadlines vary for all of our degree programs in Educational Psychology. School Psychology MEd and PhD programs have December 1 deadline only (for entry in Summer or Autumn quarters). Only Measurement, Statistics, and Research Design allows for year-round applications and four-quarter entry. *Fee:* $45.

Marshall University
Department of Psychology
Liberal Arts
One John Marshall Drive
Huntington, WV 25755-2672
Telephone: (304) 696-6446
Fax: (304) 696-2784
E-mail: *amerikan@marshall.edu*
Web: *http://www.marshall.edu/psych/psyd.htm*

Department Information:

Chairperson: Martin Amerikaner. Number of faculty: total—full-time 19, part-time 7; women—full-time 6, part-time 3; total—minority—full-time 1.

Programs and Degrees Offered:

Listed in the following order: Program area, degree type (T if terminal Master's), number awarded 7/06–6/07. Clinical PsyD (Doctor of Psychology) 4, Psychology MA/MS (Master of Arts/Science) (T) 28.

APA Accreditation: Clinical PsyD (Doctor of Psychology).

Student Applications/Admissions:

Student Applications

Clinical PsyD (Doctor of Psychology)—Applications 2007–2008, 58. Total applicants accepted 2007–2008, 8. Number full-time enrolled (new admits only) 2007–2008, 8. Number part-time enrolled (new admits only) 2007–2008, 0. Total enrolled 2007–2008 full-time, 43, part-time, 7. Openings 2008–2009, 8. The median number of years required for completion of a degree in 2006–2007 were 4. The number of students enrolled full- and part-time who were dismissed or voluntarily withdrew from this program area in 2007–2008 were 1. *Psychology MA/MS (Master of Arts/Science)*—Applications 2007–2008, 32. Total applicants accepted 2007–2008, 21. Number full-time enrolled (new admits only) 2007–2008, 11. Number part-time enrolled (new admits only) 2007–2008, 6. Total enrolled 2007–2008 full-time, 23, part-time, 34. Openings 2008–2009, 25. The median number of years required for completion of a degree in 2006–2007 were 3. The number of students enrolled full- and part-time who were dismissed or voluntarily withdrew from this program area in 2007–2008 were 2.

Admissions Requirements:

Scores: Entries appear in this order: required test or GPA, minimum score (if required), median score of students entering in 2007–2008. Master's Programs: GRE-V 400, 475; GRE-Q 400, 490; overall undergraduate GPA 3.0, 3.2; psychology GPA no minimum stated, 3.4. Applicants not meeting critieria have alternative route to admission into the MA program via completing specified graduate coursework prior to admission; please see Psychology section of the Marshall University Graduate Catalog (http://www.marshall.edu/psych) for details. Doctoral Programs: GRE-V no minimum stated, 524; GRE-Q no minimum stated, 534; overall undergraduate GPA no minimum stated, 3.23. PsyD program requires V and Q GRE, as well as transcripts showing all prievious academic grades/GPAs.

Other Criteria: (importance of criteria rated low, medium, or high): GRE/MAT scores—medium, research experience—medium, work experience—medium, extracurricular activity—medium, clinically related public service—medium, GPA—high, letters of recommendation—medium, interview—medium, statement of goals and objectives—high, undergraduate major in psychology—medium, specific undergraduate psychology courses taken—high. MA program admission is based primarily on GPA and GRE scores; PsyD program considers these, plus statement of professional goals, clinical and research experience, commitment to and understanding of rural psychological service delivery, and letters of recommendation. An interview may be required of PsyD applicants. We accept PsyD students via two routes—those with master's degrees in psychology and those who are just begining their graduate education. Criteria are similar, but weightings are a bit different for each; professional experience and demonstrated experience with rural issues are weighted more heavily in our post-MA pool. For additional information on admission requirements, go to http://www.marshall.edu/psych/psyd.html.

Student Characteristics: The following represents characteristics of students in 2007–2008 in all graduate psychology programs in the department: Female—full-time 40, part-time 24; Male—full-time 26, part-time 17; African American/Black—full-time 2, part-time 1; Hispanic/Latino(a)—full-time 0, part-time 0; Asian/Pacific Islander—full-time 1, part-time 1; American Indian/Alaska Native—full-time 1, part-time 0; Caucasian/White—full-time 61, part-time 39; Multi-ethnic—full-time 0, part-time 0; Unknown ethnicity—full-time 1, part-time 0.

Financial Information/Assistance:

Tuition for Full-Time Study: *Master's:* State residents: per academic year $4,396, $212 per credit hour; Nonstate residents: $653 per credit hour. *Doctoral:* State residents: per academic year $4,606, $239 per credit hour; Nonstate residents: per academic year $12,548, $680 per credit hour. Tuition is subject to change. Additional fees are assessed to students beyond the costs of tuition for the following: PsyD program fee $1,068 (in state), $1,449 (out-of-state). Fees prorated for part-time. Tuition costs vary by program. See the following Web site for updates and changes in tuition costs: http://www.marshall.edu/bursar.

Financial Assistance:

First-Year Students: Teaching assistantships available for first year. Research assistantships available for first year. Average amount paid per academic year: $6,000. Average number of hours worked per week: 20. Apply by ongoing. Tuition remission given: full.

Advanced Students: Teaching assistantships available for advanced students. Average amount paid per academic year: $6,000. Average number of hours worked per week: 20. Apply by April 15. Tuition remission given: full. Research assistantships available for advanced students. Average amount paid per academic year: $6,000. Average number of hours worked per week: 20. Apply by ongoing. Tuition remission given: full. Traineeships available for advanced students. Average amount paid per academic year: $6,000. Average number of hours worked per week: 20. Apply by ongoing. Tuition remission given: full.

Additional Information: Of all students currently enrolled full time, 50% benefited from one or more of the listed financial assistance programs. Application and information available online at http://www.marshall.edu/sfa/.

Internships/Practica: Doctoral Degree (PsyD Clinical): For those doctoral students for whom a professional internship was required in this program prior to graduation, (7) students applied for an internship in 2006–2007, with (7) students obtaining an internship. Of those students who obtained an internship, (7) were paid internships. Of those students who obtained an internship, (3) students placed in APA/CPA-accredited internships, (2) students placed in internships not APA/CPA-accredited, but listed with the Association of Psychology Postdoctoral and Internship Centers (APPIC), (0) students placed in internships conforming to guidelines of the Council of Directors of School Psychology Programs (CDSPP), (2) students placed in internships that were not APA/CPA-accredited, APPIC or CDSPP listed. PsyD program: 2nd-year students work in department's clinic in Huntington; 3rd-year students work at variety of sites in the Huntington community, 4th-year students work at rural placements. Some are in collaboration with primary medical facilites; some may require an overnight stay. Students must complete a full-year, full-time or 2-year, part-time predoctoral internship in order to graduate. Clinical MA: Practicum students work in Marshall's community clinic in Dunbar, WV; master's-level interns work in area mental health agencies. MA-level students interested in I/O have access to a variety of business and organizational field placements. For additional information on education and training outcomes for our programs, see the following Web site: http://www.marshall.edu/psych.

Housing and Day Care: On-campus housing is available. See the following Web site for more information: http://www.marshall.edu/residence-services/ or contact Housing Office (304) 696-6765; On-campus day care facilities are available. See the following Web site for more information: http://www.marshall.edu/coe/childdevelopment or contact Child Development Academy (304) 523-5803.

Employment of Department Graduates:

Master's Degree Graduates: Of those who graduated in the academic year 2006–2007, the following categories and numbers represent the postgraduate activities and employment of master's degree graduates: Enrolled in a psychology doctoral program (2), enrolled in a postdoctoral residency/fellowship (n/a), employed in independent practice (n/a), total from the above (master's) (2).

Doctoral Degree Graduates: Of those who graduated in the academic year 2006–2007, the following categories and numbers represent the postgraduate activities and employment of doctoral degree graduates: Enrolled in a psychology doctoral program (n/a), enrolled in another graduate/professional program (0), enrolled in a postdoctoral residency/fellowship (0), employed in independent practice (2), employed in an academic position at a university (1), employed in an academic position at a 2-year/4-year college (0), employed in other positions at a higher education institution (0), employed in a professional position in a school system (0), employed in business or industry (0), employed in government agency (0), employed in a community mental health/counseling center (1), employed in a hospital/medical center (1), still seeking employment (0), not seeking employment (0), other employment position (0), do not know (0), total from the above (doctoral) (5).

Additional Information:

Orientation, Objectives, and Emphasis of Department: Our PsyD program in Clinical Psychology (offered on our Huntington, WV campus) accepted its first students in Fall 2002 and we received APA accreditation in the spring of 2006. The program is also recognized as a designated program by the National Register/ASPPC Designation project. The program's emphasis is on preparing scholar–practitioners for rural and underserved populations in Appalachia and other rural areas. Particular foci of the doctoral program include understanding the needs and challenges of working in rural communities, preparing doctoral-level psychologists to work within these communities, and provision of services to those areas through the training program itself. A wide range of theoretical perspectives is represented on our faculty. The MA program can be individualized to address a variety of academic and professional objectives for students. There is an "area of emphasis" available in clinical psychology (based in our South Charleston, WV campus), which prepares students for entry-level clinical work at the MA level. Students can also take coursework, and do research and field placements in interest areas such as I/O psychology and a variety of disciplinary areas such as developmental, cognitive, social, and so forth. The Psychology MA program is a popular foundation program for students intending to complete Marshall's EdS program in School Psychology (contact the School Psychology program in the Graduate College of Education and Human Services for more information).

Special Facilities or Resources: Departmental and university computer facilities are available to students for clinical work and for research projects in all programs. Online library resources are excellent. Through department clinics, Clinical students are afforded the opportunity to work, under supervision, with clients from the community and university. Placements for PsyD students available at nearby community mental health centers, state hospitals, and the VA as well as at a variety of more rural sites for advanced training. MA-level students interested in I/O have access to a variety of business and organizational field placements. Faculty have a variety of active, ongoing research projects available for student collaboration.

Information for Students With Physical Disabilities: See the following Web site for more information: http://www.marshall.edu/disabled/.

Application Information:

For MA program send to Admissions Office, Marshall University Graduate College, 100 Angus Peyton Drive, South Charleston, WV 25303-1600. PsyD program: see instructions on application materials. Application available online. URL of online application: http://www.marshall.edu/psych/psydprogram/psydprogram.htm#Access_Application_Materials. Students are admitted in the Fall. January 15 deadline for PsyD program (all new PsyD students start in subsequent Fall semester); MA program has ongoing review of applicants; new MA students can begin in any semester. *Fee:* $30. $40 for nonresidents of WV.

West Virginia University

Department of Counseling, Rehabilitation Counseling and Counseling Psychology, Counseling Psychology Program
Human Resources and Education
502 Allen Hall, P.O. Box 6122
Morgantown, WV 26506-6122
Telephone: (304) 293-2227
Fax: (304) 293-4082
E-mail: *James.Bartee@mail.wvu.edu*
Web: *http://www.hre.wvu.edu/~crc/*

Department Information:

1948. Chairperson: Margaret K. Glenn. Number of faculty: total—full-time 10; women—full-time 6; faculty subject to the Americans With Disabilities Act 1.

Programs and Degrees Offered:

Listed in the following order: Program area, degree type (T if terminal Master's), number awarded 7/06–6/07. Counseling Psychology PhD (Doctor of Philosophy) 6.

APA Accreditation: Counseling PhD (Doctor of Philosophy).

Student Applications/Admissions:

Student Applications

Counseling Psychology PhD (Doctor of Philosophy)—Applications 2007–2008, 41. Total applicants accepted 2007–2008, 7. Number full-time enrolled (new admits only) 2007–2008, 7. Number part-time enrolled (new admits only) 2007–2008, 0. Total enrolled 2007–2008 full-time, 23, part-time, 14. Openings 2008–2009, 6. The median number of years required for completion of a degree in 2006–2007 were 5. The number of students enrolled full- and part-time who were dismissed or voluntarily withdrew from this program area in 2007–2008 were 0.

Admissions Requirements:

Scores: Entries appear in this order: required test or GPA, minimum score (if required), median score of students entering in 2007–2008. Doctoral Programs: GRE-V no minimum stated, 500; GRE-Q no minimum stated, 500; overall undergraduate GPA no minimum stated, 2.80; Doctoral program GRE-Analytic no minimum stated.

Other Criteria: (importance of criteria rated low, medium, or high): GRE/MAT scores—medium, research experience—medium, work experience—high, extracurricular activity—medium, clinically related public service—medium, GPA—medium, letters of recommendation—high, interview—high, statement of goals and objectives—high, goodness of fit—high. For additional information on admission requirements, go to http://www.hre.wvu.edu/crc/academic/phd_counseling.php.

Student Characteristics: The following represents characteristics of students in 2007–2008 in all graduate psychology programs in the department: Female—full-time 16, part-time 8; Male—full-time 7, part-time 6; African American/Black—full-time 1, part-time 1; Hispanic/Latino(a)—full-time 1, part-time 0; Asian/Pacific Islander—full-time 1, part-time 0; American Indian/Alaska Native—full-time 1, part-time 0; Caucasian/White—full-time 19, part-time 13; Multi-ethnic—full-time 0, part-time 0; students subject to the Americans With Disabilities Act—full-time 0, part-time 0; Unknown ethnicity—full-time 0, part-time 0; International students who hold an F-1 or J-1 Visa—full-time 1, part-time 0.

Financial Information/Assistance:

Tuition for Full-Time Study: *Master's:* State residents: per academic year $5,406, $292 per credit hour; Nonstate residents: per academic year $15,366, $840 per credit hour. *Doctoral:* State residents: per academic year $5,406, $292 per credit hour; Nonstate residents: per academic year $13,366, $840 per credit hour. See the following Web site for updates and changes in tuition costs: http://www.arc.wvu.edu/admissions/costs.html.

Financial Assistance:

First-Year Students: Teaching assistantships available for first year. Average amount paid per academic year: $8,864. Average number of hours worked per week: 20. Tuition remission given: full. Research assistantships available for first year. Average amount paid per academic year: $8,864. Average number of hours worked per week: 20. Tuition remission given: full. Fellowships and scholarships available for first year. Average amount paid per academic year: $15,000. Average number of hours worked per week: 0. Tuition remission given: full.

Advanced Students: Teaching assistantships available for advanced students. Average amount paid per academic year: $8,864. Average number of hours worked per week: 20. Tuition remission given: full. Research assistantships available for advanced students. Average amount paid per academic year: $8,864. Average number of hours worked per week: 20. Tuition remission given: full. Fellowships and scholarships available for advanced students. Average amount paid per academic year: $15,000. Average number of hours worked per week: 0. Tuition remission given: full.

Additional Information: Of all students currently enrolled full time, 72% benefited from one or more of the listed financial assistance programs. Application and information available online at http://www.wvu.edu/~finaid/.

Internships/Practica: Doctoral Degree (PhD Counseling Psychology): For those doctoral students for whom a professional internship was required in this program prior to graduation, (3) students applied for an internship in 2006–2007, with (2) students obtaining an internship. Of those students who obtained an internship, (2) were paid internships. Of those students who obtained an internship, (1) student placed in APA/CPA-accredited internships, (1) student placed in internships not APA/CPA-accredited, but listed with the Association of Psychology Postdoctoral and Internship Centers (APPIC), (0) students placed in internships conforming to guidelines of the Council of Directors of School Psychology Programs (CDSPP), (0) students placed in internships that were not APA/CPA-accredited, APPIC or CDSPP listed. The doctoral program offers a variety of opportunities for internship and practica experience. Some of the placement sites include the federal prison system, mental health agencies, employee assistant programs, private practices, VA hospitals, local school systems, university counseling center, and others.

Housing and Day Care: On-campus housing is available. There is on-campus housing at WVU and information can be obtained by calling (304) 293-5840 or going to http://www.sa.wvu.edu/housing. No on-campus day care facilities are available.

Employment of Department Graduates:

Master's Degree Graduates: Of those who graduated in the academic year 2006–2007, the following categories and numbers represent the postgraduate activities and employment of master's degree graduates: Enrolled in a postdoctoral residency/fellowship (n/a), employed in independent practice (n/a), total from the above (master's) (0).

Doctoral Degree Graduates: Of those who graduated in the academic year 2006–2007, the following categories and numbers represent the postgraduate activities and employment of doctoral degree graduates: Enrolled in a psychology doctoral program (n/a), enrolled in another graduate/professional program (0), enrolled in a postdoctoral residency/fellowship (0), employed in independent practice (0), employed in an academic position at a university (0), employed in an academic position at a 2-year/4-year college (1), employed in other positions at a higher education institution (0), employed in a professional position in a school system (0), employed in business or industry (0), employed in government agency (0), employed in a community mental health/counseling center (5), employed in a hospital/medical center (0), still seeking employment (0), not seeking employment (0), other employment position (0), do not know (0), total from the above (doctoral) (6).

Additional Information:

Orientation, Objectives, and Emphasis of Department: The department represents a variety of theoretical orientations. The objective of the department is to train professionals to serve primarily clients who are relatively normal but who are experiencing difficulties related to personal adjustment, interpersonal relationships, developmental problems, crises, academic or career stress, or decisions. The employment settings for our graduates typically include college and university counseling and testing services, community mental health agencies, clinics, hospitals, schools, rehabilitation centers, correctional centers, the United States Armed Services, and private practice.

Special Facilities or Resources: Facilities include an extensive medical center, including video equipment and computer terminals; training and observation rooms; and practicum and internship sites in a variety of settings for master's and doctoral students.

Information for Students With Physical Disabilities: See the following Web site for more information: http://www.wvu.edu/~socjust/disability.htm.

Application Information:

Send to Admissions Coordinator, Department of Counseling, Rehabilitation Counseling and Counseling Psychology, West Virginia University, P.O. Box 6122, Morgantown, WV 25606-6122. Application available online. URL of online application: http://www.hre.wvu.edu/crc/academic/cpsyappl.doc. Students are admitted in the Fall, application deadline December 1. Counseling Psychology doctoral program admits for Fall only. Application deadline is December 1. *Fee:* $50.

West Virginia University

Department of Psychology
Eberly College of Arts and Sciences
P.O. Box 6040
Morgantown, WV 26506-6040
Telephone: (304) 293-2001, ext. 31628
Fax: (304) 293-6606
E-mail: *Debra.Swinney@mail.wvu.edu*
Web: *http://www.wvu.edu/~psychology/*

Department Information:

1929. Chairperson: Michael Perone. Number of faculty: total—full-time 22, part-time 1; women—full-time 11, part-time 1.

Programs and Degrees Offered:

Listed in the following order: Program area, degree type (T if terminal Master's), number awarded 7/06–6/07. Life Span Developmental PhD (Doctor of Philosophy) 2, Behavior Analysis PhD (Doctor of Philosophy) 2, Clinical PhD (Doctor of Philosophy) 5, Professional Master's in Clinical Psychology MA/MS (Master of Arts/Science) (T) 1, Applied Behavior Analysis MA/MS (Master of Arts/Science) (T) 0.

APA Accreditation: Clinical PhD (Doctor of Philosophy).

Student Applications/Admissions:

Student Applications

Life Span Developmental PhD (Doctor of Philosophy)—Applications 2007–2008, 13. Total applicants accepted 2007–2008, 5. Number full-time enrolled (new admits only) 2007–2008, 4. Number part-time enrolled (new admits only) 2007–2008, 0. Openings 2008–2009, 6. The median number of years required for completion of a degree in 2006–2007 were 4. The number of students enrolled full- and part-time who were dismissed or voluntarily withdrew from this program area in 2007–2008 were 2. *Behavior Analysis PhD (Doctor of Philosophy)*—Applications 2007–2008, 43. Total applicants accepted 2007–2008, 5. Number full-time enrolled (new admits only) 2007–2008, 6. Number part-time enrolled (new admits only) 2007–2008, 0. Openings 2008–2009, 6. The median number of years required for completion of a degree in 2006–2007 were 5. The number of students enrolled full- and part-time who were dismissed or voluntarily withdrew from this program area in 2007–2008 were 1. *Clinical PhD (Doctor of Philosophy)*—Applications 2007–2008, 107. Total applicants accepted 2007–2008, 11. Number full-time enrolled (new admits only) 2007–2008, 9. Number part-time enrolled (new admits only) 2007–2008, 0. Openings 2008–2009, 11. The median number of years required for completion of a degree in 2006–2007 were 5. The number of students enrolled full- and part-time who were dismissed or voluntarily withdrew from this program area in 2007–2008 were 0. *Professional Master's in Clinical Psychology MA/MS (Master of Arts/Science)*—Applications 2007–2008, 16. Total applicants accepted 2007–2008, 1. Number full-time enrolled (new admits only) 2007–2008, 1. Number part-time enrolled (new admits only) 2007–2008, 0. Openings 2008–2009, 2. The median number of years required for completion of a degree in 2006–2007 were 2. The number of students enrolled full- and part-time who were dismissed or voluntarily withdrew from this program area in 2007–2008 were 0. *Applied Behavior Analysis MA/MS (Master of Arts/ Science)*—Applications 2007–2008, 0. Total applicants accepted 2007–2008, 0. Number full-time enrolled (new admits only) 2007–2008, 0. Number part-time enrolled (new admits only) 2007–2008, 0. Openings 2008–2009, 4. The number of students enrolled full- and part-time who were dismissed or voluntarily withdrew from this program area in 2007–2008 were 0.

Admissions Requirements:

Scores: Entries appear in this order: required test or GPA, minimum score (if required), median score of students entering in 2007–2008. Master's Programs: GRE-V 500; GRE-Q 500; overall undergraduate GPA 3.00; last 2 years GPA no minimum stated; psychology GPA no minimum stated. Doctoral Programs: GRE-V 500, 510; GRE-Q 500, 650; GRE-Subject (Psychology) 500, 620; overall undergraduate GPA 3.00, 3.75. The GRE Subject Test in Psychology is required for students applying to the Clinical or Clinical Child Psychology doctoral programs. The Subject Test is not required for students applying to the Behavior Analysis or Life Span Developmental Psychology doctoral programs.

Other Criteria: (importance of criteria rated low, medium, or high): GRE/MAT scores—high, research experience—high, work experience—medium, extracurricular activity—medium, clinically related public service—medium, GPA—high, letters of recommendation—high, interview—high, statement of goals and objectives—high. Match between faculty and student interests is of high importance. Only Clinical programs give high value to clinically related public service. Research experience is of medium importance for the Master's program. For additional information on admission requirements, go to http://www.wvu.edu/~psychology/graduateprogram/prospective/index.htm.

Student Characteristics: The following represents characteristics of students in 2007–2008 in all graduate psychology programs in the department: Female—full-time 47, part-time 0; Male—full-time 26, part-time 0; African American/Black—full-time 2, part-time 0; Hispanic/Latino(a)—full-time 3, part-time 0; Asian/ Pacific Islander—full-time 3, part-time 0; American Indian/ Alaska Native—full-time 0, part-time 0; Caucasian/White—full-time 63, part-time 0; Multi-ethnic—full-time 1, part-time 0; students subject to the Americans With Disabilities Act—full-time 0, part-time 0; Unknown ethnicity—full-time 1, part-time 0; International students who hold an F-1 or J-1 Visa—full-time 8, part-time 0.

Financial Information/Assistance:

Tuition for Full-Time Study: *Master's:* State residents: per academic year $5,196, $292 per credit hour; Nonstate residents: per academic year $15,064, $840 per credit hour. *Doctoral:* State residents: per academic year $5,196, $292 per credit hour; Nonstate residents: per academic year $15,064, $840 per credit hour. Tuition is subject to change. See the following Web site for updates and changes in tuition costs: http://www.arc.wvu.edu/admissions/tuition_fees.html.

Financial Assistance:

First-Year Students: Teaching assistantships available for first year. Average amount paid per academic year: $9,950. Average number of hours worked per week: 20. Apply by December 15. Tuition remission given: full. Research assistantships available for first year. Average amount paid per academic year: $9,950. Average number of hours worked per week: 20. Apply by December 15. Tuition remission given: full. Traineeships available for first year. Average amount paid per academic year: $9,950. Average number of hours worked per week: 20. Apply by December 15. Tuition remission given: full. Fellowships and scholarships available for first year. Average amount paid per academic year: $17,500. Average number of hours worked per week: 0. Apply by December 15. Tuition remission given: full.

Advanced Students: Teaching assistantships available for advanced students. Average amount paid per academic year: $10,499. Average number of hours worked per week: 20. Apply by December 15. Tuition remission given: full. Research assistantships available for advanced students. Average amount paid per academic year: $10,499. Average number of hours worked per week: 20. Apply by December 15. Tuition remission given: full. Traineeships available for advanced students. Average amount paid per academic year: $10,499. Average number of hours worked per week: 20. Apply by December 15. Tuition remission given: full. Fellowships and scholarships available for advanced students. Average amount paid per academic year: $17,500. Average number of hours worked per week: 0. Apply by December 15. Tuition remission given: full.

Additional Information: Of all students currently enrolled full time, 100% benefited from one or more of the listed financial assistance programs. Application and information available online at http://www.wvu.edu/~psychology/graduateprogram/prospective/index.htm.

Internships/Practica: Master's Degree (MA/MS Professional Master's in Clinical Psychology): An internship experience such as a final research project or "capstone" experience is required of graduates. Doctoral Degree (PhD Clinical): For those doctoral students for whom a professional internship was required in this program prior to graduation, (7) students applied for an internship in 2006–2007, with (7) students obtaining an internship. Of those students who obtained an internship, (7) were paid internships. Of those students who obtained an internship, (7) students placed in APA/CPA-accredited internships, (0) students placed in internships not APA/CPA-accredited, but listed with the Association of Psychology Postdoctoral and Internship Centers (APPIC), (0) students placed in internships conforming to guidelines of the Council of Directors of School Psychology Programs (CDSPP), (0) students placed in internships that were not APA/ CPA-accredited, APPIC or CDSPP listed. Paid clinical placements at out-of-department sites are available for doctoral clinical students who have earned master's degrees. These out-of-department practicum sites include WVU Carruth Counseling Center, "Kennedy" Federal Correctional Institution, Hopemont Hospital, Sharpe Hospital, the Robert C. Byrd Health Sciences Center, a private practice, various behavioral and community mental health agencies, and children and youth services agencies. These sites are located in Morgantown, and across the state and region. Stipends for practicum range from $8,250 to $15,000, require 16 hours of work per week, and last 12 months.

Housing and Day Care: On-campus housing is available. See the following Web site for more information: http://www.housing.wvu.edu/. No on-campus day care facilities are available.

Employment of Department Graduates:

Master's Degree Graduates: Of those who graduated in the academic year 2006–2007, the following categories and numbers represent the postgraduate activities and employment of master's degree graduates: Enrolled in a postdoctoral residency/fellowship (n/a), employed in independent practice (n/a), employed in a community mental health/counseling center (1), total from the above (master's) (1).

Doctoral Degree Graduates: Of those who graduated in the academic year 2006–2007, the following categories and numbers represent the postgraduate activities and employment of doctoral degree graduates: Enrolled in a psychology doctoral program (n/a), enrolled in a postdoctoral residency/fellowship (5), employed in an academic position at a university (2), employed in a community mental health/counseling center (1), employed in a hospital/medical center (1), do not know (2), total from the above (doctoral) (11).

Additional Information:

Orientation, Objectives, and Emphasis of Department: The Psychology Department offers the Doctor of Philosophy degree in Behavior Analysis and Life Span Developmental, Clinical Child, and Clinical Psychology, and terminal Professional Master's degrees in Applied Behavior Analysis and Clinical Psychology. The department employs a junior colleague model of training, in which graduate students participate fully in research, teaching, and service activities. The Behavior Analysis doctoral program trains students in basic research, theory, and applications of behavioral psychology. These three areas of study are integrated in the Behavior Analysis curriculum; however, a student may emphasize either basic or applied research. The Master's degree program in Applied Behavior Analysis trains students in the applications of behavior principles and concepts in situations of daily life. The Life Span Developmental program emphasizes cognitive and social/personality development across the life span. It combines breadth of exposure across a variety of perspectives on the life span with depth and rigor in research training and the opportunity to specialize in an age period such as infancy, childhood, adolescence, or adulthood and old age. The Master's and PhD Clinical programs have a behavioral/cognitive behavioral orientation. The Clinical doctoral programs train scientist–practitioners who function effectively in academic, medical center, or clinical applied settings. Specializations in developmental psychology, behavior analysis, and health psychology are available. The Clinical Professional master's program is designed to train practitioners with a terminal Master's degree to work in rural areas.

Special Facilities or Resources: The department moved into the new Life Sciences Building in July 2002. This building has modern animal research quarters for work with rats, pigeons, and other species. There are several computer-based laboratories and other laboratories for studies of learning in humans and animals, behavioral pharmacology, and neuropsychology. There are additional facilities for human research in learning, cognition, small group processes, developmental psychology, social behavior, and psychophysiology. Clinical practicum opportunities are available through the department's Quin Curtis Center for Psychological Service, Training, and Research, as well as in numerous mental health agencies throughout the state. Videotaping and direct observation equipment and facilities are available. The West Virginia University Medical Center provides facilities for research and training in such departments and areas as behavioral medicine and psychiatry, pediatrics, neurology, and dentistry. Local preschools and public schools have been cooperative in providing access to children and facilities for child development research, local businesses and other agencies offer sites for practice and research in applied behavior analysis, local senior centers and homes provide access to older adult populations, and the University's Center on Aging–Education Unit and Center for Women's Studies facilitate research related to their purviews. The University maintains an extensive network of computer facilities, and the department provides a computer for every graduate student.

Information for Students With Physical Disabilities: See the following Web site for more information: http://www.wvu.edu/~socjust/disability/.

Application Information:

Send to Departmental Admissions Committee, Department of Psychology, West Virginia University, P.O. Box 6040, Morgantown, WV 26506-6040. Application available online. URL of online application: http://www.wvu.edu/~psychology/graduateprogram/prospective/index.htm. Students are admitted in the Fall, application deadline December 15. Professional Master of Arts in Clinical Psychology and Master of Arts in Applied Behavior Analysis application deadline is March 1. *Fee:* $50.

Marquette University

Department of Counseling and Educational Psychology
School of Education
561 North 15th Street, 146 Schroeder Complex
Milwaukee, WI 53201-1881
Telephone: (414) 288-5790
Fax: (414) 288-6100
E-mail: *Todd.campbell@marquette.edu*
Web: *http://www.marquette.edu/coep*

Department Information:

1996. Chairperson: Todd C. Campbell. Number of faculty: total—full-time 4, part-time 6; women—full-time 3; ; women minority—full-time 1.

Programs and Degrees Offered:

Listed in the following order: Program area, degree type (T if terminal Master's), number awarded 7/06–6/07. Counseling MA/MS (Master of Arts/Science) (T) 30, Counseling Psychology PhD (Doctor of Philosophy) 6.

APA Accreditation: Counseling PhD (Doctor of Philosophy).

Student Applications/Admissions:

Student Applications

Counseling MA/MS (Master of Arts/Science)—Applications 2007–2008, 80. Total applicants accepted 2007–2008, 45. Number full-time enrolled (new admits only) 2007–2008, 30. Number part-time enrolled (new admits only) 2007–2008, 6. Total enrolled 2007–2008 full-time, 61, part-time, 20. Openings 2008–2009, 40. The median number of years required for completion of a degree in 2006–2007 were 2. The number of students enrolled full- and part-time who were dismissed or voluntarily withdrew from this program area in 2007–2008 were 1. *Counseling Psychology PhD (Doctor of Philosophy)*—Applications 2007–2008, 48. Total applicants accepted 2007–2008, 6. Number full-time enrolled (new admits only) 2007–2008, 6. Number part-time enrolled (new admits only) 2007–2008, 0. Total enrolled 2007–2008 full-time, 27, part-time, 12. Openings 2008–2009, 6. The median number of years required for completion of a degree in 2006–2007 were 6. The number of students enrolled full- and part-time who were dismissed or voluntarily withdrew from this program area in 2007–2008 were 2.

Admissions Requirements:

Scores: Entries appear in this order: required test or GPA, minimum score (if required), median score of students entering in 2007–2008. Master's Programs: GRE-V no minimum stated, 470; GRE-Q no minimum stated, 560; overall undergraduate GPA no minimum stated, 3.4; Master's GRE-Analytical no minimum stated, 4.5. Median score for GRE Writing = 4.5; Please note that we do not have minimum GPA or GRE cutoff scores, but review applications in their entirety. Doctoral Programs: GRE-V no minimum stated, 535; GRE-Q no minimum stated, 610; overall undergraduate GPA no minimum stated, 3.7. Median Score for GRE Writing = 4.5; Please note that we do not have minimum GPA or GRE cutoff scores, but review applications in their entirety.

Other Criteria: (importance of criteria rated low, medium, or high): GRE/MAT scores—medium, research experience—medium, work experience—medium, extracurricular activity—medium, clinically related public service—medium, GPA—high, letters of recommendation—high, interview—high, statement of goals and objectives—high, undergraduate major in psychology—low, specific undergraduate psychology courses taken—low. Applicants' goals and objectives, interviews, and letters of recommendation are important for admission into all our master's and doctoral programs. Research experience is much more important for admission into our PhD program. For additional information on admission requirements, go to http://www.marquette.edu/education/pages/programs/coep/.

Student Characteristics: The following represents characteristics of students in 2007–2008 in all graduate psychology programs in the department: Female—full-time 70, part-time 16; Male—full-time 20, part-time 5; African American/Black—full-time 2, part-time 0; Hispanic/Latino(a)—full-time 5, part-time 1; Asian/Pacific Islander—full-time 1, part-time 3; American Indian/Alaska Native—full-time 0, part-time 0; Caucasian/White—full-time 80, part-time 15; Multi-ethnic—full-time 0, part-time 0; students subject to the Americans With Disabilities Act—full-time 2, part-time 1; Unknown ethnicity—full-time 0, part-time 0; International students who hold an F-1 or J-1 Visa—full-time 2, part-time 2.

Financial Information/Assistance:

Tuition for Full-Time Study: *Master's:* State residents: $595 per credit hour; Nonstate residents: $595 per credit hour. *Doctoral:* State residents: $595 per credit hour; Nonstate residents: $595 per credit hour. See the following Web site for updates and changes in tuition costs: http://www.grad.mu.edu/future/tuition.shtml.

Financial Assistance:

First-Year Students: Teaching assistantships available for first year. Average amount paid per academic year: $6,000. Average number of hours worked per week: 10. Apply by February 15. Tuition remission given: full. Research assistantships available for first year. Average amount paid per academic year: $6,000. Average number of hours worked per week: 10. Apply by February 15. Tuition remission given: full. Fellowships and scholarships available for first year. Average amount paid per academic year: $0. Average number of hours worked per week: 0. Apply by February 15. Tuition remission given: partial.

Advanced Students: Teaching assistantships available for advanced students. Average amount paid per academic year: $6,500. Average number of hours worked per week: 10. Apply by February 15. Tuition remission given: partial. Research assistantships available for advanced students. Average amount paid per academic year: $6,500. Average number of hours worked per week: 10. Apply by February 15. Tuition remission given: full. Traineeships available for advanced students. Average amount paid per academic year: $13,000. Average number of hours worked per week: 20. Apply by February 15. Tuition remission given: full and partial. Fellowships and scholarships available for advanced students. Average amount paid per academic year: $13,000. Average number of hours worked per week: 0. Apply by varies. Tuition remission given: full and partial.

Additional Information: Of all students currently enrolled full time, 30% benefited from one or more of the listed financial assistance programs. Application and information available online at http://www.marquette.edu/grad.

Internships/Practica: We work with a wide range of inpatient and outpatient agencies and educational institutions serving a broad range of clients from children to seniors and from relatively minor adjustment issues to serious psychopathology. We currently work with approximately 60 agencies and schools and continually try to find additional sites that offer superior clinical experience and supervision. We have have two departmental clinics: the 7Cs Community Counseling Clinic and the Behavior Clinic. Please see our Web site at http://www.marquette.edu/education/pages/programs/coep/centers.shtml for more information.

Housing and Day Care: On-campus housing is available. See the following Web site for more information: http://www.grad.mu.edu/resources/stures.shtml. On-campus day care facilities are available. Child care information is available by calling (414) 288-5655.

Employment of Department Graduates:

Master's Degree Graduates: Of those who graduated in the academic year 2006–2007, the following categories and numbers represent the postgraduate activities and employment of master's degree graduates: Enrolled in a psychology doctoral program (6), enrolled in another graduate/professional program (2), enrolled in a postdoctoral residency/fellowship (n/a), employed in independent practice (n/a), employed in other positions at a higher education institution (3), employed in a professional position in a school system (11), employed in business or industry (1), employed in a community mental health/counseling center (19), employed in a hospital/medical center (2), total from the above (master's) (44).

Doctoral Degree Graduates: Of those who graduated in the academic year 2006–2007, the following categories and numbers represent the postgraduate activities and employment of doctoral degree graduates: Enrolled in a psychology doctoral program (n/a), enrolled in a postdoctoral residency/fellowship (2), employed in an academic position at a university (4), employed in other positions at a higher education institution (1), employed in a community mental health/counseling center (1), employed in a hospital/medical center (5), other employment position (1), total from the above (doctoral) (14).

Additional Information:

Orientation, Objectives, and Emphasis of Department: Our Master's in Counseling and PhD in Counseling Psychology programs are based on a comprehensive biopsychosocial approach to understanding human behavior. We believe that a sensitivity to biological, psychological, social, multicultural, and developmental influences on behavior increases students' effectiveness both as practitioners and as researchers. We use a generalist approach that includes broad preparation in the diverse areas needed to practice competently as psychological scientists and practitioners in today's health care systems. The master's program in Counseling includes school counseling and community counseling (three focus areas: addiction and mental health, adult, and child/adolescent).

Special Facilities or Resources: Our faculty, and Marquette University as a whole, are committed to offering high-quality education. Our coursework, practica, research activities, and other training opportunities are all designed to provide very current and comprehensive preparation. Our student body is small, so students receive substantial individual attention. We are also committed to developing students' competencies to work with diverse multicultural groups, and we welcome applications from individuals with diverse backgrounds. All of the full-time faculty are engaged in a variety of research projects with which students may become involved. In addition, department faculty are associated with two research centers that provide a variety of excellent opportunities for research and professional training: The Center for Addiction and Behavioral Health Research and the Integrative Neuroscience Research Center. Two community-based clinics are closely allied with the department and provide counseling and research opportunities for our students. The Behavior Clinic focuses on children 0–5 years of age and their parents. The 7Cs Community Counseling Clinic focuses on adults with addiction and other behavioral health issues.

Information for Students With Physical Disabilities: See the following Web site for more information: http://www.marquette.edu/oses/disabilityservices/.

Application Information:

Send to Graduate School, P.O. Box 1881, Milwaukee, WI 53201. Application available online. URL of online application: http://www.grad.mu.edu/index.shtml. Students are admitted in the Fall. The application deadline for the PhD program is December 1, and Febraury 1 for the master's programs. *Fee:* $40. Fee waived for Marquette Alumni.

Marquette University

Department of Psychology
Arts and Sciences
P.O. Box 1881
Milwaukee, WI 53201-1881
Telephone: (414) 288-7218
Fax: (414) 288-5333
E-mail: *michael.wierzbicki@marquette.edu*
Web: *http://www.marquette.edu/psyc*

Department Information:

1952. Chairperson: Michael J. Wierzbicki. Number of faculty: total—full-time 17; women—full-time 8; total—minority—full-time 1.

Programs and Degrees Offered:

Listed in the following order: Program area, degree type (T if terminal Master's), number awarded 7/06–6/07. Clinical Psychology MA/MS (Master of Arts/Science) (T) 1, Clinical Psychology PhD (Doctor of Philosophy) 6.

APA Accreditation: Clinical PhD (Doctor of Philosophy).

Student Applications/Admissions:

Student Applications

Clinical Psychology MA/MS (Master of Arts/Science)—Applications 2007–2008, 15. Total applicants accepted 2007–2008, 5. Number full-time enrolled (new admits only) 2007–2008, 5. The median number of years required for completion of a degree in 2006–2007 were 2. The number of students enrolled full- and part-time who were dismissed or voluntarily withdrew from this program area in 2007–2008 were 1. *Clinical Psychology PhD (Doctor of Philosophy)*—Applications 2007–2008, 90. Total applicants accepted 2007–2008, 11. Number full-time enrolled (new admits only) 2007–2008, 8. Number part-time enrolled (new admits only) 2007–2008, 0. Openings 2008–2009, 8. The median number of years required for completion of a degree in 2006–2007 were 7. The number of students enrolled full- and part-time who were dismissed or voluntarily withdrew from this program area in 2007–2008 were 0.

Admissions Requirements:

Scores: Entries appear in this order: required test or GPA, minimum score (if required), median score of students entering in 2007–2008. Master's Programs: GRE-V 500, 550; GRE-Q 500, 570; GRE-Subject (Psychology) 550, 570; overall undergraduate GPA 3.2, 3.4. Doctoral Programs: GRE-V 550, 550; GRE-Q 550, 610; GRE-Subject (Psychology) 500, 660; overall undergraduate GPA 3.40, 3.8.

Other Criteria: (importance of criteria rated low, medium, or high): GRE/MAT scores—high, research experience—high, work experience—low, clinically related public service—medium, GPA—medium, letters of recommendation—high, interview—high, statement of goals and objectives—high, undergraduate major in psychology—medium, specific undergraduate psychology courses taken—high. MS program places less emphasis on research experience. For additional information on admission requirements, go to http://www.mu.edu/psyc.

Student Characteristics: The following represents characteristics of students in 2007–2008 in all graduate psychology programs in the department: Female—full-time 34, part-time 0; Male—full-time 15, part-time 0; African American/Black—full-time 2, part-time 0; Hispanic/Latino(a)—full-time 1, part-time 0; Asian/Pacific Islander—full-time 1, part-time 0; American Indian/Alaska Native—full-time 1, part-time 0; Caucasian/White—full-time 43, part-time 0; Multi-ethnic—full-time 1, part-time 0; students subject to the Americans With Disabilities Act—full-time 0, part-time 0; Unknown ethnicity—full-time 0, part-time 0; International students who hold an F-1 or J-1 Visa—full-time 1, part-time 0.

Financial Information/Assistance:

Tuition for Full-Time Study: *Master's:* State residents: $840 per credit hour; Nonstate residents: $840 per credit hour. *Doctoral:* State residents: $840 per credit hour; Nonstate residents: $840 per credit hour. Tuition is subject to change. See the following Web site for updates and changes in tuition costs: http://www.grad.mu.edu.

Financial Assistance:

First-Year Students: Teaching assistantships available for first year. Average amount paid per academic year: $12,900. Average number of hours worked per week: 20. Apply by December 15. Tuition remission given: full. Research assistantships available for first year. Average amount paid per academic year: $12,900. Average number of hours worked per week: 20. Apply by December 15. Tuition remission given: full. Fellowships and scholarships available for first year. Average amount paid per academic year: $12,900. Average number of hours worked per week: 0. Apply by December 15. Tuition remission given: full and partial.

Advanced Students: Teaching assistantships available for advanced students. Average amount paid per academic year: $12,900. Average number of hours worked per week: 20. Apply by December 15. Tuition remission given: full. Research assistantships available for advanced students. Average amount paid per academic year: $12,900. Average number of hours worked per week: 20. Apply by December 15. Tuition remission given: full. Traineeships available for advanced students. Average amount paid per academic year: $12,900. Average number of hours worked per week: 8. Apply by December 15. Tuition remission given: partial. Fellowships and scholarships available for advanced students. Average amount paid per academic year: $15,000. Average number of hours worked per week: 0. Apply by December 15. Tuition remission given: full.

Additional Information: Of all students currently enrolled full time, 60% benefited from one or more of the listed financial assistance programs. Application and information available online at http://www.grad.mu.edu.

Internships/Practica: Doctoral Degree (PhD Clinical Psychology): For those doctoral students for whom a professional internship was required in this program prior to graduation, (4) students applied for an internship in 2006–2007, with (3) students obtaining an internship. Of those students who obtained an internship, (3) were paid internships. Of those students who obtained an internship, (2) students placed in APA/CPA-accredited internships, (1) student placed in internships not APA/CPA accredited, but listed with the Association of Psychology Postdoctoral and Internship Centers (APPIC), (0) students placed in internships conforming to guidelines of the Council of Directors of School Psychology Programs (CDSPP), (0) students placed in internships that were not APA/CPA-accredited, APPIC or CDSPP listed. Doctoral and terminal master's students obtain supervised clinical experience throughout their training. Practica are offered both in the department's training clinic, the Center for Psychological Services, and in community agencies. The department's training clinic provides assessment and intervention services to members of the general community under the supervision of licensed clinical faculty members. Students have averaged over 750 hours in the clinic, and over 2,000 hours in preinternship practicum experiences. Marquette University's urban location provides a wealth of training opportunities in the community. Recent practicum experiences have included placements in agencies that provided training in neuropsychological assessment, geropsychology, behavioral medicine, pediatric health, and family therapy. Doctoral students are required to complete a 2,000-hour internship. To date, students have completed APA-approved internships in settings located in the Milwaukee area as well as eight different states.

Housing and Day Care: On-campus housing is available. See the following Web site for more information: http://www.grad.mu.edu. On-campus day care facilities are available.

Employment of Department Graduates:

Master's Degree Graduates: Of those who graduated in the academic year 2006–2007, the following categories and numbers represent the postgraduate activities and employment of master's degree graduates: Enrolled in a postdoctoral residency/fellowship (n/a), employed in independent practice (n/a), total from the above (master's) (0).

Doctoral Degree Graduates: Of those who graduated in the academic year 2006–2007, the following categories and numbers represent the postgraduate activities and employment of doctoral degree graduates: Enrolled in a psychology doctoral program (n/a), enrolled in another graduate/professional program (0), enrolled in a postdoctoral residency/fellowship (5), employed in independent practice (0), employed in an academic position at a university (0), employed in an academic position at a 2-year/4-year college (0), employed in other positions at a higher education institution (0), employed in a professional position in a school system (0), employed in business or industry (0), employed in government agency (0), employed in a community mental health/counseling center (1), employed in a hospital/medical center (0), still seeking employment (0), not seeking employment (0), other employment position (0), do not know (0), total from the above (doctoral) (6).

Additional Information:

Orientation, Objectives, and Emphasis of Department: The Clinical Psychology program offers courses and training leading to the degrees of Doctor of Philosophy (PhD) and Master of Science (MS) in Clinical Psychology. All doctoral students acquire a Master of Science degree as they progress toward the doctoral degree. Students in the terminal master's program typically accept employment after completion of the program, but some go on to doctoral study. The doctoral program is approved by the American Psychological Association to train scientist–professionals. Students receive a solid foundation in scientific areas of psychology and in the historical foundations of psychology. Training in research skills such as statistics, measurement, and research methods ensures competence in conducting empirical research and in critically evaluating one's own and others' clinical and empirical work. Students become competent in professional practice skills such as assessment, interventions, and consultation. Supervised clinical experiences are planned throughout the curriculum. Graduates of the doctoral program are prepared to practice as clinical psychologists, consultants, teachers, researchers, and administrators.

Special Facilities or Resources: The department is located in completely refurbished and modern quarters that include a psychology clinic, an undergraduate teaching laboratory, and ample space for both faculty and student research. A full range of computer services is available at no charge to students. Located in a large metropolitan area, Marquette University is within easy commuting distance to a variety of hospitals and agencies in which training and research opportunities maybe available.

Information for Students With Physical Disabilities: See the following Web site for more information: http://www.grad.mu.edu.

Application Information:

Send to Graduate School, 305 Holthusen Hall, Marquette University, 1324 West Wisconsin Avenue, Milwaukee, WI 53201-1881. Application available online. URL of online application: http://www.grad.mu.edu/future/apply.shtml. Students are admitted in the Fall, application deadline December 15. *Fee:* $50. Waived for Marquette University alumni. Waived for evidence of financial need.

Wisconsin School of Professional Psychology

Professional School
9120 West Hampton Avenue, Suite 212
Milwaukee, WI 53225
Telephone: (414) 464-9777
Fax: (414) 358-5590
E-mail: *kathleenrusch@sbcglobal.net*
Web: *http://www.wspp.edu*

Department Information:

1980. President: Kathleen M. Rusch, PhD. Number of faculty: total—full-time 6, part-time 24; women—full-time 4, part-time 10; minority—part-time 2.

Programs and Degrees Offered:

Listed in the following order: Program area, degree type (T if terminal Master's), number awarded 7/06–6/07. Clinical PsyD (Doctor of Psychology) 2.

APA Accreditation: Clinical PsyD (Doctor of Psychology).

Student Applications/Admissions:

Student Applications

Clinical PsyD (Doctor of Psychology)—Applications 2007–2008, 20. Total applicants accepted 2007–2008, 15. Number full-time enrolled (new admits only) 2007–2008, 6. Number part-time enrolled (new admits only) 2007–2008, 6. Total enrolled 2007–2008 full-time, 27, part-time, 38. Openings 2008–2009, 15. The median number of years required for completion of a degree in 2006–2007 were 6. The number of students enrolled full- and part-time who were dismissed or voluntarily withdrew from this program area in 2007–2008 were 1.

Admissions Requirements:

Scores: Entries appear in this order: required test or GPA, minimum score (if required), median score of students entering in 2007–2008. Master's Programs: GRE-V 450, 500; GRE-Q 450, 520; GRE-Subject (Psychology) 500, 520; overall undergraduate GPA 3.0, 3.5; last 2 years GPA 3.2, 3.6; psychology GPA 3.2, 3.6. Doctoral Programs: GRE-V 450, 500; GRE-Q 450, 520; GRE-Subject (Psychology) 500, 550; overall undergraduate GPA 3.0, 3.5; psychology GPA 3.2, 3.6.

Other Criteria: (importance of criteria rated low, medium, or high): GRE/MAT scores—medium, research experience—low, work experience—high, extracurricular activity—medium, clinically related public service—high, GPA—medium, letters of recommendation—high, interview—high, statement of goals and objectives—high, essay—high, undergraduate major in psychology—medium, specific undergraduate psychology courses taken—high.

Student Characteristics: The following represents characteristics of students in 2007–2008 in all graduate psychology programs in the department: Female—full-time 20, part-time 32; Male—

full-time 7, part-time 6; African American/Black—full-time 0, part-time 6; Hispanic/Latino(a)—full-time 0, part-time 0; Asian/Pacific Islander—full-time 1, part-time 0; American Indian/Alaska Native—full-time 0, part-time 0; Caucasian/White—full-time 26, part-time 32; Multi-ethnic—full-time 0, part-time 0; students subject to the Americans With Disabilities Act—full-time 0, part-time 1; Unknown ethnicity—full-time 0, part-time 0.

Financial Information/Assistance:

Tuition for Full-Time Study: *Master's:* State residents: $675 per credit hour; Nonstate residents: $675 per credit hour. *Doctoral:* State residents: $675 per credit hour; Nonstate residents: $675 per credit hour. Tuition is subject to change. Additional fees are assessed to students beyond the costs of tuition for the following: $50 materials fee for all assessment courses.

Financial Assistance:

First-Year Students: Fellowships and scholarships available for first year. Average amount paid per academic year: $3,000. Average number of hours worked per week: 0. Apply by February 15. Tuition remission given: partial.

Advanced Students: Traineeships available for advanced students. Average number of hours worked per week: 12. Tuition remission given: partial. Fellowships and scholarships available for advanced students. Average amount paid per academic year: $1,000. Average number of hours worked per week: 0. Apply by February 15. Tuition remission given: partial.

Additional Information: Of all students currently enrolled full time, 4% benefited from one or more of the listed financial assistance programs. Application and information available online at http://www.wspp.edu.

Internships/Practica: Doctoral Degree (PsyD Clinical): For those doctoral students for whom a professional internship was required in this program prior to graduation, (10) students applied for an internship in 2006–2007, with (10) students obtaining an internship. Of those students who obtained an internship, (9) were paid internships. Of those students who obtained an internship, (3) students placed in APA/CPA-accredited internships, (7) students placed in internships not APA/CPA-accredited, but listed with the Association of Psychology Postdoctoral and Internship Centers (APPIC), (0) students placed in internships conforming to guidelines of the Council of Directors of School Psychology Programs (CDSPP), (0) students placed in internships that were not APA/CPA-accredited, APPIC or CDSPP listed. WSPP has an on-site training clinic, the Psychology Center, which is designed to serve two purposes: to provide supervised training to students and to provide quality clinical services to an inner-city multicultural disadvantaged population. The Center also maintains contracts and affiliations with a number of local service agencies to provide on-site services. Regardless of whether on- or off-site, all practica are supervised by WSPP faculty to ensure quality of supervision and communication with our DCT. Some 40 supervisors, all licensed and most National Register listed, are readily available. For assessment practica, WSPP maintains a library of psychological tests available for student use free of charge. Thus, all students are guaranteed ample practicum opportunities (the program requires 2,000 hours) without having to search for sites or supervisors. This high level of clinical training has led to our 100% internship placement rate to date.

Housing and Day Care: No on-campus housing is available. No on-campus day care facilities are available.

Employment of Department Graduates:

Master's Degree Graduates: Of those who graduated in the academic year 2006–2007, the following categories and numbers represent the postgraduate activities and employment of master's degree graduates: Enrolled in a psychology doctoral program (6), enrolled in another graduate/professional program (0), enrolled in a postdoctoral residency/fellowship (n/a), employed in independent practice (n/a), employed in an academic position at a university (0), employed in an academic position at a 2-year/4-year college (0), employed in other positions at a higher education institution (0), employed in a professional position in a school system (0), employed in business or industry (0), employed in government agency (0), employed in a community mental health/counseling center (0), employed in a hospital/medical center (0), still seeking employment (0), not seeking employment (0), other employment position (0), do not know (0), total from the above (master's) (6).

Doctoral Degree Graduates: Of those who graduated in the academic year 2006–2007, the following categories and numbers represent the postgraduate activities and employment of doctoral degree graduates: Enrolled in a psychology doctoral program (n/a), enrolled in a postdoctoral residency/fellowship (0), employed in independent practice (1), employed in an academic position at a university (0), employed in an academic position at a 2-year/4-year college (0), employed in other positions at a higher education institution (0), employed in a professional position in a school system (0), employed in business or industry (0), employed in government agency (1), employed in a community mental health/counseling center (0), employed in a hospital/medical center (0), still seeking employment (0), not seeking employment (0), other employment position (0), do not know (0), total from the above (doctoral) (2).

Additional Information:

Orientation, Objectives, and Emphasis of Department: The Wisconsin School of Professional Psychology has as its goal the provision of a doctoral-level education that emphasizes the acquisition of the traditional skills that defined the professional in the past, while staying open to new developments as they emerge. Our program balances theoretical and practical coursework, taking its impetus from the American Psychological Association's Vail Conference. The school's curriculum was developed in accord with APA norms and is continually evaluated to assure compliance with the requirements of that body. WSPP trains students toward competence in the following areas: self-awareness, assessment, research and evaluation, ethics and professional standards, management and supervision, relationship, intervention, respect for diversity, consultation, social responsibility, and community service. In its training philosophy, the school emphasizes clarity of verbal expression in written and oral communication, the development of clinical acumen, and an appreciation of the link between scientific data and clinical practice. Our program's small size and large faculty create abundant opportunities for mentorship with practicing psychologists in an apprentice-like setting.

Special Facilities or Resources: The Wisconsin School of Professional Psychology maintains a Training Clinic that includes facilities for research and practicum work associated with clinical courses. The Training Center houses an outpatient mental health clinic, which serves a primarily inner-city culturally diverse population, as well as provides opportunities for supervised experience with a wide range of clinical problems and populations. The center offers services to the community on a sliding fee basis. Supervision provided by faculty.

Application Information:
Send to Wisconsin School of Professional Psychology, 9120 West Hampton Avenue, Milwaukee, WI 53225. Application available online. URL of online application: http://www.wspp.edu. Students are admitted in the Fall, application deadline April 15; Spring, application deadline October 15. *Fee:* $75.

Wisconsin, University of, Eau Claire

Department of Psychology
Arts and Sciences
University of Wisconsin-Eau Claire
Eau Claire, WI 54702
Telephone: (715) 836-5733
Fax: (715) 836-2214
E-mail: *lozarb@uwec.edu*
Web: *http://www.psyc.uwec.edu/eds.htm*

Department Information:
1965. Chairperson: Lori Bica. Number of faculty: total—full-time 16, part-time 4; women—full-time 9, part-time 4.

Programs and Degrees Offered:
Listed in the following order: Program area, degree type (T if terminal Master's), number awarded 7/06–6/07. School Psychology EdS/MEd (School Psychology) 7.

Student Applications/Admissions:
Student Applications
School Psychology EdS/MEd (School Psychology)—Applications 2007–2008, 40. Total applicants accepted 2007–2008, 13. Number full-time enrolled (new admits only) 2007–2008, 8. Number part-time enrolled (new admits only) 2007–2008, 0. Total enrolled 2007–2008 full-time, 22. Openings 2008–2009, 8. The median number of years required for completion of a degree in 2006–2007 were 3. The number of students enrolled full- and part-time who were dismissed or voluntarily withdrew from this program area in 2007–2008 were 0.

Admissions Requirements:
Scores: Entries appear in this order: required test or GPA, minimum score (if required), median score of students entering in 2007–2008. Master's Programs: GRE-V 400, 420; GRE-Q no minimum stated, 580; overall undergraduate GPA 3.0, 3.56. Doctoral Programs: GRE-V no minimum stated; GRE-Q no minimum stated; GRE-Subject (Psychology) no minimum stated; MAT no minimum stated; overall undergraduate GPA no minimum stated; last 2 years GPA no minimum stated; psychology GPA no minimum stated.
Other Criteria: (importance of criteria rated low, medium, or high): GRE/MAT scores—high, research experience—medium, work experience—medium, extracurricular activity—medium, clinically related public service—medium, GPA—high, letters of recommendation—high, interview—high, statement of goals and objectives—high. For additional information on admission requirements, go to http://www.psyc.uwec.edu/eds.htm.

Student Characteristics: The following represents characteristics of students in 2007–2008 in all graduate psychology programs in the department: Female—full-time 18, part-time 0; Male—full-time 4, part-time 0; African American/Black—full-time 0, part-time 0; Hispanic/Latino(a)—full-time 0, part-time 0; Asian/Pacific Islander—full-time 1, part-time 0; American Indian/Alaska Native—full-time 0, part-time 0; Caucasian/White—full-time 21, part-time 0; students subject to the Americans With Disabilities Act—full-time 1, part-time 0; Unknown ethnicity—full-time 0, part-time 0.

Financial Information/Assistance:
Tuition for Full-Time Study: *Master's:* State residents: per academic year $5,005, $430 per credit hour; Nonstate residents: per academic year $17,480, $984 per credit hour. Tuition is subject to change. See the following Web site for updates and changes in tuition costs: http://www.uwec.edu/gradadmiss.

Financial Assistance:
First-Year Students: Teaching assistantships available for first year. Average amount paid per academic year: $5,005. Average number of hours worked per week: 10. Apply by March 1. Fellowships and scholarships available for first year. Average amount paid per academic year: $500. Apply by March 1.
Advanced Students: Teaching assistantships available for advanced students. Average amount paid per academic year: $5,005. Average number of hours worked per week: 10. Apply by March 1. Fellowships and scholarships available for advanced students. Average amount paid per academic year: $500. Apply by March 1.
Additional Information: Of all students currently enrolled full time, 95% benefited from one or more of the listed financial assistance programs. Application and information available online at http://www.uwec.edu/gradadmiss/.

Internships/Practica: Internships are required for the Educational Specialist degree and comprise the 3rd year of training. Students must complete a year of full-time practice as school psychologists under the supervision of an appropriately credentialed school psychologist. Students may enroll in the internship upon completion of all requirements except the thesis. A more detailed description of the internship requirements are available at the school psychology program Web site: http://www.psyc.uwec.edu/eds.htm.

Housing and Day Care: No on-campus housing is available. On-campus day care facilities are available. See the following Web site for more information: http://www.uwec.edu/Admin/Children; e-mail: children@uwec.edu.

Employment of Department Graduates:
Master's Degree Graduates: Of those who graduated in the academic year 2006–2007, the following categories and numbers represent the postgraduate activities and employment of master's degree graduates: Enrolled in a postdoctoral residency/fellowship (n/a), employed in independent practice (n/a), employed in a professional position in a school system (10), total from the above (master's) (10).

Doctoral Degree Graduates: Of those who graduated in the academic year 2006–2007, the following categories and numbers represent the postgraduate activities and employment of doctoral degree graduates: Enrolled in a psychology doctoral program (n/a), total from the above (doctoral) (0).

Additional Information:

Orientation, Objectives, and Emphasis of Department: The primary goals of the EdS School Psychology training program focus on preparation of a broadly skilled school psychology professional, one trained to meet the many and diverse challenges of practice in a rapidly changing work setting. Training in the delivery of evaluation and intervention (counseling, consultation, training, and research) services is eclectic, drawing heavily from behavioral (social learning, operant, and cognitive), clinical, developmental, and educational (regular and special education) theoretical foundations. Professional training prepares the practitioner to work with individuals from early childhood/preschool through youth and adult ages providing services related to exceptional educational, at risk, and/or regular education needs. Three training strands (diagnostics, research, and intervention) have been developed, which make available extensive "applied training" opportunities. Twelve practicas and a 3rd-year internship have been structured to provide extensive supervised, professional training experiences (over 2,000 hours), with two practica beginning during the student's first semester of enrollment. Faculty supervisors have a training emphasis and appropriate professional license/certification in the areas of assigned supervision (e.g., clinical, behavioral, school, counseling). The program has two unique features: the Human Development Center and an ongoing collaborative relationship with the Lac du Flambeau American Indian community.

Special Facilities or Resources: Extensive on-campus and field site training opportunities are available. Two interdisciplinary clinics—the Human Development Center (Psychology: School Psychology; Special Education: Learning Disabilities and Early Childhood; Communication Disorders; and Elementary Education: Reading) and the Psychological Services Center (Psychology School: Psychology and Nursing)—provide on-campus training in diagnostics and intervention services. Area schools, residential facilities for developmentally disabled, and emotionally disturbed youth and adults, and clinics offer an extensive array of additional supervised training settings. In addition, the program has a continuing collaborative relationship with the Lac du Flambeau American Indian community, which offers opportunities for short-term or semester-long practicums.

Information for Students With Physical Disabilities: See the following Web site for more information: http://www.uwec.edu/SSD; Email: bayerlam@uwec.edu.

Application Information:

Send to Office of Admissions, UW—Eau Claire, Eau Claire, WI 54702-4004. Application available online. URL of online application: http://www.apply.wisconsin.edu/graduate.eau. Students are admitted in the Spring, application deadline March 1. *Fee:* $45. Wisconsin law does not permit exemption or waiver of the application fee.

Wisconsin, University of, La Crosse

Department of Psychology/School Psychology
College of Liberal Studies
1725 State Street, 341 Graff Main Hall
La Crosse, WI 54601
Telephone: (608) 785-8441
Fax: (608) 785-8443
E-mail: *dixon.robe@uwlax.edu*
Web: *http://www.uwlax.edu/Graduate/psychology/*

Department Information:

1967. Director: Robert J. Dixon. Number of faculty: total—full-time 17, part-time 6; women—full-time 13, part-time 2; total—minority—full-time 1.

Programs and Degrees Offered:

Listed in the following order: Program area, degree type (T if terminal Master's), number awarded 7/06–6/07. School Psychology EdS/MEd (School Psychology) 13.

Student Applications/Admissions:

Student Applications

School Psychology EdS/MEd (School Psychology)—Applications 2007–2008, 47. Total applicants accepted 2007–2008, 18. Number full-time enrolled (new admits only) 2007–2008, 8. Total enrolled 2007–2008 full-time, 15, part-time, 32. Openings 2008–2009, 12. The median number of years required for completion of a degree in 2006–2007 were 3. The number of students enrolled full- and part-time who were dismissed or voluntarily withdrew from this program area in 2007–2008 were 2.

Admissions Requirements:

Scores: Entries appear in this order: required test or GPA, minimum score (if required), median score of students entering in 2007–2008. Master's Programs: GRE-V no minimum stated, 440; GRE-Q no minimum stated, 560; overall undergraduate GPA 2.85, 3.58; last 2 years GPA no minimum stated, 3.78; psychology GPA no minimum stated, 3.73. The GRE Analytical score of 5.0 refers to the Analytical Writing score. The GRE Psychology Subject Test in Psychology is not required but strongly recommended for the following applicants: If your GPA for the last 2 years is below 3.25, or if you have graduated without majoring in psychology.

Other Criteria: (importance of criteria rated low, medium, or high): GRE/MAT scores—medium, research experience—medium, work experience—medium, extracurricular activity—medium, clinically related public service—high, GPA—high, letters of recommendation—high, interview—high, statement of goals and objectives—high, undergraduate major in psychology—low, specific undergraduate psychology courses taken—low.

Student Characteristics: The following represents characteristics of students in 2007–2008 in all graduate psychology programs in the department: Female—full-time 12, part-time 27; Male—full-time 3, part-time 5; African American/Black—full-time 0, part-time 0; Hispanic/Latino(a)—full-time 0, part-time 0; Asian/Pacific Islander—full-time 0, part-time 1; American Indian/Alaska Native—full-time 0, part-time 0; Caucasian/White—

full-time 15, part-time 32; Multi-ethnic—full-time 0, part-time 0; students subject to the Americans With Disabilities Act—full-time 0, part-time 1; Unknown ethnicity—full-time 0, part-time 0.

Financial Information/Assistance:

Tuition for Full-Time Study: *Master's:* State residents: per academic year $7,035, $387 per credit hour; Nonstate residents: per academic year $17,645, $976 per credit hour. Tuition is subject to change. Additional fees are assessed to students beyond the costs of tuition for the following: Special course fees may be assessed for certain courses for supplemental materials and/or equipment.

Financial Assistance:

First-Year Students: Research assistantships available for first year. Average amount paid per academic year: $6,386. Average number of hours worked per week: 14. Apply by March 1.

Advanced Students: Research assistantships available for advanced students. Average amount paid per academic year: $6,386. Average number of hours worked per week: 14. Apply by March 1.

Additional Information: Of all students currently enrolled full time, 17% benefited from one or more of the listed financial assistance programs.

Internships/Practica: The School Psychology program prepares graduate students for certification as School Psychologists through academic coursework, 700 hours of supervised school practica, and a 1 year, 1,200-hour school internship. Graduate students are placed in local schools as early and intensively as possible. During their second, third, and fourth semesters students spend 2 days per week working in local schools under the direct supervision of experienced school psychologists. During these school practica students develop professional skills in assessment, consultation, intervention, counseling, and case management. Many of the core courses require projects that are completed in the schools during practica.

Housing and Day Care: On-campus housing is available. Campus housing is available for graduate students in Reuter Hall. This new residence hall will house 380 upper class students in 95 suites. Each suite will have four private bedrooms, a bathroom, living room, and full kitchen. Students interested in living in this hall should contact the Office of Residence Life (608-785-8075) or e-mail Sue Townsend (townsend.susa@uwlax.edu) for further information and sign-up procedures. On-campus day care facilities are available. Child Care Center: (608) 785-8813.

Employment of Department Graduates:

Master's Degree Graduates: Of those who graduated in the academic year 2006–2007, the following categories and numbers represent the postgraduate activities and employment of master's degree graduates: Enrolled in a postdoctoral residency/fellowship (n/a), employed in independent practice (n/a), employed in a professional position in a school system (9), total from the above (master's) (9).

Doctoral Degree Graduates: Of those who graduated in the academic year 2006–2007, the following categories and numbers represent the postgraduate activities and employment of doctoral degree graduates: Enrolled in a psychology doctoral program (n/a), total from the above (doctoral) (0).

Additional Information:

Orientation, Objectives, and Emphasis of Department: The emphasis of this program is to train school psychologists who are effective teachers, parents, and school consultants. The program also emphasizes a pupil services model, which addresses the educational and mental health needs of all children. The School Psychology knowledge base includes areas of Professional School Psychology, Educational Psychology, Psychological Foundations, Educational Foundations, and Mental Health. To provide psychological services in education, graduates of the School Psychology program must also have considerable knowledge of curriculum, special education, and pupil services. Graduates of the program are employed in public schools or educational agencies that serve public schools.

Personal Behavior Statement: In the initial letter sent to the incoming students they will receive information regarding the criminal background check and the ethical statement that mirrors the Wisconsin licensure requirements.

Special Facilities or Resources: Extensive fieldwork in local schools is a key to professional training. Faculty work closely with field supervisors and observe student performance in the field.

Information for Students With Physical Disabilities: See the following Web site for more information: http://www.uwlax.edu/drs/.

Application Information:

Send to School Psychology Admissions, 341 Graff Main Hall, University of Wisconsin—La Crosse, 1725 State Street, La Crosse, WI 54601. Application available online. URL of online application: http://www.uwlax.edu/graduate/psychology/. Students are admitted in the Fall, application deadline January 15. *Fee:* $45.

Wisconsin, University of, Madison

Department of Counseling Psychology, Counseling Psychology Program
School of Education
Education Building, Room 321, 1000 Bascom Mall
Madison, WI 53706
Telephone: (608) 262-0461, (608) 263-2746
Fax: (608) 265-3347
E-mail: *mgarity@education.wisc.edu*
Web: *http://www.education.wisc.edu/cp*

Department Information:

1964. Chairperson: Mary Lee Nelson. Number of faculty: total—full-time 8, part-time 2; women—full-time 4, part-time 2; total—minority—full-time 3, part-time 1; women minority—full-time 1, part-time 1.

Programs and Degrees Offered:

Listed in the following order: Program area, degree type (T if terminal Master's), number awarded 7/06–6/07. Counseling MA/MS (Master of Arts/Science) (T) 23, Counseling Psychology PhD (Doctor of Philosophy) 9.

APA Accreditation: Counseling PhD (Doctor of Philosophy).

Student Applications/Admissions:

Student Applications

Counseling MA/MS (Master of Arts/Science)—Applications 2007–2008, 164. Total applicants accepted 2007–2008, 21. Number full-time enrolled (new admits only) 2007–2008, 17. Total enrolled 2007–2008 full-time, 36, part-time, 5. Openings 2008–2009, 18. The median number of years required for completion of a degree in 2006–2007 were 2. The number of students enrolled full- and part-time who were dismissed or voluntarily withdrew from this program area in 2007–2008 were 0. *Counseling Psychology PhD (Doctor of Philosophy)*—Applications 2007–2008, 96. Total applicants accepted 2007–2008, 11. Number full-time enrolled (new admits only) 2007–2008, 8. Number part-time enrolled (new admits only) 2007–2008, 0. Total enrolled 2007–2008 full-time, 55, part-time, 2. Openings 2008–2009, 8. The median number of years required for completion of a degree in 2006–2007 were 10. The number of students enrolled full- and part-time who were dismissed or voluntarily withdrew from this program area in 2007–2008 were 0.

Admissions Requirements:

Scores: Entries appear in this order: required test or GPA, minimum score (if required), median score of students entering in 2007–2008. Master's Programs: GRE-V no minimum stated; GRE-Q no minimum stated; last 2 years GPA 3.0, 3.4. Doctoral Programs: GRE-V no minimum stated, 550; GRE-Q no minimum stated, 570.

Other Criteria: (importance of criteria rated low, medium, or high): GRE/MAT scores—medium, research experience—high, work experience—medium, extracurricular activity—high, clinically related public service—high, GPA—medium, letters of recommendation—high, interview—high, statement of goals and objectives—high. For master's: research low, no interview required. All other criteria the same.

Student Characteristics: The following represents characteristics of students in 2007–2008 in all graduate psychology programs in the department: Female—full-time 68, part-time 6; Male—full-time 23, part-time 1; African American/Black—full-time 10, part-time 2; Hispanic/Latino(a)—full-time 15, part-time 0; Asian/Pacific Islander—full-time 11, part-time 0; American Indian/Alaska Native—full-time 1, part-time 0; Caucasian/White—full-time 52, part-time 5; Multi-ethnic—full-time 1, part-time 0; students subject to the Americans With Disabilities Act—full-time 0, part-time 0; Unknown ethnicity—full-time 1, part-time 0; International students who hold an F-1 or J-1 Visa—full-time 2, part-time 0.

Financial Information/Assistance:

Tuition for Full-Time Study: *Master's:* State residents: per academic year $9,643, $604 per credit hour; Nonstate residents: per academic year $24,913, $1,558 per credit hour. *Doctoral:* State residents: per academic year $9,643, $604 per credit hour; Nonstate residents: per academic year $24,913, $1,558 per credit hour. Tuition is subject to change. See the following Web site for updates and changes in tuition costs: http://www.registrar.wisc.edu.

Financial Assistance:

First-Year Students: Teaching assistantships available for first year. Average amount paid per academic year: $14,000. Average number of hours worked per week: 13. Apply by January 5. Tuition remission given: full. Research assistantships available for first year. Average amount paid per academic year: $14,000. Average number of hours worked per week: 13. Apply by January 5. Tuition remission given: full. Fellowships and scholarships available for first year. Average amount paid per academic year: $14,000. Average number of hours worked per week: 13. Apply by January 5. Tuition remission given: full.

Advanced Students: Teaching assistantships available for advanced students. Average amount paid per academic year: $14,000. Average number of hours worked per week: 13. Tuition remission given: full. Research assistantships available for advanced students. Average amount paid per academic year: $14,000. Average number of hours worked per week: 13. Tuition remission given: full. Fellowships and scholarships available for advanced students. Average amount paid per academic year: $14,000. Average number of hours worked per week: 13. Tuition remission given: full.

Additional Information: Of all students currently enrolled full time, 35% benefited from one or more of the listed financial assistance programs.

Internships/Practica: Doctoral Degree (PhD Counseling Psychology): For those doctoral students for whom a professional internship was required in this program prior to graduation, (4) students applied for an internship in 2006–2007, with (4) students obtaining an internship. Of those students who obtained an internship, (4) were paid internships. Of those students who obtained an internship, (3) students placed in APA/CPA-accredited internships, (0) students placed in internships not APA/CPA-accredited, but listed with the Association of Psychology Postdoctoral and Internship Centers (APPIC), (0) students placed in internships conforming to guidelines of the Council of Directors of School Psychology Programs (CDSPP), (1) student placed in internships that were not APA/CPA-accredited, APPIC or CDSPP listed. Both master's and doctoral students are required to take at least two semesters of practica. For doctoral students (and some master's students), local sites include Dane County Community Mental Health Agency, Mendota Mental Health Institute, University of Wisconsin Counseling and Consultation Services, Veteran's Administration Hospital, and Family Therapy, Inc. Master's students may pursue practica in three types of settings: public schools, student services offices and counseling centers in higher education, and community mental health agencies and private clinics. The majority of practicum placements are in the Madison area but some are placed in nearby metropolitan areas in Wisconsin such as Milwaukee and Green Bay, as well as in rural communities served by regional mental health clinics.

Housing and Day Care: On-campus housing is available. See the following Web site for more information: http://www.housing.wisc.edu/. On-campus day care facilities are available.

Employment of Department Graduates:

Master's Degree Graduates: Of those who graduated in the academic year 2006–2007, the following categories and numbers represent the postgraduate activities and employment of master's degree graduates: Enrolled in a psychology doctoral program (5), enrolled in a postdoctoral residency/fellowship (n/a), employed in independent practice (n/a), total from the above (master's) (5). ***Doctoral Degree Graduates:*** Of those who graduated in the academic year 2006–2007, the following categories and numbers represent the postgraduate activities and employment of doctoral degree graduates: Enrolled in a psychology doctoral program (n/a), employed in other positions at a higher education institution (2), employed in government agency (2), still seeking employment (3), other employment position (3), total from the above (doctoral) (10).

Additional Information:

Orientation, Objectives, and Emphasis of Department: The master's and doctoral programs are intended to provide a closely integrated didactic experimental curriculum for the preparation of counseling professionals. The master's degree strongly emphasizes service delivery, and its practica/internship components reflect that emphasis. The doctoral degree emphasizes the integration of counseling and psychological theory and practice with substantive development of research skills in the domains encompassed by counseling psychology. The PhD program in counseling psychology is APA-accredited utilizing the scientist–practitioner model. Students are prepared for academic, service-delivery, research, and administrative positions in professional psychology. The Department infuses principles of multiculturalism throughout the curriculum.

Special Facilities or Resources: The department possesses excellent computer facilities including multimedia production. Also, two counseling psychologists employed at the University Counseling Service are adjunct professors in the department and provide us with ongoing linkage with that service for practica and internships. We also have very up-to-date computer software assessment resources. The department, together with departments of Rehabilitation Psychology, Special Education, and School Psychology, utilizes an interdisciplinary training center that provides professional training practices.

Information for Students With Physical Disabilities: See the following Web site for more information: http://www.jumpgate.acadsvcs.wisc.edu/~mcburney.

Application Information:

Send to Department of Counseling Psychology, Graduate Admissions, UW—Madison, 321 Education Building, 1000 Bascom Mall, Madison, WI 53706. Application available online. URL of online application: https://www.gradsch.wisc.edu/eapp/eapp.pl. Students are admitted in the Fall, application deadline for PhD is December 15; Master's, February 1. For the Summer, application deadlines are the same. *Fee:* $45.

Wisconsin, University of, Madison

Department of Educational Psychology, School Psychology Program
1025 West Johnson Street
Madison, WI 53706-1796
Telephone: (608) 262-3432
Fax: (608) 262-0843
E-mail: *edpsych@wisc.edu*
Web: *http://www.education.wisc.edu/edpsych/index.html*

Department Information:

1960. Chairperson: Ronald C. Serlin. Number of faculty: total—full-time 8; women—full-time 3; total—minority—full-time 1; women minority—full-time 1.

Programs and Degrees Offered:

Listed in the following order: Program area, degree type (T if terminal Master's), number awarded 7/06–6/07. School Psychology PhD (Doctor of Philosophy) 5, Quantitative PhD (Doctor of Philosophy) 2.

APA Accreditation: School PhD (Doctor of Philosophy).

Student Applications/Admissions:

Student Applications

School Psychology PhD (Doctor of Philosophy)—Applications 2007–2008, 57. Total applicants accepted 2007–2008, 10. Number full-time enrolled (new admits only) 2007–2008, 7. Openings 2008–2009, 10. The median number of years required for completion of a degree in 2006–2007 were 6. The number of students enrolled full- and part-time who were dismissed or voluntarily withdrew from this program area in 2007–2008 were 1. *Quantitative PhD (Doctor of Philosophy)*—Applications 2007–2008, 17. Total applicants accepted 2007–2008, 6. Number full-time enrolled (new admits only) 2007–2008, 4. Total enrolled 2007–2008 full-time, 11. Openings 2008–2009, 3. The median number of years required for completion of a degree in 2006–2007 were 6. The number of students enrolled full- and part-time who were dismissed or voluntarily withdrew from this program area in 2007–2008 were 0.

Admissions Requirements:

Scores: Entries appear in this order: required test or GPA, minimum score (if required), median score of students entering in 2007–2008. Doctoral Programs: GRE-V no minimum stated, 570; GRE-Q no minimum stated, 660; overall undergraduate GPA 3.00.

Other Criteria: (importance of criteria rated low, medium, or high): GRE/MAT scores—medium, research experience—medium, work experience—medium, extracurricular activity—low, clinically related public service—medium, GPA—medium, letters of recommendation—high, interview—high, statement of goals and objectives—high.

Student Characteristics: The following represents characteristics of students in 2007–2008 in all graduate psychology programs in the department: Female—full-time 29, part-time 0; Male—full-time 12, part-time 0; African American/Black—full-time 2, part-time 0; Hispanic/Latino(a)—full-time 2, part-time 0; Asian/Pacific Islander—full-time 5, part-time 0; American Indian/Alaska Native—full-time 0, part-time 0; Caucasian/White—full-time 32, part-time 0; students subject to the Americans With Disabilities Act—full-time 0, part-time 0; Unknown ethnicity—full-time 0, part-time 0; International students who hold an F-1 or J-1 Visa—full-time 4, part-time 0.

Financial Information/Assistance:

Tuition for Full-Time Study: *Master's:* State residents: per academic year $9,642, $604 per credit hour; Nonstate residents: per academic year $24,912, $1,559 per credit hour. *Doctoral:* State residents: per academic year $9,642, $604 per credit hour; Nonstate residents: per academic year $24,912, $1,559 per credit hour. Tuition is subject to change. See the following Web site for updates and changes in tuition costs: http://www.registrar.wisc.edu/.

Financial Assistance:

First-Year Students: Teaching assistantships available for first year. Average amount paid per academic year: $12,894. Average number of hours worked per week: 20. Apply by December 1. Tuition remission given: full. Research assistantships available for first year. Average amount paid per academic year: $16,029. Average number of hours worked per week: 20. Apply by December 1. Tuition remission given: full. Traineeships available for first year. Apply by December 1. Tuition remission given: full. Fellowships and scholarships available for first year. Average amount paid per academic year: $17,570. Average number of hours worked per week: 0. Apply by December 1. Tuition remission given: full.

Advanced Students: Teaching assistantships available for advanced students. Average amount paid per academic year: $13,401. Average number of hours worked per week: 20. Apply by December 1. Tuition remission given: full. Research assistantships available for advanced students. Average amount paid per academic year: $16,029. Average number of hours worked per week: 20. Apply by December 1. Tuition remission given: full. Traineeships available for advanced students. Apply by December 1. Tuition remission given: full. Fellowships and scholarships available for advanced students. Average amount paid per academic year: $17,570. Average number of hours worked per week: 0. Apply by December 1. Tuition remission given: full.

Additional Information: Of all students currently enrolled full time, 76% benefited from one or more of the listed financial assistance programs. Application and information available online at http://www.wisc.edu/grad.

Internships/Practica: Doctoral Degree (PhD School Psychology): For those doctoral students for whom a professional internship was required in this program prior to graduation, (6) students applied for an internship in 2006–2007, with (6) students obtaining an internship. Of those students who obtained an internship, (3) were paid internships. Of those students who obtained an internship, (0) students placed in APA/CPA-accredited internships, (3) students placed in internships not APA/CPA accredited, but listed with the Association of Psychology Postdoctoral and Internship Centers (APPIC), (0) students placed in internships conforming to guidelines of the Council of Directors of School Psychology Programs (CDSPP), (3) students placed in internships that were not APA/CPA-accredited, APPIC or CDSPP listed. The School Psychology program admits students interested in obtaining a PhD. Students working toward this goal complete a two-semester clinical practicum experience during year 2 (200-hour minimum) and a two-semester field practicum during year 3 (400-hour minimum). This practicum experience is provided by the department. After the master's, students are required to complete either an APA-approved internship or establish one of their own in a school (public or private), clinic, or hospital that is approved by the program (minimum 200 hours) to complete their PhD requirements. The Wisconsin Internship Consortium in Professional School Psychology (WICPSP) is also administered through the School Psychology program. The primary focus of the predoctoral internship program is to provide advanced training for graduate students from a wide variety of cooperating sites where an internship is provided over several rotations. This internship is implemented according to Ethical Principles of Psychologists (APA, 1992), and the criteria published by the National Register of Health Service Providers and the National Association of School Psychologists are also followed. Criteria endorsed by the Council of Directors of School Psychology are also met.

Housing and Day Care: On-campus housing is available. See the following Web site for more information: http://www.housing.wisc.edu. On-campus day care facilities are available. See the following Web site for more information: http://www.housing.wisc.edu/partners/childcare.

Employment of Department Graduates:

Master's Degree Graduates: Of those who graduated in the academic year 2006–2007, the following categories and numbers represent the postgraduate activities and employment of master's degree graduates: Enrolled in a psychology doctoral program (5), enrolled in a postdoctoral residency/fellowship (n/a), employed in independent practice (n/a), total from the above (master's) (5).

Doctoral Degree Graduates: Of those who graduated in the academic year 2006–2007, the following categories and numbers represent the postgraduate activities and employment of doctoral degree graduates: Enrolled in a psychology doctoral program (n/a), enrolled in another graduate/professional program (0), employed in an academic position at a university (1), employed in an academic position at a 2-year/4-year college (1), employed in other positions at a higher education institution (0), employed in a professional position in a school system (3), employed in business or industry (1), total from the above (doctoral) (6).

Additional Information:

Orientation, Objectives, and Emphasis of Department: The School Psychology program, within the Department of Educational Psychology, prepares professional psychologists to use knowledge of the behavioral sciences in ways that enhance the learning and adjustment of both normal and exceptional children, their families, and their teachers. A balanced emphasis is placed on developing competencies necessary for functioning in both applied settings such as schools and community agencies, and in research positions in institutions of higher education. The program focus is the study of psychological and educational principles that influence the adjustment of individuals from birth to 21 years. Students are required to demonstrate competencies in the substantive content areas of psychological and educational theory and practice.

Personal Behavior Statement: For all programs leading to a certificate or license to teach or requiring field placement (e.g., student teaching practica, counseling practica and internships, and school psychology internships), applicants for admission must disclose, among other things, whether they have ever been charged with or convicted of any crime and whether licensure has ever been denied or revoked in any state for reasons other than insufficient credits or courses. The existence of a criminal record or denial of revocation does not constitute an automatic bar to admission and will be considered only as they substantially relate to the duties and responsibilities of the programs and eventual licensure. Students who are denied admission or removed from such a placement are entitled to appeal that decision. Information about the appeals process is available in department offices, of the Office of Student Services, http://www.education.wisc.edu/edpsych.index.html.

Special Facilities or Resources: The Educational and Psychological Training Center serves advanced graduate students in Educational Psychology. It provides diagnostic and treatment services for children and adolescents experiencing a variety of learning and behavior problems. The Laboratory of Experimental Design provides assistance to students and faculty in the design and analysis of research. Members of the laboratory include graduate students and faculty in the quantitative area.

Information for Students With Physical Disabilities: See the following Web site for more information: http://www.education.wisc.edu/edpsych/index.html.

Application Information:
Send to Graduate Admissions Coordinator, Education Psychology, 1025 West Johnson Street, Madison, WI 53706-1796. Application available online. URL of online application: http://www.wisc.edu/grad. Students are admitted in the Fall, application deadline December 1. *Fee:* $45.

Wisconsin, University of, Madison

Department of Psychology
W. J. Brogden Psychology Building
1202 West Johnson Street
Madison, WI 53706
Telephone: (608) 262-1041
Fax: (608) 262-4029
E-mail: *gradinfo@psych.wisc.edu*
Web: *http://www.psych.wisc.edu/*

Department Information:
1888. Chairperson: Joseph P. Newman. Number of faculty: total—full-time 31; women—full-time 13; total—minority—full-time 3; women minority—full-time 2.

Programs and Degrees Offered:
Listed in the following order: Program area, degree type (T if terminal Master's), number awarded 7/06–6/07. Biology of Brain and Behavior PhD (Doctor of Philosophy) 0, Clinical PhD (Doctor of Philosophy) 1, Cognitive and Cognitive Neurosciences PhD (Doctor of Philosophy) 1, Developmental PhD (Doctor of Philosophy) 0, Social Psychology and Personality PhD (Doctor of Philosophy) 0, Individualized Graduate Major PhD (Doctor of Philosophy) 2, Perception PhD (Doctor of Philosophy) 0.

APA Accreditation: Clinical PhD (Doctor of Philosophy).

Student Applications/Admissions:
Student Applications
Biology of Brain and Behavior PhD (Doctor of Philosophy)—Applications 2007–2008, 19. Total applicants accepted 2007–2008, 0. Number full-time enrolled (new admits only) 2007–2008, 0. Number part-time enrolled (new admits only) 2007–2008, 0. Openings 2008–2009, 2. The number of students enrolled full- and part-time who were dismissed or voluntarily withdrew from this program area in 2007–2008 were 0. *Clinical PhD (Doctor of Philosophy)*—Applications 2007–2008, 176. Total applicants accepted 2007–2008, 12. Number full-time enrolled (new admits only) 2007–2008, 4. Number part-time enrolled (new admits only) 2007–2008, 0. Openings 2008–2009, 3. The median number of years required for completion of a degree in 2006–2007 were 7. The number of students enrolled full- and part-time who were dismissed or voluntarily withdrew from this program area in 2007–2008 were 0. *Cognitive and Cognitive Neurosciences PhD (Doctor of Philosophy)*—Applications 2007–2008, 49. Total applicants accepted 2007–2008, 8. Number full-time enrolled (new admits only) 2007–2008, 4. Number part-time enrolled (new admits only) 2007–2008, 0. Openings 2008–2009, 3. The median number of years required for completion of a degree in 2006–2007 were 5. The number of students enrolled full- and part-time who were dismissed or voluntarily withdrew from this program area in 2007–2008 were 0. *Developmental PhD (Doctor of Philosophy)*—Applications 2007–2008, 27. Total applicants accepted 2007–2008, 2. Number full-time enrolled (new admits only) 2007–2008, 0. Total enrolled 2007–2008 full-time, 9. Openings 2008–2009, 2. *Social Psychology and Personality PhD (Doctor of Philosophy)*—Applications 2007–2008, 66. Total applicants accepted 2007–2008, 6. Number full-time enrolled (new admits only) 2007–2008, 2. Number part-time enrolled (new admits only) 2007–2008, 0. Openings 2008–2009, 3. The number of students enrolled full- and part-time who were dismissed or voluntarily withdrew from this program area in 2007–2008 were 0. *Individualized Graduate Major PhD (Doctor of Philosophy)*—Applications 2007–2008, 13. Total applicants accepted 2007–2008, 4. Number full-time enrolled (new admits only) 2007–2008, 4. Number part-time enrolled (new admits only) 2007–2008, 0. Openings 2008–2009, 5. The median number of years required for completion of a degree in 2006–2007 were 7. *Perception PhD (Doctor of Philosophy)*—Applications 2007–2008, 4. Total applicants accepted 2007–2008, 0. Number full-time enrolled (new admits only) 2007–2008, 0. Number part-time enrolled (new admits only) 2007–2008, 0. The number of students enrolled full- and part-time who were dismissed or voluntarily withdrew from this program area in 2007–2008 were 0.

Admissions Requirements:
Scores: Entries appear in this order: required test or GPA, minimum score (if required), median score of students entering in 2007–2008. Doctoral Programs: GRE-V no minimum stated; GRE-Q no minimum stated; overall undergraduate GPA 3.00; Doctoral program GRE-Analytic no minimum stated. GRE Subject test is strongly recommended, but not required.
Other Criteria: (importance of criteria rated low, medium, or high): GRE/MAT scores—high, research experience—high, work experience—low, extracurricular activity—low, clinically related public service—low, GPA—high, letters of recommendation—high, interview—high, statement of goals and objectives—high. For additional information on admission requirements, go to http://psych.wisc.edu/gradstudies/NewAdmission.html.

Student Characteristics: The following represents characteristics of students in 2007–2008 in all graduate psychology programs in the department: Female—full-time 59, part-time 0; Male—full-time 30, part-time 0; African American/Black—full-time 3, part-time 0; Hispanic/Latino(a)—full-time 1, part-time 0; Asian/Pacific Islander—full-time 2, part-time 0; American Indian/Alaska Native—full-time 2, part-time 0; Caucasian/White—full-time 81, part-time 0; Multi-ethnic—full-time 0, part-time 0; students subject to the Americans With Disabilities Act—

full-time 1, part-time 0; Unknown ethnicity—full-time 0, part-time 0; International students who hold an F-1 or J-1 Visa—full-time 3, part-time 0.

Financial Information/Assistance:

Tuition for Full-Time Study: *Doctoral:* State residents: per academic year $4,821; Nonstate residents: per academic year $12,456. Tuition is subject to change. Additional fees are assessed to students beyond the costs of tuition for the following: student fees. See the following Web site for updates and changes in tuition costs: http://www.registrar.wisc.edu/students/fees_tuition/tuition.php.

Financial Assistance:

First-Year Students: Teaching assistantships available for first year. Average amount paid per academic year: $17,196. Average number of hours worked per week: 20. Apply by January 5. Tuition remission given: full. Research assistantships available for first year. Average amount paid per academic year: $19,032. Average number of hours worked per week: 20. Apply by January 5. Tuition remission given: full. Traineeships available for first year. Average amount paid per academic year: $20,772. Average number of hours worked per week: 20. Apply by January 5. Tuition remission given: full. Fellowships and scholarships available for first year. Average amount paid per academic year: $17,570. Apply by January 5. Tuition remission given: full.

Advanced Students: Teaching assistantships available for advanced students. Average amount paid per academic year: $20,640. Average number of hours worked per week: 20. Tuition remission given: full. Research assistantships available for advanced students. Average amount paid per academic year: $19,032. Average number of hours worked per week: 20. Tuition remission given: full. Traineeships available for advanced students. Average number of hours worked per week: 20. Tuition remission given: full. Fellowships and scholarships available for advanced students. Average amount paid per academic year: $17,570. Tuition remission given: full.

Additional Information: Of all students currently enrolled full time, 100% benefited from one or more of the listed financial assistance programs. Application and information available online at http://info.gradsch.wisc.edu/admin/admissions/appinstr.html.

Internships/Practica: Doctoral Degree (PhD Clinical): For those doctoral students for whom a professional internship was required in this program prior to graduation, (5) students applied for an internship in 2006–2007, with (4) students obtaining an internship. Of those students who obtained an internship, (4) were paid internships. Of those students who obtained an internship, (3) students placed in APA/CPA-accredited internships, (1) student placed in internships not APA/CPA-accredited, but listed with the Association of Psychology Postdoctoral and Internship Centers (APPIC), (0) students placed in internships conforming to guidelines of the Council of Directors of School Psychology Programs (CDSPP), (0) students placed in internships that were not APA/CPA-accredited, APPIC or CDSPP listed. Clinical Psychology graduate students are required to complete a minimum of 400 hours of practicum experience, of which at least 150 hours are in direct service experience and at least 75 hours are in formally scheduled supervision. Each student will complete a 160-hour clerkship at a preapproved site that is designed to expose students to diverse clinical populations and the practice of clinical psychology in an applied setting. Also, a 1-year internship is required.

Housing and Day Care: On-campus housing is available. See the following Web site for more information: http://www.housing.wisc.edu. On-campus day care facilities are available. See the following Web site for more information: http://www.housing.wisc.edu/occfr.

Employment of Department Graduates:

Master's Degree Graduates: Of those who graduated in the academic year 2006–2007, the following categories and numbers represent the postgraduate activities and employment of master's degree graduates: Enrolled in a postdoctoral residency/fellowship (n/a), employed in independent practice (n/a), total from the above (master's) (0).

Doctoral Degree Graduates: Of those who graduated in the academic year 2006–2007, the following categories and numbers represent the postgraduate activities and employment of doctoral degree graduates: Enrolled in a psychology doctoral program (n/a), total from the above (doctoral) (0).

Additional Information:

Orientation, Objectives, and Emphasis of Department: The psychology PhD program is characterized by the following goals: emphasis both on extensive academic training in general psychology and on intensive research training in the student's particular area of concentration, a wide offering of content courses and seminars permitting the student considerable freedom in working out a program of study in collaboration with the major professor, and early and continuing commitment to research. Students are expected to become competent scholars and creative scientists in their own areas of concentration.

Special Facilities or Resources: The department has an extraordinary array of research facilities. Virtually all laboratories are fully computer controlled, and the department's general-purpose facilities are freely available to all graduate students. The Brogden and the Harlow Primate Laboratory have special facilities for housing animals, as well as for behavioral, pharmacological, anatomical, immunological, and physiological studies. We are well-equipped for studies of visual, auditory, and language perception and other areas of cognitive psychology. In addition, the Psychology Department Research and Training Clinic is housed in the Brogden Building. Many of the faculty and graduate students are affiliated with the Institute of Aging, the Waisman Center on Mental Retardation and Human Development, the Wisconsin Regional Primate Research Center, the Health Emotions Center, the Neuroscience Training Program, the Keck Neuroimaging Center, the Hearing Training Program, the Institute for Research on Poverty, the NSF National Consortium on Violence Research, and the Women's Studies Research Center. There are strong ties to the departments of Anatomy, Anthropology, Communicative Disorders, Educational Psychology, Entomology, Immunology, Industrial Engineering, Ophthalmology, Psychiatry, Sociology, Wildlife Ecology, Zoology, the Mass Communication Research Center, the Institute for Research on Poverty, and the Survey Research Laboratory.

Information for Students With Physical Disabilities: See the following Web site for more information: http://www.wisc.edu/adac/uw.html.

Application Information:
Supplementary materials should be sent to Graduate Admissions, Department of Psychology, University of Wisconsin, 1202 West Johnson Street, Madison, WI 53706. Application available online. URL of online application: http://www.info.gradsch.wisc.edu/admin/admissions/appinstr.html. Students are admitted in the Fall, application deadline December 15. *Fee:* $45. Similar to GRE fee waiver: http://www.education.wisc.edu/elpa/admissions/gen_adm.html.

Wisconsin, University of, Madison

Human Development and Family Studies
School of Human Ecology
1430 Linden Drive
Madison, WI 53706
Telephone: (608) 263-2381
Fax: (608) 265-1172
E-mail: *hdfs@mail.sohe.wisc.edu*
Web: *http://www.sohe.wisc.edu/departments/hdfs*

Department Information:
1903. Chairperson: Linda J. Roberts. Number of faculty: total—full-time 13; women—full-time 8; total—minority—full-time 3; women minority—full-time 2.

Programs and Degrees Offered:
Listed in the following order: Program area, degree type (T if terminal Master's), number awarded 7/06–6/07. Human Ecology: Human Development and Family Studies PhD (Doctor of Philosophy) 3, Human Ecology: Human Development and Family Studies MA/MS (Master of Arts/Science) 8.

Student Applications/Admissions:

Student Applications

Human Ecology: Human Development and Family Studies PhD (Doctor of Philosophy)—Applications 2007–2008, 10. Total applicants accepted 2007–2008, 4. Number full-time enrolled (new admits only) 2007–2008, 1. Number part-time enrolled (new admits only) 2007–2008, 0. Total enrolled 2007–2008 full-time, 21, part-time, 2. Openings 2008–2009, 3. The median number of years required for completion of a degree in 2006–2007 were 6. The number of students enrolled full- and part-time who were dismissed or voluntarily withdrew from this program area in 2007–2008 were 0. *Human Ecology: Human Development and Family Studies MA/MS (Master of Arts/Science)*—Applications 2007–2008, 23. Total applicants accepted 2007–2008, 9. Number full-time enrolled (new admits only) 2007–2008, 4. Number part-time enrolled (new admits only) 2007–2008, 0. Total enrolled 2007–2008 full-time, 7, part-time, 2. Openings 2008–2009, 3. The median number of years required for completion of a degree in 2006–2007 were 3. The number of students enrolled full- and part-time who were dismissed or voluntarily withdrew from this program area in 2007–2008 were 0.

Admissions Requirements:

Scores: Entries appear in this order: required test or GPA, minimum score (if required), median score of students entering in 2007–2008. Master's Programs: GRE-V no minimum stated, 524; GRE-Q no minimum stated, 600; overall undergraduate GPA 3.0, 3.53. Doctoral Programs: GRE-V no minimum stated, 600; GRE-Q no minimum stated, 727; overall undergraduate GPA 3.0, 3.34.

Other Criteria: (importance of criteria rated low, medium, or high): GRE/MAT scores—medium, research experience—medium, work experience—low, GPA—high, letters of recommendation—high, statement of goals and objectives—high, fit with faculty interest—high. For additional information on admission requirements, go to http://info.gradsch.wisc.edu/admin/admissions/index.html or http://www.sohe.wisc.edu/departments/hdf.

Student Characteristics: The following represents characteristics of students in 2007–2008 in all graduate psychology programs in the department: Female—full-time 24, part-time 4; Male—full-time 4, part-time 0; African American/Black—full-time 1, part-time 0; Hispanic/Latino(a)—full-time 3, part-time 1; Asian/Pacific Islander—full-time 9, part-time 0; American Indian/Alaska Native—full-time 0, part-time 0; Caucasian/White—full-time 15, part-time 3; Multi-ethnic—full-time 0, part-time 0; Unknown ethnicity—full-time 0, part-time 0; International students who hold an F-1 or J-1 Visa—full-time 6, part-time 0.

Financial Information/Assistance:

Tuition for Full-Time Study: *Master's:* State residents: $604 per credit hour; Nonstate residents: $1,558 per credit hour. *Doctoral:* State residents: $604 per credit hour; Nonstate residents: $1,558 per credit hour. Tuition is subject to change. See the following Web site for updates and changes in tuition costs: http://www.registrar.wisc.edu/students/fees_tuition/tuition.php.

Financial Assistance:

First-Year Students: Teaching assistantships available for first year. Average amount paid per academic year: $8,595. Average number of hours worked per week: 13. Apply by January 10. Tuition remission given: full. Research assistantships available for first year. Average amount paid per academic year: $12,688. Average number of hours worked per week: 13. Apply by varies. Tuition remission given: full. Fellowships and scholarships available for first year. Apply by January 10.

Advanced Students: Teaching assistantships available for advanced students. Average amount paid per academic year: $10,317. Average number of hours worked per week: 13. Apply by January 10. Tuition remission given: full. Research assistantships available for advanced students. Average amount paid per academic year: $12,688. Average number of hours worked per week: 13. Apply by varies. Tuition remission given: full. Fellowships and scholarships available for advanced students. Apply by January 10.

Additional Information: Of all students currently enrolled full time, 80% benefited from one or more of the listed financial assistance programs. Application and information available online at http://whyuwmadison.gradsch.wisc.edu/academic/academics.html.

Internships/Practica: No information provided.

Housing and Day Care: On-campus housing is available. See the following Web site for more information: http://www.whyuwmadison.gradsch.wisc.edu/life/housing.html. On-campus day care facilities are available. University provides a childcare assistance subsidy. See the following Web site for more information: http://www.housing.wisc.edu/partners/childcare/.

Employment of Department Graduates:

Master's Degree Graduates: Of those who graduated in the academic year 2006–2007, the following categories and numbers represent the postgraduate activities and employment of master's degree graduates: Enrolled in another graduate/professional program (5), enrolled in a postdoctoral residency/fellowship (n/a), employed in independent practice (n/a), employed in government agency (1), do not know (2), total from the above (master's) (8).

Doctoral Degree Graduates: Of those who graduated in the academic year 2006–2007, the following categories and numbers represent the postgraduate activities and employment of doctoral degree graduates: Enrolled in a psychology doctoral program (n/a), employed in an academic position at a university (1), do not know (2), total from the above (doctoral) (3).

Additional Information:

Orientation, Objectives, and Emphasis of Department: The UW Human Development and Family Studies Graduate Program provides opportunities for advanced study and research on human development and families across the life span. Two assumptions are basic to the philosophy and organization of the program. First, we can only understand individual development within its social context, and families are an essential component of this context. Second, we can only understand families within their larger social context—historical change, social class, ethnicity, and public policy. The program offers courses on development in infancy, childhood, adolescence, adulthood, and old age. Other courses focus on family relationships, process, and diversity. The faculty bring the perspectives of many different disciplines and methodologies to their work. Faculty and students never lose sight, however, of the connections among human development, family life, and the broader sociohistorical context.

Special Facilities or Resources: Because the department has joint faculty in UW Extension, students often work in the community doing community-based research and outreach projects. Departmental faculty have affiliated appointments with research centers and other programs on campus, which students have access to. The Family Interaction Lab in the department provides a naturalitic homelike setting for unobtrusive videotaping of interactions. A control room is located adjacent to the interaction room for camera control, taping, editing, dubing, and coding of videotapes. The UW Preschool Laboratory is adjacent to the department.

Information for Students With Physical Disabilities: See the following Web site for more information: http://www.mcburney.wisc.edu/services.

Application Information:

Send to Graduate Admissions, Human Development and Family Studies, Graduate Program, University of Wisconsin—Madison, 1430 Linden Drive, Madison, WI 53706. Application available online. URL of online application: https://www.gradsch.wisc.edu/eapp/eapp.pl. Students are admitted in the Fall, application deadline January 10. *Fee:* $56.

Wisconsin, University of, Milwaukee

Department of Psychology
College of Letters and Science
P.O. Box 413
Milwaukee, WI 53201-0413
Telephone: (414) 229-4747
Fax: (414) 229-5219
E-mail: *suelima@uwm.edu*
Web: *http://www.uwm.edu/Dept/Psychology*

Department Information:

1956. Chairperson: David Osmon. Number of faculty: total—full-time 22; women—full-time 6; total—minority—full-time 1.

Programs and Degrees Offered:

Listed in the following order: Program area, degree type (T if terminal Master's), number awarded 7/06–6/07. Experimental Behavior Analysis MA/MS (Master of Arts/Science) (T) 0, Experimental Health Psychology MA/MS (Master of Arts/Science) (T) 0, Experimental PhD (Doctor of Philosophy) 4, Clinical PhD (Doctor of Philosophy) 10.

APA Accreditation: Clinical PhD (Doctor of Philosophy).

Student Applications/Admissions:

Student Applications

Experimental Behavior Analysis MA/MS (Master of Arts/Science)—Applications 2007–2008, 10. Total applicants accepted 2007–2008, 0. Number full-time enrolled (new admits only) 2007–2008, 0. Number part-time enrolled (new admits only) 2007–2008, 0. Openings 2008–2009, 2. The number of students enrolled full- and part-time who were dismissed or voluntarily withdrew from this program area in 2007–2008 were 0. *Experimental Health Psychology MA/MS (Master of Arts/Science)*—Applications 2007–2008, 26. Total applicants accepted 2007–2008, 4. Number full-time enrolled (new admits only) 2007–2008, 4. Number part-time enrolled (new admits only) 2007–2008, 0. Openings 2008–2009, 4. The number of students enrolled full- and part-time who were dismissed or voluntarily withdrew from this program area in 2007–2008 were 0. *Experimental PhD (Doctor of Philosophy)*—Applications 2007–2008, 15. Total applicants accepted 2007–2008, 11. Number full-time enrolled (new admits only) 2007–2008, 5. Number part-time enrolled (new admits only) 2007–2008, 0. Openings 2008–2009, 5. The median number of years required for completion of a degree in 2006–2007 were 6. The number of students enrolled full- and part-time who were dismissed or voluntarily withdrew from this program area in 2007–2008 were 2. *Clinical PhD (Doctor of Philosophy)*—Applications 2007–2008, 109. Total applicants accepted 2007–2008, 10. Number full-time enrolled (new admits only) 2007–2008, 6. Number part-time enrolled (new admits only) 2007–2008, 0. Openings 2008–2009, 5. The median number of years required for completion of a degree in 2006–2007 were 6. The number of students enrolled full- and part-time who were dismissed or voluntarily withdrew from this program area in 2007–2008 were 0.

Admissions Requirements:

Scores: Entries appear in this order: required test or GPA, minimum score (if required), median score of students entering

in 2007–2008. Master's Programs: GRE-V no minimum stated, 480; GRE-Q no minimum stated, 595; GRE-Subject (Psychology) no minimum stated, 630; overall undergraduate GPA 3.00, 3.54; last 2 years GPA no minimum stated, 3.44; psychology GPA no minimum stated, 3.55. Doctoral Programs: GRE-V no minimum stated, 520; GRE-Q no minimum stated, 655; GRE-Subject (Psychology) no minimum stated, 710; overall undergraduate GPA 3.00, 3.55; last 2 years GPA no minimum stated, 3.69; psychology GPA no minimum stated, 3.65. For the Experimental Doctoral Program: GRE V+Q minimum is 800.

Other Criteria: (importance of criteria rated low, medium, or high): GRE/MAT scores—high, research experience—medium, work experience—low, extracurricular activity—low, clinically related public service—low, GPA—high, letters of recommendation—high, interview—high, statement of goals and objectives—high. No interview is required for admission to the doctoral program in Experimental Psychology, but an interview is required for admission to the doctoral program in Clinical Psychology. For additional information on admission requirements, go to http://www.uwm.edu/Dept/Psychology/gradapp.html.

Student Characteristics: The following represents characteristics of students in 2007–2008 in all graduate psychology programs in the department: Female—full-time 44, part-time 0; Male—full-time 30, part-time 0; African American/Black—full-time 2, part-time 0; Hispanic/Latino(a)—full-time 6, part-time 0; Asian/Pacific Islander—full-time 6, part-time 0; American Indian/Alaska Native—full-time 0, part-time 0; Caucasian/White—full-time 60, part-time 0; Multi-ethnic—full-time 0, part-time 0; students subject to the Americans With Disabilities Act—full-time 0, part-time 0; Unknown ethnicity—full-time 0, part-time 0; International students who hold an F-1 or J-1 Visa—full-time 4, part-time 0.

Financial Information/Assistance:

Tuition for Full-Time Study: *Master's:* State residents: per academic year $9,253, $779 per credit hour; Nonstate residents: per academic year $23,619, $1,677 per credit hour. *Doctoral:* State residents: per academic year $9,253, $779 per credit hour; Nonstate residents: per academic year $23,619, $1,677 per credit hour. Tuition is subject to change. See the following Web site for updates and changes in tuition costs: http://www.bfs.uwm.edu/fees/.

Financial Assistance:

First-Year Students: Teaching assistantships available for first year. Average amount paid per academic year: $11,044. Average number of hours worked per week: 20. Apply by December 31. Tuition remission given: full. Research assistantships available for first year. Average amount paid per academic year: $17,000. Average number of hours worked per week: 20. Apply by December 31. Tuition remission given: full. Fellowships and scholarships available for first year. Average amount paid per academic year: $9,000. Average number of hours worked per week: 0. Apply by December 31. Tuition remission given: full.

Advanced Students: Teaching assistantships available for advanced students. Average amount paid per academic year: $11,965. Average number of hours worked per week: 20. Apply by December 31. Tuition remission given: full. Research assistantships available for advanced students. Average amount paid per academic year: $17,000. Average number of hours worked per week: 20. Apply by December 31. Tuition remission given: full. Fellowships and scholarships available for advanced students. Average amount paid per academic year: $14,000. Average number of hours worked per week: 0. Apply by December 31. Tuition remission given: full.

Additional Information: Of all students currently enrolled full time, 81% benefited from one or more of the listed financial assistance programs. Application and information available online at http://www.uwm.edu/Dept/Psychology/gradapp.html.

Internships/Practica: Master's Degree (MA/MS Experimental Behavior Analysis): An internship experience such as a final research project or "capstone" experience is required of graduates. Master's Degree (MA/MS Experimental Health Psychology): An internship experience such as a final research project or "capstone" experience is required of graduates. Doctoral Degree (PhD Clinical): For those doctoral students for whom a professional internship was required in this program prior to graduation, (6) students applied for an internship in 2006–2007, with (6) students obtaining an internship. Of those students who obtained an internship, (6) were paid internships. Of those students who obtained an internship, (6) students placed in APA/CPA-accredited internships, (0) students placed in internships not APA/CPA-accredited, but listed with the Association of Psychology Postdoctoral and Internship Centers (APPIC), (0) students placed in internships conforming to guidelines of the Council of Directors of School Psychology Programs (CDSPP), (0) students placed in internships that were not APA/CPA-accredited, APPIC or CDSPP listed. Numerous training sites in the greater Milwaukee area are used for clinical training practica, providing students with excellent training in clinical psychology, including neuropsychology and health psychology. These training experiences equip Clinical doctoral students to compete for nationally recognized predoctoral internships.

Housing and Day Care: On-campus housing is available. See the following Web site for more information: http://www4.uwm.edu/Dept/housing/. On-campus day care facilities are available. See the following Web site for more information: http://www4.uwm.edu/ccc/.

Employment of Department Graduates:

Master's Degree Graduates: Of those who graduated in the academic year 2006–2007, the following categories and numbers represent the postgraduate activities and employment of master's degree graduates: Enrolled in a postdoctoral residency/fellowship (n/a), employed in independent practice (n/a), total from the above (master's) (0).

Doctoral Degree Graduates: Of those who graduated in the academic year 2006–2007, the following categories and numbers represent the postgraduate activities and employment of doctoral degree graduates: Enrolled in a psychology doctoral program (n/a), enrolled in a postdoctoral residency/fellowship (7), employed in an academic position at a university (1), employed in an academic position at a 2-year/4-year college (3), employed in a community mental health/counseling center (2), employed in a hospital/medical center (1), total from the above (doctoral) (14).

Additional Information:

Orientation, Objectives, and Emphasis of Department: The department has a PhD program in Clinical Psychology (which includes earning the MS), a PhD program in Experimental Psychology (which includes earning the MS), and terminal Experimental MS programs in Health Psychology and Behavior Analysis. The Experimental PhD program offers specialization in behavior analysis, cognition and perception, developmental psychology, health and social psychology, and neuroscience. Regardless of the specialty area, the goal of the program is to provide the students with an understanding of psychology as a scientific discipline and to prepare them for careers in research and teaching. The Clinical program follows the Boulder model, in which students are trained as both scientists and practitioners through integration of research, practical experience, and coursework in personality theory, psychopathology, assessment, and psychotherapy. A predoctoral internship is required. Although a Clinical student may emphasize either the basic or applied aspect of psychology, the goal of the program is excellence in both areas. Students in the Clinical as well as the Experimental program are directly involved in research under the direction of their major professor, during each semester in the department.

Special Facilities or Resources: The department moved to a completely remodeled building in September 1985, which contains a separate research laboratory for each member of the faculty and specifically designed quarters for teaching laboratory courses. Faculty have computers in their offices, as well as in their laboratories. Special construction, air conditioning, and ventilation were included in the teaching and research laboratories to accommodate work with animal subjects and human participants. There is also a mechanical and woodworking shop and an electronics shop, supervised by a full-time technician. The department training clinic is housed in a separate wing of the building with its own offices, clerical staff, research space, clinic rooms, and full-time director.

Information for Students With Physical Disabilities: See the following Web site for more information: http://www4.uwm.edu/sac/.

Application Information:

Send to Chairperson, Graduate Admissions Committee, Department of Psychology, P.O. Box 413, Milwaukee, WI 53201-0413. Application available online. URL of online application: http://www.uwm.edu/Dept/Psychology/gradapp.html. Students are admitted in the Fall, application deadline December 31. The application deadline is December 5 for the doctoral program in Clinical Psychology. Note that two separate applications are required: one to the Psychology Department and one to the Graduate School. *Fee:* $45. Application fee for foreign students is $85. International applicants should consult the following Web site: http://www.uwm.edu/Dept/CIE.

Wisconsin, University of, Milwaukee (2007 data)

Educational Psychology
Education
2400 East Hartford IP0413
Milwaukee, WI 53211
Telephone: (414) 229-4767
Fax: (414) 229-4939
E-mail: *psmith@uwm.edu*
Web: *http://www.uwm.edu/Dept/EdPsych*

Department Information:

1965. Chairperson: Anthony A. Hains, PhD Number of faculty: total—full-time 24, part-time 13; women—full-time 15, part-time 9.

Programs and Degrees Offered:

Listed in the following order: Program area, degree type (T if terminal Master's), number awarded 7/06–6/07. Counseling MA/MS (Master of Arts/Science) 72, School EdS/MEd (School Psychology) 7, Research Methodology MA/MS (Master of Arts/Science) 3, Learning and Development MA/MS (Master of Arts/Science) (T) 2, Counseling Psychology PhD (Doctor of Philosophy) 4, School Psychology PhD (Doctor of Philosophy) 4, Learning and Development PhD (Doctor of Philosophy) 1, Research Methodology PhD (Doctor of Philosophy) 2.

APA Accreditation: Counseling PhD (Doctor of Philosophy). School PhD (Doctor of Philosophy).

Student Applications/Admissions:

Student Applications

Counseling MA/MS (Master of Arts/Science)—Applications 2007–2008, 211. Total applicants accepted 2007–2008, 77. Number full-time enrolled (new admits only) 2007–2008, 22. Number part-time enrolled (new admits only) 2007–2008, 55. Total enrolled 2007–2008 full-time, 89, part-time, 235. Openings 2008–2009, 65. The median number of years required for completion of a degree in 2006–2007 were 4. The number of students enrolled full- and part-time who were dismissed or voluntarily withdrew from this program area in 2007–2008 were 4. *School EdS/MEd (School Psychology)*—Applications 2007–2008, 42. Total applicants accepted 2007–2008, 13. Number full-time enrolled (new admits only) 2007–2008, 17. Number part-time enrolled (new admits only) 2007–2008, 2. Total enrolled 2007–2008 full-time, 26, part-time, 27. Openings 2008–2009, 14. The median number of years required for completion of a degree in 2006–2007 were 4. The number of students enrolled full- and part-time who were dismissed or voluntarily withdrew from this program area in 2007–2008 were 1. *Research Methodology MA/MS (Master of Arts/Science)*—Applications 2007–2008, 15. Total applicants accepted 2007–2008, 5. Number full-time enrolled (new admits only) 2007–2008, 5. Number part-time enrolled (new admits only) 2007–2008, 0. Openings 2008–2009, 5. The median number of years required for completion of a degree in 2006–2007 were 2. The number of students enrolled full- and part-time who were dismissed or voluntarily withdrew from this program area in 2007–2008 were 0. *Learning and Development MA/MS (Master of Arts/Science)*—Applications 2007–2008, 7. Total applicants accepted 2007–2008, 4. Number full-time enrolled (new admits only) 2007–2008, 2. Number part-time enrolled (new admits only) 2007–2008, 2. Total enrolled 2007–2008 full-time, 10, part-time, 1. Openings 2008–2009, 5. The median number of years required for completion of a degree in 2006–2007 were 2. The number of students enrolled full- and part-time who were dismissed or voluntarily withdrew from this program area in 2007–2008 were 0. *Counseling Psychology PhD (Doctor of Philosophy)*—Applications 2007–2008, 27. Total applicants accepted 2007–2008, 7. Number full-time enrolled (new admits only) 2007–2008, 6. Number part-time enrolled (new admits only) 2007–2008, 0. Openings 2008–2009, 6. The median number of years required for completion of a degree in 2006–2007 were 5. The number of students enrolled full- and part-time who were dismissed or voluntarily withdrew from this program area in 2007–2008 were 0. *School Psychology PhD (Doctor of Philosophy)*—Applications 2007–2008, 22. Total applicants accepted

2007–2008, 4. Number full-time enrolled (new admits only) 2007–2008, 4. Number part-time enrolled (new admits only) 2007–2008, 0. Openings 2008–2009, 5. The median number of years required for completion of a degree in 2006–2007 were 5. The number of students enrolled full- and part-time who were dismissed or voluntarily withdrew from this program area in 2007–2008 were 0. *Learning and Development PhD (Doctor of Philosophy)*—Applications 2007–2008, 3. Total applicants accepted 2007–2008, 1. Number full-time enrolled (new admits only) 2007–2008, 1. Number part-time enrolled (new admits only) 2007–2008, 0. Openings 2008–2009, 2. The median number of years required for completion of a degree in 2006–2007 were 4. The number of students enrolled full- and part-time who were dismissed or voluntarily withdrew from this program area in 2007–2008 were 0. *Research Methodology PhD (Doctor of Philosophy)*—Applications 2007–2008, 7. Total applicants accepted 2007–2008, 2. Number full-time enrolled (new admits only) 2007–2008, 2. Number part-time enrolled (new admits only) 2007–2008, 0. Openings 2008–2009, 2. The median number of years required for completion of a degree in 2006–2007 were 4. The number of students enrolled full- and part-time who were dismissed or voluntarily withdrew from this program area in 2007–2008 were 0.

Admissions Requirements:

Scores: Entries appear in this order: required test or GPA, minimum score (if required), median score of students entering in 2007–2008. Master's Programs: overall undergraduate GPA 2.75, 3.6; last 2 years GPA 3.00, 3.8. Doctoral Programs: GRE-V no minimum stated; GRE-Q no minimum stated; GRE-Subject (Psychology) no minimum stated; overall undergraduate GPA 3.00, 3.5; Doctoral program GRE-Analytic no minimum stated; 40th percentile GRE-V, 30th percentile GRE-Q.

Other Criteria: (importance of criteria rated low, medium, or high): GRE/MAT scores—medium, research experience—high, work experience—low, clinically related public service—medium, GPA—high, letters of recommendation—high, interview—high, statement of goals and objectives—high, Research Interests—high. For additional information on admission requirements, go to http://www.soe.uwm.edu/pages/welcome/Departments/Educational_Psychology.

Student Characteristics: The following represents characteristics of students in 2007–2008 in all graduate psychology programs in the department: Female—full-time 124, part-time 158; Male—full-time 83, part-time 105; African American/Black—full-time 41, part-time 17; Hispanic/Latino(a)—full-time 9, part-time 2; Asian/Pacific Islander—full-time 5, part-time 2; American Indian/Alaska Native—full-time 1, part-time 0; Caucasian/White—full-time 145, part-time 227; Multi-ethnic—full-time 1, part-time 0; students subject to the Americans With Disabilities Act—full-time 4, part-time 1; Unknown ethnicity—full-time 5, part-time 15.

Financial Information/Assistance:

Tuition for Full-Time Study: *Master's:* State residents: per academic year $7,402, $475 per credit hour; Nonstate residents: per academic year $21,700, $1,300 per credit hour. *Doctoral:* State residents: per academic year $7,402, $475 per credit hour; Nonstate residents: per academic year $21,700, $1,300 per credit hour. Tuition is subject to change. See the following Web site for updates and changes in tuition costs: http://www.uwm.edu.

Financial Assistance:

First-Year Students: Teaching assistantships available for first year. Average amount paid per academic year: $8,500. Average number of hours worked per week: 20. Apply by rolling. Tuition remission given: full. Research assistantships available for first year. Average amount paid per academic year: $9,500. Average number of hours worked per week: 20. Apply by rolling. Tuition remission given: full. Fellowships and scholarships available for first year. Average amount paid per academic year: $8,000. Average number of hours worked per week: 20. Apply by rolling. Tuition remission given: full.

Advanced Students: Teaching assistantships available for advanced students. Average amount paid per academic year: $9,000. Average number of hours worked per week: 20. Apply by rolling. Tuition remission given: full. Research assistantships available for advanced students. Average amount paid per academic year: $10,000. Average number of hours worked per week: 20. Apply by rolling. Tuition remission given: full. Fellowships and scholarships available for advanced students. Average amount paid per academic year: $10,000. Average number of hours worked per week: 20. Apply by rolling. Tuition remission given: full.

Additional Information: Of all students currently enrolled full time, 65% benefited from one or more of the listed financial assistance programs. Application and information available online at http://www.soe.uwm.edu/pages/welcome/Departments/Educational_Psychology.

Internships/Practica: Students are placed in a variety of educational, business, and community settings as part of their graduate training.

Housing and Day Care: On-campus housing is available. See the following Web site for more information: http://www.uwm.edu/Dept/. On-campus day care facilities are available through Sanburg Child Care. See the following Web site for more information: http://www.uwm.edu/Dept/CCC.

Employment of Department Graduates:

Master's Degree Graduates: Of those who graduated in the academic year 2006–2007, the following categories and numbers represent the postgraduate activities and employment of master's degree graduates: Enrolled in a postdoctoral residency/fellowship (n/a), employed in independent practice (n/a), total from the above (master's) (0).

Doctoral Degree Graduates: Of those who graduated in the academic year 2006–2007, the following categories and numbers represent the postgraduate activities and employment of doctoral degree graduates: Enrolled in a psychology doctoral program (n/a), total from the above (doctoral) (0).

Additional Information:

Orientation, Objectives, and Emphasis of Department: The department has one MS program with majors in Community Counseling, School Counseling, School Psychology (also EdS), Research Methods, as well as Learning and Development. PhD program in Educational Psychology includes Research Methods, Learning and Development, School Psychology, and Counseling Psychology. The PhD programs in School Psychology and Counseling Psychology follow the model of training outlined by the

American Psychological Association. The programs are based on the scientist–practitioner model, in which students are trained as psychological scientists with specializations in school or counseling psychology. A strong, multicultural perspective undergirds the programs, with an emphasis on the contextual factors in student's work, and both provide unique training in the psychological, social, and educational needs of multiethnic populations within an urban psychosocial context. Students gain the knowledge, skills, and attitudes to work in a heterogeneous environment. Students are prepared to work in academic, service, delivery, research, and administrative positions.

Special Facilities or Resources: The department possesses excellent computer facilities. The department enjoys a strong collaborative relationship with the Department of Psychology, working together in an on-campus psychology clinic. We also have strong linkages to urban community and school partners, which provide students with a diverse set of research and practice opportunities.

Information for Students With Physical Disabilities: See the following Web site for more information: http://www.uwm.edu/DSAD/SAC.

Application Information:
For MS and EdS send to Department of Educational Psychology, UW—Milwaukee, P.O. Box 413, Milwaukee, WI 53201; for PhD send to Application Chair, Department of Educational Psychology, UW—Milwaukee, P.O. Box 413, Milwaukee, WI 53201. Application available online. URL of online application: http://www.uwm.edu/Dept/Grad_Sch/Prospective/. Students are admitted in the Fall, application deadline January 15. Admission once per academic year for Counseling and School Psychology programs. Research Methods and Learning and Development program have rolling admissions and will consider applications at anytime. *Fee:* $45.

Wisconsin, University of, Oshkosh

Department of Psychology
College of Letters and Science
800 Algoma Boulevard
Oshkosh, WI 54901
Telephone: (414) 424-2300
Fax: (414) 424-1204
E-mail: *kochj@uwosh.edu*
Web: *http://www.uwosh.edu/departments/psychology/*

Department Information:
1959. Chairperson: James Koch. Number of faculty: total—full-time 11, part-time 6; women—full-time 4, part-time 5.

Programs and Degrees Offered:
Listed in the following order: Program area, degree type (T if terminal Master's), number awarded 7/06–6/07. Experimental Psychology MA/MS (Master of Arts/Science) (T) 3, Industrial/Organizational Psychology MA/MS (Master of Arts/Science) (T) 7.

Student Applications/Admissions:
Student Applications
Experimental Psychology MA/MS (Master of Arts/Science)—Applications 2007–2008, 8. Total applicants accepted 2007–2008, 7. Number full-time enrolled (new admits only) 2007–2008, 5. Number part-time enrolled (new admits only) 2007–2008, 0. Openings 2008–2009, 10. The median number of years required for completion of a degree in 2006–2007 were 2. The number of students enrolled full- and part-time who were dismissed or voluntarily withdrew from this program area in 2007–2008 were 1. *Industrial/Organizational Psychology MA/MS (Master of Arts/Science)*—Applications 2007–2008, 25. Total applicants accepted 2007–2008, 12. Number full-time enrolled (new admits only) 2007–2008, 8. Number part-time enrolled (new admits only) 2007–2008, 0. Openings 2008–2009, 9. The median number of years required for completion of a degree in 2006–2007 were 2.

Admissions Requirements:
Scores: Entries appear in this order: required test or GPA, minimum score (if required), median score of students entering in 2007–2008. Master's Programs: GRE-V no minimum stated; GRE-Q no minimum stated; overall undergraduate GPA no minimum stated; last 2 years GPA no minimum stated; Master's GRE-Analytical no minimum stated.
Other Criteria: (importance of criteria rated low, medium, or high): GRE/MAT scores—medium, research experience—medium, work experience—low, extracurricular activity—low, GPA—medium, letters of recommendation—medium, statement of goals and objectives—medium. Students in the Industrial/Organizational emphasis are required to submit a two-to-three page personal statement covering the origins of their interest in working in Industrial/Organizational Psychology, relevant experience (work or volunteer) in this field, and any other relevant personal information. Students in the Experimental emphasis are required to submit a one-to-two page personal statement. This statement should include reasons for wanting to come to UW Oshkosh and areas of research interest. The admissions committee is particularly interested in details about research experience, including class projects, assistantships, presentations, or other research experiences. If there were any extenuating circumstances leading to low performance in any aspect as an undergraduate or on GRE exams, it would be appropriate to comment on these in the personal statement.

Student Characteristics: The following represents characteristics of students in 2007–2008 in all graduate psychology programs in the department: Female—full-time 18, part-time 2; Male—full-time 8, part-time 1; African American/Black—full-time 1, part-time 0; Hispanic/Latino(a)—full-time 1, part-time 0; Asian/Pacific Islander—full-time 0, part-time 0; American Indian/Alaska Native—full-time 0, part-time 0; Caucasian/White—full-time 24, part-time 3; Multi-ethnic—full-time 0, part-time 0; students subject to the Americans With Disabilities Act—full-time 0, part-time 0; Unknown ethnicity—full-time 0, part-time 0.

Financial Information/Assistance:
Tuition for Full-Time Study: *Master's:* State residents: per academic year $6,246, $347 per credit hour; Nonstate residents: per academic year $16,848, $936 per credit hour.

Financial Assistance:
First-Year Students: Research assistantships available for first year. Average number of hours worked per week: 14. Fellowships and scholarships available for first year.

Advanced Students: Research assistantships available for advanced students. Average number of hours worked per week: 14. Fellowships and scholarships available for advanced students.

Additional Information: Of all students currently enrolled full time, 75% benefited from one or more of the listed financial assistance programs. Application and information available online at http://www.uwosh.edu/gradstudies/financialinfo/index.php.

Internships/Practica: Industrial/Organizational students participate in practica in years 1 and 2. Some students also have the opportunity to do internships.

Housing and Day Care: On-campus housing is available. Contact the Residence Life office: (920) 424-3212. On-campus day care facilities are available. Contact the Children's Learning and Care Center, the on-campus child care facility, at (920) 424-0260 for more information.

Employment of Department Graduates:

Master's Degree Graduates: Of those who graduated in the academic year 2006–2007, the following categories and numbers represent the postgraduate activities and employment of master's degree graduates: Enrolled in a psychology doctoral program (3), enrolled in another graduate/professional program (0), enrolled in a postdoctoral residency/fellowship (n/a), employed in independent practice (n/a), employed in an academic position at a university (0), employed in an academic position at a 2-year/4-year college (0), employed in other positions at a higher education institution (0), employed in a professional position in a school system (0), employed in business or industry (4), employed in government agency (0), employed in a community mental health/counseling center (0), employed in a hospital/medical center (0), still seeking employment (0), not seeking employment (0), other employment position (1), do not know (0), total from the above (master's) (8).

Doctoral Degree Graduates: Of those who graduated in the academic year 2006–2007, the following categories and numbers represent the postgraduate activities and employment of doctoral degree graduates: Enrolled in a psychology doctoral program (n/a), total from the above (doctoral) (0).

Additional Information:

Orientation, Objectives, and Emphasis of Department: The program offers a master's degree in psychology with emphases in industrial/organizational and experimental psychology. All students are required to take core courses dealing with psychological methods and statistical analysis. Classes are small. Students in the I/O emphasis take two semesters of a practicum course that involves experience working with organizations in the local area. Students in the experimental emphasis take several content courses and conduct collaborative research with faculty.

Special Facilities or Resources: Practicum placements are available for research in local agencies and industries. Animal and human laboratories are also available.

Information for Students With Physical Disabilities: See the following Web site for more information: http://www.tts.uwosh.edu/dean/disabilities.htm.

Application Information:

Send to Office of Graduate Studies, University of Wisconsin, Oshkosh, 800 Algoma Boulevard, Oshkosh, WI 54901. Application available online. URL of online application: http://www.apps9.uwex.edu/pls/ea/Apply.Graduate?app_type=G&src=OSH&srcu=OSH&uw=OSH. Students are admitted in the Spring, application deadline March 15. Application deadline is for I/O program. The Experimental program has rolling admissions. *Fee:* $45.

Wisconsin, University of, Stout

Psychology Department / Applied Psychology
College of Education, Health and Human Sciences
McCalmont Hall 317
Menomonie, WI 54751-0790
Telephone: (715) 232-2451
Fax: (715) 232-5303
E-mail: *gorbatenkok@uwstout.edu*
Web: *http://www.uwstout.edu/programs/msap/*

Department Information:

1982. Program Director MSAP; Program Director MFT: Dr. Kristina Gorbatenko-Roth, Dr. Bruce Kuehl. Number of faculty: total—full-time 14, part-time 7; women—full-time 5, part-time 4; total—minority—full-time 3, part-time 1; women minority—part-time 1.

Programs and Degrees Offered:

Listed in the following order: Program area, degree type (T if terminal Master's), number awarded 7/06–6/07. Applied Psychology MA/MS (Master of Arts/Science) (T) 10, Marriage and Family Therapy MA/MS (Master of Arts/Science).

Student Applications/Admissions:

Student Applications

Applied Psychology MA/MS (Master of Arts/Science)—Applications 2007–2008, 21. Total applicants accepted 2007–2008, 17. Number full-time enrolled (new admits only) 2007–2008, 14. Number part-time enrolled (new admits only) 2007–2008, 1. Total enrolled 2007–2008 full-time, 29, part-time, 1. Openings 2008–2009, 25. The median number of years required for completion of a degree in 2006–2007 were 2. The number of students enrolled full- and part-time who were dismissed or voluntarily withdrew from this program area in 2007–2008 were 2. *Marriage and Family Therapy MA/MS (Master of Arts/Science).*

Admissions Requirements:

Scores: Entries appear in this order: required test or GPA, minimum score (if required), median score of students entering in 2007–2008. Master's Programs: overall undergraduate GPA 3.0, 3.38. The MSAP program and the UW—Stout require a 3.0 undergraduate GPA for nonprobationary admission. The MFT program requires a 2.75 undergraduate GPA to be considered for admission.

Other Criteria: (importance of criteria rated low, medium, or high): research experience—high, work experience—high, extracurricular activity—medium, clinically related public service—medium, GPA—high, letters of recommendation—high, statement of goals and objectives—high, applied experience—high, undergraduate major in psychology—low, specific undergraduate psychology courses taken—medium, GRE/MAT scores (MSAP = none, MFT = none); research experience (MSAP = high, MFT = low); work experience (MSAP = high, MFT = high); extracurricular activity (MSAP = medium, MFT = medium); clinically related public service (MSAP = low, MFT = medium); GPA (MSAP = high, MFT = medium); letters of recommendation (MSAP = high, MFT = high); interview (MSAP = none, MFT = high); statement of goals and objectives (MSAP = high, MFT = high); undergraduate major in psychology (MSAP = low); specific undergraduate psychology courses taken (MSAP = medium); other applied experience (MSAP = high, MFT = none). For additional information on admission requirements, go to http://www.uwstout.edu/programs/grad.shtml.

Student Characteristics: The following represents characteristics of students in 2007–2008 in all graduate psychology programs in the department: Female—full-time 19, part-time 1; Male—full-time 9, part-time 0; African American/Black—full-time 1, part-time 0; Hispanic/Latino(a)—full-time 1, part-time 0; Asian/Pacific Islander—full-time 1, part-time 0; American Indian/Alaska Native—full-time 0, part-time 0; Caucasian/White—full-time 24, part-time 1; Unknown ethnicity—full-time 0, part-time 0; International students who hold an F-1 or J-1 Visa—full-time 1, part-time 0.

Financial Information/Assistance:

Tuition for Full-Time Study: *Master's:* State residents: per academic year $8,000, $331 per credit hour; Nonstate residents: per academic year $13,383, $557 per credit hour. Tuition is subject to change. See the following Web site for updates and changes in tuition costs: http://www.uwstout.edu/stubus/.

Financial Assistance:

First-Year Students: Teaching assistantships available for first year. Average amount paid per academic year: $5,000. Average number of hours worked per week: 13. Apply by none. Research assistantships available for first year. Average amount paid per academic year: $4,000. Average number of hours worked per week: 10. Apply by none.

Advanced Students: Teaching assistantships available for advanced students. Average amount paid per academic year: $5,000. Average number of hours worked per week: 13. Apply by none. Research assistantships available for advanced students. Average amount paid per academic year: $4,000. Average number of hours worked per week: 10. Apply by none.

Additional Information: Of all students currently enrolled full time, 50% benefited from one or more of the listed financial assistance programs. Application and information available online at http://www.uwstout.edu/grad/finance.html and http://www.uwstout.edu/finaid/.

Internships/Practica: Master's Degree (MA/MS Applied Psychology): An internship experience such as a final research project or "capstone" experience is required of graduates. UW—Stout has a reputation for its experiential-based curriculum. Approximately 700 students annually are in co-op or internship placements. The institution has an extensive network of business and industry contacts for the internship experience that is organized through the Placement and Co-op Services office. MSAP students are encouraged to seek out placement sites early in their program work. MFT is a 2-year, full time program. The 2nd year consists primarily of a clinical practicum in which students work with clients in both an on-campus and off-campus therapy clinic. Supervision is provided by four faculty who are also American Association for Marriage and Family Therapy Approved Supervisors. For additional information on education and training outcomes for our programs, see the following Web site: MSAP: http://www.uwstout.edu/programs/msap/; MFT: http://www.uwstout.edu/programs/msmft.

Housing and Day Care: On-campus housing is available. See the following Web site for more information: http://www.uwstout.edu/housing/. Contact Housing at (715) 232-1121; On-campus day care facilities are available. For information about child care services, contact the Child and Family Study Center, UW—Stout, Menomonie, WI 54751; phone (715) 232-1478 or e-mail cfsc@uwstout.edu.

Employment of Department Graduates:

Master's Degree Graduates: Of those who graduated in the academic year 2006–2007, the following categories and numbers represent the postgraduate activities and employment of master's degree graduates: Enrolled in a psychology doctoral program (5), enrolled in another graduate/professional program (0), enrolled in a postdoctoral residency/fellowship (n/a), employed in independent practice (n/a), employed in an academic position at a 2-year/4-year college (2), employed in other positions at a higher education institution (5), employed in a professional position in a school system (1), employed in business or industry (42), employed in a community mental health/counseling center (5), other employment position (3), total from the above (master's) (63).

Doctoral Degree Graduates: Of those who graduated in the academic year 2006–2007, the following categories and numbers represent the postgraduate activities and employment of doctoral degree graduates: Enrolled in a psychology doctoral program (n/a), total from the above (doctoral) (0).

Additional Information:

Orientation, Objectives, and Emphasis of Department: The MS in Applied Psychology (MSAP) is a 2-year program designed around a core of psychological theories, principles, and research methods. Students choose from among three concentration areas: industrial/organizational psychology, program evaluation, and applied research nonclinical health psychology. Dual concentrations in industrial/organizational psychology and program evaluation as well as program evaluation and health psychology are common. The MSAP program is designed to provide students with the knowledge, experience, skills, and abilities to apply theories and methods to the identification of and solution to a variety a variety of 21st century, real-world problems in business and industry, health care, and nonprofit organizations. A majority of classes incorporate real-world, hands-on learning opportunities that involve extensive group work and communication with external stakeholders. Numerous opportunities exist outside of formal courses for additional applied experience. The purpose of the MS MFT program is to train marriage and family therapists. The program is accredited by the Commission on Accreditation for Marriage and Family Therapy Education. It focuses primarily on systemic and relational theory and technique in the treatment of couple and family issues, including clinical symptoms. Graduates meet the educational requirements for becoming licensed in most states, including Wisconsin and Minnesota.

Special Facilities or Resources: The university has numerous consulting relationships with local and regional businesses and industries, health-related organizations, governmental agencies, and nonprofit organizations. MSAP students utilize the latest multimedia hardware and software to perform both quantitative and qualitative analyses. Several facilities and labs within the College of Human Development and the Psychology Department will receive or have received lab modernization funds. One of the most unique aspects of the MFT program is the on-campus Clinical Services Center facility in which all MFT students work with clients from the community under direct supervision of the MFT clinical faculty. One-way mirrors and audio-visual support is customary in the CSC. See the following Web site for more information: http://www.uwstout.edu/chd/csc.

Information for Students With Physical Disabilities: See the following Web site for more information: http://www.uwstout.edu/disability/.

Application Information:
Send to Program Director MSAP or Program Director MFT, and also the UW—Stout Graduate School. Application available online. URL of online application: http://www.uwstout.edu/programs/grad.shtml. Students are admitted in the Fall, application deadline February 1; Spring, application deadline October 1; programs have rolling admissions. All students applying to the graduate study at UW—Stout must apply to both the university-level Graduate School and also to a specific graduate program (the MSAP program or the MFT program). The MSAP program, the MFT program, and the Graduate School each have separate application materials. The MFT program admits students one time per year and applications are due February 1. Students who are admitted start school the following Fall semester. MSAP applications deadlines are February 1 for admission the following Fall semester and October 1 for admission the following Spring semester. *Fee:* $45.

Wyoming, University of
Department of Psychology
Arts and Sciences
Department 3415, 1000 East University Avenue
Laramie, WY 82071
Telephone: (307) 766-6303
Fax: (307) 766-2926
E-mail: *cpepper@uwyo.edu*
Web: *http://www.uwyo.edu/psychology*

Department Information:
1909. Chairperson: Carolyn Pepper. Number of faculty: total—full-time 15; women—full-time 7; total—minority—full-time 1; women minority—full-time 1.

Programs and Degrees Offered:
Listed in the following order: Program area, degree type (T if terminal Master's), number awarded 7/06–6/07. Clinical PhD (Doctor of Philosophy) 7, Developmental PhD (Doctor of Philosophy) 0, General PhD (Doctor of Philosophy) 2, Psychology and Law PhD (Doctor of Philosophy) 1.

APA Accreditation: Clinical PhD (Doctor of Philosophy).

Student Applications/Admissions:
Student Applications
Clinical PhD (Doctor of Philosophy)—Applications 2007–2008, 88. Total applicants accepted 2007–2008, 8. Number full-time enrolled (new admits only) 2007–2008, 5. Openings 2008–2009, 5. The median number of years required for completion of a degree in 2006–2007 were 10. The number of students enrolled full- and part-time who were dismissed or voluntarily withdrew from this program area in 2007–2008 were 0. *Developmental PhD (Doctor of Philosophy)*—Applications 2007–2008, 7. Total applicants accepted 2007–2008, 0. Number full-time enrolled (new admits only) 2007–2008, 0. Openings 2008–2009, 2. The number of students enrolled full- and part-time who were dismissed or voluntarily withdrew from this program area in 2007–2008 were 0. *General PhD (Doctor of Philosophy)*—Applications 2007–2008, 14. Total applicants accepted 2007–2008, 2. Number full-time enrolled (new admits only) 2007–2008, 2. Openings 2008–2009, 2. The median number of years required for completion of a degree in 2006–2007 were 8. The number of students enrolled full- and part-time who were dismissed or voluntarily withdrew from this program area in 2007–2008 were 0. *Psychology and Law PhD (Doctor of Philosophy)*—Applications 2007–2008, 3. Total applicants accepted 2007–2008, 0. Number full-time enrolled (new admits only) 2007–2008, 0. Total enrolled 2007–2008 full-time, 6. Openings 2008–2009, 2. The median number of years required for completion of a degree in 2006–2007 were 5. The number of students enrolled full- and part-time who were dismissed or voluntarily withdrew from this program area in 2007–2008 were 1.

Admissions Requirements:
Scores: Entries appear in this order: required test or GPA, minimum score (if required), median score of students entering in 2007–2008. Doctoral Programs: GRE-V 500, 591; GRE-Q 550, 647; GRE-Subject (Psychology) 550, 637; overall undergraduate GPA 3.00, 3.57.
Other Criteria: (importance of criteria rated low, medium, or high): GRE/MAT scores—high, research experience—high, work experience—low, extracurricular activity—low, clinically related public service—medium, GPA—medium, letters of recommendation—high, interview—high, statement of goals and objectives—high. Work Experience is relevant to the Clinical Program only. For additional information on admission requirements, go to http://uwadmnweb.uwyo.edu/psychology/grad.asp.

Student Characteristics: The following represents characteristics of students in 2007–2008 in all graduate psychology programs in the department: Female—full-time 27, part-time 0; Male—full-time 16, part-time 0; African American/Black—full-time 0, part-time 0; Hispanic/Latino(a)—full-time 1, part-time 0; Asian/Pacific Islander—full-time 2, part-time 0; American Indian/Alaska Native—full-time 1, part-time 0; Caucasian/White—full-time 39, part-time 0; Multi-ethnic—full-time 0, part-time 0; students subject to the Americans With Disabilities Act—full-time 0, part-time 0; Unknown ethnicity—full-time 0, part-time 0; International students who hold an F-1 or J-1 Visa—full-time 1, part-time 0.

Financial Information/Assistance:
Tuition for Full-Time Study: *Master's:* State residents: per academic year $3,936, $164 per credit hour; Nonstate residents: per academic year $11,280, $470 per credit hour. *Doctoral:* State residents: per academic year $3,936, $164 per credit hour; Nonstate residents: per academic year $11,280, $470 per credit hour. See the following Web site for updates and changes in tuition costs: http://www.uwyo.edu/sfa.

Financial Assistance:
First-Year Students: Teaching assistantships available for first year. Average amount paid per academic year: $10,696. Average number of hours worked per week: 20. Tuition remission given: full. Research assistantships available for first year. Average amount paid per academic year: $10,696. Average number of hours worked per week: 20. Tuition remission given: full. Fellowships and scholarships available for first year. Average amount paid per academic year: $2,000. Average number of hours worked per week: 0.
Advanced Students: Teaching assistantships available for advanced students. Average amount paid per academic year: $14,886. Average number of hours worked per week: 20. Tuition remission given: full. Research assistantships available for advanced students. Average number of hours worked per week: 20. Tuition remission given: full.
Additional Information: Of all students currently enrolled full time, 100% benefited from one or more of the listed financial assistance programs.

Internships/Practica: Doctoral Degree (PhD Clinical): For those doctoral students for whom a professional internship was required in this program prior to graduation, (3) students applied for an internship in 2006–2007, with (3) students obtaining an internship. Of those students who obtained an internship, (3) were paid internships. Of those students who obtained an internship, (3) students placed in APA/CPA-accredited internships, (0) students placed in internships not APA/CPA-accredited, but listed with the Association of Psychology Postdoctoral and Internship Centers (APPIC), (0) students placed in internships conforming to guidelines of the Council of Directors of School Psychology Programs (CDSPP), (0) students placed in internships that were not APA/CPA-accredited, APPIC or CDSPP listed. Given Wyoming's large geographic area (approximately 100,000 square miles) and small population (approximately 500,000), we arrange practica and clerkships for Clinical students in various settings throughout the state. Clerkships are typically conducted in the summer for extended periods of time. Practica and clerkships include a variety of clinical populations such as children, adolescents, adults, and elderly people. They occur in a range of placements including outpatient mental health centers, inpatient hospitals, VA Medical Centers, and residential programs. Specialty experiences include forensic evaluation, substance abuse training, and parent training. For additional information on education and training outcomes for our programs, see the following Web site: http://www.uwadmnweb.uwyo.edu/psychology/clinicalinternship.asp.

Housing and Day Care: On-campus housing is available. See the following Web site for more information: http://www.uwadmnweb.uwyo.edu/reslife-dining/. On-campus day care facilities are available. Two facilities are available on campus. See the following Web site for more information: http://www.uwyo.edu/Family/Child_Care/C_Care_Center.htm and http://www.uwyo.edu/Family/Child_Care/cdcnewpg.htm. The university is also building a large Child Care center and it will open in 2006. Other quality child care are available in the local community.

Employment of Department Graduates:

Master's Degree Graduates: Of those who graduated in the academic year 2006–2007, the following categories and numbers represent the postgraduate activities and employment of master's degree graduates: Enrolled in a postdoctoral residency/fellowship (n/a), employed in independent practice (n/a), total from the above (master's) (0).

Doctoral Degree Graduates: Of those who graduated in the academic year 2006–2007, the following categories and numbers represent the postgraduate activities and employment of doctoral degree graduates: Enrolled in a psychology doctoral program (n/a), employed in government agency (1), employed in a community mental health/counseling center (1), employed in a hospital/medical center (3), still seeking employment (2), total from the above (doctoral) (7).

Additional Information:

Orientation, Objectives, and Emphasis of Department: The University of Wyoming is the only 4-year university in the state of Wyoming. The Psychology Department has a broad undergraduate teaching mission and has one of the largest number of majors in the College of Arts and Sciences. The graduate curriculum provides breadth of training in psychology and permits specialization in various content areas. The Clinical Psychology PhD program is based on the scientist–practitioner model with an emphasis on training in integrated behavioral health care. Some Clinical students may also pursue a concentration in developmental psychology, psychology and law, or social–personality with experimental graduate program faculty. The goal of the Clinical program is to provide students with the knowledge base and broad conceptual skills necessary for professional practice and/or research in a variety of settings. The PhD program in Experimental Psychology provides students with broad training that can be used in a variety of academic and applied settings. Students may concentrate in Developmental Psychology or they may complete their concentration in Social Psychology. Students in any of the programs may pursue a Psychology and Law concentration. All programs contain opportunities for both applied and basic research training.

Special Facilities or Resources: The department has approximately 24,000 square feet of laboratory, office, and clinic space in a science complex with direct access to the university's science library; and various computer labs. Faculty laboratories range from wet laboratories designed for the biological aspects of human behavior to labs designed to assess mock jurors and jury decision making. The Psychology Clinic has ample space for individual or small group assessment and treatment. These facilities also have observation mirrors and videotape recording capability.

Information for Students With Physical Disabilities: See the following Web site for more information: http://www.uwyo.edu/seo.

Application Information:

Send to Graduate Admissions Committee, Department of Psychology, University of Wyoming, Department 3415, 1000 East University Avenue, Laramie, WY 82071. Application available online. URL of online application: http://www.uwyo.edu/psychology. Students are admitted in the Fall, application deadline January 15. *Fee:* $50. There is no fee for applying to the program. Only students who are accepted into and are officially entering the program are charged the fee.

Acadia University
Department of Psychology
18 University Avenue
Wolfville, NS B4P 2R6
Telephone: (902) 585-1301
Fax: (902) 585-1078
E-mail: *peter.horvath@acadiau.ca*
Web: *http://www.ace.acadiau.ca/science/psyc/GRAD/Home.htm*

Department Information:
1926. Head: Dr. Doug Symons. Number of faculty: total—full-time 12, part-time 3; women—full-time 6, part-time 1; total—minority—full-time 1, part-time 1.

Programs and Degrees Offered:
Listed in the following order: Program area, degree type (T if terminal Master's), number awarded 7/06–6/07. Clinical MA/MS (Master of Arts/Science) (T) 5.

Student Applications/Admissions:
Student Applications
Clinical MA/MS (Master of Arts/Science)—Applications 2007–2008, 43. Total applicants accepted 2007–2008, 5. Number full-time enrolled (new admits only) 2007–2008, 5. Total enrolled 2007–2008 full-time, 10. Openings 2008–2009, 5. The median number of years required for completion of a degree in 2006–2007 were 2. The number of students enrolled full- and part-time, who were dismissed or voluntarily withdrew from this program area in 2007–2008 were 0.

Admissions Requirements:
Scores: Entries appear in this order: required test or GPA, minimum score (if required), median score of students entering in 2007–2008. Master's Programs: GRE-V 500, 500; GRE-Q 500, 640; overall undergraduate GPA 3.50, 3.60; psychology GPA 3.50.
Other Criteria: (importance of criteria rated low, medium, or high): GRE/MAT scores—high, research experience—high, work experience—medium, extracurricular activity—medium, clinically related public service—medium, GPA—high, letters of recommendation—high, interview—high, statement of goals and objectives—high, undergraduate major in psychology—high.

Student Characteristics: The following represents characteristics of students in 2007–2008 in all graduate psychology programs in the department: Female—full-time 8, part-time 0; Male—full-time 2, part-time 0; African American/Black—full-time 0, part-time 0; Hispanic/Latino(a)—full-time 0, part-time 0; Asian/Pacific Islander—full-time 0, part-time 0; American Indian/Alaska Native—full-time 0, part-time 0; Caucasian/White—full-time 10, part-time 0; students subject to the Americans With Disabilities Act—full-time 0, part-time 0; Unknown ethnicity—full-time 0, part-time 0; International students who hold an F-1 or J-1 Visa—full-time 0, part-time 0.

Financial Information/Assistance:
Tuition for Full-Time Study: *Master's:* State residents: per academic year $7,211. Tuition is subject to change. See the following Web site for updates and changes in tuition costs: http://www.acadiau.ca/fees/Tuition_Fees.htm.

Financial Assistance:
First-Year Students: Teaching assistantships available for first year. Average amount paid per academic year: $12. Average number of hours worked per week: 10. Apply by February 1.
Advanced Students: Teaching assistantships available for advanced students. Average amount paid per academic year: $8,000. Average number of hours worked per week: 10.
Additional Information: Of all students currently enrolled full time, 60% benefited from one or more of the listed financial assistance programs. Application and information available online at http://www.acadiau.ca/admissions/gradPrograms.htm.

Internships/Practica: Master's Degree (Clinical): An internship experience such as a final research project or "capstone" experience is required of graduates. Two 150-hour internships are mandatory in intervention and assessment. Internship in community psychology is available.

Housing and Day Care: On-campus housing is available. See the following Web site for more information: http://www.ask.acadiau.ca. No on-campus day care facilities are available.

Employment of Department Graduates:
Master's Degree Graduates: Of those who graduated in the academic year 2006–2007, the following categories and numbers represent the postgraduate activities and employment of master's degree graduates: Enrolled in a psychology doctoral program (3), enrolled in a postdoctoral residency/fellowship (n/a), employed in independent practice (n/a), employed in a community mental health/counseling center (2), total from the above (master's) (5).
Doctoral Degree Graduates: Of those who graduated in the academic year 2006–2007, the following categories and numbers represent the postgraduate activities and employment of doctoral degree graduates: Enrolled in a psychology doctoral program (n/a), total from the above (doctoral) (0).

Additional Information:
Orientation, Objectives, and Emphasis of Department: The department's principle objective is to train MS students in clinical psychology. The department's orientation is eclectic although there is an emphasis on cognitive approaches to problems in psychology. Master's-level registration as a psychologist is available in all Maritime Provinces in Canada. Our curriculum is also highly respected, and graduates going on to doctoral programs elsewhere have had full recognition of coursework in all instances. We are registered with CAMPP.

Special Facilities or Resources: The department is part of the cooperative Clinical PhD program of Dalhousie University.

Application Information:
Send to Admissions Office, Acadia University, Wolfville, NS, B4P 2R6. Application available online. URL of online application: http://

www.acadiau.ca/admissions/admission_form/GRADApp-Form.pdf. Students are admitted in the Fall, application deadline February 1. *Fee:* $50. Note: All dollar amounts specified in this entry are Canadian dollars.

Alberta, University of

Department of Psychology
P217 Biological Sciences Building
Edmonton, AB T6G 2E9
Telephone: (708) 492-5216
Fax: (708) 492-1768
E-mail: *douglas.grant@ualberta.ca*
Web: *http://www.psych.ualberta.ca*

Department Information:

1961. Chair: Douglas S. Grant. Number of faculty: total—full-time 32; women—full-time 8; total—minority—full-time 2.

Programs and Degrees Offered:

Listed in the following order: Program area, degree type (T if terminal Master's), number awarded 7/06–6/07. Master's Program MA/MS (Master of Arts/Science) 1, Doctoral Program PhD (Doctor of Philosophy) 6.

Student Applications/Admissions:

Student Applications

Master's Program MA/MS (Master of Arts/Science)—Applications 2007–2008, 31. Total applicants accepted 2007–2008, 9. Number full-time enrolled (new admits only) 2007–2008, 6. Total enrolled 2007–2008 full-time, 27. Openings 2008–2009, 5. The median number of years required for completion of a degree in 2006–2007 were 3. The number of students enrolled full- and part-time, who were dismissed or voluntarily withdrew from this program area in 2007–2008 were 0. *Doctoral Program PhD (Doctor of Philosophy)*—Applications 2007–2008, 22. Total applicants accepted 2007–2008, 12. Number full-time enrolled (new admits only) 2007–2008, 5. Total enrolled 2007–2008 full-time, 33. Openings 2008–2009, 5. The median number of years required for completion of a degree in 2006–2007 were 6. The number of students enrolled full- and part-time, who were dismissed or voluntarily withdrew from this program area in 2007–2008 were 1.

Admissions Requirements:

Scores: Entries appear in this order: required test or GPA, minimum score (if required), median score of students entering in 2007–2008. Master's Programs: GRE-V no minimum stated; GRE-Q no minimum stated; last 2 years GPA 3.0. Doctoral Programs: GRE-V no minimum stated; GRE-Q no minimum stated; last 2 years GPA 3.0.

Other Criteria: (importance of criteria rated low, medium, or high): GRE/MAT scores—high, research experience—high, work experience—low, extracurricular activity—low, GPA—high, letters of recommendation—high, statement of goals and objectives—high. For additional information on admission requirements, go to http://www.psych.ualberta.ca/graduate/gradprospect.html.

Student Characteristics: The following represents characteristics of students in 2007–2008 in all graduate psychology programs in the department: Female—full-time 33, part-time 0; Male—full-time 27, part-time 0; African American/Black—full-time 0, part-time 0; Hispanic/Latino(a)—full-time 0, part-time 0; Asian/Pacific Islander—full-time 13, part-time 0; American Indian/Alaska Native—full-time 1, part-time 0; Caucasian/White—full-time 46, part-time 0; students subject to the Americans With Disabilities Act—full-time 0, part-time 0; Unknown ethnicity—full-time 0, part-time 0; International students who hold an F-1 or J-1 Visa—full-time 14, part-time 0.

Financial Information/Assistance:

Tuition for Full-Time Study: *Master's:* State residents: per academic year $4,249; Nonstate residents: per academic year $7,840. *Doctoral:* State residents: per academic year $4,249; Nonstate residents: per academic year $7,840. Tuition is subject to change. See the following Web site for updates and changes in tuition costs: http://www.gradstudies.ualberta.ca/regfees/index.htm.

Financial Assistance:

First-Year Students: Teaching assistantships available for first year. Average amount paid per academic year: $22,690. Average number of hours worked per week: 12. Apply by January 15. Research assistantships available for first year. Average amount paid per academic year: $22,690. Average number of hours worked per week: 12. Apply by January 15. Fellowships and scholarships available for first year. Average number of hours worked per week: 3. Apply by January 15. Tuition remission given: full and partial.

Advanced Students: Teaching assistantships available for advanced students. Average amount paid per academic year: $23,330. Average number of hours worked per week: 12. Apply by January 15. Research assistantships available for advanced students. Average amount paid per academic year: $23,330. Average number of hours worked per week: 12. Apply by January 15. Fellowships and scholarships available for advanced students. Average number of hours worked per week: 3. Apply by January 15. Tuition remission given: full and partial.

Additional Information: Of all students currently enrolled full time, 95% benefited from one or more of the listed financial assistance programs. Application and information available online at http://www.psych.ualberta.ca/graduate/gradprospect.html.

Internships/Practica: No information provided.

Housing and Day Care: On-campus housing is available. See the following Web site for more information: http://www.uofaweb.ualberta.ca/residences/. Contact Housing and Food Services, (780) 492-4281, (800) 615-4807, housing@ualberta.ca. On-campus day care facilities are available. There are a number of child care agencies. Please ask the Psychology Graduate Assistant for current telephone numbers for child care on campus.

Employment of Department Graduates:

Master's Degree Graduates: Of those who graduated in the academic year 2006–2007, the following categories and numbers represent the postgraduate activities and employment of master's degree graduates: Enrolled in another graduate/professional program (1), enrolled in a postdoctoral residency/fellowship (n/a), employed in independent practice (n/a), employed in an academic position at a university (1), not seeking employment (1), total from the above (master's) (3).

Doctoral Degree Graduates: Of those who graduated in the academic year 2006–2007, the following categories and numbers represent the postgraduate activities and employment of doctoral degree graduates: Enrolled in a psychology doctoral program (n/a), enrolled in a postdoctoral residency/fellowship (2), employed in a professional position in a school system (1), employed in a government agency (1), total from the above (doctoral) (4).

Additional Information:

Orientation, Objectives, and Emphasis of Department: The goal of the graduate program is to train competent and independent researchers who will make significant contributions to the discipline of psychology. The program entails early and sustained involvement in research and ensures that students attain expertise in focal and related domains. The program offers training that leads to degrees in a range of research areas, including Behavior, Systems, and Cognitive Neuroscience; Cognition; Comparative Cognition and Behavior Developmental Science; and Social and Cultural Psychology. Recent PhD graduates from the department have successfully found positions in universities and colleges, branches of government, and industry. A reasonably close match between the research interests of prospective students and faculty members is essential because the program involves apprenticeship-style training. Although many faculty members conduct research on problems that have practical and social significance, we do not have programs in clinical, counseling, or industrial/organizational psychology.

Special Facilities or Resources: The department maintains a number of specialized support facilities for staff and student use including an electronics shop, labs for teaching and research use, and an instructional technology lab to support teaching. In addition, the department maintains a psychology reading room and a small facility for photographic needs. Department computing resources include approximately 300 computers used in research and a further 40 computers used for administration and instructional needs. All staff and student computers have network capability on the department and campus networks. Technical assistance for research, teaching, and administrative needs is provided by department technical staff. For research services, the department maintains a fully equipped electronics shop staffed by technicians who design, build, and maintain custom laboratory equipment and data acquisition devices for laboratory applications. The shop contains a variety of professional equipment for electronics and fabrication work and stocks supplies for research and equipment needs. Technical staff also provide a full range of assistance with equipment selection and ordering, equipment repair, and new equipment configuration and setup. Other resources include the University Teaching Program, which improves the teaching skills of graduate students through workshops and practica, and the Community–University Partnership, which facilitates community- and school-based research.

Information for Students With Physical Disabilities: See the following Web site for more information: http://www.ualberta.ca/ssds.

Application Information:

Send to Graduate Program Assistant, Department of Psychology, P-217D Biological Sciences, University of Alberta, Edmonton, AB Canada T6G 2E9. Application available online. URL of online application: http://www.psych.ualberta.ca/graduate/AppInfo.html. Students are admitted in the Fall, application deadline January 15. The department admits approximately 10 graduate students per year. Students holding an undergraduate degree are admitted either to the Master's program or directly to the PhD program; upon successful completion of the Master's degree they would normally continue in the PhD program. Students holding a qualifying Master's Degree are admitted directly to the PhD program. *Fee:* $100. Note: All dollar amounts specified in this entry are Canadian dollars.

British Columbia, University of

Department of Psychology
2136 West Mall, Kenny Psychology Building
Vancouver, BC V6T 1Z4
Telephone: (604) 822-3144
Fax: (604) 822-6923
E-mail: *gradsec@psych.ubc.ca*
Web: *http://www.psych.ubc.ca*

Department Information:

1951. Head: Eric Eich. Number of faculty: total—full-time 46, part-time 26; women—full-time 20, part-time 13.

Programs and Degrees Offered:

Listed in the following order: Program area, degree type (T if terminal Master's), number awarded 7/06–6/07. Behavioral Neuroscience PhD (Doctor of Philosophy) 0, Clinical PhD (Doctor of Philosophy) 4, Forensic PhD (Doctor of Philosophy) 1, Developmental PhD (Doctor of Philosophy) 0, Cognitive Science PhD (Doctor of Philosophy) 2, Social/Personality PhD (Doctor of Philosophy) 0, Quantitative Methods PhD (Doctor of Philosophy) 0, Health PhD (Doctor of Philosophy) 0.

APA Accreditation: Clinical PhD (Doctor of Philosophy).

CPA Accreditation: Clinical PhD (Doctor of Philosophy).

Student Applications/Admissions:

Student Applications

Behavioral Neuroscience PhD (Doctor of Philosophy)—Applications 2007–2008, 10. Total applicants accepted 2007–2008, 3. Number full-time enrolled (new admits only) 2007–2008, 0. Number part-time enrolled (new admits only) 2007–2008, 0. Openings 2008–2009, 6. The number of students enrolled full- and part-time, who were dismissed or voluntarily withdrew from this program area in 2007–2008 were 0. *Clinical PhD (Doctor of Philosophy)*—Applications 2007–2008, 125. Total applicants accepted 2007–2008, 7. Number full-time enrolled (new admits only) 2007–2008, 4. Number part-time enrolled (new admits only) 2007–2008, 0. Openings 2008–2009, 8. The median number of years required for completion of a degree in 2006–2007 were 6. The number of students enrolled full- and part-time, who were dismissed or voluntarily withdrew from this program area in 2007–2008 were 0. *Forensic PhD (Doctor of Philosophy)*—Applications 2007–2008, 0. Total applicants accepted 2007–2008, 0. Number full-time enrolled (new admits only) 2007–2008, 0. Number part-time enrolled (new admits only) 2007–2008, 0. The median number of years required for completion of a degree in 2006–2007 were 6. The number of students enrolled full- and part-time, who were dismissed or voluntarily withdrew from this program area in 2007–2008 were 2. *Developmental PhD (Doctor of Philosophy)*—Applications 2007–2008, 20. Total applicants accepted 2007–2008, 2. Number full-time enrolled (new admits only) 2007–2008, 1. Number part-time enrolled (new admits only) 2007–2008, 0. Openings 2008–2009, 7. The number of students enrolled full- and part-time, who were dismissed or voluntarily withdrew from this program area in 2007–2008 were 0. *Cognitive Science PhD (Doctor of Philosophy)*—Applications 2007–2008, 22. Total applicants accepted 2007–2008, 8. Number full-time enrolled (new admits only) 2007–2008, 2. Number part-time enrolled (new admits only) 2007–2008, 0. Openings 2008–2009, 8. The median number of years required for completion of a degree in 2006–2007 were 6. The number of students enrolled full- and part-time, who were dismissed or voluntarily withdrew from this program area in 2007–2008 were 1. *Social/Personality PhD (Doctor of Philosophy)*—Applications 2007–2008, 55. Total applicants accepted 2007–2008, 11. Number full-time enrolled (new admits only) 2007–2008, 9. Number part-time enrolled (new admits only) 2007–2008, 0. Openings 2008–2009, 8. The number of students enrolled full- and part-time, who were dismissed or voluntarily withdrew from this program area in 2007–2008 were 3. *Quantitative Methods PhD (Doctor of Philosophy)*—Applications 2007–2008, 6. Total applicants accepted 2007–2008, 1. Number full-time enrolled (new admits only) 2007–2008, 0. Number part-time enrolled (new admits only) 2007–2008, 0. Openings 2008–2009, 4. The number of students enrolled full- and part-time, who were dismissed or voluntarily withdrew from this program area in 2007–2008 were 0. *Health PhD (Doctor of Philosophy)*—Applications 2007–2008, 9. Total applicants accepted 2007–2008, 2. Number full-time enrolled (new admits only) 2007–2008, 2. Number part-time enrolled (new admits only) 2007–2008, 0. Openings 2008–2009, 6. The number of students enrolled full- and part-time, who were dismissed or voluntarily withdrew from this program area in 2007–2008 were 0.

Admissions Requirements:

Scores: Entries appear in this order: required test or GPA, minimum score (if required), median score of students entering in 2007–2008. Master's Programs: GRE-V 580; GRE-Q 740; GRE-Subject (Psychology) 690; last 2 years GPA B+. Doctoral Programs: GRE-V 580; GRE-Q 740; GRE-Subject (Psychology) 690.

Other Criteria: (importance of criteria rated low, medium, or high): GRE/MAT scores—medium, research experience—high, clinically related public service—low, GPA—high, letters of recommendation—high, interview—medium, statement of goals and objectives—high, undergraduate major in psychology—high, specific undergraduate psychology courses taken—medium. For additional information on admission requirements, go to http://www.psych.ubc.ca/grad-pgm/admissions.psy.

Student Characteristics: The following represents characteristics of students in 2007–2008 in all graduate psychology programs in the department: Female—full-time 69, part-time 0; Male—full-time 33, part-time 0; Caucasian/White—full-time 0, part-time 0; Unknown ethnicity—full-time 102, part-time 0.

Financial Information/Assistance:

Tuition for Full-Time Study: *Master's:* State residents: per academic year $3,939; Nonstate residents: per academic year $3,939. *Doctoral:* State residents: per academic year $3,939; Nonstate residents: per academic year $3,939. Tuition is subject to change. See the following Web site for updates and changes in tuition costs: http://www.grad.ubc.ca/apply/tuition/.

Financial Assistance:

First-Year Students: Teaching assistantships available for first year. Average amount paid per academic year: $10,700. Average number of hours worked per week: 12. Apply by January 15. Research assistantships available for first year. Average amount paid per academic year: $5,000. Apply by January 15. Fellowships and scholarships available for first year. Average amount paid per academic year: $17,500. Apply by January 15.

Advanced Students: Teaching assistantships available for advanced students. Average amount paid per academic year: $11,120. Average number of hours worked per week: 12. Apply by January 15. Research assistantships available for advanced students. Average amount paid per academic year: $5,000. Apply by January 15. Fellowships and scholarships available for advanced students. Average amount paid per academic year: $20,000. Apply by September 15.

Additional Information: Of all students currently enrolled full time, 100% benefited from one or more of the listed financial assistance programs. Application and information available online at http://www.psych.ubc.ca/grad-pgm/admissions.psy.

Internships/Practica: Doctoral Degree (PhD Clinical): For those doctoral students for whom a professional internship was required in this program prior to graduation, (2) students applied for an internship in 2006–2007, with (2) students obtaining an internship. Of those students who obtained an internship, (2) were paid internships. Of those students who obtained an internship, (2) students placed in APA/CPA-accredited internships, (0) students placed in internships not APA/CPA-accredited, but listed with the Association of Psychology Postdoctoral and Internship Centers (APPIC), (0) students placed in internships conforming to guidelines of the Council of Directors of School Psychology Programs (CDSPP), (0) students placed in internships that were not APA/CPA-accredited, APPIC or CDSPP listed. A 4-month practicum in an approved agency is required of Clinical students during the summer after the 2nd or 3rd year of the program or during the 3rd year. A 1-year internship at a mental health agency accredited by CPA or APA is required for the PhD in Clinical Psychology. For additional information on education and training outcomes for our programs, see the following Web site: http://www.psych.ubc.ca/grad-pgm/areasspec.psy?contid=101306171911.

Housing and Day Care: On-campus housing is available. See the following Web site for more information: http://www.grad.ubc.ca/apply/housing. On-campus day care facilities are available. See the following Web site for more information: http://www.childcare.ubc.ca.

Employment of Department Graduates:

Master's Degree Graduates: Of those who graduated in the academic year 2006–2007, the following categories and numbers represent the postgraduate activities and employment of master's degree graduates: Enrolled in a psychology doctoral program (13), enrolled in another graduate/professional program (1), enrolled in a postdoctoral residency/fellowship (n/a), employed in independent practice (n/a), employed in a hospital/medical center (1), other employment position (1), total from the above (master's) (16).

Doctoral Degree Graduates: Of those who graduated in the academic year 2006–2007, the following categories and numbers represent the postgraduate activities and employment of doctoral degree graduates: Enrolled in a psychology doctoral program (n/a), enrolled in a postdoctoral residency/fellowship (3), employed in independent practice (1), employed in an academic position at a 2-year/4-year college (1), employed in a hospital/medical center (2), total from the above (doctoral) (7).

Additional Information:

Orientation, Objectives, and Emphasis of Department: The department is organized into eight subject content areas with which faculty and graduate students are affiliated. Graduate training emphasizes a high degree of research competence and, from the beginning of the program, students are involved in increasingly independent research activities.

Special Facilities or Resources: The department is housed in an attractive building of about 90,000 square feet, designed for psychological research. The department has well-equipped research facilities including a psychology clinic, observational galleries, and animal, psychophysiological, perceptual, cognitive, and social/personality laboratories.

Information for Students With Physical Disabilities: See the following Web site for more information: http://www.students.ubc.ca/access/drc.cfm.

Application Information:

Send to Graduate Secretary, Department of Psychology, University of British Columbia, Vancouver, BC, Canada V6T 1Z4. Application available online. URL of online application: http://www.grad.ubc.ca/apply/online/. Students are admitted in the Fall, application deadline January 15. *Fee:* $90. The application fee for international applicants is $150. The application fee is waived for international applicants whose correspondence address is located in one of the world's 50 least developed countries, as declared by the United Nations. Note: All dollar amounts specified in this entry are Canadian dollars.

Calgary, University of (2007 data)

Department of Psychology
2500 University Drive, NW
Calgary, AB T2N 1N4
Telephone: (403) 220-5561
Fax: (403) 282-8249
E-mail: *bhbland@ucalgary.ca*
Web: *http://www.psych.ucalgary.ca*

Department Information:

1964. Head: Dr. Keith Dobson. Number of faculty: total—full-time 31; women—full-time 9.

Programs and Degrees Offered:

Listed in the following order: Program area, degree type (T if terminal Master's), number awarded 7/06–6/07. Psychology PhD (Doctor of Philosophy) 7, Clinical Psychology PhD (Doctor of Philosophy) 4.

Student Applications/Admissions:

Student Applications

Psychology PhD (Doctor of Philosophy)—Applications 2007–2008, 54. Total applicants accepted 2007–2008, 12. Number full-time enrolled (new admits only) 2007–2008, 11. Openings 2008–2009, 13. The median number of years required for completion of a degree in 2006–2007 were 3. The number of students enrolled full- and part-time, who were dismissed or voluntarily withdrew from this program area in 2007–2008 were 0. *Clinical Psychology PhD (Doctor of Philosophy)*—Applications 2007–2008, 70. Total applicants accepted 2007–2008, 7. Number full-time enrolled (new admits only) 2007–2008, 7. Openings 2008–2009, 8. The median number of years required for completion of a degree in 2006–2007 were 3. The number of students enrolled full- and part-time, who were dismissed or voluntarily withdrew from this program area in 2007–2008 were 0.

Admissions Requirements:

Scores: Entries appear in this order: required test or GPA, minimum score (if required), median score of students entering in 2007–2008. Master's Programs: GRE-V no minimum stated; GRE-Q no minimum stated; last 2 years GPA no minimum stated. Clinical Psychology, GPA of 3.7 (A-) over the last 2 years of study. Psychology, GPA of 3.4 (B+) over the last 2 years of study. Doctoral Programs: GRE-V no minimum stated; GRE-Q no minimum stated; last 2 years GPA no minimum stated.

Other Criteria: (importance of criteria rated low, medium, or high): GRE/MAT scores—medium, research experience—high, work experience—medium, extracurricular activity—low, clinically related public service—medium, GPA—high, letters of recommendation—high, interview—medium, statement of goals and objectives—medium, research proposal—high.

Student Characteristics: The following represents characteristics of students in 2007–2008 in all graduate psychology programs in the department: Female—full-time 55, part-time 0; Male—full-time 18, part-time 0; African American/Black—full-time 0, part-time 0; Hispanic/Latino(a)—full-time 0, part-time 0; Asian/Pacific Islander—full-time 4, part-time 0; American Indian/Alaska Native—full-time 0, part-time 0; Caucasian/White—full-time 69, part-time 0; students subject to the Americans With Disabilities Act—full-time 0, part-time 0; Unknown ethnicity—full-time 0, part-time 0.

Financial Information/Assistance:

Tuition for Full-Time Study: *Master's:* State residents: per academic year $5,249; Nonstate residents: per academic year $9,796. *Doctoral:* State residents: per academic year $5,249; Nonstate residents: per academic year $9,796. Tuition is subject to change. See the following Web site for updates and changes in tuition costs: http://www.grad.ucalgary.ca.

Financial Assistance:

First-Year Students: Teaching assistantships available for first year. Average amount paid per academic year: $13,000. Average number of hours worked per week: 12. Research assistantships available for first year. Average amount paid per academic year: $4,100. Fellowships and scholarships available for first year. Average amount paid per academic year: $15,000. Apply by January 15.

Advanced Students: Teaching assistantships available for advanced students. Average amount paid per academic year: $13,000. Average number of hours worked per week: 12. Research assistantships available for advanced students. Average amount paid per academic year: $4,100. Fellowships and scholarships available for advanced students. Average amount paid per academic year: $15,000. Apply by January 15.

Additional Information: Of all students currently enrolled full time, 100% benefited from one or more of the listed financial assistance programs. Application and information available online at http://www.grad.ucalgary.ca/Funding/.

Internships/Practica: Internships are available at several settings, including Foothills Hospital and Children's Hospital.

Housing and Day Care: On-campus housing is available. See the following Web site for more information: http://www.ucalgary.ca/residence/. On-campus day care facilities are available.

Employment of Department Graduates:

Master's Degree Graduates: Of those who graduated in the academic year 2006–2007, the following categories and numbers represent the postgraduate activities and employment of master's degree graduates: Enrolled in a psychology doctoral program (10), enrolled in another graduate/professional program (1), enrolled in a postdoctoral residency/fellowship (n/a), employed in independent practice (n/a), total from the above (master's) (11).

Doctoral Degree Graduates: Of those who graduated in the academic year 2006–2007, the following categories and numbers represent the postgraduate activities and employment of doctoral degree graduates: Enrolled in a psychology doctoral program (n/a), enrolled in a postdoctoral residency/fellowship (1), employed in independent practice (2), employed in an academic position at a university (2), employed in other positions at a higher education institution (1), employed in business or industry (3), employed in a community mental health/counseling center (1), employed in a hospital/medical center (4), total from the above (doctoral) (14).

Additional Information:

Orientation, Objectives, and Emphasis of Department: This is a research-oriented department with a strong focus on applied problems. We offer both a Clinical Psychology and a Psychology program. Specific research programs in psychology include: behavioral neuroscience, cognition and cognitive development (CCD), industrial/organizational psychology (I/O), social psychology, perception aging and cognitive ergonomics (PACE), and theoretical psychology.

Application Information:

Send to Graduate Programs Administrator, Department of Psychology, 2500 University Drive NW, University of Calgary, Calgary, AB T2N1N4 Canada. Application available online. URL of online application: http://www.psych.ucalgary.ca. Students are admitted in the Fall, application deadline January 15; Winter, application deadline October 15; Spring, application deadline January 15. The Clinical and Industrial/Organizational Psychology programs only accept students for a start date in September. The application deadline for these programs is January 15 only. *Fee:* $100. Note: All dollar amounts specified in this entry are Canadian dollars.

Carleton University

Department of Psychology
Faculty of Arts and Social Sciences
1125 Colonel By Drive
Ottawa, ON K1S 5B6
Telephone: (613) 520-2647
Fax: (613) 520-3667
E-mail: *janet_mantler@carleton.ca*
Web: *http://www.carleton.ca/psychology/*

Department Information:

1952. Chairperson: Janet Mantler. Number of faculty: total—full-time 46; women—full-time 19.

Programs and Degrees Offered:

Listed in the following order: Program area, degree type (T if terminal Master's), number awarded 7/06–6/07. MA/MS (Master of Arts/Science) (T) 29, Neuroscience MA/MS (Master of Arts/Science) 9, PhD (Doctor of Philosophy) 6.

Student Applications/Admissions:

Student Applications

MA/MS (Master of Arts/Science)—Applications 2007–2008, 178. Total applicants accepted 2007–2008, 67. Number full-time enrolled (new admits only) 2007–2008, 35. Number part-time enrolled (new admits only) 2007–2008, 2. Total enrolled 2007–2008 full-time, 69, part-time, 8. Openings 2008–2009, 38. The median number of years required for completion of a degree in 2006–2007 were 2. The number of students enrolled full- and part-time, who were dismissed or voluntarily withdrew from this program area in 2007–2008 were 0. *Neuroscience MA/MS (Master of Arts/Science)*—Applications 2007–2008, 25. Total applicants accepted 2007–2008, 18. Number full-time enrolled (new admits only) 2007–2008, 10. Openings 2008–2009, 18. The median number of years required for completion of a degree in 2006–2007 were 2. The number of students enrolled full- and part-time, who were dismissed or voluntarily withdrew from this program area in 2007–2008 were 0. *PhD (Doctor of Philosophy)*—Applications 2007–2008, 28. Total applicants accepted 2007–2008, 23. Number full-time enrolled (new admits only) 2007–2008, 11. Total enrolled 2007–2008 full-time, 58, part-time, 10. Openings 2008–2009, 7. The median number of years required for completion of a degree in 2006–2007 were 4. The number of students enrolled full- and part-time, who were dismissed or voluntarily withdrew from this program area in 2007–2008 were 0.

Admissions Requirements:

Scores: Entries appear in this order: required test or GPA, minimum score (if required), median score of students entering in 2007–2008. Master's Programs: last 2 years GPA 9, 10.7; psychology GPA 9. Doctoral Programs: last 2 years GPA 10; psychology GPA 10, 10.8.

Other Criteria: (importance of criteria rated low, medium, or high): research experience—high, work experience—low, extracurricular activity—low, clinically related public service—low, GPA—high, letters of recommendation—high, statement of goals and objectives—high, undergraduate major in psychology—high, specific undergraduate psychology courses taken—high. For additional information on admission requirements, go to http://www.carleton.ca/psychology/graduate/ma/index.html.

Student Characteristics: The following represents characteristics of students in 2007–2008 in all graduate psychology programs in the department: Female—full-time 108, part-time 13; Male—full-time 37, part-time 5; Asian/Pacific Islander—full-time 13, part-time 2; American Indian/Alaska Native—full-time 1, part-time 0; Caucasian/White—full-time 131, part-time 16; students subject to the Americans With Disabilities Act—full-time 0, part-time 0; Unknown ethnicity—full-time 0, part-time 0; International students who hold an F-1 or J-1 Visa—full-time 1, part-time 0.

Financial Information/Assistance:

Tuition for Full-Time Study: *Master's:* State residents: per academic year $6,848; Nonstate residents: per academic year $14,628. *Doctoral:* State residents: per academic year $6,848; Nonstate residents: per academic year $14,628. Tuition is subject to change. See the following Web site for updates and changes in tuition costs: http://www.carleton.ca/fees.

Financial Assistance:

First-Year Students: Teaching assistantships available for first year. Average amount paid per academic year: $9,084. Average number of hours worked per week: 10. Apply by January 15. Tuition remission given: partial. Research assistantships available for first year. Average amount paid per academic year: $2,500. Apply by January 15. Fellowships and scholarships available for first year. Average amount paid per academic year: $2,500. Apply by January 15.

Advanced Students: Teaching assistantships available for advanced students. Average amount paid per academic year: $9,084. Average number of hours worked per week: 10. Apply by January 15. Tuition remission given: partial. Research assistantships available for advanced students. Average amount paid per academic year: $3,500. Apply by January 15. Fellowships and scholarships available for advanced students. Average amount paid per academic year: $6,000. Apply by January 15.

Additional Information: Of all students currently enrolled full time, 45% benefited from one or more of the listed financial assistance programs. Application and information available online at http://www.carleton.ca/psychology/graduate/funding/index.html.

Internships/Practica: N/A.

Housing and Day Care: On-campus housing is available. See the following Web site for more information: http://www.carleton.ca/housing/. On-campus day care facilities are available. E-mail cbccc@ncf.ca or call (613) 520-2715.

Employment of Department Graduates:

Master's Degree Graduates: Of those who graduated in the academic year 2006–2007, the following categories and numbers represent the postgraduate activities and employment of master's degree graduates: Enrolled in a psychology doctoral program (14), enrolled in another graduate/professional program (2), enrolled in a postdoctoral residency/fellowship (n/a), employed in independent practice (n/a), employed in an academic position at a university (1), employed in a professional position in a school system (2), employed in business or industry (7), employed in a government agency (9), employed in a hospital/medical center (2), still seeking employment (1), other employment position (6), total from the above (master's) (44).

Doctoral Degree Graduates: Of those who graduated in the academic year 2006–2007, the following categories and numbers represent the postgraduate activities and employment of doctoral degree graduates: Enrolled in a psychology doctoral program (n/a), employed in a government agency (2), total from the above (doctoral) (2).

Additional Information:

Orientation, Objectives, and Emphasis of Department: The program is strongly research-oriented, although practical courses such as quantitative methods, testing, and behavior modification are available. This degree however does not offer training in applied areas (e.g. clinical, educational, counseling psychology, etc.).

Information for Students With Physical Disabilities: See the following Web site for more information: http://www.carleton.ca/paulmenton/.

Application Information:

Send to Graduate Studies Administrator, B-557 Loeb Building. URL of online application: http://www.carleton.ca/psychology/graduate. Students are admitted in the Fall, application deadline January 15; Winter, application deadline November 1. *Fee:* $75. Note: All dollar amounts specified in this entry are Canadian dollars.

Concordia University

Department of Psychology
7141 Sherbrooke Street West
Montreal, QC H4B 1R6
Telephone: (514) 848-2424, (2205)
Fax: (514) 848-4545
E-mail: *Shirley.Black@concordia.ca*
Web: *http://www.psychology.concordia.ca*

Department Information:

1963. Chairperson: Jean-Roch Laurence, PhD. Number of faculty: total—full-time 34, part-time 19; women—full-time 13, part-time 5; total—minority—full-time 2; women minority—full-time 1.

Programs and Degrees Offered:

Listed in the following order: Program area, degree type (T if terminal Master's), number awarded 7/06–6/07. Clinical Profile PhD (Doctor of Philosophy) 7, General Profile PhD (Doctor of Philosophy) 3.

APA Accreditation: Clinical PhD (Doctor of Philosophy).

CPA Accreditation: Clinical PhD (Doctor of Philosophy).

Student Applications/Admissions:

Student Applications

Clinical Profile PhD (Doctor of Philosophy)—Applications 2007–2008, 173. Total applicants accepted 2007–2008, 14. Number full-time enrolled (new admits only) 2007–2008, 11. Number part-time enrolled (new admits only) 2007–2008, 0. Openings 2008–2009, 11. The median number of years required for completion of a degree in 2006–2007 were 8. The number of students enrolled full- and part-time, who were dismissed or voluntarily withdrew from this program area in 2007–2008 were 4. *General Profile PhD (Doctor of Philosophy)*—Applications 2007–2008, 52. Total applicants accepted 2007–2008, 14. Number full-time enrolled (new admits only) 2007–2008, 8. Number part-time enrolled (new admits only) 2007–2008, 0. Openings 2008–2009, 11. The median number of years required for completion of a degree in 2006–2007 were 5. The number of students enrolled full- and part-time, who were dismissed or voluntarily withdrew from this program area in 2007–2008 were 7.

Admissions Requirements:

Scores: Entries appear in this order: required test or GPA, minimum score (if required), median score of students entering in 2007–2008. Master's Programs: overall undergraduate GPA 3.00, 3.81; psychology GPA no minimum stated. GREs: Not required, but highly recommended. Concordia = 4.30 grading scale. Minimum: 3.00 = B, Median: 3.81 = Between an A- and an A. Doctoral Programs: overall undergraduate GPA 3.00. Most students are admitted at the MA level. GREs: Not required, but highly recommended. Concordia = 4.30 grading scale.

Other Criteria: (importance of criteria rated low, medium, or high): GRE/MAT scores—low, research experience—high, work experience—medium, extracurricular activity—low, clinically related public service—medium, GPA—medium, letters of recommendation—high, interview—medium, statement of goals and objectives—high, undergraduate major in psychology—high, specific undergraduate psychology courses taken—medium. General Profile does not require clinically related service. Thesis Supervisor is required for admission to graduate program. For additional information on admission requirements, go to http://psychology.concordia.ca.

Student Characteristics: The following represents characteristics of students in 2007–2008 in all graduate psychology programs in the department: Female—full-time 94, part-time 0; Male—full-time 35, part-time 0; African American/Black—full-time 2, part-time 0; Hispanic/Latino(a)—full-time 4, part-time 0; Asian/Pacific Islander—full-time 6, part-time 0; American Indian/Alaska Native—full-time 1, part-time 0; Caucasian/White—full-time 108, part-time 0; Multi-ethnic—full-time 2, part-time 0; students subject to the Americans With Disabilities Act—full-time 0, part-time 0; Unknown ethnicity—full-time 0, part-time 0; International students who hold an F-1 or J-1 Visa—full-time 6, part-time 0.

Financial Information/Assistance:

Tuition for Full-Time Study: *Master's:* State residents: per academic year $3,100; Nonstate residents: per academic year $10,500. *Doctoral:* State residents: per academic year $3,100; Nonstate residents: per academic year $9,700. Tuition is subject to change. Tuition costs vary by program. See the following Web site for updates and changes in tuition costs: http://www.tuitionandfees.concordia.ca.

Financial Assistance:

First-Year Students: Teaching assistantships available for first year. Average amount paid per academic year: $3,750. Average number of hours worked per week: 10. Apply by August 1. Research assistantships available for first year. Average amount paid per academic year: $11,250. Average number of hours worked per week: 10. Fellowships and scholarships available for first year. Average amount paid per academic year: $20,000. Apply by October.

Advanced Students: Teaching assistantships available for advanced students. Average amount paid per academic year: $7,500. Average number of hours worked per week: 10. Apply by August 1. Research assistantships available for advanced students. Average amount paid per academic year: $7,500. Average number of hours worked per week: 10. Fellowships and scholarships available for advanced students. Average amount paid per academic year: $21,200. Apply by October.

Additional Information: Of all students currently enrolled full time, 74% benefited from one or more of the listed financial assistance programs. Application and information available online at http://graduatestudies.concordia.ca/awards.

Internships/Practica: Doctoral Degree (Clinical Profile): For those doctoral students for whom a professional internship was required in this program prior to graduation, (10) students applied for an internship in 2006–2007, with (10) students obtaining an internship. Of those students who obtained an internship, (6) were paid internships. Of those students who obtained an internship, (6) students placed in APA/CPA-accredited internships, (4) students placed in internships not APA/CPA-accredited, but listed with the Association of Psychology Postdoctoral and Internship Centers (APPIC), (0) students placed in internships conforming to guidelines of the Council of Directors of School Psychology Programs (CDSPP), (0) students placed in internships that were not APA/CPA-accredited, APPIC or CDSPP listed. Clinical students complete a variety of practica and internships while in program residence. All Clinical students receive extensive practicum experience in psychotherapy and assessment in our on-campus training clinic, the Applied Psychology Center (APC). APC clients are seen by graduate students under the supervision of clinical faculty. The types of services offered by the APC reflect the interests of clinical supervisors and students, and may include individual, family, or marital psychotherapy; behavior therapy for sexual or phobic difficulties; and treatment of child disorders. During the Summer of their 2nd year, students also complete a full-time practicum at a mental health facility in the Montreal area. During their final year in the program, students complete their full-time, predoctoral clinical internships. Recent students have undertaken predoctoral internships at a variety of mental health facilities across Canada and the United States. All students are encouraged to seek internship positions in settings accredited by either the Canadian or American Psychological Associations.

Housing and Day Care: No on-campus housing is available. On-campus day care facilities are available. See the following Web site for more information: http://deanofstudents.concordia.ca/childcare/index/shtml. Contact Sir George campus (514) 848-2424, ext. 8789; Loyola campus: (514) 848-2424, ext. 7788.

Employment of Department Graduates:

Master's Degree Graduates: Of those who graduated in the academic year 2006–2007, the following categories and numbers represent the postgraduate activities and employment of master's degree graduates: Enrolled in a psychology doctoral program (16), enrolled in another graduate/professional program (0), enrolled in a postdoctoral residency/fellowship (n/a), employed in independent practice (n/a), employed in an academic position at a university (0), employed in an academic position at a 2-year/4-year college (0), employed in other positions at a higher education institution (0), employed in a professional position in a school system (0), employed in business or industry (0), employed in a government agency (0), employed in a community mental health/counseling center (0), employed in a hospital/medical center (0), still seeking employment (0), not seeking employment (0), other employment position (0), do not know (1), total from the above (master's) (17).

Doctoral Degree Graduates: Of those who graduated in the academic year 2006–2007, the following categories and numbers represent the postgraduate activities and employment of doctoral degree graduates: Enrolled in a psychology doctoral program (n/a), enrolled in another graduate/professional program (0), enrolled in a postdoctoral residency/fellowship (2), employed in independent practice (2), employed in an academic position at a university (1), employed in an academic position at a 2-year/4-year college (0), employed in other positions at a higher education institution (0), employed in a professional position in a school system (0), employed in business or industry (0), employed in a government agency (0), employed in a community mental health/counseling center (3), employed in a hospital/medical center (0), still seeking employment (0), other employment position (0), do not know (1), total from the above (doctoral) (10).

Additional Information:

Orientation, Objectives, and Emphasis of Department: Graduate education in both Experimental and Clinical Psychology is strongly research oriented and intended for students who are planning to complete the PhD degree. The research program for all students is based on an apprentice-type model. An outstanding feature of graduate education at Concordia is that students pursuing only research studies and students pursuing research and clinical studies may conduct their research in the laboratory of any faculty member. A wide variety of contemporary research areas are represented, ranging from behavioral neurobiology, to cognitive and developmental science, and to applied interventions with humans. Research findings from numerous areas are integrated in an effort to solve problems associated with appetitive motivation and drug dependence, memory and aging, human cognition and development, developmental psychobiology, adult and child psychopathology, and sexual dysfunctions, to name several examples. Clinical training is based on the scientist–practitioner model. That is, clinical students meet the same research requirements as other students, and receive extensive professional training in the delivery of psychological services. Students may choose to specialize their clinical training with children or adults.

Special Facilities or Resources: The department has extensive animal and human research facilities that are supported by provincial, federal, and U.S. granting agencies as well as various internal and private sector funds. Research laboratories are well equipped. The department also contains two research centers that are jointly funded by the Government of Quebec and the University, the Center for Studies in Behavioral Neurobiology, and the Center for Research in Human Development. Both centers coordinate multidisciplinary research programs, provide state-of-the-art laboratory equipment, and sponsor colloquia by specialists from other universities in North America and abroad. All graduate students benefit from activities supported by the research centers.

Information for Students With Physical Disabilities: See the following Web site for more information: http://www.advocacy.concordia.ca/disabled/disabled.html.

Application Information:

Send to Concordia University, Graduate Admissions Application Centre, P.O. Box 2002, Station H, Montréal, Québec H3G 2V4, Canada. Application available online. URL of online application: http://www.concordia.ca. Students are admitted in the Fall, application deadline December 15. Psychology graduate program information and research interests are available online at http://psychology.concordia.ca, then choose "Graduate Programmes (MA and PhD)". *Fee:* $75. Note: All dollar amounts specified in this entry are Canadian dollars.

Dalhousie University

Department of Psychology
Life Sciences Centre
Halifax, NS B3H 4J1
Telephone: (902) 494-3839
Fax: (902) 494-6585
E-mail: *REBROWN@dal.ca*
Web: *http://www.dal.ca/psychology*

Department Information:

1863. Chair: Richard Brown. Number of faculty: total—full-time 10, part-time 2; women—full-time 15, part-time 1.

Programs and Degrees Offered:

Listed in the following order: Program area, degree type (T if terminal Master's), number awarded 7/06–6/07. Clinical PhD (Doctor of Philosophy) 4, Experimental Animal PhD (Doctor of Philosophy) 2, Experimental Human PhD (Doctor of Philosophy) 1, Neuroscience MA/MS (Master of Arts/Science) 1, Experimental Animal MA/MS (Master of Arts/Science) 0, Neuroscience PhD (Doctor of Philosophy) 0, Experimental Human MA/MS (Master of Arts/Science) 4.

APA Accreditation: Clinical PhD (Doctor of Philosophy).

Student Applications/Admissions:

Student Applications

Clinical PhD (Doctor of Philosophy)—Applications 2007–2008, 102. Total applicants accepted 2007–2008, 6. Number full-time enrolled (new admits only) 2007–2008, 6. Number part-time enrolled (new admits only) 2007–2008, 0. Openings 2008–2009, 6. The median number of years required for completion of a degree in 2006–2007 were 5. The number of students enrolled full- and part-time, who were dismissed or voluntarily withdrew from this program area in 2007–2008 were 0. *Experimental Animal PhD (Doctor of Philosophy)*—Applications 2007–2008, 15. Total applicants accepted 2007–2008, 2. Number full-time enrolled (new admits only) 2007–2008, 3. Openings 2008–2009, 2. The median number of years required for completion of a degree in 2006–2007 were 5. The number of students enrolled full- and part-time, who were dismissed or voluntarily withdrew from this program area in 2007–2008 were 0. *Experimental Human PhD (Doctor of Philosophy)*—Applications 2007–2008, 20. Total applicants accepted 2007–2008, 4. Number full-time enrolled (new admits only) 2007–2008, 2. Number part-time enrolled (new admits only) 2007–2008, 0. Openings 2008–2009, 6. The median number of years required for completion of a degree in 2006–2007 were 4. The number of students enrolled full- and part-time, who were dismissed or voluntarily withdrew from this program area in 2007–2008 were 0. *Neuroscience MA/MS (Master of Arts/Science)*—Applications 2007–2008, 10. Total applicants accepted 2007–2008, 2. Number full-time enrolled (new admits only) 2007–2008, 2. Number part-time enrolled (new admits only) 2007–2008, 0. Openings 2008–2009, 2. The median number of years required for completion of a degree in 2006–2007 were 2. The number of students enrolled full- and part-time, who were dismissed or voluntarily withdrew from this program area in 2007–2008 were 0. *Experimental Animal MA/MS (Master of Arts/Science)*—Applications 2007–2008, 10. Total applicants accepted 2007–2008, 0. Number full-time enrolled (new admits only) 2007–2008, 0. Total enrolled 2007–2008 full-time, 1. The median number of years required for completion of a degree in 2006–2007 were 2. The number of students enrolled full- and part-time, who were dismissed or voluntarily withdrew from this program area in 2007–2008 were 0. *Neuroscience PhD (Doctor of Philosophy)*—Applications 2007–2008, 8. Total applicants accepted 2007–2008, 4. Number full-time enrolled (new admits only) 2007–2008, 4. Number part-time enrolled (new admits only) 2007–2008, 0. The median number of years required for completion of a degree in 2006–2007 were 5. The number of students enrolled full- and part-time, who were dismissed or voluntarily withdrew from this program area in 2007–2008 were 0. *Experimental Human MA/MS (Master of Arts/Science)*—Applications 2007–2008, 12. Total applicants accepted 2007–2008, 4. Number full-time enrolled (new admits only) 2007–2008, 4. Number part-time enrolled (new admits only) 2007–2008, 0. Openings 2008–2009, 2. The median number of years required for completion of a degree in 2006–2007 were 2. The number of students enrolled full- and part-time, who were dismissed or voluntarily withdrew from this program area in 2007–2008 were 0.

Admissions Requirements:

Scores: Entries appear in this order: required test or GPA, minimum score (if required), median score of students entering in 2007–2008. Master's Programs: GRE-V 600; GRE-Q 600; GRE-Subject (Psychology) 600. Doctoral Programs: GRE-V 600; GRE-Q 600; overall undergraduate GPA 3.70.

Other Criteria: (importance of criteria rated low, medium, or high): research experience—high, work experience—low, extracurricular activity—low, clinically related public service—low, GPA—high, letters of recommendation—high, interview—medium, statement of goals and objectives—high, undergraduate major in psychology—high, specific undergraduate psychology courses taken—high. Clinically related public service is high for Clinical program.

Student Characteristics: The following represents characteristics of students in 2007–2008 in all graduate psychology programs in the department: Female—full-time 49, part-time 0; Male—full-time 11, part-time 0; African American/Black—full-time 1, part-time 0; Hispanic/Latino(a)—full-time 0, part-time 0; Asian/Pacific Islander—full-time 4, part-time 0; American Indian/Alaska Native—full-time 1, part-time 0; Caucasian/White—full-time 0, part-time 0; students subject to the Americans With Disabilities Act—full-time 0, part-time 0; Unknown ethnicity—full-time 0, part-time 0.

Financial Information/Assistance:

Tuition for Full-Time Study: *Master's:* State residents: per academic year $6,270. *Doctoral:* State residents: per academic year $6,552. Tuition is subject to change. See the following Web site for updates and changes in tuition costs: http://www.dal.ca/studentaccounts.

Financial Assistance:

First-Year Students: Teaching assistantships available for first year. Average amount paid per academic year: $2,284. Average number of hours worked per week: 10. Fellowships and scholarships available for first year.

Advanced Students: Fellowships and scholarships available for advanced students.

Additional Information: Of all students currently enrolled full time, 100% benefited from one or more of the listed financial assistance programs. Application and information available online at http://www.dal.ca/Psychology.

Internships/Practica: Doctoral Degree (Clinical): For those doctoral students for whom a professional internship was required in this program prior to graduation, (5) students applied for an internship in 2006–2007, with (5) students obtaining an internship. Of those students who obtained an internship, (5) were paid internships. Of those students who obtained an internship, (5) students placed in APA/CPA-accredited internships, (0) students placed in internships not APA/CPA-accredited, but listed with the Association of Psychology Postdoctoral and Internship Centers (APPIC), (0) students placed in internships conforming to guidelines of the Council of Directors of School Psychology Programs (CDSPP), (0) students placed in internships that were not APA/CPA-accredited, APPIC or CDSPP listed. Description of practica for APA Practicum training is integrated into the Clinical Psychology PhD curriculum, to complement knowledge and skills developed through course work, to provide opportunities to master specific assessment and intervention techniques, and to ensure that students meet expectations with regard to core competencies. Brief practica are incorporated into a number of the core clinical courses; however, the majority of praticum hours are accumulated through community placements, under the supervision of registered psychologists. Dalhousie is situated in close proximity to a variety of excellent health care facilities, including the IWK Health Centre, the QEII Health Centre, the Nova Scotia Hospital, the Canadian Forces Hospital at CFB Stadacona, and the East Coast Forensic Hospital. Under the guidance of the Field Placement Coordinator, students select and complete a program of practicum placements designed to meet their individual training needs. Students are required to complete a minimum of 600 hours of formal practicum training, but it is recognized that additional practicum hours (for a total of about 1,000–1,200 hours) are often necessary to ensure a competitive internship application.

Housing and Day Care: On-campus housing is available. See the following Web site for more information: http://www.dal.ca. On-campus day care facilities are available.

Employment of Department Graduates:

Master's Degree Graduates: Of those who graduated in the academic year 2006–2007, the following categories and numbers represent the postgraduate activities and employment of master's degree graduates: Enrolled in a psychology doctoral program (1), enrolled in another graduate/professional program (1), enrolled in a postdoctoral residency/fellowship (n/a), employed in independent practice (n/a), employed in an academic position at a university (5), employed in an academic position at a 2-year/4-year college (0), employed in other positions at a higher education institution (0), employed in a professional position in a school system (0), employed in business or industry (0), employed in a government agency (0), employed in a community mental health/counseling center (0), employed in a hospital/medical center (2), still seeking employment (0), other employment position (0), do not know (0), total from the above (master's) (9).

Doctoral Degree Graduates: Of those who graduated in the academic year 2006–2007, the following categories and numbers represent the postgraduate activities and employment of doctoral degree graduates: Enrolled in a psychology doctoral program (n/a), enrolled in another graduate/professional program (0), enrolled in a postdoctoral residency/fellowship (3), employed in independent practice (0), employed in an academic position at a university (0), employed in an academic position at a 2-year/4-year college (0), employed in other positions at a higher education institution (0), employed in a professional position in a school system (0), employed in business or industry (0), employed in a government agency (0), employed in a community mental health/counseling center (0), employed in a hospital/medical center (2), still seeking employment (0), other employment position (1), do not know (4), total from the above (doctoral) (10).

Additional Information:

Orientation, Objectives, and Emphasis of Department: The Department of Psychology offers graduate training leading to MS and PhD degrees in Psychology and in Psychology/Neuroscience, and to a PhD in Clinical Psychology. Our graduate programs emphasize training for research. They are best described as "apprenticeship" programs in which students work closely with a faculty member who has agreed to supervise the student's research. Compared with many other graduate programs, we place less emphasis on course work and greater emphasis on research, scholarship, and independent thinking. The graduate programs in psychology/neuroscience are coordinated by the Psychology Department and an interdisciplinary Neuroscience Program Committee with representation from the Departments of Anatomy, Biochemistry, Pharmacology, Physiology and Biophysics, and Psychology. Master's-level students in Psychogy and Psychology/Neuroscience are expected to advance into the corresponding PhD programs. We do not have a "terminal" Master's program. The PhD program in Clinical Psychology is cooperatively administered by the Psychology Department and the Clinical Program Committee with representation from Acadia University, Dalhousie University, Mount Saint Vincent University, Saint Mary's University, and professional psychologists from the teaching hospitals. It is a structured 5-year program that follows the scientist–practitioner model. The department does not offer a Master's degree in Clinical Psychology. During the first 4 years of the Clinical Psychology program, students complete required courses, conduct supervised and thesis research, and gain clinical experience through field placements. In the 5th year, students are placed in a full-year clinical internship.

Special Facilities or Resources: The department of psychology is located in the Life Sciences Centre, which also contains the departments of biology, earth sciences, and oceanography. The psychology building contains very extensive laboratory areas, some with circulating seawater aquaria, and is designed for research with a range of animal groups (humans, cats, birds, fish, invertebrates) using a range of research techniques in behavior, electrophysiology, neuroanatomy, immunocytochemistry, neurogenetics, and so forth. The department also houses an electronics and woodworking shop, an animal care facility, a surgical facility, a computer lab for word processing, communications, and access to a mainframe; specific neuroscience facilities are in close proximity to hospitals.

Application Information:

Send to Graduate Program Secretary, Psychology Department, Dalhousie University, Halifax, NS B3H 4J1. URL of online application: http://www.registrar.dal.ca/prospective/graduateapp.html. Students are admitted in the Fall, application deadline January 1. *Fee:* $70. Note: All dollar amounts specified in this entry are Canadian dollars.

Guelph, University of

Department of Psychology
College of Social and Applied Human Sciences
4th Floor MacKinnon Extension
Guelph, ON N1G 2W1
Telephone: (519) 824-4120 ext. 53508
Fax: (519) 837-8629
E-mail: *marmurek@psy.uoguelph.ca*
Web: *http://www.psychology.uoguelph.ca*

Department Information:

1966. Chairperson: Harvey H. C. Marmurek. Number of faculty: total—full-time 14; women—full-time 14; ; women minority—full-time 2.

Programs and Degrees Offered:

Listed in the following order: Program area, degree type (T if terminal Master's), number awarded 7/06–6/07. Neuroscience and Applied Cognitive Science PhD (Doctor of Philosophy) 0, Industrial/Organizational PhD (Doctor of Philosophy) 1, Applied Social PhD (Doctor of Philosophy) 0, Clinical Psychology: Applied Developmental Emphasis PhD (Doctor of Philosophy) 1, Neuroscience and Applied Cognitive Science MA/MS (Master of Arts/Science) 2, Applied Social MA/MS (Master of Arts/Science) 3, Clinical Psychology: Applied Develpmental Emphasis MA/MS (Master of Arts/Science) 5, Industrial/Organizational MA/MS (Master of Arts/Science) 3.

Student Applications/Admissions:

Student Applications

Neuroscience and Applied Cognitive Science PhD (Doctor of Philosophy)—Applications 2007–2008, 9. Total applicants accepted 2007–2008, 5. Number full-time enrolled (new admits only) 2007–2008, 1. Number part-time enrolled (new admits only) 2007–2008, 0. Openings 2008–2009, 3. The median number of years required for completion of a degree in 2006–2007 were 4. The number of students enrolled full- and part-time, who were dismissed or voluntarily withdrew from this program area in 2007–2008 were 0. *Industrial/Organizational PhD (Doctor of Philosophy)*—Applications 2007–2008, 9. Total applicants accepted 2007–2008, 2. Number full-time enrolled (new admits only) 2007–2008, 2. Number part-time enrolled (new admits only) 2007–2008, 0. Total enrolled 2007–2008 full-time, 10, part-time, 2. Openings 2008–2009, 3. The median number of years required for completion of a degree in 2006–2007 were 2. The number of students enrolled full- and part-time, who were dismissed or voluntarily withdrew from this program area in 2007–2008 were 1. *Applied Social PhD (Doctor of Philosophy)*—Applications 2007–2008, 10. Total applicants accepted 2007–2008, 4. Number full-time enrolled (new admits only) 2007–2008, 2. Number part-time enrolled (new admits only) 2007–2008, 0. Total enrolled 2007–2008 full-time, 14, part-time, 1. Openings 2008–2009, 3. The median number of years required for completion of a degree in 2006–2007 were 5. The number of students enrolled full- and part-time, who were dismissed or voluntarily withdrew from this program area in 2007–2008 were 1. *Clinical Psychology: Applied Developmental Emphasis PhD (Doctor of Philosophy)*—Applications 2007–2008, 17. Total applicants accepted 2007–2008, 3. Number full-time enrolled (new admits only) 2007–2008, 1. Number part-time enrolled (new admits only) 2007–2008, 0. Total enrolled 2007–2008 full-time, 22, part-time, 3. Openings 2008–2009, 4. The median number of years required for completion of a degree in 2006–2007 were 5. The number of students enrolled full- and part-time, who were dismissed or voluntarily withdrew from this program area in 2007–2008 were 0. *Neuroscience and Applied Cognitive Science MA/MS (Master of Arts/Science)*—Applications 2007–2008, 15. Total applicants accepted 2007–2008, 6. Number full-time enrolled (new admits only) 2007–2008, 6. Number part-time enrolled (new admits only) 2007–2008, 0. Openings 2008–2009, 5. The median number of years required for completion of a degree in 2006–2007 were 2. The number of students enrolled full- and part-time, who were dismissed or voluntarily withdrew from this program area in 2007–2008 were 0. *Applied Social MA/MS (Master of Arts/Science)*—Applications 2007–2008, 27. Total applicants accepted 2007–2008, 5. Number full-time enrolled (new admits only) 2007–2008, 5. Number part-time enrolled (new admits only) 2007–2008, 0. Openings 2008–2009, 5. The median number of years required for completion of a degree in 2006–2007 were 2. The number of students enrolled full- and part-time, who were dismissed or voluntarily withdrew from this program area in 2007–2008 were 0. *Clinical Psychology: Applied Develpmental Emphasis MA/MS (Master of Arts/Science)*—Applications 2007–2008, 103. Total applicants accepted 2007–2008, 6. Number full-time enrolled (new admits only) 2007–2008, 6. Number part-time enrolled (new admits only) 2007–2008, 0. Openings 2008–2009, 5. The median number of years required for completion of a degree in 2006–2007 were 2. The number of students enrolled full- and part-time, who were dismissed or voluntarily withdrew from this program area in 2007–2008 were 0. *Industrial/Organizational MA/MS (Master of Arts/Science)*—Applications 2007–2008, 34. Total applicants accepted 2007–2008, 5. Number full-time enrolled (new admits only) 2007–2008, 5. Number part-time enrolled (new admits only) 2007–2008, 0. Openings 2008–2009, 5. The median number of years required for completion of a degree in 2006–2007 were 2. The number of students enrolled full- and part-time, who were dismissed or voluntarily withdrew from this program area in 2007–2008 were 0.

Admissions Requirements:

Scores: Entries appear in this order: required test or GPA, minimum score (if required), median score of students entering in 2007–2008. Master's Programs: GRE-V no minimum stated, 580; GRE-Q no minimum stated, 625; GRE-Subject (Psychology) no minimum stated, 670; last 2 years GPA no minimum stated, 3.75; psychology GPA no minimum stated, 3.80. Doctoral Programs: GRE-V no minimum stated, 620; GRE-Q no minimum stated, 590; GRE-Subject (Psychology) no minimum stated, 660.

Other Criteria: (importance of criteria rated low, medium, or high): GRE/MAT scores—high, research experience—high, work experience—medium, extracurricular activity—low, clinically related public service—low, GPA—high, letters of recommendation—high, interview—high, statement of goals and objectives—high. For additional information on admission requirements, go to http://www.psychology.uoguelph.ca.

Student Characteristics: The following represents characteristics of students in 2007–2008 in all graduate psychology programs in the department: Female—full-time 72, part-time 6; Male—full-time 23, part-time 0; African American/Black—full-time 2, part-time 0; Hispanic/Latino(a)—full-time 0, part-time 0; Asian/Pacific Islander—full-time 4, part-time 0; American Indian/Alaska Native—full-time 0, part-time 0; Caucasian/White—full-time 86, part-time 6; Multi-ethnic—part-time 0; students subject to the Americans With Disabilities Act—full-time 0, part-time 0; Unknown ethnicity—full-time 0, part-time 0; International students who hold an F-1 or J-1 Visa—full-time 3, part-time 0.

Financial Information/Assistance:

Tuition for Full-Time Study: *Master's:* State residents: per academic year $5,823; Nonstate residents: per academic year $17,469. *Doctoral:* State residents: per academic year $5,823; Nonstate residents: per academic year $17,469. Tuition is subject to change. See the following Web site for updates and changes in tuition costs http://www.uoguelph.ca/registrar/studentfinance/index.cfm?app=tuition&level=gr.

Financial Assistance:

First-Year Students: Teaching assistantships available for first year. Average amount paid per academic year: $12,767. Average number of hours worked per week: 10. Fellowships and scholarships available for first year. Average amount paid per academic year: $1,500.

Advanced Students: Teaching assistantships available for advanced students. Average amount paid per academic year: $12,767. Average number of hours worked per week: 10. Fellowships and scholarships available for advanced students. Average amount paid per academic year: $3,500.

Additional Information: Of all students currently enrolled full time, 95% benefited from one or more of the listed financial assistance programs. Application and information available online at http://www.psychology.uoguelph.ca.

Internships/Practica: Doctoral Degree (PhD Clinical Psychology: Applied Developmental Emphasis): For those doctoral students for whom a professional internship was required in this program prior to graduation, (3) students applied for an internship in 2006–2007, with (3) students obtaining an internship. Of those students who obtained an internship, (3) were paid internships. Of those students who obtained an internship, (2) students placed in APA/CPA-accredited internships, (0) students placed in internships not APA/CPA-accredited, but listed with the Association of Psychology Postdoctoral and Internship Centers (APPIC), (0) students placed in internships conforming to guidelines of the Council of Directors of School Psychology Programs (CDSPP), (1) students placed in internships that were not APA/CPA-accredited, APPIC or CDSPP listed. For Clinical Psychology: Applied Developmental Emphasis students work 2 days per week with the psychological services staff at local public school boards. During a later semester, they are placed 4 days a week in a service facility for atypical children. Five students have been selected for accredited internship placements. For the Applied Social Psychology, students select practica in settings that include community health facilities, correctional and medical treatment settings, and private consulting firms. Industrial/Organizational and Applied Cognitive Science practica take place in industrial, governmental, and military settings.

Housing and Day Care: On-campus housing is available. See the following Web site for more information: http://www.housing.uoguelph.ca/home.cfm. On-campus day care facilities are available. See the following Web site for more information: http://www.uoguelph.ca/studentaffairs/childcare/home/.

Employment of Department Graduates:

Master's Degree Graduates: Of those who graduated in the academic year 2006–2007, the following categories and numbers represent the postgraduate activities and employment of master's degree graduates: Enrolled in a psychology doctoral program (8), enrolled in another graduate/professional program (1), enrolled in a postdoctoral residency/fellowship (n/a), employed in independent practice (n/a), employed in an academic position at a 2-year/4-year college (1), other employment position (3), total from the above (master's) (13).

Doctoral Degree Graduates: Of those who graduated in the academic year 2006–2007, the following categories and numbers represent the postgraduate activities and employment of doctoral degree graduates: Enrolled in a psychology doctoral program (n/a), employed in a community mental health/counseling center (1), total from the above (doctoral) (1).

Additional Information:

Orientation, Objectives, and Emphasis of Department: The Department of Psychology offers graduate programs leading to a Master of Arts and a Doctor of Philosophy in four fields: Neuroscience and Applied Cognitive Science, Applied Social Psychology, Clinical Psychology: Applied Developmental Emphasis, and Industrial/Organizational Psychology. The four fields follow a scientist–practitioner model and provide training in both research and professional skills, as well as a firm grounding in theory and research in relevant content areas. The PhD Clinical program is accredited by the Canadian Psychological Association. See http://www.psychology.uoguelph.ca for more information.

Special Facilities or Resources: Faculty offices and laboratories are located mainly in the MacKinnon Building, and Blackwood Hall. Graduate students have office space in Blackwood Hall and the Axelrod Building. The department is well supported with computer facilities. These include a microcomputer laboratory and extensive microcomputer support for research, teaching, data analysis, and word processing. Facilities for animal research include a fully equipped surgery room and physiological recording equipment. For research with human subjects, the department possesses portable videorecording equipment, observation rooms and experimental chambers. All of these facilities are supplemented by excellent workshop and technical support. The Centre for Psychological Services is a nonprofit organization associated with the Department of Psychology at the University of Guelph. The Centre provides high-quality psychological services at a reasonable cost, working with families and the community. The Centre is involved in training students in Clinical Psychology: Applied Developmental Emphasis and offers workshops and presentations to professionals in the community. G-CORI is a nonprofit consulting and research organization that hires students in Applied Social and Industrial/Organizational Psychology, allowing them to utilize the knowledge gained in their courses. A new building for faculty offices was recently completed.

Information for Students With Physical Disabilities: See the following Web site for more information: http://www.psychology.uoguelph.ca.

Application Information:

Send to Graduate Secretary, Department of Psychology, University of Guelph, Guelph, Ontario N1G 2W1, Canada. Telephone: (519) 824-4120, ext. 53508. Application available online. URL of online application: http://www.horizon.ouac.on.ca/webapp/account.d2w/report?ident=ACCOUNT_DSP&merchant_rn=810327&action_id=choose. Students are admitted in the Fall, application deadline December 15. All applications are reviewed in January. Interviews to take place in February. Offers to follow in March. Notification of Nonadmission May–June. *Fee:* $85. Deferral fee: $85. Note: All dollar amounts specified in this entry are Canadian dollars.

Manitoba, University of

Psychology Graduate Office
P514 Duff Roblin Building
Winnipeg, MB R3T 2N2
Telephone: (204) 474-6377
Fax: (204) 474-7917
E-mail: *Psyc_grad_office@umanitoba.ca*
Web: *http://www.umanitoba.ca/faculties/arts/psychology*

Department Information:

1947. Head: Harvey J. Keselman. Number of faculty: total—full-time 37, part-time 4; women—full-time 13.

Programs and Degrees Offered:

Listed in the following order: Program area, degree type (T if terminal Master's), number awarded 7/06–6/07. Applied Behavioural Analysis PhD (Doctor of Philosophy) 3, Brain and Cognitive Sciences PhD (Doctor of Philosophy) 4, Clinical PhD (Doctor of Philosophy) 8, Developmental PhD (Doctor of Philosophy) 0, Methodology PhD (Doctor of Philosophy) 0, Social/Personality PhD (Doctor of Philosophy) 1, School Psychology MA/MS (Master of Arts/Science) 6.

APA Accreditation: Clinical PhD (Doctor of Philosophy).

CPA Accreditation: Clinical PhD (Doctor of Philosophy).

Student Applications/Admissions:

Student Applications

Applied Behavioural Analysis PhD (Doctor of Philosophy)—Applications 2007–2008, 22. Total applicants accepted 2007–2008, 7. Number full-time enrolled (new admits only) 2007–2008, 7. Number part-time enrolled (new admits only) 2007–2008, 0. Openings 2008–2009, 2. The median number of years required for completion of a degree in 2006–2007 were 4. The number of students enrolled full- and part-time, who were dismissed or voluntarily withdrew from this program area in 2007–2008 were 0. *Brain and Cognitive Sciences PhD (Doctor of Philosophy)*—Applications 2007–2008, 12. Total applicants accepted 2007–2008, 1. Number full-time enrolled (new admits only) 2007–2008, 1. Number part-time enrolled (new admits only) 2007–2008, 0. Openings 2008–2009, 3. The median number of years required for completion of a degree in 2006–2007 were 2. The number of students enrolled full- and part-time, who were dismissed or voluntarily withdrew from this program area in 2007–2008 were 0. *Clinical PhD (Doctor of Philosophy)*—Applications 2007–2008, 67. Total applicants accepted 2007–2008, 5. Number full-time enrolled (new admits only) 2007–2008, 5. Number part-time enrolled (new admits only) 2007–2008, 0. Openings 2008–2009, 5. The median number of years required for completion of a degree in 2006–2007 were 4. The number of students enrolled full- and part-time, who were dismissed or voluntarily withdrew from this program area in 2007–2008 were 0. *Developmental PhD (Doctor of Philosophy)*—Applications 2007–2008, 3. Total applicants accepted 2007–2008, 0. Number full-time enrolled (new admits only) 2007–2008, 0. Number part-time enrolled (new admits only) 2007–2008, 0. Openings 2008–2009, 3. The number of students enrolled full- and part-time, who were dismissed or voluntarily withdrew from this program area in 2007–2008 were 0. *Methodology PhD (Doctor of Philosophy)*—Applications 2007–2008, 1. Total applicants accepted 2007–2008, 0. Number full-time enrolled (new admits only) 2007–2008, 0. Number part-time enrolled (new admits only) 2007–2008, 0. Openings 2008–2009, 3. The number of students enrolled full- and part-time, who were dismissed or voluntarily withdrew from this program area in 2007–2008 were 0. *Social/Personality PhD (Doctor of Philosophy)*—Applications 2007–2008, 19. Total applicants accepted 2007–2008, 3. Number full-time enrolled (new admits only) 2007–2008, 3. Number part-time enrolled (new admits only) 2007–2008, 0. Openings 2008–2009, 4. The median number of years required for completion of a degree in 2006–2007 were 2. The number of students enrolled full- and part-time, who were dismissed or voluntarily withdrew from this program area in 2007–2008 were 0. *School Psychology MA/MS (Master of Arts/Science)*—Applications 2007–2008, 34. Total applicants accepted 2007–2008, 10. Number full-time enrolled (new admits only) 2007–2008, 10. Number part-time enrolled (new admits only) 2007–2008, 0. Total enrolled 2007–2008 full-time, 22, part-time, 1. Openings 2008–2009, 7. The median number of years required for completion of a degree in 2006–2007 were 2. The number of students enrolled full- and part-time, who were dismissed or voluntarily withdrew from this program area in 2007–2008 were 1.

Admissions Requirements:

Scores: Entries appear in this order: required test or GPA, minimum score (if required), median score of students entering in 2007–2008. Master's Programs: GRE-V no minimum stated, 554; GRE-Q no minimum stated, 602; last 2 years GPA 3.0, 4.00. Doctoral Programs: GRE-V no minimum stated, 460; GRE-Q no minimum stated, 532.

Other Criteria: (importance of criteria rated low, medium, or high): GRE/MAT scores—high, research experience—high, work experience—medium, extracurricular activity—low, clinically related public service—medium, GPA—high, letters of recommendation—medium, interview—low, statement of goals and objectives—low, undergraduate major in psychology—high, specific undergraduate psychology courses taken—medium. For additional information on admission requirements, go to http://www.umanitoba.ca/psychology.

Student Characteristics: The following represents characteristics of students in 2007–2008 in all graduate psychology programs in the department: Female—full-time 110, part-time 1; Male—full-time 26, part-time 0; Caucasian/White—full-time 0, part-time 0; Unknown ethnicity—full-time 0, part-time 0.

Financial Information/Assistance:

Tuition for Full-Time Study: *Master's:* State residents: per academic year $4,177. *Doctoral:* State residents: per academic year $4,177. Tuition is not available at this time. Tuition is subject to change. See the following Web site for updates and changes in tuition costs including international student fees: http://www.umanitoba.ca/graduate_studies. Higher tuition cost for this program: School Psychology is a 2-year program, fees are currently approximately $4,177 per year.

Financial Assistance:

First-Year Students: Teaching assistantships available for first year. Average number of hours worked per week: 12. Apply by TBA. Research assistantships available for first year. Apply by TBA. Fellowships and scholarships available for first year. Apply by various.

Advanced Students: Teaching assistantships available for advanced students. Average number of hours worked per week: 12. Apply by TBA. Research assistantships available for advanced students. Apply by TBA. Fellowships and scholarships available for advanced students. Apply by various.

Additional Information: Of all students currently enrolled full time, 60% benefited from one or more of the listed financial assistance programs. Application and information available online at http://www.umanitoba.ca/psychology.

Internships/Practica: Doctoral Degree (PhD Clinical): For those doctoral students for whom a professional internship was required in this program prior to graduation, (5) students applied for an internship in 2006–2007, with (4) students obtaining an internship. Of those students who obtained an internship, (4) were paid internships. Of those students who obtained an internship, (4) students placed in APA/CPA-accredited internships, (0) students placed in internships not APA/CPA-accredited, but listed with the Association of Psychology Postdoctoral and Internship Centers (APPIC), (0) students placed in internships conforming to guidelines of the Council of Directors of School Psychology Programs (CDSPP), (0) students placed in internships that were not APA/CPA-accredited, APPIC or CDSPP listed. Clinical students have access to practica at our Psychological Service Center. A limited number of practica within the community are available for senior graduate students. However, the department does not offer an internship program.

Housing and Day Care: On-campus housing is available. See the following Web site for more information: http://www.umanitoba.ca/student/housing. On-campus day care facilities are available. See the following Web site for more information: http://www.umanitoba.ca/student/resource/playcare.

Employment of Department Graduates:

Master's Degree Graduates: Of those who graduated in the academic year 2006–2007, the following categories and numbers represent the postgraduate activities and employment of master's degree graduates: Enrolled in a psychology doctoral program (11), enrolled in another graduate/professional program (2), enrolled in a postdoctoral residency/fellowship (n/a), employed in independent practice (n/a), total from the above (master's) (13).

Doctoral Degree Graduates: Of those who graduated in the academic year 2006–2007, the following categories and numbers represent the postgraduate activities and employment of doctoral degree graduates: Enrolled in a psychology doctoral program (n/a), enrolled in a postdoctoral residency/fellowship (1), employed in other positions at a higher education institution (1), employed in a government agency (2), employed in a hospital/medical center (1), other employment position (2), do not know (1), total from the above (doctoral) (9).

Additional Information:

Orientation, Objectives, and Emphasis of Department: The primary purpose of our program is to provide training in several specialized areas of psychology for individuals desiring to advance their level of knowledge, their research skills, and their applied capabilities. The MA program is designed to provide a broad foundation, as well as specialized skills, in the scientific approach to psychology. The PhD program provides a higher degree of specialization coupled with more intensive training in research and application. Specialized areas of training within the department include applied behavioral analysis, brain and cognitive sciences, clinical, developmental, methodology, school, and social/personality.

Special Facilities or Resources: Basic research facilities are housed in over 100 dedicated research rooms. We host a large computer lab maintained by a crew of three excellent computer technicians, integrated animal care facilities under the supervision of a dedicated animal care technician, and a field station at which avian behavior may be studied. These resources are augmented by collaborative relationships we have with other university departments, local hospitals, St. Amant Centre, and the National Research Council: Institute for Biodiagnostics.

Information for Students With Physical Disabilities: See the following Web site for more information: http://www.umanitoba.ca.

Application Information:

Send to Linda Inglis, Graduate Program Coordinator, Psychology Graduate Office, P514 Duff Roblin Building, University of Manitoba, Winnipeg, MB R3T 2N2. Application available online. URL of online application: http://www.umanitoba.ca/faculties/graduate_studies/prospective/admissions/newapp.pdf. Students are admitted in the Winter, application deadline January 15. *Fee:* $75. Application fee for international students is $90. Note: All dollar amounts specified in this entry are Canadian dollars.

McGill University (2007 data)

Department of Educational and Counselling Psychology
Faculty of Education
3700 McTavish Street
Montreal, QC H3A 1Y2
Telephone: (514) 398-4242
Fax: (514) 398-6968
E-mail: *samantha.ryan@mcgill.ca*
Web: *http://www.education.mcgill.ca/ecp*

Department Information:

1965. Chair: Susanne P. Lajoie. Number of faculty: total—full-time 26, part-time 36; women—full-time 12, part-time 27.

Programs and Degrees Offered:

Listed in the following order: Program area, degree type (T if terminal Master's), number awarded 7/06–6/07. Counseling PhD (Doctor of Philosophy) 1, Educational PhD (Doctor of Philosophy) 6, School/Applied Child PhD (Doctor of Philosophy) 7.

APA Accreditation: Counseling PhD (Doctor of Philosophy). School PhD (Doctor of Philosophy).

Student Applications/Admissions:

Student Applications

Counseling PhD (Doctor of Philosophy)—Applications 2007–2008, 19. Total applicants accepted 2007–2008, 6. Number full-time enrolled (new admits only) 2007–2008, 4. Openings 2008–2009, 6. The median number of years required for completion of a degree in 2006–2007 were 7. The number of students enrolled full- and part-time, who were dismissed or voluntarily withdrew from this program area in 2007–2008 were 0. *Educational PhD (Doctor of Philosophy)*—Applications 2007–2008, 7. Total applicants accepted 2007–2008, 3. Number full-time enrolled (new admits only) 2007–2008, 1. Total enrolled 2007–2008 full-time, 46. Openings 2008–2009, 13. The median number of years required for completion of a degree in 2006–2007 were 7. The number of students enrolled full- and part-time, who were dismissed or voluntarily withdrew from this program area in 2007–2008 were 1. *School/Applied Child PhD (Doctor of Philosophy)*—Applications 2007–2008, 6. Total applicants accepted 2007–2008, 2. Number full-time enrolled (new admits only) 2007–2008, 2. Number part-time enrolled (new admits only) 2007–2008, 0. Openings 2008–2009, 9. The median number of years required for completion of a degree in 2006–2007 were 7. The number of students enrolled full- and part-time, who were dismissed or voluntarily withdrew from this program area in 2007–2008 were 0.

Admissions Requirements:

Scores: Entries appear in this order: required test or GPA, minimum score (if required), median score of students entering in 2007–2008. Master's Programs: GRE-V 500, 600; GRE-Q 500, 600; GRE-Subject (Psychology) 500, 600; overall undergraduate GPA 3.0, 3.5; last 2 years GPA 3.0, 3.3; psychology

GPA 3.0, 3.3. GREs are required only in School/Applied Child, Applied Developmental Psychology, and Counselling Psychology—there is no minimum cutoff. Doctoral Programs: GRE-V 500, 600; GRE-Q 500, 600; GRE-Subject (Psychology) 500, 600; overall undergraduate GPA 3.0. As for master's, no minimums.

Other Criteria: (importance of criteria rated low, medium, or high): research experience—medium, work experience—medium, extracurricular activity—medium, clinically related public service—medium, GPA—high, letters of recommendation—high, interview—medium, statement of goals and objectives—high. Relative weight of these criteria varies across program areas.

Student Characteristics: The following represents characteristics of students in 2007–2008 in all graduate psychology programs in the department: Female—full-time 166, part-time 73; Male—full-time 27, part-time 13; Caucasian/White—full-time 0, part-time 0; Unknown ethnicity—full-time 0, part-time 0.

Financial Information/Assistance:

Tuition for Full-Time Study: *Master's:* State residents: per academic year $3,099, $103 per credit hour; Nonstate residents: per academic year $11,641, $388 per credit hour. *Doctoral:* State residents: per academic year $3,099, $103 per credit hour; Nonstate residents: per academic year $10,951, $365 per credit hour. Tuition is subject to change. Tuition costs vary by program. See the following Web site for updates and changes in tuition costs: http://www.mcgill.ca/student-accounts/fees/tuition/gradfees/.

Financial Assistance:

First-Year Students: Teaching assistantships available for first year. Average amount paid per academic year: $2,235. Average number of hours worked per week: 3. Apply by September 1. Research assistantships available for first year. Average amount paid per academic year: $4,000. Average number of hours worked per week: 5.

Advanced Students: Teaching assistantships available for advanced students. Average amount paid per academic year: $4,200. Average number of hours worked per week: 6. Apply by March 15. Research assistantships available for advanced students. Average amount paid per academic year: $8,000. Average number of hours worked per week: 10. Fellowships and scholarships available for advanced students.

Additional Information: Of all students currently enrolled full time, 10% benefited from one or more of the listed financial assistance programs.

Internships/Practica: All students in the Professional Psychology programs, the MA (nonthesis) and PhD in Counseling Psychology, the MEd, and MA in Educational Psychology (Special Education and Gifted Education option), and the MA (School/Applied Child Psychology option) and PhD in School/Applied Child Psychology are required to complete internships. According to the program option these may be in mental health facilities, community social service agencies, schools, psychoeducational clinics, and so forth. In some internships, more than one setting is advised or required. New internship opportunities are regularly added, and students are welcome to seek out those that may especially suit their needs, subject to program approval.

Housing and Day Care: No on-campus housing is available. No on-campus day care facilities are available.

Employment of Department Graduates:

Master's Degree Graduates: Of those who graduated in the academic year 2006–2007, the following categories and numbers represent the postgraduate activities and employment of master's degree graduates: Enrolled in a postdoctoral residency/fellowship (n/a), employed in independent practice (n/a), total from the above (master's) (0).

Doctoral Degree Graduates: Of those who graduated in the academic year 2006–2007, the following categories and numbers represent the postgraduate activities and employment of doctoral degree graduates: Enrolled in a psychology doctoral program (n/a), total from the above (doctoral) (0).

Additional Information:

Orientation, Objectives, and Emphasis of Department: There are six broad areas of major graduate-level specialization: Counseling Psychology, Applied Developmental Psychology, Instructional Psychology, Applied Cognitive Psychology, Health Professions Education, Special Populations, and School/Applied Child Psychology. Minors are available in most of these topics that bridge the majors (e.g., computer applications, special/integrated education, gifted education, adult/professional, higher education, or psychology of gender) or topics proposed by students and approved by the department. A substantial base in research methods and statistics is provided and adjusted to students' entering competence. Graduate students in professional school psychology normally enter the Master's and are considered for transfer to the PhD (if that is their goal) after three semesters for a further 3 years of training. Graduate studies directed toward research, academic, and leadership careers follow a similar enrollment pattern except that the program normally requires 1 year less at the doctoral level. Students are welcome to take selected courses in other departments and at other Quebec universities.

Special Facilities or Resources: The Department has the Laboratory for Applied Cognitive Science, Summer Program in Gifted Education, Teaching and Learning Services, International Centre for Youth Gambling Problems and High-Risk Behavior, Neuroscience Lab for Resarch and Education in Developmental Disorders, Psychoeducational and Counselling Clinic, Psychoeducational Assessment Library, educational computer labs, and the Educational Media Centre.

Information for Students With Physical Disabilities: See the following Web site for more information: http://www.mcgill.ca/stuserv.

Application Information:

Send to Diane Bernier, Program Coordinator, Professional Psychology Graduate Programs; Geri Norton, Program Coordinator, Professional Educational Psychology Graduate Programs. Application available on-line. URL of online application: http://www.mcgill.ca/applying/graduate. Students are admitted in the Fall, application deadline January 10 and February 1; Spring, application deadline February 1; Summer, application deadline February 1. School/Applied Child Psychology deadline is January 10; Counselling Psychology February 1. Special circumstances may be examined on an individual basis. *Fee:* $80. Note: All dollar amounts specified in this entry are Canadian dollars.

McGill University
Department of Psychology
1205 Avenue Docteur Penfield
Montreal, QC H3A 1B1
Telephone: (514) 398-6124
Fax: (514) 398-4896
E-mail: *giovanna.locascio@mcgill.ca*
Web: *http://www.psych.mcgill.ca*

Department Information:

1922. Chair: Keith Franklin. Number of faculty: total—full-time 38, part-time 11; women—full-time 10, part-time 6.

Programs and Degrees Offered:

Listed in the following order: Program area, degree type (T if terminal Master's), number awarded 7/06–6/07. Clinical PhD (Doctor of Philosophy) 8, Experimental PhD (Doctor of Philosophy) 10.

APA Accreditation: Clinical PhD (Doctor of Philosophy).

CPA Accreditation: Clinical PhD (Doctor of Philosophy). Clinical PhD (Doctor of Philosophy).

Student Applications/Admissions:

Student Applications

Clinical PhD (Doctor of Philosophy)—Applications 2007–2008, 145. Total applicants accepted 2007–2008, 10. Number full-time enrolled (new admits only) 2007–2008, 8. Number part-time enrolled (new admits only) 2007–2008, 0. Openings 2008–2009, 10. The median number of years required for completion of a degree in 2006–2007 were 6. The number of students enrolled full- and part-time, who were dismissed or voluntarily withdrew from this program area in 2007–2008 were 0. *Experimental PhD (Doctor of Philosophy)*—Applications 2007–2008, 82. Total applicants accepted 2007–2008, 23. Number full-time enrolled (new admits only) 2007–2008, 13. Number part-time enrolled (new admits only) 2007–2008, 0. Openings 2008–2009, 15. The median number of years required for completion of a degree in 2006–2007 were 5. The number of students enrolled full- and part-time, who were dismissed or voluntarily withdrew from this program area in 2007–2008 were 0.

Admissions Requirements:

Scores: Entries appear in this order: required test or GPA, minimum score (if required), median score of students entering in 2007–2008. Master's Programs: GRE-V no minimum stated; GRE-Q no minimum stated; GRE-Subject (Psychology) no minimum stated; overall undergraduate GPA no minimum stated; last 2 years GPA no minimum stated; psychology GPA no minimum stated. Refer to our Graduate Program Brochure on our Web site: http://www.psych.mcgill.ca. Doctoral Programs: GRE-V no minimum stated; GRE-Q no minimum stated; GRE-Subject (Psychology) no minimum stated; overall undergraduate GPA no minimum stated; last 2 years GPA no minimum stated; psychology GPA no minimum stated. Refer to our Graduate Program Brochure on our Web site: http://www.psych.mcgill.ca.

Other Criteria: (importance of criteria rated low, medium, or high): GRE/MAT scores—high, research experience—high, work experience—medium, extracurricular activity—low, clinically related public service—medium, GPA—high, letters of recommendation—high, interview—medium, statement of goals and objectives—high, undergraduate major in psychology—medium, specific undergraduate psychology courses taken—high. Refer to our Graduate Program Brochure on our Web site: http://www.psych.mcgill.ca.

Student Characteristics: The following represents characteristics of students in 2007–2008 in all graduate psychology programs in the department: Female—full-time 73, part-time 0; Male—full-time 33, part-time 0; Caucasian/White—full-time 0, part-time 0; Unknown ethnicity—full-time 0, part-time 0; International students who hold an F-1 or J-1 Visa—full-time 19, part-time 0.

Financial Information/Assistance:

Tuition for Full-Time Study: *Master's:* State residents: per academic year $3,300; Nonstate residents: per academic year $13,200. *Doctoral:* State residents: per academic year $3,300; Nonstate residents: per academic year $11,918. Tuition is subject to change. See the following Web site for updates and changes in tuition costs: http://www.psych.mcgill.ca. Note: Non-Quebec Canadians for Master's approximately $7,300.00.

Financial Assistance:

First-Year Students: Teaching assistantships available for first year. Apply by n/a. Fellowships and scholarships available for first year. Apply by n/a.

Advanced Students: Teaching assistantships available for advanced students. Apply by n/a. Fellowships and scholarships available for advanced students. Apply by n/a.

Additional Information: Of all students currently enrolled full time, 100% benefited from one or more of the listed financial assistance programs. Application and information available online at http://ww2.mcgill.ca/StuServ/.

Internships/Practica: Doctoral Degree (Clinical): For those doctoral students for whom a professional internship was required in this program prior to graduation, (8) students applied for an internship in 2006–2007, with (8) students obtaining an internship. Of those students who obtained an internship, (8) were paid internships. Of those students who obtained an internship, (8) students placed in APA/CPA-accredited internships, (0) students placed in internships not APA/CPA-accredited, but listed with the Association of Psychology Postdoctoral and Internship Centers (APPIC), (0) students placed in internships conforming to guidelines of the Council of Directors of School Psychology Programs (CDSPP), (0) students placed in internships that were not APA/CPA-accredited, APPIC or CDSPP listed. The majority of students in our Clinical program complete their internships within Montreal, especially at McGill-affiliated hospitals. These include three large and two small general hospitals, a large psychiatric hospital, and a large children's hospital, where a wide range of assessment and treatment skills can be acquired. Specialized, advanced training is provided at other institutions in the areas of neuropsychology, hearing impairments, orthopedic disabilities, and rehabilitation. One advantage of having a local internship is that it facilitates the integration of the student's clinical and research activities. In addition, the department is able to monitor the quality of the training at the placements. All placements have active, ongoing commitments to research. Students have also completed internships at a wide variety of settings in other parts of Canada, the United States, and Europe. Settings outside Montreal must meet with staff approval.

Housing and Day Care: On-campus housing is available at McGill Residences and Student Housing. See the following Web site for more information: http://www.mcgill.ca/residences/, e-mail: housing.residences@mcgill.ca For off-campus housing, http://www.mcgill.ca/offcampus/, e-mail: offcampus.housing@mcgill.ca. On-campus day care facilities are available at McGill Child Care Centre. See the following Web site for more information: http://www.mcgill.ca/daycare/, or telephone (514) 398-6943.

Employment of Department Graduates:

Master's Degree Graduates: Of those who graduated in the academic year 2006–2007, the following categories and numbers represent the postgraduate activities and employment of master's degree graduates: Enrolled in another graduate/professional program (3), enrolled in a postdoctoral residency/fellowship (n/a), employed in independent practice (n/a), total from the above (master's) (3).

Doctoral Degree Graduates: Of those who graduated in the academic year 2006–2007, the following categories and numbers represent the postgraduate activities and employment of doctoral degree graduates: Enrolled in a psychology doctoral program (n/a), enrolled in a postdoctoral residency/fellowship (4), employed in an academic position at a university (8), employed in a hospital/medical center (7), total from the above (doctoral) (19).

Additional Information:

Orientation, Objectives, and Emphasis of Department: McGill University's Department of Psychology offers graduate work leading to the PhD degree. The program in Experimental Psychology includes the areas of cognitive science (perception, learning, and language), developmental, social, personality, quantitative, and behavioral neuroscience. A program in Clinical Psychology (accredited by APA and CPA) is also offered. The basic purpose of the graduate program is to provide the student with an environment in which he or she is free to develop skills and expertise that will serve during a professional career in teaching, research, or clinical service as a psychologist. Individually conceived and conducted research in the student's area of interest is the singlemost important activity of all graduate students in the department.

Application Information:

Send to Giovanna LoCascio, Graduate Program Coordinator, Department of Psychology, 1205 Docteur Penfield Avenue, Montreal, Quebec H3A 1B1. Application available online. Students are admitted in the Fall, application deadline December 1. Note: Students are required to apply online. All supporting documents must be submitted by the deadline to the Psychology Department. *Fee:* $80. Note: All dollar amounts specified in this entry are Canadian dollars.

Montreal, University of

Department of Psychology
P.O. Box 6128, Succursale Centre-Ville
Montreal, QC H3C 3J7
Telephone: (514) 343-6503
Fax: (514) 343-2285
E-mail: *michel.sabourin@umontreal.ca*
Web: *http://www.psy.umontreal.ca/*

Department Information:

1942. Chairperson: Dr. Michel Sabourin. Number of faculty: total—full-time 48, part-time 1; women—full-time 22.

Programs and Degrees Offered:

Listed in the following order: Program area, degree type (T if terminal Master's), number awarded 7/06–6/07. Clinical PhD (Doctor of Philosophy) 17, Experimental PhD (Doctor of Philosophy) 15, Industrial/Organizational PhD (Doctor of Philosophy) 1, Clinical Neuropsychology PhD (Doctor of Philosophy) 3.

CPA Accreditation: Clinical PhD (Doctor of Philosophy). Combination PhD (Doctor of Philosophy).

Student Applications/Admissions:

Student Applications

Clinical PhD (Doctor of Philosophy)—Applications 2007–2008, 102. Total applicants accepted 2007–2008, 17. Number full-time enrolled (new admits only) 2007–2008, 17. Total enrolled 2007–2008 full-time, 105. Openings 2008–2009, 16. The median number of years required for completion of a degree in 2006–2007 were 6. The number of students enrolled full- and part-time, who were dismissed or voluntarily withdrew from this program area in 2007–2008 were 0. *Experimental PhD (Doctor of Philosophy)*—Applications 2007–2008, 30. Total applicants accepted 2007–2008, 8. Number full-time enrolled (new admits only) 2007–2008, 8. Openings 2008–2009, 20. The median number of years required for completion of a degree in 2006–2007 were 4. *Industrial/Organizational PhD (Doctor of Philosophy)*—Applications 2007–2008, 21. Total applicants accepted 2007–2008, 5. Number full-time enrolled (new admits only) 2007–2008, 5. Total enrolled 2007–2008 full-time, 23. Openings 2008–2009, 5. The median number of years required for completion of a degree in 2006–2007 were 6. *Clinical Neuropsychology PhD (Doctor of Philosophy)*—Applications 2007–2008, 30. Total applicants accepted 2007–2008, 12. Number full-time enrolled (new admits only) 2007–2008, 12. Total enrolled 2007–2008 full-time, 63. Openings 2008–2009, 8. The median number of years required for completion of a degree in 2006–2007 were 6.

Admissions Requirements:

Scores: Entries appear in this order: required test or GPA, minimum score (if required), median score of students entering in 2007–2008. Master's Programs: psychology GPA no minimum stated, 3.5.

Other Criteria: (importance of criteria rated low, medium, or high): research experience—high, extracurricular activity—low, clinically related public service—low, GPA—high, letters of recommendation—low, interview—low, statement of goals and objectives—medium, specific undergraduate psychology courses taken—high.

Student Characteristics: The following represents characteristics of students in 2007–2008 in all graduate psychology programs in the department: Female—full-time 212, part-time 0; Male—full-time 52, part-time 0; African American/Black—full-time 3, part-time 0; Hispanic/Latino(a)—full-time 12, part-time 0; Asian/Pacific Islander—full-time 0, part-time 0; American Indian/Alaska Native—full-time 0, part-time 0; Caucasian/White—full-time 239, part-time 0; Multi-ethnic—full-time 10, part-time 0; Unknown ethnicity—full-time 0, part-time 0.

Financial Information/Assistance:

Tuition for Full-Time Study: *Master's:* State residents: per academic year $2,758; Nonstate residents: per academic year $10,800. *Doctoral:* State residents: per academic year $2,758; Nonstate residents: per academic year $10,800.

Financial Assistance:

First-Year Students: Teaching assistantships available for first year. Average amount paid per academic year: $2,000. Apply by variable. Research assistantships available for first year. Average amount paid per academic year: $2,000. Apply by variable. Fellowships and scholarships available for first year. Average amount paid per academic year: $5,000. Apply by December.

Advanced Students: Teaching assistantships available for advanced students. Average amount paid per academic year: $5,000. Apply by variable. Research assistantships available for advanced students. Average amount paid per academic year: $5,000. Apply by variable. Fellowships and scholarships available for advanced students. Average amount paid per academic year: $8,000. Apply by December.

Additional Information: Of all students currently enrolled full time, 68% benefited from one or more of the listed financial assistance programs.

Internships/Practica: The PhD programs offer internships in clinical, neuropsychology, and industrial/organizational psychology, in collaboration with general and psychiatric hospitals, correctional facilities, schools, industry, and governmental agencies.

Housing and Day Care: On-campus housing is available. See the following Web site for more information: http://www.logement.umontreal.ca. On-campus day care facilities are available.

Employment of Department Graduates:

Master's Degree Graduates: Of those who graduated in the academic year 2006–2007, the following categories and numbers represent the postgraduate activities and employment of master's degree graduates: Enrolled in a postdoctoral residency/fellowship (n/a), employed in independent practice (n/a), total from the above (master's) (0).

Doctoral Degree Graduates: Of those who graduated in the academic year 2006–2007, the following categories and numbers represent the postgraduate activities and employment of doctoral degree graduates: Enrolled in a psychology doctoral program (n/a), total from the above (doctoral) (0).

Additional Information:

Orientation, Objectives, and Emphasis of Department: In several subfields, the department offers a complete graduate curriculum that is oriented either toward scientific research (MS and PhD programs), at both the human and animal levels, or toward professional training (PhD, clinical, neuropsychology and industrial) programs. Because of its large faculty, the department presents most current theoretical perspectives and methodological approaches. The emphasis is placed on the development of the student's capacity for critical judgment, scientific analysis, and conceptual organization. With regard to professional training, the emphasis is placed on the integration of theory and practice, in both diagnosis and intervention.

Special Facilities or Resources: Because of the academic background of its faculty, our department provides the students with the opportunity of contact with both the North American and European scientific and professional traditions. The department has also organized clinical services for the general community; in this service several PhD students receive part of their professional training. Finally, the department lists on its Web site the current research of the faculty.

Information for Students With Physical Disabilities: See the following Web site for more information: http://www.umontreal.ca.

Application Information:

Send to Department Chair. Application available online. URL of online application: http://www.etudes.umontreal.ca/admission/index.html. Students are admitted in the Fall, application deadline February 1; Winter, application deadline October 15; Summer, application deadline February 1. *Fee:* $50. Note: All dollar amounts specified in this entry are Canadian dollars.

New Brunswick, University of

Department of Psychology
P.O. Box 4400
Fredericton, NB E3B 5A3
Telephone: (506) 453-4707
Fax: (506) 447-3063
E-mail: *hsears@unb.ca*
Web: *http://www.unbf.ca/psychology*

Department Information:

1966. Chairperson: E. Sandra Byers. Number of faculty: total—full-time 14; women—full-time 9.

Programs and Degrees Offered:

Listed in the following order: Program area, degree type (T if terminal Master's), number awarded 7/06–6/07. Clinical PhD (Doctor of Philosophy) 0, Experimental and Applied PhD (Doctor of Philosophy) 2.

APA Accreditation: Clinical PhD (Doctor of Philosophy).

CPA Accreditation: Clinical PhD (Doctor of Philosophy).

Student Applications/Admissions:

Student Applications

Clinical PhD (Doctor of Philosophy)—Applications 2007–2008, 52. Total applicants accepted 2007–2008, 6. Number full-time enrolled (new admits only) 2007–2008, 5. Number part-time enrolled (new admits only) 2007–2008, 0. Openings 2008–2009, 6. The number of students enrolled full- and part-time, who were dismissed or voluntarily withdrew from this program area in 2007–2008 were 0. *Experimental and Applied PhD (Doctor of Philosophy)*—Applications 2007–2008, 13. Total applicants accepted 2007–2008, 3. Number full-time enrolled (new admits only) 2007–2008, 1. Number part-time enrolled (new admits only) 2007–2008, 0. Total enrolled 2007–2008 full-time, 11, part-time, 1. Openings 2008–2009, 6. The median number of years required for completion of a degree in 2006–2007 were 9. The number of students enrolled full- and part-time, who were dismissed or voluntarily withdrew from this program area in 2007–2008 were 1.

Admissions Requirements:

Scores: Entries appear in this order: required test or GPA, minimum score (if required), median score of students entering in 2007–2008. Doctoral Programs: GRE-V no minimum stated, 600; GRE-Q no minimum stated, 600; GRE-Subject (Psychology) no minimum stated, 600; overall undergraduate GPA 3.7, 3.7. Admission to the Clinical program requires a minimum CGPA of 3.7 (equivalent to A- average). The minimum CGPA for admission to the Experimental and Applied program is 3.5 (both are on a 4.3 scale).

Other Criteria: (importance of criteria rated low, medium, or high): GRE/MAT scores—medium, research experience—high, work experience—medium, extracurricular activity—low, clinically related public service—low, GPA—high, letters of recommendation—high, interview—high, statement of goals and objectives—high. More emphasis is placed on research experience for students admitted to the Experimental and Applied program. A telephone interview is required for applicants to both of our programs. For additional information on admission requirements, go to http://www.unbf.ca/arts//psychology/graduate/grad-admin.html.

Student Characteristics: The following represents characteristics of students in 2007–2008 in all graduate psychology programs in the department: Female—full-time 40, part-time 1; Male—full-time 5, part-time 0; African American/Black—full-time 1, part-time 0; Hispanic/Latino(a)—full-time 1, part-time 0; Asian/Pacific Islander—full-time 1, part-time 0; American Indian/Alaska Native—full-time 0, part-time 0; Caucasian/White—full-time 40, part-time 1; Multi-ethnic—full-time 2, part-time 0; students subject to the Americans With Disabilities Act—full-time 0, part-time 0; Unknown ethnicity—full-time 0, part-time 0; International students who hold an F-1 or J-1 Visa—full-time 1, part-time 0.

Financial Information/Assistance:

Tuition for Full-Time Study: *Doctoral:* State residents: per academic year $6,126; Nonstate residents: per academic year $10,497. Tuition is subject to change.

Financial Assistance:

First-Year Students: Teaching assistantships available for first year. Average amount paid per academic year: $4,000. Average number of hours worked per week: 8. Apply by January 15. Fellowships and scholarships available for first year. Average amount paid per academic year: $8,000. Apply by January 15.

Advanced Students: Teaching assistantships available for advanced students. Average amount paid per academic year: $4,400. Average number of hours worked per week: 8. Apply by January 15. Fellowships and scholarships available for advanced students. Average amount paid per academic year: $8,800. Apply by January 15.

Additional Information: Of all students currently enrolled full time, 33% benefited from one or more of the listed financial assistance programs.

Internships/Practica: Students in the Clinical program have completed practica in the following types of local agencies: mental health clinic, general hospital, university counseling services, psychiatric hospital, or school system.

Housing and Day Care: On-campus housing is available. See the following Web site for more information: http://www.unb.ca/residence/reslife.html. On-campus day care facilities are available.

Employment of Department Graduates:

Master's Degree Graduates: Of those who graduated in the academic year 2006–2007, the following categories and numbers represent the postgraduate activities and employment of master's degree graduates: Enrolled in a postdoctoral residency/fellowship (n/a), employed in independent practice (n/a), total from the above (master's) (0).

Doctoral Degree Graduates: Of those who graduated in the academic year 2006–2007, the following categories and numbers represent the postgraduate activities and employment of doctoral degree graduates: Enrolled in a psychology doctoral program (n/a), enrolled in another graduate/professional program (0), enrolled in a postdoctoral residency/fellowship (0), employed in independent practice (0), employed in an academic position at a university (2), employed in an academic position at a 2-year/4-year college (0), employed in other positions at a higher education institution (0), employed in a professional position in a school system (0), employed in business or industry (0), employed in a government agency (0), employed in a community mental health/counseling center (0), employed in a hospital/medical center (0), still seeking employment (0), other employment position (0), do not know (0), total from the above (doctoral) (2).

Additional Information:

Orientation, Objectives, and Emphasis of Department: The Department of Psychology offers an integrated MA/PhD degree designed to provide extensive specialized study in either Clinical Psychology or Experimental and Applied Psychology. The Clinical program provides graduates both with sufficient skills in assessment, treatment, and outcome evaluation to initiate careers in service settings under appropriate supervision, and with the knowledge and training needed for an academic career. The Experimental and Applied Program emphasizes individual training and the development of skills to equally prepare the student for a research-oriented career in applied and academic settings.

Special Facilities or Resources: The department occupies Keirstead Hall, which is well supplied with research equipment. The facilities include laboratories for research in human learning, cognition and perception, and development, as well as physiological psychology and neuropsychology; a direct line to the computer center; space for research and teaching in clinical, community, behavior therapy, biofeedback, and other areas of applied or clinical psychology.

Information for Students With Physical Disabilities: Building is wheelchair accessible.

Application Information:
Send to School of Graduate Studies, University of New Brunswick, P.O. Box 4400, Fredericton, New Brunswick, Canada E3B 5A3. Application available online. URL of online application: http://www.unbf.ca/arts//psychology/graduate/gradapp.html. Students are admitted in the Fall, application deadline January 15. *Fee:* $50. The School of Graduate Studies offers fee waivers to selected applicants on the basis of academic merit. Note: All dollar amounts specified in this entry are Canadian dollars.

Ottawa, University of

School of Psychology
Lamoureux Hall, 145 Jean-Jacques Lussier
Ottawa, ON K1N 6N5
Telephone: (613) 562-5800 ext. 4197
Fax: (613) 562-5147
E-mail: *mcote@uottawa.ca*
Web: *http://www.grad.uottawa.ca/programs/doctorates/psy*

Department Information:
1941. Director and Associate Dean: Pierre Gosselin. Number of faculty: total—full-time 47, part-time 34; women—full-time 17, part-time 34.

Programs and Degrees Offered:
Listed in the following order: Program area, degree type (T if terminal Master's), number awarded 7/06–6/07. Clinical PhD (Doctor of Philosophy) 10, Experimental PhD (Doctor of Philosophy) 10.

APA Accreditation: Clinical PhD (Doctor of Philosophy).

Student Applications/Admissions:
Student Applications
Clinical PhD (Doctor of Philosophy)—Applications 2007–2008, 193. Total applicants accepted 2007–2008, 17. Number full-time enrolled (new admits only) 2007–2008, 16. Number part-time enrolled (new admits only) 2007–2008, 0. Total enrolled 2007–2008 full-time, 88, part-time, 3. Openings 2008–2009, 16. The median number of years required for completion of a degree in 2006–2007 were 6. The number of students enrolled full- and part-time, who were dismissed or voluntarily withdrew from this program area in 2007–2008 were 0. *Experimental PhD (Doctor of Philosophy)*—Applications 2007–2008, 44. Total applicants accepted 2007–2008, 18. Number full-time enrolled (new admits only) 2007–2008, 17. Number part-time enrolled (new admits only) 2007–2008, 0. Total enrolled 2007–2008 full-time, 51, part-time, 1. Openings 2008–2009, 14. The median number of years required for completion of a degree in 2006–2007 were 5. The number of students enrolled full- and part-time, who were dismissed or voluntarily withdrew from this program area in 2007–2008 were 1.

Other Criteria: (importance of criteria rated low, medium, or high): research experience—high, work experience—low, extracurricular activity—low, clinically related public service—medium, GPA—high, letters of recommendation—high, interview—medium, statement of goals and objectives—high, bilingualism (French/English)—high. Bilingualism is more important for the Clinical program than for the Experimental Program. Language that courses will be taken in (Clinical program only); Clinical French stream and Clinical English Stream. For additional information on admission requirements, go to http://www.etudesup.uottawa.ca/default.aspx?tabid=1727&monControl=Admission&ProgId=579.

Student Characteristics: The following represents characteristics of students in 2007–2008 in all graduate psychology programs in the department: Female—full-time 120, part-time 4; Male—full-time 16, part-time 0; African American/Black—full-time 0, part-time 0; Hispanic/Latino(a)—full-time 0, part-time 0; Asian/Pacific Islander—full-time 4, part-time 0; American Indian/Alaska Native—full-time 0, part-time 0; Caucasian/White—full-time 132, part-time 4; Multi-ethnic—full-time 0, part-time 0; students subject to the Americans With Disabilities Act—full-time 0, part-time 0; Unknown ethnicity—full-time 0, part-time 0.

Financial Information/Assistance:
Tuition for Full-Time Study: *Doctoral:* State residents: per academic year $5,601, $212 per credit hour; Nonstate residents: per academic year $13,693, $451 per credit hour. See the following Web site for updates and changes in tuition costs: http://www.uottawa.ca/academic/info/regist/fees/fees2007_en.htm.

Financial Assistance:
First-Year Students: Teaching assistantships available for first year. Average amount paid per academic year: $9,000. Average number of hours worked per week: 10. Apply by June. Research assistantships available for first year. Average amount paid per academic year: $9,000. Average number of hours worked per week: 10. Apply by June. Fellowships and scholarships available for first year. Average amount paid per academic year: $9,000. Apply by March.
Advanced Students: Teaching assistantships available for advanced students. Average amount paid per academic year: $9,000. Average number of hours worked per week: 10. Apply by June. Research assistantships available for advanced students. Average amount paid per academic year: $9,000. Average number of hours worked per week: 10. Apply by June. Traineeships available for advanced students. Average amount paid per academic year: $28,000. Average number of hours worked per week: 30. Apply by October. Fellowships and scholarships available for advanced students. Average amount paid per academic year: $9,000. Apply by October.
Additional Information: Of all students currently enrolled full time, 95% benefited from one or more of the listed financial assistance programs. Application and information available online at http://www.socialsciences.uottawa.ca/psy/eng/graduate_programs.asp.

Internships/Practica: Doctoral Degree (Clinical): For those doctoral students for whom a professional internship was required in this program prior to graduation, (8) students applied for an internship in 2006–2007, with (8) students obtaining an internship. Of those students who obtained an internship, (8) were paid internships. Of those students who obtained an internship, (8) students placed in APA/CPA-accredited internships, (0) students placed in internships not APA/CPA-accredited, but listed with the Association of Psychology Postdoctoral and Internship Centers (APPIC), (0) students placed in internships conforming to guidelines of the Council of Directors of School Psychology Programs (CDSPP), (0) students placed in internships that were not APA/CPA-accredited, APPIC or CDSPP listed. Internships, required of all Clinical program students, take place in accredited external settings in Canada and the United States as well as in local, approved training units. There is one internal training unit: the Centre for Psychological Services. There are 18 external units providing practicum training: Children's Hospital of Eastern Ontario, Ottawa Hospital, Brockville Psychiatric Hospital, Centre Hospitalier Pierre Janet, Montfort Hospital, Ottawa-Carleton Detention Centre, Conseil des Ecoles Catholiques de Langue Francaise, Center for the Treatment of Sexual Abuse and Childhood Trauma, Crossroads Children's Centre, Royal Ottawa Hospital, The Rehabilitation Centre, The Children's Aid Society of Ottawa-Carleton, Catholic School Board of Eastern Ontario, Ottawa Mindfulness Clinical, Western Quebec School Board and Centre Psychosocial de Vanier. External research internships for the Experimental program within the University of Ottawa take place in the departments of Sociology, Physiotherapy, Epidemiology, Faculties of Education, and Administration. External research internships for the Experimental program are: Royal Ottawa Hospital, Ottawa General Hospital, Children's Hospital of Eastern Ontario, Department of Psychology at Carleton University, Communications Research Center of Canada, Federal Government of Canada (Animal Care), Canadian Armed Forces, ENAP, Ministry of Health, and NORTEL.

Housing and Day Care: On-campus housing is available. See the following Web site for more information: http://www.uottawa.ca/students/housing/. On-campus day care facilities are available. See the following Web site for more information: http://www.communitylife.uottawa.ca/en/campus-service.php.

Employment of Department Graduates:

Master's Degree Graduates: Of those who graduated in the academic year 2006–2007, the following categories and numbers represent the postgraduate activities and employment of master's degree graduates: Enrolled in a postdoctoral residency/fellowship (n/a), employed in independent practice (n/a), total from the above (master's) (0).

Doctoral Degree Graduates: Of those who graduated in the academic year 2006–2007, the following categories and numbers represent the postgraduate activities and employment of doctoral degree graduates: Enrolled in a psychology doctoral program (n/a), enrolled in a postdoctoral residency/fellowship (3), employed in independent practice (3), employed in an academic position at a university (1), employed in a government agency (3), employed in a hospital/medical center (6), other employment position (1), do not know (3), total from the above (doctoral) (20).

Additional Information:

Orientation, Objectives, and Emphasis of Department: The objective of the program in Experimental Psychology is to train researchers in behavioral neurophysiology, neuroimaging, psychopharmacology, psychophysiology, human and animal cognition, perception, learning, language, sleep and dreams, social, cognitive and emotional development, personality, intergroup relations, motivation, and the social psychology of health, sports, and work. Training in behavioral neuroscience may also be provided through the Behavioural Neurosciences Specialization Program, which is a collaborative program coordinated by the University of Ottawa and Carleton University. The purpose of the Clinical Psychology program is to provide doctoral training in the area of clinical psychology and prepare students to work with adults and children. Professional training includes exposure to cognitive–behavioral, experiential, systemic–interpersonal, and community consultation approaches. Thesis supervisors within the Clinical program have special expertise in areas such as social development of children, behavior problems and mental health problems in children and adolescents, depression, psychotherapy, marital therapy, family psychology, community psychology, neuropsychology, health psychology, and program evaluation. Clinical students may also elect to choose a thesis supervisor from the Experimental program, and vice versa, or adjunct professors/clinical professors who are members of the faculty of Graduate and Postdoctoral Studies.

Special Facilities or Resources: Community Services Research Unit, for research related to evaluating and improving community agency programs; a sleep lab with two bedrooms. The School of Psychology has a training unit, the Centre for Psychological Services, which offers assessment and treatment for adults, children, families, and couples. The Centre for Research on Educational and Community Services provides program evaluation and consultation services to local social services agencies.

Information for Students With Physical Disabilities: See the following Web site for more information: http://www.web.sass.uottawa.ca/access/.

Application Information:

Send to Graduate Program Administrator, School of Psychology, University of Ottawa, Lamoureux Hall, 145 Jean-Jacques Lussier Street, Ottawa, K1N 6N5, Canada. Application available online. URL of online application: http://www.grad.uottawa.ca/apply. Students are admitted in the Fall, application deadline January 3. Experimental Program: second deadline, May 15. *Fee:* $75. Note: All dollar amounts specified in this entry are Canadian dollars.

Quebec at Montreal, University of

Department of Psychology
C.P. 8888, Succursale Centre-Ville
Montreal, QC H3C 3P8
Telephone: (514) 987-4804
Fax: (514) 987-7953
E-mail: *doctorat.psycho@uqam.ca*
Web: *http://www.psycho.uqam.ca/*

Department Information:

1969. Chairperson: Luc Reid. Number of faculty: total—full-time 52; women—full-time 23; total—minority—full-time 2; women minority—full-time 2.

Programs and Degrees Offered:

Listed in the following order: Program area, degree type (T if terminal Master's), number awarded 7/06–6/07. Community PhD

(Doctor of Philosophy) 2, Development PhD (Doctor of Philosophy) 10, Education PhD (Doctor of Philosophy) 7, I/O PhD (Doctor of Philosophy) 1, Neuropsychology PhD (Doctor of Philosophy) 7, Psychodynamic PhD (Doctor of Philosophy) 4, Social PhD (Doctor of Philosophy) 0, Behavioral PhD (Doctor of Philosophy) 5.

Student Applications/Admissions:

Student Applications

Community PhD (Doctor of Philosophy)—Applications 2007–2008, 11. Total applicants accepted 2007–2008, 8. Number full-time enrolled (new admits only) 2007–2008, 8. Number part-time enrolled (new admits only) 2007–2008, 0. The median number of years required for completion of a degree in 2006–2007 were 6. The number of students enrolled full- and part-time, who were dismissed or voluntarily withdrew from this program area in 2007–2008 were 0. *Development PhD (Doctor of Philosophy)*—Applications 2007–2008, 35. Total applicants accepted 2007–2008, 20. Number full-time enrolled (new admits only) 2007–2008, 16. Number part-time enrolled (new admits only) 2007–2008, 0. The median number of years required for completion of a degree in 2006–2007 were 6. The number of students enrolled full- and part-time, who were dismissed or voluntarily withdrew from this program area in 2007–2008 were 2. *Education PhD (Doctor of Philosophy)*—Applications 2007–2008, 28. Total applicants accepted 2007–2008, 8. Number full-time enrolled (new admits only) 2007–2008, 7. Number part-time enrolled (new admits only) 2007–2008, 0. The median number of years required for completion of a degree in 2006–2007 were 6. The number of students enrolled full- and part-time, who were dismissed or voluntarily withdrew from this program area in 2007–2008 were 3. *I/O PhD (Doctor of Philosophy)*—Applications 2007–2008, 15. Total applicants accepted 2007–2008, 8. Number full-time enrolled (new admits only) 2007–2008, 6. Number part-time enrolled (new admits only) 2007–2008, 0. The median number of years required for completion of a degree in 2006–2007 were 6. The number of students enrolled full- and part-time, who were dismissed or voluntarily withdrew from this program area in 2007–2008 were 0. *Neuropsychology PhD (Doctor of Philosophy)*—Applications 2007–2008, 24. Total applicants accepted 2007–2008, 13. Number full-time enrolled (new admits only) 2007–2008, 9. The median number of years required for completion of a degree in 2006–2007 were 6. The number of students enrolled full- and part-time, who were dismissed or voluntarily withdrew from this program area in 2007–2008 were 1. *Psychodynamic PhD (Doctor of Philosophy)*—Applications 2007–2008, 58. Total applicants accepted 2007–2008, 24. Number full-time enrolled (new admits only) 2007–2008, 22. The median number of years required for completion of a degree in 2006–2007 were 6. The number of students enrolled full- and part-time, who were dismissed or voluntarily withdrew from this program area in 2007–2008 were 3. *Social PhD (Doctor of Philosophy)*—Applications 2007–2008, 11. Total applicants accepted 2007–2008, 5. Number full-time enrolled (new admits only) 2007–2008, 5. Number part-time enrolled (new admits only) 2007–2008, 0. The median number of years required for completion of a degree in 2006–2007 were 6. The number of students enrolled full- and part-time, who were dismissed or voluntarily withdrew from this program area in 2007–2008 were 0. *Behavioral PhD (Doctor of Philosophy)*—Applications 2007–2008, 56. Total applicants accepted 2007–2008, 23. Number full-time enrolled (new admits only) 2007–2008, 18. Number part-time enrolled (new admits only) 2007–2008, 0. The median number of years required for completion of a degree in 2006–2007 were 6. The number of students enrolled full- and part-time, who were dismissed or voluntarily withdrew from this program area in 2007–2008 were 1.

Admissions Requirements:

Scores: Entries appear in this order: required test or GPA, minimum score (if required), median score of students entering in 2007–2008. Master's Programs: n/a. Doctoral Programs: overall undergraduate GPA 76%; psychology GPA no minimum stated. Minimum score required is 3.2, 4.3.

Other Criteria: (importance of criteria rated low, medium, or high): research experience—low, work experience—low, extracurricular activity—low, clinically related public service—low, GPA—high, letters of recommendation—high, interview—low, statement of goals and objectives—high.

Student Characteristics: The following represents characteristics of students in 2007–2008 in all graduate psychology programs in the department: Female—full-time 405, part-time 0; Male—full-time 92, part-time 0; African American/Black—full-time 1, part-time 0; Hispanic/Latino(a)—full-time 2, part-time 0; Asian/Pacific Islander—full-time 1, part-time 0; American Indian/Alaska Native—full-time 0, part-time 0; Caucasian/White—full-time 493, part-time 0; Unknown ethnicity—full-time 0, part-time 0.

Financial Information/Assistance:

Financial Assistance:

First-Year Students: No information provided.

Advanced Students: No information provided.

Additional Information: Of all students currently enrolled full time, 20% benefited from one or more of the listed financial assistance programs. Application and information available online at http://www.etudier.uqam.ca/financier.htm.

Internships/Practica: Internship settings include about 12 Montreal general and psychiatric hospitals, 7 community settings, 6 Montreal school boards, 4 university study centers as well as a number of private centers or clinics. Internships typically cover about 1,600–2,000 hours of supervised clinical work, including assessment procedures, multidisciplinary seminars, and various types of therapy with various orientations. Some settings also provide training in clinical observation and research.

Housing and Day Care: On-campus housing is available. Telephone: (514) 987-6669; Fax: (514) 987-0344. On-campus day care facilities are available.

Employment of Department Graduates:

Master's Degree Graduates: Of those who graduated in the academic year 2006–2007, the following categories and numbers represent the postgraduate activities and employment of master's degree graduates: Enrolled in a postdoctoral residency/fellowship (n/a), employed in independent practice (n/a), total from the above (master's) (0).

Doctoral Degree Graduates: Of those who graduated in the academic year 2006–2007, the following categories and numbers represent the postgraduate activities and employment of doctoral

degree graduates: Enrolled in a psychology doctoral program (n/a), total from the above (doctoral) (0).

Additional Information:

Special Facilities or Resources: Our department offers the following technical support to staff and graduate students: a consultant statistician, a consultant computer programmer, and a resident visual artist who designs and creates professional quality visual stimuli for research. He also prepares graphics for articles, posters, and the thesis. All labs are equipped with personal computers. Students have access to these computers and the mainframe university computer. The university offers support services for handicapped students. Please note that the teaching language in our university is French, though the majority of the literature in psychology is English. Some professors may require the students to write papers in French. Students must obtain permission to write the thesis in English. Courses in French conversation and composition are offered by the university.

Information for Students With Physical Disabilities: Intégration des personnes handicapées: (514) 987-3148.

Application Information:
Send to Registrariat Service de l'admission, Université du Québec à Montréal, Case Postale 8888, Succursale Centre-ville, Montréal Québec, Canada, H3C 3P8. Application available online. URL of online application: http://www.regis.uqam.ca/pdf/formulaires/F177_2_3.pdf. Students are admitted in the Fall, application deadline February 15. *Fee:* $55. Note: All dollar amounts specified in this entry are Canadian dollars.

Queen's University

Department of Psychology
Humphrey Hall, 62 Arch Street
Kingston, ON K7L 3N6
Telephone: (613) 533-6004
Fax: (613) 533-2499
E-mail: *psychead@queensu.ca*
Web: *http://www.psyc.queensu.ca*

Department Information:
1949. Head: V. L. Quinsey. Number of faculty: total—full-time 32; women—full-time 16.

Programs and Degrees Offered:
Listed in the following order: Program area, degree type (T if terminal Master's), number awarded 7/06–6/07. Brain, Behavior, and Cognitive Science PhD (Doctor of Philosophy) 2, Clinical PhD (Doctor of Philosophy) 3, Social/Personality PhD (Doctor of Philosophy) 2, Developmental PhD (Doctor of Philosophy) 2, Brain, Behavior, and Cognitive Science MA/MS (Master of Arts/Science) 4, Clinical MA/MS (Master of Arts/Science) 6, Developmental MA/MS (Master of Arts/Science) 2, Social/Personality MA/MS (Master of Arts/Science) 7.

APA Accreditation: Clinical PhD (Doctor of Philosophy).

CPA Accreditation: Clinical PhD (Doctor of Philosophy).

Student Applications/Admissions:
Student Applications
Brain, Behavior, and Cognitive Science PhD (Doctor of Philosophy)—Applications 2007–2008, 1. Total applicants accepted 2007–2008, 0. Number full-time enrolled (new admits only) 2007–2008, 0. Number part-time enrolled (new admits only) 2007–2008, 0. Total enrolled 2007–2008 full-time, 10, part-time, 1. Openings 2008–2009, 8. The median number of years required for completion of a degree in 2006–2007 were 4. The number of students enrolled full- and part-time, who were dismissed or voluntarily withdrew from this program area in 2007–2008 were 0. *Clinical PhD (Doctor of Philosophy)*—Applications 2007–2008, 11. Total applicants accepted 2007–2008, 1. Number full-time enrolled (new admits only) 2007–2008, 1. Number part-time enrolled (new admits only) 2007–2008, 0. Total enrolled 2007–2008 full-time, 21, part-time, 2. Openings 2008–2009, 7. The median number of years required for completion of a degree in 2006–2007 were 7. The number of students enrolled full- and part-time, who were dismissed or voluntarily withdrew from this program area in 2007–2008 were 2. *Social/Personality PhD (Doctor of Philosophy)*—Applications 2007–2008, 2. Total applicants accepted 2007–2008, 2. Number full-time enrolled (new admits only) 2007–2008, 1. Number part-time enrolled (new admits only) 2007–2008, 0. Openings 2008–2009, 5. The median number of years required for completion of a degree in 2006–2007 were 4. The number of students enrolled full- and part-time, who were dismissed or voluntarily withdrew from this program area in 2007–2008 were 1. *Developmental PhD (Doctor of Philosophy)*—Applications 2007–2008, 3. Total applicants accepted 2007–2008, 71. Number full-time enrolled (new admits only) 2007–2008, 3. Number part-time enrolled (new admits only) 2007–2008, 0. Openings 2008–2009, 6. The median number of years required for completion of a degree in 2006–2007 were 5. The number of students enrolled full- and part-time, who were dismissed or voluntarily withdrew from this program area in 2007–2008 were 0. *Brain, Behavior, and Cognitive Science MA/MS (Master of Arts/Science)*—Applications 2007–2008, 21. Total applicants accepted 2007–2008, 10. Number full-time enrolled (new admits only) 2007–2008, 3. Number part-time enrolled (new admits only) 2007–2008, 0. Openings 2008–2009, 8. The median number of years required for completion of a degree in 2006–2007 were 2. The number of students enrolled full- and part-time, who were dismissed or voluntarily withdrew from this program area in 2007–2008 were 1. *Clinical MA/MS (Master of Arts/Science)*—Applications 2007–2008, 102. Total applicants accepted 2007–2008, 11. Number full-time enrolled (new admits only) 2007–2008, 6. Number part-time enrolled (new admits only) 2007–2008, 0. Openings 2008–2009, 7. The median number of years required for completion of a degree in 2006–2007 were 2. The number of students enrolled full- and part-time, who were dismissed or voluntarily withdrew from this program area in 2007–2008 were 2. *Developmental MA/MS (Master of Arts/Science)*—Applications 2007–2008, 18. Total applicants accepted 2007–2008, 10. Number full-time enrolled (new admits only) 2007–2008, 3. Number part-time enrolled (new admits only) 2007–2008, 0. Openings 2008–2009, 6. The median number of years required for completion of a degree in 2006–2007 were 2. The number of students enrolled full- and part-time, who were dismissed or voluntarily withdrew from this program area in 2007–2008 were 0. *Social/Personality MA/MS (Master of Arts/Science)*—

Applications 2007–2008, 35. Total applicants accepted 2007–2008, 6. Number full-time enrolled (new admits only) 2007–2008, 3. Number part-time enrolled (new admits only) 2007–2008, 0. Openings 2008–2009, 5. The median number of years required for completion of a degree in 2006–2007 were 2. The number of students enrolled full- and part-time, who were dismissed or voluntarily withdrew from this program area in 2007–2008 were 0.

Admissions Requirements:

Scores: Entries appear in this order: required test or GPA, minimum score (if required), median score of students entering in 2007–2008. Master's Programs: GRE-V no minimum stated, 584; GRE-Q no minimum stated, 704; overall undergraduate GPA no minimum stated; last 2 years GPA no minimum stated; psychology GPA no minimum stated. Upper second class honours degree is required. Doctoral Programs: GRE-V no minimum stated, 584; GRE-Q no minimum stated, 704; overall undergraduate GPA no minimum stated; last 2 years GPA no minimum stated; psychology GPA no minimum stated.

Other Criteria: (importance of criteria rated low, medium, or high): GRE/MAT scores—high, research experience—medium, work experience—low, extracurricular activity—low, clinically related public service—low, GPA—high, letters of recommendation—high, statement of goals and objectives—high, supervisor availability—high, undergraduate major in psychology—high. For additional information on admission requirements, go to http://psyc.queensu.ca/gradbeta1/prostuforms.html.

Student Characteristics: The following represents characteristics of students in 2007–2008 in all graduate psychology programs in the department: Female—full-time 66, part-time 3; Male—full-time 19, part-time 0; Asian/Pacific Islander—full-time 6, part-time 0; Caucasian/White—full-time 79, part-time 3; students subject to the Americans With Disabilities Act—full-time 0, part-time 0; Unknown ethnicity—full-time 0, part-time 0; International students who hold an F-1 or J-1 Visa—full-time 5, part-time 0.

Financial Information/Assistance:

Tuition for Full-Time Study: *Master's:* State residents: per academic year $6,078; Nonstate residents: per academic year $11,449. *Doctoral:* State residents: per academic year $6,078; Nonstate residents: per academic year $11,449. Tuition is subject to change. See the following Web site for updates and changes in tuition costs: http://www.queensu.ca/registrar/fees/index.html.

Financial Assistance:

First-Year Students: Teaching assistantships available for first year. Average amount paid per academic year: $8,970. Average number of hours worked per week: 10. Apply by n/a. Fellowships and scholarships available for first year. Average amount paid per academic year: $20,000. Average number of hours worked per week: 0. Apply by October.

Advanced Students: Teaching assistantships available for advanced students. Average amount paid per academic year: $8,970. Average number of hours worked per week: 10. Apply by n/a. Fellowships and scholarships available for advanced students. Average amount paid per academic year: $20,000. Average number of hours worked per week: 0. Apply by October.

Additional Information: Of all students currently enrolled full time, 90% benefited from one or more of the listed financial assistance programs. Application and information available online at http://www.queensu.ca/sgsr/Prospectivestudents/thinkingofapplying.html.

Internships/Practica: Doctoral Degree (PhD Clinical): For those doctoral students for whom a professional internship was required in this program prior to graduation, (4) students applied for an internship in 2006–2007, with (4) students obtaining an internship. Of those students who obtained an internship, (4) were paid internships. Of those students who obtained an internship, (4) students placed in APA/CPA-accredited internships, (0) students placed in internships not APA/CPA-accredited, but listed with the Association of Psychology Postdoctoral and Internship Centers (APPIC), (0) students placed in internships conforming to guidelines of the Council of Directors of School Psychology Programs (CDSPP), (0) students placed in internships that were not APA/CPA-accredited, APPIC or CDSPP listed. Clinical program students must complete a predoctoral internship in an approved setting under the primary supervision of a registered psychologist. Students are expected to seek placement in a CPA/APA approved site.

Housing and Day Care: On-campus housing is available. See the following Web site for more information: http://www.queensu.ca/dsao/housing/ah1.htm. On-campus day care facilities are available. See the following Web site for more information: http://www.queensu.ca/dsao/daycare/centre/index2.htm.

Employment of Department Graduates:

Master's Degree Graduates: Of those who graduated in the academic year 2006–2007, the following categories and numbers represent the postgraduate activities and employment of master's degree graduates: Enrolled in a psychology doctoral program (10), enrolled in another graduate/professional program (0), enrolled in a postdoctoral residency/fellowship (n/a), employed in independent practice (n/a), employed in an academic position at a university (0), employed in an academic position at a 2-year/4-year college (0), employed in other positions at a higher education institution (0), employed in a professional position in a school system (0), employed in business or industry (0), employed in a government agency (0), employed in a community mental health/counseling center (0), employed in a hospital/medical center (0), still seeking employment (0), do not know (0), total from the above (master's) (10).

Doctoral Degree Graduates: Of those who graduated in the academic year 2006–2007, the following categories and numbers represent the postgraduate activities and employment of doctoral degree graduates: Enrolled in a psychology doctoral program (n/a), enrolled in a postdoctoral residency/fellowship (0), employed in independent practice (0), employed in an academic position at a university (6), employed in an academic position at a 2-year/4-year college (0), employed in other positions at a higher education institution (0), employed in a professional position in a school system (0), employed in business or industry (0), employed in a government agency (2), employed in a community mental health/counseling center (0), employed in a hospital/medical center (3), still seeking employment (0), other employment position (0), do not know (3), total from the above (doctoral) (14).

Additional Information:

Orientation, Objectives, and Emphasis of Department: All programs stress empirical research. The Brain, Behavior, and Cognitive Science program, the Developmental program, and the Social/Personality program emphasize research skills and scholarship, preparing students for either academic positions or for research positions in government, industry, and the like. The Clinical program is based on a scientist–practitioner model of training that emphasizes the integration of research and clinical skills in the understanding, assessment, treatment, and prevention of psychological problems.

Special Facilities or Resources: Extensive computer and laboratory facilities are available to graduate students for research and clinical experience. Financial assistance is available in the form of federal, provincial, and university fellowships, scholarships, and bursaries. For 2007–2008, incoming Master's students received a minimum of $18,000, PhD students received a minimum of $21,000. A portion of this guaranteed minimum is in the form of a teaching assistantship.

Information for Students With Physical Disabilities: See the following Web site for more information: http://www.queensu.ca/dsao/resource.htm.

Application Information:

Send to The Registrar, School of Graduate Studies and Research, Gordon Hall, Queen's University, Kingston, ON, Canada K7L 3N6. Application available online. URL of online application: http://www.queensu.ca/sgsr/prospectivestudents/thinkingof applying.html. Students are admitted in the Fall, application deadline January 15. *Fee:* $85. Not applicable. Note: All dollar amounts specified in this entry are Canadian dollars.

Regina, University of

Department of Psychology
3737 Wascana Parkway
Regina, SK S4S 0A2
Telephone: (306) 585-4157
Fax: (306) 585-5429
E-mail: *william.smythe@uregina.ca*
Web: *http://www.uregina.ca/arts/psychology/*

Department Information:

1965. Department Head: William Smythe. Number of faculty: total—full-time 20; women—full-time 10; total—minority—full-time 1.

Programs and Degrees Offered:

Listed in the following order: Program area, degree type (T if terminal Master's), number awarded 7/06–6/07. Clinical MA/MS (Master of Arts/Science) (T) 3, Clinical PhD (Doctor of Philosophy) 2, Experimental and Applied Psychology MA/MS (Master of Arts/Science) (T) 3, Experimental and Applied Psychology PhD (Doctor of Philosophy) 0.

CPA Accreditation: Clinical PhD (Doctor of Philosophy).

Student Applications/Admissions:

Student Applications

Clinical MA/MS (Master of Arts/Science)—Applications 2007–2008, 38. Total applicants accepted 2007–2008, 6. Number full-time enrolled (new admits only) 2007–2008, 6. Openings 2008–2009, 5. The median number of years required for completion of a degree in 2006–2007 were 2. The number of students enrolled full- and part-time, who were dismissed or voluntarily withdrew from this program area in 2007–2008 were 0. *Clinical PhD (Doctor of Philosophy)*—Applications 2007–2008, 7. Total applicants accepted 2007–2008, 5. Number full-time enrolled (new admits only) 2007–2008, 4. Number part-time enrolled (new admits only) 2007–2008, 0. Openings 2008–2009, 5. The median number of years required for completion of a degree in 2006–2007 were 4. The number of students enrolled full- and part-time, who were dismissed or voluntarily withdrew from this program area in 2007–2008 were 1. *Experimental and Applied Psychology MA/MS (Master of Arts/Science)*—Applications 2007–2008, 14. Total applicants accepted 2007–2008, 2. Number full-time enrolled (new admits only) 2007–2008, 2. Number part-time enrolled (new admits only) 2007–2008, 0. Openings 2008–2009, 4. The median number of years required for completion of a degree in 2006–2007 were 2. The number of students enrolled full- and part-time, who were dismissed or voluntarily withdrew from this program area in 2007–2008 were 0. *Experimental and Applied Psychology PhD (Doctor of Philosophy)*—Applications 2007–2008, 4. Total applicants accepted 2007–2008, 2. Number full-time enrolled (new admits only) 2007–2008, 1. Number part-time enrolled (new admits only) 2007–2008, 0. Openings 2008–2009, 5. The median number of years required for completion of a degree in 2006–2007 were 4. The number of students enrolled full- and part-time, who were dismissed or voluntarily withdrew from this program area in 2007–2008 were 0.

Admissions Requirements:

Scores: Entries appear in this order: required test or GPA, minimum score (if required), median score of students entering in 2007–2008. Master's Programs: GRE-V no minimum stated; GRE-Q no minimum stated; GRE-Subject (Psychology) no minimum stated; overall undergraduate GPA no minimum stated; psychology GPA no minimum stated. For all GRE scores the 40th percentile is considered to be the minimu score accepted. Doctoral Programs: GRE-V no minimum stated; GRE-Q no minimum stated; GRE-Subject (Psychology) no minimum stated; overall undergraduate GPA no minimum stated; psychology GPA no minimum stated. Submission of GRE scores is optional for applicants who hold a Master's degree from a Canadian University.

Other Criteria: (importance of criteria rated low, medium, or high): GRE/MAT scores—high, research experience—medium, work experience—low, extracurricular activity—low, clinically related public service—medium, GPA—high, letters of recommendation—high, statement of goals and objectives—high, undergraduate major in psychology—high, specific undergraduate psychology courses taken—low. For additional information on admission requirements, go to http://www.uregina.ca/arts/psychology/forms/Graduate%20Program%20Brochure%20-%20June%202007.pdf.

Student Characteristics: The following represents characteristics of students in 2007–2008 in all graduate psychology programs

in the department: Female—full-time 43, part-time 0; Male—full-time 8, part-time 0; African American/Black—full-time 1, part-time 0; Hispanic/Latino(a)—full-time 0, part-time 0; Asian/Pacific Islander—full-time 2, part-time 0; American Indian/Alaska Native—full-time 3, part-time 0; Caucasian/White—full-time 38, part-time 0; Multi-ethnic—full-time 2, part-time 0; students subject to the Americans With Disabilities Act—full-time 0, part-time 0; Unknown ethnicity—full-time 3, part-time 0; International students who hold an F-1 or J-1 Visa—full-time 2, part-time 0.

Financial Information/Assistance:

Tuition for Full-Time Study: *Master's:* State residents: $166 per credit hour; Nonstate residents: $166 per credit hour. *Doctoral:* State residents: per academic year $2,999; Nonstate residents: per academic year $2,999. See the following Web site for updates and changes in tuition costs: http://www.uregina.ca/presoff/vpadmin/policymanual/students/90200501.html.

Financial Assistance:

First-Year Students: Teaching assistantships available for first year. Average amount paid per academic year: $4,206. Average number of hours worked per week: 7. Apply by June 15. Research assistantships available for first year. Average amount paid per academic year: $4,500. Average number of hours worked per week: 7. Apply by February 28. Fellowships and scholarships available for first year. Average amount paid per academic year: $5,000. Average number of hours worked per week: 0. Apply by June 15.

Advanced Students: Teaching assistantships available for advanced students. Average amount paid per academic year: $4,794. Average number of hours worked per week: 7. Apply by June 15. Research assistantships available for advanced students. Average amount paid per academic year: $5,000. Average number of hours worked per week: 7. Apply by February 28. Fellowships and scholarships available for advanced students. Average amount paid per academic year: $6,000. Average number of hours worked per week: 0. Apply by June 15.

Additional Information: Of all students currently enrolled full time, 60% benefited from one or more of the listed financial assistance programs. Application and information available online at http://www.uregina.ca/gradstudies/main/financial_aid.shtml.

Internships/Practica: Master's Degree (Clinical): An internship experience such as a final research project or "capstone" experience is required of graduates. Master's Degree (MA/MS Experimental and Applied Psychology): An internship experience such as a final research project or "capstone" experience is required of graduates. Doctoral Degree (PhD Clinical): For those doctoral students for whom a professional internship was required in this program prior to graduation, (2) students applied for an internship in 2006–2007, with (2) students obtaining an internship. Of those students who obtained an internship, (2) were paid internships. Of those students who obtained an internship, (2) students placed in APA/CPA-accredited internships, (0) students placed in internships not APA/CPA-accredited, but listed with the Association of Psychology Postdoctoral and Internship Centers (APPIC), (0) students placed in internships conforming to guidelines of the Council of Directors of School Psychology Programs (CDSPP), (0) students placed in internships that were not APA/CPA-accredited, APPIC or CDSPP listed. A wide array of community resources are available and well utilized in providing practicum and internship training. The department cannot guarantee placement in these facilities, but our record of supplying these has been perfect in the past.

Housing and Day Care: On-campus housing is available. See the following Web site for more information: http://www.uregina.ca/residences/. On-campus day care facilities are available. Wascana Co-Operative Day Care (306) 585-5311.

Employment of Department Graduates:

Master's Degree Graduates: Of those who graduated in the academic year 2006–2007, the following categories and numbers represent the postgraduate activities and employment of master's degree graduates: Enrolled in a psychology doctoral program (4), enrolled in another graduate/professional program (0), enrolled in a postdoctoral residency/fellowship (n/a), employed in independent practice (n/a), employed in an academic position at a university (1), employed in an academic position at a 2-year/4-year college (0), employed in other positions at a higher education institution (0), employed in a professional position in a school system (0), employed in business or industry (0), employed in a government agency (1), employed in a community mental health/counseling center (0), employed in a hospital/medical center (0), still seeking employment (0), not seeking employment (0), other employment position (0), do not know (0), total from the above (master's) (6).

Doctoral Degree Graduates: Of those who graduated in the academic year 2006–2007, the following categories and numbers represent the postgraduate activities and employment of doctoral degree graduates: Enrolled in a psychology doctoral program (n/a), enrolled in another graduate/professional program (0), enrolled in a postdoctoral residency/fellowship (0), employed in independent practice (0), employed in an academic position at a university (1), employed in an academic position at a 2-year/4-year college (0), employed in other positions at a higher education institution (0), employed in a professional position in a school system (0), employed in business or industry (0), employed in a government agency (0), employed in a community mental health/counseling center (0), employed in a hospital/medical center (1), still seeking employment (0), other employment position (0), do not know (0), total from the above (doctoral) (2).

Additional Information:

Orientation, Objectives, and Emphasis of Department: Teaching and research are oriented toward clinical, social, and applied approaches. The majority of graduate students are in Clinical psychology. Faculty orientation is eclectic. Cognitive behavioral and humanistic approaches are represented. Neuropsychology is also well represented.

Special Facilities or Resources: The department has clinical and counseling rooms for research purposes, a small testing library, permanent space for faculty research, and observation rooms and computer labs.

Information for Students With Physical Disabilities: See the following Web site for more information: http://www.uregina.ca/studserv/disability/index.shtml.

Application Information:

Send to Dean, Faculty of Graduate Studies and Research, University of Regina, 3737 Wascana Parkway, Regina, SK S4S 0A2. Application available online. URL of online application: https://www.dataware.cc.uregina.ca/app/Misc/introduction.cfm. Students are admitted in the Fall, application deadline February 15. *Fee:* $85. Note: All dollar amounts specified in this entry are Canadian dollars.

Ryerson University

Department of Psychology
350 Victoria Street
Toronto, ON M5B 2K3
Telephone: (416) 979-5000
Fax: (416) 979-5273
E-mail: *mantony@ryerson.ca*
Web: *http://www.ryerson.ca/psychology*

Department Information:

1974. Chairperson: Jean-Paul Boudreau. Number of faculty: total—full-time 24, part-time 9; women—full-time 12, part-time 7; total—minority—full-time 1; women minority—full-time 1.

Programs and Degrees Offered:

Listed in the following order: Program area, degree type (T if terminal Master's), number awarded 7/06–6/07. Clinical Psychology MA/MS (Master of Arts/Science) 0, Psychological Science MA/MS (Master of Arts/Science) 0, Clinical Psychology (launches Fall 2009) PhD (Doctor of Philosophy) 0, Psychological Science (launches Fall 2009) PhD (Doctor of Philosophy) 0.

Student Applications/Admissions:

Student Applications

Clinical Psychology MA/MS (Master of Arts/Science)—Applications 2007–2008, 150. Total applicants accepted 2007–2008, 13. Number full-time enrolled (new admits only) 2007–2008, 13. Number part-time enrolled (new admits only) 2007–2008, 0. Openings 2008–2009, 10. The median number of years required for completion of a degree in 2006–2007 were 2. The number of students enrolled full- and part-time, who were dismissed or voluntarily withdrew from this program area in 2007–2008 were 0. *Psychological Science MA/MS (Master of Arts/Science)*—Applications 2007–2008, 30. Total applicants accepted 2007–2008, 11. Number full-time enrolled (new admits only) 2007–2008, 13. Number part-time enrolled (new admits only) 2007–2008, 0. Openings 2008–2009, 6. The median number of years required for completion of a degree in 2006–2007 were 2. The number of students enrolled full- and part-time, who were dismissed or voluntarily withdrew from this program area in 2007–2008 were 0. *Clinical Psychology (Launches Fall 2009) PhD (Doctor of Philosophy)*—Applications 2007–2008, 0. Total applicants accepted 2007–2008, 0. Number full-time enrolled (new admits only) 2007–2008, 0. Number part-time enrolled (new admits only) 2007–2008, 0. The median number of years required for completion of a degree in 2006–2007 were 4. The number of students enrolled full- and part-time, who were dismissed or voluntarily withdrew from this program area in 2007–2008 were 0. *Psychological Science (Launches Fall 2009) PhD (Doctor of Philosophy)*—Applications 2007–2008, 0. Total applicants accepted 2007–2008, 0. Number full-time enrolled (new admits only) 2007–2008, 0. Number part-time enrolled (new admits only) 2007–2008, 0. The median number of years required for completion of a degree in 2006–2007 were 3. The number of students enrolled full- and part-time, who were dismissed or voluntarily withdrew from this program area in 2007–2008 were 0.

Admissions Requirements:

Scores: Entries appear in this order: required test or GPA, minimum score (if required), median score of students entering in 2007–2008. Master's Programs: GRE-V no minimum stated; GRE-Q no minimum stated; overall undergraduate GPA no minimum stated; last 2 years GPA no minimum stated. Note that the GRE requirements for the Psychological Science Field are currently under review. Check departmental Web site for updated requirements. GRE Subject test is recommended, but not required. Doctoral Programs: GRE-V no minimum stated; GRE-Q no minimum stated; overall undergraduate GPA no minimum stated; last 2 years GPA no minimum stated. Program launches in Fall 2009. Minimum and median scores are not yet available.

Other Criteria: (importance of criteria rated low, medium, or high): GRE/MAT scores—medium, research experience—high, work experience—medium, extracurricular activity—low, clinically related public service—low, GPA—high, letters of recommendation—high, interview—high, statement of goals and objectives—high, undergraduate major in psychology—medium, specific undergraduate psychology courses taken—medium. Undergraduate major in psychology is recommended for both fields, and is especially important for the Clinical Psychology field. For additional information on admission requirements, go to http://www.ryerson.ca/psychology/graduate/admissions/.

Student Characteristics: The following represents characteristics of students in 2007–2008 in all graduate psychology programs in the department: Female—full-time 21, part-time 0; Male—full-time 3, part-time 0; African American/Black—full-time 0, part-time 0; Hispanic/Latino(a)—full-time 0, part-time 0; Asian/Pacific Islander—full-time 3, part-time 0; American Indian/Alaska Native—full-time 0, part-time 0; Caucasian/White—full-time 21, part-time 0; Multi-ethnic—full-time 0, part-time 0; students subject to the Americans With Disabilities Act—full-time 0, part-time 0; Unknown ethnicity—full-time 0, part-time 0; International students who hold an F-1 or J-1 Visa—full-time 1, part-time 0.

Financial Information/Assistance:

Financial Assistance:

First-Year Students: Teaching assistantships available for first year. Average amount paid per academic year: $9,165. Average number of hours worked per week: 10. Research assistantships available for first year. Average amount paid per academic year: $9,165. Average number of hours worked per week: 10. Fellowships and scholarships available for first year. Average amount paid per academic year: $7,000. Average number of hours worked per week: 0.

Advanced Students: Teaching assistantships available for advanced students. Average amount paid per academic year: $9,165. Average number of hours worked per week: 10. Research assistantships available for advanced students. Average amount paid per academic year: $9,165. Average number of hours worked per week: 10. Fellowships and scholarships available for advanced students. Average amount paid per academic year: $7,000. Average number of hours worked per week: 0.

Additional Information: Of all students currently enrolled full time, 100% benefited from one or more of the listed financial assistance programs. Application and information available online at http://www.ryerson.ca/psychology/graduate/admissions/.

Internships/Practica: Our Clinical Psychology students have been successful at securing practicum placements at top training centers, including Baycrest, Bellwood Health Services, the Centre for Addiction and Mental Health, Hamilton Health Sciences, Humber River Regional Hospital, North York General Hospital, St. Joseph's Healthcare Hamilton, Toronto General Hospital, Ryerson Centre for Student Development and Counselling, Toronto Rehabilitation Institute, and others. With a focus on breadth and depth training in applied research methodology, possible practicum placements for the Psychological Science students include both internal sites such as the research labs of faculty in the Ryerson Department of Psychology as well as external sites such as the Centre for Addiction and Mental Health, Kunin-Lunenfeldt Applied Research, MultiHealth Systems (MHS), Rotman Research Institute, Health Canada, Defense Research and Development Canada, and Transport Canada.

Housing and Day Care: No on-campus housing is available. On-campus day care facilities are available. See the following Web site for more information: http://www.ryerson.ca/ece/ELC.html.

Employment of Department Graduates:

Master's Degree Graduates: Of those who graduated in the academic year 2006–2007, the following categories and numbers represent the postgraduate activities and employment of master's degree graduates: Enrolled in a postdoctoral residency/fellowship (n/a), employed in independent practice (n/a), total from the above (master's) (0).

Doctoral Degree Graduates: Of those who graduated in the academic year 2006–2007, the following categories and numbers represent the postgraduate activities and employment of doctoral degree graduates: Enrolled in a psychology doctoral program (n/a), total from the above (doctoral) (0).

Additional Information:

Orientation, Objectives, and Emphasis of Department: Launched in Fall of 2007, Canada's newest graduate program in psychology offers students opportunities to study in either Clinical Psychology (CPA accreditation anticipated in the next few years) or Psychological Science. The Psycholological Science stream offers opportunities to specialize in research areas that include neuroscience, social psychology, developmental psychology, cognition and perception, or history and theory. The graduate program in Psychology offers an innovative curriculum that is anchored in applied experimental and clinical research. Trained at some of the top universities in Canada, the United States, and around the world, the core faculty (including 17 hired since 2005) bring a rigorous and student-centered approach to scientific and clinical training. Based in a department known for career-focused learning and student development, the program takes advantage of its downtown Toronto location, with proximity to major sites for practicum training and clinical research, and offers students access to world-class training opportunities.

Special Facilities or Resources: The department has also developed a new state-of-the-art lab facility that includes over 10,000 square feet of research space. This new space has been built from the ground up to serve the research and training needs of our psychology graduate students and faculty. We are also planning to develop a fully equipped, in-house training clinic to meet the requirements of our Clinical Psychology program.

Information for Students With Physical Disabilities: See the following Web site for more information: http://www.ryerson.ca/studentservices/accesscentre/.

Application Information:

Send to Graduate Admissions Office, School of Graduate Studies, Ryerson University, 350 Victoria Street, Toronto, Ontario M5B 2K3 Canada. Application available online. URL of online application: http://www.ryerson.ca/psychology/graduate/admissions/. Students are admitted in the Fall, application deadline December 15; programs have rolling admissions. *Fee:* $90. Note: All dollar amounts specified in this entry are Canadian dollars.

Saint Mary's University

Department of Psychology
923 Robie Street
Halifax, NS B3H 3C3
Telephone: (902) 420-5846
Fax: (902) 496-8287
E-mail: *vic.catano@smu.ca*
Web: *http://www.smu.ca/academic/science/psych/*

Department Information:

1966. Chairperson: Victor Catano. Number of faculty: total—full-time 11, part-time 7; women—full-time 6, part-time 3.

Programs and Degrees Offered:

Listed in the following order: Program area, degree type (T if terminal Master's), number awarded 7/06–6/07. Applied Industrial/Organizational Psychology MA/MS (Master of Arts/Science) (T) 5, Industrial/Organizational Psychology PhD (Doctor of Philosophy) 0.

Student Applications/Admissions:

Student Applications

Applied Industrial/Organizational Psychology MA/MS (Master of Arts/Science)—Applications 2007–2008, 30. Total applicants accepted 2007–2008, 11. Number full-time enrolled (new admits only) 2007–2008, 8. Number part-time enrolled (new admits only) 2007–2008, 0. Total enrolled 2007–2008 full-time, 21, part-time, 2. Openings 2008–2009, 8. The median number of years required for completion of a degree in 2006–2007 were 2. The number of students enrolled full- and part-time, who were dismissed or voluntarily withdrew from this program area in 2007–2008 were 1. *Industrial/Organizational Psychology PhD (Doctor of Philosophy)*—Applications 2007–2008, 8. Total applicants accepted 2007–2008, 5. Number full-time enrolled (new admits only) 2007–2008, 1. Number part-time enrolled (new admits only) 2007–2008, 4. Total enrolled 2007–2008 full-time, 6, part-time, 4. Openings 2008–2009, 3. The number of students enrolled full- and part-time, who were dismissed or voluntarily withdrew from this program area in 2007–2008 were 0.

Admissions Requirements:

Scores: Entries appear in this order: required test or GPA, minimum score (if required), median score of students entering in 2007–2008. Master's Programs: GRE-V 500; GRE-Q 500; GRE-Subject (Psychology) 500, 640; overall undergraduate GPA 3.00, 3.33; last 2 years GPA no minimum stated; psychology GPA no minimum stated. Doctoral Programs: GRE-V no minimum stated; GRE-Q no minimum stated; GRE-Subject (Psychology) no minimum stated; overall undergraduate GPA no minimum stated; last 2 years GPA no minimum stated; psychology GPA no minimum stated.

Other Criteria: (importance of criteria rated low, medium, or high): GRE/MAT scores—high, research experience—high, work experience—low, extracurricular activity—low, GPA—high, letters of recommendation—medium, statement of goals and objectives—high, undergraduate major in psychology—high, specific undergraduate psychology courses taken—low.

Student Characteristics: The following represents characteristics of students in 2007–2008 in all graduate psychology programs in the department: Female—full-time 18, part-time 5; Male—full-time 9, part-time 3; African American/Black—full-time 0, part-time 0; Hispanic/Latino(a)—full-time 0, part-time 0; Asian/Pacific Islander—full-time 0, part-time 0; American Indian/Alaska Native—full-time 0, part-time 0; Caucasian/White—full-time 24, part-time 8; Multi-ethnic—full-time 1, part-time 0; students subject to the Americans With Disabilities Act—full-time 0, part-time 0; Unknown ethnicity—full-time 0, part-time 0.

Financial Information/Assistance:

Tuition for Full-Time Study: *Master's:* State residents: per academic year $3,700; Nonstate residents: per academic year $7,048. *Doctoral:* State residents: per academic year $5,000; Nonstate residents: per academic year $7,232. Tuition is subject to change. See the following Web site for updates and changes in tuition costs: http://www.fgsr.smu.ca/grad_pro_fin.html.

Financial Assistance:

First-Year Students: Teaching assistantships available for first year. Average amount paid per academic year: $5,000. Average number of hours worked per week: 13. Apply by February 1. Research assistantships available for first year. Average amount paid per academic year: $7,500. Average number of hours worked per week: 10. Apply by no deadline. Traineeships available for first year. Average amount paid per academic year: $9,000. Average number of hours worked per week: 40. Apply by March. Fellowships and scholarships available for first year. Average amount paid per academic year: $7,200. Average number of hours worked per week: 0. Apply by February 1.

Advanced Students: Teaching assistantships available for advanced students. Average amount paid per academic year: $5,000. Average number of hours worked per week: 13. Apply by June 1. Research assistantships available for advanced students. Average amount paid per academic year: $7,500. Average number of hours worked per week: 10. Apply by no deadline. Traineeships available for advanced students. Average amount paid per academic year: $8,000. Average number of hours worked per week: 10. Apply by no deadline. Fellowships and scholarships available for advanced students. Average amount paid per academic year: $15,000. Average number of hours worked per week: 0. Apply by June 1.

Additional Information: Of all students currently enrolled full time, 100% benefited from one or more of the listed financial assistance programs. Application and information available online at http://fgsr.smu.ca/grad_pro_app.html.

Internships/Practica: Masters' students are required to complete a supervised full-time, paid internship (minimum of 500 hours) in the summer following their 1st year or part-time during their 2nd year. Placements are available in a variety of government agencies, human resource departments, research agencies, and private consulting firms. Salaries range from $6,000 to $13,000 for the 4 months.

Housing and Day Care: On-campus housing is available. See the following Web site for more information: http://www.smu.ca/administration/resoffic/welcome.html. On-campus day care facilities are available. See the following Web site for more information: http://www.smu.ca/administration/studentservices/daycare.html.

Employment of Department Graduates:

Master's Degree Graduates: Of those who graduated in the academic year 2006–2007, the following categories and numbers represent the postgraduate activities and employment of master's degree graduates: Enrolled in a psychology doctoral program (3), enrolled in another graduate/professional program (1), enrolled in a postdoctoral residency/fellowship (n/a), employed in independent practice (n/a), employed in an academic position at a university (0), employed in an academic position at a 2-year/4-year college (0), employed in other positions at a higher education institution (0), employed in a professional position in a school system (0), employed in business or industry (3), employed in a government agency (1), employed in a community mental health/counseling center (0), employed in a hospital/medical center (0), still seeking employment (0), other employment position (0), do not know (0), total from the above (master's) (8).

Doctoral Degree Graduates: Of those who graduated in the academic year 2006–2007, the following categories and numbers represent the postgraduate activities and employment of doctoral degree graduates: Enrolled in a psychology doctoral program (n/a), total from the above (doctoral) (0).

Additional Information:

Orientation, Objectives, and Emphasis of Department: Master's Program: Students will acquire a background in theory and research that is consistent with the scientist–practitioner model, preparing themselves for employment and/or continued graduate education. Full-time students normally require 2 years to complete the program. Part-time students may take 2 to 4 years longer. Masters' students are normally provided with financial support for 2 years. PhD Program: Students will acquire a background in theory and research that is consistent with the scientist–practitioner model, preparing them for an academic career or a career in consulting and/or industry. Full-time students normally require 3 years to complete the program, but may complete it in 2 years. PhD students are normally provided with financial support for 3 years.

Special Facilities or Resources: General research laboratories, graduate computer lab, small-group research space, graduate student offices, and a tests and measurements library that includes psychological test batteries are available. Support systems include audiovisual equipment, computer facilities, and a technical workshop. Students may be involved in the CN Centre for Occupational Health and Safety, as well as the Centre for Leadership Excellence.

Application Information:
Send to Faculty of Graduate Studies and Research, Saint Mary's University, Halifax, Nova Scotia, Canada B3H 3C3. Application available online. URL of online application: http://www.fgsr.smu.ca/GraduateStudies/Admissions/Science.aspx. Students are admitted in the Fall, application deadline February 1. *Fee:* $70. Note: All dollar amounts specified in this entry are Canadian dollars.

Saskatchewan, University of

Department of Psychology
Arts and Science
9 Campus Drive
Saskatoon, SK S7N 5A5
Telephone: (306) 966-6657
Fax: (306) 966-6630
E-mail: *angela.jeon@usask.ca*
Web: *http://www.usask.ca/psychology/*

Department Information:
1946. Head: Valerie Thompson. Number of faculty: total—full-time 12, part-time 6; women—full-time 10, part-time 5.

Programs and Degrees Offered:
Listed in the following order: Program area, degree type (T if terminal Master's), number awarded 7/06–6/07. Applied Social MA/MS (Master of Arts/Science) (T) 3, Clinical PhD (Doctor of Philosophy) 5, Applied Social PhD (Doctor of Philosophy) 1, Basic Behavioural Science PhD (Doctor of Philosophy) 1, Culture and Human Development PhD (Doctor of Philosophy) 0.

CPA Accreditation: Clinical PhD (Doctor of Philosophy).

Student Applications/Admissions:
Student Applications
Applied Social MA/MS (Master of Arts/Science)—Applications 2007–2008, 27. Total applicants accepted 2007–2008, 3. Number full-time enrolled (new admits only) 2007–2008, 2. Number part-time enrolled (new admits only) 2007–2008, 0. Openings 2008–2009, 4. The median number of years required for completion of a degree in 2006–2007 were 6. The number of students enrolled full- and part-time, who were dismissed or voluntarily withdrew from this program area in 2007–2008 were 0. *Clinical PhD (Doctor of Philosophy)*—Applications 2007–2008, 65. Total applicants accepted 2007–2008, 5. Number full-time enrolled (new admits only) 2007–2008, 5. Number part-time enrolled (new admits only) 2007–2008, 0. Openings 2008–2009, 5. The median number of years required for completion of a degree in 2006–2007 were 9. The number of students enrolled full- and part-time, who were dismissed or voluntarily withdrew from this program area in 2007–2008 were 1. *Applied Social PhD (Doctor of Philosophy)*—Applications 2007–2008, 3. Total applicants accepted 2007–2008, 1. Number full-time enrolled (new admits only) 2007–2008, 1. Number part-time enrolled (new admits only) 2007–2008, 0. Openings 2008–2009, 2. The median number of years required for completion of a degree in 2006–2007 were 7. The number of students enrolled full- and part-time, who were dismissed or voluntarily withdrew from this program area in 2007–2008 were 0. *Basic Behavioural Science PhD (Doctor of Philosophy)*—Applications 2007–2008, 13. Total applicants accepted 2007–2008, 2. Number full-time enrolled (new admits only) 2007–2008, 2. Number part-time enrolled (new admits only) 2007–2008, 0. Total enrolled 2007–2008 full-time, 17, part-time, 4. Openings 2008–2009, 3. The median number of years required for completion of a degree in 2006–2007 were 4. The number of students enrolled full- and part-time, who were dismissed or voluntarily withdrew from this program area in 2007–2008 were 1. *Culture and Human Development PhD (Doctor of Philosophy)*—Applications 2007–2008, 15. Total applicants accepted 2007–2008, 3. Number full-time enrolled (new admits only) 2007–2008, 3. Total enrolled 2007–2008 full-time, 3. Openings 2008–2009, 3. The median number of years required for completion of a degree in 2006–2007 were 4. The number of students enrolled full- and part-time, who were dismissed or voluntarily withdrew from this program area in 2007–2008 were 0.

Admissions Requirements:
Scores: Entries appear in this order: required test or GPA, minimum score (if required), median score of students entering in 2007–2008. Master's Programs: GRE-V no minimum stated, 560; GRE-Q no minimum stated, 608; GRE-Subject (Psychology) no minimum stated, 704; last 2 years GPA no minimum stated, 86.6; psychology GPA no minimum stated, 86.6. GRE median scores are those for the Applied Social program only. Averages are for Applied Social program only. Doctoral Programs: GRE-V no minimum stated, 565; GRE-Q no minimum stated, 685; GRE-Subject (Psychology) no minimum stated, 696; last 2 years GPA no minimum stated; psychology GPA no minimum stated. GRE median scores are for Clinical admission only. Students applying for admission to a Basic Behavioural Science (BBS) program do not require GRE scores. Averages for Clinical admission were 85.8% last 2 years; 85.1% psychology students are admitted directly into a MA/PhD transfer program without an MA degree, thus no MA averages. Averages for BBS admission were 84.3% last 2 years; 84.4% psychology students are admitted directly into a MA/PhD transfer program without an MA degree, thus no MA averages. The one student admitted to a BBS PhD degree had an average of 92.3% on MA courses.
Other Criteria: (importance of criteria rated low, medium, or high): GRE/MAT scores—medium, research experience—high, work experience—medium, extracurricular activity—low, clinically related public service—low, GPA—high, letters of recommendation—high, interview—high, statement of goals and objectives—high. GRE scores are not required for the Basic Behavioural Science (BBS) application. For additional information on admission requirements, go to http://www.usask.ca/psychology/.

Student Characteristics: The following represents characteristics of students in 2007–2008 in all graduate psychology programs in the department: Female—full-time 68, part-time 0; Male—full-time 15, part-time 0; African American/Black—full-time 0, part-time 0; Hispanic/Latino(a)—full-time 0, part-time 0; Asian/Pacific Islander—full-time 0, part-time 0; American Indian/Alaska Native—full-time 0, part-time 0; Caucasian/White—

full-time 0, part-time 0; Multi-ethnic—full-time 0, part-time 0; students subject to the Americans With Disabilities Act—full-time 0, part-time 0; Unknown ethnicity—full-time 0, part-time 0.

Financial Information/Assistance:

Tuition for Full-Time Study: *Master's:* State residents: per academic year $3,611; Nonstate residents: per academic year $3,611. *Doctoral:* State residents: per academic year $3,611; Nonstate residents: per academic year $3,611. Tuition is subject to change. See the following Web site for updates and changes in tuition costs: http://www.usask.ca/cgsr/.

Financial Assistance:

First-Year Students: Fellowships and scholarships available for first year. Average amount paid per academic year: $16,000.

Advanced Students: Fellowships and scholarships available for advanced students. Average amount paid per academic year: $16,000.

Additional Information: Of all students currently enrolled full time, 80% benefited from one or more of the listed financial assistance programs. Application and information available online at http://www.usask.ca/psychology/.

Internships/Practica: Master's Degree (Applied Social): An internship experience such as a final research project or "capstone" experience is required of graduates. Full-time internships and practicum training concurrent with coursework are required at the MA and PhD levels in both Clinical and Applied Social programs. In the Clinical program, 4-month MA internship placements are available at a number of hospital and outpatient clinics throughout the province. At the PhD level, 12-month internships have been arranged in larger clinical settings with diversified client populations in Canada and the United States. The Applied Social program requires 4-month applied research internships at both the MA and PhD levels. Practicum and internship placements are arranged in a wide variety of government, institutional, and business settings. One internship placement was in an APA, APPIC accredited setting; one was in an APA, APPIC, CCPPP accredited setting; two were in an APPIC, CPA and CCPPP accredited setting; one was in a CCPPP setting.

Housing and Day Care: On-campus housing is available. See the following Web site for more information: http://www.students.usask.ca/campuslife/housing/. On-campus day care facilities are available. See the following Web site for more information: http://www.students.usask.ca/support/childcare/.

Employment of Department Graduates:

Master's Degree Graduates: Of those who graduated in the academic year 2006–2007, the following categories and numbers represent the postgraduate activities and employment of master's degree graduates: Enrolled in a postdoctoral residency/fellowship (n/a), employed in independent practice (n/a), employed in other positions at a higher education institution (1), total from the above (master's) (1).

Doctoral Degree Graduates: Of those who graduated in the academic year 2006–2007, the following categories and numbers represent the postgraduate activities and employment of doctoral degree graduates: Enrolled in a psychology doctoral program (n/a), enrolled in another graduate/professional program (1), employed in an academic position at a 2-year/4-year college (1), employed in a government agency (1), employed in a community mental health/counseling center (2), total from the above (doctoral) (5).

Additional Information:

Orientation, Objectives, and Emphasis of Department: All graduate programs are small and highly selective. The Clinical program focuses on PhD training, based on a scientist–practitioner model with an eclectic theoretical perspective. The goal is to train people who will be able to function in a wide variety of community, agency, academic, and research settings. The applied social program attempts to train people at the MA and PhD level for researcher consultant positions in applied (MA) or academic (PhD) settings. Areas of concentration include program development and evaluation, group processes, and organizational development. The basic behavioral science programs are individually structured, admitting a few students to work with active research supervisors, most frequently in physiological, neuropsychology, cognitive psychology, or culture and development.

Special Facilities or Resources: The department has a Psychological Services Centre, an animal lab, a cognitive science lab with access to fMRI facilities. There are also numerous microcomputers, excellent mainframe computer facilities, and a good research library. The Women's Studies Research Unit promotes scholarly research by, for, and about women, providing a source of support for all women studying, teaching, researching, and working on campus.

Information for Students With Physical Disabilities: See the following Web site for more information: http://www.students.usask.ca/disability/.

Application Information:

Send to Graduate Chair, University of Saskatchewan, Department of Psychology, 9 Campus Drive, Saskatoon, SK Canada S7N 5A5. Application available online. URL of online application: http://www.usask.ca/psychology/. Students are admitted in the Fall, application deadline December 15. *Fee:* $75. Note: All dollar amounts specified in this entry are Canadian dollars.

Sherbrooke, University of (2007 data)

Department of Psychology
2500 Boulevard de l'Universite
Sherbrooke, QC J1K 2R1
Telephone: (819) 821-7222
Fax: (819) 821-7925
E-mail: *Monique.Bacon@USherbrooke.ca*
Web: *http://www.usherb.ca*

Department Information:

1967. Chairperson: Claude Charbonneau. Number of faculty: total—full-time 17; women—full-time 9.

Programs and Degrees Offered:

Listed in the following order: Program area, degree type (T if terminal Master's), number awarded 7/06–6/07. Human Relations MA/MS (Master of Arts/Science) (T) 11, Psychology PsyD (Doctor of Psychology) 0.

Student Applications/Admissions:

Student Applications

Human Relations MA/MS (Master of Arts/Science)—Applications 2007–2008, 4. Total applicants accepted 2007–2008, 4. Number full-time enrolled (new admits only) 2007–2008, 4. The median number of years required for completion of a degree in 2006–2007 were 3. The number of students enrolled full- and part-time, who were dismissed or voluntarily withdrew from this program area in 2007–2008 were 0. *Psychology PsyD (Doctor of Psychology)*—Applications 2007–2008, 131. Total applicants accepted 2007–2008, 72. Number full-time enrolled (new admits only) 2007–2008, 23. Number part-time enrolled (new admits only) 2007–2008, 32. Total enrolled 2007–2008 full-time, 73, part-time, 32. Openings 2008–2009, 40. The median number of years required for completion of a degree in 2006–2007 were 4. The number of students enrolled full- and part-time, who were dismissed or voluntarily withdrew from this program area in 2007–2008 were 10.

Admissions Requirements:

Scores: Entries appear in this order: required test or GPA, minimum score (if required), median score of students entering in 2007–2008. Doctoral Programs: overall undergraduate GPA 3.2, 3.8.

Other Criteria: (importance of criteria rated low, medium, or high): work experience—medium, extracurricular activity—medium, GPA—high, letters of recommendation—low, interview—high, statement of goals and objectives—high.

Student Characteristics: The following represents characteristics of students in 2007–2008 in all graduate psychology programs in the department: Female—full-time 72, part-time 16; Male—full-time 15, part-time 16; African American/Black—full-time 2, part-time 0; Hispanic/Latino(a)—full-time 0, part-time 0; Asian/Pacific Islander—full-time 0, part-time 0; American Indian/Alaska Native—full-time 0, part-time 0; Caucasian/White—full-time 85, part-time 32; Multi-ethnic—full-time 0, part-time 0; students subject to the Americans With Disabilities Act—full-time 0, part-time 0; Unknown ethnicity—full-time 0, part-time 0.

Financial Information/Assistance:

Tuition for Full-Time Study: *Doctoral:* State residents: $1,914 per credit hour; Nonstate residents: $8,784 per credit hour. See the following Web site for updates and changes in tuition costs: http://www.usherb.ca.

Financial Assistance:

First-Year Students: Teaching assistantships available for first year. Average amount paid per academic year: $1,350. Average number of hours worked per week: 3.

Advanced Students: Teaching assistantships available for advanced students. Average amount paid per academic year: $1,350. Average number of hours worked per week: 3. Research assistantships available for advanced students. Average amount paid per academic year: $5,000. Average number of hours worked per week: 7. Fellowships and scholarships available for advanced students. Average amount paid per academic year: $1,300.

Additional Information: Of all students currently enrolled full time, 75% benefited from one or more of the listed financial assistance programs. Application and information available online at http://www.usherb.ca.

Internships/Practica: All internships or practica are limited to students enrolled in our graduate program.

Housing and Day Care: On-campus housing is available. See the following Web site for more information: http://www.usherb.ca. On-campus day care facilities are available.

Employment of Department Graduates:

Master's Degree Graduates: Of those who graduated in the academic year 2006–2007, the following categories and numbers represent the postgraduate activities and employment of master's degree graduates: Enrolled in a postdoctoral residency/fellowship (n/a), employed in independent practice (n/a), do not know (11), total from the above (master's) (11).

Doctoral Degree Graduates: Of those who graduated in the academic year 2006–2007, the following categories and numbers represent the postgraduate activities and employment of doctoral degree graduates: Enrolled in a psychology doctoral program (n/a), total from the above (doctoral) (0).

Additional Information:

Orientation, Objectives, and Emphasis of Department: Our department presents itself as a professional school of psychology. It offers an undergraduate program in general psychology and a 4-year graduate program (PsyD) in counseling or organizational psychology. The determinants of the program are the need to develop, as a practician, competencies in the following areas: evaluation, intervention, consultation, interpersonal relations, ethics, management, and supervision. Students who choose to develop their competencies in psychotherapy have the opportunity to explore their values, interests, and skills in relation to three approaches: humanist–positive, psychodynamic, cognitive–behavioral. Those who wish to intervene in organizational psychology develop a system's approach and focus on cooperative relationships, based on the belief in human potential and the need to involve an organization's human resources in change processes that affect them. Professional skills are developed in practicum situations and finally in a full-year internship. Applied research is integrated into the program and the curriculum requires the production of a thesis.

Special Facilities or Resources: Our department is a small one with 17 faculty teachers. The professorial resources are directly available to students, and the training and supervision are highly personalized. The department offers a community service of individual counseling through its intervention center, which is also the ground for research. We are affiliated with the local center for health and social services as well as the geriatric institution where colleages from the department cooperate in research programs and where one of our teachers has a well-structured laboratory for research on sleeping patterns.

Information for Students With Physical Disabilities: See the following Web site for more information: http://www.usherbrooke.ca.

Application Information:

Send to Bureau du Registraire, Universite de Sherbrooke, Sherbrooke, Quebec, J1K 2R1. Application available online. URL of online application: http://www.usherbrooke.ca. Students are admitted in the Fall, application deadline February 1. *Fee:* $50. Note: All dollar amounts specified in this entry are Canadian dollars.

Simon Fraser University

Department of Psychology
8888 University Drive
Burnaby, BC V5A 1S6
Telephone: (778) 782-3354
Fax: (778) 782-3427
E-mail: *turner@sfu.ca*
Web: *http://www.psyc.sfu.ca/*

Department Information:

1965. Chair, Department of Psychology: Daniel Weeks. Number of faculty: total—full-time 40; women—full-time 11.

Programs and Degrees Offered:

Listed in the following order: Program area, degree type (T if terminal Master's), number awarded 7/06–6/07. Experimental Psychology PhD (Doctor of Philosophy) 4, Clinical Psychology PhD (Doctor of Philosophy) 8.

APA Accreditation: Clinical PhD (Doctor of Philosophy).

CPA Accreditation: Clinical PhD (Doctor of Philosophy).

Student Applications/Admissions:

Student Applications

Experimental Psychology PhD (Doctor of Philosophy)—Applications 2007–2008, 81. Total applicants accepted 2007–2008, 12. Number full-time enrolled (new admits only) 2007–2008, 12. Total enrolled 2007–2008 full-time, 43. Openings 2008–2009, 5. The median number of years required for completion of a degree in 2006–2007 were 4. The number of students enrolled full- and part-time, who were dismissed or voluntarily withdrew from this program area in 2007–2008 were 0. *Clinical Psychology PhD (Doctor of Philosophy)*—Applications 2007–2008, 163. Total applicants accepted 2007–2008, 8. Number full-time enrolled (new admits only) 2007–2008, 8. Total enrolled 2007–2008 full-time, 55. Openings 2008–2009, 7. The median number of years required for completion of a degree in 2006–2007 were 5. The number of students enrolled full- and part-time, who were dismissed or voluntarily withdrew from this program area in 2007–2008 were 0.

Admissions Requirements:

Scores: Entries appear in this order: required test or GPA, minimum score (if required), median score of students entering in 2007–2008. Master's Programs: GRE-V no minimum stated, 605; GRE-Q no minimum stated, 690; GRE-Subject (Psychology) no minimum stated, 750; overall undergraduate GPA no minimum stated, 3.89; psychology GPA no minimum stated, 3.98. GRE-Subject (Psychology) required for Clinical applicants only. Applicants must have a minimum CGPA of 3.23/4.00. Doctoral Programs: GRE-V no minimum stated, 570; GRE-Q no minimum stated, 660; GRE-Subject (Psychology) no minimum stated, 750; overall undergraduate GPA no minimum stated, 3.73; psychology GPA no minimum stated, 3.91. GRE-Subject (Psychology) required for Clinical applicants only. Applicants must have minimum CGPA of 3.23/4.00.

Other Criteria: (importance of criteria rated low, medium, or high): GRE/MAT scores—high, research experience—high, work experience—low, extracurricular activity—low, clinically related public service—low, GPA—high, letters of recommendation—high, interview—high, statement of goals and objectives—high, undergraduate major in psychology—high, specific undergraduate psychology courses taken—medium. Interview is more relevant to admission to clinical program. For additional information on admission requirements, go to http://www.psyc.sfu.ca/grad/.

Student Characteristics: The following represents characteristics of students in 2007–2008 in all graduate psychology programs in the department: Female—full-time 71, part-time 0; Male—full-time 27, part-time 0; African American/Black—part-time 0; Hispanic/Latino(a)—part-time 0; Asian/Pacific Islander—part-time 0; American Indian/Alaska Native—part-time 0; Caucasian/White—full-time 0, part-time 0; Unknown ethnicity—full-time 0, part-time 0.

Financial Information/Assistance:

Tuition for Full-Time Study: *Master's:* State residents: per academic year $4,515; Nonstate residents: per academic year $4,515. *Doctoral:* State residents: per academic year $4,515; Nonstate residents: per academic year $4,515. Tuition is subject to change. See the following Web site for updates and changes in tuition costs: http://www.students.sfu.ca/fees/gradfees.html.

Financial Assistance:

First-Year Students: Teaching assistantships available for first year. Average amount paid per academic year: $16,098. Average number of hours worked per week: 15. Research assistantships available for first year. Fellowships and scholarships available for first year. Average amount paid per academic year: $6,250. Apply by March 15.

Advanced Students: Teaching assistantships available for advanced students. Average amount paid per academic year: $19,008. Average number of hours worked per week: 15. Research assistantships available for advanced students. Fellowships and scholarships available for advanced students. Average amount paid per academic year: $6,250. Apply by March 15.

Additional Information: Of all students currently enrolled full time, 100% benefited from one or more of the listed financial assistance programs. Application and information available online at http://www.psyc.sfu.ca/grad.

Internships/Practica: Doctoral Degree (PhD Clinical Psychology, three specialty streams): For those doctoral students for whom a professional internship was required in this program prior to graduation, (5) students applied for an internship in 2006–2007, with (5) students obtaining an internship. Of those students who obtained an internship, (5) were paid internships. Of those students who obtained an internship, (4) students placed in APA/CPA-accredited internships, (0) students placed in internships not APA/CPA-accredited, but listed with the Association of Psychology Postdoctoral and Internship Centers (APPIC), (0) students placed in internships conforming to guidelines of the Council of Directors of School Psychology Programs (CDSPP), (1) students placed in internships that were not APA/CPA accredited, APPIC or CDSPP listed. Students in the Clinical program are required to complete an MA practicum and a PhD internship. The practica are coordinated by the Director of Clinical Training, and take place primarily in local multidisciplinary community settings under the overall supervision of psychology personnel. Internships are all external to the program.

Housing and Day Care: On-campus housing is available. See the following Web site for more information: http://www.students.sfu.ca/residences/. On-campus day care facilities are available. See the following Web site for more information: http://www.sfu.ca/childcare-society/.

Employment of Department Graduates:

Master's Degree Graduates: Of those who graduated in the academic year 2006–2007, the following categories and numbers represent the postgraduate activities and employment of master's degree graduates: Enrolled in a psychology doctoral program (10), enrolled in a postdoctoral residency/fellowship (n/a), employed in independent practice (n/a), employed in business or industry (1), employed in a government agency (2), total from the above (master's) (13).

Doctoral Degree Graduates: Of those who graduated in the academic year 2006–2007, the following categories and numbers represent the postgraduate activities and employment of doctoral degree graduates: Enrolled in a psychology doctoral program (n/a), enrolled in another graduate/professional program (0), enrolled in a postdoctoral residency/fellowship (2), employed in independent practice (0), employed in an academic position at a university (1), employed in an academic position at a 2-year/4-year college (2), employed in other positions at a higher education institution (0), employed in a professional position in a school system (0), employed in business or industry (0), employed in a government agency (0), employed in a community mental health/counseling center (2), employed in a hospital/medical center (5), total from the above (doctoral) (12).

Additional Information:

Orientation, Objectives, and Emphasis of Department: The department has a mainstream, empirical orientation. The objectives of our undergraduate program are to produce majors who have a broad exposure to the various fields of psychology, and to produce honors students who, in addition, have received higher level training in research methods and have completed an honors research project. The department offers graduate work leading to master's and doctoral degrees in clinical or experimental psychology. Within the Clinical and Experimental programs, all graduate students work on topics from one of the following general research areas: cognitive and biological psychology, developmental psychology, law and forensic psychology, social psychology, and theory and methods. The Clinical program subscribes to the scientist–practitioner model of training, and offers specializations in child clinical psychology, clinical forensic psychology, and clinical neuropsychology. In cooperation with the University of British Columbia, Law and Forensic Psychology students are allowed leave from one university to complete degree requirements in the other in order to obtain both PhD and LLB degrees.

Special Facilities or Resources: The Psychology department has numerous technical resources available to its members. A Microcomputer Lab houses 18 workstations running Windows XP and hosts a variety of statistical packages (SPSS, SAS, Lisrel, MathCAD, Systat), productivity packages (Microsoft Office, Acrobat, Write-N-Cite), Internet packages (Firefox, Thunderbird, secure file transfer programs), and other utility programs. Although the University provides central e-mail service, the department provides in-house file storage, printing, scanning, photocopying, and teleconferencing resources. One conference room with an LCD projector and workstation is available for presentations (colloquia, thesis defences, etc.). Other portable multimedia equipment include LCD projectors, VCRs, and audiorecording devices. Students normally receive office space in the research laboratories of their supervisors. Most faculty labs have computers and printers for graduate and honours students. Neuroscience labs for animal studies are equipped for physiological and behavioral research, as well as advanced microscopy and image analysis. The department's array of technical and information technologies are managed and maintained by a five-member IT staff. The Clinical program operates a separate training clinic with a full-time director and office coordinator, and staffed by Clinical students. It has an extensive test library, audio- videorecording capabilities, and presentation projection facilities. The library has excellent resources including online databases in psychology; interlibrary loans of books and journals are readily accessible.

Information for Students With Physical Disabilities: See the following Web site for more information: http://www.students.sfu.ca/csd/.

Application Information:

Send to Anita Turner, Graduate Program Assistant, Psychology Department, Simon Fraser University, 8888 University Drive, Burnaby, BC V5A 1S6. Application available online. URL of online application: http://www.sfu.ca/gradstudents/applicants/. Students are admitted in the Fall, application deadline January 5. The application materials should be sent in one complete package. Reference forms and letters should be in sealed envelopes and signed by the referee. The graduate application check list must be included with the application materials. *Fee:* $75. Note: All dollar amounts specified in this entry are Canadian dollars.

Toronto, University of

Department of Psychology
100 Saint George Street
Toronto, ON M5S 3G3
Telephone: (416) 978-3404
Fax: (416) 976-4811
E-mail: *chair@psych.utoronto.ca*
Web: *http://www.psych.utoronto.ca*

Department Information:

1891. Chairperson: Peter Herman. Number of faculty: total—full-time 74, part-time 38; women—full-time 24, part-time 12; total—minority—full-time 2, part-time 1; women minority—full-time 1.

Programs and Degrees Offered:

Listed in the following order: Program area, degree type (T if terminal Master's), number awarded 7/06–6/07. Behavioral Neuroscience MA/MS (Master of Arts/Science) 20, Behavioral Neuroscience PhD (Doctor of Philosophy) 2, Cognition/Perception MA/MS (Master of Arts/Science) 20, Cognition/Perception PhD (Doctor of Philosophy) 3, Developmental MA/MS (Master of Arts/Science) 6, Social/Personality/Abnormal MA/MS (Master of Arts/Science) 5, Developmental PhD (Doctor of Philosophy) 1, Social/Personality/Abnormal PhD (Doctor of Philosophy) 3.

Student Applications/Admissions:

Student Applications

Behavioral Neuroscience MA/MS (Master of Arts/Science)—Applications 2007–2008, 30. Total applicants accepted 2007–2008, 8. Number full-time enrolled (new admits only) 2007–2008, 4. Total enrolled 2007–2008 full-time, 6. Openings 2008–2009, 10. The median number of years required for completion of a degree in 2006–2007 was 1. The number of students enrolled full- and part-time, who were dismissed or voluntarily withdrew from this program area in 2007–2008 were 0. *Behavioral Neuroscience PhD (Doctor of Philosophy)*—Applications 2007–2008, 9. Total applicants accepted 2007–2008, 2. Number full-time enrolled (new admits only) 2007–2008, 1. Total enrolled 2007–2008 full-time, 36. Openings 2008–2009, 10. The median number of years required for completion of a degree in 2006–2007 were 10. The number of students enrolled full- and part-time, who were dismissed or voluntarily withdrew from this program area in 2007–2008 were 0. *Cognition/Perception MA/MS (Master of Arts/Science)*—Applications 2007–2008, 60. Total applicants accepted 2007–2008, 12. Number full-time enrolled (new admits only) 2007–2008, 12. Total enrolled 2007–2008 full-time, 13. Openings 2008–2009, 10. The median number of years required for completion of a degree in 2006–2007 was 1. The number of students enrolled full- and part-time, who were dismissed or voluntarily withdrew from this program area in 2007–2008 were 0. *Cognition/Perception PhD (Doctor of Philosophy)*—Applications 2007–2008, 7. Total applicants accepted 2007–2008, 2. Number full-time enrolled (new admits only) 2007–2008, 1. Total enrolled 2007–2008 full-time, 43. Openings 2008–2009, 10. The median number of years required for completion of a degree in 2006–2007 were 5. The number of students enrolled full- and part-time, who were dismissed or voluntarily withdrew from this program area in 2007–2008 were 0. *Developmental MA/MS (Master of Arts/Science)*—Applications 2007–2008, 28. Total applicants accepted 2007–2008, 5. Number full-time enrolled (new admits only) 2007–2008, 4. Total enrolled 2007–2008 full-time, 4. Openings 2008–2009, 10. The median number of years required for completion of a degree in 2006–2007 was 1. The number of students enrolled full- and part-time, who were dismissed or voluntarily withdrew from this program area in 2007–2008 were 0. *Social/Personality/Abnormal MA/MS (Master of Arts/Science)*—Applications 2007–2008, 90. Total applicants accepted 2007–2008, 11. Number full-time enrolled (new admits only) 2007–2008, 8. Total enrolled 2007–2008 full-time, 8. Openings 2008–2009, 10. The median number of years required for completion of a degree in 2006–2007 was 1. The number of students enrolled full- and part-time, who were dismissed or voluntarily withdrew from this program area in 2007–2008 were 0. *Developmental PhD (Doctor of Philosophy)*—Applications 2007–2008, 5. Total applicants accepted 2007–2008, 2. Number full-time enrolled (new admits only) 2007–2008, 0. Total enrolled 2007–2008 full-time, 7. Openings 2008–2009, 10. The median number of years required for completion of a degree in 2006–2007 were 6. The number of students enrolled full- and part-time, who were dismissed or voluntarily withdrew from this program area in 2007–2008 were 0. *Social/Personality/Abnormal PhD (Doctor of Philosophy)*—Applications 2007–2008, 12. Total applicants accepted 2007–2008, 1. Number full-time enrolled (new admits only) 2007–2008, 1. Total enrolled 2007–2008 full-time, 19. Openings 2008–2009, 10. The median number of years required for completion of a degree in 2006–2007 were 4.

Admissions Requirements:

Scores: Entries appear in this order: required test or GPA, minimum score (if required), median score of students entering in 2007–2008. Master's Programs: GRE-V 500, 600; GRE-Q 500, 725; last 2 years GPA 3.7, 4. Doctoral Programs: GRE-V 500, 600; GRE-Q 500, 725; last 2 years GPA 3.7, 4.

Other Criteria: (importance of criteria rated low, medium, or high): GRE/MAT scores—high, research experience—high, work experience—low, extracurricular activity—low, GPA—high, letters of recommendation—high, interview—high, statement of goals and objectives—high, undergraduate major in psychology—medium, specific undergraduate psychology courses taken—medium.

Student Characteristics: The following represents characteristics of students in 2007–2008 in all graduate psychology programs in the department: Female—full-time 92, part-time 0; Male—full-time 44, part-time 0; African American/Black—full-time 5, part-time 0; Hispanic/Latino(a)—full-time 2, part-time 0; Asian/Pacific Islander—full-time 9, part-time 0; American Indian/Alaska Native—full-time 1, part-time 0; Caucasian/White—full-time 94, part-time 0; Multi-ethnic—full-time 9, part-time 0; students subject to the Americans With Disabilities Act—full-time 1, part-time 0; Unknown ethnicity—full-time 16, part-time 0; International students who hold an F-1 or J-1 Visa—full-time 22, part-time 0.

Financial Information/Assistance:

Tuition for Full-Time Study: *Master's:* State residents: per academic year $6,914; Nonstate residents: per academic year $14,358. *Doctoral:* State residents: per academic year $6,914; Nonstate residents: per academic year $14,358. Tuition is subject to change. See the following Web site for updates and changes in tuition costs: http://www.sgs.utoronto.ca/current/fees/index.asp.

Financial Assistance:

First-Year Students: Teaching assistantships available for first year. Average amount paid per academic year: $6,000. Average number of hours worked per week: 10. Apply by June 1. Traineeships available for first year. Average amount paid per academic year: $6,000. Apply by December 15. Fellowships and scholarships available for first year. Average amount paid per academic year: $10,414. Apply by December 15.

Advanced Students: Teaching assistantships available for advanced students. Average amount paid per academic year: $6,000. Average number of hours worked per week: 10. Apply by June 1. Traineeships available for advanced students. Average amount paid per academic year: $6,000. Apply by December 15. Fellowships and scholarships available for advanced students. Average amount paid per academic year: $10,414. Apply by December 15.

Additional Information: Of all students currently enrolled full time, 100% benefited from one or more of the listed financial assistance programs. Application and information available online at http://www.psych.utoronto.ca.

Internships/Practica: No information provided.

Housing and Day Care: On-campus housing is available. See the following Web site for more information: http://www.sgs.utoronto.

ca/prospective/housing/index.asp. On-campus day care facilities are available.

Employment of Department Graduates:

Master's Degree Graduates: Of those who graduated in the academic year 2006–2007, the following categories and numbers represent the postgraduate activities and employment of master's degree graduates: Enrolled in a psychology doctoral program (28), enrolled in a postdoctoral residency/fellowship (n/a), employed in independent practice (n/a), total from the above (master's) (28).

Doctoral Degree Graduates: Of those who graduated in the academic year 2006–2007, the following categories and numbers represent the postgraduate activities and employment of doctoral degree graduates: Enrolled in a psychology doctoral program (n/a), enrolled in another graduate/professional program (3), employed in an academic position at a university (2), employed in a hospital/medical center (1), do not know (3), total from the above (doctoral) (9).

Additional Information:

Orientation, Objectives, and Emphasis of Department: The purpose of graduate training at the University of Toronto is to prepare students for careers in teaching and research. Teaching and research apprenticeships, therefore, constitute a large portion of such training. Research training is supplemented by courses and seminars. In some cases the courses are designed to provide up-to-date fundamental background information in psychology. The bulk of instruction, however, takes place in informal seminars; these provide an opportunity for the discussion of theoretical issues, the formulation of research problems, and the review of current developments in specific research areas. In the past, most of our graduates have entered academic careers. More recently, graduates have also taken research and managerial positions in research institutes, hospitals, government agencies, and industrial corporations.

Special Facilities or Resources: The department has modern laboratories at the St. George, Erindale, and Scarborough campuses, as well as a fully equipped electronic workshop. Students have access to an extensive computer system including the university's central computer, the department's Sun computer, and many advanced microcomputers. The department has close ties to several medical hospitals, as well as the Clarke Psychiatric Hospital, Baycrest Center, and the Rotman Research Institute at the Center and the Addiction Research Foundation.

Information for Students With Physical Disabilities: See the following Web site for more information: http://www.sa.utoronto.ca/area.php?waid=5.

Application Information:

Send to Graduate Studies, Department of Psychology, University of Toronto, 100 Saint George Street, Toronto, Ontario, Canada M5S 3G3. Application available online. URL of online application: http://www.psych.utoronto.ca. Students are admitted in the Fall, application deadline December 15. *Fee:* $90. Note: All dollar amounts specified in this entry are Canadian dollars.

Victoria, University of

Department of Psychology
P.O. Box 3050 STN CSC
Victoria, BC V8W 3P5
Telephone: (250) 721-7525
Fax: (250) 721-8929
E-mail: *psychair@uvic.ca*
Web: *http://www.web.uvic.ca/psyc/*

Department Information:

1963. Chair: Elizabeth Brimacombe. Number of faculty: total—full-time 30, part-time 3; women—full-time 14, part-time 2; minority—part-time 1.

Programs and Degrees Offered:

Listed in the following order: Program area, degree type (T if terminal Master's), number awarded 7/06–6/07. Clinical Neuropsychology PhD (Doctor of Philosophy) 2, Cognition and Brain Science PhD (Doctor of Philosophy) 2, Experimental Neuropsychology PhD (Doctor of Philosophy) 0, Social PhD (Doctor of Philosophy) 2, Clinical Life Span PhD (Doctor of Philosophy) 1, Life Span Development and Aging PhD (Doctor of Philosophy) 1.

APA Accreditation: Clinical PhD (Doctor of Philosophy).

CPA Accreditation: Clinical PhD (Doctor of Philosophy). Clinical PhD (Doctor of Philosophy).

Student Applications/Admissions:

Student Applications

Clinical Neuropsychology PhD (Doctor of Philosophy)—Applications 2007–2008, 39. Total applicants accepted 2007–2008, 4. Openings 2008–2009, 4. The median number of years required for completion of a degree in 2006–2007 were 7. The number of students enrolled full- and part-time, who were dismissed or voluntarily withdrew from this program area in 2007–2008 were 0. *Cognition and Brain Science PhD (Doctor of Philosophy)*—Applications 2007–2008, 11. Total applicants accepted 2007–2008, 1. Number full-time enrolled (new admits only) 2007–2008, 3. Openings 2008–2009, 2. The median number of years required for completion of a degree in 2006–2007 were 5. The number of students enrolled full- and part-time, who were dismissed or voluntarily withdrew from this program area in 2007–2008 were 0. *Experimental Neuropsychology PhD (Doctor of Philosophy)*—Applications 2007–2008, 9. Total applicants accepted 2007–2008, 2. Number full-time enrolled (new admits only) 2007–2008, 1. Openings 2008–2009, 2. The median number of years required for completion of a degree in 2006–2007 were 6. The number of students enrolled full- and part-time, who were dismissed or voluntarily withdrew from this program area in 2007–2008 were 0. *Social PhD (Doctor of Philosophy)*—Applications 2007–2008, 37. Total applicants accepted 2007–2008, 2. Number full-time enrolled (new admits only) 2007–2008, 1. Openings 2008–2009, 3. The median number of years required for completion of a degree in 2006–2007 were 6. The number of students enrolled full- and part-time, who were dismissed or voluntarily withdrew from this program area in 2007–2008 were 0. *Clinical Life Span PhD (Doctor of Philosophy)*—Applications 2007–2008, 84. Total applicants accepted 2007–2008, 9. Number full-time enrolled (new admits only) 2007–2008, 3. Total enrolled 2007–2008 full-time, 18. Openings 2008–2009, 6. The median number of years required for completion of a degree in 2006–2007 were 6. The number of students enrolled full- and part-time, who were dismissed or voluntarily withdrew from this program area in 2007–2008 were 0. *Life Span Development and Aging PhD (Doctor of Philosophy)*—Applications 2007–2008, 27. Total applicants accepted 2007–2008, 1. Total enrolled 2007–2008 full-time, 7. Openings 2008–2009, 4. The median number of years required for completion of a degree in 2006–2007 were 6. The number of students enrolled full- and part-time, who were dismissed or voluntarily withdrew from this program area in 2007–2008 were 0.

Admissions Requirements:

Scores: Entries appear in this order: required test or GPA, minimum score (if required), median score of students entering in 2007–2008. Master's Programs: GRE-V no minimum stated, 560; GRE-Q no minimum stated, 609; last 2 years GPA 5.00, 7.77. Note: UVic GPAs are on a scale of 1 to 9. Doctoral Programs: GRE-V no minimum stated, 560; GRE-Q no minimum stated, 609. Note: UVic GPAs are on a scale of 1 to 9.
Other Criteria: (importance of criteria rated low, medium, or high): GRE/MAT scores—high, research experience—high, work experience—medium, extracurricular activity—medium, clinically related public service—medium, GPA—high, letters of recommendation—high, interview—high, statement of goals and objectives—high. Group interview required for Clinical programs only.

Student Characteristics: The following represents characteristics of students in 2007–2008 in all graduate psychology programs in the department: Female—full-time 59, part-time 0; Male—full-time 14, part-time 0; African American/Black—full-time 1, part-time 0; Hispanic/Latino(a)—full-time 1, part-time 0; Asian/Pacific Islander—full-time 8, part-time 0; American Indian/Alaska Native—full-time 1, part-time 0; Caucasian/White—full-time 47, part-time 0; Multi-ethnic—part-time 0; Unknown ethnicity—full-time 12, part-time 0.

Financial Information/Assistance:

Tuition for Full-Time Study: *Master's:* State residents: per academic year $4,664; Nonstate residents: per academic year $5,550. *Doctoral:* State residents: per academic year $4,664; Nonstate residents: per academic year $5,550. Tuition is subject to change. See the following Web site for updates and changes in tuition costs: http://www.registrar.uvic.ca/grad/continuing/fees/tuitionandfees.html.

Financial Assistance:

First-Year Students: Teaching assistantships available for first year. Average amount paid per academic year: $4,500. Research assistantships available for first year. Average amount paid per academic year: $4,500. Fellowships and scholarships available for first year. Average amount paid per academic year: $15,000.

Advanced Students: Teaching assistantships available for advanced students. Average amount paid per academic year: $4,500. Research assistantships available for advanced students. Average amount paid per academic year: $4,500. Fellowships and scholarships available for advanced students. Average amount paid per academic year: $15,000.

Additional Information: Of all students currently enrolled full time, 95% benefited from one or more of the listed financial assistance programs. Application and information available online at http://registrar.uvic.ca/safa/.

Internships/Practica: Internships and practica for students in the Clinical program are arranged through the Clinical program.

Housing and Day Care: On-campus housing is available. See the following Web site for more information: On- and off-campus housing: http://www.hfcs.uvic.ca/. On-campus day care facilities are available. See the following Web site for more information: Day care: http://www.stas.uvic.ca/dayc/.

Employment of Department Graduates:

Master's Degree Graduates: Of those who graduated in the academic year 2006–2007, the following categories and numbers represent the postgraduate activities and employment of master's degree graduates: Enrolled in a psychology doctoral program (9), enrolled in another graduate/professional program (0), enrolled in a postdoctoral residency/fellowship (n/a), employed in independent practice (n/a), total from the above (master's) (9).
Doctoral Degree Graduates: Of those who graduated in the academic year 2006–2007, the following categories and numbers represent the postgraduate activities and employment of doctoral degree graduates: Enrolled in a psychology doctoral program (n/a), enrolled in another graduate/professional program (0), enrolled in a postdoctoral residency/fellowship (3), employed in independent practice (6), employed in an academic position at a university (4), employed in a community mental health/counseling center (5), employed in a hospital/medical center (6), total from the above (doctoral) (24).

Additional Information:

Orientation, Objectives, and Emphasis of Department: The graduate program in psychology emphasizes the training of research competence, and, in the case of neuropsychology and life span, the acquisition of clinical skills. The department's orientation is strongly empirical, and students are expected to develop mastery of appropriate methods and design as well as of specific content areas of psychology. The program is directed toward the PhD degree, although students must obtain a master's degree as part of the normal requirements. Formal programs of study, involving a coordinated sequence of courses, are offered for both Experimental and Clinical Neuropsychology (up to but not including a clinical internship), Life Span Development and Aging, and Clinical Life Span Development. Individual programs of study may be designed according to the interests of individual students and faculty members in such areas as social psychology, environmental psychology, experimental and applied behavior analysis, psychopathology, cognition, and human psychophysiology.

Special Facilities or Resources: Fully equipped facilities include a psychology clinic operating as an outpatient service and teaching clinic; large observation rooms with audio- and videorecording equipment for the study of group interaction and other social processes; microcomputer-based cognition laboratories; experimental rooms with one-way mirrors; electrophysiological recording rooms; and specialized labs for the study of visual and auditory perception. We have recently constructed a new Brain and Cognition Laboratory featuring two state-of-the-art event-related potential (ERP) systems. The department enjoys good community contact with local hospitals (general, rehabilitation, and extended care), schools, and private and government agencies, which provide sites for both research and practicum experiences.

Information for Students With Physical Disabilities: See the following Web site for more information: http://www.rcsd.uvic.ca/.

Application Information:
Send to Graduate Admissions and Records, University of Victoria, P.O. Box 3025, STN CSC, Victoria, BC V8W 3P2 Canada. Courier address: Graduate Admissions and Records, University of Victoria, Room A255, Second Floor, University Centre, 3800 Finnerty Road (Ring Road), Victoria, BC V8P 5C2 Canada. Application available online. URL of online application: http://www.registrar.uvic.ca/grad/. Students are admitted in the Fall, application deadline January 1. *Fee:* $100. $125 if any postsecondary transcripts come from institutions outside of Canada. Note: All dollar amounts specified in this entry are Canadian dollars.

Waterloo, University of (2007 data)

Department of Psychology
200 University Avenue West
Waterloo, ON N2L 3G1
Telephone: (519) 888-4567
Fax: (519) 746-8631
E-mail: *mjdixon@watarts.uwaterloo.ca*
Web: *http://www.psychology.uwaterloo.ca/*

Department Information:
1963. Chairperson: Michael Dixon. Number of faculty: total—full-time 34, part-time 12; women—full-time 12, part-time 8.

Programs and Degrees Offered:
Listed in the following order: Program area, degree type (T if terminal Master's), number awarded 7/06–6/07. Industrial/Organizational PhD (Doctor of Philosophy) 2, Social PhD (Doctor of Philosophy) 2, Cognitive PhD (Doctor of Philosophy) 1, Behavioral Neuroscience PhD (Doctor of Philosophy) 3, Clinical PhD (Doctor of Philosophy) 4, Developmental PhD (Doctor of Philosophy) 1, Industrial/Organizational MA/MS (Master of Arts/Science) (T) 3, Developmental MA/MS (Master of Arts/Science) (T) 3.

APA Accreditation: Clinical PhD (Doctor of Philosophy).

Student Applications/Admissions:
Student Applications
Industrial/Organizational PhD (Doctor of Philosophy)—Applications 2007–2008, 22. Total applicants accepted 2007–2008, 5. Number full-time enrolled (new admits only) 2007–2008, 4. Total enrolled 2007–2008 full-time, 8, part-time, 1. Openings 2008–2009, 3. *Social PhD (Doctor of Philosophy)*—Applications 2007–2008, 30. Total applicants accepted 2007–2008, 10. Number full-time enrolled (new admits only) 2007–2008, 7. Openings 2008–2009, 5. *Cognitive PhD (Doctor of Philosophy)*—Applications 2007–2008, 10. Total applicants accepted 2007–2008, 9. Number full-time enrolled (new admits only) 2007–2008, 7. Total enrolled 2007–2008 full-time, 16. Openings 2008–2009, 5. *Behavioral Neuroscience PhD (Doctor of Philosophy)*—Applications 2007–2008, 15. Total applicants accepted 2007–2008, 17. Number full-time enrolled (new admits only) 2007–2008, 2. Total enrolled 2007–2008 full-time, 11, part-time, 2. Openings 2008–2009, 6. *Clinical PhD (Doctor of Philosophy)*—Applications 2007–2008, 134. Total applicants accepted 2007–2008, 7. Number full-time enrolled (new admits only) 2007–2008, 6. Total enrolled 2007–2008 full-time, 20, part-time, 3. Openings 2008–2009, 5. *Developmental PhD (Doctor of Philosophy)*—Applications 2007–2008, 13. Total applicants accepted 2007–2008, 3. Number full-time enrolled (new admits only) 2007–2008, 0. Total enrolled 2007–2008 full-time, 3, part-time, 2. Openings 2008–2009, 3. *Industrial/Organizational MA/MS (Master of Arts/Science)*—Applications 2007–2008, 9. Total applicants accepted 2007–2008, 4. Number full-time enrolled (new admits only) 2007–2008, 2. Total enrolled 2007–2008 full-time, 8. Openings 2008–2009, 4. *Developmental MA/MS (Master of Arts/Science)*—Applications 2007–2008, 8. Total applicants accepted 2007–2008, 4. Number full-time enrolled (new admits only) 2007–2008, 4. Total enrolled 2007–2008 full-time, 4. Openings 2008–2009, 5.

Admissions Requirements:
Scores: Entries appear in this order: required test or GPA, minimum score (if required), median score of students entering in 2007–2008. Master's Programs: GRE-V no minimum stated; GRE-Q no minimum stated; overall undergraduate GPA 3.00; last 2 years GPA 3.00. Doctoral Programs: GRE-V no minimum stated; GRE-Q no minimum stated; overall undergraduate GPA 3.00; last 2 years GPA 3.00.
Other Criteria: (importance of criteria rated low, medium, or high): GRE/MAT scores—high, research experience—medium, work experience—low, clinically related public service—medium, GPA—high, letters of recommendation—high, interview—medium, statement of goals and objectives—low. For additional information on admission requirements, go to http://www.grad.uwaterloo.ca/students/applicrequirements.asp.

Student Characteristics: The following represents characteristics of students in 2007–2008 in all graduate psychology programs in the department: Female—full-time 62, part-time 6; Male—full-time 32, part-time 2; African American/Black—full-time 0, part-time 0; Hispanic/Latino(a)—full-time 0, part-time 0; Asian/Pacific Islander—full-time 0, part-time 0; American Indian/Alaska Native—full-time 0, part-time 0; Caucasian/White—full-time 0, part-time 0; Unknown ethnicity—full-time 0, part-time 0.

Financial Information/Assistance:
Tuition for Full-Time Study: *Master's:* State residents: per academic year $6,439; Nonstate residents: per academic year $15,799. *Doctoral:* State residents: per academic year $6,439; Nonstate residents: per academic year $15,799. Tuition is subject to change. See the following Web site for updates and changes in tuition costs: http://www.adm.uwaterloo.ca/infofin/students/stdfees.htm.

Financial Assistance:

First-Year Students: Teaching assistantships available for first year. Research assistantships available for first year. Fellowships and scholarships available for first year.

Advanced Students: Teaching assistantships available for advanced students. Research assistantships available for advanced students. Fellowships and scholarships available for advanced students.

Additional Information: Of all students currently enrolled full time, 100% benefited from one or more of the listed financial assistance programs.

Internships/Practica: The Applied Master's program requires a 4-month supervised Internship. The Clinical program requires a 4-month practicum during the program of study and a 12-month internship at the conclusion of the academic program. Most practicum placements are with local hospitals, schools or industries.

Housing and Day Care: On-campus housing is available. See the following Web site for more information: http://www.housing.uwaterloo.ca. On-campus day care facilities are available. See the following Web site for more information: http://www.studentservices.uwaterloo.ca/childcare/.

Employment of Department Graduates:

Master's Degree Graduates: Of those who graduated in the academic year 2006–2007, the following categories and numbers represent the postgraduate activities and employment of master's degree graduates: Enrolled in a psychology doctoral program (1), enrolled in a postdoctoral residency/fellowship (n/a), employed in independent practice (n/a), do not know (2), total from the above (master's) (3).

Doctoral Degree Graduates: Of those who graduated in the academic year 2006–2007, the following categories and numbers represent the postgraduate activities and employment of doctoral degree graduates: Enrolled in a psychology doctoral program (n/a), enrolled in a postdoctoral residency/fellowship (7), employed in independent practice (1), employed in an academic position at a university (3), employed in a community mental health/counseling center (1), employed in a hospital/medical center (1), do not know (2), total from the above (doctoral) (15).

Additional Information:

Orientation, Objectives, and Emphasis of Department: There is a strong emphasis on research in all six divisions of the PhD program, and MA/MS students are prepared for careers in applied psychology in a variety of areas. Students are involved either through participation in ongoing faculty research or through development of their own ideas; course work is intended to provide students with general knowledge and intensive preparation in their area of concentration and for some of the programs, the blending of theory and practice is experience in internship and practicum arrangements.

Special Facilities or Resources: Within a large four-story building, extensive laboratory facilities are available for animal and human research. Additional educational and resource centers operate in conjunction with academic and research programs; Animal Care, Preschool, two Assessment Clinics, and mechanical and electronics shops. Research requiring special populations is often carried out at community institutions under the supervision of faculty members. Considerable investment has been made to technical services including excellent computer facilities and consulting personnel who are available for student research and courses.

Information for Students With Physical Disabilities: See the following Web site for more information: http://www.studentservices.uwaterloo.ca/disabilities/.

Application Information:

Send to Graduate Studies Office, University of Waterloo, 200 University Avenue West, Waterloo, ON N2L 3G1. Application available online. URL of online application: http://www.grad.uwaterloo.ca/students/applyingonline.asp. Students are admitted in the Fall, application deadline December 15. The December 15 deadline applies to the Clinical and Social programs only. All other programs have a deadline of January 15. *Fee:* $75. Note: All dollar amounts specified in this entry are Canadian dollars.

Western Ontario, The University of

Department of Psychology
Social Science Centre, 1151 Richmond Street North
London, ON N6A 5C2
Telephone: (519) 661-2064
Fax: (519) 661-3961
E-mail: *vmvandom@uwo.ca*
Web: *http://www.psychology.uwo.ca*

Department Information:

1931. Chairperson: Klaus-Peter Ossenkopp. Number of faculty: total—full-time 56, part-time 35; women—full-time 11, part-time 16.

Programs and Degrees Offered:

Listed in the following order: Program area, degree type (T if terminal Master's), number awarded 7/06–6/07. Clinical PhD (Doctor of Philosophy) 3, Cognition and Perception PhD (Doctor of Philosophy) 0, Developmental PhD (Doctor of Philosophy) 1, Industrial/Organizational PhD (Doctor of Philosophy) 1, Personality and Measurement PhD (Doctor of Philosophy) 0, Behavioral and Cognitive Neuroscience PhD (Doctor of Philosophy) 3, Social PhD (Doctor of Philosophy) 0.

CPA Accreditation: Clinical PhD (Doctor of Philosophy).

Student Applications/Admissions:

Student Applications

Clinical PhD (Doctor of Philosophy)—Applications 2007–2008, 121. Total applicants accepted 2007–2008, 16. Number full-time enrolled (new admits only) 2007–2008, 11. Number part-time enrolled (new admits only) 2007–2008, 0. Total enrolled 2007–2008 full-time, 35, part-time, 4. Openings 2008–2009, 4. The median number of years required for completion of a degree in 2006–2007 were 6. The number of students enrolled full- and part-time, who were dismissed or voluntarily withdrew from this program area in 2007–2008 were 0. *Cognition and Perception PhD (Doctor of Philosophy)*—Applications 2007–2008, 9. Total applicants accepted 2007–2008, 6. Number full-time enrolled (new admits only) 2007–

2008, 3. Number part-time enrolled (new admits only) 2007–2008, 0. Total enrolled 2007–2008 full-time, 17, part-time, 3. Openings 2008–2009, 3. The number of students enrolled full- and part-time, who were dismissed or voluntarily withdrew from this program area in 2007–2008 were 1. *Developmental PhD (Doctor of Philosophy)*—Applications 2007–2008, 10. Total applicants accepted 2007–2008, 4. Number full-time enrolled (new admits only) 2007–2008, 2. Number part-time enrolled (new admits only) 2007–2008, 0. Total enrolled 2007–2008 full-time, 11, part-time, 1. Openings 2008–2009, 2. The median number of years required for completion of a degree in 2006–2007 were 5. The number of students enrolled full- and part-time, who were dismissed or voluntarily withdrew from this program area in 2007–2008 were 2. *Industrial/Organizational PhD (Doctor of Philosophy)*—Applications 2007–2008, 36. Total applicants accepted 2007–2008, 6. Number full-time enrolled (new admits only) 2007–2008, 2. Number part-time enrolled (new admits only) 2007–2008, 0. Total enrolled 2007–2008 full-time, 17, part-time, 2. Openings 2008–2009, 5. The median number of years required for completion of a degree in 2006–2007 were 6. The number of students enrolled full- and part-time, who were dismissed or voluntarily withdrew from this program area in 2007–2008 were 0. *Personality and Measurement PhD (Doctor of Philosophy)*—Applications 2007–2008, 5. Total applicants accepted 2007–2008, 1. Number full-time enrolled (new admits only) 2007–2008, 4. Number part-time enrolled (new admits only) 2007–2008, 1. Total enrolled 2007–2008 full-time, 29, part-time, 1. Openings 2008–2009, 1. The number of students enrolled full- and part-time, who were dismissed or voluntarily withdrew from this program area in 2007–2008 were 0. *Behavioral and Cognitive Neuroscience PhD (Doctor of Philosophy)*—Applications 2007–2008, 17. Total applicants accepted 2007–2008, 10. Number full-time enrolled (new admits only) 2007–2008, 9. Number part-time enrolled (new admits only) 2007–2008, 0. Total enrolled 2007–2008 full-time, 29, part-time, 1. Openings 2008–2009, 5. The median number of years required for completion of a degree in 2006–2007 were 5. The number of students enrolled full- and part-time, who were dismissed or voluntarily withdrew from this program area in 2007–2008 were 0. *Social PhD (Doctor of Philosophy)*—Applications 2007–2008, 37. Total applicants accepted 2007–2008, 5. Number full-time enrolled (new admits only) 2007–2008, 1. Number part-time enrolled (new admits only) 2007–2008, 0. Openings 2008–2009, 5. The number of students enrolled full- and part-time, who were dismissed or voluntarily withdrew from this program area in 2007–2008 were 0.

Admissions Requirements:

Scores: Entries appear in this order: required test or GPA, minimum score (if required), median score of students entering in 2007–2008. Doctoral Programs: GRE-V 530; GRE-Q 560. The Psychology Subject Graduate Record Examination score is no longer required, although it is still recommended.

Other Criteria: (importance of criteria rated low, medium, or high): GRE/MAT scores—high, research experience—high, work experience—low, extracurricular activity—low, clinically related public service—low, GPA—high, letters of recommendation—high, interview—medium, statement of goals and objectives—high. An applicant is accepted into our program to work with individual faculty members. The department gives preference to applicants who have a high potential for success in graduate school and who also share research interests with prospective faculty supervisors. Whereas most of our applicants have an Honour's degree in Psychology, we give full consideration to applicants with an undergraduate Honour's degree (or its equivalent) in other relevant areas. An Honour's degree in Psychology (or its equivalent) is required for admission into the Clinical MS. A Master's degree in Psychology (with content that is primarily Clinical) is required for admission into the Clinical PhD. These requirements reflect the clinical accreditation regulations of the Canadian Psychological Association. For additional information on admission requirements, go to http://www.psychology.uwo.ca.

Student Characteristics: The following represents characteristics of students in 2007–2008 in all graduate psychology programs in the department: Female—full-time 81, part-time 7; Male—full-time 50, part-time 5; African American/Black—full-time 0, part-time 0; Hispanic/Latino(a)—full-time 0, part-time 0; Asian/Pacific Islander—full-time 0, part-time 0; American Indian/Alaska Native—full-time 0, part-time 0; Caucasian/White—full-time 0, part-time 0; Unknown ethnicity—full-time 0, part-time 0.

Financial Information/Assistance:

Tuition for Full-Time Study: *Doctoral:* State residents: per academic year $6,600; Nonstate residents: per academic year $14,500. Tuition is subject to change. See the following Web site for updates and changes in tuition costs: http://www.studentservices.uwo.ca.

Financial Assistance:

First-Year Students: Teaching assistantships available for first year. Average amount paid per academic year: $11,374. Average number of hours worked per week: 10. Tuition remission given: partial. Fellowships and scholarships available for first year. Average amount paid per academic year: $9,000. Tuition remission given: partial.

Advanced Students: Teaching assistantships available for advanced students. Average amount paid per academic year: $11,374. Average number of hours worked per week: 10. Tuition remission given: partial. Fellowships and scholarships available for advanced students. Average amount paid per academic year: $12,000. Tuition remission given: partial.

Additional Information: Of all students currently enrolled full time, 85% benefited from one or more of the listed financial assistance programs. Application and information available online at http://www.psychology.uwo.ca.

Internships/Practica: Clinical Psychology students complete a 1-year internship (CPA accredited) near the end of their doctoral training. Students in Industrial/Organizational Psychology typically meet professional training requirements through a combination of practica courses and placements.

Housing and Day Care: On-campus housing is available. See the following Web site for more information: http://www.uwo.ca/hfs/. On-campus day care facilities are available. See the following Web site for more information: Western Graduate Students With Families: http://grad.uwo.ca/current_students/family_friendly.htm; Flexible Child Care: http://www.usc.uwo.ca/flexcare/; Western Y Child Care Centre: http://www.westerndaycare.com/; Mary J.

Wright University Laboratory Preschool: http://www.thelab school.uwo.ca/.

Employment of Department Graduates:

Master's Degree Graduates: Of those who graduated in the academic year 2006–2007, the following categories and numbers represent the postgraduate activities and employment of master's degree graduates: Enrolled in a postdoctoral residency/fellowship (n/a), employed in independent practice (n/a), total from the above (master's) (0).

Doctoral Degree Graduates: Of those who graduated in the academic year 2006–2007, the following categories and numbers represent the postgraduate activities and employment of doctoral degree graduates: Enrolled in a psychology doctoral program (n/a), enrolled in a postdoctoral residency/fellowship (1), employed in independent practice (1), employed in an academic position at a university (3), employed in a professional position in a school system (1), employed in a hospital/medical center (1), total from the above (doctoral) (8).

Additional Information:

Orientation, Objectives, and Emphasis of Department: The department is organized into seven subject content areas, with initial graduate selection procedures administered by area faculty and area committees. Applicants must indicate an area of interest. The department is research intensive and is oriented toward training researchers. Graduate students are expected to be continually involved in research as well as to complete required courses and comprehensive exams. The Clinical Psychology program adopts the scientist–practitioner model, where both research and professional skills are developed.

Special Facilities or Resources: Currently, facilities for experimental research in the nine-story research wing of the Social Science Centre include animal laboratories, rooms specially designed for research with human participants in behavioral and cognitive neuroscience, clinical, cognition and pereption, developmental, industrial/organizational, personality and measurement, and social psychology and, in addition, a preschool for observation and research into child development, early childhood education, curricula, materials, and teaching methods. In September 2007, along with the Mary J. Wright University Laboratory Preschool, faculty and graduate students in the Clinical and Developmental areas moved to three renovated buildings in another area of Western's campus (Westminster College). A broad range of equipment is available, and additional special equipment necessary for a student's research may be obtained. Facilities to aid in running experiments include sophisticated general and dedicated laboratory computers. An engineering shop, an audiovisual unit, a workshop, and electronic consultants are available. The department also has easy access to the Social Science Network and Data Services. In addition to the Student Development Centre and the Psychological Services in the University Hospital on campus, potential field settings (and sources of subjects for research) include a wide variety of schools, and a large number of psychiatric, and general hospitals, and specialized centers for research and treatment with children, adolescents, and adults.

Information for Students With Physical Disabilities: See the following Web site for more information: http://www.sdc.uwo.ca/.

Application Information:

Send to The Graduate Office, Department of Psychology, Social Science Centre, The University of Western Ontario, 1151 Richmond Street, London, Ontario, Canada N6A 5C2. Application available online. URL of online application: http://www.grad.uwo.ca/. Students are admitted in the Fall, application deadline January 15. *Fee:* $50. There is a possibility that the application fee will rise in 2009. Note: All dollar amounts specified in this entry are Canadian dollars.

Wilfrid Laurier University

Department of Psychology
75 University Avenue, West
Waterloo, ON N2L 3C5
Telephone: (519) 884-1970
Fax: (519) 746-7605
E-mail: *rsharkey@wlu.ca*
Web: *http://www.wlu.ca/homepage.php?grp_id=44*

Department Information:

1956. Chairperson: Dr. Mark Pancer. Number of faculty: total—full-time 33, part-time 17; women—full-time 13, part-time 11; total—minority—full-time 2, part-time 3; women minority—full-time 1, part-time 1.

Programs and Degrees Offered:

Listed in the following order: Program area, degree type (T if terminal Master's), number awarded 7/06–6/07. Community Psychology MA/MS (Master of Arts/Science) (T) 4, Community Psychology PhD (Doctor of Philosophy) 0, Social and Developmental MA/MS (Master of Arts/Science) (T) 4, Social and Developmental PhD (Doctor of Philosophy) 1, Brain and Cognition PhD (Doctor of Philosophy) 0, Brain and Cognition MA/MS (Master of Arts/Science) (T) 3.

Student Applications/Admissions:

Student Applications

Community Psychology MA/MS (Master of Arts/Science)—Applications 2007–2008, 28. Total applicants accepted 2007–2008, 6. Number full-time enrolled (new admits only) 2007–2008, 6. Number part-time enrolled (new admits only) 2007–2008, 1. Total enrolled 2007–2008 full-time, 18, part-time, 3. Openings 2008–2009, 7. The median number of years required for completion of a degree in 2006–2007 were 2. The number of students enrolled full- and part-time, who were dismissed or voluntarily withdrew from this program area in 2007–2008 were 0. *Community Psychology PhD (Doctor of Philosophy)*—Applications 2007–2008, 4. Total applicants accepted 2007–2008, 1. Number full-time enrolled (new admits only) 2007–2008, 1. Number part-time enrolled (new admits only) 2007–2008, 0. Openings 2008–2009, 3. The number of students enrolled full- and part-time, who were dismissed or voluntarily withdrew from this program area in 2007–2008 were 0. *Social and Developmental MA/MS (Master of Arts/Science)*—Applications 2007–2008, 58. Total applicants accepted 2007–2008, 6. Number full-time enrolled (new admits only) 2007–2008, 6. Openings 2008–2009, 7. The median number of years required for completion of a degree in 2006–2007 were 2. The number of students enrolled full- and part-time, who were dismissed or voluntarily withdrew from this program area in

2007–2008 were 0. *Social and Developmental PhD (Doctor of Philosophy)*—Applications 2007–2008, 12. Total applicants accepted 2007–2008, 4. Number full-time enrolled (new admits only) 2007–2008, 4. Number part-time enrolled (new admits only) 2007–2008, 0. Openings 2008–2009, 3. The median number of years required for completion of a degree in 2006–2007 were 4. The number of students enrolled full- and part-time, who were dismissed or voluntarily withdrew from this program area in 2007–2008 were 0. *Brain and Cognition PhD (Doctor of Philosophy)*—Applications 2007–2008, 0. Total applicants accepted 2007–2008, 0. Number full-time enrolled (new admits only) 2007–2008, 0. Number part-time enrolled (new admits only) 2007–2008, 0. Openings 2008–2009, 3. The number of students enrolled full- and part-time, who were dismissed or voluntarily withdrew from this program area in 2007–2008 were 0. *Brain and Cognition MA/MS (Master of Arts/Science)*—Applications 2007–2008, 20. Total applicants accepted 2007–2008, 6. Number full-time enrolled (new admits only) 2007–2008, 6. Number part-time enrolled (new admits only) 2007–2008, 0. Openings 2008–2009, 7. The median number of years required for completion of a degree in 2006–2007 were 2. The number of students enrolled full- and part-time, who were dismissed or voluntarily withdrew from this program area in 2007–2008 were 0.

Admissions Requirements:

Scores: Entries appear in this order: required test or GPA, minimum score (if required), median score of students entering in 2007–2008. Master's Programs: last 2 years GPA 8.0, 10.0. GPA of 8.0 is the equivalent of a B, and 10.0 is the equivalent of an A-. GRE General Test is strongly recommended for Social/Developmental and required for Brain/Cognition. GRE General Test is not required for Community. Doctoral Programs: overall undergraduate GPA 10.0. GPA of 10.0 is the equivalent of a A-. GRE General Test is strongly recommended for Social/Developmental and required for Brain/Cognition. GRE General Test is not required for Community.

Other Criteria: (importance of criteria rated low, medium, or high): research experience—medium, work experience—low, extracurricular activity—low, clinically related public service—low, GPA—high, letters of recommendation—high, interview—medium, statement of goals and objectives—high.

Student Characteristics: The following represents characteristics of students in 2007–2008 in all graduate psychology programs in the department: Female—full-time 48, part-time 2; Male—full-time 20, part-time 1; African American/Black—full-time 4, part-time 0; Hispanic/Latino(a)—full-time 0, part-time 0; Asian/Pacific Islander—full-time 2, part-time 1; American Indian/Alaska Native—full-time 1, part-time 0; Caucasian/White—full-time 61, part-time 2; Multi-ethnic—full-time 0, part-time 0; students subject to the Americans With Disabilities Act—full-time 0, part-time 0; Unknown ethnicity—full-time 0, part-time 0.

Financial Information/Assistance:

Tuition for Full-Time Study: *Master's:* State residents: per academic year $5,914; Nonstate residents: per academic year $13,293. *Doctoral:* State residents: per academic year $5,914; Nonstate residents: per academic year $13,293. Tuition is subject to change. See the following Web site for updates and changes in tuition costs: http://www.wlu.ca/page.php?grp_id=36&p=654.

Financial Assistance:

First-Year Students: No information provided.

Advanced Students: No information provided.

Additional Information: Of all students currently enrolled full time, 0% benefited from one or more of the listed financial assistance programs. Application and information available online at http://www.wlu.ca/page.php?grp_id=36&p=600.

Internships/Practica: No information provided.

Housing and Day Care: On-campus housing is available. See the following Web site for more information: http://www.wlu.ca/~wwwhouse. On-campus day care facilities are available. Contact the Abwunza Child Care Centre at abwunzacc@kwymca.org for more information.

Employment of Department Graduates:

Master's Degree Graduates: Of those who graduated in the academic year 2006–2007, the following categories and numbers represent the postgraduate activities and employment of master's degree graduates: Enrolled in a postdoctoral residency/fellowship (n/a), employed in independent practice (n/a), total from the above (master's) (0).

Doctoral Degree Graduates: Of those who graduated in the academic year 2006–2007, the following categories and numbers represent the postgraduate activities and employment of doctoral degree graduates: Enrolled in a psychology doctoral program (n/a), total from the above (doctoral) (0).

Additional Information:

Orientation, Objectives, and Emphasis of Department: Graduate students can obtain an MA, MS, or PhD in one of the three fields: Brain and Cognition, Social and Developmental Psychology, and Community Psychology. The objective of the MA, MS, and PhD programs in the fields of Brain and Cognition, and Social and Developmental Psychology is to develop competence in designing, conducting, and evaluating research in the fields of brain and cognition or in social and developmental Psychology. Five half-credit courses and a thesis constitute the degree requirements in these MA/MS programs. The purpose of these programs is to prepare students for doctoral studies or for employment in an environment requiring research skills. Students in good standing can be considered for admission to the PhD programs in these area, which involve seven half-credit courses, two comprehensive papers, and a dissertation. In the field of Community Psychology, the objective is to train scientist–practitioners with skills in community collaboration. Students receive training in theory, research, and practice that will enable them to analyze the implications of social change for the delivery of community services. Six half-credit courses and a thesis are required for the MA degree. Students who complete this program are prepared for either doctoral-level training or for employment in community research and service. Students in good standing can be considered for admission to the PhD program in this area, which involves six half-credit courses, two comprehensive papers, and a dissertation.

Special Facilities or Resources: The department has free unlimited access to the university computer, microprocessors, extensive electromechanical equipment, full-time electronics research associate, full-time field supervisor, and access to a wide variety of field settings for research and consultation.

Information for Students With Physical Disabilities: See the following Web site for more information: http://www.mylaurier.ca/accessible/home.htm.

Application Information:
Send to Rita Sharkey, Graduate Program Assistant, Psychology Department, Wilfrid Laurier University, 75 University Avenue West, Waterloo, ON N2L 3C5. Application available online. URL of online application: http://www.wlu.ca/page.php?grp_id=36&p=600. Students are admitted in the Fall, application deadline February 1. *Fee:* $75. Note: All dollar amounts specified in this entry are Canadian dollars.

Windsor, University of

Psychology
Faculty of Arts and Social Sciences
401 Sunset Avenue
Windsor, ON N9B 3P4
Telephone: (519) 253-3000, ext. 2215
Fax: (519) 973-7021
E-mail: *paivio@uwindsor.ca*
Web: *http://www.uwindsor.ca/psychology*

Department Information:
1944. Head: Sandra Paivio. Number of faculty: total—full-time 32; women—full-time 18; total—minority—full-time 2.

Programs and Degrees Offered:
Listed in the following order: Program area, degree type (T if terminal Master's), number awarded 7/06–6/07. Applied Social PhD (Doctor of Philosophy) 1, Clinical (Adult, Child, Neuropsychology) PhD (Doctor of Philosophy) 12.

APA Accreditation: Clinical PhD (Doctor of Philosophy).

CPA Accreditation: Clinical PhD (Doctor of Philosophy).

Student Applications/Admissions:
Student Applications
Applied Social PhD (Doctor of Philosophy)—Applications 2007–2008, 20. Total applicants accepted 2007–2008, 11. Number full-time enrolled (new admits only) 2007–2008, 4. Number part-time enrolled (new admits only) 2007–2008, 0. Openings 2008–2009, 5. The median number of years required for completion of a degree in 2006–2007 were 7. The number of students enrolled full- and part-time, who were dismissed or voluntarily withdrew from this program area in 2007–2008 were 6. *Clinical (Adult, Child, Neuropsychology) PhD (Doctor of Philosophy)*—Applications 2007–2008, 158. Total applicants accepted 2007–2008, 25. Number full-time enrolled (new admits only) 2007–2008, 10. Number part-time enrolled (new admits only) 2007–2008, 0. Openings 2008–2009, 12. The median number of years required for completion of a degree in 2006–2007 were 8. The number of students enrolled full- and part-time, who were dismissed or voluntarily withdrew from this program area in 2007–2008 were 0.

Admissions Requirements:
Scores: Entries appear in this order: required test or GPA, minimum score (if required), median score of students entering in 2007–2008. Master's Programs: Students are accepted directly into PhD program. See Doctoral Program requirements below. Doctoral Programs: GRE-V 60%; GRE-Q 60%; GRE-Subject (Psychology) 60%; overall undergraduate GPA 3.3; last 2 years GPA 3.3; psychology GPA 3.3. GRE numbers indicated above reflect percentile rankings not raw scores.
Other Criteria: (importance of criteria rated low, medium, or high): GRE/MAT scores—high, research experience—medium, work experience—low, extracurricular activity—low, clinically related public service—medium, GPA—high, letters of recommendation—high, interview—medium, statement of goals and objectives—medium, honors thesis—high, undergraduate major in psychology—high, specific undergraduate psychology courses taken—high. For additional information on admission requirements, go to http://www.uwindsor.ca/psychology.

Student Characteristics: The following represents characteristics of students in 2007–2008 in all graduate psychology programs in the department: Female—full-time 93, part-time 0; Male—full-time 17, part-time 0; Caucasian/White—full-time 0, part-time 0; Unknown ethnicity—full-time 0, part-time 0.

Financial Information/Assistance:
Tuition for Full-Time Study: *Doctoral:* State residents: per academic year $6,000; Nonstate residents: per academic year $13,800. Tuition is subject to change. See the following Web site for updates and changes in tuition costs: http://www.prospectives.uwindsor.ca/.

Financial Assistance:
First-Year Students: Teaching assistantships available for first year. Average amount paid per academic year: $8,727. Average number of hours worked per week: 10. Apply by January 15. Research assistantships available for first year. Average number of hours worked per week: 10. Fellowships and scholarships available for first year. Average amount paid per academic year: $6,000. Apply by January 15. Tuition remission given: full.
Advanced Students: Teaching assistantships available for advanced students. Average amount paid per academic year: $9,724. Average number of hours worked per week: 10. Research assistantships available for advanced students. Average number of hours worked per week: 10. Fellowships and scholarships available for advanced students. Average amount paid per academic year: $6,000. Tuition remission given: full.
Additional Information: Of all students currently enrolled full time, 90% benefited from one or more of the listed financial assistance programs.

Internships/Practica: Doctoral Degree (PhD Clinical; Adult, Child, Neuropsychology): For those doctoral students for whom a professional internship was required in this program prior to graduation, (7) students applied for an internship in 2006–2007, with (7) students obtaining an internship. Of those students who obtained an internship, (7) were paid internships. Of those students who obtained an internship, (6) students placed in APA/CPA-accredited internships, (0) students placed in internships not APA/CPA-accredited, but listed with the Association of Psychology Postdoctoral and Internship Centers (APPIC), (0) students placed in internships conforming to guidelines of the Council of Directors of School Psychology Programs (CDSPP), (1) student placed in internships that were not APA/CPA accredited,

APPIC or CDSPP listed. A wide variety of clinical practica are available in the Windsor–Detroit area, and Clinical students obtain additional Summer practicum positions across the country. Students are placed in predoctoral internships throughout Canada and the United States. Applied Social students obtain practica and internships in business and industry, community, and health-related agencies.

Housing and Day Care: On-campus housing is available. See the following Web site for more information: http://www.uwindsor.ca/residence. On-campus day care facilities are available. There is a day care centre very close to the University. Great Beginnings Day Care Centre (519) 253-5235.

Employment of Department Graduates:

Master's Degree Graduates: Of those who graduated in the academic year 2006–2007, the following categories and numbers represent the postgraduate activities and employment of master's degree graduates: Enrolled in a psychology doctoral program (15), enrolled in a postdoctoral residency/fellowship (n/a), employed in independent practice (n/a), total from the above (master's) (15). ***Doctoral Degree Graduates:*** Of those who graduated in the academic year 2006–2007, the following categories and numbers represent the postgraduate activities and employment of doctoral degree graduates: Enrolled in a psychology doctoral program (n/a), enrolled in a postdoctoral residency/fellowship (1), employed in independent practice (3), employed in an academic position at a university (2), employed in other positions at a higher education institution (1), employed in a government agency (1), employed in a community mental health/counseling center (2), employed in a hospital/medical center (3), total from the above (doctoral) (13).

Additional Information:

Orientation, Objectives, and Emphasis of Department: Graduate offerings are divided into two areas: Clinical and Applied social. Students applying for the Clinical program apply directly into specialty areas of adult clinical, child clinical, or clinical neuropsychology. Each of the areas combines theoretical, substantive, and methodological course work with a variety of applied training experiences. The mission of the graduate programs in the Department of Psychology is to provide graduate students with a foundation of theory, research, and practice to enable them to conduct research and/or apply psychology in a variety of settings including universities, private practice, schools, health and medical organizations, social service agencies, businesses, and basic and applied research firms.

Special Facilities or Resources: The Department of Psychology's PhD program is unique in that all areas of specialization (Applied Social, Clinical Neuropsychology, Adult Clinical, and Child Clinical) have an applied focus. Applied training and research resources include the Psychological Services Centre, the Child Study Centre, the Emotion–Cognition Research Laboratory, Health Research Centre for the Study of Violence Against Women, the Student Counselling Centre, and the Psycholinguistics and Neurolinguistics Laboratory. There are faculty–student research groups in the areas of eating disorders, trauma and psychotherapy, problem gambling, computer-mediated communication, feminist research, emotional competence, culture and diversity, health psychology, neuropsychoanalysis, aging, forgiveness, applied memory, multicultural and counselling research, and autism. The department is affiliated with the Summit Centre for Preschool Children With Autism. The university campus has wireless computer access throughout. Researchers have access to a participant pool and Web-based participant recruitment as well as systems that allow for Web-based data collection.

Information for Students With Physical Disabilities: See the following Web site for more information: http://www.uwindsor.ca/sn (Special Needs Office).

Application Information:

Send to Office of the Registrar, Graduate Studies Division, University of Windsor, 401 Sunset Avenue, Windsor, Ontario, Canada N9B 3P4. Application available online. URL of online application: http://www.uwindsor.ca/registrar. Students are admitted in the Fall, application deadline January 15. *Fee:* $55. U.S. equivalent for application fee varies according to the exchange rate on the day of online application. Note: All dollar amounts specified in this entry are Canadian dollars.

York University

Graduate Program in Psychology
4700 Keele Street, Behavioural Science Building
Toronto, ON M3J 1P3
Telephone: (416) 736-5290
Fax: (416) 736-5814
E-mail: *suzmac@yorku.ca*
Web: *http://www.yorku.ca/health/psyc/graduate/graduate.htm*

Department Information:

1963. Director, Graduate Program in Psychology: Dr. Suzanne MacDonald. Number of faculty: total—full-time 84, part-time 7; women—full-time 39, part-time 2; total—minority—full-time 8, part-time 2; women minority—full-time 3, part-time 1.

Programs and Degrees Offered:

Listed in the following order: Program area, degree type (T if terminal Master's), number awarded 7/06–6/07. Brain, Behavior, and Cognitive Sciences PhD (Doctor of Philosophy) 5, Clinical PhD (Doctor of Philosophy) 20, Clinical Developmental PhD (Doctor of Philosophy) 8, Developmental and Cognitive Processes PhD (Doctor of Philosophy) 4, History and Theory PhD (Doctor of Philosophy) 2, Social/Personality PhD (Doctor of Philosophy) 8.

APA Accreditation: Clinical PhD (Doctor of Philosophy). Clinical PhD (Doctor of Philosophy).

CPA Accreditation: Clinical PhD (Doctor of Philosophy). Clinical PhD (Doctor of Philosophy).

Student Applications/Admissions:

Student Applications

Brain, Behavior, and Cognitive Sciences PhD (Doctor of Philosophy)—Applications 2007–2008, 17. Total applicants accepted 2007–2008, 9. Number full-time enrolled (new admits only) 2007–2008, 6. Number part-time enrolled (new admits only) 2007–2008, 0. Total enrolled 2007–2008 full-time, 23, part-time, 2. Openings 2008–2009, 10. The median number of years required for completion of a degree in 2006–2007 were 6. The number of students enrolled full- and part-time, who were dismissed or voluntarily withdrew from this program area in 2007–2008 were 2. *Clinical PhD (Doctor of Philosophy)*—Applications 2007–2008, 150. Total applicants accepted 2007–2008, 13. Number full-time enrolled (new admits only) 2007–2008, 12. Number part-time enrolled (new admits only) 2007–2008, 0. Total enrolled 2007–2008 full-time, 55, part-time, 11. Openings 2008–2009, 8. The median number of years required for completion of a degree in 2006–2007 were 6. The number of students enrolled full- and part-time, who were dismissed or voluntarily withdrew from this program area in 2007–2008 were 1. *Clinical Developmental PhD (Doctor of Philosophy)*—Applications 2007–2008, 96. Total applicants accepted 2007–2008, 18. Number full-time enrolled (new admits only) 2007–2008, 10. Number part-time enrolled (new admits only) 2007–2008, 0. Total enrolled 2007–2008 full-time, 52, part-time, 8. Openings 2008–2009, 8. The median number of years required for completion of a degree in 2006–2007 were 6. The number of students enrolled full- and part-time, who were dismissed or voluntarily withdrew from this program area in 2007–2008 were 4. *Developmental and Cognitive Processes PhD (Doctor of Philosophy)*—Applications 2007–2008, 13. Total applicants accepted 2007–2008, 8. Number full-time enrolled (new admits only) 2007–2008, 2. Number part-time enrolled (new admits only) 2007–2008, 0. Total enrolled 2007–2008 full-time, 25, part-time, 3. Openings 2008–2009, 7. The median number of years required for completion of a degree in 2006–2007 were 6. The number of students enrolled full- and part-time, who were dismissed or voluntarily withdrew from this program area in 2007–2008 were 4. *History and Theory PhD (Doctor of Philosophy)*—Applications 2007–2008, 4. Total applicants accepted 2007–2008, 3. Number full-time enrolled (new admits only) 2007–2008, 1. Number part-time enrolled (new admits only) 2007–2008, 0. Total enrolled 2007–2008 full-time, 10, part-time, 1. Openings 2008–2009, 3. The median number of years required for completion of a degree in 2006–2007 were 6. The number of students enrolled full- and part-time, who were dismissed or voluntarily withdrew from this program area in 2007–2008 were 0. *Social/Personality PhD (Doctor of Philosophy)*—Applications 2007–2008, 47. Total applicants accepted 2007–2008, 10. Number full-time enrolled (new admits only) 2007–2008, 4. Number part-time enrolled (new admits only) 2007–2008, 0. Total enrolled 2007–2008 full-time, 29, part-time, 3. Openings 2008–2009, 7. The median number of years required for completion of a degree in 2006–2007 were 6. The number of students enrolled full- and part-time, who were dismissed or voluntarily withdrew from this program area in 2007–2008 were 1.

Admissions Requirements:

Scores: Entries appear in this order: required test or GPA, minimum score (if required), median score of students entering in 2007–2008. Master's Programs: GRE-V no minimum stated; GRE-Q no minimum stated; GRE-Subject (Psychology) N/A, N/A; last 2 years GPA no minimum stated. Students are ranked, and GRE scores figure prominently in the rankings. The two Clinical areas are most discriminatory in terms of GRE scores. The nonclinical areas do not require the GRE-Subject if applicants have completed a 4-year psychology degree. Doctoral Programs: GREs are not required by any of the six areas in the program if the applicants have previously completed a MA/MS degree.

Other Criteria: (importance of criteria rated low, medium, or high): GRE/MAT scores—high, research experience—high, work experience—medium, clinically related public service—low, GPA—high, letters of recommendation—high, statement of goals and objectives—medium, undergraduate major in psychology—medium, specific undergraduate psychology courses taken—low. The non-Clinical areas place no weight on clinically related public service. For additional information on admission requirements, go to http://www.yorku.ca/grads/cal/psy.htm.

Student Characteristics: The following represents characteristics of students in 2007–2008 in all graduate psychology programs in the department: Female—full-time 159, part-time 25; Male—full-time 35, part-time 3; Caucasian/White—full-time 0, part-time 0; Unknown ethnicity—full-time 194, part-time 28; International students who hold an F-1 or J-1 Visa—full-time 10, part-time 0.

Financial Information/Assistance:

Tuition for Full-Time Study: *Master's:* State residents: per academic year $5,441; Nonstate residents: per academic year $11,928. *Doctoral:* State residents: per academic year $5,441; Nonstate residents: per academic year $11,928. Tuition is subject to change. See the following Web site for updates and changes in tuition costs: http://www.yorku.ca/osfs/gradfeesmain.shtml.

Financial Assistance:

First-Year Students: Teaching assistantships available for first year. Average amount paid per academic year: $12,000. Average number of hours worked per week: 10. Research assistantships available for first year. Average amount paid per academic year: $10,000. Average number of hours worked per week: 10. Traineeships available for first year. Fellowships and scholarships available for first year. Average amount paid per academic year: $4,000.

Advanced Students: Teaching assistantships available for advanced students. Average amount paid per academic year: $14,000. Average number of hours worked per week: 10. Research assistantships available for advanced students. Average number of hours worked per week: 10. Fellowships and scholarships available for advanced students.

Additional Information: Of all students currently enrolled full time, 100% benefited from one or more of the listed financial assistance programs. Application and information available online at http://www.yorku.ca/graduatestudents.

Internships/Practica: Doctoral internships are available; practicum work is done on a half-time basis during the academic year and, when possible, full-time during the Summer. Research practica, and a clinical practicum as part of the Clinical area's program, are done on campus. Clinical internships are available in the York Counseling and Development Center and a variety of hospitals, clinics, and counseling centers in the city and elsewhere. Descriptions of the program and of faculty research interests are available on the Web.

Housing and Day Care: On-campus housing is available. See the following Web site for more information: http://www.yorku.ca/stuhouse/yorkapts/rates.htm. For general inquiries (416) 736-5152 or e-mail: yorkapts@yorku.ca. On-campus day care facilities are available. Contact Child Care Centre, 90 Atkinson Road, Room 128, M3J 2S5, Toronto, Ontario; telephone (416) 736-5190 for general information; e-mail daycare@yorku.ca. Lee Wiggins Childcare Centre, Room 201, Student Centre Building, 4700 Keele Street, Toronto, Ontario M3J 1P3; telephone: (416) 736-5959; e-mail: lpowell@yorku.ca.

Employment of Department Graduates:

Master's Degree Graduates: Of those who graduated in the academic year 2006–2007, the following categories and numbers represent the postgraduate activities and employment of master's degree graduates: Enrolled in a psychology doctoral program (24), enrolled in another graduate/professional program (2), enrolled in a postdoctoral residency/fellowship (n/a), employed in independent practice (n/a), do not know (2), total from the above (master's) (28).

Doctoral Degree Graduates: Of those who graduated in the academic year 2006–2007, the following categories and numbers represent the postgraduate activities and employment of doctoral degree graduates: Enrolled in a psychology doctoral program (n/a), enrolled in a postdoctoral residency/fellowship (4), employed in independent practice (1), employed in an academic position at a university (4), employed in an academic position at a 2-year/4-year college (0), employed in other positions at a higher education institution (0), employed in a professional position in a school system (1), employed in business or industry (0), employed in a government agency (0), employed in a community mental health/counseling center (3), employed in a hospital/medical center (4), still seeking employment (0), other employment position (2), do not know (0), total from the above (doctoral) (19).

Additional Information:

Orientation, Objectives, and Emphasis of Department: Strength and depth are emphasized in the areas of brain, behavior and cognitive science (learning, perception, physiological, psychometrics); clinical; clinical development; developmental cognitive processes; history and theory; and social/personality. The department attempts to prepare students as researchers and practitioners in a given area. Most students admitted to the MA but are accepted on the assumption that they will continue into PhD studies.

Special Facilities or Resources: The department has a vivarium, wet laboratories, shop facilities for woodwork and photography, substantial computing facilities, audiovisual equipment including VCRs, and observational laboratories with two-way mirrors.

Information for Students With Physical Disabilities: See the following Web site for more information: http://www.yorku.ca or visit http://www.studentsaffairs.yorku.ca/opd.

Application Information:

Send to Admissions Office, Student Services Centre, York University, 4700 Keele Street, Toronto, Ontario M3J 1P3, Canada. Application available online. URL of online application: http://www.yorku.ca/graduatestudents. Students are admitted in the Fall, application deadline December 15. *Fee:* $80. Foreign students' tuition fees are usually subsidized by the Faculty of Graduate Studies, to bring the fee in line with the domestic tuition fee. This subsidization is often maintained as the student continues in the program beyond the 1st year as well. Note: All dollar amounts specified in this entry are Canadian dollars.

INDEX OF PROGRAMS BY AREA OF STUDY OFFERED

B

Behavioral Psychology
American University (PhD)
Auburn University (MA/MS—terminal)
Boston College (PhD)
Boston University (MA/MS—terminal)
Bowling Green State University (PhD)
California State University, Sacramento (MA/MS—terminal)
California, University of, Davis (PhD)
Carnegie Mellon University (PhD)
Cincinnati, University of (EdS/MEd, PhD)
City University of New York (PhD)
City University of New York: Graduate Center (PhD)
City University of New York: Graduate School and University Center (PhD)
Claremont Graduate University (MA/MS—terminal, PhD)
Colorado, University of, Boulder (PhD)
Cornell University (PhD)
Drexel University (MA/MS—terminal)
Eastern Michigan University (MA/MS—terminal)
Florida Institute of Technology (MA/MS, MA/MS—terminal)
Florida International University (MA/MS—terminal)
Florida State University (MA/MS—terminal)
Florida, University of (PhD)
Georgia Southern University (PsyD)
Georgia State University (PhD)
Hofstra University (PhD)
Illinois State University (MA/MS—terminal)
Indiana University (PhD)
Iowa, University of (PhD)
Jacksonville State University (MA/MS—terminal)
Kansas, University of (MA/MS, PhD)
Long Island University (Other)
Manitoba, University of (PhD)
Maryland, University of, Baltimore County (MA/MS—terminal)
Michigan State University (PhD)
Middle Tennessee State University (MA/MS—terminal)
Minnesota State University—Mankato (MA/MS)
Mississippi State University (PhD)
Missouri, University of, St. Louis (PhD)
Nevada, University of, Reno (PhD)
North Carolina, University of, Wilmington (MA/MS—terminal)
Northeastern University (MA/MS—terminal)
Pacific University (MA/MS—terminal)
Pacific, University of the (MA/MS)
Quebec at Montreal, University of (PhD)
Saskatchewan, University of (PhD)
Southern California, University of, Keck School of Medicine (PhD)
State University of New York at Buffalo (PhD)
State University of New York, Binghamton University (PhD)
State University of New York, College at Brockport (MA/MS—terminal)
Syracuse University (PhD)
Tennessee, University of, Knoxville (PhD)
Texas, University of, Austin (PhD)
Toronto, University of (MA/MS, PhD)
Utah State University (PhD)
Washington University in St. Louis (PhD)
Washington, University of (PhD)
West Virginia University (PhD)
Western Michigan University (MA/MS—terminal, PhD)
Wisconsin, University of, Milwaukee (MA/MS—terminal)

Biological Psychology
Arizona, University of (PhD)
British Columbia, University of (PhD)
California, University of, Berkeley (PhD)
Chicago, University of (PhD)
City University of New York: Graduate School and University Center (PhD)
Colorado, University of, Boulder (PhD)
Delaware, University of (PhD)
George Mason University (MA/MS—terminal, PhD)
Humboldt State University (MA/MS—terminal)
Illinois, University of, Chicago (PhD)
Johns Hopkins University (PhD)
Louisiana State University (PhD)
Maine, University of (PhD)
Miami University (Ohio) (PhD)
Michigan, University of (PhD)
Minnesota, University of (PhD)
Nebraska, University of, Omaha (MA/MS)
New Orleans, University of (PhD)
North Carolina, University of, Chapel Hill (PhD)
Pittsburgh, University of (PhD)
Purdue University (PhD)
Rutgers University—New Brunswick (PhD)
Stony Brook University (PhD)
Texas, University of, Austin (PhD)
Virginia Commonwealth University (PhD)
Virginia Polytechnic Institute and State University (PhD)
Washington State University (PhD)
Washington, University of (PhD)
Wayne State University (PhD)
Western Ontario, The University of (PhD)
Wisconsin, University of, Madison (PhD)

C

Child and Adolescent Psychology
Alabama, University of, at Birmingham (PhD)
Alfred University (EdS/MEd, PsyD)
Alliant International University: Fresno/Sacramento (PsyD)
Alliant International University: Irvine (MA/MS—terminal, PsyD)
Alliant International University: Los Angeles (MA/MS—terminal)
Alliant International University: Sacramento (MA/MS—terminal, PsyD)
Alliant International University: San Diego (MA/MS—terminal, PsyD)
Arcadia University (MA/MS—terminal)
Argosy University/Orange County (PsyD)
Boston College (PhD)
Bowling Green State University (PhD)
California, University of, Davis (MA/MS—terminal)
Central Florida, University of (PhD)
Delaware, University of (PhD)
Denver, University of (MA/MS, PhD)
DePaul University (PhD)
Detroit–Mercy, University of (MA/MS—terminal)
Florida International University (PhD)
Illinois State University (MA/MS—terminal)
Illinois, University of, Urbana–Champaign (PhD)
Indianapolis, University of (PsyD)
John F. Kennedy University (MA/MS—terminal)
Lewis University (MA/MS)
Loyola University of Chicago (PhD)
Maine, University of (PhD)
Maryland, University of (PhD)
McGill University (PhD)
Minnesota, University of (PhD)
New Orleans, University of (PhD)
Ohio State University, The (PhD)
Ohio University (PhD)
Pennsylvania State University (PhD)
Rhode Island, University of, Chafee Social Sciences Center (MA/MS—terminal, PhD)
Seattle Pacific University (PhD)
Southern Illinois University, at Carbondale (PhD)
Southern Mississippi, The University of (PhD)
State University of New York at Buffalo (MA/MS—terminal, Other)
Temple University (PhD)
Texas A&M University (PhD)
Texas, University of, Austin (PhD)
Toledo, University of (PhD)
Tulane University (PhD)
University of Human Psychology (PhD)
Utah State University (PhD)
Utah, University of (PhD)
Vanderbilt University (PhD)
Vanderbilt University, Peabody College (PhD)
Victoria, University of (PhD)

Virginia Commonwealth University (PhD)
Washington State University (PhD)
Washington, University of (PhD)
Wayne State University (MA/MS—terminal)
Wheaton College (PsyD)
Wisconsin, University of, Milwaukee (PhD)
Yeshiva University (PsyD)
York University (PhD)

Clinical Psychology

Abilene Christian University (MA/MS—terminal)
Acadia University (MA/MS—terminal)
Adelphi University (PhD)
Adler School of Professional Psychology (PsyD)
Alabama, University of (PhD)
Alabama, University of, at Birmingham (PhD)
Alaska, University of, Anchorage (MA/MS—terminal)
Alaska, University of, Fairbanks/Anchorage (PhD)
Alliant International University: Fresno/Sacramento (PhD, PsyD)
Alliant International University: San Francisco (PhD, PsyD, Respecialization Diploma)
Alliant International University: Los Angeles (PhD, PsyD)
Alliant International University: San Diego (PhD, PsyD, Respecialization Diploma)
American International College (MA/MS—terminal)
American University (PhD)
Antioch University New England (PsyD)
Antioch University, Santa Barbara (MA/MS—terminal, PsyD)
Appalachian State University (MA/MS—terminal)
Argosy University, Hawaii Campus (MA/MS—terminal, PsyD)
Argosy University/American School of Professional Psychology, Schaumburg Campus (MA/MS—terminal, PsyD)
Argosy University/Atlanta (MA/MS—terminal, PsyD)
Argosy University/Dallas Campus (MA/MS—terminal, PsyD)
Argosy University/Orange County (MA/MS—terminal)
Argosy University/Phoenix, American School of Professional Psychology (MA/MS—terminal, PsyD)
Argosy University/San Francisco Bay Area (MA/MS—terminal, PsyD)
Argosy University/Seattle (MA/MS—terminal)
Argosy University/Tampa (PsyD)
Argosy University/Twin Cities (PsyD)
Argosy University/Washington, D.C. (MA/MS—terminal, PsyD)
Arizona State University (PhD)
Arizona, University of (PhD)
Arkansas, University of (PhD)
Auburn University (PhD)
Auburn University at Montgomery (MA/MS—terminal)
Augusta State University (MA/MS—terminal)
Azusa Pacific University (MA/MS, MA/MS—terminal, PsyD)
Ball State University (MA/MS—terminal)
Barry University (MA/MS—terminal)
Baylor University (PsyD)
Benedictine University (MA/MS—terminal)
Boston University (PhD)
Brigham Young University (PhD)
British Columbia, University of (PhD)
Bryn Mawr College (PhD)
Calgary, University of (PhD)
California Institute of Integral Studies (PsyD)
California Lutheran University (MA/MS—terminal)
California State University, Dominguez Hills (MA/MS—terminal)
California State University, Fullerton (MA/MS—terminal)
California State University, Northridge (MA/MS—terminal)
California, University of, Berkeley (PhD)
California, University of, Los Angeles (PhD)
Carlos Albizu University (PhD, PsyD)
Carlos Albizu University, Miami Campus (PsyD)
Case Western Reserve University (PhD)
Catholic University of America, The (PhD)
Central Florida, University of (MA/MS—terminal, PhD)
Central Michigan University (PhD)
Chestnut Hill College (MA/MS—terminal, PsyD)
Cincinnati, University of (PhD)
Citadel, The (MA/MS—terminal)
City University of New York: Brooklyn College (MA/MS—terminal)
City University of New York: Graduate Center (PhD)
City University of New York: Graduate School and University Center (PhD)
City University of New York: John Jay College of Criminal Justice (MA/MS—terminal, PhD)
Clark University (PhD)
Cleveland State University (MA/MS—terminal)
Colorado, University of, at Colorado Springs (MA/MS—terminal, PhD)
Colorado, University of, Boulder (PhD)
Colorado, University of, Denver (MA/MS—terminal, PhD)
Concordia University (PhD)
Connecticut, University of (PhD)
Dalhousie University (PhD)
Dayton, University of (MA/MS—terminal)
Denver, University of (PhD, PsyD)
Detroit–Mercy, University of (MA/MS—terminal, PhD)
Duke University (PhD)
Duquesne University (PhD)
East Carolina University (PhD)
East Tennessee State University (PhD)
Eastern Illinois University (MA/MS—terminal)
Eastern Kentucky University (MA/MS—terminal)
Eastern Michigan University (MA/MS—terminal, PhD)
Edinboro University of Pennsylvania (MA/MS—terminal)
Emory University (PhD)
Emporia State University (MA/MS—terminal)
Fairleigh Dickinson University, Metropolitan Campus (PhD)
Fielding Graduate University (PhD, Respecialization Diploma)
Florida Institute of Technology (PsyD)
Florida State University (PhD)
Florida, University of (PhD)
Fordham University (PhD)
Forest Institute of Professional Psychology (MA/MS—terminal, PsyD)
Fort Hays State University (MA/MS—terminal)
Francis Marion University (MA/MS—terminal)
Fuller Theological Seminary (PhD, PsyD)
Gallaudet University (PhD)
George Fox University (PsyD)
George Washington University (PhD, PsyD)
Georgia Southern University (MA/MS—terminal, PsyD)
Georgia State University (PhD)
Georgia, University of (PhD)
Guelph, University of (MA/MS, PhD)
Hartford, University of (MA/MS—terminal, PsyD)
Harvard University (PhD)
Hawaii, University of, Manoa (PhD)
Hofstra University (PhD)
Houston, University of (PhD)
Idaho State University (PhD)
Illinois Institute of Technology (PhD)
Illinois State University (MA/MS—terminal)
Illinois, University of, Chicago (PhD)
Immaculata University (PsyD)
Indiana State University (PsyD)
Indiana University (PhD)
Indiana University of Pennsylvania (PsyD)
Indiana University–Purdue University Indianapolis (PhD)
Indianapolis, University of (MA/MS)
Institute for the Psychological Sciences (MA/MS—terminal)
Iowa, University of (PhD)
James Madison University (MA/MS—terminal, PsyD)
John F. Kennedy University (PsyD)
Kansas, University of (PhD)
Kent State University (PhD)
Kentucky, University of (PhD)
La Verne, University of (PsyD)
Lamar University—Beaumont (MA/MS—terminal)
Loma Linda University (PhD, PsyD)
Long Island University (MA/MS—terminal, PhD, PsyD)

Louisiana State University (PhD)
Louisiana, University of, Monroe (MA/MS)
Louisville, University of (PhD)
Loyola College (MA/MS—terminal, PsyD)
Loyola University of Chicago (PhD)
Maine, University of (PhD)
Manitoba, University of (PhD)
Marquette University (MA/MS—terminal, PhD)
Marshall University (MA/MS—terminal, PsyD)
Maryland, University of (PhD)
Maryland, University of, Baltimore County (PhD)
Marywood University (PsyD)
Massachusetts School of Professional Psychology (Respecialization Diploma)
Massachusetts, University of (PhD)
Massachusetts, University of, Boston (PhD)
Massachusetts, University of, Dartmouth (MA/MS—terminal)
McGill University (PhD)
Memphis, University of (PhD)
Miami University (Ohio) (PhD)
Michigan School of Professional Psychology (MA/MS—terminal, PsyD)
Michigan State University (PhD)
Michigan, University of (PhD)
Middle Tennessee State University (MA/MS—terminal)
Midwestern State University (MA/MS—terminal)
Midwestern University (MA/MS, PsyD)
Millersville University (MA/MS—terminal)
Minnesota, University of (PhD)
Mississippi State University (MA/MS—terminal)
Mississippi, University of (PhD)
Missouri State University (MA/MS—terminal)
Missouri, University of, Columbia (PhD)
Missouri, University of, St. Louis (PhD)
Montana, The University of (PhD)
Montreal, University of (PhD)
Morehead State University (Kentucky) (MA/MS—terminal)
Murray State University (MA/MS—terminal)
Nebraska, University of, Lincoln (PhD)
Nevada, University of, Las Vegas (PhD)
Nevada, University of, Reno (PhD)
New Brunswick, University of (PhD)
New Mexico Highlands University (MA/MS—terminal)
New Mexico, University of (PhD)
New York University (MA/MS—terminal, PhD)
North Carolina, University of, at Greensboro (PhD)
North Carolina, University of, Chapel Hill (PhD)
North Carolina, University of, Charlotte (MA/MS—terminal, PhD)
North Carolina, University of, Wilmington (MA/MS—terminal)
North Dakota State University (MA/MS—terminal)
North Dakota, University of (PhD)
North Florida, University of (MA/MS—terminal)
North Texas, University of (PhD)
Northern Illinois University (PhD)
Northern Iowa, University of (MA/MS—terminal)
Northwestern University (PhD)
Northwestern University, Feinberg School of Medicine (PhD)
Nova Southeastern University (PhD, PsyD)
Ohio State University, The (PhD)
Oklahoma State University (PhD)
Old Dominion University (PsyD)
Oregon, University of (PhD)
Ottawa, University of (PhD)
Pace University (PsyD)
Pacific Graduate School of Psychology (Other, PhD, PsyD)
Pacific Graduate School of Psychology & Stanford University School of Medicine, Department of Psychiatry and Behavioral Sciences (PsyD)
Pacific University (PsyD)
Pacific, University of the (MA/MS)
Pacifica Graduate Institute (PhD)
Penn State Harrisburg (MA/MS—terminal)
Pennsylvania State University (PhD)
Pennsylvania, University of (MA/MS—terminal, Other, PhD)
Pepperdine University (MA/MS—terminal, PsyD)
Philadelphia College of Osteopathic Medicine (MA/MS—terminal, Other, PsyD, Respecialization Diploma)
Phillips Graduate Institute (PsyD)
Pittsburg State University (MA/MS—terminal)
Pittsburgh, University of (PhD)
Puerto Rico, University of (MA/MS, PhD)
Purdue University (PhD)
Quebec at Montreal, University of (PhD)
Queen's University (MA/MS, PhD)
Radford University (MA/MS—terminal)
Regent University (PsyD)
Regina, University of (MA/MS—terminal, PhD)
Rhode Island, University of, Chafee Social Sciences Center (PhD)
Rochester, University of (PhD)
Roger Williams University (MA/MS—terminal)
Roosevelt University (MA/MS—terminal, PsyD)
Rowan University (MA/MS)
Rutgers University—New Brunswick (PhD)
Rutgers—The State University of New Jersey (PsyD)
Ryerson University (MA/MS, PhD)
Saint Francis, University of (MA/MS—terminal)
Saint Louis University (PhD)
Saint Michael's College (MA/MS—terminal)
Sam Houston State University (MA/MS—terminal, PhD)
San Diego State University/University of California, San Diego Joint Doctoral Program in Clinical Psychology (PhD)
San Francisco State University (MA/MS—terminal)
San Jose State University (MA/MS—terminal)
Saskatchewan, University of (PhD)
Seattle University (MA/MS—terminal)
Sham University (PhD)
Sherbrooke, University of (PsyD)
Simon Fraser University (PhD)
South Carolina, University of (PhD)
South Dakota, University of (PhD)
South Florida, University of (PhD)
Southern California, University of (PhD)
Southern Illinois University Edwardsville (MA/MS—terminal)
Southern Illinois University, at Carbondale (PhD)
Southern Methodist University (PhD)
Southern Mississippi, The University of (PhD)
Southern Oregon University (MA/MS)
Spalding University (PsyD)
Springfield College (EdS/MEd, MA/MS—terminal)
St. John's University (PhD)
St. Mary's University (MA/MS—terminal)
State University of New York at Buffalo (PhD)
State University of New York, Binghamton University (PhD)
State University of New York, College at Brockport (MA/MS—terminal)
State University of New York, University at Albany (PhD)
Stony Brook University (PhD)
Suffolk University (PhD, Respecialization Diploma)
Syracuse University (PhD)
Teachers College, Columbia University (MA/MS—terminal, PhD)
Temple University (PhD)
Tennessee, University of, Knoxville (PhD)
Texas A&M University (PhD)
Texas A&M University—Commerce (MA/MS—terminal)
Texas of the Permian Basin, The University of (MA/MS—terminal)
Texas Southwestern Medical Center at Dallas, University of (PhD)
Texas Tech University (PhD)
Texas, University of, Austin (PhD)
Texas, University of, El Paso (MA/MS—terminal)
Texas, University of, Pan American (MA/MS—terminal)
Texas, University of, Tyler (MA/MS—terminal)
The Chicago School of Professional Psychology (MA/MS—terminal, PsyD, Respecialization Diploma)
The New School for Social Research (PhD)
Toledo, University of (PhD)
Towson University (MA/MS—terminal)
Tulsa, University of (MA/MS—terminal, PhD)
Uniformed Services University of the Health Sciences (PhD)
Utah, University of (PhD)

Valdosta State University (MA/MS—terminal)
Vanderbilt University (PhD)
Vanderbilt University, Peabody College (PhD)
Vanguard University of Southern California (MA/MS—terminal)
Vermont, University of (PhD)
Victoria, University of (PhD)
Virginia Consortium Program in Clinical Psychology (PsyD)
Virginia Polytechnic Institute and State University (PhD)
Virginia State University (MA/MS—terminal)
Virginia, University of (PhD)
Walden University (PhD)
Washburn University (MA/MS—terminal)
Washington University in St. Louis (PhD)
Washington, University of (PhD)
Waterloo, University of (PhD)
West Chester University of Pennsylvania (MA/MS—terminal)
West Virginia University (MA/MS—terminal, PhD)
Western Carolina University (MA/MS—terminal)
Western Illinois University (MA/MS—terminal)
Western Kentucky University (MA/MS—terminal)
Western Michigan University (PhD)
Western Ontario, The University of (PhD)
Wheaton College (MA/MS—terminal, PsyD)
Wichita State University (PhD)
William Paterson University (MA/MS—terminal)
Windsor, University of (PhD)
Wisconsin School of Professional Psychology (PsyD)
Wisconsin, University of, Madison (PhD)
Wisconsin, University of, Milwaukee (PhD)
Wright Institute (PsyD)
Wright State University (PsyD)
Wyoming, University of (PhD)
Xavier University (PsyD)
Yale University (PhD)
York University (PhD)

Cognitive Psychology

Alabama, University of (PhD)
Arizona State University (PhD)
Arizona, University of (PhD)
Armandos School of hard knocks (PhD)
Auburn University (PhD)
Ball State University (MA/MS—terminal)
Boston College (PhD)
Bowling Green State University (PhD)
Brandeis University (PhD)
British Columbia, University of (PhD)
Brown University (PhD)
California, University of, Berkeley (PhD)
California, University of, Davis (PhD)
California, University of, Irvine (PhD)
California, University of, Los Angeles (PhD)
California, University of, Riverside (PhD)
California, University of, Santa Cruz (PhD)
Carleton University (MA/MS)
Carnegie Mellon University (PhD)
Catholic University of America, The (MA/MS—terminal, PhD)
Chicago, University of (PhD)
City University of New York: Brooklyn College (PhD)
City University of New York: Graduate School and University Center (PhD)
Claremont Graduate University (MA/MS—terminal, PhD)
Clemson University (PhD)
Colorado State University (PhD)
Colorado, University of, Boulder (PhD)
Columbia University (EdS/MEd, PhD)
Connecticut, University of (PhD)
Cornell University (PhD)
Dayton, University of (MA/MS—terminal)
Delaware, University of (PhD)
Denver, University of (PhD)
DePaul University (PhD)
Duke University (PhD)
Emory University (PhD)
Florida State University (PhD)
Florida, University of (PhD)
Georgia Institute of Technology (PhD)
Georgia State University (PhD)
Georgia, University of (PhD)
Guelph, University of (MA/MS, PhD)
Harvard University (PhD)
Hawaii, University of, Manoa (PhD)
Houston, University of (PhD)
Illinois State University (MA/MS—terminal)
Illinois, University of, Chicago (PhD)
Illinois, University of, Urbana–Champaign (PhD)
Indiana University (PhD)
Iowa State University (PhD)
Iowa, University of (PhD)
Johns Hopkins University (PhD)
Kansas State University (PhD)
Kansas, University of (PhD)
Lehigh University (PhD)
Louisiana State University (PhD)
Manitoba, University of (PhD)
Maryland, University of (PhD)
Massachusetts, University of (PhD)
Miami University (Ohio) (PhD)
Michigan State University (PhD)
Michigan, University of (PhD)
Minnesota, University of (PhD)
Mississippi State University (PhD)
Missouri, University of, Columbia (PhD)
Montana State University (MA/MS)
Montreal, University of (PhD)
Nebraska, University of, Lincoln (PhD)
Nebraska, University of, Omaha (MA/MS)
Nevada, University of, Las Vegas (PhD)
New Hampshire, University of (PhD)
New Mexico State University (MA/MS—terminal, PhD)
New Mexico, University of (PhD)
New York University, Graduate School of Arts and Science (PhD)
North Carolina, University of, at Greensboro (PhD)
North Carolina, University of, Chapel Hill (PhD)
Northeastern University (PhD)
Northern Illinois University (PhD)
Northwestern University (PhD)
Notre Dame, University of (PhD)
Ohio State University, The (PhD)
Ohio University (PhD)
Oregon, University of (PhD)
Pennsylvania State University (PhD)
Pittsburgh, University of (PhD)
Purdue University (PhD)
Quebec at Montreal, University of (PhD)
Rice University (PhD)
Rutgers University—New Brunswick (PhD)
Rutgers University—Newark Campus (PhD)
Saint Louis University (PhD)
Saskatchewan, University of (PhD)
South Florida, University of (PhD)
Southern California, University of (PhD)
Southern Illinois University, at Carbondale (PhD)
Stanford University (PhD)
State University of New York at Buffalo (PhD)
State University of New York, Binghamton University (PhD)
State University of New York, University at Albany (PhD)
Stony Brook University (PhD)
Syracuse University (PhD)
Temple University (PhD)
Tennessee, University of, Knoxville (PhD)
Texas A&M University (PhD)
Texas A&M University—Commerce (MA/MS—terminal, PhD)
Texas Tech University (PhD)
Toledo, University of (PhD)
Toronto, University of (MA/MS, PhD)
Utah, University of (PhD)
Vanderbilt University (PhD)
Vanderbilt University, Peabody College (PhD)
Victoria, University of (PhD)
Virginia, University of (PhD)
Washington State University (PhD)
Washington University in St. Louis (PhD)
Washington, University of (Other, PhD)
Waterloo, University of (PhD)
Western Ontario, The University of (PhD)
Wilfrid Laurier University (MA/MS—terminal, PhD)
Wisconsin, University of, Madison (PhD)
Yale University (PhD)
Yeshiva University (PsyD)
York University (PhD)

Community Psychology

Alaska, University of, Fairbanks/Anchorage (PhD)
Arizona State University (MA/MS—terminal)
Boston College (PhD)
California, University of, Berkeley (PhD)
Central Connecticut State University (MA/MS—terminal)
DePaul University (PhD)

East Central University (MA/MS—terminal)
Fayetteville State University (MA/MS—terminal)
George Mason University (PhD)
George Washington University (PhD)
Georgia State University (PhD)
Hawaii, University of, Manoa (PhD)
Illinois, University of, Chicago (PhD)
Illinois, University of, Urbana–Champaign (PhD)
La Verne, University of (PsyD)
Lamar University—Beaumont (MA/MS—terminal)
Maryland, University of, Baltimore County (PhD)
Marywood University (MA/MS—terminal)
Massachusetts School of Professional Psychology (MA/MS—terminal)
Massachusetts, University of, Lowell (MA/MS—terminal)
Metropolitan State University (MA/MS—terminal)
Michigan State University (PhD)
New Haven, University of (MA/MS)
New York University (PhD)
North Carolina State University (PhD)
North Carolina, University of, Charlotte (MA/MS—terminal)
Oklahoma, University of (Other)
Portland State University (PhD)
Quebec at Montreal, University of (PhD)
Rutgers—The State University of New Jersey, Graduate School of Applied and Professional Psychology (PsyD)
Sage Colleges, The (MA/MS—terminal)
Sonoma State University (MA/MS—terminal)
South Carolina, University of (PhD)
Southern Mississippi, The University of (MA/MS—terminal)
State University of New York at Buffalo (MA/MS—terminal)
Temple University (MA/MS—terminal)
Texas A&M International University (MA/MS—terminal)
Vanderbilt University, Peabody College (PhD)
Virginia, University of (PhD)
West Virginia University (MA/MS—terminal)
Western Illinois University (MA/MS—terminal)
Wichita State University (PhD)
Wilfrid Laurier University (MA/MS—terminal, PhD)

Comparative Psychology

California, University of, Davis (PhD)
Oklahoma, University of (PhD)
York University (PhD)

Consulting Psychology

Alliant International University: San Diego (PhD)
Alliant International University: San Francisco (PhD)
Fairleigh Dickinson University, Madison (MA/MS—terminal)
Massachusetts School of Professional Psychology (MA/MS—terminal)
New Haven, University of (MA/MS—terminal)
Northern Colorado, University of (PhD)
Wayne State University (MA/MS—terminal, PhD)

Counseling Psychology

Abilene Christian University (MA/MS—terminal)
Adelphi University (MA/MS—terminal)
Adler School of Professional Psychology (MA/MS—terminal)
Akron, University of (PhD)
Alaska Pacific University (MA/MS—terminal)
Angelo State University (MA/MS—terminal)
Arcadia University (MA/MS—terminal)
Argosy University, Hawaii Campus (MA/MS—terminal)
Argosy University/Orange County (EdD, MA/MS—terminal)
Argosy University/Phoenix, American School of Professional Psychology (MA/MS—terminal)
Argosy University/Seattle (MA/MS—terminal)
Argosy University/Twin Cities (MA/MS—terminal)
Argosy University/Washington, DC (EdD, MA/MS—terminal)
Arizona State University (PhD)
Assumption College (MA/MS—terminal)
Auburn University (PhD)
Auburn University at Montgomery (MA/MS—terminal)
Avila University (MA/MS—terminal)
Ball State University (MA/MS—terminal, PhD)
Baltimore, University of (MA/MS—terminal)
Boston College (MA/MS—terminal, PhD)
Brigham Young University (PhD)
California Lutheran University (MA/MS—terminal)
California Polytechnic State University (MA/MS—terminal)
California State University, Bakersfield (MA/MS—terminal)
California State University, Chico (MA/MS—terminal)
California State University, Sacramento (MA/MS—terminal)
Carlos Albizu University, Miami Campus (MA/MS—terminal)
Central Arkansas, University of (MA/MS—terminal)
Central Oklahoma, University of (MA/MS—terminal)
Central Washington University (MA/MS—terminal, Other)
Chestnut Hill College (MA/MS—terminal)
Citadel, The (MA/MS—terminal)
City University of New York: Brooklyn College (MA/MS—terminal)
City University of New York: John Jay College of Criminal Justice (MA/MS)
Colorado State University (PhD)
Denver, University of (MA/MS—terminal, PhD)
Fairleigh Dickinson University, Madison (MA/MS—terminal)
Florida International University (MA/MS—terminal)
Florida State University (MA/MS—terminal, PhD)
Florida, University of (PhD)
Fordham University (PhD)
Forest Institute of Professional Psychology (MA/MS—terminal)
Francis Marion University (MA/MS—terminal)
Frostburg State University (MA/MS—terminal)
Georgia, University of (PhD)
Georgian Court University (MA/MS—terminal)
Goddard College (MA/MS—terminal)
Houston Baptist University (MA/MS—terminal)
Houston, University of (Other, PhD)
Humboldt State University (MA/MS—terminal)
Illinois State University (MA/MS—terminal)
Illinois, University of, Urbana–Champaign (PhD)
Immaculata University (MA/MS, MA/MS—terminal)
Indiana State University (MA/MS—terminal, PhD)
Indiana University (PhD)
Indianapolis, University of (MA/MS)
Iowa State University (PhD)
Iowa, University of (PhD)
James Madison University (EdS/MEd, Other)
John F. Kennedy University (MA/MS—terminal)
Kansas, University of (MA/MS—terminal, PhD)
Kentucky, University of (MA/MS, PhD)
La Verne, University of (MA/MS—terminal)
LaSalle University (Other)
Lehigh University (Other, PhD)
Lesley University (MA/MS, MA/MS—terminal, Other, Respecialization Diploma)
Lewis & Clark College, Graduate School of Education and Counseling (EdS/MEd, MA/MS—terminal)
Lewis University (MA/MS)
Louisiana State University in Shreveport (MA/MS—terminal)
Louisiana Tech University (MA/MS—terminal, PhD)
Louisiana, University of, Lafayette (MA/MS—terminal)
Loyola College (MA/MS—terminal)
Loyola University of Chicago (PhD)
Marist College (MA/MS)
Marquette University (MA/MS—terminal)

Maryland, University of (PhD)
Marywood University (MA/MS—terminal)
McGill University (PhD)
Memphis, University of (PhD)
Miami, University of (PhD)
Midwestern State University (MA/MS—terminal)
Millersville University (MA/MS—terminal, Other)
Minnesota, University of (MA/MS—terminal, PhD)
Missouri, University of, Columbia (EdS/MEd, MA/MS—terminal, PhD)
Missouri, University of, Kansas City (PhD)
Morehead State University (Kentucky) (MA/MS—terminal)
Mount St. Mary's College (MA/MS—terminal)
Nebraska, University of, Lincoln (PhD)
New York University (MA/MS—terminal, PhD)
North Dakota, University of (PhD)
North Florida, University of (MA/MS—terminal)
North Texas, University of (PhD)
Northeastern University (MA/MS—terminal, PhD)
Northern Arizona University (PhD)
Northern Colorado, University of (MA/MS—terminal, PsyD)
Notre Dame, University of (PhD)
Nova Southeastern University (MA/MS—terminal)
Ohio State University, The (PhD)
Oklahoma State University (PhD)
Oklahoma, University of (Other, PhD)
Oregon, University of (PhD)
Our Lady of the Lake University (MA/MS—terminal)
Pennsylvania State University (PhD)
Pennsylvania, University of (MA/MS, MA/MS—terminal, Other)
Puget Sound, University of (Other)
Radford University (PsyD)
Roosevelt University (MA/MS—terminal)
Rowan University (MA/MS)
Rutgers—The State University of New Jersey, New Brunswick (EdD, Other)
Sage Colleges, The (MA/MS—terminal, Other)
Saint Francis, University of (MA/MS, MA/MS—terminal, Other)
Saint Mary's University of Minnesota (MA/MS—terminal)
Santa Clara University (MA/MS, MA/MS—terminal)
Seton Hall University (MA/MS—terminal, PhD)
Sonoma State University (MA/MS—terminal)
Southern Illinois University, at Carbondale (PhD)
Southern Mississippi, The University of (PhD)
Southern Oregon University (MA/MS)
St. Cloud State University (MA/MS—terminal)
St. Thomas, University of (MA/MS—terminal, PsyD)
State University of New York at Buffalo (MA/MS—terminal, Other, PhD)
State University of New York at New Paltz (MA/MS—terminal)
State University of New York, University of Albany (MA/MS, PhD)
Teachers College, Columbia University (Other, PhD)
Temple University (MA/MS—terminal)
Tennessee, University of, Knoxville (PhD)
Texas A&M International University (MA/MS—terminal)
Texas A&M University (PhD)
Texas A&M University—Kingsville (MA/MS—terminal)
Texas Tech University (PhD)
Texas, University of, Austin (PhD)
Texas, University of, Tyler (MA/MS—terminal)
Towson University (MA/MS—terminal)
Utah, University of (MA/MS—terminal, PhD)
Valparaiso University (MA/MS—terminal)
Virginia, University of (PhD)
Walden University (PhD)
Walla Walla University (MA/MS—terminal)
Washington State University (Other, PhD)
West Florida, The University of (MA/MS—terminal)
West Virginia University (PhD)
Western Michigan University (MA/MS—terminal, PhD)
Wheaton College (MA/MS—terminal)
William Paterson University (MA/MS—terminal)
Wisconsin, University of, Madison (MA/MS—terminal, PhD)
Wisconsin, University of, Milwaukee (PhD)
Wisconsin, University of, Stout (MA/MS)
Yeshiva University (MA/MS—terminal)

D

Developmental Psychology

Alabama, University of (PhD)
Alabama, University of, at Birmingham (PhD)
American International College (EdD)
Arizona State University (PhD)
Ball State University (MA/MS—terminal, PhD)
Boston College (MA/MS—terminal, PhD)
Boston University (PhD)
Bowling Green State University (PhD)
Brandeis University (MA/MS—terminal, PhD)
British Columbia, University of (PhD)
Bryn Mawr College (PhD)
California State University, Northridge (MA/MS—terminal)
California, University of (PhD)
California, University of, Berkeley (PhD)
California, University of, Davis (PhD)
California, University of, Los Angeles (PhD)
California, University of, Riverside (PhD)
California, University of, Santa Cruz (PhD)
Carnegie Mellon University (PhD)
Catholic University of America, The (PhD)
Chicago, University of (PhD)
City University of New York: Graduate School and University Center (PhD)
Claremont Graduate University (MA/MS—terminal, PhD)
Clark University (PhD)
Cleveland State University (PhD)
Connecticut, University of (PhD)
Denver, University of (PhD)
DePaul University (PhD)
Duke University (PhD)
Duquesne University (PhD)
Florida International University (PhD)
Florida State University (PhD)
Florida, University of (PhD)
Fordham University (PhD)
George Mason University (MA/MS—terminal, PhD)
Georgia State University (PhD)
Georgia, University of (PhD)
Guelph, University of (MA/MS, PhD)
Harvard University (PhD)
Hawaii, University of, Manoa (PhD)
Illinois State University (MA/MS—terminal)
Illinois, University of, Urbana–Champaign (PhD)
Indiana University (PhD)
Iowa, University of (PhD)
Johns Hopkins University (PhD)
Kansas, University of (PhD)
Lesley University (Other)
Louisiana State University (PhD)
Loyola University of Chicago (PhD)
Manitoba, University of (PhD)
Maryland, University of (PhD)
Maryland, University of, Baltimore County (PhD)
Massachusetts, University of (PhD)
Miami, University of (PhD)
Michigan, University of (PhD)
Millersville University (MA/MS, Other)
Minnesota, University of (PhD)
Missouri, University of, Columbia (PhD)
Nebraska, University of, Lincoln (PhD)
Nebraska, University of, Omaha (MA/MS, MA/MS—terminal, PhD)
New Hampshire, University of (PhD)
New Mexico, University of (PhD)
New York University (PhD)
North Carolina State University (PhD)
North Carolina, University of, at Greensboro (PhD)
North Carolina, University of, Chapel Hill (PhD)
North Florida, University of (MA/MS—terminal)
Northern Illinois University (PhD)
Northwestern University (PhD)
Notre Dame, University of (PhD)
Ohio State University, The (PhD)
Oklahoma State University (PhD)

Old Dominion University (PhD)
Oregon, University of (PhD)
Pennsylvania State University (PhD)
Pennsylvania, University of (MA/MS, PhD)
Pittsburgh, University of (PhD)
Portland State University (PhD)
Purdue University (PhD)
Quebec at Montreal, University of (PhD)
Queen's University (MA/MS, PhD)
Rochester, University of (PhD)
Rutgers University—New Brunswick (PhD)
Saint Louis University (PhD)
San Francisco State University (MA/MS—terminal)
Southern California, University of (PhD)
Stanford University (PhD)
Temple University (PhD)
Texas A&M University (PhD)
Texas of the Permian Basin, The University of (MA/MS—terminal)
Texas, University of, Austin (PhD)
The New School for Social Research (PhD)
Toronto, University of (MA/MS, PhD)
Tulane University (PhD)
Utah, University of (PhD)
Vanderbilt University (PhD)
Vanderbilt University, Peabody College (PhD)
Victoria, University of (PhD)
Virginia Commonwealth University (PhD)
Virginia Polytechnic Institute and State University (PhD)
Virginia, University of (PhD)
Washington University in St. Louis (PhD)
Washington, University of (PhD)
Waterloo, University of (MA/MS—terminal, PhD)
Wayne State University (MA/MS—terminal, PhD)
West Virginia University (PhD)
Western Michigan University (MA/MS—terminal)
Western Ontario, The University of (PhD)
Wilfrid Laurier University (MA/MS—terminal, PhD)
Wisconsin, University of, Madison (PhD)
Wisconsin, University of, Milwaukee (MA/MS—terminal)
Wyoming, University of (PhD)
Yale University (PhD)
York University (PhD)

E

Educational Psychology

Alliant International University: Irvine (MA/MS—terminal), PsyD)
Alliant International University: Los Angeles (MA/MS—terminal, PsyD)
Alliant International University: San Diego (MA/MS—terminal, PsyD)
Alliant International University: San Francisco (MA/MS—terminal, PsyD)
American International College (EdD, MA/MS)
Arizona State University (Other)
Ball State University (MA/MS—terminal, PhD)
City University of New York: Graduate School and University Center (PhD)
Colorado, University of, Boulder (MA/MS—terminal, PhD)
East Carolina University (MA/MS—terminal)
Fordham University (PhD)
Hawaii, University of (Other, PhD)
Houston, University of (Other, PhD)
Illinois, University of, Urbana–Champaign (PhD)
Indiana University (MA/MS, PhD)
Iowa, University of (PhD)
Kansas, University of (EdS/MEd, MA/MS—terminal, Other, PhD)
Kean University (MA/MS)
Kentucky, University of (MA/MS—terminal, PhD)
Louisiana Tech University (MA/MS—terminal)
Maryland, University of (PhD)
McGill University (PhD)
Michigan, University of (PhD)
Mississippi State University (PhD)
Missouri, University of, Columbia (EdS/MEd, MA/MS—terminal, PhD)
New York University (MA/MS—terminal)
Northern Arizona University (PhD)
Northern Colorado, University of (MA/MS—terminal, PhD)
Oklahoma State University (PhD)
Oklahoma, University of (Other, PhD)
Pennsylvania State University (PhD)
Quebec at Montreal, University of (PhD)
Rutgers—The State University of New Jersey, New Brunswick (EdD, Other, PhD)
State University of New York at Buffalo (MA/MS—terminal, PhD)
State University of New York, University of Albany (MA/MS, PhD)
Temple University (MA/MS—terminal, PhD)
Tennessee, University of, Knoxville (PhD)
Texas A&M International University (MA/MS—terminal)
Texas A&M University—Commerce (PhD)
Texas Tech University (PhD)
Texas, University of, Austin (MA/MS—terminal, Other, PhD)
Utah, University of (EdS/MEd, MA/MS—terminal, Other)
Virginia State University (MA/MS—terminal)
Walden University (PhD)
Washington State University (Other, PhD)
Wayne State University (PhD)
Wisconsin, University of, Madison (PhD)

Environmental Psychology

City University of New York: Graduate School and University Center (PhD)
Humboldt State University (MA/MS—terminal)
New York University (PhD)

Experimental Psychology (Applied)

Akron, University of (MA/MS)
Auburn University (MA/MS—terminal)
Avila University (MA/MS—terminal)
Calgary, University of (PhD)
California State University, Long Beach (MA/MS—terminal)
Catholic University of America, The (MA/MS—terminal, PhD)
Central Florida, University of (PhD)
Central Michigan University (PhD)
Central Washington University (MA/MS—terminal)
Cincinnati, University of (PhD)
City University of New York: John Jay College of Criminal Justice (PhD)
Clemson University (PhD)
Cleveland State University (MA/MS—terminal)
Embry-Riddle Aeronautical University (MA/MS—terminal)
Florida International University (PhD)
Florida, University of (PhD)
Fort Hays State University (MA/MS—terminal)
Georgia Institute of Technology (MA/MS—terminal, PhD)
Idaho, University of (MA/MS—terminal)
Kansas State University (PhD)
Memphis, University of (PhD)
Mississippi State University (MA/MS—terminal)
Missouri State University (MA/MS—terminal)
New Brunswick, University of (PhD)
New Mexico State University (MA/MS—terminal, PhD)
North Carolina, University of, Wilmington (MA/MS—terminal)
North Texas, University of (PhD)
Regina, University of (MA/MS—terminal, PhD)
Rice University (PhD)
Ryerson University (MA/MS, PhD)
Southeastern Louisiana University (MA/MS—terminal)
State University of New York, University at Albany (PhD)
Tennessee, University of, Chattanooga (MA/MS—terminal)
Texas, University of, Arlington (PhD)
Washington College (MA/MS—terminal)
Wichita State University (PhD)
Wyoming, University of (PhD)

Experimental Psychology (General)

Alabama, University of, at Huntsville (MA/MS—terminal)
Alberta, University of (MA/MS, PhD)
American University (MA/MS—terminal)
Appalachian State University (MA/MS—terminal)
Arkansas, University of (PhD)
Augusta State University (MA/MS—terminal)
Brown University (PhD)
Bucknell University (MA/MS—terminal)
Calgary, University of (PhD)

California State University, Bakersfield (MA/MS—terminal)
California State University, Fullerton (MA/MS—terminal)
California State University, Northridge (MA/MS)
California State University, San Marcos (MA/MS—terminal)
California, University of, Irvine (PhD)
California, University of, San Diego (PhD)
California, University of, Santa Barbara (PhD)
Carnegie Mellon University (PhD)
Case Western Reserve University (PhD)
Central Connecticut State University (MA/MS—terminal)
Central Michigan University (MA/MS, MA/MS—terminal)
Central Oklahoma, University of (MA/MS)
Central Washington University (MA/MS—terminal)
Chicago, University of (PhD)
Cincinnati, University of (PhD)
City University of New York: Brooklyn College (MA/MS—terminal)
College of William and Mary (MA/MS—terminal)
Colorado, University of, at Colorado Springs (MA/MS—terminal)
Dalhousie University (MA/MS, PhD)
Eastern Kentucky University (MA/MS—terminal)
Eastern Michigan University (MA/MS—terminal)
Embry-Riddle Aeronautical University (MA/MS—terminal)
Emporia State University (MA/MS—terminal)
Fayetteville State University (MA/MS—terminal)
Florida Atlantic University (MA/MS—terminal, PhD)
Fort Hays State University (MA/MS—terminal)
Georgia Institute of Technology (PhD)
Georgia Southern University (MA/MS—terminal)
Hartford, University of (MA/MS—terminal)
Harvard University (PhD)
Idaho State University (MA/MS—terminal)
Idaho, University of (MA/MS—terminal)
Indiana State University (MA/MS—terminal)
Iona College (MA/MS—terminal)
Jacksonville State University (MA/MS—terminal)
Kent State University (PhD)
Kentucky, University of (PhD)
Loma Linda University (MA/MS—terminal, PhD)
Long Island University (MA/MS—terminal)
Louisiana, University of, Lafayette (MA/MS—terminal)
Louisiana, University of, Monroe (MA/MS—terminal)
Louisville, University of (PhD)
Maine, University of (MA/MS)
Marietta College (MA/MS—terminal)
Marist College (MA/MS—terminal)
Massachusetts, University of, Dartmouth (MA/MS—terminal)
McGill University (PhD)
Middle Tennessee State University (MA/MS—terminal)
Mississippi State University (MA/MS—terminal)
Mississippi, University of (PhD)
Missouri State University (MA/MS—terminal)
Montana, The University of (PhD)
Montreal, University of (PhD)
Morehead State University (Kentucky) (MA/MS—terminal)
Murray State University (MA/MS—terminal)
Nebraska, University of, Lincoln (PhD)
Nevada, University of, Reno (PhD)
New Hampshire, University of (PhD)
New York University, Graduate School of Arts and Science (PhD)
North Carolina, University of, Wilmington (MA/MS—terminal)
North Dakota, University of (PhD)
Northern Michigan University (MA/MS)
Old Dominion University (MA/MS—terminal)
Ottawa, University of (PhD)
Queen's University (MA/MS, PhD)
Radford University (MA/MS—terminal)
Regina, University of (PhD)
Rutgers University—New Brunswick (PhD)
Ryerson University (MA/MS, PhD)
Saint Joseph's University (MA/MS—terminal)
Saint Louis University (PhD)
Sam Houston State University (MA/MS—terminal)
San Jose State University (MA/MS—terminal)
Seton Hall University (MA/MS—terminal)
Sham University (MA/MS)
Shippensburg University (MA/MS—terminal)
Simon Fraser University (PhD)
South Alabama, University of (MA/MS—terminal)
South Carolina, University of (PhD)
Southeastern Louisiana University (MA/MS—terminal)
Southern Connecticut State University (MA/MS—terminal)
Southern Mississippi, The University of (PhD)
St. John's University (MA/MS—terminal)
State University of New York at New Paltz (MA/MS—terminal)
Stony Brook University (PhD)
Syracuse University (PhD)
Tennessee, University of, Knoxville (MA/MS—terminal, PhD)
Texas A&M University—Commerce (MA/MS—terminal)
Texas Tech University (PhD)
Texas, University of, Arlington (PhD)
Texas, University of, Austin (PhD)
Texas, University of, Pan American (MA/MS—terminal)
Towson University (MA/MS—terminal)
Tufts University (PhD)
Utah State University (PhD)
Utah, University of (PhD)
Vermont, University of (PhD)
Victoria, University of (PhD)
Villanova University (MA/MS—terminal)
Wake Forest University (MA/MS—terminal)
Walden University (PhD)
Washington College (MA/MS—terminal)
West Chester University of Pennsylvania (MA/MS—terminal)
West Florida, The University of (MA/MS—terminal)
Western Carolina University (MA/MS—terminal)
Western Illinois University (MA/MS—terminal)
Western Kentucky University (MA/MS—terminal)
Wisconsin, University of, Madison (PhD)
Wisconsin, University of, Oshkosh (MA/MS—terminal)
Wyoming, University of (PhD)
Xavier University (MA/MS—terminal)

F

Family Psychology

Alliant International University: Irvine (MA/MS—terminal), PsyD)
Alliant International University: Los Angeles (MA/MS—terminal)
Alliant International University: Sacramento (MA/MS—terminal, PsyD)
Alliant International University: San Diego (MA/MS—terminal, PhD, PsyD)
Antioch University, Santa Barbara (PsyD)
Argosy University/Orange County (EdD, MA/MS—terminal)
Argosy University/Twin Cities (MA/MS—terminal)
Arizona State University (MA/MS—terminal, PhD)
Azusa Pacific University (MA/MS, PsyD)
California, University of, Riverside (PhD)
Fuller Theological Seminary (PhD, PsyD)
James Madison University (Other)
Lewis & Clark College, Graduate School of Education and Counseling (MA/MS—terminal)
North Carolina State University (PhD)
Northern Colorado, University of (MA/MS)
Old Dominion University (PsyD)
Pepperdine University (MA/MS—terminal)
Portland State University (PhD)
Springfield College (EdS/MEd)
Texas Woman's University (PhD)
Texas, University of, Tyler (MA/MS—terminal)
Vanguard University of Southern California (MA/MS—terminal)
Wayne State University (PhD)
Wheaton College (MA/MS—terminal)

Forensic Psychology
Alliant International University: Fresno (PhD, PsyD)
Alliant International University: Los Angeles (PsyD)
Alliant International University: Sacramento (PsyD)
American International College (MA/MS—terminal)
Argosy University/Orange County (MA/MS—terminal, PsyD)
Argosy University/Phoenix, American School of Professional Psychology (MA/MS—terminal)
Argosy University/Washington, DC (MA/MS—terminal)
Arizona, University of (PhD)
Baltimore, University of (MA/MS—terminal)
British Columbia, University of (PhD)
Carleton University (MA/MS—terminal, PhD)
City University of New York: John Jay College of Criminal Justice (MA/MS, MA/MS—terminal, PhD)
Denver, University of (MA/MS—terminal)
Drexel University (PhD)
Fairleigh Dickinson University, Metropolitan Campus (MA/MS—terminal)
Marymount University (MA/MS—terminal)
Massachusetts School of Professional Psychology (PsyD)
Missouri State University (MA/MS—terminal)
Roger Williams University (MA/MS—terminal)
Sage Colleges, The (Other)
Saskatchewan, University of (MA/MS—terminal, PhD)
The Chicago School of Professional Psychology (MA/MS—terminal)
Valparaiso University (MA/MS)
Washburn University (MA/MS—terminal)
Widener University (Other)
Wisconsin School of Professional Psychology (PsyD

G

Gender Psychology
Alliant International University: Irvine (PsyD)
Goddard College (MA/MS—terminal)
Hawaii, University of, Manoa (PhD)
Texas Woman's University (PhD)

General Psychology (Theory, History, and Philosophy)
Adelphi University (MA/MS—terminal)
Alliant International University: Fresno/Sacramento (PhD, PsyD)
Angelo State University (MA/MS—terminal)
Arizona, University of (PhD)
Boston University (MA/MS—terminal, PhD)
Brigham Young University (MA/MS—terminal)
California State University, Bakersfield (MA/MS—terminal)
California State University, Long Beach (MA/MS—terminal)
California State University, Sacramento (MA/MS—terminal)
Carlos Albizu University (PhD, PsyD)
Central Oklahoma, University of (MA/MS—terminal)
Connecticut College (MA/MS—terminal)
DePaul University (MA/MS—terminal)
Drexel University (MA/MS—terminal)
Fairleigh Dickinson University, Metropolitan Campus (MA/MS—terminal)
Goddard College (MA/MS—terminal)
Governors State University (MA/MS—terminal)
Indiana University–Purdue University Indianapolis (PhD)
Long Island University (MA/MS—terminal)
Marist College (MA/MS—terminal)
Marshall University (MA/MS—terminal)
Marywood University (MA/MS—terminal)
Memphis, University of (MA/MS—terminal)
New Mexico Highlands University (MA/MS—terminal)
New York University, Graduate School of Arts and Science (MA/MS—terminal)
North Florida, University of (MA/MS—terminal)
Pace University (MA/MS—terminal)
Pacific Graduate School of Psychology (MA/MS—terminal)
Pennsylvania, University of (PhD)
Pittsburg State University (MA/MS—terminal)
Purdue University (PhD)
Rhode Island College (MA/MS—terminal)
Sam Houston State University (MA/MS—terminal)
Sham University (MA/MS)
Southern Connecticut State University (MA/MS—terminal)
State University of New York at Buffalo (MA/MS—terminal)
State University of New York at New Paltz (MA/MS—terminal)
Stephen F. Austin State University (MA/MS—terminal)
Texas, University of, El Paso (MA/MS—terminal, PhD)
The New School for Social Research (MA/MS—terminal)
Walden University (MA/MS—terminal)
Wesleyan University (MA/MS—terminal)
West Chester University of Pennsylvania (MA/MS—terminal)
West Florida, The University of (MA/MS—terminal)
West Texas A & M University (MA/MS—terminal)
Yeshiva University (MA/MS—terminal)

Geropsychology
Akron, University of (PhD)
Cleveland State University (PhD)
Colorado, University of, at Colorado Springs (PhD)
North Carolina State University (PhD)
Sham University (PhD)
West Virginia University (PhD)
Yeshiva University (PsyD)

H

Health Psychology
Alabama, University of, at Birmingham (PhD)
Alliant International University: Los Angeles (PsyD)
Appalachian State University (MA/MS—terminal)
British Columbia, University of (PhD)
California, University of (PhD)
California, University of, Irvine (PhD)
California, University of, Los Angeles (PhD)
California, University of, Riverside (PhD)
Carleton University (MA/MS—terminal, PhD)
Carnegie Mellon University (PhD)
Central Connecticut State University (MA/MS)
Cincinnati, University of (PhD)
City University of New York: Graduate School and University Center (PhD)
Claremont Graduate University (MA/MS—terminal)
Clemson University (PhD)
Colorado, University of, Boulder (PhD)
Colorado, University of, Denver (PhD)
Connecticut, University of (PhD)
Cornell University (PhD)
Denver, University of (PhD)
Drexel University (PhD)
Duke University (PhD)
George Fox University (PsyD)
George Washington University (PhD)
Guelph, University of (MA/MS, PhD)
Houston, University of (PhD)
Indianapolis, University of (PsyD)
Iowa, University of (PhD)
Kansas State University (Other)
Kansas, University of (PhD)
Kent State University (PhD)
Kentucky, University of (PhD)
Marquette University (PhD)
Massachusetts School of Professional Psychology (PsyD)
Midwestern University (PsyD)
Missouri, University of, Kansas City (PhD)
New Mexico State University (PhD)
New Mexico, University of (PhD)
North Carolina State University (PhD)
North Carolina, University of, Charlotte (PhD)
North Dakota State University (PhD)
North Texas, University of (PhD)
Northern Arizona University (MA/MS—terminal)

Ohio State University, The (PhD)
Ohio University (PhD)
Old Dominion University (PhD)
Our Lady of the Lake University (PsyD)
Pittsburgh, University of (PhD)
Rhode Island, University of, Chafee Social Sciences Center (PhD)
Rosalind Franklin University of Medicine and Science (PhD)
Rutgers University—New Brunswick (PhD)
Seattle Pacific University (PhD)
Southern California, University of, Keck School of Medicine (PhD)
Stony Brook University (PhD)
Syracuse University (PhD)
Texas State University-San Marcos (MA/MS—terminal)
Texas, University of, Arlington (PhD)
Texas, University of, El Paso (PhD)
The New School for Social Research (MA/MS—terminal)
Uniformed Services University of the Health Sciences (PhD)
Utah, University of (PhD)
Virginia Commonwealth University (PhD)
Walden University (PhD)
Wayne State University (PhD)
Wisconsin, University of, Milwaukee (MA/MS—terminal, PhD)
Wisconsin, University of, Stout (MA/MS—terminal)
Yeshiva University (PhD)

I

Industrial/Organizational Psychology

Akron, University of (MA/MS—terminal), MA/MS—terminal, PhD)
Alliant International University: Fresno/Sacramento (MA/MS—terminal, PsyD)
Alliant International University: Los Angeles (MA/MS—terminal, PhD, Respecialization Diploma)
Alliant International University: San Diego (MA/MS—terminal, PhD, Respecialization Diploma)
Alliant International University: San Francisco (MA/MS—terminal, PhD, Respecialization Diploma)
Angelo State University (MA/MS—terminal)
Appalachian State University (MA/MS—terminal)
Arizona State University (MA/MS—terminal)
Auburn University (PhD)
Austin Peay State University (MA/MS—terminal)
Baltimore, University of (MA/MS—terminal)
Bowling Green State University (PhD)
California State University, Long Beach (MA/MS—terminal)
California State University, Sacramento (MA/MS—terminal
Carlos Albizu University, Miami Campus (MA/MS—terminal)
Carnegie Mellon University (PhD)
Central Florida, University of (MA/MS—terminal, PhD)
Central Michigan University (MA/MS—terminal, PhD)
City University of New York: Brooklyn College (MA/MS—terminal)
City University of New York: Graduate School and University Center (PhD)
Claremont Graduate University (MA/MS—terminal, PhD)
Clemson University (PhD)
Cleveland State University (MA/MS—terminal)
Colorado State University (PhD)
Connecticut, University of (PhD)
DePaul University (PhD)
East Carolina University (MA/MS—terminal)
Eastern Kentucky University (MA/MS—terminal)
Emporia State University (MA/MS—terminal)
Fairleigh Dickinson University, Madison (MA/MS—terminal)
Florida Institute of Technology (MA/MS—terminal, PhD)
Florida International University (PhD)
George Mason University (MA/MS—terminal, PhD)
Georgia Institute of Technology (PhD)
Georgia, University of (PhD)
Goddard College (MA/MS—terminal)
Hartford, University of (MA/MS—terminal)
Hofstra University (MA/MS—terminal, PhD)
Houston, University of (PhD)
Idaho, University of (MA/MS—terminal)
Illinois Institute of Technology (MA/MS—terminal, PhD)
Illinois State University (MA/MS—terminal)
Illinois, University of, Urbana–Champaign (MA/MS—terminal)
Indiana University–Purdue University Indianapolis (MA/MS—terminal)
Iona College (MA/MS—terminal)
John F. Kennedy University (MA/MS—terminal)
Kansas State University (MA/MS—terminal, Other, PhD)
Lamar University—Beaumont (MA/MS—terminal)
Louisiana State University (PhD)
Louisiana Tech University (MA/MS—terminal)
Maryland, University of (PhD)
Michigan State University (PhD)
Middle Tennessee State University (MA/MS—terminal)
Minnesota State University—Mankato (MA/MS—terminal)
Minnesota, University of (PhD)
Missouri State University (MA/MS—terminal)
Missouri, University of, St. Louis (PhD)
Montreal, University of (PhD)
Nebraska, University of, Omaha (MA/MS, MA/MS—terminal, PhD)
Nevada, University of, Reno (PhD)
New Haven, University of (MA/MS—terminal)
New York University, Graduate School of Arts and Science (MA/MS—terminal)
North Carolina State University (PhD)
North Carolina, University of, Charlotte (PhD)
Northern Illinois University (PhD)
Northern Iowa, University of (MA/MS—terminal)
Northern Michigan University (MA/MS—terminal)
Ohio State University, The (PhD)
Ohio University (PhD)
Old Dominion University (PhD)
Pennsylvania State University (PhD)
Portland State University (PhD)
Puerto Rico, University of (MA/MS—terminal, PhD)
Purdue University (PhD)
Quebec at Montreal, University of (PhD)
Radford University (MA/MS—terminal)
Rice University (PhD)
Roosevelt University (MA/MS—terminal)
Rutgers—The State University of New Jersey, Graduate School of Applied and Professional Psychology (PsyD)
Saint Louis University (PhD)
Saint Mary's University (MA/MS—terminal, PhD)
San Diego State University (MA/MS—terminal)
San Francisco State University (MA/MS—terminal)
San Jose State University (MA/MS—terminal)
Sherbrooke, University of (PsyD)
Sonoma State University (MA/MS)
South Florida, University of (PhD)
Southeastern Louisiana University (Other)
Southern Illinois University Edwardsville (MA/MS—terminal)
Southern Illinois University, at Carbondale (PhD)
Springfield College (MA/MS—terminal)
St. Cloud State University (MA/MS—terminal)
St. Mary's University (MA/MS—terminal)
State University of New York, University at Albany (MA/MS—terminal, PhD)
Temple University (MA/MS—terminal)
Tennessee, University of, Chattanooga (MA/MS—terminal)
Tennessee, University of, Knoxville (PhD)
Texas A&M University (PhD)
Texas, University of, Arlington (PhD)
The Chicago School of Professional Psychology (MA/MS—terminal, PsyD)
Towson University (MA/MS)
Tulsa, University of (MA/MS—terminal, Other, PhD)
Valdosta State University (MA/MS—terminal)
Victoria, University of (PhD)

Virginia Polytechnic Institute and State University (PhD)
Walden University (MA/MS, MA/MS—terminal, PhD)
Waterloo, University of (MA/MS—terminal, PhD)
Wayne State University (MA/MS—terminal)
West Chester University of Pennsylvania (MA/MS—terminal)
West Florida, The University of (MA/MS—terminal)
Western Kentucky University (MA/MS—terminal)
Western Michigan University (MA/MS—terminal, PhD)
Western Ontario, The University of (PhD)
Windsor, University of (PhD)
Wisconsin, University of, Oshkosh (MA/MS—terminal)
Wisconsin, University of, Stout (MA/MS—terminal)
Wright State University (PhD)
Xavier University (MA/MS—terminal)

M

Multicultural Psychology

Alliant International University: San Francisco (PhD), PsyD)
Alliant International University: Los Angeles (PhD)
California, University of, Santa Barbara (PhD)
Denver, University of (PsyD)
Fayetteville State University (MA/MS—terminal)
Fordham University (Other)
Goddard College (MA/MS—terminal)
Hawaii, University of, Manoa (PhD)
John F. Kennedy University (PsyD)
Marquette University (PhD)
Massachusetts, University of, Boston (MA/MS—terminal)
Massachusetts, University of, Lowell (MA/MS—terminal)
Memphis, University of (PhD)
New Mexico State University (EdS/MEd, PhD)
Our Lady of the Lake University (PsyD)
Pennsylvania, University of (PhD)
Quebec at Montreal, University of (PhD)
Utah State University (PhD)
Yale University (PhD)

N

Neuropsychology

Arizona, University of (PhD)
Boston University (PhD)
Brigham Young University (PhD)
Chicago, University of (PhD)
City University of New York: Graduate Center (PhD)
City University of New York: Graduate School and University Center (PhD)
Concordia University (PhD)
Connecticut, University of (PhD)
Delaware, University of (PhD)
Drexel University (PhD)
Duke University (PhD)
Fielding Graduate University (Other)
George Washington University (PhD)
Georgia State University (PhD)
Houston, University of (PhD)
Idaho, University of (PhD)
Michigan State University (PhD)
Montreal, University of (PhD)
New Mexico, University of (PhD)
Quebec at Montreal, University of (PhD)
Rice University (PhD)
Rosalind Franklin University of Medicine and Science (PhD)
San Diego State University (MA/MS)
South Florida, University of (PhD)
Temple University (PhD)
Texas Woman's University (PhD)
Utah, University of (PhD)
Victoria, University of (PhD)
Virginia Consortium Program in Clinical Psychology (PsyD)
Washington State University (PhD)
Wayne State University (PhD)
Yeshiva University (PhD, PsyD)

Neuroscience

Alabama, University of, at Birmingham (PhD)
American University (PhD)
Arizona State University (PhD)
Arizona, University of (PhD)
Baylor University (PhD)
Bowling Green State University (PhD)
Brandeis University (PhD)
Brigham Young University (PhD)
British Columbia, University of (PhD)
Brown University (PhD)
California, University of, Davis (PhD)
California, University of, Riverside (PhD)
California, University of, Santa Barbara (PhD)
Carleton University (MA/MS)
City University of New York (PhD)
City University of New York: Brooklyn College (PhD)
City University of New York: Graduate Center (PhD)
City University of New York: Graduate School and University Center (PhD)
Colorado, University of, Boulder (PhD)
Concordia University (PhD)
Connecticut, University of (PhD)
Cornell University (PhD)
Dalhousie University (MA/MS, PhD)
Dartmouth College (PhD)
Delaware, University of (PhD)
Denver, University of (PhD)
Duke University (PhD)
Emory University (PhD)
Florida State University (PhD)
Florida, University of (PhD)
George Washington University (PhD)
Georgia, University of (PhD)
Guelph, University of (MA/MS, PhD)
Hawaii, University of, Manoa (PhD)
Houston, University of (PhD)
Idaho, University of (PhD)
Illinois, University of, Urbana–Champaign (PhD)
Indiana University (PhD)
Iowa, University of (PhD)
Johns Hopkins University (PhD)
Kansas State University (PhD)
Kansas, University of (PhD)
Manitoba, University of (PhD)
Maryland, University of (PhD)
Massachusetts, University of (MA/MS—terminal)
Miami, University of (PhD)
Missouri, University of, Columbia (PhD)
Missouri, University of, St. Louis (PhD)
Nebraska, University of, Omaha (MA/MS, PhD)
Nevada, University of, Las Vegas (PhD)
Nevada, University of, Reno (PhD)
New Hampshire, University of (PhD)
North Dakota State University (PhD)
Northeastern University (PhD)
Northern Illinois University (PhD)
Oregon, University of (PhD)
Pittsburgh, University of (PhD)
Quebec at Montreal, University of (PhD)
Saint Louis University (PhD)
Seton Hall University (MA/MS—terminal)
South Carolina, University of (PhD)
Southern California, University of (PhD)
Southern Illinois University, at Carbondale (PhD)
Stanford University (PhD)
State University of New York at Buffalo (PhD)
State University of New York, Binghamton University (PhD)
Stony Brook University (PhD)
Texas A&M University (PhD)
Texas Christian University (PhD)
Texas, University of, Austin (PhD)
Toronto, University of (MA/MS, PhD)
Tulane University (PhD)
Vanderbilt University (PhD)
Victoria, University of (PhD)
Virginia, University of (PhD)
Washington, University of (PhD)
Waterloo, University of (PhD)
Wayne State University (PhD)
Wilfrid Laurier University (MA/MS—terminal, PhD)
Wisconsin, University of, Madison (PhD)
Wisconsin, University of, Milwaukee (PhD)
Yale University (PhD)
York University (PhD)

O

Other

Abilene Christian University (MA/MS)
Adelphi University (MA/MS—terminal)
Appalachian State University (MA/MS—terminal, Other)
Arcadia University (MA/MS—terminal)

Argosy University, Hawaii Campus (MA/MS—terminal, Respecialization Diploma)
Argosy University/Dallas Campus (MA/MS—terminal)
Argosy University/Twin Cities (PsyD)
Arizona State University (MA/MS—terminal, Other, PhD)
Auburn University (EdS/MEd, Other, PhD)
Austin Peay State University (MA/MS—terminal)
Avila University (MA/MS—terminal)
Azusa Pacific University (MA/MS—terminal)
Boston College (MA/MS—terminal)
Brown University (PhD)
California State University, Chico (MA/MS—terminal)
California State University, Long Beach (MA/MS—terminal)
California State University, Northridge (MA/MS—terminal)
California, University of, Los Angeles (PhD)
California, University of, Santa Barbara (PhD)
Carlos Albizu University, Miami Campus (MA/MS—terminal)
Carnegie Mellon University (PhD)
Catholic University of America, The (MA/MS—terminal)
Central Arkansas, University of (MA/MS—terminal)
City University of New York: Brooklyn College (MA/MS—terminal)
City University of New York: Graduate School and University Center (PhD)
Claremont Graduate University (MA/MS—terminal, PhD)
Cleveland State University (MA/MS—terminal)
Colorado State University (PhD)
Concordia University (PhD)
Connecticut, University of (PhD)
Denver, University of (MA/MS—terminal, PhD)
Duquesne University (Other, PhD)
East Tennessee State University (MA/MS—terminal, PhD)
Fielding Graduate University (PhD)
Florida International University (PhD)
Fordham University (PhD)
Gallaudet University (Other, PhD)
Geneva College (MA/MS)
George Mason University (MA/MS—terminal, PhD)
Georgia Institute of Technology (MA/MS—terminal, PhD)
Georgian Court University (MA/MS—terminal)
Gonzaga University (MA/MS—terminal)
Guelph, University of (MA/MS, PhD)
Harvard University (PhD)
Hawaii, University of, Manoa (PhD)
Houston Baptist University (MA/MS—terminal)
Houston, University of (Other)
Idaho, University of (MA/MS—terminal)
Illinois, University of, Urbana–Champaign (MA/MS—terminal, Other, PhD)
Illinois, University of, Urbana–Champaign (MA/MS—terminal, PhD)
Immaculata University (MA/MS, MA/MS—terminal)
Iona College (MA/MS—terminal)
Jacksonville State University (MA/MS—terminal)
James Madison University (EdS/MEd, MA/MS—terminal, PhD)
La Verne, University of (MA/MS—terminal)
LaSalle University (Other)
Lesley University (MA/MS, MA/MS—terminal, Other, Respecialization Diploma)
Lewis University (MA/MS—terminal)
Long Island University (Other)
Louisiana Tech University (MA/MS—terminal)
Louisiana, University of, Lafayette (MA/MS—terminal)
Loyola University of Chicago (MA/MS—terminal, Other)
Marquette University (MA/MS—terminal)
Marymount University (MA/MS—terminal)
Massachusetts, University of (PhD)
Massachusetts, University of, Boston (EdS/MEd, MA/MS—terminal)
Miami, University of (MA/MS—terminal, PhD)
Middle Tennessee State University (Other)
Millersville University (Other)
Minnesota, University of (PhD)
Mississippi State University (PhD)
Missouri, University of, Kansas City (MA/MS—terminal, Other)
New Hampshire, University of (PhD)
New Mexico State University (MA/MS—terminal, PhD)
New Mexico, University of (PhD)
New Orleans, University of (PhD)
North Carolina State University (PhD)
North Dakota State University (PhD)
North Dakota, University of (MA/MS—terminal)
Northeastern University (MA/MS—terminal, Other, PhD)
Northern Arizona University (MA/MS—terminal, Other)
Northern Iowa, University of (MA/MS)
Northern Michigan University (MA/MS—terminal)
Northwestern University (PhD)
Nova Southeastern University (MA/MS—terminal)
Ohio State University, The (PhD)
Oklahoma State University (PhD)
Oklahoma, University of (MA/MS—terminal, Other, PhD)
Old Dominion University (PhD)
Oregon, University of (MA/MS—terminal)
Our Lady of the Lake University (MA/MS—terminal)
Pacific University (MA/MS—terminal)
Penn State Harrisburg (MA/MS—terminal)
Pennsylvania State University, The (PhD)
Pepperdine University (MA/MS—terminal)
Philadelphia College of Osteopathic Medicine (EdS/MEd, MA/MS—terminal, Other, PsyD)
Pittsburg State University (MA/MS—terminal)
Pittsburgh, University of (MA/MS, PhD)
Portland State University (PhD)
Puerto Rico, University of (MA/MS—terminal, PhD)
Purdue University (PhD)
Regent University (PsyD)
Rensselaer Polytechnic Institute (PhD)
Rice University (PhD)
Roberts Wesleyan College (MA/MS—terminal)
Saint Francis, University of (MA/MS, Other)
Saint Mary's University of Minnesota (MA/MS—terminal, Other)
Sam Houston State University (MA/MS—terminal)
San Diego State University (MA/MS—terminal)
San Diego State University/University of California, San Diego Joint Doctoral Program in Clinical Psychology (PhD)
San Francisco State University (MA/MS—terminal)
Saskatchewan, University of (PhD)
Saybrook Graduate School and Research Center (MA/MS, PhD)
South Alabama, University of (MA/MS—terminal)
South Dakota, University of (PhD)
Springfield College (EdS/MEd, MA/MS—terminal)
St. Cloud State University (MA/MS—terminal)
State University of New York at Buffalo (MA/MS—terminal, PhD)
State University of New York at New Paltz (MA/MS—terminal)
State University of New York, University of Albany (Other)
Temple University (MA/MS—terminal)
Texas A&M International University (MA/MS—terminal)
Texas Tech University (PhD)
Texas, University of, Austin (Other, PhD)
Texas, University of, Tyler (MA/MS—terminal)
The New School for Social Research (MA/MS—terminal)
Tulsa, University of (MA/MS—terminal, Other, PhD)
Utah State University (MA/MS—terminal)
Valdosta State University (Other)
Vanderbilt University (Other, PhD)
Virginia, University of (PhD)
Washington, University of (PhD)
West Florida, The University of (MA/MS—terminal)
West Georgia, University of (MA/MS—terminal, PsyD)
West Virginia University (MA/MS—terminal, PhD)

Western Carolina University (MA/MS—terminal)
Western Ontario, The University of (PhD)
Wichita State University (PhD)
Widener University (Other)
Windsor, University of (PhD)
Wisconsin, University of, Madison (MA/MS, PhD)
Wisconsin, University of, Milwaukee (MA/MS, MA/MS—terminal, PhD)
Wright State University (PhD)
Wyoming, University of (PhD)
York University (PhD)

P

Personality Psychology
British Columbia, University of (PhD)
Brown University (PhD)
California, University of, Berkeley (PhD)
California, University of, Davis (PhD)
Cornell University (PhD)
Florida State University (PhD)
Illinois, University of, Chicago (PhD)
Michigan State University (PhD)
Michigan, University of (PhD)
Minnesota, University of (PhD)
Missouri, University of, Columbia (PhD)
Northeastern University (PhD)
Northwestern University (PhD)
Oklahoma, University of (PhD)
Oregon, University of (PhD)
Rochester, University of (PhD)
Texas Tech University (PhD)
Washington University in St. Louis (PhD)
Western Ontario, The University of (PhD)
Wisconsin, University of, Madison (PhD)

Physiological Psychology
Alabama, University of, at Birmingham (PhD)
Boston University (PhD)
Brown University (PhD)
Florida, University of (PhD)
Hawaii, University of, Manoa (PhD)
Nebraska, University of, Lincoln (PhD)
Nebraska, University of, Omaha (PhD)
New Orleans, University of (PhD)
Ohio University (PhD)
Oklahoma, University of (PhD)
Texas A&M University (PhD)
Tulane University (PhD)
Widener University (PsyD)

Psychoanalytic Psychology
Adelphi University (Other, PhD)
City University of New York: Graduate School and University Center (PhD)
Delaware, University of (PhD)
Detroit–Mercy, University of (PhD)
George Washington University (PsyD)
Quebec at Montreal, University of (PhD)
Sonoma State University (MA/MS)
The New School for Social Research (PhD)

Psycholinguistics
Claremont Graduate University (PhD)
Delaware, University of (PhD)
Denver, University of (PhD)
Illinois, University of, Urbana–Champaign (PhD)
Iowa, University of (PhD)
New Hampshire, University of (PhD)
Northeastern University (PhD)

Psychopharmacology
Alliant International University: San Francisco (MA/MS—terminal)
Argosy University, Hawaii Campus (Other)
Auburn University (PhD)
Fairleigh Dickinson University, Metropolitan Campus (MA/MS—terminal)
Iowa, University of (PhD)
Massachusetts School of Professional Psychology (MA/MS—terminal)
Nebraska, University of, Lincoln (PhD)
State University of New York, Binghamton University (PhD)

Q

Quantitative Psychology
Arizona State University (PhD)
British Columbia, University of (PhD)
California, University of (PhD)
California, University of, Davis (PhD)
California, University of, Los Angeles (PhD)
Georgia Institute of Technology (PhD)
Georgia, University of (PhD)
Hawaii, University of, Manoa (PhD)
Illinois State University (MA/MS—terminal)
Illinois, University of, Urbana–Champaign (PhD)
Illinois, University of, Urbana–Champaign (MA/MS—terminal)
Iowa, University of (MA/MS, PhD)
James Madison University (MA/MS—terminal)
Kansas, University of (Other, PhD)
Manitoba, University of (PhD)
Middle Tennessee State University (MA/MS—terminal)
Minnesota, University of (PhD)
Missouri, University of, Columbia (PhD)
Nebraska, University of, Lincoln (PhD)
New Mexico, University of (PhD)
North Carolina State University (PhD)
North Carolina, University of, Chapel Hill (PhD)
Notre Dame, University of (PhD)
Ohio State University, The (PhD)
Ohio University (PhD)
Purdue University (PhD)
Rhode Island, University of, Chafee Social Sciences Center (PhD)
Southern California, University of (PhD)
State University of New York, University of Albany (PhD)
Tennessee, University of, Knoxville (PhD)
Texas of the Permian Basin, The University of (MA/MS—terminal)
Utah, University of (PhD)
Vanderbilt University (PhD)
Vanderbilt University, Peabody College (PhD)
Virginia, University of (PhD)
Washington, University of (PhD)
Wisconsin, University of, Madison (PhD)
Wisconsin, University of, Milwaukee (MA/MS, PhD)

R

Rehabilitation Psychology
Illinois Institute of Technology (MA/MS—terminal)
St. Cloud State University (MA/MS—terminal)
State University of New York at Buffalo (MA/MS—terminal)

S

School Psychology
Abilene Christian University (MA/MS—terminal)
Adelphi University (MA/MS—terminal)
Adler School of Professional Psychology (MA/MS)
Alabama, University of, at Huntsville (MA/MS—terminal)
Alfred University (EdS/MEd, PsyD)
Alliant International University: Irvine (MA/MS—terminal, PsyD)
Alliant International University: Los Angeles (MA/MS—terminal, PsyD)
Alliant International University: San Diego (MA/MS—terminal, PsyD)
Alliant International University: San Francisco (MA/MS—terminal, PsyD)
Appalachian State University (Other)
Arcadia University (MA/MS—terminal)
Argosy University, Hawaii Campus (MA/MS—terminal)
Argosy University/Phoenix, American School of Professional Psychology (MA/MS—terminal, PsyD)
Arizona State University (PhD)
Auburn University (EdS/MEd, PhD)
Augusta State University (MA/MS—terminal)
Austin Peay State University (EdS/MEd)
Ball State University (EdS/MEd, MA/MS, PhD)
Barry University (MA/MS, Other)
Brigham Young University (EdS/MEd)
California State University, Chico (MA/MS—terminal)
California, University of, Berkeley (PhD)
California, University of, Santa Barbara (EdS/MEd)
Carlos Albizu University (PhD)
Central Arkansas, University of (MA/MS—terminal, PhD)
Central Michigan University (Other, PhD)
Central Washington University (EdS/MEd)
Cincinnati, University of (EdS/MEd, PhD)

Citadel, The (EdS/MEd)
City University of New York: Brooklyn College (MA/MS)
Cleveland State University (Other)
Columbia University (EdS/MEd, PhD)
Connecticut, University of (MA/MS, PhD)
Denver, University of (EdS/MEd, MA/MS, PhD)
Duquesne University (Other, PhD)
East Carolina University (MA/MS—terminal, PhD)
East Central University (MA/MS—terminal)
Eastern Illinois University (Other)
Eastern Kentucky University (EdS/MEd)
Emporia State University (EdS/MEd)
Fairleigh Dickinson University, Metropolitan Campus (MA/MS—terminal, PsyD)
Florida State University (EdS/MEd, PhD)
Fordham University (Other, PhD)
Fort Hays State University (EdS/MEd)
Francis Marion University (MA/MS—terminal)
Gallaudet University (Other)
George Mason University (MA/MS—terminal)
Georgia, University of (PhD)
Georgian Court University (MA/MS—terminal)
Hartford, University of (MA/MS)
Hofstra University (PsyD)
Houston, University of (PhD)
Humboldt State University (MA/MS—terminal)
Illinois State University (Other, PhD)
Immaculata University (MA/MS—terminal, PsyD)
Indiana State University (EdS/MEd, Other, PhD)
Indiana University (EdS/MEd, PhD)
Institute of Transpersonal Psychology (PhD)
Iona College (MA/MS—terminal)
Iowa, University of (PhD)
James Madison University (EdS/MEd, PsyD)
Kansas, University of (EdS/MEd, PhD)
Kent State University (EdS/MEd, PhD)
Kentucky, University of (MA/MS, PhD)
Lehigh University (EdS/MEd, PhD)
Lewis & Clark College, Graduate School of Education and Counseling (EdS/MEd)
Louisiana State University (PhD)
Louisiana State University in Shreveport (EdS/MEd)
Louisiana, University of, Monroe (EdS/MEd)
Manitoba, University of (MA/MS)
Marist College (MA/MS—terminal)
Maryland, University of (PhD)
Marywood University (EdS/MEd)
Massachusetts School of Professional Psychology (MA/MS)
McGill University (PhD)
Memphis, University of (MA/MS—terminal, PhD)
Middle Tennessee State University (EdS/MEd)
Millersville University (MA/MS)
Minnesota State University—Mankato (PsyD)
Minnesota State University Moorhead (EdS/MEd)
Minnesota, University of (EdS/MEd, PhD)
Minot State University (EdS/MEd)
Mississippi State University (PhD)
Missouri, University of, Columbia (EdS/MEd, MA/MS, PhD)
Montana, The University of (MA/MS—terminal, PhD)
Nebraska, University of, Lincoln (PhD)
Nebraska, University of, Omaha (EdS/MEd, MA/MS)
New Mexico State University (EdS/MEd)
New York University (PhD, PsyD)
North Carolina State University (PhD)
Northeastern University (MA/MS, PhD)
Northern Arizona University (MA/MS—terminal, PhD)
Northern Colorado, University of (EdS/MEd, PhD, Respecialization Diploma)
Northern Illinois University (PhD)
Nova Southeastern University (Other)
Ohio State University (MA/MS—terminal, PhD)
Oklahoma State University (EdS/MEd, PhD)
Oklahoma, University of (Other)
Our Lady of the Lake University (MA/MS—terminal)
Pace University (EdS/MEd, PsyD)
Pennsylvania State University (PhD)
Pennsylvania, University of (MA/MS)
Philadelphia College of Osteopathic Medicine (EdS/MEd, MA/MS—terminal, PsyD, Respecialization Diploma)
Pittsburg State University (EdS/MEd)
Radford University (EdS/MEd)
Rhode Island, University of, Chafee Social Sciences Center (MA/MS—terminal, PhD)
Roberts Wesleyan College (MA/MS—terminal)
Rutgers—The State University of New Jersey, Graduate School of Applied and Professional Psychology (PsyD)
Sam Houston State University (MA/MS—terminal)
San Francisco State University (MA/MS—terminal)
Seton Hall University (MA/MS—terminal)
Sonoma State University (MA/MS—terminal)
South Carolina, University of (PhD)
South Florida, University of (EdS/MEd, PhD)
Southern Illinois University Edwardsville (EdS/MEd, MA/MS—terminal)
Southern Mississippi, The University of (PhD)
Springfield College (Other)
St. John's University (MA/MS—terminal, PsyD)
State University of New York at Buffalo (MA/MS—terminal, PhD)
State University of New York, College at Plattsburgh (MA/MS—terminal)
State University of New York, University of Albany (Other, PsyD)
Syracuse University (PhD)
Temple University (MA/MS, PhD)
Tennessee, University of, Knoxville (PhD)
Texas A&M University (PhD)
Texas A&M University—Commerce (MA/MS—terminal)
Texas Woman's University (PhD)
Texas, University of, Austin (PhD)
Texas, University of, Tyler (MA/MS—terminal)
The Chicago School of Professional Psychology (EdS/MEd)
Towson University (MA/MS)
Trinity University (MA/MS—terminal)
Tufts University (MA/MS)
Tulane University (PhD)
Utah State University (MA/MS—terminal)
Valdosta State University (EdS/MEd)
Virginia, University of (PhD)
Walden University (PhD)
Washington, University of (EdS/MEd, PhD)
Wayne State University (MA/MS)
West Texas A&M University (MA/MS—terminal)
Western Carolina University (MA/MS—terminal)
Western Illinois University (Other)
Western Kentucky University (EdS/MEd)
Widener University (PsyD)
Winthrop University (Other)
Wisconsin, University of, Eau Claire (EdS/MEd)
Wisconsin, University of, La Crosse (EdS/MEd)
Wisconsin, University of, Madison (PhD)
Wisconsin, University of, Milwaukee (EdS/MEd, PhD)

Social Psychology

Alabama, University of (PhD)
American University (MA/MS—terminal)
Arizona State University (PhD)
Arizona, University of (PhD)
Ball State University (MA/MS—terminal)
Baylor University (PhD)
Boston College (PhD)
Brandeis University (MA/MS—terminal, PhD)
Brigham Young University (PhD)
British Columbia, University of (PhD)
Brown University (PhD)
California, University of, Berkeley (PhD)
California, University of, Davis (PhD)
California, University of, Irvine (PhD)
California, University of, Los Angeles (PhD)
California, University of, Riverside (PhD)
California, University of, Santa Barbara (PhD)
California, University of, Santa Cruz (PhD)
Chicago, University of (PhD)
City University of New York: Graduate School and University Center (PhD)

Sport Psychology

ALPHABETICAL INDEX OF INSTITUTIONS